Baseball america®
2013 ALMANAC

BASEBALL AMERICA INC. · DURHAM, N.C.

EDITOR'S NOTE: Major league statistics are based on final, unofficial 2012 averages. >> The organization statistics, which begin on page 43, include all players who participated in at least one game during the 2012 season. >> Pitchers' batting statistics are not included, nor are the pitching statistics of field players who pitched in less than two games. >> For players who played with more than one team in the same league, the player's cumulative statistics appear on the line immediately after the player's statistics with each team. >> Innings pitched have been rounded off to the nearest full inning.

BaseBall america
2013 ALMANAC

Editor
WILL LINGO

Photo Editor
NATHAN RODE

Assistant Editors
BEN BADLER, JIM CALLIS, J.J. COOPER, MATT EDDY,
CONOR GLASSEY, AARON FITT, JOSH LEVENTHAL,
JOHN MANUEL, NATHAN RODE, JIM SHONERD

Editorial Assistants
PAT HICKEY, ANDREW KRAUSE, CLINT LONGENECKER,
JOHN SANDBERG, PETER WARDELL

Database and Application Development
BRENT LEWIS, TIM COLLINS

Design & Production
SARA HIATT MCDANIEL, LINWOOD WEBB

Contributing Writer
TOM HAUDRICOURT

Programming & Technical Development
BRENT LEWIS

Cover Photo
MIGUEL CABRERA BY TOMASSO DEROSA

DISTRIBUTED BY SIMON & SCHUSTER ISBN-13: 978-1-932391-43-5

STATISTICS PROVIDED BY MAJOR LEAGUE BASEBALL ADVANCED MEDIA AND COMPILED BY BASEBALL AMERICA

BaseBall america

PRESIDENT/PUBLISHER Lee Folger

EDITORIAL
EDITORS IN CHIEF Will Lingo, John Manuel
EXECUTIVE EDITOR Jim Callis
MANAGING EDITOR J.J. Cooper
NEWS EDITOR Josh Leventhal
NATIONAL WRITER Aaron Fitt
ASSOCIATE EDITOR Matt Eddy
ASSISTANT EDITORS Ben Badler, Conor Glassey,
Nathan Rode, Jim Shonerd

PRODUCTION
DESIGN & PRODUCTION DIRECTOR Sara Hiatt McDaniel
MULTIMEDIA MANAGER Linwood Webb
PRODUCTION MANAGER Inna Cazares

ADVERTISING
DIRECTOR OF ADVERTISING Ryan Johnson
DIRECT MARKETING MANAGER Ximena Caceres
MARKETPLACE MANAGER Kristopher M. Lull
ADVERTISING SALES EXECUTIVE Edward Richards

BUSINESS
CUSTOMER SERVICE Ronnie McCabe, Jocelyn Dantini
MANAGER, FINANCE Susan Callahan
FINANCIAL ADMINISTRATOR Hailey Carpenter
TECHNOLOGY MANAGER Brent Lewis
TECHNOLOGY ASSISTANT Tim Collins

WHERE TO DIRECT QUESTIONS
ADVERTISING: advertising@baseballamerica.com
BUSINESS BEAT: joshleventhal@baseballamerica.com
COLLEGES: aaronfitt@baseballamerica.com
DESIGN/PRODUCTION: production@baseballamerica.com
DRAFT: johnmanuel@baseballamerica.com
HIGH SCHOOLS: nathanrode@baseballamerica.com
INDEPENDENT LEAGUES: jjcooper@baseballamerica.com
MAJOR LEAGUES: jimcallis@baseballamerica.com
MINOR LEAGUES: willlingo@baseballamerica.com
PHOTOS: photos@baseballamerica.com
PROSPECTS: benbadler@baseballamerica.com
REPRINTS: production@baseballamerica.com
SUBSCRIPTIONS/CUSTOMER SERVICE:
customerservice@baseballamerica.com
WEBSITE: customerservice@baseballamerica.com

GrindMedia

GRINDMEDIA MANAGEMENT
SVP, GROUP PUBLISHER Norb Garrett
norb.garrett@grindmedia.com
VP, DIGITAL Greg Morrow
greg.morrow@grindmedia.com
PRODUCTION DIRECTOR Kasey Kelley
kasey.kelley@grindmedia.com
EDITORIAL DIRECTOR—DIGITAL Chris Mauro
chris.mauro@grindmedia.com
FINANCE DIRECTOR Adam Miner
adam.miner@grindmedia.com

ADVERTISING SALES
SALES STRATEGY MGR/PRINT & EVENTS
Chris Engelsman chris.engelsman@grindmedia.com
SALES STRATEGY MGR/DIGITAL Elisabeth Murray
elisabeth.murray@grindmedia.com

DIGITAL
DIRECTOR OF ENGINEERING Jeff Kimmel
jeff.kimmel@grindmedia.com
SENIOR PRODUCT MANAGER Rishi Kumar
rishi.kumar@grindmedia.com
SENIOR PRODUCT MANAGER Marc Bartell
marc.bartell@grindmedia.com
CREATIVE DIRECTOR Peter Tracy
peter.tracy@grindmedia.com

MARKETING AND EVENTS
DIRECTOR OF EVENT OPERATIONS Sean Nielsen
sean.nielsen@grindmedia.com

FACILITIES
MANAGER Randy Ward randy.ward@grindmedia.com
OFFICE COORDINATOR Ruth Hosea
ruth.hosea@grindmedia.com
ARCHIVIST Thomas Voehringer
thomas.voehringer@sorc.com

SOURCE INTERLINK MEDIA

**OFFICERS OF SOURCE INTERLINK
COMPANIES, INC.**
PRESIDENT AND CHIEF EXECUTIVE OFFICER
Michael Sullivan
EVP, CHIEF FINANCIAL OFFICER John Bode
EVP, CHIEF ADMINISTRATIVE OFFICER
Stephanie Justice

SOURCE INTERLINK MEDIA, LLC
PRESIDENT Chris Argentieri
CHIEF CREATIVE OFFICER Alan Alpanian
SVP, FINANCE Dan Bednar
VP, SINGLE COPY SALES AND MARKETING Chris Butler
EVP, ENTHUSIAST AUTOMOTIVE Doug Evans
SVP, NEW PRODUCT DEVELOPMENT Howard Lim
CHIEF CONTENT OFFICER Angus MacKenzie
SVP, MANUFACTURING AND PRODUCTION
Kevin Mullan
SVP, CONSUMER MEDIA AND INTEGRATED SALES
Eric Schwab

DIGITAL MEDIA
CHIEF TECHNOLOGY OFFICER, DIGITAL MEDIA
Raghu Bala
SVP, DIGITAL MARKETING Craig Buccola
SVP, DIGITAL PRODUCT DEVELOPMENT Todd Busby
SVP, DIGITAL PRODUCT DEVELOPMENT Tom Furukawa
VP, DIGITAL PRODUCT DEVELOPMENT Dan Hong
**VP, DIGITAL ADVERTISING PRODUCTS AND
OPERATIONS** Jung Park

**CONSUMER MARKETING, ENTHUSIAST
MEDIA SUBSCRIPTION COMPANY, INC.**
VP, CONSUMER MARKETING Tom Slater
VP, RETENTION AND OPERATIONS FULFILLMENT
Donald T. Robinson III

TABLE OF CONTENTS

BILL NICHOLS

MAJOR
LEAGUES

Cabrera captures first Triple Crown in 45 years

BY TOM HAUDRICOURT

After perhaps the most exciting final day of the regular season in major league history the previous year, baseball fans could not be so lucky as to bear witness to a repeat of that drama in 2012, could they?

Well, actually . . .

Not only did the final day provide compelling baseball theater on a team level, it also presented historic ramifications on a personal level, thanks to Tigers third baseman Miguel Cabrera, who became the first Triple Crown winner since 1967.

The playoff races also presented some surprising entrants. The upstart Nationals won a best-in-baseball 98 games and claimed their first National League East title, giving the nation's Capital its first playoff stage since 1933, when President Franklin D. Roosevelt was in his first year in the White House.

Up Interstate 95 some 40 miles or so, the Orioles ended a drought not nearly as long as their beltway rivals. The Nationals never had made the postseason as a franchise dating to their days as the Montreal Expos, but neither had the once-mighty Orioles been to the postseason since 1997. Baltimore's dry spell ended when it claimed one of two American League wild-card berths after chasing the Yankees to the wire for the East title.

Neither of those stories was as shocking as what the never-say-die Athletics pulled off in the AL West, however. Five games behind the two-time defending AL-champion Rangers with just nine to play, Oakland roared back to win the division by sweeping Texas in a final three-game series, including a 12-5 romp on the final day.

The A's occupied the top spot in the division only one day, but it was the only day that mattered—the final day. Texas held at least a share of the lead on all but three days of the season, but in the end they settled for second place and a wild-card berth.

Oakland, 13 games out on June 30, became just the fifth team in major league history to erase a deficit at least that large to earn a division or league crown. Oakland became the third club to win a division title or pennant while spending only one day in first place, joining the 1951 New York Giants and 2006 Twins.

Triple Crown winner Miguel Cabrera's 44 home runs and 139 RBIs led the majors

The A's, who pulled off an amazing 14 walk-off victories, finished with a 94-68 record, a 20-game improvement over the previous season despite operating with a $55 million payroll, second lowest in the majors. The big-spending Rangers couldn't hold them off, and the even bigger-spending Angels had to settle for third place in the division.

Not to be denied, Oakland overcame an early four-run deficit on the final day to win going away.

"I dreamt it. I truly believed it deep in my heart," said A's closer Grant Balfour, who wrapped up all three games of the season-ending sweep of the disbelieving Rangers.

Making the comeback all the more stunning, Oakland relied on an all-rookie rotation down the stretch after righthander Brandon McCarthy and lefty Brett Anderson were lost to injuries and veteran righty Bartolo Colon to a suspension for a performance-enhancing substance.

"You don't get through a season with the record we have and get lucky 162 times," A's general manager Billy Beane said, "so I think the talent of these guys needs to be recognized.

"We wanted to create a team that had a chance to get better from the first day forward. That was the expectation set. We just didn't know where we were going to start from, and, in fairness, maybe we were a little further ahead when we started than maybe anyone anticipated."

The Rangers did not recover from their shocking collapse, bowing out in the one-game wild-card playoff at home to the Orioles.

Crashing The Party

Few gave the Nationals a chance to win the powerful NL East and no one picked the Orioles as a potential playoff club in the AL. Yet Washington took charge of its division behind a potent pitching staff led by 24-year-old ace righthander Stephen Strasburg, and Baltimore chased New York to the wire in the AL East.

Heading into the final day of the season, an Orioles win combined with a Yankees loss would have forced a one-game playoff for the AL East division title. New York prevailed, however, when it won 14-2 and completed its three-game sweep of the free-falling Red Sox; the Orioles fell to the Rays 4-1.

The biggest moment in that division battle happened in Game No. 161 when the Yankees' Raul Ibanez socked a pinch-hit, game-tying home run in the ninth inning against the Red Sox, then won the game with a 12th-inning single to allow New York to maintain its one-game advantage.

DIAMOND IMAGES

The Nationals' decision to shut down ace Stephen Strasburg generated debate

"It's not how many times you get knocked down. It's how many times you get back up," Ibanez said of the tense battle with Baltimore.

The Orioles knew a thing or two about continuing to fight. They went 29-9 in one-run games, the third-best winning percentage (.763) in major league history. And talk about continuing to battle? After losing its first two extra-inning games of the season, Baltimore won a major league-record 16 in a row to finish the season.

The Nationals' run to the playoffs was not nearly as dramatic. Under the steady hand of 69-year-old manager Davey Johnson, and featuring the deepest pitching staff in the league, Washington held off the hard-charging Braves to claim the NL East and unseat the aging Phillies.

No team representing Washington had advanced to the postseason since the 1933 Senators won the AL pennant. The Nationals franchise began life as the Montreal Expos in 1969, relocated to D.C. in 2005 and bided time in outdated RFK Stadium until Nationals Park opened in '08.

Washington made news by calling up 19-year-old phenom outfielder Bryce Harper at the end of April, but it was a decision made with Strasburg, the organization's other No. 1 overall draft pick, that created controversy and generated endless debate. General manager Mike Rizzo and Johnson announced that Strasburg would be shut down after reaching an innings limit, rendering him

TRIPLE CROWN WINNERS

By edging Josh Hamilton and Curtis Granderson for the American League lead in home runs, Miguel Cabrera joined a select group of Triple Crown winners, every one of his predecessors a Hall of Famer. Forty-five years had elapsed since Carl Yastrzemski won baseball's last Triple Crown, and in the interim, baseball had expanded by 10 teams while adding two full rounds of playoffs prior to the World Series.

Year	Lge	Player, Team	AVG	HR	RBI
2012	AL	Miguel Cabrera, Tigers	.330	44	139
1967	AL	Carl Yastrzemski, Red Sox	.326	44	121
1966	AL	Frank Robinson, Orioles	.316	49	122
1956	AL	Mickey Mantle, Yankees	.353	52	130
1947	AL	Ted Williams, Red Sox	.343	32	114
1942	AL	Ted Williams, Red Sox	.356	36	137
1937	NL	Joe Medwick, Cardinals	.374	31	154
1934	AL	Lou Gehrig, Yankees	.363	49	165
1933	AL	Jimmie Foxx, Athletics	.356	48	163
1933	NL	Chuck Klein, Phillies	.368	28	120
1925	NL	Rogers Hornsby, Cardinals	.403	39	143
1922	NL	Rogers Hornsby, Cardinals	.401	42	152
1909	AL	Ty Cobb, Tigers	.377	9	107
1901	AL	Nap Lajoie, Athletics	.426	14	125

unavailable for the postseason.

The franchise that had waited more than four decades to make the postseason had opted to voluntarily shut down its ace in October. The move had Strasburg's long-term interests in mind—he missed most of 2011 while rehabbing from Tommy John surgery—though many considered the gesture overprotective.

The imposed ceiling turned out to be 160 innings. Strasburg went 15-6, 3.16 in 28 starts with 197 strikeouts in 159⅓ innings, and then he pitched no more. Strasburg publicly decried the decision, but the judgment of his bosses prevailed.

"I'm not sure any of us understand, but it's the right thing to do," Johnson said. "They way I look at things, the job that (ownership) and the front office have done building this organization, I don't look at this as the only chance you're going to get to be in the postseason, the World Series."

"I know (Strasburg) will be unhappy about it," Rizzo said. "He is an ultra-competitor. We have taken that out of his hands. This is a developmental decision and it ultimately falls on the doorstop of the general manager."

Cabrera Joins Select Company

The Tigers, preseason favorites in the AL Central after lavishing $214 million on free agent first baseman Prince Fielder, had anything but a cakewalk in the division. Detroit chased the White Sox all season, finally overtaking them in the final weeks of what became a division-or-bust playoff run.

A secondary, but more-compelling subplot came to the fore during the Tigers' chase of the White Sox. With a finishing flourish, Cabrera put himself in position to win the first Triple Crown since Red Sox left fielder Carl Yastrzemski accomplished the feat in 1967.

Cabrera built a comfortable cushion in the RBI department, but only late in the season did he separate himself from Angels rookie sensation Mike Trout in the chase for the AL batting title. But would Cabrera be able to overtake the Rangers' Josh Hamilton and the Yankees' Curtis Granderson, a pair of hard-hitting center fielders, for the AL home run title?

Cabrera, who moved from first base to third to accommodate Fielder, ultimately finished with 44 homers, edging out Hamilton and Granderson by one. He batted an even .330 and finished with 139 RBIs to lead the AL in average, home runs and RBIs and become baseball's 15th Triple Crown winner.

In fact, Cabrera won his second consecutive

AL batting title and led the majors in homers and RBIs, both of which established personal bests.

"It's an unbelievable feeling," Cabrera said after

CONTINUED ON PAGE 12

PLAYER AND ROOKIE OF THE YEAR

Trout triumphs twice over

BY JERRY CRASNICK

Of all the captivating storylines in baseball this season, from Miguel Cabrera's Triple Crown to the startling resurgence of ball in Baltimore and Oakland, the long-term ramifications are most profound in Anaheim, where a precocious outfielder expedited the learning curve and staked his claim among the game's elite.

The Angels went a disappointing 89-73 to finish out of the playoff picture, but Mike Trout's coming-out party was a sight to behold. He became the first player in major league history to surpass 30 homers, 45 stolen bases and 125 runs in a season. Trout finished three runs short of Joe DiMaggio's American League rookie record of 132 runs scored in 1936, and he fell one steal short of joining Barry Bonds and Eric Davis as the third player in history to pull off a 30-50. At one point, Trout bagged 30 steals in a row without being caught.

American League rookie of the year? Trout sewed that one up by winning the rookie of the month award in May, June, July and August. In the process, he turned the Athletics' Yoenis Cespedes, the Rangers' Yu Darvish and other worthy candidates into innocent bystanders.

Trout's all-around performance was stunning enough to put him right in the thick of the American League MVP debate with Cabrera, who won the first Triple Crown since Carl Yastrzemski in 1967. Traditionalists favor Cabrera, but Trout has garnered widespread support through a rare combination of offense,

Mike Trout's all-around exploits earned him Player and Rookie of the Year honors

LARRY GOREN

baserunning and superb defense in center field.

Trout's performance earned him another first, becoming the only player to win the Baseball America Rookie of the Year and Major League Player of the Year awards in the same season.

"The most remarkable thing was the way you felt every day, because it was remarkable every day," Angels general manager Jerry Dipoto said. "To see someone of his age and experience level come up and play as consistently well as he did and be the guy who stirred it up. It's fascinating that someone has the trait to be able stand up against the best players in world and overcome. Mike set a tone all year long. He played every day, every inning of every game. The electricity on the bases and the defensive prowess were tough to look past. I mean, every day.

"It was the ball you thought was going to drop in that Trout was there to catch. It was bringing back homers. They weren't just simple, 'Jump up on the yellow stripe.' It was two feet over the wall where it looked like his arm was going to disconnect from his body and then bringing the ball back. He put together a speed-power combination that I don't know if we've seen in the game.

PREVIOUS POY WINNERS

2002	Alex Rodriguez, ss, Rangers
2003	Barry Bonds, of, Giants
2004	Barry Bonds, of, Giants
2005	Albert Pujols, 1b, Cardinals
2006	Johan Santana, lhp, Twins
2007	Alex Rodriguez, ss, Yankees
2008	C.C. Sabathia, lhp, Indians/Brewers
2009	Joe Mauer, c, Twins
2010	Roy Halladay, rhp, Phillies
2011	Matt Kemp, of, Dodgers

Full list: BaseballAmerica.com/awards

"And he handled everything with such an unusual degree of humility, it really stood out to everyone around him. There's that old baseball adage, 'He plays the game the right way.' I would venture to say that every player who played with or against Mike or any staff that came across him felt the same way. You saw it when he made the All-Star Game and went into Kansas City and people were coming to see him—rather than vice versa. That's kind of remarkable for a 20-year-old guy."

Red Sox special assistant Eddie Bane, who selected Trout with the 25th pick in the 2009 draft in a previous role as Angels scouting director, points to Trout, Cespedes, the Nationals' Bryce Harper, the Rangers' Jurickson Profar and a passel of good young pitchers as players who will set a standard for excellence and fan appeal in the game moving forward.

"It's a nice time for another golden age in baseball," Bane said.

Amazingly, both Harper and Trout began their seasons in anonymity, navigating the final step of the apprenticeship process in Triple-A. In a fitting coincidence, they both received their big promotions to the majors on April 27.

Trout started out in Salt Lake City after a spring that was interrupted by a viral infection and a shoulder inflammation. But the enthusiasm was already building in Anaheim based on an encouraging cameo in 2011.

"He's not scared," teammate Torii Hunter said in March. "That's what I like—the heart he has. We would see this guy battling, fouling balls off and getting to 3-2 counts. He'd have a 10-pitch at-bat and strike out and we were like, 'Wow, that's impressive.'"

The Angels were 6-14 when they released veteran Bobby Abreu and put out an all-points bulletin for Trout, who was hitting .403 in 20 games in the Pacific Coast League.

The kid displayed a knack for producing big moments. The Angels made a trip to Camden Yards in late June, and Trout made a jaw-dropping catch to steal a home run from J.J. Hardy with dozens of friends and family members from back home in New Jersey watching from the stands. He went 9-for-17 with a 1.409 OPS against Felix Hernandez, and homered twice in 17 at-bats against Darvish. Bane, in hindsight, figured the kid might hit .285 with 15 homers and 20 stolen bases. Trout blew past those numbers in a heartbeat.

Two displays of all-around play from Trout stand out for Dipoto. In September, the Angels were driving for a playoff berth when they hosted the Tigers in Anaheim. Trout led off back-to-back games with homers off Justin Verlander and Anibal Sanchez, and Los Angeles swept the series.

Then there was the speed. During the Angels' final home series against Texas, he hit a routine grounder to the left of Gold Glove third baseman Adrian Beltre that didn't turn out to be quite so routine. Beltre took a mini-pirouette and threw a rocket across the field, and the call could have gone either way at first base.

Last year, Trout and Harper were playing catch in the outfield as teammates with the Scottsdale Scorpions in the Arizona Fall League. Now they're friends and texting buddies who revel in each other's success. If things work out according to plan, they'll spend the next 15 years hanging out at the All-Star Game each July.

"He's an unbelievable talent," the 19-year-old Harper said of Trout. "He's got that sixth tool—that mentality of playing ball and taking that mental side and playing the game he knows how to play. He has a really long career ahead of him. I'm happy for the things he's doing this year.

"I can't wait until I'm 20."

Let the record show that Harper turned 20 on Oct. 16, and Trout turned 21 all the way back on Aug. 21. They still have a few things to learn on the way to fulfilling their promise. But when the talent is this profound, the next pleasant surprise is just another lineup card away. The new faces of baseball have figured it out in a hurry, as bookends in a new golden age.

PREVIOUS ROY WINNERS	
2002	Eric Hinske, 3b, Blue Jays
2003	Brandon Webb, rhp, Diamondbacks
2004	Khalil Greene, ss, Padres
2005	Huston Street, rhp, Athletics
2006	Justin Verlander, rhp, Tigers
2007	Ryan Braun, 3b, Brewers
2008	Geovany Soto, c, Cubs
2009	Andrew McCutchen, of, Pirates
2010	Jason Heyward, of, Braves
2011	Jeremy Hellickson, rhp, Rays

Full list: BaseballAmerica.com/awards

CONTINUED FROM PAGE 9

clinching the feat on the final day of the season. "I can't describe the feeling right now. It was hard the last two days because everybody talked about it. I just had to focus. I had to go out there and do the job."

Cabrera joined an elite group of crown winners that included Hall of Famers such as Mickey Mantle, Ted Williams and Lou Gehrig. Because he achieved his feat amid a flurry of exciting playoff races, some wondered if it received the warranted level of attention. Tigers manager Jim Leyland said Cabrera, his reserved veteran slugger, deserved to bask in the glow of a special feat.

"I would say without question he's enjoyed it," Leyland said. "I doubt very much, knowing him, that he necessarily enjoys all the extra attention and all the extra conversations he's had to have. It's kind of out of his realm in personality, to be honest with you."

A sidelight to Cabrera carving his niche in the record books was the national debate as to who deserved the AL's true Most Valuable Player award. Many sided with the Triple Crown winner; others leaned to the dynamic Trout, who set the game on its ear with an incredible across-the-board performance after being promoted by the Angels at age 20 in late April.

Trout showed that he could do anything on a baseball field, his youth no disadvantage. He hit .326/.399/.564 in 559 at-bats, smacked 30 homers, 27 doubles and eight triples; stole 49 bases in 54 attempts and played center field in a fashion that generated one video highlight after another

of leaping, home run-robbing catches. Trout led the majors with 129 runs scored and 49 steals while finishing runner-up to Cabrera in the AL batting race.

Trout became the first major leaguer to hit 30 home runs, score 125 runs and steal 45 bases in a season. Only Joe DiMaggio (132 in 1936), Lloyd Waner (133 in 1927) and Ted Williams (131 in 1939) scored more runs as rookies.

Trout obviously set the bar ridiculously high for his career, but Angels manager Mike Scioscia said he didn't think future expectations would overwhelm one of the most talented young players to reach the majors in recent years.

"Mike is not doing anything he's not capable of," Scioscia said. "He's playing to his potential at a very young age. His challenge will be consistency. He has the ability to do what he did this year for a long time, and that's what's exciting about him."

Hamilton ceded the home run title to Cabrera but nevertheless had the most impressive power display of the season on May 8 in Baltimore. That day he slugged four home runs and a double, setting an AL record with 18 total bases, one shy of the big league record set by the Dodgers' Shawn Green on May 23, 2002.

All four homers were two-run shots, and three went out to center field at Orioles Park at Camden Yards.

"It's tough to hit four home runs in (batting practice) and he did it in a game," said awestruck Orioles catcher Matt Wieters.

Diamondbacks second baseman Aaron Hill also turned in a personal accomplishment that was rather stunning. Hill hit for the cycle twice, the

AMERICAN LEAGUE STANDINGS

EAST	W	L	PCT	GB	Manager	General Manager	Attendance	Average	Last Penn.
New York Yankees	95	67	.586	—	Joe Girardi	Brian Cashman	3,542,406	43,733	2009
* Baltimore Orioles	93	69	.574	2	Buck Showalter	Dan Duquette	2,102,240	26,611	1983
Tampa Bay Rays	90	72	.556	5	Joe Maddon	Andrew Friedman	1,559,681	19,255	2008
Toronto Blue Jays	73	89	.451	22	John Farrell	Alex Anthopoulos	2,099,663	25,922	1993
Boston Red Sox	69	93	.426	26	Bobby Valentine	Ben Cherington	3,043,003	37,568	2007
CENTRAL	W	L	PCT	GB	Manager	General Manager	Attendance	Average	Last Penn.
Detroit Tigers	88	74	.543	—	Jim Leyland	Dave Dombrowski	3,028,033	37,383	2012
Chicago White Sox	85	77	.525	3	Robin Ventura	Ken Williams	1,965,955	24,271	2005
Kansas City Royals	72	90	.444	16	Ned Yost	Dayton Moore	1,739,859	21,748	1985
Cleveland Indians	68	94	.420	20	Manny Acta/S. Alomar Jr.	Chris Antonetti	1,603,596	19,797	1997
Minnesota Twins	66	96	.407	22	Ron Gardenhire	Terry Ryan	2,776,354	34,276	1991
WEST	W	L	PCT	GB	Manager	General Manager	Attendance	Average	Last Penn.
Oakland Athletics	94	68	.580	—	Bob Melvin	Billy Beane	1,679,013	20,729	1990
* Texas Rangers	93	69	.574	1	Ron Washington	Jon Daniels	3,460,280	42,720	2011
Los Angeles Angels	89	73	.549	5	Mike Scioscia	Jerry Dipoto	3,061,770	37,800	2002
Seattle Mariners	75	87	.463	19	Eric Wedge	Jack Zduriencik	1,721,920	21,258	Never

*Wild card

PLAYOFFS—Wild Card: Orioles defeated Rangers 5-1 in one-game playoff. **Division Series:** Yankees defeated Orioles 3-2 and Tigers defeated Athletics 3-2 in best-of-five series. **League Championship Series:** Tigers defeated Yankees 4-0 in best-of-seven series.

first player to do that in one season since Babe Herman of the Brooklyn Robins in 1931.

Even more amazing, Hill pulled off his two cycles within 11 days of each other, on June 18 at home against the Mariners and on June 29 in Milwaukee against the Brewers.

"He's a good hitter, and there are plenty of good hitters who don't hit for the cycle twice in 11 days," Brewers lefthander Randy Wolf said. "The cycle is one of those crazy things that is part luck, part skill, and he has done it twice."

Refusing To Knuckle Under

Harper and Trout headed a list of heralded newcomers that also included rookies such as A's outfielder Yoenis Cespedes, Rangers righty Yu Darvish, D-backs lefty Wade Miley and Orioles third baseman Manny Machado. Yet it was 37-year-old knuckleballer R.A. Dickey of the Mets who captured the imagination of fans throughout baseball perhaps as much as any player.

Dickey, whose career appeared stalled until he experienced a control breakthrough in 2010, rushed from the gate with a fury, going 11-1, 2.00 through his first 14 starts. In early June, he pitched back-to-back one-hitters, the first pitcher to do so in the NL in 68 years and only the 11th pitcher since 1900 to allow one hit or fewer in consecutive complete games.

Along the way, Dickey went 44⅔ innings without allowing an earned run, and as a reward he made his first all-star team.

"This guys is just amazing with that pitch, just amazing," Mets manager Terry Collins said.

Dickey finished at 20-6, 2.73 and led the NL with 233⅔ innings, 230 strikeouts, five complete games and three shutouts. As if that weren't amazing enough, Dickey revealed after his final start that he had pitched much of the season with an abdominal tear that would require surgery.

The Batting Title That Wasn't

While Cabrera, Trout and others battled for the AL batting crown, the NL race took an unexpected, unprecedented turn. On Aug. 15, the commissioner's office announced that Giants left fielder Melky Cabrera had been suspended for 50 games for testing positive for high levels of synthetic testosterone, a banned substance under the game's drug program.

At the time of the suspension, Cabrera—named the MVP of the All-Star Game—led the majors with 159 hits and ranked second in the NL with a .346 average. The case reached a new level of sordidness when the New York Daily News reported that an associate of Cabrera set up a fake Web site, purportedly selling substances that the player claimed were responsible for his positive test. That plot was uncovered by an MLB investigation.

As Pirates center fielder Andrew McCutchen fell behind Cabrera in the batting race, many questioned whether MLB ought to allow a known PED user to win the batting title. At the time of his suspension, Cabrera had 501 plate appearances, one short of qualifying.

However, under official baseball rule 10.22 (a),

NATIONAL LEAGUE STANDINGS

EAST	W	L	PCT	GB	Manager	General Manager	Attendance	Average	Last Penn.
Washington Nationals	98	64	.605	—	Davey Johnson	Mike Rizzo	2,370,794	30,010	Never
*Atlanta Braves	94	68	.580	4	Fredi Gonzalez	Frank Wren	2,420,171	29,879	1999
Philadelphia Phillies	81	81	.500	17	Charlie Manuel	Ruben Amaro Jr.	3,565,718	44,021	2009
New York Mets	74	88	.457	24	Terry Collins	Sandy Alderson	2,242,803	28,035	2000
Miami Marlins	69	93	.426	29	Ozzie Guillen	Larry Beinfest	2,219,444	27,401	2003
CENTRAL	W	L	PCT	GB	Manager	General Manager	Attendance	Average	Last Penn.
Cincinnati Reds	97	65	.599	—	Dusty Baker	Walt Jocketty	2,347,251	28,978	1990
*St. Louis Cardinals	88	74	.543	9	Mike Matheny	John Mozeliak	3,262,109	40,273	2011
Milwaukee Brewers	83	79	.512	14	Ron Roenicke	Doug Melvin	2,831,385	34,955	^1982
Pittsburgh Pirates	79	83	.488	18	Clint Hurdle	Neal Huntington	2,091,918	26,149	1979
Chicago Cubs	61	101	.377	36	Dale Sveum	Jed Hoyer	2,882,756	35,590	1945
Houston Astros	55	107	.340	42	B. Mills/T. DeFrancesco	Jeff Luhnow	1,607,733	19,849	2005
WEST	W	L	PCT	GB	Manager	General Manager	Attendance	Average	Last Penn.
San Francisco Giants	94	68	.580	—	Bruce Bochy	Brian Sabean	3,377,371	41,696	2012
Los Angeles Dodgers	86	76	.531	8	Don Mattingly	Ned Colletti	3,324,246	41,040	1988
Arizona Diamondbacks	81	81	.500	13	Kirk Gibson	Kevin Towers	2,177,617	26,884	2001
San Diego Padres	76	86	.469	18	Bud Black	Josh Byrnes	2,123,721	26,219	1998
Colorado Rockies	64	98	.395	30	Jim Tracy	Dan O'Dowd	2,630,458	32,475	2007

*Wild card ^American League

PLAYOFFS—Wild Card: Cardinals defeated Braves 6-3 in one-game playoff. **Division Series:** Cardinals defeated Nationals 3-2 and Giants defeated Reds 3-2 in best-of-five series. **League Championship Series:** Giants defeated Cardinals 4-3 in best-of-seven series.

plate appearances can be added to a player's total until he has enough to qualify. If his batting average still holds up, he is declared the batting champ. Cabrera's average would have held at .346 even with an additional 0-for-1 on his ledger.

Much to the relief of MLB and many fans, Cabrera, in a savvy public relations move, filed a request with the Players Association and MLB that Rule 10.22 (a) not be applied to his average. That disqualified him from the batting race—but had MLB opened a Pandora's box by not applying an official rule in a uniform fashion?

"After giving this matter the consideration it deserves, I have decided that Major League Baseball will comply with Mr. Cabrera's request," Commissioner Bud Selig said in a press release. "I respect his gesture as a sign of his regret and his desire to move forward, and I believe that, under these circumstances, the outcome is appropriate."

"I know that changing the rules midseason can present problems," Cabrera said, "(but) I thank the Players Association and Major League Baseball for finding a way to grant my request."

As fate would have it, Giants catcher Buster Posey won the batting crown with a .336 average.

No-Hitters No Problem

Despite the quantity of individual offensive exploits in 2012, pitchers again provided the most quality. The overall major league batting average held steady at .255, even as 19.8 percent of all plate appearances resulted in a strikeout—an all-

Johan Santana tossed the first no-hitter in the 51-year history of the Mets on June 1

time high—and the cumulative on-base percentage (.319) reached its lowest point since 1988.

Pitchers established a new record with three perfect games in one season, and they tied a record with seven no-hitters in all. Over a remarkable 13-day period beginning on June 1, fans were treated to three no-hitters—and each was notewor-

NO LACK FOR NO-HITTERS

After witnessing three no-hitters in 2011 and six more in 2010 (counting Roy Halladay's playoff no-no), baseball fans were treated to a record-tying seven no-hitters in 2012. Among those no-nos were a record three perfect games [PG], thrown in chronological order by righthanders Philip Humber (White Sox), Matt Cain (Giants) and Felix Hernandez (Mariners).

Three of the season's no-hitters (including two perfect games) were thrown at Seattle's Safeco Field, and all were memorable— Humber's for its sheer unlikeliness, Kevin Millwood's for the fact that it featured six pitchers, and Hernandez's perfecto because he had so little margin for error in a 1-0 game.

In his June 13 masterpiece against the Astros, Cain tied Sandy Koufax for both most strikeouts (14) and highest Game Score (101, where 50 is about average) in a perfect game.

Pitcher, Team	Date	Opponent	Score	IP	H	R	ER	BB	SO	HBP	BF	Pitches	Game Score
Philip Humber, White Sox [PG]	April 21	@Mariners	4-0	9	0	0	0	0	9	0	27	96	96
Jered Weaver, Angels	May 2	Twins	9-0	9	0	0	0	1	9	0	29	121	95
* Johan Santana, Mets	June 1	Cardinals	8-0	9	0	0	0	5	8	0	32	134	90
** Kevin Millwood, Mariners	June 8	Dodgers	1-0	6	0	0	0	1	6	0	18	68	77
Matt Cain, Giants [PG]	June 13	Astros	10-0	9	0	0	0	0	14	0	27	125	101
Felix Hernandez, Mariners [PG]	Aug. 15	Rays	1-0	9	0	0	0	0	12	0	27	113	99
Homer Bailey, Reds	Sept. 28	@Pirates	1-0	9	0	0	0	1	10	0	28	115	96

* Santana threw the first no-hitter in the 51-year history of the Mets franchise.

** Millwood pitched the first six innings of the Mariners' six-pitcher no-hitter, leaving his start with a groin strain. Relievers Charlie Furbush ($^2/_3$ inning), Stephen Pryor ($^1/_3$), Lucas Luetge ($^1/_3$), Brandon League ($^2/_3$) and Tom Wilhelmsen (one) completed the final three innings.

ALL-ROOKIE TEAM 2012

Pos	PLAYER, TEAM	AGE	AB	AVG	OBP	SLG	2B	HR	RBI	SB	RUNDOWN
C	Wilin Rosario, Rockies	23	396	.270	.312	.530	19	28	71	4	Just missed 30 HR, but incredible power for rookie
1B	* Anthony Rizzo, Cubs	23	337	.285	.342	.463	15	15	48	3	Hit 38 homers between Triple-A Iowa and Chicago
2B	Donovan Solano, Marlins	24	285	.295	.342	.375	11	2	28	7	Minor league FA replaced Omar Infante post-trade
SS	Zack Cozart, Reds	27	561	.246	.288	.399	33	15	35	4	Reds love the glove, but on-base must improve
3B	Todd Frazier, Reds	26	422	.273	.331	.498	26	19	67	3	Secret weapon subbed for 3B Rolen, 1B Votto
CF	Mike Trout, Angels	21	559	.326	.399	.564	27	30	83	49	First 30-40 rookie led MLB in steals and runs (129)
OF	Yoenis Cespedes, Athletics	26	487	.292	.356	.505	25	23	82	16	Helped lead A's power surge; .909 second-half OPS
OF	* Bryce Harper, Nationals	19	533	.270	.340	.477	26	22	59	18	One of best-ever seasons by a teenager
DH	* Yonder Alonso, Padres	25	549	.273	.348	.393	39	9	62	3	More contact, power in tough park down stretch

Pos	PITCHER, TEAM	AGE	W	L	SV	ERA	IP	SO	BB	RUNDOWN
SP	* Wei-Yin Chen, Orioles	27	12	11	0	4.02	193	154	57	Stayed healthy, won Game Two of ALDS vs. Yankees
SP	Yu Darvish, Rangers	26	16	9	0	3.90	191	221	89	Second in MLB with 10.4 SO/9; 5-1, 2.35 in final 8 starts
SP	Mike Fiers, Brewers	27	9	10	0	3.74	128	135	36	Atypical journey culminates with strong rookie season
SP	* Wade Miley, D-backs	25	16	11	0	3.33	195	144	37	Led rookie starters in wins, innings, ERA and WHIP (1.18)
SP	Jarrod Parker, Athletics	23	13	8	0	3.47	181	140	63	Fronted all-rookie rotation for Athletics down stretch
RP	Ryan Cook, Athletics	25	6	2	14	2.09	73	80	27	Began Athletics career with 21 scoreless appearances
RP	* Robbie Ross, Rangers	23	6	0	0	2.22	65	47	23	Groundball-oriented southpaw held lefties to .613 OPS
CL	Kelvin Herrera, Royals	22	4	3	3	2.35	84	77	21	Led rookie relievers in innings, average velo (98.5 mph)

*Bats/throws lefthanded

thy in its own right beyond the fact that one team collected zero hits.

On June 1, Mets lefthander Johan Santana tossed a no-hitter against the potent Cardinals lineup, becoming the first pitcher in franchise history to throw a no-no and leaving the Padres as the only team without one.

Santana had missed the previous season following shoulder surgery, and Collins didn't want him to throw many more than 100 pitches. As it turned out, Santana required a career-high 134.

"I just couldn't take him out," said Collins, well aware of the club's no-hit history.

Santana benefited from a missed call. In the sixth inning, Cardinals right fielder Carlos Beltran scorched a liner that replays show hit the white chalk on the third-base line and should have been ruled fair, but umpire Adrian Johnson called it foul and Beltran then grounded out.

One week later, the Mariners used teamwork to throw a no-hitter against the Dodgers. Six pitchers combined to hold Los Angeles without a hit in a tense 1-0 victory at Seattle's Safeco Field. Starter Kevin Millwood departed after six innings with a slight groin injury, turning things over to Charlie Furbush (two outs), Stephen Pryor (one), Lucas Luetge (one), Brandon League (two) and Tom Wilhelmsen (three) to record the final nine outs.

The Mariners combined bid tied the major league record for the most pitchers used in a no-hitter, accomplished previously in 2003 by the Astros, and it was the 10th combined no-hitter in big league history.

On June 13, Giants righthander Matt Cain needed no help from his bullpen to make history. He pitched the first perfect game in franchise history, and as the Giants romped the hapless Astros 10-0. Cain struck out a career-high 14 batters as the sellout crowd of 42,298 at San Francisco's AT&T Park roared its approval.

Cain received a huge assist from right fielder Gregor Blanco, who raced deep in the gap in right-center in the seventh inning to haul in a drive from Jordan Schafer, making a diving grab before landing with a belly flop on the warning track.

"I still don't know how he caught that ball," Giants manager Bruce Bochy said after the game.

Cain, however, was not the first pitcher to throw a perfect game in 2012—though he was a much likelier candidate. On April 12, White Sox righthander Philip Humber turned the trick against the Mariners in Seattle.

"I don't know what my name is doing on that list," a humbled Humber said after the 4-0 victory. "It's an awesome feeling. People are telling me I've got to get this (uniform) for the Hall of Fame. I've been to the Hall of Fame, and to think something of mine is going to be theirs is pretty awesome."

A first-round pick by the Mets in 2004 who went to the Twins as part of a deal for Santana, Humber landed with the White Sox only after being waived by the A's and Royals.

A mild controversy surrounded the final out of Humber's perfecto. With the count 3-2 on Mariners shortstop Brendan Ryan, Humber fired a slider off the outside corner that sailed past catcher A.J. Pierzynski as Ryan tried to check his swing. Much to Ryan's dismay, umpire Brian Runge said he offered at the pitch and Pierzynski tracked down the ball and fired to first for the final out.

The perfect game did not launch Humber to a banner season. He lost his rotation spot in August and finished the season at 5-5, 6.44 in 26 games (16 starts).

The third perfecto of the season also took place at Seattle's Safeco Field but did not come from an unlikely source. Mariners righthander Felix Hernandez retired all 27 Rays hitters he faced on Aug. 15, accomplishing a feat that many considered inevitable one day.

Hernandez had no margin for error in the 1-0 white-knuckle victory against Tampa Bay. He struck out third baseman Sean Rodriguez looking to end the game before getting mobbed by his teammates. Hernandez's gem was the 23rd perfect game in major league history, yet the fifth since May 2010.

"I don't have any words to explain this," the 26-year-old Hernandez said after Mariners fans witnessed their third no-hit game of the season. "I realized in the third (inning). I was like, 'Wow, nobody on base.'

"When I came out for the ninth, I was a little nervous, but you gotta make your pitches."

Thus the Mariners became the first team in history to pitch a perfect game and have one pitched against them in the same season. But it was an all-too-familiar experience for Tampa Bay, which managed no hits in a game for the fifth time—one of those instances being a perfect game thrown by White Sox lefty Mark Buehrle in 2009.

Two other pitchers tossed no-hit games in 2012. Angels righthander Jered Weaver accomplished the feat on May 2 against the Twins, and Reds righty Homer Bailey turned the trick against the fading Pirates on Sept. 29, giving him the Reds' first no-hitter since Tom Browning's perfect game in 1988.

Mounting Casualty List

As far as the medical staffs of major league clubs were concerned, 2012 was the Year of the Injury. Many star-caliber players were lost for significant amounts of time, beginning in spring training when Cardinals righthander Chris Carpenter went down with a neck issue that sidelined him until the final week of the season.

Both of the 2011 runners-up for MVP endured injury-riddled follow-up campaigns. Dodgers center fielder Matt Kemp lost considerable time with hamstring issues and later injured a shoulder, while Red Sox center fielder Jacoby Ellsbury went down with a dislocated shoulder.

Rays third baseman Evan Longoria sat three

NATIONAL LEAGUE BEST TOOLS

A Baseball America survey of National League managers, conducted at midseason 2012, ranked players with the best tools.

BEST HITTER
1. Joey Votto, Reds
2. Andrew McCutchen, Pirates
3. Matt Kemp, Dodgers

BEST POWER
1. Giancarlo Stanton, Marlins
2. Ryan Braun, Brewers
3. Matt Kemp, Dodgers

BEST BUNTER
1. Juan Pierre, Phillies
2. Michael Bourn, Braves
3. Emilio Bonifacio, Marlins

BEST STRIKE-ZONE JUDGMENT
1. Joey Votto, Reds
2. David Wright, Mets
3. Todd Helton, Rockies

BEST HIT-AND-RUN ARTIST
1 (tie). Placido Polanco, Phillies
1 (tie). Martin Prado, Braves
3. Willie Bloomquist, Dbacks

BEST BASERUNNER
1. Michael Bourn, Braves
2. Emilio Bonifacio, Marlins
3. Shane Victorino, Phillies

FASTEST BASERUNNER
1. Michael Bourn, Braves
2. Dee Gordon, Dodgers
3. Tony Campana, Cubs

MOST EXCITING PLAYER
1. Andrew McCutchen, Pirates
2. Matt Kemp, Dodgers
3. Giancarlo Stanton, Marlins

BEST PITCHER
1. Clayton Kershaw, Dodgers
2. Matt Cain, Giants
3. Stephen Strasburg, Nationals

BEST FASTBALL
1. Aroldis Chapman, Reds
2. Craig Kimbrel, Braves
3. Stephen Strasburg, Nationals

BEST CURVEBALL
1. Clayton Kershaw, Dodgers
2. Gio Gonzalez, Nationals
3. Adam Wainwright, Cardinals

BEST SLIDER
1. Craig Kimbrel, Braves
2. Sergio Romo, Giants
3. Matt Cain, Giants

BEST CHANGEUP
1. Cole Hamels, Phillies
2. Johan Santana, Mets
3. Stephen Strasburg, Nationals

BEST CONTROL
1. Cliff Lee, Phillies
2. Roy Halladay, Phillies
3. Matt Cain, Giants

BEST PICKOFF MOVE
1. Mark Buehrle, Marlins
2. Chris Capuano, Dodgers
3. Clayton Richard, Padres

BEST RELIEVER
1. Craig Kimbrel, Braves
2. Aroldis Chapman, Reds
3. Joel Hanrahan, Pirates

BEST DEFENSIVE CATCHER
1. Yadier Molina, Cardinals
2. Carlos Ruiz, Phillies
3. Brian McCann, Braves

BEST DEFENSIVE 1B
1. Joey Votto, Reds
2. Adam LaRoche, Nationals
3. James Loney, Dodgers

BEST DEFENSIVE 2B
1. Brandon Phillips, Reds
2. Darwin Barney, Cubs
3. Danny Espinosa, Nationals

BEST DEFENSIVE 3B
1. Ryan Zimmerman, Nationals
2. David Wright, Mets
3. Chase Headley, Padres

BEST DEFENSIVE SS
1. Troy Tulowitzki, Rockies
2. Ian Desmond, Nationals
3. Jose Reyes, Marlins

BEST INFIELD ARM
1. Ian Desmond, Nationals
2 (tie). Rafael Furcal, Cardinals
2 (tie). Troy Tulowitzki, Rockies

BEST DEFENSIVE OF
1. Michael Bourn, Braves
2. Andrew McCutchen, Pirates
3. Drew Stubbs, Reds

BEST OUTFIELD ARM
1. Carlos Gonzalez, Rockies
2. Rick Ankiel, Nationals
3. Jay Bruce, Reds

BEST MANAGER
1. Bruce Bochy, Giants
2. Davey Johnson, Nationals
3. Clint Hurdle, Pirates

months with a hamstring injury. Rockies shortstop Troy Tulowitzki missed most of the second half with a groin tear that required surgery. As the season progressed, Phillies righthander Roy Halladay (strained lat) joined the ranks of the severely injured.

Yankees closer Mariano Rivera blew out a knee while shagging balls during BP in Kansas City on May 3. Lost for the remainder of the season, the 42-year-old vowed not to have his career end by injury.

"He's been (shagging) and no one ever said a word," Yankees manager Joe Girardi said. "That's part of who he is. You take that away from him and he may not be the same guy, the same pitcher."

One doesn't see many ACL tears in baseball, but the Brewers lost two starters to that injury on the same West Coast trip in early May. First baseman Mat Gamel went down chasing a foul pop and veteran shortstop Alex Gonzalez blew out his knee on a slide into second base.

Sputtering Start For Pujols

The Angels made the biggest offseason splash by signing 32-year-old free agent first baseman Albert Pujols away from the Cardinals with a 10-year, $240 million contract. While many wondered about the wisdom of such a long pact, no one expected Pujols to do a pratfall at the opening bell.

With the scrutiny and pressure growing day by day, Pujols went the entire month of April without a home run, a first for his storied career. He finally ended the national nightmare on May 6 by driving a pitch from Blue Jays rookie righthander Drew Hutchison out of the park in his 28th game and 111th at-bat.

Angels right fielder Torii Hunter arranged for an empty dugout to await Pujols after the homer, making light of the long wait. The crowd at Angel

Stadium roared for a curtain call, but Pujols, booed earlier in the game for striking out, declined.

"This game is about making adjustments and being patient," Pujols said after the game. "Every player, whether a position player or a pitcher, goes through it where sometimes you try to do too much."

It's only human to want to live up to a big contract, and Pujols pressed so hard to do so that he came out of his game for several weeks. He finished the season with career lows in terms of average (.285), on-base percentage (.343), slugging (.516), homers (30) and walks (52).

On the same day that Pujols finally hit his first homer, the Orioles won a 17-inning marathon against the Red Sox by a 9-6 score. Baltimore DH Chris Davis went 0-for-8 in that game, but he picked up the win after pitching two scoreless innings of relief when manager Buck Showalter ran out of pitchers. (The righty-throwing Davis sat 90-92 mph as a pitcher at Navarro (Texas) JC in 2005 and '06.)

The Red Sox also ran out of arms and turned to outfielder Darnell McDonald, who took the loss when he surrendered a three-run homer to Orioles center fielder Adam Jones in the 17th. It was the first time two position players ended a game on the mound since Oct. 4, 1925, when the Tigers' Ty Cobb and the St. Louis Browns' George Sisler closed out the second game of a doubleheader on the last day of the season.

CONTINUED ON PAGE 19

DRUG SUSPENSIONS

Major league players—or at least those who tested positive for a banned substance while on a 40-man roster—set a dubious distinction in 2012, racking up more suspensions for performance-enhancer use (seven) than in any season since 2007 (eight). What's more, the list of penalized players was the most prominent in the eight-year history of the drug-testing program.

Yasmani Grandal

Player	Pos	Team	Date	Suspension	Substance
Guillermo Mota	RHP	Giants	May 7	100 games*	clenbuterol
Freddy Galvis	2B	Phillies	June 19	50 games	clostebol metabolite
Marlon Byrd	CF	Free Agent	June 25	50 games	tamoxifen
Melky Cabrera	LF	Giants	Aug. 15	50 games	testosterone
Bartolo Colon	RHP	Athletics	Aug. 22	50 games	testosterone
Ryan Adams	2B	Orioles	Nov. 2	25 games	amphetamine
Yasmani Grandal	C	Padres	Nov. 7	50 games	testosterone

* Penalty for second career violation of baseball's joint drug prevention and treatment program

Three of the biggest names all tested positive for elevated levels of testosterone:

■ The Giants' Melky Cabrera won MVP honors at the All-Star Game and might have won the National League batting title (.346 through 459 at-bats) and picked up a second World Series ring had he not been busted.

■ Athletics righthander Bartolo Colon was in the midst Year Two of his career renaissance—the 39-year-old went 10-9, 3.43 in 24 starts—when he failed his test.

■ Padres switch-hitting rookie catcher Yasmani Grandal ranked as the No. 9 prospect in the Triple-A Pacific Coast League and turned in a successful half-season in San Diego, batting .297/.394/.469 with eight homers in 192 at-bats. He topped all first-year backstops (min. 200 plate appearances) in average, on-base, walk rate (13.7 percent) and strikeout rate (17.3).

LARRY GOREN

ORGANIZATION OF THE YEAR

Reds return to relevance

BY J.J. COOPER

Baseball's oldest professional club is finally relevant again.

The Reds' season ended earlier than they would have liked after the Giants rallied to win three do-or-die games in the National League Division Series, but that was only a dour ending to what was a sensational season in Cincinnati.

The Reds finished the season with a 97-65 record, second best in baseball. It was the team's most wins since the Big Red Machine won 102 games in 1976.

When the Reds beat San Francisco in Game One of their division series, it marked the club's first playoff win since 1990, when the team last won the World Series. After missing the playoffs for 14 consecutive years, Cincinnati now has made the cut in two of the past three years. And after signing first baseman Joey Votto and second baseman Brandon Phillips to contract extensions prior to the 2012 season, the club appears poised to return to the playoffs multiple times.

As a small-market team, Cincinnati has managed to turn itself into a consistent playoff threat without relying on free agency. Outfielder Ryan Ludwick was the only significant contributor to the 2012 club acquired on the free agent market, and he was signed to a bargain-basement $2 million one-year contract.

The Reds fielded three homegrown starting pitchers and six homegrown regular position players. Closer Aroldis Chapman, signed by the Reds out of Cuba, went 5-5, 1.51 with 38 saves

Joey Votto's knee injury didn't slow the Reds' run to 97 wins—most since 1976

ED WOLFSTEIN

and 122 strikeouts in 72 innings pitched.

The rest of the lineup and rotation was filled out by players the club had acquired in trades, including a December 2011 blockbuster that sent prospects Yonder Alonso, Yasmani Grandal and Brad Boxberger along with righthander Edinson Volquez to the Padres for righthander Mat Latos. Latos immediately stepped into the Reds' rotation as No. 2 starter.

Because of that emphasis on building a successful team through player development and scouting, the Reds are the Baseball America Organization of the Year for 2012.

"This city and the fan base here had been neglected for a while," Reds general manager Walt Jocketty said. "They hadn't had any winning teams. This is a great baseball city. They hadn't won here in a long time. Fans weren't sure what direction the organization was going. Now they see with the direction the ownership group and we are taking: We want to win and are built to win.

"Whenever we had a problem (in 2012) someone stepped in. Now there is a great feeling in the clubhouse that this is a team that can win and will continue to win."

PREVIOUS WINNERS	
2002	Minnesota Twins
2003	Florida Marlins
2004	Minnesota Twins
2005	Atlanta Braves
2006	Los Angeles Dodgers
2007	Colorado Rockies
2008	Tampa Bay Rays
2009	Philadelphia Phillies
2010	San Francisco Giants
2011	St. Louis Cardinals

Full list: BaseballAmerica.com/awards

CONTINUED FROM PAGE 17

No Day At The Beach

All the way across the country from Anaheim, an entire organization got off to a staggering start. The Marlins, finally in their long-awaited, retractable-roof ballpark, showed that honeymoons can end before the ink dries on the lease agreement.

Perhaps it was an omen when the Cardinals ruined the debut of Marlins Park by winning 4-1 in the season opener. But that was nothing compared to the firestorm created a few days later when new manager Ozzie Guillen made remarks sympathetic to Cuban dictator Fidel Castro, resulting in a five-game suspension for Guillen.

Protestors who formed outside of the new ballpark thought the suspension wasn't enough, calling for the firing of Guillen.

"I feel as though I have betrayed the Latino people," Guillen told reporters at a packed, nationally-televised news conference. "I'm very embarrassed, very sad and I'm very, very, very sorry."

Matters only got worse from there for the Marlins. Closer Heath Bell, signed to a three-year, $27 million deal as a free agent over the winter, blew one lead after another, forcing Guillen to demote him in the bullpen pecking order. Miami never got going and eventually began to retool the roster in July by trading Hanley Ramirez (and the $31.5 million owed him in 2013-14) to the Dodgers.

The Marlins continued to clear the deck in July, trading second baseman Omar Infante and right-hander Anibal Sanchez to the Tigers, first baseman Gaby Sanchez to the Pirates and righty reliever Edward Mujica to the Cardinals. Following the season, Miami swallowed $8 million to deal Bell to the D-backs as part of a three-team deal that returned only struggling high Class A shortstop Yordy Cabrera from the A's. In November, the Marlins sent shortstop Jose Reyes, lefthander Mark Buehrle, righthander Josh Johnson, center fielder Emilio Bonifacio and catcher John Buck to the Blue Jays for shortstop Yunel Escobar, righthander Henderson Alvarez, catcher Jeff Mathis and four prospects: outfielder Jake Marisnick, lefthander Justin Nicolino, shortstop Adeiny Hechavarria and righthander Anthony DeSclafani.

Instead of competing for the NL East crown, the Marlins sunk to last place, losing 93 games. Putting a bad product on the field tempered the enthusiasm of Miami fans, and the club ended up with a season attendance of 2.2 million, a huge jump from previous seasons but last among the 11 new ballparks to open since 2001.

DIAMOND IMAGES

Red Sox manager Bobby Valentine went one-and-done after a 93-loss season

"What went wrong?" Guillen said. "Everything. I've never seen a team lose in more different ways than the way we lost. Just name it and we did it. Bases loaded—nothing. No pitching, no catching, no managing.

"Maybe we learned from the experience it's not about 'new' and expectations. It's about how people perform on the field. We had to figure out the right people, the right players to perform on the field."

The search will continue in 2013 with new manager Mike Redmond after the Marlins fired Guillen in late October. He had three years and $7.5 million left on his contract.

Crying In Their Chowder

Up the Atlantic coast, another veteran team with a new manager and high expectations hit the skids almost from the start. Many worried that it would be oil and water with Bobby Valentine in Boston if the Red Sox struggled. Sure enough, they started 1-5.

With Valentine piloting the club and first-year GM Ben Cherington on board, optimists dreamed of the franchise's first playoff appearance since 2009. Instead, the team imploded and lost 93 games—the first 90-loss Red Sox team since 1966—costing Valentine his job.

CONTINUED ON PAGE 21

MAJOR LEAGUE *ALL-STARS*

ANDREW WOOLLEY

Ryan Braun hit a career-high 41 homers and repeated as NL leader in OPS (.987)

LARRY GOREN

David Price led the AL with 20 wins and a 2.56 ERA while striking out 8.7 per nine

FIRST TEAM

Pos.	Player, Team	AVG	OBP	SLG	AB	R	H	2B	3B	HR	RBI	BB	SO	SB	CS
C	Buster Posey, Giants	.336	.408	.549	530	78	178	39	1	24	103	69	96	1	1
1B	* Prince Fielder, Tigers	.313	.412	.528	581	83	182	33	1	30	108	85	84	1	0
2B	* Robinson Cano, Yankees	.313	.379	.550	627	105	196	48	1	33	94	61	96	3	2
3B	Miguel Cabrera, Tigers	.330	.393	.606	622	109	205	40	0	44	139	66	98	4	1
SS	Ian Desmond, Nationals	.292	.335	.511	513	72	150	33	2	25	73	30	113	21	6
CF	Mike Trout, Angels	.326	.399	.564	559	129	182	27	8	30	83	67	139	49	5
OF	Ryan Braun, Brewers	.319	.391	.595	598	108	191	36	3	41	112	63	128	30	7
OF	Andrew McCutchen, Pirates	.327	.400	.553	593	107	194	29	6	31	96	70	132	20	12
DH	Edwin Encarnacion, Blue Jays	.280	.384	.557	542	93	152	24	0	42	110	84	94	13	3

Pos.	Pitcher, Team	W	L	ERA	G	GS	SV	IP	H	R	ER	HR	BB	SO	WHIP
SP	R.A. Dickey, Mets	20	6	2.73	34	33	0	234	192	78	71	24	54	230	1.05
SP	* Gio Gonzalez, Nationals	21	8	2.89	32	32	0	199	149	69	64	9	76	207	1.13
SP	* Clayton Kershaw, Dodgers	14	9	2.53	33	33	0	228	170	70	64	16	63	229	1.02
SP	* David Price, Rays	20	5	2.56	31	31	0	211	173	63	60	16	59	205	1.10
SP	Justin Verlander, Tigers	17	8	2.64	33	33	0	238	192	81	70	19	60	239	1.06
RP	Craig Kimbrel, Braves	3	1	1.01	63	0	42	63	27	7	7	3	14	116	0.65

SECOND TEAM

Pos.	Player, Team	AVG	OBP	SLG	AB	R	H	2B	3B	HR	RBI	BB	SO	SB	CS
C	Yadier Molina, Cardinals	.315	.373	.501	505	65	159	28	0	22	76	45	55	12	3
1B	* Joey Votto, Reds	.337	.474	.567	374	59	126	44	0	14	56	94	85	5	3
2B	# Ben Zobrist, Rays	.270	.377	.471	560	88	151	39	7	20	74	97	103	14	9
3B	# Chase Headley, Padres	.286	.376	.498	604	95	173	31	2	31	115	86	157	17	6
SS	Derek Jeter, Yankees	.316	.362	.429	683	99	216	32	0	15	58	45	90	9	4
CF	* Josh Hamilton, Rangers	.285	.354	.577	562	103	160	31	2	43	128	60	162	7	4
OF	Giancarlo Stanton, Marlins	.290	.361	.608	449	75	130	30	1	37	86	46	143	6	2
OF	Josh Willingham, Twins	.260	.366	.524	519	85	135	30	1	35	110	76	141	3	2
DH	Adrian Beltre, Rangers	.321	.359	.561	604	95	194	33	2	36	102	36	82	1	0

Pos.	Pitcher, Team	W	L	ERA	G	GS	SV	IP	H	R	ER	HR	BB	SO	WHIP
SP	Johnny Cueto, Reds	19	9	2.78	33	33	0	217	205	73	67	15	49	170	1.17
SP	Zack Greinke, Brewers/Angels	15	5	3.48	34	34	0	212	200	84	82	18	54	200	1.20
SP	Felix Hernandez, Mariners	13	9	3.06	33	33	0	232	209	84	79	14	56	223	1.14
SP	* Chris Sale, White Sox	17	8	3.05	30	29	0	192	167	66	65	19	51	192	1.14
SP	Stephen Strasburg, Nationals	15	6	3.16	28	28	0	159	136	62	56	15	48	197	1.15
RP	Fernando Rodney, Rays	2	2	0.60	76	0	48	75	43	9	5	2	15	76	0.78

*Bats/throws lefthanded. #Switch-hitter.

EXECUTIVE OF THE YEAR

The chief architect of two World Series winners in the last three years, Giants general manager Brian Sabean mastered all player-procurement disciplines to build the 2012 champs.

San Francisco signed and developed the likes of Buster Posey, Pablo Sandoval, Matt Cain, Tim Lincecum, Madison Bumgarner and Sergio Romo. Sabean traded for Marco Scutaro and Hunter Pence during the 2012 season—after buying low on Angel Pagan and Melky Cabrera in the offseason—while pro scouting efforts yielded the likes of Ryan Vogelsong, Gregor Blanco and Santiago Casilla

Brian Sabean

PREVIOUS WINNERS

2002: Billy Beane, Athletics	**2007:** Jack Zduriencik, Brewers
2003: Brian Sabean, Giants	**2008:** Theo Epstein, Red Sox
2004: Terry Ryan, Twins	**2009:** Dan O'Dowd, Rockies
2005: Mark Shapiro, Indians	**2010:** Jon Daniels, Rangers
2006: Dave Drombowski, Tigers	**2011:** Doug Melvin, Brewers

Full list: BaseballAmerica.com/awards

MANAGER OF THE YEAR

Orioles manager Buck Showalter didn't have the most talented roster in the AL East at his disposal, yet he mixed and matched his way to a shocking 93 wins and a wild-card playoff berth, the franchise's first playoff appearance in 15 years. In winning 16 of 18 extra-inning games and 29 of 38 one-run contests, Baltimore pursued the division-champion Yankees to the final wekend.

Buck Showalter

The keys to the Orioles' success: a deep, talented bullpen; a power-oriented offense (only the Yankees hit more homers) and strong two-way players at catcher (Matt Wieters), shortstop (J.J. Hardy) and in center field (Adam Jones).

PREVIOUS WINNERS

2002: Mike Scioscia, Angels	**2007:** Terry Francona, Red Sox
2003: Jack McKeon, Marlins	**2008:** Ron Gardenhire, Twins
2004: Bobby Cox, Braves	**2009:** Mike Scioscia, Angels
2005: Ozzie Guillen, White Sox	**2010:** Bobby Cox, Braves
2006: Jim Leyland, Tigers	**2011:** Joe Maddon, Rays

Full list: BaseballAmerica.com/awards

CONTINUED FROM PAGE 19

Equally as shocking as Valentine's one-and-done tenure was management's decision to blow up the roster, beginning with the trade of team-icon third baseman Kevin Youkilis to the White Sox in June. The boldest move was yet to come, with Boston pulling off a blockbuster trade with the Dodgers that sent first baseman Adrian Gonzalez, righthander Josh Beckett, injured left fielder Carl Crawford and utilityman Nick Punto to Los Angeles while clearing more than $260 million off the books and yielding live-armed righthanders Rubby de la Rosa and Allen Webster plus three others.

Gonzalez and Crawford had been heralded additions in December 2010 but the former didn't meet expectations and the latter didn't stay healthy.

"As we look forward to this offseason, we felt like the opportunity to build what we need . . . required more of a bold move to give us an opportunity to really reshape the roster, reshape the team," said Cherington, whose roster also was devastated by serious injuries to key players.

"It was a difficult thing to do, to trade away four players like this."

The Red Sox selected Valentine's replacement in late October, hiring manager John Farrell away from the division-rival Blue Jays. Because Farrell, the Red Sox pitching coach from 2007-10, had a year remaining on his Toronto contract, the two sides agreed on a minor trade—shortstop Mike Aviles to the Blue Jays; reliever David Carpenter to the Red Sox—to settle the matter of compensation.

Gentlemen, Start Your Wallets

Beleaguered Dodgers owner Frank McCourt accomplished his goal of selling the franchise by Opening Day. That much was no surprise, though the purchase price of $2.15 billion far outstripped the total for any previous United States professional franchise.

Guggenheim Baseball Management placed the winning bid for the franchise plus the surrounding land and the parking lot of Dodger Stadium. The purchasing group was led by Mark Walter, controlling partner for global financial services firm

Guggenheim Partners, but also included longtime baseball executive Stan Kasten, who previously spearheaded the Braves and Nationals franchises, and former Los Angeles Lakers basketball star Magic Johnson.

Just like that, one of the founding franchises in the NL was reborn and re-energized, ending the disappointment and bitterness that marked the McCourt regime.

Selig spoke for Dodgers fans everywhere when he welcomed the new ownership group, in particular the involvement of Johnson.

"I believe that a man of Magic's remarkable stature and experience can play an integral role for one of the game's most historic franchises, in a city where he is revered," Selig said.

"The interest in this franchise and its historic sale price are profound illustrations of the great overall health of our industry."

The franchise had been thrown into financial turmoil by the divorce of McCourt and former wife Jamie, who had helped run the Dodgers. That ugliness had paralyzed the once-proud team, but the new owners promised to do whatever it took to restore Los Angeles to glory.

The group put its money where its mouth was by taking on hefty salary commitments and surrendering young talent to add a long list of veterans: shortstop Hanley Ramirez and lefty reliever Randy Choate from the Marlins, righty reliever Brandon League from the Mariners, outfielder Shane Victorino and righthander Joe Blanton from the Phillies and Adrian Gonzalez, Josh Beckett, Carl Crawford and Nick Punto from the Red Sox.

Despite the acquisitions, the Dodgers failed to make the playoffs, though they weren't eliminated from winning the second NL wild card until the penultimate day of the season.

Beat Goes On In Pittsburgh

When the Pirates made it through the 110th game of the season with a 62-46 record, the end of their unprecedented losing streak appeared near at hand. The Pirates had suffered 19 consecutive losing seasons—a record for North American team sports—and nobody in the organization wanted to make it an even 20.

No team that far over .500 at that stage of the season had finished with a losing record. The Pirates had been winning with a modest offense sparked by ultra-talented center fielder Andrew McCutchen and a strong pitching staff led by offseason acquisition A.J. Burnett. Pittsburgh remained in the hunt in the NL Central while also leading the wild-card race.

GEORGE GOJKOVICH

Despite Andrew McCutchen's exploits, the Pirates endured a 20th straight lost year

Then, as if the spigot had been turned off, the Pirates began to lose games at a worrisome pace. They slipped back toward .500, and whispers of yet another losing season created a self-fulfilling prophecy.

As Pittsburgh slipped from playoff contention, the focus shifted to finishing above .500—but they couldn't right the ship. The Pirates skidded to a 79-83 finish that doomed the franchise to a 20th consecutive losing season.

"I came out in the middle of the season and said we weren't going to have the same result, because we had better depth, better players, better leadership," general manager Neal Huntington said. "Yet we had the same slide.

"I wouldn't say it's been more concerning (than 2011). Losing is losing, and we're all tired of it."

Huntington attempted to fortify the Pirates roster before the trade deadline, picking up Astros lefty Wandy Rodriguez as well as reliever Chad Qualls, right fielder Travis Snider and first baseman Gaby Sanchez. Those moves proved to be insufficient to stave off a horrendous collapse, and Huntington was second-guessed for not doing more.

Yet another losing record cast a pall over the strides made on the club, particularly on the offensive side of things, where McCutchen turned in an

CONTINUED ON PAGE 24

NL routs AL for third straight

All-star MVP Melky Cabrera went 2-for-3 with a homer, two runs and two RBIs

KANSAS CITY

Sometimes, scoring only one run off Tigers ace Justin Verlander can be a chore. Imagine the surprise on the American League bench when the National League broke through for five first-inning runs against Verlander en route to an 8-0 romp at Kauffman Stadium.

The win marked the third consecutive victory for the NL, which had gone the previous 13 years without winning even one All-Star Game. The fact that it was over almost before it began made it all the more noteworthy.

After Brewers left fielder Ryan Braun put the NL on the board with an RBI double, Giants third baseman Pablo Sandoval struck the big blow with a bases-loaded triple. Afterward, Verlander made a somewhat stunning admission, saying he was more focused on the radar gun than making pitches.

"I know the fans don't want to see me throw 90 (mph) and try to hit the corners," he said. "They like to see the 100-mile-an-hour fastball."

Giants center fielder Melky Cabrera, who singled in the first inning ahead of Braun's double, later homered and earned game MVP honors. In August, he would be suspended for 50 games for testing positive for synthetic testosterone, a performance-enhancing substance.

In an unusual twist, Tony La Russa managed the NL, even though the long-time Cardinals skipper had retired after St. Louis won the 2011 World Series. With home-field advantage in the World Series at stake, La Russa took his job seriously, going all-out to win.

The game featured the appearances of rookie sensations Mike Trout of the Angels and Bryce Harper of the Nationals. But the feel-good moment came when Braves icon Chipper Jones, in his final All-Star Game appearance, came to the plate as a pinch-hitter in the sixth inning and dribbled a hit through the right side.

Jones broke into a wide grin as he reached first base, knowing he had been lucky rather than good.

"Forty years old and an infield hit in the All-Star Game," Jones later said with a laugh. "It's actually the way I scripted it."

ALL-STAR GAME

JULY 10, 2012

National League 8, American League 0

NATIONAL	AB	R	H	BI	AMERICAN	AB	R	H	BI
Gonzalez, C, dh	2	0	0	0	Jeter, ss	2	0	1	0
a-Holliday, ph-dh	1	1	1	1	1-Cabrera, A, ph-ss	1	0	0	0
c-Jones, C, ph-dh	1	0	1	0	Cano, 2b	2	0	1	0
e-Bourn, ph-dh	1	0	0	0	2-Kinsler, ph-2b	2	0	0	0
Cabrera, Me, cf	3	2	2	2	Hamilton, lf	2	0	0	0
McCutchen, A, cf	2	0	1	0	Trout, lf	1	0	1	0
Braun, lf	3	1	2	1	Bautista, rf	1	0	0	0
Bruce, rf	2	0	0	0	Trumbo, rf	2	0	0	0
Votto, 1b	3	0	0	0	Fielder, 1b	2	0	0	0
Freese, 1b	1	0	0	0	Konerko, 1b	0	0	0	0
LaHair, 1b	1	0	0	0	Mauer, 1b	1	0	1	0
Beltran, rf	1	1	0	0	Beltre, A, 3b	2	0	0	0
b-Harper, ph-lf	1	0	0	0	Cabrera, Mi, 3b	1	0	0	0
Posey, c	2	1	0	0	Andrus, 3b	1	0	0	0
Ruiz, c	1	0	0	0	Ortiz, dh	2	0	1	0
Sandoval, P, 3b	2	1	1	3	3-Butler, ph-dh	2	0	0	0
Wright, D, 3b	2	0	0	0	Napoli, c	2	0	1	0
Uggla, 2b	3	0	1	1	Wieters, c	2	0	0	0
Altuve, 2b	1	0	0	0	Granderson, cf	2	0	0	0
Furcal, ss	3	1	1	0	Jones, Ad, cf	1	0	0	0
d-Castro, S, ph-ss	1	0	0	0					
TOTAL	**37**	**8**	**10**	**8**		**31**	**0**	**6**	**0**

National	500	300	000—8
American	000	000	000—0

a-singled for Gonzalez, C in the 4th. b-walked for Beltran in the 5th. c-singled for Holliday in the 6th. d-flied out for Furcal in the 8th. e-struck out for Jones, C in the 8th. 1-walked for Jeter in the 5th. 2-flied out for Cano in the 5th. 3-grounded out for Ortiz in the 7th.

LOB—American 8, National 5. **2B**—Bruan (1). **3B**—Sandoval, P (1), Furcal (1), Braun (1). **HR**—Cabrera, Me (1). **SB**—Trout (1).

NATIONAL	IP	H	R	ER	BB	SO	AMERICAN	IP	H	R	ER	BB	SO
Cain (W)	2	1	0	0	0	1	Verlander (L)	1	4	5	5	2	2
Gonzalez, Gi	1	0	0	0	0	1	Nathan	1	0	0	0	0	0
Strasburg	1	1	0	0	1	0	Price	1	0	0	0	0	0
Kershaw	1	2	0	0	1	0	Harrison	1	4	3	3	0	0
Dickey	1	1	0	0	0	1	Weaver	1	0	0	0	1	0
Hamels	1	0	0	0	0	0	Sale	1	2	0	0	0	1
Kimbrel	⅔	0	0	0	0	2	Cook, R	1	0	0	0	0	2
Chapman	⅓	0	0	0	1	1	Johnson, Ji	1	0	0	0	0	1
Miley	⅓	1	0	0	0	0	Rodney	1	0	0	0	0	0
Hanrahan	⅓	0	0	0	0	1							
Papelbon	⅓	0	0	0	0	0							

T—2:59. **A**—40,933.

MVP-caliber season (.327/.400/.553, 31 homers, 20 steals) and 2008 first-round third baseman Pedro Alvarez slugged 30 homers.

Not-So-Fond Farewell

The 2012 season figured to be a transitional one for the Astros, with new owner Jim Crane and the team playing their last year in the NL Central before switching leagues in 2013 and joining the potent AL West. But much like the previous season, things quickly spiraled out of control for the undermanned club.

With the team headed for a second consecutive 100-loss season, Houston took an everything-must-go approach, leading to the trades of starting pitchers Rodriguez and J.A. Happ, closer Brett Myers, first baseman Carlos Lee and third baseman Chris Johnson. The trades made the Astros the youngest team in the majors, and they played like it, finishing with 107 defeats.

The Astros fired manager Brad Mills in mid-August, sending coaches Mike Barnett and Bobby Meacham out the door with him. Triple-A Oklahoma City manager Tony DeFrancesco stepped in as interim skipper—though he didn't last long. First-year Houston GM Jeff Luhnow hired Nationals third-base coach Bo Porter to manage the Astros before the 2012 season had even concluded.

"We really feel good about the players who are going to be part of this organization," Luhnow said. "At the big league level, we've accomplished a full year of evaluation. We've seen, as expected, some players take a step forward—like (righthander Lucas) Harrell, (second baseman Jose) Altuve, (third baseman Matt) Dominguez and (center fielder Justin) Maxwell—all players who are forcing themselves to be part of our future plan."

It seemed fitting that the Astros finished the season with a series in Chicago against the Cubs, the NL Central's other rebuilding team. Before that series was done, the Cubs joined Houston in the 100-loss club (61-101), the first at the Friendly Confines since 1966.

In their first year under new manager Dale Sveum, the Cubs used 53 players, a club record, including 20 rookies—the most for Chicago since 1974. Leading the charge of newcomers was highly regarded first baseman Anthony Rizzo, promoted at midseason amid much fanfare.

Change was the order of the day in Wrigley. Outfielders Marlon Byrd and Reed Johnson, catcher Geovany Soto, righthander Ryan Dempster and

ACTIVE LEADERS

Career leaders among players who played in a game in 2012. Batters require 3,000 plate appearances and pitchers 1,000 innings to qualify for percentage titles.

BATTERS			PITCHERS		
AVG	Albert Pujols	.325	ERA	Mariano Rivera	2.21
OBP	Todd Helton	.419	SO/9	Kerry Wood	10.32
SLG	Albert Pujols	.608	BB/9	Roy Halladay	1.86
OPS	Albert Pujols	1.022	HR/9	Mariano Rivera	0.48
R	Alex Rodriguez	1,898	W	Jamie Moyer	269
H	Derek Jeter	3,304	L	Jamie Moyer	209
2B	Todd Helton	570	SV	Mariano Rivera	608
3B	Carl Crawford	114	IP	Jamie Moyer	4,074
HR	Alex Rodriguez	647	SO	Jamie Moyer	2,441
RBI	Alex Rodriguez	1,950	BB	Jamie Moyer	1,155
BB	Jim Thome	1,747	AVG	Mariano Rivera	.210
SO	Jim Thome	2,548	G	Mariano Rivera	1,051
XBH	Alex Rodriguez	1,189	GS	Jamie Moyer	638
SB	Juan Pierre	591	HR	Jamie Moyer	522

lefty Paul Maholm got traded, and Kerry Wood retired in May. The Cubs dismissed hitting coach Rudy Jaramillo in June.

"We're going to do what we need to do to put ourselves in a position to be a contending team, year in and year out," first-year Cubs team president Theo Epstein said, "and that means no shortcuts and taking the long approach.

"When you acquire young players and trade for prospects, it's pretty obvious it's not a quick road, (but) I think it'll be a rewarding journey."

Phillies, Brewers Wave White Flag

The Phillies and Brewers, two teams expected to contend for the playoffs in the NL, foundered badly in the first half and appeared headed nowhere. Accordingly, both clubs looked to move veterans for young talent at the trade deadline.

The Phillies dealt two-thirds of their starting outfield, sending Hunter Pence to the Giants and Shane Victorino to the Dodgers. They decided to keep lefthander Cole Hamels, signing the ace lefty to a six-year, $144 million extension, the second-largest deal for a pitcher in history.

"I wanted to give the Phillies every opportunity," Hamels said. "It's very hard to leave a place you've had so many great memories and have been able to enjoy so much good, and you know there's so much more good to come."

The Brewers tried to lure their ace righthander Zack Greinke into staying, offering him more than $100 million, but when he made it clear he wanted to explore the free agent market, Milwaukee dealt him to the Angels for three prospects, including shortstop Jean Segura.

"It was a tough one because I'm very fond of

Zack, not only as a player but as a person," Brewers GM Doug Melvin said. "He's one of my favorite players I've ever been associated with. That makes it a little tougher. We had to make a decision and turn the page."

Oddly enough, the Phillies and Brewers both started playing better after making those trades. Each club jumped into the chase for the second wild-card berth in the NL before falling short. Milwaukee salvaged a winning season (83-79) but Philly could do no better than break even at 81-81.

Braun Under The Microscope

The season began on a controversial note for Brewers left fielder Ryan Braun, the reigning NL MVP. Word leaked over the winter that he had failed a drug test administered during the 2011 playoffs, testing positive for elevated testosterone. The supposedly confidential process played out publicly, and Braun eventually got the failed test overthrown on appeal to avoid a 50-game suspension at the season's outset.

The commissioner's office issued a statement vehemently disagreeing with the decision of arbitrator Shyam Das, who ruled the collection process had been compromised by an undocumented chain of custody. MLB later fired Das, though Braun resolutely maintained his innocence.

That development put Braun in the position of having to produce or else have people question the validity of his MVP performance. With fans booing him roundly on the road, Braun responded to that pressure and adversity by putting together another elite performance.

Braun led the NL with 41 home runs—a career high—108 runs scored, a .987 OPS and 356 total bases while batting .319/.391/.595 with 112 RBIs in 598 at-bats.

"I knew from the beginning it was going to be challenging, and certainly it was," Braun said. "But for the most part I feel like I handled everything well. I feel like I was able to keep my composure, compete every day and ultimately contribute to a lot of our success as a team, and that's something I'm proud of."

Santo, Larkin Elected To Hall

It was an emotional day in Cooperstown during Hall of Fame induction ceremonies when the late Ron Santo's widow Vicki gave an acceptance speech that left tears in the eyes of most in attendance.

"Words cannot express my sorrow that Ron Santo didn't live to see this day, that he's not here to give this speech," she said of the long-time Cubs

Former Reds shortstop Barry Larkin gained entry to the Hall of Fame on his third ballot

third baseman, who passed away on Dec. 3, 2010. The Hall of Fame Veterans Committee finally inducted Santo a year later.

"This is not a sad day, not at all. This is a very happy day. It's an incredible day for an incredible man, a man who lived an extraordinary life to its fullest. Indeed, he had a wonderful life."

Santo spent five decades with the Cubs organization, first as a player and later as a revered broadcaster, refusing to let his Type 1 diabetes define him as a person. The nine-time all-star hit .277/.362/.464 with 342 home runs and 1,331 RBIs while serving as the preeminent third baseman in the NL during the 1960s.

Former Reds shortstop Barry Larkin, who played his entire 19-year career with Cincinnati, also found it impossible to rein in his emotions while giving his acceptance speech.

In his third year on the ballot, Larkin was the lone player elected by the Baseball Writers Association of America. The 1995 NL MVP batted .295/.371/.444 for his career and served as one of the game's top power-speed threats with 198 home runs and 379 stolen bases. He made 12 all-star teams and won nine Silver Slugger awards in the 13 seasons from 1988 to 2000.

Larkin's Reds pulled off one of the great World Series upsets in history, sweeping the heavily-favored A's in 1990.

ARIZONA DIAMONDBACKS

A.J. Pollock	April 18
Pat Corbin	April 30
Trevor Bauer	June 28
Ryan Wheeler	July 20
Jake Elmore	Aug. 11
Tyler Skaggs	Aug. 22
Adam Eaton	Sept. 4
Tyler Graham	Sept. 7

ATLANTA BRAVES

Tyler Pastornicky	April 7
Andrelton Simmons	June 2
Luis Avilan	July 14

BALTIMORE ORIOLES

Ryan Flaherty	April 7
Wei-Yin Chen	April 10
Luis Exposito	May 4
Stuart Pomeranz	May 7
Xavier Avery	May 13
Miguel Gonzalez	May 29
Joe Mahoney	July 7
Miguel Socolovich	July 14
Steve Johnson	July 15
Manny Machado	Aug. 9
Dylan Bundy	Sept. 23
L.J. Hoes	Sept. 25

BOSTON RED SOX

Che-Hsuan Lin	April 14
Will Middlebrooks	May 2
Mauro Gomez	May 13

CHICAGO CUBS

Lendy Castillo	April 10
Adrian Cardenas	May 7
Blake Parker	May 17
Blake Lalli	May 18
Jeff Beliveau	July 22
Alberto Cabrera	Aug. 1
Brett Jackson	Aug. 5
Josh Vitters	Aug. 5
Brooks Raley	Aug. 7
Chris Rusin	Aug. 21
Jaye Chapman	Sept. 4

CHICAGO WHITE SOX

Nate Jones	April 8
Jose Quintana	May 7
Jordan Danks	June 7
Leyson Septimo	June 29
Brian Omogrosso	July 3
Pedro Hernandez	July 18
Deunte Heath	Sept. 1

CINCINNATI REDS

J.J. Hoover	April 25
Mike Costanzo	May 13
Kris Negron	June 7
Todd Redmond	Aug. 18
Henry Rodriguez	Sept. 2
Denis Phipps	Sept. 3
Didi Gregorius	Sept. 5
Pedro Villarreal	Sept. 5
Tony Cingrani	Sept. 9

CLEVELAND INDIANS

Juan Diaz	May 25
Scott Barnes	May 30
Cody Allen	July 20
Thomas Neal	Sept. 2

COLORADO ROCKIES

Christian Friedrich	May 9
Edwar Cabrera	June 27
Josh Rutledge	July 13
Matt McBride	Aug. 4
Will Harris	Aug. 13
Rob Scahill	Sept. 11
Rafael Ortega	Sept. 30

DETROIT TIGERS

Drew Smyly	April 12
Thad Weber	April 22
Luke Putkonen	April 29
Quintin Berry	May 23
Casey Crosby	June 1
Bryan Holaday	June 6
Jose Ortega	June 8
Hernan Perez	June 9
Darin Downs	July 3
Avisail Garcia	Aug. 31

HOUSTON ASTROS

Marwin Gonzalez	April 6
Rhiner Cruz	April 7
Dallas Keuchel	June 17
Mickey Storey	Aug. 3
Brandon Barnes	Aug. 7

KANSAS CITY ROYALS

Irving Falu	May 6
Will Smith	May 23
Clint Robinson	June 8
Ryan Verdugo	July 17
David Lough	Sept. 1
Jake Odorizzi	Sept. 23

LOS ANGELES ANGELS

David Carpenter	April 13
Kole Calhoun	May 22
Jean Segura	July 24
Steve Geltz	Aug. 16
Nick Maronde	Sept. 2
Drew Taylor	Sept. 27

LOS ANGELES DODGERS

Scott Van Slyke	May 9
Elian Herrera	May 15
Ivan De Jesus Jr.	May 20
Alex Castellanos	May 31
Shawn Tolleson	June 7
Stephen Fife	July 17
Josh Wall	July 22
Paco Rodriguez	Sept. 9

MIAMI MARLINS

Dan Jennings	April 30
Kevin Mattison	May 12
Donovan Solano	May 21
Rob Brantly	Aug. 14
A.J. Ramos	Sept. 4
Tom Koehler	Sept. 5

MILWAUKEE BREWERS

Norichika Aoki	April 6
Wily Peralta	April 22
Tyler Thornburg	June 19
Jeff Bianchi	July 13
Jim Henderson	July 26

MINNESOTA TWINS

Brian Dozier	May 7
Cole De Vries	May 24
Tyler Robertson	June 26
Chris Herrmann	Sept. 16

NEW YORK METS

Kirk Nieuwenhuis	April 7
Jeremy Hefner	April 23
Jordany Valdespin	April 23
Zach Lutz	April 24
Robert Carson	May 18
Elvin Ramirez	June 3
Josh Edgin	July 13
Matt Harvey	July 26
Collin McHugh	Aug. 23
Jeurys Familia	Sept. 4

NEW YORK YANKEES

David Phelps	April 8
D.J. Mitchell	May 1
Adam Warren	June 29

Melky Mesa	Sept. 22

OAKLAND ATHLETICS

Yoenis Cespedes	March 28
Pedro Figueroa	April 21
Sean Doolittle	June 5
Derek Norris	June 21
A.J. Griffin	June 24
Dan Straily	Aug. 3

PHILADELPHIA PHILLIES

Freddy Galvis	April 5
Jake Diekman	May 15
B.J. Rosenberg	June 9
Phillippe Aumont	Aug. 23
Tyler Cloyd	Aug. 29
Steven Lerud	Aug. 30
Darin Ruf	Sept. 14
Tyson Brummett	Oct. 3

PITTSBURGH PIRATES

Matt Hague	April 7
Gorkys Hernandez	May 21
Jordy Mercer	May 29
Starling Marte	July 26
Kyle McPherson	Aug. 20
Justin Wilson	Aug. 20
Brock Holt	Sept. 1
Bryan Morris	Sept. 14

ST. LOUIS CARDINALS

Erik Komatsu	April 6
Matt Adams	May 20
Chuckie Fick	May 26
Sam Freeman	June 1
Joe Kelly	June 10
Barret Browning	June 30
Trevor Rosenthal	July 18
Ryan Jackson	Aug. 11
Shelby Miller	Sept. 5

SAN DIEGO PADRES

Joe Wieland	April 14
Miles Mikolas	May 5
Yasmani Grandal	June 2
Brad Boxberger	June 10
Nick Vincent	June 26
Eddy Rodriguez	Aug. 2
Cory Burns	Aug. 4
Tommy Layne	Aug. 14
Andrew Werner	Aug. 22

Casey Kelly	Aug. 27
Ali Solis	Sept. 16

SAN FRANCISCO GIANTS

Dan Otero	April 7
Charlie Culberson	May 13
Francisco Peguero	Aug. 25
Jean Machi	Sept. 3

SEATTLE MARINERS

Munenori Kawasaki	April 7
Lucas Luetge	April 7
Erasmo Ramirez	April 9
Hisashi Iwakuma	April 20
Stephen Pryor	June 2
Carter Capps	Aug. 3
Luis Jimenez	Sept. 4
Carlos Triunfel	Sept. 7

TAMPA BAY RAYS

Stephen Vogt	April 6
Chris Archer	June 20

TEXAS RANGERS

Robbie Ross	April 8
Yu Darvish	April 9
Tanner Scheppers	June 7
Justin Grimm	June 16
Martin Perez	June 27
Mike Olt	Aug. 2
Jurickson Profar	Sept. 2
Wilmer Font	Sept. 18

TORONTO BLUE JAYS

Evan Crawford	April 15
Drew Hutchison	April 21
Yan Gomes	May 17
Sam Dyson	July 5
Aaron Loup	July 14
Anthony Gose	July 17
Moises Sierra	July 31
Adeiny Hechavarria	Aug. 4
Chad Jenkins	Aug. 7

WASHINGTON NATIONALS

Bryce Harper	April 28
Tyler Moore	April 29
Sandy Leon	May 14
Jhonatan Solano	May 29
Eury Perez	Sept. 1
Christian Garcia	Sept. 4

Bryce Harper

ED WOLFSTEIN

CLUB BATTING

	AVG	G	AB	R	H	2B	3B	HR	RBI	BB	SO	SB	CS	OBP	SLG
Los Angeles	.274	162	5536	767	1518	273	22	187	732	449	1113	134	33	.332	.433
Texas	.273	162	5590	808	1526	303	32	200	780	478	1103	91	44	.334	.446
Detroit	.268	162	5476	726	1467	279	39	163	698	511	1103	59	23	.335	.422
Kansas City	.265	162	5636	676	1492	295	37	131	643	404	1032	132	38	.317	.400
New York	.265	162	5524	804	1462	280	13	245	774	565	1176	93	27	.337	.453
Boston	.260	162	5604	734	1459	339	16	165	695	428	1197	97	31	.315	.415
Minnesota	.260	162	5562	701	1448	270	30	131	667	505	1069	135	37	.325	.390
Chicago	.255	162	5518	748	1409	228	29	211	726	461	1203	109	43	.318	.422
Cleveland	.251	162	5525	667	1385	266	24	136	635	555	1087	110	44	.324	.381
Baltimore	.247	162	5560	712	1375	270	16	214	677	480	1315	58	29	.311	.417
Toronto	.245	162	5487	716	1346	247	22	198	677	473	1251	123	41	.309	.407
Tampa Bay	.240	162	5398	697	1293	250	30	175	665	571	1323	134	44	.317	.394
Oakland	.238	162	5527	713	1315	267	32	195	676	550	1387	122	32	.310	.404
Seattle	.234	162	5494	619	1285	241	27	149	584	466	1259	104	35	.296	.369

CLUB PITCHING

	ERA	G	CG	SHO	SV	IP	H	R	ER	HR	BB	SO	AVG
Tampa Bay	3.19	162	7	15	50	1460	1233	577	518	139	469	1383	.228
Oakland	3.48	162	1	13	47	1470	1360	614	569	147	462	1136	.245
Detroit	3.75	162	9	8	40	1431	1409	670	596	151	438	1318	.256
Seattle	3.76	162	8	11	43	1457	1359	651	608	166	449	1166	.248
New York	3.85	162	6	9	51	1445	1401	668	618	190	431	1318	.253
Baltimore	3.90	162	1	10	55	1483	1433	705	642	184	481	1177	.252
Texas	3.99	162	7	10	43	1442	1378	707	639	175	446	1286	.250
Chicago	4.02	162	6	11	37	1446	1365	676	646	186	503	1246	.250
Los Angeles	4.02	162	6	16	38	1433	1339	699	640	186	483	1157	.246
Kansas City	4.30	162	2	12	44	1451	1504	746	693	163	542	1177	.270
Toronto	4.64	162	5	11	29	1444	1439	784	745	204	574	1142	.261
Boston	4.70	162	6	4	35	1443	1449	806	754	190	529	1176	.262
Minnesota	4.77	162	3	6	35	1439	1536	832	762	198	465	943	.274
Cleveland	4.78	162	2	6	43	1442	1503	845	766	174	543	1086	.268

CLUB FIELDING

	PCT	PO	A	E	DP			PCT	PO	A	E	DP
Chicago	.988	4337	1578	70	154		Baltimore	.983	4449	1680	106	151
Seattle	.988	4370	1570	72	155		Boston	.983	4329	1687	101	159
New York	.987	4336	1471	74	135		Detroit	.983	4292	1481	99	127
Texas	.986	4326	1496	85	136		Minnesota	.983	4316	1785	107	188
Cleveland	.984	4326	1665	96	157		Oakland	.982	4410	1568	111	135
Los Angeles	.984	4300	1578	98	141		Kansas City	.981	4354	1624	113	171
Toronto	.984	4331	1737	101	167		Tampa Bay	.981	4379	1641	114	155

INDIVIDUAL BATTING LEADERS (MINIMUM 2.7 PA/TEAM GAME)

	AVG	G	AB	R	H	2B	3B	HR	RBI	BB	SO	SB
Miguel Cabrera, Detroit	.330	161	622	109	205	40	0	44	139	66	98	4
Mike Trout, Los Angeles	.326	139	559	129	182	27	8	30	83	67	139	49
Adrian Beltre, Texas	.321	156	604	95	194	33	2	36	102	36	82	1
Joe Mauer, Minnesota	.319	147	545	81	174	31	4	10	85	90	88	8
Derek Jeter, New York	.316	159	683	99	216	32	0	15	58	45	90	9
Prince Fielder, Detroit	.313	162	581	83	182	33	1	30	108	85	84	1
Torii Hunter, Los Angeles	.313	140	534	81	167	24	1	16	92	38	133	9
Billy Butler, Kansas City	.313	161	614	72	192	32	1	29	107	54	111	2
Robinson Cano, New York	.313	161	627	105	196	48	1	33	94	61	96	3
David Murphy, Texas	.304	147	457	65	139	29	3	15	61	54	74	10

INDIVIDUAL PITCHING LEADERS (MINIMUM 0.8 IP/TEAM GAME)

	W	L	ERA	G	GS	CG	SHO	SV	IP	H	R	ER	BB	SO
David Price, Tampa Bay	20	5	2.56	31	31	2	1	0	211	173	63	16	59	205
Justin Verlander, Detroit	17	8	2.64	33	33	6	1	0	238	192	81	19	60	239
Jered Weaver, Los Angeles	20	5	2.81	30	30	3	2	0	189	147	63	20	45	142
Chris Sale, Chicago	17	8	3.05	30	29	1	0	0	192	167	66	19	51	192
Felix Hernandez, Seattle	13	9	3.06	33	33	5	5	0	232	209	84	14	56	223
Jeremy Hellickson, T.B.	10	11	3.10	31	31	0	0	0	177	163	68	25	59	124
Matt Harrison, Texas	18	11	3.29	32	32	4	2	0	213	210	82	22	59	133
Hiroki Kuroda, New York	16	11	3.32	33	33	3	2	0	220	205	86	25	51	167
Jake Peavy, Chicago	11	12	3.37	32	32	4	1	0	219	191	88	27	49	194
C.C. Sabathia, New York	15	6	3.38	28	28	2	0	0	200	184	89	22	44	197

AWARD WINNERS

Selected by Baseball Writers Association of America

MOST VALUABLE PLAYER

Player	1st	2nd	3rd	Total
Miguel Cabrera, Detroit	22	6	—	362
Mike Trout, Los Angeles	6	21	1	281
Adrian Beltre, Texas	—	1	16	210
Robinson Cano, New York	—	—	6	149
Josh Hamilton, Texas	—	—	—	127
Adam Jones, Baltimore	—	—	1	120
Derek Jeter, New York	—	—	2	77
Justin Verlander, Detroit	—	—	—	58
Prince Fielder, Detroit	—	—	—	56
Yoenis Cespedes, Oakland	—	—	—	41
Edwin Encarnacion, Toronto	—	—	—	33
David Price, Tampa Bay	—	—	1	26
Fernando Rodney, Tampa Bay	—	—	—	24
Jim Johnson, Baltimore	—	—	1	22
Alex Rios, Chicago	—	—	—	17
Josh Reddick, Oakland	—	—	—	14
Albert Pujols, Los Angeles	—	—	—	8
Ben Zobrist, Tampa Bay	—	—	—	7
Joe Mauer, Minnesota	—	—	—	6
Rafael Soriano, New York	—	—	—	5
Matt Wieters, Baltimore	—	—	—	4
Felix Hernandez, Seattle	—	—	—	2
Jered Weaver, Los Angeles	—	—	—	2
Raul Ibanez, New York	—	—	—	1

CY YOUNG AWARD

Pitcher	1st	2nd	3rd	Total
David Price, Tampa Bay	14	13	1	153
Justin Verlander, Detroit	13	13	2	149
Jered Weaver, Los Angeles	—	2	14	70
Felix Hernandez, Seattle	—	5	41	
Fernando Rodney, Tampa Bay	1	—	5	38
Chris Sale, Chicago	—	—	1	17
Jim Johnson, Baltimore	—	—	—	5
Matt Harrison, Texas	—	—	—	2
Yu Darvish, Texas	—	—	—	1

ROOKIE OF THE YEAR

Player	1st	2nd	3rd	Total
Mike Trout, Los Angeles	28	—	—	140
Yoenis Cespedes, Oakland	—	19	6	63
Yu Darvish, Texas	—	9	19	46
Wei-Yin Chen, Baltimore	—	—	2	2
Jarrod Parker, Oakland	—	—	1	1

MANAGER OF THE YEAR

Manager	1st	2nd	3rd	Total
Bob Melvin, Oakland	16	12	—	116
Buck Showalter, Baltimore	12	16	—	108
Robin Ventura, Chicago	—	—	12	12
Joe Maddon, Tampa Bay	—	—	7	7
Joe Girardi, New York	—	—	5	5
Jim Leyland, Detroit	—	—	2	2
Ron Washington, Texas	—	—	2	2

GOLD GLOVE WINNERS

Selected by AL managers

C—Matt Wieters, Baltimore. 1B—Mark Teixeira, New York. 2B—Robinson Cano, New York. 3B—Adrian Belte, Texas. SS—J.J. Hardy, Baltimore. LF—Alex Gordon, Kansas City. CF—Adam Jones, Baltimore. RF—Josh Reddick, Oakland. P—Jeremy Hellickson, Rays; and Jake Peavy, Chicago (tie).

SILVER SLUGGER AWARDS

Selected by AL managers, coaches

C—A.J. Pierzynski, Chicago. 1B—Prince Fielder, Detroit. 2B—Robinson Cano, New York. 3B—Miguel Cabrera, Detroit. SS—Derek Jeter, New York. OF—Josh Hamilton, Texas; Mike Trout, Los Angeles; and Josh Willingham, Minnesota. DH—Billy Butler, Kansas City.

DEPARTMENT LEADERS

BATTING

GAMES
Prince Fielder, Detroit	162
Adam Jones, Baltimore	162
Ichiro Suzuki, Sea/N.Y.	162
4 players	161

AT-BATS
Derek Jeter, New York	683
J.J. Hardy, Baltimore	663
Ian Kinsler, Texas	655
Adam Jones, Baltimore	648
Alex Gordon, Kansas City	642

PLATE APPEARANCES
Derek Jeter, New York	740
Ian Kinsler, Texas	731
Alex Gordon, Kansas City	721
J.J. Hardy, Baltimore	713
Elvis Andrus, Texas	711

RUNS
Mike Trout, Los Angeles	129
Miguel Cabrera, Detroit	109
Robinson Cano, New York	105
Ian Kinsler, Texas	105
Josh Hamilton, Texas	103
Austin Jackson, Detroit	103
Adam Jones, Baltimore	103

HITS
Derek Jeter, New York	216
Miguel Cabrera, Detroit	205
Robinson Cano, New York	196
Adrian Beltre, Texas	194
Billy Butler, Kansas City	192

TOTAL BASES
Miguel Cabrera, Detroit	377
Robinson Cano, New York	345
Adrian Beltre, Texas	339
Adam Jones, Baltimore	327
Josh Hamilton, Texas	324

DOUBLES
Alex Gordon, Kansas City	51
Albert Pujols, Los Angeles	50
Robinson Cano, New York	48
Nelson Cruz, Texas	45
Shin-Soo Choo, Cleveland	43

TRIPLES
Austin Jackson, Detroit	10
Elvis Andrus, Texas	9
Alex Rios, Chicago	8
Mike Trout, Los Angeles	8
Jemile Weeks, Oakland	8

EXTRA-BASE HITS
Miguel Cabrera, Detroit	84
Robinson Cano, New York	82
Albert Pujols, Los Angeles	80
Josh Hamilton, Texas	76
Adam Jones, Baltimore	74

HOME RUNS
Miguel Cabrera, Detroit	44
Curtis Granderson, New York	43
Josh Hamilton, Texas	43
Edwin Encarnacion, Toronto	42
Adam Dunn, Chicago	41

RUNS BATTED IN
Miguel Cabrera, Detroit	139
Josh Hamilton, Texas	128
Edwin Encarnacion, Toronto	110
Josh Willingham, Minnesota	110
Prince Fielder, Detroit	108

Robinson Cano

SACRIFICES
Elvis Andrus, Texas	17
Bobby Wilson, Los Angeles	13
Jayson Nix, New York	9
Jemile Weeks, Oakland	9
6 players	8

SACRIFICE FLIES
Mark Teixeira, New York	12
Justin Morneau, Minnesota	10
Adrian Beltre, Texas	9
Josh Hamilton, Texas	9
3 players	8

HIT BY PITCH
Prince Fielder, Detroit	17
Kevin Youkilis, Bos., Chi.	17

Shin-Soo Choo, Cleveland	14
Josh Willingham, Minnesota	14
2 players	13

WALKS
Adam Dunn, Chicago	105
Ben Zobrist, Tampa Bay	97
Carlos Santana, Cleveland	91
Joe Mauer, Minnesota	90
Carlos Pena, Tampa Bay	87

STOLEN BASES
Mike Trout, Los Angeles	49
Rajai Davis, Toronto	46
Ben Revere, Minnesota	40
Coco Crisp, Oakland	39
Alcides Escobar, Kansas City	35

CAUGHT STEALING
Rajai Davis, Toronto	13
Alejandro De Aza, Chicago	12
Elvis Andrus, Texas	10
5 players	9

STOLEN-BASE PERCENTAGE
Quintin Berry, Detroit	100%
Alexi Casilla, Minnesota	95.5%
Desmond Jennings, T.B.	93.9%
Mike Trout, Los Angeles	90.7%
Coco Crisp, Oakland	90.7%

STRIKEOUTS
Adam Dunn, Chicago	222
Curtis Granderson, New York	195
Carlos Pena, Tampa Bay	182
Chris Davis, Baltimore	169
B.J. Upton, Tampa Bay	169

TOUGHEST TO STRIKE OUT
(AT-BATS PER STRIKEOUT)
Ichiro Suzuki, Sea/N.Y.	10.31
Michael Brantley, Cleveland	9.86
Ben Revere, Minnesota	9.46
Dustin Pedroia, Boston	9.38
Michael Young, Texas	8.73

GROUNDED INTO DOUBLE PLAYS
Miguel Cabrera, Detroit	28
Howie Kendrick, Los Angeles	26
Michael Young, Texas	26
Derek Jeter, New York	24
Joe Mauer, Minnesota	23

MULTI-HIT GAMES
Miguel Cabrera, Detroit	64
Derek Jeter, New York	64
Robinson Cano, New York	60
Alex Gordon, Kansas City	60
3 players	56

ON-BASE PERCENTAGE
Joe Mauer, Minnesota	.416
Prince Fielder, Detroit	.412
Mike Trout, Los Angeles	.399
Miguel Cabrera, Detroit	.393
Edwin Encarnacion, Toronto	.384

SLUGGING PERCENTAGE
Miguel Cabrera, Detroit	.606
Josh Hamilton, Texas	.577
Mike Trout, Los Angeles	.564
Adrian Beltre, Texas	.561
Edwin Encarnacion, Toronto	.557

ON-BASE-PLUS-SLUGGING
Miguel Cabrera, Detroit	.999
Mike Trout, Los Angeles	.963
Edwin Encarnacion, Toronto	.941
Prince Fielder, Detroit	.940
Josh Hamilton, Texas	.930

LOWEST AVERAGE
Carlos Pena, Tampa Bay	.197
Adam Dunn, Chicago	.204
Justin Smoak, Seattle	.217
Jemile Weeks, Oakland	.221
Mark Reynolds, Baltimore	.221

PITCHING

WINS
David Price, Tampa Bay	20
Jered Weaver, Los Angeles	20
Matt Harrison, Texas	18
Chris Sale, Chicago	17
Justin Verlander, Detroit	17

Josh Hamilton

ED WOLFSTEIN

ANDREW WOOLLEY

LOSSES

Ubaldo Jimenez, Cleveland	17
Luke Hochevar, Kansas City	16
Justin Masterson, Cleveland	15
Henderson Alvarez, Toronto	14
Bruce Chen, Kansas City	14
Jon Lester, Boston	14
Rickey Romero, Toronto	14

GAMES

Boone Logan, New York	80
Kelvin Herrera, Kansas City	76
Joel Peralta, Tampa Bay	76
Fernando Rodney, Tampa Bay	76
Grant Balfour, Oakland	75

GAMES STARTED

Bruce Chen, Kansas City	34
Justin Masterson, Cleveland	34
C.J. Wilson, Los Angeles	34
6 players	33

GAMES FINISHED

Jose Valverde, Detroit	67
Fernando Rodney, Tampa Bay	65
Jim Johnson, Baltimore	63
Joe Nathan, Texas	62
Alfredo Aceves, Boston	55

COMPLETE GAMES

Justin Verlander, Detroit	6
Felix Hernandez, Seattle	5
Matt Harrison, Texas	4
Jake Peavy, Chicago	4
5 players	3

SHUTOUTS

Felix Hernandez, Seattle	5
Brandon Morrow, Toronto	3
Hiroki Kuroda, New York	2
Matt Harrison, Texas	2
James Shields, Tampa Bay	2
Jered Weaver, Los Angeles	2

SAVES

Jim Johnson, Baltimore	51
Fernando Rodney, Tampa Bay	48
Rafael Soriano, New York	42
Chris Perez, Cleveland	39
Joe Nathan, Texas	37

INNINGS PITCHED

Justin Verlander, Detroit	238.1
Felix Hernandez, Seattle	232
James Shields, Tampa Bay	227.2
Hiroki Kuroda, New York	219.2

Justin Verlander

DIAMOND IMAGES

Jake Peavy, Chicago	219

HITS ALLOWED

Rick Porcello, Detroit	226
Henderson Alvarez, Toronto	216
Jon Lester, Boston	216
Bruce Chen, Kansas City	215
Justin Masterson, Cleveland	212

RUNS ALLOWED

Luke Hochevar, Kansas City	127
Justin Masterson, Cleveland	122
Ricky Romero, Toronto	122
Jon Lester, Boston	117
Ubaldo Jimenez, Cleveland	116

HOME RUNS ALLOWED

Ervin Santana, Los Angeles	39
Phil Hughes, New York	35
Jason Vargas, Seattle	35
Bruce Chen, Kansas City	33
Derek Holland, Texas	32
Tommy Hunter, Baltimore	32

WALKS

Ricky Romero, Toronto	105

Ubaldo Jimenez, Cleveland	95
C.J. Wilson, Los Angeles	91
Yu Darvish, Texas	89
Justin Masterson, Cleveland	88

WALKS PER NINE INNINGS

Scott Diamond, Minnesota	1.61
Tommy Milone, Oakland	1.71
Dan Haren, Los Angeles	1.94
C.C. Sabathia, New York	1.98
Jake Peavy, Chicago	2.01

HIT BATTERS

Gavin Floyd, Chicago	14
Luke Hochevar, Kansas City	13
Justin Masterson, Cleveland	13
Clay Buchholz, Boston	12
Felix Hernandez, Seattle	12

STRIKEOUTS

Justin Verlander, Detroit	239
Max Scherzer, Detroit	231
Felix Hernandez, Seattle	223
James Shields, Tampa Bay	223
Yu Darvish, Texas	221

STRIKEOUTS PER NINE INNINGS

Max Scherzer, Detroit	11.08
Yu Darvish, Texas	10.40
Justin Verlander, Detroit	9.03
Chris Sale, Chicago	9.00
Matt Moore, Tampa Bay	8.88

STRIKEOUTS PER NINE INNINGS (RELIEVERS)

Steve Delabar, Sea/Tor	12.55
Greg Holland, Kansas City	12.22
David Robertson, New York	12.02
Tim Collins, Kansas City	12.01
Joel Peralta, Tampa Bay	11.28

DOUBLE PLAYS

Henderson Alvarez, Toronto	30
Clay Buchholz, Boston	27
Matt Harrison, Texas	27
Jon Lester, Boston	27
2 players	26

PICKOFFS

Ricky Romero, Toronto	8
Travis Blackley, Oakland	7
Tommy Milone, Oakland	6
Chris Sale, Chicago	6
2 players	5

WILD PITCHES

Ubaldo Jimenez, Cleveland	16
Justin Masterson, Cleveland	14
Felix Hernandez, Seattle	13
Hiroki Kuroda, New York	13
Francisco Liriano, Minn., Chi.	11

WALKS-PLUS-HITS PER INNING

Jered Weaver, Los Angeles	1.02
Justin Verlander, Detroit	1.06
Jake Peavy, Chicago	1.10
David Price, Tampa Bay	1.10
Chris Sale, Chicago	1.14

OPPONENT AVERAGE

Jered Weaver, Los Angeles	.214
Justin Verlander, Detroit	.217
Yu Darvish, Texas	.220
David Price, Tampa Bay	.226
Jake Peavy, Chicago	.234

WORST ERA

Ricky Romero, Toronto	5.77
Luke Hochevar, Kansas City	5.73
Ubaldo Jimenez, Cleveland	5.40
Ervin Santana, Los Angeles	5.16
Bruce Chen, Kansas City	5.07

FIELDING

PITCHER

PCT	Six players tied at	1.000
PO	Clay Buchholz, Boston	29
A	Henderson Alvarez, Toronto	35
E	Aaron Cook, Boston	5
	Rick Porcello, Detroit	5
	James Shields, Tampa Bay	5
DP	Sam Deduno, Minnesota	5

CATCHER

PCT	Jose Molina, Tampa Bay	.994
PO	Matt Wieters, Baltimore	994
A	A.J. Pierzynski, Chicago	71
E	Matt Wieters, Baltimore	10
DP	Jose Molina, Tampa Bay	8
	A.J. Pierzynski, Chicago	8
PB	Alex Avila, Detroit	10
	Carlos Santana, Cleveland	10

FIRST BASE

PCT	Mark Teixeira, New York	.999
PO	Prince Fielder, Detroit	1,256
A	Casey Kotchman, Cleveland	108
E	Prince Fielder, Detroit	11
DP	Eric Hosmer, Kansas City	132

SECOND BASE

PCT	Dustin Pedroia, Boston	.992
PO	Robinson Cano, New York	285
A	Jason Kipnis, Cleveland	440
E	Ian Kinsler, Texas	18
DP	Gordon Beckham, Chicago	110

THIRD BASE

PCT	Adrian Beltre, Texas	.974
PO	Miguel Cabrera, Detroit	127
	Mike Moustakas, Kansas City	127
A	Mike Moustakas, Kansas City	312

E	Brett Lawrie, Toronto	17
	Trevor Plouffe, Minnesota	17
DP	Mike Moustakas, Kansas City	41

SHORTSTOP

PCT	J.J. Hardy, Baltimore	.992
PO	J.J. Hardy, Baltimore	244
A	J.J. Hardy, Baltimore	529
E	Asdrubal Cabrera, Cleveland	19
	Alcides Escobar, Kansas City	19
DP	J.J. Hardy, Baltimore	113

OUTFIELD

PCT	Four players tied at	1.000
PO	Adam Jones, Baltimore	439
A	Jeff Francoeur, Kansas City	19
E	Rajai Davis, Toronto	8
	Adam Jones, Baltimore	8
DP	Torii Hunter, Los Angeles	5

MAJOR LEAGUES

CLUB BATTING

	AVG	G	AB	R	H	2B	3B	HR	RBI	BB	SO	SB	CS	OBP	SLG
Colorado	.274	162	5577	758	1526	306	52	166	716	450	1213	100	40	.330	.436
St. Louis	.271	162	5622	765	1526	290	37	159	732	533	1192	91	37	.338	.421
San Francisco	.269	162	5558	718	1495	287	57	103	675	483	1097	118	39	.327	.397
Washington	.261	162	5615	731	1468	301	25	194	688	479	1325	105	35	.322	.428
Arizona	.259	162	5462	734	1416	307	33	165	710	539	1266	93	51	.328	.418
Milwaukee	.259	162	5557	776	1442	300	39	202	741	466	1240	158	39	.325	.437
Philadelphia	.255	162	5544	684	1414	271	28	158	659	454	1094	116	23	.317	.400
Los Angeles	.252	162	5438	637	1369	269	23	116	607	481	1156	104	44	.317	.374
Cincinnati	.251	162	5477	669	1377	296	30	172	636	481	1266	87	27	.315	.411
New York	.249	162	5450	650	1357	286	21	139	625	503	1250	79	38	.316	.386
Atlanta	.247	162	5425	700	1341	263	30	149	660	567	1289	101	32	.320	.389
San Diego	.247	162	5422	651	1339	272	43	121	610	539	1238	155	46	.319	.380
Miami	.244	162	5437	609	1327	261	39	137	576	484	1228	149	41	.308	.382
Pittsburgh	.243	162	5412	651	1313	241	37	170	620	444	1354	73	52	.304	.395
Chicago	.240	162	5411	613	1297	265	36	137	570	447	1235	94	45	.302	.378
Houston	.236	162	5407	583	1276	238	28	146	545	463	1365	105	46	.302	.371

CLUB PITCHING

	ERA	G	CG	SHO	SV	IP	H	R	ER	HR	BB	SO	AVG
Washington	3.33	162	3	9	51	1468	1296	594	543	129	497	1325	.237
Cincinnati	3.34	162	9	12	56	1453	1356	588	540	152	427	1248	.247
Los Angeles	3.34	162	2	10	40	1450	1277	597	538	122	539	1276	.238
Atlanta	3.42	162	5	16	47	1445	1310	600	549	145	464	1232	.243
San Francisco	3.68	162	5	14	53	1451	1361	649	593	142	489	1237	.248
St. Louis	3.71	162	4	10	42	1463	1420	648	603	134	436	1218	.255
Philadelphia	3.83	162	5	11	42	1451	1387	680	618	178	409	1385	.251
Pittsburgh	3.86	162	2	10	45	1433	1357	674	615	153	490	1192	.249
Arizona	3.93	162	4	9	39	1434	1432	688	626	155	417	1200	.261
San Diego	4.01	162	4	11	43	1435	1356	710	640	162	539	1205	.248
Miami	4.09	162	5	7	38	1441	1448	724	655	133	495	1113	.263
New York	4.09	162	7	13	36	1434	1368	709	651	161	488	1240	.251
Milwaukee	4.22	162	0	9	44	1454	1458	733	682	169	525	1402	.261
Chicago	4.51	162	1	9	28	1414	1399	759	708	175	573	1128	.259
Houston	4.56	162	3	11	31	1423	1493	794	721	173	540	1170	.270
Colorado	5.22	162	0	7	36	1422	1637	890	824	198	566	1144	.290

CLUB FIELDING

	PCT	PO	A	E	DP		PCT	PO	A	E	DP
Atlanta	.986	4336	1654	86	147	Philadelphia	.983	4354	1560	101	118
Arizona	.985	4301	1676	90	146	St. Louis	.983	4388	1754	107	149
Cincinnati	.985	4359	1602	89	113	Chicago	.982	4241	1583	105	148
Washington	.985	4405	1632	94	134	Pittsburgh	.982	4300	1656	112	126
Los Angeles	.984	4349	1669	98	138	Houston	.981	4270	1729	118	132
Miami	.983	4322	1649	103	154	San Francisco	.981	4353	1639	115	134
Milwaukee	.983	4361	1532	99	133	Colorado	.980	4266	1718	122	139
New York	.983	4302	1502	101	135	San Diego	.980	4304	1655	121	97

INDIVIDUAL BATTING LEADERS (MINIMUM 2.7 PA/TEAM GAME)

	AVG	G	AB	R	H	2B	3B	HR	RBI	BB	SO	SB
Buster Posey, San Francisco	.336	148	530	78	178	39	1	24	103	69	96	1
Andrew McCutchen, Pittsburgh	.327	157	593	107	194	29	6	31	96	70	132	20
Ryan Braun, Milwaukee	.319	154	598	108	191	36	3	41	112	63	128	30
Yadier Molina, St. Louis	.315	138	505	65	159	28	0	22	76	45	55	12
Jordan Pacheco, Colorado	.309	132	475	51	147	32	3	5	54	22	61	7
Allen Craig, St. Louis	.307	119	469	76	144	35	0	22	92	37	89	2
Marco Scutaro, Colorado/S.F.	.306	156	620	87	190	32	4	7	74	40	49	9
David Wright, New York	.306	156	581	91	178	41	2	21	93	81	112	15
John Jay, St. Louis	.305	117	443	70	135	22	4	4	40	34	71	19
Carlos Gonzalez, Colorado	.303	135	518	89	157	31	5	22	85	56	115	20

INDIVIDUAL PITCHING LEADERS (MINIMUM 0.8 IP/TEAM GAME)

	W	L	ERA	G	GS	CG	SHO	SV	IP	H	R	ER	BB	SO
Clayton Kershaw, L.A.	14	9	2.53	33	33	2	2	0	228	170	70	64	63	229
R.A. Dickey, New York	20	6	2.73	34	33	5	3	0	234	192	78	24	54	230
Johnny Cueto, Cincinnati	19	9	2.78	33	33	2	0	0	217	205	73	15	49	170
Matt Cain, San Francisco	16	5	2.79	32	32	2	2	0	219	177	73	21	51	193
Kyle Lohse, St. Louis	16	3	2.86	33	33	0	0	0	211	192	74	19	38	143
Gio Gonzalez, Washington	21	8	2.89	32	32	2	1	0	199	149	69	9	76	207
Jordan Zimmermann, Wash.	12	8	2.94	32	32	0	0	0	196	186	69	18	43	153
Cole Hamels, Philadelphia	17	6	3.05	31	31	2	0	0	215	190	80	24	52	216
Cliff Lee, Philadelphia	6	9	3.16	30	30	0	0	0	211	207	79	26	28	207
Wade Miley, Arizona	16	11	3.33	32	29	0	0	0	195	193	79	14	37	144

AWARD WINNERS

Selected by Baseball Writers Association of America

MOST VALUABLE PLAYER

Player	1st	2nd	3rd	Total
Buster Posey, San Francisco	27	4	1	422
Ryan Braun, Milwaukee	3	15	10	285
Andrew McCutchen, Pittsburgh	—	6	13	245
Yadier Molina, St. Louis	2	6	8	241
Chase Headley, San Diego	—	—	—	127
David Wright, New York	—	—	—	86
Adam LaRoche, Washington	—	—	—	86
Craig Kimbrel, Atlanta	—	1	—	73
Aramis Ramirez, Milwaukee	—	—	—	47
Jay Bruce, Cincinnati	—	—	—	46
Matt Holliday, St. Louis	—	—	—	34
Aroldis Chapman, Cincinnati	—	—	—	20
Brandon Phillips, Cincinnati	—	—	—	18
Joey Votto, Cincinnati	—	—	—	16
R.A. Dickey, New York	—	—	—	16
Clayton Kershaw, Los Angeles	—	—	—	15
Ian Desmond, Washington	—	—	—	15
Michael Bourn, Washington	—	—	—	12
Allen Craig, St. Louis	—	—	—	10
Gio Gonzalez, Washington	—	—	—	8
Alfonso Soriano, Chicago	—	—	—	8
Kris Medlen, Atlanta	—	—	—	8
Martin Prado, Atlanta	—	—	—	8
Ryan Zimmerman, Washington	—	—	—	7
Giancarlo Stanton, Miami	—	—	—	7
Carlos Beltran, St. Louis	—	—	—	6
Aaron Hill, Arizona	—	—	—	6
Carlos Ruiz, Philadelphia	—	—	—	4
Jason Heyward, Atlanta	—	—	—	4
Johnny Cueto, Cincinnati	—	—	—	2
Bryce Harper, Washington	—	—	—	2
Chipper Jones, Atlanta	—	—	—	1
Miguel Montero, Arizona	—	—	—	1
Angel Pagan, San Francisco	—	—	—	1
Hunter Pence, San Francisco	—	—	—	1

CY YOUNG AWARD

Pitcher	1st	2nd	3rd	Total
R.A. Dickey, New York	27	5		209
Clayton Kershaw, Los Angeles	2	11	10	96
Gio Gonzalez, Washington	1	12	6	93
Johnny Cueto, Cincinnati	1	4	10	75
Craig Kimbrel, Atlanta	1	—	5	41
Matt Cain, San Francisco	—	—	1	22
Kyle Lohse, St. Louis	—	—	—	6
Aroldis Chapman, Cincinnati	—	—	1	1
Cole Hamels, Philadelphia	—	—	1	1

ROOKIE OF THE YEAR

Player	1st	2nd	3rd	Total
Bryce Harper, Washington	16	8	8	112
Wade Miley, Arizona	12	13	6	105
Todd Frazier, Cincinnati	3	7	9	45
Wilin Rosario, Colorado	1	2	1	12
Norichika Aoki, Milwaukee	—	2	5	11
Yonder Alonso, San Diego	—	—	1	1
Matt Carpenter, St. Louis	—	—	1	1
Jordan Pacheco, Colorado	—	—	1	1

MANAGER OF THE YEAR

Manager	1st	2nd	3rd	Total
Davey Johnson, Washington	23	4	4	131
Dusty Baker, Cincinnati	5	14	10	77
Bruce Bochy, San Francisco	4	10	11	61
Fredi Gonzalez, Atlanta	—	4	5	17
Bud Black, San Diego	—	—	1	1
Mike Matheny, St. Louis	—	—	1	1

GOLD GLOVE WINNERS
Selected by NL managers

C—Yadier Molina, St. Louis. 1B—Andy LaRoche, Washington. 2B—Darwin Barney, Chicago. 3B—Chase Headley, San Diego. SS—Jimmy Rollins, Philadelphia. LF—Carlos Gonzalez, Colorado. CF—Andrew McCutchen, Pittsburgh. RF—Jason Heyward, Atlanta. P—Mark Buehrle, Miami.

SILVER SLUGGER AWARDS
Selected by NL managers, coaches

C—Buster Posey, San Francisco. 1B—Adam LaRoche, Washington. 2B—Aaron Hill, Arizona. 3B—Chase Headley, San Diego. SS—Ian Desmond, Washington. OF—Ryan Braun, Milwaukee; Jay Bruce, Cincinnati; and Andrew McCutchen, Pittsburgh. P—Stephen Strasburg, Washington.

BATTING

GAMES
Starlin Castro, Chicago	162
Chase Headley, San Diego	161
Danny Espinosa, Washington	160
Hunter Pence, Phi./S.F.	160
Jose Reyes, Miami	160

AT-BATS
Starlin Castro, Chicago	646
Jose Reyes, Miami	642
Jimmy Rollins, Philadelphia	632
Michael Bourn, Atlanta	624
Marco Scutaro, Colo/S.F.	620

PLATE APPEARANCES
Jose Reyes, Miami	716
Michael Bourn, Atlanta	703
Chase Headley, San Diego	699
Jimmy Rollins, Philadelphia	699
Starlin Castro, Chicago	691

RUNS
Ryan Braun, Milwaukee	108
Andrew McCutchen, Pitt.	107
Justin Upton, Arizona	107
Jimmy Rollins, Philadelphia	102
Bryce Harper, Washington	98

HITS
Andrew McCutchen, Pitt.	194
Ryan Braun, Milwaukee	191
Marco Scutaro, Colo/S.F.	190
Martin Prado, Atlanta	186
Aaron Hill, Arizona	184
Jose Reyes, Miami	184

TOTAL BASES
Ryan Braun, Milwaukee	356
Andrew McCutchen, Pitt.	328
Aaron Hill, Arizona	318
Aramis Ramirez, Milwaukee	308
Chase Headley, San Diego	301

DOUBLES
Aramis Ramirez, Milwaukee	50
Aaron Hill, Arizona	44
Joey Votto, Cincinnati	44
Paul Goldschmidt, Arizona	43
Martin Prado, Atlanta	42

TRIPLES
Angel Pagan, San Francisco	15
Starlin Castro, Chicago	12
Jose Reyes, Miami	12
Dexter Fowler, Colorado	11
Michael Bourn, Atlanta	10
Melky Cabrera, San Francisco	10
Tyler Colvin, Colorado	10

EXTRA-BASE HITS
Ryan Braun, Milwaukee	80
Aramis Ramirez, Milwaukee	80
Aaron Hill, Arizona	76
Jay Bruce, Cincinnati	74
Corey Hart, Milwaukee	69
Adam LaRoche, Washington	69

HOME RUNS
Ryan Braun, Milwaukee	41
Giancarlo Stanton, Miami	37
Jay Bruce, Cincinnati	34
Adam LaRoche, Washington	33
Carlos Beltran, St. Louis	32
Ike Davis, New York	32
Alfonso Soriano, Chicago	32

Buster Posey

RUNS BATTED IN
Chase Headley, San Diego	115
Ryan Braun, Milwaukee	112
Alfonso Soriano, Chicago	108
Aramis Ramirez, Milwaukee	105
Hunter Pence, Phi./S.F.	104

SACRIFICES
Johnny Cueto, Cincinnati	17
Juan Pierre, Philadelphia	17
Clayton Kershaw, L.A.	14
Chris Capuano, Los Angeles	13
Kyle Lohse, St. Louis	12

SACRIFICE FLIES
Freddie Freeman, Atlanta	9
Paul Goldschmidt, Arizona	9
Adam LaRoche, Washington	9
Buster Posey, San Francisco	9
Martin Prado, Atlanta	9
Marco Scutaro, San Francisco	9

HIT BY PITCH
Carlos Quentin, San Diego	17
Carlos Ruiz, Philadelphia	16
Jon Jay, St. Louis	15
3 players	13

WALKS
Dan Uggla, Atlanta	94
Joey Votto, Cincinnati	94
Chase Headley, San Diego	86
David Wright, New York	81
Matt Holliday, St. Louis	75

STOLEN BASES
Everth Cabrera, San Diego	44
Michael Bourn, Atlanta	42
Jose Reyes, Miami	40
Shane Victorino, Phi./L.A.	39
Carlos Gomez, Milwaukee	37
Juan Pierre, Philadelphia	37

CAUGHT STEALING
Michael Bourn, Atlanta	13
Starlin Castro, Chicago	13
Andrew McCutchen, Pitt.	12
Jose Tabata, Pittsburgh	12
2 players	11

STOLEN-BASE PERCENTAGE
Everth Cabrera, San Diego	91.7%
Emilio Bonifacio, New York	90.9%
Tony Campana, Chicago	90.9%
Shane Victorino, Phi./L.A.	86.7%
Carlos Gomez, Milwaukee	86%

STRIKEOUT
Danny Espinosa, Washington	189
Pedro Alvarez, Pittsburgh	180
Rickie Weeks, Milwaukee	169
Dan Uggla, Atlanta	168
Drew Stubbs, Cincinnati	166

TOUGHEST TO STRIKE OUT
(AT-BATS PER STRIKEOUT)
Marco Scutaro, Colo/S.F.	12.65
Jose Reyes, Miami	11.46
Carlos Lee, Hou/Mia	11.22
Norichika Aoki, Milwaukee	9.45
Darwin Barney, Chicago	9.45

GROUNDED INTO DOUBLE PLAYS
Ryan Zimmerman, Washington	20
David Freese, St. Louis	19
Brandon Phillips, Cincinnati	19
Buster Posey, San Francisco	19
Martin Prado, Atlanta	19

MULTI-HIT GAMES
Martin Prado, Atlanta	60
Ryan Braun, Milwaukee	56
Marco Scutaro, Colo/S.F.	56
Matt Holliday, St. Louis	55
Andrew McCutchen, Pitt.	53

ON-BASE PERCENTAGE
Joey Votto, Cincinnati	.474
Buster Posey, San Francisco	.408
Andrew McCutchen, Pitt.	.400
Ryan Braun, Milwaukee	.391
David Wright, New York	.391

SLUGGING PERCENTAGE
Giancarlo Stanton, Miami	.608
Ryan Braun, Milwaukee	.595
Andrew McCutchen, Pitt.	.553
Buster Posey, San Francisco	.549
Aramis Ramirez, Milwaukee	.540

ON-BASE-PLUS-SLUGGING
Ryan Braun, Milwaukee	.987
Buster Posey, San Francisco	.957
Andrew McCutchen, Pitt.	.953
Aramis Ramirez, Milwaukee	.901
David Wright, New York	.883

LOWEST AVERAGE
Drew Stubbs, Cincinnati	.213
Dan Uggla, Atlanta	.220
Ike Davis, New York	.227
Rickie Weeks, Milwaukee	.230
Cameron Maybin, San Diego	.243

PITCHING

WINS
Gio Gonzalez, Washington	21

Giancarlo Stanton

DEPARTMENT LEADERS

R.A. Dickey

TOMASSO DeROSA

R.A. Dickey, New York	20
Johnny Cueto, Cincinnati	19
Lance Lynn, St. Louis	18
Cole Hamels, Philadelphia	17

LOSSES

Tim Lincecum, San Francisco	15
Erik Bedard, Pittsburgh	14
Josh Johnson, Miami	14
Clayton Richard, San Diego	14
9 players	13

GAMES

Matt Belisle, Colorado	80
Shawn Camp, Chicago	80
Randy Choate, Mia/L.A.	80
Mitchell Boggs, St. Louis	78
Francisco Rodriguez, Mil.	78

GAMES STARTED

12 players	33

GAMES FINISHED

Jonathan Papelbon, Phil.	64
Jason Motte, St. Louis	58
Joel Hanrahan, Pittsburgh	57
Craig Kimbrel, Atlanta	56
John Axford, Milwaukee	54

COMPLETE GAMES

R.A. Dickey, New York	5
Ricky Nolasco, Miami	3
Adam Wainwright, St. Louis	3
13 players	2

SHUTOUTS

R.A. Dickey, New York	3
Matt Cain, San Francisco	2
Cole Hamels, Philadelphia	2
Clayton Kershaw, L.A.	2
Ricky Nolasco, Miami	2
Johan Santana, New York	2
Adam Wainwright, St. Louis	2

SAVES

Craig Kimbrel, Atlanta	42
Jason Motte, St. Louis	42
Aroldis Chapman, Cincinnati	38
Jonathan Papelbon, Phil.	38
Joel Hanrahan, Pittsburgh	36

INNINGS PITCHED

R.A. Dickey, New York	233.2
Clayton Kershaw, L.A.	227.2
Matt Cain, San Francisco	219.1
Clayton Richard, San Diego	218.2

Johnny Cueto, Cincinnati	217

HITS ALLOWED

Clayton Richard, San Diego	228
Ian Kennedy, Arizona	216
Ricky Nolasco, Miami	214
Bronson Arroyo, Cincinnati	209
Joe Blanton, Phi./L.A.	207
Cliff Lee, Philadelphia	207

RUNS ALLOWED

Tim Lincecum, San Francisco	111
Clayton Richard, San Diego	110
Joe Blanton, Phi./L.A.	106
Ian Kennedy, Arizona	101
Ricky Nolasco, Miami	100

HOME RUNS ALLOWED

Clayton Richard, San Diego	31
Joe Blanton, Phi./L.A.	29
Ian Kennedy, Arizona	28
Tommy Hanson, Atlanta	27
Bronson Arroyo, Cincinnati	26
Homer Bailey, Cincinnati	26
Mark Buehrle, Miami	26
Yovani Gallardo, Milwaukee	26
Mike Leake, Cincinnati	26
Cliff Lee, Philadelphia	26

Mike Minor, Atlanta	26

WALKS

Edinson Volquez, San Diego	105
Tim Lincecum, San Francisco	90
Aaron Harang, Los Angeles	85
Yovani Gallardo, Milwaukee	81
Lucas Harrell, Houston	78

WALKS PER NINE INNINGS

Cliff Lee, Philadelphia	1.19
Bronson Arroyo, Cincinnati	1.56
Joe Blanton, Phi./L.A.	1.60
Kyle Lohse, St. Louis	1.62
Wade Miley, Arizona	1.71

HIT BATTERS

Ian Kennedy, Arizona	14
Johnny Cueto, Cincinnati	12
Trevor Cahill, Arizona	11
Paul Maholm, Chi/Atl	11
Lance Lynn, St. Louis	10
Carlos Zambrano, Miami	10

STRIKEOUTS

R.A. Dickey, New York	230
Clayton Kershaw, L.A.	229
Cole Hamels, Philadelphia	216
Gio Gonzalez, Washington	207

Cliff Lee, Philadelphia	207

STRIKEOUTS PER NINE INNINGS

Gio Gonzalez, Washington	9.35
Jeff Samardzija, Chicago	9.27
Lance Lynn, St. Louis	9.20
Tim Lincecum, San Francisco	9.19
Clayton Kershaw, L.A.	9.05

STRIKEOUTS PER NINE INNINGS (RELIEVERS)

Craig Kimbrel, Atlanta	16.66
Aroldis Chapman, Cincinnati	15.32
Kenley Jansen, Los Angeles	13.71
David Hernandez, Arizona	12.91
John Axford, Milwaukee	12.07

DOUBLE PLAYS

R.A. Dickey, New York	25
Trevor Cahill, Arizona	23
Jake Westbrook, St. Louis	23
Clayton Richard, San Diego	22
4 players	21

PICKOFFS

Clayton Kershaw, L.A.	11
Johnny Cueto, Cincinnati	9
R.A. Dickey, New York	5
Cole Hamels, Philadelphia	5
8 players	4

WILD PITCHES

Tim Lincecum, San Francisco	17
Jaime Garcia, St. Louis	12
8 players	10

WALKS-PLUS-HITS PER INNING

Clayton Kershaw, L.A.	1.02
Matt Cain, San Francisco	1.04
R.A. Dickey, New York	1.05
Kyle Lohse, St. Louis	1.09
Madison Bumgarner, S.F.	1.11

OPPONENT AVERAGE

Gio Gonzalez, Washington	.206
Clayton Kershaw, L.A.	.210
Matt Cain, San Francisco	.222
R.A. Dickey, New York	.226
Mat Latos, Cincinnati	.230

WORST ERA

Tim Lincecum, San Francisco	5.18
Joe Blanton, Phi./L.A.	4.71
Bud Norris, Houston	4.65
Mike Leake, Cincinnati	4.58
Tommy Hanson, Atlanta	4.48

FIELDING

PITCHER

PCT	10 players tied at	1.000
PO	Josh Johnson, Miami	25
	Mike Leake, Cincinnati	25
A	Mark Buehrle, Miami	47
E	Clayton Richard, San Diego	6
DP	R.A. Dickey, New York	6

CATCHER

		PCT
Brian McCann, Atlanta		.998
PO	Miguel Montero, Arizona	1,008
A	Yadier Molina, St. Louis	88
E	Wilin Rosario, Colorado	13
DP	A.J. Ellis, Los Angeles	12
	Yadier Molina, St. Louis	12
PB	Wilin Rosario, Colorado	21

FIRST BASE

PCT	Carlos Lee, Houston/Miami	.995

PO	Freddie Freeman, Atlanta	1,295
A	Joey Votto, Cincinnati	116
E	Yonder Alonso, San Diego	12
	Freddie Freeman, Atlanta	12
DP	Freddie Freeman, Atlanta	122

SECOND BASE

PCT	Darwin Barney, Chicago	.997
PO	Darwin Barney, Chicago	311
A	Aaron Hill, Arizona	487
E	Rickie Weeks, Milwaukee	16
DP	Dan Uggla, Atlanta	103

THIRD BASE

PCT	Aramis Ramirez, Milwaukee	.977
PO	David Wright, New York	107
A	Chase Headley, San Diego	315
E	Pedro Alvarez, Pittsburgh	27
DP	David Freese, St. Louis	29

SHORTSTOP

PCT	Jimmy Rollins, Philadelphia	.978
PO	Starlin Castro, Chicago	266
A	Starlin Castro, Chicago	465
E	Starlin Castro, Chicago	27
DP	Jose Reyes, Miami	105

OUTFIELD

PCT	Jon Jay, St. Louis	1.000
PO	Michael Bourn, Atlanta	383
A	Jason Kubel, Arizona	14
E	Bryce Harper, Washington	7
	Hunter Pence, Philadelphia/S.F.	7
	Giancarlo Stanton, Miami	7
	Will Venable, San Diego	7
DP	Alfonso Soriano, Chicago	6

Third baseman Pablo Sandoval joined historic company when he homered three times—twice off Justin Verlander—in Game One of the World Series, setting his Giants on course for a sweep

Giants win second Series title in three years

BY TOM HAUDRICOURT

The Giants had no business making it to the 2012 World Series. Teams just don't win six straight games while facing elimination in the postseason to advance to the title round.

Yet, that's exactly what San Francisco did to move beyond the National League Division Series against the Reds and the Championship Series against the Cardinals.

After escaping the NL playoffs by the skin of their teeth in both rounds, the Giants, naturally, swept the Tigers in the World Series.

That's how unpredictable the 2012 postseason was, from beginning to end. Even San Francisco manager Bruce Bochy had trouble believing his club was taking home the big trophy for the second time in three years.

"I'm a little numb, really," Bochy said. "To be world champions in two out of the last three years, it's amazing. Believe me, I know how difficult it is to get."

The Giants fell behind the Reds two games to none in the NLDS, losing both games at home, before traveling to Cincinnati for the remaining three games. Baseball's new one-game wild-card playoff games, added after the regular-season schedule was announced, muddled the Division Series format for the 2012 season. Teams with home-field advantage opened on the road and used the 2-3 format instead of the traditional 2-2-1.

No team ever had been put in the position of having to win three consecutive road games to advance beyond the DS round, yet that's exactly what the Giants did, stunning the favored Reds. San Francisco then fell behind the defending World Series-champion Cardinals three games to one in the NLCS, only to win three elimination games in a row once again.

The Giants needed no desperate escape acts once they got to the World Series. They simply swept the Tigers, who in turn had stunningly swept the punchless Yankees in the ALCS. Detroit mustered very little offense against Giants pitchers in the Series, scoring six times in four games and hitting .159 as a team.

The Giants finished the year with one of the greatest postseason runs ever, winning seven in a row—something they never did during the regular season—while allowing just seven runs to the Cardinals and Tigers. The starting pitchers went 6-0, 0.99 over that span.

The Tigers should have known they were in trouble when ace righthander Justin Verlander got tagged for five runs in four innings in Game One. Giants third baseman Pablo Sandoval did most of the damage with a pair of homers, and he later added a third against reliever Al Alburquerque to become just the fourth player in World Series history to hit three in a game, joining the likes of Babe Ruth (twice), Reggie Jackson and Albert Pujols.

"The guy had one of those unbelievable World Series nights that they'll be talking about for years," Tigers manager Jim Leyland said. "He just had one of those nights when he hit whatever we pitched to him."

In a surprising twist, Giants lefty Barry Zito out-pitched Verlander, the reigning AL MVP and Cy Young award winner, despite his status as Public Enemy No. 1 among many San Francisco fans. He went 58-69, 4.47 in his first six seasons of a seven-year, $126 million deal, yet Zito kept the Giants alive in the NLCS, winning Game Five against St. Louis, and limited the Tigers to one run in 5⅔ innings in the Series opener.

The Giants had home-field advantage in the Series because, in a case of déjà vu, Verlander got tagged for five first-inning runs in the All-Star Game as the NL cruised to an 8-0 victory. Sandoval accounted for three of those runs with a bases-clearing triple.

The Tigers never recovered from their opening loss. The Giants pitched shutouts in the next two games, winning by identical 2-0 scores. No team had tossed back-to-back shutouts in the Series since 1966, when the Orioles blanked the Dodgers over the final three games of the Baltimore sweep.

Through the first three games, the Giants had led every inning of the Series. Detroit finally showed some life in Game Four when third baseman and Triple Crown winner Miguel Cabrera smacked a two-run home run in the second inning off righty Matt Cain to put the Tigers on top 2-1. It was Detroit's first lead of the Series and ended the Giants' remarkable streak of 56 innings without trailing.

That lead would be short-lived, however. Catcher Buster Posey put San Francisco back on top with a two-run homer in the sixth, and the Giants eventually prevailed 4-3 in 10 innings. Second baseman Marco Scutaro drove home Ryan Theriot, that game's DH, with a single off Detroit lefty Phil Coke, thrust into the closer's role after Jose Valverde melted down in the earlier rounds of the postseason.

The Giants acquired Scutaro at the trade deadline from the Rockies, and the journeyman infielder caught fire in the postseason, winning MVP honors in the NLCS against the Cardinals for hitting .500 with four RBIs in seven games.

"He had one more left in him, and it was the biggest one we needed," Cain said.

The Giants pitching staff proved so deep that two-time Cy Young award winner Tim Lincecum pitched out of the bullpen. Furthermore, San Francisco held the powerful 1-2 punch of Cabrera and first baseman Prince Fielder in check, and that normally dynamic duo batted a combined .148 (4-for-27) with Fielder going 1-for-14 with zero RBIs.

"We didn't hit enough," Leyland said. "There was no doubt about it. They swept us."

Wild-Card Playoff Games Debut

Neither the Giants nor the Tigers had to contend with the new one-game play-in for the teams that capture the two wild-card berths in each league. For the first time, the top-seeded wild card team could go one and out, and that's exactly what happened to both the Rangers in the AL and the Braves in the NL.

In what became the farewell for franchise icon Chipper Jones, the Braves melted down in a 6-3 loss to St. Louis. Atlanta committed three errors, including a crucial one by Jones, the third baseman, but the game will be remembered always for a controversial infield-fly rule call in the eighth inning that helped short-circuit a Braves rally. Turner Field fans littered the field with debris, creating a 19-minute delay.

The Braves took the unusual step of protesting the game, with the belief that left-field umpire Sam Holbrook's call on shortstop Andrelton Simmons' fly that fell to the ground in shallow left was incorrect. The commissioner's office denied the protest, and the Braves' season was done after they had won 94 games, the same number as the eventual champion Giants.

"Unfortunately, I feel that I'm the one to blame," said Jones, who threw away a double-play grounder in the fourth inning that led to a three-run rally against previously unbeaten starter Kris Medlen.

As for the infield-fly ruling, Jones said, "That one play didn't cost us the game. Three errors cost us the game. We just dug ourselves too big a hole."

The Rangers' one-game exit was perhaps even more stunning, not just because they offered little fight in a 5-1 loss to Baltimore. Texas just never seemed to recover from ceding the AL West to the Athletics by wasting a five-game lead with nine to play, and they could not regroup against the determined Orioles.

CLIFF WELCH
Delmon Young

The Rangers hoped to return to the World Series for a third consecutive year and avenge the heart-wrenching loss to the Cardinals in 2011, but they never got started in the postseason.

"It's frustrating to get to the World Series and lose, but I would definitely rather get there and lose than be at this point and lose," left fielder David Murphy said.

Division Series Drama

The Nationals and Reds finished with the best records in the NL during the regular season, winning 98 and 97 games, respectively, but in the temporary 2-3 format in the Division Series, both teams opened on the road. The Reds put themselves in fantastic position by winning both games in San Francisco, while the Nationals—playing in the postseason for the first time—split in St. Louis.

Both teams would be the victims of tremendous comebacks by their opponents. The Giants did it over a period of three games, sweeping the stunned Reds in their own ballpark. The Cardinals' comeback was consolidated into Game Five in Nationals Park.

Cincinnati appeared primed to win in three games when righthander Homer Bailey throttled the Giants in the first half of Game Three. Despite striking out 16 times, the Giants eventually prevailed 2-1 in 10 innings, benefitting from an error by veteran third baseman Scott Rolen.

That victory was the springboard the Giants needed to take all three games in Cincy, including a 6-4 decision in Game Five spurred by Posey's grand slam off righty Mat Latos.

Down two games to one, the Nationals regained momentum in their series when right fielder Jayson Werth struck a walk-off homer in the bottom of the ninth inning of Game Four. Washington won that game 2-1, then raced to a 6-0 lead after three innings in Game Five.

St. Louis narrowed the deficit to two runs and trailed 7-5 heading into the ninth, when the Cardinals plated four runs against closer Drew Storen and beat the disbelieving Nationals 9-7. Second baseman Daniel Descalso and rookie shortstop Pete Kozma delivered key hits in the rally.

"They don't quit, and it's hard to beat a team that doesn't quit," Cardinals manager Mike Matheny said.

The Athletics had no quit in them, either, as the Tigers discovered in their Division Series. DH Seth Smith and center fielder Coco Crisp delivered huge hits off Valverde to cap a three-run rally in Game Four to stave off elimination and force a deciding fifth game in Oakland.

The Tigers had the great equalizer in Game Five, however, in Verlander, who pitched a four-hitter with 11 strikeouts to end the Athletics' dreams of advancing. Verlander was the difference in the series, winning the first game and the last.

YEAR	CHAMPIONSHIP SERIES	ALCS MVP	DIVISION SERIES 1	DIVISION SERIES 2
2012	Detroit 4, New York 0	Delmon Young, of, Detroit	New York 3, Baltimore* 2	Detroit 3, Oakland 2
2011	Texas 4, Detroit 2	Nelson Cruz, of, Texas	Detroit 3, New York 2	Texas 3, Tampa Bay* 1
2010	Texas 4, New York 2	Josh Hamilton, of, Texas	Texas 3, Tampa Bay 2	New York* 3, Minnesota 0
2009	New York 4, Los Angeles 2	C.C. Sabathia, lhp, New York	New York 3, Minnesota 0	Los Angeles 3, Boston* 0
2008	Tampa Bay 4, Boston 3	Matt Garza, rhp, Tampa Bay	Boston* 3, Los Angeles 1	Tampa Bay 3, Chicago 1
2007	Boston 4, Cleveland 3	Josh Beckett, rhp, Boston	Boston 3, Los Angeles 0	Cleveland 3, New York* 1
2006	Detroit 4, Oakland 0	Placido Polanco, 2b, Detroit	Detroit* 3, New York 1	Oakland 3, Minnesota 0
2005	Chicago 4, Los Angeles 1	Paul Konerko, 1b, Chicago	Chicago 3, Boston* 0	Los Angeles 3, New York 2
2004	Boston 4, New York 3	David Ortiz, dh, Boston	Boston* 3, Anaheim 0	New York 3, Minnesota 1
2003	New York 4, Boston 3	Mariano Rivera, rhp, New York	New York 3, Minnesota 1	Boston* 3, Oakland 2
2002	Anaheim 4, Minnesota 1	Adam Kennedy, 2b, Anaheim	Anaheim* 3, New York 1	Minnesota 3, Oakland 2
2001	New York 4, Seattle 1	Andy Pettitte, lhp, New York	Seattle 3, Cleveland 2	New York 3, Oakland* 2
2000	New York 4, Seattle 2	David Justice, of, New York	New York 3, Oakland 2	Seattle* 3, Chicago 0
1999	New York 4, Boston 1	Orlando Hernandez, rhp, New York	Boston* 3, Cleveland 2	New York 3, Texas 0
1998	New York 4, Cleveland 2	David Wells, lhp, New York	Cleveland 3, Boston* 1	New York 3, Texas 0
1997	Cleveland 4, Baltimore 2	Marquis Grissom, of, Cleveland	Cleveland 3, New York* 2	Baltimore 3, Seattle 1
1996	New York 4, Baltimore 1	Bernie Williams, of, New York	Baltimore* 3, Cleveland 1	New York 3, Texas 1
1995	Cleveland 4, Seattle 2	Orel Hershiser, rhp, Cleveland	Cleveland 3, Boston 0	Seattle 3, New York* 2

AMERICAN LEAGUE CHAMPIONS, 1995–2012

American League postseason results in Wild Card Era, 1995-present, where (*) denotes wild card playoff entrant.

In the other ALDS, Eastern Division rivals Baltimore and New York waged battle. The Yankees didn't claim the division title until the final day of the season, and they had an equally hard time putting away the Orioles in the first round. The two teams played to a two-all draw through four games, which made for a bit of playoff history. For the first time in 18 seasons of the three-round playoff format, all four Division Series went the full five games.

The Yankees had their ace C.C. Sabathia for Game Five, and that made the difference in a 3-1 victory. Fortunate that a long drive by Baltimore's Nate McLouth went just foul in the sixth inning, Sabathia pitched a four-hitter for his first complete game in the postseason as well as the Yankees' first in 12 years.

BILL NICHOLS

Marco Scutaro

Giants, Tigers Prevail In LCS Round

All the drama in the Tigers-Yankees ALCS belonged on New York's side—and all of it was bad.

It began in Game One when Valverde blew a 4-0 ninth-inning lead that marked his last appearance as Detroit's closer. Yankees DH Raul Ibanez, who helped the Yankees win the AL East with a pinch-hit homer against the Red Sox, struck again with a two-run blast after Ichiro Suzuki hit a two-run shot to get New York on the board.

The Tigers eventually prevailed 6-4 in 12 innings, but the defeat was even more costly for the Yankees because shortstop Derek Jeter suffered a fractured left ankle trying to make a play up the middle. The injury knocked him out for the year and required offseason surgery. Jeter's injury was an omen of things to come for New York, which fell into a deep freeze at the plate and never recovered.

Manager Joe Girardi benched slumping third baseman Alex Rodriguez three times, creating a firestorm around the highest-paid player in the game. But the rest of the lineup remained hapless, including normally stout second baseman Robinson Cano, who saw his postseason slump reach 29 hitless at-bats at one point.

As a result of the team-wide slump, the Yankees were swept in a postseason series for the first time in 32 years. They scored in only three of 39 innings during the series, batting .157. They lost the Game Four finale 8-1 when Sabathia got shelled for 11 hits and six runs in just 3⅔ innings.

Over in the NLCS, the early chatter centered on a take-out slide of Scutaro by Cardinals left fielder Matt Holliday in Game Two, a late hit behind the bag that left the Giants second baseman gimpy. San Francisco shook that off to roll to a 7-1 victory that evened the series and sent it to St. Louis.

The Cardinals reached the verge of a second straight World Series appearance, going up three games to one, but they never quite made it. The much-maligned Zito, whom the Giants left off their postseason roster in 2010, tossed 7⅔ scoreless innings in a 5-0 victory that sent the series back to San Francisco.

Back home in front of their raucous fans, the Giants won Games Six and Seven by scores of 6-1 and 9-0, meaning they steam-rolled the Cardinals by a combined score of 20-1 over the final three contests.

"These guys never quit," Bochy said. "They just kept believing and got it done."

NATIONAL LEAGUE CHAMPIONS, 1995–2012

National League postseason results in Wild Card Era, 1995-present, where (*) denotes wild card playoff entrant.

YEAR	CHAMPIONSHIP SERIES	NLCS MVP	DIVISION SERIES	DIVISION SERIES
2012	San Francisco 4, St. Louis 3	Marco Scutaro, 2b, San Francisco	St. Louis* 3, Washington 2	San Francisco 3, Cincinnati 2
2011	St. Louis 4, Milwaukee 2	David Freese, 3b, St. Louis	St. Louis* 3, Philadelphia 2	Milwaukee 3, Arizona 2
2010	San Francisco 4, Philadelphia 2	Cody Ross, of, San Francisco	Philadelphia 3, Cincinnati 0	San Francisco 3, Atlanta* 1
2009	Philadelphia 4, Los Angeles 1	Ryan Howard, 1b, Philadelphia	Los Angeles 3, St. Louis 0	Philadelphia 3, Colorado* 1
2008	Philadelphia 4, Los Angeles 1	Cole Hamels, lhp, Philadelphia	Los Angeles 3, Chicago 0	Philadelphia 3, Milwaukee* 1
2007	Colorado 4, Arizona 0	Matt Holliday, of, Colorado	Arizona 3, Chicago 0	Colorado* 3, Philadelphia 0
2006	St. Louis 4, New York 3	Jeff Suppan, rhp, St. Louis	New York 3, Los Angeles* 0	St. Louis 3, San Diego 1
2005	Houston 4, St. Louis 2	Roy Oswalt, rhp, Houston	St. Louis 3, San Diego 0	Houston* 3, Atlanta 1
2004	St. Louis 4, Houston 3	Albert Pujols, 1b, St. Louis	St. Louis 3, Los Angeles 1	Houston* 3, Atlanta 2
2003	Florida 4, Chicago 3	Ivan Rodriguez, c, Florida	Florida* 3, San Francisco 1	Chicago 3, Atlanta 2
2002	San Francisco 4, St. Louis 1	Benito Santiago, c, San Francisco	San Francisco* 3, Atlanta 2	St. Louis 3, Arizona 0
2001	Arizona 4, Atlanta 1	Craig Counsell, ss, Arizona	Atlanta 3, Houston 0	Arizona 3, St. Louis* 2
2000	New York 4, St. Louis 1	Mike Hampton, lhp, New York	St. Louis 3, Atlanta 0	New York* 3, San Francisco 1
1999	Atlanta 4, New York 2	Eddie Perez, c, Atlanta	Atlanta 3, Houston 1	New York* 3, Arizona 1
1998	San Diego 4, Atlanta 2	Sterling Hitchcock, lhp, San Diego	Atlanta 3, Chicago* 0	San Diego 3, Houston 1
1997	Florida 4, Atlanta 2	Livan Hernandez, rhp, Florida	Florida* 3, San Francisco 0	Atlanta 3, Houston 0
1996	Atlanta 4, St. Louis 3	Javy Lopez, c, Atlanta	Atlanta 3, Los Angeles* 0	St. Louis 3, San Diego 0
1995	Atlanta 4, Cincinnati 0	Mike Devereaux, of, Atlanta	Atlanta 3, Colorado* 1	Cincinnati 3, Los Angeles 0

BILL NICHOLS

Bruce Bochy added his name to the list of managers to win multiple World Series

Year	Winner	Loser	Result
1903	Boston (AL)	Pittsburgh (NL)	5-3
1904	NO SERIES		
1905	New York (NL)	Philadelphia (AL)	4-1
1906	Chicago (AL)	Chicago (NL)	4-2
1907	Chicago (NL)	Detroit (AL)	4-0
1908	Chicago (NL)	Detroit (AL)	4-1
1909	Pittsburgh (NL)	Detroit (AL)	4-3
1910	Philadelphia (AL)	Chicago (NL)	4-1
1911	Philadelphia (AL)	New York (NL)	4-2
1912	Boston (AL)	New York (NL)	4-3-1
1913	Philadelphia (AL)	New York (NL)	4-1
1914	Boston (NL)	Philadelphia (AL)	4-0
1915	Boston (AL)	Philadelphia (NL)	4-1
1916	Boston (AL)	Brooklyn (NL)	4-1
1917	Chicago (AL)	New York (NL)	4-2
1918	Boston (AL)	Chicago (NL)	4-2
1919	Cincinnati (NL)	Chicago (AL)	5-3
1920	Cleveland (AL)	Brooklyn (NL)	5-2
1921	New York (NL)	New York (AL)	5-3
1922	New York (NL)	New York (AL)	4-0
1923	New York (AL)	New York (NL)	4-2
1924	Washington (AL)	New York (NL)	4-3
1925	Pittsburgh (NL)	Washington (AL)	4-3
1926	St. Louis (NL)	New York (AL)	4-3
1927	New York (AL)	Pittsburgh (NL)	4-0
1928	New York (AL)	St. Louis (NL)	4-0
1929	Philadelphia (AL)	Chicago (NL)	4-1
1930	Philadelphia (AL)	St. Louis (NL)	4-2
1931	St. Louis (NL)	Philadelphia (AL)	4-3
1932	New York (AL)	Chicago (NL)	4-0
1933	New York (NL)	Washington (AL)	4-1
1934	St. Louis (NL)	Detroit (AL)	4-3
1935	Detroit (AL)	Chicago (NL)	4-2
1936	New York (AL)	New York (NL)	4-2
1937	New York (AL)	New York (NL)	4-1
1938	New York (AL)	Chicago (NL)	4-0
1939	New York (AL)	Cincinnati (NL)	4-0
1940	Cincinnati (NL)	Detroit (AL)	4-3
1941	New York (AL)	Brooklyn (NL)	4-1
1942	St. Louis (NL)	New York (AL)	4-1
1943	New York (AL)	St. Louis (NL)	4-1
1944	St. Louis (NL)	St. Louis (AL)	4-2
1945	Detroit (AL)	Chicago (NL)	4-3
1946	St. Louis (NL)	Boston (AL)	4-3
1947	New York (AL)	Brooklyn (NL)	4-3
1948	Cleveland (AL)	Boston (NL)	4-2
1949	New York (AL)	Brooklyn (NL)	4-1
1950	New York (AL)	Philadelphia (NL)	4-0
1951	New York (AL)	New York (NL)	4-2
1952	New York (AL)	Brooklyn (NL)	4-3
1953	New York (AL)	Brooklyn (NL)	4-2
1954	New York (NL)	Cleveland (AL)	4-0
1955	Brooklyn (NL)	New York (AL)	4-3
1956	New York (AL)	Brooklyn (NL)	4-3
1957	Milwaukee (NL)	New York (AL)	4-3
1958	New York (AL)	Milwaukee (NL)	4-3
1959	Los Angeles (NL)	Chicago (AL)	4-2
1960	Pittsburgh (NL)	New York (AL)	4-3
1961	New York (AL)	Cincinnati (NL)	4-1
1962	New York (AL)	San Francisco (NL)	4-3
1963	Los Angeles (NL)	New York (AL)	4-0
1964	St. Louis (NL)	New York (AL)	4-3

Year	Winner	Loser	Result
1965	Los Angeles (NL)	Minnesota (AL)	4-3
1966	Baltimore (AL)	Los Angeles (NL)	4-0
1967	St. Louis (NL)	Boston (AL)	4-3
1968	Detroit (AL)	St. Louis (NL)	4-3
1969	New York (NL)	Baltimore (AL)	4-1
1970	Baltimore (AL)	Cincinnati (NL)	4-1
1971	Pittsburgh (NL)	Baltimore (AL)	4-3
1972	Oakland (AL)	Cincinnati (NL)	4-3
1973	Oakland (AL)	New York (NL)	4-3
1974	Oakland (AL)	Los Angeles (NL)	4-1
1975	Cincinnati (NL)	Boston (AL)	4-3
1976	Cincinnati (NL)	New York (AL)	4-0
1977	New York (AL)	Los Angeles (NL)	4-2
1978	New York (AL)	Los Angeles (NL)	4-2
1979	Pittsburgh (NL)	Baltimore (AL)	4-3
1980	Philadelphia (NL)	Kansas City (AL)	4-2
1981	Los Angeles (NL)	New York (AL)	4-2
1982	St. Louis (NL)	Milwaukee (AL)	4-3
1983	Baltimore (AL)	Philadelphia (NL)	4-1
1984	Detroit (AL)	San Diego (NL)	4-1
1985	Kansas City (AL)	St. Louis (NL)	4-3
1986	New York (NL)	Boston (AL)	4-3
1987	Minnesota (AL)	St. Louis (NL)	4-3
1988	Los Angeles (NL)	Oakland (AL)	4-1
1989	Oakland (AL)	San Francisco (NL)	4-0
1990	Cincinnati (NL)	Oakland (AL)	4-0
1991	Minnesota (AL)	Atlanta (NL)	4-3
1992	Toronto (AL)	Atlanta (NL)	4-2
1993	Toronto (AL)	Philadelphia (NL)	4-2
1994	NO SERIES		
1995	Atlanta (NL)	Cleveland (AL)	4-2
1996	New York (AL)	Atlanta (NL)	4-2
1997	Florida (NL)	Cleveland (AL)	4-3
1998	New York (AL)	San Diego (NL)	4-0
1999	New York (AL)	Atlanta (NL)	4-0
2000	New York (AL)	New York (NL)	4-1
2001	Arizona (NL)	New York (AL)	4-3
2002	Anaheim (AL)	San Francisco (NL)	4-3
2003	Florida (NL)	New York (AL)	4-2
2004	Boston (AL)	St. Louis (NL)	4-0
2005	Chicago (AL)	Houston (NL)	4-0
2006	St. Louis (NL)	Detroit (AL)	4-1
2007	Boston (AL)	Colorado (NL)	4-0
2008	Philadelphia (NL)	Tampa Bay (AL)	4-1
2009	New York (AL)	Philadelphia (NL)	4-2
2010	San Francisco (NL)	Texas (AL)	4-1
2011	St. Louis (NL)	Texas (AL)	4-3
2012	San Francisco (NL)	Detroit (AL)	4-0

WORLD SERIES BOX SCORES

GAME ONE October 24
SAN FRANCISCO 8, DETROIT 3

DETROIT	AB	R	H	BI	BB	SO	SAN FRAN	AB	R	H	BI	BB	SO
Jackson, A, cf	4	1	2	0	0	1	Pagan, cf	4	2	2	0	0	0
Infante, 2b	4	0	1	0	0	1	Scutaro, 2b	4	2	2	2	0	0
Cabrera, Mi, 3b	3	0	1	1	1	1	Sandoval, 3b	4	3	4	4	0	0
Fielder, 1b	4	0	1	0	0	0	Arias, 3b	0	0	0	0	0	0
Young, D, lf	4	1	2	0	0	0	Posey, c	4	0	2	1	0	1
Peralta, ss	4	1	1	2	0	2	Pence, rf	4	0	0	0	0	3
Garcia, A, rf	3	0	0	0	0	1	Belt, 1b	3	1	0	0	1	1
c-Dirks, ph	1	0	0	0	0	0	Blanco, lf	4	0	0	0	0	3
Avila, c	3	0	0	1	1	0	Crawford, ss	4	0	0	0	0	0
Verlander, p	1	0	0	0	0	0	Zito, p	2	0	1	1	0	1
a-Worth, ph	1	0	0	0	0	1	Lincecum, p	1	0	0	0	0	0
Alburquerque, p	0	0	0	0	0	0	1-Huff, ph	1	0	0	0	0	0
b-Berry, ph	1	0	0	0	0	0	Mijares, p	0	0	0	0	0	0
Valverde, p	0	0	0	0	0	0	Kontos, p	0	0	0	0	0	0
Benoit, p	0	0	0	0	0	0	Affeldt, p	0	0	0	0	0	0
Porcello, p	0	0	0	0	0	0							
d-Santiago, ph	1	0	0	0	0	0							
TOTAL	**34**	**3**	**8**	**3**	**2**	**8**		**35**	**8**	**11**	**8**	**1**	**10**

Detroit	000	001	002—3
San Francisco	103	110	20x—8

a-Struck out for Verlander in the 5th. b-Grounded out for Alburquerque in the 7th. c-Grounded out for Garcia, A in the 9th. d-Grounded into a forceout for Porcello in the 9th.

1-Grounded out for Lincecum in the 8th.

LOB—Tigers 6, Giants 4. **2B**—Jackson, A (1), Pagan 2 (2). **HR**—Peralta (1), Sandoval 3 (3). **GIDP**—Young, D.

DETROIT	IP	H	R	ER	BB	SO	SAN FRAN	IP	H	R	ER	BB	SO
Verlander (L)	4	6	5	5	1	4	Zito (W)	5⅔	6	1	1	1	3
Alburquerque	2	1	1	1	0	2	Lincecum	2⅓	0	0	0	0	5
Valverde	⅓	4	2	2	0	1	Mijares	⅓	0	0	0	0	0
Benoit	⅔	0	0	0	0	2	Kontos	⅓	2	2	2	1	0
Porcello	1	0	0	0	0	1	Affeldt	⅓	0	0	0	0	0

WP—Benoit.
T—3:26. **A**—42,855.

GAME TWO October 25
SAN FRANCISCO 2, DETROIT 0

DETROIT	AB	R	H	BI	BB	SO	SAN FRAN	AB	R	H	BI	BB	SO
Jackson, A, cf	3	0	0	0	1	3	Pagan, cf	3	1	0	0	1	1
Infante, 2b	4	0	1	0	0	2	Scutaro, 2b	4	0	0	0	0	1
Cabrera, Mi, 3b	2	0	0	1	0	0	Sandoval, 3b	3	0	1	0	1	0
Fielder, 1b	2	0	0	0	0	0	Romo, p	0	0	0	0	0	0
Young, D, lf	3	0	1	0	0	0	Posey, c	3	0	1	0	1	0
Kelly, lf-rf	0	0	0	0	0	0	Pence, rf	3	1	1	1	0	0
Peralta, ss	3	0	0	0	0	0	Belt, 1b	3	0	0	0	1	2
Garcia, A, rf	2	0	0	0	0	0	Blanco, lf	3	0	2	0	0	0
a-Dirks, ph-rf	1	0	0	0	0	0	Crawford, ss	2	0	0	0	1	0
Dotel, p	0	0	0	0	0	0	Bumgarner, p	2	0	0	0	0	1
Coke, p	0	0	0	0	0	0	1-Theriot, ph	1	0	0	0	0	1
Laird, c	3	0	0	0	0	1	Casilla, p	0	0	0	0	0	0
Fister, p	2	0	0	0	0	1	Arias, 3b	0	0	0	0	0	0
Smyly, p	0	0	0	0	0	0							
Berry, lf	1	0	0	0	0	0							
TOTAL	**26**	**0**	**2**	**0**	**2**	**9**		**27**	**2**	**5**	**1**	**5**	**6**

Detroit	000	000	000—0
San Francisco	000	000	11x—2

a-Grounded out for Garcia, A in the 8th.
1-Struck out for Bumgarner in the 7th.

LOB—Tigers 2, Giants 7. **2B**—Young, D (1). **SF**—Pence. **GIDP**—Fielder, Crawford. **SB**—Pagan (1). **CS**—Infante (1). **PO**—Infante. **A**—Blanco.

GAME THREE October 27
SAN FRANCISCO 2, DETROIT 0

SAN FRAN	AB	R	H	BI	BB	SO	DETROIT	AB	R	H	BI	BB	SO
Pagan, cf	4	0	0	0	0	1	Jackson, A, cf	2	0	1	0	2	0
Scutaro, 2b	4	0	0	0	0	1	Berry, lf	3	0	0	1	2	
Sandoval, 3b	4	0	2	0	0	0	Cabrera, Mi, 3b	4	0	1	0	0	0
Arias, 3b	0	0	0	0	0	0	Fielder, 1b	4	0	0	0	0	2
Posey, c	4	0	0	0	0	2	Young, D, rf	3	0	0	0	1	0
Pence, rf	3	1	2	0	1	0	Dirks, rf	3	0	0	1	1	
Belt, 1b	4	0	0	0	0	3	Peralta, ss	4	0	0	0	0	0
Blanco, lf	4	1	1	1	0	1	Avila, c	4	0	1	0	0	1
Sanchez, H, dh	4	0	0	0	3		Infante, 2b	4	0	2	0	0	1
Crawford, ss	3	0	2	1	0	1							
TOTAL	**34**	**2**	**7**	**2**	**1**	**12**		**31**	**0**	**5**	**0**	**5**	**7**

San Francisco	020	000	000—2
Detroit	000	000	000—0

LOB—Giants 6, Tigers 9. **2B**—Sandoval (1). **3B**—Blanco (1). **SB**—Pence (1), Crawford (1). **GIDP**—Fielder, Berry. **E**—Crawford (1), Jackson, A (1).

SAN FRAN	IP	H	R	ER	BB	SO	DETROIT	IP	H	R	ER	BB	SO
Vogelsong (W)	5⅔	5	0	0	4	3	Sanchez, An (L)	7	6	2	2	1	8
Lincecum	2⅓	0	0	0	1	3	Benoit	1	1	0	0	0	1
Romo (S)	1	0	0	0	0	1	Coke	1	0	0	0	0	3

WP—Sanchez, An.
T—3:25. **A**—42,262.

GAME FOUR October 28
SAN FRANCISCO 4, DETROIT 3 (10 INNINGS)

SAN FRAN	AB	R	H	BI	BB	SO	DETROIT	AB	R	H	BI	BB	SO
Pagan, cf	5	0	0	0	0	2	Jackson, A, cf	4	1	0	0	1	2
Scutaro, 2b	4	1	2	1	1	0	Berry, lf	3	0	0	0	0	0
Sandoval, 3b	5	0	1	0	0	2	a-Garcia, A, ph-rf	0	0	0	1	0	
Arias, 3b	0	0	0	0	0	0	b-Kelly, ph	1	0	0	0	0	1
Posey, c	4	1	1	2	0	2	Cabrera, Mi, 3b	4	1	1	2	1	3
Pence, rf	4	1	1	0	0	3	Fielder, 1b	4	0	0	0	0	2
Belt, 1b	3	0	1	1	1	1	Young, D, dh	4	1	2	1	0	2
Blanco, lf	4	0	1	0	0	0	Dirks, rf-lf	4	0	1	0	0	1
Theriot, dh	4	1	1	0	0	1	Peralta, ss	4	0	0	0	0	1
Crawford, ss	3	0	1	0	0	0	Infante, 2b	3	0	1	0	0	0
							c-Worth, pr-2b	0	0	0	0	0	0
							Laird, c	4	0	0	0	0	0
TOTAL	**36**	**4**	**9**	**4**	**2**	**13**		**35**	**3**	**5**	**3**	**3**	**12**

San Francisco	010	002	000 1—4
Detroit	002	001	000 0—3

a-Walked for Berry in the 8th. b-Struck out for Garcia, A in the 10th. c-Ran for Infante in the 9th.

LOB—Giants 5, Tigers 6. **2B**—Pence (1). **3B**—Belt (1). **HR**—Posey (1), Cabrera, Mi (1), Young, D (1). **SH**—Crawford. **GIDP**—Sandoval. **CS**—Belt (1).

SAN FRAN	IP	H	R	ER	BB	SO	DETROIT	IP	H	R	ER	BB	SO
Cain	7	5	3	3	2	5	Scherzer	6⅓	7	3	3	1	8
Affeldt	1⅔	0	0	0	1	4	Smyly	⅓	0	0	0	0	0
Casilla (W)	⅓	0	0	0	0	0	Dotel	1⅓	0	0	0	1	1
Romo (S)	1	0	0	0	0	3	Coke (L)	2	2	1	1	0	4

HBP—Infante (by Casilla).
T—3:34. **A**—42,152.

The following continues under Game Two's pitching lines at top-right:

DETROIT	IP	H	R	ER	BB	SO	SAN FRAN	IP	H	R	ER	BB	SO
Fister (L)	6	4	1	1	1	3	Bumgarner (W)	7	2	0	0	2	8
Smyly	1⅓	1	1	1	3	2	Casilla	1	0	0	0	0	0
Dotel	⅓	0	0	0	1	0	Romo (S)	1	0	0	0	0	1
Coke	⅓	0	0	0	0	1							

Fister pitched to 1 batter in the 7th.
IBB—Sandoval (by Smyly). **HBP**—Fielder (by Bumgarner).
T—3:05. **A**—42,982.

AMERICAN LEAGUE WILD CARD GAME

TEXAS RANGERS VS·BALTIMORE ORIOLES

BALTIMORE ORIOLES

PLAYER, POS	AVG	G	AB	R	H	2B	3B	HR	RBI	BB	SO	SB
Robert Andino, 2b	1.000	1	1	2	1	1	0	0	0	0	0	0
Endy Chavez, rf	—	1	0	0	0	0	0	0	0	0	0	0
Chris Davis, rf	.250	1	4	0	1	0	0	0	0	0	3	0
Ryan Flaherty, 2b	.333	1	3	0	1	0	0	0	0	0	1	0
Lew Ford, dh	—	1	0	1	0	0	0	0	0	0	0	0
J.J. Hardy, ss	.400	1	5	1	2	0	0	0	1	0	1	0
Adam Jones, cf	.000	1	3	0	0	0	0	0	1	0	0	0
Manny Machado, 3b	.333	1	3	0	1	0	0	0	1	0	1	0
Nate McLouth, lf	.250	1	4	1	1	0	0	0	2	0	0	1
Mark Reynolds, 1b	.000	1	3	0	0	0	0	0	0	0	2	1
Jim Thome, dh	.333	1	3	0	1	0	0	0	0	1	1	0
Matt Wieters, c	.000	1	4	0	0	0	0	0	0	0	2	0
Totals	**.242**	**1**	**33**	**5**	**8**	**1**	**0**	**0**	**5**	**1**	**12**	**2**

PITCHER	W	L	ERA	G	GS	SV	IP	H	R	ER	BB	SO
Jim Johnson	0	0	0.00	1	0	0	1.0	2	0	0	1	0
Brian Matusz	0	0	0.00	1	0	0	0.1	0	0	0	0	1
Darren O'Day	0	0	0.00	1	0	0	2.0	1	0	0	0	1
Joe Saunders	1	0	1.59	1	1	0	5.2	6	1	1	1	4
Totals	**1**	**0**	**1.00**	**1**	**1**	**0**	**9**	**9**	**1**	**1**	**2**	**6**

TEXAS RANGERS

PLAYER, POS	AVG	G	AB	R	H	2B	3B	HR	RBI	BB	SO	SB
Elvis Andrus, ss	.500	1	4	0	2	0	0	0	0	0	0	0
Adrian Beltre, 3b	.000	1	4	0	0	0	0	0	0	0	0	0
Nelson Cruz, rf	.500	1	4	0	2	0	0	0	0	0	0	0
Craig Gentry, cf	.000	1	2	0	0	0	0	0	0	0	0	0
Josh Hamilton, lf	.000	1	4	0	0	0	0	0	0	0	2	0
Ian Kinsler, 2b	.667	1	3	1	2	0	0	0	0	1	0	0
Mitch Moreland, ph	.000	1	1	0	0	0	0	0	0	0	1	0
David Murphy, lf	.000	1	2	0	0	0	0	0	0	0	0	0
Mike Napoli, c	.000	1	3	0	0	0	0	0	0	1	2	0
Jurickson Profar, ph	1.000	1	1	0	1	0	0	0	0	0	0	0
Geovany Soto, c	.000	1	2	0	0	0	0	0	0	0	1	0
Michael Young, 1b	.500	1	4	0	2	0	0	0	0	0	0	0
Totals	**.265**	**1**	**34**	**1**	**9**	**0**	**0**	**0**	**0**	**2**	**6**	**0**

PITCHER	W	L	ERA	G	GS	SV	IP	H	R	ER	BB	SO
Yu Darvish	0	1	2.70	1	1	0	6.2	5	3	2	0	7
Derek Holland	0	0	0.00	1	0	0	0.1	1	0	0	0	1
Joe Nathan	0	0	18.00	1	0	0	1.0	2	2	2	1	1
Koji Uehara	0	0	0.00	1	0	0	1.0	0	0	0	0	3
Totals	**0**	**1**	**4.00**	**1**	**1**	**0**	**9**	**8**	**5**	**4**	**1**	**12**

E—O'Day, Reynolds, Holland, Young. DP—Baltimore 3. LOB—Baltimore 6, Texas 8. SB—McLouth, Reynolds. SH—Machado. SF—Jones, McLouth. HBP—Reynolds (by Darvish). WP—Holland.

SCORE BY INNINGS

Baltimore	100	001	102—5
Texas	100	000	000—1

AMERICAN LEAGUE DIVISION SERIES

NEW YORK YANKEES VS BALTIMORE ORIOLES

BALTIMORE ORIOLES

PLAYER, POS	AVG	G	AB	R	H	2B	3B	HR	RBI	BB	SO	SB
Robert Andino, 2b	.364	5	11	1	4	0	0	0	0	0	2	0
Endy Chavez, rf	.000	3	1	0	0	0	0	0	0	0	1	0
Chris Davis, rf	.200	5	20	1	4	0	0	0	2	1	6	0
Ryan Flaherty, 2b	.250	3	8	1	2	0	0	1	1	0	1	0
Lew Ford, dh	.375	3	8	1	3	1	0	0	1	0	0	0
J.J. Hardy, ss	.136	5	22	0	3	2	0	0	1	1	4	0
Adam Jones, cf	.087	5	23	0	2	0	0	0	0	0	6	0
Manny Machado, 3b	.125	5	16	2	2	1	0	1	1	2	5	0
Nate McLouth, lf	.318	5	22	2	7	1	0	1	3	1	3	2
Mark Reynolds, 1b	.158	5	19	0	3	0	0	0	1	1	8	0
Jim Thome, dh	.083	3	12	0	1	0	0	0	0	0	4	0
Matt Wieters, c	.150	5	20	2	3	1	0	0	0	2	2	0
Totals	**.187**	**5**	**182**	**10**	**34**	**6**	**0**	**3**	**10**	**8**	**42**	**2**

PITCHER	W	L	ERA	G	GS	SV	IP	H	R	ER	BB	SO
Luis Ayala	0	0	0.00	1	0	0	0.1	2	0	0	0	1
Wei-Yin Chen	1	0	1.42	1	1	0	6.1	8	2	1	1	3
Miguel Gonzalez	0	0	1.29	1	1	0	7.0	5	1	1	0	8
Jason Hammel	0	1	3.18	2	2	0	11.1	8	4	4	6	11
Tommy Hunter	0	0	0.00	2	0	0	1.1	0	0	0	0	1
Jim Johnson	0	1	10.38	4	0	2	4.1	6	6	5	0	4
Brian Matusz	0	1	2.08	5	0	0	4.1	2	1	1	2	5
Darren O'Day	0	0	0.00	4	0	0	5.0	0	0	0	1	4
Troy Patton	0	0	4.50	3	0	0	2.0	3	1	1	2	3
Joe Saunders	0	0	1.59	1	1	0	5.2	3	1	1	4	5
Pedro Strop	1	0	0.00	2	0	0	2.1	1	0	0	1	2
Totals	**2**	**3**	**2.52**	**5**	**5**	**2**	**50**	**38**	**16**	**14**	**17**	**47**

NEW YORK YANKEES

PLAYER, POS	AVG	G	AB	R	H	2B	3B	HR	RBI	BB	SO	SB
Robinson Cano, 2b	.091	5	22	1	2	2	0	0	4	1	3	0
Eric Chavez, 3b	.000	3	8	0	0	0	0	0	0	0	4	0
Brett Gardner, lf	—	2	0	0	0	0	0	0	0	0	0	0
Curtis Granderson, cf	.158	5	19	1	3	0	0	1	1	1	9	1
Raul Ibanez, dh	.444	4	9	2	4	0	0	2	3	1	2	0
Derek Jeter, ss	.364	5	22	4	8	1	1	0	2	1	8	0
Russell Martin, c	.176	5	17	2	3	1	0	1	3	2	0	0
Jayson Nix, ss	.500	2	4	0	2	1	0	0	0	0	0	0
Eduardo Nunez, dh	.200	3	5	2	1	0	0	0	0	0	0	0
Alex Rodriguez, 3b	.125	4	16	1	2	0	0	0	0	2	9	0
Ichiro Suzuki, lf	.217	5	23	2	5	2	0	0	3	1	3	1
Nick Swisher, rf	.111	5	18	0	2	0	0	0	1	2	5	0
Mark Teixeira, 1b	.353	5	17	1	6	0	0	1	5	2	1	1
Totals	**.211**	**5**	**180**	**16**	**38**	**8**	**1**	**4**	**16**	**17**	**47**	**3**

PITCHER	W	L	ERA	G	GS	SV	IP	H	R	ER	BB	SO
Joba Chamberlain	0	0	0.00	1	0	0	1.0	1	0	0	0	1
Phil Hughes	0	0	1.35	1	1	0	6.2	4	1	1	3	8
Hiroki Kuroda	0	0	2.16	1	1	0	8.1	5	2	2	1	3
Boone Logan	0	0	0.00	2	0	0	0.2	0	0	0	0	1
Derek Lowe	0	0	0.00	1	0	0	0.1	0	0	0	0	0
Andy Pettitte	0	1	3.86	1	1	0	7.0	7	3	3	1	5
David Phelps	0	1	6.75	1	0	0	1.1	2	1	1	0	1
Clay Rapada	0	0	0.00	1	0	0	0.1	0	0	0	0	0
David Robertson	1	0	0.00	4	0	0	4.1	1	0	0	0	5
C.C. Sabathia	2	0	1.53	2	2	0	17.2	12	3	3	3	16
Rafael Soriano	0	0	0.00	2	0	0	3.1	2	0	0	0	2
Totals	**3**	**2**	**1.76**	**5**	**5**	**0**	**50**	**34**	**10**	**10**	**8**	**42**

E—Flaherty, Hardy (2), Reynolds, Jeter (2), Teixeira. DP—Baltimore 7, New York 3. LOB—Baltimore 31, New York 34. SB—McLouth (2), Granderson, Suzuki, Teixeira. CS—McLouth, Suzuki. SH—Andino, Machado, Jeter, Suzuki. SF—Swisher. HBP—Davis (by Kuroda), Reynolds (by Kuroda). IBB—Cano (by Matusz), Granderson (by Hammel), Teixeira (by Hammel). WP—Matusz.

SCORE BY INNINGS

Baltimore	005	021	010	000	1—10
New York	201	112	206	001	0—16

OAKLAND ATHLETICS VS DETROIT TIGERS

DETROIT TIGERS

PLAYER, POS	AVG	G	AB	R	H	2B	3B	HR	RBI	BB	SO	SB
Alex Avila, c	.250	4	12	2	3	1	0	1	1	0	6	0
Quintin Berry, lf	.300	4	10	1	3	1	0	0	0	1	3	1
Miguel Cabrera, 3b	.250	5	20	1	5	2	0	0	1	1	1	0
Andy Dirks, lf	.294	5	17	0	5	1	0	0	0	0	3	1
Prince Fielder, 1b	.190	5	21	1	4	0	0	1	2	1	2	0
Avisail Garcia, rf	.143	5	7	0	1	0	0	0	1	1	2	0
Omar Infante, 2b	.353	5	17	6	6	1	0	0	0	1	6	1
Austin Jackson, cf	.250	5	20	4	5	2	0	0	3	1	7	0
Don Kelly, dh	—	1	0	1	0	0	0	0	1	0	0	0
Gerald Laird, c	.000	2	5	0	0	0	0	0	0	0	3	0
Jhonny Peralta, ss	.294	5	17	1	5	0	0	0	1	3	1	0
Danny Worth, ss	—	1	0	0	0	0	0	0	0	0	0	0
Delmon Young, dh	.235	5	17	0	4	0	0	2	6	0	3	0
Totals	**.252**	**5**	**163**	**17**	**41**	**8**	**0**	**2**	**11**	**7**	**39**	**4**

PITCHER	W	L	ERA	G	GS	SV	IP	H	R	ER	BB	SO
Al Alburquerque	1	0	0.00	2	0	0	1.1	0	0	0	0	1
Joaquin Benoit	0	0	6.00	3	0	0	3.0	4	2	2	1	2
Phil Coke	0	0	0.00	3	0	0	1.2	1	0	0	2	1
Octavio Dotel	0	0	0.00	2	0	0	1.0	0	0	0	1	2
Doug Fister	0	0	2.57	1	1	0	7.0	6	2	2	2	8
Rick Porcello	0	0	0.00	1	0	0	0.1	0	0	0	0	0
Anibal Sanchez	0	1	2.84	1	1	0	6.1	5	2	2	2	3
Max Scherzer	0	0	0.00	1	1	0	5.1	3	1	0	1	8
Jose Valverde	0	1	16.20	2	0	1	1.2	4	3	3	0	3
Justin Verlander	2	0	0.56	2	2	0	16.0	7	1	1	5	22
Totals	3	2	2.06	5	5	1	43.2	30	11	10	14	50

OAKLAND ATHLETICS

PLAYER, POS	AVG	G	AB	R	H	2B	3B	HR	RBI	BB	SO	SB
Yoenis Cespedes, lf	.316	5	19	1	6	1	0	0	2	2	2	2
Coco Crisp, cf	.182	5	22	3	4	0	0	1	2	0	2	0
Josh Donaldson, 3b	.294	5	17	1	5	1	0	0	0	1	4	0
Stephen Drew, ss	.211	5	19	0	4	2	0	0	1	2	7	0
Jonny Gomes, ph	.000	1	1	0	0	0	0	0	0	0	0	0
George Kottaras, c	.000	4	4	0	0	0	0	0	0	0	2	0
Brandon Moss, 1b	.133	5	15	0	2	0	0	0	2	7	0
Derek Norris, c	.083	5	12	0	1	0	0	0	0	0	6	0
Cliff Pennington, 2b	.286	5	14	1	4	0	0	0	1	3	4	0
Josh Reddick, rf	.118	5	17	2	2	0	0	1	1	1	10	0
Seth Smith, dh	.133	5	15	3	2	1	0	1	3	3	6	0
Totals	.194	5	155	11	30	5	0	3	10	14	50	2

PITCHER	W	L	ERA	G	GS	SV	IP	H	R	ER	BB	SO
Brett Anderson	1	0	0.00	1	1	0	6.0	2	0	0	2	6
Grant Balfour	0	1	5.40	2	0	1	1.2	3	1	1	1	2
Jerry Blevins	0	0	0.00	3	0	0	3.2	1	0	0	0	6
Ryan Cook	1	0	8.10	4	0	0	3.1	4	3	3	1	4
Sean Doolittle	0	0	3.38	3	0	0	2.2	5	3	1	0	5
A.J. Griffin	0	0	3.60	1	1	0	5.0	7	2	2	1	3
Tommy Milone	0	0	1.50	1	1	0	6.0	5	1	1	1	6
Pat Neshek	0	0	0.00	1	0	0	0.2	0	0	0	0	1
Jarrod Parker	0	2	4.26	2	2	0	12.2	14	7	6	2	11
Evan Scribner	0	0	0.00	1	0	0	2.0	0	0	0	0	3
Totals	2	3	2.89	5	5	1	43.2	41	17	14	7	39

E—Fielder, Crisp, Drew, Parker. **DP**—Detroit 2, Oakland 6. **LOB**—Detroit 30, Oakland 30. **SB**—Berry, Dirks, Infante, Peralta, Cespedes (2). **CS**—Young, Norris. **SH**—Berry, Dirks, Infante, Jackson, Kottaras. **SF**—Kelly. **HBP**—Cabrera (by Cook), Laird (by Milone), Young (by Parker), Moss (by Fister), Smith (by Fister). **IBB**—Fielder (by Balfour). **WP**—Benoit, Scherzer, Cook, Milone, Parker (2).

SCORE BY INNINGS

Detroit	105	110	621—17
Oakland	201	011	123—11

AMERICAN LEAGUE CHAMPIONSHIP SERIES

NEW YORK YANKEES VS- DETROIT TIGERS

DETROIT TIGERS

PLAYER, POS	AVG	G	AB	R	H	2B	3B	HR	RBI	BB	SO	SB
Alex Avila, c	.200	3	10	0	2	0	0	0	0	4	0	0
Quintin Berry, lf	.250	3	8	2	2	1	0	0	0	0	1	1
Miguel Cabrera, 3b	.313	4	16	3	5	1	0	1	4	3	2	0
Andy Dirks, lf	.222	4	18	0	4	1	0	0	1	1	5	0
Prince Fielder, 1b	.235	4	17	1	4	0	0	0	1	2	5	0
Avisail Garcia, rf	.455	4	11	0	5	1	0	0	3	0	1	1
Omar Infante, 2b	.222	4	18	3	4	0	0	0	0	1	3	1
Austin Jackson, cf	.353	4	17	3	6	1	1	1	2	3	0
Don Kelly, dh	—	1	0	1	0	0	0	0	0	0	0	0
Gerald Laird, c	.125	2	8	0	1	0	0	0	0	0	1	0
Jhonny Peralta, ss	.389	4	18	3	7	1	0	2	3	1	3	0
Delmon Young, dh	.353	4	17	3	6	1	0	2	6	2	5	0
Totals	.291	4	158	19	46	7	1	6	19	12	30	3

PITCHER	W	L	ERA	G	GS	SV	IP	H	R	ER	BB	SO
Joaquin Benoit	0	0	0.00	1	0	0	0.2	1	0	0	0	0
Phil Coke	0	0	0.00	4	0	2	5.2	3	0	0	0	4
Octavio Dotel	0	0	0.00	2	0	0	2.1	0	0	0	2	3
Doug Fister	0	0	0.00	1	1	0	6.1	6	0	0	4	5
Anibal Sanchez	1	0	0.00	1	1	0	7.0	3	0	0	3	7

	W	L	ERA	G	GS	SV	IP	H	R	ER	BB	SO
Max Scherzer	1	0	1.59	1	1	0	5.2	2	1	1	2	10
Drew Smyly	1	0	0.00	2	0	0	2.1	1	0	0	0	2
Jose Valverde	0	0	54.00	1	0	0	0.2	3	4	4	1	2
Justin Verlander	1	0	1.08	1	1	0	8.1	3	1	1	0	3
Totals	4	0	1.38	4	4	2	39	22	6	6	12	36

NEW YORK YANKEES

PLAYER, POS	AVG	G	AB	R	H	2B	3B	HR	RBI	BB	SO	SB
Robinson Cano, 2b	.056	4	18	0	1	0	0	0	0	0	3	0
Eric Chavez, 3b	.000	3	8	0	0	0	0	0	0	0	4	0
Brett Gardner, lf	.000	3	8	0	0	0	0	0	0	0	1	2
Curtis Granderson, cf	.000	4	11	0	0	0	0	0	0	2	7	1
Raul Ibanez, dh	.231	4	13	1	3	1	0	1	2	3	4	0
Derek Jeter, ss	.200	1	5	0	1	0	0	0	0	1	2	0
Russell Martin, c	.143	4	14	1	2	0	0	0	0	3	0
Jayson Nix, ss	.000	4	4	0	0	0	0	0	0	1	1	0
Eduardo Nunez, ss	.333	2	6	2	2	0	1	1	1	0	1	0
Alex Rodriguez, 3b	.111	3	9	0	1	0	0	0	0	0	3	0
Chris Stewart, c	—	1	0	0	0	0	0	0	0	0	0	0
Ichiro Suzuki, lf	.353	4	17	1	6	0	0	1	2	1	2	0
Nick Swisher, rf	.250	3	12	0	3	2	0	0	1	1	5	0
Mark Teixeira, 1b	.200	4	15	1	3	1	0	0	0	3	1	0
Totals	.157	4	140	6	22	4	1	3	6	12	36	4

PITCHER	W	L	ERA	G	GS	SV	IP	H	R	ER	BB	SO
Joba Chamberlain	0	0	0.00	3	0	0	1.1	3	0	0	0	0
Cody Eppley	0	0	0.00	4	0	0	3.2	4	0	0	1	4
Phil Hughes	0	1	3.00	1	1	0	3.0	3	1	1	3	1
Hiroki Kuroda	0	1	3.52	1	1	0	7.2	5	3	3	0	11
Boone Logan	0	0	0.00	3	0	0	3.0	3	0	0	0	1
Derek Lowe	0	0	16.20	2	0	0	1.2	3	3	3	0	1
Andy Pettitte	0	0	2.70	1	1	0	6.2	7	2	2	3	5
David Phelps	0	1	9.00	2	0	0	2.0	5	3	2	1	1
Clay Rapada	0	0	0.00	4	0	0	1.1	0	0	0	2	1
David Robertson	0	0	4.50	2	0	0	2.0	2	1	1	0	2
C.C. Sabathia	0	1	12.27	1	1	0	3.2	11	6	5	2	3
Rafael Soriano	0	0	0.00	1	0	0	1.0	0	0	0	0	0
Totals	0	4	4.14	4	4	0	37	46	19	17	12	30

E—Fielder, Infante, Sanchez, Chavez, Nunez, Teixeira. **DP**—Detroit 1, New York 2. **LOB**—Detroit 40, New York 29. **SB**—Berry, Garcia, Infante, Gardner (2), Granderson, Nunez. **CS**—Ibanez. **IBB**—Cabrera (by Pettitte), Young (by Rapada), Ibanez (by Sanchez).

SCORE BY INNINGS

Detroit	101	512	250	002—19
New York	000	001	005	000—6

NATIONAL LEAGUE WILD CARD GAME

ATLANTA BRAVES VS- ST- LOUIS CARDINALS

ST. LOUIS CARDINALS

PLAYER, POS	AVG	G	AB	R	H	2B	3B	HR	RBI	BB	SO	SB
Carlos Beltran, rf	.250	1	4	1	1	0	0	0	0	1	0
Matt Carpenter, 3b	1.000	1	1	0	1	0	0	0	1	0	0	0
Adron Chambers, pr	—	1	0	1	0	0	0	0	0	0	0	0
Allen Craig, 1b	.500	1	4	1	2	1	0	0	1	0	0	0
Daniel Descalso, 2b	.000	1	3	0	0	0	0	0	0	0	0	0
David Freese, 3b	.000	1	2	0	0	0	0	0	0	1	0	0
Matt Holliday, lf	.667	1	3	2	2	0	0	1	1	0	0	0
Jon Jay, cf	.000	1	4	0	0	0	0	0	0	0	1	0
Pete Kozma, ss	.000	1	4	1	0	0	0	0	0	0	2	0
Kyle Lohse, p	.000	1	2	0	0	0	0	0	0	0	1	0
Yadier Molina, c	.000	1	4	0	0	0	0	0	1	0	0	0
Shane Robinson, lf	.000	1	1	0	0	0	0	0	0	1	0	0
Totals	.188	1	32	6	6	1	0	1	5	0	5	0

PITCHER	W	L	ERA	G	GS	SV	IP	H	R	ER	BB	SO
Mitchell Boggs	0	0	0.00	1	0	0	0.2	1	0	0	1	0
Kyle Lohse	1	0	3.18	1	1	0	5.2	6	2	2	1	6
Lance Lynn	0	0	0.00	1	0	0	1.0	0	0	0	0	0
Jason Motte	0	0	0.00	1	0	1	1.1	2	0	0	1	1
Edward Mujica	0	0	13.50	1	0	0	0.2	2	1	1	0	0
Marc Rzepczynski	0	0	0.00	1	0	0	0.1	1	0	0	0	0
Totals	1	0	3.00	1	1	1	9	12	3	3	3	7

ATLANTA BRAVES

PLAYER, POS	AVG	G	AB	R	H	2B	3B	HR	RBI	BB	SO	SB
Michael Bourn, cf	.200	1	5	0	1	0	0	0	1	0	2	0
Jose Constanza, ph	1.000	1	1	1	1	0	1	0	0	0	0	0
Freddie Freeman, 1b	.750	1	4	0	3	1	0	0	0	1	1	0
Jason Heyward, rf	.200	1	5	0	1	0	0	0	0	0	1	0
Chipper Jones, 3b	.200	1	5	0	1	0	0	0	0	0	1	0
Brian McCann, ph	—	1	0	0	0	0	0	0	0	0	1	0
Kris Medlen, p	.000	1	2	0	0	0	0	0	0	0	1	0
Tyler Pastornicky, pr	—	1	0	0	0	0	0	0	0	0	0	0
Martin Prado, lf	.200	1	5	0	1	0	0	0	0	0	1	0
David Ross, c	.750	1	4	1	3	0	0	1	2	0	0	0
Andrelton Simmons, ss	.250	1	4	1	0	0	0	0	0	1	0	0
Dan Uggla, 2b	.000	1	4	1	0	0	0	0	0	1	0	0
Totals	**.308**	**1**	**39**	**3**	**12**	**2**	**1**	**1**	**3**	**3**	**7**	**0**

PITCHER	W	L	ERA	G	GS	SV	IP	H	R	ER	BB	SO
Chad Durbin	0	0	—	1	0	0	0.0	0	1	0	0	0
Craig Kimbrel	0	0	0.00	1	0	0	1.0	0	0	0	0	1
Kris Medlen	0	1	2.84	1	1	0	6.1	3	5	2	0	4
Eric O'Flaherty	0	0	0.00	1	0	0	1.0	2	0	0	0	0
Jonny Venters	0	0	0.00	1	0	0	0.2	1	0	0	0	0
Totals	**0**	**1**	**2.00**	**1**	**1**	**0**	**9**	**6**	**6**	**2**	**0**	**5**

E—Jones, Simmons, Uggla. DP—Atlanta 2. LOB—St. Louis 2, Atlanta 12. SH—Descalso. SF—Freese. HBP—Holliday (by Medlen).

SCORE BY INNINGS
St. Louis	000 301 200—6
Atlanta	020 000 100—3

NATIONAL LEAGUE DIVISION SERIES

WASHINGTON NATIONALS VS ST. LOUIS CARDINALS

ST. LOUIS CARDINALS

PLAYER, POS	AVG	G	AB	R	H	2B	3B	HR	RBI	BB	SO	SB
Carlos Beltran, rf	.444	5	18	5	8	3	0	2	4	5	1	1
Chris Carpenter, p	.667	1	3	0	2	1	0	0	0	0	1	0
Matt Carpenter, ph	.000	5	4	0	0	0	0	0	0	0	3	0
Adron Chambers, pr	—	2	0	1	0	0	0	0	0	0	0	0
Allen Craig, 1b	.316	5	19	2	6	2	0	1	3	4	6	0
Tony Cruz, c	—	1	0	0	0	0	0	0	0	0	0	0
Daniel Descalso, 2b	.316	5	19	7	6	1	0	2	6	1	5	1
David Freese, 3b	.421	5	19	3	8	3	0	0	1	3	5	0
Jaime Garcia, p	—	1	0	0	0	0	0	0	0	0	0	0
Matt Holliday, lf	.190	5	21	2	4	1	0	0	4	2	6	0
Jon Jay, cf	.200	5	20	4	4	0	1	0	4	2	5	2
Pete Kozma, ss	.250	5	16	4	4	1	0	1	5	5	5	0
Kyle Lohse, p	.000	1	2	0	0	0	0	0	0	0	1	0
Yadier Molina, c	.118	5	17	3	2	0	0	0	1	5	1	0
Jason Motte, p	.000	2	1	0	0	0	0	0	0	0	1	0
Shane Robinson, ph	.000	3	1	1	0	0	0	0	0	1	0	0
Skip Schumaker, ph	.000	4	4	0	0	0	0	0	1	0	1	0
Adam Wainwright, p	.000	2	2	0	0	0	0	0	0	1	2	0
Totals	**.265**	**5**	**166**	**32**	**44**	**12**	**1**	**6**	**29**	**29**	**43**	**4**

PITCHER	W	L	ERA	G	GS	SV	IP	H	R	ER	BB	SO
Mitchell Boggs	0	1	0.00	4	0	0	3.2	3	2	0	1	2
Chris Carpenter	1	0	0.00	1	1	0	5.2	7	0	0	2	2
Jaime Garcia	0	0	4.50	1	1	0	2.0	2	1	1	3	3
Joe Kelly	0	0	0.00	3	0	0	3.2	0	0	0	1	3
Kyle Lohse	0	0	1.29	1	1	0	7.0	2	1	1	1	5
Lance Lynn	1	1	8.10	3	0	0	3.1	4	3	3	2	6
Jason Motte	1	0	3.00	2	0	0	3.0	3	1	1	0	1
Edward Mujica	0	0	3.00	3	0	0	3.0	3	1	1	1	1
Trevor Rosenthal	0	0	0.00	3	0	0	3.1	1	0	0	0	6
Marc Rzepczynski	0	0	0.00	1	0	0	0.1	1	0	0	0	1
Fernando Salas	0	0	0.00	1	0	0	1.0	0	0	0	0	1
Adam Wainwright	0	0	7.88	2	2	0	8.0	13	7	7	3	15
Totals	**3**	**2**	**2.86**	**5**	**5**	**0**	**44**	**39**	**16**	**14**	**14**	**46**

WASHINGTON NATIONALS

PLAYER, POS	AVG	G	AB	R	H	2B	3B	HR	RBI	BB	SO	SB
Roger Bernadina, ph	.000	4	2	0	0	0	0	0	0	2	1	0
Ian Desmond, ss	.368	5	19	2	7	1	0	0	0	0	3	0
Ross Detwiler, p	.000	1	1	0	0	0	0	0	0	0	1	0
Danny Espinosa, 2b	.067	5	15	0	1	0	0	0	0	2	7	0
Gio Gonzalez, p	.000	2	3	0	0	0	0	0	0	1	2	0
Bryce Harper, cf	.130	5	23	2	3	1	1	1	2	0	8	0
Edwin Jackson, p	.000	2	1	0	0	0	0	0	0	0	0	0
Adam LaRoche, 1b	.176	5	17	4	3	0	0	2	2	4	3	0
Steve Lombardozzi, ph	.333	3	3	0	1	0	0	0	0	0	0	0
Tyler Moore, ph	1.000	1	1	0	1	0	0	0	2	0	0	0
Michael Morse, lf	.263	5	19	2	5	0	0	1	2	0	4	0
Kurt Suzuki, c	.235	5	17	0	4	0	0	0	2	2	4	0
Chad Tracy, ph	.000	5	4	0	0	0	0	0	0	0	1	0
Jayson Werth, rf	.238	5	21	3	5	1	0	1	1	3	6	0
Ryan Zimmerman, 3b	.381	5	21	3	8	1	0	2	4	0	6	0
Jordan Zimmermann, p	1.000	2	1	0	1	0	0	0	1	0	0	0
Totals	**.232**	**5**	**168**	**16**	**39**	**4**	**1**	**7**	**16**	**14**	**46**	**0**

PITCHER	W	L	ERA	G	GS	SV	IP	H	R	ER	BB	SO
Sean Burnett	0	0	27.00	2	0	0	1.0	3	4	3	1	1
Tyler Clippard	0	0	3.00	3	0	0	3.0	1	1	1	1	5
Ross Detwiler	0	0	0.00	1	1	0	6.0	3	1	0	3	2
Christian Garcia	0	0	3.38	2	0	0	2.2	2	1	1	4	4
Gio Gonzalez	0	0	4.50	2	2	0	10.0	6	5	5	11	10
Michael Gonzalez	0	0	9.00	1	0	0	1.0	1	1	1	0	1
Tom Gorzelanny	0	0	0.00	1	0	0	0.1	1	0	0	0	0
Edwin Jackson	0	1	7.50	2	1	0	6.0	9	5	5	3	6
Ryan Mattheus	1	0	6.00	3	0	0	3.0	3	2	2	1	0
Craig Stammen	0	0	9.00	4	0	0	3.0	5	3	3	2	3
Drew Storen	1	1	9.00	4	0	1	4.0	3	4	4	3	6
Jordan Zimmermann	0	1	11.25	2	1	0	4.0	7	5	5	0	5
Totals	**2**	**3**	**6.14**	**5**	**5**	**1**	**44**	**44**	**32**	**30**	**29**	**43**

E—Freese, Kozma, Desmond, Espinosa, LaRoche, Morse, Zimmerman. DP—St. Louis 2, Washington 5. LOB—St. Louis 41, Washington 37. SB—Beltran, Descalso, Jay (2). CS—Freese. SH—Descalso, Jay, Lohse, Lynn, Espinosa (2). SF—Beltran, Descalso, Jay, Zimmerman. HBP—Holliday (by Stammen), Kozma (by Stammen), Molina (by Stammen). IBB—Craig (by C.Garcia), Freese (by Detwiler). WP—Wainwright, G.Gonzalez 2.

SCORE BY INNINGS
St. Louis	192 322 274—32
Washington	333 020 131—16

CINCINNATI REDS VS SAN FRANCISCO GIANTS

SAN FRANCISCO GIANTS

PLAYER, POS	AVG	G	AB	R	H	2B	3B	HR	RBI	BB	SO	SB
Joaquin Arias, ss	.500	4	6	3	3	2	0	0	0	0	1	0
Brandon Belt, 1b	.077	5	13	0	1	0	0	0	0	2	7	0
Gregor Blanco, lf	.286	5	14	3	4	1	0	1	2	1	5	0
Madison Bumgarner, p	.000	1	1	0	0	0	0	0	0	0	1	0
Matt Cain, p	.000	2	4	0	0	0	0	0	0	0	4	0
Brandon Crawford, ss	.182	5	11	1	2	0	1	0	1	3	4	0
Aubrey Huff, ph	.000	3	3	0	0	0	0	0	0	0	1	0
Tim Lincecum, p	.000	2	2	0	0	0	0	0	0	0	0	0
Xavier Nady, lf	.000	4	5	0	0	0	0	0	0	1	3	0
Angel Pagan, cf	.150	5	20	3	3	1	0	1	4	2	3	0
Hunter Pence, rf	.200	5	20	4	4	0	0	0	0	3	1	0
Buster Posey, c	.211	5	19	3	4	0	0	2	5	3	4	0
Sergio Romo, p	.000	3	1	0	0	0	0	0	0	0	1	0
Hector Sanchez, c	.500	1	2	1	1	0	0	0	0	2	1	0
Pablo Sandoval, 3b	.333	5	21	2	7	2	0	1	3	0	2	0
Marco Scutaro, 2b	.150	5	20	2	3	1	0	0	1	2	0	0
Ryan Theriot, ph	.000	2	2	0	0	0	0	0	0	0	1	0
Ryan Vogelsong, p	—	1	0	0	0	0	0	0	0	0	0	0
Barry Zito, p	.000	1	1	0	0	0	0	0	0	0	0	0
Totals	**.194**	**5**	**165**	**18**	**32**	**7**	**1**	**5**	**16**	**16**	**39**	**1**

PITCHER	W	L	ERA	G	GS	SV	IP	H	R	ER	BB	SO
Jeremy Affeldt	0	0	0.00	3	0	0	3.2	3	0	0	1	2
Madison Bumgarner	0	1	8.31	1	1	0	4.1	7	4	4	1	4
Matt Cain	1	1	5.06	2	2	0	10.2	11	6	6	3	9
Santiago Casilla	0	0	2.70	5	0	0	3.1	6	2	1	1	5
George Kontos	0	0	0.00	4	0	0	3.2	2	0	0	0	2
Tim Lincecum	1	0	1.42	2	0	0	6.1	3	1	1	0	8
Javier Lopez	0	0	0.00	2	0	0	0.2	0	0	0	0	0
Jose Mijares	0	0	81.00	2	0	0	0.1	2	3	3	1	1
Guillermo Mota	0	0	18.00	2	0	0	1.0	4	2	2	0	2
Sergio Romo	1	0	2.08	3	0	1	4.1	2	1	1	1	1

	W	L	ERA	G	GS	SV	IP	H	R	ER	BB	SO
Ryan Vogelsong	0	0	1.80	1	1	0	5.0	3	1	1	3	5
Barry Zito	0	0	6.75	1	1	0	2.2	4	2	2	4	4
Totals	3	2	4.11	5	5	1	46	47	22	21	15	43

CINCINNATI REDS

PLAYER, POS	AVG	G	AB	R	H	2B	3B	HR	RBI	BB	SO	SB
Bronson Arroyo, p	.000	1	4	0	0	0	0	0	0	0	2	0
Homer Bailey, p	.000	2	3	0	0	0	0	0	0	0	0	0
Jay Bruce, rf	.263	5	19	2	5	2	0	1	4	2	2	0
Miguel Cairo, ph	.000	3	2	0	0	0	0	0	0	0	0	0
Zack Cozart, ss	.238	5	21	2	5	0	0	0	0	2	5	0
Johnny Cueto, p	—	1	0	0	0	0	0	0	0	0	0	0
Todd Frazier, 3b	.167	4	6	0	1	0	0	0	1	1	2	0
Ryan Hanigan, c	.200	4	15	3	3	0	0	0	3	0	3	0
Chris Heisey, lf	.000	4	3	1	0	0	0	0	0	0	1	0
Mat Latos, p	.000	2	2	0	0	0	0	0	0	0	1	0
Mike Leake, p	.500	1	2	0	1	0	0	0	0	0	0	0
Ryan Ludwick, lf	.333	5	18	4	6	0	0	3	4	4	5	0
Dioner Navarro, c	.250	2	4	0	1	0	0	0	0	1	2	0
Xavier Paul, ph	.333	3	3	1	1	0	0	0	0	0	1	0
Brandon Phillips, 2b	.375	5	24	1	9	3	0	1	7	0	4	1
Scott Rolen, 3b	.250	4	16	1	4	0	0	0	1	1	4	0
Drew Stubbs, cf	.211	5	19	4	4	1	1	0	1	0	3	0
Wilson Valdez, cf	.000	2	1	0	0	0	0	0	0	0	0	0
Joey Votto, 1b	.389	5	18	3	7	0	0	0	4	5	0	0
Totals	.261	5	180	22	47	6	1	5	21	15	43	1

PITCHER	W	L	ERA	G	GS	SV	IP	H	R	ER	BB	SO
Jose Arredondo	0	0	20.25	2	0	0	1.1	4	3	3	2	0
Bronson Arroyo	1	0	0.00	1	1	0	7.0	1	0	0	1	4
Homer Bailey	0	0	1.29	1	1	0	7.0	1	1	1	1	10
Jonathan Broxton	0	1	0.00	3	0	0	3.0	4	1	0	1	4
Aroldis Chapman	0	0	3.00	3	0	0	3.0	2	1	1	2	3
Johnny Cueto	0	0	0.00	1	1	0	0.1	0	0	0	0	1
J.J. Hoover	0	0	0.00	2	0	0	2.2	0	0	0	2	0
Mat Latos	0	1	6.48	2	1	0	8.1	11	7	6	2	5
Mike Leake	0	1	10.38	1	1	0	4.1	6	5	5	2	1
Sam LeCure	1	0	0.00	3	0	0	4.0	2	0	0	2	5
Sean Marshall	0	0	0.00	3	0	0	4.0	0	0	0	3	3
Alfredo Simon	0	0	0.00	1	0	0	1.0	1	0	0	1	1
Totals	2	3	3.13	5	5	0	46	32	18	16	18	39

E—Lincecum, Sandoval, Cozart, Rolen (2). **DP**—San Francisco 4, Cincinnati 3. **LOB**—San Francisco 30, Cincinnati 39. **SB**—Pence, Phillips. **CS**—Pagan, Bruce. **SH**—Scutaro, Vogelsong. **SF**—Pagan, Sandoval, Phillips. **HBP**—Blanco (by Bailey), Bruce (by Affeldt), Cozart (by Cain), Hanigan (by Cain). **IBB**—Crawford (by LeCure), Ludwick (by Affeldt). **WP**—Casilla, Arredondo, Chapman (2).

SCORE BY INNINGS

San Francisco	121	081	301	1—18
Cincinnati	213	422	053	0—22

NATIONAL LEAGUE CHAMPIONSHIP SERIES

SAN FRANCISCO GIANTS VS. ST. LOUIS CARDINALS

ST. LOUIS CARDINALS

PLAYER, POS	AVG	G	AB	R	H	2B	3B	HR	RBI	BB	SO	SB
Carlos Beltran, rf	.300	6	20	2	6	3	0	1	2	2	3	2
Chris Carpenter, p	.500	2	2	0	1	1	0	0	1	0	1	0
Matt Carpenter, 1b	.333	3	9	3	3	1	0	1	2	3	2	0
Adron Chambers, ph	.000	4	2	0	0	0	0	0	0	0	0	0
Allen Craig, 1b	.125	7	24	1	3	1	0	0	2	1	6	0
Tony Cruz, ph	.000	1	0	0	0	0	0	0	0	0	1	0
Daniel Descalso, 2b	.200	7	25	2	5	1	0	0	0	1	7	1
David Freese, 3b	.192	7	26	2	5	2	0	1	2	1	7	0
Matt Holliday, lf	.200	6	25	1	5	0	0	0	2	0	4	1
Jon Jay, cf	.207	7	29	3	6	1	0	0	3	1	5	0
Pete Kozma, ss	.227	7	22	3	5	1	0	0	3	7	1	
Kyle Lohse, p	.000	2	3	0	0	0	0	0	0	0	0	0
Lance Lynn, p	.000	2	2	0	0	0	0	0	0	0	1	0
Yadier Molina, c	.393	7	28	2	11	1	0	0	2	0	1	0
Shane Robinson, ph	.000	6	6	0	0	0	0	0	0	1	2	0
Skip Schumaker, ph	.000	5	5	0	0	0	0	0	0	0	2	0
Adam Wainwright, p	.000	1	1	0	0	0	0	0	0	1	0	0
Totals	.217	7	230	19	50	12	0	3	19	15	49	5

PITCHER	W	L	ERA	G	GS	SV	IP	H	R	ER	BB	SO
Joaquin Benoit	0	0	0.00	1	0	0	0.2	1	0	0	0	0
Mitchell Boggs	0	0	5.40	4	0	0	3.1	4	2	2	2	3
Chris Carpenter	0	2	4.50	2	2	0	8.0	12	10	4	4	7
Joe Kelly	0	0	4.50	4	0	0	4.0	6	2	2	3	2
Kyle Lohse	1	1	7.04	2	2	0	7.2	13	6	6	6	3
Lance Lynn	0	1	4.91	2	2	0	7.1	9	8	4	4	9
Shelby Miller	0	0	5.40	2	0	0	3.1	4	2	2	1	4
Jason Motte	0	0	2.25	3	0	2	4.0	2	1	1	0	0
Edward Mujica	1	0	0.00	5	0	0	4.0	4	0	0	0	3
Trevor Rosenthal	0	0	0.00	4	0	0	5.1	1	0	0	2	9
Marc Rzepczynski	0	0	6.75	3	0	0	1.1	1	1	1	1	2
Fernando Salas	0	0	3.86	4	0	0	4.2	3	2	2	0	4
Adam Wainwright	1	0	1.29	1	1	0	7.0	4	1	1	0	5
Totals	3	4	3.75	7	7	2	60	63	35	25	23	51

SAN FRANCISCO GIANTS

PLAYER, POS	AVG	G	AB	R	H	2B	3B	HR	RBI	BB	SO	SB
Joaquin Arias, 3b	.000	4	2	0	0	0	0	0	0	0	0	0
Brandon Belt, 1b	.304	6	23	6	7	1	1	1	2	2	5	1
Gregor Blanco, lf	.182	7	22	6	4	1	1	0	2	6	3	0
Madison Bumgarner, p	.000	1	1	0	0	0	0	0	0	0	1	0
Matt Cain, p	.400	2	5	0	2	0	0	0	1	0	3	0
Brandon Crawford, ss	.217	7	23	2	5	1	0	0	5	3	7	0
Aubrey Huff, ph	.200	6	5	1	1	0	0	0	0	1	1	0
Tim Lincecum, p	.000	2	1	0	0	0	0	0	0	0	1	0
Angel Pagan, cf	.242	7	33	4	8	0	1	1	2	1	5	0
Hunter Pence, rf	.179	7	28	4	5	1	0	1	3	1	8	0
Buster Posey, c	.154	7	26	1	4	0	0	0	1	4	6	0
Hector Sanchez, c	.000	2	5	0	0	0	0	0	0	0	3	0
Pablo Sandoval, 3b	.310	7	29	4	9	2	0	2	6	2	4	0
Marco Scutaro, 2b	.500	7	28	6	14	3	0	0	4	2	1	0
Ryan Theriot, ph	.667	3	3	0	2	0	0	0	3	1	0	0
Ryan Vogelsong, p	.200	2	5	1	1	1	0	0	1	0	2	0
Barry Zito, p	.500	1	2	0	1	0	0	0	0	1	0	1
Totals	.261	7	241	35	63	10	3	5	31	23	51	1

PITCHER	W	L	ERA	G	GS	SV	IP	H	R	ER	BB	SO
Jeremy Affeldt	0	0	0.00	5	0	0	4.2	2	0	0	1	4
Madison Bumgarner	0	1	14.73	1	1	0	3.2	8	6	6	1	2
Matt Cain	1	1	2.19	2	2	0	12.1	11	3	3	2	6
Santiago Casilla	0	0	0.00	4	0	0	2.1	2	0	0	0	3
George Kontos	0	0	13.50	3	0	0	1.1	2	2	2	0	0
Tim Lincecum	0	1	5.40	2	1	0	6.2	6	4	4	4	4
Javier Lopez	0	0	0.00	3	0	0	2.1	0	0	0	2	4
Jose Mijares	0	0	0.00	3	0	0	2.0	1	0	0	1	3
Guillermo Mota	0	0	27.00	1	0	0	0.2	2	2	2	0	1
Sergio Romo	0	0	0.00	4	0	0	3.1	2	0	0	0	3
Ryan Vogelsong	2	0	1.29	2	2	0	14.0	8	2	2	3	13
Barry Zito	1	0	0.00	1	1	0	7.2	6	0	0	1	6
Totals	4	3	2.80	7	7	0	61.0	50	19	19	15	49

E—Carpenter, Holliday, Jay, Kozma (2), Lynn, Blanco, Cain, Sandoval (2). **DP**—St. Louis 3, San Francisco 2. **LOB**—St. Louis 48, San Francisco 52. **SB**—Beltran (2), Descalso, Holliday, Kozma, Belt. **CS**—Kozma. **SH**—Wainwright, Cain, Vogelsong, Zito. **SF**—Craig. **HBP**—Craig (by Vogelsong), Holliday (by Cain), Jay (by Cain). **IBB**—Descalso (by Cain), Kozma (by Zito), Crawford (by Carpenter), Posey (by Lohse). **WP**—Affeldt, Casilla, Romo.

SCORE BY INNINGS

St. Louis	232	423	300—19	
San Francisco	366	(12)00	152—35	

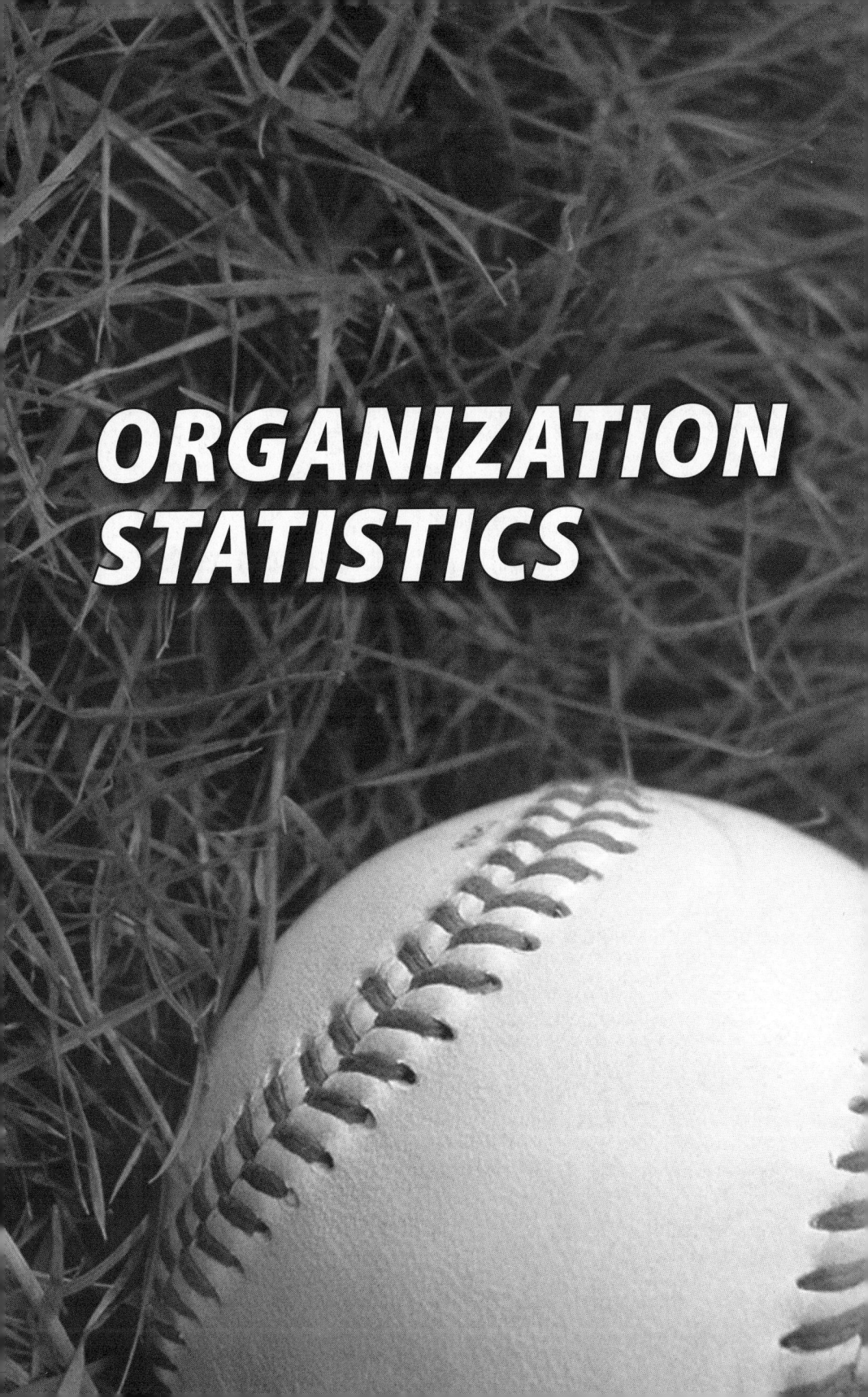

ORGANIZATION STATISTICS

Arizona Diamondbacks

SEASON IN A SENTENCE: After a surprise play-off run in 2011, the Diamondbacks never seemed to get untracked in 2012, meandering around .500 all season and finishing the season at 81-81 and 13 games out of first place in the National League West.

HIGH POINT: Arizona didn't see first place in the NL West after April 10, but the apex of the season probably came on Aug. 3, with a 4-2 win over the Phillies that was the team's fourth straight and capped a strong run of pitching performances by Trevor Cahill, Wade Miley, Pat Corbin and Ian Kennedy. The Diamondbacks were four games over .500 at that point and just two games out of the division lead.

LOW POINT: The team went 11-17 in May and finished the month 10 1/2 games out of first place, a hole Arizona was never able to really dig itself out of, leading to a sell-off of veteran players by the end of the season.

NOTABLE ROOKIES: Lefthander Wade Miley was one of the best rookie starting pitchers in the game, symbolic of an organization deep in young pitching. Lefthander Pat Corbin also held down a rotation spot for much of the season as injuries struck Josh Collmenter and Daniel Hudson. Tyler Skaggs and Trevor Bauer made their major league debuts but will make more significant contributions in the future.

KEY TRANSACTIONS: Arizona spent a lot of time on the phone with Oakland. Before the 2012 season the Diamondbacks sent a package of players highlighted by Jarrod Parker to the Athletics for Craig Breslow and Trevor Cahill. Once the season didn't seem destined for the playoffs in August, Arizona sent Stephen Drew to the A's and Joe Saunders to the Orioles for young players, and after the season ended the team traded Chris Young to the A's in a three-way deal that netted Cliff Pennington from Oakland and Heath Bell from the Marlins.

DOWN ON THE FARM: Most Diamondbacks farm teams were below .500 for the season, but Triple-A Reno was a bright spot, winning not only the Pacific Coast League title but also the Triple-A National Championship. Center fielder Adam Eaton was the team's driving force, batting .375 between Double-A and Triple-A to lead the minors. The ability to call on players like Bauer, Corbin, Miley and Skaggs highlighted the strength of the system's pitching talent.

OPENING DAY PAYROLL: $74.3 million (24th)

PLAYERS OF THE YEAR

MAJOR LEAGUE	MINOR LEAGUE
Wade Miley lhp	**Adam Eaton** of
16-11, 3.33	(Double-A/Triple-A)
144 SO/37 BB	.375/.456/.523
All-star as rookie	Led minors in batting

ORGANIZATION LEADERS

BATTING		*Minimum 250 PA
MAJORS		
* AVG	Aaron Hill	.302
* OPS	Aaron Hill	.882
HR	Jason Kubel	30
RBI	Jason Kubel	90
MINORS		
* AVG	Adam Eaton, Mobile/Reno	.375
* OBP	Adam Eaton, Mobile/Reno	.456
* SLG	Ryan Wheeler, Reno	.572
R	Adam Eaton, Mobile/Reno	130
H	Adam Eaton, Mobile/Reno	198
TB	Adam Eaton, Mobile/Reno	276
2B	Adam Eaton, Mobile/Reno	47
3B	Tom Belza, South Bend	10
3B	Ender Inciarte, South Bend/Visalia	10
HR	Jonathan Griffin, Visalia/Mobile	28
RBI	Jonathan Griffin, Visalia/Mobile	102
BB	Jake Elmore, Reno	74
SO	Matt Helm, South Bend	148
SB	Ender Inciarte, South Bend/Visalia	46

PITCHING		#Minimum 75 IP
MAJORS		
W	Wade Miley	16
# ERA	Wade Miley	3.33
SO	Ian Kennedy	187
SV	J.J. Putz	32
MINORS		
W	Trevor Bauer, Mobile/Reno	12
	Archie Bradley, South Bend	12
L	Derek Eitel, Mobile	11
	Joe Martinez, Reno	11
# ERA	Trevor Bauer, Mobile/Reno	2.42
G	Sam Demel, Reno	56
GS	Four tied at	27
SV	Jonathan Albaladejo, Reno	25
IP	David Holmberg, Visalia/Mobile	173.1
BB	Archie Bradley, South Bend	84
SO	Trevor Bauer, Mobile/Reno	157
# AVG	Archie Bradley, South Bend	.181

General Manager: Kevin Towers. **Farm Director:** Mike Bell. **Scouting Director:** Ray Montgomery.

Class	Team	League	W	L	PCT	Finish	Manager
Majors	Arizona Diamondbacks	National	81	81	.500	t-8th (16)	Kirk Gibson
Triple-A	Reno Aces	Pacific Coast	81	63	.563	3rd (16)	Brett Butler
Double-A	Mobile BayBears	Southern	69	71	.493	t-6th (10)	Turner Ward
High A	Visalia Rawhide	California	64	76	.457	9th (10)	Jason Hardtke
Low A	South Bend Silver Hawks	Midwest	67	73	.479	13th (16)	Mark Haley
Short-season	Yakima Bears	Northwest	36	40	.474	5th (8)	Audo Vicente
Rookie	Missoula Osprey	Pioneer	41	35	.539	4th (8)	Andy Green
Rookie	AZL Diamondbacks	Arizona	27	29	.482	8th (13)	Hector De La Cruz
Overall 2012 Minor League Record			385	387	.499	19th (30)	

ORGANIZATION STATISTICS

ARIZONA DIAMONDBACKS

NATIONAL LEAGUE

Batting	B-T	HT	WT	DOB	AVG	vLH	vRH	G	AB	R	H	2B	3B	HR	RBI	BB	HBP	SH	SF	SO	SB	CS	SLG	OBP
Bell, Josh	B-R	6-3	230	11-13-86	.173	.083	.200	21	52	3	9	2	0	1	4	4	0	0	0	14	0	0	.269	.232
Blanco, Henry	R-R	5-11	220	8-29-71	.188	.162	.222	21	64	6	12	3	0	1	7	3	0	0	0	18	1	0	.281	.224
Bloomquist, Willie	R-R	5-11	185	11-27-77	.302	.317	.295	80	324	47	98	21	5	0	23	12	0	0	2	55	7	10	.398	.325
Blum, Geoff	B-R	6-3	220	4-26-73	.143	.000	.160	17	28	1	4	0	0	0	1	2	0	0	1	7	0	0	.143	.194
Drew, Stephen	L-R	6-0	190	3-16-83	.193	.189	.194	40	135	17	26	8	1	2	12	19	0	0	1	35	0	1	.311	.290
Eaton, Adam	L-L	5-8	185	12-6-88	.259	.313	.226	22	85	19	22	3	2	2	5	14	3	1	0	15	2	3	.412	.382
Elmore, Jake	R-R	5-10	180	6-15-87	.191	.158	.204	30	68	1	13	4	0	0	5	5	0	0	6	0	0	.250	.247
Goldschmidt, Paul	R-R	6-3	230	9-10-87	.286	.343	.257	145	514	82	147	43	1	20	82	60	4	0	9	130	18	3	.490	.359
Graham, Tyler	R-R	6-0	185	1-25-84	.000	.000	.000	10	2	1	0	0	0	0	0	0	0	0	0	2	0	1	.000	.000
Hill, Aaron	R-R	5-11	205	3-21-82	.302	.271	.316	156	609	93	184	44	6	26	85	52	4	1	2	86	14	5	.522	.360
Jacobs, Mike	L-R	6-3	215	10-30-80	.211	.400	.143	13	19	4	4	1	0	0	2	4	0	0	0	6	0	0	.263	.348
Johnson, Chris	R-R	6-3	220	10-1-84	.286	.281	.289	44	147	12	42	7	2	7	35	8	1	1	3	40	1	0	.503	.321
2-team total (92 Houston)					.281	—	—	136	488	48	137	28	5	15	76	31	4	1	4	132	5	1	.451	.326
Kubel, Jason	L-R	6-0	220	5-25-82	.253	.234	.264	141	506	75	128	30	4	30	90	57	2	0	6	151	1	1	.506	.327
McDonald, John	R-R	5-9	180	9-24-74	.249	.318	.214	70	197	16	49	9	0	6	22	12	1	2	0	33	0	1	.386	.295
Montero, Miguel	L-R	5-11	215	7-9-83	.286	.259	.299	141	486	65	139	25	2	15	88	73	12	0	2	130	0	0	.438	.391
Nieves, Wil	R-R	5-11	190	9-25-77	.306	.278	.333	16	36	4	11	1	0	1	3	1	0	1	0	8	0	1	.417	.324
2-team total (16 Colorado)					.301	—	—	32	83	7	25	3	0	2	8	4	0	1	1	17	0	1	.410	.330
Overbay, Lyle	L-L	6-2	235	1-28-77	.292	.214	.305	45	96	11	28	9	0	2	10	12	0	0	1	26	0	0	.448	.367
2-team total (20 Atlanta)					.259	—	—	65	116	12	30	10	0	2	10	13	0	0	1	34	0	0	.397	.331
Parra, Gerardo	L-L	5-11	200	5-6-87	.273	.256	.278	133	385	58	105	21	2	7	36	33	4	6	2	77	15	9	.392	.335
Pollock, A.J.	R-R	6-1	195	12-5-87	.247	.269	.207	31	81	8	20	4	1	2	8	9	0	1	2	11	1	2	.395	.315
Ransom, Cody	R-R	6-3	205	2-17-76	.269	.357	.220	26	78	11	21	7	0	5	16	7	3	0	0	30	0	0	.551	.352
2-team total (64 Milwaukee)					.220	—	—	90	246	29	54	14	0	11	42	30	3	3	0	109	0	1	.411	.312
Roberts, Ryan	R-R	5-11	185	9-19-80	.250	.269	.239	83	252	28	63	9	0	6	34	22	0	2	4	45	6	3	.357	.306
Schmidt, Konrad	R-R	5-10	230	8-2-84	.000	—	.000	4	7	1	0	0	0	0	2	1	0	0	0	2	0	0	.000	.125
Upton, Justin	R-R	6-2	205	8-25-87	.280	.275	.282	150	554	107	155	24	4	17	67	63	5	0	6	121	18	8	.430	.355
Wheeler, Ryan	L-R	6-3	235	7-10-88	.239	.067	.266	50	109	11	26	6	1	1	10	9	0	0	1	22	1	0	.339	.294
Young, Chris	R-R	6-2	190	9-5-83	.231	.267	.210	101	325	36	75	24	0	14	41	36	2	0	0	79	8	3	.434	.311

Pitching	B-T	HT	WT	DOB	W	L	ERA	G	GS	CG	SV	IP	H	R	ER	HR	BB	SO	AVG	vLH	vRH	K/9	BB/9
Albaladejo, Jonathan	R-R	6-5	255	10-30-82	0	0	9.00	3	0	0	0	3	5	3	3	1	0	2	.385	.333	.500	6.00	0.00
Albers, Matt	L-R	6-0	225	1-20-83	1	1	2.57	23	0	0	0	21	16	7	6	3	7	19	.213	.212	.214	8.14	3.00
Bauer, Trevor	R-R	6-1	185	1-17-91	1	2	6.06	4	4	0	0	16	14	13	11	2	13	17	.230	.281	.172	9.37	7.16
Bergesen, Brad	L-R	6-2	210	9-25-85	2	1	3.64	19	0	0	0	30	29	14	12	2	7	18	.266	.326	.222	5.46	2.12
Breslow, Craig	L-L	6-0	190	8-8-80	2	0	2.70	40	0	0	0	43	38	15	13	5	13	42	.233	.243	.226	8.72	2.70
Cahill, Trevor	R-R	6-4	220	3-1-88	13	12	3.78	32	32	2	0	200	184	93	84	16	74	156	.250	.253	.246	7.02	3.33
Collmenter, Josh	R-R	6-2	235	2-7-86	5	3	3.69	28	11	0	0	90	92	39	37	13	22	80	.264	.313	.215	7.97	2.19
Corbin, Pat	L-L	6-2	185	7-19-89	6	8	4.54	22	17	0	1	107	117	56	54	14	25	86	.280	.325	.269	7.23	2.10
Demel, Sam	R-R	6-0	205	10-23-85	0	1	9.00	1	0	0	0	1	2	1	1	0	1	0	.500	.000	.667	0.00	9.00
Hernandez, David	R-R	6-2	230	5-13-85	2	3	2.50	72	0	0	4	68	48	21	19	4	22	98	.190	.240	.145	12.91	2.90
Hudson, Daniel	R-R	6-3	225	3-9-87	3	2	7.35	9	9	0	0	45	62	37	37	9	12	37	.332	.340	.321	7.35	2.38
Kennedy, Ian	R-R	6-0	190	12-19-84	15	12	4.02	33	33	1	0	208	216	101	93	28	55	187	.266	.265	.267	8.08	2.38
Lindstrom, Matt	R-R	6-2	220	2-11-80	0	0	2.53	12	0	0	0	11	10	3	3	0	2	10	.238	.167	.292	8.44	1.69
Martinez, Joe	L-R	6-2	190	2-26-83	0	0	9.00	1	0	0	0	1	2	1	1	0	0	1	.400	.500	.333	9.00	0.00
Miley, Wade	L-L	6-0	220	11-13-86	16	11	3.33	32	29	0	0	195	193	79	72	14	37	144	.255	.200	.270	6.66	1.71
Paterson, Joe	R-L	6-1	210	5-19-86	0	0	37.13	6	0	0	0	3	15	11	11	2	3	0	.652	.500	.769	0.00	10.13
Putz, J.J.	R-R	6-5	250	2-22-77	1	5	2.82	57	0	0	32	54	41	18	17	4	11	65	.223	.219	.227	10.77	1.82
Saito, Takashi	L-R	6-2	200	2-14-70	0	0	6.75	16	0	0	0	12	17	14	9	4	5	11	.321	.261	.367	8.25	3.75
Saunders, Joe	L-L	6-3	210	6-16-81	6	10	4.22	21	21	1	0	130	146	68	61	17	31	89	.280	.207	.303	6.16	2.15
Shaw, Bryan	B-R	6-1	210	11-8-87	1	6	3.49	64	0	0	2	59	60	29	23	4	24	41	.273	.333	.211	6.22	3.64
Skaggs, Tyler	L-L	6-3	195	7-13-91	1	3	5.83	6	6	0	0	29	30	20	19	6	13	21	.256	.167	.273	6.44	3.99

	B-T	HT	WT	DOB	W	L	ERA	G	GS	CG	SV	IP	H	R	ER	HR	BB	SO	AVG	vLH	vRH	K/9	BB/9
Zagurski, Mike	L-L	6-0	225	1-27-83	0	0	5.54	45	0	0	0	37	37	24	23	5	19	34	.272	.298	.253	8.20	4.58
Ziegler, Brad	R-R	6-4	210	10-10-79	6	1	2.49	77	0	0	0	69	54	21	19	2	21	42	.228	.268	.211	5.50	2.75

Fielding

Catcher	PCT	G	PO	A	E	DP	PB
Blanco	.987	21	141	14	2	5	2
Montero	.992	139	1008	78	9	8	5
Nieves	.983	12	56	3	1	0	1
Schmidt	1.000	2	11	3	0	0	1

First Base	PCT	G	PO	A	E	DP
Goldschmidt	.995	139	1234	65	7	106
Jacobs	.967	4	26	3	1	4
Overbay	.995	21	170	14	1	26
Wheeler	1.000	4	21	1	0	1

Second Base	PCT	G	PO	A	E	DP
Bloomquist	.500	1	1	0	1	0
Elmore	1.000	5	3	6	0	3
Hill	.992	153	264	487	6	94

McDonald	1.000	4	6	10	0	2
Roberts	1.000	8	14	18	0	8

Third Base	PCT	G	PO	A	E	DP
Bell	.960	12	6	18	1	1
Bloomquist	.963	11	5	21	1	1
Blum	1.000	6	1	13	0	2
Johnson	.938	39	17	74	6	7
McDonald	1.000	5	2	3	0	0
Ransom	.902	18	8	29	4	5
Roberts	.957	60	37	118	7	8
Wheeler	.959	23	11	36	2	4

Shortstop	PCT	G	PO	A	E	DP
Bloomquist	.982	64	85	139	4	31
Drew	.977	36	40	88	3	25

	PCT	G	PO	A	E	DP
Elmore	.973	17	22	50	2	9
McDonald	.995	54	67	142	1	31
Ransom	1.000	7	8	14	0	4

Outfield	PCT	G	PO	A	E	DP
Bloomquist	—	2	0	0	0	0
Eaton	.975	21	37	2	1	1
Graham	—	2	0	0	0	0
Kubel	.995	125	185	14	1	3
Parra	.980	109	189	8	4	1
Pollock	1.000	25	58	0	0	0
Roberts	1.000	1	1	0	0	0
Upton	.984	149	309	6	5	2
Young	.990	87	201	4	2	1

RENO ACES   TRIPLE-A
PACIFIC COAST LEAGUE

Batting	B-T	HT	WT	DOB	AVG	vLH	vRH	G	AB	R	H	2B	3B	HR	RBI	BB	HBP	SH	SF	SO	SB	CS	SLG	OBP
Bell, Josh	B-R	6-3	230	11-13-86	.311	.330	.304	85	328	60	102	25	2	12	75	33	3	0	7	70	3	4	.509	.372
Blum, Geoff	B-R	6-3	220	4-26-73	.237	.167	.250	12	38	5	9	3	0	1	8	10	1	0	0	5	0	0	.395	.408
Bortnick, Tyler	R-R	5-11	185	7-3-87	.212	.256	.194	39	132	11	28	7	0	2	12	14	1	4	0	26	5	2	.311	.293
Budde, Ryan	R-R	5-11	210	8-15-79	.184	.233	.174	56	174	20	32	10	0	1	24	21	0	3	3	53	3	0	.259	.268
Clevlen, Brent	R-R	6-1	205	10-27-83	.377	.429	.357	37	77	17	29	5	2	3	17	8	0	0	1	24	3	0	.610	.430
Drew, Stephen	L-R	6-0	190	3-16-83	.250	.000	.281	9	36	6	9	1	1	2	5	4	0	0	0	6	0	0	.500	.325
Eaton, Adam	L-L	5-8	185	12-6-88	.381	.387	.379	119	488	119	186	46	5	7	45	53	15	5	1	68	38	10	.539	.456
Elmore, Jake	R-R	5-10	180	6-15-87	.344	.388	.330	108	419	95	144	30	9	1	73	74	5	7	6	54	32	8	.465	.442
Frey, Evan	L-L	6-0	170	6-7-86	.240	.200	.250	39	104	19	25	3	1	1	7	19	0	1	0	25	3	2	.317	.358
Gillespie, Cole	R-R	6-2	200	6-20-84	.308	.361	.294	126	441	85	136	35	4	13	66	59	4	0	6	80	11	8	.494	.390
Graham, Tyler	R-R	6-0	185	1-25-84	.115	.083	.135	26	61	7	7	0	2	1	6	8	2	1	0	12	1	1	.230	.239
2-team total (5 Fresno)					.150	—		31	80	10	12	1	2	1	6	9	2	1	0	13	2	1	.250	.253
Harbin, Taylor	R-R	5-9	171	2-13-86	.308	.343	.297	127	478	73	147	43	3	5	70	21	6	3	5	52	18	1	.441	.341
Jacobs, Mike	L-R	6-3	215	10-30-80	.279	.206	.298	101	333	59	93	15	0	18	60	44	0	0	1	83	2	2	.486	.362
Kaczrowski, Dan	R-R	5-9	170	6-17-87	.000	—	.000	1	1	0	0	0	0	0	0	0	0	0	0	0	0	0	.000	.000
Kuhn, Tyler	L-R	5-10	185	9-9-86	.264	.400	.228	23	72	11	19	4	1	2	7	3	0	1	0	11	1	1	.431	.293
LaPensee, Ryan	R-R	6-3	190	8-10-88	.286	.000	.286	5	7	0	2	0	0	0	1	0	0	0	0	0	0	0	.286	.286
Manzella, Tommy	R-R	6-2	200	4-16-83	.100	.000	.125	15	40	2	4	1	0	0	2	2	0	1	0	21	0	0	.125	.143
McMurray, Chris	R-R	6-1	195	10-12-86	.000	—	.000	1	3	0	0	0	0	0	0	0	0	0	0	0	0	0	.000	.000
Pollock, A.J.	R-R	6-1	195	12-5-87	.318	.273	.331	106	428	65	136	25	3	3	52	32	5	2	4	52	21	8	.411	.369
Ransom, Cody	R-R	6-2	205	2-17-76	.294	.429	.259	10	34	5	10	2	0	2	9	6	0	0	0	14	0	0	.529	.400
Reed, Mark	L-R	5-11	180	4-13-86	.171	.400	.133	22	35	8	6	1	0	0	4	4	0	1	0	13	0	0	.200	.256
Ruiz, Randy	R-R	6-3	250	10-19-77	.331	.295	.343	49	181	35	60	9	1	14	53	19	2	0	3	47	3	1	.624	.395
Ryal, Rusty	R-R	6-2	200	3-16-83	.241	.244	.240	64	191	24	46	9	1	4	29	6	4	0	4	49	4	0	.361	.273
Schmidt, Konrad	R-R	5-10	200	8-2-84	.277	.359	.252	93	332	43	92	24	0	7	47	25	8	4	5	69	2	0	.413	.338
Strieby, Ryan	R-R	6-5	235	8-9-85	.200	.000	.250	3	5	0	1	0	0	0	1	0	0	0	0	3	0	0	.200	.333
Sutil, Wladimir	R-R	5-10	155	10-31-84	.211	.100	.333	14	19	2	4	1	0	0	4	0	0	2	0	1	0	0	.263	.211
Wheeler, Ryan	L-R	6-3	235	7-10-88	.351	.302	.366	93	362	56	127	27	4	15	90	26	2	0	9	67	3	1	.572	.388
Winfree, David	R-R	6-3	235	8-5-86	.263	.167	.293	28	99	18	26	7	1	2	15	8	1	0	3	22	0	0	.414	.315
Young, Chris	R-R	6-2	190	9-5-83	.000	—	.000	1	2	0	0	0	0	0	1	0	0	0	0	1	0	0	.000	.000

Pitching	B-T	HT	WT	DOB	W	L	ERA	G	GS	CG	SV	IP	H	R	ER	HR	BB	SO	AVG	vLH	vRH	K/9	BB/9
Albaladejo, Jonathan	R-R	6-5	255	10-30-82	5	3	3.65	49	0	0	25	57	46	23	23	8	23	60	.224	.223	.225	9.53	3.65
Bauer, Trevor	R-R	6-1	185	1-17-91	5	1	2.85	14	14	1	0	82	74	28	26	8	35	97	.241	.222	.258	10.65	3.84
Bergesen, Brad	L-R	6-2	210	9-25-85	0	0	0.00	1	1	0	0	4	1	0	0	0	1	3	.091	.000	.167	7.36	2.45
Brewer, Charles	R-R	6-3	205	4-7-88	11	7	5.99	24	24	2	0	134	177	110	89	26	34	104	.318	.319	.318	7.00	2.29
Cabrera, Daniel	R-R	6-7	225	5-28-81	1	1	3.00	3	3	0	0	18	15	6	6	3	2	12	.224	.150	.333	6.00	1.00
Capaul, Alex	R-R	6-2	210	11-2-88	0	0	16.20	1	0	0	0	2	4	5	3	1	2	1	.400	.333	.429	5.40	10.80
Capellan, Victor	R-R	6-2	195	7-24-89	2	0	0.00	6	0	0	0	9	3	0	0	0	6	4	.107	.083	.125	4.15	6.23
Corbin, Pat	L-L	6-2	185	7-19-89	3	2	3.44	9	9	0	0	52	57	24	20	4	15	55	.274	.208	.294	9.46	2.58
DeMark, Mike	R-R	6-0	210	5-20-83	5	5	4.19	53	1	0	0	69	80	44	32	5	20	63	.287	.313	.265	8.26	2.62
Demel, Sam	R-R	6-0	205	10-23-85	1	4	4.07	56	0	0	1	66	60	34	30	11	22	75	.237	.240	.235	10.18	2.98
Enright, Barry	R-R	6-3	220	3-30-86	8	6	5.87	21	21	1	0	110	118	74	72	19	51	72	.283	.277	.289	5.87	4.16
2-team total (8 Salt Lake)					13	7	4.86	29	29	2	0	163	160	93	88	22	70	102	—	—	—	5.63	3.87
Flynn, Conrad	R-R	6-3	190	11-18-88	1	0	6.43	1	1	0	0	7	9	6	5	1	2	2	.300	.250	.318	2.57	2.57
Gorgen, Matt	R-R	5-10	210	1-27-87	1	2	3.00	20	0	0	0	27	27	12	9	4	7	22	.252	.289	.226	7.33	2.33
Henry, Bryan	R-R	6-3	205	2-15-85	2	1	4.70	15	2	0	0	44	50	24	23	8	14	20	.294	.364	.250	4.09	2.86
Hudson, Daniel	R-R	6-3	225	3-9-87	1	0	3.60	1	1	0	0	5	5	2	2	0	1	2	.278	.286	.273	3.60	1.80
Jakubauskas, Chris	R-R	6-2	215	12-22-78	2	3	4.18	18	7	0	0	52	57	31	24	4	14	28	.286	.330	.248	4.88	2.44
2-team total (3 Las Vegas)					2	3	4.64	21	7	0	0	54	61	35	28	2	16	28	—	—	—	4.64	2.65
Kroenke, Zach	R-L	6-2	215	4-21-84	6	5	5.67	32	17	0	0	119	150	87	75	12	36	59	.311	.242	.342	4.46	2.72
Lane, Jason	R-L	6-2	225	12-22-76	2	0	7.59	15	0	0	0	21	33	19	18	2	6	18	.351	.447	.286	7.59	2.53

Name		HT	WT	DOB	W	L	ERA	G	GS	CG	SV	IP	H	R	ER	HR	BB	SO	AVG	vLH	vRH	K/9	BB/9
Layne, Tommy	L-L	6-3	185	11-2-84	0	2	10.35	5	4	0	0	20	30	24	23	4	9	14	.337	.125	.456	6.30	4.05
2-team total (5 Tucson)					0	5	9.00	10	9	0	0	42	58	44	42	8	24	33	—	—	—	7.07	5.14
Lewis, Jensen	R-R	6-3	220	5-16-84	7	2	3.65	52	0	0	4	57	50	27	23	7	20	43	.236	.276	.208	6.83	3.18
Martinez, Joe	L-R	6-2	190	2-26-83	10	11	5.39	27	27	1	0	155	206	104	93	15	49	99	.325	.369	.284	5.74	2.84
Paterson, Joe	R-L	6-1	210	5-19-86	2	2	4.15	48	0	0	2	43	41	20	20	7	16	40	.248	.191	.316	8.31	3.32
Saito, Takashi	L-R	6-2	210	2-14-70	0	1	10.13	4	0	0	0	3	7	3	3	1	1	2	.467	.400	.500	6.75	3.38
Shaw, Bryan	B-R	6-1	210	11-8-87	0	0	2.25	8	0	0	2	8	6	2	2	0	2	10	.207	.200	.214	11.25	2.25
Sinclair, Taylor	L-L	6-3	180	12-23-85	0	2	10.61	16	1	0	0	19	26	26	22	4	16	7	.329	.303	.348	3.38	7.71
Skaggs, Tyler	L-L	6-3	195	7-13-91	4	2	2.91	9	9	0	0	53	49	22	17	4	16	45	.253	.296	.228	7.69	2.73
Stange, Daniel	R-R	6-1	229	12-22-85	0	0	23.63	3	0	0	0	3	8	8	7	0	5	2	.615	.571	.667	6.75	16.88
2-team total (2 Tucson)					0	0	15.75	5	0	0	0	4	9	9	7	0	8	3	—	—	—	6.75	18.00
Tomko, Brett	R-R	6-4	220	4-7-73	0	0	5.40	2	2	0	0	10	13	6	6	3	4	4	.325	.385	.214	3.60	3.60
Woodall, Bryan	R-R	6-1	200	10-24-86	2	1	8.28	21	0	0	1	25	35	24	23	3	14	22	.333	.408	.268	7.92	5.04
Zagurski, Mike	L-L	6-0	225	1-27-83	0	0	2.00	6	0	0	0	9	3	2	2	1	2	7	.103	.100	.105	7.00	2.00

Fielding

Catcher	PCT	G	PO	A	E	DP	PB
Budde	.992	54	349	42	3	2	7
McMurray	1.000	1	7	1	0	0	0
Reed	.978	9	39	5	1	1	1
Schmidt	.988	90	597	65	8	8	7

First Base	PCT	G	PO	A	E	DP
Bell	1.000	10	77	2	0	4
Jacobs	.989	74	610	35	7	54
Ruiz	.990	37	285	24	3	25
Ryal	.952	2	19	1	1	2
Strieby	1.000	1	5	2	0	1
Wheeler	.996	32	258	21	1	24

Second Base	PCT	G	PO	A	E	DP
Bortnick	.975	22	45	73	3	15
Elmore	.989	39	78	108	2	24
Harbin	.980	59	122	176	6	37
Kuhn	1.000	10	14	21	0	4
Manzella	1.000	2	4	4	0	0

Third Base	PCT	G	PO	A	E	DP
Ryal	.970	22	36	62	3	13
Bell	.875	59	36	83	17	1
Blum	.941	10	5	11	1	1
Bortnick	1.000	11	3	11	0	0
Elmore	1.000	6	3	16	0	2
Harbin	.884	13	11	27	5	4
Kaczrowski	1.000	1	0	3	0	0
Kuhn	1.000	2	3	5	0	0
Manzella	1.000	1	0	1	0	0
Ransom	.667	1	1	1	1	0
Ryal	.864	10	9	10	3	2
Wheeler	.951	49	25	92	6	7

Shortstop	PCT	G	PO	A	E	DP
Bortnick	1.000	5	3	6	0	1
Drew	1.000	9	13	22	0	6
Elmore	.979	60	81	149	5	21
Harbin	.967	57	78	158	8	39

Outfield	PCT	G	PO	A	E	DP
Manzella	.971	11	14	19	1	3
Ransom	.975	9	12	27	1	6
Sutil	.929	9	5	8	1	2
Clevlen	.974	19	36	1	1	1
Eaton	.980	118	283	13	6	3
Elmore	1.000	5	4	0	0	0
Frey	1.000	36	66	6	0	0
Gillespie	.983	119	216	10	4	3
Graham	.939	15	29	2	2	0
Kuhn	1.000	7	14	0	0	0
LaPensee	1.000	2	3	0	0	0
Pollock	.983	106	230	6	4	3
Reed	—	2	0	0	0	0
Ryal	1.000	12	20	1	0	0
Sutil	1.000	2	1	0	0	0
Wheeler	1.000	10	4	0	0	0
Winfree	.960	20	23	1	1	0
Young	1.000	1	1	0	0	0

MOBILE BAYBEARS
DOUBLE-A
SOUTHERN LEAGUE

Batting	B-T	HT	WT	DOB	AVG	vLH	vRH	G	AB	R	H	2B	3B	HR	RBI	BB	HBP	SH	SF	SO	SB	CS	SLG	OBP
Arbelo, Yazy	L-R	6-4	229	4-7-88	.208	.157	.227	64	183	15	38	8	0	6	21	22	2	0	3	67	0	1	.350	.295
Borchering, Bobby	B-R	6-2	205	10-25-90	.130	.133	.129	21	77	4	10	0	0	2	8	3	2	0	0	27	0	1	.208	.183
Clevlen, Brent	R-R	6-1	205	10-27-83	.260	.316	.229	67	223	45	58	15	3	10	39	30	1	1	4	64	3	1	.489	.345
Comerota, Jimmy	R-R	6-1	175	12-1-86	.000	—	.000	2	4	0	0	0	0	0	0	0	0	0	0	0	0	0	.000	.000
Davidson, Matt	R-R	6-2	225	3-26-91	.261	.339	.234	135	486	81	127	28	2	23	76	69	15	0	5	126	3	4	.469	.367
Drew, Stephen	L-R	6-0	190	3-16-83	.200	1.000	.000	3	10	2	2	0	0	0	0	4	0	0	0	1	0	0	.200	.556
Easley, Ed	R-R	6-0	205	12-21-85	.265	.242	.283	67	204	18	54	7	0	2	23	31	0	0	4	30	1	1	.328	.356
Eaton, Adam	L-L	5-8	185	12-6-88	.300	.353	.261	11	40	11	12	1	0	0	3	6	5	0	0	8	6	1	.325	.451
Frey, Evan	L-L	6-0	170	6-7-86	.236	.300	.236	95	360	47	92	14	3	0	23	50	2	1	2	50	29	7	.311	.348
Gilbert, Archie	R-R	5-8	185	7-8-83	.231	.241	.226	30	91	7	21	3	0	0	7	4	1	0	0	8	3	.264	.271
Greene, Kyle	L-R	6-1	200	5-26-86	.211	.261	.200	70	123	15	26	3	1	1	15	9	2	0	1	39	0	1	.276	.274
Griffin, Jon	R-R	6-7	250	4-29-89	.438	.667	.300	5	16	2	7	1	0	2	4	1	0	0	0	1	0	0	.875	.471
Kaczrowski, Dan	R-R	5-9	170	6-17-87	.225	.303	.177	83	200	21	45	6	0	1	21	33	1	4	1	21	7	6	.270	.336
Krauss, Marc	L-R	6-2	235	10-5-87	.283	.252	.296	104	346	75	98	29	2	15	61	73	9	0	5	91	6	4	.509	.416
Linton, Ollie	L-L	5-8	160	4-7-86	.053	.000	.091	7	19	1	1	0	0	1	1	3	0	0	0	4	0	1	.211	.182
Mangini, Matt	L-R	6-4	230	12-21-85	.293	.286	.296	17	41	5	12	5	0	0	11	8	1	0	1	6	0	0	.415	.412
Marte, Alfredo	R-R	6-0	190	3-31-89	.294	.298	.292	113	398	68	117	25	3	20	75	34	11	0	3	72	6	6	.523	.363
Nick, David	R-R	6-2	180	2-3-90	.249	.241	.252	123	458	49	114	23	2	5	43	28	4	3	3	85	13	5	.341	.296
Owings, Chris	R-R	5-10	180	8-12-91	.263	.258	.264	69	297	35	78	10	3	6	28	11	1	1	0	69	4	3	.377	.291
Perez, Rossmel	B-R	5-9	200	8-26-89	.270	.293	.263	80	263	23	71	10	0	0	20	35	3	5	5	19	4	1	.308	.356
Strieby, Ryan	R-R	6-5	235	8-9-85	.208	.158	.235	34	106	9	22	2	0	3	13	18	4	0	2	29	1	1	.311	.338
Sutil, Wladimir	R-R	5-10	155	10-31-84	.223	.205	.231	89	251	29	56	14	1	1	31	27	6	2	6	28	6	7	.299	.307
Torrez, Raoul	R-R	5-10	180	3-16-88	.169	.135	.196	35	83	12	14	4	0	2	9	9	1	0	0	31	3	1	.289	.258

Pitching	B-T	HT	WT	DOB	W	L	ERA	G	GS	CG	SV	IP	H	R	ER	HR	BB	SO	AVG	vLH	vRH	K/9	BB/9
Anderson, Chase	R-R	6-1	175	11-30-87	5	4	2.86	21	21	0	0	104	91	35	33	9	25	97	.238	.237	.238	8.39	2.16
Bauer, Trevor	R-R	6-1	185	1-17-91	7	1	1.68	8	8	0	0	48	33	12	9	1	26	60	.192	.200	.186	11.17	4.84
Bolsinger, Mike	R-R	6-2	209	1-29-88	4	3	3.82	15	15	0	0	78	82	40	33	5	38	64	.283	.256	.304	7.42	4.40
Brewer, Charles	R-R	6-3	205	4-7-88	0	0	4.15	3	3	0	0	17	19	9	8	2	2	13	.268	.267	.268	6.75	1.04
Corbin, Pat	L-L	6-2	185	7-19-89	2	0	1.67	4	4	0	0	27	22	5	5	0	8	25	.234	.211	.240	8.33	2.67
De La Rosa, Eury	L-L	5-9	167	2-24-90	4	4	2.84	53	0	0	8	63	47	20	20	3	17	68	.206	.178	.225	9.66	2.42
Eitel, Derek	R-R	6-4	200	11-21-87	8	11	4.37	27	25	0	0	150	167	87	73	17	52	91	.286	.285	.287	5.45	3.11
Flynn, Conrad	R-R	6-3	190	11-18-88	0	1	3.00	4	2	0	0	12	14	6	4	0	0	5	.280	.278	.281	3.75	0.00
Gorgen, Matt	R-R	5-10	210	1-27-87	1	2	2.83	28	0	0	7	35	29	12	11	0	18	49	.218	.364	.138	12.60	4.63
Hagens, Bradin	R-R	6-3	210	5-12-89	0	0	3.97	2	2	0	0	11	9	5	5	2	2	5	.214	.227	.200	3.97	1.59

	B-T	HT	WT	DOB	W	L	ERA	G	GS	CG	SV	IP	H	R	ER	HR	BB	SO	AVG	vLH	vRH	K/9	BB/9
Henry, Bryan	R-R	6-3	205	2-15-85	1	1	5.19	15	1	0	1	35	52	22	20	7	7	18	.347	.344	.349	4.67	1.82
Hernandez, Gaby	R-R	6-3	215	5-21-86	0	8	6.26	14	10	0	0	65	74	50	45	11	25	58	.290	.254	.326	8.07	3.48
Holmberg, David	R-L	6-4	219	7-19-91	5	5	3.60	15	15	0	0	95	104	45	38	8	23	67	.281	.247	.293	6.35	2.18
Lorin, Brett	L-R	6-7	245	3-31-87	3	10	6.40	29	18	0	0	103	127	83	73	12	35	70	.304	.305	.303	6.14	3.07
Marshall, Evan	R-R	6-2	220	4-18-90	6	3	3.51	42	0	0	16	49	55	24	19	2	16	27	.284	.333	.248	4.99	2.96
Munson, Kevin	R-R	6-1	215	1-3-89	3	5	6.28	44	0	0	3	53	55	40	37	3	27	64	.266	.303	.237	10.87	4.58
Ortega, Yonata	R-R	6-1	220	11-11-86	2	2	6.88	42	0	0	1	52	57	49	40	8	40	51	.277	.345	.230	8.77	6.88
Santana, Frank	R-R	6-2	200	2-21-89	0	0	0.00	1	0	0	0	1	1	0	0	0	1	1	.250	.000	.333	9.00	9.00
Schultz, Bo	R-R	6-3	215	9-25-85	2	3	2.11	17	0	0	0	21	20	8	5	0	7	13	.244	.317	.171	5.48	2.95
Sinclair, Taylor	L-L	6-3	180	12-23-85	1	0	1.47	12	1	0	0	18	13	4	3	0	5	7	.191	.143	.213	3.44	2.45
Skaggs, Tyler	L-L	6-3	195	7-13-91	5	4	2.84	13	13	0	0	70	63	27	22	8	21	71	.241	.214	.249	9.17	2.71
Smith, Eric	R-R	6-3	220	10-15-88	3	2	4.29	30	0	0	0	42	38	22	20	1	28	23	.247	.318	.193	4.93	6.00
Tomko, Brett	R-R	6-4	220	4-7-73	2	0	2.70	2	2	0	0	10	10	3	3	0	1	7	.256	.357	.200	6.30	2.70
Woodall, Bryan	R-R	6-1	200	10-24-86	5	1	5.14	27	0	0	0	42	51	24	24	3	11	41	.297	.318	.274	8.79	2.36

Fielding

Catcher	PCT	G	PO	A	E	DP	PB
Easley	.989	64	473	48	6	3	4
Perez	.990	80	510	95	6	4	4

First Base	PCT	G	PO	A	E	DP
Arbelo	.985	51	362	26	6	32
Easley	1.000	3	28	4	0	1
Greene	.980	16	86	11	2	8
Griffin	1.000	4	35	7	0	6
Krauss	.980	30	212	28	5	19
Mangini	1.000	9	67	3	0	3
Strieby	1.000	30	219	15	0	29
Torrez	1.000	11	66	6	0	6

Second Base	PCT	G	PO	A	E	DP
Comerota	1.000	2	3	3	0	2

	PCT	G	PO	A	E	DP	PB
Kaczrowski	.983	18	32	26	1	7	
Nick	.972	115	211	243	13	59	
Sutil	.929	6	7	6	1	3	
Torrez	.939	7	14	17	2	4	

Third Base	PCT	G	PO	A	E	DP
Davidson	.921	127	101	227	28	21
Greene	—	1	0	0	0	0
Kaczrowski	1.000	9	6	7	0	0
Mangini	1.000	2	0	3	0	1
Torrez	1.000	6	3	8	0	1

Shortstop	PCT	G	PO	A	E	DP
Drew	1.000	2	4	2	0	1
Kaczrowski	.941	18	23	41	4	6
Owings	.974	67	131	205	9	47

	PCT	G	PO	A	E	DP
Sutil	.932	58	70	123	14	25
Torrez	.875	3	1	6	1	0

Outfield	PCT	G	PO	A	E	DP
Borchering	.939	20	30	1	2	0
Clevlen	.966	62	137	6	5	3
Eaton	1.000	11	22	2	0	0
Frey	.975	92	225	8	6	0
Gilbert	1.000	22	37	2	0	0
Kaczrowski	1.000	19	35	1	0	0
Krauss	.970	77	124	4	4	0
Linton	.889	7	8	0	1	0
Mangini	1.000	2	2	0	0	0
Marte	.983	110	226	5	4	3
Sutil	.923	11	12	0	1	0
Torrez	—	1	0	0	0	0

VISALIA RAWHIDE

HIGH CLASS A

CALIFORNIA LEAGUE

Batting	B-T	HT	WT	DOB	AVG	vLH	vRH	G	AB	R	H	2B	3B	HR	RBI	BB	HBP	SH	SF	SO	SB	CS	SLG	OBP
Arbelo, Yazy	L-R	6-4	229	4-7-88	.261	.237	.270	55	207	37	54	8	1	21	50	20	2	0	2	57	0	2	.614	.329
Bell, Carter	R-R	6-1	195	6-12-90	.259	.281	.252	81	282	30	73	11	1	4	36	26	4	3	2	43	0	2	.348	.328
Borchering, Bobby	B-R	6-2	205	10-25-90	.277	.234	.291	81	307	47	85	23	1	18	60	28	4	0	5	96	0	2	.534	.340
Bourgeois, Marc	L-R	5-11	205	3-15-89	.364	.000	.571	3	11	1	4	2	2	0	3	1	0	0	0	4	1	0	.909	.417
Broxton, Keon	R-R	6-3	195	5-7-90	.267	.266	.268	130	490	84	131	24	1	19	62	40	4	0	2	136	21	8	.437	.326
Freeman, Mike	L-R	6-0	192	8-4-87	.309	.285	.318	135	537	91	166	24	5	3	59	60	2	6	5	88	30	4	.389	.377
Gilbert, Archie	R-R	5-8	185	7-8-83	.169	.133	.179	18	71	5	12	0	1	2	7	3	1	2	1	5	0	1	.282	.211
Gomez, Raywilly	B-R	5-11	192	1-23-90	.273	.306	.263	91	300	30	82	19	0	4	31	38	0	3	4	35	0	0	.377	.351
Griffin, Jon	R-R	6-7	250	4-29-89	.300	.346	.283	128	487	87	146	19	3	26	98	49	4	0	8	107	0	0	.511	.363
Groff, Eric	R-R	5-11	195	1-25-88	.194	.086	.225	46	155	13	30	2	0	6	18	10	1	4	1	62	4	1	.323	.246
Henry, Bryan	R-R	6-3	220	2-15-85	.172	.167	.174	8	29	2	5	0	0	0	3	4	0	0	0	5	0	0	.172	.273
Inciarte, Ender	L-L	5-11	160	10-29-90	.319	.384	.291	62	248	46	79	12	5	1	17	22	2	6	1	32	28	8	.419	.377
Kim, Jae Yun	R-R	6-1	185	9-16-90	.120	.200	.067	10	25	2	3	1	0	0	1	0	1	1	1	7	0	0	.160	.148
LaPensee, Ryan	R-R	6-3	190	8-10-88	.263	.301	.249	95	334	39	88	16	3	4	36	20	5	5	3	62	8	2	.365	.312
Mateo, Wagner	L-L	6-2	194	3-8-89	.263	.429	.226	10	38	3	10	3	0	0	2	5	0	0	0	13	0	1	.342	.349
Montilla, Gerson	R-R	5-10	168	11-13-89	.282	.305	.271	60	259	43	73	13	1	10	31	14	1	5	0	39	3	2	.456	.321
Owings, Chris	R-R	5-10	180	8-12-91	.324	.340	.319	59	241	51	78	16	2	11	24	13	2	0	1	63	8	3	.544	.362
Torrez, Raoul	R-R	5-10	180	3-16-88	.227	.309	.182	47	154	20	35	4	0	3	18	12	3	4	1	53	1	0	.312	.294
Valencia, Chris	L-R	6-2	195	4-25-87	.213	.111	.237	30	94	8	20	4	0	0	8	4	1	4	1	33	4	4	.255	.279
Van Winkle, Tyson	R-R	6-1	190	2-2-88	.260	.288	.245	42	150	19	39	8	0	3	19	12	1	1	1	32	0	0	.373	.317
Weber, Garrett	R-R	5-10	165	3-29-89	.297	.303	.295	100	394	59	117	23	1	14	65	23	4	5	3	67	1	1	.467	.340
Williams, Jake	B-L	6-1	190	1-7-89	.174	.200	.167	6	23	1	4	1	0	0	2	1	0	0	0	8	0	0	.217	.208
Young, Chris	R-R	6-2	190	9-5-83	.308	.333	.286	3	13	3	4	3	0	1	7	0	0	0	0	4	0	0	.769	.308

Pitching	B-T	HT	WT	DOB	W	L	ERA	G	GS	CG	SV	IP	H	R	ER	HR	BB	SO	AVG	vLH	vRH	K/9	BB/9
Belfiore, Mike	R-L	6-2	220	10-3-88	0	0	2.37	12	0	0	1	19	13	5	5	2	5	28	.197	.150	.217	13.26	2.37
Bolsinger, Mike	R-R	6-2	209	1-29-88	3	2	2.37	7	7	0	0	38	31	15	10	1	13	49	.215	.263	.184	11.61	3.08
Capellan, Victor	R-R	6-2	195	7-24-89	0	2	8.00	13	0	0	0	18	28	19	16	4	6	21	.341	.345	.340	10.50	3.00
Carreras, Alexander	L-L	6-1	200	1-9-90	1	3	9.95	4	4	0	0	13	20	18	14	3	6	12	.333	.385	.319	8.53	4.26
Chafin, Andrew	R-L	6-2	205	6-17-90	6	6	4.93	30	22	0	0	122	112	74	67	12	69	150	.241	.250	.237	11.04	5.08
Cooper, Blake	R-R	5-11	190	3-30-88	3	7	3.38	48	0	0	5	56	56	28	21	2	21	59	.253	.292	.227	9.48	3.38
Erben, Jeremy	R-R	5-11	195	9-15-87	1	1	5.18	40	0	0	0	49	45	28	28	13	26	68	.243	.145	.324	12.58	4.81
Flynn, Conrad	R-R	6-3	190	11-18-88	1	1	7.20	12	4	0	0	40	48	33	32	10	17	41	.289	.232	.330	9.23	3.83
Gerdeman, Ross	R-R	6-3	210	11-7-89	0	1	18.90	1	1	0	0	3	9	7	7	2	1	4	.474	.417	.571	10.80	2.70
Hagens, Bradin	R-R	6-3	210	5-12-89	3	4	3.88	35	11	0	0	95	83	48	41	4	49	82	.240	.240	.240	7.77	4.64
Hernandez, Ray	R-R	6-1	190	9-1-88	6	9	5.76	30	21	0	0	134	160	99	86	27	46	137	.289	.286	.292	9.18	3.08
Holmberg, David	R-L	6-4	219	7-19-91	6	3	2.99	12	12	0	0	78	62	31	26	6	14	86	.214	.257	.199	9.88	1.61
Johnson, D.J.	L-R	6-4	235	8-30-89	2	3	6.55	21	0	0	3	22	26	16	16	6	11	28	.292	.250	.333	11.45	4.91
Medlinger, Donny	R-R	6-1	165	9-29-90	0	0	3.00	2	0	0	0	3	2	1	1	0	4	5	.200	.000	.222	15.00	12.00

Name	B-T	HT	WT	DOB	W	L	ERA	G	GS	CG	SV	IP	H	R	ER	HR	BB	SO	AVG	vLH	vRH	K/9	BB/9
Meo, Anthony	R-R	6-2	185	2-19-90	9	8	4.11	26	25	0	0	140	134	78	64	15	71	153	.251	.251	.251	9.84	4.56
Paredes, Willy	R-R	6-3	180	2-2-89	3	4	6.46	10	10	0	0	47	62	44	34	3	18	27	.304	.286	.315	5.13	3.42
Rosario, Diogenes	R-R	6-2	179	9-1-88	2	0	4.85	42	0	0	0	59	53	40	32	4	40	68	.235	.253	.222	10.31	6.07
Saito, Takashi	L-R	6-2	200	2-14-70	0	0	0.00	1	1	0	0	1	1	0	0	0	1	0	.333	.500	.000	0.00	9.00
Schultz, Bo	R-R	6-3	215	9-25-85	4	2	4.50	29	0	0	11	34	41	21	17	3	10	36	.295	.291	.298	9.53	2.65
Schuster, Patrick	R-L	6-1	182	10-30-90	4	5	4.90	47	2	0	1	64	56	37	35	5	32	67	.240	.263	.225	9.37	4.48
Shields, Jeff	R-R	6-3	205	2-22-90	1	3	9.99	6	4	0	0	24	37	27	27	1	15	11	.346	.325	.358	4.07	5.55
Siemens, Taylor	L-L	6-5	200	7-1-89	5	7	4.84	16	16	0	0	89	105	58	48	13	34	87	.297	.287	.302	8.76	3.43
Simmons, Seth	R-R	5-9	170	6-14-88	0	2	6.94	9	0	0	0	12	13	10	9	3	4	18	.277	.429	.154	13.89	3.09
Smith, Eric	R-R	6-3	220	10-15-88	1	2	3.72	13	0	0	2	19	17	8	8	1	10	16	.258	.320	.220	7.45	4.66
Winkler, Kyle	R-R	5-11	195	6-18-90	3	1	5.44	31	0	0	0	43	51	34	26	2	24	38	.293	.250	.324	7.95	5.02

Fielding

Catcher	PCT	G	PO	A	E	DP	PB
Gomez	.991	89	742	74	7	3	10
Henry	.986	8	66	3	1	0	1
Kim	1.000	10	68	14	0	0	2
Van Winkle	.985	42	354	35	6	3	14

First Base	PCT	G	PO	A	E	DP
Arbelo	.955	15	120	8	6	11
Bell	.982	6	53	2	1	2
Griffin	.991	110	906	63	9	95
Mateo	.979	4	42	4	1	3
Williams	1.000	6	51	2	0	3

Second Base	PCT	G	PO	A	E	DP
Freeman	.974	48	92	132	6	33

	PCT	G	PO	A	E	DP
Groff	.945	13	17	35	3	6
Montilla	.964	58	104	166	10	48
Torrez	1.000	3	7	11	0	2
Weber	.957	20	24	43	3	9

Third Base	PCT	G	PO	A	E	DP
Bell	.915	75	20	130	14	13
Groff	.839	24	5	42	9	3
Torrez	1.000	12	6	13	0	2
Weber	.912	32	11	72	8	9

Shortstop	PCT	G	PO	A	E	DP
Freeman	.954	81	119	236	17	50
Owings	.943	55	84	147	14	30
Torrez	1.000	5	5	11	0	3

	PCT	G	PO	A	E	DP
Weber	1.000	1	1	0	0	0

Outfield	PCT	G	PO	A	E	DP
Borchering	.967	73	83	4	3	1
Bourgeois	1.000	3	4	0	0	0
Broxton	.977	128	244	8	6	3
Gilbert	.957	18	21	1	1	0
Inciarte	.976	60	123	1	3	0
LaPensee	.986	87	133	5	2	0
Montilla	1.000	1	2	1	0	0
Torrez	.930	27	40	0	3	0
Valencia	.982	28	53	2	1	0
Young	1.000	2	6	0	0	0

SOUTH BEND SILVER HAWKS — LOW CLASS A
MIDWEST LEAGUE

Batting	B-T	HT	WT	DOB	AVG	vLH	vRH	G	AB	R	H	2B	3B	HR	RBI	BB	HBP	SH	SF	SO	SB	CS	SLG	OBP
Aguila, Roidany	R-R	5-10	175	10-22-90	.254	.256	.253	103	378	51	96	24	1	7	51	24	3	1	6	65	0	0	.378	.299
Belza, Tom	L-R	6-0	190	7-31-89	.260	.168	.286	130	511	76	133	18	10	9	80	56	4	5	6	98	12	2	.387	.334
Billigen, Brian	R-R	6-0	170	5-11-90	.250	.364	.176	8	28	2	7	1	0	1	5	2	0	0	0	4	0	1	.393	.300
Bourgeois, Marc	L-R	5-11	205	3-15-89	.249	.234	.252	92	346	45	86	17	5	10	48	23	1	1	5	74	3	3	.413	.293
Court, Ryan	R-R	6-2	210	5-28-88	.264	.326	.246	102	383	64	101	24	2	8	53	38	9	3	4	111	6	1	.399	.341
Ellison, Chris	L-R	6-2	189	12-16-88	.240	.219	.247	136	562	90	135	23	6	5	58	55	5	4	9	123	12	4	.329	.309
Gallego, Niko	R-R	6-0	150	12-29-88	.220	.235	.215	61	200	20	44	9	2	0	12	10	5	5	0	35	4	5	.285	.274
Groff, Eric	R-R	5-11	195	1-25-88	.295	.395	.274	64	251	31	74	19	1	4	34	7	1	0	2	46	5	2	.426	.314
Helm, Matt	R-R	6-1	210	9-1-90	.271	.330	.254	135	520	67	141	36	1	10	76	58	7	0	5	148	11	4	.402	.349
Henry, Bryan	R-R	6-3	220	6-9-89	.259	.286	.250	23	85	7	22	1	0	1	10	3	0	1	0	23	1	0	.306	.284
Inciarte, Ender	L-L	5-11	160	10-29-90	.293	.298	.292	65	225	36	66	16	5	1	30	31	0	5	3	31	18	4	.422	.375
Jamieson, Sean	R-R	6-0	193	3-2-89	.327	.222	.348	14	55	8	18	5	0	1	7	9	1	0	0	14	5	1	.473	.431
2-team total (119 Burlington)					.244	—	—	133	504	79	123	30	5	11	56	75	15	6	7	106	30	7	.389	.354
Jenkins, Kerry	R-R	6-1	210	5-17-89	.294	.320	.287	64	238	34	70	14	4	4	38	10	15	3	4	50	2	2	.437	.356
Jones, Zach	R-R	5-10	170	11-1-88	.143	.167	.133	14	42	4	6	1	0	0	2	4	0	0	0	14	0	0	.167	.217
Montilla, Gerson	R-R	5-10	168	11-13-89	.293	.268	.302	67	263	39	77	23	3	4	42	32	2	0	2	38	7	4	.449	.371
Navarro, Raul	R-R	5-10	170	2-5-92	.249	.229	.253	60	221	32	55	3	3	0	16	22	4	1	2	31	6	3	.290	.325
Parr, Josh	R-R	5-11	170	9-11-89	.189	.143	.204	44	148	19	28	7	1	0	8	9	2	1	3	33	7	4	.250	.248
Pena, Fidel	R-R	5-10	180	7-19-91	.261	.233	.270	72	264	33	69	14	1	2	24	23	6	3	0	57	9	3	.345	.334
Stone, Bobby	L-L	6-2	220	11-14-89	.144	.136	.147	24	90	8	13	6	0	2	14	5	0	0	1	33	0	0	.278	.188
Van Winkle, Tyson	R-R	6-1	190	2-2-88	.174	.286	.125	6	23	2	4	0	0	0	1	0	0	0	0	5	0	0	.174	.174

Pitching	B-T	HT	WT	DOB	W	L	ERA	G	GS	CG	SV	IP	H	R	ER	HR	BB	SO	AVG	vLH	vRH	K/9	BB/9
Barbosa, Andrew	R-L	6-8	205	11-18-87	2	5	4.82	11	11	0	0	52	58	38	28	5	27	60	.278	.324	.255	10.32	4.64
Barrett, Jake	R-R	6-3	230	7-22-91	0	3	5.84	25	0	0	0	25	28	18	16	2	13	25	.283	.314	.250	9.12	4.74
Bradley, Archie	R-R	6-4	225	8-10-92	12	6	3.84	27	27	0	0	136	87	64	58	6	84	152	.181	.192	.171	10.06	5.56
Bradley, J.R.	R-R	6-3	185	6-9-92	7	8	5.98	28	19	0	0	117	149	89	78	15	45	60	.310	.308	.313	4.60	3.45
Capaul, Alex	R-R	6-2	210	11-2-88	1	4	5.68	17	3	0	2	38	45	28	24	4	18	18	.302	.253	.351	4.26	2.84
Darrah, Jesse	L-R	6-2	190	3-28-90	8	5	4.65	31	18	0	0	120	120	69	62	12	40	87	.258	.282	.232	6.53	3.00
Fleck, Kaleb	R-R	6-2	190	1-24-89	4	2	2.73	24	0	0	3	30	28	10	9	0	16	19	.257	.228	.288	5.76	4.85
Flynn, Conrad	R-R	6-3	190	11-18-88	1	1	5.04	5	4	0	0	25	29	14	14	5	6	19	.296	.284	.323	6.84	2.16
Green, Tyler	R-R	6-1	185	11-24-91	4	9	3.78	26	20	0	1	126	132	67	53	8	60	75	.273	.247	.301	5.34	4.27
Hessler, Keith	L-L	6-4	215	3-15-89	2	5	3.20	39	7	0	1	90	86	40	32	3	44	75	.261	.285	.246	7.50	4.40
Hogben, Kable	R-R	6-3	190	7-6-90	4	3	3.93	41	0	0	2	69	62	35	30	3	19	50	.241	.314	.180	6.55	2.49
Johnson, D.J.	L-R	6-4	235	8-30-89	2	4	3.08	21	0	0	4	26	25	12	9	1	7	32	.243	.286	.204	10.94	2.39
Paredes, Willy	R-R	6-3	180	2-2-89	2	1	2.98	29	1	0	3	48	35	16	16	1	10	42	.203	.195	.211	7.82	1.86
Pedrotty, John	L-L	6-4	220	11-28-90	5	6	6.28	17	17	0	0	90	102	67	63	11	40	62	.288	.269	.301	6.18	3.99
Perry, Blake	R-R	6-5	190	2-3-92	0	1	8.10	6	3	0	0	13	9	14	12	1	19	13	.191	.133	.294	8.78	12.83
Sample, Mat	R-R	6-5	200	8-16-88	4	1	4.57	43	0	0	6	67	74	39	34	0	32	64	.285	.287	.282	8.60	4.30
Santana, Frank	R-R	6-2	200	2-21-89	1	0	3.10	12	0	0	0	20	19	8	7	1	6	15	.250	.244	.257	6.64	2.66
Shields, Jeff	R-R	6-3	205	2-22-90	0	5	4.05	8	8	0	0	47	51	25	21	2	10	24	.282	.333	.240	4.63	1.93
Siemens, Taylor	L-L	6-5	200	7-1-89	4	1	4.14	16	2	0	1	37	38	22	17	3	10	30	.260	.316	.225	7.30	2.43
Simmons, Seth	R-R	5-9	170	6-14-88	4	3	1.76	37	0	0	1	66	44	15	13	2	35	80	.195	.237	.152	10.85	4.75

ARIZONA DIAMONDBACKS

Fielding

Catcher	PCT	G	PO	A	E	DP	PB
Aguila	.980	83	569	71	13	11	8
Henry	.962	16	119	7	5	2	1
Jones	.967	12	79	9	3	2	0
Pena	1.000	26	196	31	0	2	1
Van Winkle	.970	5	28	4	1	0	1

First Base	PCT	G	PO	A	E	DP
Belza	.997	30	283	24	1	27
Court	.980	15	135	11	3	17
Helm	.988	73	669	64	9	62
Stone	.981	24	233	19	5	26

Second Base	PCT	G	PO	A	E	DP
Belza	1.000	1	0	1	0	0

Gallego	.938	17	25	50	5	12
Groff	.965	53	88	163	9	37
Montilla	.980	56	103	192	6	43
Navarro	1.000	3	4	8	0	1
Pena	.987	14	31	47	1	10

Third Base	PCT	G	PO	A	E	DP
Court	.937	84	69	169	16	15
Gallego	1.000	2	4	7	0	0
Groff	1.000	6	2	9	0	1
Helm	.890	49	23	98	15	10

Shortstop	PCT	G	PO	A	E	DP
Gallego	.961	38	64	131	8	33
Jamieson	.971	11	16	18	1	6

Navarro	.968	50	57	155	7	29
Parr	.949	44	78	144	12	32

Outfield	PCT	G	PO	A	E	DP
Belza	.980	87	141	7	3	4
Billigen	.895	8	17	0	2	0
Bourgeois	.993	77	127	11	1	3
Ellison	.972	132	227	19	7	1
Gallego	1.000	1	2	0	0	0
Inciarte	.982	64	159	6	3	1
Jenkins	1.000	54	94	7	0	1

YAKIMA BEARS   SHORT-SEASON

NORTHWEST LEAGUE

Batting	B-T	HT	WT	DOB	AVG	vLH	vRH	G	AB	R	H	2B	3B	HR	RBI	BB	HBP	SH	SF	SO	SB	CS	SLG	OBP
Abreu, Jesus	R-R	5-10	155	4-14-92	.188	.214	.176	17	48	3	9	1	0	0	3	7	1	0	0	16	0	0	.208	.304
Comerota, Jimmy	R-R	6-1	175	12-1-86	.206	.219	.203	53	180	17	37	3	1	1	19	22	2	0	3	23	4	3	.250	.295
Cooper, Shaun	R-R	5-11	190	10-8-89	.213	.222	.211	67	230	31	49	11	4	6	29	37	9	1	1	67	4	4	.374	.343
Freeman, Ronnie	R-R	6-1	195	1-8-91	.273	.344	.256	46	165	13	45	10	0	0	16	9	8	0	0	25	0	0	.333	.341
Ginther, Mark	R-R	6-3	200	12-4-89	.195	.211	.192	62	215	24	42	11	1	4	21	16	3	0	1	49	1	0	.312	.260
House, Jacob	L-L	6-3	210	6-27-89	.281	.280	.281	36	139	15	39	8	1	2	13	8	2	0	1	38	2	0	.396	.327
Jenkins, Kerry	R-R	6-1	210	5-17-89	.100	.000	.125	5	20	4	2	0	0	0	1	1	2	0	0	6	0	0	.100	.217
Kim, Jae Yun	R-R	6-1	185	9-16-90	.214	.000	.231	4	14	1	3	1	0	0	1	0	0	1	0	5	0	0	.286	.250
Lang, Michael	R-R	5-11	185	1-13-89	.258	.258	.258	55	194	35	50	10	3	6	17	12	5	0	0	51	6	2	.433	.318
Loftus, Joe	R-R	6-3	210	8-7-89	.223	.412	.180	52	184	20	41	12	1	3	28	25	4	0	2	40	7	0	.348	.326
Mateo, Wagner	L-L	6-2	190	3-30-93	.194	.250	.178	49	186	13	36	8	1	0	12	15	2	0	1	85	3	2	.247	.260
McConnell, Adam	R-R	6-0	187	1-24-90	.240	.400	.200	7	25	2	6	1	0	0	0	0	0	0	0	7	0	0	.280	.240
Medrano, Kevin	L-R	6-1	155	5-21-90	.341	.383	.332	64	264	33	90	8	4	0	24	14	1	2	1	30	13	5	.402	.375
Parr, Josh	R-R	5-11	170	9-11-89	.235	.195	.243	68	251	34	59	15	0	6	32	18	12	5	3	49	14	5	.367	.313
Perez-Ramos, Yogey	L-L	6-3	197	10-29-88	.285	.304	.281	35	137	16	39	4	2	1	12	10	1	0	1	14	1	3	.365	.336
Poma, Danny	R-R	6-1	200	2-23-89	.228	.306	.211	58	202	34	46	4	1	2	22	16	11	3	2	21	8	5	.287	.316
Rodriguez, Steven	L-R	6-1	200	1-8-90	.242	.389	.210	27	99	7	24	7	0	1	14	9	0	0	2	22	0	1	.343	.300
Zabala, Henry	R-R	6-1	175	10-20-89	.125	.000	.143	3	8	2	1	0	0	1	2	2	0	0	0	1	0	0	.500	.300

Pitching	B-T	HT	WT	DOB	W	L	ERA	G	GS	CG	SV	IP	H	R	ER	HR	BB	SO	AVG	vLH	vRH	K/9	BB/9
Acosta, Victor	R-R	5-11	175	3-10-90	2	2	1.34	26	0	0	2	47	39	11	7	1	18	30	.227	.219	.231	5.74	3.45
Brewer, Chase	R-R	6-4	220	2-1-90	0	1	6.75	5	0	0	0	8	12	7	6	0	6	7	.353	.231	.429	7.88	6.75
Burgos, Enrique	R-R	6-4	200	11-23-90	2	3	2.35	25	0	0	4	38	28	11	10	1	19	40	.201	.250	.172	9.39	4.46
Capaul, Alex	R-R	6-2	210	11-2-88	1	0	3.38	2	2	0	0	11	12	5	4	1	2	8	.293	.400	.231	6.75	1.69
Capellan, Victor	R-R	6-2	195	7-24-89	4	2	2.36	21	0	0	2	34	32	13	9	3	10	39	.244	.280	.222	10.22	2.62
Carreras, Alexander	L-L	6-1	200	1-9-90	8	5	2.96	15	15	0	0	82	79	36	27	5	36	55	.256	.133	.278	6.04	3.95
Fermin, Jose	R-R	6-1	160	4-14-90	0	1	4.22	2	2	0	0	11	8	5	5	1	6	8	.205	.120	.357	6.75	5.06
Forslund, Blake	R-R	6-4	215	2-16-90	1	4	7.18	23	0	0	1	31	36	31	25	3	22	26	.286	.333	.240	7.47	6.32
Gibbs, Jeff	R-R	6-4	185	4-23-91	0	0	20.25	2	1	0	0	1	1	3	3	0	5	2	.200	.000	.333	13.50	33.75
Hively, R.J.	R-R	6-2	205	11-27-88	1	0	1.76	23	0	0	4	31	21	8	6	1	8	28	.189	.224	.161	8.22	2.35
Jose, Jose	L-L	6-2	175	7-21-90	2	3	1.65	24	0	0	0	33	15	11	6	1	21	37	.135	.139	.133	10.19	5.79
Locante, Will	L-L	6-1	190	2-2-90	0	1	4.50	9	0	0	3	10	7	7	5	0	8	11	.189	.150	.235	9.90	7.20
O'Neill, Bobby	R-R	6-3	220	7-15-89	0	0	2.25	5	1	0	0	8	10	2	2	1	4	6	.303	.222	.400	6.75	4.50
Owings, Kyle	R-R	6-1	215	1-4-90	1	4	4.17	15	6	0	0	58	63	35	27	4	18	30	.283	.243	.317	4.63	2.78
Pena, Miguel	R-R	6-0	160	9-18-90	0	0	3.38	2	2	0	0	5	5	3	2	1	7	3	.250	.167	.375	5.06	11.81
Perry, Blake	R-R	6-5	190	2-3-92	5	1	2.37	13	12	1	0	68	52	22	18	4	17	58	.207	.219	.197	7.64	2.24
Platt, Austin	R-R	6-3	190	3-5-92	1	4	9.12	7	2	0	0	26	39	26	26	3	15	13	.371	.370	.373	4.56	5.26
Santana, Frank	R-R	6-2	200	2-23-89	0	2	3.12	11	0	0	0	17	16	7	6	1	5	20	.239	.263	.229	10.38	2.60
Stultz, Derrick	R-R	6-3	220	3-23-89	1	2	3.69	9	7	0	0	32	31	15	13	1	11	17	.248	.254	.242	4.83	3.13
Thomas, Chris	R-R	6-2	175	12-21-89	0	0	6.75	4	0	0	0	4	7	3	3	0	2	3	.389	.250	.429	6.75	4.50
Watts, Daniel	L-L	6-3	190	10-26-89	4	5	2.23	15	15	0	0	77	72	31	19	2	16	52	.242	.222	.248	6.10	1.88
Wheeler, Cody	L-L	5-11	160	8-19-89	3	0	1.87	14	11	0	0	43	36	13	9	0	14	41	.226	.174	.235	8.52	2.91

Fielding

Catcher	PCT	G	PO	A	E	DP	PB
Freeman	.989	45	343	32	4	3	2
Kim	.972	4	32	3	1	0	1
Rodriguez	.995	27	172	27	1	1	7

First Base	PCT	G	PO	A	E	DP
Comerota	1.000	17	111	11	0	13
House	.994	18	161	15	1	8
Mateo	.974	44	352	30	10	31

Second Base	PCT	G	PO	A	E	DP
Abreu	.944	15	28	40	4	8
Comerota	.955	4	6	15	1	5

McConnell	.960	4	15	9	1	5
Medrano	.984	28	50	72	2	12
Parr	.963	27	71	83	6	13

Third Base	PCT	G	PO	A	E	DP
Abreu	1.000	1	0	2	0	0
Comerota	.947	16	10	44	3	0
Ginther	.907	60	46	101	15	7
McConnell	1.000	2	2	2	0	0

Shortstop	PCT	G	PO	A	E	DP
McConnell	—	1	0	0	0	0
Medrano	.944	36	52	99	9	12

Parr	.955	40	80	113	9	26

Outfield	PCT	G	PO	A	E	DP
Comerota	.958	16	20	3	1	0
Cooper	.984	42	60	2	1	0
Jenkins	1.000	5	3	0	0	0
Lang	.964	53	128	5	5	0
Loftus	.989	44	83	4	1	1
Perez-Ramos	.929	16	26	0	2	0
Poma	1.000	57	127	5	0	0

AZL DIAMONDBACKS — ROOKIE

ARIZONA LEAGUE

Batting	B-T	HT	WT	DOB	AVG	vLH	vRH	G	AB	R	H	2B	3B	HR	RBI	BB	HBP	SH	SF	SO	SB	CS	SLG	OBP
Bianco, Justin	L-R	5-11	195	8-24-92	.274	.333	.250	24	84	15	23	5	2	0	11	10	2	1	0	26	8	3	.381	.365
Billigen, Brian	R-R	6-0	170	5-11-90	.327	.250	.355	30	104	30	34	5	3	1	17	24	2	0	1	24	11	5	.462	.458
Bloomquist, Willie	R-R	5-11	185	11-27-77	.333	.333	.333	4	9	3	3	1	1	0	4	1	0	0	0	1	0	0	.667	.400
Bolivar, Anderson	B-R	5-11	165	9-9-92	.247	.385	.217	20	73	13	18	3	1	1	14	4	1	0	1	8	0	0	.356	.291
Castillo, William	R-R	5-10	158	7-11-92	.303	.217	.340	43	152	29	46	5	2	0	20	15	2	6	0	23	14	4	.362	.373
Flores, Rudy	L-R	6-3	205	12-12-90	.400	.000	.571	3	10	3	4	1	0	0	4	2	0	0	0	1	1	0	.500	.500
Fuller, Ryan	R-R	6-1	205	5-2-90	.252	.333	.225	32	107	13	27	5	2	1	8	9	5	0	1	33	2	1	.364	.336
Garcia, Bubu	R-R	5-10	190	3-17-94	.139	.111	.148	11	36	2	5	0	0	0	4	1	0	0	0	10	0	0	.139	.162
Glenn, Alex	L-L	5-11	175	6-11-91	.244	.308	.216	36	127	24	31	4	4	4	23	18	5	3	0	41	8	3	.433	.360
Graham, Tyler	R-R	6-0	185	1-25-84	.273	.571	.133	8	22	3	6	2	1	0	5	9	0	0	0	4	3	0	.455	.484
Jones, Zach	R-R	5-10	170	11-1-88	.273	.500	.222	3	11	0	3	1	0	0	3	0	0	0	0	2	0	0	.364	.273
Leonard, John	R-R	6-0	159	6-25-92	.182	.125	.214	14	44	3	8	2	0	0	2	1	0	1	0	14	1	0	.227	.200
Linton, Ollie	L-L	5-8	160	4-7-86	.214	.000	.250	4	14	1	3	1	0	0	4	1	1	0	1	2	0	1	.286	.294
Llewellyn, Phildrick	B-R	6-1	205	9-25-93	.240	.353	.195	38	121	12	29	7	1	0	14	18	0	4	1	41	4	1	.314	.336
Lopez, B.J.	R-R	5-9	185	9-29-94	.071	.000	.077	9	14	2	1	0	0	0	0	6	1	0	0	9	2	0	.071	.381
McDonald, John	R-R	5-9	180	9-24-74	.000	.000	.000	3	8	1	0	0	0	0	1	3	1	0	0	1	0	0	.000	.333
Munoz, Joe	R-R	6-3	195	12-28-93	.260	.234	.270	47	173	25	45	4	2	2	20	16	1	3	0	53	4	4	.341	.326
Santiago, Alan	L-R	6-1	170	7-24-90	.222	.143	.273	7	18	6	4	1	0	0	0	5	1	0	0	7	0	0	.278	.417
Smith, Damion	L-R	6-3	170	2-14-94	.222	.125	.255	23	63	9	14	1	0	0	7	16	0	0	0	30	3	1	.238	.380
Taylor, Chuck	B-L	5-9	185	9-21-93	.234	.224	.238	52	205	41	48	7	2	0	16	20	3	4	1	55	16	7	.288	.310
Trahan, Stryker	L-R	6-1	215	4-25-94	.281	.229	.303	49	167	29	47	11	3	5	25	40	2	0	2	48	8	1	.473	.422
Velazquez, Andrew	B-R	5-8	175	7-14-94	.319	.138	.379	29	116	33	37	8	5	1	20	18	1	1	3	35	20	3	.500	.406
Walding, Miles	R-R	6-1	175	3-19-89	.188	.286	.146	24	69	8	13	2	1	0	7	8	0	0	0	23	2	3	.246	.273
Williams, Jake	B-L	6-1	190	1-2-91	.217	.346	.167	28	92	10	20	3	1	0	13	15	1	0	0	36	1	1	.272	.333

Pitching	B-T	HT	WT	DOB	W	L	ERA	G	GS	CG	SV	IP	H	R	ER	HR	BB	SO	AVG	vLH	vRH	K/9	BB/9
Brewer, Chase	R-R	6-4	220	2-1-90	1	0	11.12	5	0	0	0	6	8	7	7	2	1	10	.333	.182	.462	15.88	1.59
Collmenter, Josh	R-R	6-2	235	2-7-86	0	0	0.00	3	3	0	0	8	5	0	0	0	0	11	.179	.286	.071	12.38	0.00
Eckels, Ben	R-R	6-0	175	1-29-94	4	3	4.13	11	9	0	0	52	50	31	24	1	23	56	.248	.202	.280	9.63	3.96
Gibbs, Jeff	R-R	6-4	185	4-23-91	0	4	12.66	10	7	0	0	21	24	37	30	2	35	18	.282	.243	.313	7.59	14.77
Guzman, Francisco	L-L	6-5	190	7-2-89	2	2	5.09	8	1	0	1	18	20	13	10	0	7	16	.290	.385	.233	8.15	3.57
Hamilton, Tanner	R-R	6-3	210	11-29-88	1	0	6.26	15	0	0	1	23	28	16	16	0	11	32	.308	.250	.339	12.52	4.30
Hernandez, Luis	R-R	6-2	187	6-22-92	4	4	4.71	13	12	1	0	65	62	44	34	4	28	53	.247	.228	.260	7.34	3.88
Locante, Will	L-L	6-1	190	2-2-90	0	1	5.02	13	0	0	6	14	14	14	8	1	4	21	.241	.188	.262	13.19	2.51
Marino, Harry	R-L	6-0	180	7-14-90	2	0	2.60	16	0	0	0	17	13	5	5	0	10	19	.210	.000	.265	9.87	5.19
Medlinger, Donny	R-R	6-1	165	9-29-90	1	0	0.38	18	0	0	4	24	14	4	1	0	5	29	.169	.179	.164	11.03	1.90
Meyerchick, Eric	R-R	6-1	200	2-13-90	3	2	5.48	18	0	0	2	23	28	16	14	2	8	23	.301	.314	.293	9.00	3.13
Owings, Kyle	R-R	6-1	215	1-4-90	0	0	4.50	2	0	0	0	4	3	2	2	0	0	5	.214	.500	.167	11.25	0.00
Parra, Geordy	R-R	6-2	165	9-6-93	1	4	5.45	12	7	0	0	40	52	32	24	3	19	37	.311	.315	.310	8.39	4.31
Platt, Austin	R-R	6-3	190	3-5-92	2	3	4.46	7	5	0	0	36	35	23	18	3	14	38	.246	.213	.272	9.41	3.47
Potter, Andrew	R-R	6-0	208	2-9-94	3	0	4.33	13	2	0	0	54	50	30	26	2	25	43	.248	.268	.233	7.17	4.17
Pulley, Jonathan	R-R	6-2	215	5-20-93	2	4	5.30	15	4	0	0	37	41	29	22	4	15	42	.266	.250	.275	10.13	3.62
Saito, Takashi	L-R	6-2	200	2-14-70	0	0	0.00	4	4	0	0	4	2	0	0	0	4	6	.154	.000	.200	9.00	0.00
Saunders, Joe	L-L	6-3	210	6-16-81	0	1	6.23	1	1	0	0	4	3	5	3	0	5	7	.176	.000	.214	14.54	10.38
Triana, Karl	R-R	6-0	180	10-7-92	1	0	0.00	1	1	0	0	5	4	1	0	0	0	10	.190	—	.190	18.00	0.00
Urbina, Elroy	L-L	6-1	180	7-22-89	0	1	4.21	17	0	0	0	26	33	21	12	0	17	16	.314	.304	.317	5.61	5.96

Fielding

Catcher	PCT	G	PO	A	E	DP	PB
Bolivar	1.000	9	50	7	0	0	3
Jones	1.000	1	8	0	0	0	1
Llewellyn	.984	8	56	7	1	0	1
Lopez	1.000	1	7	3	0	1	1
Trahan	.972	40	328	56	11	2	18

First Base	PCT	G	PO	A	E	DP
Flores	1.000	3	27	0	0	3
Llewellyn	.992	29	243	15	2	16
Williams	.988	27	241	14	3	19

Second Base	PCT	G	PO	A	E	DP
Castillo	.968	24	41	79	4	16

	PCT	G	PO	A	E	DP
Leonard	.933	9	12	16	2	2
Velazquez	.951	26	39	77	6	13

Third Base	PCT	G	PO	A	E	DP
Castillo	.970	12	6	26	1	1
Fuller	.855	31	24	47	12	7
Garcia	.500	2	0	2	2	1
Walding	1.000	15	5	28	0	1

Shortstop	PCT	G	PO	A	E	DP
Bloomquist	1.000	4	2	2	0	0
Leonard	.938	6	5	10	1	2
McDonald	1.000	3	7	7	0	5
Munoz	.882	45	58	129	25	23

	PCT	G	PO	A	E	DP
Velazquez	.917	3	7	4	1	0
Walding	1.000	2	1	2	0	0

Outfield	PCT	G	PO	A	E	DP
Bianco	.950	24	35	3	2	2
Billigen	.941	27	46	2	3	0
Glenn	.964	31	50	4	2	1
Graham	1.000	5	8	0	0	0
Linton	1.000	3	3	1	0	0
Santiago	1.000	7	7	0	0	0
Smith	.958	21	23	0	1	0
Taylor	.965	51	78	4	3	0
Walding	.857	5	5	1	1	0

MISSOULA OSPREY — ROOKIE

PIONEER LEAGUE

Batting	B-T	HT	WT	DOB	AVG	vLH	vRH	G	AB	R	H	2B	3B	HR	RBI	BB	HBP	SH	SF	SO	SB	CS	SLG	OBP
Abreu, Jesus	R-R	5-10	155	4-14-92	.000	—	.000	2	1	0	0	0	0	0	1	0	0	0	0	1	0	0	.000	.500
Almadova, Breland	R-R	6-1	195	10-18-90	.306	.316	.301	64	255	38	78	17	4	1	28	22	5	1	2	41	11	3	.416	.370
Bianco, Justin	L-R	5-11	195	8-24-92	.194	.190	.195	27	98	10	19	4	0	3	17	7	0	2	1	40	4	0	.327	.245
Bream, Tyler	R-B	6-3	210	10-26-89	.272	.222	.290	46	169	27	46	12	2	3	26	14	1	0	4	37	2	2	.420	.330
Brito, Socrates	L-L	6-2	197	9-6-92	.312	.268	.327	69	279	47	87	15	5	4	39	21	1	0	4	73	15	9	.444	.357
Dultz, Kevin	R-R	6-2	215	7-17-88	.194	.143	.208	23	31	5	6	2	0	1	4	6	1	0	0	9	0	1	.355	.342

Batting	B-T	HT	WT	DOB	AVG	vLH	vRH	G	AB	R	H	2B	3B	HR	RBI	BB	HBP	SH	SF	SO	SB	CS	SLG	OBP
Flores, Rudy	L-R	6-3	205	12-12-90	.296	.271	.306	46	169	22	50	11	1	3	32	20	4	0	1	51	1	0	.426	.381
Glenn, Alex	L-L	5-11	175	6-11-91	.300	.077	.362	17	60	12	18	1	3	6	17	8	0	0	1	18	1	0	.717	.377
Gutierrez, Yosbel	R-R	5-10	170	1-20-93	.322	.242	.354	32	115	16	37	9	1	2	15	15	7	0	1	25	3	0	.470	.428
Koeneman, Kyle	R-R	6-1	220	8-26-88	.171	.444	.077	12	35	4	6	3	0	1	5	7	3	0	0	13	1	1	.343	.356
Lamb, Jake	L-R	6-3	195	10-9-90	.329	.303	.336	67	280	47	92	22	5	9	57	24	7	0	4	51	8	2	.539	.390
Leonard, John	R-R	6-0	159	6-25-92	.172	.269	.137	31	99	13	17	1	0	0	4	13	1	1	0	16	1	3	.182	.274
Linton, Ty	R-R	6-3	195	1-17-91	.238	.245	.235	42	168	26	40	7	1	4	19	6	1	0	1	62	1	3	.363	.267
Marzilli, Evan	L-L	5-11	175	3-13-91	.332	.491	.278	51	211	40	70	10	1	0	15	21	4	0	0	35	6	3	.389	.403
McConnell, Adam	R-R	6-0	187	1-24-90	.250	.364	.190	12	32	5	8	2	0	0	5	6	0	0	1	9	1	1	.313	.359
Perez, Michael	L-R	5-11	180	8-7-92	.293	.323	.282	58	225	43	66	16	5	10	60	20	5	0	4	72	0	1	.542	.358
Pulfer, Daniel	R-R	5-9	195	2-16-90	.285	.184	.318	55	200	32	57	10	3	2	27	13	9	3	5	23	6	0	.395	.348
Ruiz, Pedro	B-R	5-11	165	8-30-91	.313	.344	.303	65	249	58	78	12	4	2	19	43	2	5	0	69	20	6	.418	.418
Velazquez, Andrew	B-R	5-8	175	7-14-94	.220	.111	.244	14	50	9	11	0	2	0	4	5	0	0	1	12	2	0	.300	.286

Pitching	B-T	HT	WT	DOB	W	L	ERA	G	GS	CG	SV	IP	H	R	ER	HR	BB	SO	AVG	vLH	vRH	K/9	BB/9
Barbosa, Andrew	R-L	6-8	205	11-18-87	1	0	0.41	4	4	0	0	22	9	1	1	0	9	28	.130	.208	.089	11.45	3.68
Blake, Michael	L-L	5-11	190	8-4-90	0	1	6.00	17	0	0	1	24	24	18	16	4	22	37	.264	.259	.266	13.88	8.25
Camacho, Yiomar	R-R	6-1	172	2-24-90	3	4	4.91	13	13	0	0	62	70	43	34	5	25	61	.283	.226	.326	8.81	3.61
Capper, Chris	R-R	6-1	203	2-5-91	3	2	3.77	24	0	0	1	43	44	22	18	6	14	44	.265	.288	.247	9.21	2.93
Gerdeman, Ross	R-R	6-3	210	11-7-89	5	5	5.06	16	15	0	0	89	97	58	50	6	35	62	.284	.340	.239	6.27	3.54
Geyer, Cody	R-R	5-11	215	5-4-92	0	1	22.50	2	0	0	0	2	5	5	5	1	3	2	.500	.750	.333	9.00	13.50
O'Neill, Bobby	R-R	6-3	220	7-15-89	0	0	18.00	4	0	0	0	4	11	9	8	1	3	1	.500	.333	.700	2.25	6.75
Pack, Chris	R-R	6-3	215	8-23-87	6	2	5.42	15	14	0	0	76	83	55	46	10	29	55	.282	.302	.267	6.48	3.42
Price, Dexter	R-R	6-7	220	8-8-90	3	2	5.31	22	0	0	1	39	47	30	23	2	17	28	.301	.281	.315	6.46	3.92
Ray, Jared	R-R	6-3	190	2-25-89	3	5	4.10	13	12	0	0	64	57	34	29	4	22	58	.239	.298	.201	8.20	3.11
Rivera, Michael	R-R	6-0	230	10-15-90	2	2	5.81	19	0	0	0	31	25	21	20	5	13	37	.219	.212	.226	10.74	3.77
Smith, Patrick	R-R	6-2	170	1-29-90	2	1	5.36	23	0	0	1	44	52	30	26	4	18	47	.294	.261	.315	9.69	3.71
Spilker, Vince	R-R	6-3	215	8-23-90	1	0	3.92	18	0	0	6	21	17	9	9	1	8	28	.227	.219	.233	12.19	3.48
Stevens, Chase	R-R	5-10	186	8-15-90	3	2	3.21	26	0	0	0	34	23	13	12	7	17	59	.189	.289	.130	15.77	4.54
Thomas, Chris	R-R	6-2	175	12-21-89	2	1	3.09	13	4	0	0	32	28	12	11	2	8	30	.235	.216	.250	8.44	2.25
Thompson, Justin	R-R	6-1	200	12-4-89	2	2	1.69	25	0	0	8	32	23	10	6	2	10	47	.200	.298	.132	13.22	2.81
Triana, Karl	R-R	6-0	180	10-7-92	5	5	5.64	14	14	0	0	67	78	48	42	8	28	59	.291	.282	.298	7.93	3.76

Fielding

Catcher	PCT	G	PO	A	E	DP	PB
Dultz	1.000	15	69	7	0	1	2
Gutierrez	.989	20	166	17	2	1	10
Perez	.986	52	433	62	7	8	4

First Base	PCT	G	PO	A	E	DP
Bream	.989	32	262	17	3	17
Dultz	1.000	3	21	3	0	0
Flores	.983	36	319	24	6	33
Koeneman	.989	9	82	4	1	7

Second Base	PCT	G	PO	A	E	DP
Leonard	.963	17	31	48	3	8
McConnell	.913	5	8	13	2	2

Pulfer	.967	45	75	128	7	30	
Ruiz	1.000	9	19	34	0	6	
Velazquez	.970	6	16	16	1	4	

Third Base	PCT	G	PO	A	E	DP
Abreu	—	1	0	0	0	0
Bream	.857	8	6	12	3	0
Lamb	.963	64	43	141	7	13
McConnell	.818	4	5	4	2	1
Pulfer	1.000	1	3	2	0	0

Shortstop	PCT	G	PO	A	E	DP
Leonard	.957	15	24	43	3	12
McConnell	.833	2	4	1	1	0

Pulfer	.889	2	3	5	1	1	
Ruiz	.888	55	78	161	30	26	
Velazquez	.897	8	6	20	3	3	

Outfield	PCT	G	PO	A	E	DP
Almadova	.990	52	90	8	1	0
Bianco	.905	21	36	2	4	0
Brito	.961	65	90	8	4	2
Glenn	.895	15	17	0	2	0
Linton	.970	32	31	1	1	0
Marzilli	.963	47	77	2	3	0
Pulfer	1.000	3	1	0	0	0

DSL DIAMONDBACKS   ROOKIE
DOMINICAN SUMMER LEAGUE

Batting	B-T	HT	WT	DOB	AVG	vLH	vRH	G	AB	R	H	2B	3B	HR	RBI	BB	HBP	SH	SF	SO	SB	CS	SLG	OBP
Andujar, Omar	L-R	6-0	190	8-9-94	.190	.000	.308	10	21	2	4	0	0	0	1	10	0	0	0	6	0	1	.190	.452
2-team total (25 Diamondbacks/Reds)					.121	—	—	35	91	5	11	2	0	0	2	21	2	0	0	34	0	2	.143	.298
Becerra, Ifran	L-R	5-10	155	6-13-91	.246	.188	.267	19	61	12	15	0	1	1	7	17	1	0	1	17	4	4	.328	.413
2-team total (28 White Sox)					.274	—	—	47	135	28	37	4	3	3	24	28	2	0	5	34	14	7	.415	.394
Carrasco, Cesar	R-R	6-2	185	10-3-93	.261	.250	.265	69	257	42	67	6	2	2	37	38	4	0	4	54	3	4	.323	.360
Ceballos, Pablo	R-R	5-10	170	3-5-95	.231	.286	.167	7	13	5	3	0	0	1	3	2	3	0	0	1	0	0	.462	.444
Cordoba, Aldahir	R-R	5-10	170	9-5-94	.152	.063	.180	28	66	7	10	0	0	0	1	12	6	0	0	26	4	6	.152	.333
Garcia, Raul	R-R	6-0	159	12-14-94	.277	.277	.277	64	231	33	64	18	2	6	40	23	8	1	4	61	5	4	.450	.357
Garcia, Yorman	R-R	6-1	175	3-17-94	.277	.320	.259	62	260	39	72	10	5	0	22	17	6	5	1	46	25	11	.354	.335
Heredia, Juan	R-R	5-11	145	7-4-92	.250	.200	.269	47	148	24	37	8	1	0	12	35	4	4	0	24	11	7	.318	.406
2-team total (17 Diamondbacks/Reds)					.250	—	—	64	196	28	49	12	2	0	13	51	6	5	0	37	14	9	.332	.419
Liriano, Jesse	R-R	6-0	175	10-9-91	.205	.417	.111	15	39	7	8	0	0	0	2	6	1	0	0	17	2	3	.205	.326
2-team total (25 Diamondbacks/Reds)					.200	—	—	40	115	14	23	2	2	0	8	11	3	0	1	39	5	6	.252	.285
Mejias, Ronny	B-R	6-0	170	5-9-94	.219	.133	.249	63	237	34	52	10	2	1	20	35	0	6	3	50	7	2	.291	.316
Queliz, Jose	R-R	6-3	200	8-7-92	.250	.250	.250	46	156	23	39	6	3	0	30	10	2	1	3	25	1	0	.346	.298
Ramirez, Freddy	R-R	6-0	170	6-27-92	.255	.150	.282	31	98	14	25	7	1	0	12	9	5	1	1	18	1	3	.347	.345
Rosario, Yeisson	L-L	6-0	185	9-20-92	.243	.186	.267	64	235	32	57	11	1	1	21	34	5	2	1	43	4	6	.311	.349
Samboy, Raul	R-R	5-11	165	9-25-93	.214	.154	.228	17	70	8	15	3	1	1	8	2	1	0	2	12	1	2	.329	.240
2-team total (46 Diamondbacks/Reds)					.244	—	—	63	246	22	60	10	1	1	18	12	3	1	3	53	7	10	.305	.284
Silvestre, Valentino	R-R	5-11	177	10-15-93	.205	.316	.172	25	83	10	17	6	0	1	7	11	2	2	1	26	0	0	.313	.309
Sosa, Maximo	R-R	6-2	191	3-10-92	.223	.240	.218	63	206	27	46	10	1	6	34	28	7	0	6	52	2	4	.369	.328
Vargas, Ranfy	R-R	6-2	210	11-16-92	.214	.194	.221	36	117	25	25	9	2	0	15	21	2	1	0	35	3	1	.325	.343

Pitching	B-T	HT	WT	DOB	W	L	ERA	G	GS	CG	SV	IP	H	R	ER	HR	BB	SO	AVG	vLH	vRH	K/9	BB/9
Basora, Anthony	L-L	6-4	203	2-17-95	1	0	1.08	3	1	0	0	17	9	2	2	1	3	18	.158	.188	.146	9.72	1.62
2-team total (10 Diamondbacks/Reds)					2	7	3.07	13	11	0	0	59	55	26	20	1	16	49	—	—	—	7.52	2.45
Benitez, Anfernee	L-L	6-1	176	7-24-95	4	2	2.25	15	13	0	0	72	59	24	18	2	21	49	.228	.333	.198	6.13	2.63
Bracho, Silvino	R-R	5-11	179	7-17-92	3	0	0.32	22	0	0	8	28	20	2	1	0	5	30	.202	.154	.233	9.64	1.61
Cardenas, David	R-R	5-11	160	1-17-92	0	0	0.00	3	0	0	0	4	4	4	0	0	3	1	.250	.000	.308	2.25	6.75
Castillo, Jesus	R-R	6-2	165	8-27-95	2	4	5.40	14	8	0	0	47	57	31	28	3	17	41	.311	.250	.351	7.91	3.28
Cespedes, Christian	R-R	6-2	155	12-22-93	3	3	2.08	21	0	0	0	35	19	14	8	1	19	51	.162	.130	.183	13.24	4.93
Encarnacion, Virgilio	R-R	6-2	190	2-8-92	2	3	3.42	20	0	0	1	26	23	18	10	0	12	27	.228	.229	.226	9.23	4.10
Fermin, Jose	R-R	6-1	160	4-14-94	5	2	1.72	14	14	0	0	73	57	25	14	0	22	71	.218	.205	.228	8.71	2.70
Hernandez, Carlos	R-R	5-11	170	4-26-94	7	3	1.68	14	14	0	0	70	53	19	13	1	38	67	.213	.239	.193	8.66	4.91
Leal, Erick	R-R	6-3	180	3-17-95	6	2	2.44	14	12	1	0	70	58	26	19	1	11	70	.221	.218	.224	9.00	1.41
Moya, Gabriel	L-L	6-0	175	1-9-95	1	2	2.55	15	0	0	0	25	16	8	7	0	10	30	.188	.375	.169	10.95	3.65
Parra, Geordy	R-R	6-2	165	9-6-93	1	0	4.50	3	3	0	0	16	19	10	8	3	2	17	.279	.333	.229	9.56	1.13
Penalo, Yeudis	R-R	6-2	190	9-15-93	1	1	2.77	11	0	0	2	13	8	4	4	0	6	8	.182	.053	.280	5.54	4.15
Solis, Jency	R-R	6-1	180	2-22-93	2	3	3.38	22	0	0	6	35	36	15	13	0	6	25	.263	.277	.250	6.49	1.56
Velez, Roger	L-L	6-2	192	12-17-94	2	2	6.89	11	5	0	0	33	42	27	25	1	12	32	.307	.286	.309	8.82	3.31
2-team total (3 Diamondbacks/Reds)					3	3	5.85	14	8	0	0	48	56	34	31	1	16	50	—	—	—	9.44	3.02

Fielding

Catcher	PCT	G	PO	A	E	DP	PB
Andujar	1.000	6	47	6	0	0	2
Ceballos	.976	7	38	1	1	0	0
Queliz	.986	36	296	49	5	5	3
Ramirez	.996	28	198	34	1	1	8

First Base	PCT	G	PO	A	E	DP
Andujar	1.000	2	2	1	0	0
Carrasco	.988	21	160	10	2	14
Heredia	.984	6	58	2	1	2
Liriano	1.000	7	43	3	0	0
Mejias	.982	8	51	3	1	2

	PCT	G	PO	A	E	DP
Vargas	.979	33	300	29	7	23
Second Base	PCT	G	PO	A	E	DP
Garcia	.942	57	117	141	16	27
Heredia	.889	2	4	4	1	1
Liriano	1.000	1	1	2	0	1
Mejias	.978	11	22	23	1	5
Samboy	.857	2	5	1	1	0

Third Base	PCT	G	PO	A	E	DP
Carrasco	.864	44	28	86	18	5
Mejias	.846	21	8	36	8	4
Silvestre	.913	9	3	18	2	1

Shortstop	PCT	G	PO	A	E	DP
Heredia	.926	37	68	83	12	17
Mejias	.903	24	28	65	10	8
Samboy	.915	11	14	29	4	5

Outfield	PCT	G	PO	A	E	DP
Becerra	.950	17	15	4	1	0
Cordoba	.921	21	34	1	3	1
Garcia	.935	62	109	6	8	2
Heredia	.500	2	1	0	1	0
Rosario	.966	63	107	7	4	1
Sosa	.948	49	69	4	4	2

DSL DIAMONDBACKS/REDS

ROOKIE

DOMINICAN SUMMER LEAGUE

Batting	B-T	HT	WT	DOB	AVG	vLH	vRH	G	AB	R	H	2B	3B	HR	RBI	BB	HBP	SH	SF	SO	SB	CS	SLG	OBP
Andujar, Omar	L-R	6-0	190	8-9-94	.100	.056	.115	25	70	3	7	2	0	0	1	11	2	0	0	28	0	1	.129	.241
2-team total (10 Diamondbacks)					.121	—	—	35	91	5	11	2	0	0	2	21	2	0	0	34	0	2	.143	.298
Chavez, Alberti	R-R	5-10	170	7-21-95	.314	.179	.358	46	159	14	50	11	1	0	16	12	0	1	3	18	9	4	.396	.356
De Luna, Jose	R-R	6-3	194	3-11-94	.132	.226	.096	33	114	6	15	1	1	0	5	7	2	0	0	23	0	4	.158	.195
Duque, Andres	R-R	6-3	176	2-9-92	.215	.262	.203	56	200	11	43	6	2	0	13	4	5	1	0	31	1	2	.265	.249
Guerrero, Raynay	R-R	6-4	190	2-24-93	.180	.118	.202	45	128	9	23	7	0	2	9	7	4	0	1	33	0	0	.281	.243
Heredia, Juan	R-R	5-11	145	7-4-92	.250	.500	.214	17	48	4	12	4	1	0	1	16	2	1	0	13	3	2	.375	.455
2-team total (47 Diamondbacks)					.250	—	—	64	196	28	49	12	2	0	13	51	6	5	0	37	14	9	.332	.419
Jimenez, Olvis	L-L	6-4	175	5-18-94	.137	.143	.135	39	124	5	17	4	0	0	6	13	3	1	0	38	2	2	.169	.236
Jordan, Jose	L-R	5-10	160	9-21-94	.194	.182	.198	57	170	15	33	9	0	0	10	23	3	4	1	39	2	8	.247	.299
Liriano, Jesse	R-R	6-0	175	10-9-91	.197	.238	.182	25	76	7	15	2	2	0	6	5	2	0	1	22	3	3	.276	.262
2-team total (15 Diamondbacks)					.200	—	—	40	115	14	23	2	2	0	8	11	3	0	1	39	5	6	.252	.285
Mejia, Cesar	L-R	6-1	165	12-8-94	.213	.227	.210	40	127	6	27	6	1	0	7	18	2	1	0	44	3	6	.276	.320
Mier y Teran, Jonniel	R-R	6-1	170	3-30-94	.202	.240	.191	39	114	13	23	5	4	0	4	7	3	0	1	48	6	1	.316	.264
Peralta, Henderson	B-R	6-0	195	6-4-91	.219	.225	.216	51	151	15	33	4	1	1	8	18	4	0	1	32	6	5	.278	.316
Peraza, Juan Carlos	R-R	6-2	197	3-12-93	.122	.074	.136	35	115	9	14	7	0	0	10	11	3	0	0	43	0	1	.183	.217
Raga, Jose	R-R	5-11	190	11-20-93	.188	.000	.273	5	16	1	3	0	0	0	1	0	0	0	0	4	0	0	.188	.235
2-team total (29 Reds)					.139	—	—	34	101	7	14	1	0	0	5	6	3	1	0	21	1	0	.149	.209
Rivas, Jefry	R-R	6-1	175	9-6-92	.189	.133	.211	31	106	4	20	5	1	0	7	8	0	0	2	19	4	1	.255	.241
Samboy, Raul	R-R	5-11	155	9-25-93	.256	.227	.265	46	176	14	45	7	0	0	10	10	2	1	1	41	6	8	.295	.302
2-team total (17 Diamondbacks)					.244	—	—	63	246	22	60	10	1	1	18	12	3	1	3	53	7	10	.305	.284
Valor, Geraldo	R-R	5-10	155	5-2-94	.255	.179	.284	31	102	9	26	3	0	0	12	15	3	1	3	15	6	2	.284	.358
2-team total (26 Diamondbacks)					.238	—	—	57	185	26	44	4	1	0	18	26	5	3	4	31	11	4	.270	.341
Velazquez, Nestor	R-R	5-11	170	5-28-93	.207	.250	.194	50	174	26	36	1	0	0	11	19	2	4	0	38	5	9	.213	.292

Pitching	B-T	HT	WT	DOB	W	L	ERA	G	GS	CG	SV	IP	H	R	ER	HR	BB	SO	AVG	vLH	vRH	K/9	BB/9
Arias, Junior	R-R	6-3	170	11-10-93	2	1	5.45	15	3	0	1	38	46	36	23	1	15	39	.301	.294	.303	9.24	3.55
Aybar, Manuel	R-R	6-3	185	1-6-93	1	8	4.40	13	13	0	0	57	42	36	28	2	31	53	.209	.292	.163	8.32	4.87
Basora, Anthony	L-L	6-4	203	2-17-95	1	7	3.86	10	10	0	0	42	46	24	18	0	13	31	.282	.318	.277	6.64	2.79
2-team total (3 Diamondbacks)					2	7	3.07	13	11	0	0	59	55	26	20	1	16	49	—	—	—	7.52	2.45
Beard, Eliezer	R-R	6-4	202	4-23-91	2	5	2.08	8	6	0	0	35	35	16	8	0	9	32	.267	.271	.265	8.31	2.34
2-team total (1 Reds)					2	5	2.13	9	7	0	0	38	39	17	9	0	11	35	—	—		8.29	2.61
Castillo, Luis	R-R	6-2	180	3-10-95	0	9	4.48	14	14	0	0	60	84	36	30	2	13	36	.333	.274	.363	5.37	1.94
Cuevas, Israel	R-R	6-1	178	9-19-93	2	3	3.67	14	0	0	1	27	23	15	11	0	22	22	.228	.233	.225	7.33	7.33
Damian, Pedro	R-R	6-1	170	11-29-92	0	1	1.29	3	3	0	0	14	9	6	2	0	9	17	.170	.111	.182	10.93	5.79
2-team total (10 Diamondbacks)					1	3	3.27	13	13	0	0	44	33	28	16	1	32	43	—	—		8.80	6.55
De Leon, John	R-R	6-4	205	10-13-93	0	0	7.84	20	0	0	0	21	21	27	18	0	32	14	.256	.261	.254	6.10	13.94
Heredia, Jose	L-L	6-3	200	6-12-92	0	0	9.31	14	0	0	0	10	11	15	10	0	27	10	.306	.333	.303	9.31	25.14
Hernandez, Joyce	R-R	6-2	170	10-28-92	0	0	7.48	15	0	0	0	22	30	21	18	3	14	17	.319	.370	.299	7.06	5.82

Lara, Jean	R-R	6-3	200	4-15-93	1	4	4.02	13	5	0	0	31	25	19	14	1	25	25	.219	.238	.208	7.18	7.18
Montilla, Franklin	R-R	6-4	203	6-28-94	0	0	9.00	1	0	0	0	1	1	1	1	0	0	0	.250	.333	.000	0.00	0.00
Morales, Pablo	R-R	6-2	190	3-22-95	0	1	10.80	5	0	0	0	5	7	11	6	1	8	3	.333	.500	.294	5.40	14.40
Munoz, Jose	R-R	6-1	180	4-4-92	2	2	2.60	19	0	0	5	45	37	17	13	0	18	37	.230	.278	.206	7.40	3.60
Ortiz, Enmanuel	R-R	6-4	195	3-4-93	1	4	9.12	20	0	0	0	25	40	36	25	1	18	14	.370	.333	.389	5.11	6.57
Patino, Carlos	R-R	6-1	160	4-8-93	0	1	1.59	12	0	0	4	34	22	9	6	0	6	25	.185	.196	.178	6.62	1.59
2-team total (7 Reds)					1	1	2.15	19	0	0	5	59	42	17	14	1	9	52	—	—	—	7.98	1.38
Ramirez, Bernardo	R-R	6-2	180	2-2-93	2	4	1.28	12	12	0	0	56	40	19	8	0	20	47	.204	.173	.223	7.51	3.20
Ramirez, Harold	R-R	6-0	197	9-19-92	0	0	6.75	7	0	0	0	11	9	9	8	1	12	14	.225	.083	.286	11.81	10.13
2-team total (4 Reds)					0	0	5.02	11	0	0	0	14	12	13	8	1	16	16	—	—	—	10.05	10.05
Sarrameda, Ramon	R-R	6-3	180	7-8-91	1	1	1.72	6	0	0	0	16	14	8	3	1	5	15	.233	.333	.190	8.62	2.87
2-team total (11 Reds)					4	2	1.61	17	0	0	0	50	41	15	9	3	10	36	—	—	—	6.44	1.79
Suarez, Jose	L-L	6-3	180	5-1-91	0	0	13.50	12	0	0	0	13	22	25	20	0	17	11	.373	.667	.320	7.43	11.48
Velez, Roger	L-L	6-2	192	12-17-94	1	1	3.60	3	3	0	0	15	14	7	6	0	4	18	.250	.167	.260	10.80	2.40
2-team total (11 Diamondbacks)					3	3	5.85	14	8	0	0	48	56	34	31	1	16	50	—	—	—	9.44	3.02
Zapata, John	R-R	5-11	190	8-11-92	0	1	2.41	13	0	0	1	19	14	10	5	0	10	19	.187	.182	.189	9.16	4.82
2-team total (6 Reds)					0	3	4.25	19	0	0	1	30	30	20	14	0	14	26	—	—	—	7.89	4.25

Fielding

Catcher	PCT	G	PO	A	E	DP	PB
Andujar	.948	15	75	16	5	0	8
Peralta	.971	45	326	43	11	2	11
Peraza	.962	14	85	15	4	1	13
Raga	.960	4	18	6	1	0	1

First Base	PCT	G	PO	A	E	DP
Andujar	.930	8	53	0	4	1
Jordan	.982	7	51	5	1	4
Liriano	.984	17	120	4	2	9
Mejia	—	1	0	0	0	0
Peraza	.948	18	152	12	9	9
Rivas	.987	9	70	4	1	10
Velazquez	.974	17	100	14	3	9

Second Base	PCT	G	PO	A	E	DP
Chavez	.903	7	15	13	3	1
Heredia	—	1	0	0	0	0

	PCT	G	PO	A	E	DP
Jordan	.970	40	92	103	6	21
Liriano	.500	1	1	0	1	0
Mejia	1.000	4	4	3	0	0
Samboy	.800	1	4	0	1	0
Valor	.970	13	31	34	2	8
Velazquez	.959	8	22	25	2	6

Third Base	PCT	G	PO	A	E	DP
Chavez	.769	6	5	5	3	1
Mejia	.792	19	17	21	10	1
Rivas	.900	22	26	37	7	1
Samboy	1.000	3	2	7	0	0
Valor	—	1	0	0	0	0
Velazquez	.964	25	22	58	3	5

Shortstop	PCT	G	PO	A	E	DP
Chavez	.925	11	23	26	4	4
Heredia	1.000	1	1	3	0	0

	PCT	G	PO	A	E	DP
Heredia	.918	13	30	37	6	7
Jordan	1.000	1	0	2	0	0
Samboy	.890	32	48	81	16	12
Valor	.924	15	22	39	5	6

Outfield	PCT	G	PO	A	E	DP
Chavez	.930	18	37	3	3	0
De Luna	.889	31	52	4	7	0
Duque	.940	56	95	14	7	3
Guerrero	.935	42	55	3	4	1
Heredia	1.000	2	4	0	0	0
Jimenez	.881	29	53	6	8	0
Liriano	.857	6	6	0	1	0
Mier y Teran	.958	39	42	4	2	0
Rivas	—	1	0	0	0	0
Velazquez	1.000	2	1	0	0	0

Atlanta Braves

SEASON IN A SENTENCE: The Braves were able to erase the memory of 2011's collapse by returning to the playoffs and giving Chipper Jones a victory lap, though the playoff trip ended abruptly with a loss to the Cardinals in the first National League Wild Card Game.

HIGH POINT: Atlanta was in playoff contention all season, though it was usually assumed to be the wild card with Washington out in front in the NL East. But the Braves closed particularly strong, going 19-8 in September and getting within three games of the Nationals at the end of the month. The final home game was a 6-2 win over the Mets, with a crowd of 50,000-plus on hand to watch Jones' farewell and Craig Kimbrel's 42nd save.

LOW POINT: You could argue that the Wild Card Game was both a high point and a low point, as Turner Field was sold out and excited in a way that hadn't been seen in awhile. The game was full of twists and turns, including a botched infield-fly rule call that Braves fans will always remember, and the season ultimately ended with a 6-3 loss to the Cardinals.

NOTABLE ROOKIES: The Braves opened the season with one rookie shortstop, Tyler Pastornicky, but finished it with another, Andrelton Simmons. Simmons actually drew more attention in spring training, but the Braves thought he needed more seasoning and Pastornicky would be steadier. When Pastornicky was batting .248 at the end of May, however, they sent him down and called Simmons up. He batted .289/.335/.416 with strong defense and looks like he'll be there for years to come. Randall Delgado had a 4.37 ERA in 17 starts and will be counted on to win a rotation spot to open 2013.

KEY TRANSACTIONS: Atlanta played a pat hand through the season, making only minor adjustments such as bringing in Reed Johnson and Paul Maholm from the Cubs and Jeff Baker from the Tigers. The most significant transaction will be Jones' retirement after 18 years in the middle of the lineup.

DOWN ON THE FARM: Braves farm clubs had an aggregate winning percentage of .461, one of the worst marks in baseball, and Double-A Mississippi and Triple-A Gwinnett were particularly bad, finishing an aggregate 35 games under .500. Braves farmhands made only one appearance on Baseball America's classification all-star teams: Mississippi catcher Evan Gattis, who batted .258/.343/.522.

OPENING DAY PAYROLL: $83.3 million (16th)

ORGANIZATION LEADERS

BATTING		*Minimum 250 AB
MAJORS		
* AVG	Martin Prado	.301
* OPS	Jason Heyward	.814
HR	Jason Heyward	27
RBI	Freddie Freeman	94
MINORS		
* AVG	Jose Constanza, Gwinnett	.314
* OBP	Chris Garcia, Lynchburg	.408
* SLG	Ernesto Mejia, Gwinnett	.502
R	Nick Ahmed, Lynchburg	84
H	Ernesto Mejia, Gwinnett	152
TB	Ernesto Mejia, Gwinnett	258
2B	Nick Ahmed, Lynchburg	36
3B	Kyle Kubitza, Rome	9
HR	Ernesto Mejia, Gwinnett	24
RBI	Ernesto Mejia, Gwinnett	92
BB	Chris Garcia, Lynchburg	85
SO	Adam Milligan, Mississippi/Lynchburg	172
SB	Luis Durango, Gwinnett	46

PITCHING		#Minimum 75 IP
MAJORS		
W	Tim Hudson	16
# ERA	Tim Hudson	3.62
SO	Tommy Hanson	161
SV	Craig Kimbrel	42
MINORS		
W	Gus Schlosser, Lynchburg	13
L	Three tied at	11
# ERA	J.R. Graham, Lynchburg/Mississippi	2.80
G	Dusty Hughes, Gwinnett	54
	Andrew Russell, Mississippi/Gwinnett	54
GS	Six tied at	27
SV	Juan Jaime, Lynchburg	18
IP	Gus Schlosser, Lynchburg	165.1
BB	David Hale, Mississippi	67
SO	Aaron Northcraft, Lynchburg	160
# AVG	J.R. Graham, Lynchburg/Mississippi	.228

2012 PERFORMANCE

General Manager: Frank Wren. **Farm Director:** Ronnie Richardson. **Scouting Director:** Tony DeMacio.

Class	Team	League	W	L	PCT	Finish	Manager
Majors	Atlanta Braves	National	94	68	.580	t-3rd (16)	Fredi Gonzalez
Triple-A	Gwinnett Braves	International	62	82	.431	12th (14)	Dave Brundage
Double-A	Mississippi Braves	Southern	62	77	.446	10th (10)	Aaron Holbert
High A	Lynchburg Hillcats	Carolina	72	68	.514	3rd (8)	Luis Salazar
Low A	Rome Braves	South Atlantic	62	76	.449	t-10th (14)	Randy Ingle
Rookie	Danville Braves	Appalachian	36	28	.563	4th (10)	Jonathan Schuerholz
Rookie	GCL Braves	Gulf Coast	21	37	.362	14th (14)	Rocket Wheeler
Overall 2012 Minor League Record			315	368	.461	25th (30)	

ORGANIZATION STATISTICS

ATLANTA BRAVES
NATIONAL LEAGUE

Batting	B-T	HT	WT	DOB	AVG	vLH	vRH	G	AB	R	H	2B	3B	HR	RBI	BB	HBP	SH	SF	SO	SB	CS	SLG	OBP
Baker, Jeff	R-R	6-2	210	6-21-81	.105	.167	.000	14	19	1	2	0	0	0	1	1	0	0	0	10	0	0	.105	.150
2-team total (54 Chicago)					.248	—	—	68	153	17	38	10	1	4	21	9	0	0	2	38	4	1	.405	.287
Boscan, J.C.	R-R	6-2	215	12-26-79	.200	.333	.143	6	10	0	2	0	0	0	2	0	0	0	0	1	0	0	.200	.200
Bourn, Michael	L-R	5-11	180	12-27-82	.274	.273	.275	155	624	96	171	26	10	9	57	70	3	2	4	155	42	13	.391	.348
Constanza, Jose	L-L	5-9	150	9-1-83	.250	.182	.262	37	76	8	19	2	0	0	4	8	0	2	0	21	5	2	.276	.321
Diaz, Matt	R-R	6-0	215	3-3-78	.222	.269	.100	51	108	10	24	6	0	2	13	9	0	0	1	21	0	0	.333	.280
Francisco, Juan	L-R	6-2	245	6-24-87	.234	.189	.245	93	192	17	45	11	0	9	32	11	1	0	1	70	1	1	.432	.278
Freeman, Freddie	L-R	6-5	225	9-12-89	.259	.237	.276	147	540	91	140	33	2	23	94	64	7	0	9	129	2	0	.456	.340
Heyward, Jason	L-L	6-5	240	8-9-89	.269	.224	.300	158	587	93	158	30	6	27	82	58	2	0	3	152	21	8	.479	.335
Hinske, Eric	L-R	6-2	235	8-5-77	.197	.118	.209	91	132	16	26	7	1	2	13	14	0	0	1	41	0	0	.311	.272
Janish, Paul	R-R	6-2	200	10-12-82	.186	.194	.181	55	167	18	31	6	1	0	9	17	2	0	0	30	1	0	.234	.269
Johnson, Reed	R-R	5-10	180	12-8-76	.270	.299	.212	43	100	7	27	5	0	0	4	3	2	0	0	18	0	1	.320	.305
2-team total (76 Chicago)					.290	—	—	119	269	30	78	14	3	3	20	13	6	0	0	61	2	2	.398	.337
Jones, Chipper	B-R	6-4	210	4-24-72	.287	.298	.278	112	387	58	111	23	0	14	62	57	1	0	3	51	1	0	.455	.377
McCann, Brian	L-R	6-3	230	2-20-84	.230	.236	.227	121	439	44	101	14	0	20	67	44	1	0	3	76	3	0	.399	.300
Overbay, Lyle	L-L	6-2	235	1-28-77	.100	—	.100	20	20	1	2	1	0	0	1	0	0	0	0	8	0	0	.150	.143
2-team total (45 Arizona)					.259	—	—	65	116	12	30	10	0	2	10	13	0	0	1	34	0	0	.397	.331
Pastornicky, Tyler	R-R	5-11	190	12-13-89	.243	.196	.265	76	169	21	41	6	1	2	13	10	1	7	1	32	2	0	.325	.287
Prado, Martin	R-R	6-1	190	10-27-83	.301	.323	.290	156	617	81	186	42	6	10	70	58	2	4	9	69	17	4	.438	.359
Ross, David	R-R	6-2	205	3-19-77	.256	.241	.268	62	176	18	45	7	0	9	23	18	0	0	2	60	1	0	.449	.321
Simmons, Andrelton	R-R	6-2	170	9-4-89	.289	.305	.280	49	166	17	48	8	2	3	19	12	1	0	3	21	1	0	.416	.335
Uggla, Dan	R-R	5-11	205	3-11-80	.220	.220	.220	154	523	86	115	29	0	19	78	94	10	0	3	168	4	3	.384	.348
Wilson, Jack	R-R	6-0	200	12-29-77	.169	.194	.150	40	71	4	12	1	1	0	4	2	0	3	1	12	0	0	.211	.189

Pitching	B-T	HT	WT	DOB	W	L	ERA	G	GS	CG	SV	IP	H	R	ER	HR	BB	SO	AVG	vLH	vRH	K/9	BB/9
Avilan, Luis	L-L	6-2	220	7-19-89	1	0	2.00	31	0	0	0	36	27	9	8	1	10	33	.211	.180	.231	8.25	2.50
Batista, Miguel	R-R	6-1	210	2-19-71	0	0	3.00	5	0	0	0	6	5	2	2	1	2	2	.227	.400	.083	3.00	3.00
2-team total (30 New York)					1	3	4.61	35	5	0	0	53	58	30	27	6	33	36	—	—	—	6.15	5.64
Beachy, Brandon	R-R	6-3	215	9-3-86	5	5	2.00	13	13	1	0	81	49	24	18	6	29	68	.171	.148	.189	7.56	3.22
Delgado, Randall	R-R	6-3	200	2-9-90	4	9	4.37	18	17	0	0	93	89	48	45	8	42	76	.256	.263	.250	7.38	4.08
Durbin, Chad	R-R	6-2	220	12-3-77	4	1	3.10	76	0	0	1	61	52	25	21	9	28	49	.231	.274	.206	7.23	4.13
Gearrin, Cory	R-R	6-3	200	4-14-86	0	1	1.80	22	0	0	0	20	17	4	4	1	5	20	.233	.345	.159	9.00	2.25
Hanson, Tommy	R-R	6-6	220	8-28-86	13	10	4.48	31	31	0	0	175	183	95	87	27	71	161	.271	.295	.245	8.30	3.66
Hernandez, Livan	R-R	6-2	245	2-20-75	1	1	4.94	18	0	0	1	31	40	17	17	5	8	19	.331	.333	.328	5.52	2.32
2-team total (26 Milwaukee)					4	1	6.42	44	0	0	1	67	84	48	48	15	16	48	—	—	—	6.42	2.14
Hudson, Tim	R-R	6-1	175	7-14-75	16	7	3.62	28	28	1	0	179	168	77	72	12	48	102	.248	.235	.263	5.13	2.41
Jurrjens, Jair	R-R	6-1	200	1-29-86	3	4	6.89	11	10	0	0	48	72	40	37	8	18	19	.350	.345	.355	3.54	3.35
Kimbrel, Craig	R-R	5-11	205	5-28-88	3	1	1.01	63	0	0	42	63	27	7	7	3	14	116	.126	.116	.136	16.66	2.01
Maholm, Paul	L-L	6-2	220	6-25-82	4	5	3.54	11	11	1	0	69	63	29	27	8	19	59	.241	.180	.256	7.73	2.49
2-team total (21 Chicago)					13	11	3.67	32	31	1	0	189	178	80	77	20	53	140	—	—	—	6.67	2.52
Martinez, Cristhian	R-R	6-1	185	3-6-82	5	4	3.91	54	0	0	1	74	80	33	32	6	19	65	.277	.241	.311	7.94	2.32
Medlen, Kris	B-R	5-10	190	10-7-85	10	1	1.57	50	12	2	1	138	103	26	24	6	23	120	.208	.208	.207	7.83	1.50
Minor, Mike	R-L	6-4	205	12-26-87	11	10	4.12	30	30	0	0	179	151	88	82	26	56	145	.232	.239	.230	7.28	2.81
Moylan, Peter	R-R	6-2	225	12-2-78	1	0	1.80	8	0	0	1	5	3	3	1	1	2	2	.167	.500	.125	3.60	3.60
O'Flaherty, Eric	L-L	6-2	220	2-5-85	3	0	1.73	64	0	0	0	57	47	14	11	3	19	46	.229	.113	.291	7.22	2.98
Sheets, Ben	R-R	6-1	220	7-18-78	4	4	3.47	9	9	0	0	49	52	21	19	6	13	35	.275	.265	.292	6.39	2.37
Teheran, Julio	R-R	6-2	175	1-27-91	0	0	5.68	2	1	0	0	6	5	4	4	0	1	5	.217	.125	.267	7.11	1.42
Varvaro, Anthony	R-R	6-0	195	10-31-84	1	1	5.40	12	0	0	0	17	16	11	10	2	9	21	.250	.273	.226	11.34	4.86
Venters, Jonny	L-L	6-3	195	3-20-85	5	4	3.22	66	0	0	0	59	61	23	21	6	28	69	.270	.250	.281	10.59	4.30

Fielding

Catcher	PCT	G	PO	A	E	DP	PB
Boscan	.974	6	37	1	1	0	0
McCann	.998	114	845	51	2	4	6
Ross	.995	54	366	27	2	4	4

First Base	PCT	G	PO	A	E	DP
Freeman	.991	146	1295	74	12	122
Hinske	.981	15	95	8	2	6
Overbay	1.000	2	20	0	0	0
Prado	1.000	4	35	7	0	8

Second Base	PCT	G	PO	A	E	DP
Baker	1.000	1	0	1	0	0
Pastornicky	1.000	3	3	5	0	1
Prado	1.000	10	8	20	0	4
Uggla	.984	152	258	471	12	103
Wilson	.857	2	1	5	1	1

Third Base	PCT	G	PO	A	E	DP
Francisco	.935	49	20	67	6	9

Jones	.953	103	41	181	11	8
Prado	.980	25	13	35	1	6

Shortstop	PCT	G	PO	A	E	DP
Janish	.991	55	63	166	2	34
Pastornicky	.948	47	43	84	7	21
Prado	1.000	5	2	8	0	4
Simmons	.987	49	67	158	3	31
Wilson	.986	29	21	49	1	14

Outfield	PCT	G	PO	A	E	DP
Baker	1.000	4	4	0	0	0
Bourn	.995	153	383	3	2	0
Constanza	1.000	25	41	2	0	0
Diaz	1.000	24	50	2	0	2
Heyward	.986	156	335	11	5	4
Hinske	1.000	10	9	0	0	0
Johnson	.966	33	28	0	1	0
Prado	.984	119	179	9	3	1

GWINNETT BRAVES   TRIPLE-A

INTERNATIONAL LEAGUE

Batting	B-T	HT	WT	DOB	AVG	vLH	vRH	G	AB	R	H	2B	3B	HR	RBI	BB	HBP	SH	SF	SO	SB	CS	SLG	OBP
Boscan, J.C.	R-R	6-2	215	12-26-79	.189	.290	.150	70	222	22	42	12	0	3	23	19	4	4	1	59	1	0	.284	.264
Constanza, Jose	L-L	5-9	150	9-1-83	.314	.282	.324	88	344	54	108	10	4	1	27	36	2	8	2	43	14	6	.375	.380
DeLome, Collin	L-R	6-2	195	12-18-85	.125	.000	.167	6	16	4	2	1	0	0	0	1	1	0	5	0	0	.188	.176
Durango, Luis	B-R	5-9	155	4-23-86	.289	.303	.282	132	499	68	144	13	5	0	45	50	0	14	2	90	46	16	.335	.352
Friday, Brian	R-R	5-11	190	12-16-85	.170	.143	.179	30	88	12	15	3	0	2	8	11	0	0	0	19	3	0	.273	.263
2-team total (66 Indianapolis)					.213	—		96	282	38	60	13	2	2	33	34	4	2	1	57	10	6	.294	.305
Gartrell, Stefan	R-R	6-3	230	1-14-84	.251	.260	.247	122	418	67	105	22	1	20	55	50	3	0	1	123	10	0	.452	.335
Gotay, Ruben	B-R	5-11	175	12-25-82	.243	.220	.252	57	181	31	44	8	1	5	22	31	1	0	0	46	1	0	.381	.357
Harrilchak, Cory	L-L	5-10	175	10-27-87	.000	.000	.000	2	8	1	0	0	0	0	0	1	0	0	0	3	0	0	.000	.111
Kroeger, Josh	L-L	6-3	230	8-31-82	.323	.333	.321	31	96	13	31	7	0	2	12	17	1	0	0	11	2	1	.458	.430
2-team total (64 Pawtucket)					.266	—		95	334	47	89	24	0	11	37	39	1	0	4	54	3	6	.437	.341
Marrero, Christian	L-L	6-1	185	7-30-86	.247	.318	.227	68	194	22	48	14	1	4	29	29	1	2	1	40	6	5	.392	.347
2-team total (8 Indianapolis)					.241	—		76	216	26	52	14	1	5	35	34	1	3	1	44	6	6	.384	.345
McGill, Shawn	R-R	6-4	195	2-29-84	.143	.167	.130	17	35	6	5	0	0	0	2	2	0	0	1	6	1	1	.143	.184
Mejia, Ernesto	R-R	6-5	245	12-2-85	.296	.276	.303	133	514	73	152	32	1	24	92	34	8	0	3	132	10	4	.502	.347
Overbay, Lyle	L-L	6-2	235	1-28-77	.273	.000	.400	7	22	3	6	3	0	0	3	6	0	0	0	6	0	0	.409	.429
Paiml, Greg	R-R	6-0	185	8-3-84	.212	.154	.237	29	85	11	18	4	0	0	7	6	0	2	1	22	2	0	.259	.261
Parraz, Jordan	R-R	6-3	215	10-8-84	.288	.444	.220	34	118	14	34	6	1	2	9	11	3	1	0	26	5	1	.407	.364
Pastornicky, Tyler	R-R	5-11	190	12-13-89	.268	.387	.238	38	153	15	41	15	1	1	20	11	1	0	2	21	3	3	.399	.317
Pie, Felix	L-L	6-2	185	2-8-85	.285	.324	.275	96	333	39	95	26	7	6	51	23	5	0	3	46	16	0	.459	.338
Ryal, Rusty	R-R	6-2	200	3-16-83	.287	.130	.333	28	101	9	29	8	0	2	12	5	2	0	0	24	3	0	.426	.333
Sutton, Drew	B-R	6-3	200	6-30-83	.270	.302	.255	38	137	19	37	10	2	0	15	20	4	1	2	34	2	3	.372	.374
2-team total (12 Indianapolis)					.241	—		50	158	21	38	11	2	0	16	24	5	1	2	31	3	3	.335	.354
Terdoslavich, Joey	B-R	6-0	200	9-9-88	.180	.197	.173	53	194	19	35	4	0	4	20	19	0	1	1	50	3	0	.263	.252
Tiffee, Terry	B-R	6-2	225	4-21-79	.299	.364	.274	34	117	9	35	9	0	2	21	3	0	0	1	13	0	1	.427	.314
Wilson, Jack	R-R	6-0	200	12-29-77	.188	.278	.152	19	64	7	12	4	0	0	6	4	1	1	2	9	1	2	.250	.239
Wilson, Josh	R-R	6-0	175	3-26-81	.241	.258	.233	122	407	46	98	26	3	5	43	34	6	1	4	97	7	4	.356	.306
Yepez, Jose	R-R	6-0	205	6-19-81	.264	.246	.269	79	254	21	67	16	1	3	30	26	11	0	3	37	2	1	.370	.354
Zawadzki, Lance	B-R	5-10	180	5-26-85	.231	.192	.240	48	147	12	34	5	1	3	17	7	1	2	0	31	3	1	.340	.271

Pitching	B-T	HT	WT	DOB	W	L	ERA	G	GS	CG	SV	IP	H	R	ER	HR	BB	SO	AVG	vLH	vRH	K/9	BB/9
Batista, Miguel	R-R	6-1	210	2-19-71	1	1	3.38	6	4	0	0	24	19	9	9	2	10	21	.216	.174	.262	7.88	3.75
Buchter, Ryan	L-L	6-4	230	2-13-87	0	2	10.13	9	0	0	0	8	10	13	9	1	17	5	.303	.333	.292	5.63	19.13
Bullock, Billy	R-R	6-6	225	2-27-88	0	0	11.07	14	0	0	0	20	33	25	25	4	23	26	.355	.372	.340	11.51	10.18
Carlyle, Buddy	L-R	6-3	210	12-21-77	5	4	3.43	33	1	0	0	76	81	33	29	5	14	73	.279	.289	.270	8.64	1.66
Carrasco, D.J.	R-R	6-4	215	4-12-77	1	0	12.60	5	0	0	0	5	10	7	7	0	5	3	.435	.500	.364	5.40	9.00
2-team total (2 Buffalo)					1	0	9.00	7	0	0	0	8	12	8	8	1	5	4	—	—	—	4.50	5.63
Chapman, Jaye	R-R	6-0	195	5-22-87	3	6	3.52	40	0	0	7	54	46	31	21	3	29	60	.232	.298	.173	10.06	4.86
Cordier, Erik	R-R	6-4	230	2-25-86	1	1	4.38	8	4	0	0	25	27	15	12	1	21	15	.297	.310	.286	5.47	7.66
Delgado, Randall	R-R	6-3	200	2-9-90	4	3	4.06	8	8	1	0	44	47	20	20	6	21	51	.275	.289	.263	10.35	4.26
Flande, Yohan	L-L	6-2	180	1-27-86	6	11	4.21	29	27	0	0	148	153	75	69	11	55	106	.270	.279	.266	6.46	3.35
Gearrin, Cory	R-R	6-3	200	4-14-86	3	3	2.30	39	0	0	9	55	43	21	14	0	22	66	.215	.221	.211	10.87	3.62
Gilmartin, Sean	L-L	6-2	190	5-8-90	1	2	4.78	7	7	0	0	38	41	22	20	6	13	25	.273	.176	.323	5.97	3.11
Hanson, Tommy	R-R	6-6	220	8-28-86	1	0	0.00	1	1	0	0	5	3	0	0	0	2	5	.176	.200	.143	9.00	3.60
Hudson, Tim	R-R	6-1	175	7-14-75	2	0	0.84	2	2	0	0	11	8	2	1	0	5	8	.190	.263	.130	6.75	4.22
Hughes, Dusty	L-L	5-10	190	6-29-82	3	2	3.31	54	0	4	0	65	68	30	24	2	37	55	.269	.252	.284	7.58	5.10
Junge, Eric	R-R	6-5	220	1-5-77	6	8	4.66	19	18	1	0	104	126	67	54	7	37	64	.299	.320	.276	5.52	3.19
Jurrjens, Jair	R-R	6-1	200	1-29-86	4	6	4.98	14	14	1	0	72	79	47	40	10	16	39	.273	.259	.288	4.85	1.99
Leach, Brent	L-L	6-5	215	11-18-82	0	1	189.00	1	1	0	0	0	3	7	7	1	4	1	.750	.500	1.000	27.00	108.00
Lugo, Jose	L-L	6-1	180	4-10-84	2	6	6.50	20	7	0	0	62	79	48	45	5	37	58	.315	.340	.297	8.37	5.34
McCurry, Cole	L-L	6-2	180	9-25-85	1	2	4.88	17	0	0	0	28	20	15	15	1	15	17	.208	.135	.254	5.53	4.88
2-team total (2 Norfolk)					1	2	4.59	19	0	0	1	33	26	17	17	1	17	23	—	—	—	6.21	4.59
Medlen, Kris	B-R	5-10	190	10-7-85	0	2	4.73	3	3	0	0	13	15	7	7	2	6	12	.288	.280	.296	8.10	4.05
Moylan, Peter	R-R	6-2	225	12-2-78	0	0	5.68	12	0	0	0	13	18	8	8	1	5	13	.327	.435	.250	9.24	3.55
Redmond, Todd	R-R	6-3	215	5-17-85	6	6	3.58	18	18	1	0	106	107	50	42	11	28	96	.262	.293	.229	8.18	2.38
2-team total (8 Louisville)					8	11	3.63	26	25	1	0	149	150	71	60	18	39	136	—	—	—	8.23	2.36
Rice, Jason	R-R	5-10	190	5-13-86	1	1	3.38	16	0	0	0	19	20	10	7	0	15	18	.263	.250	.273	8.68	7.23
Rodriguez, Daniel	L-L	6-0	185	12-11-84	0	0	1.50	2	1	0	0	6	5	2	1	1	7	4	.238	.167	.267	6.00	10.50
Russell, Adam	R-R	6-8	255	4-14-83	3	3	7.28	31	0	0	1	38	52	34	31	1	26	37	.335	.353	.322	8.69	6.10
Russell, Andrew	R-R	6-0	202	4-27-84	1	1	1.75	20	0	0	2	26	19	6	5	1	11	13	.218	.242	.204	4.56	3.86
Swaggerty, Ben	L-L	6-1	185	8-8-82	0	0	4.32	6	0	0	0	8	7	5	4	2	6	9	.219	.231	.211	9.72	6.48

ATLANTA BRAVES

	B-T	HT	WT	DOB	W	L	ERA	G	GS	CG	SV	IP	H	R	ER	HR	BB	SO	AVG	vLH	vRH	K/9	BB/9
Teheran, Julio	R-R	6-2	175	1-27-91	7	9	5.08	26	26	1	0	131	146	81	74	18	43	97	.289	.276	.304	6.66	2.95
Varvaro, Anthony	R-R	6-0	195	10-31-84	0	2	2.23	33	1	0	6	44	39	12	11	1	24	47	.231	.291	.178	9.54	4.87
Venters, Jonny	L-L	6-3	195	3-20-85	0	0	0.00	1	1	0	0	1	0	0	0	0	0	0	.000	.000	.000	0.00	0.00

Fielding

Catcher	PCT	G	PO	A	E	DP	PB
Boscan	.989	70	559	50	7	13	10
McGill	.982	8	53	1	1	0	1
Yepez	.994	75	468	34	3	5	8

First Base	PCT	G	PO	A	E	DP
Gotay	1.000	2	6	0	0	0
Kroeger	.977	5	39	3	1	6
Marrero	1.000	36	260	27	0	29
Mejia	.991	95	719	62	7	71
Overbay	1.000	6	46	2	0	3
Sutton	1.000	1	6	1	0	2
Tiffee	1.000	5	52	2	0	9

Second Base	PCT	G	PO	A	E	DP
Friday	.975	19	31	48	2	11
Gotay	1.000	6	5	19	0	2
Paiml	.971	7	10	23	1	4

	PCT	G	PO	A	E	DP	PB
Pastornicky	1.000	9	13	15	0	3	
Ryal	.989	18	33	53	1	16	
Sutton	.971	30	57	78	4	22	
Wilson	.967	25	45	71	4	20	
Zawadzki	.964	42	68	92	6	25	

Third Base	PCT	G	PO	A	E	DP
Friday	1.000	2	1	1	0	0
Gotay	.954	47	32	72	5	6
Ryal	.957	11	7	15	1	3
Sutton	.923	7	4	8	1	0
Terdoslavich	.831	50	36	72	22	8
Tiffee	.957	25	14	30	2	3
Wilson	1.000	9	8	12	0	1
Zawadzki	.500	2	1	0	1	0

Shortstop	PCT	G	PO	A	E	DP
Friday	.969	12	9	22	1	6

	PCT	G	PO	A	E	DP
Paiml	.933	19	38	60	7	20
Pastornicky	.958	29	45	70	5	22
Wilson	.963	12	18	34	2	7
Wilson	.951	85	107	183	15	39
Zawadzki	1.000	2	1	0	0	0

Outfield	PCT	G	PO	A	E	DP
Constanza	.973	80	180	3	5	1
DeLome	1.000	5	12	0	0	0
Durango	.990	130	282	13	3	3
Gartrell	.974	83	147	5	4	1
Harrilchak	1.000	2	5	0	0	0
Kroeger	.962	21	25	0	1	0
Marrero	.950	16	18	1	1	0
Parraz	.981	30	52	1	1	0
Pie	.989	85	165	9	2	0
Ryal	1.000	3	6	1	0	0

MISSISSIPPI BRAVES

DOUBLE-A

SOUTHERN LEAGUE

Batting	B-T	HT	WT	DOB	AVG	vLH	vRH	G	AB	R	H	2B	3B	HR	RBI	BB	HBP	SH	SF	SO	SB	CS	SLG	OBP
Bethancourt, Christian	R-R	6-2	219	9-2-91	.243	.259	.238	71	268	30	65	5	1	2	26	11	2	4	3	45	8	6	.291	.275
Carrithers, Alden	L-R	5-9	165	11-14-84	.315	.341	.306	74	165	27	52	6	0	0	10	35	0	3	1	21	9	3	.352	.433
Christian, Jason	L-R	6-3	185	6-16-87	.219	.208	.221	55	155	20	34	3	1	0	6	20	3	2	1	32	2	0	.252	.318
Cunningham, Todd	B-R	6-0	200	3-20-89	.309	.267	.324	120	466	77	144	23	6	3	51	38	4	8	3	51	24	8	.403	.364
Gac, Ian	R-R	6-3	240	8-10-85	.247	.244	.248	75	255	26	63	27	1	7	35	31	5	0	1	85	4	3	.443	.339
Gattis, Evan	R-R	6-4	230	8-18-86	.258	.371	.231	49	182	24	47	13	4	9	37	20	4	0	1	29	1	1	.522	.343
Gosselin, Phil	R-R	6-1	190	10-30-88	.242	.231	.245	128	484	55	117	23	3	3	46	46	9	4	4	90	12	4	.320	.317
Harrilchak, Cory	L-L	5-10	175	10-27-87	.179	.032	.220	53	140	11	25	10	0	0	18	18	3	0	3	31	9	1	.250	.280
Jones, Mycal	R-R	5-10	170	5-30-87	.141	.125	.145	28	85	11	12	0	0	0	9	1	3	0	0	25	7	5	.141	.232
Kennelly, Matt	R-R	6-1	210	3-21-89	.254	.264	.250	62	197	20	50	13	1	1	22	21	5	0	1	26	3	0	.345	.339
Kleinknecht, Barrett	R-R	6-0	200	8-10-88	.219	.219	.219	49	128	15	28	11	0	0	16	14	2	2	3	23	2	2	.305	.299
Landoni, Emerson	B-R	5-11	180	2-19-89	.273	.400	.167	4	11	1	3	0	0	0	0	0	0	0	0	2	0	0	.273	.273
Leonard, Joe	R-R	6-5	215	8-26-88	.263	.253	.265	124	426	56	112	22	3	9	66	48	5	3	5	88	6	2	.392	.341
Maldonado, Brahiam	R-R	5-11	205	9-18-85	.094	.083	.100	10	32	1	3	0	0	0	2	0	0	0	7	0	0	.094	.147
2-team total (72 Chattanooga)					.247	—	—	82	243	27	60	11	3	7	21	14	5	0	0	52	4	0	.403	.302
Marrero, Christian	L-L	6-1	185	7-30-86	.250	.222	.263	11	28	4	7	1	0	1	6	6	1	1	1	7	1	0	.393	.389
McGill, Shawn	R-R	6-4	195	2-29-84	.143	.333	.111	6	21	1	3	0	0	1	3	0	0	0	0	3	0	0	.286	.143
Milligan, Adam	L-R	6-3	230	3-14-88	.176	.130	.190	30	102	4	18	5	0	1	9	8	2	1	1	38	0	0	.255	.248
Paiml, Greg	R-R	6-0	185	8-3-84	.139	.000	.200	31	72	4	10	1	0	0	2	8	1	1	0	27	0	0	.153	.235
2-team total (27 Birmingham)					.205	—	—	58	161	15	33	6	1	0	11	12	1	1	1	53	4	2	.255	.263
Parraz, Jordan	R-R	6-3	215	10-8-84	.208	.500	.111	7	24	4	5	1	0	0	3	4	1	0	0	6	0	0	.250	.345
Pedroza, Jaime	B-R	5-8	167	9-12-86	.193	.244	.162	35	109	17	21	6	0	4	6	11	2	1	0	35	1	0	.358	.279
Simmons, Andrelton	R-R	6-2	170	9-4-89	.293	.324	.286	44	174	29	51	9	2	3	21	20	3	4	2	20	10	2	.420	.372
Smith, Tim	L-L	6-3	225	6-14-86	.279	.333	.256	55	165	22	46	6	1	2	22	13	5	0	2	26	3	1	.364	.346
Stevens, Bobby	R-R	6-0	190	3-30-87	.200	.250	.167	14	30	1	6	1	0	1	6	4	2	1	2	10	0	0	.333	.316
Terdoslavich, Joey	B-R	6-0	200	9-9-88	.315	.354	.301	78	298	43	94	24	5	5	51	27	3	0	5	62	4	0	.480	.372
Ware, L.V.	R-R	5-10	185	3-18-87	.190	.286	.143	5	21	0	4	0	0	0	1	0	0	0	0	5	1	1	.190	.227
Wiley, Keenan	L-L	6-0	175	4-27-87	.237	.176	.254	111	372	40	88	14	2	1	35	40	1	6	2	82	15	6	.293	.311

Pitching	B-T	HT	WT	DOB	W	L	ERA	G	GS	CG	SV	IP	H	R	ER	HR	BB	SO	AVG	vLH	vRH	K/9	BB/9
Avilan, Luis	L-L	6-2	220	7-19-89	3	6	3.23	16	12	0	1	61	50	27	22	7	31	55	.224	.189	.242	8.07	4.55
Buchter, Ryan	L-L	6-4	230	2-13-87	3	1	1.31	35	0	0	4	41	24	7	6	1	19	50	.168	.170	.167	10.89	4.14
Bullock, Billy	R-R	6-6	225	2-27-88	1	2	3.89	26	0	0	1	39	30	20	17	3	33	41	.216	.260	.191	9.38	7.55
Butts, Brett	R-R	6-1	205	4-24-86	1	2	12.41	11	0	0	0	12	19	17	17	5	8	13	.358	.348	.367	8.03	5.84
Cordier, Erik	R-R	6-4	230	2-25-86	0	2	20.25	5	0	0	0	4	8	9	9	0	5	6	.421	.333	.500	13.50	11.25
Gilmartin, Sean	L-L	6-2	190	5-8-90	5	8	3.54	20	20	3	0	119	111	49	47	9	26	86	.248	.189	.270	6.49	1.96
Graham, J.R.	R-R	6-0	185	1-14-90	3	1	3.18	9	9	0	0	45	35	17	16	2	17	42	.210	.250	.169	8.34	3.38
Hale, David	R-R	6-2	210	3-27-87	8	4	3.77	27	27	0	0	146	121	66	61	11	67	124	.228	.215	.239	7.66	4.14
Jones, Chris	L-L	6-2	202	9-19-88	2	5	3.90	45	0	0	2	60	69	29	26	1	19	61	.285	.244	.306	9.15	2.85
Lamm, Mark	R-R	6-4	215	3-8-88	2	7	3.92	50	0	0	10	60	64	30	26	3	20	53	.274	.262	.282	7.99	3.02
Leach, Brent	L-L	6-5	215	11-18-82	2	4	2.81	17	5	0	0	48	45	21	15	3	23	40	.251	.242	.257	7.50	4.31
Lugo, Jose	L-L	6-1	180	4-10-84	3	4	3.02	12	9	1	0	63	52	23	21	4	27	50	.229	.189	.248	7.18	3.88
Masters, Chris	L-L	6-0	225	10-1-87	1	1	4.76	12	5	0	0	28	26	16	15	4	24	28	.250	.200	.275	8.89	7.62
McCurry, Cole	L-L	6-2	180	9-25-85	0	0	9.00	1	0	0	0	1	1	1	1	0	1	1	.250	.000	.500	9.00	9.00
Moran, Gary	R-R	6-8	255	5-29-85	5	10	2.91	29	23	2	1	161	153	73	52	7	42	117	.253	.255	.252	6.55	2.35
Moylan, Peter	R-R	6-2	225	12-2-78	1	0	0.00	1	0	0	1	3	0	0	0	0	1	2	.000	.000	.000	6.75	0.00
Rasmus, Cory	R-R	6-1	220	11-6-87	3	5	3.68	50	0	0	7	59	45	24	24	3	32	62	.220	.214	.224	9.51	4.91
Russell, Andrew	R-R	6-0	202	4-27-84	5	1	2.35	34	0	0	0	38	29	12	10	1	17	31	.215	.341	.154	7.28	3.99
Sheets, Ben	R-R	6-1	220	7-18-78	0	1	5.06	2	2	0	0	11	12	7	6	0	1	10	.279	.053	.458	8.44	0.84

Player	B-T	HT	WT	DOB	W	L	ERA	G	GS	CG	SV	IP	H	R	ER	HR	BB	SO	AVG	SLG	OBP
Shreve, Chase	L-L	6-3	180	7-12-90	2	1	3.93	11	0	0	0	18	17	8	8	1	16	16	.243	.308	.205	7.85	7.85
Spruill, Zeke	B-R	6-5	190	9-11-89	9	11	3.67	27	27	1	0	162	158	81	66	8	46	106	.260	.279	.242	5.90	2.56
Sullivan, Richard	L-L	6-3	235	4-14-87	0	1	7.00	5	0	0	0	9	10	7	7	1	5	13	.278	.417	.208	13.00	5.00
Tarsi, Mike	R-L	6-8	202	8-11-86	2	0	1.89	14	0	0	1	19	15	5	4	2	7	19	.214	.206	.222	9.00	3.32
Wilson, Andrew	R-R	6-2	180	7-30-87	0	0	12.83	9	0	0	0	13	21	20	19	1	12	6	.350	.360	.343	4.05	8.10

Fielding

Catcher	PCT	G	PO	A	E	DP	PB
Bethancourt	.985	69	473	55	8	6	5
Gattis	.982	17	102	10	2	1	1
Kennelly	.995	57	404	32	2	5	0
Kleinknecht	1.000	1	1	0	0	0	0
McGill	.982	5	50	4	1	0	0

First Base	PCT	G	PO	A	E	DP
Christian	1.000	2	11	2	0	2
Gac	.992	64	535	56	5	58
Kennelly	1.000	1	11	1	0	1
Kleinknecht	.962	6	48	3	2	4
Leonard	.955	3	19	2	1	2
Marrero	1.000	1	2	0	0	0
Stevens	1.000	1	3	0	0	0
Terdoslavich	.983	68	586	47	11	66

Second Base	PCT	G	PO	A	E	DP
Carrithers	1.000	13	18	27	0	5
Christian	.857	5	3	3	1	2
Gosselin	.973	120	217	316	15	81

	PCT	G	PO	A	E	DP	PB
Kleinknecht	1.000	7	14	19	0	5	
Landoni	1.000	3	1	8	0	2	
Paiml	1.000	4	6	6	0	1	
Pedroza	1.000	3	2	4	0	2	
Stevens	—	1	0	0	0	0	

Third Base	PCT	G	PO	A	E	DP
Carrithers	1.000	12	9	11	0	1
Christian	.909	6	1	9	1	0
Kleinknecht	1.000	12	7	14	0	3
Leonard	.964	115	60	210	10	24
Paiml	1.000	2	1	6	0	1
Pedroza	.900	4	2	7	1	1
Terdoslavich	.824	6	5	9	3	0

Shortstop	PCT	G	PO	A	E	DP
Christian	.935	40	70	103	12	25
Kleinknecht	.987	15	26	49	1	13
Landoni	1.000	1	2	3	0	1
Paiml	.956	21	26	60	4	13
Pedroza	.975	24	53	64	3	25

Simmons	.983	44	84	151	4	32

Outfield	PCT	G	PO	A	E	DP
Carrithers	.979	33	44	3	1	2
Christian	—	1	0	0	0	0
Cunningham	.981	113	197	6	4	4
Gattis	.977	30	40	2	1	0
Gosselin	1.000	7	6	0	0	0
Harrilchak	.973	41	68	4	2	2
Jones	1.000	27	52	3	0	1
Maldonado	1.000	5	10	0	0	0
Marrero	1.000	9	15	1	0	0
Milligan	1.000	24	34	0	0	0
Paiml	1.000	1	1	0	0	0
Parraz	1.000	6	7	0	0	0
Smith	.980	37	46	3	1	1
Stevens	1.000	10	7	2	0	0
Ware	.960	5	24	0	1	0
Wiley	.985	103	190	7	3	3

LYNCHBURG HILLCATS　　　　HIGH CLASS A

CAROLINA LEAGUE

Batting	B-T	HT	WT	DOB	AVG	vLH	vRH	G	AB	R	H	2B	3B	HR	RBI	BB	HBP	SH	SF	SO	SB	CS	SLG	OBP
Ahmed, Nick	R-R	6-3	205	3-15-90	.269	.241	.274	130	506	84	136	36	4	6	49	49	4	10	2	102	40	10	.391	.337
Brewer, Dan	R-R	5-11	195	7-19-87	.260	.231	.266	40	154	23	40	8	1	2	16	19	1	1	1	29	8	4	.364	.343
Comer, Chad	R-R	6-2	220	8-29-88	.168	.250	.153	36	101	2	17	3	0	0	4	10	2	3	0	23	0	0	.198	.257
Dalfonso, Jakob	L-R	6-3	200	1-25-90	.222	1.000	.176	5	18	2	4	0	0	0	1	0	0	0	0	3	0	0	.222	.263
Garcia, Chris	L-R	6-2	225	11-25-87	.285	.271	.287	125	411	56	117	25	1	11	59	85	2	0	2	92	3	4	.431	.408
Gattis, Evan	R-R	6-4	230	8-18-86	.385	.455	.357	21	78	14	30	7	0	9	29	10	4	0	2	12	1	1	.821	.468
Hefflinger, Robby	R-R	6-4	220	1-3-90	.228	.185	.240	37	123	14	28	8	0	4	11	18	2	1	0	47	1	1	.390	.336
Jones, Mycal	R-R	5-10	170	5-30-87	.253	.265	.251	102	383	45	97	27	3	3	30	34	9	9	2	64	22	8	.363	.327
La Stella, Tommy	L-R	5-11	185	1-31-89	.302	.360	.290	85	298	43	90	22	5	5	56	36	11	3	10	24	13	2	.460	.386
Landoni, Emerson	B-R	5-11	185	2-19-89	.217	.235	.213	67	198	22	43	6	1	3	20	14	2	4	1	33	1	7	.303	.274
Lipka, Matt	R-R	6-1	195	4-15-92	.271	.209	.288	51	199	32	54	5	1	2	13	20	1	5	4	32	12	6	.337	.335
McGill, Shawn	R-R	6-4	195	2-29-84	.222	.222	.222	14	45	7	10	4	0	1	8	4	2	1	1	6	2	1	.378	.308
Milligan, Adam	L-R	6-3	230	3-14-88	.255	.217	.264	91	337	45	86	21	2	15	49	20	6	0	3	134	3	0	.463	.306
Query, Ryan	R-R	5-11	190	8-24-87	.259	.333	.222	9	27	2	7	3	0	1	5	1	0	0	4	0	0	.481	.394
Rohm, David	R-R	6-3	215	1-22-90	.238	.304	.226	85	281	27	67	19	3	2	26	15	2	6	5	57	2	2	.349	.277
Rose, Kyle	R-R	6-0	165	5-24-89	.226	.267	.217	33	84	12	19	4	2	0	4	8	2	3	0	18	5	3	.321	.309
Salcedo, Edward	R-R	6-3	195	7-30-91	.240	.284	.230	130	471	65	113	26	2	17	61	33	4	2	1	130	23	14	.412	.295
Schlehuber, Braeden	R-R	6-2	205	1-7-88	.270	.308	.262	87	289	36	78	17	4	8	42	9	17	2	2	47	1	2	.439	.328
Smith, Tim	L-L	6-3	225	6-14-86	.320	.167	.341	15	50	10	16	4	0	1	6	9	3	1	0	6	0	2	.460	.452
Snitker, Troy	R-R	6-2	210	12-5-88	.000	—	.000	1	3	0	0	0	0	0	0	0	0	0	0	1	0	0	.000	.000
Spina, Mike	R-R	6-1	220	12-17-86	.222	.444	.194	26	81	5	18	7	1	1	12	12	2	0	0	26	1	1	.370	.337
Stevens, Bobby	R-R	6-0	190	3-30-87	.200	.273	.190	32	95	17	19	7	0	2	8	5	3	2	1	22	3	2	.337	.260
2-team total (51 Frederick)					.250	—	—	83	280	42	70	14	0	8	24	13	6	4	1	69	8	4	.386	.297
Ware, L.V.	R-R	5-10	180	3-18-87	.167	.286	.091	11	36	2	6	0	0	0	2	1	0	1	3	0	9	1	3	.167	.231
Weaver, Matt	R-R	6-0	175	1-27-90	.216	.296	.196	87	278	25	60	9	2	10	32	14	3	2	0	110	2	3	.371	.261

Pitching	B-T	HT	WT	DOB	W	L	ERA	G	GS	CG	SV	IP	H	R	ER	HR	BB	SO	AVG	vLH	vRH	K/9	BB/9
Brewer, Caleb	R-R	6-3	205	2-2-89	1	1	4.44	29	0	0	0	47	50	28	23	3	29	35	.281	.339	.254	6.75	5.59
Butts, Brett	R-R	6-1	205	4-24-86	0	1	2.25	6	0	0	1	8	7	2	2	0	0	10	.241	.200	.263	11.25	0.00
Chaffee, Matt	L-L	6-0	185	12-19-88	3	1	3.99	45	0	0	6	56	58	34	25	10	27	65	.255	.333	.251	10.38	4.31
Cornely, John	R-R	6-1	195	5-17-89	0	0	0.00	4	0	0	1	7	1	0	0	0	2	13	.045	.000	.056	15.95	2.45
Delgado, Dimaster	L-L	6-2	180	3-9-89	7	7	3.92	24	24	0	0	129	144	63	56	7	39	80	.288	.296	.287	5.60	2.73
Graham, J.R.	R-R	6-0	185	1-14-90	9	1	2.63	17	17	1	0	103	88	34	30	6	17	68	.236	.287	.207	5.96	1.49
Harper, Ryne	R-R	6-3	215	3-27-89	2	1	1.83	27	0	0	0	44	40	9	9	0	13	49	.244	.313	.216	9.95	2.64
Jaime, Juan	R-R	6-1	230	8-2-87	1	3	3.16	42	0	0	18	51	31	19	18	4	33	73	.173	.127	.194	12.80	5.79
Lee, Mike	R-R	6-7	220	11-18-86	3	3	3.93	11	9	0	0	55	54	27	24	2	16	42	.260	.284	.248	6.87	2.62
Marshall, Ian	R-R	6-3	215	3-3-87	1	4	5.34	21	0	0	2	29	41	17	17	4	11	24	.342	.308	.351	7.53	3.45
Martin, Cody	R-R	6-2	210	9-4-89	12	7	2.93	22	19	1	0	107	93	49	35	7	34	123	.235	.264	.225	10.31	2.85
Masters, Chris	L-L	6-0	225	10-1-87	0	3	5.40	7	5	0	0	30	28	19	18	5	12	22	.252	.167	.263	6.60	3.60
McCurry, Cole	L-L	6-2	180	9-25-85	0	0	5.40	4	0	0	1	5	8	4	3	0	2	2	.381	.000	.400	3.60	3.60
Northcraft, Aaron	R-R	6-4	225	5-28-90	10	11	3.98	27	27	2	0	152	143	83	67	4	53	160	.247	.246	.247	9.49	3.15
Pacheco, Ronan	L-L	6-6	170	7-29-88	0	4	7.82	12	5	0	0	25	42	32	22	3	27	24	.362	.619	.305	8.53	9.59
Schlosser, Gus	R-R	6-4	220	10-20-88	13	7	3.38	27	27	1	0	165	156	73	62	9	33	139	.252	.306	.227	7.57	1.80
Shreve, Chase	L-L	6-3	180	7-12-90	4	4	2.15	32	0	0	1	46	44	16	11	2	17	41	.262	.231	.271	8.02	3.33

Sims, Blaine	L-L	6-0	185	3-10-89	1	3	4.42	39	2	0	1	71	82	43	35	6	28	52	.292	.164	.323	6.56	3.53	
Weber, Ryan	R-R	6-0	170	8-12-90	2	4	3.38	19	5	0	2	45	50	20	17	1	7	40	.276	.344	.242	7.94	1.39	
Wilson, Andrew	R-R	6-2	180	7-30-87	3	3	1.70	32	0	0	1	48	33	10	9	1	12	45	.195	.228	.179	8.50	2.27	

Fielding

Catcher	PCT	G	PO	A	E	DP	PB
Comer	.986	36	255	23	4	1	2
Gattis	.989	10	77	11	1	1	4
McGill	.969	10	87	6	3	0	3
Query	.957	6	39	6	2	0	0
Schlehuber	.987	84	629	71	9	5	7
Snitker	1.000	1	10	1	0	0	0

First Base	PCT	G	PO	A	E	DP
Dalfonso	1.000	3	25	0	0	4
Garcia	.992	104	918	47	8	90
Spina	.986	17	137	5	2	10
Weaver	.989	25	173	8	2	20

Second Base	PCT	G	PO	A	E	DP
La Stella	.975	75	141	177	8	54

	PCT	G	PO	A	E	DP
Landoni	.966	43	55	88	5	23
Stevens	1.000	5	6	9	0	2
Weaver	.971	27	34	67	3	12

Third Base	PCT	G	PO	A	E	DP
Dalfonso	1.000	1	0	2	0	0
Landoni	.920	13	4	19	2	2
Salcedo	.891	120	79	265	42	19
Stevens	1.000	5	4	11	0	0
Weaver	.906	9	8	21	3	2

Shortstop	PCT	G	PO	A	E	DP
Ahmed	.963	128	211	457	26	99
Landoni	.976	13	13	28	1	7
Weaver	.900	2	4	5	1	1

Outfield	PCT	G	PO	A	E	DP
Brewer	.971	40	64	2	2	0
Dalfonso	1.000	1	3	0	0	0
Gattis	1.000	3	4	0	0	0
Hefflinger	1.000	32	42	2	0	0
Jones	.984	102	179	9	3	2
Lipka	1.000	50	96	6	0	1
Milligan	.971	42	64	3	2	0
Rohm	.987	77	147	4	2	1
Rose	.935	32	42	1	3	0
Smith	1.000	4	7	0	0	0
Stevens	.917	22	19	3	2	0
Ware	.923	11	11	1	1	0
Weaver	1.000	32	36	1	0	0

ROME BRAVES

LOW CLASS A

SOUTH ATLANTIC LEAGUE

Batting	B-T	HT	WT	DOB	AVG	vLH	vRH	G	AB	R	H	2B	3B	HR	RBI	BB	HBP	SH	SF	SO	SB	CS	SLG	OBP
Abreu, Abner	R-R	6-3	187	10-24-89	.207	.429	.176	19	58	2	12	3	0	0	3	1	0	0	0	15	3	0	.259	.220
Anselment, Chase	L-R	6-1	208	10-15-90	.218	.231	.214	49	165	25	36	5	1	7	20	17	1	0	2	40	3	1	.388	.292
Beckwith, William	R-L	6-2	220	8-19-90	.291	.283	.294	106	381	52	111	26	0	15	78	33	9	0	2	92	17	9	.478	.360
Brownsten, Cory	R-R	6-0	210	6-3-88	.206	.225	.198	77	238	27	49	10	1	1	16	23	3	5	1	45	4	0	.269	.283
Clabough, K.C.	R-R	5-11	180	10-24-88	.083	.000	.100	9	24	1	2	0	0	0	1	2	1	0	0	4	0	0	.083	.185
Dalfonso, Jakob	L-R	6-3	200	1-25-90	.200	.259	.172	25	85	6	17	4	1	0	9	6	2	0	0	19	1	0	.271	.269
De Los Santos, Fernando	R-R	6-1	180	1-18-90	.242	.246	.241	74	231	27	56	11	0	7	23	12	2	6	1	61	2	1	.381	.285
DeSantiago, Nick	L-R	5-11	215	4-17-91	.173	.063	.200	24	81	9	14	3	0	0	11	0	2	0	23	1	0	.210	.272	
Drury, Brandon	R-R	6-2	190	8-21-92	.229	.187	.243	123	445	47	102	22	3	6	51	20	7	3	5	73	3	4	.333	.270
Fleming, Kurt	B-R	6-1	185	8-30-91	.139	.400	.097	12	36	1	5	1	1	0	6	4	2	0	0	7	0	1	.222	.262
Heffley, Ross	R-R	5-7	180	1-21-90	.296	.266	.312	62	233	42	69	13	1	4	24	18	0	7	1	36	10	3	.412	.345
Hefflinger, Robby	R-R	6-4	220	1-3-90	.284	.353	.256	84	296	44	84	21	1	12	58	38	1	0	5	81	7	1	.483	.362
Jones, Chipper	B-R	6-4	210	4-24-72	.250	.000	1.000	2	4	0	1	0	0	0	1	2	0	0	0	1	0	0	.250	.500
Kubitza, Kyle	L-R	6-3	190	7-15-90	.239	.302	.217	128	448	68	107	24	9	9	59	73	5	1	4	127	18	11	.393	.349
Larsson, Chase	L-L	6-2	230	11-10-88	.303	.400	.286	12	33	3	10	4	1	0	3	8	0	1	1	8	1	1	.485	.429
Marte, Felix	R-R	6-1	180	11-14-90	.231	.231	.232	36	121	6	28	7	0	0	12	4	2	0	2	50	0	1	.289	.264
Miranda, Sergio	B-R	5-9	193	3-5-87	.241	.250	.239	25	83	8	20	3	1	0	6	10	1	5	1	16	1	0	.301	.326
Mueller, Tony	R-R	6-0	190	2-22-90	.266	.302	.251	115	421	69	112	8	0	0	31	42	2	17	1	71	29	11	.285	.335
Query, Ryan	R-R	5-11	190	8-24-87	.210	.158	.227	46	157	16	33	5	0	2	14	7	2	2	1	36	0	1	.280	.251
Reyes, Elmer	R-R	5-11	150	11-26-90	.251	.255	.249	112	379	49	95	26	6	5	36	15	10	10	2	64	5	5	.391	.296
Reyes, Gerardo	R-R	5-10	170	2-7-91	.077	.000	.095	8	26	1	2	0	0	0	2	0	0	0	5	0	0	.077	.143	
Robbins, Logan	R-R	6-0	190	8-4-89	.167	.111	.182	13	42	6	7	4	0	0	1	8	2	0	0	13	5	1	.262	.327
Sanchez, Edison	R-R	6-4	195	11-1-90	.180	.200	.213	31	100	8	18	5	1	0	7	17	2	0	1	42	1	0	.250	.308
Skinner, Will	R-R	6-0	210	6-9-89	.246	.265	.238	105	354	44	87	25	2	9	49	36	5	1	1	107	14	3	.404	.323
Walker, Kirk	R-R	6-1	170	12-23-88	.273	.500	.222	4	11	1	3	0	0	0	1	1	0	0	0	4	0	0	.273	.333

Pitching	B-T	HT	WT	DOB	W	L	ERA	G	GS	CG	SV	IP	H	R	ER	HR	BB	SO	AVG	vLH	vRH	K/9	BB/9
Briceno, Rafael	R-R	6-2	175	10-29-90	3	6	6.55	14	13	0	0	67	95	57	49	7	19	40	.332	.347	.321	5.35	2.54
Cornely, John	R-R	6-1	195	5-17-89	1	3	3.51	39	0	0	7	51	46	20	20	5	36	81	.230	.250	.216	14.20	6.31
Filak, Dave	R-R	6-4	220	11-24-89	5	9	5.67	26	18	1	1	102	110	77	64	6	51	102	.275	.301	.256	9.03	4.51
Garcia, Bryam	R-R	5-10	190	11-16-88	0	1	3.38	15	0	0	0	29	27	14	11	2	22	23	.239	.395	.160	7.06	6.75
Gil, Yean Carlos	R-R	6-2	160	10-12-90	0	2	5.79	5	0	0	2	14	12	9	9	1	8	11	.222	.190	.247	7.07	5.14
Harper, Ryne	R-R	6-2	215	3-27-89	0	2	4.32	15	0	0	5	25	30	12	12	5	7	41	.294	.298	.291	14.76	2.52
Holland, Adam	R-R	6-5	225	12-15-89	5	9	4.04	17	15	1	0	85	82	42	38	5	37	46	.255	.286	.233	4.89	3.93
Hudson, Tim	R-R	6-1	175	7-14-75	0	2	7.71	2	2	0	0	7	13	7	6	0	1	1	.419	.294	.571	1.29	1.29
Hyatt, Nathan	R-R	6-0	185	9-26-90	0	1	1.23	11	0	0	3	15	10	3	2	0	5	23	.196	.235	.176	14.11	3.07
Lucas, Joe	R-R	6-5	190	4-23-89	0	1	9.75	7	0	0	0	12	23	18	13	1	6	7	.371	.346	.389	5.25	4.50
Marshall, Ian	R-R	6-3	215	3-3-87	1	1	3.86	11	0	0	1	16	19	9	7	2	6	18	.297	.310	.286	9.92	3.31
Miller, Jarrett	R-R	6-1	195	9-28-89	5	3	4.11	16	7	0	0	50	49	24	23	1	30	54	.257	.264	.250	9.66	5.36
Moore, Navery	R-R	6-2	212	8-10-90	8	3	3.86	26	13	0	0	103	83	46	44	3	45	84	.221	.257	.200	7.36	3.94
Moylan, Peter	R-R	6-2	225	12-2-78	0	1	9.00	4	0	0	0	4	5	4	4	0	2	3	.313	.750	.167	6.75	4.50
Pacheco, Ronan	L-L	6-6	170	7-29-88	3	0	2.65	18	0	0	1	34	31	13	10	0	14	32	.242	.250	.240	8.47	3.71
Perez, Carlos	L-L	6-2	195	11-20-91	0	3	12.79	7	4	0	0	19	33	28	27	3	19	12	.379	.556	.333	5.68	9.00
Peterson, Dave	R-R	6-5	205	1-4-90	4	1	1.93	20	0	0	8	28	21	10	6	0	11	33	.198	.244	.164	7.39	3.54
Rivera, Wilson	R-R	6-1	195	10-30-89	2	0	2.88	36	0	0	0	56	45	21	18	2	37	70	.218	.173	.244	11.18	5.91
Rohrbough, Cole	L-L	6-3	205	5-23-87	1	0	5.23	10	0	0	0	10	9	6	6	1	6	12	.225	.182	.241	10.45	5.23
Ross, Greg	R-R	6-3	200	9-6-89	7	9	4.60	25	21	1	0	131	146	78	67	10	40	106	.280	.277	.282	7.28	2.75
Scoggin, Patrick	R-R	6-4	230	2-21-91	0	0	0.00	1	0	0	0	1	2	0	0	1	0	0	.400	.333	.500	0.00	9.00
Silva, Ernesto	R-R	6-4	180	2-5-92	0	6	6.53	13	5	0	0	51	65	47	37	3	25	29	.317	.281	.333	5.12	4.41
Starn, David	L-L	6-0	190	5-19-90	1	2	5.50	10	8	0	0	34	37	24	21	2	20	28	.280	.276	.282	7.34	5.24
Talley, Matt	L-L	6-6	225	8-8-89	0	0	3.24	4	0	0	0	8	14	8	3	1	6	6	.368	.000	.438	6.48	6.48

	B-T	HT	WT	DOB	W	L	ERA	G	GS CG SV	IP	H	R	ER HR	BB	SO	AVG	vLH vRH	K/9	BB/9
2-team total (7 Kannapolis)					1	0	2.29	11	0 0 0	20	23	10	5 2	11	10	—	— —	4.58	5.03
Thomas, Ian	L-L	6-4	210	4-20-87	5	0	3.15	26	0 0 6	46	45	19	16 4	15	58	.254	.255 .254	11.43	2.96
Weber, Ryan	R-R	6-0	170	8-12-90	5	5	5.88	16	11 0 0	72	86	52	47 4	16	54	.294	.281 .303	6.75	2.00
Williamson, Fabian	R-L	6-2	175	10-20-88	2	4	4.29	14	8 0 0	50	51	31	24 5	31	36	.260	.196 .280	6.44	5.54
Wood, Alex	L-L	6-4	215	1-12-91	4	3	2.22	13	13 0 0	53	39	18	13 1	14	52	.206	.250 .188	8.89	2.39
Wright, Clint	R-R	6-6	239	4-29-90	0	0	8.22	4	0 0 0	8	6	7	7 1	2	6	.222	.273 .188	7.04	2.35

Fielding

Catcher	PCT	G	PO	A	E	DP	PB
Brownsten	.981	76	547	83	12	5	3
DeSantiago	.989	22	176	10	2	3	2
Query	.983	46	316	33	6	2	4

First Base	PCT	G	PO	A	E	DP
Beckwith	.987	75	640	32	9	60
Dalfonso	.954	7	60	2	3	5
Drury	.998	55	468	28	1	43
Hefflinger	.857	1	5	1	1	0
Sanchez	1.000	2	15	1	0	1

Second Base	PCT	G	PO	A	E	DP
Clabough	1.000	5	8	10	0	1
De Los Santos	.960	34	58	87	6	26
Drury	1.000	2	4	3	0	1
Heffley	.981	59	106	201	6	40

Third Base	PCT	G	PO	A	E	DP
Beckwith	1.000	1	0	1	0	0
De Los Santos	.900	7	3	6	1	1
Drury	.925	44	18	80	8	11
Jones	.500	2	0	1	1	0
Kubitza	.915	90	55	161	20	15

Shortstop	PCT	G	PO	A	E	DP
Clabough	.929	4	9	4	1	2
De Los Santos	.915	30	37	71	10	8
Drury	1.000	1	1	0	0	0
Miranda	1.000	1	1	1	0	0

Miranda	.929	24	34	58	7	14	
Reyes	1.000	8	17	17	0	1	
Robbins	.945	12	24	45	4	12	
Walker	1.000	3	3	11	0	2	

Reyes	.947	111	153	334	27	66	

Outfield	PCT	G	PO	A	E	DP
Abreu	1.000	18	31	0	0	0
Anselment	.987	42	74	3	1	0
Dalfonso	.923	13	23	1	2	0
De Los Santos	—	2	0	0	0	0
Fleming	1.000	11	22	0	0	0
Hefflinger	.947	70	84	5	5	0
Larsson	1.000	11	22	3	0	1
Marte	.962	35	74	1	3	0
Mueller	.977	112	209	7	5	1
Sanchez	1.000	22	29	0	0	0
Skinner	.963	93	173	10	7	1
Walker	—	1	0	0	0	0

DANVILLE BRAVES   ROOKIE

APPALACHIAN LEAGUE

Batting	B-T	HT	WT	DOB	AVG	vLH	vRH	G	AB	R	H	2B	3B	HR	RBI	BB	HBP	SH	SF	SO	SB	CS	SLG	OBP
Alcantara, Aris	R-R	6-2	170	5-5-90	.276	.415	.236	47	185	24	51	14	1	5	41	9	4	1	3	32	7	2	.443	.318
Brown, Blake	R-R	6-0	185	6-30-91	.201	.163	.213	53	179	27	36	6	1	4	20	25	4	2	0	72	10	4	.313	.313
DeSantiago, Nick	L-R	5-11	215	4-17-91	.263	.100	.288	24	76	15	20	0	0	0	14	15	2	0	0	20	0	0	.395	.398
Elander, Josh	R-R	6-1	215	3-19-91	.260	.243	.267	36	123	19	32	6	2	4	19	16	5	0	1	19	3	1	.439	.366
Fleming, Kurt	B-R	6-1	185	8-30-91	.247	.333	.211	26	81	13	20	6	0	0	9	6	1	0	2	23	0	3	.321	.300
Franco, Carlos	R-R	6-2	170	12-20-91	.271	.194	.292	50	166	35	45	6	3	2	20	37	2	0	1	36	6	5	.380	.408
Garcia, Eric	L-R	5-11	175	2-18-91	.194	.286	.167	17	62	10	12	2	1	0	6	11	1	0	1	13	3	1	.258	.320
Hyams, Levi	L-R	6-2	205	10-6-89	.254	.194	.270	45	177	33	45	10	0	5	28	20	0	2	3	38	7	3	.395	.369
Kalenkosky, Casey	R-R	6-0	204	10-28-89	.241	.182	.267	34	108	17	26	10	0	2	14	18	4	0	0	30	1	0	.389	.369
Luna, Ronald	R-R	6-0	145	8-18-92	.292	.327	.277	43	161	24	47	6	0	1	18	5	2	3	1	25	6	0	.348	.320
Marte, Felix	R-R	6-1	180	11-14-90	.262	.302	.250	50	187	30	49	5	2	8	27	20	2	0	1	64	3	2	.439	.338
Moranda, Seth	R-R	6-2	180	9-26-92	.250	.250	.250	5	16	1	4	0	0	0	2	0	0	1	0	5	0	0	.250	.250
Moses, Trenton	R-R	6-3	230	2-9-89	.298	.400	.274	38	131	19	39	10	0	3	18	8	4	0	2	28	0	0	.443	.352
Peraza, Jose	R-R	5-11	167	4-30-94	.281	.125	.305	32	121	21	34	4	0	1	18	9	4	2	0	18	15	2	.339	.351
Reyes, Gerardo	R-R	5-10	170	2-7-91	.214	.385	.138	11	42	3	9	1	0	0	4	2	0	2	1	6	2	0	.238	.244
Robbins, Logan	R-R	6-0	190	8-4-89	.207	.111	.232	33	87	12	18	3	0	1	11	13	2	2	2	26	7	3	.276	.317
Sanchez, Edison	R-R	6-4	195	11-1-90	.256	.361	.229	47	176	27	45	12	4	5	23	12	4	0	2	43	0	2	.455	.314
Snitker, Troy	R-R	6-2	210	12-5-88	.274	.222	.291	25	73	15	20	7	0	1	7	10	1	2	0	24	0	0	.411	.369
Tewell, Tyler	L-R	5-11	185	7-17-91	.286	.000	.308	4	14	1	4	3	0	0	3	0	0	0	0	3	0	0	.500	.286

Pitching	B-T	HT	WT	DOB	W	L	ERA	G	GS CG SV	IP	H	R	ER HR	BB	SO	AVG	vLH vRH	K/9	BB/9
Briceno, Rafael	R-R	6-2	175	10-29-90	3	3	6.45	13	5 0 0	38	48	34	27 3	13	39	.304	.268 .324	9.32	3.11
Cabrera, Mauricio	R-R	6-2	180	9-22-93	2	2	2.97	12	12 0 0	58	45	23	19 3	23	48	.213	.233 .203	7.49	3.59
Castillo, Eduardo	R-R	6-2	170	7-27-90	3	3	6.86	13	7 0 0	41	49	32	31 3	10	26	.295	.250 .318	5.75	2.21
Fitzgerald, Jeremy	R-R	6-0	175	2-4-91	1	0	2.45	16	0 0 2	22	16	7	6 2	11	21	.203	.200 .204	8.59	4.50
Garcia, Bryam	R-R	5-10	190	11-16-88	0	1	2.16	12	0 0 6	17	14	4	4 0	9	24	.226	.389 .159	12.96	4.86
Geronimo, Ignacio	R-R	6-1	170	6-1-91	0	0	4.91	6	0 0 0	7	11	7	4 1	3	8	.324	.211 .467	9.82	3.68
Hashem, Mike	L-L	6-1	220	10-13-88	3	1	6.75	16	0 0 0	20	20	18	15 2	12	10	.253	.077 .288	4.50	5.40
Hyatt, Nathan	R-R	6-0	185	9-26-90	2	0	1.80	7	0 0 3	10	3	2	2 0	3	14	.100	.083 .111	12.60	2.70
Jadofsky, Zach	R-R	6-3	210	6-17-90	0	1	1.95	15	0 0 1	28	23	6	6 1	4	18	.237	.364 .200	5.86	1.30
LaFreniere, Frank	R-R	6-5	185	6-2-90	5	2	4.02	12	12 0 0	65	79	34	29 5	17	39	.302	.281 .312	5.40	2.35
Perez, Carlos	L-L	6-2	195	11-20-91	3	2	2.05	16	0 0 0	31	20	9	7 0	15	50	.182	.250 .167	14.67	4.40
Perez, Williams	R-R	6-0	185	5-21-91	4	3	4.15	13	9 0 1	56	54	31	26 5	9	54	.245	.351 .192	8.63	1.44
Robertson, Charlie	L-R	6-5	190	4-30-90	0	1	4.66	7	0 0 0	10	14	10	5 0	3	5	.333	.421 .261	4.66	2.79
Rohde, Brandon	L-L	6-3	215	9-14-89	0	1	13.50	3	0 0 0	3	4	5	5 1	2	6	.286	.000 .400	16.20	5.40
Scoggin, Patrick	R-R	6-4	230	2-21-91	0	0	0.00	3	0 0 1	6	2	0	0 0	7	10	.143	.077	11.12	0.00
Silva, Ernesto	R-R	6-4	180	2-5-92	5	1	3.80	11	11 0 0	64	64	32	27 7	9	23	.267	.295 .257	3.23	1.27
Simmons, Shae	R-R	5-9	180	9-3-90	0	2	3.48	9	0 0 2	10	11	7	4 0	8	21	.256	.200 .273	18.29	6.97
Sims, Luke	R-R	6-2	195	5-10-94	2	4	4.33	8	8 0 0	27	26	14	13 2	12	29	.243	.222 .250	9.67	4.00
Talley, Matt	L-L	6-6	225	8-8-89	1	0	12.00	5	0 0 0	6	9	8	8 1	7	2	.360	.286 .389	10.50	10.50
2-team total (2 Bristol)					1	0	6.55	7	0 0 0	11	14	8	8 1	12	9	—	— —	7.36	9.82
Wilson, Alex	R-R	6-5	200	4-3-91	1	1	2.73	15	0 0 2	26	29	10	8 1	5	28	.269	.235 .284	9.57	1.71
Wright, Clint	R-R	6-6	239	4-29-90	1	0	1.74	12	0 0 0	21	17	8	4 0	7	20	.218	.250 .210	8.71	3.05

Fielding

Catcher	PCT	G	PO	A	E	DP	PB
DeSantiago	.978	24	172	10	4	1	7

Elander	.978	22	160	17	4	1	4
Snitker	.979	23	174	12	4	2	3

Tewell	1.000	1	7	0	0	0

ATLANTA BRAVES

First Base	PCT	G	PO	A	E	DP
Alcantara	.992	41	358	23	3	30
Kalenkosky	1.000	26	223	11	0	28

Second Base	PCT	G	PO	A	E	DP
Hyams	.975	45	70	123	5	31
Luna	.891	12	17	24	5	3
Reyes	.985	10	29	38	1	8

Third Base	PCT	G	PO	A	E	DP
Franco	.911	42	30	93	12	15
Moranda	.571	2	1	3	3	1
Moses	.881	26	12	47	8	3

Shortstop	PCT	G	PO	A	E	DP
Garcia	.932	16	28	54	6	10
Luna	.926	30	34	92	10	17
Moranda	1.000	3	3	1	0	1

	PCT	G	PO	A	E	DP
Peraza	.914	17	22	63	8	13

Outfield	PCT	G	PO	A	E	DP
Brown	.979	50	95	0	2	1
Fleming	.949	25	34	3	2	0
Marte	.962	50	71	4	3	1
Robbins	.932	27	52	3	4	0
Sanchez	.973	46	69	4	2	2

GCL BRAVES   ROOKIE

GULF COAST LEAGUE

Batting	B-T	HT	WT	DOB	AVG	vLH	vRH	G	AB	R	H	2B	3B	HR	RBI	BB	HBP	SH	SF	SO	SB	CS	SLG	OBP
Arno, Robinson	R-R	6-4	216	3-13-93	.240	.185	.261	31	96	7	23	7	0	4	15	10	2	0	1	34	1	0	.438	.321
Black, Justin	R-R	6-0	195	5-20-93	.182	.235	.163	41	132	15	24	2	1	2	7	19	2	3	1	54	3	4	.258	.292
Clabough, K.C.	R-R	5-11	180	10-24-88	.246	.316	.217	28	65	13	16	4	0	0	4	6	9	0	1	11	7	1	.308	.383
Daniel, Emmanuel	R-R	6-1	165	12-25-91	.192	.105	.222	29	73	4	14	1	0	1	5	1	1	1	0	16	2	3	.247	.213
de la Rosa, Bryan	R-R	5-8	193	3-26-94	.162	.214	.148	29	68	5	11	1	0	1	3	2	1	1	1	30	0	1	.221	.194
Dodig, Mike	L-R	6-4	210	7-8-93	.174	.081	.211	37	132	10	23	5	1	2	11	8	1	0	2	37	2	0	.273	.224
Garcia, Eric	L-R	5-11	175	2-18-91	.253	.240	.258	24	87	14	22	5	0	3	13	15	2	0	0	22	2	3	.414	.375
Garcia, Hector	B-R	6-2	170	6-9-92	.288	.231	.302	21	66	5	19	3	0	0	7	7	1	0	0	16	2	1	.333	.365
Gattis, Evan	R-R	6-4	230	8-18-86	.500	1.000	.455	4	12	2	6	0	0	0	1	1	0	0	0	2	0	0	.500	.538
Gomez, Victor	R-R	6-1	215	1-10-89	.000	.000	—	1	1	0	0	0	0	0	0	0	0	0	0	0	0	0	.000	.000
La Stella, Tommy	L-R	5-11	185	1-31-89	.231	.200	.250	5	13	4	3	0	1	1	3	4	1	0	0	1	0	0	.615	.444
Larsson, Chase	L-L	6-2	230	11-10-88	.333	.250	.375	5	12	1	4	0	0	0	1	5	0	0	0	2	2	0	.333	.529
Laumann, Jackson	R-R	6-3	220	9-21-93	.252	.333	.232	34	119	9	30	5	0	1	10	7	1	0	0	27	0	1	.319	.299
Lien, Connor	R-R	6-3	205	3-15-94	.228	.250	.221	48	149	30	34	4	2	0	11	19	10	1	1	49	15	3	.282	.352
Livesay, Cody	L-L	6-0	160	7-6-93	.228	.050	.288	27	79	14	18	1	0	0	5	13	0	1	1	24	5	2	.241	.333
Madrid, Luis	R-R	6-0	165	3-11-93	.216	.273	.192	39	111	12	24	4	0	0	8	6	6	1	0	12	0	0	.252	.293
Meneses, Joey	R-R	6-0	190	5-6-92	.303	.391	.263	41	145	13	44	5	5	0	14	9	3	0	2	29	2	4	.407	.352
Moranda, Seth	R-R	6-2	180	9-26-92	.244	.438	.200	27	86	11	21	1	0	0	5	12	6	0	0	22	2	1	.256	.375
Nunez, Anthony	R-R	6-3	205	2-2-90	.275	.167	.321	23	40	5	11	3	0	0	4	4	0	0	1	12	2	0	.350	.341
Parraz, Jordan	R-R	6-3	215	10-8-84	.250	.333	.222	3	12	1	3	0	0	0	2	0	0	0	0	1	1	0	.250	.250
Peraza, Jose	R-R	5-11	165	4-30-94	.318	.336	.318	21	85	17	27	3	3	0	10	4	0	3	0	6	10	3	.424	.348
Sanchez, Carlos	R-R	6-0	178	11-5-93	.244	.250	.240	28	78	7	19	5	0	0	6	7	1	0	1	14	2	2	.308	.310
Sanchez, Fernelys	B-R	6-3	210	3-1-94	.155	.333	.093	17	58	6	9	1	0	1	5	9	0	0	0	32	3	1	.224	.269
Tewell, Tyler	L-R	5-11	185	7-17-91	.312	.370	.288	35	93	12	29	6	1	3	24	3	0	1	1	13	1	1	.495	.323
Vargas, Angel	R-R	6-0	205	2-16-88	.140	.000	.182	17	43	4	6	1	0	0	2	7	2	1	1	24	3	0	.163	.283

Pitching	B-T	HT	WT	DOB	W	L	ERA	G	GS	CG	SV	IP	H	R	ER	HR	BB	SO	AVG	vLH	vRH	K/9	BB/9
Avendano, Magdiel	R-R	6-1	155	9-11-93	1	1	4.86	15	0	0	3	17	17	11	9	1	3	14	.236	.222	.241	7.56	1.62
Barczycowski, Chris	R-R	6-8	250	2-11-92	0	0	9.53	11	0	0	0	11	26	14	12	1	6	10	.456	.400	.486	7.94	4.76
Cordier, Erik	R-R	6-4	230	2-25-86	0	0	0.00	4	1	0	0	4	0	0	0	0	0	0	.000	.000	.000	14.73	14.73
Dillon, Jaden	R-R	5-11	180	1-9-90	0	2	3.19	12	8	0	0	42	50	22	15	3	10	37	.292	.327	.276	7.87	2.13
Drake, Donovan	R-R	6-0	200	9-29-88	2	3	1.42	11	0	0	1	25	27	13	4	2	8	24	.273	.292	.267	8.53	2.84
Espinosa, Abraham	R-R	6-1	175	6-3-93	3	6	3.80	11	8	0	0	47	45	26	20	4	15	37	.250	.226	.263	7.04	2.85
Estrella, Roberto	R-R	6-2	175	8-14-92	2	5	6.23	11	8	0	0	43	56	36	30	3	15	30	.311	.333	.299	6.23	3.12
Flores, Mike	R-R	6-9	235	8-28-93	1	0	4.41	11	0	0	0	16	13	11	8	0	15	13	.200	.217	.190	7.16	8.27
Garcia, Elvin	L-L	5-11	175	5-14-90	2	2	4.18	12	0	0	1	28	30	15	13	3	2	25	.261	.222	.278	8.04	0.64
Holland, Adam	R-R	6-5	225	12-15-89	1	1	6.35	4	2	0	0	6	5	4	4	0	4	2	.250	.250	.250	6.35	6.35
Kimbrel, Matt	R-R	6-0	190	3-13-90	1	1	4.61	8	0	0	0	14	16	7	7	0	2	9	.281	.167	.333	5.93	1.32
McKague, Kevin	R-R	6-5	240	12-24-88	0	0	15.19	5	0	0	0	5	7	12	9	1	4	5	.318	.182	.455	8.44	6.75
Merejo, Luis	L-L	6-0	175	10-8-94	0	5	4.61	10	8	0	0	41	38	25	21	1	9	53	.245	.265	.236	11.63	1.98
Montenegro, Jorge	R-R	6-0	170	1-24-91	2	2	4.89	15	4	0	0	35	38	27	19	0	20	39	.268	.314	.242	10.03	5.14
Moylan, Peter	R-R	6-2	225	12-2-78	0	0	7.71	4	3	0	0	5	4	4	4	1	1	4	.250	.286	.222	7.71	1.93
Otero, Andy	L-L	5-9	160	6-3-92	0	0	0.00	2	0	0	0	3	2	0	0	0	0	3	.182	.000	.250	9.00	0.00
Rodgers, Chad	L-L	6-3	185	11-23-87	0	2	5.14	7	3	0	0	7	9	10	4	0	4	10	.290	.333	.263	12.86	5.14
Rohde, Brandon	L-L	6-3	215	9-14-89	0	0	1.31	15	0	0	3	21	13	4	3	1	3	23	.171	.269	.120	10.02	1.31
Ruiz, Reymi	R-R	6-0	175	1-27-91	0	2	29.25	4	0	0	0	4	15	16	13	2	3	3	.536	.571	.524	6.75	6.75
Schils, Steven	R-R	6-2	220	8-14-90	0	1	63.00	3	0	0	0	1	1	8	7	0	9	1	.200	.000	.250	9.00	81.00
Scoggin, Patrick	R-R	6-4	230	2-21-91	0	0	0.00	6	0	0	2	8	3	0	0	0	1	9	.120	.250	.000	10.57	1.17
Simmons, Shae	R-R	5-9	180	9-3-90	2	0	0.00	7	1	0	0	14	5	1	0	0	8	15	.109	.059	.138	9.42	5.02
Sims, Luke	R-R	6-2	195	5-10-94	0	0	1.29	3	3	0	0	7	2	2	1	1	1	10	.091	.125	.071	12.86	1.29
Tate, Richie	R-R	6-6	225	4-11-92	1	2	2.62	16	0	0	3	34	19	15	10	3	16	20	.165	.146	.176	5.24	4.19
Ubiera, Andry	R-R	6-0	170	5-22-93	2	2	4.04	12	9	0	0	49	54	24	22	2	17	48	.276	.269	.279	8.82	3.12
Wright, Clint	R-R	6-6	239	4-29-90	1	0	0.00	2	0	0	0	2	0	0	0	0	0	2	.000	.000	.000	9.00	0.00

Fielding

Catcher	PCT	G	PO	A	E	DP	PB
de la Rosa	.947	28	139	22	9	3	13
Gomez	1.000	1	1	0	0	0	0
Nunez	1.000	18	57	10	0	2	1
Sanchez	.967	27	156	20	6	2	5
Tewell	.980	21	85	13	2	1	4

First Base	PCT	G	PO	A	E	DP
Arno	.964	30	198	16	8	10

	.983	31	221	15	4	15
Laumann	.983	31	221	15	4	15
Nunez	.962	4	23	2	1	1

Second Base	PCT	G	PO	A	E	DP
Clabough	.985	18	24	41	1	5
Garcia	1.000	1	1	2	0	1
La Stella	1.000	4	9	8	0	0
Madrid	.977	38	50	76	3	13
Vargas	.870	7	8	12	3	0

Third Base	PCT	G	PO	A	E	DP
Clabough	1.000	3	2	0	0	0
Dodig	.837	33	26	46	14	3
Moranda	.929	12	10	29	3	4
Vargas	.680	10	7	10	8	0

Shortstop	PCT	G	PO	A	E	DP
Clabough	1.000	3	4	11	0	0
Garcia	.949	23	44	67	6	12

Moranda	.870	15	18	29	7	8
Peraza	.916	17	38	38	7	7

Outfield	PCT	G	PO	A	E	DP
Black	.939	35	61	1	4	1
Daniel	.938	25	27	3	2	1

Garcia	.971	17	33	1	1	1
Gattis	1.000	4	5	0	0	0
Larsson	1.000	5	8	0	0	0
Lien	.977	44	82	4	2	2
Livesay	1.000	23	43	1	0	0

Meneses	.977	27	41	1	1	0
Parraz	.875	3	7	0	1	0
Sanchez	1.000	1	1	0	0	0
Sanchez	.933	9	14	0	1	0

DSL BRAVES   ROOKIE

DOMINICAN SUMMER LEAGUE

Batting	B-T	HT	WT	DOB	AVG	vLH	vRH	G	AB	R	H	2B	3B	HR	RBI	BB	HBP	SH	SF	SO	SB	CS	SLG	OBP
Aybar, Yunior	R-R	5-11	173	9-20-91	.200	.500	.154	10	15	4	3	0	0	0	0	4	0	0	0	3	0	0	.200	.368
Bernal, Iosif	R-R	6-3	200	10-22-94	.259	.267	.257	48	139	20	36	11	0	1	26	21	8	0	2	48	6	0	.360	.382
Camargo, Johan	R-R	6-0	160	12-13-93	.343	.235	.366	59	198	38	68	14	1	2	26	25	7	10	1	27	6	3	.455	.433
Castro, Carlos	R-R	6-1	195	5-24-94	.254	.375	.235	22	59	7	15	6	0	0	8	1	2	0	3	10	1	0	.356	.277
Chin, Gerald	L-R	5-10	160	5-29-93	.291	.385	.273	21	79	14	23	1	4	0	3	7	0	0	1	14	2	2	.405	.345
Cleofa, Nisandro	R-R	5-11	180	10-25-93	.171	.333	.148	40	70	12	12	0	1	0	5	6	2	1	0	20	3	1	.200	.256
De La Cruz, Alexander	R-R	6-1	185	8-22-91	.198	.156	.208	54	162	17	32	4	1	0	15	7	6	5	0	32	0	0	.235	.257
Diaz, Eugenio	R-R	6-2	200	11-7-94	.318	.389	.300	32	88	5	28	3	0	0	10	7	1	0	0	28	0	0	.352	.375
Gomez, Gustavo	R-R	6-1	170	7-19-91	.226	.000	.250	18	31	1	7	0	0	0	1	3	0	0	0	9	0	0	.226	.294
Henriquez, Isael	R-R	6-0	180	12-15-93	.306	.333	.296	11	36	9	11	0	1	0	7	5	2	0	1	15	2	1	.361	.409
Heredia, Jesus	R-R	6-2	175	1-21-95	.036	.000	.048	32	28	3	1	0	0	0	2	0	0	1	11	2	1	.036	.100
McKenzie, Ibrahim	R-R	6-2	185	2-8-94	.257	.235	.262	61	206	22	53	8	2	6	26	16	12	1	0	50	2	4	.403	.346
Monasterio, Luis	R-R	6-0	170	11-11-94	.250	.241	.252	47	136	21	34	3	1	0	19	19	3	6	0	41	4	4	.287	.354
Morel, Jose	R-R	6-1	170	8-2-93	.198	.205	.196	63	197	23	39	5	2	3	28	32	1	3	1	54	3	4	.289	.312
Obregon, Omar	B-R	5-10	150	4-18-94	.269	.000	.325	48	93	21	25	2	0	0	5	21	3	6	0	19	7	6	.290	.419
Palacios, Cristian	B-R	6-0	155	1-25-94	.163	.200	.152	29	43	10	7	1	0	0	8	2	5	1	0	17	2	2	.186	.280
Piloto, Alejandro	R-R	6-0	185	4-8-92	.333	.500	.286	11	36	4	12	1	0	0	4	2	1	0	0	8	7	3	.361	.385
Reyes, Victor	L-R	6-3	170	10-5-94	.296	.360	.285	52	162	40	48	3	0	0	33	31	5	1	3	39	12	6	.315	.418
Rivero, Miguel	B-R	6-1	175	6-14-94	.292	.321	.284	42	137	24	40	4	3	0	19	14	4	0	3	30	3	2	.365	.367
Tielman, Juruengelo	R-R	6-1	210	5-11-93	.238	.094	.289	40	122	13	29	8	0	0	10	11	1	0	0	33	2	1	.303	.305
Zuniga, Fernan	R-R	5-11	170	3-9-95	.267	.000	.308	14	15	4	4	0	0	0	2	2	1	0	0	7	0	0	.267	.389

Pitching	B-T	HT	WT	DOB	W	L	ERA	G	GS	CG	SV	IP	H	R	ER	HR	BB	SO	AVG	vLH	vRH	K/9	BB/9
Caballero, Ahmed	R-R	6-2	145	8-25-94	0	1	7.41	16	0	0	0	17	21	18	14	0	22	7	.313	.294	.320	3.71	11.65
Cabrera, Ray	R-R	6-0	170	10-18-94	2	0	5.02	9	0	0	1	14	11	9	8	1	9	14	.212	.353	.143	8.79	5.65
Concepcion, Miguel	L-L	5-11	165	9-29-94	0	0	3.38	4	0	0	0	3	2	1	0	2	2	.231	.000	.300	6.75	6.75
Constanzo, Victor	R-R	6-2	170	12-18-92	0	0	17.36	5	1	0	0	5	12	11	9	0	11	2	.462	.375	.500	3.86	21.21
Cordero, Daniel	R-R	6-0	180	6-7-93	0	1	4.15	4	4	0	0	17	19	9	8	1	2	19	.275	.421	.220	9.87	1.04
Flores, Michael	L-L	6-0	180	8-8-92	5	3	1.71	14	14	0	0	63	49	22	12	0	23	67	.217	.220	.216	9.57	3.29
Gonzalez, Francisco	R-R	6-0	170	9-21-94	1	4	4.91	12	9	0	0	48	49	33	26	2	29	32	.269	.308	.254	6.04	5.48
Jones, Jesus	R-R	6-2	165	5-31-95	1	3	5.68	17	2	0	0	38	39	26	24	5	28	20	.283	.319	.264	4.74	6.63
Leiva, Darrel	R-R	6-1	185	7-31-94	3	1	5.63	10	0	0	1	16	21	11	10	2	6	9	.318	.286	.327	5.06	3.38
Leon, Nelson	L-L	6-0	175	6-29-95	1	3	4.29	10	8	0	0	36	31	19	17	1	15	35	.238	.375	.219	8.83	3.79
Liranzo, Jesus	R-R	6-2	175	3-7-95	0	0	9.00	1	0	0	0	1	1	1	1	0	2	2	.250	.000	.333	18.00	18.00
Matos, David	L-L	6-3	185	5-9-94	0	0	81.00	2	0	0	0	0	1	5	3	0	4	1	.500	.000	.500	27.00	108.00
Medina, Cesar	R-R	6-3	180	6-16-94	0	0	3.38	6	0	0	0	8	7	3	3	0	6	2	.226	.250	.211	2.25	6.75
Medina, Enrique	L-L	5-11	180	3-5-92	3	1	2.97	19	1	0	0	36	27	21	12	1	14	21	.203	.333	.186	5.20	3.41
Paulino, Richard	R-R	6-2	175	3-28-95	1	3	8.55	7	6	0	0	20	19	24	19	0	18	16	.279	.261	.289	7.20	8.10
Rivero, Adrian	L-L	6-3	185	5-30-91	0	1	3.58	10	4	0	1	28	22	12	11	0	14	26	.232	.222	.233	8.46	4.55
Rodriguez, Rafael	R-R	6-1	180	9-22-92	0	1	1.48	21	0	0	0	24	18	9	4	1	16	13	.220	.091	.267	4.81	5.92
Rosario, Jose	R-R	6-1	160	2-22-94	6	3	2.25	17	5	0	2	56	46	15	14	1	20	40	.229	.323	.184	6.43	3.21
Saldeno, Jesus	R-R	6-0	170	10-28-92	2	2	4.15	15	6	0	0	35	25	19	16	1	33	27	.225	.297	.189	7.01	8.57
Sauceda, Ramon	R-R	6-1	185	8-19-92	8	1	3.27	17	1	0	1	41	45	17	15	2	9	31	.274	.171	.309	6.75	1.96
Zavala, Jorge	R-R	6-4	200	6-10-94	2	1	3.07	16	3	0	1	41	35	18	14	0	17	38	.233	.209	.253	8.34	3.73

Fielding

Catcher	PCT	G	PO	A	E	DP	PB
Castro	.967	11	66	21	3	0	2
De La Cruz	.977	53	330	44	9	2	8
Diaz	1.000	2	4	4	0	0	1
Zuniga	1.000	13	40	7	0	0	0

4 First Base	PCT	G	PO	A	E	DP
De La Cruz	1.000	1	5	0	0	2
Diaz	.985	12	61	3	1	6
McKenzie	.979	61	434	35	10	45

Second Base	PCT	G	PO	A	E	DP
Aybar	.895	7	9	8	2	2
Chin	.965	21	46	36	3	9

	PCT	G	PO	A	E	DP
Gomez	.875	4	4	3	1	1
Monasterio	.968	45	94	90	6	26
Obregon	1.000	1	1	0	0	0

Third Base	PCT	G	PO	A	E	DP
Camargo	.877	44	37	70	15	10
Gomez	.818	7	3	6	2	0
Tielman	.926	35	26	49	6	8

Shortstop	PCT	G	PO	A	E	DP
Camargo	.943	26	40	60	6	10
Monasterio	—	1	0	0	0	0
Obregon	.939	47	52	87	9	16
Palacios	.820	15	16	25	9	4

Outfield	PCT	G	PO	A	E	DP
Aybar	—	1	0	0	0	0
Bernal	.932	48	81	1	6	0
Cleofa	.973	36	36	0	1	0
Diaz	1.000	4	1	0	0	0
Henriquez	1.000	11	14	1	0	0
Heredia	.850	31	15	2	3	0
Morel	.941	61	133	10	9	4
Palacios	—	4	0	0	0	0
Piloto	1.000	11	18	1	0	1
Rivero	.968	41	55	5	2	2

ATLANTA BRAVES

Baltimore Orioles

SEASON IN A SENTENCE: Who'da thunk it?

HIGH POINT: After the baseball world had waited all season for the Orioles to collapse, they clinched their first playoff berth since 1997 on Sept. 30 after beating the Red Sox 6-3 and then watching the Angels lose later that day. They contended for the American League East title until the last but ultimately fell two games short of the Yankees and won a wild card spot. And then, amazingly, things got better, as Baltimore got a sterling effort from Joe Saunders and the bullpen to end the Rangers' season 5-1 in Arlington, taking the first-ever American League Wild Card Game.

LOW POINT: While the five-game loss to the Yankees in an AL Division Series was a bitter disappointment, it would be hard to call it a low point after all the team achieved. The emotional low may have come when Nick Markakis, who had already recovered from a broken hamate bone early in the season and ignited the lineup from the leadoff spot, broke his thumb early in September. It looked like it might submarine the Orioles' chances, but true to the way the season went, other players stepped up and the team kept chugging along.

NOTABLE ROOKIES: Taiwanese lefthander Wei-Yin Chen was a key acquisition for the rotation, making 32 starts and going 12-11, 4.02, with a win over the Yankees in the Division Series as well. But calling up 20-year-old Manny Machado in August was a transformational move for the team, as he solidified the infield defense at third base and energized the lineup. It looks like he'll be manning the left side of the infield in Baltimore for years.

KEY TRANSACTIONS: Chen and Machado were the marquee moves, but first-year general manager Dan Duquette showed no shyness in shaking up the Orioles' roster, and he made several moves that paid dividends. Most notably the team signed Miguel Gonzalez to a minor league deal in March, and he ended up as one of the team's best starters down the stretch. Other contributors were Ryan Flaherty, acquired in the Rule 5 draft; Jason Hammel, acquired from the Rockies for Jeremy Guthrie before the season; and Nate McLouth, picked up in a minor league deal in June.

DOWN ON THE FARM: The story begins and ends with Dylan Bundy, the game's best pitching prospect. In his professional debut, he went 9-3, 2.08 at three minor league levels before earning a callup in September to fortify Baltimore's bullpen.

OPENING DAY PAYROLL: $81.4 million (19th)

PLAYERS OF THE YEAR

MAJOR LEAGUE	MINOR LEAGUE
Adam Jones	**Dylan Bundy**
of	rhp
.287/.334/.505	(Lo A/Hi A/Double-A)
32 HR, 16 SB	9-3, 2.08
Won 2nd Gold Glove	119 SO/28 BB/104 IP

ORGANIZATION LEADERS

BATTING		*Minimum 250 AB
MAJORS		
* AVG	Adam Jones	.287
* OPS	Adam Jones	.839
HR	Chris Davis	33
RBI	Chris Davis	85
MINORS		
* AVG	Ty Kelly, Norfolk/Frederick/Bowie	.327
* OBP	Ty Kelly, Norfolk/Frederick/Bowie	.425
* SLG	Brandon Waring, Bowie/Norfolk	.504
R	Brandon Waring, Bowie/Norfolk	82
H	Ty Kelly, Norfolk/Frederick/Bowie	154
TB	Ty Kelly, Norfolk/Frederick/Bowie	220
2B	Robbie Widlansky, Bowie	35
3B	Alexander Mercedes, DSL/GCL/Aberdeen	10
HR	Brandon Waring, Bowie/Norfolk	24
RBI	Robbie Widlansky, Bowie	83
BB	Brenden Webb, Delmarva/Frederick	98
SO	Jai Miller, Bowie/Norfolk	159
SB	Glynn Davis, Delmarva/Frederick	37

PITCHING		#Minimum 75 IP
MAJORS		
W	Wei-Yin Chen	12
# ERA	Wei-Yin Chen	4.02
SO	Wei-Yin Chen	154
SV	Jim Johnson	51
MINORS		
W	Zach Clark, Bowie/Norfolk	15
L	Tim Berry, Delmarva/Frederick/Bowie	13
# ERA	Zach Clark, Bowie/Norfolk	2.79
G	David Walters, Norfolk/Frederick	46
GS	Jason Berken, Norfolk	26
	Zach Clark, Bowie/Norfolk	26
SV	Kyler Newby, Norfolk/Bowie	20
IP	Zach Clark, Bowie/Norfolk	167.2
BB	Parker Bridwell, Delmarva	63
	Williams Louico, Delmarva	63
SO	Tyler Wilson, Delmarva/Frederick	143
# AVG	Richard Zagone, Frederick/Bowie/Norfolk	.224

2012 PERFORMANCE

General Manager: Dan Duquette. **Farm Director:** John Stockstill. **Scouting Director:** Gary Rajsich.

Class	Team	League	W	L	PCT	Finish	Manager
Majors	Baltimore Orioles	American	93	69	.574	t-3rd (14)	Buck Showalter
Triple-A	Norfolk Tides	International	74	70	.514	7th (14)	Ron Johnson
Double-A	Bowie Baysox	Eastern	78	64	.549	3rd (12)	Gary Kendall
High A	Frederick Keys	Carolina	62	77	.446	8th (8)	Orlando Gomez
Low A	Delmarva Shorebirds	South Atlantic	52	86	.377	14th (14)	Ryan Minor
Short-season	Aberdeen IronBirds	New York-Penn	28	48	.368	14th (14)	Gary Allenson
Rookie	GCL Orioles	Gulf Coast	25	35	.417	12th (14)	Ramon Sambo
Overall 2012 Minor League Record			319	380	.456	27th (30)	

ORGANIZATION STATISTICS

BALTIMORE ORIOLES

AMERICAN LEAGUE

Batting	B-T	HT	WT	DOB	AVG	vLH	vRH	G	AB	R	H	2B	3B	HR	RBI	BB	HBP	SH	SF	SO	SB	CS	SLG	OBP
Andino, Robert	R-R	6-0	195	4-25-84	.211	.216	.208	127	384	41	81	13	1	7	28	37	2	7	1	100	5	5	.305	.283
Avery, Xavier	L-L	6-0	190	1-1-90	.223	.125	.244	32	94	14	21	6	1	1	6	11	0	2	0	23	6	3	.340	.305
Betemit, Wilson	B-R	6-2	220	11-2-81	.261	.140	.302	102	341	41	89	19	0	12	40	31	1	0	3	103	0	1	.422	.322
Chavez, Endy	L-L	6-0	170	2-7-78	.203	.185	.206	64	158	15	32	6	0	2	12	6	1	4	0	24	3	2	.278	.236
Davis, Chris	L-R	6-3	230	3-17-86	.270	.265	.271	139	515	75	139	20	0	33	85	37	7	0	3	169	2	3	.501	.326
Exposito, Luis	R-R	6-3	210	1-20-87	.056	.143	.000	9	18	2	1	0	0	0	3	0	0	0	0	5	0	0	.056	.190
Flaherty, Ryan	L-R	6-3	210	7-27-86	.216	.250	.213	77	153	15	33	2	1	6	19	6	3	3	1	43	1	0	.359	.258
Ford, Lew	R-R	6-0	200	8-12-76	.183	.224	.091	25	71	7	13	3	0	3	4	7	0	1	0	13	1	0	.352	.256
Hall, Bill	R-R	6-0	210	12-28-79	.222	.143	.500	7	9	2	2	0	0	1	1	5	0	0	0	7	0	0	.556	.500
Hardy, J.J.	R-R	6-1	190	8-19-82	.238	.277	.225	158	663	85	158	30	2	22	68	38	3	7	2	106	0	1	.389	.282
Hoes, L.J.	R-R	6-0	190	3-5-90	.000	—	.000	2	1	0	0	0	0	0	0	0	0	0	0	0	0	0	.000	.000
Johnson, Nick	L-L	6-3	235	9-19-78	.207	.250	.200	38	87	9	18	4	0	4	11	11	4	0	0	26	2	0	.391	.324
Jones, Adam	R-R	6-3	225	8-1-85	.287	.292	.285	162	648	103	186	39	3	32	82	34	13	0	2	126	16	7	.505	.334
Machado, Manny	R-R	6-3	185	7-6-92	.262	.280	.255	51	191	24	50	8	3	7	26	9	0	1	1	38	2	0	.445	.294
Mahoney, Joe	L-L	6-6	240	2-1-87	.000	—	.000	2	4	0	0	0	0	0	0	0	0	0	0	0	0	0	.000	.000
Markakis, Nick	L-L	6-1	190	11-17-83	.298	.313	.291	104	420	59	125	28	3	13	54	42	4	0	5	51	1	1	.471	.363
McLouth, Nate	L-R	5-11	180	10-28-81	.268	.217	.289	55	209	35	56	12	1	7	18	22	2	2	1	43	12	1	.435	.342
Paulino, Ronny	R-R	6-3	250	4-21-81	.254	.207	.294	20	63	5	16	3	0	0	5	1	0	0	0	9	0	0	.302	.266
Pearce, Steve	R-R	5-11	210	4-13-83	.254	.294	.216	28	71	8	18	4	0	3	14	8	0	2	2	17	0	1	.437	.321
2-team total (12 New York)					.229	—	—	40	96	14	22	4	0	4	18	13	0	2	2	25	0	1	.396	.315
Quintanilla, Omar	L-R	5-9	185	10-24-81	.232	.333	.188	36	99	12	23	3	0	3	12	8	0	1	2	25	0	1	.354	.284
Reimold, Nolan	R-R	6-4	205	10-12-83	.313	.313	.314	16	67	10	21	6	0	5	10	2	0	0	0	14	1	0	.627	.333
Reynolds, Mark	R-R	6-2	220	8-3-83	.221	.227	.219	135	457	65	101	26	0	23	69	73	6	0	2	159	1	3	.429	.335
Roberts, Brian	B-R	5-9	175	10-9-77	.182	.250	.167	17	66	2	12	0	0	0	5	5	0	1	2	12	1	1	.182	.233
Teagarden, Taylor	R-R	6-0	215	12-21-83	.158	.154	.161	22	57	4	9	3	0	2	9	5	0	2	0	23	0	0	.316	.226
Thome, Jim	L-R	6-4	250	8-27-70	.257	.125	.269	28	101	8	26	5	0	3	10	14	0	0	0	40	0	0	.396	.348
Tolleson, Steve	R-R	5-11	185	11-1-83	.183	.192	.158	29	71	4	13	2	1	0	6	4	0	1	0	17	1	0	.310	.227
Wieters, Matt	B-R	6-5	240	5-21-86	.249	.323	.224	144	526	67	131	27	1	23	83	60	4	0	3	112	3	0	.435	.329

Pitching	B-T	HT	WT	DOB	W	L	ERA	G	GS	CG	SV	IP	H	R	ER	HR	BB	SO	AVG	vLH	vRH	K/9	BB/9
Arrieta, Jake	R-R	6-4	225	3-6-86	3	9	6.20	24	18	0	0	115	122	82	79	16	35	109	.272	.291	.249	8.56	2.75
Ayala, Luis	R-R	6-2	175	1-12-78	5	5	2.64	66	0	0	1	75	81	27	22	7	14	51	.272	.284	.262	6.12	1.68
Berken, Jason	R-R	6-0	205	11-27-83	0	0	18.00	1	0	0	0	1	6	7	2	2	1	0	.667	.500	.714	0.00	9.00
Britton, Zach	L-L	6-3	195	12-22-87	5	3	5.07	12	11	0	0	60	61	37	34	6	32	53	.260	.235	.273	7.91	4.77
Bundy, Dylan	B-R	6-1	195	11-15-92	0	0	0.00	2	0	0	0	2	1	0	0	0	1	0	.200	.500	.000	0.00	5.40
Chen, Wei-Yin	L-L	6-0	195	7-21-85	12	11	4.02	32	32	0	0	193	186	97	86	29	57	154	.250	.232	.257	7.19	2.66
Eveland, Dana	L-L	6-1	235	10-29-83	0	1	4.73	14	2	0	0	32	32	18	17	3	13	18	.256	.239	.265	5.01	3.62
Gonzalez, Miguel	R-R	6-1	170	5-27-84	9	4	3.25	18	15	0	0	105	92	38	38	13	35	77	.235	.250	.220	6.58	2.99
Gregg, Kevin	R-R	6-6	245	6-20-78	3	2	4.95	40	0	0	0	40	30	26	24	6	24	37	.291	.286	.295	7.63	4.95
Hammel, Jason	R-R	6-6	225	9-2-82	8	6	3.43	20	20	1	0	118	104	48	45	9	42	113	.234	.203	.266	8.62	3.20
Hunter, Tommy	R-R	6-3	250	7-3-86	7	8	5.45	33	20	0	0	134	161	85	81	32	27	77	.302	.294	.311	5.18	1.82
Johnson, Jim	R-R	6-6	240	6-27-83	2	1	2.49	71	0	0	51	69	55	21	19	3	15	41	.220	.225	.214	5.37	1.97
Johnson, Steve	R-R	6-1	220	8-31-87	4	0	2.11	12	4	0	0	38	23	9	9	4	18	46	.174	.169	.179	10.80	4.23
Lindstrom, Matt	R-R	6-3	220	2-11-80	1	0	2.72	34	0	0	0	36	35	14	11	2	12	30	.254	.321	.207	7.43	2.97
Matusz, Brian	L-L	6-4	200	2-11-87	6	10	4.87	34	16	0	0	98	112	61	53	15	41	81	.284	.175	.327	7.44	3.77
O'Day, Darren	R-R	6-4	220	10-22-82	7	1	2.28	69	0	0	0	67	49	17	17	6	14	69	.202	.207	.200	9.27	1.88
Patton, Troy	B-L	6-1	180	9-3-85	1	0	2.43	54	0	0	0	56	45	15	15	5	12	49	.215	.212	.219	7.92	1.94
Phillips, Zach	L-L	6-1	190	9-21-86	0	0	6.00	6	0	0	0	6	7	4	4	2	3	5	.280	.417	.154	7.50	4.50
Pomeranz, Stu	R-R	6-7	220	12-17-84	0	0	3.00	3	0	0	0	6	7	2	2	1	1	3	.280	.250	.294	4.50	1.50
Romero, J.C.	B-L	5-11	205	6-4-76	0	0	6.75	5	0	0	0	4	7	4	3	1	1	3	.368	.444	.300	2.25	2.25
Saunders, Joe	L-L	6-3	210	6-16-81	3	3	3.63	7	7	0	0	45	49	20	18	4	8	23	.283	.178	.320	4.63	1.61
Socolovich, Miguel	R-R	6-1	190	7-24-86	0	0	6.97	6	0	0	0	10	11	8	8	2	6	6	.268	.296	.214	5.23	5.23
Strop, Pedro	R-R	6-0	215	6-13-85	5	2	2.44	70	0	0	3	66	52	18	18	2	37	58	.217	.252	.184	7.87	5.02
Tillman, Chris	R-R	6-5	210	4-15-88	9	3	2.93	15	15	0	0	86	66	38	28	12	24	66	.207	.216	.192	6.91	2.51
Wolf, Randy	L-L	6-0	205	8-22-76	2	0	5.28	5	2	0	0	15	17	9	9	2	7	8	.304	.222	.342	4.70	4.11

Fielding

Catcher	PCT	G	PO	A	E	DP	PB
Exposito	1.000	9	43	3	0	0	1
Paulino	1.000	11	62	4	0	1	3
Teagarden	1.000	21	110	7	0	0	1
Wieters	.991	134	994	52	10	7	5

First Base	PCT	G	PO	A	E	DP
Betemit	.992	15	123	6	1	10
Davis	.989	38	342	28	4	37
Flaherty	1.000	3	3	0	0	1
Johnson	.982	5	51	3	1	7
Mahoney	1.000	2	10	0	0	0
Reynolds	.995	108	926	40	5	84

Second Base	PCT	G	PO	A	E	DP
Andino	.973	108	183	286	13	66
Flaherty	.989	28	36	56	1	13
Quintanilla	.966	32	38	77	4	13

	PCT	G	PO	A	E	DP	PB
Roberts	.987	17	30	48	1	9	
Tolleson	1.000	4	7	6	0	2	

Third Base	PCT	G	PO	A	E	DP
Andino	1.000	15	8	13	0	1
Flaherty	.941	17	2	14	1	1
Machado	.967	51	44	102	5	4
Reynolds	.850	15	10	24	6	5
Tolleson	.879	12	2	27	4	0

Shortstop	PCT	G	PO	A	E	DP
Andino	1.000	2	4	7	0	4
Flaherty	—	1	0	0	0	0
Hardy	.992	158	244	529	6	113
Quintanilla	1.000	7	7	7	0	2
Tolleson	1.000	3	1	1	0	1

Outfield	PCT	G	PO	A	E	DP
Andino	—	2	0	0	0	0
Avery	.962	28	49	1	2	0
Betemit	.889	5	8	0	1	0
Chavez	.975	57	75	2	2	0
Davis	.977	41	82	3	2	0
Flaherty	.964	24	27	0	1	0
Ford	1.000	18	27	2	0	0
Hall	1.000	2	1	0	0	0
Hoes	—	1	0	0	0	0
Jones	.982	162	439	7	8	0
Markakis	.990	102	187	3	2	0
McLouth	.990	55	94	1	1	0
Pearce	1.000	25	36	1	0	0
Reimold	.897	15	26	0	3	0
Tolleson	1.000	7	11	0	0	0

NORFOLK TIDES   TRIPLE-A
INTERNATIONAL LEAGUE

Batting	B-T	HT	WT	DOB	AVG	vLH	vRH	G	AB	R	H	2B	3B	HR	RBI	BB	HBP	SH	SF	SO	SB	CS	SLG	OBP
Adams, Ryan	R-R	5-11	185	4-21-87	.224	.261	.201	65	232	26	52	18	0	4	20	27	3	1	1	60	2	2	.353	.312
Andino, Robert	R-R	6-0	195	4-25-84	.333	.000	.375	2	9	1	3	0	0	0	2	1	0	0	0	1	0	0	.333	.400
Antonelli, Matt	R-R	6-1	195	4-8-85	.204	.300	.178	29	93	11	19	4	0	1	7	19	3	1	0	23	1	2	.280	.357
2-team total (15 Scranton/W-B)					.201	—	—	44	154	22	31	5	1	2	11	24	4	1	0	32	1	2	.286	.324
Avery, Xavier	L-L	6-0	190	1-1-90	.236	.206	.247	102	390	57	92	13	5	8	34	51	5	9	3	106	22	7	.356	.330
Barfield, Josh	R-R	6-0	190	12-17-82	.000	.000	.000	4	8	0	0	0	0	0	0	1	0	0	0	3	0	0	.000	.111
Beerer, Scott	R-R	6-1	200	7-4-82	.215	.294	.188	18	65	6	14	2	1	0	7	2	1	0	0	5	0	0	.277	.250
Bell, Josh	B-R	6-3	230	11-13-86	.094	.111	.087	9	32	2	3	2	0	1	3	7	0	0	0	8	0	1	.250	.256
Britton, Buck	L-R	6-1	163	5-16-86	.100	.000	.143	3	10	0	1	0	0	0	0	0	0	0	0	3	0	0	.100	.100
Chavez, Endy	L-L	6-0	170	2-7-78	.149	.000	.226	15	47	2	7	3	0	0	4	2	1	1	2	6	0	0	.213	.192
Davis, Blake	L-R	5-11	170	12-22-83	.251	.196	.271	108	355	33	89	17	4	3	38	25	1	6	3	61	6	0	.346	.299
De San Miguel, Allan	R-R	5-9	200	2-1-88	.000	—	.000	1	3	0	0	0	0	0	0	0	0	0	0	1	0	0	.000	.000
Exposito, Luis	R-R	6-3	210	1-20-87	.268	.310	.252	55	205	26	55	11	1	6	23	18	0	0	1	35	0	2	.420	.326
2-team total (3 Pawtucket)					.265	—	—	58	215	27	57	13	1	6	24	19	0	0	1	37	0	2	.419	.323
Flaherty, Ryan	L-R	6-3	210	7-27-86	.289	.083	.385	9	38	5	11	1	1	2	3	2	1	0	0	9	0	0	.526	.341
Ford, Lew	R-R	6-0	200	8-12-76	.331	.291	.342	62	242	35	80	14	3	11	40	23	1	0	1	43	8	2	.550	.390
Hall, Bill	R-R	6-0	210	12-28-79	.246	.314	.215	90	342	38	84	18	0	15	45	26	1	0	1	141	2	1	.430	.300
Hester, John	R-R	6-4	230	9-14-83	.265	.200	.292	10	34	7	9	4	0	1	1	3	1	0	0	8	0	0	.471	.342
Hoes, L.J.	R-R	6-0	190	3-5-90	.300	.287	.306	82	317	54	95	14	4	3	38	34	4	1	1	43	8	7	.397	.374
Hoffmann, Jamie	R-R	6-3	235	8-20-84	.254	.279	.244	110	366	49	93	19	2	11	44	54	1	0	6	74	9	2	.407	.347
Joseph, Caleb	R-R	6-3	180	6-18-86	.206	.185	.220	22	68	6	14	4	1	0	7	8	0	0	0	10	0	0	.294	.289
Kelly, Ty	L-R	6-0	185	7-20-88	.278	.333	.259	11	36	3	10	1	0	1	2	4	0	0	0	3	1	0	.389	.350
Mahoney, Joe	L-L	6-6	240	2-1-87	.265	.276	.260	132	491	54	130	29	1	10	56	35	6	0	4	95	4	2	.389	.319
McLouth, Nate	L-L	5-11	180	10-28-81	.244	.208	.258	47	180	29	44	5	2	10	33	18	5	3	3	26	5	0	.461	.325
Miller, Jai	R-R	6-3	200	1-17-85	.196	.264	.167	53	179	20	35	10	1	8	21	27	3	0	2	95	3	1	.397	.308
Paulino, Ronny	R-R	6-3	250	4-21-81	.287	.216	.323	40	150	13	43	9	1	1	15	13	0	0	1	25	0	0	.380	.341
Richardson, Antoan	B-R	5-8	165	10-8-83	.160	.100	.200	9	25	4	4	0	0	0	0	7	0	2	0	6	1	0	.160	.344
Roberts, Brian	R-R	5-9	175	10-9-77	.238	.400	.188	5	21	2	5	2	0	0	1	2	0	0	0	4	0	0	.333	.304
Robinson, Chris	R-R	6-0	220	5-12-84	.232	.250	.225	52	177	18	41	10	2	0	18	15	3	0	3	27	0	2	.311	.298
Rojas, Carlos	R-R	6-1	186	1-11-84	.208	.240	.198	39	106	8	22	2	0	0	7	9	0	2	0	20	0	0	.226	.270
Starr, Sammie	R-R	5-8	165	5-31-88	.000	.000	—	1	4	0	0	0	0	0	0	0	0	0	0	2	0	0	.000	.000
Stevens, Bobby	R-R	6-0	190	3-30-87	.111	.000	.250	3	9	0	1	1	0	0	0	1	0	0	0	1	0	0	.222	.200
Tejada, Miguel	R-R	5-9	220	5-25-74	.259	.261	.259	36	135	10	35	5	0	1	18	11	3	0	2	16	1	0	.296	.325
Thomas, Scott	L-R	5-11	202	5-21-86	.143	.000	.167	5	14	2	2	0	0	0	0	0	0	0	0	5	0	0	.143	.143
Tolleson, Steve	R-R	5-11	185	11-1-83	.278	.365	.236	50	162	15	45	8	0	1	21	23	0	3	5	32	3	2	.346	.358
Waring, Brandon	R-R	6-4	195	1-2-86	.248	.300	.226	66	234	44	58	12	0	13	33	23	10	0	3	86	0	1	.466	.337
Wheeler, Zelous	R-R	5-10	220	1-16-87	.231	.000	.316	14	52	6	12	2	0	1	3	5	1	1	0	8	0	1	.327	.310

Pitching	B-T	HT	WT	DOB	W	L	ERA	G	GS	CG	SV	IP	H	R	ER	HR	BB	SO	AVG	vLH	vRH	K/9	BB/9
Arrieta, Jake	R-R	6-4	225	3-6-86	5	4	4.02	10	10	1	0	56	46	25	25	3	28	54	.223	.246	.208	8.68	4.50
Bascom, Tim	R-R	6-1	205	1-4-85	0	0	3.68	4	0	0	0	15	8	6	6	1	11	12	.163	.240	.083	7.36	6.75
Beaulac, Eric	R-R	6-5	190	11-13-86	1	0	0.00	3	1	0	0	5	2	1	0	0	6	1	.118	.250	.000	1.69	10.13
Bergesen, Brad	L-R	6-2	210	9-25-85	4	3	4.03	22	10	0	1	80	90	42	36	10	23	41	.288	.320	.258	4.59	2.58
Berken, Jason	R-R	6-0	205	11-27-83	5	6	3.50	26	26	1	0	144	160	73	56	10	39	98	.286	.283	.289	6.13	2.44
Bischoff, Matt	R-R	6-0	190	5-21-87	0	1	6.00	1	1	0	0	3	4	3	2	0	1	2	.286	.286	.286	6.00	3.00
Britton, Zach	L-L	6-3	195	12-22-87	4	2	4.91	9	9	0	0	51	49	29	28	5	20	37	.249	.171	.269	6.49	3.51
Burke, Greg	R-R	6-4	215	9-21-82	2	1	1.53	21	0	0	3	35	25	8	6	1	11	30	.195	.185	.203	7.64	2.80
Clark, Zach	R-R	6-0	195	7-11-83	5	2	1.75	8	7	1	0	46	38	10	9	1	16	32	.228	.228	.227	6.22	3.11
Egan, Pat	R-R	6-7	230	10-25-84	1	1	1.65	8	0	0	0	16	9	3	3	0	1	12	.158	.200	.135	6.61	0.55
Eveland, Dana	L-L	6-1	235	10-29-83	5	5	2.79	14	14	0	0	84	82	32	26	4	28	55	.254	.242	.259	5.89	3.00
Eyre, Willie	R-R	6-0	235	7-21-78	1	3	7.92	21	0	0	0	25	33	22	22	2	15	20	.320	.326	.317	7.20	5.40
Fowler, Zach	L-L	6-4	205	2-27-89	2	0	4.50	3	0	0	0	8	9	4	4	0	4	5	.290	.308	.278	5.63	4.50

Pitching	B-T	HT	WT	DOB	W	L	ERA	G	GS	CG	SV	IP	H	R	ER	HR	BB	SO	AVG	vLH	vRH	SO/9	BB/9
Gamboa, Eddie	R-R	6-2	195	12-21-84	1	1	7.02	4	3	0	0	17	20	13	13	4	5	9	.299	.303	.294	4.86	2.70
George, Chris	L-L	6-2	200	9-16-79	0	1	11.25	4	1	0	0	8	13	10	10	2	5	5	.361	.250	.393	5.63	5.63
Gleason, Sean	L-R	6-0	190	8-21-85	0	0	7.20	3	0	0	0	5	9	6	4	1	3	3	.360	.400	.300	5.40	5.40
Gonzalez, Miguel	R-R	6-1	170	5-27-84	3	2	1.61	14	6	0	1	45	22	12	8	1	10	53	.143	.147	.139	10.68	2.01
Hunter, Tommy	R-R	6-3	250	7-3-86	2	1	4.66	3	3	1	0	19	20	10	10	2	5	14	.267	.260	.280	6.52	2.33
Johnson, Steve	R-R	6-1	220	8-31-87	4	8	2.86	19	14	1	0	91	66	38	29	7	31	86	.202	.266	.145	8.47	3.05
Link, Jon	R-R	6-0	205	3-23-84	1	2	3.48	18	0	0	3	21	23	12	8	2	7	16	.280	.333	.225	6.97	3.05
Loomis, Andy	L-L	5-10	175	11-25-85	0	0	2.79	6	0	0	0	10	15	4	3	0	2	8	.333	.333	.333	7.45	1.86
Matusz, Brian	L-L	6-4	200	2-11-87	2	1	4.21	10	6	1	1	47	43	24	22	2	15	32	.242	.258	.233	6.13	2.87
McCurry, Cole	L-L	6-2	180	9-25-85	0	0	3.18	2	0	0	1	6	6	2	2	0	2	6	.273	.125	.357	9.53	3.18
2-team total (17 Gwinnett)					1	2	4.59	19	0	0	1	33	26	17	17	1	17	23	—	—	—	6.21	4.59
Moyer, Jamie	L-L	6-0	185	11-18-62	1	1	1.69	3	3	0	0	16	11	4	3	1	0	16	.180	.250	.156	9.00	0.00
Neshek, Pat	B-R	6-3	210	9-4-80	3	2	2.66	35	0	0	11	44	42	13	13	1	7	49	.251	.324	.202	10.02	1.43
Newby, Kyler	R-R	6-4	225	2-22-85	0	0	0.00	1	0	0	1	1	1	0	0	0	1	0	.250	1.000	.000	9.00	9.00
Petersime, Zach	R-R	6-3	175	1-19-89	0	3	3.86	5	3	0	0	16	16	8	7	2	6	13	.250	.188	.313	7.16	3.31
Phillips, Zach	L-L	6-1	190	9-21-86	2	2	3.17	42	0	0	7	54	56	22	19	2	22	45	.269	.325	.237	7.50	3.67
Pineiro, Joel	R-R	6-0	200	9-25-78	1	0	3.65	2	2	0	0	12	10	5	5	0	0	9	.227	.176	.259	6.57	0.00
Pomeranz, Stu	R-R	6-7	220	12-17-84	0	0	0.00	5	0	0	2	10	2	0	0	0	2	15	.065	.063	.067	13.50	1.80
Romero, J.C.	B-L	5-11	205	6-4-76	1	0	2.51	11	1	0	2	14	10	4	4	0	5	13	.192	.207	.174	8.16	3.14
2-team total (8 Columbus)					1	0	2.74	25	1	0	3	23	14	7	7	3	8	20	—	—	—	7.83	3.13
Rundles, Rich	L-L	6-5	210	6-3-81	1	0	2.03	4	1	0	0	13	6	5	3	0	5	13	.130	.214	.094	8.78	3.38
Socolovich, Miguel	R-R	6-1	190	7-24-86	4	0	1.90	28	0	0	2	52	33	13	11	4	14	52	.179	.224	.148	9.00	2.42
Tillman, Chris	R-R	6-5	210	4-15-88	8	8	3.63	16	15	1	0	89	85	36	36	5	30	92	.249	.230	.273	9.27	3.02
Villarreal, Oscar	L-R	6-0	215	11-22-81	3	4	2.88	37	2	0	1	69	62	30	22	1	27	49	.243	.254	.233	6.42	3.54
Viola, Pedro	L-L	6-1	185	6-29-83	0	0	7.80	11	0	0	0	15	14	14	13	4	15	17	.250	.238	.257	10.20	9.00
Wada, Tsuyoshi	L-L	5-11	180	2-21-81	0	1	20.25	1	1	0	0	3	6	6	6	1	4	1	.429	.250	.500	3.38	13.50
Walters, David	R-R	6-3	190	8-13-87	0	0	11.57	1	0	0	0	2	3	3	3	1	1	1	.333	.000	.600	3.86	3.86
Willis, Dontrelle	L-L	6-4	225	1-12-82	0	3	8.53	4	1	0	0	6	10	8	6	0	4	4	.345	.333	.348	5.68	5.68
Zagone, Rick	L-L	6-4	215	9-30-86	2	0	0.00	4	2	0	1	20	9	0	0	0	7	16	.138	.250	.102	7.08	3.10

Fielding

Catcher	PCT	G	PO	A	E	DP	PB
De San Miguel	1.000	1	3	0	0	0	0
Exposito	.980	45	313	36	7	8	4
Hester	.970	10	60	5	2	1	1
Joseph	1.000	20	156	14	0	2	4
Paulino	.995	29	204	13	1	5	5
Robinson	.997	40	287	20	1	0	1
Thomas	.963	5	25	1	1	1	1

First Base	PCT	G	PO	A	E	DP
Antonelli	1.000	1	14	2	0	1
Bell	1.000	1	7	0	0	0
Britton	1.000	1	9	1	0	4
Flaherty	1.000	2	9	1	0	0
Hall	.923	1	12	0	1	2
Hoffmann	.963	6	24	2	1	0
Mahoney	.998	128	1086	80	2	105
Robinson	.964	3	25	2	1	0
Waring	1.000	10	93	4	0	8

Second Base	PCT	G	PO	A	E	DP
Adams	.945	56	95	146	14	30
Andino	.909	2	5	5	1	3
Antonelli	.966	7	17	11	1	1
Davis	.978	10	14	30	1	7
Flaherty	1.000	2	7	8	0	2
Hall	.991	27	49	66	1	12
Hoffmann	—	1	0	0	0	0
Kelly	.889	6	7	17	3	5
Roberts	1.000	5	5	11	0	3
Rojas	1.000	33	54	88	0	25
Stevens	1.000	3	3	5	0	0
Tolleson	1.000	2	5	7	0	0
Wheeler	1.000	5	10	17	0	3

Third Base	PCT	G	PO	A	E	DP
Adams	1.000	1	4	3	0	1
Antonelli	.944	15	8	26	2	2
Barfield	—	1	0	0	0	0
Bell	1.000	3	3	3	0	0
Britton	1.000	1	0	2	0	0
Flaherty	1.000	2	0	1	0	0
Hall	.857	26	19	47	11	4
Kelly	.909	4	4	6	1	0
Tejada	.972	30	19	51	2	2
Tolleson	.941	8	6	10	1	2
Waring	.928	51	38	91	10	13
Wheeler	.893	7	5	20	3	2

Shortstop	PCT	G	PO	A	E	DP
Antonelli	.857	1	3	3	1	2
Davis	.985	98	114	274	6	64
Hall	.800	1	2	2	1	1
Rojas	.944	6	4	13	1	3
Starr	1.000	1	0	3	0	0
Tejada	1.000	3	3	5	0	2
Tolleson	.942	41	44	101	9	19
Wheeler	1.000	3	3	4	0	1

Outfield	PCT	G	PO	A	E	DP
Antonelli	1.000	2	2	0	0	0
Avery	.972	102	199	7	6	2
Beerer	.895	10	17	0	2	0
Bell	1.000	1	3	0	0	0
Britton	1.000	1	1	0	0	0
Chavez	1.000	15	23	0	0	0
Davis	1.000	1	1	0	0	0
Flaherty	1.000	5	9	0	0	0
Ford	.981	25	50	1	1	1
Hall	1.000	6	17	0	0	0
Hoes	.983	80	172	5	3	1
Hoffmann	.984	91	181	3	3	0
Mahoney	1.000	1	3	0	0	0
McLouth	.989	45	91	0	1	0
Miller	.972	49	101	3	3	1
Richardson	1.000	8	20	0	0	0

BOWIE BAYSOX   DOUBLE-A

EASTERN LEAGUE

Batting	B-T	HT	WT	DOB	AVG	vLH	vRH	G	AB	R	H	2B	3B	HR	RBI	BB	HBP	SH	SF	SO	SB	CS	SLG	OBP
Adair, Travis	L-R	5-10	180	12-23-87	.164	.095	.178	40	122	9	20	2	0	1	12	10	0	2	1	21	2	1	.205	.226
Baez, Edgardo	R-R	6-2	190	7-12-85	.167	.000	.500	3	6	0	1	0	0	0	1	0	0	0	1	1	0	.167	.286
Baker, Aaron	L-R	6-2	220	9-10-87	.429	—	.429	2	7	1	3	1	0	0	4	2	0	0	0	2	0	0	.571	.556
Barfield, Josh	R-R	6-0	190	12-17-82	.267	.295	.254	80	285	41	76	19	1	1	30	23	0	0	3	30	17	6	.351	.318
Betemit, Wilson	B-R	6-2	220	11-2-81	.250	.000	.500	2	8	1	2	0	0	1	4	0	0	0	0	1	0	0	.625	.250
Britton, Buck	L-R	6-1	163	5-16-86	.294	.330	.282	99	377	54	111	23	1	9	54	37	1	4	2	60	5	5	.432	.357
Bumbry, Steve	L-L	5-11	185	4-4-88	.170	.087	.200	29	88	6	15	4	0	1	6	10	0	0	0	23	1	1	.250	.255
Chavez, Endy	L-L	6-0	170	2-7-78	.200	.000	.250	3	10	3	2	0	0	0	2	0	0	0	0	0	0	0	.200	.333
De San Miguel, Allan	R-R	5-9	200	2-1-88	.225	.182	.236	31	111	13	25	8	1	4	18	15	0	0	1	33	1	0	.423	.315
Flacco, Mike	R-R	6-6	212	1-17-87	.091	.200	.000	4	11	0	1	0	0	0	0	0	0	0	0	4	0	0	.091	.091
Hoes, L.J.	R-R	6-0	190	3-5-90	.265	.182	.298	51	196	25	52	9	3	2	16	31	1	1	0	33	12	5	.372	.368
Hughes, Rhyne	L-L	6-2	215	9-9-83	.278	.231	.294	75	266	50	74	19	1	13	51	41	0	2	4	74	4	1	.504	.370
Joseph, Caleb	R-R	6-3	180	6-18-86	.272	.318	.251	80	279	38	76	17	1	12	48	29	3	2	4	60	2	0	.470	.343
Kelly, Ty	L-R	6-0	185	7-20-88	.308	.353	.289	46	172	24	53	11	2	1	27	21	2	1	3	28	1	0	.413	.384

Name	B-T	HT	WT	DOB	AVG	vLH	vRH	OBP	G	AB	R	H	2B	3B	HR	RBI	BB	SO	SB	CS	?	?	SLG	OBP
Machado, Manny	R-R	6-3	185	7-6-92	.266	.303	.253	109	402	60	107	26	5	11	59	48	6	1	2	70	13	4	.438	.352
Markakis, Nick	L-L	6-1	190	11-17-83	.300	—	.300	3	10	4	3	1	0	2	4	2	0	0	0	2	0	0	1.000	.417
Miller, Jai	R-R	6-3	200	1-17-85	.195	.244	.170	44	133	12	26	5	0	4	17	18	0	0	2	64	2	1	.323	.288
Reynolds, Mark	R-R	6-2	220	8-3-83	.143	.000	.167	2	7	0	1	0	0	0	0	0	2	0	0	0	4	0	0	.143	.333
Richardson, Antoan	R-R	5-8	165	10-8-83	.279	.169	.311	90	290	68	81	4	4	1	15	61	7	8	1	60	26	5	.331	.415
Roberts, Brian	B-R	5-9	175	10-9-77	.250	.000	.250	7	16	4	4	3	0	1	3	4	0	0	1	3	0	0	.625	.381
Rojas, Carlos	R-R	6-1	186	1-11-84	.296	.154	.429	9	27	2	8	1	0	0	2	2	0	1	0	6	0	1	.333	.345
2-team total (10 Akron)					.175	—		19	57	4	10	1	0	0	4	8	0	3	0	11	0	1	.193	.277
Rooney, Michael	R-R	5-11	172	8-7-88	.333	.000	.400	2	6	1	2	0	0	0	0	0	0	0	0	0	0	0	.333	.333
Ruettiger, John	L-L	6-1	195	9-21-89	.240	.200	.250	9	25	2	6	0	0	0	1	4	0	0	0	3	2	0	.240	.345
Schoop, Jonathan	R-R	6-1	195	10-16-91	.245	.308	.218	124	485	68	119	24	1	14	56	50	9	6	5	103	5	3	.386	.324
Schutz, Kipp	L-L	6-4	205	3-21-88	.077	.000	.100	5	13	0	1	0	0	0	1	1	0	0	0	2	0	0	.077	.143
Stevens, Bobby	R-R	6-0	190	3-30-87	.000	.000	.000	2	7	0	0	0	0	0	0	0	0	0	0	0	0	0	.000	.000
Teagarden, Taylor	R-R	6-0	215	12-21-83	.286	.000	.333	3	7	1	2	1	0	0	0	3	0	0	0	3	0	0	.429	.500
Thomas, Scott	L-R	5-11	202	3-31-85	.231	.000	.250	5	13	1	3	1	0	0	0	1	0	0	1	0	0	0	.308	.286
Townsend, Tyler	L-R	6-3	215	5-14-88	.247	.222	.261	21	73	11	18	2	0	6	13	10	0	0	0	24	0	0	.521	.337
Ward, Brian	R-R	5-11	210	10-17-85	.217	.319	.175	50	161	18	35	5	0	1	12	24	2	2	1	24	4	0	.267	.324
Waring, Brandon	R-R	6-4	195	1-2-86	.276	.302	.265	52	185	38	51	16	1	11	30	27	8	1	1	56	2	0	.551	.389
Welty, Ronnie	R-R	6-3	204	1-19-88	.286	.261	.298	37	140	23	40	11	2	8	30	3	1	1	1	38	1	1	.564	.303
Wheeler, Zelous	R-R	5-10	220	1-16-87	.275	.242	.288	97	334	48	92	18	2	13	44	38	10	3	4	63	5	1	.458	.363
Widlansky, Robbie	L-R	6-2	210	11-6-84	.316	.300	.322	128	469	71	148	35	1	8	83	64	7	2	2	74	11	3	.446	.404

Pitching	B-T	HT	WT	DOB	W	L	ERA	G	GS	CG	SV	IP	H	R	ER	HR	BB	SO	AVG	vLH	vRH	K/9	BB/9
Bascom, Tim	R-R	6-1	205	1-4-85	6	6	4.41	23	21	0	0	120	121	65	59	9	45	88	.264	.266	.263	6.58	3.37
Belfiore, Mike	R-L	6-2	220	10-3-88	5	1	2.85	28	0	0	2	47	43	20	15	2	21	50	.239	.160	.269	9.51	3.99
Berry, Ryan	R-R	6-0	192	8-3-88	0	0	0.00	1	0	0	0	3	1	0	0	0	1	0	.111	.000	.250	3.00	0.00
Berry, Tim	L-L	6-3	180	3-18-91	0	1	37.80	1	1	0	0	2	7	9	7	0	2	4	.583	1.000	.500	21.60	10.80
Britton, Zach	L-L	6-3	195	12-22-87	1	0	0.75	2	2	0	0	12	8	4	1	0	3	11	.186	.167	.194	8.25	2.25
Bundy, Dylan	B-R	6-1	195	11-15-92	2	0	3.24	3	3	0	0	17	14	7	6	1	8	13	.230	.269	.200	7.02	4.32
Bundy, Bobby	R-R	6-2	215	1-13-90	2	11	6.25	17	17	0	0	81	98	66	56	7	35	64	.301	.292	.306	7.14	3.90
Burke, Greg	R-R	6-4	215	9-21-82	1	0	1.53	23	0	0	14	29	21	6	5	0	4	20	.191	.250	.162	6.14	1.23
Bywater, Matt	L-L	6-2	190	6-15-89	1	0	0.00	1	1	0	0	5	2	0	0	0	0	3	.118	.000	.167	5.40	0.00
Clark, Zach	R-R	6-0	195	7-11-83	10	5	3.19	20	19	1	0	121	112	47	43	8	38	66	.248	.261	.240	4.90	2.82
Drake, Oliver	R-R	6-4	215	1-13-87	1	1	1.50	3	3	0	0	18	8	4	3	1	4	15	.125	.158	.077	7.50	2.00
Egan, Pat	R-R	6-7	230	10-25-84	3	0	1.60	31	0	0	2	51	50	13	9	1	12	41	.266	.239	.282	7.28	2.13
Gamboa, Eddie	R-R	6-2	195	12-21-84	8	4	3.33	23	13	0	1	92	103	41	34	4	17	71	.295	.268	.315	6.95	1.66
Gleason, Sean	L-R	6-0	190	8-21-85	2	1	5.97	17	4	0	1	38	50	31	25	5	12	30	.325	.379	.284	7.17	2.87
Gurka, Jason	L-L	6-0	170	1-10-88	2	3	3.60	12	0	0	1	20	19	8	8	3	12	22	.250	.150	.286	9.90	5.40
Hinton, Robert	R-R	6-1	205	8-13-84	1	1	3.34	41	0	1	1	59	61	28	22	4	14	60	.263	.314	.233	9.10	2.12
Hunter, Tommy	R-R	6-3	250	7-3-86	1	0	0.00	2	1	1	1	10	3	0	0	0	1	6	.091	.071	.105	5.40	0.90
Lindstrom, Matt	R-R	6-3	220	2-11-80	0	0	3.86	2	1	0	0	2	4	3	1	0	1	1	.364	.400	.333	3.86	3.86
Loomis, Andy	L-L	5-10	175	11-25-85	0	1	5.63	10	1	0	1	16	20	13	10	3	3	16	.299	.000	.357	9.00	1.69
McCurry, Cole	L-L	6-2	180	9-25-85	0	7	6.46	11	9	0	0	46	55	35	33	5	22	26	.301	.200	.320	5.09	4.30
Newby, Kyler	R-R	6-4	225	2-22-85	5	4	2.44	42	0	0	19	55	38	18	15	1	21	74	.191	.206	.183	12.04	3.42
Pelzer, Wynn	R-R	6-1	205	6-23-86	0	2	9.00	3	0	0	0	3	3	3	3	0	2	4	.364	.333	.375	12.00	6.00
Petrini, Chris	R-L	6-0	205	2-11-87	6	3	2.62	24	0	0	1	69	59	24	20	3	12	67	.229	.203	.278	8.78	2.88
Pettit, Jake	L-L	6-1	185	10-28-86	11	3	3.86	24	21	0	0	124	114	57	53	16	24	86	.251	.234	.255	6.26	1.75
Pomeranz, Stu	R-R	6-7	220	12-17-84	0	0	0.00	5	0	0	1	13	7	2	0	0	1	20	.149	.095	.192	13.50	0.68
Schrader, Clay	L-R	5-11	200	4-28-90	1	0	2.74	19	0	0	1	23	15	7	7	1	24	17	.192	.097	.255	6.65	9.39
Tillman, Chris	R-R	6-5	210	4-15-88	0	1	8.10	1	1	0	0	3	4	3	3	0	2	2	.308	.667	.200	5.40	5.40
Viola, Pedro	L-L	6-1	185	6-29-83	0	2	3.34	25	0	0	4	32	23	12	12	3	8	50	.198	.250	.182	13.92	2.23
Wolf, Ross	R-R	6-0	180	10-18-82	0	0	6.75	7	0	0	1	8	12	6	6	2	2	7	.353	.308	.381	7.88	2.25
Wright, Mike	R-R	6-5	195	1-3-90	5	3	4.91	12	12	0	0	62	71	38	34	7	17	45	.289	.351	.250	6.50	2.45
Zagone, Rick	L-L	6-4	215	9-30-86	4	4	4.86	11	11	0	0	67	61	41	36	6	26	39	.252	.311	.239	5.27	3.51

Fielding

Catcher	PCT	G	PO	A	E	DP	PB
De San Miguel	1.000	31	209	10	0	0	5
Joseph	.994	61	401	60	3	5	9
Teagarden	1.000	2	11	2	0	0	0
Thomas	1.000	4	9	2	0	0	1
Ward	.986	50	368	45	6	4	1

First Base	PCT	G	PO	A	E	DP
Betemit	1.000	1	8	0	0	2
Britton	1.000	4	46	5	0	7
Flacco	1.000	2	20	0	0	3
Hughes	.997	63	576	25	2	61
Rojas	1.000	1	1	1	0	0
Townsend	.946	11	101	5	6	6
Waring	.997	37	356	18	1	31
Widlansky	.991	27	217	9	2	24

Second Base	PCT	G	PO	A	E	DP
Adair	.984	17	21	41	1	7
Barfield	1.000	4	6	11	0	4
Britton	.991	28	40	68	1	21

(Second Base, cont.)	PCT	G	PO	A	E	DP
Kelly	1.000	5	7	14	0	3
Roberts	.923	7	10	14	2	5
Rojas	1.000	3	6	8	0	3
Rooney	.889	3	3	5	1	2
Schoop	.970	88	161	253	13	68

Third Base	PCT	G	PO	A	E	DP
Adair	1.000	5	2	9	0	1
Betemit	1.000	1	0	1	0	0
Britton	.950	15	5	33	2	2
Kelly	.934	21	16	41	4	4
Machado	.857	2	1	5	1	0
Reynolds	.857	5	1	5	1	0
Rojas	.900	5	1	17	2	1
Waring	.923	4	5	7	1	0
Wheeler	.931	91	58	210	20	23

Shortstop	PCT	G	PO	A	E	DP
Barfield	1.000	1	1	0	0	0
Machado	.954	104	151	308	22	68
Schoop	.948	39	48	99	8	31

(Outfield)	PCT	G	PO	A	E	DP
Wheeler	1.000	2	1	0	0	0

Outfield	PCT	G	PO	A	E	DP
Adair	.955	14	19	2	1	0
Baez	1.000	3	5	0	0	0
Barfield	.991	65	107	1	1	0
Britton	1.000	45	58	8	0	1
Bumbry	.951	29	39	0	2	0
Chavez	1.000	3	2	1	0	0
Hoes	.991	50	114	2	1	1
Kelly	.991	17	21	0	0	0
Markakis	1.000	2	4	1	0	0
Miller	.973	43	106	3	3	0
Richardson	.986	87	203	3	3	2
Ruettiger	1.000	9	11	1	0	0
Schutz	1.000	5	7	0	0	0
Stevens	—	1	0	0	0	0
Welty	.957	34	65	2	3	0
Widlansky	1.000	48	57	3	0	1

CAROLINA LEAGUE

Batting	B-T	HT	WT	DOB	AVG	vLH	vRH	G	AB	R	H	2B	3B	HR	RBI	BB	HBP	SH	SF	SO	SB	CS	SLG	OBP
Adair, Travis	L-R	5-10	180	12-23-87	.285	.333	.281	41	130	18	37	6	0	1	10	17	0	1	1	17	7	2	.354	.365
Baker, Aaron	L-R	6-2	220	9-10-87	.266	.269	.266	89	319	44	85	18	3	22	72	36	6	1	2	77	7	3	.549	.350
Bernadina, Roderick	R-R	6-1	162	8-10-92	.077	—	.077	4	13	1	1	0	0	1	4	0	0	0	0	2	0	0	.308	.077
Boss, Torsten	L-R	6-0	190	12-27-90	.143	—	.143	2	7	1	1	0	0	0	0	0	1	0	0	2	0	0	.143	.250
Bumbry, Steve	L-L	5-11	185	4-4-88	.249	.167	.261	64	229	30	57	20	2	7	32	27	4	1	1	85	12	2	.445	.337
Dalles, Justin	R-R	6-2	205	12-30-88	.234	.389	.183	41	145	14	34	8	0	2	11	11	2	0	0	31	0	0	.331	.297
Davis, Adam	R-R	6-0	205	12-15-89	.417	1.000	.300	4	12	4	5	1	0	0	2	1	0	1	1	1	0	0	.500	.429
Davis, Glynn	R-R	6-3	170	12-7-91	.256	.235	.262	22	82	11	21	1	1	0	4	12	1	2	0	25	8	1	.293	.358
De San Miguel, Allan	R-R	5-9	200	2-1-88	.260	.462	.231	30	104	16	27	7	0	2	17	12	4	0	1	29	3	1	.385	.355
Flacco, Mike	R-R	6-6	212	1-17-87	.218	.324	.189	103	344	42	75	15	1	8	35	31	5	1	4	58	7	7	.337	.289
Kelly, Ty	L-R	6-0	185	7-20-88	.346	.354	.344	76	263	47	91	17	0	9	41	54	3	2	2	41	2	3	.513	.460
Kolodny, Tyler	R-R	6-3	206	3-9-88	.139	.250	.125	13	36	2	5	2	0	0	3	3	1	0	0	14	2	0	.194	.262
Mosby, Michael	R-R	6-0	195	10-30-89	.234	.262	.225	82	261	22	61	16	3	4	35	26	3	5	2	76	2	6	.364	.308
Mummey, Trent	L-L	5-10	185	1-5-89	.228	.184	.238	72	259	40	59	14	1	4	22	35	2	5	1	35	15	7	.336	.323
Nowak, Jeremy	B-R	6-0	205	3-17-88	.281	.358	.264	117	452	61	127	26	1	7	44	40	2	4	3	117	8	5	.389	.340
Oliveira, Joe	R-R	6-0	195	9-30-87	.209	.325	.183	72	220	23	46	8	1	2	14	30	2	4	1	42	7	3	.282	.308
Pena, Jerome	B-R	5-11	185	11-6-88	.308	.222	.319	20	78	12	24	7	0	1	4	6	1	1	0	20	4	0	.436	.365
Planeta, Mike	R-R	6-4	182	10-17-89	.138	.000	.160	17	58	3	8	2	0	1	3	4	0	2	1	22	3	3	.224	.190
Rooney, Michael	R-R	5-11	172	8-7-88	.136	.143	.134	52	118	15	16	5	0	0	9	13	3	7	0	33	8	3	.178	.239
Rosa, Garabez	R-R	6-2	166	10-12-89	.245	.258	.242	108	363	37	89	16	2	7	45	10	4	10	2	87	4	5	.358	.272
Ruettiger, John	L-L	6-1	195	9-21-89	.274	.259	.275	64	234	38	64	10	0	1	12	35	2	5	0	32	16	8	.329	.373
Schutz, Kipp	L-L	6-4	205	3-21-88	.304	.500	.274	41	135	15	41	6	0	2	21	13	1	1	0	30	1	1	.393	.369
Starr, Sammie	R-R	5-8	165	5-31-88	.250	—	.250	2	4	0	1	0	0	0	1	0	0	0	0	2	0	0	.250	.250
Stevens, Bobby	R-R	6-0	190	3-30-87	.276	.281	.275	51	185	25	51	7	0	6	16	8	3	2	0	47	5	2	.411	.316
2-team total (32 Lynchburg)					.250	—	—	83	280	42	70	14	0	8	24	13	6	4	1	69	8	4	.386	.29
Stifler, Jason	R-R	6-0	215	8-12-86	.000	.000	—	1	1	0	0	0	0	0	0	0	0	0	0	0	0	0	.000	.000
Sweeney, Matt	L-R	6-3	215	4-4-88	.250	.200	.260	33	116	15	29	11	0	2	13	10	0	0	1	22	0	1	.397	.307
Thomas, Scott	L-R	5-11	202	3-21-85	.194	—	.194	11	31	1	6	0	0	0	2	0	0	0	1	10	0	1	.194	.188
Townsend, Tyler	L-R	6-3	215	5-14-88	.254	.364	.229	33	118	14	30	5	0	3	18	15	1	0	2	31	0	1	.373	.338
Tremblay, Chris	R-R	5-10	185	11-13-86	.127	.100	.133	18	55	2	7	1	0	1	4	2	0	0	0	17	4	0	.200	.158
Webb, Brenden	L-L	6-3	190	2-24-90	.270	.333	.265	23	74	14	20	6	1	3	13	11	3	1	1	30	1	3	.500	.382
Welty, Ronnie	R-R	6-3	204	1-19-88	.415	.545	.381	13	53	12	22	7	3	3	17	1	2	0	0	10	3	0	.830	.446

Pitching	B-T	HT	WT	DOB	W	L	ERA	G	GS	CG	SV	IP	H	R	ER	HR	BB	SO	AVG	vLH	vRH	K/9	BB/9
Baker, David	R-R	6-4	195	4-17-91	0	1	16.88	5	0	0	0	8	20	15	15	5	3	7	.488	.500	.484	7.88	3.38
Beaulac, Eric	R-R	6-5	190	11-13-86	3	2	3.38	15	0	0	1	32	25	14	12	3	18	31	.217	.263	.208	8.72	5.06
Berry, Ryan	R-R	6-0	192	8-3-88	2	4	3.36	36	0	0	11	67	67	32	25	3	21	43	.259	.242	.264	5.78	2.82
Berry, Tim	L-L	6-3	180	3-18-91	5	5	4.32	15	13	0	0	75	83	44	36	6	20	61	.285	.392	.263	7.32	2.40
Bischoff, Matt	R-R	6-0	190	5-21-87	0	0	2.89	16	0	0	1	28	22	10	9	5	6	28	.210	.238	.202	9.00	1.93
Bundy, Dylan	B-R	6-1	195	11-15-92	6	3	2.84	12	12	0	0	57	48	20	18	5	18	66	.233	.339	.193	10.42	2.84
Bywater, Matt	L-L	6-2	190	6-15-89	1	2	5.67	19	5	0	0	46	57	32	29	7	14	37	.302	.242	.314	7.24	2.74
Copeland, Scott	R-R	6-3	210	12-15-87	3	8	6.88	18	18	1	0	86	118	79	66	11	38	64	.330	.355	.321	6.67	3.96
Erbe, Brandon	R-R	6-4	190	12-25-87	2	3	6.82	19	1	0	0	30	32	27	23	4	24	30	.274	.278	.272	8.90	7.12
Esquivel, Jaime	R-R	6-2	190	5-25-92	0	0	0.00	1	0	0	0	2	1	0	0	0	0	2	.125	.500	.000	9.00	0.00
Fowler, Zach	L-L	6-4	205	2-27-89	0	1	6.55	7	0	0	0	11	17	8	8	2	2	10	.362	.333	.368	8.18	1.64
Gamboa, Eddie	R-R	6-2	195	12-21-84	1	0	0.00	2	1	0	0	9	2	0	0	0	6	6	.074	.000	.125	6.23	0.00
Gausman, Kevin	R-R	6-4	185	1-6-91	0	1	6.00	3	3	0	0	9	10	6	6	3	1	8	.278	.545	.160	8.00	1.00
Gurka, Jason	L-L	6-0	170	1-10-88	1	2	2.18	20	1	0	1	45	30	12	11	1	12	43	.191	.267	.173	8.54	2.38
Hammel, Jason	R-R	6-6	225	9-2-82	1	0	0.00	1	1	0	0	5	3	0	0	0	1	7	.158	.000	.214	12.60	1.80
Haughian, Nick	L-L	6-0	205	1-1-87	0	0	18.00	4	0	0	0	3	4	7	6	1	3	1	.286	.000	.364	3.00	9.00
Howard, Trent	L-L	6-2	200	10-16-89	4	10	4.83	21	18	0	0	101	110	71	54	15	26	70	.280	.271	.282	6.26	2.32
Jones, Devin	R-R	6-2	170	7-24-90	7	1	2.80	9	9	2	0	55	53	18	17	5	12	29	.255	.333	.238	4.77	1.98
Loomis, Andy	L-L	5-10	175	11-25-85	1	1	2.63	26	0	0	3	38	36	14	11	0	13	35	.255	.032	.318	8.36	3.11
Melendez, Oscar	R-R	6-0	170	9-15-86	1	0	7.00	13	0	0	0	18	19	16	14	2	18	12	.271	.211	.294	6.00	9.00
Moore, Justin	R-R	6-3	190	7-26-89	0	4	9.17	10	6	0	0	36	58	40	37	6	11	13	.360	.400	.340	3.22	2.72
Moreau, Nathan	L-L	6-3	223	9-15-86	0	0	15.00	2	1	0	0	3	6	6	5	1	7	3	.400	.500	.385	9.00	21.00
Moreland, Kenny	R-R	5-11	200	4-2-86	2	3	3.94	14	0	0	0	32	33	16	14	5	6	19	.268	.316	.247	5.34	1.69
Petrini, Chris	R-L	6-0	205	2-11-87	0	1	1.88	8	0	0	1	14	6	3	3	0	9	14	.122	.091	.132	8.79	5.65
Schrader, Clay	L-R	5-11	200	4-28-90	1	1	1.29	23	0	0	4	35	20	7	5	0	27	51	.165	.231	.134	13.11	6.94
Simon, Kyle	R-R	6-5	225	8-18-90	2	8	3.96	14	14	0	0	73	86	47	32	8	21	49	.293	.310	.280	6.07	2.60
Walters, David	R-R	6-3	190	8-13-87	3	6	3.55	45	0	0	12	58	61	27	23	8	15	51	.269	.333	.253	7.87	2.31
Wilkins, Bobby	R-R	6-4	225	8-20-89	1	0	0.00	1	0	0	0	2	2	1	0	0	0	2	.333	.000	.333	9.00	0.00
Wilson, Tyler	R-R	6-2	185	9-25-89	7	7	3.49	19	19	0	0	111	95	49	43	12	19	114	.228	.286	.205	9.24	1.54
Wright, Mike	R-R	6-5	195	1-3-90	5	2	2.91	8	8	0	0	46	47	16	15	3	5	35	.266	.222	.285	6.80	0.97
Zagone, Rick	L-L	6-4	215	9-30-86	3	1	2.91	13	9	0	0	56	44	20	18	5	27	35	.219	.154	.235	5.66	4.37

Fielding

Catcher	PCT	G	PO	A	E	DP	PB
Dalles	.992	37	223	31	2	5	2
Davis	.923	4	22	2	2	0	1
De San Miguel	.984	27	168	17	3	0	0
Oliveira	.990	72	522	60	6	3	9
Thomas	.979	8	46	1	1	0	3

First Base	PCT	G	PO	A	E	DP
Baker	.989	59	505	26	6	55
De San Miguel	1.000	3	22	0	0	3
Flacco	.992	61	479	45	4	46
Kolodny	1.000	2	9	0	0	2
Sweeney	.938	2	15	0	1	0

BALTIMORE ORIOLES

Townsend	.985	23	191	9	3	15
Second Base	**PCT**	**G**	**PO**	**A**	**E**	**DP**
Adair	.978	22	37	51	2	13
Boss	1.000	1	1	3	0	0
Kelly	.989	55	119	143	3	37
Mosby	1.000	1	0	1	0	0
Pena	.975	20	32	47	2	15
Rooney	.977	24	40	44	2	14
Starr	1.000	2	1	2	0	0
Stevens	.981	20	47	54	2	14
Tremblay	.950	5	6	13	1	2
Third Base	**PCT**	**G**	**PO**	**A**	**E**	**DP**
Adair	.902	17	7	39	5	3
Baker	—	1	0	0	0	0

Boss	1.000	1	2	4	0	1
Flacco	1.000	1	0	1	0	0
Kelly	.917	16	9	35	4	6
Kolodny	—	1	0	0	0	0
Mosby	.920	82	45	174	19	14
Rosa	—	1	0	0	0	0
Sweeney	.844	27	14	51	12	4
Shortstop	**PCT**	**G**	**PO**	**A**	**E**	**DP**
Adair	.500	3	0	1	1	0
Mosby	—	1	0	0	0	0
Rooney	.959	23	35	59	4	15
Rosa	.953	107	173	332	25	59
Tremblay	.943	13	18	48	4	8

Outfield	**PCT**	**G**	**PO**	**A**	**E**	**DP**
Bernadina	1.000	4	8	0	0	0
Bumbry	.971	63	91	10	3	2
Davis	.977	22	39	3	1	1
Flacco	.750	8	2	1	1	0
Kelly	1.000	5	9	1	0	0
Kolodny	1.000	10	18	1	0	0
Mummey	.975	68	151	4	4	1
Nowak	.969	91	150	4	5	0
Planeta	1.000	16	34	1	0	1
Ruettiger	.984	63	117	4	2	1
Schutz	1.000	27	27	1	0	0
Stevens	.977	31	39	4	1	0
Webb	1.000	13	21	1	0	0
Welty	1.000	13	24	1	0	0

DELMARVA SHOREBIRDS

LOW CLASS A

SOUTH ATLANTIC LEAGUE

Batting	B-T	HT	WT	DOB	AVG	vLH	vRH	G	AB	R	H	2B	3B	HR	RBI	BB	HBP	SH	SF	SO	SB	CS	SLG	OBP
Bernadina, Roderick	R-R	6-1	162	8-10-92	.298	.265	.314	31	104	8	31	4	0	2	12	9	3	2	0	21	3	1	.394	.371
Caronia, Anthony	L-R	6-0	170	5-22-91	.100	.000	.133	7	20	0	2	0	0	0	0	1	0	0	0	7	1	0	.100	.143
Chavez, Endy	L-L	6-0	170	2-7-78	.111	.000	.125	3	9	2	1	0	0	0	1	2	0	0	0	1	0	0	.111	.273
Dalles, Justin	R-R	6-2	205	12-30-88	.329	.389	.308	20	70	13	23	5	0	4	12	11	0	0	2	13	0	0	.571	.410
Davis, Adam	R-R	6-0	205	12-15-89	.200	.225	.185	35	105	11	21	2	0	3	13	7	4	1	0	30	2	0	.305	.276
Davis, Glynn	R-R	6-3	170	12-7-91	.252	.280	.239	101	397	53	100	16	2	0	25	51	6	6	5	91	29	9	.302	.342
Delmonico, Nicky	L-R	6-2	196	7-12-92	.249	.175	.278	95	338	49	84	22	0	11	54	47	7	0	1	73	8	1	.411	.351
Esposito, Jason	R-R	6-2	200	7-19-90	.209	.257	.188	123	473	52	99	13	2	5	51	26	8	1	4	113	8	3	.277	.260
Givens, Mychal	R-R	6-1	190	5-13-90	.243	.237	.246	100	337	43	82	15	0	2	27	39	5	6	1	49	13	8	.306	.330
Herbst, Lucas	L-L	5-10	185	9-9-90	.136	.333	.086	13	44	4	6	1	0	2	6	2	1	0	0	5	0	1	.295	.191
Hoppy, Kyle	L-L	6-0	195	5-8-91	.117	.100	.120	16	60	5	7	1	0	1	6	4	0	0	0	13	0	1	.183	.172
Knight, Austin	B-R	5-11	195	2-13-90	.111	.167	.000	5	9	1	1	0	0	0	1	0	0	0	0	3	0	0	.222	.200
Leonora, Dudley	R-R	6-1	154	12-15-91	.163	.071	.200	16	49	3	8	2	0	0	3	0	1	0	1	11	0	0	.204	.212
Lino, Gabriel	R-R	6-3	200	5-17-93	.218	.172	.236	56	206	28	45	13	0	4	18	16	3	0	2	64	1	1	.340	.282
2-team total (37 Lakewood)					.222	—	—	93	338	44	75	23	0	7	32	30	5	0	2	97	1	3	.352	.293
Lorenzo, Gregory	R-R	6-0	160	5-31-91	.333	.348	.327	19	72	13	24	2	2	1	3	1	3	1	0	22	6	2	.458	.368
Marin, Adrian	R-R	6-0	165	3-8-94	.286	.444	.167	6	21	5	6	0	0	0	2	1	1	0	0	2	2	0	.286	.348
Narron, Connor	R-R	6-3	195	11-12-91	.232	.232	.232	119	439	49	102	21	1	10	58	39	5	0	3	101	2	3	.353	.300
Ohlman, Michael	R-R	6-4	205	12-14-90	.304	.339	.286	51	171	27	52	16	2	2	28	33	1	0	4	27	0	1	.456	.411
Pena, Jerome	B-R	5-11	185	11-6-88	.250	.331	.208	21	80	13	20	4	1	1	8	8	1	1	0	19	3	0	.363	.326
Planeta, Mike	R-R	6-4	182	10-17-89	.272	.221	.300	78	294	43	80	19	2	1	27	23	1	9	1	78	12	0	.361	.326
Roberts, Brian	B-R	5-9	175	10-9-77	.200	.500	.000	2	5	0	1	0	0	0	0	1	0	0	0	1	0	0	.200	.333
Rooney, Michael	R-R	5-11	172	8-7-88	.067	.000	.111	3	15	0	1	1	0	0	0	0	0	0	0	5	0	0	.133	.067
Ruettiger, John	L-L	6-1	195	9-21-89	.305	.161	.365	26	105	17	32	6	0	0	13	13	0	0	1	20	10	1	.362	.378
Russell, Steel	L-R	6-0	192	9-5-90	.333	—	.333	1	3	0	1	0	0	0	0	0	0	0	0	0	0	0	.333	.333
Sawyer, Wynston	R-R	6-1	181	11-14-91	.221	.228	.218	86	289	26	64	14	0	2	49	39	4	0	5	52	2	1	.291	.318
Starr, Sammie	R-R	5-8	165	5-31-88	.238	.245	.236	106	369	42	88	25	2	4	41	34	14	2	3	59	9	3	.350	.324
Teagarden, Taylor	R-R	6-2	215	12-21-83	.333	1.000	.143	3	9	0	3	2	0	0	3	2	0	0	1	5	0	0	.556	.417
Velleggia, Joe	R-R	6-7	246	7-23-88	.208	.214	.200	6	24	2	5	2	0	1	4	1	0	0	0	8	0	0	.417	.240
Webb, Brenden	L-L	6-3	190	2-24-90	.251	.211	.267	101	311	51	78	23	4	11	48	87	7	1	3	108	18	3	.457	.422
Winegardner, Tommy	B-R	5-10	189	3-11-90	.174	.087	.206	28	86	7	15	2	0	0	2	3	0	0	1	29	1	0	.198	.226

Pitching	B-T	HT	WT	DOB	W	L	ERA	G	GS	CG	SV	IP	H	R	ER	HR	BB	SO	AVG	vLH	vRH	K/9	BB/9
Baker, David	R-R	6-4	195	4-17-91	2	3	4.66	21	0	0	2	37	38	23	19	2	18	30	.271	.286	.262	7.36	4.42
Beal, Jesse	B-R	6-6	210	7-12-90	2	4	4.70	27	0	0	3	59	71	42	31	4	19	45	.290	.294	.287	6.83	2.88
Beaulac, Eric	R-R	6-5	190	11-13-86	0	1	5.79	4	0	0	0	5	8	3	3	0	6	7	.364	.500	.313	13.50	11.57
Berry, Tim	L-L	6-3	180	3-18-91	2	7	5.02	10	10	0	0	52	60	38	29	3	17	44	.282	.300	.275	7.62	2.94
Bischoff, Matt	R-R	6-0	190	5-21-87	0	0	11.37	6	0	0	0	6	14	8	8	1	4	5	.452	.385	.500	7.11	5.68
Bridwell, Parker	R-R	6-4	190	8-2-91	5	9	5.98	23	22	1	0	114	122	82	76	15	63	71	.281	.285	.278	5.59	4.96
Bundy, Dylan	B-R	6-1	195	11-15-92	1	0	0.00	8	8	0	0	30	5	2	0	0	2	40	.053	.047	.059	12.00	0.60
Bywater, Matt	L-L	6-2	190	6-15-89	1	1	1.56	8	0	0	0	17	8	4	3	1	5	9	.143	.118	.154	4.67	2.60
Chalas, Miguel	R-R	6-0	170	6-27-92	9	8	5.02	24	21	0	0	113	128	76	63	11	43	76	.293	.298	.289	6.05	3.42
Coffey, Cameron	L-L	6-5	215	9-20-90	0	0	4.50	1	0	0	0	2	2	1	1	1	2	0	.250	.000	.286	0.00	9.00
Cowan, Jake	L-R	6-4	195	6-30-88	1	0	2.22	13	0	0	5	28	22	13	7	0	26	23	.227	.163	.278	7.31	8.26
Davies, Zach	R-R	6-0	150	2-7-93	5	7	3.86	25	17	0	1	114	109	52	49	11	46	91	.255	.242	.266	7.16	3.62
Escat, Gene	R-R	6-2	195	9-3-89	3	2	3.96	18	0	0	1	25	24	13	11	3	8	23	.258	.286	.241	8.28	2.88
Fowler, Zach	L-L	6-4	205	2-27-89	0	1	3.18	20	0	0	2	45	43	20	16	3	13	42	.242	.145	.293	8.34	2.58
Guzman, Juan	R-R	6-0	160	2-25-91	1	3	7.08	5	3	0	0	20	30	19	16	4	9	21	.345	.325	.362	9.30	3.98
Howard, Trent	L-L	6-2	200	10-16-89	2	0	1.93	6	0	0	0	23	21	7	5	1	7	16	.247	.250	.246	6.17	2.70
Jones, Devin	R-R	6-2	170	7-4-90	1	6	2.65	19	0	0	3	54	49	20	16	1	11	51	.241	.267	.222	8.45	1.82
Louico, Williams	R-R	6-2	180	4-10-90	0	7	6.06	23	12	0	1	68	60	59	46	4	63	45	.233	.276	.197	5.93	8.30
McCracken, Jason	R-R	6-4	225	9-4-91	1	0	1.08	5	0	0	1	8	12	1	1	0	2	6	.343	.294	.389	6.48	2.16
Moore, Justin	R-R	6-3	190	7-26-89	1	2	5.14	3	3	0	0	14	14	12	8	2	6	7	.275	.333	.233	4.50	3.86
Nivar, Jose	B-R	6-1	170	2-28-89	0	3	10.95	10	0	0	0	12	17	18	15	0	17	13	.304	.190	.371	9.49	12.41
Palsha, Ryan	R-R	6-1	180	5-17-90	0	0	5.68	10	0	0	0	13	11	8	8	2	11	16	.234	.217	.250	11.37	7.82

	B-T	HT	WT	DOB	W	L	ERA	G	GS	CG	SV	IP	H	R	ER	HR	BB	SO	AVG	vLH	vRH	K/9	BB/9
Petersime, Zach	R-R	6-3	175	1-19-89	0	0	2.78	10	0	0	5	23	19	7	7	0	7	10	.241	.222	.256	3.97	2.78
Rivera, Jorge	L-L	6-0	200	10-30-90	0	0	27.00	1	0	0	0	1	1	2	2	0	3	0	.333	.000	.500	0.00	40.50
Rodriguez, Eduardo	L-L	6-2	175	4-7-93	5	7	3.70	22	22	1	0	107	103	56	44	4	30	73	.251	.252	.251	6.14	2.52
Schmarzo, Alex	R-R	6-3	200	2-28-89	0	1	6.14	8	0	0	1	15	16	10	10	1	4	17	.271	.333	.207	10.43	2.45
Taylor, Matt	R-L	6-1	185	4-1-91	5	7	4.33	23	12	2	1	96	103	59	46	7	41	85	.273	.236	.288	8.00	3.86
Wilkins, Bobby	R-R	6-4	225	8-20-89	0	0	1.59	9	0	0	0	11	7	5	2	0	3	4	.167	.235	.120	3.18	2.38
Wilson, Tyler	R-R	6-2	185	9-25-89	3	3	5.06	6	6	0	0	32	30	19	18	4	11	29	.252	.211	.290	8.16	3.09
Wooten, Eric	L-L	6-3	180	3-18-90	2	3	3.46	11	2	0	1	39	37	20	15	4	6	30	.242	.265	.231	6.92	1.38

Fielding

Catcher	PCT	G	PO	A	E	DP	PB
Dalles	1.000	10	87	3	0	1	1
Davis	.959	27	151	11	7	0	10
Lino	.970	51	359	34	12	6	14
Ohlman	.990	14	89	9	1	2	6
Russell	1.000	1	3	0	0	0	0
Sawyer	.984	40	239	14	4	0	10
Teagarden	1.000	2	9	1	0	0	0

First Base	PCT	G	PO	A	E	DP
Delmonico	.978	57	453	32	11	38
Narron	.989	51	437	34	5	37
Sawyer	.987	35	295	14	4	29

Second Base	PCT	G	PO	A	E	DP
Caronia	1.000	4	6	11	0	2
Delmonico	.928	31	51	91	11	22

	PCT	G	PO	A	E	DP
Leonora	.974	11	15	22	1	2
Pena	.967	21	36	51	3	15
Roberts	1.000	2	3	6	0	1
Rooney	1.000	1	4	6	0	3
Starr	.981	56	91	169	5	32
Winegardner	.963	19	28	49	3	8

Third Base	PCT	G	PO	A	E	DP
Esposito	.919	119	83	213	26	15
Leonora	.900	5	5	13	2	1
Narron	.857	7	3	9	2	2
Starr	.963	10	8	18	1	2

Shortstop	PCT	G	PO	A	E	DP
Caronia	1.000	3	4	4	0	2
Givens	.942	89	153	255	25	59
Marin	1.000	6	5	17	0	2

	PCT	G	PO	A	E	DP
Starr	.940	39	62	111	11	19
Winegardner	.909	4	3	7	1	2

Outfield	PCT	G	PO	A	E	DP
Bernadina	.956	31	63	2	3	2
Chavez	1.000	2	2	0	0	0
Davis	.965	100	210	13	8	7
Herbst	.966	13	25	3	1	0
Hoppy	1.000	12	15	1	0	1
Knight	1.000	4	6	0	0	0
Lorenzo	.917	19	43	1	4	0
Narron	.982	46	52	4	1	1
Planeta	.986	77	139	5	2	0
Ruettiger	.959	24	47	0	2	0
Webb	.982	100	207	13	4	1

ABERDEEN IRONBIRDS   SHORT-SEASON

NEW YORK-PENN LEAGUE

Batting	B-T	HT	WT	DOB	AVG	vLH	vRH	G	AB	R	H	2B	3B	HR	RBI	BB	HBP	SH	SF	SO	SB	CS	SLG	OBP
Adams, Ryan	R-R	5-11	185	4-21-87	.333	—	.333	2	6	0	2	0	0	0	1	2	0	0	0	1	0	0	.333	.500
Baker, Aaron	L-R	6-2	220	9-10-87	.250	—	.250	1	4	0	1	1	0	0	0	0	0	0	0	2	0	0	.500	.250
Bernadina, Roderick	R-R	6-1	162	8-10-92	.259	.243	.266	30	116	19	30	5	1	0	14	9	1	0	2	19	4	0	.319	.313
Boss, Torsten	L-R	6-0	190	12-27-90	.257	.237	.264	65	237	33	61	14	4	5	27	30	8	0	0	53	9	3	.414	.360
Bream, Doug	L-L	6-2	205	5-30-89	.260	.143	.279	15	50	7	13	5	0	1	11	1	3	1	0	2	0	0	.420	.315
Caronia, Anthony	L-R	6-0	170	5-22-91	.233	.250	.228	33	103	13	24	1	2	1	7	12	1	0	1	26	10	4	.311	.316
Davis, Adam	R-R	6-0	205	12-15-89	.000	.000	.000	1	3	0	0	0	0	0	0	0	0	0	0	1	0	0	.000	.000
Edman, Cameron	R-R	6-3	205	6-17-88	.211	.268	.189	42	152	14	32	9	0	4	24	9	1	0	2	40	0	0	.349	.256
Herbst, Lucas	L-L	5-10	185	9-9-90	.270	.179	.292	38	141	21	38	7	4	1	16	2	4	1	3	23	2	2	.397	.293
Hernandez, Manuel	R-R	6-1	190	8-19-92	.180	.222	.171	15	50	3	9	3	0	0	4	4	4	0	2	12	0	1	.240	.283
Howard, Will	L-L	6-3	170	1-6-89	.217	.102	.246	65	240	21	52	8	0	0	20	18	1	2	4	50	13	3	.250	.270
Hutter, Joel	R-R	6-1	210	2-28-90	.257	.264	.254	64	245	22	63	16	1	0	30	21	1	0	1	30	3	0	.331	.317
Kalush, Scott	R-R	6-1	215	3-22-90	.138	.242	.082	35	94	7	13	1	0	0	5	18	1	2	0	30	1	2	.149	.283
Kimmel, Sam	L-R	6-0	185	11-3-89	.282	.231	.292	47	163	21	46	4	3	3	18	14	3	1	2	20	9	3	.399	.346
Leonora, Dudley	R-R	6-1	154	12-15-91	.200	.211	.188	12	35	1	7	2	0	0	3	2	0	0	0	5	0	0	.257	.243
Lorenzo, Gregory	R-R	6-0	160	5-31-91	.317	.250	.333	9	41	8	13	1	0	0	6	1	2	1	0	5	6	1	.341	.364
Mercedes, Alexander	R-R	6-0	160	3-20-92	.267	.750	.091	3	15	0	4	1	0	0	0	0	0	0	0	3	0	0	.333	.267
Ortiz, Roberto	R-R	6-1	195	10-28-88	.169	.148	.188	16	59	6	10	4	0	0	8	5	0	0	1	17	3	0	.237	.231
Pena, Jerome	B-R	5-11	185	11-6-88	.319	.250	.355	13	47	6	15	0	2	1	8	5	3	0	2	12	1	1	.468	.404
Perez, Pedro	R-R	5-11	170	5-8-91	.107	.182	.059	8	28	1	3	1	0	0	3	2	0	0	0	9	0	0	.143	.167
Richards, Kris	R-R	6-0	190	12-6-89	.077	.250	.000	4	13	0	1	0	0	0	1	0	0	0	0	5	0	0	.077	.143
Roberts, Brian	B-R	5-9	175	10-9-77	.000	.000	.000	1	4	1	0	0	0	0	0	1	0	0	0	2	0	0	.000	.200
Segui, Cory	R-R	6-1	200	12-20-91	.100	.000	.125	3	10	1	1	0	0	0	1	2	0	0	0	6	0	0	.100	.308
Simpson, Creede	R-R	6-2	185	9-8-89	.234	.164	.258	62	239	29	56	6	3	5	28	22	1	1	2	60	4	0	.347	.299
Townsend, Tyler	L-R	6-3	215	5-14-88	.429	.667	.250	4	14	3	6	4	0	0	1	0	0	1	0	1	0	0	.571	.500
Vega, Anthony	L-R	6-0	190	12-6-90	.194	.113	.218	64	232	34	45	7	5	4	17	33	4	3	1	69	14	2	.319	.304
Velleggia, Joe	R-R	6-7	246	7-23-88	.107	.091	.118	7	28	3	3	2	1	0	1	0	0	0	0	10	0	0	.250	.138
Veloz, Hector	R-R	6-2	192	2-1-94	.219	.182	.238	8	32	3	7	2	0	0	1	0	1	0	0	11	0	0	.281	.242
Walker, Christian	R-R	6-0	220	3-28-91	.284	.286	.283	22	81	12	23	5	0	2	9	10	2	0	0	14	2	1	.420	.376
Weems, Chase	L-R	6-2	190	1-17-89	.190	.000	.211	11	21	2	4	2	0	1	2	0	1	0	0	8	0	0	.429	.227
Welty, Ronnie	R-R	6-3	204	1-19-88	.700	.750	.667	3	10	5	7	2	0	2	8	5	0	0	0	1	0	0	1.500	.800
Winegardner, Tommy	R-R	5-10	189	3-31-90	.194	.100	.238	9	36	3	7	1	0	1	3	0	3	0	2	6	2	0	.355	.342

Pitching	B-T	HT	WT	DOB	W	L	ERA	G	GS	CG	SV	IP	H	R	ER	HR	BB	SO	AVG	vLH	vRH	K/9	BB/9
Beck, Sander	R-R	6-3	215	10-3-90	4	3	2.44	17	0	0	1	44	28	18	12	4	21	59	.177	.153	.198	11.98	4.26
Blackmar, Mark	R-R	6-3	215	4-28-92	4	3	3.57	14	7	0	0	63	65	33	25	1	23	29	.272	.295	.261	4.14	3.29
Coffey, Cameron	L-L	6-5	215	9-20-90	3	5	5.23	13	7	0	0	53	55	37	31	4	23	33	.274	.333	.256	5.57	3.88
Escat, Gene	R-R	6-2	195	9-3-89	0	0	2.35	7	0	0	0	8	6	2	2	0	5	5	.231	.429	.158	5.87	5.87
Esquivel, Jaime	R-R	6-2	190	5-25-92	2	3	7.20	8	4	0	0	25	28	24	20	2	19	29	.275	.306	.258	10.44	6.84
Fernandez, Jesse	R-R	6-2	225	1-24-90	0	1	2.79	10	0	0	0	19	20	6	6	0	11	15	.270	.273	.268	6.98	5.12
Gausman, Kevin	R-R	6-4	185	1-6-91	0	0	0.00	2	2	0	0	6	1	0	0	0	5	8	.053	.000	.071	7.50	0.00
Guzman, Juan	R-R	6-0	160	2-25-91	2	0	1.66	7	7	0	0	38	27	12	7	3	11	43	.190	.230	.160	10.18	2.61
Hader, Josh	L-L	6-3	160	4-7-94	0	0	0.00	5	0	0	0	8	2	0	0	0	2	13	.074	.000	.087	14.04	2.16
Jimenez, Enrico	L-L	6-3	195	2-7-89	0	2	5.63	8	0	0	0	16	17	14	10	1	18	10	.258	.417	.222	5.63	10.13
Kline, Branden	R-R	6-3	195	9-29-91	0	0	4.50	4	4	0	0	12	12	7	6	1	4	12	.273	.474	.120	9.00	3.00

Pitching (cont.)	B-T	HT	WT	DOB	W	L	ERA	G	GS	CG	SV	IP	H	R	ER	HR	BB	SO	AVG	vLH	vRH	K/9	BB/9
McCracken, Jason	R-R	6-4	225	9-4-91	1	1	2.53	5	0	0	0	11	10	4	3	0	1	1	.263	.316	.211	0.84	0.84
Medina, Jhondaniel	R-R	5-11	158	2-8-93	0	0	9.00	1	0	0	0	4	3	4	4	0	3	3	.200	.000	.214	6.75	6.75
Nivar, Jose	B-R	6-1	170	2-28-89	2	3	4.68	20	0	0	2	33	25	23	17	0	30	27	.214	.359	.141	7.44	8.27
Palsha, Ryan	R-R	6-1	180	5-17-90	0	0	11.25	2	0	0	0	4	7	5	5	1	3	1	.412	.000	.538	2.25	6.75
Parry, Bennett	L-L	6-6	225	8-7-91	0	3	2.63	11	0	0	1	27	24	12	8	0	12	26	.242	.185	.264	8.56	3.95
Petersime, Zach	R-R	6-3	175	1-19-89	0	0	3.00	1	0	0	0	3	4	1	1	0	0	0	.364	1.000	.222	0.00	0.00
Pinales, Elias	R-R	6-4	155	11-7-92	0	0	9.53	3	0	0	0	6	8	6	6	0	4	9	.320	.000	.364	14.29	6.35
Richardson, David	R-R	5-11	170	1-31-91	3	4	5.58	15	12	0	0	61	63	45	38	3	37	54	.268	.272	.265	7.92	5.43
Rivera, Jorge	L-L	6-0	200	10-30-90	1	3	3.26	8	8	0	0	30	21	13	11	0	21	34	.194	.143	.213	10.09	6.23
Rutledge, Lex	L-L	6-1	195	6-28-91	0	3	9.49	6	6	0	0	12	16	17	13	1	13	12	.291	.250	.302	8.76	9.49
Salas, Domingo	R-R	6-2	155	5-11-91	0	0	0.00	1	0	0	0	1	1	2	0	0	2	1	.200	.000	.333	9.00	18.00
Santana, Alexander	B-R	5-11	170	8-26-91	1	0	0.00	1	0	0	0	4	1	0	0	0	2	3	.083	.000	.143	6.75	4.50
Schmarzo, Alex	R-R	6-3	200	2-28-89	0	0	1.77	10	0	0	1	20	11	4	4	1	4	15	.157	.161	.154	6.64	1.77
Severino, Janser	R-R	6-2	140	9-16-91	0	0	0.00	3	0	0	1	3	1	0	0	1	4		.111	.000	.143	13.50	3.38
Vader, Sebastian	R-R	6-4	175	6-3-92	1	8	3.71	14	13	0	0	70	77	36	29	1	24	49	.274	.284	.267	6.27	3.07
Wager, Brady	R-R	6-3	190	11-17-90	0	2	5.06	6	6	0	0	27	30	20	15	2	6	18	.286	.258	.297	6.08	2.03
Ward, Dustin	L-L	6-0	175	2-27-90	0	0	12.00	3	0	0	0	6	11	8	8	0	7	10	.393	.375	.400	15.00	10.50
Wilkins, Bobby	R-R	6-4	225	8-20-89	1	1	4.66	12	0	0	1	19	25	13	10	2	7	22	.298	.333	.278	10.24	3.26
Wise, Ken	R-R	6-6	225	4-7-90	1	2	5.63	10	0	0	0	16	15	13	10	0	19	11	.250	.286	.219	6.19	10.69

Fielding

Catcher	PCT	G	PO	A	E	DP	PB
Davis	.889	1	7	1	1	0	0
Kalush	.981	35	280	34	6	0	11
Kimmel	.976	30	180	27	5	2	11
Perez	.959	8	40	7	2	0	1
Weems	1.000	9	47	4	0	1	3

First Base	PCT	G	PO	A	E	DP
Bream	.990	12	98	3	1	6
Edman	.992	41	329	40	3	34
Leonora	1.000	1	2	0	0	0
Townsend	1.000	3	22	1	0	2
Velleggia	1.000	3	29	1	0	4
Veloz	.943	3	31	2	2	2
Walker	.981	17	144	11	3	17

Second Base	PCT	G	PO	A	E	DP
Adams	.917	2	4	7	1	3
Caronia	.926	9	13	12	2	1
Leonora	1.000	1	0	3	0	0
Pena	.973	12	33	39	2	12
Richards	1.000	1	4	3	0	1
Roberts	1.000	1	1	2	0	1
Simpson	.963	47	91	120	8	35
Winegardner	1.000	4	8	5	0	1

Third Base	PCT	G	PO	A	E	DP
Boss	.932	57	38	98	10	4
Caronia	1.000	6	2	14	0	0
Leonora	1.000	10	9	13	0	0
Segui	.875	3	1	6	1	0
Veloz	.833	2	1	4	1	1

Shortstop	PCT	G	PO	A	E	DP
Caronia	.933	16	20	36	4	8
Hutter	.940	55	104	180	18	42
Richards	.941	3	5	11	1	5
Winegardner	.955	3	6	15	1	3

Outfield	PCT	G	PO	A	E	DP
Bernadina	.952	29	56	4	3	0
Herbst	1.000	31	45	4	0	0
Hernandez	1.000	15	17	3	0	0
Howard	.969	63	123	4	4	1
Lorenzo	.947	9	18	0	1	0
Mercedes	.833	3	5	0	1	0
Ortiz	1.000	13	16	1	0	0
Simpson	1.000	3	4	0	0	0
Vega	.985	63	127	1	2	0
Welty	1.000	2	3	0	0	0

GCL ORIOLES   ROOKIE
GULF COAST LEAGUE

Batting	B-T	HT	WT	DOB	AVG	vLH	vRH	G	AB	R	H	2B	3B	HR	RBI	BB	HBP	SH	SF	SO	SB	CS	SLG	OBP
Adams, Ryan	R-R	5-11	185	4-21-87	.167	.000	.333	2	6	1	1	0	0	0	1	0	0	0	1	0	0		.167	.286
Aguilar, Andres	R-R	5-11	175	1-12-94	.234	.310	.207	37	111	14	26	5	0	0	6	4	2	0	2	5	2	1	.279	.298
Balog, Nik	L-L	6-3	220	10-14-89	.376	.200	.414	28	85	9	32	12	1	0	10	6	2	0	0	10	0	0	.541	.430
Bleeker, Derrick	R-R	6-5	220	3-11-91	.238	.400	.216	14	42	3	10	2	1	0	2	4	0	0	0	9	2	0	.333	.304
Capellan, Byron	R-R	5-11	150	8-9-93	.203	.200	.204	42	133	15	27	6	0	0	6	6	2	4	1	13	2	1	.248	.246
Caronia, Anthony	L-R	6-0	170	5-22-91	.500	.400	.571	3	12	1	6	0	0	0	3	0	1	0	0	2	1	1	.500	.538
Chavez, Endy	L-L	6-0	170	2-7-78	.000	—	.000	1	4	0	0	0	0	0	0	0	0	0	0	2	0	0	.000	.000
Exposito, Luis	R-R	6-3	210	1-20-87	.235	.333	.182	5	17	1	4	0	0	0	1	0	0	0	0	0	0	0	.235	.235
Frantini, Brett	R-R		210	2-7-90	.000	.000	.000	3	5	1	0	0	0	0	0	1	0	0	0	3	0	0	.000	.286
Graham, Jack	R-R	5-10	190	10-23-89	.118	.200	.083	17	34	0	4	0	0	0	0	4	1	0	0	16	0	0	.118	.231
Hernandez, Manuel	R-R	6-1	190	8-19-92	.234	.241	.232	46	154	17	36	6	1	3	19	12	5	0	2	36	1	2	.344	.306
Hunnicutt, Ray	R-R	5-11	180	12-17-93	.170	.167	.171	27	94	10	16	1	0	1	6	13	4	0	1	23	9	2	.213	.295
Kalush, Scott	R-R	6-1	215	3-22-90	—	—	—	1	0	0	0	0	0	0	0	0	0	0	0	0	0	0	—	—
Lartiguez, Oswill	R-R	6-1	179	8-11-92	.170	.500	.081	16	47	4	8	1	0	0	2	3	0	0	0	7	0	0	.191	.220
Lorenzo, Gregory	R-R	6-0	160	5-31-91	.316	.333	.310	25	76	9	24	4	3	2	7	3	5	0	0	15	4	3	.526	.381
Marin, Adrian	R-R	6-0	165	3-8-94	.287	.297	.284	47	178	24	51	7	3	0	13	11	3	1	0	34	6	1	.360	.339
Mercedes, Alexander	R-R	6-0	160	3-20-92	.185	.200	.176	7	27	3	5	0	0	0	2	0	2	0	2	3	1		.185	.241
Murphy, Tanner	L-R	6-1	190	7-4-92	.188	.067	.222	22	69	4	13	2	0	0	6	7	0	2	0	9	0	0	.217	.263
Ohlman, Michael	R-R	6-4	205	12-14-90	.276	.286	.273	8	29	5	8	3	0	1	3	2	0	0	0	10	1	0	.483	.323
Pellegrino, Dan	R-R	5-11	190	11-2-88	.194	.000	.226	16	36	1	7	2	0	0	4	3	2	0	1	9	0	0	.250	.286
Richards, Kris	R-R	6-0	190	12-6-89	.127	.000	.165	37	118	11	15	4	0	1	14	14	4	4	2	39	4	1	.186	.239
Richards, Tommy	R-R	5-11	195	4-27-90	.221	.208	.225	34	113	14	25	5	0	0	6	5	2	2	3	16	2	2	.265	.260
Russell, Steel	L-R	6-0	192	9-5-90	.180	.240	.165	39	128	7	23	2	1	0	11	9	1	0	2	22	0	0	.211	.236
Segui, Cory	R-R	6-0	200	12-20-91	.133	.000	.333	5	15	1	2	0	0	0	1	1	0	0	1	5	0	0	.133	.176
Simmons, Jalen	R-R	6-4	195	3-16-93	.172	.071	.205	38	116	11	20	5	1	1	9	8	3	0	1	52	2	2	.259	.242
Teagarden, Taylor	R-R	6-0	215	12-21-83	.125	.333	.000	3	8	0	1	0	0	0	0	2	1	0	0	2	0	0	.125	.364
Townsend, Tyler	L-R	6-3	215	5-14-88	.152	.143	.154	10	33	3	5	1	0	3	8	3	0	0	0	12	0	0	.455	.222
Veloz, Hector	R-R	6-2	192	2-1-94	.281	.320	.271	34	121	14	34	9	2	3	18	8	3	0	1	30	0	0	.463	.338
Welty, Ronnie	R-R	6-3	204	1-19-88	.200	.000	.222	3	10	1	2	1	0	0	0	2	0	0	0	3	0	0	.300	.333

Pitching	B-T	HT	WT	DOB	W	L	ERA	G	GS	CG	SV	IP	H	R	ER	HR	BB	SO	AVG	vLH	vRH	K/9	BB/9
Figuereo, Jose	R-R	6-1	190	3-23-92	0	0	3.93	16	0	0	6	18	16	8	8	0	11	16	.239	.241	.237	7.85	5.40
Green, Chris	R-R	6-3	225	6-5-89	1	0	0.00	3	0	0	0	5	2	0	0	0	0	10	.125	.400	.000	18.00	0.00

	B-T	HT	WT	DOB	W	L	ERA	G	GS	CG	SV	IP	H	R	ER	HR	BB	SO	AVG	vLH	vRH	K/9	BB/9
Grendell, Kevin	L-L	6-2	185	8-22-93	0	4	7.27	7	7	0	0	17	17	15	14	2	11	29	.254	.200	.263	15.06	5.71
Grim, Nick	R-R	6-3	190	1-16-91	0	0	11.74	6	0	0	0	8	12	10	10	0	9	4	.414	.412	.417	4.70	10.57
Hader, Josh	L-L	6-3	160	4-7-94	2	0	2.66	12	0	0	2	20	12	7	6	2	7	35	.174	.167	.176	15.49	3.10
Lin, Yi-Hsiang	L-L	6-0	175	12-16-92	0	5	6.68	11	5	0	0	32	40	35	24	1	16	22	.294	.200	.310	6.12	4.45
Lindstrom, Matt	R-R	6-3	220	2-11-80	0	0	4.50	2	2	0	0	2	2	1	1	0	0	2	.250	.250	.250	9.00	0.00
McAdams, Sean	R-R	6-6	210	11-17-93	3	0	6.27	13	0	0	0	19	24	16	13	0	12	20	.304	.412	.222	9.64	5.79
McCracken, Jason	R-R	6-4	225	9-4-91	2	2	3.43	5	4	0	0	21	18	9	8	0	10	15	.231	.125	.304	6.43	4.29
Medina, Jhondaniel	R-R	5-11	158	2-8-93	1	3	3.72	10	7	0	2	46	33	20	19	2	17	47	.205	.190	.214	9.20	3.33
Parry, Bennett	L-L	6-6	225	8-7-91	1	1	2.79	4	3	0	0	19	13	6	6	1	2	26	.186	.150	.200	12.10	0.93
Pinales, Elias	L-L	6-4	155	11-7-92	2	3	2.48	8	7	0	0	36	30	13	10	1	9	33	.233	.056	.261	8.17	2.23
Pineiro, Joel	R-R	6-0	200	9-25-78	0	0	2.25	3	3	0	0	12	9	4	3	0	1	10	.205	.176	.222	7.50	0.75
Pintar, Jake	L-R	6-7	200	2-13-94	0	2	3.57	11	0	0	0	18	19	8	7	2	9	11	.279	.240	.302	5.60	4.58
Porter, Duke	L-L	6-4	185	11-19-91	0	0	1.80	6	0	0	0	10	6	2	2	0	4	5	.162	.000	.194	4.50	3.60
Rennie, Luc	R-R	6-2	200	2-26-94	1	1	3.04	12	0	0	1	27	24	10	9	0	9	27	.245	.333	.206	9.11	3.04
Rosan, Joe	R-R	6-0	190	2-25-91	0	0	0.00	3	0	0	0	4	1	0	0	1	4	.077	.000	.100	9.00	2.25
Rutledge, Lex	L-L	6-1	195	6-28-91	0	1	1.64	6	0	0	0	11	9	6	2	0	3	13	.220	.250	.212	10.64	2.45
Salas, Domingo	R-R	6-2	170	5-11-91	3	2	3.96	12	5	0	1	36	45	18	16	1	14	34	.310	.403	.241	8.42	3.47
Santana, Alexander	B-R	5-11	170	8-26-91	3	1	3.38	6	6	0	0	29	23	15	11	0	12	33	.217	.185	.228	10.13	3.68
Schreurs, Ron	L-L	6-6	205	7-14-92	0	0	0.00	2	0	0	0	3	0	0	0	0	1	3	.000	.000	.000	9.00	3.00
Severino, Janser	R-R	6-2	140	9-16-91	1	5	4.89	13	4	0	0	39	41	25	21	0	11	38	.268	.262	.272	8.84	2.56
Torres, Dennis	R-R	6-3	200	5-17-90	0	0	0.00	2	0	0	0	2	2	0	0	0	0	2	.222	.250	.200	7.71	0.00
Wager, Brady	R-R	6-3	190	11-17-90	0	2	4.26	6	3	0	0	13	15	8	6	0	5	12	.288	.385	.192	8.53	3.55
Wooten, Eric	L-L	6-3	180	3-18-90	2	0	0.00	3	2	0	0	14	7	0	0	0	3	15	.149	.353	.033	9.64	1.93
Yermal, Joe	R-R	6-7	205	8-27-88	0	2	1.42	5	2	0	1	13	12	4	2	0	0	9	.250	.063	.344	6.39	0.00

Fielding

Catcher	PCT	G	PO	A	E	DP	PB
Exposito	1.000	3	20	6	0	0	3
Frantini	1.000	2	8	1	0	0	0
Graham	1.000	9	41	4	0	0	5
Kalush	1.000	1	1	0	0	0	0
Murphy	.994	19	152	22	1	1	4
Pellegrino	1.000	7	33	5	0	0	1
Russell	.981	29	232	29	5	2	12
Teagarden	1.000	2	8	3	0	0	0

First Base	PCT	G	PO	A	E	DP
Balog	.991	27	204	11	2	14
Graham	—	1	0	0	0	0
Ohlman	1.000	2	17	3	0	1
Pellegrino	1.000	3	15	3	0	1
Richards	.986	18	133	6	2	9
Russell	1.000	3	12	1	0	2

	PCT	G	PO	A	E	DP
Schreurs	1.000	5	39	3	0	2
Townsend	1.000	7	45	3	0	2
Veloz	.875	1	7	0	1	1

Second Base	PCT	G	PO	A	E	DP
Adams	1.000	1	1	1	0	0
Capellan	.976	14	16	24	1	4
Caronia	.933	3	5	9	1	0
Mercedes	.875	7	3	11	2	1
Richards	1.000	7	14	14	0	3
Richards	.967	30	47	71	4	11

Third Base	PCT	G	PO	A	E	DP
Capellan	.955	12	4	17	1	2
Richards	.931	11	6	21	2	0
Richards	1.000	3	3	3	0	1
Segui	.917	5	3	8	1	1

	PCT	G	PO	A	E	DP
Veloz	.877	32	21	50	10	4

Shortstop	PCT	G	PO	A	E	DP
Capellan	.958	15	8	38	2	6
Marin	.944	42	53	100	9	16
Richards	1.000	4	5	6	0	1

Outfield	PCT	G	PO	A	E	DP
Aguilar	.983	33	56	3	1	1
Bleeker	1.000	9	13	0	0	0
Chavez	1.000	1	2	0	0	0
Hernandez	.971	38	64	3	2	0
Hunnicutt	.970	27	64	0	2	0
Lartiguez	.913	16	19	2	2	0
Lorenzo	.981	24	51	1	1	0
Simmons	.925	36	46	3	4	2
Welty	1.000	2	5	0	0	0

DSL ORIOLES   ROOKIE

DOMINICAN SUMMER LEAGUE

Batting	B-T	HT	WT	DOB	AVG	vLH	vRH	G	AB	R	H	2B	3B	HR	RBI	BB	HBP	SH	SF	SO	SB	CS	SLG	OBP
Alexander, Rochendiad	R-R	6-3	189	11-10-94	.210	.160	.232	22	81	11	17	4	0	0	4	5	2	0	0	28	3	3	.259	.273
Cabrera, Jacniel	R-R	5-11	140	6-11-95	.183	.263	.154	31	71	12	13	0	0	0	4	8	4	2	0	22	7	3	.183	.301
Duran, Brailyn	R-R	6-3	170	11-10-93	.186	.256	.158	42	140	15	26	7	1	2	19	8	2	2	2	36	3	3	.293	.237
Fajardo, Daniel	R-R	6-1	170	11-19-94	.175	.227	.160	33	97	5	17	3	0	0	6	6	0	2	0	18	1	1	.206	.223
Labrador, Alexander	R-R	6-2	190	10-27-94	.177	.143	.196	34	79	9	14	0	0	0	6	10	1	4	0	19	4	2	.177	.278
Lamas, Sergio	B-R	6-0	176	11-26-93	.244	.222	.255	33	82	15	20	6	0	0	9	18	3	1	0	25	1	6	.317	.398
Larez, Carlos	R-R	5-11	160	5-11-93	.220	.148	.255	41	82	14	18	2	1	0	7	14	6	7	0	24	8	4	.268	.373
Ledesma, Ronarsy	R-R	5-11	170	4-19-93	.343	.397	.322	68	245	35	84	18	8	2	41	26	15	1	5	43	19	10	.506	.430
Magallanes, Neomar	R-R	5-11	180	8-13-92	.000	.000	.000	10	14	0	0	0	0	0	0	1	1	0	0	4	0	0	.000	.125
Martinez, Rockny	B-R	6-2	175	7-14-92	.218	.139	.253	63	234	25	51	6	3	1	17	16	9	7	1	50	12	4	.282	.292
Medina, Victor	R-R	6-0	180	11-20-94	.189	.122	.217	48	164	16	31	12	1	1	13	5	3	2	3	50	0	3	.293	.223
Mena, Kelvin	R-R	6-0	200	6-1-93	.185	.244	.164	55	157	20	29	8	1	1	12	34	7	2	0	58	4	1	.268	.354
Mercedes, Alexander	R-R	6-0	160	3-20-92	.289	.177	.341	63	246	36	71	3	10	1	21	27	4	9	1	23	23	12	.394	.367
Mora, Ivan	R-R	6-1	171	7-22-94	.234	.289	.211	47	128	18	30	8	2	0	14	4	4	5	3	31	8	4	.328	.273
Pezzarossi, Paolo	R-R	6-1	200	3-27-93	.100	.063	.114	19	60	3	6	1	0	0	4	0	1	0	0	30	1	0	.117	.156
Pichardo, Miguel	L-L	6-1	160	10-21-94	.198	.190	.202	49	126	22	25	6	1	1	7	31	2	1	2	50	3	1	.286	.360
Taveras, Junior	R-R	5-10	187	12-28-92	.358	.263	.387	26	81	8	29	7	1	0	20	5	2	0	2	4	1	0	.469	.400
Vargas, Yariel	R-R	6-0	180	3-29-94	.182	.000	.200	4	11	3	2	0	0	0	1	0	0	0	0	2	0	0	.182	.400
Vasquez, Oscar	B-R	5-11	150	11-22-93	.267	.175	.304	62	221	45	59	7	4	1	30	31	2	4	1	40	18	7	.348	.361

Pitching	B-T	HT	WT	DOB	W	L	ERA	G	GS	CG	SV	IP	H	R	ER	HR	BB	SO	AVG	vLH	vRH	K/9	BB/9
Alvarado, Cristian	R-R	6-2	165	9-20-94	2	3	3.68	13	13	0	0	66	58	31	27	1	21	51	.237	.255	.223	6.95	2.86
Aquino, Wilmer	L-L	5-9	170	12-5-91	3	4	2.92	14	14	0	0	71	59	39	23	0	41	73	.226	.269	.215	9.25	5.20
Bolivar, Miguel	R-R	6-0	180	11-2-94	3	3	5.23	17	0	0	0	33	38	25	19	0	21	18	.279	.317	.250	4.96	5.79
Cuevas, Yanuel	R-R	5-11	180	10-25-93	0	0	0.00	1	0	0	0	1	0	0	0	0	1	0	.000	.000	.000	0.00	9.00
Duran, Elvis	R-R	6-7	235	6-11-94	0	0	6.75	6	0	0	0	8	12	9	6	2	7	8	.333	.400	.286	9.00	7.88
Floranus, Wendell	R-R	6-0	158	4-16-95	6	6	4.69	14	11	1	1	63	68	40	33	3	14	41	.272	.239	.299	5.83	1.99
Garcia, Miguel	R-R	6-1	180	3-24-93	4	3	2.82	12	12	1	0	73	66	27	23	2	17	54	.246	.213	.274	6.63	2.09

Gomez, Carlos	L-L	6-3	190	2-12-94	0	0	9.00	12	0	0	0	13	18	15	13	0	16	12	.316	.667	.275	8.31	11.08
Isenia, Jonatan	R-R	6-2	180	3-31-93	0	1	1.47	13	0	0	0	18	14	7	3	0	3	10	.209	.208	.209	4.91	1.47
Jimenez, Francisco	R-R	6-1	160	10-4-94	3	0	1.52	11	0	0	1	30	23	12	5	0	12	16	.211	.271	.164	4.85	3.64
Marrugo, Yeizer	R-R	6-0	170	10-1-94	1	2	1.44	13	2	0	1	25	12	7	4	0	20	20	.141	.077	.196	7.20	7.20
Mercedes, Daniel	R-R	6-4	180	5-12-92	2	2	1.29	23	0	0	9	35	32	15	5	0	9	28	.242	.231	.250	7.20	2.31
Moreno, Rafael	R-R	6-0	200	2-11-95	2	3	3.86	14	12	0	1	65	56	34	28	3	22	59	.230	.263	.198	8.13	3.03
Perez, Julio	R-R	6-2	175	1-16-92	1	1	3.32	18	0	0	1	22	18	16	8	0	19	14	.222	.156	.265	5.82	7.89
Pinales, Elias	L-L	6-4	155	11-7-92	1	1	5.85	5	5	0	0	20	20	14	13	1	9	22	.250	.500	.222	9.90	4.05
Salas, Johan	R-R	6-2	195	11-11-94	3	3	3.49	13	1	0	0	28	32	16	11	1	14	16	.283	.283	.284	5.08	4.45
Santana, Alexander	B-R	5-11	170	8-26-91	2	3	1.86	12	0	0	2	29	14	10	6	0	10	38	.147	.184	.123	11.79	3.10

Fielding

Catcher	PCT	G	PO	A	E	DP	PB
Fajardo	.985	32	170	27	3	0	8
Labrador	.990	33	185	20	2	2	14
Magallanes	.966	5	25	3	1	0	1
Taveras	.948	18	103	25	7	0	4

First Base	PCT	G	PO	A	E	DP
Magallanes	1.000	2	3	0	0	0
Medina	.981	26	188	21	4	20
Mena	.980	52	409	31	9	29
Mercedes	1.000	4	13	0	0	0
Taveras	1.000	2	5	0	0	0

Second Base	PCT	G	PO	A	E	DP
Cabrera	1.000	10	12	22	0	0
Lamas	1.000	6	6	8	0	3
Mercedes	.971	18	48	53	3	12
Vasquez	.923	45	64	116	15	14

Third Base	PCT	G	PO	A	E	DP
Ledesma	.888	67	56	127	23	8
Pichardo	.900	6	5	4	1	0

Shortstop	PCT	G	PO	A	E	DP
Cabrera	.918	18	27	40	6	3
Lamas	.917	20	35	53	8	12

	PCT	G	PO	A	E	DP
Pichardo	.901	45	76	107	20	23

Outfield	PCT	G	PO	A	E	DP
Alexander	.951	22	38	1	2	0
Duran	.954	40	59	3	3	2
Lamas	—	1	0	0	0	0
Larez	.984	33	53	7	1	1
Martinez	.971	54	65	3	2	1
Medina	1.000	4	5	1	0	0
Mercedes	.975	31	72	6	2	1
Mora	.969	39	61	1	2	0
Pezzarossi	1.000	9	13	0	0	0
Vargas	1.000	3	4	0	0	0

Boston Red Sox

SEASON IN A SENTENCE: For the Red Sox, 2012 was as embarrassing as 2011 was painful.

HIGH POINT: Four days after new manager Bobby Valentine left Jon Lester in to give up 11 runs to the Blue Jays on July 22, players met with owner John Henry and president Larry Lucchino to blast the manager. At that point, the Red Sox were on the fringe of wild-card contention with a 49-50 record. Yes, this passes for a high point in the Red Sox' worst season since 1965.

LOW POINT: The Red Sox went on a pronounced slide after the meeting that prompted a fire sale, which provides flexibility for the future but destroyed the present. They won just nine of their last 36 games, finishing at 69-93. Boston fired Valentine the day after the end of the season and traded Mike Aviles to get manager John Farrell from the Blue Jays. Ben Cherington, who was promoted to take over from departed GM Theo Epstein, hadn't wanted to hire Valentine in the first place, but ownership pushed him on Cherington. Concerns that Valentine's outspoken personality wouldn't mesh well with a veteran club quickly came true. He alienated many of his players by calling out Aviles during spring training and Kevin Youkilis in April.

NOTABLE ROOKIES: In the midst of all the bad news, young players did provide positive developments in Boston, with Will Middlebrooks homering 15 times in 75 games and fellow rookie Felix Doubront tying for the team lead with 11 victories.

KEY TRANSACTIONS: When Boston dropped 16 of 27 games at the end of July and into August, ownership and Cherington decided to blow up the roster. The Red Sox shipped Adrian Gonzalez and Carl Crawford, who joined the club in blockbuster moves three days apart in December 2010, to the Dodgers, along with Josh Beckett and Nick Punto. Boston shed $261 million in salary commitments and acquired a pair of quality arms in Rubby de la Rosa and Allen Webster, along with James Loney, Jerry Sands and Ivan DeJesus Jr. The club also jettisoned Youkilis to the White Sox in June.

DOWN ON THE FARM: Shortstop Xander Bogaerts continued to develop rapidly while several 2011 draft picks (outfielder Jackie Bradley, righthander Matt Barnes, lefthander Henry Owens, catcher Blake Swihart) provided intriguing early returns. Triple-A Pawtucket also won the International League title.

OPENING DAY PAYROLL: $173.2 million (3rd)

PLAYERS OF THE YEAR

MAJOR LEAGUE	MINOR LEAGUE
Dustin Pedroia 2b	**Xander Bogaerts** ss
.290/.347/.449	(High A/Double-A)
15 HR/20 SB	.307/.373/.523
Led team in R, H, 2B	20 HR at age 19

ORGANIZATIONAL LEADERS

BATTING   *Minimum 250 AB

MAJORS

* AVG	Adrian Gonzalez	.300
* OPS	Adrian Gonzalez	.812
HR	Jarrod Saltalamacchia	25
RBI	Adrian Gonzalez	86

MINORS

* AVG	J.C. Linares, Portland/Pawtucket	.316
* OBP	Jackie Bradley, Salem/Portland	.430
* SLG	Mauro Gomez, Pawtucket	.589
R	Jackie Bradley, Salem/Portland	90
H	Keury De La Cruz, Greenville/Salem	153
TB	Keury De La Cruz, Greenville/Salem	266
2B	Travis Shaw, Salem/Portland	44
3B	Keury De La Cruz, Greenville/Salem	8
	Raymel Flores, DSL Red Sox	8
HR	Mauro Gomez, Pawtucket	24
RBI	Keury De La Cruz, Greenville/Salem	87
BB	Jackie Bradley, Salem/Portland	87
SO	Bryce Brentz, Portland/Pawtucket	136
SB	Garin Cecchini, Greenville	51

PITCHING   #Minimum 75 IP

MAJORS

W	Clay Buchholz	11
	Felix Doubront	11
# ERA	Clay Buchholz	4.56
SO	Felix Doubront	167
SV	Alfredo Aceves	25

MINORS

W	Billy Buckner, Portland/Pawtucket	12
	Henry Owens, Greenville	12
L	Drake Britton, Salem/Portland	12
	Chris Hernandez, Portland/Pawtucket	12
# ERA	Matt Barnes, Greenville/Salem	2.86
G	Tyler Lockwood, Salem/Greenville	48
GS	Billy Buckner, Portland/Pawtucket	27
SV	Michael Olmsted, Salem/Portland	19
IP	Billy Buckner, Portland/Pawtucket	153
BB	Jason Garcia, Greenville	67
SO	Matt Barnes, Greenville/Salem	133
# AVG	Matt Barnes, Greenville/Salem	.225

2012 PERFORMANCE

General Manager: Ben Cherington. **Farm Director:** Ben Crockett. **Scouting Director:** Amiel Sawdaye.

Class	Team	League	W	L	PCT	Finish	Manager
Majors	Boston Red Sox	American	69	93	.426	12th (14)	Bobby Valentine
Triple-A	Pawtucket Red Sox	International	79	65	.549	4th (14)	Arnie Beyeler
Double-A	Portland Sea Dogs	Eastern	68	73	.482	8th (12)	Kevin Boles
High A	Salem Red Sox	Carolina	68	69	.496	4th (8)	Billy McMillon
Low A	Greenville Drive	South Atlantic	66	73	.475	9th (14)	Carlos Febles
Short-season	Lowell Spinners	New York-Penn	36	40	.474	6th (14)	Bruce Crabbe
Rookie	GCL Red Sox	Gulf Coast	34	26	.567	5th (14)	George Lombard
Overall 2012 Minor League Record			351	346	.504	17th (30)	

ORGANIZATION STATISTICS

BOSTON RED SOX

AMERICAN LEAGUE

Batting	B-T	HT	WT	DOB	AVG	vLH	vRH	G	AB	R	H	2B	3B	HR	RBI	BB	HBP	SH	SF	SO	SB	CS	SLG	OBP
Anderson, Lars	L-L	6-4	215	9-25-87	.125	.000	.143	6	8	1	1	0	0	0	0	0	0	0	0	3	0	0	.125	.125
Aviles, Mike	R-R	5-10	205	3-13-81	.250	.286	.236	136	512	57	128	28	0	13	60	23	2	3	6	77	14	6	.381	.282
Byrd, Marlon	R-R	6-0	215	8-30-77	.270	.357	.207	34	100	9	27	2	0	1	7	2	1	1	2	21	0	2	.320	.286
Ciriaco, Pedro	R-R	6-0	170	9-27-85	.293	.304	.289	76	259	33	76	15	2	2	19	8	0	5	0	47	16	3	.390	.315
Crawford, Carl	L-L	6-2	215	8-5-81	.282	.282	.282	31	117	23	33	10	2	3	19	3	2	1	2	22	5	0	.479	.306
De Jesus Jr., Ivan	R-R	5-11	200	5-1-87	.000	.000	.000	8	8	0	0	0	0	0	0	0	0	0	0	6	0	0	.000	.000
Ellsbury, Jacoby	L-L	6-1	195	9-11-83	.271	.292	.259	74	303	43	82	18	0	4	26	19	0	0	1	43	14	3	.370	.313
Gomez, Mauro	R-R	6-2	230	9-7-84	.275	.229	.315	37	102	14	28	5	2	2	17	8	0	0	1	26	0	0	.422	.324
Gonzalez, Adrian	L-L	6-2	225	5-8-82	.300	.302	.298	123	484	63	145	37	0	15	86	31	5	0	7	81	0	0	.469	.343
Iglesias, Jose	R-R	5-11	185	1-5-90	.118	.172	.077	25	68	5	8	2	0	1	2	4	3	2	0	16	1	0	.191	.200
Kalish, Ryan	L-L	6-0	215	3-28-88	.229	.333	.210	36	96	12	22	3	0	5	6	0	0	1	26	3	2	.260	.272
Lavarnway, Ryan	R-R	6-4	225	8-7-87	.157	.180	.146	46	153	11	24	8	0	2	12	11	0	0	2	41	0	0	.248	.211
Lillibridge, Brent	R-R	5-11	185	9-18-83	.125	.091	.200	10	16	0	2	0	0	0	0	0	0	0	0	5	0	0	.125	.125
3-team total (49 Chicago, 43 Cleveland)					.195	—	—	102	190	25	37	6	0	3	10	11	4	1	3	71	13	2	.274	.250
Lin, Che-Hsuan	R-R	6-0	180	9-21-88	.250	.333	.000	9	12	1	3	0	0	0	0	0	0	0	0	5	0	0	.250	.250
Loney, James	L-L	6-3	220	5-7-84	.230	.118	.253	30	100	5	23	2	0	2	8	5	0	0	1	12	0	0	.310	.264
McDonald, Darnell	R-R	5-11	205	11-17-78	.214	.214	.214	38	84	17	18	7	0	2	9	12	0	2	1	17	1	1	.369	.309
2-team total (4 New York)					.205	—	—	42	88	17	18	7	0	2	9	12	0	2	1	19	1	1	.352	.297
Middlebrooks, Will	R-R	6-4	225	9-9-88	.288	.300	.282	75	267	34	77	14	0	15	54	13	3	0	3	70	4	1	.509	.325
Nava, Daniel	B-L	5-10	200	2-22-83	.243	.185	.269	88	267	38	65	21	0	6	33	37	9	2	2	63	3	0	.390	.352
Ortiz, David	L-L	6-4	250	11-18-75	.318	.320	.317	90	324	65	103	26	0	23	60	56	0	0	3	51	0	1	.611	.415
Pedroia, Dustin	R-R	5-8	165	8-17-83	.290	.305	.283	141	563	81	163	39	3	15	65	48	5	1	6	60	20	6	.449	.347
Podsednik, Scott	L-L	6-0	185	3-18-76	.302	.395	.280	63	199	19	60	7	0	1	12	6	1	8	2	35	8	2	.352	.322
Punto, Nick	B-R	5-9	190	11-8-77	.200	.111	.215	65	125	14	25	6	0	1	10	19	0	2	2	33	5	0	.272	.301
Quiroz, Guillermo	R-R	6-1	215	11-29-81	.000	.000	.000	2	2	0	0	0	0	0	0	0	0	0	0	1	0	0	.000	.000
Repko, Jason	R-R	5-11	200	12-27-80	.091	.000	.167	5	11	0	1	0	0	0	0	0	0	0	0	4	0	0	.091	.091
Ross, Cody	R-L	5-10	195	12-23-80	.267	.295	.256	130	476	70	127	34	1	22	81	42	3	1	6	129	2	3	.481	.326
Saltalamacchia, Jarrod	B-R	6-4	235	5-2-85	.222	.170	.230	121	405	55	90	17	1	25	59	38	1	0	4	139	0	1	.454	.288
Shoppach, Kelly	R-R	6-0	220	4-29-80	.250	.250	.250	48	140	16	35	12	2	5	17	11	5	2	0	62	1	0	.471	.327
Spears, Nate	L-R	5-11	175	5-3-85	.000	—	.000	4	4	0	0	0	0	0	0	0	0	0	0	3	0	0	.000	.000
Sweeney, Ryan	L-L	6-4	225	2-20-85	.260	.100	.277	63	204	22	53	19	2	0	16	12	1	1	1	43	0	0	.373	.303
Valencia, Danny	R-R	6-2	220	9-19-84	.143	.267	.000	10	28	1	4	0	0	1	4	0	0	0	1	6	0	0	.250	.138
2-team total (34 Minnesota)					.188	—	—	44	154	14	29	6	1	3	21	3	0	0	4	38	0	1	.299	.199
Youkilis, Kevin	R-R	6-1	220	3-15-79	.233	.256	.224	42	146	25	34	7	1	4	14	14	4	0	1	39	0	0	.377	.315
2-team total (80 Chicago)					.235	—	—	122	438	72	103	15	2	19	60	51	17	0	3	108	0	0	.409	.336

Pitching	B-T	HT	WT	DOB	W	L	ERA	G	GS	CG	SV	IP	H	R	ER	HR	BB	SO	AVG	vLH	vRH	K/9	BB/9
Aceves, Alfredo	R-R	6-3	220	12-8-82	2	10	5.36	69	0	0	25	84	80	51	50	11	31	75	.254	.269	.239	8.04	3.32
Albers, Matt	L-R	6-0	225	1-20-83	2	0	2.29	40	0	0	0	39	30	14	10	6	15	25	.204	.222	5.72	3.43
Atchison, Scott	R-R	6-2	200	3-29-76	2	1	1.58	42	0	0	0	51	42	10	9	2	9	36	.223	.188	.252	6.31	1.58
Bailey, Andrew	R-R	6-3	240	5-31-84	1	1	7.04	19	0	0	6	15	21	12	12	2	8	14	.318	.364	.273	8.22	4.70
Bard, Daniel	R-R	6-4	215	6-25-85	5	6	6.22	17	10	0	0	59	60	42	41	9	43	38	.271	.260	.286	5.76	6.52
Beato, Pedro	R-R	6-4	220	10-27-86	1	0	4.70	4	0	0	0	8	6	4	4	0	3	7	.222	.214	.231	8.22	3.52
Beckett, Josh	R-R	6-5	225	5-15-80	5	11	5.23	21	21	0	0	127	131	75	74	16	38	94	.266	.279	.249	6.64	2.69
Bowden, Michael	R-R	6-3	215	9-9-86	0	0	3.00	2	0	0	0	3	2	1	1	1	1	3	.200	.250	.167	9.00	3.00
Breslow, Craig	L-L	6-0	190	8-8-80	1	0	2.70	23	0	0	0	20	14	7	6	0	9	19	.206	.184	.233	8.55	4.05
Buchholz, Clay	L-R	6-3	190	8-14-84	11	8	4.56	29	29	2	0	189	187	104	96	25	64	129	.263	.266	.260	6.13	3.04
Carpenter, Chris	R-R	6-4	220	12-26-85	1	0	9.00	8	0	0	0	6	7	6	6	1	10	2	.318	.600	.083	3.00	15.00
Cook, Aaron	R-R	6-3	215	2-8-79	4	11	5.65	18	18	1	0	94	117	66	59	11	16	20	.304	.340	.261	1.91	2.01
Doubront, Felix	L-L	6-2	165	10-23-87	11	10	4.86	29	29	0	0	161	162	95	87	24	71	167	.259	.259	.259	9.34	3.97
Germano, Justin	R-R	6-2	210	8-6-82	0	0	0.00	1	0	0	0	6	5	0	0	0	2	7	.227	.200	.250	11.12	3.18
Hill, Rich	L-L	6-5	220	3-11-80	1	0	1.83	25	0	0	0	20	17	4	4	0	11	21	.236	.205	.273	9.61	5.03
Lester, Jon	L-L	6-4	240	1-7-84	9	14	4.82	33	33	3	0	205	216	117	110	25	68	166	.273	.259	.278	7.28	2.98
Matsuzaka, Daisuke	R-R	6-0	185	9-13-80	1	7	8.28	11	11	0	0	46	58	43	42	11	20	41	.307	.333	.280	8.08	3.94

Melancon, Mark	R-R	6-2	215	3-28-85	0	2	6.20	41	0	0	1	45	45	31	31	8	12	41	.256	.291	.227	8.20	2.40
Miller, Andrew	L-L	6-7	210	5-21-85	3	2	3.35	53	0	0	0	40	28	15	15	3	20	51	.194	.149	.263	11.38	4.46
Morales, Franklin	L-L	6-0	210	1-24-86	3	4	3.77	37	9	0	1	76	64	38	32	11	30	76	.224	.184	.245	8.96	3.54
Mortensen, Clayton	R-R	6-4	185	4-10-85	1	1	3.21	26	0	0	0	42	32	15	15	7	19	41	.212	.179	.238	8.79	4.07
Padilla, Vicente	R-R	6-0	230	9-27-77	4	1	4.50	56	0	0	1	50	59	26	25	7	15	51	.298	.280	.314	9.18	2.70
Stewart, Zach	R-R	6-2	205	9-28-86	0	2	22.24	2	2	0	0	6	17	14	14	4	0	3	.515	.600	.444	4.76	0.00
2-team total (18 Chicago)					1	4	8.58	20	3	0	0	36	58	40	34	14	4	19	—	—	—	4.79	1.01
Tazawa, Junichi	R-R	5-11	180	6-6-86	1	1	1.43	37	0	0	1	44	37	7	7	1	5	45	.227	.234	.222	9.20	1.02
Thomas, Justin	L-L	6-3	220	1-18-84	0	0	7.71	7	0	0	0	5	10	4	4	0	2	4	.476	.333	.583	7.71	3.86
2-team total (4 New York)					0	0	8.22	11	0	0	0	8	12	7	7	1	3	7	—	—	—	8.22	3.52

Fielding

Catcher	PCT	G	PO	A	E	DP	PB
Lavarnway	.990	28	183	11	2	0	0
Quiroz	1.000	1	1	0	0	0	1
Saltalamacchia	.991	104	715	41	7	3	6
Shoppach	.987	46	294	18	4	0	4

First Base	PCT	G	PO	A	E	DP
Anderson	1.000	2	4	0	0	0
Gomez	.992	16	112	14	1	13
Gonzalez	.998	115	949	104	2	100
Lillibridge	1.000	2	8	1	0	0
Loney	1.000	28	212	19	0	21
Ortiz	1.000	7	54	2	0	4
Punto	1.000	5	4	1	0	0
Saltalamacchia	1.000	1	1	0	0	0
Youkilis	1.000	13	81	9	0	12

Second Base	PCT	G	PO	A	E	DP
Aviles	1.000	2	1	3	0	0
Ciriaco	1.000	16	13	29	0	1

	PCT	G	PO	A	E	DP/PB
De Jesus Jr.	.750	5	2	1	1	1
Pedroia	.992	139	228	392	5	100
Punto	.980	15	21	28	1	7
Spears	1.000	1	0	1	0	0

Third Base	PCT	G	PO	A	E	DP
Aviles	1.000	1	0	3	0	0
Ciriaco	.930	35	28	79	8	9
De Jesus Jr.	—	1	0	0	0	0
Gomez	.778	9	7	7	4	0
Middlebrooks	.949	72	32	134	9	13
Punto	.982	26	11	45	1	6
Spears	1.000	1	1	1	0	0
Valencia	1.000	10	5	10	0	0
Youkilis	.960	33	20	52	3	3

Shortstop	PCT	G	PO	A	E	DP
Aviles	.975	128	207	369	15	89
Ciriaco	.980	12	15	35	1	9
De Jesus Jr.	1.000	1	1	1	0	1

	PCT	G	PO	A	E	DP
Iglesias	.980	24	27	71	2	16
Punto	1.000	6	8	19	0	1

Outfield	PCT	G	PO	A	E	DP
Anderson	1.000	4	1	0	0	0
Byrd	.973	34	70	1	2	0
Ciriaco	1.000	7	7	0	0	0
Crawford	.977	30	42	0	1	0
Ellsbury	.982	73	164	2	3	1
Gonzalez	.905	18	18	1	2	1
Kalish	.939	32	62	0	4	0
Lillibridge	1.000	7	7	0	0	0
Lin	1.000	9	6	0	0	0
McDonald	.983	31	57	2	1	0
Nava	.983	79	111	5	2	0
Podsednik	.989	57	88	3	1	0
Repko	1.000	4	12	0	0	0
Ross	.995	116	198	9	1	2
Spears	—	2	0	0	0	0
Sweeney	.983	61	111	3	2	2

PAWTUCKET RED SOX — TRIPLE-A
INTERNATIONAL LEAGUE

Batting	B-T	HT	WT	DOB	AVG	vLH	vRH	G	AB	R	H	2B	3B	HR	RBI	BB	HBP	SH	SF	SO	SB	CS	SLG	OBP
Anderson, Lars	L-L	6-4	215	9-25-87	.259	.261	.258	93	340	49	88	22	2	9	52	56	0	0	5	89	1	0	.415	.359
2-team total (18 Columbus)					.250	—	—	111	396	53	99	27	2	9	59	65	2	0	7	107	1	0	.396	.353
Bermudez, Ronald	R-R	6-1	165	6-6-88	.163	.143	.172	17	43	5	7	1	1	0	2	2	1	0	1	11	1	0	.233	.213
Brentz, Bryce	R-R	6-0	190	12-30-88	.118	.400	.000	5	17	0	2	0	0	0	0	1	0	0	0	6	0	0	.118	.167
Butler, Daniel	R-R	5-10	190	10-17-86	.233	.238	.231	22	73	8	17	5	0	3	11	9	0	0	1	20	0	0	.425	.313
Ciriaco, Pedro	R-R	6-0	170	9-27-85	.301	.329	.291	64	276	41	83	13	2	4	21	6	2	3	2	49	14	8	.406	.318
Crawford, Carl	L-L	6-2	215	8-5-81	.333	.500	.300	3	12	2	4	0	0	0	1	1	0	0	0	1	1	0	.333	.385
De Jesus Jr., Ivan	R-R	5-11	200	5-1-87	.385	.500	.350	7	26	5	10	1	0	0	0	2	0	0	0	3	1	0	.423	.429
Dent, Ryan	R-R	6-0	190	3-15-89	.214	.400	.111	5	14	2	3	1	0	0	1	2	0	1	0	5	0	0	.286	.313
Ellsbury, Jacoby	L-L	6-1	195	9-11-83	.125	—	.125	2	8	1	1	0	0	0	0	0	0	0	0	1	0	0	.125	.125
Exposito, Luis	R-R	6-3	210	1-20-87	.200	.250	.167	3	10	1	2	2	0	0	1	1	0	0	0	2	0	0	.400	.273
2-team total (55 Norfolk)					.265	—	—	58	215	27	57	13	1	6	24	19	0	0	1	37	0	2	.419	.323
Gomez, Mauro	R-R	6-2	230	9-7-84	.310	.317	.307	100	387	65	120	34	1	24	74	35	3	0	1	88	1	0	.589	.371
Hassan, Alex	R-R	6-3	195	4-1-88	.256	.200	.274	94	312	39	80	13	0	7	46	55	8	0	4	70	1	1	.365	.377
Hazelbaker, Jeremy	L-R	6-3	190	8-14-87	.267	.111	.333	7	30	2	8	3	0	0	3	0	1	0	1	8	3	0	.367	.281
Hee, Jonathan	B-R	6-0	180	8-11-85	.253	.232	.264	64	198	13	50	11	1	2	21	16	6	1	2	40	2	3	.348	.324
Iglesias, Jose	R-R	5-11	185	1-5-90	.266	.253	.270	88	353	46	94	9	1	1	23	27	2	9	5	46	12	3	.306	.318
Kalish, Ryan	L-L	6-0	215	3-28-88	.261	.267	.259	27	111	18	29	5	0	4	14	13	0	1	1	30	7	2	.414	.336
Kroeger, Josh	L-L	6-3	230	8-31-82	.244	.188	.266	64	238	34	58	17	0	9	25	20	0	0	4	43	1	5	.429	.303
2-team total (31 Gwinnett)					.266	—	—	95	334	47	89	24	0	11	37	39	1	0	4	54	3	6	.437	.341
LaRoche, Andy	R-R	6-1	195	9-13-83	.264	.244	.270	50	182	23	48	15	0	7	25	18	3	0	1	24	1	1	.462	.338
2-team total (46 Columbus)					.251	—	—	96	327	41	82	20	0	12	41	38	4	0	1	52	1	1	.422	.335
Lavarnway, Ryan	R-R	6-4	225	8-7-87	.295	.370	.272	83	319	52	94	22	0	8	43	40	4	0	4	62	1	0	.439	.376
Lin, Che-Hsuan	R-R	6-0	180	9-21-88	.247	.189	.270	113	396	42	98	11	5	2	30	42	3	2	2	65	15	4	.316	.323
Linares, Juan Carlos	R-R	5-11	190	9-7-84	.297	.310	.294	52	202	24	60	11	1	8	29	7	2	1	4	36	0	0	.480	.321
McDonald, Darnell	R-R	5-11	205	11-17-78	.190	.200	.188	6	21	2	4	3	0	0	2	1	0	1	0	6	0	0	.333	.217
2-team total (31 Scranton/W-B)					.194	—	—	37	129	20	25	4	0	3	9	15	2	0	1	35	1	2	.295	.286
Middlebrooks, Will	R-R	6-4	225	9-9-88	.333	.345	.328	24	93	18	31	3	1	9	27	7	0	0	0	18	3	1	.677	.380
Nava, Daniel	B-L	5-10	200	2-22-83	.313	.286	.324	29	99	20	31	7	1	4	18	16	4	0	1	15	1	1	.525	.425
Podsednik, Scott	L-L	6-0	185	3-18-76	.281	.313	.274	25	89	10	25	2	1	1	11	8	0	2	3	13	4	2	.360	.330
2-team total (23 Lehigh Valley)					.242	—	—	48	165	23	40	3	1	1	15	16	1	2	3	25	10	3	.291	.308
Repko, Jason	R-R	5-11	200	12-27-80	.225	.364	.163	47	178	30	40	6	4	7	26	15	3	1	2	40	4	3	.421	.293
Rivera, Mike	R-R	6-1	220	9-8-76	.250	.290	.239	43	140	7	35	5	0	3	18	8	5	0	1	35	0	1	.350	.312
Rodriguez, Reynaldo	R-R	6-0	195	2-7-86	.186	.083	.226	12	43	8	8	3	0	0	4	4	1	0	1	12	1	0	.256	.265
Ross, Cody	R-L	5-10	195	12-23-80	.143	.000	.250	2	7	1	1	0	0	0	0	0	1	0	0	0	0	0	.143	.333
Spears, Nate	L-R	5-11	175	7-8-84	.240	.231	.243	108	346	46	83	16	4	10	38	43	3	3	0	86	3	2	.396	.329
Spring, Matt	R-R	6-2	215	11-7-84	.333	.333	.333	2	9	1	3	1	0	0	1	0	0	0	0	4	1	0	.444	.333
Thomas, Tony	R-R	5-10	180	7-10-86	.242	.267	.230	68	223	35	54	10	2	10	30	22	1	0	4	64	12	1	.439	.308
Valencia, Danny	R-R	6-2	220	9-19-84	.306	.357	.286	13	49	3	15	3	0	1	8	3	1	0	0	12	0	2	.429	.358

	B-T	HT	WT	DOB	AVG	vLH	vRH	G	AB	R	H	2B	3B	HR	RBI	BB	HBP	SH	SF	SO	SB	CS	SLG	OBP
2-team total (69 Rochester)					.259	—	—	82	317	33	82	20	1	8	45	18	1	0	1	52	1	4	.404	.300
Youkilis, Kevin	R-R	6-1	220	3-15-79	.364	.000	.400	4	11	1	4	2	0	0	1	3	0	0	0	4	0	1	.545	.500

Pitching	B-T	HT	WT	DOB	W	L	ERA	G	GS	CG	SV	IP	H	R	ER	HR	BB	SO	AVG	vLH	vRH	K/9	BB/9
Atchison, Scott	R-R	6-2	200	3-29-76	0	0	13.50	2	1	0	0	2	3	3	3	1	0	2	.333	.500	.286	9.00	0.00
Bailey, Andrew	R-R	6-3	240	5-31-84	0	0	0.00	3	0	0	0	3	1	0	0	0	0	4	.091	.000	.143	10.80	0.00
Bard, Daniel	R-R	6-4	215	6-25-85	3	2	7.03	31	1	0	0	32	31	29	25	2	29	32	.254	.238	.271	9.00	8.16
Beato, Pedro	R-R	6-4	220	10-27-86	0	0	0.00	4	0	0	1	5	1	1	0	0	4	7	.067	.143	.000	12.60	7.20
2-team total (24 Buffalo)					4	4	3.64	28	1	0	1	42	33	22	17	7	15	34	—	—	—	7.29	3.21
Buchholz, Clay	L-R	6-3	190	8-14-84	0	0	0.00	1	1	0	0	2	1	0	0	0	2	3	.125	.000	.200	11.57	7.71
Buckner, Billy	R-R	6-2	205	8-27-83	8	6	3.91	17	17	1	0	97	87	48	42	12	36	59	.239	.253	.226	5.49	3.35
Carpenter, Chris	R-R	6-4	220	12-26-85	1	0	1.15	16	0	0	4	16	7	2	2	1	8	17	.137	.200	.097	9.77	4.60
Cook, Aaron	R-R	6-3	215	2-8-79	3	0	2.41	6	6	2	0	37	33	12	10	1	12	16	.237	.192	.288	3.86	2.89
De La Torre, Jose	R-R	5-9	175	10-17-85	1	0	2.45	12	0	0	2	18	15	5	5	2	3	16	.227	.296	.179	7.85	1.47
2-team total (7 Columbus)					2	0	2.79	19	0	0	2	29	24	9	9	2	5	32	—	—	—	9.93	1.55
Duckworth, Brandon	R-R	6-2	215	1-23-76	9	2	3.17	21	18	0	0	111	110	43	39	12	35	93	.263	.221	.302	7.56	2.85
Fields, Josh	R-R	6-0	185	8-19-85	1	0	0.00	10	0	0	4	14	8	0	0	0	2	19	.174	.200	.154	12.51	1.32
Figueroa, Nelson	R-R	6-1	185	5-18-74	5	3	3.77	8	6	1	0	43	34	19	18	3	12	33	.217	.232	.205	6.91	2.51
2-team total (17 Scranton/W-B)					12	5	3.89	25	15	2	0	116	113	54	50	11	37	69	—	—	—	5.37	2.88
Germano, Justin	R-R	6-2	210	8-6-82	9	4	2.40	17	16	1	0	105	82	33	28	15	13	72	.211	.200	.220	6.17	1.11
Hernandez, Chris	L-L	6-1	185	12-14-88	1	4	3.59	8	7	0	0	43	40	18	17	4	17	30	.252	.216	.269	6.33	3.59
Hill, Rich	L-L	6-5	220	3-11-80	1	0	1.13	8	0	0	0	8	3	1	1	1	2	10	.111	.000	.176	11.25	2.25
Huntzinger, Brock	R-R	6-3	200	7-2-88	0	0	6.00	2	0	0	0	3	4	2	2	0	1	4	.308	.500	.222	12.00	3.00
Inman, Will	R-R	6-0	215	2-6-87	1	3	2.23	35	0	0	6	48	35	14	12	3	34	60	.203	.231	.181	11.17	6.33
Kehrt, Jeremy	R-R	6-2	190	12-21-85	0	0	7.20	2	1	0	0	5	7	4	4	1	1	3	.350	.364	.333	5.40	1.80
Latimer, Will	L-L	6-3	190	12-4-85	0	2	6.30	5	0	0	0	10	13	7	7	4	4	5	.317	.167	.435	4.50	3.60
MacDonald, Mike	R-R	6-1	215	10-29-81	0	1	4.50	1	1	0	0	4	7	2	2	1	1	6	.389	.500	.357	13.50	2.25
Mathis, Doug	R-R	6-3	220	6-7-83	7	6	4.07	19	18	0	0	102	116	56	46	12	36	59	.286	.323	.251	5.22	3.19
Matsuzaka, Daisuke	R-R	6-0	185	9-13-80	1	3	3.18	11	11	0	0	51	42	23	18	6	17	41	.220	.228	.211	7.24	3.00
Melancon, Mark	R-R	6-2	215	3-28-85	0	0	0.83	21	0	0	11	22	15	2	2	0	3	27	.185	.140	.237	11.22	1.25
Miller, Andrew	L-L	6-7	210	5-21-85	0	0	5.73	10	0	0	1	11	4	7	7	1	14	23	.105	.063	.136	18.82	11.45
Mock, Garrett	R-R	6-4	230	4-25-83	3	2	3.33	35	0	0	5	49	49	18	18	5	23	53	.274	.286	.263	9.80	4.25
Mortensen, Clayton	R-R	6-4	185	4-10-85	5	3	1.91	24	0	0	2	38	21	11	8	3	15	36	.160	.179	.147	8.60	3.58
Ohlendorf, Ross	R-R	6-4	240	8-8-82	4	3	4.61	10	10	0	0	53	57	28	27	5	15	37	.277	.259	.296	6.32	2.56
Pena Jr., Tony	R-R	6-2	185	3-23-81	1	9	4.75	32	12	0	0	91	108	50	48	11	30	62	.305	.333	.280	6.13	2.97
Prior, Mark	R-R	6-5	230	9-7-80	1	0	3.96	19	0	0	1	25	15	11	11	4	23	38	.172	.214	.133	13.68	8.28
Spoone, Chorye	R-R	6-1	215	9-16-85	1	1	2.79	14	0	0	0	19	18	8	6	2	20	10	.254	.385	.178	4.66	9.31
Stewart, Zach	R-R	6-2	205	9-28-86	3	5	3.94	11	11	0	0	59	58	26	26	6	14	42	.252	.261	.244	6.37	2.12
Tazawa, Junichi	R-B	5-11	180	6-6-86	3	2	2.55	25	0	0	4	42	34	18	12	2	17	56	.211	.270	.161	11.91	3.61
Thomas, Justin	L-L	6-3	220	1-18-84	0	0	3.38	4	0	0	0	5	5	2	2	0	0	5	.238	.400	.091	8.44	0.00
2-team total (30 Scranton/W-B)					2	1	3.45	34	6	0	1	63	54	25	24	3	20	54	—	—	—	7.76	2.87
Wilson, Alex	R-R	6-0	215	11-3-86	5	3	3.72	40	3	0	1	73	76	40	30	3	33	78	.270	.316	.228	9.66	4.09
Wright, Steve	R-R	6-1	200	8-30-84	0	1	3.15	4	4	0	0	20	19	10	7	1	5	16	.238	.323	.184	7.20	2.25

Fielding

Catcher	PCT	G	PO	A	E	DP	PB
Butler	1.000	22	155	12	0	0	5
Exposito	1.000	3	23	1	0	1	3
Lavarnway	.991	80	590	49	6	2	8
Rivera	.997	39	278	30	1	3	1
Spring	1.000	2	23	0	0	0	0

First Base	PCT	G	PO	A	E	DP
Anderson	.990	66	565	46	6	51
Gomez	.986	52	397	36	6	44
LaRoche	1.000	11	78	3	0	6
Rivera	1.000	1	10	0	0	0
Rodriguez	.977	10	78	7	2	6
Spears	1.000	5	46	4	0	5

Second Base	PCT	G	PO	A	E	DP
Ciriaco	.964	23	38	68	4	19
De Jesus Jr.	1.000	6	8	10	0	1
Dent	1.000	2	3	3	0	1
Hee	.986	32	57	84	2	20
LaRoche	1.000	6	6	14	0	2

	PCT	G	PO	A	E	DP
Spears	.988	35	67	103	2	16
Thomas	.977	46	87	121	5	23
Third Base	PCT	G	PO	A	E	DP
Ciriaco	.750	3	3	3	2	0
Dent	1.000	1	1	3	0	2
Gomez	.938	8	7	8	1	0
Hee	1.000	15	9	21	0	0
LaRoche	1.000	28	22	41	0	3
Middlebrooks	.978	24	14	31	1	6
Rivera	1.000	2	0	1	0	0
Spears	.970	62	42	117	5	13
Valencia	.903	12	5	23	3	2
Youkilis	1.000	3	1	4	0	1
Shortstop	PCT	G	PO	A	E	DP
Ciriaco	.971	37	53	113	5	23
De Jesus Jr.	.857	1	0	6	1	0
Dent	1.000	1	1	4	0	1
Hee	.986	18	34	39	1	7
Iglesias	.966	88	119	252	13	52

	PCT	G	PO	A	E	DP
Spears	—	1	0	0	0	0
Outfield	PCT	G	PO	A	E	DP
Anderson	1.000	16	22	0	0	0
Bermudez	1.000	12	17	0	0	0
Brentz	1.000	4	9	0	0	0
Crawford	1.000	3	5	0	0	0
Ellsbury	1.000	2	5	0	0	0
Hassan	.994	88	170	4	1	1
Hazelbaker	1.000	4	7	0	0	0
Kalish	.976	20	40	1	1	1
Kroeger	.991	54	110	2	1	0
Lin	.985	110	247	9	4	3
Linares	.988	41	74	5	1	1
McDonald	1.000	4	3	0	0	0
Nava	1.000	19	30	0	0	0
Podsednik	1.000	18	32	2	0	1
Repko	1.000	42	104	2	0	1
Ross	.667	1	2	0	1	0
Spears	1.000	3	5	0	0	0
Thomas	1.000	8	16	1	0	0

PORTLAND SEA DOGS

DOUBLE-A

EASTERN LEAGUE

Batting	B-T	HT	WT	DOB	AVG	vLH	vRH	G	AB	R	H	2B	3B	HR	RBI	BB	HBP	SH	SF	SO	SB	CS	SLG	OBP
Bermudez, Ronald	R-R	6-1	165	6-6-88	.278	.282	.277	47	158	15	44	9	1	2	15	7	1	0	1	29	4	3	.386	.311
Bogaerts, Xander	R-R	6-3	175	10-1-92	.326	.258	.361	23	92	12	30	10	0	5	17	1	3	0	1	21	1	1	.598	.351
Bradley, Jackie	L-R	5-10	180	4-19-90	.271	.293	.260	61	229	37	62	16	2	6	29	35	4	0	3	49	8	3	.437	.373
Brentz, Bryce	R-R	6-0	190	12-30-88	.296	.311	.291	122	456	62	135	30	1	17	76	40	4	0	4	130	7	5	.478	.355
Butler, Daniel	R-R	5-10	190	10-17-86	.251	.216	.260	73	247	29	62	14	2	6	26	31	7	0	0	42	0	0	.397	.351

Player	B-T	HT	WT	DOB	AVG	vLH	vRH	G	AB	R	H	2B	3B	HR	RBI	BB	HBP	SH	SF	SO	SB	CS	SLG	OBP
Crawford, Carl	L-L	6-2	215	8-5-81	.400	.333	.429	3	10	2	4	0	1	0	1	2	0	0	0	1	1	0	.600	.500
Dent, Ryan	R-R	6-0	190	3-15-89	.237	.256	.229	83	266	40	63	6	0	3	22	29	2	6	3	60	4	2	.293	.313
Ellsbury, Jacoby	L-L	6-1	195	9-11-83	.222	.000	.286	2	9	1	2	1	0	0	0	0	0	0	0	1	0	0	.333	.222
Gentile, Zach	L-R	5-8	165	11-1-86	.241	.172	.260	41	133	16	32	7	0	0	15	11	3	5	1	19	3	1	.293	.311
Gibson, Derrik	R-R	6-1	170	12-5-89	.225	.212	.229	115	405	43	91	13	3	0	26	44	3	1	2	93	14	5	.272	.304
Hazelbaker, Jeremy	L-R	6-3	190	8-14-87	.273	.274	.272	114	436	77	119	21	6	19	64	35	9	6	2	114	33	11	.479	.338
Hedman, Drew	L-L	6-2	200	7-20-86	.127	.125	.127	22	71	8	9	3	0	4	7	9	2	0	1	28	0	0	.338	.241
Hee, Jonathan	B-R	6-0	180	8-15-85	.150	.250	.083	7	20	1	3	1	0	0	2	4	2	0	1	7	0	0	.200	.333
Hernandez, Jayson	R-R	5-10	200	9-2-88	.190	.200	.188	7	21	0	4	1	0	0	3	1	0	0	0	6	0	0	.238	.227
Hissey, Pete	L-L	6-1	180	1-17-90	.250	.227	.259	70	236	21	59	14	1	1	27	17	1	1	4	47	15	5	.331	.298
Johns, Bryan	R-R	5-9	180	11-18-88	.143	.000	.250	2	7	1	1	0	0	0	0	0	0	0	0	3	1	0	.143	.143
Kalish, Ryan	L-L	6-0	215	3-28-88	.222	.000	.250	3	9	0	2	1	0	0	4	0	0	0	0	1	0	0	.333	.462
Linares, Juan Carlos	R-R	5-11	190	9-7-84	.333	.306	.342	58	210	34	70	17	1	8	33	22	4	0	2	30	0	1	.538	.403
Meneses, Heiker	R-R	5-9	160	7-1-91	.197	.259	.180	41	127	12	25	1	1	1	10	13	2	3	0	33	1	3	.244	.282
Natoli, Nick	R-R	6-1	195	1-17-88	.151	.045	.196	24	73	4	11	3	0	1	5	1	0	1	0	16	0	0	.192	.271
Rodriguez, Reynaldo	R-R	6-0	195	2-7-86	.257	.225	.267	90	327	45	84	27	3	16	49	35	4	0	2	81	6	3	.505	.334
Shaw, Travis	L-R	6-4	225	4-16-90	.227	.205	.239	31	110	13	25	13	0	3	12	21	1	0	1	34	1	1	.427	.353
Smith, Marquez	R-R	5-10	205	3-20-85	.293	.342	.275	71	280	43	82	22	1	8	37	23	4	3	4	52	1	0	.464	.350
Spring, Matt	R-R	6-2	215	11-7-84	.197	.182	.203	60	198	16	39	8	0	7	22	23	3	0	0	74	0	2	.343	.290
Sweeney, Ryan	L-L	6-4	225	2-20-85	.143	.000	.167	2	7	0	1	0	0	0	0	0	0	0	0	0	0	0	.143	.143
Tejeda, Oscar	R-R	6-1	170	12-26-89	.262	.308	.247	51	202	18	53	12	0	5	31	9	1	0	2	41	2	1	.396	.294
2-team total (54 Altoona)					.253	—	—	105	400	41	101	25	1	8	59	24	2	2	7	83	5	1	.380	.293
Vazquez, Christian	R-R	5-9	195	8-21-90	.205	.167	.218	20	73	11	15	4	0	0	5	8	0	0	1	9	0	0	.260	.280
Vitek, Kolbrin	R-R	6-2	195	4-1-89	.242	.203	.260	46	186	14	45	13	1	1	10	10	1	0	0	47	0	0	.339	.284
Wilkerson, Shannon	R-R	6-0	198	7-20-88	.264	.269	.262	24	91	8	24	5	0	0	6	5	1	0	0	16	3	0	.319	.309

Pitching	B-T	HT	WT	DOB	W	L	ERA	G	GS	CG	SV	IP	H	R	ER	HR	BB	SO	AVG	vLH	vRH	K/9	BB/9
Bailey, Andrew	R-R	6-3	240	5-31-84	0	0	9.00	1	0	0		1	3	1	1	0	0	2	.500	.750	.000	18.00	0.00
Balcom-Miller, Chris	R-R	6-2	210	3-3-89	4	5	4.41	26	12	0	0	86	79	46	42	9	49	61	.262	.271	.254	6.41	5.15
Britton, Drake	L-L	6-2	200	5-22-89	4	7	3.72	16	16	0	0	85	86	41	35	3	38	76	.266	.309	.255	8.08	4.04
Buckner, Billy	R-R	6-2	205	8-27-83	4	3	3.20	10	10	1	0	56	51	20	20	6	17	51	.243	.271	.224	8.15	2.72
Carlson, Jesse	L-L	6-0	160	12-31-80	0	0	27.00	1	0	0		1	5	3	3	0	0	1	.714	1.000	.667	9.00	0.00
Carpenter, Chris	R-R	6-4	220	12-26-85	0	0	4.50	1	1	0	0	2	2	1	1	0	0	3	.250	.250		13.50	0.00
Clay, Caleb	R-R	6-2	180	2-15-88	3	3	4.61	34	1	0	9	66	76	37	34	12	19	61	.288	.287	.288	8.28	2.58
Duarte, Marco	R-R	6-2	185	8-19-86	1	0	3.18	6	0	0	1	17	15	6	6	2	9	10	.231	.240	.225	9.24	4.76
Fields, Josh	R-R	6-0	185	8-19-85	3	3	2.62	32	0	0	8	45	30	14	13	4	16	59	.185	.200	.175	11.89	3.22
Hernandez, Chris	L-L	6-1	185	12-14-88	4	8	3.13	18	18	0	0	104	102	46	36	7	36	60	.260	.246	.262	5.21	3.13
Hill, Rich	L-L	6-5	220	3-11-80	0	0	0.00	1	0	0		1	0	0	0	0	1	1	.000	.000		9.00	0.00
Huntzinger, Brock	R-R	6-3	200	7-2-88	4	5	3.93	38	4	0	6	71	60	35	31	4	24	55	.227	.191	.255	6.97	3.04
Kehrt, Jeremy	R-R	6-2	190	12-21-85	8	3	4.15	25	14	0	0	108	125	56	50	10	31	66	.290	.301	.282	5.48	2.58
Kurcz, Aaron	R-R	6-0	175	8-8-90	3	4	3.04	29	0	0	4	50	42	21	17	4	27	72	.221	.207	.231	12.87	4.83
Latimer, Will	L-L	6-3	190	12-4-85	2	3	4.81	22	2	0	0	49	53	26	26	5	17	38	.283	.267	.289	7.03	3.14
Lee, Mike	R-R	6-7	220	11-18-86	0	0	7.00	4	0	0	0	9	16	8	7	0	4	4	.390	.400	.385	4.00	4.00
MacDonald, Mike	R-R	6-1	215	10-29-81	3	2	4.62	10	9	0	0	51	53	27	26	2	12	34	.277	.286	.270	6.04	2.13
Martin, Chris	R-R	6-7	175	6-2-86	3	6	4.48	23	12	0	0	76	83	42	38	4	18	65	.275	.215	.320	7.66	2.12
Matsuzaka, Daisuke	R-R	6-0	185	9-13-80	0	0	1.93	1	1	0	0	5	3	1	1	0	2	7	.143	.150	.250	13.50	3.86
Mortensen, Clayton	R-R	6-4	185	4-10-85	0	0	18.00	1	0	0		1	3	2	2	0	1	0	.500	.500	.500	0.00	9.00
Olmsted, Michael	R-R	6-6	245	5-2-87	1	2	0.00	14	0	0	3	20	11	5	0	0	7	31	.155	.167	.146	13.95	3.15
Pimentel, Stolmy	R-R	6-5	165	2-1-90	6	7	4.59	22	22	1	0	116	115	66	59	9	42	86	.259	.285	.240	6.69	3.27
Portice, Eammon	R-R	6-2	185	6-18-85	0	1	4.76	9	0	0	0	17	18	9	9		7	15	.273	.240	.293	7.94	3.71
Pressly, Ryan	R-R	6-3	175	12-15-88	2	2	2.93	14	0	0	0	28	23	9	9	2	10	21	.232	.293	.190	6.83	3.25
Ranaudo, Anthony	R-R	6-7	231	9-9-89	1	3	6.69	9	9	0	0	38	41	29	28	4	27	27	.283	.220	.326	6.45	6.45
Rosario, Charle	R-R	5-10	158	7-23-88	2	1	8.40	8	0	0	2	15	19	16	14	5	10	17	.322	.375	.286	10.20	6.00
Spoone, Chorye	R-R	6-1	215	9-16-85	2	1	4.15	12	0	0	0	22	19	12	10	1	14	17	.238	.226	.245	7.06	5.82
2-team total (16 New Hampshire)					2	3	3.65	28	1	0	0	44	33	21	18	2	29	32	—	—	—	6.50	5.89
Urquidez, Jason	R-R	6-0	175	9-12-82	4	2	2.85	17	2	0	0	52	52	17	15	3	11	36	.284	.271	.292	6.85	2.09
Webster, Allen	R-R	6-3	185	2-10-90	0	1	8.00	2	2	0	0	9	13	8	8	1	4	12	.325	.267	.360	12.00	4.00
Workman, Brandon	R-R	6-4	195	8-13-88	3	1	3.96	5	5	0	0	25	23	12	11	2	5	23	.247	.297	.214	8.28	1.80
Wright, Steve	R-R	6-1	200	8-30-84	1	0	1.50	1	1	0	0	6	5	1	1	0	2	2	.238	.273	.200	3.00	3.00
2-team total (20 Akron)					10	6	2.44	21	21	1	0	122	91	45	33	8	64	103	—	—	—	7.62	4.73

Fielding

Catcher	PCT	G	PO	A	E	DP	PB
Butler	.990	72	468	49	5	4	3
Hernandez	.968	3	27	3	1	0	0
Spring	.988	50	372	32	5	1	8
Vazquez	.983	20	159	17	3	2	4

First Base	PCT	G	PO	A	E	DP
Dent	1.000	1	3	0	0	1
Gentile	1.000	1	5	1	0	2
Hedman	.993	16	145	6	1	12
Hee	1.000	2	22	1	0	2
Rodriguez	.993	87	704	48	5	72
Shaw	.993	30	267	24	2	35
Spring	.988	11	80	2	1	10

Second Base	PCT	G	PO	A	E	DP
Dent	.979	56	114	162	6	47
Gentile	.982	34	68	95	3	23
Gibson	.000	1	0	0	1	0
Hee	1.000	3	5	4	0	1
Johns	1.000	2	2	3	0	0
Meneses	.993	28	73	68	1	16
Natoli	.882	7	13	17	4	3
Smith	.984	13	23	37	1	12

Third Base	PCT	G	PO	A	E	DP
Dent	.964	13	8	19	1	3
Gentile	.875	1	2	5	1	0
Gibson	.970	12	3	29	1	1
Hee	1.000	2	0	4	0	0
Meneses	.826	8	6	13	4	2
Natoli	.951	14	12	46	3	2
Rodriguez	—	1	0	0	0	0
Shaw	1.000	1	2	0	0	0
Smith	.956	55	38	135	8	17
Vitek	.929	41	17	88	8	9

Shortstop	PCT	G	PO	A	E	DP
Bogaerts	.962	21	29	71	4	16
Dent	.935	13	23	35	4	7
Gibson	.962	100	122	281	16	59
Meneses	.920	8	15	31	4	8
Natoli	.909	3	4	6	1	2

Outfield	PCT	G	PO	A	E	DP
Bermudez	1.000	45	88	2	0	1
Bradley	.973	48	108	2	3	0
Brentz	.969	83	146	10	5	4
Crawford	1.000	3	2	0	0	0
Dent	—	2	0	0	0	0

	PCT	G	PO	A	E	DP
Ellsbury	1.000	2	3	0	0	0
Gentile	.923	5	12	0	1	0
Hazelbaker	.953	76	111	10	6	1
Hedman	1.000	4	10	0	0	0
Hissey	.973	66	103	6	3	1
Kalish	1.000	3	6	0	0	0

	PCT	G	PO	A	E	DP
Linares	1.000	48	77	6	0	0
Sweeney	—	1	0	0	0	0
Tejeda	.982	34	53	1	1	0
Wilkerson	.983	22	56	1	1	0

SALEM RED SOX　　　　　　　　　　　　　　　　　　HIGH CLASS A
CAROLINA LEAGUE

Batting	B-T	HT	WT	DOB	AVG	vLH	vRH	G	AB	R	H	2B	3B	HR	RBI	BB	HBP	SH	SF	SO	SB	CS	SLG	OBP
Almanzar, Michael	R-R	6-3	190	12-2-90	.300	.257	.312	124	454	62	136	36	0	12	54	33	7	0	4	77	10	4	.458	.353
Blair, Carson	R-R	6-1	190	10-18-89	.206	.290	.187	51	165	25	34	11	3	3	24	21	2	0	3	48	2	3	.364	.298
Bogaerts, Xander	R-R	6-3	175	10-1-92	.302	.253	.315	104	384	59	116	27	3	15	64	43	5	1	2	85	4	4	.505	.378
Bradley, Jackie	L-R	5-10	180	4-19-90	.359	.321	.371	67	234	53	84	26	2	3	34	52	10	0	8	40	16	6	.526	.480
Chester, David	R-R	6-5	270	3-31-89	.360	.500	.333	7	25	4	9	1	0	1	5	1	0	0	1	7	0	0	.520	.370
Coyle, Sean	R-R	5-8	175	1-17-92	.249	.253	.249	116	437	60	109	31	2	9	63	29	15	0	3	116	16	0	.391	.316
De La Cruz, Keury	L-L	5-11	170	11-28-91	.280	.286	.278	6	25	1	7	2	0	1	6	1	0	0	0	2	1	1	.480	.308
Gentile, Zach	L-R	5-8	165	11-1-86	.346	.400	.333	8	26	6	9	3	0	0	5	7	0	0	0	4	1	0	.462	.485
Hedman, Drew	L-L	6-2	200	7-20-86	.247	.200	.260	62	190	31	47	13	3	5	33	34	3	0	4	52	10	0	.426	.364
Hernandez, Jayson	R-R	5-10	200	9-2-88	.125	.333	.088	12	40	2	5	3	0	0	1	1	0	0	0	10	0	0	.200	.146
Ibarra, Adalberto	L-R	5-10	205	4-3-87	.275	.262	.278	75	247	31	68	15	1	0	25	38	8	1	2	39	8	4	.344	.386
Jacobs, Brandon	R-R	6-1	225	12-8-90	.252	.394	.213	114	437	62	110	30	0	13	61	39	8	0	3	128	17	9	.410	.322
Johns, Bryan	R-R	5-9	180	11-18-88	.143	—	.143	2	7	1	1	0	0	0	0	1	0	0	0	3	0	0	.143	.250
Johnson, Matty	B-R	5-8	165	4-10-88	.265	.257	.267	48	155	28	41	10	1	1	17	21	1	2	2	23	5	6	.361	.352
Kalish, Ryan	L-L	6-0	215	3-28-88	.333	.000	.400	3	12	3	4	0	0	1	1	0	0	0	0	3	1	1	.583	.333
Kang, James	R-R	5-9	175	10-19-87	.190	.192	.189	49	116	11	22	4	3	0	6	13	2	1	3	39	2	3	.276	.276
LeBlanc, Lucas	R-R	6-2	200	5-7-89	.200	.308	.172	41	125	16	25	8	1	0	9	10	5	4	1	33	1	4	.280	.284
Marquis, Matt	R-R	6-0	200	2-22-90	.152	.286	.115	10	33	2	5	1	0	0	1	2	0	1	0	14	1	0	.182	.200
Meneses, Heiker	R-R	5-9	160	7-1-91	.272	.383	.237	62	250	35	68	16	4	2	32	9	7	5	2	55	18	11	.392	.313
Renfroe, David	R-R	6-3	200	11-16-90	.182	.500	.138	10	33	2	6	1	0	0	5	3	1	0	1	7	0	1	.212	.263
Sanchez, Felix	B-R	6-0	165	6-2-90	.262	.326	.235	46	145	16	38	6	1	1	13	10	5	1	2	42	25	4	.338	.327
Shaw, Travis	L-R	6-4	225	4-16-90	.305	.340	.291	99	354	69	108	31	3	16	73	59	7	0	3	81	11	2	.545	.411
Vazquez, Christian	R-R	5-9	195	8-21-90	.266	.286	.261	81	293	43	78	17	0	7	41	40	4	3	2	70	2	2	.396	.360
Wilkerson, Shannon	R-R	6-0	198	7-20-88	.269	.299	.261	100	386	50	104	19	5	4	42	20	1	7	6	72	29	7	.376	.303

Pitching	B-T	HT	WT	DOB	W	L	ERA	G	GS	CG	SV	IP	H	R	ER	HR	BB	SO	AVG	vLH	vRH	K/9	BB/9
Barnes, Matt	R-R	6-4	205	6-17-90	5	5	3.58	20	20	1	0	93	85	42	37	6	25	91	.250	.248	.251	8.81	2.42
Bayer, Jeremiah	R-R	6-2	200	12-26-85	1	3	4.24	20	0	0	1	40	49	28	19	3	9	43	.288	.417	.238	9.60	2.01
Britton, Drake	L-L	6-2	200	5-22-89	3	5	5.80	18	0	0	0	45	42	35	29	5	19	42	.246	.313	.230	8.40	3.80
Castillo, Yeiper	R-R	6-3	158	9-6-88	3	4	3.17	11	11	0	0	60	44	24	21	3	25	49	.213	.198	.223	7.39	3.77
Celestino, Miguel	R-R	6-6	205	10-10-89	7	9	4.68	26	26	0	0	135	129	75	70	18	44	93	.255	.284	.243	6.22	2.94
Couch, Keith	L-R	6-2	210	11-5-89	11	9	3.46	28	28	2	0	146	152	65	56	9	34	109	.270	.277	.267	6.73	2.10
Duarte, Marco	R-R	6-2	185	8-19-86	1	2	3.24	15	0	0	1	25	24	11	9	3	8	25	.250	.281	.234	9.00	2.88
Flores, Ruben	R-R	6-4	170	5-19-84	1	0	2.72	19	0	0	2	36	25	14	11	5	8	31	.197	.135	.222	7.68	1.98
Gleason, Mike	R-R	6-2	200	3-12-88	1	1	5.13	22	0	0	3	47	52	28	27	6	16	33	.280	.296	.273	6.27	3.04
Hill, Rich	L-L	6-5	220	3-11-80	0	0	0.00	3	3	0	0	4	1	0	0	0	1	8	.077	.000	.091	18.00	2.25
Jones, Andrew	R-R	6-3	185	5-1-89	5	4	3.35	39	0	0	4	75	89	32	28	3	9	53	.293	.313	.284	6.33	1.08
Kehrt, Jeremy	R-R	6-2	190	12-21-85	0	1	4.50	2	2	0	0	10	9	6	5	0	2	5	.225	.125	.250	4.50	1.80
Latimer, Will	L-L	6-0	190	12-4-85	2	1	7.15	5	0	0	0	11	15	9	9	2	5	12	.306	.100	.359	9.53	3.97
Lockwood, Tyler	R-R	6-0	180	12-9-87	0	0	6.75	4	0	0	0	8	13	7	6	1	2	2	.361	.200	.423	2.25	2.25
Matsuzaka, Daisuke	R-R	6-0	185	9-13-80	0	1	6.75	1	1	0	0	4	6	3	3	2	0	3	.333	—	.333	6.75	0.00
McCarthy, Mike	R-R	6-3	185	11-18-87	2	1	2.55	5	4	0	0	25	25	9	7	1	4	20	.263	.258	.266	7.30	1.46
Olmsted, Michael	R-R	6-6	245	5-2-87	0	2	2.29	33	0	0	16	39	25	13	10	1	8	61	.175	.212	.154	13.96	1.83
Pressly, Ryan	R-R	6-3	175	12-15-88	5	3	6.28	20	12	0	0	76	86	58	53	9	26	61	.287	.300	.281	7.22	3.08
Rivera, Manuel	L-L	6-0	170	9-19-89	5	5	6.06	28	6	0	2	85	95	65	57	15	46	59	.286	.271	.290	6.27	4.89
Rosario, Charle	R-R	5-10	158	7-23-88	4	2	4.91	20	2	0	2	51	55	30	28	5	15	36	.284	.206	.325	6.31	2.63
Ruiz, Pete	R-R	6-3	205	8-21-87	5	2	3.14	27	0	0	5	49	47	17	17	3	16	51	.250	.237	.256	9.43	2.96
Swinson, Scott	R-R	6-2	190	3-11-88	0	2	8.36	6	1	0	0	14	18	15	13	3	7	11	.321	.286	.343	7.07	4.50
Workman, Brandon	R-R	6-4	195	8-13-88	7	7	3.40	20	20	0	0	114	104	47	43	10	20	107	.244	.250	.241	8.47	1.58

Fielding

Catcher	PCT	G	PO	A	E	DP	PB
Blair	.983	36	217	20	4	0	7
Hernandez	.974	11	63	12	2	0	2
Ibarra	.969	17	109	15	4	1	2
Vazquez	.987	76	577	110	9	6	8

First Base	PCT	G	PO	A	E	DP
Almanzar	.994	19	157	9	1	8
Chester	1.000	3	32	0	0	2
Hedman	.991	35	297	17	3	24
Ibarra	1.000	1	12	0	0	3
Renfroe	1.000	8	69	4	0	6
Shaw	.984	79	649	43	11	64

Second Base	PCT	G	PO	A	E	DP
Coyle	.967	111	177	290	16	67
Gentile	1.000	5	15	21	0	10
Kang	.973	12	17	19	1	4
Meneses	.976	16	39	43	2	8

Third Base	PCT	G	PO	A	E	DP
Almanzar	.948	102	52	205	14	26
Gentile	.750	3	2	4	2	0
Johns	1.000	1	1	2	0	1
Kang	.872	18	9	25	5	3
Meneses	.941	14	9	23	2	1
Renfroe	.800	2	2	6	2	1
Shaw	.947	10	12	24	2	4

Shortstop	PCT	G	PO	A	E	DP
Bogaerts	.958	98	130	262	17	47
Johns	1.000	1	2	3	0	0
Kang	.884	17	10	28	5	5
Meneses	.986	32	56	84	2	22

Outfield	PCT	G	PO	A	E	DP
Bradley	.973	67	142	1	4	1
De La Cruz	1.000	6	14	0	0	0
Hedman	.913	15	19	2	2	0
Jacobs	.973	107	171	11	5	1
Johnson	1.000	46	78	5	0	2
Kalish	1.000	1	4	0	0	0
Kang	1.000	2	2	1	0	0

LeBlanc	.988	37	75	5	1	1		Sanchez	.943	38	48	2	3	0			
Marquis	.947	10	17	1	1	1		Wilkerson	.996	100	223	3	1	0			

GREENVILLE DRIVE

LOW CLASS A

SOUTH ATLANTIC LEAGUE

Batting	B-T	HT	WT	DOB	AVG	vLH	vRH	G	AB	R	H	2B	3B	HR	RBI	BB	HBP	SH	SF	SO	SB	CS	SLG	OBP
Cecchini, Garin	L-R	6-2	200	4-20-91	.305	.223	.338	118	455	84	139	38	4	4	62	61	7	0	3	90	51	6	.433	.394
De La Cruz, Keury	L-L	5-11	170	11-28-91	.308	.320	.304	116	474	71	146	35	8	19	81	26	6	0	0	101	19	7	.536	.352
Escobar, Leonel	R-R	5-10	175	9-4-90	.194	.125	.217	11	31	3	6	3	0	0	3	3	0	1	0	7	0	0	.290	.265
Garcia, Jose	R-R	5-11	165	4-23-91	.251	.239	.256	91	346	61	87	15	2	7	33	45	2	4	3	88	25	9	.367	.338
Guerrero, Dreily	B-R	5-11	162	10-12-90	.210	.200	.213	18	62	7	13	2	0	0	7	3	1	2	0	21	0	0	.242	.258
Johns, Bryan	R-R	5-9	180	11-18-88	.232	.200	.243	74	241	33	56	17	0	0	19	50	5	3	3	56	5	4	.303	.371
Koback, Cody	R-R	6-1	185	4-20-90	.260	.237	.269	89	331	37	86	12	2	4	37	19	11	5	1	85	19	4	.344	.320
LeBlanc, Lucas	R-R	6-2	200	5-7-89	.264	.214	.291	34	121	16	32	6	0	3	15	9	5	1	2	31	1	3	.388	.336
Marquis, Matt	R-R	6-0	200	2-22-90	.235	.156	.286	37	115	14	27	6	1	1	10	12	4	0	0	40	0	1	.330	.328
Moanaroa, Boss	L-R	6-0	200	7-12-91	.262	.269	.260	110	359	48	94	20	1	5	49	77	4	0	8	113	1	1	.365	.391
Natoli, Nick	R-R	6-1	195	1-17-88	.228	.268	.211	48	136	27	31	10	0	1	13	30	3	3	1	34	8	0	.324	.376
Ramos, Henry	B-R	6-2	187	4-15-92	.254	.238	.303	122	441	61	112	24	4	8	63	44	4	5	0	101	12	10	.381	.327
Renfroe, David	R-R	6-3	200	11-16-90	.256	.311	.234	96	355	49	91	27	0	10	64	33	7	0	2	69	4	0	.417	.330
Repko, Jason	R-R	5-11	200	12-27-80	.273	.167	.313	7	22	5	6	0	1	1	2	6	1	0	0	10	1	0	.500	.448
Swihart, Blake	B-R	6-1	175	4-3-92	.262	.232	.271	92	344	44	90	17	4	7	53	26	0	0	8	68	6	2	.395	.307
Turocy, Drew	L-L	6-3	190	12-26-88	.282	.319	.270	81	291	36	82	18	1	2	29	18	2	1	2	61	8	3	.371	.326
Vinicio, Jose	B-R	5-11	150	7-10-93	.277	.203	.305	70	256	37	71	9	3	3	32	13	4	3	2	56	24	11	.371	.320
Weems, Jordan	L-R	6-3	175	11-7-92	.201	.193	.205	86	298	33	60	11	0	0	29	44	2	1	0	87	4	1	.238	.308

Pitching	B-T	HT	WT	DOB	W	L	ERA	G	GS	CG	SV	IP	H	R	ER	HR	BB	SO	AVG	vLH	vRH	K/9	BB/9
Barnes, Matt	R-R	6-4	205	6-17-90	2	0	0.34	5	5	0	0	27	12	1	1	0	4	42	.130	.128	.132	14.18	1.35
Brahney, Kevin	L-L	6-5	220	8-8-88	2	1	10.00	14	0	0	0	27	40	31	30	4	8	28	.348	.424	.317	9.33	2.67
Carpenter, Chris	R-R	6-4	220	12-26-85	0	0	4.50	2	2	0	0	2	1	1	1	0	1	4	.143	.000	.333	18.00	4.50
Castillo, Yeiper	R-R	6-3	158	9-6-88	5	4	3.92	17	11	0	2	78	73	39	34	7	37	70	.249	.310	.211	8.08	4.27
Cervenka, Hunter	L-L	6-1	215	1-3-90	0	3	8.04	9	0	0	0	16	15	17	14	1	12	24	.254	.176	.286	13.79	6.89
Chavez, Dylan	L-L	6-3	190	4-16-91	1	2	9.00	15	0	0	0	22	29	22	22	2	10	20	.319	.200	.364	8.18	4.09
Diaz, Luis	R-R	6-3	210	4-9-92	3	8	6.01	20	17	0	0	91	117	66	61	8	28	62	.315	.247	.364	6.11	2.76
Erasmus, Justin	R-R	5-10	175	1-22-90	1	3	9.24	26	0	0	3	50	70	51	51	13	16	38	.329	.370	.303	6.89	2.90
Garcia, Jason	R-R	6-0	185	11-21-92	6	6	6.16	28	22	0	2	115	135	85	79	8	67	95	.297	.231	.336	7.41	5.23
Hill, Rich	L-L	6-5	220	3-11-80	0	0	4.50	2	2	0	0	2	2	1	1	0	0	5	.250	.500	.167	22.50	0.00
Kraus, Kyle	R-R	5-11	185	1-19-90	0	0	3.18	6	2	0	0	17	19	6	6	2	2	15	.284	.316	.231	7.94	1.06
Lockwood, Tyler	R-R	6-0	180	12-9-87	5	3	3.46	44	0	0	9	65	70	29	25	4	27	52	.268	.250	.279	7.20	3.74
McCarthy, Mike	R-R	6-3	185	11-18-87	3	4	3.66	26	4	0	1	64	55	29	26	1	24	51	.235	.253	.224	7.17	3.38
Miller, Andrew	L-L	6-7	210	5-21-85	0	0	0.00	2	1	0	0	2	2	0	0	0	0	3	.286	.000	.400	13.50	0.00
Ogando, Nefi	R-R	6-2	185	6-3-89	4	4	3.70	38	0	0	2	75	72	34	31	3	34	54	.248	.188	.280	6.45	4.06
Ott, Matty	R-R	6-1	190	4-20-90	4	3	3.54	39	0	0	5	84	68	42	33	12	27	65	.219	.214	.222	6.96	2.89
Owens, Henry	L-L	6-6	190	7-21-92	12	5	4.87	23	22	0	0	102	100	58	55	10	47	130	.256	.365	.230	11.51	4.16
Pena, Mickey	L-L	6-2	175	10-24-90	8	7	2.95	20	19	0	0	101	95	43	33	7	21	91	.253	.333	.230	8.14	1.88
Ramirez, Noe	R-R	6-3	180	12-22-89	2	7	4.15	16	16	0	0	85	89	43	39	12	19	82	.277	.216	.312	8.72	2.02
Rosario, Charle	R-R	5-10	158	7-23-88	1	0	4.80	7	0	0	0	15	12	8	8	2	4	17	.211	.143	.250	10.20	2.40
Striz, Nate	R-R	6-2	220	10-15-88	2	3	3.34	23	0	0	0	30	19	11	11	2	12	43	.183	.229	.159	13.04	3.64
Swinson, Scott	R-R	6-2	190	3-11-88	4	0	1.74	14	4	0	0	52	47	14	10	0	12	34	.240	.210	.254	5.92	2.09
Vellette, Raynel	R-R	6-2	165	6-10-91	0	1	4.00	4	0	0	0	9	8	4	4	1	7	9	.250	.333	.217	9.00	7.00
Wilson, Tyler	R-R	6-5	192	12-24-89	0	1	5.91	13	0	0	1	21	26	17	14	6	11	10	.299	.276	.310	4.22	4.64
Younginer, Madison	R-R	6-4	195	11-3-90	1	8	7.29	13	12	0	0	54	72	52	44	8	30	44	.323	.297	.344	7.29	4.97

Fielding

Catcher	PCT	G	PO	A	E	DP	PB
Escobar	1.000	10	67	6	0	1	4
Swihart	.988	66	517	45	7	7	3
Weems	.993	68	511	38	4	2	10

First Base	PCT	G	PO	A	E	DP
Moanaroa	.988	96	757	51	10	78
Natoli	1.000	1	1	1	0	0
Renfroe	.995	51	386	17	2	35

Second Base	PCT	G	PO	A	E	DP
Garcia	.974	77	154	221	10	54

	PCT	G	PO	A	E	DP
Guerrero	1.000	3	3	10	0	3
Johns	.977	60	104	156	6	38
Natoli	1.000	3	8	6	0	3

Third Base	PCT	G	PO	A	E	DP
Cecchini	.944	99	53	184	14	19
Natoli	.955	7	5	16	1	3
Renfroe	.955	36	18	67	4	4

Shortstop	PCT	G	PO	A	E	DP
Garcia	.860	12	18	25	7	4
Guerrero	.983	15	22	35	1	9

	PCT	G	PO	A	E	DP
Johns	.838	11	10	21	6	6
Natoli	.951	36	51	85	7	19
Vinicio	.924	70	110	196	25	44

Outfield	PCT	G	PO	A	E	DP
De La Cruz	.947	95	149	12	9	0
Koback	.988	86	159	8	2	2
LeBlanc	.947	28	52	2	3	1
Marquis	1.000	26	35	4	0	0
Ramos	.965	118	237	11	9	3
Repko	1.000	3	7	0	0	0
Turocy	.978	75	124	9	3	2

LOWELL SPINNERS

SHORT-SEASON

NEW YORK-PENN LEAGUE

Batting	B-T	HT	WT	DOB	AVG	vLH	vRH	G	AB	R	H	2B	3B	HR	RBI	BB	HBP	SH	SF	SO	SB	CS	SLG	OBP
Betts, Mookie	R-R	5-9	156	10-7-92	.267	.338	.234	71	251	34	67	8	1	0	31	32	3	2	4	30	20	4	.307	.352
Chester, David	R-R	6-5	270	3-31-89	.232	.263	.215	43	164	23	38	8	0	9	28	22	1	0	1	37	0	1	.445	.324
Colorado, Jose	L-R	6-1	170	8-26-90	.050	.000	.067	6	20	0	1	0	0	0	0	3	1	1	0	9	1	0	.050	.208
Davies, Jake	L-L	6-0	220	9-15-89	.254	.258	.253	34	122	10	31	5	1	0	13	9	1	0	2	27	0	1	.311	.306
Gedman, Matt	L-R	6-2	205	9-26-88	.206	.211	.205	44	155	18	32	4	0	3	21	12	3	0	2	19	3	0	.290	.273

BOSTON RED SOX

	B-T	HT	WT	DOB	AVG	vLH	vRH	G	AB	R	H	2B	3B	HR	RBI	BB	HBP	SH	SF	SO	SB	CS	SLG	OBP
Guerrero, Dreily	B-R	5-11	162	10-12-90	.274	.392	.217	41	157	17	43	8	0	0	13	15	0	2	3	44	11	5	.325	.331
Heller, Kevin	R-R	5-10	195	9-12-89	.333	.429	.294	7	24	3	8	2	0	2	3	2	0	1	0	7	2	0	.667	.385
Iglesias, Jose	R-R	5-11	185	1-5-90	.375	.667	.200	2	8	1	3	1	0	0	0	1	0	0	0	1	1	0	.500	.444
Jerez, Williams	L-L	6-4	190	5-16-92	.241	.212	.260	23	83	6	20	3	0	0	5	3	1	0	0	13	3	1	.277	.276
Johnson, Matty	B-R	5-8	165	4-10-88	.191	.200	.189	12	47	7	9	0	0	0	1	5	0	0	0	13	4	0	.191	.269
Kapstein, Zach	R-R	6-2	195	5-28-92	.160	.206	.128	26	81	9	13	3	0	0	2	7	3	0	0	31	0	0	.198	.253
Mager, Kevin	R-R	6-2	185	5-16-89	.200	.000	.286	3	10	0	2	0	0	0	0	0	0	0	0	4	0	0	.200	.200
Marquis, Matt	R-R	6-0	200	2-22-90	.226	.222	.227	32	115	12	26	3	2	3	16	14	2	1	0	48	6	1	.365	.321
Marrero, Deven	R-R	6-1	194	8-25-90	.268	.286	.259	64	246	45	66	14	3	2	24	34	1	2	1	48	24	6	.374	.358
Miller, Mike	R-R	5-9	170	9-27-89	.261	.265	.260	66	264	39	69	14	1	1	15	29	1	1	0	35	21	3	.333	.337
Minnich, Nathan	L-R	6-3	245	7-21-90	.136	.063	.179	12	44	2	6	0	0	0	3	4	3	0	0	13	0	0	.136	.255
Moore, Nick	B-R	6-2	200	12-9-92	.115	.000	.143	7	26	0	3	0	0	0	1	2	0	1	0	12	0	0	.115	.179
Perez, Oscar	R-R	6-1	185	11-9-91	.148	.269	.119	42	135	10	20	7	0	0	11	6	1	2	3	32	0	1	.200	.186
Perkins, Kendrick	L-R	6-2	225	9-12-91	.223	.159	.250	42	148	24	33	6	1	4	16	17	3	0	1	60	3	1	.358	.314
Reyes, Roberto	R-R	6-3	240	8-1-90	.167	.222	.133	9	24	1	4	0	0	0	2	0	0	0	0	14	0	0	.167	.167
Roberson, Tim	R-R	5-10	190	7-19-89	.203	.226	.184	21	69	5	14	2	0	2	7	5	0	0	2	17	0	0	.319	.250
Rondon, Cleuluis	R-R	6-0	155	4-13-94	.000	—	.000	2	4	0	0	0	0	0	0	0	0	0	0	1	0	0	.000	.000
Schwindenhammer, Seth	L-R	6-2	205	7-1-91	.073	.100	.065	13	41	4	3	0	1	2	8	4	0	0	0	24	0	0	.268	.156
Tavarez, Aneury	L-R	5-9	175	4-14-92	.272	.303	.259	62	213	19	58	9	4	4	24	11	7	3	1	59	6	3	.408	.328
Thompson, Jason	B-R	6-1	180	7-30-90	.231	.182	.267	10	26	3	6	0	0	0	2	3	1	0	1	9	1	0	.231	.323
Vinicio, Jose	B-R	5-11	150	7-10-93	.000	.000	.000	2	8	0	0	0	0	0	0	0	0	0	0	2	0	0	.000	.000
Vitek, Kolbrin	R-R	6-2	195	4-1-89	.250	.500	.167	2	8	1	2	1	0	0	1	0	0	0	0	2	0	0	.375	.250
Watkins, J.T.	R-R	6-0	190	8-30-89	.200	.286	.161	17	45	4	9	1	0	1	4	3	3	0	0	13	0	1	.289	.294

Pitching	B-T	HT	WT	DOB	W	L	ERA	G	GS	CG	SV	IP	H	R	ER	HR	BB	SO	AVG	vLH	vRH	K/9	BB/9
Augliera, Mike	R-R	6-0	200	6-8-90	1	3	4.42	15	14	0	0	39	42	21	19	2	3	43	.280	.281	.280	10.01	0.70
Brahney, Kevin	L-L	6-5	220	8-8-88	0	0	2.57	5	0	0	1	7	7	2	2	0	4	8	.280	.286	.278	10.29	5.14
Chavez, Dylan	L-L	6-3	190	4-16-91	0	2	6.00	4	0	0	0	6	8	10	4	0	0	7	.296	.333	.286	10.50	0.00
Cuevas, William	R-R	6-0	160	10-14-90	8	2	1.40	15	6	0	0	77	55	12	12	4	15	72	.204	.189	.217	8.38	1.75
Dahlstrand, Jacob	R-R	6-5	205	3-26-92	4	4	4.42	12	6	0	0	55	49	32	27	1	32	26	.245	.229	.256	4.25	5.24
Gomez, Sergio	R-R	6-3	155	8-24-93	0	0	3.60	1	1	0	0	5	4	2	2	1	1	4	.211	.333	.154	7.20	1.80
Good, Zach	L-L	6-3	185	6-8-92	0	6	6.34	10	6	0	0	33	31	35	23	0	37	13	.265	.364	.242	3.58	
10.19 Haley, Justin	R-R	6-5	230	6-16-91	0	1	1.89	13	12	0	0	33	23	11	7	1	16	33	.200	.122	.243	8.91	4.32
Johnson, Brian	L-L	6-3	225	12-7-90	0	0	0.00	4	4	0	0	6	2	0	0	0	1	4	.111	.500	.063	6.35	1.59
Kapteyn, Braden	R-R	6-4	225	3-24-89	0	1	1.82	19	0	0	7	35	12	8	7	0	23	35	.107	.136	.088	9.09	5.97
Kraus, Kyle	R-R	5-11	185	1-19-90	0	0	2.61	10	0	0	3	10	10	5	3	0	2	8	.233	.235	.231	6.97	1.74
Larson, Greg	R-R	6-8	225	9-25-89	1	2	2.76	15	0	0	2	33	30	13	10	1	12	27	.242	.298	.208	7.44	3.31
Light, Pat	R-R	6-5	195	3-29-91	0	2	2.37	12	12	0	0	30	27	9	8	1	5	30	.243	.244	.243	8.90	1.48
Maddox, Austin	R-R	6-2	220	5-13-91	0	0	0.00	1	1	0	0	3	2	0	0	1	4	.200	.000	.250	12.00	3.00
Marin, Leandro	R-R	5-11	165	11-9-88	2	2	9.28	9	0	0	0	11	13	16	11	0	13	14	.302	.412	.231	11.81	10.97
Montas, Francellis	R-R	6-2	185	3-21-93	0	0	0.00	1	1	0	0	4	5	1	0	0	1	4	.357	.250	.400	9.82	2.45
Ortega, Yunior	R-R	5-11	170	8-10-91	2	4	3.76	20	1	0	4	55	58	26	23	3	10	45	.274	.348	.220	7.36	1.64
Schmeltzer, Jadd	R-R	6-4	240	12-27-88	2	3	6.14	12	0	0	0	22	31	16	15	0	10	13	.344	.414	.311	5.32	4.09
Taveras, Francisco	L-L	6-0	180	5-23-90	6	3	1.99	15	1	0	0	68	46	21	15	0	31	59	.190	.111	.213	7.81	4.10
Vellette, Raynel	R-R	6-2	165	6-10-91	4	3	3.56	16	8	0	0	78	60	34	31	6	41	55	.212	.261	.168	6.32	4.71
Wilson, Tyler	R-R	6-5	192	12-24-89	5	1	5.32	15	0	0	0	47	49	30	28	2	15	31	.258	.275	.252	5.89	2.85
Younginer, Madison	R-R	6-4	195	11-3-90	0	0	4.09	3	3	0	0	11	8	5	5	1	7	4	.205	.294	.136	3.27	5.73

Fielding

Catcher	PCT	G	PO	A	E	DP	PB
Perez	.994	42	279	46	2	3	9
Reyes	.976	7	40	1	1	0	3
Roberson	.993	19	132	13	1	4	3
Watkins	.991	15	101	14	1	0	1

First Base	PCT	G	PO	A	E	DP
Chester	.985	36	297	29	5	26
Davies	.996	32	232	20	1	18
Gedman	1.000	1	8	2	0	2
Mager	1.000	1	7	0	0	0
Minnich	.958	7	67	2	3	9

Second Base	PCT	G	PO	A	E	DP
Betts	.969	58	123	154	9	37
Guerrero	.947	5	14	22	2	8

	PCT	G	PO	A	E	DP
Miller	1.000	6	9	10	0	5
Thompson	.968	9	11	19	1	4

Third Base	PCT	G	PO	A	E	DP
Gedman	.913	34	44	51	9	4
Guerrero	.773	9	6	11	5	0
Miller	.979	29	30	63	2	6
Moore	.952	6	7	13	1	3
Vitek	.667	1	0	2	1	1

Shortstop	PCT	G	PO	A	E	DP
Betts	.917	13	24	42	6	10
Iglesias	1.000	1	4	7	0	1
Marrero	.939	29	55	84	9	17
Miller	.967	31	57	62	4	19
Rondon	1.000	2	3	1	0	1

	PCT	G	PO	A	E	DP
Vinicio	1.000	2	0	2	0	0

Outfield	PCT	G	PO	A	E	DP
Colorado	.895	6	17	0	2	0
Guerrero	.979	26	45	2	1	0
Heller	.917	7	11	0	1	0
Jerez	.964	23	52	1	2	0
Johnson	.967	12	28	1	1	0
Kapstein	.941	18	16	0	1	0
Mager	—	1	0	0	0	0
Marquis	.975	32	77	2	2	1
Perkins	.932	41	66	3	5	1
Schwindenhammer	1.000	12	18	0	0	0
Tavarez	.974	58	109	4	3	0

GCL RED SOX

ROOKIE

GULF COAST LEAGUE

Batting	B-T	HT	WT	DOB	AVG	vLH	vRH	G	AB	R	H	2B	3B	HR	RBI	BB	HBP	SH	SF	SO	SB	CS	SLG	OBP
Aguero, Ynoel	B-R	5-10	170	12-7-90	.143	.000	.222	5	14	3	2	2	0	0	2	1	0	0	1	6	0	0	.286	.188
Bishop, Beau	R-R	6-2	200	7-6-93	.189	.158	.206	16	53	9	10	1	0	0	6	3	0	0	0	16	0	0	.208	.232
Briscoe, Keaton	L-R	6-0	190	5-13-91	.160	.118	.182	33	100	18	16	2	1	0	14	19	0	2	3	40	3	1	.200	.287
Colorado, Jose	L-R	6-1	170	8-26-90	.286	.215	.325	53	185	33	53	17	1	1	30	28	3	1	4	35	15	6	.405	.382
Conklin, Iseha	R-R	5-11	180	9-11-92	.205	.176	.218	38	112	13	23	5	1	1	13	8	5	2	2	44	2	1	.295	.283
Coste, Carlos	R-R	6-2	186	5-11-93	.136	.167	.125	12	22	2	3	0	0	0	2	0	0	0	0	11	0	0	.136	.208
Crawford, Carl	L-L	6-2	215	8-5-81	.214	.222	.200	5	14	2	3	1	0	0	0	5	0	0	0	4	0	1	.286	.421

Name	B-T	HT	WT	DOB	AVG	vLH	vRH	G	AB	R	H	2B	3B	HR	RBI	BB	HBP	SH	SF	SO	SB	CS	SLG	OBP
Davies, Jake	L-L	6-0	220	9-15-89	.279	.212	.343	20	68	12	19	7	0	1	9	9	1	0	0	9	1	0	.426	.372
Ellsbury, Jacoby	L-L	6-1	195	9-11-83	.200	.167	.250	4	10	3	2	1	0	1	3	4	0	0	0	3	0	0	.600	.429
Heller, Kevin	R-R	5-10	195	9-12-89	.263	.286	.258	12	38	11	10	3	0	0	2	6	0	0	0	8	0	1	.342	.364
Lin, Tzu-Wei	L-R	5-9	155	2-15-94	.255	.167	.309	29	110	21	28	5	1	0	16	16	0	1	3	28	4	2	.318	.341
Lopez, Deiner	B-R	6-0	165	5-30-94	.267	.340	.212	37	116	17	31	8	0	0	12	10	3	2	0	25	7	2	.336	.341
Loya, Jesus	L-R	6-0	170	6-15-92	.425	.455	.389	12	40	4	17	3	0	0	7	0	0	0	0	2	4	0	.500	.425
Mager, Kevin	R-R	6-2	185	5-16-89	.205	.224	.191	32	117	7	24	6	1	0	17	9	4	1	0	22	0	1	.274	.285
Meyers, Mike	R-R	6-1	175	12-28-93	.337	.214	.391	30	92	12	31	10	0	1	10	7	0	1	0	36	2	0	.478	.384
Minnich, Nathan	L-R	6-3	245	7-21-90	.232	.219	.238	27	95	13	22	5	1	0	17	21	1	0	3	34	0	0	.305	.367
Moore, Nick	B-R	6-2	200	12-9-92	.251	.176	.299	50	175	33	44	6	2	3	24	32	1	1	2	46	7	1	.360	.367
Pineda, Jeremias	B-R	5-11	175	11-16-90	.421	.354	.459	36	133	20	56	9	3	0	22	5	2	1	1	22	14	7	.534	.447
2-team total (16 Twins)					.365	—	—	52	192	28	70	9	4	1	25	11	3	1	1	38	23	9	.469	.406
Rodriguez, Miguel	R-R	6-2	227	10-8-90	.183	.115	.209	31	93	9	17	6	0	0	10	7	1	1	1	23	1	0	.247	.245
Rondon, Cleuluis	R-R	6-0	155	4-13-94	.231	.250	.218	47	182	19	42	10	6	0	16	9	2	3	3	42	2	2	.352	.270
Sopilka, David	R-R	6-0	170	8-30-93	.196	.184	.203	31	107	9	21	2	0	0	8	8	1	0	0	17	0	0	.215	.259
Thompson, Shaq	R-R	6-2	225	4-21-94	.000	.000	.000	13	39	3	0	0	0	0	1	8	0	0	0	37	1	1	.000	.170
Vitek, Kolbrin	R-R	6-2	195	4-1-89	.273	.000	.333	4	11	4	3	1	0	0	2	2	0	0	1	0	0	0	.364	.357

Pitching	B-T	HT	WT	DOB	W	L	ERA	G	GS	CG	SV	IP	H	R	ER	HR	BB	SO	AVG	vLH	vRH	K/9	BB/9
Alcantara, Mario	R-R	6-2	170	12-27-92	3	2	5.15	13	12	0	0	44	44	27	25	4	35	38	.268	.293	.255	7.83	7.21
Aro, Jonathan	R-R	6-0	172	10-10-90	3	4	4.66	11	4	0	0	39	45	21	20	4	9	34	.294	.278	.303	7.91	2.09
Bailey, Andrew	R-R	6-3	240	5-31-84	0	0	0.00	2	2	0	0	2	2	0	0	1	4		.286	1.000	.167	18.00	4.50
Bastardo, Luis	R-R	6-1	165	5-14-90	2	0	4.70	7	0	0	1	8	13	5	4	0	4	7	.382	.600	.345	8.22	4.70
Betancourt, Ricardo	L-L	6-2	175	9-9-92	4	3	2.31	11	3	0	0	39	38	15	10	2	8	25	.259	.182	.281	5.77	1.85
Bonnelly, Sully	R-R	6-2	215	10-16-92	1	0	3.34	12	0	0	1	30	27	11	11	2	16	23	.245	.290	.228	6.98	4.85
Buttrey, Ty	L-R	6-5	210	3-31-93	0	0	1.80	4	3	0	0	5	5	2	1	0	1	5	.278	.400	.231	9.00	1.80
Callahan, Jamie	R-R	6-2	205	8-24-94	1	0	5.19	5	4	0	0	9	8	5	5	0	3	7	.258	.200	.286	7.27	3.12
Carpenter, Chris	R-R	6-4	220	12-26-85	0	0	4.50	2	1	0	0	2	1	1	1	0	1	1	.167	.000	.200	4.50	4.50
Ethington, Willie	R-R	6-3	190	12-8-93	0	0	2.89	6	1	0	0	9	14	3	3	0	3	8	.359	.385	.346	7.71	2.89
Fernandez, Jeffry	R-R	6-3	180	3-25-93	0	0	5.68	2	1	0	0	6	10	5	4	0	3	3	.357	.222	.421	4.26	4.26
Gomez, Sergio	R-R	6-3	155	8-24-93	5	4	2.83	12	8	0	0	57	44	22	18	4	10	56	.210	.117	.247	8.79	1.57
Hill, Rich	L-L	6-5	220	3-11-80	0	1	13.50	2	1	0	0	1	0	2	2	0	2	3	.000	—	.000	20.25	13.50
Jimenez, Ellis	R-R	6-2	175	6-26-92	3	1	2.18	9	2	0	1	33	30	9	8	1	6	26	.248	.302	.218	7.09	1.64
Kukuk, Cody	L-L	6-4	200	4-10-93	2	0	0.90	5	0	0	0	10	3	2	1	0	3	16	.086	.200	.067	14.40	2.70
Maddox, Austin	R-R	6-2	220	5-13-91	0	1	1.80	3	3	0	0	5	4	1	1	0	1	4	.222	.000	.308	7.20	1.80
Melendez, Oscar	R-R	6-1	150	10-13-93	1	1	4.83	12	0	0	1	32	38	20	17	0	11	23	.295	.311	.286	6.54	3.13
Montas, Francellis	R-R	6-2	185	3-21-93	1	5	3.98	12	9	0	0	41	34	22	18	0	12	41	.228	.292	.198	9.07	2.66
Pena, Mickey	L-L	6-2	175	10-24-90	0	1	4.50	1	0	0	0	4	3	2	2	0	1	4	.214	.000	.250	9.00	2.25
Pinales, Carlos	R-R	6-1	180	4-5-92	4	1	1.52	16	0	0	3	41	32	12	7	2	1	34	.205	.250	.183	7.40	0.22
Reyes, Pedro	L-L	6-0	155	5-28-93	0	1	15.43	2	0	0	0	2	3	5	4	0	5	0	.333	.000	.375	0.00	19.29
Ruiz, Pete	R-R	6-3	205	8-21-87	0	0	9.00	2	1	0	0	3	6	4	3	1	0	3	.400	.600	.300	9.00	0.00
Scott, Robby	B-L	6-3	220	8-29-89	0	0	0.44	14	0	0	1	20	13	2	1	0	5	23	.188	.200	.188	10.18	2.21
Spalding, Matt	R-R	5-11	190	10-22-92	1	1	2.70	8	4	0	0	20	11	10	6	1	12	15	.177	.294	.133	6.75	5.40
Striz, Nate	R-R	6-2	220	10-15-88	0	0	0.00	1	0	0	0	2	1	0	0	0	1	3	.143	1.000	.000	13.50	4.50
Swinson, Scott	R-R	6-2	190	3-11-88	0	0	0.00	2	0	0	0	3	0	0	0	0	0	1	.000	.000	.000	3.00	0.00
Wendelken, J.B.	R-R	6-0	190	3-24-93	2	0	1.27	13	0	0	2	21	11	3	3	0	3	28	.147	.080	.180	11.81	1.27
Williams, Stephen	R-R	6-5	210	8-10-92	0	0	0.00	2	0	0	0	3	0	0	0	0	1	1	.000	.000	.000	3.00	3.00
Younginer, Madison	R-R	6-4	195	11-3-90	0	0	4.50	1	1	0	0	2	1	1	1	0	0	3	.143	.000	.167	13.50	0.00

Fielding

Catcher	PCT	G	PO	A	E	DP	PB
Bishop	.982	14	97	10	2	0	5
Coste	.955	7	20	1	1	0	0
Rodriguez	.991	18	103	11	1	2	5
Sopilka	.993	31	227	45	2	2	8

First Base	PCT	G	PO	A	E	DP
Davies	.993	19	128	11	1	19
Mager	.989	9	83	7	1	6
Minnich	.982	26	204	11	4	16
Rodriguez	.980	7	47	1	1	9

Second Base	PCT	G	PO	A	E	DP
Briscoe	1.000	8	21	10	0	1

	PCT	G	PO	A	E	DP
Lopez	.986	33	69	71	2	18
Mager	1.000	2	2	2	0	0
Meyers	.935	18	34	38	5	15

Third Base	PCT	G	PO	A	E	DP
Briscoe	.767	8	7	16	7	3
Mager	.950	7	8	11	1	4
Moore	.879	46	37	79	16	9
Vitek	1.000	2	2	3	0	0

Shortstop	PCT	G	PO	A	E	DP
Lin	.902	17	16	39	6	8
Lopez	.700	2	2	5	3	2
Meyers	1.000	5	3	5	0	1

	PCT	G	PO	A	E	DP
Rondon	.949	41	61	125	10	25

Outfield	PCT	G	PO	A	E	DP
Aguero	1.000	5	7	1	0	1
Briscoe	1.000	16	20	1	0	0
Colorado	.982	52	105	4	2	0
Conklin	.971	35	64	4	2	0
Crawford	1.000	4	6	0	0	0
Ellsbury	1.000	2	5	0	0	0
Heller	.950	12	17	2	1	0
Loya	.923	10	11	1	1	0
Mager	.957	13	20	2	1	0
Pineda	.971	33	64	4	2	2
Thompson	1.000	12	22	1	0	1

DSL RED SOX
ROOKIE
DOMINICAN SUMMER LEAGUE

Batting	B-T	HT	WT	DOB	AVG	vLH	vRH	G	AB	R	H	2B	3B	HR	RBI	BB	HBP	SH	SF	SO	SB	CS	SLG	OBP
Almengo, Osvaldo	R-R	6-2	180	10-1-92	.177	.154	.186	35	96	11	17	3	1	1	15	9	4	0	2	32	0	0	.260	.270
Amaya, Anthony	L-L	5-10	160	5-1-94	.232	.295	.204	62	198	28	46	11	1	2	21	22	12	4	1	38	10	9	.328	.343
Andujar, Ricardo	B-R	6-0	160	8-6-92	.225	.269	.198	48	138	17	31	2	3	0	10	25	5	1	1	33	6	4	.283	.361
Del Rosario, Robert	R-R	5-11	185	7-25-92	.238	.260	.230	67	260	36	62	10	3	3	38	30	1	0	3	50	20	4	.335	.316
Duncan, Roberto	R-R	6-3	175	2-18-93	.219	.222	.218	62	196	42	43	9	2	5	29	39	12	4	1	53	6	1	.362	.379
Estrella, Junior	R-R	5-9	170	3-29-93	.286	.214	.314	14	49	6	14	5	0	0	7	10	0	0	0	16	4	2	.388	.407
Flores, Raymel	B-R	5-9	155	9-22-94	.254	.205	.277	37	138	26	35	3	8	0	18	23	9	1	1	40	4	3	.391	.392

Name	B-T	HT	WT	DOB	AVG	vLH	vRH	G	AB	R	H	2B	3B	HR	BB	SO	SB	CS	HBP	SO	BB	...	OBP	SLG
Garcia, Andres	R-R	5-9	155	3-12-94	.224	.190	.242	69	245	46	55	7	4	0	26	56	6	9	7	37	15	8	.286	.373
Margot, Manuel	R-R	5-11	170	9-28-94	.285	.314	.270	68	260	49	74	10	7	4	45	36	8	0	5	25	33	9	.423	.382
Paulino, Diory	R-R	6-0	170	7-13-94	.125	.000	.200	2	8	0	1	0	0	0	0	0	0	0	0	3	0	0	.125	.125
Peralta, Aneudis	R-R	5-11	195	8-21-93	.249	.206	.270	61	209	31	52	18	1	0	26	35	6	2	2	39	2	3	.344	.369
Segovia, Kevin	R-R	6-0	170	1-1-95	.167	.118	.200	17	42	8	7	1	0	0	4	7	2	3	0	19	0	0	.190	.314
Suarez, Alixon	R-R	6-1	180	7-25-94	.270	.232	.292	63	226	41	61	15	4	4	28	39	11	0	2	41	2	3	.425	.399
Titts, Gregori	L-R	5-10	150	6-23-95	.150	.174	.135	23	60	9	9	0	0	0	2	9	1	2	0	14	3	1	.150	.271
Urena, Pablo	R-R	6-0	175	10-17-94	.185	.229	.167	36	119	6	22	4	0	0	7	7	7	3	1	34	1	1	.218	.269
Valenzuela, Luis	L-R	5-10	150	8-25-93	.133	.125	.136	9	30	4	4	0	2	0	3	4	0	0	0	5	0	0	.267	.235

Pitching	B-T	HT	WT	DOB	W	L	ERA	G	GS	CG	SV	IP	H	R	ER	HR	BB	SO	AVG	vLH	vRH	K/9	BB/9
Abreu, William	R-R	6-0	200	1-2-92	2	0	1.96	12	0	0	0	23	17	10	5	0	16	10	.202	.259	.175	3.91	6.26
Betancourt, Ricardo	L-L	6-2	175	9-9-92	1	0	1.50	2	0	0	0	6	7	1	1	1	0	5	.280	.250	.286	7.50	0.00
Bonnelly, Sully	R-R	6-2	215	10-14-92	0	0	0.00	4	2	1	0	0	2	4	.154	.000	.200	9.82	4.91
Espitia, Jose	R-R	6-2	180	9-16-93	0	0	1.50	2	2	0	0	6	3	1	1	0	1	8	.136	.333	.063	12.00	1.50
Florian, Wildyn	R-R	6-1	185	10-29-92	0	0	7.53	10	0	0	1	14	17	15	12	0	9	6	.279	.227	.308	3.77	5.65
Garcia, Carlos	L-L	6-0	170	12-15-94	1	3	6.23	13	0	0	1	30	38	29	21	2	15	19	.302	.333	.299	5.64	4.45
Garcia, Edwar	R-R	6-4	175	11-19-93	1	2	4.04	14	14	0	0	49	44	33	22	1	30	33	.238	.250	.229	6.06	5.51
Gonzalez, William	R-R	6-2	180	6-16-93	0	0	3.68	6	0	0	0	7	6	3	3	0	8	7	.214	.364	.118	8.59	9.82
Heras, Keivin	R-R	6-1	160	9-21-94	6	1	2.03	13	13	0	0	62	46	15	14	2	20	30	.206	.194	.212	4.35	2.90
Martinez, Enfember	R-R	5-11	140	8-30-95	3	0	1.69	12	0	0	3	32	26	6	6	2	5	14	.218	.243	.207	3.94	1.41
Mercedes, Simon	R-R	6-4	200	2-17-92	0	0	0.00	1	1	0	0	4	4	0	0	0	2	4	.250	—	.250	9.00	4.50
Ortega, Luis	L-L	5-10	155	4-20-93	6	3	2.12	13	13	1	0	59	55	22	14	1	16	29	.241	.217	.244	4.40	2.43
Osorio, Edwin	R-R	6-2	175	10-20-93	1	0	5.40	7	0	0	0	8	9	8	5	0	7	2	.281	.333	.261	2.16	7.56
Pacheco, Edinxon	R-R	6-4	180	1-6-94	0	0	8.44	4	0	0	0	5	6	5	5	1	4	4	.261	.500	.211	6.75	6.75
Perez, Randy	L-R	5-10	165	4-1-94	5	3	3.97	15	12	0	1	57	53	28	25	0	27	43	.252	.313	.242	6.83	4.29
Pimentel, Yankory	R-R	6-2	210	9-29-93	1	0	2.76	12	0	0	1	33	28	13	10	1	15	30	.228	.167	.247	8.27	4.13
Pinales, Carlos	R-R	6-1	180	4-5-92	1	0	0.00	2	0	0	0	4	2	0	0	0	1	2	.143	.000	.222	4.15	2.08
Ramirez, Victor	R-R	6-1	190	5-12-95	3	0	1.32	13	0	0	4	48	31	15	7	0	13	29	.178	.205	.169	5.48	2.45
Ramos, Luis	L-L	6-1	180	6-5-95	0	3	9.90	9	0	0	0	10	13	14	11	1	6	7	.302	.400	.289	6.30	5.40
Rodriguez, Javier	L-L	6-2	165	5-1-95	0	1	9.00	4	0	0	0	3	6	5	3	0	5	1	.429	.667	.364	3.00	15.00
Romero, Dioscar	R-R	6-3	230	4-17-95	5	4	2.69	15	15	1	0	60	48	31	18	0	23	47	.214	.212	.215	7.01	3.43
Taveras, German	R-R	6-2	180	2-15-93	0	1	5.88	16	0	0	1	26	26	20	17	1	15	17	.271	.250	.281	5.88	5.19
Torrealba, Jervis	L-L	6-0	165	6-9-95	2	5	4.40	15	0	0	1	45	51	31	22	0	16	22	.290	.333	.283	4.40	3.20
Vasquez, Leonel	R-R	6-0	150	2-10-91	3	3	2.10	23	0	0	9	26	27	7	6	0	11	27	.273	.217	.289	9.47	3.86

Fielding

Catcher	PCT	G	PO	A	E	DP	PB
Segovia	1.000	11	45	9	0	0	2
Suarez	.986	53	320	39	5	0	9
Urena	.982	10	51	4	1	1	4

First Base	PCT	G	PO	A	E	DP
Almengo	1.000	1	9	3	0	2
Duncan	.988	55	530	31	7	38
Suarez	1.000	3	21	0	0	2
Urena	.981	12	94	9	2	12

Second Base	PCT	G	PO	A	E	DP
Andujar	1.000	2	2	1	0	0

	PCT	G	PO	A	E	DP
Garcia	.970	69	151	204	11	46
Valenzuela	.750	1	2	1	1	0

Third Base	PCT	G	PO	A	E	DP
Andujar	.818	10	6	12	4	1
Duncan	.842	5	2	14	3	1
Estrella	.870	8	7	13	3	1
Peralta	.888	48	39	119	20	9
Valenzuela	.846	3	2	9	2	1

Shortstop	PCT	G	PO	A	E	DP
Andujar	.897	34	53	95	17	18
Duncan	.667	1	1	1	1	0

	PCT	G	PO	A	E	DP
Estrella	.875	4	2	12	2	0
Flores	.921	30	47	105	13	18
Paulino	1.000	2	2	7	0	0
Valenzuela	.929	3	7	6	1	1

Outfield	PCT	G	PO	A	E	DP
Almengo	.821	23	21	2	5	0
Amaya	.953	61	97	4	5	2
Andujar	—	1	0	0	0	0
Del Rosario	.984	58	116	8	2	2
Margot	.984	65	175	5	3	0
Titts	1.000	17	18	1	0	0

Chicago Cubs

SEASON IN A SENTENCE: The hiring of Theo Epstein has the organization clearly pointed toward the future, but the present was pretty lousy.

HIGH POINT: In a season when the Cubs were never above .500 and lost 101 games, they at least had a heartwarming moment when Kerry Wood retired on May 19, striking out the White Sox's Dayan Viciedo in his last outing and walking off the mound to a raucous reception. Wood, 34, battled health issues all season.

LOW POINT: The Cubs had only one month when they were better than .500, going 15-10 in June, and they collapsed after that, finishing the season on an 18-42 slide. Perhaps the true low is that even after going 61-101 Chicago won't have the No. 1 pick in the 2013 draft because the Astros were even worse.

NOTABLE ROOKIES: Chicago had plenty of opportunity for young players in 2012, though the only one who looks like a definite part of the future is first baseman Anthony Rizzo, who was acquired from the Padres in January. He batted .285/.342/.463 after getting called up in late June and eventually took over first base from fellow rookie Brian LaHair. LaHair got off to a blazing start, batting .313/.400/.592 on June 1, but tailed off and ended the season coming off the bench or playing right field. Top prospect Brett Jackson also made his big league debut, but he struck out 59 times in 120 at-bats. Even though the pitching staff ranked 14th in the National League in ERA, no rookies pitched significant innings.

KEY TRANSACTIONS: The new Cubs administration got busy right away making over both the front office and the roster, but the project is still very much a work in progress. Veterans such as Jeff Baker, Marlon Byrd, Sean Marshall, Geovany Soto and Carlos Zambrano were jettisoned for prospects or younger major leaguers, and in many cases even those players have since been turned over, such as Chris Volstad coming in a trade with the Marlins and then going on a waiver claim to the Royals. The only acquisitions that appear to have potential long-term significance are Rizzo and Travis Wood, acquired from the Reds for Marshall.

DOWN ON THE FARM: Only the Double-A Tennessee and Rookie-level Arizona League squads had winning records, but shortstop Javier Baez was the best prospect in the low Class A Midwest League, and outfielder Albert Almora highlighted what looks like a strong 2012 draft class.

OPENING DAY PAYROLL: $88.2 million (15th)

PLAYERS OF THE YEAR

RODGER WOOD

MAJOR LEAGUE	MINOR LEAGUE
Jeff Samardzija rhp	**Javier Baez** ss
9-13, 3.81	(Low A/High A)
180 SO/56 BB	.294/.346/.543
2nd in NL in SO/9	Top prospect in MWL

ORGANIZATION LEADERS

BATTING		*Minimum 250 AB
MAJORS		
* AVG	Starlin Castro	.283
* OPS	Alfonso Soriano	.821
HR	Alfonso Soriano	32
RBI	Alfonso Soriano	108
MINORS		
* AVG	Josh Vitters, Iowa	.304
* OBP	John Andreoli, Daytona	.402
* SLG	Josh Vitters, Iowa	.513
R	Logan Watkins, Tennessee	93
H	Rubi Silva, Daytona/Tennessee	148
TB	Greg Rohan, Daytona/Tennessee/Iowa	242
2B	Greg Rohan, Daytona/Tennessee/Iowa	38
3B	Rubi Silva, Daytona/Tennessee	14
HR	Anthony Rizzo, Iowa	23
RBI	Justin Bour, Tennessee	110
BB	Zeke DeVoss, Peoria	82
SO	Brett Jackson, Iowa	158
SB	John Andreoli, Daytona	55

PITCHING		#Minimum 75 IP
MAJORS		
W	Paul Maholm	9
# ERA	Jeff Samardzija	3.81
SO	Jeff Samardzija	180
SV	Carlos Marmol	20
MINORS		
W	Nick Struck, Tennessee	14
L	Brooks Raley, Tennessee/Iowa	10
	Nick Struck, Tennessee	10
# ERA	P.J. Francescon, Peoria/Daytona	3.01
G	Brian Schlitter, Daytona/Tennessee	50
GS	Dallas Beeler, Tennessee	27
SV	Frank Batista, Iowa/Tennessee	24
IP	Eric Jokisch, Daytona/Tennessee	159.1
BB	Austin Kirk, Daytona/Tennessee	60
SO	Nick Struck, Tennessee	123
# AVG	Matt Loosen, Daytona	.202

General Manager: Theo Epstein. **Farm Director:** Oneri Fleita. **Scouting Director:** Tim Wilken.

Class	Team	League	W	L	PCT	Finish	Manager
Majors	Chicago Cubs	National	61	101	.377	15th (16)	Dale Sveum
Triple-A	Iowa Cubs	Pacific Coast	53	87	.379	16th (16)	Dave Bialas
Double-A	Tennessee Smokies	Southern	72	68	.514	4th (10)	Buddy Bailey
High A	Daytona Cubs	Florida State	59	74	.444	9th (12)	Brian Harper
Low A	Peoria Chiefs	Midwest	63	75	.457	14th (16)	Casey Kopitzke
Short-season	Boise Hawks	Northwest	37	39	.487	4th (8)	Mark Johnson
Rookie	AZL Cubs	Arizona	37	19	.661	2nd (13)	Bobby Mitchell
Overall 2012 Minor League Record			321	362	.470	24th (30)	

ORGANIZATION STATISTICS

CHICAGO CUBS

NATIONAL LEAGUE

Batting	B-T	HT	WT	DOB	AVG	vLH	vRH	G	AB	R	H	2B	3B	HR	RBI	BB	HBP	SH	SF	SO	SB	CS	SLG	OBP
Baker, Jeff	R-R	6-2	210	6-21-81	.269	.275	.256	54	134	16	36	10	1	4	20	8	0	0	2	28	4	1	.448	.306
2-team total (14 Atlanta)					.248	—	—	68	153	17	38	10	1	4	21	9	0	0	2	38	4	1	.405	.287
Barney, Darwin	R-R	5-10	185	11-8-85	.254	.257	.252	156	548	73	139	26	4	7	44	33	3	1	5	58	6	1	.354	.299
Byrd, Marlon	R-R	6-0	215	8-30-77	.070	.143	.056	13	43	1	3	0	0	0	2	3	1	0	0	10	0	1	.070	.149
Campana, Tony	L-L	5-8	165	5-30-86	.264	.229	.273	89	174	26	46	6	0	0	5	11	0	7	0	43	30	3	.299	.308
Cardenas, Adrian	L-R	6-0	205	10-10-87	.183	.250	.179	45	60	5	11	6	0	0	2	7	0	0	0	13	0	0	.283	.269
Castillo, Welington	R-R	5-10	210	4-24-87	.265	.476	.195	52	170	16	45	11	0	5	22	17	2	0	1	51	0	0	.418	.337
Castro, Starlin	R-R	6-0	190	3-24-90	.283	.293	.280	162	646	78	183	29	12	14	78	36	4	0	5	100	25	13	.430	.323
Clevenger, Steve	L-R	6-0	195	4-5-86	.201	.069	.224	69	199	16	40	12	0	1	16	16	0	0	0	39	0	1	.276	.260
DeJesus, David	L-L	5-11	190	12-20-79	.263	.149	.289	148	506	76	133	28	8	9	50	61	9	2	4	89	7	8	.403	.350
DeWitt, Blake	L-R	5-11	195	8-20-85	.138	—	.138	18	29	1	4	1	0	0	1	0	0	0	1	2	0	0	.172	.133
Hill, Koyie	B-R	6-1	210	3-9-79	.179	.150	.211	11	39	3	7	1	0	1	0	1	0	0	0	7	0	0	.205	.179
Jackson, Brett	L-R	6-2	210	8-2-88	.175	.167	.176	44	120	14	21	6	1	4	9	22	0	0	0	59	3	0	.342	.303
Johnson, Reed	R-R	5-10	180	12-8-76	.302	.321	.282	76	169	23	51	9	3	3	16	10	4	0	0	43	2	1	.444	.355
2-team total (43 Atlanta)					.290	—	—	119	269	30	78	14	3	3	20	13	6	0	0	61	2	2	.398	.337
LaHair, Bryan	L-R	6-5	240	11-5-82	.259	.063	.291	130	340	42	88	17	0	16	40	39	0	0	1	124	4	2	.450	.334
Lalli, Blake	L-R	6-1	205	5-12-83	.133	.000	.182	6	15	1	2	0	0	0	2	1	0	0	0	3	0	0	.133	.188
Mather, Joe	R-R	6-4	215	7-23-82	.209	.202	.216	103	225	18	47	11	0	5	19	14	1	1	2	46	5	2	.324	.256
Recker, Anthony	R-R	6-2	240	8-29-83	.167	.125	.200	9	18	1	3	1	0	1	4	2	1	0	0	2	0	0	.389	.286
Rizzo, Anthony	L-L	6-3	220	8-8-89	.285	.208	.318	87	337	44	96	15	0	15	48	27	3	0	1	62	3	2	.463	.342
Sappelt, Dave	R-R	5-9	195	1-2-87	.275	.440	.182	26	69	8	19	6	0	2	8	7	1	1	0	9	0	0	.449	.351
Soriano, Alfonso	R-R	6-1	195	1-7-76	.262	.260	.263	151	561	68	147	33	2	32	108	44	7	0	3	153	6	2	.499	.322
Soto, Geovany	R-R	6-1	220	1-20-83	.199	.235	.184	52	176	26	35	6	1	6	14	19	2	0	0	35	0	0	.347	.284
Stewart, Ian	L-R	6-3	215	4-5-85	.201	.179	.207	55	179	16	36	5	2	5	17	21	2	0	0	46	0	3	.335	.292
Valbuena, Luis	L-R	5-10	195	11-30-85	.219	.196	.225	90	265	26	58	20	0	4	28	36	0	0	2	55	0	2	.340	.310
Vitters, Josh	R-R	6-2	200	8-27-89	.121	.111	.130	36	99	7	12	2	0	2	5	7	2	0	1	33	2	0	.202	.193

Pitching	B-T	HT	WT	DOB	W	L	ERA	G	GS	CG	SV	IP	H	R	ER	HR	BB	SO	AVG	vLH	vRH	K/9	BB/9
Asencio, Jairo	R-R	6-2	180	5-5-84	0	0	3.07	12	0	0	0	15	12	6	5	1	11	8	.214	.269	.167	4.91	6.75
Beliveau, Jeff	L-L	6-1	195	1-17-87	1	0	4.58	22	0	0	0	18	21	9	5	12	17	.292	.360	.255	8.66	6.11
Berken, Jason	R-R	6-0	205	11-27-83	0	3	4.82	4	4	0	0	19	23	14	10	3	6	11	.303	.273	.326	5.30	2.89
Bowden, Michael	R-R	6-3	215	9-9-86	0	0	2.95	30	0	0	0	37	30	12	12	4	16	29	.227	.208	.238	7.12	3.93
Cabrera, Alberto	R-R	6-4	210	10-25-88	1	1	5.40	25	0	0	0	22	16	15	13	1	18	27	.205	.133	.250	11.22	7.48
Camp, Shawn	R-R	6-0	205	11-18-75	3	6	3.59	80	0	0	2	78	79	32	31	7	21	54	.261	.263	.259	6.26	2.43
Castillo, Lendy	R-R	6-1	170	4-8-89	0	1	7.88	13	0	0	0	16	24	16	14	2	12	13	.343	.423	.295	7.31	6.75
Chapman, Jaye	R-R	6-0	195	5-24-87	0	1	3.75	14	0	0	0	12	8	5	5	0	10	12	.200	.125	.250	9.00	7.50
Coleman, Casey	L-R	6-0	185	7-3-87	0	2	7.40	17	1	0	0	24	37	20	20	5	12	16	.349	.435	.283	5.92	4.44
Corpas, Manny	R-R	6-3	210	12-3-82	0	2	5.01	48	0	0	0	47	50	27	26	7	16	28	.273	.328	.248	5.40	3.09
Dempster, Ryan	R-R	6-2	215	5-3-77	5	5	2.25	16	16	0	0	104	81	28	26	9	27	83	.210	.197	.221	7.18	2.34
Dolis, Rafael	R-R	6-4	215	1-10-88	2	4	6.39	34	0	0	4	38	40	29	27	5	23	24	.278	.141	.388	5.68	5.45
Garza, Matt	R-R	6-4	215	11-26-83	5	7	3.91	18	18	0	0	104	90	48	45	15	32	96	.236	.247	.224	8.33	2.78
Germano, Justin	R-R	6-2	210	8-6-82	2	10	6.75	13	12	0	0	64	81	52	48	7	19	45	.309	.281	.325	6.33	2.67
Hinshaw, Alex	L-L	6-2	175	10-31-82	0	0	135.00	2	0	0	0	4	5	5	3	1	0	.800	.000	1.000	0.00	27.00
2-team total (31 San Diego)					1	1	6.04	33	0	0	0	28	27	19	19	8	21	36	—	—	—	11.44	6.67
Lopez, Rodrigo	R-R	6-1	185	12-14-75	0	1	5.68	4	0	0	0	6	8	6	4	0	5	2	.320	.300	.333	2.84	7.11
Maholm, Paul	L-L	6-2	220	6-25-82	9	6	3.74	21	20	0	0	120	115	51	50	12	34	81	.256	.304	.240	6.06	2.54
2-team total (11 Atlanta)					13	11	3.67	32	31	1	0	189	178	80	77	20	53	140	—	—	—	6.67	2.52
Maine, Scott	L-L	6-3	215	2-2-85	1	1	4.79	21	0	0	0	21	17	11	11	2	12	26	.230	.130	.275	11.32	5.23
Marmol, Carlos	R-R	6-2	215	10-14-82	3	3	3.42	61	0	0	20	55	40	24	21	4	45	72	.200	.221	.177	11.71	7.32
Parker, Blake	R-R	6-3	225	6-19-85	0	0	6.00	7	0	0	0	6	10	7	4	3	5	6	.370	.143	.450	9.00	7.50
Raley, Brooks	L-L	6-3	185	6-29-88	1	2	8.14	5	5	0	0	24	33	23	22	7	11	16	.317	.214	.333	5.92	4.07
Rusin, Chris	L-L	6-2	195	10-22-86	2	3	6.37	7	7	0	0	30	38	22	21	4	11	21	.314	.273	.330	6.37	3.34
Russell, James	L-L	6-4	200	1-8-86	7	1	3.25	77	0	0	2	69	67	28	25	5	23	55	.255	.262	.250	7.14	2.99
Samardzija, Jeff	R-R	6-5	225	1-23-85	9	13	3.81	28	28	1	0	175	157	79	74	20	56	180	.240	.241	.239	9.27	2.89
Socolovich, Miguel	R-R	6-1	190	7-24-86	0	0	4.50	6	0	0	0	6	4	3	1	3	6	.182	.100	.250	9.00	4.50

	B-T	HT	WT	DOB	W	L	ERA	G	GS	CG	SV	IP	H	R	ER	HR	BB	SO	AVG	vLH	vRH	K/9	BB/9
Volstad, Chris	R-R	6-8	230	9-23-86	3	12	6.31	21	21	0	0	111	137	81	78	16	43	61	.306	.283	.322	4.93	3.48
Wells, Randy	R-R	6-5	230	8-28-82	1	2	5.34	12	4	0	0	29	35	18	17	1	24	14	.313	.353	.279	4.40	7.53
Wood, Kerry	R-R	6-5	210	6-16-77	0	2	8.31	10	0	0	0	9	8	8	8	1	11	6	.267	.214	.313	6.23	11.42
Wood, Travis	R-L	5-11	175	2-6-87	6	13	4.27	26	26	0	0	156	133	80	74	25	54	119	.232	.195	.241	6.87	3.12

Fielding

Catcher	PCT	G	PO	A	E	DP	PB
Castillo	.981	49	345	24	7	2	4
Clevenger	.988	51	319	18	4	0	4
Hill	.988	11	71	8	1	0	0
Lalli	1.000	4	20	0	0	0	0
Recker	.969	5	27	4	1	0	0
Soto	.982	52	356	25	7	2	1

First Base	PCT	G	PO	A	E	DP
Baker	.987	20	143	7	2	11
Castillo	—	1	0	0	0	0
Clevenger	1.000	9	31	3	0	3
LaHair	.994	58	445	18	3	44
Lalli	1.000	2	4	0	0	1
Mather	1.000	2	3	1	0	0
Recker	1.000	1	7	0	0	2
Rizzo	.995	85	685	46	4	76

Second Base	PCT	G	PO	A	E	DP
Baker	1.000	8	6	11	0	3
Barney	.997	155	311	418	2	96
Cardenas	1.000	12	16	15	0	2
DeWitt	1.000	4	12	8	0	2
Valbuena	1.000	5	2	4	0	1

Third Base	PCT	G	PO	A	E	DP
Cardenas	.500	1	1	1	2	0
Clevenger	—	1	0	0	0	0
Mather	.870	18	2	18	3	3
Stewart	.955	52	21	86	5	4
Valbuena	.963	82	45	137	7	18
Vitters	.926	29	9	41	4	4

Shortstop	PCT	G	PO	A	E	DP
Barney	.923	3	4	8	1	2

Castro	.964	162	266	465	27	97

Outfield	PCT	G	PO	A	E	DP
Baker	1.000	15	20	0	0	0
Byrd	.972	13	35	0	1	0
Campana	1.000	69	91	1	0	0
Cardenas	1.000	3	1	0	0	0
DeJesus	.993	143	262	8	2	1
DeWitt	1.000	1	1	0	0	0
Jackson	.979	39	94	0	2	0
Johnson	.987	53	74	3	1	1
LaHair	.967	36	59	0	2	0
Mather	1.000	56	91	0	0	0
Sappelt	1.000	21	37	2	0	1
Soriano	.996	145	253	12	1	6

IOWA CUBS

PACIFIC COAST LEAGUE

TRIPLE-A

Batting	B-T	HT	WT	DOB	AVG	vLH	vRH	G	AB	R	H	2B	3B	HR	RBI	BB	HBP	SH	SF	SO	SB	CS	SLG	OBP
Adduci, Jim	L-L	6-2	210	5-15-85	.306	.370	.277	42	147	27	45	9	2	2	17	17	1	3	2	40	7	4	.435	.377
Amaya, Gioskar	R-R	5-11	175	12-13-92	1.000	—	1.000	1	1	1	1	0	0	0	0	0	0	0	0	0	0	0	2.000	1.000
Amezaga, Alfredo	B-R	5-11	165	1-16-78	.274	.266	.278	113	398	65	109	17	2	6	42	37	1	1	2	60	12	3	.372	.336
Apodaca, Juan	R-R	5-11	180	7-15-86	.280	.295	.273	52	132	10	37	9	0	1	18	22	1	0	0	26	0	0	.371	.387
Campana, Tony	L-L	5-8	165	5-30-86	.280	.220	.304	37	143	24	40	2	1	1	4	12	1	8	1	34	18	7	.329	.338
Cardenas, Adrian	L-R	6-0	205	10-10-87	.300	.319	.292	65	243	30	73	22	4	3	32	33	1	1	4	32	5	0	.461	.381
Castillo, Wellington	R-R	5-10	210	4-24-87	.260	.233	.272	44	146	22	38	6	0	6	22	23	5	0	2	37	0	0	.425	.375
Clevenger, Steve	L-R	6-0	195	4-5-86	.462	1.000	.417	5	13	5	6	2	0	1	3	2	0	0	0	0	0	0	.846	.533
DeWitt, Blake	L-R	5-11	195	8-20-85	.127	.034	.164	30	102	5	13	3	0	0	5	14	2	0	0	23	0	0	.157	.246
Esposito, Brian	R-R	6-1	210	2-24-79	.225	.231	.222	41	120	6	27	6	0	0	8	6	1	0	0	28	0	0	.275	.268
Frazier, Jeff	R-R	6-3	195	8-10-82	.275	.150	.327	27	69	6	19	4	0	1	7	5	1	0	2	12	0	0	.377	.325
Gonzalez, Edgar	R-R	6-0	180	6-14-78	.286	.143	.333	9	28	1	8	1	1	0	3	2	0	0	0	4	1	0	.393	.333
Hernandez, Diory	R-R	6-0	185	4-8-84	.241	.213	.265	60	158	10	38	9	1	2	13	9	0	1	2	20	1	0	.348	.278
2-team total (32 Oklahoma City)					.223	—	—	92	202	15	45	9	1	2	15	13	1	3	3	33	2	1	.307	.269
Jackson, Brett	L-R	6-2	210	8-2-88	.256	.279	.246	106	407	66	104	22	12	15	47	47	6	2	5	158	27	5	.479	.338
Lalli, Blake	L-R	6-1	205	5-12-83	.259	.218	.276	93	301	33	78	20	0	7	40	17	0	0	6	54	0	1	.395	.293
2-team total (4 Sacramento)					.256	—	—	97	316	34	81	20	0	8	41	18	0	0	6	55	0	2	.396	.291
Mota, Jonathan	R-R	6-0	200	6-1-87	.235	.000	.308	7	17	3	4	1	1	1	5	1	0	0	0	3	0	0	.588	.278
Recker, Anthony	R-R	6-2	240	8-29-83	.286	.000	.286	3	7	1	2	1	0	0	2	0	0	0	0	2	0	0	.429	.444
2-team total (52 Sacramento)					.266	—	—	55	207	30	55	8	0	9	29	30	1	0	0	58	3	1	.435	.361
Rizzo, Anthony	L-L	6-3	220	8-8-89	.342	.313	.356	70	257	48	88	18	2	23	62	23	4	0	0	52	2	2	.696	.405
Rohan, Greg	R-R	6-0	205	5-11-86	.290	.370	.263	27	107	11	31	5	0	4	24	7	0	0	1	18	0	0	.449	.330
Samson, Nate	R-R	6-1	190	8-19-87	.280	.385	.243	19	50	8	14	1	0	0	3	3	1	0	0	4	0	1	.300	.333
Sappelt, Dave	R-R	5-9	195	1-2-87	.266	.331	.236	133	500	50	133	26	4	7	54	36	2	6	6	73	15	6	.376	.314
Soto, Geovany	R-R	6-1	220	1-20-83	.188	.200	.167	5	16	1	3	2	0	0	0	1	0	0	0	5	0	0	.313	.235
Tolbert, Matt	B-R	6-0	185	5-4-82	.240	.209	.251	113	329	38	79	16	1	1	13	34	2	8	2	66	9	5	.304	.313
Valbuena, Luis	L-R	5-10	195	11-30-85	.303	.264	.324	58	211	38	64	17	1	8	31	28	1	0	6	50	1	1	.507	.378
Vitters, Josh	R-R	6-2	205	8-27-89	.304	.331	.290	110	415	54	126	32	2	17	68	30	5	0	2	77	6	3	.513	.356
Wright, Ty	R-R	6-0	200	2-26-85	.287	.313	.272	68	230	34	66	19	0	5	33	18	4	1	1	45	3	2	.435	.348

Pitching	B-T	HT	WT	DOB	W	L	ERA	G	GS	CG	SV	IP	H	R	ER	HR	BB	SO	AVG	vLH	vRH	K/9	BB/9
Asencio, Jairo	R-R	6-2	180	5-5-84	0	1	1.35	13	0	0	5	13	6	4	2	1	4	13	.130	.238	.040	8.78	2.70
Batista, Frank	R-R	5-10	170	4-26-89	0	0	5.87	6	0	0	0	8	9	6	5	1	4	5	.300	.333	.267	5.87	4.70
Beliveau, Jeff	L-L	6-1	195	1-17-87	4	5	3.89	37	0	0	0	44	44	21	19	4	18	52	.260	.267	.257	10.64	3.68
Berlind, Dan	R-R	6-7	215	12-3-87	0	0	108.00	1	0	0	0	0	3	4	4	0	2	0	.750	.667	1.000	0.00	54.00
Bowden, Michael	R-R	6-3	215	9-9-86	3	2	2.76	23	0	0	2	33	19	12	10	2	17	35	.167	.184	.154	9.64	4.68
Cabrera, Alberto	R-R	6-4	210	10-25-88	2	0	4.19	13	0	0	0	19	29	13	9	4	4	39	.341	.333	13.50	1.86
Caridad, Esmailin	R-R	5-10	195	10-28-83	1	4	3.03	44	2	0	0	65	52	28	22	4	29	65	.214	.195	.231	8.95	3.99
Chapman, Jaye	R-R	6-0	195	5-22-87	0	2	7.71	8	0	0	0	9	11	8	8	0	7	10	.306	.231	.348	9.64	6.75
Coleman, Casey	L-R	6-0	185	7-3-87	2	4	4.34	13	11	0	0	58	53	29	28	4	25	52	.247	.252	.240	8.07	3.88
Corpas, Manny	R-R	6-3	210	12-3-82	0	2	4.01	19	0	0	0	34	30	16	15	4	9	19	.240	.317	.161	5.08	2.41
De La Cruz, Frankie	R-R	5-11	210	3-12-84	1	6	3.80	27	14	0	0	95	91	47	40	6	58	57	.253	.200	.300	5.42	5.51
Dolis, Rafael	R-R	6-4	215	1-10-88	0	1	2.51	13	0	0	3	14	15	4	4	1	6	14	.278	.348	.226	8.79	3.77
Harris, Ty'Relle	R-R	6-4	205	12-12-86	2	3	4.88	8	5	0	0	31	32	19	17	3	10	26	.268	.288	.250	7.47	2.87
Hatley, Marcus	R-R	6-5	220	3-26-88	1	0	8.22	12	0	0	0	15	14	14	14	0	10	18	.237	.367	.103	10.57	5.87
Jackson, Jay	R-R	6-1	195	10-27-87	3	7	6.57	37	9	0	0	86	105	67	63	14	43	76	.309	.317	.301	7.92	4.48
Lindsay, Shane	R-R	6-2	230	1-25-85	0	0	—	1	0	0	0	0	1	4	4	0	4	0	1.000	.000	1.000	—	—
2-team total (8 Albuquerque)					0	1	9.00	9	0	0	0	9	9	9	9	0	16	8	—	—	—	8.00	16.00

Name	B-T	HT	WT	DOB	W	L	ERA	G	GS	CG	SV	IP	H	R	ER	HR	BB	SO	AVG	vLH	vRH	K/9	BB/9
Lopez, Rodrigo	R-R	6-1	185	12-14-75	2	5	5.28	18	15	0	0	73	84	47	43	8	26	55	.295	.294	.296	6.75	3.19
MacDougal, Mike	B-R	6-4	180	3-5-77	1	2	7.85	19	0	0	1	18	31	18	16	3	16	11	.388	.341	.436	5.40	7.85
Maine, Scott	L-L	6-3	215	2-2-85	4	2	2.88	28	0	0	5	34	21	12	11	1	13	29	.168	.209	.146	7.60	3.41
Marmol, Carlos	R-R	6-2	215	10-14-82	0	0	0.00	2	0	0	0	2	1	0	0	0	2	4	.143	.167	.000	18.00	9.00
McClung, Seth	L-R	6-6	280	2-7-81	1	2	6.32	4	3	0	0	16	24	14	11	3	10	16	.338	.533	.195	9.19	5.74
2-team total (21 Nashville)					3	15	6.35	25	23	1	0	119	145	96	84	19	70	96	—	—	—	7.26	5.29
Negrin, Yoanner	R-R	5-11	190	4-29-84	0	1	3.60	3	3	0	0	15	20	7	6	1	4	9	.333	.522	.216	5.40	2.40
Parker, Blake	R-R	6-3	225	6-19-85	1	1	3.42	21	0	0	6	24	16	9	9	3	6	22	.190	.257	.143	8.37	2.28
Raley, Brooks	L-L	6-3	185	6-29-88	4	8	3.62	14	14	1	0	82	87	39	33	7	28	69	.272	.233	.286	7.57	3.07
Ramirez, Horacio	L-L	6-1	220	11-24-79	0	1	4.58	3	0	0	0	18	22	9	9	2	5	6	.314	.455	.250	2.04	2.55
Robertson, Nate	R-L	6-2	225	9-3-77	0	2	8.10	14	0	0	0	20	30	19	18	6	4	15	.337	.242	.393	6.75	1.80
2-team total (9 Las Vegas)					0	3	8.07	23	2	0	0	29	43	28	26	8	8	20	—	—	—	6.21	2.48
Rowland-Smith, Ryan	L-L	6-3	240	1-26-83	3	6	3.94	30	8	0	0	78	75	43	34	6	41	62	.253	.245	.256	7.18	4.75
Rusin, Chris	L-L	6-2	195	10-22-86	8	9	4.55	25	25	0	0	140	146	81	71	17	53	94	.267	.228	.285	6.03	3.40
Searle, Ryan	R-R	6-0	190	6-22-89	1	0	0.00	2	0	0	0	7	4	0	0	0	2	5	.174	.133	.250	6.75	2.70
Socolovich, Miguel	R-R	6-1	190	7-24-86	0	0	5.40	3	0	0	0	3	3	2	1	0	5	5	.231	.250	.222	13.50	0.00
Volstad, Chris	R-R	6-8	230	9-23-86	3	5	5.17	12	12	0	0	71	86	48	41	7	19	52	.296	.324	.266	6.56	2.40
Wells, Randy	R-R	6-5	230	8-28-82	3	3	7.89	9	9	0	0	43	52	39	38	6	18	29	.295	.283	.310	6.02	3.74
Wood, Travis	R-L	5-11	175	2-6-87	3	3	4.57	7	7	0	0	41	48	22	21	5	11	39	.294	.250	.318	8.49	2.40

Fielding

Catcher	PCT	G	PO	A	E	DP	PB
Apodaca	.989	41	248	12	3	1	1
Castillo	.974	41	277	24	8	1	5
Clevenger	1.000	4	20	1	0	0	1
Esposito	.992	33	222	21	2	0	3
Lalli	1.000	29	189	18	0	2	4
Recker	1.000	2	12	0	0	0	0
Soto	1.000	4	25	2	0	0	0

First Base	PCT	G	PO	A	E	DP
DeWitt	1.000	7	44	5	0	5
Frazier	1.000	2	12	1	0	0
Gonzalez	1.000	1	6	2	0	0
Hernandez	.966	3	24	4	1	3
Lalli	.991	41	301	33	3	29
Rizzo	.986	66	564	66	9	53
Rohan	.993	18	127	6	1	14
Samson	1.000	2	11	1	0	1
Vitters	.974	9	71	4	2	8

Second Base	PCT	G	PO	A	E	DP
Amaya	—	1	0	0	0	0

	PCT	G	PO	A	E	DP
Amezaga	.965	35	61	106	6	22
Cardenas	.983	52	91	145	4	25
DeWitt	1.000	7	9	17	0	3
Hernandez	1.000	17	42	33	0	12
Lalli	—	1	0	0	0	0
Samson	.970	7	11	21	1	2
Tolbert	1.000	21	29	62	0	16
Valbuena	1.000	9	20	27	0	8

Third Base	PCT	G	PO	A	E	DP
Amezaga	1.000	3	2	2	0	0
Cardenas	.944	7	6	11	1	0
DeWitt	.500	2	1	1	2	0
Hernandez	.939	24	14	32	3	5
Lalli	—	1	0	0	0	0
Mota	1.000	1	0	1	0	0
Rohan	.913	12	6	15	2	1
Samson	1.000	2	1	3	0	0
Tolbert	—	1	0	0	0	0
Valbuena	1.000	5	5	6	0	2
Vitters	.913	95	57	162	21	14

Shortstop	PCT	G	PO	A	E	DP
Amezaga	.935	43	65	109	12	27
Cardenas	.900	3	2	7	1	2
Hernandez	.800	1	3	1	1	1
Tolbert	.967	58	74	134	7	28
Valbuena	.974	44	62	125	5	22

Outfield	PCT	G	PO	A	E	DP
Adduci	.986	40	70	1	1	0
Amezaga	1.000	22	23	1	0	0
Campana	.955	37	81	4	4	0
DeWitt	.960	13	22	2	1	0
Frazier	1.000	14	28	0	0	0
Gonzalez	1.000	5	2	1	0	0
Jackson	.978	103	221	1	5	0
Lalli	—	1	0	0	0	0
Mota	1.000	5	8	0	0	0
Samson	1.000	4	3	0	0	0
Sappelt	.986	129	265	12	4	3
Tolbert	1.000	24	36	1	0	0
Wright	.978	52	83	6	2	1

TENNESSEE SMOKIES — DOUBLE-A

SOUTHERN LEAGUE

Batting	B-T	HT	WT	DOB	AVG	vLH	vRH	G	AB	R	H	2B	3B	HR	RBI	BB	HBP	SH	SF	SO	SB	CS	SLG	OBP
Adduci, Jim	L-L	6-2	210	5-15-85	.294	.270	.302	84	252	40	74	12	1	5	27	31	0	7	3	47	11	3	.409	.367
Apodaca, Juan	R-R	5-11	180	7-15-86	.309	.391	.276	31	81	12	25	8	0	1	11	18	2	0	2	14	1	1	.444	.437
Bour, Justin	L-R	6-4	250	5-28-88	.283	.273	.287	138	506	64	143	36	0	17	110	62	3	0	6	115	4	1	.455	.360
Brenly, Mike	R-R	6-3	230	10-14-86	.227	.275	.210	84	269	24	61	13	0	6	28	26	0	5	0	59	1	2	.342	.295
Burgess, Michael	L-L	5-11	195	10-20-88	.259	.230	.267	119	332	41	86	22	1	10	43	45	2	1	1	63	0	0	.422	.350
Castillo, Welington	R-R	5-10	210	4-24-87	.364	.000	.500	5	11	3	4	0	0	2	6	5	1	0	0	3	0	0	.909	.588
Cerda, Matt	L-R	5-9	165	6-20-90	.266	.214	.281	85	259	38	69	10	2	3	15	54	1	0	1	59	4	0	.355	.394
Flores, Luis	R-R	5-10	195	11-2-86	.167	.211	.151	26	72	4	12	3	0	1	11	16	1	2	1	13	0	0	.250	.322
Ha, Jae-Hoon	R-R	6-1	185	10-29-90	.273	.365	.243	121	465	63	127	28	3	6	47	50	8	3	3	96	11	5	.385	.352
Harrington, Dustin	R-R	5-11	180	11-14-88	.256	.231	.269	24	39	5	10	2	1	0	1	1	0	2	0	12	0	0	.359	.275
Lake, Junior	R-R	6-2	215	3-27-90	.279	.242	.290	103	405	56	113	26	3	10	50	35	4	2	2	105	21	12	.432	.341
Mota, Jonathan	R-R	6-0	200	6-1-87	.293	.278	.300	21	58	8	17	4	0	3	10	5	0	0	0	16	0	0	.517	.349
Noble, Chad	R-R	6-1	210	11-18-87	.121	.100	.125	19	58	3	7	1	0	0	9	3	0	0	1	18	0	0	.138	.161
Perez, Nelson	L-R	6-3	215	11-16-87	.205	.094	.242	43	127	16	26	6	1	5	17	13	1	0	1	35	1	2	.402	.282
Recker, Anthony	R-R	6-2	240	8-29-83	.200	.000	.273	4	15	1	3	1	0	1	4	0	0	0	0	7	0	0	.467	.200
Ridling, Rebel	R-R	6-4	230	5-22-86	.190	.203	.185	68	226	25	43	7	1	8	36	28	0	0	5	55	2	2	.336	.274
Rohan, Greg	R-R	6-0	205	5-11-86	.263	.190	.284	28	95	13	25	10	0	5	17	12	3	0	0	19	0	0	.526	.364
Samson, Nate	R-R	6-1	190	8-19-87	.271	.328	.247	75	210	27	57	12	0	2	14	15	0	2	2	32	4	0	.357	.317
Silva, Rubi	L-R	5-11	180	6-25-89	.263	.158	.295	20	80	8	21	0	3	2	13	2	0	0	1	17	3	0	.413	.277
Soto, Elliot	R-R	5-9	160	8-21-89	.220	.273	.189	82	209	16	46	5	4	0	15	27	1	5	2	45	2	3	.282	.310
Szczur, Matt	R-R	6-1	195	7-20-89	.210	.156	.225	35	143	24	30	7	4	2	6	14	1	0	0	29	4	2	.357	.285
Watkins, Logan	L-R	5-11	170	8-29-89	.281	.221	.301	133	488	93	137	20	11	9	52	76	7	14	3	97	28	7	.422	.383
Wright, Ty	R-R	6-0	200	2-26-85	.429	.000	.462	5	14	2	6	1	0	1	4	0	0	0	1	0	0	0	.714	.400

Pitching	B-T	HT	WT	DOB	W	L	ERA	G	GS	CG	SV	IP	H	R	ER	HR	BB	SO	AVG	vLH	vRH	K/9	BB/9
Antigua, Jeffry	R-L	6-1	170	6-23-90	1	1	3.83	20	2	0	1	40	41	17	17	6	13	40	.270	.412	.198	9.00	2.93
Batista, Frank	R-R	5-10	170	4-26-89	2	0	2.22	43	0	0	24	53	38	14	13	6	21	39	.199	.202	.196	6.66	3.59
Beeler, Dallas	R-R	6-5	205	6-12-89	6	7	4.24	27	27	1	0	136	166	74	64	11	48	70	.305	.338	.280	4.63	3.18
Berlind, Dan	R-R	6-7	215	12-3-87	0	2	13.50	7	0	0	0	8	15	12	12	0	8	5	.405	.438	.381	5.63	9.00

Name	B-T	HT	WT	DOB	W	L	ERA	G	GS	CG	SV	IP	H	R	ER	HR	BB	SO	AVG	vLH	vRH	K/9	BB/9
Brigham, Jake	R-R	6-3	210	2-10-88	0	2	19.64	2	2	0	0	4	11	9	8	1	4	3	.500	.455	.545	7.36	9.82
Cabrera, Alberto	R-R	6-4	210	10-25-88	2	1	2.52	23	0	0	5	36	30	15	10	2	10	45	.217	.274	.171	11.36	2.52
Castillo, Lendy	R-R	6-1	170	4-8-89	0	0	3.00	2	2	0	0	3	3	1	1	0	2	2	.273	.250	.333	6.00	6.00
Chapman, Jaye	R-R	6-0	195	5-22-87	0	0	0.00	2	0	0	0	2	0	0	0	0	0	2	.000	.000	.000	9.00	0.00
Dolis, Rafael	R-R	6-4	215	1-10-88	0	0	0.00	2	0	0	2	0	0	0	0	0	0	2	.250	.250	.250	9.00	0.00
Harman, Casey	L-L	6-1	210	3-17-89	1	4	4.88	34	2	0	0	55	69	35	30	10	11	43	.300	.313	.293	6.99	1.79
Harris, Ty'Relle	R-R	6-4	235	12-12-86	0	2	3.68	14	2	0	0	29	31	14	12	1	16	19	.274	.310	.236	5.83	4.91
Hatley, Marcus	R-R	6-5	220	3-26-88	3	1	3.40	28	0	0	4	45	36	18	17	3	20	46	.232	.246	.223	9.20	4.00
Jokisch, Eric	R-L	6-2	185	7-29-89	7	2	2.91	18	17	1	0	105	86	35	34	7	33	63	.226	.219	.229	5.40	2.83
Kirk, Austin	L-L	6-1	200	5-22-90	2	0	3.09	5	4	1	0	23	18	9	8	3	12	13	.220	.160	.246	5.01	4.63
McNutt, Trey	R-R	6-4	220	8-2-89	9	8	4.26	34	17	0	0	95	93	58	45	12	45	66	.251	.254	.247	6.25	4.26
Negrin, Yoanner	R-R	5-11	190	4-29-84	1	0	0.00	1	1	0	0	5	1	0	0	1	4	.067	.143	.000	7.20	1.80
Raley, Brooks	L-L	6-3	185	6-29-88	2	2	3.51	8	8	0	0	49	47	19	19	2	12	29	.260	.300	.252	5.36	2.22
Rhee, Dae-Eun	L-R	6-2	190	3-23-89	9	8	4.81	27	26	0	0	142	168	93	76	18	51	78	.298	.312	.286	4.93	3.22
Rhoderick, Kevin	R-R	6-1	190	8-19-88	2	8	4.99	44	0	0	8	58	49	37	32	5	47	53	.230	.189	.263	8.27	7.34
Rosscup, Zach	L-L	6-2	205	6-9-88	0	1	4.84	11	1	0	0	22	14	12	12	1	19	29	.179	.143	.193	11.69	7.66
Rusin, Chris	L-L	6-2	195	10-22-86	0	0	0.00	1	1	0	0	3	0	0	0	0	0	1	.000	.000	.000	3.00	0.00
Schlitter, Brian	R-R	6-5	235	12-21-85	3	4	3.00	29	0	0	6	42	43	19	14	2	11	44	.264	.320	.216	9.43	2.36
Searle, Ryan	R-R	6-6	190	6-22-89	1	2	4.07	8	2	0	0	24	26	14	11	2	11	17	.277	.386	.180	6.29	4.07
Struck, Nick	R-R	5-11	185	10-7-89	14	10	3.18	28	26	0	0	156	140	69	55	14	44	123	.238	.240	.236	7.11	2.54
Weathers, Casey	R-R	6-1	205	6-10-85	4	2	6.62	31	0	0	0	34	25	26	25	2	53	29	.208	.164	.246	7.68	14.03
Weismann, Scott	R-R	6-0	190	2-8-90	0	0	0.00	2	0	0	0	5	2	0	0	2	1	.133	.000	.286	1.93	3.86
Zeller, Joe	R-R	5-10	190	10-17-87	0	0	0.00	1	0	0	0	1	0	0	0	0	1	.000	.000	.000	9.00	0.00
Zych, Tony	R-R	6-3	190	8-7-90	2	1	4.38	20	0	0	0	25	26	12	12	1	12	28	.268	.370	.176	10.22	4.38

Fielding

Catcher	PCT	G	PO	A	E	DP	PB
Apodaca	.995	25	188	6	1	1	1
Brenly	.996	74	467	44	2	4	7
Castillo	1.000	3	8	4	0	0	1
Flores	.979	24	127	16	3	0	1
Noble	1.000	17	96	12	0	0	0
Recker	1.000	3	22	2	0	0	0

First Base	PCT	G	PO	A	E	DP
Bour	.985	128	1109	67	18	91
Brenly	1.000	3	11	1	0	2
Castillo	1.000	2	14	0	0	0
Ridling	.992	15	107	14	1	12
Rohan	1.000	2	13	1	0	0

Second Base	PCT	G	PO	A	E	DP
Cerda	.951	11	12	27	2	3
Harrington	1.000	9	6	11	0	3
Samson	.989	21	35	54	1	15
Soto	.989	24	40	49	1	8
Watkins	.987	95	187	272	6	47

Third Base	PCT	G	PO	A	E	DP
Cerda	.910	64	53	108	16	13
Harrington	.929	6	2	11	1	0
Lake	.899	29	17	54	8	4
Mota	.880	10	7	15	3	1
Rohan	.952	15	11	29	2	6
Samson	.973	33	15	57	2	2
Soto	—	1	0	0	0	0

Shortstop	PCT	G	PO	A	E	DP
Lake	.921	72	82	199	24	29
Mota	1.000	2	1	2	0	1

	PCT	G	PO	A	E	DP
Soto	.976	47	67	137	5	25
Watkins	.972	29	30	74	3	16

Outfield	PCT	G	PO	A	E	DP
Adduci	.994	77	163	7	1	1
Bour	.667	3	2	0	1	0
Burgess	.993	92	135	9	1	1
Ha	.978	116	250	12	6	2
Mota	1.000	7	10	0	0	0
Perez	.979	35	46	0	1	0
Ridling	.984	42	55	5	1	0
Rohan	.895	11	13	4	2	2
Samson	1.000	10	7	1	0	0
Silva	.960	20	44	4	2	1
Szczur	.988	34	75	5	1	1
Watkins	1.000	17	18	1	0	1
Wright	1.000	5	2	2	0	1

DAYTONA CUBS   HIGH CLASS A
FLORIDA STATE LEAGUE

Batting	B-T	HT	WT	DOB	AVG	vLH	vRH	G	AB	R	H	2B	3B	HR	RBI	BB	HBP	SH	SF	SO	SB	CS	SLG	OBP
Alcantara, Arismendy	B-R	5-10	160	10-29-91	.302	.308	.299	85	331	47	100	13	7	7	51	19	2	2	5	61	25	4	.447	.339
Andreoli, John	R-R	6-1	215	6-9-90	.289	.267	.302	121	412	68	119	17	8	1	25	75	4	3	2	89	55	20	.376	.402
Baez, Javier	R-R	6-1	205	12-1-92	.188	.143	.203	23	80	9	15	3	1	4	13	5	1	0	0	21	4	2	.400	.244
Bonne, Elieser	R-R	6-2	180	2-17-87	.275	.299	.264	102	353	34	97	17	2	3	40	10	1	2	5	71	24	13	.360	.293
Burruel, Sergio	L-R	5-11	210	7-22-91	.244	.200	.269	14	41	3	10	3	0	0	1	3	1	0	0	10	0	0	.317	.311
Cerda, Matt	L-R	5-9	165	6-20-90	.165	.129	.185	26	85	13	14	3	0	0	9	19	0	0	1	11	3	0	.200	.314
Davis, Taylor	R-R	5-11	185	11-28-89	.223	.194	.242	52	157	15	35	8	0	2	26	21	1	0	2	24	3	2	.312	.315
Frias, Vladimir	B-R	6-2	170	9-6-86	.316	.250	.333	15	38	2	12	2	0	0	1	4	1	0	0	8	3	2	.368	.395
Giansanti, Anthony	R-R	5-11	200	9-28-88	.091	.000	.111	5	11	2	1	0	0	0	0	0	0	0	0	5	0	0	.091	.091
Gibbs, Micah	B-R	5-11	223	7-27-88	.200	.313	.140	62	185	25	37	4	1	4	16	33	6	0	1	68	3	0	.297	.338
Harrington, Dustin	R-R	5-11	180	11-14-88	.198	.157	.229	42	121	12	24	4	3	0	8	4	0	1	1	33	1	0	.281	.222
Jones, Richard	L-R	6-0	215	1-31-88	.224	.197	.236	59	210	20	47	12	2	0	28	8	5	0	3	61	0	0	.300	.265
Lopez, Rafael	L-R	5-9	190	10-2-87	.269	.235	.282	35	119	18	32	10	0	2	12	13	0	0	1	14	1	0	.403	.338
Noble, Chad	R-R	6-1	210	11-18-87	.188	.159	.209	49	154	17	29	7	1	0	16	9	1	4	5	32	1	1	.253	.231
Perez, Nelson	L-R	6-3	215	11-16-87	.278	.253	.289	79	263	45	73	14	5	11	46	41	5	0	4	94	8	4	.494	.380
Ridling, Rebel	R-R	6-4	230	5-22-86	.238	.288	.213	63	235	29	56	16	0	5	31	22	0	0	3	38	3	2	.370	.300
Rohan, Greg	R-R	6-0	205	5-11-86	.285	.257	.300	75	291	40	83	23	1	12	65	24	6	0	2	41	0	0	.495	.350
Saunders, Tim	R-R	6-0	180	5-17-90	.310	.417	.267	12	42	8	13	3	0	0	4	4	0	0	1	13	4	1	.381	.362
Silva, Rubi	L-R	5-11	180	6-25-89	.302	.270	.321	111	420	48	127	15	11	3	61	13	2	4	6	75	7	18	.412	.322
Soto, Elliot	R-R	5-9	160	8-21-89	.231	.267	.182	9	26	3	6	2	0	0	1	2	0	0	0	2	0	1	.308	.286
Szczur, Matt	R-R	6-1	195	7-20-89	.295	.288	.298	78	295	68	87	19	4	2	34	47	4	2	4	50	38	12	.407	.394
Torreyes, Ronald	R-R	5-9	140	9-2-92	.264	.279	.255	115	421	62	111	25	3	6	47	32	10	5	6	29	13	4	.385	.326
Villanueva, Christian	R-R	5-11	160	6-19-91	.250	.381	.206	25	84	14	21	5	0	4	9	10	1	0	0	24	5	2	.452	.337

Pitching	B-T	HT	WT	DOB	W	L	ERA	G	GS	CG	SV	IP	H	R	ER	HR	BB	SO	AVG	vLH	vRH	K/9	BB/9
Burke, Kyler	L-L	6-3	205	4-20-88	1	7	4.92	12	9	0	0	57	64	37	31	5	22	39	.275	.306	.261	6.19	3.49
Castillo, Lendy	R-R	6-1	170	4-8-89	0	0	0.00	1	1	0	0	4	3	1	0	0	1	4	.200	.182	.250	9.00	2.25
Cates, Zach	R-R	6-3	200	12-17-89	0	6	10.50	7	7	0	0	24	42	33	28	0	13	10	.389	.302	.473	3.75	4.88

	B-T	HT	WT	DOB	W	L	ERA	G	GS	CG	SV	IP	H	R	ER	HR	BB	SO	AVG	vLH	vRH	K/9	BB/9
Cervenka, Hunter	L-L	6-1	215	1-3-90	0	0	3.86	11	0	0	0	19	21	10	8	2	11	19	.288	.136	.353	9.16	5.30
Del Valle, Frank	L-L	5-11	190	9-16-89	5	5	3.26	22	15	0	0	99	70	47	36	14	30	84	.194	.197	.193	7.61	2.72
Figueroa, Eduardo	R-R	6-1	185	11-30-88	4	5	2.90	37	5	0	2	78	61	28	25	8	29	59	.218	.257	.192	6.84	3.36
Francescon, Patrick	R-R	5-11	185	1-4-89	3	6	3.75	17	17	1	0	84	83	42	35	8	24	53	.257	.266	.250	5.68	2.57
Harman, Casey	L-L	6-1	210	3-17-89	0	0	0.00	5	0	0	0	9	4	0	0	0	2	5	.129	.083	.158	4.82	1.93
Harris, Ty'Relle	R-R	6-4	235	12-12-86	2	1	2.53	16	0	0	0	21	12	8	6	3	13	22	.154	.156	.152	9.28	5.48
Hendricks, Kyle	R-R	6-3	190	12-7-89	1	0	4.24	5	4	0	0	17	17	8	8	3	3	11	.254	.192	.293	5.82	1.59
Iannazzo, Matt	L-L	5-9	170	1-8-90	0	0	0.00	3	0	0	0	5	3	0	0	0	2	2	.158	.143	.167	3.38	3.38
Jokisch, Eric	R-L	6-2	185	7-29-89	3	4	3.48	9	9	0	0	54	55	24	21	4	16	52	.267	.293	.252	8.61	2.65
Kirk, Austin	L-L	6-1	200	5-22-90	7	3	3.13	22	21	0	0	129	120	50	45	3	48	78	.244	.281	.225	5.43	3.34
Loosen, Matt	R-R	6-2	205	4-10-89	11	5	4.07	23	23	0	0	113	83	58	51	8	46	110	.202	.231	.176	8.79	3.67
Lorick, Jeff	L-L	6-0	195	12-18-87	2	4	4.58	31	0	0	2	39	44	24	20	1	18	41	.295	.211	.348	9.38	4.12
Morris, A.J.	R-R	6-2	185	12-1-86	5	2	2.24	39	0	0	7	52	36	17	13	1	15	42	.189	.205	.176	7.22	2.58
Schlitter, Brian	R-R	6-5	235	12-21-85	0	1	2.00	21	0	0	2	27	27	9	6	1	2	19	.260	.262	.258	6.33	0.67
Searle, Ryan	R-R	6-0	190	6-22-89	6	3	4.22	32	3	0	1	60	59	29	28	5	20	49	.257	.216	.282	7.39	3.02
Simpson, Hayden	R-R	6-0	170	5-20-89	2	3	6.98	14	4	0	1	39	51	32	30	5	29	16	.325	.286	.356	3.72	6.75
Spencer, Matt	L-L	6-4	230	1-27-86	0	1	8.76	11	0	0	0	12	12	12	12	0	16	8	.250	.333	.200	5.84	11.68
Suarez, Larry	R-R	6-4	245	12-20-89	0	3	13.50	10	0	0	0	11	23	16	16	1	8	3	.434	.364	.484	2.53	6.75
Wallach, Brett	R-R	6-5	205	12-2-88	0	0	8.18	7	0	0	0	11	19	11	10	1	5	8	.365	.450	.313	6.55	4.09
Weismann, Scott	R-R	6-0	190	2-8-90	3	5	5.63	32	0	0	4	46	49	32	29	7	16	44	.269	.316	.236	8.55	3.11
Whitenack, Robert	R-R	6-5	185	11-20-88	1	6	5.96	15	15	0	0	51	70	42	34	4	27	31	.332	.348	.313	5.44	4.73
Zeller, Joe	R-R	5-10	190	10-17-87	0	1	3.66	17	0	0	0	32	29	16	13	0	13	29	.248	.241	.254	8.16	3.66
Zych, Tony	R-R	6-3	190	8-7-90	3	3	3.19	27	0	0	6	37	32	16	13	0	7	36	.239	.260	.226	8.84	1.72

Fielding

Catcher	PCT	G	PO	A	E	DP	PB
Burruel	.967	14	77	11	3	0	2
Davis	.990	13	95	7	1	2	1
Gibbs	.985	46	306	26	5	2	1
Lopez	.981	22	141	18	3	3	5
Noble	.990	47	286	20	3	2	3

First Base	PCT	G	PO	A	E	DP
Davis	.985	10	60	7	1	6
Gibbs	1.000	2	16	1	0	0
Jones	.982	44	332	40	7	26
Lopez	1.000	1	8	0	0	0
Noble	1.000	3	23	3	0	5
Ridling	.985	53	412	42	7	36
Rohan	.991	27	198	14	2	10

Second Base	PCT	G	PO	A	E	DP
Alcantara	.833	1	1	4	1	1
Cerda	1.000	1	1	0	0	0

Frias	1.000	3	6	3	0	1
Harrington	1.000	10	16	31	0	6
Silva	.961	28	53	71	5	10
Soto	1.000	2	6	5	0	2
Torreyes	.976	91	160	211	9	46

Third Base	PCT	G	PO	A	E	DP
Alcantara	.833	8	2	18	4	0
Cerda	.908	22	16	43	6	7
Davis	.912	16	10	21	3	3
Frias	1.000	2	2	6	0	1
Harrington	.959	28	13	34	2	2
Rohan	.920	42	33	71	9	3
Saunders	.800	2	0	4	1	0
Villanueva	.958	24	10	59	3	5

Shortstop	PCT	G	PO	A	E	DP
Alcantara	.903	71	98	182	30	34
Baez	.976	23	30	52	2	12

Frias	1.000	1	2	3	0	0
Harrington	1.000	1	3	1	0	0
Saunders	.958	11	14	32	2	9
Soto	.960	7	8	16	1	3
Torreyes	.978	20	38	50	2	5

Outfield	PCT	G	PO	A	E	DP
Andreoli	.971	117	219	13	7	2
Bonne	.967	97	172	5	6	1
Frias	1.000	6	9	0	0	0
Giansanti	.800	4	4	0	1	0
Harrington	1.000	2	4	0	0	0
Perez	.955	51	101	5	5	0
Ridling	1.000	2	1	0	0	0
Silva	.983	71	163	13	3	2
Szczur	.994	58	153	3	1	0

PEORIA CHIEFS
MIDWEST LEAGUE
LOW CLASS A

Batting	B-T	HT	WT	DOB	AVG	vLH	vRH	G	AB	R	H	2B	3B	HR	RBI	BB	HBP	SH	SF	SO	SB	CS	SLG	OBP
Baez, Javier	R-R	6-1	205	12-1-92	.333	.388	.317	57	213	41	71	10	5	12	33	9	10	0	3	48	20	3	.596	.383
Balaguert, Yasiel	R-R	6-2	215	1-2-93	.208	.286	.190	39	149	10	31	5	0	1	18	5	0	0	1	49	0	1	.262	.232
Burruel, Sergio	L-R	5-11	210	7-22-91	.250	.214	.260	39	128	12	32	6	0	0	18	12	0	4	0	28	1	0	.297	.314
Cabezas, Yaniel	R-R	5-11	185	4-19-89	.197	.173	.205	58	208	14	41	5	1	1	15	10	0	3	1	34	1	1	.245	.233
Chen, Pin-Chieh	L-R	6-1	170	7-3-91	.259	.241	.266	127	464	75	120	15	10	2	51	62	3	3	7	78	36	14	.347	.345
Cuneo, Ryan	L-R	6-3	190	10-10-88	.252	.256	.250	38	143	11	36	6	1	4	23	18	2	0	2	25	0	0	.392	.339
Darvill, Wes	L-R	6-2	175	9-10-91	.224	.242	.217	116	447	49	100	16	6	3	35	39	1	5	4	83	11	6	.306	.285
Davis, Taylor	R-R	5-11	185	11-28-89	.338	.313	.347	18	65	5	22	4	2	1	12	8	0	0	3	8	0	0	.508	.395
DeVoss, Zeke	B-R	5-10	175	7-17-90	.249	.287	.235	125	465	88	116	24	7	6	38	82	20	10	4	118	35	16	.370	.382
Easterling, Taiwan	R-R	5-11	195	2-24-89	.243	.321	.222	70	268	29	65	17	2	4	28	21	9	3	3	76	18	10	.366	.316
Geiger, Dustin	R-R	6-2	180	12-2-91	.251	.316	.228	75	303	42	76	14	0	17	53	20	4	0	5	79	1	1	.465	.301
Giansanti, Anthony	R-R	5-11	200	9-18-86	.296	.333	.288	25	98	9	29	5	0	0	12	8	0	0	0	16	1	2	.347	.349
Golden, Reggie	R-R	5-10	210	10-10-91	.192	.111	.235	7	26	1	5	0	0	0	1	1	0	0	0	9	1	0	.192	.250
Gonzalez, Eduardo	L-L	5-10	170	2-9-92	.217	.286	.196	17	60	6	13	2	2	1	6	6	1	0	0	17	0	1	.367	.299
Hernandez, Marco	L-R	6-0	170	9-6-92	.210	.213	.209	43	157	18	33	2	3	2	12	9	0	2	3	40	2	1	.299	.249
Hoilman, Paul	R-R	6-4	230	2-11-89	.237	.310	.209	109	413	48	98	30	5	8	61	50	6	0	4	155	1	0	.392	.326
Krist, Chadd	R-R	5-11	190	1-28-90	.253	.224	.267	40	150	18	38	15	1	4	23	15	2	1	3	33	0	1	.447	.324
Lopez, Rafael	L-R	5-9	190	10-2-87	.265	.179	.308	31	117	14	31	7	1	0	12	17	0	1	3	13	1	0	.342	.350
Rademacher, Bijan	L-L	6-0	200	6-15-91	.221	.125	.268	35	122	16	27	7	1	0	11	10	0	3	0	26	2	1	.295	.280
Rogers, Jacob	L-R	6-5	195	8-23-89	.300	.273	.308	16	50	13	15	0	2	5	13	9	1	0	0	14	1	1	.420	.493
Saunders, Tim	R-R	6-0	180	5-17-90	.321	.300	.328	20	81	12	26	5	1	2	12	8	1	0	2	21	8	0	.481	.380
Soler, Jorge	R-R	6-3	205	2-25-92	.338	.333	.339	20	80	14	27	5	0	3	15	6	2	0	0	6	4	1	.513	.398
Zapata, Oliver	B-R	5-9	180	1-5-91	.225	.223	.225	109	369	40	83	9	0	4	29	40	4	6	4	93	19	13	.282	.305
Zapenas, Brad	R-R	5-9	185	12-8-89	.273	.211	.293	24	77	13	21	3	0	0	3	14	0	1	0	16	1	1	.312	.385

Pitching	B-T	HT	WT	DOB	W	L	ERA	G	GS	CG	SV	IP	H	R	ER	HR	BB	SO	AVG	vLH	vRH	K/9	BB/9
Antigua, Jeffry	R-L	6-1	170	6-23-90	2	3	2.63	14	4	0	0	41	33	19	12	5	11	38	.217	.097	.248	8.34	2.41
Berg, Justin	R-R	6-3	225	6-7-84	0	3	5.40	13	0	0	0	27	36	29	16	0	14	17	.308	.341	.288	5.74	4.73

Name	B-T	HT	WT	DOB	W	L	ERA	G	GS	CG	SV	IP	H	R	ER	HR	BB	SO	AVG	vLH	vRH	K/9	BB/9
Burke, Kyler	L-L	6-3	205	4-20-88	2	2	2.31	15	10	0	1	74	57	27	19	5	22	52	.211	.288	.193	6.32	2.68
Cates, Zach	R-R	6-3	200	12-17-89	0	3	5.45	9	9	0	0	38	49	26	23	1	13	31	.314	.327	.307	7.34	3.08
Cervenka, Hunter	L-L	6-1	215	1-3-90	3	0	2.54	15	0	0	1	28	23	13	8	1	10	28	.225	.136	.250	8.89	3.18
Concepcion, Gerardo	L-L	6-2	180	2-29-92	2	6	7.39	12	12	0	0	52	70	52	43	6	30	28	.329	.270	.341	4.82	5.16
Cruz, Willengton	R-L	6-2	170	8-8-90	1	4	6.75	13	4	0	0	40	44	34	30	7	21	30	.277	.295	.270	6.75	4.73
Francescon, Patrick	R-R	5-11	185	1-4-89	5	1	1.86	9	9	0	0	53	28	15	11	5	14	42	.155	.123	.169	7.09	2.36
Jensen, Michael	R-R	6-1	185	12-10-90	11	5	3.47	26	26	0	0	140	117	71	54	6	40	115	.217	.189	.237	7.39	2.57
Levitt, Pete	R-R	6-5	235	4-24-89	0	1	1.99	14	0	0	1	23	23	13	5	0	12	25	.256	.188	.293	9.93	4.76
Liria, Luis	B-R	6-2	170	1-15-90	2	5	4.55	39	0	0	5	59	50	36	30	3	46	52	.242	.189	.260	7.89	6.98
Lorick, Jeff	L-L	6-0	195	12-18-87	0	0	0.52	15	0	0	0	17	9	1	1	0	8	25	.148	.125	.156	12.98	4.15
McDonald, Sheldon	L-L	5-11	205	11-5-88	1	3	1.89	33	0	0	0	62	45	20	13	3	16	57	.205	.170	.216	8.27	2.32
McKirahan, Andrew	R-L	6-2	195	2-8-90	0	0	1.80	9	0	0	2	10	6	2	2	0	4	11	.176	.143	.185	9.90	3.60
Pena, Felix	R-R	6-2	186	2-25-90	0	0	4.50	6	0	0	0	10	9	5	5	1	5	10	.237	.091	.296	9.00	4.50
Perakslis, Steve	R-R	6-1	185	1-15-91	0	0	9.00	1	0	0	0	1	3	1	1	0	0	1	.750	.000	.750	9.00	0.00
Peralta, Starling	R-R	6-4	180	11-11-90	5	8	3.44	20	17	0	0	99	80	55	38	11	42	86	.217	.269	.193	7.79	3.81
Reed, Austin	R-R	6-3	200	10-31-91	5	8	3.65	38	0	0	1	62	67	32	25	4	24	49	.283	.268	.289	7.15	3.50
Rosario, Jose	R-R	6-1	170	8-29-90	6	8	4.22	20	20	0	0	111	125	59	52	7	34	95	.276	.316	.254	7.70	2.76
Rosscup, Zach	R-L	6-2	205	6-9-88	2	0	0.00	3	0	0	0	7	3	0	0	0	0	12	.125	.167	.111	14.73	0.00
Shafer, Bryce	R-R	6-0	180	11-14-88	1	2	4.63	23	0	0	0	35	34	20	18	3	19	36	.262	.244	.271	9.26	4.89
Socorro, Kenny	R-R	5-9	175	6-2-89	1	0	0.00	1	0	0	0	2	0	0	0	0	1	0	.000	.000	.000	4.50	0.00
Spencer, Matt	L-L	6-4	230	1-27-86	1	0	0.00	1	0	0	0	2	0	0	0	0	0	3	.000	.000	.000	13.50	0.00
Suarez, Larry	R-R	6-4	245	12-20-89	3	2	4.15	30	0	0	5	43	48	24	20	2	21	38	.281	.228	.307	7.89	4.36
Thomas, Charles	R-R	6-4	250	7-2-88	0	0	6.75	2	0	0	0	3	2	2	2	0	3	5	.273	.000	.333	16.88	10.13
Wang, Yao-Lin	R-R	6-0	180	2-5-91	4	5	3.92	37	9	0	12	78	72	43	34	7	27	82	.241	.265	.225	9.46	3.12
Weismann, Scott	R-R	6-0	190	2-8-90	0	0	3.52	5	0	0	0	8	8	3	3	0	0	7	.258	.250	.267	8.22	0.00
Wells, Ben	R-R	6-2	220	9-10-92	3	2	3.27	12	8	0	1	44	48	23	16	0	12	36	.274	.318	.248	7.36	2.45
Zeller, Joe	R-R	5-10	190	10-17-87	3	4	3.75	11	10	0	0	60	69	33	25	4	12	22	.292	.309	.282	3.30	1.80

Fielding

Catcher	PCT	G	PO	A	E	DP	PB
Burruel	.996	29	215	29	1	1	5
Cabezas	1.000	42	317	40	0	1	5
Davis	.989	11	78	9	1	0	0
Giansanti	.960	2	21	3	1	0	0
Krist	.986	28	200	17	3	1	5
Lopez	.987	27	202	29	3	1	7

First Base	PCT	G	PO	A	E	DP
Burruel	1.000	1	8	0	0	0
Cabezas	1.000	1	4	0	0	1
Cuneo	.983	24	202	23	4	23
Geiger	.971	11	84	15	3	4
Hoilman	.978	87	781	63	19	53
Rogers	.964	16	144	15	6	10

Second Base	PCT	G	PO	A	E	DP
Darvill	.919	18	37	42	7	8
DeVoss	.950	119	255	277	28	57
Zapenas	.909	2	7	3	1	1

Third Base	PCT	G	PO	A	E	DP
Darvill	.883	55	26	125	20	6
Geiger	.897	53	38	110	17	12
Giansanti	.895	10	9	25	4	2
Saunders	.833	6	6	9	3	1
Zapenas	.932	18	17	38	4	7

Shortstop	PCT	G	PO	A	E	DP
Baez	.941	52	75	166	15	22
Darvill	.935	33	44	114	11	11
Hernandez	.953	42	61	141	10	21
Saunders	.903	14	9	47	6	3

Outfield	PCT	G	PO	A	E	DP
Balaguert	1.000	30	30	4	0	0
Chen	.966	122	249	7	9	1
Cuneo	1.000	10	10	0	0	0
Darvill	1.000	5	9	0	0	0
Easterling	.955	68	121	7	6	1
Giansanti	.952	10	17	3	1	2
Golden	.938	6	15	0	1	0
Gonzalez	.960	15	24	0	1	0
Hoilman	1.000	3	3	0	0	0
Rademacher	.978	29	41	3	1	0
Soler	.977	19	41	1	1	0
Zapata	.990	103	190	9	2	2

BOISE HAWKS   SHORT-SEASON

NORTHWEST LEAGUE

Batting	B-T	HT	WT	DOB	AVG	vLH	vRH	G	AB	R	H	2B	3B	HR	RBI	BB	HBP	SH	SF	SO	SB	CS	SLG	OBP
Almora, Albert	R-R	6-1	170	4-16-94	.292	.261	.310	9	65	9	19	7	0	1	6	0	0	0	0	0	0	1	.446	.292
Amaya, Gioskar	R-R	5-11	175	12-13-92	.298	.378	.268	69	272	61	81	6	12	8	33	33	6	2	4	65	15	5	.496	.381
Batista, Xavier	R-R	6-3	190	1-18-92	.198	.300	.154	51	167	22	33	11	0	4	17	19	1	0	0	54	0	2	.335	.283
Bruno, Stephen	R-R	5-9	165	11-17-90	.361	.410	.346	67	252	51	91	19	3	3	37	18	20	0	2	47	2	7	.496	.442
Candelario, Jeimer	R-R	6-1	180	11-24-93	.281	.388	.246	71	278	34	78	14	0	6	47	26	3	0	3	55	2	1	.396	.345
Contreras, Willson	R-R	6-1	175	5-13-92	.273	.319	.256	64	249	32	68	10	1	3	39	11	5	0	1	54	3	2	.357	.316
Dunston Jr., Shawon	L-R	6-2	170	2-5-93	.185	.300	.164	19	65	10	12	4	1	1	2	4	2	0	0	14	1	2	.323	.254
Escobar, Carlos	R-R	5-11	185	12-31-90	.235	.286	.216	19	51	8	12	6	0	1	9	10	0	0	1	12	0	1	.412	.355
Garsez, Izaac	L-L	6-1	210	1-24-90	.228	.167	.239	25	79	17	18	3	3	1	7	7	4	0	2	28	2	1	.380	.315
Gonzalez, Eduardo	L-L	5-10	170	2-9-92	.143	.200	.133	10	35	2	5	0	0	0	3	0	0	2	0	6	2	1	.143	.143
Gonzalez, Gregori	R-R	5-9	170	7-11-89	1.000	—	1.000	1	1	0	1	0	0	0	1	0	0	0	0	0	0	0	1.000	1.000
Hernandez, Marco	L-R	6-0	170	9-6-92	.286	.220	.305	67	269	39	77	12	4	5	38	10	0	2	2	36	8	3	.416	.310
Inoa, Brian	B-R	5-10	170	2-21-92	.250	.500	.167	3	8	2	2	1	0	0	0	0	0	0	0	1	0	0	.375	.250
Kim, Dong-Yub	R-R	6-4	200	7-24-90	.250	.242	.253	33	112	16	28	8	0	5	14	4	2	0	0	33	3	0	.455	.288
Krist, Chadd	R-R	5-11	190	1-28-90	.328	.143	.386	16	58	9	19	4	0	0	6	4	0	0	1	5	0	0	.397	.365
Marra, Justin	L-R	5-10	190	1-18-93	.600	.500	.667	2	5	1	3	0	0	0	1	0	0	0	0	0	0	0	.600	.667
Martin, Trey	R-R	6-2	188	12-11-92	.270	.196	.291	57	204	26	55	5	4	3	23	13	2	9	1	48	6	5	.377	.318
Rademacher, Bijan	L-L	6-0	205	6-15-91	.396	.333	.409	14	53	9	21	6	0	1	8	2	0	0	1	7	0	1	.566	.411
Rymel, Lance	R-R	6-0	195	5-2-90	.188	.231	.176	25	64	10	12	4	0	2	10	3	2	3	0	11	0	0	.344	.246
Shoulders, Rock	L-R	6-2	225	9-26-91	.250	.195	.263	63	208	29	52	11	0	10	37	28	1	0	0	69	0	0	.447	.342
Vogelbach, Dan	L-R	6-0	250	12-17-92	.322	.333	.319	37	143	23	46	9	1	10	31	23	2	0	0	34	0	1	.608	.423

Pitching	B-T	HT	WT	DOB	W	L	ERA	G	GS	CG	SV	IP	H	R	ER	HR	BB	SO	AVG	vLH	vRH	K/9	BB/9
Ackerman, Hunter	L-L	6-0	190	10-24-90	1	1	7.66	9	0	0	1	22	27	22	19	2	11	28	.293		.323	11.28	4.43
Amlung, Justin	R-R	6-0	174	5-21-90	0	1	6.00	6	6	0	0	12	19	8	8	3	4	6	.404	.389	.414	4.50	3.00
Arias, Jose	R-R	6-5	220	1-17-91	4	2	3.25	14	13	0	0	64	61	26	23	3	19	46	.258	.247	.266	6.50	2.69
Bremer, Tyler	R-R	6-2	210	12-7-89	0	1	4.80	8	0	0	1	15	17	8	8	3	5	12	.288	.318	.270	7.20	3.00

	B-T	HT	WT	DOB	W	L	ERA	G	GS	CG	SV	IP	H	R	ER	HR	BB	SO	AVG	vLH	vRH	K/9	BB/9
Cruz, Willengton	R-L	6-2	170	8-8-90	2	4	6.46	11	4	0	0	31	36	24	22	3	18	25	.310	.333	.304	7.34	5.28
Dickson, Ian	R-R	6-5	205	9-16-90	3	3	5.60	15	15	0	0	63	69	47	39	7	25	48	.275	.228	.307	6.89	3.59
Diplan, Rafael	R-R	6-1	190	10-27-91	3	3	4.37	19	0	0	1	35	36	25	17	2	22	24	.254	.264	.247	6.17	5.66
Dorris, Nathan	L-L	6-3	185	12-9-90	1	1	1.93	9	0	0	4	14	12	3	3	0	7	13	.235	.188	.257	8.36	4.50
Hamann, Mike	R-R	6-3	165	1-1-91	0	0	5.91	7	0	0	1	11	11	7	7	0	2	6	.262	.235	.280	5.06	1.69
Heesch, Michael	R-L	6-5	245	5-15-90	3	1	2.66	12	0	0	0	24	25	8	7	0	1	19	.258	.231	.268	7.23	0.38
Iannazzo, Matt	L-L	5-9	170	1-8-90	1	1	8.49	7	0	0	1	12	20	12	11	0	3	11	.385	.545	.341	8.49	2.31
Johnson, Pierce	R-R	6-3	170	5-10-91	0	0	4.50	4	4	0	0	8	10	5	4	0	3	12	.323	.300	.333	13.50	3.38
Jung, Su-Min	R-R	6-2	190	4-1-90	1	1	3.51	16	1	0	0	26	19	11	10	1	18	25	.196	.162	.217	8.77	6.31
Levitt, Pete	R-R	6-5	235	4-24-89	1	2	8.04	10	0	0	1	16	21	15	14	1	6	5	.313	.391	.273	2.87	3.45
Orozco, Eddie	R-R	6-2	195	4-11-89	2	1	1.95	19	0	0	6	28	19	6	6	0	11	31	.190	.111	.234	10.08	3.58
Paulino, Amaury	R-R	6-1	175	8-31-91	0	2	11.74	3	0	0	0	8	11	10	10	0	6	5	.344	.313	.375	5.87	7.04
Pena, Felix	R-R	6-2	186	2-25-90	4	2	3.43	15	0	0	0	63	60	33	24	5	22	42	.243	.306	.201	6.00	3.14
Pichardo, Roderick	R-R	5-10	180	9-24-90	0	2	5.94	12	0	0	0	17	17	12	11	0	10	16	.266	.222	.297	8.64	5.40
Pugliese, James	R-R	6-3	195	8-12-92	1	5	5.37	15	11	0	0	60	78	46	36	8	22	51	.307	.275	.329	7.61	3.28
Scott, Tayler	R-R	6-3	165	6-1-92	5	1	2.52	15	15	0	0	71	66	30	20	0	29	43	.245	.238	.250	5.43	3.66
Shafer, Bryce	R-R	6-0	180	11-14-88	1	1	0.77	10	0	0	2	12	11	4	1	1	8	11	.262	.118	.360	8.49	6.17
Simpson, Hayden	R-R	6-0	170	5-20-89	2	4	6.18	15	1	0	2	44	51	39	30	6	22	47	.276	.228	.311	9.69	4.53
Smith, Brian	L-L	6-0	170	12-12-92	1	0	0.00	3	0	0	0	8	6	0	0	0	4	9	.214	.273	.176	10.57	4.70
Spencer, Matt	L-L	6-4	230	1-27-86	1	0	2.08	3	0	0	0	4	3	2	1	0	4	6	.176	.167	.182	12.46	8.31
Zeller, Joe	R-R	5-10	190	10-17-87	0	0	1.59	2	0	0	0	6	5	1	1	0	0	2	.250	.273	.222	3.18	0.00

Fielding

Catcher	PCT	G	PO	A	E	DP	PB
Contreras	.976	39	254	29	7	1	8
Escobar	.971	14	94	6	3	1	0
Krist	1.000	9	49	11	0	0	0
Marra	1.000	1	12	0	0	0	0
Rymel	.968	23	146	6	5	1	0

First Base	PCT	G	PO	A	E	DP
Candelario	1.000	2	2	0	0	0
Contreras	.983	6	56	2	1	9
Shoulders	.992	42	351	34	3	18
Vogelbach	.989	29	255	15	3	17

Second Base	PCT	G	PO	A	E	DP
Amaya	.968	59	110	165	9	30
Bruno	.944	17	41	60	6	10
Contreras	1.000	1	1	2	0	0
Gonzalez	1.000	1	1	0	0	0

Third Base	PCT	G	PO	A	E	DP
Bruno	.920	19	12	34	4	2
Candelario	.891	59	39	124	20	11
Contreras	—	1	0	0	0	0

Shortstop	PCT	G	PO	A	E	DP
Bruno	.899	14	19	43	7	6
Hernandez	.926	63	103	171	22	22

Outfield	PCT	G	PO	A	E	DP
Almora	1.000	15	39	1	0	0
Batista	.921	47	68	2	6	0
Bruno	1.000	7	7	1	0	0
Contreras	1.000	16	32	2	0	0
Dunston Jr.	1.000	17	33	1	0	1
Garsez	.897	23	34	1	4	1
Gonzalez	1.000	10	17	1	0	0
Kim	.976	29	41	0	1	0
Martin	.985	57	127	3	2	2
Rademacher	.880	13	21	1	3	0
Shoulders	.917	7	9	2	1	0

AZL CUBS   ROOKIE

ARIZONA LEAGUE

Batting	B-T	HT	WT	DOB	AVG	vLH	vRH	G	AB	R	H	2B	3B	HR	RBI	BB	HBP	SH	SF	SO	SB	CS	SLG	OBP
Almora, Albert	R-R	6-1	170	4-16-94	.347	.500	.298	18	75	18	26	5	1	1	13	2	1	0	2	8	5	1	.480	.363
Baez, Jeffrey	R-R	6-0	180	10-30-93	.222	.000	.286	6	18	0	4	0	0	2	1	0	0	0	5	1	0	.222	.263
Balaguert, Yasiel	R-R	6-2	215	1-2-93	.235	.321	.207	32	115	16	27	4	2	2	15	10	0	0	3	27	1	1	.357	.289
Bote, David	R-R	5-11	170	4-7-93	.232	.290	.213	38	125	16	29	7	3	1	14	19	4	1	1	32	5	2	.360	.349
Carhart, Ben	R-R	5-10	200	1-21-90	.353	.444	.308	35	136	28	48	9	1	1	21	15	2	0	2	14	1	1	.456	.419
Crawford, Rashad	B-R	6-3	185	10-15-93	.167	.100	.200	9	30	6	5	0	0	0	3	7	0	0	0	9	4	0	.167	.324
Cuneo, Ryan	L-R	6-3	190	10-10-88	.000	.000	—	1	2	0	0	0	0	0	0	0	0	0	0	0	0	0	.000	.000
Dunston Jr., Shawon	L-R	6-2	170	2-5-93	.286	.333	.265	39	161	30	46	6	4	2	24	18	1	2	2	33	4	2	.410	.357
Escobar, Carlos	R-R	6-2	185	12-31-90	.231	.000	.353	8	26	4	6	3	0	0	3	5	1	0	1	12	1	0	.346	.364
Garsez, Izaac	L-L	6-1	210	1-24-90	.273	.176	.316	13	55	10	15	1	3	1	8	7	0	0	0	16	4	1	.455	.355
Giansanti, Anthony	R-R	5-11	200	9-28-88	.200	.500	.167	6	20	4	4	1	0	1	7	3	0	0	0	2	0	0	.400	.304
Gonzalez, Gregori	R-R	5-9	170	7-11-94	.444	.500	.333	3	9	2	4	1	0	0	2	2	0	0	1	2	1	2	0	.556	.500
Gretzky, Trevor	L-L	6-4	190	9-14-92	.304	.148	.352	35	115	17	35	1	1	0	10	12	1	3	1	24	4	0	.330	.372
Lockhart, Daniel	L-R	5-11	165	11-4-92	.221	.286	.194	45	190	31	42	5	4	1	20	18	4	1	0	27	11	3	.305	.302
Lopez, Rafael	L-R	5-9	190	10-23-87	.467	.200	.600	4	15	5	7	2	1	0	4	1	1	0	0	4	0	0	.733	.529
Marra, Justin	L-L	5-10	190	1-18-93	.322	.150	.371	29	90	20	29	11	1	0	14	21	3	0	2	19	0	1	.467	.457
Martin, Trey	R-R	6-2	188	12-11-92	.448	.429	.455	7	29	5	13	5	1	0	6	2	2	0	0	3	2	0	.690	.515
Mineo, Alberto	L-R	5-10	170	7-23-94	.157	.200	.129	17	51	8	8	0	0	0	3	10	0	1	0	14	1	1	.157	.295
Penalver, Carlos	R-R	6-0	170	7-18-94	.273	.305	.258	49	183	27	50	7	1	0	20	19	1	0	2	31	7	4	.322	.341
Petit, Wilfredo	B-R	5-11	165	2-9-93	.100	.500	.000	4	10	1	1	0	0	0	0	1	0	0	0	2	0	0	.100	.182
Rademacher, Bijan	L-L	6-0	200	6-15-91	.333	.333	.333	3	12	3	4	1	0	1	1	0	0	0	0	2	2	0	.667	.333
Rogers, Jacob	R-R	6-5	195	8-23-89	.341	.300	.362	26	88	19	30	11	1	2	17	15	1	0	0	32	1	1	.557	.442
Rosario, Neftali	R-R	5-11	193	7-22-93	.214	.231	.207	14	42	8	9	3	0	0	7	5	0	0	0	11	1	0	.286	.298
Saunders, Tim	R-R	6-0	180	5-17-90	.493	.520	.478	17	71	23	35	5	0	3	17	5	2	0	1	11	5	2	.690	.532
Schlecht, Garrett	L-L	6-2	190	2-15-93	.252	.212	.267	35	119	21	30	6	1	1	16	20	1	1	2	32	8	2	.345	.359
Soler, Jorge	R-R	6-3	205	2-25-92	.241	.444	.139	14	54	14	13	2	0	2	10	6	1	0	0	13	8	0	.389	.328
Vogelbach, Dan	L-R	6-0	250	12-17-92	.324	.371	.299	24	102	16	33	12	2	7	31	12	0	0	1	14	1	0	.686	.391

Pitching	B-T	HT	WT	DOB	W	L	ERA	G	GS	CG	SV	IP	H	R	ER	HR	BB	SO	AVG	vLH	vRH	K/9	BB/9
Ackerman, Hunter	L-L	6-1	190	10-24-90	1	0	0.90	4	3	0	0	10	5	1	1	0	3	10	.147	.143	.148	9.00	2.70
Adrian, Daniel	R-R	6-1	175	12-7-90	0	1	3.27	13	0	0	0	22	20	15	8	1	15	21	.233	.267	.214	8.59	6.14
Amlung, Justin	R-R	6-0	174	5-21-90	0	0	0.00	3	0	0	0	6	2	0	0	0	1	6	.100	.143	.077	9.00	1.50
Berg, Justin	R-R	6-3	225	6-7-84	0	0	14.54	3	2	0	0	4	9	10	7	0	4	2	.391	.286	.438	4.15	8.31
Blackburn, Paul	R-R	6-2	185	12-4-93	2	0	3.48	9	6	0	0	21	23	11	8	2	7	13	.284	.214	.321	5.66	3.05
Bremer, Tyler	R-R	6-2	210	12-7-89	0	1	11.57	2	0	0	0	2	4	3	3	0	0	0	.400	.600	.200	0.00	0.00

Name	B-T	HT	WT	DOB	W	L	ERA	G	GS	CG	SV	IP	H	R	ER	HR	BB	SO	AVG	vLH	vRH	K/9	BB/9
Cales, David	R-R	5-11	205	7-27-87	0	0	13.50	1	1	0	0	1	2	1	1	0	2	1	.500	1.000	.000	13.50	27.00
Castillo, Lendy	R-R	6-1	170	4-8-89	0	0	0.69	4	4	0	0	13	7	1	1	0	3	16	.156	.286	.097	11.08	2.08
Cates, Zach	R-R	6-3	200	12-17-89	0	0	2.70	1	1	0	0	3	4	1	1	0	1	5	.308	.500	.222	13.50	2.70
Collado, Juan	R-R	6-1	175	4-4-90	1	0	0.00	2	0	0	0	4	0	0	0	0	1	4	.000	.000	.000	9.82	2.45
Dolis, Rafael	R-R	6-4	215	1-10-88	1	1	6.35	5	0	0	0	6	7	5	4	0	2	5	.292	.300	.286	7.94	3.18
Dorris, Nathan	L-L	6-3	185	12-9-90	1	0	1.80	7	0	0	1	10	8	3	2	0	4	8	.222	.200	.231	7.20	3.60
Elias, Ethan	R-R	6-3	180	4-27-93	1	2	3.90	13	4	0	0	30	38	18	13	1	6	22	.311	.324	.307	6.60	1.80
Estevez, Ricardo	R-R	6-0	180	4-11-84	0	0	0.00	1	1	0	0	2	3	1	0	0	0	1	.375	.400	.333	5.40	0.00
Garcia, Ramon	R-R	6-2	170	8-2-91	1	0	13.50	1	0	0	0	1	3	2	2	1	0	1	.500	.600	.000	6.75	0.00
Hamann, Mike	R-R	6-3	165	1-1-91	0	0	0.00	1	0	0	0	1	0	0	0	0	1	2	.000	.000	.000	18.00	9.00
Hartman, Ryan	R-R	6-3	180	5-10-92	1	1	8.10	11	0	0	2	17	30	21	15	0	9	13	.395	.292	.442	7.02	4.86
Heesch, Michael	R-L	6-5	245	5-15-90	0	0	0.00	2	0	0	1	2	1	0	0	0	0	3	.143	.000	.250	13.50	0.00
Henrie, David	R-R	6-5	190	1-18-91	4	1	5.32	7	0	0	0	22	26	16	13	3	4	19	.289	.280	.292	7.77	1.64
Hoffner, Corbin	R-R	6-5	235	7-30-93	0	1	0.71	7	1	0	0	13	15	9	1	0	4	13	.288	.292	.286	9.24	2.84
Iannazzo, Matt	L-L	5-9	170	1-8-90	0	1	1.13	4	0	0	0	8	6	2	1	0	4	12	.222	.000	.240	13.50	4.50
Jimenez, Alvido	R-R	6-1	160	11-22-91	3	4	2.64	15	1	0	1	31	19	13	9	2	7	30	.174	.267	.109	8.80	2.05
Johnson, Pierce	R-R	6-3	170	5-10-91	0	0	0.00	2	2	0	0	3	4	0	0	0		2	.364	.400	.333	6.00	0.00
Jung, Su-Min	R-R	6-2	190	4-1-90	0	0	0.00	1	1	0	0	3	1	0	0	0	1	3	.100	.000	.250	9.00	3.00
Kim, Jin-Young	R-R	6-1	190	4-16-92	0	1	1.53	14	0	0	2	18	18	3	8	0	4	14	.250	.276	.233	7.13	2.04
Lang, Trey	R-R	6-3	225	5-18-92	0	0	3.29	7	3	0	0	14	16	6	5	1	2	11	.286	.261	.303	7.24	1.32
Lindsay, Shane	R-R	6-2	230	1-25-85	0	0	3.38	3	0	0	0	5	4	2	2	0	4	7	.211	.100	.333	11.81	6.75
Maltos-Garcia, Arturo	R-R	6-1	190	8-2-91	2	0	5.89	12	0	0	0	18	11	12	12	3	12	20	.175	.125	.226	9.82	5.89
Maples, Dillon	R-R	6-2	195	5-9-92	0	1	4.35	6	4	0	0	10	6	7	5	0	10	12	.162	.071	.217	10.45	8.71
Martin, Chad	R-R	6-7	230	5-17-90	4	2	5.06	14	0	0	1	16	17	10	9	0	9	17	.262	.444	.191	9.56	5.06
Martinez-Pumarino, Carlos	R-R	6-4	230	4-2-91	5	0	3.53	14	1	0	0	43	36	22	17	1	14	44	.225	.241	.216	9.14	2.91
McNeil, Ryan	R-R	6-3	210	2-1-94	1	0	1.35	8	6	0	0	20	19	3	3	1	10	18	.264	.353	.184	8.10	4.50
Orozco, Eddie	R-R	6-2	195	4-11-89	1	0	0.00	1	0	0	0	1	1	0	0	0	0	2	.200	.000	.250	18.00	0.00
Padron, Loiger	R-R	6-0	180	1-31-91	4	0	2.54	12	0	0	0	28	24	12	8	2	12	31	.224	.304	.164	9.85	3.81
Perakslis, Steve	R-R	6-1	185	1-15-91	4	0	3.20	15	0	0	2	25	23	13	9	0	6	26	.230	.176	.258	9.24	2.13
Prieto, Anthony	L-L	5-11	170	11-16-93	0	1	2.33	10	7	0	0	19	9	5	5	0	12	11	.145	.154	.143	5.12	5.59
Rakkar, Jasvir	R-R	6-2	200	4-27-91	0	0	2.70	7	0	0	1	10	10	3	3	0	5	13	.256	.263	.250	11.70	4.50
Rosscup, Zach	R-L	6-2	205	6-9-88	0	0	0.00	1	0	0	0	2	0	0	0	0	4		.000	—	.000	21.60	0.00
Smith, Brian	L-L	6-0	170	12-12-92	0	1	1.72	7	3	0	0	16	7	3	3	0	6	13	.135	.250	.114	7.47	3.45
Underwood, Duane	R-R	6-2	205	7-20-94	0	1	5.19	5	5	0	0	7	6	5		1	6	7	.206	.308	.143	7.27	6.23
Wells, Ben	R-R	6-2	220	9-10-92	0	0	0.00	1	0	0	0	1	0	0	0		1	3	.000	.000	—	27.00	9.00
York, Tony	R-R	6-3	190	2-18-90	0	0	16.20	2	0	0	0	2	4	3	3	0	0		.444	.667	.333	0.00	0.00

Fielding

Catcher	PCT	G	PO	A	E	DP	PB
Escobar	1.000	6	51	3	0	0	0
Lopez	.917	2	10	1	1	0	0
Marra	.990	24	178	19	2	1	6
Mineo	.972	14	91	15	3	0	3
Petit	.972	4	28	7	1	0	0
Rosario	.972	13	92	11	3	0	5

First Base	PCT	G	PO	A	E	DP
Carhart	1.000	5	28	0	0	7
Giansanti	1.000	2	18	1	0	1
Gretzky	.976	14	117	6	3	9
Rogers	.966	15	138	5	5	11
Schlecht	.875	1	6	1	1	1
Vogelbach	.995	21	203	10	1	17

Second Base	PCT	G	PO	A	E	DP
Bote	.958	16	25	44	3	5

	PCT	G	PO	A	E	DP
Gonzalez	1.000	1	1	1	0	0
Lockhart	.944	33	73	97	10	16
Penalver	.964	5	13	14	1	4
Saunders	1.000	3	5	8	0	2

Third Base	PCT	G	PO	A	E	DP
Bote	.864	9	5	14	3	2
Carhart	.941	26	16	48	4	3
Giansanti	.857	3	1	5	1	1
Lockhart	.857	9	4	8	2	3
Rogers	.667	2	2	2	2	0
Saunders	.909	8	3	27	3	6

Shortstop	PCT	G	PO	A	E	DP
Bote	.939	11	12	34	3	2
Lockhart	1.000	1	2	1	0	0
Penalver	.937	42	67	141	14	27
Saunders	1.000	2	4	8	0	1

Outfield	PCT	G	PO	A	E	DP
Almora	.974	18	34	3	1	1
Baez	.917	5	9	2	1	1
Balaguert	.968	25	27	3	1	1
Crawford	.833	8	19	1	4	0
Dunston Jr.	.974	38	72	2	2	0
Garsez	.917	12	20	2	2	0
Gonzalez	1.000	2	3	0	0	0
Gretzky	.909	15	10	0	1	0
Martin	1.000	7	14	0	0	0
Rademacher	1.000	2	3	0	0	0
Rogers	1.000	3	3	0	0	0
Saunders	1.000	3	6	0	0	0
Schlecht	.889	26	28	4	4	2
Soler	1.000	9	11	0	0	0

DSL CUBS1

ROOKIE

DOMINICAN SUMMER LEAGUE

Batting	B-T	HT	WT	DOB	AVG	vLH	vRH	G	AB	R	H	2B	3B	HR	RBI	BB	HBP	SH	SF	SO	SB	CS	SLG	OBP
Alcala, Roney	B-R	6-1	190	2-15-94	.303	.340	.293	59	231	43	70	13	2	5	43	13	3	0	5	32	8	4	.442	.341
Baez, Jeffrey	R-R	6-0	180	10-30-93	.291	.297	.289	48	172	40	50	10	4	3	28	18	8	1	3	35	28	9	.448	.378
Calero, Arnaldo	R-R	6-1	175	11-16-93	.269	.150	.303	54	182	21	49	10	1	3	23	11	1	0	0	44	7	9	.385	.314
Caro, Roberto	R-R	6-0	185	9-25-93	.327	.190	.360	32	107	25	35	3	2	0	9	18	0	4	0	22	8	2	.393	.424
2-team total (23 Cubs 2)					.314	—	—	55	191	47	60	5	6	0	18	32	2	7	0	29	15	8	.403	.418
Cuevas, Varonex	B-R	6-0	165	7-24-92	.276	.419	.245	54	170	25	47	6	1	0	12	16	2	1	1	33	12	9	.324	.344
De La Cruz, Steven	R-R	6-0	183	12-13-93	.357	.143	.429	10	28	4	10	4	0	0	5	1	0	0	0	2	0	1	.500	.379
2-team total (2 Cubs 2)					.303	—	—	12	33	4	10	4	0	0	5	1	0	0	0	5	0	1	.424	.324
Emeterio, Jenner	R-R	6-1	170	3-19-93	.283	.390	.246	45	159	27	45	8	2	2	20	24	2	2	2	32	12	7	.396	.380
Gonzalez, Antonio	B-R	5-10	170	1-27-94	.269	.200	.286	8	26	5	7	1	2	0	5	6	0	0	0	3	2	2	.462	.406
2-team total (40 Cubs 2)					.237	—	—	48	131	19	31	4	2	0	14	18	3	1	0	32	12	7	.298	.342
Gonzalez, Leonardo	R-R	6-1	178	2-17-95	.215	.250	.208	30	93	10	20	4	0	0	8	10	2	0	0	19	1	2	.258	.305
Mercedes, Enderson	R-R	6-2	180	12-4-92	.172	.190	.167	29	87	14	15	4	0	5	9	11	4	0	1	48	1	1	.391	.291
2-team total (17 Cubs 2)					.169	—	—	46	118	20	20	5	0	6	14	18	5	0	1	65	1	3	.364	.303
Ortega, John	B-R	5-11	152	5-4-94	.184	.313	.159	47	98	19	18	1	1	0	11	26	2	1	1	11	6	7	.214	.362

	B-T	HT	WT	DOB	AVG	vLH	vRH	G	AB	R	H	2B	3B	HR	RBI	BB	HBP	SH	SF	SO	SB	CS	SLG	OBP
Paniagua, Jose	R-R	6-2	180	6-7-94	.211	.194	.215	48	171	20	36	5	2	2	16	10	1	2	1	46	3	8	.298	.257
Paula, Adonis	R-R	6-1	185	6-21-94	.186	.233	.172	37	129	16	24	4	2	1	11	9	5	0	0	36	4	2	.271	.266
Petit, Wilfredo	B-R	5-11	165	2-9-93	.200	.179	.206	51	175	17	35	7	2	1	18	11	2	2	0	22	4	2	.280	.255
Ramirez, Carlos	R-L	5-9	185	5-27-92	.258	.087	.294	38	132	16	34	9	1	0	19	11	4	1	1	14	0	2	.341	.331
Rico, Miguel	R-R	6-2	204	9-15-93	.239	.139	.268	48	159	17	38	5	1	1	17	15	11	0	3	40	4	2	.302	.340
Sanchez, Francisco	R-R	6-1	170	12-17-93	.196	.170	.206	53	194	29	38	5	3	5	24	10	3	0	4	64	7	5	.330	.242

Pitching

	B-T	HT	WT	DOB	W	L	ERA	G	GS	CG	SV	IP	H	R	ER	HR	BB	SO	AVG	vLH	vRH	K/9	BB/9
Abreu, Gilberto	R-R	6-2	180	8-8-93	0	0	2.45	2	2	0	0	4	2	2	1	0	3	3	.154	.000	.200	7.36	7.36
Adrian, Daniel	R-R	6-1	175	12-7-90	0	1	4.15	4	2	0	0	13	12	8	6	1	9	13	.250	.077	.314	9.00	6.23
Bautista, Jonathan	R-R	6-3	190	11-19-92	0	1	2.92	8	0	0	0	12	8	4	0	6	8	.157	.174	.143	5.84	4.38	
2-team total (7 Cubs 2)					0	1	3.43	15	0	0	0	21	16	12	8	1	11	15	—	—	—	6.43	4.71
Bermudez, Harrinson	R-R	6-4	190	3-6-95	0	0	6.11	9	0	0	0	18	18	16	12	0	9	10	.269	.292	.256	5.09	4.58
Cabreja, Enger	R-R	6-2	180	1-28-92	1	2	6.91	8	1	0	0	14	15	14	11	1	11	16	.254	.240	.265	10.05	6.91
Carrillo, Francisco	R-R	6-0	190	3-15-90	1	4	1.60	18	0	0	4	39	33	16	7	0	10	48	.219	.212	.224	10.98	2.29
Castro, Javier	R-R	6-0	160	2-10-92	0	1	3.14	6	4	0	0	14	9	5	5	0	5	8	.170	.091	.226	5.02	3.14
De la Cruz, Juancito	R-R	6-3	170	1-21-93	1	1	6.30	10	0	0	0	20	26	16	14	2	20	19	.333	.333	.333	8.55	9.00
De la Cruz, Michael	R-R	6-2	180	11-28-89	0	0	9.00	2	2	0	0	2	1	2	2	0	4	1	.200	.000	.333	4.50	18.00
Diaz, Andin	L-L	6-0	182	9-2-92	1	4	5.16	10	2	0	1	23	23	17	13	1	10	17	.261	.429	.230	6.75	3.97
Fuentes, Manuel	L-L	6-1	168	6-6-92	1	0	3.57	14	0	0	0	23	14	13	9	0	26	20	.179	.083	.197	7.94	10.32
Guillen, Luis	R-R	6-1	150	12-16-93	0	1	3.24	3	3	0	0	8	2	4	3	0	1	6	.077	.154	.000	6.48	1.08
Hernandez, Jeffry	R-R	6-5	215	1-19-95	1	3	4.58	8	4	0	0	20	25	17	10	0	8	15	.321	.179	.400	6.86	3.66
Leyba, Richard	L-L	6-4	210	10-25-91	0	0	17.61	5	0	0	0	8	19	15	15	4	6	10	.463	.800	.417	11.74	7.04
Martinez, Eric	R-R	6-2	185	1-25-90	4	6	4.08	21	0	0	4	40	45	24	18	1	7	23	.298	.255	.320	5.22	1.59
Mejias, Angel	L-L	6-3	180	10-30-93	4	2	2.58	13	11	1	0	70	56	26	20	1	23	57	.223	.133	.243	7.36	2.97
Mercado, Hendry	R-R	6-3	170	3-21-94	0	1	24.75	8	1	0	1	12	22	34	33	3	18	4	.423	.261	.552	3.00	13.50
Paulino, Jose	L-L	6-2	165	4-9-95	2	6	4.18	15	7	0	0	60	54	41	28	4	20	60	.224	.235	.222	8.95	2.98
Perez, Hector	R-R	6-1	157	6-25-93	2	0	4.50	12	10	0	0	50	49	28	25	2	23	47	.254	.297	.227	8.46	4.14
Rodriguez, Carlos A.	L-L	5-11	178	7-18-95	5	3	2.01	14	12	0	0	72	52	27	16	2	20	73	.197	.149	.207	9.17	2.51
Severino, Carlos	R-R	6-0	180	8-1-91	6	1	2.79	18	1	0	2	42	41	28	13	3	22	39	.252	.235	.263	8.36	4.71
Villalba, Luis	L-L	6-2	182	10-28-92	3	1	1.93	10	8	0	0	47	33	13	10	1	20	37	.200	.118	.209	7.14	3.86

Fielding

Catcher	PCT	G	PO	A	E	DP	PB
De La Cruz	.960	5	19	5	1	0	0
Gonzalez	.978	20	109	25	3	2	10
Ortega	1.000	1	2	0	0	0	0
Petit	.981	41	306	48	7	2	4
Ramirez	.990	12	87	15	1	1	4

First Base	PCT	G	PO	A	E	DP
Alcala	.985	36	252	15	4	17
Calero	1.000	1	3	0	0	0
Cuevas	1.000	2	12	0	0	0
Gonzalez	1.000	2	12	0	0	0
Paula	.942	12	91	7	6	6
Petit	1.000	7	40	2	0	1
Ramirez	.957	7	44	1	2	4
Rico	.974	15	137	13	4	10

Second Base	PCT	G	PO	A	E	DP
Cuevas	.923	30	56	76	11	13
Emeterio	.886	11	19	20	5	5
Gonzalez	.939	7	13	18	2	3
Ortega	.882	29	51	54	14	7
Sanchez	.857	3	5	7	2	0

Third Base	PCT	G	PO	A	E	DP
Alcala	.930	15	13	27	3	2
Cuevas	.862	12	6	19	4	1
Ortega	1.000	2	2	1	0	0
Paula	.855	20	11	42	9	2
Petit	1.000	1	0	1	0	0
Rico	.896	32	20	66	10	8
Sanchez	.500	1	0	1	1	0

Shortstop	PCT	G	PO	A	E	DP
Cuevas	.947	13	14	22	2	1
Emeterio	.882	21	39	51	12	6
Gonzalez	—	1	0	0	0	0
Ortega	—	1	0	0	0	0
Sanchez	.868	43	72	105	27	13

Outfield	PCT	G	PO	A	E	DP
Alcala	.842	12	14	2	3	0
Baez	1.000	46	105	4	0	1
Calero	.956	50	61	4	3	0
Caro	.969	30	58	4	2	2
Emeterio	1.000	8	11	0	0	0
Gonzalez	1.000	2	2	0	0	0
Mercedes	.918	28	44	1	4	0
Ortega	.750	3	3	0	1	0
Paniagua	.957	46	64	3	3	1
Sanchez	.000	1	0	0	1	0

DSL CUBS2   ROOKIE

DOMINICAN SUMMER LEAGUE

Batting	B-T	HT	WT	DOB	AVG	vLH	vRH	G	AB	R	H	2B	3B	HR	RBI	BB	HBP	SH	SF	SO	SB	CS	SLG	OBP
Acosta, Luis	R-R	6-2	195	11-28-94	.197	.176	.204	61	203	26	40	10	1	3	28	25	3	0	1	89	10	4	.300	.293
Arcila, Delbis	L-L	6-3	190	4-30-93	.258	.286	.248	62	217	30	56	15	3	2	29	36	4	1	1	50	5	6	.382	.372
Caro, Roberto	B-R	6-0	185	9-25-93	.298	.333	.283	23	84	22	25	2	4	0	9	14	2	3	0	7	7	6	.417	.410
2-team total (32 Cubs 1)					.314	—	—	55	191	47	60	5	6	0	18	32	2	7	0	29	15	8	.403	.418
Castillo, Erick	B-R	5-11	180	2-25-93	.180	.118	.191	42	111	12	20	7	0	0	10	13	7	4	1	13	0	2	.243	.303
Contreras, Edwin	L-L	6-0	190	12-13-93	.224	.250	.220	38	98	9	22	4	0	0	11	7	0	0	0	29	1	1	.265	.276
De La Cruz, Steven	R-R	6-0	183	12-13-93	.000	.000	.000	2	5	0	0	0	0	0	0	0	0	0	0	3	0	0	.000	.000
2-team total (10 Cubs 1)					.303	—	—	12	33	4	10	4	0	0	5	1	0	0	0	5	0	1	.424	.324
Encarnacion, Kelvin	B-R	6-0	175	11-23-91	.308	.250	.331	52	172	38	53	6	3	5	31	39	5	3	1	27	12	10	.465	.447
Flete, Bryant	B-R	5-10	146	1-31-93	.296	.216	.317	60	179	32	53	5	7	1	14	33	5	3	0	26	10	9	.419	.419
Gonzalez, Antonio	B-R	6-0	170	1-27-94	.229	.161	.257	40	105	14	24	3	0	0	9	12	3	1	0	29	10	5	.257	.325
2-team total (8 Cubs 1)					.237	—	—	48	131	19	31	4	2	0	14	18	3	1	0	32	12	7	.298	.342
Malave, Mark	B-R	6-3	185	1-5-95	.229	.167	.249	62	227	25	52	11	0	0	21	32	2	0	1	49	5	0	.278	.328
Marcano, Antonio	L-R	6-2	187	10-18-94	.245	.283	.236	63	220	28	54	9	5	0	18	34	2	2	1	38	6	5	.332	.350
Mercedes, Enderson	R-R	6-2	180	12-4-92	.161	.143	.167	17	31	6	5	1	0	1	5	7	1	0	0	17	0	2	.290	.333
2-team total (29 Cubs 1)					.169	—	—	46	118	20	20	5	0	6	14	18	5	0	1	65	1	3	.364	.303
Ortiz, Dalfis	B-R	5-10	160	2-10-92	.261	.143	.284	40	88	19	23	4	0	0	6	21	0	2	1	21	5	5	.307	.400
Pena, Jhonny	B-R	5-10	190	5-24-92	.294	.500	.237	48	119	16	35	6	0	2	25	33	5	1	2	26	5	1	.395	.459
Puente, Jeffry	L-R	5-10	170	4-21-92	.227	.182	.236	53	128	23	29	7	2	0	16	18	5	1	0	21	15	8	.313	.344
Ubiera, Shamil	R-R	6-0	190	9-28-92	.297	.328	.287	66	249	48	74	24	1	4	41	17	9	0	3	47	14	8	.450	.360
Valerio, Antonio	R-R	5-11	170	3-21-91	.077	.000	.111	5	13	0	1	0	0	0	3	0	0	0	0	3	0	0	.077	.077
Vargas, Eufran	R-R	5-11	178	7-14-94	.172	.154	.178	29	58	5	10	1	0	0	6	13	3	0	1	18	0	2	.190	.347

Pitching

Pitching	B-T	HT	WT	DOB	W	L	ERA	G	GS	CG	SV	IP	H	R	ER	HR	BB	SO	AVG	vLH	vRH	K/9	BB/9
Araujo, Pedro	R-R	6-3	214	7-2-93	5	2	2.72	13	8	0	0	53	50	21	16	1	12	47	.245	.250	.244	7.98	2.04
Baldayaque, Jesus	R-R	6-2	195	4-17-92	0	2	4.29	11	0	0	0	21	24	13	10	0	11	9	.289	.308	.286	3.86	4.71
Bautista, Jonathan	R-R	6-3	190	11-19-92	0	0	4.15	7	0	0	1	9	8	4	4	1	5	7	.242	.182	.273	7.27	5.19
2-team total (8 Cubs 1)					0	1	3.43	15	0	0	1	21	16	12	8	1	11	15	—	—	—	6.43	4.71
Brazoban, Pedro	R-R	6-2	163	7-13-92	0	0	4.50	3	0	0	0	6	10	3	3	0	2	5	.385	.600	.333	7.50	3.00
Colinas, Augusto	L-L	6-0	178	12-20-92	1	0	3.38	13	0	0	1	16	11	6	6	1	10	11	.196	.286	.184	6.19	5.63
Diaz, Alberto	L-L	5-9	157	6-12-91	2	2	2.51	18	0	0	4	32	20	10	9	3	19	28	.194	.182	.196	7.79	5.29
Diaz, Jorge	R-R	6-6	190	1-20-92	1	2	3.00	12	7	0	0	36	36	17	12	1	12	24	.273	.188	.300	6.00	3.00
Eregua, Greyfer	R-R	5-11	160	10-15-93	3	2	3.48	10	9	0	0	44	39	20	17	3	8	36	.247	.231	.252	7.36	1.64
Figueroa, Frailyn	L-L	6-2	203	6-14-95	2	1	5.40	11	1	0	0	18	25	16	11	1	9	13	.342	.222	.359	6.38	4.42
Frias, Alexander	R-R	6-4	180	5-29-92	1	1	5.23	16	0	0	2	21	21	15	12	2	11	10	.263	.313	.250	4.35	4.79
Garcia, Victor	L-L	6-2	175	4-1-92	3	1	2.34	17	0	0	2	35	24	12	9	1	12	39	.195	.143	.202	10.13	3.12
Morel, Yomar	R-R	6-1	180	11-18-93	1	0	2.84	11	0	0	0	25	30	12	8	0	7	24	.294	.357	.284	8.53	2.49
Padron, Loiger	R-R	6-0	180	1-31-91	0	1	4.09	4	2	0	0	11	15	5	5	1	7	10	.357	.500	.313	8.18	5.73
Pereyra, Jesus	R-R	6-2	175	7-24-93	0	3	4.97	17	1	0	1	29	29	19	16	4	14	16	.264	.355	.228	4.97	4.34
Pieters, Chris	L-L	6-3	183	3-21-94	2	5	6.00	14	6	0	0	33	27	28	22	1	47	24	.237	.111	.248	6.55	12.82
Reyes, Amalio	R-R	6-2	175	5-22-91	1	6	2.95	16	10	0	0	64	52	33	21	3	13	44	.224	.286	.201	6.19	1.83
Salazar, Victor	R-R	6-3	178	1-21-93	4	2	3.55	16	0	0	1	33	30	19	13	3	19	37	.252	.192	.269	10.09	5.18
Santana, Alex	R-R	6-1	170	10-23-93	1	3	2.88	13	12	0	0	59	51	30	19	2	14	51	.231	.185	.250	7.74	2.12
Torrez, Daury	R-R	6-3	170	6-11-93	6	3	1.21	14	13	0	0	75	57	14	10	6	4	50	.213	.213	.214	6.03	0.48

Fielding

Catcher	PCT	G	PO	A	E	DP	PB
Castillo	.974	41	244	53	8	2	4
De La Cruz	1.000	2	6	3	0	0	0
Pena	.990	22	87	13	1	0	3
Puente	.667	1	1	1	0	0	
Valerio	.971	5	33	1	1	0	0
Vargas	.973	24	123	21	4	2	5

First Base	PCT	G	PO	A	E	DP
Arcila	.982	44	413	23	8	23
Encarnacion	—	1	0	0	0	0
Gonzalez	1.000	1	1	0	0	0
Malave	1.000	1	8	0	0	2
Pena	.985	18	130	5	2	12
Puente	.984	15	117	9	2	11
Vargas	1.000	1	2	0	0	1

Second Base	PCT	G	PO	A	E	DP
Flete	.933	34	72	82	11	15
Gonzalez	.958	22	34	58	4	8
Ortiz	.949	21	38	36	4	9
Puente	.974	12	18	19	1	5

Third Base	PCT	G	PO	A	E	DP
Acosta	.900	4	0	9	1	0
Flete	.800	1	1	3	1	0
Gonzalez	.000	1	0	0	1	0
Malave	.962	54	46	157	8	13
Ortiz	.967	10	10	19	1	1
Puente	.889	10	4	20	3	2

Shortstop	PCT	G	PO	A	E	DP
Acosta	.889	52	63	121	23	20
Flete	.877	19	30	34	9	6

	PCT	G	PO	A	E	DP
Gonzalez	.933	4	7	7	1	1
Malave	.941	4	7	9	1	1
Puente	—	1	0	0	0	0

Outfield	PCT	G	PO	A	E	DP
Acosta	1.000	1	3	1	0	1
Arcila	.923	21	20	4	2	0
Caro	1.000	14	31	0	0	0
Contreras	.875	16	13	1	2	0
Encarnacion	.989	45	89	5	1	1
Flete	1.000	3	8	0	0	0
Gonzalez	1.000	2	1	0	0	0
Marcano	.974	59	69	5	2	0
Mercedes	.875	16	6	1	1	0
Puente	.750	7	3	0	1	0
Ubiera	.941	57	88	8	6	1

Chicago White Sox

SEASON IN A SENTENCE: Chicago's win-now approach almost worked, as the White Sox led the American League Central until a September slump gave Detroit a chance to overtake them.

HIGH POINT: The White Sox beat Detroit 5-4 in a rescheduled game on Sept. 17 to extend their division lead to three games with just 15 to play. With three games against the Royals, Chicago appeared on track to put the division away.

LOW POINT: Instead, the White Sox lost two of three to the Royals and then were swept by the Angels. Even after that, Chicago still led the division, but a 1-2 series against hapless Cleveland showed the team had run out of gas. Chicago went 4-11 over its final 15 games.

NOTABLE ROOKIES: The White Sox's bullpen was in large part made up of hard-throwing youngsters. Nate Jones, Hector Santiago and Brian Omogrosso helped get the Sox to rookie closer Addison Reed (3-2, 4.75 with 25 saves). But no rookie was more effective or more surprising than lefthander Jose Quintana. Signed as a minor league free agent who had never pitched above Class A, Quintana quickly earned a spot in the rotation, going 6-6, 3.76.

KEY TRANSACTIONS: General manager Kenny Williams did what he could to keep the White Sox in the pennant race. Chicago picked up Kevin Youkilis to bolster the club's on-base abilities. Nearer the trade deadline, Chicago picked up lefthander Francisco Liriano and righthander Brett Myers to bolster the pitching staff. Myers (3-4, 3.12) was generally effective, but Liriano (3-2, 5.40) struggled. None of the players the Sox traded away are considered frontline prospects. More siginficantly, Williams moved up to an executive vice president role after the season, with longtime assistant Rick Hahn taking over as GM.

DOWN ON THE FARM: The White Sox had plenty of highlights. Triple-A Charlotte and high Class A Winston-Salem both had the best records in their leagues before losing in the finals of their league playoffs. On the other end of the spectrum, Rookie-level Bristol went 19-46. First-round pick Courtney Hawkins handled being placed on the fast track and already ranks as the organization's top prospect. While many first-round high school picks spent the year in Rookie leagues, Hawkins quickly jumped to low Class A Kannapolis and finished the season helping the Winston-Salem club in the playoffs.

OPENING DAY PAYROLL: $96.9 million (11th)

PLAYERS OF THE YEAR

MAJOR LEAGUE	MINOR LEAGUE
Chris Sale	**Carlos Sanchez**
lhp	**ss/2b**
17-8, 3.05	(Hi A/AA/AAA)
192 SO/51 BB	.323/.378/.403
4th in AL in ERA, SO/9	CL batting champion

ORGANIZATION LEADERS

BATTING		*Minimum 250 AB
MAJORS		
* AVG	Alex Rios	.304
* OPS	Paul Konerko	.857
HR	Adam Dunn	41
RBI	Adam Dunn	96
MINORS		
* AVG	Carlos Sanchez, W-S/Birmingham/Charlotte	.323
* OBP	Brady Shoemaker, W-S/Birmingham	.416
* SLG	Dan Johnson, Charlotte	.492
R	Brady Shoemaker, W-S/Birmingham	91
H	Carlos Sanchez, W-S/Birmingham/Charlotte	169
TB	Trayce Thompson, W-S/Birmingham/Charlotte	249
2B	Brady Shoemaker, W-S/Birmingham	35
3B	Jared Mitchell, Birmingham/Charlotte	13
HR	Dan Johnson, Charlotte	28
RBI	Trayce Thompson, W-S/Birmingham/Charlotte	96
BB	Dan Johnson, Charlotte	94
SO	Jared Mitchell, Birmingham/Charlotte	179
SB	Keenyn Walker, Kannapolis/Winston-Salem	56

PITCHING		#Minimum 75 IP
MAJORS		
W	Chris Sale	17
# ERA	Chris Sale	3.05
SO	Jake Peavy	194
SV	Addison Reed	29
MINORS		
W	Charles Leesman, Charlotte	12
L	Nestor Molina, Charlotte/Birmingham	11
	Jefferson Olacio, Kannapolis/Bristol	11
# ERA	Charles Leesman, Charlotte	2.47
G	Steven Upchurch, Kannapolis/Winston-Salem	43
GS	Jake Petricka, Winston-Salem/Birmingham	29
SV	Ryan Kussmaul, Birmingham/Charlotte	13
IP	Charles Shirek, Charlotte	170.1
BB	Jake Petricka, Winston-Salem/Birmingham	81
SO	Scott Snodgress, Kannapolis/Winston-Salem	128
# AVG	Scott Snodgress, Kannapolis/Winston-Salem	.217

General Manager: Ken Williams. **Farm Director:** Buddy Bell. **Scouting Director:** Doug Laumann.

Class	Team	League	W	L	PCT	Finish	Manager
Majors	Chicago White Sox	American	85	77	.525	8th (14)	Robin Ventura
Triple-A	Charlotte Knights	International	83	61	.576	3rd (14)	Joel Skinner
Double-A	Birmingham Barons	Southern	63	76	.453	9th (10)	Bobby Magallanes
High A	Winston-Salem Dash	Carolina	87	51	.630	1st (8)	Tommy Thompson
Low A	Kannapolis Intimidators	South Atlantic	61	78	.439	t-12th (14)	Julio Vinas
Rookie	Bristol White Sox	Appalachian	19	46	.292	10th (10)	Pete Rose
Rookie	Great Falls Voyagers	Pioneer	40	36	.526	5th (8)	Ryan Newman
Overall 2012 Minor League Record			353	348	.504	18th (30)	

ORGANIZATION STATISTICS

CHICAGO WHITE SOX

AMERICAN LEAGUE

Batting	B-T	HT	WT	DOB	AVG	vLH	vRH	G	AB	R	H	2B	3B	HR	RBI	BB	HBP	SH	SF	SO	SB	CS	SLG	OBP
Beckham, Gordon	R-R	6-0	190	9-16-86	.234	.227	.236	151	525	62	123	24	0	16	60	40	7	8	2	89	5	4	.371	.296
Danks, Jordan	L-R	6-4	210	8-7-86	.224	.179	.256	50	67	12	15	1	0	1	4	6	0	0	2	16	3	1	.284	.280
De Aza, Alejandro	L-L	6-0	190	4-11-84	.281	.248	.291	131	524	81	147	29	6	9	50	47	9	4	1	109	26	12	.410	.349
Dunn, Adam	L-R	6-6	285	11-9-79	.204	.191	.211	151	539	87	110	19	0	41	96	105	1	0	4	222	2	1	.468	.333
Escobar, Eduardo	B-R	5-10	165	1-5-89	.207	.333	.159	36	87	14	18	4	1	0	3	9	0	1	0	23	2	0	.276	.281
2-team total (14 Minnesota)					.214	—	—	50	131	18	28	4	1	0	9	11	1	2	1	31	3	0	.260	.278
Flowers, Tyler	R-R	6-4	245	1-24-86	.213	.269	.179	52	136	19	29	6	0	7	13	12	4	1	0	56	2	1	.412	.296
Fukudome, Kosuke	L-R	6-0	200	4-26-77	.171	.250	.162	24	41	2	7	1	0	0	4	8	0	0	2	9	0	1	.195	.294
Gimenez, Hector	B-R	5-10	225	9-28-82	.455	.800	.167	5	11	1	5	0	0	0	1	0	0	0	0	3	0	0	.455	.455
Hudson, Orlando	B-R	6-0	190	12-12-77	.197	.125	.227	51	137	10	27	3	3	2	17	12	0	3	0	24	3	1	.307	.262
Johnson, Dan	L-R	6-2	210	8-10-79	.364	.400	.353	14	22	8	8	1	0	3	6	9	0	0	0	3	0	0	.818	.548
Konerko, Paul	R-R	6-2	220	3-5-76	.298	.271	.307	144	533	66	159	22	0	26	75	56	7	0	2	83	0	0	.486	.371
Lillibridge, Brent	R-R	5-11	185	9-18-83	.175	.080	.237	49	63	10	11	1	0	0	2	4	1	1	1	26	7	2	.190	.232
3-team total (10 Boston, 43 Cleveland)					.195	—	—	102	190	25	37	6	0	3	10	11	4	1	3	71	13	2	.274	.250
Lopez, Jose	R-R	6-0	205	11-24-83	.217	.364	.083	15	23	2	5	1	0	0	1	0	0	0	0	6	0	0	.261	.250
2-team total (66 Cleveland)					.246	—	—	81	236	18	58	14	0	4	28	9	0	0	3	41	0	1	.356	.270
Morel, Brent	R-R	6-2	220	4-21-87	.177	.200	.170	35	113	14	20	2	0	0	5	7	0	5	0	39	4	1	.195	.225
Olmedo, Ray	B-R	5-11	165	5-31-81	.244	.143	.296	20	41	8	10	2	0	0	1	0	0	1	0	9	0	0	.293	.244
Pierzynski, A.J.	L-R	6-3	235	12-30-76	.278	.248	.287	135	479	68	133	18	4	27	77	28	8	1	4	78	0	0	.501	.326
Ramirez, Alexei	R-R	6-2	180	9-22-81	.265	.290	.258	158	593	59	157	24	4	9	73	16	4	4	4	77	20	7	.364	.287
Rios, Alex	R-R	6-5	215	2-18-81	.304	.293	.308	157	605	93	184	37	8	25	91	26	4	0	5	92	23	6	.516	.334
Viciedo, Dayan	R-R	5-11	240	3-10-89	.255	.350	.225	147	505	64	129	18	1	25	78	28	6	0	4	120	0	2	.444	.300
Wise, Dewayne	L-L	6-0	200	2-24-78	.258	.173	.297	45	163	20	42	7	1	5	22	9	1	0	3	40	12	4	.405	.295
2-team total (55 New York)					.259	—	—	100	224	31	58	10	2	8	30	11	1	0	3	52	19	4	.429	.293
Youkilis, Kevin	R-R	6-1	220	3-15-79	.236	.284	.218	80	292	47	69	8	1	15	46	37	13	0	2	69	0	0	.425	.346
2-team total (42 Boston)					.235	—	—	122	438	72	103	15	2	19	60	51	17	0	3	108	0	0	.409	.336

Pitching	B-T	HT	WT	DOB	W	L	ERA	G	GS	CG	SV	IP	H	R	ER	HR	BB	SO	AVG	vLH	vRH	K/9	BB/9
Axelrod, Dylan	R-R	6-0	195	7-30-85	2	2	5.47	14	7	0	0	51	56	32	31	8	21	40	.275	.277	.273	7.06	3.71
Bruney, Brian	R-R	6-3	235	2-17-82	1	0	0.00	1	0	0	0	1	0	0	0	0	2	0	.000	.000	.000	18.00	18.00
Crain, Jesse	R-R	6-1	215	7-5-81	2	3	2.44	51	0	0	0	48	29	14	13	5	23	60	.171	.232	.129	11.25	4.31
Danks, John	L-L	6-1	215	4-15-85	3	4	5.70	9	9	0	0	54	57	35	34	7	23	30	.273	.307	.248	5.03	3.86
Floyd, Gavin	R-R	6-6	235	1-27-83	12	11	4.29	29	29	0	0	168	166	84	80	22	63	144	.259	.291	.226	7.71	3.38
Heath, Deunte	R-R	6-4	215	8-8-85	0	0	4.50	3	0	0	0	2	1	1	1	1	1	1	.167	.000	.333	4.50	4.50
Hernandez, Pedro	L-L	5-10	200	4-12-89	0	1	18.00	1	1	0	0	4	12	8	8	3	1	2	.500	.667	.400	4.50	2.25
Humber, Phil	R-R	6-3	210	12-21-82	5	5	6.44	26	16	1	0	102	113	74	73	23	44	85	.276	.302	.243	7.50	3.88
Jones, Nathan	R-R	6-5	185	1-28-86	8	0	2.39	65	0	0	0	72	67	19	19	4	32	65	.256	.170	.304	8.16	4.02
Liriano, Francisco	L-L	6-2	215	10-26-83	3	2	5.40	12	11	0	0	57	54	34	34	7	32	58	.251	.254	.250	9.21	5.08
2-team total (22 Minnesota)					6	12	5.34	34	28	0	0	157	143	97	93	19	87	167	—	—	—	9.59	5.00
Marinez, Jhan	R-R	6-1	200	8-12-88	0	0	0.00	2	0	0	0	3	2	0	0	0	2	1	.250	.333	.200	3.38	6.75
Myers, Brett	R-R	6-4	240	8-17-80	3	4	3.12	35	0	0	9	35	30	13	12	4	9	21	.238	.225	.244	5.45	2.34
Ohman, Will	L-L	6-2	225	8-13-77	0	2	6.41	32	0	0	0	27	23	19	19	6	5	13	.228	.186	.286	4.39	1.69
Omogrosso, Brian	R-R	6-4	230	4-26-84	0	0	2.57	17	0	0	0	21	20	6	6	3	9	18	.247	.281	.224	7.71	3.86
Peavy, Jake	R-R	6-1	195	5-31-81	11	12	3.37	32	32	4	0	219	191	88	82	27	49	194	.234	.252	.210	7.97	2.01
Quintana, Jose	L-L	6-0	215	1-24-89	6	6	3.76	25	22	0	0	136	142	62	57	14	42	81	.275	.252	.284	5.35	2.77
Reed, Addison	R-R	6-4	220	12-27-88	3	2	4.75	62	0	0	29	55	57	30	29	6	18	54	.266	.293	.243	8.84	2.95
Sale, Chris	L-L	6-6	180	3-30-89	17	8	3.05	30	29	1	0	192	167	66	65	19	51	192	.235	.233	.236	9.00	2.39
Santiago, Hector	R-L	6-0	210	12-16-87	4	1	3.33	42	4	0	4	70	54	26	26	10	40	79	.211	.211	.211	10.11	5.12
Septimo, Leyson	L-L	6-1	195	7-7-85	0	2	5.02	21	0	0	0	14	8	8	8	3	6	14	.157	.161	.150	8.79	3.77
Stewart, Zach	R-R	6-2	205	9-28-86	1	2	6.00	18	1	0	0	30	41	26	20	10	4	16	.320	.286	.347	4.80	1.20
2-team total (2 Boston)					1	4	8.58	20	3	0	0	36	58	40	34	14	4	19	—	—	—	4.79	1.01
Stults, Eric	L-L	6-0	225	12-9-79	0	0	2.70	2	1	0	0	7	6	2	2	0	4	2	.240	.222	.250	5.40	5.40
Thornton, Matt	L-L	6-6	240	9-15-76	4	10	3.46	74	0	0	3	65	63	27	25	4	17	53	.257	.256	.258	7.34	2.35
Veal, Donnie	L-L	6-4	240	9-18-84	0	0	1.38	24	0	0	1	13	5	2	2	0	4	19	.111	.094	.154	13.15	2.77

CHICAGO WHITE SOX

Fielding

Catcher	PCT	G	PO	A	E	DP	PB
Flowers	.994	49	324	29	2	5	1
Gimenez	1.000	3	16	0	0	0	0
Pierzynski	.994	126	899	71	6	8	8

First Base	PCT	G	PO	A	E	DP
Dunn	.995	52	387	34	2	31
Flowers	1.000	2	10	1	0	2
Johnson	1.000	3	12	1	0	2
Konerko	.999	105	818	60	1	96
Lillibridge	1.000	20	32	3	0	3
Lopez	1.000	3	4	0	0	0
Youkilis	1.000	13	36	0	0	8

Second Base	PCT	G	PO	A	E	DP
Beckham	.990	149	280	411	7	110

Escobar	1.000	6	10	8	0	1
Hudson	1.000	11	19	30	0	11
Olmedo	1.000	2	4	6	0	2

Third Base	PCT	G	PO	A	E	DP
Escobar	.969	22	4	27	1	3
Hudson	.944	29	17	51	4	6
Lillibridge	1.000	6	5	8	0	3
Lopez	1.000	11	4	9	0	2
Morel	.962	33	25	51	3	2
Olmedo	1.000	10	4	10	0	0
Youkilis	.965	78	42	125	6	17

Shortstop	PCT	G	PO	A	E	DP
Escobar	.933	4	3	11	1	1
Olmedo	.875	5	2	5	1	1

Ramirez	.982	158	227	434	12	93

Outfield	PCT	G	PO	A	E	DP
Danks	1.000	41	44	0	0	0
De Aza	.991	130	326	4	3	1
Dunn	1.000	5	8	0	0	0
Escobar	1.000	1	2	0	0	0
Fukudome	1.000	15	22	0	0	0
Gimenez	1.000	2	1	0	0	0
Lillibridge	1.000	21	17	0	0	0
Rios	.980	156	333	9	7	2
Viciedo	.992	131	233	13	2	0
Wise	1.000	45	90	2	0	0

CHARLOTTE KNIGHTS — TRIPLE-A

INTERNATIONAL LEAGUE

Batting	B-T	HT	WT	DOB	AVG	vLH	vRH	G	AB	R	H	2B	3B	HR	RBI	BB	HBP	SH	SF	SO	SB	CS	SLG	OBP
Baisley, Jeff	R-R	6-3	225	12-19-82	.250	.267	.244	16	56	4	14	3	0	1	5	5	2	0	1	14	0	0	.357	.328
2-team total (10 Toledo)					.183	—	—	26	93	5	17	4	0	1	8	7	3	0	2	16	0	0	.258	.257
Castro, Jose	B-R	5-8	170	11-5-86	.174	.200	.167	8	23	4	4	1	0	0	1	0	1	1	0	5	0	0	.217	.208
Danks, Jordan	L-R	6-4	210	8-7-86	.317	.327	.313	64	218	37	69	17	1	8	30	44	0	0	2	66	6	3	.514	.428
De Aza, Alejandro	L-L	6-0	190	4-11-84	.250	.091	.444	5	20	3	5	1	0	1	2	1	0	0	0	3	0	0	.450	.286
Espino, Damaso	R-R	6-1	210	5-8-83	.000	.000	.000	3	7	0	0	0	0	0	0	1	0	1	0	1	0	0	.000	.125
Fukudome, Kosuke	L-R	6-0	200	4-26-77	.154	.222	.000	4	13	0	2	0	0	0	3	0	0	0		4	0	0	.154	.313
2-team total (39 Scranton/W-B)					.264	—	—	43	140	17	37	5	1	2	16	40	1	0	1	29	1	1	.357	.429
Gallagher, Jimmy	L-L	6-1	195	9-3-85	.225	.161	.243	82	276	29	62	15	2	1	28	32	1	1	4	54	4	1	.304	.304
Garcia, Drew	B-R	6-1	175	4-22-86	.234	.167	.262	99	364	43	85	18	2	5	49	28	5	6	5	83	4	3	.335	.294
Gimenez, Hector	B-R	5-10	225	9-28-82	.259	.259	.259	99	375	50	97	22	2	14	57	37	0	4	2	89	2	1	.440	.324
Golson, Greg	R-R	6-0	190	9-17-85	.276	.275	.277	109	449	67	124	29	7	6	52	17	5	7	2	114	20	2	.412	.309
Greene, Justin	R-R	6-0	185	10-10-85	.238	.185	.267	56	185	28	44	6	1	6	25	17	2	0	1	50	12	4	.378	.307
Hudson, Orlando	B-R	6-0	190	12-17-77	.313	.200	.364	5	16	1	5	1	0	0	1	0	0	0		2	0		.375	.353
Jackson, Conor	R-R	6-2	215	5-7-82	.277	.233	.293	88	318	44	88	23	0	9	41	41	4	0	3	43	5	1	.434	.363
Johnson, Dan	L-R	6-2	210	8-10-79	.267	.222	.289	137	476	77	127	21	1	28	85	94	7	0	10	94	1	0	.492	.388
Kuhn, Tyler	L-R	5-10	185	9-9-86	.273	.281	.270	103	417	65	114	26	4	4	36	20	3	5	4	66	6	4	.384	.309
Loman, Seth	L-R	6-4	225	12-16-85	.273	.400	.167	4	11	1	3	0	0	0	2	0	0			4	0	0	.273	.385
Lopez, Jose	R-R	6-0	205	11-24-83	.306	.250	.324	13	49	7	15	5	0	1	10	6	0	0		8	0	0	.469	.382
2-team total (6 Columbus)					.375	—	—	19	72	8	27	9	0	1	14	7	0	0	0	10	0	0	.542	.430
Manzella, Tommy	R-R	6-2	200	4-16-83	.171	.214	.148	14	41	4	7	3	0	0	6	2	1	1		14	0	0	.244	.205
Martinez, Ozzie	R-R	5-10	200	5-7-88	.178	.234	.153	60	214	15	38	11	0	0	13	10	2	4	0	34	4	0	.229	.221
McPherson, Dallas	L-R	6-4	225	7-23-80	.253	.237	.259	61	229	35	58	12	0	12	47	28	1	0	2	83	2	1	.463	.335
2-team total (20 Indianapolis)					.265	—	—	81	306	45	81	16	1	17	62	37	1	0	2	115	3	1	.490	.344
Mitchell, Jared	L-L	6-0	205	10-13-88	.231	.143	.258	36	121	18	28	11	1	1	13	16	2	1	1	53	1	1	.364	.329
Morel, Brent	R-R	6-2	220	4-21-87	.194	.222	.186	34	124	12	24	4	0	1	10	8	0	0	0	28	0	0	.250	.242
Olmedo, Ray	B-R	5-11	165	5-31-81	.273	.238	.288	80	275	24	75	15	1	0	19	27	1	7	0	42	9	3	.335	.340
Phegley, Josh	R-R	5-10	215	2-12-88	.266	.295	.254	102	394	40	105	22	1	6	48	20	4	0	3	60	3	0	.373	.306
Saladino, Tyler	R-R	6-0	190	7-20-89	.224	.250	.216	15	49	9	11	2	0	0	6	4	1	0		16	1	0	.265	.296
Sanchez, Carlos	R-R	5-11	175	6-29-92	.256	.214	.280	11	39	4	10	2	0	0	0	0	0	6		0	0		.308	.256
Shelton, Kyle	R-R	6-0	184	5-15-86	.200	.200	.200	8	20	1	4	1	0	1	2	1	0	0		5	0	0	.400	.304
Short, Brandon	R-R	6-0	190	9-9-88	.333	.000	.500	2	6	0	2	0	0	0	2	0	1	0		0	0	0	.333	.429
Thompson, Trayce	R-R	6-3	195	3-15-91	.167	.222	.111	6	18	1	3	2	0	0	2	0	0			6	1	0	.278	.250
Wise, Dewayne	L-L	6-0	200	2-24-78	.161	.143	.167	7	31	3	5	1	1	0	3	1	0	0	1	8	1	0	.258	.182
2-team total (21 Scranton/W-B)					.280	—	—	28	107	20	30	8	1	4	13	10	0	0	1	24	3	0	.486	.339

Pitching	B-T	HT	WT	DOB	W	L	ERA	G	GS	CG	SV	IP	H	R	ER	HR	BB	SO	AVG	vLH	vRH	K/9	BB/9
Axelrod, Dylan	R-R	6-0	195	7-30-85	7	5	2.88	16	16	1	0	97	81	34	31	8	31	92	.230	.283	.193	8.54	2.88
Ballinger, J.R.	R-R	6-1	190	4-2-88	0	0	7.71	2	0	0	0	5	4	6	4	1	4	2	.235	.333	.182	3.86	7.71
Bruney, Brian	R-R	6-3	235	2-17-82	2	3	1.70	25	4	0	11	37	22	7	7	1	13	37	.171	.259	.107	9.00	3.16
Carroll, Scott	R-R	6-4	215	9-24-84	2	3	3.78	9	8	0	0	48	39	21	20	6	18	36	.224	.207	.241	6.80	3.40
2-team total (25 Louisville)					4	6	4.74	34	8	0	0	87	90	47	46	10	34	63	—	—	—	6.49	3.50
Carter, Anthony	L-R	6-3	210	4-4-86	4	6	4.60	39	1	0	2	63	71	39	32	6	22	54	.282	.261	.298	7.76	3.16
Castro, Simon	R-R	6-5	230	4-9-88	1	1	4.32	5	5	0	0	25	32	13	12	2	6	16	.303	.304	.327	5.76	2.16
Crain, Jesse	R-R	6-1	215	7-5-81	0	0	0.00	2	2	0	0	2	0	0	0	0	0	3	.000	.000	.000	13.50	0.00
Danks, John	L-L	6-1	215	4-15-85	0	0	2.25	1	1	0	0	4	4	3	1	0	1	1	.267	.000	.286	2.25	2.25
Doyle, Terry	R-R	6-4	260	11-2-85	6	3	2.83	12	11	1	0	76	53	25	24	5	18	71	.199	.191	.206	8.37	2.12
Heath, Deunte	R-R	6-4	215	8-8-85	4	3	1.48	36	4	0	3	67	47	13	11	4	20	74	.190	.212	.176	9.94	2.69
Hernandez, Pedro	L-L	5-10	200	4-12-89	1	0	3.71	3	2	0	0	17	18	8	7	1	3	17	.281	.240	.308	9.00	1.59
2-team total (4 Rochester)					1	2	4.46	7	6	0	0	34	43	18	17	2	4	28	—	—	—	7.34	1.05
Humber, Phil	R-R	6-3	210	12-21-82	0	1	5.68	2	2	0	0	6	8	4	4	1	4	4	.308	.250	.333	5.68	5.68
Infante, Greg	R-R	6-2	215	7-10-87	4	1	3.66	20	0	0	1	32	30	18	13	1	16	20	.254	.220	.273	5.63	4.50
Kloess, Brandon	R-R	6-2	195	12-9-84	3	0	1.61	13	1	0	1	28	27	6	5	1	12	26	.252	.217	.279	8.36	3.86
Kussmaul, Ryan	R-R	6-4	185	9-19-86	0	0	18.00	1	0	0	0	1	4	2	2	0	0	0	.667	.750	.500	0.00	0.00

Pitching	B-T	HT	WT	DOB	W	L	ERA	G	GS	CG	SV	IP	H	R	ER	HR	BB	SO	AVG	vLH	vRH	K/9	BB/9
Leesman, Charlie	L-L	6-4	210	3-10-87	12	10	2.47	26	26	0	0	135	129	54	37	8	52	103	.255	.271	.251	6.87	3.47
Lindsay, Shane	R-R	6-2	230	1-25-85	1	1	7.48	15	0	0	0	22	16	20	18	2	28	25	.219	.200	.237	10.38	11.63
Marinez, Jhan	R-R	6-1	200	8-12-88	4	2	2.86	40	0	0	4	63	39	24	20	5	30	65	.177	.184	.173	9.29	4.29
Molina, Nestor	R-R	6-1	180	1-9-89	0	1	13.50	1	1	0	0	4	9	6	6	2	1	4	.450	.444	.455	9.00	2.25
Moskos, Daniel	R-L	6-1	210	4-28-86	1	1	4.43	17	0	0	2	20	26	12	10	2	14	21	.313	.382	.265	9.30	6.20
2-team total (14 Indianapolis)					2	3	4.19	31	0	0	2	34	39	18	16	2	22	32	—	—	—	8.39	5.77
Olsen, Scott	L-L	6-4	210	1-12-84	0	0	2.25	2	2	0	0	4	3	1	1	1	2	2	.214	.250	.200	4.50	4.50
Omogrosso, Brian	R-R	6-4	230	4-26-84	0	2	4.56	33	0	0	9	47	43	25	24	3	12	59	.240	.225	.253	11.22	2.28
Remenowsky, Dan	R-R	6-5	245	4-7-86	2	1	3.86	11	1	0	1	21	26	9	9	3	5	21	.310	.342	.283	9.00	2.14
Rienzo, Andre	R-R	6-3	160	7-5-88	0	0	0.00	1	1	0	0	7	5	1	0	0	2	10	.227	.250	.167	13.50	2.70
Rodriguez, Santos	L-L	6-5	180	1-2-88	0	0	3.68	5	0	0	0	7	7	3	3	0	2	9	.250	.333	.188	11.05	2.45
Santiago, Hector	R-L	6-0	210	12-16-87	1	0	0.00	3	3	0	0	15	9	0	0	0	6	13	.188	.083	.222	7.98	3.68
Septimo, Leyson	L-L	6-1	195	7-7-85	2	1	1.31	24	0	0	1	34	16	5	5	1	20	43	.139	.089	.171	11.27	5.24
Shirek, Charlie	R-R	6-3	205	10-25-85	11	5	3.65	28	26	1	0	170	172	79	69	18	29	117	.260	.253	.267	6.18	1.53
Stults, Eric	L-L	6-0	225	12-9-79	1	1	2.20	5	5	0	0	29	25	7	7	0	10	26	.243	.167	.266	8.16	3.14
Veal, Donnie	L-L	6-4	240	9-18-84	7	3	2.08	35	0	0	2	52	40	17	12	0	23	61	.211	.242	.195	10.56	3.98
Whisler, Wes	L-L	6-5	240	4-7-83	0	1	6.35	5	0	0	0	6	6	6	4	1	2	2	.231	.091	.333	3.18	3.18
Zaleski, Matt	R-R	6-1	205	12-2-81	7	6	3.70	25	22	1	0	129	131	56	53	12	51	77	.273	.301	.252	5.37	3.56

Fielding

Catcher	PCT	G	PO	A	E	DP	PB
Espino	1.000	3	23	1	0	0	0
Gimenez	.984	47	339	27	6	5	4
Phegley	.996	96	772	59	3	5	12

First Base	PCT	G	PO	A	E	DP
Gallagher	.992	32	252	11	2	27
Gimenez	.995	20	173	11	1	18
Jackson	1.000	3	31	5	0	1
Johnson	.995	89	728	40	4	78
Loman	1.000	4	28	1	0	2
McPherson	1.000	2	18	0	0	1
Shelton	1.000	1	5	1	0	0

Second Base	PCT	G	PO	A	E	DP
Castro	1.000	5	10	18	0	5
Garcia	.987	85	129	241	5	54
Hudson	1.000	4	4	6	0	3
Kuhn	.980	30	56	94	3	17
Lopez	.826	5	8	11	4	4
Martinez	.833	1	2	3	1	0

	PCT	G	PO	A	E	DP
Olmedo	.989	17	38	54	1	13
Saladino	1.000	1	1	4	0	0
Sanchez	1.000	1	1	2	0	1

Third Base	PCT	G	PO	A	E	DP
Baisley	.904	16	17	30	5	5
Castro	1.000	2	0	4	0	0
Gimenez	1.000	1	0	2	0	0
Jackson	.932	15	13	28	3	2
Johnson	.941	15	5	27	2	1
Kuhn	.977	17	6	36	1	3
Lopez	1.000	6	4	13	0	1
Manzella	1.000	7	4	13	0	2
McPherson	.926	28	10	40	4	4
Morel	.954	26	4	58	3	4
Olmedo	.958	19	16	30	2	4
Shelton	.800	3	2	2	1	0

Shortstop	PCT	G	PO	A	E	DP
Castro	1.000	1	1	1	0	1
Garcia	.949	14	23	33	3	9

	PCT	G	PO	A	E	DP
Manzella	1.000	5	7	11	0	5
Martinez	.937	59	92	162	17	31
Olmedo	.960	41	61	105	7	29
Saladino	.973	14	30	43	2	14
Sanchez	1.000	10	18	28	0	11

Outfield	PCT	G	PO	A	E	DP
Danks	1.000	64	141	4	0	0
De Aza	1.000	3	6	0	0	0
Fukudome	1.000	4	9	2	0	0
Gallagher	.990	49	98	2	1	1
Golson	.970	102	212	13	7	3
Greene	.990	54	90	6	1	2
Jackson	1.000	65	119	9	0	0
Kuhn	1.000	47	75	7	0	3
Mitchell	.984	36	60	1	1	0
Olmedo	1.000	2	4	0	0	0
Shelton	1.000	4	3	0	0	0
Short	1.000	2	2	0	0	0
Thompson	.938	6	15	0	1	0
Wise	.900	5	9	0	1	0

BIRMINGHAM BARONS

DOUBLE-A

SOUTHERN LEAGUE

Batting	B-T	HT	WT	DOB	AVG	vLH	vRH	G	AB	R	H	2B	3B	HR	RBI	BB	HBP	SH	SF	SO	SB	CS	SLG	OBP
Castro, Jose	B-R	5-8	170	11-5-86	.181	.167	.183	22	72	8	13	3	0	0	1	5	1	1	0	3	0	2	.222	.244
Ciolli, Nick	L-R	6-2	215	12-6-87	.000	.000	.000	3	11	0	0	0	0	0	0	0	0	0	0	3	0	0	.000	.000
Dubler, Kevin	L-R	6-1	200	2-18-87	.214	.500	.167	5	14	2	3	0	0	0	1	4	1	0	0	4	0	0	.429	.267
Espino, Damaso	R-R	6-1	210	5-8-83	.284	.414	.226	66	229	20	65	8	0	0	23	22	1	2	1	30	1	0	.319	.348
Gallagher, Jimmy	L-L	6-1	195	9-3-85	.295	.200	.345	11	44	6	13	1	0	1	4	5	0	0	0	8	2	0	.386	.367
Garcia, Drew	B-R	6-1	175	4-22-86	.316	.400	.291	33	133	17	42	10	3	1	26	11	1	5	1	19	1	2	.459	.370
Gaston, Jon	L-R	6-0	215	10-13-86	.204	.182	.211	17	49	5	10	2	0	2	5	6	1	0	1	20	2	0	.367	.298
Gilmore, Jon	R-R	6-3	195	8-23-88	.180	.139	.198	33	122	16	22	6	0	0	10	11	1	1	1	43	0	0	.230	.252
Gonzalez, Miguel	R-R	5-11	180	12-3-90	.214	.318	.167	22	70	5	15	1	0	0	7	7	1	2	0	16	0	0	.229	.295
Greene, Justin	R-R	6-0	185	10-10-85	.281	.333	.258	39	135	21	38	10	3	2	13	21	0	1	1	35	14	1	.444	.376
Haddow, Mark	R-R	6-2	220	12-2-87	.118	.000	.133	5	17	0	2	0	0	0	1	1	0	0	0	5	0	0	.118	.211
Loman, Seth	L-R	6-4	225	12-16-85	.276	.269	.278	115	413	55	114	21	3	16	58	45	13	0	2	90	0	2	.458	.364
Martinez, Jose	R-R	6-5	170	7-25-88	.248	.193	.266	114	436	54	108	15	1	5	42	41	2	2	1	87	6	3	.321	.315
Mitchell, Jared	L-L	6-0	205	10-13-88	.240	.227	.244	94	334	51	80	13	12	10	54	62	7	3	2	126	20	5	.440	.368
Morrison, Erik	R-R	6-0	190	10-23-85	.271	.293	.264	84	295	41	80	12	0	6	42	21	3	1	2	57	2	1	.373	.324
Oester, Jake	R-R	6-1	190	7-22-86	.210	.270	.184	37	124	13	26	8	0	0	23	17	4	1	2	36	0	0	.274	.320
Paiml, Greg	R-R	6-0	185	8-3-84	.258	.143	.294	27	89	11	23	5	1	0	9	4	0	1	0	26	4	2	.337	.287
2-team total (31 Mississippi)					.205	—	—	58	161	15	33	6	1	0	11	12	1	1	1	53	4	2	.255	.263
Saladino, Tyler	R-R	6-0	190	7-20-89	.237	.231	.239	112	418	71	99	15	4	4	39	75	8	2	6	91	38	8	.321	.359
Sanchez, Carlos	R-R	5-11	175	6-29-92	.370	.375	.368	30	119	17	44	9	1	0	13	10	2	1	1	22	7	5	.462	.424
Shoemaker, Brady	R-R	6-0	200	5-10-87	.254	.218	.269	56	189	30	48	12	1	4	26	45	5	0	1	59	2	1	.392	.408
Short, Brandon	R-R	6-0	190	9-9-88	.214	.000	.265	10	42	5	9	2	0	0	1	2	0	0	0	7	1	0	.262	.250
Sierra, Luis	L-R	5-11	150	7-23-87	.242	.194	.251	64	219	23	53	12	2	0	24	24	2	1	1	36	0	2	.315	.321
Smith, Corey	R-R	6-1	200	4-15-82	.286	.237	.300	65	259	38	74	19	1	8	39	23	6	0	1	43	1	1	.459	.356
Thompson, Trayce	R-R	6-3	195	3-15-91	.280	.267	.286	14	50	10	14	1	1	3	6	8	0	0	0	16	2	0	.520	.379
Wagner, Daniel	L-R	6-0	185	7-12-88	.270	.167	.294	19	63	6	17	3	1	0	7	5	0	1	0	7	4	2	.349	.324
Wilkins, Andy	L-R	6-2	225	9-13-88	.239	.223	.245	116	435	68	104	28	1	17	69	63	1	0	3	94	6	4	.425	.335
Williams Jr., Kenny	B-R	6-0	180	5-22-86	.250	.125	.278	77	260	36	65	18	3	4	30	26	2	3	2	55	5	3	.388	.321

CHICAGO WHITE SOX

Pitching	B-T	HT	WT	DOB	W	L	ERA	G	GS	CG	SV	IP	H	R	ER	HR	BB	SO	AVG	vLH	vRH	K/9	BB/9
Arroyo, Spencer	L-L	6-2	166	8-9-88	6	4	4.59	12	12	0	0	69	76	41	35	7	31	36	.280	.233	.304	4.72	4.06
Bachanov, Jon	R-R	6-4	230	1-30-89	0	1	11.42	9	1	0	0	9	12	12	11	2	15	9	.316	.412	.238	9.35	15.58
Bayne, Cameron	R-R	6-2	195	2-14-88	7	10	6.43	20	20	0	0	106	124	83	76	13	58	50	.296	.286	.306	4.23	4.91
Bellamy, Kyle	R-R	6-5	220	10-25-87	1	2	4.68	16	0	0	0	25	27	17	13	2	16	14	.276	.348	.212	5.04	5.76
Buch, Ryan	R-R	6-3	205	11-8-87	0	0	0.00	2	0	0	1	4	1	0	0	0	2	2	.091	.000	.167	4.50	4.50
Carroll, Scott	R-R	6-4	215	9-24-84	0	0	0.00	1	1	0	0	5	1	0	0	0	2	2	.067	.111	.000	3.60	3.60
Castro, Simon	R-R	6-5	230	4-9-88	6	4	3.70	15	15	0	0	90	89	50	37	4	21	72	.254	.304	.209	7.20	2.10
Griffith, Nevin	R-R	6-3	210	3-23-89	1	2	6.59	32	1	0	1	55	45	43	40	2	56	41	.231	.169	.283	6.75	9.22
Gunter, Michael	R-R	6-1	190	7-5-90	0	0	2.70	2	0	0	1	3	2	1	1	0	1	4	.167	.200	.143	10.80	2.70
Heidenreich, Matt	L-R	6-5	185	1-17-91	1	2	5.89	3	3	0	0	18	27	14	12	1	5	9	.338	.436	.244	4.42	2.45
Hernandez, Pedro	L-L	5-10	200	4-12-89	7	2	2.75	12	12	0	0	69	68	21	21	6	18	37	.260	.194	.284	4.85	2.36
Humber, Phil	R-R	6-3	210	12-21-82	1	0	1.50	1	1	0	0	6	2	1	1	0	0	5	.111	.125	.100	7.50	0.00
Hunt, Leroy	R-R	6-6	240	11-28-87	2	3	4.39	29	0	0	0	55	57	28	27	2	34	32	.274	.320	.234	5.20	5.53
Infante, Greg	R-R	6-2	215	7-10-87	0	0	0.00	1	0	0	0	1	0	0	0	0	0	1	.000	.000	.000	9.00	0.00
Kloess, Brandon	R-R	6-2	195	12-9-84	3	3	3.35	24	2	0	3	46	35	23	17	0	18	44	.207	.271	.162	8.67	3.55
Kussmaul, Ryan	R-R	6-4	185	9-19-86	2	1	1.11	37	0	0	13	57	30	9	7	3	24	61	.152	.126	.176	9.63	3.79
Mabee, Henry	R-R	6-4	230	7-10-85	4	2	0.79	17	0	0	2	34	26	5	3	1	12	25	.217	.174	.243	6.55	3.15
McCully, Nick	R-R	5-11	195	9-5-88	2	4	4.75	16	7	1	0	55	50	30	29	5	31	42	.242	.293	.200	6.87	5.07
Molina, Nestor	R-R	6-1	180	1-9-89	6	10	4.26	22	21	0	0	123	156	60	58	7	26	84	.312	.354	.273	6.16	1.91
Petricka, Jake	R-R	6-5	210	6-5-88	3	3	5.46	10	10	0	0	58	63	35	35	7	35	27	.290	.299	.282	4.21	5.46
Quintana, Jose	L-L	6-0	215	1-24-89	1	3	2.77	9	9	0	0	49	43	17	15	1	14	41	.240	.250	.237	7.58	2.59
Remenowsky, Dan	R-R	6-5	245	4-7-86	1	3	2.15	25	1	0	3	46	21	12	11	1	22	54	.138	.109	.159	10.57	4.30
Rienzo, Andre	R-R	6-3	160	7-5-88	4	3	3.27	13	13	1	0	72	56	31	26	2	33	72	.209	.263	.138	9.04	4.14
Rodriguez, Santos	L-L	6-5	180	1-2-88	2	4	2.81	37	0	0	8	64	33	22	20	6	33	60	.153	.225	.110	8.44	4.64
Sanchez, Salvador	R-R	6-6	195	9-13-85	1	1	4.24	16	0	0	0	23	17	19	11	2	17	12	.210	.222	.200	4.63	6.56
Umberger, Dustin	R-R	6-0	190	2-10-87	0	0	1.80	2	0	0	0	5	4	1	1	0	1	1	.235	.167	.273	16.20	0.00
Wickswat, Matt	L-L	6-2	210	8-4-86	2	8	9.68	21	8	0	0	53	72	65	57	3	61	34	.332	.273	.364	5.77	10.36
Zaleski, Matt	R-R	6-1	205	12-2-81	0	1	4.09	2	2	0	0	11	10	5	5	1	5	7	.256	.063	.391	5.73	4.09

Fielding

Catcher	PCT	G	PO	A	E	DP	PB
Dubler	1.000	1	4	0	0	0	0
Espino	.998	62	395	46	1	1	3
Gonzalez	.988	22	139	19	2	4	3
Sierra	.987	55	355	36	5	2	14
Saladino	.989	20	36	52	1		13
Sanchez	.986	14	32	37	1		9
Sierra	1.000	5	6	8	0		3
Wagner	.918	19	23	44	6		6
Sanchez	1.000	11	22	39	0		7

First Base	PCT	G	PO	A	E	DP
Loman	.991	47	394	27	4	42
Oester	1.000	2	12	0	0	0
Sierra	—	1	0	0	0	0
Smith	1.000	1	13	0	0	1
Wilkins	.992	93	804	60	7	68

Second Base	PCT	G	PO	A	E	DP
Castro	1.000	18	31	46	0	6
Garcia	.977	27	58	67	3	19
Morrison	.974	32	55	97	4	18
Paiml	.926	11	17	33	4	10

Third Base	PCT	G	PO	A	E	DP
Morrison	.967	42	22	67	3	4
Oester	.971	33	17	50	2	10
Sanchez	.900	4	1	8	1	0
Smith	.917	62	44	144	17	17
Wilkins	.917	5	4	7	1	0

Shortstop	PCT	G	PO	A	E	DP
Castro	.917	4	4	7	1	3
Garcia	.933	7	9	19	2	3
Morrison	.938	12	14	31	3	5
Paiml	.974	15	28	46	2	9
Saladino	.948	93	131	270	22	51

Outfield	PCT	G	PO	A	E	DP
Ciolli	1.000	3	13	0	0	0
Gallagher	1.000	10	16	2	0	0
Gaston	.967	12	29	0	1	0
Gilmore	1.000	12	17	0	0	0
Greene	.978	39	86	4	2	0
Haddow	1.000	5	5	1	0	0
Martinez	.978	114	213	10	5	4
Mitchell	.949	90	216	9	12	1
Morrison	—	1	0	0	0	0
Shoemaker	1.000	46	92	2	0	1
Short	1.000	10	18	1	0	0
Thompson	.964	14	25	2	1	1
Williams Jr.	.987	70	155	2	2	1

WINSTON-SALEM DASH — HIGH CLASS A

CAROLINA LEAGUE

Batting	B-T	HT	WT	DOB	AVG	vLH	vRH	G	AB	R	H	2B	3B	HR	RBI	BB	HBP	SH	SF	SO	SB	CS	SLG	OBP
Black, Dan	L-R	6-5	240	7-2-87	.315	.382	.291	129	499	82	157	29	2	17	88	64	3	0	5	92	5	2	.483	.392
Blanke, Mike	R-R	6-4	230	10-17-88	.240	.316	.216	91	338	46	81	24	0	10	50	27	3	3	0	66	0	0	.399	.303
Ciolli, Nick	L-R	6-2	215	12-6-87	.280	.256	.288	46	168	29	47	10	1	4	26	11	3	1	1	48	7	2	.423	.333
Curley, Chris	R-R	6-0	185	8-25-87	.417	.500	.375	3	12	4	5	1	1	0	1	0	0	0	0	4	0	0	.667	.417
Dowdy, Jeremy	R-R	6-2	215	7-13-90	.222	.200	.235	13	27	4	6	2	0	0	2	0	0	0	1	4	0	0	.296	.214
Earley, Michael	R-R	6-0	200	3-15-88	.291	.300	.288	124	454	76	132	27	7	13	73	34	10	3	2	73	7	6	.467	.352
Eveland, Kyle	R-R	5-10	175	4-11-87	.111	.000	.143	4	9	3	1	0	0	0	1	1	0	0	0	2	0	0	.111	.200
Gonzalez, Miguel	R-R	5-11	180	12-3-90	.247	.171	.273	50	162	20	40	9	0	1	16	12	2	6	2	24	0	1	.321	.303
Haddow, Mark	R-R	6-2	220	12-2-87	.000	—	.000	4	10	1	0	0	0	0	1	1	0	1	1	2	0	0	.000	.083
Hankerd, Cyle	R-R	6-3	215	1-24-85	.325	.355	.315	74	265	55	86	24	4	15	51	16	25	0	3	46	6	2	.615	.411
Hawkins, Courtney	R-R	6-3	220	11-12-93	.294	.286	.300	5	17	3	5	2	0	1	2	0	0	1	0	2	0	1	.588	.294
Herbek, David	R-R	6-2	182	4-2-89	.313	.393	.293	47	144	24	45	9	2	5	23	17	3	3	4	37	2	3	.507	.387
Jarrad, D.J.	R-R	6-1	170	2-15-89	.167	—	.167	2	6	1	1	0	0	0	0	1	0	0	0	3	0	0	.167	.286
Johnson, Michael	L-R	5-9	175	10-28-88	.111	.000	.143	9	18	3	2	0	0	0	1	3	0	1	0	6	0	0	.111	.238
Morel, Brent	R-R	6-2	220	4-21-87	.227	.125	.286	7	22	2	5	4	0	0	0	2	0	0	0	4	0	0	.409	.292
Oester, Jake	R-R	6-1	190	7-22-86	.252	.212	.271	34	103	13	26	7	0	1	13	13	1	1	0	36	2	1	.350	.342
Rice, Bill	L-R	5-11	185	9-7-88	.154	—	.154	4	13	1	2	1	0	0	0	5	0	0	0	2	1	0	.231	.154
Sanchez, Carlos	R-R	5-11	175	6-29-92	.315	.268	.332	92	365	58	115	14	6	1	42	31	7	7	6	64	19	10	.395	.374
Semien, Marcus	R-R	6-1	190	9-17-90	.273	.316	.257	107	418	80	114	31	5	14	59	55	5	6	3	97	11	5	.471	.362
Shelton, Kyle	R-R	6-0	184	5-15-86	.313	.308	.316	9	32	6	10	2	1	2	6	1	1	0	0	8	0	1	.625	.353
Shoemaker, Brady	R-R	6-0	200	5-10-87	.331	.314	.338	78	284	61	94	23	0	13	59	30	16	0	2	54	2	1	.549	.422
Short, Brandon	R-R	6-0	190	9-9-88	.297	.333	.280	10	37	4	11	2	0	0	7	8	1	1	2	13	0	1	.351	.417
Silverio, Juan	R-R	6-1	175	4-18-91	.243	.286	.228	78	263	36	64	20	3	8	51	15	2	1	4	67	4	4	.433	.285

Batting	B-T	HT	WT	DOB	AVG	vLH	vRH	G	AB	R	H	2B	3B	HR	RBI	BB	HBP	SH	SF	SO	SB	CS	SLG	OBP
Smith, Kevan	R-R	6-4	240	6-28-88	.273	.300	.263	22	77	8	21	4	2	3	23	5	1	0	3	17	0	0	.494	.314
Thompson, Trayce	R-R	6-3	195	3-15-91	.254	.208	.272	116	449	77	114	28	5	22	90	45	6	2	8	144	18	3	.486	.325
Wagner, Daniel	L-R	6-0	185	7-12-88	.264	.294	.256	88	322	57	85	13	0	2	34	31	1	9	3	41	30	5	.323	.328
Walker, Keenyn	B-R	6-3	195	8-12-90	.238	.205	.250	37	143	31	34	7	1	3	16	24	0	0	1	50	17	4	.364	.345
Wilson, Ross	R-R	5-11	185	11-9-88	.190	.188	.190	25	79	11	15	3	1	0	6	11	2	0	3	21	0	0	.253	.295

Pitching	B-T	HT	WT	DOB	W	L	ERA	G	GS	CG	SV	IP	H	R	ER	HR	BB	SO	AVG	vLH	vRH	K/9	BB/9
Arroyo, Spencer	L-L	6-2	166	8-9-88	5	3	4.33	14	14	0	0	73	72	37	35	6	32	59	.261	.389	.230	7.31	3.96
Bachanov, Jon	R-R	6-4	230	1-30-89	7	2	3.95	23	9	0	0	66	52	33	29	4	43	55	.226	.257	.212	7.50	5.86
Ballinger, J.R.	R-R	6-1	190	4-2-88	3	3	3.83	31	0	0	0	49	47	24	21	3	25	29	.240	.308	.206	5.29	4.56
Bassitt, Chris	R-R	6-5	205	2-22-89	5	4	3.66	38	10	0	4	91	74	45	37	6	54	75	.218	.257	.200	7.42	5.34
Bellamy, Kyle	R-R	6-5	220	10-25-87	0	0	1.65	18	0	0	4	27	18	9	5	0	8	29	.182	.135	.210	9.55	2.63
Blough, Bryan	R-R	6-1	190	8-29-89	2	0	3.93	10	0	0	0	18	19	8	8	3	7	17	.268	.292	.255	8.35	3.44
Buch, Ryan	R-R	6-3	205	11-8-87	4	5	6.21	22	10	0	0	62	74	50	43	7	27	63	.292	.310	.283	9.10	3.90
Burnside, Paul	R-R	6-4	225	11-20-86	0	0	16.88	4	0	0	0	3	3	5	5	0	3		.000		.300	16.88	16.88
Collop, Justin	R-R	6-1	185	5-30-88	9	4	4.17	31	16	0	0	121	131	59	56	14	38	80	.279	.290	.273	5.95	2.83
Heidenreich, Matt	L-R	6-5	185	1-17-91	8	2	3.57	15	15	2	0	93	88	42	37	12	13	62	.246	.230	.257	5.98	1.25
Hudelson, James	R-R	6-4	215	5-16-90	0	0	0.00	2	0	0	0	2	1	0	0	0	1	3	.143	.000	.143	13.50	4.50
Hunt, Leroy	R-R	6-6	240	11-28-87	0	0	2.35	12	0	0	7	15	13	4	4	0	3	21	.232	.300	.194	12.33	1.76
Johnson, Erik	R-R	6-3	240	12-30-89	4	3	2.74	8	8	0	0	49	43	19	15	0	10	48	.230	.288	.203	8.76	1.82
Marin, Terance	R-R	6-1	170	8-21-89	5	6	2.42	33	0	0	7	67	66	34	18	3	12	69	.254	.256	.253	9.27	1.61
McCray, Stephen	L-R	6-3	230	10-6-87	9	3	3.30	25	17	0	0	117	97	53	43	11	43	91	.226	.235	.222	6.98	3.30
McCully, Nick	R-R	5-11	195	9-5-88	4	3	2.89	24	0	0	5	37	25	15	12	3	18	48	.191	.265	.146	11.57	4.34
Moran, Kevin	R-R	6-4	195	7-7-89	0	0	27.00	1	0	0	0	1	0	2	2	0	4	0	.000	.000	.000	0.00	54.00
Negus, Phil	R-R	6-2	205	11-10-87	0	1	5.40	3	0	0	0	7	10	5	4	0	2	9	.333	.231	.412	12.15	2.70
Peterson, Max	L-L	6-2	210	6-27-88	0	0	9.00	4	0	0	0	3	4	3	3	0	0	3	.308	.000	.444	9.00	0.00
Petricka, Jake	R-R	6-5	210	6-5-88	5	5	5.33	19	19	0	0	83	93	58	49	2	46	84	.284	.284	.284	9.15	5.01
Rienzo, Andre	R-R	6-3	160	7-5-88	3	0	1.08	4	0	0	0	25	17	3	3	0	7	31	.193	.244	.149	11.16	2.52
Sanchez, Salvador	R-R	6-6	195	9-13-85	0	0	0.00	3	0	0	0	4	2	0	0	0	4	3	.154	.500	.091	9.00	0.00
Snodgrass, Scott	L-L	6-5	210	9-20-89	4	0	1.50	8	0	0	0	42	26	10	7	2	15	44	.176	.185	.174	9.43	3.21
Thompson, Taylor	R-R	6-5	225	6-18-87	2	1	2.44	33	0	0	12	44	26	13	12	2	13	57	.169	.256	.135	11.57	2.64
Upchurch, Steven	R-R	6-4	180	9-14-89	4	1	3.08	27	3	0	0	61	50	27	21	3	17	49	.225	.239	.219	7.19	2.49
Vance, Kevin	R-R	6-0	208	7-8-90	1	0	1.66	11	0	0	0	22	19	5	4	3	5	29	.235	.370	.167	12.05	2.08
Walters, Blair	L-L	6-0	200	11-8-89	1	3	7.01	5	5	0	0	26	38	20	20	3	4	24	.345	.333	.351	8.42	1.40
Wickswat, Matt	L-L	6-2	210	8-4-86	1	1	7.82	7	1	0	0	13	15	11	11	0	11	13	.313	.364	.297	9.24	7.82
Wilson, Jake	R-R	6-0	195	8-12-87	1	1	3.60	4	0	0	0	5	4	2	2	0	6	5	.211	.000	.222	9.00	10.80

Fielding

Catcher	PCT	G	PO	A	E	DP	PB
Black	—	1	0	0	0	0	0
Blanke	.987	76	611	53	9	5	4
Dowdy	.974	7	33	4	1	0	0
Gonzalez	.984	47	336	44	6	1	4
Smith	.985	16	126	6	2	1	2

First Base	PCT	G	PO	A	E	DP
Black	.989	125	1018	108	12	93
Dowdy	1.000	2	1	0	0	0
Hankerd	1.000	12	105	12	0	10
Johnson	.955	3	20	1	1	1
Shelton	1.000	1	1	2	0	0

Second Base	PCT	G	PO	A	E	DP
Eveland	—	1	0	0	0	0
Herbek	1.000	7	11	16	0	2
Johnson	—	1	0	0	0	0
Oester	1.000	2	3	3	0	1
Sanchez	.980	45	85	114	4	29

	PCT	G	PO	A	E	DP
Semien	.959	24	54	64	5	21
Shelton	1.000	1	0	4	0	0
Wagner	.977	65	104	146	6	29
Wilson	1.000	1	1	2	0	0

Third Base	PCT	G	PO	A	E	DP
Curley	1.000	3	4	7	0	1
Eveland	1.000	2	0	5	0	1
Herbek	.927	21	9	42	4	2
Johnson	1.000	2	1	10	0	1
Morel	.800	5	2	2	1	0
Oester	.929	31	13	52	5	3
Shelton	1.000	2	1	3	0	0
Silverio	.887	70	46	143	24	12
Wagner	.778	10	6	15	6	3
Wilson	1.000	3	2	7	0	0

Shortstop	PCT	G	PO	A	E	DP
Herbek	.950	15	13	44	3	6
Jarrad	1.000	2	2	5	0	0

	PCT	G	PO	A	E	DP
Sanchez	.948	47	55	128	10	28
Semien	.943	80	104	211	19	40

Outfield	PCT	G	PO	A	E	DP
Black	—	1	0	0	0	0
Ciolli	.963	39	74	3	3	0
Dowdy	—	1	0	0	0	0
Earley	.973	101	168	9	5	2
Haddow	1.000	4	9	0	0	0
Hankerd	.983	30	54	4	1	0
Hawkins	1.000	4	10	0	0	0
Rice	1.000	2	5	0	0	0
Shoemaker	.972	68	101	5	3	1
Short	1.000	6	7	0	0	0
Silverio	1.000	4	10	0	0	0
Thompson	.982	115	265	8	5	0
Wagner	1.000	4	8	0	0	0
Walker	.986	36	68	3	1	1
Wilson	1.000	16	22	2	0	0

KANNAPOLIS INTIMIDATORS — LOW CLASS A
SOUTH ATLANTIC LEAGUE

Batting	B-T	HT	WT	DOB	AVG	vLH	vRH	G	AB	R	H	2B	3B	HR	RBI	BB	HBP	SH	SF	SO	SB	CS	SLG	OBP
Barraza, Jose	L-R	6-1	220	7-28-94	.000	—	.000	1	4	0	0	0	0	0	0	0	0	0	0	1	0	0	.000	.000
Buckner, Grant	R-R	6-2	215	3-21-88	.254	.254	.254	109	414	51	105	19	1	6	59	44	6	3	6	109	8	5	.348	.330
Curley, Chris	R-R	6-0	185	8-25-87	.271	.241	.284	49	192	29	52	9	1	11	29	10	5	0	2	48	7	1	.500	.321
De Pinto, Joe	R-R	6-1	190	4-3-89	.237	.169	.272	75	262	35	62	11	3	0	23	28	3	3	3	39	5	3	.302	.314
DeMichele, Joey	L-R	5-11	185	2-5-91	.261	.231	.272	58	234	30	61	12	7	5	29	19	1	2	0	54	5	4	.436	.319
Douglas, Andrew	R-R	6-0	210	5-27-89	.172	.143	.186	25	64	6	11	3	0	0	6	15	2	0	0	23	2	2	.219	.346
Dubler, Kevin	L-R	6-1	200	2-18-87	.229	.333	.207	10	35	3	8	1	0	2	5	5	0	0	1	10	0	0	.429	.317
Eveland, Kyle	R-R	5-10	175	4-11-87	.125	.000	.200	2	8	0	1	0	0	0	0	1	0	0	0	2	0	1	.125	.222
Haddow, Mark	R-R	6-2	220	12-2-87	.306	.369	.281	108	392	69	120	21	4	7	57	51	4	7	4	85	6	2	.434	.388
Hankerd, Cyle	R-R	6-3	215	1-24-85	.438	.286	.480	9	32	11	14	3	0	5	14	5	3	0	1	7	0	0	1.000	.537
Harvard, Justin	L-R	6-3	196	10-28-87	.190	.250	.175	22	79	12	15	3	0	1	16	4	1	0	3	30	2	0	.266	.230
Hawkins, Courtney	R-R	6-3	220	11-12-93	.308	.350	.289	16	65	11	20	5	2	4	15	4	1	1	1	17	3	2	.631	.352
Heisler, Adam	L-R	5-10	165	6-7-88	.259	.189	.283	35	143	19	37	5	1	1	10	10	0	0	1	26	15	2	.329	.305
Herbek, David	R-R	6-2	182	4-2-89	.214	.203	.221	43	145	28	31	10	0	0	9	21	5	3	2	27	3	3	.283	.329

Name	B-T	HT	WT	DOB	AVG	vLH	vRH	G	AB	R	H	2B	3B	HR	RBI	BB	HBP	SH	SF	SO	SB	CS	OBP	SLG
Jacquot, Jimmy	R-R	6-1	195	6-15-88	.125	.000	.250	2	8	1	1	0	0	0	0	0	0	0	0	3	0	0	.125	.125
Jarrad, D.J.	R-R	6-1	170	2-15-89	.171	.250	.140	24	70	6	12	2	0	0	1	4	1	0	0	18	1	0	.200	.227
Johnson, Michael	L-R	5-9	175	10-28-88	.160	.150	.164	25	81	11	13	3	1	0	4	13	0	1	0	25	1	3	.222	.277
Kuhn, Collin	R-R	6-0	195	11-27-88	.172	.160	.179	20	64	4	11	1	0	0	6	8	6	3	0	23	2	3	.188	.321
Marjama, Mike	R-R	6-2	205	7-20-89	.306	.333	.288	23	85	6	26	5	0	1	8	4	0	1	0	14	1	2	.400	.337
Medina, Martin	R-R	6-0	200	3-24-90	.256	.300	.239	71	250	25	64	11	0	3	25	24	1	6	2	67	3	3	.336	.321
Pangilinan, Leighton	L-R	6-3	230	3-6-91	.225	.246	.217	121	444	52	100	22	3	8	56	38	10	2	3	127	7	2	.342	.299
Pena, Gary	R-R	5-11	178	3-10-92	.218	.186	.229	65	216	18	47	7	0	4	27	8	2	3	1	62	1	2	.306	.251
Pugh, Tillman	R-R	6-0	190	2-19-89	.250	.250	.250	9	32	6	8	2	0	0	2	0	0	1	0	12	3	0	.313	.294
2-team total (17 Savannah)					.143	—	—	26	91	12	13	2	0	1	2	7	0	2	0	37	7	0	.198	.204
Ravelo, Rangel	R-R	6-2	210	4-24-92	.290	.313	.281	76	290	32	84	19	3	2	39	20	7	3	7	38	6	1	.397	.343
Rice, Bill	L-R	5-11	185	9-7-88	.293	.228	.315	60	225	35	66	9	3	2	15	21	2	1	0	29	13	5	.387	.359
Robinson, Kyle	R-R	6-3	210	12-2-88	.143	.111	.154	10	35	1	5	1	0	1	3	1	0	0	0	16	0	0	.257	.167
Smith, Kevan	R-R	6-4	240	6-28-88	.282	.252	.295	86	340	48	96	26	0	7	60	25	9	1	4	62	0	1	.421	.344
Walker, Keenyn	B-R	6-3	195	8-12-90	.282	.235	.303	74	266	53	75	15	5	1	39	50	1	1	2	93	39	11	.387	.395
Wilson, Ross	R-R	5-11	185	11-9-88	.279	.260	.287	62	244	52	68	12	3	7	33	43	13	1	3	55	8	2	.439	.409

Pitching	B-T	HT	WT	DOB	W	L	ERA	G	GS	CG	SV	IP	H	R	ER	HR	BB	SO	AVG	vLH	vRH	K/9	BB/9
Ballinger, J.R.	R-R	6-1	190	4-2-88	0	0	0.00	1	0	0	0	1	0	0	0	0	0	1	.000	.000	—	13.50	0.00
Blough, Bryan	R-R	6-1	190	8-29-89	2	6	4.23	32	6	0	6	66	73	36	31	6	9	58	.286	.330	.257	7.91	1.23
Brase, Stew	R-R	6-3	195	1-20-89	4	7	5.96	38	1	0	1	74	111	68	49	2	41	47	.346	.328	.356	5.72	4.99
Buch, Ryan	R-R	6-3	205	11-8-87	2	0	0.90	3	1	0	0	10	10	1	1	0	2	12	.270	.294	.250	10.80	1.80
Casey, Jarrett	R-L	6-0	185	10-27-87	5	8	5.81	33	9	0	1	91	100	63	59	12	44	62	.277	.297	.270	6.11	4.34
Cose, Jake	B-R	6-5	195	8-28-90	0	0	0.00	1	1	0	0	3	2	0	0	0	0	4	.200	.000	.250	12.00	0.00
Devenski, Chris	R-R	6-3	195	11-13-90	6	5	4.23	19	8	0	2	62	63	31	29	8	19	54	.266	.276	.258	7.88	2.77
2-team total (5 Lexington)					8	7	3.86	24	13	1	2	91	86	42	39	9	35	92	—	—	—	9.10	3.46
Hanna, Chris	R-L	6-1	180	3-7-92	2	3	4.30	7	5	0	0	38	39	21	18	4	8	27	.257	.333	.233	6.45	1.91
2-team total (16 Hickory)					3	3	4.46	23	5	0	2	77	86	43	38	10	17	57	—	—	—	6.69	2.00
Jaye, Myles	B-R	6-3	170	12-28-91	4	7	6.04	17	17	0	0	79	102	60	53	6	39	65	.318	.341	.302	7.41	4.44
Johnson, Erik	R-R	6-3	240	12-30-89	2	2	2.30	9	9	0	0	43	39	15	11	3	19	39	.235	.268	.218	8.16	3.98
Kibby, Todd	L-L	6-4	240	8-31-91	0	0	3.00	1	1	0	0	6	4	2	2	0	2	5	.200	.429	.077	7.50	3.00
Lane, Matt	R-L	6-6	195	8-11-90	4	5	4.55	32	17	0	0	121	145	81	61	6	41	93	.303	.248	.325	6.94	3.06
Leyer, Euclides	R-R	6-2	172	12-28-92	2	1	5.02	5	5	0	0	29	27	16	16	2	11	17	.250	.283	.218	5.34	3.45
Lopez, Adam	R-R	6-5	195	2-21-90	0	0	0.00	2	0	0	1	3	0	0	0	0	0	6	.000	.000	.000	16.20	0.00
Marin, Terance	R-R	6-1	190	8-21-89	2	1	1.21	9	0	0	3	22	11	4	3	0	8	22	.151	.125	.163	8.87	3.22
McCray, Stephen	L-R	6-3	230	10-6-87	0	2	2.30	6	1	0	0	16	10	4	4	1	3	14	.182	.217	.156	8.04	1.72
Mustain, Mitch	R-R	6-2	225	2-24-89	1	0	4.82	8	0	0	0	9	8	5	5	0	10	2	.222	.385	.130	1.93	9.64
Olacio, Jefferson	L-L	6-7	230	1-16-94	1	5	5.35	15	5	0	0	37	43	31	22	3	26	34	.287	.333	.269	8.27	6.32
Parrent, Brandon	L-L	6-3	215	7-14-90	2	2	7.34	8	8	0	0	34	40	30	28	2	22	21	.303	.310	.301	5.50	5.77
Peterson, Max	L-L	6-2	210	6-27-88	1	1	1.33	13	0	0	4	20	18	3	3	0	4	24	.247	.316	.204	10.62	1.77
Sanchez, Salvador	R-R	6-6	195	9-13-85	0	0	0.00	1	0	0	0	1	0	0	0	0	0	1	.000	.000	.000	9.00	0.00
Snodgrass, Scott	L-L	6-5	210	9-20-89	3	3	3.64	19	19	0	0	99	86	49	40	4	49	84	.233	.259	.222	7.64	4.45
Soptic, Jeff	R-R	6-6	210	4-8-91	3	2	5.40	27	0	0	4	43	26	26	26	1	29	36	.176	.226	.147	7.48	6.02
Talley, Matt	L-L	6-6	225	8-8-89	1	0	1.59	7	0	0	0	11	9	2	2	1	5	4	.225	.154	.259	3.18	3.97
2-team total (4 Rome)					1	0	2.29	11	0	0	0	20	23	10	5	2	11	10	—	—	—	4.58	5.03
Umberger, Dustin	R-R	6-0	190	2-10-87	1	2	4.39	15	0	0	4	27	25	16	13	2	10	35	.252	.250	.254	11.81	3.38
Upchurch, Steven	R-R	6-4	180	9-14-89	1	1	3.28	16	0	0	3	25	27	11	9	1	11	16	.278	.256	.293	5.84	4.01
Van Skike, Jason	R-R	6-4	195	4-10-89	4	2	4.75	22	0	0	3	42	34	25	22	2	22	36	.218	.237	.206	7.78	4.75
Vance, Kevin	R-R	6-0	208	7-8-90	4	2	3.05	19	9	0	0	80	70	34	27	4	28	70	.236	.261	.219	7.91	3.16
Walters, Blair	L-L	6-0	200	11-8-89	3	3	2.88	13	13	0	0	72	61	27	23	6	18	69	.226	.174	.244	8.63	2.25
Webb, Daniel	R-R	6-3	210	8-18-89	1	8	5.81	31	4	0	3	62	73	51	40	2	27	50	.293	.308	.283	7.26	3.92

Fielding

Catcher	PCT	G	PO	A	E	DP	PB
Barraza	1.000	1	7	2	0	1	0
Dubler	1.000	6	48	7	0	1	0
Jacquot	.900	1	9	0	1	0	1
Marjama	.993	19	128	23	1	1	4
Medina	.981	54	370	49	8	4	7
Smith	.996	60	400	68	2	6	9

First Base	PCT	G	PO	A	E	DP
Buckner	.988	18	147	14	2	13
Hankern	1.000	1	8	0	0	2
Medina	1.000	9	76	2	0	6
Pangilinan	.983	108	916	58	17	72
Ravelo	.976	6	39	2	1	3
Robinson	1.000	3	28	2	0	4

Second Base	PCT	G	PO	A	E	DP
De Pinto	.889	17	36	44	10	6
DeMichele	.990	57	121	169	3	35
Eveland	.750	1	1	2	1	1

	PCT	G	PO	A	E	DP
Herbek	.986	18	33	39	1	12
Jarrad	1.000	3	4	12	0	0
Johnson	.952	17	26	34	3	7
Wilson	.952	33	69	70	7	12

Third Base	PCT	G	PO	A	E	DP
Buckner	.921	45	33	84	10	8
Curley	.932	14	13	28	3	9
De Pinto	.877	25	18	46	9	6
Jarrad	1.000	2	3	0	0	0
Johnson	.600	2	1	2	2	0
Medina	1.000	2	4	0	0	0
Ravelo	.918	54	46	110	14	10

Shortstop	PCT	G	PO	A	E	DP
Curley	.936	27	44	88	9	16
Eveland	.857	1	2	4	1	0
Herbek	.925	28	49	75	10	14
Jarrad	.957	20	20	46	3	7
Johnson	1.000	2	3	2	0	0

	PCT	G	PO	A	E	DP
Pena	.949	65	83	160	13	30
Wilson	.750	6	3	9	4	0

Outfield	PCT	G	PO	A	E	DP
Buckner	.939	31	44	2	3	0
Douglas	.976	23	39	2	1	1
Haddow	.964	106	227	12	9	5
Hankern	1.000	2	2	0	0	0
Harvard	1.000	21	39	2	0	0
Hawkins	1.000	16	33	2	0	1
Heisler	1.000	32	50	0	0	0
Johnson	1.000	1	3	0	0	0
Kuhn	1.000	19	18	3	0	2
Pugh	1.000	9	19	0	0	0
Rice	.977	57	118	8	3	0
Robinson	1.000	7	13	1	0	0
Walker	.978	74	176	5	4	1
Wilson	.959	28	45	2	2	0

BRISTOL SOX — ROOKIE
APPALACHIAN LEAGUE

Batting	B-T	HT	WT	DOB	AVG	vLH	vRH	G	AB	R	H	2B	3B	HR	RBI	BB	HBP	SH	SF	SO	SB	CS	SLG	OBP
Ayala, Sammy	L-R	6-2	195	7-12-94	.202	.231	.197	24	84	12	17	3	0	1	5	5	2	0	1	23	0	1	.274	.261
Barnum, Keon	L-L	6-5	225	1-16-93	.279	.364	.250	13	43	6	12	1	0	3	8	5	0	0	1	13	0	0	.512	.347
Barraza, Jose	L-R	6-1	220	7-28-94	.175	.103	.198	36	120	13	21	2	3	0	8	13	1	1	0	53	0	1	.242	.261
Basto, Nick	R-R	6-1	180	4-1-94	.238	.235	.239	59	210	12	50	4	2	1	21	12	6	0	6	51	0	1	.290	.291
Brown, Jake	L-R	5-11	185	2-15-90	.247	.250	.246	50	170	19	42	7	1	0	12	26	2	2	1	39	10	2	.300	.352
De Pinto, Joe	R-R	6-1	190	4-3-89	.313	.000	.333	4	16	2	5	3	0	0	4	1	1	0	0	1	0	0	.500	.389
DeMichele, Joey	L-R	5-11	185	2-5-91	.348	.385	.333	12	46	7	16	4	3	2	9	3	2	1	0	8	3	0	.696	.412
Douglas, Andrew	R-R	6-0	210	5-27-89	.237	.500	.222	13	38	6	9	4	1	1	4	6	2	0	1	13	3	1	.474	.362
Dowdy, Jeremy	R-R	6-2	215	7-13-90	.412	.333	.429	5	17	2	7	2	1	0	3	2	0	0	1	2	0	0	.647	.450
Farris, Cory	L-R	6-0	190	12-29-89	.158	.091	.171	40	139	8	22	5	0	1	12	8	0	0	0	44	0	2	.216	.204
Grabe, Eric	R-R	5-10	190	8-8-89	.357	.429	.333	42	140	24	50	13	2	2	21	19	3	0	1	24	2	0	.521	.442
Hall, Thurman	R-R	6-0	190	2-12-93	.180	.000	.200	23	61	4	11	0	1	0	2	8	2	1	0	21	2	1	.213	.296
Hawkins, Courtney	R-R	6-3	220	11-12-93	.272	.161	.302	38	147	25	40	8	1	3	16	7	3	0	2	37	8	2	.401	.314
Hayes, Dustin	R-R	6-2	180	11-21-91	.000	.000	.000	2	2	0	0	0	0	0	0	1	0	0	0	2	0	0	.000	.333
Kiser, Kale	B-R	5-10	185	3-31-90	.262	.282	.256	55	195	41	51	16	5	4	18	21	15	0	2	38	7	0	.456	.373
Nikorak, Steve	R-R	6-2	215	9-3-89	.147	.208	.134	39	136	10	20	2	2	1	12	3	1	1	1	47	0	0	.213	.170
Ramirez, Juan	R-R	6-4	196	8-28-90	.209	.171	.221	44	139	15	29	6	3	1	12	3	5	2	1	49	1	1	.317	.250
Rosario, Angel	R-R	5-10	175	12-14-91	.262	.000	.333	13	42	2	11	4	0	0	4	5	1	0	0	8	0	1	.357	.354
Stoner, Zach	L-R	6-3	200	12-16-93	.171	.375	.121	30	82	6	14	2	0	0	3	15	4	0	0	34	0	0	.195	.327
Thompson, William	R-R	6-3	210	1-30-90	.300	.333	.273	7	20	2	6	1	0	0	4	1	0	0	0	5	0	0	.350	.440
Williams, Alex	L-R	6-6	260	10-1-89	.233	.216	.236	58	202	18	47	11	0	4	23	21	4	0	3	65	0	1	.347	.313

Pitching	B-T	HT	WT	DOB	W	L	ERA	G	GS	CG	SV	IP	H	R	ER	HR	BB	SO	AVG	vLH	vRH	K/9	BB/9
Bautista, Jose	L-L	6-1	175	3-31-92	0	0	1.35	2	2	0	0	7	1	1	1	0	5	8	.053	.000	.059	10.80	6.75
Boydston, Adam	R-L	6-1	190	10-20-88	0	2	5.75	12	1	0	0	20	30	13	13	1	9	21	.357	.250	.375	9.30	3.98
Brito, Jose	R-R	6-0	175	10-10-90	0	3	8.15	15	0	0	0	18	19	21	16	1	15	13	.264	.227	.280	6.62	7.64
Bucciferro, Tony	R-R	6-3	200	12-27-89	0	0	2.57	6	0	0	0	7	4	3	2	1	0	5	.154	.083	.214	6.43	0.00
Castro, Simon	R-R	6-5	230	4-9-88	0	0	4.50	1	1	0	0	2	1	1	1	0	0	0	.429	.000	.500	0.00	0.00
Cose, Jake	B-R	6-5	195	8-28-90	3	6	4.38	12	12	0	0	62	65	39	30	2	21	64	.261	.313	.237	9.34	3.06
Diaz, Evandert	R-R	6-3	190	5-20-92	1	1	11.57	6	0	0	0	12	24	17	15	3	8	7	.414	.250	.500	5.40	6.17
Guerrero, Jordan	L-L	6-3	165	5-31-94	0	1	3.00	7	0	0	0	9	10	3	3	0	4	6	.294	.333	.286	6.00	4.00
Gunter, Michael	R-R	6-1	190	7-5-90	0	0	2.70	7	0	0	1	7	9	4	2	0	1	12	.300	.364	.263	16.20	1.35
Hanna, Chris	R-L	6-1	180	3-7-92	0	0	9.95	4	1	0	0	6	8	7	7	2	2	4	.320	.400	.300	5.68	2.84
Hansen, Kyle	R-R	6-8	200	4-20-91	0	0	1.93	5	0	0	2	5	2	1	1	0	4	8	.133	.500	.077	15.43	7.71
Haselden, David	R-R	6-3	230	10-31-89	1	2	3.24	5	5	0	0	25	24	16	9	3	0	20	.240	.237	.242	7.20	0.00
Hudelson, James	R-R	6-4	215	5-16-90	1	3	5.86	21	0	0	2	28	30	20	18	1	14	25	.265	.276	.262	8.13	4.55
Jaffe, Eric	R-R	6-3	220	6-16-91	1	1	7.36	12	0	0	2	11	11	14	9	0	9	9	.250	.235	.259	7.36	7.36
Kibby, Todd	L-L	6-4	240	8-31-91	5	4	2.79	11	11	2	0	71	59	30	22	2	21	69	.223	.267	.217	8.75	2.66
Leyer, Euclides	R-R	6-2	172	12-28-92	0	4	4.95	7	7	1	0	40	41	27	22	4	10	45	.253	.250	.255	10.13	2.25
Lopez, Adam	R-R	6-5	195	2-21-90	1	0	3.27	11	0	0	0	11	14	5	4	0	6	14	.318	.250	.357	11.45	4.91
Matos, Darwin	R-R	6-0	170	8-4-90	0	1	3.00	4	3	0	0	21	18	8	7	0	14	19	.234	.077	.314	8.14	6.00
Moran, Kevin	R-R	6-4	195	7-7-89	0	1	54.00	5	0	0	0	2	1	15	12	0	13	2	.143	.000	.167	9.00	58.50
Mustain, Mitch	R-R	6-2	225	2-27-88	1	2	4.50	11	0	0	1	14	15	7	7	1	4	10	.273	.278	.270	6.43	2.57
Olacio, Jefferson	L-L	6-7	230	1-16-94	2	6	5.03	12	12	1	0	59	57	38	33	4	38	55	.254	.323	.244	8.39	5.80
Olsen, Scott	L-L	6-4	210	1-12-84	0	1	9.00	1	1	0	0	1	1	1	1	0	0	1	.250	—	.250	9.00	0.00
Sanchez, Leopoldo	R-R	6-1	180	6-5-91	1	4	5.07	14	8	0	0	55	62	36	31	6	16	49	.282	.268	.290	8.02	2.62
Sanchez, Salvador	R-R	6-6	195	9-13-85	0	0	0.00	2	0	0	0	2	1	0	0	0	0	3	.143	.000	.333	13.50	0.00
Santiago, Anthony	R-R	5-11	200	9-22-89	0	2	7.62	8	1	0	0	13	10	12	11	3	12	6	.213	.273	.194	4.15	8.31
Talley, Matt	L-L	6-6	225	8-8-89	0	0	0.00	2	0	0	0	5	5	0	0	0	5	2	.313	1.000	.267	3.60	9.00
2-team total (5 Danville)					1	0	6.55	7	0	0	0	11	14	8	8	1	12	9	—		—	7.36	9.82
Thompson, Taylor	R-R	6-5	225	6-18-87	0	0	0.00	1	0	0	0	1	1	0	0	0	0	2	.250	.000	.333	18.00	0.00
Throne, Storm	R-R	6-7	215	9-3-90	2	2	8.38	15	0	0	0	19	32	19	18	1	15	13	.364	.458	.328	6.05	6.98

Fielding

Catcher	PCT	G	PO	A	E	DP	PB
Ayala	.968	16	116	4	4	1	3
Barraza	.965	26	199	24	8	0	17
Dowdy	.972	4	34	1	1	0	1
Rosario	.987	10	71	7	1	0	4
Stoner	1.000	10	62	4	0	0	2

First Base	PCT	G	PO	A	E	DP
Barnum	.963	10	72	7	3	2
Nikorak	1.000	4	37	6	0	2
Williams	.987	51	421	25	6	37

Second Base	PCT	G	PO	A	E	DP
Brown	.982	40	63	99	3	18
DeMichele	.975	12	14	25	1	4
Grabe	1.000	17	25	35	0	11

Third Base	PCT	G	PO	A	E	DP
De Pinto	.882	4	2	13	2	0
Grabe	.923	21	15	45	5	6
Nikorak	.913	34	13	71	8	5
Thompson	.950	7	6	13	1	2

Shortstop	PCT	G	PO	A	E	DP
Basto	.892	58	67	132	24	22
Brown	.909	10	13	17	3	5

Outfield	PCT	G	PO	A	E	DP
Douglas	1.000	11	20	1	0	1
Farris	.939	35	57	5	4	0
Hall	.974	23	36	2	1	1
Hawkins	.971	35	66	2	2	1
Hayes	1.000	2	1	0	0	0
Kiser	.987	54	73	3	1	1
Ramirez	.959	44	90	3	4	0

GREAT FALLS VOYAGERS — ROOKIE
PIONEER LEAGUE

Batting	B-T	HT	WT	DOB	AVG	vLH	vRH	G	AB	R	H	2B	3B	HR	RBI	BB	HBP	SH	SF	SO	SB	CS	SLG	OBP
Barroso, Yoandy	R-R	6-2	190	11-26-88	.300	.324	.290	62	230	38	69	15	2	2	44	34	6	1	2	52	2	1	.409	.401

Name	B-T	HT	WT	DOB	AVG	vLH	vRH	G	AB	R	H	2B	3B	HR	RBI	BB	HBP	SH	SF	SO	SB	CS	SLG	OBP
Douglas, Andrew	R-R	6-0	210	5-27-89	.176	.333	.091	4	17	3	3	1	0	0	1	3	0	0	0	8	1	1	.235	.300
Fisher, Zac	L-R	6-2	190	12-13-91	.218	.050	.256	36	110	21	24	7	1	2	10	17	1	0	0	10	0	0	.355	.328
Hayes, Dustin	R-R	6-2	180	11-21-91	.130	.000	.167	10	23	2	3	0	1	0	1	2	0	0	0	11	1	0	.217	.200
Heisler, Adam	L-R	5-10	165	6-7-88	.269	.368	.214	25	108	20	29	9	3	0	12	11	0	1	1	13	10	2	.407	.333
Jarrad, D.J.	R-R	6-1	170	2-15-89	.370	.375	.368	6	27	4	10	0	1	0	3	0	0	0	0	4	0	0	.444	.370
Jirschele, Justin	L-R	5-11	195	4-15-90	.267	.132	.315	42	146	26	39	6	1	0	27	20	2	1	2	21	0	0	.322	.359
Johnson, Micah	B-R	5-11	190	12-18-90	.273	.247	.284	69	271	49	74	10	5	4	25	43	1	3	0	74	19	6	.391	.375
Johnson, Michael	L-R	5-9	175	10-28-88	.252	.179	.269	38	147	26	37	5	2	2	14	25	0	1	2	44	3	2	.354	.356
Marjama, Mike	R-R	6-2	205	7-20-89	.250	.333	.190	9	36	4	9	2	1	1	9	1	0	0	1	4	0	1	.444	.263
McCarthy, Thomas	R-R	6-1	205	7-25-90	.302	.190	.346	41	149	21	45	9	1	1	18	12	4	2	2	28	1	1	.396	.365
Mercedes, Daurys	R-R	6-1	165	2-26-90	.198	.244	.182	51	162	29	32	4	4	1	17	22	4	2	1	62	3	4	.290	.307
Mosier, Bryce	R-R	6-2	200	5-21-93	.293	.417	.241	12	41	7	12	2	0	0	1	4	0	1	0	10	0	0	.341	.356
Nikorak, Steve	R-R	6-2	215	9-3-89	.207	.000	.286	7	29	7	6	0	0	0	2	6	1	1	0	0	6	0	0	.414	.258
Palmeiro, Patrick	R-R	6-3	210	3-6-90	.219	.259	.198	42	160	21	35	7	1	2	20	10	1	0	2	42	0	0	.313	.266
Robinson, Kyle	R-R	6-3	210	12-2-88	.326	.327	.326	49	187	30	61	18	3	2	44	24	2	0	4	43	1	0	.487	.401
Rosario, Angel	R-R	5-10	175	12-14-91	.239	.176	.260	18	67	5	16	6	0	1	16	3	2	3	1	8	0	0	.373	.288
Ruiz, Abe	L-R	6-4	210	3-29-90	.240	.179	.265	27	96	13	23	7	0	0	11	10	3	0	2	23	0	1	.313	.324
Salgado, Brad	R-R	6-1	185	7-15-91	.161	.235	.133	37	124	22	20	5	2	1	11	23	5	3	1	53	0	0	.258	.314
Tanner, Brent	L-R	6-2	225	10-1-87	.280	.290	.276	65	243	37	68	17	4	4	42	32	4	1	3	54	0	0	.432	.369
Voight, Zach	R-R	6-0	185	8-26-90	.339	.467	.295	20	59	12	20	6	0	0	9	26	1	2	2	16	0	1	.441	.534
Williams, Tyler	R-R	6-2	205	1-5-91	.255	.333	.233	44	165	23	42	6	0	4	15	10	5	1	0	80	0	1	.364	.317

Pitching	B-T	HT	WT	DOB	W	L	ERA	G	GS	CG	SV	IP	H	R	ER	HR	BB	SO	AVG	vLH	vRH	K/9	BB/9
Beck, Chris	R-R	6-3	210	9-4-90	4	3	4.69	15	6	0	0	40	51	27	21	3	12	36	.319	.347	.294	8.03	2.68
Bollinger, Ryan	L-L	6-6	185	2-4-91	4	3	3.56	17	3	0	1	48	61	21	19	1	9	36	.310	.338	.294	6.75	1.69
Bowling, Cal	R-R	6-2	195	10-22-89	1	1	4.34	13	0	0	1	19	17	9	9	1	6	16	.243	.172	.293	7.71	4.34
Brennan, Brandon	R-R	6-4	220	7-26-91	3	2	4.34	14	7	0	0	37	44	27	18	2	16	31	.297	.316	.278	7.47	3.86
Casey, J.C.	R-R	6-3	174	12-13-88	4	7	3.46	15	15	0	0	75	81	39	29	3	26	55	.280	.313	.255	6.57	3.11
Dvorsky, Joe	R-R	6-2	200	9-9-88	2	1	2.08	22	0	0	5	35	37	11	8	0	4	35	.274	.308	.243	9.09	1.04
Hansen, Kyle	R-R	6-8	200	4-20-91	0	0	40.50	1	0	0	0	1	2	3	3	0	1	0	.667	1.000	.500	0.00	13.50
Hardin, Brandon	R-R	6-0	200	2-17-90	2	1	3.41	22	0	0	4	34	40	22	13	1	9	40	.282	.377	.225	10.49	2.36
Isler, Zach	R-R	6-4	235	10-31-90	3	2	4.50	18	1	0	0	44	52	25	22	2	12	33	.304	.303	.306	6.75	2.45
Linza, Keegan	R-R	6-6	230	11-10-88	5	3	4.78	16	16	0	0	79	99	50	42	3	6	57	.306	.294	.317	6.49	0.68
McGinnis, Cory	L-R	6-0	180	12-24-89	1	2	4.60	17	3	0	0	45	51	28	23	4	18	42	.285	.311	.267	8.40	3.60
Merkley, Brett	R-R	5-11	165	8-15-87	1	2	3.70	18	0	0	6	24	31	10	10	2	9	18	.304	.318	.293	6.66	3.33
Parrent, Brandon	L-L	6-3	215	7-14-90	2	5	5.21	14	13	0	0	48	55	37	28	3	25	37	.278	.273	.280	6.89	4.66
Putman, David	R-R	6-1	205	2-28-90	2	1	2.73	19	0	0	2	26	25	9	8	1	12	41	.240	.143	.306	14.01	4.10
Royse, Thomas	R-R	6-5	210	9-7-88	0	1	4.35	5	5	0	0	21	32	15	10	1	2	14	.360	.256	.457	6.10	0.87
Toney, Zach	L-L	6-3	230	3-20-89	2	0	4.44	18	4	0	0	47	42	27	23	2	25	58	.236	.309	.191	11.19	4.82
Virgili, Andrew	R-R	6-2	205	1-30-90	4	2	4.09	18	3	0	0	51	44	25	23	1	21	44	.240	.286	.202	7.82	3.73

Fielding

Catcher	PCT	G	PO	A	E	DP	PB
Fisher	.979	35	257	19	6	1	2
Marjama	1.000	7	44	11	0	1	1
Mosier	.961	8	44	5	2	1	0
Rosario	.986	18	126	20	2	0	6
Tanner	.977	14	106	23	3	1	1

First Base	PCT	G	PO	A	E	DP
Johnson	1.000	1	7	0	0	0
Nikorak	1.000	2	21	1	0	2
Palmeiro	.983	5	52	5	1	7
Robinson	1.000	2	15	1	0	3
Ruiz	.985	23	187	12	3	17
Tanner	.978	49	450	30	11	45

Second Base	PCT	G	PO	A	E	DP
Jirschele	.937	21	26	63	6	11
Johnson	.957	43	78	145	10	39
Johnson	.954	13	14	48	3	7
Mercedes	1.000	1	0	1	0	0
Voight	1.000	2	5	4	0	2

Third Base	PCT	G	PO	A	E	DP
Johnson	1.000	2	1	2	0	0
McCarthy	.896	38	27	59	10	7
Nikorak	.917	3	3	8	1	1
Palmeiro	1.000	4	4	6	0	0
Williams	.870	31	24	63	13	5

Shortstop	PCT	G	PO	A	E	DP
Jarrad	.870	6	2	18	3	2

	PCT	G	PO	A	E	DP
Jirschele	.959	20	34	59	4	12
Johnson	.800	1	1	3	1	1
Salgado	.896	33	54	93	17	19
Voight	.956	18	28	59	4	19

Outfield	PCT	G	PO	A	E	DP
Barroso	.963	58	98	7	4	2
Douglas	1.000	4	10	0	0	0
Hayes	1.000	4	2	0	0	0
Heisler	1.000	25	39	4	0	1
Johnson	.973	23	33	3	1	0
Mercedes	.978	48	88	2	2	0
Palmeiro	1.000	28	40	6	0	2
Robinson	.941	44	59	5	4	1

DSL WHITE SOX   ROOKIE

DOMINICAN SUMMER LEAGUE

Batting	B-T	HT	WT	DOB	AVG	vLH	vRH	G	AB	R	H	2B	3B	HR	RBI	BB	HBP	SH	SF	SO	SB	CS	SLG	OBP
Abreu, Julio	R-R	6-6	210	10-29-91	.143	.167	.139	14	42	3	6	1	0	0	4	3	2	1	0	11	1	0	.167	.234
Ariza, Jose	R-R	6-2	183	12-23-93	.116	.125	.114	16	43	6	5	1	1	0	2	7	1	0	0	20	0	0	.186	.255
Becerra, Ifran	L-R	5-10	155	6-13-91	.297	.294	.298	28	74	16	22	4	2	2	17	11	1	0	4	17	10	3	.486	.378
2-team total (19 Diamondbacks)					.274			47	135	28	37	4	3	3	24	28	2	0	5	34	14	7	.415	.394
Buda, Maurizo	R-R	6-1	175	1-7-92	.267	.222	.288	60	195	26	52	10	1	2	29	37	6	4	4	49	1	0	.359	.393
De Jesus, Jhan	R-R	6-2	165	1-30-92	.114	.095	.122	25	70	4	8	0	0	0	1	9	0	0	0	19	1	0	.114	.215
Fernandez, Andelson	R-R	6-2	170	2-22-91	—	—	—	1	0	1	0	0	0	0	0	0	0	0	0	0	0	0	—	—
Garcia, Humberto	B-R	5-10	165	5-20-94	.186	.250	.164	48	156	20	29	2	4	1	13	14	5	0	0	33	10	8	.269	.274
Garcia, Joxelier	R-R	5-10	185	4-30-94	.231	.214	.235	22	65	5	15	2	0	0	6	9	0	1	1	13	0	1	.262	.320
Gonzalez, Carlos	R-R	6-2	172	8-30-93	.209	.180	.220	58	191	18	40	7	0	0	21	31	3	0	3	63	0	3	.246	.325
Guerrero, Sandy	R-R	6-1	180	10-14-92	.208	.213	.206	47	149	17	31	1	1	2	21	14	4	2	0	37	5	0	.268	.293
Pizzoli, Franco	R-R	5-9	170	2-1-94	.282	.390	.240	58	209	24	59	4	4	0	23	18	6	2	1	20	1	3	.340	.355
Polanco, Luis	R-R	6-3	190	9-30-91	.360	.333	.375	9	25	3	9	2	0	0	4	3	3	1	0	2	1	0	.440	.484
Ramos, Roger	R-R	6-2	174	10-9-94	.185	.167	.191	40	124	8	23	7	0	0	7	7	3	1	0	44	10	0	.242	.246

Rocha, Jaider	R-R	6-1	185	5-23-93	.227	.125	.271	55	185	36	42	10	2	0	24	26	5	1	2	38	4	1	.303	.335
Rodriguez, Antonio	R-R	6-0	180	5-7-95	.238	.143	.286	8	21	2	5	1	0	0	2	1	0	0	0	7	1	0	.286	.273
Santana, Vladimir	R-R	6-0	165	1-24-91	.277	.300	.271	63	173	29	48	7	0	1	11	34	3	1	0	45	12	4	.335	.405
Santos, Jeffy	B-R	6-2	150	1-4-93	.238	.197	.254	63	239	32	57	4	2	0	19	26	1	4	3	52	8	4	.272	.312
Valdez, Bradley	L-R	6-0	195	12-11-94	.187	.200	.183	36	123	14	23	5	0	0	6	11	3	1	1	34	1	2	.228	.268
Velasquez, Victor	B-R	5-11	195	2-5-95	.264	.275	.260	49	174	27	46	4	3	0	14	18	5	0	2	32	10	9	.322	.347

Pitching	B-T	HT	WT	DOB	W	L	ERA	G	GS	CG	SV	IP	H	R	ER	HR	BB	SO	AVG	vLH	vRH	K/9	BB/9
Arias, Feny	L-L	6-0	175	5-6-91	3	3	2.19	15	6	0	0	53	48	21	13	0	21	59	.234	.200	.241	9.96	3.54
Arteaga, Luis	R-R	6-1	185	10-19-94	0	0	3.62	12	10	0	0	37	33	17	15	1	11	27	.237	.304	.193	6.51	2.65
Diaz, Carlos	L-L	6-0	186	1-1-94	0	3	3.94	17	1	0	0	30	29	20	13	2	18	19	.266	.286	.263	5.76	5.46
Diaz, Evandert	R-R	6-3	190	5-20-92	0	0	4.12	5	3	0	0	20	25	13	9	0	10	10	.347	.435	.306	4.58	4.58
Jaquez, Juan	R-R	6-4	164	12-30-89	2	7	3.68	15	0	0	0	37	37	21	15	1	15	22	.272	.320	.244	5.40	3.68
Leyer, Robin	R-R	6-2	175	3-13-93	1	4	3.12	13	13	0	0	52	62	35	18	0	17	31	.292	.235	.342	5.37	2.94
Magallanes, Yensi	L-L	6-0	185	2-2-93	5	0	1.27	23	0	0	0	43	27	8	6	0	21	39	.188	.111	.205	8.23	4.43
Matos, Darwin	R-R	6-0	170	8-4-90	1	1	3.61	12	9	0	0	42	31	18	17	1	16	53	.201	.146	.226	11.27	3.40
Mora, Hansel	R-R	6-4	185	8-10-94	0	1	2.70	8	3	0	0	17	16	8	5	0	7	13	.246	.174	.286	7.02	3.78
Nieves, Wilce	R-R	6-0	175	5-12-92	5	5	2.23	22	0	0	3	48	50	18	12	0	8	21	.276	.315	.250	3.91	1.49
Ortiz, Braulio	R-R	6-5	205	12-20-91	3	3	3.93	16	8	0	1	50	54	31	22	1	20	37	.276	.341	.225	6.62	3.58
Peralta, Yelmison	R-R	6-0	190	3-3-95	0	5	7.26	12	12	0	0	31	29	33	25	2	33	20	.242	.235	.246	5.81	9.58
Rodriguez, Wilmy	R-R	6-4	225	11-8-90	1	4	8.46	11	4	0	0	22	31	29	21	0	18	18	.341	.182	.431	7.25	7.25
Valerio, Kelvis	R-R	6-1	160	9-26-91	5	2	1.43	25	0	0	6	44	32	13	7	2	15	38	.209	.214	.206	7.77	3.07
Vargas, Ivan	R-R	6-3	190	8-14-91	0	2	5.46	18	0	0	0	30	35	24	18	0	18	15	.302	.233	.342	4.55	5.46

Fielding

Catcher	PCT	G	PO	A	E	DP	PB
Ariza	.961	16	84	14	4	0	3
Garcia	.961	18	108	15	5	0	4
Pizzoli	.985	43	287	44	5	1	11

First Base	PCT	G	PO	A	E	DP
Abreu	1.000	6	38	1	0	2
Guerrero	.968	38	268	31	10	32
Pizzoli	1.000	7	66	2	0	5
Polanco	.970	9	62	3	2	1
Rocha	1.000	2	3	0	0	1
Valdez	.985	16	125	6	2	5

Second Base	PCT	G	PO	A	E	DP
Becerra	1.000	2	1	4	0	1
Garcia	.968	39	100	84	6	22
Guerrero	1.000	1	0	1	0	0
Santana	.944	3	6	11	1	2
Velasquez	.957	31	71	85	7	11

Third Base	PCT	G	PO	A	E	DP
Becerra	1.000	5	2	2	0	1
Gonzalez	.890	51	39	107	18	6
Guerrero	1.000	6	3	10	0	0
Santana	.750	3	0	3	1	0
Valdez	.767	8	8	15	7	1
Velasquez	.852	10	7	16	4	2

Shortstop	PCT	G	PO	A	E	DP
Santana	.833	2	1	4	1	0
Santos	.923	62	118	158	23	23
Velasquez	1.000	10	9	25	0	5

Outfield	PCT	G	PO	A	E	DP
Becerra	.967	14	29	0	1	0
Buda	1.000	42	51	3	0	0
De Jesus	.952	23	38	2	2	0
Ramos	.929	36	62	3	5	0
Rocha	.922	49	77	6	7	0
Rodriguez	1.000	7	12	0	0	0
Santana	.955	55	100	5	5	2

Cincinnati Reds

SEASON IN A SENTENCE: Until the Giants eliminated them in the National League Division Series, 2012 was the best Reds season in decades, as 97 wins represented the club's most since the Big Red Machine.

HIGH POINT: Todd Frazier's groundout scored Scott Rolen to give Cincinnati a 5-4 win on Aug. 4. Its 22nd win in 25 games helped build an insurmountable lead in the NL Central. Even more impressively, most of the run came with Joey Votto on the disabled list with a knee injury.

LOW POINT: After taking a 2-0 lead on the Giants in their NL Division Series, the Reds lost the next two games at home. But it was Game Five where the Reds hit rock bottom. Starter Mat Latos was chased in a six-run fifth, and while the Reds did rally to bring the winning run to the plate in the ninth, San Francisco won its third of six do-or-die games on its way to winning the World Series.

NOTABLE ROOKIES: Frazier came to spring training without a starting job. He left without one either, but because of his versatility he was able to play regularly at several positions. When Rolen was hurt, Frazier played third base. When Votto was hurt, he played first, and he also saw time in left field. Wherever he played, Frazier hit (.273/.331/.498). Catcher Devin Mesoraco started the season as a regular but hit .212/.288/.352, earning a demotion to Triple-A Louisville.

KEY TRANSACTIONS: The Reds brought in free agent closer Ryan Madson, who blew out his elbow in spring training and never threw a regular season pitch. Free agent outfielder Ryan Ludwick proved to be a bargain, however. Signed for $2 million, he batted .275/.346/.531 with 26 home runs. The Reds dipped into the depth of their farm system, trading Yonder Alonso, Yasmani Grandal, Brad Boxberger and Edinson Volquez to the Padres to add Latos, who went 14-4, 3.48. By trading third baseman Juan Francisco to the Braves, the Reds picked up reliever J.J. Hoover who went 1-0, 2.05 in 31 innings.

DOWN ON THE FARM: Shortstop Billy Hamilton set a new single-season minor league stolen base record with 155 steals, a clear highlight in a year when several teams struggled. Triple-A Louisville has been one of the better clubs in the International League in recent years, but with much of that talent now in Cincinnati the Bats went 51-93. Low Class A Dayton posted the second-worst record in the Midwest League.

OPENING DAY PAYROLL: $82.2 million (17th)

ORGANIZATION LEADERS

BATTING		*Minimum 250 AB
MAJORS		
* AVG	Brandon Phillips	.281
* OPS	Jay Bruce	.841
HR	Jay Bruce	34
RBI	Jay Bruce	99
MINORS		
* AVG	Steve Selsky, Dayton/Bakersfield	.317
* OBP	Billy Hamilton, Bakersfield/Pensacola	.410
* SLG	Steve Selsky, Dayton/Bakersfield	.515
R	Billy Hamilton, Bakersfield/Pensacola	112
H	Billy Hamilton, Bakersfield/Pensacola	159
TB	Steve Selsky, Dayton/Bakersfield	255
2B	Steve Selsky, Dayton/Bakersfield	32
	Ryan Wright, Dayton/Bakersfield	32
3B	Billy Hamilton, Bakersfield/Pensacola	14
HR	Donald Lutz, AZL Reds/Bakersfield/Pensacola	22
RBI	Travis Mattair, Bakersfield	82
BB	Billy Hamilton, Bakersfield/Pensacola	86
SO	Juan Duran, Bakersfield	151
SB	Billy Hamilton, Bakersfield/Pensacola	155

PITCHING		#Minimum 75 IP
MAJORS		
W	Johnny Cueto	19
# ERA	Johnny Cueto	2.78
SO	Mat Latos	185
SV	Aroldis Chapman	38
MINORS		
W	Tony Cingrani, Bakersfield/Pensacola	10
	Sean Gallagher, Louisville	10
L	Pedro Villarreal, Pensacola/Louisville	14
# ERA	Tony Cingrani, Bakersfield/Pensacola	1.73
G	Justin Freeman, Pensacola	57
GS	Three tied at	28
SV	Carlos Contreras, Dayton/Bakersfield	20
IP	Stalin Gerson, Dayton/Bakersfield	151.2
	Chad Reineke, Louisville	151.2
BB	Tim Crabbe, Pensacola/Bakersfield	81
SO	Tony Cingrani, Bakersfield/Pensacola	172
#AVG	Tony Cingrani, Bakersfield/Pensacola	.191

General Manager: Walt Jocketty. **Farm Director:** Bill Bavasi. **Scouting Director:** Chris Buckley.

Class	Team	League	W	L	PCT	Finish	Manager
Majors	Cincinnati Reds	National	97	65	.599	2nd (16)	Dusty Baker
Triple-A	Louisville Bats	International	51	93	.354	14th (14)	David Bell
Double-A	Pensacola Blue Wahoos	Southern	68	70	.493	t-6th (10)	Jim Riggleman
High A	Bakersfield Blaze	California	72	68	.514	5th (10)	Ken Griffey
Low A	Dayton Dragons	Midwest	60	78	.435	15th (16)	Delino DeShields
Rookie	AZL Reds	Arizona	18	38	.321	12th (13)	Jose Nieves
Rookie	Billings Mustangs	Pioneer	42	34	.553	3rd (8)	Pat Kelly
Overall 2012 Minor League Record			311	381	.449	29th (30)	

ORGANIZATION STATISTICS

CINCINNATI REDS

NATIONAL LEAGUE

Batting	B-T	HT	WT	DOB	AVG	vLH	vRH	G	AB	R	H	2B	3B	HR	RBI	BB	HBP	SH	SF	SO	SB	CS	SLG	OBP
Bruce, Jay	L-L	6-3	225	4-3-87	.252	.225	.263	155	560	89	141	35	5	34	99	62	4	0	7	155	9	3	.514	.327
Cairo, Miguel	R-R	6-1	225	5-4-74	.187	.239	.163	70	150	9	28	7	2	1	13	4	1	0	1	20	4	0	.280	.212
Costanzo, Mike	L-R	6-3	215	9-9-83	.056	—	.056	17	18	0	1	0	0	0	1	1	0	0	2	10	0	0	.056	.095
Cozart, Zack	R-R	6-0	195	8-12-85	.246	.265	.240	138	561	72	138	33	4	15	35	31	3	2	3	113	4	0	.399	.288
Frazier, Todd	R-R	6-3	215	2-12-86	.273	.298	.262	128	422	55	115	26	6	19	67	36	3	0	4	103	3	2	.498	.331
Gregorius, Didi	L-R	6-1	185	2-18-90	.300	.500	.278	8	20	1	6	0	0	0	2	0	0	1	0	5	0	0	.300	.300
Hanigan, Ryan	R-R	6-0	210	8-16-80	.274	.329	.259	112	317	25	87	14	0	2	24	44	3	4	3	37	0	0	.338	.365
Harris, Willie	L-R	5-9	195	6-22-78	.114	—	.114	25	44	5	5	4	0	0	2	3	0	1	0	8	1	1	.205	.170
Heisey, Chris	R-R	6-0	220	12-14-84	.265	.274	.262	120	347	44	92	16	5	7	31	18	7	3	0	81	6	3	.401	.315
Ludwick, Ryan	R-L	6-3	215	7-13-78	.275	.263	.280	125	422	53	116	28	1	26	80	42	5	1	2	97	0	1	.531	.346
Mesoraco, Devin	R-R	6-1	225	6-19-88	.212	.308	.183	54	165	17	35	8	0	5	14	17	1	0	1	33	1	1	.352	.288
Navarro, Dioner	B-R	5-9	205	2-9-84	.290	.200	.327	24	69	6	20	3	1	2	12	2	0	1	1	12	0	0	.449	.306
Negron, Kris	R-R	6-0	195	2-1-86	.250	1.000	.000	4	4	2	1	0	0	0	1	0	0	0	0	2	0	0	.250	.400
Paul, Xavier	L-R	5-9	200	2-25-85	.314	.000	.325	55	86	8	27	5	1	2	7	9	0	1	0	18	4	2	.465	.379
Phillips, Brandon	R-R	6-0	200	6-28-81	.281	.269	.286	147	580	86	163	30	1	18	77	28	8	3	4	79	15	2	.429	.321
Phipps, Denis	R-R	6-3	210	7-22-85	.300	.000	.500	8	10	4	3	1	0	1	2	1	0	0	0	4	0	0	.700	.364
Rodriguez, Henry	B-R	5-10	150	2-9-90	.214	—	.214	12	14	0	3	1	0	0	2	2	0	0	0	2	0	0	.286	.313
Rolen, Scott	R-R	6-4	245	4-4-75	.245	.234	.249	92	294	26	72	17	2	8	39	30	3	0	3	62	2	1	.398	.318
Stubbs, Drew	R-R	6-4	205	10-4-84	.213	.283	.186	136	493	75	105	13	2	14	40	42	2	6	1	166	30	7	.333	.277
Valdez, Wilson	R-R	5-11	170	5-20-78	.206	.308	.169	77	194	15	40	4	0	0	15	8	0	5	1	36	3	1	.227	.236
Votto, Joey	L-R	6-3	225	9-10-83	.337	.288	.359	111	374	59	126	44	0	14	56	94	5	0	2	85	5	3	.567	.474

Pitching	B-T	HT	WT	DOB	W	L	ERA	G	GS	CG	SV	IP	H	R	ER	HR	BB	SO	AVG	vLH	vRH	K/9	BB/9
Arredondo, Jose	R-R	6-0	190	3-12-84	6	2	2.95	66	0	0	1	61	50	26	20	7	34	62	.225	.165	.277	9.15	5.02
Arroyo, Bronson	R-R	6-4	195	2-24-77	12	10	3.74	32	32	1	0	202	209	86	84	26	35	129	.267	.287	.245	5.75	1.56
Bailey, Homer	R-R	6-3	225	5-3-86	13	10	3.68	33	33	2	0	208	206	97	85	26	52	168	.256	.245	.265	7.27	2.25
Bray, Bill	L-L	6-3	230	6-5-83	0	0	5.19	14	0	0	0	9	6	5	5	2	14	7	.222	.000	.375	7.27	14.54
Broxton, Jonathan	R-R	6-4	300	6-16-84	3	3	2.82	25	0	0	4	22	20	7	7	1	3	20	.241	.147	.306	8.06	1.21
Chapman, Aroldis	L-L	6-4	200	2-28-88	5	5	1.51	68	0	0	38	72	35	13	12	4	23	122	.141	.108	.155	15.32	2.89
Cingrani, Tony	L-L	6-4	200	7-5-89	0	0	1.80	3	0	0	0	5	4	1	1	1	2	9	.200	.200	.200	16.20	3.60
Cueto, Johnny	R-R	5-10	215	2-15-86	19	9	2.78	33	33	2	0	217	205	73	67	15	49	170	.252	.279	.220	7.05	2.03
Hoover, J.J.	R-R	6-3	230	8-13-87	1	0	2.05	28	0	0	1	31	17	7	7	2	13	31	.160	.120	.196	9.10	3.82
Latos, Mat	R-R	6-6	235	12-9-87	14	4	3.48	33	33	2	0	209	179	81	81	25	64	185	.230	.252	.208	7.95	2.75
Leake, Mike	R-R	6-0	180	11-12-87	8	9	4.58	30	30	2	0	179	201	97	91	26	41	116	.287	.296	.276	5.83	2.06
LeCure, Sam	R-R	6-1	210	5-4-84	3	3	3.14	48	0	0	0	57	46	22	20	3	23	61	.221	.208	.232	9.58	3.61
Marshall, Sean	L-L	6-7	220	8-30-82	5	5	2.51	73	0	0	9	61	55	18	17	3	16	74	.232	.173	.273	10.92	2.36
Ondrusek, Logan	R-R	6-8	230	2-13-85	5	2	3.46	63	0	0	2	55	51	23	21	8	31	39	.246	.190	.285	6.42	5.10
Redmond, Todd	R-R	6-3	215	5-17-85	0	1	10.80	1	1	0	0	3	7	4	4	1	5	2	.412	.364	.500	5.40	13.50
Simon, Alfredo	R-R	6-6	260	5-8-81	3	2	2.66	36	0	0	1	61	65	22	18	2	22	52	.275	.267	.283	7.67	3.25
Villarreal, Pedro	R-R	6-1	225	12-9-87	0	0	0.00	1	0	0	0	1	0	0	0	0	0	1	.000	.000	.000	9.00	0.00

Fielding

Catcher	PCT	G	PO	A	E	DP	PB
Hanigan	.995	110	781	48	4	6	3
Mesoraco	.997	53	368	24	1	1	3
Navarro	.993	21	131	9	1	0	1

First Base	PCT	G	PO	A	E	DP
Cairo	.994	24	156	14	1	7
Costanzo	.900	2	9	0	1	0
Frazier	.994	39	315	21	2	30
Votto	.994	109	850	116	6	69

Second Base	PCT	G	PO	A	E	DP
Cairo	.974	8	15	22	1	7
Harris	.963	7	8	18	1	4

Third Base	PCT	G	PO	A	E	DP
Cairo	.870	13	8	12	3	1
Frazier	.968	73	45	105	5	4
Harris	1.000	1	0	2	0	1
Rolen	.948	87	45	139	10	6
Valdez	.900	14	5	13	2	1

Shortstop	PCT	G	PO	A	E	DP
Cozart	.975	138	204	349	14	68
Gregorius	1.000	6	8	10	0	4

	PCT	G	PO	A	E	DP
Phillips	.992	146	241	391	5	73
Rodriguez	1.000	2	5	5	0	2
Valdez	.976	22	14	27	1	3

	PCT	G	PO	A	E	DP
Valdez	.990	33	47	54	1	15

Outfield	PCT	G	PO	A	E	DP
Bruce	.981	154	297	8	6	1
Frazier	1.000	7	12	0	0	0
Harris	1.000	1	1	0	0	0
Heisey	.984	101	181	4	3	0
Ludwick	.995	108	191	0	1	0
Negron	—	1	0	0	0	0
Paul	1.000	18	15	2	0	0
Phipps	1.000	2	4	0	0	0
Stubbs	.982	135	272	5	5	1
Valdez	1.000	5	6	0	0	0

INTERNATIONAL LEAGUE

Batting	B-T	HT	WT	DOB	AVG	vLH	vRH	G	AB	R	H	2B	3B	HR	RBI	BB	HBP	SH	SF	SO	SB	CS	SLG	OBP
Costanzo, Mike	L-R	6-3	215	9-9-83	.262	.167	.297	96	313	41	82	18	1	9	38	43	2	0	0	79	0	4	.412	.355
Dorn, Danny	L-L	6-2	205	7-20-84	.230	.206	.239	69	226	26	52	14	1	7	24	28	4	0	4	65	1	2	.394	.321
2-team total (47 Toledo)					.252	—	—	116	393	50	99	25	2	14	49	50	8	0	5	108	5	2	.433	.344
Frazier, Todd	R-R	6-3	215	2-12-86	.231	.286	.200	10	39	4	9	2	0	1	7	2	0	0	0	11	3	0	.359	.268
Gathright, Joey	L-R	5-10	175	4-27-81	.299	.361	.279	40	147	9	44	7	0	0	16	7	4	2	1	29	4	2	.347	.346
Gregorius, Didi	L-R	6-1	185	2-18-90	.243	.225	.254	48	185	25	45	10	3	6	23	12	0	4	1	31	0	2	.427	.288
Harris, Willie	L-R	5-9	195	6-22-78	.224	.263	.206	74	250	22	56	13	0	3	20	23	3	1	2	52	4	3	.312	.295
Janish, Paul	R-R	6-2	200	10-12-82	.237	.281	.214	49	169	27	40	12	1	4	11	20	4	1	0	26	0	1	.391	.332
Jones, Daryl	L-L	6-0	180	6-25-87	.187	.192	.185	27	91	16	17	5	1	3	9	11	1	1	0	31	7	1	.363	.282
Mesoraco, Devin	R-R	6-1	225	6-19-88	.167	.100	.250	5	18	0	3	1	0	0	0	1	0	0	0	2	0	0	.222	.211
Miller, Corky	R-R	6-1	255	3-18-76	.235	.292	.213	89	243	20	57	8	0	7	29	57	5	5	3	46	2	1	.354	.386
Navarro, Dioner	B-R	5-9	205	2-9-84	.319	.350	.306	62	207	24	66	12	0	5	32	23	2	2	6	24	0	0	.449	.382
Negron, Kris	R-R	6-0	195	2-1-86	.218	.213	.221	74	284	34	62	13	2	6	20	22	6	5	2	77	17	3	.342	.287
Paul, Xavier	L-R	5-9	200	2-25-85	.480	.375	.529	6	25	4	12	2	0	1	4	1	0	0	0	5	3	0	.680	.500
2-team total (60 Syracuse)					.332	—	—	66	238	34	79	18	1	9	48	20	2	3	0	46	9	3	.529	.388
Peacock, Brian	R-R	6-1	185	8-26-84	.203	.273	.170	32	69	7	14	4	0	2	8	5	0	0	1	19	0	1	.348	.253
Perez, Felix	L-L	6-2	190	11-14-84	.301	.271	.312	116	392	46	118	25	1	4	35	23	6	6	1	63	5	5	.401	.348
Perez, Yordanys	B-R	6-1	200	4-12-84	.000	.000	.000	3	8	0	0	0	0	0	0	0	1	0	0	4	0	0	.000	.111
Phillips, P.J.	R-R	6-3	170	9-23-86	.143	.167	.125	4	14	0	2	0	0	0	1	0	0	0	1	3	0	1	.143	.133
Phipps, Denis	R-R	6-3	210	7-22-85	.221	.197	.236	92	357	48	79	19	0	15	45	33	4	2	2	103	4	2	.401	.293
Puckett, Cody	R-R	5-9	189	4-3-87	.219	.184	.236	91	310	38	68	12	1	9	45	25	2	0	5	81	8	1	.352	.278
Rhinehart, Bill	L-L	6-0	202	11-22-84	.233	.231	.234	92	292	32	68	14	1	8	26	31	2	0	1	64	1	3	.370	.310
Rodriguez, Henry	B-R	5-10	150	2-9-90	.244	.247	.242	51	213	23	52	10	0	3	20	6	0	1	1	35	5	4	.333	.264
Rojas, Miguel	R-R	5-11	197	2-24-89	.186	.100	.212	44	129	9	24	3	0	1	7	7	0	7	1	16	0	0	.233	.226
Rolen, Scott	R-R	6-4	245	4-4-75	.333	.333	.333	2	6	1	2	0	0	1	3	0	0	0	0	2	0	0	.833	.333
Soto, Neftali	R-R	6-2	200	2-28-89	.245	.220	.259	122	465	55	114	30	0	14	59	41	5	0	1	116	2	1	.400	.313
Valaika, Chris	R-R	6-0	215	8-14-85	.223	.171	.253	85	291	30	65	14	2	6	29	15	4	2	4	63	2	3	.347	.268
Votto, Joey	L-R	6-3	225	9-10-83	.167	.250	.000	2	6	1	1	0	0	1	0	1	0	0	0	4	0	0	.667	.167

Pitching	B-T	HT	WT	DOB	W	L	ERA	G	GS	CG	SV	IP	H	R	ER	HR	BB	SO	AVG	vLH	vRH	K/9	BB/9
Allen, James	R-R	6-1	197	11-20-89	0	0	12.00	1	0	0	0	3	8	4	4	0	3	1	.533	.417	1.000	3.00	9.00
Atilano, Luis	R-R	6-2	220	5-10-85	0	1	15.43	1	1	0	0	2	5	4	4	0	2	0	.500	.000	.714	0.00	7.71
Brackman, Andrew	R-R	6-10	230	12-4-85	1	3	9.87	5	5	0	0	17	18	19	19	3	16	13	.269	.280	.262	6.75	8.31
Bray, Bill	L-L	6-3	230	6-5-83	1	0	9.00	14	0	0	0	12	17	14	12	1	12	10	.327	.200	.406	7.50	9.00
Carroll, Scott	R-R	6-4	215	9-24-84	2	3	5.90	25	0	0	0	40	51	26	26	4	16	27	.319	.317	.321	6.13	3.63
2-team total (9 Charlotte)					4	6	4.74	34	8	0	0	87	90	47	46	10	34	63	—	—	—	6.49	3.50
Christiani, Nick	R-R	6-0	190	7-17-87	2	5	3.34	54	0	0	1	73	84	34	27	4	29	35	.299	.369	.258	4.33	3.59
Feierabend, Ryan	L-L	6-3	225	8-22-85	1	4	6.75	7	7	0	0	36	45	29	26	11	17	26	.321	.323	.321	6.49	4.41
Fisher, Carlos	R-R	6-4	220	2-22-83	0	2	4.61	52	0	0	0	66	57	36	34	6	57	64	.237	.257	.221	8.68	7.73
Francis, Jeff	L-L	6-5	220	1-8-81	3	6	3.72	12	12	1	0	77	84	33	32	6	18	65	.286	.299	.279	7.56	2.09
Gallagher, Sean	R-R	6-2	220	12-30-85	10	9	4.92	26	26	0	0	139	134	78	76	18	75	84	.261	.272	.251	5.44	4.86
Gustafson, Tim	R-R	6-3	210	12-29-84	5	7	5.56	18	18	0	0	87	101	59	54	13	42	58	.294	.314	.276	5.98	4.33
Hoover, J.J.	R-R	6-3	230	8-13-87	4	0	1.22	30	0	0	13	37	15	9	5	1	12	55	.121	.109	.128	13.38	2.92
Joseph, Donnie	L-L	6-3	190	11-1-87	4	1	2.86	18	0	0	5	22	22	8	7	0	9	22	.259	.174	.290	9.00	3.68
Judy, Josh	R-R	6-4	210	2-9-86	2	2	6.99	40	0	0	1	57	68	44	44	6	30	56	.302	.372	.252	8.89	4.76
Mahay, Ron	L-L	6-2	200	6-28-71	1	0	4.50	14	1	0	0	18	21	10	9	0	10	16	.284	.333	.255	8.00	5.00
Masset, Nick	R-R	6-4	235	5-17-82	0	1	8.10	6	2	0	0	7	7	6	6	0	3	9	.259	.400	.083	12.15	4.05
Obispo, Wirfin	R-R	6-1	160	9-26-84	0	1	6.05	10	3	0	0	19	19	14	13	0	15	14	.271	.326	.185	6.52	6.98
Ohman, Will	L-L	6-2	225	8-13-77	0	1	4.09	15	0	0	0	11	17	5	5	0	10	17	.354	.400	.321	13.91	8.18
Ondrusek, Logan	R-R	6-8	230	2-13-85	0	1	9.00	3	0	0	0	4	8	4	4	1	4	5	.421	.375	.455	11.25	9.00
Redmond, Todd	R-R	6-3	215	5-17-85	2	5	3.77	8	7	0	0	43	43	21	18	7	11	40	.261	.243	.274	8.37	2.30
2-team total (18 Gwinnett)					8	11	3.63	26	25	1	0	149	150	71	60	18	39	136	—	—	—	8.23	2.36
Reineke, Chad	R-R	6-6	230	4-9-82	5	11	4.57	27	26	0	0	152	174	86	77	16	45	108	.293	.277	.305	6.41	2.67
Smith, Jordan	R-R	6-4	225	2-4-86	3	3	4.76	51	0	0	13	57	67	31	30	2	16	36	.295	.327	.270	5.72	2.54
Texeira, Kanekoa	R-R	6-2	190	2-6-86	3	3	2.72	34	3	0	1	56	47	19	17	2	27	35	.232	.209	.250	5.59	4.31
Tomko, Brett	R-R	6-4	220	4-7-73	0	6	3.78	12	12	0	0	67	66	28	28	4	33	48	.261	.278	.244	6.48	4.46
Villarreal, Pedro	R-R	6-1	225	12-9-87	3	12	4.61	20	20	0	0	113	129	70	58	9	32	81	.285	.275	.293	6.43	2.54
Webb, Travis	L-L	6-4	205	8-2-84	2	6	4.81	54	1	0	0	58	47	34	31	7	34	67	.221	.186	.244	10.40	5.28

Fielding

Catcher	PCT	G	PO	A	E	DP	PB
Mesoraco	.963	5	24	2	1	0	1
Miller	.995	77	513	45	3	8	9
Navarro	.992	49	355	34	3	2	5
Peacock	.986	26	127	10	2	0	1

First Base	PCT	G	PO	A	E	DP
Costanzo	.983	14	97	17	2	12
Dorn	1.000	21	150	20	0	13
Miller	1.000	2	2	0	0	0
Perez	—	1	0	0	0	0
Soto	.989	113	931	88	11	100

	PCT	G	PO	A	E	DP
Votto	.938	2	15	0	1	4
Second Base	**PCT**	**G**	**PO**	**A**	**E**	**DP**
Gregorius	1.000	3	4	8	0	1
Harris	.981	23	36	67	2	13
Janish	1.000	3	7	10	0	4
Negron	1.000	15	35	47	0	10
Puckett	.982	40	63	104	3	22
Rodriguez	.988	18	38	43	1	12
Rojas	1.000	3	3	13	0	2
Valaika	.952	54	92	107	10	34

Third Base	PCT	G	PO	A	E	DP
Costanzo	.932	65	31	106	10	10
Frazier	.955	8	7	14	1	2
Harris	.935	15	7	22	2	2
Janish	1.000	3	1	6	0	0
Negron	.968	18	18	43	2	3
Rodriguez	.941	28	16	64	5	8
Rolen	1.000	2	0	2	0	1
Soto	1.000	1	0	1	0	0
Valaika	.925	16	9	28	3	1

Shortstop	PCT	G	PO	A	E	DP
Gregorius	.980	42	83	114	4	35
Harris	1.000	5	4	9	0	0
Janish	.975	43	51	102	4	19
Negron	.953	21	28	54	4	14
Rodriguez	.935	7	12	17	2	2
Rojas	.988	37	65	94	2	27
Valaika	1.000	2	3	3	0	1

Outfield	PCT	G	PO	A	E	DP
Costanzo	1.000	3	7	0	0	0
Dorn	.981	36	49	3	1	0
Frazier	—	1	0	0	0	0
Gathright	1.000	36	72	0	0	0
Harris	.978	26	43	1	1	0
Jones	.945	22	50	2	3	0
Negron	1.000	24	50	3	0	0
Paul	1.000	6	7	0	0	0

	PCT	G	PO	A	E	DP
Peacock	—	1	0	0	0	0
Perez	.979	101	221	16	5	5
Perez	1.000	3	5	0	0	0
Phillips	1.000	4	8	0	0	0
Phipps	.973	91	211	8	6	1
Puckett	.964	48	75	5	3	0
Rhinehart	.982	69	103	4	2	0
Soto	—	1	0	0	0	0

PENSACOLA BLUE WAHOOS   DOUBLE-A

SOUTHERN LEAGUE

Batting	B-T	HT	WT	DOB	AVG	vLH	vRH	G	AB	R	H	2B	3B	HR	RBI	BB	HBP	SH	SF	SO	SB	CS	SLG	OBP
Barnhart, Tucker	B-R	5-10	185	1-7-91	.200	.184	.207	41	130	10	26	4	1	2	12	11	0	1	0	22	1	1	.292	.262
Berset, Chris	B-R	6-0	195	1-27-88	.227	.400	.083	7	22	3	5	0	0	0	1	3	1	0	0	3	0	0	.227	.346
Costanzo, Mike	L-R	6-3	215	9-9-83	.333	.167	.375	11	30	8	10	2	0	3	13	10	0	0	0	11	0	1	.700	.500
Ewing, James	R-R	6-0	190	10-27-86	.000	.000	.000	5	6	0	0	0	0	0	0	1	0	0	0	1	0	0	.000	.143
Fellhauer, Josh	L-L	5-11	175	3-24-88	.314	.231	.324	117	338	50	106	20	2	4	41	54	2	3	2	54	6	4	.420	.409
Fleury, Mark	L-R	6-0	189	5-4-88	.160	.158	.161	68	187	25	30	10	0	1	17	36	3	6	4	72	1	1	.230	.300
Greene, Brodie	R-R	6-1	195	9-25-87	.244	.277	.228	124	435	46	106	22	3	3	46	43	7	7	4	70	12	4	.329	.319
Gregorius, Didi	L-R	6-1	185	2-18-90	.278	.250	.291	81	316	45	88	11	8	1	31	29	4	7	3	49	3	4	.373	.344
Guzman, Joel	R-R	6-7	225	11-24-84	.263	.288	.250	65	236	26	62	10	0	7	35	24	0	1	2	44	1	2	.394	.328
Hamilton, Billy	B-R	6-1	160	9-9-90	.286	.306	.278	50	175	33	50	4	5	1	15	36	0	1	1	43	51	16	.383	.406
Hill, Koyie	B-R	6-1	210	3-9-79	.195	.125	.240	14	41	5	8	3	0	1	5	3	0	0	0	10	0	0	.341	.250
Hunt, Stephen	L-L	6-0	190	1-11-89	.213	.143	.225	28	47	4	10	1	0	0	4	8	0	1	1	14	0	0	.234	.321
LaMarre, Ryan	R-L	6-2	205	11-21-88	.263	.270	.261	133	482	68	127	22	3	5	32	60	10	4	2	119	30	10	.353	.356
Lutz, Donald	L-R	6-3	235	2-6-89	.242	.225	.248	40	149	17	36	5	1	5	15	13	3	0	0	32	1	3	.389	.315
Means, Andrew	R-R	6-1	214	9-11-86	.244	.239	.247	76	156	18	38	4	1	3	10	17	3	1	0	29	4	1	.340	.330
Mills, Beau	L-R	6-3	220	8-15-86	.272	.186	.294	60	206	21	56	14	1	10	31	20	3	2	1	38	2	1	.495	.343
Peacock, Brian	R-R	6-1	185	8-26-84	.304	.171	.447	25	79	7	24	3	0	0	8	5	0	1	0	25	0	1	.342	.345
Perez, Juan	L-R	6-0	180	11-1-91	.000	.000	.000	3	3	0	0	0	0	0	0	1	0	0	0	2	0	0	.000	.250
Perez, Yordanys	B-R	6-1	200	4-12-84	.225	.147	.242	68	187	13	42	7	1	4	29	7	2	3	2	36	0	3	.337	.258
Phillips, P.J.	R-R	6-3	170	9-23-86	.198	.198	.198	68	172	12	34	8	0	2	15	11	0	2	0	47	5	1	.279	.246
Puckett, Cody	R-R	5-9	189	4-3-87	.268	.256	.275	37	123	18	33	4	1	7	21	21	0	1	1	38	1	0	.488	.372
Rhinehart, Bill	L-L	6-0	202	11-22-84	.150	.286	.077	6	20	2	3	3	0	0	2	1	0	0	0	9	0	0	.300	.190
Rodriguez, Henry	B-R	5-10	150	2-9-90	.348	.327	.363	33	132	19	46	6	2	1	5	9	0	1	2	18	3	0	.439	.385
Rojas, Miguel	R-R	5-11	197	2-24-89	.210	.208	.211	58	143	14	30	1	0	0	10	16	1	0	0	17	2	3	.217	.294
Smith, Bryson	R-R	6-1	195	12-17-88	.307	.316	.302	50	153	16	47	5	5	1	31	3	5	1	4	23	4	1	.425	.333
Vidal, David	R-R	5-11	185	10-23-89	.230	.214	.236	97	335	42	77	21	1	11	39	28	4	6	4	90	0	2	.397	.294

Pitching	B-T	HT	WT	DOB	W	L	ERA	G	GS	CG	SV	IP	H	R	ER	HR	BB	SO	AVG	vLH	vRH	K/9	BB/9
Atilano, Luis	R-R	6-2	220	5-10-85	0	1	3.00	1	0	0	0	3	3	1	1	0	3	3	.200	.250	.167	9.00	9.00
Cingrani, Tony	L-L	6-4	200	7-5-89	5	3	2.12	16	15	1	0	89	59	24	21	7	39	101	.192	.207	.186	10.18	3.93
Corcino, Daniel	R-R	5-11	205	8-26-90	8	8	3.01	26	26	0	0	143	111	61	48	9	65	126	.216	.191	.234	7.91	4.08
Crabbe, Tim	R-R	6-4	195	2-20-88	3	6	4.90	18	18	0	0	86	81	49	47	9	66	93	.252	.232	.268	9.69	6.88
De La Rosa, Wilkin	L-L	6-0	185	2-21-85	1	1	2.49	46	0	0	1	43	36	14	12	3	27	41	.224	.215	.229	8.52	5.61
Freeman, Justin	R-R	6-1	170	10-22-86	4	7	2.91	57	0	0	16	68	49	22	22	7	16	68	.198	.210	.190	9.00	2.12
Griffin, Michael	R-R	5-9	200	10-1-83	1	1	7.94	4	0	0	0	6	7	5	5	1	5	4	.318	.500	.214	6.35	7.94
Gustafson, Tim	R-R	6-3	210	12-29-84	2	2	5.04	14	7	0	0	45	47	29	25	4	16	34	.275	.217	.306	6.85	3.22
Hayes, Drew	R-R	6-1	190	9-3-87	2	3	3.41	56	1	0	1	63	53	24	24	3	38	64	.235	.169	.273	9.09	5.40
Joseph, Donnie	L-L	6-3	190	11-1-87	4	2	0.89	26	0	0	13	30	13	4	3	1	8	46	.129	.097	.143	13.65	2.37
Lotzkar, Kyle	L-R	6-4	205	10-24-89	4	6	5.21	18	17	0	0	86	77	56	50	12	53	96	.238	.276	.214	10.01	5.53
Manno, Chris	L-L	6-3	170	11-4-88	1	1	3.78	50	0	0	2	50	51	26	21	5	22	51	.266	.250	.275	9.18	3.96
Miller, Erik	R-R	6-3	210	4-9-90	0	0	0.00	3	0	0	0	2	1	0	0	0	2	1	.200	.000	.333	5.40	10.80
Obispo, Wirfin	R-R	6-1	190	9-26-84	5	2	2.23	25	10	0	0	77	42	20	19	8	28	77	.163	.233	.106	9.04	3.29
Partch, Curtis	R-R	6-5	227	2-13-87	7	4	4.73	45	4	0	6	70	75	38	37	7	33	64	.274	.302	.256	8.19	4.22
Pearl, Brian	L-R	6-1	190	5-17-88	1	3	7.01	23	0	0	0	26	35	21	20	3	13	21	.347	.306	.369	7.36	4.56
Ravin, Josh	R-R	6-4	220	1-21-88	1	3	5.25	20	0	0	0	24	23	16	14	3	20	22	.256	.233	.277	8.25	7.50
Rogers, Chad	R-R	5-11	175	8-3-89	3	1	1.99	6	6	0	0	32	27	7	7	2	6	22	.241	.255	.228	6.54	1.71
Serrano, Mark	L-R	6-1	185	9-14-85	7	4	3.95	41	9	0	0	93	90	43	41	11	30	95	.251	.255	.249	9.16	2.89
Sulbaran, Juan Carlos	R-R	6-2	220	11-9-89	7	7	4.04	19	19	0	0	105	101	49	47	17	54	111	.261	.247	.271	9.54	4.64
Tanner, Clayton	R-L	6-2	205	12-5-87	1	3	4.08	30	0	0	1	29	22	13	13	0	14	22	.210	.196	.220	6.91	4.40
Villarreal, Pedro	R-R	6-1	225	12-9-87	1	2	3.57	6	6	0	0	35	31	16	14	2	6	26	.240	.279	.206	6.62	1.53

Fielding

Catcher	PCT	G	PO	A	E	DP	PB
Barnhart	.989	41	314	40	4	3	6
Berset	.975	7	76	3	2	0	0
Fleury	.980	65	530	49	12	8	8
Hill	1.000	11	93	9	0	0	0
Peacock	.995	23	194	13	1	2	0

First Base	PCT	G	PO	A	E	DP
Costanzo	.989	8	81	5	1	3
Fleury	1.000	2	3	0	0	0
Guzman	.989	52	343	20	4	30
Hunt	.982	7	50	4	1	5
Lutz	.981	14	102	3	2	9
Mills	.995	55	391	39	2	30
Perez	.982	8	52	2	1	5
Rhinehart	1.000	1	5	0	0	0
Rojas	1.000	4	12	1	0	1

Second Base	PCT	G	PO	A	E	DP
Ewing	1.000	1	1	2	0	0
Greene	.973	119	183	249	12	42
Phillips	1.000	5	3	5	0	1
Puckett	—	1	0	0	0	0
Rodriguez	1.000	1	4	0	0	1
Rojas	.990	25	40	57	1	17

Third Base	PCT	G	PO	A	E	DP
Costanzo	1.000	2	0	5	0	0
Phillips	.833	5	0	5	1	0
Puckett	1.000	4	0	5	0	0

	PCT	G	PO	A	E	DP
Rodriguez	.976	29	21	62	2	4
Rojas	1.000	14	13	6	0	2
Vidal	.986	95	60	152	3	11
Shortstop	**PCT**	**G**	**PO**	**A**	**E**	**DP**
Greene	1.000	4	6	10	0	1
Gregorius	.953	80	121	165	14	34
Hamilton	.968	48	69	110	6	21
Perez	1.000	1	1	1	0	0

	PCT	G	PO	A	E	DP
Phillips	—	1	0	0	0	0
Rojas	.927	9	8	30	3	3
Outfield	**PCT**	**G**	**PO**	**A**	**E**	**DP**
Fellhauer	.994	106	166	13	1	1
Guzman	—	1	0	0	0	0
Hunt	1.000	7	8	0	0	0
LaMarre	.983	130	274	20	5	3
Lutz	.982	31	52	2	1	0

	PCT	G	PO	A	E	DP
Means	.986	58	70	3	1	1
Mills	—	1	0	0	0	0
Perez	1.000	29	31	1	0	0
Phillips	.968	44	60	1	2	1
Puckett	1.000	34	47	1	0	0
Rhinehart	1.000	4	8	2	0	1
Smith	.971	43	65	2	2	0

BAKERSFIELD BLAZE   HIGH CLASS A

CALIFORNIA LEAGUE

Batting	B-T	HT	WT	DOB	AVG	vLH	vRH	G	AB	R	H	2B	3B	HR	RBI	BB	HBP	SH	SF	SO	SB	CS	SLG	OBP
Barnhart, Tucker	B-R	5-10	185	1-7-91	.278	.158	.326	59	198	26	55	12	1	4	22	29	1	2	1	45	0	2	.409	.371
Berset, Chris	B-R	6-0	195	1-27-88	.217	.200	.225	49	161	22	35	8	0	5	19	22	3	0	2	27	1	2	.360	.319
Bowe, Theo	L-R	5-9	160	8-5-90	.314	.276	.325	96	373	65	117	13	2	3	39	45	5	6	4	72	58	28	.383	.391
Christian, Jason	L-R	6-3	185	6-16-87	.250	.000	.300	5	12	2	3	0	0	0	1	4	0	0	0	4	0	0	.250	.438
D'Anna, Dominic	L-R	6-1	215	12-23-88	.277	.343	.258	84	300	56	83	19	3	7	45	52	5	0	6	77	3	0	.430	.386
Duran, Juan	R-R	6-7	205	9-2-91	.237	.220	.245	106	422	47	100	16	2	12	57	26	5	0	5	151	3	2	.370	.286
Ewing, James	R-R	6-0	190	10-27-86	.177	.209	.151	30	96	8	17	3	0	0	16	13	4	1	0	25	0	0	.208	.301
Hamilton, Billy	B-R	6-1	160	9-9-90	.323	.320	.325	82	337	79	109	18	9	1	30	50	2	2	1	70	104	21	.439	.413
Hunt, Stephen	L-L	6-0	190	1-11-89	.205	.097	.228	50	176	12	36	8	1	2	20	18	3	1	2	28	0	1	.295	.286
Lohman, Devin	R-R	6-1	185	4-14-89	.257	.329	.229	130	494	80	127	23	3	14	70	60	15	3	3	108	34	9	.401	.353
Lutz, Donald	L-R	6-3	235	2-6-89	.265	.200	.292	63	253	42	67	18	3	17	51	19	4	0	1	71	7	2	.561	.325
Mattair, Travis	R-R	6-5	210	12-21-88	.274	.268	.277	126	492	73	135	31	3	19	82	50	4	0	4	119	3	6	.465	.344
Matthews, Jaren	L-L	6-2	215	2-20-89	.220	.231	.218	25	91	6	20	6	1	1	11	4	1	1	0	23	3	2	.319	.260
Means, Andrew	R-R	6-1	214	9-11-86	.270	.429	.233	11	37	5	10	1	1	1	8	3	0	0	0	12	2	1	.432	.325
Muller, Kurt	R-R	5-10	170	7-7-89	.262	.328	.232	55	183	31	48	16	2	2	24	17	2	3	3	25	15	8	.404	.327
Rodriguez, Yorman	R-R	6-2	184	8-15-92	.156	.265	.089	23	90	7	14	4	0	0	3	0	0	1		39	4	0	.200	.181
Selsky, Steve	R-R	6-1	205	7-20-89	.348	.388	.335	69	267	52	93	21	3	15	48	26	10	0	4	62	13	2	.618	.420
Smith, Bryson	R-R	6-1	195	12-17-88	.313	.264	.338	57	211	35	66	8	1	5	38	13	10	1	3	38	3	7	.431	.376
Terry, Joe	L-R	5-11	185	12-18-89	.333	.333	.333	6	21	3	7	1	0	0	2	1	0	0	0	5	0	0	.381	.364
Vasquez, Niko	R-R	6-0	170	2-26-89	.235	.244	.231	66	238	35	56	18	2	4	22	30	1	3	0	40	1	0	.378	.323
Vicioso, Danny	R-R	6-0	190	10-27-88	.290	.273	.296	33	131	11	38	9	1	3	16	3	0	0	0	30	1	1	.443	.306
Vidal, David	R-R	5-11	185	10-23-89	.281	.195	.325	35	121	20	34	7	0	7	21	13	2	0	1	26	3	0	.512	.358
Wright, Ryan	R-R	6-1	195	12-3-89	.271	.276	.269	23	96	17	26	5	2	5	16	2	1	0	3	17	3	1	.521	.284

Pitching	B-T	HT	WT	DOB	W	L	ERA	G	GS	CG	SV	IP	H	R	ER	HR	BB	SO	AVG	vLH	vRH	K/9	BB/9
Brackman, Andrew	R-R	6-10	230	12-4-85	1	3	5.52	29	3	0	1	46	47	32	28	5	26	32	.278	.232	.310	6.31	5.12
Cingrani, Tony	L-L	6-4	200	7-5-89	5	1	1.11	10	10	0	0	57	39	13	7	2	13	71	.189	.237	.170	11.28	2.06
Contreras, Carlos	R-R	6-0	165	1-8-91	1	0	2.70	9	0	0	4	10	9	5	3	1	5	12	.225	.158	.286	10.80	4.50
Crabbe, Tim	R-R	6-4	195	2-20-88	5	2	3.28	10	10	0	0	58	46	23	21	5	15	60	.215	.277	.159	9.36	2.34
De La Rosa, Wilkin	L-L	6-0	185	2-21-85	0	0	1.04	7	0	0	2	9	11	3	1	0	2	8	.344	.286	.389	8.31	2.08
De Los Santos, Abel	R-R	6-1	215	5-17-92	0	0	81.00	1	0	0	0		3	4	3	0	2	1	.750	.500	1.000	27.00	54.00
Dennhardt, Mike	R-R	6-1	205	6-1-90	0	0	4.05	5	0	0	1	7	6	3	3	2	3	2	.250	.333	.200	2.70	4.05
Doyle, Pat	R-R	6-2	205	5-12-88	9	5	5.73	39	5	0	1	82	94	59	52	15	23	69	.289	.292	.288	7.60	2.53
French, Justice	R-R	6-4	215	8-2-89	1	2	3.94	22	6	0	0	59	68	29	26	5	23	30	.291	.314	.277	4.55	3.49
Gerson, Starlin	R-R	6-4	175	8-26-88	2	1	6.30	4	4	0	0	20	25	14	14	6	0	17	.301	.293	.310	7.65	0.00
Griffin, Michael	R-R	5-9	200	10-1-83	2	4	5.53	37	0	0	0	42	48	27	26	3	37	50	.294	.284	.302	10.63	7.87
Holdzkom, John	R-R	6-7	225	10-19-87	0	1	5.19	6	1	0	0	9	6	5	5	0	13	10	.194	.200	.188	10.38	13.50
Howell, Blaine	L-L	5-11	210	10-2-88	1	2	4.84	27	0	0	0	35	43	24	19	2	19	25	.299	.293	.302	6.37	4.84
Joyce, Chris	L-L	6-0	195	12-25-89	4	4	6.10	31	0	0	1	38	49	34	26	6	22	33	.306	.262	.337	7.75	5.17
Kiel, Ryan	L-L	6-4	230	6-26-87	0	0	3.38	2	0	0	0	3	2	1	1	1	2	4	.200	.000	.333	13.50	6.75
Lotzkar, Kyle	L-R	6-4	205	10-24-89	3	0	2.39	5	5	0	0	26	22	8	7	2	10	27	.224	.235	.219	9.23	3.42
Martinez, Porfirio	R-R	5-10	175	11-29-89	0	0	13.50	1	0	0	0	1	2	2	2		2	0	.333	.000	.500	0.00	13.50
McMyne, Kyle	R-R	5-11	220	10-18-89	2	3	7.02	35	0	0	6	41	47	36	32	8	28	31	.287	.284	.289	6.80	6.15
Moran, Jimmy	R-R	6-1	180	9-6-90	0	0	0.00	1	0	0	0	1	0	0	0	0	0	0	.000	.000	.000	0.00	0.00
Partch, Curtis	R-R	6-5	227	2-13-87	0	0	1.50	7	0	0	2	12	7	2	2	1	3	15	.167	.273	.129	11.25	2.25
Pearl, Brian	L-R	6-1	190	5-17-88	1	1	1.31	28	0	0	13	34	25	8	5	1	8	41	.202	.160	.230	10.75	2.10
Pinckard, Brooks	L-R	6-1	190	8-15-88	1	5	7.20	34	0	0	2	45	47	37	36	9	39	33	.280	.212	.324	6.60	7.80
Ravin, Josh	R-R	6-4	220	1-21-88	0	0	6.00	3	0	0	0	3	4	3	2	1	4	6	.267	.200	.400	12.00	6.00
Renken, Daniel	R-R	6-3	190	7-5-89	6	9	5.93	28	28	0	0	143	167	106	94	22	57	125	.293	.293	.293	7.89	3.60
Robles, Tanner	L-L	6-4	205	2-24-89	3	3	2.50	7	7	0	0	36	33	11	10	3	13	35	.239	.205	.253	8.75	3.25
Rogers, Chad	R-R	5-11	175	8-3-89	6	4	3.15	21	21	0	0	111	113	48	39	11	29	88	.263	.305	.234	7.11	2.34
Smith, Josh	R-R	6-2	220	8-7-87	9	8	3.80	27	27	1	0	147	143	71	62	15	46	140	.254	.269	.240	8.57	2.82
Walczak, Jamie	R-R	6-2	195	5-4-87	4	5	5.65	39	13	0	2	100	110	70	63	17	46	120	.275	.301	.257	10.76	4.13
Wolford, Dan	R-R	6-2	210	8-19-88	6	5	6.19	48	0	0	2	68	73	48	47	12	37	66	.278	.278	.277	8.69	4.87

Fielding

Catcher	PCT	G	PO	A	E	DP	PB
Barnhart	.986	59	492	81	8	8	7
Berset	.978	49	387	54	10	1	2
Vicioso	.975	33	230	38	7	1	6

First Base	PCT	G	PO	A	E	DP
D'Anna	.990	73	639	50	7	48

	PCT	G	PO	A	E	DP
Hunt	.984	24	180	8	3	10
Lutz	.978	24	216	3	5	17
Mattair	.990	23	180	21	2	19

Second Base	PCT	G	PO	A	E	DP
Ewing	.938	16	26	35	4	7
Lohman	.971	65	121	178	9	38

	PCT	G	PO	A	E	DP
Muller	.750	1	2	4	2	1
Terry	1.000	3	5	5	0	1
Vasquez	.960	38	65	101	7	13
Wright	.971	20	42	57	3	9

Third Base	PCT	G	PO	A	E	DP
Ewing	1.000	1	1	2	0	1

Mattair	.939	95	71	175	16	8
Terry	1.000	1	0	2	0	0
Vasquez	.980	18	20	29	1	5
Vidal	.894	31	23	53	9	5
Shortstop	**PCT**	**G**	**PO**	**A**	**E**	**DP**
Hamilton	.935	77	120	242	25	46
Lohman	.934	61	90	149	17	25

Vasquez	1.000	4	5	8	0	2
Outfield	**PCT**	**G**	**PO**	**A**	**E**	**DP**
Bowe	.962	92	197	5	8	3
Christian	1.000	2	1	0	0	0
Duran	.908	77	114	5	12	1
Ewing	1.000	8	11	2	0	0
Hunt	.947	12	16	2	1	1

Lutz	.964	28	27	0	1	0
Matthews	.914	22	30	2	3	0
Means	1.000	11	21	0	0	0
Muller	.966	41	81	3	3	0
Rodriguez	.891	22	39	2	5	0
Selsky	.992	62	113	8	1	3
Smith	.973	54	106	2	3	2

DAYTON DRAGONS　　　　　　　　　　　　　　　LOW CLASS A

MIDWEST LEAGUE

Batting	B-T	HT	WT	DOB	AVG	vLH	vRH	G	AB	R	H	2B	3B	HR	RBI	BB	HBP	SH	SF	SO	SB	CS	SLG	OBP
Arias, Junior	R-R	6-2	178	1-9-92	.208	.258	.190	97	361	52	75	11	3	7	35	20	3	3	1	96	28	7	.313	.255
Bowe, Theo	L-R	5-9	160	8-5-90	.186	.364	.160	24	86	8	16	1	2	0	2	12	0	2	0	19	12	1	.244	.286
Buckley, Sean	R-R	6-4	220	9-3-89	.244	.293	.231	116	426	46	104	28	1	14	68	33	7	0	3	139	1	2	.413	.307
Cairo, Miguel	R-R	6-1	225	5-4-74	.000	.000	.000	3	10	0	0	0	0	0	0	0	0	1	0	2	0	0	.000	.000
Dailey, Brandon	R-R	5-10	170	2-10-92	.191	.219	.177	26	94	10	18	6	0	1	7	6	0	2	0	22	2	1	.287	.240
Diaz, Sammy	R-R	5-11	170	2-28-91	.266	.136	.306	27	94	16	25	3	1	1	16	13	0	2	1	18	6	0	.351	.352
Dickinson, Spencer	R-R	5-10	180	9-3-89	.143	.000	.189	16	49	4	7	0	0	0	3	10	0	0	0	12	1	1	.143	.288
Ewing, James	R-R	6-0	190	10-27-86	.182	.125	.235	9	33	1	6	2	0	0	1	5	0	0	0	4	1	1	.242	.289
Gonzalez, Yovan	R-R	5-10	186	11-11-89	.230	.208	.237	92	317	37	73	12	0	5	42	19	1	5	5	55	2	3	.315	.272
Maddox, Robert	L-L	6-2	195	10-18-88	.143	.000	.182	3	14	1	2	0	0	0	1	0	0	0	0	5	0	0	.143	.143
Muller, Kurt	R-R	5-10	170	7-7-89	.329	.278	.345	19	76	17	25	3	0	4	10	4	7	0	0	10	7	2	.526	.414
O'Shea, Nick	R-R	6-3	220	1-29-89	.208	.333	.168	74	265	24	55	12	0	4	28	7	1	2	0	68	0	0	.298	.231
Perez, Juan	L-R	6-0	180	11-1-91	.253	.266	.250	125	482	64	122	27	8	9	51	51	11	7	4	88	24	14	.398	.336
Rodriguez, Yorman	R-R	6-2	184	8-15-92	.271	.255	.276	65	258	35	70	17	3	6	44	12	2	2	2	61	7	5	.430	.307
Selsky, Steve	R-R	6-1	205	7-20-89	.281	.266	.287	59	228	27	64	11	3	3	26	12	3	1	2	49	5	1	.395	.322
Sierra, Jefry	R-R	5-10	165	4-16-90	.241	.346	.193	71	257	33	62	7	2	0	27	6	0	1	2	62	16	7	.284	.257
Silva, Juan	L-L	6-0	190	1-8-91	.271	.250	.277	118	380	58	103	24	3	8	42	69	3	5	8	109	25	12	.413	.380
Stubbs, Drew	R-R	6-4	205	10-4-84	.100	.000	.125	3	10	0	1	0	0	0	1	1	0	0	0	2	0	0	.100	.182
Terry, Joe	L-R	5-11	185	12-18-89	.255	.119	.286	83	321	44	82	15	4	6	36	23	5	2	6	51	22	7	.383	.310
Vicioso, Danny	R-R	6-0	190	10-27-88	.234	.375	.161	29	94	6	22	6	0	0	4	7	1	0	1	24	1	1	.298	.291
Votto, Joey	L-R	6-3	225	9-10-83	.200	.000	.200	3	5	1	1	0	0	0	1	3	0	0	1	1	0	0	.200	.444
Waldrop, Kyle	L-L	6-3	190	12-22-89	.284	.227	.299	117	416	59	118	21	6	8	50	38	4	7	4	77	10	6	.421	.346
Wrenn, Taylor	L-R	5-11	175	12-22-89	.400	.500	.375	3	10	2	4	1	0	0	3	0	0	0	0	1	0	0	.500	.400
Wright, Ryan	R-R	6-1	195	12-3-89	.285	.274	.289	102	389	53	111	27	6	5	50	32	3	2	2	51	14	1	.424	.343

Pitching	B-T	HT	WT	DOB	W	L	ERA	G	GS	CG	SV	IP	H	R	ER	HR	BB	SO	AVG	vLH	vRH	K/9	BB/9
Allen, James	R-R	6-1	197	11-20-89	8	4	3.72	33	11	0	0	114	99	51	47	6	32	95	.231	.216	.248	7.52	2.53
Bray, Bill	L-L	6-3	230	6-5-83	1	0	0.00	2	0	0	0	3	0	0	0	1	4	.000	.000	.000	13.50	3.38
Contreras, Carlos	R-R	6-0	165	1-8-91	0	1	3.20	40	0	0	16	51	29	22	18	6	19	51	.158	.195	.125	9.06	3.38
Dennhardt, Mike	R-R	6-1	205	6-1-90	2	3	2.27	29	0	0	1	48	40	16	12	3	6	28	.215	.234	.196	5.29	1.13
French, Justice	R-R	6-4	215	8-2-89	3	2	3.31	6	6	0	0	33	33	14	12	3	9	31	.264	.315	.225	8.54	2.48
Gerson, Starlin	R-R	6-4	175	8-26-88	6	8	3.76	24	24	0	0	132	142	68	55	21	28	100	.267	.270	.264	6.84	1.91
Gonzalez, Carlos	R-R	6-1	195	6-12-90	3	3	3.14	20	6	0	1	52	46	24	18	4	19	47	.238	.286	.182	8.19	3.31
Green, Cole	R-R	6-0	220	5-4-89	1	0	8.68	19	0	0	0	28	30	30	27	3	22	17	.270	.240	.295	5.46	7.07
Guillon, Ismael	L-L	6-3	185	2-13-92	2	0	2.55	4	4	0	0	25	22	8	7	2	7	27	.247	.200	.278	9.85	2.55
Jensen, Dan	R-R	6-8	225	7-25-89	7	10	5.00	37	8	0	1	90	102	64	50	8	37	49	.273	.293	.254	4.90	3.70
Johnson, Jacob	R-R	6-4	215	9-12-90	2	5	5.36	18	18	0	0	89	111	68	53	12	21	60	.293	.265	.327	6.07	2.12
Kemp, Ryan	R-R	6-4	210	9-26-90	3	5	3.99	46	0	0	5	65	76	34	29	4	24	49	.290	.294	.286	6.75	3.31
Kiel, Ryan	L-L	6-4	230	6-26-87	0	0	0.00	2	0	0	0	5	3	0	0	0	4	1	.167	.200	.125	7.20	0.00
Lucas, Sean	R-L	6-2	200	4-6-89	0	0	2.35	5	0	0	0	8	10	4	2	1	2	5	.286	.250	.333	5.87	2.35
Masset, Nick	R-R	6-4	235	5-17-82	0	0	0.00	1	1	0	0	1	1	0	0	0	0	0	.250	.333	.000	0.00	0.00
McMyne, Kyle	R-R	5-11	220	10-18-89	3	2	2.59	18	0	0	2	24	20	7	7	1	8	22	.215	.289	.146	8.14	2.96
Miller, Erik	R-R	6-3	210	4-9-90	0	3	14.18	9	0	0	0	13	26	24	21	0	13	10	.433	.500	.382	6.75	8.78
Moran, Jimmy	R-R	6-1	180	6-7-90	2	3	4.81	24	0	0	0	39	46	28	21	2	19	31	.288	.325	.247	7.09	4.35
Mugarian, Wes	R-R	6-5	185	9-18-91	3	3	5.55	12	6	0	0	49	59	38	30	7	16	43	.296	.327	.267	7.95	2.96
Muhammad, El'Hajj	R-R	6-2	200	7-7-91	0	3	3.23	38	0	0	2	53	47	20	19	6	27	48	.246	.237	.255	8.15	4.58
O'Rear, Lucas	L-R	6-7	240	11-24-88	1	2	5.54	30	0	0	0	50	57	40	31	5	33	41	.288	.297	.278	7.33	5.90
Pinckard, Brooks	L-R	6-1	190	8-15-88	0	0	0.00	6	0	0	2	10	4	0	0	0	11	.114	.056	.176	9.90	0.00
Quezada, Radhames	R-R	6-2	175	7-6-90	5	9	3.35	22	22	0	0	99	88	47	37	10	56	74	.248	.242	.246	6.70	5.07
Robles, Tanner	L-L	6-4	205	2-24-89	5	5	4.45	16	16	0	0	85	87	50	42	5	33	57	.266	.252	.274	6.04	3.49
Stephenson, Robert	R-R	6-2	190	2-24-93	2	4	4.19	8	8	0	0	34	32	23	16	4	15	35	.246	.240	.255	9.17	3.93
Tuttle, Daniel	R-R	6-1	175	8-21-90	1	3	5.03	8	8	0	0	34	35	23	19	3	12	20	.273	.338	.193	5.29	3.18

Fielding

Catcher	PCT	G	PO	A	E	DP	PB
Gonzalez	.989	92	629	83	8	12	6
O'Shea	.989	50	309	42	4	5	10
Vicioso	.909	2	10	0	1	0	0

First Base	PCT	G	PO	A	E	DP
Buckley	.990	97	824	62	9	71
Maddox	1.000	2	23	0	0	1
O'Shea	.990	23	178	18	2	16
Vicioso	.995	21	165	17	1	10

Votto	1.000	3	7	3	0	2

Second Base	PCT	G	PO	A	E	DP
Dailey	.913	7	9	12	2	3
Diaz	.969	5	12	19	1	5
Dickinson	1.000	4	4	11	0	3
Ewing	1.000	1	0	3	0	1
Terry	.950	31	47	105	8	17
Wrenn	1.000	2	4	8	0	0
Wright	.977	90	164	296	11	47

Third Base	PCT	G	PO	A	E	DP
Arias	.877	95	82	174	36	12
Cairo	1.000	2	0	1	0	0
Dailey	.926	12	3	22	2	1
Diaz	.875	13	15	20	5	2
Dickinson	.667	3	1	3	2	1
Ewing	1.000	4	3	7	0	0
Terry	.912	13	11	20	3	0

CINCINNATI REDS

Shortstop	PCT	G	PO	A	E	DP
Dailey	.813	7	4	22	6	0
Diaz	.897	8	16	19	4	3
Ewing	1.000	3	5	6	0	2
Perez	.943	122	212	348	34	81
Wrenn	1.000	1	1	1	0	0

Outfield	PCT	G	PO	A	E	DP
Bowe	.985	22	66	1	1	0
Buckley	.875	5	7	0	1	0
Diaz	—	1	0	0	0	0
Dickinson	1.000	8	12	1	0	0
Muller	1.000	19	52	0	0	1

Rodriguez	.969	58	92	2	3	0
Selsky	.990	48	100	1	1	1
Sierra	.965	64	129	9	5	3
Silva	.987	98	222	7	3	4
Stubbs	1.000	3	4	0	0	1
Waldrop	.974	100	182	9	5	1

AZL REDS
ARIZONA LEAGUE

ROOKIE

CINCINNATI REDS

Batting	B-T	HT	WT	DOB	AVG	vLH	vRH	G	AB	R	H	2B	3B	HR	RBI	BB	HBP	SH	SF	SO	SB	CS	SLG	OBP
Aldazoro, Argenis	L-L	6-2	160	9-17-92	.213	.259	.203	43	160	20	34	7	4	5	17	6	1	0	0	38	3	3	.400	.246
Arias, Brayan	R-R	6-2	180	11-27-91	.295	.154	.315	31	105	16	31	5	1	1	16	3	3	1	2	20	4	1	.390	.327
Bueno, Ronald	B-R	5-10	154	10-4-92	.417	.000	.556	5	12	3	5	1	1	0	3	4	0	1	0	1	1	.667	.563
Estevez, Wilfrel	R-R	6-0	177	8-11-90	.269	.174	.292	38	119	15	32	8	0	2	21	5	1	0	1	22	3	2	.387	.302
Flores, Ponceano	R-R	6-1	182	4-6-90	.273	.200	.294	8	22	7	6	0	1	0	0	1	2	0	0	6	1	1	.364	.360
Guzman, Aldi	R-R	6-4	235	2-20-93	.100	.250	.063	7	20	0	2	0	0	0	0	1	0	0	0	14	1	0	.100	.143
Hargreaves, Elliott	L-L	5-10	175	4-1-94	.220	.500	.171	12	41	5	9	2	1	0	3	4	0	0	1	7	3	2	.317	.283
Kennelly, Josh	R-R	6-2	180	2-9-94	.243	.429	.200	14	37	7	9	3	0	1	5	8	1	0	0	11	0	0	.405	.391
Lopez, Jhimmy	R-R	6-0	216	8-19-92	.227	.250	.224	30	110	11	25	10	0	2	18	9	0	0	0	27	0	1	.373	.286
Lutz, Donald	L-R	6-3	235	2-6-89	.643	1.000	.545	4	14	3	9	2	2	0	5	3	0	0	0	4	0	0	1.071	.706
Matthews, Adam	R-R	6-1	195	4-10-90	.325	.176	.350	32	117	21	38	7	2	2	19	16	1	1	1	24	2	2	.470	.407
Morillo, Julio	R-R	5-11	176	12-27-92	.157	.125	.163	15	51	3	8	1	0	0	4	1	0	0	0	3	0	0	.176	.173
Ortiz, Jose	R-R	5-11	205	6-11-94	.359	.333	.367	13	39	10	14	5	1	0	6	8	1	0	1	10	3	0	.538	.469
Paula, Daniel	R-R	5-11	180	11-22-92	.341	.250	.351	25	85	13	29	6	1	0	16	7	0	0	0	8	4	3	.435	.391
Peterson, Brent	R-R	6-0	180	10-20-92	.291	.227	.303	38	141	28	41	4	3	1	15	15	5	0	1	29	15	5	.383	.377
Phipps, Denis	R-R	6-3	210	7-22-85	.400	.333	.412	5	20	6	8	0	1	2	5	0	1	0	0	5	0	0	.800	.429
Rachal, Avain	R-R	6-0	195	2-11-94	.297	.143	.317	33	118	27	35	6	4	0	9	12	1	0	1	24	5	1	.415	.364
Rahier, Tanner	R-R	6-2	205	10-12-93	.192	.172	.195	51	193	21	37	9	1	4	30	21	0	1	4	43	5	2	.311	.266
Reynoso, Jonathan	R-R	6-3	177	1-7-93	.311	.387	.296	50	190	37	59	7	3	2	16	6	1	4	4	23	30	9	.411	.328
Rodriguez, Henry	B-R	5-10	150	2-9-90	.235	.250	.231	5	17	1	4	1	0	0	1	1	0	0	0	2	0	0	.294	.278
Valaika, Chris	R-R	6-0	215	8-14-85	.100	.500	.000	3	10	1	1	0	0	1	1	1	0	0	0	0	0	0	.400	.182
Valdelamar, Jose	R-R	5-11	186	1-10-90	.161	.000	.185	19	62	8	10	3	0	2	10	4	0	0	0	25	1	0	.306	.212
Valor, Humberto	R-R	6-1	185	9-9-92	.263	.280	.260	44	156	20	41	6	1	0	16	8	5	4	0	24	13	5	.314	.320
Washington, Ty	R-R	5-9	160	9-1-93	.270	.167	.294	17	63	9	17	0	2	2	9	9	0	2	2	12	6	2	.429	.351

Pitching	B-T	HT	WT	DOB	W	L	ERA	G	GS	CG	SV	IP	H	R	ER	HR	BB	SO	AVG	vLH	vRH	K/9	BB/9
Clarke, Mitch	R-L	6-2	220	8-29-90	0	0	4.50	1	1	0	0	2	1	1	1	0	0	3	.143	.000	.250	13.50	0.00
Covington, Vaughn	L-R	6-5	210	11-15-93	0	2	7.88	15	3	0	0	24	31	31	21	2	22	21	.292	.293	.292	7.88	8.25
De Los Santos, Abel	R-R	6-1	215	5-17-92	1	1	2.86	17	0	0	4	22	20	10	7	1	12	36	.233	.231	.234	14.73	4.91
Diaz, Pedro	R-R	6-0	180	4-29-93	1	6	5.72	14	12	0	0	46	60	34	29	3	14	43	.303	.333	.282	8.47	2.76
Fennell, Ryan	R-R	6-4	220	4-23-90	0	0	0.00	5	0	0	0	6	3	1	0	0	3	1	.143	.182	.100	4.50	4.50
Garrett, Amir	L-L	6-5	210	5-3-92	0	2	5.79	7	5	0	0	14	14	14	9	1	12	13	.255	.267	.250	8.36	7.71
Guzman, Jose	R-R	6-3	178	9-8-91	0	2	5.71	11	1	0	0	17	11	11	11	3	9	17	.180	.088	.296	8.83	4.67
Housey, Joey	R-R	6-3	190	10-15-89	0	0	3.09	11	0	0	0	12	10	6	4	1	3	15	.227	.417	.156	11.57	2.31
Howell, Blaine	L-L	5-11	210	10-2-88	0	0	18.00	1	0	0	0	1	2	3	2	1	1	1	.333	.500	.250	9.00	9.00
Joyce, Chris	L-L	6-0	195	12-25-89	1	0	0.00	4	0	0	1	7	3	0	0	0	1	7	.125	.200	.105	14.85	1.35
Lewis-Walker, Robert	R-R	6-3	195	4-7-93	0	2	5.30	16	0	0	0	19	28	17	11	2	5	18	.350	.343	.356	8.68	2.41
Masset, Nick	R-R	6-4	235	5-17-82	0	0	0.00	2	2	0	0	2	0	0	0	0	0	5	.000	.000	.000	22.50	0.00
McCaffrey, Richard	L-L	6-1	205	12-31-90	1	0	4.44	11	0	0	0	24	31	14	12	0	4	25	.304	.313	.300	9.25	1.48
Moran, Luke	R-R	6-2	200	3-6-92	2	3	4.75	14	5	0	0	36	41	24	19	4	9	42	.279	.317	.250	10.50	2.25
Moscot, Jon	R-R	6-4	205	8-15-91	0	1	0.00	2	1	0	0	2	3	1	0	0	5	1	.273	.333	.250	3.86	19.29
Muehring, Austin	R-R	6-3	185	5-18-91	0	1	7.53	15	0	0	0	14	20	15	12	3	14	10	.333	.429	.250	6.28	8.79
Peralta, Wandy	L-L	6-1	205	7-27-91	3	6	6.55	14	4	0	0	45	62	47	33	3	22	40	.307	.220	.343	7.94	4.37
Pineda, Lorgi	R-R	6-1	173	10-31-91	0	1	9.31	10	4	0	0	10	14	15	10	1	9	12	.341	.389	.304	11.17	8.38
Redan, Ibrahin	R-R	6-3	185	12-11-93	0	0	10.80	5	0	0	0	5	7	8	6	1	5	3	.304	.333	.286	5.40	9.00
Salter, Austin	R-R	6-4	205	9-5-91	3	1	2.15	15	3	0	0	38	32	17	9	2	11	38	.218	.229	.208	9.08	2.63
Saunders, Mike	R-R	6-2	210	3-7-91	3	0	1.47	13	2	0	1	31	32	10	5	0	16	23	.267	.318	.237	6.75	4.70
Stephens, Jackson	R-R	6-3	205	5-11-94	1	1	4.64	20	0	0	2	21	23	12	11	2	3	22	.274	.250	.292	9.28	1.27
Taveras, Werleen	R-R	5-11	200	11-9-90	0	0	9.00	3	0	0	0	4	4	4	4	0	4	4	.267	.250	.273	9.00	9.00
Tomko, Brett	R-R	6-4	220	4-7-73	0	1	47.25	1	1	0	0	1	9	8	7	0	0	1	.692	.333	.800	6.75	0.00
Travieso, Nick	R-R	6-2	215	1-31-94	0	2	4.71	8	8	0	0	21	20	11	11	3	5	14	.250	.231	.268	6.00	2.14
Williams, Jose	R-R	6-5	200	2-17-91	1	4	5.60	13	7	0	0	45	48	32	28	2	20	22	.274	.314	.248	4.40	4.00

Fielding

Catcher	PCT	G	PO	A	E	DP	PB
Kennelly	.980	12	91	7	2	1	1
Morillo	1.000	13	105	10	0	0	5
Ortiz	.955	9	74	10	4	1	1
Paula	.985	23	177	16	3	1	10

	PCT	G	PO	A	E	DP
Kennelly	—	1	0	0	0	0
Lopez	.961	27	207	12	9	15
Lutz	.833	1	5	0	1	0
Morillo	1.000	2	2	0	0	0
Rachal	.933	3	28	0	2	3
Valor	.667	1	1	1	1	0

	PCT	G	PO	A	E	DP
Rachal	.899	23	36	53	10	9
Rahier	—	1	0	0	0	0
Rodriguez	1.000	1	4	2	0	1
Valaika	1.000	1	0	4	0	0
Valor	.931	13	18	36	4	5
Washington	.909	14	15	25	4	5

First Base	PCT	G	PO	A	E	DP
Aldazoro	.986	8	67	6	1	5
Estevez	.977	12	83	1	2	6
Flores	.982	8	51	4	1	5
Guzman	.947	2	16	2	1	1

Second Base	PCT	G	PO	A	E	DP
Lopez	—	1	0	0	0	0
Matthews	1.000	1	2	0	0	0
Peterson	.939	11	23	23	3	5

Third Base	PCT	G	PO	A	E	DP
Bueno	1.000	2	0	1	0	0
Lopez	—	1	0	0	0	0
Rahier	.888	47	45	98	18	7

Rodriguez	1.000	3	0	7	0 0
Valaika	1.000	2	2	2	0 0
Valor	.875	6	1	6	1 0

Shortstop	PCT	G	PO	A	E DP
Bueno	.900	3	1	8	1 1
Peterson	.879	27	43	73	16 15
Rachal	—	1	0	0	0 0

Valor	.959	26	26	67	4	11
Washington	.917	5	4	7	1	0

Outfield	PCT	G	PO	A	E	DP
Aldazoro	.877	31	48	2	7	0
Arias	.973	25	34	2	1	1
Estevez	.971	21	33	0	1	0
Guzman	1.000	1	2	0	0	0

Hargreaves	1.000	10	15	2	0 0
Lutz	1.000	2	0	1	0 0
Matthews	.894	25	39	3	5 2
Phipps	1.000	4	5	1	0 0
Reynoso	.972	50	102	4	3 1
Valdelamar	.810	14	16	1	4 0

BILLINGS MUSTANGS   ROOKIE
PIONEER LEAGUE

Batting	B-T	HT	WT	DOB	AVG	vLH	vRH	G	AB	R	H	2B	3B	HR	RBI	BB	HBP	SH	SF	SO	SB	CS	SLG	OBP
Amaral, Beau	L-L	5-11	170	2-11-91	.295	.255	.306	57	234	55	69	10	3	1	24	17	6	0	2	27	20	2	.376	.355
Dailey, Brandon	R-R	5-10	170	2-10-92	.308	.239	.336	46	159	29	49	10	5	5	24	9	3	3	1	48	5	1	.528	.355
Diaz, Sammy	B-R	5-11	170	2-28-91	.219	.188	.229	17	64	10	14	3	0	0	6	7	2	1	0	7	0	1	.266	.315
Dickinson, Spencer	R-R	5-10	180	9-3-89	.365	.333	.378	15	52	13	19	4	0	1	9	9	0	1	1	8	1	2	.500	.452
Gelalich, Jeff	L-R	6-1	180	3-16-91	.244	.056	.275	35	127	27	31	7	2	2	9	14	4	0	1	42	4	1	.378	.336
Gomez, Wagner	B-R	6-1	180	12-2-91	.201	.094	.235	48	134	19	27	6	1	3	21	21	3	2	0	40	1	1	.328	.323
Lentz, Matt	L-R	6-3	220	1-10-89	.240	.125	.263	29	96	11	23	7	2	1	12	5	3	0	2	37	2	1	.385	.292
Maddox, Robert	L-L	6-2	195	10-18-88	.251	.341	.226	53	187	32	47	5	1	13	37	20	2	0	2	42	3	0	.497	.327
Matthews, Jon	R-R	6-1	195	4-6-91	.179	.222	.158	37	112	18	20	2	2	1	12	11	2	0	1	31	18	4	.259	.262
May, Brennan	R-R	5-10	190	9-25-90	.323	.111	.409	8	31	3	10	5	1	0	3	1	0	0	0	16	0	1	.548	.344
Mejias-Brean, Seth	R-R	6-2	210	4-5-91	.313	.333	.308	46	179	35	56	12	2	8	40	21	2	0	1	29	6	0	.536	.389
Morillo, Julio	R-R	5-11	176	12-27-92	.167	.250	.139	16	48	5	8	2	0	0	2	3	1	1	0	9	0	0	.208	.231
Pigott, Daniel	R-R	6-2	205	10-4-89	.308	.273	.330	38	146	22	45	8	2	3	31	6	4	0	2	28	2	1	.452	.348
Ramirez, Robert	L-R	6-1	170	7-19-92	.232	.275	.215	50	181	23	42	6	3	2	28	11	2	0	2	47	11	4	.331	.281
Rosa, Gabriel	R-R	6-4	185	7-2-93	.179	.158	.186	21	78	8	14	6	0	0	5	1	0	0	1	25	2	0	.256	.188
Sanchez, Carlos	L-L	5-10	175	4-4-91	.308	.284	.318	61	237	37	73	15	12	8	55	13	3	2	4	41	2	0	.574	.346
Sosa, Fray	R-R	6-1	205	8-29-89	.253	.269	.245	25	79	15	20	8	0	0	14	6	5	1	0	11	1	0	.354	.344
Vincej, Zach	R-R	6-0	165	5-1-91	.336	.394	.318	38	143	27	48	10	1	0	17	9	7	0	4	23	4	4	.434	.393
Winker, Jesse	L-L	6-3	195	8-17-93	.338	.333	.340	62	228	42	77	16	3	5	35	40	4	2	1	50	1	3	.500	.443
Wrenn, Taylor	L-R	5-11	175	12-22-89	.274	.278	.274	35	113	17	31	5	1	0	12	12	3	1	0	14	3	4	.336	.359

Pitching	B-T	HT	WT	DOB	W	L	ERA	G	GS	CG	SV	IP	H	R	ER	HR	BB	SO	AVG	vLH	vRH	K/9	BB/9
Adames, Jesus	R-R	6-4	235	1-25-91	1	0	4.39	18	0	0	1	27	25	16	13	4	14	25	.250	.244	.254	8.44	4.73
Amezcua, Tony	R-R	6-0	185	5-27-91	3	5	4.65	15	2	0	0	50	46	38	26	5	24	48	.231	.233	.229	8.58	4.29
Becker, Nolan	R-L	6-6	225	6-13-91	0	1	8.44	13	0	0	0	16	27	22	15	0	14	20	.380	.364	.388	11.25	7.88
Bender, Joel	L-L	6-4	205	8-3-91	3	4	6.75	15	5	0	0	52	71	46	39	3	25	42	.324	.264	.354	7.27	4.33
Chacin, Alejandro	R-R	6-0	200	6-24-93	4	2	3.41	20	0	0	1	29	28	16	11	2	15	29	.262	.207	.282	9.00	4.66
Cisco, Drew	L-R	6-0	185	7-29-91	4	1	3.39	15	15	0	0	58	60	27	22	4	7	45	.267	.295	.239	6.94	1.08
Fennell, Ryan	R-R	6-4	220	4-23-90	0	0	19.29	2	1	0	0	2	5	5	5	1	2	3	.455	.000	.625	11.57	7.71
Garrett, Amir	L-L	6-5	210	5-3-92	0	0	0.00	2	2	0	0	6	4	0	0	0	1	5	.211	.333	.154	7.50	1.50
Gonzalez, Carlos	R-R	6-1	195	6-12-90	1	0	0.00	1	0	0	0	4	0	0	0	0	0	4	.000	.000	.000	0.00	0.00
Guillon, Ismael	L-L	6-3	185	2-13-92	4	1	2.29	11	10	0	0	51	39	16	13	1	24	63	.210	.348	.164	11.12	4.24
Housey, Joey	R-R	6-3	190	10-15-89	0	2	27.00	2	0	0	0	2	4	5	5	0	1	1	.444	.667	.333	5.40	5.40
Klimesh, Ben	R-R	6-2	215	5-14-90	0	3	6.99	13	0	0	1	28	38	27	22	5	13	38	.319	.364	.293	12.07	4.13
Langfield, Dan	R-R	6-2	196	1-21-91	3	0	2.68	15	5	0	0	37	27	12	11	1	17	54	.197	.235	.174	13.14	4.14
Lucas, Sean	R-L	6-2	200	4-6-89	3	1	2.25	20	0	0	6	24	20	8	6	1	3	24	.222	.229	.218	9.00	1.13
McCaffrey, Richard	L-L	6-1	205	12-31-90	0	0	3.86	1	0	0	0	2	5	2	1	0	1	2	.500	1.000	.444	7.71	3.86
Miller, Erik	R-R	6-3	210	4-9-90	1	1	9.20	16	0	0	1	15	15	16	15	1	18	16	.278	.267	.282	9.82	11.05
Moran, Jimmy	R-R	6-1	180	6-7-90	1	1	2.37	18	0	0	3	19	19	6	5	0	5	22	.257	.440	.163	10.42	2.37
Moscot, Jon	R-R	6-4	205	8-15-91	0	1	2.88	10	10	0	0	25	19	11	8	2	6	26	.213	.293	.146	9.36	2.16
Mugarian, Wes	R-R	6-0	185	9-18-91	1	1	3.21	3	3	0	0	14	16	6	5	2	2	7	.286	.296	.276	4.50	1.29
O'Rear, Lucas	L-R	6-7	240	11-24-88	1	0	3.38	2	1	0	0	5	6	2	2	0	1	0	.273	.308	.222	0.00	1.69
Ramos, Carlos	R-R	6-0	176	11-4-90	1	1	7.12	18	0	0	0	30	43	29	24	0	12	30	.323	.308	.333	8.90	3.56
Remer, Jordan	L-L	6-2	210	3-19-90	0	0	5.50	21	0	0	0	18	14	11	11	0	19	19	.219	.240	.205	9.50	9.50
Romano, Sal	L-R	6-2	220	10-12-93	5	6	5.32	15	15	0	0	64	74	45	38	1	23	52	.288	.337	.256	7.27	3.22
Routt, Nick	L-L	6-4	215	8-28-90	1	1	4.76	18	0	0	0	23	22	16	12	0	17	22	.253	.182	.296	8.74	6.75
Salter, Austin	R-R	6-4	205	9-5-91	1	0	7.11	3	0	0	0	6	8	5	5	1	4	8	.308	.222	.500	11.37	5.68
Saunders, Mike	R-R	6-1	200	3-7-91	0	0	7.59	5	0	0	0	11	17	9	9	1	3	8	.354	.348	.360	6.75	2.53
Stephenson, Robert	R-R	6-2	190	2-24-93	1	0	2.05	7	7	0	0	31	22	11	7	2	8	37	.195	.200	.190	10.86	2.35
Wiley, Mo	R-R	6-4	230	12-11-89	3	2	2.45	17	0	0	9	18	13	6	5	3	6	26	.200	.333	.105	12.76	2.95

Fielding

Catcher	PCT	G	PO	A	E	DP	PB
Gomez	.972	45	347	37	11	2	13
Morillo	.976	16	146	16	4	1	1
Sosa	.964	24	164	26	7	2	9

First Base	PCT	G	PO	A	E	DP
Maddox	.971	23	189	12	6	17
Sanchez	.991	58	494	32	5	44

Second Base	PCT	G	PO	A	E	DP
Dailey	.940	20	25	54	5	8
Diaz	1.000	2	5	5	0	1
Ramirez	.938	25	38	67	7	11

Wrenn	.957	31	63	94	7	23

Third Base	PCT	G	PO	A	E	DP
Dickinson	.667	2	1	1	1	0
Mejias-Brean	.904	45	29	94	13	7
Ramirez	.930	20	10	43	4	4
Rosa	.829	11	9	20	6	1

Shortstop	PCT	G	PO	A	E	DP
Dailey	.905	24	40	46	9	9
Diaz	.938	12	19	41	4	8
Rosa	.894	9	15	27	5	6
Vincej	.974	37	52	100	4	20

Wrenn	1.000	1	2	3	0	1

Outfield	PCT	G	PO	A	E	DP
Amaral	.960	56	91	6	4	4
Diaz	.909	4	10	0	1	0
Dickinson	.958	14	20	3	1	1
Gelalich	.933	34	38	4	3	0
Lentz	.786	16	11	0	3	0
Matthews	.907	28	46	3	5	1
May	.900	5	9	0	1	0
Pigott	1.000	28	24	0	0	0
Rosa	—	1	0	0	0	0
Winker	.950	53	74	2	4	0

DOMINICAN SUMMER LEAGUE

ROOKIE

Batting	B-T	HT	WT	DOB	AVG	vLH	vRH	G	AB	R	H	2B	3B	HR	RBI	BB	HBP	SH	SF	SO	SB	CS	SLG	OBP
Aquino, Aristides	R-R	6-4	190	4-22-94	.197	.217	.190	65	239	28	47	11	0	3	26	24	4	3	4	65	5	8	.280	.277
Ariza, Jorge	L-R	6-0	185	7-20-91	.178	.200	.175	19	45	6	8	2	0	0	3	4	3	1	2	8	0	0	.222	.278
Baez, Ariel	R-R	6-0	183	1-22-91	.242	.229	.246	47	161	12	39	9	2	1	27	16	3	1	2	37	4	1	.342	.319
Bueno, Ronald	B-R	5-10	154	10-4-92	.233	.281	.216	33	120	25	28	4	3	2	10	25	2	2	0	14	12	3	.367	.374
Burgos, Deyvi	L-L	6-2	185	7-16-92	.187	.205	.181	53	171	19	32	6	2	1	17	27	3	6	3	46	6	4	.263	.304
Duarte, Jose	R-R	6-2	190	4-23-93	.195	.156	.210	40	113	14	22	1	3	0	10	15	2	4	0	39	4	1	.257	.300
Farinez, Rusbel	R-R	5-9	150	4-27-92	.256	.283	.245	58	223	35	57	9	2	0	32	28	3	3	3	34	11	6	.314	.342
Florentino, Oviel	B-R	6-1	160	2-3-94	.232	.229	.234	41	142	22	33	2	1	0	16	24	2	2	1	39	3	3	.261	.349
Garcia, Kevin W	R-R	6-1	177	6-19-93	.264	.226	.274	66	239	35	63	13	8	1	44	41	8	3	8	40	9	5	.397	.378
Mendez, Miguel	L-R	5-10	160	4-16-93	.299	.257	.310	51	164	35	49	5	4	1	14	27	5	3	0	13	9	5	.396	.413
Raga, Jose	R-R	5-11	190	11-20-93	.129	.136	.127	29	85	6	11	1	0	0	5	5	3	1	0	17	1	0	.141	.204
2-team total (5 Diamondbacks/Reds)					.139	—	—	34	101	7	14	1	0	0	5	6	3	1	0	21	1	0	.149	.209
Rodriguez, Johan	R-R	6-0	165	11-8-90	.208	.125	.250	6	24	3	5	0	0	0	2	2	0	0	0	2	1	0	.208	.269
Soto, Junior	R-R	5-11	188	9-27-91	.240	.467	.183	21	75	10	18	2	1	1	11	13	1	1	1	10	1	1	.333	.356
Suero, Jonathan	B-R	6-0	170	2-28-93	.274	.255	.280	59	212	38	58	5	2	2	14	25	9	5	3	50	17	10	.344	.369
Valdelamar, Jose	R-R	5-11	186	1-10-90	.250	.667	.111	4	12	2	3	1	0	0	1	0	0	0	0	2	0	0	.333	.250
Valor, Geraldo	R-R	5-10	155	5-2-94	.217	.273	.197	26	83	17	18	1	1	0	6	11	2	2	1	16	5	2	.253	.320
2-team total (31 Diamondbacks/Reds)					.238	—	—	57	185	26	44	4	1	0	18	26	5	3	4	31	11	4	.270	.341

Pitching	B-T	HT	WT	DOB	W	L	ERA	G	GS	CG	SV	IP	H	R	ER	HR	BB	SO	AVG	vLH	vRH	K/9	BB/9
Beard, Eliezer	R-R	6-4	202	4-23-91	0	0	2.70	1	1	0	0	3	4	1	1	0	2	3	.286	.400	.222	8.10	5.40
2-team total (8 Diamondbacks/Reds)					2	5	2.13	9	7	0	0	38	39	17	9	0	11	35	—	—	—	8.29	2.61
Bohorquez, Fabian	R-R	6-2	198	11-28-90	0	0	2.64	16	0	0	1	31	22	12	9	0	16	28	.198	.209	.191	8.22	4.70
Cantalizo, Eury	R-R	6-2	185	9-24-91	7	2	1.50	20	3	0	1	54	37	12	9	0	12	55	.189	.200	.181	9.17	2.00
Castellano, Josue	L-L	6-0	190	1-13-92	5	2	3.51	25	0	0	10	26	29	15	10	0	10	27	.287	.636	.244	9.47	3.51
Damian, Pedro	R-R	6-1	170	11-29-92	1	2	4.20	10	10	0	0	30	24	22	14	1	23	26	.222	.239	.210	7.80	6.90
2-team total (3 Diamondbacks/Reds)					1	3	3.27	13	13	0	0	44	33	28	16	1	32	43	—	—	—	8.80	6.55
De Sousa, Jose	L-L	6-0	180	5-15-92	2	3	2.03	21	0	0	2	31	23	18	7	1	16	32	.197	.231	.192	9.29	4.65
Encarnacion, Carlos	R-R	6-3	180	11-15-93	1	1	11.42	14	0	0	0	17	22	27	22	1	29	14	.297	.256	.343	7.27	15.06
Marquez, Soid F	R-R	6-3	165	1-3-95	0	3	5.64	9	9	0	0	30	31	24	19	2	13	17	.267	.256	.273	5.04	3.86
Martinez, Jairo	L-L	6-1	175	3-21-93	6	1	3.32	17	0	0	2	38	37	20	14	2	16	38	.257	.364	.237	9.00	3.79
Martinez, Juan	L-L	6-2	175	7-15-92	2	1	2.42	18	6	0	1	52	47	20	14	0	20	52	.246	.214	.252	9.00	3.46
Morillo, JR	L-L	5-11	167	10-30-91	2	1	3.33	16	0	0	1	46	42	20	17	0	13	39	.255	.200	.264	7.63	2.54
Parra, Jesus	R-R	5-11	175	4-14-91	4	0	0.83	13	0	0	2	22	14	3	2	0	7	20	.184	.138	.213	8.31	2.91
Patino, Carlos	R-R	6-1	160	4-8-93	1	0	2.92	7	0	0	1	25	20	8	8	1	3	27	.220	.118	.281	9.85	1.09
2-team total (12 Diamondbacks/Reds)					1	1	2.15	19	0	0	5	59	42	17	14	1	9	52	—	—	—	7.98	1.38
Ramirez, Harold	R-R	6-0	197	9-19-92	0	0	0.00	4	0	0	0	4	3	4	0	0	4	2	.214	.125	.333	4.91	9.82
2-team total (7 Diamondbacks/Reds)					0	0	5.02	11	0	0	0	14	12	13	8	1	16	16	—	—	—	10.05	10.05
Romero, Franderlin	R-R	6-1	190	2-21-91	2	5	1.67	14	14	0	0	65	41	19	12	1	17	48	.186	.149	.209	6.68	2.37
Rosario, Jose	L-L	6-4	209	3-19-91	2	2	3.20	14	14	0	0	51	38	26	18	0	23	44	.210	.200	.212	7.82	4.09
Sarrameda, Ramon	R-R	6-3	180	7-8-91	3	1	1.56	11	0	0	6	35	27	7	6	2	5	21	.221	.306	.164	5.45	1.30
2-team total (6 Diamondbacks/Reds)					4	2	1.61	17	0	0	6	50	41	15	9	3	10	36	—	—	—	6.44	1.79
Torrealba, Julio	L-L	6-1	190	4-24-90	2	3	4.26	15	12	0	0	51	37	26	24	2	29	41	.208	.241	.201	7.28	5.15
Zapata, John	R-R	5-11	190	8-11-92	0	2	7.36	6	0	0	0	11	16	10	9	0	4	7	.348	.292	.409	5.73	3.27
2-team total (13 Diamondbacks/Reds)					0	3	4.25	19	0	0	1	30	30	20	14	0	14	26	—	—	—	7.89	4.25

Fielding

Catcher	PCT	G	PO	A	E	DP	PB
Ariza	.968	19	131	21	5	0	1
Duarte	.974	36	226	33	7	0	10
Raga	.953	28	174	28	10	0	8
Soto	1.000	2	7	1	0	0	0

First Base	PCT	G	PO	A	E	DP
Baez	.964	40	346	27	14	24
Burgos	.971	12	95	5	3	8
Duarte	1.000	3	28	0	0	2
Rodriguez	1.000	2	19	1	0	0
Soto	.984	15	121	6	2	11
Suero	1.000	1	8	0	0	0
Valdelamar	1.000	1	8	0	0	1

Second Base	PCT	G	PO	A	E	DP
Bueno	1.000	9	16	10	0	3
Farinez	.939	12	17	29	3	4
Mendez	.955	42	80	112	9	24
Rodriguez	1.000	2	4	2	0	3
Suero	.974	7	18	19	1	4
Valor	.828	5	5	19	5	1

Third Base	PCT	G	PO	A	E	DP
Baez	1.000	2	1	1	0	0
Bueno	.912	12	9	22	3	2
Farinez	.913	25	27	57	8	9
Rodriguez	1.000	1	0	2	0	0
Suero	.910	32	33	68	10	6
Valor	1.000	2	1	2	0	0

Shortstop	PCT	G	PO	A	E
DP Bueno	.968	15	19	42	2	8
Florentino	.860	32	45	78	20	10
Rodriguez	1.000	1	2	4	0	1
Suero	.933	11	20	22	3	0
Valor	.900	15	24	48	8	7

Outfield	PCT	G	PO	A	E	DP
Aquino	.930	65	99	8	8	1
Burgos	.981	39	48	3	1	0
Farinez	1.000	14	16	1	0	0
Fernandez	.985	32	62	4	1	1
Garcia	1.000	62	114	4	0	0
Rodriguez	.500	1	1	0	1	0
Valdelamar	1.000	1	1	0	0	0

DOMINICAN SUMMER LEAGUE

ROOKIE

Batting	B-T	HT	WT	DOB	AVG	vLH	vRH	G	AB	R	H	2B	3B	HR	RBI	BB	HBP	SH	SF	SO	SB	CS	SLG	OBP
Andujar, Omar	L-R	6-0	190	8-9-94	.100	.056	.115	25	70	3	7	2	0	0	1	11	2	0	0	28	0	1	.129	.241
2-team total (10 Diamondbacks)					.121	—	—	35	91	5	11	2	0	0	2	21	2	0	0	34	0	2	.143	.298
Chavez, Alberti	R-R	5-10	170	7-21-95	.314	.179	.358	46	159	14	50	11	1	0	16	12	0	1	3	18	9	4	.396	.356
De Luna, Jose	R-R	6-3	194	3-11-94	.132	.226	.096	33	114	6	15	1	1	0	5	7	2	0	0	23	0	4	.158	.195
Duque, Andres	R-R	6-3	176	2-9-92	.215	.262	.203	56	200	11	43	6	2	0	13	4	5	1	0	31	1	2	.265	.249

	B-T	HT	WT	DOB	AVG	vLH	vRH	G	AB	R	H	2B	3B	HR	RBI	BB	HBP	SH	SF	SO	SB	CS	OBP	SLG
Guerrero, Raynay	R-R	6-4	190	2-24-93	.180	.118	.202	45	128	9	23	7	0	2	9	7	4	0	1	33	0	0	.281	.243
Heredia, Juan	R-R	5-11	145	7-4-92	.250	.500	.214	17	48	4	12	4	1	0	1	16	2	1	0	13	3	2	.375	.455
2-team total (47 Diamondbacks)					.250	—	—	64	196	28	49	12	2	0	13	51	6	5	0	37	14	9	.332	.419
Jimenez, Olvis	L-L	6-4	175	5-18-94	.137	.143	.135	39	124	5	17	4	0	0	6	13	3	1	0	38	2	2	.169	.236
Jordan, Jose	L-R	5-10	160	9-21-94	.194	.182	.198	57	170	15	33	9	0	0	10	23	3	4	1	39	2	8	.247	.299
Liriano, Jesse	R-R	6-0	175	10-9-91	.197	.238	.182	25	76	7	15	2	2	0	6	5	2	0	1	22	3	3	.276	.262
2-team total (15 Diamondbacks)					.200	—	—	40	115	14	23	2	2	0	8	11	3	0	1	39	5	6	.252	.285
Mejia, Cesar	L-R	6-1	165	12-8-94	.213	.227	.210	40	127	6	27	6	1	0	7	18	2	1	0	44	3	6	.276	.320
Mier y Teran, Jonniel	R-R	6-1	170	3-30-94	.202	.240	.191	39	114	13	23	5	4	0	4	7	3	0	1	48	6	1	.316	.264
Peralta, Henderson	B-R	6-0	195	6-4-91	.219	.225	.216	51	151	15	33	4	1	1	8	18	4	0	1	32	6	5	.278	.316
Peraza, Juan Carlos	R-R	6-2	197	3-12-93	.122	.074	.136	35	115	9	14	7	0	0	10	11	3	0	0	43	0	1	.183	.217
Raga, Jose	R-R	5-11	190	11-20-93	.188	.000	.273	5	16	1	3	0	0	0	0	1	0	0	0	4	0	0	.188	.235
2-team total (29 Reds)					.139	—	—	34	101	7	14	1	0	0	5	6	3	1	0	21	1	0	.149	.209
Rivas, Jefry	R-R	6-1	175	9-6-92	.189	.133	.211	31	106	4	20	5	1	0	7	8	0	0	2	19	4	1	.255	.241
Samboy, Raul	R-R	5-11	155	9-25-93	.256	.227	.265	46	176	14	45	7	0	0	10	16	2	1	1	41	6	8	.295	.302
2-team total (17 Diamondbacks)					.244	—	—	63	246	22	60	10	1	1	18	12	3	1	3	53	7	10	.305	.284
Valor, Geraldo	R-R	5-10	155	5-2-94	.255	.179	.284	31	102	9	26	3	0	0	12	15	3	1	3	15	6	2	.284	.358
2-team total (26 Reds)					.238	—	—	57	185	26	44	4	1	0	18	26	5	3	4	31	11	4	.270	.341
Velazquez, Nestor	R-R	5-11	170	5-28-93	.207	.250	.194	50	174	26	36	1	0	0	11	19	2	4	0	38	5	9	.213	.292

Pitching	B-T	HT	WT	DOB	W	L	ERA	G	GS	CG	SV	IP	H	R	ER	HR	BB	SO	AVG	vLH	vRH	K/9	BB/9
Arias, Junior	R-R	6-3	170	11-10-93	2	1	5.45	15	3	0	1	38	46	36	23	1	15	39	.301	.294	.303	9.24	3.55
Aybar, Manuel	R-R	6-3	185	1-6-93	1	8	4.40	13	13	0	0	57	42	36	28	2	31	53	.209	.292	.163	8.32	4.87
Basora, Anthony	L-L	6-4	203	2-17-95	1	7	3.86	10	10	0	0	42	46	24	18	0	13	31	.282	.318	.277	6.64	2.79
2-team total (3 Diamondbacks)					2	7	3.07	13	11	0	0	59	55	26	20	1	16	49	—	—	—	7.52	2.45
Beard, Eliezer	R-R	6-4	202	4-23-91	2	5	2.08	8	6	0	0	35	35	16	8	0	9	32	.267	.271	.265	8.31	2.34
2-team total (1 Reds)					2	5	2.13	9	7	0	0	38	39	17	9	0	11	35	—	—	—	8.29	2.61
Castillo, Luis	R-R	6-2	180	3-10-95	0	9	4.48	14	14	0	0	60	84	36	30	2	13	36	.333	.274	.363	5.37	1.94
Cuevas, Israel	R-R	6-1	178	9-19-93	2	3	3.67	14	0	0	1	27	23	15	11	0	22	22	.228	.233	.225	7.33	7.33
Damian, Pedro	R-R	6-1	170	11-29-92	0	1	1.29	3	3	0	0	14	9	6	2	0	9	17	.170	.111	.182	10.93	5.79
2-team total (10 Reds)					1	3	3.27	13	13	0	0	44	33	28	16	1	32	43	—	—	—	8.80	6.55
De Leon, John	R-R	6-4	205	10-13-93	0	0	7.84	20	0	0	0	21	21	27	18	0	32	14	.256	.261	.254	6.10	13.94
Heredia, Jose	L-L	6-3	200	6-12-92	0	0	9.31	14	0	0	0	10	11	15	10	0	27	10	.306	.333	.303	9.31	25.14
Hernandez, Joyce	R-R	6-2	170	10-28-92	0	0	7.48	15	0	0	0	22	30	21	18	3	14	17	.319	.370	.299	7.06	5.82
Lara, Jean	R-R	6-3	200	4-15-93	1	4	4.02	13	5	0	0	31	25	19	14	1	25	25	.219	.238	.208	7.18	7.18
Montilla, Franklin	R-R	6-4	203	6-28-94	0	0	9.00	1	0	0	0	1	1	1	1	0	0	0	.250	.333	.000	0.00	0.00
Morales, Pablo	R-R	6-2	190	3-22-95	0	1	10.80	5	0	0	0	5	7	11	6	1	8	3	.333	.500	.294	5.40	14.40
Munoz, Jose	R-R	6-1	180	4-4-92	2	2	2.60	19	0	0	5	45	37	17	13	0	18	37	.230	.278	.206	7.40	3.60
Ortiz, Enmanuel	R-R	6-4	195	3-4-93	1	4	9.12	20	0	0	0	25	40	36	25	1	18	14	.370	.338	.389	5.11	6.57
Patino, Carlos	R-R	6-1	160	4-8-93	0	1	1.59	12	0	0	4	34	22	9	6	0	6	25	.185	.196	.178	6.62	1.59
2-team total (7 Reds)					1	1	2.15	19	0	0	5	59	42	17	14	1	9	52	—	—	—	7.98	1.38
Ramirez, Bernardo	R-R	6-2	180	2-2-93	2	4	1.28	12	12	0	0	56	40	19	8	0	20	47	.204	.173	.223	7.51	3.20
Ramirez, Harold	R-R	6-0	197	9-19-92	0	0	6.75	7	0	0	0	11	9	9	8	1	12	14	.225	.083	.286	11.81	10.13
2-team total (4 Reds)					0	0	5.02	11	0	0	0	14	12	13	8	1	16	16	—	—	—	10.05	10.05
Sarrameda, Ramon	R-R	6-3	180	7-8-91	1	1	1.72	6	0	0	0	16	14	8	3	1	5	15	.233	.333	.190	8.62	2.87
2-team total (11 Reds)					4	2	1.61	17	0	0	0	50	41	15	9	3	10	36	—	—	—	6.44	1.79
Suarez, Jose	L-L	6-3	180	5-1-91	0	0	13.50	12	0	0	0	13	22	25	20	0	17	11	.373	.667	.320	7.43	11.48
Velez, Roger	L-L	6-2	192	12-17-94	1	1	3.60	3	3	0	0	15	14	7	6	0	4	18	.250	.167	.260	10.80	2.40
2-team total (11 Diamondbacks)					3	3	5.85	14	8	0	0	48	56	34	31	1	16	50	—	—	—	9.44	3.02
Zapata, John	R-R	5-11	190	8-11-92	0	1	2.41	13	0	0	1	19	14	10	5	0	10	19	.187	.182	.189	9.16	4.82
2-team total (6 Reds)					0	3	4.25	19	0	0	1	30	30	20	14	0	14	26	—	—	—	7.89	4.25

Fielding

Catcher	PCT	G	PO	A	E	DP	PB
Andujar	.948	15	75	16	5	0	8
Peralta	.971	45	326	43	11	2	11
Peraza	.962	14	85	15	4	1	13
Raga	.960	4	18	6	1	0	1

First Base	PCT	G	PO	A	E	DP
Andujar	.930	8	53	0	4	1
Jordan	.982	7	51	5	1	4
Liriano	.984	17	120	4	2	9
Mejia	—	1	0	0	0	0
Peraza	.948	18	152	12	9	9
Rivas	.987	9	70	4	1	10
Velazquez	.974	17	100	14	3	9

Second Base	PCT	G	PO	A	E	DP
Chavez	.903	7	15	13	3	1
Heredia	—	1	0	0	0	0

	PCT	G	PO	A	E	DP
Jordan	.970	40	92	103	6	21
Liriano	.500	1	1	0	1	0
Mejia	1.000	4	4	3	0	0
Samboy	.800	1	4	0	1	0
Valor	.970	13	31	34	2	8
Velazquez	.959	8	22	25	2	6

Third Base	PCT	G	PO	A	E	DP
Chavez	.769	6	5	5	3	1
Mejia	.792	19	17	21	10	1
Rivas	.900	22	26	37	7	1
Samboy	1.000	3	2	7	0	0
Valor	—	1	0	0	0	0
Velazquez	.964	24	21	58	3	5

Shortstop	PCT	G	PO	A	E	DP
Chavez	.925	11	23	26	4	4
Heredia	1.000	1	1	3	0	0

	PCT	G	PO	A	E	DP
Heredia	.918	13	30	37	6	7
Jordan	1.000	1	0	2	0	0
Samboy	.890	32	48	81	16	12
Valor	.924	15	22	39	5	6

Outfield	PCT	G	PO	A	E	DP
Chavez	.930	18	37	3	3	0
De Luna	.889	31	52	4	7	0
Duque	.940	56	95	14	7	3
Guerrero	.935	42	55	3	4	1
Heredia	1.000	2	4	0	0	0
Jimenez	.881	29	53	6	8	0
Liriano	.857	6	6	0	1	0
Mier y Teran	.958	39	42	4	2	0
Rivas	—	1	0	0	0	0
Velazquez	1.000	2	1	1	0	0

Cleveland Indians

SEASON IN A SENTENCE: Only the Rockies had a higher team ERA than the Indians, who crumbled in the second half for their fifth straight season without cracking a .500 record.

HIGH POINT: After beating the Mariners 6-5 in 11 innings on May 17, the Indians increased their lead in the American League Central to four games, their biggest lead of the season. Even then, however, a productive offense masked a pitching staff that gave up too many runs.

LOW POINT: Through the first 100 games of the season, the Indians were a .500 team, but they finished the season on an 18-44 slide, including a stretch in which they lost 15 of their last 16 games in August. They went 5-24 for the month, getting outscored 179-96. The rotation was a disaster, with Justin Masterson regressing and Ubaldo Jimenez and Derek Lowe unable to recapture their peak form. The offense was inconsistent, and again Grady Sizemore didn't play an inning due to injury.

NOTABLE ROOKIES: Righthander Zach McAllister made 22 starts in the big leagues, where his 4.24 ERA was the lowest among the seven pitchers who made the most starts for the Indians in 2012. Righthanded reliever Cody Allen, who is still rookie-eligible for 2013, zipped to the big leagues after being drafted out of High Point in the 23rd round in 2011.

KEY TRANSACTIONS: After giving up significant talent to bring in Jimenez in 2011, when a good early start had also proved to be a mirage, the Indians didn't make any big deals in 2012. They purchased Rockies righthander Esmil Rogers in June and he was one of Cleveland's better relievers in the second half, posting a 3.06 ERA in 53 innings with 53 strikeouts and 12 walks. After the season, Cleveland traded him to the Blue Jays for Mike Aviles and Yan Gomes.

DOWN ON THE FARM: Francisco Lindor earned raves from scouts who saw him in the low Class A Midwest League, where he showed he was one of the best defensive shortstops in the minors with an advanced approach at the plate. Dorssys Paulino, a Dominican shortstop signed on July 2, 2011 for $1.1 million, had a terrific pro debut in the Rookie-level Arizona League, showing a compact stroke from the right side. The upper levels of the minors remained thin, however, with little help coming from the farm in 2012 and not much expected to contribute in 2013.

OPENING DAY PAYROLL: $78.4 million (21st)

PLAYERS OF THE YEAR

MAJOR LEAGUE
Shin-Soo Choo
of
.283/.373/.441
16 HR, 43 2B, 21 SB
10th in AL in OBP

MINOR LEAGUE
Russ Canzler
of
(Triple-A)
.265/.328/.487
22 HR, 79 RBIs

ORGANIZATION LEADERS

BATTING		*Minimum 250 AB
MAJORS		
* AVG	Michael Brantley	.288
* OPS	Shin-Soo Choo	.814
HR	Carlos Santana	18
RBI	Jason Kipnis	76
	Carlos Santana	76
MINORS		
* AVG	Tim Fedroff, Akron/Columbus	.316
	Jordan Smith, Lake County	.316
* OBP	Thomas Neal, Akron	.400
* SLG	Jared Goedert, Akron/Columbus	.502
R	Francisco Lindor, Lake County	83
H	Tim Fedroff, Akron/Columbus	148
	Jordan Smith, Lake County	148
TB	Russ Canzler, Columbus	237
2B	Russ Canzler, Columbus	36
3B	Tim Fedroff, Akron/Columbus	10
HR	Russ Canzler, Columbus	22
RBI	Russ Canzler, Columbus	79
BB	Cord Phelps, Columbus	71
SO	Nick Weglarz, Akron	140
SB	Todd Hankins, Lake County/Carolina	33
PITCHING		#Minimum 75 IP
MAJORS		
W	Justin Masterson	11
# ERA	Justin Masterson	4.93
SO	Justin Masterson	159
SV	Chris Perez	39
MINORS		
W	T.J. McFarland, Akron/Columbus	16
L	Michael Goodnight, Carolina	13
# ERA	Steven Wright, Akron	2.49
G	Preston Guilmet, Akron	50
GS	Elvis Araujo, Lake County	28
	Mike Rayl, Akron/Carolina	28
SV	Preston Guilmet, Akron	24
IP	T.J. McFarland, Akron/Columbus	163
BB	Michael Goodnight, Carolina	76
SO	Corey Kluber, Columbus	128
# AVG	Steven Wright, Akron	.207

General Manager: Chris Antonetti. **Farm Director:** Ross Atkins. **Scouting Director:** Brad Grant.

Class	Team	League	W	L	PCT	Finish	Manager
Majors	Cleveland Indians	American	68	94	.420	13th (14)	Manny Acta
Triple-A	Columbus Clippers	International	75	69	.521	6th (14)	Mike Sarbaugh
Double-A	Akron Aeros	Eastern	82	59	.582	1st (12)	Chris Tremie
High A	Carolina Mudcats	Carolina	63	77	.450	7th (8)	Edwin Rodriguez
Low A	Lake County Captains	Midwest	71	68	.511	7th (16)	David Wallace
Short-season	Mahoning Valley Scrappers	New York-Penn	30	45	.400	t-11th (14)	Ted Kubiak
Rookie	AZL Indians	Arizona	31	25	.554	t-6th (13)	Anthony Medrano
Overall 2012 Minor League Record			352	343	.506	12th (30)	

ORGANIZATION STATISTICS

CLEVELAND INDIANS

AMERICAN LEAGUE

Batting	B-T	HT	WT	DOB	AVG	vLH	vRH	G	AB	R	H	2B	3B	HR	RBI	BB	HBP	SH	SF	SO	SB	CS	SLG	OBP
Brantley, Michael	L-L	6-2	200	5-15-87	.288	.265	.299	149	552	63	159	37	4	6	60	53	0	0	4	56	12	9	.402	.348
Cabrera, Asdrubal	B-R	6-0	180	11-13-85	.270	.286	.263	143	555	70	150	35	1	16	68	52	6	1	2	99	9	4	.423	.338
Canzler, Russ	R-R	6-2	220	4-11-86	.269	.393	.215	26	93	9	25	3	0	3	11	4	0	0	0	22	0	0	.398	.299
Carlin, Luke	B-R	5-10	195	12-20-80	.214	.000	.333	4	14	2	3	1	0	0	1	0	0	0	0	3	1	0	.286	.214
Carrera, Ezequiel	L-L	5-10	185	6-11-87	.272	.333	.245	48	147	20	40	6	3	2	11	8	1	1	1	35	8	1	.395	.312
Chisenhall, Lonnie	L-R	6-2	190	10-4-88	.268	.184	.298	43	142	16	38	6	1	5	16	8	1	0	0	27	2	1	.430	.311
Choo, Shin-Soo	L-L	5-11	205	7-13-82	.283	.199	.327	155	598	88	169	43	2	16	67	73	14	0	1	150	21	7	.441	.373
Cunningham, Aaron	R-R	5-11	195	4-24-86	.175	.179	.172	72	97	5	17	4	0	1	7	9	0	3	0	25	0	3	.247	.245
Damon, Johnny	L-L	6-2	205	11-5-73	.222	.205	.227	64	207	25	46	6	2	4	19	17	0	0	0	27	4	0	.329	.281
Diaz, Juan	B-R	6-4	200	12-12-88	.267	.000	.364	5	15	4	4	0	0	0	1	1	0	0	0	5	0	0	.267	.353
Donald, Jason	R-R	6-1	195	9-4-84	.202	.175	.224	43	124	18	25	2	1	2	11	5	3	1	2	40	4	0	.282	.246
Duncan, Shelley	R-R	6-5	225	9-29-79	.203	.212	.193	81	232	29	47	10	0	11	31	28	1	0	3	59	1	2	.388	.288
Hafner, Travis	L-R	6-3	240	6-3-77	.228	.197	.241	66	219	23	50	6	2	12	34	32	9	0	3	47	0	0	.438	.346
Hannahan, Jack	L-R	6-2	210	3-4-80	.244	.167	.270	105	287	23	70	16	0	4	29	27	2	1	1	63	0	2	.341	.312
Kipnis, Jason	L-R	5-11	185	4-3-87	.257	.215	.280	152	591	86	152	22	4	14	76	67	5	3	6	109	31	7	.379	.335
Kotchman, Casey	L-L	6-3	220	2-22-83	.229	.221	.231	142	463	46	106	12	0	12	55	26	7	3	1	49	3	0	.333	.280
LaPorta, Matt	R-R	6-2	215	1-8-85	.241	.286	.174	22	58	2	14	2	0	1	5	1	1	0	0	17	0	0	.328	.267
Lillibridge, Brent	R-R	5-11	185	9-18-83	.216	.255	.183	43	111	15	24	5	0	3	8	7	3	0	2	40	6	0	.342	.276
3-team total (10 Boston, 49 Chicago)					.195	—	—	102	190	25	37	6	0	3	10	11	4	1	3	71	13	2	.274	.250
Lopez, Jose	R-R	6-0	205	11-24-83	.249	.265	.238	66	213	16	53	13	0	4	28	8	0	0	3	35	0	1	.366	.272
2-team total (15 Chicago)					.246	—	—	81	236	18	58	14	0	4	28	9	0	0	3	41	0	1	.356	.270
Marson, Lou	R-R	6-1	200	6-26-86	.226	.221	.229	70	195	27	44	8	2	0	13	36	1	2	1	44	4	2	.287	.348
Neal, Thomas	R-R	6-2	200	8-17-87	.217	.154	.300	9	23	2	5	1	0	0	2	1	0	0	0	6	0	0	.261	.250
Phelps, Cord	B-R	6-2	200	1-24-87	.212	.400	.130	14	33	2	7	0	0	1	5	1	0	0	0	10	0	0	.303	.235
Rottino, Vinny	R-R	6-1	215	4-7-80	.107	.071	.143	18	28	4	3	1	0	1	2	1	0	2	1	8	1	0	.250	.133
Santana, Carlos	B-R	5-11	200	4-8-86	.252	.272	.243	143	507	72	128	27	2	18	76	91	3	0	8	101	3	5	.420	.365

Pitching	B-T	HT	WT	DOB	W	L	ERA	G	GS	CG	SV	IP	H	R	ER	HR	BB	SO	AVG	vLH	vRH	K/9	BB/9
Accardo, Jeremy	R-R	6-1	200	12-8-81	0	0	4.58	26	0	0	0	35	38	19	18	3	16	28	.288	.220	.342	7.13	4.08
2-team total (1 Oakland)					0	0	4.82	27	0	0	0	37	42	21	20	3	16	29	—	—	—	6.99	3.86
Allen, Cody	R-R	6-1	210	11-20-88	0	1	3.72	27	0	0	0	29	29	12	12	2	15	27	.266	.240	.288	8.38	4.66
Asencio, Jairo	R-R	6-2	180	5-5-84	1	1	5.96	18	0	0	0	26	27	17	17	4	8	21	.273	.261	.283	7.36	2.81
Barnes, Scott	L-L	6-4	200	9-5-87	0	0	4.26	16	0	0	0	19	17	9	9	1	7	16	.236	.200	.262	7.58	3.32
Gomez, Jeanmar	R-R	6-3	200	2-10-88	5	8	5.96	20	17	0	0	91	95	66	60	15	34	47	.273	.258	.285	4.67	3.38
Hagadone, Nick	L-L	6-5	230	1-1-86	1	0	6.39	27	0	0	1	25	26	18	18	4	15	26	.263	.200	.315	9.24	5.33
Heredia, Roberto	R-R	6-4	230	8-30-80	0	3	7.53	3	3	0	0	14	17	15	12	4	3	2	.304	.364	.217	1.26	1.88
Herrmann, Frank	L-R	6-4	220	5-30-84	0	0	2.33	15	0	0	0	19	12	5	5	1	4	14	.179	.138	.211	6.52	1.86
Huff, David	L-L	6-2	215	8-22-84	3	1	3.38	6	4	0	0	27	30	14	10	5	5	19	.280	.333	.254	6.41	1.69
Jimenez, Ubaldo	R-R	6-5	210	1-22-84	9	17	5.40	31	31	0	0	177	190	116	106	25	95	143	.273	.272	.272	7.28	4.84
Kluber, Corey	R-R	6-4	215	4-10-86	2	5	5.14	12	12	0	0	63	76	44	36	9	18	54	.295	.301	.286	7.71	2.57
Lowe, Derek	R-R	6-6	230	6-1-73	8	10	5.52	21	21	1	0	119	156	79	73	8	45	41	.321	.353	.294	3.10	3.40
2-team total (17 New York)					9	11	5.11	38	21	1	1	143	180	88	81	10	51	55	—	—	—	3.47	3.22
Maine, Scott	L-L	6-3	215	2-2-85	1	2	10.50	9	0	0	0	6	13	7	7	3	6	6	.464	.333	.526	9.00	4.50
Masterson, Justin	R-R	6-6	250	3-22-85	11	15	4.93	34	34	1	0	206	212	122	113	18	88	159	.269	.296	.236	6.94	3.84
McAllister, Zach	R-R	6-6	240	12-8-87	6	8	4.24	22	22	0	0	125	133	78	59	19	38	110	.268	.243	.299	7.90	2.73
Perez, Chris	R-R	6-4	230	7-1-85	0	4	3.59	61	0	0	39	58	49	25	23	6	16	59	.222	.181	.267	9.21	2.50
Perez, Rafael	L-L	6-3	195	5-15-82	1	0	3.52	8	0	0	0	8	5	3	3	1	4	4	.185	.231	.143	4.70	4.70
Pestano, Vinnie	R-R	6-0	200	2-20-85	3	3	2.57	70	0	0	2	70	53	20	20	7	24	76	.207	.241	.168	9.77	3.09
Rogers, Esmil	R-R	6-1	190	8-14-85	3	1	3.06	44	0	0	0	53	47	19	18	5	12	54	.237	.255	.220	9.17	2.04
Seddon, Chris	L-L	6-4	220	10-13-83	1	1	3.67	17	2	0	0	34	35	15	14	2	13	18	.265	.229	.286	4.72	3.41
Sipp, Tony	L-L	6-0	190	7-12-83	1	2	4.42	63	0	0	1	55	47	29	27	9	23	51	.228	.209	.250	8.35	3.76
Smith, Joe	R-R	6-2	205	3-22-84	7	4	2.96	72	0	0	0	67	53	22	22	4	25	53	.213	.218	.209	7.12	3.36
Tomlin, Josh	R-R	6-1	190	10-19-84	5	8	6.36	21	16	0	0	103	126	74	73	18	25	56	.301	.303	.299	4.88	2.18
Wheeler, Dan	R-R	6-3	220	12-10-77	0	0	8.76	12	0	0	0	12	17	12	12	3	7	2	.327	.520	.148	1.46	5.11

CLEVELAND INDIANS

Fielding

Catcher	PCT	G	PO	A	E	DP	PB
Carlin	1.000	4	32	1	0	0	1
Marson	.996	69	433	18	2	3	2
Rottino	1.000	2	5	0	0	0	0
Santana	.990	100	628	65	7	3	10

First Base	PCT	G	PO	A	E	DP
Canzler	.982	8	52	2	1	5
Duncan	1.000	1	1	0	0	0
Hannahan	.909	2	9	1	1	3
Kotchman	.995	137	1099	108	6	114
LaPorta	1.000	11	56	6	0	5
Lillibridge	—	1	0	0	0	0
Lopez	1.000	11	56	2	0	2
Santana	.989	21	160	13	2	21

Second Base	PCT	G	PO	A	E	DP
Donald	.920	8	7	16	2	5

	PCT	G	PO	A	E	DP	PB
Kipnis	.991	146	241	440	6	94	
Lillibridge	.933	6	6	8	1	2	
Lopez	1.000	4	2	4	0	1	
Phelps	1.000	5	4	12	0	2	

Third Base	PCT	G	PO	A	E	DP
Chisenhall	.921	30	16	54	6	7
Donald	.846	12	5	17	4	1
Hannahan	.949	96	63	180	13	18
Lillibridge	.950	12	6	13	1	1
Lopez	.959	39	14	56	3	7
Phelps	—	1	0	0	0	0

Shortstop	PCT	G	PO	A	E	DP
Cabrera	.971	136	223	408	19	99
Diaz	.944	5	8	9	1	4
Donald	.968	10	13	17	1	4
Hannahan	1.000	7	4	6	0	1

	PCT	G	PO	A	E	DP
Lillibridge	.887	21	14	33	6	5
Phelps	1.000	1	2	6	0	3

Outfield	PCT	G	PO	A	E	DP
Brantley	.997	144	336	5	1	3
Canzler	1.000	11	20	1	0	0
Carrera	.991	47	112	1	1	0
Choo	.993	154	293	7	2	1
Cunningham	1.000	70	65	4	0	1
Damon	.980	56	99	1	2	0
Donald	1.000	7	12	0	0	0
Duncan	.976	57	78	4	2	0
Lillibridge	1.000	7	7	0	0	0
Lopez	—	1	0	0	0	0
Neal	.923	8	11	1	1	1
Rottino	1.000	12	14	1	0	0
Santana	1.000	1	2	0	0	0

COLUMBUS CLIPPERS   TRIPLE-A
INTERNATIONAL LEAGUE

Batting	B-T	HT	WT	DOB	AVG	vLH	vRH	G	AB	R	H	2B	3B	HR	RBI	BB	HBP	SH	SF	SO	SB	CS	SLG	OBP
Anderson, Lars	L-L	6-4	215	9-25-87	.196	.143	.204	18	56	4	11	5	0	0	7	9	2	0	2	18	0	0	.286	.319
2-team total (93 Pawtucket)					.250	—	—	111	396	53	99	27	2	9	59	65	2	0	7	107	1	0	.396	.353
Canzler, Russ	R-R	6-2	220	4-11-86	.265	.277	.260	130	487	68	129	36	3	22	79	46	2	0	4	128	2	4	.487	.328
Carlin, Luke	R-R	5-10	195	12-20-80	.252	.192	.273	62	206	23	52	10	0	3	27	34	1	1	2	26	0	1	.345	.358
Carrera, Ezequiel	L-L	5-10	185	6-11-87	.294	.297	.293	97	394	65	116	19	6	6	42	29	3	9	3	60	26	7	.419	.345
Chisenhall, Lonnie	L-R	6-2	190	10-4-88	.314	.265	.348	30	118	16	37	12	0	4	17	4	2	0	0	18	0	0	.517	.341
Copeland, Ben	L-L	6-1	190	12-17-83	.242	.167	.259	10	33	2	8	1	0	2	3	0	0	0	0	5	0	0	.455	.242
Crowe, Trevor	B-R	5-10	190	11-17-83	.250	.214	.267	38	132	20	33	7	1	3	12	17	1	0	2	24	8	3	.386	.336
Cunningham, Aaron	R-R	5-11	195	4-24-86	.203	.250	.190	22	74	6	15	4	0	2	5	8	0	2	0	21	0	0	.338	.280
Diaz, Juan	B-R	6-4	200	12-12-88	.306	.176	.345	19	72	12	22	5	2	1	11	4	0	0	0	18	0	0	.458	.342
Donald, Jason	R-R	6-1	195	9-4-84	.277	.317	.265	65	256	46	71	18	3	6	31	30	6	3	1	58	5	5	.441	.365
Fedroff, Tim	L-R	5-11	220	2-4-87	.325	.291	.333	69	265	52	86	14	5	9	32	31	1	4	3	45	9	0	.517	.393
Gallas, Anthony	R-R	6-2	210	12-14-87	.308	.333	.300	6	13	2	4	1	0	0	2	1	0	0	0	3	0	0	.385	.400
Goedert, Jared	R-R	6-1	205	5-25-85	.279	.349	.255	86	326	54	91	17	0	14	60	28	0	0	5	72	0	1	.460	.331
Hafner, Travis	L-R	6-3	240	6-3-77	.100	.000	.167	3	10	0	1	0	0	0	1	0	1	0	1	2	0	0	.100	.167
Hannahan, Jack	L-R	6-2	210	3-4-80	.000	.000	.000	1	4	0	0	0	0	0	0	1	0	0	0	2	0	0	.000	.000
Hernandez, Michel	R-R	6-0	215	8-12-78	.105	.167	.077	6	19	2	2	1	0	0	1	4	0	0	0	2	0	1	.158	.261
Huffman, Chad	R-R	6-1	215	4-29-85	.282	.200	.317	67	234	34	66	22	0	6	33	23	2	1	1	58	1	0	.453	.350
LaPorta, Matt	R-R	6-2	215	1-8-85	.264	.294	.252	101	375	56	99	19	1	19	62	44	9	0	6	81	0	3	.472	.350
LaRoche, Andy	R-R	6-1	195	9-13-83	.234	.250	.228	46	145	18	34	5	0	5	16	20	1	0	0	29	0	0	.372	.331
2-team total (50 Pawtucket)					.251	—	—	96	327	41	82	20	0	12	41	38	4	0	1	52	1	1	.422	.335
Lopez, Jose	R-R	6-0	205	11-24-83	.522	.600	.500	5	23	1	12	4	0	0	4	1	0	0	0	2	0	0	.696	.542
2-team total (13 Charlotte)					.375	—	—	19	72	8	27	9	0	1	14	7	0	0	0	10	0	0	.542	.430
Mills, Beau	L-R	6-3	220	8-15-86	.197	.333	.160	39	127	13	25	4	0	7	21	7	1	0	3	34	0	0	.394	.239
Pagnozzi, Matt	R-R	6-2	215	11-10-82	.224	.312	.185	78	245	27	55	12	0	7	32	33	5	5	4	71	0	0	.359	.324
Petit, Gregorio	R-R	5-10	195	12-10-84	.260	.250	.263	111	377	51	98	24	0	10	45	29	6	6	4	75	1	2	.403	.320
Phelps, Cord	B-R	6-2	200	1-23-87	.276	.290	.271	135	503	82	139	34	3	16	62	71	4	1	3	94	9	4	.451	.368
Rohlinger, Ryan	R-R	6-0	195	10-7-83	.308	.000	.500	4	13	3	4	0	0	1	4	1	0	0	0	1	0	0	.538	.357
Rottino, Vinny	R-R	6-1	215	4-7-80	.291	.291	.291	60	234	38	68	18	1	5	41	22	3	0	6	33	9	3	.440	.351
2-team total (36 Buffalo)					.297	—	—	96	374	60	111	28	2	9	66	34	4	0	8	53	14	6	.455	.355
Spilborghs, Ryan	R-R	6-1	200	9-5-79	.250	.360	.191	21	72	12	18	3	0	1	13	10	1	0	2	18	0	0	.333	.341
Tolentino, Patric	R-R	6-4	220	7-18-89	.000	—	.000	1	1	0	0	0	0	0	0	0	0	0	0	1	0	0	.000	.000
Toole, Justin	R-R	6-0	180	9-10-86	.333	.222	.444	6	18	2	6	1	0	0	2	0	2	0	1	0	0	.389	.333

Pitching	B-T	HT	WT	DOB	W	L	ERA	G	GS	CG	SV	IP	H	R	ER	HR	BB	SO	AVG	vLH	vRH	K/9	BB/9
Accardo, Jeremy	R-R	6-1	200	12-8-81	0	2	2.76	13	0	0	4	16	12	7	5	0	7	16	.207	.118	.244	8.82	3.86
Allen, Cody	R-R	6-1	210	11-20-88	3	2	2.27	24	0	0	2	32	22	8	8	3	9	35	.195	.133	.235	9.95	2.56
Ambriz, Hector	R-R	6-2	235	5-24-84	0	1	3.55	20	1	0	1	33	29	14	13	3	17	25	.240	.255	.230	6.82	4.64
Barnes, Scott	L-L	6-4	200	9-5-87	2	3	3.98	31	3	0	2	52	37	26	23	1	23	67	.196	.269	.156	11.60	3.98
Berger, Eric	L-L	6-2	205	4-22-86	2	6	5.50	26	13	0	0	88	92	55	54	16	29	78	.266	.263	.267	7.95	2.95
Cook, Cole	R-R	6-6	220	10-18-88	0	0	0.00	4	2	0	0	9	6	0	0	0	4	10	.200	.235	.179	7.50	3.00
De La Torre, Jose	R-R	5-9	175	10-17-85	1	0	3.38	7	0	0	0	11	9	4	4	0	2	16	.237	.000	.300	13.50	1.69
2-team total (12 Pawtucket)					2	0	2.79	19	0	0	2	29	24	9	9	2	5	32	—	—	—	9.93	1.55
Espino, Paolo	R-R	5-10	190	1-10-87	0	1	6.75	2	2	0	0	7	10	8	5	2	4	5	.333	.400	.267	6.75	5.40
Gomez, Jeanmar	R-R	6-3	200	2-10-88	6	5	4.41	11	11	1	0	69	75	39	34	6	17	54	.273	.241	.303	7.01	2.21
Hagadone, Nick	L-L	6-5	230	1-1-86	0	0	0.00	5	0	0	0	7	4	0	0	1	7	.167	.143	.176	8.59	1.23
Heredia, Roberto	R-R	6-4	230	8-30-80	1	0	4.50	2	2	0	0	12	13	6	6	0	3	7	.271	.346	.182	5.25	2.25
Herrmann, Frank	L-R	6-4	220	5-30-84	3	2	4.78	42	0	0	8	53	58	31	28	8	15	58	.282	.284	.280	9.91	2.56
Huff, David	L-L	6-2	215	8-1-84	7	6	4.97	24	22	2	0	134	155	78	74	27	34	79	.288	.300	.284	5.31	2.28
Kluber, Corey	R-R	6-4	215	4-10-86	11	7	3.59	21	21	1	0	125	121	62	50	9	49	128	.251	.255	.248	9.19	3.52
Landis, Kyle	R-R	6-1	185	5-30-86	0	0	6.00	1	0	0	0	3	2	2	2	1	2	.182	.167	.200	6.00	3.00
Langwell, Matt	R-R	6-2	225	5-6-86	4	0	3.29	32	0	0	0	55	49	21	20	0	22	63	.238	.264	.217	10.37	3.62
Lee, Chen	R-R	5-11	190	10-21-86	2	0	2.57	5	0	0	0	7	5	2	2	1	1	8	.208	.667	.143	10.29	1.29

	B-T	HT	WT	DOB	W	L	ERA	G	GS	CG	SV	IP	H	R	ER	HR	BB	SO	AVG	vLH	vRH	K/9	BB/9
Maine, Scott	L-L	6-3	215	2-2-85	0	0	0.00	2	0	0	0	2	2	0	0	0	0	0	.286	.500	.200	0.00	0.00
McAllister, Zach	R-R	6-6	240	12-8-87	5	2	2.98	11	11	0	0	63	59	27	21	5	19	52	.251	.248	.254	7.39	2.70
McFarland, T.J.	L-L	6-3	209	6-8-89	8	6	4.82	17	17	1	0	103	112	55	55	9	33	55	.279	.320	.261	4.82	2.89
Murata, Toru	L-R	6-0	175	5-20-85	0	1	5.87	2	2	0	0	8	8	5	5	1	2	5	.286	.417	.188	5.87	2.35
Packer, Matt	L-L	6-0	200	8-28-87	1	4	5.50	6	6	0	0	34	45	21	21	6	14	23	.321	.290	.346	6.03	3.67
Perez, Rafael	L-L	6-3	195	5-15-82	0	0	0.00	2	0	0	0	2	1	0	0	0	1	1	.167	.333	.000	4.50	4.50
Price, Bryan	R-R	6-4	210	11-13-86	0	1	6.63	13	0	0	0	19	27	14	14	2	12	17	.321	.349	.293	8.05	5.68
Ray, Chris	R-R	6-3	210	1-12-82	2	4	2.75	33	0	0	11	36	33	16	11	1	17	30	.246	.255	.241	7.50	4.25
Romero, J.C.	B-L	5-11	205	6-4-76	0	0	3.12	8	0	0	1	9	4	3	3	3	3	7	.138	.154	.125	7.27	3.12
2-team total (17 Norfolk)					1	0	2.74	25	1	0	3	23	14	7	7	3	8	20	—	—	—	7.83	3.13
Schwinden, Chris	R-R	6-3	215	9-22-86	1	2	5.87	3	3	0	0	15	16	11	10	4	6	5	.258	.282	.217	2.93	3.52
3-team total (21 Buffalo, 1 Scranton/W-B)					9	9	3.21	25	23	2	0	126	126	54	45	11	37	99	—	—	—	7.07	2.64
Seddon, Chris	L-L	6-4	220	10-13-83	11	5	3.44	20	20	1	0	123	112	55	47	16	27	108	.246	.194	.261	7.90	1.98
Slowey, Kevin	R-R	6-3	205	5-4-84	3	3	5.14	8	8	0	0	49	52	31	28	7	13	34	.271	.277	.268	6.24	2.39
Sturdevant, Tyler	R-L	6-0	185	12-20-85	0	3	6.30	18	0	0	0	20	29	14	14	5	9	15	.349	.361	.340	6.75	4.05
Tejeda, Robinson	R-R	6-2	245	3-24-82	0	0	18.00	1	0	0	0	1	3	2	2	1	0	1	.500	.000	.750	9.00	0.00
Van Mil, Loek	R-R	7-1	260	9-15-84	0	0	6.48	6	0	0	0	8	12	6	6	1	7	4	.343	.154	.455	4.32	7.56
Wheeler, Dan	R-R	6-3	220	12-10-77	3	3	2.32	36	0	0	5	43	38	14	11	4	13	30	.235	.303	.188	6.33	2.74

Fielding

Catcher	PCT	G	PO	A	E	DP	PB
Carlin	.992	62	472	35	4	4	2
Hernandez	1.000	6	42	3	0	0	0
Pagnozzi	.993	76	512	56	4	7	3
Rottino	1.000	2	15	0	0	0	1

First Base	PCT	G	PO	A	E	DP
Anderson	.993	14	137	9	1	13
Canzler	.986	47	373	38	6	40
Goedert	1.000	11	75	4	0	6
LaPorta	.989	52	439	26	5	44
Mills	1.000	16	130	6	0	9
Petit	1.000	1	6	0	0	0
Rottino	1.000	9	71	2	0	9
Tolentino	1.000	1	1	0	0	0

Second Base	PCT	G	PO	A	E	DP
Donald	.976	10	18	23	1	3

	PCT	G	PO	A	E	DP
Phelps	.991	132	254	322	5	88
Rohlinger	1.000	2	6	3	0	2
Toole	1.000	1	2	3	0	1

Third Base	PCT	G	PO	A	E	DP
Canzler	.929	8	6	20	2	3
Chisenhall	.935	27	18	68	6	5
Donald	.944	7	5	12	1	0
Goedert	.925	42	28	70	8	5
LaRoche	.926	30	22	53	6	3
Lopez	.867	5	4	9	2	1
Petit	.964	30	13	67	3	5
Rohlinger	1.000	1	0	3	0	0

Shortstop	PCT	G	PO	A	E	DP
Diaz	.989	19	30	58	1	13
Donald	.954	33	47	97	7	25
LaRoche	.921	10	9	26	3	7

	PCT	G	PO	A	E	DP
Petit	.966	82	116	253	13	52
Rohlinger	1.000	1	1	3	0	1
Toole	.944	5	5	12	1	2

Outfield	PCT	G	PO	A	E	DP
Canzler	.963	47	78	1	3	0
Carrera	.973	94	212	2	6	1
Copeland	1.000	10	25	1	0	0
Crowe	1.000	31	58	1	0	0
Cunningham	1.000	22	59	0	0	0
Donald	1.000	17	34	2	0	0
Fedroff	1.000	68	115	3	0	2
Gallas	.875	5	6	1	1	0
Goedert	.931	15	27	0	2	0
Huffman	.988	54	80	0	1	0
LaPorta	1.000	25	29	1	0	0
Rottino	.966	41	83	2	3	0
Spilborghs	1.000	17	28	0	0	0

CLEVELAND INDIANS

AKRON AEROS   DOUBLE-A
EASTERN LEAGUE

Batting	B-T	HT	WT	DOB	AVG	vLH	vRH	G	AB	R	H	2B	3B	HR	RBI	BB	HBP	SH	SF	SO	SB	CS	SLG	OBP
Abraham, Adam	R-R	6-0	228	3-27-87	.259	.286	.248	108	379	63	98	28	1	13	54	44	6	2	3	80	2	4	.441	.343
Aguilar, Jesus	R-R	6-3	257	6-30-90	.292	.333	.278	20	72	12	21	6	0	3	13	13	1	0	1	24	0	0	.500	.402
Bellows, Kyle	R-R	6-2	204	8-19-88	.243	.333	.199	59	202	26	49	10	0	5	29	27	0	1	0	42	3	1	.366	.332
Casas, Jordan	L-R	5-11	180	3-17-88	.000	.000	.000	3	5	0	0	0	0	0	0	0	0	0	0	0	0	0	.000	.000
Chen, Chun	R-R	5-11	210	11-1-88	.308	.301	.311	108	399	62	123	30	1	5	43	56	2	0	2	101	6	3	.426	.394
Copeland, Ben	L-L	6-1	190	12-17-83	.189	.132	.209	46	148	22	28	7	2	1	15	11	0	3	1	33	12	1	.284	.244
Crowe, Trevor	B-R	5-10	190	11-17-83	.333	.250	.364	4	15	1	5	2	0	0	1	2	0	0	0	0	0	0	.467	.412
Diaz, Juan	B-R	6-4	200	12-12-88	.259	.101	.316	96	371	51	96	24	2	11	52	25	3	4	2	95	1	3	.423	.309
Fedroff, Tim	L-R	5-11	220	2-4-87	.305	.238	.336	54	203	27	62	9	5	3	22	30	1	4	1	33	5	6	.443	.396
Goedert, Jared	R-R	6-1	205	5-25-85	.395	.357	.415	35	124	19	49	10	1	5	17	20	0	0	1	20	0	0	.613	.476
Henry, Jordan	L-R	6-3	175	6-13-88	.278	.360	.258	73	248	33	69	6	1	0	16	33	1	6	2	31	8	4	.310	.363
Hernandez, Michel	R-R	6-0	215	8-12-78	.208	.182	.220	46	144	7	30	10	0	1	15	6	3	1	0	19	1	0	.299	.255
Holt, Tyler	R-R	5-10	187	3-10-89	.250	.244	.251	55	216	29	54	5	2	0	12	24	1	6	1	41	13	4	.292	.326
Lawson, Matt	R-R	6-0	195	11-18-85	.327	.289	.338	60	196	20	64	17	3	1	23	6	4	3		30	7	4	.459	.408
Neal, Thomas	R-R	6-2	227	8-17-87	.314	.304	.317	117	405	77	127	24	1	12	51	46	14	3	2	71	11	8	.467	.400
Perez, Roberto	R-R	6-0	227	12-23-88	.212	.242	.204	95	283	31	60	16	2	1	31	49	6	7	4	67	0	1	.293	.336
Rohlinger, Ryan	R-R	6-0	195	10-7-83	.235	.217	.241	108	353	44	83	14	0	7	48	51	6	8	7	59	2	2	.334	.336
Rojas, Carlos	R-R	6-1	186	1-11-84	.067	.000	.100	10	30	2	2	0	0	0	2	6	0	2	0	5	0	0	.067	.222
2-team total (9 Bowie)					.175	—	—	19	57	4	10	1	0	0	4	8	0	3	0	11	0	1	.193	.277
Stoneburner, Davis	R-R	6-0	175	1-14-85	.198	.158	.211	102	313	26	62	17	3	0	26	25	6	4	3	75	13	4	.272	.268
Tice, Jeremie	R-R	6-1	219	9-25-86	.262	.267	.260	16	65	5	17	5	0	1	11	4	2	0	1	20	0	0	.385	.319
Tolentino, Patric	R-R	6-4	220	7-18-89	.125	.286	.059	9	24	1	3	1	0	0	0	2	0	0	0	8	0	0	.167	.192
Toole, Justin	R-R	6-0	180	9-10-86	.080	—	.080	8	25	0	2	0	0	1	0	1	1	1	0	4	0	0	.080	.115
Weglarz, Nick	L-L	6-3	240	12-16-87	.239	.217	.246	109	368	47	88	22	0	14	58	58	6	0	4	140	3	1	.413	.349

Pitching	B-T	HT	WT	DOB	W	L	ERA	G	GS	CG	SV	IP	H	R	ER	HR	BB	SO	AVG	vLH	vRH	K/9	BB/9
Allen, Cody	R-R	6-1	210	11-20-88	0	0	1.17	5	0	0	1	8	2	1	1	1	0	0	.080	.100	.067	11.74	0.00
Armstrong, Shawn	R-R	6-2	210	9-11-90	1	0	0.89	17	0	0	3	20	12	2	2	0	12	22	.176	.269	.119	9.74	5.31
Berger, Eric	L-L	6-2	205	4-22-86	0	3	4.37	5	5	0	0	23	22	16	11	3	8	21	.244	.188	.257	8.34	3.18
Brach, Brett	R-R	6-2	205	3-29-88	5	7	3.65	19	18	0	0	94	106	45	38	8	35	49	.294	.346	.254	4.71	3.36
Bryson, Rob	R-R	6-1	200	12-11-87	5	5	2.62	43	0	0	2	65	45	20	19	4	43	76	.195	.281	.141	10.47	5.92
Cook, Cole	R-R	6-6	220	10-18-88	0	0	2.08	3	0	0	0	4	4	1	1	0	1	4	.235	.167	.273	8.31	2.08
De La Torre, Jose	R-R	5-9	175	10-17-85	7	1	2.80	27	1	0	2	45	33	16	14	0	19	42	.212	.189	.232	8.40	3.80
Espino, Paolo	R-R	5-10	190	1-10-87	7	3	3.09	22	20	0	0	116	116	42	40	7	34	106	.265	.275	.256	8.20	2.63

Name	B-T	HT	WT	DOB	W	L	ERA	G	GS	CG	SV	IP	H	R	ER	HR	BB	SO	AVG	vLH	vRH	K/9	BB/9
Flores, Jose	R-R	6-3	250	6-4-89	0	1	2.70	6	0	0	0	7	6	4	2	0	2	4	.231	.200	.273	5.40	2.70
Guilmet, Preston	R-R	6-2	200	7-27-87	2	2	2.39	50	0	0	24	53	41	14	14	4	13	51	.211	.200	.219	8.72	2.22
Haley, Trey	R-R	6-3	180	6-21-90	3	1	1.76	9	0	0	0	15	10	5	3	0	11	23	.189	.250	.138	13.50	6.46
House, T.J.	R-L	6-2	215	9-29-89	8	5	3.98	23	23	1	0	124	114	59	55	7	44	90	.246	.243	.246	6.51	3.18
Huff, David	L-L	6-2	215	8-22-84	0	0	0.00	1	1	0	0	4	1	0	0	1	3		.083	.000	.111	6.75	2.25
Jimenez, Francisco	L-L	5-11	164	10-2-88	0	1	12.27	1	1	0	0	4	7	5	5	0	1	2	.389	.250	.429	4.91	2.45
Landis, Kyle	R-R	6-1	185	5-30-86	6	4	3.55	41	0	0	2	66	67	26	26	5	13	55	.271	.233	.299	7.50	1.77
Langwell, Matt	R-R	6-2	225	5-6-86	0	0	0.63	10	0	0	3	14	10	2	1	0	5	18	.217	.263	.185	11.30	3.14
McFarland, T.J.	L-L	6-3	209	6-8-89	8	2	2.69	10	10	1	0	60	61	18	18	1	12	41	.272	.286	.269	6.12	1.79
Murata, Toru	L-R	6-0	175	5-20-85	3	1	2.60	24	8	0	0	66	59	22	19	1	19	59	.244	.276	.219	8.09	2.60
Packer, Matt	L-L	6-0	200	8-28-87	2	1	2.41	3	3	0	0	19	20	8	5	2	1	12	.270	.333	.254	5.79	0.48
Perez, Rafael	L-L	6-3	195	5-15-82	0	0	0.00	3	1	0	0	4	2	0	0	0	0	6	.154	.000	.222	0.00	0.00
Price, Bryan	R-R	6-4	210	11-13-86	2	3	3.02	27	0	0	4	51	44	20	17	6	12	46	.239	.253	.229	8.17	2.13
Radeke, Mason	R-R	6-1	175	6-13-86	1	1	1.50	3	1	0	0	6	5	4	1	2	2	2	.208	.222	.200	3.00	3.00
Rayl, Mike	L-L	6-5	180	11-1-88	0	1	15.00	1	1	0	0	3	8	7	5	1	2	0	.444	.400	.462	0.00	6.00
Rondon, Hector	R-R	6-3	180	2-26-88	0	0	2.25	2	0	0	0	4	4	1	1	0	1	3	.286	.429	.143	6.75	2.25
Salazar, Danny	R-R	6-0	190	1-11-90	4	0	1.85	6	6	0	0	34	25	8	7	1	8	23	.203	.190	.215	6.09	2.12
Soto, Giovanni	L-L	6-3	180	5-18-91	6	9	3.93	22	22	2	0	121	111	62	53	10	49	100	.247	.265	.240	7.42	3.63
Stowell, Bryce	R-R	6-2	205	9-23-86	2	1	3.72	25	0	0	2	29	23	13	12	5	9	44	.217	.231	.209	13.66	2.79
Sturdevant, Tyler	R-L	6-0	185	12-20-85	0	0	3.72	6	0	0	0	10	10	5	4	1	3	10	.278	.308	.261	9.31	2.79
Van Mil, Loek	R-R	7-1	260	9-15-84	1	1	1.94	27	0	0	0	46	34	11	10	2	11	40	.204	.145	.245	7.77	2.14
Wright, Steve	R-R	6-1	200	8-30-84	9	6	2.49	20	20	1	0	116	86	44	32	8	62	101	.207	.249	.172	7.86	4.82
2-team total (1 Portland)					10	6	2.44	21	21	1	0	122	91	45	33	8	64	103	—	—	—	7.62	4.73

Fielding

Catcher	PCT	G	PO	A	E	DP	PB
Chen	1.000	8	51	4	0	1	1
Hernandez	.990	44	259	36	3	2	5
Perez	.990	95	699	92	8	6	25
Tolentino	1.000	5	23	1	0	2	0

First Base	PCT	G	PO	A	E	DP
Abraham	1.000	58	468	37	0	55
Aguilar	1.000	13	106	9	0	9
Chen	.995	62	547	42	3	57
Goedert	1.000	1	7	1	0	0
Rohlinger	1.000	1	1	0	0	0
Stoneburner	1.000	4	38	2	0	5
Tice	1.000	1	10	1	0	1
Tolentino	1.000	2	11	1	0	0
Toole	1.000	6	44	2	0	5

Second Base	PCT	G	PO	A	E	DP
Abraham	1.000	1	0	2	0	0

	PCT	G	PO	A	E	DP
Lawson	.982	59	93	179	5	41
Rohlinger	.993	33	51	83	1	22
Stoneburner	.984	55	115	139	4	39
Toole	.800	2	5	3	2	1

Third Base	PCT	G	PO	A	E	DP
Abraham	.939	16	11	20	2	1
Bellows	.953	59	31	111	7	10
Goedert	1.000	5	0	9	0	3
Lawson	1.000	1	0	1	0	0
Rohlinger	.983	50	33	84	2	11
Rojas	.941	6	4	12	1	1
Stoneburner	.867	14	5	21	4	2
Toole	—	1	0	0	0	0

Shortstop	PCT	G	PO	A	E	DP
Diaz	.955	96	127	301	20	63
Rohlinger	1.000	24	33	61	0	22
Rojas	.875	4	8	13	3	3

	PCT	G	PO	A	E	DP
Stoneburner	.949	23	27	47	4	10

Outfield	PCT	G	PO	A	E	DP
Abraham	1.000	2	1	0	0	0
Casas	1.000	3	3	0	0	0
Copeland	1.000	45	84	4	0	1
Crowe	1.000	4	5	1	0	0
Fedroff	.980	50	97	3	2	0
Goedert	1.000	24	33	1	0	0
Henry	.986	69	136	5	2	2
Holt	.982	55	102	7	2	3
Neal	.996	102	220	2	1	0
Stoneburner	.889	10	8	0	1	0
Tice	1.000	11	12	2	0	0
Weglarz	.958	73	92	0	4	0

CAROLINA MUDCATS   HIGH CLASS A
CAROLINA LEAGUE

Batting	B-T	HT	WT	DOB	AVG	vLH	vRH	G	AB	R	H	2B	3B	HR	RBI	BB	HBP	SH	SF	SO	SB	CS	SLG	OBP
Aguilar, Jesus	R-R	6-3	257	6-30-90	.277	.305	.272	107	368	63	102	25	2	12	58	45	9	0	5	91	0	1	.454	.365
Bradley, Mark	L-L	5-9	160	8-30-90	.195	.125	.212	12	41	2	8	0	0	0	1	3	0	0	0	11	0	2	.195	.250
Cannon, Tyler	B-R	6-0	191	8-30-87	.267	.339	.249	88	288	36	77	21	1	1	27	27	2	0	3	72	1	0	.358	.331
Casas, Jordan	L-R	5-11	180	3-17-88	.000	—	.000	2	4	0	0	0	0	0	0	1	0	0	0	1	1	0	.000	.200
Childs, Dwight	R-R	6-2	190	7-23-88	.138	.158	.135	44	130	9	18	4	0	2	16	6	2	4	1	39	1	0	.215	.187
Cid, Delvi	R-R	6-2	170	7-09-88	.281	.387	.250	95	274	50	77	18	4	5	29	21	5	8	0	80	32	10	.431	.343
Gallas, Anthony	R-R	6-2	210	12-14-87	.250	.269	.245	107	376	48	94	30	4	8	51	27	4	0	3	85	2	3	.415	.305
Greenwell, Bo	L-L	6-0	185	10-15-88	.310	.125	.340	46	171	19	53	10	2	2	17	19	3	2	1	32	5	1	.427	.387
Hankins, Todd	R-R	5-11	180	11-24-88	.218	.235	.213	24	78	9	17	4	1	3	11	9	2	0	0	28	3	1	.410	.315
Holt, Tyler	R-R	5-10	187	3-10-89	.263	.310	.252	81	316	48	83	10	7	0	22	38	4	4	0	62	16	8	.339	.349
Lowery, Jake	L-R	5-10	200	7-21-90	.222	.233	.219	59	203	20	45	15	0	2	25	28	0	1	1	71	0	1	.325	.315
Moncrief, Carlos	L-R	6-1	210	11-3-88	.249	.267	.246	101	353	57	88	23	4	15	53	46	3	3	2	126	17	2	.465	.339
Monsalve, Alex	R-R	6-2	225	4-22-92	.233	.160	.253	34	116	10	27	4	0	1	6	7	1	1	1	17	1	0	.293	.280
Rodriguez, Ronny	R-R	6-0	170	4-17-92	.264	.303	.255	126	454	67	120	20	4	19	66	19	5	3	2	88	7	7	.452	.300
Tice, Jeremie	R-R	6-1	219	9-25-86	.282	.400	.253	52	181	33	51	18	0	12	47	20	6	0	1	44	0	0	.580	.370
Toole, Justin	R-R	6-0	180	9-10-86	.241	.233	.243	83	270	24	65	6	3	1	18	12	4	5	1	46	5	3	.296	.282
Urshela, Giovanny	R-R	6-0	197	10-11-91	.278	.197	.295	114	439	50	122	30	1	14	59	16	7	5	8	60	1	1	.446	.309
Washington, LeVon	L-L	5-11	170	7-26-91	.071	.000	.111	4	14	2	1	0	0	0	1	1	0	0	0	3	0	0	.071	.133
Wolters, Tony	L-R	5-10	165	6-9-92	.260	.264	.259	125	485	66	126	30	8	8	58	36	8	5	3	104	5	9	.404	.320

Pitching	B-T	HT	WT	DOB	W	L	ERA	G	GS	CG	SV	IP	H	R	ER	HR	BB	SO	AVG	vLH	vRH	K/9	BB/9
Allen, Cody	R-R	6-1	210	11-20-88	0	0	0.00	2	0	0	0	4	1	0	0	0	0	8	.077	.000	.118	18.00	0.00
Armstrong, Shawn	R-R	6-2	210	9-11-90	1	3	2.06	26	0	0	1	44	31	10	10	0	23	52	.205	.196	.210	10.72	4.74
Blair, Kyle	R-R	6-2	236	9-27-88	5	2	5.95	22	3	0	0	59	56	42	39	8	33	44	.245	.311	.213	6.71	5.03
Brach, Brett	R-R	6-2	190	3-29-88	0	1	4.45	9	4	0	0	28	29	15	14	1	11	16	.276	.320	.263	5.08	3.49
Colon, Joseph	R-R	6-0	167	2-18-90	1	2	7.53	3	3	0	0	14	21	17	12	3	7	11	.344	.375	.333	6.91	4.40
Cook, Clayton	R-R	6-3	175	7-23-90	1	0	2.31	3	3	0	0	12	5	3	3	0	7	8	.122	.111	.125	6.17	5.40
Cook, Cole	R-R	6-6	220	10-18-88	0	1	2.74	14	1	0	3	23	19	10	7	3	10	18	.221	.222	.220	7.04	3.91
Cooper, Jordan	R-R	6-2	190	5-10-89	9	7	3.54	29	7	0	1	94	101	43	37	8	16	75	.281	.302	.273	7.18	1.53

Name	B-T	HT	WT	DOB	W	L	ERA	G	GS	CG	SV	IP	H	R	ER	HR	BB	SO	AVG	vLH	vRH	K/9	BB/9
Dickerson, Dale	R-R	6-2	210	9-11-86	5	2	4.38	30	1	0	1	39	35	24	19	1	33	29	.245	.340	.198	6.69	7.62
Ehlert, Clayton	R-R	6-1	195	11-2-87	1	0	9.00	2	0	0	0	2	2	4	2	0	4	4	.286	.333	.250	18.00	18.00
Flores, Jose	R-R	6-3	250	6-4-89	1	2	2.37	36	0	0	15	38	35	14	10	0	13	35	.245	.171	.269	8.29	3.08
Goodnight, Michael	R-R	6-4	215	6-10-89	2	13	4.64	28	27	0	0	145	151	89	75	8	76	101	.278	.299	.265	6.25	4.71
Haley, Trey	R-R	6-3	180	6-21-90	0	0	1.04	12	0	0	2	17	8	4	2	0	6	16	.133	.111	.143	8.31	3.12
House, T.J.	R-L	6-2	215	9-29-89	2	0	1.44	4	4	0	0	25	17	9	4	1	6	26	.189	.267	.173	9.36	2.16
Hubbard, Antwonie	R-R	6-3	250	7-30-88	0	0	0.00	1	0	0	0	1	0	0	0	0	0	0	.000	.000	.000	0.00	0.00
Jimenez, Francisco	L-L	5-11	164	10-2-88	8	8	5.19	26	21	1	0	113	131	71	65	9	57	64	.300	.253	.309	5.11	4.55
Johnson, Jeff	R-R	6-0	185	2-9-90	0	2	4.15	9	0	0	1	17	13	8	8	1	3	18	.217	.158	.244	9.35	1.56
Martin, Josh	R-R	6-5	230	12-30-89	0	1	5.06	3	0	0	0	5	6	3	3	2	1	4	.286	.400	.182	6.75	1.69
Martinez, Fabio	R-R	6-3	190	10-29-89	0	2	8.53	8	0	0	0	6	5	7	6	0	8	7	.217	.250	.200	9.95	11.37
Murata, Toru	L-R	6-0	175	5-20-85	0	0	0.00	1	0	0	0	1	1	0	0	0	1	2	.200	.000	.250	13.50	6.75
Nixon, Robert	R-R	6-1	190	11-1-88	1	0	5.40	14	0	0	1	30	33	19	18	1	10	26	.277	.367	.247	7.80	3.00
Packer, Matt	L-L	6-0	200	8-28-87	1	0	0.00	2	2	0	0	8	3	0	0	0	1	7	.125	.250	.063	7.88	1.13
Petter, Kyle	L-L	6-0	180	4-5-90	1	1	5.59	17	0	0	0	29	29	20	18	2	22	26	.271	.269	.272	8.07	6.83
Rayl, Mike	L-L	6-5	180	11-1-88	10	9	4.28	27	27	0	0	149	144	76	71	13	57	95	.259	.256	.260	5.73	3.44
Reichenbach, J.D.	L-L	6-2	180	8-29-87	5	7	5.14	38	0	0	1	63	68	43	36	5	30	48	.279	.295	.275	6.86	4.29
Roberts, Will	L-R	6-5	195	8-17-90	5	10	5.68	24	19	1	0	122	146	83	77	10	30	77	.296	.350	.265	5.68	2.21
Salazar, Danny	R-R	6-0	190	1-11-90	1	2	2.68	16	16	0	0	54	46	17	16	3	19	53	.237	.219	.246	8.89	3.19
Sides, Steven	R-R	6-4	215	6-22-89	2	1	3.52	21	0	0	5	31	26	15	12	1	23	38	.241	.346	.207	11.15	6.75
Sturdevant, Tyler	R-L	6-0	185	12-20-85	1	0	0.00	5	0	0	0	7	2	0	0	0	2	3	.095	.000	.154	3.86	2.57
Suarez, Benny	R-R	6-0	190	9-28-91	0	1	5.40	2	2	0	0	7	8	4	4	0	2	3	.296	.500	.211	4.05	2.70

Fielding

Catcher

Catcher	PCT	G	PO	A	E	DP	PB
Cannon	.984	28	167	20	3	4	4
Childs	.980	42	253	34	6	2	1
Lowery	.978	49	309	39	8	3	5
Monsalve	.959	29	187	23	9	0	3
Toole	1.000	1	2	0	0	0	0

First Base

First Base	PCT	G	PO	A	E	DP
Aguilar	.996	104	836	80	4	95
Cannon	.991	15	106	8	1	8
Childs	1.000	1	1	1	0	0
Tice	.970	8	62	3	2	2
Toole	1.000	21	138	9	0	12
Urshela	1.000	1	1	0	0	0

Second Base

Second Base	PCT	G	PO	A	E	DP
Cannon	.889	1	6	2	1	1
Hankins	.800	5	4	4	2	2
Rodriguez	.977	45	95	119	5	33
Toole	.993	31	77	62	1	20
Wolters	.950	63	122	179	16	42

Third Base

Third Base	PCT	G	PO	A	E	DP
Cannon	.846	16	1	32	6	6
Cid	—	1	0	0	0	0
Hankins	1.000	2	1	1	0	0
Rodriguez	—	1	0	0	0	0
Toole	.870	18	7	13	3	0
Urshela	.964	113	55	212	10	11
Wolters	—	1	0	0	0	0

Shortstop

Shortstop	PCT	G	PO	A	E	DP
Hankins	—	1	0	0	0	0
Rodriguez	.924	80	110	229	28	49
Toole	1.000	1	0	1	0	0
Wolters	.971	61	92	178	8	42

Outfield

Outfield	PCT	G	PO	A	E	DP
Bradley	1.000	12	21	2	0	1
Cannon	—	1	0	0	0	0
Casas	1.000	1	10	0	0	0
Cid	.957	85	148	6	7	2
Gallas	.965	80	131	8	5	1
Greenwell	1.000	39	74	3	0	0
Hankins	1.000	13	30	2	0	0
Holt	.990	80	197	9	2	1
Moncrief	.987	100	225	6	3	3
Nixon	1.000	1	1	0	0	0
Tice	1.000	8	9	1	0	0
Toole	1.000	6	7	0	0	0
Washington	.900	4	9	0	1	0

LAKE COUNTY CAPTAINS

LOW CLASS A

MIDWEST LEAGUE

Batting	B-T	HT	WT	DOB	AVG	vLH	vRH	G	AB	R	H	2B	3B	HR	RBI	BB	HBP	SH	SF	SO	SB	CS	SLG	OBP
Bartolone, Nick	R-R	5-10	153	10-22-90	.179	.167	.184	18	56	6	10	1	0	0	7	4	0	0	0	12	0	2	.196	.233
Bradley, Mark	L-L	5-9	160	8-30-90	.240	.500	.118	11	25	5	6	0	0	0	1	2	0	0	0	11	1	0	.240	.296
Casas, Jordan	L-R	5-11	180	3-17-88	.238	.286	.231	29	105	13	25	0	0	0	6	3	2	2	1	21	5	0	.295	.293
Castillo, Leonardo	R-R	6-2	190	7-9-93	.216	.222	.215	116	425	37	92	21	5	4	48	19	4	5	4	88	1	0	.318	.254
Garcia, Robel	B-R	6-0	168	3-28-93	.210	.214	.209	63	233	24	49	12	1	3	23	27	2	2	0	68	2	2	.309	.298
Hankins, Todd	R-R	5-11	180	11-18-90	.243	.303	.223	78	268	40	65	11	5	2	26	34	3	1	2	79	30	3	.343	.332
Hannahan, Jack	L-R	6-2	210	3-4-80	.125	.000	.143	2	8	0	1	0	0	0	0	0	0	0	0	4	0	0	.125	.125
Lavisky, Alex	R-R	6-1	200	1-13-91	.246	.324	.224	93	342	44	84	18	0	12	49	34	2	3	4	95	2	0	.404	.314
Lindor, Francisco	B-R	5-11	175	11-14-93	.257	.288	.249	122	490	83	126	24	3	6	42	61	11	4	1	78	27	12	.355	.352
Lowery, Alex	L-R	5-10	200	7-21-90	.248	.224	.257	39	137	25	34	0	2	7	28	24	0	3	1	39	1	0	.504	.358
MacPhee, Zack	B-R	5-9	175	2-13-90	.222	.192	.230	75	239	27	53	6	3	2	26	33	2	5	2	49	2	6	.297	.319
Medina, Yhoxian	R-R	5-10	165	5-11-90	.214	.250	.208	19	56	5	12	1	0	0	2	7	0	1	1	11	0	1	.232	.297
Monsalve, Alex	R-R	6-2	225	4-22-92	.265	.300	.258	73	283	36	75	17	1	7	36	23	3	1	3	35	1	2	.406	.324
Myles, Bryson	R-R	5-11	230	9-18-89	.290	.221	.314	102	369	40	107	20	2	3	59	33	7	4	5	85	20	12	.379	.355
Ramirez, Jose	R-R	5-9	165	9-17-92	.354	.382	.344	67	277	54	98	13	4	3	27	24	1	8	3	26	15	6	.462	.403
Rodriguez, Luigi	B-R	5-11	160	11-13-92	.268	.243	.275	117	463	75	124	21	5	11	48	50	1	3	4	133	24	9	.406	.338
Sabourin, Jerrud	L-L	6-2	210	11-2-89	.297	.240	.311	130	472	60	140	26	2	3	66	51	7	1	7	77	4	0	.379	.369
Santana, Carlos	B-R	5-11	200	4-8-86	.250	—	.250	1	4	1	1	0	0	1	2	0	0	0	0	0	0	0	1.000	.250
Smith, Jordan	L-R	6-4	205	7-5-90	.316	.315	.317	116	468	70	148	23	7	9	74	35	5	1	4	52	9	3	.453	.367
Tolentino, Patric	R-R	6-4	220	7-18-89	.200	.143	.212	13	40	4	8	2	0	2	7	4	1	0	0	13	0	0	.400	.289
Valerio, Charlie	R-R	6-0	204	11-7-90	.000	.000	.000	3	11	0	0	0	0	0	1	0	0	0	0	5	0	0	.000	.083
Washington, LeVon	L-R	5-11	170	7-26-91	.440	.400	.450	6	25	8	11	1	0	0	1	6	1	0	0	8	0	3	.480	.563

Pitching	B-T	HT	WT	DOB	W	L	ERA	G	GS	CG	SV	IP	H	R	ER	HR	BB	SO	AVG	vLH	vRH	K/9	BB/9
Anderson, Cody	R-R	6-4	220	9-14-90	4	7	3.20	24	23	0	0	98	92	40	35	8	29	72	.249	.242	.255	6.59	2.65
Araujo, Elvis	L-L	6-6	215	7-15-91	7	10	5.00	28	28	1	0	135	141	89	75	7	61	111	.270	.271	.269	7.40	4.07
Armstrong, Shawn	R-R	6-2	210	9-11-90	0	0	0.00	2	0	0	0							4	.091	.167	.000	9.82	4.91
Blair, Kyle	R-R	6-2	236	9-27-88	0	2	12.08	5	1	0	0	13	15	17	17	4	4	13	.288	.241	.348	9.24	2.84
Carmona, Manuel	R-R	6-0	190	6-21-92	0	1	4.09	34	0	0	1	51	41	25	23	2	31	36	.230	.253	.211	6.39	5.51
Colon, Joseph	R-R	6-0	167	2-18-90	8	8	2.90	19	19	0	0	112	100	44	36	6	32	72	.246	.235	.255	5.80	2.58
Cook, Cole	R-R	6-6	220	10-18-88	2	3	3.46	22	0	0	2	39	39	24	15	2	11	32	.255	.257	.253	7.38	2.54

Name	B-T	HT	WT	DOB	W	L	ERA	G	GS	CG	SV	IP	H	R	ER	HR	BB	SO	AVG	vLH	vRH	K/9	BB/9
Cooper, Jordan	R-R	6-2	190	5-10-89	0	1	0.00	2	0	0	0	2	4	1	0	0	0	1	.400	.444	.000	3.86	0.00
De Los Santos, Xavier	R-R	6-0	180	10-13-88	0	0	13.50	3	0	0	1	2	2	2	0	2	3	.333	.500	.250	20.25	13.50
DeJesus, Luis	R-R	6-3	173	12-16-91	0	1	7.50	4	0	0	1	12	15	11	10	2	6	12	.288	.316	.273	9.00	4.50
Guerrero, Harold	L-L	6-4	235	5-21-90	0	0	11.57	3	0	0	0	2	2	3	3	0	4	7	.222	.000	.400	27.00	15.43
Head, Louis	R-R	6-0	170	4-23-90	2	0	3.78	15	0	0	0	33	38	21	14	6	7	28	.275	.236	.318	7.56	1.89
Heredia, Roberto	R-R	6-4	230	8-30-80	1	1	3.65	2	2	0	0	12	12	7	5	5	1	13	.250	.333	.185	9.49	0.73
Hubbard, Antwonie	R-R	6-3	250	7-30-88	1	0	2.21	13	0	0	0	20	14	7	5	4	8	13	.209	.074	.300	5.75	3.54
Jimenez, Danny	L-L	6-2	205	9-23-89	2	4	5.28	9	7	1	0	46	45	30	27	5	12	33	.262	.241	.280	6.46	2.35
Johnson, Jeff	R-R	6-0	185	2-9-90	4	3	3.92	36	0	0	15	41	32	20	18	1	18	57	.208	.246	.180	12.41	3.92
Morimando, Shawn	L-L	5-11	170	11-20-92	7	6	3.59	22	22	1	0	110	96	51	44	11	52	69	.239	.200	.263	5.63	4.24
Nervis, Joshua	R-R	6-3	230	10-25-88	0	0	4.09	4	0	0	1	11	9	5	5	1	6	6	.237	.188	.273	4.91	4.91
Nixon, Robert	R-R	6-1	190	11-1-88	1	1	3.12	21	0	0	1	52	54	24	18	1	25	42	.274	.273	.275	7.27	4.33
Pasquale, Nick	R-R	6-0	190	10-27-90	3	0	2.17	9	2	0	0	29	25	8	7	1	1	17	.238	.255	.220	5.28	0.31
Penny, Cody	R-R	6-3	195	5-15-91	4	1	1.59	9	0	0	0	17	10	3	3	1	4	16	.169	.161	.179	8.47	2.12
Petter, Kyle	L-L	6-0	180	4-5-90	2	0	1.65	18	0	0	0	33	14	6	6	1	21	37	.130	.154	.116	10.19	5.79
Radeke, Mason	R-R	6-1	175	6-13-90	7	6	3.38	28	12	0	1	109	91	49	41	11	24	117	.220	.265	.185	9.63	1.98
Roberts, Will	L-R	6-5	195	8-17-90	2	1	2.90	5	5	0	0	31	26	14	10	1	8	13	.220	.268	.177	3.77	2.32
Sides, Steven	R-R	6-4	215	6-22-89	1	0	1.05	18	0	0	1	34	19	4	4	0	11	37	.157	.130	.179	9.70	2.88
Sterling, Felix	R-R	6-3	200	3-15-93	4	8	6.58	24	18	0	1	93	104	87	68	15	40	71	.280	.266	.294	6.87	3.87
Tejeda, Enosil	R-R	6-0	175	6-21-89	3	1	1.23	18	0	0	8	22	13	3	3	0	6	15	.176	.241	.133	6.14	2.45
Valera, Francisco	R-R	6-1	170	10-19-89	6	3	5.35	41	0	0	0	76	75	46	45	9	28	58	.260	.322	.216	6.90	3.33

Fielding

Catcher	PCT	G	PO	A	E	DP	PB
Lavisky	.990	65	466	54	5	2	7
Lowery	.995	25	172	21	1	2	7
Monsalve	.986	46	316	43	5	3	7
Tolentino	.976	6	34	6	1	1	0
Valerio	.667	1	1	1	0	0	1

First Base	PCT	G	PO	A	E	DP
Castillo	.981	13	97	7	2	5
Sabourin	.993	128	1092	89	8	108
Valerio	1.000	2	20	0	0	3

Second Base	PCT	G	PO	A	E	DP
Bartolone	1.000	1	2	2	0	0
Garcia	.958	59	121	178	13	40
Hankins	.976	19	36	45	2	11

	PCT	G	PO	A	E	DP
Medina	1.000	4	5	9	0	1
Ramirez	.993	62	111	170	2	31

Third Base	PCT	G	PO	A	E	DP
Bartolone	.750	1	1	2	1	0
Castillo	.889	104	84	172	32	14
Garcia	.667	1	1	1	1	0
Hankins	.891	29	16	41	7	5
Hannahan	1.000	2	0	7	0	0
Medina	.882	10	9	21	4	1

Shortstop	PCT	G	PO	A	E	DP
Bartolone	.958	11	22	24	2	9
Garcia	.833	1	1	4	1	0
Hankins	.833	2	4	6	2	1
Lindor	.968	120	192	349	18	77

	PCT	G	PO	A	E	DP
Medina	1.000	4	7	7	0	4
Ramirez	1.000	2	4	7	0	1

Outfield	PCT	G	PO	A	E	DP
Bartolone	1.000	2	3	0	0	0
Bradley	1.000	10	9	2	0	0
Casas	1.000	26	63	0	0	0
Hankins	.981	25	44	7	1	1
MacPhee	.993	69	138	4	1	1
Medina	1.000	2	1	0	0	0
Myles	.954	88	164	1	8	0
Rodriguez	.971	107	225	8	7	3
Sabourin	1.000	1	2	0	0	0
Smith	.984	96	177	6	3	2
Washington	1.000	6	8	0	0	0

MAHONING VALLEY SCRAPPERS   SHORT-SEASON

NEW YORK-PENN LEAGUE

Batting	B-T	HT	WT	DOB	AVG	vLH	vRH	G	AB	R	H	2B	3B	HR	RBI	BB	HBP	SH	SF	SO	SB	CS	SLG	OBP
Bradley, Mark	L-L	5-9	160	8-30-90	.264	.294	.250	16	53	8	14	1	0	0	1	13	0	0	0	16	3	3	.283	.409
Campbell, Andrew	R-R	6-0	155	2-18-92	.167	.091	.200	21	72	7	12	0	0	1	8	6	1	0	1	20	3	0	.208	.238
Frazar, Evan	R-R	6-0	185	3-17-91	.256	.167	.290	38	129	11	33	4	0	2	16	8	2	1	0	36	2	3	.333	.309
Garcia, Robel	B-R	6-0	168	3-28-93	.227	.264	.211	56	181	24	41	12	0	0	16	23	0	4	1	44	3	1	.293	.312
Gonzalez, Erik	R-R	6-1	165	8-31-91	.220	.207	.224	60	214	30	47	9	1	2	18	11	2	3	0	50	9	1	.299	.264
Haase, Eric	R-R	5-10	180	12-18-92	.091	.143	.000	3	11	1	1	0	0	0	0	1	0	0	0	4	0	0	.091	.167
Jones, Hunter	R-R	6-2	185	8-17-91	.230	.317	.180	52	174	17	40	5	2	0	11	12	1	6	0	41	3	3	.282	.283
Kelly, Jairo	B-R	6-0	170	9-20-92	.212	.234	.203	42	170	16	36	5	2	1	19	11	5	1	0	68	2	3	.282	.280
Lucas, Jeremy	R-R	6-1	205	1-10-91	.250	.250	.250	29	88	10	22	6	0	2	8	16	1	2	2	14	1	0	.386	.364
Martinez, Jorge	B-R	6-2	170	3-29-93	.188	.100	.227	9	32	4	6	3	0	1	6	2	0	0	1	9	0	0	.375	.229
Naquin, Tyler	L-R	6-2	175	4-24-91	.270	.314	.255	36	137	22	37	11	2	0	13	17	7	0	0	26	4	3	.380	.379
Nilsson, Mitch	B-R	5-11	165	5-24-91	.197	.059	.245	20	66	4	13	4	0	0	3	5	0	1	0	27	0	0	.258	.254
Paulino, Dorssys	R-R	6-0	175	11-21-94	.271	.227	.297	15	59	5	16	5	0	1	8	3	0	0	0	14	2	1	.407	.306
Ramirez, Jose	B-R	5-9	165	9-17-92	.364	.500	.333	3	11	2	4	2	0	0	1	0	1	0	0	2	1	0	.545	.417
Romero, Juan	R-R	6-1	175	6-16-93	.186	.200	.180	42	140	17	26	3	2	7	25	8	2	0	1	66	0	4	.386	.238
Sever, Jon	R-R	5-11	187	8-12-90	.274	.389	.218	46	164	16	45	10	1	1	20	21	4	0	1	37	1	2	.366	.368
Siliga, Aaron	L-L	5-10	180	8-24-92	.203	.231	.192	61	237	27	48	7	4	0	15	13	0	1	0	49	6	2	.266	.244
Stock, Richard	R-R	6-2	190	2-8-91	.295	.231	.327	22	78	9	23	7	0	0	4	3	3	0	0	17	1	0	.385	.345
Valerio, Charlie	B-R	6-0	204	11-7-90	.269	.288	.261	53	197	25	53	12	1	5	35	22	2	0	3	48	5	3	.416	.344
Vick, Logan	L-R	5-11	185	10-22-90	.181	.136	.200	22	72	7	13	3	0	0	3	11	0	2	1	15	3	0	.222	.302
Wendle, Joe	L-R	5-11	190	4-26-90	.327	.347	.318	61	245	32	80	15	4	4	37	15	5	0	2	25	4	1	.469	.375

Pitching	B-T	HT	WT	DOB	W	L	ERA	G	GS	CG	SV	IP	H	R	ER	HR	BB	SO	AVG	vLH	vRH	K/9	BB/9
Aviles, Robbie	L-R	6-4	200	12-17-91	0	2	5.12	15	5	0	1	39	47	22	22	4	13	17	.305	.258	.341	3.96	3.03
Davenport, Geoff	L-L	6-1	180	3-14-90	2	3	3.41	15	7	0	0	61	62	27	23	3	20	33	.267	.288	.261	4.90	2.97
DeJesus, Luis	R-R	6-3	173	12-16-91	4	2	2.02	14	14	1	0	80	57	24	18	5	17	52	.197	.168	.213	5.83	1.90
Encarnacion, Luis	R-R	6-3	170	10-25-91	0	2	4.73	21	0	0	0	27	20	14	14	5	24	36	.211	.256	.173	12.15	8.10
Guerrero, Harold	L-L	6-4	235	5-21-90	1	0	4.91	4	0	0	0	4	5	2		0	3	7	.250	.500	.214	17.18	7.36
Head, Louis	R-R	6-0	170	4-23-90	0	2	2.03	7	0	0	3	13	10	4	3	0	1	15	.204	.136	.259	10.13	0.68
Homblert, Rafael	R-R	6-5	178	9-4-91	3	2	2.35	24	0	0	2	31	36	10	8	1	8	21	.300	.349	.278	6.16	2.35
Lee, Jacob	R-R	6-1	190	10-25-89	4	2	3.12	16	8	0	0	43	38	18	15	1	12	47	.221	.203	.232	9.76	2.49
Martin, Josh	R-R	6-5	230	12-30-89	4	1	4.14	14	3	0	0	37	23	21	15	4	12	41	.219	.215	.221	8.08	2.96
Merritt, Ryan	L-L	6-0	160	2-21-92	3	4	4.09	14	14	0	0	66	82	42	30	3	17	40	.304	.379	.283	5.45	2.32

Name	B-T	HT	WT	DOB	W	L	ERA	G	GS	CG	SV	IP	H	R	ER	HR	BB	SO	AVG	vLH	vRH	K/9	BB/9
Morel, Luis	R-R	6-0	170	11-19-92	2	6	4.89	12	9	0	0	50	59	36	27	1	28	49	.286	.265	.301	8.88	5.07
Paredes, Alexis	R-R	6-3	175	1-24-92	0	0	1.93	3	0	0	0	5	3	2	1	0	5	2	.188	.333	.154	3.86	9.64
Pasquale, Nick	R-R	6-0	190	10-27-90	0	0	4.32	4	0	0	1	8	9	4	4	0	1	7	.273	.273	.273	7.56	1.08
Penny, Cody	R-R	6-3	195	5-15-91	0	2	3.05	13	0	0	2	21	17	8	7	0	8	18	.230	.250	.211	7.84	3.48
Peoples, Scott	R-R	6-5	195	9-5-91	1	1	2.28	16	0	0	0	24	17	8	6	1	8	21	.200	.296	.155	7.99	3.04
Sisco, Jake	R-R	6-3	185	12-9-91	1	6	5.03	15	15	0	0	77	81	49	43	6	30	45	.273	.252	.284	5.26	3.51
Stokes, Jim	R-R	6-6	225	10-9-90	1	4	5.61	18	0	0	0	26	28	25	16	2	17	18	.277	.189	.328	6.31	5.96
Tejeda, Enosil	R-R	6-0	175	6-21-89	2	0	1.74	8	0	0	3	10	8	3	2	0	4	10	.216	.333	.160	8.71	3.48
Wagoner, Jack	R-R	6-1	205	6-20-89	3	5	4.36	24	0	0	2	33	35	23	16	2	16	34	.265	.292	.250	9.27	4.36

Fielding

Catcher	PCT	G	PO	A	E	DP	PB
Haase	.963	3	24	2	1	1	0
Lucas	1.000	27	168	16	0	0	6
Nilsson	1.000	1	6	0	0	0	1
Stock	.947	16	96	12	6	2	4
Valerio	.980	32	214	30	5	2	7

First Base	PCT	G	PO	A	E	DP
Frazar	.988	29	240	7	3	23
Gonzalez	.988	27	226	19	3	14
Nilsson	.961	12	98	1	4	5
Sever	1.000	1	7	1	0	3
Valerio	.981	9	97	5	2	14

Second Base	PCT	G	PO	A	E	DP
Garcia	.955	37	61	89	7	22
Ramirez	1.000	2	2	7	0	0
Sever	.960	6	10	14	1	4
Wendle	.972	32	54	85	4	19

Third Base	PCT	G	PO	A	E	DP
Frazar	1.000	5	5	11	0	1
Gonzalez	.896	24	20	66	10	11
Martinez	.625	7	4	6	6	0
Sever	.913	19	15	27	4	2
Wendle	.892	21	14	52	8	4

Shortstop	PCT	G	PO	A	E	DP
Garcia	.929	19	24	55	6	14

	PCT	G	PO	A	E	DP
Kelly	.923	42	51	105	13	15
Paulino	.915	15	18	36	5	5
Ramirez	1.000	1	1	6	0	0

Outfield	PCT	G	PO	A	E	DP
Bradley	.971	14	33	0	1	0
Campbell	.865	21	31	1	5	0
Gonzalez	1.000	8	18	2	0	1
Jones	.978	52	83	6	2	1
Naquin	.978	34	88	3	2	1
Romero	.954	32	60	2	3	1
Siliga	.981	61	152	4	3	2
Vick	1.000	18	35	1	0	0

AZL INDIANS
ROOKIE

ARIZONA LEAGUE

Batting	B-T	HT	WT	DOB	AVG	vLH	vRH	G	AB	R	H	2B	3B	HR	RBI	BB	HBP	SH	SF	SO	SB	CS	SLG	OBP
Battaglia, Ryan	R-R	6-1	202	6-29-92	.214	.077	.239	29	84	22	18	4	2	3	19	22	2	0	2	34	1	1	.417	.382
Bautista, Claudio	R-R	5-11		11-29-93	.273	.273	.273	37	132	30	36	6	2	6	22	19	2	1	2	31	8	1	.485	.368
Booth, Tyler	L-L	6-0	155	10-27-92	.268	.444	.231	36	157	19	42	11	2	3	22	15	5	0	0	40	6	0	.420	.287
Boscan, Manuel	R-R	6-0	160	3-10-93	.274	.222	.283	24	62	10	17	2	0	0	8	5	1	0	3	8	4	2	.306	.324
Brown, Mark	L-L	5-9	160	9-11-91	.159	.000	.184	24	44	10	7	0	1	0	5	16	0	2	0	18	2	1	.205	.383
Campbell, Andrew	L-R	6-0	155	2-18-92	.182	.000	.242	12	44	10	8	1	1	0	5	5	0	0	0	15	3	0	.250	.265
Cervenka, Martin	R-R	6-1	175	8-3-92	.240	.300	.231	26	75	7	18	3	0	0	12	14	0	0	2	21	0	1	.280	.352
De Jesus, Victor	R-R	6-2	170	1-13-93	.206	.000	.259	14	34	3	7	0	0	0	3	4	0	0	1	13	2	0	.206	.282
Haase, Eric	R-R	5-10	180	12-18-92	.282	.261	.288	28	103	16	29	11	2	3	22	5	0	0	1	29	1	0	.515	.312
Hamilton, Nick	B-R	6-1	200	11-19-89	.240	.500	.190	17	50	12	12	1	1	0	4	10	2	1	0	8	2	0	.300	.387
Herrera, Juan	R-R	5-11	165	6-28-93	.283	.296	.279	39	138	28	39	11	2	0	15	26	1	1	2	35	8	2	.391	.395
Kelly, Jairo	B-R	6-0	170	9-20-92	.240	.400	.200	7	25	6	6	1	0	0	2	2	0	0	0	11	3	0	.280	.296
Lin, Chia-Ching	L-R	6-0	180	1-4-92	.250	.250	.250	16	36	2	9	0	0	0	3	7	0	0	0	16	0	2	.306	.372
Lora, Felix	R-R	6-3	190	6-18-93	.095	.143	.071	11	21	1	2	0	0	1	1	2	0	0	0	8	0	0	.238	.174
Martinez, Jorge	B-R	6-2	170	3-29-93	.347	.265	.365	46	190	31	66	14	3	7	39	16	1	0	4	44	4	0	.563	.393
McClure, D'vone	R-R	6-1	175	1-22-94	.211	.118	.233	24	90	15	19	4	0	1	12	11	2	2	2	19	2	1	.289	.305
Medina, Yhoxian	R-R	5-10	165	5-11-90	.176	.000	.188	16	34	6	6	1	0	0	4	9	3	1	0	7	1	1	.206	.391
Paulino, Dorssys	R-R	6-0	175	11-21-94	.355	.500	.324	41	172	42	61	14	6	6	30	15	0	0	1	31	9	1	.610	.404
Rodriguez, Nelson	R-R	6-2	225	6-12-94	.229	.357	.211	32	109	19	25	7	3	4	17	24	2	0	1	41	0	0	.459	.375
Ruiz, Brian	R-R	6-3	180	9-11-92	.147	.167	.143	15	34	2	5	1	0	0	2	6	0	0	0	11	1	1	.176	.194
Santander, Anthony	B-R	6-2	187	10-19-94	.305	.276	.312	43	154	27	47	15	1	4	32	13	7	0	2	37	6	3	.494	.381
Schubert, Josh	R-R	6-4	210	1-25-94	.225	.294	.214	36	120	20	27	4	0	0	20	18	7	0	1	49	3	0	.258	.356
Washington, LeVon	L-R	5-11	170	7-26-91	.444	.333	.500	3	9	3	4	0	0	0	2	1	0	0	0	2	1	0	.444	.500

Pitching	B-T	HT	WT	DOB	W	L	ERA	G	GS	CG	SV	IP	H	R	ER	HR	BB	SO	AVG	vLH	vRH	K/9	BB/9
Baker, Dylan	R-R	6-2	215	4-6-92	0	1	4.13	8	8	0	0	24	20	16	11	1	15	30	.255	.280	.246	11.25	5.63
Brown, Mitch	R-R	6-1	195	4-13-94	2	0	3.58	8	8	0	0	28	24	16	11	3	10	26	.204	.258	.179	8.46	3.25
Chiang, Shao-Ching	R-R	6-0	175	11-10-93	0	0	9.00	1	1	0	0	1	2	1	1	0	0	0	.500	1.000	.333	0.00	0.00
Cleto, Jeffry	R-R	6-3	190	6-14-91	1	1	9.28	14	0	0	0	21	29	28	22	4	14	16	.319	.459	.222	6.75	5.91
Encarnacion, Estevenson	R-R	6-4	186	6-4-90	4	2	4.93	20	0	0	2	35	28	22	19	1	23	28	.219	.200	.226	7.27	5.97
Encarnacion, Isaias	L-L	6-4	200	7-10-91	0	0	8.64	8	0	0	0	8	12	10	8	0	15	13	.343	.200	.400	14.04	16.20
Haley, Trey	R-R	6-3	180	6-21-90	1	0	7.50	4	0	0	0	6	8	5	5	0	2	10	.320	.429	.278	15.00	3.00
Hamrick, Caleb	R-R	6-2	210	9-25-93	0	1	3.24	5	0	0	0	8	3	3	0	2	6		.241	.214	.267	6.48	2.16
Howard, Dillon	R-R	6-4	210	7-1-92	1	7	7.90	12	10	0	0	41	65	53	36	3	18	35	.348	.342	.351	7.68	3.95
Jimenez, Danny	L-L	6-2	205	9-23-89	0	0	0.00	2	0	0	0	3	0	0	0	0	0	3	.000	.000	.000	9.00	0.00
Lovegrove, Kieran	R-R	6-4	185	7-28-94	0	2	6.00	8	7	0	0	21	28	16	14	1	9	18	.318	.344	.304	7.71	3.86
Lovera, Yeiker	R-R	6-0	175	1-23-93	2	1	8.03	7	1	0	0	12	20	12	11	2	6	13	.351	.321	.379	9.49	4.38
Lugo, Luis	L-L	6-5	200	3-5-94	2	4	4.50	11	10	0	0	42	38	30	21	4	21	51	.242	.250	.239	10.93	4.50
Morel, Luis	R-R	6-0	170	11-19-92	1	1	3.07	4	3	0	0	15	15	8	5	1	3	19	.246	.160	.306	11.66	1.84
Nervis, Joshua	R-R	6-3	230	10-25-88	1	0	1.52	13	0	0	3	24	14	4	4	1	8	34	.167	.217	.148	12.93	3.04
Packer, Matt	L-L	6-0	200	8-28-87	0	0	1.93	3	3	0	0	5	5	3	1	0	0	5	.263	.333	.231	9.64	0.00
Paredes, Alexis	R-R	6-3	175	1-24-92	4	1	2.95	17	0	0	4	40	30	18	13	2	17	44	.205	.173	.223	9.98	3.86
Pasquale, Nick	R-R	6-0	190	10-27-90	1	1	6.23	4	2	0	0	13	17	12	9	1	3	14	.321	.333	.314	5.54	2.08
Polanco, Anderson	L-L	6-3	190	9-6-92	1	2	6.35	12	0	0	0	23	24	20	16	5	21	26	.273	.375	.234	10.32	8.34
Puerta, Breily	R-R	5-10	180	6-17-92	4	1	3.60	18	0	0	3	35	33	15	14	2	15	35	.244	.227	.253	9.00	3.86
Rondon, Hector	R-R	6-3	180	2-26-88	0	0	0.00	2	2	0	0	3	0	0	0	0	1	6	.000	.000	.000	18.00	3.00
Santana, Juan	R-R	6-2	170	7-2-93	0	0	7.43	16	0	0	0	27	31	26	22	1	18	17	.290	.318	.270	5.74	6.08

CLEVELAND INDIANS

	B-T	HT	WT	DOB	W	L	ERA	G	GS	CG	SV	IP	H	R	ER	HR	BB	SO	AVG	vLH	vRH	K/9	BB/9
Sterling, Felix	R-R	6-3	200	3-15-93	3	0	1.66	6	0	0	2	22	14	8	4	0	7	31	.177	.182	.174	12.88	2.91
Suarez, Benny	R-R	6-0	190	9-28-91	1	0	4.19	9	1	0	1	19	18	10	9	2	10	19	.247	.200	.264	8.84	4.66
White, Walker	R-R	5-11	185	11-9-91	2	0	2.70	7	0	0	0	13	11	5	4	1	5	15	.234	.333	.211	10.13	3.38

Fielding

Catcher	PCT	G	PO	A	E	DP	PB
Battaglia	.935	8	67	5	5	2	6
Boscan	1.000	5	8	0	0	0	1
Cervenka	.986	26	185	31	3	4	8
Haase	.973	25	185	35	6	0	11
Rodriguez	.971	3	28	5	1	1	4

First Base	PCT	G	PO	A	E	DP
Battaglia	.975	17	152	5	4	13
Boscan	.971	13	96	4	3	5
Hamilton	1.000	2	15	4	0	1
Rodriguez	.979	28	225	12	5	19

Second Base	PCT	G	PO	A	E	DP
Bautista	.933	30	55	85	10	18

	PCT	G	PO	A	E	DP
Hamilton	1.000	1	0	1	0	0
Herrera	.951	21	35	63	5	9
Kelly	.667	2	3	1	2	0
Medina	.923	4	8	16	2	4

Third Base	PCT	G	PO	A	E	DP
Hamilton	.810	11	2	15	4	0
Herrera	.920	9	10	13	2	1
Martinez	.905	37	24	81	11	6

Shortstop	PCT	G	PO	A	E	DP
Bautista	.929	7	4	9	1	0
Herrera	.897	9	11	24	4	7
Kelly	.833	6	5	10	3	3
Medina	.956	11	17	26	2	5

	PCT	G	PO	A	E	DP
Paulino	.868	31	46	86	20	16

Outfield	PCT	G	PO	A	E	DP
Booth	.984	32	55	6	1	0
Brown	1.000	20	18	0	0	0
Campbell	.905	11	18	1	2	0
De Jesus	.786	13	10	1	3	0
Lin	1.000	9	14	0	0	0
Lora	1.000	9	9	1	0	0
McClure	.927	22	37	1	3	1
Ruiz	1.000	10	12	1	0	0
Santander	1.000	39	49	4	0	1
Schubert	.852	31	43	3	8	1
Washington	1.000	2	3	0	0	0

DSL INDIANS   ROOKIE

DOMINICAN SUMMER LEAGUE

Batting	B-T	HT	WT	DOB	AVG	vLH	vRH	G	AB	R	H	2B	3B	HR	RBI	BB	HBP	SH	SF	SO	SB	CS	SLG	OBP
Acosta, Wilkin	L-L	6-0	185	10-8-92	.063	.000	.091	7	16	5	1	0	1	0	0	6	1	0	0	4	3	0	.188	.348
Cabral, Victor	R-R	6-2	180	11-5-93	.289	.268	.301	64	235	37	68	12	4	2	33	21	11	2	0	32	8	3	.400	.375
Calderon, Kevin	R-R	5-11	180	4-4-94	.186	.152	.208	31	86	5	16	2	0	1	9	7	1	3	0	17	2	1	.244	.255
Castillo, Amauri	R-R	6-2	197	4-4-93	.202	.136	.236	56	193	19	39	8	0	3	22	7	2	1	0	41	0	0	.290	.238
Castillo, Ivan	B-R	5-11	150	5-30-95	.236	.231	.238	65	216	28	51	6	0	1	14	21	2	6	1	32	16	6	.278	.308
De La Cruz, Juan	B-R	6-1	195	8-5-93	.247	.245	.248	59	174	16	43	11	1	1	26	21	2	4	3	26	2	3	.339	.330
Depen, Michael	R-R	6-3	186	6-16-92	.281	.280	.281	50	171	23	48	14	3	3	29	14	5	3	1	39	10	10	.450	.351
Diaz, Rainel	R-R	6-0	175	8-16-94	.143	.143	.143	15	21	2	3	0	0	0	1	0	0	0	0	7	0	0	.143	.143
Lunar, Henry	R-R	5-10	170	11-18-93	.286	.000	.500	5	7	0	2	0	0	0	0	0	0	0	0	0	4	0	1	.286	.286
Mejia, Joel	R-R	5-11	157	4-7-93	.263	.298	.244	41	137	28	36	4	5	0	7	17	2	2	2	29	17	6	.365	.348
Mendoza, Yonathan	B-R	5-11	167	2-10-94	.287	.270	.293	43	136	23	39	3	0	0	11	22	4	3	0	10	11	6	.309	.401
Miguel, Francisco	R-R	6-3	206	3-24-95	.179	.172	.182	33	84	8	15	3	0	1	2	9	0	0	0	29	1	2	.250	.258
Moncion, Juan Carlos	L-L	6-2	210	10-24-93	.204	.200	.206	55	201	19	41	11	0	2	30	19	6	2	3	42	4	4	.289	.288
Sancez, Omar	B-R	6-1	179	2-10-95	.197	.196	.197	59	183	19	36	9	2	0	13	20	7	2	2	47	14	6	.268	.297
Santana, Andri	B-R	6-2	180	7-23-92	.325	.273	.346	39	114	20	37	3	1	2	12	17	2	1	1	45	10	9	.421	.418
Soto, Fidias	R-R	6-2	185	1-13-93	.167	.133	.185	30	42	8	7	3	0	2	5	13	8	0	0	20	2	4	.381	.444
Valdez, Ordomar	B-R	5-9	150	4-27-94	.284	.317	.271	62	218	43	62	4	4	0	16	41	3	6	1	36	25	16	.339	.403

Pitching	B-T	HT	WT	DOB	W	L	ERA	G	GS	CG	SV	IP	H	R	ER	HR	BB	SO	AVG	vLH	vRH	K/9	BB/9
Alcantara, Martin	R-R	5-11	180	9-14-91	1	3	1.56	22	0	0	10	35	27	14	6	1	17	29	.209	.263	.200	7.53	4.41
Aquino, Luis	R-R	6-1	185	6-30-93	1	1	3.80	17	1	0	0	24	24	15	10	0	13	10	.267	.333	.253	3.80	4.94
Arias, Jesus	R-R	6-1	185	9-29-93	2	1	7.98	12	0	0	0	15	11	13	13	0	14	10	.229	.333	.265	6.14	8.59
Beras, Jesus	R-R	6-3	188	1-8-93	0	0	12.71	12	0	0	0	11	16	21	16	0	14	8	.320	.333	.316	6.35	11.12
Diaz, Carlos	L-L	6-3	190	2-3-92	2	5	1.59	11	11	0	0	51	28	16	9	3	25	49	.162	.167	.161	8.65	4.41
Estrella, Edward	R-R	6-1	170	1-24-94	4	0	1.85	22	0	0	2	39	35	9	8	1	11	16	.250	.407	.212	3.69	2.54
Garcia, Juan	R-R	6-1	183	12-3-93	0	1	2.20	13	0	0	0	16	14	5	4	0	12		.255	.222	.261	6.61	6.06
Gomez, Luis	L-L	6-0	195	9-15-92	2	0	0.56	14	8	0	1	48	25	9	3	0	11	46	.152	.083	.158	8.57	2.05
Manzueta, Cristian	L-L	6-5	205	10-30-94	0	1	3.38	12	5	0	0	21	12	9	8	0	17	15	.182	.000	.182	6.33	7.17
Marte, Juan	R-R	6-4	175	6-24-94	0	1	7.02	13	0	0	1	17	22	13	13	0	5	8	.324	.545	.281	4.32	2.70
Nivar, Juan	R-R	6-1	170	9-24-92	4	1	1.36	10	10	0	0	46	26	11	7	1	13	54	.163	.118	.175	10.49	2.53
Pineda, Edgar	L-L	5-10	155	9-7-94	1	0	5.14	12	0	0	0	14	9	10	8	0	15	13	.188	.000	.196	8.36	9.64
Placido, Anderson	L-L	6-0	190	9-24-93	6	1	1.97	13	11	0	0	59	47	18	13	1	29	49	.232	.154	.237	7.43	4.40
Puello, Johan	R-R	5-11	165	1-5-94	0	6	3.75	14	3	0	0	24	25	20	10	2	17	15	.258	.333	.244	5.63	6.38
Ramirez, Anvioris	L-L	6-1	165	3-10-88	1	1	3.38	9	0	0	1	16	13	8	6	0	6	9	.220	.000	.228	5.06	3.38
Rivas, Alejandro	R-R	6-1	205	8-21-91	1	0	5.27	13	0	0	1	14	12	8	8	2	11	12	.240	.182	.256	7.90	7.24
Rodriguez, Ramon	R-R	5-11	176	3-1-94	5	4	2.75	20	4	0	1	52	51	24	16	3	18	37	.267	.323	.256	6.36	3.10
Vincent, Junior	R-R	6-2	190	2-28-95	0	1	4.50	7	1	0	0	10	13	8	5	1	3	7	.317	.286	.324	6.30	2.70
Vizcaya, Anthony	R-R	6-0	180	10-24-93	3	2	0.94	13	12	0	0	67	38	13	7	0	19	33	.167	.192	.163	4.43	2.55
Zapata, Jose	R-R	6-4	200	5-21-93	2	6	4.82	15	4	0	0	28	19	20	15	1	19	14	.190	.438	.143	4.50	6.11

Fielding

Catcher	PCT	G	PO	A	E	DP	PB
Calderon	.978	30	151	28	4	0	3
De La Cruz	.985	45	229	41	4	3	8
Diaz	.983	15	54	4	1	0	3
Lunar	1.000	5	21	0	0	0	1

First Base	PCT	G	PO	A	E	DP
Castillo	1.000	5	28	1	0	0
De La Cruz	.990	10	101	2	1	4
Mendoza	1.000	1	3	0	0	1
Moncion	.985	52	493	28	8	42
Sancez	.973	7	68	5	2	8

Second Base	PCT	G	PO	A	E	DP
Mendoza	.964	14	24	30	2	8
Valdez	.970	60	161	167	10	40

Third Base	PCT	G	PO	A	E	DP
Castillo	.936	53	31	129	11	11
De La Cruz	—	1	0	0	0	0
Mendoza	.947	24	18	53	4	6

Shortstop	PCT	G	PO	A	E	DP
Castillo	.944	65	104	232	20	34
Mendoza	.939	8	13	18	2	2

Outfield	PCT	G	PO	A	E	DP
Acosta	1.000	7	8	2	0	1
Cabral	.980	39	45	3	1	1
Depen	.947	47	53	1	3	1
Mejia	.985	37	58	6	1	0
Miguel	.918	32	42	3	4	1
Sancez	.942	37	47	2	3	0
Santana	1.000	14	11	1	0	0
Soto	.974	25	35	2	1	0
Valdez	—	1	0	0	0	0

Colorado Rockies

SEASON IN A SENTENCE: When your general manager and farm director switch jobs midseason, and that's the *second-most* unconventional move of the season, it's a good sign that things didn't go as planned.

HIGH POINT: Any playoff hopes had long since been forgotten, but the Rockies went 17-11 in August (the only winning month of the season) including a five-game winning streak from Aug. 19-Aug. 24 when the pitching staff allowed two runs or fewer in every game.

LOW POINT: In mid-June, Colorado went on a 1-12 bender that led the team to go to a four-man rotation with a flexible 75-pitch limit—its most unconventional move of the season—and eventually led general manager Dan O'Dowd and assistant GM Bill Geivett, who oversaw scouting and player development, to swap roles, although they kept the same titles.

NOTABLE ROOKIES: With shortstop Troy Tulowitzki lost for much of the season with a groin injury, Josh Rutledge stepped and in an ably filled the role, batting .274/.306/.469 in 277 at-bats. Catcher Wilin Rosario hit 28 home runs as the club's everyday catcher while throwing out 32 percent of basestealers. Drew Pomeranz, acquired from the Indians in last year's Ubaldo Jimenez deal, did not have as easy a time making the transition to Coors Field. Pomeranz went 2-9, 4.93.

KEY TRANSACTIONS: Before the season, the Rockies sent righthander Jason Hammel to the Orioles for righthander Jeremy Guthrie. Hammel turned into an ace for the Orioles, while Guthrie fell apart in Colorado. The Rockies then exchanged problems with the Royals, sending Guthrie to Kansas City for lefthander Jonathan Sanchez. Sanchez went 0-3, 9.53 in three starts before he was placed on the disabled list.

DOWN ON THE FARM: Low Class A Asheville was one of the best teams in the minors all season, going 88-42 overall and then claiming its first outright South Atlantic League championship since 1984. David Dahl, the club's 2012 first-round pick, was the Rookie-level Pioneer League MVP despite being one of its youngest players. Short-season Tri-Cities was the only team that didn't finish with a winning record. The year ended on a down note with the firing of longtime Asheville manager Joe Mikulik, however. He had managed the team for 13 years and won SAL manager of the year honors four times, including 2012.

OPENING DAY PAYROLL: $78.1 million (22nd)

PLAYERS OF THE YEAR

MAJOR LEAGUE	MINOR LEAGUE
Dexter Fowler of	**Christian Bergman** rhp
.300/.389/.474	(High Class A)
11 3B, 53 RBIs	16-5, 3.65
7th in NL in OBP	Cal Lg. pitcher of year

ORGANIZATION LEADERS

BATTING		*Minimum 250 PA
MAJORS		
* AVG	Jordan Pacheco	.309
* OPS	Carlos Gonzalez	.881
HR	Wilin Rosario	28
RBI	Carlos Gonzalez	85
MINORS		
* AVG	Matt McBride, Colorado Springs	.344
* OBP	Kyle Parker, Modesto	.415
* SLG	Andrew Brown, Colorado Springs	.597
R	Trevor Story, Asheville	96
H	Corey Dickerson, Modesto/Tulsa	154
TB	Corey Dickerson, Modesto/Tulsa	274
2B	Trevor Story, Asheville	43
3B	David Dahl, Grand Junction	10
HR	Andrew Brown, Colorado Springs	24
	Jared Clark, Modesto	24
RBI	Andrew Brown, Colorado Springs	98
BB	Jared Clark, Modesto	89
SO	Jared Clark, Modesto	128
SB	Rafael Ortega, Modesto	36

PITCHING		#Minimum 75 IP
MAJORS		
W	Rex Brothers	8
# ERA	Josh Roenicke	3.25
SO	Rex Brothers	83
SV	Rafael Betancourt	31
MINORS		
W	Christian Bergman, Modesto	16
L	Parker Frazier, Tulsa	14
# ERA	Tyler Anderson, Asheville	2.47
G	Coty Woods, Tulsa/Colo. Springs	61
GS	Rob Scahill, Colorado Springs	29
SV	Coty Woods, Tulsa/Colo. Springs	27
IP	Parker Frazier, Tulsa	167
BB	Tyler Matzek, Modesto	95
SO	Rob Scahill, Colorado Springs	159
# AVG	Edwar Cabrera, Tulsa/Colo. Springs	.195

General Manager: Dan O'Dowd. **Farm Director:** Jeff Bridich. **Scouting Director:** Bill Schmidt.

Class	Team	League	W	L	PCT	Finish	Manager
Majors	Colorado Rockies	National	64	98	.395	14th (16)	Jim Tracy
Triple-A	Colorado Springs Sky Sox	Pacific Coast	75	69	.521	7th (16)	Stu Cole
Double-A	Tulsa Drillers	Texas	75	64	.540	4th (8)	Duane Espy
High A	Modesto Nuts	California	73	67	.521	4th (10)	Lenn Sakata
Low A	Asheville Tourists	South Atlantic	88	52	.629	1st (14)	Joe Mikulik
Short-season	Tri-City Dust Devils	Northwest	32	44	.421	t-6th (8)	Fred Ocasio
Rookie	Grand Junction Rockies	Pioneer	43	33	.566	2nd (8)	Tony Diaz
Overall 2012 Minor League Record			386	329	.540	2nd (30)	

ORGANIZATION STATISTICS

COLORADO ROCKIES
NATIONAL LEAGUE

Batting	B-T	HT	WT	DOB	AVG	vLH	vRH	G	AB	R	H	2B	3B	HR	RBI	BB	HBP	SH	SF	SO	SB	CS	SLG	OBP
Blackmon, Charlie	L-L	6-3	210	7-1-86	.283	.348	.267	42	113	15	32	8	0	2	9	4	3	1	0	17	1	2	.407	.325
Brown, Andrew	R-R	6-0	185	9-10-84	.232	.275	.208	46	112	14	26	7	0	5	11	12	0	0	2	34	2	2	.429	.302
Colvin, Tyler	L-L	6-3	210	9-5-85	.290	.270	.297	136	420	62	122	27	10	18	72	21	2	2	1	117	7	3	.531	.327
Cuddyer, Michael	R-R	6-2	220	3-27-79	.260	.258	.261	101	358	53	93	30	2	16	58	32	0	0	4	78	8	3	.489	.317
Field, Tommy	R-R	5-9	175	2-22-87	.000	.000	.000	2	2	0	0	0	0	0	0	0	1	0	0	1	0	0	.000	.333
Fowler, Dexter	B-R	6-4	190	3-22-86	.300	.315	.293	143	454	72	136	18	11	13	53	68	0	6	2	128	12	5	.474	.389
Giambi, Jason	L-R	6-3	250	1-8-71	.225	.296	.194	60	89	7	20	4	0	1	8	20	2	0	2	24	0	0	.303	.372
Gonzalez, Carlos	L-L	6-1	220	10-17-85	.303	.266	.325	135	518	89	157	31	5	22	85	56	2	0	3	115	20	5	.510	.371
Helton, Todd	L-R	6-2	220	8-20-73	.238	.184	.268	69	240	31	57	16	1	7	37	39	1	0	3	44	1	1	.400	.343
Hernandez, Ramon	R-R	6-0	220	5-20-76	.217	.152	.239	52	184	16	40	10	0	5	28	6	2	2	2	32	0	1	.353	.247
Herrera, Jonathan	B-R	5-9	180	11-3-84	.262	.231	.272	86	225	29	59	9	1	3	12	16	2	7	0	39	4	1	.351	.317
LeMahieu, D.J.	R-R	6-4	205	7-13-88	.297	.233	.320	81	229	26	68	12	4	2	22	13	0	3	2	42	1	2	.410	.332
McBride, Matt	R-R	6-2	215	5-23-85	.205	.194	.213	31	78	8	16	2	0	2	11	1	1	0	1	17	0	0	.308	.222
Nelson, Chris	R-R	5-11	205	9-3-85	.301	.307	.299	111	345	45	104	21	3	9	53	27	1	2	2	84	2	1	.458	.352
Nieves, Wil	R-R	5-11	190	9-25-77	.298	.500	.279	16	47	3	14	2	0	1	5	3	0	0	1	9	0	0	.404	.333
2-team total (16 Arizona)					.301	—	—	32	83	7	25	3	0	2	8	4	0	1	1	17	0	1	.410	.330
Ortega, Rafael	L-R	5-11	160	5-15-91	.500	.000	1.000	2	4	0	2	0	0	0	1	0	0	1	0	2	1	0	.500	.667
Pacheco, Jordan	R-R	6-1	200	1-30-86	.309	.351	.294	132	475	51	147	32	3	5	54	22	3	1	4	61	7	2	.421	.341
Rosario, Wilin	R-R	5-11	215	2-23-89	.270	.348	.239	117	396	67	107	19	0	28	71	25	1	0	4	99	4	5	.530	.312
Rutledge, Josh	R-R	6-1	190	4-21-89	.274	.247	.286	73	277	37	76	20	5	8	37	9	4	0	1	54	7	0	.469	.306
Scutaro, Marco	R-R	5-10	185	10-30-75	.271	.257	.276	95	377	47	102	16	3	4	30	27	4	4	3	35	7	3	.361	.324
2-team total (61 San Francisco)					.306	—	—	156	620	87	190	32	4	7	74	40	4	10	9	49	9	4	.405	.348
Tulowitzki, Troy	R-R	6-3	215	10-10-84	.287	.173	.333	47	181	33	52	8	2	8	27	19	2	0	1	19	2	2	.486	.360
Young Jr., Eric	B-R	5-10	180	5-25-85	.316	.383	.291	98	174	36	55	7	2	4	15	13	4	5	0	31	14	2	.448	.377

Pitching	B-T	HT	WT	DOB	W	L	ERA	G	GS	CG	SV	IP	H	R	ER	HR	BB	SO	AVG	vLH	vRH	K/9	BB/9
Belisle, Matt	R-R	6-4	225	6-6-80	3	8	3.71	80	0	0	3	80	91	36	33	5	18	69	.282	.313	.259	7.76	2.03
Betancourt, Rafael	R-R	6-2	220	4-29-75	1	4	2.81	60	0	0	31	58	53	19	18	6	12	57	.241	.304	.186	8.90	1.87
Brothers, Rex	L-L	6-0	210	12-18-87	8	2	3.86	75	0	0	0	68	63	33	29	5	37	83	.251	.206	.282	11.04	4.92
Cabrera, Edwar	L-L	6-0	175	10-20-87	0	2	11.12	2	2	0	0	6	9	9	7	3	7	5	.346	.333	.353	7.94	11.12
Chacin, Jhoulys	R-R	6-3	225	1-7-88	3	5	4.43	14	14	0	0	69	80	35	34	10	32	45	.288	.293	.282	5.87	4.17
Chatwood, Tyler	R-R	6-0	185	12-16-89	5	6	5.43	19	12	0	1	65	74	43	39	9	33	41	.290	.311	.268	5.71	4.59
De La Rosa, Jorge	L-L	6-1	220	4-5-81	0	2	9.28	3	3	0	0	11	17	14	11	5	2	6	.340	.125	.381	5.06	1.69
Ekstrom, Mike	R-R	6-0	190	8-30-83	0	0	6.32	15	0	0	0	16	21	11	11	1	2	9	.328	.524	.233	5.17	1.15
Escalona, Edgmer	R-R	6-4	235	10-6-86	0	1	6.04	22	0	0	0	22	23	16	15	5	7	21	.264	.242	.278	8.46	2.82
Francis, Jeff	L-L	6-5	220	1-8-81	6	7	5.58	24	24	0	0	113	145	71	70	15	22	76	.316	.270	.329	6.05	1.75
Friedrich, Christian	R-L	6-4	215	7-8-87	5	8	6.17	16	16	0	0	85	102	61	58	14	30	74	.303	.288	.307	7.87	3.19
Guthrie, Jeremy	R-R	6-1	205	4-8-79	3	9	6.35	19	15	0	0	91	122	72	64	21	31	45	.324	.355	.289	4.47	3.08
Harris, Will	R-R	6-4	225	8-28-84	1	1	8.15	20	0	0	0	18	27	18	16	3	6	19	.342	.265	.400	9.68	3.06
Moscoso, Guillermo	R-R	6-1	200	11-14-83	3	2	6.12	23	3	0	0	50	67	34	34	8	19	47	.321	.304	.333	8.46	3.42
Moyer, Jamie	L-L	6-0	185	11-18-62	2	5	5.70	10	10	0	0	54	75	40	34	11	18	36	.328	.333	.325	6.04	3.02
Nicasio, Juan	R-R	6-3	230	8-31-86	2	3	5.28	11	11	0	0	58	72	37	34	7	22	54	.313	.299	.325	8.38	3.41
Ottavino, Adam	L-R	6-5	230	11-22-85	5	1	4.56	53	0	0	0	79	76	42	40	9	34	81	.253	.286	.232	9.23	3.87
Outman, Josh	L-L	6-1	200	9-14-84	1	3	8.19	27	7	0	0	41	47	37	37	7	20	40	.290	.197	.347	8.85	4.43
Pomeranz, Drew	R-L	6-5	240	11-22-88	2	9	4.93	22	22	0	0	97	97	57	53	14	46	83	.261	.169	.287	7.73	4.28
Putnam, Zach	R-R	6-1	225	7-3-87	0	0	0.00	2	0	0	0	2	3	0	0	0	1	0	.429	.250	.667	0.00	4.50
Reynolds, Matt	L-L	6-5	240	10-2-84	3	1	4.40	71	0	0	0	57	65	31	28	11	17	51	.291	.269	.311	8.01	2.67
Roenicke, Josh	R-R	6-3	200	8-4-82	4	2	3.25	63	0	0	1	89	85	40	32	9	43	54	.259	.231	.278	5.48	4.36
Rogers, Esmil	R-R	6-1	190	8-14-85	0	2	8.06	23	0	0	0	26	36	23	23	2	18	29	.324	.235	.400	10.17	6.31
Sanchez, Jonathan	L-L	6-0	200	11-19-82	0	3	9.53	3	3	0	0	11	17	13	12	3	9	9	.370	.333	.375	7.15	7.15
Scahill, Rob	R-R	6-2	220	2-15-87	0	0	1.04	6	0	0	0	9	7	1	1	0	3	4	.233	.111	.286	4.15	3.12
Torres, Carlos	R-R	6-1	185	10-22-82	5	3	5.26	31	0	0	0	53	49	31	31	2	26	42	.257	.225	.279	7.13	4.42
White, Alex	R-R	6-3	215	8-29-88	2	9	5.51	23	20	0	0	98	114	66	60	13	51	64	.288	.285	.291	5.88	4.68

Fielding

Catcher	PCT	G	PO	A	E	DP	PB
Hernandez	.994	46	336	17	2	4	1
Nieves	.989	12	84	7	1	2	0
Pacheco	.968	5	29	1	1	0	0
Rosario	.983	105	694	78	13	5	21

First Base	PCT	G	PO	A	E	DP
Colvin	.989	31	167	7	2	11
Cuddyer	.991	26	217	15	2	22
Giambi	1.000	13	86	3	0	7
Helton	.997	67	566	57	2	53
Hernandez	1.000	2	1	0	0	0
LeMahieu	1.000	1	1	0	0	0
McBride	.967	8	59	0	2	3
Nieves	1.000	2	1	0	0	0
Pacheco	.988	43	324	10	4	26
Rosario	.889	1	8	0	1	1

Second Base	PCT	G	PO	A	E	DP
Field	1.000	1	1	0	0	0
Herrera	1.000	19	26	32	0	6
LeMahieu	.994	67	105	204	2	33
Nelson	.989	21	39	54	1	13
Rutledge	1.000	7	15	18	0	4
Scutaro	.983	72	139	205	6	45

Third Base	PCT	G	PO	A	E	DP
Herrera	1.000	13	7	13	0	2
LeMahieu	1.000	9	2	8	0	0
Nelson	.931	92	45	118	12	14
Pacheco	.948	82	21	142	9	15
Rosario	.500	3	0	1	1	0

Shortstop	PCT	G	PO	A	E	DP
Herrera	.981	42	53	101	3	15

	PCT	G	PO	A	E	DP
LeMahieu	—	2	0	0	0	0
Nelson	1.000	1	1	0	0	0
Rutledge	.956	57	83	157	11	33
Scutaro	.977	27	40	89	3	17
Tulowitzki	.964	47	76	140	8	31

Outfield	PCT	G	PO	A	E	DP
Blackmon	1.000	33	54	4	0	2
Brown	.967	33	55	3	2	0
Colvin	.984	94	179	8	3	1
Cuddyer	.977	74	122	6	3	3
Fowler	.978	131	257	4	6	2
Gonzalez	.982	131	207	7	4	0
McBride	1.000	12	20	0	0	0
Ortega	1.000	1	3	0	0	0
Young Jr.	1.000	34	64	0	0	0

COLORADO SPRINGS SKY SOX   TRIPLE-A

PACIFIC COAST LEAGUE

Batting	B-T	HT	WT	DOB	AVG	vLH	vRH	G	AB	R	H	2B	3B	HR	RBI	BB	HBP	SH	SF	SO	SB	CS	SLG	OBP
Blackmon, Charlie	L-L	6-3	210	7-1-86	.303	.241	.336	59	228	55	69	18	4	5	34	29	3	2	2	42	10	0	.482	.385
Brown, Andrew	R-R	6-0	185	9-10-84	.308	.284	.316	100	390	81	120	33	4	24	98	37	2	1	8	100	3	1	.597	.364
Castillo, Wilkin	R-R	6-0	200	6-1-84	.253	.348	.216	74	233	27	59	8	3	4	34	7	1	5	4	29	4	1	.365	.273
Cesario, Jimmy	L-R	5-11	200	10-15-85	.247	.273	.242	34	77	10	19	3	0	1	10	5	1	1	0	16	0	1	.325	.301
Cuddyer, Michael	R-R	6-2	220	3-27-79	.667	.667	.667	2	9	4	6	1	0	1	3	0	0	0	0	1	0	1	1.111	.667
Culberson, Charlie	R-R	6-1	200	4-10-89	.336	.351	.330	30	125	17	42	11	1	2	12	1	1	0	1	18	6	2	.488	.344
2-team total (91 Fresno)					.263	—	—	121	476	70	125	25	7	12	65	21	5	2	4	94	14	4	.420	.298
Field, Tommy	R-R	5-9	175	2-22-87	.246	.233	.252	121	435	74	107	31	6	8	49	41	5	8	4	76	4	0	.400	.315
Giambi, Jason	L-R	6-3	250	1-8-71	.333	—	.333	2	6	0	2	1	0	0	0	0	0	0	0	2	0	0	.500	.333
Harris, Brendan	R-R	6-1	200	8-26-80	.317	.237	.345	106	357	73	113	33	4	9	63	52	7	1	7	44	2	3	.507	.407
Hernandez, Ramon	R-R	6-0	220	5-20-76	.167	.250	.125	4	12	2	2	0	0	1	4	1	1	0	0	1	0	0	.417	.286
Herrera, Jonathan	B-R	5-9	180	11-3-84	.167	.000	.222	4	12	1	2	1	0	0	0	0	0	0	0	1	0	0	.250	.167
Iribarren, Hernan	L-R	6-1	195	6-29-84	.302	.344	.289	111	381	62	115	18	4	1	40	42	1	7	5	59	20	3	.378	.368
LeMahieu, D.J.	R-R	6-4	205	7-13-88	.314	.269	.330	61	255	33	80	14	2	1	31	23	0	0	2	29	13	6	.396	.368
McBride, Matt	R-R	6-2	215	5-23-85	.344	.374	.335	108	439	73	151	42	6	10	87	19	1	0	10	47	0	1	.535	.365
Nelson, Chris	R-R	5-11	205	9-3-85	.294	.300	.290	13	51	12	15	4	1	0	8	2	1	0	0	12	1	1	.412	.333
Nieves, Wil	R-R	5-11	190	9-25-77	.306	.353	.286	34	111	15	34	4	0	3	16	6	0	4	2	20	1	1	.423	.336
Pacheco, Jordan	R-R	6-1	200	1-30-86	.433	.583	.400	17	67	10	29	4	0	3	10	3	3	1	0	5	1	0	.627	.479
Pettit, Chris	R-R	6-0	200	8-15-84	.278	.250	.300	6	18	2	5	1	0	0	1	2	0	0	0	4	0	0	.333	.350
Roberts, Brandon	L-R	6-0	190	11-9-84	.282	.317	.274	82	238	44	67	15	3	0	25	22	3	3	2	25	13	4	.370	.347
Santos, Omir	R-R	6-0	215	4-29-81	.311	.333	.300	38	119	12	37	9	0	2	21	2	0	1	1	17	0	0	.437	.320
Tarleton, Dallas	L-R	5-11	200	8-5-87	.300	.167	.333	9	30	5	9	1	0	0	7	2	0	0	0	10	0	0	.333	.344
Tracy, Chad	R-R	6-3	210	7-4-85	.269	.220	.287	133	454	61	122	38	0	12	82	34	5	1	4	112	1	4	.432	.324
Tulowitzki, Troy	R-R	6-3	215	10-10-84	.353	.000	.400	6	17	3	6	1	0	2	4	0	0	0	0	4	0	0	.765	.389
Wheeler, Tim	L-R	6-4	215	1-21-88	.303	.269	.316	92	379	67	115	27	4	2	37	29	3	3	1	69	7	7	.412	.357
Wood, Brandon	R-R	6-3	205	3-2-85	.259	.288	.247	119	401	56	104	28	1	10	64	28	5	0	4	97	2	0	.409	.313

Pitching	B-T	HT	WT	DOB	W	L	ERA	G	GS	CG	SV	IP	H	R	ER	HR	BB	SO	AVG	vLH	vRH	K/9	BB/9
Bergmann, Jason	R-R	6-3	220	9-25-81	3	3	6.98	28	0	0	4	40	58	34	31	5	16	33	.339	.341	.337	7.43	3.60
Bibens-Dirkx, Austin	R-R	6-1	210	4-29-85	1	1	13.89	7	0	0	0	12	20	18	18	2	12	10	.392	.467	.286	7.71	9.26
Brooks, Ricky	R-R	6-3	180	7-18-84	0	4	9.00	14	4	0	0	32	46	36	32	6	19	20	.341	.406	.273	5.63	5.34
Brothers, Rex	L-L	6-0	210	12-18-87	0	0	1.69	4	0	0	1	5	3	1	1	0	3	13	.167	.125	.200	21.94	5.06
Cabrera, Edwar	L-L	6-0	175	10-20-87	3	1	3.41	6	6	1	0	32	26	18	12	6	12	39	.224	.229	.222	11.08	3.41
Chacin, Jhoulys	R-R	6-3	225	1-7-88	1	1	2.63	2	2	0	0	14	10	4	4	1	5	5	.208	.227	.192	3.29	3.29
Chatwood, Tyler	R-R	6-0	185	12-16-89	0	2	5.79	9	9	0	0	37	52	26	24	2	19	30	.327	.313	.342	7.47	4.58
De La Rosa, Jorge	L-L	6-1	220	4-5-81	0	1	9.45	2	2	0	0	7	9	8	7	3	3	5	.310	.333	.294	6.75	4.05
Dodson, Stephen	R-R	6-5	200	8-29-85	3	3	4.26	30	0	0	0	38	52	23	18	0	15	22	.327	.390	.268	5.21	3.55
Ekstrom, Mike	R-R	6-0	190	8-30-83	3	1	2.53	43	0	0	1	57	47	17	16	0	18	57	.224	.189	.250	9.00	2.84
Escalona, Edgmer	R-R	6-4	235	10-6-86	3	3	2.93	32	0	0	4	40	37	18	13	2	17	40	.240	.179	.287	9.00	3.83
Friedrich, Christian	R-L	6-4	215	7-8-87	2	1	3.00	5	5	1	0	30	23	12	10	1	4	27	.213	.242	.200	8.10	1.20
Gomez, Kennil	R-R	6-3	170	4-8-88	1	0	5.89	11	0	0	0	18	16	12	12	2	12	14	.229	.257	.200	6.87	5.89
Gomez, Leuris	R-R	6-0	170	10-20-86	1	0	0.00	1	0	0	0	2	2	0	0	0	2	1	.250	.200	.333	9.00	0.00
Gonzalez, Edgar	R-R	6-2	210	2-23-83	3	3	5.40	15	7	0	0	47	54	32	28	5	11	40	.284	.289	.280	7.71	2.12
2-team total (2 Oklahoma City)					4	3	4.37	17	9	0	0	60	60	34	29	5	13	48	—	—	—	7.24	1.96
Harris, Will	R-R	6-4	225	8-28-84	2	0	1.02	13	0	0	0	18	9	2	2	0	1	20	.145	.132	.167	10.19	0.51
Hynick, Brandon	R-R	6-3	205	3-7-85	1	2	7.29	5	4	0	0	21	31	17	17	2	6	14	.348	.366	.333	6.00	2.57
Johnson, Tyler	B-L	6-2	200	6-7-81	0	1	7.15	8	0	0	0	11	13	9	9	0	11	6	.317	.211	.409	4.76	8.74
Junge, Eric	R-R	6-5	220	1-5-77	0	0	8.44	5	2	0	0	16	27	15	15	2	5	10	.375	.391	.346	5.63	2.81
Marquez, Jeff	R-R	6-2	190	8-10-84	1	0	6.75	2	0	0	0	5	3	2	2	1	2	2	.385	.333	.400	6.75	6.75
2-team total (17 Tacoma)					5	8	6.69	19	14	0	0	79	113	64	59	11	36	47	—	—	—	5.33	4.08
Merklinger, Dan	L-L	6-1	195	11-19-85	0	0	0.00	3	2	0	0	7	6	0	0	0	7	4	.250	.250	.250	5.14	9.00
Molleken, Dustin	L-R	6-4	230	8-21-84	3	0	5.18	40	0	0	1	49	58	33	28	5	18	36	.299	.275	.320	6.66	3.33

COLORADO ROCKIES

Name	B-T	HT	WT	DOB	W	L	ERA	G	GS	CG	SV	IP	H	R	ER	HR	BB	SO	AVG	vLH	vRH	K/9	BB/9
Moscoso, Guillermo	R-R	6-1	200	11-14-83	8	6	6.13	18	18	0	0	98	127	68	67	14	26	85	.318	.305	.332	7.78	2.38
Ottavino, Adam	L-R	6-5	230	11-22-85	0	0	3.20	13	0	0	0	20	22	8	7	2	7	25	.268	.256	.282	11.44	3.20
Outman, Josh	L-L	6-1	200	9-14-84	0	0	0.00	2	0	0	0	2	1	1	0	0	0	1	.167	.000	.250	4.50	0.00
Pomeranz, Drew	L-R	6-5	240	11-22-88	4	4	2.51	9	9	0	0	47	52	23	13	2	20	46	.274	.231	.296	8.87	3.86
Putnam, Zach	R-R	6-1	225	7-3-87	3	4	4.15	49	0	0	12	61	73	35	28	5	27	49	.298	.311	.285	7.27	4.01
Ring, Royce	L-L	6-0	220	12-21-80	0	0	1.17	11	0	0	0	8	6	1	1	1	3	7	.214	.174	.400	8.22	3.52
Riordan, Cory	R-R	6-4	200	5-25-86	3	3	4.88	13	9	0	1	55	61	32	30	3	9	37	.284	.283	.284	6.02	1.46
Scahill, Rob	R-R	6-2	220	2-15-87	9	11	5.68	29	29	1	0	152	168	109	96	11	74	159	.280	.257	.305	9.41	4.38
Schmidt, Nick	L-L	6-5	245	10-10-85	7	3	5.68	12	11	0	0	65	80	45	41	5	31	47	.310	.343	.298	6.51	4.29
Sexton, Tim	R-R	6-6	185	6-10-87	0	0	6.00	1	0	0	0	3	4	2	2	0	1	1	.333	.667	.222	3.00	3.00
Simons, Zach	L-R	6-3	205	5-23-85	0	0	10.32	9	0	0	0	11	20	19	13	3	5	14	.377	.409	.355	11.12	3.97
Torres, Carlos	R-R	6-1	185	10-22-82	5	4	3.98	14	13	0	0	61	62	30	27	6	25	59	.265	.254	.275	8.70	3.69
Torres, Joe	L-L	6-2	195	9-3-82	0	0	7.11	13	0	0	0	13	18	11	10	0	11	15	.333	.269	.393	10.66	7.82
Wells, Jared	R-R	6-4	200	10-31-81	0	0	5.96	19	0	0	0	23	29	16	15	3	16	18	.299	.311	.288	7.15	6.35
White, Alex	R-R	6-3	215	8-29-88	3	4	3.71	11	11	0	0	61	54	28	25	3	23	45	.238	.222	.257	6.68	3.41
Williamson, Joey	R-R	6-2	210	1-28-86	1	1	7.62	10	1	0	0	13	20	12	11	1	6	12	.351	.382	.304	8.31	4.15
Woods, Coty	R-R	6-2	190	3-14-88	1	2	7.40	23	0	0	11	21	34	18	17	4	11	13	.374	.419	.333	5.66	4.79

Fielding

Catcher	PCT	G	PO	A	E	DP	PB
Castillo	.983	64	505	31	9	2	10
Hernandez	1.000	4	14	0	0	0	1
McBride	1.000	8	54	5	0	0	1
Nieves	.993	31	248	25	2	2	1
Pacheco		4	19	1	0	0	0
Santos	1.000	35	185	17	0	3	5
Tarleton	.984	9	57	6	1	1	0

First Base	PCT	G	PO	A	E	DP
Brown	1.000	1	2	0	0	0
Cuddyer	1.000	1	9	0	0	2
Giambi	1.000	1	7	0	0	0
McBride	.993	36	261	31	2	29
Tracy	.993	101	820	62	6	75
Wood	.980	12	92	7	2	11

Second Base	PCT	G	PO	A	E	DP
Castillo	.500	2	1	0	1	0
Cesario	1.000	6	11	6	0	1

	PCT	G	PO	A	E	DP
Culberson	.988	28	59	99	2	20
Harris	.944	9	8	26	2	8
Herrera	1.000	4	2	8	0	2
Iribarren	.993	29	68	83	1	21
LeMahieu	.980	52	95	148	5	28
Nelson	1.000	2	3	7	0	2
Wood	.970	22	35	62	3	12

Third Base	PCT	G	PO	A	E	DP
Castillo	1.000	1	1	1	0	0
Cesario	.900	2	1	8	1	0
Harris	.901	71	24	113	15	10
Iribarren	.923	8	4	8	1	2
LeMahieu	.889	7	5	11	2	0
Nelson	.950	9	6	13	1	2
Pacheco	.846	13	5	17	4	2
Wood	.898	43	20	68	10	5

Shortstop	PCT	G	PO	A	E	DP
Field	.952	117	179	302	24	66

	PCT	G	PO	A	E	DP
Harris	.967	8	9	20	1	1
Iribarren	.930	10	17	23	3	7
LeMahieu	1.000	1	2	7	0	2
Tulowitzki	.800	4	3	5	2	1
Wood	.983	17	18	41	1	12

Outfield	PCT	G	PO	A	E	DP
Blackmon	.984	57	119	5	2	2
Brown	.953	95	168	15	9	4
Castillo	1.000	2	1	0	0	0
Cesario	1.000	6	6	0	0	0
Cuddyer	1.000	1	3	0	0	0
Harris	.981	61	101	5	2	1
McBride	.980	61	95	4	2	2
Pettit	1.000	4	6	3	0	0
Roberts	.992	63	120	2	1	1
Wheeler	.964	91	154	8	6	3
Wood	1.000	8	16	0	0	0

TULSA DRILLERS

DOUBLE-A

TEXAS LEAGUE

Batting	B-T	HT	WT	DOB	AVG	vLH	vRH	G	AB	R	H	2B	3B	HR	RBI	BB	HBP	SH	SF	SO	SB	CS	SLG	OBP
Arenado, Nolan	R-R	6-1	205	4-16-91	.285	.379	.258	134	516	55	147	36	1	12	56	39	7	1	10	58	0	2	.428	.337
Cesario, Jimmy	L-R	5-11	200	10-15-85	.245	.200	.257	59	192	26	47	9	1	5	23	9	4	2	1	32	2	1	.380	.291
Crousset, Juan	L-L	5-11	193	4-30-90	.235	.000	.267	7	17	1	4	1	0	0	2	2	0	0	0	7	0	0	.294	.316
Davis, Lars	L-R	6-3	205	11-7-85	.287	.283	.287	90	307	34	88	12	0	9	43	22	3	3	0	75	1	0	.414	.340
Dickerson, Corey	L-R	6-2	210	5-20-89	.274	.311	.263	67	266	40	73	16	3	13	38	18	2	0	3	51	7	3	.504	.322
Giambi, Jason	L-R	6-3	250	1-8-71	.429	.429	—	3	7	1	3	0	0	0	1	1	0	0	0	2	0	0	.429	.500
Gonzalez, Jose	R-R	6-1	165	6-23-87	.230	.259	.216	51	174	20	40	7	0	1	12	11	2	3	1	40	1	2	.287	.282
Herrera, Jonathan	B-R	5-9	180	11-3-84	.176	.000	.214	5	17	2	3	0	0	1	1	0	0	2	0	0	0	0	.353	.176
Matthes, Kent	R-R	6-2	215	1-8-87	.214	.270	.198	94	336	44	72	18	2	17	40	22	6	2	2	86	0	2	.432	.273
Mitchell, Mike	R-R	6-1	200	8-24-85	.236	.267	.227	127	462	41	109	14	4	4	33	19	6	5	2	95	22	13	.310	.274
Nina, Angelys	R-R	5-11	165	11-16-88	.269	.326	.252	118	412	45	111	19	2	6	52	27	2	1	3	67	9	4	.369	.315
Paulsen, Ben	L-R	6-4	205	10-27-87	.255	.214	.264	120	436	58	111	18	3	13	53	37	2	0	3	113	1	4	.399	.314
Pettit, Chris	R-R	6-0	200	8-15-84	.293	.150	.368	19	58	11	17	4	0	3	8	3	0	1	1	18	1	0	.517	.323
Roling, Kiel	R-R	6-3	240	1-23-87	.261	.214	.278	84	268	38	70	15	0	13	48	21	0	0	2	77	1	1	.463	.313
Rutledge, Josh	R-R	6-1	190	4-21-89	.306	.429	.272	87	356	57	109	27	3	13	35	14	5	0	4	69	14	4	.508	.338
Schaeffer, Warren	R-R	6-0	180	1-28-85	.189	.160	.197	80	222	31	42	7	0	1	15	10	9	3	1	55	2	0	.232	.250
Torres, Tim	B-R	6-2	180	11-12-83	.226	.190	.235	101	292	42	66	15	2	3	23	45	2	0	2	87	14	4	.322	.331
Tulowitzki, Troy	R-R	6-3	215	10-10-84	.300	.300	—	3	10	1	3	1	0	1	2	0	0	0	0	2	0	0	.700	.300
Zuanich, Mike	R-R	6-4	225	7-10-86	.233	.300	.202	60	189	20	44	6	0	7	24	20	6	0	1	57	1	1	.376	.324

Pitching	B-T	HT	WT	DOB	W	L	ERA	G	GS	CG	SV	IP	H	R	ER	HR	BB	SO	AVG	vLH	vRH	K/9	BB/9
Cabrera, Edwar	L-L	6-0	175	10-20-87	8	4	2.94	15	15	0	0	98	65	35	32	15	23	82	.186	.215	.175	7.53	2.11
Chacin, Jhoulys	R-R	6-3	225	1-7-88	0	0	6.00	2	2	0	0	9	9	6	6	1	2	7	.257	.300	.240	7.00	2.00
Chatwood, Tyler	R-R	6-0	185	12-16-89	1	1	3.00	4	4	0	0	24	17	9	8	2	7	22	.198	.273	.172	8.25	2.63
De La Rosa, Jorge	L-L	6-1	220	4-5-81	0	0	9.00	2	2	0	0	5	5	5	5	1	3	5	.381	.000	.471	9.00	5.40
Frazier, Parker	R-R	6-5	159	11-11-88	5	14	3.88	27	27	0	0	167	182	79	72	19	40	93	.285	.289	.282	5.01	2.16
Gardner, Joe	R-R	6-4	220	3-18-88	8	8	3.97	28	23	0	1	138	129	68	61	13	39	99	.244	.273	.225	6.44	2.54
Harris, Will	R-R	6-4	225	8-28-84	2	1	2.62	31	0	0	1	34	26	12	10	2	12	46	.205	.180	.221	12.06	3.15
Houston, Dan	R-R	6-3	205	10-24-86	10	10	3.74	27	27	0	0	161	174	75	67	16	38	96	.279	.278	.279	5.36	2.12
Hynick, Brandon	R-R	6-3	205	3-7-85	7	3	2.11	12	12	0	0	81	70	21	19	6	18	51	.232	.211	.241	5.67	2.00
Jacobson, Brett	R-R	6-6	205	11-9-86	0	0	9.64	5	0	0	0	7	5	5	5	1	7	10	.350	.625	.167	19.29	13.50
Johnson, Tyler	B-L	6-2	200	6-7-81	0	0	8.44	5	0	0	0	5	9	6	5	0	3	8	.375	.455	.308	13.50	5.06
Marbry, Michael	R-R	6-3	185	9-3-84	4	2	4.02	49	0	0	0	62		31	29	10	20	35	.248	.294	.224	4.85	2.77

	B-T	HT	WT	DOB	W	L	ERA	G	GS	CG	SV	IP	H	R	ER	HR	BB	SO	AVG	vLH	vRH	K/9	BB/9
Outman, Josh	L-L	6-1	200	9-14-84	2	5	3.63	14	11	0	0	69	64	32	28	4	30	71	.252	.185	.275	9.22	3.89
Pomeranz, Drew	R-L	6-5	240	11-22-88	0	0	0.00	1	1	0	0	4	4	0	0	1	4		.235	.000	.250	9.00	2.25
Ring, Royce	L-L	6-0	220	12-21-80	1	0	1.08	9	0	0	0	8	6	1	1	1	2	6	.200	.267	.133	6.48	2.16
Riordan, Cory	R-R	6-4	200	5-25-86	3	2	3.66	20	1	0	0	39	40	17	16	6	8	29	.272	.241	.292	6.64	1.83
Schmidt, Nick	L-L	6-5	245	10-10-85	5	3	3.29	14	14	0	0	82	74	31	30	9	15	73	.239	.181	.261	8.01	1.65
Sexton, Tim	R-R	6-6	185	6-10-87	3	1	5.26	19	0	0	0	26	25	16	15	3	5	28	.260	.258	.262	9.82	1.75
2-team total (4 NW Arkansas)					4	1	4.78	23	0	0	0	32	33	19	17	3	7	33	—	—	—	9.28	1.97
Simons, Zach	L-R	6-3	205	5-23-85	5	2	1.93	33	0	0	0	47	32	11	10	4	24	33	.204	.208	.202	6.36	4.63
Solbach, Michael	R-R	6-3	185	7-31-85	0	0	0.00	10	0	0	2	8	2	0	0	0	3	9	.074	.111	.056	9.72	3.24
Sullivan, Josh	R-R	6-4	205	7-5-84	1	2	2.76	60	0	0	17	62	56	27	19	3	24	63	.241	.276	.221	9.15	3.48
Torres, Joe	L-L	6-2	195	9-3-82	4	0	2.35	17	0	0	1	15	12	5	4	2	6	21	.226	.217	.233	12.33	3.52
Williamson, Joey	R-R	6-2	210	1-28-86	3	2	1.87	36	0	0	1	43	36	13	9	1	24	53	.228	.250	.214	11.01	4.98
Woods, Coty	R-R	6-2	190	3-14-88	3	2	0.76	38	0	0	16	36	26	4	3	1	8	34	.205	.190	.212	8.58	2.02
Yacko, Kurt	R-R	5-11	180	8-22-87	0	1	15.43	2	0	0	0	2	3	4	4	1	2	4	.333	.500	.200	15.43	7.71

Fielding

Catcher	PCT	G	PO	A	E	DP	PB
Davis	.999	88	625	51	1	10	14
Gonzalez	.993	51	378	39	3	2	6
Rutledge	.981	22	41	60	2	12	
Schaeffer	.949	9	8	29	2	7	
Torres	1.000	5	7	12	0	2	
Schaeffer	.974	64	81	213	8	55	
Torres	1.000	3	5	10	0	3	
Tulowitzki	1.000	2	0	2	0	0	

First Base	PCT	G	PO	A	E	DP
Giambi	1.000	2	7	0	0	0
Paulsen	.990	99	969	40	10	94
Roling	.994	40	337	24	2	29
Zuanich	1.000	3	34	3	0	3

Second Base	PCT	G	PO	A	E	DP
Cesario	.976	27	44	80	3	23
Herrera	1.000	2	3	2	0	0
Nina	.984	82	156	225	6	54

Third Base	PCT	G	PO	A	E	DP
Arenado	.952	133	90	362	23	36
Cesario	1.000	4	2	4	0	1
Schaeffer	1.000	1	0	2	0	0
Torres	1.000	3	3	10	0	1

Shortstop	PCT	G	PO	A	E	DP
Herrera	1.000	2	1	5	0	0
Nina	1.000	11	11	32	0	3
Rutledge	.978	67	88	179	6	33

Outfield	PCT	G	PO	A	E	DP
Cesario	1.000	1	1	0	0	0
Crousset	.833	6	5	0	1	0
Dickerson	.978	67	81	6	2	2
Matthes	.971	91	157	8	5	4
Mitchell	.983	124	283	6	5	2
Pettit	.963	16	25	1	1	0
Torres	1.000	79	128	13	0	3
Zuanich	1.000	43	75	1	0	0

MODESTO NUTS
HIGH CLASS A
CALIFORNIA LEAGUE

Batting

	B-T	HT	WT	DOB	AVG	vLH	vRH	G	AB	R	H	2B	3B	HR	RBI	BB	HBP	SH	SF	SO	SB	CS	SLG	OBP
Adames, Cristhian	B-R	6-0	160	7-26-91	.280	.286	.278	115	418	59	117	21	7	2	54	47	3	11	6	82	4	2	.378	.352
Beuerlein, Drew	B-R	6-0	205	1-13-88	.400	.400	.400	3	10	4	4	2	0	1	2	1	0	1	0	1	0	0	.900	.455
Clark, Jared	R-R	6-4	215	5-9-86	.236	.242	.234	122	432	76	102	27	0	24	95	89	5	1	5	128	2	2	.465	.369
Cleary, Delta	B-R	6-3	180	8-14-89	.277	.333	.254	57	253	42	70	11	3	2	32	19	0	3	4	56	9	6	.368	.322
Crousset, Juan	L-L	5-11	193	4-30-90	.289	.289	.290	79	304	53	88	18	4	10	49	26	2	2	3	72	4	1	.474	.346
Dickerson, Corey	L-R	6-2	210	5-22-89	.338	.377	.326	60	240	43	81	24	4	9	43	25	1	0	4	42	9	5	.583	.396
Frawley, Casey	R-R	5-11	170	9-17-87	.158	.143	.161	8	38	7	6	2	0	1	5	3	0	1	0	7	0	0	.289	.220
Garneau, Dustin	R-R	6-1	215	8-13-87	.243	.190	.256	86	300	35	73	18	3	6	29	40	2	2	4	41	2	3	.383	.332
Gomez, Hector	R-R	6-2	180	3-5-88	.375	.000	.500	3	8	2	3	0	1	0	3	2	0	0	0	4	1	0	.625	.500
Langfels, Jayson	R-R	6-2	205	8-17-88	.280	.231	.295	81	275	44	77	16	6	4	51	29	8	3	3	82	5	3	.425	.362
Laurent, Chandler	R-R	5-10	180	10-17-87	.177	.139	.188	48	164	22	29	11	2	1	23	17	1	2	3	65	8	4	.287	.254
Massanari, Bryce	R-R	6-2	215	4-29-86	.232	.071	.299	26	95	13	22	5	0	2	15	6	4	0	1	39	0	0	.347	.302
Ortega, Rafael	L-R	5-11	160	5-15-91	.283	.264	.290	114	495	81	140	23	8	6	60	46	4	4	7	93	36	18	.410	.344
Parker, Kyle	R-R	6-0	200	9-30-89	.308	.250	.323	102	390	86	120	18	6	23	73	66	6	0	1	88	1	2	.562	.415
Ramirez, Michael	R-R	5-10	165	4-27-90	.214	.200	.222	4	14	0	3	1	0	0	1	1	0	0		4	1	0	.286	.313
Robinson, Scott	R-R	6-0	185	7-6-88	.152	.111	.167	11	33	3	5	0	1	0	0	2	2	1	0	11	3	2	.212	.243
Smalling, Tim	R-R	6-3	207	10-14-87	.274	.259	.278	68	259	38	71	14	4	2	33	28	1	4	3	53	5	1	.382	.344
Tanos, Brett	R-R	5-11	175	10-6-88	.275	.287	.272	111	403	75	111	22	5	6	51	78	5	4	5	81	10	6	.400	.395
Tarleton, Dallas	L-R	5-11	200	8-5-87	.279	.200	.297	58	222	32	62	13	3	6	29	24	2	2	4	58	0	0	.446	.349
Tracy, Mark	R-R	6-4	220	1-1-88	.264	.324	.248	41	163	24	43	12	0	6	24	11	0	1	0	45	1	1	.448	.310
Velazquez, Helder	R-R	6-3	165	10-14-88	.252	.306	.230	80	250	32	63	17	0	7	39	15	9	5	6	58	4	2	.404	.311
Wong, Joey	L-R	5-10	175	4-12-88	.247	.250	.247	24	89	11	22	3	1	1	15	6	3	1	1	14	0	2	.337	.313

Pitching

	B-T	HT	WT	DOB	W	L	ERA	G	GS	CG	SV	IP	H	R	ER	HR	BB	SO	AVG	vLH	vRH	K/9	BB/9
Bennigson, Craig	R-L	6-2	230	3-21-87	0	3	4.91	40	2	0	2	77	87	46	42	8	20	55	.282	.207	.323	6.43	2.34
Bergman, Christian	R-R	6-1	180	5-4-88	16	5	3.65	27	27	0	0	163	161	73	66	16	37	121	.259	.257	.261	6.69	2.05
Chacin, Jhoulys	R-R	6-3	225	1-7-88	0	1	19.29	1	1	0	0	2	7	5	5	0	0	1	.583	.667	.500	3.86	0.00
De La Rosa, Jorge	L-L	6-1	220	4-5-81	0	0	4.76	2	2	0	0	6	7	4	3	0	3	7	.292	.286	.294	11.12	4.76
Froneberger, Isaiah	L-L	5-10	200	6-23-89	7	4	2.84	53	0	0	10	76	67	26	24	1	39	78	.240	.248	.235	9.24	4.62
Gomez, Kennil	R-R	6-1	180	4-8-88	4	5	5.97	14	14	0	0	66	85	52	44	10	28	32	.320	.356	.296	4.34	3.80
Gomez, Leuris	R-R	6-0	170	10-20-86	4	1	5.14	22	16	0	1	98	103	63	56	12	35	97	.270	.226	.300	8.91	3.21
Gonzalez, Juan	R-R	6-2	206	4-5-90	6	13	6.03	27	26	1	0	134	178	109	90	12	54	96	.328	.314	.336	6.43	3.62
Guthrie, Jeremy	R-R	6-1	205	4-8-79	1	1	0.00	1	1	0	0	4	3	0	0	0	1	4	.200	.200	.200	9.00	2.25
Hungerman, Josh	L-L	6-3	195	9-8-86	0	0	5.73	6	0	0	0	11	15	12	7	0	10	7	.326	.500	.214	5.73	8.18
Hynick, Brandon	R-R	6-3	205	3-7-85	1	2	3.74	5	5	0	0	34	25	16	14	1	1	22	.198	.190	.206	5.88	0.27
Jorgenson, Adam	R-R	6-0	185	9-10-85	1	0	1.86	31	0	0	16	29	23	8	6	1	7	41	.205	.310	.143	12.72	2.17
Kern, Bruce	R-R	5-11	175	4-24-88	0	0	0.00	2	0	0	1	2	1	0	0	0	0	4	.167	.250	.000	21.60	0.00
Matzek, Tyler	L-L	6-3	210	10-19-90	6	8	4.62	28	28	0	0	142	134	85	73	7	95	153	.246	.261	.240	9.67	6.01
Mueller, Josh	R-R	6-4	215	1-18-89	5	1	3.18	12	8	0	1	51	47	18	18	3	21	36	.254	.328	.212	6.35	3.71
Outman, Josh	L-L	6-1	200	9-14-84	0	0	0.00	1	1	0	0	1	0	0	0	0	0	1	.000	.000	.000	9.00	0.00
Padilla, Roberto	L-L	6-3	200	6-29-90	3	1	4.87	8	1	0	0	20	28	11	11	3	14	6	.333	.323	.340	2.66	6.20
Parker, Geoff	R-R	6-3	245	3-22-89	1	0	3.46	9	0	0	0	13	11	6	5	2	3	12	.224	.267	.206	8.31	2.08

Name	B-T	HT	WT	DOB	W	L	ERA	G	GS	CG	SV	IP	H	R	ER	HR	BB	SO	AVG	vLH	vRH	K/9	BB/9
Perez, Juan	R-R	6-0	190	5-30-89	1	0	10.50	6	0	0	0	6	8	7	7	2	7	3	.308	.333	.300	4.50	10.50
Rankin, Will	R-R	6-0	192	5-1-89	0	0	2.70	4	0	0	0	7	6	2	2	0	4	7	.250	.333	.222	9.45	5.40
Rose, Chad	R-R	6-2	200	2-17-88	4	7	4.26	54	0	0	0	74	60	45	35	6	44	80	.220	.230	.214	9.73	5.35
Schnaitmann, Nick	R-R	6-6	190	11-16-89	5	4	3.92	52	0	0	1	85	87	42	37	5	39	65	.272	.313	.249	6.88	4.13
Sitton, Kraig	L-L	6-5	190	7-13-88	1	2	3.08	41	0	0	0	50	62	26	17	4	17	22	.315	.338	.299	3.99	3.08
Slaats, Josh	R-R	6-5	225	12-22-88	1	2	7.91	8	8	0	0	33	45	30	29	4	25	32	.336	.420	.286	8.73	6.82
Solbach, Michael	R-R	6-3	185	7-31-85	0	0	0.00	7	0	0	1	8	4	0	0	0	2	9	.148	.200	.118	10.57	2.35
Wolford, Mike	R-R	6-3	200	5-24-89	0	0	2.45	2	0	0	0	4	3	1	1	0	3	0	.250	.200	.286	0.00	7.36
Yacko, Kurt	R-R	5-11	180	8-22-87	6	4	3.64	45	0	0	1	59	68	24	24	7	14	50	.293	.264	.312	7.58	2.12

Fielding

Catcher	PCT	G	PO	A	E	DP	PB
Beuerlein	1.000	3	17	0	0	0	1
Garneau	.992	86	652	67	6	7	12
Massanari	1.000	8	46	8	0	0	2
Ramirez	1.000	4	19	2	0	0	0
Tarleton	.994	44	311	34	2	1	5

First Base	PCT	G	PO	A	E	DP
Clark	.989	76	574	43	7	64
Massanari	1.000	9	72	3	0	12
Tracy	.985	24	182	20	3	23
Velazquez	.984	41	297	16	5	26

Second Base	PCT	G	PO	A	E	DP
Frawley	1.000	6	15	19	0	3

	PCT	G	PO	A	E	DP
Gomez	—	1	0	0	0	0
Smalling	.973	43	84	98	5	25
Tanos	.980	75	170	172	7	59
Velazquez	.960	17	30	42	3	12
Wong	1.000	4	6	10	0	4

Third Base	PCT	G	PO	A	E	DP
Langfels	.940	80	64	154	14	20
Tanos	.888	29	32	47	10	6
Velazquez	.878	17	13	23	5	3
Wong	1.000	19	13	39	0	6

Shortstop	PCT	G	PO	A	E	DP
Adames	.966	115	184	327	18	72
Frawley	1.000	2	3	7	0	2

	PCT	G	PO	A	E	DP
Gomez	1.000	1	0	4	0	1
Smalling	.958	22	32	60	4	12
Velazquez	1.000	3	10	9	0	4
Wong	.923	2	3	9	1	4

Outfield	PCT	G	PO	A	E	DP
Cleary	.968	57	114	7	4	1
Crousset	.958	74	130	6	6	0
Dickerson	.933	48	95	2	7	0
Laurent	.962	48	96	4	4	0
Ortega	.993	111	274	19	2	2
Parker	.967	77	140	5	5	0
Robinson	1.000	10	22	0	0	0

ASHEVILLE TOURISTS

SOUTH ATLANTIC LEAGUE

LOW CLASS A

Batting	B-T	HT	WT	DOB	AVG	vLH	vRH	G	AB	R	H	2B	3B	HR	RBI	BB	HBP	SH	SF	SO	SB	CS	SLG	OBP
Beuerlein, Drew	B-R	6-0	205	1-13-88	.000	.000	.000	5	16	0	0	0	0	0	0	1	0	0	6	0	0	.000	.111
Casteel, Ryan	R-R	6-1	205	6-6-91	.279	.291	.273	71	251	28	70	24	2	2	28	19	1	0	0	44	6	2	.414	.332
Cleary, Delta	B-R	6-3	180	8-14-89	.304	.286	.311	60	237	47	72	13	2	4	35	30	3	7	0	43	14	7	.426	.389
Featherston, Taylor	R-R	6-1	185	10-8-89	.299	.253	.314	105	378	75	113	30	4	12	53	53	8	1	4	87	15	4	.495	.393
Herrera, Rosell	B-R	6-3	180	10-16-92	.202	.197	.204	63	213	22	43	8	2	1	26	21	0	1	2	49	6	3	.272	.271
Humphries, Brian	L-R	6-3	195	3-20-90	.287	.321	.272	115	436	79	125	27	6	2	55	36	1	8	7	70	9	6	.390	.338
Kandilas, David	R-R	6-2	185	9-14-90	.266	.220	.286	83	278	47	74	22	2	4	49	38	4	3	2	54	19	3	.403	.360
Laurent, Chandler	R-R	5-10	180	10-17-87	.188	.143	.206	13	48	3	9	2	1	1	4	3	0	0	1	20	0	2	.333	.231
Massey, Tyler	L-L	6-0	205	7-21-89	.292	.321	.280	104	394	72	115	21	3	10	71	35	2	3	3	77	22	7	.437	.350
Mende, Sam	R-R	6-3	195	1-9-90	.281	.311	.269	112	430	76	121	38	3	12	68	29	12	3	5	91	23	8	.467	.340
Ribera, Jordan	L-R	6-0	225	12-22-88	.280	.297	.273	65	250	38	70	23	4	10	48	19	1	0	2	62	0	1	.524	.331
Riggins, Harold	R-R	6-2	240	3-6-90	.302	.258	.319	87	328	63	99	23	0	19	76	37	11	0	3	104	8	5	.546	.388
Rivera, Jose	R-R	5-10	170	4-18-90	.257	.373	.212	65	210	29	54	14	1	2	30	12	5	7	1	21	2	4	.362	.311
Simon, Jared	R-R	6-1	210	3-3-89	.266	.233	.280	114	413	70	110	23	1	14	58	34	15	1	3	113	5	3	.429	.342
Story, Trevor	R-R	6-1	175	11-15-92	.277	.215	.301	122	477	96	132	43	6	18	63	60	9	0	2	121	15	3	.505	.367
Swanner, Will	R-R	6-2	185	9-10-91	.302	.289	.306	88	325	60	98	24	1	16	61	38	7	1	1	101	3	3	.529	.385
Wong, Joey	L-R	5-10	175	4-12-88	.250	.077	.302	14	56	7	14	0	4	0	4	4	0	1	0	11	2	2	.393	.300

Pitching	B-T	HT	WT	DOB	W	L	ERA	G	GS	CG	SV	IP	H	R	ER	HR	BB	SO	AVG	vLH	vRH	K/9	BB/9
Alsup, Ben	R-R	6-3	180	9-9-88	14	5	3.63	24	24	1	0	156	150	68	63	9	46	90	.255	.273	.241	5.19	2.65
Anderson, Tyler	L-L	6-4	215	12-30-89	12	3	2.47	20	20	2	0	120	102	43	33	5	28	81	.232	.222	.235	6.06	2.09
Bennigson, Craig	R-L	6-2	230	3-21-87	0	0	1.23	3	0	0	0	7	3	1	1	0	2	5	.125	.125	.125	6.14	2.45
Brewer, Russell	R-R	6-0	200	2-25-88	1	3	2.09	47	0	0	3	60	38	19	14	5	15	76	.175	.193	.164	11.34	2.24
Gagnon, Tyler	R-R	6-2	175	3-22-89	0	0	2.60	7	2	0	1	17	13	5	5	1	8	18	.259		.167	6.75	4.15
Gillingham, Alex	R-R	6-3	200	10-17-89	6	8	3.66	19	19	1	0	123	122	58	50	5	28	83	.260	.255	.264	6.07	2.05
Gonzalez, Nelson	R-R	6-1	168	2-15-90	8	4	4.12	51	0	0	4	63	66	38	29	3	25	63	.269	.245	.287	8.95	3.55
Hernandez, Jefri	R-R	6-1	170	4-27-91	5	1	4.42	53	0	0	21	59	68	32	29	1	17	32	.292	.351	.250	4.88	2.59
Jensen, Chris	R-R	6-4	200	9-30-90	12	3	4.28	25	25	0	0	145	148	81	69	14	50	95	.262	.268	.257	5.90	3.10
Mayo, Vianney	R-R	6-2	200	4-6-90	4	7	4.78	19	19	1	0	96	101	61	51	10	36	73	.269	.271	.267	6.84	3.38
Parker, Geoff	R-R	6-3	245	3-22-89	4	3	4.02	28	5	0	1	56	46	27	25	8	21	53	.220	.241	.208	8.52	3.38
Perez, Juan	R-R	6-0	190	5-30-89	0	0	0.00	2	0	0	0	2	2	0	0	0	0	0	.250	.000	.333	0.00	0.00
Rankin, Will	R-R	6-0	192	5-1-89	1	1	2.20	15	0	0	0	16	10	4	4	1	5	9	.185	.273	.125	4.96	2.76
Reid, Taylor	R-R	6-3	215	6-8-89	2	0	10.71	14	0	0	0	19	27	26	23	4	17	9	.321	.300	.341	4.19	7.91
Roberts, Kenny	L-L	6-1	200	3-9-88	4	1	1.85	50	0	0	0	68	53	16	14	4	9	56	.211	.156	.236	7.41	1.19
Suarez, Rafael	R-R	6-0	200	5-14-89	2	2	5.40	29	1	0	0	47	61	31	28	5	12	30	.310	.277	.333	5.79	2.31
Willoughby, Seth	R-R	6-2	195	6-28-90	0	0	3.00	3	0	0	0	3	4	1	1	0	3	3	.333	.500	.250	9.00	0.00
Winkler, Danny	R-R	6-1	200	2-2-90	11	10	4.46	25	25	0	0	145	152	80	72	16	47	136	.269	.311	.240	8.42	2.91
Wolford, Mike	R-R	6-3	200	5-24-89	2	1	3.63	12	0	0	0	17	16	10	7	1	4	8	.250	.333	.217	4.15	2.08

Fielding

Catcher	PCT	G	PO	A	E	DP	PB
Beuerlein	1.000	3	13	1	0	0	0
Casteel	.981	66	404	52	9	3	5
Swanner	.984	75	505	35	9	5	14

First Base	PCT	G	PO	A	E	DP
Casteel	1.000	1	7	0	0	1

	PCT	G	PO	A	E	DP
Massey	.974	25	210	17	6	19
Mende	1.000	2	16	0	0	2
Ribera	.991	51	497	44	5	35
Riggins	.995	64	603	47	3	52

Second Base	PCT	G	PO	A	E	DP
Featherston	.967	61	101	194	10	41

	PCT	G	PO	A	E	DP
Mende	.978	21	39	51	2	15
Rivera	.968	64	93	151	8	23
Wong	1.000	4	8	12	0	3

Third Base	PCT	G	PO	A	E	DP
Featherston	.941	16	12	36	3	1
Herrera	.971	29	16	50	2	3

Mende	.948	78	68	153	12	11
Story	.969	21	15	48	2	3
Wong	1.000	2	2	5	0	0
Shortstop	**PCT**	**G**	**PO**	**A**	**E**	**DP**
Featherston	.952	20	26	54	4	7

Herrera	.935	29	36	94	9	19
Story	.949	85	117	290	22	51
Wong	.949	8	14	23	2	6
Outfield	**PCT**	**G**	**PO**	**A**	**E**	**DP**
Cleary	.993	59	138	3	1	1

Humphries	.996	112	214	9	1	2
Kandilas	.992	68	118	6	1	2
Laurent	.958	13	20	3	1	0
Massey	.969	72	112	12	4	0
Simon	.974	104	165	20	5	6

TRI-CITY DUST DEVILS   SHORT-SEASON

NORTHWEST LEAGUE

Batting	B-T	HT	WT	DOB	AVG	vLH	vRH	G	AB	R	H	2B	3B	HR	RBI	BB	HBP	SH	SF	SO	SB	CS	SLG	OBP
Aguilera, Anthony	R-R	6-0	215	10-30-86	.198	.158	.208	31	96	12	19	4	0	0	7	7	1	3	3	17	0	0	.240	.252
Argyropoulos, Matt	R-R	6-2	195	8-24-88	.250	.258	.248	42	152	15	38	6	0	2	24	8	2	1	5	45	4	0	.329	.287
Berggren, Jarod	R-R	6-2	190	10-31-89	.205	.231	.200	27	88	10	18	1	1	1	6	8	1	2	0	25	1	1	.273	.278
Beuerlein, Drew	B-R	6-0	205	1-13-88	.176	.000	.231	5	17	0	3	0	0	0	1	3	1	0	0	3	0	0	.176	.333
Blackmon, Charlie	L-L	6-3	210	7-1-86	.237	.231	.239	17	59	8	14	5	0	1	3	7	3	0	0	10	3	0	.373	.348
De La Cruz, Robert	R-R	5-11	189	10-10-89	.214	.259	.197	28	98	7	21	1	0	0	4	10	1	0	0	26	2	2	.224	.294
De Leon, Miguel	R-R	6-2	195	8-5-91	.200	.167	.207	54	205	19	41	6	0	4	30	17	5	0	2	74	1	0	.288	.275
Herrera, Rosell	B-R	6-3	180	10-16-92	.284	.222	.297	47	194	30	55	6	2	1	30	14	1	0	2	34	7	3	.351	.332
Hutcheson, Pat	L-R	5-10	185	10-9-89	.196	.240	.189	50	168	11	33	2	2	0	18	8	1	7	0	37	4	3	.232	.237
Jones, Derek	L-L	6-0	210	6-3-90	.191	.167	.197	68	235	29	45	13	5	1	22	33	7	2	3	87	9	7	.302	.306
Mehrten, Alec	R-R	6-3	190	7-24-90	.244	.238	.246	28	90	11	22	3	0	0	12	7	4	2	3	15	0	0	.278	.317
Murphy, Tom	R-R	6-1	220	4-3-91	.288	.263	.293	55	212	26	61	13	3	6	38	14	7	1	2	52	1	1	.462	.349
Osborne, Zach	R-R	5-8	170	2-4-90	.259	.364	.240	42	143	24	37	7	1	0	16	16	2	5	0	7	5	3	.322	.342
Pirkle, Richard	R-R	6-1	190	8-16-88	.435	.800	.333	9	23	7	10	0	0	0	2	4	3	0	0	7	1	0	.435	.567
Ramirez, Michael	R-R	5-10	165	4-27-90	.214	.167	.222	14	42	6	9	4	0	0	3	2	3	2	0	12	0	1	.310	.298
Ribera, Jordan	L-R	6-0	225	12-22-88	.324	.333	.323	9	34	4	11	4	0	0	6	5	0	0	0	7	0	1	.441	.410
Roja, Yafistel	B-R	5-11	150	10-26-91	.241	.171	.260	49	162	10	39	2	1	0	11	8	0	4	0	37	13	3	.265	.276
Shepherd, Jaron	L-R	6-1	175	10-30-88	—	—	.000	1	0	0	0	0	0	0	0	1	0	0	0	0	0	0	—	1.000
Sosa, Francisco	R-R	6-4	180	2-27-90	.275	.341	.261	68	251	35	69	14	2	4	36	24	8	5	2	57	21	2	.394	.354
Thomas, Dillon	L-L	6-1	195	12-10-92	.214	.000	.237	24	84	11	18	3	0	0	14	13	0	0	0	26	6	3	.250	.347
Von Tungeln, Kyle	L-L	5-9	175	9-18-90	.258	.323	.242	44	151	33	39	10	3	1	20	34	4	2	3	36	7	3	.384	.401
Wong, Joey	L-R	5-10	175	4-12-88	.207	.000	.222	9	29	5	6	1	0	0	1	5	3	1	0	5	1	1	.241	.378

Pitching	B-T	HT	WT	DOB	W	L	ERA	G	GS	CG	SV	IP	H	R	ER	HR	BB	SO	AVG	vLH	vRH	K/9	BB/9
Arrowood, Ryan	R-R	6-3	190	8-24-90	4	3	2.26	20	5	0	0	52	38	15	13	2	14	55	.205	.224	.195	9.58	2.44
Blank, Trent	R-R	6-2	175	8-31-89	1	0	3.34	16	0	0	0	30	32	14	11	2	4	28	.267	.296	.242	8.49	1.21
Brown, Andrew	R-R	6-2	195	11-11-89	0	1	4.76	9	0	0	0	11	15	7	6	0	7	6	.341	.294	.370	4.76	5.56
Broyles, Shane	R-R	6-1	180	8-19-91	5	3	3.69	13	11	0	0	68	64	33	28	4	11	60	.242	.232	.248	7.90	1.45
Dennis, Chris	R-R	6-0	180	3-31-89	2	2	2.11	23	0	0	1	43	30	10	10	3	18	46	.196	.137	.225	9.70	3.80
Federico, Eric	R-R	5-11	175	9-4-87	0	0	0.00	8	0	0	0	14	6	0	0	0	5	8	.128	.050	.185	5.02	3.14
Flemer, Matt	R-R	6-2	210	11-22-90	3	3	2.12	15	0	0	1	30	18	8	7	2	7	23	.176	.158	.188	6.98	2.12
Gagnon, Tyler	R-R	6-2	175	3-22-89	2	2	3.24	6	4	0	0	25	31	10	9	1	3	16	.301	.275	.317	5.76	1.08
Hart, Brook	L-R	6-5	220	4-19-89	4	1	2.84	20	0	0	3	25	26	10	8	0	7	22	.260	.258	.261	7.82	2.49
Hughes, Ben	R-R	6-5	215	11-29-89	3	5	4.40	14	14	0	0	72	77	42	35	3	25	61	.272	.204	.318	7.66	3.14
Hungerman, Josh	L-L	6-3	195	9-8-86	0	3	3.77	9	0	0	0	14	13	11	6	0	6	22	.232	.105	.297	13.81	3.77
Oakes, T.J.	R-R	6-2	210	7-15-90	1	2	4.41	11	11	0	0	49	64	29	24	4	7	38	.318	.349	.296	6.98	1.29
Padilla, Roberto	L-L	6-3	200	6-29-90	2	4	5.18	9	9	0	0	40	39	27	23	1	19	27	.258	.255	.260	6.08	4.28
Paulencu, Adam	R-R	6-4	205	11-17-90	0	0	8.10	3	0	0	0	3	6	3	3	0	4	4	.429	.000	.545	10.80	10.80
Rankin, Will	R-R	6-0	192	5-1-89	0	0	0.00	6	0	0	5	5	6	0	0	0	0	4	.273	.429	.200	6.75	0.00
Reid, Taylor	R-R	6-3	215	6-8-89	0	1	9.61	16	1	0	0	20	26	21	21	0	17	12	.329	.333	.327	5.49	7.78
Slaats, Josh	R-R	6-5	225	12-22-88	0	3	4.30	12	7	0	0	38	34	22	18	1	23	31	.239	.233	.244	7.41	5.50
Tago, Peter	R-R	6-2	170	7-5-92	2	7	5.47	14	14	0	0	72	68	48	44	4	39	37	.249	.232	.259	4.60	4.85
Willoughby, Seth	R-R	6-2	195	6-28-90	2	1	1.44	21	0	0	8	25	18	5	4	1	4	27	.200	.143	.236	9.72	1.44
Wolford, Mike	R-R	6-3	200	5-24-89	1	2	6.10	15	0	0	0	21	34	22	14	2	11	16	.358	.324	.377	6.97	4.79

Fielding

Catcher	PCT	G	PO	A	E	DP	PB
Aguilera	.990	27	191	16	2	4	3
Murphy	.980	37	269	23	6	2	6
Pirkle	1.000	5	22	3	0	0	6
Ramirez	1.000	14	84	13	0	1	3

First Base	PCT	G	PO	A	E	DP
Argyropoulos	.983	13	112	3	2	3
Beuerlein	1.000	3	24	3	0	1
De Leon	.982	50	447	31	9	36
Hutcheson	1.000	1	9	1	0	1
Jones	1.000	1	14	1	0	1
Ribera	1.000	9	82	13	0	5

Second Base	PCT	G	PO	A	E	DP
Hutcheson	.986	17	27	46	1	6
Osborne	.984	18	29	34	1	7
Roja	.961	46	55	116	7	17

Third Base	PCT	G	PO	A	E	DP
Argyropoulos	.908	26	30	49	8	4
Hutcheson	.957	27	20	47	3	3
Mehrten	.894	27	16	43	7	2
Osborne	1.000	2	1	1	0	0

Shortstop	PCT	G	PO	A	E	DP
Herrera	.905	44	45	136	19	17
Hutcheson	.941	4	9	7	1	1

Mehrten	1.000	1	2	1	0	0
Osborne	.956	23	37	72	5	13
Wong	.970	9	7	25	1	4

Outfield	PCT	G	PO	A	E	DP
Berggren	.912	22	29	2	3	0
Blackmon	1.000	10	18	1	0	0
De La Cruz	1.000	13	25	1	0	0
Jones	.984	65	119	8	2	2
Roja	1.000	2	2	0	0	0
Shepherd	—	1	0	0	0	0
Sosa	.937	62	114	5	8	1
Thomas	1.000	24	50	2	0	1
Von Tungeln	.988	39	83	1	1	0

COLORADO ROCKIES

GRAND JUNCTION ROCKIES   ROOKIE

PIONEER LEAGUE

Batting	B-T	HT	WT	DOB	AVG	vLH	vRH	G	AB	R	H	2B	3B	HR	RBI	BB	HBP	SH	SF	SO	SB	CS	SLG	OBP
Beuerlein, Drew	B-R	6-0	205	1-13-88	.125	.250	.000	2	8	2	1	0	0	0	1	0	0	0	0	3	0	0	.125	.222
Briceno, Jose	R-R	6-0	195	9-19-92	.391	.444	.357	7	23	5	9	0	0	2	5	2	1	0	0	2	0	0	.652	.462
Ciriaco, Juan	R-R	5-9	155	7-6-90	.268	.315	.245	56	220	32	59	6	3	0	21	11	1	7	2	36	15	4	.323	.303
Cowell, Chris	R-R	6-4	215	12-23-89	.271	.333	.239	21	70	9	19	5	0	2	6	7	1	0	0	31	0	0	.429	.346
Dahl, David	L-R	6-2	185	4-1-94	.379	.346	.391	67	280	62	106	22	10	9	57	21	2	1	2	42	12	7	.625	.423
De Leon, Miguel	R-R	6-2	195	8-5-91	.222	.222	.222	5	18	4	4	1	0	2	8	2	0	0	1	6	0	0	.611	.286
Galvez, Cesar	B-R	5-9	145	7-24-91	.340	.412	.306	13	53	10	18	0	1	0	4	3	0	3	0	8	6	2	.377	.375
Garvey, Ryan	R-R	6-1	190	3-30-93	.304	.500	.237	29	102	18	31	7	2	5	19	15	2	0	2	33	2	2	.559	.397
Graeter, Ashley	R-R	6-1	190	10-3-89	.294	.289	.296	40	163	27	48	12	0	1	28	10	2	2	2	35	3	2	.387	.339
Helton, Todd	L-L	6-2	220	8-20-73	.600	—	.600	2	5	0	3	0	0	0	2	1	0	0	0	0	0	0	.600	.667
McLeod, Jeremy	R-R	6-0	195	12-26-90	.270	.500	.185	12	37	4	10	2	0	0	1	3	0	1	0	12	2	0	.324	.325
Newton, Kyle	R-R	5-11	185	7-3-90	.000	.000	.000	1	4	0	0	0	0	0	0	1	0	0	0	0	0	0	.000	.000
Osborne, Zach	R-R	5-8	170	4-20-90	.227	.167	.250	6	22	4	5	1	0	0	1	0	1	0	0	1	0	0	.273	.261
Pena, Franmy	B-R	5-10	175	6-8-92	.125	.167	.107	16	40	5	5	2	0	1	5	2	3	0	0	13	0	0	.250	.222
Popick, Jeff	R-R	6-4	220	6-17-89	.350	.381	.337	41	137	33	48	12	1	6	30	19	3	2	3	37	2	1	.584	.432
Prime, Corelle	R-R	6-5	200	2-18-94	.283	.263	.292	36	127	17	36	7	0	1	11	18	1	1	0	34	0	0	.362	.377
Ramirez, Michael	R-R	5-10	165	4-27-90	.255	.067	.344	14	47	7	12	2	0	0	4	4	3	1	0	8	0	1	.298	.352
Rodriguez, Wilfredo	R-R	6-2	200	1-25-94	.319	.255	.348	43	166	26	53	14	1	2	27	13	1	2	1	23	1	1	.452	.370
Stolz, Jason	R-R	6-2	200	3-21-90	.260	.254	.262	54	204	33	53	13	2	2	24	14	4	0	0	46	5	4	.373	.320
Thomore, Carl	R-R	6-2	212	1-13-93	.208	.238	.185	15	48	11	10	1	1	1	6	11	1	1	0	16	0	1	.333	.367
Waldrip, Ben	L-L	6-6	245	6-27-90	.217	.170	.234	48	184	24	40	8	0	10	33	15	2	0	1	53	0	1	.424	.282
Wessinger, Matt	R-R	6-0	180	9-20-90	.274	.162	.322	63	248	53	68	8	3	4	27	28	3	6	3	57	22	8	.379	.351
White, Max	L-L	6-2	175	10-10-93	.200	.244	.184	50	170	30	34	5	3	4	18	29	2	1	1	72	6	5	.335	.322
Yan, Julian	R-R	6-2	180	11-27-91	.282	.422	.236	66	255	50	72	13	1	16	57	21	9	1	1	82	9	4	.529	.357

Pitching	B-T	HT	WT	DOB	W	L	ERA	G	GS	CG	SV	IP	H	R	ER	HR	BB	SO	AVG	vLH	vRH	K/9	BB/9
Aquino, Jayson	L-L	6-1	170	11-22-92	4	0	1.87	7	7	0	0	43	32	13	9	2	11	36	.203	.259	.191	7.48	2.28
Butler, Eddie	B-R	6-2	180	3-13-91	7	1	2.13	13	12	0	0	68	59	18	16	1	13	55	.230	.226	.234	7.32	1.73
Carasiti, Matt	R-R	6-3	205	7-23-91	3	4	4.37	14	14	0	0	68	80	45	33	6	20	34	.295	.320	.273	4.50	2.65
De La Rosa, Jorge	L-L	6-1	220	4-5-81	0	0	0.00	1	1	0	0	3	3	0	0	0	0	5	.250	.000	.273	15.00	0.00
Fernandez, Raul	R-R	6-2	180	6-22-90	1	1	3.52	30	0	0	2	31	28	16	12	3	6	27	.231	.246	.217	7.92	1.76
Gonzalez, Rayan	R-R	6-3	175	10-18-90	0	3	6.75	22	0	0	0	24	33	25	18	3	15	27	.308	.241	.377	10.13	5.63
Jemiola, Zach	L-R	6-3	200	4-6-94	0	0	12.91	5	0	0	0	8	14	12	11	3	6	5	.378	.421	.333	5.87	7.04
Jiminian, Johendi	R-R	6-3	165	10-14-92	2	4	7.71	14	13	0	0	47	60	47	40	5	33	28	.311	.347	.274	5.40	6.36
Johnson, Patrick	R-R	5-10	170	8-14-88	1	2	4.46	26	3	0	0	40	46	24	20	5	20	53	.284	.258	.302	11.83	4.46
Mason, Mike	R-L	6-3	190	4-3-90	3	0	6.15	18	0	0	0	26	26	21	18	3	12	24	.257	.231	.267	8.20	4.10
Meaux, Jesse	R-R	6-4	210	8-8-89	3	0	6.49	23	0	0	4	26	32	19	19	7	6	28	.302	.359	.269	9.57	2.05
Mejia, Jordan	R-R	6-2	190	4-6-91	1	2	4.71	18	0	0	0	21	22	14	11	2	12	17	.286	.306	.268	7.29	5.14
Mejias, Alving	R-R	6-0	200	12-26-91	7	6	5.21	15	8	0	0	57	74	35	33	2	15	37	.315	.327	.305	5.84	2.37
Mueller, Josh	R-R	6-4	215	1-18-89	2	3	8.38	6	6	0	0	29	42	30	27	3	8	17	.339	.314	.356	5.28	2.48
Oberg, Scott	R-R	6-2	205	3-13-90	0	2	2.33	25	0	0	13	27	20	9	7	2	6	29	.196	.188	.204	9.67	2.00
Roliard, Kyle	L-L	6-5	190	2-6-90	0	1	3.38	19	0	0	0	21	20	9	8	1	17	15	.253	.250	.254	6.33	7.17
Seise, Anthony	R-L	6-1	188	2-23-93	0	0	14.46	9	0	0	0	9	11	16	15	3	19	5	.306	.333	.296	4.82	18.32
Stuart, Shawn	R-R	6-3	210	12-26-88	5	2	3.07	20	2	0	0	41	38	18	14	6	11	45	.245	.265	.230	9.88	2.41
Vargas, Jonathan	L-L	6-2	150	5-29-89	0	0	6.43	6	0	0	0	7	9	6	5	1	5	7	.300	.286	.304	9.00	6.43
Warner, Ryan	L-R	6-7	195	1-21-94	3	0	7.00	14	10	0	0	45	63	39	35	9	13	36	.333	.323	.344	7.20	2.60

Fielding

Catcher	PCT	G	PO	A	E	DP	PB
Beuerlein	1.000	1	8	0	0	0	3
Briceno	.950	3	15	4	1	0	0
Cowell	.993	17	120	13	1	0	2
Pena	.974	12	64	12	2	0	1
Ramirez	.983	13	103	13	2	2	4
Rodriguez	.992	34	233	29	2	2	9

First Base	PCT	G	PO	A	E	DP
De Leon	.958	2	21	2	1	3
Helton	1.000	2	7	1	0	0
Prime	.981	26	236	28	5	31
Waldrip	.983	48	436	23	8	36

Second Base	PCT	G	PO	A	E	DP
Ciriaco	.950	55	99	185	15	43
Galvez	1.000	3	5	7	0	2
Wessinger	.955	19	43	63	5	21

Third Base	PCT	G	PO	A	E	DP
Graeter	.875	38	34	71	15	15
Newton	.500	1	0	2	2	0
Stolz	.954	20	19	43	3	5
Wessinger	.915	18	18	36	5	2

Shortstop	PCT	G	PO	A	E	DP
Galvez	.900	9	21	24	5	6

Graeter	1.000	2	1	5	0	1
Osborne	.966	6	13	15	1	2
Stolz	.931	34	56	105	12	26
Wessinger	.898	27	38	77	13	13

Outfield	PCT	G	PO	A	E	DP
Dahl	.967	62	116	2	4	1
Garvey	.903	19	25	3	3	0
McLeod	.778	10	6	1	2	0
Popick	.983	34	54	3	1	1
Thomore	.846	12	10	1	2	1
White	.941	36	61	3	4	1
Yan	.952	64	108	12	6	2

DSL ROCKIES   ROOKIE

DOMINICAN SUMMER LEAGUE

Batting	B-T	HT	WT	DOB	AVG	vLH	vRH	G	AB	R	H	2B	3B	HR	RBI	BB	HBP	SH	SF	SO	SB	CS	SLG	OBP
Daza, Yonathan	R-R	6-2	190	2-28-94	.213	.200	.218	53	150	22	32	3	1	1	10	5	7	6	0	22	3	2	.267	.272
De La Cruz, Jose	R-R	6-0	160	6-12-92	.221	.154	.227	49	123	15	26	8	1	0	14	14	5	6	2	49	3	3	.293	.313
Derkes, Marcos	B-R	6-0	155	9-12-91	.304	.359	.288	47	171	37	52	12	2	0	18	29	12	3	1	31	16	12	.398	.437
Dilone, Miguel	L-R	6-2	175	7-8-93	.319	.241	.345	65	226	45	72	19	6	1	37	30	1	1	3	24	15	7	.469	.396
Garcia, Dawin	B-R	6-1	0	8-28-93	.092	.286	.069	24	65	3	6	1	0	0	5	4	0	1	1	19	0	1	.108	.143
Garcia, Henry	R-R	6-2	195	9-21-93	.234	.175	.256	57	231	30	54	15	1	3	38	8	7	0	2	57	6	1	.346	.278

	B-T	HT	WT	DOB	AVG	vLH	vRH	G	AB	R	H	2B	3B	HR	RBI	BB	HBP	SH	SF	SO	SB	CS	OBP	SLG
Jean, Luis	R-R	6-1	150	8-17-94	.302	.275	.315	52	162	38	49	3	2	0	17	25	7	5	0	12	6	5	.346	.418
Jimenez, Emerson	L-R	6-1	160	12-16-94	.261	.229	.274	65	238	23	62	9	1	0	16	9	1	6	1	42	13	4	.307	.289
Jimenez, Wilkyns	R-R	6-2	180	7-18-95	.263	.154	.320	35	114	12	30	1	0	0	15	5	0	5	0	15	0	2	.272	.294
Marte, Hamlet	R-R	5-10	180	2-3-94	.178	.083	.197	27	73	9	13	2	0	0	2	10	0	2	0	16	1	3	.205	.277
Pena, Franmy	B-R	5-10	175	6-8-92	.313	.143	.444	4	16	0	5	2	0	0	5	1	0	0	0	1	1	0	.438	.353
Reyes, Randy	R-R	6-0	175	9-4-92	.250	.167	.300	10	32	6	8	0	0	0	0	1	0	0	0	8	0	1	.250	.273
Richardson, Denzel	R-R	6-2	174	1-7-94	.211	.182	.218	35	109	13	23	4	1	0	8	6	1	1	1	34	4	6	.266	.256
Roble, Jonathan	B-R	5-11	170	4-25-92	.105	.333	.078	18	57	4	6	3	0	0	6	4	2	0	0	20	0	3	.158	.190
Rosario, Jairo	R-R	5-10	175	1-21-93	.241	.292	.218	47	158	18	38	5	1	1	11	12	1	2	0	26	3		.304	.298
Soriano, Wilson	R-R	5-9	140	12-31-91	.354	.362	.351	66	229	39	81	14	4	0	24	21	6	21	1	13	27	14	.450	.420
Tapia, Raimel	L-L	6-2	160	2-4-94	.316	.235	.349	63	237	31	75	9	1	0	35	20	8	3	4	35	13	11	.363	.383

Pitching	B-T	HT	WT	DOB	W	L	ERA	G	GS	CG	SV	IP	H	R	ER	HR	BB	SO	AVG	vLH	vRH	K/9	BB/9
Aquino, Jayson	L-L	6-1	170	11-22-92	6	1	1.52	9	9	2	0	65	45	12	11	1	9	74	.191	.152	.198	10.25	1.25
Brazoban, Huascar	R-R	6-3	155	10-15-89	1	0	3.71	18	0	0	2	17	18	11	7	1	15	15	.281	.280	.282	7.94	7.94
Estevez, Carlos	R-R	6-4	210	12-28-92	3	3	4.14	12	9	1	0	54	53	31	25	3	13	38	.259	.298	.225	6.29	2.15
Guerrero, Hector	R-R	6-2	195	11-19-92	0	0	47.25	2	0	0	0	1	4	7	7	0	3	1	.571	.000	.800	6.75	20.25
Herrera, Alvin	R-R	6-1	165	3-15-93	0	1	2.79	9	0	0	0	10	8	3	3	1	8	6	.242	.357	.158	5.59	7.45
Jesus, Francis	R-R	6-0	160	12-19-94	0	0	13.50	2	0	0	0	1	2	4	2	0	3	0	.286	.333	.250	0.00	20.25
Leon, Carlos	R-R	6-2	195	4-10-92	0	1	11.81	5	0	0	0	5	9	8	7	0	3	3	.375	.500	.200	5.06	5.06
Lezama, Angel	R-R	6-0	164	3-1-94	5	4	2.51	12	12	0	0	61	58	35	17	2	9	69	.240	.286	.200	10.18	1.33
Martinez, David	R-R	6-0	150	2-14-95	3	1	1.77	13	3	0	0	41	31	13	8	2	6	29	.204	.206	.202	6.42	1.33
Medrano, Andres	R-R	6-0	190	4-10-92	2	2	4.01	20	0	0	8	25	24	13	11	0	12	8	.250	.283	.220	2.92	4.38
Medrano, Julio	R-R	6-2	175	11-3-92	0	1	6.14	3	1	0	0	7	11	7	5	0	1	5	.344	.200	.409	6.14	1.23
Montilla, Manuel	R-R	6-4	205	9-7-91	7	3	1.54	28	0	0	9	41	29	11	7	0	7	30	.203	.185	.213	6.59	1.54
Padron, Yohan	L-L	5-11	185	4-8-94	0	0	3.86	4	0	0	0	2	1	1	1	0	3	2	.143	.000	.143	7.71	11.57
Palacios, Javier	R-R	6-1	165	9-29-93	3	1	1.70	22	0	0	0	37	38	14	7	3	4	25	.259	.300	.237	6.08	0.97
Payamps, Joel	R-R	6-2	170	4-7-94	1	2	3.02	12	12	0	0	60	43	26	20	1	16	38	.196	.169	.215	5.73	2.41
Polanco, Carlos	R-R	6-2	175	2-18-94	0	1	6.35	4	0	0	0	6	6	4	4	0	3	3	.250	.167	.333	4.76	4.76
Rodriguez, Helmis	L-L	5-11	155	6-10-94	4	1	1.82	12	12	0	0	74	60	22	15	3	12	53	.221	.158	.231	6.45	1.46
Santana, Jhonriz	R-R	6-1	165	4-22-93	0	0	0.90	10	0	0	0	10	4	1	0	5	5	.244	.222	.261	4.50	4.50
Senzatela, Antonio	R-R	6-1	180	1-21-95	5	2	0.72	13	12	0	0	63	40	10	5	0	14	35	.179	.200	.168	5.03	2.01
Villarroel, Hector	L-L	6-3	150	8-12-95	0	1	6.00	13	0	0	0	12	14	10	8	0	8	14	.286	.400	.256	10.50	6.00
Yan, Carlos	R-R	6-5	192	1-28-91	1	2	2.13	18	0	0	2	25	23	12	6	1	7	14	.232	.282	.200	4.97	2.49

Fielding

Catcher	PCT	G	PO	A	E	DP	PB
Jimenez	1.000	13	62	11	0	0	4
Marte	.977	21	112	14	3	1	1
Pena	.969	3	27	4	1	0	0
Rosario	.982	47	293	37	6	0	20

First Base	PCT	G	PO	A	E	DP
De La Cruz	.979	20	133	8	3	11
Dilone	1.000	1	9	1	0	0
Garcia	.987	56	526	23	7	32
Jean	1.000	1	6	0	0	2
Jimenez	1.000	1	3	0	0	0

Second Base	PCT	G	PO	A	E	DP
Dilone	.944	56	100	136	14	23
Garcia	.960	5	11	13	1	3
Garcia	1.000	1	1	3	0	0
Jean	.970	14	28	37	2	6
Soriano	1.000	1	3	0	0	0

Third Base	PCT	G	PO	A	E	DP
De La Cruz	.857	25	11	43	9	3
Garcia	1.000	2	0	2	0	0
Jean	.878	22	15	50	9	6
Soriano	.926	38	41	84	10	10

Shortstop	PCT	G	PO	A	E	DP
Garcia	.912	8	7	24	3	2
Jean	.778	4	6	1	2	0
Jimenez	.867	65	78	164	37	19

Outfield	PCT	G	PO	A	E	DP
Daza	.978	51	82	5	2	1
De La Cruz	1.000	1	1	0	0	0
Derkes	.959	46	91	3	4	3
Richardson	.958	31	43	3	2	1
Roble	.909	13	10	0	1	0
Soriano	.969	31	61	2	2	0
Tapia	.922	61	100	6	9	1

COLORADO ROCKIES

Detroit Tigers

SEASON IN A SENTENCE: Despite being in first place in the American League Central for just 34 days and finishing with the seventh-best record (88-74) in the AL, the Tigers returned to the playoffs in 2012, making back-to-back trips to the postseason for the first time since 1934-35.

HIGH POINT: The end of the season was a roller-coaster ride for Tigers fans. Tied with the White Sox for the division lead with eight games left, the Tigers finished with a 6-2 kick. Detroit needed all five games to beat the Athletics in an AL Division Series, then swept the Yankees in the AL Championship Series. On an individual basis, Miguel Cabrera won baseball's first Triple Crown since 1967.

LOW POINT: Five days off after sweeping the Yankees seemed to break the Tigers' late momentum, and they were swept in the World Series by the red-hot Giants. The Tigers' bats were tame in the series, as they scored just six runs over the four games.

NOTABLE ROOKIES: Outfielder Quintin Berry signed as a minor league free agent and played well down the stretch, hitting .258/.330/.354 with solid defense and 21 stolen bases. Righthander Drew Smyly started 18 games, going 4-3, 3.99 with 94 strikeouts and 34 walks over 99 innings. Outfielder Avisail Garcia made the postseason roster after making his major league debut on Aug. 31 and started against lefthanders. He will still be rookie-eligible in 2013 and should be a significant contributor.

KEY TRANSACTIONS: Owner Mike Ilitch continues to spend the money to win, and the team signed free agent Prince Fielder to a nine-year, $214 million contract heading into the season. Fielder, Cabrera and Verlander account for nearly half of the Tigers' payroll. Detroit has been astute at trading prospects for useful big leaguers in recent seasons, and this year's key trade came when the team sent former righthander Jacob Turner, catcher Rob Brantly and lefthander Brian Flynn to the Marlins for Anibal Sanchez and Omar Infante. The teams also made history by becoming the first clubs to trade competitive-balance lottery picks.

DOWN ON THE FARM: Top prospect Nick Castellanos was the MVP of the Futures Game after going 3-for-4 with a home run and a walk. Righthander Bruce Rondon regularly touches triple digits and ranked third in the minors with 29 saves.

OPENING DAY PAYROLL: $132.3 million (5th)

PLAYERS OF THE YEAR

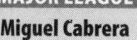

MAJOR LEAGUE	MINOR LEAGUE
Miguel Cabrera	**Nick Castellanos**
3b	**3b/of**
.330/.393/.606	(High A/Double-A)
44 HR, 139 RBIs	.320/.365/.451
Won AL triple crown	32 2B, 10 HR

ORGANIZATION LEADERS

BATTING		*Minimum 250 AB
MAJORS		
* AVG	Miguel Cabrera	.330
* OPS	Miguel Cabrera	.999
HR	Miguel Cabrera	44
RBI	Miguel Cabrera	139
MINORS		
* AVG	Dean Green, West Michigan/Lakeland	.322
* OBP	Ben Guez, Erie/Toledo	.403
* SLG	Dean Green, West Michigan/Lakeland	.508
R	Eugenio Suarez, West Michigan	82
H	Nick Castellanos, Lakeland/Erie	172
TB	Nick Castellanos, Lakeland/Erie	242
2B	Tyler Collins, Lakeland	35
2B	Aaron Westlake, West Michigan	35
3B	Avisail Garcia, Lakeland/Erie	8
HR	Brad Eldred, Toledo	24
RBI	Jordan Lennerton, Erie	82
BB	Jordan Lennerton, Erie	79
SO	James Robbins, Lakeland	171
SB	Hernan Perez, Lakeland	27

PITCHING		#Minimum 75 IP
MAJORS		
W	Justin Verlander	17
# ERA	Justin Verlander	2.64
SO	Justin Verlander	239
SV	Jose Valverde	35
MINORS		
W	Wilsen Palacios, West Michigan	12
	Luis Angel Sanz, West Michigan/Lakeland	12
L	James Avery, Erie	13
L	Ramon Garcia, Toledo/Erie	13
# ERA	Thomas Collier, West Michigan	2.74
G	Bruce Rondon, Lakeland/Erie/Toledo	52
GS	Kyle Ryan, West Michigan	28
SV	Bruce Rondon, Lakeland/Erie/Toledo	29
IP	Ramon Garcia, Toledo/Erie	159.1
BB	Alex Burgos, Lakeland	88
BB	Andrew Oliver, Toledo	88
SO	Adam Wilk, Toledo	128
# AVG	Adam Wilk, Toledo	.221

2012 PERFORMANCE

General Manager: Dave Dombrowski. **Farm Director:** Dan Lunetta. **Scouting Director:** David Chadd.

Class	Team	League	W	L	PCT	Finish	Manager
Majors	Detroit Tigers	American	88	74	.543	7th (14)	Jim Leyland
Triple-A	Toledo Mud Hens	International	60	84	.417	13th (14)	Phil Nevin
Double-A	Erie SeaWolves	Eastern	57	84	.404	12th (12)	Chris Cron
High A	Lakeland Flying Tigers	Florida State	73	58	.557	3rd (12)	Dave Huppert
Low A	West Michigan Whitecaps	Midwest	72	68	.514	6th (16)	Ernie Young
Short-season	Connecticut Tigers	New York-Penn	35	40	.467	t-7th (14)	Andrew Graham
Rookie	GCL Tigers	Gulf Coast	36	24	.600	t-1st (14)	Basilio Cabrera
Overall 2012 Minor League Record			333	358	.482	23rd (30)	

ORGANIZATION STATISTICS

DETROIT TIGERS
AMERICAN LEAGUE

Batting	B-T	HT	WT	DOB	AVG	vLH	vRH	G	AB	R	H	2B	3B	HR	RBI	BB	HBP	SH	SF	SO	SB	CS	SLG	OBP
Avila, Alex	L-R	5-11	210	1-29-87	.243	.176	.262	116	367	42	89	21	2	9	48	61	2	2	2	104	2	0	.384	.352
Baker, Jeff	R-R	6-2	210	6-21-81	.200	.154	.333	15	35	1	7	2	0	0	4	2	0	0	0	10	0	0	.257	.243
Berry, Quintin	L-L	6-0	175	11-21-84	.258	.214	.268	94	291	44	75	10	6	2	29	25	7	6	1	80	21	0	.354	.330
Boesch, Brennan	L-L	6-4	235	4-12-85	.240	.230	.244	132	470	52	113	22	2	12	54	26	5	0	2	104	6	3	.372	.286
Cabrera, Miguel	R-R	6-4	240	4-18-83	.330	.314	.335	161	622	109	205	40	0	44	139	66	3	0	6	98	4	1	.606	.393
Dirks, Andy	L-L	6-0	195	1-24-86	.322	.274	.336	88	314	56	101	18	5	8	35	23	2	3	2	53	1	1	.487	.370
Eldred, Brad	R-R	6-6	270	7-12-80	.188	.000	.300	5	16	1	3	1	1	0	1	0	0	0	0	6	0	0	.375	.235
Fielder, Prince	L-R	5-11	275	5-9-84	.313	.289	.328	162	581	83	182	33	1	30	108	85	17	0	7	84	1	0	.528	.412
Garcia, Avisail	R-R	6-4	240	6-12-91	.319	.333	.294	23	47	7	15	0	0	0	3	3	1	0	0	10	0	2	.319	.373
Holaday, Bryan	R-R	6-0	205	11-19-87	.250	.500	.125	6	12	3	3	1	0	0	0	0	0	1	0	2	0	0	.333	.250
Infante, Omar	R-R	5-11	195	12-26-81	.257	.328	.226	64	226	27	58	7	5	4	20	9	0	4	2	23	7	2	.385	.283
Inge, Brandon	R-R	5-11	190	5-19-77	.100	.154	.000	9	20	2	2	1	0	1	2	0	0	0	0	6	0	0	.300	.100
2-team total (74 Oakland)					.218			83	303	33	66	14	0	12	54	24	1	0	3	91	0	1	.383	.275
Jackson, Austin	R-R	6-1	185	2-1-87	.300	.289	.305	137	543	103	163	29	10	16	66	67	2	2	3	134	12	9	.479	.377
Kelly, Don	L-R	6-4	190	2-15-80	.186	.083	.198	75	113	14	21	2	1	1	7	14	0	0	2	22	2	0	.248	.276
Laird, Gerald	R-R	6-1	225	11-13-79	.282	.204	.382	63	174	24	49	8	1	2	11	14	1	1	1	21	0	0	.374	.337
Peralta, Jhonny	R-R	6-2	215	5-28-82	.239	.214	.249	150	531	58	127	32	3	13	63	49	2	1	2	105	1	2	.384	.305
Perez, Hernan	R-R	6-1	185	3-26-91	.500	.000	1.000	2	2	1	1	0	0	0	0	0	0	0	0	0	0	0	.500	.500
Raburn, Ryan	R-R	6-0	185	4-17-81	.171	.165	.175	66	205	14	35	14	0	1	12	13	2	1	1	53	1	1	.254	.226
Santiago, Ramon	B-R	5-11	185	8-31-79	.206	.140	.228	93	228	19	47	7	1	2	17	20	5	5	1	39	1	0	.272	.283
Santos, Omir	R-R	6-0	215	4-29-81	.125	.000	.200	3	8	0	1	0	0	0	0	1	0	0	1	1	0	0	.125	.111
Thomas, Clete	L-R	5-11	195	11-14-83	—	—	—	3	0	1	0	0	0	0	0	0	0	0	0	0	0	0	—	—
2-team total (12 Minnesota)					.143	—	—	15	28	3	4	1	0	1	4	0	1	0	0	16	0	0	.286	.172
Worth, Danny	R-R	6-1	185	9-30-85	.216	.297	.135	43	74	9	16	3	0	0	3	13	0	2	1	23	0	0	.257	.330
Young, Delmon	R-R	6-3	240	9-14-85	.267	.308	.247	151	574	54	153	27	1	18	74	20	7	0	7	112	0	2	.411	.296
Young, Matt	L-R	5-8	175	10-3-82	.100	.000	.100	5	10	2	1	1	0	0	1	0	1	0	0	9	0	0	.200	.182

Pitching	B-T	HT	WT	DOB	W	L	ERA	G	GS	CG	SV	IP	H	R	ER	HR	BB	SO	AVG	vLH	vRH	K/9	BB/9
Alburquerque, Al	R-R	6-0	195	6-10-86	0	0	0.68	8	0	0	0	13	6	1	1	0	8	18	.133	.136	.130	12.15	5.40
Balester, Collin	R-R	6-5	200	6-6-86	2	0	6.50	11	0	0	0	18	14	14	13	5	11	12	.209	.250	.186	6.00	5.50
Below, Duane	L-L	6-3	220	11-15-85	2	1	3.88	27	1	0	0	46	49	25	20	6	8	29	.280	.304	.260	5.63	1.55
Benoit, Joaquin	R-R	6-3	220	7-26-77	5	3	3.68	73	0	0	2	71	59	31	29	14	22	84	.228	.237	.217	10.65	2.79
Coke, Phil	L-L	6-1	210	7-19-82	2	3	4.00	66	0	0	1	54	71	28	24	5	18	51	.324	.263	.396	8.50	3.00
Crosby, Casey	R-L	6-5	225	9-17-88	1	1	9.49	3	3	0	0	12	15	13	13	2	11	9	.313	.250	.344	6.57	8.03
Dotel, Octavio	R-R	6-0	230	11-25-73	5	3	3.57	57	0	0	1	58	50	23	23	3	12	62	.230	.288	.197	9.62	1.86
Downs, Darin	R-L	6-3	210	12-26-84	2	1	3.48	18	0	0	0	21	18	8	8	1	9	20	.237	.171	.293	8.71	3.92
Fister, Doug	R-R	6-8	210	2-4-84	10	10	3.45	26	26	2	0	162	156	73	62	15	37	137	.249	.270	.220	7.63	2.06
Marte, Luis	R-R	5-11	200	8-26-86	1	0	2.82	13	0	0	0	22	19	7	7	4	9	19	.229	.281	.196	7.66	3.63
Ortega, Jose	R-R	5-11	185	10-12-88	0	0	3.38	2	0	0	0	3	3	1	1	1	1	4	.250	.000	.429	13.50	3.38
Porcello, Rick	R-R	6-5	200	12-27-88	10	12	4.59	31	31	0	0	176	226	101	90	14	44	107	.310	.325	.294	5.46	2.25
Putkonen, Luke	R-R	6-6	210	5-10-86	0	2	3.94	12	0	0	1	16	19	7	7	0	8	10	.302	.333	.267	5.63	4.50
Sanchez, Anibal	R-R	5-11	205	2-27-84	4	6	3.74	12	12	1	0	75	81	36	31	8	15	57	.275	.260	.295	6.87	1.81
Scherzer, Max	R-R	6-3	220	7-27-84	16	7	3.74	32	32	0	0	188	179	82	78	23	60	231	.256	.292	.201	11.08	2.88
Schlereth, Daniel	L-L	6-0	200	5-9-86	0	0	10.29	6	0	0	0	7	14	10	8	3	5	6	.412	.231	.524	7.71	6.43
Smyly, Drew	L-L	6-3	190	6-13-89	4	3	3.99	23	18	0	0	99	93	49	44	12	33	94	.247	.224	.258	8.52	2.99
Turner, Jacob	R-R	6-5	210	5-21-91	1	1	8.03	3	3	0	0	12	17	11	11	4	7	7	.321	.182	.419	5.11	5.11
Valverde, Jose	R-R	6-4	255	3-24-78	3	4	3.78	71	0	0	35	69	59	34	29	3	27	48	.229	.257	.193	6.26	3.52
Verlander, Justin	R-R	6-5	225	2-20-83	17	8	2.64	33	33	6	0	238	192	81	70	19	60	239	.217	.213	.222	9.03	2.27
Villareal, Brayan	R-R	6-0	170	5-10-87	3	5	2.63	50	0	0	0	55	38	20	16	3	28	66	.201	.190	.206	10.87	4.61
Weber, Thad	R-R	6-2	205	9-28-84	0	1	9.00	2	0	0	0	4	10	4	4	0	2	1	.455	.500	.429	2.25	4.50
Wilk, Adam	L-L	6-2	180	12-9-87	0	3	8.18	3	3	0	0	11	21	11	10	4	3	7	.412	.417	.410	5.73	2.45

Fielding

Catcher	PCT	G	PO	A	E	DP	PB
Avila	.994	113	897	57	6	7	10
Holaday	1.000	6	25	2	0	1	0
Laird	.990	56	393	22	4	2	2
Santos	.913	3	21	0	2	0	2

First Base	PCT	G	PO	A	E	DP
Cabrera	1.000	2	4	0	0	1
Fielder	.992	159	1256	105	11	113
Kelly	1.000	8	30	2	0	3

Second Base	PCT	G	PO	A	E	DP
Infante	.966	61	84	174	9	27
Inge	.966	6	11	17	1	3
Kelly	—	1	0	0	0	0
Perez	1.000	1	1	0	0	0

	PCT	G	PO	A	E	DP
Raburn	.971	32	36	63	3	13
Santiago	.996	71	75	149	1	32
Worth	.989	31	36	50	1	13
Young	1.000	2	1	1	0	1

Third Base	PCT	G	PO	A	E	DP
Baker	.875	4	3	4	1	1
Cabrera	.966	154	127	243	13	31
Infante	.500	6	0	1	1	0
Inge	1.000	2	0	1	0	1
Kelly	1.000	3	1	3	0	0
Santiago	.833	6	0	5	1	0
Worth	1.000	5	0	1	0	0

Shortstop	PCT	G	PO	A	E	DP
Peralta	.988	149	229	359	7	75

	PCT	G	PO	A	E	DP
Santiago	.922	20	13	34	4	4
Worth	1.000	3	2	7	0	3

Outfield	PCT	G	PO	A	E	DP
Baker	1.000	12	10	0	0	0
Berry	.988	87	167	2	2	0
Boesch	.989	121	167	5	2	1
Dirks	.973	72	107	1	3	0
Garcia	1.000	21	23	1	0	1
Jackson	.997	137	339	5	1	1
Kelly	.955	59	61	3	3	0
Raburn	.979	51	44	2	1	0
Thomas	—	3	0	0	0	0
Young	.947	31	35	1	2	0
Young	1.000	4	7	0	0	0

TOLEDO MUD HENS   TRIPLE-A
INTERNATIONAL LEAGUE

Batting	B-T	HT	WT	DOB	AVG	vLH	vRH	G	AB	R	H	2B	3B	HR	RBI	BB	HBP	SH	SF	SO	SB	CS	SLG	OBP
Avila, Alex	L-R	5-11	210	1-29-87	.429	.333	.500	3	7	0	3	0	0	0	1	1	0	0	0	3	0	0	.429	.500
Baisley, Jeff	R-R	6-3	225	12-19-82	.081	.100	.074	10	37	1	3	1	0	0	3	2	1	0	1	2	0	0	.108	.146
2-team total (16 Charlotte)					.183	—	—	26	93	5	17	4	0	1	8	7	3	0	2	16	0	0	.258	.257
Berry, Quintin	L-L	6-0	175	11-21-84	.270	.333	.246	39	159	18	43	8	0	0	11	22	3	2	1	46	19	3	.321	.368
Bishop, Rawley	R-R	6-3	205	11-19-85	.143	.250	.118	6	21	1	3	1	0	0	1	3	0	0	1	8	0	1	.190	.240
Brantly, Rob	L-R	6-2	205	7-14-89	.254	.294	.240	36	130	11	33	4	0	0	6	7	1	0	1	25	0	0	.285	.295
Ciriaco, Audy	R-R	6-3	195	6-16-87	.224	.277	.208	102	348	43	78	16	0	12	35	17	1	3	0	74	17	7	.374	.262
Corcino, Edgar	B-R	6-2	190	6-7-92	.250	—	.250	3	4	0	1	0	0	0	0	0	0	1	0	1	0	0	.250	.250
Davis, Brad	R-R	6-1	190	12-09-82	.327	.357	.317	15	55	9	18	3	0	0	9	5	1	0	0	9	0	0	.382	.393
Diaz, Argenis	R-R	6-0	190	2-12-87	.253	.239	.257	111	356	33	90	12	0	0	32	27	0	1	4	64	12	7	.287	.302
Dirks, Andy	L-L	6-0	195	1-24-86	.216	.250	.200	10	37	4	8	1	0	2	5	4	0	0	0	8	2	0	.405	.293
Dlugach, Brent	R-R	6-4	200	7-23-83	.169	.105	.196	25	65	8	11	2	0	2	8	7	1	5	1	19	2	0	.292	.257
Dorn, Danny	L-L	6-2	205	7-20-84	.281	.256	.290	47	167	24	47	11	1	7	25	22	4	0	1	43	4	0	.485	.376
2-team total (69 Louisville)					.252	—	—	116	393	50	99	25	2	14	49	50	8	0	5	108	5	2	.433	.344
Eldred, Brad	R-R	6-6	270	7-12-80	.305	.321	.301	63	236	49	72	18	1	24	65	24	3	0	2	73	5	0	.695	.374
Frazier, Jeff	R-R	6-3	195	8-10-82	.190	.200	.186	23	79	6	15	4	0	1	5	1	0	0	0	24	0	0	.278	.200
Guez, Ben	R-R	5-11	180	1-24-87	.284	.294	.280	82	292	43	83	20	6	6	37	33	12	2	1	76	11	6	.455	.379
Head, Jerad	R-R	6-0	210	11-15-82	.268	.286	.259	85	295	50	79	18	0	12	38	29	11	0	2	64	9	1	.451	.353
Henry, Justin	L-R	6-3	180	4-30-85	.300	.340	.291	131	476	72	143	14	5	1	38	54	3	5	5	65	22	12	.357	.372
Holaday, Bryan	R-R	6-0	205	11-19-87	.240	.310	.219	75	250	18	60	12	1	2	25	22	5	3	2	43	2	0	.320	.312
Inge, Brandon	R-R	5-11	190	5-19-77	.111	.250	.000	3	9	1	1	0	0	0	0	3	1	0	0	1	0	0	.111	.385
Iorg, Cale	R-R	6-2	185	9-6-85	.157	.125	.167	47	134	9	21	7	1	1	6	6	0	1	0	45	2	2	.246	.193
Jackson, Austin	R-R	6-1	185	2-1-87	.125	—	.125	2	8	0	1	0	0	0	1	0	0	0	0	2	0	1	.125	.222
Johnson, Jamie	L-R	5-9	180	4-26-87	.222	1.000	.152	10	36	4	8	0	1	0	2	5	0	0	0	3	3	1	.278	.317
Kelly, Don	L-R	6-4	190	2-15-80	.233	.381	.173	20	73	8	17	2	0	1	12	12	0	0	0	17	4	1	.301	.341
Lindsey, John	R-R	6-2	255	1-30-77	.270	.303	.257	65	233	33	63	17	0	15	47	29	7	0	2	59	0	0	.536	.365
Maggard, Zach	R-R	5-11	181	8-2-88	.222	.000	.250	3	9	1	2	0	0	1	2	0	0	0	0	3	0	0	.556	.222
Patterson, Eric	L-R	6-0	170	4-8-83	.244	.245	.244	64	221	23	54	6	2	2	23	41	2	1	2	58	13	3	.317	.365
Pounds, Bryan	R-R	6-0	195	10-4-85	.132	.300	.071	12	38	6	5	0	1	2	5	1	0	1	0	9	0	1	.342	.154
Raburn, Ryan	R-R	6-0	185	4-17-81	.250	.286	.239	15	60	8	15	2	0	4	12	5	1	0	0	15	1	0	.483	.318
Reina, Adolfo	R-R	6-0	210	1-22-90	.250	.500	.000	1	4	1	1	0	0	1	2	0	0	0	0	2	0	0	1.000	.250
Santos, Omir	R-R	6-2	215	4-29-81	.310	.375	.294	23	84	7	26	7	1	0	9	2	0	0	3	17	0	1	.417	.315
Strieby, Ryan	R-R	6-5	235	8-9-85	.195	.185	.198	88	334	41	65	17	2	13	52	37	3	0	2	108	0	0	.374	.279
Worth, Danny	R-R	6-1	185	9-30-85	.264	.327	.244	60	216	30	57	15	2	5	24	31	4	2	2	58	10	5	.421	.364
Young, Matt	L-R	5-8	175	10-3-82	.212	.207	.213	96	293	44	62	6	5	1	24	68	3	3	2	68	16	4	.276	.363

Pitching	B-T	HT	WT	DOB	W	L	ERA	G	GS	CG	SV	IP	H	R	ER	HR	BB	SO	AVG	vLH	vRH	K/9	BB/9
Alburquerque, Al	R-R	6-0	195	6-10-86	1	0	1.69	9	0	0	0	11	9	2	2	1	4	18	.225	.182	.278	15.19	3.38
Balester, Collin	R-R	6-5	210	6-10-86	1	1	3.64	31	0	0	1	47	38	20	19	7	12	45	.224	.267	.189	8.62	2.30
Below, Duane	L-L	6-3	220	11-15-85	1	2	6.23	4	4	0	0	17	24	12	12	3	12	7	.353	.438	.327	3.63	6.23
Bootcheck, Chris	R-R	6-5	210	10-24-78	2	5	4.06	41	0	0	17	44	39	25	20	1	26	53	.228	.267	.198	10.76	5.28
Brown, Brooks	L-R	6-3	210	6-20-85	4	4	4.90	29	19	0	0	112	125	67	61	11	58	81	.291	.290	.292	6.51	4.66
Crosby, Casey	R-L	6-5	225	9-17-88	7	9	4.01	22	22	2	0	126	112	63	56	12	65	112	.238	.221	.245	8.02	4.66
Downs, Darin	R-L	6-3	210	12-26-84	0	2	2.15	25	0	0	0	29	25	8	7	0	8	33	.234	.159	.286	10.13	2.45
Fister, Doug	L-R	6-8	210	2-4-84	0	0	0.00	1	1	0	0	4	2	0	0	0	1	5	.143	.143	.143	11.25	2.25
Garcia, Ramon	L-L	6-2	165	10-30-84	1	3	8.46	7	6	0	0	28	41	29	26	1	11	15	.350	.480	.315	4.88	3.58
Hoffman, Matt	L-L	6-2	225	11-8-88	1	2	3.69	43	0	0	0	46	55	28	19	4	16	32	.289	.317	.269	6.22	3.11
Marte, Luis	R-R	5-11	200	8-26-86	3	2	3.70	18	0	0	2	24	20	10	10	1	10	27	.222	.256	.196	9.99	3.70
Miner, Zach	R-R	6-4	215	3-12-82	2	0	2.50	23	0	0	2	36	23	10	10	3	20	16	.180	.115	.239	4.00	5.00
Ni, Fu-Te	L-L	6-0	170	11-14-82	2	2	4.56	7	5	0	0	24	27	12	12	5	14	14	.287	.231	.309	5.32	5.32
Oliver, Andy	L-L	6-3	210	12-3-87	5	9	4.88	28	19	0	0	118	103	70	64	7	88	112	.235	.228	.238	8.54	6.71
Ortega, Jose	R-R	5-11	185	10-12-88	5	8	5.74	45	0	0	1	63	76	44	40	4	51	68	.311	.309	.313	9.77	7.32
Putkonen, Luke	R-R	6-6	210	5-10-86	3	3	4.92	24	2	0	0	57	68	37	31	3	20	46	.304	.255	.338	7.31	3.18
Robowski, Ryan	L-L	5-11	175	2-3-88	0	2	4.38	7	0	0	0	12	11	7	6	0	5	8	.244	.259	.222	5.84	3.65

Pitcher																						
Rondon, Bruce	R-R	6-2	190	12-9-90	1	0	2.25	9	0	0	2	8	5	3	2	1	7	9	.167	.294	.000	10.13	7.88
Schlereth, Daniel	L-L	6-0	200	5-9-86	0	0	10.80	3	0	0	0	2	3	2	2	0	4	2	.375	.667	.200	10.80	21.60
Smyly, Drew	L-L	6-3	190	6-13-89	0	2	6.11	7	7	0	0	18	22	13	12	3	8	25	.310	.318	.306	12.74	4.08
Teufel, Shawn	L-L	6-3	215	7-16-86	1	1	5.40	2	2	0	0	10	11	8	6	1	8	5	.282	.182	.321	4.50	7.20
Turner, Jacob	R-R	6-5	210	5-21-91	4	2	3.16	10	10	1	0	63	52	23	22	2	24	40	.229	.219	.239	5.74	3.45
Villareal, Brayan	R-R	6-0	170	5-10-87	0	0	1.29	8	0	0	1	14	5	2	2	1	7	22	.125	.143	.115	14.14	4.50
Waite, Rob	R-R	6-3	210	1-9-87	2	3	4.76	31	2	0	1	57	69	38	30	2	26	29	.303	.301	.303	4.61	4.13
Weber, Thad	R-R	6-2	205	9-28-84	7	11	4.20	22	21	1	0	129	123	62	60	16	31	97	.251	.270	.232	6.78	2.17
Wilk, Adam	L-L	6-2	180	12-9-87	7	11	2.77	24	24	3	0	150	123	61	46	13	28	128	.221	.219	.222	7.70	1.68
Wood, Austin	L-L	6-2	195	11-2-86	0	0	5.68	11	0	0	0	13	19	10	8	1	12	18	.333	.133	.405	12.79	8.53

Fielding

Catcher	PCT	G	PO	A	E	DP	PB
Avila	1.000	2	10	0	0	0	0
Brantly	.971	30	189	12	6	2	4
Davis	.991	15	111	4	1	0	1
Holaday	.987	74	565	47	8	5	4
Maggard	.938	3	13	2	1	0	0
Reina	1.000	1	7	2	0	1	0
Santos	.985	23	180	12	3	3	2

First Base	PCT	G	PO	A	E	DP
Baisley	1.000	1	15	0	0	0
Bishop	1.000	2	20	2	0	3
Dorn	.990	47	367	30	4	35
Eldred	.982	14	105	5	2	5
Kelly	1.000	1	5	0	0	3
Lindsey	.983	6	53	4	1	6
Raburn	1.000	2	11	1	0	1
Strieby	.994	73	623	65	4	65

Second Base	PCT	G	PO	A	E	DP
Diaz	.985	16	36	28	1	13
Dlugach	.963	20	32	45	3	10
Henry	.991	25	50	61	1	19

Inge	1.000	2	5	7	0	1
Iorg	.965	30	36	74	4	18
Patterson	.954	19	33	29	3	11
Pounds	1.000	1	1	0	1	0
Raburn	.977	11	21	21	1	7
Worth	1.000	31	60	67	0	13
Young	.968	15	26	34	2	7

Third Base	PCT	G	PO	A	E	DP
Baisley	.882	7	2	13	2	0
Bishop	.800	1	1	3	1	0
Ciriaco	.954	76	56	151	10	17
Corcino	1.000	3	1	2	0	0
Dlugach	1.000	1	1	2	0	0
Henry	.968	37	20	71	3	8
Kelly	.973	14	12	24	1	2
Pounds	.958	10	3	20	1	7
Worth	.857	10	4	14	3	0

Shortstop	PCT	G	PO	A	E	DP
Ciriaco	.967	24	31	58	3	11
Diaz	.974	93	116	252	10	60
Dlugach	.875	4	4	3	1	0

Iorg	.944	11	14	20	2	0
Worth	.935	20	24	62	6	14

Outfield	PCT	G	PO	A	E	DP
Berry	.978	39	87	1	2	1
Bishop	1.000	1	2	0	0	0
Dirks	1.000	8	10	0	0	0
Dorn	1.000	1	1	0	0	0
Eldred	1.000	2	2	0	0	0
Frazier	.875	22	21	0	3	0
Guez	.986	82	140	4	2	2
Head	.972	79	124	13	4	3
Henry	.977	72	171	1	4	0
Iorg	.909	9	10	0	1	0
Jackson	1.000	2	6	0	0	0
Johnson	1.000	10	23	0	0	0
Kelly	1.000	7	14	0	0	0
Patterson	.987	45	75	3	1	0
Raburn	1.000	7	13	1	0	0
Worth	—	1	0	0	0	0
Young	.986	80	137	5	2	1

ERIE SEAWOLVES

DOUBLE-A

EASTERN LEAGUE

Batting	B-T	HT	WT	DOB	AVG	vLH	vRH	G	AB	R	H	2B	3B	HR	RBI	BB	HBP	SH	SF	SO	SB	CS	SLG	OBP
Bishop, Rawley	R-R	6-3	205	11-19-85	.246	.277	.236	117	410	46	101	21	2	8	51	43	6	2	5	100	15	8	.366	.323
Brantly, Rob	L-R	6-2	205	7-14-89	.311	.375	.297	46	180	16	56	16	1	3	24	12	2	0	1	17	0	3	.461	.359
Castellanos, Nick	R-R	6-4	210	3-4-92	.264	.377	.233	79	322	35	85	15	1	7	25	14	2	0	3	76	5	4	.382	.296
De Los Santos, Carlos	B-R	6-0	177	11-1-90	.000	—	.000	2	2	0	0	0	0	0	0	0	0	0	0	1	0	0	.000	.000
Dlugach, Brent	R-R	6-4	200	3-3-83	.261	.750	.158	7	23	2	6	2	0	0	4	0	0	0	0	10	1	1	.348	.370
Douglas, Brandon	R-R	6-0	200	8-27-85	.263	.328	.240	131	471	56	124	23	3	3	48	42	6	7	3	74	13	4	.344	.330
Fields, Daniel	L-R	6-1	201	1-23-91	.264	.214	.272	29	106	13	28	4	0	2	7	13	2	0	1	21	9	1	.358	.352
Garcia, Avisail	R-R	6-4	240	6-12-91	.312	.333	.306	55	215	31	67	9	3	6	22	7	4	0	0	38	9	4	.465	.345
Gaynor, Wade	R-R	6-3	225	4-19-88	.229	.250	.217	13	35	10	8	1	0	2	9	6	0	0	0	8	1	0	.429	.341
Guez, Ben	R-R	5-11	180	1-24-87	.308	.333	.300	26	78	22	24	4	0	3	11	20	7	1	1	17	4	2	.474	.481
Johnson, Jamie	L-R	5-9	180	4-26-87	.281	.255	.289	116	427	60	120	18	1	2	37	55	0	4	9	48	11	6	.342	.356
Jones, Corey	L-R	6-0	190	9-14-87	.243	.241	.243	76	235	19	57	14	2	3	21	13	6	4	2	45	3	5	.357	.297
Lennerton, Jordan	L-L	6-2	217	2-16-86	.269	.209	.290	139	495	73	133	34	1	21	82	79	2	0	6	141	2	4	.469	.368
McCann, James	B-R	6-2	210	6-13-90	.200	.204	.199	64	220	15	44	12	0	2	19	8	0	1	1	44	2	2	.282	.227
Murrian, John	R-R	6-2	215	6-15-88	.254	.294	.212	20	67	9	17	4	0	1	9	4	1	0	1	11	0	0	.358	.301
Plagman, Tony	L-L	6-2	211	8-14-87	.229	.246	.225	112	393	43	90	28	2	13	56	27	12	1	5	98	11	3	.410	.295
Pounds, Bryan	R-R	6-0	195	10-4-85	.201	.197	.204	58	169	20	34	5	0	5	16	19	2	0	2	40	3	3	.349	.286
Rockett, Michael	R-R	6-1	180	7-26-87	.246	.259	.233	65	171	22	42	5	4	4	18	3	1	0	1	49	3	1	.392	.261
Romero, Niuman	B-R	6-1	190	1-24-85	.300	.290	.303	135	523	73	157	28	4	9	67	54	5	5	6	65	19	5	.421	.367
Sanz, Luis	R-R	5-10	165	2-23-91	.130	.154	.125	24	69	5	9	2	1	0	3	4	1	1	0	8	1	1	.188	.189
Thigpen, Wes	R-R	6-0	200	6-20-89	.400	.667	.286	3	10	1	4	3	0	0	1	0	0	0	0	1	0	0	.700	.400
Wyatt, Brent	B-R	5-10	185	1-25-85	.212	.000	.233	11	33	6	7	1	0	1	3	0	1	0	1	3	1	0	.242	.278

Pitching	B-T	HT	WT	DOB	W	L	ERA	G	GS	CG	SV	IP	H	R	ER	HR	BB	SO	AVG	vLH	vRH	K/9	BB/9
Avery, James	R-R	6-0	210	6-10-84	10	13	4.73	27	27	1	0	158	186	91	83	14	53	114	.301	.311	.293	6.49	3.02
Carrillo, Cesar	R-R	6-3	170	4-29-84	1	3	9.00	6	5	0	0	20	29	22	20	3	12	11	.337	.306	.360	4.95	5.40
Clark, Tyler	B-R	6-2	185	1-4-89	0	0	7.36	7	0	0	0	7	8	8	6	1	6	6	.276	.308	.250	8.59	7.36
Cooper, Patrick	R-R	6-3	204	8-25-89	3	10	5.10	23	17	1	0	109	119	65	62	12	35	72	.280	.333	.244	5.93	2.88
De La Cruz, Kelvin	L-L	6-5	190	8-1-88	5	8	4.92	30	18	2	0	115	115	65	63	16	50	92	.265	.324	.247	7.18	3.90
Faulk, Kenny	L-L	6-0	210	5-27-87	1	0	4.53	40	0	0	4	58	58	29	29	5	32	68	.259	.183	.303	10.61	4.99
Flynn, Brian	L-L	6-8	240	4-19-90	0	1	9.00	1	1	0	0	5	8	5	5	1	2	3	.381	.500	.353	5.40	3.60
Garcia, Ramon	L-L	6-2	165	10-30-84	9	10	3.96	22	21	2	0	132	139	63	58	20	29	87	.268	.261	.271	5.95	1.98
Gayhart, Jared	L-R	6-3	195	10-29-86	1	6	4.58	35	9	0	0	92	91	50	47	11	34	99	.256	.238	.270	9.65	3.31
Kopp, Michael	R-R	6-3	205	10-22-85	1	1	6.12	17	1	0	0	32	43	23	22	5	15	24	.323	.306	.333	6.68	4.18
Miner, Zach	R-R	6-4	215	3-12-82	0	0	9.00	1	0	0	0	2	4	2	2	0	2	1	.500	.400	.667	4.50	9.00
Morrison, Mike	R-R	6-1	210	12-17-87	4	3	3.14	40	0	0	4	63	46	24	22	6	40	72	.205	.183	.216	10.29	5.71
Robowski, Ryan	L-L	5-11	175	2-3-88	1	1	3.32	25	0	0	2	43	35	18	16	5	11	41	.226	.204	.238	8.52	2.28

Rondon, Bruce	R-R	6-2	190	12-9-90	0	1	0.83	21	0	0	12	22	15	4	2	1	9	23	.195	.286	.119	9.55	3.74
Samuels, Zach	L-R	6-2	180	10-8-86	3	1	5.04	16	0	0	0	25	21	14	14	3	21	26	.236	.235	.236	9.36	7.56
Segovia, Zack	R-R	6-2	245	4-11-83	5	6	5.98	12	12	1	0	65	83	49	43	11	22	30	.311	.328	.294	4.18	3.06
Sorensen, Mark	R-R	6-3	205	2-21-86	1	2	12.00	6	2	0	0	12	22	18	16	3	8	7	.386	.400	.375	5.25	6.00
Stohr, Tyler	L-R	6-2	210	9-19-86	2	1	2.19	23	0	0	1	25	18	6	6	1	24	20	.207	.172	.224	7.30	8.76
Voss, Jay	L-L	6-4	195	4-22-87	0	3	6.10	3	3	0	0	10	17	9	7	1	4	8	.386	.462	.355	6.97	3.48
Waite, Rob	R-R	6-3	210	1-9-87	1	1	4.64	10	1	0	0	21	18	11	11	4	5	14	.234	.097	.326	5.91	2.11
Weinhardt, Robbie	R-R	6-2	205	12-8-85	1	2	2.73	44	0	0	7	66	57	21	20	6	26	56	.234	.294	.201	7.64	3.55
Wesson, Jared	L-L	6-5	190	1-30-86	7	11	5.90	24	24	0	0	119	139	84	78	17	57	84	.298	.279	.304	6.35	4.31
Wood, Austin	L-L	6-2	195	11-2-86	1	0	2.61	9	0	0	0	10	10	6	3	0	4	9	.256	.231	.269	7.84	3.48

Fielding

Catcher	PCT	G	PO	A	E	DP	PB
Brantly	.989	36	253	25	3	2	1
McCann	.994	64	437	34	3	4	7
Murrian	.981	19	141	18	3	1	0
Sanz	.988	24	145	21	2	0	1
Thigpen	1.000	3	14	1	0	0	1

First Base	PCT	G	PO	A	E	DP
Bishop	1.000	17	96	6	0	6
Gaynor	1.000	2	4	0	0	0
Lennerton	.998	128	1000	64	2	96

Second Base	PCT	G	PO	A	E	DP
De Los Santos	1.000	2	0	1	0	1
Douglas	.978	119	249	291	12	79

	PCT	G	PO	A	E	DP
Jones	.988	22	37	46	1	15
Romero	1.000	1	1	4	0	2

Third Base	PCT	G	PO	A	E	DP
Bishop	.965	48	45	94	5	11
Castellanos	.974	27	19	55	2	3
Dlugach	.938	6	3	12	1	3
Gaynor	1.000	3	2	4	0	0
Jones	.966	31	9	47	2	2
Pounds	.948	37	23	68	5	6

Shortstop	PCT	G	PO	A	E	DP
Dlugach	1.000	1	2	1	0	1
Douglas	.955	9	9	12	1	4
Jones	—	1	0	0	0	0

	PCT	G	PO	A	E	DP
Romero	.977	134	191	358	13	64

Outfield	PCT	G	PO	A	E	DP
Bishop	.922	30	47	0	4	0
Castellanos	.980	51	96	3	2	1
Fields	.969	28	61	1	2	0
Garcia	1.000	52	136	4	0	1
Gaynor	1.000	8	12	1	0	0
Guez	1.000	24	47	2	0	2
Johnson	.993	102	266	11	2	2
Plagman	.993	77	130	7	1	0
Rockett	.963	63	97	8	4	2
Wyatt	.957	10	20	2	1	1

LAKELAND FLYING TIGERS

HIGH CLASS A

FLORIDA STATE LEAGUE

Batting	B-T	HT	WT	DOB	AVG	vLH	vRH	G	AB	R	H	2B	3B	HR	RBI	BB	HBP	SH	SF	SO	SB	CS	SLG	OBP
Casali, Curt	R-R	6-2	220	11-9-88	.250	.222	.268	46	160	18	40	13	0	1	18	11	6	2	0	28	0	0	.350	.322
Castellanos, Nick	R-R	6-4	210	3-4-92	.405	.356	.423	55	215	37	87	17	3	3	32	22	3	0	3	42	3	2	.553	.461
Castillo, Luis	R-R	5-11	160	5-15-89	.238	.303	.203	86	311	36	74	18	0	1	28	31	1	14	3	62	2	3	.305	.306
Collins, Tyler	L-L	5-11	205	6-6-90	.290	.259	.305	126	473	68	137	35	5	7	66	58	6	0	5	64	20	3	.429	.371
Corcino, Edgar	B-R	6-2	190	6-7-92	.400	.500	.000	2	5	1	2	0	0	1	1	0	0	0	1	0	0	1.000	.400
Durham, Lance	L-R	5-11	210	2-20-88	.125	.000	.154	5	16	0	2	0	0	0	0	0	0	0	7	0	0	.125	.125
Fields, Daniel	L-R	6-1	201	1-23-91	.266	.227	.288	62	244	31	65	11	4	1	26	19	1	0	3	55	14	7	.357	.318
Garcia, Avisail	R-R	6-4	240	6-12-91	.289	.270	.299	67	266	47	77	8	5	8	36	11	5	0	5	57	14	4	.447	.324
Gaynor, Wade	R-R	6-3	225	4-19-88	.254	.275	.245	105	370	55	94	18	5	14	65	50	9	1	4	88	10	3	.443	.353
Green, Dean	L-R	6-4	255	6-30-89	.348	.395	.330	38	141	16	49	11	2	3	36	7	8	0	0	25	2	0	.518	.410
Guida, Jordan	R-R	5-9	185	9-22-88	.000	.000	.000	1	2	1	0	0	0	0	0	0	1	1	0	0	0	0	.000	.500
Holm, Jeff	L-L	6-3	220	10-17-88	.333	.667	.267	6	18	2	6	0	0	0	2	0	0	0	2	1	0	.333	.400
Iorg, Cale	R-R	6-2	185	9-6-85	.192	.250	.143	7	26	6	5	1	0	0	1	1	2	0	0	6	1	0	.231	.276
Jones, Corey	L-R	6-0	190	9-14-87	.063	.000	.083	5	16	2	1	1	0	0	0	1	0	0	0	3	0	0	.125	.118
Lemon, Marcus	L-R	5-11	173	6-3-88	.324	.377	.309	81	281	47	91	19	3	3	29	28	2	7	1	40	10	4	.445	.388
Machado, Dixon	R-R	6-0	140	2-22-92	.195	.222	.183	119	421	59	82	16	1	2	37	51	1	16	1	61	23	5	.252	.283
Maggard, Zach	R-R	5-11	181	8-2-88	.176	.000	.214	5	17	2	3	0	0	1	0	0	0	0	5	0	0	.353	.176
McCann, James	B-R	6-2	210	6-13-90	.288	.188	.330	45	160	24	46	10	0	0	20	10	5	0	2	29	3	0	.350	.345
Perez, Hernan	R-R	6-1	185	3-26-91	.261	.307	.239	124	441	50	115	11	4	5	44	24	2	6	6	70	27	4	.338	.298
Perry, Matt	L-R	6-2	182	7-17-87	.100	.000	.167	15	20	3	2	0	0	0	0	5	0	0	0	8	0	0	.100	.280
Reina, Adolfo	R-R	6-0	210	1-22-90	.298	.231	.329	39	121	12	36	6	0	3	17	6	0	1	3	25	0	0	.421	.323
Robbins, James	L-L	6-0	225	9-26-90	.237	.221	.245	124	455	51	108	29	2	11	62	37	1	1	2	171	4	1	.382	.295
Rockett, Michael	R-R	6-1	180	7-26-87	.253	.250	.254	25	87	9	22	7	1	2	6	2	0	2	0	22	0	0	.425	.270
Sanz, Luis	R-R	5-10	165	2-23-91	.195	.182	.200	11	41	3	8	1	0	0	3	4	0	1	0	6	0	0	.220	.261
Schotts, Austin	R-R	5-11	180	9-16-93	.333	.667	.333	2	3	1	1	0	0	0	0	0	0	0	1	0	1	0	.333	.333
Soares, Ryan	R-R	6-1	195	7-10-87	.100	.000	.125	3	10	1	1	0	0	0	0	1	0	0	0	3	0	0	.100	.182
Thigpen, Wes	R-R	6-0	200	5-20-89	.000	.000	.000	3	7	0	0	0	0	0	0	0	0	0	0	3	0	0	.000	.000

Pitching	B-T	HT	WT	DOB	W	L	ERA	G	GS	CG	SV	IP	H	R	ER	HR	BB	SO	AVG	vLH	vRH	K/9	BB/9
Alburquerque, Al	R-R	6-0	195	6-10-86	0	0	5.40	4	3	0	0	3	5	2	2	1	1	9	.333	.300	.400	24.30	2.70
Bennett, Daniel	B-R	6-4	220	12-28-88	2	1	3.86	7	0	0	0	12	8	6	5	1	7	12	.195	.333	.138	9.26	5.40
Burgos, Alex	L-L	5-11	195	12-1-90	8	10	4.90	25	23	0	0	121	115	76	66	6	88	78	.270	.288	.262	5.79	6.53
Carrillo, Cesar	R-R	6-3	170	4-29-84	2	3	4.50	6	5	0	0	32	32	16	16	2	9	22	.274	.289	.264	6.19	2.53
Clark, Tyler	B-R	6-2	185	1-4-89	6	1	0.63	31	0	0	9	43	19	4	3	1	17	59	.137	.130	.140	12.45	3.59
Cooper, Patrick	R-R	6-3	204	8-25-89	1	0	2.53	5	0	0	1	11	14	3	3	0	1	7	.359	.500	.296	5.91	0.84
Crouse, Matt	L-L	6-4	185	7-1-90	8	2	1.91	38	2	0	6	71	49	18	15	4	25	47	.198	.187	.202	5.99	3.18
Eichhorn, Kevin	R-R	6-0	175	2-6-90	3	2	4.00	8	8	0	0	45	57	22	20	1	7	25	.306	.313	.301	5.00	1.40
Felix, Julio	R-R	6-1	185	2-23-92	0	0	9.00	1	0	0	0	2	1	1	1	0	0	0	.400	1.000	.250	0.00	0.00
Flynn, Brian	L-L	6-8	240	4-19-90	8	4	3.71	18	18	0	0	102	113	47	42	5	32	84	.280	.263	.287	7.41	2.82
Knudson, Guido	R-R	6-1	185	8-5-89	0	1	4.28	15	0	0	0	27	30	17	13	3	6	27	.270	.316	.247	8.89	1.98
Larez, Victor	R-R	6-3	160	5-28-87	4	1	1.72	35	0	0	2	68	48	23	13	2	29	59	.200	.222	.187	7.81	3.84
Little, Matt	R-R	5-11	180	3-19-88	4	5	3.95	34	0	0	3	57	50	27	25	2	30	56	.244	.259	.233	8.84	4.74
Marte, Luis	R-R	5-11	200	8-26-86	0	0	0.00	1	1	0	0	2	1	0	0	0	0	3	.143	.000	1.67	13.50	0.00
Mercedes, Melvin	R-R	6-3	190	11-2-90	0	0	0.00	1	0	0	0	1	0	0	0	0	0	1	.250	.333	.000	0.00	9.00
Rondon, Bruce	R-R	6-2	190	12-9-90	1	0	1.93	22	0	0	15	23	12	5	5	1	10	34	.152	.214	.118	13.11	3.86

Name	B-T	HT	WT	DOB	W	L	ERA	G	GS	CG	SV	IP	H	R	ER	HR	BB	SO	AVG	vLH	vRH	K/9	BB/9
Samuels, Zach	L-R	6-2	180	10-8-86	0	0	0.00	2	0	0	1	2	0	1	0	0	1	1	.000	.000	.000	4.50	4.50
Sanz, Luis	R-R	6-1	173	11-19-87	11	3	3.46	23	16	0	0	114	107	53	44	9	40	91	.251	.249	.252	7.16	3.15
Saupold, Warwick	R-R	6-1	195	1-16-90	2	2	3.77	7	5	0	0	31	32	15	13	2	11	24	.264	.238	.278	6.97	3.19
Schlereth, Daniel	L-L	6-0	200	5-9-86	0	0	1.13	8	6	0	0	8	6	1	1	0	7	9	.207	.000	.300	10.13	7.88
Sorensen, Mark	R-R	6-3	205	2-21-86	0	1	4.50	2	2	0	0	12	11	6	6	1	0	2	.262	.318	.200	1.50	0.00
Stroud, Brian	R-R	6-4	215	10-18-88	1	4	4.02	10	10	0	0	47	44	22	21	3	19	23	.250	.274	.233	4.40	3.64
Teufel, Shawn	L-L	6-3	215	7-16-86	5	7	6.64	22	18	1	0	107	137	82	79	12	52	64	.320	.311	.324	5.38	4.37
Todd, Jade	R-L	6-2	190	3-22-90	0	0	0.00	1	0	0	0	1	0	0	0	0	0	0	.000	—	.000	0.00	0.00
Turner, Jacob	R-R	6-5	210	5-21-91	1	2	1.66	4	4	0	0	22	17	8	4	1	7	17	.218	.219	.217	7.06	2.91
VerHagen, Drew	R-R	6-6	230	10-22-90	0	3	3.67	8	6	0	0	27	20	13	11	0	14	17	.206	.190	.218	5.67	4.67
Wesson, Jared	L-L	6-5	190	1-30-86	0	1	3.79	3	3	0	0	19	20	9	8	0	6	14	.274	.333	.255	6.63	2.84
White, Tyler	R-R	6-2	197	8-8-89	2	3	5.37	31	0	0	1	55	46	35	33	1	25	66	.231	.225	.235	10.73	4.07
Woolley, Ryan	R-R	6-1	190	2-11-88	4	2	3.88	27	1	0	1	56	49	27	24	0	25	47	.241	.225	.254	7.60	4.04

Fielding

Catcher	PCT	G	PO	A	E	DP	PB
Casali	.982	41	293	42	6	1	3
Guida	1.000	1	6	1	0	0	0
McCann	.983	45	303	35	6	5	5
Reina	.983	35	210	21	4	3	7
Sanz	.988	11	73	9	1	0	1
Thigpen	1.000	3	18	1	0	0	0

First Base	PCT	G	PO	A	E	DP
Durham	.833	1	5	0	1	0
Gaynor	1.000	3	20	1	0	0
Perry	1.000	5	36	2	0	2
Robbins	.994	122	1063	83	7	93

Second Base	PCT	G	PO	A	E	DP
Corcino	—	1	0	0	0	0

	PCT	G	PO	A	E	DP
Iorg	1.000	5	4	13	0	4
Jones	1.000	1	1	3	0	1
Lemon	1.000	14	26	39	0	9
Perez	.979	111	180	287	10	58
Perry	1.000	1	0	1	0	0
Soares	.875	2	4	3	1	1

Third Base	PCT	G	PO	A	E	DP
Castellanos	.902	51	23	97	13	6
Gaynor	.959	77	50	138	8	13
Lemon	1.000	1	0	1	0	0
Perry	—	4	0	0	0	0
Rockett	1.000	1	0	3	0	0
Soares	.667	1	0	2	1	0

Shortstop	PCT	G	PO	A	E	DP
Iorg	1.000	1	0	1	0	0
Machado	.966	118	186	318	18	62
Perez	.951	15	24	34	3	6

Outfield	PCT	G	PO	A	E	DP
Castillo	.984	81	172	7	3	1
Collins	.986	115	198	9	3	0
Fields	.992	60	121	3	1	1
Garcia	.955	65	136	11	7	1
Gaynor	.944	10	13	4	1	1
Holm	1.000	6	15	0	0	0
Lemon	.974	38	68	7	2	1
Rockett	1.000	24	57	10	0	3
Schotts	—	1	0	0	0	0

WEST MICHIGAN WHITECAPS

LOW CLASS A

MIDWEST LEAGUE

Batting	B-T	HT	WT	DOB	AVG	vLH	vRH	G	AB	R	H	2B	3B	HR	RBI	BB	HBP	SH	SF	SO	SB	CS	SLG	OBP
Casali, Curt	R-R	6-2	220	11-9-88	.288	.216	.308	48	170	25	49	12	0	8	25	27	6	2	1	18	2	1	.500	.402
Castillo, Luis	R-R	5-11	160	5-15-89	.280	.286	.278	12	50	12	14	4	2	2	11	3	0	2	2	6	0	1	.560	.309
Corcino, Edgar	B-R	6-2	190	6-7-92	.219	.235	.214	19	73	9	16	1	1	2	6	6	0	2	0	20	0	1	.342	.278
De Los Santos, Carlos	B-R	6-0	177	11-1-90	.238	.000	.263	14	21	4	5	0	1	0	1	1	1	1	0	5	1	0	.333	.304
Durham, Lance	L-R	5-11	210	2-20-88	.238	.286	.225	51	164	21	39	12	3	5	25	40	1	0	1	64	1	0	.439	.388
Green, Dean	L-R	6-4	255	6-30-89	.306	.321	.301	58	219	34	67	16	0	9	38	23	6	1	4	39	0	3	.502	.381
Guida, Jordan	R-R	5-9	185	9-22-88	.000	.000	—	1	2	0	0	0	0	0	0	0	0	0	0	1	0	0	.000	.000
Holm, Jeff	L-L	6-3	220	10-17-88	.254	.250	.255	40	118	15	30	4	1	1	11	19	1	2	0	9	4	0	.331	.362
Kaline, Colin	B-R	5-10	150	4-26-89	.171	.061	.214	41	117	12	20	1	0	0	3	15	1	4	0	29	0	1	.179	.271
King, Jason	B-R	6-0	216	6-14-89	.253	.284	.244	90	340	43	86	25	2	7	37	25	4	4	5	52	4	1	.400	.307
Krizan, Jason	L-R	6-0	185	8-26-89	.244	.187	.263	110	365	38	89	20	1	4	40	50	1	5	5	48	5	3	.337	.333
Leyland, Patrick	R-R	6-2	210	10-11-91	.237	.179	.258	68	257	18	61	10	0	2	24	3	2	7	2	33	0	0	.300	.250
Loy, Brandon	R-R	6-0	190	5-3-90	.240	.314	.218	134	499	71	120	21	5	2	39	45	1	15	6	119	21	4	.315	.301
Maggard, Zach	R-R	5-11	181	8-2-88	.193	.029	.250	40	135	17	26	8	1	4	20	6	2	4	0	52	0	0	.356	.238
McVaney, Jeff	R-R	6-2	210	10-9-89	.250	.261	.247	56	220	34	55	13	4	4	29	11	5	1	2	39	1	0	.400	.298
Moya, Steven	L-R	6-7	229	9-8-91	.288	.393	.253	59	243	28	70	14	3	9	47	11	1	1	2	59	5	3	.481	.319
Perry, Matt	L-R	6-2	182	7-17-87	.125	.286	.059	7	24	4	3	0	0	0	0	3	1	0	0	8	2	0	.125	.250
Purroy, Gabriel	R-R	5-9	160	4-16-92	.173	.087	.195	34	110	5	19	4	0	1	12	7	2	1	0	22	0	2	.236	.233
Reaves, Jared	R-R	5-10	185	7-20-90	.200	.000	.250	5	15	1	3	0	0	0	0	0	0	0	0	5	0	0	.200	.200
Smith, Pat	L-L	6-0	170	10-11-91	.071	.167	.045	8	28	3	2	0	0	1	3	1	0	0	0	8	0	0	.179	.103
Suarez, Eugenio	B-R	6-0	170	7-18-91	.288	.325	.276	135	511	82	147	34	5	6	67	65	15	5	7	116	21	9	.409	.380
Vasquez, Danry	L-R	6-3	169	1-8-94	.162	.143	.167	29	99	5	16	3	0	1	7	7	1	2	3	20	0	0	.222	.218
Westlake, Aaron	L-R	6-4	235	12-27-88	.249	.333	.219	123	465	56	116	35	2	9	69	47	2	2	2	105	4	1	.391	.320
Wright, Chad	L-R	5-10	198	7-27-89	.256	.178	.279	131	523	73	134	19	4	4	40	44	9	12	3	68	21	13	.331	.323

Pitching	B-T	HT	WT	DOB	W	L	ERA	G	GS	CG	SV	IP	H	R	ER	HR	BB	SO	AVG	vLH	vRH	K/9	BB/9
Avila, Nick	R-R	6-2	220	8-29-88	2	3	5.37	34	0	0	2	59	90	46	41	5	24	47	.339	.321	.317	6.16	3.15
Bennett, Daniel	B-R	6-4	220	12-28-88	5	2	2.68	39	0	0	11	40	42	15	12	1	17	49	.266	.356	.188	10.93	3.79
Carreno, Josue	R-R	6-1	170	6-26-91	9	8	3.23	27	27	0	0	139	129	55	50	5	28	119	.246	.267	.224	7.69	1.81
Clinard, Will	R-R	6-4	225	11-3-89	1	1	2.96	14	0	0	2	24	27	10	8	1	7	20	.276	.188	.360	7.40	2.59
Collier, Tommy	R-R	6-2	205	12-3-89	9	8	2.74	24	24	1	0	125	112	44	38	5	37	84	.247	.249	.245	6.06	2.67
Ferrell, Jeff	R-R	6-3	185	11-23-90	7	5	3.91	23	16	0	1	92	76	44	40	9	29	81	.224	.209	.243	7.92	2.84
Kelley, Tim	L-R	6-6	230	10-11-87	0	5	12.00	10	1	0	0	18	29	27	24	1	11	14	.367	.385	.358	7.00	5.50
Knudson, Guido	R-R	6-1	185	8-5-89	0	0	0.00	1	0	0	0	3	1	0	0	0	0	3	.091	.000	.143	0.00	0.00
Lebron, Ramon	R-R	6-1	190	1-2-89	0	0	5.18	26	0	0	1	33	24	21	19	1	39	33	.209	.241	.180	9.00	10.64
Mercedes, Melvin	R-R	6-3	190	11-2-90	0	3	2.80	37	0	0	9	64	54	25	20	3	23	43	.230	.278	.189	6.02	3.22
Palacios, Wilsen	R-R	6-3	180	12-15-89	12	9	3.70	23	23	0	0	129	133	60	53	5	23	77	.270	.242	.300	5.37	1.60
Ryan, Kyle	L-L	6-5	180	8-2-91	7	8	3.74	28	28	1	0	159	176	85	66	11	59	106	.281	.262	.295	5.96	3.34
Sanz, Luis	R-R	6-1	173	11-19-87	1	0	0.00	2	0	0	0	2	0	0	0	0	2	4	.176	.375	.000	6.75	3.38
Saupold, Warwick	R-R	6-1	195	1-16-90	2	1	2.79	28	1	0	2	58	58	25	18	3	10	58	.260	.239	.281	9.00	1.55
Smith, Brennan	R-R	6-3	200	8-4-89	3	4	3.86	19	15	0	0	84	78	37	36	8	22	58	.251	.269	.232	6.21	2.36

Smith, Chad	R-R	6-3	215	10-2-89	0	2	4.38	8	5	0	0	25	23	12	12	2	6	17	.250	.288	.200	6.20	2.19
Smith, Slade	R-R	6-2	185	9-26-90	2	1	3.59	20	0	0	1	48	60	22	19	2	15	34	.319	.344	.295	6.42	2.83
Teufel, Shawn	L-L	6-3	215	7-16-86	0	1	9.00	1	0	0	0	4	7	4	4	0	2	3	.412	.250	.462	6.75	4.50
Todd, Jade	R-L	6-2	190	3-22-90	6	2	1.65	44	0	0	2	60	39	11	11	3	19	71	.191	.155	.224	10.65	2.85
Torrealba, Michael	R-R	5-11	150	11-19-89	5	5	3.01	46	0	0	5	75	57	31	25	2	31	81	.210	.236	.188	9.76	3.74
White, Tyler	R-R	6-2	197	8-8-89	1	0	0.00	1	0	0	0	2	2	0	0	0	1	1	.250	.000	.250	4.50	4.50
Woolley, Ryan	R-R	6-1	190	2-11-88	0	0	1.23	4	0	0	0	7	4	1	1	0	2	8	.160	.000	.250	9.82	2.45

Fielding

Catcher	PCT	G	PO	A	E	DP	PB
Casali	.995	46	358	27	2	1	1
Guida	1.000	1	6	0	0	0	1
Leyland	.970	23	150	9	5	1	3
Maggard	.986	40	244	37	4	5	5
Purroy	.962	34	261	20	11	1	3

First Base	PCT	G	PO	A	E	DP
Durham	1.000	9	81	9	0	5
Green	.986	15	123	14	2	10
Holm	1.000	12	84	6	0	7
Leyland	.976	13	112	9	3	10
Loy	1.000	1	4	0	0	0
Westlake	.987	96	873	60	12	73

Second Base	PCT	G	PO	A	E	DP
Corcino	1.000	1	1	3	0	0

	PCT	G	PO	A	E	DP
De Los Santos	1.000	5	5	6	0	2
Kaline	.976	13	14	27	1	7
Loy	.977	111	145	318	11	64
Reaves	.944	3	4	13	1	2
Suarez	1.000	15	19	44	0	5

Third Base	PCT	G	PO	A	E	DP
Corcino	.902	19	18	28	5	1
De Los Santos	1.000	1	3	6	0	1
Kaline	.983	26	14	43	1	2
King	.924	90	61	157	18	9
Perry	.938	7	4	11	1	1
Westlake	1.000	1	1	0	0	0

Shortstop	PCT	G	PO	A	E	DP
Loy	.963	24	36	68	4	13
Reaves	1.000	1	1	3	0	1

Suarez	.971	119	257	349	18	80

Outfield	PCT	G	PO	A	E	DP
Castillo	.967	12	28	1	1	0
Durham	.857	4	5	1	1	0
Holm	.923	27	35	1	3	0
Krizan	.981	106	195	7	4	1
Loy	1.000	2	2	0	0	0
McVaney	1.000	55	81	1	0	0
Moya	.990	57	98	6	1	0
Smith	1.000	8	16	1	0	0
Vasquez	.938	28	43	2	3	0
Wright	.997	130	331	7	1	2

CONNECTICUT TIGERS

SHORT-SEASON

NEW YORK-PENN LEAGUE

Batting	B-T	HT	WT	DOB	AVG	vLH	vRH	G	AB	R	H	2B	3B	HR	RBI	BB	HBP	SH	SF	SO	SB	CS	SLG	OBP
Aguasvivas, Juaner	R-R	6-4	248	9-15-89	.220	.148	.243	61	227	16	50	18	1	3	29	11	2	0	4	73	1	0	.348	.258
Corcino, Edgar	B-R	6-2	190	6-7-92	.179	.184	.176	42	140	21	25	2	6	1	12	15	2	2	2	44	4	4	.300	.264
Cortez, Luis	R-R	6-0	155	1-8-92	.119	.167	.106	20	59	3	7	3	0	0	4	2	3	0	0	18	1	0	.169	.188
De Los Santos, Carlos	B-R	6-0	177	11-1-90	.245	.083	.297	14	49	6	12	0	0	0	5	4	0	1	2	10	8	1	.245	.291
Dean, Jordan	R-R	5-10	170	8-12-90	.200	.265	.180	44	145	14	29	3	3	0	15	14	0	2	1	34	11	5	.262	.269
Gomez, Edwin	B-R	6-3	175	8-26-91	.133	.143	.125	5	15	1	2	0	0	0	2	1	0	0	0	3	0	0	.133	.188
Hanover, Tyler	R-R	5-7	170	8-25-89	.269	.364	.246	57	219	22	59	11	0	2	14	16	1	4	0	28	6	1	.347	.322
Harrison, Brett	R-R	6-0	185	6-9-92	.156	.250	.135	19	64	8	10	3	1	0	5	1	1	2	0	29	0	1	.234	.182
Kirksey, Zach	L-R	6-1	207	2-17-89	.194	.095	.209	48	155	16	30	4	1	6	27	10	11	1	2	55	10	4	.348	.287
McVaney, Jeff	R-R	6-2	210	1-16-90	.288	.417	.250	15	52	5	15	3	0	0	5	6	5	0	0	8	0	0	.346	.413
Neil, Charlie	B-R	6-5	195	2-1-90	.160	.154	.162	20	50	5	8	0	0	1	8	1	1	0	21	1	1	.160	.288
Pickar, Bennett	R-R	6-1	185	9-14-90	.205	.154	.215	52	156	12	32	4	1	1	8	20	1	2	1	47	0	0	.263	.298
Reaves, Jared	R-R	5-10	185	7-20-90	.240	.250	.238	55	208	32	50	13	1	2	10	13	6	3	0	37	3	3	.341	.304
Remes, Tim	R-R	6-0	205	6-17-92	.103	.111	.100	14	39	2	4	1	0	0	1	10	1	1	0	19	1	0	.128	.300
Smith, Pat	L-L	6-0	170	10-11-91	.232	.240	.230	62	224	23	52	11	1	3	25	20	2	3	2	59	6	2	.330	.298
Stewart, Jake	R-R	6-2	195	11-20-90	.218	.204	.221	66	262	43	57	11	1	7	21	19	0	2	3	66	11	6	.347	.268
Thigpen, Wes	R-R	6-0	200	6-20-89	.130	.333	.100	7	23	2	3	0	0	0	1	1	0	0	0	5	1	0	.130	.167
Travis, Devon	R-R	5-9	183	2-21-91	.280	.300	.274	25	93	17	26	2	2	3	11	8	3	2	1	10	3	1	.441	.352
Vasquez, Danry	L-R	6-3	169	1-8-94	.311	.197	.345	72	289	36	90	16	2	2	35	13	1	5	2	45	6	4	.401	.341

Pitching	B-T	HT	WT	DOB	W	L	ERA	G	GS	CG	SV	IP	H	R	ER	HR	BB	SO	AVG	vLH	vRH	K/9	BB/9
Barrett, Tyler	R-L	6-2	210	6-23-89	0	2	36.00	3	0	0	0	2	9	8	8	0	4	8	.600	.375	.857	18.00	9.00
Briceno, Endrys	R-R	6-4	150	2-7-92	4	3	5.15	12	12	0	0	58	60	37	33	3	22	30	.269	.244	.286	4.68	3.43
Clinard, Will	R-R	6-4	225	11-3-89	2	1	1.38	7	0	0	2	13	8	3	2	0	2	19	.174	.154	.182	13.15	1.38
Davenport, Matt	R-R	6-8	200	10-11-89	2	1	0.77	16	0	0	2	23	14	2	2	0	4	22	.182	.160	.192	8.49	1.54
De La Rosa, Edgar	R-R	6-6	215	11-20-90	4	4	3.10	15	15	0	0	73	66	32	25	3	35	54	.242	.279	.216	6.69	4.33
Duffey, Jack	L-L	6-2	190	4-18-92	1	3	2.60	7	5	0	0	28	27	9	8	0	9	16	.260	.148	.299	5.20	2.93
Gillies, Charlie	R-R	6-2	200	8-30-90	0	4	3.40	12	12	0	0	42	31	22	16	1	17	42	.195	.215	.175	8.93	3.61
Heckaman, Eric	R-R	6-2	215	5-14-88	1	2	3.32	18	1	0	1	38	31	17	14	2	23	33	.220	.226	.215	7.82	5.45
Kelley, Tim	L-R	6-6	230	10-11-87	1	4	3.88	17	9	0	0	49	47	23	21	6	13	40	.257	.237	.271	7.40	2.40
Lebron, Ramon	R-R	6-1	190	1-2-89	1	1	5.74	9	0	0	0	16	11	13	10	3	9	16	.200	.333	.135	9.19	5.17
Lo, Hua-Wei	L-L	5-11	165	12-1-94	2	4	3.21	10	10	0	0	48	45	26	17	3	17	27	.253	.143	.287	5.10	3.21
Longstreth, Ryan	L-L	6-1	205	4-16-90	0	1	6.23	9	2	0	0	17	23	13	12	1	5	9	.319	.167	.370	4.67	2.60
Nesbitt, Angel	R-R	6-1	175	12-4-90	4	3	4.71	20	0	0	0	36	49	23	19	1	11	23	.336	.403	.286	5.70	2.72
Nieves, Efrain	L-L	6-0	169	11-15-89	4	1	2.79	21	0	0	3	42	28	13	13	2	8	42	.181	.060	.238	9.00	1.71
Phillips, Alex	L-L	6-4	205	5-11-90	1	0	2.51	18	0	0	1	32	28	10	9	1	6	29	.235	.250	.231	8.07	1.67
Robertson, Montreal	R-R	6-4	220	6-19-90	0	4	4.69	11	9	0	0	48	42	29	25	2	20	33	.239	.274	.214	6.19	3.75
Rogers, Joe	L-L	6-1	205	2-18-91	2	1	2.28	18	0	0	3	24	20	7	6	0	12	28	.220	.115	.262	10.65	4.56
Sabol, Jake	R-R	6-5	220	8-11-88	0	1	15.63	4	0	0	0	6	14	12	11	1	4	1	.438	.571	.182	1.42	5.68
Scantling, Hunter	R-R	6-8	275	9-12-89	2	0	1.23	13	0	0	2	22	7	3	3	1	6	21	.100	.067	.109	8.59	2.45
Smith, Chad	R-R	6-3	215	10-2-89	0	0	1.42	2	0	0	2	6	3	1	1	0	2	8	.143	.000	.200	11.37	2.84
Smith, Slade	R-R	6-2	185	9-26-90	0	0	3.00	2	0	0	0	3	2	1	1	0	0	5	.182	.286	.000	15.00	0.00
Turley, Josh	L-L	6-0	185	8-26-90	4	1	1.06	12	0	0	0	34	23	5	4	0	5	25	.193	.205	.188	6.62	1.32

Fielding

Catcher	PCT	G	PO	A	E	DP	PB
Neil	1.000	9	45	5	0	0	4
Pickar	.981	52	319	44	7	2	17
Remes	1.000	14	101	9	0	1	9
Thigpen	.981	7	44	9	1	1	4

DETROIT TIGERS

First Base	PCT	G	PO	A	E	DP
Aguasvivas	.986	61	579	34	9	53
Corcino	.993	15	129	8	1	15
Cortez	1.000	2	12	0	0	1
Harrison	1.000	1	4	0	0	1

Second Base	PCT	G	PO	A	E	DP
Corcino	1.000	1	2	2	0	2
Cortez	1.000	6	11	19	0	5
De Los Santos	.941	11	11	37	3	8
Dean	.946	24	45	61	6	13
Hanover	.974	9	16	22	1	5

	PCT	G	PO	A	E	DP
Reaves	1.000	1	4	3	0	2
Travis	.969	23	54	70	4	14

Third Base	PCT	G	PO	A	E	DP
Corcino	.900	23	16	47	7	3
Dean	1.000	1	0	3	0	1
Hanover	.927	36	22	79	8	8
Harrison	.813	15	7	19	6	0

Shortstop	PCT	G	PO	A	E	DP
Cortez	.881	12	19	40	8	8
De Los Santos	.818	1	5	4	2	3

	PCT	G	PO	A	E	DP
Dean	.949	11	20	36	3	8
Reaves	.966	51	77	181	9	35

Outfield	PCT	G	PO	A	E	DP
Gomez	.857	5	5	1	1	0
Kirksey	1.000	13	19	0	0	0
McVaney	1.000	12	17	1	0	0
Neil	1.000	2	1	0	0	0
Smith	.992	62	119	4	1	1
Stewart	.970	63	124	4	4	2
Vasquez	.985	71	120	11	2	4

GCL TIGERS

ROOKIE

GULF COAST LEAGUE

Batting	B-T	HT	WT	DOB	AVG	vLH	vRH	G	AB	R	H	2B	3B	HR	RBI	BB	HBP	SH	SF	SO	SB	CS	SLG	OBP
Allen, Andrew	R-R	6-1	225	7-10-89	.213	.300	.189	17	47	7	10	2	0	0	4	4	2	0	0	15	0	0	.255	.302
Brown, Rashad	L-L	5-11	180	12-17-93	.250	.095	.291	30	100	16	25	3	3	0	10	7	2	1	0	29	4	2	.340	.312
Castro, Harold	L-R	6-0	145	11-30-93	.311	.271	.324	51	193	24	60	14	2	1	21	10	1	9	3	25	15	3	.420	.343
Cortez, Luis	R-R	6-0	155	1-8-92	.217	.000	.278	6	23	4	5	1	0	1	4	0	0	0	0	9	0	0	.391	.217
De Los Santos, Carlos	R-R	6-0	177	11-1-90	.276	.333	.261	8	29	5	8	0	0	0	2	0	0	1	0	5	1	1	.276	.276
Delgado, Alwin	R-R	6-3	175	11-3-92	.236	.167	.256	31	110	16	26	6	2	2	11	9	1	2	0	25	2	3	.382	.300
Driggers, D.J.	R-R	6-3	195	6-28-92	.160	.136	.167	28	94	11	15	5	1	0	5	6	4	0	0	35	3	2	.234	.240
Gibson, Tyler	L-R	6-2	190	6-17-93	.167	.133	.177	52	186	30	31	6	2	2	16	30	4	1	0	68	18	7	.253	.295
Gonzalez, David	R-R	5-9	140	12-1-93	.243	.286	.231	39	136	19	33	5	1	0	16	22	0	4	0	20	6	2	.294	.348
Green, Dean	L-R	6-4	255	6-30-89	.094	.000	.136	9	32	1	3	0	0	0	5	4	0	0	1	5	0	0	.094	.189
Guida, Jordan	R-R	5-9	185	9-22-88	.467	.250	.545	5	15	6	7	2	0	0	2	1	0	0	0	4	1	0	.600	.556
Hanover, Tyler	R-R	5-7	170	8-25-89	.364	.000	.444	4	11	3	4	1	0	1	5	4	1	0	1	1	4	0	.727	.529
Harrison, Brett	R-R	6-0	185	6-9-92	.173	.150	.179	32	98	10	17	3	0	3	11	7	4	1	0	39	0	1	.296	.257
Jensen, Cory	B-R	5-11	185	9-29-89	.178	.333	.130	29	90	7	16	4	0	1	11	12	3	2	3	14	4	1	.256	.287
Kapstein, Jacob	B-R	6-2	215	2-24-94	.152	.300	.087	14	33	4	5	2	0	0	4	4	0	0	0	13	1	1	.212	.243
Longley, Andrew	R-R	6-3	215	10-5-88	.236	.263	.230	33	106	9	25	8	1	2	17	7	6	1	0	30	1	0	.387	.319
Paulino, Miguel	R-R	6-1	185	11-3-93	.154	.000	.160	12	26	2	4	0	0	0	1	3	0	0	0	13	0	0	.154	.241
Remes, Tim	R-R	6-0	205	6-17-92	.221	.167	.237	24	77	15	17	7	0	1	10	17	1	2	1	23	0	0	.351	.365
Salgado, Ismael	R-R	6-1	165	1-11-93	.209	.167	.222	44	129	15	27	8	2	0	8	9	1	4	0	33	5	2	.302	.266
Schotts, Austin	R-R	5-11	180	9-16-93	.310	.270	.322	40	155	31	48	11	3	3	21	12	2	5	3	41	15	4	.452	.360
Soledad, Jose	R-R	5-11	165	7-22-92	.266	.333	.246	26	79	6	21	4	1	1	7	4	0	1	0	18	3	2	.380	.301
Ustariz, Jesus	R-R	6-1	192	4-26-93	.282	.219	.298	50	163	21	46	13	1	2	20	26	2	1	4	25	1	1	.411	.379

Pitching	B-T	HT	WT	DOB	W	L	ERA	G	GS	CG	SV	IP	H	R	ER	HR	BB	SO	AVG	vLH	vRH	K/9	BB/9
Carmichael, Nick	R-R	6-6	220	4-13-90	3	1	2.22	10	10	0	0	45	40	13	11	2	14	38	.244	.234	.248	7.66	2.82
Carr, Josh	R-R	6-4	210	11-26-89	5	2	2.70	15	6	0	0	47	47	16	14	0	9	39	.269	.324	.234	7.52	1.74
Ehlers, Logan	L-L	6-1	190	10-30-91	0	0	1.10	5	3	0	0	16	9	2	2	0	3	16	.167	.000	.191	8.82	1.65
Espinal, Yoel	R-R	6-2	200	11-7-92	1	1	6.89	13	0	0	0	31	25	25	24	3	24	26	.216	.184	.231	7.47	6.89
Felix, Julio	R-R	6-1	185	2-23-92	4	2	4.11	17	0	0	2	35	29	18	16	2	8	29	.225	.313	.173	7.46	2.06
Harrison, Drew	R-R	6-4	260	1-22-91	2	0	0.79	8	0	0	1	11	5	1	1	0	6	12	.135	.167	.120	9.53	4.76
Hidalgo, Luis	R-R	6-1	170	1-18-91	0	4	5.08	18	0	0	0	44	38	27	25	3	15	46	.236	.265	.223	9.34	3.05
Jamison, Preston	L-L	6-6	225	3-2-93	0	0	4.40	7	4	0	0	14	9	7	7	2	11	14	.184	.063	.242	8.79	6.91
John, Jordan	R-L	6-3	200	7-5-90	0	0	0.00	3	0	0	0	4	1	0	0	0	5		.091	.000	.100	12.27	0.00
Lo, Hua-Wei	L-L	5-11	165	12-1-90	0	0	1.93	4	3	0	0	19	10	4	4	0	2	18	.152	.056	.188	8.68	0.96
Longstreth, Ryan	L-L	6-1	206	4-16-90	3	0	3.07	11	0	0	0	15	7	5	5	0	7	21	.259	.200	.279	12.89	4.30
Lopez, Yorfrank	R-R	6-3	170	12-1-90	5	3	2.32	15	7	0	0	54	44	15	14	3	12	57	.219	.220	.218	9.44	1.99
Miner, Zach	R-R	6-4	215	3-12-82	0	0	2.25	3	0	0	0	4	2	1	1	0	0	6	.133	.200	.100	13.50	0.00
Paulino, David	R-R	6-5	180	2-6-94	1	0	2.25	3	1	0	0	4	1	1	1	0	3	5	.083	.000	.091	11.25	6.75
Perez, Fernando	R-R	6-3	181	12-17-93	5	4	4.24	12	10	0	0	47	36	28	22	1	19	43	.213	.276	.161	8.29	3.66
Randall, Hudson	R-R	6-4	185	9-22-90	0	1	3.00	7	1	0	1	12	11	4	4	0	3	8	.239	.211	.259	6.00	2.25
Sabol, Jake	R-R	6-5	220	8-11-88	0	0	54.00	1	0	0	0	1	7	6	6	0	1	2	.700	.500	1.000	18.00	9.00
Smith, Chad	R-R	6-3	215	10-2-89	1	0	0.61	4	3	0	0	15	14	2	1	0	6	15	.250	.263	.243	14.11	3.68
Solano, Gregorio	R-R	6-3	180	7-9-92	5	2	3.95	19	0	0	0	43	47	23	19	4	13	33	.278	.283	.276	6.85	2.70
Stroud, Brian	R-R	6-4	215	10-18-88	0	1	10.13	2	2	0	0	5	9	6	6	0	3	3	.391	.375	.400	5.06	5.06
Thompson, Jake	R-R	6-4	235	1-31-94	1	2	1.91	7	7	0	0	28	14	6	6	1	10	31	.149	.200	.125	9.85	3.18
Valdez, Jose	R-R	6-1	167	3-1-90	0	1	0.82	23	0	0	15	22	15	3	2	0	10	28	.188	.258	.143	11.45	4.09
VerHagen, Drew	R-R	6-6	230	10-22-90	0	0	2.25	2	0	0	0	4	5	2	1	0	0	2	.313	.600	.182	4.50	0.00

Fielding

Catcher	PCT	G	PO	A	E	DP	PB
Guida	1.000	5	26	4	0	0	1
Kapstein	1.000	4	14	0	0	0	1
Longley	.990	32	263	20	3	3	6
Remes	.991	24	198	19	2	0	5

First Base	PCT	G	PO	A	E	DP
Allen	.970	10	64	0	2	8
Soledad	.974	11	71	3	2	5
Ustariz	.993	47	393	28	3	37

Second Base	PCT	G	PO	A	E	DP
Castro	.959	48	92	120	9	29
Delgado	.667	1	0	2	1	1
Hanover	.909	2	2	8	1	1
Jensen	.980	11	17	32	1	7

Third Base	PCT	G	PO	A	E	DP
Cortez	1.000	2	0	5	0	0
Delgado	.931	13	5	22	2	1
Hanover	.833	2	0	5	1	0
Harrison	.951	31	20	57	4	7

	PCT	G	PO	A	E	DP
Jensen	.923	11	7	29	3	3
Soledad	.923	6	2	10	1	0
Ustariz	1.000	1	1	0	0	0

Shortstop	PCT	G	PO	A	E	DP
Cortez	.905	4	6	13	2	3
De Los Santos	1.000	8	17	23	0	6
Delgado	.917	11	16	28	4	5
Gonzalez	.969	38	53	101	5	24
Jensen	.750	2	4	2	2	1

Outfield	PCT	G	PO	A	E	DP
Brown	.950	27	34	4	2	0
Driggers	.967	25	28	1	1	0

Gibson	.988	51	78	2	1	1
Jensen	1.000	3	2	0	0	0
Kapstein	1.000	2	1	0	0	0

Paulino	.938	11	14	1	1	0
Salgado	1.000	41	67	2	0	0
Schotts	.940	32	44	3	3	0

DSL TIGERS
DOMINICAN SUMMER LEAGUE

ROOKIE

Batting	B-T	HT	WT	DOB	AVG	vLH	vRH	G	AB	R	H	2B	3B	HR	RBI	BB	HBP	SH	SF	SO	SB	CS	SLG	OBP
Acevedo, Sandy	L-L	6-0	170	12-25-92	.280	.259	.291	51	164	30	46	6	6	5	27	27	8	5	2	47	8	6	.482	.403
Chavez, Albertin	R-R	5-10	172	1-21-92	.237	.333	.207	13	38	3	9	1	0	0	8	5	0	1	1	6	3	2	.263	.318
Contreras, Francisco	R-R	6-1	180	12-3-92	.220	.169	.242	61	214	28	47	9	1	0	20	27	6	3	3	35	7	9	.271	.320
Crafort, Samuel	B-R	6-0	147	7-31-93	.210	.180	.224	45	157	26	33	6	3	1	6	39	2	3	0	61	15	1	.306	.374
Felipe, Eurys	B-R	5-10	150	3-9-94	.205	.273	.179	13	39	7	8	1	0	0	6	6	0	2	0	15	5	0	.231	.311
Hidalgo, Gregoris	R-R	5-10	160	12-18-93	.192	.381	.115	24	73	9	14	4	1	1	7	12	0	0	1	18	5	3	.315	.302
Joseph, Manuel	R-R	5-11	160	5-16-94	.295	.203	.344	53	200	31	59	10	3	4	33	22	4	5	4	32	7	7	.435	.370
Oses, Omar	R-R	5-11	159	5-25-93	.181	.100	.209	43	116	21	21	3	0	1	8	12	3	7	1	40	7	8	.233	.273
Ovalles, Victor	R-R	6-4	195	6-23-93	.255	.316	.232	38	137	15	35	8	0	0	17	11	3	0	1	23	1	2	.314	.322
Pena, Lenny	L-R	6-3	195	3-27-92	.238	.167	.274	64	235	27	56	10	2	3	37	19	13	1	3	51	1	1	.336	.326
Pena, Yerison	B-R	6-1	180	7-18-91	.298	.327	.279	43	141	28	42	4	5	2	20	35	2	3	2	37	6	5	.440	.439
Rodriguez, Sandy	R-R	6-1	180	10-19-94	.183	.179	.186	24	71	6	13	0	0	0	3	7	0	1	0	22	0	4	.183	.256
Santana, Felix A.	R-R	5-10	180	8-29-91	.224	.211	.229	48	143	23	32	3	1	2	11	11	7	1	2	25	16	6	.301	.307
Santana, Felix	R-R	5-10	180	8-19-94	.234	.235	.233	56	197	25	46	8	0	1	20	21	5	4	3	61	5	3	.289	.319
Valdez, Ignacio	R-R	6-3	195	7-16-95	.234	.233	.234	29	107	10	25	6	1	0	10	5	1	0	1	35	4	3	.308	.272
Yance, Anderson	L-L	5-11	160	7-25-92	.218	.167	.233	14	55	9	12	2	0	0	3	1	0	0	0	2	2	2	.255	.317

Pitching	B-T	HT	WT	DOB	W	L	ERA	G	GS	CG	SV	IP	H	R	ER	HR	BB	SO	AVG	vLH	vRH	K/9	BB/9
Alcantara, Juan	R-R	6-4	195	7-30-94	4	2	3.97	17	3	0	1	45	40	24	20	0	16	28	.242	.204	.259	5.56	3.18
Baez, Sandy	R-R	6-2	180	11-25-93	0	3	5.21	10	9	0	0	38	43	31	22	1	12	42	.293	.395	.257	9.95	2.84
Burgos, Cesar	R-R	6-2	185	3-1-93	3	2	2.27	23	0	0	3	32	34	11	8	2	9	24	.281	.206	.310	6.82	2.56
Chavez, Emanuel	R-R	6-3	175	1-19-95	1	4	4.15	14	8	1	1	48	29	27	22	2	27	33	.181	.163	.189	6.23	5.10
Ciriaco, Ricardo	R-R	6-0	220	8-18-92	2	2	2.38	14	7	0	0	53	42	19	14	0	15	34	.215	.190	.227	5.77	2.55
Falcon, Juan	R-R	6-3	200	3-7-92	6	3	2.18	23	0	0	1	45	25	18	11	0	30	31	.162	.244	.133	6.15	5.96
Guzman, Jesus	L-L	6-3	175	1-2-91	4	1	2.01	24	0	0	0	45	27	13	10	3	9	54	.174	.222	.168	10.88	1.81
Jacobs, Vijandrick	L-L	5-10	185	2-20-94	0	0	2.35	7	3	0	0	15	10	9	4	0	18	18	.182	.200	.180	10.57	7.04
Lara, Carlos	R-R	6-2	170	3-2-94	2	5	2.43	16	13	0	0	59	57	27	16	0	14	48	.254	.295	.233	7.28	2.12
Manzanillo, Rafael	R-R	6-6	190	10-24-91	1	2	6.04	15	5	0	0	25	24	23	17	0	34	22	.270	.240	.281	7.82	12.08
Minier, Gregorio	R-R	6-0	170	2-20-92	0	0	9.82	4	0	0	0	4	2	4	4	0	7	2	.167	.250	.125	4.91	17.18
Montero, Miguel	R-R	6-3	170	12-4-92	2	2	14.00	13	1	0	0	18	25	33	28	1	24	12	.333	.320	.340	6.00	12.00
Morillo, Gregory	R-R	6-2	180	3-4-92	0	1	4.30	13	0	0	0	23	14	11	11	2	14	23	.187	.292	.137	9.00	5.48
Obispo, Janry	R-R	6-3	205	10-10-93	4	4	4.67	14	7	0	0	44	43	26	23	2	14	32	.256	.321	.226	6.50	2.84
Paniagua, Adrian	R-R	6-0	195	5-1-91	0	1	16.20	3	0	0	0	2	4	6	3	0	3	1	.400	.000	.571	5.40	16.20
Rosario, Harold	R-R	5-11	198	10-23-92	1	1	4.40	16	8	0	0	47	42	24	23	0	20	53	.251	.246	.255	10.15	3.83

Fielding

Catcher	PCT	G	PO	A	E	DP	PB
Oses	.972	18	120	21	4	3	8
Rodriguez	.961	20	150	23	7	0	5
Santana	.988	33	213	36	3	0	8

First Base	PCT	G	PO	A	E	DP
Acevedo	.960	4	23	1	1	2
Contreras	1.000	2	6	0	0	2
Ovalles	1.000	2	8	0	0	1
Pena	.983	62	557	33	10	44
Rodriguez	1.000	2	7	1	0	0
Santana	1.000	1	6	0	0	0

Second Base	PCT	G	PO	A	E	DP
Chavez	1.000	1	1	0	0	0

Contreras	1.000	1	4	3	0	2
Felipe	1.000	8	21	23	0	7
Hidalgo	.969	16	27	35	2	9
Pena	.968	42	86	97	6	18

Third Base	PCT	G	PO	A	E	DP
Contreras	.911	60	63	151	21	14
Hidalgo	.000	1	0	0	1	0
Joseph	—	1	0	0	0	0
Ovalles	.500	1	0	1	1	0
Pena	.750	3	4	5	3	0
Pena	.833	3	3	2	1	0

Shortstop	PCT	G	PO	A	E	DP
Chavez	1.000	11	16	26	0	4

Felipe	.833	1	2	3	1	0
Hidalgo	.750	5	3	3	2	1
Joseph	.957	52	78	167	11	29

Outfield	PCT	G	PO	A	E	DP
Acevedo	.986	48	66	4	1	0
Crafort	.962	42	69	7	3	2
Joseph	1.000	1	1	0	0	0
Oses	1.000	21	23	0	0	0
Santana	1.000	1	1	1	0	0
Santana	.981	48	50	2	1	1
Valdez	.912	28	52	0	5	0
Yance	1.000	14	18	1	0	0

VSL TIGERS
VENEZUELAN SUMMER LEAGUE

ROOKIE

Batting	B-T	HT	WT	DOB	AVG	vLH	vRH	G	AB	R	H	2B	3B	HR	RBI	BB	HBP	SH	SF	SO	SB	CS	SLG	OBP
Alvarado, Davi	R-R	5-8	154	3-19-95	.202	.174	.211	35	94	14	19	3	1	0	4	8	2	3	0	9	3	3	.255	.279
Betancourt, Javier	R-R	5-10	173	5-8-95	.333	.321	.337	32	123	24	41	6	0	3	15	10	3	1	2	16	4	5	.455	.391
Castillo, Eliezer	R-R	6-0	169	1-10-95	.232	.167	.252	48	155	19	36	5	0	1	19	7	10	1	1	37	3	5	.284	.306
Chavez, Albertin	R-R	5-10	172	1-21-92	.284	.200	.309	34	88	24	25	5	1	0	8	18	6	0	1	13	5	3	.364	.434
Fuentes, Steven	B-R	5-11	178	10-21-94	.257	.372	.230	59	226	23	58	8	4	2	25	18	3	1	2	47	8	8	.354	.317
Montero, Jhosua	R-R	5-11	190	1-15-94	.205	.250	.191	34	117	13	24	4	0	0	10	3	1	1	2	20	2	3	.239	.228
Navarro, Franklin	R-R	5-10	181	10-17-94	.315	.227	.335	62	241	31	76	19	1	4	33	16	2	0	2	51	2	2	.452	.360
Ovalles, Jose	R-R	5-10	190	8-2-93	.259	.286	.250	50	170	22	44	17	0	5	21	17	9	1	0	32	4	2	.447	.357
Padron, Victor	L-R	5-8	160	7-5-94	.273	.500	.237	15	44	5	12	1	1	0	2	9	1	0	0	4	3	0	.341	.407
Perez, Arvicent	R-R	5-8	186	1-14-94	.289	.211	.308	34	97	8	28	5	1	1	15	5	3	0	2	11	3	0	.392	.336
Perez, Carlos	R-R	6-0	155	2-16-94	.255	.263	.253	54	196	30	50	8	1	6	25	14	5	2	0	42	1	2	.398	.321
Tenia, Gabriel	R-R	6-0	203	1-18-93	.228	.231	.228	55	184	21	42	10	1	5	22	16	9	2	0	54	0	0	.375	.321

Tovar, Orvin	R-R	5-11	180	8-6-93	.281	.235	.292	68	253	43	71	17	2	9	53	28	3	0	2	28	8	2	.470	.357
Yance, Anderson	L-L	5-11	160	7-25-92	.227	.259	.219	43	141	22	32	9	1	1	11	14	2	0	0	23	4	2	.326	.306
Zambrano, Jose	B-R	5-6	151	11-4-93	.342	.400	.332	60	225	37	77	12	0	1	34	20	5	4	2	16	12	4	.409	.405

Pitching	B-T	HT	WT	DOB	W	L	ERA	G	GS	CG	SV	IP	H	R	ER	HR	BB	SO	AVG	vLH	vRH	K/9	BB/9
Belisario, Johan	R-R	5-11	155	8-13-93	1	7	4.91	13	13	0	0	62	85	43	34	4	10	43	.336	.333	.337	6.21	1.44
Camaripano, Junior	L-L	6-2	175	12-21-93	2	3	8.71	16	0	0	0	21	22	23	20	0	10	16	.275	.267	.277	6.97	4.35
Castro, Anthony	R-R	6-1	158	4-13-95	1	2	3.38	13	13	0	0	53	40	32	20	2	30	46	.212	.246	.195	7.76	5.06
Cedeno, Cruz	R-R	6-1	150	10-14-93	0	0	4.15	4	0	0	0	4	4	2	2	0	3	3	.286	.143	.429	6.23	6.23
Cedeno, Luis	R-R	6-1	185	10-2-93	1	4	6.12	16	7	0	1	43	56	33	29	8	15	23	.322	.396	.289	4.85	3.16
Fuentes, Jose	R-R	6-0	168	6-10-94	1	5	4.47	13	10	0	0	48	56	31	24	5	25	34	.296	.273	.309	6.33	4.66
Gutierrez, Alfred	R-R	6-0	163	6-12-95	0	1	8.31	9	0	0	0	17	17	18	16	2	10	17	.262	.350	.222	8.83	5.19
Hidrogo, Eudis	L-L	6-1	198	6-6-95	5	0	1.33	11	1	0	0	27	19	5	4	0	12	26	.200	.467	.150	8.67	4.00
Jimenez, Eduardo	R-R	6-1	182	4-4-95	0	5	3.61	13	7	0	1	42	46	20	17	1	16	30	.286	.239	.304	6.38	3.40
Medina, Jose	R-R	6-2	195	9-24-92	2	2	6.62	18	1	0	0	35	44	29	26	8	11	20	.310	.220	.359	5.09	2.80
Pina, Edgar	R-R	5-10	204	3-5-93	2	3	3.00	27	0	0	13	30	36	16	10	1	12	22	.310	.342	.295	6.60	3.60
Robles, Reinaldo	R-R	6-1	191	1-7-95	1	3	5.59	13	4	0	0	29	35	23	18	4	19	17	.297	.179	.354	5.28	5.90
Rodriguez, Jose	R-R	5-11	180	12-30-92	3	0	4.40	13	7	0	1	47	49	29	23	5	24	34	.263	.111	.326	6.51	4.60
Rodriguez, Luis	R-R	6-1	160	5-11-92	0	0	8.64	7	0	0	0	8	13	9	8	1	7	9	.333	.385	.308	9.72	7.56
Rojas, Eduardo	R-R	6-2	175	1-7-94	0	0	7.16	12	0	0	0	16	16	14	13	1	16	2	.254	.318	.220	1.10	8.82
Sanchez, Jairo	R-R	5-11	204	8-11-92	0	0	18.00	1	0	0	0	1	3	2	2	0	0	1	.500	.000	.600	9.00	0.00
Sanchez, Julio	R-R	5-11	162	9-21-91	2	2	3.52	18	0	0	1	23	23	11	9	0	13	14	.271	.333	.236	5.48	5.09
Vasquez, Angel	R-R	6-5	190	10-8-93	3	3	6.06	14	7	0	0	52	76	45	35	6	18	20	.344	.375	.326	3.46	3.12
Verastegui, Adenson	R-R	5-11	196	2-19-93	6	0	3.51	18	0	0	0	33	32	16	13	2	19	24	.256	.214	.277	6.48	5.13

Fielding

Catcher	PCT	G	PO	A	E	DP	PB
Chavez	1.000	1	1	0	0	0	0
Navarro	.988	36	205	43	3	0	4
Ovalles	.986	21	114	26	2	1	2
Perez	.940	16	64	15	5	0	2
Tenia	.867	3	13	0	2	0	1

First Base	PCT	G	PO	A	E	DP
Chavez	.967	8	56	2	2	11
Ovalles	.977	19	155	13	4	12
Tenia	.990	46	382	12	4	36

Second Base	PCT	G	PO	A	E	DP
Alvarado	.954	23	52	51	5	12
Betancourt	.977	21	34	51	2	13

	PCT	G	PO	A	E	DP
Castillo	1.000	1	2	5	0	1
Chavez	1.000	5	6	13	0	0
Fuentes	.958	5	13	10	1	4
Zambrano	.972	25	51	53	3	12

Third Base	PCT	G	PO	A	E	DP
Alvarado	.750	2	2	1	1	1
Castillo	.889	37	42	54	12	6
Chavez	.944	7	5	12	1	2
Fuentes	.910	22	22	49	7	4
Zambrano	.897	10	8	18	3	5

Shortstop	PCT	G	PO	A	E	DP
Alvarado	.714	2	2	3	2	1
Betancourt	.879	8	13	16	4	3

	PCT	G	PO	A	E	DP
Castillo	.979	9	15	32	1	7
Chavez	1.000	1	1	0	0	0
Fuentes	.931	33	67	108	13	20
Zambrano	.951	27	36	81	6	14

Outfield	PCT	G	PO	A	E	DP
Chavez	.941	10	15	1	1	0
Montero	.955	34	56	7	3	2
Padron	.958	14	22	1	1	0
Perez	.991	53	99	10	1	6
Tovar	.982	68	147	13	3	2
Yance	.932	42	62	7	5	2

DETROIT TIGERS

Houston Astros

SEASON IN A SENTENCE: The Astros had the worst year in franchise history at the big league level—for the second consecutive season—with a 4-33 stretch in the second half leading to the firing of manager Brad Mills in August.

HIGH POINT: Rookie righthander Lucas Harrell provided two: He beat Clayton Kershaw and the Dodgers on May 25 to get the Astros within a game of .500 at 22-23, and threw a shutout to beat the Padres 1-0 on June 27. The 1 hour, 58 minute affair left the Astros 32-43, six games ahead of the last-place Cubs.

LOW POINT: Of course there were many in a 107-loss season. After Harrell's shutout of the Padres, Houston went on a 4-33 skid, as general manager Jeff Luhnow traded off veterans—Carlos Lee, Chris Johnson, Wandy Rodriguez and Brett Myers chief among them—for prospects. The Giants' Matt Cain struck out 14 and tossed a perfect game against the Astros on June 13. A 12-game losing streak from July 17-28 was the longest in franchise history.

NOTABLE ROOKIES: The Astros gave plenty of them a try. Harrell, a 27-year-old who previously had three brief callups with the White Sox, wound up as their top pitcher and was later joined in the rotation by lefthander Dallas Keuchel. Two Rule 5 draftees, infielder Marwin Gonzalez and righthander Rhiner Cruz, also got plenty of chances. Houston may have found a keeper in former Marlins third baseman Matt Dominguez, a 22-year-old who hit .284/.310/.477 in 31 games.

KEY TRANSACTIONS: The trades of Johnson, Lee, Myers and Rodriguez brought more quantity than quality. The Astros also remade their front office under Luhnow, firing Bobby Heck, who had overseen the club's drafts since 2008. Heck's final draft started with the No. 1 overall pick, and the Astros selected shortstop Carlos Correa while also signing righthander Lance McCullers Jr. as a supplemental first-rounder. Luhnow hired Bo Porter as the new big league manager in September, with former big leaguer Quinton McCracken taking over as farm director.

DOWN ON THE FARM: After finishing with the worst cumulative record in the minors in three of the last four seasons, the Astros fielded winning teams in the minors. Lancaster won the high Class A California League championship, and Corpus Christi had the Double-A Texas League's best record.

OPENING DAY PAYROLL: $60.7 million (28th)

PLAYERS OF THE YEAR

MAJOR LEAGUE	MINOR LEAGUE
Lucas Harrell	**Jonathan Singleton**
rhp	**1b**
11-11, 3.76	(Double-A)
140 SO/78 BB	.284/.396/.497
Led NL P in Field Pct.	27 2B, 21 HR

ORGANIZATION LEADERS

BATTING		*Minimum 250 AB
MAJORS		
* AVG	Jose Altuve	.290
* OPS	Jose Altuve	.739
HR	Justin Maxwell	18
RBI	J.D. Martinez	55
MINORS		
* AVG	Brandon Barnes, Corpus Christi/Okla. City	.321
* OBP	Jon Singleton, Corpus Christi	.396
* SLG	Brad Snyder, Okla. City	.550
R	Delino DeShields Jr., Lexington/Lancaster	113
H	Jimmy Paredes, Okla. City	161
TB	George Springer, Lancaster/Corpus Christi	266
2B	Brandon Barnes, Corpus Christi/Okla. City	39
3B	George Springer, Lancaster/Corpus Christi	10
HR	Mike Hessman, Okla. City	35
RBI	Erik Castro, Lancaster	108
	Zachary Johnson, Lexington	108
BB	Jon Singleton, Corpus Christi	88
SO	Telvin Nash, Lancaster	198
SB	Delino DeShields Jr., Lexington/Lancaster	101

PITCHING		#Minimum 75 IP
MAJORS		
W	Lucas Harrell	11
# ERA	Lucas Harrell	3.76
SO	Bud Norris	165
SV	Brett Myers	19
MINORS		
W	Bobby Doran, Lancaster/Corpus Christi	14
	Michael Foltynewicz, Lexington	14
L	Three tied at	10
# ERA	Nick Tropeano, Lexington/Lancaster	3.02
G	Jason Stoffel, Corpus Christi	56
GS	Ross Seaton, Okla. City /Corpus Christi	29
SV	Jason Stoffel, Corpus Christi	27
IP	Ross Seaton, Okla. City /Corpus Christi	169.1
BB	Jose Cisnero, Corpus Christi/Okla. City	64
SO	Nick Tropeano, Lexington/Lancaster	166
# AVG	Jarred Cosart, Corpus Christi/Okla. City	.250
	Michael Foltynewicz, Lexington	.250

2012 PERFORMANCE

General Manager: Jeff Luhnow. **Farm Director:** Fred Nelson. **Scouting Director:** Bobby Heck.

Class	Team	League	W	L	PCT	Finish	Manager
Majors	Houston Astros	National	55	107	.340	16th (16)	Brad Mills/Tony DeFrancesco
Triple-A	Oklahoma City RedHawks	Pacific Coast	78	65	.545	6th (16)	Tony DeFrancesco/Tom Lawless
Double-A	Corpus Christi Hooks	Texas	81	59	.579	1st (8)	Keith Bodie
High A	Lancaster JetHawks	California	74	66	.529	3rd (10)	Rodney Linares
Low A	Lexington Legends	South Atlantic	69	69	.500	7th (14)	Ivan De Jesus
Short-season	Tri-City ValleyCats	New York-Penn	51	25	.671	2nd (14)	Stubby Clapp
Rookie	Greeneville Astros	Appalachian	36	32	.529	t-5th (10)	Omar Lopez
Rookie	GCL Astros	Gulf Coast	28	31	.475	9th (14)	Ed Romero
Overall 2012 Minor League Record			417	347	.546	1st (30)	

ORGANIZATION STATISTICS

HOUSTON ASTROS

NATIONAL LEAGUE

Batting	B-T	HT	WT	DOB	AVG	vLH	vRH	G	AB	R	H	2B	3B	HR	RBI	BB	HBP	SH	SF	SO	SB	CS	SLG	OBP
Altuve, Jose	R-R	5-5	170	5-6-90	.290	.359	.264	147	576	80	167	34	4	7	37	40	6	4	4	74	33	11	.399	.340
Barnes, Brandon	R-R	6-2	205	5-15-86	.204	.234	.176	43	98	8	20	3	0	1	7	5	1	1	0	29	1	1	.265	.250
Bixler, Brian	R-R	6-1	195	10-22-82	.193	.262	.130	36	88	11	17	6	0	2	7	7	0	1	0	36	3	0	.330	.253
Bogusevic, Brian	L-L	6-3	220	2-18-84	.203	.156	.213	146	355	39	72	9	2	7	28	41	7	0	1	96	15	4	.299	.297
Buck, Travis	L-R	6-2	230	11-18-83	.216	.286	.209	33	74	7	16	5	1	0	6	6	1	0	0	18	0	0	.311	.284
Castro, Jason	L-R	6-3	215	6-18-87	.257	.148	.286	87	257	29	66	15	2	6	29	31	1	2	4	61	0	0	.401	.334
Corporan, Carlos	B-R	6-2	220	1-7-84	.269	.222	.283	27	78	5	21	2	0	4	13	4	1	1	1	19	0	1	.449	.310
Dominguez, Matt	R-R	6-1	215	8-28-89	.284	.250	.294	31	109	14	31	2	2	5	16	4	0	0	0	17	0	0	.477	.310
Downs, Matt	R-R	6-1	190	3-19-84	.202	.184	.225	91	178	15	36	4	1	8	16	8	4	1	0	38	2	4	.371	.253
Francisco, Ben	R-R	6-1	185	10-23-81	.247	.185	.276	31	85	5	21	4	0	2	5	5	0	0	0	23	0	0	.365	.289
Gonzalez, Marwin	B-R	6-1	195	3-14-89	.234	.113	.276	80	205	21	48	13	0	2	12	13	0	1	0	29	3	3	.327	.280
Greene, Tyler	R-R	6-2	190	8-17-83	.246	.417	.206	39	126	18	31	6	0	7	11	6	0	0	1	39	3	2	.460	.278
2-team total (77 St. Louis)					.230	—	—	116	305	34	70	15	2	11	30	19	1	2	3	95	12	4	.400	.274
Johnson, Chris	R-R	6-3	220	10-1-84	.279	.213	.297	92	341	36	95	21	3	8	41	23	3	0	1	92	4	1	.428	.329
2-team total (44 Arizona)					.281	—	—	136	488	48	137	28	5	15	76	31	4	1	4	132	5	1	.451	.326
Laird, Brandon	R-R	6-1	215	9-11-87	.257	.211	.313	17	35	2	9	1	0	1	4	2	0	0	0	8	0	0	.371	.297
Lee, Carlos	R-R	6-2	270	6-20-76	.287	.136	.332	66	258	24	74	15	1	5	29	19	0	0	0	17	0	0	.411	.336
2-team total (81 Miami)					.264	—	—	147	550	53	145	27	1	9	77	58	1	0	6	49	3	0	.365	.332
Lowrie, Jed	B-R	6-0	180	4-17-84	.244	.184	.265	97	340	43	83	16	0	16	42	43	2	0	2	65	2	0	.438	.331
Martinez, Fernando	L-R	6-1	205	10-10-88	.237	.077	.257	41	118	12	28	7	1	6	14	6	5	0	1	34	0	1	.466	.300
Martinez, J.D.	R-R	6-3	205	8-21-87	.241	.255	.235	113	395	34	95	14	3	11	55	40	1	0	2	96	0	2	.375	.311
Maxwell, Justin	R-R	6-5	235	11-6-83	.229	.272	.208	124	315	46	72	13	3	18	53	32	3	0	2	114	9	4	.460	.304
Moore, Scott	L-R	6-2	195	11-17-83	.259	.182	.263	72	201	23	52	11	0	9	26	16	7	1	3	56	0	1	.448	.330
Paredes, Jimmy	B-R	6-3	200	11-25-88	.189	.063	.224	24	74	7	14	1	1	0	3	6	0	0	2	21	2	1	.230	.244
Pearce, Steve	R-R	5-11	210	4-13-83	.254	.235	.261	21	63	2	16	4	1	0	8	7	3	0	2	16	1	1	.349	.347
Schafer, Jordan	L-L	6-1	190	9-4-86	.211	.100	.232	106	313	40	66	10	2	4	23	36	3	6	1	106	27	9	.294	.297
Snyder, Chris	R-R	6-4	240	2-12-81	.176	.169	.181	76	221	23	39	8	0	7	26	43	3	1	0	70	0	0	.308	.295
Wallace, Brett	L-R	6-2	260	8-26-86	.253	.273	.247	66	229	24	58	10	1	9	24	18	6	0	1	73	0	0	.424	.323

Pitching	B-T	HT	WT	DOB	W	L	ERA	G	GS	CG	SV	IP	H	R	ER	HR	BB	SO	AVG	vLH	vRH	K/9	BB/9
Abad, Fernando	L-L	6-2	215	12-17-85	0	6	5.09	37	6	0	0	46	57	27	26	6	19	38	.311	.277	.331	7.43	3.72
Ambriz, Hector	L-R	6-2	235	5-24-84	1	1	4.19	18	0	0	0	19	14	9	9	0	11	22	.206	.174	.222	10.24	5.12
Carpenter, David	R-R	6-2	215	7-15-85	0	2	6.02	30	0	0	0	30	43	21	20	4	14	27	.341	.417	.295	8.19	4.25
Cedeno, Xavier	L-L	6-1	205	8-26-86	0	1	3.77	44	0	0	1	31	30	15	13	3	14	36	.254	.213	.298	10.45	4.06
Cordero, Francisco	R-R	6-3	245	5-11-75	0	3	19.80	6	0	0	0	5	13	11	11	2	4	5	.481	.625	.421	9.00	7.20
Cruz, Rhiner	R-R	6-2	205	11-1-86	1	1	6.05	52	0	0	0	55	65	38	37	8	29	46	.297	.315	.285	7.53	4.75
Del Rosario, Enerio	R-R	6-2	190	10-16-85	0	0	9.00	19	0	0	0	19	34	21	19	1	7	11	.395	.425	.370	5.21	3.32
Fick, Chuckie	R-R	6-5	185	11-20-85	0	1	4.30	18	0	0	0	23	24	13	11	4	17	17	.286	.400	.237	6.65	6.65
2-team total (2 St. Louis)					0	1	4.38	20	0	0	0	25	27	14	12	4	18	17	—	—	—	6.20	6.57
Galarraga, Armando	R-R	6-3	230	1-15-82	0	4	6.75	5	5	0	0	24	28	20	18	6	18	17	.286	.244	.321	6.38	6.75
Gonzalez, Edgar	R-R	6-2	210	2-23-83	3	1	5.04	6	6	0	0	25	23	14	14	3	8	18	.240	.279	.208	6.48	2.88
Happ, J.A.	L-L	6-6	195	10-19-82	7	9	4.83	18	18	0	0	104	112	58	56	17	39	98	.275	.266	.278	8.45	3.36
Harrell, Lucas	B-R	6-2	210	6-3-85	11	11	3.76	32	32	1	0	194	185	90	81	13	78	140	.253	.248	.258	6.51	3.62
Keuchel, Dallas	L-L	6-3	210	1-1-88	3	8	5.27	16	16	1	0	85	93	56	50	14	39	38	.286	.250	.296	4.01	4.11
Lopez, Wilton	R-R	6-0	205	7-19-83	6	3	2.17	64	0	0	10	66	61	18	16	4	8	54	.250	.231	.261	7.33	1.09
Lyles, Jordan	R-R	6-4	210	10-19-90	5	12	5.09	25	25	1	0	141	159	97	80	20	42	99	.279	.300	.263	6.30	2.67
Lyon, Brandon	R-R	6-1	200	8-10-79	0	2	3.25	37	0	0	0	36	37	13	13	3	11	35	.262	.250	.268	8.75	2.75
Myers, Brett	R-R	6-4	240	8-17-80	0	4	3.52	35	0	0	19	31	35	17	12	4	6	20	.285	.318	.246	5.87	1.76
Norris, Bud	R-R	6-0	230	3-2-85	7	13	4.65	29	29	0	0	168	165	90	87	23	66	165	.254	.263	.245	8.82	3.53
Rodriguez, Aneury	R-R	6-4	250	12-13-87	0	0	3.00	1	1	0	0	6	2	2	2	2	2	6	.105	.000	.182	9.00	3.00
Rodriguez, Fernando	R-R	6-3	235	6-18-84	2	10	5.37	71	0	0	0	70	68	45	42	10	34	78	.252	.226	.266	9.98	4.35
Rodriguez, Wandy	R-L	5-10	195	1-18-79	7	9	3.79	21	21	0	0	131	134	66	55	13	32	89	.260	.266	.258	6.13	2.20
2-team total (13 Pittsburgh)					12	13	3.76	34	33	0	0	206	205	99	86	21	56	139	—	—	—	6.08	2.45

Name	B-T	HT	WT	DOB	W	L	ERA	G	GS	CG	SV	IP	H	R	ER	HR	BB	SO	AVG	vLH	vRH	K/9	BB/9
Storey, Mickey	R-R	6-2	185	3-16-86	0	1	3.86	26	0	0	0	30	27	14	13	2	10	34	.237	.167	.269	10.09	2.97
Valdez, Jose	R-R	6-4	200	1-22-83	0	0	2.25	12	0	0	0	12	12	4	3	1	8	10	.261	.222	.286	7.50	6.00
Weiland, Kyle	L-R	6-4	195	9-12-86	0	3	6.62	3	3	0	0	18	24	13	13	5	7	13	.333	.343	.324	6.62	3.57
Wright, Wesley	R-L	5-11	180	1-28-85	2	2	3.27	77	0	0	1	52	45	20	19	4	17	54	.226	.198	.269	9.29	2.92

Fielding

Catcher	PCT	G	PO	A	E	DP	PB
Castro	.989	79	525	40	6	6	8
Corporan	.989	24	164	23	2	3	2
Snyder	.994	72	498	39	3	5	3

First Base	PCT	G	PO	A	E	DP
Downs	.981	25	135	16	3	10
Johnson	1.000	6	42	3	0	2
Laird	1.000	4	21	0	0	1
Lee	.995	65	576	44	3	46
Moore	.993	19	136	9	1	10
Pearce	.987	10	76	2	1	7
Snyder	.000	1	0	0	1	0
Wallace	.986	58	455	39	7	41

Second Base	PCT	G	PO	A	E	DP
Altuve	.984	147	257	410	11	83
Bixler	1.000	5	5	16	0	0
Downs	1.000	3	5	9	0	2
Gonzalez	1.000	6	5	15	0	1
Greene	1.000	4	8	9	0	3
Moore	1.000	6	11	17	0	3
Paredes	.857	5	5	13	3	2

Third Base	PCT	G	PO	A	E	DP
Bixler	1.000	4	1	5	0	1
Dominguez	.987	31	18	59	1	9
Downs	.912	18	5	26	3	1
Gonzalez	1.000	14	2	16	0	0
Johnson	.940	88	56	149	13	8
Laird	.923	8	2	10	1	0
Moore	.900	28	9	36	5	3
Wallace	.833	8	2	8	2	3

Shortstop	PCT	G	PO	A	E	DP
Bixler	1.000	8	8	11	0	4
Downs	—	1	0	0	0	0
Gonzalez	.971	47	55	112	5	19
Greene	.953	34	38	84	6	15
Lowrie	.980	93	102	284	8	48

Outfield	PCT	G	PO	A	E	DP
Barnes	1.000	37	65	3	0	1
Bixler	1.000	12	15	0	0	0
Bogusevic	.975	121	187	5	5	3
Buck	.976	21	40	1	1	0
Downs	1.000	13	8	1	0	0
Francisco	.968	26	29	1	1	0
Johnson	—	1	0	0	0	0
Martinez	1.000	37	49	1	0	0
Martinez	.986	100	131	9	2	0
Maxwell	.990	95	185	5	2	2
Moore	1.000	17	22	0	0	0
Paredes	.923	16	23	1	2	0
Pearce	1.000	11	12	1	0	0
Schafer	.989	87	178	4	2	1
Wright	—	1	0	0	0	0

HOUSTON ASTROS

OKLAHOMA CITY REDHAWKS — TRIPLE-A

PACIFIC COAST LEAGUE

Batting	B-T	HT	WT	DOB	AVG	vLH	vRH	G	AB	R	H	2B	3B	HR	RBI	BB	HBP	SH	SF	SO	SB	CS	SLG	OBP
Bailey, Adam	L-L	6-1	195	3-6-88	.000	.000	.000	2	7	0	0	0	0	0	0	0	0	0	0	1	0	0	.000	.000
Barnes, Brandon	R-R	6-2	205	5-15-86	.323	.356	.303	62	235	51	76	19	1	5	38	23	1	2	2	49	14	4	.477	.383
Bixler, Brian	R-R	6-1	195	10-22-82	.269	.244	.281	75	249	43	67	12	1	3	19	27	3	1	1	59	11	2	.361	.346
Buck, Travis	L-R	6-2	230	11-18-83	.359	.300	.386	22	64	9	23	4	0	1	6	5	1	1	0	8	0	0	.469	.414
Castro, Jason	L-R	6-3	215	6-18-87	.462	.333	.571	4	13	1	6	1	0	1	2	2	0	0	0	1	0	0	.769	.533
Corporan, Carlos	B-R	6-2	220	1-7-84	.286	.244	.313	68	206	35	59	15	0	6	31	15	6	0	2	46	2	0	.447	.349
DeLome, Collin	L-R	6-2	195	12-18-85	.176	.500	.133	10	17	2	3	1	0	0	0	2	1	0	0	5	1	0	.235	.300
Dominguez, Matt	R-R	6-1	215	8-28-89	.298	.344	.270	45	161	21	48	10	0	2	23	11	2	1	2	21	0	0	.398	.347
2-team total (78 New Orleans)					.257	—	—	123	447	48	115	24	0	9	69	34	3	3	5	52	0	1	.371	.311
Downs, Matt	R-R	6-1	190	3-19-84	.267	.143	.345	24	90	14	24	2	0	3	15	8	3	0	1	20	3	2	.389	.343
Fernandez, Jair	R-R	6-1	220	12-10-86	.125	.000	.200	2	8	0	1	0	0	0	2	0	1	0	0	4	0	0	.125	.222
Goebbert, Jake	L-L	6-0	205	9-24-87	.133	.000	.200	16	30	2	4	1	0	0	1	5	0	0	0	7	0	0	.167	.257
Gonzalez, Marwin	B-R	6-1	195	3-14-89	.333	.556	.267	13	39	2	13	4	0	1	10	3	1	0	0	7	0	0	.513	.395
Hernandez, Diory	R-R	6-0	185	4-8-84	.159	.211	.120	32	44	5	7	0	0	0	2	4	1	0	1	13	1	1	.159	.240
2-team total (60 Iowa)					.223	—	—	92	202	15	45	9	1	2	15	13	1	1	3	33	2	1	.307	.269
Hessman, Mike	R-R	6-5	215	3-5-78	.231	.301	.193	123	441	73	102	19	0	35	78	40	6	0	5	136	0	1	.512	.301
Krauss, Marc	L-R	6-2	235	10-5-87	.123	.118	.125	22	57	3	7	0	0	0	2	6	0	2	1	20	1	1	.123	.203
Kreke, Jordan	R-R	6-1	205	5-21-87	.273	.238	.304	21	44	9	12	3	1	0	3	2	3	0	0	8	1	0	.386	.347
Lowrie, Jed	B-R	6-0	180	4-17-84	.500	1.000	.400	2	6	1	3	0	0	0	3	1	0	0	1	1	0	0	.500	.500
Martinez, Fernando	L-R	6-1	205	10-10-88	.314	.273	.333	90	341	55	107	23	2	13	62	24	6	0	2	85	1	2	.507	.367
Martinez, Jose	R-R	5-11	175	1-24-86	.205	.227	.196	23	73	5	15	2	1	0	9	4	3	1	1	9	2	0	.260	.272
Martinez, J.D.	R-R	6-3	205	8-21-87	.233	.294	.196	23	90	6	21	6	0	0	4	4	0	0	1	17	0	1	.300	.263
Maxwell, Justin	R-R	6-5	235	11-6-83	.200	—	.200	3	10	1	2	1	0	0	0	0	0	0	0	3	0	0	.300	.200
Moore, Scott	L-R	6-2	195	11-17-83	.318	.296	.329	73	245	47	78	26	1	10	54	35	6	1	4	51	3	3	.555	.410
Paredes, Jimmy	B-R	6-3	200	11-25-88	.318	.282	.336	124	507	92	161	28	7	13	59	22	3	2	2	101	37	10	.477	.348
Powell, Landon	B-R	6-3	265	3-19-82	.251	.284	.238	79	239	35	60	6	0	8	38	36	2	1	1	56	0	0	.377	.353
Ruggiano, Justin	R-R	6-2	205	4-12-82	.325	.243	.363	39	117	21	38	13	1	5	29	18	0	0	2	24	5	3	.581	.409
Sanchez, Angel	R-R	6-1	205	9-20-83	.320	.345	.307	107	344	48	110	13	1	5	45	40	2	8	4	25	7	3	.407	.390
Schafer, Jordan	L-L	6-1	190	9-4-86	.154	.250	.000	4	13	2	2	0	0	0	2	0	0	0	1	2	0	0	.154	.267
Shuck, J.B.	L-L	5-11	205	6-18-87	.298	.262	.312	115	315	49	94	11	3	0	33	39	0	2	2	20	12	8	.352	.374
Simunic, Andy	R-R	6-0	170	8-7-85	.000	.000	.000	8	9	0	0	0	0	0	0	1	0	1	0	4	0	0	.000	.100
Snyder, Brad	L-L	6-3	220	5-25-82	.304	.286	.314	122	362	65	110	23	3	20	66	40	3	0	3	108	16	10	.550	.375
Wallace, Brett	L-R	6-2	260	8-26-86	.300	.354	.275	86	310	54	93	16	0	16	57	27	13	0	1	87	0	1	.506	.379
Wallace, Chris	R-R	6-0	220	4-27-88	.270	.188	.333	15	37	4	10	3	0	0	7	5	0	0	0	9	0	0	.351	.357

Pitching	B-T	HT	WT	DOB	W	L	ERA	G	GS	CG	SV	IP	H	R	ER	HR	BB	SO	AVG	vLH	vRH	K/9	BB/9
Abad, Fernando	L-L	6-2	215	12-17-85	2	0	3.90	13	3	0	2	28	33	12	12	3	7	28	.303	.324	.293	9.11	2.28
Abreu, Juan	R-R	6-0	185	4-8-85	2	3	7.09	38	0	0	5	46	46	37	36	12	34	54	.264	.250	.277	10.64	6.70
2-team total (4 Las Vegas)					2	3	6.80	42	0	0	5	49	50	38	37	13	36	59	—	—		10.84	6.61
Ambriz, Hector	L-R	6-2	235	5-24-84	1	1	3.33	18	0	0	2	24	28	9	9	1	11	18	.304	.296	.316	6.66	4.07
Aristil, Jonnathan	R-R	6-1	190	11-30-86	0	0	6.75	21	0	0	0	29	38	24	22	5	11	26	.322	.361	.281	7.98	3.38
Bass, Brian	R-R	6-2	215	1-6-82	5	5	5.56	17	13	0	0	78	105	59	48	9	34	46	.326	.341	.307	5.33	3.94
Buchanan, Jake	R-R	6-0	200	9-24-89	0	1	10.13	3	1	0	0	8	17	10	9	1	5	5	.459	.550	.353	5.63	5.63
Carpenter, David	R-R	6-2	215	7-15-85	1	0	2.08	7	0	0	3	9	7	2	2	1	0	6	.212	.188	.235	6.23	0.00
2-team total (16 Las Vegas)					1	1	3.08	23	0	0	4	26	21	10	9	2	7	25	—	—		8.54	2.39
Cedeno, Xavier	L-L	6-1	205	8-26-86	2	0	2.28	22	0	0	1	28	27	16	7	0	9	25	.250	.104	.367	8.13	2.93
Cisnero, Jose	R-R	6-3	185	4-11-89	4	1	4.54	8	8	0	0	40	52	23	20	1	18	32	.329	.359	.288	7.26	4.08

Player	B-T	HT	WT	DOB																			
Clemens, Paul	R-R	6-4	195	2-14-88	8	8	6.73	20	20	0	0	102	145	82	76	16	32	68	.341	.300	.385	6.02	2.83
Cosart, Jarred	R-R	6-3	180	5-25-90	1	2	2.60	6	5	0	0	28	26	10	8	0	13	24	.250	.269	.231	7.81	4.23
Cruz, Rhiner	R-R	6-2	205	11-1-86	0	0	5.40	2	0	0	0	2	1	2	1	0	1	3	.200	.000	.333	16.20	5.40
Del Rosario, Enerio	R-R	6-2	190	10-16-85	4	1	5.01	36	0	0	1	41	43	25	23	5	20	18	.265	.337	.178	3.92	4.35
Fick, Chuckie	R-R	6-5	185	11-20-85	1	1	9.82	5	0	0	1	4	3	4	4	0	2	3	.231	.286	.167	7.36	4.91
2-team total (42 Memphis)					2	2	5.09	47	0	0	3	46	52	27	26	6	15	23	—	—		4.50	2.93
Flores, Adalberto	R-R	6-7	225	11-4-86	6	1	7.54	37	0	0	0	45	61	39	38	10	21	33	.326	.278	.371	6.55	4.17
Galarraga, Armando	R-R	6-3	230	1-15-82	3	2	4.12	9	9	0	0	44	37	20	20	7	18	31	.226	.233	.218	6.39	3.71
Gonzalez, Edgar	R-R	6-2	210	2-23-83	1	0	0.69	2	2	0	0	13	6	2	1	0	2	8	.136	.158	.120	5.54	1.38
2-team total (15 Colorado Springs)					4	3	4.37	17	9	0	0	60	60	34	29	5	13	48	—	—		7.24	1.96
Hamburger, Mark	R-R	6-4	195	2-5-87	1	1	4.71	17	0	0	0	21	21	12	11	2	12	15	.256	.325	.190	6.43	5.14
3-team total (21 Round Rock, 5 Tucson)					1	5	6.20	43	4	0	2	78	104	57	54	11	36	63	—	—		7.24	4.14
Hicks, Chris	R-R	6-4	205	2-17-87	0	0	5.14	6	0	0	0	7	9	4	4	0	2	10	.321	.273	.353	12.86	2.57
Keuchel, Dallas	L-L	6-3	210	1-1-88	6	7	3.90	16	16	2	0	92	92	46	40	5	20	50	.264	.255	.267	4.87	1.95
Lopez, Wilton	R-R	6-0	205	7-19-83	0	0	13.50	2	0	0	0	2	4	4	3	2	0	1	.364	.000	.500	4.50	0.00
Lyles, Jordan	R-R	6-4	210	10-19-90	5	0	3.54	7	7	0	0	41	41	16	16	2	8	33	.272	.235	.301	7.30	1.77
Mock, Garrett	R-R	6-4	230	4-25-83	0	0	5.54	12	0	0	1	13	15	8	8	1	5	15	.300	.360	.240	10.38	3.46
Musick, Wes	L-L	6-0	190	12-30-86	1	2	3.64	6	6	0	0	30	32	15	12	1	9	15	.278	.364	.244	4.55	2.73
Norris, Bud	R-R	6-0	230	3-2-85	1	0	3.60	1	1	0	0	5	3	2	2		3	7	.167	.222	.111	12.60	5.40
Oberholtzer, Brett	L-L	6-2	230	7-1-89	5	7	4.52	15	15	0	0	90	105	48	45	13	19	69	.292	.274	.300	6.93	1.91
Owens, Rudy	L-L	6-3	230	12-18-87	2	3	4.34	8	8	0	0	46	43	23	22	7	14	23	.243	.245	.242	4.53	2.76
Perez, Sergio	R-R	6-3	230	12-5-84	4	2	4.54	40	4	0	0	75	79	41	38	8	37	59	.274	.274	.275	7.05	4.42
Rodriguez, Aneury	R-R	6-4	250	12-13-87	4	7	6.60	29	13	0	0	93	130	71	68	10	44	75	.336	.372	.301	7.28	4.27
Sanches, Brian	R-R	6-1	190	8-8-78	2	3	6.57	12	0	0	0	12	16	9	9	3	2	10	.302	.344	.238	7.30	1.46
Seaton, Ross	L-R	6-4	213	9-18-89	0	1	3.09	4	4	0	0	23	24	11	8	2	7	11	.258	.213	.304	4.24	2.70
Sosa, Henry	R-R	6-1	210	7-28-85	2	0	5.12	6	6	0	0	32	37	21	18	2	10	21	.287	.347	.204	5.97	2.84
Storey, Mickey	R-R	6-2	185	3-16-86	7	4	3.05	38	2	0	2	65	62	24	22	8	14	72	.248	.310	.194	9.97	1.94
Valdez, Jose	R-R	6-4	200	1-22-83	0	5	4.95	46	0	0	21	44	53	27	24	5	12	59	.282	.333	.238	12.16	2.47

Fielding

Catcher	PCT	G	PO	A	E	DP	PB
Castro	1.000	4	24	2	0	0	1
Corporan	.998	67	398	47	1	3	8
Fernandez	.950	2	17	2	1	0	0
Powell	.992	76	476	46	4	7	7
Wallace	.988	11	76	3	1	0	2

First Base	PCT	G	PO	A	E	DP
Downs	.973	10	64	9	2	8
Hessman	.996	105	838	63	4	67
Moore	1.000	10	84	8	0	9
Ruggiano	1.000	1	1	0	0	0
Shuck	1.000	1	12	1	0	2
Wallace	.991	29	210	19	2	23

Second Base	PCT	G	PO	A	E	DP
Bixler	1.000	8	12	17	0	3
Downs	1.000	9	22	28	0	3
Hernandez	1.000	5	3	4	0	1
Kreke	1.000	1	1	2	0	0
Martinez	1.000	12	20	38	0	12
Moore	1.000	3	2	10	0	1

	PCT	G	PO	A	E	DP
Paredes	.959	102	173	289	20	50
Sanchez	.969	23	33	62	3	16

Third Base	PCT	G	PO	A	E	DP
Bixler	.917	12	1	21	2	1
Dominguez	.947	45	32	75	6	7
Downs	.800	5	2	2	1	0
Hernandez	1.000	5	2	7	0	2
Kreke	.857	5	1	5	1	1
Martinez	1.000	1	0	1	0	0
Moore	.964	43	30	78	4	12
Sanchez	1.000	3	0	1	0	0
Wallace	.923	47	27	93	10	9

Shortstop	PCT	G	PO	A	E	DP
Bixler	.969	35	57	97	5	28
Gonzalez	.941	10	17	15	2	4
Hernandez	.960	11	9	15	1	3
Kreke	.966	12	12	16	1	3
Lowrie	1.000	2	2	3	0	0
Martinez	.962	11	24	26	2	7
Sanchez	.960	78	118	193	13	39

	PCT	G	PO	A	E	DP
Simunic	1.000	4	3	3	0	1
Wallace	.912	9	14	17	3	1

Outfield	PCT	G	PO	A	E	DP
Barnes	.983	60	172	2	3	1
Bixler	.969	18	29	2	1	0
Buck	1.000	11	11	0	0	0
DeLome	.889	6	8	0	1	0
Downs	1.000	4	5	0	0	0
Goebbert	1.000	9	7	0	0	0
Hernandez	1.000	1	2	0	0	0
Krauss	1.000	17	31	2	0	0
Martinez	.986	76	130	8	2	2
Martinez	1.000	19	22	2	0	0
Maxwell	1.000	3	8	0	0	0
Moore	1.000	12	20	0	0	0
Paredes	.981	21	50	1	1	0
Ruggiano	.983	34	57	2	1	0
Schafer	1.000	4	6	0	0	0
Shuck	.987	91	143	7	2	3
Snyder	.979	106	180	6	4	0

CORPUS CHRISTI HOOKS

DOUBLE-A

TEXAS LEAGUE

Batting	B-T	HT	WT	DOB	AVG	vLH	vRH	G	AB	R	H	2B	3B	HR	RBI	BB	HBP	SH	SF	SO	SB	CS	SLG	OBP
Bailey, Adam	L-L	6-1	195	3-6-88	.258	.300	.250	49	132	13	34	13	0	2	20	9	0	0	2	26	2	0	.402	.301
Barnes, Brandon	R-R	6-2	205	5-15-86	.317	.348	.305	44	164	30	52	20	0	7	31	14	3	0	2	42	7	2	.567	.377
Borchering, Bobby	B-R	6-2	205	10-25-90	.189	.179	.194	30	95	11	18	5	1	4	18	10	2	0	2	36	1	1	.389	.275
Buck, Travis	R-R	6-2	230	11-18-83	.143	.000	.188	7	21	3	3	2	0	0	3	4	0	0	0	9	0	0	.238	.280
Castro, Jason	L-R	6-3	215	6-18-87	.800	.750	1.000	3	5	1	4	2	0	0	2	0	0	0	0	0	0	0	1.200	.857
Fernandez, Jair	R-R	6-1	220	12-10-86	.269	.300	.257	56	186	28	50	10	0	6	29	15	6	0	1	34	0	0	.419	.341
Garcia, Rene	R-R	6-0	200	3-4-84	.333	.167	.381	9	27	2	9	1	0	0	2	1	2	0	0	3	0	1	.370	.379
Goebbert, Jake	L-L	6-0	205	9-24-87	.304	.333	.296	114	368	71	112	23	6	9	53	55	5	2	3	57	5	3	.473	.399
Grossman, Robbie	B-L	6-0	205	9-16-89	.267	.375	.233	36	135	22	36	8	2	3	11	18	5	1	1	43	4	1	.422	.371
Heath, Ben	R-R	6-2	220	10-7-88	.217	.400	.167	9	23	2	5	2	0	0	1	0	0	1	7	0	0		.304	.240
Hernandez, Enrique	R-R	5-11	170	8-24-91	.247	.077	.279	23	81	7	20	2	1	1	3	4	2	1	0	9	2	2	.309	.299
Hinze, Kody	R-R	6-0	225	7-29-87	.212	.244	.198	83	260	34	55	7	0	11	40	33	1	0	4	82	1	2	.365	.299
Krauss, Marc	L-R	6-2	235	10-5-87	.414	.300	.474	7	29	11	12	2	0	5	16	6	0	0	0	5	1	0	1.000	.514
Kreke, Jordan	R-R	6-1	205	11-25-86	.190	.115	.207	50	137	15	26	4	1	1	11	4	2	0	2	45	9	2	.255	.221
Lee, Carlos	R-R	6-2	270	6-20-76	.500	.500	.500	3	10	1	5	0	0	1	2	0	0	0	0	2	0	0	.800	.500
Locke, Drew	R-R	6-1	205	2-28-83	.295	.288	.298	68	261	40	77	16	1	8	46	21	1	0	2	48	1	2	.456	.347
Martinez, Jose	R-R	5-11		1-24-86	.304	.361	.287	107	425	75	129	21	4	13	75	36	6	0	5	40	3	1	.464	.362
Maxwell, Justin	R-R	6-5	235	11-6-83	.250	—	.250	2	8	2	2	1	0	0	1	0	0	0	0	5	0	0	.375	.333
McCurdy, Ryan	R-R	5-10	175	12-28-87	.200	.000	.246	29	75	7	15	3	1	1	9	7	5	3	1	4	0	0	.307	.307
Muren, Drew	L-R	6-6	195	11-22-88	.291	.233	.313	33	110	19	32	6	2	1	6	8	1	2	1	18	5	6	.409	.342
Orloff, Ben	R-R	5-11	174	4-26-87	.295	.292	.296	39	122	16	36	5	1	0	15	8	5	4	1	6	3	1	.352	.360

	B-T	HT	WT	DOB	AVG	vLH	vRH	G	AB	R	H	2B	3B	HR	RBI	BB	HBP	SH	SF	SO	SB	CS	SLG	OBP
Simunic, Andy	R-R	6-0	170	8-7-85	.297	.341	.284	106	391	59	116	11	1	2	37	29	5	5	5	65	15	4	.345	.349
Singleton, Jonathan	L-L	6-2	235	9-18-91	.284	.232	.304	131	461	94	131	27	4	21	79	88	1	0	5	131	7	2	.497	.396
Springer, George	R-R	6-3	200	9-19-89	.219	.333	.190	22	73	8	16	3	0	2	5	6	1	1	0	25	4	2	.342	.288
Steele, T.J.	R-R	6-3	205	9-21-86	.141	.111	.159	26	71	10	10	1	1	2	7	4	0	2	1	27	2	0	.268	.184
2-team total (26 San Antonio)					.200	—	—	52	155	18	31	4	2	2	17	9	2	2	1	44	5	3	.290	.251
Thompson, Jose	R-R	6-2	180	5-14-87	.119	.100	.125	18	42	1	5	1	0	0	1	0	2	0	0	17	0	0	.143	.159
Villar, Jonathan	B-R	6-1	195	5-2-91	.261	.265	.259	86	326	54	85	7	2	11	50	35	4	8	4	87	39	8	.396	.336
Wallace, Chris	R-R	6-0	220	4-27-88	.251	.245	.253	63	199	26	50	14	0	5	29	19	5	3	1	60	3	0	.397	.330
Wates, Austin	R-R	6-1	179	9-2-88	.304	.259	.317	95	359	58	109	16	4	7	48	31	11	6	2	71	17	11	.429	.375
Wikoff, Brandon	L-R	5-8	171	4-5-88	.190	.000	.235	22	63	7	12	2	0	0	2	9	1	3	1	6	1	0	.222	.297

Pitching	B-T	HT	WT	DOB	W	L	ERA	G	GS	CG	SV	IP	H	R	ER	HR	BB	SO	AVG	vLH	vRH	K/9	BB/9
Abreu, Erick	R-R	6-1	170	8-9-83	10	4	4.14	36	3	0	2	76	68	40	35	13	25	67	.239	.212	.257	7.93	2.96
Aristil, Jonnathan	R-R	6-1	160	11-30-86	0	1	4.32	8	0	0	0	17	20	8	8	4	3	21	.303	.333	.289	11.34	1.62
Buchanan, Jake	R-R	6-0	200	9-24-89	5	9	4.96	27	19	0	0	134	171	85	74	11	33	83	.310	.301	.317	5.56	2.21
Chapman, Kevin	L-L	6-3	220	2-19-88	6	3	2.64	49	0	0	2	58	49	19	17	2	32	59	.226	.200	.241	9.16	4.97
Cisnero, Jose	R-R	6-3	185	4-11-89	9	6	3.40	20	20	2	0	109	93	44	41	7	46	116	.227	.218	.233	9.61	3.81
Clemens, Paul	R-R	6-4	195	2-14-88	3	2	3.46	7	7	0	0	42	41	18	16	7	11	37	.255	.265	.247	7.99	2.38
Cosart, Jarred	R-R	6-3	180	5-25-90	5	5	3.52	15	15	0	0	87	83	37	34	3	38	68	.250	.253	.247	7.03	3.93
Doran, Bobby	R-R	6-6	235	3-21-89	6	2	4.83	10	10	0	0	54	61	29	29	6	16	43	.284	.337	.248	7.17	2.67
Flores, Adalberto	R-R	6-7	225	11-4-86	1	1	7.65	13	0	0	0	20	27	17	17	4	5	22	.321	.313	.327	9.90	2.25
Heidenreich, Matt	L-R	6-5	185	1-17-91	3	1	3.93	8	7	0	0	34	39	22	15	2	7	26	.277	.262	.289	6.82	1.83
Hicks, Chris	R-R	6-4	205	2-17-87	0	1	9.82	2	0	0	0	4	3	4	4	1	0	1	.200	.000	.250	2.45	0.00
Leon, Arcenio	R-R	6-1	225	9-22-86	3	2	4.38	44	0	0	2	64	60	36	31	6	33	58	.251	.323	.200	8.20	4.66
Musick, Wes	L-L	6-0	190	12-30-86	0	1	3.00	3	1	0	0	12	9	4	4	0	6	14	.214	.077	.276	10.50	4.50
Oberholtzer, Brett	L-L	6-2	230	7-1-89	5	3	4.21	13	13	0	0	77	81	41	36	11	21	68	.267	.206	.285	7.95	2.45
Rasmussen, Rob	R-L	5-9	160	4-2-89	4	4	4.80	11	10	0	0	54	58	30	29	6	18	44	.276	.329	.250	7.29	2.98
Seaton, Ross	L-R	6-4	213	9-18-89	8	8	4.07	25	25	1	0	146	155	75	66	17	31	106	.271	.302	.250	6.53	1.91
Sogard, Alex	L-L	6-3	215	7-25-87	3	1	3.86	33	0	0	0	56	60	28	23	3	25	35	.291	.333	.264	5.87	4.19
Stoffel, Jason	R-R	6-2	225	9-15-88	2	1	2.33	56	0	0	27	58	41	16	15	3	16	57	.196	.127	.226	8.84	2.48
Villar, Henry	R-R	5-11	180	5-24-87	4	2	4.68	25	2	0	1	50	50	26	26	8	8	30	.266	.247	.279	5.40	1.44
Wojciechowski, Asher	R-R	6-4	235	12-21-88	2	2	2.06	8	8	0	0	44	30	14	10	0	14	34	.190	.236	.165	7.01	2.89
Zeid, Josh	R-R	6-5	210	3-24-87	2	0	5.59	47	0	0	1	56	57	35	35	6	20	66	.263	.258	.266	10.54	3.20

Fielding

Catcher	PCT	G	PO	A	E	DP	PB
Castro	1.000	3	11	2	0	2	0
Fernandez	.995	51	348	36	2	4	2
Garcia	.983	9	52	5	1	0	1
Heath	.981	9	49	4	1	1	1
McCurdy	.983	27	159	15	3	0	2
Wallace	.989	59	420	31	5	3	9

First Base	PCT	G	PO	A	E	DP
Goebbert	1.000	1	0	0	0	0
Hinze	.996	32	257	13	1	32
Kreke	1.000	1	8	0	0	0
Lee	1.000	2	6	0	0	0
Locke	1.000	4	32	1	0	2
Singleton	.988	113	926	78	12	88

Second Base	PCT	G	PO	A	E	DP
Hernandez	.982	23	50	59	2	16
Kreke	1.000	4	3	3	0	0

	PCT	G	PO	A	E	DP
Martinez	.988	106	212	291	6	77
Simunic	1.000	2	1	2	0	0
Thompson	.938	3	9	6	1	2
Wikoff	.958	7	8	15	1	5

Third Base	PCT	G	PO	A	E	DP
Borchering	.940	23	12	35	3	8
Fernandez	1.000	3	0	7	0	1
Hinze	.500	1	0	1	0	0
Kreke	.938	25	16	45	4	3
Simunic	.952	84	50	147	10	14
Thompson	.895	9	6	11	2	0
Wikoff	.933	12	5	23	2	3

Shortstop	PCT	G	PO	A	E	DP
Kreke	1.000	3	1	6	0	0
Orloff	.981	38	52	107	3	21
Simunic	1.000	23	26	71	0	14
Villar	.938	85	94	272	24	53

	PCT	G	PO	A	E	DP
Wikoff	1.000	1	1	3	0	0

Outfield	PCT	G	PO	A	E	DP
Bailey	.978	25	39	5	1	0
Barnes	.962	41	95	5	4	2
Buck	1.000	5	5	0	0	0
Goebbert	.978	89	170	6	4	2
Grossman	.986	35	71	1	1	0
Krauss	1.000	7	12	1	0	0
Kreke	1.000	8	8	1	0	0
Locke	1.000	58	121	5	0	0
Maxwell	1.000	2	3	0	0	0
Muren	.969	32	61	2	2	1
Simunic	1.000	2	8	1	0	1
Singleton	.955	19	21	0	1	0
Springer	1.000	20	39	0	0	0
Steele	.976	23	40	1	1	0
Wates	.974	88	147	5	4	2

LANCASTER JETHAWKS   HIGH CLASS A

CALIFORNIA LEAGUE

Batting	B-T	HT	WT	DOB	AVG	vLH	vRH	G	AB	R	H	2B	3B	HR	RBI	BB	HBP	SH	SF	SO	SB	CS	SLG	OBP
Adamson, Daniel	R-R	5-11	210	9-15-87	.083	.000	.100	4	12	1	1	0	0	1	1	0	0	0	0	10	0	0	.333	.083
Aplin, Andrew	L-L	6-0	190	3-21-91	.260	.281	.250	24	104	19	27	4	2	3	13	4	0	0	0	16	4	3	.423	.287
Bailey, Adam	L-L	6-1	195	3-6-88	.279	.277	.280	47	179	28	50	13	0	8	25	13	0	1	1	40	2	2	.486	.326
Castro, Erik	L-R	6-4	200	11-13-87	.285	.261	.293	128	485	87	138	27	1	27	108	78	3	0	7	162	4	4	.511	.382
DeShields, Delino	R-R	5-9	210	8-16-92	.237	.250	.231	24	97	17	23	2	3	2	9	13	2	1	1	23	18	5	.381	.336
Epps, Chris	L-R	6-2	172	12-10-88	.285	.388	.239	46	158	35	45	6	6	10	32	25	0	0	3	46	3	3	.589	.376
Garcia, Rene	R-R	6-0	200	3-21-90	.279	.266	.285	60	215	23	60	13	0	0	22	6	4	3	2	24	1	1	.340	.308
Heath, Ben	R-R	6-2	220	10-7-88	.298	.316	.291	50	191	26	57	9	0	5	29	13	1	0	0	51	1	0	.424	.346
Hernandez, Enrique	R-R	5-11	170	8-24-91	.275	.293	.269	100	378	52	104	25	7	5	49	22	3	5	3	43	4	2	.418	.318
Hogue, Grant	R-R	6-1	190	6-26-86	.361	.471	.327	43	144	40	52	8	3	0	17	17	0	4	3	22	27	2	.458	.421
King, Emilio	R-R	6-0	212	8-17-89	—	—	—	2	0	0	0	0	0	0	0	0	0	0	0	0	0	0	—	—
McCurdy, Ryan	R-R	5-10	175	12-28-87	.667	—	.667	2	3	0	2	0	0	0	0	0	0	1	0	0	0	0	.667	.750
Meyer, Jonathan	R-R	6-1	195	11-1-90	.272	.287	.266	129	504	78	137	24	2	8	57	31	3	1	4	101	4	3	.375	.315
Mier, Jio	R-R	6-1	195	8-26-90	.292	.319	.282	46	171	28	50	9	1	3	25	29	1	2	1	34	6	3	.409	.396
Moon, Chan	L-R	6-0	160	3-23-91	.188	.143	.200	10	32	2	6	0	0	0	1	0	0	1	0	15	0	2	.188	.188
Muren, Drew	L-R	6-6	195	11-22-88	.321	.154	.400	21	81	16	26	2	0	2	13	7	1	0	1	19	5	1	.420	.378
Nash, Telvin	R-R	6-1	248	2-20-91	.224	.260	.212	106	393	61	88	19	0	29	75	47	7	0	2	198	0	1	.494	.316
Orloff, Brian	R-R	5-11	174	4-26-87	.288	.215	.309	77	285	40	82	8	0	0	29	32	4	6	5	22	7	3	.316	.362
Pena, Roberto	R-R	6-0	180	6-8-92	.213	.409	.132	21	75	10	16	4	0	1	11	5	0	2	1	15	0	0	.307	.259

	B-T	HT	WT	DOB	AVG	vLH	vRH	G	AB	R	H	2B	3B	HR	RBI	BB	HBP	SH	SF	SO	SB	CS	SLG	OBP
Perez, Carlos	R-R	6-0	195	10-27-90	.318	.318	.318	26	88	11	28	6	1	0	10	6	1	2	0	17	0	1	.409	.368
Santana, Domingo	R-R	6-5	228	8-5-92	.302	.288	.307	119	457	87	138	26	6	23	97	55	9	0	4	148	7	1	.536	.385
Springer, George	R-R	6-3	200	9-19-89	.316	.316	.316	106	401	137	137	18	10	22	82	56	6	0	5	131	28	6	.557	.398
Todd, Alex	R-R	6-2	190	8-15-89	.286	.333	.261	54	185	36	53	11	1	3	21	16	13	1	2	46	4	2	.405	.380
Valenzuela, Rafael	L-R	6-1	175	10-20-87	.284	.222	.305	73	275	45	78	14	4	6	35	24	4	1	1	48	11	4	.429	.349

Pitching	B-T	HT	WT	DOB	W	L	ERA	G	GS	CG	SV	IP	H	R	ER	HR	BB	SO	AVG	vLH	vRH	K/9	BB/9
Alaniz, R.J.	R-R	6-4	175	6-14-91	6	2	5.04	17	17	0	0	100	113	58	56	12	26	70	.288	.281	.293	6.30	2.34
Cain, Colton	L-L	6-3	255	2-5-91	2	2	5.55	7	7	0	0	36	41	24	22	4	18	25	.287	.217	.337	6.31	4.54
Chowning, Jason	R-R	6-2	178	10-17-87	0	1	14.54	7	0	0	0	9	16	14	14	1	11	13	.400	.421	.381	13.50	11.42
Clark, Kirk	R-R	6-2	202	7-19-88	4	4	5.36	35	0	0	8	40	44	25	24	6	22	22	.282	.333	.247	4.91	4.91
De Leon, Jorge	R-R	6-0	185	8-15-87	2	9	7.70	40	14	0	6	88	116	88	75	11	44	60	.320	.304	.335	6.16	4.52
Doran, Bobby	R-R	6-6	235	3-21-89	8	4	3.57	17	17	0	0	103	95	50	41	8	30	72	.244	.250	.236	6.27	2.61
Dydalewicz, Brad	L-L	6-1	180	3-24-90	1	0	6.13	28	0	0	0	40	51	30	27	4	18	22	.315	.237	.359	4.99	4.08
Garcia, Gabriel	L-L	5-11	140	5-11-89	1	0	5.84	9	0	0	0	12	18	8	8	3	4	11	.333	.333	.333	8.03	2.92
Grimmett, Zach	R-R	6-3	185	2-5-90	3	6	8.21	23	10	0	1	83	123	80	76	21	25	66	.348	.369	.333	7.13	2.70
Lo, Chia-Jen	R-R	5-11	185	4-7-86	0	0	1.42	11	0	0	0	19	14	3	3	1	4	20	.222	.200	.242	9.47	1.89
Long, Kenny	L-L	6-1	155	1-28-89	1	0	1.13	12	0	0	2	8	3	1	1	0	2	18	.115	.056	.250	20.25	2.25
Martinez, David	R-R	6-2	180	8-4-87	9	5	4.38	27	26	0	0	160	181	90	78	19	33	114	.285	.307	.263	6.40	1.85
Musick, Wes	L-L	6-0	190	12-30-86	3	1	2.51	5	5	1	0	32	27	10	9	4	7	26	.235	.235	.235	7.24	1.95
Perez, Tyson	R-R	6-3	215	12-27-89	9	5	5.03	21	21	1	0	120	149	73	67	19	32	79	.308	.321	.294	5.93	2.40
Quevedo, Carlos	R-R	6-1	222	9-30-89	2	4	2.03	15	0	0	3	31	23	7	7	4	10	37	.207	.240	.180	10.74	2.90
Robinson, Andrew	R-R	6-1	185	2-13-88	4	5	4.33	44	0	0	6	60	54	41	29	4	26	74	.233	.288	.182	11.04	3.88
Sogard, Alex	L-L	6-3	215	7-25-87	0	2	2.81	6	0	0	0	16	12	7	5	0	8	17	.197	.167	.226	9.56	4.50
Streilein, Brian	R-R	6-4	218	11-3-88	2	3	7.78	26	0	0	1	42	52	36	36	4	16	33	.313	.247	.371	7.13	3.46
Trinidad, Jose	R-R	5-11	150	7-13-87	8	4	3.59	41	3	0	0	76	77	37	32	8	33	43	.269	.250	.289	5.09	3.91
Tropeano, Nick	R-R	6-4	205	8-27-90	6	3	3.31	12	12	0	0	71	72	37	26	8	21	69	.265	.248	.278	8.79	2.67
Urckfitz, Pat	L-L	6-4	200	7-21-88	0	3	3.66	45	0	0	8	66	69	31	27	5	21	62	.265	.257	.272	8.41	2.85
Walters, Blair	L-L	6-0	200	11-8-89	3	3	7.62	8	8	0	0	39	49	36	33	8	15	34	.301	.290	.309	7.85	3.46

Fielding

Catcher	PCT	G	PO	A	E	DP	PB
Garcia	.984	60	381	59	7	4	7
Heath	.989	39	250	32	3	6	8
McCurdy	1.000	2	12	0	0	0	0
Pena	.971	21	147	19	5	0	0
Perez	.996	26	196	31	1	3	1

First Base	PCT	G	PO	A	E	DP
Castro	.990	66	541	46	6	65
Nash	.976	9	77	5	2	7
Valenzuela	.994	67	624	36	4	49

Second Base	PCT	G	PO	A	E	DP
DeShields	.955	24	45	60	5	14
Hernandez	.971	99	222	281	15	71

Moon	1.000	2	1	2	0	0
Orloff	1.000	8	15	25	0	3
Todd	.947	17	24	47	4	14

Third Base	PCT	G	PO	A	E	DP
Castro	.800	2	1	3	1	0
Meyer	.954	128	102	250	17	24
Orloff	1.000	3	3	9	0	1
Todd	1.000	7	1	12	0	0
Valenzuela	.750	3	0	3	1	0

Shortstop	PCT	G	PO	A	E	DP
Mier	.954	44	76	133	10	28
Moon	1.000	8	8	21	0	4
Orloff	.972	63	95	182	8	45

Todd	.949	31	48	100	8	17

Outfield	PCT	G	PO	A	E	DP
Adamson	1.000	3	2	0	0	0
Aplin	.985	23	64	1	1	0
Bailey	.987	45	72	5	1	1
Epps	.980	28	45	3	1	0
Hernandez	1.000	6	13	1	0	0
Hogue	.966	39	80	6	3	2
King	—	2	0	0	0	0
Muren	.976	21	37	3	1	0
Nash	.940	49	77	2	5	1
Santana	.953	114	189	12	10	2
Springer	.992	103	237	7	2	0

LEXINGTON LEGENDS
SOUTH ATLANTIC LEAGUE

LOW CLASS A

Batting	B-T	HT	WT	DOB	AVG	vLH	vRH	G	AB	R	H	2B	3B	HR	RBI	BB	HBP	SH	SF	SO	SB	CS	SLG	OBP
Alvarez, Luis	R-R	5-11	230	2-28-90	.264	.222	.273	17	53	7	14	1	1	2	8	3	2	0	0	13	1	0	.434	.328
Austin, Jay	L-L	5-11	170	8-10-90	.255	.294	.235	15	51	7	13	1	1	0	4	7	1	0	0	4	5	0	.314	.356
Burnett, Tyler	L-R	6-0	205	5-9-89	.178	.000	.235	12	45	4	8	1	0	1	2	7	0	0	0	12	1	0	.267	.288
DeShields, Delino	R-R	5-9	210	8-16-92	.298	.345	.281	111	440	96	131	22	5	10	52	70	7	4	2	108	83	14	.439	.401
Duffy, Matt	R-R	6-3	227	2-6-89	.280	.308	.269	134	492	73	138	32	1	16	70	48	41	0	6	106	6	3	.447	.387
Epps, Chris	L-R	6-2	172	12-10-88	.226	.120	.250	36	133	17	30	6	0	3	17	15	2	0	1	39	5	1	.338	.311
Fernandez, Jose	R-R	6-1	170	5-20-93	.258	.267	.255	20	66	14	17	7	0	1	10	8	0	0	1	19	2	0	.409	.333
Fontana, Nolan	L-R	5-11	190	6-6-91	.225	.188	.235	49	151	37	34	9	1	2	25	65	3	2	1	44	12	2	.338	.464
Genoves, Ernesto	R-R	5-11	203	6-4-91	.000	.000	.000	1	2	0	0	0	0	0	0	0	0	0	0	0	0	0	.000	.000
Gominsky, Justin	R-R	6-4	185	8-26-89	.241	.255	.235	94	332	37	80	15	1	2	36	34	5	7	3	69	13	4	.310	.318
Hamblin, Miles	L-R	6-3	200	10-28-88	.333	.000	.500	2	3	2	1	0	0	1	1	1	0	0	0	0	0	0	1.333	.500
Hernandez, Teoscar	R-R	6-2	180	10-15-92	.240	.000	.300	8	25	2	6	2	0	1	5	3	0	1	1	12	1	0	.440	.310
Hinson, John	L-R	6-1	180	9-13-88	.339	.267	.364	15	59	12	20	4	0	2	11	1	0	1	0	17	4	1	.508	.350
Howick, Jimmy	R-R	6-2	185	8-26-90	.179	.200	.169	29	95	18	17	4	0	2	10	11	0	3	0	22	2	1	.284	.264
Johnson, Zach	R-R	5-11	200	6-16-88	.238	.221	.245	134	508	63	121	38	1	15	108	75	10	0	14	92	0	1	.406	.339
King, Emilio	R-R	6-0	212	8-17-89	.135	.091	.154	20	74	6	10	3	0	0	5	8	0	0	0	31	0	0	.176	.220
Kreke, Jordan	R-R	6-1	205	5-21-87	.190	.150	.211	15	58	4	11	1	0	0	2	3	1	3	0	16	2	2	.207	.242
Kvasnicka, Mike	L-R	6-2	180	11-8-88	.232	.221	.236	88	345	46	80	15	1	15	53	19	2	0	1	86	1	2	.412	.275
McCurdy, Ryan	R-R	5-10	175	12-28-87	.185	.238	.159	24	65	9	12	4	0	0	7	12	8	1	1	10	3	1	.246	.372
Meredith, Brandon	R-R	6-2	225	12-19-89	.278	.256	.286	86	316	54	88	19	4	15	48	43	8	1	2	86	12	3	.506	.377
Moon, Chan	L-R	6-0	160	3-23-91	.257	.270	.250	62	214	27	55	13	1	3	30	28	0	7	3	57	13	5	.369	.339
Morales, Jobduan	R-R	5-10	180	6-7-91	.270	.313	.255	17	63	4	17	2	0	6	5	0	0	2	16	0	0	.302	.294
Moronta, Cristian	R-R	5-10	185	12-5-89	.278	.500	.250	5	18	3	5	3	0	0	4	2	0	0	0	6	0	0	.444	.350
Muren, Drew	L-R	6-6	195	11-22-88	.279	.202	.308	48	183	25	51	12	1	3	17	11	3	2	3	29	4	5	.404	.325
Pena, Roberto	R-R	6-0	210	6-8-91	.255	.250	.243	61	220	21	54	12	0	2	22	10	1	5	3	43	1	2	.327	.290
Scott, Jordan	L-R	6-2	180	9-22-91	.230	.239	.227	110	404	55	93	13	2	1	43	57	2	12	5	81	13	11	.280	.325
Sosa, Ruben	B-R	5-7	170	9-23-90	.280	.111	.327	44	125	25	35	3	2	0	9	17	0	2	1	26	13	2	.336	.364

	B-T	HT	WT	DOB	AVG	vLH	vRH	G	AB	R	H	2B	3B	HR	RBI	BB	HBP	SH	SF	SO	SB	CS	SLG	OBP
Todd, Alex	R-R	6-2	190	8-15-89	.306	.318	.302	22	85	16	26	4	1	1	13	10	2	1	1	13	0	0	.412	.388
Wierzbicki, Jesse	R-R	6-3	200	11-24-88	.250	.111	.316	8	28	7	7	1	1	1	5	2	2	2	5	1	0		.464	.344

Pitching	B-T	HT	WT	DOB	W	L	ERA	G	GS	CG	SV	IP	H	R	ER	HR	BB	SO	AVG	vLH	vRH	K/9	BB/9
Bushue, Tanner	R-R	6-4	180	6-20-91	0	3	18.82	6	3	0	0	11	27	25	23	4	6	10	.466	.533	.393	8.18	4.91
Chowning, Jason	R-R	6-2	178	10-17-87	1	2	0.66	19	0	0	10	27	12	7	2	2	9	40	.128	.222	.069	13.17	2.96
Cruz, Luis	L-L	5-9	170	9-10-90	9	8	4.05	28	24	0	0	147	152	74	66	12	47	135	.263	.282	.254	8.28	2.88
Devenski, Chris	R-R	6-3	195	11-13-90	2	2	3.07	5	5	1	0	29	23	11	10	1	16	38	.225	.244	.213	11.66	4.91
2-team total (19 Kannapolis)					8	7	3.86	24	13	1	2	91	86	42	39	9	35	92	—	—		9.10	3.46
Diaz, Dayan	R-R	5-10	156	2-10-89	5	4	1.85	41	0	0	19	58	40	14	12	1	30	64	.197	.184	.207	9.87	4.63
Dufek, Jonas	R-R	6-5	215	6-30-88	6	5	5.47	25	24	0	0	127	147	89	77	16	37	117	.288	.306	.272	8.31	2.63
Foltynewicz, Mike	R-R	6-4	200	10-7-91	14	4	3.14	27	27	0	0	152	145	65	53	11	62	125	.250	.271	.233	7.40	3.67
Ford, Blake	L-R	6-5	215	5-16-88	0	0	13.50	2	0	0	0	2	5	3	3	0	2	1	.455	.600	.333	4.50	9.00
Galarraga, Armando	R-R	6-3	230	1-15-82	0	0	2.25	1	1	0	0	4	4	1	1	0	2	0	.250	.500	.100	0.00	4.50
Garcia, Gabriel	L-L	5-11	140	5-11-89	1	2	5.03	21	0	0	0	39	41	25	22	6	10	27	.265	.245	.275	6.18	2.29
Gouvea, Murillo	R-R	6-2	200	9-15-88	2	7	3.71	50	0	0	4	78	62	36	32	12	29	87	.222	.231	.215	10.08	3.36
Grills, Evan	L-L	6-4	205	6-13-92	4	1	4.92	37	0	0	0	71	81	40	39	11	23	42	.287	.283	.290	5.30	2.90
Hallock, Kyle	L-L	6-2	185	8-6-88	1	1	10.23	7	6	0	0	22	40	27	25	7	13	15	.404	.478	.382	6.14	5.32
Lambson, Mitchell	L-L	6-1	198	7-20-90	1	2	2.72	19	0	0	0	36	30	12	11	2	10	42	.217	.231	.209	10.40	2.48
Ordosgoitti, Luis	R-R	6-4	180	9-22-92	5	5	5.42	19	19	0	0	103	133	69	62	13	26	77	.316	.381	.263	6.73	2.27
Perez, Juri	R-R	5-11	203	8-8-90	2	1	4.18	5	3	2	0	24	22	16	11	1	12	21	.265	.132	.378	7.99	4.56
Pettus, Nate	R-R	6-1	209	10-9-88	1	6	5.86	31	0	0	0	63	71	43	41	6	37	48	.292	.325	.264	6.86	5.29
Quevedo, Carlos	R-R	6-1	222	9-30-89	4	3	3.88	25	4	0	4	56	55	26	24	6	6	59	.257	.304	.221	9.54	0.97
Quezada, Euris	R-R	6-6	210	4-6-89	1	2	4.62	14	0	0	1	25	29	16	13	0	18	20	.290	.211	.339	7.11	6.39
Rodriguez, Richard	R-R	6-4	185	3-4-90	0	0	3.00	1	1	0	0	3	3	1	1	0	1	4	.250	.000	.333	12.00	3.00
Rollins, David	L-L	6-1	195	12-21-89	1	3	3.48	6	6	0	0	31	27	14	12	5	9	25	.241	.333	.197	7.26	2.61
Shirley, Tommy	R-L	6-5	220	11-11-88	2	4	3.06	16	1	0	1	35	32	13	12	2	16	45	.237	.302	.207	11.46	4.08
Tropeano, Nick	R-R	6-4	205	8-27-90	6	4	2.78	15	14	0	0	87	77	29	27	3	26	97	.238	.187	.270	10.00	2.68
Zuloaga, Scott	R-L	6-4	200	9-20-89	0	1	10.50	5	0	0	0	6	8	8	7	2	4	4	.308	.333	.300	6.00	6.00

Fielding

Catcher	PCT	G	PO	A	E	DP	PB
Alvarez	.978	16	108	26	3	2	5
Genoves	—	1	0	0	0	0	
Hamblin	1.000	2	7	0	0	0	
Kvasnicka	.987	26	204	26	3	4	11
McCurdy	1.000	24	180	18	0	1	1
Morales	.991	10	105	7	1	0	1
Moronta	.980	5	45	4	1	1	
Pena	.993	61	476	59	4	5	4

First Base	PCT	G	PO	A	E	DP
Burnett	.972	7	62	7	2	4
Duffy	1.000	8	67	10	0	7
Johnson	.988	119	1038	77	13	77
Morales	1.000	2	17	1	0	4
Wierzbicki	.971	4	33	1	1	7

Second Base	PCT	G	PO	A	E	DP
DeShields	.960	108	183	278	19	44

Hinson	.824	5	4	10	3	0
Kreke	1.000	1	2	1	0	0
Moon	.964	23	28	53	3	18
Sosa	.923	13	16	20	3	2
Todd	1.000	2	5	6	0	2

Third Base	PCT	G	PO	A	E	DP
Burnett	1.000	1	1	0	0	0
Duffy	.938	117	82	207	19	14
Fernandez	.778	4	1	6	2	1
Hinson	.857	6	5	13	3	1
Kreke	.917	10	5	17	2	1
Moon	.923	5	2	10	1	1
Wierzbicki	.714	2	2	3	2	0

Shortstop	PCT	G	PO	A	E	DP
Fernandez	.837	10	15	21	7	4
Fontana	.974	48	92	135	6	33
Howick	.922	29	39	67	9	13

Kreke	.889	2	4	4	1	1
Moon	.938	35	48	102	10	16
Todd	.958	19	33	59	4	10

Outfield	PCT	G	PO	A	E	DP
Austin	.963	10	25	1	1	0
Epps	.942	30	48	1	3	0
Gominsky	.971	93	183	15	6	5
Hernandez	1.000	8	7	1	0	0
King	1.000	20	30	3	0	1
Kreke	1.000	2	2	0	0	0
Kvasnicka	.983	38	54	4	1	2
Meredith	.987	53	75	2	1	1
Muren	.990	48	95	2	1	0
Scott	.995	108	210	10	1	1
Sosa	1.000	11	15	1	0	0

TRI-CITY VALLEYCATS
SHORT-SEASON

NEW YORK-PENN LEAGUE

Batting	B-T	HT	WT	DOB	AVG	vLH	vRH	G	AB	R	H	2B	3B	HR	RBI	BB	HBP	SH	SF	SO	SB	CS	SLG	OBP
Aplin, Andrew	L-L	6-0	190	3-21-91	.348	.383	.333	44	164	38	57	9	5	4	25	24	5	1	2	22	20	7	.537	.441
Batista, Jean	B-R	6-2	180	11-15-91	.306	.200	.333	12	49	7	15	4	0	0	3	6	0	1	1	12	2	1	.388	.300
Cokinos, M.P.	R-R	6-2	215	6-18-90	.320	.306	.326	36	125	18	40	4	1	3	18	9	2	1	2	14	1	1	.440	.370
Davidson, Chase	L-R	6-5	222	1-14-90	.156	.200	.148	9	32	4	5	1	0	1	5	3	0	0	0	9	1	0	.281	.229
Dineen, Ryan	L-R	6-2	205	3-2-91	.217	.232	.213	66	230	31	50	6	2	2	23	28	5	3	1	69	7	1	.287	.314
Elkins, Austin	B-R	5-11	185	12-21-90	.272	.274	.271	66	254	45	69	13	2	5	25	30	5	7	0	47	18	4	.398	.360
Gominsky, Justin	R-R	6-4	185	8-26-89	.167	.000	.176	5	18	1	3	1	0	0	4	0	0	0	0	3	0	0	.222	.167
Gulbransen, Dan	L-R	5-11	205	1-5-91	.218	.150	.235	58	206	31	45	8	1	6	37	26	5	2	3	41	7	0	.354	.317
Heineman, Tyler	B-R	5-11	205	6-19-91	.358	.333	.366	55	193	33	69	14	0	0	26	26	9	3	2	12	6	2	.430	.452
Johnson, Neiko	R-R	5-9	165	2-2-88	.215	.216	.214	43	149	24	32	3	2	1	10	23	4	3	1	31	15	7	.282	.333
King, Emilio	R-R	6-0	212	8-17-89	.200	.122	.236	41	130	18	26	7	2	4	17	6	3	2	1	46	1	0	.377	.250
McKinney, Jarrod	R-R	5-11	205	10-14-89	.224	.261	.209	48	161	22	36	5	1	5	25	18	4	2	3	55	4	4	.360	.312
Morales, Jobduan	B-R	5-10	180	6-7-91	.292	.257	.305	37	130	25	38	7	1	5	28	15	1	0	1	28	1	2	.477	.367
Moronta, Cristian	R-R	5-10	185	12-5-89	.200	.500	.125	3	10	0	2	0	0	0	1	0	0	0	0	5	0	0	.200	.200
Sclafani, Joe	B-R	5-9	185	4-22-90	.271	.290	.264	70	266	39	72	9	3	1	36	33	4	4	4	40	16	3	.338	.355
Tucker, Preston	L-L	6-0	217	7-6-90	.321	.371	.308	42	165	32	53	7	0	8	38	18	2	0	2	16	1	2	.509	.390
Wierzbicki, Jesse	R-R	6-3	200	11-24-88	.297	.254	.311	70	256	46	76	11	3	5	40	29	6	0	4	50	19	5	.422	.376

Pitching	B-T	HT	WT	DOB	W	L	ERA	G	GS	CG	SV	IP	H	R	ER	HR	BB	SO	AVG	vLH	vRH	K/9	BB/9
Ballew, Travis	R-R	6-0	160	5-1-91	5	1	1.62	23	0	0	3	39	23	9	7	2	17	44	.174	.276	.146	10.15	3.92
Bircher, Joe	L-L	6-4	205	3-27-90	3	4	3.32	13	13	0	0	65	76	30	24	6	20	42	.292	.306	.288	5.82	2.77
Cotton, Jamaine	R-R	6-2	185	9-27-90	2	1	3.31	23	0	0	0	33	31	16	12	3	15	32	.250	.300	.234	8.82	4.13
Day, Lance	R-R	6-1	200	10-4-89	6	1	2.73	11	8	0	0	53	52	19	16	2	8	34	.250	.247	.252	5.81	1.37

Name	B-T	HT	WT	DOB	W	L	ERA	G	GS	CG	SV	IP	H	R	ER	HR	BB	SO	AVG	vLH	vRH	K/9	BB/9
Ford, Blake	L-R	6-5	215	5-16-88	0	3	2.28	27	0	0	14	28	20	10	7	0	14	24	.192	.206	.186	7.81	4.55
Holmes, Brian	L-L	6-4	205	1-30-91	7	2	2.57	13	12	1	0	67	39	22	19	4	25	65	.165	.180	.160	8.78	3.38
Long, Kenny	L-L	6-1	155	1-28-89	1	1	1.88	17	0	0	2	14	4	3	3	0	5	20	.089	.000	.200	12.56	3.14
Meiners, Jeremiah	L-L	6-0	200	8-16-88	4	2	1.98	20	0	0	2	41	30	12	9	0	11	41	.199	.205	.196	9.00	2.41
Minaya, Juan	R-R	6-4	185	9-18-90	2	2	4.66	17	2	0	0	37	34	21	19	0	17	31	.238	.227	.242	7.61	4.17
Neely, John	R-R	6-2	195	7-9-90	0	1	3.12	22	0	0	4	40	45	18	14	2	11	37	.285	.217	.313	8.26	2.45
Perez, Juri	R-R	5-11	203	8-8-90	2	2	1.81	9	8	0	0	50	41	13	10	1	15	39	.222	.197	.234	7.07	2.72
Propst, Brad	R-R	6-1	180	3-18-89	1	0	8.56	11	0	0	0	14	25	15	13	3	3	12	.403	.190	.512	7.90	1.98
Quezada, Euris	R-R	6-6	210	4-6-89	0	0	0.00	6	0	0	0	9	6	0	0	2	10	.171	.125	.185	9.64	1.93
Rodgers, Brady	R-R	6-2	187	9-17-90	7	2	2.89	12	12	0	0	62	60	26	20	5	11	49	.251	.207	.279	7.07	1.59
Shirley, Tommy	R-L	6-5	220	11-11-88	1	0	1.29	3	0	0	0	7	6	2	1	0	1	8	.214	.167	.227	10.29	1.29
Velasquez, Vincent	B-R	6-3	185	6-7-92	4	1	3.35	9	9	0	0	46	37	19	17	2	17	51	.223	.246	.210	10.05	3.35
West, Aaron	R-R	6-1	195	6-11-90	6	2	2.04	12	12	0	0	62	50	15	14	3	9	59	.218	.198	.232	8.61	1.31
Zuloaga, Scott	R-L	6-4	200	9-20-89	0	0	0.00	8	0	0	0	5	4	0	0	0	0	0	.211	.091	.375	7.20	0.00

Fielding

Catcher	PCT	G	PO	A	E	DP	PB
Cokinos	1.000	19	137	4	0	0	1
Heineman	.997	37	275	35	1	2	3
Morales	.984	22	179	11	3	1	4
Moronta	1.000	2	11	4	0	0	0

First Base	PCT	G	PO	A	E	DP
Batista	1.000	3	21	3	0	2
Cokinos	1.000	3	15	1	0	4
Morales	1.000	5	54	1	0	6
Tucker	1.000	2	18	1	0	3
Wierzbicki	.995	67	562	47	3	36

Second Base	PCT	G	PO	A	E	DP
Batista	.667	1	0	2	1	0
Elkins	.959	64	117	167	12	30
Johnson	1.000	14	26	29	0	10

Third Base	PCT	G	PO	A	E	DP
Batista	.600	4	1	5	4	0
Dineen	.915	66	52	131	17	9
Johnson	.810	6	5	12	4	3
Wierzbicki	.714	3	2	3	2	1

Shortstop	PCT	G	PO	A	E	DP
Batista	.952	4	6	14	1	3
Elkins	1.000	2	1	6	0	1
Johnson	1.000	1	1	1	0	0
Sclafani	.945	70	89	184	16	30

Outfield	PCT	G	PO	A	E	DP
Aplin	.989	43	89	5	1	1
Gominsky	.909	5	8	2	1	0
Gulbransen	.963	54	76	1	3	0
Johnson	.976	21	40	0	1	0
King	.942	38	77	4	5	1
McKinney	.983	40	54	4	1	2
Tucker	1.000	34	50	3	0	0

GREENEVILLE ASTROS ROOKIE

APPALACHIAN LEAGUE

Batting	B-T	HT	WT	DOB	AVG	vLH	vRH	G	AB	R	H	2B	3B	HR	RBI	BB	HBP	SH	SF	SO	SB	CS	SLG	OBP
Alvarez, Luis	R-R	5-11	230	2-28-90	.294	.000	.357	6	17	3	5	1	0	2	3	2	0	0	0	4	0	0	.706	.368
Batista, Jean	R-R	6-2	180	11-15-91	.321	.170	.369	51	196	30	63	19	2	6	36	7	1	1	2	31	6	2	.531	.345
Blasik, Brian	R-R	5-11	180	3-15-90	.318	.345	.309	55	217	29	69	14	3	1	43	11	1	5	5	25	6	1	.424	.346
Correa, Carlos	R-R	6-4	190	9-22-94	.371	.600	.333	11	35	5	13	3	1	1	3	5	0	1	0	8	1	0	.600	.450
Fernandez, Jose	R-R	6-1	170	5-20-93	.184	.400	.107	14	38	4	7	1	0	0	1	8	1	0	0	13	2	0	.211	.340
Genoves, Ernesto	R-R	5-11	203	6-4-91	.235	.133	.274	48	162	27	38	13	0	5	25	17	2	0	3	29	2	1	.407	.310
Gingras, Ricky	L-R	6-2	205	10-18-90	.190	.211	.185	29	100	7	19	2	0	3	17	4	0	1	0	17	0	0	.300	.221
Howick, Jimmy	R-R	6-2	185	8-26-90	.201	.179	.209	45	149	17	30	7	0	1	14	10	3	1	1	33	2	0	.268	.264
Ibanez, Angel	L-R	6-2	220	9-10-90	.264	.321	.247	60	227	30	60	10	1	0	21	15	1	3	2	32	3	3	.317	.310
Joyce, Terrell	R-R	6-3	230	5-29-92	.273	.169	.311	58	220	31	60	14	0	7	27	19	1	0	1	66	2	1	.432	.332
Magee, Josh	R-R	5-10	160	10-1-91	.241	.250	.238	12	29	3	7	2	0	0	1	1	0	1	0	4	4	2	.310	.267
Martinez, Mike	R-R	6-0	215	12-5-89	.277	.057	.336	48	166	26	46	8	0	3	23	22	3	1	3	31	1	0	.380	.366
Monzon, Jose	R-R	6-0	170	12-30-91	.214	.182	.226	45	117	16	25	2	0	2	11	14	1	1	1	36	4	0	.282	.301
Moronta, Cristian	R-R	5-10	185	12-5-89	.429	—	.429	6	7	0	3	1	0	0	1	0	0	1	1	0	0		.571	.444
Ovando, Ariel	L-L	6-4	190	9-15-93	.287	.259	.297	59	223	34	64	13	2	6	35	22	0	0	1	67	0	0	.444	.350
Ruiz, Rio	L-R	6-1	180	5-22-94	.220	.250	.214	15	50	8	11	3	1	1	7	4	1	0	0	10	0	0	.380	.291
Sosa, Ruben	B-R	5-7	170	9-23-90	.077	.000	.111	4	13	4	1	0	0	0	1	1	0	0	0	2	2	0	.077	.200
Toney, D'Andre	R-R	5-10	170	1-24-92	.252	.184	.271	59	230	43	58	8	0	3	18	25	10	5	0	60	15	5	.326	.351
Wik, Marc	L-R	5-11	195	7-18-92	.235	.250	.231	40	119	22	28	3	1	1	11	21	2	2	0	46	3	6	.286	.359

Pitching	B-T	HT	WT	DOB	W	L	ERA	G	GS	CG	SV	IP	H	R	ER	HR	BB	SO	AVG	vLH	vRH	K/9	BB/9
Bushue, Tanner	R-R	6-4	180	6-20-91	1	3	5.65	16	0	0	0	29	32	26	18	3	21	34	.286	.243	.307	10.67	6.59
Comer, Kevin	R-R	6-3	205	8-1-92	0	1	9.00	2	1	0	0	6	10	6	6	2	2	5	.370	.429	.350	7.50	3.00
2-team total (10 Bluefield)					3	4	4.56	12	8	0	0	49	53	31	25	6	10	34	—	—	—	6.20	1.82
Dando, Zach	R-R	6-3	175	1-4-91	4	0	3.18	19	0	0	1	34	34	16	12	0	9	32	.250	.293	.232	8.47	2.38
Dimock, Michael	R-R	6-2	194	10-26-89	0	0	4.20	20	0	0	4	30	26	15	14	0	9	36	.230	.241	.226	10.80	2.70
Feliz, Michael	R-R	6-4	210	9-28-93	1	1	5.13	6	6	0	0	26	28	16	15	1	14	28	.269	.189	.313	9.57	4.78
Garcia, Christian	R-R	6-2	175	9-24-93	2	0	4.19	18	0	0	0	34	34	16	16	4	14	30	.260	.217	.282	7.86	3.67
Gonzalez, Erick	R-R	6-1	175	1-10-92	0	0	0.00	2	0	0	0	2	1	0	0	0	0	4	.000	.000	.000	4.50	0.00
Hardoin, Zack	L-L	5-10	190	7-11-88	0	0	3.38	8	0	0	0	11	9	4	4	2	4	11	.237	.167	.250	9.28	3.38
Hauschild, Mike	R-R	6-3	210	1-22-90	2	2	1.78	19	1	0	3	30	22	6	6	0	9	39	.202	.194	.205	11.57	2.67
Houser, Adrian	R-R	6-4	205	2-2-93	3	4	4.19	11	11	0	0	58	53	28	27	1	23	54	.245	.227	.253	8.38	3.57
Jankowski, Jordan	R-R	6-1	210	5-17-89	4	0	2.23	23	0	0	4	32	25	8	8	1	10	53	.205	.417	.116	14.75	2.78
Lambson, Mitchell	L-L	6-1	198	7-20-90	1	0	0.00	4	0	0	1	10	4	0	0	0	0	12	.118	.000	.154	11.17	0.00
Lee, Chris	L-L	6-3	175	8-17-92	1	2	11.42	5	3	0	0	9	13	15	11	1	9	9	.361	.333	.370	9.35	9.35
McCullers Jr., Lance	L-R	6-1	190	10-2-93	0	3	4.80	4	4	0	0	17	17	10	9	1	12	18	.182	.188	.179	10.20	6.00
Minor, Daniel	R-R	5-11	188	2-9-91	3	2	2.75	11	11	0	0	59	51	23	18	3	10	48	.229	.276	.212	7.32	1.53
Musgrove, Joe	R-R	6-5	230	12-4-92	0	1	7.00	4	0	0	0	9	14	7	7	0	4	10	.359	.400	.333	10.00	4.00
2-team total (2 Bluefield)					0	1	4.24	6	1	0	0	17	19	8	8	0	4	19	—	—	—	10.06	2.12
Propst, Brad	R-R	6-1	180	3-18-89	1	0	1.00	6	0	0	0	9	6	1	1	1	3	10	.194	.111	.227	10.00	3.00
Quezada, Euris	R-R	6-6	210	4-6-89	3	3	2.65	10	0	0	2	17	16	9	5	0	2	19	.242	.190	.267	10.06	1.06
Ramirez, Francis	R-R	6-5	205	1-12-92	5	4	4.05	13	13	0	0	53	49	28	24	3	29	59	.250	.284	.233	9.96	4.89
Rodriguez, Richard	R-R	6-4	185	3-4-90	2	1	3.90	8	0	0	0	32	27	18	14	3	9	37	.218	.265	.200	10.30	2.51
Tiburcio, Frederick	R-R	6-3	192	11-1-90	3	5	4.47	12	11	2	0	58	52	34	29	5	27	55	.229	.217	.237	8.49	4.17

	B-T	HT	WT	DOB	W	L	ERA	G	GS	CG	SV	IP	H	R	ER	HR	BB	SO	AVG	vLH	vRH	K/9	BB/9
Walter, Andrew	R-R	6-4	200	10-18-90	0	0	2.75	13	0	0	0	20	18	6	6	3	11	27	.240	.150	.273	12.36	5.03
Zuloaga, Scott	R-L	6-4	200	9-20-89	0	0	2.13	20	0	0	0	13	10	4	3	0	4	16	.200	.158	.226	11.37	2.84

Fielding

Catcher	PCT	G	PO	A	E	DP	PB
Alvarez	.972	4	27	8	1	1	2
Genoves	.991	45	401	31	4	3	3
Gingras	.995	22	169	25	1	1	2
Moronta	1.000	5	24	0	0	0	1

First Base	PCT	G	PO	A	E	DP
Alvarez	—	1	0	0	0	0
Batista	.987	26	216	7	3	18
Fernandez	1.000	1	0	1	0	0
Ibanez	1.000	4	31	1	0	4
Magee	1.000	1	7	0	0	0
Martinez	.994	42	348	8	2	25

Second Base	PCT	G	PO	A	E	DP
Batista	.964	11	24	29	2	4

Blasik	.981	48	76	132	4	26
Fernandez	1.000	2	2	4	0	0
Howick	1.000	5	6	10	0	2
Magee	1.000	4	4	11	0	2
Sosa	1.000	1	2	1	0	1
Wik	.875	2	4	3	1	0

Third Base	PCT	G	PO	A	E	DP
Blasik	1.000	5	2	16	0	2
Ibanez	.907	53	24	83	11	9
Magee	1.000	2	0	4	0	0
Ruiz	.950	9	6	13	1	1

Shortstop	PCT	G	PO	A	E	DP
Batista	.930	13	19	47	5	11
Correa	.977	11	15	27	1	8

Fernandez	.875	8	11	24	5	1
Howick	.953	39	42	100	7	11

Outfield	PCT	G	PO	A	E	DP
Blasik	—	1	0	0	0	0
Ibanez	—	1	0	0	0	0
Joyce	.953	39	38	3	2	0
Monzon	.971	44	65	2	2	0
Ovando	.945	52	66	3	4	1
Sosa	1.000	1	1	0	0	0
Toney	.959	57	116	2	5	0
Wik	.938	24	28	2	2	0

GCL ASTROS — ROOKIE

GULF COAST LEAGUE

Batting	B-T	HT	WT	DOB	AVG	vLH	vRH	G	AB	R	H	2B	3B	HR	RBI	BB	HBP	SH	SF	SO	SB	CS	SLG	OBP
Carnahan, Jon	R-R	6-3	225	9-14-89	.250	.200	.269	13	36	3	9	2	0	0	2	2	0	0	0	4	0	1	.306	.289
Correa, Carlos	R-R	6-4	190	9-22-94	.232	.324	.207	39	155	23	36	11	1	2	9	7	1	0	0	36	5	1	.355	.270
De La Rosa, Luis	B-R	6-1	162	1-2-92	.149	.231	.118	27	47	9	7	1	2	1	6	6	2	1	2	15	2	0	.319	.263
Diaz, Kenny	R-R	5-9	175	5-9-92	.194	.222	.182	19	31	2	6	0	0	0	2	1	1	3	0	6	0	0	.194	.242
Gomez, Edwin	B-R	6-3	175	8-26-91	.260	.182	.284	31	96	10	25	7	1	1	12	5	1	2	0	25	0	1	.385	.304
Gonzalez, Alfredo	R-R	6-1	190	7-13-92	.244	.350	.214	27	90	13	22	3	1	0	6	3	4	1	0	10	5	0	.300	.299
Gonzalez, Wallace	R-R	6-5	240	2-11-93	.256	.233	.263	41	125	15	32	6	2	2	19	5	2	1	0	40	1	0	.384	.295
Hernandez, Teoscar	R-R	6-2	180	10-15-92	.243	.206	.252	51	177	25	43	11	2	4	18	19	3	0	1	54	10	1	.395	.325
Marte, Ydarqui	R-R	6-1	188	10-10-92	.210	.083	.240	33	62	11	13	3	0	1	5	1	0	3	0	17	1	0	.306	.222
Martone, Luca	B-R	5-8	150	10-21-92	.091	.000	.100	10	11	0	1	0	0	0	1	0	0	0	0	2	0	0	.091	.231
Mejia, Yonathan	R-R	6-2	175	9-19-92	.239	.265	.234	52	188	16	45	4	0	2	23	12	0	2	1	33	3	2	.293	.284
Mier, Jio	R-R	6-2	180	8-26-90	.214	.286	.143	5	14	1	3	1	0	0	2	1	0	0	1	0	0	0	.286	.250
Moronta, Cristian	R-R	5-10	185	12-5-89	.000	—	.000	2	3	0	0	0	0	0	0	0	0	1	0	0	0	0	.000	.250
Phillips, Brett	L-R	6-0	175	5-30-94	.251	.220	.261	54	175	26	44	7	6	0	13	28	4	8	4	48	7	5	.360	.360
Polanco, Franny	R-R	6-1	185	12-20-91	.122	.000	.152	18	41	0	5	1	0	0	3	2	1	0	0	8	1	0	.146	.182
Redinger, Kyle	R-R	6-3	205	12-19-91	.167	.500	.071	13	18	0	3	0	0	0	3	1	0	0	0	6	1	0	.167	.211
Reynolds, Javaris	L-L	6-1	190	1-24-93	.214	.429	.143	11	28	3	6	0	0	0	4	4	1	0	0	7	1	2	.214	.333
Rivera, Darwin	R-R	5-11	180	10-27-91	.310	.390	.289	57	200	24	62	14	0	4	29	19	3	0	3	44	0	2	.440	.373
Ruiz, Rio	L-R	6-1	180	5-22-94	.271	.231	.288	23	85	13	23	8	2	0	11	12	0	0	0	22	2	0	.412	.361
Santana, Juan	R-R	6-1	176	8-16-94	.268	.209	.285	56	194	16	52	12	0	0	24	10	2	4	1	22	5	1	.330	.309
Schafer, Jordan	L-L	6-1	190	9-4-86	.500	—	.500	1	2	0	1	0	0	0	0	0	0	0	0	0	0	0	.500	.500
Silfa, Yoel	R-R	5-11	160	7-8-93	.281	.500	.231	12	32	7	9	1	0	0	6	4	0	1	0	7	0	0	.313	.361
Solano, Jose	R-R	6-2	175	3-15-92	.169	.167	.170	24	59	6	10	1	1	1	2	4	2	3	0	20	2	2	.271	.246
Vizcaino, Kelvin	R-R	6-0	175	9-30-92	.087	.000	.100	10	23	2	2	0	0	0	0	1	0	0	0	9	2	1	.087	.125
Wates, Austin	R-R	6-1	179	9-2-88	.556	1.000	.500	3	9	2	5	0	0	1	2	0	0	0	0	2	0	0	.889	.556

Pitching	B-T	HT	WT	DOB	W	L	ERA	G	GS	CG	SV	IP	H	R	ER	HR	BB	SO	AVG	vLH	vRH	K/9	BB/9
Abreu, Alan	R-R	6-3	185	6-14-90	1	2	2.70	14	0	0	0	20	17	7	6	0	15	8	.236	.207	.256	3.60	6.75
Barrios, Agapito	R-R	6-2	167	11-30-93	1	5	3.28	11	5	0	0	49	51	25	18	1	8	26	.266	.283	.259	4.74	1.46
Batista, Ricardo	L-L	6-1	170	8-19-91	1	0	1.71	14	1	0	0	21	13	5	4	0	17	18	.191	.214	.175	7.71	7.29
Culbreth, Brandon	R-R	6-4	200	7-27-92	1	3	5.91	10	4	0	0	32	37	27	21	1	18	22	.278	.255	.293	6.19	5.06
De Leon, Ambiorix	L-L	6-3	185	8-7-91	1	2	3.74	17	0	0	0	22	27	12	9	1	6	17	.290	.250	.308	7.06	2.49
Feliz, Michael	R-R	6-4	210	9-28-93	5	0	1.64	7	3	0	0	38	25	8	7	2	9	35	.185	.151	.207	8.22	2.11
Franco, Enderson	R-R	6-2	190	12-29-92	3	2	4.86	10	7	1	0	50	69	31	27	2	8	37	.329	.302	.351	6.66	1.44
Frias, Edison	R-R	6-1	178	12-18-90	4	1	2.14	10	5	0	0	46	44	17	11	1	15	32	.256	.246	.261	6.22	2.91
Gonzalez, Erick	R-R	6-1	175	1-10-92	2	0	1.80	19	0	0	10	25	24	7	5	0	9	14	.267	.250	.278	5.04	3.24
Guduan, Reymin	L-L	6-4	185	3-16-92	1	1	5.40	8	3	0	0	18	26	11	11	1	16	16	.342	.316	.351	7.85	7.85
Gustave, Jandel	R-R	6-2	160	10-12-92	2	1	5.79	10	4	0	0	28	24	23	18	0	27	22	.224	.267	.208	7.07	8.68
Hallock, Kyle	L-L	6-2	185	8-6-88	0	2	3.12	5	5	0	0	9	10	4	3	0	3	7	.294	.467	.158	7.27	3.12
Holley, Krishawn	R-R	6-0	195	2-8-92	1	1	0.68	7	1	0	0	13	8	1	1	1	1	8	.167	.200	.152	5.40	0.68
Lo, Chia-Jen	R-R	5-11	185	4-7-86	0	1	0.00	8	5	0	0	11	5	2	0	0	2	11	.128	.143	.120	9.00	1.64
McCullers Jr., Lance	L-R	6-1	190	10-2-93	1	1	1.64	4	4	0	0	11	10	2	2	0	2	12	.227	.125	.286	9.82	1.64
Mojica, Juan	R-R	6-4	190	2-13-89	0	3	11.30	11	0	0	0	14	17	19	18	1	8	15	.283	.360	.229	9.42	5.02
Montero, Jose	R-R	6-4	190	1-22-93	1	2	5.03	13	1	0	0	20	21	13	11	0	11	13	.288	.318	.275	5.95	5.03
Quintero, Rodney	R-R	6-2	215	1-18-90	0	3	5.93	12	0	0	0	14	13	11	9	0	13	14	.245	.286	.219	9.22	8.56
Rivera, Raul	R-R	6-3	185	2-5-91	2	1	2.00	12	6	0	1	36	36	11	8	2	4	35	.255	.218	.279	8.75	1.00
Sanchez, Gera	R-R	6-0	170	6-8-89	2	0	1.88	10	0	0	2	14	15	4	3	0	6	16	.288	.304	.276	10.05	3.77
Valdez, Jose	R-R	6-4	200	1-22-83	0	0	0.00	5	5	0	0	5	2	0	0	0	1	7	.111	.000	.182	12.60	1.80
Walter, Andrew	R-R	6-4	200	10-18-90	0	0	0.00	2	0	0	0	4	1	0	0	0	1	6	.083	.333	.000	13.50	2.25

Fielding

Catcher	PCT	G	PO	A	E	DP	PB
Carnahan	1.000	12	65	5	0	0	2
Diaz	.987	19	69	5	1	3	0
Gonzalez	.995	26	181	22	1	2	9
Moronta	1.000	1	6	0	0	0	0
Polanco	.989	18	80	13	1	1	4

First Base	PCT	G	PO	A	E	DP
Gomez	.971	20	159	7	5	20
Mejia	.970	38	275	16	9	34
Redinger	.966	11	28	0	1	5
Rivera	.880	3	21	1	3	1

Second Base	PCT	G	PO	A	E	DP
Martone	.941	8	6	10	1	3
Santana	.982	33	65	100	3	27
Silfa	.927	12	22	29	4	9
Solano	.932	16	27	42	5	12

Third Base	PCT	G	PO	A	E	DP
Diaz	—	1	0	0	0	0
Redinger	.600	3	1	2	2	0
Rivera	.887	49	35	83	15	18
Ruiz	1.000	7	10	14	0	2
Solano	.786	5	4	7	3	1

Shortstop	PCT	G	PO	A	E	DP
Correa	.936	36	56	106	11	24
Mier	.875	4	1	6	1	0
Santana	.921	24	31	62	8	17

Outfield	PCT	G	PO	A	E	DP
De La Rosa	.933	20	28	0	2	0
Gomez	.857	9	11	1	2	1
Gonzalez	.976	31	40	1	1	0
Hernandez	.957	48	98	12	5	5
Marte	.947	25	18	0	1	0
Phillips	.961	53	117	7	5	2
Reynolds	.882	10	15	0	2	0
Schafer	1.000	1	1	0	0	0
Vizcaino	1.000	10	11	0	0	0
Wates	1.000	3	5	0	0	0

DSL ASTROS

ROOKIE

DOMINICAN SUMMER LEAGUE

Batting	B-T	HT	WT	DOB	AVG	vLH	vRH	G	AB	R	H	2B	3B	HR	RBI	BB	HBP	SH	SF	SO	SB	CS	SLG	OBP
Avea, Marlon	R-R	6-1	195	8-31-93	.204	.143	.231	35	93	14	19	4	0	2	8	4	7	1	1	14	4	0	.312	.286
Cesar, Randy	R-R	6-1	180	1-11-95	.213	.203	.217	59	202	17	43	6	0	1	16	23	5	3	1	37	2	1	.257	.307
Coa, Pedro	R-R	6-2	190	12-21-92	.256	.240	.262	37	90	11	23	2	0	1	7	8	1	4	1	5	0	5	.311	.320
Cortorreal, Jean Carlos	R-R	6-1	170	7-17-94	.201	.238	.186	55	144	21	29	2	3	0	16	17	0	1	0	30	2	4	.257	.286
De La Cruz, Johan	R-R	6-2	190	1-3-93	.181	.289	.129	56	138	13	25	2	0	3	17	18	6	1	4	27	8	2	.261	.295
Laguna, Mesac	R-R	6-2	185	1-12-92	.248	.333	.215	68	246	29	61	13	0	6	23	20	5	4	2	24	7	4	.374	.315
Medina, Michael	R-R	6-0	190	10-3-93	.113	.118	.111	27	62	5	7	2	1	0	1	1	3	0	0	31	1	2	.177	.167
Mejia, Brauly	R-R	6-0	185	10-28-94	.250	.160	.288	36	84	10	21	2	1	0	4	5	4	1	0	25	7	3	.298	.323
Michelena, Arturo	R-R	5-11	165	10-15-94	.202	.161	.216	34	119	12	24	2	2	0	12	5	0	4	0	18	5	3	.252	.234
Murillo, Cristian	L-L	6-1	165	6-1-93	.182	.146	.198	56	132	28	24	5	0	0	10	40	2	5	2	34	5	6	.220	.375
Pena, Brian	R-R	6-1	185	6-14-94	.183	.190	.180	28	71	4	13	1	0	0	4	11	1	1	2	18	0	1	.197	.294
Reynoso, Jarico	R-R	5-10	170	1-14-93	.241	.245	.239	58	187	25	45	3	2	0	12	16	7	3	0	46	17	10	.278	.324
Reynoso, Luis	R-R	6-1	170	9-2-94	.281	.288	.277	50	171	23	48	11	0	1	17	27	1	1	0	31	8	3	.363	.382
Roa, Hector	R-R	6-0	195	3-1-95	.221	.222	.221	33	122	11	27	4	1	4	14	7	0	2	3	41	1	2	.369	.258
Santana, Edward	R-R	6-0	170	10-20-94	—	—	—	2	0	0	0	0	0	0	0	0	0	0	0	0	0	0	—	—
Serrano, Frederick	R-R	6-2	190	8-29-94	.209	.193	.216	56	182	10	38	7	0	3	14	18	4	1	1	67	0	2	.297	.293
Silfa, Yoel	R-R	5-11	160	7-8-93	.180	.185	.179	56	194	21	35	6	0	0	14	13	2	3	1	29	3	3	.211	.238

Pitching	B-T	HT	WT	DOB	W	L	ERA	G	GS	CG	SV	IP	H	R	ER	HR	BB	SO	AVG	vLH	vRH	K/9	BB/9
Abad, Luis	R-R	6-3	165	4-18-94	0	4	7.96	14	5	0	0	26	18	26	23	3	31	27	.207	.375	.169	9.35	10.73
Angulo, Yoiner	R-R	6-1	175	10-7-91	0	1	4.50	2	2	0	0	2	2	1	1	0	0	0	.286	.250	.333	0.00	0.00
Arauz, Harold	R-R	6-2	185	5-29-95	1	1	4.30	8	5	0	0	15	19	9	7	0	3	15	.297	.357	.280	9.20	1.84
Arias, Johan	R-R	6-0	170	1-1-92	1	2	4.53	17	5	0	2	46	60	28	23	1	17	32	.317	.310	.321	6.31	3.35
Baso, Xavier	R-R	6-0	190	1-12-91	0	0	2.57	6	6	0	0	7	5	2	2	1	2	7	.208	.500	.150	9.00	2.57
Castillo, Jesus	R-R	6-3	175	10-24-91	0	1	2.38	6	0	0	0	11	3	6	3	1	13	10	.086	.000	.115	7.94	10.32
Chevalier, Rayderson	R-R	6-1	165	1-31-95	3	3	6.44	15	5	0	0	43	48	40	31	3	23	40	.284	.318	.279	8.31	4.78
Colon, Frangy	R-R	6-2	170	11-18-93	0	4	4.81	18	0	0	0	39	39	30	21	2	14	29	.255	.143	.288	6.64	3.20
De Los Santos, Samil	R-R	6-4	175	1-8-94	2	3	2.50	12	9	0	0	58	42	21	16	1	20	63	.197	.295	.172	9.83	3.12
Delis, Juan	R-R	6-1	195	5-29-94	1	0	3.69	17	0	0	0	32	18	22	13	0	26	26	.175	.111	.188	7.39	7.39
Franzua, Geronimo	L-L	6-1	170	9-25-93	0	0	8.10	12	1	0	0	13	12	19	12	1	31	12	.235	.000	.250	8.10	20.93
Hernandez, Elieser	R-R	6-1	170	5-3-95	1	4	4.11	12	8	1	2	35	37	18	16	0	8	25	.280	.225	.304	6.43	2.06
Hernandez, Juan	R-R	6-3	170	1-24-93	0	4	3.78	13	11	0	0	48	47	23	20	1	25	40	.258	.240	.265	7.55	4.72
Hurtado, Erick	L-L	6-4	190	11-21-94	0	1	7.36	6	0	0	0	11	10	9	9	2	9	11	.238	.000	.244	9.00	7.36
Mesa, Victor	R-R	6-2	170	11-26-93	1	4	4.33	18	0	4	0	35	40	26	17	2	15	19	.290	.350	.265	4.84	3.82
Rodriguez, Rauldison	R-R	5-11	160	10-21-93	0	0	3.18	10	0	0	1	11	10	7	4	1	10	14	.222	.250	.212	11.12	7.94
Saucedo, Javier	L-L	5-11	160	9-28-93	5	4	3.21	17	1	0	0	48	38	22	17	3	25	33	.232	.167	.237	6.23	4.72
Villarroel, Edwin	L-L	6-3	165	5-18-95	4	7	2.25	14	11	0	0	68	68	39	17	1	24	22	.260	.368	.251	2.91	3.18
Yonquelys, Martinez	R-R	6-0	180	4-23-93	2	3	4.43	18	0	0	1	41	45	25	20	2	25	38	.290	.152	.328	8.41	5.53

Fielding

Catcher	PCT	G	PO	A	E	DP	PB
Avea	.983	33	183	49	4	0	8
Coa	.960	26	136	31	7	2	4
Medina	1.000	1	1	0	0	0	0
Pena	.989	23	157	27	2	2	8

First Base	PCT	G	PO	A	E	DP
Avea	1.000	1	1	0	0	0
Cesar	1.000	3	13	0	0	0
Coa	1.000	6	25	4	0	4
Cortorreal	1.000	2	4	0	0	1
Laguna	.989	40	259	18	3	25
Medina	.972	14	67	3	2	9
Pena	1.000	3	2	0	0	0
Roa	.991	12	107	6	1	8
Serrano	.991	17	106	4	1	2

Second Base	PCT	G	PO	A	E	DP
Coa	1.000	2	3	5	0	1
Cortorreal	.962	31	54	47	4	11
Michelena	.938	8	17	13	2	2
Reynoso	.946	12	24	29	3	8
Silfa	.940	28	55	55	7	18

Third Base	PCT	G	PO	A	E	DP
Cesar	.881	53	47	130	24	13
Coa	1.000	1	1	3	0	0
Cortorreal	1.000	3	3	4	0	0
Roa	.833	2	3	7	2	0
Silfa	.974	14	11	27	1	2

Shortstop	PCT	G	PO	A	E	DP
Coa	1.000	1	1	3	0	0

	PCT	G	PO	A	E	DP
Cortorreal	.862	6	11	14	4	0
Michelena	.930	23	38	69	8	11
Reynoso	.892	34	73	93	20	11
Silfa	.920	13	21	25	4	6

Outfield	PCT	G	PO	A	E	DP
Cortorreal	1.000	4	1	1	0	0
De La Cruz	.933	43	41	1	3	0
Laguna	.981	37	49	2	1	1
Mejia	.900	22	26	1	3	0
Murillo	.949	52	74	0	4	0
Reynoso	.968	55	117	3	4	2
Roa	1.000	12	28	0	0	0
Santana	1.000	2	1	0	0	0
Serrano	.846	20	21	1	4	0

Kansas City Royals

SEASON IN A NUTSHELL: Our Time was the Royals' marketing slogan, but it proved to be a mirage as the loss of three pitchers to Tommy John surgery gutted an already thin pitching staff.

HIGH POINT: On April 10, after one trip through the rotation, the Royals were 3-2 with a series win over the Angels. It would be the last time the Royals would be over .500.

LOW POINT: The season was over almost before it started. Just six games into the season, the Royals began a 12-game losing streak. Kansas City actually had a winning record in two of the next three months, but a 6-15 April was an impossible handicap to overcome.

NOTABLE ROOKIES: After a wave of promotions in 2011, there were fewer opportunities for rookies in 2012. Reliever Kelvin Herrera proved to be the hardest thrower in baseball, with a fastball that sat at 98 mph and often touched 100. He provided 84 quality innings out of the bullpen and should step into an even more significant role in 2013. Jarrod Dyson was supposed to be a backup outfielder, but injuries meant he started more than 100 games in the outfield, hitting .260/.328/.322 with 30 steals. Utility infielder Irving Falu was a surprising callup after spending parts of 10 seasons in the minor league system.

KEY TRANSACTIONS: The Royals shipped outfielder Melky Cabrera to the Giants for lefthander Jonathan Sanchez before the season, and it couldn't have turned out worse. Before being suspended for performance-enhancing drugs, Cabrera was an MVP candidate, while an unhappy Sanchez went 1-6, 7.76 in 12 starts before being shipped to the Rockies for Jeremy Guthrie. Guthrie worked out much better, going 5-3, 3.16 in 14 starts with Kansas City. At the trade deadline, the Royals sent closer Jonathan Broxton to the Reds for lefthander Donnie Joseph and righthander J.C. Sulbaran.

DOWN ON THE FARM: Wil Myers put together one of the best seasons a Royals farmhand has ever had. He hit 37 home runs on his way to winning Baseball America's Minor League Player of the Year award. No farm team won a minor league title in 2012, but two did make their league championship series. Myers and the Triple-A Omaha Storm Chasers fell to Reno in four games in a best-of-five series. Rookie-level Burlington, led by 2011 first-round pick Bubba Starling, fell in extra innings in the deciding game of the Appalachian League finals.

OPENING DAY PAYROLL: $60.9 million (27th)

PLAYERS OF THE YEAR

MAJOR LEAGUE	MINOR LEAGUE
Alex Gordon	**Wil Myers**
of	of/3b
.294/.368/.455	(Double-A/Triple-A)
Led AL with 51 2B	.314/.387/.600
2nd cons. Gold Glove	BA Minor League POY

ORGANIZATION LEADERS

BATTING		*Minimum 250 AB
MAJORS		
* AVG	Billy Butler	.313
* OPS	Billy Butler	.883
HR	Billy Butler	29
RBI	Billy Butler	107
MINORS		
* AVG	Irving Falu, Omaha	.329
* OBP	Johnny Giavotella, Omaha	.404
* SLG	Wil Myers, NW Arkansas/Omaha	.600
R	Wil Myers, NW Arkansas/Omaha	98
H	Wil Myers, NW Arkansas/Omaha	164
TB	Wil Myers, NW Arkansas/Omaha	313
2B	Clint Robinson, Omaha	37
3B	David Lough, Omaha	11
HR	Wil Myers, NW Arkansas/Omaha	37
RBI	Wil Myers, NW Arkansas/Omaha	109
BB	Clint Robinson, Omaha	79
SO	Brett Eibner, Wilmington	165
SB	Terrance Gore, Burlington	36

PITCHING		#Minimum 75 IP
MAJORS		
W	Bruce Chen	11
# ERA	Luis Mendoza	4.23
SO	Luke Hochevar	144
SV	Jonathan Broxton	23
MINORS		
W	Jake Odorizzi, NW Arkansas/Omaha	15
L	Noel Arguelles, NW Arkansas	14
# ERA	Edwin Carl, Kane County/Wilmington	2.90
G	Brandon Sisk, Omaha	50
GS	Jason Adam, Wilmington	27
GS	Aaron Brooks, Kane County	27
GS	Mike Montgomery, Omaha/NW Arkansas	27
SV	Patrick Keating, AZL/NW Arkansas	9
SV	Sam Runion, Wilmington/NW Arkansas	9
SV	John Walter, Burlington	9
IP	Jason Adam, Wilmington	158
BB	Chris Dwyer, NW Arkansas/Omaha	68
SO	Jake Odorizzi, NW Arkansas/Omaha	135
# AVG	Ryan Verdugo, Omaha	.227

General Manager: Dayton Moore. **Farm Director:** Scott Sharp. **Scouting Director:** Lonnie Goldberg.

Class	Team	League	W	L	PCT	Finish	Manager
Majors	Kansas City Royals	American	72	90	.444	11th (14)	Ned Yost
Triple-A	Omaha Storm Chasers	Pacific Coast	83	61	.576	2nd (16)	Mike Jirschele
Double-A	Northwest Arkansas Naturals	Texas	58	81	.417	8th (8)	Brian Poldberg
High A	Wilmington Blue Rocks	Carolina	66	74	.471	5th (8)	Vance Wilson
Low A	Kane County Cougars	Midwest	68	72	.486	10th (16)	Brian Buchanan
Rookie	Idaho Falls Chukars	Pioneer	35	41	.461	t-6th (8)	Omar Ramirez
Rookie	Burlington Royals	Appalachian	41	25	.621	2nd (10)	Tommy Shields
Rookie	AZL Royals	Arizona	23	32	.418	9th (13)	Darryl Kennedy
Overall 2012 Minor League Record			374	386	.492	22nd (30)	

ORGANIZATION STATISTICS

KANSAS CITY ROYALS

AMERICAN LEAGUE

Batting	B-T	HT	WT	DOB	AVG	vLH	vRH	G	AB	R	H	2B	3B	HR	RBI	BB	HBP	SH	SF	SO	SB	CS	SLG	OBP
Abreu, Tony	B-R	5-9	200	11-13-84	.257	.207	.293	22	70	5	18	2	1	1	15	2	1	0	1	13	0	0	.357	.284
Betancourt, Yuniesky	R-R	5-11	205	1-31-82	.228	.247	.215	57	215	21	49	14	1	7	36	9	0	1	3	25	0	1	.400	.256
Bourgeois, Jason	R-R	5-9	195	1-4-82	.258	.265	.231	30	62	10	16	2	1	0	5	4	0	0	0	4	5	4	.323	.303
Butler, Billy	R-R	6-1	240	4-18-86	.313	.331	.306	161	614	72	192	32	1	29	107	54	7	0	4	111	2	1	.510	.373
Cain, Lorenzo	R-R	6-2	200	4-13-86	.266	.306	.247	61	222	27	59	9	2	7	31	15	3	0	4	56	10	0	.419	.316
Dyson, Jarrod	L-R	5-9	165	8-15-84	.260	.206	.275	102	292	52	76	8	5	0	9	30	1	4	3	56	30	5	.322	.328
Escobar, Alcides	R-R	6-1	190	12-16-86	.293	.277	.299	155	605	68	177	30	7	5	52	27	8	8	0	100	35	5	.390	.331
Falu, Irving	B-R	5-10	180	6-6-83	.341	.385	.322	24	85	14	29	6	1	0	7	4	0	2	0	9	0	2	.435	.371
Francoeur, Jeff	R-R	6-4	210	1-8-84	.235	.225	.239	148	561	58	132	26	3	16	49	34	7	0	1	119	4	7	.378	.287
Getz, Chris	L-R	5-11	185	8-30-83	.275	.229	.291	64	189	22	52	10	3	0	17	11	0	8	2	17	9	3	.360	.312
Giavotella, Johnny	R-R	5-8	185	7-10-87	.238	.203	.259	53	181	21	43	7	1	1	15	8	0	0	0	35	3	0	.304	.270
Gordon, Alex	L-R	6-1	220	2-10-84	.294	.248	.320	161	642	93	189	51	5	14	72	73	3	0	3	140	10	5	.455	.368
Hosmer, Eric	L-L	6-4	230	10-24-89	.232	.220	.238	152	535	65	124	22	2	14	60	56	2	0	5	95	16	1	.359	.304
Lough, David	L-L	5-11	185	1-20-86	.237	.167	.245	20	59	9	14	2	1	0	2	4	1	0	1	9	1	0	.305	.292
Maier, Mitch	L-R	6-3	210	6-30-82	.172	.176	.170	32	64	8	11	1	1	2	7	8	0	1	1	24	2	0	.313	.260
Moore, Adam	R-R	6-3	220	5-8-84	.182	.500	.000	4	11	1	2	1	0	1	2	1	0	0	0	3	0	0	.545	.250
Moustakas, Mike	L-R	6-0	215	9-11-88	.242	.254	.236	149	563	69	136	34	1	20	73	39	7	0	5	124	5	2	.412	.296
Pena, Brayan	B-R	5-9	230	1-7-82	.236	.265	.222	68	212	16	50	10	1	2	25	9	0	1	4	24	0	1	.321	.262
Perez, Salvador	R-R	6-3	245	5-10-90	.301	.358	.279	76	289	38	87	16	0	11	39	12	1	0	3	27	0	0	.471	.328
Pina, Manny	R-R	6-0	215	6-5-87	.000	.000	.000	1	2	0	0	0	0	0	0	0	0	0	0	0	0	0	.000	.000
Quintero, Humberto	R-R	5-9	215	8-2-79	.232	.152	.257	43	138	7	32	12	0	1	19	4	1	0	1	28	0	1	.341	.257
Robinson, Clint	L-L	6-5	240	2-16-85	.000	.000	.000	4	4	0	0	0	0	0	0	0	0	0	0	2	0	0	.000	.000

Pitching	B-T	HT	WT	DOB	W	L	ERA	G	GS	CG	SV	IP	H	R	ER	HR	BB	SO	AVG	vLH	vRH	K/9	BB/9
Adcock, Nate	R-R	6-4	225	2-25-88	0	3	2.34	12	2	0	0	35	37	13	9	4	13	22	.282	.237	.319	5.71	3.38
Broxton, Jonathan	R-R	6-4	300	6-16-84	1	2	2.27	35	0	0	23	36	36	11	9	1	14	25	.273	.258	.286	6.31	3.53
Bueno, Francisley	L-L	5-11	200	3-5-81	1	1	1.56	18	0	0	0	17	16	4	3	0	2	7	.246	.263	.222	3.63	1.04
Chen, Bruce	L-L	6-2	210	6-19-77	11	14	5.07	34	34	0	0	192	215	114	108	33	47	140	.281	.314	.271	6.57	2.21
Coleman, Louis	R-R	6-4	205	4-4-86	0	0	3.71	42	0	0	0	51	41	23	21	10	26	65	.219	.235	.210	11.47	4.59
Collins, Tim	L-L	5-7	165	8-21-89	5	4	3.36	72	0	0	0	70	55	29	26	8	34	93	.216	.239	.196	12.01	4.39
Colon, Roman	R-R	6-5	245	8-13-79	0	0	6.75	3	0	0	0	8	12	6	6	0	3	3	.353	.385	.333	3.38	3.38
Crow, Aaron	R-R	6-3	190	11-10-86	3	1	3.48	73	0	0	2	65	54	27	25	4	22	65	.231	.188	.255	9.05	3.06
Duffy, Danny	L-L	6-3	200	12-21-88	2	2	3.90	6	6	0	0	28	26	13	12	2	18	28	.252	.192	.273	9.11	5.86
Guthrie, Jeremy	R-R	6-1	205	4-8-79	5	3	3.16	14	14	0	0	91	84	37	32	9	19	56	.248	.239	.256	5.54	1.88
Herrera, Kelvin	R-R	5-10	190	12-31-89	4	3	2.35	76	0	0	3	84	79	24	22	4	21	77	.250	.275	.235	8.22	2.24
Hochevar, Luke	R-R	6-5	220	9-15-83	8	16	5.73	32	32	2	0	185	202	127	118	27	61	144	.281	.298	.261	6.99	2.96
Holland, Greg	R-R	5-10	195	11-20-85	7	4	2.96	67	0	0	16	67	58	22	22	2	34	91	.234	.194	.264	12.22	4.57
Hottovy, Tommy	L-L	6-1	195	7-9-81	0	0	2.89	9	0	0	0	9	11	3	3	2	5	6	.306	.250	.375	5.79	4.82
Jeffress, Jeremy	R-R	6-0	195	9-21-87	0	0	6.75	13	0	0	0	13	19	14	10	0	13	13	.317	.192	.412	8.78	8.78
Mazzaro, Vin	R-R	6-2	220	9-27-86	4	3	5.73	18	6	0	0	44	55	29	28	3	19	26	.318	.329	.311	5.32	3.89
Mendoza, Luis	R-R	6-3	240	10-31-83	8	10	4.23	30	25	0	0	166	176	84	78	15	59	104	.278	.292	.263	5.64	3.20
Mijares, Jose	L-L	6-0	230	10-29-84	2	2	2.56	51	0	0	0	39	36	13	11	3	13	37	.248	.214	.295	8.61	3.03
Odorizzi, Jake	R-R	6-2	185	3-27-90	0	1	4.91	2	2	0	0	7	8	4	4	1	4	4	.267	.280	.000	4.91	4.91
Paulino, Felipe	R-R	6-2	270	10-5-83	3	1	1.67	7	7	0	0	38	31	8	7	3	15	39	.223	.190	.273	9.32	3.58
Sanchez, Jonathan	L-L	6-0	200	11-19-82	1	6	7.76	12	12	0	0	53	65	47	46	8	44	36	.302	.250	.323	6.08	7.43
Smith, Will	L-L	6-5	240	7-10-89	6	9	5.32	16	16	0	0	90	111	54	53	12	33	59	.313	.356	.295	5.92	3.31
Teaford, Everett	L-L	6-0	165	5-15-84	1	4	4.99	18	5	0	0	61	68	34	34	11	21	35	.285	.300	.275	5.14	3.08
Verdugo, Ryan	L-L	6-0	195	4-10-87	0	1	32.40	1	1	0	0	2	8	6	6	1	2	2	.615	.500	.714	10.80	10.80

Fielding

Catcher	PCT	G	PO	A	E	DP	PB
Moore	.923	3	11	1	1	0	1
Pena	.989	52	344	18	4	4	5

	PCT	G	PO	A	E	DP	PB
Perez	.993	74	522	53	4	4	3
Pina	1.000	1	4	0	0	0	0
Quintero	.985	43	310	28	5	5	2

First Base	PCT	G	PO	A	E	DP
Butler	.982	20	147	15	3	18
Hosmer	.993	148	1183	103	9	132
Pena	1.000	3	8	0	0	0

KANSAS CITY ROYALS

Second Base	PCT	G	PO	A	E	DP
Abreu	.981	11	19	32	1	10
Betancourt	.975	46	89	107	5	40
Falu	.982	14	19	37	1	9
Getz	.983	61	95	143	4	40
Giavotella	.967	45	84	93	6	21

Third Base	PCT	G	PO	A	E	DP
Abreu	1.000	6	3	10	0	2

	PCT	G	PO	A	E	DP
Betancourt	1.000	8	3	11	0	1
Falu	.895	5	4	13	2	1
Moustakas	.967	149	127	312	15	41

Shortstop	PCT	G	PO	A	E	DP
Abreu	1.000	4	5	5	0	3
Betancourt	.800	1	1	3	1	1
Escobar	.972	155	242	408	19	97
Falu	1.000	5	6	9	0	3

Outfield	PCT	G	PO	A	E	DP
Bourgeois	.940	24	44	3	3	1
Cain	.974	60	144	3	4	1
Dyson	.976	88	231	8	6	4
Francoeur	.985	147	242	19	4	3
Gordon	.994	160	319	17	2	3
Hosmer	.667	3	1	1	1	0
Lough	.968	17	30	0	1	0
Maier	1.000	22	38	0	0	0

OMAHA STORM CHASERS TRIPLE-A

PACIFIC COAST LEAGUE

Batting	B-T	HT	WT	DOB	AVG	vLH	vRH	G	AB	R	H	2B	3B	HR	RBI	BB	HBP	SH	SF	SO	SB	CS	SLG	OBP
Abreu, Tony	B-R	5-9	200	11-13-84	.322	.363	.305	103	429	60	138	36	5	9	73	14	4	4	2	69	7	2	.492	.347
Betancourt, Yuniesky	R-R	5-11	205	1-31-82	.625	.500	.750	2	8	1	5	0	0	1	5	0	0	0	0	0	0	0	1.000	.625
Bourgeois, Jason	R-R	5-9	195	1-4-82	.243	.379	.186	60	222	41	54	7	1	3	8	21	2	2	0	24	7	5	.324	.314
Cain, Lorenzo	R-R	6-2	200	4-13-86	.321	.333	.320	7	28	4	9	3	0	1	6	2	0	0	1	4	0	0	.536	.355
Clark, Cody	R-R	6-3	200	9-14-81	.180	.115	.203	72	205	23	37	6	0	4	22	17	2	12	4	39	0	0	.268	.246
Colon, Christian	R-R	6-1	180	3-14-90	.412	.667	.357	5	17	4	7	1	0	1	5	2	0	0	2	1	0	0	.647	.429
Dyson, Jarrod	L-R	5-9	165	8-15-84	.333	.273	.366	15	63	12	21	3	3	0	5	4	0	4	0	5	7	1	.476	.373
Eigsti, Ryan	R-R	6-1	205	8-24-85	.167	.000	.182	11	12	1	2	0	0	0	0	1	0	2	0	3	0	0	.167	.231
2-team total (10 Las Vegas)					.158	—		21	38	1	6	1	0	0	3	3	0	2	0	10	0	0	.184	.220
Evans, Terry	R-R	6-4	210	1-19-82	.283	.353	.256	22	60	10	17	2	0	3	11	5	1	0	0	21	0	0	.467	.348
Falu, Irving	B-R	5-10	180	6-6-83	.329	.287	.343	88	365	69	120	22	3	7	50	28	0	11	2	41	21	6	.463	.375
Getz, Chris	L-R	5-11	185	8-30-83	.279	.133	.357	11	43	7	12	2	1	0	8	4	0	0	0	4	1	0	.372	.340
Giavotella, Johnny	R-R	5-8	185	7-10-87	.323	.320	.324	89	362	67	117	20	2	10	71	46	0	4	0	40	7	1	.472	.404
Kouzmanoff, Kevin	R-R	6-1	210	7-25-81	.262	.261	.262	56	210	19	55	15	2	0	31	13	0	2	3	40	1	1	.352	.301
Lough, David	L-L	5-11	185	1-20-86	.275	.232	.292	130	491	69	135	19	11	10	69	25	8	14	6	65	26	4	.420	.317
Maier, Mitch	L-R	6-3	210	6-30-82	.288	.273	.293	38	132	25	38	4	1	4	17	21	1	0	2	31	2	1	.424	.385
Mertins, Kurt	R-R	5-10	188	4-22-86	.259	.250	.261	28	58	11	15	1	0	2	7	2	0	0	1	9	1	0	.379	.279
Moore, Adam	R-R	6-3	220	5-8-84	.296	.233	.318	35	115	18	34	8	0	3	22	14	3	1	2	24	2	0	.443	.381
2-team total (24 Tacoma)					.259	—		59	201	28	52	13	0	6	33	19	3	2	4	38	2	0	.413	.326
Myers, Wil	R-R	6-3	205	12-10-90	.304	.284	.311	99	388	66	118	15	5	24	79	45	3	0	3	98	2	2	.554	.378
Navarro, Rey	B-R	5-10	175	12-22-89	.300	.333	.286	17	60	7	18	3	0	1	8	1	1	0	7	1	0		.400	.391
Perez, Salvador	R-R	6-3	245	5-10-90	.340	.500	.278	12	50	11	17	2	0	0	5	2	0	1	0	5	0	0	.380	.365
Ramirez, Max	R-R	5-11	175	10-11-84	.300	.312	.295	110	387	59	116	16	0	17	77	47	3	1	7	82	0	0	.473	.374
Robinson, Clint	L-L	6-5	240	2-16-85	.292	.260	.306	131	487	70	142	37	1	13	67	79	3	0	1	65	1	0	.452	.393
Robinson, Derrick	B-L	5-11	185	9-28-87	.268	.224	.279	116	422	73	113	12	3	2	28	50	2	8	6	84	23	9	.325	.344
Romak, Jamie	R-R	6-2	220	9-30-85	.147	.000	.185	11	34	5	5	2	0	0	2	2	1	0	0	8	0	0	.206	.216
2-team total (31 Memphis)					.247	—		42	146	14	36	10	1	0	14	10	2	1	2	32	0	0	.329	.300
Seratelli, Anthony	B-R	6-0	205	2-27-83	.299	.222	.320	115	384	64	115	17	3	17	66	44	3	4	9	92	15	4	.492	.374

Pitching	B-T	HT	WT	DOB	W	L	ERA	G	GS	CG	SV	IP	H	R	ER	HR	BB	SO	AVG	vLH	vRH	K/9	BB/9
Adcock, Nate	R-R	6-4	225	2-25-88	8	6	5.53	19	18	0	0	99	116	67	61	5	30	60	.297	.324	.264	5.44	2.72
Bueno, Francisley	L-L	5-11	200	3-5-81	1	4	2.75	35	0	0	6	56	43	23	17	5	15	54	.211	.200	.217	8.73	2.43
Coleman, Louis	R-R	6-4	205	4-4-86	0	2	3.20	11	1	0	3	20	13	7	7	1	8	26	.183	.147	.216	11.90	3.66
Colon, Roman	R-R	6-5	245	8-13-79	4	2	3.09	40	1	0	7	67	66	31	23	7	28	59	.257	.214	.293	7.93	3.76
Davis, Doug	R-L	6-4	215	9-21-75	9	4	4.66	20	16	1	0	106	124	57	55	12	38	88	.296	.323	.283	7.45	3.22
Dwyer, Chris	R-L	6-3	215	4-10-88	3	4	6.97	9	9	1	0	50	73	41	39	10	24	33	.349	.271	.388	5.90	4.29
Gutierrez, Juan	R-R	6-3	260	7-14-83	0	1	8.18	10	0	0	0	11	13	10	10	2	3	7	.289	.333	.250	5.73	2.45
Hardy, Blaine	L-L	6-2	220	3-14-87	3	2	3.79	30	0	0	1	55	68	24	23	6	22	45	.318	.357	.299	7.41	3.62
Hollingsworth, Ethan	R-R	6-2	200	5-4-87	2	3	6.44	11	2	0	0	29	45	24	21	2	10	18	.357	.422	.290	5.52	3.07
Hottovy, Tommy	L-L	6-1	195	7-9-81	2	2	2.52	41	0	0	7	50	42	18	14	6	16	61	.221	.147	.270	10.98	2.88
Jeffress, Jeremy	R-R	6-0	195	9-21-87	5	4	4.97	37	0	0	2	58	52	34	32	4	25	61	.246	.287	.218	9.47	3.88
Joseph, Donnie	L-L	6-3	190	11-1-87	1	0	4.15	11	0	0	2	17	21	9	8	1	13	19	.296	.250	.326	9.87	6.75
Mariot, Michael	R-R	6-0	190	11-8-87	0	0	2.25	2	0	0	0	8	6	2	2	0	3	6	.214	.308	.133	3.38	3.38
Marks, Justin	L-L	6-3	195	1-12-88	0	1	48.60	1	1	0	0	2	7	9	9	0	3	0	.636	1.000	.500	0.00	16.20
Mazzaro, Vin	R-R	6-2	220	9-27-86	2	2	3.63	22	8	0	5	67	69	28	27	4	20	62	.279	.240	.322	8.33	2.69
Montgomery, Mike	L-L	6-4	200	7-1-89	3	6	5.69	17	17	1	0	92	110	74	58	12	43	67	.298	.326	.283	6.58	4.22
O'Sullivan, Sean	R-R	6-2	240	9-1-87	5	4	6.75	17	5	0	1	53	76	43	40	6	16	26	.339	.318	.360	4.39	3.88
2-team total (14 Las Vegas)					14	7	4.23	31	19	0	1	143	153	82	67	11	46	70	—	—	—	4.42	2.90
Odorizzi, Jake	R-R	6-2	185	3-27-90	11	3	2.93	19	18	0	0	107	105	41	35	12	40	88	.254	.229	.279	7.38	3.35
Sanchez, Jonathan	L-L	6-0	200	11-19-82	1	1	6.75	3	3	0	0	13	14	10	10	5	7	13	.264	.313	.243	8.78	4.73
Sisk, Brandon	L-L	6-2	220	7-13-85	3	2	2.54	50	0	0	8	67	59	19	19	8	32	73	.234	.240	.231	9.76	4.28
Smith, Will	R-L	6-5	240	7-10-89	4	4	3.61	15	15	0	0	90	104	44	36	8	22	74	.290	.316	.274	7.43	2.21
Teaford, Everett	L-L	6-0	165	5-15-84	4	0	1.09	7	6	0	0	33	24	4	4	2	8	25	.207	.174	.229	6.82	2.18
Verdugo, Ryan	L-L	6-0	195	4-10-87	12	4	3.75	27	24	0	0	137	114	60	57	19	67	118	.227	.214	.233	7.77	4.41

Fielding

Catcher	PCT	G	PO	A	E	DP	PB
Clark	.994	71	479	41	3	2	3
Eigsti	.946	10	33	2	2	0	0
Moore	.997	35	261	30	1	1	3
Perez	.981	8	47	5	1	0	0

	PCT	G	PO	A	E	DP	PB
Ramirez	.989	39	250	20	3	5	3

First Base	PCT	G	PO	A	E	DP
Maier	1.000	9	63	5	0	7
Ramirez	1.000	11	72	4	0	16
Robinson	.985	102	775	55	13	89

	PCT	G	PO	A	E	DP
Romak	.984	6	57	5	1	6
Seratelli	.995	27	185	9	1	18

Second Base	PCT	G	PO	A	E	DP
Abreu	1.000	4	8	17	0	5
Betancourt	1.000	2	2	4	0	1

	PCT	G	PO	A	E	DP
Colon	—	1	0	0	0	0
Falu	1.000	8	13	24	0	6
Getz	1.000	9	16	21	0	7
Giavotella	.983	79	139	205	6	54
Mertins	1.000	14	13	18	0	4
Navarro	1.000	17	35	43	0	14
Seratelli	.935	21	35	52	6	18

Third Base	PCT	G	PO	A	E	DP
Falu	.938	35	23	52	5	3
Giavotella	.833	4	3	7	2	1
Kouzmanoff	.965	55	36	101	5	8

	PCT	G	PO	A	E	DP
Mertins	.933	8	5	9	1	2
Myers	.935	13	8	21	2	3
Seratelli	.937	37	26	63	6	4

Shortstop	PCT	G	PO	A	E	DP
Abreu	.958	97	156	275	19	71
Colon	1.000	4	9	8	0	4
Falu	.976	32	44	78	3	26
Seratelli	.958	12	30	38	3	8

Outfield	PCT	G	PO	A	E	DP
Bourgeois	1.000	55	119	8	0	1

	PCT	G	PO	A	E	DP
Cain	1.000	5	11	0	0	0
Dyson	.977	14	40	2	1	0
Evans	1.000	16	34	3	0	0
Falu	1.000	11	28	1	0	0
Lough	.979	125	313	8	7	1
Maier	.972	25	66	3	2	0
Mertins	1.000	1	2	0	0	0
Myers	.981	70	152	3	3	0
Robinson	—	1	0	0	0	0
Robinson	.986	108	204	3	3	1
Seratelli	.933	9	14	0	1	0

NORTHWEST ARKANSAS NATURALS DOUBLE-A

TEXAS LEAGUE

Batting	B-T	HT	WT	DOB	AVG	vLH	vRH	G	AB	R	H	2B	3B	HR	RBI	BB	HBP	SH	SF	SO	SB	CS	SLG	OBP
Betancourt, Yuniesky	R-R	5-11	205	1-31-82	.333	.000	.417	4	15	1	5	1	0	1	4	0	0	0	0	3	0	0	.600	.333
Cain, Lorenzo	R-R	6-2	200	4-13-86	.208	.000	.294	7	24	4	5	1	0	1	1	0	0	0	0	6	0	0	.375	.208
Colon, Christian	R-R	6-1	180	5-14-89	.289	.338	.272	73	273	33	79	9	2	5	27	31	2	7	2	27	12	6	.392	.364
Duncan, Eric	L-R	6-3	210	12-7-84	.267	.138	.291	52	187	21	50	6	2	4	24	8	2	2	1	45	3	1	.385	.303
Espinal, Yowill	R-R	6-0	170	4-1-91	.158	.200	.143	7	19	1	3	0	0	0	2	0	0	0	6	2	0	.158	.238
Evans, Terry	R-R	6-4	210	1-19-82	.190	.333	.133	6	21	1	4	3	0	0	1	3	0	0	1	7	0	0	.333	.280
Fletcher, Brian	R-R	6-0	190	10-26-88	.256	.293	.249	65	254	32	65	11	2	10	34	15	9	0	2	96	6	3	.433	.318
Jenkins, Ryan	R-R	6-2	215	1-26-87	.240	.276	.230	43	129	10	31	9	0	0	13	6	0	1	0	28	0	0	.310	.274
Kendall, Jason	R-R	6-0	190	6-26-74	.333	1.000	.000	2	3	1	1	0	0	0	0	0	0	0	0	0	0	0	.333	.333
Kouzmanoff, Kevin	R-R	6-1	210	7-25-81	.300	.450	.270	34	120	10	36	10	0	2	15	4	1	0	2	19	1	0	.433	.323
Liberto, Michael	R-R	5-7	170	6-21-88	.238	.176	.250	39	101	14	24	2	0	0	12	2	0	0	2	29	1	2	.257	.319
Lisson, Mario	R-R	6-2	220	5-31-84	.247	.299	.234	116	376	40	93	24	2	11	52	45	8	3	3	83	20	4	.410	.338
McClure, Alex	B-R	6-0	185	6-16-89	.212	.286	.200	61	193	14	41	5	2	1	9	7	3	6	1	60	6	6	.275	.250
Merrifield, Whit	R-R	6-1	175	1-24-89	.260	.238	.267	24	96	12	25	2	1	1	8	8	0	1	1	19	3	2	.333	.314
Mertins, Kurt	R-R	5-10	188	4-22-86	.205	.258	.167	25	73	6	15	2	0	0	4	5	3	1	2	10	1	2	.233	.277
Myers, Wil	R-R	6-3	205	12-10-90	.343	.362	.333	35	134	32	46	11	1	13	30	16	1	0	1	42	4	1	.731	.414
Navarro, Rey	B-R	5-10	175	12-22-89	.250	.233	.255	109	400	51	100	14	3	3	39	30	4	9	6	41	9	4	.323	.305
Orlando, Paulo	R-R	6-2	210	11-1-85	.279	.190	.301	116	420	54	117	18	2	6	40	30	4	3	5	57	21	6	.374	.329
Pina, Manny	R-R	6-0	215	6-5-87	.260	.300	.252	43	131	9	34	3	0	5	20	24	5	0	2	30	0	0	.397	.389
Prades, Yem	R-R	6-2	194	3-8-88	.269	.290	.263	118	495	71	133	30	3	8	44	11	4	8	4	114	14	7	.390	.288
Rodriguez, Julio	R-R	6-1	225	8-3-89	.234	.289	.221	67	201	20	47	9	0	1	17	7	5	6	1	31	0	0	.294	.276
Schoop, Sharlon	R-R	6-2	190	4-15-87	.267	.282	.262	50	165	18	44	7	0	7	19	7	2	1	1	41	1	1	.436	.341
Testa, Carlo	L-L	6-3	218	12-16-86	.245	.261	.241	113	364	51	89	16	4	15	54	40	3	3	5	109	12	4	.434	.320
Theriot, Ben	L-R	6-1	190	12-8-87	.261	.200	.278	8	23	1	6	0	0	0	3	2	0	1	1	8	0	0	.261	.308
Van Stratten, Nick	R-R	6-1	185	5-22-85	.284	.174	.306	44	134	12	38	6	2	0	14	4	4	5	0	18	3	1	.358	.324
Whittleman, John	L-R	6-2	195	2-11-87	.220	.260	.207	93	305	45	67	18	1	15	44	67	1	0	3	109	1	1	.433	.359

Pitching	B-T	HT	WT	DOB	W	L	ERA	G	GS	CG	SV	IP	H	R	ER	HR	BB	SO	AVG	vLH	vRH	K/9	BB/9
Arguelles, Noel	L-L	6-3	225	1-12-90	4	14	6.41	25	25	0	0	119	146	95	85	12	66	59	.307	.349	.295	4.45	4.98
Baumann, Buddy	L-L	5-10	175	12-9-87	3	2	4.12	32	0	0	2	59	47	31	27	7	33	58	.220	.208	.225	8.85	5.03
Dennick, Ryan	L-L	6-0	185	11-06-87	6	5	4.62	30	3	0	4	74	65	45	38	9	30	72	.230	.223	.234	8.76	3.65
Dobies, Andrew	L-L	6-1	180	4-20-83	0	0	5.40	2	0	0	0	5	4	3	3	1	3	4	.211	.000	.333	7.20	5.40
Dwyer, Chris	R-L	6-3	215	4-10-88	5	8	5.25	17	16	0	0	86	79	57	50	13	44	71	.242	.221	.248	7.46	4.62
Gutierrez, Juan	R-R	6-3	260	7-14-83	0	0	9.00	5	0	0	3	5	8	5	5	2	2	5	.348	.333	.364	9.00	3.60
Hardy, Blaine	L-L	6-2	220	3-14-87	1	1	2.61	10	0	0	3	21	17	8	6	3	9	13	.230	.167	.260	5.66	3.92
Holland, Greg	R-R	5-10	195	11-20-85	0	1	0.00	2	2	0	0	2	1	1	0	0	0	3	.143	.000	.250	13.50	0.00
Hollingsworth, Ethan	R-R	6-2	200	5-4-87	3	8	4.17	23	6	0	2	73	80	37	34	6	20	48	.285	.284	.285	5.89	2.45
Jeffress, Jeremy	R-R	6-0	195	9-21-87	0	0	0.00	1	0	0	1	1	0	0	0	0	1	3	.000		.000	20.25	6.75
Keating, Patrick	R-R	6-0	200	6-9-87	2	2	4.79	32	0	0	9	41	40	30	22	7	18	39	.247	.180	.277	8.49	3.92
Keck, Jon	L-L	6-6	215	6-18-88	2	2	4.04	28	0	0	0	42	38	21	19	2	27	42	.252	.250	.253	8.93	5.74
Lafferty, Brendan	L-L	6-3	180	5-27-86	1	1	4.77	43	0	0	1	60	55	36	32	9	40	71	.240	.143	.297	10.59	5.97
Marimon, Sugar Ray	R-R	6-1	168	9-30-88	3	6	4.59	12	12	0	0	67	66	34	34	9	29	36	.264	.272	.259	4.86	3.92
Mariot, Michael	R-R	6-0	190	10-20-88	6	3	3.40	31	14	0	1	114	111	48	43	12	30	81	.258	.271	.249	6.41	2.38
Marks, Justin	L-L	6-3	195	1-12-88	3	5	3.80	17	17	0	0	85	79	39	36	8	38	73	.250	.262	.246	7.70	4.01
Melville, Tim	R-R	6-5	210	10-9-89	2	1	7.71	6	5	0	0	23	27	22	20	4	15	19	.293	.311	.277	7.33	5.79
Montgomery, Mike	L-L	6-4	200	7-1-89	2	6	6.67	10	10	0	0	58	69	44	43	12	21	44	.299	.370	.266	6.83	3.26
Odorizzi, Jake	R-R	6-2	185	3-27-90	4	2	3.32	7	7	0	0	38	27	15	14	2	10	47	.191	.204	.184	11.13	2.37
Paukovits, Bryan	R-R	6-7	240	6-29-87	2	0	5.01	29	0	0	0	56	67	38	31	4	27	45	.302	.318	.295	7.28	4.37
Paulino, Felipe	R-R	6-2	270	10-5-83	1	0	4.05	3	3	0	0	13	12	6	6	3	14	16	.231	.316	.182	9.45	2.70
Pimentel, Elisaul	R-R	6-2	170	7-10-88	2	5	6.17	17	7	0	0	54	64	40	37	7	21	40	.302	.357	.275	6.67	3.50
Rogers, Nick	R-R	6-2	225	10-2-87	0	2	10.24	10	0	0	0	10	10	11	11	1	16	8	.278	.167	.333	7.45	14.90
Runion, Sam	R-R	6-4	220	11-9-88	1	0	2.30	10	0	0	3	16	13	4	4	0	4	11	.241	.130	.323	6.32	2.30
Sexton, Tim	R-R	6-6	185	6-10-87	1	0	2.84	4	0	0	0	6	8	3	2	0	2	5	.308	.250	.333	7.11	2.84
2-team total (19 Tulsa)					4	1	4.78	23	0	0	0	32	33	19	17	3	7	33	—	—	—	9.28	1.97
Sulbaran, Juan Carlos	R-R	6-2	220	11-9-89	0	4	7.62	6	6	0	0	26	33	25	22	7	22	24	.295	.360	.242	8.31	7.62
Ventura, Yordano	R-R	5-11	140	6-3-91	1	2	4.60	6	6	0	0	29	23	16	15	1	13	25	.221	.200	.241	7.67	3.99
Volz, Kendal	R-R	6-5	225	12-2-87	3	1	2.19	10	0	0	6	25	16	7	6	0	11	16	.188	.182	.190	5.84	4.01

Fielding

Catcher	PCT	G	PO	A	E	DP	PB
Jenkins	.997	41	283	21	1	3	1
Kendall	.889	2	7	1	1	0	0
Pina	.993	37	235	43	2	1	2
Rodriguez	.977	65	374	51	10	9	14
Theriot	.971	8	66	2	2	1	0

First Base	PCT	G	PO	A	E	DP
Duncan	.929	4	26	0	2	0
Kouzmanoff	1.000	6	54	1	0	8
Lisson	.990	63	485	32	5	52
Schoop	1.000	19	124	4	0	10
Whittleman	.988	62	480	24	6	48

Second Base	PCT	G	PO	A	E	DP
Betancourt	1.000	2	0	8	0	1
Colon	1.000	17	41	47	0	14
Espinal	1.000	1	1	0	0	0
Liberto	1.000	6	11	9	0	1
Lisson	1.000	5	7	15	0	3

	PCT	G	PO	A	E	DP
McClure	1.000	1	3	4	0	2
Merrifield	.980	24	37	62	2	16
Mertins	.929	3	4	9	1	1
Navarro	.975	76	157	198	9	54
Schoop	.982	14	25	29	1	4

Third Base	PCT	G	PO	A	E	DP
Duncan	.969	29	14	49	2	6
Espinal	.923	4	2	10	1	1
Kouzmanoff	1.000	5	1	16	0	3
Liberto	.985	26	27	37	1	6
Lisson	.924	45	31	102	11	19
Mertins	.947	18	5	31	2	2
Myers	1.000	2	0	1	0	1
Navarro	1.000	12	11	29	0	4
Schoop	.958	8	4	19	1	3

Shortstop	PCT	G	PO	A	E	DP
Colon	.926	54	66	148	17	23
Espinal	.900	2	2	7	1	0

	PCT	G	PO	A	E	DP
Liberto	.833	3	1	4	1	1
McClure	.976	60	78	161	6	37
Navarro	.901	23	24	58	9	11
Schoop	.935	6	12	17	2	2

Outfield	PCT	G	PO	A	E	DP
Cain	1.000	5	10	0	0	0
Evans	1.000	4	5	0	0	0
Fletcher	.970	49	63	1	2	0
Lisson	1.000	4	10	0	0	0
Mertins	—	1	0	0	0	0
Myers	1.000	33	91	4	0	1
Orlando	.983	103	215	10	4	2
Prades	.989	114	275	5	3	1
Schoop	.500	1	2	0	2	0
Testa	.986	78	137	5	2	2
Van Stratten	.976	42	71	9	2	4

WILMINGTON BLUE ROCKS   HIGH CLASS A

CAROLINA LEAGUE

Batting	B-T	HT	WT	DOB	AVG	vLH	vRH	G	AB	R	H	2B	3B	HR	RBI	BB	HBP	SH	SF	SO	SB	CS	SLG	OBP
Adams, Lane	R-R	6-2	198	11-13-89	.240	.294	.222	68	262	37	63	10	1	6	25	21	2	0	0	64	8	4	.355	.302
Beltre, Geulin	B-R	6-0	185	10-27-90	.243	.272	.233	117	412	40	100	14	5	5	37	32	4	12	1	98	16	12	.337	.303
Bonilla, Jose	R-R	5-10	188	8-4-88	.210	.277	.183	53	167	18	35	3	1	3	18	28	3	1	1	51	3	0	.293	.332
Calixte, Orlando	R-R	5-11	160	2-3-92	.281	.288	.279	63	256	38	72	17	4	4	28	15	3	2	2	65	8	3	.426	.326
Cuthbert, Cheslor	R-R	6-1	190	11-16-92	.240	.245	.238	124	475	47	114	18	0	7	59	37	2	0	3	80	6	3	.322	.296
David, Kevin	R-R	6-1	205	4-10-88	.251	.300	.234	58	187	24	47	9	1	3	23	11	5	1	3	48	2	0	.358	.306
Eibner, Brett	R-R	6-3	195	12-2-88	.196	.210	.192	120	423	60	83	26	5	15	53	57	5	1	0	165	5	2	.388	.299
Elder, Chris	L-R	5-11	205	7-5-88	.231	.000	.273	4	13	0	3	0	1	0	3	1	0	0	0	3	0	0	.385	.286
Fields, Matt	R-R	6-5	235	7-8-85	.281	.322	.268	67	253	41	71	10	2	17	41	32	3	0	1	94	3	1	.538	.367
Fletcher, Brian	R-R	6-0	190	10-26-88	.289	.310	.282	67	246	27	71	15	0	5	25	19	6	0	1	51	5	2	.411	.353
Franco, Angel	R-R	5-10	155	5-23-90	.266	.239	.272	106	357	40	95	16	3	3	35	33	2	18	0	45	10	4	.353	.332
Graterol, Juan	R-R	6-1	170	2-14-89	.301	.311	.298	61	196	26	59	12	0	2	18	7	4	4	0	24	0	2	.393	.338
Hernandez, Roman	R-R	6-0	195	1-9-88	.223	.315	.186	74	256	31	57	10	1	0	15	19	2	4	1	55	1	7	.270	.281
Liberto, Michael	R-R	5-7	170	6-21-88	.286	.200	.333	6	14	1	4	0	0	0	2	0	0	0	1	0	1	0	.286	.375
McClure, Alex	B-R	6-0	185	6-16-89	.222	.229	.219	58	194	15	43	5	0	0	19	15	3	4	1	51	5	4	.247	.286
Merrifield, Whit	R-R	6-1	175	1-24-89	.258	.247	.261	101	380	59	98	20	3	8	36	41	4	10	5	69	25	5	.389	.333
Morales, Adrian	R-R	5-8	180	11-18-88	.000	.000	.000	1	3	0	0	0	0	0	1	0	0	0	0	1	0	0	.000	.000
Piterson, Luis	R-R	5-11	155	2-22-91	.272	.317	.255	54	147	16	40	7	0	0	13	7	2	7	4	29	9	1	.320	.306
Swab, Kenny	R-R	6-2	215	8-20-88	.094	.167	.077	10	32	2	3	1	0	0	3	1	1	0	0	12	0	0	.125	.194
Van Stratten, Nick	R-R	6-1	185	5-22-85	.366	.353	.370	21	71	14	26	4	1	1	13	5	3	0	0	8	4	0	.493	.430
Watts, Murray	L-R	6-7	270	10-9-87	.229	.182	.234	31	105	8	24	4	0	4	15	12	0	0	1	42	0	1	.400	.305

Pitching	B-T	HT	WT	DOB	W	L	ERA	G	GS	CG	SV	IP	H	R	ER	HR	BB	SO	AVG	vLH	vRH	K/9	BB/9
Adam, Jason	R-R	6-4	219	8-4-91	7	12	3.53	27	27	0	0	158	148	73	62	18	36	123	.251	.271	.240	7.01	2.05
Billo, Greg	R-R	6-4	220	7-15-90	5	4	4.35	12	10	0	0	60	55	31	29	4	20	56	.240	.276	.218	8.40	3.00
Boruff, Chase	L-R	6-2	195	7-27-88	1	8	7.48	28	4	0	4	49	65	51	41	6	21	45	.316	.317	.315	8.21	3.83
Carl, Edwin	R-R	6-0	210	8-31-88	2	2	4.00	22	0	0	2	54	53	25	24	4	14	56	.261	.257	.263	9.33	2.33
Cruz, Antonio	L-L	5-11	200	10-7-91	1	2	3.48	15	0	0	0	21	16	8	8	0	17	15	.222	.143	.241	6.53	7.40
Dennick, Ryan	L-L	6-0	185	1-10-87	2	1	4.57	6	1	0	0	22	26	11	11	2	6	17	.313	.333	.308	7.06	2.49
Ferguson, Andy	R-R	6-1	195	9-2-88	4	2	2.97	10	10	0	0	64	64	21	21	5	9	59	.271	.350	.231	8.34	1.27
Garrido, Santiago	R-R	6-1	195	9-29-88	3	2	3.00	9	3	0	1	24	27	8	8	1	9	21	.290	.291	.291	7.88	3.38
Graffeo, Nick	R-R	6-2	190	12-14-87	0	3	3.75	23	0	0	0	36	31	19	15	2	14	32	.225	.220	.227	8.00	3.50
Keck, Jon	L-L	6-6	215	6-18-88	2	1	1.61	11	0	0	0	22	15	4	4	1	12	15	.197	.294	.169	6.04	4.84
Marimon, Sugar Ray	R-R	6-1	168	9-30-88	4	2	2.12	14	9	0	1	68	51	16	16	5	18	60	.206	.163	.232	7.94	2.38
Melgarejo, Thomas	L-L	6-2	220	1-10-87	0	0	3.12	9	0	0	0	17	18	6	6	2	5	12	.269	.238	.283	6.23	2.60
Perez, Leondy	R-R	6-1	190	8-19-89	5	4	3.74	19	12	0	2	75	90	42	31	3	14	49	.290	.361	.252	5.91	1.69
Pimentel, Elisaul	R-R	6-2	170	7-10-88	3	3	3.00	9	8	1	0	51	39	20	17	3	15	47	.209	.281	.177	8.29	2.65
Pounders, Brooks	R-R	6-4	270	9-26-90	6	4	4.32	16	15	0	0	83	87	41	40	5	25	75	.269	.359	.227	8.10	2.70
Ridings, Matt	R-R	6-0	190	10-17-87	6	2	2.74	15	10	0	0	66	51	24	20	7	12	54	.209	.216	.206	7.40	1.64
Rogers, Nick	R-R	6-2	225	10-2-87	3	4	2.40	29	0	0	8	41	35	15	11	2	22	44	.235	.286	.210	9.58	4.79
Runion, Sam	R-R	6-4	220	11-9-88	3	1	2.36	27	0	0	6	50	54	15	13	1	12	39	.338	.250	.250	7.07	2.17
Sample, Tyler	L-R	6-7	245	6-27-89	1	9	5.84	28	15	0	0	99	104	77	64	14	53	91	.267	.276	.261	8.30	4.83
Stueve, Andrew	R-R	6-0	190	4-7-89	0	1	7.36	2	0	0	0	7	6	6	6	0	2	4	.214	.273	.176	4.91	2.45
Ventura, Yordano	R-R	5-11	140	6-3-91	3	5	3.30	16	16	0	0	76	66	32	28	7	28	98	.229	.194	.250	11.55	3.30
White, Cole	R-R	6-1	199	1-22-88	3	1	4.37	18	0	0	0	35	34	21	17	1	25	28	.266	.224	.291	7.20	6.43
Yambati, Robinson	R-R	6-3	185	1-15-91	2	1	2.16	17	0	0	5	25	22	7	6	0	10	31	.234	.214	.242	11.16	3.60

Fielding

Catcher	PCT	G	PO	A	E	DP	PB
Bonilla	.979	45	336	29	8	3	7
David	.993	55	383	47	3	5	4

	PCT	G	PO	A	E	DP	PB
Graterol	.997	35	262	28	1	1	1
Jones	.969	3	25	6	1	0	0
Swab	1.000	8	69	10	0	0	2

First Base	PCT	G	PO	A	E	DP
Fields	.990	55	454	21	5	45
Fletcher	.986	41	317	25	5	25

Graterol	.994	21	147	7	1	14
Kuebler	1.000	19	142	10	0	11
Watts	1.000	8	65	0	0	3
Second Base	**PCT**	**G**	**PO**	**A**	**E**	**DP**
Franco	.977	69	124	174	7	44
Liberto	1.000	1	3	3	0	2
Merrifield	.976	51	85	118	5	23
Piterson	.972	26	49	57	3	12
Third Base	**PCT**	**G**	**PO**	**A**	**E**	**DP**
Cuthbert	.925	120	56	192	20	19

Franco	.846	14	9	24	6	2
Kuebler	1.000	2	2	0	0	0
Morales	1.000	1	0	1	0	1
Piterson	1.000	4	7	10	0	2
Shortstop	**PCT**	**G**	**PO**	**A**	**E**	**DP**
Calixte	.924	63	66	191	21	31
Franco	.947	5	6	12	1	2
Liberto	1.000	2	1	5	0	2
McClure	.960	57	64	151	9	24
Piterson	.970	17	23	42	2	9

Outfield	**PCT**	**G**	**PO**	**A**	**E**	**DP**
Adams	.994	62	154	4	1	1
Beltre	.964	105	196	20	8	7
Eibner	.977	114	246	5	6	4
Elder	1.000	4	7	0	0	0
Fletcher	.958	16	23	0	1	0
Hernandez	.962	66	123	3	5	1
Merrifield	.978	44	86	4	2	0
Piterson	1.000	1	1	0	0	0
Van Stratten	.941	14	14	2	1	0

KANE COUNTY COUGARS
MIDWEST LEAGUE

LOW CLASS A

KANSAS CITY ROYALS

Batting	B-T	HT	WT	DOB	AVG	vLH	vRH	G	AB	R	H	2B	3B	HR	RBI	BB	HBP	SH	SF	SO	SB	CS	SLG	OBP
Adams, Lane	R-R	6-2	198	11-13-89	.298	.274	.311	67	262	40	78	13	4	5	44	21	2	2	4	48	11	1	.435	.349
Antonio, Mike	R-R	6-2	190	10-26-91	.213	.206	.217	123	464	51	99	23	2	5	64	32	4	1	10	79	6	2	.304	.265
Aparicio, Julio	R-R	6-2	175	1-4-90	.265	.292	.250	52	189	16	50	5	1	4	17	13	3	3	1	46	1	1	.365	.320
Bonifacio, Jorge	R-R	6-1	192	6-4-93	.282	.274	.285	105	412	54	116	20	6	10	61	30	4	2	0	84	6	3	.432	.336
Calixte, Orlando	R-R	5-11	160	2-3-92	.241	.266	.228	62	228	31	55	13	4	10	34	21	0	3	2	44	2	5	.465	.303
David, Kevin	R-R	6-1	205	4-10-88	.203	.286	.152	23	74	9	15	1	1	0	3	4	1	1	0	17	0	0	.243	.253
Davis, Runey	R-R	6-0	185	1-2-89	.241	.308	.188	23	58	12	14	6	0	2	10	12	0	1	1	29	2	1	.448	.366
Elder, Chris	L-R	5-11	205	7-5-88	.237	.111	.260	18	59	7	14	7	1	1	12	5	1	0	0	13	0	0	.441	.308
Escobar, Edul	R-R	5-11	185	6-2-90	.180	.188	.175	38	128	8	23	6	0	1	9	6	1	1	1	26	1	0	.250	.221
Espinal, Yowill	R-R	6-0	170	4-1-91	.281	.263	.289	21	57	9	16	0	0	0	4	7	0	3	0	17	0	2	.281	.359
Espy, Dean	R-R	6-1	210	10-30-89	.255	.245	.261	82	290	33	74	15	0	3	27	16	3	1	1	62	6	0	.338	.300
Ferguson, Tim	R-R	6-1	190	10-25-88	.283	.291	.279	112	375	47	106	18	4	5	40	35	2	3	1	50	14	9	.392	.346
Lane, Travis	R-R	6-2	215	8-10-90	.000	.000	.000	1	3	0	0	0	0	0	0	0	0	0	0	1	0	0	.000	.000
Llanos, Alex	R-R	6-1	160	9-21-90	.280	.221	.304	68	261	30	73	12	1	1	23	9	1	3	4	47	8	7	.345	.308
Lopez, Jack	R-R	5-9	165	12-16-92	.222	.256	.208	64	261	30	58	9	2	0	16	14	4	8	1	43	14	4	.272	.271
Mateo, Danny	B-R	6-1	178	8-10-91	.262	.220	.281	131	515	73	135	20	10	8	61	43	6	2	2	103	3	1	.386	.325
Moreno, Henry	R-R	6-2	162	6-6-89	.197	.164	.224	44	152	10	30	11	0	1	13	8	2	0	3	50	0	0	.289	.242
Shin, Jin-Ho	R-R	6-2	200	10-20-91	.181	.222	.164	27	94	13	17	5	0	1	8	5	0	1	0	35	1	0	.266	.222
Swab, Kenny	R-R	6-2	215	8-20-88	.231	.293	.202	58	182	20	42	9	1	2	12	17	4	2	1	42	0	0	.324	.309
Trapp, Justin	R-R	5-10	165	10-7-90	.272	.318	.248	117	467	75	127	20	9	12	50	46	13	2	2	115	24	9	.430	.352
Watts, Murray	L-R	6-7	270	10-9-87	.212	.103	.231	56	189	33	40	12	1	9	28	24	0	0	1	54	0	0	.429	.299

Pitching	B-T	HT	WT	DOB	W	L	ERA	G	GS	CG	SV	IP	H	R	ER	HR	BB	SO	AVG	vLH	vRH	K/9	BB/9
Alexander, Scott	L-L	6-2	190	7-10-89	2	3	2.55	10	6	0	0	35	34	21	10	2	16	31	.252	.205	.275	7.90	4.08
Baez, Angel	R-R	6-3	196	2-14-91	6	5	3.17	16	15	1	0	77	65	36	27	5	31	83	.220	.268	.197	9.74	3.64
Brazoban, Jose	R-R	5-9	165	5-28-93	1	1	14.54	3	0	0	0	4	5	8	7	0	5	2	.313	.143	.444	4.15	10.38
Brickhouse, Bryan	R-R	6-0	195	6-6-92	3	3	5.61	10	10	0	0	51	50	39	32	3	23	40	.249	.222	.267	7.01	4.03
Brooks, Aaron	R-R	6-4	220	4-27-90	9	12	4.98	27	27	1	0	154	191	99	85	18	26	120	.304	.317	.295	7.03	1.52
Brown, Rudy	L-L	6-4	225	6-16-88	3	0	2.95	25	1	0	1	43	43	15	14	1	11	40	.267	.300	.252	8.44	2.32
Cantrell, Eric	R-R	6-4	210	7-25-89	0	0	14.54	4	0	0	0	4	10	7	7	2	3	3	.435	.143	.563	6.23	6.23
Carl, Edwin	R-R	6-0	210	8-31-88	5	2	1.92	12	11	0	0	61	60	17	13	6	13	46	.260	.281	.246	6.79	1.92
Culver, Malcom	R-R	6-1	205	2-9-90	2	1	3.69	37	0	0	6	63	57	28	26	1	34	52	.250	.238	.257	7.39	4.83
Dooley, Gates	R-R	6-0	205	8-22-88	2	3	5.56	25	0	0	3	55	66	37	34	2	23	33	.308	.297	.314	5.40	3.76
Fassold, Cody	R-R	6-2	230	10-2-88	1	3	2.83	26	0	0	2	48	30	15	15	4	21	57	.178	.203	.164	10.76	3.97
Ferguson, Andy	R-R	6-1	195	9-2-88	0	1	1.93	2	2	0	0	9	10	4	2	0	5	7	.256	.231	.269	6.75	4.82
Garrido, Santiago	R-R	6-1	195	10-4-88	3	0	0.68	6	3	0	0	26	14	4	2	0	9	15	.156	.114	.182	5.13	3.08
Giovenco, Mike	R-R	6-6	235	1-4-88	5	3	4.34	32	2	0	2	56	52	31	27	4	38	50	.255	.316	.219	8.04	6.11
Graffeo, Nick	R-R	6-2	190	12-14-87	0	1	3.42	18	0	0	8	24	20	12	9	5	15	23	.230	.250	.222	8.75	5.70
Melville, Tim	R-R	6-5	210	10-9-89	0	1	4.50	2	2	0	0	6	7	3	3	1	3	4	.280	.250	.286	6.00	4.50
Mitchell, Jason	R-R	6-2	185	3-13-88	4	7	4.65	31	10	0	3	101	112	68	52	6	38	82	.279	.270	.284	7.33	3.40
Moen, Kellen	B-R	6-2	185	5-30-88	4	10	5.25	30	20	0	1	123	134	83	72	16	32	121	.271	.270	.272	8.83	2.34
Pounders, Brooks	R-R	6-4	270	9-26-90	3	2	3.38	12	8	0	0	51	52	32	19	2	19	57	.252	.279	.239	10.13	3.38
Ridings, Matt	R-R	6-0	180	10-17-87	4	3	2.43	21	0	0	2	37	33	17	10	0	6	39	.232	.241	.227	9.49	1.46
Smith, Kyle	R-R	6-0	170	9-10-92	4	3	2.94	13	13	0	0	67	62	26	22	3	20	87	.241	.217	.258	11.63	2.67
Stueve, Andrew	R-R	6-0	190	4-7-89	2	2	8.10	9	0	0	0	13	21	12	12	2	5	9	.362	.333	.387	6.08	3.38
Triggs, Andrew	R-R	6-4	210	3-6-89	1	1	1.70	20	0	0	4	42	31	13	8	2	9	48	.193	.250	.158	10.20	1.91
White, Cole	R-R	6-2	195	1-22-88	0	0	9.00	3	0	0	0	5	5	5	5	1	5	6	.263	.250	.273	10.80	9.00
Yambati, Robinson	R-R	6-3	185	1-15-91	2	1	3.22	16	4	0	2	45	40	21	16	1	17	33	.231	.135	.273	6.65	3.43
Zimmer, Kyle	R-R	6-3	215	9-13-91	2	3	2.43	6	6	0	0	30	34	15	8	1	8	29	.301	.273	.313	8.80	2.43

Fielding

Catcher	PCT	G	PO	A	E	DP	PB
David	.985	23	181	21	3	0	1
Escobar	.974	38	279	25	8	0	6
Lane	1.000	1	9	0	0	0	0
Shin	.980	27	202	38	5	3	5
Swab	.988	58	438	61	6	5	14
First Base	**PCT**	**G**	**PO**	**A**	**E**	**DP**	
Espy	.990	79	601	67	7	41	
Moreno	.992	30	244	17	2	18	

Swab	1.000	1	2	0	0	0
Watts	.985	35	317	9	5	26
Second Base	**PCT**	**G**	**PO**	**A**	**E**	**DP**
Espinal	.950	6	5	14	1	1
Espy	1.000	1	0	1	0	0
Mateo	.912	40	95	103	19	26
Trapp	.947	94	142	255	22	40
Third Base	**PCT**	**G**	**PO**	**A**	**E**	**DP**
Antonio	.876	89	44	160	29	19

Bonifacio	1.000	1	1	2	0	1
Espinal	1.000	2	0	5	0	0
Mateo	.882	51	39	66	14	7
Shortstop	**PCT**	**G**	**PO**	**A**	**E**	**DP**
Antonio	.929	7	10	16	2	3
Calixte	.910	60	81	172	25	29
Espinal	.932	12	15	26	3	2
Lopez	.945	64	89	187	16	28

Outfield	PCT	G	PO	A	E	DP
Adams	.973	64	140	3	4	0
Antonio	.500	1	1	0	1	0
Aparicio	.963	48	99	4	4	0

	PCT	G	PO	A	E	DP
Bonifacio	.978	96	168	11	4	2
Davis	1.000	21	41	3	0	0
Elder	.962	17	25	0	1	0
Ferguson	.986	110	205	7	3	1

	PCT	G	PO	A	E	DP
Llanos	.964	67	128	6	5	1
Trapp	1.000	1	0	2	0	0

BURLINGTON ROYALS   ROOKIE
APPALACHIAN LEAGUE

Batting	B-T	HT	WT	DOB	AVG	vLH	vRH	G	AB	R	H	2B	3B	HR	RBI	BB	HBP	SH	SF	SO	SB	CS	SLG	OBP
Arteaga, Humberto	R-R	6-1	160	1-23-94	.274	.326	.261	58	234	40	64	13	3	2	29	9	6	10	3	31	7	3	.380	.313
Conner, Cameron	L-L	6-2	185	1-16-88	.200	.200	.200	7	10	4	2	1	0	0	2	1	1	0	0	5	1	1	.300	.333
Diekroeger, Kenny	R-R	6-2	190	11-5-90	.208	.200	.210	52	202	21	42	6	1	8	33	18	1	0	1	60	5	0	.366	.275
Elder, Chris	L-R	5-11	205	7-5-88	.263	.308	.254	26	80	13	21	5	2	1	7	15	2	0	0	10	1	0	.413	.392
Ford, Fred	R-R	6-5	200	4-10-92	.248	.378	.213	62	214	38	53	11	1	13	35	36	3	0	1	83	5	5	.491	.362
Gallagher, Cameron	R-R	6-3	210	12-6-92	.276	.300	.271	36	127	13	35	10	0	3	15	10	1	0	1	16	1	3	.425	.331
Gore, Terrance	R-R	5-7	165	6-8-91	.256	.237	.259	61	227	50	58	4	2	0	13	36	9	4	0	52	36	2	.291	.379
Hudak, Alex	L-R	5-11	200	4-7-90	.344	.571	.315	19	61	9	21	8	0	1	7	7	2	0	0	12	1	2	.525	.429
Leonard, Patrick	R-R	6-4	225	10-20-92	.251	.224	.258	62	235	37	59	9	3	14	46	30	2	0	1	55	6	2	.494	.340
Maggi, Beau	L-R	6-1	208	11-11-90	.202	.182	.207	41	109	16	22	4	2	0	8	24	1	0	0	33	3	1	.275	.351
Marquez, Alex	R-R	5-11	190	12-10-92	.143	.200	.125	21	42	1	6	0	0	0	4	3	3	2	1	7	0	0	.143	.245
Morales, Adrian	R-R	5-8	180	11-18-88	.170	.320	.116	31	94	11	16	3	0	1	8	7	3	0	1	14	5	1	.234	.248
Moreno, Henry	R-R	6-2	162	6-6-89	.375	.250	.429	14	40	6	15	4	0	3	9	3	2	0	0	11	0	0	.700	.444
Rodriguez, Jose	B-R	5-8	165	11-5-92	.218	.278	.203	35	87	6	19	3	2	0	7	7	1	4	0	13	3	1	.299	.284
Starling, Bubba	R-R	6-4	180	8-3-92	.275	.250	.282	53	200	35	55	8	2	10	33	28	3	0	1	70	10	1	.485	.371
Threlkeld, Mark	R-R	6-3	205	5-2-90	.283	.333	.271	62	219	37	62	18	3	10	40	15	3	0	3	40	1	2	.530	.333

Pitching	B-T	HT	WT	DOB	W	L	ERA	G	GS	CG	SV	IP	H	R	ER	HR	BB	SO	AVG	vLH	vRH	K/9	BB/9
Bangs, Parker	R-R	6-4	210	12-22-87	0	1	30.38	2	0	0	0	3	4	9	9	1	5	1	.400	.500	.375	3.38	16.88
Binford, Christian	R-R	6-7	215	12-20-92	2	3	2.03	8	8	0	0	40	40	12	9	1	4	31	.252	.250	.252	6.98	0.90
Caramo, Yender	R-R	6-0	175	8-25-91	5	3	3.30	13	11	0	0	71	72	30	26	5	5	47	.260	.208	.278	5.96	0.63
Conroy, Patrick	L-L	6-4	218	1-14-92	5	2	4.13	13	11	0	1	61	59	31	28	6	22	43	.254	.333	.243	6.34	3.25
Edelen, Brian	R-R	6-2	200	3-7-88	0	0	7.20	5	0	0	0	5	6	5	4	0	4	4	.316	.000	.462	7.20	7.20
Fairchild, Austin	R-L	6-0	195	3-25-94	0	0	22.50	3	1	0	0	2	2	5	5	1	5	2	.250	.000	.286	9.00	22.50
Hernandez, Danny	R-R	6-1	180	4-14-89	5	2	4.15	12	12	0	0	65	64	32	30	8	7	61	.258	.273	.251	8.45	0.97
Junis, Jake	R-R	6-3	210	9-16-92	2	2	4.15	7	6	0	0	35	39	20	16	2	5	22	.283	.250	.300	5.71	1.30
Karlik, Joe	R-R	6-3	190	4-13-89	0	0	3.38	5	0	0	0	8	7	3	3	1	2	3	.241	.182	.278	3.38	2.25
Mack, Tyler	R-R	6-4	205	9-3-90	2	0	2.08	4	2	0	0	13	4	3	3	2	6	10	.093	.067	.107	6.92	4.15
Martinez, Josiel	L-L	5-10	160	11-9-91	1	3	2.74	12	1	0	1	23	28	9	7	0	7	18	.311	.286	.316	7.04	2.74
Morales, Julio	R-R	6-1	172	11-22-88	1	1	3.75	13	1	0	0	24	19	10	10	2	14	20	.211	.267	.183	7.50	5.25
Peterson, Mark	R-R	6-0	190	9-7-90	6	0	1.16	18	0	0	0	31	20	7	4	2	5	19	.187	.158	.193	5.52	1.45
Rassi, Lincoln	R-R	6-1	180	3-21-90	1	1	7.71	13	0	0	2	23	21	20	20	4	13	30	.247	.200	.267	11.57	5.01
Rodgers, Colin	L-L	6-0	180	12-2-93	3	1	2.05	11	11	0	0	48	40	19	11	2	16	25	.226	.192	.232	4.66	2.98
Rodriguez, Freddy	R-R	6-3	188	12-1-90	2	2	5.80	15	2	0	0	36	47	26	23	0	11	21	.318	.220	.355	5.30	2.78
Rodriguez, Jose	R-R	6-2	192	9-18-92	0	0	0.00	1	0	0	0	2	0	1	0	0	1	2	.000	.000	.000	9.00	4.50
Stueve, Andrew	R-R	6-0	190	4-7-89	0	1	6.00	6	0	0	0	12	16	8	8	2	1	12	.308	.357	.289	9.00	0.75
Stumpf, Daniel	L-L	6-2	200	1-4-91	2	1	1.55	19	0	0	5	29	20	6	5	1	8	34	.190	.227	.181	10.55	2.48
Tomchick, Ben	R-R	6-6	205	12-17-89	1	1	3.21	8	0	0	0	14	11	6	5	0	6	14	.212	.000	.262	9.00	3.86
Walter, John	R-R	6-5	225	5-20-91	3	1	2.63	21	0	0	9	27	17	10	8	1	7	35	.177	.167	.181	11.52	2.30

Fielding

Catcher	PCT	G	PO	A	E	DP	PB
Gallagher	.991	30	191	19	2	1	2
Maggi	.988	29	149	12	2	0	4
Marquez	.983	18	100	17	2	2	4

First Base	PCT	G	PO	A	E	DP
Marquez	1.000	2	4	2	0	0
Morales	1.000	1	11	1	0	1
Moreno	1.000	9	55	2	0	3
Rodriguez	1.000	1	9	0	0	0
Threlkeld	.993	58	527	30	4	46

Second Base	PCT	G	PO	A	E	DP
Diekroeger	.971	36	50	82	4	20
Morales	.936	9	20	24	3	6
Rodriguez	.945	22	36	50	5	17
Threlkeld	1.000	1	3	1	0	0

Third Base	PCT	G	PO	A	E	DP
Leonard	.929	55	37	145	14	11
Morales	.978	12	12	33	1	3
Threlkeld	—	1	0	0	0	0

Shortstop	PCT	G	PO	A	E	DP
Arteaga	.965	58	54	192	9	30
Diekroeger	.956	10	13	30	2	6

Outfield	PCT	G	PO	A	E	DP
Conner	1.000	3	5	0	0	0
Elder	1.000	19	21	1	0	0
Ford	.964	53	100	6	4	2
Gore	.960	61	142	2	6	0
Hudak	1.000	11	17	1	0	0
Rodriguez	1.000	2	2	0	0	0
Starling	.972	53	132	6	4	3

AZL ROYALS   ROOKIE
ARIZONA LEAGUE

Batting	B-T	HT	WT	DOB	AVG	vLH	vRH	G	AB	R	H	2B	3B	HR	RBI	BB	HBP	SH	SF	SO	SB	CS	SLG	OBP
Allen, Jerrell	R-R	6-2	180	9-6-92	.211	.188	.219	36	128	16	27	7	2	1	13	16	4	2	0	31	4	3	.320	.318
Brown, Bobby	L-R	6-3	200	10-14-89	.250	.267	.246	22	72	12	18	3	0	0	6	2	0	1		21	3	0	.292	.321
Colon, Christian	R-R	6-1	180	5-14-89	.364	.375	.357	7	22	6	8	3	0	0	4	4	1	0	0	0	1	1	.500	.481
Donato, Mark	L-L	6-2	225	11-18-91	.253	.206	.267	38	154	24	39	13	3	3	27	11	1	0	1	34	0	0	.435	.305
Escalera-Maldonado, Alfredo	R-R	5-8	180	2-17-95	.303	.333	.293	30	119	26	36	3	2	0	11	5	3	0	1	29	2	1	.361	.344
Estades, Ariel	L-R	5-11	150	4-27-94	.250	.316	.233	29	92	18	23	2	2	0	10	11	0	1	0	31	8	2	.315	.330
Gonzalez, Pedro	R-R	6-2	162	1-28-92	.283	.222	.302	33	113	12	32	10	2	2	21	8	2	0	3	19	0	0	.460	.333
Goris, Diego	R-R	6-2	165	12-8-90	.425	.421	.426	18	80	14	34	6	3	3	19	2	2	0	2	10	0	0	.688	.442
Harper, Lance	B-R	6-1	205	7-17-90	.318	.400	.304	22	66	13	21	2	0	0	6	7	1	0	0	20	1	2	.348	.392

	B-T	HT	WT	DOB	AVG	vLH	vRH	G	AB	R	H	2B	3B	HR	RBI	BB	HBP	SH	SF	SO	SB	CS	SLG	OBP
Holloway, Marsalis	R-R	5-10	160	9-18-92	.118	.222	.080	13	34	3	4	0	0	0	1	5	0	1	0	13	3	0	.118	.231
Hudak, Alex	L-R	5-11	200	4-7-90	.188	.250	.175	14	48	4	9	5	0	0	4	4	0	0	1	19	0	0	.292	.245
Johnson, Chad	R-R	6-1	175	5-31-94	.260	.167	.290	38	123	29	32	10	1	1	23	26	0	0	2	34	0	0	.382	.384
Meade, Ryan	R-R	6-3	215	6-25-89	.182	.250	.143	3	11	2	2	2	0	0	1	2	0	0	0	2	0	0	.364	.308
Patino, Alfredo	R-R	6-0	175	5-18-93	.209	.160	.224	34	110	23	23	1	0	0	6	12	2	1	0	27	6	3	.218	.298
Pina, Manny	R-R	6-0	215	6-5-87	.462	.500	.455	6	13	3	6	2	0	0	5	6	1	0	1	2	0	0	.615	.619
Ramos, Mauricio	R-R	6-1	160	2-2-92	.283	.375	.252	48	191	20	54	9	3	2	31	13	2	0	2	35	0	1	.393	.332
Rivera, Alexis	L-L	6-2	225	6-17-94	.341	.295	.356	48	176	35	60	7	4	3	34	23	2	0	5	29	9	3	.477	.413
Torres, Ramon	R-R	5-10	155	1-22-93	.316	.265	.333	49	193	47	61	5	4	3	27	23	0	9	2	25	17	8	.430	.385
Urena, Lewis	R-R	5-8	145	5-6-91	.176	.154	.180	24	74	6	13	2	0	0	6	8	0	3	0	11	3	0	.203	.256
Villegas, Luis	R-R	5-10	170	12-2-92	.232	.167	.243	29	82	15	19	4	1	1	7	13	4	0	2	15	1	1	.341	.356

Pitching	B-T	HT	WT	DOB	W	L	ERA	G	GS	CG	SV	IP	H	R	ER	HR	BB	SO	AVG	vLH	vRH	K/9	BB/9
Alexander, Scott	L-L	6-2	190	7-10-89	0	1	0.00	1	1	0	0	0	0	1	0	0	0	0	.000	.000	.000	0.00	0.00
Almonte, Miguel	R-R	6-2	160	4-4-93	2	1	2.33	6	2	0	0	27	22	13	7	0	5	28	.212	.235	.200	9.33	1.67
Brazoban, Jose	R-R	5-9	165	5-28-93	1	3	3.38	13	0	0	3	16	18	11	6	0	4	19	.273	.280	.268	10.69	2.25
Castillo, Darwin	R-R	6-4	180	10-27-92	2	0	4.76	12	0	0	2	23	26	22	12	1	16	23	.286	.333	.259	9.13	6.35
Cruz, Antonio	L-L	5-11	200	10-7-91	0	1	5.79	3	0	0	0	5	3	3	3	0	1	7	.176	.250	.154	13.50	1.93
Deshazier, Torey	R-R	6-0	160	9-16-93	1	3	7.86	13	2	0	0	34	41	34	30	2	21	43	.291	.333	.264	11.27	5.50
Durden, Andrew	R-R	6-0	200	11-27-88	0	0	7.50	6	0	0	2	6	9	5	5	1	1	8	.346	.364	.333	12.00	1.50
Fairchild, Austin	R-L	6-0	195	3-25-94	0	2	48.60	3	2	0	0	2	2	11	9	0	11	3	.333	.000	.500	16.20	59.40
Garrido, Santiago	R-R	6-1	195	10-4-89	0	0	0.00	2	0	0	0	2	3	0	0	0	0	1	.375	.333	.400	5.40	0.00
Giovenco, Mike	R-R	6-6	235	1-4-88	0	1	0.00	3	1	0	0	3	3	2	0	0	3	1	.273	.250	.286	3.00	9.00
Goudeau, Ashton	R-R	6-6	205	7-23-92	1	1	3.97	13	0	0	1	34	31	18	15	1	16	43	.240	.214	.260	11.38	4.24
Guevara, Cruz	L-L	6-0	155	5-29-94	1	0	6.75	14	0	0	1	19	23	18	14	0	15	21	.295	.241	.327	10.13	7.23
Gutierrez, Juan	R-R	6-3	260	7-14-83	0	1	17.36	4	4	0	0	5	11	10	9	2	1	6	.458	.417	.500	11.57	1.93
Halley, Shane	B-R	6-1	200	9-28-89	0	1	13.50	2	1	0	0	1	3	3	2	0	0	1	.429	1.000	.200	6.75	0.00
Haynes, Hunter	L-L	6-1	175	2-12-94	3	3	7.82	14	4	0	0	36	50	41	31	5	24	34	.321	.306	.327	8.58	6.06
Karlik, Joe	R-R	6-3	190	4-13-89	0	0	0.00	4	0	0	0	3	1	0	0	0	2	2	.125	.000	.200	6.75	6.75
Keating, Patrick	R-R	6-0	220	6-9-87	0	0	1.93	3	1	0	0	5	3	1	1	0	0	8	.176	.250	.111	15.43	0.00
Lamb, John	L-L	6-4	200	7-10-90	0	0	6.35	4	4	0	0	6	6	4	4	0	2	6	.250	.333	.200	9.53	3.18
Lopez, Joe	R-R	5-10	180	3-20-90	0	1	15.00	3	0	0	0	3	7	7	5	0	4	3	.438	.250	.625	9.00	12.00
Lovvorn, Zach	R-R	6-0	185	5-26-94	0	3	8.34	14	8	0	0	50	64	50	46	3	27	39	.312	.400	.267	7.07	4.89
Lumpkins, Stephen	R-L	6-8	225	4-16-90	0	0	19.64	5	0	0	0	4	7	8	8	0	11	2	.438	.143	.667	4.91	27.00
Marks, Justin	L-L	6-3	195	1-12-88	0	0	1.80	2	1	0	0	5	4	1	1	0	3	8	.211	.200	.214	14.40	5.40
Melville, Tim	R-R	6-5	210	10-9-89	0	0	0.00	2	2	0	0	5	2	1	0	0	1	7	.118	.000	.286	12.60	1.80
Newberry, Jake	R-R	6-2	195	11-20-94	1	0	2.81	11	0	0	0	16	13	6	5	1	8	12	.232	.321	.143	6.75	4.50
Nina, Aroni	R-R	6-4	178	4-9-90	3	2	5.14	9	4	0	0	35	33	23	20	3	21	43	.243	.261	.224	11.06	5.40
Perez, Leondy	R-R	6-1	190	8-19-89	0	0	1.00	3	3	0	0	9	1	1	1	0	3	9	.212	.111	.333	9.00	1.00
Rodriguez, Jose	R-R	6-2	192	9-18-92	0	0	4.15	9	0	0	0	13	14	9	6	1	10	4	.269	.269	.269	2.77	6.92
Sons, Dylan	L-L	6-3	176	7-15-93	3	3	6.14	14	6	0	1	44	58	36	30	3	28	28	.320	.391	.296	5.73	5.73
Stephenson, Niklas	R-R	6-2	195	11-16-93	0	0	5.63	7	0	0	0	8	11	6	5	1	3	3	.333	.400	.304	3.38	3.38
Tenuta, Matt	L-L	6-4	208	12-16-93	3	5	4.58	13	1	0	1	39	51	29	20	1	21	30	.325	.409	.292	6.86	4.81
Ventura, Yordano	R-R	5-11	140	6-3-91	0	0	2.45	1	1	0	0	4	3	1	1	0	1	7	.214	.500	.100	17.18	2.45
White, Cole	R-R	6-2	195	1-22-88	1	0	0.00	2	1	0	0	2	0	0	0	0	0	4	.000	.000	.000	18.00	0.00
Witt, Christian	R-R	6-4	245	10-11-88	0	0	9.64	3	0	0	0	5	15	18	5	1	4	4	.484	.400	.563	7.71	7.71
Zimmer, Kyle	R-R	6-3	215	9-13-91	1	0	0.90	3	3	0	0	10	5	1	1	0	0	13	.152	.214	.105	11.70	0.00

Fielding

Catcher	PCT	G	PO	A	E	DP	PB
Gonzalez	.973	17	124	19	4	2	3
Johnson	.995	24	166	23	1	1	9
Pina	.975	6	34	5	1	0	1
Villegas	.980	17	131	14	3	0	4

First Base	PCT	G	PO	A	E	DP
Brown	.976	20	154	8	4	11
Donato	.991	38	330	18	3	42
Meade	1.000	2	16	0	0	0

Second Base	PCT	G	PO	A	E	DP
Colon	.933	3	5	9	1	3

Goris	.917	9	14	41	5	9
Patino	.946	29	47	75	7	15
Urena	.948	18	28	45	4	13

Third Base	PCT	G	PO	A	E	DP
Goris	.950	7	8	11	1	1
Patino	1.000	5	2	6	0	1
Ramos	.905	48	26	88	12	8

Shortstop	PCT	G	PO	A	E	DP
Colon	1.000	2	0	8	0	1
Goris	.500	1	0	1	1	0
Torres	.910	49	69	133	20	33

	PCT	G	PO	A	E	DP
Urena	.900	6	7	11	2	3

Outfield	PCT	G	PO	A	E	DP
Allen	.925	36	45	4	4	3
Brown	1.000	2	5	0	0	0
Escalera-Maldonado	.925	29	48	1	4	0
Estades	.860	29	35	2	6	0
Harper	.857	18	17	1	3	0
Holloway	1.000	12	13	1	0	1
Hudak	.968	13	29	1	1	0
Rivera	.921	44	54	4	5	1

IDAHO FALLS CHUKARS   ROOKIE

PIONEER LEAGUE

Batting	B-T	HT	WT	DOB	AVG	vLH	vRH	G	AB	R	H	2B	3B	HR	RBI	BB	HBP	SH	SF	SO	SB	CS	SLG	OBP
Alcantara, Ysmelin	R-R	6-2	180	5-13-90	.208	.235	.198	33	120	14	25	4	2	2	14	9	2	2	0	33	0	1	.325	.275
Aparicio, Julio	R-R	6-2	175	1-4-90	.583	1.000	.444	3	12	2	7	1	0	0	6	1	1	0	0	0	0	0	.667	.643
Bates, Sam	L-R	6-4	215	2-15-90	.222	.000	.250	5	18	3	4	1	0	1	3	0	0	0	0	3	0	0	.444	.222
Bello, Rainier	B-R	5-10	165	6-1-92	.255	.255	.255	54	212	25	54	17	2	7	37	5	4	0	1	51	0	2	.453	.284
Blanco, Jerico	R-R	6-1	160	5-25-92	.274	.281	.272	39	113	18	31	6	3	0	15	7	3	1	0	23	0	1	.381	.333
Chapman, Ethan	L-R	6-0	180	1-5-90	.313	.403	.288	67	281	58	88	9	9	1	29	32	1	2	2	43	25	7	.420	.383
Cuckovich, Nicholas	R-R	6-2	200	10-8-91	.280	.338	.260	66	246	44	69	12	8	3	43	33	6	1	2	68	9	2	.431	.376
DelGuidice, Nick	R-R	5-11	180	6-1-89	.287	.378	.256	47	174	29	50	15	2	3	22	15	2	1	1	21	0	0	.448	.349
Garcia, Carlos	R-R	6-0	176	3-18-92	.273	.383	.228	59	209	42	57	8	0	2	20	23	2	5	2	31	10	7	.340	.347
Goris, Diego	R-R	6-2	165	12-8-90	.286	.271	.292	40	154	27	44	8	1	10	32	2	1	2	1	22	0	0	.545	.297

KANSAS CITY ROYALS

Name	B-T	HT	WT	DOB	AVG	vLH	vRH	G	AB	R	H	2B	3B	HR	RBI	BB	HBP	SH	SF	SO	SB	CS	SLG	OBP
Hernandez, Elier	R-R	6-3	200	11-21-94	.208	.164	.226	60	250	30	52	10	4	0	34	14	2	1	0	66	2	0	.280	.256
Lane, Travis	R-R	6-2	215	8-10-90	.152	.118	.172	14	46	7	7	2	2	0	3	5	2	0	0	15	0	0	.283	.264
Lopez, Jack	R-R	5-9	165	12-16-92	.385	.333	.400	3	13	6	5	0	1	0	3	2	0	0	0	1	1	0	.538	.467
Martinez, Adrian	R-R	6-1	158	1-12-91	.195	.250	.182	28	82	10	16	0	1	0	8	6	2	1	0	18	0	1	.220	.267
Mondesi, Adalberto	B-R	6-1	165	7-27-95	.290	.345	.268	50	207	35	60	7	2	3	30	19	1	1	4	65	11	2	.386	.346
Morin, Parker	L-R	5-11	195	7-2-91	.267	.156	.300	55	195	30	52	10	3	4	21	8	2	0	1	36	1	0	.410	.301
Schlehuber, Jared	R-R	6-3	220	12-24-88	.286	.239	.315	37	119	14	34	10	0	5	19	12	1	0	0	26	0	0	.496	.356
Shin, Jin-Ho	R-R	6-2	200	10-20-91	.274	.279	.273	60	226	33	62	13	1	7	33	16	4	0	3	53	0	0	.434	.329
Smith, Tyler	R-R	6-0	200	7-5-88	.273	.125	.667	5	11	2	3	0	0	1	1	0	0	0	0	3	0	0	.545	.273

Pitching	B-T	HT	WT	DOB	W	L	ERA	G	GS	CG	SV	IP	H	R	ER	HR	BB	SO	AVG	vLH	vRH	K/9	BB/9
Allen, Kevin	R-R	6-1	205	3-31-91	2	1	4.76	19	0	0	6	28	31	19	15	2	11	30	.272	.313	.242	9.53	3.49
Brickhouse, Bryan	R-R	6-0	195	6-6-92	0	0	37.80	1	1	0	0	2	5	7	7	1	3	1	.500	.400	.600	5.40	16.20
Cruz, Fernando	B-R	6-2	205	3-28-90	4	3	6.88	20	0	0	3	35	49	30	27	2	17	38	.333	.388	.288	9.68	4.33
Durden, Andrew	R-R	6-0	200	11-27-88	1	0	21.94	4	0	0	0	5	12	13	13	2	8	4	.462	.333	.529	6.75	13.50
Ferguson, Andy	R-R	6-1	195	9-2-88	2	0	1.14	4	4	0	0	24	16	3	3	2	6	21	.188	.161	.204	7.99	2.28
Hall, Cory	R-R	6-2	232	5-12-88	2	1	2.15	21	0	0	5	29	23	7	7	1	12	35	.209	.128	.254	10.74	3.68
Hentges, Chase	R-R	6-5	195	5-15-90	0	1	16.43	6	0	0	0	8	19	20	14	1	12	5	.463	.526	.409	5.87	14.09
Killen, John	L-L	6-7	185	8-20-90	0	0	10.45	10	0	0	0	10	14	12	12	2	15	11	.318	.250	.344	9.58	13.06
Lamb, John	L-L	6-4	200	7-10-90	0	1	7.36	2	2	0	0	7	9	6	6	2	2	8	.300	.750	.231	9.82	2.45
Lewis, Sam	R-R	6-4	195	10-9-91	2	0	3.86	4	0	0	0	7	9	6	3	1	3	3	.300	.375	.214	3.86	3.86
Lopez, Joe	R-R	5-10	180	3-20-90	2	1	2.72	18	0	0	3	36	40	15	11	2	9	36	.288	.346	.253	8.92	2.23
Middendorf, Dave	R-L	6-3	235	1-23-89	2	1	5.18	22	0	0	3	42	59	29	24	1	11	27	.343	.286	.371	5.83	2.38
Mills, Alec	R-R	6-4	185	11-30-91	1	4	4.62	17	7	0	3	51	58	33	26	7	17	50	.278	.295	.263	8.88	3.02
Nina, Aroni	R-R	6-4	178	4-9-90	0	2	6.84	5	5	0	0	25	28	22	19	1	8	22	.283	.340	.217	7.92	2.88
Patton, Spencer	R-R	6-1	185	2-20-88	0	7	6.32	16	8	0	0	57	67	43	40	4	21	84	.295	.306	.287	13.26	3.32
Schulz, Clayton	L-L	6-2	180	6-7-90	5	7	6.07	14	13	0	0	70	89	50	47	2	30	61	.317	.246	.336	7.88	3.88
Selman, Sam	R-L	6-3	165	11-14-90	5	4	2.09	13	12	0	0	60	45	21	14	1	22	89	.204	.164	.217	13.28	3.28
Smith, Kyle	R-R	6-0	170	9-10-92	1	0	1.80	1	1	0	0	5	3	1	1	0	1	11	.167	.222	.111	19.80	1.80
Sneed, Zeb	R-R	6-4	195	3-19-91	2	2	7.43	13	12	0	0	53	63	49	44	3	28	47	.294	.260	.322	7.93	4.73
Strahm, Matt	R-L	6-4	180	11-12-91	1	3	5.64	19	0	0	0	30	34	29	19	1	17	42	.268	.351	.233	12.46	5.04
Stueve, Andrew	R-R	6-0	190	4-7-89	0	0	5.48	9	0	0	2	23	31	15	14	2	4	20	.310	.389	.266	7.83	1.57
Triggs, Andrew	R-R	6-4	210	3-16-89	0	0	2.45	2	0	0	0	4	4	2	1	0	1	3	.267	.000	.400	7.36	2.45
Williams, Ali	R-R	6-2	185	7-8-89	3	3	5.25	14	11	0	0	60	65	40	35	6	22	67	.269	.241	.294	10.05	3.30

Fielding

Catcher	PCT	G	PO	A	E	DP	PB
Lane	.978	13	109	22	3	4	4
Morin	.990	24	181	24	2	3	10
Shin	.986	41	358	58	6	2	10
Smith	.957	4	22	0	1	0	0

First Base	PCT	G	PO	A	E	DP
Bello	.977	47	384	40	10	25
Cuckovich	1.000	2	2	0	0	0
Schlehuber	.997	35	275	19	1	23

Second Base	PCT	G	PO	A	E	DP
Cuckovich	.889	2	2	6	1	1

	PCT	G	PO	A	E	DP
DelGuidice	1.000	9	13	29	0	3
Garcia	.963	57	81	128	8	26
Goris	.980	7	19	29	1	5
Martinez	1.000	3	1	4	0	0

Third Base	PCT	G	PO	A	E	DP
Cuckovich	.865	43	24	72	15	10
DelGuidice	.966	26	14	42	2	3
Goris	.958	8	4	19	1	1
Martinez	1.000	1	1	0	0	0

Shortstop	PCT	G	PO	A	E	DP
DelGuidice	1.000	7	7	25	0	2

	PCT	G	PO	A	E	DP
Lopez	.923	2	3	9	1	1
Martinez	.904	24	26	68	10	13
Mondesi	.902	47	72	139	23	20

Outfield	PCT	G	PO	A	E	DP
Alcantara	.947	28	33	3	2	1
Aparicio	1.000	3	5	0	0	0
Bates	1.000	3	3	1	0	0
Blanco	1.000	35	46	5	0	0
Chapman	.986	67	127	12	2	2
Cuckovich	.931	17	27	0	2	0
Goris	1.000	23	20	1	0	1
Hernandez	.907	60	104	3	11	1

DSL ROYALS   ROOKIE

DOMINICAN SUMMER LEAGUE

Batting	B-T	HT	WT	DOB	AVG	vLH	vRH	G	AB	R	H	2B	3B	HR	RBI	BB	HBP	SH	SF	SO	SB	CS	SLG	OBP
Bautista, Ismael	R-R	5-11	160	12-8-94	.243	.154	.292	11	37	6	9	1	0	1	4	4	0	2	2	7	3	2	.351	.302
Bueno, Misael	R-R	6-1	190	8-10-93	.220	.333	.171	13	50	7	11	2	3	1	7	2	1	1	1	10	0	1	.440	.259
Cano, Cristian	R-R	6-2	170	2-9-94	.291	.217	.313	58	196	36	57	9	2	1	26	41	5	2	4	39	9	7	.372	.419
Castellano, Angelo	R-R	6-0	170	1-13-95	.248	.289	.235	52	153	19	38	3	1	0	10	25	4	11	1	19	4	6	.281	.366
Flores, Jeckson	R-R	5-11	145	10-28-93	.224	.242	.217	65	228	55	51	9	1	0	24	42	11	8	2	37	13	9	.272	.367
Franco, Wander	R-R	6-0	156	12-12-94	.311	.329	.303	66	235	45	73	13	5	2	38	44	7	0	2	30	13	7	.434	.431
Giron, Jose	R-R	5-11	155	6-27-93	.218	.204	.225	58	174	38	38	5	3	1	11	24	5	9	1	24	10	8	.299	.328
Gomez, Brawlun	R-R	6-2	185	8-5-92	.191	.134	.216	62	215	32	41	6	5	3	21	29	4	8	2	70	8	11	.307	.296
Gonzalez, Cesar	R-R	6-3	185	11-20-93	.238	.268	.229	57	181	25	43	7	1	0	30	12	9	9	4	28	2	3	.287	.311
Lara, Luis	R-R	5-11	188	5-1-94	.266	.313	.238	40	128	18	34	5	2	1	17	14	3	2	3	29	1	0	.359	.345
Melo, Eddy	R-R	6-2	180	8-28-93	.269	.259	.272	63	216	22	58	10	4	0	41	29	3	4	2	55	5	5	.352	.360
Santa, Johan	R-R	5-11	178	3-27-92	.305	.229	.337	48	118	18	36	8	3	2	20	21	3	3	2	24	7	6	.475	.417
Solano, Jose	R-R	6-1	170	8-17-93	.228	.206	.237	64	219	30	50	6	3	0	19	15	4	3	1	47	8	8	.283	.289
Tovar, Roberto	B-R	6-1	180	11-16-94	.206	.217	.200	32	68	8	14	4	2	0	7	9	1	2	0	15	0	2	.324	.308

Pitching	B-T	HT	WT	DOB	W	L	ERA	G	GS	CG	SV	IP	H	R	ER	HR	BB	SO	AVG	vLH	vRH	K/9	BB/9
Almonte, Miguel	R-R	6-2	160	4-4-93	6	1	1.44	10	10	0	0	50	34	15	8	2	8	46	.194	.095	.226	8.28	1.44
Arias, Yojensy	L-L	6-3	180	7-29-93	0	0	4.22	9	0	0	0	11	12	9	5	0	8	5	.293	.400	.278	4.22	6.75
Cepin, Reinaldo	L-L	6-1	160	1-10-94	0	0	4.12	10	2	0	0	20	20	12	9	0	15	14	.278	.000	.303	6.41	6.86
Crisostomo, Branly	R-R	6-1	180	10-25-94	2	3	3.06	11	5	0	0	35	26	15	12	4		23	.205	.261	.192	5.86	1.02
Diaz, Elvis	R-R	6-3	185	2-6-93	2	2	7.23	12	0	0	2	24	24	21	19	2	5	15	.258	.182	.282	5.70	1.90
Diaz, Frankelis	R-R	6-0	190	9-25-91	0	0	9.00	1	0	0	0	1	2	1	1	0	0	1	.400	.000	.500	9.00	0.00
Encarnacion, Felix	R-R	6-3	185	11-2-93	1	1	10.05	11	0	0	0	14	22	17	16	2	6	4	.373	.318	.405	2.51	3.77

Feliz, Igol	R-R	6-3	195	5-31-93	5	2	2.84	19	1	0	1	44	35	19	14	1	18	28	.216	.341	.174	5.68	3.65
Fernandez, Pedro	R-R	6-0	175	5-25-94	3	2	1.93	12	10	0	0	51	44	15	11	0	14	49	.237	.262	.229	8.59	2.45
Garces, Sandy	L-L	6-0	170	10-15-93	4	2	2.62	13	13	0	0	58	47	27	17	6	10	39	.220	.286	.212	6.02	1.54
Machado, Andres	R-R	6-0	175	4-22-93	2	1	2.87	15	3	0	4	38	37	14	12	1	19	27	.270	.294	.262	6.45	4.54
Melendez, Cesar	R-R	6-1	162	3-20-95	0	0	4.05	4	0	0	0	7	10	3	3	0	3	0	.345	.500	.320	0.00	4.05
Melgar, Luis	R-R	6-3	153	2-5-92	3	3	2.45	15	12	0	0	66	49	23	18	5	14	39	.203	.136	.225	5.32	1.91
Munoz, Jairo	R-R	6-0	180	8-12-91	1	1	4.94	12	1	0	1	24	25	15	13	1	11	18	.263	.318	.247	6.85	4.18
Ortiz, Jesus	R-R	5-10	170	1-6-91	5	0	2.70	16	0	0	2	27	22	11	8	2	13	26	.232	.154	.261	8.78	4.39
Pena, Yimauri	R-R	6-2	160	10-15-93	1	3	5.06	10	5	0	0	27	30	17	15	2	13	14	.283	.241	.299	4.73	4.39
Polanco, Adelso	R-R	6-3	165	12-20-93	3	1	3.30	14	2	0	3	30	28	12	11	1	5	12	.252	.154	.282	3.60	1.50
Rios, Ronny	R-R	6-2	195	10-18-91	3	1	3.38	14	3	0	1	35	32	19	13	1	17	14	.237	.170	.273	3.63	4.41
Rosario, Harol	R-R	6-3	197	9-15-92	0	1	3.34	17	1	0	6	32	34	17	12	2	10	26	.270	.219	.287	7.24	2.78
Tatis, Yerinson	R-R	6-4	177	1-1-94	0	2	3.09	10	0	0	0	12	14	6	4	0	6	4	.304	.200	.355	3.09	4.63
Viloria, Alejandro	L-L	6-0	165	6-15-95	0	1	14.54	6	0	0	0	4	4	7	7	0	10	2	.286	.000	.333	4.15	20.77

Fielding

Catcher	PCT	G	PO	A	E	DP	PB
Gonzalez	.980	46	260	37	6	0	13
Lara	.978	24	113	19	3	0	9
Melo	1.000	8	37	6	0	0	1
Tovar	.833	5	5	0	1	0	1

First Base	PCT	G	PO	A	E	DP
Castellano	1.000	4	33	5	0	3
Gonzalez	.983	8	55	4	1	3
Melo	.993	53	414	22	3	30
Tovar	.986	19	142	3	2	5

Second Base	PCT	G	PO	A	E	DP
Cano	.961	38	66	105	7	12

	PCT	G	PO	A	E	DP
Castellano	1.000	3	7	8	0	2
Flores	.956	13	29	36	3	5
Santa	.960	23	41	56	4	11

Third Base	PCT	G	PO	A	E	DP
Cano	—	2	0	0	0	0
Castellano	.938	38	26	80	7	3
Franco	.897	33	33	71	12	5
Santa	.500	1	1	0	1	0

Shortstop	PCT	G	PO	A	E	DP
Bautista	.922	11	19	28	4	3
Castellano	.667	1	1	3	2	0
Flores	.938	54	93	166	17	25

	PCT	G	PO	A	E	DP
Franco	1.000	3	3	10	0	2
Santa	.920	6	10	13	2	1

Outfield	PCT	G	PO	A	E	DP
Bueno	.846	12	21	1	4	0
Cano	.977	22	38	4	1	0
Giron	.984	58	118	6	2	1
Gomez	.969	61	118	8	4	1
Melo	1.000	8	6	1	0	0
Solano	.957	59	104	6	5	0

Los Angeles Angels

SEASON IN A SENTENCE: Mike Trout had a rookie season for the ages to become the first person to win Baseball America's Major League Player of the Year and Rookie of the Year awards in the same season, but it wasn't enough for the Angels to make the playoffs.

HIGH POINT: The Angels called up Trout for his first game of the season on April 28 and not only did he immediately produce, but he also energized the lineup as a whole. Trout hit .326/.399/.564, leading the American League with 129 runs and 49 stolen bases while being caught just five times.

LOW POINT: The Angels finished with an 89-win season, but an 8-15 start put them nine games back in the American League West by the end of April, a hole that proved insurmountable. Newly signed free agent Albert Pujols was part of that slow start, batting .217/.265/.304 at the end of April, though he came around after Trout joined the lineup.

NOTABLE ROOKIES: Trout didn't just have one of the greatest rookie seasons of all-time, he had one of the best seasons ever, and arguably the best season since Barry Bonds in the early 2000s. Righthander Garrett Richards pitched in 30 games (including nine starts) for the Angels, finishing with a 4.69 ERA in 71 innings with 47 strikeouts and 34 walks.

KEY TRANSACTIONS: The Angels had a thin farm system to begin with and traded away three of their top prospects in shortstop Jean Segura and righthanders Johnny Hellweg and Ariel Pena to pick up Zack Greinke at the trade deadline. Greinke pitched well for the Angels, but he became a free agent after the season. In May, the Angels also traded righthander Donn Roach and second baseman Alexi Amarista to the Padres for righthander Ernesto Frieri, who became a dominant reliever. In 54 innings, he had a 2.32 ERA with 80 strikeouts and 26 walks.

DOWN ON THE FARM: A combination of trades, Trout reaching the big leagues by age 19 and surrendering their top two picks in the 2012 draft to sign Pujols and C.J. Wilson led to the Angels having one of baseball's thinnest farm systems by the end of the year. It showed on the field, as Angels affiliates posted a .449 winning percentage, worst in baseball. The most notable standout was Kaleb Cowart, a third baseman who hit .276/.358/.452 between the low Class A Midwest League and high Class A California League.

OPENING DAY PAYROLL: $154.5 million (4th)

PLAYERS OF THE YEAR

MAJOR LEAGUE	MINOR LEAGUE
Mike Trout	**Kaleb Cowart**
of	3b
.326/.399/.564	(Low A/High A)
49 SB, 129 R	.276/.358/.452
BA Major League POY	16 HR, 103 RBIs

ORGANIZATION LEADERS

BATTING		*Minimum 250 AB
MAJORS		
* AVG	Mike Trout	.326
* OPS	Mike Trout	.963
HR	Mark Trumbo	32
RBI	Albert Pujols	105
MINORS		
* AVG	Luis Jimenez, Salt Lake	.309
* OBP	Paul McAnulty, Salt Lake/Arkansas	.373
* SLG	C.J. Cron, Inland Empire	.516
R	Kaleb Cowart, Cedar Rapids/Inland Empire	90
H	Randal Grichuk, Inland Empire	160
TB	C.J. Cron, Inland Empire	271
2B	Luis Jimenez, Salt Lake	38
3B	Ryan Jones, Cedar Rapids/Inland Empire	12
HR	C.J. Cron, Inland Empire	27
RBI	C.J. Cron, Inland Empire	123
BB	Paul McAnulty, Salt Lake/Arkansas	73
SO	Chevy Clarke, Cedar Rapids/Orem	130
SB	Travis Witherspoon, Inland Empire/Arkansas	34

PITCHING		#Minimum 75 IP
MAJORS		
W	Jered Weaver	20
# ERA	Jered Weaver	2.81
SO	C.J. Wilson	173
SV	Ernesto Frieri	23
MINORS		
W	Matt Shoemaker, Salt Lake	11
	Greg Smith, Arkansas/Salt Lake	11
L	Ryan Crowley, Inland Empire/Cedar Rapids	14
# ERA	AJ Schugel, Arkansas	2.89
G	Kevin Johnson, Salt Lake/Arkansas	56
GS	Matt Shoemaker, Salt Lake	29
SV	Ty Kelley, Cedar Rapids/Inland Empire	19
IP	Matt Shoemaker, Salt Lake	176.2
BB	Austin Wood, Cedar Rapids	72
SO	Matt Shoemaker, Salt Lake	124
# AVG	Ariel Pena, Arkansas	.222

General Manager: Jerry Dipoto. **Farm Director:** Mike LaCassa. **Scouting Director:** Ric Wilson.

Class	Team	League	W	L	PCT	Finish	Manager
Majors	Los Angeles Angels	American	89	73	.549	6th (14)	Mike Scioscia
Triple-A	Salt Lake Bees	Pacific Coast	73	71	.507	10th (16)	Keith Johnson
Double-A	Arkansas Travelers	Texas	62	78	.443	6th (8)	Mike Micucci
High A	Inland Empire 66ers	California	66	74	.471	8th (10)	Bill Haselman
Low A	Cedar Rapids Kernels	Midwest	53	86	.381	16th (16)	Jamie Burke
Rookie	Orem Owlz	Pioneer	35	41	.461	t-6th (8)	Tom Kotchman
Rookie	AZL Angels	Arizona	23	33	.411	10th (13)	Brent Del Chiaro
Overall 2012 Minor League Record			312	383	.449	30th (30)	

ORGANIZATION STATISTICS

LOS ANGELES ANGELS
AMERICAN LEAGUE

Batting	B-T	HT	WT	DOB	AVG	vLH	vRH	G	AB	R	H	2B	3B	HR	RBI	BB	HBP	SH	SF	SO	SB	CS	SLG	OBP
Abreu, Bobby	L-R	6-0	220	3-11-74	.208	.500	.182	8	24	1	5	3	0	0	5	2	0	0	1	5	0	0	.333	.259
Amarista, Alexi	L-R	5-7	150	4-6-89	—	—	—	1	0	1	0	0	0	0	0	0	0	0	0	0	0	0	—	—
Aybar, Erick	B-R	5-10	180	1-14-84	.290	.336	.274	141	517	67	150	31	5	8	45	22	5	7	2	61	20	4	.416	.324
Bourjos, Peter	R-R	6-1	185	3-31-87	.220	.232	.212	101	168	27	37	7	0	3	19	15	3	6	3	44	3	1	.315	.291
Calhoun, Kole	L-L	5-10	190	10-14-87	.174	.000	.222	21	23	2	4	1	0	0	1	2	0	0	0	6	1	0	.217	.240
Callaspo, Alberto	B-R	5-9	200	4-19-83	.252	.306	.229	138	457	55	115	20	0	10	53	56	0	3	4	59	4	3	.361	.331
Conger, Hank	B-R	6-1	220	1-29-88	.167	—	.167	7	18	0	3	0	0	0	1	1	1	1	0	0	0	0	.167	.238
Hester, John	R-R	6-4	230	9-14-83	.212	.216	.208	39	85	14	18	1	0	3	4	8	1	1	0	25	0	0	.329	.287
Hunter, Torii	R-R	6-2	225	7-18-75	.313	.340	.303	140	534	81	167	24	1	16	92	38	8	1	3	133	9	1	.451	.365
Iannetta, Chris	R-R	6-0	230	4-8-83	.240	.208	.249	79	221	27	53	6	1	9	26	29	2	0	1	60	1	3	.398	.332
Izturis, Maicer	B-R	5-8	170	9-12-80	.256	.231	.265	100	289	35	74	11	0	2	20	25	2	3	0	38	17	2	.315	.320
Kendrick, Howard	R-R	5-10	205	7-12-83	.287	.309	.278	147	550	57	158	32	3	8	67	29	4	6	5	115	14	6	.400	.325
Langerhans, Ryan	L-L	6-3	220	2-20-80	.000	.000	.000	2	1	0	0	0	0	0	0	0	0	1	0	1	0	0	.000	.000
Morales, Kendrys	B-R	6-1	225	6-20-83	.273	.229	.280	134	484	61	132	26	1	22	73	31	4	0	3	116	0	1	.467	.320
Pujols, Albert	R-R	6-3	230	1-16-80	.285	.290	.283	154	607	85	173	50	0	30	105	52	5	0	6	76	8	1	.516	.343
Romine, Andrew	B-R	6-1	190	12-24-85	.412	.333	.429	12	17	2	7	0	0	1	3	0	1	0	0	3	1	0	.412	.500
Segura, Jean	R-R	5-10	165	3-17-90	.000	.000	.000	1	3	0	0	0	0	0	0	0	0	0	0	2	0	0	.000	.000
Trout, Mike	R-R	6-1	210	8-7-91	.326	.267	.346	139	559	129	182	27	8	30	83	67	6	0	7	139	49	5	.564	.399
Trumbo, Mark	R-R	6-4	225	1-16-86	.268	.266	.269	144	544	66	146	19	3	32	95	36	4	0	2	153	4	5	.491	.317
Wells, Vernon	R-R	6-1	230	12-8-78	.230	.227	.232	77	243	36	56	9	0	11	29	16	1	0	2	35	3	1	.403	.279
Wilson, Bobby	R-R	6-0	220	4-8-83	.211	.220	.207	75	171	19	36	5	0	3	13	15	1	13	1	33	0	0	.292	.277

Pitching	B-T	HT	WT	DOB	W	L	ERA	G	GS	CG	SV	IP	H	R	ER	HR	BB	SO	AVG	vLH	vRH	K/9	BB/9
Carpenter, David	R-R	6-3	180	9-1-87	1	2	4.76	28	0	0	0	40	42	21	21	6	17	28	.276	.308	.253	6.35	3.86
Cassevah, Bobby	R-R	6-3	220	9-11-85	1	0	7.20	4	0	0	0	5	5	4	4	2	6	2	.263	.333	.200	3.60	10.80
Downs, Scott	L-L	6-2	215	3-17-76	1	1	3.15	57	0	0	9	46	43	17	16	3	17	32	.246	.190	.297	6.31	3.35
Enright, Barry	R-R	6-3	220	3-30-86	0	0	14.73	3	0	0	0	4	7	6	6	1	1	0	.368	.273	.500	0.00	2.45
Frieri, Ernesto	R-R	6-2	200	7-19-85	4	2	2.32	56	0	0	23	54	26	15	14	7	26	80	.140	.069	.202	13.25	4.31
Geltz, Steve	R-R	5-10	170	11-1-87	0	0	4.50	2	0	0	0	2	2	1	1	0	3	1	.286	.500	.200	4.50	13.50
Greinke, Zack	R-R	6-2	200	10-21-83	6	2	3.53	13	13	0	0	89	80	35	35	11	26	78	.242	.235	.250	7.86	2.62
Haren, Dan	R-R	6-5	215	9-17-80	12	13	4.33	30	30	1	0	177	190	95	85	28	38	142	.275	.234	.320	7.23	1.94
Hawkins, LaTroy	R-R	6-5	220	12-21-72	2	3	3.64	48	0	0	1	42	45	20	17	5	13	23	.280	.214	.351	4.93	2.79
Isringhausen, Jason	R-R	6-3	235	9-7-72	3	2	4.14	50	0	0	0	46	44	22	21	7	19	31	.251	.241	.260	6.11	3.74
Jepsen, Kevin	R-R	6-3	235	7-26-84	3	2	3.02	49	0	0	2	45	39	17	15	3	12	38	.244	.286	.205	7.66	2.42
Maronde, Nick	B-L	6-3	205	9-5-89	0	0	1.50	12	0	0	0	6	6	1	1	0	3	7	.261	.385	.100	10.50	4.50
Mills, Brad	L-L	6-0	185	3-5-85	1	0	0.00	1	1	0	0	5	3	0	0	0	6	6	.167	.500	.125	10.80	0.00
Pauley, David	R-R	6-2	215	6-17-83	0	1	4.35	5	0	0	0	10	16	6	5	1	3	4	.356	.250	.414	3.48	2.61
2-team total (5 Toronto)					0	1	6.48	10	0	0	0	17	27	13	12	2	5	6	—	—	—	3.24	2.70
Richards, Garrett	R-R	6-3	215	5-27-88	4	3	4.69	30	9	0	1	71	77	46	37	7	34	47	.280	.321	.239	5.96	4.31
Santana, Ervin	R-R	6-2	185	12-12-82	9	13	5.16	30	30	1	0	178	165	109	102	39	61	133	.239	.262	.213	6.72	3.08
Takahashi, Hisanori	L-L	5-10	175	4-2-75	0	3	4.93	42	0	0	0	42	39	24	23	6	10	41	.242	.255	.224	8.79	2.14
Taylor, Drew	R-L	6-2	195	8-18-86	0	0	11.57	3	0	0	0	2	3	3	3	0	4	0	.300	.000	.600	0.00	15.43
Thompson, Rich	R-R	6-1	210	7-1-84	0	1	15.43	2	0	0	0	2	5	4	4	1	1	3	.417	.333	.500	11.57	3.86
2-team total (1 Oakland)					0	1	12.00	3	0	0	0	3	6	4	4	1	1	3	—	—	—	9.00	3.00
Walden, Jordan	R-R	6-5	235	11-16-87	3	2	3.46	45	0	0	1	39	35	15	15	3	18	48	.229	.171	.286	11.08	4.15
Weaver, Jered	R-R	6-7	210	10-4-82	20	5	2.81	30	30	3	0	189	147	63	59	20	45	142	.214	.199	.235	6.77	2.15
Williams, Jerome	R-R	6-3	240	12-4-81	6	8	4.58	32	15	1	1	138	139	73	70	17	35	98	.263	.263	.264	6.41	2.29
Wilson, C.J.	L-L	6-1	210	11-18-80	13	10	3.83	34	34	0	0	202	181	102	86	19	91	173	.239	.217	.246	7.70	4.05

Fielding

Catcher	PCT	G	PO	A	E	DP	PB
Conger	.981	7	48	4	1	0	0
Hester	1.000	38	195	9	0	2	1
Iannetta	.996	78	495	35	2	3	8

	PCT	G	PO	A	E	DP	PB
Wilson	.991	72	420	32	4	6	2

First Base	PCT	G	PO	A	E	DP
Kendrick	1.000	2	4	1	0	0
Morales	.995	28	199	13	1	18

	PCT	G	PO	A	E	DP
Pujols	.994	120	1013	97	7	95
Trumbo	1.000	21	145	5	0	8
Wilson	1.000	4	10	2	0	1

LOS ANGELES ANGELS

Second Base	PCT	G	PO	A	E	DP
Izturis	1.000	29	26	68	0	14
Kendrick	.979	143	238	407	14	81
Romine	—	1	0	0	0	0

Third Base	PCT	G	PO	A	E	DP
Callaspo	.963	131	77	235	12	19
Izturis	.912	30	12	40	5	4
Pujols	1.000	3	1	3	0	2
Romine	.000	1	0	0	1	0

Trumbo	.714	8	5	5	4	0

Shortstop	PCT	G	PO	A	E	DP
Aybar	.975	139	232	359	15	86
Izturis	.944	26	29	56	5	8
Romine	.967	8	9	20	1	6
Segura	1.000	1	1	5	0	0

Outfield	PCT	G	PO	A	E	DP
Abreu	1.000	7	11	0	0	0

Bourjos	.994	90	164	2	1	1
Calhoun	1.000	16	13	0	0	0
Hunter	.984	134	240	14	4	5
Kendrick	.667	2	2	0	1	0
Langerhans	—	2	0	0	0	0
Trout	.988	139	340	3	4	1
Trumbo	.980	97	144	4	3	0
Wells	.993	74	137	0	1	0

SALT LAKE BEES   TRIPLE-A

PACIFIC COAST LEAGUE

Batting	B-T	HT	WT	DOB	AVG	vLH	vRH	G	AB	R	H	2B	3B	HR	RBI	BB	HBP	SH	SF	SO	SB	CS	SLG	OBP
Aldridge, Cory	L-R	6-1	225	6-13-79	.215	.182	.222	72	251	39	54	8	0	20	49	22	0	0	3	91	6	3	.486	.275
Amarista, Alexi	L-S	5-7	150	4-6-89		.300	.263	18	77	11	21	6	2	0	12	3	0	0	3	6	1	0	.403	.289
2-team total (11 Tucson)					.278	—	—	29	126	17	35	7	2	1	18	4	0	1	3	12	4	0	.389	.293
Bourjos, Peter	R-R	6-1	185	3-31-87	.310	.600	.250	7	29	4	9	1	3	0	3	3	0	0	0	6	0	0	.552	.375
Calhoun, Kole	L-L	5-10	190	10-14-87	.298	.282	.303	105	410	79	122	30	7	14	73	44	5	0	4	88	12	3	.507	.369
Cantu, Jorge	R-R	6-3	205	1-30-82	.291	.286	.292	21	86	12	25	5	0	4	22	2	0	0	2	11	0	0	.488	.300
Conger, Hank	B-R	6-1	220	1-29-88	.295	.238	.313	67	264	48	78	17	0	10	42	19	3	0	2	49	2	0	.473	.347
Crowe, Trevor	B-R	5-10	190	11-17-83	.301	.154	.328	42	163	26	49	10	3	0	16	15	0	0	3	28	10	6	.399	.354
Deeds, Doug	L-L	6-2	195	6-2-81	.292	.276	.297	91	332	58	97	21	7	5	35	26	2	5	1	76	5	1	.443	.346
Diaz, Robinson	R-R	5-11	215	9-19-83	.285	.111	.336	46	158	25	45	10	1	4	31	5	1	1	1	9	2	1	.437	.309
2-team total (7 Round Rock)					.290	—	—	53	183	28	53	12	1	4	33	6	1	1	1	10	2	1	.432	.314
Heether, Adam	R-R	6-0	195	1-14-82	.220	.133	.239	27	82	12	18	4	0	4	11	6	1	0	1	17	4	0	.415	.278
Heid, Drew	L-R	5-10	175	12-14-87	.224	.214	.229	25	76	9	17	3	0	1	7	14	0	1	0	13	4	1	.303	.344
Hester, John	R-R	6-4	230	9-14-83	.217	.263	.205	26	92	7	20	4	2	3	13	9	0	2	2	32	0	1	.402	.282
Iannetta, Chris	R-R	6-0	230	4-8-83	.273	.250	.286	6	22	3	6	2	0	0	2	3	0	0	0	7	0	0	.364	.360
Jimenez, Luis	R-R	6-1	205	1-18-88	.309	.328	.303	122	485	78	150	38	2	16	85	19	2	5	6	70	17	7	.495	.334
Langerhans, Ryan	L-L	6-3	220	2-20-80	.250	.300	.234	96	336	59	84	21	6	11	54	63	1	0	1	113	6	4	.446	.369
Long, Matt	L-R	5-11	175	4-30-87	.282	.333	.268	98	347	54	98	19	8	9	46	34	2	3	7	63	15	6	.461	.344
Lucas, Ed	R-R	6-3	205	5-21-82	.262	.214	.243	118	412	61	108	20	2	12	52	28	6	4	3	82	5	4	.408	.316
McAnulty, Paul	L-R	5-11	225	2-24-81	.247	.250	.246	80	275	44	68	23	1	15	56	48	1	0	2	73	1	2	.502	.359
Mulroy, Sam	R-R	5-11	202	10-11-89	1.000	—	1.000	1	1	1	1	0	0	0	0	0	0	0	0	0	0	0	1.000	1.000
Navarro, Efren	L-L	6-0	200	5-14-86	.294	.254	.307	141	528	79	155	35	1	7	74	36	3	0	10	70	3	2	.403	.336
Romine, Andrew	B-R	6-1	190	12-24-85	.285	.282	.286	87	351	57	100	11	7	4	39	24	4	7	2	46	23	10	.390	.336
Rosario, Alberto	R-R	5-10	190	1-10-87	.221	.167	.255	21	77	6	17	3	0	1	8	4	1	1	0	17	4	1	.299	.268
Swift, Jimmy	R-R	6-2	190	12-21-87	.500	—	.500	1	2	0	1	0	1	0	1	0	0	0	0	1	0	0	1.500	.500
Trout, Mike	R-R	6-1	210	8-7-91	.403	.400	.404	20	77	21	31	4	5	1	13	11	1	1	3	16	6	1	.623	.467
Wells, Vernon	R-R	6-1	230	12-8-78	.308	.500	.222	7	26	2	8	1	0	2	3	0	2	0	0	6	3	0	.577	.357
Wilson, Bobby	R-R	6-0	220	4-8-83	.286	.333	.250	2	7	0	2	0	0	0	0	0	0	0	0	1	0	0	.286	.286

Pitching	B-T	HT	WT	DOB	W	L	ERA	G	GS	CG	SV	IP	H	R	ER	HR	BB	SO	AVG	vLH	vRH	K/9	BB/9
Bell, Trevor	L-R	6-2	205	10-12-86	1	6	8.27	10	10	0	0	37	62	44	34	7	24	19	.376	.407	.345	4.62	5.84
Berg, Jeremy	R-R	6-0	180	7-17-86	2	2	3.97	46	1	0	0	70	70	33	31	8	19	68	.259	.317	.223	8.70	2.43
Brasier, Ryan	R-R	6-0	205	8-26-87	7	3	4.37	55	0	0	13	60	66	30	29	1	24	54	.286	.287	.285	8.15	3.62
Carpenter, David	R-R	6-3	180	9-1-87	0	0	2.75	15	0	0	1	20	10	6	6	2	8	14	.149	.167	.135	6.41	3.66
Cassevah, Bobby	R-R	6-3	220	9-11-85	4	1	6.22	44	0	0	10	46	60	33	32	3	19	28	.311	.321	.304	5.44	3.69
Enright, Barry	R-R	6-3	220	3-30-86	5	1	2.73	8	8	1	0	53	42	19	16	3	19	30	.222	.241	.209	5.13	3.25
2-team total (21 Reno)					13	7	4.86	29	29	2	0	163	160	93	88	22	70	102	—	—	—	5.63	3.87
Geltz, Steve	R-R	5-10	170	11-1-87	0	1	5.08	25	0	0	5	34	29	19	19	4	14	33	.236	.250	.224	8.82	3.74
Graham, Caleb	R-R	6-3	220	1-18-87	0	0	27.00	1	0	0	0	1	2	3	3	2	1	1	.400	.667	.000	9.00	9.00
Hawkins, LaTroy	R-R	6-5	220	12-21-72	0	0	0.00	2	1	0	0	2	1	0	0	0	1	1	.143	.250	.000	4.50	4.50
Hurley, Eric	R-R	6-4	195	9-17-85	7	8	5.81	18	18	0	0	98	107	71	63	11	38	70	.286	.287	.285	6.45	3.50
Jepsen, Kevin	R-R	6-3	235	7-26-84	2	2	3.24	20	0	0	2	25	18	9	9	1	9	35	.202	.243	.173	12.60	3.24
Johnson, Kevin	L-R	6-4	240	8-19-88	1	2	5.68	20	0	0	2	25	37	18	16	4	5	13	.349	.339	.360	4.62	1.78
McKiernan, Eddie	R-R	5-11	160	3-21-89	5	3	7.35	13	10	0	0	64	86	52	52	9	20	38	.323	.380	.285	5.37	2.83
Meyer, Matt	L-L	6-4	220	1-17-85	1	2	6.26	51	0	0	0	42	46	34	29	3	41	38	.291	.263	.321	8.21	8.86
Mills, Brad	L-L	6-0	185	3-5-85	5	10	5.86	21	19	0	0	109	133	73	71	13	40	67	.306	.264	.328	5.53	3.30
Pauley, David	R-R	6-2	215	6-17-83	2	0	1.76	9	5	0	0	31	27	8	6	4	7	21	.231	.246	.217	6.16	2.05
2-team total (11 Tacoma)					3	2	2.43	20	7	1	0	59	62	19	16	7	15	41	—	—	—	6.22	2.28
Richards, Garrett	R-R	6-3	215	5-27-88	7	3	4.21	14	14	0	0	77	87	36	36	5	35	65	.289	.306	.274	7.60	4.09
Rincon, Juan	R-R	5-11	210	1-23-79	0	1	3.12	17	3	0	1	26	21	11	9	3	18	23	.228	.162	.273	7.96	6.23
Rodriguez, Francisco	R-R	6-1	220	2-26-83	2	3	6.35	40	1	0	0	51	57	37	36	6	31	28	.288	.341	.250	4.94	5.47
Russell, Adam	R-R	6-8	255	4-14-83	0	0	6.75	12	0	0	0	11	14	9	8	1	8	9	.318	.320	.316	7.59	6.75
Shoemaker, Matt	R-R	6-2	225	9-27-86	11	10	5.65	29	29	1	0	177	229	123	111	25	45	124	.318	.340	.298	6.32	2.29
Smith, Greg	L-L	6-1	190	12-22-83	9	10	3.97	22	21	0	0	138	136	67	61	18	38	83	.257	.295	.245	5.40	2.47
Takahashi, Hisanori	L-L	5-10	175	4-2-75	0	0	0.00	1	0	0	0	1	0	0	0	0	0	0	.000	—	.000	0.00	0.00
Taylor, Drew	R-L	6-2	195	8-18-86	1	0	3.50	16	0	0	0	18	16	7	7	3	11	17	.229	.207	.244	8.50	5.50
Van Mil, Loek	R-R	7-1	260	9-4-84	1	0	6.30	8	0	0	0	10	12	10	7	1	5	5	.286	.292	.280	4.50	4.50
Walden, Jordan	R-R	6-5	235	11-16-87	0	1	6.75	3	0	0	0	3	3	4	2	0	0	3	.300	.250	.333	10.13	0.00
White, Sean	R-R	6-4	210	4-25-81	0	1	8.12	29	2	0	1	38	52	34	34	2	24	21	.329	.324	.333	5.02	5.73
Williams, Jerome	R-R	6-3	240	12-4-81	0	1	7.88	2	2	0	0	8	13	9	7	1	0	8	.361	.286	.409	9.00	0.00

Fielding

Catcher	PCT	G	PO	A	E	DP	PB
Conger	.980	59	364	32	8	5	2
Diaz	.976	42	230	14	6	1	1
Hester	.984	25	175	13	3	2	0
Iannetta	1.000	4	13	1	0	0	0
Rosario	.988	21	141	17	2	2	2
Wilson	1.000	2	9	4	0	0	0

First Base	PCT	G	PO	A	E	DP
Calhoun	1.000	3	19	1	0	2
Langerhans	1.000	1	10	1	0	1
McAnulty	1.000	5	41	0	0	3
Navarro	.997	140	1215	93	4	120

Second Base	PCT	G	PO	A	E	DP
Amarista	.974	8	15	22	1	5
Cantu	.973	12	5	31	1	4

	PCT	G	PO	A	E	DP
Heether	.976	11	17	24	1	3
Long	.968	84	163	228	13	63
Lucas	.982	25	38	69	2	10
Romine	.979	10	19	27	1	7

Third Base	PCT	G	PO	A	E	DP
Amarista	1.000	6	3	16	0	0
Cantu	.929	7	6	7	1	0
Heether	1.000	2	0	5	0	0
Jimenez	.947	118	90	264	20	29
Romine	.968	13	8	22	1	1
Swift	—	1	0	0	0	0

Shortstop	PCT	G	PO	A	E	DP
Amarista	1.000	8	6	4	0	1
Long	1.000	1	1	1	0	0
Lucas	.965	77	151	258	15	61

	PCT	G	PO	A	E	DP
Romine	.984	64	118	190	5	44

Outfield	PCT	G	PO	A	E	DP
Aldridge	.982	58	108	2	2	1
Amarista	1.000	1	1	0	0	0
Bourjos	1.000	4	8	1	0	1
Calhoun	.987	101	218	11	3	2
Crowe	.990	40	96	6	1	2
Deeds	.992	73	123	3	1	1
Heether	1.000	13	14	0	0	0
Heid	1.000	23	52	3	0	0
Langerhans	.990	88	183	7	2	1
Long	.973	15	36	0	1	0
Lucas	1.000	14	24	0	0	0
McAnulty	1.000	4	5	1	0	0
Trout	1.000	13	21	0	0	0
Wells	1.000	5	8	0	0	0

ARKANSAS TRAVELERS

DOUBLE-A

TEXAS LEAGUE

Batting	B-T	HT	WT	DOB	AVG	vLH	vRH	G	AB	R	H	2B	3B	HR	RBI	BB	HBP	SH	SF	SO	SB	CS	SLG	OBP
Auer, Tyson	R-R	6-0	188	10-24-85	.143	.273	.105	15	49	4	7	2	1	0	1	1	1	0	0	13	0	1	.224	.176
Castillo, Angel	R-R	6-3	195	6-7-89	.183	.202	.174	99	273	35	50	9	1	6	24	22	5	3	2	87	8	6	.289	.255
Cruz, Jeremy	R-R	6-1	225	4-19-87	.269	.200	.313	9	26	1	7	2	0	1	0	2	0	0	8	0	1	.346	.322	
Gutierrez, Adrian	R-R	6-2	205	12-31-90	.000	.000	.000	5	14	1	0	0	0	0	0	0	0	0	6	0	0	.000	.000	
Haerther, Casey	R-R	6-2	210	10-5-87	.271	.295	.262	124	487	39	132	21	1	10	56	12	1	0	3	64	1	0	.380	.288
Heether, Adam	R-R	6-0	195	1-14-82	.207	.217	.202	40	140	18	29	4	0	2	18	18	4	1	0	32	1	1	.279	.315
Heid, Drew	L-R	5-10	175	12-14-87	.190	.500	.175	14	42	4	8	0	0	0	4	1	1	0	0	5	2	0	.190	.227
Hernandez, Brian	R-R	6-1	195	11-25-88	.249	.294	.236	65	233	19	58	10	0	1	19	24	3	2	2	58	2	2	.305	.324
Jimenez, Jose	L-R	5-10	240	1-2-87	.116	.000	.172	14	43	1	5	1	0	0	2	3	0	0	0	10	0	0	.140	.174
Kiniry, Rian	L-R	6-0	180	12-12-86	.142	.115	.154	60	169	22	24	6	2	1	20	15	0	3	2	46	9	2	.219	.210
Long, Matt	L-R	5-11	175	4-30-87	.278	.270	.283	27	97	16	27	7	1	3	18	15	1	0	3	27	8	3	.464	.371
Lopez, Roberto	R-R	6-0	195	10-1-85	.258	.289	.247	137	524	58	135	36	1	16	80	38	13	0	5	69	5	7	.422	.321
McAnulty, Paul	L-R	5-11	225	2-24-81	.279	.212	.299	40	140	26	39	5	0	10	27	25	4	0	1	31	0	2	.529	.400
Mount, Ryan	L-R	6-0	190	8-17-86	.236	.324	.204	71	254	23	60	13	1	5	26	18	1	0	5	57	3	2	.354	.284
Osuna, Renny	R-R	6-0	172	4-24-85	.258	.262	.257	124	476	64	123	24	1	3	43	36	2	6	3	52	19	6	.332	.311
Perez, Darwin	B-R	5-10	160	7-27-89	.214	.183	.225	126	407	51	87	14	3	6	36	44	3	3	3	98	15	8	.307	.293
Ramirez, Carlos	R-R	5-11	210	3-19-88	.204	.197	.206	85	275	29	56	12	1	2	23	33	11	2	2	55	4	0	.276	.312
Rosario, Alberto	R-R	5-10	190	1-10-87	.221	.341	.180	50	163	14	36	7	0	1	17	6	3	1	1	32	1	3	.282	.260
Segura, Jean	R-R	5-10	165	3-17-90	.294	.328	.279	94	374	50	110	10	5	7	40	23	8	6	3	57	33	13	.404	.346
Swift, Jimmy	R-R	6-2	190	12-21-87	.232	.138	.265	71	224	21	52	8	0	3	12	12	3	4	0	63	3	4	.308	.280
Witherspoon, Travis	R-R	6-2	190	4-16-89	.202	.114	.226	54	208	28	42	9	2	6	21	24	1	1	1	54	9	4	.351	.286
Yarbrough, Alex	B-R	5-11	180	8-3-91	.111	.200	.077	5	18	1	2	1	0	0	0	0	0	0	0	3	0	0	.167	.111

Pitching	B-T	HT	WT	DOB	W	L	ERA	G	GS	CG	SV	IP	H	R	ER	HR	BB	SO	AVG	vLH	vRH	K/9	BB/9
Arenas, Orangel	R-R	6-0	200	3-31-89	5	11	5.26	27	24	1	0	140	176	90	82	17	43	81	.316	.361	.282	5.19	2.76
Berg, Jeremy	R-R	6-0	180	7-17-86	0	0	0.00	2	0	0	0	4	4	0	0	0	0	6	.286	.500	.125	13.50	0.00
Boshers, Buddy	L-L	6-3	205	5-9-88	1	0	3.75	19	0	0	0	24	28	10	10	3	5	27	.292	.348	.240	10.13	1.88
Carmona, Ysmael	R-R	6-0	170	2-12-85	0	1	1.93	4	0	0	0	5	4	1	1	1	3	5	.235	.167	.273	9.64	5.79
Chaffee, Ryan	R-R	6-2	195	5-18-88	5	1	2.72	37	0	0	0	43	24	15	13	3	27	56	.164	.234	.131	11.72	5.65
Geltz, Steve	R-R	5-10	170	11-1-87	3	0	0.36	21	0	0	6	25	13	1	1	0	6	37	.148	.171	.132	13.14	2.13
Graham, Caleb	R-R	6-3	220	1-18-87	2	2	2.50	48	0	0	1	58	42	17	16	3	17	66	.204	.276	.176	10.30	2.65
Grube, Jarrett	R-R	6-4	220	11-5-81	3	3	2.98	8	7	0	0	45	42	16	15	2	5	40	.249	.294	.229	7.94	0.99
Hellweg, Johnny	R-R	6-9	210	10-29-88	5	10	3.38	21	21	1	0	120	105	52	45	8	60	88	.245	.258	.235	6.62	4.51
Johnson, Kevin	L-R	6-4	240	8-19-88	1	4	2.37	36	0	0	16	38	35	13	10	3	11	18	.250	.313	.197	4.26	2.61
Maronde, Nick	B-L	6-3	205	9-5-89	3	2	3.34	7	5	0	0	32	39	13	12	1	3	21	.300	.258	.313	5.85	0.84
McKiernan, Eddie	R-R	5-11	160	3-21-89	4	5	5.05	18	6	0	2	52	58	32	29	5	19	38	.280	.329	.255	6.62	3.31
Oye, Matt	R-R	6-5	230	2-25-86	4	6	3.85	34	15	0	4	112	113	57	48	10	40	75	.263	.258	.267	6.01	3.20
Pena, Ariel	R-R	6-3	190	5-20-89	6	6	2.99	19	19	1	0	114	95	43	38	14	42	111	.222	.241	.209	8.74	3.31
Piazza, Mike	R-R	6-4	205	11-24-86	5	5	3.53	39	10	0	0	107	93	45	42	7	35	90	.236	.299	.196	7.57	2.94
Robinson, Dakota	L-L	6-3	190	6-5-88	2	3	5.76	43	0	0	0	50	59	33	32	7	24	38	.294	.364	.239	6.84	4.32
Russell, Adam	R-R	6-8	255	4-14-83	0	0	0.00	1	0	0	0	1	0	0	0	0	0	3	.000	—	.000	27.00	.00
Scholl, Chris	R-R	5-11	195	10-27-87	2	1	6.53	33	0	0	0	40	56	37	29	7	9	37	.322	.333	.315	8.33	2.03
Schugel, A.J.	R-R	6-1	190	6-27-89	6	8	2.89	27	27	0	0	140	117	54	45	9	55	109	.232	.237	.229	6.99	3.53
Smith, Greg	L-L	6-1	190	12-22-83	2	1	4.37	6	6	1	0	35	44	19	17	5	7	23	.310	.321	.307	5.91	1.80
Taylor, Drew	R-L	6-2	195	8-18-86	2	4	4.61	37	0	0	2	41	44	22	21	4	14	39	.273	.250	.292	8.56	3.07
Tillman, Daniel	R-R	6-1	185	3-14-89	1	5	12.10	20	0	0	0	19	23	27	26	3	19	21	.303	.333	.283	9.78	8.84

Fielding

Catcher	PCT	G	PO	A	E	DP	PB
Gutierrez	1.000	5	33	5	0	0	2
Jimenez	.974	13	71	4	2	1	3
Ramirez	.988	82	592	68	8	6	4
Rosario	.990	49	331	52	4	4	9

First Base	PCT	G	PO	A	E	DP
Haerther	.985	50	377	16	6	30
Heether	.938	4	30	0	2	3
Hernandez	.889	1	7	1	1	1
Jimenez	1.000	1	7	1	0	0

	PCT	G	PO	A	E	DP
Lopez	.997	56	371	21	1	34
McAnulty	.988	29	230	13	3	21
Osuna	1.000	1	10	0	0	1
Swift	1.000	15	117	7	0	19

Second Base	PCT	G	PO	A	E	DP
Long	1.000	3	7	3	0	2
Osuna	.984	65	146	156	5	50
Perez	.985	59	119	145	4	33
Segura	1.000	2	8	9	0	4
Swift	.975	10	15	24	1	4
Yarbrough	.926	5	13	12	2	5

Third Base	PCT	G	PO	A	E	DP
Heether	.879	11	6	23	4	4
Hernandez	.978	64	43	131	4	12

Osuna	.932	53	46	92	10	6
Perez	1.000	2	0	2	0	0
Swift	.882	14	9	21	4	3

Shortstop	PCT	G	PO	A	E	DP
Perez	.986	63	86	193	4	37
Segura	.951	80	111	237	18	43
Swift	—	1	0	0	0	0

Outfield	PCT	G	PO	A	E	DP
Auer	1.000	15	25	1	0	0
Castillo	.990	94	195	4	2	2

Cruz	1.000	7	12	0	0	0
Heether	1.000	14	23	0	0	0
Heid	.966	13	25	3	1	0
Kiniry	1.000	57	127	9	0	2
Long	1.000	23	47	3	0	2
Lopez	.966	92	164	6	6	0
Mount	.960	51	95	2	4	0
Osuna	1.000	1	4	0	0	0
Swift	.964	27	48	6	2	1
Witherspoon	.978	54	132	3	3	0

INLAND EMPIRE 66ERS

HIGH CLASS A

CALIFORNIA LEAGUE

Batting	B-T	HT	WT	DOB	AVG	vLH	vRH	G	AB	R	H	2B	3B	HR	RBI	BB	HBP	SH	SF	SO	SB	CS	SLG	OBP
Almanzar, Jean	B-R	5-7	150	2-7-89	.227	.265	.214	113	383	40	87	10	5	1	35	14	0	10	2	49	3	1	.287	.253
Bandy, Jett	R-R	6-4	210	3-26-90	.247	.253	.245	94	324	42	80	22	1	7	46	20	15	3	3	51	1	1	.386	.318
Brewer, Brandon	L-R	5-9	170	4-2-90	.229	.167	.247	44	105	17	24	6	0	0	8	11	1	5	0	20	0	0	.286	.308
Cowart, Kaleb	B-R	6-3	195	6-2-92	.259	.313	.241	69	263	48	68	15	4	7	49	45	2	1	4	67	5	3	.426	.366
Cron Jr., C.J.	R-R	6-4	235	1-5-90	.293	.313	.287	129	525	73	154	32	2	27	123	17	11	0	4	72	3	4	.516	.327
Cruz, Jeremy	R-R	6-1	225	4-19-87	.280	.273	.283	21	82	9	23	5	1	3	11	3	1	0	0	19	0	1	.476	.314
Giovinazzo, Chris	R-R	6-0	205	11-30-88	.129	.200	.075	21	70	4	9	0	2	1	4	7	0	1	0	19	2	1	.229	.208
Gomez, Rolando	L-R	5-7	145	6-18-89	.281	.246	.290	86	331	51	93	19	6	3	37	32	3	3	1	75	18	7	.402	.349
Gowens, Brennan	L-R	6-0	195	3-14-90	.198	.212	.194	76	263	22	52	7	1	2	26	23	1	1	2	58	4	5	.255	.263
Grichuk, Randal	R-R	6-1	195	8-13-91	.298	.353	.279	135	537	79	160	30	9	18	71	23	9	2	4	92	16	6	.488	.335
Heid, Drew	L-R	5-10	175	12-14-87	.285	.355	.266	75	284	60	81	16	0	5	25	43	3	4	1	46	12	8	.394	.384
Hernandez, Brian	L-R	6-1	195	11-25-88	.292	.304	.287	65	240	29	70	9	1	3	33	17	8	0	2	33	2	3	.375	.356
Jimenez, Jose	L-R	5-10	240	1-2-87	.248	.222	.255	62	210	22	52	6	0	3	14	20	0	3	1	39	1	1	.319	.312
Jones, Ryan	L-L	6-0	192	5-19-88	.249	.217	.258	57	205	30	51	14	7	1	28	23	2	3	3	50	1	2	.400	.326
Lindsey, Taylor	L-R	6-0	195	12-2-91	.289	.233	.306	134	547	79	158	26	6	9	58	29	5	4	4	66	8	6	.408	.328
Lugo, Carlos	R-R	6-0	190	11-20-89	.000	.000	.000	1	3	0	0	0	0	0	0	0	0	0	0	2	0	0	.000	.000
Mitchell, Gary	L-R	6-4	235	4-3-89	.158	.200	.143	5	19	1	3	1	0	0	1	2	0	0	0	7	1	0	.211	.238
Pacione, Ricky	B-R	5-9	185	4-25-89	.227	.133	.244	35	97	9	22	3	1	0	7	11	2	1	2	14	1	1	.278	.313
Swift, Jimmy	R-R	6-2	190	12-21-87	.252	.364	.203	34	107	14	27	5	2	2	12	10	2	1	0	28	2	1	.393	.328
Ware, Landis	R-R	5-11	170	10-8-88	.333	.375	.000	4	9	1	3	1	0	0	1	0	0	0	0	4	0	1	.444	.333
Wilson, Bobby	R-R	6-0	220	4-8-83	.000	—	.000	1	2	0	0	0	0	0	0	0	0	0	0	0	0	0	.000	.000
Witherspoon, Travis	R-R	6-2	190	4-16-89	.319	.297	.327	67	270	52	86	10	5	7	27	33	3	0	0	52	25	7	.470	.399

Pitching	B-T	HT	WT	DOB	W	L	ERA	G	GS	CG	SV	IP	H	R	ER	HR	BB	SO	AVG	vLH	vRH	K/9	BB/9
Batista, Lay	R-R	6-2	180	8-4-89	6	7	3.82	29	16	0	0	113	111	61	48	12	53	80	.255	.249	.262	6.37	4.22
Boshers, Buddy	L-L	6-3	205	5-9-88	4	2	2.52	26	0	0	1	39	30	15	11	4	16	48	.201	.159	.233	10.98	3.66
Burkard, Alex	L-L	6-8	215	1-4-89	3	0	3.21	30	1	0	0	56	53	26	20	5	28	36	.249	.250	.248	5.79	4.50
Cassevah, Bobby	R-R	6-3	220	9-11-85	0	0	1.80	5	0	0	1	5	4	1	1	1	2	4	.235	.400	.167	7.20	3.60
Cendejas, Eric	R-R	6-0	175	1-28-88	4	5	2.87	47	0	0	5	63	60	24	20	2	7	48	.243	.289	.213	6.89	1.01
Chaffee, Ryan	R-R	6-2	195	5-18-88	2	0	2.38	18	0	0	7	23	17	6	6	2	9	28	.218	.200	.233	11.12	3.57
Correa, Manuarys	R-R	6-3	170	1-5-89	9	10	4.31	31	25	1	0	165	191	85	79	13	26	111	.288	.289	.286	6.05	1.42
Crowley, Ryan	L-L	6-3	190	11-15-90	1	8	7.76	14	12	0	0	63	93	59	54	8	26	54	.342	.346	.340	7.76	3.73
Diemer, Brian	R-R	6-5	240	3-25-88	0	2	14.29	4	4	0	0	11	20	18	18	2	6	6	.370	.483	.240	4.76	4.76
Flores, Manuel	L-L	6-2	170	6-1-87	2	1	3.96	47	0	0	0	50	56	31	27	1	27	54	.241	.204	.271	7.92	3.96
George, Bryant	R-R	5-10	185	7-17-88	3	2	4.69	43	0	0	2	56	66	36	29	1	30	48	.295	.330	.264	7.76	4.85
Giardina, Carmine	L-L	6-3	225	2-20-88	1	0	4.12	13	0	0	0	20	12	9	9	2	13	32	.171	.162	.182	14.64	5.95
Haren, Dan	R-R	6-5	215	9-17-80	0	0	3.60	1	1	0	0	5	7	2	2	0	0	2	.350	.500	.200	3.60	0.00
Hawkins, LaTroy	R-R	6-5	220	12-21-72	0	0	9.00	1	0	0	0	1	2	1	1	1	0	2	.400	.333	.500	18.00	0.00
Holtman, Johnny	R-R	6-5	225	1-11-88	0	1	15.43	2	0	0	0	2	6	4	4	1	6	1	.462	.400	.500	3.86	0.00
Hurst, Kyle	R-R	6-4	230	8-23-85	0	0	6.00	10	0	0	0	18	21	12	12	3	11	16	.296	.250	.333	8.00	5.50
Jimenez, Eswarlin	L-L	6-1	187	11-27-91	1	1	2.75	3	3	0	0	20	23	7	6	2	1	14	.307	.258	.341	6.20	0.46
Kehrer, Tyler	L-L	6-3	210	3-28-88	2	3	5.82	33	0	0	0	39	39	28	25	4	39	37	.273	.280	.269	8.61	9.08
Kelley, Ty	R-R	6-4	220	8-18-88	2	0	1.20	12	0	0	5	15	11	2	2	1	7	20	.216	.179	.261	12.00	4.20
Lopez, Baudilio	R-R	6-1	190	11-20-90	2	2	7.68	15	4	0	0	36	56	32	31	6	15	24	.366	.460	.300	5.94	3.72
Maronde, Nick	B-L	6-3	205	9-5-89	3	1	1.82	10	10	0	0	59	40	13	12	4	14	60	.187	.137	.213	9.10	2.12
Martinez, Fabio	R-R	6-3	190	10-29-89	0	5	10.72	8	8	0	0	23	26	32	27	2	32	23	.283	.375	.182	9.13	12.71
Meade, Aaron	B-L	6-2	185	5-2-88	1	2	7.52	5	5	0	0	20	23	17	17	3	7	18	.280	.280	.281	7.97	3.10
Nabors, Kevin	R-R	6-3	220	8-12-85	1	3	6.00	22	0	0	0	24	31	19	16	3	15	30	.298	.342	.273	11.25	5.63
Reckling, Trevor	L-L	6-2	205	5-22-89	0	1	18.90	4	2	0	0	7	6	19	14	0	15	5	.240	.200	.250	6.75	20.25
Reynolds, Danny	R-R	6-0	170	5-2-91	1	3	5.45	6	0	0	0	33	39	23	20	3	8	25	.298	.315	.276	6.82	2.18
Roach, Donn	R-R	6-1	200	12-14-89	5	0	2.16	6	6	0	0	42	36	11	10	1	3	29	.228	.212	.247	6.26	0.65
2-team total (8 Lake Elsinore)					10	1	1.94	14	13	0	0	88	77	26	19	2	14	73	—	—	—	7.44	1.43
Robinson, Dakota	L-L	6-3	190	6-5-88	0	0	0.00	3	0	0	2	3	1	0	0	0	1	3	.111	.250	.000	12.00	3.00
Russell, Max	L-L	6-2	210	9-21-88	6	12	7.11	27	25	1	0	133	200	131	105	26	41	83	.346	.336	.351	5.62	2.77
Smith, Andrew	R-R	6-3	205	11-5-88	5	2	4.30	10	0	0	0	59	65	30	28	6	14	41	.281	.336	.226	6.29	2.15
Tillman, Daniel	R-R	6-1	185	3-14-89	1	1	1.88	22	0	0	8	24	10	9	5	0	14	31	.127	.132	.122	11.63	5.25
Williams, Jerome	R-R	6-3	240	12-4-81	1	0	3.27	2	2	0	0	11	4	4	4	1	1	9	.250	.375	.100	7.36	0.82

Fielding																				

Catcher	PCT	G	PO	A	E	DP	PB
Bandy	.986	83	544	78	9	6	5

Jimenez	.988	54	368	44	5	5	3
Lugo	1.000	1	7	0	0	0	0

Pacione	.981	15	96	9	2	0	2
Wilson	1.000	1	4	0	0	0	0

First Base	PCT	G	PO	A	E	DP
Almanzar	.980	9	47	1	1	5
Bandy	.988	10	79	5	1	2
Cron Jr.	.978	95	794	58	19	60
Cruz	1.000	7	64	4	0	6
Hernandez	1.000	8	56	3	0	6
Jimenez	.972	8	67	2	2	7
Mitchell	1.000	2	6	0	0	0
Swift	.992	14	119	5	1	5

Second Base	PCT	G	PO	A	E	DP
Almanzar	.931	4	13	14	2	4
Brewer	.966	11	10	18	1	3
Gomez	.963	5	7	19	1	1
Lindsey	.973	123	226	388	17	69

Pacione	1.000	2	0	2	0	0
Ware	1.000	2	1	3	0	0

Third Base	PCT	G	PO	A	E	DP
Almanzar	.905	10	7	12	2	2
Brewer	1.000	8	4	10	0	1
Cowart	.954	62	40	125	8	9
Gomez	1.000	5	4	4	0	1
Hernandez	.967	51	38	107	5	10
Swift	.875	12	7	14	3	2

Shortstop	PCT	G	PO	A	E	DP
Almanzar	.964	93	141	236	14	38
Brewer	.941	16	18	30	3	7
Gomez	.922	41	54	112	14	19

Swift	.600	2	0	3	2	1

Outfield	PCT	G	PO	A	E	DP
Brewer	.800	6	4	0	1	0
Cruz	.933	9	14	0	1	0
Giovinazzo	.962	15	24	1	1	0
Gowens	.988	71	158	4	2	0
Grichuk	.977	133	285	9	7	2
Heid	.962	73	118	9	5	1
Hernandez	—	1	0	0	0	0
Jones	.980	50	93	7	2	2
Mitchell	1.000	4	9	1	0	0
Pacione	.889	9	7	1	1	0
Witherspoon	.984	66	172	9	3	2

CEDAR RAPIDS KERNELS

LOW CLASS A

MIDWEST LEAGUE

Batting	B-T	HT	WT	DOB	AVG	vLH	vRH	G	AB	R	H	2B	3B	HR	RBI	BB	HBP	SH	SF	SO	SB	CS	SLG	OBP
Baker, Abel	L-R	6-1	200	10-26-90	.246	.129	.277	85	293	31	72	11	1	6	40	24	2	1	2	52	0	0	.352	.305
Borenstein, Zach	L-R	6-0	205	7-23-90	.266	.200	.287	79	293	42	78	25	3	11	50	27	6	0	1	60	13	5	.485	.339
Bushyhead, Caleb	L-R	5-11	185	8-2-89	.222	.500	.200	9	27	2	6	1	0	0	1	1	0	1	0	7	1	1	.259	.250
Clarke, Chevy	B-R	5-11	200	1-9-92	.190	.221	.177	77	269	38	51	9	2	6	27	22	11	3	2	79	11	3	.305	.276
Cowart, Kaleb	B-R	6-3	195	6-2-92	.293	.277	.300	66	263	42	77	16	3	9	54	22	3	0	3	44	9	4	.479	.348
Hairgrove, Trevor	R-R	6-1	185	9-16-89	.221	.240	.214	105	362	36	80	18	1	3	30	17	4	5	5	69	1	2	.301	.260
Hall, Frazier	L-R	6-4	220	6-3-88	.254	.261	.252	126	456	56	116	21	0	13	50	40	8	0	6	88	0	1	.386	.322
Jones, Ryan	L-L	6-0	192	5-19-88	.295	.327	.283	58	207	30	61	9	5	4	27	24	2	2	1	40	3	4	.444	.372
Linares, Raul	B-R	5-11	160	10-4-90	.333	.333	—	1	3	1	1	1	0	0	0	0	0	0	0	0	0	0	.667	.333
Lugo, Carlos	R-R	6-0	190	11-20-89	.167	.207	.143	28	78	8	13	3	0	0	2	10	2	3	0	20	0	2	.205	.278
Martinez, Drew	L-L	5-10	170	4-4-89	.250	.364	.231	42	156	19	39	4	1	0	12	9	3	1	1	24	14	3	.288	.302
Mitchell, Gary	R-R	6-4	235	4-3-89	.245	.224	.252	87	302	50	74	15	2	14	46	42	3	0	1	102	9	1	.447	.342
Moesquit, Kevin	R-R	5-10	180	6-20-91	.237	.264	.228	108	413	55	98	18	0	2	31	43	6	3	4	70	16	10	.295	.315
Parks, Jarrod	R-R	6-1	190	5-24-88	.063	.000	.067	5	16	0	1	1	0	0	0	0	0	0	0	7	0	0	.125	.063
Scioscia, Matt	R-R	6-2	220	9-20-88	.234	.235	.233	75	274	28	64	10	0	3	26	10	4	2	0	54	1	2	.303	.271
Soto, Wendell	B-R	5-9	170	5-11-92	.216	.231	.209	51	167	20	36	7	0	5	23	14	1	1	1	42	4	3	.347	.279
Stamets, Eric	R-R	6-0	185	9-25-91	.274	.182	.301	62	248	34	68	13	1	1	20	15	3	1	0	35	7	2	.347	.323
Workman, Andy	R-R	6-1	200	11-16-88	.278	.268	.282	117	428	65	119	19	5	11	68	28	10	1	11	73	9	3	.423	.329
Wright, Zach	R-R	6-1	205	1-10-90	.268	.400	.217	52	179	30	48	7	1	6	23	28	6	1	0	28	1	2	.419	.385
Yarbrough, Alex	B-R	5-11	180	8-3-91	.287	.250	.298	58	244	35	70	12	9	0	27	10	2	1	0	20	9	2	.410	.320

Pitching	B-T	HT	WT	DOB	W	L	ERA	G	GS	CG	SV	IP	H	R	ER	HR	BB	SO	AVG	vLH	vRH	K/9	BB/9
Alvarez, R.J.	R-R	6-1	180	6-8-91	3	2	3.29	23	0	0	0	27	22	16	10	2	11	38	.216	.270	.185	12.51	3.62
Batista, Lay	R-R	6-2	180	8-4-89	1	0	1.13	2	0	0	1	8	4	2	1	0	2	5	.143	.000	.160	5.63	2.25
Bedrosian, Cam	R-R	6-0	205	10-2-91	3	11	6.31	21	21	0	0	83	91	61	58	5	52	48	.286	.311	.274	5.23	5.66
Carlin, Junior	L-L	6-2	165	6-4-88	0	1	6.39	8	0	0	0	13	10	9	9	2	8	12	.227	.000	.256	8.53	5.68
Clevinger, Mike	R-R	6-4	217	12-21-90	1	1	3.73	8	8	0	0	41	37	18	17	3	13	34	.243	.186	.280	7.46	2.85
Crowley, Ryan	L-L	6-3	190	11-15-90	2	6	3.80	13	13	0	0	73	80	37	31	8	14	55	.283	.176	.306	6.75	1.72
DeJiulio, Frank	R-R	6-3	185	8-22-89	4	7	6.65	34	10	0	1	91	99	74	67	18	48	65	.282	.331	.256	6.45	4.76
Diaz, Jairo	R-R	6-0	195	5-27-91	2	7	7.70	13	13	0	0	69	99	63	59	8	29	45	.343	.386	.319	5.87	3.78
Diemer, Brian	R-R	6-5	240	3-25-89	0	0	20.25	1	1	0	0	3	7	8	6	2	2	2	.438	.571	.333	6.75	6.75
Fernandez, Arjenis	R-R	6-4	195	7-29-93	0	1	16.20	1	1	0	0	3	5	7	6	1	3	3	.357	.333	.400	8.10	8.10
Giardina, Carmine	L-L	6-3	225	2-20-88	3	5	3.99	33	0	0	0	50	42	24	22	5	27	58	.235	.130	.280	10.51	4.89
Jimenez, Eswarlin	L-L	6-1	187	11-21-91	7	5	3.51	21	17	0	0	97	113	45	38	4	19	59	.310	.239	.327	5.46	1.76
Johnson, Michael	L-L	6-2	190	2-5-91	5	7	5.28	34	12	0	0	106	104	65	62	11	45	83	.261	.215	.275	7.07	3.83
Kelley, Ty	R-R	6-4	220	8-18-88	4	1	1.81	38	0	0	14	45	31	12	9	1	15	41	.196	.176	.206	8.26	3.02
Lodge, Brandon	R-R	6-2	185	8-3-88	1	0	4.41	11	0	0	0	16	20	11	8	1	9	9	.294	.375	.250	4.96	4.96
Meade, Aaron	B-L	6-2	185	5-2-88	2	3	3.16	27	6	0	0	63	53	27	22	2	23	45	.228	.204	.236	6.46	3.30
Melioris, Joe	R-R	6-11	270	5-29-90	3	3	4.10	40	1	0	1	83	82	47	38	7	28	61	.257	.272	.256	6.59	3.02
Mutz, Nick	R-R	6-1	190	6-15-90	0	1	11.81	9	0	0	1	11	26	15	14	6	6	5	.520	.556	.500	4.22	5.06
Negrete, Jake	R-R	6-3	190	3-8-90	0	0	9.39	6	0	0	0	8	11	8	8	1	6	7	.324	.444	.188	7.04	7.04
Odom, Logan	L-R	6-6	240	8-2-89	1	5	5.58	41	0	0	0	60	62	38	37	5	35	46	.268	.277	.264	6.94	5.28
Reynolds, Danny	R-R	6-0	170	5-2-91	1	3	2.91	11	10	1	0	53	45	19	17	4	20	35	.237	.239	.236	5.98	3.42
Riedie, Shane	R-R	6-5	230	1-5-90	1	1	7.15	6	0	0	0	11	14	11	9	2	7	4	.298	.286	.308	3.18	5.56
Scoggins, Reid	R-R	6-3	210	7-18-90	0	0	5.63	3	0	0	0	3	3	3	2	0	4	5	.231	.000	.375	18.90	10.80
Tromblee, Stephen	L-L	5-10	205	4-3-89	4	4	4.01	46	0	0	5	61	60	30	27	6	17	63	.260	.279	.253	9.35	2.52
Wood, Austin	R-R	6-4	225	7-11-90	5	12	4.30	26	26	0	0	128	125	68	61	4	72	109	.264	.281	.255	7.68	5.08

Fielding

Catcher	PCT	G	PO	A	E	DP	PB
Baker	.987	68	459	57	7	4	3
Lugo	.995	26	164	21	1	4	2
Scioscia	1.000	2	15	4	0	0	2
Wright	.986	46	300	49	5	3	9

First Base	PCT	G	PO	A	E	DP
Hairgrove	.969	8	60	2	2	4

Hall	.991	108	937	70	9	101	
Mitchell	.979	13	89	6	2	11	
Scioscia	.982	12	102	9	2	9	

Second Base	PCT	G	PO	A	E	DP
Hairgrove	1.000	9	21	27	0	11
Moesquit	.978	69	130	176	7	52
Parks	1.000	4	12	5	0	2

Yarbrough	.982	58	115	159	5	44

Third Base	PCT	G	PO	A	E	DP
Borenstein	.667	2	2	0	1	1
Bushyhead	1.000	2	3	5	0	0
Cowart	.961	63	45	153	8	17
Hairgrove	.961	47	36	86	5	11
Moesquit	.937	28	18	56	5	7

Parks	1.000	1	0	2	0	0
Shortstop	**PCT**	**G**	**PO**	**A**	**E**	**DP**
Bushyhead	.875	7	12	16	4	3
Hairgrove	.931	19	30	51	6	18
Linares	1.000	1	1	3	0	1
Moesquit	.920	5	3	20	2	5

Soto	.966	51	72	157	8	34
Stamets	.969	61	84	201	9	36
Outfield	**PCT**	**G**	**PO**	**A**	**E**	**DP**
Borenstein	.950	72	101	14	6	2
Clarke	.974	77	177	7	5	4
Hairgrove	.912	16	30	1	3	0

Jones	.980	49	86	12	2	0
Martinez	1.000	40	75	3	0	1
Mitchell	.970	51	92	6	3	2
Moesquit	.917	6	10	1	1	0
Workman	.978	115	263	6	6	1

AZL ANGELS

ROOKIE

ARIZONA LEAGUE

LOS ANGELES ANGELS

Batting	B-T	HT	WT	DOB	AVG	vLH	vRH	G	AB	R	H	2B	3B	HR	RBI	BB	HBP	SH	SF	SO	SB	CS	SLG	OBP
Amaral, Blake	R-R	6-1	210	10-31-90	.176	.150	.188	20	68	12	12	3	1	1	14	2	5	0	1	24	4	1	.294	.250
Auer, Tyson	R-R	6-0	188	10-24-85	.318	.250	.357	5	22	4	7	2	0	0	2	0	0	0	0	4	2	0	.409	.375
Beltran, Glenn	R-R	6-2	220	12-23-91	.264	.293	.254	41	163	15	43	5	3	1	14	10	2	0	1	40	1	1	.350	.313
Bolden, Ryan	R-L	6-2	195	9-17-91	.133	.095	.143	32	98	18	13	2	1	2	6	21	1	0	1	40	2	2	.235	.289
Capote, Joel	R-R	5-11	180	12-8-89	.367	.500	.300	9	30	7	11	2	0	1	6	5	1	1	0	3	3	0	.533	.472
Cruz, Jeremy	R-R	6-1	225	4-19-87	.000	.000	.000	1	4	0	0	0	0	0	0	0	0	0	0	2	0	0	.000	.000
Dalton, Ryan	R-R	6-1	200	7-24-91	.218	.200	.225	29	110	18	24	11	0	1	14	11	4	2	2	28	0	0	.345	.307
Davis, Quinten	R-R	185	8-1-92	.242	.300	.225	39	132	13	32	6	1	0	4	14	1	1	0	40	3	2	.303	.323
Eaves, Kody	L-R	6-0	175	7-8-92	.261	.133	.308	42	165	25	43	7	5	2	19	16	2	1	3	34	6	0	.400	.328
Gutierrez, Adrian	R-R	6-2	205	12-31-90	.267	.125	.429	6	15	1	4	0	0	0	2	0	0	0	1	0	0	.267	.267
Linares, Raul	B-R	5-11	160	10-4-90	.180	.231	.167	20	61	4	11	0	2	0	6	4	1	0	0	19	5	0	.246	.242
Livingston, Zac	R-R	6-2	209	9-30-89	.214	.250	.200	9	14	1	3	1	0	0	0	0	0	1	0	2	0	0	.286	.214
Martinez, Sandy	B-R	5-11	180	7-18-92	.293	.167	.338	27	92	11	27	5	0	0	10	13	2	0	0	8	0	0	.348	.393
Mendez, Samir	R-R	6-1	215	7-13-92	.217	.154	.238	26	106	8	23	2	0	0	16	4	0	0	1	20	0	1	.236	.243
Patterson, Chase	R-R	5-11	185	9-11-93	.190	.214	.182	18	58	8	11	3	0	0	5	4	2	1	1	31	0	0	.241	.262
Pizarro, Pedro	R-R	5-10	205	12-19-93	.176	.000	.214	15	51	6	9	2	0	0	3	2	2	0	0	15	0	2	.216	.236
Rondon, Jose	R-R	6-1	160	3-3-94	.260	.300	.246	48	192	26	50	13	2	1	20	14	2	3	2	24	5	5	.365	.314
Ross, Chance	R-R	6-0	180	2-28-90	.284	.318	.269	23	74	9	21	3	2	0	12	9	2	1	1	11	3	0	.378	.372
Sneed, James	L-L	5-10	170	2-2-89	.243	.255	.239	50	185	26	45	5	1	0	20	25	4	4	0	32	7	8	.281	.346
Toribio, Pedro	R-R	5-10	158	7-21-90	.379	.350	.395	30	116	29	44	7	5	0	7	4	0	1	1	17	1	5	.526	.397
Ware, Landis	R-R	5-11	170	10-8-88	.324	.300	.333	21	74	11	24	9	1	0	16	9	2	1	2	16	3	0	.473	.402
Whitley, Jackson	L-L	6-3	220	9-5-92	.227	.045	.273	32	110	13	25	5	1	1	16	23	1	0	0	31	0	1	.318	.366

Pitching	B-T	HT	WT	DOB	W	L	ERA	G	GS	CG	SV	IP	H	R	ER	HR	BB	SO	AVG	vLH	vRH	K/9	BB/9
Almonte, Yency	B-R	6-3	185	6-4-94	0	0	6.00	3	0	0	0	3	5	3	2	0	1	0	.357	.200	.444	0.00	3.00
Alvarado, Josh	R-R	6-0	180	12-20-87	0	0	9.53	4	0	0	0	6	6	6	6	0	5	5	.286	.500	.235	7.94	7.94
Bell, Trevor	L-R	6-2	205	10-12-86	0	0	3.09	3	3	0	0	12	11	5	4	1	3	8	.250	.200	.292	6.17	2.31
Boyd, Jake	R-R	6-3	200	1-6-90	1	0	4.05	10	0	0	3	13	14	6	6	1	5	13	.275	.346	.200	8.78	3.38
Bush, Garrett	R-R	6-4	190	10-11-90	0	1	3.00	5	0	0	0	6	2	3	2	0	12	6	.100	.111	.091	9.00	18.00
Carlin, Junior	L-L	6-2	165	6-4-88	3	0	4.09	8	0	0	0	11	6	5	5	1	7	18	.146	.000	.188	14.73	5.73
Collins, Matt	R-R	6-5	208	1-13-89	0	1	5.92	11	2	0	0	24	37	22	16	1	8	20	.349	.273	.403	7.40	2.96
Da Silva, Alex	R-R	6-2		8-28-91	0	0	14.40	4	0	0	0	5	9	8	8	0	5	2	.429	.364	.500	3.60	9.00
Dellatorre, Nic	R-L	5-11	195	8-28-91	1	3	6.84	8	5	0	0	25	34	22	19	1	6	15	.315	.476	.276	5.40	2.16
Fernandez, Arjenis	R-R	6-4	195	7-29-93	3	2	4.68	13	12	0	0	60	56	32	31	5	22	33	.248	.316	.198	4.98	3.32
Hatcher, Kenny	R-R	6-1	205	5-4-90	0	3	6.64	19	0	0	2	20	25	16	15	0	7	19	.325	.259	.360	8.41	3.10
Hurst, Kyle	R-R	6-4	230	8-23-85	1	1	20.25	2	0	0	0	3	7	6	6	1	2	2	.500	.429	.571	6.75	6.75
Hurtado, Daniel	R-R	6-3	180	7-25-92	2	5	4.71	15	5	0	0	36	44	33	19	2	17	21	.289	.319	.265	5.20	4.21
LeBarron, Zachary	L-L	6-3	200	6-18-90	4	3	2.70	14	13	0	0	67	63	32	20	2	20	53	.245	.198	.269	7.16	2.70
Love, Brandon	L-L	6-3	195	3-6-90	1	5	4.53	14	9	0	0	56	53	35	28	3	17	49	.247	.209	.264	7.92	2.75
Maronde, Nick	B-L	6-3	205	9-5-89	0	1	1.13	3	3	0	0	8	3	4	1	0	2	9	.107	.167	.063	10.13	2.25
Mutz, Nick	R-R	6-1	190	6-15-90	0	3	10.45	9	0	0	0	10	14	17	12	0	3	8	.292	.333	.267	6.97	2.61
Pena, Tony	R-R	6-2	240	1-9-82	0	0	0.00	2	2	0	0	2	2	0	0	0	0	2	.286	.333	.250	9.00	0.00
Powell, Robbie	R-R	6-0	180	2-7-90	0	0	0.00	3	0	0	1	4	2	0	0	0	0	7	.143	.167	.125	15.75	0.00
Ramirez, Orlando	R-R	6-1	170	5-4-92	0	1	6.48	13	0	0	0	17	23	13	12	1	3	9	.315	.258	.357	4.86	1.62
Santos, Edward	R-R	6-2	220	10-22-89	1	1	2.64	20	0	0	6	31	24	11	9	0	13	33	.211	.229	.197	9.68	3.82
Scoggins, Reid	R-R	6-3	210	7-18-90	1	0	4.24	15	0	0	0	17	13	12	8	0	14	34	.210	.095	.268	18.00	7.41
Smith, Andrew	R-R	6-3	205	11-5-88	0	1	1.76	5	1	0	0	15	9	7	3	0	4	14	.155	.154	.156	8.22	2.35
Sookee, Aaron	R-R	6-3	172	6-5-91	0	2	5.68	6	0	0	0	13	16	11	8	0	3	10	.302	.355	.227	7.11	2.13
Spomer, Kurt	B-R	6-2	215	7-10-89	5	0	3.12	20	0	0	0	35	42	16	12	2	7	29	.307	.263	.338	7.53	1.82
Vargas-Vila, Daniel	R-R	6-1	205	6-7-89	0	1	17.18	1	1	0	0	4	12	7	7	1	1	2	.571	.333	.750	4.91	2.45

Fielding

Catcher	PCT	G	PO	A	E	DP	PB
Gutierrez	1.000	5	15	0	0	0	1
Livingston	1.000	8	24	5	0	0	1
Martinez	.975	27	168	28	5	3	4
Patterson	.954	16	109	16	6	2	7
Pizarro	.960	14	81	15	4	1	3

First Base	PCT	G	PO	A	E	DP
Mendez	.977	22	203	11	5	11
Ross	.972	3	34	1	1	3
Whitley	.967	32	303	24	11	27

Second Base	PCT	G	PO	A	E	DP
Eaves	.952	37	64	94	8	22

Linares	1.000	3	8	8	0	2
Rondon	1.000	1	1	5	0	1
Toribio	.872	9	14	20	5	6
Ware	.958	8	19	27	2	6

Third Base	PCT	G	PO	A	E	DP
Dalton	.865	22	16	48	10	3
Linares	.886	14	13	26	5	2
Rondon	.857	2	2	4	1	0
Ross	.951	20	15	43	3	4
Ware	.750	1	1	2	1	0

Shortstop	PCT	G	PO	A	E	DP
Eaves	1.000	1	0	5	0	0

Linares	1.000	2	1	3	0	0
Rondon	.932	43	77	141	16	26
Toribio	.903	13	19	46	7	9

Outfield	PCT	G	PO	A	E	DP
Amaral	.929	8	13	0	1	0
Auer	1.000	4	14	0	3	0
Beltran	.970	38	59	5	2	0
Bolden	.949	29	36	1	2	1
Capote	1.000	9	16	0	0	0
Cruz	1.000	1	2	0	0	0
Davis	.983	39	57	2	1	1
Sneed	.941	50	91	5	6	0

170 · Baseball America 2013 Almanac

BaseballAmerica.com

Batting

Batting	B-T	HT	WT	DOB	AVG	vLH	vRH	G	AB	R	H	2B	3B	HR	RBI	BB	HBP	SH	SF	SO	SB	CS	SLG	OBP
Bemboom, Anthony	L-R	6-2	190	1-18-90	.250	.281	.239	40	124	15	31	3	0	2	20	16	1	0	1	21	1	0	.323	.338
Bolaski, Michael	R-R	6-3	185	2-5-92	.286	.290	.284	60	224	37	64	9	4	7	32	23	2	0	1	54	3	0	.455	.356
Bushyhead, Caleb	L-R	5-11	185	8-2-89	.289	.269	.295	41	121	17	35	6	3	0	15	15	1	5	1	20	2	1	.388	.370
Capote, Joel	R-R	5-11	180	12-8-89	.335	.407	.312	56	224	45	75	16	5	4	33	35	6	2	2	33	8	10	.504	.434
Clarke, Chevy	B-R	5-11	200	1-9-92	.271	.348	.244	53	177	34	48	11	0	3	26	31	4	7	2	51	11	1	.384	.388
Davis, Quinten	R-R	6-1	185	8-1-92	.120	.167	.105	12	25	4	3	0	1	0	4	3	0	0	0	8	2	0	.200	.214
Gutierrez, Adrian	R-R	6-2	205	12-31-90	.294	.300	.292	10	34	8	10	1	0	2	7	2	0	1	1	5	0	0	.500	.324
Hinkle, Wade	L-L	6-0	225	9-5-89	.338	.419	.314	72	266	62	90	21	0	15	57	43	11	0	5	52	1	1	.586	.443
Johnson, Kyle	R-R	6-0	180	11-9-89	.289	.323	.273	33	97	18	28	6	0	1	12	9	3	4	0	9	7	0	.381	.367
Johnson, Sherman	L-R	5-10	178	7-15-90	.269	.283	.265	54	182	38	49	12	2	3	20	49	2	6	1	40	8	1	.407	.427
Livingston, Zac	R-R	6-2	209	9-30-89	.226	.188	.243	17	53	7	12	2	0	1	7	1	1	3	0	18	0	0	.321	.255
Lugo, Carlos	R-R	6-0	190	11-20-89	.278	.143	.364	9	18	1	5	2	0	0	3	0	0	0	0	3	0	0	.389	.278
Martinez, Drew	L-L	5-10	170	4-4-89	.286	.100	.326	16	56	18	16	2	1	0	7	8	0	2	2	5	3	0	.357	.364
Mulroy, Sam	R-R	5-11	202	10-11-89	.161	.294	.103	20	56	8	9	3	0	1	5	7	2	1	0	14	3	0	.268	.277
Parks, Jarrod	R-R	6-1	190	5-24-88	.275	.174	.316	25	80	20	22	5	0	4	19	14	5	1	1	21	1	1	.488	.410
Ray, Andrew	R-R	6-1	195	5-1-91	.283	.305	.273	46	180	23	51	18	3	6	36	5	0	0	1	43	0	0	.517	.301
Rondon, Jose	R-R	6-1	160	3-3-94	.300	.250	.313	6	20	4	6	1	1	0	1	2	0	1	1	3	1	0	.450	.348
Snyder, Mike	R-R	6-4	235	6-17-90	.332	.342	.328	70	277	42	92	25	3	8	59	28	3	0	5	53	3	1	.531	.393
Soto, Wendell	S-R	5-9	170	5-11-92	.329	.241	.356	59	234	45	77	18	5	4	37	20	2	4	4	51	8	1	.500	.381
Walsh, Jonathan	B-R	6-2	208	11-14-90	.300	.356	.281	64	230	54	69	16	4	9	45	46	1	1	5	46	1	0	.522	.411

Pitching

Pitching	B-T	HT	WT	DOB	W	L	ERA	G	GS	CG	SV	IP	H	R	ER	HR	BB	SO	AVG	vLH	vRH	K/9	BB/9
Adams, Austin	R-R	6-2	180	5-5-91	0	1	5.46	25	0	0	4	28	22	20	17	4	15	31	.220	.143	.262	9.96	4.82
Baker, Garrett	L-L	6-5	215	8-1-89	4	2	3.58	21	0	0	1	38	42	20	15	3	11	37	.276	.277	.276	8.84	2.63
Boyd, Jake	R-R	6-3	200	1-6-90	2	1	2.14	15	0	0	2	21	23	9	5	0	8	13	.267	.235	.288	5.57	3.43
Bush, Garrett	R-R	6-4	190	10-11-90	0	1	39.00	5	0	0	0	3	9	13	13	1	8	4	.500	.556	.444	12.00	24.00
DeLoach, Tyler	R-L	6-6	240	4-12-91	0	0	6.75	12	0	0	0	12	13	9	9	0	16	15	.277	.222	.310	11.25	12.00
Diaz, Jairo	R-R	6-0	195	5-27-91	5	6	5.30	14	14	0	0	75	93	57	44	5	23	61	.304	.328	.287	7.35	2.77
Efferson, Brandon	R-R	5-11	175	11-25-88	0	1	6.03	19	4	0	1	37	46	29	25	2	10	30	.307	.347	.287	7.23	2.41
Krehbiel, Joe	R-R	6-2	185	12-20-92	2	2	5.12	22	0	0	0	32	38	21	18	2	10	34	.292	.321	.273	9.66	2.84
Lodge, Brandon	R-R	6-2	185	8-3-88	0	0	3.60	4	0	0	0	10	10	5	4	1	2	10	.256	.417	.185	9.00	1.80
Lopez, Baudilio	R-R	6-1	190	11-20-90	0	2	12.32	8	3	0	0	19	35	26	26	4	11	11	.398	.405	.391	5.21	5.21
Lowery, Pat	R-R	6-5	195	4-2-90	0	4	9.15	15	6	0	0	41	64	46	42	1	19	26	.356	.366	.349	5.66	4.14
Morin, Mike	R-R	6-4	175	5-3-91	2	2	4.93	24	0	0	4	35	34	23	19	2	14	29	.262	.268	.257	7.53	3.63
Newcomb, Aaron	R-R	6-3	190	3-2-90	3	1	4.85	15	7	0	0	43	47	25	23	1	5	34	.287	.320	.258	7.17	1.05
O'Grady, Chris	L-L	6-4	220	4-17-90	3	3	5.87	13	0	0	0	15	18	15	10	0	10	14	.295	.308	.286	8.22	5.87
Perez, Gabriel	R-R	6-0	185	6-3-91	8	1	5.06	15	15	0	0	80	80	45	45	4	25	78	.257	.262	.253	8.78	2.81
Powell, Robbie	R-R	6-0	180	2-7-90	1	2	4.26	21	0	0	4	25	19	14	12	3	5	23	.216	.229	.208	8.11	1.78
Ramirez, Orlando	R-R	6-1	170	5-4-92	0	0	6.35	4	0	0	0	6	8	4	4	0	4	5	.348	.500	.316	7.94	6.35
Riedie, Shane	R-R	6-5	230	1-5-90	0	0	2.16	3	0	0	0	8	8	3	2	0	1	2	.267	.300	.250	2.16	1.08
Rodriguez, Nataniel	L-L	5-10	185	8-27-90	3	4	7.53	13	5	0	0	29	37	26	24	3	20	32	.311	.405	.268	10.05	6.28
Roth, Michael	L-L	6-1	210	2-15-90	0	2	4.91	11	9	0	0	22	23	13	12	2	11	21	.274	.172	.327	8.59	4.50
Santiago, Yancarlos	L-L	6-0	180	1-23-91	1	3	5.91	15	1	0	0	35	40	26	23	2	15	25	.282	.238	.300	6.43	3.86
Santos, Edward	R-R	6-2	220	10-22-89	0	0	0.00	1	0	0	0	2	2	0	0	0	2	1	.286	.333	.250	5.40	10.80
Sappington, Mark	R-R	6-5	209	11-17-90	1	1	5.15	15	12	0	0	37	31	25	21	3	16	34	.231	.226	.236	8.35	3.93
Sookee, Aaron	R-R	6-3	172	6-5-91	0	2	5.02	11	0	0	0	14	10	10	8	0	11	10	.196	.313	.143	6.28	6.91

Fielding

Catcher	PCT	G	PO	A	E	DP	PB
Bemboom	.986	39	238	47	4	1	8
Gutierrez	1.000	10	62	13	0	0	2
Livingston	.992	17	109	16	1	1	4
Lugo	.976	7	38	2	1	0	0
Mulroy	1.000	18	103	9	0	0	6

First Base	PCT	G	PO	A	E	DP
Hinkle	.978	67	573	37	14	64
Parks	1.000	2	11	0	0	1
Snyder	.990	12	91	9	1	7

Second Base	PCT	G	PO	A	E	DP
Bushyhead	.939	13	30	32	4	10

Johnson	.976	53	95	153	6	36
Parks	.974	16	32	44	2	9

Third Base	PCT	G	PO	A	E	DP
Bolaski	.832	44	32	77	22	7
Bushyhead	.857	13	11	7	3	1
Johnson	.500	1	0	1	1	
Parks	1.000	5	1	5	0	1
Snyder	.883	24	17	36	7	4

Shortstop	PCT	G	PO	A	E	DP
Bushyhead	.943	15	29	37	4	9
Johnson	1.000	1	1	0	0	0
Rondon	.962	6	7	18	1	4

Soto	.942	58	93	182	17	42

Outfield	PCT	G	PO	A	E	DP
Bushyhead	—	1	0	0	0	0
Capote	.991	55	107	5	1	0
Clarke	.978	51	84	5	2	0
Davis	1.000	11	15	0	0	0
Johnson	.979	32	42	4	1	0
Martinez	.909	15	18	2	2	1
Mulroy	—	1	0	0	0	0
Ray	.943	29	32	1	2	0
Walsh	.885	56	73	4	10	1

Batting

Batting	B-T	HT	WT	DOB	AVG	vLH	vRH	G	AB	R	H	2B	3B	HR	RBI	BB	HBP	SH	SF	SO	SB	CS	SLG	OBP
Alberto, Ranyelmy	R-R	6-2	175	5-27-94	.246	.116	.280	59	207	28	51	7	5	1	24	22	2	2	1	39	6	6	.343	.323
Almao, Angel	R-R	5-10	145	11-5-94	.242	.259	.236	30	99	14	24	1	0	0	5	15	2	0	0	19	3	4	.253	.353
Aquino, Bladimir	R-R	6-0	190	7-3-93	.232	.286	.214	18	56	4	13	2	0	0	6	5	0	0	1	16	0	0	.268	.290
De La Cruz, Ercilio	B-R	5-11	160	10-28-92	.182	.400	.143	11	33	2	6	0	0	0	2	6	0	1	0	10	1	2	.182	.308
Dionicio, Ismael	B-R	5-10	165	7-19-91	.300	.250	.313	59	203	29	61	7	2	0	27	34	5	7	0	33	21	15	.355	.413
Espinoza, Luis	R-R	6-3	180	1-13-94	.133	.000	.148	14	30	2	4	0	0	0	1	1	0	0	0	9	0	0	.133	.161

	B-T	HT	WT	DOB	AVG	vLH	vRH	G	AB	R	H	2B	3B	HR	RBI	BB	HBP	SH	SF	SO	SB	CS	OBP	SLG
Fernandez, Jesus	R-R	6-1	185	3-6-94	.221	.091	.246	23	68	5	15	0	0	0	9	10	1	1	1	26	1	1	.221	.325
Herrera, Jose	B-R	6-0	155	1-14-93	.212	.188	.218	49	156	23	33	4	2	0	14	17	6	2	2	22	2	4	.263	.309
Jolly, Luis	R-R	6-2	180	3-21-93	.163	.083	.176	35	80	18	13	3	1	1	9	15	8	3	2	33	1	4	.263	.343
Mateo, Steven	R-R	6-2	188	8-19-92	.169	.182	.167	28	71	17	12	3	0	0	5	19	3	3	1	24	4	0	.211	.362
Montilla, Angel	R-R	6-1	170	4-18-93	.208	.241	.200	52	149	18	31	5	3	3	20	7	14	3	0	41	13	5	.342	.306
Moreno, Juan	R-R	6-1	160	11-17-94	.173	.125	.182	20	52	3	9	0	0	0	4	5	1	3	1	7	1	1	.173	.254
Perez, Ayendy	L-R	5-9	160	9-10-93	.261	.356	.234	60	203	40	53	5	4	0	23	36	8	7	2	41	14	8	.325	.390
Salcedo, Erick	B-R	5-10	155	6-28-93	.240	.138	.260	56	175	30	42	5	0	0	22	33	2	13	3	25	7	4	.269	.362
Santana, Gabriel	R-R	6-2	180	8-18-95	.240	.421	.198	31	100	18	24	3	0	0	10	10	4	0	1	17	0	2	.270	.330
Tovar, Luis	R-R	6-0	155	6-2-94	.071	.000	.077	17	28	1	2	0	0	0	0	3	1	0	0	12	0	1	.071	.188
Villavicencio, Gabriel	R-R	6-0	190	10-3-92	.212	.242	.202	41	132	13	28	6	0	0	14	15	3	5	2	23	4	3	.258	.303
Vivas, Enyelber	R-R	6-1	175	8-26-92	.224	.364	.200	43	152	16	34	5	0	0	22	17	2	6	1	27	1	1	.257	.308

Pitching	B-T	HT	WT	DOB	W	L	ERA	G	GS	CG	SV	IP	H	R	ER	HR	BB	SO	AVG	vLH	vRH	K/9	BB/9
Alcantara, Alfonso	R-R	6-2	190	4-3-93	5	4	2.13	14	14	0	0	72	51	27	17	0	40	77	.199	.143	.218	9.63	5.00
Campos, Alexis	R-R	6-1	160	6-23-92	3	3	2.77	22	0	0	8	26	22	13	8	0	11	27	.224	.313	.182	9.35	3.81
De La Cruz, Miguel	R-R	6-1	175	8-5-92	0	0	7.36	8	0	0	1	11	13	9	9	0	10	10	.302	.214	.345	8.18	8.18
DeLeon, Ernesto	R-R	6-6	230	11-24-91	0	0	4.35	8	0	0	0	10	7	7	5	0	10	5	.194	.083	.250	4.35	8.71
Fernandez, Arjenis	R-R	6-4	195	7-29-93	1	0	2.57	3	3	0	0	14	7	4	4	0	7	10	.156	.250	.121	6.43	4.50
Guerra, Angel	R-R	6-1	180	2-2-93	8	2	2.09	15	15	0	0	90	79	23	21	1	15	68	.239	.227	.243	6.77	1.49
Lopez, Eduar	R-R	6-0	180	2-21-95	2	1	3.54	12	11	0	0	53	42	24	21	5	23	83	.212	.200	.217	14.01	3.88
Melo, Ivan	L-L	6-1	165	7-21-94	2	3	2.79	15	15	0	0	68	64	28	21	1	32	55	.258	.350	.240	7.32	4.26
Mendoza, Jose	R-R	6-2	165	7-29-94	1	1	2.45	7	3	0	0	22	16	7	6	0	7	16	.205	.125	.241	6.55	2.86
Paredes, Eduardo	R-R	6-1	170	3-6-95	3	3	1.56	22	0	0	8	35	26	13	6	0	8	45	.206	.220	.200	11.68	2.08
Pimentel, Yunior	L-L	6-4	180	9-9-94	0	0	2.38	6	0	0	0	11	10	3	3	0	9	11	.238	.125	.265	8.74	7.15
Reinoso, Yordany	R-R	6-1	185	10-16-93	0	0	2.63	8	0	0	0	14	11	4	4	1	7	14	.224	.000	.275	9.22	4.61
Reyes, Jose	R-R	6-2	160	2-3-93	0	0	2.70	12	0	0	0	20	11	6	6	1	11	10	.164	.190	.152	4.95	4.50
Rodriguez, Ramon	R-R	6-0	180	9-20-93	3	3	1.86	16	1	0	1	39	26	9	8	1	18	43	.193	.200	.189	10.01	4.19
Rosario, Edisson	L-L	6-0	180	8-13-94	0	1	4.00	5	0	0	0	9	7	4	4	0	1	4	.206	.111	.240	4.00	1.00
Santana, Francisco	L-L	5-10	155	2-1-93	5	2	1.47	17	2	0	3	49	34	13	8	0	15	46	.210	.292	.196	8.45	2.76
Valdez, Alexander	R-R	6-0	175	1-28-94	4	1	6.12	17	0	0	1	25	26	21	17	1	10	28	.255	.276	.247	10.08	3.60

Fielding

Catcher	PCT	G	PO	A	E	DP	PB
Alberto	1.000	1	6	1	0	0	0
Aquino	.923	5	29	7	3	0	0
Fernandez	.994	19	148	18	1	0	8
Santana	.938	5	29	1	2	0	5
Vivas	.979	39	325	41	8	2	9
Dionicio	.971	46	94	108	6		25
Herrera	1.000	2	2	0	0		1
Mateo	1.000	1	1	0	0		0
Moreno	1.000	5	5	5	0		3
Salcedo	1.000	1	1	0	0		0

First Base	PCT	G	PO	A	E	DP
Alberto	1.000	1	9	1	0	1
De La Cruz	.967	9	86	2	3	12
Dionicio	1.000	10	90	2	0	4
Espinoza	1.000	1	1	0	0	0
Mateo	.977	11	83	3	2	5
Villavicencio	.991	39	307	20	3	27

Second Base	PCT	G	PO	A	E	DP
Almao	.940	16	32	31	4	6

Third Base	PCT	G	PO	A	E	DP
Alberto	1.000	1	0	4	0	0
Dionicio	1.000	1	1	0	0	0
Herrera	.933	47	36	104	10	8
Mateo	.848	9	11	17	5	1
Moreno	.905	8	6	13	2	0
Salcedo	1.000	1	3	0	0	0
Villavicencio	1.000	1	0	1	0	0

Shortstop	PCT	G	PO	A	E	DP
Almao	.889	12	17	31	6	8

	PCT	G	PO	A	E	DP
Moreno	.905	6	9	10	2	1
Salcedo	.938	48	86	139	15	26

Outfield	PCT	G	PO	A	E	DP
Alberto	.953	55	78	4	4	1
Aquino	—	1	0	0	0	0
De La Cruz	—	2	0	0	0	0
Espinoza	1.000	7	5	0	0	0
Herrera	1.000	2	1	0	0	0
Jolly	.951	26	36	3	2	0
Montilla	.981	46	52	1	1	0
Perez	.991	58	90	15	1	1
Tovar	1.000	11	9	0	0	0

Los Angeles Dodgers

SEASON IN A SENTENCE: Finally escaping the turmoil of the Frank McCourt era, the Dodgers didn't hesitate to flex their new financial muscle and spent much of the first half of the season atop the National League West before fading in the second half.

HIGH POINT: The Dodgers' best moment came before the season started, when they announced in late March that a group led by Stan Kasten and Magic Johnson would take control of the franchise after submitting a massive $2 billion bid, finally allowing the team to turn the page on the McCourt era.

LOW POINT: The Dodgers were the victims of a combined no-hitter at Seattle on June 8, as six Mariners pitchers did the job and provided a sign of things to come. The Dodgers finished 13th in the National League in scoring, not helped by losing Matt Kemp for two months in the middle of the season due to injury. Worst of all was when the Dodgers went to San Francisco June 25-27 and were shut out by the rival Giants in all three games, the first time in franchise history they were shut out for an entire series.

NOTABLE ROOKIES: Few rookies saw significant action other than a handful of relievers. Righthanders Josh Lindblom and Shawn Tolleson each made at least 40 appearances, though Lindblom and another young arm (Nate Eovaldi) were among the players traded away as the Dodgers tried to stay in contention. Lefthander Paco Rodriguez, a second-round pick in June, became the first 2012 draftee to reach the majors, making several crucial relief appearances down the stretch and posting a 1.35 ERA.

KEY TRANSACTIONS: Following the sale of the team, Dodgers moved aggressively to strengthen their roster. The first headliner came when they traded for Hanley Ramirez from Miami in July. Then in August, they pulled a massive nine-player deal with the Red Sox, bringing in Josh Beckett, Carl Crawford, Adrian Gonzalez and Nick Punto. They also brought in Joe Blanton and Shane Victorino in separate trades with the Phillies.

DOWN ON THE FARM: Veteran righthander John Ely won the pitching triple crown in the Triple-A Pacific Coast League. Rookie-level Ogden posted the best record in the Pioneer League, and the Dodgers' domestic affiliates' cumulative .528 winning percentage was among the best in baseball.

OPENING DAY PAYROLL: $95.1 million (12th)

2012 PERFORMANCE

General Manager: Ned Colletti. **Farm Director:** De Jon Watson. **Scouting Director:** Logan White.

Class	Team	League	W	L	PCT	Finish	Manager
Majors	Los Angeles Dodgers	National	86	76	.531	6th (16)	Don Mattingly
Triple-A	Albuquerque Isotopes	Pacific Coast	80	64	.556	4th (16)	Lorenzo Bundy
Double-A	Chattanooga Lookouts	Southern	73	65	.529	3rd (10)	Carlos Subero
High A	Rancho Cucamonga Quakes	California	68	72	.486	7th (10)	Juan Bustabad
Low A	Great Lakes Loons	Midwest	67	73	.479	12th (16)	John Shoemaker
Rookie	Ogden Raptors	Pioneer	44	32	.579	1st (8)	Damon Berryhill
Rookie	AZL Dodgers	Arizona	34	21	.618	3rd (13)	Matt Martin
Overall 2012 Minor League Record			366	327	.528	5th (30)	

ORGANIZATION STATISTICS

LOS ANGELES DODGERS
NATIONAL LEAGUE

Batting	B-T	HT	WT	DOB	AVG	vLH	vRH	G	AB	R	H	2B	3B	HR	RBI	BB	HBP	SH	SF	SO	SB	CS	SLG	OBP
Abreu, Bobby	L-R	6-0	220	3-11-74	.246	.256	.243	92	195	28	48	8	1	3	19	35	0	0	0	51	6	2	.344	.361
Castellanos, Alex	R-R	5-11	195	8-4-86	.174	.000	.400	16	23	3	4	0	1	1	3	0	1	0	1	8	0	0	.391	.200
Cruz, Luis	R-R	6-2	220	2-10-84	.297	.302	.294	78	283	26	84	20	0	6	40	9	2	1	1	34	2	1	.431	.322
De Jesus Jr., Ivan	R-R	5-11	200	5-1-87	.273	.158	.429	23	33	5	9	3	0	0	4	3	0	0	1	7	1	1	.364	.324
Ellis, A.J.	R-R	6-3	215	4-9-81	.270	.224	.285	133	423	44	114	20	1	13	52	65	7	6	4	107	0	0	.414	.373
Ellis, Mark	R-R	5-10	190	6-6-77	.258	.321	.228	110	415	62	107	21	1	7	31	40	7	2	0	70	5	0	.364	.333
Ethier, Andre	L-L	6-2	205	4-10-82	.284	.222	.325	149	556	79	158	36	1	20	89	50	9	0	3	124	2	2	.460	.351
Federowicz, Tim	R-R	5-10	215	8-5-87	.333	—	.333	3	3	0	1	0	0	0	1	0	0	0	0	2	0	0	.333	.500
Gonzalez, Adrian	L-L	6-2	225	5-8-82	.297	.379	.241	36	145	12	43	10	1	3	22	11	0	0	1	29	2	0	.441	.344
Gordon, Dee	L-R	5-11	160	4-22-88	.228	.172	.255	87	303	38	69	9	2	1	17	20	3	2	2	62	32	10	.281	.280
Gwynn Jr., Tony	L-R	5-11	195	10-4-82	.232	.209	.243	103	259	29	60	8	4	0	17	16	0	2	0	52	13	6	.293	.276
Hairston Jr., Jerry	R-R	5-10	190	5-29-76	.273	.293	.260	78	238	19	65	13	1	4	26	23	3	1	2	27	1	2	.387	.342
Herrera, Elian	B-R	5-10	190	2-1-85	.251	.265	.244	67	187	26	47	10	1	1	17	23	2	2	0	50	4	2	.332	.340
Kemp, Matt	R-R	6-4	225	9-23-84	.303	.363	.276	106	403	74	122	22	2	23	69	40	3	0	3	103	9	4	.538	.367
Kennedy, Adam	L-R	5-11	195	1-10-76	.262	.233	.268	86	168	22	44	8	1	2	16	23	1	4	5	33	1	1	.357	.345
Loney, James	L-L	6-3	220	5-7-84	.254	.240	.259	114	334	32	85	18	0	4	33	23	0	1	1	39	0	3	.344	.302
Punto, Nick	B-R	5-9	190	11-8-77	.286	.714	.179	22	35	6	10	1	0	0	6	0	2	0	9	1	0	.314	.390
Ramirez, Hanley	R-R	6-2	230	12-23-83	.271	.275	.269	64	251	30	68	11	2	10	44	17	3	0	1	60	7	3	.450	.324
2-team total (93 Miami)					.257	—	—	157	604	79	155	29	4	24	92	54	6	0	3	132	21	7	.437	.322
Rivera, Juan	R-R	6-2	220	7-3-78	.244	.260	.232	109	312	30	76	14	0	9	47	18	3	0	6	35	1	3	.375	.286
Sands, Jerry	R-R	6-4	225	9-28-87	.174	.158	.250	9	23	2	4	2	0	0	1	1	0	0	0	9	0	0	.261	.208
Sellers, Justin	R-R	5-10	155	2-1-86	.205	.174	.238	19	44	6	9	3	1	1	2	5	0	1	0	14	0	0	.386	.286
Treanor, Matt	R-R	6-0	200	3-3-76	.175	.218	.125	36	103	11	18	3	1	2	10	14	2	1	2	29	1	1	.282	.281
Uribe, Juan	R-R	6-0	240	3-22-79	.191	.143	.222	66	162	15	31	9	0	2	17	13	2	1	1	37	0	1	.284	.258
Van Slyke, Scott	R-R	6-5	250	7-24-86	.167	.154	.179	27	54	4	9	2	0	2	7	2	0	1	0	14	1	0	.315	.196
Victorino, Shane	B-R	5-9	190	11-30-80	.245	.333	.204	53	208	26	51	12	2	2	15	18	4	4	1	31	15	2	.351	.316
2-team total (101 Philadelphia)					.255	—	—	154	595	72	152	29	7	11	55	53	6	9	3	80	39	6	.383	.321

Pitching	B-T	HT	WT	DOB	W	L	ERA	G	GS	CG	SV	IP	H	R	ER	HR	BB	SO	AVG	vLH	vRH	K/9	BB/9
Beckett, Josh	R-R	6-5	225	5-15-80	2	3	2.93	7	7	0	0	43	43	16	14	5	14	38	.257	.282	.236	7.95	2.93
Belisario, Ronald	R-R	6-3	245	12-31-82	8	1	2.54	68	0	0	1	71	47	22	20	3	29	69	.187	.250	.142	8.75	3.68
Billingsley, Chad	R-R	6-1	240	7-29-84	10	9	3.55	25	25	0	0	150	148	66	59	11	45	128	.257	.260	.255	7.70	2.71
Blanton, Joe	R-R	6-3	235	12-11-80	2	4	4.99	10	10	0	0	58	66	32	32	7	16	51	.291	.306	.279	7.96	2.50
2-team total (21 Philadelphia)					10	13	4.71	31	30	2	0	191	207	106	100	29	34	166	—	—	—	7.82	1.60
Capuano, Chris	L-L	6-3	215	8-19-78	12	12	3.72	33	33	0	0	198	188	91	82	25	54	162	.254	.231	.260	7.35	2.45
Choate, Randy	L-L	6-1	205	9-5-75	0	0	4.05	36	0	0	0	13	13	7	6	1	9	11	.255	.171	.600	7.43	6.08
2-team total (44 Miami)					0	0	3.03	80	0	0	1	39	29	18	13	1	18	38	—	—	—	8.84	4.19
Coffey, Todd	R-R	6-4	240	9-9-80	1	0	4.66	23	0	0	0	19	17	11	10	1	9	18	.239	.167	.277	8.38	4.19
De La Rosa, Rubby	R-R	5-11	205	3-4-89	0	0	27.00	1	0	0	0	1	0	2	2	0	2	0	.000	.000	.000	0.00	27.00
Elbert, Scott	L-L	6-2	225	8-13-85	1	1	2.20	43	0	0	0	33	27	8	8	3	13	29	.231	.271	.170	7.99	3.58
Ely, John	R-R	6-2	200	5-13-86	0	2	20.25	2	0	0	0	3	6	6	6	0	4	3	.462	.375	.600	10.13	13.50
Eovaldi, Nate	R-R	6-2	215	2-13-90	1	6	4.15	10	10	0	0	56	63	27	26	5	20	34	.289	.349	.202	5.43	3.20
2-team total (12 Miami)					4	13	4.30	22	22	0	0	119	133	59	57	10	47	78	—	—	—	5.88	3.54
Fife, Stephen	R-R	6-3	220	10-4-86	0	2	2.70	5	5	0	0	27	25	8	8	2	12	20	.255	.224	.286	6.75	4.05
Guerra, Javy	R-R	6-1	200	10-31-85	2	3	2.60	45	0	0	8	45	44	13	13	1	23	37	.265	.314	.229	7.40	4.60
Guerrier, Matt	R-R	6-3	195	8-2-78	0	2	3.86	16	0	0	0	14	8	6	6	3	7	9	.174	.316	.074	5.79	4.50
Harang, Aaron	R-R	6-7	260	5-9-78	10	10	3.61	31	31	0	0	180	167	85	72	14	85	131	.246	.260	.233	6.56	4.26
Jansen, Kenley	B-R	6-5	260	9-30-87	5	3	2.35	65	0	0	25	65	33	18	17	6	22	99	.146	.147	.145	13.71	3.05
Kershaw, Clayton	L-L	6-3	220	3-19-88	14	9	2.53	33	33	2	0	228	170	70	64	16	63	229	.210	.181	.216	9.05	2.49
League, Brandon	R-R	6-2	210	3-16-83	2	1	2.30	28	0	0	6	27	17	7	7	0	14	27	.183	.176	.186	8.89	4.61
Lilly, Ted	L-L	6-0	190	1-4-76	5	1	3.14	8	8	0	0	49	36	23	17	3	19	31	.203	.209	.201	5.73	3.51
Lindblom, Josh	R-R	6-4	240	6-15-87	2	2	3.02	48	0	0	0	48	42	16	16	9	18	43	.241	.253	.232	8.12	3.40
2-team total (26 Philadelphia)					3	5	3.55	74	0	0	1	71	61	31	28	13	35	70	—	—	—	8.87	4.44

Player	B-T	HT	WT	DOB	W	L	ERA	G	GS	CG	SV	IP	H	R	ER	HR	BB	SO	AVG	vLH	vRH	K/9	BB/9
MacDougal, Mike	B-R	6-4	180	3-5-77	0	0	7.94	7	0	0	0	6	9	5	5	0	6	4	.346	.182	.467	6.35	9.53
Rodriguez, Paco	L-L	6-3	215	4-16-91	0	1	1.35	11	0	0	0	7	3	1	1	0	4	6	.136	.143	.125	8.10	5.40
Tolleson, Shawn	R-R	6-2	220	1-19-88	3	1	4.30	40	0	0	0	38	30	19	18	4	20	39	.221	.316	.152	9.32	4.78
Wall, Josh	R-R	6-6	220	1-21-87	1	0	4.76	7	0	0	0	6	3	3	3	1	1	4	.158	.000	.250	6.35	1.59
Wright, Jamey	R-R	6-6	235	12-24-74	5	3	3.72	66	0	0	0	68	72	35	28	2	30	54	.270	.252	.283	7.18	3.99

Fielding

Catcher	PCT	G	PO	A	E	DP	PB
Ellis	.995	131	1007	87	6	12	11
Federowicz	1.000	2	13	0	0	0	0
Treanor	.989	35	261	21	3	3	0

First Base	PCT	G	PO	A	E	DP
Gonzalez	.997	36	315	33	1	34
Hairston Jr.	—	1	0	0	0	0
Kennedy	1.000	3	3	1	0	0
Loney	.992	105	703	55	6	64
Rivera	.985	54	301	19	5	20
Sands	1.000	1	9	1	0	1
Van Slyke	1.000	5	23	4	0	2

Second Base	PCT	G	PO	A	E	DP
Cruz	1.000	2	5	9	0	2
De Jesus Jr.	1.000	7	5	9	0	2
Ellis	.994	110	211	274	3	59
Hairston Jr.	.973	30	44	66	3	16

Third Base	PCT	G	PO	A	E	DP
Cruz	.984	51	29	92	2	9
De Jesus Jr.	.750	5	1	2	1	0
Hairston Jr.	.947	32	15	56	4	2
Herrera	.968	20	10	20	1	3
Kennedy	.967	39	20	68	3	5
Punto	1.000	5	0	1	0	0
Ramirez	1.000	8	3	15	0	0
Sellers	1.000	7	2	5	0	2
Uribe	.963	46	21	84	4	7

Shortstop	PCT	G	PO	A	E	DP
Cruz	.981	24	44	58	2	12
Gordon	.946	79	127	186	18	38

	PCT	G	PO	A	E	DP
Herrera	.978	13	21	23	1	7
Kennedy	.958	16	35	33	3	3
Punto	1.000	11	15	23	0	7
Sellers	1.000	3	1	1	0	0

	PCT	G	PO	A	E	DP
Hairston Jr.	.667	2	1	1	1	0
Herrera	1.000	2	1	0	0	0
Ramirez	.974	57	72	150	6	35
Sellers	.975	9	17	22	1	4
Uribe	.800	1	2	2	1	0

Outfield	PCT	G	PO	A	E	DP
Abreu	.984	47	59	2	1	0
Castellanos	.917	13	11	0	1	0
Ethier	.988	147	238	3	3	1
Gwynn Jr.	.994	90	149	6	1	0
Hairston Jr.	.973	18	35	1	1	0
Herrera	.980	32	48	1	1	1
Kemp	.995	105	208	7	1	1
Kennedy	—	1	0	0	0	0
Rivera	1.000	46	52	3	0	0
Sands	1.000	7	8	0	0	0
Van Slyke	1.000	21	22	1	0	1
Victorino	.991	53	110	2	1	1

ALBUQUERQUE ISOTOPES

TRIPLE-A

PACIFIC COAST LEAGUE

Batting	B-T	HT	WT	DOB	AVG	vLH	vRH	G	AB	R	H	2B	3B	HR	RBI	BB	HBP	SH	SF	SO	SB	CS	SLG	OBP
Abreu, Bobby	L-R	6-0	220	3-11-74	.353	.400	.333	5	17	2	6	1	0	0	3	0	0	0	.412	.450
Angle, Matt	L-R	5-10	180	9-10-85	.303	.240	.325	115	393	62	119	18	5	5	47	41	6	5	2	82	13	3	.412	.376
Baisley, Jeff	R-R	6-3	225	12-19-82	.284	.307	.273	62	225	37	64	15	2	8	41	20	4	0	5	46	0	1	.476	.346
Bard, Josh	B-R	6-3	225	3-30-78	.331	.362	.311	45	148	19	49	9	0	6	32	6	0	1	0	19	0	0	.514	.355
Becker, Joe	R-R	5-10	184	11-8-85	.202	.139	.233	51	109	13	22	4	1	0	15	13	0	4	0	16	1	0	.257	.287
Castellanos, Alex	R-R	5-11	195	8-4-86	.328	.299	.342	94	344	74	113	25	7	17	52	46	11	2	4	85	16	8	.590	.420
Cavazos-Galvez, Brian	R-R	6-0	215	5-17-87	.354	.377	.339	57	178	33	63	11	3	7	32	5	2	1	1	24	1	1	.567	.376
Cilladi, Steve	R-R	5-9	182	3-15-87	.000	—	.000	1	1	0	0	0	0	0	0	0	0	0	0	1	0	0	.000	.000
Cruz, Luis	R-R	6-2	220	2-10-84	.318	.433	.266	74	289	46	92	31	3	8	46	13	1	0	2	34	1	2	.529	.348
De Jesus Jr., Ivan	R-R	5-11	200	5-1-87	.295	.319	.288	60	224	32	66	12	3	3	33	14	1	0	4	53	1	1	.415	.333
Federowicz, Tim	R-R	5-10	215	8-5-87	.294	.376	.261	115	412	71	121	34	1	11	76	52	3	1	7	91	0	1	.461	.371
Fields, Josh	R-R	6-2	220	12-14-82	.322	.368	.300	133	490	96	158	32	5	13	71	59	2	3	7	116	9	4	.488	.392
Gordon, Dee	L-R	5-11	160	4-22-88	.267	.333	.200	8	30	3	8	0	1	0	1	2	0	0	0	3	2	1	.333	.313
Gwynn Jr., Tony	L-R	5-11	195	10-4-82	.338	.333	.341	19	68	12	23	4	1	0	7	8	1	2	0	12	4	1	.426	.416
Hairston Jr., Jerry	R-R	5-10	195	5-29-76	.000	.000	.000	2	6	0	0	0	0	0	0	0	0	0	0	0	0	0	.000	.000
Henson, Tyler	R-R	6-1	205	12-15-87	.284	.311	.271	53	141	25	40	9	1	5	20	21	0	3	1	47	1	1	.468	.374
Herrera, Elian	B-R	5-10	190	2-1-85	.341	.429	.297	64	273	50	93	20	10	3	40	17	2	3	2	47	11	7	.520	.381
Kemp, Matt	R-R	6-4	225	9-23-84	.500	.200	.636	4	16	6	8	2	0	2	6	0	0	0	0	2	0	0	1.000	.500
Kennedy, Adam	L-R	195	1-10-76	.500	—	.500	1	4	0	2	0	0	0	0	0	0	0	0	0	0	0	.500	.500
Martinez, Ozzie	R-R	5-10	200	5-7-88	.255	.265	.250	39	102	8	26	3	0	0	8	6	0	2	0	14	0	0	.275	.296
Miles, Aaron	B-R	5-8	180	12-15-76	.235	.172	.282	18	68	7	16	2	1	1	7	6	0	1	0	8	0	0	.338	.297
Oeltjen, Trent	L-L	6-1	205	2-28-83	.294	.270	.303	112	402	72	118	22	8	13	61	35	7	6	6	106	14	9	.485	.356
Ogle, Tyler	R-R	5-11	193	8-9-90	1.000	1.000	1.000	1	3	0	3	0	0	0	4	1	0	0	0	0	0	0	1.000	1.000
Rivera, Juan	R-R	6-2	220	7-3-78	.400	—	.400	2	5	2	2	0	0	1	3	1	1	0	0	2	0	0	1.000	.571
Russell, Kyle	L-L	6-5	195	5-27-86	.111	.000	.125	7	18	4	2	0	0	0	2	0	0	0	0	4	0	0	.111	.200
Sands, Jerry	R-R	6-4	225	9-28-87	.296	.294	.297	119	452	84	134	17	4	26	107	59	3	0	8	106	1	0	.524	.375
Sellers, Justin	R-R	5-10	155	2-1-86	.286	.000	.333	2	7	1	2	1	0	0	1	0	0	0	1	2	0	0	.429	.250
Van Slyke, Scott	R-R	6-5	250	7-24-86	.327	.275	.349	95	358	68	117	34	1	18	67	46	3	0	4	64	5	3	.578	.404
Zawadzki, Lance	B-R	5-10	180	5-26-85	.000	.000	.000	5	13	1	0	0	0	0	0	1	0	1	0	4	0	0	.000	.071
2-team total (8 Memphis)					.200	—	—	13	45	3	9	1	1	0	3	2	0	1	0	10	1	0	.267	.234

Pitching	B-T	HT	WT	DOB	W	L	ERA	G	GS	CG	SV	IP	H	R	ER	HR	BB	SO	AVG	vLH	vRH	K/9	BB/9
Antonini, Mike	R-L	6-1	210	8-6-85	2	7	5.71	30	13	0	0	87	105	64	55	17	39	57	.297	.242	.326	5.92	4.05
Barcelo, Lorenzo	R-R	6-4	230	8-10-77	0	0	6.00	1	0	0	0	3	6	2	2	0	1	1	.400	.375	.429	3.00	0.00
Belisario, Ronald	R-R	6-3	245	12-31-82	0	0	0.00	2	0	0	0	2	2	2	0	0	2	0	.286	.333	.250	0.00	10.80
Corcoran, Tim	R-R	6-2	205	4-15-78	0	0	21.60	3	0	0	0	3	8	8	8	2	4	2	.500	.444	.571	5.40	10.80
Ely, John	R-R	6-3	205	5-13-86	14	7	3.20	27	27	1	0	169	150	68	60	18	36	165	.238	.245	.227	8.80	1.92
Felix, Francisco	R-R	5-11	205	7-28-83	1	1	7.94	7	1	0	0	17	24	16	15	4	9	6	.364	.349	.391	3.18	4.76
Fife, Stephen	R-R	6-3	220	10-4-86	11	4	4.66	25	24	0	0	135	157	85	70	13	44	93	.290	.251	.337	6.18	2.93
Guerra, Javy	R-R	6-1	200	10-31-85	0	0	8.31	3	0	0	0	4	7	4	4	1	1	3	.368	.417	.286	6.23	2.08
Guzman, Angel	R-R	6-3	190	12-14-81	2	1	4.43	23	0	0	2	22	27	12	11	2	6	17	.307	.362	.244	6.85	2.42
Johnson, Blake	R-R	6-5	200	6-14-85	3	1	5.74	21	5	0	0	42	45	28	27	6	13	32	.265	.267	.262	6.80	2.76
Leach, Brent	L-L	6-5	215	11-18-82	1	2	7.02	10	0	0	1	17	26	16	13	3	8	16	.347	.241	.413	8.64	4.32
Ledezma, Wil	L-L	6-4	225	1-21-81	3	3	6.99	38	0	0	3	37	43	30	29	7	21	48	.279	.254	.295	11.57	5.06
Lindsay, Shane	R-R	6-2	230	1-25-85	0	1	5.00	8	0	0	0	9	8	5	5	0	8	8	.242	.176	.313	8.00	12.00

Name	B-T	HT	WT	DOB	W	L	ERA	G	GS	CG	SV	IP	H	R	ER	HR	BB	SO	AVG	vLH	vRH	K/9	BB/9
2-team total (1 Iowa)					0	1	9.00	9	0	0	0	9	9	9	9	0	16	8	—	—	—	8.00	16.00
Loop, Derrick	R-L	6-3	220	12-11-83	11	4	4.88	34	13	0	0	103	101	61	56	11	44	67	.259	.258	.259	5.84	3.83
Montgomery, Bret	R-R	6-6	250	8-6-85	1	1	3.31	9	1	0	0	16	14	10	6	1	9	6	.246	.333	.167	3.31	4.96
Nieve, Fernando	R-R	6-0	220	7-15-82	7	9	5.96	25	24	0	0	119	162	91	79	19	38	107	.324	.298	.353	8.07	2.87
Parisi, Mike	R-R	6-3	215	4-18-83	1	1	2.72	9	9	0	0	43	39	13	13	2	11	37	.250	.293	.188	7.74	2.30
Rice, Scott	L-L	6-6	225	9-21-81	2	3	4.40	54	0	0	9	59	58	33	29	3	22	47	.256	.193	.292	7.13	3.34
Savage, Will	R-R	6-4	210	8-25-84	10	7	5.59	30	24	0	0	142	179	98	88	19	40	67	.317	.320	.313	4.26	2.54
St. Clair, Cole	L-L	6-5	225	7-30-86	3	3	4.24	41	3	0	0	81	85	46	38	4	30	35	.274	.270	.277	3.90	3.35
Threets, Erick	L-L	6-5	240	11-4-81	2	2	5.19	18	0	0	1	17	16	11	10	2	11	12	.246	.154	.308	6.23	5.71
2-team total (34 Sacramento)					6	4	2.79	52	0	0	4	61	51	20	19	2	30	43	—	—	—	6.31	4.40
Tolleson, Shawn	R-R	6-2	220	1-19-88	0	1	4.82	8	0	0	0	9	8	5	5	1	1	15	.222	.158	.294	14.46	0.96
Troncoso, Ramon	R-R	6-2	215	2-16-83	4	1	6.67	45	0	0	1	59	77	48	44	6	26	40	.316	.350	.283	6.07	3.94
Tucker, Ryan	R-R	6-1	215	12-6-86	0	0	4.50	4	0	0	0	4	6	2	2	0	0	4	.353	.333	.364	9.00	0.00
Vasquez, Luis	R-R	6-4	175	4-3-86	0	1	16.88	9	0	0	0	8	9	15	15	1	9	7	.300	.417	.222	7.88	10.13
Wall, Josh	R-R	6-6	220	1-21-87	2	1	4.53	55	0	0	28	54	50	30	27	7	20	52	.242	.262	.221	8.72	3.35

Fielding

Catcher	PCT	G	PO	A	E	DP	PB
Bard	.989	39	251	21	3	1	1
Federowicz	.985	108	662	101	12	5	3
Ogle	1.000	1	3	2	0	0	0

First Base	PCT	G	PO	A	E	DP
Baisley	.978	37	339	25	8	36
Bard	.750	2	3	0	1	0
Cavazos-Galvez	—	1	0	0	0	0
Fields	.989	37	260	19	3	23
Rivera	1.000	1	1	0	0	0
Sands	.983	44	370	29	7	34
Van Slyke	.978	39	338	22	8	35

Second Base	PCT	G	PO	A	E	DP
Becker	1.000	14	17	27	0	5
Castellanos	.968	50	91	148	8	37
Cruz	1.000	1	3	2	0	0
De Jesus Jr.	.983	43	60	118	3	26
Fields	1.000	4	4	14	0	1
Hairston Jr.	1.000	1	1	0	0	0
Henson	.941	9	10	22	2	4
Herrera	1.000	22	37	52	0	15
Martinez	1.000	5	10	18	0	5
Miles	.940	10	22	25	3	7
Zawadzki	1.000	1	2	6	0	0

Third Base	PCT	G	PO	A	E	DP
Baisley	.976	20	8	32	1	3
Becker	.957	15	6	16	1	3
Castellanos	.949	34	16	58	4	3
Cruz	1.000	2	2	3	0	0
De Jesus Jr.	.875	6	4	10	2	0
Fields	.953	70	40	123	8	16
Hairston Jr.	—	1	0	0	0	0
Henson	.833	3	1	4	1	0
Herrera	.923	6	5	7	1	0
Kennedy	1.000	1	0	2	0	0
Martinez	1.000	1	0	2	0	1
Miles	.833	4	3	2	1	1

Shortstop	PCT	G	PO	A	E	DP
Becker	.957	10	16	29	2	5
Cruz	.965	72	110	196	11	38
De Jesus Jr.	.938	9	21	24	3	5
Gordon	.939	8	11	20	2	9
Herrera	.934	25	49	65	8	24
Martinez	.934	28	30	69	7	10
Miles	.909	4	6	14	2	3
Sellers	1.000	2	8	10	0	4
Zawadzki	1.000	3	3	6	0	1

Outfield	PCT	G	PO	A	E	DP
Abreu	1.000	2	3	0	0	0
Angle	1.000	111	267	9	0	2
Castellanos	1.000	4	3	0	0	0
Cavazos-Galvez	.974	47	69	6	2	1
Cruz	—	1	0	0	0	0
De Jesus Jr.	—	3	0	0	0	0
Fields	.900	4	9	0	1	0
Gwynn Jr.	.963	15	26	0	1	0
Hairston Jr.	1.000	1	2	0	0	0
Henson	.985	30	64	2	1	0
Herrera	1.000	15	21	2	0	0
Kemp	1.000	2	3	0	0	0
Oeltjen	.985	101	193	5	3	2
Rivera	1.000	2	1	0	0	0
Russell	1.000	3	2	0	0	0
Sands	.994	79	149	11	1	3
Van Slyke	.960	57	91	5	4	1

CHATTANOOGA LOOKOUTS

DOUBLE-A

SOUTHERN LEAGUE

Batting	B-T	HT	WT	DOB	AVG	vLH	vRH	G	AB	R	H	2B	3B	HR	RBI	BB	HBP	SH	SF	SO	SB	CS	SLG	OBP
Baez, Pedro	R-R	6-2	195	3-11-88	.216	.236	.209	78	273	41	59	13	4	4	36	33	9	0	2	64	5	3	.337	.319
Becker, Joe	R-R	5-10	184	11-8-85	.283	.091	.343	19	46	8	13	1	0	1	3	7	1	0	0	6	1	0	.370	.389
Buss, Nick	L-R	6-2	195	12-15-86	.272	.242	.282	132	492	70	134	24	10	8	57	38	5	19	4	71	19	13	.411	.328
Cavazos-Galvez, Brian	R-R	6-0	215	5-17-87	.167	.278	.133	20	78	11	13	3	0	4	11	6	1	1	1	17	5	0	.359	.233
Coyle, Bobby	L-L	6-1	215	3-6-89	.324	.263	.389	13	37	4	12	0	1	1	5	3	0	1	0	9	1	1	.459	.375
Denker, Travis	R-R	5-9	205	8-5-85	.228	.317	.192	64	206	23	47	13	0	4	25	21	4	0	4	48	4	1	.350	.306
Erickson, Gorman	B-R	6-4	220	3-11-88	.234	.303	.200	94	274	25	64	15	1	3	25	44	3	6	1	56	1	2	.328	.345
Henson, Tyler	R-R	6-1	205	12-15-87	.133	.000	.154	5	15	2	2	0	0	0	2	5	0	0	1	6	0	0	.133	.333
Jackson, Anthony	B-R	5-8	175	6-17-84	.240	.182	.271	48	129	21	31	3	2	0	4	14	3	0	1	24	12	3	.295	.327
Lemmerman, Jake	R-R	6-1	192	5-4-89	.233	.327	.197	116	373	52	87	29	2	7	46	53	13	8	2	94	8	0	.378	.347
Maldonado, Brahiam	R-R	5-11	205	9-18-85	.270	.338	.238	72	211	26	57	11	3	2	21	14	5	0	0	45	4	0	.450	.325
2-team total (10 Mississippi)					.247	—	—	82	243	27	60	11	3	7	21	14	5	0	0	52	4	0	.403	.302
Nunez, Luis	R-R	5-11	160	11-21-86	.257	.209	.271	123	405	57	104	23	5	11	65	40	1	7	8	54	22	6	.420	.319
Ponte, Angelo	R-R	5-11	215	12-16-86	.200	.000	.250	1	5	0	1	0	0	0	0	0	0	0	0	2	0	0	.200	.333
Retherford, C.J.	R-R	5-10	195	8-14-85	.250	.283	.232	44	148	13	37	6	2	3	20	10	4	0	2	20	2	0	.378	.311
Russell, Kyle	L-L	6-5	195	6-27-86	.262	.128	.289	74	229	38	60	18	1	11	44	41	4	0	3	69	4	2	.493	.379
Smith, Blake	L-R	6-2	225	12-9-87	.267	.274	.264	133	461	69	123	29	4	13	65	64	3	0	2	134	14	6	.432	.358
Vazquez, Jan	B-R	5-10	165	4-29-91	.176	.143	.200	6	17	4	3	1	0	0	1	4	0	1	1	4	0	0	.235	.318
Wallach, Matt	L-R	6-1	210	2-17-86	.232	.000	.267	59	168	22	39	3	0	4	17	24	4	5	1	35	2	0	.321	.340
Wise, J.T.	R-R	6-0	210	6-2-86	.278	.288	.273	121	418	59	116	41	1	9	70	62	6	0	2	125	1	0	.445	.377
Ynoa, Rafael	R-R	6-0	180	8-7-87	.278	.306	.267	113	421	58	117	23	4	0	37	58	1	9	4	70	23	8	.352	.364

Pitching	B-T	HT	WT	DOB	W	L	ERA	G	GS	CG	SV	IP	H	R	ER	HR	BB	SO	AVG	vLH	vRH	K/9	BB/9
Aguasviva, Geison	L-L	6-2	166	8-3-87	2	5	2.53	50	0	0	1	64	42	21	18	3	28	40	.189	.186	.190	5.63	3.94
Ames, Steven	R-R	6-1	205	3-15-88	3	3	1.56	54	0	0	18	63	52	11	11	2	13	72	.222	.290	.177	10.23	1.85
Bawcom, Logan	R-R	6-2	200	11-2-88	3	3	2.60	27	0	0	13	35	30	10	10	1	16	36	.236	.219	.254	9.35	4.15
2-team total (12 Jackson)					5	3	2.39	39	0	0	19	49	36	13	13	2	31	51	—	—	—	9.37	5.69
De La Rosa, Rubby	R-R	5-11	205	3-4-89	0	0	27.00	2	0	0	0	1	3	3	3	1	0	0	.500	.500	.500	0.00	9.00
Dominguez, Jose	R-R	6-0	160	8-7-90	0	1	1.29	5	0	0	1	7	2	1	1	0	0	9	.095	.250	.000	11.57	0.00
Eadington, Eric	R-L	6-2	220	2-9-88	1	2	5.73	9	0	0	0	11	13	8	7	0	4	11	.289	.278	.296	9.00	3.27
Elbert, Scott	L-L	6-2	225	8-13-85	0	0	0.00	3	0	0	0	2	0	0	0	0	0	6	.000	.000	.000	27.00	0.00

Eovaldi, Nate	R-R	6-2	215	2-13-90	2	2	3.09	9	8	0	0	35	30	12	12	2	13	30	.244	.276	.215	7.71	3.34
Felix, Francisco	R-R	5-11	205	7-28-83	0	0	0.00	1	0	0	0	1	0	0	0	0	1	0	.000	.000	.000	0.00	9.00
Johnson, Blake	R-R	6-5	200	6-14-85	2	3	3.38	21	0	0	1	29	25	15	11	2	15	22	.227	.255	.203	6.75	4.60
Lee, Zach	R-R	6-4	190	9-13-91	4	3	4.25	13	13	0	0	66	69	37	31	6	22	51	.272	.333	.224	6.99	3.02
Magill, Matt	R-R	6-3	190	11-10-89	11	8	3.75	26	26	0	0	146	127	71	61	8	61	168	.232	.265	.202	10.33	3.75
Martin, Ethan	R-R	6-2	195	6-6-89	8	6	3.58	20	20	0	0	118	89	48	47	5	61	112	.214	.260	.171	8.54	4.65
Miller, Aaron	L-L	6-3	200	9-18-87	6	6	4.45	25	25	0	0	121	117	64	60	10	71	110	.261	.221	.276	8.16	5.27
Montgomery, Bret	R-R	6-6	250	8-6-85	0	0	45.00	1	0	0	0	1	4	5	5	1	2	2	.571	1.000	.400	18.00	18.00
Patterson, Red	R-R	6-3	210	5-11-87	7	1	3.07	47	0	0	0	70	70	29	24	2	32	71	.255	.287	.237	9.09	4.09
Portice, Eammon	R-R	6-2	185	6-18-85	1	0	5.40	8	0	0	0	10	10	7	6	2	5	8	.244	.350	.143	7.20	4.50
Redding, JonMichael	R-R	6-1	195	11-16-87	2	1	6.10	4	0	0	0	10	10	7	7	0	8	9	.256	.300	.211	7.84	6.97
Reed, Chris	L-L	6-4	195	5-20-90	0	4	4.84	12	11	0	0	35	31	19	19	2	20	29	.242	.209	.259	7.39	5.09
Rodriguez, Paco	L-L	6-3	215	4-16-91	1	0	1.32	15	0	0	3	14	7	2	2	0	6	22	.149	.174	.125	14.49	3.95
Roemer, Wes	R-R	6-0	205	10-7-86	4	2	2.73	23	0	0	1	53	50	22	16	3	17	46	.251	.279	.230	7.86	2.91
Santiago, Andres	R-R	6-2	200	10-26-89	1	2	2.77	6	4	0	0	26	21	11	8	1	13	26	.221	.152	.286	9.00	4.50
Smith, Steve	R-R	6-2	215	5-15-86	0	0	0.00	6	0	0	0	7	3	0	0	0	2	5	.130	.000	.167	6.75	2.70
Solano, Javier	R-R	6-0	177	3-31-90	3	0	2.73	38	0	0	0	63	58	20	19	4	17	60	.251	.252	.250	8.62	2.44
Tolleson, Shawn	R-R	6-2	220	1-19-88	0	0	1.38	11	0	0	5	13	8	2	2	2	4	19	.178	.211	.154	13.15	2.77
Vasquez, Luis	R-R	6-4	175	4-3-86	2	2	5.80	34	1	0	0	45	55	31	29	1	28	32	.304	.349	.265	6.40	5.60
von Schamann, Duke	R-R	6-5	220	6-3-91	1	0	1.80	1	1	0	0	5	3	1	1	0	1	0	.188	.000	.231	0.00	1.80
Webster, Allen	R-R	6-3	185	2-10-90	6	8	3.55	27	22	0	0	122	120	63	48	1	57	117	.260	.278	.244	8.65	4.22
Withrow, Chris	R-R	6-4	220	4-1-89	3	3	4.65	22	7	0	2	60	52	34	31	3	36	64	.233	.265	.207	9.60	5.40

Fielding

Catcher	PCT	G	PO	A	E	DP	PB
Erickson	.996	86	677	54	3	7	7
Ponte	1.000	1	13	0	0	0	0
Vazquez	1.000	6	58	4	0	1	0
Wallach	.991	49	413	33	4	7	5
Wise	1.000	4	29	5	0	1	0

First Base	PCT	G	PO	A	E	DP
Cavazos-Galvez	1.000	6	32	0	0	5
Denker	1.000	30	219	19	0	25
Nunez	.991	17	97	8	1	10
Wallach	1.000	2	8	0	0	3
Wise	.988	104	786	52	10	75

Second Base	PCT	G	PO	A	E	DP
Becker	.962	6	8	17	1	4
Denker	.983	16	21	36	1	4
Jackson	.875	3	5	2	1	2
Lemmerman	.985	28	58	73	2	20
Nunez	.968	55	90	123	7	28
Ynoa	.970	59	105	154	8	37

Third Base	PCT	G	PO	A	E	DP
Baez	.960	74	38	130	7	9
Becker	.778	5	4	3	2	0
Denker	1.000	12	3	10	0	0
Lemmerman	1.000	1	1	0	0	0
Nunez	.984	35	13	48	1	7
Retherford	.953	36	19	63	4	12

Shortstop	PCT	G	PO	A	E	DP
Becker	1.000	2	0	4	0	0
Lemmerman	.957	83	102	233	15	48
Nunez	.889	5	1	7	1	2
Ynoa	.959	59	82	153	10	43

Outfield	PCT	G	PO	A	E	DP
Buss	.985	131	246	16	4	4
Cavazos-Galvez	.952	15	19	1	1	0
Coyle	1.000	10	7	0	0	0
Henson	1.000	5	9	0	0	0
Jackson	1.000	39	65	3	0	0
Maldonado	.977	54	81	5	2	0
Nunez	.962	25	22	3	1	0
Russell	.976	55	81	2	2	1
Smith	.975	127	225	13	6	3
Wallach	—	1	0	0	0	0

RANCHO CUCAMONGA QUAKES — *HIGH CLASS A*

CALIFORNIA LEAGUE

Batting	B-T	HT	WT	DOB	AVG	vLH	vRH	G	AB	R	H	2B	3B	HR	RBI	BB	HBP	SH	SF	SO	SB	CS	SLG	OBP
Aguilar, Alexis	R-R	5-11	162	6-17-91	.255	.273	.250	58	192	25	49	8	0	1	15	10	3	2	1	35	8	2	.313	.301
Akins, Nick	R-R	6-1	220	12-25-87	.245	.229	.254	29	102	13	25	4	0	2	8	5	1	1	0	20	1	0	.343	.287
Angulo, Selme	L-R	5-10	190	2-12-85	.000	—	.000	1	2	0	0	0	0	0	0	0	0	0	0	1	0	0	.000	.000
Baez, Pedro	R-R	6-2	195	3-11-88	.228	.167	.235	50	184	19	42	14	1	7	23	14	2	0	2	44	2	1	.429	.287
Becker, Joe	R-R	5-10	184	11-8-85	.313	.286	.333	4	16	2	5	0	0	0	0	0	0	0	0	4	0	0	.313	.313
Cavazos-Galvez, Brian	R-R	6-0	215	5-17-87	.346	.294	.371	12	52	14	18	2	1	3	11	2	0	0	0	4	4	2	.596	.370
Coyle, Bobby	L-L	6-1	215	3-6-89	.378	.361	.382	56	201	34	76	17	2	8	32	11	0	0	1	18	3	1	.602	.408
Delmonico, Tony	R-R	6-0	194	4-27-87	.188	.263	.156	21	64	2	12	3	1	0	9	13	2	0	1	24	0	1	.266	.338
Domecus, Steve	R-R	6-3	220	6-29-87	.277	.412	.242	22	83	14	23	7	1	0	8	7	4	0	0	14	2	0	.386	.362
Ellis, Mark	R-R	5-10	190	6-6-77	.286	.500	.125	4	14	3	4	0	0	0	3	2	0	0	0	3	0	0	.286	.375
Ethier, Andre	L-L	6-2	205	4-10-82	.000	.000	.000	2	4	0	0	0	0	0	1	1	0	0	0	1	0	0	.000	.200
Gallagher, Austin	L-R	6-5	210	11-16-88	.283	.216	.304	105	374	58	106	27	1	15	74	58	3	0	1	82	2	5	.481	.383
Garcia, Jonathan	R-R	5-11	175	11-11-91	.233	.250	.228	95	378	54	88	18	2	12	41	15	3	1	3	134	2	3	.386	.266
Grider, Casio	R-R	6-1	165	8-17-87	.217	.243	.209	51	152	23	33	7	2	2	11	9	6	4	1	41	7	1	.329	.286
Guerrero, Pedro	R-R	6-3	185	12-3-88	.150	.125	.167	7	20	2	3	1	0	0	0	0	0	1	0	7	0	0	.200	.150
Henson, Tyler	R-R	6-1	205	12-15-87	.192	.121	.227	29	99	14	19	8	1	3	14	11	1	0	1	33	3	2	.384	.277
Jacobs, Chris	R-R	6-5	257	11-25-88	.273	.359	.243	87	300	49	82	15	0	17	49	31	6	0	0	103	2	1	.493	.353
Kemp, Matt	R-R	6-4	225	9-23-84	.429	.600	.333	4	14	2	6	1	0	0	4	2	0	0	0	4	0	0	.500	.500
Kennedy, Adam	L-R	5-11	195	1-10-76	.250	.000	.286	5	16	4	4	0	1	0	1	1	0	0	0	4	0	0	.375	.294
Landry, Leon	L-R	5-11	185	9-20-89	.328	.309	.335	80	345	63	113	26	15	8	51	14	5	7	5	52	20	9	.559	.358
2-team total (24 High Desert)					.341	—	—	104	449	88	153	34	18	13	76	19	6	7	6	66	27	11	.584	.371
Maynard, Pratt	L-R	6-0	215	11-19-89	.214	.200	.217	9	28	1	6	0	0	0	3	4	0	0	1	6	1	0	.214	.303
Mirabal, Charlie	R-R	5-11	180	4-2-87	.191	.186	.193	70	204	26	39	5	3	0	14	12	1	7	0	34	7	2	.245	.240
O'Brien, Chris	B-R	6-0	219	7-24-89	.252	.358	.213	80	302	33	76	11	3	7	44	23	2	0	4	54	1	0	.377	.305
Page, Jarrad	B-R	6-1	205	10-19-84	.040	.250	.000	8	25	0	1	0	0	0	1	1	0	0	1	6	1	1	.040	.074
2-team total (30 San Jose)					.156	—	—	38	135	16	21	3	2	1	10	10	0	0	2	47	6	2	.230	.211
Pederson, Joc	L-L	6-1	185	4-21-92	.313	.330	.309	110	434	96	136	26	4	18	70	51	10	2	2	81	26	14	.516	.396
Pericht, Mike	R-R	6-5	235	5-23-88	.265	.189	.291	40	147	24	39	9	0	10	28	14	5	0	1	54	0	0	.531	.347
Puig, Yasiel	R-R	6-3	215	12-7-90	.327	.538	.256	14	52	10	17	2	0	1	4	6	1	0	0	8	7	4	.423	.407
Retherford, C.J.	R-R	5-10	195	8-14-85	.343	.316	.352	74	286	49	98	19	2	20	72	21	7	3	5	42	9	4	.633	.395
Rivera, Juan	R-R	6-2	220	7-3-78	.143	—	.143	2	7	1	1	0	0	1	2	0	0	0	0	1	0	0	.571	.143

Batting	B-T	HT	WT	DOB	AVG	vLH	vRH	G	AB	R	H	2B	3B	HR	RBI	BB	HBP	SH	SF	SO	SB	CS	SLG	OBP
Sellers, Justin	R-R	5-10	155	2-1-86	.286	.000	.333	3	7	1	2	1	1	0	0	1	0	0	0	1	1	0	.714	.375
Songco, Angelo	L-R	6-0	190	9-9-88	.218	.292	.207	46	188	20	41	7	0	6	20	13	3	0	1	50	1	1	.351	.278
Suarez, Gabe	R-R	6-0	170	12-14-84	.261	.375	.246	19	69	11	18	5	0	0	6	6	0	2	0	24	1	2	.333	.320
Uribe, Juan	R-R	6-0	240	3-22-79	.300	.500	.000	3	10	1	3	0	1	1	3	0	0	0	1	4	0	0	.800	.273
Vazquez, Jan	B-R	5-10	165	4-29-91	.242	.273	.236	20	66	7	16	1	0	0	6	5	2	1	0	10	4	0	.258	.315
Wingo, Scott	L-R	5-11	175	3-25-89	.246	.229	.251	109	353	53	87	12	7	2	33	56	15	10	6	77	13	8	.337	.367

Pitching	B-T	HT	WT	DOB	W	L	ERA	G	GS	CG	SV	IP	H	R	ER	HR	BB	SO	AVG	vLH	vRH	K/9	BB/9
Acosta, Ryan	R-R	6-2	170	11-4-88	4	2	4.30	28	5	0	0	67	66	39	32	8	28	79	.255	.265	.244	10.61	3.76
Bawcom, Logan	R-R	6-2	200	11-2-88	1	1	0.64	12	0	0	7	14	4	1	1	0	6	24	.087	.067	.097	15.43	3.86
Belisario, Ronald	R-R	6-3	245	12-31-82	0	1	12.00	1	0	0	0	3	6	4	4	0	0	1	.429	.500	.375	3.00	0.00
Cabrera, Freddie	R-R	6-5	210	1-25-90	1	3	6.35	40	1	0	1	67	88	56	47	9	27	43	.317	.322	.313	5.81	3.65
Coffey, Todd	R-R	6-4	240	9-9-80	0	1	4.50	2	2	0	0	2	3	1	1	0	0	1	.375	.500	.250	4.50	0.00
Cone, Derek	R-R	6-5	210	6-20-90	0	0	4.50	1	0	0	0	2	1	1	1	0	0	0	.143	.250	.000	0.00	0.00
De La Rosa, Rubby	R-R	5-11	205	3-4-89	1	0	0.00	3	2	0	0	9	4	0	0	0	3	9	.138	.211	.000	9.00	3.00
Eadington, Eric	R-L	6-2	220	2-9-88	2	1	3.29	35	0	0	21	38	36	14	14	0	15	39	.261	.196	.305	9.16	3.52
Frias, Carlos	R-R	6-4	170	11-13-89	0	1	12.71	3	1	0	0	6	9	8	8	0	8	5	.375	.500	.313	7.94	12.71
Garcia, Onelki	L-L	6-3	220	8-2-89	0	0	0.00	1	0	0	0	2	0	0	0	0	1	4	.000	.000	.000	18.00	0.00
Garcia, Yimi	R-R	6-1	175	8-18-90	2	1	2.53	9	0	0	2	11	7	5	3	0	5	22	.175	.316	.048	18.56	4.22
Gould, Garrett	R-R	6-4	190	7-19-91	5	10	5.75	27	23	0	0	130	140	91	83	19	54	123	.275	.204	.331	8.52	3.74
Guerra, Javy	R-R	6-1	200	10-31-85	0	0	4.50	2	2	0	0	2	1	1	1	0	0	1	.125	.250	.000	4.50	0.00
Guerrier, Matt	R-R	6-3	195	8-2-78	0	0	3.60	5	3	0	0	5	3	2	2	0	0	5	.176	.167	.182	9.00	0.00
Hawksworth, Blake	R-R	6-3	195	3-1-83	0	0	4.50	2	2	0	0	2	1	1	1	0	0	2	.125	.250	.000	9.00	0.00
Lee, Zach	R-R	6-4	190	9-13-91	2	3	4.55	12	12	0	0	55	60	31	28	9	10	52	.270	.288	.261	8.46	1.63
Lilly, Ted	L-L	6-0	190	1-4-76	0	1	5.73	4	4	0	0	11	10	8	7	3	2	7	.238	.083	.300	5.73	1.64
Martin, Jarret	L-L	6-4	227	8-14-89	0	1	12.27	2	2	0	0	4	4	5	5	2	3	2	.286	.500	.200	4.91	7.36
Martinez, Brandon	R-R	6-4	150	11-25-90	4	5	7.24	21	16	0	1	83	110	75	67	11	46	62	.321	.354	.291	6.70	4.97
McGough, Scott	R-R	6-0	170	10-31-89	3	5	3.99	35	0	0	5	47	45	23	21	3	26	48	.249	.264	.239	9.13	4.94
Montgomery, Bret	R-R	6-6	250	8-6-85	0	0	5.45	27	0	0	1	33	34	24	20	4	11	28	.264	.254	.273	7.64	3.00
Noriega, Juan	R-R	5-7	145	9-3-90	0	0	11.37	6	0	0	0	6	13	9	8	1	3	8	.433	.563	.286	11.37	4.26
O'Sullivan, Ryan	R-R	6-2	190	9-5-90	3	2	3.57	14	0	0	0	18	21	12	7	2	8	12	.292	.382	.211	6.11	4.08
Portice, Eammon	R-R	6-2	185	10-18-85	1	2	4.26	23	0	0	0	38	43	19	18	2	18	40	.297	.325	.262	9.47	4.26
Purpura, Robert	R-R	6-0	185	2-26-87	2	1	8.64	7	0	0	0	8	11	8	8	2	7	6	.306	.438	.200	6.48	7.56
Redding, JonMichael	R-R	6-1	195	11-16-87	9	7	4.42	25	17	0	0	130	149	76	64	10	48	102	.287	.294	.282	7.04	3.31
Reed, Chris	L-L	6-4	195	11-4-90	1	4	3.09	7	6	0	0	35	25	12	12	1	14	38	.203	.235	.191	9.77	3.60
Roberts, Jordan	L-L	6-2	200	1-5-86	8	0	3.67	38	1	0	0	88	100	40	36	7	29	66	.284	.264	.295	6.72	2.95
Rodriguez, Juan	R-R	6-5	195	12-12-88	2	1	2.89	8	0	0	0	9	9	4	3	0	10	15	.250	.364	.200	14.46	9.64
Sanchez, Angel	R-R	6-3	177	11-28-89	6	12	6.58	27	23	0	0	130	157	106	95	26	51	103	.300	.261	.333	7.13	3.53
Santiago, Andres	R-R	6-2	200	10-26-89	5	3	3.96	16	14	0	0	86	69	41	38	6	27	96	.214	.205	.223	10.01	2.81
Smith, Steve	R-R	6-2	215	5-15-86	4	2	4.25	34	0	0	3	55	52	35	26	5	21	46	.248	.236	.256	7.53	3.44
Stem, Craig	R-R	6-5	215	1-5-90	0	1	18.00	3	0	0	0	2	4	4	4	2	2	2	.444	.750	.200	9.00	9.00
Thomas, Mike	L-L	6-2	185	1-6-89	0	0	3.18	10	0	0	0	11	9	5	4	1	5	10	.265	.190	.217	7.94	3.97
Wilborn, Greg	L-L	6-2	175	6-3-87	1	1	9.18	13	2	0	0	17	17	19	17	1	18	18	.274	.304	.256	9.72	9.72
Zocchi, P.J.	R-R	5-11	195	6-19-85	1	0	16.20	3	0	0	0	3	9	7	6	1	0	6	.429	.375	.462	16.20	0.00

Fielding

Catcher	PCT	G	PO	A	E	DP	PB
Angulo	1.000	1	1	0	0	0	0
Domecus	.965	17	128	11	5	1	2
Maynard	1.000	9	71	6	0	1	0
O'Brien	.994	72	567	61	4	4	8
Pericht	.996	28	197	25	1	1	6
Vazquez	.969	20	140	14	5	2	1

First Base	PCT	G	PO	A	E	DP
Gallagher	.996	55	449	29	2	40
Jacobs	.993	53	427	29	3	33
Rivera	1.000	2	2	1	0	1
Songco	.984	34	275	29	5	31

Second Base	PCT	G	PO	A	E	DP
Aguilar	1.000	2	2	7	0	1
Ellis	1.000	3	1	7	0	0
Grider	.800	1	2	6	2	2
Henson	.952	12	24	36	3	5
Kennedy	1.000	2	2	5	0	0
Mirabal	1.000	2	1	6	0	0
Retherford	.957	5	13	9	1	3

	PCT	G	PO	A	E	DP
Suarez	.986	12	32	36	1	9
Wingo	.960	109	184	322	21	60

Third Base	PCT	G	PO	A	E	DP
Aguilar	1.000	4	2	2	0	0
Baez	.893	50	29	80	13	4
Becker	.889	4	2	8	1	0
Delmonico	1.000	14	5	29	0	2
Guerrero	1.000	2	0	2	0	0
Kennedy	.800	2	1	3	1	0
Mirabal	—	1	0	0	0	0
Retherford	.961	71	51	146	8	18
Uribe	1.000	2	5	7	0	2

Shortstop	PCT	G	PO	A	E	DP
Aguilar	.909	48	66	104	17	23
Grider	.896	33	37	83	14	15
Guerrero	.870	5	4	16	3	1
Mirabal	.962	62	85	168	10	25
Sellers	1.000	1	3	2	0	0
Suarez	.857	2	4	2	1	1

Outfield	PCT	G	PO	A	E	DP
Aguilar	1.000	3	1	1	0	0
Akins	.929	23	50	2	4	0
Cavazos-Galvez	.947	11	18	0	1	0
Coyle	1.000	35	42	0	0	0
Delmonico	1.000	7	7	0	0	0
Domecus	.917	4	11	0	1	0
Ethier	1.000	2	1	0	0	0
Gallagher	1.000	19	34	3	0	0
Garcia	.985	92	182	12	3	4
Grider	1.000	15	20	0	0	0
Guerrero	1.000	1	1	0	0	0
Henson	1.000	15	28	1	0	0
Kemp	1.000	3	4	0	0	0
Landry	.994	79	154	6	1	0
Page	1.000	2	3	0	0	0
Pederson	.991	109	220	9	2	3
Puig	1.000	8	10	0	0	0
Rivera	1.000	2	4	0	0	0
Suarez	1.000	5	13	0	0	0

GREAT LAKES LOONS

LOW CLASS A

MIDWEST LEAGUE

Batting	B-T	HT	WT	DOB	AVG	vLH	vRH	G	AB	R	H	2B	3B	HR	RBI	BB	HBP	SH	SF	SO	SB	CS	SLG	OBP
Akins, Nick	R-R	6-1	220	12-25-87	.238	.171	.257	55	189	31	45	10	1	8	24	28	5	0	2	48	10	6	.429	.348
Arredondo, Jesus Alberto	L-R	6-0	180	2-20-91	.254	.224	.261	102	394	47	100	24	5	0	30	28	3	9	4	41	13	8	.340	.305
Baldwin III, James	L-R	6-3	190	10-10-91	.209	.191	.214	123	440	62	92	18	8	7	40	45	7	4	0	177	53	8	.334	.293
Bosnik, Jesse	L-R	6-2	205	7-23-88	.239	.243	.238	106	372	47	89	17	2	8	44	26	2	0	3	67	21	4	.360	.290

Name	B-T	HT	WT	DOB	AVG	vLH	vRH	G	AB	R	H	2B	3B	HR	RBI	BB	HBP	SH	SF	SO	SB	CS	OBP	SLG
Boudreaux, Justin	R-R	6-1	190	10-3-89	.144	.286	.092	31	104	13	15	3	2	0	8	12	3	0	1	32	4	2	.212	.250
Cuevas, Noel	R-R	6-2	187	10-2-91	.227	.269	.218	40	150	14	34	5	2	2	18	8	4	1	1	25	7	1	.327	.282
Dickson, O'Koyea	R-R	5-11	215	2-9-90	.272	.300	.264	106	386	63	105	27	1	17	48	46	14	0	5	65	11	6	.479	.366
Edge, Andrew	R-R	6-2	225	12-31-87	.421	.500	.412	7	19	1	8	1	1	0	2	3	1	0	0	8	1	0	.579	.522
Guerrero, Pedro	R-R	6-3	185	12-3-88	.225	.159	.246	90	293	38	66	15	3	10	42	16	5	7	5	91	7	1	.399	.273
Hunt, Jeff	L-R	6-2	190	2-13-91	.237	.300	.219	42	135	17	32	7	0	6	23	11	1	4	2	46	1	1	.422	.295
Maynard, Pratt	L-R	6-0	215	11-19-89	.252	.268	.248	81	282	34	71	18	0	3	34	30	1	0	3	48	6	2	.348	.323
Morales, Delvis	B-R	6-1	146	8-29-90	.160	.071	.192	38	106	12	17	1	1	0	8	14	1	4	0	26	3	2	.189	.264
Ogle, Tyler	R-R	5-11	193	8-9-90	.210	.263	.186	18	62	10	13	1	0	3	7	6	3	0	0	16	0	0	.371	.310
Pericht, Mike	R-R	6-5	235	5-23-88	.186	.091	.219	14	43	5	8	3	0	1	2	7	3	0	0	18	1	0	.326	.340
Schebler, Scott	L-R	6-1	208	10-6-90	.260	.237	.267	137	515	67	134	32	8	6	67	30	10	2	3	99	17	11	.388	.312
Shines, Devin	R-L	5-9	185	5-15-89	.219	.227	.217	30	105	12	23	4	0	3	12	8	2	0	0	27	2	2	.343	.287
Songco, Angelo	L-R	6-0	190	9-9-88	.175	.120	.189	34	120	15	21	5	0	6	20	14	4	0	1	26	0	0	.367	.281
Suarez, Gabe	R-R	6-0	170	12-14-84	.333	.400	.313	7	21	4	7	0	0	0	2	4	1	0	0	2	2	0	.333	.462
Sweeney, Darnell	B-R	6-1	150	2-1-91	.291	.308	.286	51	199	34	58	8	4	5	23	24	2	3	1	41	17	4	.447	.372
Taylor, Kevin	L-R	6-0	200	7-13-91	.240	.273	.230	51	183	22	44	6	1	2	19	9	2	3	0	25	4	5	.317	.284
Vazquez, Jan	B-R	5-10	165	4-29-91	.267	.200	.287	40	131	11	35	5	0	1	9	8	4	0	2	35	1	0	.328	.324
Winker, Joey	L-L	6-1	190	8-28-89	.225	.196	.234	114	426	57	96	31	2	11	64	36	5	0	7	110	8	2	.385	.289

Pitching

Pitching	B-T	HT	WT	DOB	W	L	ERA	G	GS	CG	SV	IP	H	R	ER	HR	BB	SO	AVG	vLH	vRH	K/9	BB/9
Araujo, Victor	R-R	5-11	171	11-9-89	0	0	5.40	1	1	0	0	5	4	5	3	2	3	3	.211	.300	.111	5.40	5.40
Brown, Geoff	L-L	6-1	200	1-20-89	1	1	5.14	3	0	0	0	7	12	6	4	0	3	4	.387	.429	.375	5.14	3.86
Campbell, James	R-R	6-1	195	9-20-91	0	1	2.40	9	2	0	0	15	10	4	4	0	6	13	.189	.192	.185	7.80	3.60
Carela, Danny	R-R	6-3	225	9-18-87	2	1	2.57	7	0	0	1	7	4	2	2	0	5	9	.160	.333	.000	11.57	6.43
Cash, Ralston	R-R	6-1	197	8-20-91	1	6	6.42	9	8	0	0	41	45	33	29	4	24	29	.278	.277	.278	6.42	5.31
Coulombe, Danny	L-L	5-10	185	10-26-89	0	1	3.72	20	0	0	1	19	15	8	8	0	17	29	.217	.238	.185	13.50	7.91
Diaz, Amalio	R-R	6-2	170	9-10-86	1	0	3.27	5	0	0	0	11	14	4	4	1	5	5	.350	.353	.348	4.09	4.09
Dominguez, Jose	R-R	6-0	160	8-7-90	4	3	5.25	33	5	0	4	72	77	51	42	4	47	78	.268	.319	.224	9.75	5.88
Eadington, Eric	R-L	6-2	220	2-9-88	1	0	3.06	11	0	0	5	18	16	6	6	1	1	22	.235	.194	.270	13.75	0.51
Garcia, Yimi	R-R	6-1	175	8-18-90	4	4	3.02	40	0	0	14	42	42	19	14	0	17	60	.253	.278	.234	12.96	3.67
Gomez, Gustavo	R-R	6-2	210	5-24-91	8	8	5.63	24	24	0	0	110	122	77	69	8	55	77	.281	.281	.281	6.28	4.49
Griggs, Scott	R-R	6-3	185	5-13-91	1	0	3.86	8	0	0	0	12	7	5	5	0	13	14	.175	.300	.050	10.80	10.03
Hershiser, Jordan	R-R	6-8	245	9-15-88	0	0	3.60	3	0	0	0	5	5	2	2	0	3	2	.263	.250	.273	3.60	5.40
Laney, Matt	L-L	6-4	235	9-2-88	2	2	4.34	15	6	0	0	46	41	25	22	2	28	38	.244	.250	.242	7.49	5.52
Lima, Joel	R-R	6-0	165	8-7-89	2	0	4.52	28	3	0	0	78	79	43	39	13	22	22	.266	.275		6.03	2.55
Martin, Jarret	L-L	6-4	227	8-14-89	4	5	4.29	16	16	0	0	78	63	45	37	4	48	78	.221	.211	.226	9.04	5.56
Martinez, Brandon	R-R	6-4	150	11-25-90	1	4	7.04	5	5	0	0	23	30	19	18	4	9	10	.309	.393	.275	3.91	3.52
Mateo, Jackson	R-R	6-0	193	8-22-92	0	1	6.75	1	1	0	0	4	5	3	3	0	2	3	.333	.000	.417	6.75	4.50
Noriega, Juan	R-R	5-7	145	9-3-90	3	2	2.78	38	0	0	1	68	59	24	21	3	23	49	.238	.263	.216	6.49	3.04
O'Sullivan, Ryan	R-R	6-2	190	9-5-90	5	4	2.92	15	9	0	0	71	52	32	23	3	23	43	.201	.212	.191	5.45	2.92
Ozoria, Arismendy	R-R	6-0	195	8-7-90	8	8	4.51	26	25	0	0	116	124	73	58	9	50	77	.273	.255	.292	5.99	3.89
Rodriguez, Juan	R-R	6-5	195	12-12-88	3	0	7.45	21	0	0	2	29	21	26	24	4	31	32	.198	.222	.180	9.93	9.62
Rodriguez, Paco	L-L	6-3	215	4-16-91	0	0	0.00	6	0	0	2	6	4	0	0	0	0	10	.182	.250	.167	15.00	0.00
Sanchez, Raydel	R-R	6-0	205	3-11-90	3	8	4.64	27	14	0	0	95	93	58	49	17	33	61	.258	.241	.273	5.78	3.13
Shelton, Matt	R-R	6-4	205	11-30-88	3	5	2.81	43	0	0	2	67	56	33	21	5	25	70	.215	.265	.177	9.36	3.34
Stem, Craig	R-R	6-5	215	1-5-90	0	0	0.00	7	0	0	1	11	5	0	0	1	11		.128	.174	.063	8.74	0.79
Sulbaran, Miguel	L-L	5-10	165	3-19-94	0	1	15.00	2	2	0	0	6	13	11	10	2	4	3	.464	.556	.421	4.50	6.00
Thomas, Mike	L-L	6-2	185	1-6-89	4	2	1.24	37	0	0	5	51	35	11	7	1	27	63	.190	.136	.233	11.12	4.76
von Schamann, Duke	R-R	6-5	220	6-3-91	4	4	3.22	12	12	1	0	67	59	29	24	3	13	42	.233	.272	.195	5.64	1.75
West, Jason	R-R	5-11	185	7-30-88	0	0	2.22	14	0	0	1	24	16	9	6	0	16	12	.195	.114	.255	4.44	5.92
Wilborn, Greg	L-L	6-2	175	6-3-87	2	2	4.54	7	7	0	0	38	30	20	19	5	25	37	.226	.170	.263	8.84	5.97

Fielding

Catcher	PCT	G	PO	A	E	DP	PB
Edge	.976	5	39	1	1	0	1
Maynard	.990	77	561	59	6	4	4
Ogle	.989	12	83	6	1	0	1
Pericht	.965	13	100	11	4	1	4
Vazquez	.980	39	265	33	6	1	6

First Base	PCT	G	PO	A	E	DP
Bosnik	1.000	19	121	7	0	12
Dickson	.978	71	603	72	15	37
Shines	1.000	1	2	0	0	0
Songco	.981	22	198	10	4	16
Winker	.977	38	314	24	8	22

Second Base	PCT	G	PO	A	E	DP
Arredondo	.966	78	121	246	13	43
Bosnik	1.000	2	1	2	0	1
Boudreaux	1.000	1	0	3	0	0
Guerrero	.983	31	47	69	2	11
Suarez	1.000	1	2	3	0	1
Taylor	.974	36	57	95	4	17

Third Base	PCT	G	PO	A	E	DP
Bosnik	.910	86	75	167	24	11
Boudreaux	.848	15	6	22	5	3
Guerrero	.944	15	6	28	2	3
Hunt	.880	28	17	56	10	5
Suarez	.750	3	0	3	1	0
Taylor	1.000	4	0	1	0	0

Shortstop	PCT	G	PO	A	E	DP
Arredondo	—	1	0	0	0	0
Boudreaux	.918	15	17	28	4	5
Guerrero	.948	45	64	120	10	24
Morales	.948	37	46	100	8	15
Sweeney	.923	49	59	108	14	14

Outfield	PCT	G	PO	A	E	DP
Akins	.975	46	74	4	2	0
Arredondo	—	1	0	0	0	0
Baldwin III	.968	122	300	7	10	4
Boudreaux	1.000	1	2	1	0	0
Cuevas	.988	39	83	0	1	1
Dickson	1.000	5	5	0	0	0
Guerrero	—	1	0	0	0	0
Hunt	—	1	0	0	0	0
Morales	1.000	1	2	0	0	0
Schebler	.978	130	216	11	5	1
Shines	.946	24	34	1	2	0
Suarez	1.000	1	2	0	0	0
Winker	.990	65	95	3	1	1

ARIZONA LEAGUE

LOS ANGELES DODGERS

Batting	B-T	HT	WT	DOB	AVG	vLH	vRH	G	AB	R	H	2B	3B	HR	RBI	BB	HBP	SH	SF	SO	SB	CS	SLG	OBP
Alexander, Theo	L-R	6-1	195	8-25-94	.237	.320	.206	27	93	11	22	1	0	0	9	6	0	2	0	36	1	0	.247	.283
Babitt, Zach	L-R	5-7	160	9-1-89	.254	.235	.262	16	59	11	15	1	0	0	6	13	0	1	0	6	4	1	.271	.389
Cannon, John	R-R	6-0	180	5-11-90	.225	.320	.174	24	71	17	16	3	1	1	11	12	1	0	1	14	1	1	.338	.341
Cavazos-Galvez, Brian	R-R	6-0	215	5-17-87	.389	.000	.389	6	18	4	7	4	0	1	4	0	0	0	0	3	2	0	.778	.389
Chaplin, Jake	L-L	6-0	180	1-27-90	.250	.500	.000	1	4	0	1	0	0	0	2	0	0	0	0	1	0	0	.250	.250
Chigbogu, Justin	L-L	6-1	240	7-8-94	.200	.152	.220	32	115	18	23	4	0	3	12	14	0	0	2	50	2	3	.313	.282
Cowen, Austin	R-R	5-11	195	9-15-89	.280	.500	.211	13	25	3	7	1	0	0	2	1	0	0	1	7	0	0	.320	.296
Cuevas, Noel	R-R	6-2	187	10-2-91	.295	.476	.239	23	88	22	26	5	1	0	12	9	4	0	2	9	22	4	.375	.379
Curletta, Joey	R-R	6-4	225	3-8-94	.149	.286	.117	25	74	5	11	2	0	0	6	7	2	0	2	25	0	0	.176	.235
Edge, Andrew	R-R	6-2	225	12-31-87	.208	.333	.190	16	48	8	10	5	0	0	3	7	2	0	0	15	1	0	.313	.333
Embree, Corey	R-R	6-3	218	7-12-92	.320	.250	.333	24	75	12	24	5	4	0	18	10	2	1	1	15	1	1	.493	.409
Franco, Bladimir	R-R	6-1	172	2-4-91	.253	.167	.266	26	91	12	23	5	0	6	19	5	0	1	0	34	0	0	.505	.292
Henderson, Josh	L-L	6-0	184	11-16-93	.208	.125	.250	8	24	3	5	2	0	0	6	1	0	0	1	5	1	0	.292	.231
Hoenecke, Paul	L-R	6-1	180	7-8-90	.382	.281	.406	41	165	29	63	21	4	5	38	11	0	0	2	22	2	1	.648	.416
Jackson, Anthony	B-R	5-8	175	6-17-84	.289	.375	.267	11	38	12	11	0	1	2	7	12	2	0	1	6	3	1	.500	.472
Jarrin, Stefan	R-R	5-10	170	8-27-90	.209	.143	.229	26	91	13	19	3	1	3	9	11	2	0	1	24	1	1	.363	.305
O'Connell, Sean	L-R	6-4	181	12-12-91	—	—	—	1	0	1	0	0	0	0	0	1	0	0	0	0	0	0	—	1.000
Oeltjen, Trent	L-L	6-1	205	2-28-83	.400	.500	.333	1	5	1	2	0	0	0	1	0	0	0	0	0	0	0	.400	.400
Ogle, Tyler	R-R	5-11	193	8-9-90	.483	.333	.521	16	60	22	29	9	0	5	24	11	0	0	0	12	1	1	.883	.563
Oguisten, Faustino	R-R	6-2	165	1-17-91	.214	.000	.231	5	14	2	3	0	0	0	1	0	0	0	0	6	2	1	.214	.267
Pena, Gregory	B-R	6-0	175	12-16-91	.270	.250	.277	29	63	18	17	0	0	3	9	0	0	0	15	7	2	.270	.361
Pericht, Mike	R-R	6-5	235	5-23-88	.135	.000	.172	10	37	5	5	2	1	1	6	3	1	0	0	19	0	0	.324	.220
Puig, Yasiel	R-R	6-3	215	12-7-90	.400	.000	.440	9	30	10	12	0	3	4	11	6	0	0	7	1	1	1.000	.500
Rivas, Webster	R-R	6-0	195	8-8-90	.208	.500	.182	7	24	1	5	0	0	0	1	2	1	0	0	7	0	0	.208	.296
Rodriguez, Leo	R-R	5-11	160	12-11-91	.217	.188	.227	35	120	25	26	4	1	1	15	12	5	2	1	24	3	1	.292	.312
Santana, Alex	R-R	6-4	200	8-21-93	.240	.278	.231	26	96	12	23	3	1	1	12	11	0	0	1	41	4	1	.323	.315
Scavuzzo, Jacob	R-R	6-4	185	1-15-94	.220	.143	.246	24	82	11	18	3	1	1	5	5	2	1	0	27	7	2	.317	.281
Sgromolo, John	L-L	6-0	210	8-9-90	.310	.526	.259	27	100	19	31	7	1	1	17	11	0	0	1	16	0	0	.430	.375
Valentin, Jesmuel	B-R	5-10	174	5-12-94	.211	.167	.224	43	152	34	32	6	2	2	18	35	1	4	5	24	5	2	.316	.352

Pitching	B-T	HT	WT	DOB	W	L	ERA	G	GS	CG	SV	IP	H	R	ER	HR	BB	SO	AVG	vLH	vRH	K/9	BB/9
Angeles, Aris	R-R	6-0	179	9-9-89	2	0	4.50	16	1	0	0	26	31	13	13	2	10	22	.287	.282	.290	7.62	3.46
Araujo, Victor	R-R	5-11	171	11-9-89	4	2	6.88	13	11	0	0	54	64	47	41	9	18	48	.287	.313	.277	8.05	3.02
Bermudez, Jhosue	L-L	6-0	195	4-21-93	1	1	4.70	3	2	0	0	8	8	5	4	1	3	3	.276	.125	.333	3.52	3.52
Bird, Zach	R-R	6-3	177	7-14-94	1	2	4.54	10	10	0	0	40	36	24	20	2	17	46	.237	.275	.218	10.44	3.86
Caughel, Lindsey	R-R	6-3	190	8-13-90	2	2	3.18	7	0	0	0	17	18	10	6	2	3	14	.261	.238	.271	7.41	1.59
De La Rosa, Rubby	R-R	5-11	205	3-4-89	0	0	0.00	1	1	0	0	3	1	0	0	0	0	3	.100	.167	.000	9.00	0.00
Garcia, Alan	R-R	6-4	253	12-25-90	0	0	6.00	2	0	0	1	3	2	2	2	0	0	4	.182	.000	.250	12.00	0.00
Hershiser, Jordan	R-R	6-8	245	9-15-88	2	1	2.55	15	0	0	0	18	18	13	5	1	7	20	.237	.238	.236	10.19	3.57
Jones, Travis	R-R	6-2	200	5-23-89	1	2	4.15	20	0	0	4	22	21	15	10	0	5	27	.244	.294	.212	11.22	2.08
Martinez, Jonathan	R-R	6-1	170	6-27-94	3	0	3.05	13	12	0	0	59	59	28	20	3	16	59	.253	.263	.248	9.00	2.44
Mateo, Jackson	R-R	6-0	193	8-22-92	4	0	2.72	16	1	0	0	36	34	16	11	3	20	29	.248	.255	.244	7.18	4.95
Mesa, Luis	R-R	6-4	170	7-13-90	0	2	9.00	3	0	0	0	6	10	6	6	2	1	2	.385	.444	.353	3.00	1.50
Perez, Ricky	R-R	5-11	185	5-24-90	1	1	8.46	19	0	0	9	22	33	23	21	1	9	27	.351	.310	.369	10.88	3.63
Robinson, Joe	R-R	6-2	190	9-19-90	1	1	2.08	3	0	0	1	4	5	2	1	1	1	3	.313	.250	.333	6.23	2.08
Sulbaran, Miguel	L-L	5-10	165	3-19-94	6	3	2.51	11	11	0	0	57	57	23	16	2	9	62	.251	.278	.243	9.73	1.41
Takano, Kazuya	R-R	6-1	170	11-10-92	1	1	3.77	8	0	0	0	14	10	6	6	1	10	14	.196	.077	.237	8.79	6.28
Taveras, Samuel	R-R	6-5	175	9-20-89	2	1	3.57	16	0	0	0	23	20	11	9	3	9	14	.230	.259	.217	5.56	3.57
Unzue, Alfredo	L-L	6-1	175	8-16-85	0	0	0.00	4	0	0	0	3	2	0	0	0	3	5	.182	.500	.111	13.50	8.10
Velasquez, Abdiel	R-R	6-3	184	3-4-93	0	1	13.50	1	1	0	0	2	3	3	3	0	1	1	.375	.500	.250	4.50	4.50
Villa, Francisco	R-R	6-0	194	4-1-92	1	1	4.15	8	0	0	0	13	20	15	6	2	7	6	.357	.500	.300	4.15	4.85
Welch, Riley	R-R	6-0	160	9-12-90	0	0	0.00	3	0	0	0	6	2	0	0	0	0	7	.100	.222	.000	10.50	0.00
Wilborn, Greg	L-L	6-2	175	6-3-87	1	0	2.25	3	1	0	0	8	7	2	2	0	3	8	.241	.000	.304	9.00	3.38

Fielding

Catcher	PCT	G	PO	A	E	DP	PB
Cannon	.989	24	170	18	2	0	9
Cowen	1.000	4	7	0	0	0	0
Edge	.968	16	109	13	4	1	0
O'Connell	—	1	0	0	0	0	0
Ogle	.976	6	37	4	1	0	1
Pericht	1.000	9	76	9	0	0	1
Rivas	.980	7	40	9	1	1	0

First Base	PCT	G	PO	A	E	DP
Chaplin	1.000	1	10	1	0	0
Chigbogu	.977	15	117	12	3	9
Hoenecke	.995	23	193	14	1	13
Rodriguez	—	1	0	0	0	0
Sgromolo	.994	20	154	5	1	13

Second Base	PCT	G	PO	A	E	DP
Babitt	.929	16	30	35	5	7
Jarrin	.962	25	38	62	4	10
Oguisten	1.000	1	4	3	0	2
Rodriguez	.984	15	24	39	1	4

Third Base	PCT	G	PO	A	E	DP
Cowen	—	1	0	0	0	0
Franco	.938	23	11	50	4	3
Hoenecke	—	1	0	0	0	0
Rodriguez	.783	8	5	13	5	2
Santana	.852	26	17	29	8	1

Shortstop	PCT	G	PO	A	E	DP
Oguisten	.750	3	0	6	2	1
Rodriguez	.935	13	19	24	3	4

Valentin	.907	43	78	116	20	23

Outfield	PCT	G	PO	A	E	DP
Alexander	.950	26	37	1	2	0
Cavazos-Galvez	1.000	4	8	1	0	0
Cuevas	.976	22	36	5	1	0
Curletta	.944	25	31	3	2	0
Embree	1.000	23	26	4	0	1
Henderson	1.000	7	7	0	0	0
Hoenecke	.600	13	3	0	2	0
Jackson	1.000	11	34	0	0	0
Oeltjen	—	1	0	0	0	0
Pena	.939	27	31	0	2	0
Puig	.750	4	6	0	2	0
Scavuzzo	.962	22	50	1	2	0

OGDEN RAPTORS

ROOKIE

PIONEER LEAGUE

Batting	B-T	HT	WT	DOB	AVG	vLH	vRH	G	AB	R	H	2B	3B	HR	RBI	BB	HBP	SH	SF	SO	SB	CS	SLG	OBP
Boudreaux, Justin	R-R	6-1	190	10-3-89	.236	.250	.233	44	165	34	39	12	1	3	28	18	8	1	1	42	5	1	.376	.339
Capellan, Jose	R-R	6-0	190	10-10-90	.338	.455	.302	34	139	21	47	15	3	1	20	6	0	2	2	30	1	0	.511	.361
Cowen, Austin	R-R	5-11	195	9-15-89	.364	.250	.429	6	22	6	8	2	0	1	6	1	2	0	1	1	0	0	.591	.423
Cuevas, Noel	R-R	6-2	187	10-2-91	.340	.222	.366	13	50	15	17	4	1	0	8	7	1	0	2	6	6	2	.460	.417
Ethel, J.J.	R-R	6-2	180	5-22-89	.216	.364	.154	13	37	10	8	4	0	2	10	5	2	0	1	10	0	0	.486	.333
Ethier, Devon	R-R	6-0	165	6-4-90	.169	.077	.188	26	77	9	13	5	0	0	6	6	2	1	1	31	3	1	.234	.244
Franco, Bladimir	R-R	6-1	172	2-4-91	.282	.316	.275	29	110	15	31	5	1	2	12	13	2	0	0	39	2	3	.400	.368
Hoenecke, Paul	L-R	6-1	180	7-8-90	.500	—	.500	3	4	1	2	2	0	0	2	1	0	0	0	1	0	0	1.000	.600
Holland, Malcolm	R-R	5-11	165	6-18-92	.244	.241	.244	60	193	46	47	6	0	0	15	54	6	2	1	47	44	9	.275	.421
Morales, Delvis	B-R	6-1	146	8-29-90	.341	.300	.352	30	135	21	46	9	2	0	15	13	1	5	0	26	9	5	.437	.403
Nam, Tae-Hyeok	R-R	6-0	209	3-13-91	.252	.290	.241	38	139	20	35	9	1	4	16	12	1	0	0	50	0	0	.417	.316
Ogle, Tyler	R-R	5-11	193	8-9-90	.258	.000	.308	8	31	9	8	2	0	0	5	4	1	0	1	5	0	0	.419	.351
Rathjen, Jeremy	R-R	6-6	190	1-28-90	.324	.353	.318	68	262	67	85	17	1	9	53	48	10	2	3	55	16	8	.500	.443
Santana, Alex	R-R	6-4	200	8-21-93	.269	.273	.268	24	93	14	25	8	1	1	19	4	1	1	3	29	1	2	.409	.297
Seager, Corey	L-R	6-3	195	4-27-94	.309	.333	.302	46	175	34	54	9	2	8	33	21	2	1	3	33	8	2	.520	.383
Shines, Devin	R-L	5-9	185	5-15-89	.304	.241	.321	35	138	30	42	10	1	8	34	10	5	1	6	41	8	0	.565	.358
Smith, Eric	L-R	6-1	190	10-10-90	.336	.298	.347	63	256	55	86	17	7	3	55	33	7	0	6	32	2	1	.492	.417
Stover, Pat	R-R	6-4	210	9-12-90	.270	.271	.269	45	178	24	48	3	1	2	19	19	5	0	3	54	1	6	.331	.351
Sweeney, Darnell	B-R	6-1	150	2-1-91	.303	.250	.320	16	66	12	20	1	2	0	10	9	1	0	3	8	10	2	.379	.380
Thompson, Kevin	R-R	6-3	185	9-16-88	.218	.118	.238	30	101	13	22	5	0	1	16	6	6	1	1	26	5	1	.297	.298
Valdez, Jesus	R-R	6-3	180	3-27-92	.324	.214	.351	70	281	54	91	19	2	9	62	31	8	0	2	58	4	2	.502	.404

Pitching	B-T	HT	WT	DOB	W	L	ERA	G	GS	CG	SV	IP	H	R	ER	HR	BB	SO	AVG	vLH	vRH	K/9	BB/9
Campbell, James	R-R	6-1	195	9-20-91	0	0	9.82	3	0	0	0	4	6	5	4	1	3	5	.353	.143	.500	12.27	7.36
Caughel, Lindsey	R-R	6-3	190	8-13-90	3	2	3.38	8	7	1	0	43	33	19	16	2	8	29	.213	.202	.225	6.12	1.69
Cone, Derek	R-R	6-5	210	6-20-90	1	1	9.35	18	4	0	0	35	41	38	36	5	32	25	.297	.345	.263	6.49	8.31
Cotton, Jharel	R-R	6-1	197	1-19-92	1	0	1.20	5	1	0	0	15	9	2	2	0	3	20	.180	.250	.133	12.00	1.80
Coulombe, Danny	L-L	5-10	185	10-26-89	0	0	1.50	3	0	0	0	6	3	2	1	0	1	8	.125	.200	.105	12.00	1.50
De Aza, Carlos	R-R	6-3	178	5-4-90	0	5	7.86	14	4	0	0	26	35	31	23	5	12	18	.307	.368	.246	6.15	4.10
Downing, Gregg	L-L	5-10	175	11-8-90	3	0	5.33	21	3	0	2	54	64	34	32	8	20	39	.292	.313	.284	6.50	3.33
Drowne, Mike	R-L	5-10	175	7-28-88	4	1	5.15	20	0	0	0	37	47	28	21	2	26	27	.320	.205	.361	6.63	6.38
Frias, Carlos	R-R	6-4	170	11-13-89	7	4	4.15	15	15	0	0	78	83	49	36	5	21	67	.269	.306	.236	7.73	2.42
Garcia, Alan	R-R	6-4	253	12-25-90	1	1	5.75	16	0	0	3	20	22	13	13	2	13	24	.289	.286	.292	10.62	5.75
Gonzalez, Sawil	R-R	6-2	170	3-24-90	2	1	3.79	16	0	0	3	19	12	11	8	2	7	33	.174	.167	.178	15.63	3.32
Griggs, Scott	R-R	6-3	185	5-13-91	0	0	4.09	11	0	0	5	11	5	7	5	0	8	18	.135	.200	.091	14.73	6.55
Hermsen, Jake	R-L	6-0	205	11-16-89	1	6	4.24	12	12	0	0	51	64	37	24	1	16	37	.288	.241	.304	6.53	2.82
Jones, Owen	R-R	6-1	190	6-12-89	1	2	4.28	24	0	0	7	27	32	15	13	3	4	28	.283	.246	.321	9.22	1.32
Jones, Travis	R-R	6-2	200	5-23-89	0	1	2.70	2	0	0	0	3	4	2	1	0	2	2	.286	.000	.444	5.40	5.40
Laney, Matt	L-L	6-4	235	9-2-88	3	3	6.70	11	11	0	0	48	66	49	36	6	23	30	.324	.267	.340	5.59	4.28
Martinez, Jonathan	R-R	6-1	170	6-27-94	0	1	6.00	2	2	0	0	9	13	7	6	2	3	9	.333	.375	.304	9.00	3.00
Mesa, Luis	R-R	6-4	170	7-13-90	1	1	6.95	8	3	0	0	22	33	20	17	0	12	12	.344	.360	.326	4.91	4.91
Nishijimi, Kazuki	L-L	6-1	190	11-23-89	8	1	4.56	16	0	0	0	57	54	34	24	6	12	30	.292	.323	.277	5.70	2.28
Reckling, Matthew	R-R	6-4	210	3-24-89	0	0	27.00	1	0	0	0	1	2	2	2	1	1	1	.400	.500	.333	13.50	13.50
Stem, Craig	R-R	6-5	215	1-5-90	3	1	4.73	17	1	0	0	27	19	17	14	1	17	26	.209	.135	.259	8.78	5.74
Stripling, Ross	R-R	6-3	190	11-23-89	1	0	1.24	14	12	0	0	36	26	7	5	0	6	37	.197	.164	.231	9.17	1.49
Sulbaran, Miguel	L-L	5-10	165	3-19-94	0	1	5.40	1	1	0	0	5	5	3	3	1	1	4	.278	.000	.357	7.20	1.80
von Schamann, Duke	R-R	6-5	220	6-3-91	0	0	0.00	2	0	0	0	3	1	0	0	0	2	2	.100	.000	.167	6.00	0.00
Welch, Riley	R-R	6-0	160	9-12-90	0	0	15.43	2	0	0	0	2	6	4	4	2	2	1	.500	.333	.556	3.86	7.71
West, Jason	R-R	5-11	185	7-30-88	3	0	5.02	22	0	0	0	38	47	34	21	3	21	34	.309	.318	.302	8.12	5.02

Fielding

Catcher	PCT	G	PO	A	E	DP	PB
Capellan	.987	33	265	28	4	2	5
Cowen	1.000	5	31	3	0	0	1
Ethel	.948	8	53	2	3	0	0
Ogle	.900	2	14	4	2	0	0
Smith	.991	29	203	17	2	1	7

First Base	PCT	G	PO	A	E	DP
Ethel	1.000	2	2	2	0	1
Hoenecke	.929	2	11	2	1	0
Nam	.988	35	319	12	4	29
Valdez	.983	42	368	31	7	38

Second Base	PCT	G	PO	A	E	DP
Boudreaux	.959	13	28	42	3	13

	PCT	G	PO	A	E	DP
Holland	.919	36	56	114	15	22
Morales	.956	25	48	83	6	18
Sweeney	.909	2	3	7	1	0

Third Base	PCT	G	PO	A	E	DP
Boudreaux	.917	9	5	17	2	1
Franco	.894	27	15	61	9	6
Santana	.761	22	19	32	16	5
Thompson	.926	20	9	54	5	4

Shortstop	PCT	G	PO	A	E	DP
Boudreaux	.914	14	23	41	6	8
Morales	.960	5	9	15	1	4
Seager	.916	44	68	117	17	27
Sweeney	.921	13	16	42	5	10

	PCT	G	PO	A	E	DP
Thompson	1.000	2	2	3	0	1

Outfield	PCT	G	PO	A	E	DP
Cuevas	.947	13	35	1	2	0
Ethier	.912	26	31	0	3	0
Holland	1.000	24	52	2	0	1
Rathjen	.962	66	119	8	5	2
Shines	.950	34	53	4	3	3
Stover	.951	45	75	2	4	1
Thompson	1.000	8	10	0	0	0
Valdez	1.000	20	31	5	0	1

DSL DODGERS　　　　　　　　　　　ROOKIE

DOMINICAN SUMMER LEAGUE

Batting	B-T	HT	WT	DOB	AVG	vLH	vRH	G	AB	R	H	2B	3B	HR	RBI	BB	HBP	SH	SF	SO	SB	CS	SLG	OBP
Alcantara, Luis	R-R	6-1	185	10-23-92	.271	.353	.245	27	70	10	19	3	0	0	6	3	2	1	1	10	2	3	.314	.316
Almarante, Bernys	R-R	6-0	185	9-12-93	.000	—	.000	2	3	0	0	0	0	0	0	0	0	0	0	1	0	0	.000	.000
Capellan, Yensys	R-R	6-2	190	10-4-93	.276	.273	.277	46	163	23	45	9	2	2	30	20	1	1	1	27	2	2	.393	.357
Chales, Jorlin	B-R	5-9	155	7-7-94	.200	.500	.000	2	5	1	1	1	0	0	1	0	0	0	0	2	0	0	.400	.200
Cordero, Josmar	R-R	5-10	175	9-10-91	.362	.350	.367	60	229	50	83	19	1	6	47	14	9	2	1	20	9	5	.533	.419
De La Cruz, Detriano	R-R	6-3	195	11-27-91	.250	.167	.273	9	28	6	7	2	0	0	1	1	0	2	0	10	0	0	.321	.276
Gomez, Rafael	B-R	6-0	170	1-5-95	.175	.214	.163	29	63	6	11	0	0	0	4	15	2	1	0	27	3	1	.175	.350
Infante, Jorky	R-R	6-0	155	2-24-91	.275	.271	.276	61	222	28	61	5	4	0	19	26	4	5	5	30	12	6	.333	.354
Javier, Jose Luis	R-R	5-10	160	10-31-92	.242	.216	.252	65	198	35	48	8	2	1	19	21	5	5	2	55	15	7	.318	.327
Jimenez, Jhoanel	B-R	5-11	185	6-19-90	.250	.000	.500	2	4	2	1	0	0	0	0	3	0	0	0	0	0	0	.250	.571
Linares, Jonathan	R-R	6-0	160	4-29-93	.301	.378	.277	49	156	27	47	15	1	1	27	18	6	2	3	20	3	0	.429	.388
Martinez, Vladimir	R-R	6-2	173	6-26-92	.250	.200	.270	25	88	14	22	2	0	0	7	10	0	0	0	8	1	4	.273	.327
Nunez, Gerson	R-R	5-11	178	12-21-90	.333	.294	.348	54	189	28	63	6	3	1	31	8	5	7	2	34	9	3	.413	.373
Perez, Jesus	R-R	6-1	180	7-19-93	.224	.353	.189	55	161	20	36	4	1	1	19	14	1	5	1	32	4	6	.280	.288
Rodriguez, Arce	R-R	6-0	191	12-10-92	.352	.231	.390	15	54	11	19	4	0	0	6	7	2	0	1	9	3	1	.426	.438
Rojas, Jeffry	B-R	6-0	170	8-18-92	.327	.381	.315	38	113	10	37	3	1	1	18	8	8	0	2	6	2	5	.398	.405
Romano, Albert	B-R	6-1	171	7-14-95	.185	.000	.263	8	27	1	5	1	0	0	4	2	0	0	1	2	1	0	.222	.233
Rosario, Martin	R-R	5-10	182	12-29-91	.218	.258	.203	34	110	8	24	3	0	0	7	7	1	3	0	29	1	0	.245	.271
Santana, Melvin	R-R	5-10	160	10-4-91	.315	.333	.309	64	232	51	73	11	7	3	26	29	1	8	3	34	13	6	.461	.389
Subero, Luis	R-R	5-11	185	3-21-95	.217	.000	.263	11	23	1	5	0	0	0	4	0	0	1	1	0	1	0	.217	.208
Tejeda, Claudio	R-R	6-0	170	12-29-92	.226	.211	.231	47	146	22	33	6	0	0	13	26	4	6	2	26	4	6	.267	.354
Urena, Daury	R-R	6-1	170	4-10-91	.261	.000	.316	8	23	6	6	1	0	0	0	0	0	1	0	0	2	0	.304	.292

Pitching	B-T	HT	WT	DOB	W	L	ERA	G	GS	CG	SV	IP	H	R	ER	HR	BB	SO	AVG	vLH	vRH	K/9	BB/9
Alcantara, Geuris	R-R	6-2	185	5-29-92	5	1	4.55	19	0	0	1	30	33	18	15	2	9	13	.292	.208	.315	3.94	2.73
Beras, Leonel	L-L	6-0	155	7-18-88	5	4	3.59	15	12	0	0	78	77	39	31	4	22	95	.259	.241	.261	11.01	2.55
Bermudez, Jhosue	L-L	6-0	195	4-21-93	5	2	3.28	10	9	0	0	47	38	19	17	0	21	35	.232	.000	.242	6.75	4.05
Binns, Simon	R-R	6-3	170	7-13-93	1	0	9.35	4	0	0	0	9	10	9	9	1	4	5	.286	.286	.286	5.19	4.15
Bock, Edinson	R-R	6-2	190	4-15-94	1	4	5.06	15	7	0	0	37	33	23	21	2	20	31	.246	.250	.245	7.47	4.82
Canelo, Willie	L-L	6-2	180	5-27-92	1	1	2.04	14	0	0	0	18	13	8	4	1	9	15	.200	.000	.206	7.64	4.58
Chavez, Giordanny	R-R	6-3	185	4-19-91	0	0	2.25	2	1	0	0	4	6	3	1	0	2	0	.353	.000	.375	0.00	4.50
De La Rosa, Ricardo	R-R	6-0	184	4-19-91	0	6	5.56	21	0	0	9	23	28	16	14	0	8	23	.311	.238	.333	9.13	3.18
De Paula, Luis	L-L	6-1	170	4-23-92	1	1	2.72	12	6	0	0	36	31	20	11	0	17	35	.230	.000	.250	8.67	4.21
Diaz, Jose Agusto	R-R	5-11	185	1-15-91	4	1	1.49	15	10	2	2	73	54	15	12	3	6	59	.205	.170	.212	7.31	0.74
Jean, Elou	R-R	5-11	205	4-29-92	0	0	0.00	1	0	0	0	1	0	0	0	0	0	0	.000	—	.000	0.00	0.00
Jimenez, Luis	R-R	6-0	178	5-28-93	4	2	4.56	12	1	0	1	24	26	19	12	1	9	15	.277	.417	.229	5.70	3.42
Lantigua, Daniel	R-R	6-3	180	5-29-92	0	0	9.35	9	0	0	0	9	13	10	9	0	9	6	.342	.286	.355	6.23	9.35
Munoz, Bryan	R-R	6-2	180	7-26-95	1	0	1.80	8	0	0	1	10	9	2	2	1	5	12	.243	.250	.241	10.80	4.50
Pena, Ariel	R-R	6-4	208	1-8-92	0	1	15.43	5	0	0	0	5	7	12	8	4	1	5	.350	.000	.438	1.93	15.43
Querales, Mario	R-R	6-1	175	11-15-94	1	4	5.16	15	6	0	1	30	37	25	17	0	19	10	.308	.429	.272	3.03	5.76
Sandoval, Nelson	R-R	6-0	190	2-26-94	2	1	4.08	12	1	0	0	18	14	11	8	1	13	11	.222	.238	.214	5.60	6.62
Serrano, Wellington	L-L	6-0	190	9-5-94	0	0	0.00	2	0	0	0	2	1	0	0	0	3	1	.167	.000	.000	4.50	13.50
Shellon, Andrew	R-R	6-2	150	1-6-93	0	0	0.00	1	0	0	0	3	2	0	0	0	2	0	.200	.500	.125	6.00	0.00
Silverio, Luis	L-L	6-3	190	6-6-91	3	2	3.22	19	6	0	1	45	42	23	16	1	16	26	.253	.083	.266	5.24	3.22
Tamarez, Moises	R-R	6-3	195	3-6-93	0	0	2.70	3	1	0	0	7	7	6	2	0	0	3	.259	—	.259	4.05	0.00
Teodo, Wascar	R-R	6-4	190	6-25-94	3	0	1.67	16	6	0	0	54	35	12	10	2	19	42	.183	.240	.163	7.00	3.17
Velasquez, Abdiel	R-R	6-3	184	3-4-93	0	1	2.45	6	4	0	0	22	17	7	6	0	4	11	.213	.100	.229	4.50	1.64

Fielding

Catcher	PCT	G	PO	A	E	DP	PB
Alcantara	1.000	7	16	1	0	0	2
Cordero	.977	25	142	28	4	1	6
Jimenez	1.000	2	8	4	0	0	0
Linares	1.000	27	132	35	0	1	1
Rojas	1.000	1	1	0	0	0	0
Rosario	.977	26	136	36	4	1	4
Subero	.941	8	25	7	2	1	3

First Base	PCT	G	PO	A	E	DP
Alcantara	1.000	1	1	0	0	0
Cordero	.984	45	340	29	6	31
Linares	.995	26	179	5	1	12
Rojas	.978	10	80	7	2	3
Rosario	1.000	2	8	1	0	1
Subero	—	1	0	0	0	0

Second Base	PCT	G	PO	A	E	DP
Chales	1.000	2	2	2	0	0
Infante	1.000	1	2	3	0	1
Javier	.933	6	16	12	2	2
Martinez	.972	7	17	18	1	7
Santana	.935	56	121	110	16	20
Tejeda	.944	8	7	10	1	3

Third Base	PCT	G	PO	A	E	DP
Capellan	.881	21	14	60	10	2
Infante	.933	10	10	18	2	0
Perez	.846	5	2	9	2	1
Rojas	.932	24	19	49	5	2
Tejeda	.795	24	18	40	15	4

Shortstop	PCT	G	PO	A	E	DP
Almarante	1.000	2	1	3	0	0
Gomez	.860	21	25	49	12	7
Infante	.960	7	7	17	1	2
Javier	.908	39	49	80	13	14
Romano	.846	8	12	21	6	3
Santana	1.000	1	0	1	0	1
Tejeda	1.000	13	7	20	0	5

Outfield	PCT	G	PO	A	E	DP
Alcantara	—	1	0	0	0	0
Alcantara	.950	18	14	5	1	0
De La Cruz	.952	9	20	0	1	0
Gomez	—	2	0	0	0	0
Infante	.958	47	87	5	4	1
Javier	.968	28	29	1	1	0
Linares	—	1	0	0	0	0
Martinez	1.000	12	15	0	0	0
Nunez	.950	48	110	5	6	1
Perez	.962	50	72	3	3	0
Rojas	1.000	1	2	0	0	0
Rosario	.889	6	5	3	1	0
Tejeda	1.000	13	15	1	0	0
Urena	1.000	8	3	0	0	0

Miami Marlins

SEASON IN A SENTENCE: The Marlins opened their new ballpark with a splash, signing free agents Heath Bell, Mark Buehrle and Jose Reyes and sending prospects to the White Sox in order to pry Ozzie Guillen away to be their manager, but by season's end Miami was mired in last place and Bell and Guillen were on their way out of town.

HIGH POINT: The Marlins definitely won the offseason, generating national attention not only for the high-profile free agents but for shiny new Marlins Park, which had a contemporary feel in contrast to the retro ballpark trend of the last 20 years. The Marlins' national profile reached a point it hadn't seen since the club won its last World Series title in 2003.

LOW POINT: Unfortunately for Miami, the team eventually had to take the field, and there it never lived up to expectations. Just five games into the season, Guillen was forced to apologize for statements he made about Fidel Castro that angered many Cuban emigrees in the community. It was all downhill from there, as a solid May was quickly forgotten during an awful June that saw Bell lose his closer job. From June 1 on, the Marlins were 40-71.

NOTABLE ROOKIES: A midseason sell-off brought in young talent to a team that began the season with no notable rookies. Righthanders Nate Eovaldi (3-7, 4.43) and Jacob Turner (1-4, 3.38) both earned spots in the rotation. Lefthander Dan Jennings was reasonably effective working out of the bullpen in short stints.

KEY TRANSACTIONS: It's hard to find an offseason move that paid off handsomely for the Marlins, and by midseason the team was ready to unload payroll. Third baseman Hanley Ramirez was traded to the Dodgers in a deal that brought back Eovaldi. First baseman Gaby Sanchez was sent to the Pirates, and righthander Anibal Sanchez was sent to the Tigers for Turner. Bell went to the Diamondbacks after the season.

DOWN ON THE FARM: Righthander Jose Fernandez, the club's first-round pick in 2011, was one of the breakout stars of 2012, dominating at low Class A Greensboro and high Class A Jupiter. In Jupiter, he was paired with center fielder Christian Yelich, who hit for average and power while playing an excellent center field. Those two clubs also were Miami's most successful on the field. Greensboro went 80-59 before falling in the South Atlantic League championship series.

OPENING DAY PAYROLL: $118.1 million (7th)

PLAYERS OF THE YEAR

AMANDA WILLIAMS

MAJOR LEAGUE	MINOR LEAGUE
Giancarlo Stanton of	**Jose Fernandez** rhp
.290/361/.608	(Low A/High A)
37 HR, 30 2B	14-1, 1.75
Led NL in SLG	Led minors in WHIP

ORGANIZATION LEADERS

BATTING		*Minimum 250 AB
MAJORS		
* AVG	Jose Reyes	.287
* OPS	Jose Reyes	.780
HR	Giancarlo Stanton	37
RBI	Giancarlo Stanton	86
MINORS		
* AVG	Mike Cervenak, New Orleans	.340
* OBP	Mike Cervenak, New Orleans	.408
* SLG	Christian Yelich, Jupiter	.519
R	Marcell Ozuna, Jupiter	89
H	Austin Barnes, Greensboro	152
TB	Marcell Ozuna, Jupiter	233
2B	Austin Barnes, Greensboro	36
3B	Donnie Webb, Jacksonville	8
HR	Luke Montz, New Orleans	29
RBI	Marcell Ozuna, Jupiter	95
BB	Jake Smolinski, Jacksonville	78
SO	Kyle Jensen, Jacksonville	162
SB	Kevin Mattison, New Orleans	26

PITCHING		#Minimum 75 IP
MAJORS		
W	Mark Buehrle	13
# ERA	Mark Buehrle	3.74
SO	Josh Johnson	165
SV	Heath Bell	19
MINORS		
W	Jose Fernandez, Greensboro/Jupiter	14
L	Tom Koehler, New Orleans	11
	Graham Taylor, Jacksonville	11
# ERA	Jose Fernandez, Greensboro/Jupiter	1.75
G	A.J. Ramos, Jacksonville	55
GS	Four players tied at	27
SV	Michael Brady, Jupiter	22
IP	Tom Koehler, New Orleans	151
BB	Brad Hand, New Orleans	75
SO	Jose Fernandez, Greensboro/Jupiter	158
# AVG	Jose Fernandez, Greensboro/Jupiter	.191

General Manager: Larry Beinfest. **Farm Director:** Marty Scott. **Scouting Director:** Stan Meek.

Class	Team	League	W	L	PCT	Finish	Manager
Majors	Miami Marlins	National	69	93	.426	13th (16)	Ozzie Guillen
Triple-A	New Orleans Zephyrs	Pacific Coast	73	67	.521	8th (16)	Ron Hassey
Double-A	Jacksonville Suns	Southern	70	70	.500	5th (10)	Andy Barkett
High A	Jupiter Hammerheads	Florida State	74	62	.544	5th (12)	Andy Haines
Low A	Greensboro Grasshoppers	South Atlantic	80	59	.576	3rd (14)	Dave Berg
Short-season	Jamestown Jammers	New York-Penn	35	40	.467	t-7th (14)	Angel Espada
Rookie	GCL Marlins	Gulf Coast	29	30	.492	7th (14)	Jorge Hernandez
Overall 2012 Minor League Record			361	328	.524	8th (30)	

ORGANIZATION STATISTICS

MIAMI MARLINS
NATIONAL LEAGUE

Batting	B-T	HT	WT	DOB	AVG	vLH	vRH	G	AB	R	H	2B	3B	HR	RBI	BB	HBP	SH	SF	SO	SB	CS	SLG	OBP
Bonifacio, Emilio	B-R	5-11	205	4-23-85	.258	.210	.282	64	244	30	63	3	4	1	11	25	1	4	0	52	30	3	.316	.330
Brantly, Rob	L-R	6-2	205	7-14-89	.290	.200	.313	31	100	14	29	8	0	3	8	13	0	0	0	16	1	1	.460	.372
Buck, John	R-R	6-2	230	7-7-80	.192	.162	.206	106	343	29	66	15	1	12	41	49	3	1	2	103	0	0	.347	.297
Coghlan, Chris	L-R	6-0	190	6-18-85	.140	.050	.164	39	93	10	13	1	0	1	10	9	0	1	2	12	0	2	.183	.212
Cousins, Scott	L-L	6-1	195	1-22-85	.163	.000	.194	53	86	7	14	4	1	1	3	4	0	2	0	24	1	1	.267	.200
Dobbs, Greg	L-R	6-1	210	7-2-78	.285	.279	.286	120	319	26	91	13	2	5	39	14	2	0	7	53	4	2	.386	.313
Green, Nick	R-R	5-11	185	9-10-78	.174	.182	.167	7	23	1	4	3	0	0	1	0	1	0	0	6	0	0	.304	.208
Greenberg, Adam	L-R	5-9	180	2-21-81	.000	—	.000	1	1	0	0	0	0	0	0	0	0	0	0	1	0	0	.000	.000
Hayes, Brett	R-R	6-0	200	2-13-84	.202	.156	.220	39	114	7	23	6	0	3	4	0	0	0	49	1	0	.254	.229
Hernandez, Gorkys	R-R	6-0	190	9-7-87	.212	.185	.231	45	132	16	28	2	3	3	11	12	2	1	0	37	5	2	.341	.288
2-team total (25 Pittsburgh)					.192	—	—	70	156	18	30	2	3	3	13	13	3	1	0	42	7	2	.301	.267
Infante, Omar	R-R	5-11	195	12-26-81	.287	.309	.278	85	328	42	94	23	2	8	33	12	1	4	2	42	10	1	.442	.312
Kearns, Austin	R-R	6-3	240	5-20-80	.245	.196	.340	87	147	21	36	6	0	4	16	22	6	0	0	44	2	1	.367	.366
Lee, Carlos	R-R	6-2	270	6-20-76	.243	.256	.238	81	292	29	71	12	0	4	48	39	1	0	6	32	3	0	.325	.328
2-team total (66 Houston)					.264	—	—	147	550	53	145	27	1	9	77	58	1	0	6	49	3	0	.365	.332
Mattison, Kevin	L-L	6-1	195	9-20-85	.000	.000	.000	3	5	0	0	0	0	0	0	0	0	0	0	2	0	0	.000	.000
Morrison, Logan	L-L	6-3	240	8-25-87	.230	.213	.236	93	296	30	68	15	1	11	36	31	4	0	3	58	1	0	.399	.308
Murphy, Donnie	R-R	5-10	190	3-10-83	.216	.128	.275	52	116	13	25	6	2	3	12	9	2	1	1	35	1	1	.379	.281
Petersen, Bryan	L-R	6-0	190	4-9-86	.195	.137	.211	84	241	29	47	9	3	0	17	25	1	5	1	58	8	2	.257	.272
Ramirez, Hanley	R-R	6-2	230	12-23-83	.246	.253	.244	93	353	49	87	18	2	14	48	37	3	0	2	72	14	4	.428	.322
2-team total (64 Los Angeles)					.257	—	—	157	604	79	155	29	4	24	92	54	6	0	3	132	21	7	.437	.322
Reyes, Jose	B-R	6-1	195	6-11-83	.287	.277	.291	160	642	86	184	37	12	11	57	63	0	5	6	56	40	11	.433	.347
Ruggiano, Justin	R-R	6-2	205	4-12-82	.313	.330	.305	91	288	38	90	23	1	13	36	29	0	1	1	84	14	8	.535	.374
Sanchez, Gaby	R-R	6-2	230	9-2-83	.202	.241	.186	55	183	12	37	10	0	3	17	12	0	0	1	36	1	0	.306	.250
2-team total (50 Pittsburgh)					.217	—	—	105	299	30	65	16	0	7	30	25	1	0	1	56	1	0	.341	.279
Solano, Donovan	R-R	5-9	190	12-17-87	.295	.291	.297	93	285	29	84	11	3	2	28	21	2	3	5	58	7	0	.375	.342
Stanton, Giancarlo	R-R	6-5	245	11-8-89	.290	.302	.285	123	449	75	130	30	1	37	86	46	5	0	1	143	6	2	.608	.361
Velazquez, Gil	R-R	6-2	185	10-17-79	.232	.263	.216	19	56	2	13	1	0	0	2	1	0	0	0	11	0	0	.250	.246

Pitching	B-T	HT	WT	DOB	W	L	ERA	G	GS	CG	SV	IP	H	R	ER	HR	BB	SO	AVG	vLH	vRH	K/9	BB/9
Bell, Heath	R-R	6-2	260	9-29-77	4	5	5.09	73	0	0	19	64	70	38	36	5	29	59	.282	.239	.317	8.34	4.10
Buehrle, Mark	L-L	6-2	245	3-23-79	13	13	3.74	31	31	1	0	202	197	88	84	26	40	125	.258	.217	.271	5.56	1.78
Choate, Randy	L-L	6-1	205	9-5-75	0	0	2.49	44	0	0	1	25	16	11	7	0	9	27	.178	.150	.233	9.59	3.20
2-team total (36 Los Angeles)					0	0	3.03	80	0	0	1	39	29	18	13	1	18	38	—	—	—	8.84	4.19
Cishek, Steve	R-R	6-6	215	6-18-86	5	2	2.69	68	0	0	15	64	54	26	19	3	29	68	.230	.279	.185	9.61	4.10
Dunn, Mike	L-L	6-0	220	5-23-85	0	3	4.91	60	0	0	1	44	49	31	24	3	29	47	.283	.293	.272	9.61	5.93
Eovaldi, Nate	R-R	6-2	215	2-13-90	3	7	4.43	12	12	0	0	63	70	32	31	5	27	44	.279	.290	.264	6.29	3.86
2-team total (10 Los Angeles)					4	13	4.30	22	22	0	0	119	133	59	57	10	47	78	—	—	—	5.88	3.54
Gaudin, Chad	R-R	5-10	185	3-24-83	4	2	4.54	46	0	0	0	69	72	39	35	6	26	57	.274	.322	.232	7.40	3.38
Hand, Brad	L-L	6-3	220	3-20-90	0	1	17.18	1	1	0	0	4	6	7	7	1	6	3	.353	.500	.308	7.36	14.73
Hatcher, Chris	R-R	6-2	200	1-12-85	0	0	4.30	11	0	0	0	15	17	9	7	3	6	10	.288	.357	.226	6.14	3.68
Jennings, Daniel	L-L	6-3	215	4-17-87	1	0	1.89	22	0	0	0	19	18	5	4	2	11	8	.247	.282	.206	3.79	5.21
Johnson, Josh	L-R	6-7	250	1-31-84	8	14	3.81	31	31	0	0	191	180	84	81	14	65	165	.252	.263	.238	7.76	3.06
Koehler, Tom	R-R	6-3	225	6-29-86	0	1	5.40	8	1	0	0	13	15	8	8	4	5	13	.278	.250	.294	8.78	1.35
LeBlanc, Wade	L-L	6-2	215	8-7-84	2	5	3.67	25	9	0	0	69	71	30	28	7	19	43	.275	.280	.273	5.64	2.49
Mujica, Edward	R-R	6-3	225	5-10-84	0	3	4.38	41	0	0	2	39	36	21	19	6	9	26	.240	.270	.211	6.00	2.08
2-team total (29 St. Louis)					0	3	3.03	70	0	0	2	65	56	24	22	7	12	47	—	—	—	6.47	1.65
Nolasco, Ricky	R-R	6-2	215	12-13-82	12	13	4.48	31	31	3	0	191	214	100	95	18	47	125	.285	.299	.270	5.89	2.21
Ramos, A.J.	R-R	5-10	210	9-20-86	0	0	3.86	11	0	0	0	9	8	4	4	2	4	13	.229	.118	.333	12.54	3.86
Rosario, Sandy	R-R	6-1	210	8-22-85	0	0	18.00	4	0	0	0	3	8	6	6	0	0	2	.471	.400	.571	6.00	0.00
Sanchez, Anibal	R-R	5-11	205	2-27-84	5	7	3.94	19	19	0	0	121	119	59	53	12	33	110	.259	.229	.288	8.18	2.45
Turner, Jacob	R-R	6-5	210	5-21-91	1	4	3.38	7	7	0	0	43	33	21	16	5	9	29	.208	.192	.221	6.12	1.90
Webb, Ryan	R-R	6-5	230	2-5-86	4	3	4.03	65	0	0	0	60	72	30	27	2	20	44	.295	.314	.282	6.56	2.98
Zambrano, Carlos	B-R	6-4	275	6-1-81	7	10	4.49	35	20	1	0	132	123	75	66	9	75	95	.251	.244	.257	6.46	5.10

Fielding

Catcher	PCT	G	PO	A	E	DP	PB
Brantly	.990	28	191	16	2	1	6
Buck	.991	105	715	57	7	4	7
Hayes	.980	33	221	21	5	1	1

First Base	PCT	G	PO	A	E	DP
Dobbs	.993	18	127	7	1	10
Kearns	1.000	2	14	1	0	2
Lee	.996	80	643	60	3	68
Morrison	.994	21	148	26	1	18
Sanchez	.996	54	442	47	2	45

Second Base	PCT	G	PO	A	E	DP
Bonifacio	.952	15	19	40	3	7
Green	1.000	2	1	7	0	3
Infante	.982	83	149	278	8	71

Murphy	1.000	13	16	25	0	3
Solano	.992	58	88	166	2	28

Third Base	PCT	G	PO	A	E	DP
Dobbs	.828	36	13	35	10	1
Green	.800	3	2	6	2	1
Murphy	.967	22	9	20	1	1
Ramirez	.954	90	66	122	9	20
Solano	.900	10	5	13	2	2
Velazquez	.959	17	16	31	2	3

Shortstop	PCT	G	PO	A	E	DP
Green	1.000	1	2	3	0	1
Murphy	1.000	2	3	4	0	2
Reyes	.973	160	226	419	18	105
Solano	1.000	5	1	5	0	2

Outfield	PCT	G	PO	A	E	DP
Bonifacio	.991	51	111	1	1	0
Coghlan	1.000	32	54	0	0	0
Cousins	1.000	36	44	0	0	0
Dobbs	1.000	37	43	0	0	0
Hernandez	1.000	35	83	1	0	0
Kearns	.989	34	90	0	1	0
Mattison	—	1	0	0	0	0
Morrison	.959	59	89	4	4	2
Petersen	.992	72	115	4	1	1
Ruggiano	.984	85	180	3	3	0
Solano	1.000	10	13	0	0	0
Stanton	.974	117	257	6	7	1

NEW ORLEANS ZEPHYRS

PACIFIC COAST LEAGUE

TRIPLE-A

MIAMI MARLINS

Batting	B-T	HT	WT	DOB	AVG	vLH	vRH	G	AB	R	H	2B	3B	HR	RBI	BB	HBP	SH	SF	SO	SB	CS	SLG	OBP
Aguila, Chris	R-R	5-11	200	2-23-79	.254	.330	.209	84	260	23	66	12	0	6	25	29	4	1	1	60	2	1	.369	.337
Armstrong, Cole	L-R	6-3	210	8-24-83	.207	.294	.185	37	82	7	17	6	0	2	8	12	1	1	0	26	0	0	.354	.316
Bowman, Shawn	R-R	6-3	225	12-9-84	.333	.395	.275	22	78	10	26	4	0	3	8	1	0	0	0	15	0	0	.500	.342
Brantly, Rob	L-R	6-2	205	7-14-89	.365	.240	.481	14	52	7	19	4	2	1	11	1	1	0	0	9	0	0	.558	.389
Cervenak, Mike	R-R	5-11	195	8-17-76	.340	.325	.347	101	371	61	126	22	0	13	57	43	3	0	5	49	1	2	.504	.408
Coghlan, Chris	L-R	6-0	190	6-18-85	.284	.364	.248	84	317	42	90	21	3	7	31	46	2	0	3	44	10	2	.435	.375
Cousins, Scott	L-L	6-1	195	1-22-85	.296	.265	.309	61	233	36	69	13	2	7	36	24	2	1	2	58	14	3	.459	.364
Davis, Brad	R-R	6-1	190	12-29-82	.067	.500	.000	9	15	1	1	0	0	0	0	0	0	0	0	3	0	0	.133	.125
2-team total (39 Tucson)					.146	—		46	144	15	21	8	1	2	12	11	0	0	1	37	4	0	.257	.205
Dominguez, Jeff	B-R	6-1	185	7-31-86	.207	.267	.167	39	111	8	23	4	0	1	4	4	0	1	0	24	0	0	.270	.235
Dominguez, Matt	R-R	6-1	215	8-28-89	.234	.213	.243	78	286	27	67	14	0	7	46	23	1	2	3	31	0	1	.357	.291
2-team total (45 Oklahoma City)					.257	—		123	447	48	115	24	0	9	69	34	3	3	5	52	0	1	.371	.311
Duarte, Jose	R-R	5-10	165	3-7-85	.233	.290	.172	21	60	3	14	1	0	1	4	9	0	0	0	11	1	1	.300	.333
Green, Nick	R-R	5-11	185	9-10-78	.344	.378	.326	63	212	44	73	16	1	12	47	15	5	1	2	36	2	2	.599	.397
Gutierrez, Chris	R-R	5-9	185	3-12-84	.100	.333	.000	4	10	2	1	0	0	1	2	2	0	0	0	2	0	0	.400	.250
Hayes, Brett	R-R	6-0	200	2-13-84	.356	.364	.351	16	59	9	21	4	0	3	8	3	1	0	0	11	0	0	.576	.397
Holm, Steve	R-R	6-0	205	10-21-79	.135	.083	.160	13	37	3	5	2	0	1	2	5	1	0	0	8	0	0	.270	.256
Jefferies, Jake	L-R	6-2	215	10-30-87	.133	.000	.167	6	15	1	2	1	0	0	2	2	0	1	0	2	0	1	.200	.235
Lambin, Chase	B-R	6-2	195	7-7-79	.253	.235	.262	89	249	24	63	7	3	8	32	19	3	5	7	53	0	4	.402	.306
Lasater, Ben	R-R	6-3	195	5-25-84	.268	.000	.324	10	41	6	11	1	0	1	6	1	1	0	1	9	2	1	.366	.295
Lopez, Alfredo	R-R	5-10	160	10-7-89	.111	.200	.000	4	9	2	1	0	0	0	1	1	0	0	0	2	0	0	.111	.200
Mattison, Kevin	L-L	6-1	195	9-20-85	.241	.291	.218	121	482	80	116	23	6	13	41	44	6	3	3	145	26	12	.394	.310
Montz, Luke	R-R	6-1	230	7-7-83	.222	.248	.208	123	370	55	82	14	0	29	74	45	3	0	2	101	1	3	.495	.310
Murphy, Donnie	R-R	5-10	190	3-10-83	.302	.250	.329	33	106	21	32	6	0	13	25	14	4	0	1	28	1	0	.726	.400
Pedroza, Sergio	L-R	6-1	180	2-23-84	.106	.067	.118	28	66	4	7	2	0	3	5	4	0	0	1	17	1	1	.227	.213
Petersen, Bryan	L-R	6-0	190	4-9-86	.321	.309	.327	64	243	45	78	8	2	3	28	20	5	0	3	43	8	7	.407	.380
Quintero, Humberto	R-R	5-9	215	8-2-79	.133	.000	.182	5	15	1	2	0	0	0	3	2	0	0	0	3	0	0	.133	.235
2-team total (25 Nashville)					.245	—		30	110	10	27	8	0	1	15	3	2	1	1	24	0	0	.345	.276
Sammons, Clint	R-R	6-1	210	5-15-83	.188	.097	.215	43	138	11	26	3	0	6	15	5	1	1	2	40	0	0	.341	.219
Sanchez, Gaby	R-R	6-2	230	9-2-83	.302	.370	.281	34	116	20	35	7	0	5	18	22	5	0	1	23	2	2	.491	.431
Solano, Donovan	R-R	5-9	190	12-17-87	.262	.244	.270	36	141	14	37	7	1	0	14	10	4	4	1	27	4	0	.326	.327
Velazquez, Gil	R-R	6-2	185	10-17-79	.312	.360	.292	110	398	52	124	15	1	4	42	49	4	8	2	50	6	8	.384	.391

Pitching	B-T	HT	WT	DOB	W	L	ERA	G	GS	CG	SV	IP	H	R	ER	HR	BB	SO	AVG	vLH	vRH	K/9	BB/9
Bramhall, Bobby	L-L	5-11	190	7-13-85	0	0	13.50	1	0	0	0	1	1	2	2	0	2	0	.667	1.000	.500	0.00	27.00
Delaney, Rob	L-R	6-2	250	9-8-84	3	1	2.29	44	0	0	1	63	58	17	16	2	18	46	.244	.228	.261	6.57	2.57
Dunn, Mike	L-L	6-0	220	5-23-85	1	1	4.58	12	0	0	0	18	19	11	9	0	7	24	.275	.267	.282	12.23	3.57
Glover, Gary	R-R	6-4	225	12-3-76	2	3	4.17	43	0	0	0	69	66	37	32	10	26	64	.249	.264	.231	8.35	3.39
Hand, Brad	L-L	6-3	220	3-20-90	11	7	4.00	27	27	0	0	148	129	72	66	15	75	141	.238	.218	.249	8.56	4.55
Hatcher, Chris	R-R	6-2	200	1-12-85	1	0	0.77	37	0	0	11	47	33	6	4	1	15	45	.196	.192	.200	8.62	2.87
Jennings, Daniel	L-L	6-3	215	4-17-87	1	3	3.14	42	0	0	2	52	48	19	18	2	16	48	.253	.266	.236	2.79
Jones, Beau	L-L	6-1	205	8-25-86	2	1	7.54	22	0	0	0	23	23	19	19	5	20	17	.274	.154	.378	6.75	7.94
Kaminska, Kyle	L-R	6-4	180	10-5-88	0	1	6.23	2	0	0	0	4	5	3	3	0	0	2	.278	.286	.273	4.15	0.00
Koehler, Tom	R-R	6-2	225	6-29-86	12	11	4.17	28	27	0	0	151	154	80	70	15	61	138	.268	.274	.260	8.23	3.64
Lazo, Raudel	L-L	5-10	175	4-12-89	0	0	0.00	1	0	0	0	1	0	0	0	0	0	0	.000	.000	—	0.00	0.00
LeBlanc, Wade	L-L	6-2	215	8-7-84	5	5	3.74	16	16	0	0	99	91	43	41	10	20	91	.243	.313	.214	8.30	1.82
Link, Jon	R-R	6-0	205	3-23-84	1	0	0.75	11	0	0	7	12	5	1	1	0	5	10	.125	.214	.077	7.50	3.75
Madden, Corey	R-R	6-0	205	3-30-84	0	0	0.00	1	0	0	0	1	0	0	0	0	2	.000	.000	18.00	0.00
Martin, J.D.	R-R	6-4	220	1-2-83	9	9	5.95	29	21	1	0	130	168	91	86	18	17	89	.316	.315	.316	6.16	1.18
Oviedo, Juan Carlos	R-R	6-2	190	3-15-82	0	0	0.00	1	0	0	0	1	0	0	0	0	1	0	.000	.000	1.000	0.00	27.00
Poveda, Omar	R-R	6-3	235	9-28-87	4	3	4.90	12	11	0	0	61	65	35	33	11	34	61	.273	.261	.290	9.05	5.04
Ray, Robert	R-R	6-3	205	1-21-84	2	2	3.48	33	0	0	1	54	49	25	21	5	20	45	.243	.255	.229	7.45	3.31
Reed, Evan	R-R	6-4	250	12-31-85	2	3	7.16	23	0	0	1	33	43	27	26	2	16	27	.312	.319	.303	7.44	4.41
Rosario, Sandy	R-R	6-1	210	8-22-85	0	2	1.04	25	0	0	16	26	20	4	3	0	2	24	.215	.192	.244	8.31	0.69
Sanabia, Alex	R-R	6-2	205	9-8-88	6	7	4.06	17	17	1	0	89	92	44	40	11	24	63	.266	.290	.238	6.39	2.44

Schmidt, Josh	R-R	6-4	175	11-14-82	0	0	2.77	6	0	0	0	13	11	4	4	1	9	15	.234	.333	.154 10.38 6.23
Turner, Jacob	R-R	6-5	210	5-21-91	2	0	1.98	5	5	0	0	27	27	6	6	2	12	16	.267	.222	.319 5.27 3.95
Varner, Rett	R-R	6-4	185	2-3-88	0	0	0.00	2	0	0	0	2	1	0	0	0	1	1	.167	.333	.000 4.50 4.50
Villanueva, Elih	R-R	6-0	240	7-27-86	9	8	3.90	32	16	0	1	113	120	57	49	11	44	83	.274	.298	.245 6.61 3.50
Webb, Ryan	R-R	6-5	230	2-5-86	2	0	1.59	3	0	0	0	6	3	1	1	0	1	1	.158	.100	.222 1.59 1.59

Fielding

Catcher	PCT	G	PO	A	E	DP	PB
Armstrong	.990	25	182	12	2	1	0
Brantly	.982	13	95	14	2	2	1
Davis	1.000	7	21	4	0	0	0
Hayes	.964	15	102	6	4	1	2
Holm	.988	11	75	6	1	0	0
Jefferies	1.000	5	35	0	0	0	0
Montz	.981	40	247	15	5	0	4
Quintero	1.000	5	34	2	0	0	0
Sammons	.984	41	274	28	5	0	1

First Base	PCT	G	PO	A	E	DP
Cervenak	.997	50	336	29	1	39
Dominguez	.952	4	19	1	1	5
Lasater	.990	10	88	8	1	7
Montz	.995	52	378	31	2	36
Sanchez	.993	31	249	26	2	24

Second Base	PCT	G	PO	A	E	DP
Dominguez	1.000	19	28	36	0	8

	PCT	G	PO	A	E	DP	PB
Green	.987	31	48	99	2	19	
Gutierrez	1.000	3	9	5	0	4	
Lambin	.964	50	78	109	7	22	
Lopez	1.000	1	0	1	0	0	
Murphy	1.000	19	37	37	0	15	
Solano	.979	18	29	64	2	13	
Velazquez	.959	15	25	46	3	11	

Third Base	PCT	G	PO	A	E	DP
Bowman	.951	20	19	20	2	1
Cervenak	.944	22	13	21	2	2
Dominguez	.942	78	53	125	11	15
Green	.833	10	8	7	3	1
Lambin	.976	19	13	28	1	3
Murphy	—	1	0	0	0	0

Shortstop	PCT	G	PO	A	E	DP
Dominguez	.862	8	9	16	4	3
Green	.964	17	20	34	2	12
Gutierrez	.833	1	0	5	1	0

	PCT	G	PO	A	E	DP
Lopez	1.000	2	3	0	0	0
Murphy	.964	11	20	34	2	8
Solano	.983	17	21	38	1	10
Velazquez	.968	88	141	223	12	60

Outfield	PCT	G	PO	A	E	DP
Aguila	.974	68	146	4	4	1
Cervenak	.950	8	19	0	1	0
Coghlan	.995	82	175	7	1	0
Cousins	.976	61	118	4	3	1
Duarte	1.000	18	33	0	0	0
Lambin	1.000	4	2	1	0	0
Mattison	.994	119	300	10	2	2
Montz	.500	4	2	0	2	0
Pedroza	.962	15	21	4	1	0
Petersen	.985	60	122	8	2	0

JACKSONVILLE SUNS

DOUBLE-A

SOUTHERN LEAGUE

Batting	B-T	HT	WT	DOB	AVG	vLH	vRH	G	AB	R	H	2B	3B	HR	RBI	BB	HBP	SH	SF	SO	SB	CS	SLG	OBP
Black, Danny	L-R	6-2	170	8-19-88	.265	.400	.241	8	34	5	9	3	0	0	2	3	0	0	1	11	2	1	.353	.316
Bowman, Shawn	R-R	6-3	225	12-9-84	.227	.215	.231	96	343	33	78	18	0	8	45	31	4	0	3	105	1	1	.350	.297
Ceballos, Jose	R-R	6-0	190	12-27-88	.000	.000	—	1	1	0	0	0	0	0	0	0	0	0	0	1	0	0	.000	.000
Cox, Zack	L-R	6-0	215	5-9-89	.253	.200	.277	24	95	14	24	6	1	1	13	10	0	0	1	27	0	0	.368	.321
Dominguez, Jeff	B-R	6-1	185	7-31-86	.252	.236	.257	68	222	26	56	14	2	4	22	20	2	1	2	48	8	5	.387	.317
Duarte, Jose	R-R	5-10	165	3-7-85	.234	.260	.221	63	145	21	34	6	0	2	11	25	0	2	1	23	3	3	.317	.345
Dudley, Aaron	L-R	6-3	193	2-17-88	.231	.167	.242	16	39	4	9	1	0	1	7	2	1	0	0	10	0	0	.333	.286
Duran, German	R-R	5-10	185	8-3-84	.212	.286	.192	11	33	6	7	1	0	3	8	3	0	0	1	8	0	2	.515	.270
Gran, Paul	R-R	5-11	182	4-7-86	.239	.221	.245	114	368	49	88	16	4	5	29	45	19	1	6	106	10	7	.345	.347
Gutierrez, Chris	R-R	5-9	185	3-12-84	.248	.227	.255	118	420	50	104	26	0	3	45	48	12	2	4	85	6	4	.331	.339
Jefferies, Jake	L-R	6-2	215	10-30-87	.233	.083	.266	42	133	18	31	6	0	2	13	12	0	2	0	21	0	1	.323	.297
Jensen, Kyle	R-L	6-3	255	5-20-88	.234	.227	.236	132	445	70	104	21	2	24	84	69	3	0	4	162	1	1	.452	.338
Krick, Taylor	R-R	6-1	215	3-31-88	.188	.000	.250	7	16	1	3	0	0	0	1	3	1	1	0	3	0	0	.188	.350
Lasater, Ben	R-R	6-3	195	5-25-84	.288	.286	.303	49	168	15	50	13	0	3	21	18	1	0	1	43	0	0	.429	.367
Lopez, Alfredo	R-R	5-10	160	10-7-89	.231	.238	.227	25	65	9	15	0	0	0	10	9	1	2	0	10	3	4	.231	.333
Mitchell, Russ	R-R	5-11	200	2-15-85	.163	.158	.164	24	80	4	13	3	0	0	10	14	0	1	0	20	0	0	.200	.287
Ortiz, Jaime	L-L	6-1	220	7-14-88	.188	.000	.214	14	32	2	6	0	0	1	4	7	0	1	1	3	0	0	.281	.325
Patterson, Ryan	R-R	5-11	205	5-2-83	.244	.244	.244	52	168	23	41	12	0	3	16	10	0	2	1	25	3	2	.369	.285
Pertusati, Danny	R-R	6-1	185	4-27-90	.300	.250	.318	38	120	20	36	6	2	4	18	13	4	1	0	22	1	0	.483	.387
Poulk, Dallas	L-R	5-11	175	5-16-88	.241	.111	.267	17	54	4	13	2	0	0	7	6	0	1	2	13	0	0	.278	.306
Skipworth, Kyle	L-R	6-4	225	3-1-90	.217	.154	.242	116	420	59	91	16	2	21	63	36	6	0	5	143	1	1	.414	.285
Smith, Curt	R-R	5-10	210	9-9-86	.261	.179	.295	96	268	41	70	17	2	9	48	20	4	1	6	59	3	3	.440	.315
Smolinski, Jake	R-R	6-0	205	2-9-89	.257	.320	.237	112	408	71	105	24	3	7	42	78	10	2	2	74	9	4	.382	.388
Webb, Donnie	B-R	5-11	210	4-30-86	.242	.250	.240	103	285	49	69	11	8	7	42	43	5	6	6	81	7	9	.411	.345

Pitching	B-T	HT	WT	DOB	W	L	ERA	G	GS	CG	SV	IP	H	R	ER	HR	BB	SO	AVG	vLH	vRH	K/9	BB/9
Alvarez, Jose	L-L	5-10	180	5-6-89	6	9	4.22	25	24	3	0	136	141	66	64	8	26	70	.274	.247	.287	4.62	1.72
Andrelczyk, Pete	R-R	6-1	185	11-10-85	0	0	0.00	1	0	0	0	1	0	0	0	0	1	2	.000	.000	.000	18.00	9.00
Bramhall, Bobby	L-L	5-11	190	7-13-85	1	2	3.23	28	1	0	0	61	50	23	22	4	18	61	.221	.200	.235	8.95	2.64
Camineiro, Arquimedes	R-R	6-4	245	6-16-87	0	0	3.06	12	0	0	2	18	16	6	6	0	10	17	.242	.192	.275	8.66	5.09
Cargill, Collin	R-R	6-2	190	10-6-87	2	0	2.45	9	0	0	0	11	5	3	3	0	3	9	.143	.167	.130	7.36	2.45
Conley, Jordan	R-R	6-1	180	7-19-86	2	3	3.24	16	0	0	0	25	27	11	9	3	4	25	.276	.227	.315	9.00	1.44
Dayton, Grant	L-L	6-2	200	11-25-87	2	1	4.15	7	0	0	0	13	12	6	6	2	4	19	.245	.389	.161	13.15	2.77
Evans, Bryan	R-R	6-3	205	2-26-87	7	8	4.66	29	27	0	0	135	131	78	70	13	62	97	.259	.271	.247	6.45	4.12
Flynn, Brian	L-L	6-8	240	4-19-90	3	0	3.80	8	0	0	0	45	48	22	19	3	13	32	.273	.255	.279	6.40	2.60
Kaminska, Kyle	L-R	6-4	180	10-5-88	6	3	5.11	31	0	0	1	49	70	31	28	9	9	42	.332	.289	.368	7.66	1.64
Korpi, Wade	R-L	5-11	185	3-10-86	1	1	5.32	17	0	0	0	22	28	18	13	1	8	24	.298	.225	.352	9.82	3.27
Leverton, James	R-L	6-2	185	5-13-86	3	0	3.36	23	0	0	1	56	49	23	21	4	20	53	.238	.220	.250	8.47	3.20
Link, Jon	R-R	6-0	205	3-23-84	1	0	6.00	3	0	0	1	3	5	4	2	0	1	2	.385	.800	.125	6.00	3.00
Madden, Corey	R-R	6-0	205	3-30-84	2	1	2.61	15	0	0	0	21	19	7	6	1	6	17	.250	.278	.225	7.40	2.61
Montgomery, Matt	R-R	6-4	210	7-21-87	0	1	4.76	1	1	0	0	6	8	3	3	0	4	2	.348	.273	.417	3.18	3.18
Neal, Zach	R-R	6-3	220	11-9-88	4	6	3.80	21	10	0	0	69	77	36	29	4	12	45	.288	.297	.282	5.90	1.57
Neil, Matthew	R-R	6-6	225	9-5-86	2	7	4.78	19	19	0	0	92	106	57	49	11	17	66	.286	.314	.264	6.43	1.66
O'Gara, Joey	R-R	6-7	205	4-20-88	1	1	0.77	2	2	0	0	9	4	1	1	0	2	9	.209	.130	.300	6.94	1.54
Oaks, Alan	R-R	6-3	225	4-4-88	1	2	6.55	4	1	0	0	11	12	8	8	2	6	10	.279	.375	.158	8.18	4.91
Ojala, Mike	R-R	6-3	195	8-24-87	0	1	4.08	12	0	0	0	18	18	11	8	2	6	13	.265	.250	.286	6.62	3.06

MIAMI MARLINS

	B-T	HT	WT	DOB	W	L	ERA	G	GS	CG	SV	IP	H	R	ER	HR	BB	SO	AVG	vLH	vRH	K/9	BB/9
Olmos, Edgar	L-L	6-5	180	4-12-90	0	1	0.54	9	1	0	0	17	8	1	1	0	16	13	.145	.087	.188	7.02	8.64
Parcell, Garrett	R-R	6-5	220	7-12-84	0	1	7.62	10	0	0	0	13	16	11	11	2	8	11	.314	.350	.290	7.62	5.54
Poveda, Omar	R-R	6-3	235	9-28-87	6	3	4.71	14	14	0	0	71	84	42	37	5	23	53	.302	.338	.270	6.75	2.93
Ramos, A.J.	R-R	5-10	210	9-20-86	3	3	1.44	55	0	0	21	69	36	14	11	3	21	89	.151	.191	.116	11.67	2.75
Reed, Evan	R-R	6-4	250	12-31-85	3	1	2.34	27	0	0	12	35	24	10	9	1	11	43	.195	.173	.211	11.16	2.86
Rosario, Sandy	R-R	6-1	210	8-22-85	0	0	4.50	2	0	0	1	2	3	1	1	1	1	4	.333	.333	.333	18.00	4.50
Schmidt, Josh	R-R	6-4	175	11-14-82	5	3	3.83	37	0	0	1	42	33	19	18	1	27	41	.217	.293	.170	8.72	5.74
Squires, Chris	R-R	6-2	195	3-29-88	0	1	7.11	10	0	0	1	13	19	12	10	2	7	13	.352	.333	.367	9.24	4.97
Taylor, Graham	L-L	6-3	225	5-25-84	9	11	3.97	26	26	2	0	147	169	71	65	18	34	86	.287	.277	.291	5.25	2.08
Varner, Rett	R-R	6-4	185	2-3-88	0	0	2.61	6	0	0	0	10	13	3	3	1	3	7	.295	.417	.250	6.10	2.61

Fielding

Catcher	PCT	G	PO	A	E	DP	PB
Jefferies	.976	34	231	16	6	0	2
Krick	1.000	6	36	4	0	0	1
Skipworth	.991	103	725	81	7	10	8

First Base	PCT	G	PO	A	E	DP
Dominguez	1.000	12	83	7	0	8
Dudley	.971	4	32	2	1	2
Duran	.967	4	28	1	1	6
Lasater	.989	45	337	27	4	33
Mitchell	.994	18	138	15	1	12
Ortiz	1.000	11	65	5	0	6
Smith	.993	60	410	33	3	34

Second Base	PCT	G	PO	A	E	DP
Dominguez	.992	27	53	64	1	21
Duran	.944	4	9	8	1	5

	PCT	G	PO	A	E	DP
Gran	.972	91	160	193	10	46
Gutierrez	1.000	1	2	0	0	0
Lopez	1.000	17	36	42	0	10
Pertusati	1.000	2	2	4	0	0
Poulk	.930	14	26	27	4	5

Third Base	PCT	G	PO	A	E	DP
Bowman	.945	89	66	175	14	21
Cox	.897	24	10	51	7	5
Dominguez	1.000	1	0	2	0	0
Duran	—	1	0	0	0	0
Gran	.977	18	11	32	1	3
Krick	1.000	1	1	0	0	0
Mitchell	.882	5	3	12	2	2
Smith	.800	5	6	2	2	0

Shortstop	PCT	G	PO	A	E	DP
Black	1.000	8	10	32	0	6
Dominguez	.966	14	24	32	2	6
Gran	1.000	1	1	2	0	0
Gutierrez	.950	114	181	272	24	59
Lopez	1.000	6	7	13	0	2

Outfield	PCT	G	PO	A	E	DP
Dominguez	.938	11	15	0	1	0
Duarte	.990	48	99	4	1	2
Jensen	.982	114	207	17	4	6
Lopez	1.000	2	4	0	0	0
Patterson	.980	47	95	4	2	1
Pertusati	1.000	34	76	1	0	0
Smith	1.000	1	4	0	0	0
Smolinski	.982	111	205	9	4	2
Webb	.985	88	193	2	3	0

MIAMI MARLINS

JUPITER HAMMERHEADS — HIGH CLASS A

FLORIDA STATE LEAGUE

Batting	B-T	HT	WT	DOB	AVG	vLH	vRH	G	AB	R	H	2B	3B	HR	RBI	BB	HBP	SH	SF	SO	SB	CS	SLG	OBP
Barber, Blake	R-R	5-10	180	4-4-90	.156	.200	.120	16	45	6	7	1	0	0	2	3	2	1	1	13	1	1	.178	.235
Behar, Jose	R-R	6-1	200	4-30-89	.250	.000	.400	4	8	1	2	0	0	1	1	1	0	0	0	1	0	0	.625	.333
Black, Danny	L-R	6-2	170	8-19-88	.314	.372	.273	78	293	38	92	16	4	0	30	27	3	5	2	68	17	7	.396	.375
Bonifacio, Emilio	B-R	5-11	205	4-23-85	.167	.300	.100	9	30	6	5	1	0	0	4	6	0	0	0	9	3	1	.200	.306
Canha, Mark	R-R	6-2	195	2-15-89	.293	.331	.268	114	406	65	119	24	3	6	68	54	9	1	8	75	1	3	.411	.382
Dayleg, Terrence	R-R	6-0	170	9-19-87	.242	.175	.275	37	120	12	29	2	1	1	13	5	0	4	0	20	0	0	.300	.272
Dudley, Aaron	L-R	6-3	193	2-17-88	.268	.237	.281	64	205	23	55	11	2	2	30	20	1	0	3	36	2	1	.371	.332
Fisher, Ryan	L-R	6-3	195	4-24-88	.254	.215	.274	103	355	46	90	26	4	5	50	34	8	1	6	86	3	1	.392	.328
Galloway, Isaac	R-R	6-2	190	10-10-89	.223	.180	.247	39	139	15	31	7	0	2	13	3	1	1	1	48	2	0	.317	.243
Hernandez, Yeison	B-R	5-10	190	6-29-92	.237	.250	.227	11	38	5	9	2	0	0	2	1	2	0	0	5	1	0	.289	.293
Kearns, Austin	R-R	6-3	240	5-20-80	.167	.000	.250	3	6	1	1	0	0	0	1	1	1	0	0	0	0	0	.167	.375
Krick, Taylor	R-R	6-1	215	3-31-88	.300	.336	.264	81	250	30	75	16	1	0	38	35	11	5	2	51	2	5	.372	.406
Lopez, Alfredo	R-R	5-10	160	10-7-89	.280	.308	.253	50	157	23	44	8	1	1	18	22	2	1	1	22	9	2	.363	.374
Main, Michael	R-R	6-1	170	12-14-88	.200	.333	.000	4	10	2	2	0	0	0	2	0	0	0	1	0	0	0	.200	.333
McConkey, Brian	L-R	6-2	210	12-17-88	.223	.184	.243	34	112	10	25	2	1	1	15	10	1	0	0	26	0	0	.286	.293
Murphy, Donnie	R-R	5-10	190	3-10-83	.353	.750	.231	4	17	4	6	1	1	1	6	0	0	0	1	3	0	0	.706	.333
Ozuna, Marcell	R-R	6-2	190	11-12-90	.266	.218	.294	129	489	89	130	27	2	24	95	44	3	0	3	116	8	3	.476	.328
Perio, Noah	L-R	6-0	170	11-14-91	.248	.195	.274	119	463	50	115	22	2	1	40	27	4	4	4	68	6	4	.311	.293
Pertusati, Danny	R-R	6-1	185	4-27-90	.232	.283	.192	70	224	23	52	10	0	2	11	16	5	3	3	29	5	3	.304	.294
Poulk, Dallas	L-R	5-11	175	5-16-88	.211	.160	.238	86	279	30	59	14	1	2	29	41	2	1	2	73	6	5	.290	.315
Realmuto, J.T.	R-R	6-1	190	3-18-91	.256	.279	.240	123	446	63	114	16	0	8	46	37	7	3	6	64	13	5	.345	.319
Smith, Rand	R-R	6-0	190	6-11-87	.171	.211	.125	18	35	3	6	1	0	0	2	5	0	0	0	8	0	0	.200	.275
Stanton, Giancarlo	R-R	6-5	245	11-8-89	.313	.250	.333	4	16	2	5	1	0	2	5	0	0	0	0	1	0	0	.750	.313
Yelich, Christian	L-R	6-4	189	12-5-91	.330	.313	.342	106	397	76	131	29	5	12	48	49	0	1	0	85	20	6	.519	.404

Pitching	B-T	HT	WT	DOB	W	L	ERA	G	GS	CG	SV	IP	H	R	ER	HR	BB	SO	AVG	vLH	vRH	K/9	BB/9
Barnes, Blake	R-R	6-1	180	7-9-90	0	0	4.15	6	0	0	0	9	8	5	4	3	2	10	.229	.125	.259	10.38	2.08
Brady, Mike	R-R	6-0	200	3-21-87	2	4	3.38	50	0	0	22	53	54	20	20	4	7	64	.260	.272	.248	10.80	1.18
Bramhall, Bobby	L-L	5-11	190	7-13-85	0	0	0.00	1	0	0	0	3	1	0	0	0	1	2	.100	.333	.000	5.40	2.70
Caminero, Arquimedes	R-R	6-4	245	6-16-87	1	0	0.44	19	0	0	1	21	12	2	1	0	9	27	.160	.147	.171	11.76	3.92
Cargill, Collin	R-R	6-2	190	10-6-87	0	0	1.69	18	0	0	1	21	21	8	4	0	14	15	.269	.379	.204	6.33	5.91
Conley, Adam	L-L	6-3	185	5-24-90	4	2	4.44	12	12	0	0	53	59	29	26	0	19	51	.282	.270	.288	8.72	3.25
Conley, Jordan	R-R	6-1	180	7-19-86	5	0	1.61	32	0	0	0	45	25	8	8	3	14	39	.160	.185	.133	7.86	2.82
Dayton, Grant	L-L	6-2	190	11-25-87	2	5	2.10	31	6	0	2	60	48	19	14	1	18	71	.214	.222	.211	10.65	2.70
Donatello, Sean	R-R	6-2	205	8-24-90	1	2	6.75	8	0	0	0	16	23	12	12	0	10	13	.329	.344	.316	7.31	5.63
Fernandez, Jose	R-R	6-3	215	7-31-92	7	1	1.96	11	11	0	0	55	38	12	12	0	17	59	.193	.202	.184	9.65	2.78
Higgins, Tyler	R-R	6-3	200	4-22-91	1	1	2.36	16	0	0	0	27	21	10	7	3	7	19	.210	.200	.200	6.41	2.36
James, Chad	L-L	6-3	180	1-23-91	6	10	4.87	24	23	0	0	115	138	80	62	9	50	80	.299	.295	.300	6.28	3.92
Lazo, Raudel	L-L	5-10	175	4-12-89	7	1	2.44	41	0	0	3	59	53	17	16	4	16	61	.243	.176	.273	9.31	2.44
Leverton, James	R-L	6-2	185	5-13-86	1	2	4.50	8	0	0	0	12	15	6	6	0	4	14	.300	.300	.300	10.50	3.00
Lowell, Collin	L-L	6-4	235	10-25-90	0	0	1.80	1	1	0	0	5	4	1	1	1	1	5	.235	.000	.267	9.00	1.80
McGough, Scott	R-R	6-0	170	10-31-89	2	1	3.24	15	0	0	1	17	19	7	6	0	4	8	.297	.310	.286	4.32	2.16
Merkling, Patrick	L-L	6-1	165	3-21-91	0	1	9.00	4	0	0	0	4	5	5	4	1	3	3	.313	.500	.200	6.75	6.75

Name	B-T	HT	WT	DOB	W	L	ERA	G	GS	CG	SV	IP	H	R	ER	HR	BB	SO	AVG	vLH	vRH	K/9	BB/9
Morey, Robert	R-R	6-1	185	11-27-88	8	3	3.84	18	16	0	0	89	97	46	38	4	29	57	.277	.276	.279	5.76	2.93
Mujica, Edward	R-R	6-3	225	5-10-84	0	0	0.00	2	2	0	0	3	0	0	0	0	0	2	.000	.000	.000	6.00	0.00
Neal, Zach	R-R	6-3	220	11-9-88	4	1	1.21	9	0	0	0	45	41	7	6	2	10	33	.244	.237	.250	6.65	2.01
Neil, Matthew	R-R	6-6	225	9-5-86	6	0	2.06	8	8	0	0	44	39	14	10	3	11	28	.236	.314	.152	5.77	2.27
Oaks, Alan	R-R	6-3	225	4-4-88	1	2	6.17	17	2	0	0	35	45	27	24	4	15	30	.302	.328	.282	7.71	3.86
Ojala, Mike	R-R	6-3	195	8-24-87	3	5	4.82	29	0	0	0	47	47	25	25	8	18	42	.267	.278	.260	8.10	3.47
Oliver, Dejai	R-R	6-2	200	8-28-90	0	0	12.27	4	0	0	0	7	11	10	10	1	4	8	.344	.211	.538	9.82	4.91
Olmos, Edgar	L-L	6-5	180	4-12-90	1	5	4.33	24	13	0	0	89	83	50	43	5	48	78	.248	.255	.245	7.86	4.84
Oviedo, Juan Carlos	R-R	6-2	190	3-15-82	0	1	3.38	2	2	0	0	3	1	1	1	0	1	2	.100	.000	.167	6.75	3.38
Rasmussen, Rob	R-L	5-9	160	4-2-89	4	7	3.90	16	16	0	0	88	83	52	38	6	36	75	.250	.253	.249	7.70	3.70
Rodriguez, Jose	R-R	6-1	195	9-24-90	0	0	3.38	2	0	0	0	5	5	2	2	0	1	3	.263	.200	.333	5.06	1.69
Rosario, Sandy	R-R	6-1	210	8-22-85	0	0	7.36	4	2	0	0	4	3	3	3	1	2	1	.214	.000	.333	2.45	4.91
Squires, Chris	R-R	6-2	195	3-29-88	3	2	2.60	21	0	0	0	45	36	17	13	2	14	34	.220	.200	.234	6.80	2.80
Stone, Dane	R-R	6-7	225	6-14-91	0	0	3.46	9	0	0	0	13	12	5	5	1	3	21	.240	.333	.154	14.54	2.08
Tamares, Joel	R-R	6-2	155	8-13-90	1	0	0.00	1	0	0	0	1	0	0	0	0	0	0	.000	.000	.000	0.00	0.00
Varner, Rett	R-R	6-4	185	2-3-88	4	6	3.87	21	14	0	0	88	104	52	38	2	22	57	.294	.315	.276	5.81	2.24

Fielding

Catcher	PCT	G	PO	A	E	DP	PB
Behar	1.000	2	12	2	0	0	0
Canha	1.000	1	9	1	0	0	0
Dudley	1.000	10	52	4	0	0	1
Krick	.993	38	250	22	2	1	7
Realmuto	.981	95	686	73	15	4	9

First Base	PCT	G	PO	A	E	DP
Canha	.988	90	716	57	9	64
Dayleg	1.000	1	1	0	0	0
Dudley	.980	22	137	8	3	11
Krick	1.000	7	63	2	0	4
McConkey	1.000	22	164	11	0	12
Realmuto	1.000	1	3	0	0	0

Second Base	PCT	G	PO	A	E	DP
Barber	1.000	4	5	13	0	4
Hernandez	.944	3	5	12	1	3
Lopez	1.000	10	18	28	0	2

	PCT	G	PO	A	E	DP
Murphy	1.000	1	2	3	0	1
Perio	.975	112	209	289	13	62
Pertusati	1.000	2	1	3	0	0
Poulk	.923	8	11	13	2	2

Third Base	PCT	G	PO	A	E	DP
Barber	.846	8	4	7	2	0
Canha	.944	11	2	15	1	1
Fisher	.901	81	48	153	22	12
Krick	.939	17	14	32	3	4
Lopez	.889	21	6	34	5	2
Murphy	1.000	1	2	0	0	0
Poulk	.722	6	3	10	5	0

Shortstop	PCT	G	PO	A	E	DP
Barber	1.000	4	4	5	0	0
Black	.955	77	119	202	15	37
Dayleg	.918	37	46	89	12	19
Hernandez	1.000	8	5	17	0	3

	PCT	G	PO	A	E	DP
Lopez	1.000	3	2	6	0	1
Murphy	1.000	1	1	1	0	0
Poulk	.918	16	21	35	5	6

Outfield	PCT	G	PO	A	E	DP
Bonifacio	1.000	9	16	0	0	0
Dudley	—	1	0	0	0	0
Galloway	.986	37	68	0	1	0
Kearns	—	2	0	0	0	0
Krick	.955	20	18	3	1	0
Lopez	.950	12	18	1	1	1
Main	.909	4	10	0	1	0
Ozuna	.986	122	276	10	4	2
Pertusati	.976	66	116	6	3	0
Poulk	.965	53	79	4	3	0
Smith	.970	14	30	2	1	0
Stanton	.667	2	2	0	1	0
Yelich	.979	99	226	3	5	1

GREENSBORO GRASSHOPPERS — LOW CLASS A
SOUTH ATLANTIC LEAGUE

Batting	B-T	HT	WT	DOB	AVG	vLH	vRH	G	AB	R	H	2B	3B	HR	RBI	BB	HBP	SH	SF	SO	SB	CS	SLG	OBP
Adams, Joshua	R-R	5-11	185	3-7-89	.264	.291	.248	127	489	60	129	33	0	14	84	45	4	2	6	96	1	2	.417	.327
Barnes, Austin	R-R	5-10	190	12-28-89	.318	.335	.308	123	478	76	152	36	3	12	65	59	9	17	3	61	9	2	.481	.401
Caldwell, Tony	R-R	5-10	195	12-2-88	.238	.246	.233	45	147	18	35	3	1	1	12	17	3	2	1	29	1	1	.293	.327
Dayleg, Terrence	R-R	6-0	170	9-19-87	.219	.248	.201	72	265	33	58	9	0	3	26	15	6	4	3	55	0	0	.287	.273
Gimenez, Wilfredo	R-R	6-0	180	12-18-90	.266	.259	.271	87	323	36	86	11	2	2	24	22	0	2	2	43	0	0	.331	.311
Goetz, Ryan	L-R	5-10	185	5-16-88	.273	.301	.256	96	384	53	105	18	5	5	40	43	3	5	5	54	2	1	.385	.347
Gomez, Anthony	R-R	6-0	190	11-26-90	.182	.000	.222	6	22	3	4	1	0	0	0	2	0	0	0	2	0	0	.227	.250
Hernandez, Yeison	R-R	5-10	150	6-29-92	.211	.571	.000	5	19	1	4	0	0	0	1	1	0	1	0	0	0	0	.211	.250
Keys, Brent	L-R	6-1	210	7-14-90	.335	.301	.357	95	370	72	124	21	3	5	51	34	4	11	3	30	18	5	.449	.394
Lopez, Alfredo	R-R	5-10	160	10-7-89	.250	.286	.214	9	28	6	7	1	0	0	1	1	3	1	0	4	1	1	.286	.344
McIntyre, Ryan	L-R	6-1	190	5-26-90	.268	.288	.253	88	314	44	84	16	4	6	32	26	6	4	0	61	5	7	.401	.335
Nola, Austin	R-R	6-0	180	12-28-89	.217	.230	.211	50	175	20	38	10	0	1	16	24	1	4	1	26	5	2	.291	.313
Rieger, Ryan	L-L	6-2	205	8-10-90	.237	.230	.242	108	388	46	92	25	1	7	53	67	3	0	2	99	3	1	.361	.352
Schultz, John	L-L	5-11	195	5-3-89	.309	.333	.295	51	188	22	58	9	1	3	15	23	1	0	2	29	3	2	.415	.383
Senne, Aaron	L-L	6-2	180	11-5-87	.284	.260	.299	84	342	40	97	16	2	10	53	26	5	1	1	78	1	2	.430	.342
Smith, Rand	R-R	6-0	190	6-11-87	.265	.277	.256	48	155	24	41	5	1	1	20	21	1	2	1	36	3	1	.329	.354
Smith, Matt	R-R	6-3	230	12-13-87	.279	.273	.283	90	340	63	95	15	1	20	74	35	7	0	1	104	0	1	.506	.358
Wooster, James	L-L	6-1	200	6-19-90	.260	.213	.285	97	366	52	95	21	2	11	47	33	0	2	2	94	3	6	.418	.319

Pitching	B-T	HT	WT	DOB	W	L	ERA	G	GS	CG	SV	IP	H	R	ER	HR	BB	SO	AVG	vLH	vRH	K/9	BB/9
Brice, Austin	R-R	6-4	205	6-19-92	8	6	4.35	25	19	0	3	110	96	63	53	13	68	122	.237	.254	.224	10.01	5.58
Cargill, Collin	R-R	6-2	190	10-6-87	0	1	1.54	9	0	0	2	12	11	3	2	0	6	12	.239	.429	.156	9.26	4.63
Conley, Adam	L-L	6-3	185	5-24-90	7	3	2.78	14	14	0	0	74	58	30	23	4	24	84	.213	.231	.209	10.17	2.91
Cravey, Kevin	R-R	6-1	180	8-15-87	10	0	1.01	33	0	0	5	53	37	8	6	1	12	42	.194	.176	.203	7.09	2.03
Esch, Jacob	R-R	6-4	190	3-27-90	1	3	3.13	6	4	0	0	32	27	15	11	1	11	26	.231	.077	.308	7.39	3.13
Fernandez, Jose	R-R	6-3	215	7-31-92	7	0	1.59	14	14	0	0	79	51	16	14	2	18	99	.189	.232	.158	11.28	2.05
Heaney, Andrew	L-L	6-3	180	6-5-91	1	2	4.95	4	4	0	0	20	25	15	11	0	4	21	.287	.231	.297	9.45	1.80
Hodges, Josh	R-R	6-7	235	6-24-91	8	10	3.65	27	26	1	0	148	147	72	60	14	56	98	.264	.261	.266	5.96	3.41
Lowell, Charlie	L-L	6-4	235	10-25-90	5	5	4.35	23	21	0	0	110	90	59	53	9	59	117	.224	.225	.224	9.60	4.84
Lyman, Scott	R-R	6-4	215	3-21-90	3	6	5.30	15	12	0	0	75	78	47	44	7	44	62	.275	.325	.240	7.47	5.30
Mincey, Brad	R-R	6-0	190	12-9-88	3	2	2.73	45	0	0	7	69	65	27	21	2	17	58	.244	.233	.252	7.53	2.21
Nappo, Greg	L-L	6-0	190	8-25-88	4	4	2.77	40	3	0	3	78	58	26	24	6	24	103	.201	.221	.193	11.88	2.77
Nygren, James	R-R	6-0	195	3-8-89	6	2	4.97	42	0	0	10	76	77	49	42	5	31	44	.269	.319	.235	5.21	3.67
Oliver, Dejai	R-R	6-2	200	8-28-90	2	2	5.03	29	0	0	1	54	46	31	30	6	30	57	.230	.217	.239	9.56	5.03
Omahen, John	R-R	6-0	190	3-15-89	1	5	5.24	36	0	0	1	67	84	44	39	10	24	41	.305	.269	.329	5.51	3.22
Reed, Frankie	L-L	6-2	185	2-12-88	2	0	4.15	5	0	0	0	9	7	4	4	0	3	7	.219	.182	.238	7.27	3.12

Name	B-T	HT	WT	DOB	W	L	ERA	G	GS	CG	SV	IP	H	R	ER	HR	BB	SO	AVG	vLH	vRH	K/9	BB/9
Rodriguez, Jose	R-R	6-1	195	9-24-90	2	0	5.68	5	0	0	0	6	8	6	4	0	9	6	.286	.182	.353	8.53	12.79
Shafer, Chris	R-R	6-2	245	5-16-89	1	2	8.31	7	0	0	0	13	22	13	12	1	3	10	.400	.364	.424	6.92	2.08
Urena, Jose	R-R	6-3	172	9-12-91	9	6	3.38	27	22	1	2	138	143	67	52	13	29	101	.266	.299	.241	6.57	1.89
Wittgren, Nick	R-R	6-3	210	5-29-91	0	0	0.00	6	0	0	0	2	6	1	0	0	0	1	13	.053	.143	.000	19.50	1.50

Fielding

Catcher	PCT	G	PO	A	E	DP	PB
Barnes	.972	16	121	17	4	0	1
Caldwell	.988	42	286	31	4	3	9
Gimenez	.987	84	717	72	10	4	13

First Base	PCT	G	PO	A	E	DP
Dayleg	1.000	8	57	1	0	3
Rieger	.992	88	785	49	7	75
Senne	.976	25	192	14	5	18
Smith	.985	23	188	11	3	19

Second Base	PCT	G	PO	A	E	DP
Barnes	.981	104	195	311	10	73
Dayleg	1.000	1	2	2	0	1
Goetz	.984	26	57	68	2	14

	PCT	G	PO	A	E	DP
Gomez	1.000	4	7	14	0	1
Hernandez	1.000	2	4	3	0	1
Lopez	.950	4	9	10	1	5

Third Base	PCT	G	PO	A	E	DP
Adams	.936	126	64	230	20	27
Dayleg	.778	4	1	6	2	0
Gimenez	1.000	1	0	1	0	0
Goetz	.955	9	3	18	1	3
Gomez	.750	1	0	3	1	1
Lopez	1.000	1	1	1	0	0

Shortstop	PCT	G	PO	A	E	DP
Dayleg	.935	60	81	180	18	34
Goetz	.917	24	28	83	10	12

	PCT	G	PO	A	E	DP
Gomez	1.000	1	1	3	0	0
Hernandez	.938	3	7	8	1	0
Lopez	.875	4	2	5	1	1
Nola	.966	49	89	141	8	30

Outfield	PCT	G	PO	A	E	DP
Goetz	1.000	38	56	1	0	0
Keys	.975	95	184	8	5	3
McIntyre	.988	81	157	11	2	5
Schultz	1.000	42	52	1	0	0
Senne	.988	53	82	1	1	0
Smith	.973	39	72	0	2	0
Wooster	.947	76	107	0	6	0

JAMESTOWN JAMMERS

SHORT-SEASON

NEW YORK-PENN LEAGUE

Batting	B-T	HT	WT	DOB	AVG	vLH	vRH	G	AB	R	H	2B	3B	HR	RBI	BB	HBP	SH	SF	SO	SB	CS	SLG	OBP
Behar, Jose	R-R	6-1	200	4-30-89	.170	.240	.143	26	88	3	15	5	0	0	8	7	1	0	0	21	0	0	.227	.240
Copeland, Kolby	L-R	6-0	190	2-5-94	.227	.000	.238	6	22	5	5	0	1	0	3	0	0	0	2	2	0	.318	.320	
Dewitt, Kentrell	L-R	5-11	180	3-20-91	.197	.125	.230	40	127	16	25	11	1	2	16	14	1	1	0	50	6	1	.346	.282
Dice, Brian	R-R	6-1	190	10-8-87	.146	.071	.185	13	41	3	6	1	0	1	1	2	0	0	0	17	0	0	.244	.186
Flynn, Cameron	L-R	6-0	195	2-24-90	.214	.280	.186	27	84	9	18	5	0	1	14	7	1	1	1	24	0	1	.310	.280
Gomez, Anthony	R-R	6-0	190	11-26-90	.269	.279	.264	51	193	26	52	3	2	2	28	13	3	3	3	10	6	3	.337	.321
Hernandez, Yeison	B-R	5-10	150	6-29-92	.235	.216	.241	43	149	17	35	8	1	0	10	11	2	5	0	18	2	2	.302	.296
Juengel, Matt	R-R	6-2	185	1-13-90	.218	.211	.221	46	179	25	39	3	4	1	16	13	6	0	0	26	2	1	.296	.293
Keefer, Cody	L-R	6-1	185	11-6-90	.343	.389	.327	18	70	13	24	4	0	0	9	5	1	1	0	11	0	1	.400	.395
Main, Michael	R-R	6-1	170	12-14-88	.276	.314	.266	41	163	18	45	8	1	2	20	14	2	0	1	18	5	5	.374	.339
Martinez, Juancito	R-R	6-1	170	6-10-89	.254	.158	.289	60	209	27	53	8	2	3	21	11	2	5	2	58	15	3	.354	.295
Mendoza, Pedro	R-R	6-0	148	5-11-91	.246	.278	.235	34	134	11	33	6	0	0	11	3	0	1	2	9	2	0	.291	.259
Munoz, Felix	L-L	6-1	193	4-7-92	.224	.212	.228	35	125	13	28	5	0	2	14	4	2	0	1	32	0	0	.312	.258
Nola, Austin	R-R	6-0	180	12-28-89	.189	.227	.161	15	53	2	10	0	0	2	7	0	1	1	3	0	1		.189	.279
Othman, Sharif	B-R	6-0	195	3-23-88	.181	.188	.179	37	116	15	21	5	1	2	11	9	0	1	0	25	1	0	.293	.240
Peralta, Rony	L-R	6-0	160	8-19-90	.183	.050	.219	35	93	8	17	8	0	0	4	11	0	3	0	23	1	1	.269	.269
Perez, Yefri	R-R	5-11	150	2-24-91	.280	.238	.297	45	143	18	40	8	0	1	16	8	2	1	1	12	4	5	.357	.325
Romero, Avery	R-R	5-11	195	5-11-93	.381	.500	.368	7	21	3	8	0	0	0	4	3	0	1	0	1	0	1	.381	.458
Rosa, Viosergy	L-L	6-3	185	6-16-90	.279	.353	.253	61	197	22	55	12	0	3	25	46	1	0	3	45	0	0	.386	.413
Solorzano, Jesus	R-R	6-0	190	8-8-90	.314	.371	.291	59	210	36	66	13	3	8	27	17	5	0	3	49	7	6	.519	.374
Vaughn, Michael	R-R	6-2	190	12-19-90	.176	.000	.205	13	51	3	9	3	0	0	3	2	0	0	0	10	0	0	.353	.176

Pitching	B-T	HT	WT	DOB	W	L	ERA	G	GS	CG	SV	IP	H	R	ER	HR	BB	SO	AVG	vLH	vRH	K/9	BB/9
Berglund, Bryan	R-R	6-4	180	11-2-90	0	1	3.09	10	0	0	0	12	11	4	4	0	9	8	.250	.368	.160	6.17	6.94
Cargill, Collin	R-R	6-2	190	10-6-87	0	0	2.25	2	0	0	0	4	4	2	1	0	1	3	.267	.250	.273	6.75	2.25
Del Orbe, Ramon	R-R	5-11	190	2-17-92	3	5	3.69	15	14	0	0	76	63	36	31	3	30	49	.227	.226	.227	5.83	3.57
Donatello, Sean	R-R	6-2	205	8-24-90	1	2	2.56	15	2	0	1	32	31	10	9	1	6	18	.258	.298	.233	5.12	1.71
Ellington, Brian	R-R	6-4	200	8-4-90	2	0	2.40	18	0	0	0	30	20	11	8	2	25	33	.187	.162	.200	9.90	7.50
Esch, Jacob	R-R	6-4	190	3-27-90	3	0	3.16	10	2	0	1	37	31	15	13	3	13	27	.233	.178	.261	6.57	3.16
Hope, Mason	R-R	6-3	190	7-27-90	3	4	2.90	14	14	0	0	71	72	33	23	1	27	53	.267	.320	.234	6.69	3.41
Logan, Blake	R-R	6-1	245	1-12-92	1	2	1.74	9	0	0	0	31	31	12	6	1	7	29	.261	.243	.268	8.42	2.03
Manzueta, Jheyson	R-R	6-2	162	12-5-89	2	0	1.29	21	0	0	3	35	23	8	5	2	13	43	.176	.158	.189	11.06	3.34
McCarthy, Casey	R-R	6-4	215	4-13-90	0	0	1.23	3	0	0	1	7	4	3	1	0	2	14	.143	.200	.111	17.18	2.45
Merkling, Patrick	L-L	6-1	165	3-21-91	1	0	0.00	3	0	0	0	7	4	0	0	0	2	8	.154	.111	.176	10.29	2.57
Milroy, Matt	L-R	6-2	185	10-5-90	2	3	4.11	9	8	0	0	35	31	21	16	3	23	30	.233	.245	.226	7.71	5.91
Newell, Ryan	R-R	6-2	215	6-18-91	2	2	5.29	10	3	0	0	17	14	10	10	1	16	16	.233	.150	.275	8.47	8.47
Reed, Frankie	L-L	6-1	185	2-12-88	2	1	2.45	16	0	0	3	29	19	9	8	0	6	34	.181	.162	.191	10.43	1.84
Reyes, Helpi	R-R	6-1	200	7-27-92	3	7	4.19	15	14	0	0	67	49	40	31	2	34	57	.203	.200	.206	7.70	4.59
Rodriguez, Jose	R-R	6-1	195	9-24-90	2	2	1.33	14	0	0	0	27	19	7	4	0	11	28	.188	.179	.194	9.33	3.67
Smith, Mason	L-L	6-2	190	1-22-90	1	0	10.38	5	0	0	0	9	15	10	10	2	6	5	.385	.429	.360	5.19	6.23
Steckenrider, Drew	R-R	6-5	215	1-10-91	1	2	3.72	10	8	0	0	36	28	20	15	0	25	38	.217	.159	.247	9.41	6.19
Wittgren, Nick	R-R	6-3	210	5-29-91	0	2	1.46	17	0	0	11	25	24	4	4	0	4	34	.250	.265	.242	12.41	1.46
Wright, Beau	L-L	6-2	255	1-2-91	4	4	3.70	18	2	0	0	41	35	27	17	2	23	40	.234	.341	.183	8.71	5.01

Fielding

Catcher	PCT	G	PO	A	E	DP	PB
Behar	.979	26	201	30	5	4	7
Dice	1.000	10	60	6	0	1	4
Othman	.989	37	238	27	3	0	11
Vaughn	.988	8	81	3	1	2	6

First Base	PCT	G	PO	A	E	DP
Munoz	.990	24	191	15	2	19

	PCT	G	PO	A	E	DP
Rosa	.985	55	500	26	8	46

Second Base	PCT	G	PO	A	E	DP
Gomez	.966	28	46	95	5	16
Hernandez	.842	4	5	11	3	5
Mendoza	.964	5	10	17	1	4
Peralta	.961	11	18	31	2	8
Perez	.969	45	50	76	4	13

	PCT	G	PO	A	E	DP
Romero	.929	3	5	8	1	3

Third Base	PCT	G	PO	A	E	DP
Juengel	.901	36	33	85	13	12
Mendoza	.987	25	22	54	1	6
Nola	1.000	5	2	11	0	1
Peralta	.857	7	4	8	2	0
Romero	.857	5	2	8	0	1

Shortstop	PCT	G	PO	A	E	DP
Gomez	.969	21	31	64	3	11
Hernandez	.915	37	43	119	15	13
Nola	.947	9	14	22	2	8
Peralta	.978	12	18	26	1	8

Outfield	PCT	G	PO	A	E	DP
Copeland	1.000	6	7	1	0	0
Dewitt	.909	30	29	1	3	1
Flynn	.974	25	34	3	1	1
Keefer	1.000	13	15	1	0	0

Main	.963	40	71	6	3	2
Martinez	.968	59	116	6	4	1
Solorzano	.949	59	89	4	5	1

GCL MARLINS — ROOKIE

GULF COAST LEAGUE

Batting	B-T	HT	WT	DOB	AVG	vLH	vRH	G	AB	R	H	2B	3B	HR	RBI	BB	HBP	SH	SF	SO	SB	CS	SLG	OBP
Acosta, Pedro	R-R	6-2	213	7-11-90	.280	.167	.295	33	100	10	28	5	1	1	13	10	2	0	1	15	0	0	.380	.354
Barber, Blake	R-R	5-10	180	4-4-90	.385	.538	.354	23	78	6	30	2	1	4	10	2	1	1	0	10	3	1	.590	.407
Burke, Connor	R-R	6-1	195	8-20-92	.176	.182	.175	24	68	8	12	2	1	0	3	7	1	2	0	24	0	0	.235	.263
Castillo, Felix	R-R	5-11	191	7-16-91	.197	.167	.203	29	76	10	15	1	0	0	1	8	4	1	0	8	0	0	.211	.307
Castro, Victor	R-R	6-1	198	1-10-92	.203	.231	.197	23	79	10	16	4	0	1	7	2	0	0	2	20	0	0	.291	.217
Ceballos, Jose	R-R	6-0	190	12-27-88	.345	.500	.302	16	55	7	19	1	0	2	10	2	2	0	1	11	0	0	.473	.383
Claussen, Patrick	L-R	5-11	190	4-12-90	.213	.267	.203	31	94	12	20	4	0	1	5	12	7	1	1	20	0	1	.287	.342
Copeland, Kolby	L-R	6-0	190	2-5-94	.286	.257	.291	56	217	34	62	14	6	0	34	16	0	1	3	27	2	6	.406	.331
Cordova, Rehiner	B-R	6-0	150	1-11-94	.284	.308	.281	32	102	16	29	3	0	0	9	11	2	3	0	20	4	1	.314	.365
Cruz, David	R-R	6-0	201	1-23-92	.152	.100	.167	20	46	5	7	1	0	0	6	7	3	0	0	20	1	2	.174	.304
Dean, Austin	R-R	6-1	190	10-14-93	.223	.261	.216	47	148	15	33	11	0	2	15	24	3	4	3	35	2	2	.338	.337
Duran, Carlos	L-R	6-1	192	5-24-92	.160	.000	.222	10	25	2	4	0	0	0	0	1	1	1	0	2	0	0	.160	.222
Flynn, Cameron	L-R	6-0	195	2-24-90	.375	.250	.417	10	32	3	12	2	2	0	7	5	1	0	1	6	1	0	.563	.462
Keefer, Cody	L-R	6-1	185	11-6-90	.289	.500	.268	13	45	6	13	2	1	1	9	9	0	0	0	10	1	0	.444	.407
Keene, Bubba	R-R	6-4	190	3-19-93	.000	—	.000	2	5	0	0	0	0	0	0	0	0	0	0	4	0	0	.000	.000
Lasater, Ben	R-R	6-3	195	5-25-84	.250	.000	.278	6	20	3	5	2	0	0	3	5	0	0	0	6	0	0	.350	.400
Main, Michael	R-R	6-1	170	12-14-88	.340	.333	.341	11	47	10	16	2	1	0	7	4	0	0	0	4	1	2	.426	.392
McConkey, Brian	L-R	6-2	210	12-17-88	.205	.143	.219	12	39	4	8	2	0	0	3	9	2	0	0	14	0	2	.256	.380
Miller, Ron	R-R	5-11	205	1-7-94	.182	.222	.171	40	132	14	24	7	2	4	14	6	2	0	2	51	0	0	.356	.225
Ortiz, Luis	B-R	5-10	161	3-14-92	.255	.261	.254	42	153	26	39	6	1	2	10	14	2	3	0	23	18	0	.346	.325
Rivera, Christian	R-R	5-10	165	2-10-94	.215	.385	.182	29	79	14	17	5	0	0	4	20	3	2	1	24	4	2	.278	.388
Romero, Avery	R-R	5-11	195	5-11-93	.223	.235	.221	33	121	8	27	6	0	3	15	10	6	0	2	21	0	1	.347	.309
Sappelt, Eddie	B-R	5-11	175	7-16-94	.111	.000	.125	12	18	4	2	0	0	0	1	2	0	1	0	6	3	0	.111	.200
Vaughn, Michael	R-R	6-2	190	12-19-90	.277	.286	.276	26	83	9	23	4	0	0	9	5	2	0	1	27	1	0	.325	.330
Vigil, Rodrigo	R-R	6-0	164	1-3-93	.200	.667	.162	11	40	2	8	2	0	0	3	1	1	0	0	6	1	0	.250	.238
Yelich, Christian	L-R	6-4	189	12-5-91	.250	—	.250	1	4	0	1	0	0	0	0	0	0	0	0	0	0	0	.250	.250

Pitching	B-T	HT	WT	DOB	W	L	ERA	G	GS	CG	SV	IP	H	R	ER	HR	BB	SO	AVG	vLH	vRH	K/9	BB/9
Adames, Jose	R-R	6-2	165	1-17-93	1	1	5.40	12	0	0	0	15	19	9	9	2	12	7	.306	.409	.250	4.20	7.20
Barnes, Blake	R-R	6-1	180	7-9-90	0	1	0.00	9	0	0	0	10	7	2	0	0	2	9	.200	.250	.174	7.84	1.74
Battisto, A.J.	R-R	6-0	193	9-30-83	0	0	0.00	1	1	0	0	1	0	0	0	0	0	1	.000	.000	.000	9.00	0.00
Beltre, Andy	R-R	6-4	195	7-6-93	1	5	2.96	12	9	0	0	49	46	21	16	1	19	41	.247	.263	.240	7.58	3.51
Cavanerio, Jorgan	R-R	6-1	155	8-18-94	3	2	5.13	11	9	0	0	47	61	33	27	4	13	35	.310	.302	.313	6.65	2.47
De La Rosa, Esmerling	R-R	6-2	199	5-15-91	2	3	2.76	13	0	0	0	16	13	8	5	0	13	18	.213	.353	.159	9.92	7.16
Del Pozo, Miguel	L-L	6-1	180	10-14-92	1	2	4.02	18	3	0	1	31	27	15	14	1	23	32	.225	.158	.238	9.19	6.61
Fox, Hayden	R-L	6-4	200	3-1-91	2	2	4.45	12	5	0	1	32	26	19	16	1	19	38	.218	.115	.247	10.58	5.29
Garcia, Jarlin	L-L	6-2	170	1-18-93	1	1	3.60	12	4	0	0	40	38	32	16	2	14	32	.242	.263	.235	7.20	3.15
Garcia, Michael	R-R	6-2	165	3-25-91	0	0	2.57	6	0	0	0	7	10	2	2	0	4	2	.357	.231	.467	2.57	5.14
German, Domingo	R-R	6-2	175	8-4-92	2	0	1.61	13	0	0	0	22	17	5	4	0	16	29	.215	.217	.214	11.69	6.45
Gil, Daniel	R-R	6-5	185	12-15-87	0	0	0.00	3	0	0	1	4	2	0	0	0	3		.154	.200	.125	6.75	0.00
Heaney, Andrew	L-L	6-3	180	6-5-91	0	0	2.57	2	2	0	0	7	7	2	2	0	2	9	.259	.000	.304	11.57	2.57
Higgins, Tyler	R-R	6-3	230	4-22-91	1	0	3.24	7	0	0	3	8	4	3	3	0	5	8	.143	.250	.100	8.64	5.40
Jackson, Justin	R-R	6-4	201	12-14-88	4	2	2.39	11	6	0	0	38	30	11	10	2	7	25	.210	.232	.195	5.97	1.67
Johnson, Graham	R-R	6-6	215	10-13-89	1	1	9.00	7	2	0	0	7	10	7	7	1	2	2	.357	.308	.400	9.00	2.57
Lyman, Scott	R-R	6-4	215	3-21-90	0	1	15.00	1	1	0	0	3	6	5	5	0	4	3	.429	.500	.417	9.00	12.00
Madden, Corey	R-R	6-0	205	3-30-84	0	0	0.00	2	1	0	0	2	0	0	0	0	0	4	.000	.000	.000	18.00	0.00
McCarthy, Casey	R-R	6-4		4-13-90	1	0	2.53	14	0	0	0	21	20	7	6	0	3	22	.253	.267	.245	9.28	1.27
Merkling, Patrick	L-L	6-1	165	3-21-91	0	1	3.38	10	0	0	0	16	14	8	6	0	6	17	.237	.188	.256	9.56	3.38
Newell, Ryan	R-R	6-2	215	6-18-91	0	2	2.70	5	4	0	0	8	7	3	0	7	11		.222	.063	.350	9.90	6.30
Oaks, Jason	R-R	6-3	225	4-4-88	0	0	4.50	3	1	0	0	4	6	2	2	0	1	5	.333	.333	.333	11.25	2.25
Ravago, Robert	R-R	6-1	180	9-4-90	2	1	3.00	21	0	0	7	27	24	11	9	0	7	20	.245	.333	.200	6.67	2.33
Rogers, Jared	R-R	6-7	198	5-9-88	2	2	5.40	10	9	0	0	28	39	21	17	3	13	19	.315	.341	.301	6.04	4.13
Sanabia, Alex	R-R	6-2	205	9-8-88	0	0	0.00	1	1	0	0	3	4	0	0	0	0	3	.308	.600	.125	9.00	0.00
Smith, Chipper	L-L	6-2	195	1-22-90	1	0	0.00	9	1	0	1	17	8	3	0	1	2	14	.136	.071	.156	7.27	1.04
Stone, Dane	R-R	6-7	225	6-14-91	1	0	1.00	10	0	0	0	18	9	5	2	0	3	26	.141	.095	.163	13.00	1.50
Tamares, Joel	R-R	6-2	155	8-13-90	2	0	2.19	8	0	0	0	12	9	4	3	0	6	11	.205	.333	.156	8.03	4.38
Zawacki, Brett	R-R	6-1	190	5-2-89	0	0	0.00	3	0	0	0	4	0	0	0	0	1	4	.133	.143	.125	8.31	2.08

Fielding

Catcher	PCT	G	PO	A	E	DP	PB
Acosta	.933	2	13	1	1	0	1
Castillo	.977	29	186	22	5	3	2
Ceballos	1.000	7	38	4	0	0	0
Cruz	.974	16	102	9	3	0	3
Vaughn	.961	18	112	11	5	1	2

First Base	PCT	G	PO	A	E	DP
Acosta	.977	15	120	7	3	10
Burke	1.000	1	3	0	0	0
Castro	.944	2	15	2	1	0
Claussen	.971	9	66	2	2	10
Duran	.983	10	55	4	1	6
Lasater	.967	5	28	1	1	1
McConkey	1.000	9	78	3	0	7
Miller	.940	18	120	6	8	11
Sappelt	1.000	1	2	0	0	0

Second Base	PCT	G	PO	A	E	DP
Barber	.970	7	22	10	1	1
Cordova	—	1	0	0	0	0

MIAMI MARLINS

Ortiz	.957	37	81	96	8	24
Romero	.983	12	26	31	1	7
Vigil	.900	5	5	13	2	2

Third Base	PCT	G	PO	A	E	DP
Barber	.976	12	9	31	1	4
Claussen	.836	20	16	35	10	2
Cordova	—	1	0	0	0	0
Miller	.786	10	8	14	6	2
Ortiz	1.000	1	1	1	0	0

Romero	.938	17	11	34	3	3
Vigil	.800	4	4	0	1	0

Shortstop	PCT	G	PO	A	E	DP
Barber	.500	1	1	1	2	0
Cordova	.976	29	31	89	3	13
Rivera	.921	28	38	79	10	16
Romero	1.000	4	7	9	0	3

Outfield	PCT	G	PO	A	E	DP
Burke	.944	18	16	1	1	1

Castro	.935	19	27	2	2	1
Claussen	1.000	3	6	0	0	0
Copeland	.957	54	86	3	4	2
Dean	.972	47	70	0	2	0
Flynn	1.000	10	17	0	0	0
Keefer	.968	13	28	2	1	1
Keene	1.000	2	5	0	0	0
Main	1.000	11	27	1	0	0
Sappelt	1.000	8	9	0	0	0
Yelich	.500	1	1	0	1	0

DSL MARLINS

MIAMI MARLINS

ROOKIE

DOMINICAN SUMMER LEAGUE

Batting	B-T	HT	WT	DOB	AVG	vLH	vRH	G	AB	R	H	2B	3B	HR	RBI	BB	HBP	SH	SF	SO	SB	CS	SLG	OBP
Almonte, Erwin	L-L	6-0	170	2-22-95	.250	.347	.209	65	244	19	61	12	1	1	25	14	4	0	0	37	1	1	.320	.302
Avello, Roger	R-R	6-2	189	12-5-94	.220	.304	.195	34	100	16	22	4	1	1	9	13	3	1	0	25	6	2	.310	.328
Castro, Victor	R-R	6-1	198	1-10-92	.385	.200	.500	4	13	4	5	0	1	0	2	4	2	0	0	2	2	0	.538	.579
De La Cruz, Dionicio	R-R	6-2	175	1-31-94	.202	.212	.197	62	198	30	40	7	0	2	17	19	5	3	4	50	7	3	.268	.283
De Leon, Miguel	R-R	5-10	160	5-9-93	.213	.300	.165	44	141	9	30	6	0	0	9	12	3	1	0	27	1	0	.255	.288
Gonzalez, Randy	L-L	6-3	180	7-18-94	.130	.091	.167	7	23	2	3	1	0	0	1	2	0	0	0	8	0	0	.174	.200
Jimenez, Joel	R-R	5-11	189	4-30-92	.265	.239	.284	32	113	14	30	6	1	1	11	10	1	0	1	18	1	0	.363	.328
Leon, Alsy	R-R	5-11	178	2-12-94	.202	.175	.216	34	114	12	23	4	1	1	9	9	1	1	0	7	2	0	.281	.266
Lopez, Javier	R-R	6-2	180	9-13-94	.208	.217	.203	50	207	24	43	10	0	1	13	16	2	0	0	47	4	7	.271	.271
Made, Pedro	B-R	6-2	160	9-29-94	.169	.230	.137	57	178	19	30	2	3	0	11	24	2	2	0	68	14	4	.213	.275
Molina, Leudy	L-R	6-0	160	11-20-94	.219	.100	.262	33	114	11	25	6	3	0	13	16	1	0	0	40	3	2	.325	.321
Mota, Juan	R-R	6-1	167	9-17-92	.246	.238	.250	52	195	18	48	4	1	0	10	14	2	2	2	19	3	1	.277	.300
Peguero, Alinson	R-R	6-2	175	4-13-94	.200	.333	.167	5	15	0	3	0	0	0	2	1	0	0	0	6	0	0	.200	.250
Pujols, Wildert	L-L	6-1	175	6-7-94	.276	.295	.266	48	170	26	47	10	4	0	26	14	5	0	2	29	13	4	.382	.346
Reyes, Angel	R-R	6-0	175	5-6-95	.221	.188	.229	29	86	11	19	4	1	0	6	9	3	2	0	19	1	0	.291	.316
Salgado, Rafael	R-R	5-11	175	7-15-93	.238	.259	.227	50	164	19	39	5	1	0	13	19	1	1	2	24	8	8	.280	.317
Silva, Geral	R-R	6-1	155	10-29-94	.123	.143	.116	21	57	4	7	0	0	0	4	6	0	0	0	21	3	0	.123	.206
Vigil, Rodrigo	R-R	6-0	164	1-3-93	.268	.364	.233	12	41	4	11	1	0	0	6	4	2	0	1	7	1	0	.341	.354
Ynoa, Christopher	R-R	6-1	175	1-28-93	.234	.238	.232	41	141	14	33	5	3	0	17	17	2	2	0	42	9	4	.312	.325

Pitching	B-T	HT	WT	DOB	W	L	ERA	G	GS	CG	SV	IP	H	R	ER	HR	BB	SO	AVG	vLH	vRH	K/9	BB/9
Adames, Jose	R-R	6-2	165	1-17-93	1	0	2.78	5	1	0	0	23	22	12	7	0	10	16	.272	.357	.226	6.35	3.97
Almonte, Jefferies	R-R	6-2	190	5-29-92	1	7	3.72	15	9	0	1	58	59	38	24	1	25	33	.260	.216	.288	5.12	3.88
Arias, Jesus	L-L	5-9	150	4-16-93	2	0	1.77	5	2	1	0	20	14	5	4	1	3	19	.192	.222	.188	8.41	1.33
Arias, Juan	R-R	6-2	170	12-30-94	1	3	5.23	12	0	0	0	21	24	18	12	2	10	11	.289	.306	.277	4.79	4.35
Batman, Jean	L-L	6-2	190	10-23-92	0	0	19.64	4	1	0	0	4	5	8	8	0	14	3	.385	.000	.417	7.36	34.36
Brito, Cesar	L-L	6-1	180	10-7-93	0	1	8.00	10	1	0	0	18	23	17	16	2	10	9	.303	.200	.318	4.50	5.00
Castellanos, Gabriel	L-L	6-1	165	12-28-93	2	6	5.98	15	6	0	0	44	51	43	29	1	30	37	.288	.348	.279	7.63	6.18
Cuello, Pedro	R-R	6-3	175	6-29-94	0	0	9.45	4	0	0	0	7	7	9	7	0	6	3	.280	.222	.313	4.05	8.10
De La Cruz, Angel	R-R	6-4	170	10-18-93	2	2	3.95	14	7	0	0	43	48	31	19	1	22	24	.279	.250	.290	4.98	4.57
De La Rosa, Leurys	R-R	6-2	160	11-5-94	0	1	7.71	3	3	0	0	12	14	11	10	2	4	7	.292	.100	.342	5.40	3.09
Diaz, Jose	R-R	6-2	180	5-7-93	2	2	2.84	14	7	0	2	44	41	19	14	1	22	27	.243	.245	.242	5.48	4.47
Jean, Victor	R-R	6-2	185	4-25-94	0	3	3.12	14	6	0	2	49	45	27	17	3	19	34	.239	.220	.246	6.24	3.49
Mendoza, Yeims	R-R	6-2	155	2-27-93	1	4	4.76	15	0	0	3	28	28	24	15	2	23	23	.248	.087	.289	7.31	7.31
Osoria, Aneury	R-R	6-2	170	11-15-93	1	4	8.86	10	4	0	0	21	26	28	21	1	20	17	.299	.333	.281	7.17	8.44
Perez, Yonqueli	R-R	6-4	175	6-6-93	0	2	2.22	10	0	0	0	24	12	15	6	1	27	19	.146	.156	.140	7.03	9.99
Ramos, Felix	B-L	6-0	175	12-2-93	2	3	5.32	17	3	0	1	47	43	36	28	1	29	25	.256	.304	.248	4.75	5.51
Romero, Derlin	R-R	6-2	175	10-8-94	1	0	8.18	8	0	0	0	11	14	11	10	0	7	6	.326	.235	.385	4.91	5.73
Santamaria, Rigoberto	R-R	6-2	195	4-27-94	3	6	2.36	14	13	1	0	80	73	32	21	2	17	61	.239	.255	.236	6.86	1.91

Fielding

Catcher	PCT	G	PO	A	E	DP	PB
De Leon	1.000	1	7	0	0	0	0
Jimenez	.989	29	148	30	2	0	3
Leon	.993	22	120	29	1	2	9
Reyes	.962	28	151	24	7	3	7
Ynoa	1.000	1	2	0	0	0	0

First Base	PCT	G	PO	A	E	DP
Almonte	.980	24	184	10	4	16
De Leon	.958	14	89	2	4	9
Jimenez	.971	8	60	6	2	6
Leon	1.000	9	80	3	0	6
Mota	.978	26	206	16	5	21
Ynoa	1.000	2	13	1	0	1

Second Base	PCT	G	PO	A	E	DP
Made	.894	8	25	17	5	3
Mota	.950	4	11	8	1	2
Salgado	.961	42	87	109	8	30
Vigil	.952	11	26	34	3	7
Ynoa	.961	13	27	22	2	5

Third Base	PCT	G	PO	A	E	DP
De Leon	.886	20	16	54	9	5
Made	.778	7	4	10	4	1
Molina	.838	33	27	56	16	4
Mota	.900	6	5	13	2	0
Silva	—	1	0	0	0	0
Ynoa	.917	15	6	27	3	3

Shortstop	PCT	G	PO	A	E	DP
Lopez	.869	35	47	106	23	17

Made	.875	6	5	9	2	0
Salgado	.880	5	6	16	3	1
Silva	.929	16	35	43	6	8
Ynoa	.919	11	7	27	3	7

Outfield	PCT	G	PO	A	E	DP
Almonte	.948	35	50	5	3	0
Avello	.927	33	51	0	4	0
Castro	.875	4	5	2	1	1
De La Cruz	.800	2	4	0	1	0
De La Cruz	.972	62	132	8	4	2
Gonzalez	.667	4	2	0	1	0
Made	.960	37	45	3	2	2
Peguero	1.000	4	4	0	0	0
Pujols	.919	45	95	7	9	4

Milwaukee Brewers

SEASON IN A SENTENCE: The Brewers closed strong in their first season without Prince Fielder, but couldn't overcome a slow start and finished five games out of the playoffs.

HIGH POINT: The Brewers were 47-56 at the end of July but closed the season on a 36-23 run, including a six-game winning streak at the end of September. The streak included a sweep of the Pirates topped off by a game when third baseman Aramis Ramirez had a home run and Ryan Braun had an RBI on his way to 112 for the season. Braun bounced back from his offseason steroid questions with another huge season, virtually duplicating his numbers from 2011.

LOW POINT: The Brewers didn't lead the National League Central at any point during the season, but they completely took themselves out of division contention in June and July. They closed July losing nine of 11 games, including a seven-game losing streak that featured sweeps by the Phillies and Reds.

NOTABLE ROOKIES: Mike Fiers has taken an unlikely path, as an NCAA Division II player who was a 22nd-round pick and a minor league reliever, but he ended up leading NL rookie starters with 9.5 strikeouts per nine innings. He has an average fastball but fools batters with a deceptive delivery and strong offspeed stuff. When the Brewers traded Zack Greinke to the Angels, Jean Segura was one of the key players they received, and they plugged him right into the major league lineup at shortstop. Japanese veteran Norichika Aoki was solid in his first season in the United States, batting .288/.355/.433 and playing mostly in right field.

KEY TRANSACTIONS: When the season looked lost—and knowing his contract was about to expire—the Brewers sent Greinke to the Angels for three prospects: Segura and righthanders Johnny Hellweg and Ariel Pena. Their major moves before the season to try to replace Fielder's bat, signing Ramirez and Aoki, both worked out well and the team led the NL in both runs and home runs.

DOWN ON THE FARM: Brewers affiliates had a collective .459 winning percentage, with only low Class A Wisconsin finishing with a winning record. Hunter Morris had a standout season in Double-A, winning Southern League player of the year honors after leading the league with 28 home runs and being voted the league's best defensive first baseman. Hiram Burgos was the top pitcher, going 10-4, 1.95 between three levels.

OPENING DAY PAYROLL: $97.7 million (10th)

PLAYERS OF THE YEAR

MAJOR LEAGUE	MINOR LEAGUE
Ryan Braun	**Hunter Morris**
of	1b
.319/.391/.595	(Double-A)
41 HR, 112 RBIs	.303/.357/.563
Led NL in OPS, TB	28 HR, 113 RBIs

ORGANIZATION LEADERS

BATTING		*Minimum 250 AB
MAJORS		
* AVG	Ryan Braun	.319
* OPS	Ryan Braun	.986
HR	Ryan Braun	41
RBI	Ryan Braun	112
MINORS		
* AVG	Jordan Brown, Nashville	.306
* OBP	Jason Rogers, Wisconsin/Brevard County	.405
* SLG	Hunter Morris, Huntsville	.563
R	Chadwin Stang, Wisconsin	85
H	Hunter Morris, Huntsville	158
TB	Hunter Morris, Huntsville	294
2B	Hunter Morris, Huntsville	40
3B	Ben McMahan, Wisconsin	11
HR	Hunter Morris, Huntsville	28
RBI	Hunter Morris, Huntsville	113
BB	Jason Rogers, Wisconsin/Brevard County	79
SO	Nick Ramirez, Wisconsin	144
	Chadwin Stang, Wisconsin	144
SB	Reggie Keen, Brevard County	45

PITCHING		#Minimum 75 IP
MAJORS		
W	Yovani Gallardo	16
# ERA	Yovani Gallardo	3.66
SO	Yovani Gallardo	204
SV	John Axford	35
MINORS		
W	Three tied at	11
L	Seth McClung, Nashville	13
# ERA	Hiram Burgos, Brevard/Huntsville/Nashville	1.95
G	Robert Wooten, Huntsville/Nashville	57
GS	David Goforth, Wisconsin	28
	Wily Peralta, Nashville	28
SV	Casey Medlen, Brevard County	22
IP	Hiram Burgos, Brevard/Huntsville/Nashville	171
BB	Wily Peralta, Nashville	78
SO	Hiram Burgos, Brevard/Huntsville/Nashville	153
# AVG	Hiram Burgos, Brevard/Huntsville/Nashville	.210

2012 PERFORMANCE

General Manager: Doug Melvin. **Farm Director:** Reid Nichols. **Scouting Director:** Bruce Seid.

Class	Team	League	W	L	PCT	Finish	Manager
Majors	Milwaukee Brewers	National	83	79	.512	7th (16)	Ron Roenicke
Triple-A	Nashville Sounds	Pacific Coast	67	77	.465	12th (16)	Mike Guerrero
Double-A	Huntsville Stars	Southern	65	74	.468	8th (10)	Darnell Coles
High A	Brevard County Manatees	Florida State	63	72	.467	8th (12)	Joe Ayrault
Low A	Wisconsin Timber Rattlers	Midwest	78	61	.561	3rd (16)	Matt Erickson
Rookie	AZL Brewers	Arizona	19	37	.339	11th (13)	Tony Diggs
Rookie	Helena Brewers	Pioneer	24	52	.316	8th (8)	Jeff Isom
Overall 2012 Minor League Record			316	373	.459	26th (30)	

ORGANIZATION STATISTICS

MILWAUKEE BREWERS

NATIONAL LEAGUE

Batting	B-T	HT	WT	DOB	AVG	vLH	vRH	G	AB	R	H	2B	3B	HR	RBI	BB	HBP	SH	SF	SO	SB	CS	SLG	OBP
Aoki, Norichika	L-R	5-9	180	1-5-82	.288	.270	.299	151	520	81	150	37	4	10	50	43	13	7	5	55	30	8	.433	.355
Bianchi, Jeff	R-R	5-11	180	10-5-86	.188	.091	.234	33	69	8	13	2	0	3	9	4	0	2	1	13	0	0	.348	.230
Braun, Ryan	R-R	6-1	200	11-17-83	.319	.363	.305	154	598	108	191	36	3	41	112	63	11	0	5	128	30	7	.595	.391
Conrad, Brooks	B-R	5-10	190	1-16-80	.075	.111	.045	25	40	2	3	0	0	2	6	3	0	0	1	16	0	0	.225	.136
Farris, Eric	R-R	5-9	180	3-3-86	.125	.000	.333	13	8	1	1	0	0	0	1	0	0	0	0	2	1	0	.125	.222
Gamel, Mat	L-R	6-0	225	7-26-85	.246	.286	.236	21	69	10	17	2	1	1	6	4	1	0	1	15	3	0	.348	.293
Gomez, Carlos	R-R	6-4	210	12-4-85	.260	.261	.260	137	415	72	108	19	4	19	51	20	8	6	3	98	37	6	.463	.305
Gonzalez, Alex	R-R	6-1	210	2-15-77	.259	.211	.274	24	81	8	21	4	0	4	15	6	2	0	0	15	1	1	.457	.326
Green, Taylor	L-R	5-11	195	11-2-86	.184	.200	.184	58	103	8	19	7	0	3	14	10	2	0	2	24	0	0	.340	.265
Hart, Corey	R-R	6-6	235	3-24-82	.270	.290	.265	149	562	91	152	35	4	30	83	44	11	2	3	151	5	0	.507	.334
Ishikawa, Travis	L-L	6-3	225	9-24-83	.257	.286	.250	94	152	19	39	12	1	4	30	13	4	4	1	42	0	0	.428	.329
Izturis, Cesar	B-R	5-9	180	2-10-80	.235	.174	.259	57	162	9	38	6	2	2	11	3	0	4	0	13	1	1	.333	.248
2-team total (5 Washington)					.241	—	—	62	166	13	40	7	2	2	11	3	0	4	0	13	1	1	.343	.254
Kottaras, George	L-R	6-0	200	5-10-83	.209	.111	.221	58	86	10	18	4	0	3	12	29	0	1	0	24	0	0	.360	.409
Lucroy, Jonathan	R-R	6-0	195	6-13-86	.320	.400	.292	96	346	46	101	17	4	12	58	22	4	1	3	44	4	1	.513	.368
Maldonado, Martin	R-R	6-1	225	8-16-86	.266	.250	.271	78	233	22	62	9	0	8	30	17	2	4	0	56	1	1	.408	.321
Maysonet, Edwin	R-R	6-1	180	10-17-81	.250	.118	.302	30	60	7	15	1	1	4	3	1	2	0	9	1	0	.350	.297
Morgan, Nyjer	L-L	5-10	185	7-2-80	.239	.263	.237	122	289	44	69	5	3	3	16	20	6	7	0	63	12	5	.308	.302
Ramirez, Aramis	R-R	6-1	205	6-25-78	.300	.338	.288	149	570	92	171	50	3	27	105	44	12	0	4	82	9	2	.540	.360
Ransom, Cody	R-R	6-3	205	2-17-76	.196	.220	.183	64	168	18	33	7	0	6	26	23	0	3	0	79	0	1	.345	.293
2-team total (26 Arizona)					.220	—	—	90	246	29	54	14	0	11	42	30	3	3	0	109	0	1	.411	.312
Schafer, Logan	L-L	6-1	180	9-8-86	.304	.000	.350	16	23	3	7	1	2	0	5	1	0	0	1	3	0	1	.522	.320
Segura, Jean	R-R	5-10	165	3-17-90	.264	.086	.319	44	148	19	39	4	3	0	14	13	0	1	1	21	7	1	.331	.321
Torrealba, Yorvit	R-R	5-11	200	7-19-78	.000	.000	.000	5	5	0	0	0	0	0	0	1	0	0	0	2	0	0	.000	.167
Weeks, Rickie	R-R	5-10	220	9-13-82	.230	.248	.224	157	588	85	135	29	4	21	63	74	13	0	2	169	16	3	.400	.328

Pitching	B-T	HT	WT	DOB	W	L	ERA	G	GS	CG	SV	IP	H	R	ER	HR	BB	SO	AVG	vLH	vRH	K/9	BB/9
Axford, John	R-R	6-5	210	4-1-83	5	8	4.67	75	0	0	35	69	61	42	36	10	39	93	.229	.225	.234	12.07	5.06
Chulk, Vinnie	R-R	6-2	200	12-19-78	1	0	10.00	7	0	0	0	9	17	10	10	0	4	10	.386	.368	.400	10.00	4.00
Dillard, Tim	R-R	6-4	220	7-19-83	0	2	4.38	34	0	0	0	37	45	21	18	3	14	29	.302	.340	.281	7.05	3.41
Estrada, Marco	R-R	5-11	200	7-5-83	5	7	3.64	29	23	0	0	138	129	62	56	18	29	143	.247	.247	.246	9.30	1.89
Fiers, Mike	R-R	6-3	195	6-15-85	9	10	3.74	23	22	0	0	128	125	56	53	12	36	135	.254	.265	.242	9.52	2.54
Gallardo, Yovani	R-R	6-2	210	2-27-86	16	9	3.66	33	33	0	0	204	185	86	83	26	81	204	.243	.256	.230	9.00	3.57
Greinke, Zack	R-R	6-2	200	10-21-83	9	3	3.44	21	21	0	0	123	120	49	47	7	28	122	.254	.259	.248	8.93	2.05
Henderson, Jim	L-R	6-5	190	10-21-82	1	3	3.52	36	0	0	3	31	26	12	12	1	13	45	.230	.294	.177	13.21	3.82
Hernandez, Livan	R-R	6-2	245	2-20-75	3	0	7.68	26	0	0	0	36	44	31	31	10	8	29	.306	.315	.296	7.18	1.98
2-team total (18 Atlanta)					4	1	6.42	44	0	0	1	67	84	48	48	15	16	48	—	—	—	6.42	2.14
Kintzler, Brandon	R-R	5-10	185	8-1-84	3	0	3.78	14	0	0	0	17	18	7	7	1	7	14	.277	.290	.265	7.56	3.78
Loe, Kameron	R-R	6-8	245	9-10-81	6	5	4.61	70	0	0	2	68	78	41	35	9	20	55	.284	.307	.267	7.24	2.63
Marcum, Shaun	R-R	6-0	195	12-14-81	7	4	3.70	21	21	0	0	124	116	57	51	16	41	109	.245	.263	.227	7.91	2.98
McClendon, Mike	R-R	6-5	225	4-3-85	0	0	6.43	9	0	0	0	14	20	11	10	1	5	4	.345	.357	.333	2.57	3.21
Narveson, Chris	L-L	6-3	205	12-20-81	1	1	7.00	2	2	0	0	9	10	8	7	2	4	5	.294	.286	.300	5.00	4.00
Parra, Manny	L-L	6-3	205	10-30-82	2	3	5.06	62	0	0	0	59	62	39	33	3	35	61	.265	.229	.296	9.36	5.37
Peralta, Wily	R-R	6-2	240	5-8-89	2	1	2.48	5	5	0	0	29	24	8	8	0	11	23	.242	.265	.220	7.14	3.41
Perez, Juan	R-R	6-0	170	9-3-78	0	1	5.14	10	0	0	0	7	6	4	4	2	8	10	.231	.154	.308	12.86	10.29
Rodriguez, Francisco	R-R	6-0	195	1-7-82	2	7	4.38	78	0	0	3	72	65	37	35	8	31	72	.241	.224	.260	9.00	3.88
Rogers, Mark	R-R	6-2	225	1-30-86	3	1	3.92	7	7	0	0	39	36	17	17	5	14	41	.243	.253	.232	9.46	3.23
Stinson, Josh	R-R	6-4	210	3-14-88	0	0	0.96	6	1	0	0	9	7	1	1	1	5	3	.212	.222	.200	2.89	4.82
Thornburg, Tyler	R-R	6-0	190	9-29-88	0	0	4.50	8	3	0	0	22	24	11	11	8	7	20	.279	.268	.289	8.18	2.86
Veras, Jose	R-R	6-6	240	10-20-80	5	4	3.63	72	0	0	1	67	61	29	27	5	40	79	.239	.260	.220	10.61	5.37
Wolf, Randy	L-L	6-0	205	8-22-76	3	10	5.69	25	24	0	0	142	179	94	90	21	45	96	.314	.274	.325	6.07	2.85

Fielding

Catcher	PCT	G	PO	A	E	DP	PB
Kottaras	1.000	27	162	7	0	0	1
Lucroy	.991	88	714	34	7	4	2
Maldonado	.990	69	523	47	6	6	2
Torrealba	1.000	2	3	0	0	0	0

First Base	PCT	G	PO	A	E	DP
Conrad	1.000	7	35	1	0	1
Gamel	.979	20	134	8	3	15
Green	1.000	18	110	10	0	10
Hart	.995	103	733	64	4	67
Ishikawa	.993	43	269	17	2	21
Izturis	1.000	1	2	0	0	0
Kottaras	1.000	6	10	0	0	2
Maldonado	1.000	4	9	0	0	1
Ransom	1.000	1	1	0	0	0

Second Base	PCT	G	PO	A	E	DP
Bianchi	1.000	4	1	2	0	0

	PCT	G	PO	A	E	DP
Conrad	1.000	4	5	10	0	1
Farris	1.000	2	1	0	0	0
Green	1.000	4	0	6	0	0
Izturis	—	1	0	0	0	0
Maysonet	.929	3	3	10	1	2
Ransom	1.000	6	7	14	0	4
Weeks	.974	152	236	374	16	78

Third Base	PCT	G	PO	A	E	DP
Bianchi	1.000	6	3	3	0	0
Conrad	1.000	2	0	1	0	0
Gamel	—	1	0	0	0	0
Green	.900	13	6	12	2	2
Izturis	1.000	3	1	6	0	1
Maysonet	1.000	1	0	1	0	0
Ramirez	.977	143	71	222	7	14
Ransom	.943	17	4	29	2	3

Shortstop	PCT	G	PO	A	E	DP
Bianchi	.980	14	14	34	1	7
Conrad	—	1	0	0	0	0
Gonzalez	.970	24	30	67	3	17
Izturis	.981	45	42	112	3	16
Maysonet	.959	18	25	46	3	14
Ransom	.984	41	43	84	2	20
Segura	.939	43	64	91	10	20

Outfield	PCT	G	PO	A	E	DP
Aoki	.988	133	231	8	3	2
Braun	.979	151	276	6	6	1
Farris	—	1	0	0	0	0
Gomez	.981	128	255	9	5	4
Hart	.976	53	80	0	2	0
Ishikawa	—	3	0	0	0	0
Morgan	1.000	86	153	2	0	1
Schafer	1.000	9	17	0	0	0

NASHVILLE SOUNDS   TRIPLE-A

PACIFIC COAST LEAGUE

Batting	B-T	HT	WT	DOB	AVG	vLH	vRH	G	AB	R	H	2B	3B	HR	RBI	BB	HBP	SH	SF	SO	SB	CS	SLG	OBP
Almonte, Erick	R-R	6-2	245	2-1-78	.200	.179	.213	34	75	10	15	3	0	0	5	9	0	1	0	18	0	1	.240	.286
Bianchi, Jeff	R-R	5-11	180	10-5-86	.317	.309	.322	73	249	33	79	13	1	5	19	22	1	5	1	48	11	5	.438	.374
Brown, Jordan	L-L	6-0	205	12-18-83	.306	.306	.306	104	359	43	110	22	1	8	37	22	1	4	2	49	2	3	.440	.346
Buller, Dayton	R-R	6-0	190	6-22-81	.248	.353	.194	37	101	9	25	6	1	3	9	10	0	2	0	32	0	0	.416	.315
Conrad, Brooks	B-R	5-10	190	1-16-80	.405	.424	.390	21	74	17	30	5	1	10	28	11	0	0	0	15	0	1	.905	.482
Davis, Khris	R-R	6-0	195	12-21-87	.310	.357	.282	32	113	23	35	12	0	4	24	20	3	0	4	27	1	0	.522	.414
Farris, Eric	R-R	5-9	180	3-3-86	.286	.287	.285	131	483	63	138	21	1	7	31	27	6	4	8	56	35	13	.377	.329
Gibbons, Jay	L-L	6-0	195	3-2-77	.204	.171	.228	34	98	15	20	5	0	6	11	9	1	0	1	15	0	0	.439	.275
Gindl, Caleb	L-L	5-9	205	8-31-88	.261	.250	.268	127	452	54	118	27	5	12	50	37	2	2	4	98	4	1	.423	.317
Gonzalez, Andy	R-R	6-3	215	12-15-81	.221	.238	.209	87	280	30	62	17	1	8	38	33	2	0	4	54	3	2	.375	.304
Green, Taylor	L-R	5-11	195	11-2-86	.273	.273	.273	77	282	24	77	17	0	7	29	28	3	0	0	57	1	3	.408	.345
Halton, Sean	R-R	6-5	265	6-7-87	.274	.288	.262	119	358	48	98	23	3	17	57	43	5	0	6	81	0	2	.497	.354
Ishikawa, Travis	L-L	6-3	225	9-24-83	.222	.222	.222	6	18	1	4	3	0	0	5	3	0	0	0	2	0	0	.389	.333
Izturis, Cesar	B-R	5-9	180	12-10-80	.083	.167	.000	4	12	1	1	0	0	0	0	1	0	0	1	1	0	0	.083	.083
Jaramillo, Jason	R-R	6-0	215	10-9-82	.188	.149	.209	41	133	7	25	3	0	2	12	14	2	0	2	25	2	1	.256	.272
2-team total (11 Sacramento)					.198	—	—	52	172	10	34	5	0	2	17	18	3	0	2	35	2	1	.262	.282
Lucroy, Jonathan	R-R	6-0	195	6-13-86	.429	.500	.333	2	7	4	3	0	0	0	1	0	1	0	0	1	1	0	.429	.500
Maldonado, Martin	R-R	6-1	225	8-16-86	.198	.267	.176	35	121	10	24	6	0	4	13	9	4	1	3	37	0	2	.347	.270
Maysonet, Edwin	R-R	6-1	180	10-17-81	.208	.174	.222	69	231	20	48	13	2	3	19	16	4	5	3	45	2	1	.320	.268
Patterson, Corey	L-R	5-10	180	8-13-79	.251	.195	.278	117	363	46	91	20	4	10	39	15	3	4	2	78	18	3	.410	.285
Phillips, Paul	R-R	5-11	200	4-15-77	.209	.167	.240	14	43	2	9	0	0	2	4	0	0	1		7	0	0	.209	.271
2-team total (17 Las Vegas)					.278	—	—	31	97	7	27	2	0	0	6	9	1	3	1	12	0	1	.299	.343
Quintero, Humberto	R-R	5-9	215	8-2-79	.263	.308	.232	25	95	9	25	8	0	1	12	1	2	1	1	21	0	0	.379	.283
2-team total (5 New Orleans)					.245	—	—	30	110	10	27	8	0	1	15	3	2	1	1	24	0	0	.345	.276
Sanchez, Juan	R-R	5-11	170	1-16-87	.100	.000	.143	6	10	0	1	0	0	0	0	0	0	0	0	3	0	0	.100	.100
Schafer, Logan	L-L	6-1	180	9-8-86	.278	.265	.286	124	464	72	129	23	9	11	40	29	10	7	3	72	16	7	.438	.332
Statia, Hainley	B-R	5-10	180	1-19-86	.279	.270	.283	49	129	16	36	5	0	0	16	12	0	0	2	26	1	0	.318	.336
Williams, Adrian	R-R	6-0	175	1-3-91	.333	1.000	.000	3	6	1	2	0	0	0	0	0	0	0	0	3	0	0	.333	.429

Pitching	B-T	HT	WT	DOB	W	L	ERA	G	GS	CG	SV	IP	H	R	ER	HR	BB	SO	AVG	vLH	vRH	K/9	BB/9
Baker, Brian	R-R	6-5	190	1-10-83	4	4	4.36	25	21	1	0	109	117	57	53	15	53	86	.277	.306	.246	7.08	4.36
Burgos, Hiram	R-R	6-1	210	8-4-87	2	2	2.91	8	8	0	0	46	39	18	15	4	15	35	.224	.217	.232	6.80	2.91
Butler, Josh	R-R	6-5	205	12-11-84	0	3	4.67	4	4	0	0	17	14	10	9	1	11	9	.226	.265	.179	4.67	5.71
Chulk, Vinnie	R-R	6-2	200	1-19-78	3	0	1.75	16	0	0	1	26	17	7	5	2	9	25	.187	.188	.186	8.77	3.16
De Los Santos, Fautino	R-R	6-2	225	2-15-86	1	0	1.98	11	0	0	0	14	17	3	3	0	4	17	.315	.321	.308	11.20	2.63
2-team total (28 Sacramento)					2	3	5.80	39	0	0	0	50	66	33	32	2	20	60	—	—		10.87	3.62
Dillard, Tim	R-R	6-4	220	7-19-83	1	1	9.42	14	0	0	0	14	28	16	15	4	8	15	.418	.414	.421	5.65	5.02
Estrada, Marco	R-R	5-11	200	7-5-83	0	0	1.13	2	2	0	0	8	7	1	1	0	5	5	.241	.200	.333	5.63	5.63
Fiers, Mike	R-R	6-3	195	6-15-85	1	3	4.42	10	10	1	0	55	49	28	27	6	18	49	.243	.263	.224	8.02	2.95
Garate, Victor	L-L	6-1	210	9-25-84	3	5	7.78	29	0	0	0	39	52	35	34	4	22	40	.329	.410	.278	9.15	5.03
Hand, Donovan	R-R	6-4	210	3-3-84	3	3	3.84	44	3	0	0	80	90	35	34	7	18	54	.292	.301	.284	6.10	2.03
Henderson, Jim	L-R	6-5	190	10-21-82	4	3	1.69	35	0	0	15	48	36	10	9	2	22	56	.214	.233	.200	10.50	4.13
Kintzler, Brandon	R-R	5-10	185	8-1-84	0	1	1.54	8	0	0	0	12	8	2	2	0	2	11	.200	.278	.136	8.49	1.54
Lowe, Johnnie	R-R	6-5	220	3-21-85	4	0	3.55	19	0	0	0	33	32	13	13	6	21	20	.256	.258	.254	5.45	5.73
McClendon, Mike	R-R	6-5	225	4-3-85	4	3	4.19	33	0	0	5	43	40	24	20	2	18	27	.255	.280	.232	5.65	3.77
McClung, Seth	L-R	6-6	280	2-7-81	2	13	6.36	21	20	1	0	103	121	82	73	16	60	80	.294	.322	.269	6.97	5.23
2-team total (4 Iowa)					3	15	6.35	25	23	1	0	119	145	96	84	19	70	96	—	—		7.26	5.29
Meadows, Dan	L-L	6-6	220	11-3-87	0	0	4.42	13	0	0	0	15	11	8	7	0	8	10	.250	.222	.268	7.36	4.91
Peralta, Wily	R-R	6-2	240	5-8-89	7	11	4.66	28	28	1	0	147	154	79	76	9	78	143	.275	.262	.286	8.78	4.79
Perez, Juan	R-L	6-0	170	9-3-78	4	2	3.60	38	0	0	0	40	32	17	16	3	20	54	.224	.215	.231	12.15	4.50
Rivas, Amaury	R-R	6-2	215	12-20-85	5	8	5.24	50	2	0	1	67	72	42	39	7	32	39	.280	.282	.279	5.24	4.30

MILWAUKEE BREWERS

Rogers, Mark	R-R	6-2	225	1-30-86	6	6	4.72	18	18	0	0	95	92	52	50	13	49	74	.258	.269	.247	6.99	4.63
Sanchez, Jesus	R-R	5-11	202	9-24-87	4	1	1.71	20	0	0	0	26	23	6	5	0	9	23	.242	.269	.209	7.86	3.08
Stetter, Mitch	L-L	6-4	220	1-16-81	0	1	4.70	10	0	0	0	8	6	4	4	0	6	12	.222	.222	.222	14.09	7.04
Thornburg, Tyler	R-R	6-0	190	9-29-88	2	3	3.58	8	8	0	0	38	38	16	15	1	13	42	.264	.233	.315	10.04	3.11
Vargas, Claudio	R-R	6-4	235	6-19-78	7	1	3.69	20	20	0	0	110	112	48	45	11	32	84	.269	.270	.267	6.89	2.63
Wooten, Rob	R-R	6-4	190	7-21-85	0	2	3.93	40	0	0	7	53	49	23	23	4	16	49	.247	.292	.206	8.37	2.73

Fielding

Catcher	PCT	G	PO	A	E	DP	PB
Buller	.992	31	225	15	2	0	4
Jaramillo	.987	41	283	17	4	2	3
Lucroy	1.000	2	18	0	0	0	6
Maldonado	.980	34	262	30	6	3	6
Phillips	.988	14	78	7	1	0	2
Quintero	.991	25	205	26	2	4	1

First Base	PCT	G	PO	A	E	DP
Almonte	.967	10	54	5	2	8
Brown	.994	41	273	35	2	32
Conrad	.955	3	18	3	1	2
Green	1.000	6	30	1	0	4
Halton	.992	100	755	63	7	94
Ishikawa	1.000	4	22	3	0	4

Second Base	PCT	G	PO	A	E	DP
Conrad	1.000	10	16	24	0	8
Farris	.988	110	201	292	6	82

		G	PO	A	E	DP	PB
Green	1.000	9	11	28	0	1	
Maysonet	1.000	7	13	19	0	7	
Sanchez	—	1	0	0	0	0	
Statia	1.000	16	27	30	0	8	
Williams	.857	1	1	5	1	0	

Third Base	PCT	G	PO	A	E	DP
Almonte	.917	7	2	9	1	2
Conrad	1.000	1	2	1	0	0
Gonzalez	.952	74	41	119	8	14
Green	.945	57	35	102	8	15
Halton	1.000	1	1	2	0	0
Maysonet	1.000	6	3	7	0	2
Statia	.944	8	4	13	1	4

Shortstop	PCT	G	PO	A	E	DP
Bianchi	.986	69	96	190	4	52
Farris	.962	10	15	35	2	7
Gonzalez	1.000	4	5	10	0	5

		G	PO	A	E	DP
Izturis	1.000	3	5	9	0	2
Maysonet	.973	50	66	116	5	23
Statia	.981	17	15	38	1	8

Outfield	PCT	G	PO	A	E	DP
Almonte	1.000	4	2	0	0	0
Brown	.986	43	66	2	1	0
Conrad	1.000	2	3	0	0	0
Davis	1.000	29	42	0	0	0
Farris	1.000	13	20	1	0	0
Gibbons	.977	27	40	3	1	1
Gindl	1.000	123	223	12	0	3
Gonzalez	—	1	0	0	0	0
Maysonet	.900	7	9	0	1	0
Patterson	.983	98	169	4	3	0
Sanchez	1.000	3	2	0	0	0
Schafer	.990	120	289	8	3	4
Statia	—	1	0	0	0	0

HUNTSVILLE STARS   DOUBLE-A

SOUTHERN LEAGUE

Batting	B-T	HT	WT	DOB	AVG	vLH	vRH	G	AB	R	H	2B	3B	HR	RBI	BB	HBP	SH	SF	SO	SB	CS	SLG	OBP
Bianchi, Jeff	R-R	5-11	180	10-5-86	.351	.333	.354	19	77	11	27	4	0	0	6	6	0	2	0	11	3	1	.403	.398
Bolivar, Domnit	R-R	5-11	165	5-12-89	.198	.152	.227	78	207	16	41	6	0	3	19	17	1	4	2	50	5	4	.271	.260
Cline, Matt	R-R	5-10	188	10-18-85	.162	.188	.152	45	111	8	18	2	0	1	3	10	1	4	0	17	0	1	.207	.238
Davis, Kentrail	L-R	5-9	210	6-29-88	.274	.287	.269	122	438	55	120	22	7	7	41	54	3	2	1	121	19	11	.404	.357
Davis, Khris	R-R	6-0	195	12-21-87	.383	.515	.337	44	128	23	49	9	0	8	23	20	5	1	0	33	2	2	.641	.484
De La Rosa, Anderson	R-R	5-11	195	8-1-84	.228	.235	.225	64	224	18	51	9	2	6	24	13	3	4	0	53	0	0	.366	.279
Gennett, Scooter	L-R	5-9	164	5-1-90	.293	.241	.315	133	533	66	156	30	2	5	44	28	3	6	3	71	11	5	.385	.330
Gibbons, Jay	L-L	6-0	195	3-2-77	.316	.217	.358	24	76	6	24	8	0	0	10	13	2	0	0	10	1	0	.421	.429
Gonzalez, Andy	R-R	6-3	215	12-15-81	.301	.263	.316	42	133	25	40	4	5	1	19	35	1	0	2	24	1	1	.444	.444
Haydel, Lee	L-L	5-11	180	7-15-87	.284	.325	.277	109	282	39	80	4	2	2	14	27	1	4	2	60	10	6	.333	.346
Jaramillo, Jason	B-R	6-0	215	10-9-82	.258	.265	.256	34	120	14	31	8	0	0	12	14	0	0	0	19	0	0	.325	.336
Kjeldgaard, Brock	R-R	6-5	235	1-22-86	.234	.310	.207	48	158	24	37	9	0	8	29	28	1	0	2	43	1	3	.443	.349
Krieger, Scott	R-R	6-0	215	1-30-87	.300	.200	.360	15	40	3	12	1	0	1	5	3	0	0	0	10	1	0	.400	.349
Manzella, Tommy	R-R	6-2	200	4-16-83	.252	.290	.237	62	218	22	55	7	0	1	28	27	1	5	1	57	3	4	.298	.336
Mittelstaedt, T.J.	L-R	5-10	185	2-13-88	.189	.100	.217	44	122	16	23	7	0	4	12	24	0	0	2	37	3	0	.344	.318
Morris, Hunter	L-R	6-2	200	10-7-88	.303	.266	.318	136	522	77	158	40	6	28	113	40	6	0	3	117	2	1	.563	.357
Prince, Josh	R-R	6-0	180	1-26-88	.251	.287	.238	137	505	74	127	28	3	7	55	74	3	6	7	130	41	18	.360	.346
Reed, Michael	R-R	6-0	190	11-18-92	.000	.000	.000	3	7	0	0	0	0	0	0	0	0	1	0	3	0	0	.000	.000
Sanchez, Juan	R-R	5-11	170	1-16-87	.189	.257	.161	46	122	7	23	5	0	1	10	9	2	2	0	22	0	2	.254	.256
Segura, Jean	R-R	5-10	165	3-17-90	.433	.286	.478	8	30	7	13	3	0	0	4	4	1	1	1	4	4	0	.533	.500
Statia, Hainley	B-R	5-10	180	1-19-86	.244	.297	.221	59	213	23	52	10	0	0	12	22	2	0	0	29	6	2	.291	.321
Weisenburger, Adam	R-R	5-10	185	12-13-88	.187	.149	.207	47	139	14	26	3	0	2	13	16	6	1	2	36	0	1	.252	.294

Pitching	B-T	HT	WT	DOB	W	L	ERA	G	GS	CG	SV	IP	H	R	ER	HR	BB	SO	AVG	vLH	vRH	K/9	BB/9
Anundsen, Evan	R-R	6-3	215	12-17-88	5	8	4.85	28	24	1	0	119	134	71	64	9	45	67	.286	.265	.302	5.08	3.41
Baker, Brian	R-R	6-5	190	1-10-83	0	1	2.08	2	2	0	0	13	7	6	3	0	10	.156	.143	.167	6.92	1.38
Blanks, Bradley	R-R	6-4	185	3-17-85	1	2	4.35	14	0	0	1	21	20	10	10	2	10	19	.260	.320	.231	8.27	4.35
Burgos, Hiram	R-R	6-1	210	8-4-87	6	1	1.94	13	13	1	0	83	68	21	18	3	28	77	.230	.300	.175	8.32	3.02
Butler, Josh	R-R	6-5	205	12-11-84	0	0	4.60	4	0	0	0	8	7	4	4	2	4	.341	.400	.286	4.00	2.00
Byrd, Darren	R-R	6-3	200	10-24-86	3	5	2.59	50	0	0	6	73	58	27	21	2	36	71	.215	.186	.236	8.75	4.44
Dillard, Tim	R-R	6-4	220	7-19-83	0	0	5.40	3	0	0	0	5	5	3	3	0	1	8	.250	.375	.167	14.40	1.80
Garman, Brian	L-L	5-10	180	7-19-86	1	0	3.00	24	0	0	0	24	29	12	8	0	8	17	.319	.377	.276	6.38	3.00
Heckathorn, Kyle	R-R	6-6	225	6-17-88	5	11	4.75	35	17	0	0	119	127	67	63	7	38	88	.275	.251	.294	6.64	2.87
Hellweg, Johnny	R-R	6-9	210	10-29-88	2	1	2.70	7	2	0	0	20	16	7	6	0	15	17	.222	.290	.171	7.65	6.75
Kintzler, Brandon	R-R	5-10	185	8-1-84	0	2	3.28	31	0	0	9	36	35	15	13	1	12	20	.269	.288	.254	5.05	3.03
Lowe, Johnnie	R-R	6-5	220	3-21-85	4	4	5.26	11	10	0	0	53	54	36	31	5	30	40	.260	.304	.318	6.79	5.09
Manzanillo, Santo	R-R	6-0	205	12-20-88	0	4	6.08	12	0	0	1	13	13	10	9	2	10	10	.260	.280	.240	6.75	6.75
Marzec, Eric	R-R	6-0	190	1-13-88	1	1	7.53	10	0	0	0	14	15	12	12	2	10	18	.259	.250	.265	11.30	6.28
Meadows, Dan	L-L	6-6	220	11-3-87	1	5	4.18	33	3	0	0	52	45	25	24	4	22	34	.253	.191	.291	5.92	3.83
Mercedes, Roque	R-R	6-3	185	10-28-86	1	1	13.50	9	0	0	0	14	24	21	21	2	12	12	.381	.538	.250	7.71	7.71
Merklinger, Dan	L-L	6-1	195	11-19-85	4	7	6.50	24	18	0	0	62	57	50	45	9	51	63	.244	.211	.254	9.10	7.36
Nelson, Jimmy	R-R	6-6	245	6-5-89	2	4	3.91	10	10	0	0	46	34	25	20	2	37	42	.206	.240	.178	8.22	7.24
Pena, Ariel	R-R	6-3	190	5-20-89	0	2	7.24	7	7	0	0	32	30	26	26	3	25	29	.255	.355	.316	8.07	6.40
Sanchez, Jesus	R-R	5-11	202	9-24-87	3	2	1.59	32	0	0	11	45	34	8	8	2	13	41	.213	.216	.209	8.14	2.58
Seidel, R.J.	R-R	6-5	200	9-3-87	3	2	3.34	39	4	0	1	67	62	31	25	6	31	53	.245	.217	.265	7.08	4.14

MILWAUKEE BREWERS

	B-T	HT	WT	DOB	W	L	ERA	G	GS	CG	SV	IP	H	R	ER	HR	BB	SO	AVG	vLH	vRH	K/9	BB/9
Stetter, Mitch	L-L	6-4	220	1-16-81	1	0	1.99	31	0	0	0	23	12	5	5	1	10	28	.160	.111	.233	11.12	3.97
Stinson, Josh	R-R	6-4	210	3-14-88	11	9	3.16	29	24	1	1	145	167	70	51	7	71	91	.291	.260	.321	5.64	4.40
Thornburg, Tyler	R-R	6-0	190	9-29-88	8	1	3.00	13	13	0	0	75	57	36	25	6	24	71	.212	.243	.180	8.52	2.88
Valiquette, Philippe	L-L	6-1	205	2-14-87	0	1	8.49	11	0	0	0	12	19	13	11	3	6	4	.404	.368	.429	3.09	4.63
Williamson, Brandon	R-R	6-2	180	4-22-89	0	0	5.00	2	2	0	0	9	9	6	5	2	3	7	.250	.154	.304	7.00	3.00
Wooten, Rob	R-R	6-4	190	7-21-85	3	0	1.74	17	0	0	8	21	18	4	4	1	7	21	.228	.321	.176	9.15	3.05

Fielding

Catcher	PCT	G	PO	A	E	DP	PB
De La Rosa	.980	64	431	65	10	2	15
Jaramillo	.986	34	262	20	4	4	6
Weisenburger	.982	45	292	39	6	9	8

First Base	PCT	G	PO	A	E	DP
Bolivar	1.000	2	11	0	0	1
Cline	1.000	1	5	0	0	1
Gibbons	1.000	2	13	1	0	0
Morris	.995	136	1198	55	6	112

Second Base	PCT	G	PO	A	E	DP
Bolivar	1.000	7	10	10	0	3
Cline	1.000	1	2	4	0	1
Gennett	.970	127	239	377	19	81
Mittelstaedt	.967	8	12	17	1	2

Third Base	PCT	G	PO	A	E	DP
Bolivar	.854	17	16	25	7	5
Cline	.919	27	20	48	6	4
Gonzalez	.967	40	27	89	4	8
Mittelstaedt	.896	17	11	32	5	3
Prince	.833	4	1	4	1	0
Sanchez	.906	14	9	20	3	1
Statia	.965	31	20	62	3	6

Shortstop	PCT	G	PO	A	E	DP
Bianchi	.946	18	23	47	4	10
Bolivar	.927	19	40	49	7	11
Cline	.929	6	11	15	2	4
Manzella	.969	61	83	168	8	39
Prince	.938	3	6	9	1	2
Sanchez	.846	5	8	14	4	5

	PCT	G	PO	A	E	DP
Segura	1.000	8	15	26	0	5
Statia	.973	23	37	73	3	16

Outfield	PCT	G	PO	A	E	DP
Cline	1.000	1	2	0	0	0
Davis	.991	120	208	9	2	4
Davis	.967	28	56	2	2	0
Gibbons	1.000	13	24	1	0	0
Haydel	.990	69	99	4	1	1
Kjeldgaard	1.000	45	67	2	0	1
Krieger	1.000	6	3	1	0	0
Mittelstaedt	.900	6	8	1	1	0
Prince	.975	128	266	11	7	2
Reed	1.000	2	7	1	0	1
Sanchez	1.000	18	29	1	0	0

BREVARD COUNTY MANATEES

HIGH CLASS A

FLORIDA STATE LEAGUE

Batting	B-T	HT	WT	DOB	AVG	vLH	vRH	G	AB	R	H	2B	3B	HR	RBI	BB	HBP	SH	SF	SO	SB	CS	SLG	OBP
Berberet, Parker	R-R	6-3	205	10-20-89	.247	.204	.267	46	154	16	38	9	0	2	12	15	2	1	2	34	0	3	.344	.318
Dean, Brent	R-R	6-1	210	7-26-86	.239	.192	.268	19	67	4	16	0	0	0	7	1	0	0	0	15	1	0	.239	.250
Dishon, Johnny	R-R	5-11	193	3-21-89	.203	.200	.204	48	153	12	31	6	2	0	9	15	1	4	1	50	17	5	.268	.276
Gomez, Hector	R-R	6-2	180	3-5-88	.105	.036	.146	23	76	9	8	3	1	1	8	4	3	1	1	19	0	0	.211	.179
Hawn, Cody	L-R	6-1	195	8-11-88	.214	.175	.236	125	463	57	99	27	1	12	69	38	2	0	5	103	4	4	.354	.274
Keen, Reggie	R-R	5-10	180	12-2-87	.252	.230	.265	125	472	53	119	20	4	3	35	33	1	20	4	89	45	19	.331	.300
Kjeldgaard, Brock	R-R	6-5	235	1-22-86	.183	.128	.215	32	104	20	19	5	0	4	15	14	4	0	1	49	1	0	.346	.301
Krieger, Scott	R-R	6-0	215	1-30-87	.248	.262	.241	39	129	25	32	7	1	2	19	9	4	1	0	32	6	1	.364	.317
Mittelstaedt, T.J.	L-R	5-10	185	2-13-88	.258	.269	.251	76	275	44	71	17	7	9	46	42	2	4	1	84	14	9	.469	.359
Paciorek, Joey	R-R	6-2	225	9-20-88	.239	.186	.259	47	155	11	37	8	1	1	26	9	3	0	5	38	2	2	.323	.285
Reed, Michael	R-R	6-0	190	11-18-92	.281	.333	.261	11	32	5	9	0	0	0	5	8	0	1	0	8	3	0	.281	.425
Rogers, Jason	R-R	6-2	250	3-13-88	.300	.269	.316	67	233	33	70	11	0	5	23	42	4	0	0	42	7	1	.412	.416
Romero, Franklin	R-R	5-11	180	6-24-88	.219	.200	.229	93	301	32	66	7	1	1	22	6	5	5	1	87	18	6	.259	.246
Sanchez, Juan	R-R	5-11	170	1-16-87	.205	.200	.209	23	73	8	15	2	0	1	6	4	2	0	2	14	2	0	.274	.259
Shaw, Nick	R-R	5-11	160	8-25-88	.250	.232	.259	125	452	70	113	24	3	3	45	69	7	16	2	90	9	7	.336	.357
Velazquez, Miguel	R-R	6-2	205	5-15-88	.178	.277	.122	36	129	8	23	7	1	3	13	8	2	0	3	26	0	3	.318	.232
Vucinich, Shea	R-R	6-1	185	12-1-88	.249	.309	.216	122	422	48	105	25	1	5	59	50	47	12	4	97	15	7	.353	.339
Walker, Mike	L-R	6-3	215	6-12-88	.280	.242	.301	129	460	64	129	24	1	12	75	54	6	2	3	123	10	4	.415	.361
Weisenburger, Adam	R-R	5-10	185	12-13-88	.260	.143	.333	23	73	8	19	2	1	0	6	11	2	1	0	13	1	1	.315	.372
Zarraga, Shawn	R-R	6-0	260	1-21-89	.292	.250	.321	28	96	11	28	6	1	2	18	9	6	0	1	6	2	2	.438	.384

Pitching	B-T	HT	WT	DOB	W	L	ERA	G	GS	CG	SV	IP	H	R	ER	HR	BB	SO	AVG	vLH	vRH	K/9	BB/9
Arnett, Eric	R-R	6-5	230	1-25-88	1	0	3.56	33	0	0	1	61	54	30	24	4	31	61	.241	.263	.224	9.05	4.60
Bradley, Jed	L-L	6-4	225	6-12-90	5	10	5.53	20	20	1	0	107	136	76	66	9	43	60	.311	.238	.342	5.03	3.61
Bucci, Nick	R-R	6-2	180	7-16-90	2	2	1.99	6	6	0	0	32	25	8	7	3	15	37	.210	.222	.203	10.52	4.26
Burgos, Hiram	R-R	6-1	210	8-4-87	2	1	0.87	7	6	0	0	41	21	5	4	1	6	41	.150	.200	.122	8.93	1.31
Gagnon, Drew	R-R	6-4	195	6-26-90	1	2	2.82	11	11	1	0	67	56	25	21	3	18	49	.229	.211	.243	6.58	2.42
Garman, Brian	L-L	5-10	180	7-19-88	3	3	1.88	22	1	0	0	38	31	12	8	4	12	46	.215	.208	.220	10.80	2.82
Hall, Brooks	R-R	6-5	200	6-26-90	4	3	4.33	16	13	0	1	69	72	41	33	7	35	40	.273	.302	.244	5.24	4.59
Harvey, Seth	L-R	6-2	205	1-20-88	3	0	3.24	16	0	0	0	25	16	9	9	1	15	28	.184	.184	.184	10.08	5.40
Holle, Greg	R-R	6-8	240	11-16-88	3	7	3.94	43	0	0	5	62	56	32	27	1	13	37	.242	.284	.213	5.40	1.90
Jungmann, Taylor	R-R	6-6	210	12-18-89	11	6	3.53	26	26	1	0	153	159	70	60	7	46	99	.267	.309	.224	5.82	2.71
Keeling, Thomas	L-L	6-3	185	3-30-88	4	5	5.64	40	0	0	0	53	52	39	33	5	30	52	.257	.246	.263	8.89	5.13
Kintzler, Brandon	R-R	5-10	185	8-1-84	0	1	3.00	6	0	0	0	6	7	2	2	0	3	9	.292	.357	.200	13.50	4.50
Marzec, Eric	R-R	6-0	190	1-13-88	1	2	2.45	23	2	0	2	37	33	15	10	2	13	31	.239	.286	.200	7.61	3.19
Medlen, Casey	R-R	6-0	155	8-4-89	3	4	2.98	46	0	0	22	54	52	23	18	2	17	63	.246	.214	.268	10.44	2.82
Miller, Matt	R-R	6-2	180	7-7-90	1	2	7.20	4	4	0	0	20	33	19	16	2	5	20	.371	.370	.371	9.00	2.25
Moye, Andy	R-R	6-5	180	9-11-87	5	3	5.13	12	11	0	0	60	59	37	34	7	21	45	.250	.323	.200	6.79	3.17
Nelson, Jimmy	R-R	6-6	245	6-5-89	4	4	2.21	13	13	1	0	81	63	24	20	3	25	77	.216	.270	.152	8.52	2.77
Ross, Austin	R-R	6-2	200	8-12-88	0	0	1.54	3	3	0	0	12	8	2	2	0	4	9	.186	.188	.185	6.94	3.09
Toledo, Tommy	R-R	6-3	190	12-13-88	2	1	6.05	11	0	0	0	19	23	13	13	1	13	13	.295	.351	.244	6.05	6.05
Valiquette, Philippe	L-L	6-1	205	2-14-87	0	0	4.00	5	0	0	0	9	10	4	4	1	4	6	.303	.286	.316	6.00	4.00
Wawrzasek, Stosh	R-R	6-0	251	8-30-90	0	0	5.40	6	0	0	0	7	5	5	4	1	2	3	.200	.000	.294	4.05	2.70
Whalen, Connor	L-L	6-3	195	4-19-88	0	2	6.94	9	0	0	0	12	16	10	9	1	7	12	.348	.375	.333	9.26	5.40
Williams, Alan	L-L	6-3	195	3-5-90	4	4	3.06	26	0	0	0	35	40	14	12	1	12	35	.294	.234	.326	8.92	3.06
Williamson, Brandon	R-R	6-2	180	4-22-89	4	10	5.65	20	19	0	0	94	113	72	59	13	31	64	.297	.330	.265	6.13	2.97

Fielding

Catcher	PCT	G	PO	A	E	DP	PB
Berberet	.989	42	236	24	3	2	6
Dean	.978	11	85	5	2	0	1
Paciorek	.986	39	262	20	4	3	4
Weisenburger	.973	23	167	16	5	1	3
Zarraga	.977	24	197	13	5	0	2

First Base	PCT	G	PO	A	E	DP
Berberet	1.000	1	4	0	0	0
Hawn	.992	79	716	27	6	47
Rogers	.988	40	316	25	4	27
Walker	.987	17	149	8	2	13

Second Base	PCT	G	PO	A	E	DP
Mittelstaedt	.978	10	14	30	1	3

	PCT	G	PO	A	E	DP
Shaw	.986	19	29	40	1	6
Vucinich	.974	107	217	298	14	63

Third Base	PCT	G	PO	A	E	DP
Hawn	1.000	1	0	4	0	0
Mittelstaedt	.945	27	17	52	4	9
Paciorek	1.000	2	1	4	0	2
Sanchez	.917	4	2	9	1	1
Vucinich	.974	13	7	31	1	1
Walker	.920	90	57	174	20	11

Shortstop	PCT	G	PO	A	E	DP
Gomez	.941	21	27	69	6	8
Sanchez	1.000	8	8	20	0	3
Shaw	.959	107	143	320	20	50

	PCT	G	PO	A	E	DP
Vucinich	1.000	3	7	6	0	1

Outfield	PCT	G	PO	A	E	DP
Dishon	.989	47	79	7	1	2
Keen	.984	125	239	10	4	0
Kjeldgaard	1.000	29	45	2	0	1
Krieger	1.000	25	40	2	0	1
Mittelstaedt	.952	39	74	6	4	1
Reed	1.000	11	18	0	0	0
Rogers	.966	18	26	2	1	0
Romero	.974	89	176	9	5	0
Sanchez	.960	12	21	3	1	2
Velazquez	.929	17	26	0	2	0

WISCONSIN TIMBER RATTLERS

LOW CLASS A

MIDWEST LEAGUE

Batting	B-T	HT	WT	DOB	AVG	vLH	vRH	G	AB	R	H	2B	3B	HR	RBI	BB	HBP	SH	SF	SO	SB	CS	SLG	OBP
Berberet, Parker	R-R	6-3	205	10-20-89	.261	.200	.268	14	46	6	12	1	0	0	6	9	0	0	1	11	3	1	.283	.375
Dishon, Johnny	R-R	5-11	193	3-21-89	.220	.282	.193	48	127	19	28	4	2	1	9	24	3	2	1	38	11	4	.307	.355
Garfield, Cameron	R-R	6-1	195	5-23-91	.298	.319	.284	66	225	33	67	18	0	11	33	27	5	0	0	42	3	1	.524	.385
Garza, Mike	R-R	6-1	195	3-11-90	.209	.255	.185	38	139	12	29	7	0	1	16	3	3	3	3	31	1	5	.281	.236
George, Carlos	R-R	6-2	165	2-6-89	.233	.253	.228	75	266	28	62	10	1	2	21	6	2	3	3	71	9	8	.301	.253
Gomez, Carlos	R-R	6-4	210	12-4-85	.154	.000	.200	4	13	2	2	0	0	1	3	1	0	0	0	4	0	0	.385	.214
Haniger, Mitch	R-R	6-2	180	12-23-90	.286	.375	.242	14	49	9	14	4	0	1	8	7	1	0	1	13	1	0	.429	.379
Hopkins, Greg	R-R	6-1	200	11-22-88	.269	.248	.282	104	394	45	106	21	1	9	50	17	6	1	7	73	7	9	.396	.304
Lucroy, Jonathan	R-R	6-0	195	6-13-86	.333	.500	.167	4	12	0	4	1	0	0	2	1	0	0	0	1	0	0	.417	.385
Macias, Brandon	R-R	5-10	185	10-10-88	.288	.269	.295	127	468	83	135	35	2	8	63	58	21	9	4	73	11	12	.423	.388
McMahan, Ben	R-R	6-0	201	10-14-89	.287	.274	.293	109	414	64	119	21	11	15	68	29	2	1	3	129	9	5	.500	.335
Neda, Rafael	R-R	6-1	215	10-12-88	.229	.274	.204	74	227	13	52	9	1	1	16	22	5	3	0	36	0	1	.291	.311
Ramirez, Nick	L-L	6-3	225	8-1-89	.248	.194	.276	96	383	46	95	28	0	16	70	26	1	0	4	144	0	0	.446	.295
Rivera, Yadiel	R-R	6-2	175	5-2-92	.247	.293	.229	127	465	60	115	26	5	12	49	26	4	6	5	119	7	3	.402	.290
Roberts, Tyler	R-R	6-0	226	10-25-90	.185	.179	.188	31	92	9	17	3	0	4	11	10	0	0	0	30	0	0	.348	.265
Roenicke, Lance	R-R	6-1	190	6-8-88	.245	.262	.232	42	143	21	35	5	0	2	14	5	4	2	3	37	7	4	.322	.284
Rogers, Jason	R-R	6-2	250	3-13-88	.301	.333	.288	66	239	39	72	24	1	6	43	37	1	0	2	46	5	0	.485	.394
Stang, Chad	R-R	6-2	190	3-26-89	.270	.268	.271	127	481	85	130	24	9	10	47	43	4	9	3	144	26	10	.420	.333
Walla, Max	L-L	5-11	195	4-12-91	.234	.125	.261	101	355	58	83	13	2	7	41	47	2	3	2	107	12	10	.341	.325
Williams, Adrian	R-R	6-0	175	1-3-91	.153	.214	.133	43	118	11	18	1	0	0	7	17	1	7	1	39	5	3	.161	.263

Pitching	B-T	HT	WT	DOB	W	L	ERA	G	GS	CG	SV	IP	H	R	ER	HR	BB	SO	AVG	vLH	vRH	K/9	BB/9
Barnes, Jacob	R-R	6-2	230	4-14-90	4	7	3.84	25	7	0	3	94	87	46	40	10	46	83	.251	.259	.243	7.98	4.42
Cravy, Tyler	R-R	6-3	194	7-13-89	2	5	3.38	24	0	0	3	51	45	24	19	5	15	53	.231	.218	.239	9.41	2.66
Gagnon, Drew	R-R	6-4	195	6-26-90	6	1	2.83	14	14	0	0	83	67	26	26	6	19	65	.219	.230	.212	7.08	2.07
Goforth, David	R-R	6-0	188	10-11-88	10	8	4.66	28	28	0	0	151	154	91	78	16	63	93	.269	.265	.272	5.56	3.76
Harvey, Seth	L-R	6-2	205	1-20-88	4	0	2.66	22	0	0	13	24	22	8	7	1	8	32	.244	.205	.283	12.17	3.04
Lasker, Maverick	R-R	6-2	190	2-17-90	0	0	7.98	6	0	0	1	15	18	14	13	1	13	9	.310	.421	.256	5.52	7.98
Lintz, Seth	R-R	6-1	170	2-7-90	0	1	11.00	6	0	0	0	9	15	13	11	3	7	3	.375	.375	.375	3.00	7.00
Manzanillo, Santo	R-R	6-0	205	12-20-88	2	1	7.50	4	0	0	0	6	5	5	5	1	5	2	.263	.125	.364	3.00	7.50
Marcum, Shaun	R-R	6-0	195	12-14-81	1	0	2.84	3	3	0	0	13	9	5	4	1	3	10	.191	.240	.136	7.11	2.13
Miller, Matt	R-R	6-6	220	1-30-89	10	7	3.68	22	22	0	0	132	132	61	54	8	38	95	.267	.263	.269	6.48	2.59
Moye, Andy	R-R	6-5	180	9-11-87	3	0	1.45	8	7	0	0	37	25	8	6	1	8	33	.191	.154	.227	7.96	1.93
Peterson, Stephen	L-L	6-3	210	11-6-87	3	2	3.27	25	0	0	3	41	29	16	15	1	27	35	.196	.217	.186	7.62	5.88
Pierce, Chad	R-R	6-1	215	11-20-87	7	5	3.47	27	12	0	2	125	112	51	48	10	41	115	.239	.155	.301	8.30	2.96
Semmelhack, Eric	R-R	6-5	230	1-7-91	2	3	6.16	10	5	0	0	31	37	23	21	3	15	22	.296	.404	.231	6.46	4.40
Shackelford, Kevin	R-R	6-5	215	4-7-89	3	5	4.06	27	3	0	5	64	70	30	29	4	23	43	.283	.282	.285	6.02	3.22
Strong, Mike	L-L	6-0	194	11-17-88	1	1	2.76	21	0	0	3	42	30	18	13	2	26	60	.195	.137	.223	12.76	5.53
Suter, Brent	R-L	6-5	195	8-29-89	0	0	2.08	3	0	0	2	9	11	4	2	0	3	8	.306	.385	.261	8.31	3.12
Thompson, Chad	R-R	6-7	207	2-6-91	5	2	4.31	18	18	0	0	86	69	42	41	11	37	74	.221	.226	.217	7.77	3.89
Toledo, Tommy	R-R	6-3	190	12-31-89	7	1	1.95	21	0	0	6	37	20	11	8	3	11	31	.157	.208	.122	7.54	2.68
Wawrzasek, Stosh	R-R	6-0	251	8-30-90	0	1	2.61	15	0	0	3	31	23	9	9	1	9	30	.205	.246	.164	8.71	2.61
West, Will	L-L	6-4	170	7-23-92	1	1	6.20	5	5	0	0	20	29	15	14	0	10	15	.345	.300	.351	6.64	4.43
White, Michael	R-R	6-6	190	9-11-89	0	0	7.98	7	0	0	1	15	23	16	13	1	9	7	.359	.333	.372	4.30	5.52
Williams, Alan	L-L	6-3	195	3-5-90	0	0	9.00	3	0	0	1	8							.095	.200	.063	11.37	9.95
Williams, Mark	R-R	6-4	225	8-12-89	7	10	3.88	27	14	1	2	116	111	58	50	7	42	90	.255	.312	.208	6.98	3.26
Williamson, Brandon	R-R	6-2	180	4-22-89	0	0	4.50	1	1	0	0	6	4	3	3	1	2	3	.182	.133	.286	4.50	3.00

Fielding

Catcher	PCT	G	PO	A	E	DP	PB
Berberet	1.000	5	31	5	0	0	1
Garfield	.978	49	328	36	8	4	7
Lucroy	.941	3	14	2	1	0	0
Neda	.989	74	476	53	6	4	4
Roberts	.990	26	175	18	2	2	3

First Base	PCT	G	PO	A	E	DP
Berberet	1.000	4	35	4	0	2
Garza	1.000	2	25	1	0	1
Hopkins	.995	20	175	18	1	16
Ramirez	.994	88	774	63	5	59
Rogers	.992	29	217	21	2	19

	PCT	G	PO	A	E	DP
Walla	1.000	3	3	0	0	1

Second Base	PCT	G	PO	A	E	DP
George	.961	57	87	161	10	32
Hopkins	.996	60	102	155	1	27
Macias	.895	5	4	13	2	1
Williams	.958	23	35	56	4	6

Third Base	PCT	G	PO	A	E	DP
Garza	.922	20	11	36	4	3
Hopkins	.905	17	9	29	4	6
Macias	.957	102	65	200	12	13

Shortstop	PCT	G	PO	A	E	DP
Macias	1.000	1	2	4	0	1
Rivera	.962	126	216	348	22	71

	PCT	G	PO	A	E	DP
Williams	.966	13	18	39	2	5
Outfield	PCT	G	PO	A	E	DP
Dishon	1.000	45	96	7	0	2
Garza	—	1	0	0	0	0
George	1.000	10	22	0	0	0
Gomez	1.000	3	4	0	0	0
Haniger	.957	12	21	1	1	0
McMahan	.955	98	180	12	9	3
Roenicke	.984	26	61	1	1	0
Rogers	1.000	14	22	0	0	0
Stang	.993	125	257	8	2	4
Walla	.951	95	169	7	9	0
Williams	1.000	3	6	0	0	0

AZL BREWERS ROOKIE
ARIZONA LEAGUE

Batting	B-T	HT	WT	DOB	AVG	vLH	vRH	G	AB	R	H	2B	3B	HR	RBI	BB	HBP	SH	SF	SO	SB	CS	SLG	OBP
Andrade, Joe	L-R	5-10	195	4-21-90	.417	—	.417	5	12	0	5	3	0	0	3	0	0	0	1	0	0		.667	.417
Brennan, Taylor	R-R	6-0	210	1-31-92	.159	.000	.189	34	107	17	17	3	1	1	20	32	2	0	0	51	6	0	.290	.362
Coulter, Clint	R-R	6-3	210	7-30-93	.302	.325	.295	49	169	37	51	3	3	5	33	37	6	0	2	40	3	5	.444	.439
Davis, Khris	R-R	6-0	195	12-21-87	.368	.125	.545	6	19	7	7	0	0	3	5	2	1	0	0	7	1	1	.842	.455
Dowell, Malcolm	R-R	6-0	190	4-21-93	.268	.290	.262	44	138	21	37	2	1	0	18	18	5	1	1	37	8	2	.297	.370
Garcia, Jose	R-R	6-3	195	3-5-91	.220	.167	.244	18	59	12	13	1	1	2	9	3	1	1	1	17	1	0	.373	.266
Harris, Jalen	R-R	6-2	210	7-7-92	.172	.167	.173	31	122	13	21	1	3	0	12	12	0	0	0	38	2	1	.230	.246
Hinojosa, Dionis	R-R	6-1	180	8-14-90	.258	.320	.242	37	120	21	31	6	1	0	16	9	2	0	0	39	10	2	.350	.321
Houle, Dustin	R-R	6-1	205	11-9-93	.206	.140	.227	47	175	19	36	10	0	1	19	13	3	2	1	33	0	1	.280	.271
Jenkins, Renaldo	R-R	6-0	190	3-1-93	.299	.429	.277	29	97	16	29	3	2	0	12	11	0	1	0	13	8	1	.371	.370
Kjeldgaard, Brock	R-R	6-5	235	1-22-86	.000	.000	.000	1	4	0	0	0	0	0	0	0	0	0	0	1	0	0	.000	.000
Mejia, Deyvi	R-R	6-0	195	11-3-89	.255	.308	.238	17	55	10	14	3	1	2	16	0	1	0	0	16	0	0	.455	.268
Ortega, Angel	R-R	6-2	170	9-11-93	.242	.256	.237	46	178	26	43	6	2	1	16	11	0	2	1	24	9	4	.315	.284
Pena, Jose	R-R	6-2	192	3-3-93	.299	.375	.281	40	167	30	50	9	7	5	31	13	1	0	2	39	1	1	.527	.350
Rivera, Edgardo	L-R	6-0	155	4-12-94	.262	.174	.282	32	126	26	33	6	0	0	13	19	0	2	1	36	9	1	.310	.356
Sermo, Jose	R-R	6-0	190	3-22-91	.284	.220	.303	45	183	26	52	7	4	4	28	11	3	0	0	41	6	4	.432	.335
Sharkey, Alan	L-L	6-1	185	11-8-93	.240	.278	.229	41	154	26	37	6	0	0	21	18	1	0	1	17	6	2	.279	.322
Taylor, Tyrone	R-R	6-0	185	1-22-94	.389	.250	.406	8	36	11	14	5	3	0	6	1	0	0	1	3	3	1	.694	.395

Pitching	B-T	HT	WT	DOB	W	L	ERA	G	GS	CG	SV	IP	H	R	ER	HR	BB	SO	AVG	vLH	vRH	K/9	BB/9
Armold, Jonathan	R-R	6-2	200	1-15-89	0	2	3.64	12	0	0	0	30	34	20	12	2	13	32	.281	.250	.304	9.71	3.94
Banda, Anthony	L-L	6-3	175	8-10-93	2	3	5.83	14	4	0	0	42	54	41	27	3	24	43	.309	.321	.303	9.29	5.18
Blaski, Austin	R-R	6-3	200	8-2-90	0	0	3.93	12	0	0	0	18	20	11	8	1	7	17	.299	.429	.205	8.35	3.44
Bucci, Nick	R-R	6-2	180	7-16-90	1	1	1.64	4	4	0	0	11	7	3	2	1	0	7	.179	.133	.208	5.73	0.00
Butler, Josh	R-R	6-5	205	12-11-84	0	0	4.50	4	2	0	0	6	6	4	3	1	0	4	.261	.125	.333	6.00	0.00
Chulk, Vinnie	R-R	6-2	200	12-19-78	0	0	0.00	2	1	0	0	2	0	0	0	0	0	4	.000	.000	.000	4.50	0.00
Dicent, Joel	R-R	6-3	176	8-4-91	3	4	5.19	14	8	0	1	52	55	34	30	3	30	43	.274	.261	.283	7.44	5.19
Fasano, Ryan	R-R	6-1	195	11-10-89	0	0	3.38	10	0	0	1	19	22	8	7	0	3	20	.286	.320	.269	9.64	1.45
Francisco, Juan	R-R	6-5	180	12-15-90	4	2	6.43	13	2	0	0	42	63	41	30	5	18	35	.352	.323	.368	7.50	3.86
Hall, Austin	R-R	6-4	210	9-21-88	2	2	4.41	13	3	0	0	33	38	23	16	3	13	31	.275	.340	.225	8.54	3.58
Keller, Daniel	R-R	6-5	190	6-30-92	0	4	9.33	14	5	0	0	45	76	58	47	4	19	30	.362	.316	.400	5.96	3.77
Lamontagne, Andre	B-R	6-1	203	3-24-86	0	1	11.25	3	3	0	0	4	5	5	5	1	4	5	.357	.000	.500	11.25	9.00
Lasker, Maverick	R-R	6-2	190	2-17-90	0	1	6.75	6	0	0	0	12	10	11	9	0	13	8	.213	.250	.194	6.00	9.75
Lavandero, Alex	L-R	6-3	180	11-21-93	0	2	15.43	11	0	0	0	12	20	26	20	3	20	8	.357	.429	.314	6.17	15.43
Lopez, Jorge	R-R	6-4	165	2-10-93	1	3	5.33	7	3	0	2	25	27	22	15	2	12	20	.270	.324	.242	7.11	4.26
Mangum, Taylor	R-R	6-1	190	3-4-89	1	1	0.79	5	0	0	0	11	10	2	1	0	6	11	.222	.278	.185	8.74	4.76
Manzanillo, Santo	R-R	6-0	205	12-20-88	0	1	10.13	2	0	0	0	3	4	5	3	0	0	2	.333	1.000	.200	6.75	0.00
Otterman, David	R-L	6-3	210	5-15-91	0	0	0.00	2	2	0	0	3	2	0	0	0	1	4	.182	.000	.182	12.00	3.00
Quintana, Zachary	R-R	5-11	180	4-15-94	3	4	5.82	13	4	0	1	43	44	30	28	3	22	39	.293	.311	.211	8.10	4.57
Reyes, Eduard	R-R	6-0	174	8-23-90	0	3	2.70	7	4	0	0	30	26	13	9	0	10	33	.241	.256	.232	9.90	3.00
Rivero, Francisco	R-R	6-2	204	3-11-91	0	1	2.25	6	5	0	0	8	9	2	2	0	1	5	.265	.222	.280	5.63	1.13
Saba, Yefri	R-R	6-2	152	9-7-91	0	0	13.14	7	0	0	0	12	21	19	18	2	10	9	.382	.414	.346	6.57	7.30
Sosa, Carlos	R-R	6-6	236	9-6-91	2	2	3.54	15	0	0	1	20	18	10	8	3	4	20	.240	.265	.220	8.85	1.77

Fielding

Catcher	PCT	G	PO	A	E	DP	PB
Andrade	1.000	5	23	2	0	1	2
Coulter	.966	26	200	25	8	3	21
Garcia	.909	3	8	2	1	0	0
Houle	.980	28	177	21	4	4	13
Mejia	.966	6	20	8	1	0	0

First Base	PCT	G	PO	A	E	DP
Harris	.991	12	108	5	1	1
Mejia	1.000	3	26	0	0	2
Sharkey	.976	41	334	35	9	29

Second Base	PCT	G	PO	A	E	DP
Brennan	1.000	2	2	6	0	0
Jenkins	.918	19	42	48	8	11
Sermo	.954	36	73	94	8	17

Third Base	PCT	G	PO	A	E	DP
Brennan	.857	32	23	43	11	2
Harris	.850	19	13	38	9	5
Sermo	.733	6	2	9	4	1

Shortstop	PCT	G	PO	A	E	DP
Jenkins	.829	9	10	24	7	3

	PCT	G	PO	A	E	DP
Ortega	.926	46	78	121	16	21
Sermo	.733	3	4	7	4	2

Outfield	PCT	G	PO	A	E	DP
Davis	1.000	6	7	0	0	0
Dowell	.935	43	71	1	5	0
Garcia	.941	15	28	4	2	1
Hinojosa	.971	36	62	4	2	1
Kjeldgaard	1.000	1	2	0	0	0
Pena	.907	40	60	8	7	3
Rivera	.927	32	50	1	4	0

HELENA BREWERS ROOKIE
PIONEER LEAGUE

Batting	B-T	HT	WT	DOB	AVG	vLH	vRH	G	AB	R	H	2B	3B	HR	RBI	BB	HBP	SH	SF	SO	SB	CS	SLG	OBP
Andrade, Joe	L-R	5-10	195	4-21-90	.170	.273	.139	13	47	7	8	3	0	0	5	8	0	0	0	14	1	0	.234	.291
Berard, Kevin	R-R	5-10	170	12-3-91	.152	.227	.123	23	79	8	12	3	0	0	2	2	1	0		27	5	0	.190	.193
Eshleman, Paul	R-R	6-3	220	9-3-90	.250	.469	.194	40	156	16	39	9	0	4	22	3	2	0	5	47	0	0	.385	.265

Name	B-T	HT	WT	DOB	AVG	vLH	vRH	G	AB	R	H	2B	3B	HR	RBI	BB	HBP	SH	SF	SO	SB	CS	SLG	OBP
Garza, Mike	R-R	6-1	195	3-11-90	.407	.500	.381	19	81	7	33	4	2	2	13	5	0	0	0	10	5	2	.580	.442
Giacalone, Adam	L-R	6-2	218	12-22-91	.317	.353	.304	69	259	33	82	17	1	3	32	35	0	1	3	66	3	5	.425	.394
Hernandez, Yonki	B-R	5-10	160	10-5-90	.250	.171	.281	38	124	23	31	2	1	1	10	14	0	4	0	39	14	2	.306	.326
Jenkins, Renaldo	R-R	6-0	190	3-1-93	.200	.200	.200	4	15	2	3	1	0	0	0	2	0	0	0	3	2	0	.267	.294
Martinez, Andres	R-R	6-2	188	1-26-92	.241	.313	.214	21	58	6	14	6	1	1	9	1	1	2	0	28	4	1	.431	.267
McFarland, Chris	R-R	6-0	190	11-24-92	.301	.214	.330	72	282	48	85	17	1	6	42	23	3	3	2	79	15	6	.433	.358
Mondesi, Raul	R-R	5-10	180	8-23-92	.231	.239	.228	68	273	43	63	12	6	5	32	14	6	4	1	87	8	4	.374	.282
Nemeth, Michael	L-R	6-1	200	4-4-89	.235	.120	.286	25	81	7	19	2	0	0	8	18	0	0	3	13	0	0	.259	.363
Pena, Jose	R-R	6-2	192	3-3-93	.306	.318	.302	21	85	18	26	4	3	3	15	4	1	0	2	17	1	1	.529	.337
Quiles, Emmanuel	R-R	5-11	186	10-26-89	.249	.188	.270	49	185	21	46	11	1	3	30	7	0	1	2	39	1	1	.368	.273
Reed, Michael	R-R	6-0	190	11-18-92	.246	.227	.252	48	179	29	44	5	1	1	20	24	1	3	1	58	11	1	.302	.337
Rodriguez, Alfredo	R-R	6-0	175	5-26-90	.281	.204	.300	72	267	30	75	13	2	1	36	34	9	6	1	45	7	10	.356	.379
Roenicke, Lance	R-R	6-1	190	6-8-88	.538	.000	.583	3	13	1	7	1	0	0	5	1	0	0	0	1	0	0	.615	.571
Sanchez, Ruben	L-L	6-2	198	8-20-91	.267	.295	.259	56	202	30	54	8	3	2	18	13	1	1	0	44	15	4	.366	.315
Taylor, Tyrone	R-R	6-0	185	1-22-94	.385	.467	.333	10	39	11	15	4	0	2	5	5	1	0	0	8	3	2	.641	.467
Turay, Michael	R-R	5-10	175	1-6-90	.255	.302	.238	46	165	23	42	11	1	4	14	10	2	1	1	42	0	2	.406	.303
Williams, Adrian	R-R	6-0	175	1-3-91	.125	.167	.111	9	24	3	3	0	0	0	1	9	0	2	0	9	2	1	.125	.364

Pitching	B-T	HT	WT	DOB	W	L	ERA	G	GS	CG	SV	IP	H	R	ER	HR	BB	SO	AVG	vLH	vRH	K/9	BB/9
Armold, Jonathan	R-R	6-2	200	1-15-89	0	0	0.00	3	0	0	0	3	5	0	0	0	1	3	.357	.500	.300	8.10	2.70
Fasano, Ryan	R-R	6-1	195	11-10-89	1	1	7.20	2	0	0	0	5	8	4	4	0	3	2	.364	.400	.333	3.60	5.40
Francisco, Mike	R-L	6-4	224	8-4-88	1	1	4.97	20	0	0	1	29	33	16	16	1	11	21	.284	.231	.312	6.52	3.41
Gainey, Preston	R-R	6-3	205	2-13-91	0	4	8.05	12	7	0	0	38	46	39	34	8	21	31	.289	.324	.259	7.34	4.97
Gibbard, Ryan	R-R	6-3	220	11-28-89	1	5	5.27	14	10	0	0	55	60	36	32	3	13	39	.279	.274	.284	6.42	2.14
Glynn, Elliott	L-L	6-1	160	1-13-89	2	2	8.51	15	0	0	0	24	28	28	23	5	21	24	.292	.222	.319	8.88	7.77
Lorenzo, Leonard	R-R	6-0	190	7-16-91	2	7	5.48	14	12	0	0	64	73	46	39	7	26	64	.293	.264	.320	9.00	3.66
Magnifico, Damien	R-R	6-1	185	5-24-91	0	3	5.82	9	1	0	0	22	21	17	14	2	15	25	.250	.275	.227	10.38	6.23
Mangum, Taylor	R-R	6-1	190	3-4-89	1	1	5.40	9	0	0	1	15	15	10	9	1	6	12	.273	.261	.281	7.20	3.60
Otterman, David	R-L	6-3	210	5-15-91	0	1	9.00	4	1	0	0	10	13	13	10	0	4	7	.295	.353	.259	6.30	3.60
Pierce, Joel	L-R	6-4	200	12-21-92	0	1	7.36	16	1	0	0	26	31	26	21	2	17	22	.298	.295	.300	7.71	5.96
Ruiz, Manuel	L-L	6-5	175	12-12-88	0	1	8.27	13	0	0	1	16	13	15	15	2	24	23	.217	.350	.150	12.67	13.22
Schaub, Mike	R-R	6-2	180	5-31-92	1	3	7.28	15	5	0	0	51	59	48	41	10	34	35	.295	.275	.316	6.22	6.04
Semmelhack, Eric	R-R	6-5	230	1-7-91	1	3	4.02	6	0	0	0	31	27	17	14	1	9	20	.229	.261	.184	5.74	2.59
Suter, Brent	R-L	6-5	195	8-29-89	4	2	3.92	11	2	0	0	44	49	22	19	4	8	42	.290	.281	.295	8.66	1.65
Viramontes, Martin	R-R	6-5	225	7-12-89	2	6	6.27	16	0	0	1	37	44	31	26	1	27	53	.295	.296	.295	12.78	6.51
Wagner, Tyler	R-R	6-3	195	11-24-91	1	4	7.77	14	13	0	0	49	63	51	42	6	22	47	.304	.298	.308	8.69	4.07
Wall, Taylor	L-L	6-2	190	1-8-90	3	1	3.98	14	10	0	0	54	65	32	24	3	20	40	.313	.366	.285	6.63	3.31
West, Will	L-L	6-4	170	7-23-92	0	4	7.84	8	0	0	0	41	64	40	36	3	16	35	.362	.365	.360	7.62	3.48
Whalen, Connor	L-L	6-3	195	4-19-88	1	0	2.35	22	0	0	7	31	29	11	8	0	13	36	.236	.275	.217	10.57	3.82
White, Michael	R-R	6-6	190	9-11-89	3	2	4.71	14	0	0	1	21	24	11	11	0	12	22	.300	.324	.283	9.43	5.14

Fielding

Catcher

	PCT	G	PO	A	E	DP	PB
Andrade	.968	4	26	4	1	1	1
Eshleman	.975	29	243	25	7	2	7
Quiles	.979	33	242	37	6	2	8
Turay	.969	14	83	11	3	1	4
McFarland	.939	65	100	179	18		41
Williams	.927	8	10	28	3		6
Rodriguez	.940	72	112	232	22		51

First Base

	PCT	G	PO	A	E	DP
Giacalone	.989	69	650	53	8	59
Nemeth	.984	7	55	5	1	7

Second Base

	PCT	G	PO	A	E	DP
Berard	.933	2	6	8	1	1
Jenkins	.875	4	3	11	2	1

Third Base

	PCT	G	PO	A	E	DP
Berard	.875	14	10	18	4	2
Garza	.896	19	18	25	5	3
Jenkins	1.000	2	1	0	0	0
Martinez	.894	16	12	30	5	4
Nemeth	.944	8	3	14	1	0
Turay	.847	21	8	42	9	2

Shortstop

	PCT	G	PO	A	E	DP
Berard	.864	5	6	13	3	2

Outfield

	PCT	G	PO	A	E	DP
Berard	1.000	1	1	0	0	0
Glynn	—	1	0	0	0	0
Hernandez	.944	38	50	1	3	0
Mondesi	.946	67	111	11	7	1
Pena	.875	21	34	1	5	1
Reed	.966	47	80	4	3	2
Roenicke	1.000	3	3	0	0	0
Sanchez	.911	50	71	1	7	0
Taylor	.929	5	13	0	1	0
Williams	—	1	0	0	0	0

DSL BREWERS ROOKIE

DOMINICAN SUMMER LEAGUE

Batting	B-T	HT	WT	DOB	AVG	vLH	vRH	G	AB	R	H	2B	3B	HR	RBI	BB	HBP	SH	SF	SO	SB	CS	SLG	OBP
Belonis, Carlos	R-R	6-3	175	8-19-94	.259	.308	.244	47	174	28	45	6	2	2	22	12	4	0	1	54	25	9	.351	.319
Castillo, Francisco	R-R	5-11	170	6-4-93	.272	.250	.278	53	206	34	56	3	2	1	14	22	3	3	2	28	30	8	.320	.348
Colatosti, Raphachel	R-R	6-1		7-3-93	.221	.146	.241	59	199	32	44	4	0	1	19	27	9	3	2	34	14	3	.256	.338
De La Cruz, Yunior	R-R	6-0	195	12-23-89	.191	.120	.211	38	115	12	22	4	0	0	14	15	1	4	5	16	0	0	.226	.279
De Leon, Juan	R-R	6-4	217	2-27-92	.209	.150	.225	30	91	14	19	4	0	4	13	9	2	0	0	31	0	0	.385	.294
Dicent, Jose	R-R	6-2	176	10-1-90	.234	.231	.235	53	175	17	41	4	1	1	16	30	6	3	2	40	7	2	.286	.362
Martinez, Kevin	B-R	5-10	180	1-11-95	.143	.053	.163	37	105	8	15	2	0	0	6	15	1	0	3	23	2	0	.162	.256
Matos, Sthervin	R-R	6-1	185	2-13-94	.184	.000	.206	12	38	3	7	0	0	0	1	6	2	0	0	10	2	1	.184	.326
Mejia, Natanael	R-R	6-0	175	7-10-92	.262	.143	.294	27	65	5	17	2	0	1	3	6	1	0	1	8	0	2	.338	.329
Mendoza, Alejandro	R-R	5-11	160	2-12-92	.237	.186	.250	63	207	34	49	3	0	1	23	30	8	6	1	54	13	7	.266	.354
Ortiz, Juan	L-R	6-1	175	9-20-94	.229	.205	.234	62	214	28	49	11	1	3	24	27	5	0	1	58	18	7	.332	.328
Otano, Leudi	R-R	5-11	180	2-21-91	.273	.000	.286	11	22	5	6	3	1	0	2	6	0	0	0	9	1	0	.500	.429
Pena, Carlos	R-R	5-11	190	9-28-92	.223	.222	.224	31	103	17	23	6	1	4	21	11	1	1	2	16	0	1	.417	.302
Rubio, Elvis	R-R	6-3	215	7-2-94	.242	.114	.275	60	211	30	51	12	0	2	27	27	8	0	1	44	6	2	.327	.348
Santana, Yunior	R-R	6-3	210	9-10-93	.175	.086	.204	46	143	16	25	1	0	3	16	20	0	1	1	64	7	2	.245	.274

Pitching	B-T	HT	WT	DOB	W	L	ERA	G	GS	CG	SV	IP	H	R	ER	HR	BB	SO	AVG	vLH	vRH	K/9	BB/9
Arias, Doni	R-R	6-3	187	7-26-92	0	1	5.40	13	0	0	1	13	18	10	8	0	12	14	.305	.316	.300	9.45	8.10
De La Cruz, Joan	L-L	6-3	175	9-30-94	0	2	5.40	9	1	0	0	12	11	8	7	0	6	14	.250	.667	.184	10.80	4.63
Diaz, Miguel	R-R	6-1	175	11-28-94	0	3	4.62	15	1	0	1	25	27	20	13	0	15	21	.278	.226	.303	7.46	5.33
Diaz, Victor	R-R	6-1	170	10-6-93	0	1	1.90	13	0	0	0	24	16	8	5	2	14	26	.208	.217	.204	9.89	5.32
Flores, Junior	R-R	6-1	175	10-13-94	1	3	7.92	17	0	0	1	25	24	24	22	1	19	21	.264	.172	.306	7.56	6.84
Gomez, Milton	R-R	6-1	172	4-22-94	3	6	3.51	13	10	0	0	56	67	33	22	1	20	46	.290	.284	.293	7.35	3.20
Lopez, Jorge	R-R	6-4	165	2-10-93	0	1	4.76	5	3	0	0	23	22	14	12	0	10	26	.256	.286	.235	10.32	3.97
Montano, Eliezer	L-L	6-7	170	10-21-91	1	4	4.54	13	4	0	1	40	44	28	20	3	20	36	.289	.286	.290	8.17	4.54
Ortega, Jorge	R-R	6-1	165	6-20-93	6	5	2.54	13	13	1	0	78	81	32	22	0	13	53	.270	.211	.304	6.12	1.50
Padilla, Marcos	L-L	6-2	175	1-1-94	0	0	10.38	8	0	0	0	9	8	11	10	0	11	6	.267	.000	.286	6.23	11.42
Paulino, Felix	R-R	5-11	165	5-21-91	4	0	3.50	13	0	0	0	18	22	11	7	0	6	18	.293	.357	.255	9.00	3.00
Peguero, Pedro	R-R	6-6	215	8-10-93	0	1	27.00	3	2	0	0	2	1	6	6	0	5	1	.200	.500	.000	4.50	22.50
Reyes, Eduard	R-R	6-0	174	8-23-90	3	1	1.39	8	8	0	0	45	37	20	7	1	11	51	.215	.197	.225	10.13	2.18
Rizzo, Gian	R-R	6-1	160	9-5-93	3	0	1.08	11	10	1	0	50	46	12	6	0	6	52	.241	.257	.231	9.36	1.08
Santiago, Juan	L-L	5-11	176	12-23-90	2	4	1.49	12	8	0	1	54	40	14	9	1	22	65	.207	.167	.211	10.77	3.64
Tejada, Melvin	R-R	6-3	175	1-24-95	1	1	2.96	15	0	1	0	27	21	13	9	0	15	24	.214	.273	.185	7.90	4.94
Torres, Joshua	R-R	6-0	160	4-26-94	0	2	5.68	9	0	0	0	13	10	8	8	2	6	8	.213	.214	.212	5.68	4.26
Torrez, Orlando	R-R	6-3	195	4-14-92	1	1	7.71	6	3	0	0	12	11	11	10	0	9	11	.239	.133	.290	8.49	6.94
Ventura, Angel	R-R	6-2	185	4-7-93	1	3	7.12	13	2	0	1	30	46	32	24	2	13	27	.354	.361	.351	8.01	3.86

Fielding

Catcher	PCT	G	PO	A	E	DP	PB
De La Cruz	.976	21	151	14	4	0	6
Martinez	.965	9	48	7	2	1	6
Mejia	.974	24	160	28	5	1	5
Pena	.970	22	175	17	6	1	5

First Base	PCT	G	PO	A	E	DP
De La Cruz	.969	15	119	6	4	13
De Leon	.980	19	139	8	3	8
Dicent	.992	14	116	6	1	6
Martinez	.987	9	69	6	1	8
Mendoza	1.000	9	58	3	0	5
Rubio	.956	8	59	6	3	5

Second Base	PCT	G	PO	A	E	DP
Castillo	1.000	1	5	3	0	1

	PCT	G	PO	A	E	DP
Colatosti	.960	12	23	25	2	3
Martinez	.800	2	2	2	1	1
Mendoza	.961	52	96	128	9	26
Otano	.750	5	8	4	4	0

Third Base	PCT	G	PO	A	E	DP
Colatosti	.914	20	12	41	5	2
De Leon	.750	1	1	2	1	1
Dicent	.930	38	19	61	6	2
Matos	.833	8	7	8	3	1
Mendoza	.833	2	3	7	2	1
Otano	1.000	1	3	3	0	0
Rubio	1.000	1	2	0	0	0

Shortstop	PCT	G	PO	A	E	DP
Belonis	.885	33	44	72	15	11

	PCT	G	PO	A	E	DP
Castillo	.947	4	6	12	1	1
Colatosti	.942	31	57	88	9	21
Dicent	.000	1	0	0	1	0
Mendoza	.941	4	5	11	1	0

Outfield	PCT	G	PO	A	E	DP
Belonis	—	1	0	0	0	0
Castillo	.937	48	72	2	5	0
Dicent	1.000	5	4	1	0	0
Martinez	—	1	0	0	0	0
Mendoza	—	1	0	0	0	0
Ortiz	.933	60	77	7	6	0
Otano	.833	7	4	1	1	0
Padilla	—	1	0	0	0	0
Rubio	.943	49	63	3	4	0
Santana	.929	36	37	2	3	1

Minnesota Twins

SEASON IN A SENTENCE: Losing has become the norm again for the Twins, as they followed the 99-loss 2011 debacle with a 96-loss snore of a season that was over when they lost their first four games and 15 of their first 20 in April.

HIGH POINT: Other than strong seasons by Joe Mauer and free-agent signee Josh Willingham, though, that was about it for the good news in the Twin Cities. Recent farm products such as Trevor Plouffe (24 homers, second on the team), Ben Revere (.333 OBP, 40 steals) and Chris Parmelee (.755 OPS in his final 26 games) showed signs they could be low-cost contributors.

LOW POINT: The team dropped 90 games in consecutive seasons for the first time in 12 years. When that happened in 1999-2000, the Twins had the lowest payroll in baseball. This time, they had the highest (2011) and third-highest (2012) payrolls in franchise history. The losing has affected attendance at Target Field, which dropped nearly 400,000 to 2.8 million fans in 2011. Minnesota's problems start on the mound. Twins starters posted a 5.40 ERA, worst in the American League. Twelve pitchers made five or more starts, and only Former Rule 5 draftee Scott Diamond and perhaps Cole DeVries earned spots in the 2013 rotation.

NOTABLE ROOKIES: The team's pitching imploded almost immediately and the season became an audition for young players, some of whom responded. Diamond turned out to be the team's top starter at 12-9, 3.54, and DeVries (4.11 ERA) and Liam Hendriks (5.59 ERA) each made 16 starts. In addition to Parmelee, infielder Brian Dozier played in 84 games, though he batted .234/.271/.332.

KEY TRANSACTIONS: Even though it was a lost year, the Twins did not have a big midseason sell-off, with the only notable deal coming when they sent Francisco Liriano to the White Sox for two prospects.

DOWN ON THE FARM: Minnesota's top pitching prospect, Kyle Gibson, made his way back from Tommy John surgery and could factor into the 2013 big league rotation after a strong performance in the Arizona Fall League. In the first year of baseball's new draft system, Minnesota had the largest signing pool for the first 10 rounds at $12.4 million and spent nearly half of that on its top pick, outfielder Byron Buxton. The No. 2 overall selection helped lead Elizabethton to the Rookie-level Appalachian League title.

OPENING DAY PAYROLL: $94.1 million (13th)

PLAYERS OF THE YEAR

MAJOR LEAGUE

Josh Willingham
of
.260/.366/.524
35 HR, 110 RBIs
3rd in AL in RBIs

MINOR LEAGUE

Oswaldo Arcia
of
(High A/Double-A)
.320/.388/.539
17 HR, 98 RBIs

ORGANIZATION LEADERS

BATTING		*Minimum 250 AB
MAJORS		
* AVG	Joe Mauer	.319
* OPS	Josh Willingham	.890
HR	Josh Willingham	35
RBI	Josh Willingham	110
MINORS		
* AVG	Oswaldo Arcia, Fort Myers/New Britain	.320
* OBP	Oswaldo Arcia, Fort Myers/New Britain	.388
* SLG	Oswaldo Arcia, Fort Myers/New Britain	.539
R	Aaron Hicks, New Britain	100
H	Oswaldo Arcia, Fort Myers/New Britain	150
TB	Oswaldo Arcia, Fort Myers/New Britain	253
2B	Chris Colabello, New Britain	37
3B	Adonis Pacheco, DSL Twins	12
HR	Miguel Sano, Beloit	28
RBI	Miguel Sano, Beloit	100
BB	Miguel Sano, Beloit	80
SO	Miguel Sano, Beloit	144
SB	Aaron Hicks, New Britain	32

PITCHING		#Minimum 75 IP
MAJORS		
W	Scott Diamond	12
# ERA	Scott Diamond	3.54
SO	Francisco Liriano	109
SV	Glen Perkins	16
MINORS		
W	Jason Wheeler, Beloit	14
L	Madison Boer, Beloit/Fort Myers	12
L	Logan Darnell, New Britain	12
L	Steven Hirschfeld, Rochester/New Britain	12
# ERA	B.J. Hermsen, Fort Myers/New Britain	2.88
G	Bruce Pugh, Fort Myers/New Britain	48
G	Caleb Thielbar, Fort Myers/N.B./Rochester	48
GS	Logan Darnell, New Britain	28
GS	Pat Dean, Fort Myers	28
GS	Steven Hirschfeld, Rochester/New Britain	28
SV	Corey Williams, Beloit	17
IP	B.J. Hermsen, Fort Myers/New Britain	162.2
BB	Matthew Summers, Beloit/Fort Myers	59
SO	Jason Wheeler, Beloit	115
# AVG	B.J. Hermsen, Fort Myers/New Britain	.258

General Manager: Terry Ryan. **Farm Director:** Jim Rantz. **Scouting Director:** Deron Johnson.

Class	Team	League	W	L	PCT	Finish	Manager
Majors	Minnesota Twins	American	66	96	.407	14th (14)	Ron Gardenhire
Triple-A	Rochester Red Wings	International	72	72	.500	8th (14)	Gene Glynn
Double-A	New Britain Rock Cats	Eastern	75	67	.528	5th (12)	Jeff Smith
High A	Fort Myers Miracle	Florida State	60	75	.444	10th (12)	Jake Mauer
Low A	Beloit Snappers	Midwest	77	63	.550	4th (16)	Nelson Prada
Rookie	Elizabethton Twins	Appalachian	43	22	.662	1st (10)	Ray Smith
Rookie	GCL Twins	Gulf Coast	33	27	.550	6th (14)	Ramon Borrego
Overall 2012 Minor League Record			360	326	.525	6th (30)	

ORGANIZATION STATISTICS

MINNESOTA TWINS

AMERICAN LEAGUE

Batting	B-T	HT	WT	DOB	AVG	vLH	vRH	G	AB	R	H	2B	3B	HR	RBI	BB	HBP	SH	SF	SO	SB	CS	SLG	OBP
Burroughs, Sean	L-R	6-1	195	9-12-80	.118	.000	.143	10	17	0	2	1	0	0	1	1	0	0	0	3	0	0	.176	.167
Butera, Drew	R-R	6-1	200	8-9-83	.198	.118	.234	42	111	7	22	6	0	1	5	9	2	0	0	26	0	0	.279	.270
Carroll, Jamey	R-R	5-11	175	2-18-74	.268	.338	.240	138	470	65	126	18	1	1	40	52	4	7	4	65	9	5	.317	.343
Carson, Matt	R-R	6-2	200	7-1-81	.227	.238	.222	26	66	3	15	1	0	0	4	2	0	0	1	21	0	0	.242	.246
Casilla, Alexi	B-R	5-9	180	7-20-84	.241	.296	.224	106	299	33	72	17	2	1	30	16	3	3	5	52	21	1	.321	.282
Doumit, Ryan	B-R	6-1	220	4-3-81	.275	.247	.288	134	484	56	133	34	1	18	75	29	7	0	8	98	0	0	.461	.320
Dozier, Brian	R-R	5-11	190	5-15-87	.234	.256	.227	84	316	33	74	11	1	6	33	16	1	4	3	58	9	2	.332	.271
Escobar, Eduardo	B-R	5-10	165	1-5-89	.227	.385	.161	14	44	4	10	0	0	0	6	2	1	1	1	8	1	0	.227	.271
2-team total (36 Chicago)					.214	—	—	50	131	18	28	4	1	0	9	11	1	2	1	31	3	0	.260	.278
Florimon, Pedro	B-R	6-2	180	12-10-86	.219	.255	.200	43	137	16	30	5	2	1	10	10	0	3	0	30	3	1	.307	.272
Herrmann, Chris	L-R	6-0	200	11-24-87	.056	.000	.083	7	18	0	1	0	0	0	1	1	0	0	0	5	0	0	.056	.105
Hughes, Luke	R-R	5-11	205	8-2-84	.200	.167	.250	4	10	0	2	0	0	0	2	0	0	0	1	4	1	0	.200	.182
2-team total (4 Oakland)					.130	—	—	8	23	0	3	0	0	0	2	0	0	0	1	10	1	0	.130	.125
Komatsu, Erik	L-L	5-10	175	10-1-87	.219	.250	.214	15	32	2	7	0	0	0	1	4	0	0	1	3	0	0	.219	.297
Mastroianni, Darin	R-R	5-11	190	8-26-85	.252	.288	.227	77	163	22	41	3	2	3	17	18	1	3	1	45	21	3	.350	.328
Mauer, Joe	L-R	6-5	230	4-19-83	.319	.287	.336	147	545	81	174	31	4	10	85	90	2	1	3	88	8	4	.446	.416
Morneau, Justin	L-R	6-4	220	5-15-81	.267	.232	.290	134	505	63	135	26	2	19	77	49	6	0	10	102	1	0	.440	.333
Nishioka, Tsuyoshi	B-R	6-1	175	7-27-84	.000	—	.000	3	12	0	0	0	0	0	1	1	0	0	1	1	0	0	.000	.071
Parmelee, Chris	L-L	6-1	230	2-24-88	.229	.245	.223	64	192	18	44	10	2	5	20	13	4	0	1	52	0	0	.380	.290
Plouffe, Trevor	R-R	6-2	205	6-15-86	.235	.242	.232	119	422	56	99	19	1	24	55	37	4	0	2	92	1	3	.455	.301
Revere, Ben	L-R	5-9	170	5-3-88	.294	.314	.284	124	511	70	150	13	6	0	32	29	3	6	4	54	40	9	.342	.333
Span, Denard	L-L	6-0	210	2-27-84	.283	.301	.275	128	516	71	146	38	4	4	41	47	0	4	1	62	17	6	.395	.342
Thomas, Clete	L-R	5-11	195	11-14-83	.143	.167	.136	12	28	2	4	1	0	1	4	0	1	0	0	16	0	0	.286	.172
2-team total (3 Detroit)					.143	—	—	15	28	3	4	1	0	1	4	0	1	0	0	16	0	0	.286	.172
Valencia, Danny	R-R	6-2	220	9-19-84	.198	.211	.193	34	126	13	25	6	1	2	17	3	0	0	3	32	0	1	.310	.212
2-team total (10 Boston)					.188	—	—	44	154	14	29	6	1	3	21	3	0	0	4	38	0	1	.299	.199
Willingham, Josh	R-R	6-2	230	2-17-79	.260	.231	.273	145	519	85	135	30	1	35	110	76	14	0	6	141	3	2	.524	.366

Pitching	B-T	HT	WT	DOB	W	L	ERA	G	GS	CG	SV	IP	H	R	ER	HR	BB	SO	AVG	vLH	vRH	K/9	BB/9
Blackburn, Nick	R-R	6-4	240	2-24-82	4	9	7.39	19	19	0	0	99	143	81	81	23	26	42	.340	.376	.311	3.83	2.37
Burnett, Alex	R-R	6-0	220	7-26-87	4	4	3.52	67	0	0	0	72	71	33	28	4	26	36	.257	.215	.279	4.52	3.27
Burton, Jared	R-R	6-5	225	6-2-81	3	2	2.18	64	0	0	5	62	41	21	15	5	16	55	.186	.235	.154	7.98	2.32
Capps, Matt	R-R	6-2	260	9-3-83	1	4	3.68	30	0	0	14	29	28	13	12	5	4	18	.241	.175	.305	5.52	1.23
Deduno, Samuel	R-R	6-3	190	7-2-83	6	5	4.44	15	15	0	0	79	69	40	39	10	53	57	.241	.256	.221	6.49	6.04
DeVries, Cole	R-R	6-2	180	2-12-85	5	5	4.11	17	16	0	0	88	88	48	40	16	18	58	.252	.236	.266	5.95	1.85
Diamond, Scott	L-L	6-3	220	7-30-86	12	9	3.54	27	27	1	0	173	184	76	68	17	31	90	.274	.291	.268	4.68	1.61
Duensing, Brian	L-L	6-0	205	2-22-83	4	12	5.12	55	11	0	0	109	126	71	62	10	27	69	.288	.250	.310	5.70	2.23
Fien, Casey	R-R	6-2	205	10-21-83	2	1	2.06	35	0	0	0	35	25	9	8	3	9	32	.195	.173	.211	8.23	2.31
Gray, Jeff	R-R	6-2	210	11-19-81	6	1	5.71	49	0	0	0	52	58	34	33	9	22	26	.278	.317	.252	4.50	3.81
Hendriks, Liam	R-R	6-1	205	2-10-89	1	8	5.59	16	16	1	0	85	106	61	53	17	26	50	.305	.257	.357	5.27	2.74
Liriano, Francisco	L-L	6-2	215	10-26-83	3	10	5.31	22	17	0	0	100	89	63	59	12	55	109	.239	.195	.251	9.81	4.95
2-team total (12 Chicago)					6	12	5.34	34	28	0	0	157	143	97	93	19	87	167	—	—	—	9.59	5.00
Maloney, Matt	L-L	6-4	210	1-16-84	1	0	8.18	9	0	0	0	11	17	10	10	2	1	5	.347	.389	.323	4.09	0.82
Manship, Jeff	R-R	6-2	210	1-16-85	0	0	7.89	12	0	0	0	22	29	19	19	4	7	12	.326	.238	.404	4.98	2.91
Marquis, Jason	L-R	6-1	220	8-21-78	2	4	8.47	7	7	0	0	34	52	33	32	9	14	12	.371	.360	.389	3.18	3.71
Oliveros, Lester	R-R	6-0	225	5-28-88	0	0	5.40	1	0	0	0	2	1	1	1	0	1	1	.167	.000	.333	5.40	5.40
Pavano, Carl	R-R	6-5	265	1-8-76	2	5	6.00	11	11	0	0	63	80	46	42	9	8	33	.313	.319	.305	4.71	1.14
Perdomo, Luis	R-R	6-0	170	4-27-84	0	0	3.18	15	0	0	0	17	15	8	6	0	12	8	.238	.156	.323	4.24	6.35
Perkins, Glen	L-L	6-0	205	3-2-83	3	1	2.56	70	0	0	16	70	57	25	20	8	16	78	.222	.192	.241	9.98	2.05
Robertson, Tyler	L-L	6-5	255	12-23-87	2	2	5.40	40	0	0	0	25	21	16	15	4	14	26	.223	.190	.290	9.36	5.04
Swarzak, Anthony	R-R	6-4	210	9-10-85	3	6	5.03	44	5	0	0	97	106	57	54	15	31	62	.284	.254	.309	5.77	2.89
Vasquez, Esmerling	R-R	6-1	200	11-7-83	0	2	5.68	6	6	0	0	32	32	20	20	2	19	14	.274	.361	.179	3.98	5.40
Waldrop, Kyle	R-R	6-5	220	10-27-85	0	1	2.53	17	0	0	0	21	27	6	6	2	6	7	.318	.237	.383	2.95	2.53
Walters, P.J.	R-R	6-4	215	3-12-85	2	5	5.69	12	12	1	0	62	71	41	39	12	22	42	.291	.318	.261	6.13	3.21

Fielding

Catcher	PCT	G	PO	A	E	DP	PB
Butera	.996	41	242	15	1	2	4
Doumit	.994	59	290	22	2	3	2
Herrmann	1.000	3	9	0	0	0	1
Mauer	.993	74	425	25	3	5	1

First Base	PCT	G	PO	A	E	DP
Burroughs	1.000	1	4	0	0	1
Doumit	1.000	1	3	0	0	0
Hughes	1.000	1	10	0	0	0
Mauer	.993	30	265	17	2	22
Morneau	.994	99	879	72	6	105
Parmelee	.994	38	296	25	2	43
Plouffe	1.000	3	14	0	0	2

Second Base	PCT	G	PO	A	E	DP
Carroll	.981	66	115	194	6	46
Casilla	.980	96	178	263	9	81

	PCT	G	PO	A	E	DP	PB
Escobar	1.000	8	18	27	0	7	
Hughes	.923	3	5	7	1	0	
Mastroianni	—	1	0	0	0	0	
Nishioka	.895	3	6	11	2	6	
Plouffe	1.000	4	5	8	0	2	

Third Base	PCT	G	PO	A	E	DP
Burroughs	1.000	3	3	5	0	1
Carroll	.957	44	25	63	4	10
Casilla	1.000	4	0	4	0	1
Escobar	1.000	3	0	5	0	0
Hughes	—	1	0	0	0	0
Plouffe	.935	95	64	180	17	14
Valencia	.959	34	21	73	4	9

Shortstop	PCT	G	PO	A	E	DP
Carroll	.989	37	53	120	2	29
Dozier	.964	83	111	287	15	70

	PCT	G	PO	A	E	DP
Escobar	1.000	6	7	15	0	4
Florimon	.965	43	69	125	7	26
Plouffe	.500	1	0	1	1	0

Outfield	PCT	G	PO	A	E	DP
Carson	1.000	22	25	3	0	1
Doumit	.933	22	42	0	3	0
Herrmann	1.000	2	1	0	0	0
Komatsu	.947	9	17	1	1	0
Mastroianni	.971	61	100	2	3	0
Parmelee	1.000	19	30	1	0	0
Plouffe	.964	17	25	2	1	0
Revere	1.000	121	274	8	0	3
Span	.989	125	339	6	4	3
Thomas	1.000	11	19	1	0	0
Willingham	.984	119	237	6	4	2

ROCHESTER RED WINGS

INTERNATIONAL LEAGUE

TRIPLE-A

Batting	B-T	HT	WT	DOB	AVG	vLH	vRH	G	AB	R	H	2B	3B	HR	RBI	BB	HBP	SH	SF	SO	SB	CS	SLG	OBP
Bates, Aaron	R-R	6-4	230	3-10-84	.238	.333	.200	28	84	7	20	4	0	0	10	18	1	0	0	19	0	0	.286	.379
Benson, Joe	R-R	6-1	215	3-5-88	.179	.200	.171	28	95	9	17	3	2	2	8	11	1	0	1	27	4	0	.316	.269
Bigley, Evan	R-R	6-1	200	3-9-87	.207	.216	.204	39	140	11	29	7	0	3	20	5	1	0	3	37	1	1	.321	.235
Burroughs, Sean	L-R	6-1	195	9-12-80	.271	.203	.296	67	221	23	60	14	0	1	18	16	2	1	0	25	2	0	.348	.326
Butera, Drew	R-R	6-1	200	8-9-83	.279	.200	.303	15	43	6	12	3	0	1	5	3	0	1	1	9	0	0	.419	.319
Carson, Matt	R-R	6-2	200	7-1-81	.282	.292	.278	115	422	64	119	28	2	14	53	37	6	2	2	106	9	5	.457	.347
Chang, Ray	R-R	6-1	195	8-24-83	.241	.319	.213	89	266	27	64	8	0	0	17	20	5	2	2	39	3	3	.271	.304
Dinkelman, Brian	L-R	5-11	195	11-10-83	.252	.244	.254	74	246	32	62	13	3	4	32	26	5	2	0	46	5	5	.378	.336
Dozier, Brian	R-R	5-11	190	5-15-87	.232	.200	.241	48	181	15	42	11	1	2	17	14	1	1	3	34	3	2	.337	.286
Escobar, Eduardo	B-R	5-10	165	1-5-89	.217	.111	.255	35	138	19	30	3	3	1	9	8	0	4	1	26	3	1	.304	.259
Florimon, Pedro	B-R	6-2	180	12-10-86	.251	.273	.244	83	311	38	78	16	2	3	27	23	3	7	1	89	6	7	.344	.308
Hollimon, Michael	B-R	6-1	195	6-14-82	.223	.231	.220	59	166	21	37	7	2	5	14	21	0	1	3	50	2	0	.380	.305
Lehmann, Danny	R-R	5-11	185	9-5-85	.237	1.000	.216	14	38	7	9	4	0	0	8	1	1	0	0	7	0	0	.342	.383
Mastroianni, Darin	R-R	5-11	190	8-26-85	.346	.400	.333	20	78	10	27	2	2	0	11	5	1	1	0	14	10	1	.423	.393
Nishioka, Tsuyoshi	B-R	6-1	175	7-27-84	.258	.279	.250	101	392	42	101	18	1	2	34	32	1	5	1	53	7	3	.324	.315
Parmelee, Chris	L-L	6-1	230	2-24-88	.338	.354	.329	64	228	45	77	17	1	17	49	51	1	0	2	52	1	1	.645	.457
Plouffe, Trevor	R-R	6-2	205	6-15-86	.000	.000	.000	2	8	0	0	0	0	0	0	1	0	0	0	2	0	0	.000	.111
Ramirez, Wilkin	R-R	6-2	190	10-25-85	.276	.214	.298	98	370	39	102	18	1	15	54	18	5	0	3	97	7	7	.451	.316
Revere, Ben	L-R	5-9	170	5-3-88	.330	.235	.351	23	94	9	31	1	0	0	6	4	1	1	1	6	2	2	.340	.360
Rivera, Rene	R-R	5-10	230	7-31-83	.226	.238	.221	95	288	31	65	14	1	10	34	30	4	4	0	62	0	1	.385	.307
Rizzotti, Matt	L-L	6-5	265	12-24-85	.246	.182	.259	22	69	1	17	4	0	0	6	2	0	0	0	18	0	0	.304	.268
Thomas, Clete	L-R	6-1	195	11-14-83	.232	.222	.235	109	393	47	91	22	5	12	47	27	1	3	2	109	15	4	.405	.281
Thurston, Joe	L-R	5-11	225	9-29-79	.093	.154	.067	15	43	4	4	0	0	1	2	5	0	1	0	12	0	0	.163	.184
2-team total (11 Lehigh Valley)					.139	—	—	26	72	9	10	1	0	2	4	12	1	0	1	16	1	0	.236	.267
Tosoni, Rene	L-R	6-0	200	7-2-86	.167	.300	.143	21	66	7	11	2	0	0	5	9	0	1	0	16	3	0	.197	.267
Towles, J.R.	R-R	6-2	205	2-11-84	.214	.237	.208	52	168	24	36	14	0	1	10	12	4	3	2	36	2	4	.315	.280
Valencia, Danny	R-R	6-2	220	9-19-84	.250	.309	.230	69	268	30	67	17	1	7	37	15	0	0	1	40	1	2	.399	.289
2-team total (13 Pawtucket)					.259	—	—	82	317	33	82	20	1	8	45	18	1	0	1	52	1	4	.404	.300

Pitching	B-T	HT	WT	DOB	W	L	ERA	G	GS	CG	SV	IP	H	R	ER	HR	BB	SO	AVG	vLH	vRH	K/9	BB/9
Blackburn, Nick	R-R	6-4	240	2-24-82	3	7	2.70	7	7	1	0	37	42	16	11	2	9	11	.302	.261	.343	2.70	2.21
Bromberg, David	L-R	6-5	245	9-14-87	1	2	2.75	5	2	0	0	20	17	6	6	0	10	16	.236	.310	.186	7.32	4.58
Deduno, Samuel	R-R	6-3	190	7-2-83	1	2	2.14	9	9	0	0	42	27	13	10	2	22	46	.185	.150	.227	9.86	4.71
DeVries, Cole	R-R	6-2	180	12-21-84	3	5	4.37	12	12	0	0	70	75	37	34	7	10	50	.273	.256	.289	6.43	1.29
Diamond, Scott	L-L	6-3	220	7-30-86	4	1	2.60	6	6	0	0	35	35	12	10	1	7	26	.269	.294	.260	6.75	1.82
Fien, Casey	R-R	6-2	205	10-21-83	2	5	4.30	33	0	0	9	46	39	23	22	5	14	42	.228	.192	.258	8.22	2.74
French, Luke	L-L	6-4	220	3-13-85	1	5	6.42	19	14	0	0	74	90	54	53	11	40	49	.303	.295	.307	5.93	4.84
Gibson, Kyle	R-R	6-6	210	10-23-87	0	2	9.45	2	2	0	0	7	11	7	7	1	6	11	.367	.364	.368	13.50	1.35
Guerra, Deolis	R-R	6-5	245	4-17-89	2	3	4.87	29	0	0	0	57	59	33	31	7	21	56	.268	.287	.254	8.79	3.30
Gutierrez, Carlos	R-R	6-3	230	9-22-86	2	2	5.06	10	0	0	0	16	13	9	9	2	3	20	.217	.286	.156	11.25	1.69
Hendriks, Liam	R-R	6-1	205	2-10-89	9	3	3.20	16	16	1	0	106	76	28	26	5	28	82	.201	.204	.197	6.94	2.37
Hernandez, Pedro	L-L	5-10	200	4-12-89	0	2	5.19	4	4	0	0	17	25	10	10	1	1	11	.342	.278	.364	5.71	0.52
2-team total (3 Charlotte)					1	2	4.46	7	6	0	0	34	43	18	17	2	4	28	—	—	—	7.34	1.05
Hirschfeld, Steve	R-R	6-5	226	9-8-85	1	3	7.07	6	6	0	0	28	42	24	22	3	7	13	.347	.389	.286	4.18	2.25
Hurley, Eric	R-R	6-4	195	9-17-85	0	1	14.14	5	4	0	0	14	28	22	22	5	6	10	.406	.333	.426	6.43	3.86
Lanigan, Bobby	R-R	6-4	220	5-5-87	6	2	4.69	22	0	0	1	40	40	25	21	3	17	21	.260	.300	.234	4.69	3.79
Maloney, Matt	L-L	6-4	210	1-16-84	0	4	9.38	8	6	0	0	24	46	33	25	5	7	16	.400	.541	.333	6.00	2.63
Manship, Jeff	R-R	6-2	210	1-16-85	6	3	2.91	22	11	0	0	80	79	27	26	5	35	52	.263	.248	.275	5.83	3.92
Martis, Shairon	R-R	6-1	225	3-30-87	4	3	5.22	10	10	0	0	59	64	35	34	8	17	39	.276	.257	.290	5.98	2.61
2-team total (4 Indianapolis)					4	3	5.51	14	10	0	0	67	72	43	41	12	21	46	—	—	—	6.18	2.82
Oliveros, Lester	R-R	6-0	225	5-28-88	1	2	3.07	19	0	0	6	29	24	10	10	2	8	35	.229	.279	.194	10.74	2.45
Perdomo, Luis	R-R	6-0	170	4-27-84	4	1	2.43	19	0	0	7	33	27	9	9	4	6	25	.218	.226	.211	6.75	1.62

Name	B-T	HT	WT	DOB	W	L	ERA	G	GS	CG	SV	IP	H	R	ER	HR	BB	SO	AVG	vLH	vRH	K/9	BB/9
Robertson, Tyler	L-L	6-5	255	12-23-87	2	2	3.77	33	0	0	2	29	26	18	12	2	13	33	.230	.167	.288	10.36	4.08
Sattler, Dan	R-R	6-3	190	11-11-83	1	0	2.38	7	0	0	1	11	5	3	3	1	4	11	.128	.083	.148	8.74	3.18
Slama, Anthony	R-R	6-3	200	1-6-84	1	0	1.24	31	0	0	14	36	26	6	5	1	18	56	.195	.173	.210	13.87	4.46
Thielbar, Caleb	L-L	6-0	200	1-31-87	3	1	3.57	25	1	0	1	40	42	19	16	5	16	32	.266	.219	.298	7.14	3.57
Thompson, Daryl	R-R	6-0	205	11-2-85	1	5	4.71	9	9	0	0	42	47	24	22	3	25	30	.296	.315	.279	6.43	5.36
Turpen, Dan	R-R	6-4	245	8-17-86	0	0	4.74	13	0	0	2	19	16	15	10	1	15	15	.235	.217	.244	7.11	7.11
Vasquez, Esmerling	R-R	6-1	200	11-7-83	9	6	2.78	31	8	1	0	100	74	33	31	8	39	98	.210	.240	.186	8.79	3.50
Waldrop, Kyle	R-R	6-5	220	10-27-85	0	0	3.34	24	0	0	4	35	35	14	13	1	13	16	.263	.328	.208	4.11	3.34
Walters, P.J.	R-R	6-4	215	3-12-85	3	3	4.01	14	14	1	0	58	67	28	26	7	15	47	.288	.371	.228	7.25	2.31
Wise, Brendan	L-R	6-2	190	1-9-86	2	3	5.64	29	3	0	1	53	85	43	33	3	25	34	.374	.425	.325	5.81	4.27

Fielding

Catcher	PCT	G	PO	A	E	DP	PB
Butera	1.000	14	95	10	0	0	1
Lehmann	.990	14	95	5	1	1	0
Rivera	.984	81	543	62	10	7	14
Towles	.991	44	294	21	3	1	1

First Base	PCT	G	PO	A	E	DP
Bates	.980	20	135	12	3	17
Burroughs	.997	32	284	19	1	28
Chang	1.000	9	56	3	0	5
Hollimon	.983	10	54	3	1	4
Parmelee	.997	62	540	63	2	54
Rivera	1.000	7	32	2	0	3
Rizzotti	.979	15	84	11	2	11
Tosoni	.900	1	7	2	1	3

Second Base	PCT	G	PO	A	E	DP
Burroughs	1.000	2	2	6	0	3
Chang	.978	22	38	52	2	13

	PCT	G	PO	A	E	DP
Dinkelman	.976	9	13	27	1	4
Dozier	.938	4	12	3	1	1
Escobar	.946	9	14	21	2	4
Hollimon	.964	7	12	15	1	3
Mastroianni	1.000	5	7	10	0	0
Nishioka	.978	87	164	240	9	61
Thurston	.971	13	26	42	2	10

Third Base	PCT	G	PO	A	E	DP
Burroughs	.960	11	6	18	1	3
Chang	.947	53	27	80	6	11
Dinkelman	1.000	1	0	1	0	0
Escobar	1.000	17	9	17	0	2
Hollimon	.898	19	14	30	5	5
Plouffe	1.000	2	2	4	0	0
Valencia	.947	56	30	95	7	8

Shortstop	PCT	G	PO	A	E	DP
Chang	1.000	1	2	4	0	0

	PCT	G	PO	A	E	DP
Dozier	.962	42	49	104	6	30
Escobar	.974	10	16	21	1	4
Florimon	.976	83	133	233	9	51
Nishioka	.953	15	20	41	3	6
Thurston	1.000	1	1	2	0	2

Outfield	PCT	G	PO	A	E	DP
Benson	1.000	26	56	1	0	0
Bigley	1.000	34	60	3	0	1
Butera	.500	1	1	0	1	0
Carson	.985	105	185	11	3	2
Dinkelman	1.000	25	39	1	0	0
Hollimon	1.000	16	24	2	0	1
Mastroianni	1.000	16	21	1	0	0
Ramirez	.989	86	176	7	2	1
Revere	1.000	20	46	0	0	0
Thomas	.983	105	227	5	4	2
Tosoni	.968	14	28	2	1	0
Towles	1.000	2	2	0	0	0

NEW BRITAIN ROCK CATS   DOUBLE-A

EASTERN LEAGUE

Batting	B-T	HT	WT	DOB	AVG	vLH	vRH	G	AB	R	H	2B	3B	HR	RBI	BB	HBP	SH	SF	SO	SB	CS	SLG	OBP
Arcia, Oswaldo	L-R	6-0	210	5-9-91	.328	.329	.328	69	262	54	86	20	5	10	67	28	5	0	4	62	3	2	.557	.398
Benson, Joe	R-R	6-1	215	3-5-88	.184	.121	.204	37	141	13	26	6	1	3	20	13	3	0	0	43	4	3	.305	.268
Beresford, James	R-R	6-1	162	1-19-89	.266	.269	.265	114	369	38	98	12	3	0	25	35	1	7	1	53	3	3	.314	.330
Bigley, Evan	R-R	6-1	200	3-9-87	.268	.211	.288	88	347	42	93	19	3	12	66	20	2	2	1	85	3	3	.444	.311
Colabello, Chris	R-R	6-4	210	10-24-83	.284	.274	.288	134	496	78	141	37	1	19	98	47	13	0	5	94	0	0	.478	.358
De Los Santos, Estarlin	B-R	5-10	185	1-20-87	.216	.147	.241	100	287	38	62	9	1	2	24	17	7	4	0	59	8	6	.275	.277
Dolenc, Mark	R-R	6-3	218	11-8-84	.168	.212	.150	46	113	9	19	1	0	1	3	4	1	2	0	40	4	4	.204	.203
Florimon, Pedro	B-R	6-2	180	12-10-86	.283	.345	.262	30	113	11	32	4	0	2	8	11	0	3	0	28	7	1	.372	.347
Hanson, Nate	R-R	6-0	190	4-28-87	.276	.273	.278	101	351	40	97	16	1	7	50	16	5	2	8	41	2	2	.387	.311
Herrmann, Chris	L-R	6-0	200	11-24-87	.276	.325	.259	127	490	91	135	25	1	10	61	58	1	1	6	89	2	1	.392	.350
Hicks, Aaron	B-R	6-2	185	10-2-89	.286	.283	.287	129	472	100	135	21	11	13	61	79	1	3	8	116	32	11	.460	.384
Lehmann, Danny	R-R	5-11	185	9-5-85	.165	.227	.147	33	97	6	16	4	0	0	6	17	2	0	0	20	0	1	.206	.302
Mastroianni, Darin	R-R	5-11	190	8-26-85	.143	.286	.107	9	35	6	5	1	0	0	4	0	1	0	11	4	1	.171	.231
Pinto, Josmil	R-R	5-11	230	3-31-89	.298	.273	.306	12	47	8	14	4	1	2	9	4	1	0	0	10	0	5	.553	.365
Ramirez, Wilkin	R-R	6-2	190	10-25-85	.388	.231	.444	11	49	12	19	3	3	4	7	2	0	0	0	10	2	0	.816	.412
Rizzotti, Matt	L-L	6-5	265	12-24-85	.225	.190	.235	32	102	9	23	6	0	2	11	22	0	0	2	25	1	0	.343	.357
Rohlfing, Dan	R-R	6-0	190	2-12-89	.252	.295	.235	46	163	15	41	12	1	0	8	9	1	0	0	37	0	2	.337	.295
Romero, Deibinson	R-R	6-1	200	9-24-86	.267	.293	.258	138	469	62	125	23	1	19	78	60	10	0	9	95	2	0	.441	.356
Roof, Shawn	R-R	5-10	175	8-3-84	.214	.156	.235	50	117	18	25	3	0	0	7	6	2	2	0	21	6	0	.239	.264
Tosoni, Rene	L-R	6-0	200	7-2-86	.233	.183	.252	60	223	19	52	10	3	1	19	18	2	3	1	32	2	1	.318	.296

Pitching	B-T	HT	WT	DOB	W	L	ERA	G	GS	CG	SV	IP	H	R	ER	HR	BB	SO	AVG	vLH	vRH	K/9	BB/9
Albers, Andrew	R-L	6-1	195	10-6-85	4	3	3.75	19	17	0	0	98	111	41	41	7	12	73	.297	.292	.298	6.68	1.10
Bromberg, David	L-R	6-5	245	9-14-87	3	2	3.75	28	8	1	0	72	68	31	30	5	35	68	.249	.262	.240	8.50	4.38
Darnell, Logan	L-L	6-2	210	2-2-89	11	12	5.08	28	28	0	0	156	193	91	88	22	47	98	.308	.343	.298	5.65	2.71
French, Luke	L-L	6-4	220	9-13-85	4	1	2.10	9	9	1	0	56	35	14	13	4	17	27	.187	.265	.170	4.37	2.75
Gonzalez, Jose	L-L	5-9	166	2-3-90	2	2	3.38	13	0	0	0	16	9	9	6	1	8	17	.161	.318	.059	9.56	4.50
Guerra, Deolis	R-R	6-5	245	4-17-89	2	0	0.71	7	0	0	1	13	5	1	1	0	1	15	.119	.091	.129	10.66	0.71
Hauser, Matt	R-R	6-2	195	3-30-88	0	0	3.38	10	0	0	1	16	18	7	6	3	4	8	.290	.318	.275	4.50	2.25
Hermsen, B.J.	R-R	6-5	235	12-1-89	11	6	3.22	22	22	1	0	140	145	59	50	12	25	75	.269	.338	.219	4.83	1.61
Hirschfeld, Steve	R-R	6-5	226	9-8-85	8	9	4.44	22	22	1	0	118	141	63	58	16	29	81	.299	.302	.298	6.20	2.22
Ibarra, Edgar	L-L	6-0	189	5-31-89	2	1	6.15	14	0	0	0	34	40	27	23	6	15	28	.303	.250	.317	7.49	4.01
Jacobson, Brett	R-R	6-6	205	11-9-86	0	3	7.50	18	0	0	0	42	44	41	35	4	45	28	.284	.286	.283	5.36	9.64
Lanigan, Bobby	R-R	6-4	220	5-5-87	1	3	3.86	22	0	0	3	30	36	15	13	3	4	28	.288	.244	.310	8.31	1.19
Marquis, Jason	L-R	6-1	220	8-21-78	1	0	1.93	2	2	0	0	14	12	3	3	1	0	11	.240	.158	.290	7.07	0.00
Martin, Blake	L-L	6-2	182	6-19-86	4	5	4.68	39	10	1	0	77	72	43	40	7	35	73	.254	.257	.252	8.53	4.09
Martis, Shairon	R-R	6-1	225	3-30-87	1	1	5.68	4	3	0	0	19	23	13	12	2	5	11	.303	.343	.268	5.21	2.37
2-team total (11 Altoona)					7	3	4.85	15	11	0	0	72	68	40	39	9	24	41	—	—		5.10	2.99
Oliveros, Lester	R-R	6-0	225	5-28-88	1	1	1.42	13	0	0	2	19	10	3	3	0	7	16	.164	.273	.103	7.58	3.32
Perdomo, Luis	R-R	6-0	170	4-27-84	4	4	2.75	26	0	0	2	39	27	13	12	0	16	43	.191	.178	.198	9.84	3.66

	B-T	HT	WT	DOB	W	L	ERA	G	GS	CG	SV	IP	H	R	ER	HR	BB	SO	AVG	vLH	vRH	K/9	BB/9
Popham, Marty	R-R	6-6	235	8-4-87	1	1	4.02	9	0	0	0	16	18	8	7	1	3	16	.286	.345	.235	9.19	1.72
Pugh, Bruce	R-R	6-3	180	7-18-88	4	2	1.50	31	0	0	9	42	26	8	7	2	23	48	.182	.174	.186	10.29	4.93
Sattler, Dan	R-R	6-3	190	11-11-83	1	0	2.03	5	0	0	1	13	10	3	3	1	4	4	.208	.333	.152	2.70	2.70
Thielbar, Caleb	L-L	6-0	200	1-31-87	2	0	1.80	16	0	0	4	25	18	5	5	1	3	26	.198	.125	.224	9.36	1.08
Thompson, Aaron	L-L	6-3	200	2-28-87	3	8	5.23	22	13	0	0	86	115	54	50	9	22	45	.334	.352	.328	4.71	2.30
Thompson, Brad	R-R	6-1	190	1-31-82	0	1	10.29	4	1	0	0	7	16	9	8	1	0	5	.457	.563	.368	6.43	0.00
Turpen, Dan	R-R	6-4	245	8-17-86	3	2	4.25	33	0	0	5	53	52	28	25	4	23	59	.255	.246	.259	10.02	3.91
Watts, Dakota	R-R	6-5	201	11-16-87	2	0	2.67	24	0	0	2	34	31	13	10	1	16	27	.242	.267	.229	7.22	4.28
Wimmers, Alex	L-R	6-2	195	11-1-88	0	0	4.15	1	1	0	0	4	6	2	2	1	2	3	.316	.333	.308	6.23	4.15

Fielding

Catcher	PCT	G	PO	A	E	DP	PB
Herrmann	.995	83	585	36	3	8	4
Lehmann	.988	33	213	25	3	0	1
Pinto	1.000	2	10	1	0	0	0
Rohlfing	.994	29	150	15	1	1	2

First Base	PCT	G	PO	A	E	DP
Colabello	.996	124	999	82	4	98
Hanson	.991	12	98	9	1	12
Rizzotti	.984	8	58	3	1	4
Tosoni	.667	1	2	0	1	0

Second Base	PCT	G	PO	A	E	DP
Beresford	.996	53	104	124	1	27
De Los Santos	.989	28	37	49	1	9

	PCT	G	PO	A	E	DP
Hanson	.993	44	56	87	1	19
Roof	.954	40	66	99	8	22

Third Base	PCT	G	PO	A	E	DP
De Los Santos	.900	7	2	7	1	0
Hanson	.939	17	4	27	2	2
Herrmann	—	1	0	0	0	0
Romero	.945	132	77	234	18	23

Shortstop	PCT	G	PO	A	E	DP
Beresford	.966	60	91	162	9	31
De Los Santos	.950	55	93	136	12	35
Florimon	.981	30	48	107	3	22
Roof	1.000	1	2	0	0	0

Outfield	PCT	G	PO	A	E	DP
Arcia	.965	59	129	8	5	0
Benson	1.000	34	73	6	0	3
Bigley	.995	82	193	16	1	2
De Los Santos	1.000	6	9	0	0	0
Dolenc	1.000	36	59	1	0	0
Hanson	1.000	9	11	0	0	0
Herrmann	.979	27	41	5	1	1
Hicks	.975	118	306	10	8	2
Mastroianni	1.000	9	14	2	0	0
Ramirez	1.000	7	16	0	0	0
Rohlfing	.955	11	21	0	1	0
Tosoni	1.000	46	80	8	0	1

FORT MYERS MIRACLE HIGH CLASS A
FLORIDA STATE LEAGUE

Batting	B-T	HT	WT	DOB	AVG	vLH	vRH	G	AB	R	H	2B	3B	HR	RBI	BB	HBP	SH	SF	SO	SB	CS	SLG	OBP
Arcia, Oswaldo	L-R	6-0	210	5-9-91	.309	.210	.352	55	207	22	64	16	3	7	31	23	1	1	3	45	1	3	.517	.376
Benson, Joe	R-R	6-1	215	3-5-88	.303	.308	.300	8	33	7	10	3	0	1	8	5	0	0	0	9	4	0	.485	.395
Goncalves, Jonathan	R-R	5-11	159	5-13-89	.225	.200	.234	27	89	10	20	5	0	0	13	10	1	0	1	24	2	2	.281	.307
Gonzales, Mike	L-R	6-6	270	6-16-88	.244	.149	.285	72	225	28	55	12	0	6	27	30	5	1	5	69	0	0	.378	.340
Hidalgo, Anderson	R-R	5-9	192	9-5-88	.236	.228	.240	84	288	34	68	13	1	3	38	22	5	4	3	52	1	0	.319	.299
Knudson, Kyle	R-R	6-3	210	9-12-87	.253	.226	.266	56	190	24	48	11	0	0	18	30	6	2	1	41	0	0	.311	.370
Leer, Andy	R-R	6-2	200	1-3-88	.186	.130	.215	92	269	35	50	9	0	3	27	39	5	3	4	90	4	5	.253	.297
Liddle, Steven	L-L	6-1	205	11-24-87	.198	.314	.151	34	121	20	24	3	0	5	21	12	2	0	1	25	1	1	.347	.279
Mejia, Aderlin	B-R	5-11	170	5-12-92	.111	.000	.200	5	9	4	1	0	0	0	0	2	0	0	0	2	0	0	.111	.273
Michael, Levi	B-R	5-10	180	2-9-91	.246	.315	.212	117	431	58	106	14	4	2	38	56	8	11	6	82	6	0	.311	.339
Morales, Angel	R-R	6-1	180	11-24-89	.220	.203	.229	112	363	56	80	8	5	7	35	45	4	4	4	115	12	3	.328	.310
Ortiz, Danny	L-L	5-11	166	1-5-90	.269	.240	.283	97	375	55	101	24	5	8	35	22	3	3	2	67	4	4	.424	.313
Perez, Jairo	R-R	5-10	160	6-10-88	.265	.235	.280	65	238	39	63	13	1	6	30	23	10	0	3	28	4	2	.403	.350
Pinto, Josmil	R-R	5-11	230	3-31-89	.295	.300	.293	93	349	45	103	22	2	12	51	39	0	0	5	63	0	0	.473	.361
Ramirez, Wilkin	R-R	6-2	190	10-25-85	.267	.500	.111	4	15	1	4	0	0	0	0	1	0	0	0	5	0	0	.267	.313
Rams, Danny	R-R	6-2	230	12-19-88	.227	.289	.182	68	229	36	52	8	2	6	32	38	1	1	1	94	0	2	.358	.338
Ray, Lance	L-R	6-1	194	9-2-89	.234	.230	.236	108	367	42	86	21	1	13	66	50	3	1	5	81	5	1	.403	.327
Rohlfing, Dan	R-R	6-0	190	2-12-89	.218	.255	.202	45	165	10	36	8	0	1	19	17	2	1	2	34	0	1	.285	.296
Santana, Daniel	B-R	5-11	173	11-7-90	.286	.271	.294	121	507	70	145	21	9	8	60	29	5	3	3	77	17	11	.410	.320
Tosoni, Rene	L-R	6-0	200	7-2-86	.231	.000	.300	4	13	2	3	1	0	1	2	1	0	0	0	3	0	0	.538	.286

Pitching	B-T	HT	WT	DOB	W	L	ERA	G	GS	CG	SV	IP	H	R	ER	HR	BB	SO	AVG	vLH	vRH	K/9	BB/9
Achter, A.J.	R-R	6-5	205	8-27-88	2	1	0.79	19	0	0	6	34	21	8	3	0	3	37	.168	.167	.169	9.70	0.79
Baker, Scott	R-R	6-4	215	9-19-81	0	0	54.00	1	1	0	0	0	2	2	2	0	0	0	.667	.500	1.000	0.00	0.00
Boer, Madison	R-R	6-4	215	7-18-89	7	10	6.41	22	19	0	0	111	147	88	79	15	32	66	.322	.314	.329	5.35	2.59
Bowen, Ricky	R-R	6-3	178	8-6-87	4	6	2.95	46	0	0	5	76	77	30	25	3	29	67	.269	.275	.265	7.90	3.42
Capps, Matt	R-R	6-2	260	9-3-83	1	0	0.00	2	1	0	0	2	1	1	0	0	0	1	.143	.250	.000	4.50	0.00
Davis, Tony	B-L	5-11	185	1-16-88	2	0	15.19	5	0	0	0	5	10	9	9	1	3	4	.357	.063	.750	6.75	5.06
Dean, Pat	L-L	6-1	180	5-25-89	10	8	3.99	28	28	0	0	153	177	74	68	11	33	81	.289	.287	.290	4.70	1.94
Dempster, Clint	L-L	6-0	180	8-29-89	0	1	4.58	11	0	0	0	20	23	10	10	2	14	15	.288	.308	.278	6.86	6.41
Fuentes, Nelvin	L-L	6-0	206	4-7-89	4	0	3.21	30	0	0	0	62	59	29	22	5	16	62	.250	.321	.215	9.05	2.34
Garcia, Jhon	R-R	6-1	216	5-19-87	1	5	3.80	11	7	0	0	43	46	23	18	4	14	28	.275	.268	.281	5.91	2.95
Gibson, Kyle	R-R	6-6	210	10-23-87	0	0	2.57	2	2	0	0	7	6	2	2	1	1	7	.231	.214	.250	9.00	1.29
Gonzalez, Jose	L-L	5-9	166	2-3-90	2	4	4.85	25	2	0	0	52	46	32	28	7	13	51	.237	.174	.272	8.83	2.25
Hauser, Matt	R-R	6-2	195	3-30-88	4	2	2.88	31	6	0	1	72	60	27	23	2	28	58	.226	.209	.244	7.25	3.50
Hermsen, B.J.	R-R	6-5	235	12-1-89	1	0	0.78	4	4	0	0	23	16	2	2	1	5	12	.190	.143	.257	4.70	1.96
Ibarra, Edgar	L-L	6-0	189	5-31-89	1	3	3.60	18	0	0	2	45	49	28	18	1	16	41	.272	.246	.286	8.20	3.20
Munoz, Miguel	R-R	6-2	182	8-4-88	2	7	4.66	28	6	0	1	64	70	37	33	7	25	49	.282	.302	.268	6.93	3.53
Nelson, Cole	L-L	6-7	235	7-14-89	5	8	6.26	23	14	0	2	82	115	67	57	5	49	66	.328	.277	.349	7.24	5.38
O'Rourke, Ryan	R-L	6-3	217	4-30-88	0	1	5.50	9	0	0	0	18	22	13	11	1	6	16	.297	.167	.339	8.00	2.00
Pavano, Carl	R-R	6-5	265	1-8-76	0	0	1.80	2	2	0	0	5	4	1	1	0	1	3	.211	.222	.200	5.40	0.00
Popham, Marty	R-R	6-6	235	8-4-87	3	2	5.04	15	12	0	0	70	80	41	39	4	29	48	.293	.313	.275	6.20	3.75
Pugh, Bruce	R-R	6-3	180	7-18-88	1	3	2.60	17	0	0	5	28	29	15	8	2	8	24	.266	.333	.190	7.81	2.60
Salcedo, Adrian	R-R	6-4	175	2-5-91	0	1	6.39	8	7	0	0	25	33	24	18	1	15	14	.314	.250	.400	4.97	5.33
Sattler, Dan	R-R	6-3	190	11-11-83	0	0	1.80	3	0	0	1	5	3	1	1	0	2	5	.176	.250	.000	9.00	3.60
Soliman, Manuel	R-R	6-2	185	8-11-89	0	1	5.40	2	2	0	0	5	7	3	3	1	5	5	.333	.250	.444	9.00	1.50

	B-T	HT	WT	DOB	W	L	ERA	G	GS	CG	SV	IP	H	R	ER	HR	BB	SO	AVG	vLH	vRH	K/9	BB/9
Stuifbergen, Tom	R-R	6-3	261	9-26-88	6	7	5.09	15	14	1	0	74	103	50	42	5	12	39	.326	.382	.265	4.72	1.45
Summers, Matt	R-R	6-1	205	8-17-89	2	3	4.81	9	8	0	0	39	46	24	21	7	25	26	.307	.253	.373	5.95	5.72
Thielbar, Caleb	L-L	6-0	200	1-31-87	1	1	0.00	7	0	0	1	12	4	1	0	0	2	16	.100	.000	.167	11.68	1.46
Tonkin, Mike	R-R	6-7	220	11-19-89	1	1	2.97	22	0	0	6	30	24	12	10	2	11	44	.212	.227	.203	13.05	3.26
Waldrop, Kyle	R-R	6-5	220	10-27-85	0	0	0.00	4	0	0	0	4	2	0	0	0	1	5	.143	.200	.000	11.25	2.25
Watts, Dakota	R-R	6-5	201	11-16-87	0	0	0.87	7	0	0	1	10	4	1	1		2	9	.121	.158	.071	7.84	1.74

Fielding

Catcher	PCT	G	PO	A	E	DP	PB
Knudson	.994	45	306	28	2	2	9
Leer	1.000	1	4	1	0	0	0
Pinto	.988	56	361	42	5	5	1
Rams	1.000	2	6	1	0	0	3
Rohlfing	1.000	35	226	33	0	5	4

First Base	PCT	G	PO	A	E	DP
Gonzales	.986	63	465	20	7	45
Leer	1.000	27	192	15	0	14
Liddle	.993	34	263	15	2	22
Ray	.981	20	140	11	3	10
Rohlfing	1.000	4	35	2	0	2

Second Base	PCT	G	PO	A	E	DP
Leer	.974	35	70	82	4	18

	PCT	G	PO	A	E	DP
Mejia	1.000	1	0	2	0	0
Michael	.975	65	110	167	7	41
Perez	.956	8	21	22	2	6
Santana	.947	32	61	82	8	20

Third Base	PCT	G	PO	A	E	DP
Hidalgo	.945	64	61	111	10	9
Knudson	.000	1	0	0	1	0
Leer	.936	30	23	50	5	3
Mejia	1.000	3	2	6	0	0
Perez	.901	42	29	71	11	2

Shortstop	PCT	G	PO	A	E	DP
Michael	.962	53	73	155	9	29
Santana	.950	85	123	216	18	39

Outfield	PCT	G	PO	A	E	DP
Arcia	.983	51	110	8	2	2
Benson	1.000	8	23	0	0	0
Goncalves	1.000	27	57	2	0	1
Hidalgo	1.000	1	2	0	0	0
Leer	1.000	1	2	0	0	0
Morales	.984	108	303	7	5	1
Ortiz	.996	96	214	8	1	1
Perez	1.000	3	6	0	0	0
Ramirez	1.000	4	9	0	0	0
Rams	.944	36	50	1	3	0
Ray	.977	73	124	5	3	1
Rohlfing	1.000	1	1	0	0	0
Santana	1.000	2	5	0	0	0
Tosoni	1.000	4	5	0	0	0

BELOIT SNAPPERS

MIDWEST LEAGUE

LOW CLASS A

Batting	B-T	HT	WT	DOB	AVG	vLH	vRH	G	AB	R	H	2B	3B	HR	RBI	BB	HBP	SH	SF	SO	SB	CS	SLG	OBP
Bryant, Adam	R-R	5-11	170	5-21-89	.243	.265	.237	75	296	32	72	10	2	1	32	14	2	3	3	56	2	5	.301	.279
Goncalves, Jonathan	R-R	5-11	159	5-13-89	.278	.205	.300	86	306	42	85	16	4	2	31	39	8	6	4	50	14	9	.376	.370
Grimes, Tyler	R-R	5-10	187	7-3-90	.202	.171	.211	105	322	50	65	17	3	7	30	43	11	3	2	99	7	6	.339	.315
Knudson, Kyle	R-R	6-3	210	9-12-87	.250	.333	.234	18	56	3	14	3	0	1	9	6	0	2	0	9	0	0	.357	.323
Koch, Matt	R-R	6-0	210	11-21-88	.253	.265	.250	89	304	47	77	23	2	8	39	35	11	7	2	106	1	3	.421	.349
Leachman, Drew	R-R	6-3	200	4-21-89	.272	.283	.269	107	415	51	113	13	4	5	46	44	6	1	2	64	10	6	.359	.349
Liddle, Steven	L-L	6-1	205	11-24-87	.283	.172	.325	32	106	16	30	12	1	3	14	24	1	0	1	24	2	1	.500	.417
Lin, Wang-Wei	L-R	6-0	191	6-28-88	.232	.177	.244	102	353	54	82	14	5	4	30	49	12	9	3	70	12	7	.334	.343
Ortiz, Danny	L-L	5-11	166	1-5-90	.299	.316	.294	22	87	8	26	4	0	2	13	4	1	2	0	15	3	4	.414	.337
Pettersen, Adam	R-R	5-9	170	11-19-88	.248	.228	.256	93	319	51	79	13	2	2	35	28	4	12	5	53	12	2	.320	.312
Rhodes, Rory	R-R	6-7	200	7-28-91	.189	.200	.183	26	90	12	17	3	0	2	13	10	0	0	3	27	1	3	.289	.262
Roberts, Nate	L-L	6-1	200	2-25-89	.299	.240	.312	76	281	60	84	18	3	4	33	44	23	3	1	37	27	8	.427	.433
Rodriguez, Jairo	R-R	5-11	180	8-24-88	.265	.209	.279	64	215	20	57	12	0	2	20	18	3	6	1	40	0	0	.349	.329
Rosario, Eddie	L-R	6-0	170	9-28-91	.296	.247	.309	95	392	60	116	32	4	12	50	31	1	0	5	69	11	11	.490	.345
Sano, Miguel	R-R	6-3	195	5-11-93	.258	.261	.258	129	457	75	118	28	4	28	100	80	8	0	8	144	8	3	.521	.373
Vargas, Kennys	B-R	6-5	215	8-1-90	.318	.296	.323	41	154	22	49	10	1	11	36	28	1	0	3	41	0	0	.610	.419
Wickens, Stephen	R-R	5-10	170	3-5-89	.284	.219	.299	49	169	31	48	10	0	2	26	29	8	5	1	26	7	5	.379	.411
Williams, J.D.	B-R	5-11	183	11-20-90	.234	.233	.234	97	359	60	84	16	2	6	39	39	2	5	2	115	23	9	.340	.311

Pitching	B-T	HT	WT	DOB	W	L	ERA	G	GS	CG	SV	IP	H	R	ER	HR	BB	SO	AVG	vLH	vRH	K/9	BB/9
Achter, A.J.	R-R	6-5	205	8-27-88	3	1	2.48	18	1	0	0	40	33	17	11	5	12	49	.226	.250	.214	11.03	2.70
Atherton, Tim	R-R	6-2	195	11-7-89	1	2	3.10	26	0	0	0	49	30	19	17	3	36	59	.176	.196	.168	10.76	6.57
Baxendale, D.J.	R-R	6-2	190	12-8-90	0	0	1.64	11	0	0	2	11	12	3	2	0	1	15	.279	.333	.258	12.27	0.82
Boer, Madison	R-R	6-4	215	11-9-89	2	2	3.58	5	5	0	0	28	26	13	11	1	10	20	.252	.222	.276	6.51	3.25
Carter, Bart	L-L	6-1	208	7-8-87	1	1	7.90	20	0	0	0	27	39	27	24	4	12	35	.328	.286	.345	11.52	3.95
Dempster, Clint	L-L	6-0	180	8-29-89	2	3	2.21	30	0	0	4	37	30	10	9	3	14	33	.226	.229	.224	8.10	3.44
Evans, Steven	L-L	6-4	210	8-9-89	0	0	4.00	4	0	0	0	9	8	4	4	0	5	12	.235	.250	.227	12.00	5.00
Fuentes, Nelvin	L-L	6-0	206	4-7-89	0	0	2.45	7	0	0	0	11	8	3	3	0	4	15	.195	.111	.219	12.27	3.27
Gallant, Dallas	R-R	6-3	195	1-25-89	1	0	2.53	9	0	0	1	11	6	4	3	0	8	14	.167	.300	.115	11.81	6.75
Gruver, Steven	L-L	6-2	205	6-30-89	7	8	3.61	30	18	0	0	115	126	61	46	8	29	68	.282	.233	.297	5.34	2.28
Hurlbut, David	L-L	6-3	180	11-24-89	6	6	2.76	25	15	0	1	111	105	47	34	5	25	85	.249	.200	.261	6.89	2.03
Johnson, Cole	R-R	6-3	200	10-6-89	3	1	1.71	16	5	0	0	42	37	10	8	2	11	48	.230	.200	.253	10.29	2.36
Jones, Tyler	R-R	6-4	215	9-5-89	5	5	4.67	18	16	0	0	87	90	58	45	5	35	102	.263	.283	.247	10.59	3.63
Jones, Zack	R-R	6-1	185	12-4-90	0	0	3.21	12	0	0	4	14	9	7	5	1	7	25	.184	.333	.097	16.07	4.50
Kimes, Corey	L-L	6-4	240	5-2-90	2	0	4.34	9	0	0	0	19	19	10	9	1	11	12	.271	.050	.360	5.79	5.30
Melotakis, Mason	R-L	6-3	190	6-28-91	3	1	2.08	13	0	0	1	17	15	6	4	3	4	24	.221	.160	.256	12.46	2.08
O'Rourke, Ryan	R-L	6-3	217	4-30-88	2	5	5.59	29	2	0	0	56	61	38	35	7	16	56	.272	.161	.310	8.95	2.56
Rogers, Taylor	L-L	6-3	170	12-17-90	2	2	2.70	9	4	0	0	33	33	18	10	5	12	35	.248	.250	.248	9.45	3.24
Shibuya, Tim	R-R	6-1	190	9-14-89	3	6	5.59	17	15	1	0	74	88	62	46	9	23	47	.283	.326	.247	6.81	1.82
Summers, Matt	R-R	6-1	205	8-17-89	9	4	3.55	19	18	1	0	109	103	56	43	9	34	71	.249	.275	.234	5.86	2.81
Tomshaw, Matthew	L-L	6-2	200	12-17-88	4	6	3.02	20	14	0	0	86	85	40	29	4	17	66	.261	.246	.265	6.88	1.77
Tonkin, Mike	R-R	6-7	220	11-19-89	3	0	1.38	22	0	0	6	39	29	8	6	3	9	53	.206	.213	.202	12.23	2.08
Wheeler, Jason	L-L	6-8	265	10-27-90	14	6	3.45	27	27	0	0	157	170	75	60	12	43	115	.281	.271	.288	6.61	2.47
Williams, Corey	L-L	6-1	190	7-4-90	4	4	3.47	47	0	0	0	62	55	29	24	5	33	68	.234	.179	.251	9.82	4.76

Fielding

Catcher	PCT	G	PO	A	E	DP	PB
Knudson	.993	18	135	12	1	0	4
Koch	.981	70	522	53	11	4	6
Rodriguez	.983	58	461	50	9	5	10

First Base	PCT	G	PO	A	E	DP
Bryant	.990	33	282	29	3	30

	PCT	G	PO	A	E	DP
Koch	1.000	1	1	0	0	1
Leachman	.986	22	188	17	3	22
Liddle	.988	29	218	19	3	16
Rhodes	.976	26	227	15	6	16
Sano	1.000	1	7	0	0	0
Vargas	.990	33	281	15	3	32

Second Base	PCT	G	PO	A	E	DP
Bryant	1.000	11	21	26	0	8
Grimes	.949	18	37	37	4	13
Pettersen	.975	39	60	97	4	24
Rosario	.957	67	156	176	15	48
Wickens	1.000	8	8	23	0	3

Third Base	PCT	G	PO	A	E	DP
Bryant	.800	1	0	4	1	0
Goncalves	1.000	1	0	1	0	0
Grimes	.000	1	0	0	1	0
Pettersen	.904	19	12	35	5	7
Sano	.884	125	70	249	42	18
Vargas	1.000	1	2	5	0	0
Wickens	—	1	0	0	0	0

Shortstop	PCT	G	PO	A	E	DP
Bryant	.962	20	14	61	3	10
Grimes	.932	77	106	211	23	41
Pettersen	.964	15	22	59	3	12

	PCT	G	PO	A	E	DP
Wickens	.931	32	50	98	11	17

Outfield	PCT	G	PO	A	E	DP
Goncalves	.994	78	153	4	1	0
Leachman	.978	56	86	4	2	2
Liddle	—	1	0	0	0	0
Lin	.955	94	167	1	8	0
Ortiz	.975	19	38	1	1	0
Pettersen	1.000	16	23	0	0	0
Roberts	.964	70	131	3	5	0
Rosario	.951	19	38	1	2	0
Williams	.980	83	143	7	3	0

ELIZABETHTON TWINS · ROOKIE

APPALACHIAN LEAGUE

Batting	B-T	HT	WT	DOB	AVG	vLH	vRH	G	AB	R	H	2B	3B	HR	RBI	BB	HBP	SH	SF	SO	SB	CS	SLG	OBP
Altobelli, Bo	R-R	6-1	200	2-6-91	.230	.200	.232	18	61	6	14	2	0	0	6	4	0	2	0	11	0	0	.262	.277
Arias, Jhonatan	R-R	5-10	180	2-18-89	.301	.353	.291	30	103	14	31	6	0	1	11	7	0	1	2	15	0	1	.388	.339
Buxton, Byron	R-R	6-1	188	12-18-93	.286	.250	.295	21	77	16	22	6	1	1	6	8	2	0	0	15	7	0	.429	.368
Cross, Kelly	B-R	6-3	205	3-21-92	.050	.167	.000	6	20	2	1	0	0	0	1	3	0	0	0	6	0	0	.050	.174
Goodrum, Niko	B-R	6-3	170	2-28-92	.242	.359	.218	58	227	38	55	12	8	4	38	38	1	0	3	56	6	3	.419	.349
Harrison, Travis	R-R	6-1	215	10-17-92	.301	.289	.304	60	219	39	66	12	4	5	27	24	7	0	3	51	3	0	.461	.383
Hendricks, Joshua	R-R	6-3	217	11-9-91	.222	.353	.198	29	108	9	24	9	0	1	13	10	1	0	1	38	0	0	.333	.292
Hicks, D.J.	L-R	6-5	228	4-2-90	.270	.333	.260	31	115	21	31	7	0	4	25	19	2	0	0	37	1	0	.435	.382
Jimenez, Romy	R-R	6-2	170	5-14-91	.347	.500	.320	35	118	31	41	12	1	8	35	19	1	0	1	25	0	1	.669	.439
Kepler, Max	L-L	6-4	180	2-10-93	.297	.286	.299	59	232	40	69	16	5	10	49	27	8	0	2	33	7	0	.539	.387
Mention, Kelvin	L-L	5-11	198	2-18-92	.182	.000	.188	19	66	11	12	2	0	1	7	5	3	1	0	16	1	0	.258	.270
Pimentel, Candido	B-R	5-11	160	7-19-90	.330	.391	.323	56	215	45	71	10	3	1	22	26	1	5	0	42	16	7	.419	.405
Polanco, Jorge	B-R	5-11	165	7-5-93	.318	.281	.326	51	173	35	55	15	2	5	27	20	3	3	5	26	6	3	.514	.388
Quesada, Michael	R-R	6-0	180	2-1-90	.234	.308	.216	18	64	13	15	5	0	0	10	8	1	0	0	16	0	0	.313	.329
Rhodes, Rory	R-R	6-7	200	7-28-91	.262	.333	.246	44	168	29	44	8	2	6	26	17	2	0	1	48	1	1	.440	.335
Walker, Adam Brett	R-R	6-4	225	10-18-91	.250	.256	.249	58	232	44	58	7	4	14	45	19	1	0	0	76	4	0	.496	.310
Wickens, Stephen	R-R	5-10	170	3-5-89	.424	.600	.348	10	33	8	14	2	2	0	4	5	1	0	1	7	1	1	.606	.500

Pitching	B-T	HT	WT	DOB	W	L	ERA	G	GS	CG	SV	IP	H	R	ER	HR	BB	SO	AVG	vLH	vRH	K/9	BB/9
Arevalo, Ricardo	R-R	6-3	210	2-28-91	1	3	5.25	13	12	0	0	48	43	33	28	6	26	49	.232	.176	.265	9.19	4.88
Bard, Luke	R-R	6-3	195	11-13-90	0	0	0.00	4	0	0	1	3	2	0	0	0	2	4	.200	.000	.286	12.00	6.00
Baxendale, D.J.	R-R	6-2	190	12-8-90	0	0	0.00	6	0	0	0	8	1	0	0	1	16	.042	.000	.056	18.78	1.17
Berrios, J.O.	R-R	6-0	187	5-27-94	2	0	1.29	3	3	0	0	14	8	2	2	1	22	.163	.211	.133	14.14	0.64
Boyd, Hudson	R-R	6-2	235	10-18-92	2	5	2.95	13	13	0	0	58	63	33	19	7	23	36	.270	.348	.240	5.59	3.57
Burris, Josh	B-R	5-10	175	11-28-91	7	0	1.75	18	0	0	0	36	24	10	7	1	21	40	.190	.205	.184	10.00	5.25
Chargois, J.T.	R-R	6-3	200	12-3-90	0	0	1.69	12	0	0	5	16	10	4	3	0	5	22	.182	.118	.211	12.38	2.81
Duffey, Tyler	R-R	6-3	210	12-27-90	2	0	1.42	12	0	0	2	19	10	3	3	1	2	27	.154	.174	.143	12.79	0.95
Evans, Steven	L-L	6-4	210	8-9-89	2	0	5.40	10	0	0	0	10	13	6	6	0	5	12	.295	.500	.250	10.80	4.50
Ferreira, Andrew	R-L	6-2	200	10-22-90	2	0	1.80	10	0	0	0	7	2	2	0	0	13	.206	.200	.208	11.70	6.30
Gallant, Dallas	R-R	6-3	195	1-25-89	0	0	0.00	5	0	0	1	6	3	0	0	0	8	.143	.000	.176	12.00	0.00
Herr, Tyler	R-R	6-8	220	10-8-90	3	0	2.56	21	0	0	1	32	27	9	9	2	12	29	.243	.345	.207	8.24	3.41
Huber, Travis	R-R	6-3	226	6-13-90	1	0	7.71	9	0	0	1	14	18	12	12	2	8	10	.300	.240	.343	6.43	5.14
Jones, Zack	R-R	6-1	185	12-4-90	0	0	0.00	6	0	0	0	6	2	0	0	0	4	9	.100	.167	.071	13.50	6.00
Kimes, Corey	L-L	6-4	240	5-2-90	3	0	2.51	8	0	0	0	29	25	9	8	3	8	18	.225	.346	.188	5.65	2.51
Lee, Brett	L-L	6-4	200	9-20-90	4	0	2.68	16	4	0	0	44	39	17	13	3	12	48	.236	.226	.239	9.89	2.47
Mata, Angel	R-R	6-2	190	12-3-92	4	3	3.38	13	13	0	0	53	31	23	20	7	34	55	.171	.140	.185	9.28	5.74
Mazza, Chris	R-R	6-4	175	10-17-89	3	1	3.45	9	0	0	0	16	15	8	6	1	1	15	.242	.158	.279	8.62	0.57
Melotakis, Mason	R-L	6-3	190	6-28-91	1	1	1.35	7	0	0	0	7	2	2	1	0	2	10	.091	.000	.118	13.50	2.70
Merck, Kaleb	R-R	6-0	200	2-17-90	3	2	4.07	16	0	0	2	24	24	12	11	2	6	28	.255	.200	.275	10.36	2.22
Nunez, Luis	L-L	5-11	160	5-28-90	0	2	5.09	14	0	0	0	23	15	15	13	1	17	21	.181	.150	.190	8.22	6.65
Powell, Christian	L-R	6-5	210	7-3-91	1	0	5.74	10	0	0	1	16	18	11	10	0	9	14	.290	.273	.300	11.49	4.02
Robb, Hein	L-L	6-0	185	5-12-92	2	4	3.73	13	8	0	0	41	47	26	17	4	14	38	.280	.195	.307	8.34	3.07
Rogers, Taylor	L-L	6-3	170	12-17-90	2	1	1.80	6	6	0	0	30	20	7	6	2	5	39	.187	.167	.191	11.70	1.50

Fielding

Catcher	PCT	G	PO	A	E	DP	PB
Altobelli	.993	18	131	11	1	1	10
Arias	.989	27	244	32	3	2	5
Cross	1.000	6	45	8	0	0	2
Quesada	.994	17	139	21	1	3	7

First Base	PCT	G	PO	A	E	DP
Hendricks	.988	21	152	7	2	14
Hicks	.989	20	171	12	2	16
Rhodes	.996	25	216	15	1	20

Second Base	PCT	G	PO	A	E	DP
Pimentel	.973	26	44	66	3	14
Polanco	.983	35	73	102	3	21
Wickens	1.000	6	13	22	0	3

Third Base	PCT	G	PO	A	E	DP
Goodrum	.762	7	2	14	5	1
Harrison	.832	59	29	90	24	8

Shortstop	PCT	G	PO	A	E	DP
Goodrum	.945	50	66	156	13	30
Polanco	.909	15	18	32	5	9

	PCT	G	PO	A	E	DP
Wickens	1.000	2	4	6	0	2

Outfield	PCT	G	PO	A	E	DP
Buxton	.935	17	28	1	2	0
Jimenez	.978	34	42	2	1	1
Kepler	.989	50	87	2	1	0
Mention	1.000	17	18	0	0	0
Pimentel	.925	22	36	1	3	0
Polanco	—	1	0	0	0	0
Rhodes	1.000	4	6	0	0	0
Walker	.950	53	90	6	5	1
Wickens	1.000	1	1	0	0	0

GCL TWINS — ROOKIE

GULF COAST LEAGUE

Batting	B-T	HT	WT	DOB	AVG	vLH	vRH	G	AB	R	H	2B	3B	HR	RBI	BB	HBP	SH	SF	SO	SB	CS	SLG	OBP
Benson, Joe	R-R	6-1	215	3-5-88	.375	1.000	.286	3	8	1	3	1	0	0	0	1	0	0	0	2	1	1	.500	.444
Buxton, Byron	R-R	6-1	188	12-18-93	.216	.111	.262	27	88	17	19	4	3	4	14	11	3	0	0	26	4	3	.466	.324
Compton, Brian	R-R	6-2	195	9-29-89	.130	.182	.083	8	23	2	3	1	0	0	1	1	0	1	0	3	0	0	.174	.167
Cross, Kelly	B-R	6-3	205	3-21-92	.197	.231	.190	23	76	7	15	1	0	1	4	5	0	0	1	26	0	0	.250	.244
Fernandez, Jorge	B-R	6-3	188	3-30-94	.263	.300	.246	30	99	9	26	2	0	0	10	3	1	1	1	27	1	0	.283	.288
Haar, Bryan	R-R	6-3	200	12-9-89	.250	.308	.229	44	148	12	37	9	1	1	14	13	3	0	2	35	3	3	.345	.319
Hurt, Will	R-R	5-11	175	12-22-93	.141	.129	.149	27	78	5	11	0	0	0	3	7	1	1	0	23	1	2	.141	.221
Larson, Zach	R-R	6-2	185	10-8-93	.250	.286	.231	15	40	4	10	1	1	0	2	3	1	1	0	10	3	0	.325	.318
Licon, Joel	R-R	5-10	180	12-21-90	.250	.220	.261	49	160	19	40	8	2	2	21	17	5	2	2	42	5	2	.363	.337
Mejia, Aderlin	B-R	5-11	170	5-12-92	.324	.222	.360	48	170	27	55	13	0	1	20	14	1	3	4	13	11	7	.418	.370
Murphy, Jonathan	R-R	6-1	195	6-23-90	.216	.211	.218	52	171	29	37	9	1	2	22	15	3	1	2	41	13	7	.316	.288
Ortiz, Kelvin	R-R	6-1	178	10-19-91	.221	.200	.231	42	113	18	25	6	2	2	8	14	8	1	1	37	8	2	.363	.346
Pimentel, Javier	R-R	6-2	175	3-13-94	.198	.148	.213	36	121	10	24	7	0	1	13	2	2	0	1	34	1	1	.281	.222
Pineda, Jeremias	B-R	5-11	175	11-16-90	.237	.286	.211	16	59	8	14	0	1	1	3	6	1	0	0	16	9	2	.322	.318
2-team total (36 Red Sox)					.365	—	—	52	192	28	70	9	4	1	25	11	3	1	1	38	23	9	.469	.406
Ramirez, Jose	R-R	5-10	165	9-6-91	.234	.220	.240	50	145	18	34	3	1	0	13	10	3	5	2	33	3	5	.269	.294
Rodriguez, Dereck	R-R	6-1	160	6-5-92	.263	.231	.274	30	99	13	26	8	0	3	12	11	2	0	0	31	6	2	.434	.348
Rosario, Eddie	L-R	6-0	170	9-28-91	.368	.143	.500	5	19	2	7	3	0	1	4	1	0	0	0	2	0	0	.684	.400
Santy, Bryan	R-R	6-1	200	6-28-90	.296	.412	.243	19	54	7	16	5	0	0	7	9	3	1	1	9	1	3	.389	.418
Tosoni, Rene	L-R	6-0	200	7-2-86	.316	.000	.375	5	19	4	6	4	0	0	5	1	0	0	0	2	1	0	.526	.350
Wade, Logan	B-R	6-1	189	11-13-91	.234	.158	.267	39	124	12	29	6	4	1	10	12	0	2	0	29	2	2	.371	.301
Younis, Jacob	B-R	5-8	190	7-10-93	.139	.167	.133	12	36	4	5	0	0	0	2	2	2	0	0	6	1	1	.139	.225

Pitching	B-T	HT	WT	DOB	W	L	ERA	G	GS	CG	SV	IP	H	R	ER	HR	BB	SO	AVG	vLH	vRH	K/9	BB/9
Albers, Andrew	R-L	6-1	195	10-6-85	1	0	1.93	2	1	0	0	5	4	1	1	0	3	3	.222	.000	.286	5.79	5.79
Bard, Luke	R-R	6-3	195	11-13-90	0	0	6.75	3	0	0	0	4	3	3	3	0	5	3	.231	.286	.167	6.75	11.25
Berrios, J.O.	R-R	6-0	187	5-27-94	1	0	1.08	8	1	0	4	17	7	2	2	0	3	27	.121	.161	.074	14.58	1.62
Bromberg, David	L-R	6-5	245	9-14-87	0	0	18.00	2	1	0	0	2	6	5	4	0	1	3	.500	.714	.200	13.50	4.50
Chen, Hung Yi	R-R	5-10	190	9-25-92	2	3	3.41	16	0	0	0	29	25	11	11	2	5	26	.236	.286	.203	8.07	1.55
De La Cruz, Melciades	R-R	6-1	190	5-12-93	1	4	2.32	18	0	0	6	31	24	14	8	0	14	34	.209	.244	.186	9.87	4.06
Gibbons, Sam	L-R	6-4	190	12-12-93	4	1	2.29	10	6	0	0	35	28	10	9	1	8	22	.228	.194	.239	5.60	2.04
Gibson, Kyle	R-R	6-6	210	10-23-87	0	0	2.45	9	7	0	0	15	9	4	4	1	4	16	.176	.133	.194	9.82	2.45
Goldsmith, Carson	R-R	6-3	200	7-25-90	0	0	6.75	3	0	0	0	4	3	4	3	0	5	5	.231	.000	.300	11.25	11.25
Higginbotham, Trent	R-R	6-2	185	5-16-92	1	2	7.71	14	0	0	2	23	24	21	20	0	19	15	.282	.282	.283	5.79	7.33
Jorge, Felix	R-R	6-2	170	1-2-94	0	3	2.34	12	7	0	1	35	30	11	9	0	12	37	.221	.238	.213	9.61	3.12
Landa, Yorman	R-R	6-0	175	6-11-94	1	3	2.43	10	0	0	0	33	23	13	9	0	15	27	.204	.194	.207	7.29	5.40
Lo, Kuo Hua	R-R	5-10	195	10-28-92	2	0	1.13	11	6	0	0	40	24	6	5	0	7	33	.171	.216	.155	7.49	1.59
Malinowski, Austin	R-L	6-4	210	11-30-92	3	2	2.27	11	6	0	0	32	35	13	8	0	11	32	.278	.217	.313	9.09	3.13
Martinez, Andre	L-L	6-0	185	6-22-93	0	1	4.50	6	3	0	0	14	12	8	7	0	9	11	.231	.182	.244	7.07	5.79
Mazza, Chris	R-R	6-4	175	10-17-89	2	1	0.60	9	0	0	1	15	12	4	1	0	1	13	.214	.217	.212	7.80	0.60
Montanez, Josue	L-L	6-2	195	1-15-92	2	0	0.36	8	4	0	0	25	13	5	1	0	8	30	.149	.143	.151	10.80	2.88
Muren, Alex	R-R	6-3	195	11-6-91	3	2	1.46	15	0	0	4	25	12	5	4	0	9	12	.143	.120	.153	4.38	3.28
Ramirez, Gerardo	R-R	6-2	165	1-17-94	4	1	6.62	12	0	0	0	18	24	13	13	0	10	13	.343	.375	.326	6.62	5.09
Rosario, Randy	L-L	6-0	160	5-18-94	2	1	1.64	10	7	0	0	38	19	12	7	0	19	42	.147	.200	.124	9.86	4.46
Salcedo, Adrian	R-R	6-4	175	2-5-91	0	1	3.38	3	2	0	0	5	7	6	2	0	1	4	.292	.273	.308	6.75	1.69
Sanudo, Gonzalo	R-R	6-3	215	11-20-92	2	0	2.00	15	2	0	4	36	34	8	8	0	2	33	.252	.225	.263	8.25	0.50
Slama, Anthony	R-R	6-3	200	1-6-84	0	0	3.38	2	0	0	0	3	2	1	1	0	1	3	.222	.000	.250	10.13	3.38
Solbach, Markus	R-R	6-5	195	8-26-91	2	1	5.82	11	0	0	0	17	27	15	11	2	1	14	.370	.517	.273	7.41	0.53
Tomshaw, Matthew	L-L	6-2	200	12-17-88	0	0	0.00	2	0	0	0	3	2	0	0	0	0	1	.182	.000	.222	3.00	0.00
Wimmers, Alex	L-R	6-2	195	11-1-88	0	1	40.50	1	1	0	0	1	4	3	3	0	1	0	.800	1.000	.750	0.00	13.50

Fielding

Catcher	PCT	G	PO	A	E	DP	PB
Compton	1.000	7	45	3	0	0	3
Cross	.976	21	144	16	4	0	3
Fernandez	.986	25	194	19	3	4	10
Santy	.978	11	79	11	2	0	4

First Base	PCT	G	PO	A	E	DP
Fernandez	1.000	3	22	1	0	1
Haar	.989	40	341	23	4	30
Mejia	1.000	5	31	1	0	2
Pimentel	.987	11	72	4	1	7
Tosoni	1.000	1	7	0	0	1
Wade	1.000	4	36	3	0	3

Second Base	PCT	G	PO	A	E	DP
Hurt	.947	5	5	13	1	2
Licon	.938	10	22	23	3	7
Mejia	.889	2	5	3	1	2
Ramirez	.959	32	38	80	5	18
Rosario	1.000	4	4	6	0	0
Wade	.944	11	10	24	2	3
Younis	1.000	3	2	8	0	1

Third Base	PCT	G	PO	A	E	DP
Licon	.951	22	12	46	3	5
Mejia	.929	18	18	21	3	3
Pimentel	.857	16	7	11	3	1
Ramirez	1.000	7	6	11	0	1

Shortstop	PCT	G	PO	A	E	DP
Hurt	.959	17	20	50	3	8
Licon	1.000	2	5	5	0	2
Mejia	.980	24	34	62	2	15
Ramirez	.977	10	16	27	1	4
Wade	.872	10	7	27	5	4

Outfield	PCT	G	PO	A	E	DP
Benson	1.000	1	2	0	0	0
Buxton	.955	22	41	1	2	1
Larson	1.000	14	21	1	0	0
Licon	.941	10	15	1	1	0
Murphy	.988	48	76	3	1	0
Ortiz	1.000	35	44	1	0	1
Pimentel	1.000	3	3	0	0	0
Pineda	.968	16	27	3	1	1
Ramirez	—	1	0	0	0	0
Rodriguez	.980	28	45	5	1	2
Rosario	—	1	0	0	0	0
Tosoni	1.000	4	6	0	0	0
Wade	1.000	5	5	0	0	0
Younis	1.000	6	9	0	0	0

DOMINICAN SUMMER LEAGUE

Batting	B-T	HT	WT	DOB	AVG	vLH	vRH	G	AB	R	H	2B	3B	HR	RBI	BB	HBP	SH	SF	SO	SB	CS	SLG	OBP
Amarante, Junior	L-L	5-11	185	3-21-95	.175	.152	.184	41	120	16	21	2	2	0	6	10	4	2	0	40	4	2	.225	.261
Andrade, Jorge	B-R	5-10	170	12-7-94	.236	.182	.273	39	110	17	26	3	0	2	11	12	3	3	0	26	4	4	.318	.328
Arias, Victor	B-R	5-11	170	3-26-91	.179	.067	.220	37	112	13	20	4	1	0	11	6	3	2	1	29	7	4	.232	.238
Baez, Dubal	R-R	6-0	175	6-14-93	.263	.289	.250	38	118	22	31	5	0	0	11	16	7	2	1	23	8	4	.305	.380
Boni, Junior	R-R	6-0	175	2-5-91	.202	.250	.188	33	104	12	21	5	1	0	10	18	2	1	0	22	6	2	.269	.331
Ciprian, Ernesto	R-R	6-2	175	2-9-91	.270	.278	.266	49	163	20	44	5	4	2	21	25	2	0	2	39	6	4	.387	.370
Concepcion, Eddy	B-R	5-11	185	1-25-93	.241	.229	.247	41	145	20	35	6	2	2	19	20	0	0	1	27	4	4	.352	.331
Gonzalez, Luis	B-R	5-11	180	10-10-94	.182	.288	.133	45	165	22	30	3	0	2	18	17	2	1	1	32	5	4	.236	.265
Martinez, Carlos	R-R	5-11	170	4-6-94	.168	.103	.191	48	149	15	25	7	0	0	17	17	5	1	4	46	3	6	.215	.269
Mateo, Francis	L-L	5-11	185	4-24-93	.215	.143	.250	43	149	16	32	7	0	3	16	12	3	1	0	53	1	2	.322	.287
Pacheco, Adonis	L-L	5-11	175	7-14-91	.322	.397	.291	61	211	42	68	9	12	4	34	28	4	1	2	40	18	5	.536	.408
Polanco, Joel	R-R	5-11	175	8-15-92	.254	.319	.218	39	134	23	34	15	1	0	17	18	7	1	1	27	6	2	.381	.369
Silva, Jhon	B-R	5-11	160	6-5-93	.243	.176	.300	14	37	9	9	1	0	0	5	9	1	0	0	9	2	3	.270	.404
Valera, Rafael P	R-R	5-11	180	8-15-94	.244	.191	.274	40	131	23	32	3	1	0	12	22	3	1	1	29	8	4	.282	.363
Vielma, Engelb	R-R	5-11	155	6-22-94	.268	.340	.234	44	157	24	42	4	3	0	19	18	4	0	2	27	16	5	.331	.354
Ynfante, Gabriel A.	B-R	5-11	158	11-15-94	.231	.361	.181	47	130	20	30	1	1	0	12	27	7	4	1	41	8	2	.254	.388
Ynojoso, Jonatan	B-R	5-11	150	10-23-92	.174	.229	.155	42	132	23	23	6	2	0	5	16	2	1	0	33	8	4	.250	.273

Pitching	B-T	HT	WT	DOB	W	L	ERA	G	GS	CG	SV	IP	H	R	ER	HR	BB	SO	AVG	vLH	vRH	K/9	BB/9
Abreu, Jose	R-R	5-11	170	7-13-92	1	2	2.25	14	7	0	1	40	35	17	10	1	9	23	.236	.245	.232	5.18	2.03
Arias, Pedro	R-R	6-2	190	2-4-94	0	1	10.13	5	0	0	0	5	7	9	6	0	8	6	.333	.286	.357	10.13	13.50
Defrank, Damian	R-R	6-3	200	2-1-95	0	4	3.06	14	14	0	0	53	53	24	18	0	16	27	.275	.250	.289	4.58	2.72
Florentino, Yeison	R-R	6-3	180	1-16-92	0	0	4.50	4	0	0	1	6	10	6	3	0	0	4	.323	.400	.286	6.00	0.00
Gonzalez, Miguel	R-R	6-1	180	10-12-94	1	4	2.01	12	12	0	0	45	36	25	10	1	20	35	.211	.194	.220	7.05	4.03
Jimenez, Jadison	L-L	6-0	180	3-19-94	8	3	3.58	20	0	0	1	38	30	18	15	2	23	22	.222	.143	.231	5.26	5.50
Jimenez, Jose	R-R	6-3	215	12-12-91	0	3	6.17	13	4	0	0	23	28	20	16	1	19	18	.304	.211	.370	6.94	7.33
Martinez, Edgar	R-R	6-0	145	9-1-90	3	0	4.98	21	1	0	6	34	50	21	19	1	7	31	.357	.298	.398	8.13	1.83
Perez, Sebastian	R-R	6-1	175	5-17-95	1	1	5.64	14	0	0	0	22	25	21	14	1	12	7	.294	.313	.283	2.82	4.84
Ramirez, Jose	R-R	6-1	170	8-19-92	1	0	5.11	15	0	0	1	25	31	23	14	2	11	24	.301	.357	.262	8.76	4.01
Reyes, Reudis	R-R	6-4	175	3-18-93	0	5	6.25	23	0	0	0	40	44	37	28	0	24	13	.282	.326	.264	2.90	5.36
Romero, Fernando	R-R	6-0	215	12-24-94	1	4	4.65	14	6	0	0	31	26	19	16	0	14	28	.224	.179	.247	8.13	4.06
Silva, Argenis	R-R	6-0	190	7-24-95	4	0	4.76	21	1	0	1	40	37	24	21	1	31	29	.237	.208	.250	6.58	7.03
Subero, Junior	R-R	6-0	180	3-14-92	5	3	1.43	12	12	1	0	63	50	16	10	1	9	54	.216	.213	.219	7.71	1.29
Vargas, Javier	R-R	6-1	185	1-28-93	2	4	2.45	15	10	0	1	51	43	23	14	0	14	28	.224	.200	.238	4.91	2.45
Villasana, Elias	R-R	6-1	190	3-22-93	2	1	7.26	23	2	0	1	40	41	35	32	0	35	35	.266	.250	.279	7.94	7.94
Zarzuela, Ezequiel	R-R	6-1	170	11-18-90	2	1	6.23	6	0	0	0	9	11	6	6	0	2	9	.306	.364	.280	9.35	2.08
Zoquiel, Reyson	L-L	5-11	175	11-5-93	0	3	6.34	23	1	0	4	33	36	28	23	1	35	37	.277	.067	.304	10.19	9.64

Fielding

Catcher	PCT	G	PO	A	E	DP	PB
Arias	.667	1	2	0	1	0	3
Concepcion	.987	22	128	19	2	1	8
Gonzalez	.989	25	161	24	2	1	11
Polanco	.985	27	162	32	3	1	7

First Base	PCT	G	PO	A	E	DP
Arias	.994	21	151	16	1	15
Ciprian	1.000	1	2	0	0	0
Concepcion	1.000	12	89	7	0	6
Gonzalez	.961	15	142	5	6	6
Martinez	.968	5	54	6	2	4
Mateo	1.000	1	2	0	0	0
Pacheco	1.000	8	52	2	0	2
Polanco	.989	11	85	5	1	3
Valera	1.000	4	28	1	0	2
Ynfante	.968	5	28	2	1	2

Second Base	PCT	G	PO	A	E	DP
Andrade	.896	25	31	55	10	7

Arias	1.000	2	6	4	0	0
Baez	.941	5	6	10	1	1
Valera	.965	12	24	31	2	7
Vielma	1.000	6	8	15	0	3
Ynfante	.960	18	20	28	2	6
Ynojoso	.956	16	22	43	3	3

Third Base	PCT	G	PO	A	E	DP
Andrade	1.000	1	1	0	0	0
Arias	.914	9	14	18	3	4
Baez	.750	2	2	1	1	0
Martinez	.890	42	38	83	15	3
Valera	.846	11	8	25	6	1
Ynfante	1.000	13	8	26	0	1

Shortstop	PCT	G	PO	A	E	DP
Andrade	.727	3	6	2	3	1
Arias	.778	2	2	5	2	0
Baez	1.000	2	3	2	0	0
Valera	.778	3	2	5	2	0

Vielma	.899	35	57	103	18	9
Ynfante	.822	11	15	22	8	3
Ynojoso	.933	23	34	63	7	10

Outfield	PCT	G	PO	A	E	DP
Amarante	.927	38	73	3	6	1
Andrade	1.000	1	1	0	0	0
Arias	—	2	0	0	0	0
Baez	.959	21	42	5	2	0
Boni	1.000	7	13	0	0	0
Ciprian	.938	47	53	8	4	1
Mateo	.933	36	54	2	4	1
Pacheco	.957	52	106	6	5	2
Polanco	—	1	0	0	0	0
Silva	1.000	14	19	2	0	1
Valera	.929	12	13	0	1	0
Ynojoso	.923	6	10	2	1	0

New York Mets

SEASON IN A SENTENCE: Mets win totals have waned from 79 to 77 to 74 in three seasons as the franchise continues to pare payroll, which has declined an estimated 37 percent from a high-water mark of $149 million in 2009.

HIGH POINT: Lefty Johan Santana threw the first no-hitter in the franchise's 51 seasons on June 1, holding the Cardinals in check with eight strikeouts in an 8-0 win. Santana also threw a career-high 134 pitches, worked around five walks and benefited from the third-base umpire's generous foul call on a Carlos Beltran line drive.

LOW POINT: A nine-game home losing streak in September (to the division-rival Braves, Nationals and Phillies, no less) destroyed any semblance of goodwill following the Mets' surprising first-half record of 46-40. At the depths of their despair, New York went a club-record 16 consecutive home games without scoring more than three runs.

NOTABLE ROOKIES: Righthander Matt Harvey, the seventh overall pick in the 2010 draft, limited the Diamondbacks to three hits in 5 1/3 shutout innings on July 26. He struck out 11, the most in a debut since the Nationals' Stephen Strasburg fanned 14 on June 8, 2010. Harvey made 30 starts between Triple-A Buffalo and New York and went 10-10, 3.35 with 182 strikeouts, 74 walks and 139 hits in 169 innings. The Mets filled out their bullpen in the second half with power-armed rookies such as righthander Jeurys Familia and lefties Robert Carson and Josh Edgin.

KEY TRANSACTIONS: General manager Sandy Alderson had no encore for the 2011 trade deadline acquisition of righthander Zack Wheeler. In fact, the organization's most notable 2012 transactions barely registered. The Mets traded righty reliever Pedro Beato to the Red Sox for catcher Kelly Shoppach in August. They signed Dominican shortstop German "Amed" Rosario for $1.75 million on July 2, establishing a club bonus record for an international amateur. In November, they released free agent flop Jason Bay, deferring some of the $21 million he's owed in 2013 while reclaiming a roster spot.

DOWN ON THE FARM: Harvey and Wheeler ranked as the top pitching prospects in the Triple-A International and Double-A Eastern leagues, respectively, lending hope that the organization's return to relevancy could arrive via pitching. High Class A St. Lucie had the best record in the Florida State League but lost out in the playoffs.

OPENING DAY PAYROLL: $93.3 million (14th)

PLAYERS OF THE YEAR

MAJOR LEAGUE

R.A. Dickey
rhp
20-6, 2.73
230 SO/54 BB
Led NL in IP, SO

MINOR LEAGUE

Zack Wheeler
rhp
(Double-A/Triple-A)
12-8, 3.26
148 SO/149 IP

ORGANIZATION LEADERS

BATTING		*Minimum 250 AB
MAJORS		
* AVG	David Wright	.306
* OPS	David Wright	.883
HR	Ike Davis	32
RBI	David Wright	93
MINORS		
* AVG	T.J. Rivera, Savannah/St. Lucie	.320
* OBP	Camden Maron, Savannah	.403
* SLG	Fred Lewis, Buffalo	.482
R	Matt Den Dekker, Binghamton/Buffalo	84
H	T.J. Rivera, Savannah/St. Lucie	165
TB	Matt Den Dekker, Binghamton/Buffalo	244
2B	Dustin Lawley, Savannah	35
3B	Matt Den Dekker, Binghamton/Buffalo	8
HR	Aderlin Rodriguez, Savannah/St. Lucie	24
RBI	Aderlin Rodriguez, Savannah/St. Lucie	83
BB	Valentino Pascucci, Buffalo	87
SO	Matt Den Dekker, Binghamton/Buffalo	154
SB	Alonzo Harris, St. Lucie	40

PITCHING		#Minimum 75 IP
MAJORS		
W	R.A. Dickey	20
# ERA	R.A. Dickey	2.73
SO	R.A. Dickey	230
SV	Frank Francisco	23
MINORS		
W	Gonzalez Germen, St. Lucie/Buff./Binghamton	12
	Zack Wheeler, Binghamton/Buffalo	12
L	Mark Cohoon, Buffalo/Binghamton	12
	Gonzalez Germen, St. Lucie/Buff./Binghamton	12
# ERA	Tyler Pill, Savannah/St. Lucie	2.31
G	Fernando Cabrera, Buffalo	57
GS	Jeurys Familia, Buffalo	28
SV	Fernando Cabrera, Buffalo	22
IP	Mark Cohoon, Buffalo/Binghamton	154.2
BB	Jeurys Familia, Buffalo	73
SO	Zack Wheeler, Binghamton/Buffalo	148
# AVG	Rafael Montero, Savannah/St. Lucie	.212

2012 PERFORMANCE

General Manager: Sandy Alderson. **Farm Director:** Adam Wogan. **Scouting Director:** Tom Tanous.

Class	Team	League	W	L	PCT	Finish	Manager
Majors	New York Mets	National	74	88	.457	12th (16)	Terry Collins
Triple-A	Buffalo Bisons	International	67	76	.469	10th (14)	Wally Backman
Double-A	Binghamton Mets	Eastern	68	74	.479	9th (12)	Pedro Lopez
High A	St. Lucie Mets	Florida State	83	52	.615	1st (12)	Ryan Ellis
Low A	Savannah Sand Gnats	South Atlantic	69	67	.507	6th (14)	Luis Rojas
Short-season	Brooklyn Cyclones	New York-Penn	45	31	.592	4th (14)	Rich Donnelly
Rookie	Kingsport Mets	Appalachian	23	43	.348	9th (10)	Jose Leger
Overall 2012 Minor League Record			355	343	.509	11th (30)	

ORGANIZATION STATISTICS

NEW YORK METS
NATIONAL LEAGUE

Batting	B-T	HT	WT	DOB	AVG	vLH	vRH	G	AB	R	H	2B	3B	HR	RBI	BB	HBP	SH	SF	SO	SB	CS	SLG	OBP
Baxter, Mike	L-R	6-0	195	12-7-84	.263	.053	.288	89	179	26	47	14	2	3	17	25	5	0	2	45	5	3	.413	.365
Bay, Jason	R-R	6-2	210	9-20-78	.165	.172	.158	70	194	21	32	2	0	8	20	19	0	0	2	58	5	1	.299	.237
Cedeno, Ronny	R-R	6-0	195	2-2-83	.259	.277	.236	78	166	18	43	11	1	4	22	17	1	2	0	35	0	1	.410	.332
Davis, Ike	L-L	6-4	230	3-22-87	.227	.174	.253	156	519	66	118	26	0	32	90	61	1	0	3	141	0	2	.462	.308
Duda, Lucas	L-R	6-4	255	2-3-86	.239	.239	.240	121	401	43	96	15	0	15	57	51	4	0	3	120	1	0	.389	.329
Hairston, Scott	R-R	6-0	205	5-25-80	.263	.286	.239	134	377	52	99	25	3	20	57	19	1	0	1	83	8	2	.504	.299
Johnson, Rob	R-R	6-1	220	7-22-82	.250	.227	.267	17	52	3	13	2	0	0	4	4	0	1	1	10	0	0	.288	.298
Lewis, Fred	L-R	6-2	205	12-9-80	.150	.000	.158	18	20	2	3	0	0	0	0	4	1	0	0	5	0	0	.150	.320
Lutz, Zach	R-R	6-1	220	6-3-86	.091	.000	.250	7	11	1	1	0	0	0	0	0	0	0	0	5	0	0	.091	.091
Murphy, Daniel	L-R	6-2	205	4-1-85	.291	.283	.294	156	571	62	166	40	3	6	65	36	1	0	4	82	10	2	.403	.332
Nickeas, Mike	R-R	6-0	215	2-13-83	.174	.217	.122	47	109	8	19	3	0	1	13	8	2	2	1	27	0	0	.229	.242
Nieuwenhuis, Kirk	L-R	6-3	215	8-7-87	.252	.180	.271	91	282	40	71	12	1	7	28	25	2	3	2	98	4	4	.376	.315
Quintanilla, Omar	L-R	5-9	185	10-24-81	.257	.125	.296	29	70	13	18	5	0	1	4	8	2	0	0	17	0	0	.371	.350
Rottino, Vinny	R-R	6-1	215	4-7-80	.182	.200	.125	18	33	8	6	1	0	2	5	6	0	0	0	9	3	0	.394	.308
Satin, Josh	R-R	6-2	200	12-23-84	.000	—	.000	1	1	0	0	0	0	0	0	0	0	0	0	1	0	0	.000	.000
Shoppach, Kelly	R-R	6-0	220	4-29-80	.203	.216	.190	28	79	7	16	2	0	3	10	5	3	0	0	27	0	0	.342	.276
Tejada, Ruben	R-R	5-11	185	10-27-89	.289	.320	.273	114	464	53	134	26	0	1	25	27	5	3	2	73	4	4	.351	.333
Thole, Josh	L-R	6-1	215	10-28-86	.234	.211	.241	104	321	24	75	15	0	1	21	27	1	4	1	50	0	0	.290	.294
Torres, Andres	B-R	5-10	195	1-26-78	.230	.286	.194	132	374	47	86	17	7	3	35	52	3	1	2	90	13	5	.337	.327
Turner, Justin	R-R	6-0	210	11-23-84	.269	.241	.295	94	171	20	46	13	1	2	19	9	4	0	1	24	1	1	.392	.319
Valdespin, Jordany	L-R	6-0	190	12-23-87	.241	.226	.244	94	191	28	46	9	1	8	26	10	2	3	0	44	10	3	.424	.286
Wright, David	R-R	6-0	210	12-20-82	.306	.320	.300	156	581	91	178	41	2	21	93	81	5	0	5	112	15	10	.492	.391

Pitching	B-T	HT	WT	DOB	W	L	ERA	G	GS	CG	SV	IP	H	R	ER	HR	BB	SO	AVG	vLH	vRH	K/9	BB/9
Acosta, Manny	B-R	6-4	215	5-1-81	1	3	6.46	45	0	0	1	47	48	38	34	7	25	46	.259	.253	.264	8.75	4.75
Batista, Miguel	R-R	6-1	210	2-19-71	1	3	4.82	30	5	0	0	47	53	28	25	5	31	34	.290	.308	.272	6.56	5.98
2-team total (5 Atlanta)					1	3	4.61	35	5	0	0	53	58	30	27	6	33	36	—	—	—	6.15	5.64
Beato, Pedro	R-R	6-4	220	10-27-86	0	0	10.38	7	0	0	0	4	5	5	5	1	2	5	.278	.667	.200	10.38	4.15
Byrdak, Tim	L-L	5-11	190	10-31-73	2	2	4.40	56	0	0	0	31	18	16	15	2	18	34	.180	.154	.229	9.98	5.28
Carrasco, D.J.	R-R	6-4	215	4-12-77	0	0	7.36	4	0	0	0	4	6	3	3	2	0	3	.353	.286	.400	7.36	0.00
Carson, Robert	L-L	6-4	240	1-23-89	0	0	4.73	17	0	0	0	13	13	7	7	2	4	5	.260	.286	.227	3.38	2.70
Dickey, R.A.	R-R	6-2	215	10-29-74	20	6	2.73	34	33	5	0	234	192	78	71	24	54	230	.226	.237	.218	8.86	2.08
Edgin, Josh	L-L	6-1	225	12-17-86	1	2	4.56	34	0	0	0	26	19	14	13	5	10	30	.204	.164	.263	10.52	3.51
Egbert, Jack	L-R	6-3	220	5-12-83	0	0	0.00	1	0	0	0	1	0	0	0	0	0	0	.000	.000	.000	0.00	0.00
Familia, Jeurys	R-R	6-4	230	10-10-89	0	0	5.84	8	1	0	0	12	10	8	8	0	9	10	.233	.316	.167	7.30	6.57
Francisco, Frank	R-R	6-2	250	9-11-79	1	3	5.53	48	0	0	23	42	47	27	26	5	21	47	.269	.273	.264	9.99	4.46
Gee, Dillon	R-R	6-1	205	4-28-86	6	7	4.10	17	17	0	0	110	108	56	50	12	29	97	.256	.287	.219	7.96	2.38
Hampson, Justin	L-L	6-1	205	5-24-80	0	0	1.80	13	0	0	0	10	6	4	2	0	5	4	.194	.150	.273	3.60	4.50
Harvey, Matt	R-R	6-4	225	3-27-89	3	5	2.73	10	10	0	0	59	42	19	18	5	26	70	.200	.212	.185	10.62	3.94
Hefner, Jeremy	R-R	6-4	215	3-11-86	4	7	5.09	26	13	0	0	94	110	55	53	9	18	62	.287	.302	.272	5.96	1.73
McHugh, Collin	R-R	6-2	195	6-19-87	0	4	7.59	8	4	0	0	21	27	21	18	5	8	17	.314	.361	.280	7.17	3.38
Mejia, Jenrry	R-R	6-0	205	10-11-89	1	2	5.63	5	3	0	0	16	20	10	10	2	9	8	.313	.267	.353	4.50	5.06
Niese, Jon	L-L	6-4	215	10-27-86	13	9	3.40	30	30	0	0	190	174	77	72	22	49	155	.241	.243	.240	7.33	2.32
Olson, Garrett	R-L	6-1	205	10-18-83	0	0	108.00	1	0	0	0	0	3	4	4	0	1	0	.750	1.000	.500	0.00	27.00
Parnell, Bobby	R-R	6-4	200	9-8-84	5	4	2.49	74	0	0	7	69	65	24	19	4	20	61	.249	.235	.261	8.00	2.62
Pelfrey, Mike	R-R	6-7	250	1-14-84	0	0	2.29	3	3	0	0	20	24	5	5	0	4	13	.300	.298	.303	5.95	1.83
Ramirez, Elvin	R-R	6-3	210	10-10-87	0	1	5.48	20	0	0	0	21	24	13	13	1	20	22	.296	.250	.351	9.28	8.44
Ramirez, Ramon	R-R	5-11	200	8-31-81	3	4	4.24	58	0	0	1	64	58	33	30	4	35	52	.247	.273	.224	7.35	4.95
Rauch, Jon	R-R	6-11	290	9-27-78	3	7	3.59	73	0	0	4	58	45	28	23	7	12	42	.209	.262	.176	6.55	1.87
Santana, Johan	L-L	6-0	210	3-13-79	6	9	4.85	21	21	2	0	117	117	65	63	17	39	111	.258	.281	.251	8.54	3.00
Schwinden, Chris	R-R	6-3	215	9-22-86	0	1	12.46	3	2	0	0	9	15	13	12	4	3	1	.357	.429	.286	1.04	3.12
Young, Chris	R-R	6-10	260	5-25-79	4	9	4.15	20	20	0	0	115	119	58	53	16	36	80	.269	.278	.261	6.26	2.82

Fielding

Catcher	PCT	G	PO	A	E	DP	PB
Johnson	1.000	17	130	6	0	0	2
Nickeas	.993	45	280	20	2	3	8
Shoppach	.966	27	160	11	6	3	4
Thole	.992	100	690	50	6	3	18

First Base	PCT	G	PO	A	E	DP
Davis	.994	148	1156	71	8	106
Duda	.960	6	20	4	1	1
Lutz	.917	1	10	1	1	0
Murphy	1.000	12	46	4	0	5
Rottino	1.000	7	36	2	0	6
Turner	.982	11	53	2	1	6

Second Base	PCT	G	PO	A	E	DP
Cedeno	.974	28	29	45	2	9

	PCT	G	PO	A	E	DP
Murphy	.974	138	228	325	15	69
Quintanilla	1.000	2	1	0	0	0
Turner	.982	14	29	26	1	7
Valdespin	1.000	16	19	19	0	9

Third Base	PCT	G	PO	A	E	DP
Cedeno	1.000	3	1	1	0	0
Rottino	1.000	2	0	1	0	0
Turner	1.000	11	5	8	0	1
Wright	.974	155	107	267	10	20

Shortstop	PCT	G	PO	A	E	DP
Cedeno	.972	27	18	52	2	10
Quintanilla	.975	23	24	55	2	12
Tejada	.974	112	164	280	12	72
Turner	1.000	10	9	20	0	5

	PCT	G	PO	A	E	DP
Valdespin	.727	4	3	5	3	2
Wright	1.000	1	0	2	0	0

Outfield	PCT	G	PO	A	E	DP
Baxter	.988	63	81	3	1	2
Bay	.983	65	113	2	2	0
Duda	.977	105	164	5	4	0
Hairston	.994	108	152	1	1	0
Lewis	1.000	6	4	0	0	0
Nieuwenhuis	.978	83	174	0	4	0
Rottino	1.000	8	6	0	0	0
Torres	.993	124	261	6	2	1
Valdespin	1.000	39	60	1	0	0

BUFFALO BISONS

TRIPLE-A

INTERNATIONAL LEAGUE

Batting	B-T	HT	WT	DOB	AVG	vLH	vRH	G	AB	R	H	2B	3B	HR	RBI	BB	HBP	SH	SF	SO	SB	CS	SLG	OBP
Baxter, Mike	L-R	6-0	195	12-7-84	.375	.250	.438	6	24	2	9	1	0	0	3	2	1	0	0	7	0	0	.417	.444
Bay, Jason	R-R	6-2	210	9-20-78	.300	—	.300	3	10	2	3	0	0	0	0	4	0	0	0	3	1	0	.300	.500
Blaquiere, Jean Luc	R-R	6-0	196	2-27-86	.176	.154	.190	13	34	4	6	1	0	0	2	7	0	0	0	14	0	0	.206	.317
Cedeno, Ronny	R-R	6-0	195	2-2-83	.172	.111	.200	7	29	2	5	0	0	0	1	1	0	0	0	6	0	0	.172	.200
den Dekker, Matt	L-L	6-1	205	8-10-87	.220	.239	.214	77	295	37	65	10	4	9	47	14	2	1	5	90	11	2	.373	.256
Duda, Lucas	L-R	6-4	255	2-3-86	.260	.214	.279	25	96	12	25	4	0	3	8	10	0	0	1	21	0	0	.396	.327
Emaus, Brad	R-R	6-0	205	3-28-86	.212	.275	.171	73	203	14	43	9	0	4	18	23	2	3	1	30	2	1	.315	.297
Fisher, Michael	B-R	6-2	188	3-22-85	.169	.115	.212	30	59	5	10	1	0	0	2	3	0	1	0	6	1	0	.186	.210
Johnson, Rob	R-R	6-1	205	7-22-82	.207	.163	.223	45	164	20	34	7	1	4	15	9	1	0	3	26	3	2	.335	.253
Kazmar, Sean	R-R	5-9	180	8-5-84	.138	.083	.176	11	29	2	4	1	0	0	2	1	0	3	0	10	0	0	.172	.167
Lewis, Fred	L-R	6-2	205	12-9-80	.294	.217	.319	108	419	80	123	26	7	13	45	57	1	0	0	113	25	8	.482	.379
Loewen, Adam	L-L	6-4	235	4-9-84	.227	.222	.228	59	207	32	47	10	0	8	26	30	1	0	0	55	4	1	.391	.328
Lutz, Zach	R-R	6-1	220	6-3-86	.299	.321	.293	72	244	34	73	16	1	10	35	42	5	1	2	75	0	0	.496	.410
Martin, Dustin	L-L	6-2	215	4-4-84	.257	.125	.273	28	74	13	19	7	0	1	8	4	0	0	1	20	2	0	.392	.291
May, Lucas	R-R	6-0	205	10-24-84	.215	.234	.208	75	256	25	55	19	3	3	25	10	1	0	2	74	2	1	.348	.245
Navarro, Oswaldo	R-R	6-0	200	10-2-84	.230	.235	.184	42	100	7	21	4	1	2	11	5	1	2	1	19	0	1	.330	.252
Nickeas, Mike	R-R	6-0	215	2-13-83	.364	.214	.404	22	66	10	24	6	0	1	6	0	0	1	2	9	0	0	.500	.405
Nieuwenhuis, Kirk	L-R	6-3	215	8-7-87	.182	—	.182	5	11	0	2	1	0	0	1	2	0	0	0	4	1	0	.273	.308
Pascucci, Valentino	R-R	6-6	265	11-17-78	.217	.202	.222	123	383	57	83	17	0	17	62	87	0	1	3	148	0	1	.394	.359
Quintanilla, Omar	L-R	5-9	185	10-24-81	.282	.167	.317	48	156	18	44	11	2	6	27	14	1	1	0	27	1	3	.494	.345
Reyes, Raul	L-L	6-0	195	12-30-86	.250	.161	.280	51	124	16	31	5	0	1	10	19	1	1	0	42	1	2	.315	.354
Rodriguez, Josh	R-R	6-0	185	12-18-84	.265	.254	.268	65	257	30	68	14	1	8	32	22	3	3	2	56	3	5	.420	.327
Rottino, Vinny	R-R	6-1	215	4-7-80	.307	.333	.299	36	140	22	43	10	1	4	25	12	1	0	2	20	5	3	.479	.361
2-team total (60 Columbus)					.297			96	374	60	111	28	2	9	66	34	4	0	8	53	14	6	.455	.355
Satin, Josh	R-R	6-2	200	12-23-84	.286	.223	.303	131	441	72	126	25	1	14	60	77	3	0	6	109	3	4	.442	.391
Scales, Bobby	R-R	6-0	185	10-4-77	.339	.323	.346	32	109	16	37	10	0	2	9	22	2	2	0	18	2	2	.486	.459
Tejada, Ruben	R-R	5-11	185	10-27-89	.200	.143	.231	6	20	3	4	1	0	0	2	1	0	0	0	3	0	0	.250	.238
Thole, Josh	L-R	6-1	215	10-28-86	.200	.250	.000	2	5	0	1	0	0	0	0	0	0	0	0	0	0	0	.200	.200
Torres, Andres	B-R	5-10	195	1-26-78	.143	.000	.167	2	7	1	1	0	0	0	0	2	0	1	0	3	1	0	.143	.333
Tuiasosopo, Matt	R-R	6-2	230	5-10-86	.242	.304	.222	131	418	47	101	14	0	12	57	51	5	4	3	117	3	4	.361	.329
Turner, Justin	R-R	6-0	210	11-23-84	.250	—	.250	2	8	0	2	0	0	0	0	0	0	0	0	0	0	0	.250	.250
Valdespin, Jordany	L-R	6-0	190	12-23-87	.285	.208	.299	39	151	22	43	2	1	5	23	10	1	0	1	22	10	8	.411	.331
Wimberly, Corey	B-R	5-8	170	10-26-83	.301	.291	.308	39	133	28	40	3	1	0	4	14	15	3	1	1	15	7	6	.376	.382

Pitching	B-T	HT	WT	DOB	W	L	ERA	G	GS	CG	SV	IP	H	R	ER	HR	BB	SO	AVG	vLH	vRH	K/9	BB/9
Acosta, Manny	B-R	6-4	215	5-1-81	0	1	2.25	17	0	0	0	28	24	12	7	1	4	25	.233	.244	.224	8.04	1.29
Beato, Pedro	R-R	6-4	220	10-27-86	4	4	4.14	37	1	0	0	37	32	21	17	7	11	27	.234	.212	.247	6.57	2.68
2-team total (4 Pawtucket)					4	4	3.64	28	1	0	1	42	33	22	17	7	15	34	—	—	—	7.29	3.21
Cabrera, Fernando	R-R	6-4	225	11-16-81	4	5	4.10	57	0	0	22	66	70	34	31	9	35	60	.264	.313	.227	7.94	4.63
Carpenter, Drew	R-R	6-3	230	5-18-85	0	0	1.93	5	0	0	0	5	5	1	1	0	6	.263	.429	.167	11.57	0.00
Carrasco, D.J.	R-R	6-4	215	4-12-77	0	0	3.00	2	0	0	0	3	2	1	1	0	1	.182	.000	.286	3.00	0.00
2-team total (5 Gwinnett)					1	0	9.00	7	0	0	0	8	12	8	8	1	5	4	—	—	—	4.50	5.63
Carson, Robert	L-L	6-4	240	1-23-89	0	0	1.72	10	0	0	1	16	16	4	3	1	6	15	.276	.263	.282	8.62	3.45
Cohoon, Mark	L-L	6-2	195	9-15-87	0	1	14.63	2	2	0	0	8	16	13	13	2	3	4	.400	.385	.429	4.50	3.38
Edgin, Josh	L-L	6-1	225	12-17-86	3	2	3.89	35	0	0	1	37	34	19	16	0	18	40	.241	.220	.256	9.73	4.38
Egbert, Jack	L-R	6-3	220	5-12-83	3	4	5.40	27	1	0	0	40	47	30	24	4	9	25	.288	.326	.266	6.08	2.03
Familia, Jeurys	R-R	6-4	230	10-10-89	9	9	4.73	28	28	1	0	137	145	84	72	8	73	128	.267	.263	.271	8.41	4.80
Germen, Gonzalez	R-R	6-1	175	9-23-87	1	0	5.14	1	1	0	0	7	7	4	4	0	2	3	.259	.200	.333	3.86	2.57
Hampson, Justin	L-L	6-1	205	5-24-80	4	3	2.33	51	0	0	4	66	63	20	17	5	22	59	.251	.289	.227	8.09	3.02
Harvey, Matt	R-R	6-4	230	3-27-89	7	5	3.68	20	20	0	0	110	97	46	45	9	48	112	.233	.225	.240	9.16	3.93
Hefner, Jeremy	R-R	6-4	215	3-11-86	5	2	2.77	10	9	0	0	62	55	25	19	4	10	37	.239	.222	.257	5.40	1.46
Herrera, Danny Ray	L-L	5-6	165	10-21-84	0	0	1.50	3	0	0	0	1	6	3	1	1	1	3	.150	.200	.133	7.50	4.50
Holt, Brad	R-R	6-4	194	10-13-86	0	0	10.13	6	0	0	1	5	11	6	6	0	4	3	.407	.375	.421	5.06	6.75
James, Chuck	L-L	6-0	190	11-9-81	0	1	4.57	18	0	0	0	22	19	11	11	2	9	22	.232	.346	.179	9.14	3.74

Name	B-T	HT	WT	DOB	W	L	ERA	G	GS	CG	SV	IP	H	R	ER	HR	BB	SO	AVG	vLH	vRH	K/9	BB/9
McHugh, Collin	R-R	6-2	195	6-19-87	2	4	3.42	13	13	0	0	74	60	32	28	8	29	70	.216	.236	.199	8.55	3.54
Mejia, Jenrry	R-R	6-0	205	10-11-89	3	4	3.54	26	10	0	0	74	75	38	29	4	24	39	.263	.248	.275	4.76	2.93
Nitkowski, C.J.	L-L	6-3	210	3-9-73	0	2	7.53	15	0	0	1	14	24	15	12	1	8	13	.375	.276	.457	8.16	5.02
Olson, Garrett	R-L	6-1	205	10-18-83	4	7	4.63	34	21	0	0	122	133	70	63	11	53	107	.277	.274	.278	7.87	3.90
Owen, Dylan	R-R	5-11	185	7-12-86	4	9	6.28	28	10	0	1	76	83	60	53	13	42	36	.283	.278	.286	4.26	4.97
Patterson, Scott	R-R	6-7	225	6-20-79	0	1	21.60	2	0	0	0	2	7	4	4	0	0	2	.636	.333	.750	10.80	0.00
Ramirez, Edgar	R-R	6-4	250	11-30-83	0	1	5.14	4	0	0	0	7	7	5	4	1	4	4	.241	.417	.118	5.14	5.14
Ramirez, Elvin	R-R	6-3	210	10-10-87	3	1	2.36	33	0	0	1	42	26	14	11	2	25	41	.177	.219	.145	8.79	5.36
Ramirez, Ramon	R-R	5-11	200	8-31-81	0	1	40.50	1	0	0	0	1	4	3	3	0	1	0	.800	.750	1.000	0.00	13.50
Rodriguez, Armando	R-R	6-3	250	1-28-88	0	0	2.08	1	1	0	0	4	3	1	1	0	2	2	.188	.333	.100	4.15	4.15
Schwinden, Chris	R-R	6-3	215	9-22-86	8	6	2.70	21	19	2	0	107	102	39	32	7	30	92	.249	.216	.279	7.76	2.53
3-team total (3 Columbus, 1 Scranton/W-B)					9	9	3.21	25	23	2	0	126	126	54	45	11	37	99	—	—	—	7.07	2.64
Stevens, Jeff	R-R	6-2	205	9-5-83	1	1	3.32	34	0	0	1	41	44	21	15	5	18	33	.277	.193	.324	7.30	3.98
Wheeler, Zack	R-R	6-4	185	5-30-90	2	2	3.27	6	6	1	0	33	23	13	12	2	16	31	.205	.135	.267	8.45	4.36
Young, Chris	R-R	6-10	260	5-25-79	0	0	0.00	1	1	0	0	6	2	0	0	0	3	2	.095	.000	.154	3.00	4.50

Fielding

Catcher	PCT	G	PO	A	E	DP	PB
Blaquiere	.943	11	78	4	5	0	0
Johnson	.986	45	332	28	5	2	4
May	.990	71	458	43	5	4	10
Nickeas	.969	22	172	16	6	2	1
Rottino	.950	3	19	0	1	0	0
Thole	1.000	1	5	0	0	0	0

First Base	PCT	G	PO	A	E	DP
Duda	1.000	2	14	1	0	1
Fisher	1.000	6	24	0	0	3
Loewen	.988	39	309	19	4	18
Lutz	.986	10	73	0	1	6
May	.926	3	24	1	2	2
Pascucci	.984	20	118	9	2	12
Satin	.995	79	609	42	3	53
Tuiasosopo	1.000	10	24	0	0	1

Second Base	PCT	G	PO	A	E	DP
Cedeno	1.000	2	3	5	0	1
Emaus	.972	59	95	148	7	34
Fisher	.950	5	6	13	1	0
Navarro	.900	6	4	5	1	0
Rodriguez	1.000	1	1	3	0	1
Satin	.981	36	62	96	3	17
Scales	.989	27	46	48	1	5
Tuiasosopo	.900	3	4	5	1	0
Turner	1.000	1	0	2	0	0
Valdespin	.943	22	34	49	5	10

Third Base	PCT	G	PO	A	E	DP
Emaus	.909	7	3	7	1	0
Fisher	.929	8	5	8	1	1
Lutz	.975	56	31	87	3	5
Navarro	.964	15	4	23	1	1
Satin	1.000	9	0	7	0	0
Scales	—	1	0	0	0	0
Tuiasosopo	.956	70	51	123	8	13

Shortstop	PCT	G	PO	A	E	DP
Cedeno	.923	5	8	16	2	5
Kazmar	.911	11	18	33	5	10
Navarro	.907	16	14	35	5	7
Quintanilla	.974	48	57	130	5	21
Rodriguez	.932	64	96	180	20	31
Scales	1.000	3	3	5	0	1
Tejada	1.000	6	5	13	0	3
Tuiasosopo	1.000	1	0	2	0	0
Turner	1.000	1	0	4	0	0
Valdespin	1.000	1	1	2	0	0

Outfield	PCT	G	PO	A	E	DP
Baxter	1.000	5	7	2	0	0
Bay	1.000	2	2	0	0	0
den Dekker	.990	76	185	9	2	2
Duda	1.000	22	36	2	0	0
Lewis	.975	106	193	6	5	0
Loewen	.905	19	37	1	4	0
Martin	.951	25	39	0	2	0
Nieuwenhuis	1.000	4	10	0	0	0
Pascucci	1.000	42	62	1	0	0
Reyes	.976	49	79	1	2	1
Rottino	1.000	33	74	3	0	1
Scales	1.000	1	1	0	0	0
Torres	1.000	2	3	0	0	0
Tuiasosopo	1.000	54	99	4	0	1
Valdespin	1.000	15	35	0	0	0
Wimberly	.976	16	40	0	1	0

BINGHAMTON METS

DOUBLE-A

EASTERN LEAGUE

Batting	B-T	HT	WT	DOB	AVG	vLH	vRH	G	AB	R	H	2B	3B	HR	RBI	BB	HBP	SH	SF	SO	SB	CS	SLG	OBP
Baxter, Mike	L-R	6-0	195	12-7-84	.300	.667	.143	3	10	1	3	0	0	0	1	1	1	0	1	2	0	0	.300	.385
Bonfe, Joe	R-R	6-4	220	12-28-87	.318	.389	.269	19	44	7	14	1	1	0	4	6	2	0	1	13	0	3	.386	.415
Campbell, Eric	R-R	6-3	220	4-9-87	.297	.356	.276	115	394	53	117	25	2	9	50	58	6	2	5	76	10	5	.439	.391
Centeno, Juan	L-R	5-9	172	11-16-89	.285	.307	.277	79	281	29	80	12	2	0	35	23	1	4	4	43	1	1	.342	.337
den Dekker, Matt	L-L	6-1	205	8-10-87	.340	.333	.343	58	238	47	81	21	4	8	29	20	5	1	4	64	10	7	.563	.397
Dykstra, Allan	L-R	6-5	215	5-21-87	.262	.333	.227	62	191	35	50	9	0	7	25	51	4	0	2	65	1	0	.419	.423
Fernandez, Rafael	L-L	6-1	171	8-3-88	.100	.000	.143	4	10	2	1	0	0	0	1	1	1	0	1	5	0	0	.100	.231
Fisher, Michael	B-R	6-2	188	3-22-85	.238	.286	.214	6	21	3	5	0	0	1	2	2	0	0	0	5	0	1	.381	.304
Flores, Wilmer	R-R	6-3	190	8-6-91	.311	.324	.305	66	251	37	78	18	2	8	33	20	1	1	2	30	0	0	.494	.361
Gronauer, Kai	R-R	6-1	215	11-28-86	.212	.333	.155	25	85	6	18	3	0	1	6	7	1	0	0	20	2	0	.282	.280
Havens, Reese	L-R	6-1	195	10-20-86	.215	.247	.203	94	325	41	70	14	0	10	39	58	4	2	1	113	1	1	.351	.340
Kazmar, Sean	R-R	5-9	180	8-5-84	.236	.276	.219	57	195	23	46	9	2	4	21	13	3	1	1	27	0	2	.364	.292
Lagares, Juan	R-R	6-1	175	3-17-89	.283	.331	.265	130	499	69	141	29	6	4	48	37	4	2	5	93	21	10	.389	.334
Marte, Jefry	R-R	6-1	187	6-21-91	.251	.336	.220	129	462	61	116	20	3	9	58	43	6	0	2	76	9	5	.366	.322
Martin, Dustin	L-L	6-2	215	4-4-84	.286	.310	.279	72	241	41	69	12	5	6	41	36	1	2	0	58	9	6	.452	.381
Navarro, Oswaldo	R-R	6-0	200	10-2-84	.293	.304	.288	22	75	10	22	2	0	1	9	12	2	0	2	19	0	1	.360	.396
Ozga, Travis	B-R	6-2	210	12-7-86	.173	.095	.186	49	139	17	24	4	0	4	19	15	0	2	0	30	1	0	.288	.253
Pena, Francisco	R-R	6-2	230	10-12-89	.198	.194	.200	40	126	14	25	7	0	3	17	16	2	1	0	25	1	0	.325	.299
Reyes, Raul	L-L	6-0	195	12-30-86	.253	.172	.268	51	178	26	45	5	1	6	28	17	1	2	1	46	1	1	.393	.320
Rodriguez, Josh	R-R	6-0	185	12-18-84	.290	.236	.308	57	214	30	62	14	3	5	29	28	1	1	1	48	5	3	.453	.373
Sandoval, Rylan	R-R	5-10	185	8-10-87	.247	.200	.271	25	73	9	18	4	3	2	16	5	2	0	0	24	1	1	.466	.313
Tovar, Wilfredo	R-R	5-10	180	8-11-91	.254	.271	.248	57	193	20	49	11	2	0	27	11	6	3	4	22	2	1	.332	.308
Zapata, Pedro	R-R	6-4	185	10-3-87	.213	.196	.219	93	334	35	71	8	6	2	21	18	3	2	1	107	15	7	.290	.258

Pitching	B-T	HT	WT	DOB	W	L	ERA	G	GS	CG	SV	IP	H	R	ER	HR	BB	SO	AVG	vLH	vRH	K/9	BB/9
Batista, Miguel	R-R	6-1	210	2-19-71	0	1	5.14	1	1	0	0	7	4	5	4	1	4	3	.182	.333	.077	3.86	5.14
Carpenter, Drew	R-R	6-3	230	5-18-85	0	0	0.00	5	0	0	3	5	4	0	0	0	2	10	.211	.286	.167	18.00	3.60
Carson, Robert	L-L	6-4	240	1-23-89	1	2	4.79	31	0	0	9	36	45	22	19	2	15	37	.300	.188	.331	9.34	3.79
Cohoon, Mark	L-L	6-2	195	9-15-87	8	11	3.62	23	23	2	0	147	147	66	59	12	30	83	.268	.258	.271	5.09	1.84
Edgin, Josh	L-L	6-1	225	12-17-86	0	0	1.42	6	0	0	2	6	5	1	1	1	2	5	.208	.250	.200	7.11	2.84
Francisco, Frank	R-R	6-2	250	9-11-79	0	0	3.86	5	0	0	1	5	6	2	2	0	1	4	.300	.273	.333	7.71	1.93
Fraser, Ryan	R-R	6-3	190	8-27-88	2	2	3.48	26	0	0	4	34	29	14	13	1	13	25	.228	.167	.274	6.68	3.48

	B-T	HT	WT	DOB	W	L	ERA	G	GS	CG	SV	IP	H	R	ER	HR	BB	SO	AVG	vLH	vRH		
Germen, Gonzalez	R-R	6-1	175	9-23-87	8	12	4.59	20	19	0	0	120	127	72	61	11	33	97	.272	.284	.263	7.30	2.48
Gorski, Darin	L-L	6-4	210	10-6-87	9	8	4.00	25	24	0	0	140	128	68	62	20	50	118	.244	.219	.251	7.60	3.22
Holt, Brad	R-R	6-4	194	10-13-86	2	1	3.40	39	0	0	1	48	43	21	18	3	28	42	.240	.208	.262	7.93	5.29
Kaplan, Jeff	R-R	6-0	190	7-9-85	3	0	3.12	19	0	0	1	26	35	9	9	1	8	24	.327	.353	.315	8.31	2.77
Kolarek, Adam	L-L	6-3	215	1-14-89	2	0	5.68	6	0	0	1	6	10	4	4	2	4	8	.385	.333	.412	11.37	5.68
Mazzoni, Cory	R-R	6-1	190	10-19-89	5	5	4.46	14	14	2	0	81	90	45	40	9	20	56	.281	.342	.230	6.25	2.23
McHugh, Collin	R-R	6-2	195	6-19-87	5	5	2.41	12	12	0	0	75	63	21	20	4	17	65	.228	.267	.205	7.83	2.05
Mejia, Jenrry	R-R	6-0	205	10-11-89	0	0	5.63	2	2	0	0	8	11	5	5	1	3	8	.344	.385	.316	9.00	3.38
Moore, Brandon	R-R	6-3	190	1-24-86	0	2	13.09	10	0	0	0	11	17	17	16	1	10	9	.370	.474	.296	7.36	8.18
Mulvey, Kevin	R-R	6-1	205	5-26-85	0	1	5.59	13	0	0	0	19	20	13	12	2	13	14	.270	.133	.364	6.52	6.05
Nitkowski, C.J.	L-L	6-3	210	3-9-73	0	0	0.00	6	0	0	0	5	1	0	0	0	4	8	.071	.143	.000	15.43	7.71
Peavey, Greg	R-R	6-2	185	7-11-88	8	8	5.06	25	25	2	0	144	169	91	81	18	37	84	.296	.288	.301	5.25	2.31
Ramirez, Edgar	R-R	6-4	250	11-30-83	1	1	4.46	28	0	0	0	42	39	23	21	4	13	26	.244	.267	.230	5.53	2.76
Ramirez, Elvin	R-R	6-3	210	10-10-87	0	1	1.38	8	0	0	1	13	7	2	2	0	7	16	.152	.250	.118	11.08	4.85
Rodriguez, Armando	R-R	6-3	250	1-28-88	2	3	3.22	34	3	0	1	73	58	29	26	13	21	77	.217	.255	.191	9.54	2.60
Rosario, Adrian	R-R	6-4	180	9-30-89	1	2	5.83	26	0	0	3	29	35	21	19	1	29	27	.307	.460	.188	8.28	8.90
Stevens, Jeff	R-R	6-2	205	9-5-83	0	0	7.71	6	0	0	0	9	11	8	8	0	9	9	.282	.214	.320	8.68	8.68
Turgeon, Erik	R-R	6-0	170	3-25-87	1	3	7.40	17	0	0	0	24	43	25	20	5	12	22	.384	.463	.338	8.14	4.44
2-team total (1 Altoona)					2	3	6.84	18	0	0	0	26	43	25	20	5	13	22	—	—		7.52	4.44
Wheeler, Zack	R-R	6-4	185	5-30-90	10	6	3.26	19	19	1	0	116	92	46	42	2	43	117	.225	.270	.188	9.08	3.34

Fielding

Catcher	PCT	G	PO	A	E	DP	PB
Centeno	.991	79	522	52	5	5	9
Gronauer	.990	25	188	16	2	1	1
Pena	.982	39	292	27	6	2	1

First Base	PCT	G	PO	A	E	DP
Bonfe	1.000	7	45	3	0	6
Campbell	.996	56	431	32	2	63
Dykstra	.984	41	287	23	5	23
Fisher	.944	3	17	0	1	2
Flores	.982	7	51	5	1	2
Marte	.971	5	32	2	1	4
Navarro	1.000	2	20	0	0	2
Ozga	.987	28	206	22	3	21

Second Base	PCT	G	PO	A	E	DP
Fisher	1.000	2	0	3	0	0

	PCT	G	PO	A	E	DP
Flores	.990	24	39	60	1	14
Havens	.974	79	152	182	9	34
Kazmar	1.000	7	11	19	0	1
Navarro	1.000	9	16	25	0	7
Rodriguez	.973	16	37	34	2	15
Sandoval	.927	10	18	20	3	6

Third Base	PCT	G	PO	A	E	DP
Bonfe	.875	2	3	4	1	0
Campbell	1.000	1	2	4	0	1
Flores	.964	26	14	39	2	1
Marte	.939	107	51	179	15	18
Navarro	.895	6	3	14	2	2
Rodriguez	1.000	5	6	11	0	3

Shortstop	PCT	G	PO	A	E	DP
Kazmar	.941	41	64	111	11	23

	PCT	G	PO	A	E	DP
Navarro	.875	5	3	11	2	1
Rodriguez	.949	35	44	86	7	19
Sandoval	.885	7	10	13	3	2
Tovar	.965	57	98	152	9	33

Outfield	PCT	G	PO	A	E	DP
Baxter	1.000	1	1	0	0	0
Bonfe	1.000	2	3	0	0	0
Campbell	1.000	45	79	5	0	0
den Dekker	.978	56	132	2	3	2
Fernandez	1.000	2	4	0	0	0
Kazmar	.909	4	10	0	1	0
Lagares	.995	125	353	17	2	4
Martin	.975	68	153	5	4	1
Ozga	1.000	1	4	0	0	0
Reyes	1.000	43	67	1	0	1
Zapata	1.000	85	141	5	0	1

ST. LUCIE METS

HIGH CLASS A

FLORIDA STATE LEAGUE

Batting	B-T	HT	WT	DOB	AVG	vLH	vRH	G	AB	R	H	2B	3B	HR	RBI	BB	HBP	SH	SF	SO	SB	CS	SLG	OBP
Baxter, Mike	L-R	6-0	195	12-7-84	.267	.000	.444	4	15	1	4	3	0	0	4	1	1	0	0	4	0	0	.467	.353
Bay, Jason	R-R	6-2	210	9-20-78	.133	.200	.100	5	15	0	2	0	0	0	1	4	0	0	1	6	1	0	.133	.300
Bonfe, Joe	R-R	6-4	220	12-28-87	.152	.182	.136	13	33	4	5	1	0	0	3	3	2	1	0	8	1	0	.182	.263
Ceciliani, Darrell	L-L	6-1	220	6-22-90	.329	.321	.333	23	85	19	28	6	1	1	10	10	1	0	1	13	2	0	.459	.402
Cedeno, Ronny	R-R	6-0	195	2-2-83	.000	—	.000	1	4	0	0	0	0	0	0	0	0	0	0	0	0	0	.000	.000
Clark, Jonathan	L-R	6-1	180	9-28-90	.231	.167	.286	6	13	1	3	0	0	0	1	2	0	0	0	5	1	0	.231	.333
Dykstra, Allan	L-R	6-5	215	5-21-87	.258	.333	.188	9	31	3	8	3	0	0	2	8	0	0	1	11	1	0	.355	.400
Fernandez, Rafael	L-L	6-1	171	8-3-88	.242	.231	.245	64	207	29	50	14	2	7	32	20	2	1	1	57	5	1	.430	.313
Flores, Wilmer	R-R	6-3	190	8-6-91	.289	.265	.302	64	242	31	70	12	0	10	42	18	3	1	8	30	3	2	.463	.336
Forsythe, Blake	R-R	6-2	220	7-31-89	.244	.248	.242	88	295	32	72	17	2	8	42	40	5	0	5	89	0	0	.397	.339
Gomez, Gilbert	R-R	6-3	190	3-8-92	.125	.000	.200	2	8	0	1	0	0	0	0	0	0	0	0	3	0	0	.125	.125
Gronauer, Kai	R-R	6-1	215	11-28-86	.205	.231	.194	15	44	6	9	3	0	1	7	3	0	0	1	8	1	0	.341	.250
Harris, Alonzo	R-R	5-11	165	11-16-89	.287	.353	.253	116	443	74	127	23	7	8	42	44	3	2	2	66	40	11	.424	.354
Loewen, Adam	L-L	6-6	235	4-9-84	.286	.200	.333	4	14	2	4	1	0	0	1	3	0	0	0	2	0	0	.357	.412
Lucas, Richard	R-R	6-1	205	11-24-88	.251	.267	.243	124	411	71	103	26	1	8	53	60	11	2	1	128	19	4	.377	.360
Lutz, Zach	R-R	6-1	220	6-3-86	.250	.200	.267	6	20	2	5	2	0	1	8	4	0	0	2	5	0	0	.500	.346
McQueen, ZeErika	R-R	6-0	175	6-29-88	.222	.313	.150	13	36	5	8	0	0	0	2	2	0	0	0	10	1	0	.222	.263
Muno, Danny	B-R	5-11	175	2-8-89	.280	.216	.308	81	289	36	81	16	2	6	39	50	3	6	4	53	19	3	.412	.387
Nieves, Luis	R-R	5-11	160	12-15-88	.133	.000	.182	5	15	2	2	1	0	0	2	2	0	1	0	2	1	0	.200	.235
Pena, Francisco	R-R	6-2	230	10-12-89	.254	.283	.236	41	142	19	36	10	1	4	22	11	0	1	1	29	0	0	.423	.305
Puello, Cesar	R-R	6-2	195	4-1-91	.260	.304	.241	66	227	36	59	17	4	4	21	7	16	2	0	58	19	2	.423	.328
Ratliff, Sean	L-L	6-3	185	2-24-87	.136	.000	.214	7	22	1	3	1	0	0	3	1	0	0	0	10	0	0	.182	.240
Rivera, T.J.	R-R	6-1	190	10-27-88	.306	.257	.326	64	255	31	78	15	3	1	29	14	2	4	1	38	7	2	.400	.346
Rodriguez, Aderlin	R-R	6-3	210	11-18-91	.242	.340	.198	42	153	19	37	5	0	8	24	8	2	0	0	30	1	0	.431	.288
Sandoval, Rylan	R-R	5-10	185	10-23-88	.228	.167	.258	23	92	10	21	3	0	2	6	5	1	1	0	22	0	0	.326	.276
Shields, Robbie	R-R	6-1	195	12-7-87	.232	.218	.240	105	370	40	86	19	1	5	35	38	5	5	2	70	8	4	.330	.311
Taijeron, Travis	R-R	6-2	200	1-20-89	.203	.200	.204	48	158	22	32	6	0	7	21	18	5	1	0	52	2	0	.373	.304
Tejada, Ruben	R-R	5-11	185	10-27-89	.111	.333	.000	2	9	1	1	1	0	0	0	0	0	0	0	2	0	0	.222	.111
Torres, Andres	B-R	5-10	195	1-26-78	.333	.000	.364	3	12	3	4	1	0	0	1	0	0	0	0	2	0	0	.417	.333
Torres, Juan	R-R	6-1	180	10-7-88	.193	.185	.196	26	83	9	16	3	0	1	10	4	1	1	1	12	0	0	.265	.236
Tovar, Wilfredo	R-R	5-10	160	8-11-91	.284	.311	.271	65	218	31	62	17	1	1	23	29	4	4	1	17	12	7	.385	.377
Vaughn, Cory	R-R	6-3	225	5-1-89	.243	.270	.231	126	456	73	111	25	3	23	69	65	12	0	2	114	21	4	.463	.351

Pitching

Pitching	B-T	HT	WT	DOB	W	L	ERA	G	GS	CG	SV	IP	H	R	ER	HR	BB	SO	AVG	vLH	vRH	K/9	BB/9
Allen, Kyle	R-R	6-3	195	2-12-90	2	0	4.18	23	3	0	0	56	58	33	26	5	12	39	.260	.264	.257	6.27	1.93
Almonte, Yohan	R-R	6-1	150	11-9-89	7	5	6.57	19	17	0	1	86	106	68	63	4	21	57	.303	.321	.281	5.94	2.19
Beato, Pedro	R-R	6-4	220	10-27-86	0	0	0.00	3	0	0	0	4	2	0	0	1	4	.154	.000	.250	9.00	2.25
Bennett, Hamilton	R-L	6-1	180	6-26-88	7	2	2.55	41	0	0	0	60	51	29	17	3	17	54	.227	.159	.270	8.10	2.55
Carrasco, D.J.	R-R	6-4	215	4-12-77	1	0	0.00	4	2	0	0	6	1	0	0	1	4	.056	.000	.111	6.00	1.50
Church, John	R-R	6-2	235	11-4-86	2	2	2.97	37	0	0	7	58	52	25	19	3	27	53	.241	.280	.202	8.27	4.21
Cuan, Angel	L-L	5-11	150	5-29-89	6	10	4.01	23	21	0	0	114	123	57	51	10	29	83	.273	.289	.263	6.53	2.28
deGrom, Jake	L-R	6-4	185	6-19-88	3	0	2.08	4	4	0	0	22	14	5	5	1	6	18	.177	.176	.179	7.48	2.49
Fontanez, Randy	R-R	6-1	205	5-18-89	0	0	0.00	1	0	0	0	3	1	0	0	0	2	.125	.250	.000	6.00	0.00
Fraser, Ryan	R-R	6-3	190	8-27-88	3	2	2.08	19	0	0	2	30	30	7	7	1	7	18	.263	.291	.237	5.34	2.08
Fuller, Jim	L-L	5-10	180	6-1-87	0	0	1.93	3	0	0	0	5	7	1	1	0	2	5	.350	.500	.250	9.64	3.86
Germen, Gonzalez	R-R	6-1	175	9-23-87	3	0	3.04	5	4	0	0	27	25	10	9	3	8	21	.255	.306	.167	7.09	2.70
Goeddel, Erik	R-R	6-3	185	12-20-88	5	6	3.41	22	20	0	0	108	110	51	41	4	43	98	.263	.255	.273	8.14	3.57
Huchingson, Chase	L-L	6-5	197	4-14-89	8	7	4.10	24	22	0	0	121	120	64	55	6	55	102	.260	.279	.252	7.61	4.10
Kaplan, Jeff	R-R	6-0	190	7-9-85	2	0	4.50	6	0	0	2	10	12	5	5	0	2	6	.316	.292	.357	5.40	1.80
Kolarek, Adam	L-L	6-3	215	1-14-89	1	3	2.37	44	0	0	18	57	49	18	15	3	21	70	.234	.197	.256	11.05	3.32
Leathersich, Jack	R-L	5-11	205	7-14-90	2	5	4.13	26	0	0	1	48	41	25	22	3	24	76	.224	.258	.205	14.25	4.50
Mazzoni, Cory	R-R	6-1	190	10-19-89	5	1	3.25	12	12	0	0	64	64	28	23	3	16	48	.264	.268	.261	6.79	2.26
Mejia, Jenrry	R-R	6-0	205	10-11-89	1	0	2.45	2	2	0	0	11	7	3	3	1	2	8	.184	.208	.143	6.55	1.64
Montero, Rafael	R-R	6-0	170	10-17-90	5	2	2.13	8	8	1	0	51	35	13	12	2	11	56	.196	.248	.128	9.95	1.95
Pill, Tyler	R-R	6-1	185	5-29-90	6	1	2.05	11	10	0	0	61	53	17	14	2	14	51	.240	.217	.267	7.48	2.05
Ramirez, Ramon	R-R	5-11	200	8-31-81	0	0	13.50	2	1	0	0	2	5	3	3	0	0	6	.455	.500	.333	0.00	0.00
Rosario, Adrian	R-R	6-4	180	9-30-89	3	0	0.94	23	0	0	11	29	10	4	3	1	11	34	.104	.078	.133	10.67	3.45
Verrett, Logan	R-R	6-2	180	6-19-90	2	0	2.09	6	6	1	0	39	30	11	9	4	4	26	.205	.237	.171	6.05	0.93
Walters, Jeff	R-R	6-3	170	11-6-87	1	3	3.76	19	0	0	6	26	27	13	11	1	8	19	.273	.295	.255	6.49	2.73
Whitenton, Taylor	R-R	6-3	190	2-20-88	7	3	2.24	42	0	0	7	56	42	15	14	0	34	68	.208	.180	.235	10.86	5.43
Young, Chris	R-R	6-10	260	5-25-79	1	0	3.18	3	3	0	0	17	17	6	6	1	2	7	.266	.317	.174	3.71	1.06

Fielding

Catcher	PCT	G	PO	A	E	DP	PB
Forsythe	.988	81	576	67	8	3	9
Gronauer	.983	15	109	9	2	1	0
Pena	.993	36	252	33	2	2	3
Torres	.974	10	69	5	2	0	0

First Base	PCT	G	PO	A	E	DP
Bonfe	1.000	3	22	4	0	0
Dykstra	.982	6	49	5	1	2
Loewen	1.000	1	5	1	0	0
Lucas	.982	116	898	83	18	72
Rodriguez	.957	3	20	2	1	1
Torres	1.000	9	69	5	0	7

Second Base	PCT	G	PO	A	E	DP
Flores	1.000	3	5	12	0	1
Harris	—	2	0	0	0	0
Muno	.961	55	78	118	8	25
Nieves	.944	5	8	9	1	5
Rivera	1.000	11	16	26	0	4

Third Base	PCT	G	PO	A	E	DP
Sandoval	.951	15	22	36	3	6
Shields	.969	44	69	116	6	18
Tovar	1.000	2	4	8	0	1
Bonfe	—	1	0	0	0	0
Flores	.941	61	42	85	8	5
Lucas	.957	8	5	17	1	1
Lutz	1.000	5	8	7	0	3
Rodriguez	.870	37	31	49	12	7
Shields	.929	26	12	40	4	1

Shortstop	PCT	G	PO	A	E	DP
Cedeno	1.000	1	1	2	0	1
Muno	.937	18	33	41	5	8
Rivera	.933	51	58	123	13	21
Sandoval	.882	4	6	9	2	1
Shields	—	1	0	0	0	0
Tejada	1.000	2	4	1	0	0
Tovar	.964	61	85	157	9	32

Outfield	PCT	G	PO	A	E	DP
Bay	1.000	2	3	0	0	0
Bonfe	1.000	6	8	0	0	0
Ceciliani	1.000	17	34	1	0	0
Clark	1.000	4	4	0	0	0
Fernandez	1.000	48	82	3	0	0
Forsythe	—	1	0	0	0	0
Gomez	1.000	1	1	0	0	0
Harris	.985	103	251	7	4	0
Loewen	1.000	3	6	0	0	0
McQueen	1.000	11	19	1	0	0
Puello	.986	61	138	5	2	1
Ratliff	.833	6	5	0	1	0
Sandoval	1.000	2	2	0	0	0
Shields	—	1	0	0	0	0
Taijeron	.986	41	68	1	1	0
Torres	1.000	3	8	0	0	0
Vaughn	.977	114	246	9	6	1

SAVANNAH SAND GNATS

SOUTH ATLANTIC LEAGUE

LOW CLASS A

Batting

Batting	B-T	HT	WT	DOB	AVG	vLH	vRH	G	AB	R	H	2B	3B	HR	RBI	BB	HBP	SH	SF	SO	SB	CS	SLG	OBP
Brown, Brandon	R-R	6-1	180	7-28-87	.222	.204	.229	91	329	47	73	18	2	5	34	34	5	4	4	81	12	8	.334	.301
Carrillo, Xorge	R-R	6-1	220	4-12-89	.154	.211	.100	11	39	2	6	0	1	0	4	2	0	0	0	8	0	0	.231	.195
Cordero, Albert	R-R	5-11	175	1-14-90	.194	.243	.176	76	252	21	49	13	0	2	22	28	2	2	4	43	0	2	.270	.276
De La Cruz, Yucarybert	R-R	6-0	160	10-23-90	.195	.177	.203	54	200	29	39	4	1	3	19	16	1	2	1	46	8	3	.270	.257
Frenzel, Cole	L-R	6-2	208	3-13-90	.204	.160	.223	47	162	18	33	11	0	3	11	15	4	0	1	31	1	0	.327	.286
Gomez, Gilbert	R-R	6-3	190	3-8-92	.256	.266	.252	79	285	39	73	14	3	2	24	48	1	2	0	68	8	8	.347	.365
Harrison, Brian	R-R	6-2	180	12-15-88	.241	.301	.219	113	423	54	102	27	1	5	61	40	6	0	4	72	5	0	.345	.313
Honeck, Sam	L-L	6-2	210	6-19-87	.133	.000	.154	5	15	1	2	1	0	0	4	0	0	0	0	5	0	0	.200	.316
Lawley, Dustin	R-R	6-1	195	4-11-89	.261	.294	.249	129	482	77	126	35	3	14	66	50	5	0	6	122	14	4	.434	.333
Maron, Cam	L-R	6-1	175	1-20-91	.300	.258	.315	93	343	48	103	18	2	5	47	53	8	2	3	73	2	1	.408	.403
McQueen, ZeErika	R-R	6-0	175	6-29-88	.105	.000	.125	7	19	0	2	1	0	0	1	1	1	0	0	7	0	1	.158	.190
Nieves, Luis	R-R	5-11	180	7-30-88	.281	.400	.155	38	135	15	27	3	1	0	15	9	0	4	0	18	10	0	.237	.250
Pron, Greg	R-R	6-6	195	1-3-89	.240	.263	.230	112	396	38	95	21	6	2	44	27	5	2	6	112	16	0	.338	.293
Pugh, Tillman	R-R	6-0	190	2-19-89	.085	.125	.070	17	59	6	5	0	0	1	2	5	0	1	0	25	4	0	.136	.156
2-team total (9 Kannapolis)					.143	—		26	91	12	13	2	0	1	2	7	0	2	0	37	7	0	.198	.204
Reynolds, Matt	R-R	6-1	200	12-3-90	.259	.271	.253	42	158	18	41	8	0	3	13	12	7	0	2	26	5	1	.367	.335
Rivera, T.J.	R-R	6-1	190	10-27-88	.333	.293	.345	64	261	42	87	14	1	8	37	26	3	3	3	33	4	3	.487	.396
Rodriguez, Aderlin	R-R	6-3	210	11-18-91	.274	.130	.320	83	318	41	87	21	1	16	59	29	2	1	2	71	1	0	.497	.336
Taijeron, Travis	R-R	6-3	210	12-15-88	.291	.321	.282	64	230	46	67	17	3	12	44	37	7	0	3	70	4	1	.548	.401
Thurber, Charley	L-L	6-4	220	12-28-89	.223	.190	.233	99	349	29	78	15	5	3	39	37	3	1	1	109	4	3	.321	.303
Tijerina, Ismael	R-R	6-0	165	8-19-89	.137	.167	.128	19	51	4	7	1	0	0	3	6	0	3	0	10	0	1	.157	.313
Torres, Juan	R-R	6-1	180	10-7-88	.000	—	.000	1	2	0	0	0	0	0	0	0	0	0	0	0	0	0	.000	.000

Pitching	B-T	HT	WT	DOB	W	L	ERA	G	GS	CG	SV	IP	H	R	ER	HR	BB	SO	AVG	vLH	vRH	K/9	BB/9
Almonte, Yohan	R-R	6-1	150	11-9-89	0	3	9.45	3	3	0	0	13	17	14	14	5	8	7	.304	.167	.406	4.73	5.40
Bradford, Chase	R-R	6-1	185	8-5-89	4	5	2.47	37	0	0	3	51	43	21	14	3	14	41	.224	.303	.172	7.24	2.47
Camarena, Marcos	R-R	6-3	202	9-8-90	7	6	2.92	30	11	0	0	105	93	44	34	9	16	72	.237	.210	.252	6.19	1.38
Chism, T.J.	L-L	5-10	190	8-9-88	4	2	2.34	45	0	0	19	50	44	14	13	1	13	42	.235	.279	.214	7.56	2.34
deGrom, Jake	L-R	6-4	185	6-19-88	6	3	2.51	15	15	0	0	90	77	33	25	3	14	78	.225	.248	.211	7.83	1.41
Diaz, Miller	R-R	6-1	209	6-22-92	0	1	5.79	1	1	0	0	5	7	6	3	0	1	8	.333	.286	.357	15.43	1.93
Fontanez, Randy	R-R	6-1	205	5-18-89	3	4	4.90	28	1	0	0	61	70	36	33	2	17	57	.285	.257	.303	8.46	2.52
Fuller, Jim	L-L	5-10	180	6-1-87	3	5	6.15	11	10	0	0	41	41	30	28	3	14	39	.255	.255	.254	8.56	3.07
Fulmer, Michael	R-R	6-3	200	3-15-93	7	6	2.74	21	21	1	0	108	92	37	33	6	38	101	.227	.250	.211	8.39	3.16
Gant, John	R-R	6-3	175	8-6-92	0	1	10.38	1	1	0	0	4	10	5	5	1	0	5	.455	.500	.429	10.38	0.00
Gould, Jeremy	R-L	6-4	205	6-6-88	0	0	6.35	4	0	0	0	6	5	6	4	0	3	1	.263	.000	.357	1.59	4.76
Hansen, Craig	R-R	6-6	230	11-15-83	0	0	0.00	2	0	0	0	2	0	0	0	0	2	1	.000	.000	.000	4.50	9.00
Leathersich, Jack	R-L	5-11	205	7-14-90	0	1	0.75	12	0	0	1	24	10	4	2	0	8	37	.132	.300	.071	13.88	3.00
Montero, Rafael	R-R	6-0	170	10-17-90	6	3	2.52	12	12	0	0	71	61	24	20	4	8	54	.223	.250	.205	6.81	1.01
Morel, Estarlin	R-R	6-0	185	10-2-89	1	1	2.55	26	0	0	2	35	31	10	10	1	14	40	.235	.229	.238	10.19	3.57
Panteliodis, Alex	L-L	6-2	235	7-7-90	5	8	3.64	22	22	0	0	109	123	53	44	6	33	86	.288	.268	.297	7.12	2.73
Pill, Tyler	R-R	6-1	185	5-29-90	3	4	2.61	9	9	0	0	52	56	17	15	3	8	54	.279	.305	.261	9.41	1.39
Sage, Brandon	L-L	6-2	210	10-3-86	1	1	2.76	10	0	0	0	16	16	7	5	0	8	22	.254	.174	.300	12.12	4.41
Seng, Tyson	L-R	6-1	180	8-5-93	0	0	6.00	6	0	0	0	9	15	7	6	0	3	7	.357	.429	.321	7.00	3.00
Tapia, Domingo	R-R	6-4	186	12-16-91	6	5	3.98	20	19	0	0	109	92	55	48	2	32	101	.227	.259	.204	8.37	2.65
Vazquez, Carlos	L-L	5-11	180	9-3-91	6	2	2.96	41	0	0	2	79	59	29	26	4	26	75	.208	.202	.210	8.54	2.96
Verrett, Logan	R-R	6-2	180	6-19-90	3	2	3.06	11	11	1	0	65	57	32	22	7	9	67	.228	.233	.225	9.32	1.25
Walters, Jeff	R-R	6-3	170	11-6-87	3	2	0.95	17	0	0	4	28	20	7	3	0	4	30	.198	.237	.175	9.53	1.27
West, Jared	R-R	6-1	180	7-30-88	1	2	4.99	39	0	0	1	61	69	35	34	2	36	48	.299	.286	.307	7.04	5.28

Fielding

Catcher

Catcher	PCT	G	PO	A	E	DP	PB
Carrillo	.974	8	70	6	2	0	2
Cordero	.988	66	545	51	7	3	4
Maron	.988	62	459	20	6	3	4

De La Cruz	.957	27	39	73	5	12
Nieves	1.000	3	2	5	0	0
Rivera	.943	33	43	72	7	9
Tijerina	1.000	3	5	5	0	0

Reynolds	.960	37	56	110	7	24
Rivera	.945	26	30	73	6	8
Tijerina	.931	12	17	37	4	9

First Base

First Base	PCT	G	PO	A	E	DP
Cordero	1.000	1	1	0	0	0
Frenzel	.991	42	321	22	3	23
Harrison	.988	85	735	33	9	57
Honeck	1.000	4	27	3	0	1
Rodriguez	.984	7	59	3	1	1
Torres	1.000	1	2	0	0	0

Third Base

Third Base	PCT	G	PO	A	E	DP
Brown	.889	10	7	9	2	1
Harrison	.927	15	10	28	3	0
Lawley	.952	44	32	87	6	3
Rodriguez	.910	70	48	134	18	8
Tijerina	.778	4	3	4	2	0

Outfield

Outfield	PCT	G	PO	A	E	DP
Gomez	.944	75	149	3	9	0
Lawley	.985	77	124	6	2	0
McQueen	1.000	6	8	0	0	0
Pron	.979	97	178	8	4	2
Pugh	.977	15	43	0	1	0
Taijeron	.977	50	124	3	3	1
Thurber	.985	92	187	4	3	1

Second Base

Second Base	PCT	G	PO	A	E	DP
Brown	.959	73	118	164	12	42

Shortstop

Shortstop	PCT	G	PO	A	E	DP
De La Cruz	.911	26	33	59	9	12
Nieves	.973	35	45	100	4	17

BROOKLYN CYCLONES   SHORT-SEASON

NEW YORK-PENN LEAGUE

Batting	B-T	HT	WT	DOB	AVG	vLH	vRH	G	AB	R	H	2B	3B	HR	RBI	BB	HBP	SH	SF	SO	SB	CS	SLG	OBP
Boyd, Jayce	R-R	6-3	185	12-30-90	.239	.213	.250	54	201	18	48	9	1	5	19	25	0	0	2	30	1	3	.368	.320
Cecchini, Gavin	R-R	6-1	180	12-22-93	.000	.000	.000	5	5	2	0	0	0	0	0	1	0	0	0	1	0	0	.000	.167
Clark, Jonathan	L-R	6-1	180	9-28-90	.209	.250	.200	19	43	8	9	2	0	2	14	0	0	1	14	5	1	.256	.397
Concepcion, Julio	R-R	6-4	194	9-5-89	.211	.313	.171	17	57	5	12	2	0	1	3	3	1	0	0	16	1	0	.298	.262
de la Cruz, Maikis	R-R	5-11	174	9-6-90	.217	.200	.231	9	23	5	5	3	1	0	2	4	1	1	0	4	0	0	.435	.357
Evans, Phillip	R-R	5-10	190	9-16-92	.252	.281	.237	73	294	32	74	8	1	5	29	31	3	0	1	48	2	0	.337	.328
Frenzel, Cole	L-R	6-2	208	3-13-90	.342	.421	.315	19	73	11	25	4	2	1	13	7	2	0	1	11	0	0	.493	.410
Gamboa, Juan Carlos	L-R	5-7	152	4-18-91	.186	.258	.165	39	140	11	26	3	0	1	5	21	1	3	1	30	2	4	.229	.294
Glenn, Jeff	R-R	6-3	185	9-22-91	.227	.219	.232	27	88	9	20	3	0	1	5	15	1	0	0	26	0	0	.295	.346
Nimmo, Brandon	L-R	6-3	185	3-27-93	.248	.191	.279	69	266	41	66	20	2	6	40	46	7	1	1	78	1	5	.406	.372
Pina, Eudy	R-R	6-3	188	4-12-91	.261	.313	.238	61	207	23	54	13	2	5	27	21	2	0	1	55	10	2	.415	.333
Plawecki, Kevin	R-R	6-2	205	2-26-91	.250	.305	.216	61	216	26	54	8	0	7	25	28	8	0	3	24	0	0	.384	.345
Ponce, Dimas	R-R	5-11	140	5-22-92	.200	.206	.197	64	215	23	43	8	1	1	21	18	2	4	5	47	1	0	.260	.263
Reynolds, Jeff	R-R	5-10	175	7-28-89	.232	.250	.222	24	69	15	16	0	0	2	6	11	2	0	1	9	0	0	.319	.349
Rivero, Jorge	B-R	6-0	183	1-6-89	.152	.091	.182	11	33	3	5	2	0	0	2	3	0	1	0	8	0	0	.212	.222
Rodriguez, Richie	R-R	5-9	170	2-15-90	.123	.156	.098	30	106	10	13	3	0	0	6	3	2	1	0	22	0	0	.151	.203
Rohan, Eddie	R-R	6-0	205	8-15-88	.100	.250	.000	6	10	1	1	0	0	0	1	0	0	0	0	4	0	0	.100	.308
Sabol, Stefan	R-R	6-0	200	2-2-92	.241	.277	.226	60	220	25	53	17	1	5	21	30	4	0	0	58	0	1	.395	.343
Sanchez, Alex	R-R	6-3	200	11-28-90	.261	.276	.254	50	184	11	48	9	0	2	15	11	4	0	1	27	0	0	.342	.315
Zapata, Nelfi	R-R	6-0	203	12-13-90	.137	.103	.151	29	102	10	14	2	0	2	8	15	1	0	1	27	0	0	.216	.252

Pitching	B-T	HT	WT	DOB	W	L	ERA	G	GS	CG	SV	IP	H	R	ER	HR	BB	SO	AVG	vLH	vRH	K/9	BB/9
Bowman, Matt	R-R	6-0	165	5-31-91	2	2	2.45	12	1	0	3	29	26	9	8	1	2	30	.239	.229	.246	9.20	0.61
Cessa, Luis	R-R	6-3	190	4-25-92	5	4	2.49	13	13	0	0	72	64	21	20	4	13	44	.241	.257	.229	5.47	1.62
Frias, Darwin	R-R	6-0	192	2-18-92	2	2	5.14	6	0	0	0	7	9	9	4	0	6	5	.310	.375	.286	6.43	7.71
Gould, Jeremy	R-L	6-4	205	6-6-88	0	0	0.00	1	0	0	1	1	0	0	0	0	3	0	.000	.000	.000	27.00	0.00
Hansen, Craig	R-R	6-6	230	11-15-83	0	1	11.25	5	0	0	0	4	5	6	5	0	5	3	.357	.286	.429	6.75	11.25
Hilario, Julian	R-R	6-1	190	8-17-90	4	4	3.23	12	10	0	0	56	62	25	20	1	20	45	.279	.292	.271	7.28	3.23
Koch, Matt	L-R	6-3	185	11-2-90	0	2	5.01	13	2	0	0	23	25	13	13	1	7	19	.278	.231	.314	7.33	2.70
Lara, Rainy	R-R	6-4	180	3-14-91	8	3	2.91	12	12	0	0	68	53	23	22	6	12	77	.211	.254	.173	10.19	1.59

Name	B-T	HT	WT	DOB	W	L	ERA	G	GS	CG	SV	IP	H	R	ER	HR	BB	SO	AVG	vLH	vRH	K/9	BB/9
Mateo, Luis	R-R	6-3	185	3-22-90	4	5	2.45	12	12	0	0	73	57	22	20	2	9	85	.210	.263	.189	10.43	1.10
Mincone, John	L-L	6-1	215	7-23-89	2	0	1.82	20	0	0	6	30	19	6	6	1	6	29	.183	.119	.226	8.80	1.82
Peterson, Tim	R-R	6-1	190	2-22-91	1	1	6.26	15	0	0	0	23	28	17	16	5	5	23	.292	.317	.273	9.00	1.96
Robles, Hansel	R-R	5-11	185	8-13-90	6	1	1.11	12	12	0	0	73	47	14	9	0	10	66	.184	.194	.178	8.17	1.24
Ruff, Rich	R-R	6-3	215	12-14-88	0	0	13.50	2	0	0	0	1	1	2	2	0	3	0	.200	.000	.333	0.00	20.25
Santana, Johan	L-L	6-0	210	3-13-79	0	0	0.00	1	1	0	0	3	1	0	0	0	1	3	.100	1.000	.000	9.00	3.00
Sewald, Paul	R-R	6-2	190	5-26-90	0	2	1.88	16	0	0	4	29	26	7	6	2	2	35	.236	.235	.237	10.99	0.63
Taylor, Logan	R-R	6-5	205	12-13-91	2	0	0.93	13	0	0	0	19	11	3	2	0	2	19	.159	.300	.102	8.84	0.93
Urbina, Juan	L-L	6-2	170	5-31-93	0	0	3.60	3	0	0	0	5	4	2	2	0	3	5	.222	.000	.286	9.00	5.40
Vanderheiden, Tyler	R-R	6-2	174	6-27-90	2	0	0.82	25	0	0	12	22	20	4	2	0	10	22	.235	.242	.231	9.00	4.09
Wheeler, Beck	R-R	6-3	215	12-13-88	1	1	5.14	25	0	0	0	28	19	17	16	3	13	37	.188	.140	.224	11.89	4.18
Wynn, David	B-L	5-10	168	10-16-89	1	1	1.44	21	0	0	1	25	12	7	4	1	13	21	.145	.148	.143	7.56	4.68
Yanez, Ernesto	R-R	6-0	162	1-22-90	1	0	2.04	13	0	0	0	18	15	8	4	2	6	15	.224	.265	.182	7.64	3.06
Ynoa, Gabriel	R-R	6-2	158	5-26-93	5	2	2.23	13	13	0	0	77	61	25	19	1	10	64	.213	.264	.176	7.51	1.17

Fielding

Catcher	PCT	G	PO	A	E	DP	PB
Glenn	.987	19	145	11	2	0	2
Plawecki	.988	36	306	28	4	3	5
Rohan	1.000	2	3	0	0	0	
Zapata	.990	22	188	15	2	3	4

First Base	PCT	G	PO	A	E	DP
Boyd	.994	50	455	34	3	29
Frenzel	.993	16	135	5	1	9
Plawecki	1.000	1	1	0	0	0
Sanchez	.981	11	96	5	2	5

Second Base	PCT	G	PO	A	E	DP
Gamboa	.981	37	62	94	3	19
Ponce	1.000	1	1	3	0	0
Reynolds	.943	14	13	20	2	3
Rodriguez	.958	28	35	57	4	12

Third Base	PCT	G	PO	A	E	DP
Ponce	.967	63	35	110	5	7
Reynolds	.824	10	2	12	3	0
Sanchez	.759	14	3	19	7	2

Shortstop	PCT	G	PO	A	E	DP
Cecchini	1.000	2	4	6	0	1

	PCT	G	PO	A	E	DP
Evans	.963	73	115	223	13	30
Gamboa	1.000	2	5	4	0	0

Outfield	PCT	G	PO	A	E	DP
Clark	.939	17	30	1	2	0
Concepcion	.944	15	17	0	1	0
de la Cruz	.933	9	13	1	1	0
Nimmo	.994	69	152	5	1	2
Pina	.974	60	102	9	3	2
Reynolds	1.000	1	1	0	0	0
Rivero	1.000	8	10	0	0	0
Sabol	.978	57	83	4	2	1

KINGSPORT METS
APPALACHIAN LEAGUE

ROOKIE

Batting	B-T	HT	WT	DOB	AVG	vLH	vRH	G	AB	R	H	2B	3B	HR	RBI	BB	HBP	SH	SF	SO	SB	CS	SLG	OBP
Bernal, Michael	R-R	6-1	195	12-27-91	.294	.333	.286	5	17	6	5	2	0	1	6	5	0	0	0	9	0	1	.588	.455
Carpenter, Tyler	R-R	5-10	190	7-7-88	.000	—	.000	2	1	0	0	0	0	0	0	0	0	0	0	1	0	0	.000	.000
Cecchini, Gavin	R-R	6-1	180	12-22-93	.246	.233	.252	53	191	21	47	9	2	1	22	18	1	0	2	43	5	4	.330	.311
Chavez, Anthony	R-R	6-2	185	11-8-92	.233	.178	.254	56	159	27	37	6	2	1	20	15	2	0	4	52	12	4	.314	.300
Concepcion, Julio	R-R	6-4	194	9-5-89	.182	.000	.211	8	22	3	4	1	0	2	5	1	0	0	9	0	0	.500	.217
de la Cruz, Maikis	R-R	5-11	174	9-6-90	.274	.197	.302	63	223	24	61	12	5	1	30	14	3	1	6	48	9	5	.386	.317
De Leon, Jeyckol	R-R	6-2	185	7-25-90	.232	.229	.233	52	168	16	39	10	0	3	16	10	2	1	1	54	0	0	.345	.282
Diehl, Jeff	R-R	6-4	195	9-30-93	.251	.211	.272	49	171	18	43	12	4	2	21	9	1	0	1	64	0	1	.404	.291
Kaupe, Branden	B-R	5-7	175	4-10-94	.173	.162	.177	50	133	23	23	1	1	0	3	18	1	0	1	44	3	3	.195	.358
Leroux, Jon	R-R	6-1	205	9-19-90	.198	.185	.202	40	116	19	23	9	0	4	13	12	4	0	2	34	1	1	.379	.291
Machillanada, Alex	R-R	5-11	177	10-1-91	.217	.313	.182	23	60	4	13	1	0	0	6	4	1	1	0	8	0	0	.233	.277
Marquez, Brad	R-R	6-1	185	12-14-92	.267	.222	.286	9	30	4	8	1	1	0	2	2	0	0	0	6	1	2	.367	.313
Nido, Tomas	R-R	6-0	200	4-12-94	.242	.406	.185	38	124	15	30	6	0	2	15	12	1	0	3	23	1	0	.339	.307
Peguero, Eris	L-R	6-1	175	11-29-89	.273	.317	.253	37	132	13	36	1	0	2	13	7	1	0	2	30	5	3	.326	.305
Perez, Pedro	B-R	6-1	190	8-31-94	.119	.063	.154	12	42	1	5	1	1	0	1	3	0	0	0	12	0	1	.190	.178
Rivero, Jorge	B-R	6-0	183	1-6-89	.313	.289	.321	39	144	16	45	8	4	2	20	8	0	0	4	24	4	2	.465	.340
Ruiz, Yeixon	B-R	6-0	155	3-19-91	.250	.333	.208	41	144	24	36	3	0	1	16	9	1	3	0	26	4	2	.292	.299
Tuschak, Joe	L-R	6-0	185	10-17-92	.192	.200	.189	46	130	15	25	6	1	1	10	21	1	1	2	49	2	1	.277	.305
Weijgertse, Kevin	R-R	6-4	176	2-22-91	.177	.200	.167	41	96	6	17	1	0	0	4	9	1	2	0	28	0	0	.188	.255

Pitching	B-T	HT	WT	DOB	W	L	ERA	G	GS	CG	SV	IP	H	R	ER	HR	BB	SO	AVG	vLH	vRH	K/9	BB/9
Arias, Martires	R-R	6-7	207	11-10-90	2	2	2.76	12	0	0	0	16	17	11	5	2	8	18	.258	.107	.368	9.92	4.41
Baldonado, Alberto	L-L	6-2	160	2-1-93	0	2	6.75	6	2	0	0	12	8	9	9	2	8	10	.190	.125	.206	7.50	9.00
Bay, Shane	L-L	6-2	225	2-29-92	0	0	2.57	9	0	0	4	14	9	6	4	0	6	14	.184	.214	.171	9.00	3.86
Birdwell, Peter	R-R	6-4	225		1	0	3.00	2	0	0	0	3	3	2	1	0	1	3	.273	.400	.167	9.00	3.00
Budgell, Matt	R-R	6-2	150	9-30-92	1	2	0.87	12	0	0	1	21	17	7	2	0	10	16	.233	.250	.222	6.97	4.35
Carnevale, Hunter	R-R	5-11	200	8-27-88	0	0	1.50	6	0	0	2	6	6	1	1	0	4	7	.250	.444	.133	10.50	6.00
Chivilli, Cristian	R-R	6-2	200	2-19-91	1	3	6.48	10	2	0	1	25	33	23	18	3	13	18	.320	.368	.292	6.48	4.68
Diaz, Miller	R-R	6-1	209	6-22-92	2	1	3.56	11	5	0	0	43	36	26	17	2	18	45	.220	.327	.165	9.42	3.77
Dotson, Zach	L-L	6-1	180	10-30-90	0	0	40.50	2	0	0	0	1	1	5	3	0	5	0	.250	.000	.500	0.00	67.50
Estevez, Ramon	R-R	6-0	165	10-27-90	0	2	6.06	11	0	0	1	16	12	11	11	0	9	19	.214	.200	.222	10.47	4.96
Flexen, Chris	R-R	6-3	215	7-1-94	1	3	5.63	7	6	0	0	32	38	23	20	2	14	26	.286	.242	.300	7.31	3.94
Gant, John	R-R	6-3	175	8-6-92	3	3	4.55	11	11	0	0	55	62	31	28	6	19	47	.272	.282	.266	7.64	3.09
Gsellman, Robert	R-R	6-4	200	7-18-93	1	3	3.92	11	5	0	0	44	42	27	19	3	18	33	.250	.148	.298	6.80	3.71
Massie, Andrew	R-R	6-1	170	1-27-94	0	2	6.14	9	4	0	1	29	35	21	20	6	17	20	.299	.298	.300	6.14	5.22
Matz, Steve	R-L	6-2	192	5-29-91	2	1	1.55	6	6	0	0	29	16	10	5	1	17	34	.158	.143	.161	10.55	5.28
Montgomery, Christian	R-R	6-1	230	11-20-92	0	1	9.39	2	2	0	0	8	6	10	8	0	6	7	.214	.250	.188	8.22	7.04
Morris, Akeel	R-R	6-1	170	11-14-92	0	6	7.98	11	6	0	2	38	38	37	34	7	22	50	.253	.283	.240	11.74	5.17
Ortega, Flabio	R-R	6-1	170	8-19-90	1	0	2.79	8	0	0	2	10	13	3	3	1	4	6	.342	.545	.259	5.59	3.72
Oswalt, Corey	R-R	6-4	200	9-3-93	4	3	8.15	9	6	0	0	35	49	33	32	1	7	20	.329	.291	.351	5.09	1.78
Perez, Andres E.	R-R	6-2	184	2-8-91	0	1	9.82	10	0	0	1	7	10	10	8	2	4	12	.313	.400	.273	14.73	4.91
Rengel, Luis	R-R	6-2	165	3-19-90	0	0	7.66	13	0	0	1	22	27	21	19	2	8	15	.293	.310	.286	6.45	3.22
Reyes, Persio	R-R	6-2	151	3-17-93	3	6	6.18	11	11	0	0	51	66	39	35	4	18	34	.316	.310	.320	6.00	3.18

Urbina, Juan	L-L	6-2	170	5-31-93	1	0	5.11	9	0	0	0	12	9	7	7	0	16	18	.205	.100	.235	13.14	11.68
Valdez, Carlos	L-L	6-0	170	9-30-90	0	1	1.17	4	0	0	0	8	7	6	1	0	6	7	.233	.333	.222	8.22	7.04
Villasmil, Edioglis	R-R	6-2	164	4-10-92	0	1	13.06	11	0	0	0	10	13	15	15	1	12	15	.302	.286	.310	13.06	10.45
Welch, Brandon	R-R	6-1	185	8-24-91	0	0	9.00	1	0	0	0	1	2	1	1	0	0	0	.400	—	.400	0.00	0.00
Whalen, Robert	R-R	6-2	200	1-31-94	0	0	0.00	1	0	0	0	1	1	1	0	0	0	1	.333	1.000	.000	9.00	0.00

Fielding

Catcher	PCT	G	PO	A	E	DP	PB
De Leon	.958	25	168	14	8	1	4
Leroux	1.000	2	10	2	0	1	0
Machillanada	.992	22	112	20	1	1	2
Nido	.969	28	194	23	7	1	9

First Base	PCT	G	PO	A	E	DP
De Leon	.976	26	196	9	5	12
Diehl	.986	9	64	6	1	3
Leroux	.980	20	142	8	3	8
Weijgertse	1.000	28	117	16	0	9

Second Base	PCT	G	PO	A	E	DP
Kaupe	.930	49	66	94	12	15

Machillanada	—	1	0	0	0	0
Rivero	.875	2	3	4	1	1
Ruiz	.938	22	29	46	5	10

Third Base	PCT	G	PO	A	E	DP
Chavez	.846	18	5	17	4	0
Perez	.828	11	8	16	5	1
Rivero	.935	12	9	20	2	2
Ruiz	.957	20	12	32	2	2
Weijgertse	1.000	15	13	42	0	1

Shortstop	PCT	G	PO	A	E	DP
Cecchini	.964	33	51	81	5	13
Chavez	.876	36	43	91	19	13

Kaupe	.600	2	0	3	2	0
Ruiz	1.000	1	1	3	0	1

Outfield	PCT	G	PO	A	E	DP
Bernal	.667	1	2	0	1	0
Concepcion	1.000	5	3	0	0	0
de la Cruz	.964	63	132	3	5	0
Diehl	.958	28	43	3	2	1
Leroux	.909	10	10	0	1	0
Marquez	.917	9	21	1	2	0
Peguero	.952	35	75	4	4	2
Rivero	1.000	21	34	1	0	1
Tuschak	.892	41	57	1	7	0
Weijgertse	—	1	0	0	0	0

DSL METS1   ROOKIE

DOMINICAN SUMMER LEAGUE

Batting	B-T	HT	WT	DOB	AVG	vLH	vRH	G	AB	R	H	2B	3B	HR	RBI	BB	HBP	SH	SF	SO	SB	CS	SLG	OBP
Carrion, Junior	R-R	6-0	198	12-16-93	.216	.125	.247	27	97	11	21	3	1	0	7	6	3	0	0	34	6	4	.268	.283
Cruzado, Victor	B-R	5-11	178	6-3-92	.279	.333	.260	32	104	24	29	6	3	1	12	22	0	0	1	21	7	3	.423	.402
Figuera, Jose	R-R	6-2	178	6-10-93	.190	.267	.163	20	58	8	11	5	0	0	8	6	4	1	2	17	1	3	.276	.300
2-team total (14 Mets2)					.191	—	—	34	89	11	17	6	1	0	11	9	5	2	2	25	3	4	.281	.295
Garcia, Jose	B-R	6-0	200	11-3-94	.216	.205	.219	58	199	23	43	6	3	0	26	28	5	3	4	29	9	4	.276	.322
Hilario, Manuel	R-R	5-10	172	2-10-92	.269	.231	.280	34	119	22	32	4	3	2	17	14	1	0	2	24	11	0	.403	.346
2-team total (28 Mets2)					.286	—	—	62	224	45	64	13	6	4	41	30	5	0	3	42	23	2	.451	.378
Leal, Miguel	R-R	6-0	184	7-4-91	.260	.250	.263	48	123	11	32	3	0	0	15	18	5	1	5	12	5	4	.285	.364
Liriano, Victor	R-R	6-4	193	5-23-93	.167	.286	.130	24	60	6	10	0	0	0	2	2	3	0	0	17	2	1	.167	.231
2-team total (14 Mets2)					.175	—	—	38	97	7	17	0	0	0	4	4	3	3	0	29	3	2	.175	.231
Maria, Jose	R-R	5-9	194	11-30-94	.187	.278	.158	23	75	8	14	2	1	0	5	8	2	0	0	17	2	4	.240	.282
2-team total (16 Mets2)					.167	—	—	39	114	14	19	3	1	0	13	15	3	1	3	29	3	4	.211	.274
Marmolejos, Merqui	R-R	5-11	184	10-10-93	.198	.273	.177	41	101	20	20	2	2	2	11	13	2	2	2	29	3	2	.317	.297
Martinez, Jose	R-R	6-1	159	1-18-94	.206	.149	.223	67	204	28	42	15	1	1	15	18	4	3	0	50	3	10	.304	.283
Mora, John	L-L	5-10	164	5-31-93	.287	.167	.319	38	115	23	33	9	3	0	20	23	4	1	4	20	9	12	.417	.411
2-team total (26 Mets2)					.268	—	—	64	198	38	53	12	3	0	27	34	8	4	5	37	11	16	.359	.388
Moscote, Victor	R-R	6-1	155	5-10-94	.280	.250	.287	42	107	16	30	3	1	2	13	13	3	1	1	25	0	2	.383	.371
Pierre, Ysidro	B-R	6-1	171	11-30-93	.222	.237	.218	50	171	28	38	9	3	1	18	17	7	1	2	55	18	6	.327	.315
Ramos, Natanael	R-R	5-10	170	6-19-93	.270	.375	.241	12	37	4	10	0	0	3	3	1	0	1	11	1	2	.270	.333
2-team total (18 Mets2)					.224	—	—	30	76	7	17	2	0	0	9	8	1	0	2	24	1	2	.250	.299
Rodriguez, Jean	B-R	6-0	157	9-3-92	.280	.071	.330	41	143	23	40	7	3	0	14	12	0	3	2	22	6	4	.371	.331
2-team total (19 Mets2)					.270	—	—	60	200	31	54	9	3	0	19	23	0	3	2	35	8	6	.345	.342
Rojas, Hengelbert	R-R	6-1	188	10-27-93	.280	.250	.288	36	132	12	37	6	0	3	20	14	1	0	2	24	6	6	.394	.349
2-team total (24 Mets2)					.270	—	—	60	222	26	60	14	0	5	40	20	5	0	2	47	8	9	.401	.341
Rondon, Pedro	R-R	6-1	180	4-30-92	.259	.238	.267	27	81	16	21	4	0	1	11	18	5	1	1	15	13	4	.346	.419
2-team total (38 Mets2)					.231	—	—	65	216	44	50	9	0	1	22	40	7	3	4	38	18	7	.287	.363
Sierra, Johanny	R-R	6-4	180	1-3-92	.242	.243	.242	55	165	26	40	8	0	2	11	20	11	1	0	51	16	8	.327	.362
Valencia, Gregory	R-R	6-3	183	3-19-93	.164	.125	.176	55	171	18	28	6	1	1	6	25	3	0	1	60	6	5	.228	.280

Pitching	B-T	HT	WT	DOB	W	L	ERA	G	GS	CG	SV	IP	H	R	ER	HR	BB	SO	AVG	vLH	vRH	K/9	BB/9
Acosta, Octavio	R-R	6-0	165	3-20-90	0	1	2.84	3	3	0	0	6	5	3	2	0	3	8	.200	.250	.190	4.26	4.26
2-team total (1 Mets2)					0	1	1.74	4	3	0	0	10	7	4	2	0	4	7	—	—	—	6.10	3.48
Almeida, Adrian	L-L	6-0	150	2-25-95	0	3	2.50	12	12	0	0	40	35	14	11	0	24	33	.255	.500	.228	7.49	5.45
Almonte, Gaby	R-R	6-0	185	8-15-92	1	3	1.52	10	0	0	0	30	25	17	5	0	15	24	.227	.324	.178	7.28	4.55
2-team total (6 Mets2)					2	4	2.42	16	5	0	1	52	45	28	14	0	25	36	—	—	—	6.23	4.33
Alvarez, Jean	R-R	6-1	160	5-1-95	1	0	1.54	10	0	0	0	10	5	2	1	3	7	.217	.300	.154	5.40	2.31
2-team total (7 Mets2)					1	0	3.00	17	0	0	0	18	20	10	6	2	8	13	—	—	—	6.50	4.00
Bautista, Jose	R-R	5-11	158	12-11-92	3	0	4.03	18	2	0	1	29	25	14	13	1	12	25	.238	.100	.293	7.76	3.72
Berihuete, Enmanuel	R-R	6-0	174	11-5-93	0	2	10.13	6	2	0	0	8	10	11	9	0	11	10	.323	.364	.300	11.25	12.38
2-team total (11 Mets2)					1	2	9.90	17	2	0	0	20	23	24	22	1	25	17	—	—	—	7.65	11.25
Caminero, Franly	L-L	5-11	175	12-3-92	2	2	4.08	16	0	0	3	29	42	20	13	1	15	22	.356	.167	.390	6.91	4.71
Carreno, Carlos	R-R	6-0	169	8-12-95	0	0	0.00	2	1	0	0	3	6	1	0	0	1	4	.429	.000	.500	3.00	0.00
2-team total (7 Mets2)					2	1	6.75	9	1	0	0	20	30	17	15	1	8	14	—	—	—	6.30	3.60
Castillo, Yrelvis	R-R	6-4	197	7-13-91	0	2	7.36	12	2	0	0	15	15	16	12	0	11	8	.268	.200	.293	4.91	6.75
Cespedes, Jose	R-R	6-5	174	12-4-94	2	1	1.82	11	0	0	1	25	14	7	5	1	4	21	.179	.154	.192	7.66	1.46
Coronado, Carlos	R-R	5-11	176	9-26-91	2	0	1.69	16	0	0	8	21	17	5	4	0	3	21	.218	.240	.208	8.86	1.27
2-team total (11 Mets2)					4	1	2.06	27	0	0	13	35	30	10	8	0	5	26	—	—	—	6.69	1.29
Crismatt, Nabil	R-R	6-1	197	12-25-94	3	0	3.00	13	0	0	0	18	14	6	6	0	5	17	.215	.167	.234	8.50	2.50
2-team total (6 Mets2)					4	0	4.26	19	0	0	0	25	21	12	12	1	8	23	—	—	—	8.17	2.84
Debora, Nicolas	R-R	6-5	170	12-6-93	0	1	7.20	4	0	0	0	5	5	4	4	0	5	3	.300	.000	.333	5.40	9.00

Player	B-T	HT	WT	DOB	W	L	ERA	G	GS	CG	SV	IP	H	R	ER	HR	BB	SO	AVG	vLH	vRH		
Encarnacion, Jose	R-R	6-4	190	10-11-90	0	2	3.38	7	6	0	0	29	21	14	11	0	24	35	.206	.269	.184	10.74	7.36
2-team total (8 Mets2)					0	5	7.17	15	11	0	0	43	33	41	34	1	51	45	—	—		9.49	10.76
Feliz, Gabriel	L-L	5-11	160	11-12-92	0	0	2.35	6	0	0	0	8	9	3	2	0	4	5	.300	.333	.296	5.87	4.70
2-team total (9 Mets2)					0	1	2.20	15	0	0	1	16	16	5	4	1	11	10	—	—		5.51	6.06
German, Audry	R-R	5-11	163	8-16-92	1	2	4.85	7	2	0	0	13	18	17	7	1	10	5	.321	.273	.333	3.46	6.92
2-team total (11 Mets2)					4	4	5.26	18	3	0	1	38	40	33	22	2	29	25	—	—		5.97	6.93
Gonzalez, Marcos	R-R	6-0	175	10-22-92	0	0	0.96	7	0	0	1	9	10	1	1	0	2	3	.286	.333	.269	2.89	1.93
2-team total (12 Mets2)					2	1	1.82	19	0	0	3	25	23	7	5	2	4	12	—	—		4.38	1.46
Marte, Juan	R-R	6-3	208	8-29-90	0	1	0.00	5	0	0	0	5	6	9	0	0	5	4	.273	.250	.300	7.20	9.00
2-team total (6 Mets2)					2	1	1.13	11	4	0	0	24	22	14	3	0	16	12	—	—		4.50	6.00
Merilan, Claudio	R-R	6-1	184	5-3-94	2	0	2.81	19	0	0	1	32	27	19	10	1	23	20	.229	.245	.217	5.63	6.47
Molina, Marcos	R-R	6-3	188	3-8-95	2	2	3.78	9	8	0	0	33	32	17	14	0	8	19	.252	.167	.286	5.13	2.16
2-team total (5 Mets2)					5	2	3.58	14	13	0	0	55	48	25	22	0	14	40	—	—		6.51	2.28
Montero, Randi	R-R	6-2	165	11-8-92	2	1	3.86	10	1	0	1	28	22	22	12	0	9	19	.206	.156	.227	6.11	2.89
2-team total (5 Mets2)					2	2	4.03	15	1	0	1	38	30	27	17	0	14	25	—	—		5.92	3.32
Nuez, Yoryi	R-R	6-1	153	2-13-93	1	2	2.68	8	8	0	0	37	29	12	11	0	9	31	.213	.244	.198	7.54	2.19
2-team total (6 Mets2)					3	3	2.47	14	14	0	0	66	51	24	18	1	20	51	—	—		6.99	2.74
Popa, Luis	R-R	5-11	185	10-27-94	0	0	3.86	3	2	0	0	9	4	4	4	2	4	6	.133	.200	.100	5.79	3.86
Ramos, Eduard	R-R	6-2	195	2-22-92	0	1	2.78	15	0	0	0	23	16	10	7	2	21	16	.205	.158	.220	6.35	8.34
Reina, Richard	R-R	6-2	183	2-7-95	0	1	4.35	6	0	0	0	10	11	6	5	0	6	8	.282	.571	.219	6.97	5.23
2-team total (10 Mets2)					1	2	6.33	16	0	0	1	21	17	16	15	1	25	19	—	—		8.02	10.55
Reyes, Ruben	R-R	6-4	178	9-22-90	3	2	4.20	15	6	0	0	41	36	24	19	2	27	35	.235	.264	.220	7.75	5.98
Rodriguez, Euner	R-R	6-0	170	2-10-94	2	3	6.43	7	0	0	0	14	14	16	10	0	12	8	.255	.467	.175	5.14	7.71
2-team total (11 Mets2)					2	3	8.13	18	0	0	1	28	29	33	25	3	28	23	—	—		7.48	9.11
Rodriguez, Miguel	R-R	6-3	186	8-27-91	1	0	4.35	11	0	0	0	10	12	5	5	0	3	8	.293	.455	.233	6.97	2.61
2-team total (1 Mets2)					1	0	3.97	12	0	0	0	11	12	5	5	0	3	9	—	—		7.15	2.38
Rodriguez, Waldo	L-L	5-11	176	10-20-90	3	3	5.28	12	2	0	1	31	38	21	18	0	10	25	.302	.286	.305	7.34	2.93
2-team total (7 Mets2)					5	3	5.20	19	2	0	3	45	50	29	26	0	18	37	—	—		7.40	3.60
Rosario, Lenny	L-L	6-1	162	5-15-91	2	2	2.98	13	13	0	0	45	28	17	15	0	43	48	.190	.182	.192	9.53	8.54
Suazo, Randinson	R-R	6-0	190	4-19-95	0	0	6.00	4	0	0	0	3	1	2	2	0	4	1	.111	.000	.125	3.00	12.00

Fielding

Catcher	PCT	G	PO	A	E	DP	PB
Garcia	.958	48	311	75	17	5	12
Hilario	1.000	3	26	2	0	0	0
Leal	.988	16	73	9	1	0	3
Maria	.955	6	37	5	2	0	1
Moscote	.957	6	20	2	1	0	1
Ramos	1.000	6	36	4	0	0	2

First Base	PCT	G	PO	A	E	DP
Cruzado	1.000	4	18	0	0	0
Hilario	1.000	21	155	15	0	15
Leal	.993	21	142	3	1	13
Maria	1.000	10	81	5	0	10
Marmolejos	.938	7	40	5	3	3
Moscote	.991	20	107	7	1	5
Ramos	1.000	7	50	7	0	9

Second Base	PCT	G	PO	A	E	DP
Cruzado	.933	7	14	14	2	0

	PCT	G	PO	A	E	DP
Hilario	.960	9	11	13	1	3
Marmolejos	.918	23	32	35	6	8
Martinez	—	1	0	0	0	0
Ramos	1.000	1	0	1	0	0
Rodriguez	.950	28	55	58	6	15
Rondon	.974	24	55	57	3	13
Valencia	1.000	1	2	0	0	1

Third Base	PCT	G	PO	A	E	DP
Hilario	.000	1	0	0	2	0
Moscote	.911	23	16	35	5	3
Rodriguez	1.000	10	7	27	0	0
Rondon	.500	2	0	1	1	1
Valencia	.864	52	53	99	24	10

Shortstop	PCT	G	PO	A	E	DP
Martinez	.917	66	119	169	26	32
Rodriguez	.932	11	16	25	3	0
Rondon	1.000	2	4	5	0	0

Outfield	PCT	G	PO	A	E	DP
Carrion	.889	26	30	2	4	0
Cruzado	.933	12	14	0	1	0
Figuera	.931	17	25	2	2	1
Hilario	1.000	1	1	0	0	0
Leal	1.000	3	3	0	0	0
Liriano	.938	20	14	1	1	0
Marmolejos	.857	5	6	0	1	0
Mora	.949	37	70	5	4	0
Pierre	.964	48	99	8	4	1
Rojas	.934	36	51	6	4	1
Rondon	1.000	1	2	0	0	0
Sierra	.974	33	37	1	1	0
Valencia	1.000	6	7	0	0	0

DSL METS2 — ROOKIE

DOMINICAN SUMMER LEAGUE

Batting	B-T	HT	WT	DOB	AVG	vLH	vRH	G	AB	R	H	2B	3B	HR	RBI	BB	HBP	SH	SF	SO	SB	CS	SLG	OBP
Abreu, Adrian	R-R	6-0	185	6-14-91	.295	.259	.307	66	224	55	66	5	1	6	44	45	5	4	4	26	30	6	.406	.417
Canelon, Leon	R-R	5-11	150	9-10-91	.302	.246	.326	56	189	36	57	9	2	1	16	16	2	12	1	41	11	5	.386	.361
Caraballo, Oswald	R-R	6-2	180	1-5-93	.297	.347	.283	66	222	33	66	14	0	1	33	27	4	8	2	21	10	6	.374	.380
Figuera, Jose	R-R	6-2	178	6-10-93	.194	.250	.174	14	31	3	6	1	1	0	3	3	1	1	0	8	2	1	.290	.286
2-team total (20 Mets1)					.191	—	—	34	89	11	17	6	1	0	11	9	5	2	2	25	3	4	.281	.295
Hilario, Manuel	R-R	5-10	172	2-10-92	.305	.353	.282	28	105	23	32	9	3	2	24	16	4	0	1	18	12	2	.505	.413
2-team total (34 Mets1)					.286	—	—	62	224	45	64	13	6	4	41	30	5	0	3	42	23	2	.451	.378
Liriano, Victor	R-R	6-4	193	5-23-93	.189	.364	.115	14	37	1	7	0	0	0	2	2	0	3	0	12	1	1	.189	.231
2-team total (24 Mets1)					.175	—	—	38	97	7	17	0	0	0	4	4	3	3	0	29	3	2	.175	.231
Lupo, Vicente	R-R	6-0	180	11-26-93	.343	.351	.340	65	204	58	70	18	3	10	45	46	18	1	0	45	12	7	.608	.500
Maracaro, Alvin	R-R	5-9	178	2-10-93	.129	.167	.105	15	31	8	4	0	0	0	1	7	3	1	0	6	4	0	.129	.341
Maria, Jose	R-R	5-9	194	11-30-94	.128	.000	.147	16	39	6	5	1	0	0	8	7	1	1	3	12	1	0	.154	.260
2-team total (23 Mets1)					.167	—	—	39	114	14	19	3	1	0	13	15	3	1	3	29	3	4	.211	.274
Mora, John	L-L	5-10	164	5-31-93	.241	.217	.250	26	83	15	20	3	0	0	7	11	4	3	1	17	2	4	.277	.354
2-team total (38 Mets1)					.268	—	—	64	198	38	53	12	3	0	27	34	8	4	5	37	11	16	.359	.388
Ortega, Luis	R-R	5-10	187	4-5-93	.127	.059	.158	37	55	11	7	2	1	0	4	9	6	2	1	10	5	3	.200	.310
Ramos, Natanael	R-R	5-10	170	6-19-93	.179	.273	.143	18	39	3	7	2	0	0	6	5	0	0	1	13	0	0	.231	.267
2-team total (12 Mets1)					.224	—	—	30	76	7	17	2	0	0	9	8	1	0	2	24	1	2	.250	.299
Reyes, Alfredo	R-R	6-2	160	10-4-93	.232	.242	.229	62	237	30	55	10	1	0	26	17	2	3	4	49	9	3	.283	.285
Rodriguez, Dionis	R-R	6-0	183	2-15-95	.242	.267	.233	49	161	17	39	8	1	1	22	19	8	2	2	34	7	3	.323	.347

Batting	B-T	HT	WT	DOB	AVG	vLH	vRH	G	AB	R	H	2B	3B	HR	RBI	BB	HBP	SH	SF	SO	SB	CS	OBP	SLG
Rodriguez, Jean	B-R	6-0	157	9-3-92	.246	.286	.233	19	57	8	14	2	0	0	5	11	0	0	0	13	2	2	.281	.368
2-team total (41 Mets1)					.270	—	—	60	200	31	54	9	3	0	19	23	0	3	2	35	8	6	.345	.342
Rojas, Hengelbert	R-R	6-1	188	10-27-93	.256	.176	.304	24	90	14	23	8	0	2	20	6	4	0	0	23	2	3	.411	.330
2-team total (36 Mets1)					.270	—	—	60	222	26	60	14	0	5	40	20	5	0	2	47	8	9	.401	.341
Rondon, Pedro	R-R	6-1	180	4-30-92	.215	.250	.206	38	135	28	29	5	0	0	11	22	2	2	3	23	5	3	.252	.327
2-team total (27 Mets1)					.231	—	—	65	216	44	50	9	0	1	22	40	7	3	4	38	18	7	.287	.363
Sanchez, Elvis	R-R	6-2	190	2-8-94	.248	.256	.245	47	149	28	37	12	2	4	21	19	5	1	0	53	4	2	.436	.353
Urena, Jhoan	B-R	6-1	200	9-1-94	.279	.273	.281	64	262	37	73	15	3	4	34	20	2	0	4	46	12	3	.405	.330

Pitching	B-T	HT	WT	DOB	W	L	ERA	G	GS	CG	SV	IP	H	R	ER	HR	BB	SO	AVG	vLH	vRH	K/9	BB/9
Acosta, Octavio	R-R	6-0	165	3-20-90	0	0	0.00	1	0	0	0	4	1	0	0	0	1	4	.154	.250	.111	9.00	2.25
2-team total (3 Mets1)					0	1	1.74	4	3	0	0	10	7	4	2	0	4	7	—	—		6.10	3.48
Almonte, Gaby	R-R	6-0	185	8-15-92	1	1	3.63	6	5	0	1	22	20	11	9	0	10	12	.250	.257	.244	4.84	4.03
2-team total (10 Mets1)					2	4	2.42	16	5	0	1	52	45	28	14	0	25	36	—	—		6.23	4.33
Alvarez, Jean	R-R	6-1	160	5-1-95	0	0	5.68	7	0	0	0	6	10	5	4	1	5	6	.357	.364	.353	8.53	7.11
2-team total (10 Mets1)					1	0	3.00	17	0	0	0	18	20	10	6	2	8	13	—	—		6.50	4.00
Berihuete, Emmanuel	R-R	6-0	174	11-5-93	1	0	9.75	11	0	0	0	12	13	13	13	1	14	7	.295	.438	.214	5.25	10.50
2-team total (6 Mets1)					1	2	9.90	17	2	0	0	20	23	24	22	1	25	17	—	—		7.65	11.25
Canelon, Kevin	L-L	6-1	175	1-16-94	1	1	2.95	14	14	0	0	55	37	21	18	2	20	40	.181	.130	.188	6.55	3.27
Carreno, Luis	R-R	6-0	169	8-12-95	2	1	7.94	7	0	0	0	17	24	16	15	1	8	13	.364	.462	.300	6.88	4.24
2-team total (2 Mets1)					2	1	6.75	9	1	0	0	20	30	17	15	1	8	14	—	—		6.30	3.50
Celas, Jose	R-R	6-1	180	1-12-91	1	0	0.93	5	0	0	0	10	7	1	1	0	5	12	.212	.091	.273	11.17	4.66
Celis, Jorge	L-L	5-10	160	9-11-94	2	1	5.60	14	0	0	0	27	28	18	17	2	16	23	.269	.200	.281	7.57	5.27
Coronado, Carlos	R-R	5-11	176	9-26-91	2	1	2.63	11	0	0	5	14	13	5	4	0	2	5	.265	.118	.344	3.29	1.32
2-team total (16 Mets1)					4	1	2.06	27	0	0	13	35	30	10	8	0	5	26	—	—		6.69	1.29
Crismatt, Nabil	R-R	6-1	197	12-25-94	1	0	7.36	6	0	0	0	7	7	6	6	1	3	6	.318	.500	.300	7.36	3.68
2-team total (13 Mets1)					4	0	4.26	19	0	0	0	25	21	12	12	1	8	23	—	—		8.17	2.84
Encarnacion, Jose	R-R	6-4	190	10-11-90	0	3	15.53	8	5	0	0	13	12	27	23	1	27	10	.250	.214	.265	6.75	18.23
2-team total (7 Mets1)					0	5	7.17	15	11	0	0	43	33	41	34	1	51	45	—	—		9.49	10.76
Feliz, Gabriel	L-L	5-11	160	11-12-92	0	1	2.08	9	0	0	1	9	7	2	2	1	7	5	.233	.167	.250	5.19	7.27
2-team total (6 Mets1)					0	1	2.20	15	0	0	1	16	16	5	4	1	11	10	—	—		5.51	6.06
German, Audry	R-R	5-11	163	8-16-92	3	2	5.47	11	1	0	1	25	22	16	15	1	19	20	.247	.242	.250	7.30	6.93
2-team total (7 Mets1)					4	4	5.26	18	3	0	1	38	40	33	22	2	29	25	—	—		5.97	6.93
Gonzalez, Marcos	R-R	6-0	175	10-22-92	2	1	2.35	12	0	0	2	15	13	6	4	2	2	9	.220	.263	.200	5.28	1.17
2-team total (7 Mets1)					2	1	1.82	19	0	0	3	25	23	7	5	2	5	24	—	—		4.38	1.46
Gonzalez, Yoan	L-L	6-0	178	1-29-91	2	1	2.57	14	14	0	0	67	53	31	19	0	24	65	.223	.286	.212	8.78	3.24
Lugo, Jesus	R-R	6-1	165	3-31-94	4	3	3.61	18	3	0	1	47	40	23	19	0	21	49	.235	.273	.222	9.32	3.99
Marte, Juan	R-R	6-3	208	8-29-90	2	0	1.42	6	4	0	0	19	16	5	3	0	11	8	.250	.407	.135	3.79	5.21
2-team total (5 Mets1)					2	1	1.13	11	4	0	0	24	22	14	3	0	16	12	—	—		4.50	6.00
Martinez, Wimbert	R-R	6-2	175	12-18-93	5	2	2.95	16	6	0	1	61	58	21	20	1	19	43	.267	.242	.277	6.34	2.80
Molina, Marcos	R-R	6-3	188	3-8-95	3	0	3.27	5	5	0	0	22	16	8	8	0	6	21	.195	.273	.167	8.59	2.45
2-team total (9 Mets1)					5	2	3.58	14	13	0	0	55	48	25	22	0	14	40	—	—		6.51	2.28
Montero, Randi	R-R	6-2	165	11-8-92	0	1	4.50	5	0	0	0	10	8	5	5	0	5	6	.216	.000	.296	5.40	4.50
2-team total (10 Mets1)					2	2	4.03	15	1	0	1	38	30	27	17	0	14	25	—	—		5.92	3.32
Nuez, Yoryi	R-R	6-1	153	2-13-93	2	1	2.20	6	6	0	0	29	22	12	7	1	11	20	.216	.158	.250	6.28	3.45
2-team total (8 Mets1)					3	3	2.47	14	14	0	0	66	51	24	18	1	20	51	—	—		6.99	2.74
Olivo, Aneury	L-L	6-2	159	10-24-94	1	3	7.36	15	0	0	4	22	25	22	18	0	18	19	.305	.467	.269	7.77	7.36
Reina, Richard	R-R	6-2	183	2-7-95	1	1	8.18	10	0	0	0	11	6	10	10	1	19	11	.171	.167	.174	9.00	15.55
2-team total (6 Mets1)					1	2	6.33	16	0	0	1	21	17	16	15	1	25	19	—	—		8.02	10.55
Rodriguez, Euner	R-R	6-0	170	2-10-94	0	0	9.88	11	0	0	1	14	15	17	15	3	16	15	.273	.375	.231	9.88	10.54
2-team total (7 Mets1)					2	3	8.13	18	0	0	0	28	29	33	25	3	28	23	—	—		7.48	9.11
Rodriguez, Jhonaiker	R-R	6-1	178	6-26-94	3	1	4.26	12	0	0	0	19	19	16	9	0	19	18	.247	.150	.281	8.53	9.00
Rodriguez, Miguel	R-R	6-3	186	8-27-91	0	0	0.00	1	0	0	0	1	0	0	0	0	0	1	.000	—	.000	9.00	0.00
2-team total (11 Mets1)					1	0	3.97	12	0	0	0	11	12	5	5	0	3	9	—	—		7.15	2.38
Rodriguez, Ramon	R-R	5-11	169	12-27-91	3	1	2.20	18	5	0	2	49	42	24	12	0	15	28	.231	.261	.212	5.14	2.76
Rodriguez, Waldo	L-L	5-11	176	10-20-90	2	0	5.40	13	0	0	2	14	12	8	8	0	8	12	.222	.500	.200	7.53	5.02
2-team total (12 Mets1)					5	3	5.20	19	2	0	3	45	50	29	26	0	18	37	—	—		7.40	3.60
Solano, Yoseibis	R-R	6-1	190	4-22-93	0	0	16.88	4	0	0	0	3	5	5	5	1	2	2	.417	.000	.417	6.75	6.75

Fielding

Catcher	PCT	G	PO	A	E	DP	PB
Abreu	.970	27	168	25	6	0	6
Maria	.950	4	18	1	1	0	2
Ortega	1.000	2	5	0	0	0	0
Ramos	1.000	15	64	4	0	0	2
Rodriguez	.976	37	235	46	7	2	6

First Base	PCT	G	PO	A	E	DP
Abreu	.991	34	303	21	3	35
Hilario	.992	14	121	7	1	6
Maria	1.000	3	4	0	0	0
Ortega	.986	16	64	4	1	5
Sanchez	.961	22	139	9	6	13

Second Base	PCT	G	PO	A	E	DP
Canelon	.980	35	68	77	3	20
Hilario	.929	6	5	8	1	0
Maracaro	.942	12	23	26	3	6
Rodriguez	.959	16	32	39	3	9
Rondon	1.000	15	29	35	0	11

Third Base	PCT	G	PO	A	E	DP
Canelon	.926	13	7	18	2	1
Rodriguez	.500	3	0	3	3	0
Sanchez	.500	1	0	1	1	0
Urena	.906	61	37	127	17	14

Shortstop	PCT	G	PO	A	E	DP
Canelon	.930	12	25	28	4	6
Reyes	.938	62	93	179	18	26

Outfield	PCT	G	PO	A	E	DP
Abreu	.833	7	5	0	1	0
Caraballo	.993	64	130	3	1	1
Figuera	1.000	14	21	1	0	0
Hilario	1.000	4	5	1	0	0
Liriano	.929	13	26	0	2	0
Lupo	.920	54	77	4	7	0
Mora	1.000	25	41	2	0	1
Ortega	1.000	8	5	1	0	0
Rojas	.960	24	42	6	2	1
Rondon	.971	23	32	2	1	0

New York Yankees

SEASON IN A SENTENCE: Will 2012 be the turning point in Yankees history, the year when the heroes of teams that have reached the postseason in 17 of the last 18 seasons fade into the past and force the franchise to forge a new identity?

HIGH POINT: The Yankees battled the Orioles all season but ended up winning the American League East for the third time in four years, then overcame the Orioles again in a five-game AL Division Series. Derek Jeter led the majors in hits for the second time and moved into 11th place on the all-time list.

LOW POINT: When Mariano Rivera blew out his knee in May and Jeter broke his ankle in the AL Championship Series, those were low moments. But the ALCS as a whole was a study in embarrassment, as the Tigers swept the Yankees, who scored just six runs in the four games. The collapse was a team effort, but the attention focused on Alex Rodriguez, who did not play in the Division Series clincher against the Orioles, then started two of four ALCS games and ended up batting .120 (3-for-25) for the postseason, with 12 strikeouts.

NOTABLE ROOKIES: The Yankees were hoping to get contributions from Manny Banuelos and Dellin Betances, who entered the year as New York's best pitching prospects. Banuelos blew out his elbow and required Tommy John surgery, while Betances was bumped down to Double-A. The only rookie to make any kind of impact was reliever Cody Eppley, who made 59 appearances after coming from the Rangers on the waiver wire.

KEY TRANSACTIONS: The Yankees made a bold move to bolster their pitching by trading their top hitting prospect, Jesus Montero, to the Mariners, but Michael Pineda missed the entire season with a shoulder tear and 20-year-old Jose Campos worked just 25 innings before being shut down with elbow issues. The team made no blockbuster moves during the season, but picking up Ichiro Suzuki from Seattle provided a boost to the lineup.

DOWN ON THE FARM: Outfielders Mason Williams, Slade Heathcott and Tyler Austin and catcher Gary Sanchez need more time to develop but are candidates to become the first homegrown Yankees to crack the big league lineup since Brett Gardner in 2008. Triple-A Scranton/Wilkes-Barre played on the road (as the Empire State Yankees) as its home ballpark went through renovations, yet still went 84-60, and Dave Miley was Baseball America's Minor League Manager of the Year.

OPENING DAY PAYROLL: $198.0 million (1st)

PLAYERS OF THE YEAR

MAJOR LEAGUE

Robinson Cano
2b
.313/.379/.550
33 HR, 48 SB
Won 2nd Gold Glove

MINOR LEAGUE

Tyler Austin
of
(Lo A/Hi A/Double-A)
.322/.400/.559
17 HR, 23 SB

ORGANIZATION LEADERS

BATTING		*Minimum 250 AB
MAJORS		
* AVG	Derek Jeter	.316
* OPS	Robinson Cano	.929
HR	Curtis Granderson	43
RBI	Curtis Granderson	106
MINORS		
* AVG	Tyler Austin, Charleston/Tampa/Trenton	.319
* OBP	Jack Cust, Scranton/Wilkes-Barre	.400
* SLG	Tyler Austin, Charleston/Tampa/Trenton	.553
R	Tyler Austin, Charleston/Tampa/Trenton	92
H	Ramon Flores, Tampa/Trenton	158
TB	Tyler Austin, Charleston/Tampa/Trenton	231
2B	Tyler Austin, Charleston/Tampa/Trenton	35
3B	Ramon Flores, Tampa/Trenton	7
HR	Luke Murton, Trenton	25
RBI	Kyle Roller, Tampa	85
RBI	Gary Sanchez, Charleston/Tampa	85
BB	Jack Cust, Scranton/Wilkes-Barre	81
SO	Jack Cust, Scranton/Wilkes-Barre	127
SB	Abraham Almonte, GCL/Trenton	32

PITCHING		#Minimum 75 IP
MAJORS		
W	Phil Hughes	16
	Hiroki Kuroda	16
# ERA	Hiroki Kuroda	3.32
SO	C.C. Sabathia	197
SV	Rafael Soriano	42
MINORS		
W	Brett Marshall, Trenton	13
	Ramon Ortiz, Scranton/Wilkes-Barre	13
L	Bryan Mitchell, Charleston	11
# ERA	Vidal Nuno, Tampa/Trenton	2.54
G	Juan Cedeno, Scranton/Wilkes-Barre	53
GS	Three tied at	27
SV	Mark Montgomery, Tampa/Trenton	15
IP	Ramon Ortiz, Scranton/Wilkes-Barre	169.1
BB	Dellin Betances, Scranton/Trenton	99
SO	Vidal Nuno, Tampa/Trenton	126
# AVG	Bryan Mitchell, Charleston	.240

2012 PERFORMANCE

General Manager: Brian Cashman. **Farm Director:** Mark Newman. **Scouting Director:** Damon Oppenheimer.

Class	Team	League	W	L	PCT	Finish	Manager
Majors	New York Yankees	American	95	67	.586	1st (14)	Joe Girardi
Triple-A	Empire State Yankees	International	84	60	.583	2nd (14)	Dave Miley
Double-A	Trenton Thunder	Eastern	79	63	.556	2nd (12)	Tony Franklin
High A	Tampa Yankees	Florida State	65	70	.481	6th (12)	Luis Sojo
Low A	Charleston RiverDogs	South Atlantic	73	63	.537	4th (14)	Carlos Mendoza
Short-season	Staten Island Yankees	New York-Penn	30	45	.400	t-11th (14)	Justin Pope
Rookie	GCL Yankees	Gulf Coast	35	25	.583	4th (14)	Tom Nieto
Overall 2012 Minor League Record			**366**	**326**	**.529**	**3rd (30)**	

ORGANIZATION STATISTICS

NEW YORK YANKEES

AMERICAN LEAGUE

Batting	B-T	HT	WT	DOB	AVG	vLH	vRH	G	AB	R	H	2B	3B	HR	RBI	BB	HBP	SH	SF	SO	SB	CS	SLG	OBP
Cano, Robinson	L-R	6-0	210	10-22-82	.313	.239	.359	161	627	105	196	48	1	33	94	61	7	0	2	96	3	2	.550	.379
Cervelli, Francisco	R-R	6-1	205	3-6-86	.000	.000	.000	3	1	1	0	0	0	0	0	0	0	0	0	0	0	0	.000	.500
Chavez, Eric	L-R	6-1	215	12-7-77	.281	.152	.298	113	278	36	78	12	0	16	37	30	1	0	4	59	0	0	.496	.348
Dickerson, Chris	L-L	6-4	230	4-10-82	.286	1.000	.231	25	14	5	4	0	0	2	5	3	0	0	0	5	3	0	.714	.412
Gardner, Brett	L-L	5-10	185	8-24-83	.323	.857	.167	16	31	7	10	2	0	0	3	5	0	1	0	7	2	2	.387	.417
Granderson, Curtis	L-R	6-1	195	3-16-81	.232	.218	.239	160	596	102	138	18	4	43	106	75	5	1	7	195	10	3	.492	.319
Ibanez, Raul	L-R	6-2	220	6-2-72	.240	.197	.248	130	384	50	92	19	3	19	62	35	4	0	2	67	3	0	.453	.308
Jeter, Derek	R-R	6-3	195	6-26-74	.316	.364	.294	159	683	99	216	32	0	15	58	45	5	6	1	90	9	4	.429	.362
Jones, Andruw	R-R	6-1	225	4-23-77	.197	.202	.185	94	233	27	46	7	0	14	34	28	5	0	3	71	0	0	.408	.294
Martin, Russell	R-R	5-10	205	2-15-83	.211	.226	.205	133	422	50	89	18	0	21	53	53	8	2	0	95	6	1	.403	.311
McDonald, Darnell	R-R	5-11	205	11-17-78	.000	.000	—	4	4	0	0	0	0	0	0	0	0	0	0	2	0	0	.000	.000
2-team total (38 Boston)					.205	—	42	88	17	18	7	0	2	9	12	0	2	1	19	1	1	.352	.297
McGehee, Casey	R-R	6-1	220	10-12-82	.151	.189	.063	22	53	9	8	3	0	1	6	5	0	0	1	10	0	0	.264	.229
Mesa, Melky	R-R	6-1	190	1-31-87	.500	.000	1.000	3	2	0	1	0	0	0	1	0	0	0	0	0	0	0	.500	.500
Nix, Jayson	R-R	5-11	195	8-26-82	.243	.255	.228	74	177	24	43	13	0	4	18	14	2	9	0	53	6	3	.384	.306
Nunez, Eduardo	R-R	6-0	185	6-15-87	.292	.360	.205	38	89	14	26	4	1	1	11	6	1	0	4	12	11	2	.393	.330
Pearce, Steve	R-R	5-11	210	4-13-83	.160	.167	.000	12	25	6	4	0	0	1	4	5	0	0	0	8	0	0	.280	.300
2-team total (28 Baltimore)					.229	—	40	96	14	22	4	0	4	18	13	0	2	2	25	0	1	.396	.315
Pena, Ramiro	B-R	5-11	185	7-18-85	.250	.000	.333	3	4	1	1	0	0	0	0	0	0	0	0	0	0	0	.250	.250
Rodriguez, Alex	R-R	6-3	225	7-27-75	.272	.308	.256	122	463	74	126	17	1	18	57	51	10	0	5	116	13	1	.430	.353
Stewart, Chris	R-R	6-4	210	2-19-82	.241	.214	.259	55	141	15	34	8	0	1	13	10	1	3	2	21	2	0	.319	.292
Suzuki, Ichiro	L-R	5-11	170	10-22-73	.322	.397	.289	67	227	28	73	13	1	5	27	5	2	5	1	21	14	5	.454	.340
2-team total (95 Seattle)					.283	—	162	629	77	178	28	6	9	55	22	2	5	5	61	29	7	.390	.307
Swisher, Nick	B-L	5-11	200	11-25-80	.272	.270	.273	148	537	75	146	36	0	24	93	77	4	1	5	141	2	3	.473	.364
Teixeira, Mark	B-R	6-3	215	4-11-80	.251	.269	.239	123	451	66	113	27	1	24	84	54	7	0	12	83	2	1	.475	.332
Wise, Dewayne	L-L	6-0	200	2-24-78	.262	.250	.265	55	61	11	16	3	1	3	8	2	0	0	0	12	7	0	.492	.286
2-team total (45 Chicago)					.259	—	100	224	31	58	10	2	8	30	11	1	0	3	52	19	4	.429	.293

Pitching	B-T	HT	WT	DOB	W	L	ERA	G	GS	CG	SV	IP	H	R	ER	HR	BB	SO	AVG	vLH	vRH	K/9	BB/9
Aardsma, David	R-R	6-3	205	12-27-81	0	0	9.00	1	0	0	0	1	1	1	1	1	1	1	.250	.000	1.000	9.00	9.00
Chamberlain, Joba	R-R	6-2	250	9-23-85	1	0	4.35	22	0	0	0	21	26	11	10	3	6	22	.302	.226	.345	9.58	2.61
Eppley, Cody	R-R	6-5	205	10-8-85	1	2	3.33	59	0	0	0	46	46	19	17	3	17	32	.266	.352	.227	6.26	3.33
Garcia, Freddy	R-R	6-4	255	10-6-76	7	6	5.20	30	17	0	0	107	112	64	62	18	35	89	.270	.282	.256	7.46	2.93
Hughes, Phil	R-R	6-5	240	6-24-86	16	13	4.23	32	32	1	0	191	196	101	90	35	46	165	.259	.211	.308	7.76	2.16
Igarashi, Ryota	R-R	5-11	200	5-28-79	0	0	12.00	2	0	0	0	3	4	4	4	0	3	3	.308	.200	.375	9.00	9.00
2-team total (2 Toronto)					0	0	18.00	4	0	0	0	4	9	8	8	0	5	5	—	—	—	11.25	11.25
Kuroda, Hiroki	R-R	6-1	205	2-10-75	16	11	3.32	33	33	3	0	220	205	86	81	25	51	167	.249	.253	.244	6.84	2.09
Logan, Boone	R-L	6-5	215	8-13-84	7	2	3.74	80	0	0	1	55	48	23	23	6	28	68	.234	.231	.238	11.06	4.55
Lowe, Derek	R-R	6-6	230	6-1-73	1	1	3.04	17	0	0	1	24	24	9	8	2	6	14	.261	.294	.241	5.32	2.28
2-team total (21 Cleveland)					9	11	5.11	38	21	1	1	143	180	88	81	10	51	55	—	—	—	3.47	3.22
Mitchell, D.J.	R-R	6-0	160	5-13-87	0	0	3.86	4	0	0	0	5	7	2	2	1	3	2	.333	.364	.300	3.86	5.79
Nova, Ivan	R-R	6-4	225	1-12-87	12	8	5.02	28	28	0	0	170	194	100	95	28	56	153	.288	.272	.303	8.08	2.96
Pettitte, Andy	L-L	6-5	225	6-15-72	5	4	2.87	12	12	0	0	75	65	26	24	8	21	69	.232	.202	.245	8.24	2.51
Phelps, David	R-R	6-2	200	10-9-86	4	4	3.34	33	11	0	0	100	81	38	37	14	38	96	.223	.227	.220	8.67	3.43
Qualls, Chad	R-R	6-5	220	8-17-78	1	0	6.14	8	0	0	0	7	10	5	5	0	3	2	.345	.222	.400	2.45	3.68
Rapada, Clay	R-L	6-5	200	3-9-81	3	0	2.82	70	0	0	0	38	29	14	12	2	17	38	.215	.186	.303	8.92	3.99
Rivera, Mariano	R-R	6-2	195	11-29-69	1	1	2.16	9	0	0	5	8	6	2	2	0	2	8	.200	.154	.235	8.64	2.16
Robertson, David	R-R	5-11	195	4-9-85	2	7	2.67	65	0	0	2	61	52	19	18	5	19	81	.229	.208	.252	12.02	2.82
Sabathia, CC	L-L	6-7	290	7-21-80	15	6	3.38	28	28	2	0	200	184	89	75	22	44	197	.238	.224	.241	8.87	1.98
Soriano, Rafael	R-R	6-1	230	12-19-79	2	1	2.26	69	0	0	42	68	55	17	17	6	24	69	.217	.221	.214	9.18	3.19
Thomas, Justin	L-L	6-3	220	1-18-84	0	0	9.00	4	0	0	0	3	2	3	3	1	1	3	.182	.125	.333	9.00	3.00
2-team total (7 Boston)					0	0	8.22	11	0	0	0	8	12	7	7	1	3	7	—	—	—	8.22	3.52
Wade, Cory	R-R	6-2	185	5-28-83	1	1	6.46	39	0	0	0	39	46	29	28	8	8	38	.286	.278	.292	8.77	1.85
Warren, Adam	R-R	6-2	225	8-25-87	0	0	23.14	1	1	0	0	2	8	6	6	2	2	1	.533	.400	.600	3.86	7.71

Fielding

Catcher	PCT	G	PO	A	E	DP	PB
Cervelli	1.000	3	8	0	0	0	0
Martin	.994	128	924	61	6	3	9
Stewart	.990	54	379	25	4	3	8

First Base	PCT	G	PO	A	E	DP
Chavez	.982	10	49	5	1	2
McGehee	1.000	8	31	1	0	3
Pearce	1.000	9	55	0	0	7
Swisher	.989	41	255	18	3	23
Teixeira	.999	119	985	69	1	91

Second Base	PCT	G	PO	A	E	DP
Cano	.992	154	285	435	6	92
McGehee	—	1	0	0	0	0

	PCT	G	PO	A	E	DP
Nix	1.000	13	16	24	0	4
Nunez	.667	1	0	2	1	0

Third Base	PCT	G	PO	A	E	DP
Chavez	.961	64	36	86	5	5
McGehee	.944	12	10	7	1	1
Nix	.964	29	15	39	2	6
Nunez	.900	9	6	12	2	1
Rodriguez	.957	81	57	119	8	13

Shortstop	PCT	G	PO	A	E	DP
Jeter	.980	135	172	324	10	67
Nix	.983	18	24	34	1	8
Nunez	.931	16	20	34	4	7
Pena	1.000	1	0	4	0	0

Outfield	PCT	G	PO	A	E	DP
Dickerson	1.000	22	11	0	0	0
Gardner	1.000	15	14	1	0	0
Granderson	1.000	157	346	3	0	0
Ibanez	1.000	90	131	2	0	0
Jones	.988	66	81	3	1	2
McDonald	.500	4	1	0	1	0
Mesa	—	1	0	0	0	0
Nix	.917	11	11	0	1	0
Nunez	1.000	4	8	0	0	0
Suzuki	1.000	63	101	2	0	0
Swisher	.986	109	214	4	3	0
Wise	.974	53	35	2	1	0

SCRANTON/WILKES-BARRE YANKEES TRIPLE-A
INTERNATIONAL LEAGUE

Batting	B-T	HT	WT	DOB	AVG	vLH	vRH	G	AB	R	H	2B	3B	HR	RBI	BB	HBP	SH	SF	SO	SB	CS	SLG	OBP
Antonelli, Matt	R-R	6-1	195	4-8-85	.197	.115	.257	15	61	11	12	1	1	1	4	5	1	0	0	9	0	0	.295	.269
2-team total (29 Norfolk)					.201	—	—	44	154	22	31	5	1	2	11	24	4	1	0	32	1	2	.286	.324
Baker, Ryan	R-R	5-9	205	11-9-84	.500	—	.500	1	2	0	1	1	0	0	2	0	0	0	0	1	0	0	1.000	.500
Bernier, Doug	R-R	6-1	185	6-24-80	.201	.152	.219	58	174	13	35	9	0	0	10	27	0	6	1	49	1	2	.253	.307
Branyan, Russ	L-R	6-4	235	12-19-75	.309	.207	.346	33	110	19	34	5	0	11	39	26	0	0	1	31	0	0	.655	.438
Cervelli, Francisco	R-R	6-1	205	3-6-86	.246	.221	.255	99	354	43	87	15	2	2	39	39	15	3	6	82	6	0	.316	.341
Curtis, Colin	L-L	6-1	200	2-1-85	.220	.345	.182	71	250	26	55	13	2	1	23	32	1	0	3	55	12	3	.300	.308
Cust, Jack	L-R	6-1	247	1-7-79	.249	.243	.252	98	337	63	84	14	1	20	66	81	5	0	2	127	2	0	.475	.400
Dickerson, Chris	L-L	6-4	230	4-10-82	.316	.328	.312	69	266	57	84	24	4	7	25	49	1	0	5	73	17	3	.515	.417
Fukudome, Kosuke	L-R	6-0	200	4-26-77	.276	.313	.263	39	127	17	35	5	1	2	16	37	1	0	1	25	1	1	.378	.440
2-team total (4 Charlotte)					.264	—	—	43	140	17	37	5	1	2	16	40	1	0	1	29	1	1	.357	.429
Gardner, Brett	L-L	5-10	185	8-24-83	.600	.750	.000	2	5	1	3	0	1	0	0	2	0	0	0	1	0	0	1.000	.714
Garner, Cole	R-R	6-2	210	12-15-84	.258	.297	.241	64	236	27	61	13	1	6	25	16	2	1	0	75	3	1	.398	.311
Gil, Jose	R-R	6-2	205	9-4-86	.200	—	.200	1	5	0	1	0	0	0	0	0	0	0	0	0	0	0	.200	.200
Joseph, Corban	L-R	6-0	180	10-28-88	.266	.174	.299	84	327	50	87	25	2	13	56	53	0	3	3	57	0	1	.474	.366
Kruml, Ray	L-R	5-11	175	8-5-85	.225	.267	.214	24	71	6	16	3	0	1	7	4	0	0	2	22	7	2	.310	.267
Laird, Brandon	R-R	6-1	215	9-11-87	.254	.324	.227	130	503	54	128	31	2	15	77	34	7	0	6	103	1	0	.414	.307
McDonald, Darnell	R-R	5-11	205	11-17-78	.194	.316	.169	31	108	18	21	1	0	3	7	15	1	0	0	29	1	2	.287	.298
2-team total (6 Pawtucket)					.194	—	—	37	129	20	25	4	0	3	9	15	2	0	1	35	1	2	.295	.286
Mesa, Melky	R-R	6-1	190	1-31-87	.230	.250	.224	33	126	19	29	8	1	9	21	7	0	0	0	43	5	1	.524	.271
Molina, Gustavo	R-R	6-1	250	2-24-82	.174	.222	.159	29	109	7	19	5	0	4	18	4	1	1	1	29	0	0	.330	.209
Mujica, Yadil	L-R	6-1	170	1-1-85	.308	.333	.300	12	39	2	12	3	0	0	1	3	0	0	0	5	1	1	.385	.357
Musteller, Ronnier	R-R	5-10	210	8-8-84	.303	.294	.306	89	347	51	105	21	1	10	49	26	7	1	4	49	7	2	.455	.359
Nix, Jayson	R-R	5-11	195	8-26-82	.233	.375	.182	8	30	5	7	4	0	0	4	3	1	0	1	9	0	0	.367	.314
Nunez, Eduardo	R-R	6-0	185	6-15-87	.227	.282	.210	38	163	18	37	4	0	2	16	7	0	0	2	28	16	3	.288	.256
Pearce, Steve	R-R	5-11	210	4-13-83	.318	.310	.321	53	192	37	61	15	0	11	30	29	5	0	1	33	3	1	.568	.419
Pena, Ramiro	B-R	5-11	185	7-18-85	.258	.267	.255	101	360	40	93	13	3	2	29	34	3	4	3	74	1	3	.328	.325
Romine, Austin	R-R	6-0	220	11-22-88	.213	.533	.109	17	61	6	13	2	0	3	9	8	0	0	2	10	0	0	.393	.296
Russo, Kevin	R-R	5-11	190	7-8-84	.284	.368	.249	101	402	57	114	21	3	0	36	45	4	1	4	72	15	5	.351	.358
Tatum, Craig	R-R	6-1	225	3-18-83	.179	.143	.190	8	28	3	5	0	0	1	6	3	0	0	0	6	0	0	.286	.258
Wise, Dewayne	L-L	6-0	200	2-24-78	.329	.444	.265	21	76	17	25	7	0	4	10	9	0	0	0	16	2	0	.579	.400
2-team total (7 Charlotte)					.280	—	—	28	107	20	30	8	1	4	13	10	0	0	1	24	3	0	.486	.339

Pitching	B-T	HT	WT	DOB	W	L	ERA	G	GS	CG	SV	IP	H	R	ER	HR	BB	SO	AVG	vLH	vRH	K/9	BB/9
Banuelos, Manny	L-L	5-11	200	3-13-91	0	2	4.50	6	6	0	0	24	29	13	12	2	10	22	.299	.324	.283	8.25	3.75
Betances, Dellin	R-R	6-8	260	3-23-88	3	5	6.39	16	16	0	0	75	71	58	53	9	69	71	.250	.272	.230	8.56	8.32
Bulger, Jason	R-R	6-4	215	12-6-78	2	1	3.41	24	1	0	1	34	25	13	13	3	21	28	.208	.209	.208	7.34	5.50
Cedeno, Juan	L-L	6-1	200	8-19-83	3	0	2.81	53	0	0	4	64	66	23	20	5	21	57	.273	.240	.296	8.02	2.95
Claiborne, Preston	R-R	6-2	215	1-21-88	4	0	4.05	20	0	0	1	33	31	17	15	2	12	29	.254	.320	.208	7.83	3.24
Delcarmen, Manny	R-R	6-2	220	2-16-82	3	5	4.42	39	2	0	3	57	62	35	28	5	36	59	.276	.255	.291	9.32	5.68
Eppley, Cody	R-R	6-5	205	10-8-85	0	0	0.00	7	0	0	2	9	3	0	0	0	1	13	.100	.000	.167	12.54	0.96
Farquhar, Danny	R-R	5-9	180	2-17-87	0	1	0.00	1	0	0	0	2	0	0	0	0	0	1	.000	.000	.000	4.50	0.00
Figueroa, Nelson	R-R	6-1	185	5-18-74	7	2	3.96	17	9	1	0	73	79	35	32	8	25	36	.282	.301	.260	4.46	3.10
2-team total (8 Pawtucket)					12	5	3.89	25	15	2	0	116	113	54	50	11	37	69	—	—	—	5.37	2.88
Heyer, Craig	R-R	6-3	205	11-15-85	0	0	0.00	4	0	0	0	4	2	0	0	0	1	2	.133	.000	.222	4.15	2.08
Hyde, Lee	R-L	6-2	205	2-14-85	0	0	4.76	6	0	0	0	6	6	3	3	0	5	3	.286	.000	.316	4.76	7.94
Igarashi, Ryota	R-R	5-11	200	5-28-79	4	3	2.45	30	0	0	10	37	30	11	10	1	18	55	.216	.207	.222	13.50	4.42
Maine, John	R-R	6-4	200	5-8-81	8	5	4.97	16	15	0	0	80	76	51	44	7	31	66	.250	.214	.290	7.46	3.50
Meloan, Jon	R-R	6-3	225	7-11-84	0	0	0.00	1	0	0	0	2	0	0	0	0	1	1	.000	.000	.000	4.50	4.50
Miller, Adam	R-R	6-4	215	11-26-84	0	1	4.50	5	0	0	0	10	13	5	5	0	4	4	.342	.389	.300	3.60	3.60
Mitchell, D.J.	R-R	6-0	160	5-13-87	6	4	5.04	15	14	0	0	86	85	49	48	8	29	72	.261	.263	.259	7.56	3.05
O'Connor, Mike	L-L	6-3	185	8-17-80	3	6	3.73	31	15	0	0	109	117	49	45	14	28	95	.273	.252	.283	7.87	2.32
Ortiz, Ramon	R-R	6-0	175	5-23-73	13	6	3.45	27	27	1	0	169	167	75	65	18	37	104	.261	.310	.215	5.53	1.97
Perez, Kelvin	R-R	6-1	140	10-10-85	1	2	3.77	7	0	0	0	14	15	6	6	2	5	21	.263	.267	.262	13.19	3.14
Pettitte, Andy	L-L	6-5	225	6-15-72	0	1	5.40	1	1	0	0	5	8	5	3	0	2	5	.381	.333	.400	9.00	3.60

NEW YORK YANKEES

Player	B-T	HT	WT	DOB	W	L	ERA	G	GS	CG	SV	IP	H	R	ER	HR	BB	SO	AVG	vLH	vRH	K/9	BB/9
Phelps, David	R-R	6-2	200	10-9-86	1	0	0.00	1	1	0	0	7	4	0	0	0	3	7	.167	.167	.167	9.45	4.05
Robertson, David	R-R	5-11	195	4-9-85	0	0	0.00	2	1	0	0	2	0	0	0	0	0	2	.000	.000	.000	9.00	0.00
Rondon, Francisco	L-L	6-1	160	4-19-88	0	0	11.57	1	0	0	0	2	4	3	3	0	1	2	.400	1.000	.333	7.71	3.86
Schwinden, Chris	R-R	6-3	215	9-22-86	0	1	6.75	1	1	0	0	4	8	4	3	0	1	2	.400	.333	.500	4.50	2.25
3-team total (21 Buffalo, 3 Columbus)					9	9	3.21	25	23	2	0	126	126	54	45	11	37	99	—	—	—	7.07	2.64
Thomas, Justin	L-L	6-3	220	1-18-84	2	1	3.45	30	6	0	1	57	49	23	22	3	20	49	.236	.195	.260	7.69	3.14
2-team total (4 Pawtucket)					2	1	3.45	34	6	0	1	63	54	25	24	3	20	54	—	—	—	7.76	2.87
Tracy, Matt	L-L	6-3	212	11-26-88	1	0	1.80	1	1	0	0	5	3	1	1	0	3	4	.167	.500	.125	7.20	5.40
Venditte, Pat	R-B	6-1	180	6-30-85	1	1	2.77	7	0	0	0	13	11	4	4	1	6	12	.234	.167	.276	8.31	4.15
Wade, Cory	R-R	6-2	185	5-28-83	2	0	2.27	17	0	0	5	32	22	12	8	3	9	20	.190	.193	.186	5.68	2.56
Warren, Adam	R-R	6-2	225	8-25-87	7	8	3.71	26	26	2	0	153	167	64	63	11	46	107	.276	.262	.290	6.31	2.71
Whelan, Kevin	R-R	5-11	205	1-8-84	3	0	3.55	24	0	0	12	25	23	10	10	2	16	36	.242	.171	.283	12.79	5.68
Whitley, Chase	R-R	6-3	215	6-14-89	9	5	3.25	41	2	0	1	80	61	30	29	7	25	66	.213	.203	.221	7.39	2.80

Fielding

Catcher	PCT	G	PO	A	E	DP	PB
Cervelli	.993	96	702	60	5	4	15
Molina	1.000	28	205	22	0	4	1
Romine	.991	13	101	9	1	0	4
Tatum	1.000	8	49	9	0	0	2

First Base	PCT	G	PO	A	E	DP
Antonelli	.962	3	23	2	1	0
Bernier	1.000	1	11	0	0	1
Branyan	.993	31	261	23	2	24
Fukudome	1.000	22	177	14	0	13
Gil	1.000	1	7	1	0	1
Laird	.983	44	382	22	7	40
Pearce	.995	48	402	19	2	45

Second Base	PCT	G	PO	A	E	DP
Antonelli	1.000	10	13	32	0	3
Bernier	.986	14	31	39	1	17
Joseph	.969	80	152	249	13	53

	PCT	G	PO	A	E	DP
Nix	1.000	5	3	13	0	4
Pena	.986	18	32	40	1	10
Russo	1.000	20	30	45	0	13

Third Base	PCT	G	PO	A	E	DP
Bernier	.960	12	9	15	1	2
Laird	.926	79	45	117	13	8
Mujica	—	2	0	0	0	0
Mustelier	1.000	6	3	8	0	0
Nix	1.000	2	4	6	0	0
Pearce	.833	3	2	8	2	0
Pena	.975	16	9	30	1	4
Russo	.988	33	27	55	1	7

Shortstop	PCT	G	PO	A	E	DP
Antonelli	1.000	2	2	7	0	4
Bernier	.976	33	42	78	3	12
Mujica	.964	11	27	27	2	9
Nunez	.967	35	45	102	5	21

	PCT	G	PO	A	E	DP
Pena	.974	69	100	197	8	51
Outfield	PCT	G	PO	A	E	DP
Curtis	.993	68	145	3	1	1
Dickerson	.973	65	142	3	4	2
Fukudome	1.000	16	27	0	0	0
Gardner	1.000	2	1	0	0	0
Garner	.982	62	105	3	2	0
Kruml	.980	22	49	1	1	0
Laird	1.000	5	7	0	0	0
McDonald	.981	27	52	1	1	1
Mesa	1.000	32	71	0	0	0
Mustelier	.975	74	112	5	3	1
Nix	1.000	1	4	0	0	0
Pearce	—	1	0	0	0	0
Russo	.991	50	105	1	1	0
Wise	.978	21	42	2	1	0

TRENTON THUNDER — DOUBLE-A

EASTERN LEAGUE

Batting	B-T	HT	WT	DOB	AVG	vLH	vRH	G	AB	R	H	2B	3B	HR	RBI	BB	HBP	SH	SF	SO	SB	CS	SLG	OBP
Adams, David	R-R	6-1	205	5-15-87	.306	.330	.295	86	327	44	100	23	0	8	48	38	9	1	8	53	3	1	.450	.385
Almonte, Abe	B-R	5-9	205	6-27-89	.276	.169	.310	78	319	47	88	17	4	4	25	37	0	2	1	59	30	5	.392	.350
Almonte, Zoilo	B-R	6-0	205	6-10-89	.277	.213	.303	106	419	64	116	23	1	21	70	25	4	0	3	103	15	4	.487	.322
Austin, Tyler	R-R	6-2	200	9-6-91	.286	—	.286	2	7	2	2	0	0	0	1	1	0	0	0	1	0	0	.286	.375
Brewer, Dan	R-R	5-11	195	7-19-87	.221	.053	.259	27	104	6	23	4	0	1	8	7	0	0	0	25	2	1	.288	.270
Brown, Shane	R-R	5-11	197	1-11-88	.136	.143	.132	30	81	3	11	0	0	0	7	3	1	2	1	21	0	0	.136	.174
Farnham, Jeff	R-R	5-11	190	8-30-87	.192	.240	.176	30	99	14	19	4	0	1	6	14	1	2	0	26	2	0	.263	.298
Flores, Ramon	L-L	5-11	190	3-26-92	.400	—	.400	1	5	2	2	0	0	1	2	0	0	0	0	0	0	0	1.000	.400
Garcia, Adonis	R-R	5-9	190	4-12-85	.288	.333	.268	28	118	17	34	12	0	4	14	5	2	0	1	18	2	1	.492	.325
Gil, Jose	R-R	6-0	205	9-4-86	.214	.290	.188	73	248	29	53	12	0	6	32	23	3	6	4	48	6	2	.335	.284
Higashioka, Kyle	R-R	6-0	205	4-20-90	.087	.000	.105	7	23	1	2	0	0	0	2	2	0	0	1	8	0	0	.087	.154
Ibarra, Walter	B-R	5-11	180	11-1-87	.276	.306	.267	44	156	17	43	15	2	1	15	5	2	3	0	27	2	1	.417	.307
Johnson, Cody	L-R	6-4	240	8-18-88	.244	.235	.247	59	221	29	54	11	1	16	37	30	1	0	1	90	0	0	.520	.336
Joseph, Corban	L-R	6-0	180	10-28-88	.314	.273	.328	23	86	9	27	4	0	2	6	15	0	0	1	13	0	0	.430	.412
Lyerly, Rob	L-R	6-2	200	7-23-87	.176	.000	.188	5	17	2	3	0	0	2	3	2	0	0	0	7	0	0	.529	.263
Mahoney, Kevin	L-R	6-1	205	5-11-87	.248	.237	.252	90	318	42	79	15	3	11	36	35	6	0	3	73	4	0	.418	.331
Maruszak, Addison	R-R	6-1	195	12-21-86	.276	.373	.242	117	416	53	115	25	1	16	59	34	2	1	5	78	5	3	.457	.330
Medchill, Neil	L-R	6-4	220	6-25-87	.276	.200	.302	17	58	6	16	3	0	5	11	3	1	0	0	20	0	0	.586	.323
Mesa, Melky	R-R	6-1	190	1-31-87	.277	.202	.302	88	332	60	92	18	1	14	46	29	6	0	2	75	17	3	.464	.344
Molina, Gustavo	R-R	6-1	250	2-24-82	.304	.000	.333	6	23	5	7	1	0	2	6	1	0	0	0	2	0	0	.609	.333
Mujica, Yadil	L-R	6-1	170	2-4-85	.230	.222	.232	56	187	19	43	5	1	1	12	15	1	1	0	26	1	7	.283	.291
Murphy, J.R.	B-R	5-11	195	5-13-91	.231	.174	.257	43	147	23	34	12	1	4	16	16	2	0	5	32	0	0	.408	.306
Murton, Luke	R-R	6-4	222	5-21-86	.249	.216	.261	126	466	58	116	21	2	25	68	44	12	0	4	120	0	3	.464	.327
Mustelier, Ronnier	R-R	5-10	210	8-8-84	.353	.300	.366	25	102	17	36	6	2	5	20	9	2	0	1	19	3	4	.598	.412
Pirela, Jose	B-R	5-10	191	11-21-89	.293	.354	.266	82	317	56	93	19	3	8	33	26	6	7	2	48	9	3	.448	.356
Segedin, Rob	R-R	6-3	220	11-10-88	.188	.091	.212	48	165	16	31	6	0	3	13	13	2	0	2	33	0	0	.279	.253
Sublett, Damon	L-R	6-1	190	9-22-85	.214	.208	.217	22	70	12	15	4	0	1	9	13	0	0	1	20	3	0	.314	.333
Toussen, Jose	R-R	6-1	155	11-13-89	.333	.333	.000	2	3	1	1	0	0	0	0	0	0	0	0	1	0	0	.667	.333

Pitching	B-T	HT	WT	DOB	W	L	ERA	G	GS	CG	SV	IP	H	R	ER	HR	BB	SO	AVG	vLH	vRH	K/9	BB/9
Arbiso, Cory	R-R	6-3	210	4-21-86	1	1	3.34	8	0	0	0	32	38	18	12	4	12	18	.295	.267	.310	5.01	3.34
Betances, Dellin	R-R	6-8	260	3-23-88	3	4	6.51	11	10	0	0	57	73	49	41	4	30	53	.319	.377	.261	8.42	4.76
Chamberlain, Joba	R-R	6-2	250	9-23-85	1	0	0.00	1	0	0	0	1	1	0	0	0	0	3	.167	.250	.000	20.25	0.00
Claiborne, Preston	R-R	6-2	215	11-23-87	2	2	2.22	30	0	0	5	49	33	17	12	1	24	49	.195	.217	.187	9.06	4.44
Dubee, Michael	R-R	6-3	185	1-12-86	2	3	4.32	26	0	0	0	33	44	18	16	2	22	27	.326	.286	.344	7.29	5.94
2-team total (16 New Hampshire)					4	4	4.07	42	0	0	0	55	63	28	25	5	29	53	—	—	—	8.62	4.72
Farquhar, Danny	R-R	5-9	180	2-17-87	1	0	0.00	6	0	0	4	11	2	0	0	0	14	.057	.067	.050	11.45	0.00
2-team total (20 New Hampshire)					1	1	2.18	26	0	0	5	41	30	14	10	2	10	47	—	—	—	10.23	2.18

Name	T	HT	WT	DOB	W	L	ERA	G	GS	CG	SV	IP	H	R	ER	HR	BB	SO	AVG	vLH	vRH	K/9	BB/9
Feliciano, Pedro	L-L	5-10	195	8-25-76	0	0	0.00	2	0	0	0	1	0	0	0	0	2	2	.000	.000	.000	13.50	13.50
Flannery, Ryan	R-R	6-4	245	1-6-86	3	2	3.97	37	0	0	8	45	43	21	20	0	28	30	.253	.309	.226	5.96	5.56
Hall, Shaeffer	R-L	6-1	205	10-2-87	9	10	3.67	27	27	0	0	164	179	80	67	15	41	100	.279	.278	.280	5.48	2.25
Heyer, Craig	R-R	6-3	205	11-15-85	3	5	6.07	25	11	0	0	70	87	50	47	6	24	45	.312	.272	.339	5.81	3.10
Hyde, Lee	R-L	6-2	205	2-14-85	2	3	3.76	43	0	0	0	38	31	19	16	2	19	41	.223	.200	.241	9.63	4.46
Kahnle, Tommy	R-R	6-1	220	8-7-89	0	0	0.00	1	0	0	0	2	2	0	0	0	0	2	.250	.500	.167	9.00	0.00
Marshall, Brett	R-R	5-11	200	3-22-90	13	7	3.52	27	27	0	0	158	151	68	62	15	53	120	.255	.256	.255	6.82	3.01
Meloan, Jon	R-R	6-3	225	7-11-84	0	0	4.03	20	0	0	4	22	26	11	10	2	8	26	.283	.211	.333	10.48	3.22
Miller, Adam	R-R	6-4	215	11-26-84	0	3	5.08	8	8	0	0	39	57	26	22	2	13	14	.345	.346	.345	3.23	3.00
Montgomery, Mark	R-R	5-11	205	8-30-90	3	1	1.88	15	0	0	1	24	12	5	5	1	6	38	.143	.132	.152	14.25	2.25
Nuno, Vidal	L-L	5-11	195	7-26-87	9	5	2.45	20	20	0	0	114	109	40	31	10	27	100	.252	.261	.249	7.89	2.13
O'Brien, Mikey	R-R	5-11	185	3-3-90	5	7	4.20	20	19	0	0	105	110	56	49	7	39	72	.267	.292	.248	6.17	3.34
Orta, Ricky	R-R	6-2	195	11-6-84	1	0	2.25	5	0	0	0	8	4	3	2	1	3	8	.154	.000	.211	9.00	3.38
Perez, Kelvin	R-R	6-1	140	10-10-85	6	1	1.14	41	0	0	4	71	47	16	9	1	35	60	.192	.114	.229	7.57	4.42
Pettitte, Andy	L-L	6-5	225	6-15-72	0	1	5.40	1	1	0	0	5	7	4	3	0	1	3	.304	.375	.267	5.40	1.80
Phelps, David	R-R	6-2	200	10-9-86	1	0	0.00	1	1	0	0	7	1	0	0	0	1	11	.048	.125	.000	14.85	1.35
Pinder, Branden	R-R	6-3	210	1-26-89	0	0	0.00	1	0	0	0	1	1	0	0	0	0	0	.167	.000	.250	0.00	0.00
Pope, Ryan	R-R	6-3	205	5-21-86	3	6	4.64	46	4	0	8	64	84	44	33	8	14	66	.313	.313	.314	9.28	1.97
Romanski, Josh	L-L	6-0	185	10-18-86	1	2	4.97	12	3	0	0	29	36	17	16	2	9	20	.305	.303	.306	6.21	2.79
Rondon, Francisco	L-L	6-1	160	4-19-88	5	0	3.96	41	0	0	1	64	56	29	28	6	39	70	.235	.235	.236	9.90	5.51
Stoneburner, Graham	R-R	6-0	205	9-29-87	3	0	5.02	20	4	0	0	38	46	25	21	6	9	28	.305	.357	.274	6.69	2.15
Turley, Nik	L-L	6-6	230	9-11-89	1	0	5.40	1	1	0	0	5	8	3	3	0	1	1	.381	.571	.286	1.80	1.80
Whitley, Chase	R-R	6-3	215	6-14-89	0	0	0.00	0	0	0	1	4	1	0	0	0	2	7	.077	.000	.091	15.75	4.50

Fielding

Catcher	PCT	G	PO	A	E	DP	PB
Farnham	.991	30	197	25	2	2	1
Gil	.993	67	491	57	4	6	6
Higashioka	1.000	5	26	5	0	0	0
Molina	1.000	5	31	4	0	0	0
Murphy	.994	38	300	35	2	3	4

First Base	PCT	G	PO	A	E	DP
Brewer	1.000	1	3	0	0	0
Brown	1.000	3	14	2	0	2
Gil	1.000	5	27	4	0	3
Lyerly	.976	5	38	3	1	2
Mahoney	.975	14	111	8	3	7
Maruszak	1.000	7	31	0	0	2
Murton	.988	115	949	66	12	88

Second Base	PCT	G	PO	A	E	DP
Adams	.958	42	72	111	8	26
Ibarra	.977	18	38	46	2	7
Joseph	.976	15	36	45	2	12
Mahoney	.983	22	55	63	2	18

	PCT	G	PO	A	E	DP
Maruszak	.933	4	4	10	1	0
Mujica	1.000	2	2	1	0	0
Mustelier	.846	2	7	4	2	1
Pirela	.979	40	81	103	4	22
Toussen	1.000	1	3	1	0	0

Third Base	PCT	G	PO	A	E	DP
Adams	.951	23	11	47	3	4
Brown	1.000	1	0	1	0	0
Mahoney	.950	44	25	109	7	9
Maruszak	.933	38	16	67	6	5
Mujica	1.000	3	1	3	0	1
Mustelier	.925	18	9	28	3	1
Pirela	.708	11	6	11	7	1
Segedin	.919	13	6	28	3	0

Shortstop	PCT	G	PO	A	E	DP
Ibarra	.944	26	42	75	7	13
Mahoney	1.000	1	0	3	0	1
Maruszak	.952	70	92	205	15	30
Mujica	.974	50	86	137	6	33

Outfield	PCT	G	PO	A	E	DP
Almonte	.984	71	172	7	3	1
Almonte	.956	95	227	10	11	3
Austin	1.000	2	6	0	0	0
Brewer	.944	23	33	1	2	1
Brown	.952	23	20	0	1	0
Flores	1.000	1	2	0	0	0
Garcia	.983	28	56	2	1	0
Hyde	—	1	0	0	0	0
Johnson	1.000	22	31	2	0	0
Mahoney	.923	6	9	3	1	2
Medchill	.955	10	18	3	1	0
Mesa	.995	82	205	8	1	1
Murton	—	1	0	0	0	0
Mustelier	1.000	6	12	0	0	0
Pirela	1.000	28	47	1	0	0
Segedin	.968	30	53	7	2	1
Sublett	.970	17	30	2	1	1

TAMPA YANKEES   HIGH CLASS A
FLORIDA STATE LEAGUE

Batting	B-T	HT	WT	DOB	AVG	vLH	vRH	G	AB	R	H	2B	3B	HR	RBI	BB	HBP	SH	SF	SO	SB	CS	SLG	OBP
Anderson, Jake	L-R	6-0	170	12-3-91	.333	—	.333	1	3	0	1	0	0	0	0	0	0	0	0	1	0	1	.333	.333
Austin, Tyler	R-R	6-2	200	9-6-91	.321	.283	.341	36	134	20	43	13	1	2	23	12	2	0	0	28	6	0	.478	.385
Blaser, Tyson	R-R	6-2	225	12-8-87	.364	.340	.391	30	99	13	36	7	1	0	16	18	2	2	1	24	2	1	.455	.467
Branyan, Russ	L-R	6-4	235	12-19-75	.333	.000	.571	3	12	3	4	1	0	1	4	0	0	0	3	0	0		.667	.500
Brown, Shane	R-R	5-11	197	1-11-88	.241	.000	.350	9	29	0	7	2	0	0	5	5	0	0	0	3	0	0	.310	.353
De Leon, Kelvin	R-R	6-2	180	10-29-90	.114	.208	.065	21	70	2	8	0	0	0	4	8	0	0	0	20	0	0	.114	.205
Duran, Kelvin	L-L	5-11	165	11-10-90	.211	.200	.214	7	19	1	4	0	0	0	0	0	0	0	7	1	0		.211	.211
Felix, Anderson	B-R	6-0	175	5-11-92	.239	.296	.200	23	67	7	16	5	1	0	4	12	0	0	1	19	5	2	.343	.350
Flores, Ramon	L-L	5-11	190	3-26-92	.302	.286	.311	131	517	83	156	29	7	6	39	54	5	2	5	85	24	9	.420	.370
Garcia, Adonis	R-R	5-9	190	4-12-85	.236	.405	.145	29	106	11	25	7	1	1	15	9	0	0	0	18	0	2	.349	.296
Heathcott, Slade	L-L	6-1	190	9-28-90	.307	.257	.333	60	215	38	66	16	2	5	27	20	5	2	1	66	17	4	.470	.378
Higashioka, Kyle	R-R	6-0	205	4-20-90	.185	.238	.159	37	124	13	23	5	0	6	21	10	0	2	2	34	1	1	.371	.243
Lassiter, Garrison	L-R	6-1	185	12-22-89	.195	.250	.172	24	82	10	16	2	0	1	4	6	0	0	0	31	2	0	.256	.250
Mahoney, Kevin	L-R	6-1	205	5-11-87	.200	.000	.333	2	5	0	1	0	0	0	0	1	1	0	0	3	0	0	.200	.333
Medchill, Neil	L-R	6-4	220	6-25-87	.248	.225	.264	57	218	26	54	9	4	6	32	19	0		2	70	3	1	.408	.305
Mojica, Jose	R-R	6-0	145	12-26-88	.226	.193	.242	104	354	30	80	16	3	2	30	16	4	2	3	62	3	4	.305	.265
Mujica, Yadil	L-R	6-1	170	6-4-85	.136	.200	.103	14	44	5	6	0	0	0	4	1	1	0		9	1	1	.182	.224
Murphy, J.R.	B-R	5-11	195	5-13-91	.257	.248	.263	67	265	39	68	14	1	5	28	26	0	2	1	41	4	3	.374	.322
Nunez, Eduardo	R-R	6-0	185	6-15-87	.286	—	.286	2	7	2	2	0	0	0	0	0	0	0	0	1	1	0	.286	.286
Rabago, Hector	R-R	5-10	185	8-24-88	.143	.256	.076	31	105	6	15	1	0	1	7	7	3	0	1	21	0	0	.181	.216
Rodriguez, Alex	R-R	6-3	225	7-27-75	.000	.000	.000	2	7	1	0	0	0	0	0	1	0	0		4	0	0	.000	.125
Roller, Kyle	L-R	6-1	235	3-27-88	.266	.243	.278	121	418	59	111	22	5	18	85	45	16	0	3	115	4	2	.471	.357
Romine, Austin	R-R	6-0	220	11-22-88	.389	.571	.273	5	18	2	7	0	0	1	1	0	0	0		3	0	0	.556	.421
Rosario, Francisco	B-R	6-1	170	7-12-90	.333	.000	.429	3	9	0	3	0	0	0	0	0	0	0	0	3	0	0	.333	.333
Sanchez, Gary	R-R	6-2	220	12-2-92	.279	.328	.252	48	172	21	48	10	1	5	29	10	3	0	0	41	4	0	.436	.330

Name	B-T	HT	WT	DOB	AVG	vLH	vRH	G	AB	R	H	2B	3B	HR	RBI	BB	HBP	SH	SF	SO	SB	CS	SLG	OBP
Segedin, Rob	R-R	6-3	220	11-10-88	.297	.285	.305	73	290	44	86	21	1	7	41	29	3	0	4	53	9	4	.448	.362
Sosa, Eduardo	L-L	6-0	180	3-14-91	.237	.217	.247	64	241	24	57	8	3	1	17	17	4	2	1	54	8	6	.307	.297
Toussen, Jose	R-R	6-1	155	11-13-89	.193	.178	.201	81	244	25	47	14	1	0	14	14	0	5	0	49	5	4	.258	.236
Williams, Mason	L-R	6-0	150	8-21-91	.277	.318	.262	22	83	13	23	3	0	3	7	3	0	0	0	14	1	4	.422	.302
Wilson, Zach	R-R	6-1	205	8-6-90	.240	.298	.212	88	312	23	75	16	3	2	22	22	1	1	1	54	5	0	.330	.292

Pitching

Pitching	B-T	HT	WT	DOB	W	L	ERA	G	GS	CG	SV	IP	H	R	ER	HR	BB	SO	AVG	vLH	vRH	K/9	BB/9
Aardsma, David	R-R	6-3	205	12-27-81	0	0	0.00	1	1	0	0	1	0	0	0	0	1	0	.000	.000	.000	0.00	9.00
Agramonte, Kenedy	R-R	5-10	150	12-4-90	0	0	0.00	1	0	0	0	1	1	0	0	0	1	1	.250	.000	.250	9.00	9.00
Arrebato, Rigoberto	L-L	5-11	190	2-4-86	4	2	4.19	35	0	0	2	54	48	29	25	4	26	54	.239	.210	.258	9.06	4.36
Barreda, Manuel	R-R	5-11	165	10-8-88	5	3	3.95	35	0	0	0	57	50	28	25	6	32	60	.244	.289	.204	9.47	5.05
Bashore, Matt	L-L	6-2	200	4-6-88	0	0	3.60	5	0	0	0	10	13	4	4	1	7	7	.317	.250	.333	6.30	6.30
Black, Sean	R-R	6-3	185	4-23-88	2	6	6.61	25	8	0	1	63	78	49	46	5	26	53	.302	.284	.323	7.61	3.73
Bleich, Jeremy	L-L	6-2	185	6-18-87	1	1	3.86	8	2	0	0	16	20	10	7	2	5	10	.299	.313	.294	5.51	2.76
Chamberlain, Joba	R-R	6-2	250	9-23-85	0	1	2.25	3	3	0	0	4	3	2	1	1	1	1	.250	.250	—	2.25	2.25
Cotham, Caleb	R-R	6-3	215	11-6-87	2	6	4.48	15	11	0	0	62	71	33	31	4	22	44	.289	.236	.331	6.35	3.18
Cruz, Dawerd	R-R	6-1	170	12-7-88	0	0	7.71	1	0	0	0	2	6	3	2	0	1	1	.462	.455	.500	3.86	3.86
De La Cruz, Joel	R-R	6-1	190	6-9-89	0	0	0.00	1	0	0	0	2	1	0	0	0	0	2	.167	.333	.000	10.80	0.00
DeLuca, Evan	L-L	6-1	195	3-9-91	0	0	3.18	3	0	0	0	6	5	2	2	0	10	6	.238	.167	.267	9.53	15.88
Dott, Aaron	R-L	6-4	215	5-17-88	4	4	3.34	26	1	0	0	62	51	23	23	1	28	67	.223	.227	.221	9.73	4.06
Feliciano, Pedro	L-L	5-10	195	8-25-76	0	0	18.00	1	0	0	0	1	4	2	2	0	1	5	.571	.500	.600	9.00	0.00
Goody, Nick	B-R	6-1	195	7-6-91	0	0	2.25	3	0	0	0	4	4	1	1	0	1	7	.250	.250	.250	15.75	2.25
Greene, Shane	R-R	6-4	210	11-17-88	4	7	5.22	24	23	0	0	112	113	80	65	5	63	101	.265	.282	.253	8.12	5.06
Kahnle, Tommy	R-R	6-1	220	8-7-89	2	1	2.45	30	0	0	6	55	30	16	15	3	24	72	.158	.154	.162	11.78	3.93
Mascheri, Rich	L-L	5-10	190	8-7-89	1	0	6.75	2	0	0	0	3	4	2	2	0	2	1	.364	.500	.286	3.38	6.75
Mejia, Edison	R-R	6-1	185	7-2-90	0	0	6.75	1	0	0	0	1	2	1	1	0	0	2	.333	.500	.250	13.50	0.00
Mercedes, Melvin	R-R	6-3	170	8-28-89	0	0	6.00	2	0	0	0	3	4	2	2	1	1	1	.308	.333	.286	3.00	3.00
Meyers, Brad	R-R	6-6	205	9-13-85	0	1	37.80	1	0	0	0	2	8	8	7	1	0	0	.667	.400	.857	0.00	0.00
Montgomery, Mark	R-R	5-11	205	8-30-90	4	1	1.34	31	0	0	14	40	23	6	6	0	16	61	.165	.197	.141	13.61	3.57
Nuding, Zach	R-R	6-4	250	3-29-90	8	3	3.89	16	14	0	0	86	89	41	37	3	26	66	.267	.289	.250	6.93	2.73
Nuno, Vidal	L-L	5-11	195	7-26-87	1	1	2.96	11	1	0	0	24	22	11	8	2	6	26	.232	.250	.222	9.62	2.22
O'Brien, Mikey	R-R	5-11	185	3-3-90	4	1	2.92	7	6	0	0	37	31	13	12	0	13	32	.230	.250	.211	7.78	3.16
Pettitte, Andy	L-L	6-5	225	6-15-72	0	0	1.29	2	2	0	0	7	4	1	1	0	0	5	.174	.286	.125	6.43	0.00
Phelps, David	R-R	6-2	200	10-9-86	0	0	0.00	2	2	0	0	5	7	0	0	0	1	5	.350	.222	.455	8.44	1.69
Pinder, Branden	R-R	6-3	210	1-26-89	2	6	2.79	41	0	0	9	68	70	27	21	1	29	67	.262	.298	.235	8.91	3.86
Ramirez, Jose	R-R	6-1	155	1-21-90	7	6	3.19	21	18	0	0	99	92	43	35	7	30	94	.239	.240	.238	8.57	2.74
Rondon, Francisco	L-L	6-1	160	4-19-88	0	0	0.00	2	0	0	0	5	2	1	0	0	2	8	.125	.200	.091	14.40	3.60
Smith, Alex	R-R	6-3	200	9-29-89	0	0	0.00	1	0	0	0	3	3	0	0	0	1	1	.250	.273	.000	3.00	3.00
Sneed, Kramer	L-L	6-3	185	10-7-88	0	7	5.37	31	4	0	0	64	65	41	38	5	40	49	.265	.269	.263	6.93	5.65
Tracy, Matt	L-L	6-3	212	11-26-88	5	7	3.27	18	18	2	0	99	88	47	36	3	39	64	.249	.272	.239	5.82	3.55
Turley, Nik	L-L	6-6	230	9-11-89	9	5	2.89	23	21	1	0	112	97	38	36	7	44	116	.235	.263	.224	9.32	3.54

Fielding

Catcher	PCT	G	PO	A	E	DP	PB
Blaser	1.000	5	38	3	0	1	4
Higashioka	.991	24	208	23	2	3	3
Murphy	.984	59	495	47	9	8	9
Rabago	1.000	8	57	4	0	0	0
Romine	1.000	4	34	0	0	0	0
Sanchez	.986	38	265	25	4	0	8

First Base	PCT	G	PO	A	E	DP
Austin	1.000	5	33	2	0	4
Blaser	1.000	7	53	6	0	3
Branyan	1.000	1	14	0	0	1
Brown	1.000	2	12	1	0	0
Flores	1.000	2	7	1	0	0
Mahoney	1.000	1	13	3	0	1
Medchill	1.000	1	5	0	0	0
Roller	.994	119	929	89	6	77
Toussen	1.000	2	3	1	0	0

Second Base	PCT	G	PO	A	E	DP
Anderson	1.000	1	0	1	0	0
Castro	.943	51	116	150	16	27
Felix	.972	23	46	59	3	11
Lassiter	.000	1	0	0	1	0
Mahoney	—	1	0	0	0	0
Mojica	1.000	1	0	2	0	0
Mujica	1.000	3	4	7	0	2
Rabago	.957	10	21	24	2	9
Toussen	.973	49	86	94	5	20

Third Base	PCT	G	PO	A	E	DP
Brown	1.000	1	0	1	0	0
Lassiter	.897	22	8	27	4	2
Murphy	—	1	0	0	0	0
Rabago	.909	10	4	16	2	1
Rodriguez	1.000	1	0	1	0	0
Segedin	.949	16	12	25	2	4
Toussen	1.000	2	1	1	0	0
Wilson	.903	87	49	146	21	8

Shortstop	PCT	G	PO	A	E	DP
Castro	1.000	2	0	1	0	0
Lassiter	.750	1	3	3	2	1
Mojica	.963	103	120	272	15	49

	PCT	G	PO	A	E	DP
Mujica	.925	11	12	25	3	3
Nunez	1.000	2	0	4	0	0
Rabago	1.000	2	1	5	0	0
Rosario	1.000	3	0	6	0	1
Toussen	.987	16	27	47	1	11

Outfield	PCT	G	PO	A	E	DP
Austin	.952	31	56	3	3	0
Brown	1.000	5	7	1	0	0
De Leon	.960	17	24	0	1	0
Duran	1.000	5	8	0	0	0
Flores	.984	126	240	10	4	2
Garcia	.974	26	35	2	1	1
Heathcott	.961	19	47	2	2	0
Medchill	.927	33	48	3	4	0
Rabago	1.000	2	2	1	0	0
Segedin	.944	54	93	9	6	3
Sosa	.986	64	129	7	2	1
Toussen	1.000	11	25	1	0	1
Williams	1.000	22	38	2	0	2

CHARLESTON RIVERDOGS

LOW CLASS A

SOUTH ATLANTIC LEAGUE

Batting	B-T	HT	WT	DOB	AVG	vLH	vRH	G	AB	R	H	2B	3B	HR	RBI	BB	HBP	SH	SF	SO	SB	CS	SLG	OBP
Arcia, Francisco	B-R	6-0	155	9-14-89	.246	.226	.251	68	224	28	55	14	1	5	46	21	5	2	4	65	2	3	.384	.319
Austin, Tyler	R-R	6-2	200	9-6-91	.320	.247	.349	70	266	69	85	22	5	14	54	37	3	0	3	68	17	2	.598	.405
Bichette Jr., Dante	R-R	6-1	215	9-26-92	.248	.273	.238	122	471	67	117	24	3	3	46	44	7	0	0	94	3	4	.331	.322
Blaser, Tyson	R-R	6-2	225	12-8-87	.293	.296	.291	22	82	8	24	5	0	1	14	7	1	0	1	20	0	0	.390	.352
Butler, Saxon	L-L	6-2	239	5-11-90	.235	.152	.288	25	85	9	20	4	0	3	9	6	3	0	2	19	0	0	.388	.302
Castillo, Ali	R-R	5-10	165	6-19-89	.307	.234	.344	86	283	44	87	20	1	5	28	27	8	5	2	33	17	13	.438	.381
Culver, Cito	B-R	6-0	185	8-26-92	.215	.200	.221	122	466	66	100	14	6	2	40	71	4	4	5	104	22	11	.283	.321

Name	B-T	HT	WT	DOB	AVG	vLH	vRH	G	AB	R	H	2B	3B	HR	RBI	BB	HBP	SH	SF	SO	SB	CS	SLG	OBP
De Leon, Kelvin	R-R	6-2	180	10-29-90	.240	.278	.225	84	283	36	68	17	0	4	34	25	4	1	5	77	5	4	.343	.306
Felix, Anderson	B-R	6-0	175	5-11-92	.315	.238	.346	22	73	12	23	6	1	1	11	9	1	1	0	23	6	1	.466	.398
Gamel, Ben	L-L	5-11	180	5-17-92	.306	.330	.298	110	444	56	136	23	5	2	61	23	4	0	5	71	19	10	.394	.342
Gardner, Brett	L-L	5-10	185	8-24-83	.333	—	.333	1	3	1	1	0	0	0	0	0	0	0	0	0	1	1	0	.333	.333
Grice, Cody	R-R	6-0	220	1-19-90	.212	.175	.237	31	99	11	21	2	0	1	8	5	2	0	0	33	6	0	.263	.264
Gumbs, Angelo	R-R	6-0	175	10-13-92	.272	.303	.260	67	257	40	70	14	3	7	36	18	1	0	2	60	26	3	.432	.320
McCoy, Nick	R-R	5-10	180	3-2-87	.288	.300	.281	17	52	6	15	2	0	0	2	5	0	0	0	8	0	1	.327	.351
McGehee, Casey	R-R	6-1	220	10-12-82	.360	.286	.389	7	25	4	9	3	0	0	8	2	0	0	0	4	0	0	.480	.407
Nunez, Reymond	R-R	6-4	210	9-25-90	.238	.222	.244	104	378	36	90	21	0	5	47	20	6	0	1	108	3	2	.333	.286
Orozco, Jamiel	R-R	5-11	160	1-29-93	.185	.214	.154	9	27	1	5	2	0	0	1	1	0	1	0	7	0	1	.259	.214
Refsnyder, Robert	R-R	6-1	205	3-26-91	.241	.186	.272	46	162	22	39	8	0	4	22	16	3	0	1	25	11	1	.364	.319
Sanchez, Gary	R-R	6-2	220	12-2-92	.297	.359	.276	68	263	44	78	19	0	13	56	22	2	0	2	65	11	4	.517	.353
Sosa, Eduardo	L-L	6-0	180	3-14-91	.230	.184	.245	42	148	19	34	3	4	2	8	14	1	1	1	42	2	4	.345	.299
Stevenson, Casey	L-R	6-3	200	5-18-88	.300	.250	.316	66	230	38	69	10	3	5	37	18	5	1	2	39	4	2	.435	.361
Williams, Mason	L-R	6-0	150	8-21-91	.304	.347	.289	69	276	55	84	19	4	8	28	21	4	7	3	33	19	9	.489	.359

Pitching	B-T	HT	WT	DOB	W	L	ERA	G	GS	CG	SV	IP	H	R	ER	HR	BB	SO	AVG	vLH	vRH	K/9	BB/9
Allen, Scottie	R-R	6-1	170	7-3-91	4	7	4.40	26	24	0	0	125	126	71	61	9	30	97	.263	.276	.254	7.00	2.17
Arneson, Zach	R-R	6-2	190	11-17-88	1	0	0.00	1	0	0	0	2	0	0	0	0	0	1	.000	.000	.000	4.50	0.00
Arrebato, Rigoberto	L-L	5-11	190	2-4-86	0	0	4.63	6	0	0	0	12	9	6	6	2	4	14	.209	.400	.152	10.80	3.09
Bashore, Matt	L-L	6-2	200	4-6-88	1	4	3.78	11	11	0	0	50	38	24	21	0	26	42	.210	.265	.189	7.56	4.68
Black, Corey	R-R	5-11	175	8-4-91	2	2	3.80	5	5	0	0	24	18	11	10	0	5	29	.214	.316	.130	11.03	1.90
Brebbia, John	R-R	6-1	185	5-30-90	3	1	2.96	29	0	0	2	52	55	17	17	4	18	53	.281	.312	.261	9.23	3.14
Campos, Jose	R-R	6-4	195	7-27-92	3	0	4.01	5	5	0	0	25	20	12	11	2	8	26	.213	.300	.148	9.49	2.92
Checo, Mariel	R-R	6-3	190	10-16-89	7	2	4.95	28	0	0	0	40	30	25	22	5	27	47	.208	.254	.173	10.58	6.08
Cotham, Caleb	R-R	6-3	215	11-6-87	3	1	2.31	8	8	0	0	39	32	11	10	1	7	32	.225	.280	.196	7.38	1.62
De La Cruz, Joel	B-R	6-1	190	6-9-89	3	3	3.66	25	0	0	3	47	45	25	19	3	27	49	.257	.238	.268	9.45	5.21
Gerritse, Brett	R-R	6-4	220	3-4-91	4	5	3.83	24	14	0	0	94	90	44	40	4	35	70	.250	.225	.266	6.70	3.35
Goody, Nick	R-R	6-1	195	7-6-91	1	2	1.09	17	0	0	6	25	15	3	3	0	7	40	.174	.176	.173	14.59	2.55
Guerra, Pedro	R-R	6-0	180	1-9-90	4	1	1.61	36	0	0	9	56	35	10	10	2	16	61	.178	.220	.148	9.80	2.57
Lewis, Freddy	L-L	6-2	210	12-16-86	7	2	3.56	39	0	0	1	61	61	27	24	2	24	66	.257	.270	.252	9.79	3.56
Mahoney, Dan	R-R	6-3	195	2-17-88	2	0	3.39	35	0	0	6	66	72	34	25	3	24	53	.269	.257	.279	7.49	4.10
Mercedes, Melvin	R-R	6-3	170	8-28-89	1	1	9.90	5	0	0	0	10	20	11	11	2	4	6	.435	.529	.379	5.40	3.60
Mitchell, Bryan	L-R	6-2	175	4-19-91	9	11	4.58	27	26	0	0	120	107	74	61	7	72	121	.240	.235	.243	9.08	5.40
Oliver, Will	R-R	6-2	185	7-4-87	3	6	4.58	25	21	0	0	110	132	64	56	5	48	84	.301	.245	.346	6.83	3.93
Paullus, Robert	R-R	6-1	190	8-31-89	3	2	6.65	29	0	0	3	47	53	35	35	3	24	38	.288	.312	.271	7.23	4.56
Rodriguez, Wilton	R-R	6-3	195	11-6-90	1	3	6.80	13	7	0	0	44	58	39	33	10	16	33	.315	.357	.280	6.80	3.30
Rutckyj, Evan	R-L	6-5	213	1-31-92	3	2	4.50	6	0	0	0	24	22	13	12	0	14	23	.237	.304	.214	8.63	5.25
Short, Charlie	R-R	6-0	220	8-13-88	1	0	4.41	11	0	0	1	16	19	8	8	2	7	23	.292	.222	.342	12.67	3.86
Smith, Adam	R-R	6-3	200	12-15-89	1	0	5.23	8	0	0	0	10	8	6	6	0	12	9	.222	.273	.200	7.84	10.45
Varce, Zach	R-R	6-0	195	12-14-88	0	0	4.15	8	0	0	0	13	13	8	6	0	5	15	.255	.263	.250	10.38	3.46
Vargas, Cesar	R-R	6-1	160	12-30-91	0	0	3.72	2	2	0	0	10	10	4	4	1	4	8	.286	.308	.273	7.45	3.72
Wetherell, Phil	R-R	6-5	225	10-9-89	6	8	5.97	37	7	0	7	78	92	55	52	7	33	77	.290	.306	.280	8.85	3.79

Fielding

Catcher	PCT	G	PO	A	E	DP	PB
Arcia	.996	59	452	50	2	1	13
Blaser	.983	13	107	10	2	0	3
McCoy	1.000	15	124	6	0	0	1
Sanchez	.975	53	398	67	12	2	10

First Base	PCT	G	PO	A	E	DP
Austin	1.000	3	16	1	0	3
Blaser	.984	6	62	0	1	8
Butler	.995	19	188	9	1	16
McGehee	1.000	1	7	1	0	0
Nunez	.981	89	739	40	15	70
Stevenson	.974	22	166	18	5	21

Second Base	PCT	G	PO	A	E	DP
Castillo	.992	55	91	166	2	35
Felix	1.000	6	6	15	0	0
Gumbs	.974	61	118	186	8	42
Orozco	.923	7	8	16	2	5
Stevenson	.977	12	17	25	1	5

Third Base	PCT	G	PO	A	E	DP
Bichette Jr.	.938	112	85	230	21	19
Castillo	1.000	5	3	5	0	0
Felix	1.000	2	2	3	0	0
McGehee	1.000	3	0	4	0	0
Stevenson	.911	15	11	30	4	5

Shortstop	PCT	G	PO	A	E	DP
Castillo	.964	12	17	37	2	7
Culver	.958	119	194	313	22	80
Felix	.889	4	5	11	2	2
Gumbs	1.000	1	1	5	0	1
Orozco	—	1	0	0	0	0

Outfield	PCT	G	PO	A	E	DP
Austin	.991	61	102	4	1	0
Castillo	1.000	12	15	2	0	0
De Leon	.967	60	83	4	3	0
Felix	1.000	2	3	0	0	0
Gamel	.980	102	187	7	4	1
Gardner	—	1	0	0	0	0
Grice	.981	30	48	3	1	0
Refsnyder	.975	42	72	5	2	0
Sosa	.967	42	57	2	2	0
Stevenson	1.000	3	2	0	0	0
Williams	.994	66	151	2	1	0

STATEN ISLAND YANKEES
SHORT-SEASON

NEW YORK-PENN LEAGUE

Batting	B-T	HT	WT	DOB	AVG	vLH	vRH	G	AB	R	H	2B	3B	HR	RBI	BB	HBP	SH	SF	SO	SB	CS	SLG	OBP
Bird, Greg	L-R	6-3	215	11-9-92	.400	.250	.438	11	40	4	16	4	0	2	8	6	1	0	0	10	0	0	.650	.489
Butler, Saxon	L-L	6-2	239	5-11-90	.296	.273	.303	36	142	29	42	14	1	10	36	14	4	0	2	32	0	0	.620	.370
Cayones, Exicardo	L-L	6-0	183	10-9-91	.228	.167	.242	47	158	22	36	7	0	1	15	33	5	2	2	40	7	2	.291	.374
Custodio, Claudio	R-R	5-10	155	10-30-90	.253	.304	.238	62	241	33	61	10	5	1	22	14	1	9	0	58	13	1	.349	.297
Dugas, Taylor	L-L	5-8	170	12-15-89	.306	.327	.300	59	209	38	64	9	1	1	15	51	12	3	1	35	5	2	.373	.465
Duran, Matt	R-R	6-1	205	5-1-93	.221	.245	.215	61	226	24	50	12	0	3	17	14	1	0	2	57	0	0	.314	.267
Kuo, Fu-Lin	R-R	6-0	185	1-7-91	.250	.242	.252	38	136	12	34	10	0	0	16	9	9	1	2	40	0	1	.324	.333
Lopez, Daniel	R-R	6-2	175	1-17-92	.237	.175	.255	55	177	22	42	4	2	0	13	20	2	3	1	50	9	0	.282	.320
O'Brien, Peter	R-R	6-3	215	7-15-90	.202	.174	.211	48	198	27	40	8	0	10	32	10	3	0	2	61	0	1	.394	.249
Oh, Danny	L-L	6-0	190	12-28-89	.198	.095	.229	29	91	9	18	3	1	1	4	8	0	0	1	20	1	1	.286	.260
Orozco, Jamiel	R-R	5-11	160	1-29-93	.141	.056	.164	23	85	6	12	3	0	1	9	4	2	0	2	28	0	0	.212	.194

	B-T	HT	WT	DOB	AVG	vLH	vRH	G	AB	R	H	2B	3B	HR	RBI	BB	HBP	SH	SF	SO	SB	CS	SLG	OBP
Rosario, Jose	R-R	5-11	160	11-29-91	.217	.214	.218	60	230	30	50	7	1	1	19	13	3	2	0	42	13	4	.270	.268
Santana, Ravel	R-R	6-2	160	5-1-92	.216	.244	.208	60	218	22	47	7	0	3	19	25	3	0	1	68	3	1	.289	.304
Snyder, Matt	L-R	6-5	200	6-17-90	.299	.255	.316	52	187	18	56	13	1	3	34	26	5	0	1	19	0	0	.428	.397
Tejeda, Isaias	R-R	6-0	195	10-28-91	.187	.148	.200	30	107	12	20	5	1	2	12	12	0	0	1	17	0	0	.308	.267
Valera, Jackson	R-R	6-1	175	4-8-92	.157	.308	.105	13	51	4	8	0	0	0	3	1	0	0	9	0	0	.157	.218
Wilson, Wes	R-R	6-0	210	8-18-89	.262	.143	.286	10	42	5	11	3	1	0	3	1	1	1	0	8	0	1	.381	.295

Pitching

	B-T	HT	WT	DOB	W	L	ERA	G	GS	CG	SV	IP	H	R	ER	HR	BB	SO	AVG	vLH	vRH	K/9	BB/9
Aardsma, David	R-R	6-3	205	12-27-81	0	1	27.00	1	1	0	0	1	4	4	2	1	1	1	.500	1.000	.200	13.50	13.50
Arbiso, Cory	R-R	6-3	210	4-21-86	1	0	0.00	3	0	0	0	4	4	4	0	0	1	3	.235	.250	.231	6.75	2.25
Basford, Charles	R-R	6-2	210	7-16-90	2	3	5.18	18	0	0	0	24	33	17	14	2	8	22	.327	.281	.348	8.14	2.96
Benak, Andrew	R-R	6-5	225	1-31-90	5	5	3.98	16	12	0	0	61	62	30	27	2	24	35	.265	.333	.217	5.16	3.54
Black, Corey	R-R	5-11	175	8-4-91	0	0	2.28	6	6	0	0	28	22	9	7	1	8	21	.222	.355	.162	6.83	2.60
Bleich, Jeremy	L-L	6-2	185	4-8-87	0	0	2.53	5	4	0	0	11	8	3	3	1	2	7	.205	.000	.320	5.91	1.69
Checo, Mariel	R-R	6-3	190	10-16-89	0	2	4.86	11	0	0	0	17	14	12	9	2	21	13	.230	.200	.244	7.02	11.34
DeLuca, Evan	L-L	6-1	195	3-9-91	0	0	8.10	17	0	0	0	27	31	27	24	3	25	17	.298	.273	.310	5.74	8.44
Encinas, Gabe	R-R	6-3	195	12-21-91	3	7	4.97	16	15	0	0	71	73	49	39	8	39	48	.266	.291	.248	6.11	4.97
Enns, Dietrich	L-L	6-1	195	5-16-91	2	2	2.11	22	0	0	0	43	34	10	10	0	15	33	.218	.279	.195	6.96	3.16
Erickson, Eric	R-R	6-0	187	2-17-88	1	1	3.86	7	0	0	1	9	7	4	4	1	1	8	.189	.286	.130	7.71	0.96
Feliciano, Pedro	L-L	5-10	195	8-25-76	0	0	3.00	3	1	0	0	3	3	1	1	1	0	2	.231	.000	.273	6.00	0.00
Flight, Tim	L-L	6-4	195	12-27-90	1	5	5.20	13	10	0	1	45	52	32	26	2	21	37	.287	.184	.151	7.40	4.20
Garrison, Taylor	R-R	5-11	165	5-24-90	0	2	2.28	26	0	0	11	28	20	9	7	0	8	28	.192	.079	.258	9.11	2.60
Goody, Nick	B-R	6-1	195	7-6-91	0	0	0.00	3	0	0	1	3	1	0	0	1	0	5	.091	.167	.000	13.50	2.70
Haslup, Charlie	R-R	6-3	180	8-23-91	2	1	3.18	11	0	0	0	17	14	6	6	1	6	12	.219	.143	.256	6.35	3.18
Lopez, Stefan	R-R	6-2	190	6-4-91	0	0	5.68	15	0	0	0	19	28	21	12	1	5	16	.315	.379	.283	7.58	2.37
Morton, Taylor	R-R	6-3	194	12-18-91	0	3	9.13	6	4	0	0	24	28	25	24	3	20	9	.289	.333	.262	3.42	7.61
Mullee, Conor	R-R	6-3	185	2-25-88	0	0	3.60	6	0	0	0	5	3	2	2	1	1	4	.167	.000	.200	7.20	1.80
Pazos, James	R-L	6-3	230	5-5-91	2	2	1.79	28	0	0	3	40	29	9	8	0	19	39	.196	.205	.193	8.70	4.24
Rincon, Angel	R-R	6-1	180	9-26-92	1	0	5.19	2	1	0	0	9	9	5	5	1	4	2	.273	.250	.286	2.08	4.15
Romanski, Josh	L-L	6-0	185	10-18-86	0	0	0.00	5	0	0	0	7	5	1	0	0	1	8	.200	.000	.238	10.29	1.29
Rutckyj, Evan	R-L	6-5	213	1-31-92	5	6	3.72	15	14	0	0	77	80	38	32	4	35	63	.265	.250	.267	7.33	4.07
Smith, Alex	R-R	6-3	200	9-29-91	2	2	5.13	21	1	0	1	33	44	32	19	1	12	25	.303	.308	.301	6.75	3.24
Varnadore, Derek	R-R	6-3	215	7-10-90	3	5	3.55	19	6	0	0	58	50	27	23	5	12	42	.227	.268	.203	6.48	1.85
Woods, Zach	R-R	6-0	190	11-15-87	0	0	17.18	19	4	0	1	4	7	7	7	1	2	5	.389	.250	.429	12.27	4.91

Fielding

Catcher	PCT	G	PO	A	E	DP	PB
O'Brien	.981	33	226	29	5	1	8
Tejeda	.971	24	155	15	5	0	9
Valera	.966	8	52	4	2	0	1
Wilson	.988	10	76	7	1	0	1

First Base	PCT	G	PO	A	E	DP
Bird	.989	10	83	4	1	6
Butler	.985	12	124	11	2	15
Duran	.950	2	16	3	1	1
Kuo	1.000	8	73	3	0	3
Snyder	.991	45	393	29	4	35

	PCT	G	PO	A	E	DP
Valera	1.000	2	18	1	0	0

Second Base	PCT	G	PO	A	E	DP
Custodio	1.000	1	1	3	0	0
Kuo	.985	13	20	46	1	10
Orozco	.974	19	55	58	3	19
Rosario	.947	44	93	122	12	22

Third Base	PCT	G	PO	A	E	DP
Duran	.882	58	40	117	21	8
Kuo	.842	16	8	40	9	2
Orozco	.800	2	2	2	1	0

Shortstop	PCT	G	PO	A	E	DP
Custodio	.915	60	85	184	25	28
Orozco	1.000	2	1	2	0	1
Rosario	.964	15	28	53	3	12

Outfield	PCT	G	PO	A	E	DP
Cayones	.985	46	63	4	1	0
Dugas	.959	56	92	2	4	1
Lopez	.952	52	98	2	5	1
Oh	1.000	27	50	1	0	0
Santana	.964	53	104	4	4	0

GCL YANKEES   ROOKIE
GULF COAST LEAGUE

Batting	B-T	HT	WT	DOB	AVG	vLH	vRH	G	AB	R	H	2B	3B	HR	RBI	BB	HBP	SH	SF	SO	SB	CS	SLG	OBP
Alcantara, Jorge	R-R	6-1	195	8-9-91	.222	.200	.231	26	72	12	16	2	1	2	8	12	2	0	0	20	4	2	.361	.349
Almonte, Abe	B-R	5-9	205	6-27-89	.222	.000	.286	7	18	2	4	2	0	0	2	0	0	0	4	2	0	.333	.300
Anderson, Jake	L-R	6-0	170	12-3-91	.179	.000	.238	10	28	4	5	2	0	0	5	0	0	0	10	1	1	.250	.303
Andujar, Miguel	R-R	6-0	175	3-2-95	.232	.200	.244	50	177	21	41	9	0	1	19	13	1	0	0	37	1	3	.299	.288
Aune, Austin	L-R	6-2	190	9-6-94	.273	.294	.267	39	139	19	38	10	3	1	20	19	1	1	3	45	6	4	.410	.358
Austin, Tyler	R-R	6-2	200	9-6-91	.500	.000	.750	2	6	1	3	0	0	1	2	1	0	0	0	1	0	0	1.000	.571
Bird, Greg	L-R	6-3	215	11-9-92	.286	.353	.250	17	49	9	14	2	1	0	5	11	1	0	1	13	0	0	.367	.419
Breen, Chris	R-R	6-3	215	3-26-94	.274	.345	.236	25	84	12	23	6	1	0	7	3	2	0	2	17	0	1	.369	.308
Brewer, Dan	R-R	5-11	190	7-19-87	.182	.000	.250	4	11	3	2	0	0	0	2	0	0	0	4	2	1	.182	.308
Calderon, Yeicok	L-L	6-2	185	12-23-91	.270	.288	.262	44	159	24	43	3	3	8	22	21	0	0	1	52	0	2	.478	.354
de Oleo, Eduardo	R-R	5-10	180	1-25-93	.191	.091	.222	20	47	7	9	2	0	1	9	5	1	0	0	17	0	1	.298	.283
Duran, Kelvin	L-L	5-11	165	11-10-94	.200	.000	.087	26	95	10	19	3	0	1	10	7	0	2	1	22	4	1	.263	.252
Heathcott, Slade	L-L	6-1	190	9-28-90	.235	.167	.273	5	17	3	4	2	0	0	2	5	0	0	0	4	2	0	.353	.409
Ibarra, Walter	B-R	5-11	180	11-1-87	.182	.111	.231	7	22	1	4	2	0	0	0	0	0	0	0	3	0	0	.273	.182
James, Justin	L-L	6-5	230	11-24-90	.138	.000	.125	12	29	3	4	0	0	0	0	7	0	0	0	10	1	0	.138	.306
Jones, Austin	R-R	6-1	205	8-20-92	.223	.214	.226	46	148	23	33	11	0	0	12	17	1	0	0	39	0	0	.297	.307
Leonora, Ericson	R-R	5-11	174	8-25-92	.227	.200	.239	55	198	24	45	10	0	7	30	19	4	1	1	41	5	0	.384	.306
Lopez, Jerison	R-R	5-11	177	8-24-91	.321	.279	.336	48	159	26	51	13	1	0	15	15	3	0	2	26	3	1	.415	.385
Mahoney, Kevin	L-R	6-1	215	9-21-87	.250	—	.250	2	4	1	1	0	0	1	1	0	0	0	1	0	0	.750	.400
Mikolas, Nathan	L-L	6-0	200	12-30-93	.149	.250	.102	31	87	7	13	0	0	1	5	12	6	0	0	35	1	1	.184	.295
Nunez, Eduardo	R-R	6-0	185	6-15-87	.200	.250	.167	4	10	1	2	0	0	1	1	0	0	0	0	0	0	0	.500	.200
O'Brien, Peter	R-R	6-3	215	7-15-90	.357	.800	.111	4	14	2	5	2	0	0	2	0	0	0	0	1	0	0	.500	.357
Oliberto, Mikeson	R-R	5-10	164	8-23-90	.279	.188	.315	48	172	21	48	13	6	3	22	15	2	2	1	42	8	2	.477	.342

	B-T	HT	WT	DOB	AVG	vLH	vRH	G	AB	R	H	2B	3B	HR	RBI	BB	HBP	SH	SF	SO	SB	CS	SLG	OBP
Perez, Fernando	B-R	6-2	160	12-9-90	.196	.235	.176	18	51	2	10	0	0	0	2	2	0	1	0	19	0	0	.196	.226
Remedios, David	R-R	6-0	215	6-27-87	.292	.364	.270	19	48	11	14	1	0	5	12	5	3	0	0	14	0	0	.625	.393
Romine, Austin	R-R	6-0	220	11-22-88	.208	.375	.125	9	24	3	5	3	0	0	5	5	1	0	0	3	0	0	.333	.367
Rosario, Francisco	B-R	6-1	170	7-12-90	.273	.200	.310	21	44	2	12	1	0	0	0	5	1	1	0	14	3	0	.295	.360
Smith, Dalton	R-R	6-3	205	6-29-94	.208	.200	.211	8	24	0	5	1	0	0	4	4	0	0	5	0	0		.250	.321

Pitching	B-T	HT	WT	DOB	W	L	ERA	G	GS	CG	SV	IP	H	R	ER	HR	BB	SO	AVG	vLH	vRH	K/9	BB/9
Aardsma, David	R-R	6-3	205	12-27-81	0	0	0.00	3	3	0	0	5	3	1	0	0	1	7	.158	.125	.182	12.60	1.80
Agramonte, Kenedy	R-R	5-10	150	12-4-90	2	1	2.25	11	0	0	0	16	10	5	4	2	4	21	.182	.143	.195	11.81	2.25
Arbiso, Cory	R-R	6-3	210	4-21-86	0	0	6.35	4	3	0	0	6	7	4	4	0	0	6	.304	.429	.250	9.53	0.00
Arneson, Zach	R-R	6-2	190	11-17-88	0	0	4.50	2	1	0	0	2	2	1	1	0	1	3	.250	.000	.400	13.50	4.50
Bautista, Rony	L-L	6-7	200	9-17-91	4	1	3.51	12	0	0	1	41	32	19	16	1	16	48	.212	.152	.229	10.54	3.51
Bello, Yoely	L-L	6-2	150	12-16-90	2	1	5.17	12	0	0	0	16	17	10	9	1	6	14	.283	.125	.341	8.04	3.45
Beriguete, Victor	R-R	6-1	185	11-6-88	1	0	0.00	4	0	0	1	8	3	0	0	0	2	6	.115	.143	.105	6.75	2.25
Black, Corey	R-R	5-11	175	8-4-91	0	0	6.75	1	1	0	0	1	2	1	1	0	2	0	.333	.000	.500	0.00	13.50
Bleich, Jeremy	L-L	6-2	185	6-18-87	1	0	0.00	3	2	0	0	6	3	0	0	0	1	7	.136	.400	.059	11.12	1.59
Camarena, Daniel	L-L	6-0	200	11-9-92	0	0	1.02	5	3	0	0	18	8	2	2	1	0	15	.136	.176	.119	7.64	0.00
Castro, Kelvin	R-R	6-3	164	12-14-87	0	2	7.11	7	0	0	1	6	10	6	5	0	3	4	.345	.333	.350	5.68	4.26
Chamberlain, Joba	R-R	6-2	250	9-23-85	0	0	0.00	3	3	0	0	4	0	1	0	0	0	6	.000	.000	.000	13.50	0.00
Cote, Jordan	R-R	6-5	215	11-13-92	3	0	0.98	6	2	0	0	28	21	4	3	0	4	25	.204	.156	.225	8.13	1.30
Cruz, Dawerd	R-R	6-1	170	12-7-88	0	0	0.00	1	0	0	0	1	0	0	0	0	1	0	.000	—	.000	9.00	9.00
Davis, Rookie	R-R	6-3	235	4-29-93	2	1	2.65	7	1	0	0	17	17	9	5	1	4	17	.250	.381	.191	9.00	2.12
Dawe, Dayton	R-R	6-2	175	4-13-94	0	0	3.38	6	0	0	0	11	6	6	4	0	7	8	.167	.083	.208	6.75	5.91
Feliciano, Pedro	L-L	5-10	195	8-25-76	0	0	0.00	4	4	0	0	4	2	0	0	0	1	5	.143	.250	.100	11.25	2.25
Frare, Caleb	L-L	6-1	195	7-8-93	2	1	2.74	10	2	0	0	23	17	7	7	0	7	23	.227	.087	.288	9.00	2.74
Gallegos, Giovanny	R-R	6-2	175	8-14-91	0	1	1.67	12	4	0	0	27	20	7	5	1	2	22	.206	.133	.239	7.33	0.67
Hebert, Chaz	L-L	6-2	180	9-4-92	1	2	2.52	11	2	0	1	25	23	7	7	2	4	30	.242	.292	.225	10.80	1.44
Hensley, Ty	R-R	6-4	220	7-30-93	1	2	3.00	5	4	0	0	12	8	8	4	1	7	14	.174	.214	.156	10.50	5.25
Lail, Brady	R-R	6-2	175	8-9-93	1	0	1.42	5	0	0	0	13	8	3	2	0	2	10	.190	.188	.192	7.11	1.42
Maher, Joey	R-R	6-5	200	8-5-92	0	3	5.64	7	3	0	2	22	28	15	14	1	8	17	.308	.355	.283	6.85	3.22
Mascheri, Rich	L-L	5-10	190	8-7-89	0	0	0.00	3	0	0	1	4	0	0	0	0	0	6	.000	.000	.000	13.50	4.50
Mejia, Edison	R-R	6-1	185	7-2-90	1	3	3.10	19	0	0	11	20	17	8	7	1	3	20	.213	.091	.259	8.85	1.33
Mercedes, Melvin	R-R	6-3	170	8-28-89	1	2	5.14	16	1	0	2	21	29	16	12	2	8	15	.333	.458	.286	6.43	3.43
Mojica, Deivi	R-R	6-1	185	3-19-91	0	0	0.00	1	0	0	0	0	0	0	0	0	0	0	.000	—		0.00	0.00
Niebla, Luis Alberto	R-R	6-2	180	1-4-91	5	2	4.29	12	4	0	1	42	50	25	20	2	7	32	.301	.333	.286	6.86	1.50
Nuding, Zach	R-R	6-4	250	3-29-90	1	0	1.26	4	3	0	0	14	9	3	2	0	8	11	.188	.154	.200	6.91	5.02
Rincon, Angel	R-R	6-1	180	9-26-92	2	1	1.59	7	5	0	0	23	11	4	4	0	6	22	.143	.130	.148	8.74	2.37
Sharp, Hayden	R-R	6-6	195	10-30-92	1	1	3.52	8	4	0	0	23	16	14	9	1	12	20	.195	.160	.211	7.83	4.70
Smith, Adam	R-R	6-3	200	12-15-89	1	1	6.00	5	0	0	0	6	5	4	4	0	5	9	.217	.200	.222	13.50	7.50
Stoneburner, Graham	R-R	6-0	205	9-29-87	0	1	4.70	4	3	0	0	8	8	7	4	1	1	3	.276	.333	.250	3.52	1.17
Vargas, Cesar	R-R	6-1	160	12-30-91	3	2	2.97	11	2	0	2	36	36	16	12	1	8	30	.254	.159	.296	7.43	1.98

Fielding

Catcher	PCT	G	PO	A	E	DP	PB
Bird	1.000	3	23	0	0	1	1
Breen	.974	23	169	17	5	0	7
de Oleo	.960	20	103	17	5	2	2
O'Brien	1.000	3	17	2	0	0	2
Remedios	.993	19	122	14	1	1	6
Romine	.974	7	36	1	1	0	1

First Base	PCT	G	PO	A	E	DP
Alcantara	.979	12	89	3	2	5
Bird	.988	12	75	6	1	2
Jones	.989	44	332	32	4	24

Second Base	PCT	G	PO	A	E	DP
Alcantara	.900	2	6	3	1	0
Anderson	.978	10	20	24	1	5

Ibarra	1.000	6	9	8	0	1
Lopez	.981	46	67	92	3	16
Mahoney	1.000	1	2	3	0	1
Rosario	1.000	7	5	8	0	1

Third Base	PCT	G	PO	A	E	DP
Alcantara	.786	5	1	10	3	0
Andujar	.907	50	33	104	14	5
Lopez	1.000	1	0	3	0	0
Mahoney	—	1	0	0	0	0
Smith	.900	7	3	6	1	0

Shortstop	PCT	G	PO	A	E	DP
Aune	.887	31	39	79	15	14
Ibarra	1.000	1	0	2	0	0
Lopez	1.000	1	0	3	0	0

Nunez	1.000	4	1	3	0	0
Perez	.949	18	16	40	3	8
Rosario	1.000	14	15	29	0	0

Outfield	PCT	G	PO	A	E	DP
Alcantara	1.000	6	4	0	0	0
Almonte	1.000	5	4	0	0	0
Austin	1.000	1	1	0	0	0
Brewer	1.000	4	2	1	0	0
Calderon	.915	31	65	0	6	0
Duran	1.000	23	49	1	0	0
James	1.000	10	24	0	0	0
Leonora	.985	39	62	2	1	0
Mikolas	.947	30	35	1	2	0
Oliberto	.976	45	79	3	2	1

DSL YANKEES1 — ROOKIE

DOMINICAN SUMMER LEAGUE

Batting	B-T	HT	WT	DOB	AVG	vLH	vRH	G	AB	R	H	2B	3B	HR	RBI	BB	HBP	SH	SF	SO	SB	CS	SLG	OBP
Aparicio, Jesus	R-R	5-11	186	8-18-94	.167	—	.167	3	6	1	1	0	0	0	0	1	0	0	0	2	0	0	.167	.286
2-team total (18 Yankees 2)					.150	—	—	21	60	4	9	1	0	0	4	5	1	0	0	17	1	0	.167	.227
Aquino, Melvin	R-R	5-11	160	7-14-92	.241	.207	.250	42	145	24	35	15	0	2	14	10	0	0	0	39	8	0	.386	.321
Avelino, Abiatal	R-R	5-11	186	2-14-95	.302	.326	.296	57	222	46	67	11	1	1	25	27	10	3	2	34	20	2	.374	.398
Brito, Sandy	R-R	6-3	170	6-9-93	.243	.178	.260	62	218	47	53	14	6	4	25	61	0	0	0	72	12	3	.417	.409
Coa, Rainiero	R-R	5-10	170	1-3-93	.267	.000	.286	11	15	3	4	1	0	0	2	4	1	0	0	2	0	0	.333	.450
Figueroa, Jose	L-R	5-10	170	12-9-92	.382	.425	.370	58	186	44	71	12	11	3	39	18	8	1	0	25	4	9	.613	.458
Herrera, Roybell	R-R	5-11	177	12-30-90	.229	.294	.202	35	118	20	27	5	0	4	20	7	4	1	2	22	0	0	.373	.290
Javier, Jose	R-R	5-10	160	9-16-92	.329	.355	.324	52	167	39	55	8	4	2	24	22	6	1	2	32	15	6	.461	.421
Lopez, Jose	R-R	5-10	170	8-13-91	.207	.125	.220	19	58	4	12	2	0	0	3	5	0	1	0	15	0	0	.241	.290
Martini, Renzo	R-R	6-1	190	8-25-92	.290	.340	.275	60	221	43	64	22	4	5	49	28	7	0	5	27	1	3	.493	.379
Mojica, Miguel	R-R	6-2	180	8-23-92	.225	.241	.220	44	129	21	29	3	1	2	18	20	2	1	3	30	5	6	.310	.331
Pina, Julio	R-R	5-9	190	6-18-91	.160	.167	.158	10	25	3	4	0	0	0	2	4	0	0	0	9	2	1	.160	.276

	B-T	HT	WT	DOB	AVG	vLH	vRH	G	AB	R	H	2B	3B	HR	RBI	BB	HBP	SH	SF	SO	SB	CS	SLG	OBP
2-team total (11 Yankees 2)					.250	—	—	21	52	11	13	5	0	0	3	8	0	0	0	14	2	1	.346	.350
Polanco, Jose	R-R	6-1	190	5-22-91	.219	.241	.212	40	128	24	28	4	1	3	23	22	5	0	0	46	11	2	.336	.355
Polo, Rafael	R-R	6-2	165	4-2-93	.333	—	.333	1	3	3	1	0	1	0	1	2	1	0	0	0	0	0	1.000	.667
Ramos, Abraham	R-R	5-10	150	8-3-92	.324	.200	.345	13	34	6	11	1	0	0	6	4	0	1	0	6	0	2	.353	.395
2-team total (14 Yankees 2)					.235	—	—	27	68	13	16	2	0	1	8	13	0	1	0	14	1	3	.309	.358
Reyes, Allison	R-R	6-0	165	9-16-92	.333	.320	.337	41	114	16	38	14	0	0	14	9	5	1	0	16	10	4	.456	.406
Romero, Wilmer	R-R	6-1	185	12-19-93	.298	.256	.309	46	178	30	53	16	2	6	36	14	1	0	0	43	1	1	.511	.352
Tamarez, Christopher	R-R	6-2	170	10-25-93	.338	.444	.305	56	228	41	77	18	1	6	35	21	2	0	3	40	2	6	.504	.394
Valerio, Allen	R-R	6-1	173	1-11-93	.118	.000	.133	7	17	2	2	1	0	0	1	1	1	0	0	4	1	2	.176	.211
2-team total (34 Yankees 2)					.216	—	—	41	125	19	27	5	2	3	16	19	2	1	2	24	3	2	.360	.324

Pitching	B-T	HT	WT	DOB	W	L	ERA	G	GS	CG	SV	IP	H	R	ER	HR	BB	SO	AVG	vLH	vRH	K/9	BB/9
Acuna, Joaquin	R-R	6-2	185	3-7-91	3	0	5.40	13	1	0	1	32	31	20	19	2	24	19	.252	.292	.227	5.40	6.82
Alcantara, Brayan	R-R	6-1	175	8-6-92	0	0	2.45	2	0	0	0	4	4	3	1	0	4	5	.267	.667	.167	12.27	9.82
2-team total (13 Yankees 2)					0	8	6.23	15	13	0	0	43	52	50	30	2	37	36	—	—	—	7.48	7.68
Aquino, Daury	R-R	6-1	179	4-4-91	5	0	1.79	14	0	0	5	50	36	15	10	1	10	33	.200	.176	.209	5.90	1.79
Arias, Freddery	R-R	6-1	196	10-24-94	3	2	2.67	13	0	0	2	34	27	15	10	0	20	27	.221	.200	.232	7.22	5.35
Batista, Jean	R-R	6-4	175	10-27-91	0	3	6.04	13	0	0	0	28	27	23	19	1	13	24	.252	.289	.232	7.22	4.13
Burgos, Havid	L-L	6-1	188	8-6-94	5	1	4.00	12	0	0	0	27	24	19	12	1	20	26	.245	.188	.256	8.67	6.67
Canela, Erick	R-R	6-1	155	10-2-90	7	1	1.29	14	14	0	0	70	37	13	10	2	13	70	.158	.147	.164	9.00	1.67
Cedeno, Luis	R-R	5-11	154	7-14-94	1	0	0.00	8	0	0	1	9	6	0	0	0	2	10	.194	.100	.238	9.64	1.93
De Paula, Rafael	R-R	6-2	212	3-24-91	8	2	1.46	14	14	1	0	62	35	18	10	2	18	85	.162	.167	.159	12.41	2.63
Garcia, Samuel	R-R	6-0	180	3-4-93	1	1	2.93	12	0	0	1	15	11	5	5	1	4	20	.204	.261	.161	11.74	2.35
Jose, Fernando	R-R	6-2	190	11-27-92	1	0	1.29	4	1	0	0	14	11	4	2	0	10	12	.224	.364	.184	7.71	6.43
Joseph, Francis	R-R	5-10	165	10-4-93	1	0	4.00	6	0	0	0	9	7	4	4	1	2	11	.282	.167	.303	11.00	2.00
Martinez, Dallas	R-R	6-0	174	10-28-94	2	1	2.19	14	14	0	0	66	65	27	16	2	21	54	.271	.289	.261	7.40	2.88
Mateo, Andres	R-R	5-11	200	4-24-91	0	0	27.00	1	0	0	0	0	0	1	1	0	3	0	.000	.000	.000	0.00	81.00
2-team total (4 Yankees 2)					0	1	5.06	5	0	0	0	5	3	4	3	0	6	6	—	—	—	10.13	10.13
Ordaz, Rafael	R-R	6-4	201	2-17-95	0	0	4.50	1	0	0	0	2	0	3	1	0	3	0	.000	.000	.000	0.00	13.50
2-team total (13 Yankees 2)					1	1	6.69	14	0	0	0	39	56	37	29	2	22	24	—	—	—	5.54	5.08
Pena, Jose	R-R	6-0	190	3-22-91	2	1	0.99	16	0	0	8	27	20	3	3	0	2	32	.208	.163	.245	10.54	0.66
Perez, Elvin	R-R	6-4	193	8-3-90	0	0	0.00	2	0	0	0	2	1	0	0	0	2	0	.143	.000	.250	0.00	9.00
2-team total (7 Yankees 2)					0	4	2.43	9	7	0	0	37	31	14	10	1	11	22	—	—	—	5.35	2.68
Polanco, Reynaldo	R-R	6-2	178	5-20-93	4	3	2.61	13	12	0	0	52	41	25	15	1	30	50	.222	.268	.193	8.71	5.23
Rodriguez, Edwin	R-R	6-0	150	5-16-90	1	2	1.83	15	0	0	7	20	14	4	4	0	2	28	.194	.226	.171	12.81	0.92
Saavedra, Jhon	R-R	6-2	180	2-2-89	0	0	0.00	4	0	0	0	3	1	0	0	0	2	4	.111	.000	.200	13.50	6.75
2-team total (8 Yankees 2)					0	1	6.39	12	0	0	1	13	17	10	9	0	4	14	—	—	—	9.95	2.84
Severino, Luis	R-R	6-0	195	2-20-94	4	2	1.68	14	14	0	0	64	46	19	12	2	17	45	.205	.181	.217	6.30	2.38

Fielding

Catcher	PCT	G	PO	A	E	DP	PB
Aparicio	1.000	3	11	0	0	0	
Coa	1.000	8	38	9	0	0	1
Herrera	.982	23	138	30	3	1	2
Lopez	.971	19	150	15	5	0	6
Pina	1.000	1	7	0	0	0	
Vavrusa	.980	28	214	30	5	0	4

First Base	PCT	G	PO	A	E	DP
Coa	1.000	3	2	1	0	0
Herrera	1.000	5	33	0	0	3
Martini	.991	51	435	27	4	42
Mojica	.950	4	19	0	1	3
Ramos	.955	5	18	3	1	1
Valerio	1.000	2	12	0	0	1

	PCT	G	PO	A	E	DP
Vavrusa	1.000	12	103	0	0	12

Second Base	PCT	G	PO	A	E	DP
Javier	.964	51	71	117	7	24
Polo	1.000	1	2	1	0	0
Ramos	1.000	1	2	5	0	2
Reyes	.983	28	50	64	2	16

Third Base	PCT	G	PO	A	E	DP
Aquino	.888	34	27	60	11	4
Martini	.848	12	4	24	5	3
Ramos	.941	7	6	10	1	1
Reyes	.833	5	2	3	1	0
Tamarez	.902	21	16	39	6	4
Valerio	.667	1	1	1	1	1

Shortstop	PCT	G	PO	A	E	DP
Aquino	1.000	1	0	1	0	0
Avelino	.934	47	83	130	15	29
Reyes	.750	2	2	4	2	2
Tamarez	.918	21	27	62	8	10

Outfield	PCT	G	PO	A	E	DP
Brito	.968	51	86	4	3	0
Figueroa	.979	58	88	5	2	3
Mojica	.985	41	62	2	1	0
Pina	.750	9	3	0	1	0
Polanco	.919	32	32	2	3	1
Reyes	1.000	4	3	1	0	0
Romero	.978	37	40	4	1	0

DSL YANKEES2 — ROOKIE

DOMINICAN SUMMER LEAGUE

Batting	B-T	HT	WT	DOB	AVG	vLH	vRH	G	AB	R	H	2B	3B	HR	RBI	BB	HBP	SH	SF	SO	SB	CS	SLG	OBP
Aguilar, Angel	R-R	6-0	170	6-13-95	.234	.259	.221	49	171	19	40	3	0	0	11	8	4	0	0	33	1	0	.251	.284
Aparicio, Jesus	R-R	5-11	186	8-18-94	.148	.071	.175	18	54	3	8	1	0	0	4	1	0	0	0	15	1	0	.167	.220
2-team total (3 Yankees 1)					.150	—	—	21	60	4	9	1	0	0	4	5	1	0	0	17	1	0	.167	.227
Barrios, Daniel	R-R	5-11	183	4-18-95	.207	.140	.237	52	140	32	29	6	3	0	9	35	1	1	1	51	5	2	.293	.367
Castellon, Alfredo	L-R	6-2	166	6-4-93	.000	.000	.000	1	5	0	0	0	0	0	0	0	0	0	0	2	0	0	.000	.000
Castillo, Yohanny	R-R	6-1	200	7-10-93	.210	.323	.162	32	105	10	22	7	0	2	17	15	1	0	1	23	0	0	.333	.311
Cuevas, Bryan	R-R	5-10	179	10-14-93	.315	.321	.313	62	260	41	82	14	8	3	37	15	0	1	2	48	10	3	.465	.350
Gomez, Jhoan	R-R	6-0	175	2-14-93	.250	.179	.273	39	116	17	29	8	0	4	17	11	3	2	2	33	1	3	.422	.326
Liranzo, Ozzie	B-R	5-8	182	1-26-93	.250	.267	.243	19	52	10	13	4	1	0	8	10	1	0	0	12	0	2	.365	.435
Marte, Freite	R-R	5-10	174	11-23-89	.288	.324	.273	64	257	41	74	9	5	2	27	22	8	3	1	66	17	9	.385	.361
Mateo, Jorge	R-R	6-0	188	6-23-95	.255	.125	.308	14	55	15	14	2	1	1	8	12	0	1	1	11	4	1	.382	.382
Munoz, Barfil	R-R	6-1	170	5-21-94	.237	.246	.233	56	207	34	49	9	1	8	36	26	5	0	1	60	1	1	.406	.335
Noriega, Alvaro	R-R	6-0	198	11-9-94	.246	.254	.242	59	228	20	56	14	0	2	22	8	5	1	0	30	3	3	.333	.286
Pierret, Abraham	R-R	6-1	159	11-8-93	.240	.197	.259	57	208	26	50	17	3	2	21	15	2	0	0	55	5	2	.380	.298
Pina, Julio	R-R	5-9	190	6-18-91	.333	.500	.235	11	27	8	9	5	0	0	1	4	0	0	0	5	0	0	.519	.419
2-team total (10 Yankees 1)					.250	—	—	21	52	11	13	5	0	0	3	8	0	0	0	14	2	1	.346	.350

Name	B-T	HT	WT	DOB	AVG	vLH	vRH	G	AB	R	H	2B	3B	HR	RBI	BB	SO			SB	CS		OBP	SLG
Ramos, Abraham	R-R	5-10	150	8-3-92	.147	.182	.130	14	34	7	5	1	0	1	2	9	0	0	0	8	1	1	.265	.326
2-team total (13 Yankees 1)					.235	—	—	27	68	13	16	2	0	1	8	13	0	1	0	14	1	3	.309	.358
Rey, Victor	R-R	6-2	178	6-29-95	.191	.048	.255	22	68	8	13	1	0	2	9	11	2	0	0	14	1	2	.294	.321
Rodriguez, Wascar	R-R	6-2	198	10-6-94	.228	.122	.287	38	136	15	31	7	1	2	17	14	4	0	3	40	1	1	.338	.312
Valera, Junior	R-R	6-0	180	9-27-92	.255	.333	.220	50	145	17	37	5	5	0	15	22	4	2	0	32	8	3	.359	.368
Valerio, Allen	R-R	6-1	173	1-11-93	.231	.125	.276	34	108	17	25	4	2	3	16	18	1	1	2	20	2	0	.389	.341
2-team total (7 Yankees 1)					.216	—	—	41	125	19	27	5	2	3	16	19	2	1	2	24	3	2	.360	.324

Pitching	B-T	HT	WT	DOB	W	L	ERA	G	GS	CG	SV	IP	H	R	ER	HR	BB	SO	AVG	vLH	vRH	K/9	BB/9
Alcantara, Brayan	R-R	6-1	175	8-6-92	0	8	6.58	13	13	0	0	40	48	47	29	2	33	31	.306	.302	.309	7.03	7.49
2-team total (2 Yankees 1)					0	8	6.23	15	13	0	0	43	52	50	30	2	37	36	—	—	—	7.48	7.68
Bello, Hector	L-L	6-1	175	5-19-91	1	3	4.37	14	0	0	0	45	53	33	22	0	17	41	.286	.222	.297	8.14	3.38
Cabrera, Cristofer	R-R	6-0	180	12-25-92	5	4	2.84	14	14	0	0	57	37	26	18	4	28	49	.184	.224	.171	7.74	4.42
Cedeno, Moises	R-R	6-0	188	8-29-95	0	1	15.12	4	4	0	0	8	13	17	14	0	12	5	.333	.400	.292	5.40	12.96
De La Rosa, Maikel	L-L	6-2	170	11-25-90	0	1	2.45	20	0	0	4	26	27	11	7	0	10	23	.281	.200	.296	8.06	3.51
Diaz, Carlos	L-L	6-2	170	5-24-95	0	0	4.50	1	0	0	0	2	1	1	1	0	2	0	.143	.000	.167	0.00	9.00
Guzman, Raudy	R-R	6-1	211	9-27-94	2	8	4.72	14	14	0	0	55	62	44	29	2	31	35	.273	.244	.290	5.69	5.04
Juliana, Hershelon	R-R	6-1	171	2-6-93	0	1	3.07	16	1	0	2	29	27	12	10	1	18	15	.250	.256	.246	4.60	5.52
Magallanes, Kelvin	R-R	6-1	175	7-15-94	0	1	9.31	11	0	0	0	19	21	27	20	0	27	15	.276	.231	.300	6.98	12.57
Mateo, Andres	R-R	5-11	200	4-24-91	1	0	3.60	4	0	0	0	5	3	3	2	0	3	6	.214	.200	.222	10.80	5.40
2-team total (1 Yankees 1)					0	1	5.06	5	0	0	0	5	3	4	3	0	6	6	—	—	—	10.13	10.13
Ordaz, Rafael	R-R	6-4	201	2-17-95	1	1	6.81	13	0	0	0	37	56	34	28	2	19	24	.350	.345	.352	5.84	4.62
2-team total (1 Yankees 1)					1	1	6.69	14	0	0	0	39	56	37	29	2	22	24	—	—	—	5.54	5.08
Perez, Elvin	R-R	6-4	193	8-3-90	0	4	2.57	7	7	0	0	35	30	14	10	1	9	22	.238	.182	.268	5.66	2.31
2-team total (2 Yankees 1)					0	4	2.43	9	7	0	0	37	31	14	10	1	11	22	—	—	—	5.35	2.68
Pichardo, Jose	R-R	5-11	164	7-21-93	0	1	7.79	14	1	0	0	17	19	15	15	0	14	12	.297	.281	.313	6.23	7.27
Pujols, Jose	R-R	6-6	183	11-19-92	0	2	2.93	5	0	0	0	15	15	10	5	0	10	13	.242	.267	.219	7.63	5.87
Reyes, Aderlis	R-R	6-2	182	10-23-91	1	0	8.50	15	0	0	0	18	23	23	17	1	20	14	.311	.355	.279	7.00	10.00
Rivera, Eduardo	R-R	6-5	190	9-24-92	0	6	5.02	14	14	0	0	52	41	41	29	1	43	45	.220	.239	.210	7.79	7.44
Rodriguez, David	R-R	5-11	156	1-15-93	3	2	5.40	14	2	0	0	33	30	23	20	2	22	23	.244	.275	.229	6.21	5.94
Rodriguez, Ramon	R-R	6-1	170	7-23-91	0	0	4.91	3	0	0	0	4	3	2	2	0	2	3	.250	.000	.429	7.36	4.91
Saavedra, Jhon	R-R	6-2	180	2-2-90	0	1	8.10	8	0	0	0	10	16	10	9	0	2	10	.364	.250	.429	9.00	1.80
2-team total (4 Yankees 1)					0	1	6.39	12	0	0	0	13	17	10	9	0	4	14	—	—	—	9.95	2.84
Soto, Dubeny	R-R	5-11	185	10-30-88	0	2	4.50	2	0	0	0	2	4	2	1	0	1	0	.500	.600	.333	4.50	0.00

Fielding

Catcher	PCT	G	PO	A	E	DP	PB
Aparicio	.913	16	78	17	9	1	5
Castillo	1.000	4	11	1	0	0	1
Liranzo	.954	16	88	16	5	0	9
Noriega	.967	34	193	41	8	2	2
Pina	.928	11	54	10	5	0	4

First Base	PCT	G	PO	A	E	DP
Barrios	.975	5	38	1	1	4
Castellon	1.000	1	9	0	0	0
Castillo	.985	19	185	10	3	18
Gomez	.992	15	123	8	1	12
Noriega	.980	18	141	8	3	12
Ramos	.990	14	95	6	1	11
Rey	1.000	1	6	1	0	1

	PCT	G	PO	A	E	DP
Valerio	.974	4	37	0	1	2

Second Base	PCT	G	PO	A	E	DP
Aguilar	1.000	1	3	2	0	1
Barrios	.926	21	50	38	7	10
Cuevas	.961	39	87	109	8	28
Valera	.920	17	36	33	6	11
Valerio	1.000	1	2	1	0	0

Third Base	PCT	G	PO	A	E	DP
Aguilar	.839	6	8	18	5	3
Barrios	.900	20	11	25	4	2
Gomez	.875	17	12	30	6	0
Rey	.934	19	12	45	4	2
Valerio	.907	22	20	48	7	3

Shortstop	PCT	G	PO	A	E	DP
Aguilar	.890	35	52	93	18	18
Barrios	1.000	1	2	3	0	0
Cuevas	.911	18	28	54	8	9
Mateo	.957	11	16	29	2	2
Valerio	.927	13	20	31	4	10

Outfield	PCT	G	PO	A	E	DP
Gomez	1.000	6	10	1	0	0
Marte	.934	59	93	6	7	1
Munoz	.972	46	67	2	2	0
Pierret	.952	54	94	6	5	2
Rodriguez	.922	33	41	6	4	2
Valera	.942	30	44	5	3	1

NEW YORK YANKEES

Oakland Athletics

SEASON IN A SENTENCE: The Athletics staged one of the most improbable seasons in recent memory, using a roster full of rookies to overcome a 13-game deficit at the end of June, stun the Rangers and win the American League West.

HIGH POINT: The A's began opening eyes with a four-game sweep of the Yankees from July 19-22. Their story reached its climax in the final regular season series at home against Texas, which they entered trailing the Rangers by two games. Playing at home in front of raucous full houses, Oakland swept Texas to steal the division away, capped off by a 12-5 rout in the finale. The AL Division Series almost seemed like a footnote to the story, but the A's nearly stole the show there too, taking the Tigers the distance before falling to Justin Verlander in Game Five.

LOW POINT: For the A's to make their comeback, they had to hit their low point first. They endured a nine-game losing streak from May 22-June 1, which left their record at 22-30, and they fell 13 games out of first place after three straight losses to the Rangers in Arlington from June 28-30. Another lowlight came in August when Bartolo Colon, one of the few veterans in the team's rotation, was suspended 50 games for testing positive for elevated levels of testosterone.

NOTABLE ROOKIES: The A's got as many contributions from rookies as any contender in history. At times, the team used a rotation composed entirely of rookies, ranging from top prospect Jarrod Parker, who was acquired from the Diamondbacks before the season, to breakout players like A.J. Griffin and Dan Straily. In the lineup, Cuban import Yoenis Cespedes lived up to his billing by leading the team in average and slugging while hitting 23 homers.

KEY TRANSACTIONS: The A's won the derby to sign Cespedes with a four-year, $36 million deal in March. Other key contributors were brought in through trades, like Parker and reliever Ryan Cook from Arizona and lefthander Tom Milone and catcher Derek Norris from the Nationals. The A's cleared the way for Norris by sending Kurt Suzuki to Washington in another trade in August.

DOWN ON THE FARM: On his way to the majors, Straily won the minor league strikeout title with 190. Three of Oakland's six domestic affiliates reached their leagues' playoffs, including Triple-A Sacramento posting the best record in the Pacific Coast League, but none claimed a title.

OPENING DAY PAYROLL: $55.4 million (29th)

PLAYERS OF THE YEAR

MAJOR LEAGUE	MINOR LEAGUE
Josh Reddick	**Dan Straily**
of	rhp
.242/.305/.463	(Double-A/Triple-A)
32 HR, 85 RBIs	9-7, 2.78
Won first Gold Glove	190 SO led minors

ORGANIZATION LEADERS

BATTING		*Minimum 250 AB
MAJORS		
* AVG	Yoenis Cespedes	.292
* OPS	Yoenis Cespedes	.861
HR	Josh Reddick	32
RBI	Josh Reddick	85
MINORS		
* AVG	Miles Head, Stockton/Midland	.333
* OBP	Conner Crumbliss, Midland	.414
* SLG	Miles Head, Stockton/Midland	.577
R	Conner Crumbliss, Midland	94
H	Miles Head, Stockton/Midland	160
TB	Miles Head, Stockton/Midland	277
2B	Miles Head, Stockton/Midland	32
	B.A. Vollmuth, Burlington/Stockton	32
3B	Jermaine Mitchell, Sacramento	11
HR	Dusty Robinson, Burlington/Stockton	27
RBI	Miles Head, Stockton/Midland	84
BB	Conner Crumbliss, Midland	120
SO	Dusty Coleman, Midland	182
SB	Chad Oberacker, Burlington/Stockton	30

PITCHING		#Minimum 75 IP
MAJORS		
W	Jarrod Parker	13
	Tommy Milone	13
# ERA	Jarrod Parker	3.47
SO	Jarrod Parker	140
SV	Grant Balfour	24
MINORS		
W	Brad Peacock, Sacramento	12
L	Fabio Castro, Sacramento/Midland	14
# ERA	Dan Straily, Midland/Sacramento	2.78
G	Jonathan Ortiz, Midland	52
GS	Drew Granier, Burlington	28
SV	Zach Thornton, Stockton	16
IP	Drew Granier, Burlington	162.2
BB	Gary Daley, Midland	71
SO	Dan Straily, Midland/Sacramento	190
# AVG	Dan Straily, Midland/Sacramento	.202

General Manager: Billy Beane. **Farm Director:** Keith Lieppman. **Scouting Director:** Eric Kubota.

Class	Team	League	W	L	PCT	Finish	Manager
Majors	Oakland Athletics	American	94	68	.580	2nd (14)	Bob Melvin
Triple-A	Sacramento River Cats	Pacific Coast	86	58	.597	1st (16)	Darren Bush
Double-A	Midland RockHounds	Texas	64	74	.464	5th (8)	Steve Scarsone
High A	Stockton Ports	California	56	84	.400	10th (10)	Webster Garrison
Low A	Burlington Bees	Midwest	67	72	.482	11th (16)	Aaron Nieckula
Short-season	Vermont Lake Monsters	New York-Penn	33	43	.434	10th (14)	Rick Magnante
Rookie	AZL Athletics	Arizona	37	17	.685	1st (13)	Marcus Jensen
Overall 2012 Minor League Record			343	348	.496	21st (30)	

ORGANIZATION STATISTICS

OAKLAND ATHLETICS

AMERICAN LEAGUE

Batting	B-T	HT	WT	DOB	AVG	vLH	vRH	G	AB	R	H	2B	3B	HR	RBI	BB	HBP	SH	SF	SO	SB	CS	SLG	OBP
Allen, Brandon	L-R	6-2	235	2-12-86	.000	—	.000	3	7	0	0	0	0	0	0	0	0	0	0	5	0	0	.000	.000
2-team total (7 Tampa Bay)					.100	—	—	10	20	3	2	0	0	1	3	2	0	0	0	9	0	0	.250	.182
Barton, Daric	L-R	6-0	205	8-16-85	.204	.188	.210	46	113	8	23	7	0	1	6	22	1	0	0	32	1	0	.292	.338
Carter, Chris	R-R	6-4	245	12-18-86	.239	.241	.237	67	218	38	52	12	0	16	39	39	0	0	3	83	0	0	.514	.350
Cespedes, Yoenis	R-R	5-10	210	10-18-85	.292	.298	.289	129	487	70	142	25	5	23	82	43	7	0	3	102	16	4	.505	.356
Cowgill, Collin	R-L	5-9	185	5-22-86	.269	.318	.233	38	104	10	28	2	0	1	9	11	0	0	1	27	3	4	.337	.336
Crisp, Coco	B-R	5-10	185	11-1-79	.259	.248	.265	120	455	68	118	25	7	11	46	45	0	6	2	64	39	4	.418	.325
Donaldson, Josh	R-R	6-0	220	12-8-85	.241	.229	.246	75	274	34	66	16	0	9	33	14	5	0	1	61	4	1	.398	.289
Drew, Stephen	L-R	6-0	190	3-16-83	.250	.204	.272	39	152	21	38	5	0	5	16	18	0	0	2	41	1	1	.382	.326
Gomes, Jonny	R-R	6-1	225	11-22-80	.262	.299	.209	99	279	46	73	10	0	18	47	44	8	1	1	104	3	1	.491	.377
Hicks, Brandon	R-R	6-2	200	9-14-85	.172	.159	.200	22	64	8	11	5	0	3	7	6	0	0	0	31	1	0	.391	.243
Hughes, Luke	R-R	5-11	205	8-2-84	.077	.333	.000	4	13	0	1	0	0	0	0	0	0	0	0	6	0	0	.077	.077
2-team total (4 Minnesota)					.130	—	—	8	23	0	3	0	0	0	2	0	0	0	1	10	1	0	.130	.125
Inge, Brandon	R-R	5-11	190	5-19-77	.226	.216	.232	74	283	31	64	13	0	11	52	24	1	0	3	85	0	1	.389	.286
2-team total (9 Detroit)					.218	—	—	83	303	33	66	14	0	12	54	24	1	0	3	91	0	1	.383	.275
Ka'aihue, Kila	L-R	6-4	235	3-29-84	.234	.297	.209	39	128	13	30	9	0	4	14	10	1	0	0	28	1	0	.398	.295
Kottaras, George	L-R	6-0	200	5-10-83	.212	.294	.191	27	85	10	18	2	1	6	19	8	0	0	0	24	0	0	.471	.280
Moss, Brandon	L-R	6-0	210	9-16-83	.291	.293	.290	84	265	48	77	18	0	21	52	26	3	0	2	90	1	1	.596	.358
Norris, Derek	R-R	6-0	210	2-14-89	.201	.209	.195	60	209	19	42	8	1	7	34	21	1	0	1	66	5	1	.349	.276
Pennington, Cliff	B-R	5-10	193	6-15-84	.215	.168	.232	125	418	50	90	18	2	6	28	35	2	5	2	90	15	6	.311	.278
Recker, Anthony	R-R	6-2	240	8-29-83	.129	.000	.174	13	31	3	4	1	0	0	4	1	1	0	1	13	0	0	.161	.250
Reddick, Josh	L-R	6-2	180	2-19-87	.242	.237	.245	156	611	85	148	29	5	32	85	55	2	1	4	151	11	1	.463	.305
Rosales, Adam	R-R	6-1	195	5-20-83	.222	.219	.229	42	99	12	22	5	0	2	8	11	0	0	1	24	0	0	.333	.297
Smith, Seth	L-L	6-3	210	9-30-82	.240	.157	.259	125	383	55	92	23	2	14	52	50	5	0	3	98	2	2	.420	.333
Sogard, Eric	L-R	5-10	190	5-22-86	.167	.200	.159	37	102	8	17	3	1	2	7	5	0	1	0	17	2	0	.275	.206
Suzuki, Kurt	R-R	5-11	195	10-4-83	.218	.233	.212	75	262	19	57	15	0	1	18	9	3	2	2	53	1	0	.286	.250
Taylor, Michael	R-R	6-5	255	12-19-85	.143	.083	.222	6	21	2	3	1	0	0	0	0	0	0	0	10	0	0	.190	.143
Weeks, Jemile	B-R	5-9	160	1-26-87	.221	.232	.215	118	444	54	98	15	8	2	20	50	5	9	3	70	16	5	.304	.305

Pitching	B-T	HT	WT	DOB	W	L	ERA	G	GS	CG	SV	IP	H	R	ER	HR	BB	SO	AVG	vLH	vRH	K/9	BB/9
Accardo, Jeremy	R-R	6-1	200	12-8-81	0	0	9.00	1	0	0	0	2	4	2	2	0	0	1	.444	.000	.500	4.50	0.00
2-team total (26 Cleveland)					0	0	4.82	27	0	0	0	37	42	21	20	3	16	29	—	—	—	6.99	3.86
Anderson, Brett	L-L	6-4	235	2-1-88	4	2	2.57	6	6	0	0	35	29	11	10	1	7	25	.225	.219	.227	6.43	1.80
Balfour, Grant	R-R	6-2	200	12-30-77	3	2	2.53	75	0	0	24	75	41	21	21	4	28	72	.160	.157	.163	8.68	3.38
Blackley, Travis	L-L	6-3	205	11-4-82	6	4	3.86	24	15	0	0	103	91	47	44	10	30	69	.238	.231	.241	6.05	2.63
Blevins, Jerry	L-L	6-6	175	9-6-83	5	1	2.48	63	0	0	1	65	45	20	18	7	25	54	.201	.182	.219	7.44	3.44
Carignan, Andrew	R-R	5-11	235	7-23-86	1	1	4.66	11	0	0	0	10	8	5	5	0	10	8	.242	.273	.227	7.45	9.31
Chavez, Jesse	R-R	6-2	160	8-21-83	0	0	18.90	4	0	0	0	3	9	7	7	1	1	4	.474	.600	.429	8.10	2.70
2-team total (9 Toronto)					1	1	9.85	13	2	0	0	25	34	29	27	7	11	30	—	—	—	10.95	4.01
Colon, Bartolo	R-R	5-11	265	5-24-73	10	9	3.43	24	24	0	0	152	161	62	58	17	23	91	.266	.274	.257	5.38	1.36
Cook, Ryan	R-R	6-2	215	6-30-87	6	2	2.09	71	0	0	14	73	42	18	17	4	27	80	.166	.171	.162	9.82	3.31
De Los Santos, Fautino	R-R	6-2	225	2-15-86	0	0	3.00	6	0	0	0	3	7	1	1	0	3	3	.412	.250	.462	9.00	9.00
Doolittle, Sean	L-L	6-3	210	9-26-86	2	1	3.04	44	0	0	1	47	40	18	16	3	11	60	.227	.286	.195	11.41	2.09
Figueroa, Pedro	L-L	6-0	215	11-23-85	0	0	3.32	19	0	0	0	22	16	9	8	2	15	14	.216	.179	.239	5.82	6.23
Fuentes, Brian	L-L	6-4	230	8-9-75	2	2	6.84	26	0	0	5	25	30	19	19	5	10	18	.291	.265	.304	6.48	3.60
Godfrey, Graham	R-R	6-3	215	8-9-84	0	4	6.43	5	4	0	0	21	26	18	15	4	10	10	.317	.333	.290	4.29	4.29
Griffin, A.J.	R-R	6-5	230	1-28-88	7	1	3.06	15	15	0	0	82	74	29	28	10	19	64	.236	.245	.225	7.00	2.08
McCarthy, Brandon	R-R	6-7	200	7-7-83	8	6	3.24	18	18	0	0	111	115	44	40	10	24	73	.267	.288	.245	5.92	1.95
Miller, Jim	R-R	6-0	200	4-28-82	2	1	2.59	33	0	0	0	49	39	15	14	6	8	44	.217	.136	.283	8.14	4.99
Milone, Tommy	L-L	6-0	205	2-16-87	13	10	3.74	31	31	1	0	190	207	90	79	24	36	137	.278	.263	.283	6.49	1.71
Neshek, Pat	B-R	6-3	210	9-4-80	2	1	1.37	24	0	0	0	20	10	3	3	3	6	16	.147	.333	.094	7.32	2.75
Norberto, Jordan	L-L	6-0	195	12-8-86	4	1	2.77	39	0	0	1	52	37	17	16	5	22	46	.200	.225	.184	7.96	3.81
Parker, Jarrod	R-R	6-1	195	11-24-88	13	8	3.47	29	29	0	0	181	166	71	70	11	63	140	.248	.247	.248	6.95	3.13

OAKLAND ATHLETICS

	B-T	HT	WT	DOB	W	L	ERA	G	GS	CG	SV	IP	H	R	ER	HR	BB	SO	AVG	vLH	vRH	K/9	BB/9
Ross, Tyson	R-R	6-6	230	4-22-87	2	11	6.50	18	13	0	0	73	96	56	53	7	37	46	.327	.356	.297	5.65	4.54
Scribner, Evan	R-R	6-3	190	7-19-85	2	0	2.55	30	0	0	1	35	30	11	10	2	12	30	.221	.278	.183	7.64	3.06
Straily, Dan	R-R	6-2	215	12-1-88	2	1	3.89	7	7	0	0	39	36	19	17	11	16	32	.237	.271	.215	7.32	3.66
Thompson, Rich	R-R	6-1	210	7-1-84	0	0	0.00	1	0	0	0	1	1	0	0	0	0	0	.333	1.000	.000	0.00	0.00
2-team total (2 Los Angeles)					0	1	12.00	3	0	0	0	3	6	4	4	1	1	3	—	—	—	9.00	3.00

Fielding

Catcher	PCT	G	PO	A	E	DP	PB
Donaldson	.957	3	20	2	1	0	0
Kottaras	.977	27	164	8	4	0	2
Norris	.989	58	438	19	5	0	4
Recker	1.000	12	57	4	0	2	0
Suzuki	.996	75	491	37	2	4	4

First Base	PCT	G	PO	A	E	DP
Allen	1.000	3	25	2	0	1
Barton	1.000	43	319	17	0	30
Carter	.987	55	433	14	6	29
Donaldson	1.000	1	3	1	0	0
Hicks	1.000	1	3	1	0	1
Ka'aihue	.989	22	160	12	2	24
Moss	.982	55	407	24	8	38
Rosales	1.000	7	26	7	0	1

Second Base	PCT	G	PO	A	E	DP
Hicks	1.000	1	1	3	0	0
Pennington	.987	32	67	85	2	12
Rosales	1.000	21	46	41	0	14
Sogard	1.000	6	10	17	0	4
Weeks	.977	113	181	293	11	63

Third Base	PCT	G	PO	A	E	DP
Donaldson	.945	71	53	152	12	14
Hughes	.750	4	3	6	3	1
Inge	.968	74	74	140	7	17
Rosales	1.000	3	2	4	0	0
Sogard	.946	14	11	24	2	2

Shortstop	PCT	G	PO	A	E	DP
Drew	.967	39	44	102	5	17

	PCT	G	PO	A	E	DP
Hicks	.953	19	24	37	3	4
Pennington	.979	93	150	272	9	58
Rosales	1.000	11	14	27	0	3
Sogard	1.000	15	14	34	0	6

Outfield	PCT	G	PO	A	E	DP
Cespedes	.987	102	221	9	3	0
Cowgill	1.000	36	69	3	0	2
Crisp	.989	113	272	4	3	2
Gomes	.971	42	65	1	2	0
Moss	.974	23	35	2	1	0
Reddick	.982	144	310	15	6	3
Smith	.983	66	115	3	2	0
Taylor	1.000	6	14	0	0	0

SACRAMENTO RIVER CATS TRIPLE-A

PACIFIC COAST LEAGUE

Batting	B-T	HT	WT	DOB	AVG	vLH	vRH	G	AB	R	H	2B	3B	HR	RBI	BB	HBP	SH	SF	SO	SB	CS	SLG	OBP
Barton, Daric	L-R	6-0	205	8-16-85	.255	.276	.246	74	259	49	66	14	3	8	35	66	6	0	5	53	7	1	.425	.411
Carter, Chris	R-R	6-4	245	12-18-86	.279	.238	.296	72	276	48	77	19	1	12	53	38	4	0	6	74	5	1	.486	.367
Cespedes, Yoenis	R-R	5-10	210	10-18-85	.333	—	.333	3	9	1	3	0	0	0	0	1	1	0	0	1	0	0	.333	.455
Cowgill, Collin	R-L	5-9	185	5-22-86	.254	.241	.260	61	260	33	66	17	1	4	37	20	3	0	2	50	8	2	.373	.312
Donaldson, Josh	R-R	6-0	220	12-8-85	.335	.266	.366	51	209	38	70	12	2	13	45	23	1	0	1	34	5	2	.598	.402
Fiorentino, Jeff	L-R	6-1	185	4-14-83	.186	.118	.231	16	43	7	8	1	1	0	4	6	0	0	0	7	0	0	.256	.286
Galarraga, Joel	R-R	5-11	185	3-20-82	.273	.000	.333	3	11	1	3	0	0	0	0	0	0	0	0	3	0	0	.273	.273
2-team total (9 Las Vegas)					.306	—		12	36	4	11	1	1	0	3	4	0	0	0	8	1	0	.389	.375
Green, Grant	R-R	6-3	180	9-27-87	.296	.311	.290	125	524	73	155	28	6	15	75	33	2	0	3	75	13	9	.458	.338
Hicks, Brandon	R-R	6-2	200	9-14-85	.244	.302	.220	90	328	61	80	26	3	18	61	47	7	0	1	115	5	4	.506	.350
Horton, Josh	L-R	6-2	215	2-19-86	.400	.000	.500	3	10	2	4	2	0	0	2	1	0	0	0	2	0	0	.600	.455
Hughes, Luke	R-R	5-11	205	8-2-84	.235	.238	.233	35	102	16	24	6	0	2	13	14	2	0	3	28	1	2	.353	.331
2-team total (28 Las Vegas)					.275	—		67	207	36	57	15	3	5	26	27	3	1	4	60	2	2	.449	.361
Inge, Brandon	R-R	5-11	190	5-19-77	.370	.462	.286	8	27	6	10	4	0	2	9	5	0	0	0	9	0	0	.741	.469
Jaramillo, Jason	B-R	6-0	215	10-9-82	.231	.143	.250	11	39	3	9	2	0	0	5	4	1	0	0	10	0	0	.282	.318
2-team total (41 Nashville)					.198	—		52	172	10	34	5	0	2	17	18	3	0	2	35	2	1	.262	.282
Ka'aihue, Kila	L-R	6-4	235	3-29-84	.256	.309	.237	66	254	44	65	16	0	15	52	44	3	0	4	60	1	1	.496	.367
Lalli, Blake	L-R	6-1	205	5-12-83	.200	.000	.273	4	15	1	3	0	0	1	1	1	0	0	0	1	0	1	.400	.250
2-team total (93 Iowa)					.256	—		97	316	34	81	20	0	8	41	18	0	0	6	55	0	2	.396	.291
Lipkin, Ryan	R-R	6-0	205	10-8-87	.000	.000	.000	4	11	0	0	0	0	0	0	1	1	0	1	0	0	0	.000	.143
Mitchell, Jermaine	L-L	6-0	215	11-2-84	.252	.267	.246	108	409	75	103	15	11	6	38	54	5	4	2	104	15	7	.386	.345
Moss, Brandon	L-R	6-0	210	9-16-83	.286	.247	.311	51	196	32	56	11	1	15	33	22	5	0	1	40	4	0	.582	.371
Norris, Derek	R-R	6-0	210	2-14-89	.271	.271	.270	58	218	39	59	14	2	9	38	21	1	0	6	41	5	1	.477	.329
Paramore, Petey	B-R	6-2	195	10-30-86	.286	.500	.200	2	7	1	2	0	0	1	1	0	0	0	0	1	0	0	.714	.286
Parker, Steve	L-R	6-2	200	9-3-87	.256	.234	.263	99	328	43	84	13	5	7	47	32	5	5	5	93	5	1	.390	.327
Pennington, Cliff	B-R	5-10	193	6-15-84	.455	.500	.400	3	11	2	5	1	0	0	1	3	0	0	0	4	1	0	.545	.571
Peterson, Shane	L-L	6-0	195	2-11-88	.389	.318	.404	38	131	36	51	7	1	7	23	23	1	2	0	31	4	3	.618	.484
Ramirez, Manny	R-R	6-0	225	5-30-72	.302	.118	.370	17	63	8	19	3	0	0	14	5	0	0	1	17	0	0	.349	.348
Recker, Anthony	R-R	6-2	240	8-29-83	.265	.289	.258	52	200	29	53	7	0	9	29	28	1	0	0	56	3	1	.435	.358
2-team total (3 Iowa)					.266	—		55	207	30	55	8	0	9	29	30	1	0	0	58	3	1	.435	.361
Rosales, Adam	R-R	6-1	195	5-20-83	.280	.228	.301	76	275	46	77	21	1	8	47	26	2	1	6	57	4	2	.451	.340
Smith, Seth	L-L	6-3	210	9-30-82	.667	.667	.000	3	3	0	2	0	0	0	0	0	0	0	0	0	0	0	.667	.750
Sogard, Eric	L-R	5-10	190	5-22-86	.331	.271	.358	37	157	29	52	5	2	5	22	23	0	0	0	17	11	3	.484	.417
Taylor, Michael	R-R	6-5	255	12-19-85	.287	.270	.293	120	449	81	129	31	1	12	67	86	5	0	3	105	18	3	.441	.405
Timmons, Wes	R-R	6-0	180	7-12-78	.228	.289	.202	49	149	24	34	6	0	2	21	24	4	1	3	13	4	2	.309	.344
Weeks, Jemile	B-R	5-9	160	1-26-87	.333	.444	.306	10	45	5	15	4	0	0	10	6	0	0	0	8	1	0	.422	.412

Pitching	B-T	HT	WT	DOB	W	L	ERA	G	GS	CG	SV	IP	H	R	ER	HR	BB	SO	AVG	vLH	vRH	K/9	BB/9
Accardo, Jeremy	R-R	6-1	200	12-8-81	1	0	1.17	7	0	0	2	8	7	1	1	0	3	4	.233	.278	.167	4.70	3.52
Anderson, Brett	L-L	6-4	235	2-1-88	1	1	4.24	5	5	0	0	23	27	12	11	4	5	18	.290	.323	.274	6.94	1.93
Banwart, Travis	R-R	6-4	215	3-24-86	9	5	3.85	32	18	0	2	129	132	59	55	15	37	99	.264	.305	.226	6.92	2.59
Barham, Trey	L-L	6-0	215	11-7-85	0	0	13.97	6	0	0	0	10	18	15	15	2	8	6	.409	.389	.423	5.59	7.45
Billings, Bruce	R-R	6-0	200	11-18-85	7	6	3.98	25	25	0	0	133	126	63	59	15	39	117	.250	.250	.250	7.90	2.63
Carignan, Andrew	R-R	5-11	200	7-23-86	2	0	2.70	9	0	0	1	13	9	4	4	0	1	21	.184	.167	.200	14.18	0.68
Castro, Fabio	L-L	5-7	185	1-20-85	3	7	6.92	14	9	0	0	53	65	43	41	9	31	42	.297	.293	.298	7.09	5.23
Chavez, Jesse	R-R	6-2	160	8-21-83	0	0	1.80	2	1	0	1	10	8	2	2	0	2	9	.211	.200	.222	8.10	1.80
2-team total (19 Las Vegas)					8	5	3.77	21	18	1	2	105	98	47	44	10	22	95	—	—	—	8.14	1.89

				W	L	ERA	G	GS	CG	SV	IP	H	R	ER	HR	BB	SO	AVG	vLH	vRH	K/9	BB/9
De Los Santos, Fautino R-R 6-2 225 2-15-86				1	3	7.25	28	0	0	0	36	49	30	29	2	16	43	.320	.373	.279	10.75	4.00
2-team total (11 Nashville)				2	3	5.80	39	0	0	0	50	66	33	32	2	20	60	—	—		10.87	3.62
Doolittle, Sean L-L 6-3 210 9-26-86				0	0	0.00	2	0	0	0	4	1	0	0	1	0	8	.083	.000	.111	19.64	2.45
Farquhar, Danny R-R 5-9 180 2-17-87				1	2	10.13	5	0	0	0	8	10	9	9	1	6	6	.323	.222	.364	6.75	6.75
2-team total (12 Tacoma)				2	2	3.65	17	0	0	4	25	19	10	10	1	11	22	—	—		8.03	4.01
Figueroa, Pedro L-L 6-0 215 11-23-85				0	2	2.62	32	0	0	1	45	35	17	13	1	18	40	.212	.190	.225	8.06	3.63
Godfrey, Graham R-R 6-3 215 8-9-84				9	2	3.29	20	17	0	1	104	98	39	38	8	26	60	.257	.322	.201	5.19	2.25
Gray, Sonny R-R 5-11 200 11-7-89				0	0	9.00	1	1	0	0	4	10	4	4	0	1	2	.500	.500	.500	4.50	2.25
Griffin, A.J. R-R 6-5 230 1-28-88				4	2	3.07	10	10	2	0	59	48	27	20	3	11	47	.217	.207	.227	7.21	1.69
Hernandez, Carlos L-L 5-11 155 3-4-87				3	2	4.15	6	2	0	0	22	25	11	10	3	4	16	.294	.255	.342	6.65	1.66
Leon, Arnold R-R 6-1 205 9-6-88				3	0	1.77	22	0	0	0	36	26	9	7	4	15	31	.208	.246	.172	7.82	3.79
Long, Nathan R-R 6-2 210 2-9-86				0	0	45.00	1	0	0	0	1	4	5	5	0	2	1	.571	.667	.500	9.00	18.00
McCarthy, Brandon R-R 6-7 200 7-7-83				0	1	5.59	2	2	0	0	10	9	6	6	1	3	11	.250	.400	.143	10.24	2.79
Miller, Jim R-R 6-1 200 4-28-82				0	3	2.79	16	0	0	6	19	15	6	6	0	4	21	.208	.313	.125	9.78	1.86
Norberto, Jordan L-L 6-0 195 12-8-86				0	0	0.00	1	0	0	0	1	0	0	0	0	0	2	.000	—	.000	18.00	0.00
Parker, Jarrod R-R 6-1 195 11-24-88				1	0	2.18	4	4	0	0	21	22	6	5	2	6	21	.275	.281	.271	9.15	2.61
Peacock, Brad R-R 6-1 175 2-2-88				12	9	6.01	28	25	0	0	135	147	99	90	16	66	139	.275	.278	.273	9.29	4.41
Ray, Chris R-R 6-3 210 1-12-82				0	0	6.00	6	0	0	0	6	7	4	4	1	6	6	.280	.667	.158	9.00	9.00
Ross, Tyson R-R 6-6 230 4-22-87				6	2	2.99	15	13	1	0	78	69	33	26	4	29	64	.235	.253	.216	7.35	3.33
Scribner, Evan R-R 6-3 190 7-19-85				3	0	3.03	26	0	0	8	36	26	12	12	4	10	38	.203	.283	.147	9.59	2.52
Simmons, James R-R 6-3 220 9-29-86				2	0	1.80	9	0	0	0	15	12	3	3	1	8	13	.218	.194	.250	7.80	4.80
Souza, Justin R-R 6-1 185 10-22-85				3	1	6.87	36	1	0	0	58	86	51	44	12	18	26	.352	.378	.328	4.06	2.81
Straily, Dan R-R 6-2 215 12-1-88				6	3	2.03	11	11	0	0	67	40	15	15	3	19	82	.172	.235	.110	11.07	2.57
Thompson, Rich R-R 6-1 210 7-1-84				4	2	3.34	46	0	0	3	62	46	24	24	23	7	23	58	.206	.215	.198	8.42	3.34
Threets, Erick L-L 6-5 240 11-4-81				4	2	1.84	34	0	0	3	44	35	9	9	0	19	31	.226	.196	.242	6.34	3.89
2-team total (18 Albuquerque)				6	4	2.79	52	0	0	4	61	51	20	19	2	30	43	—	—		6.31	4.40
Valdez, Merkin R-R 6-3 235 11-5-81				0	1	3.75	34	0	0	5	36	33	17	15	4	17	26	.236	.246	.227	6.50	4.25
Wagner, Neil R-R 6-0 195 1-1-84				1	1	5.49	15	0	0	1	20	20	13	12	1	6	24	.263	.167	.326	10.98	2.75
2-team total (31 Tucson)				4	2	5.46	46	0	0	1	63	77	43	38	3	23	56	—	—		8.04	3.30

Fielding

Catcher	PCT	G	PO	A	E	DP	PB
Donaldson	.987	22	210	13	3	1	2
Galarraga	1.000	3	17	2	0	0	1
Jaramillo	.986	11	61	7	1	1	0
Lalli	1.000	3	18	1	0	0	0
Lipkin	1.000	4	28	1	0	0	0
Norris	.996	58	439	40	2	1	6
Paramore	1.000	2	13	1	0	0	0
Recker	.985	44	368	36	6	7	3

First Base	PCT	G	PO	A	E	DP
Barton	.989	57	487	30	6	52
Carter	.990	47	365	17	4	44
Ka'aihue	.990	22	182	12	2	20
Lalli	1.000	1	11	0	0	1
Moss	.989	13	87	6	1	4
Parker	1.000	1	5	0	0	0
Timmons	1.000	6	29	2	0	1

Second Base	PCT	G	PO	A	E	DP
Donaldson	—	1	0	0	0	0
Green	.957	19	44	68	5	15

	PCT	G	PO	A	E	DP
Hicks	1.000	30	54	66	0	18
Hughes	.982	24	47	65	2	15
Parker	—	1	0	0	0	0
Rosales	.985	13	17	47	1	9
Sogard	.989	30	76	99	2	24
Timmons	.991	25	46	64	1	14
Weeks	.938	10	13	32	3	5

Third Base	PCT	G	PO	A	E	DP
Barton	—	1	0	0	0	0
Donaldson	.966	26	20	36	2	4
Green	.968	11	12	18	1	2
Hughes	.667	2	0	2	1	0
Inge	.882	7	6	9	2	1
Ka'aihue	—	1	0	0	0	0
Parker	.930	88	49	138	14	11
Rosales	1.000	5	4	9	0	2
Sogard	1.000	3	4	7	0	0
Timmons	1.000	14	8	19	0	2

Shortstop	PCT	G	PO	A	E	DP
Donaldson	—	1	0	0	0	0

	PCT	G	PO	A	E	DP
Green	.913	19	30	33	6	11
Hicks	.969	63	119	162	9	41
Horton	1.000	3	3	5	0	1
Pennington	.923	3	5	7	1	3
Rosales	.972	57	96	146	7	38
Sogard	1.000	5	8	11	0	1

Outfield	PCT	G	PO	A	E	DP
Cespedes	.800	3	3	1	1	0
Cowgill	.979	60	141	2	3	0
Donaldson	1.000	1	1	0	0	0
Fiorentino	1.000	13	18	0	0	0
Green	.974	79	143	5	4	3
Hughes	1.000	4	3	0	0	0
Ka'aihue	.895	9	16	1	2	0
Mitchell	.984	101	239	5	4	3
Moss	.962	24	51	0	2	0
Peterson	1.000	37	48	2	0	1
Recker	1.000	3	7	0	0	0
Rosales	1.000	1	4	0	0	0
Taylor	.979	109	186	5	4	1
Timmons	1.000	3	7	0	0	0

MIDLAND ROCKHOUNDS   DOUBLE-A
TEXAS LEAGUE

Batting	B-T	HT	WT	DOB	AVG	vLH	vRH	G	AB	R	H	2B	3B	HR	RBI	BB	HBP	SH	SF	SO	SB	CS	SLG	OBP
Aliotti, Anthony	L-L	6-0	204	7-16-87	.292	.206	.319	123	455	72	133	29	1	10	76	68	3	1	4	129	0	0	.356	.385
Barfield, Jeremy	R-L	6-5	220	7-12-88	.272	.294	.264	128	482	67	131	28	1	13	64	35	4	0	7	82	1	0	.415	.322
Choice, Michael	R-R	6-0	220	11-10-89	.287	.278	.290	91	359	59	103	15	2	10	58	33	7	0	3	88	5	1	.423	.356
Coleman, Dusty	R-R	6-2	185	4-20-87	.201	.206	.200	128	427	51	86	16	4	15	59	41	10	4	4	182	9	8	.363	.284
Crumbliss, Conner	L-R	5-8	175	4-19-87	.257	.283	.249	128	470	94	121	21	6	10	45	120	9	1	5	98	24	8	.391	.414
Fabiaschi, Michael	R-R	5-11	185	8-17-88	.000	.000	.000	3	3	0	0	0	0	0	0	0	0	0	0	2	0	0	.000	.000
Freitas, David	R-R	6-3	225	3-18-89	.333	.320	.342	20	63	12	21	6	0	2	11	6	2	0	3	15	0	0	.524	.392
Gil, Leonardo	R-R	6-1	160	8-18-87	.280	.262	.287	64	211	29	59	6	2	1	21	21	2	4	1	64	3	3	.341	.349
Head, Miles	R-R	6-0	215	5-2-91	.272	.271	.273	57	213	25	58	9	2	5	28	16	5	0	0	75	0	1	.404	.338
Horton, Josh	L-R	6-2	215	2-19-86	.278	.259	.284	121	461	51	128	26	4	9	54	47	3	0	3	113	5	4	.410	.346
Hughes, Luke	R-R	5-11	205	8-2-84	.179	.000	.227	7	28	1	5	0	0	1	2	3	0	0	0	9	1	0	.286	.258
Ladendorf, Tyler	R-R	6-0	210	3-7-88	.240	.333	.208	104	416	59	100	20	1	9	54	42	11	4	3	89	7	4	.358	.324
Lipkin, Ryan	R-R	6-0	205	10-8-87	.204	.190	.208	53	191	15	39	9	0	4	17	11	4	2	1	42	1	0	.314	.227
Mesa, Eliezer	R-R	5-11	180	11-24-88	.179	.222	.158	18	56	4	10	1	2	0	7	0	1	1	2	17	1	0	.268	.186
Nunez, Juan	R-R	6-1	215	8-27-87	.000	.000	.000	2	6	0	0	0	0	0	0	1	1	0	1	2	0	0	.000	.143
Ortiz, Ryan	R-R	6-3	200	9-29-87	.167	.125	.183	44	144	19	24	5	1	2	13	21	3	1	1	40	0	0	.257	.284

OAKLAND ATHLETICS

Batting	B-T	HT	WT	DOB	AVG	vLH	vRH	G	AB	R	H	2B	3B	HR	RBI	BB	HBP	SH	SF	SO	SB	CS	SLG	OBP
Peterson, Shane	L-L	6-0	195	2-11-88	.274	.264	.279	48	157	27	43	11	3	2	23	44	3	1	0	47	9	3	.420	.441
Rizzotti, Matt	L-L	6-5	265	12-24-85	.307	.179	.351	40	150	20	46	15	0	5	27	9	1	0	0	34	0	0	.507	.350
Spina, Mike	R-R	6-1	220	12-17-86	.176	.286	.128	70	256	34	45	11	0	7	35	32	3	0	3	75	0	0	.301	.272
Taylor, Beau	L-R	6-0	200	2-13-90	.233	.150	.250	36	120	13	28	5	0	0	10	11	1	1	0	36	0	0	.275	.303

Pitching	B-T	HT	WT	DOB	W	L	ERA	G	GS	CG	SV	IP	H	R	ER	HR	BB	SO	AVG	vLH	vRH	K/9	BB/9
Barham, Trey	L-L	6-0	215	11-7-85	1	0	3.00	13	0	0	0	15	18	7	5	1	4	14	.286	.296	.278	8.40	2.40
Billings, Bruce	R-R	6-0	200	11-18-85	2	0	3.18	2	0	0	0	6	4	2	2	0	4	3	.190	.167	.200	4.76	6.35
Bowman, Josh	R-R	6-2	195	9-9-88	0	1	5.40	1	1	0	0	5	7	3	3	0	2	3	.333	.429	.286	5.40	3.60
Castro, Fabio	L-L	5-7	185	1-20-85	2	7	4.63	14	14	0	0	72	80	41	37	3	37	58	.288	.280	.289	7.25	4.63
Daley, Gary	R-R	6-3	200	11-8-85	10	10	5.11	34	18	0	2	118	130	85	67	9	71	79	.275	.257	.287	6.03	5.42
Doolittle, Sean	L-L	6-3	210	9-26-86	0	0	0.82	8	0	0	1	11	2	2	1	1	0	4	19	.056	.167	.000	15.55	3.27
Gray, Sonny	R-R	5-11	200	11-7-89	6	9	4.14	26	26	1	0	148	148	73	68	8	57	97	.263	.291	.247	5.90	3.47
Griffin, A.J.	R-R	6-5	230	1-28-88	3	1	2.49	7	7	0	0	43	31	12	12	4	7	44	.201	.141	.253	9.14	1.45
Guzman, Jose	R-R	5-11	185	11-5-87	2	1	4.50	34	0	0	0	54	55	29	27	3	20	49	.263	.260	.260	8.17	3.33
Haviland, Shawn	R-R	6-2	200	11-10-85	6	8	4.80	31	21	0	2	120	124	72	64	11	47	104	.268	.263	.272	7.80	3.53
Hernandez, Carlos	L-L	5-11	155	3-4-87	6	4	5.36	25	10	0	0	81	96	49	48	12	26	65	.303	.338	.291	7.25	2.90
Hunter, Brett	R-R	6-4	215	6-27-87	3	3	4.50	42	0	0	0	56	53	31	28	7	31	60	.254	.264	.248	9.64	4.98
Huttenlocker, A.J.	L-L	6-3	190	8-5-86	1	2	5.74	21	0	0	0	16	26	13	10	4	5	13	.361	.412	.316	7.47	2.87
Jones, Beau	R-R	6-1	205	8-25-86	2	1	3.86	20	0	0	0	23	17	11	10	1	12	19	.202	.171	.224	7.33	4.63
Krol, Ian	L-L	6-1	180	5-9-91	1	2	5.06	8	0	0	0	11	11	6	6	0	2	10	.289	.333	.269	8.44	1.69
Leon, Arnold	R-R	6-1	205	9-6-88	1	0	2.30	10	0	0	1	16	17	5	4	0	3	18	.288	.190	.342	10.34	1.72
McSwain, Matt	R-R	6-1	197	8-15-85	1	1	11.15	11	2	0	0	15	32	21	19	2	9	7	.444	.475	.406	4.11	5.28
Ortiz, Jonathan	R-R	5-10	170	10-29-85	4	6	3.75	52	0	0	15	62	58	30	26	7	18	50	.243	.200	.268	7.22	2.60
Simmons, James	R-R	6-3	220	9-29-86	1	2	3.35	30	0	0	1	48	41	18	18	3	14	37	.229	.225	.231	6.89	2.61
Smith, Murphy	R-R	6-3	210	8-25-87	6	11	4.82	27	24	0	1	140	171	91	75	8	57	83	.311	.329	.299	5.34	3.66
Smyth, Paul	R-R	5-11	210	4-1-87	1	2	4.02	44	1	0	1	69	72	33	31	8	24	53	.269	.230	.287	6.88	3.12
Straily, Dan	R-R	6-2	215	12-1-88	3	4	3.38	14	14	0	0	85	70	36	32	6	23	108	.224	.203	.237	11.39	2.43

Fielding

Catcher	PCT	G	PO	A	E	DP	PB
Freitas	.977	17	113	14	3	0	1
Lipkin	.990	53	367	28	4	1	6
Nunez	1.000	2	17	0	0	0	0
Ortiz	.972	44	323	27	10	3	5
Taylor	1.000	26	173	15	0	0	1

First Base	PCT	G	PO	A	E	DP
Aliotti	.991	102	910	87	9	95
Head	.944	2	15	2	1	1
Peterson	—	1	0	0	0	0
Rizzotti	1.000	3	23	4	0	1
Spina	.990	33	294	18	3	32

Second Base	PCT	G	PO	A	E	DP
Coleman	1.000	1	1	2	0	0

	PCT	G	PO	A	E	DP
Crumbliss	.934	14	23	34	4	6
Fabiaschi	1.000	2	3	2	0	0
Gil	.978	9	18	26	1	7
Horton	.967	52	83	151	8	38
Hughes	1.000	5	6	13	0	2
Ladendorf	.983	62	120	164	5	49

Third Base	PCT	G	PO	A	E	DP
Coleman	.971	51	21	80	3	9
Head	.951	52	28	89	6	15
Horton	.883	38	18	73	12	7
Spina	1.000	1	3	0	0	

Shortstop	PCT	G	PO	A	E	DP
Coleman	.971	127	191	411	18	84
Horton	.923	10	11	25	3	2

	PCT	G	PO	A	E	DP
Ladendorf	.885	4	11	12	3	1

Outfield	PCT	G	PO	A	E	DP
Barfield	.969	128	264	17	9	2
Choice	.962	85	172	7	7	3
Crumbliss	.984	106	175	14	3	2
Gil	—	1	0	0	0	0
Hughes	.500	2	0	1	1	0
Ladendorf	.965	41	77	5	3	1
Mesa	.966	17	28	0	1	0
Peterson	.958	44	67	2	3	0
Taylor	1.000	1	1	0	0	0

STOCKTON PORTS   HIGH CLASS A
CALIFORNIA LEAGUE

Batting	B-T	HT	WT	DOB	AVG	vLH	vRH	G	AB	R	H	2B	3B	HR	RBI	BB	HBP	SH	SF	SO	SB	CS	SLG	OBP
Cabrera, Yordy	R-R	6-1	205	9-3-90	.232	.265	.217	60	220	26	51	9	2	3	21	16	3	0	0	68	2	2	.332	.293
Cowgill, Collin	R-L	5-9	185	5-22-86	.125	.333	.000	2	8	0	1	0	0	0	0	0	0	0	0	2	0	0	.125	.125
Dixon, Rashun	R-R	6-2	210	8-27-90	.206	.250	.198	30	102	12	21	6	1	2	12	10	1	0	2	41	1	1	.343	.278
Gil, Leonardo	R-R	6-1	160	8-18-87	.000	.000	.000	6	16	1	0	0	0	0	0	3	1	0	0	10	0	0	.000	.200
Gilmartin, Michael	R-R	6-0	180	7-14-88	.256	.276	.249	118	430	58	110	18	0	9	52	47	7	2	0	98	4	3	.360	.339
Head, Miles	R-R	6-0	215	5-2-91	.382	.324	.402	67	267	57	102	23	6	18	56	23	2	0	1	55	3	0	.715	.433
Kirby-Jones, A.J.	R-R	5-10	215	10-2-88	.248	.276	.238	115	399	62	99	16	3	21	69	86	2	0	3	128	0	0	.461	.382
LeVier, Mitch	L-L	5-11	185	1-12-88	.240	.148	.261	37	146	13	35	7	0	5	18	10	1	0	1	36	1	1	.390	.291
Leyja, Nino	R-R	5-10	175	10-24-88	.211	.220	.208	48	161	19	34	7	1	2	17	15	0	2	0	47	4	2	.304	.278
Lopez, Diomendes	R-R	6-2	195	1-30-89	.286	.500	.200	5	14	3	4	2	0	1	1	1	1	0	0	6	0	0	.643	.375
Mesa, Eliezer	R-R	5-11	180	11-24-88	.130	.182	.114	13	46	4	6	0	1	0	3	0	0	0	0	12	4	0	.174	.130
Nunez, Juan	R-R	6-1	215	8-27-87	.200	.500	.125	3	10	2	2	0	0	0	1	1	0	0	0	1	0	0	.200	.273
Oberacker, Chad	L-L	5-11	195	1-14-89	.260	.218	.277	107	454	64	118	25	7	13	48	43	3	2	3	96	25	3	.432	.326
Ortiz, Ryan	R-R	6-3	200	9-29-87	.248	.262	.241	38	129	23	32	5	1	5	25	27	1	0	3	31	1	1	.419	.375
Paramore, Petey	B-R	6-2	195	10-30-86	.217	.000	.250	6	23	4	5	1	0	0	2	2	1	1	0	5	0	0	.261	.308
Pineda, Ryan	R-R	5-11	180	4-17-89	.249	.258	.246	71	237	25	59	18	1	4	28	30	5	1	1	56	4	4	.384	.344
Richard, Myrio	R-L	6-1	190	8-17-88	.253	.235	.259	72	292	32	74	14	2	3	28	29	0	2	4	40	5	1	.346	.317
Robinson, Dusty	R-R	6-0	205	9-9-89	.231	.226	.232	94	386	62	89	14	0	18	47	33	3	0	1	129	7	2	.407	.296
Stassi, Max	R-R	5-10	205	3-15-91	.268	.289	.260	84	314	48	84	18	0	15	45	27	8	0	11	83	3	1	.468	.331
Taylor, Beau	L-R	6-0	200	2-13-90	.328	.244	.353	52	195	25	64	10	2	3	34	28	1	0	2	29	0	2	.446	.412
Thompson, Tony	R-R	6-4	219	12-19-88	.276	.226	.292	94	344	48	95	22	1	11	49	38	1	0	7	61	1	1	.442	.344
Vollmuth, B.A.	R-R	6-3	215	12-23-89	.261	.215	.281	65	264	45	69	15	0	7	29	27	3	0	1	70	0	0	.398	.336
Whitaker, Josh	R-R	6-3	235	2-8-89	.259	.272	.254	99	386	62	100	16	3	20	61	33	6	1	3	122	11	5	.472	.325

Pitching

Pitching	B-T	HT	WT	DOB	W	L	ERA	G	GS	CG	SV	IP	H	R	ER	HR	BB	SO	AVG	vLH	vRH	K/9	BB/9
Anderson, Brett	L-L	6-4	235	2-1-88	0	0	9.00	1	1	0	0	2	4	2	2	0	0	0	.400	.250	.500	0.00	0.00
Bowman, Josh	R-R	6-2	195	9-9-88	6	10	3.62	25	25	0	0	147	157	76	59	14	33	127	.270	.240	.298	7.79	2.03
Brown, Jake	R-L	6-2	220	12-28-86	6	11	5.06	30	21	0	1	133	162	88	75	16	26	94	.298	.286	.302	6.35	1.76
Capra, Anthony	L-L	6-1	200	4-3-87	0	1	7.94	9	0	0	0	11	12	12	10	4	11	14	.250	.304	.200	11.12	8.74
Cole, A.J.	R-R	6-4	180	1-5-92	0	7	7.82	8	8	0	0	38	60	40	33	7	10	31	.364	.392	.337	7.34	2.37
Doolittle, Ryan	R-R	6-3	185	3-25-88	1	3	1.48	15	0	0	0	24	17	6	4	2	3	31	.193	.205	.182	11.47	1.11
Doolittle, Sean	L-L	6-3	210	9-26-86	0	0	0.87	6	0	0	0	10	5	2	1	0	2	21	.143	.111	.154	18.29	1.74
Gagnier, Drew	R-R	6-4	225	9-21-88	0	0	4.50	2	0	0	0	2	1	1	1	0	2	2	.143	.000	.200	9.00	0.00
Guzman, Jose	R-R	5-11	185	11-5-87	2	2	2.82	15	0	0	0	22	19	8	7	2	8	21	.232	.233	.231	8.46	3.22
Hassebrock, Blake	R-R	6-4	212	7-15-89	2	6	8.17	14	13	0	0	51	84	55	46	6	20	44	.367	.311	.415	7.82	3.55
Hoehn, Connor	R-R	6-1	205	7-5-89	1	2	5.86	43	0	0	1	58	58	39	38	9	40	61	.261	.245	.275	9.41	6.17
Huttenlocker, A.J.	L-L	6-3	190	8-5-86	3	1	5.40	22	1	0	1	38	47	26	23	11	8	38	.294	.358	.262	8.92	1.88
Jimenez, Deivi	R-R	6-3	205	12-30-89	0	1	3.00	1	1	0	0	3	3	1	1	0	4	.273	.429	.000	12.00	0.00
Joseph, Jonathan	R-R	6-1	180	5-17-88	0	1	9.82	7	0	0	0	11	12	13	12	2	5	16	.273	.211	.320	13.09	4.09
Krol, Ian	L-L	6-1	180	5-9-91	1	7	5.21	21	15	0	0	86	95	64	50	13	24	79	.275	.255	.283	8.24	2.50
Leon, Arnold	R-R	6-1	205	9-6-88	0	1	5.28	12	0	0	0	15	26	13	9	1	5	25	.366	.412	.324	14.67	2.93
Long, Nathan	R-R	6-2	210	2-9-86	4	4	5.14	35	8	0	1	89	121	68	51	14	27	75	.321	.340	.307	7.56	2.72
Murphy, Sean	B-R	6-6	215	8-23-88	8	8	4.80	19	19	0	0	109	98	67	58	21	35	107	.238	.200	.275	8.86	2.90
Perlman, Max	R-L	6-7	235	2-28-86	0	2	8.18	14	5	0	0	44	63	52	40	8	16	24	.332	.320	.339	4.91	3.27
Souza, Justin	R-R	6-1	185	10-22-85	1	1	3.72	8	0	0	0	10	12	4	4	1	3	11	.286	.100	.455	10.24	2.79
Thornton, Zack	R-R	6-3	213	5-19-88	4	0	4.53	48	0	0	16	54	57	33	27	5	19	70	.264	.267	.261	11.74	3.19
Treinen, Blake	R-R	6-4	215	6-30-88	7	7	4.37	24	15	1	0	103	116	60	50	11	23	92	.278	.303	.250	8.04	2.01
Urlaub, Jeff	L-L	6-2	160	4-24-87	2	2	3.86	21	0	0	0	30	21	13	13	4	8	31	.194	.184	.200	9.20	2.37
Vidal, Pedro	R-R	6-1	215	7-31-87	1	0	3.43	28	0	0	0	39	29	16	15	4	7	37	.196	.179	.210	8.47	1.60
Walz, T.J.	R-R	6-0	175	11-21-88	7	6	3.16	39	8	0	0	100	84	39	35	9	36	112	.226	.278	.188	10.11	3.25

Fielding

Catcher	PCT	G	PO	A	E	DP	PB
Lopez	.976	5	38	3	1	1	0
Nunez	.941	3	30	2	2	0	0
Ortiz	.988	29	234	19	3	0	4
Paramore	.983	6	52	7	1	3	1
Stassi	.991	66	485	51	5	8	7
Taylor	.978	35	319	29	8	1	2

First Base	PCT	G	PO	A	E	DP
Gil	1.000	3	24	4	0	2
Head	1.000	9	82	8	0	4
Kirby-Jones	.990	83	631	49	7	48
Ortiz	1.000	1	7	0	0	0
Thompson	.983	45	334	17	6	34
Vollmuth	1.000	3	9	1	0	0
Whitaker	1.000	3	15	0	0	0

Second Base	PCT	G	PO	A	E	DP
Gilmartin	.963	37	57	100	6	15
Leyja	.971	44	57	108	5	20
Pineda	.971	61	118	146	8	30
Vollmuth	1.000	1	1	0	0	0

Third Base	PCT	G	PO	A	E	DP
Gil	.667	2	2	0	1	0
Gilmartin	1.000	2	0	1	0	0
Head	.934	50	47	81	9	7
Pineda	1.000	2	1	1	0	0
Thompson	.910	30	22	49	7	5
Vollmuth	.869	59	48	104	23	8

Shortstop	PCT	G	PO	A	E	DP
Cabrera	.905	59	77	143	23	32
Gil	1.000	1	1	3	0	0
Gilmartin	.945	78	109	184	17	38
Leyja	1.000	3	4	6	0	1

Outfield	PCT	G	PO	A	E	DP
Cowgill	—	1	0	0	0	0
Dixon	.941	28	45	3	3	1
LeVier	.964	28	53	0	2	0
Mesa	.963	12	26	0	1	0
Oberacker	.976	104	243	4	6	0
Pineda	1.000	3	4	0	0	0
Richard	.984	69	122	0	2	0
Robinson	.984	92	178	9	3	0
Whitaker	.971	88	164	3	5	2

BURLINGTON BEES   LOW CLASS A

MIDWEST LEAGUE

Batting	B-T	HT	WT	DOB	AVG	vLH	vRH	G	AB	R	H	2B	3B	HR	RBI	BB	HBP	SH	SF	SO	SB	CS	SLG	OBP
Consigli, Royce	L-R	6-2	217	9-7-91	.211	.196	.214	78	256	27	54	9	4	5	22	30	0	3	2	49	4	2	.336	.292
Crocker, Bobby	R-R	6-3	220	5-1-90	.268	.350	.242	112	406	56	109	19	2	6	53	39	13	6	6	109	17	10	.369	.347
Dixon, Rashun	R-R	6-2	210	8-27-90	.238	.221	.244	77	261	53	62	8	1	12	38	49	5	0	4	102	8	6	.414	.364
Fabiaschi, Michael	R-R	5-11	185	8-17-88	.188	.281	.150	39	112	14	21	4	1	0	5	28	4	0	0	40	2	3	.241	.368
Jamieson, Sean	R-R	6-0	193	3-2-89	.234	.237	.233	119	449	71	105	25	5	10	49	66	14	6	7	92	25	6	.379	.345
2-team total (14 South Bend)					.244	—	—	133	504	79	123	30	5	11	56	75	15	6	7	106	30	7	.389	.354
Kirkland, Wade	R-R	5-10	197	4-4-89	.237	.206	.250	102	379	49	90	31	3	8	56	28	11	3	9	95	5	4	.398	.306
Landaeta, Douglas	R-R	6-1	199	11-25-88	.244	.286	.227	99	369	46	90	17	1	10	38	22	0	3	5	82	10	7	.377	.283
Lewis, Chad	R-R	6-3	200	12-10-91	.133	.167	.125	8	30	1	4	0	0	0	3	0	0	0	0	11	0	0	.133	.133
Mesa, Eliezer	R-R	5-11	180	11-24-88	.294	.295	.293	70	262	36	77	11	4	4	33	11	3	2	3	48	20	4	.412	.326
Muncy, Max	L-R	6-0	190	8-25-90	.262	.275	.170	64	229	34	63	20	2	4	23	41	1	0	3	37	3	1	.432	.383
Nester, John	R-R	6-1	210	5-28-89	.203	.207	.201	70	222	31	45	8	0	4	24	31	1	3	3	64	2	2	.293	.300
Oberacker, Chad	L-L	5-11	195	1-14-89	.317	.364	.308	16	63	14	20	5	1	2	8	1	2	0	9	5	1	.524	.403
Pan, Chih-Fang	R-R	6-0	180	3-23-89	.243	.161	.263	29	86	36	72	14	2	2	37	21	4	5	2	55	8	3	.324	.300
Pineda, Ryan	R-R	5-11	180	4-17-89	.215	.211	.220	23	79	5	17	3	1	1	7	4	1	1	0	19	1	3	.316	.262
Rickles, Nick	R-R	6-3	220	2-2-90	.220	.257	.205	95	345	33	76	19	0	6	37	17	1	6	3	73	2	3	.328	.257
Roberts, Sam	L-R	6-1	190	2-23-89	.225	.222	.226	11	40	3	9	2	1	0	3	5	0	0	0	10	0	0	.325	.311
Robinson, Dusty	R-R	6-0	205	9-9-87	.262	.226	.273	38	141	25	37	7	4	9	28	16	3	0	1	33	5	2	.560	.348
Russell, Addison	R-R	6-0	185	1-23-94	.310	.364	.298	16	58	8	18	4	2	0	9	5	1	1	1	12	5	1	.448	.369
Shipman, Aaron	L-L	6-0	175	1-27-92	.206	.185	.211	108	360	40	74	12	4	0	32	60	2	1	4	86	11	11	.261	.319
Vollmuth, B.A.	R-R	6-3	215	12-23-89	.260	.324	.237	67	265	37	69	17	1	7	44	29	3	0	3	74	7	1	.411	.337
Wooten, John	R-R	6-3	190	1-19-91	.118	.000	.133	5	17	1	2	0	1	0	1	0	1	0	1	6	0	0	.235	.158

Pitching	B-T	HT	WT	DOB	W	L	ERA	G	GS	CG	SV	IP	H	R	ER	HR	BB	SO	AVG	vLH	vRH	K/9	BB/9
Alcantara, Raul	R-R	6-3	180	12-4-92	6	11	5.08	27	17	0	0	103	119	64	58	12	38	57	.304	.313	.300	5.00	3.33
Chitwood, Logan	R-R	6-1	185	3-28-89	1	1	2.04	8	0	0	1	18	14	6	4	0	7	11	.209	.318	.156	5.60	3.57

Name	B-T	HT	WT	DOB	W	L	ERA	G	GS	CG	SV	IP	H	R	ER	HR	BB	SO	AVG	vLH	vRH	K/9	BB/9
Cole, A.J.	R-R	6-4	180	1-5-92	6	3	2.07	19	19	0	0	96	78	32	22	7	19	102	.222	.270	.192	9.60	1.79
Doolittle, Ryan	R-R	6-3	185	3-25-88	0	0	0.93	8	0	0	2	10	5	3	1	0	0	12	.147	.167	.136	11.17	0.00
Duran, Omar	L-L	6-3	209	2-26-90	0	0	7.36	3	0	0	0	4	5	3	0	4	2	.313	.333	.308	4.91	9.82	
Eppley, Nate	R-R	6-6	205	10-28-88	1	1	9.00	7	0	0	0	10	12	10	10	0	5	7	.308	.278	.333	6.30	4.50
Frankoff, Seth	R-R	6-5	200	8-27-88	5	7	4.83	36	9	0	1	104	107	61	56	11	40	84	.275	.321	.252	7.25	3.45
Granier, Drew	R-R	6-0	180	11-24-88	11	10	3.21	28	28	1	0	163	149	71	58	12	53	167	.243	.229	.250	9.24	2.93
Hassebrock, Blake	R-R	6-4	212	7-15-89	2	2	4.00	5	5	0	0	27	33	14	12	3	10	20	.295	.250	.307	6.67	3.33
House, Austin	R-R	6-4	180	1-24-91	0	0	3.38	2	0	0	0	3	2	1	1	0	1	3	.250	.000	.333	10.13	3.38
Joseph, Jonathan	R-R	6-1	180	5-17-88	1	3	4.35	34	9	0	12	83	81	51	40	7	38	73	.251	.250	.251	7.95	4.14
Kilcrease, Nathan	R-R	5-6	170	8-17-89	1	1	1.46	7	0	0	0	12	9	2	2	0	2	7	.225	.313	.167	5.11	1.46
Lamb, Chris	B-L	6-1	185	6-29-90	3	3	5.03	11	11	0	0	59	68	38	33	3	22	40	.296	.233	.310	6.10	3.36
Macias, Jose	R-R	6-2	180	7-18-89	6	6	4.39	44	7	0	9	92	104	58	45	14	21	90	.291	.325	.276	8.77	2.05
Mota, David	R-R	6-4	265	2-18-87	3	1	3.47	27	0	0	0	36	43	20	14	3	21	32	.289	.263	.304	7.93	5.20
Murphy, Sean	B-R	6-6	215	8-23-88	3	4	1.97	8	8	0	0	50	35	14	11	4	17	52	.197	.155	.217	9.30	3.04
Mye, Chaz	L-L	6-3	205	4-27-88	4	1	4.15	44	0	0	1	61	62	29	28	6	23	47	.272	.279	.269	6.97	3.41
Perlman, Max	R-L	6-7	235	2-2-88	1	3	3.92	20	5	0	2	64	58	31	28	6	16	43	.242	.295	.211	6.02	2.24
Peters, Tanner	R-R	6-0	150	8-6-90	2	6	3.16	14	12	0	0	68	58	30	24	8	18	66	.233	.208	.250	8.69	2.37
Powers, Brent	L-L	6-1	205	5-25-89	3	4	7.66	17	5	0	1	45	55	44	38	10	26	39	.313	.200	.336	7.86	5.24
Ramos, Julio	L-L	6-1	190	2-13-88	0	0	0.57	5	4	0	0	16	9	2	1	0	1	12	.167	.200	.154	6.89	0.57
Tyson, Drew	R-R	6-5	195	8-11-89	2	1	3.71	45	0	0	5	68	66	33	28	2	31	42	.253	.273	.243	5.56	4.10
Urlaub, Jeff	L-L	6-2	160	4-24-87	5	4	2.60	26	0	0	3	35	26	15	10	1	1	27	.200	.139	.223	7.01	0.26

Fielding

Catcher	PCT	G	PO	A	E	DP	PB
Nester	.984	63	493	45	9	3	8
Rickles	.986	80	566	78	9	7	8

First Base	PCT	G	PO	A	E	DP
Landaeta	.990	58	456	46	5	52
Lewis	.977	6	39	3	1	5
Muncy	.990	63	541	33	6	48
Nester	1.000	1	11	0	0	0
Rickles	.983	8	57	2	1	7
Vollmuth	.987	9	70	5	1	11

Second Base	PCT	G	PO	A	E	DP
Fabiaschi	.985	30	57	77	2	19
Jamieson	.917	4	9	13	2	8

	PCT	G	PO	A	E	DP
Kirkland	.966	12	26	30	2	5
Pan	.972	73	159	189	10	42
Pineda	1.000	15	33	47	0	18
Roberts	.956	11	20	23	2	3

Third Base	PCT	G	PO	A	E	DP
Fabiaschi	1.000	5	1	6	0	1
Kirkland	.917	76	60	151	19	17
Lewis	1.000	2	0	5	0	1
Pineda	.923	5	5	7	1	2
Vollmuth	.908	53	36	92	13	13

Shortstop	PCT	G	PO	A	E	DP
Jamieson	.960	113	189	340	22	72
Kirkland	.957	12	20	25	2	9

	PCT	G	PO	A	E	DP
Russell	.944	15	25	42	4	6

Outfield	PCT	G	PO	A	E	DP
Consigli	.978	55	83	5	2	2
Crocker	.980	103	186	9	4	2
Dixon	.976	50	80	2	2	0
Fabiaschi	1.000	1	1	0	0	0
Landaeta	1.000	26	49	2	0	0
Mesa	.989	47	89	2	1	0
Oberacker	1.000	14	21	0	0	0
Robinson	.980	24	45	3	1	1
Shipman	.985	105	189	6	3	0
Wooten	1.000	5	5	1	0	0

VERMONT LAKE MONSTERS   SHORT-SEASON

NEW YORK-PENN LEAGUE

Batting	B-T	HT	WT	DOB	AVG	vLH	vRH	G	AB	R	H	2B	3B	HR	RBI	BB	HBP	SH	SF	SO	SB	CS	SLG	OBP
Alexander, Dayton	R-R	6-1	195	2-4-91	.145	.261	.087	25	69	10	10	3	0	0	4	8	0	4	1	22	3	1	.188	.231
Booker, Austin	L-R	5-10	170	4-11-88	.253	.133	.279	50	170	17	43	6	1	0	11	21	1	4	1	30	3	5	.300	.337
Bostick, Chris	R-R	5-11	185	3-24-93	.251	.282	.240	70	279	41	70	16	4	3	29	27	4	5	1	66	12	5	.369	.325
Fabiaschi, Michael	R-R	5-11	185	8-17-88	.143	.000	.250	3	7	4	1	0	0	0	0	2	1	0	0	0	0	0	.143	.400
Lewis, Chad	R-R	6-3	200	12-10-91	.231	.125	.265	39	134	10	31	5	0	1	12	11	1	2	2	38	0	1	.291	.291
Lopez, Diomedes	R-R	6-2	195	1-30-89	.216	.231	.211	17	51	2	11	2	0	0	1	6	3	1	0	16	1	0	.255	.333
Marte, Miguel	R-R	6-3	230	8-29-89	.230	.237	.227	43	148	8	34	6	0	3	20	5	5	0	2	57	0	0	.331	.275
Mateo, Reynaldo	R-R	5-9	209	7-16-89	.247	.238	.250	21	73	7	18	4	1	2	8	6	0	3	1	32	1	0	.411	.300
Maxwell, Bruce	L-R	6-2	235	12-20-90	.254	.271	.249	61	228	22	58	14	0	0	22	26	0	1	1	35	1	0	.316	.329
Olson, Matt	L-R	6-4	236	3-29-94	.273	.000	.300	4	11	3	3	0	0	1	4	3	1	0	1	4	0	0	.545	.438
Peralta, Jensi	R-R	6-2	180	7-2-91	.100	.333	.059	8	20	4	2	0	0	0	5	0	0	0	0	8	0	1	.100	.280
Pohl, Phil	R-R	5-11	195	7-22-90	.143	—	.143	3	7	2	1	0	0	0	1	1	3	2	0	0	0	0	.143	.455
Roberts, Sam	L-R	6-1	190	2-23-89	.224	.400	.205	17	49	7	11	1	1	0	2	17	0	1	0	11	0	1	.286	.424
Robertson, Daniel	R-R	6-0	190	3-22-94	.181	.182	.181	26	94	9	17	2	0	1	8	7	0	3	0	31	1	1	.234	.238
Rojas, Kelvin	R-R	6-2	188	8-7-89	.221	.172	.238	35	113	11	25	5	0	0	9	3	0	1	2	30	0	0	.265	.237
Russell, Addison	R-R	6-0	185	1-23-94	.340	.286	.359	13	53	9	18	2	2	1	7	4	0	0	0	13	2	0	.509	.386
Solano, Wilfredo	R-R	6-2	185	1-15-93	.217	.289	.194	54	189	17	41	10	0	1	18	10	3	4	3	34	3	0	.286	.263
Stafford, Rhett	R-R	6-2	220	3-1-89	.190	.250	.167	18	58	11	11	2	0	1	5	10	0	0	0	20	0	1	.276	.309
Tanis, Jacob	R-R	6-1	200	6-30-89	.261	.190	.288	61	226	26	59	9	1	2	29	22	4	3	3	47	3	4	.336	.333
Vertigan, Brett	L-L	5-9	175	8-21-90	.266	.219	.281	67	256	34	68	15	5	1	15	24	5	6	2	31	12	5	.375	.338
Wooten, John	R-R	6-3	190	1-19-91	.286	.347	.263	67	262	27	75	16	1	4	38	16	1	2	3	44	3	6	.401	.326

Pitching	B-T	HT	WT	DOB	W	L	ERA	G	GS	CG	SV	IP	H	R	ER	HR	BB	SO	AVG	vLH	vRH	K/9	BB/9
Avila, Andres	R-R	6-0	185	6-20-90	3	4	3.82	15	12	0	0	66	68	36	28	7	16	60	.261	.315	.220	8.18	2.18
Chitwood, Logan	R-R	6-1	185	3-28-89	3	1	2.16	12	0	0	0	25	22	7	6	1	10	20	.239	.275	.212	7.20	3.60
Dull, Ryan	R-R	5-11	175	10-2-89	3	1	2.84	17	0	0	4	25	26	10	8	2	6	34	.263	.308	.233	12.08	2.13
Duran, Omar	L-L	6-3	209	2-26-90	0	1	0.44	14	0	0	0	20	4	4	1	0	20	42	.062	.125	.041	18.59	8.85
Eppley, Nate	R-R	6-6	205	10-28-88	3	0	1.98	14	0	0	2	27	16	9	6	1	7	24	.165	.133	.192	7.90	2.30
Gagnier, Drew	R-R	6-4	225	9-21-88	2	1	3.30	19	0	0	0	30	30	16	11	0	16	27	.250	.255	.247	8.10	4.80
Hall, Kris	R-R	6-3	215	6-8-91	2	0	0.99	12	4	0	0	27	17	6	3	0	14	24	.177	.220	.145	7.90	4.61
Healy, Tucker	L-R	6-1	195	6-15-90	2	0	3.07	22	0	0	3	29	26	11	10	0	13	45	.234	.293	.200	13.81	3.99
House, Austin	R-R	6-4	180	1-24-91	1	0	1.05	18	0	0	5	26	13	5	3	0	10	33	.149	.211	.102	11.57	3.51

Name	B-T	HT	WT	DOB	W	L	ERA	G	GS	CG	SV	IP	H	R	ER	HR	BB	SO	AVG	vLH	vRH	K/9	BB/9
Jimenez, Deivi	R-R	6-3	205	12-30-89	0	4	5.79	17	3	0	1	37	44	34	24	3	15	38	.291	.288	.296	9.16	3.62
Lamb, Chris	B-L	6-1	185	6-29-90	2	0	1.50	4	4	0	0	18	16	4	3	1	3	12	.242	.188	.260	6.00	1.50
Menna, J.C.	R-R	6-2	175	12-24-88	1	9	4.60	14	11	0	0	63	60	40	32	4	27	47	.249	.236	.259	6.75	3.88
Peters, Tanner	R-R	6-0	150	8-6-90	0	0	6.00	2	0	0	0	3	2	2	2	0	2	7	.182	.125	.333	21.00	6.00
Powers, Brent	L-L	6-1	205	5-25-89	0	7	5.51	16	14	0	0	64	76	44	39	7	28	57	.293	.286	.296	8.06	3.96
Pudenz, Stuart	R-R	6-5	215	9-15-90	2	1	2.59	19	0	0	0	31	21	11	9	1	9	37	.188	.216	.173	10.63	2.59
Ramos, Julio	L-L	6-1	190	2-13-88	1	1	1.80	5	3	0	0	15	13	4	3	1	2	12	.232	.368	.162	7.20	1.20
Sanburn, Nolan	R-R	6-0	175	7-21-91	0	1	3.86	7	7	0	0	19	23	10	8	2	6	19	.299	.267	.319	9.16	2.89
Streich, Seth	L-R	6-3	210	2-19-91	4	1	2.60	15	4	0	0	35	26	12	10	1	17	42	.206	.234	.190	10.90	4.41
Tanner, Cecil	R-R	6-6	240	4-23-90	0	2	9.00	4	0	0	0	5	6	5	5	1	8	6	.316	.250	.364	10.80	14.40
Vail, Tyler	R-R	6-1	208	11-3-91	3	4	4.20	12	7	0	0	56	43	29	26	2	21	55	.208	.175	.228	8.89	3.40
Wunderlich, Kurt	R-R	6-2	210	8-22-89	0	1	7.64	6	1	0	0	18	27	15	15	3	4	13	.342	.419	.292	6.62	2.04
Ynoa, Michael	R-R	6-7	210	9-24-91	1	3	6.97	8	6	0	0	21	20	18	16	2	16	19	.247	.382	.149	8.27	6.97

Fielding

Catcher	PCT	G	PO	A	E	DP	PB
Lopez	.985	14	110	18	2	3	2
Mateo	.980	10	91	7	2	0	6
Maxwell	.984	38	332	42	6	2	18
Pohl	1.000	3	30	3	0	0	0
Stafford	.969	12	86	7	3	2	4

First Base	PCT	G	PO	A	E	DP
Marte	.992	33	247	13	2	18
Olson	1.000	4	27	2	0	2
Tanis	.990	42	387	22	4	20

Second Base	PCT	G	PO	A	E	DP
Bostick	.951	53	104	150	13	22

Roberts	.939	11	19	27	3	2
Solano	1.000	13	21	36	0	5

Third Base	PCT	G	PO	A	E	DP
Lewis	.896	39	30	73	12	8
Peralta	.889	6	3	5	1	2
Robertson	.826	9	5	14	4	1
Solano	1.000	3	1	6	0	0
Tanis	.935	22	15	28	3	1

Shortstop	PCT	G	PO	A	E	DP
Bostick	.900	10	20	25	5	4
Fabiaschi	1.000	2	5	5	0	3
Robertson	.972	18	20	50	2	8

Russell	.977	12	12	30	1	2
Solano	.877	36	40	95	19	10

Outfield	PCT	G	PO	A	E	DP
Alexander	1.000	21	26	2	0	1
Booker	.988	49	79	5	1	0
Bostick	1.000	2	2	0	0	0
Marte	—	1	0	0	0	0
Rojas	.897	29	31	4	4	0
Vertigan	.976	66	118	6	3	0
Wooten	.981	62	97	6	2	0

AZL ATHLETICS

ROOKIE

ARIZONA LEAGUE

Batting	B-T	HT	WT	DOB	AVG	vLH	vRH	G	AB	R	H	2B	3B	HR	RBI	BB	HBP	SH	SF	SO	SB	CS	SLG	OBP
Alexander, Dayton	R-R	6-1	195	2-4-91	.256	.214	.280	14	39	8	10	3	0	1	8	10	0	1	0	11	4	1	.410	.408
Baez, Luis	R-R	6-3	165	5-24-91	.289	.308	.286	28	97	21	28	11	2	2	7	12	1	0	0	20	2	0	.505	.310
Boyd, B.J.	L-R	5-10	190	7-16-93	.301	.200	.317	39	143	37	43	8	4	1	20	23	1	0	0	36	16	4	.434	.401
Contreras, Franklin	R-R	6-2	165	6-10-90	.286	.333	.278	19	63	13	18	6	0	0	8	7	1	0	1	12	0	0	.381	.361
De La Cruz, Vicmal	L-L	6-0	185	11-20-93	.230	.200	.235	35	135	25	31	5	3	3	17	11	1	0	1	43	2	1	.378	.291
Hillsinger, Matt	L-R	6-3	205	4-13-90	.227	.000	.313	9	22	6	5	0	1	0	2	5	0	0	0	4	0	0	.318	.370
Kim, Seongmin	R-R	6-1	200	5-12-93	.273	.000	.333	12	22	5	6	2	0	0	1	2	1	0	0	6	0	0	.364	.360
Lewis, Chad	R-R	6-3	200	12-10-91	.243	.400	.185	10	37	6	9	0	0	2	3	0	0	0	0	10	0	0	.405	.300
Martinez, Hiram	B-R	6-1	143	9-30-92	.143	.250	.118	8	21	1	3	1	0	0	4	0	0	0	0	3	0	0	.190	.143
Mateo, Reynaldo	R-R	5-9	209	7-16-89	.400	.000	.435	19	75	20	30	8	2	5	27	5	1	0	5	18	1	0	.760	.419
Mathews, Ryan	R-R	6-4	195	8-1-89	.250	.444	.216	21	60	7	15	7	2	1	12	5	0	0	1	10	3	0	.483	.303
Maxwell, Bruce	L-R	6-2	235	12-20-90	.524	.000	.550	6	21	8	11	4	0	0	5	4	0	0	0	3	0	0	.714	.615
Mercedes, Melvin	B-R	5-8	170	1-13-92	.381	.350	.388	31	105	24	40	10	1	0	12	10	1	2	0	15	1	0	.495	.440
Nunez, Renato	R-R	6-1	185	4-4-94	.325	.333	.323	42	160	31	52	18	3	4	42	17	6	0	3	32	4	0	.550	.403
Olson, Matt	L-R	6-4	236	3-29-94	.282	.286	.282	46	177	29	50	16	1	8	41	16	2	0	2	46	0	0	.520	.345
Osorio, Luis	B-R	6-1	155	4-5-91	.208	.222	.205	18	48	7	10	0	1	0	3	4	0	1	0	16	0	1	.250	.269
Pohl, Phil	R-R	5-11	195	7-22-90	.301	.269	.310	32	113	22	34	6	2	3	17	6	8	0	1	22	1	0	.469	.375
Powell, Boog	L-L	5-10	175	1-14-93	.306	.278	.312	35	111	20	34	1	0	0	13	15	0	2	2	9	5	2	.315	.383
Richard, Myrio	R-R	6-1	190	8-27-88	.182	.500	.111	4	11	3	2	1	0	1	1	0	0	0	0	1	0	0	.545	.182
Robertson, Daniel	R-R	6-0	190	3-22-94	.297	.444	.265	29	101	25	30	10	2	4	22	16	5	1	4	15	2	0	.554	.405
Russell, Addison	R-R	6-0	185	1-23-94	.415	.250	.444	26	106	29	44	4	5	6	29	14	1	0	0	23	9	1	.717	.488
Soto, Michael	R-R	6-3	195	11-17-91	.282	.125	.310	32	103	18	29	9	2	4	23	7	0	0	2	25	1	0	.524	.321
Stafford, Rhett	R-R	6-2	220	3-1-89	.211	.500	.133	6	19	1	4	1	0	0	3	2	0	0	0	5	1	0	.263	.286
Wolfe, Chris	B-R	5-11	150	2-2-90	.229	.143	.244	21	48	12	11	5	0	0	5	11	0	1	0	11	1	1	.333	.373

Pitching	B-T	HT	WT	DOB	W	L	ERA	G	GS	CG	SV	IP	H	R	ER	HR	BB	SO	AVG	vLH	vRH	K/9	BB/9
Azor, Jose	R-R	6-2	185	10-12-88	2	1	3.32	13	0	0	1	22	19	11	8	0	13	13	.247	.286	.224	5.40	5.40
Bacus, Dakota	R-R	6-2	190	4-2-91	3	0	1.20	18	1	0	7	30	12	4	4	0	5	35	.121	.065	.170	10.50	1.50
Bahramzadeh, Kayvon	R-R	6-2	190	1-22-90	1	2	7.30	13	10	0	0	37	48	31	30	7	7	48	.312	.310	.313	11.68	1.70
Cruzado, Fernando	R-R	6-2	210	10-25-89	3	1	5.52	17	2	0	0	29	29	14	18	2	10	18	.259	.353	.218	5.52	3.07
De Young, Derek	R-R	6-0	165	12-17-91	0	0	13.50	1	0	0	0	1	1	1	1	0	2	1	.500	.000	.500	13.50	27.00
Dull, Ryan	R-R	5-11	175	10-2-89	2	0	1.42	4	0	0	1	6	3	1	1	0	3	13	.143	.200	.125	18.47	4.26
Duran, Omar	L-L	6-3	209	2-26-90	0	0	0.00	3	0	0	0	4	0	0	0	0	5	6	.000	.000	.000	12.27	0.00
Hall, Kris	R-R	6-3	215	6-8-91	1	0	4.50	2	0	0	0	2	1	1	1	0	1	3	.125	.500	.000	13.50	4.50
Hansen, Derek	R-R	6-1	215	8-21-90	2	1	4.87	13	0	0	1	20	24	12	11	1	10	24	.286	.400	.222	10.62	4.43
Hollstegge, Tyler	R-R	6-1	205	12-17-90	5	1	4.86	19	0	0	0	33	33	20	18	1	22	35	.268	.294	.250	9.45	5.94
Johnson, Tyler	R-R	6-1	195	7-18-90	5	1	3.33	14	0	0	1	27	30	14	10	1	7	21	.273	.227	.303	7.00	2.33
Kurz, Cody	R-R	6-4	225	9-13-92	0	0	4.64	17	0	0	0	21	18	13	11	1	29	9	.240	.136	.283	3.80	12.23
Massey, Taylor	L-L	6-0	200	1-14-89	1	0	3.00	17	0	0	3	24	19	9	7	3	8	27	.238	.321	.192	11.57	3.43
O'Connell, Colin	L-R	6-6	200	6-15-90	0	0	0.00	2	0	0	0	3	4	0	0	0	3	.333	.600	.143	9.00	0.00
Paulino, Gregory	R-R	6-3	180	2-4-93	4	4	5.70	14	7	0	0	60	75	41	38	6	16	56	.306	.348	.282	8.40	2.40

	B-T	HT	WT	DOB	W	L	ERA	G	GS	CG	SV	IP	H	R	ER	HR	BB	SO	AVG	vLH	vRH	K/9	BB/9
Pudenz, Stuart	R-R	6-5	215	9-15-90	0	0	0.00	2	0	0	0	2	0	0	0	0	0	3	.000	.000	.000	13.50	0.00
Sosa, Lee	R-R	6-2	205	9-3-91	1	2	4.74	18	0	0	0	25	15	14	13	0	22	29	.170	.156	.186	10.58	8.03
Streich, Seth	L-R	6-3	210	2-19-91	0	0	3.38	2	0	0	0	3	1	1	1	0	1	6	.111	.000	.200	20.25	3.38
Thomson, Matt	R-R	6-4	220	3-22-88	0	0	0.00	1	1	0	0	1	1	0	0	0	1	0	.250	.500	.000	0.00	9.00
Torres, Jose	L-L	6-2	165	9-24-93	3	1	4.33	12	12	0	0	52	52	29	25	2	29	41	.264	.222	.280	7.10	5.02
Vail, Tyler	R-R	6-1	208	11-3-91	0	0	0.93	3	3	0	0	10	5	2	1	0	1	11	.156	.176	.133	10.24	0.93
Valdez, Merkin	R-R	6-3	235	11-5-81	0	0	0.00	2	1	0	0	3	2	0	0	0	1	0	.222	.200	.250	3.00	0.00
Voiro, Vince	R-R	6-3	195	2-23-90	3	2	3.62	14	8	0	1	37	35	19	15	1	8	41	.240	.280	.219	9.88	1.93
Ynoa, Michael	R-R	6-7	210	9-24-91	0	1	5.40	6	6	0	0	10	11	7	6	1	9	6	.282	.250	.296	5.40	8.10

Fielding

Catcher	PCT	G	PO	A	E	DP	PB
Kim	.969	6	27	4	1	0	2
Mateo	.992	13	104	16	1	0	1
Maxwell	1.000	3	27	4	0	0	0
Olson	1.000	1	7	0	0	0	0
Pohl	.993	32	262	25	2	4	3
Stafford	.956	5	40	3	2	0	1

First Base	PCT	G	PO	A	E	DP
Kim	1.000	1	1	1	0	0
Mateo	.857	1	5	1	1	1
Olson	.991	36	303	24	3	36
Soto	.978	20	168	10	4	18

Second Base	PCT	G	PO	A	E	DP
Contreras	.939	17	29	48	5	14

Martinez	1.000	7	4	13	0	4
Mercedes	.976	22	35	48	2	11
Osorio	.949	16	17	20	2	5
Wolfe	.957	5	8	14	1	7

Third Base	PCT	G	PO	A	E	DP
Baez	.941	8	2	14	1	1
Lewis	.833	7	2	8	2	1
Martinez	—	1	0	0	0	0
Nunez	.900	30	8	55	7	4
Osorio	—	2	0	0	0	0
Robertson	.925	12	10	27	3	2

Shortstop	PCT	G	PO	A	E	DP
Martinez	1.000	1	0	1	0	0
Mercedes	.854	10	10	25	6	5

Robertson	.905	13	13	44	6	9
Russell	.945	21	36	50	5	13
Wolfe	.966	14	21	35	2	15

Outfield	PCT	G	PO	A	E	DP
Alexander	1.000	14	19	1	0	0
Baez	.909	21	27	3	3	1
Boyd	.986	38	68	3	1	1
De La Cruz	.953	28	38	3	2	0
Duinkerk	.957	24	20	2	1	1
Hillsinger	1.000	8	10	0	0	0
Mathews	1.000	18	19	1	0	0
Powell	.982	35	54	2	1	1
Richard	1.000	2	4	0	0	0

DSL ATHLETICS   ROOKIE

DOMINICAN SUMMER LEAGUE

Batting	B-T	HT	WT	DOB	AVG	vLH	vRH	G	AB	R	H	2B	3B	HR	RBI	BB	HBP	SH	SF	SO	SB	CS	SLG	OBP
Chavez, Jose	R-R	5-11	175	5-8-95	.250	.273	.243	35	96	8	24	4	1	0	8	9	1	2	0	18	2	3	.313	.321
De La Rosa, Anderson	R-R	6-1	180	8-12-91	.239	.185	.259	59	197	37	47	12	5	4	30	22	8	2	5	48	1	1	.411	.332
Hernandez, Luis	R-R	5-11	203	9-3-94	.070	.167	.044	19	57	4	4	0	0	0	1	6	2	1	0	24	0	0	.070	.185
Ledezma, Diego	R-R	6-5	170	8-14-90	.288	.400	.255	25	66	8	19	5	0	1	5	7	3	3	1	12	2	0	.409	.377
Martes, Mitchell	R-R	6-5	170	11-3-94	.167	.000	.188	8	18	2	3	1	0	0	1	3	0	1	0	0	0	0	.222	.286
Martinez, Hiram	B-R	6-1	143	9-30-92	.205	.364	.152	16	44	1	9	0	0	0	5	0	0	4	5	2	3	.205	.188
Martinez, Robert	R-R	6-1	180	2-8-94	.273	.286	.269	15	33	4	9	2	0	0	5	8	2	1	0	16	1	2	.333	.442
Martinez, Wilman	R-R	5-11	204	1-13-93	.204	.286	.183	34	103	9	21	3	0	0	8	8	4	0	1	17	0	2	.233	.284
Munoz, Yairo	R-R	6-1	165	1-23-95	.229	.216	.235	32	105	13	24	7	3	0	22	10	1	1	2	23	4	3	.352	.297
Osorio, Luis	B-R	6-1	155	4-5-91	.125	.182	.095	11	32	1	4	0	1	0	4	2	2	0	0	8	2	1	.188	.222
Paz, Andy	R-R	6-0	170	1-5-93	.317	.261	.339	26	82	11	26	4	2	0	7	14	0	2	0	13	1	2	.415	.417
Penalo, Rodolfo	B-R	5-7	130	8-27-92	.225	.209	.231	53	173	27	39	5	5	1	11	25	4	4	0	27	17	6	.329	.337
Pimentel, Sandber	R-R	6-3	216	9-12-94	.261	.154	.292	37	115	14	30	2	1	1	17	28	6	2	0	30	0	6	.322	.430
Raga, Argenis	R-R	6-1	176	7-22-94	.265	.258	.268	61	234	33	62	13	1	2	12	18	6	3	1	23	5	4	.355	.332
Rivas, Jesus	R-R	6-0	180	3-22-94	.199	.127	.229	54	186	23	37	10	0	3	19	13	2	4	0	41	4	1	.301	.259
Rosario, Jose	R-R	6-5	219	9-2-90	.196	.182	.202	45	153	17	30	7	0	1	17	18	1	3	1	31	2	2	.261	.283
Santana, Gabriel	R-R	6-0	165	8-23-92	.271	.317	.250	41	133	24	36	6	2	0	18	19	12	6	1	10	1	7	.346	.406
Sayegh, Jose	R-R	6-2	180	12-7-91	.105	.043	.132	31	76	1	8	3	0	0	4	5	4	0	2	26	0	3	.145	.195
Sosa, Alfredo	R-R	5-10	189	1-18-93	.177	.188	.174	27	62	9	11	0	1	0	5	14	0	1	1	28	5	2	.210	.325
Zarraga, Jonesy	R-R	6-1	170	6-3-92	.230	.185	.252	42	161	25	37	9	2	3	17	14	7	1	0	40	11	5	.366	.319

Pitching	B-T	HT	WT	DOB	W	L	ERA	G	GS	CG	SV	IP	H	R	ER	HR	BB	SO	AVG	vLH	vRH	K/9	BB/9
Alejo, Yordy	R-R	6-2	186	11-13-93	2	2	1.42	11	0	0	0	19	24	8	3	0	7	8	.320	.600	.218	3.79	3.32
Almonte, Edward	R-R	6-2	176	1-12-90	1	4	3.25	17	0	0	2	36	35	21	13	1	14	30	.265	.111	.276	7.50	3.50
Benzant, Leonel	R-R	6-6	213	12-20-91	1	6	6.30	14	10	0	1	40	46	33	28	4	18	19	.288	.308	.281	4.28	4.05
Cruzado, Fernando	R-R	6-2	210	10-25-89	3	1	5.40	4	0	0	0	12	9	7	7	1	4	7	.209	.250	.200	5.40	3.09
De Los Santos, Robinson	R-R	6-3		9-19-87	0	0	27.00	2	0	0	1	2	3	5	5	0	3	2	.375	.667	.200	10.80	16.20
Delgadillo, Yonalis	R-R	6-2	170	1-26-91	0	2	4.09	7	0	0	1	11	7	6	5	0	9	6	.189	.125	.207	4.91	7.36
Duno, Angel	R-R	6-0	180	1-10-94	2	1	1.82	19	2	0	4	40	36	12	8	0	15	26	.247	.225	.255	5.90	3.40
Ferreras, Kevin	L-L	6-0	170	7-5-93	0	1	3.12	15	0	0	0	35	30	18	12	0	25	32	.244	.000	.263	8.31	6.49
Gonzalez, Darwin	L-L	6-3	183	11-24-92	1	2	6.09	16	0	0	0	34	32	26	23	1	22	28	.258	.000	.269	7.41	5.82
Herrera, Ronald	R-R	5-10	168	5-3-95	2	4	2.47	14	14	1	0	58	66	24	16	1	20	44	.292	.281	.296	6.79	3.09
Hoyos, Renaldo	L-L	6-0	167	5-23-94	1	2	3.12	10	0	0	1	17	9	8	6	0	15	12	.173	.429	.133	6.23	7.79
Navas, Carlos	R-R	6-1	170	8-13-92	4	5	1.38	14	12	0	0	65	51	21	10	0	11	54	.229	.334	.215	7.44	1.52
Nolasco, Alex	L-L	6-4	190	9-11-90	2	3	3.35	17	0	0	2	48	43	23	18	1	17	37	.236	.333	.229	6.89	3.17
Paulino, Gregory	R-R	6-3	180	2-4-93	0	0	3.86	3	3	0	0	9	8	4	4	0	2	6	.229	.214	.238	5.79	1.93
Perez, Cristhian	R-R	6-2	180	9-13-91	4	4	1.98	14	11	0	0	68	64	22	15	1	9	46	.254	.254	.254	6.06	1.19
Rosario, Robin	R-R	6-2	180	11-3-92	0	0	1.42	8	0	0	0	13	5	2	2	0	8	6	.132	.143	.129	4.26	5.68
Suniaga, Elihoref	R-R	6-1	170	5-5-92	0	0	8.10	2	0	0	0	3	1	3	3	0	3	3	.091	.000	.125	8.10	8.10
Torres, Jose	L-L	6-2	165	9-24-93	0	0	0.00	3	2	0	0	9	6	3	0	0	3	7	.188	.000	.207	7.27	3.12
Vargas, Alejandro	R-R	5-11	160	1-29-95	1	2	7.13	13	0	0	0	18	24	14	14	2	10	15	.343	.176	.396	7.64	5.09
Veliz, Victor	L-L	5-11	170	10-6-93	2	2	4.38	13	13	0	0	51	60	30	25	3	13	35	.293	.250	.297	6.14	2.28

Fielding

Catcher	PCT	G	PO	A	E	DP	PB
Chavez	.978	15	75	12	2	0	4
Hernandez	.965	19	124	12	5	1	3
Ledezma	.964	10	47	6	2	1	1
Paz	.989	24	143	39	2	1	4
Ramirez	.964	9	41	12	2	0	8

First Base	PCT	G	PO	A	E	DP
Ledezma	.919	8	64	4	6	1
Martinez	.990	11	98	4	1	11
Osorio	1.000	4	19	1	0	2
Rivas	.956	10	60	5	3	4
Rosario	.989	42	419	21	5	38

Second Base	PCT	G	PO	A	E	DP
Chavez	1.000	8	12	12	0	0
De La Rosa	1.000	1	2	4	0	1

Second Base	PCT	G	PO	A	E	DP
Munoz	.750	2	2	1	1	0
Osorio	1.000	2	1	0	0	0
Penalo	.984	37	94	89	3	25
Raga	.953	22	50	51	5	10
Santana	1.000	5	14	11	0	1

Third Base	PCT	G	PO	A	E	DP
Chavez	1.000	1	1	1	0	1
Martinez	.968	18	16	45	2	3
Munoz	.958	6	6	17	1	1
Osorio	1.000	2	1	7	0	0
Raga	.938	26	15	61	5	3
Rivas	.900	4	2	7	1	1
Santana	.932	21	19	50	5	3

Shortstop	PCT	G	PO	A	E	DP
Martinez	.930	16	22	44	5	8

	PCT	G	PO	A	E	DP
Munoz	.892	22	22	61	10	12
Osorio	.913	4	9	12	2	1
Raga	.882	16	17	28	6	1
Santana	.929	17	27	52	6	10

Outfield	PCT	G	PO	A	E	DP
De La Rosa	.962	25	48	3	2	0
Martes	.857	8	5	1	1	0
Martinez	1.000	14	23	1	0	0
Martinez	1.000	1	1	0	0	0
Penalo	1.000	17	28	1	0	0
Pimentel	.941	23	28	4	2	1
Rivas	.900	44	59	4	7	2
Sayegh	1.000	30	32	2	0	0
Sosa	.966	25	27	1	1	0
Zarraga	.956	41	60	5	3	2

Philadelphia Phillies

SEASON IN A SENTENCE: Geared up for another run at a World Series title, the Phillies stumbled out of the gate and never got going, suddenly looking old and finishing well out of the playoffs with a .500 record.

HIGH POINT: Philadelphia beat Pittsburgh 1-0 on Opening Day, with Roy Halladay turning in a very Halladay-esque eight scoreless innings and new closer Jonathan Papelbon pitching a perfect ninth for the save. It would be the last time the Phillies were in first place in the National League East. Halladay finished the season with a 4.49 ERA, his highest in 12 seasons, and he missed seven weeks with a lat strain.

LOW POINT: The Phillies tried to hold on until Ryan Howard and Chase Utley returned from injuries, but they went into a tailspin just before the all-star break and lost 11 of 12 games, including sweeps at the hands of the Braves and Marlins. When Howard did return on July 6 he made little difference and ended up striking out 99 times in 260 at-bats, with 14 home runs. While the Phillies did push into the fringes of wild card contention late in the season, injuries ultimately did them in.

NOTABLE ROOKIES: With the second-largest payroll in baseball the Phillies were built to win now, so there were few opportunities for rookies. The team hoped Freddy Galvis would be able to hold down second base until Utley returned to action, but he was suspended after testing positive for performance-enhancing drugs in early June. He batted .226/.254/.363 but played solid defense.

KEY TRANSACTIONS: When the season went south, the Phillies sent three of their veterans to other teams around the trade deadline. Shane Victorino and Joe Blanton went to the Dodgers in separate deals, with the Phillies getting four players in return, highlighted by righthander Ethan Martin. Philadelphia also sent Hunter Pence to the Giants and got three players back, including catcher Tommy Joseph.

DOWN ON THE FARM: The story of the farm system was first baseman Darin Ruf, a 20th-round draft pick out of Creighton in 2009 who had previously labored in obscurity. Ruf batted .317/.408/.620 with 38 home runs and 104 RBIs to win Double-A Eastern League MVP honors, and he had an August for the ages, hitting 20 homers in 31 games. Reading and high Class A Clearwater were the only Phillies affiliates to finish better than .500.

OPENING DAY PAYROLL: $174.5 million (2nd)

PLAYERS OF THE YEAR

MAJOR LEAGUE	MINOR LEAGUE
Cole Hamels	**Darin Ruf**
lhp	1b
17-6, 3.05	(Double-A)
216 SO/215 IP	.317/.408/.620
3rd in NL in SO	38 HR, EL MVP

ORGANIZATION LEADERS

BATTING *Minimum 250 AB

MAJORS

* AVG	Jimmy Rollins	.250
* OPS	Jimmy Rollins	.743
HR	Jimmy Rollins	23
RBI	Jimmy Rollins	68
	Carlos Ruiz	68

MINORS

* AVG	Cody Asche, Clearwater/Reading	.324
* OBP	Darin Ruf, Reading	.408
* SLG	Darin Ruf, Reading	.620
R	Darin Ruf, Reading	93
H	Cody Asche, Clearwater/Reading	168
TB	Darin Ruf, Reading	303
2B	Jim Murphy, Clearwater	43
3B	Cesar Hernandez, Reading/Lehigh Valley	12
HR	Darin Ruf, Reading	38
RBI	Darin Ruf, Reading	104
BB	Darin Ruf, Reading	65
SO	Brian Pointer, Williamsport/Lakewood	145
SB	Roman Quinn, Williamsport	30

PITCHING #Minimum 75 IP

MAJORS

W	Cole Hamels	17
# ERA	Cole Hamels	3.05
SO	Cole Hamels	216
SV	Jonathan Papelbon	38

MINORS

W	Tyler Cloyd, Reading/Lehigh Valley	15
L	Trevor May, Reading	13
# ERA	Tyler Cloyd, Reading/Lehigh Valley	2.26
G	Tyler Knigge, Clearwater/Reading	55
GS	Trevor May, Reading	28
SV	Justin Friend, Lehigh Valley/Reading	25
IP	Tyler Cloyd, Reading/Lehigh Valley	167
BB	Trevor May, Reading	78
SO	Adam Morgan, Clearwater/Reading	169
# AVG	Tyler Cloyd, Reading/Lehigh Valley	.214

2012 PERFORMANCE

General Manager: Ruben Amaro Jr. **Farm Director:** Joe Jordan. **Scouting Director:** Marti Wolever.

Class	Team	League	W	L	PCT	Finish	Manager
Majors	Philadelphia Phillies	National	81	81	.500	t-8th (16)	Charlie Manuel
Triple-A	Lehigh Valley IronPigs	International	75	68	.524	5th (14)	Ryne Sandberg
Double-A	Reading Phillies	Eastern	76	66	.535	4th (12)	Dusty Wathan
High A	Clearwater Threshers	Florida State	72	60	.545	4th (12)	Chris Truby
Low A	Lakewood BlueClaws	South Atlantic	62	76	.449	t-10th (14)	Mickey Morandini
Short-season	Williamsport Crosscutters	New York-Penn	30	46	.395	13th (14)	Andy Tracy
Rookie	GCL Phillies	Gulf Coast	28	30	.483	8th (14)	Rolando de Armas
Overall 2012 Minor League Record			343	346	.498	20th (30)	

ORGANIZATION STATISTICS

PHILADELPHIA PHILLIES

NATIONAL LEAGUE

Batting	B-T	HT	WT	DOB	AVG	vLH	vRH	G	AB	R	H	2B	3B	HR	RBI	BB	HBP	SH	SF	SO	SB	CS	SLG	OBP
Brown, Domonic	L-L	6-5	205	9-3-87	.235	.196	.250	56	187	21	44	11	2	5	26	21	2	0	2	34	0	0	.396	.316
Fontenot, Mike	L-R	5-8	165	6-9-80	.289	.067	.329	47	97	13	28	2	0	1	5	7	1	0	0	23	0	1	.340	.343
Frandsen, Kevin	R-R	6-0	185	5-24-82	.338	.400	.308	55	195	24	66	10	3	2	14	9	5	1	0	18	0	1	.451	.383
Galvis, Freddy	B-R	5-10	170	11-14-89	.226	.267	.208	58	190	14	43	15	1	3	24	7	0	3	0	29	0	0	.363	.254
Howard, Ryan	L-L	6-4	240	11-19-79	.219	.173	.247	71	260	28	57	11	0	14	56	25	4	0	3	99	0	0	.423	.295
Kratz, Erik	R-R	6-4	255	6-15-80	.248	.256	.245	50	141	14	35	9	0	9	26	11	2	0	3	34	0	0	.504	.306
Lerud, Steve	L-R	6-1	215	10-13-84	.200	.200	.200	3	10	1	2	0	0	0	0	0	0	0	0	2	0	0	.200	.200
Luna, Hector	R-R	6-1	190	2-1-80	.226	.148	.286	28	62	5	14	2	0	2	10	4	0	0	0	14	0	0	.355	.273
Martinez, Michael	B-R	5-9	175	9-16-82	.174	.241	.115	45	115	10	20	3	0	2	7	5	0	2	0	21	0	0	.252	.208
Mayberry Jr., John	R-R	6-6	225	12-21-83	.245	.271	.229	149	441	53	108	24	0	14	46	34	2	0	2	111	1	0	.395	.301
Nix, Laynce	L-L	6-1	220	10-30-80	.246	.222	.248	70	114	13	28	10	0	3	16	12	0	0	1	42	0	0	.412	.315
Orr, Pete	L-R	6-1	195	6-8-79	.315	.000	.327	35	54	6	17	5	1	0	7	1	0	2	0	18	3	1	.444	.327
Pence, Hunter	R-R	6-4	220	4-13-83	.271	.245	.280	101	398	59	108	15	2	17	59	37	3	0	2	85	4	2	.447	.336
2-team total (59 San Francisco)					.253	—	—	160	617	87	156	26	4	24	104	56	7	1	7	145	5	2	.425	.319
Pierre, Juan	L-L	5-11	175	8-14-77	.307	.190	.329	130	394	59	121	10	6	1	25	23	4	17	1	27	37	7	.371	.351
Polanco, Placido	R-R	5-10	190	10-10-75	.257	.226	.271	90	303	28	78	15	0	2	19	18	2	4	1	25	0	0	.327	.302
Pridie, Jason	L-R	6-1	205	10-9-83	.300	—	.300	9	10	1	3	1	0	1	3	0	0	0	0	0	0	0	.700	.300
Rollins, Jimmy	B-R	5-8	180	11-27-78	.250	.218	.265	156	632	102	158	33	5	23	68	62	0	2	3	96	30	5	.427	.316
Ruf, Darin	R-R	6-3	220	7-28-86	.333	.375	.294	12	33	4	11	2	1	3	10	2	0	0	2	12	0	0	.727	.351
Ruiz, Carlos	R-R	5-10	205	1-22-79	.325	.320	.327	114	372	56	121	32	0	16	68	29	16	0	4	50	4	0	.540	.394
Schierholtz, Nate	L-R	6-2	215	2-15-84	.273	.235	.286	37	66	5	18	4	0	1	5	5	0	1	1	10	0	0	.379	.319
2-team total (77 San Francisco)					.257	—	—	114	241	20	62	8	5	6	21	23	1	1	3	46	3	2	.407	.321
Schneider, Brian	L-R	6-1	210	11-26-76	.225	.176	.236	34	89	9	20	5	0	2	7	5	3	1	0	15	0	0	.348	.289
Thome, Jim	L-R	6-4	250	8-27-70	.242	.200	.262	30	62	9	15	2	0	5	15	8	1	0	0	21	0	0	.516	.338
Utley, Chase	L-R	6-1	200	12-17-78	.256	.215	.283	83	301	48	77	15	2	11	45	43	12	0	6	43	11	1	.429	.365
Victorino, Shane	B-R	5-9	190	11-30-80	.261	.316	.242	101	387	46	101	17	5	9	40	35	2	5	2	49	24	4	.401	.324
2-team total (53 Los Angeles)					.255	—	—	154	595	72	152	29	7	11	55	53	6	9	3	80	39	6	.383	.321
Wigginton, Ty	R-R	6-0	230	10-11-77	.235	.234	.236	125	315	40	74	11	0	11	43	37	2	0	6	81	1	0	.375	.314

Pitching	B-T	HT	WT	DOB	W	L	ERA	G	GS	CG	SV	IP	H	R	ER	HR	BB	SO	AVG	vLH	vRH	K/9	BB/9
Aumont, Phillippe	L-R	6-7	260	1-7-89	0	1	3.68	18	0	0	2	15	10	6	6	0	9	14	.189	.167	.195	8.59	5.52
Bastardo, Antonio	L-L	5-11	195	9-21-85	2	5	4.33	65	0	0	1	52	40	26	25	7	26	81	.207	.169	.236	14.02	4.50
Blanton, Joe	R-R	6-3	235	12-11-80	8	9	4.59	21	20	2	0	133	141	74	68	22	18	115	.266	.288	.241	7.76	1.22
2-team total (10 Los Angeles)					10	13	4.71	31	30	2	0	191	207	106	100	29	34	166	—	—	—	7.82	1.60
Brummett, Tyson	R-R	6-0	185	8-15-84	0	0	0.00	1	0	0	0	1	2	0	0	0	0	2	.500	.500	.500	27.00	0.00
Cloyd, Tyler	R-R	6-3	190	5-16-87	2	2	4.91	6	6	0	0	33	33	18	18	8	7	30	.260	.314	.224	8.18	1.91
Contreras, Jose	R-R	6-4	255	12-6-71	1	0	5.27	17	0	0	0	14	13	10	8	1	3	15	.255	.200	.278	9.88	1.98
De Fratus, Justin	B-R	6-4	220	10-21-87	0	0	3.38	13	0	0	0	11	7	5	4	0	5	8	.179	.250	.130	6.75	4.22
Diekman, Jake	L-L	6-4	200	1-21-87	1	1	3.95	32	0	0	0	27	25	17	12	1	20	35	.234	.200	.258	11.52	6.59
Halladay, Roy	R-R	6-6	230	5-14-77	11	8	4.49	26	25	0	0	156	155	78	78	18	36	132	.261	.273	.246	7.60	2.07
Hamels, Cole	L-L	6-3	200	12-27-83	17	6	3.05	31	31	2	0	215	190	80	73	24	52	216	.237	.242	.235	9.03	2.17
Herndon, David	R-R	6-5	230	9-4-85	0	1	4.70	5	0	0	0	8	10	4	4	1	1	8	.333	.429	.250	9.39	1.17
Horst, Jeremy	L-L	6-3	215	10-1-85	2	0	1.15	32	0	0	0	31	21	8	4	1	14	40	.193	.170	.210	11.49	4.02
Kendrick, Kyle	R-R	6-3	210	8-14-84	11	12	3.90	37	25	1	0	159	154	76	69	20	49	116	.254	.238	.269	6.55	2.77
Lee, Cliff	L-L	6-3	205	8-30-78	6	9	3.16	30	30	0	0	211	207	79	74	26	28	207	.255	.263	.253	8.83	1.19
Lindblom, Josh	R-R	6-4	240	6-15-87	1	3	4.63	26	0	0	1	23	19	15	12	4	17	27	.213	.278	.170	10.41	6.56
2-team total (48 Los Angeles)					3	5	3.55	74	0	0	1	71	61	31	28	13	35	70	—	—	—	8.87	4.44
Papelbon, Jonathan	R-R	6-4	225	11-23-80	5	6	2.44	70	0	0	38	70	56	22	19	8	18	92	.216	.208	.224	11.83	2.31
Qualls, Chad	R-R	6-5	220	8-17-78	1	1	4.60	35	0	0	0	31	39	18	16	7	9	19	.302	.377	.250	5.46	2.59
2-team total (17 Pittsburgh)					1	1	5.20	52	0	0	0	45	53	29	26	7	11	25	—	—	—	5.00	2.20
Rosenberg, B.J.	R-R	6-3	220	9-17-85	1	2	6.12	22	1	0	0	25	18	17	17	4	14	24	.205	.188	.224	8.64	5.04
Sanches, Brian	R-R	6-1	190	8-8-78	0	1	9.95	6	0	0	0	6	12	7	7	4	3	5	.387	.375	.400	7.11	4.26
Savery, Joe	L-L	6-3	235	11-4-85	1	2	5.40	19	0	0	0	25	26	17	15	4	8	16	.274	.243	.293	5.76	2.88
Schwimer, Michael	R-R	6-8	240	2-19-86	2	1	4.46	35	0	0	0	34	30	18	17	3	16	36	.244	.262	.235	9.44	4.19

				W	L	ERA	G	GS	CG	SV	IP	H	R	ER	HR	BB	SO	AVG	vLH	vRH	K/9	BB/9
Stutes, Mike	R-R	6-1	185	9-4-86	0	0	6.35	6	0	0	0	6	7	6	4	0	4	5	.280	.167	.385	7.94	6.35
Valdes, Raul	L-L	5-11	190	11-27-77	3	2	2.90	27	1	0	0	31	18	10	10	3	5	35	.168	.149	.183	10.16	1.45
Worley, Vance	R-R	6-2	230	9-25-87	6	9	4.20	23	23	0	0	133	154	69	62	12	47	107	.296	.312	.280	7.24	3.18

Fielding

Catcher	PCT	G	PO	A	E	DP	PB
Kratz	.997	41	339	26	1	3	3
Lerud	1.000	3	21	0	0	0	0
Ruiz	.994	106	856	73	6	8	5
Schneider	1.000	29	197	21	0	2	1

First Base	PCT	G	PO	A	E	DP
Howard	.991	67	495	30	5	37
Luna	1.000	10	72	6	0	7
Mayberry Jr.	.995	27	175	11	1	13
Nix	.974	10	68	6	2	8
Ruf	1.000	3	16	0	0	0
Thome	.974	4	35	2	1	4
Wigginton	.991	71	421	38	4	34

Second Base	PCT	G	PO	A	E	DP
Fontenot	.951	17	28	30	3	5

	PCT	G	PO	A	E	DP
Galvis	.996	55	92	151	1	31
Martinez	.962	16	24	26	2	9
Orr	.914	13	12	20	3	4
Utley	.981	81	156	209	7	32

Third Base	PCT	G	PO	A	E	DP
Fontenot	.920	12	5	18	2	3
Frandsen	.941	52	35	76	7	4
Luna	1.000	1	1	1	0	0
Martinez	.920	10	4	19	2	2
Orr	1.000	4	1	3	0	0
Polanco	.990	80	57	148	2	10
Wigginton	.833	22	10	30	8	3

Shortstop	PCT	G	PO	A	E	DP
Galvis	1.000	5	4	18	0	3
Martinez	1.000	8	8	16	0	2

	PCT	G	PO	A	E	DP
Rollins	.978	156	204	377	13	74

Outfield	PCT	G	PO	A	E	DP
Brown	1.000	51	94	7	0	1
Luna	1.000	2	5	0	0	0
Martinez	1.000	9	9	1	0	1
Mayberry Jr.	.991	128	210	6	2	2
Nix	.970	29	32	0	1	0
Pence	.971	101	161	9	5	0
Pierre	.994	107	156	1	1	0
Pridie	1.000	2	2	0	0	0
Ruf	1.000	6	5	0	0	0
Schierholtz	1.000	33	30	0	0	0
Victorino	.996	101	232	7	1	3
Wigginton	1.000	7	13	0	0	0

LEHIGH VALLEY IRONPIGS   TRIPLE-A

INTERNATIONAL LEAGUE

Batting	B-T	HT	WT	DOB	AVG	vLH	vRH	G	AB	R	H	2B	3B	HR	RBI	BB	HBP	SH	SF	SO	SB	CS	SLG	OBP
Barnes, Jeremy	R-R	5-10	190	4-13-87	.000	.000	.000	2	2	1	0	0	0	0	0	0	1	0	0	0	2	0	0	.000	.333
Blanco, Andres	B-R	5-10	190	4-11-84	.235	.208	.247	120	413	47	97	14	1	10	40	39	2	3	4	77	6	5	.346	.301
Brown, Domonic	L-L	6-5	205	9-3-87	.286	.322	.273	60	220	33	63	13	2	5	28	17	0	0	2	42	4	6	.432	.335
Fontenot, Mike	L-R	5-8	165	6-9-80	.308	.318	.300	16	52	5	16	6	0	1	7	5	0	1	0	11	0	0	.481	.368
Fox, Jake	R-R	6-0	220	7-20-82	.290	.333	.280	9	31	3	9	4	0	0	4	0	3	0	1	6	0	0	.419	.343
2-team total (42 Indianapolis)					.247	—		51	154	18	38	14	0	2	20	13	4	0	3	30	0	0	.377	.316
Frandsen, Kevin	R-R	6-0	185	5-24-82	.302	.345	.284	99	391	38	118	34	0	1	33	14	8	2	3	31	2	4	.396	.337
Gosewisch, Tuffy	R-R	5-11	180	8-17-83	.192	.167	.207	65	213	22	41	13	0	4	20	9	5	0	1	42	0	0	.310	.241
Hernandez, Cesar	B-R	5-10	175	5-23-90	.248	.296	.234	30	121	13	30	4	1	0	6	4	0	3	1	11	5	3	.298	.270
Howard, Ryan	L-L	6-4	240	11-19-79	.417	—	.417	4	12	1	5	1	0	1	6	2	0	0	0	1	0	0	.750	.500
Hudson, Kyle	L-L	5-11	175	1-7-87	.253	.175	.275	78	296	32	75	4	1	0	17	28	0	5	0	54	15	7	.274	.318
2-team total (31 Durham)					.264	—		109	406	48	107	5	2	0	25	43	1	11	1	74	22	11	.286	.335
Hulett, Tug	R-R	5-10	185	2-28-83	.325	.313	.327	37	120	18	39	5	1	2	17	9	0	0	1	24	1	0	.433	.369
Kennelly, Tim	R-R	6-0	180	12-5-86	.189	.161	.299	17	53	3	10	2	0	1	5	2	0	2	0	9	1	0	.283	.218
Kratz, Erik	R-R	6-4	255	6-15-80	.266	.294	.256	37	124	17	33	10	0	8	30	10	3	0	4	20	0	0	.540	.326
Luna, Hector	R-R	6-1	190	2-1-80	.282	.294	.276	62	220	33	62	12	2	7	28	15	2	0	3	40	2	0	.450	.329
2-team total (4 Indianapolis)					.297	—		66	236	38	70	13	2	8	33	16	2	0	3	41	2	0	.470	.342
Martinez, Michael	B-R	5-9	175	9-16-82	.271	.474	.159	32	107	12	29	4	2	2	15	10	1	1	3	12	3	1	.402	.331
Mitchell, Derrick	R-R	6-3	210	1-5-87	.218	.147	.247	72	238	24	52	11	0	7	35	19	2	1	3	53	8	3	.353	.279
Montanez, Lou	R-R	6-1	195	12-15-81	.136	.143	.133	17	44	3	6	1	0	0	1	8	0	0	1	9	0	0	.159	.264
Nix, Laynce	L-L	6-1	220	10-30-80	.250	.286	.000	2	8	1	2	0	0	0	1	0	0	0	0	3	0	0	.250	.333
Opitz, Jake	L-R	6-0	190	7-28-86	.000	—	.000	2	2	0	0	0	0	0	0	0	0	0	0	0	0	0	.000	.000
Orr, Pete	L-R	6-1	195	6-8-79	.258	.213	.275	81	302	43	78	13	2	4	33	23	2	4	1	53	16	2	.354	.314
Overbeck, Cody	R-R	6-1	200	6-5-86	.249	.233	.255	133	458	58	114	27	2	14	71	39	1	0	3	113	0	0	.408	.307
2-team total (25 Pawtucket)					.242	—		48	165	23	40	3	1	1	15	16	1	2	3	25	10	3	.291	.308
Pridie, Jason	L-R	6-1	205	10-9-83	.298	.200	.331	49	178	17	53	7	3	5	22	16	0	0	0	38	4	0	.455	.356
Schierholtz, Nate	L-R	6-1	205	2-15-84	.118	.125	.111	4	17	1	2	0	0	0	1	0	0	0	0	3	0	0	.118	.118
Spidale, Mike	R-R	6-0	180	3-12-82	.268	.266	.269	75	228	24	61	7	0	1	8	6	2	1	0	20	7	6	.311	.291
Suomi, John	L-R	5-11	200	10-5-80	.265	.280	.263	64	196	27	52	13	0	4	18	13	0	1	0	29	1	1	.393	.311
Susdorf, Steve	L-L	6-1	195	3-28-86	.282	.178	.303	84	266	38	75	18	0	1	26	27	3	0	4	42	4	4	.361	.350
Thompson, Rich	L-R	6-3	185	4-23-79	.307	.367	.276	30	88	6	27	4	2	0	11	9	4	1	0	18	7	2	.398	.396
2-team total (63 Durham)					.310	—		93	339	47	105	17	7	2	30	29	7	9	0	53	29	7	.419	.378
Thurston, Joe	L-R	5-11	225	9-29-79	.207	.000	.240	11	29	5	6	1	0	1	2	7	1	0	0	4	1	0	.345	.378
2-team total (15 Rochester)					.139	—		26	72	9	10	1	0	2	4	12	1	0	1	16	1	0	.236	.267
Utley, Chase	L-R	6-1	200	12-17-78	.400	.000	.500	1	5	1	2	0	0	1	1	0	0	0	0	2	0	0	1.000	.400
Valle, Sebastian	R-R	6-1	205	7-24-90	.218	.200	.222	22	78	7	17	1	0	2	10	2	0	4	0	13	2	0	.397	.232

Pitching	B-T	HT	WT	DOB	W	L	ERA	G	GS	CG	SV	IP	H	R	ER	HR	BB	SO	AVG	vLH	vRH	K/9	BB/9
Aumont, Phillippe	L-R	6-7	260	1-7-89	3	1	4.26	41	0	0	15	44	34	23	21	3	34	59	.209	.230	.196	11.98	6.90
Brummett, Tyson	R-R	6-0	185	8-15-84	4	6	3.63	34	7	0	1	72	67	33	29	2	27	65	.251	.252	.250	8.13	3.38
Bush, Dave	R-R	6-2	205	11-9-79	4	3	3.16	11	11	1	0	63	69	27	22	5	8	37	.274	.224	.316	5.31	1.15
Cisco, Mike	R-R	5-11	190	5-23-87	2	0	2.67	17	0	0	0	30	27	12	9	3	11	19	.242	.243	.257	5.34	3.26
Cloyd, Tyler	R-R	6-3	190	5-16-87	12	1	2.35	22	22	1	0	142	105	39	37	14	38	93	.210	.247	.173	5.89	2.41
Cochran, Tom	L-L	6-2	195	10-16-82	9	5	3.96	25	23	0	0	127	107	63	56	10	70	106	.230	.250	.224	7.49	4.95
De Fratus, Justin	B-R	6-4	220	10-21-87	0	1	2.49	17	0	0	3	22	15	6	6	2	3	22	.203	.038	.292	9.14	1.25
Diekman, Jake	L-L	6-4	190	1-21-87	1	1	1.69	25	0	0	7	27	19	5	5	0	13	37	.196	.200	.194	12.49	4.39
Duke, Ryan	R-R	6-0	180	9-27-88	0	0	0.00	1	0	0	0	2	1	0	0	0	2	1	.143	.000	.200	9.00	9.00
Elarton, Scott	R-R	6-7	240	2-23-76	6	11	5.41	26	26	0	0	136	160	93	82	13	54	88	.290	.319	.268	5.81	3.56
Friend, Justin	R-R	6-1	200	8-26-86	2	1	4.40	12	0	0	1	14	21	8	7	1	3	13	.339	.292	.368	8.16	1.88
Gailey, Frank	L-L	5-9	190	11-18-85	0	0	9.00	1	0	0	0	3	1	1	0	0	3	1	.500	.500	.500	9.00	9.00

	B-T	HT	WT	DOB	W	L	ERA	G	GS	CG	SV	IP	H	R	ER	HR	BB	SO	AVG	vLH	vRH	K/9	BB/9
Hollands, Mario	L-L	6-5	205	8-26-88	0	2	9.24	3	3	0	0	13	21	13	13	4	4	10	.362	.462	.333	7.11	2.84
Horst, Jeremy	L-L	6-3	215	10-1-85	2	1	2.11	26	0	0	2	38	43	11	9	3	18	32	.283	.340	.257	7.51	4.23
Hyatt, Austin	R-R	6-3	205	5-23-86	2	7	6.33	11	11	0	0	54	62	45	38	10	26	35	.292	.283	.301	5.83	4.33
Misch, Pat	R-L	6-2	200	8-18-81	7	12	4.98	21	21	0	0	112	132	73	62	16	29	81	.289	.255	.304	6.51	2.33
Morillo, Juan	R-R	6-3	190	11-5-83	1	0	3.07	8	0	0	0	15	10	5	5	0	11	22	.185	.211	.171	13.50	6.75
Pettibone, Jon	L-R	6-5	200	7-19-90	4	1	2.55	7	7	1	0	42	31	12	12	0	22	32	.204	.213	.198	6.80	4.68
Purcey, David	L-L	6-5	235	4-22-82	1	4	4.37	47	1	0	0	58	57	28	28	2	33	63	.260	.265	.257	9.83	5.15
Ramirez, J.C.	R-R	6-4	250	8-16-88	3	2	4.28	29	0	0	1	40	36	19	19	3	17	34	.250	.283	.226	7.65	3.83
Rosenberg, B.J.	R-R	6-2	220	9-17-85	4	2	2.00	20	6	0	0	54	49	14	12	4	16	63	.244	.183	.301	10.50	2.67
Sanches, Brian	R-R	6-1	190	8-8-78	3	2	2.50	25	1	0	0	40	41	15	11	2	8	31	.270	.238	.292	7.03	1.82
Savery, Joe	L-L	6-3	235	11-4-85	1	1	4.24	20	0	0	2	23	27	14	11	3	9	26	.281	.393	.235	10.03	3.47
Schwimer, Michael	R-R	6-8	240	2-19-86	2	1	3.93	15	0	0	6	18	17	11	8	2	5	19	.239	.258	.225	9.33	2.45
Valdes, Raul	L-L	5-11	190	11-27-77	1	2	2.70	16	0	0	3	30	26	12	9	3	2	41	.234	.229	.237	12.30	0.60
Wright, Matt	R-R	6-4	270	3-13-82	1	1	3.09	7	4	0	0	23	18	8	8	2	7	17	.214	.214	.214	6.56	2.70

Fielding

Catcher	PCT	G	PO	A	E	DP	PB
Gosewisch	.994	59	430	31	3	8	3
Kratz	.996	31	237	17	1	0	1
Suomi	.988	35	227	16	3	1	7
Valle	.984	21	179	4	3	0	2

First Base	PCT	G	PO	A	E	DP
Fox	1.000	4	25	3	0	2
Frandsen	.984	10	58	2	1	9
Howard	1.000	3	22	3	0	2
Luna	1.000	5	23	3	0	1
Nix	1.000	1	6	0	0	0
Overbeck	.995	126	954	67	5	97
Suomi	.943	7	30	3	2	8
Susdorf	1.000	3	11	0	1	0

Second Base	PCT	G	PO	A	E	DP
Blanco	1.000	1	0	1	0	0
Fontenot	1.000	7	23	19	0	4
Frandsen	.982	81	159	214	7	60
Hernandez	.964	30	58	75	5	20

	PCT	G	PO	A	E	DP
Kennelly	1.000	1	2	2	0	0
Martinez	1.000	6	15	23	0	6
Orr	1.000	12	22	37	0	11
Thurston	.967	7	15	14	1	3
Utley	1.000	1	3	2	0	0

Third Base	PCT	G	PO	A	E	DP
Fontenot	1.000	7	6	9	0	1
Frandsen	.813	5	5	8	3	0
Hulett	.915	30	17	48	6	6
Kennelly	.923	15	8	16	2	0
Luna	.917	36	36	52	8	7
Martinez	1.000	3	3	5	0	0
Orr	.964	49	29	103	5	11
Overbeck	1.000	4	2	1	0	0

Shortstop	PCT	G	PO	A	E	DP
Blanco	.964	119	149	333	18	79
Fontenot	1.000	1	1	1	0	1
Frandsen	1.000	3	6	10	0	2
Martinez	.947	13	18	36	3	10

	PCT	G	PO	A	E	DP
Orr	.946	8	12	23	2	4

Outfield	PCT	G	PO	A	E	DP
Brown	.936	57	98	5	7	0
Fox	1.000	1	1	0	0	0
Gosewisch	—	1	0	0	0	0
Hudson	.988	75	163	5	2	3
Kennelly	—	1	0	0	0	0
Luna	1.000	1	1	0	0	0
Martinez	1.000	8	12	0	0	0
Mitchell	.994	68	161	8	1	5
Montanez	.905	12	18	1	2	1
Nix	1.000	1	4	0	0	0
Orr	1.000	14	24	0	0	0
Podsednik	.974	19	37	1	1	0
Pridie	1.000	44	76	3	0	2
Schierholtz	1.000	4	13	1	0	0
Spidale	.952	56	79	1	4	1
Susdorf	.982	64	104	5	2	0
Thompson	.983	28	58	0	1	0

READING PHILLIES

DOUBLE-A

EASTERN LEAGUE

Batting	B-T	HT	WT	DOB	AVG	vLH	vRH	G	AB	R	H	2B	3B	HR	RBI	BB	HBP	SH	SF	SO	SB	CS	SLG	OBP
Abreu, Miguel	R-R	5-10	190	11-14-84	.280	.325	.258	103	378	42	106	17	1	4	33	7	4	5	4	32	6		.362	.298
Asche, Cody	L-R	6-1	180	6-30-90	.300	.301	.300	68	263	42	79	20	3	10	47	22	3	0	1	56	1	1	.513	.360
Barnes, Jeremy	R-R	5-10	190	4-13-87	.192	.182	.200	22	52	3	10	1	0	0	3	5	1	1	1	11	0	0	.212	.271
Castro, Leandro	R-R	5-11	175	6-15-89	.287	.326	.271	133	478	66	137	35	1	10	71	7	1	8		70	13	9	.427	.316
Fox, Jake	R-R	6-0	220	7-20-82	.203	.222	.196	17	69	7	14	4	0	5	10	4	1	0	0	14	0	0	.478	.257
Gillies, Tyson	L-R	6-2	205	10-31-88	.304	.253	.326	68	276	59	84	13	8	4	24	18	11	5	1	52	8	6	.453	.369
Hanzawa, Troy	R-R	5-9	155	9-12-85	.249	.234	.255	127	413	45	103	18	6	0	44	28	3	2	9	68	4	1	.322	.296
Hernandez, Cesar	B-R	5-10	175	5-23-90	.304	.339	.289	103	411	50	125	26	11	2	51	27	0	10	2	67	16	12	.436	.345
Hill, John	L-R	6-3	205	2-11-89	.000	.000	.000	2	5	0	0	0	0	0	0	0	0	0	0	3	0	0	.000	.000
Hulett, Tug	L-R	5-10	190	1-28-83	.264	.189	.286	52	163	23	43	8	2	2	22	24	1	0	3	32	3	1	.374	.356
James, Jiwan	B-R	6-4	180	4-11-89	.249	.283	.235	111	381	55	95	14	5	6	31	21	4	4	6	115	8	8	.360	.291
Joseph, Tommy	R-R	6-1	215	7-16-91	.250	.174	.273	28	100	12	25	8	0	3	10	9	3	1	1	32	0	1	.420	.327
2-team total (80 Richmond)					.257	—	—	108	404	44	104	24	0	11	48	34	4	1	6	96	0	4	.399	.317
Kennelly, Tim	R-R	6-0	180	12-5-86	.257	.308	.150	58	183	24	47	7	1	3	19	8	0	5	5	39	1	0	.355	.281
Lerud, Steve	L-R	6-1	215	10-13-84	.235	.053	.277	35	102	7	24	7	0	0	7	13	5	0	0	11	1	0	.304	.350
Myers, D'Arby	R-R	6-3	175	12-9-88	.306	.250	.329	47	121	19	37	5	0	3	16	6	0	0	0	20	7	0	.421	.339
Opitz, Jake	L-R	6-0	190	7-28-86	.154	.000	.167	10	26	2	4	1	0	0	2	1	0	0	2	11	0	0	.192	.172
Ruf, Darin	R-R	6-3	220	7-28-86	.317	.392	.284	139	489	93	155	32	1	38	104	65	18	0	11	102	2	0	.620	.408
Spidale, Mike	R-R	6-0	180	3-12-82	.390	.318	.474	13	41	6	16	3	0	0	7	0	0	0	0	2	0	0	.463	.390
Stumpo, Bob	B-R	6-4	220	7-17-87	.174	.333	.150	9	23	2	4	1	0	0	4	0	1	0	0	2	0	0	.217	.296
Susdorf, Steve	L-L	6-1	195	7-28-86	.297	.333	.286	33	111	11	33	9	1	1	15	9	1	1	1	15	2	2	.423	.352
Tripp, Brandon	L-R	6-2	200	4-2-85	.268	.208	.283	72	228	29	61	12	1	5	27	13	7	0	4	52	2	0	.395	.321
Valle, Sebastian	R-R	6-1	205	7-24-90	.261	.273	.255	83	310	31	81	13	1	13	45	11	0	1	7	83	0	2	.435	.280

Pitching	B-T	HT	WT	DOB	W	L	ERA	G	GS	CG	SV	IP	H	R	ER	HR	BB	SO	AVG	vLH	vRH	K/9	BB/9
Bonilla, Lisalverto	R-R	6-1	164	6-6-90	2	1	1.64	21	0	0	3	33	22	6	6	1	17	46	.193	.267	.145	12.55	4.64
Brummett, Tyson	R-R	6-0	185	8-15-84	1	0	1.50	10	1	0	1	18	7	3	3	2	3	18	.117	.143	.103	9.00	1.00
Buchanan, David	R-R	6-3	190	5-11-89	3	5	3.86	12	12	1	0	72	73	36	31	7	23	40	.273	.340	.230	4.98	2.86
Cisco, Mike	R-R	5-11	190	5-23-87	3	3	1.21	23	0	0	2	45	39	12	6	2	15	40	.239	.300	.204	8.06	3.02
Cloyd, Tyler	R-R	6-3	190	5-16-87	3	0	1.80	4	4	0	0	25	22	5	5	1	5	20	.239	.212	.254	7.20	1.08
Colvin, Brody	R-R	6-3	195	8-14-90	1	4	11.02	7	7	0	0	33	43	44	40	6	23	16	.328	.349	.309	4.41	6.34
Duke, Ryan	R-R	6-0	180	9-27-88	1	0	6.52	8	0	0	0	10	9	7	7	1	7	13	.263	.286	.250	12.10	6.52
Friend, Justin	R-R	6-1	200	6-21-86	2	0	0.23	38	0	0	24	40	24	2	1	0	15	41	.178	.171	.181	9.30	3.40
Gailey, Frank	L-L	5-9	190	11-18-85	2	3	4.40	26	0	0	1	29	35	15	14	2	12	26	.310	.263	.333	8.16	3.77
Hollands, Mario	L-L	6-5	205	8-26-88	3	5	4.75	9	8	0	0	47	54	27	25	4	23	28	.293	.233	.312	5.32	4.37
Hyatt, Austin	R-R	6-3	205	5-23-86	8	5	4.62	16	16	0	0	88	92	51	45	14	26	75	.267	.268	.267	7.70	2.67

Name	B-T	HT	WT	DOB	W	L	ERA	G	GS	CG	SV	IP	H	R	ER	HR	BB	SO	AVG	vLH	vRH	K/9	BB/9
Johnson, Jay	R-L	6-2	210	12-21-89	2	1	5.02	28	0	0	0	29	33	19	16	3	18	30	.284	.219	.310	9.42	5.65
Kissock, Chris	R-R	6-4	185	5-2-85	1	1	7.56	5	0	0	0	8	14	7	7	4	4	8	.350	.500	.269	8.64	4.32
Knigge, Tyler	R-R	6-4	215	10-27-88	0	0	2.92	21	0	0	2	25	25	13	8	1	12	25	.263	.263	.263	9.12	4.38
Martin, Ethan	R-R	6-2	195	6-6-89	5	0	3.18	7	7	0	0	40	29	15	14	3	18	35	.206	.125	.247	7.94	4.08
May, Trevor	R-R	6-5	215	9-23-89	10	13	4.87	28	28	0	0	150	139	87	81	22	78	151	.249	.249	.248	9.08	4.69
Morgan, Adam	L-L	6-1	195	2-27-90	4	1	3.53	6	6	0	0	36	34	14	14	2	11	29	.260	.263	.259	7.32	2.78
Morillo, Juan	R-R	6-3	190	11-5-83	0	2	6.09	32	0	0	0	44	37	30	30	2	44	45	.230	.219	.237	9.14	8.93
Naylor, Drew	R-R	6-4	235	5-31-86	3	2	6.04	5	5	0	0	25	36	19	17	7	7	16	.333	.386	.297	5.68	2.49
Pettibone, Jon	L-R	6-5	200	7-19-90	9	7	3.30	19	19	1	0	117	115	52	43	9	27	81	.257	.228	.271	6.21	2.07
Ramirez, J.C.	R-R	6-4	250	8-16-88	0	2	3.62	16	0	0	3	27	20	14	11	3	14	18	.200	.270	.159	5.93	4.61
Rodriguez, Julio	R-R	6-4	195	8-29-90	7	7	4.23	29	22	0	0	134	121	73	63	14	76	136	.243	.275	.220	9.13	5.10
Rosenberg, B.J.	R-R	6-3	220	9-17-85	1	0	1.13	5	0	0	3	8	5	1	1	1	2	10	.167	.200	.150	11.25	2.25
Shreve, Colby	R-R	6-5	210	1-5-88	3	1	4.40	28	0	0	2	43	43	26	21	2	25	29	.259	.294	.235	6.07	5.23
Simon, Kyle	R-R	6-5	225	8-18-90	1	0	1.42	13	0	0	2	25	12	5	4	0	5	21	.133	.158	.115	7.46	1.78
Whatcott, Jordan	R-R	6-0	198	6-10-85	1	3	4.42	38	7	0	2	71	83	45	35	6	32	50	.294	.316	.283	6.31	4.04

Fielding

Catcher

Catcher	PCT	G	PO	A	E	DP	PB
Fox	1.000	2	12	1	0	0	1
Hill	1.000	2	10	1	0	1	0
Joseph	.995	24	193	9	1	1	3
Lerud	.996	31	231	20	1	4	1
Stumpo	1.000	7	51	3	0	1	2
Valle	1.000	79	589	47	0	4	9

First Base	PCT	G	PO	A	E	DP
Fox	1.000	10	72	5	0	11
Hulett	1.000	18	148	10	0	20
Joseph	1.000	2	8	1	0	0
Kennelly	.985	13	57	8	1	9
Lerud	.933	1	14	0	1	2
Opitz	1.000	2	23	1	0	1
Ruf	.995	107	758	45	4	92

	PCT	G	PO	A	E	DP
Stumpo	1.000	2	4	0	0	2
Susdorf	.971	3	32	1	1	3
Second Base	PCT	G	PO	A	E	DP
Abreu	.986	18	29	41	1	8
Hanzawa	1.000	7	15	18	0	5
Hernandez	.968	102	182	273	15	83
Hulett	.972	8	17	18	1	8
Kennelly	.875	3	6	8	2	2
Opitz	.955	4	6	15	1	6
Third Base	PCT	G	PO	A	E	DP
Abreu	.943	24	16	34	3	1
Asche	.933	67	40	114	11	10
Barnes	.923	8	3	9	1	1
Hulett	.932	18	14	27	3	3
Kennelly	.906	35	25	52	8	9

Shortstop	PCT	G	PO	A	E	DP
Abreu	.953	28	55	66	6	27
Hanzawa	.963	120	153	346	19	82
Outfield	PCT	G	PO	A	E	DP
Abreu	1.000	26	51	4	0	2
Castro	.961	125	262	11	11	2
Gillies	.987	66	144	7	2	1
James	.991	105	209	6	2	1
Kennelly	1.000	5	8	2	0	0
Myers	.981	33	53	0	1	0
Ruf	1.000	29	42	3	0	0
Spidale	1.000	10	17	0	0	0
Susdorf	1.000	7	12	1	0	0
Tripp	.938	38	58	3	4	0

CLEARWATER THRESHERS HIGH CLASS A
FLORIDA STATE LEAGUE

Batting	B-T	HT	WT	DOB	AVG	vLH	vRH	G	AB	R	H	2B	3B	HR	RBI	BB	HBP	SH	SF	SO	SB	CS	SLG	OBP
Alonso, Carlos	R-R	5-11	205	2-15-88	.278	.246	.301	93	327	44	91	12	0	4	40	35	10	3	4	49	2	1	.352	.362
Alvarez, Miguel	R-R	6-1	172	9-27-89	.178	.200	.167	27	101	6	18	1	0	0	5	2	0	1	0	33	2	2	.188	.194
Asche, Cody	L-R	6-1	180	6-30-90	.349	.311	.370	62	255	31	89	13	3	2	25	12	1	0	2	37	10	2	.447	.378
Barnes, Jeremy	R-R	5-10	190	4-13-87	.161	.171	.152	24	87	7	14	2	0	0	10	9	1	1	1	20	0	0	.184	.245
Cartwright, Albert	R-R	5-10	180	10-31-87	.257	.240	.268	105	404	60	104	20	8	5	40	32	8	2	1	91	16	8	.384	.324
Collier, Zach	L-L	6-2	185	9-8-90	.269	.222	.293	78	283	39	76	13	3	6	32	26	4	1	5	60	11	3	.399	.333
Duffy, Chris	L-R	6-2	200	12-17-87	.236	.250	.228	44	157	16	37	9	0	2	15	13	5	0	0	49	0	0	.331	.314
Duran, Edgar	R-R	5-11	155	2-10-91	.253	.242	.260	121	403	56	102	13	4	7	49	28	8	6	6	68	10	10	.357	.310
Ford, Trey	R-R	6-2	200	7-25-90	.000	.000	.000	1	4	0	0	0	0	0	0	0	0	0	0	0	0	1	.000	.000
Gillies, Tyson	L-R	6-2	205	10-31-88	.176	.222	.125	5	17	1	3	1	0	0	0	2	1	0	1	7	1	0	.235	.263
Hewitt, Anthony	R-R	6-1	190	4-27-89	.241	.253	.234	108	411	41	99	13	4	13	50	18	6	0	2	136	13	9	.387	.281
Hill, John	L-R	6-3	205	2-11-89	.091	.000	.115	14	33	4	3	1	0	1	7	0	0	1	11	0	0	.121	.244
Hillman, Drew	R-R	6-0	200	5-4-89	.223	.263	.182	53	157	20	35	10	0	5	21	7	4	1	3	30	1	0	.382	.269
Knight, Johnny	R-R	6-3	175	6-3-93	.000	—	.000	2	4	0	0	0	0	0	0	0	0	0	1	0	0	0	.000	.000
Lafrenz, Bronco	R-R	6-1	190	2-6-87	.149	.111	.172	14	47	3	7	2	0	0	2	2	0	1	0	15	0	0	.191	.184
Lavin, Peter	L-L	5-11	180	12-27-87	.269	.233	.288	116	442	68	119	23	1	6	38	34	1	2	2	72	16	5	.367	.322
Martinez, Harold	R-R	6-3	210	5-3-90	.226	.177	.259	56	195	21	44	10	1	3	15	13	1	1	1	45	2	1	.333	.276
Martinez, Michael	R-R	5-9	175	9-16-82	.333	.200	.400	4	15	4	5	1	0	0	2	1	0	0	1	0	0	.400	.375
Murphy, Jim	R-R	6-4	240	9-16-85	.274	.305	.254	125	460	75	126	43	1	17	85	53	8	0	6	123	1	2	.483	.355
Myers, D'Arby	R-R	6-3	175	12-9-88	.304	.182	.417	20	69	12	21	6	1	1	9	3	0	0	2	9	5	1	.464	.324
Nix, Laynce	L-L	6-1	220	10-30-80	.250	.000	.364	6	16	1	4	2	0	1	4	4	0	0	0	2	0	0	.563	.400
Numata, Chace	B-R	6-0	175	8-14-92	.333	.000	.500	1	3	0	1	0	0	0	0	0	0	0	0	0	0	0	.333	.333
Polanco, Placido	R-R	5-10	190	10-10-75	.417	1.000	.364	3	12	3	5	0	0	0	2	0	0	0	0	0	0	0	.417	.417
Rupp, Cameron	R-R	6-1	240	9-28-88	.267	.275	.263	104	344	32	92	22	1	10	49	40	2	2	2	77	0	0	.424	.345
Schneider, Brian	L-R	6-1	210	11-26-76	.182	.250	.143	6	22	2	4	2	0	0	2	1	0	0	0	4	0	0	.273	.217
Stassi, Brock	L-L	6-2	190	8-7-89	.222	1.000	.125	3	9	0	2	1	0	0	1	0	0	0	0	1	0	0	.333	.222
Stumpo, Bob	B-R	6-4	220	7-17-87	.270	.188	.333	11	37	2	10	4	0	0	7	1	0	0	0	8	0	0	.378	.289
Thome, Jim	L-R	6-4	250	8-27-70	.500	.000	.625	3	10	3	5	2	0	0	4	3	0	0	0	2	0	0	.700	.615
Tripp, Brandon	L-R	6-2	200	4-2-85	.257	.241	.267	36	140	15	36	9	3	1	17	5	6	0	2	35	0	0	.386	.307
Utley, Chase	L-R	6-1	200	12-17-78	.156	.100	.182	9	32	3	5	0	0	1	5	3	2	0	1	5	1	0	.250	.263

Pitching	B-T	HT	WT	DOB	W	L	ERA	G	GS	CG	SV	IP	H	R	ER	HR	BB	SO	AVG	vLH	vRH	K/9	BB/9
Aizenstadt, Andrew	R-R	6-5	185	8-4-89	0	0	0.00	1	0	0	0	1	1	1	0	0	1	3	.250	.000	.333	27.00	9.00
Arias, Gabirel	R-R	6-1	175	12-6-89	0	1	3.60	1	1	0	0	5	6	2	2	0	0	9	.300	.333	.286	16.20	0.00
Biddle, Jesse	L-L	6-4	225	10-22-91	10	6	3.22	26	26	1	0	143	129	64	51	10	54	151	.237	.225	.243	9.53	3.41
Bonilla, Lisalverto	R-R	6-1	164	6-6-90	1	1	1.35	10	0	0	1	13	9	4	2	0	4	18	.188	.250	.143	12.15	2.70
Brough, Austin	L-L	6-4	200	3-27-87	1	1	7.43	15	0	0	0	23	33	20	19	7	10	10	.330	.345	.324	3.91	3.91
Claypool, Garett	R-R	6-2	170	8-21-88	3	2	7.30	20	1	0	0	37	42	31	30	5	15	15	.284	.367	.227	10.46	3.65
Colvin, Brody	R-R	6-3	195	8-14-90	5	6	4.27	23	18	0	0	105	113	57	50	5	51	93	.285	.263	.301	7.95	4.36

PHILADELPHIA PHILLIES

Name	B-T	HT	WT	DOB	W	L	ERA	G	GS	CG	SV	IP	H	R	ER	HR	BB	SO	AVG	vLH	vRH	K/9	BB/9
Contreras, Jose	R-R	6-4	255	12-6-71	0	1	8.31	5	1	0	0	4	5	4	4	1	1	7	.263	.250	.267	14.54	2.08
De Fratus, Justin	B-R	6-4	220	10-21-87	0	0	0.00	2	1	0	0	2	2	0	0	0	0	1	.286	.667	.000	4.50	0.00
Duke, Ryan	R-R	6-0	180	9-27-88	0	1	3.24	16	0	0	0	25	22	10	9	1	8	37	.247	.265	.236	13.32	2.88
Gailey, Frank	L-L	5-9	190	11-18-85	0	0	13.50	4	0	0	0	3	7	6	5	0	2	5	.389	.500	.333	13.50	5.40
2-team total (8 Dunedin)					3	0	2.45	12	3	0	0	29	26	9	8	0	7	32	—	—	—	9.82	2.15
Garner, Perci	R-R	6-3	225	12-13-88	7	9	4.84	26	26	0	0	134	135	82	72	9	63	91	.262	.270	.256	6.11	4.23
Giles, Kenny	R-R	6-2	190	9-20-90	1	0	3.07	10	0	0	3	15	10	5	5	1	6	25	.182	.158	.194	15.34	3.68
Halladay, Roy	R-R	6-6	230	5-14-77	0	0	0.00	1	1	0	0	3	3	1	0	0	0	4	.231	.250	.200	12.00	0.00
Hollands, Mario	R-R	6-5	205	8-26-88	4	1	2.17	6	5	0	0	29	22	9	7	2	5	25	.206	.194	.211	7.76	1.55
Johnson, Jay	R-L	6-2	210	12-21-89	0	0	0.00	3	0	0	0	3	1	0	0	0	2	4	.100	.000	.125	10.80	5.40
Kinder, Andre	L-L	6-0	210	11-26-88	0	0	7.11	4	0	0	0	6	5	6	5	0	7	5	.208	.000	.294	7.11	9.95
Kissock, Chris	R-R	6-4	185	5-2-85	2	0	9.64	11	0	0	0	14	31	15	15	0	4	8	.449	.414	.475	5.14	2.57
Knigge, Tyler	R-R	6-4	215	10-27-88	4	1	0.60	34	0	0	9	45	26	3	3	0	11	45	.168	.179	.159	9.07	2.22
Morgado, Bryan	L-L	6-3	205	12-8-88	0	0	4.70	4	0	0	0	8	7	6	4	1	4	8	.250	.083	.375	9.39	4.70
Morgan, Adam	L-L	6-1	195	2-27-90	4	10	3.29	21	20	1	0	123	103	46	45	7	28	140	.227	.213	.233	10.24	2.05
Murray, Colton	R-R	6-0	195	4-22-90	0	1	2.78	19	0	0	4	23	15	11	7	1	5	28	.190	.267	.143	11.12	1.99
Naylor, Drew	R-R	6-4	235	5-31-86	0	0	4.91	2	0	0	0	4	5	2	2	0	0	7	.313	.429	.222	17.18	0.00
Neris, Hector	R-R	6-2	175	6-14-89	4	2	3.55	50	0	0	6	79	64	34	31	7	25	94	.221	.218	.222	10.75	2.86
Nesseth, Mike	R-R	6-5	225	4-19-88	2	2	2.76	21	0	0	8	29	25	12	9	0	12	16	.238	.211	.254	4.91	3.68
O'Sullivan, Ryan	R-R	6-2	190	9-5-90	2	1	2.45	6	0	0	0	11	12	3	3	0	3	6	.279	.167	.323	4.91	2.45
Rivas, Moises	R-R	6-1	169	10-15-90	0	0	3.00	1	0	0	0	3	4	2	1	0	2	3	.286	.400	.222	9.00	6.00
Rojas, Keive	R-R	6-0	170	2-26-93	0	0	0.00	1	0	0	0	1	0	0	0	0	0	2	.000	.000	.000	18.00	0.00
Rosin, Seth	R-R	6-6	250	11-2-88	0	1	3.00	3	3	0	0	12	7	5	4	0	4	7	.179	.235	.136	5.25	3.00
Santos, Felix	R-R	5-11	170	9-10-90	0	0	0.00	1	0	0	0	1	0	0	0	0	1	0	.000	.000	.000	13.50	0.00
Shreve, Colby	R-R	6-5	210	1-5-88	1	1	2.25	13	0	0	2	20	17	5	5	3	6	19	.230	.342	.111	8.55	2.70
Simon, Kyle	R-R	6-5	225	8-18-90	3	0	1.26	7	0	0	1	14	10	3	2	1	1	14	.208	.400	.071	8.79	0.63
Sosa, Juan	R-R	6-2	165	10-11-89	5	7	4.26	46	5	0	4	80	74	42	38	8	30	79	.246	.276	.224	8.85	3.36
Whatcott, Jordan	R-R	6-0	198	6-10-85	2	0	0.00	4	0	0	0	12	3	0	0	0	2	12	.081	.000	.130	9.00	1.50
Wright, Austin	L-L	6-4	235	9-26-89	11	5	3.47	27	25	0	0	148	147	73	57	11	60	133	.259	.213	.280	8.11	3.66

Fielding

Catcher	PCT	G	PO	A	E	DP	PB
Hill	.991	13	97	13	1	2	1
Lafrenz	.982	14	100	7	2	0	0
Numata	1.000	1	10	1	0	0	1
Rupp	.992	104	869	104	8	5	7
Schneider	1.000	3	18	3	0	0	1
Stumpo	.943	7	42	8	3	1	1

First Base	PCT	G	PO	A	E	DP
Duffy	1.000	1	5	0	0	0
Hillman	.974	6	34	3	1	4
Martinez	.960	6	45	3	2	1
Murphy	.990	114	979	58	11	88
Nix	.917	3	21	1	2	2
Stassi	1.000	2	17	1	0	1
Stumpo	.933	1	14	0	1	2
Tripp	.966	3	25	3	1	2

Second Base	PCT	G	PO	A	E	DP
Alonso	.983	33	47	70	2	12
Cartwright	.962	99	144	258	16	53
Ford	1.000	1	1	4	0	1
Martinez	1.000	1	2	3	0	2
Utley	1.000	4	11	7	0	2
Duran	.964	121	167	319	18	63
Martinez	1.000	1	0	5	0	1

Third Base	PCT	G	PO	A	E	DP
Alonso	.977	20	11	31	1	3
Asche	.951	61	31	104	7	7
Barnes	.500	1	1	1	2	0
Martinez	.920	50	27	88	10	7
Martinez	1.000	1	0	1	0	0
Polanco	.833	2	1	4	1	0

Shortstop	PCT	G	PO	A	E	DP
Alonso	.961	13	24	50	3	14

Outfield	PCT	G	PO	A	E	DP
Alonso	.979	28	45	2	1	0
Alvarez	.965	24	52	3	2	2
Collier	.980	74	149	1	3	0
Gillies	1.000	4	6	0	0	0
Hewitt	.912	100	199	9	20	1
Hillman	.913	18	21	0	2	0
Knight	1.000	1	1	0	0	0
Lavin	1.000	112	207	5	0	0
Martinez	1.000	1	1	0	0	0
Myers	.950	18	35	3	2	0
Tripp	.981	30	47	5	1	2

LAKEWOOD BLUECLAWS

LOW CLASS A

SOUTH ATLANTIC LEAGUE

Batting	B-T	HT	WT	DOB	AVG	vLH	vRH	G	AB	R	H	2B	3B	HR	RBI	BB	HBP	SH	SF	SO	SB	CS	SLG	OBP
Altherr, Aaron	R-R	6-5	190	1-14-91	.252	.291	.233	110	420	65	106	27	6	8	50	38	6	1	6	102	25	8	.402	.319
Alvarez, Miguel	R-R	6-1	172	9-27-89	.315	.298	.325	37	127	15	40	7	2	1	16	10	0	2	2	22	10	3	.425	.360
Carmona, William	B-R	5-11	185	3-9-91	.221	.200	.228	27	104	11	23	5	0	2	10	6	1	0	0	28	0	0	.327	.270
Carver, Tim	R-R	6-0	185	5-25-89	.210	.230	.200	50	181	21	38	8	1	1	14	18	4	5	2	24	8	2	.282	.293
Duffy, Chris	L-R	6-2	200	12-17-87	.384	.450	.346	60	216	42	83	18	0	11	56	31	4	0	2	55	2	0	.620	.466
Dugan, Kelly	R-B	6-3	195	9-18-90	.300	.291	.305	117	430	83	129	33	2	12	60	48	15	0	3	122	5	1	.470	.387
Eldemire, Gauntlett	R-R	6-3	195	2-28-89	.227	.225	.229	72	233	47	53	13	2	2	18	38	7	7	1	65	18	5	.326	.351
Ford, Trey	R-R	6-2	200	7-25-90	.157	.185	.140	22	70	6	11	0	1	1	6	11	0	0	0	21	1	0	.229	.272
Franco, Maikel	R-R	6-1	180	8-26-92	.280	.295	.273	132	503	70	141	32	3	14	84	38	7	0	6	80	3	1	.439	.336
Gillies, Tyson	L-R	6-2	205	10-31-88	.400	.250	1.000	5	5	2	2	0	0	0	2	1	0	0	0	0	0	0	.400	.625
Gonzalez, Diego	R-R	5-11	170	3-16-91	.154	.000	.207	17	39	3	6	0	0	0	2	1	1	0	0	14	4	0	.154	.175
Gonzalez, Gustavo	R-R	6-2	0	1-23-91	.181	.156	.190	36	116	9	21	0	0	0	6	7	1	1	0	24	5	0	.181	.234
Greene, Tyler	R-R	6-2	175	12-1-92	.147	.115	.163	23	75	6	11	6	0	1	7	13	0	0	1	37	2	0	.267	.270
Hill, John	L-R	6-3	205	2-11-89	.159	.143	.167	20	63	2	10	1	0	0	7	6	1	1	1	16	0	0	.175	.239
Hillman, Drew	R-R	6-0	200	5-4-89	.167	.125	.188	8	24	4	4	0	0	0	1	0	0	0	0	7	0	0	.167	.167
Howard, Ryan	L-L	6-4	240	11-19-79	.625	.000	.714	3	8	2	5	1	0	0	4	3	0	0	1	2	0	0	.750	.667
Hudson, Kyrell	R-R	6-1	180	12-6-90	.224	.364	.163	64	219	28	49	11	1	1	21	10	7	1	2	73	23	7	.297	.277
Lino, Gabriel	R-R	6-3	200	5-17-93	.227	.209	.236	37	132	16	30	10	0	3	14	14	2	0	0	33	0	2	.371	.311
2-team total (56 Delmarva)					.222	—	—	93	338	44	75	23	0	7	32	30	5	0	2	97	1	3	.352	.293
Ludy, Josh	R-R	5-10	210	4-18-90	.271	.227	.302	32	107	9	29	11	1	1	12	14	3	0	2	19	0	0	.421	.365
Malcolm, Stephen	R-R	5-11	180	4-9-90	.169	.167	.170	48	136	13	23	5	1	1	7	15	2	2	1	44	4	4	.243	.260
Martinez, Harold	R-R	6-3	210	5-3-90	.262	.318	.242	47	164	14	43	11	1	0	17	14	3	0	1	32	1	0	.341	.330
Moore, Logan	L-R	6-3	190	8-22-90	.177	.190	.173	30	96	11	17	6	0	1	11	16	4	0	0	29	0	1	.271	.319

	B-T	HT	WT	DOB	AVG	vLH	vRH	G	AB	R	H	2B	3B	HR	RBI	BB	HBP	SH	SF	SO	SB	CS	SLG	OBP
Perdomo, Carlos	R-R	5-10	168	4-25-90	.251	.268	.242	54	199	34	50	9	0	1	12	13	3	2	2	12	7	4	.312	.304
Pointer, Brian	L-L	6-0	190	1-28-92	.217	.159	.234	87	300	39	65	14	4	7	42	36	10	0	3	102	13	4	.360	.318
Stassi, Brock	L-L	6-2	190	8-7-89	.247	.267	.238	59	186	22	46	9	3	3	30	28	1	2	3	34	6	2	.376	.342
Stumpo, Bob	B-R	6-4	220	7-17-87	.258	.200	.293	36	120	11	31	4	1	1	17	20	0	1	1	20	0	2	.333	.362
Villalobos, Alejandro	R-R	5-11	170	8-20-91	.279	.317	.256	66	265	31	74	16	2	1	21	15	1	3	2	30	1	2	.366	.318

Pitching	B-T	HT	WT	DOB	W	L	ERA	G	GS	CG	SV	IP	H	R	ER	HR	BB	SO	AVG	vLH	vRH	K/9	BB/9
Arias, Gabirel	R-R	6-2	185	12-6-89	4	9	3.66	36	7	0	1	96	103	50	39	5	25	97	.272	.258	.282	9.09	2.34
Birmingham, Jim	L-L	6-5	180	8-2-88	0	0	10.57	9	0	0	0	8	8	12	9	0	10	7	.250	.235	.267	8.22	11.74
Brough, Austin	L-L	6-4	200	12-9-87	0	1	2.97	21	0	0	0	33	30	15	11	2	9	22	.236	.267	.220	5.94	2.43
Broussard, Geoff	R-R	6-0	185	9-21-90	0	0	3.00	1	0	0	0	3	3	1	1	1	3	3	.300	.400	.400	9.00	9.00
Campbell, Matt	R-R	6-2	195	9-10-87	1	3	5.60	23	0	0	3	35	31	23	22	3	20	24	.231	.250	.220	6.11	5.09
Cooper, Zach	R-R	5-10	185	1-6-90	1	3	1.13	17	0	0	4	24	15	5	3	0	9	15	.172	.171	.173	5.63	3.38
Duke, Ryan	R-R	6-0	180	9-27-88	0	2	2.79	9	0	0	3	10	11	4	3	1	3	12	.282	.333	.238	11.17	2.79
Giles, Kenny	R-R	6-2	190	9-20-90	3	3	3.61	29	6	0	5	67	54	30	27	5	44	86	.215	.209	.220	11.50	5.88
Hollands, Mario	L-L	6-5	205	8-26-88	0	1	4.57	9	0	0	0	22	25	11	11	1	7	21	.298	.192	.345	8.72	2.91
Kleven, Colin	R-R	6-5	200	4-15-91	9	8	3.99	27	27	0	0	151	151	82	67	16	41	119	.255	.276	.236	7.09	2.44
Manzanillo, Ervis	L-L	6-2	160	8-25-91	1	5	5.37	13	13	0	0	57	72	43	34	2	29	43	.306	.288	.314	6.79	4.58
Martinez, Lino	L-L	6-0	160	9-17-92	6	5	5.55	24	24	0	0	122	136	80	75	12	48	68	.280	.246	.294	5.03	3.55
Mascarello, Blake	L-L	6-1	200	6-25-89	4	1	2.64	16	0	0	1	31	34	12	9	1	7	16	.291	.205	.333	4.70	2.05
Milner, Hoby	L-L	6-2	165	1-13-91	6	3	2.59	12	12	0	0	63	52	21	18	6	22	47	.229	.196	.240	6.75	3.16
Morgado, Bryan	L-L	6-3	205	12-8-88	2	0	2.93	8	0	0	0	15	17	5	5	1	7	15	.298	.286	.880	8.80	4.11
Murray, Colton	R-R	6-0	195	4-22-90	1	3	4.30	25	0	0	4	38	45	23	18	3	16	34	.294	.339	.264	8.12	3.82
Nesseth, Mike	R-R	6-5	225	4-19-88	5	1	3.06	18	4	0	3	47	33	21	16	2	24	30	.192	.250	.141	5.74	4.60
Nichols, Chris	R-R	6-2	180	8-21-90	0	0	3.00	3	0	0	0	3	4	3	1	0	0	3	.308	.500	.143	0.00	0.00
Oviedo, Ramon	R-R	6-6	175	7-24-90	1	7	9.15	9	9	0	0	41	53	42	42	5	21	28	.321	.347	.300	6.10	4.57
Paulino, Luis	R-R	6-1	215	6-16-89	5	4	4.04	36	0	0	3	65	62	33	29	4	22	56	.253	.307	.215	7.79	3.06
Rivas, Moises	R-R	6-1	169	10-15-90	2	2	6.05	11	7	0	0	39	46	29	26	6	15	23	.309	.313	.305	5.35	3.49
Santos, Felix	R-R	5-11	170	9-10-90	0	2	1.57	11	0	0	2	23	17	7	4	0	5	25	.200	.233	.182	9.78	1.96
Sasaki, Ryan	R-L	6-5	215	10-30-90	0	1	6.60	7	0	0	0	15	18	12	11	2	12	7	.310	.435	.229	4.20	7.20
Shreve, Colby	R-R	6-5	210	1-5-88	2	1	3.60	6	0	0	0	15	12	6	6	2	7	16	.231	.160	.296	9.60	4.20
Sosa, Yari	R-R	6-0	180	9-30-90	3	2	5.07	25	2	0	2	50	55	31	28	2	21	27	.285	.250	.308	4.89	3.81
Stewart, Ethan	L-L	6-5	210	1-19-91	5	9	3.89	24	23	1	0	116	100	64	50	8	64	81	.233	.264	.220	6.30	4.98
Warner, Josh	R-R	6-3	185	10-10-92	1	0	5.19	2	2	1	0	9	11	8	5	0	5	4	.306	.400	.269	4.15	5.19

Fielding

Catcher	PCT	G	PO	A	E	DP	PB
Hill	.970	17	120	11	4	1	2
Lino	.981	37	277	27	6	2	14
Ludy	.980	25	132	13	3	1	2
Moore	.996	30	204	20	1	2	9
Stumpo	.986	31	194	21	3	4	3

First Base	PCT	G	PO	A	E	DP
Carmona	.971	9	63	5	2	8
Duffy	.994	21	149	19	1	16
Dugan	.981	25	199	11	4	17
Ford	.974	4	34	3	1	4
Hillman	1.000	4	25	0	0	3
Howard	1.000	1	8	0	0	3
Martinez	.981	32	236	25	5	21
Stassi	.990	51	356	34	4	27

Stumpo	1.000	5	37	2	0	3
Second Base	**PCT**	**G**	**PO**	**A**	**E**	**DP**
Carver	—	1	0	0	0	0
Ford	.976	11	16	25	1	7
Gonzalez	.948	20	29	63	5	10
Malcolm	.933	8	7	21	2	3
Perdomo	.976	38	65	98	4	25
Villalobos	.978	66	123	183	7	43
Third Base	**PCT**	**G**	**PO**	**A**	**E**	**DP**
Ford	.889	4	1	7	1	0
Franco	.944	122	84	186	16	17
Hillman	1.000	1	0	4	0	0
Martinez	.886	13	12	27	5	3
Shortstop	**PCT**	**G**	**PO**	**A**	**E**	**DP**
Carver	.923	49	70	121	16	27

Gonzalez	.912	16	18	34	5	6
Greene	.901	23	29	62	10	10
Malcolm	.938	37	52	84	9	19
Perdomo	.940	18	28	50	5	6
Outfield	**PCT**	**G**	**PO**	**A**	**E**	**DP**
Altherr	.996	90	253	8	1	2
Alvarez	.960	35	92	3	4	2
Dugan	.979	79	179	4	4	3
Eldemire	.987	69	151	2	2	1
Gillies	—	1	0	0	0	0
Gonzalez	.952	15	20	0	1	0
Hudson	.968	51	117	4	4	0
Malcolm	.857	3	6	0	1	0
Pointer	.969	77	124	2	4	0
Stassi	.929	9	12	1	1	0

WILLIAMSPORT CROSSCUTTERS　　　SHORT-SEASON

NEW YORK-PENN LEAGUE

Batting	B-T	HT	WT	DOB	AVG	vLH	vRH	G	AB	R	H	2B	3B	HR	RBI	BB	HBP	SH	SF	SO	SB	CS	SLG	OBP
Ford, Trey	R-R	6-2	200	7-25-90	.214	.250	.188	10	28	3	6	3	0	0	5	0	0	0	6	1	0	.321	.333
Gonzalez, Diego	R-R	5-11	170	3-16-91	.286	.400	.182	8	21	1	6	0	0	0	4	0	0	0	1	7	3	1	.286	.273
Gonzalez, Gustavo	R-R	6-2	0	1-23-91	.159	.333	.104	19	63	6	10	0	1	1	9	1	0	0	2	14	0	1	.238	.167
Greene, Larry	L-R	6-0	235	2-10-93	.272	.303	.260	70	257	36	70	22	0	2	26	41	2	0	3	78	1	2	.381	.373
Greene, Tyler	R-R	6-2	175	12-1-92	.211	.204	.213	61	218	17	46	9	2	3	19	10	1	1	3	85	2	2	.312	.246
Hoppy, Kyle	L-L	6-0	195	5-8-92	.224	.333	.191	32	116	14	26	5	0	1	11	20	1	2	0	15	4	1	.293	.343
Malcolm, Stephen	R-R	5-11	180	4-9-90	.100	.000	.105	6	20	1	2	0	0	0	1	3	0	1	0	5	1	1	.100	.217
Moore, Logan	L-R	6-3	190	8-22-90	.277	.226	.295	38	119	13	33	6	0	0	11	14	2	2	2	27	0	1	.328	.358
Numata, Chace	B-R	6-0	175	8-14-91	.233	.103	.274	43	163	22	38	4	2	2	23	13	1	3	4	22	3	1	.319	.287
Olmo, Yan	R-R	6-3	200	12-15-90	.212	.207	.214	56	203	23	43	8	2	0	18	5	5	0	1	46	5	0	.271	.248
Perkins, Cameron	R-R	6-5	195	9-27-90	.304	.355	.284	67	270	31	82	23	1	1	38	14	7	0	2	41	5	2	.407	.352
Pointer, Brian	L-L	6-0	190	1-28-92	.246	.300	.229	35	126	24	31	8	2	3	21	19	2	2	1	43	3	2	.413	.351
Quaranto, Kevin	L-R	6-3	215	5-13-88	.162	.167	.161	16	37	6	6	0	0	0	5	5	1	0	0	9	0	0	.162	.279
Quinn, Roman	B-R	5-10	170	5-14-93	.281	.347	.256	66	267	56	75	9	11	1	23	28	11	1	2	61	30	6	.408	.370
Serritella, Chris	L-R	6-3	205	2-21-90	.297	.289	.300	75	300	37	89	24	0	6	47	23	1	0	0	53	0	0	.437	.349
Stassi, Brock	L-L	6-2	190	8-7-89	.217	.400	.160	5	23	3	5	0	0	0	2	1	0	0	0	2	0	0	.217	.250
Taylor, Zach	L-R	6-3	215	5-3-91	.171	.250	.162	23	76	3	13	3	1	0	6	3	0	1	2	20	2	2	.237	.256
Tromp, Jiandido	R-R	5-11	175	9-27-93	.208	.150	.250	13	48	8	10	3	0	0	5	2	1	1	2	15	3	0	.271	.245
Walding, Mitch	L-R	6-3	190	9-10-92	.233	.167	.254	69	253	33	59	10	3	1	31	31	5	1	2	66	5	2	.308	.326

Pitching	B-T	HT	WT	DOB	W	L	ERA	G	GS	CG	SV	IP	H	R	ER	HR	BB	SO	AVG	vLH	vRH	K/9	BB/9
Aizenstadt, Andrew	R-R	6-5	185	8-4-89	0	0	1.46	7	0	0	2	12	6	4	2	0	3	15	.150	.200	.120	10.95	2.19
Birmingham, Jim	L-L	6-5	180	8-2-88	0	2	18.90	4	0	0	0	3	7	7	7	0	6	2	.438	.333	.462	5.40	16.20
Brady, Kevin	L-R	6-3	200	9-7-90	1	3	1.85	10	9	0	0	39	39	17	8	1	5	49	.258	.314	.230	11.31	1.15
Broussard, Geoff	R-R	6-0	185	9-21-90	2	1	2.35	19	0	0	7	31	31	9	8	1	5	33	.261	.244	.270	9.68	1.47
Cooper, Zach	R-R	5-10	185	1-6-90	1	0	1.69	6	0	0	2	11	8	3	2	1	6	10	.205	.250	.158	8.44	5.06
Gonzalez, Luis	L-L	6-2	170	1-17-92	0	3	4.62	16	6	0	1	51	51	32	26	2	25	46	.258	.380	.216	8.17	4.44
Guth, Jordan	R-R	6-5	200	4-7-91	2	2	5.82	11	7	0	0	34	40	25	22	4	3	18	.286	.299	.274	4.76	0.79
Hanson, Nic	R-R	6-7	210	4-15-92	2	3	7.00	19	3	0	0	45	64	42	35	6	5	29	.332	.365	.311	5.80	1.00
Inch, Steven	R-R	6-4	190	2-1-91	2	1	3.74	22	0	0	0	43	48	20	18	2	10	25	.281	.276	.283	5.19	2.08
Joaquin, Ulises	R-R	5-11	165	6-11-92	1	4	4.14	12	9	0	0	46	46	30	21	4	21	38	.253	.270	.241	7.49	4.14
Kinder, Andre	L-L	6-0	210	11-26-88	1	2	3.48	18	0	0	0	31	25	14	12	0	15	30	.225	.257	.211	8.71	4.35
Martinez, Manaure	R-R	6-1	155	12-31-91	2	2	4.91	7	6	0	0	29	30	19	16	0	15	22	.265	.320	.222	6.75	4.60
Milner, Hoby	L-L	6-2	165	1-13-91	1	0	1.59	2	1	0	0	6	2	1	1	0	2	7	.118	.000	.143	11.12	3.18
Musser, Jonathan	R-R	6-5	205	12-19-91	2	4	6.91	16	6	0	0	42	49	34	32	4	24	30	.301	.299	.302	6.48	5.18
Nichols, Chris	R-R	6-2	180	8-21-90	3	0	3.54	10	0	0	1	20	24	9	8	0	1	6	.304	.276	.320	2.66	0.44
Oviedo, Ramon	R-R	6-6	175	7-24-90	1	2	5.02	12	1	0	0	29	36	20	16	2	14	19	.308	.306	.309	5.97	4.40
Perez, Delvin	L-L	6-3	200	2-12-91	2	3	6.46	9	7	0	0	31	25	27	22	0	32	15	.227	.304	.207	4.40	9.39
Sisto, Matt	R-R	6-5	230	11-5-89	1	3	3.51	24	0	0	0	41	42	23	16	2	11	28	.264	.286	.252	6.15	2.41
Stefan, Jeb	R-R	6-4	225	4-21-90	2	4	3.94	22	6	0	2	46	46	22	20	3	16	37	.257	.268	.250	7.29	3.15
Warner, Josh	R-R	6-3	185	10-10-92	4	7	4.19	15	15	0	0	82	86	52	38	5	25	59	.264	.224	.286	6.50	2.76

Fielding

Catcher	PCT	G	PO	A	E	DP	PB
Moore	.977	35	226	26	6	1	7
Numata	.983	37	260	26	5	1	10
Quaranto	.953	6	39	2	2	0	1

First Base	PCT	G	PO	A	E	DP
Perkins	.987	23	212	16	3	16
Quaranto	1.000	2	1	0	0	0
Serritella	.977	50	398	30	10	40
Stassi	1.000	3	31	0	0	1

Second Base	PCT	G	PO	A	E	DP
Ford	.933	5	6	8	1	2

	PCT	G	PO	A	E	DP
Gonzalez	.943	19	30	53	5	11
Greene	.942	51	74	121	12	25
Malcolm	1.000	5	8	0	4	
Third Base	**PCT**	**G**	**PO**	**A**	**E**	**DP**
Ford	1.000	1	2	0	0	0
Malcolm	.667	1	1	1	1	0
Perkins	.969	11	13	18	1	2
Walding	.925	64	52	133	15	11
Shortstop	**PCT**	**G**	**PO**	**A**	**E**	**DP**
Greene	.927	11	21	30	4	
7 Quinn	.911	66	108	167	27	36

Outfield	PCT	G	PO	A	E	DP
Gonzalez	1.000	8	11	0	0	0
Greene	.971	70	126	7	4	1
Hoppy	.943	31	81	2	5	0
Olmo	.974	47	108	4	3	1
Perkins	1.000	10	22	0	0	0
Pointer	.940	34	78	1	5	1
Quaranto	—	1	0	0	0	0
Taylor	.930	20	39	1	3	0
Tromp	.968	13	27	3	1	1

GCL PHILLIES   ROOKIE
GULF COAST LEAGUE

Batting	B-T	HT	WT	DOB	AVG	vLH	vRH	G	AB	R	H	2B	3B	HR	RBI	BB	HBP	SH	SF	SO	SB	CS	SLG	OBP
Astudillo, Willians	R-R	5-9	182	10-14-91	.318	.341	.308	45	148	15	47	15	0	0	21	1	2	0	2	5	2	0	.419	.327
Bedford, Liam	R-R	5-11	175	5-13-93	.130	.000	.176	19	23	1	3	0	0	0	4	1	1	0	0	4	0	0	.130	.200
Brown, Domonic	L-L	6-5	205	9-3-87	.579	.000	.647	5	19	4	11	7	0	0	4	3	0	0	0	3	1	0	.947	.636
Cardozo, Jairo	B-R	5-11	160	1-27-94	.209	.185	.220	34	86	11	18	4	0	0	4	13	1	0	1	19	2	4	.256	.317
Carman, Chad	R-R	5-10	189	5-06	.306	.333	.297	25	49	2	15	4	1	0	4	2	3	0	0	4	0	1	.429	.370
Carmona, William	B-R	5-11	185	3-9-91	.348	.407	.323	25	92	12	32	5	3	2	20	8	0	0	2	13	0	2	.533	.392
Chavarin, Angel	L-R	6-0	176	10-22-90	.206	.059	.261	32	63	7	13	3	0	1	4	4	2	0	0	16	0	1	.302	.275
Cozens, Dylan	L-L	6-6	235	5-31-94	.255	.200	.273	50	161	24	41	11	2	5	24	21	0	1	0	44	8	2	.441	.341
Golden, Steven	R-R	6-3	180	9-12-94	.177	.125	.196	26	62	4	11	1	0	3	3	0	1	0	0	19	2	2	.226	.215
Gonzalez, Diego	R-R	5-11	170	3-16-91	.250	.333	.231	4	16	0	4	0	1	0	2	0	0	0	0	2	3	0	.375	.250
Gonzalez, Gustavo	R-R	6-2	0	1-23-91	.176	.154	.190	14	34	4	6	1	0	0	4	1	4	0	1	2	0	0	.206	.275
Green, Zach	R-R	6-3	210	3-7-94	.284	.372	.254	47	169	20	48	13	1	3	21	8	5	0	1	43	2	2	.426	.333
Knight, Johnny	R-R	6-3	175	6-3-93	.186	.083	.226	26	43	9	8	1	1	2	2	3	1	0	0	25	1	0	.395	.255
Lafrenz, Bronco	R-R	6-1	190	2-6-87	.200	.250	.167	5	10	2	2	2	0	0	2	3	0	0	1	4	0	0	.400	.357
Mitchell, Derrick	R-R	6-3	210	1-5-87	.176	.000	.250	5	17	1	3	2	0	1	3	1	0	0	0	6	0	0	.471	.222
Mora, Angelo	B-R	5-11	151	2-25-93	.271	.306	.261	40	155	20	42	7	2	0	8	9	0	0	1	32	14	5	.342	.309
Perkins, Cameron	R-R	6-5	195	9-27-90	.158	.143	.167	5	19	0	3	0	0	0	3	0	0	0	1	2	0	0	.158	.150
Pullin, Andrew	L-R	6-0	190	9-25-93	.321	.294	.330	41	140	16	45	10	0	2	13	12	7	1	0	32	3	5	.436	.403
Rodriguez, Herlis	R-R	5-11	170	7-16-94	.284	.221	.185	35	96	12	21	4	1	1	7	6	0	1	1	23	0	2	.316	.265
Silva, Francisco	R-R	5-11	155	5-12-91	.241	.273	.228	33	79	13	19	2	1	1	9	11	6	2	0	13	6	0	.329	.375
Taylor, Zach	L-R	6-3	215	5-3-91	.167	.273	.120	10	36	6	6	0	0	2	3	4	0	0	0	11	0	0	.333	.250
Tocci, Carlos	R-R	6-2	160	8-23-95	.278	.227	.293	38	97	13	27	2	0	0	9	6	2	1	1	18	9	2	.299	.330
Tromp, Jandido	R-R	5-11	175	9-27-93	.205	.222	.197	29	88	14	18	5	3	2	11	9	1	3	0	30	1	4	.398	.283
Valenzuela, Carlos	R-R	5-11	170	9-18-90	.187	.257	.167	45	155	20	29	9	2	2	17	10	4	0	1	40	1	0	.310	.253

Pitching	B-T	HT	WT	DOB	W	L	ERA	G	GS	CG	SV	IP	H	R	ER	HR	BB	SO	AVG	vLH	vRH	K/9	BB/9
Anderson, Drew	R-R	6-3	185	3-22-94	1	1	4.76	8	2	0	0	23	26	13	12	2	10	16	.289	.265	.304	6.35	3.97
Angulo, Rivar	L-L	6-3	185	7-1-91	0	1	1.66	12	0	0	0	22	12	4	4	0	15	23	.164	.143	.178	9.55	6.23
Best, Carlos	R-R	6-2	170	1-13-91	1	0	0.00	9	0	0	2	11	8	1	0	0	2	8	.205	.250	.185	6.35	1.59
Bielski, Ricky	R-R	6-3	190	10-25-94	0	1	3.07	11	0	0	0	15	16	7	5	1	7	5	.267	.250	.275	3.07	4.30
Brady, Kevin	L-R	6-3	200	9-7-90	1	0	2.45	2	1	0	0	4	2	2	1	1	2	5	.154	.143	.167	12.27	4.91
Casimiro, Ranfi	R-R	6-8	200	7-16-92	3	2	3.49	10	7	0	0	39	36	20	15	1	14	28	.252	.268	.245	6.43	3.26
Claypool, Garett	R-R	6-2	170	8-21-88	0	0	3.86	2	0	0	0	2	1	1	1	0	2	3	.125	.000	.125	11.57	7.71
De Fratus, Justin	B-R	6-4	220	10-21-87	0	0	0.00	2	1	0	0	2	1	0	0	0	0	3	.143	.000	.200	13.50	0.00
Dygestile-Therrien, Jesen	R-R	6-2	200	3-18-93	0	5	3.46	12	6	0	0	42	34	21	16	2	20	34	.225	.264	.204	7.34	4.32
Gueller, Mitch	R-R	6-3	210	11-10-93	1	5	5.27	8	6	0	0	27	26	17	16	0	12	19	.255	.300	.236	6.26	3.95

Name	B-T	HT	WT	DOB	W	L	ERA	G	GS	CG	SV	IP	H	R	ER	HR	BB	SO	AVG	vLH	vRH	K/9	BB/9
Johnson, Jay	R-L	6-2	210	12-21-89	0	0	0.00	2	0	0	0	2	1	0	0	0	0	6	.125	.000	.167	27.00	0.00
Kinder, Andre	L-L	6-0	210	11-26-88	0	0	0.00	1	0	0	0	2	1	0	0	0	0	3	.125	.000	.250	11.57	0.00
Martinez, Manaure	R-R	6-1	155	12-31-91	2	3	2.43	7	7	1	0	37	21	10	10	1	11	41	.165	.170	.163	9.97	2.68
Mascarello, Blake	L-L	6-1	200	6-25-89	0	0	0.00	2	0	0	0	2	2	0	0	0	2	4	.250	.000	.286	15.43	7.71
Mecias, Yoel	L-L	6-2	160	10-11-93	0	2	2.16	14	4	0	2	42	32	12	10	4	11	34	.206	.152	.229	7.34	2.38
Minarek, Marek	R-R	6-7	195	6-28-93	1	0	2.65	13	0	0	1	17	20	6	5	1	2	11	.290	.200	.327	5.82	1.06
Morales, Luis	R-R	6-4	212	3-16-93	1	3	5.33	13	2	0	1	25	31	16	15	2	14	22	.323	.308	.329	7.82	4.97
Morgado, Bryan	L-L	6-3	205	12-8-88	0	0	0.00	1	1	0	0	1	0	0	0	0	0	1	.000	.000	.000	9.00	0.00
Naylor, Drew	R-R	6-4	235	5-31-86	0	0	0.00	2	0	0	0	4	2	2	0	0	0	6	.133	.000	.200	13.50	0.00
Nichols, Chris	R-R	6-2	180	8-21-90	0	0	4.09	7	0	0	0	11	12	5	5	0	1	9	.293	.250	.320	7.36	0.82
Perez, Delvin	L-L	6-3	200	2-12-91	0	0	0.00	2	0	0	0	2	2	1	0	0	2	2	.286	.000	.333	9.00	9.00
Rios, Yacksel	R-R	6-3	185	6-27-93	2	2	6.60	13	4	0	0	30	44	26	22	3	9	19	.349	.286	.374	5.70	2.70
Rivas, Moises	R-R	6-1	169	10-15-90	1	0	3.00	1	0	0	0	3	0	1	1	0	1	2	.000	.000	.000	6.00	3.00
Rojas, Keive	R-R	6-0	170	2-26-93	4	1	1.67	17	0	0	0	32	22	6	6	2	7	42	.196	.250	.171	11.69	1.95
Santos, Felix	R-R	5-11	170	9-10-90	3	1	1.26	9	0	0	1	14	6	6	2	0	3	12	.125	.200	.091	7.53	1.88
Shull, Braden	L-L	6-6	215	5-8-93	0	0	0.00	1	0	0	0	0	0	0	0	0	0	0	.000	.000	.000	18.00	0.00
Vargas, Franklyn	L-L	6-4	205	8-21-94	5	3	4.70	12	11	0	0	46	38	27	24	2	26	48	.225	.273	.213	9.39	5.09
Walter, Kevin	R-R	6-5	215	5-1-92	1	0	4.91	6	3	0	0	11	19	9	6	0	3	9	.396	.267	.455	7.36	2.45
Watson, Shane	R-R	6-4	200	8-13-93	0	1	1.29	5	3	0	0	7	5	3	1	0	1	8	.200	.167	.231	10.29	1.29

Fielding

Catcher	PCT	G	PO	A	E	DP	PB
Astudillo	.995	26	155	27	1	4	4
Bedford	1.000	19	64	9	0	0	6
Carman	.967	24	102	17	4	1	2
Chavarin	.992	25	101	18	1	1	6
Lafrenz	.931	4	23	4	2	0	2

First Base	PCT	G	PO	A	E	DP
Astudillo	1.000	12	88	8	0	4
Carmona	.991	14	106	3	1	8
Chavarin	1.000	2	7	0	0	1
Perkins	1.000	2	17	2	0	2
Valenzuela	.990	30	267	20	3	14

Second Base	PCT	G	PO	A	E	DP
Cardozo	.989	23	30	61	1	11
Gonzalez	1.000	8	11	16	0	1

	PCT	G	PO	A	E	DP
Mora	.933	8	11	17	2	0
Pullin	.964	7	7	20	1	1
Silva	.935	14	29	29	4	6
Valenzuela	.933	3	7	7	1	3

Third Base	PCT	G	PO	A	E	DP
Cardozo	.889	5	0	8	1	0
Carmona	.870	10	7	13	3	0
Gonzalez	—	1	0	0	0	0
Green	.870	31	25	62	13	5
Perkins	1.000	3	3	4	0	1
Valenzuela	.970	12	7	25	1	2

Shortstop	PCT	G	PO	A	E	DP
Cardozo	1.000	3	3	5	0	1
Gonzalez	.917	3	5	6	1	0
Green	.925	9	15	22	3	0

	PCT	G	PO	A	E	DP
Mora	.958	32	63	73	6	15
Silva	.944	18	14	37	3	6

Outfield	PCT	G	PO	A	E	DP
Brown	1.000	3	2	0	0	0
Cozens	.938	38	59	2	4	0
Golden	.963	23	26	0	1	0
Gonzalez	1.000	4	8	0	0	0
Knight	1.000	22	30	2	0	0
Mitchell	1.000	3	4	0	0	0
Pullin	1.000	27	40	3	0	1
Rodriguez	.927	38	34	4	3	0
Taylor	.667	3	2	0	1	0
Tocci	.981	35	50	1	1	0
Tromp	1.000	27	36	1	0	0

DSL PHILLIES

ROOKIE

DOMINICAN SUMMER LEAGUE

Batting	B-T	HT	WT	DOB	AVG	vLH	vRH	G	AB	R	H	2B	3B	HR	RBI	BB	HBP	SH	SF	SO	SB	CS	SLG	OBP
Almonte, Marlin	R-R	5-11	180	9-28-93	.170	.208	.157	43	94	13	16	1	0	0	7	12	8	1	1	20	8	6	.181	.313
Berroa, Eladio	R-R	5-8	155	2-2-91	.207	.130	.224	44	121	12	25	2	4	1	15	16	5	4	3	27	8	4	.314	.317
Canelo, Malquin	R-R	5-10	156	9-5-94	.167	.237	.145	54	162	23	27	5	2	0	9	15	4	6	2	50	9	4	.222	.251
Cepeda, Rommel	R-R	5-11	180	11-13-91	.208	.276	.188	47	130	20	27	7	1	3	16	17	5	2	0	30	7	2	.346	.322
Contreras, Roberto	L-R	6-3	170	7-12-94	.115	.000	.133	38	104	5	12	3	0	0	4	10	6	0	0	46	1	2	.144	.233
De La Cruz, Rafael	R-R	6-2	200	7-29-91	.249	.262	.245	63	193	23	48	9	1	2	27	20	10	0	2	40	8	6	.337	.347
Hiciano, Samuel	R-R	6-1	203	1-25-94	.284	.326	.274	66	232	30	66	11	7	4	36	21	2	0	3	27	16	8	.444	.345
Marte, Olvy	B-R	5-9	154	8-8-94	.277	.314	.267	53	166	29	46	8	0	1	13	21	11	5	0	34	20	9	.343	.394
Miranda, Pedro	R-R	6-0	180	7-6-92	.271	.243	.279	53	177	22	48	4	1	0	19	15	4	4	1	27	15	7	.305	.340
Morales, Yeisson	R-R	6-3	195	4-28-92	.167	.200	.154	7	18	2	3	0	0	0	0	1	0	1	0	6	1	0	.167	.211
Nivar, Pedro	R-R	5-10	170	11-3-94	.130	.200	.111	11	23	2	3	2	0	0	1	3	1	0	0	2	1	2	.217	.259
Rios, Fernando	R-R	6-0	175	8-22-92	.256	.167	.270	17	43	5	11	2	0	0	5	0	3	1	0	14	2	1	.302	.304
Salas, Emmanuel	R-R	6-2	172	12-18-94	.191	.222	.183	43	89	10	17	1	1	0	4	13	1	1	0	28	5	2	.225	.301
Serra, Enmanuel	B-R	5-10	166	12-17-92	.254	.262	.252	60	201	26	51	9	2	0	12	31	3	4	0	22	11	8	.318	.362
Soto, Raymer	R-R	6-1	207	12-18-92	.115	.250	.104	24	52	2	6	2	0	1	5	2	2	0	1	12	0	0	.212	.175
Torres, Robinson	R-R	5-10	160	2-12-92	.274	.250	.281	59	208	26	57	7	1	0	18	7	10	4	4	25	15	5	.317	.323
Torres, Wilber	R-R	5-11	206	5-9-94	.241	.231	.243	42	133	17	32	13	0	1	16	15	4	2	1	27	6	6	.361	.333
Valdez, Hector	B-R	5-11	171	3-8-93	.146	.111	.154	24	48	3	7	1	1	0	3	3	0	1	1	10	1	0	.208	.192

Pitching	B-T	HT	WT	DOB	W	L	ERA	G	GS	CG	SV	IP	H	R	ER	HR	BB	SO	AVG	vLH	vRH	K/9	BB/9
Alejo, Francibel	L-L	6-3	170	1-21-93	5	7	3.06	13	13	1	0	79	94	38	27	3	8	46	.292	.225	.301	5.22	0.91
Cedeno, Erick	R-L	6-3	220	2-25-93	1	0	1.32	6	1	0	0	14	10	5	2	0	6	19	.208	.125	.250	12.51	3.95
Dominguez, Seranthony	R-R	6-1	183	11-25-94	4	4	3.48	15	11	0	0	67	63	32	26	5	26	40	.252	.254	.251	5.35	3.48
Dottin, Henry	R-R	6-3	170	10-10-92	0	0	5.17	11	0	0	0	16	14	11	9	0	19	13	.246	.500	.178	7.47	10.91
Emelenciano, Pedro	R-R	6-4	175	7-23-93	2	2	4.31	15	0	0	1	31	38	18	15	0	16	13	.304	.349	.280	3.73	4.60
Garcia, Elniery	L-L	6-0	155	12-24-94	2	1	4.18	8	3	0	0	24	23	14	11	1	8	19	.253	.167	.259	7.23	3.04
Lora, Pedro	L-L	6-1	190	8-11-88	4	0	2.25	19	0	0	1	36	35	14	9	1	15	39	.257	.421	.231	9.75	3.75
Lorenzo, Jorge	R-R	6-2	175	9-29-90	0	3	1.32	21	0	0	8	34	17	8	5	0	19	31	.156	.167	.151	8.21	5.03
Marte, Juan	R-R	6-4	160	5-8-90	2	1	1.08	15	0	0	2	25	16	5	3	0	13	16	.176	.176	.176	5.76	4.68
Morel, Darbin	R-R	6-3	195	7-23-93	0	0	6.14	9	0	0	0	15	15	12	10	0	8	10	.259	.353	.220	6.14	4.91
Sanchez, Feliberto	R-R	6-1	175	9-30-93	4	5	4.29	14	14	0	0	63	71	37	30	2	27	34	.296	.377	.263	4.86	3.86
Santos, Gregorio	R-R	6-3	190	3-1-93	4	3	3.55	14	14	0	0	76	84	33	30	3	29	52	.286	.260	.298	6.16	3.43
Serrano, Jorge	R-R	6-2	180	9-21-93	3	7	5.74	13	12	0	0	69	67	52	44	1	33	34	.249	.288	.224	4.43	4.30
Solano, San Lazaro	R-R	5-11	170	12-17-90	0	3	2.25	18	0	0	7	28	14	8	7	1	10	32	.149	.125	.157	10.29	3.21

Torres, Juan	R-R	6-4	197	9-11-92	1	0	10.22	10	0	0	0	12	14	16	14	2	7	14	.286	.150	.379	10.22	5.11
Valera, Masilis	R-R	6-3	182	2-5-93	0	0	6.94	11	0	0	0	12	11	9	9	0	4	4	.239	.294	.207	3.09	3.09
Vasquez, Gerard	R-R	6-2	190	6-3-94	0	0	14.14	6	0	0	0	7	7	15	11	0	12	12	.226	.231	.222	15.43	15.43

Fielding

Catcher	PCT	G	PO	A	E	DP	PB
Cepeda	.976	42	212	30	6	6	4
Rios	.955	10	53	10	3	1	0
Torres	.987	30	184	42	3	1	5

First Base	PCT	G	PO	A	E	DP
De La Cruz	.981	52	433	30	9	33
Hiciano	1.000	2	13	1	0	0
Morales	.957	6	42	3	2	3
Rios	.982	6	50	5	1	6
Soto	.982	13	52	3	1	4
Torres	.948	7	52	3	3	6

Second Base	PCT	G	PO	A	E	DP
Berroa	1.000	28	32	51	0	6

Marte	1.000	1	2	6	0	1	
Marte	.939	11	17	29	3	4	
Serra	.981	32	45	57	2	14	
Torres	.944	7	10	7	1	1	
Valdez	.930	19	21	32	4	7	

Third Base	PCT	G	PO	A	E	DP
Berroa	.898	16	11	33	5	3
De La Cruz	.960	6	6	18	1	1
Marte	1.000	1	1	2	0	0
Serra	.933	15	16	26	3	3
Torres	.896	45	42	96	16	12

Shortstop	PCT	G	PO	A	E	DP
Berroa	.857	4	3	9	2	1

Canelo	.908	53	79	137	22	21
Serra	.968	26	38	52	3	6
Torres	.750	1	2	1	1	0

Outfield	PCT	G	PO	A	E	DP
Almonte	.980	28	47	3	1	0
Contreras	.846	17	30	3	6	1
Hiciano	.952	62	97	3	5	1
Marte	.973	41	67	6	2	4
Miranda	.974	46	71	5	2	0
Nivar	.750	5	3	0	1	0
Salas	1.000	38	41	2	0	1
Serra	1.000	1	4	0	0	0
Torres	1.000	7	8	1	0	1
Valdez	1.000	2	3	0	0	0

VSL PHILLIES

VENEZUELAN SUMMER LEAGUE

ROOKIE

Batting	B-T	HT	WT	DOB	AVG	vLH	vRH	G	AB	R	H	2B	3B	HR	RBI	BB	HBP	SH	SF	SO	SB	CS	SLG	OBP
Colmenarez, Hiomarvic	R-R	5-11	175	6-7-95	.172	.200	.170	21	58	7	10	1	0	0	3	6	1	0	0	10	0	0	.190	.262
Cuicas, William	B-R	5-11	160	2-1-95	.219	.100	.240	57	201	30	44	9	3	0	15	18	3	8	1	24	7	1	.294	.291
Duran, Carlos	R-R	6-2	170	11-22-94	.204	.211	.203	52	142	21	29	7	0	1	16	15	2	2	3	35	0	4	.275	.284
Fernandez, Rafael	R-R	5-10	168	5-13-92	.337	.375	.329	44	101	13	34	4	0	3	22	13	2	1	2	11	1	1	.465	.415
Garcia, Alejandro	R-R	6-3	150	7-22-94	.128	.125	.129	32	78	8	10	1	0	1	4	6	3	1	1	18	2	1	.179	.216
Garcia, Wilson	R-R	5-11	160	1-11-94	.353	.346	.354	56	201	21	71	18	1	4	38	12	1	1	1	12	1	0	.512	.391
Herrera, Francisco	R-R	5-11	185	9-15-93	.324	.500	.305	53	182	37	59	13	0	5	33	23	7	0	4	25	1	1	.478	.412
Jimenez, Enger	R-R	6-1	165	7-4-95	.218	.235	.216	47	119	16	26	6	1	3	15	10	2	2	1	34	4	2	.361	.288
Martinez, Gustavo	R-R	5-11	155	9-22-93	.313	.323	.311	60	227	40	71	5	4	1	26	17	1	7	3	22	27	15	.383	.359
Mayorga, Jose	R-R	5-10	175	8-20-92	.284	.240	.293	48	141	13	40	8	1	1	17	19	1	3	1	16	2	4	.376	.370
Morelos, Jair	L-R	5-10	150	2-2-94	.284	.346	.274	56	190	19	54	7	2	0	18	7	1	2	3	8	1	1	.342	.308
Oberto, Wilmer	L-L	5-11	188	11-2-92	.295	.300	.294	66	217	44	64	16	1	7	35	31	14	2	4	38	6	3	.475	.410
Olivera, Deiber	R-R	5-11	155	8-25-92	.350	.185	.376	57	200	35	70	17	2	1	32	6	2	4	4	22	5	5	.470	.399
Perdomo, Alexander	B-R	5-9	155	5-24-93	.269	.316	.262	52	145	24	39	5	3	1	11	32	7	3	0	23	9	9	.366	.424
Rojo, Lucas	R-R	5-6	153	4-5-94	.354	.400	.349	18	48	10	17	5	0	1	0	4	5	1	0	5	1	0	.521	.456
Zorrilla, Freddy	R-R	6-4	195	10-19-94	.232	.286	.226	24	69	15	16	4	1	0	9	2	0	1	0	20	2	0	.319	.379

Pitching	B-T	HT	WT	DOB	W	L	ERA	G	GS	CG	SV	IP	H	R	ER	HR	BB	SO	AVG	vLH	vRH	K/9	BB/9
Arteaga, Alejandro	R-R	6-2	176	4-30-94	0	0	4.50	4	1	0	0	12	11	6	6	1	5	8	.256	.222	.280	6.00	3.75
Bermudez, Gabriel	R-R	6-3	184	6-24-93	0	1	5.40	6	0	0	0	10	8	6	6	1	9	2	.242	.300	.217	1.80	8.10
Bohorquez, Liberio	R-R	6-0	170	9-23-92	5	2	2.22	15	1	1	3	45	39	17	11	2	12	30	.224	.250	.211	6.04	2.42
Carpabire, Joseph	R-R	6-2	180	6-17-93	0	0	5.63	4	0	0	0	8	8	5	5	1	4	6	.258	.333	.227	6.75	4.50
Chavez, Jesus	L-L	6-3	175	11-22-93	0	0	4.50	2	0	0	0	4	7	4	2	0	2	3	.350	.000	.368	6.75	4.50
Diaz, Oberdan	R-L	6-1	175	1-27-95	0	3	6.20	13	0	0	1	25	38	26	17	2	17	17	.339	.556	.320	6.20	6.20
Dun, Christian	R-R	6-6	232	9-15-93	0	0	0.00	4	0	0	0	7	2	0	0	0	0	3	.087	.125	.067	4.05	0.00
Fernandez, Yeisson	L-L	6-4	170	5-17-94	3	2	4.67	8	7	0	0	35	40	20	18	0	13	17	.292	.222	.303	4.41	3.38
Gonzalez, Manuel	R-R	6-2	188	8-15-91	1	0	0.49	8	0	0	5	18	12	1	1	1	3	14	.185	.267	.160	6.87	1.47
Gonzalez, Severino	R-R	6-1	153	9-28-92	7	3	1.65	14	14	2	0	93	59	26	17	4	6	86	.179	.263	.135	8.35	0.58
Mendez, Ronald	R-R	6-5	211	2-27-93	1	4	5.70	8	7	0	0	30	35	21	19	2	12	21	.294	.389	.253	6.30	3.60
Mora, Audrys	L-L	5-11	170	6-14-93	2	0	2.16	8	0	0	0	17	20	4	4	0	6	5	.313	.333	.309	2.70	3.24
Parada, Douglas	L-L	6-1	233	2-27-93	8	2	1.82	14	14	1	0	79	53	17	16	1	10	73	.191	.053	.202	8.28	1.13
Pinto, Ricardo	R-R	6-0	165	1-20-94	7	3	2.74	15	10	0	1	69	70	34	21	4	20	39	.267	.148	.320	5.09	2.61
Rivas, Moises	R-R	6-1	169	10-15-90	5	0	1.34	8	7	0	0	47	32	13	7	0	9	36	.204	.200	.206	6.89	1.72
Suarez, Ranger	L-L	6-0	177	8-26-95	0	0	0.00	3	0	0	2	5	2	0	0	0	3	4	.125	.000	.143	7.20	5.40
Velis, Sergio	L-L	5-11	182	1-16-95	3	0	2.22	9	8	0	0	28	24	13	7	0	17	26	.226	.267	.220	8.26	5.40

Fielding

Catcher	PCT	G	PO	A	E	DP	PB
Colmenarez	.987	11	66	10	1	1	2
Fernandez	.957	15	59	8	3	0	1
Garcia	.972	24	116	25	4	1	0
Mayorga	.991	34	205	25	2	1	1

First Base	PCT	G	PO	A	E	DP
Colmenarez	1.000	1	1	1	0	0
Fernandez	1.000	7	25	2	0	4
Garcia	.992	14	115	8	1	13
Herrera	.988	33	300	20	4	22
Jimenez	1.000	1	1	0	0	0
Mayorga	1.000	5	32	1	0	3

Oberto	.982	24	210	9	4	14

Second Base	PCT	G	PO	A	E	DP
Morelos	.992	29	51	81	1	14
Olivera	1.000	2	1	2	0	0
Perdomo	.956	37	92	82	8	18
Rojo	.958	13	34	3	3	9

Third Base	PCT	G	PO	A	E	DP
Herrera	.864	12	9	29	6	2
Morelos	.900	11	7	29	4	1
Olivera	.942	52	27	134	10	12
Perdomo	1.000	1	0	1	0	0

Shortstop	PCT	G	PO	A	E	DP
Cuicas	.890	57	65	162	28	21
Morelos	.935	23	28	58	6	9
Olivera	1.000	1	0	1	0	0
Perdomo	—	1	0	0	0	0

Outfield	PCT	G	PO	A	E	DP
Duran	.948	50	69	4	4	1
Garcia	.952	30	39	1	2	0
Jimenez	.952	42	39	1	2	0
Martinez	.975	60	114	3	3	1
Oberto	.961	42	73	1	3	0
Zorrilla	.917	24	31	2	3	0

PHILADELPHIA PHILLIES

Pittsburgh Pirates

SEASON IN A SENTENCE: The Pirates pulled together a solid first half and had dreams of a return to the playoffs, but a collapse in the second half led to the team's 20th consecutive losing season.

HIGH POINT: The Pirates beat the Giants 13-2 on July 8 to improve to 48-37 and take a one-game lead over the Reds in the National League Central, looking well on their way to a .500 record, if not a playoff berth. On an individual level, outfielder Andrew McCutchen cemented his place as one of the game's brightest young stars with his best season statistically and his first Gold Glove in center field.

LOW POINT: Just like in 2011, when Pittsburgh was in first place during parts of July, again the team couldn't sustain its success through the second half. Even the run to stay above .500 fell apart, as the team endured a seven-game losing streak in September, part of a 7-21 month, and finished 79-83.

NOTABLE ROOKIES: The only rookie to make a significant contribution was righthander Jared Hughes, who went 2-2, 2.85 with 50 strikeouts and 22 walks in 76 innings out of the bullpen.

KEY TRANSACTIONS: Heading into the season, the Pirates' biggest moves were signing lefthander Erik Bedard and Rod Barajas and Clint Barmes to provide veteran stability, and trading two minor leaguers to the Yankees for A.J. Burnett. At the deadline, Pittsburgh sent thee prospects (outfielder Robbie Grossman and lefthanders Colton Cain and Rudy Owens) to the Astros for Wandy Rodriguez. They also exchanged 2006 first-rounders with the Blue Jays, trading Brad Lincoln for Travis Snider, and sent outfielder Gorkys Hernandez to the Marlins for Gaby Sanchez and minor league righthander Kyle Kaminska.

DOWN ON THE FARM: Righthanders Gerrit Cole and Jameson Taillon proved themselves as two of the top arms in the minor leagues. Cole went 9-7, 2.80, mostly between high Class A and Double-A. Taillon spent most of the season high Class A and went 9-8, 3.55 with 116 strikeouts and 38 walks over 142 innings. After signing for $5 million as a second-round pick in 2011, outfielder Josh Bell was limited to just 15 games in 2012 after having surgery on his left knee at the beginning of the season. The breakout star from the system was shortstop Alen Hanson, who had a strong season in low Class A.

OPENING DAY PAYROLL: $63.4 million (26th)

PLAYERS OF THE YEAR

MAJOR LEAGUE	MINOR LEAGUE
Andrew McCutchen of	**Alen Hanson** ss
.327/.400/.553	(Low Class A)
31 HR, 20 SB	.313/.385/.537
Won first Gold Glove	33 2B, 16 HR

ORGANIZATION LEADERS

BATTING		*Minimum 250 AB
MAJORS		
* AVG	Andrew McCutchen	.327
* OPS	Andrew McCutchen	.953
HR	Andrew McCutchen	31
RBI	Andrew McCutchen	96
MINORS		
* AVG	Brock Holt, Altoona/Indianapolis	.344
* OBP	Brock Holt, Altoona/Indianapolis	.406
* SLG	Alen Hanson, West Virginia	.528
R	Alen Hanson, West Virginia	99
H	Brock Holt, Altoona/Indianapolis	164
TB	Alen Hanson, West Virginia	258
2B	Dan Gamache, West Virginia	40
3B	Alen Hanson, West Virginia	13
3B	Starling Marte, Indianapolis/State College	13
HR	Willy Garcia, West Virginia	18
RBI	Alex Dickerson, Bradenton	90
BB	Gift Ngoepe, Bradenton	63
SO	Willy Garcia, West Virginia	131
SO	Gift Ngoepe, Bradenton	131
SB	Gregory Polanco, West Virginia	40

PITCHING		#Minimum 75 IP
MAJORS		
W	A.J. Burnett	16
# ERA	A.J. Burnett	3.51
SO	A.J. Burnett	180
SV	Joel Hanrahan	36
MINORS		
W	Rick van den Hurk, Bradenton/Indianapolis	14
L	Matt Benedict, West Virginia/Bradenton	12
# ERA	Jeff Locke, Indianapolis	2.48
G	Tim Wood, Indianapolis	54
GS	Brandon Cumpton, Altoona	27
GS	Nicholas Kingham, West Virginia	27
SV	Tim Wood, Indianapolis	21
IP	Brandon Cumpton, Altoona	152.1
BB	Ryan Hafner, West Virginia/State College	75
SO	Justin Wilson, Indianapolis	138
# AVG	Justin Wilson, Indianapolis	.189

2012 PERFORMANCE

General Manager: Neal Huntington. **Farm Director:** Kyle Stark. **Scouting Director:** Joe Delli Carri.

Class	Team	League	W	L	PCT	Finish	Manager
Majors	Pittsburgh Pirates	National	79	83	.488	10th (16)	Clint Hurdle
Triple-A	Indianapolis Indians	International	89	55	.618	1st (14)	Dean Treanor
Double-A	Altoona Curve	Eastern	72	70	.507	6th (12)	P.J. Forbes
High A	Bradenton Marauders	Florida State	60	77	.438	11th (12)	Carlos Garcia
Low A	West Virginia Power	South Atlantic	61	79	.436	t-12th (14)	Rick Sofield
Short-season	State College Spikes	New York-Penn	35	41	.461	9th (14)	Dave Turgeon
Rookie	GCL Pirates	Gulf Coast	36	24	.600	t-1st (14)	Tom Prince
Overall 2012 Minor League Record			353	346	.505	16th (30)	

ORGANIZATION STATISTICS

PITTSBURGH PIRATES

NATIONAL LEAGUE

Batting	B-T	HT	WT	DOB	AVG	vLH	vRH	G	AB	R	H	2B	3B	HR	RBI	BB	HBP	SH	SF	SO	SB	CS	SLG	OBP
Alvarez, Pedro	L-R	6-3	235	2-6-87	.244	.207	.257	149	525	64	128	25	1	30	85	57	1	0	3	180	1	0	.467	.317
Barajas, Rod	R-R	6-2	250	9-5-75	.206	.167	.217	104	321	29	66	11	0	11	31	29	7	0	4	69	0	0	.343	.283
Barmes, Clint	R-R	6-1	205	3-6-79	.229	.274	.217	144	455	34	104	16	1	8	45	20	8	8	2	106	0	2	.321	.272
Clement, Jeff	L-R	6-1	220	8-21-83	.136	—	.136	23	22	1	3	1	0	0	1	2	0	0	0	7	0	0	.182	.208
d'Arnaud, Chase	R-R	6-1	205	1-21-87	.000	.000	.000	8	6	2	0	0	0	0	1	0	0	0	0	2	1	0	.000	.000
Fryer, Eric	R-R	6-2	215	8-26-85	.250	1.000	.000	6	4	0	1	0	0	0	1	0	0	0	0	1	0	0	.250	.400
Hague, Matt	R-R	6-3	225	8-20-85	.229	.304	.191	30	70	5	16	2	0	0	7	3	1	0	0	14	1	0	.257	.270
Harrison, Josh	R-R	5-8	190	7-8-87	.233	.198	.252	104	249	34	58	9	5	3	16	10	7	7	3	37	7	3	.345	.279
Hernandez, Gorkys	R-R	6-0	190	9-7-87	.083	.000	.133	25	24	2	2	0	0	0	2	1	1	0	0	5	2	0	.083	.154
2-team total (45 Miami)					.192	—	—	70	156	18	30	2	3	3	13	13	3	1	0	42	7	2	.301	.267
Holt, Brock	L-R	5-10	170	6-11-88	.292	.267	.300	24	65	6	19	2	1	0	3	4	0	2	1	14	0	0	.354	.329
Jones, Garrett	L-L	6-4	230	6-21-81	.274	.189	.289	145	475	68	130	28	3	27	86	33	0	0	7	103	2	0	.516	.317
Marte, Starling	R-R	6-0	180	10-9-88	.257	.318	.236	47	167	18	43	3	6	5	17	8	3	2	2	50	12	5	.437	.300
McCutchen, Andrew	R-R	5-10	185	10-10-86	.327	.392	.309	157	593	107	194	29	6	31	96	70	5	0	5	132	20	12	.553	.400
McGehee, Casey	R-R	6-1	220	10-12-82	.230	.250	.222	92	265	27	61	13	1	8	35	24	2	0	2	60	1	1	.377	.297
McKenry, Mike	R-R	5-10	220	3-4-85	.233	.241	.231	88	240	25	56	14	0	12	39	29	3	0	3	73	0	0	.442	.320
McLouth, Nate	L-R	5-11	180	10-28-81	.140	.000	.157	34	57	4	8	2	0	0	2	5	0	0	0	18	0	0	.175	.210
Mercer, Jordy	R-R	6-3	200	8-27-86	.210	.100	.231	42	62	7	13	5	1	1	5	4	1	0	1	14	0	1	.371	.265
Navarro, Yamaico	R-R	5-11	215	10-31-87	.160	.222	.087	29	50	4	8	0	0	1	4	5	0	0	1	13	0	2	.220	.232
Presley, Alex	L-L	5-10	185	7-25-85	.237	.262	.232	104	346	46	82	14	7	10	25	18	2	4	0	72	9	7	.405	.279
Sanchez, Gaby	R-R	6-1	230	9-2-83	.241	.238	.243	50	116	18	28	6	0	4	13	13	1	0	0	20	0	0	.397	.323
2-team total (55 Miami)					.217	—	—	105	299	30	65	16	0	7	30	25	1	0	1	56	1	0	.341	.279
Snider, Travis	L-L	6-0	235	2-2-88	.250	.350	.231	50	128	17	32	5	1	1	9	14	1	0	2	34	2	0	.328	.324
Sutton, Drew	B-R	6-2	200	6-30-83	.243	.278	.232	24	74	10	18	8	1	1	7	4	0	0	1	26	0	1	.419	.278
Tabata, Jose	R-R	5-11	215	8-12-88	.243	.241	.244	103	333	43	81	20	3	3	16	29	6	6	0	58	8	12	.348	.315
Walker, Neil	B-R	6-3	210	9-10-85	.280	.246	.291	129	472	62	132	27	0	14	69	47	2	1	8	104	7	5	.426	.342

Pitching	B-T	HT	WT	DOB	W	L	ERA	G	GS	CG	SV	IP	H	R	ER	HR	BB	SO	AVG	vLH	vRH	K/9	BB/9
Bedard, Erik	L-L	6-1	200	3-5-79	7	14	5.01	24	24	0	0	126	129	76	70	14	56	118	.263	.218	.272	8.45	4.01
Burnett, A.J.	R-R	6-4	230	1-3-77	16	10	3.51	31	31	1	0	202	189	86	79	18	62	180	.246	.248	.245	8.01	2.76
Correia, Kevin	R-R	6-3	200	8-24-80	12	11	4.21	32	28	0	0	171	176	89	80	20	46	89	.267	.248	.284	4.68	2.42
Cruz, Juan	R-R	6-2	170	10-15-78	1	1	2.78	43	0	0	3	36	39	12	11	3	19	33	.289	.254	.316	8.33	4.79
Grilli, Jason	R-R	6-5	225	11-11-76	1	6	2.91	64	0	0	2	59	45	20	19	7	22	90	.207	.168	.241	13.81	3.38
Hanrahan, Joel	R-R	6-4	250	10-6-81	5	2	2.72	63	0	0	36	60	40	18	18	8	36	67	.187	.135	.236	10.11	5.43
Hughes, Jared	R-R	6-7	245	7-4-85	2	2	2.85	66	0	0	2	76	65	30	24	7	22	50	.226	.248	.206	5.95	2.62
Karstens, Jeff	R-R	6-3	185	9-24-82	5	4	3.97	19	15	0	0	91	89	41	40	8	15	66	.256	.243	.265	6.55	1.49
Leroux, Chris	L-R	6-6	230	4-14-84	0	0	5.56	10	0	0	0	11	11	9	7	1	2	12	.250	.143	.300	9.53	1.59
Lincoln, Brad	L-R	6-0	210	5-25-85	4	2	2.73	28	5	0	1	59	51	19	18	8	14	60	.230	.214	.244	9.10	2.12
Locke, Jeff	L-L	6-1	180	11-20-87	1	3	5.50	8	6	0	0	34	36	21	21	6	11	34	.267	.297	.255	8.91	2.88
McCutchen, Daniel	R-R	6-2	215	9-26-82	0	1	—	1	0	0	0	1	2	2	1	1	0	1	1.000	1.000	—		
McDonald, James	L-R	6-4	205	10-19-84	12	8	4.21	30	29	1	0	171	147	85	80	21	69	151	.233	.207	.260	7.95	3.63
McPherson, Kyle	B-R	6-4	220	11-11-87	0	2	2.73	10	3	0	0	26	24	8	8	3	7	21	.247	.225	.263	7.18	2.39
Meek, Evan	R-R	6-0	235	5-12-83	0	0	6.75	12	0	0	0	12	14	9	9	1	6	8	.286	.429	.179	6.00	4.50
Morris, Bryan	L-R	6-3	220	3-28-87	0	0	1.80	5	0	0	0	5	2	1	1	0	2	6	.125	.000	.200	10.80	3.60
Morton, Charlie	R-R	6-5	230	11-12-83	2	6	4.65	9	9	0	0	50	62	30	26	5	11	25	.305	.301	.310	4.47	1.97
Qualls, Chad	R-R	6-5	220	8-17-78	0	0	6.59	17	0	0	0	14	14	11	10	0	2	6	.259	.296	.222	3.95	1.32
2-team total (35 Philadelphia)					1	1	5.20	52	0	0	0	45	53	29	26	7	11	25	—	—	—	5.00	2.20
Resop, Chris	R-R	6-3	225	11-4-82	1	4	3.91	61	0	0	1	74	81	35	32	6	24	46	.276	.237	.302	5.62	2.93
Rodriguez, Wandy	R-L	5-10	195	1-18-79	5	4	3.72	13	12	0	0	75	71	33	31	8	24	50	.246	.231	.249	6.00	2.88
2-team total (21 Houston)					12	13	3.76	34	33	0	0	206	205	99	86	21	56	139	—	—	—	6.08	2.45
Slaten, Doug	L-L	6-5	215	2-4-80	0	0	2.77	10	0	0	0	13	9	4	4	1	8	6	.196	.077	.242	4.15	5.54
Takahashi, Hisanori	L-L	5-10	175	4-2-75	0	0	8.64	9	0	0	0	8	10	8	8	2	4	11	.294	.077	.429	11.88	4.32
VandenHurk, Rick	R-R	6-5	215	5-22-85	0	1	13.50	4	0	0	0	3	5	4	4	0	1	3	.357	.400	.333	10.13	3.38
Watson, Tony	L-L	6-4	210	5-30-85	5	2	3.38	68	0	0	0	53	37	21	20	5	23	53	.198	.183	.213	8.94	3.88

Wilson, Justin	L-L	6-2	220	8-18-87	0	0	1.93	8	0	0	0	5	10	1	1	0	3	7	.455	.364	.545 13.50 5.79

Fielding

Catcher	PCT	G	PO	A	E	DP	PB
Barajas	.992	99	700	41	6	4	7
McKenry	.994	81	495	41	3	1	2

First Base	PCT	G	PO	A	E	DP
Barajas	1.000	1	1	0	0	0
Barmes	—	1	0	0	0	0
Clement	1.000	1	7	1	0	0
Hague	.992	16	114	12	1	13
Jones	.991	72	500	48	5	46
McGehee	.997	77	526	44	2	48
Sanchez	.996	41	253	24	1	13

Second Base	PCT	G	PO	A	E	DP
d'Arnaud	1.000	2	1	1	0	0
Harrison	.989	28	34	52	1	5
Holt	.938	14	22	38	4	3

	PCT	G	PO	A	E	DP
Mercer	1.000	7	4	19	0	4
Navarro	1.000	1	2	3	0	1
Sutton	1.000	2	3	1	0	1
Walker	.985	125	234	361	9	76

Third Base	PCT	G	PO	A	E	DP
Alvarez	.926	145	73	264	27	23
Harrison	.955	14	5	16	1	1
McGehee	1.000	9	2	14	0	1
Mercer	—	1	0	0	0	0
Navarro	1.000	2	0	5	0	1

Shortstop	PCT	G	PO	A	E	DP
Barmes	.972	142	147	399	16	72
d'Arnaud	1.000	1	1	0	0	0
Harrison	.943	25	26	40	4	6
Mercer	.982	28	16	39	1	4

	PCT	G	PO	A	E	DP
Navarro	1.000	3	1	1	0	1
Outfield	PCT	G	PO	A	E	DP
Fryer	—	2	0	0	0	0
Harrison	1.000	13	16	1	0	0
Hernandez	1.000	21	23	0	0	0
Jones	.964	66	103	3	4	1
Marte	.958	45	66	3	3	0
McCutchen	.997	156	367	3	1	1
McLouth	1.000	16	19	0	0	0
Navarro	1.000	10	11	1	0	1
Presley	.981	90	153	2	3	1
Snider	1.000	36	65	1	0	1
Sutton	.929	16	26	0	2	0
Tabata	.983	96	166	6	3	0

INDIANAPOLIS INDIANS — TRIPLE-A

INTERNATIONAL LEAGUE

Batting	B-T	HT	WT	DOB	AVG	vLH	vRH	G	AB	R	H	2B	3B	HR	RBI	BB	HBP	SH	SF	SO	SB	CS	SLG	OBP
Boggs, Brandon	B-R	5-11	210	1-9-83	.259	.343	.228	127	409	64	106	24	5	9	57	62	4	2	4	120	6	8	.408	.359
Cabrera, Ramon	B-R	5-8	195	11-5-89	.400	1.000	.250	1	5	1	2	1	0	0	0	0	0	0	0	0	0	0	.600	.400
Clement, Jeff	L-R	6-1	220	8-21-83	.276	.281	.275	112	416	58	115	35	2	16	57	41	0	0	2	101	1	0	.486	.340
Curry, Matt	L-R	6-1	225	7-27-88	.400	1.000	.250	2	5	0	2	0	0	0	2	1	0	0	0	1	0	1	.400	.500
d'Arnaud, Chase	R-R	6-1	205	1-21-87	.252	.277	.244	98	381	63	96	24	4	6	38	37	5	3	1	93	34	5	.383	.325
Durham, Miles	R-R	6-4	205	3-21-83	.143	.182	.129	19	42	4	6	1	0	0	2	1	0	0	0	18	2	1	.167	.200
Evans, Nick	R-R	6-2	220	1-30-86	.197	.160	.217	19	71	8	14	3	0	2	9	7	0	0	2	14	0	0	.324	.263
Farrell, Jeremy	R-R	6-3	200	11-11-86	.207	.222	.200	8	29	2	6	1	0	0	3	2	1	0	0	6	0	0	.241	.281
Fox, Jake	R-R	6-0	220	7-20-82	.236	.235	.236	42	123	15	29	10	0	2	16	13	1	0	2	24	0	0	.366	.309
2-team total (9 Lehigh Valley)					.247	—	—	51	154	18	38	14	0	2	20	13	4	0	3	30	0	0	.377	.316
Friday, Brian	R-R	5-11	190	12-16-85	.232	.197	.248	66	194	26	45	10	2	0	25	23	4	2	1	38	7	6	.304	.324
2-team total (30 Gwinnett)					.213	—	—	96	282	38	60	13	2	2	33	34	4	2	1	57	10	6	.294	.305
Fryer, Eric	R-R	6-2	215	8-26-85	.204	.196	.207	65	162	14	33	7	0	0	10	10	2	1	1	38	1	0	.247	.257
Hague, Matt	R-R	6-3	225	8-20-85	.283	.319	.268	91	367	41	104	13	0	4	54	26	1	3	6	50	3	1	.351	.332
Hernandez, Anderson	B-R	5-9	190	10-30-82	.268	.272	.267	105	369	43	99	9	5	1	39	18	0	8	2	58	3	4	.328	.301
Hernandez, Gorkys	R-R	6-0	190	9-7-87	.257	.315	.240	67	237	43	61	11	2	2	25	34	2	6	2	64	13	7	.346	.353
Holt, Brock	L-R	5-10	170	6-11-88	.432	.450	.418	24	95	13	41	7	0	1	9	7	0	1	1	9	5	2	.537	.476
Larish, Jeff	L-R	6-2	200	10-11-82	.182	.077	.200	61	181	22	33	13	1	2	24	33	0	0	0	65	0	1	.298	.308
Luna, Hector	R-R	6-1	190	2-1-80	.500	.500	.500	4	16	5	8	1	0	1	5	1	0	0	0	1	0	0	.750	.529
2-team total (62 Lehigh Valley)					.297	—	—	66	236	38	70	13	2	8	33	16	2	0	3	41	2	0	.470	.342
Marrero, Christian	L-L	6-1	185	7-30-86	.182	.000	.235	8	22	4	4	0	0	1	6	5	0	1	0	4	0	1	.318	.333
2-team total (68 Gwinnett)					.241	—	—	76	216	26	52	14	1	5	35	34	1	3	1	44	6	6	.384	.345
Marte, Starling	R-R	6-0	180	10-9-88	.286	.327	.272	99	388	64	111	21	13	12	62	28	10	2	3	91	21	12	.500	.347
McPherson, Dallas	L-R	6-4	225	7-23-80	.299	.179	.367	20	77	10	23	4	1	5	15	9	0	0	0	32	1	0	.571	.372
2-team total (61 Charlotte)					.265	—	—	81	306	45	81	16	1	17	62	37	1	0	2	115	3	1	.490	.344
Mercer, Jordy	R-R	6-3	200	8-27-86	.287	.237	.307	56	209	28	60	14	1	4	27	20	4	5	3	45	3	5	.421	.357
Morales, Jose	B-R	5-11	200	2-20-83	.266	.278	.262	58	158	12	42	6	1	1	31	24	2	3	5	35	0	0	.335	.360
Navarro, Yamaico	R-R	5-11	215	10-31-87	.279	.262	.286	66	222	41	62	14	3	9	35	32	0	0	3	41	9	4	.491	.366
Perez, Miguel	R-R	6-3	235	9-25-83	.333	1.000	.000	4	6	1	2	0	0	0	0	2	0	0	0	1	0	0	.333	.500
Picart, Greg	B-R	5-11	175	9-25-85	.250	.000	.333	1	4	0	1	0	0	0	0	0	0	0	0	0	0	0	.250	.250
Presley, Alex	L-L	5-10	185	7-25-85	.307	.350	.280	40	153	24	47	3	4	5	22	24	0	1	1	26	7	2	.477	.399
Sanchez, Tony	R-R	6-0	225	5-20-88	.233	.276	.216	62	206	21	48	12	0	8	26	23	3	2	2	46	0	0	.408	.316
Sutton, Drew	B-R	6-3	200	6-30-83	.048	.000	.071	12	21	2	1	1	0	0	1	4	1	0	0	7	1	0	.095	.231
2-team total (38 Gwinnett)					.241	—	—	50	158	21	38	11	2	0	16	24	5	1	2	31	3	3	.335	.354
Tabata, Jose	R-R	5-11	215	8-12-88	.297	.333	.277	41	158	21	47	9	0	1	15	10	4	0	1	20	5	2	.354	.353
Watts, Kris	L-R	6-1	210	7-15-84	.250	.375	.188	9	24	3	6	1	0	0	4	4	0	0	0	10	0	0	.292	.357

Pitching	B-T	HT	WT	DOB	W	L	ERA	G	GS	CG	SV	IP	H	R	ER	HR	BB	SO	AVG	vLH	vRH	K/9	BB/9
Alderson, Tim	R-R	6-6	217	11-3-88	0	0	4.50	2	0	0	0	4	5	2	2	1	2	4	.294	.429	.200	9.00	4.50
Burnett, A.J.	R-R	6-4	230	1-3-77	0	1	11.25	1	1	0	0	4	7	5	5	2	4	0	.412	.571	.300	0.00	9.00
Cabrera, Daniel	R-R	6-7	225	5-28-81	6	6	4.58	20	20	1	0	108	112	57	55	6	40	71	.271	.326	.223	5.92	3.33
Cole, Gerrit	R-R	6-4	220	9-8-90	1	0	4.50	1	1	0	0	6	3	3	3	0	1	7	.273	.333	.250	10.50	1.50
Diaz, Jose R.	R-R	6-4	300	2-27-84	1	2	3.60	41	0	0	3	45	43	19	18	3	19	37	.253	.258	.250	7.40	3.80
Hughes, Jared	R-R	6-7	245	7-4-85	0	0	0.00	2	0	0	0	2	1	0	0	0	1	3	.143	.000	.200	13.50	4.50
Irwin, Phillip	R-R	6-3	220	2-2-87	3	0	2.57	4	4	0	0	21	20	8	6	1	7	28	.260	.333	.195	12.00	3.00
Johnson, Kris	L-L	6-4	170	10-14-84	5	2	4.53	20	4	0	0	46	42	25	23	7	18	33	.241	.143	.288	6.50	3.55
Karstens, Jeff	R-R	6-3	185	9-24-82	0	2	4.61	3	3	0	0	14	11	13	7	1	3	13	.216	.269	.160	8.56	1.98
Kensing, Logan	R-R	6-1	190	7-3-82	0	0	4.09	11	0	0	0	11	8	5	5	1	5	10	.205	.231	.192	8.18	4.09
Leroux, Chris	L-R	6-6	230	4-14-84	4	0	3.11	21	7	0	0	64	52	22	22	6	14	56	.222	.318	.142	7.92	1.98
Lincoln, Brad	L-R	6-0	210	5-25-85	1	0	2.25	2	0	0	0	12	10	3	3	0	0	9	.227	.227	.227	6.75	0.00
Locke, Jeff	L-L	6-1	180	11-20-87	10	5	2.48	24	24	0	0	142	126	42	39	9	43	131	.241	.197	.257	8.32	2.73

	B-T	HT	WT	DOB	W	L	ERA	G	GS	CG	SV	IP	H	R	ER	HR	BB	SO	AVG	vLH	vRH	K/9	BB/9
Martis, Shairon	R-R	6-1	225	3-30-87	0	0	7.56	4	0	0	0	8	8	8	7	4	4	7	.229	.167	.261	7.56	4.32
2-team total (10 Rochester)					4	3	5.51	14	10	0	0	67	72	43	41	12	21	46	—	—	—	6.18	2.82
McCutchen, Daniel	R-R	6-2	215	9-26-82	7	2	2.98	36	1	0	3	63	54	25	21	3	14	55	.230	.290	.190	7.82	1.99
McPherson, Kyle	B-R	6-4	220	11-11-87	0	1	0.98	3	3	0	0	18	11	3	2	1	4	17	.172	.071	.250	8.35	1.96
Meek, Evan	R-R	6-0	225	5-12-83	2	2	2.74	36	0	0	1	46	33	16	14	3	26	41	.201	.203	.200	8.02	5.09
Morris, Bryan	L-R	6-3	220	3-28-87	2	2	2.67	46	0	0	5	81	76	32	24	8	17	79	.240	.211	.263	8.78	1.89
Morton, Charlie	R-R	6-5	230	11-12-83	0	0	1.17	1	1	0	0	8	6	1	1	0	1	8	.214	.214	.214	9.39	1.17
Moskos, Daniel	R-L	6-1	210	4-28-86	1	2	3.86	14	0	0	0	14	13	6	6	0	8	11	.241	.333	.167	7.07	5.14
2-team total (17 Charlotte)					2	3	4.19	31	0	0	2	34	39	18	16	2	22	32	—	—	—	8.39	5.77
Owens, Rudy	L-L	6-3	230	12-18-87	8	5	3.14	19	19	1	0	117	112	42	41	12	25	85	.253	.225	.264	6.52	1.92
Qualls, Chad	R-R	6-5	220	8-17-78	0	0	0.00	1	1	0	0	1	0	0	0	0	0	3	.000	.000	.000	27.00	0.00
Reyes, Jo-Jo	L-L	6-2	230	11-20-84	6	2	2.67	17	9	1	0	54	51	16	16	5	13	43	.243	.153	.290	7.17	2.17
Slaten, Doug	L-L	6-5	215	2-4-80	3	3	2.11	40	0	0	0	43	30	11	10	5	13	24	.200	.143	.228	5.06	2.74
VandenHurk, Rick	R-R	6-5	215	5-22-85	13	5	2.92	21	19	0	0	123	112	46	40	8	35	113	.241	.239	.244	8.25	2.55
Welker, Duke	L-R	6-7	260	2-10-86	0	1	2.27	26	0	0	0	32	24	8	8	1	18	30	.214	.227	.206	8.53	5.12
Wilson, Justin	L-L	6-2	220	8-18-87	9	6	3.78	29	25	1	0	136	91	60	57	12	66	138	.189	.129	.214	9.15	4.38
Wood, Tim	R-R	6-0	180	11-16-82	6	6	2.19	54	0	0	21	70	55	22	17	3	23	67	.213	.232	.201	8.61	2.96

Fielding

Catcher	PCT	G	PO	A	E	DP	PB
Cabrera	1.000	1	7	1	0	0	1
Fox	1.000	1	2	0	0	0	0
Fryer	.993	40	274	15	2	1	2
Morales	.991	45	306	22	3	1	4
Perez	1.000	2	15	1	0	0	0
Sanchez	.992	59	463	33	4	1	7
Watts	1.000	7	57	5	0	0	1

First Base	PCT	G	PO	A	E	DP
Clement	.995	62	554	37	3	47
Curry	.667	1	2	0	1	1
Durham	1.000	8	38	1	0	2
Evans	.987	10	72	5	1	7
Farrell	1.000	3	10	1	0	1
Fox	.951	9	53	5	3	5
Hague	.994	41	320	19	2	33
Larish	1.000	21	161	15	0	10
Luna	—	1	0	0	0	0
McPherson	1.000	1	9	0	0	0
Navarro	1.000	3	13	1	0	0

Second Base	PCT	G	PO	A	E	DP
d'Arnaud	1.000	6	10	10	0	3
Diaz	—	1	0	0	0	0

	PCT	G	PO	A	E	DP
Friday	.993	30	56	86	1	19
Hernandez	.972	72	123	187	9	37
Holt	.973	14	30	42	2	7
Larish	1.000	1	1	0	0	0
Luna	1.000	3	4	4	0	1
Mercer	.985	11	28	37	1	5
Navarro	.966	13	20	37	2	7
Picart	1.000	1	4	4	0	2

Third Base	PCT	G	PO	A	E	DP
d'Arnaud	.857	3	1	5	1	0
Evans	.824	6	3	11	3	2
Farrell	1.000	4	2	9	0	0
Friday	.909	22	10	40	5	5
Hague	.963	50	33	97	5	5
Hernandez	.939	15	11	20	2	3
Larish	1.000	3	0	1	0	1
Luna	.800	2	1	3	1	1
McPherson	1.000	4	5	8	0	2
Mercer	1.000	10	5	20	0	5
Navarro	.942	35	31	66	6	6

Shortstop	PCT	G	PO	A	E	DP
d'Arnaud	.955	88	118	220	16	41
Friday	1.000	4	3	7	0	1

	PCT	G	PO	A	E	DP
Hernandez	1.000	12	4	24	0	2
Holt	.944	9	13	21	2	2
Larish	1.000	1	1	0	0	0
Mercer	.961	33	45	104	6	25
Navarro	1.000	2	2	1	0	1

Outfield	PCT	G	PO	A	E	DP
Boggs	.985	121	197	3	3	0
Durham	1.000	8	9	0	0	0
Evans	1.000	2	8	0	0	0
Fox	1.000	11	12	0	0	0
Fryer	1.000	13	7	0	0	0
Hernandez	1.000	2	2	1	0	0
Hernandez	.994	67	160	7	1	0
Larish	1.000	35	52	1	0	0
Marrero	1.000	6	13	0	0	0
Marte	.996	97	231	8	1	2
McPherson	1.000	9	18	0	0	0
Navarro	.938	8	12	3	1	0
Presley	1.000	40	79	2	0	0
Sutton	1.000	6	12	0	0	0
Tabata	.956	40	86	0	4	0
Watts	—	1	0	0	0	0

ALTOONA CURVE — DOUBLE-A

EASTERN LEAGUE

Batting	B-T	HT	WT	DOB	AVG	vLH	vRH	G	AB	R	H	2B	3B	HR	RBI	BB	HBP	SH	SF	SO	SB	CS	SLG	OBP
Brown, Kelson	R-R	6-3	170	11-7-87	.290	.294	.286	56	138	20	40	6	1	2	19	13	6	4	3	23	3	2	.391	.369
Cabrera, Ramon	R-S	5-8	195	11-5-89	.276	.262	.282	112	384	47	106	22	2	3	50	39	0	4	1	44	0	3	.367	.342
Chambers, Evan	R-R	5-11	210	3-24-89	.182	.500	.085	31	77	12	14	2	1	1	9	8	1	0	0	29	1	2	.273	.267
Cunningham, Jarek	R-R	6-1	195	12-25-89	.217	.220	.216	105	359	43	78	19	3	6	45	37	7	8	4	111	3	3	.337	.300
Curry, Matt	L-R	6-1	225	7-27-88	.285	.282	.287	111	396	53	113	34	5	11	76	44	1	1	8	107	4	4	.480	.352
Cutler, Charlie	L-R	6-0	200	7-29-86	.296	.364	.269	55	152	25	45	7	3	2	19	21	8	1	1	17	1	0	.421	.407
Durham, Miles	R-R	6-4	205	3-21-83	.259	.333	.232	40	135	22	35	11	2	2	14	13	0	0	4	33	6	3	.415	.316
Farrell, Jeremy	R-R	6-3	200	11-11-86	.221	.202	.233	98	298	32	66	15	1	4	25	31	12	3	0	83	3	3	.319	.320
Gonzalez, Elevys	R-R	5-11	175	10-23-89	.196	.196	.196	50	148	10	29	6	1	2	15	14	2	3	0	42	1	3	.291	.294
Grossman, Robbie	B-L	6-0	205	9-16-89	.266	.307	.242	95	350	59	93	20	4	7	36	59	4	4	0	78	9	10	.406	.378
Holt, Brock	L-R	5-10	170	6-11-88	.322	.315	.326	102	382	52	123	24	6	2	43	40	4	3	3	51	11	11	.432	.389
Lambo, Andrew	L-L	6-3	210	8-11-88	.250	.229	.263	26	92	13	23	3	1	4	16	14	0	1	1	19	0	1	.435	.346
Latimore, Quincy	R-R	5-10	175	2-3-89	.252	.280	.237	126	413	52	104	24	3	15	71	38	5	4	2	105	10	8	.433	.321
Maggi, Drew	R-R	6-0	185	5-16-89	.218	.228	.213	52	179	28	39	4	2	0	9	18	4	2	3	41	5	2	.263	.299
Marrero, Christian	L-L	6-1	185	7-30-86	.200	—	.200	5	15	2	3	0	0	1	3	0	1	0	1	6	0	0	.400	.235
Norman, Anthony	R-R	6-0	185	10-28-84	.186	.308	.152	27	59	8	11	1	2	0	3	5	1	1	1	16	1	0	.271	.258
Nunez, Gustavo	B-R	5-10	170	2-8-88	.227	.222	.231	7	22	2	5	1	0	0	3	2	0	0	0	4	1	1	.273	.292
Perez, Miguel	R-R	6-3	235	9-25-83	.250	.000	.500	1	4	0	1	0	0	0	1	0	0	0	0	2	0	0	.250	.250
Picart, Greg	B-R	5-11	175	9-25-85	.211	.333	.154	15	19	3	4	0	0	0	0	3	0	0	0	1	1	0	.211	.318
Sanchez, Tony	R-R	6-0	225	5-20-88	.277	.250	.294	40	141	22	39	14	1	0	17	18	3	0	0	33	1	1	.390	.370
Santos, Adalberto	R-R	5-11	185	9-28-87	.340	.360	.331	68	238	36	81	12	2	2	28	32	3	1	0	39	17	8	.433	.425
Stallings, Jacob	R-R	6-5	215	12-22-89	1.000	—	1.000	1	1	0	1	0	0	0	0	0	0	0	0	0	0	0	1.000	1.000
Tejeda, Oscar	R-R	6-1	170	12-26-89	.242	.292	.227	54	198	23	48	13	1	3	28	15	1	2	5	42	3	0	.364	.292
2-team total (51 Portland)					.253	—	—	105	400	41	101	25	1	8	59	24	2	2	7	83	5	1	.380	.293
Vasquez, Andy	L-R	6-1	168	10-8-87	.250	.000	.333	2	4	1	1	0	0	1	0	0	0	0	0	1	0	0	.500	.250
Welch, Stefan	L-R	6-3	175	8-12-88	.266	.196	.288	67	214	34	57	12	1	5	27	31	1	4	2	59	3	1	.402	.359

Pitching	B-T	HT	WT	DOB	W	L	ERA	G	GS	CG	SV	IP	H	R	ER	HR	BB	SO	AVG	vLH	vRH	K/9	BB/9
Alderson, Tim	R-R	6-6	217	11-3-88	5	4	4.25	26	11	0	3	85	89	45	40	7	26	62	.271	.281	.264	6.59	2.76
Baker, Nate	L-L	6-3	190	12-27-87	4	7	4.94	32	13	0	1	106	100	67	58	9	57	77	.250	.214	.262	6.56	4.85
Beckman, Ryan	R-R	6-4	185	1-2-90	0	0	0.00	1	0	0	0	0	1	0	0	0	1	1	.500	.000	1.000	27.00	27.00
Black, Vic	R-R	6-3	185	5-23-88	2	3	1.65	51	0	0	13	60	40	14	11	2	29	85	.189	.196	.183	12.75	4.35
Cofield, Kyle	R-R	6-5	220	1-23-87	0	1	5.28	11	0	0	1	15	13	10	9	3	4	15	.213	.318	.154	8.80	2.35
Cole, Gerrit	R-R	6-4	220	9-8-90	3	6	2.90	12	12	0	0	59	54	28	19	2	23	60	.239	.205	.261	9.15	3.51
Colla, Mike	R-R	6-2	220	12-23-86	5	6	3.75	37	10	0	2	96	96	49	40	11	27	75	.263	.262	.264	7.03	2.53
Cruz, Juan	R-R	6-2	170	10-15-78	0	0	13.50	2	2	0	0	1	5	2	2	0	0	2	.556	.800	.250	13.50	0.00
Cumpton, Brandon	R-R	6-2	198	11-16-88	12	11	3.84	27	27	0	0	152	149	72	65	9	46	88	.261	.272	.253	5.20	2.72
Foster, Zach	R-R	6-4	209	5-24-87	0	1	13.50	1	0	0	0	3	3	4	4	0	2	1	.250	.000	.333	3.38	6.75
Harvey, Kris	R-R	6-2	200	1-5-84	0	3	3.29	31	0	0	2	55	52	26	20	4	27	45	.249	.267	.239	7.41	4.45
Inman, Jeff	R-R	6-3	180	11-24-87	2	2	3.83	30	1	0	3	52	45	22	22	2	19	36	.230	.234	.227	6.27	3.31
Irwin, Phillip	R-R	6-3	220	2-25-87	4	7	2.93	18	16	3	0	104	97	39	34	7	17	83	.253	.250	.254	7.16	1.47
Johnson, Kris	L-L	6-4	170	10-14-84	3	2	2.09	15	9	0	1	56	50	19	13	3	24	42	.234	.159	.253	6.75	3.86
Kaminska, Kyle	L-R	6-4	180	10-5-88	1	0	3.00	4	1	0	0	12	13	4	4	0	0	11	.260	.296	.217	8.25	0.00
Karstens, Jeff	R-R	6-3	185	9-24-82	1	0	0.90	2	2	0	0	10	8	1	1	0	1	6	.222	.188	.250	5.40	0.90
Kensing, Logan	R-R	6-1	190	7-3-82	2	0	4.58	12	0	0	1	18	18	11	9	1	6	14	.257	.346	.205	7.13	3.06
Martis, Shairon	R-R	6-1	225	3-30-87	6	2	4.56	11	8	0	0	53	45	27	27	7	19	30	.231	.192	.254	5.06	3.21
2-team total (4 New Britain)					7	3	4.85	15	11	0	0	72	68	40	39	9	24	41	—	—	—	5.10	2.99
McPherson, Kyle	.B-R	6-4	220	11-11-87	3	5	4.07	9	9	0	0	49	54	26	22	5	5	46	.278	.219	.314	8.51	0.92
McSwain, Matt	R-R	6-1	197	8-15-85	4	2	4.88	19	6	0	0	55	66	35	30	2	27	41	.292	.269	.311	6.67	4.39
Poreda, Aaron	L-L	6-6	240	10-1-86	2	0	2.25	3	3	0	0	16	12	6	4	0	11	11	.211	.500	.200	6.19	6.19
Pribanic, Aaron	R-R	6-4	210	9-1-86	0	2	7.36	3	3	0	0	11	17	11	9	1	11	6	.378	.400	.367	4.91	9.00
Ramos, Jhonatan	L-L	6-0	199	8-7-89	2	1	2.61	13	0	0	0	21	19	6	6	2	6	14	.250	.304	.226	6.10	2.61
Strickland, Hunter	R-R	6-5	200	9-24-88	2	2	4.46	23	0	0	2	42	50	23	21	5	15	33	.309	.375	.265	7.02	3.19
Taillon, Jameson	R-R	6-6	225	11-18-91	3	0	1.59	3	3	0	0	17	11	3	3	0	1	18	.183	.194	.172	9.53	0.53
Townsend, Jason	R-R	6-3	190	9-17-88	2	0	0.00	3	0	0	0	10	10	0	0	0	4	3	.270	.385	.208	2.61	3.48
Turgeon, Leo	R-R	6-0	170	3-25-87	1	0	0.00	1	0	0	0	2	0	0	0	1	0	.000	.000	.000	0.00	4.50
2-team total (17 Binghamton)					2	3	6.84	18	0	0	0	26	43	25	20	5	13	22	—	—	—	7.52	4.44
Waldron, Tyler	R-R	6-2	185	5-1-89	1	2	4.05	6	6	0	0	27	26	12	12	3	11	15	.257	.167	.308	5.06	3.71
Welker, Duke	L-R	6-7	260	2-10-86	2	1	2.31	15	0	0	5	23	19	7	6	0	7	19	.221	.257	.196	7.33	2.70

Fielding

Catcher	PCT	G	PO	A	E	DP	PB
Cabrera	.994	84	571	49	4	3	4
Cutler	.988	25	154	16	2	2	0
Sanchez	.972	37	213	27	7	2	7

First Base	PCT	G	PO	A	E	DP
Curry	.991	104	955	55	9	93
Durham	1.000	6	59	2	0	10
Farrell	.993	35	284	9	2	25
Gonzalez	1.000	4	14	0	0	0
Welch	1.000	1	1	0	0	0

Second Base	PCT	G	PO	A	E	DP
Brown	.940	13	23	40	4	7
Cunningham	.977	104	210	302	12	74
Gonzalez	.976	19	28	53	2	12
Maggi	.941	4	8	8	1	1

	PCT	G	PO	A	E	DP
Picart	1.000	1	2	4	0	1
Tejeda	.973	5	18	18	1	7
Third Base	PCT	G	PO	A	E	DP
Brown	.955	29	12	51	3	12
Farrell	.876	45	26	66	13	6
Gonzalez	.886	14	7	32	5	1
Picart	1.000	4	1	4	0	0
Welch	.943	61	42	141	11	17
Shortstop	PCT	G	PO	A	E	DP
Brown	.978	13	12	32	1	6
Holt	.945	98	115	281	23	56
Maggi	.948	27	33	77	6	13
Nunez	.938	6	12	18	2	7
Picart	.889	4	4	4	1	1
Tejeda	.909	3	2	8	1	0

Outfield	PCT	G	PO	A	E	DP
Chambers	.949	20	35	2	2	1
Cutler	.917	9	20	2	2	1
Durham	.968	33	59	1	2	0
Gonzalez	1.000	5	4	0	0	0
Grossman	.989	94	176	3	2	1
Lambo	1.000	26	64	1	0	0
Latimore	.950	122	215	12	12	3
Maggi	1.000	18	36	0	0	0
Marrero	—	1	0	0	0	0
Norman	1.000	21	21	2	0	0
Santos	.936	47	71	2	5	1
Tejeda	.986	45	63	5	1	0
Vasquez	1.000	2	3	0	0	0

BRADENTON MARAUDERS

HIGH CLASS A

FLORIDA STATE LEAGUE

Batting	B-T	HT	WT	DOB	AVG	vLH	vRH	G	AB	R	H	2B	3B	HR	RBI	BB	HBP	SH	SF	SO	SB	CS	SLG	OBP
Chambers, Evan	R-R	5-11	210	3-24-89	.195	.137	.228	61	200	28	39	5	1	1	20	50	1	0	3	68	11	8	.245	.354
Diaz, Francisco	B-R	5-10	160	3-21-90	.167	.222	.148	10	36	1	6	0	0	0	2	1	0	1	0	14	0	1	.167	.211
Dickerson, Alex	L-L	6-3	235	5-26-90	.295	.310	.287	129	488	65	144	31	3	13	90	39	7	2	5	93	12	7	.451	.353
Emsley-Pai, Kawika	B-R	5-11	195	9-3-88	.167	.171	.165	47	120	19	20	6	0	1	11	35	1	4	1	33	3	0	.242	.357
Freeman, Wes	R-R	6-4	215	1-29-90	.147	.200	.116	43	150	10	22	7	1	1	9	10	1	1	3	49	1	4	.227	.201
Gonzalez, Benji	R-R	5-11	160	1-16-90	.265	.259	.270	99	294	49	78	11	3	1	20	27	2	5	3	63	8	8	.333	.330
Gonzalez, Elevys	B-R	5-11	175	10-23-89	.216	.208	.221	45	148	17	32	9	1	4	20	25	2	2	1	42	3	3	.372	.335
Grovatt, Dan	L-L	6-1	195	10-29-88	.251	.210	.271	109	390	60	98	24	5	9	38	26	3	5	2	67	15	2	.408	.302
Howard, Justin	L-L	6-0	205	8-28-87	.283	.277	.286	83	272	35	77	14	3	2	29	44	2	0	4	55	3	6	.379	.382
Maggi, Drew	R-R	6-0	185	5-16-89	.241	.200	.264	54	195	35	47	8	1	1	28	32	2	4	1	46	17	3	.308	.352
Mesa, Carlos	R-R	6-2	215	2-10-88	.223	.203	.238	51	175	15	39	4	2	4	13	7	3	1	0	63	1	2	.337	.265
Ngoepe, Gift	R-R	5-10	165	1-18-90	.232	.214	.242	124	456	66	106	11	5	9	36	63	5	11	3	131	22	14	.338	.330
Nunez, Gustavo	B-R	5-10	170	2-8-88	.294	.286	.300	5	17	1	5	1	0	0	1	0	0	0	0	3	0	0	.353	.333
Paulino, Carlos	R-R	6-0	170	9-24-89	.251	.200	.278	84	303	35	76	18	3	4	35	17	10	4	1	43	2	1	.370	.311
Rojas Jr., Mel	B-R	6-3	215	5-24-90	.245	.213	.262	130	497	61	122	12	12	6	51	35	7	4	3	107	16	8	.354	.303
Singer, Kirk	R-R	6-1	195	1-5-90	.234	.250	.223	56	197	27	46	6	2	2	20	16	1	2	2	32	5	5	.315	.292
Sosa, Junior	L-L	5-10	139	10-3-90	.171	.125	.185	10	35	2	6	1	0	0	6	0	1	0	1	0	1	0	.200	.189
Vasquez, Andy	L-R	6-1	168	10-8-87	.264	.253	.268	85	288	34	76	15	3	5	39	11	0	5	1	60	7	10	.389	.290
Welch, Stefan	L-R	6-3	175	8-12-88	.265	.205	.297	61	226	23	60	11	1	8	37	17	3	0	4	44	4	1	.429	.320

Pitching	B-T	HT	WT	DOB	W	L	ERA	G	GS	CG	SV	IP	H	R	ER	HR	BB	SO	AVG	vLH	vRH	K/9	BB/9
Benedict, Matt	R-R	6-5	220	2-3-89	0	8	8.08	14	9	1	0	49	61	51	44	5	26	22	.326	.295	.354	4.04	4.78
Burnett, A.J.	R-R	6-4	230	1-3-77	0	2	8.53	2	2	0	0	6	7	9	6	0	2	9	.259	.273	.250	12.79	2.84
Cabrera, Daniel	R-R	6-7	225	5-28-81	0	1	1.50	1	1	0	0	6	1	1	1	0	0	5	.304	.400	.125	7.50	0.00
Cain, Colton	L-L	6-3	255	2-5-91	3	5	4.20	16	16	0	0	75	68	39	35	10	25	51	.242	.275	.226	6.12	3.00
Cole, Gerrit	R-R	6-4	220	9-8-90	5	1	2.55	13	13	0	0	67	53	24	19	5	21	69	.217	.214	.220	9.27	2.82
De Leon, Emmanuel	B-R	6-1	175	12-25-90	0	1	13.50	3	0	0	0	5	8	9	8	1	2	7	.348	.429	.313	11.81	3.38
Foster, Zach	R-R	6-4	209	5-24-87	1	7	5.61	40	0	0	4	61	69	46	38	4	32	26	.283	.231	.321	3.84	4.72
Inman, Jeff	R-R	6-3	180	11-24-87	0	0	0.00	6	0	0	1	10	4	1	0	0	2	4	.125	.154	.105	3.72	1.86
Irwin, Phillip	R-R	6-3	220	2-25-87	1	0	1.80	1	1	0	0	5	2	1	1	0	0	6	.118	.100	.143	10.80	0.00
Kaminska, Kyle	L-R	6-4	180	10-5-88	2	0	1.69	3	3	0	0	16	10	3	3	0	2	11	.200	.250	.136	6.19	1.13
Kasparek, Kenn	R-R	6-10	245	9-23-85	0	6	5.05	22	6	0	1	62	73	37	35	5	20	34	.304	.404	.234	4.91	2.89
Kensing, Logan	R-R	6-1	190	7-3-82	1	1	1.69	4	0	0	0	5	1	1	1	0	4	1	.071	.000	.125	1.69	6.75
Leroux, Chris	L-R	6-6	230	4-14-84	0	1	3.00	1	1	0	0	3	2	1	1	0	1	2	.200	.000	.400	6.00	3.00
Lopez, Porfirio	L-L	5-10	160	3-24-90	2	1	2.22	12	0	0	1	28	21	10	7	2	9	18	.202	.237	.182	5.72	2.86
McCutchen, Daniel	R-R	6-2	215	9-26-82	0	0	0.00	1	0	0	0	2	1	0	0	0	1	0	.143	.250	.000	4.50	0.00
Miller, Quinton	R-R	6-1	185	11-28-89	4	4	6.34	38	0	0	5	60	67	48	42	7	32	48	.276	.311	.248	7.24	4.83
Montero, Joan	R-R	6-0	186	10-26-88	0	0	13.50	2	0	0	0	4	7	6	6	1	1	4	.476	.462	.500	9.00	2.25
Navarro, Eliecer	L-L	5-9	177	10-26-87	5	8	3.62	31	13	1	1	112	112	51	45	9	27	88	.260	.256	.266	7.07	2.17
Poytress, Josh	R-L	6-2	185	7-20-90	3	0	2.59	21	0	0	1	42	36	12	12	2	26	29	.245	.194	.282	6.26	5.62
Pribanic, Aaron	R-R	6-4	210	9-1-86	0	0	0.00	1	0	0	0	2	2	0	0	0	4	0	.250	.500	.167	0.00	21.60
Ramos, Jhonatan	L-L	6-0	199	8-7-89	6	3	4.65	25	3	0	1	60	55	33	31	5	21	37	.240	.228	.247	5.55	3.15
Sadler, Casey	R-R	6-4	200	7-13-90	4	6	3.73	32	17	0	2	130	125	63	54	7	35	93	.255	.280	.232	6.42	2.42
Salinas, Doug	R-R	6-4	195	12-5-88	0	2	5.29	19	0	0	11	17	16	11	10	2	5	10	.250	.280	.231	5.29	2.65
Strickland, Hunter	R-R	6-5	200	9-24-88	2	2	2.98	10	9	0	0	45	47	16	15	5	8	25	.272	.256	.289	4.96	1.59
Taillon, Jameson	R-R	6-6	225	11-18-91	6	8	3.82	23	23	2	0	125	109	57	53	10	37	98	.230	.196	.256	7.06	2.66
Townsend, Jason	R-R	6-3	190	9-17-88	6	2	2.23	37	0	0	4	69	60	19	17	0	21	42	.243	.242	.243	5.50	2.75
Turgeon, Erik	R-R	6-0	170	3-25-87	1	0	0.90	6	0	0	0	10	5	2	1	0	6	11	.156	.167	.150	9.90	5.40
VandenHurk, Rick	R-R	6-5	215	5-22-85	1	0	6.00	1	1	0	0	6	8	4	4	1	1	5	.320	.333	.300	7.50	1.50
Waldron, Tyler	R-R	6-2	185	5-1-89	7	8	5.09	22	20	1	0	115	143	74	65	11	29	73	.306	.341	.277	5.71	2.27

Fielding

Catcher	PCT	G	PO	A	E	DP	PB											
Diaz	1.000	10	68	6	0	1	2	Maggi	.984	44	68	117	3	25	Ngoepe	.963	117	188	351	21	71
Emsley-Pai	.997	47	249	37	1	4	4	Ngoepe	1.000	8	17	33	0	10	Nunez	.909	4	3	7	1	3
Paulino	.986	83	508	61	8	4	9	Vasquez	.976	10	13	27	1	3	Singer	.833	3	1	4	1	1

First Base	PCT	G	PO	A	E	DP
Dickerson	.985	109	1041	70	17	107
Gonzalez	1.000	1	1	0	0	0
Howard	1.000	16	111	11	0	11
Welch	1.000	15	108	9	0	17

Third Base	PCT	G	PO	A	E	DP
Gonzalez	.935	21	15	28	3	2
Gonzalez	.935	17	16	42	4	10
Singer	.928	51	36	118	12	15
Vasquez	.960	16	7	41	2	10
Welch	.912	42	36	78	11	4

Outfield	PCT	G	PO	A	E	DP
Chambers	.969	57	117	6	4	1
Freeman	1.000	27	74	2	0	0
Grovatt	.965	100	160	5	6	0
Howard	1.000	15	12	0	0	0
Mesa	1.000	47	67	6	0	1
Rojas Jr.	.986	125	273	9	4	1
Sosa	.950	9	19	0	1	0
Vasquez	.963	48	99	4	4	0

Second Base	PCT	G	PO	A	E	DP
Gonzalez	.971	67	146	193	10	55
Gonzalez	.978	15	36	54	2	13

Shortstop	PCT	G	PO	A	E	DP
Gonzalez	.976	12	11	30	1	3
Maggi	.938	8	11	19	2	8

WEST VIRGINIA POWER

LOW CLASS A

SOUTH ATLANTIC LEAGUE

Batting	B-T	HT	WT	DOB	AVG	vLH	vRH	G	AB	R	H	2B	3B	HR	RBI	BB	HBP	SH	SF	SO	SB	CS	SLG	OBP
Aponte, Francisco	B-R	5-11	135	2-9-91	.234	.186	.256	59	188	23	44	9	2	0	13	15	0	3	2	30	6	3	.303	.288
Avila, Eric	R-R	6-1	165	6-9-90	.281	.306	.268	53	185	21	52	14	1	11	35	8	2	1	2	40	1	0	.546	.315
Bell, Josh	B-R	6-4	195	8-14-92	.274	.154	.306	15	62	6	17	5	0	1	11	2	0	0	2	21	1	0	.403	.288
Carvajal, Jodaneli	S-9	160	4-20-92	.243	.250	.241	29	107	15	26	5	1	1	9	7	3	2	0	22	3	3	.336	.308
Diaz, Elias	R-R	6-1	175	11-17-90	.208	.197	.211	92	313	32	65	14	1	3	26	22	3	6	5	51	2	2	.288	.262
Diaz, Francisco	B-R	5-10	180	3-21-90	.302	.381	.262	45	126	24	38	9	0	1	17	17	4	5	5	31	0	1	.397	.388
Freeman, Wes	R-R	6-4	215	1-29-90	.000	.000	.000	1	2	0	0	0	0	0	0	0	0	0	0	1	1	0	.000	.500
Fuselier, Alex	L-R	6-0	170	9-13-89	.211	.400	.143	8	19	2	4	0	0	1	1	5	0	2	0	5	1	1	.368	.375
Gamache, Daniel	L-R	5-11	190	11-20-90	.285	.255	.294	125	449	70	128	40	5	5	52	41	6	2	4	95	7	4	.430	.350
Garcia, Willy	R-R	6-3	180	9-7-92	.240	.237	.241	122	459	57	110	17	2	18	77	32	0	1	5	131	10	8	.403	.286
Hanson, Alen	B-R	5-11	152	10-22-92	.309	.286	.318	124	489	99	151	33	13	16	62	55	4	7	3	105	35	19	.528	.381
Lashmet, Chris	R-R	6-4	230	4-25-89	.230	.276	.203	99	313	36	72	15	3	2	33	28	2	0	1	62	2	4	.316	.297
Lewis, Taylor	L-L	6-0	200	10-18-89	.244	.241	.245	66	250	42	61	7	6	4	26	22	2	4	1	61	20	4	.368	.309
Mesa, Carlos	R-R	6-2	215	2-10-88	.189	.258	.171	37	148	16	28	6	0	3	13	2	0	0	1	56	1	0	.291	.199
Osuna, Jose	R-R	6-2	213	12-12-92	.280	.233	.297	126	482	68	135	36	0	16	72	31	4	0	7	82	4	4	.454	.324
Polanco, Gregory	L-L	6-4	170	9-14-91	.325	.396	.301	116	437	84	142	26	6	16	85	44	2	1	1	64	40	15	.522	.388
Ponce, Ashley	R-R	5-11	140	11-24-91	.192	.156	.213	54	172	18	33	4	0	1	20	13	3	7	1	21	2	4	.233	.259
Schwind, Jonathan	R-R	6-0	185	5-30-90	.206	.429	.148	10	34	4	7	0	0	0	2	2	1	0	0	12	0	0	.206	.270
Singer, Kirk	R-R	6-2	170	12-1-89	.262	.273	.260	53	187	21	49	6	1	1	25	13	0	6	3	46	6	2	.321	.305
Sosa, Junior	L-L	5-10	139	10-3-90	.268	.192	.288	80	257	34	69	4	3	2	22	28	1	3	0	33	22	10	.331	.343

Pitching	B-T	HT	WT	DOB	W	L	ERA	G	GS	CG	SV	IP	H	R	ER	HR	BB	SO	AVG	vLH	vRH	K/9	BB/9
Allie, Stetson	R-R	6-2	220	3-13-91	0	1	54.00	2	1	0	0	1	4	8	6	0	11	1	.333	.500	.000	13.50	108.00
Benedict, Matt	R-R	6-5	220	2-3-89	4	4	3.42	14	14	0	0	76	72	42	29	3	23	44	.250	.277	.228	5.19	2.71
Castro, Orlando	L-L	5-11	195	3-17-92	4	6	4.76	18	10	0	1	45	48	28	24	3	17	42	.276	.238	.297	8.34	3.38

Name	B-T	HT	WT	DOB	W	L	ERA	G	GS	CG	SV	IP	H	R	ER	HR	BB	SO	AVG	vLH	vRH	K/9	BB/9
Cooper, Jordan	B-R	6-3	215	2-16-90	1	3	8.38	14	0	0	1	19	29	20	18	5	9	12	.345	.300	.386	5.59	4.19
De Leon, Emmanuel	B-R	6-1	175	12-25-90	1	5	5.08	22	0	0	4	34	32	22	19	3	24	40	.244	.276	.219	10.69	6.42
Dodson, Zack	L-L	6-2	190	7-23-90	6	6	4.86	21	21	1	0	100	111	66	54	12	40	67	.280	.270	.283	6.03	3.60
Ennis, Justin	L-L	6-1	210	4-20-88	0	0	5.79	8	0	0	0	9	15	8	6	1	5	8	.341	.294	.370	7.71	4.82
Fuesser, Zac	L-L	6-2	190	7-19-90	3	7	4.09	31	11	0	0	112	115	63	51	10	46	93	.269	.283	.262	7.45	3.69
Hafner, Ryan	R-R	6-6	205	11-22-91	0	9	8.31	21	14	0	0	61	72	61	56	5	68	29	.312	.267	.338	4.30	10.09
Jefferson, Mike	L-L	6-5	190	7-31-89	7	7	4.67	30	13	0	1	108	104	67	56	12	39	86	.246	.292	.225	7.17	3.25
Kilcrease, Nathan	R-R	5-6	170	8-17-89	0	2	1.22	30	0	0	15	37	33	8	5	1	9	35	.236	.200	.259	8.51	2.19
Kilcrease, Robert	L-L	5-11	175	3-14-89	2	2	2.80	43	0	0	3	64	48	27	20	3	25	68	.198	.138	.228	9.51	3.50
Kingham, Nick	R-R	6-5	220	11-8-91	6	8	4.39	27	27	0	0	127	115	70	62	15	36	117	.243	.243	.243	8.29	2.55
Lopez, Porfirio	L-L	5-10	160	3-24-90	2	3	5.30	14	2	0	0	36	34	24	21	3	27	35	.262	.326	.230	8.83	6.81
Ludwig, Pat	R-R	6-1	185	10-11-89	0	1	3.60	4	0	0	0	5	3	2	2	0	1	6	.176	.111	.250	10.80	1.80
Montero, Joan	R-R	6-0	186	10-26-88	3	0	8.44	18	0	0	1	32	41	30	30	6	9	20	.306	.316	.299	5.63	2.53
Payne, Vince	R-R	6-4	175	12-19-90	1	1	9.00	14	0	0	0	23	35	27	23	6	14	18	.350	.282	.393	7.04	5.48
Perez, Clario	R-R	6-1	185	8-30-92	1	1	5.84	16	0	0	2	25	24	19	16	3	14	19	.247	.267	.231	6.93	5.11
Poytress, Josh	R-L	6-2	185	7-20-90	2	0	0.79	4	0	0	0	11	5	1	1	0	3	10	.135	.300	.074	7.94	2.38
Rowland, Robby	B-R	6-4	215	12-15-91	9	5	3.30	20	19	1	0	106	110	52	39	10	23	62	.268	.265	.271	5.25	1.95
Singh, Rinku	L-L	6-2	190	8-8-88	3	1	3.00	39	0	0	1	72	72	33	24	8	18	65	.257	.286	.245	8.13	2.25
Stevenson, Trent	L-R	6-6	175	6-1-90	1	0	9.26	6	0	0	0	12	24	14	12	2	2	9	.407	.414	.400	6.94	1.54
Von Rosenberg, Zack	R-R	6-5	205	9-24-90	5	7	4.36	17	17	3	0	87	94	49	42	11	24	60	.272	.300	.252	6.23	2.49

Fielding

Catcher	PCT	G	PO	A	E	DP	PB
Diaz	.980	92	595	86	14	2	9
Diaz	.985	43	293	26	5	1	1
Schwind	.963	8	48	4	2	1	4

First Base	PCT	G	PO	A	E	DP
Lashmet	.985	39	307	31	5	13
Osuna	.983	103	876	65	16	67

Second Base	PCT	G	PO	A	E	DP
Aponte	.958	14	23	45	3	5
Carvajal	.970	16	36	29	2	6
Gamache	.960	105	211	289	21	52
Ponce	1.000	8	16	16	0	3

Third Base	PCT	G	PO	A	E	DP
Aponte	.867	10	7	19	4	1
Avila	.940	42	25	69	6	2
Carvajal	.846	8	4	18	4	2
Lashmet	.950	23	14	43	3	3
Ponce	.948	20	7	48	3	4
Singer	.925	46	42	105	12	7

Shortstop	PCT	G	PO	A	E	DP
Aponte	.971	9	13	21	1	6
Carvajal	.750	2	2	4	2	0
Hanson	.907	103	136	254	40	40
Ponce	.959	27	25	68	4	11

	PCT	G	PO	A	E	DP
Singer	1.000	7	5	21	0	2
Outfield	PCT	G	PO	A	E	DP
Aponte	.976	25	39	2	1	0
Bell	.900	14	18	0	2	1
Fuselier	1.000	8	20	0	0	0
Garcia	.973	113	205	12	6	1
Lashmet	.917	14	11	0	1	0
Lewis	.979	65	139	4	3	0
Mesa	1.000	29	60	3	0	1
Polanco	.987	98	222	12	3	0
Sosa	.993	74	131	2	1	0

STATE COLLEGE SPIKES SHORT-SEASON

NEW YORK-PENN LEAGUE

Batting	B-T	HT	WT	DOB	AVG	vLH	vRH	G	AB	R	H	2B	3B	HR	RBI	BB	HBP	SH	SF	SO	SB	CS	SLG	OBP
Aponte, Francisco	B-R	5-11	135	2-9-91	.143	—	.143	2	7	1	1	0	0	0	0	0	1	0	0	1	0	0	.143	.250
Barnes, Barrett	R-R	6-1	195	7-29-91	.288	.342	.264	38	125	16	36	6	0	5	24	17	8	1	2	21	10	6	.456	.401
Barrios, Yhonathan	B-R	5-11	179	12-1-91	.196	.219	.189	44	138	21	27	3	0	0	9	10	1	3	0	39	11	3	.217	.255
Carvajal, Jodaneli	R-R	5-9	160	4-20-92	.235	.207	.248	53	187	26	44	7	3	0	15	11	0	3	1	37	8	3	.305	.276
Crumlich, D.J.	R-R	6-0	190	4-23-90	.292	.321	.278	69	257	33	75	19	0	2	29	23	4	3	2	45	5	4	.389	.357
Diaz, Christopher	R-R	6-0	180	11-9-90	.222	.233	.217	67	239	23	53	7	2	1	20	19	4	9	3	58	9	6	.280	.287
Fortunato, Raul	R-R	6-2	190	9-5-90	.429	1.000	.385	4	14	3	6	1	1	0	1	1	0	0	0	1	1	0	.643	.467
Fuselier, Alex	L-R	6-0	170	9-13-89	.228	.250	.222	33	101	7	23	2	0	0	7	9	1	0	0	16	4	2	.248	.297
Gaffney, Tyler	R-R	6-1	225	4-20-91	.297	.375	.254	38	111	31	33	6	5	0	10	20	20	0	0	20	11	5	.441	.483
Gonzalez, Samuel	R-R	6-0	180	2-24-89	.247	.232	.256	62	194	22	48	5	2	2	26	16	7	3	5	27	3	6	.325	.320
Gourley, Walker	R-R	6-0	185	6-28-91	.253	.270	.245	64	233	28	59	13	2	1	27	13	3	9	3	42	9	5	.339	.298
Herrera, Dilson	R-R	5-10	150	3-3-94	.321	.333	.316	7	28	7	9	1	1	2	1	0	0	0	6	1	0	.536	.345
Hornback, Ryan	R-R	6-1	180	7-19-91	.291	.455	.228	22	79	8	23	4	1	0	12	4	1	1	1	18	1	1	.367	.329
Jones, Rodarrick	R-R	6-0	195	7-31-90	.128	.118	.136	14	39	3	5	2	0	0	4	3	2	1	1	9	0	0	.179	.222
Lakind, Jared	L-L	6-2	195	3-9-92	.169	.167	.170	40	124	9	21	5	0	0	8	11	0	1	1	36	1	2	.210	.235
Marte, Starling	R-R	6-0	180	10-9-88	.000	.000	.000	1	5	0	0	0	0	0	0	0	0	0	0	3	0	0	.000	.000
Nivar, Gavi	R-R	6-4	185	9-16-89	.000	.000	—	1	2	0	0	0	0	0	0	0	0	0	0	1	0	0	.000	.000
Rider, Jimmy	R-R	5-8	175	5-9-90	.119	.100	.128	20	59	6	7	1	0	0	1	8	1	1	0	12	3	0	.136	.235
Schwind, Jonathan	R-R	6-0	185	5-30-90	.118	.111	.120	11	34	2	4	0	1	0	2	2	1	1	1	7	0	0	.176	.184
Stallings, Jacob	R-R	6-5	210	12-22-89	.230	.243	.224	66	226	26	52	16	2	1	30	32	1	3	3	73	2	0	.332	.324
Trent, Derek	L-R	6-1	210	11-6-88	.237	.143	.258	15	38	5	9	3	0	1	4	1	0	0	0	13	0	0	.395	.256
Valesente, Dave	R-R	6-2	220	7-15-88	.149	.154	.147	19	47	3	7	0	0	0	4	2	1	1	0	12	1	1	.149	.200
Vasquez, Jesus	R-R	6-2	180	7-9-91	.250	.179	.282	33	124	15	31	8	1	5	10	6	0	0	0	39	3	2	.452	.285
Wood, Eric	R-R	6-2	195	11-22-92	.200	.333	.143	6	20	0	4	1	1	0	6	0	0	0	1	9	0	0	.350	.190

Pitching	B-T	HT	WT	DOB	W	L	ERA	G	GS	CG	SV	IP	H	R	ER	HR	BB	SO	AVG	vLH	vRH	K/9	BB/9
Breedlove, Lance	R-R	6-1	180	9-1-90	1	0	2.90	18	0	0	0	31	25	10	10	1	8	18	.225	.194	.240	5.23	2.32
Burnette, Jake	R-R	6-4	180	8-10-92	1	2	4.71	5	5	0	0	21	22	11	11	2	6	8	.265	.265	.265	3.43	2.57
Castro, Orlando	L-L	5-11	195	3-17-92	1	0	0.00	3	0	0	0	7	5	0	0	0	1	7	.208	.167	.222	9.45	1.35
Cooper, Jordan	B-L	6-3	215	2-16-90	1	2	4.15	11	0	0	4	13	13	8	6	0	1	11	.277	.276	.278	7.62	0.69
Creasy, Jason	R-R	6-4	185	5-13-92	0	5	5.63	14	14	0	0	54	66	39	34	3	20	29	.301	.272	.328	4.80	3.31
De Leon, Emmanuel	B-R	6-1	175	12-25-90	1	1	1.50	12	0	0	2	18	20	9	3	0	9	19	.274	.242	.300	9.50	4.50
Ennis, Justin	L-L	6-1	210	4-20-88	0	0	6.00	8	0	0	0	6	6	4	4	0	4	6	.350	.474	.238	6.00	4.00
Friend, Dalton	L-L	6-3	230	7-4-90	3	2	2.45	18	1	0	0	40	36	15	11	1	8	34	.237	.311	.206	7.59	1.79
Glasnow, Tyler	L-R	6-7	195	8-23-93	0	0	0.00	1	1	0	0	4	4	2	0	0	1	4	.267	.286	.250	9.00	2.25

Hafner, Ryan	R-R	6-6	205	11-22-91	0	2	6.08	7	0	0	0	13	16	10	9	0	7	7	.302	.143	.406	4.73	4.73
Harlan, Tom	L-L	6-6	215	3-7-90	2	6	5.19	20	0	0	0	35	44	24	20	2	11	33	.306	.381	.275	8.57	2.86
Haynes, Kyle	R-R	6-2	190	2-11-91	3	2	4.05	21	0	0	8	27	28	17	12	0	10	32	.269	.238	.290	10.80	3.38
Heredia, Luis	R-R	6-6	205	8-10-94	4	2	2.71	14	14	0	0	66	53	22	20	2	20	40	.224	.227	.220	5.43	2.71
Holmes, Clay	R-R	6-5	230	3-27-93	5	3	2.28	13	13	0	0	59	35	17	15	1	29	34	.176	.203	.158	5.16	4.40
Kleis, Kevin	R-R	6-8	225	8-31-91	1	0	3.65	9	0	0	0	12	12	5	5	0	6	10	.235	.150	.290	7.30	4.38
Kuchno, John	R-R	6-5	210	5-21-91	0	1	9.00	4	0	0	0	5	5	6	5	0	3	6	.238	.333	.111	10.80	5.40
Ludwig, Pat	R-R	6-1	185	10-11-89	3	1	1.05	14	0	0	1	26	18	5	3	0	3	21	.196	.176	.207	7.36	1.05
Montero, Joan	R-R	6-0	186	10-26-88	2	0	0.00	4	0	0	0	8	4	0	0	0	3	13	.138	.111	.182	14.04	3.24
Neverauskas, Dovydas	R-R	6-3	175	1-14-93	0	0	2.25	1	1	0	0	4	2	1	1	0	2	4	.154	.000	.250	9.00	4.50
Perez, Clario	R-R	6-1	185	8-30-92	1	3	5.94	9	4	0	1	33	38	22	22	1	10	23	.299	.296	.301	6.21	2.70
Pevny, Logan	R-R	6-3	190	1-13-92	1	1	2.08	17	0	0	1	26	23	8	6	1	11	17	.240	.333	.146	5.88	3.81
Reyes, Jo-Jo	L-L	6-2	230	11-20-84	0	0	4.50	1	0	0	0	2	3	1	1	0	0	0	.375	1.000	.286	0.00	0.00
Rodriguez, Joely	L-L	6-1	175	11-14-91	3	4	4.50	14	14	0	0	64	74	37	32	2	15	32	.298	.389	.273	4.50	2.11
Sampson, Adrian	R-R	6-3	200	10-7-91	0	1	2.95	11	9	0	0	43	38	19	14	2	17	44	.241	.209	.264	9.28	3.59
Sanchez, Isaac	R-R	6-0	170	10-14-92	0	2	13.50	3	0	0	0	4	6	6	6	0	4	2	.444	.333	.556	4.50	9.00
Smith, Josh	L-L	6-3	194	10-11-89	2	1	3.68	21	0	0	0	29	31	17	12	0	11	23	.270	.158	.325	7.06	3.38
Trepagnier, Bryton	R-R	6-5	180	9-18-91	0	0	3.38	13	0	0	0	3	5	1	1	0	2	1	.385	.667	.143	3.38	6.75

Fielding

Catcher	PCT	G	PO	A	E	DP	PB
Hornback	.968	13	79	11	3	1	1
Schwind	1.000	6	40	4	0	0	2
Stallings	.989	52	327	41	4	3	3
Trent	1.000	3	14	1	0	0	0
Valesente	.952	6	19	1	1	0	4

First Base	PCT	G	PO	A	E	DP
Gonzalez	.995	44	397	23	2	37
Gourley	1.000	1	5	0	0	0
Lakind	.973	38	334	21	10	30
Trent	1.000	1	0	1	0	0

Second Base	PCT	G	PO	A	E	DP
Aponte	.900	2	4	5	1	0
Barrios	.959	14	21	49	3	12
Carvajal	.963	45	102	130	9	33

	PCT	G	PO	A	E	DP
Crumlich	1.000	5	12	12	0	3
Gonzalez	1.000	1	1	2	0	0
Herrera	.923	5	12	24	3	5
Rider	.975	8	13	26	1	4

Third Base	PCT	G	PO	A	E	DP
Barrios	.966	22	10	47	2	6
Crumlich	.938	45	24	96	8	9
Rider	.933	6	3	11	1	0
Valesente	—	1	0	0	0	0
Wood	.875	5	2	5	1	0

Shortstop	PCT	G	PO	A	E	DP
Barrios	1.000	1	1	2	0	1
Carvajal	.783	5	4	14	5	1
Crumlich	1.000	2	2	8	0	1
Diaz	.952	67	98	218	16	35

	PCT	G	PO	A	E	DP
Rider	.750	2	1	5	2	1

Outfield	PCT	G	PO	A	E	DP
Barnes	1.000	37	65	0	0	0
Barrios	1.000	1	2	0	0	0
Crumlich	1.000	15	26	1	0	0
Fortunato	1.000	4	6	0	0	0
Fuselier	.960	28	48	0	2	0
Gaffney	.988	36	79	3	1	2
Gourley	.965	62	103	7	4	1
Jones	.885	14	21	2	3	0
Nivar	.500	1	1	0	1	0
Schwind	1.000	5	8	1	0	1
Valesente	—	3	0	0	0	0
Vasquez	.929	33	55	10	5	2

GCL PIRATES   ROOKIE
GULF COAST LEAGUE

Batting	B-T	HT	WT	DOB	AVG	vLH	vRH	G	AB	R	H	2B	3B	HR	RBI	BB	HBP	SH	SF	SO	SB	CS	SLG	OBP
Bishop, Jorge	R-R	5-10	152	3-12-91	.169	.350	.098	30	71	14	12	2	0	2	9	8	2	2	0	16	12	1	.282	.272
Child, Dylan	R-R	6-1	181	2-21-91	.152	.111	.167	15	33	4	5	1	1	0	2	3	3	1	0	9	1	0	.242	.282
Escobar, Elvis	L-L	5-10	180	9-6-94	.274	.357	.250	54	190	29	52	5	4	2	18	18	1	10	1	46	6	5	.374	.338
Espinal, Edwin	R-R	6-3	210	1-23-94	.244	.150	.261	41	131	11	32	6	1	1	14	3	0	4	0	26	0	1	.328	.261
Evans, Nick	R-R	6-2	220	1-30-86	.167	.000	.500	2	6	0	1	0	0	0	2	0	0	0	0	1	0	0	.167	.167
Herrera, Dilson	R-R	5-10	150	3-3-94	.281	.205	.300	53	199	41	56	11	4	7	27	18	0	10	0	41	11	4	.482	.341
Jhang, Jin-De	L-R	5-11	220	5-17-93	.305	.455	.274	43	128	12	39	5	2	1	23	14	2	1	0	16	1	1	.398	.382
Lambo, Andrew	L-L	6-3	210	8-11-88	.485	.400	.522	9	33	10	16	4	0	1	6	5	1	0	1	5	1	0	.697	.550
Mathisen, Wyatt	R-R	6-1	205	12-30-93	.295	.219	.318	45	139	24	41	8	0	1	15	16	7	2	3	19	10	8	.374	.388
Moroff, Max	B-R	6-0	175	5-13-93	.343	.231	.370	23	67	17	23	3	0	1	7	17	1	2	2	11	7	3	.433	.471
Myles, Candon	L-R	5-10	185	10-24-92	.279	.391	.250	34	111	15	31	2	2	0	11	15	0	1	0	24	12	5	.333	.365
Nivar, Gavi	R-R	6-4	185	9-16-89	.294	.143	.333	14	34	2	10	4	1	0	6	1	0	0	0	7	2	2	.471	.314
Nunez, Gustavo	B-R	5-10	170	1-2-88	.400	.500	.333	2	5	0	2	1	1	0	1	2	0	0	1	1	0	1	1.000	.500
Ramirez, Harold	R-R	5-11	170	9-6-94	.259	.207	.274	39	135	18	35	5	1	1	12	6	4	1	0	20	9	5	.333	.310
Rider, Jimmy	R-R	5-8	175	5-9-90	.239	.200	.250	22	71	15	17	5	0	0	6	9	2	0	1	13	2	1	.310	.337
Ross, Kevin	R-R	6-1	165	9-4-91	.233	.333	.213	21	73	9	17	3	0	1	11	2	3	1	0	10	2	4	.315	.282
Santos, Adalberto	R-R	5-11	185	9-28-87	.289	.375	.267	10	38	6	11	4	1	0	2	4	0	0	0	5	2	0	.447	.386
Schwind, Jonathan	R-R	6-0	185	5-30-90	.240	.143	.278	9	25	3	6	2	0	0	5	3	1	0	0	6	0	2	.320	.345
Urena, Luis	R-R	6-4	198	8-21-92	.200	.133	.217	47	145	18	29	7	4	5	20	12	3	2	0	65	4	5	.407	.275
Vasquez, Jesus	R-R	6-2	185	8-21-92	.246	.200	.260	23	65	11	16	3	0	2	16	5	4	1	2	17	4	5	.385	.329
Wood, Eric	R-R	6-2	195	11-22-92	.287	.345	.269	36	122	21	35	8	1	4	24	14	3	2	1	25	2	4	.467	.371

Pitching	B-T	HT	WT	DOB	W	L	ERA	G	GS	CG	SV	IP	H	R	ER	HR	BB	SO	AVG	vLH	vRH	K/9	BB/9
Brewer, Colten	R-R	6-4	200	10-29-92	1	3	3.24	8	6	0	0	25	24	12	9	3	9	18	.250	.259	.246	6.48	3.24
Cadet, Martires	L-L	6-2	170	5-9-91	3	2	2.89	14	0	0	1	28	19	12	9	2	11	31	.186	.133	.208	9.96	3.54
Campos, Luis	R-R	6-0	188	8-28-92	2	1	4.62	14	0	0	0	25	26	13	13	4	8	17	.271	.211	.310	6.04	2.84
Diaz, Axel	R-R	6-2	170	3-14-91	1	1	4.81	12	11	0	0	39	33	24	21	1	18	32	.232	.239	.229	7.32	4.12
Espinoza, Roberto	R-R	6-1	189	5-7-92	5	0	3.65	16	0	0	0	25	20	10	10	1	13	19	.227	.231	.224	6.93	4.74
Glasnow, Tyler	L-R	6-7	195	8-23-93	0	3	2.10	11	10	0	0	34	19	15	8	3	16	40	.156	.111	.182	10.49	4.19
Herrand, Jhonatan	R-R	6-5	230	9-11-91	1	2	8.10	16	0	0	0	20	22	20	18	1	32	13	.175	.120	.211	5.85	14.40
Jagoditsh, David	B-R	6-7	230	9-4-90	2	1	3.22	15	0	0	1	22	16	13	8	1	17	17	.203	.259	.173	6.85	6.85
Kleis, Kevin	R-R	6-8	225	8-31-91	0	0	3.86	4	0	0	0	5	4	2	2	1	1	1	.267	.286	.250	1.93	1.93
Lee, Wilson	L-R	6-1	180	12-11-91	4	1	3.28	15	0	0	1	25	14	11	9	1	5	22	.269	.160	.309	8.03	1.82
Lodge, Jackson	L-L	6-1	160	10-12-93	1	2	3.08	14	2	0	2	38	41	15	13	2	3	22	.287	.333	.271	5.21	0.71

	B-T	HT	WT	DOB	W	L	ERA	G	GS	CG	SV	IP	H	R	ER	HR	BB	SO	AVG	vLH	vRH		
Lopez, Cesar	R-R	6-3	210	12-3-90	3	2	4.19	11	9	0	0	43	32	22	20	5	11	24	.203	.254	.168	5.02	2.30
Lukashevich, Alexey	R-R	6-4	160	6-1-94	1	0	0.47	13	0	0	0	19	14	2	1	1	8	12	.206	.300	.167	5.68	3.79
Merejo, Aneudy	R-R	5-10	155	11-9-90	1	1	4.32	17	0	0	4	25	32	18	12	1	5	25	.302	.357	.282	9.00	1.80
Neverauskas, Dovydas	R-R	6-3	175	1-14-93	1	1	4.08	10	9	0	0	35	37	21	16	3	18	29	.268	.267	.269	7.39	4.58
Otamendi, Andy	L-L	6-0	163	5-15-93	2	0	3.98	15	3	0	1	32	28	16	14	3	8	25	.235	.282	.213	7.11	2.27
Poytress, Josh	R-L	6-2	185	7-20-90	0	0	0.00	1	0	0	0	1	0	0	0	0	0	1	.000	—	.000	9.00	0.00
Pribanic, Aaron	R-R	6-4	210	9-1-86	1	1	4.40	9	2	0	0	14	14	7	7	0	9	7	.250	.136	.324	4.40	5.65
Reyes, Jo-Jo	L-L	6-2	230	11-20-84	0	0	0.00	3	0	0	0	5	5	5	0	0	1	5	.263	.143	.333	9.00	1.80
Sanchez, Isaac	R-R	6-0	170	10-14-92	3	1	3.00	15	0	0	1	24	20	8	8	0	10	19	.227	.310	.186	7.13	3.75
Sandfort, Jon	B-R	6-6	215	8-27-94	0	1	4.80	8	8	0	0	15	11	8	8	1	10	7	.204	.240	.172	4.20	6.00
Trepagnier, Bryton	R-R	6-5	180	9-18-91	4	1	3.21	17	0	0	1	28	20	11	10	0	9	22	.200	.200	.200	7.07	2.89

Fielding

Catcher	PCT	G	PO	A	E	DP	PB
Child	.978	10	40	4	1	0	2
Jhang	1.000	36	190	26	0	0	11
Mathisen	.994	24	129	27	1	2	10
Schwind	1.000	8	43	5	0	0	2

First Base	PCT	G	PO	A	E	DP
Allie	.988	19	162	4	2	12
Child	1.000	3	14	1	0	0
Espinal	.988	29	230	22	3	22
Evans	1.000	2	20	1	0	1
Vasquez	.971	18	155	12	5	11

Second Base	PCT	G	PO	A	E	DP
Bishop	.950	6	7	12	1	3
Child	1.000	2	3	5	0	1
Herrera	.971	52	95	141	7	28
Rider	1.000	3	6	10	0	3
Ross	1.000	1	3	1	0	2

Third Base	PCT	G	PO	A	E	DP
Allie	.733	9	3	19	8	1
Bishop	1.000	2	1	2	0	1
Espinal	.947	13	9	27	2	2
Ross	.939	14	7	24	2	1
Wood	.964	30	14	67	3	4

Shortstop	PCT	G	PO	A	E	DP
Bishop	.960	20	30	42	3	5
Moroff	.958	21	18	51	3	9
Nunez	1.000	1	1	0	0	0
Rider	.969	20	22	72	3	13
Ross	.857	6	8	16	4	2

Outfield	PCT	G	PO	A	E	DP
Bishop	—		1	0	0	0
Escobar	.991	54	108	2	1	1
Lambo	1.000	8	17	1	0	0
Myles	.962	33	47	4	2	0
Nivar	1.000	11	13	3	0	1
Ramirez	1.000	38	65	1	0	0
Santos	1.000	8	14	0	0	0
Urena	.934	44	66	5	5	2
Vasquez	.833	5	5	0	1	0

DSL PIRATES1 — ROOKIE

DOMINICAN SUMMER LEAGUE

Batting	B-T	HT	WT	DOB	AVG	vLH	vRH	G	AB	R	H	2B	3B	HR	RBI	BB	HBP	SH	SF	SO	SB	CS	SLG	OBP
Adames, Yunerky	L-L	6-1	200	8-26-90	.245	.241	.247	30	106	21	26	8	2	1	19	12	2	1	0	19	5	3	.387	.333
2-team total (29 Pirates2)					.269	—	—	59	208	44	56	18	5	1	35	24	5	4	0	40	10	6	.418	.359
Aquiles, Yunior	R-R	6-3	185	11-11-93	.196	.077	.242	25	46	7	9	0	1	0	4	3	1	1	0	10	2	1	.239	.260
2-team total (32 Pirates2)					.211	—	—	57	142	23	30	2	4	0	11	15	5	3	1	47	9	6	.282	.307
Arribas, Danny	R-R	6-0	185	9-30-92	.308	.333	.297	64	224	39	69	15	0	1	37	29	5	5	8	32	8	4	.388	.387
Barrios, Gustavo	R-R	5-10	157	12-15-93	.282	.364	.250	22	39	8	11	0	1	0	2	3	1	0	0	7	2	0	.333	.349
2-team total (20 Pirates2)					.327	—	—	42	107	22	35	2	2	0	10	11	3	1	0	16	7	6	.383	.405
Benitez, Luis	B-R	5-9	153	12-8-93	.200	.206	.197	30	100	22	20	1	0	0	4	24	1	5	1	21	19	4	.210	.357
Claudio, Anthony	R-R	6-1	180	12-1-92	.400	—	.400	2	5	2	2	0	0	0	1	1	0	0	0	0	0	0	.400	.500
2-team total (35 Pirates2)					.223	—	—	37	94	16	21	2	0	0	6	12	1	0	0	19	3	2	.245	.318
De Aza, Miguel	L-L	6-0	170	11-14-92	.240	.175	.260	54	167	28	40	9	5	1	21	10	5	1	2	31	4	4	.371	.299
De La Mota, Steven	L-L	6-0	190	10-21-93	.231	.000	.300	3	13	0	3	1	0	0	2	0	0	0	0	5	1	0	.308	.231
2-team total (17 Pirates2)					.145	—	—	20	69	12	10	3	0	0	4	6	3	0	0	11	4	0	.188	.244
Esqueda, Carlos	R-R	5-8	135	12-6-91	.264	.294	.250	57	163	33	43	10	3	0	19	23	10	6	1	17	6	4	.302	.386
Garcia, Deybi	R-R	5-11	185	2-11-92	.217	.222	.215	28	83	13	18	7	2	0	6	5	1	1	0	19	0	0	.349	.283
Hurtarte, Dennis	B-R	6-2	221	6-10-93	.191	.200	.189	17	47	6	9	2	0	0	5	5	2	0	0	16	0	0	.234	.296
2-team total (30 Pirates2)					.238	—	—	47	147	15	35	8	0	0	18	15	3	0	1	39	0	3	.293	.319
Marquez, Carlos	L-R	6-2	180	4-29-93	.256	.467	.143	26	43	8	11	2	0	0	2	13	1	0	0	11	2	3	.302	.439
Montilla, Ulises	R-R	5-11	170	5-12-92	.317	.320	.316	53	186	36	59	10	5	1	43	27	5	2	6	19	15	6	.441	.406
2-team total (3 Pirates2)					.320	—	—	56	197	39	63	11	5	2	44	28	5	2	6	20	15	7	.457	.407
Morales, Tomas	R-R	6-0	190	7-30-91	.235	.345	.154	24	68	6	16	3	0	0	10	5	4	1	0	4	1	2	.279	.325
2-team total (13 Pirates2)					.258	—	—	37	93	8	24	4	0	0	13	9	4	3	0	8	1	4	.301	.349
Munoz, Carlos	L-L	5-11	225	6-29-94	.282	.182	.327	22	71	15	20	5	0	1	15	14	3	1	3	13	1	3	.394	.407
2-team total (25 Pirates2)					.261	—	—	47	134	23	35	9	1	2	27	40	7	1	4	18	3	6	.366	.443
Munoz, Edgard	R-R	5-8	150	10-31-91	.229	.292	.212	35	109	15	25	2	1	0	9	12	1	3	0	8	16	8	.266	.311
2-team total (24 Pirates2)					.239	—	—	59	188	23	45	7	1	0	15	25	3	6	1	21	24	14	.287	.336
Ozuna, Carlos	B-R	5-11	162	7-19-93	.257	.265	.252	42	152	28	39	8	3	0	21	18	2	5	0	35	13	5	.349	.343
2-team total (15 Pirates2)					.273	—	—	57	198	36	54	12	3	0	24	26	2	8	0	47	15	10	.364	.363
Padilla, Fredys	R-R	5-11	168	1-12-94	.253	.241	.259	39	87	18	22	6	1	0	7	8	4	1	0	15	2	4	.345	.343
Pena, Ramses	B-R	5-10	152	10-9-92	.226	.277	.207	53	168	34	38	8	1	1	18	27	3	4	0	41	21	6	.304	.343
Perez, Julio	R-R	6-2	220	8-19-91	.226	.167	.244	20	53	6	12	2	0	1	6	7	4	1	1	22	0	1	.321	.354
2-team total (24 Pirates2)					.244	—	—	44	123	21	30	6	0	5	14	14	7	1	1	35	2	3	.415	.352
Polo, Tito	R-R	5-11	180	8-23-94	.298	.300	.296	48	121	26	36	7	1	2	26	16	12	2	1	28	17	5	.421	.427
2-team total (7 Pirates2)					.280	—	—	55	132	27	37	7	1	2	26	16	12	4	1	32	17	7	.394	.404
Rangel, Eduardo	R-R	6-2	188	1-19-93	.257	.167	.276	14	35	2	9	0	1	0	6	5	4	1	1	6	2	2	.343	.400
2-team total (17 Pirates2)					.225	—	—	31	71	7	16	2	2	0	8	6	3	1	1	16	2	2	.338	.349
Reyes, Pablo	R-R	5-10	150	9-5-93	.267	.292	.250	17	60	9	16	7	0	0	8	8	2	1	0	5	3	2	.383	.371
2-team total (42 Pirates2)					.284	—	—	59	183	33	52	18	0	1	23	23	2	6	1	12	18	7	.399	.368
Rivera, Maximo	R-R	5-11	182	12-22-92	.318	.294	.329	31	107	26	34	4	0	1	11	3	4	3	0	14	16	5	.383	.387
2-team total (26 Pirates2)					.367	—	—	57	199	47	73	7	1	4	31	19	5	5	3	26	34	11	.472	.429
Rosario, Henry	L-L	5-9	180	4-5-93	.222	.333	.182	13	45	7	10	3	1	0	7	7	0	3	0	12	2	2	.333	.327
2-team total (36 Pirates2)					.226	—	—	49	164	26	37	6	5	3	27	29	2	6	0	44	6	9	.378	.349

Pitching

Pitching	B-T	HT	WT	DOB	W	L	ERA	G	GS	CG	SV	IP	H	R	ER	HR	BB	SO	AVG	vLH	vRH	K/9	BB/9
Basulto, Omar	L-L	6-3	190	8-24-93	5	1	1.74	17	0	0	1	47	33	17	9	2	15	44	.199	.412	.174	8.49	2.89
Beltrez, Marcus	L-L	6-0	204	10-20-92	1	1	5.73	7	0	0	1	11	7	9	7	0	8	6	.184	.333	.171	4.91	6.55
2-team total (5 Pirates2)					1	1	3.79	12	0	0	2	19	12	12	8	0	11	14	—	—	—	6.63	5.21
Calderin, Oscar	L-L	6-4	175	2-22-91	0	0	0.00	1	0	0	0	2	0	0	0	0	1	0	.000	.000	.000	0.00	4.50
2-team total (11 Pirates2)					2	0	1.96	12	0	0	2	23	20	9	5	0	7	12	—	—	—	4.70	2.74
Del Rosario, Mervin	L-L	6-3	190	3-15-92	3	2	3.43	10	10	0	0	42	40	24	16	2	10	17	.241	.240	.241	3.64	2.14
2-team total (4 Pirates2)					5	2	2.66	14	14	0	0	61	57	27	18	2	11	28	—	—	—	4.13	1.62
Ferreras, Miguel	R-R	6-5	221	9-19-91	1	0	3.65	9	0	0	0	12	11	5	5	0	9	12	.244	.250	.241	8.76	6.57
2-team total (8 Pirates2)					1	0	3.41	17	2	0	2	29	26	12	11	0	22	29	—	—	—	9.00	6.83
Grullon, Adrian	R-R	6-0	180	9-17-92	1	3	4.56	7	0	0	0	26	23	14	13	0	11	19	.242	.250	.239	6.66	3.86
2-team total (1 Pirates2)					1	4	4.23	9	8	0	0	28	23	16	13	0	13	22	—	—	—	7.16	4.23
Henriquez, Cristian	L-L	6-0	175	6-20-92	1	4	3.88	12	10	0	0	46	62	36	20	2	10	27	.318	.281	.325	5.24	1.94
2-team total (3 Pirates2)					2	4	3.03	15	12	0	0	59	67	37	20	2	14	37	—	—	—	5.61	2.12
Lopez, Jovany	L-L	5-10	155	3-11-91	3	2	2.73	16	0	0	4	26	22	15	8	2	13	27	.218	.333	.207	9.23	4.44
Lorenzo, Arquimedes	R-R	6-2	190	5-29-91	3	2	3.98	15	2	0	1	41	37	25	18	1	20	27	.236	.154	.252	5.98	4.43
Mendoza, Andres	R-R	6-2	220	6-3-92	1	0	2.48	16	0	0	0	33	27	12	9	0	14	22	.221	.200	.232	6.06	3.86
Miranda, Luylli	L-L	5-11	180	1-29-92	0	0	3.48	10	0	0	2	21	19	10	8	0	9	16	.244	.125	.257	6.97	3.92
2-team total (8 Pirates2)					2	1	3.57	18	1	0	3	45	42	20	18	1	14	41	—	—	—	8.14	2.78
Mitchell, Richard	R-R	6-2	185	7-29-95	0	0	5.52	7	0	0	0	15	16	12	9	1	8	9	.271	.222	.293	5.52	4.91
2-team total (7 Pirates2)					2	0	5.46	14	0	0	0	28	30	21	17	2	15	16	—	—	—	5.14	4.82
Paredes, Jesus	L-L	6-2	162	1-18-93	0	0	2.16	4	0	0	1	8	2	2	2	1	4	9	.077	.000	.095	9.72	4.32
2-team total (10 Pirates2)					1	1	2.40	14	0	0	3	30	22	10	8	4	16	35	—	—	—	10.50	4.80
Pimentel, Cesilio	L-L	6-2	185	1-5-93	3	3	2.75	14	6	0	3	52	47	21	16	2	18	38	.229	.188	.237	6.54	3.10
Regalado, Jose	R-R	6-3	180	11-19-91	5	1	3.45	14	10	0	1	57	63	32	22	0	16	41	.274	.277	.273	6.44	2.51
Rocha, Oderman	R-R	6-3	165	11-7-92	6	1	1.81	17	4	0	0	50	38	12	10	1	17	53	.211	.185	.222	9.60	3.08
Rodriguez, Leandro	R-R	6-3	188	7-22-93	2	2	3.65	13	10	0	0	44	39	27	18	5	14	33	.227	.235	.225	6.70	2.84
Rodriguez, Ramon	R-R	6-4	196	3-23-93	1	1	1.13	2	2	0	0	8	7	4	1	0	3	6	.233	.000	.280	6.75	3.38
2-team total (8 Pirates2)					1	5	5.10	10	10	0	0	42	55	30	24	2	13	33	—	—	—	7.02	2.76
Rosario, Miguel	R-R	6-0	182	1-30-93	0	0	4.91	1	0	0	0	4	4	2	2	0	1	3	.286	.000	.364	7.36	2.45
2-team total (2 Pirates2)					0	0	2.70	3	0	0	0	7	4	2	2	0	2	6	—	—	—	8.10	2.70
Ruiz, Carlos	R-R	6-2	169	4-13-91	5	2	3.24	17	0	0	3	33	31	15	12	0	13	26	.246	.200	.255	7.02	3.51
Santos, Luis	R-R	6-0	182	2-11-91	3	1	3.16	6	6	0	0	26	15	11	9	0	10	30	.169	.207	.150	10.52	3.51
2-team total (8 Pirates2)					6	3	2.44	14	12	0	0	63	42	24	17	0	20	74	—	—	—	10.63	2.87
Urbina, Dan	R-R	6-3	158	11-27-93	0	0	8.18	3	3	0	0	11	13	10	10	1	6	4	.295	.143	.367	3.27	4.91
2-team total (10 Pirates2)					2	2	4.42	13	12	0	0	53	51	29	26	2	24	31	—	—	—	5.26	4.08
Vera, Eduardo	R-R	6-3	177	7-3-94	0	0	5.68	4	0	0	0	6	11	5	4	0	3	6	.367	.333	.381	7.11	5.68
2-team total (12 Pirates2)					2	0	3.49	16	4	0	0	39	36	18	15	2	16	31	—	—	—	7.22	3.72

Fielding

Catcher	PCT	G	PO	A	E	DP	PB
Arribas	.985	20	111	18	2	0	3
Garcia	.993	24	142	10	1	1	1
Marquez	1.000	19	68	5	0	0	2
Morales	.981	17	91	14	2	1	4
Pena	1.000	1	4	0	0	0	4
Rangel	1.000	10	57	1	0	0	3

First Base	PCT	G	PO	A	E	DP
Adames	.987	9	71	4	1	3
Arribas	.991	22	209	14	2	14
Esqueda	1.000	1	3	0	0	0
Hurtarte	.954	11	76	7	4	5
Munoz	.995	22	198	7	1	8
Perez	.982	15	105	4	2	11

Second Base	PCT	G	PO	A	E	DP
Barrios	1.000	16	15	20	0	3
Esqueda	.950	31	57	57	6	10

Garcia	1.000	1	1	0	0	0
Marquez	1.000	1	1	4	0	1
Montilla	1.000	1	1	0	0	0
Padilla	.974	29	36	40	2	3
Pena	.984	11	35	28	1	5
Rivera	.944	3	9	8	1	0

Third Base	PCT	G	PO	A	E	DP
Arribas	.840	15	12	30	8	2
Esqueda	.911	19	16	35	5	1
Montilla	.917	41	22	121	13	7
Padilla	.500	3	1	0	1	0
Pena	1.000	5	1	4	0	0
Rivera	.714	2	0	5	2	1

Shortstop	PCT	G	PO	A	E	DP
Adames	1.000	1	1	0	0	0
Esqueda	.962	13	18	32	2	2
Ozuna	.900	41	71	128	22	21

Padilla	.667	6	1	3	2	0
Pena	.871	6	14	13	4	1
Reyes	.921	17	19	39	5	5

Outfield	PCT	G	PO	A	E	DP
Adames	.978	22	41	3	1	0
Aquiles	1.000	22	25	0	0	0
Benitez	.962	30	50	1	2	0
Claudio	1.000	1	2	1	0	0
De Aza	.912	40	49	3	5	0
De La Mota	1.000	3	4	0	0	0
Del Rosario	1.000	1	6	0	0	0
Munoz	.957	32	42	3	2	1
Pena	.978	31	44	0	1	0
Polo	.971	45	64	4	2	0
Rivera	1.000	9	10	0	0	0
Rosario	.964	13	25	2	1	0

DSL PIRATES2

DOMINICAN SUMMER LEAGUE

ROOKIE

Batting	B-T	HT	WT	DOB	AVG	vLH	vRH	G	AB	R	H	2B	3B	HR	RBI	BB	HBP	SH	SF	SO	SB	CS	SLG	OBP
Adames, Yunerky	L-L	6-1	200	8-26-90	.294	.417	.278	29	102	23	30	10	3	0	16	12	3	3	0	21	5	3	.451	.385
2-team total (30 Pirates1)					.269	—	—	59	208	44	56	18	5	1	35	24	5	4	0	40	10	6	.418	.359
Aquiles, Yunior	R-R	6-3	185	11-11-93	.219	.105	.247	32	96	16	21	2	3	0	7	12	4	2	1	37	7	5	.302	.327
2-team total (25 Pirates1)					.211	—	—	57	142	23	30	2	4	0	11	15	5	3	1	47	9	6	.282	.307
Barrios, Gustavo	R-R	5-10	157	12-15-93	.353	.143	.377	20	68	14	24	2	1	0	8	8	2	1	0	9	5	6	.412	.436
2-team total (22 Pirates1)					.327	—	—	42	107	22	35	2	2	0	10	11	3	1	0	16	7	6	.383	.405
Cerda, Reggie	R-R	6-0	185	9-10-94	.260	.400	.244	24	50	4	13	1	1	0	8	3	0	0	0	3	0	0	.320	.302
Chourio, Bealyn	R-R	1-1	92	3-31-94	—	—	—	2	0	0	0	0	0	0	0	0	0	0	0	0	0	0	—	—
Claudio, Anthony	R-R	6-1	180	12-1-92	.213	.125	.233	35	89	14	19	2	0	0	5	11	1	0	0	19	3	2	.236	.307
2-team total (2 Pirates1)					.223	—	—	37	94	16	21	2	0	0	6	12	1	0	0	19	3	2	.245	.318
De La Mota, Steven	L-L	6-0	190	10-21-93	.125	.000	.137	17	56	12	7	2	0	0	2	6	3	0	0	6	3	0	.161	.246
2-team total (3 Pirates1)					.145	—	—	20	69	12	10	3	0	0	4	6	3	0	0	11	4	0	.188	.244

Batting	B-T	HT	WT	DOB	AVG	vLH	vRH	G	AB	R	H	2B	3B	HR	RBI	BB	HBP	SH	SF	SO	SB	CS	OBP	SLG
Del Castillo, Angelo	R-R	5-10	174	2-4-92	.266	.333	.250	47	128	15	34	5	1	2	15	8	5	1	1	33	1	1	.367	.331
Galvez, Jordan	R-R	5-11	157	4-23-92	.202	.174	.208	39	124	15	25	3	2	0	6	9	3	5	0	23	6	7	.258	.272
Hurtarte, Dennis	B-R	6-2	221	6-10-93	.260	.067	.294	30	100	9	26	6	0	0	13	10	1	0	1	23	0	3	.320	.330
2-team total (17 Pirates1)					.238	—	—	47	147	15	35	8	0	0	18	15	3	0	1	39	0	3	.293	.319
Lopez, Francis	R-R	6-2	200	6-22-92	.242	.545	.182	25	66	6	16	2	0	1	11	6	2	2	0	29	1	1	.318	.324
Montilla, Ulises	R-R	5-11	170	5-12-92	.364	.500	.333	3	11	3	4	1	0	1	1	1	0	0	0	1	0	0	.727	.417
2-team total (53 Pirates1)					.320	—	—	56	197	39	63	11	5	2	44	28	5	2	6	20	15	7	.457	.407
Morales, Tomas	R-R	6-0	190	7-30-91	.320	.125	.412	13	25	2	8	1	0	0	3	4	0	2	0	4	0	2	.360	.414
2-team total (24 Pirates1)					.258	—	—	37	93	8	24	4	0	0	13	9	4	3	0	8	1	4	.301	.349
Moreno, Manuel	R-R	6-0	165	2-18-92	.300	.000	.300	9	20	1	6	0	0	0	4	2	1	0	0	3	0	0	.300	.391
Munoz, Carlos	L-L	5-11	225	6-29-94	.238	.375	.218	25	63	8	15	4	1	0	12	26	4	0	1	5	2	3	.333	.479
2-team total (22 Pirates1)					.261	—	—	47	134	23	35	9	1	1	27	40	7	1	4	18	3	6	.366	.443
Munoz, Edgard	R-R	5-8	150	10-31-91	.253	.429	.215	24	79	8	20	5	0	0	6	13	2	3	1	13	8	6	.316	.368
2-team total (35 Pirates1)					.239	—	—	59	188	23	45	7	1	0	15	25	3	6	1	21	24	14	.287	.336
Ozuna, Carlos	B-R	5-11	162	7-19-93	.326	.333	.324	15	46	8	15	4	0	0	3	8	0	3	0	12	2	5	.413	.426
2-team total (42 Pirates1)					.273	—	—	57	198	36	54	12	3	0	24	26	2	8	0	47	15	10	.364	.363
Perez, Julio	R-R	6-2	220	8-19-91	.257	.053	.333	24	70	15	18	4	0	4	8	7	3	0	0	13	2	2	.486	.350
2-team total (20 Pirates1)					.244	—	—	44	123	21	30	6	0	5	14	14	7	1	1	35	3	2	.415	.352
Polanco, Yomifer	R-R	6-1	187	2-15-93	.214	.304	.197	42	140	15	30	5	2	1	16	12	3	3	2	26	5	3	.300	.287
Polo, Tito	R-R	5-11	180	8-23-94	.091	.000	.100	7	11	1	1	0	0	0	0	0	0	2	0	4	0	2	.091	.091
2-team total (48 Pirates1)					.280	—	—	55	132	27	37	7	1	2	26	16	12	4	1	32	17	7	.394	.404
Polonia, Rodney	L-R	5-10	160	9-19-92	.215	.227	.213	47	149	18	32	7	2	0	12	10	3	5	1	21	6	3	.289	.276
Rangel, Eduardo	R-R	6-2	188	1-19-93	.194	.200	.194	17	36	5	7	2	0	1	2	3	2	2	0	10	0	0	.333	.293
2-team total (14 Pirates1)					.225	—	—	31	71	7	16	2	0	2	8	6	3	1		16	2	2	.338	.349
Reyes, Pablo	R-R	5-10	150	9-5-93	.293	.222	.305	42	123	24	36	11	0	1	15	15	0	5	1	7	15	5	.407	.367
2-team total (17 Pirates1)					.284	—	—	59	183	33	52	18	0	1	23	23	2	6	1	12	18	7	.399	.368
Reyes, Patrick	R-R	6-0	190	9-11-92	.148	.000	.190	34	81	6	12	0	0	0	6	15	3	2	0	27	0	3	.173	.303
Rivera, Maximo	R-R	5-11	182	12-22-92	.424	.429	.424	26	92	21	39	3	1	3	14	8	2	1	0	12	18	6	.576	.480
2-team total (31 Pirates1)					.367	—	—	57	199	47	73	7	1	4	31	19	5	5	3	26	34	11	.472	.429
Ronco, Jesus	R-R	5-10	171	3-31-94	.174	.167	.176	16	46	2	8	0	0	2	4	3	4	0		11	1	2	.217	.283
Rosario, Henrry	L-L	5-9	180	4-5-93	.227	.316	.210	36	119	19	27	3	4	3	20	22	2	3	0	32	4	7	.395	.357
2-team total (13 Pirates1)					.226	—	—	49	164	26	37	6	5	3	27	29	2	6	0	44	6	9	.378	.349
Salazar, Jose	R-R	6-2	174	7-11-94	.207	.174	.211	54	184	16	38	4	0	0	13	10	6	8	2	34	1	4	.228	.267

Pitching	B-T	HT	WT	DOB	W	L	ERA	G	GS	CG	SV	IP	H	R	ER	HR	BB	SO	AVG	vLH	vRH	K/9	BB/9
Almonte, Brayan	R-R	6-7	188	10-9-91	2	1	5.40	14	0	0	0	18	12	15	11	1	21	10	.203	.222	.195	4.91	10.31
Beltrez, Marcus	L-L	6-4	204	10-20-92	0	0	1.13	5	0	0	1	8	5	3	1	0	3	8	.179	.000	.192	9.00	3.38
2-team total (7 Pirates1)					1	1	3.79	12	0	0	2	19	12	12	8	0	11	14	—		—	6.63	5.21
Calderin, Oscar	L-L	6-4	175	2-22-91	2	0	2.14	11	0	0	2	21	20	9	5	0	6	12	.253	.000	.286	5.14	2.57
2-team total					2	0	1.96	12	0	0	2	23	20	9	5	0	7	12	—		—	4.70	2.74
De Aza, Remy	R-R	6-3	207	9-8-94	1	1	4.64	9	3	0	0	21	16	14	11	0	30	13	.219	.100	.264	5.48	12.66
De Leon, Christopher	R-R	6-0	158	8-2-92	1	1	2.74	16	2	0	2	46	35	15	14	1	28	51	.219	.200	.225	9.98	5.48
Del Rosario, Mervin	L-L	6-3	190	3-15-92	2	0	0.95	4	4	0	0	19	17	3	2	0	1	11	.243	.000	.246	5.21	0.47
2-team total (10 Pirates1)					5	2	2.66	14	14	0	0	61	57	27	18	2	11	28	—		—	4.13	1.62
Ferreras, Miguel	R-R	6-5	221	9-19-91	0	0	3.24	8	2	0	2	17	15	7	6	0	13	17	.259	.235	.268	9.18	7.02
2-team total (9 Pirates1)					1	0	3.41	17	2	0	2	29	26	12	11	0	22	29	—		—	9.00	6.83
Grullon, Adrian	R-R	6-0	180	9-17-92	0	1	0.00	1	0	0	0	2	0	0	2	0	3		.000	.000	.000	13.50	9.00
2-team total (8 Pirates1)					1	4	4.23	9	8	0	0	28	23	16	13	0	13	22	—		—	7.16	4.23
Gutierrez, Alexander	L-L	6-3	213	3-25-93	0	1	7.36	14	0	0	0	18	16	18	15	0	18	11	.232	.286	.226	5.40	8.84
Henriquez, Cristian	L-L	6-0	175	6-20-92	1	0	0.00	3	2	0	0	13	5	1	0	0	4	10	.116	.091	.125	6.92	2.77
2-team total (12 Pirates1)					2	4	3.03	15	12	0	0	59	67	37	20	2	14	37	—		—	5.61	2.12
Marrujo, Jose	R-R	5-10	189	9-21-92	0	2	12.46	6	0	0	2	4	7	6	6	0	3	3	.389	.429	.364	6.23	6.23
Mendoza, Jorge	R-R	6-2	160	6-27-94	3	4	4.50	16	1	0	1	34	39	23	17	1	12	15	.291	.360	.275	3.97	3.18
Miranda, Luylli	L-L	5-11	180	1-29-92	2	1	3.65	8	1	0	1	25	23	10	10	1	5	25	.242	.154	.256	9.12	1.82
2-team total (10 Pirates1)					2	1	3.57	18	1	0	3	45	42	20	18	1	14	41	—		—	8.14	2.78
Mitchell, Richard	R-R	6-2	185	7-29-95	2	0	5.40	7	0	0	0	13	14	9	8	1	7	7	.275	.222	.286	4.73	4.73
2-team total (7 Pirates1)					2	0	5.46	14	0	0	0	28	30	21	17	2	15	16	—		—	5.14	4.82
Paredes, Jesus	L-L	6-2	162	1-18-93	1	1	2.49	10	0	0	2	22	20	8	6	3	12	26	.244	.267	.239	10.80	4.98
2-team total (4 Pirates1)					1	1	2.40	14	0	0	3	30	22	10	8	4	16	35	—		—	10.50	4.80
Rico, Luis	L-L	6-1	180	11-29-93	0	1	7.04	11	9	0	0	23	25	20	18	1	21	16	.313	.333	.310	6.26	8.22
Rodriguez, Francis	R-R	6-2	172	11-28-92	1	4	5.40	16	3	0	1	33	42	29	20	2	21	24	.307	.333	.293	6.48	5.67
Rodriguez, Ramon	R-R	6-4	196	3-23-93	0	4	6.03	8	0	0	0	34	48	26	23	2	10	27	.331	.314	.336	7.08	2.62
2-team total (2 Pirates1)					1	5	5.10	10	10	0	0	42	55	30	24	2	13	33	—		—	7.02	2.76
Rosario, Miguel	R-R	6-0	182	1-30-93	0	0	0.00	2	0	0	0	3	0	0	0	1	3		.000	.000	.000	9.00	3.00
2-team total (1 Pirates1)					0	0	2.70	3	0	0	0	7	4	2	2	0	2	6	—		—	8.10	2.70
Sanchez, Angel	L-L	6-7	190	3-2-93	3	6	3.86	13	11	0	0	44	34	21	19	0	26	29	.219	.200	.222	5.89	5.28
Santiago, Cristian	R-R	6-4	232	6-14-90	2	1	4.44	15	0	0	1	26	25	17	13	3	15	14	.255	.370	.211	4.78	5.13
Santos, Luis	R-R	6-0	182	2-11-91	3	2	1.95	8	6	0	0	37	27	13	8	0	10	44	.194	.245	.163	10.70	2.43
2-team total (6 Pirates1)					6	3	2.44	14	12	0	0	63	42	24	17	0	20	74	—		—	10.63	2.87
Urbina, Dan	R-R	6-3	158	11-27-93	2	3	3.43	14	0	0	2	42	38	19	16	1	18	27	.257	.259	.255	5.79	3.86
2-team total (3 Pirates1)					2	2	4.42	13	12	0	0	53	51	29	26	2	24	31	—		—	5.26	4.08
Vera, Eduardo	R-R	6-3	177	7-3-94	2	0	3.06	12	4	0	0	32	25	13	11	2	12	26	.216	.136	.234	7.24	3.34
2-team total (4 Pirates1)					2	0	3.49	16	4	0	0	39	36	18	15	2	16	31	—		—	7.22	3.72
Vivas, Julio	R-R	6-2	227	10-1-93	4	0	2.36	17	2	0	3	42	28	13	11	0	15	37	.194	.136	.220	7.93	3.21

Fielding

Catcher	PCT	G	PO	A	E	DP	PB
Cerda	.986	19	61	7	1	0	7
Lopez	.975	23	141	17	4	0	4
Morales	.985	11	56	8	1	0	0
Rangel	1.000	14	54	4	0	0	3
Reyes	.972	32	148	25	5	0	6
Ronco	1.000	1	5	2	0	0	0

First Base	PCT	G	PO	A	E	DP
Adames	.988	11	79	3	1	7
Hurtarte	.995	23	199	4	1	13
Munoz	.990	24	201	7	2	18
Perez	.980	18	137	8	3	15
Rivera	1.000	1	1	0	0	0
Salazar	1.000	3	3	0	0	0

Second Base	PCT	G	PO	A	E	DP
Barrios	.962	11	21	29	2	8
Galvez	.964	21	32	48	3	12
Polonia	.960	45	95	95	8	16

Third Base	PCT	G	PO	A	E	DP
Aquiles	1.000	1	2	4	0	0
Galvez	.917	15	7	26	3	1
Montilla	1.000	1	0	1	0	0
Munoz	.970	9	3	29	1	1
Perez	—	1	0	0	0	0
Rangel	1.000	1	4	0	0	0
Rivera	.929	4	6	7	1	0
Ronco	.800	7	6	14	5	1
Salazar	.971	39	32	70	3	9

Shortstop	PCT	G	PO	A	E	DP
Ozuna	.945	15	19	33	3	7
Reyes	.938	38	39	96	9	14
Rivera	.000	1	0	0	2	0
Ronco	.962	4	8	17	1	4
Salazar	.962	16	23	53	3	9

Outfield	PCT	G	PO	A	E	DP
Adames	.923	11	11	1	1	0
Aquiles	.952	31	54	5	3	2
Claudio	.919	32	56	1	5	1
De La Mota	.960	13	23	1	1	1
Del Castillo	.981	44	47	5	1	1
Galvez	—	1	0	0	0	0
Montilla	1.000	1	1	0	0	0
Moreno	1.000	8	17	1	0	0
Munoz	1.000	11	16	1	0	0
Polanco	.985	35	59	5	1	0
Polo	1.000	7	13	1	0	0
Rivera	.957	13	20	2	1	0
Rosario	1.000	35	73	8	0	4
Salazar	1.000	1	2	0	0	0

St. Louis Cardinals

SEASON IN A SENTENCE: In the first season after the departures of Albert Pujols and Tony La Russa, the Cardinals returned to the playoffs and scored dramatic victories in the National League Wild Card Game and Division Series before falling to the Giants in the NL Championship Series.

HIGH POINT: After an action-packed victory over the Braves in the Wild Card Game, the Cardinals staged an entertaining Division Series with the Nationals that went the full five games. In the decisive game Washington jumped out to a 6-0 lead by the third inning. St. Louis clawed its way back but still trailed 7-5 going into the ninth. Closer Drew Storen got two outs after Carlos Beltran's leadoff double but never got the third, as two walks and singles from Daniel Descalso and Pete Kozma put the Cardinals ahead 9-7 and gave them the dramatic series win.

LOW POINT: St. Louis was in contention all year, though the Reds stretched out the lead in the NL Central by season's end. So a true low moment didn't come until the NLCS, when the Cardinals lost three straight games to the Giants after taking a 3-1 series lead. The St. Louis bats suddenly went silent, as San Francisco pitchers allowed only one run over the final three games.

NOTABLE ROOKIES: The Cardinals were a veteran-dominated team, but young players did play key complementary roles, particularly with the pitching staff. Joe Kelly made 16 starts and pitched 107 innings overall, compiling an ERA of 3.53. Hard-throwing youngsters Shelby Miller and Trevor Rosenthal came up later in the year and were key bullpen arms in the postseason, and they'll play much more prominent roles in the future. Similarly, Matt Adams, Matt Carpenter and Kozma played important roles as the team dealt with injuries.

KEY TRANSACTIONS: By far the team's biggest moves were before the season, letting Pujols depart as a free agent and seeing La Russa retire as manager, then signing Beltran. During the season the adjustments were minor, and obtaining reliever Edward Mujica from the Marlins for Zack Cox was the biggest move.

DOWN ON THE FARM: Double-A Springfield was Baseball America's Minor League Team of the Year, going 77-61 and winning the Texas League championship with a prospect-studded roster. Outfielder Oscar Taveras was the league MVP and won a league title for the third straight year.

OPENING DAY PAYROLL: $110.3 million (9th)

PLAYERS OF THE YEAR

MAJOR LEAGUE	MINOR LEAGUE
Yadier Molina	**Oscar Taveras**
c	of
.315/.373/.501	(Double-A)
22 HR, 76 RBIs	.321/.380/.572
5th cons. Gold Glove	Texas League MVP

ORGANIZATION LEADERS

BATTING		*Minimum 250 AB
MAJORS		
* AVG	Yadier Molina	.315
* OPS	Allen Craig	.876
HR	Carlos Beltran	32
RBI	Matt Holliday	102
MINORS		
* AVG	Mike O'Neill, Palm Beach/Springfield	.359
* OBP	Mike O'Neill, Palm Beach/Springfield	.458
* SLG	Oscar Taveras, Springfield	.572
R	Matt Williams, Quad Cities	89
H	Oscar Taveras, Springfield	153
TB	Oscar Taveras, Springfield	273
2B	Oscar Taveras, Springfield	37
3B	Oscar Taveras, Springfield	7
HR	Oscar Taveras, Springfield	23
RBI	Oscar Taveras, Springfield	94
BB	Greg Garcia, Springfield	80
SO	Xavier Scruggs, Springfield	150
SB	Eugenio Velez, Memphis	37

PITCHING		#Minimum 75 IP
MAJORS		
W	Lance Lynn	18
# ERA	Kyle Lohse	2.86
SO	Adam Wainwright	184
SV	Jason Motte	42
MINORS		
W	Seth Maness, Palm Beach/Springfield	14
L	Tyler Lyons, Springfield/Memphis	13
# ERA	Seth Maness, Palm Beach/Springfield	2.97
G	Adam Reifer, Memphis	58
GS	John Gast, Springfield/Memphis	28
SV	Keith Butler, Springfield	25
IP	Seth Maness, Palm Beach/Springfield	169.2
BB	Scott Gorgen, Memphis/Springfield	58
SO	Shelby Miller, Memphis	160
# AVG	Sam Gaviglio, Quad Cities	.247

General Manager: John Mozeliak. **Farm Director:** John Vuch. **Scouting Director:** Dan Kantrovitz.

Class	Team	League	W	L	PCT	Finish	Manager
Majors	St. Louis Cardinals	National	88	74	.543	5th (16)	Mike Matheny
Triple-A	Memphis Redbirds	Pacific Coast	57	87	.396	14th (16)	Ron Warner
Double-A	Springfield Cardinals	Texas	77	61	.558	3rd (8)	Mike Shildt
High A	Palm Beach Cardinals	Florida State	64	72	.471	7th (12)	Johnny Rodriguez
Low A	Quad Cities River Bandits	Midwest	68	71	.489	9th (16)	Luis Aguayo
Short-season	Batavia Muckdogs	New York-Penn	44	32	.579	5th (14)	Dann Bilardello
Rookie	Johnson City Cardinals	Appalachian	39	28	.582	3rd (10)	Oliver Marmol
Rookie	GCL Cardinals	Gulf Coast	34	24	.586	3rd (14)	Steve Turco
Overall 2012 Minor League Record			383	375	.505	15th (30)	

ORGANIZATION STATISTICS

ST. LOUIS CARDINALS

NATIONAL LEAGUE

Batting	B-T	HT	WT	DOB	AVG	vLH	vRH	G	AB	R	H	2B	3B	HR	RBI	BB	HBP	SH	SF	SO	SB	CS	SLG	OBP
Adams, Matt	L-R	6-3	230	8-31-88	.244	.150	.273	27	86	8	21	6	0	2	13	5	0	0	0	24	0	0	.384	.286
Anderson, Bryan	L-R	6-1	200	12-16-86	.250	1.000	.182	10	12	2	3	1	0	0	1	1	0	0	0	6	1	0	.333	.357
Beltran, Carlos	B-R	6-1	215	4-24-77	.269	.276	.266	151	547	83	147	26	1	32	97	65	2	1	4	124	13	6	.495	.346
Berkman, Lance	B-L	6-1	220	2-10-76	.259	.176	.281	32	81	12	21	7	1	2	7	14	2	0	0	19	2	0	.444	.381
Carpenter, Matt	L-R	6-3	200	11-26-85	.294	.265	.308	114	296	44	87	22	5	6	46	34	3	0	7	63	1	1	.463	.365
Chambers, Adron	L-L	5-10	185	10-8-86	.222	.077	.268	41	54	4	12	0	2	0	4	5	1	2	0	18	2	1	.296	.300
Craig, Allen	R-R	6-2	210	7-18-84	.307	.354	.289	119	469	76	144	35	0	22	92	37	1	0	7	89	2	1	.522	.354
Cruz, Tony	R-R	5-11	205	8-18-86	.254	.195	.282	51	126	11	32	9	1	1	11	3	0	0	2	19	0	1	.365	.267
Descalso, Daniel	L-R	5-10	190	10-19-86	.227	.309	.200	143	374	41	85	10	7	4	26	37	5	7	3	83	6	3	.324	.303
Freese, David	R-R	6-2	220	4-28-83	.293	.320	.285	144	501	70	147	25	1	20	79	57	7	0	2	122	3	3	.467	.372
Furcal, Rafael	B-R	5-8	190	10-24-77	.264	.284	.255	121	477	69	126	18	3	5	49	44	1	5	4	57	12	4	.346	.325
Greene, Tyler	R-R	6-2	190	8-17-83	.218	.245	.188	77	179	16	39	9	2	4	19	13	1	2	2	56	9	2	.358	.272
2-team total (39 Houston)					.230	—	—	116	305	34	70	15	2	11	30	19	1	2	3	95	12	4	.400	.274
Hill, Steve	R-R	5-11	200	3-14-85	.200	.333	.000	9	10	1	2	1	0	0	0	0	0	0	0	3	0	0	.300	.200
Holliday, Matt	R-R	6-4	235	1-15-80	.295	.316	.288	157	599	95	177	36	2	27	102	75	9	0	5	132	4	4	.497	.379
Jackson, Ryan	R-R	6-3	180	5-10-88	.118	.143	.100	13	17	2	2	0	0	0	0	1	0	0	0	3	0	0	.118	.167
Jay, Jon	L-L	5-11	200	3-15-85	.305	.281	.314	117	443	70	135	22	4	4	40	34	15	9	1	71	19	7	.400	.373
Komatsu, Erik	L-L	5-10	175	10-1-87	.211	1.000	.167	15	19	3	4	0	0	0	2	0	0	0	0	2	0	0	.211	.286
Kozma, Pete	R-R	6-0	170	4-11-88	.333	.333	.333	26	72	11	24	5	3	2	14	7	0	1	2	19	2	0	.569	.383
Molina, Yadier	R-R	5-11	225	7-13-82	.315	.342	.307	138	505	65	159	28	0	22	76	45	5	3	5	55	12	3	.501	.373
Robinson, Shane	R-R	5-9	160	10-30-84	.253	.256	.250	102	166	20	42	8	0	3	16	16	0	0	1	32	1	0	.355	.309
Schumaker, Skip	L-R	5-10	195	2-3-80	.276	.158	.295	107	272	37	75	14	4	1	28	27	1	0	3	50	1	1	.368	.339

Pitching	B-T	HT	WT	DOB	W	L	ERA	G	GS	CG	SV	IP	H	R	ER	HR	BB	SO	AVG	vLH	vRH	K/9	BB/9
Boggs, Mitchell	R-R	6-4	215	2-15-84	4	1	2.21	78	0	0	0	73	56	20	18	5	21	58	.211	.241	.191	7.12	2.58
Browning, Barret	L-L	6-2	205	12-28-84	1	3	5.12	22	0	0	0	19	18	11	11	2	7	11	.247	.194	.297	5.12	3.26
Carpenter, Chris	R-R	6-6	230	4-27-75	0	2	3.71	3	3	0	0	17	16	7	7	2	3	12	.242	.385	.150	6.35	1.59
Cleto, Maikel	R-R	6-3	235	5-1-89	0	0	7.00	9	0	0	0	9	13	7	7	4	2	15	.342	.280	.462	15.00	2.00
Dickson, Brandon	R-R	6-5	190	11-3-84	0	0	7.11	4	0	0	0	6	10	7	5	2	2	6	.333	.455	.263	8.53	2.84
Fick, Chuckie	R-R	6-5	185	11-20-85	0	0	5.40	2	0	0	0	2	3	1	1	0	1	0	.429	.500	.000	0.00	5.40
2-team total (18 Houston)					0	1	4.38	20	0	0	0	25	27	14	12	4	18	17	—	—	—	6.20	6.57
Freeman, Sam	R-L	5-11	170	6-24-87	0	2	5.40	24	0	0	0	20	17	13	12	2	10	18	.230	.290	.186	8.10	4.50
Fuentes, Brian	L-L	6-4	230	8-9-75	0	0	9.00	6	0	0	0	5	6	5	5	1	5	6	.300	.167	.357	10.80	9.00
Garcia, Jaime	L-L	6-2	215	7-8-86	7	7	3.92	20	20	0	0	122	136	58	53	7	30	98	.289	.260	.297	7.25	2.22
Kelly, Joe	R-R	6-1	185	6-9-88	5	7	3.53	24	16	0	0	107	112	50	42	10	36	75	.271	.318	.236	6.31	3.03
Lohse, Kyle	R-R	6-2	210	10-4-78	16	3	2.86	33	33	0	0	211	192	74	67	19	38	143	.239	.253	.226	6.10	1.62
Lynn, Lance	R-R	6-5	250	5-12-87	18	7	3.78	35	29	0	0	176	168	76	74	16	64	180	.253	.272	.237	9.20	3.27
Marte, Victor	R-R	6-2	255	11-8-80	3	2	4.91	48	0	0	0	40	51	22	22	6	14	36	.305	.318	.297	8.03	3.12
McClellan, Kyle	R-R	6-2	215	6-12-84	0	1	5.30	16	0	0	0	19	16	11	11	2	9	11	.222	.200	.238	5.30	4.34
Miller, Shelby	R-R	6-3	195	10-10-90	1	0	1.32	6	1	0	0	14	9	2	2	0	4	16	.184	.167	.194	10.54	2.63
Motte, Jason	R-R	6-0	200	6-22-82	4	5	2.75	67	0	0	42	72	49	23	22	9	17	86	.191	.122	.254	10.75	2.13
Mujica, Edward	R-R	6-3	225	5-10-84	0	0	1.03	29	0	0	0	26	20	3	3	1	3	21	.215	.195	.231	7.18	1.03
2-team total (41 Miami)					0	3	3.03	70	0	0	2	65	56	24	22	7	12	47	—	—	—	6.47	1.65
Romero, J.C.	B-L	5-11	205	6-4-76	0	0	10.13	11	0	0	0	8	14	9	9	3	5	2	.368	.353	.381	5.63	2.25
Rosenthal, Trevor	R-R	6-2	190	5-29-90	0	2	2.78	19	0	0	0	23	14	7	7	2	7	25	.175	.143	.200	9.93	2.78
Rzepczynski, Marc	L-L	6-1	205	8-29-85	1	3	4.24	70	0	0	0	47	46	22	22	7	17	33	.257	.255	.259	6.36	3.28
Salas, Fernando	R-R	6-2	200	5-30-85	1	4	4.30	65	0	0	0	59	56	28	28	5	27	60	.251	.270	.239	9.20	4.14
Sanchez, Eduardo	R-R	5-11	170	2-16-89	0	1	6.60	17	0	0	0	15	11	11	11	2	13	13	.204	.226	.174	7.80	7.80
Wainwright, Adam	R-R	6-7	230	8-30-81	14	13	3.94	32	32	3	0	199	196	96	87	15	52	184	.259	.261	.256	8.34	2.36
Westbrook, Jake	R-R	6-3	210	9-29-77	13	11	3.97	28	28	1	0	175	191	85	77	12	52	106	.282	.297	.269	5.46	2.68

Fielding

Catcher	PCT	G	PO	A	E	DP	PB
Anderson	1.000	2	9	0	0	0	0
Cruz	.993	47	255	23	2	3	3
Molina	.997	136	962	88	3	12	6

First Base	PCT	G	PO	A	E	DP
Adams	.987	24	210	12	3	13

	PCT	G	PO	A	E	DP
Anderson	.857	1	5	1	1	1
Berkman	.979	23	170	13	4	22
Carpenter	.991	44	316	12	3	32
Craig	.995	91	761	40	4	64
Cruz	1.000	2	1	1	0	2
Descalso	1.000	5	20	3	0	1
Hill	1.000	1	1	0	0	0
Molina	1.000	3	11	2	0	0
Second Base	**PCT**	**G**	**PO**	**A**	**E**	**DP**
Carpenter	1.000	5	3	4	0	2
Descalso	.986	96	137	225	5	47
Greene	.980	55	64	129	4	26

	PCT	G	PO	A	E	DP
Jackson	.929	8	2	11	1	1
Kozma	1.000	1	3	0	0	0
Schumaker	.984	61	101	143	4	35
Third Base	**PCT**	**G**	**PO**	**A**	**E**	**DP**
Carpenter	.950	33	13	44	3	3
Descalso	.926	22	8	17	2	0
Freese	.949	134	77	259	18	29
Shortstop	**PCT**	**G**	**PO**	**A**	**E**	**DP**
Descalso	.921	26	24	69	8	17
Furcal	.972	120	173	349	15	68
Greene	.957	9	8	14	1	2
Jackson	—	1	0	0	0	0

	PCT	G	PO	A	E	DP
Kozma	.965	25	22	60	3	10
Outfield	**PCT**	**G**	**PO**	**A**	**E**	**DP**
Beltran	.991	133	221	10	2	0
Carpenter	.870	21	19	1	3	0
Chambers	1.000	26	32	1	0	0
Craig	1.000	30	41	1	0	0
Greene	1.000	3	1	0	0	0
Holliday	.987	152	226	6	3	1
Jay	1.000	116	291	1	0	0
Komatsu	1.000	7	9	0	0	0
Robinson	.975	60	74	3	2	1
Schumaker	1.000	24	36	1	0	0

MEMPHIS REDBIRDS — TRIPLE-A

PACIFIC COAST LEAGUE

Batting	B-T	HT	WT	DOB	AVG	vLH	vRH	G	AB	R	H	2B	3B	HR	RBI	BB	HBP	SH	SF	SO	SB	CS	SLG	OBP
Adams, Matt	L-R	6-3	230	8-31-88	.329	.319	.333	67	258	41	85	22	0	18	50	15	0	0	3	57	3	1	.624	.362
Albitz, Vance	R-R	5-7	170	1-31-88	.295	.455	.242	13	44	6	13	2	0	1	6	5	1	0	0	5	1	1	.409	.380
Anderson, Bryan	L-R	6-1	200	12-16-86	.225	.160	.249	100	347	35	78	12	1	6	35	36	4	1	4	89	0	0	.317	.302
Bates, Aaron	R-R	6-4	230	3-10-84	.164	.294	.105	21	55	5	9	3	0	0	1	3	0	0	0	17	0	0	.218	.207
Berkman, Lance	B-L	6-1	220	2-10-76	.235	.000	.444	6	17	1	4	1	0	0	1	3	0	0	0	3	0	0	.294	.350
Canham, Mitch	L-R	6-2	205	9-25-84	.125	.077	.182	18	48	4	6	0	0	0	1	3	0	0	1	11	0	0	.125	.192
Carpenter, Matt	L-R	6-3	200	11-26-85	.143	.250	.000	3	7	1	1	0	0	0	0	2	0	0	0	2	0	0	.143	.333
Cazana, Amaury	R-R	6-1	210	9-2-78	.238	.175	.279	30	101	6	24	3	0	2	13	9	0	0	1	27	0	0	.327	.297
Chambers, Adron	L-L	5-10	185	10-8-86	.319	.306	.324	96	357	60	114	17	2	3	44	51	4	2	5	80	13	4	.403	.405
Cox, Zack	L-R	6-0	215	5-9-89	.254	.258	.252	84	299	27	76	23	0	9	30	12	5	0	0	63	1	0	.421	.294
Craig, Allen	R-R	6-2	210	7-18-84	.353	.333	.400	4	17	3	6	0	0	2	7	0	0	0	0	2	0	0	.706	.353
Curtis, Jermaine	R-R	5-11	190	7-10-87	.276	.143	.400	17	29	7	8	1	0	0	1	9	0	0	0	4	0	0	.310	.447
De La Cruz, Luis	R-R	5-9	165	5-6-89	.000	.000	.000	1	4	0	0	0	0	0	0	0	0	0	0	0	0	0	.000	.000
Derba, Nick	R-R	5-10	190	9-9-85	.138	.147	.133	36	109	8	15	3	0	1	7	12	0	0	1	33	0	0	.193	.221
Garcia, Jose	R-R	5-11	170	2-11-88	.255	.154	.289	16	51	4	13	2	0	1	4	3	2	0	0	16	1	0	.353	.321
Hamilton, Mark	L-L	6-4	220	7-29-84	.231	.215	.238	90	303	43	70	12	0	15	51	51	1	0	4	84	1	0	.419	.340
Hill, Steve	R-R	5-11	200	3-14-85	.266	.250	.274	87	301	52	80	16	0	17	52	25	3	0	2	74	0	1	.488	.326
Hunter, Cedric	L-L	6-0	185	3-10-88	.268	.255	.273	129	355	40	95	19	2	5	44	44	6	3	4	43	7	4	.375	.355
Jackson, Ryan	R-R	6-3	180	5-10-88	.272	.308	.254	117	445	60	121	23	1	10	47	43	0	12	3	75	2	0	.396	.334
Jay, Jon	L-L	5-11	200	3-15-85	.429	.429	.000	2	7	3	3	0	1	1	3	1	0	0	0	0	0	0	1.143	.500
Kozma, Pete	R-R	6-0	170	4-11-88	.232	.205	.244	131	448	61	104	16	3	11	63	41	0	4	7	74	7	4	.355	.292
Montanez, Lou	R-R	6-1	195	12-15-81	.259	.305	.238	84	263	32	68	9	0	2	25	34	5	0	4	39	1	3	.316	.350
Peterson, Brock	R-R	6-3	215	11-20-83	.250	.294	.236	21	72	10	18	3	1	5	16	8	0	0	0	17	0	1	.528	.325
Robinson, Shane	R-R	5-9	160	10-30-84	.300	.111	.365	19	70	15	21	4	2	0	3	8	2	0	0	15	5	0	.414	.388
Romak, Jamie	R-R	6-2	220	9-30-85	.277	.256	.290	31	112	9	31	8	1	0	12	8	1	1	2	24	0	0	.366	.325
2-team total (11 Omaha)					.247	—	—	42	146	14	36	10	1	0	14	10	2	1	2	32	0	0	.329	.300
Schumaker, Skip	L-R	5-10	195	2-3-80	.286	.200	.313	7	21	5	6	2	0	0	4	0	0	0	0	3	1	0	.381	.400
Swauger, Chris	L-L	6-0	195	8-11-86	.222	.200	.231	18	36	4	8	1	0	0	3	8	1	0	0	5	0	0	.250	.282
Velez, Eugenio	B-R	6-1	170	5-16-82	.280	.255	.294	136	457	70	128	34	5	11	58	51	5	2	1	99	37	9	.449	.358
Wittels, Garrett	R-R	6-1	200	5-11-90	.500	.500	.500	4	4	1	2	0	1	0	2	0	0	0	0	0	0	0	1.000	.500
Young, Matt	L-R	5-8	175	10-3-82	.442	.333	.471	13	43	7	19	2	0	0	5	3	0	0	0	12	2	0	.488	.478
Zawadzki, Lance	B-R	5-10	180	5-26-85	.281	.200	.296	8	32	2	9	1	1	0	3	1	0	0	0	6	1	0	.375	.303
2-team total (5 Albuquerque)					.200	—	—	13	45	3	9	1	1	0	3	2	0	1	0	10	1	0	.267	.234

Pitching	B-T	HT	WT	DOB	W	L	ERA	G	GS	CG	SV	IP	H	R	ER	HR	BB	SO	AVG	vLH	vRH	K/9	BB/9
Additon, Nick	L-L	6-5	215	12-16-87	3	8	4.55	16	16	0	0	87	92	47	44	10	41	81	.271	.321	.256	8.38	4.24
Blazek, Michael	R-R	6-0	180	3-16-89	0	1	10.80	2	1	0	0	5	6	4	4	1	2	1	.462	.333	.750	2.70	5.40
Broderick, Brian	R-R	6-6	205	9-1-86	3	8	7.32	20	14	0	0	79	118	78	64	13	32	55	.347	.340	.353	6.29	3.66
Browning, Barret	L-L	6-2	205	12-28-84	2	3	1.73	35	0	0	1	42	28	11	8	1	18	38	.194	.230	.169	8.21	3.89
Cleto, Maikel	R-R	6-3	235	5-1-89	2	5	5.37	45	0	0	2	54	51	35	32	4	22	66	.254	.275	.232	11.07	3.69
Dickson, Brandon	R-R	6-5	190	11-3-84	5	11	3.63	23	23	0	0	141	151	67	57	17	27	104	.271	.294	.245	6.62	1.72
Fick, Chuckie	R-R	6-5	185	11-20-85	1	1	4.68	42	0	0	2	42	49	23	22	6	13	20	.290	.329	.258	4.25	2.76
2-team total (5 Oklahoma City)					2	2	5.09	47	0	0	3	46	52	27	26	6	15	23	—	—		4.50	2.93
Freeman, Sam	R-L	5-11	170	6-24-87	2	2	2.08	27	0	0	0	30	25	7	7	3	12	27	.227	.196	.250	8.01	3.56
Garcia, Jaime	L-L	6-2	215	7-8-86	0	1	3.60	1	1	0	0	5	4	2	2	1	3	8	.222	.300	.125	14.40	5.40
Gast, John	L-L	6-1	195	2-16-89	9	5	5.10	20	20	0	0	109	124	69	62	10	42	86	.286	.268	.294	7.08	3.46
Gaub, John	R-L	6-2	210	4-28-85	0	3	6.68	33	0	0	1	32	40	24	24	5	13	32	.303	.260	.329	8.91	3.62
2-team total (5 Round Rock)					0	3	5.89	38	0	0	1	37	43	24	24	5	15	36	—	—		5.84	3.68
Gorgen, Scott	R-R	5-10	190	1-27-87	1	2	4.14	8	8	0	0	37	32	20	17	3	19	26	.237	.231	.243	6.32	4.62
Greenwood, Nick	R-L	6-1	180	9-28-87	4	3	4.40	49	4	0	0	78	87	43	38	6	23	47	.288	.260	.302	5.45	2.67
Kelly, Joe	R-R	6-1	185	6-9-88	2	5	2.86	12	12	0	0	72	75	29	23	2	21	45	.278	.275	.281	5.60	2.61
Lyons, Tyler	B-L	6-2	195	2-21-88	4	9	4.28	15	15	3	0	88	87	42	42	9	18	89	.258	.245	.264	9.07	1.83
Marte, Victor	R-R	6-2	255	11-8-80	0	2	3.00	12	0	0	3	12	9	4	4	0	7	10	.214	.222	.208	7.50	5.25
Miller, Shelby	R-R	6-3	195	10-10-90	11	10	4.74	27	27	0	0	137	138	78	72	24	50	160	.260	.274	.244	10.54	3.29
Reifer, Adam	R-R	6-2	195	6-3-86	1	4	4.90	58	0	0	2	64	64	40	35	11	20	44	.260	.293	.231	6.16	2.80
Rondon, Jorge	R-R	6-1	175	9-16-88	0	1	3.60	13	0	0	1	15	12	6	6	1	8	20	.214	.222	.207	12.00	4.80
Rosenthal, Trevor	R-R	6-2	190	5-29-90	3	3	4.20	3	3	0	0	15	11	7	7	1	5	21	.208	.222	.192	12.60	3.00
Salas, Fernando	R-R	6-2	200	5-30-85	1	0	9.00	4	0	0	1	4	6	4	4	2	0	5	.353	.222	.500	11.25	0.00

Sanchez, Eduardo	R-R	5-11	170	2-16-89	2	3	5.86	30	0	0	9	28	27	19	18	3	21	26	.252	.304	.196	8.46	6.83
Swindle, R.J.	L-L	6-3	190	7-7-83	1	1	4.76	13	0	0	0	11	12	10	6	3	3	11	.273	.261	.286	8.74	2.38
Todd, Jess	R-R	5-11	210	4-20-86	2	2	4.34	47	0	0	2	66	80	35	32	6	21	73	.300	.324	.283	9.90	2.85
Zavada, Clay	L-L	6-1	185	6-28-84	0	0	12.60	9	0	0	0	10	12	16	14	2	6	5	.279	.100	.333	4.50	5.40

Fielding

Catcher	PCT	G	PO	A	E	DP	PB
Anderson	.994	98	722	45	5	6	3
Canham	.969	10	61	2	2	0	1
De La Cruz	1.000	1	9	0	0	0	0
Derba	.993	33	249	20	2	4	2
Hill	.959	10	66	4	3	0	3

First Base	PCT	G	PO	A	E	DP
Adams	.992	59	486	37	4	46
Bates	.974	9	71	3	2	7
Berkman	.969	5	25	6	1	5
Craig	1.000	2	19	2	0	1
Derba	—	1	0	0	0	0
Hamilton	.991	14	100	5	1	8
Hill	1.000	29	207	21	0	22
Peterson	1.000	19	114	18	0	14
Romak	1.000	16	137	9	0	19
Swauger	.971	4	32	1	1	6

Second Base	PCT	G	PO	A	E	DP
Albitz	1.000	12	26	40	0	9
Curtis	.000	1	0	0	1	0

Garcia	.889	7	9	7	2	3
Jackson	1.000	13	25	25	0	9
Kozma	.976	84	148	258	10	63
Schumaker	1.000	4	3	1	0	1
Velez	1.000	34	48	75	0	20
Zawadzki	1.000	6	11	13	0	2

Third Base	PCT	G	PO	A	E	DP
Carpenter	—	1	0	0	0	0
Cox	.918	77	37	109	13	11
Curtis	.909	7	3	7	1	1
Garcia	.923	6	3	9	1	1
Hill	.902	20	15	22	4	5
Jackson	1.000	1	1	1	0	1
Velez	.838	50	22	61	16	8
Wittels	—	1	0	0	0	0

Shortstop	PCT	G	PO	A	E	DP
Garcia	1.000	2	0	4	0	1
Jackson	.973	102	160	266	12	65
Kozma	.951	45	44	92	7	18
Zawadzki	1.000	2	2	3	0	2

Outfield	PCT	G	PO	A	E	DP
Bates	.000	1	0	0	1	0
Canham	.833	7	5	0	1	0
Carpenter	1.000	2	1	0	0	0
Cazana	1.000	24	40	2	0	2
Chambers	.996	91	218	5	1	1
Curtis	1.000	3	6	0	0	0
Derba	—	1	0	0	0	0
Garcia	1.000	2	3	0	0	0
Hamilton	.986	51	72	1	1	0
Hill	.947	17	36	0	2	0
Hunter	.989	109	173	1	2	0
Jay	1.000	2	5	0	0	0
Montanez	.984	71	116	5	2	1
Robinson	1.000	18	34	0	0	0
Romak	.963	13	25	1	1	1
Schumaker	1.000	3	4	1	0	0
Swauger	.800	6	4	0	1	0
Velez	.966	55	84	2	3	0
Young	1.000	10	10	1	0	0

SPRINGFIELD CARDINALS

DOUBLE-A

TEXAS LEAGUE

Batting	B-T	HT	WT	DOB	AVG	vLH	vRH	G	AB	R	H	2B	3B	HR	RBI	BB	HBP	SH	SF	SO	SB	CS	SLG	OBP
Ahmady, Alan	R-R	5-11	200	12-14-87	.217	.500	.158	14	23	4	5	2	0	0	1	3	1	0	0	8	0	0	.304	.333
Albitz, Vance	R-R	5-7	170	1-31-88	.109	.000	.150	25	55	1	6	1	0	0	2	6	0	1	1	6	0	0	.127	.194
Carpenter, Matt	L-R	6-3	200	11-26-85	.300	.500	.250	3	10	3	3	0	0	1	3	3	0	0	0	1	0	1	.600	.462
Conley, Kyle	R-R	6-4	210	5-7-87	.226	.264	.208	46	159	23	36	8	0	9	30	18	0	0	1	49	0	0	.447	.303
Curtis, Jermaine	R-R	5-11	190	7-10-87	.313	.289	.321	96	368	61	115	19	1	1	24	47	19	5	1	51	6	1	.378	.416
Derba, Nick	R-R	5-10	190	9-9-85	.205	.308	.158	25	83	9	17	3	0	1	6	8	0	1	2	22	0	0	.277	.269
Garcia, Greg	L-R	6-0	175	8-8-89	.284	.247	.294	124	412	81	117	20	3	10	51	80	7	4	1	83	10	5	.420	.408
Garcia, Jose	R-R	5-11	170	2-11-88	.261	.211	.282	74	253	32	66	10	0	3	17	20	3	1	1	50	10	2	.336	.321
Kruml, Ray	L-R	5-11	175	8-5-85	.161	.143	.167	16	31	2	5	1	0	0	3	3	0	0	1	10	1	1	.194	.229
Melker, Adam	L-L	5-11	180	1-31-88	.278	.250	.286	126	352	50	98	14	1	10	35	36	2	5	3	75	6	3	.409	.346
O'Neill, Mike	L-L	5-9	170	2-12-88	.563	.400	.636	13	32	8	18	5	0	0	5	8	1	0	1	2	3	0	.719	.643
Perez, Audry	R-R	5-9	180	12-23-88	.263	.299	.253	81	312	28	82	12	1	4	42	6	3	1	3	58	0	0	.346	.281
Pham, Tommy	R-R	6-1	175	3-8-88	.154	.250	.129	12	39	3	6	2	0	1	3	4	0	0	0	19	0	0	.282	.233
Pritchard, Neal	R-R	6-0	195	2-21-89	.167	.000	.200	5	12	1	2	0	0	1	0	1	0	0	0	6	0	0	.417	.231
Romak, Jamie	R-R	6-2	220	9-30-85	.267	.188	.287	64	243	46	65	11	2	10	42	31	4	0	3	53	6	2	.453	.356
Rosario, Rainel	R-R	6-1	188	3-29-89	.214	.136	.265	22	56	10	12	2	0	1	6	11	0	0	0	23	1	0	.304	.343
Scruggs, Xavier	R-R	6-1	210	9-23-87	.235	.264	.225	130	452	64	106	26	1	22	91	58	9	0	3	150	8	4	.442	.331
Shaffer, Jake	L-L	6-1	190	8-16-87	.262	.250	.266	77	260	26	68	14	0	5	38	20	1	3	1	47	3	1	.373	.316
Swauger, Chris	L-L	6-0	195	8-11-86	.296	.250	.311	85	321	42	95	11	3	13	60	21	5	0	5	69	2	4	.470	.344
Tartamella, Travis	R-R	5-11	200	12-7-87	.159	.118	.173	37	132	8	21	6	0	1	7	4	2	1	0	37	0	0	.227	.196
Taveras, Oscar	L-L	6-2	180	6-19-92	.321	.305	.327	124	477	83	153	37	7	23	94	42	7	0	5	56	10	1	.572	.380
Valera, Breyvic	B-R	5-11	160	8-1-92	.200	.000	.250	3	5	2	1	0	0	0	1	0	0	0	0	0	0	0	.200	.200
Vasquez, Niko	R-R	6-0	170	2-26-89	.146	.200	.132	17	48	1	7	1	0	0	2	5	0	0	0	17	0	0	.167	.226
Wittels, Garrett	R-R	6-1	200	9-29-90	.000	.000	—	1	1	0	0	0	0	0	0	0	0	0	0	0	0	0	.000	.000
Wong, Kolten	L-R	5-9	190	10-10-90	.287	.281	.289	126	523	79	150	23	6	9	52	44	7	2	3	74	21	11	.405	.348

Pitching	B-T	HT	WT	DOB	W	L	ERA	G	GS	CG	SV	IP	H	R	ER	HR	BB	SO	AVG	vLH	vRH	K/9	BB/9
Blazek, Michael	R-R	6-0	180	3-16-89	5	8	4.16	40	7	0	0	80	61	37	37	11	34	83	.213	.229	.204	9.34	3.83
Butler, Keith	R-R	6-0	180	1-30-89	5	1	2.76	53	0	0	25	59	53	22	18	5	23	59	.242	.303	.216	9.05	3.53
Castillo, Richard	R-R	5-11	165	10-11-89	7	5	3.76	19	19	0	0	110	126	49	46	8	32	65	.297	.317	.288	5.32	2.62
Corrigan, Chris	R-R	6-2	155	12-24-87	0	1	7.36	4	0	0	0	4	6	3	3	0	2	4	.353	.400	.333	9.82	4.91
Ferrara, Anthony	R-L	6-1	175	9-2-89	0	0	4.50	3	3	0	0	10	6	6	5	0	11	10	.188	.000	.194	9.00	9.90
Fornataro, Eric	R-R	6-1	215	1-2-88	3	3	2.39	57	0	0	5	68	55	21	18	1	17	41	.226	.192	.241	5.45	2.26
Freeman, Sam	R-L	5-11	170	6-24-87	1	3	1.56	15	0	0	1	17	12	5	3	1	4	12	.190	.148	.222	6.23	2.08
Fuentes, Brian	L-L	6-4	230	8-9-75	0	0	0.00	1	0	0	0	1	0	0	0	0	0	2	.000	—	.000	18.00	0.00
Garcia, Jaime	L-L	6-2	215	7-8-86	1	0	5.23	2	2	0	0	10	8	6	6	2	0	11	.205	.125	.226	9.58	0.00
Gast, John	L-L	6-1	195	2-16-89	4	2	1.93	8	8	0	0	51	38	13	11	5	13	41	.211	.179	.220	7.19	2.28
Gorgen, Scott	R-R	5-10	190	1-27-87	5	7	4.09	21	16	0	0	92	87	49	42	7	39	93	.254	.295	.234	9.06	3.80
Hooker, Deryk	R-R	6-4	215	6-21-89	2	3	4.31	37	4	0	0	48	52	27	23	5	17	43	.281	.250	.295	8.06	3.19
Lyons, Tyler	B-L	6-2	195	2-21-88	5	4	3.92	12	12	0	0	64	70	33	28	6	19	54	.280	.174	.304	7.55	2.66
Maness, Seth	R-R	6-0	180	10-14-88	11	3	3.27	20	20	1	0	124	122	50	45	13	9	83	.253	.232	.263	6.04	0.65
Martinez, Carlos	R-R	6-0	165	9-21-91	4	3	2.90	15	14	0	0	71	62	27	23	6	22	58	.237	.266	.224	7.32	2.78
McGregor, Scott	R-R	6-2	193	12-19-86	5	2	6.86	12	11	0	0	59	74	51	45	11	18	30	.315	.344	.297	4.58	2.75
Nazario, Iden	L-L	6-0	190	3-28-89	0	0	20.25	1	0	0	0	1	3	4	3	0	2	2	.600	.500	.667	13.50	13.50

ST. LOUIS CARDINALS

Player	B-T	HT	WT	DOB	W	L	ERA	G	GS	CG	SV	IP	H	R	ER	HR	BB	SO	AVG	vLH	vRH	K/9	BB/9
Reid, Chase	L-R	6-3	215	5-17-88	0	0	5.79	8	0	0	0	19	23	12	12	5	2	8	.307	.300	.309	3.86	0.96
Rondon, Jorge	R-R	6-1	175	9-16-88	2	1	3.44	33	0	0	4	34	29	14	13	1	16	30	.238	.256	.229	7.94	4.24
Rosenthal, Trevor	R-R	6-2	190	5-29-90	8	6	2.78	17	17	0	0	94	67	33	29	6	37	83	.202	.150	.228	7.95	3.54
Schneider, Scott	R-R	6-0	175	6-7-88	0	0	12.79	8	0	0	0	13	18	18	18	1	7	7	.340	.348	.333	4.97	4.97
Siegrist, Kevin	L-L	6-5	190	7-20-89	1	2	3.62	8	5	0	0	32	26	14	13	4	9	27	.218	.176	.225	7.52	2.51
Simpson, Jesse	R-R	6-0	180	1-29-87	3	3	5.46	26	0	0	0	31	35	21	19	4	9	31	.269	.265	.271	8.90	2.59
Thomas, Kevin	R-R	6-3	215	7-8-86	5	1	4.30	45	1	0	0	73	66	40	35	10	22	73	.229	.233	.228	8.96	2.70
Wacha, Michael	R-R	6-6	195	7-1-91	0	0	1.13	4	0	0	0	8	3	1	1	0	3	17	.111	.125	.105	19.13	3.38
Whiting, Boone	R-R	6-1	175	8-20-89	0	0	1.50	2	2	0	0	12	11	2	2	0	3	9	.268	.214	.296	6.75	2.25
Wright, Justin	L-L	5-9	175	8-18-89	0	3	4.45	50	0	0	0	61	58	30	30	6	27	64	.252	.188	.277	9.49	4.01

Fielding

Catcher	PCT	G	PO	A	E	DP	PB
Derba	.985	25	189	12	3	1	2
Perez	.992	81	555	67	5	3	9
Tartamella	.997	37	280	30	1	1	6

First Base	PCT	G	PO	A	E	DP
Carpenter	1.000	2	21	1	0	2
Melker	1.000	3	15	0	0	3
Perez	1.000	1	2	0	0	0
Romak	1.000	6	63	3	0	5
Scruggs	.988	123	1180	69	15	140
Swauger	.990	11	95	5	1	8
Tartamella	—	1	0	0	0	0

Second Base	PCT	G	PO	A	E	DP
Albitz	1.000	3	8	12	0	3
Garcia	.974	18	27	47	2	14

	PCT	G	PO	A	E	DP
Pritchard	1.000	3	4	8	0	2
Valera	1.000	1	1	2	0	0
Wong	.974	123	262	370	17	111

Third Base	PCT	G	PO	A	E	DP
Albitz	1.000	7	2	17	0	1
Curtis	.951	77	40	191	12	24
Garcia	.919	34	13	66	7	7
Pritchard	1.000	1	0	1	0	0
Romak	.969	16	10	21	1	1
Valera	1.000	2	1	4	0	0
Vasquez	.957	17	16	29	2	5

Shortstop	PCT	G	PO	A	E	DP
Albitz	.917	8	9	24	3	5
Garcia	.966	119	143	425	20	92
Garcia	.928	15	14	50	5	8

	PCT	G	PO	A	E	DP
Pritchard	1.000	2	3	3	0	1

Outfield	PCT	G	PO	A	E	DP
Ahmady	1.000	5	9	0	0	0
Carpenter	1.000	1	3	0	0	0
Conley	.949	41	55	1	3	0
Garcia	1.000	11	11	1	0	0
Kruml	1.000	8	9	0	0	0
Melker	.984	104	173	6	3	1
O'Neill	1.000	11	18	0	0	0
Pham	1.000	2	4	0	0	0
Romak	.948	32	52	3	3	1
Rosario	1.000	17	25	3	0	0
Shaffer	.987	60	73	1	1	0
Swauger	.979	59	91	2	2	2
Taveras	.978	107	213	6	5	0

PALM BEACH CARDINALS

HIGH CLASS A

FLORIDA STATE LEAGUE

Batting	B-T	HT	WT	DOB	AVG	vLH	vRH	G	AB	R	H	2B	3B	HR	RBI	BB	HBP	SH	SF	SO	SB	CS	SLG	OBP
Ahmady, Alan	R-R	5-11	200	12-14-87	.299	.330	.278	76	254	33	76	24	1	4	42	37	2	0	2	44	3	2	.449	.390
Albitz, Vance	R-R	5-7	170	1-31-88	.266	.264	.268	43	124	15	33	5	0	0	13	16	2	3	3	12	6	2	.306	.352
Conley, Kyle	R-R	6-4	210	5-7-87	.154	.200	.125	4	13	1	2	0	0	1	1	1	0	0	4	0	0	.385	.267
Craig, Allen	R-R	6-2	210	7-18-84	.364	.750	.143	3	11	1	4	0	0	1	1	1	0	0	2	0	0	.636	.417
De La Cruz, Luis	R-R	5-9	165	5-6-89	.302	.330	.280	67	232	27	70	10	0	1	16	7	1	4	1	26	1	2	.358	.324
Edmondson, Chris	L-R	6-0	200	4-7-88	.256	.301	.228	123	464	58	119	18	2	9	66	34	8	0	2	82	11	4	.362	.317
Elkins, Packy	L-R	5-11	175	11-6-87	.273	.143	.297	14	44	5	12	2	0	1	7	7	2	0	2	5	3	0	.386	.382
Gil, Ronny	B-R	5-10	150	3-15-89	.224	.238	.215	121	420	45	94	24	1	1	29	27	4	5	4	97	14	6	.293	.275
Klein, Geoff	R-R	6-3	200	2-8-89	.246	.248	.246	102	353	41	87	17	0	7	34	30	2	0	0	93	2	1	.354	.309
Longmire, Nick	R-R	6-3	180	1-5-89	.189	.191	.187	84	297	32	56	11	2	3	28	16	2	1	3	87	5	5	.269	.233
Luna, Aaron	R-R	5-11	200	3-28-87	.100	.000	.143	3	10	1	1	0	0	1	3	2	0	0	0	5	0	0	.400	.250
O'Neill, Mike	L-L	5-9	190	2-12-88	.342	.319	.358	108	386	56	132	19	5	0	35	70	3	14	5	24	12	10	.417	.442
Patton, Jeremy	R-R	5-11	195	8-12-88	.192	.182	.198	43	130	12	25	3	0	0	12	18	0	1	0	29	0	0	.215	.289
Pritchard, Neal	R-R	6-0	195	2-21-89	.270	.304	.250	23	63	7	17	2	0	0	5	7	3	1	0	13	0	0	.302	.370
Rahmatulla, Tyler	R-R	5-10	190	2-26-90	.146	.103	.174	46	144	16	21	4	2	1	7	19	1	2	2	34	0	1	.222	.247
Ramsey, James	R-R	6-0	190	12-19-89	.229	.289	.194	56	210	36	48	9	3	1	14	33	1	1	2	59	10	2	.314	.333
Rasmus, Casey	L-R	6-0	175	3-29-90	.333	—	.333	1	3	0	1	0	0	0	0	0	0	0	0	0	0	0	.667	.333
Reyes, Roberto	L-L	6-0	195	5-10-89	.048	.111	.000	9	21	2	1	0	0	0	0	5	0	0	0	6	0	0	.048	.231
Rodriguez, Jonathan	R-R	6-2	205	8-21-89	.252	.244	.258	64	222	24	56	16	0	6	28	22	3	1	0	68	2	2	.405	.327
Rodriguez, Starlin	R-R	5-10	168	12-13-89	.300	.353	.270	114	430	66	129	25	6	8	48	37	14	7	1	90	16	10	.442	.373
Rosario, Rainel	R-R	6-0	188	3-29-89	.213	.224	.205	99	329	25	70	16	1	2	35	26	3	0	7	84	4	3	.286	.271
Stanley, Cody	L-R	5-10	190	12-21-88	.280	.179	.337	45	157	11	44	8	1	3	35	6	1	0	6	32	1	0	.401	.300
Swinson, Mike	R-R	6-0	195	9-24-89	.184	.212	.167	22	87	9	16	0	2	0	3	6	0	0	0	16	2	1	.230	.237
Tartamella, Travis	R-R	5-11	200	12-17-87	.150	.111	.182	8	20	0	3	1	0	0	2	2	0	0	0	4	0	0	.200	.227
Vargas, Ildemaro	R-R	6-0	170	7-16-91	.364	.100	.583	7	22	2	8	3	0	0	4	4	0	0	0	5	0	0	.500	.462
Vasquez, Niko	R-R	6-0	170	2-26-89	.217	.750	.105	7	23	3	5	1	0	0	3	4	1	0	0	5	0	0	.261	.357

Pitching	B-T	HT	WT	DOB	W	L	ERA	G	GS	CG	SV	IP	H	R	ER	HR	BB	SO	AVG	vLH	vRH	K/9	BB/9
Almarante, Jose	R-R	6-1	172	12-19-88	0	1	3.38	11	0	0	1	19	16	9	7	0	7	9	.262	.250	.273	4.34	3.38
Benes, Drew	R-R	6-2	190	11-4-88	6	8	5.31	28	16	0	0	103	117	65	61	8	36	79	.287	.269	.304	6.88	3.14
Billbrough, Logan	R-R	6-5	225	8-4-89	0	2	2.81	18	0	0	4	26	23	8	8	2	7	26	.235	.314	.190	9.12	2.45
Blair, Seth	R-R	6-2	185	3-3-89	1	3	5.40	5	5	0	0	17	18	12	10	1	14	12	.273	.282	.259	6.48	7.56
Castillo, Richard	R-R	5-11	165	10-11-89	2	3	1.86	6	2	0	0	39	22	9	8	2	10	23	.169	.120	.200	5.35	2.33
Corrigan, Chris	R-R	6-2	155	12-24-87	4	8	4.02	20	16	1	0	85	71	38	38	3	35	78	.222	.187	.262	8.26	3.71
Ferrara, Anthony	R-L	6-1	175	9-2-89	5	7	3.58	18	18	0	0	98	89	49	39	7	46	77	.245	.237	.249	7.07	4.22
Gerdel, Anderson	R-R	6-4	204	7-19-91	0	0	4.91	2	0	0	0	4	4	3	2	0	3	0	.267	.364	.000	7.36	0.00
Gillung, Nick	R-L	6-1	185	2-25-89	1	3	3.97	8	2	0	0	23	24	11	10	3	16	15	.273	.333	.246	5.96	6.35
Hald, Kyle	L-L	6-0	190	5-27-89	3	4	3.86	8	8	0	0	47	61	21	20	3	11	38	.314	.525	.260	7.33	2.12
Kiekhefer, Dean	L-L	6-0	175	6-7-89	2	2	2.24	46	0	0	14	60	61	23	15	3	4	41	.260	.227	.275	6.12	0.60
Lucas, Aiden	R-R	6-2	225	4-21-88	1	1	2.18	45	0	0	3	74	52	24	18	1	34	72	.195	.207	.186	8.72	4.12
Maness, Seth	R-R	6-0	180	10-14-88	3	1	2.15	7	7	0	0	46	45	13	11	5	1	29	.256	.234	.280	5.67	0.20
Martinez, Carlos	R-R	6-0	165	9-21-91	2	2	3.00	7	7	0	0	33	29	12	11	0	10	34	.236	.250	.218	9.27	2.73
Martinez, Ricky	R-R	6-1	195	4-20-88	0	2	9.45	10	0	0	1	13	22	16	14	0	11	8	.379	.296	.452	5.40	7.43

Name	B-T	HT	WT	DOB	W	L	ERA	G	GS	CG	SV	IP	H	R	ER	HR	BB	SO	AVG	vLH	vRH	K/9	BB/9
McGregor, Scott	R-R	6-2	193	12-19-86	0	0	2.25	2	2	0	0	8	6	3	2	0	2	3	.214	.364	.118	3.38	2.25
McInnis, Todd	R-R	6-1	165	3-26-88	4	6	4.55	22	14	0	0	89	110	59	45	13	20	60	.301	.313	.291	6.07	2.02
Miller, Travis	R-R	6-0	195	3-15-90	0	0	11.37	8	0	0	0	6	11	9	8	2	8	4	.407	.444	.389	5.68	11.37
Miranda, Danny	L-L	6-0	225	8-25-90	0	1	4.26	7	0	0	0	13	16	6	6	0	3	13	.302	.214	.333	9.24	2.13
Nazario, Iden	L-L	6-0	190	3-28-89	5	3	2.73	41	0	0	0	63	41	23	19	3	43	59	.188	.253	.154	8.47	6.18
Reid, Chase	L-R	6-3	215	5-17-88	4	6	4.71	28	0	0	5	42	47	27	22	2	18	37	.283	.347	.234	7.93	3.86
Russell, Zach	R-R	6-2	185	7-27-89	4	1	4.39	33	0	0	6	53	56	32	26	1	30	47	.262	.237	.281	7.93	5.06
Schneider, Scott	R-R	6-0	175	6-7-88	1	2	4.73	14	4	0	1	32	36	22	17	3	11	19	.279	.298	.264	5.29	3.06
Sherriff, Ryan	L-L	6-1	185	5-25-90	10	3	3.25	16	16	1	0	97	79	40	35	7	20	57	.217	.184	.230	5.29	1.86
Siegrist, Kevin	L-L	6-5	190	7-20-89	6	0	2.28	10	10	0	0	55	33	18	14	3	22	41	.173	.180	.169	6.67	3.58
Wacha, Michael	R-R	6-6	195	7-1-91	0	0	0.00	4	0	0	0	8	1	0	0	0	1	16	.040	.000	.050	18.00	1.13
Watson, Brad	R-R	6-4	185	8-8-89	0	3	6.83	7	5	0	0	28	32	22	21	4	10	20	.291	.323	.250	6.51	3.25

Fielding

Catcher	PCT	G	PO	A	E	DP	PB
De La Cruz	.978	63	393	45	10	2	13
Klein	.978	43	244	23	6	4	5
Rasmus	1.000	1	11	0	0	1	
Stanley	.980	32	230	12	5	0	3
Tartamella	.973	7	29	7	1	2	1

First Base	PCT	G	PO	A	E	DP
Ahmady	.978	7	43	2	1	3
Edmondson	.993	30	262	10	2	17
Klein	.987	49	428	19	6	27
Patton	.982	16	93	14	2	9
Pritchard	.800	1	4	0	1	0
Rodriguez	.988	46	379	32	5	38

Second Base	PCT	G	PO	A	E	DP
Albitz	1.000	19	33	57	0	12
Elkins	1.000	3	4	9	0	3

	PCT	G	PO	A	E	DP
Pritchard	1.000	5	15	12	0	4
Rahmatulla	.955	14	23	41	3	8
Rodriguez	.966	100	171	285	16	47
Vargas	.944	4	7	10	1	2

Third Base	PCT	G	PO	A	E	DP
Ahmady	.971	54	29	104	4	7
Albitz	.950	7	5	14	1	1
Elkins	1.000	11	9	19	0	1
Patton	1.000	8	1	13	0	1
Pritchard	1.000	13	14	19	0	4
Rahmatulla	.842	28	15	49	12	3
Rodriguez	.964	19	11	43	2	2
Vargas	.917	3	2	9	1	1
Vasquez	.944	7	4	13	1	2

Shortstop	PCT	G	PO	A	E	DP
Albitz	.967	15	19	40	2	6

	PCT	G	PO	A	E	DP
Gil	.939	119	164	332	32	64
Pritchard	1.000	7	8	14	0	1
Rahmatulla	.857	2	4	2	1	0
Vargas	1.000	1	2	0	0	

Outfield	PCT	G	PO	A	E	DP
Ahmady	1.000	16	28	4	0	0
Conley	1.000	3	3	0	0	0
Edmondson	1.000	62	109	2	0	0
Longmire	.989	79	172	4	2	0
Luna	.833	2	5	0	1	0
O'Neill	.978	90	174	5	4	0
Patton	1.000	2	5	1	0	0
Ramsey	1.000	53	100	6	0	3
Reyes	.846	8	9	2	2	0
Rodriguez	1.000	5	5	1	0	0
Rosario	.968	79	147	4	5	0
Swinson	.980	20	48	2	1	1

QUAD CITIES RIVER BANDITS

LOW CLASS A

MIDWEST LEAGUE

Batting	B-T	HT	WT	DOB	AVG	vLH	vRH	G	AB	R	H	2B	3B	HR	RBI	BB	HBP	SH	SF	SO	SB	CS	SLG	OBP
Apelian, Gary	R-R	6-4	206	9-22-90	.214	.222	.211	8	28	4	6	2	0	1	7	0	1	0	1	4	0	0	.393	.233
Bergin, David	R-R	6-2	235	8-25-89	.344	.500	.308	10	32	4	11	0	0	3	10	4	1	0	1	8	0	0	.625	.421
Castillo, Juan	R-R	5-11	190	12-13-89	.272	.277	.271	87	323	47	88	16	2	6	44	30	3	2	8	56	2	1	.390	.332
De La Cruz, Roberto	R-R	6-2	230	11-10-91	.207	.250	.192	62	242	21	50	9	0	5	29	5	2	1	0	67	0	2	.306	.229
Garcia, Anthony	R-R	6-0	180	1-4-92	.280	.314	.268	109	396	63	111	34	3	19	74	34	12	0	2	107	3	6	.525	.354
Hill, Virgil	R-R	5-11	186	9-9-90	.204	.311	.161	46	157	28	32	7	2	4	22	15	1	1	2	53	5	1	.350	.274
Lewis, Adam	L-R	6-0	200	4-12-89	.125	.000	.136	7	24	1	3	1	0	0	3	0	0	0		9	0	0	.167	.222
Longmire, Nick	R-R	6-3	180	1-5-89	.326	.400	.290	23	92	15	30	6	0	2	9	9	1	2		26	7	3	.457	.390
Martini, Nick	L-L	5-11	205	6-27-90	.266	.265	.266	130	482	82	128	24	4	2	52	64	10	3	4	60	11	9	.344	.361
Mateo, Luis	R-R	6-0	175	5-23-90	.257	.270	.252	113	405	70	104	22	4	12	64	27	7	3	3	105	18	6	.420	.312
Medina, Luis	L-L	6-4	230	1-1-89	.241	.202	.251	120	431	56	104	31	2	9	72	50	0	2	3	133	3	3	.385	.318
Melchionda, Anthony	R-R	6-0	195	2-17-90	.288	.297	.284	41	146	14	42	8	0	5	19	6	0	3	0	31	3	0	.445	.316
Montero, Jesus	R-R	5-10	210	6-21-91	.192	.000	.208	10	26	4	5	1	0	1	4	2	2	0	1	6	0	0	.346	.290
Patton, Jeremy	R-R	5-11	195	8-12-88	.222	.200	.227	28	90	7	20	5	0	1	15	18	1	0	1	15	0	0	.311	.355
Piscotty, Stephen	R-R	6-3	210	1-14-91	.295	.233	.311	55	210	29	62	18	1	4	27	18	9	0	0	25	3	0	.448	.376
Pritchard, Neal	R-R	6-0	195	2-21-89	.196	.130	.214	37	107	21	21	3	0	1	6	13	5	3	0	43	0	2	.252	.312
Rahmatulla, Tyler	R-R	5-10	190	2-26-90	.322	.391	.286	49	183	37	59	16	2	7	42	17	5	2	3	36	2	2	.546	.389
Rasmus, Casey	L-R	5-10	175	3-29-90	.220	.120	.240	49	150	21	33	5	1	2	9	7	0	2	1	35	5	0	.307	.253
Reyes, Roberto	L-L	6-0	195	5-10-89	.229	.220	.232	52	179	21	41	4	1	3	16	19	3	2	0	43	2	3	.313	.313
Walsh, Colin	B-R	6-0	190	9-26-89	.314	.339	.303	97	353	69	111	18	5	16	68	60	7	0	5	65	4	3	.530	.419
Walton, Jordan	L-L	5-11	185	3-13-90	.149	.000	.200	18	47	6	7	1	0	0	4	3	0	1	0	16	0	0	.170	.200
Wiley, Brett	L-R	5-10	175	11-24-91	.333	.500	.286	2	9	2	3	1	0	0	1	0	0	0	0	2	0	0	.444	.333
Williams, Matt	R-R	6-0	170	8-29-89	.269	.246	.276	131	525	89	141	32	5	6	49	48	4	8	2	91	23	12	.383	.333
Wittels, Garrett	R-R	6-1	200	5-11-90	.208	.259	.180	25	77	6	16	5	0	0	6	6	2	0	1	14	1	1	.273	.279

Pitching	B-T	HT	WT	DOB	W	L	ERA	G	GS	CG	SV	IP	H	R	ER	HR	BB	SO	AVG	vLH	vRH	K/9	BB/9
Barraclough, Kyle	R-R	6-3	225	5-23-90	0	2	4.15	11	0	0	2	17	13	9	8	0	13	21	.210	.150	.238	10.90	6.75
Billbrough, Logan	R-R	6-5	225	8-4-89	0	0	0.00	3	0	0	0	3	2	0	0	0	0	8	.182	.000		24.00	0.00
Castillo, Yunier	B-R	6-0	170	5-15-89	0	0	7.71	6	0	0	0	9	14	8	8	3	2	7	.333	.333	.333	6.75	1.93
Cole, Ethan	L-R	6-0	185	10-27-89	4	1	1.98	45	0	0	1	77	75	21	17	2	19	65	.259	.264	.256	7.56	2.21
Cornelius, Jonathan	L-L	6-1	190	5-31-88	1	2	3.27	23	8	0	0	77	83	42	28	2	18	87	.272	.242	.280	10.17	2.10
Creath, Brandon	R-R	6-3	200	2-16-89	2	3	4.50	12	0	0	0	18	17	10	9	1	8	17	.250	.167	.295	8.50	4.00
Gaviglio, Sam	R-R	6-1	200	5-22-90	9	9	3.92	23	23	0	0	133	128	74	58	12	30	113	.247	.256	.240	7.65	2.03
Hald, Kyle	L-L	6-0	190	5-27-89	4	5	3.10	16	16	1	0	90	88	40	31	4	13	77	.254	.190	.268	7.70	1.30
Hernandez, Hector	B-L	6-2	200	2-20-91	7	8	4.43	24	24	1	0	126	141	79	62	11	54	94	.285	.250	.297	6.71	3.86
Jacob, Kevin	R-R	6-6	225	3-26-89	0	1	4.85	8	0	0	0	13	12	9	7	1	9	13	.245	.172	.350	9.00	6.23
Jenkins, Tyrell	R-R	6-4	192	7-20-92	4	5	5.14	19	19	0	0	82	84	53	47	5	36	80	.267	.211	.305	8.74	3.94
Llorens, Dixon	R-R	5-10	170	11-18-92	0	1	3.98	11	0	0	2	20	14	10	9	3	5	34	.189	.304	.137	15.05	2.21
Martinez, Ricky	R-R	6-1	195	4-20-88	0	0	4.81	28	0	0	4	43	47	25	23	1	15	20	.276	.400	.209	4.19	3.14

	B-T	HT	WT	DOB	W	L	ERA	G	GS	CG	SV	IP	H	R	ER	HR	BB	SO	AVG	vLH	vRH	K/9	BB/9
McInnis, Todd	R-R	6-1	165	3-26-88	2	0	2.54	5	5	0	0	28	30	10	8	1	8	14	.278	.241	.315	4.45	2.54
Miller, Travis	R-R	6-0	195	3-15-90	3	0	2.36	18	0	0	1	27	20	8	7	0	11	22	.213	.259	.194	7.43	3.71
Miranda, Danny	L-L	6-0	225	8-25-90	4	5	3.25	38	0	0	2	53	46	21	19	4	16	48	.234	.233	.234	8.20	2.73
Paulino, Willy	R-R	6-3	172	6-21-90	2	9	5.86	28	7	0	1	66	63	61	43	11	38	67	.242	.229	.249	9.14	5.18
Polanco, Jhonny	R-R	6-3	191	4-28-92	0	0	4.50	1	1	0	0	6	8	3	3	0	3	2	.333	.000	.400	3.00	4.50
Renfro, Josh	L-L	6-0	182	8-31-89	1	0	0.00	2	0	0	0	4	1	2	0	0	1	2	.067	.000	.083	4.15	2.08
Revesz, Bob	L-L	6-4	215	7-16-88	1	1	7.90	10	0	0	0	14	18	12	12	1	3	8	.340	.364	.333	5.27	1.98
Stock, Robert	R-R	6-1	200	11-21-89	5	2	4.56	38	2	0	0	71	61	46	36	9	48	66	.233	.196	.256	8.37	6.08
Villanueva, Dail	L-L	6-3	192	1-23-90	10	7	4.29	26	23	0	0	124	127	70	59	11	50	95	.264	.216	.278	6.91	3.64
Watson, Brad	R-R	6-4	185	8-8-89	4	4	6.05	9	8	0	0	42	59	32	28	4	10	27	.337	.309	.362	5.83	2.16
Whiting, Boone	R-R	6-1	175	8-20-89	1	0	0.56	3	3	0	0	16	7	1	1	0	1	14	.130	.143	.121	7.88	0.56
Wyatt, Heath	R-R	6-2	185	8-27-88	4	7	2.24	55	0	0	20	64	53	26	16	2	20	57	.226	.301	.184	7.97	2.80

Fielding

Catcher	PCT	G	PO	A	E	DP	PB
Castillo	.983	85	609	91	12	6	23
Lewis	.952	4	39	1	2	0	1
Montero	.987	10	67	9	1	2	2
Rasmus	.986	45	308	49	5	4	7

First Base	PCT	G	PO	A	E	DP
Bergin	.947	8	70	2	4	10
De La Cruz	.974	50	418	27	12	50
Medina	.982	75	691	35	13	57
Patton	.986	15	137	8	2	11
Walsh	1.000	1	3	1	0	2

Second Base	PCT	G	PO	A	E	DP
Mateo	.980	100	171	325	10	76
Melchionda	1.000	5	8	10	0	3

	PCT	G	PO	A	E	DP
Pritchard	.974	14	33	41	2	12
Walsh	.906	26	50	46	10	13

Third Base	PCT	G	PO	A	E	DP
Mateo	1.000	5	0	11	0	0
Melchionda	.917	18	8	36	4	2
Patton	.917	9	5	17	2	2
Piscotty	.815	36	24	73	22	6
Pritchard	.898	16	10	34	5	2
Rahmatulla	.964	44	33	100	5	11
Walsh	1.000	3	1	3	0	0
Wittels	.920	15	16	30	4	3

Shortstop	PCT	G	PO	A	E	DP
Mateo	.800	4	3	13	4	1
Melchionda	.950	5	7	12	1	4

	PCT	G	PO	A	E	DP
Pritchard	.600	1	0	3	2	0
Wiley	.333	1	0	1	2	0
Williams	.947	126	197	442	36	91
Wittels	1.000	3	6	9	0	4

Outfield	PCT	G	PO	A	E	DP
Apelian	.944	8	16	1	1	1
Garcia	.967	92	108	8	4	1
Hill	.961	42	73	1	3	0
Longmire	.940	22	44	3	3	1
Martini	.982	123	257	9	5	3
Medina	.988	45	78	4	1	1
Pritchard	1.000	1	3	0	0	0
Reyes	.953	50	71	10	4	2
Walsh	.927	35	38	0	3	0
Walton	1.000	15	18	0	0	0

BATAVIA MUCKDOGS   SHORT-SEASON

NEW YORK-PENN LEAGUE

Batting	B-T	HT	WT	DOB	AVG	vLH	vRH	G	AB	R	H	2B	3B	HR	RBI	BB	HBP	SH	SF	SO	SB	CS	SLG	OBP
Apelian, Gary	R-R	6-4	206	9-22-90	.172	.172	.172	40	128	14	22	5	0	2	10	7	5	0	0	39	3	1	.258	.243
Bergin, David	R-R	6-2	235	8-25-89	.298	.133	.375	13	47	5	14	5	0	2	9	4	2	0	1	15	1	0	.532	.370
Byrd, Kolby	L-R	6-1	215	3-23-90	.222	.500	.197	26	72	8	16	4	0	0	7	6	0	1	1	16	0	0	.278	.278
Caldwell, Bruce	L-R	5-11	175	11-27-91	.167	.500	.000	2	6	0	1	0	0	0	0	0	0	0	0	2	0	0	.167	.167
De La Cruz, Roberto	R-R	6-2	230	11-10-91	.136	.077	.161	13	44	3	6	3	0	1	4	1	0	0	2	15	0	0	.273	.149
Keener, Jonathan	R-R	6-0	195	12-10-89	.238	.375	.191	37	126	11	30	4	1	2	15	6	1	1	2	34	0	0	.333	.274
Lewis, Adam	L-R	6-0	200	4-12-89	.160	.167	.158	12	25	0	4	0	0	0	1	3	0	1	0	7	0	0	.160	.250
Mateo, Leandro	B-R	5-11	170	3-17-90	.100	.500	.000	3	10	0	1	0	0	0	0	1	0	0	0	1	0	0	.100	.182
Mejia, Alex	R-R	6-1	200	1-18-91	.250	.200	.268	23	96	9	24	5	0	1	7	2	0	2	0	13	1	0	.333	.265
Melchionda, Anthony	R-R	6-1	200	12-12-88	.217	.231	.214	16	69	6	15	6	0	0	4	3	1	0	0	18	1	0	.304	.260
Montero, Jesus	R-R	5-10	210	6-21-91	.308	.467	.253	33	117	18	36	6	1	3	21	8	5	1	0	26	0	0	.453	.377
Popkins, David	L-R	6-3	215	11-16-89	.243	.143	.267	23	74	11	18	6	1	1	10	9	2	1	2	17	1	2	.392	.333
Ramos, Steve	R-R	6-0	160	7-4-90	.247	.294	.236	70	263	33	65	12	3	1	16	17	1	5	1	55	12	4	.327	.294
Rasmus, Casey	L-R	5-10	175	3-29-90	.000	.000	.000	1	3	0	0	0	0	0	0	0	0	0	0	0	0	0	.000	.000
Reyes, Roberto	L-L	6-0	195	5-10-89	.225	.200	.233	11	40	4	9	1	0	0	3	5	0	0	1	9	1	0	.250	.304
Stienstra, Danny	R-R	6-2	200	3-1-89	.345	.333	.347	37	142	20	49	7	1	3	20	11	1	2	2	11	5	1	.472	.391
Valera, Breyvic	R-R	5-11	160	8-1-92	.316	.411	.292	69	282	39	89	18	4	1	33	18	2	1	2	27	10	6	.418	.359
Vargas, Ildemaro	R-R	6-0	170	7-16-91	.083	.000	.111	3	12	0	1	0	0	0	0	0	0	0	0	6	0	0	.083	.083
Walton, Jordan	L-L	5-11	185	3-13-90	.297	.286	.300	26	74	5	22	4	0	0	8	4	3	1	0	13	0	0	.351	.358
Washington, David	L-L	6-5	200	11-20-90	.267	.147	.292	55	195	30	52	19	1	9	32	18	1	0	1	78	1	1	.513	.330
Williams Jr., Reggie	R-R	6-4	190	9-15-89	.133	.000	.148	13	30	5	4	0	0	1	3	5	0	0	0	9	1	1	.233	.257
Wilson, Jacob	R-R	5-11	180	7-29-90	.275	.368	.246	46	160	28	44	7	1	6	25	13	4	0	2	33	2	1	.444	.341
Wisdom, Patrick	R-R	6-2	210	8-27-91	.282	.320	.272	65	241	40	68	16	5	6	32	31	5	0	2	58	2	1	.465	.373
Wittels, Garrett	R-R	6-1	200	5-11-90	.254	.262	.252	47	181	23	46	13	3	1	20	13	0	2	1	36	2	3	.376	.303
Young, Matt	R-R	6-3	230	8-17-90	.246	.179	.265	55	171	30	42	9	2	3	22	23	2	1	4	61	1	3	.374	.335

Pitching	B-T	HT	WT	DOB	W	L	ERA	G	GS	CG	SV	IP	H	R	ER	HR	BB	SO	AVG	vLH	vRH	K/9	BB/9
Aldrete, Mike	R-R	5-10	165	9-30-89	0	0	3.86	4	0	0	0	5	6	2	2	0	3	3	.316	.200	.357	5.79	5.79
Almarante, Jose	R-R	6-1	172	12-19-88	1	1	2.14	13	0	0	1	21	21	9	5	1	5	21	.276	.381	.236	9.00	2.14
Baker, Corey	R-R	6-1	170	11-23-89	3	3	2.44	20	3	0	1	52	44	18	14	0	9	34	.232	.241	.224	5.92	1.57
Barraclough, Kyle	R-R	6-3	225	5-23-90	0	1	2.00	4	3	0	0	18	13	6	4	2	0	12	.200	.217	.190	6.00	0.00
Bibona, Daniel	L-L	6-0	170	6-19-88	0	1	6.43	2	2	0	0	7	9	6	5	0	4	5	.321	.000	.346	6.43	5.14
Bileckyj, Adam	L-L	6-3	205	10-17-88	0	1	4.50	3	0	0	0	4	4	3	2	0	1	4	.250	.250	.250	9.00	2.25
Castillo, Yunier	B-R	6-0	170	5-15-89	3	3	2.08	19	0	0	5	26	22	10	6	3	5	29	.229	.257	.213	10.04	1.73
Cooney, Tim	L-L	6-3	195	12-19-90	3	3	3.40	13	11	1	0	56	56	24	21	4	8	43	.268	.258	.272	6.95	1.29
Copeland, Ryan	R-L	5-11	180	6-10-88	0	0	0.00	1	0	0	0	1	1	0	0	1	1	3	.333	.500	.000	13.50	13.50
Creath, Brandon	R-R	6-2	200	2-16-89	2	2	2.76	25	0	0	6	33	27	12	10	0	14	47	.225	.238	.218	12.95	3.86
Cuda, Joey	R-R	5-9	195	9-13-89	7	1	4.15	13	13	0	0	61	64	28	28	3	11	53	.275	.263	.287	7.86	1.63
Delgado, Ramon	R-R	6-3	195	9-3-86	0	0	6.75	2	0	0	0	4	4	3	3	1	0	6	.250	.273	.200	6.75	0.00
Freeman, Ben	L-L	6-2	150	2-6-92	2	2	2.39	9	9	0	0	49	46	14	13	7	11	42	.247	.233	.250	7.71	2.02
Helisek, Kyle	L-L	6-0	170	4-23-90	4	2	3.42	12	10	0	0	55	47	24	21	1	18	33	.241	.210	.256	5.37	2.93

Name	B-T	HT	WT	DOB	W	L	ERA	G	GS	CG	SV	IP	H	R	ER	HR	BB	SO	AVG	vLH	vRH	K/9	BB/9
Heyer, Kurt	L-R	6-2	185	1-23-91	0	0	6.75	2	0	0	0	4	5	3	3	0	0	5	.313	.273	.400	11.25	0.00
Jacob, Kevin	R-R	6-6	225	3-26-89	4	1	4.36	21	0	0	0	33	24	17	16	1	14	35	.212	.243	.197	9.55	3.82
Melling, Tyler	R-L	6-2	170	9-4-88	3	1	2.01	13	13	0	0	67	67	23	15	2	4	46	.255	.318	.234	6.18	0.54
Nuernberg, Dyllon	R-R	6-1	220	5-28-91	2	1	4.70	19	0	0	2	31	26	16	16	1	13	28	.236	.205	.254	8.22	3.82
O'Shea, Ben	L-L	6-5	255	9-9-91	3	3	3.12	13	12	0	0	61	61	22	21	6	5	43	.262	.233	.272	6.38	0.74
Pasen, Jose	R-R	6-0	180	5-19-90	1	1	6.75	7	0	0	0	11	11	10	8	0	2	13	.262	.353	.200	10.97	1.69
Rein, Matt	B-L	5-11	170	5-29-88	0	0	0.00	1	0	0	0	1	2	0	0	0	0	1	.400	1.000	.250	9.00	0.00
Scanio, Joe	R-R	6-4	230	1-30-90	2	3	3.41	19	0	0	2	29	30	14	11	0	6	15	.280	.341	.242	4.66	1.86
Stoppelman, Lee	L-L	6-2	210	5-24-90	2	1	0.79	22	0	0	7	34	23	5	3	0	7	49	.183	.156	.191	12.84	1.83
Thomas, Chris	R-R	6-2	200	3-16-88	2	0	2.70	9	0	0	0	13	9	5	4	0	2	19	.191	.304	.083	12.83	1.35

Fielding

Catcher	PCT	G	PO	A	E	DP	PB
Byrd	1.000	9	51	4	0	1	3
Keener	.996	36	240	36	1	2	9
Lewis	1.000	9	48	2	0	0	1
Montero	.984	31	220	33	4	2	5
Rasmus	1.000	1	6	1	0	0	0

First Base	PCT	G	PO	A	E	DP
Bergin	.982	10	103	4	2	7
Stienstra	.996	24	222	13	1	24
Washington	.986	43	377	32	6	41

Second Base	PCT	G	PO	A	E	DP
Mateo	.867	2	7	6	2	2
Stienstra	1.000	11	12	29	0	5
Valera	.964	46	80	133	8	32

	PCT	G	PO	A	E	DP
Vargas	1.000	1	4	3	0	0
Wilson	.973	16	20	53	2	11
Wittels	1.000	2	5	5	0	0

Third Base	PCT	G	PO	A	E	DP
Wilson	.941	15	5	27	2	2
Wisdom	.969	58	42	112	5	14
Wittels	.867	4	3	10	2	0

Shortstop	PCT	G	PO	A	E	DP
Caldwell	.700	2	2	5	3	1
Mateo	—	1	0	0	0	0
Mejia	.971	22	24	75	3	15
Melchionda	.940	14	18	45	4	5
Valera	.939	13	14	32	3	8
Vargas	1.000	2	2	2	0	0

	PCT	G	PO	A	E	DP
Wittels	.939	29	38	70	7	23

Outfield	PCT	G	PO	A	E	DP
Apelian	.947	40	69	2	4	1
De La Cruz	.750	2	3	0	1	0
Melchionda	—	1	0	0	0	0
Popkins	1.000	22	35	0	0	0
Ramos	.981	69	147	9	3	1
Reyes	.955	11	20	1	1	0
Valera	1.000	4	5	1	0	0
Walton	.967	21	27	2	1	0
Williams Jr.	.895	10	17	0	2	0
Wittels	.941	10	13	3	1	2
Young	.955	52	103	2	5	1

JOHNSON CITY CARDINALS — ROOKIE

APPALACHIAN LEAGUE

Batting	B-T	HT	WT	DOB	AVG	vLH	vRH	G	AB	R	H	2B	3B	HR	RBI	BB	HBP	SH	SF	SO	SB	CS	SLG	OBP
Bean, Steve	L-R	6-2	190	9-15-93	.125	.000	.154	24	80	6	10	4	0	1	5	15	0	0	0	32	2	0	.213	.263
Bryant, Anthony	L-R	6-3	215	1-13-92	.267	.000	.333	5	15	1	4	0	0	0	4	0	0	0	0	2	2	1	.267	.267
Caldwell, Bruce	L-R	5-11	175	11-27-91	.304	.267	.308	44	148	30	45	12	1	6	26	14	1	0	3	39	2	0	.520	.361
Castillo, Ronard	R-R	6-5	200	6-16-92	.295	.300	.294	55	200	28	59	11	2	0	26	11	1	0	3	30	2	5	.370	.332
Deol, Dutch	R-R	6-3	200	10-20-92	.176	.077	.204	39	119	12	21	7	2	1	8	11	2	0	0	36	0	0	.294	.258
Ehrlich, Adam	L-R	6-1	200	12-13-92	.373	.308	.387	20	75	14	28	3	0	1	8	8	0	2	1	14	0	1	.453	.424
Jeffries, Lance	R-R	5-9	185	3-28-93	.220	.154	.236	45	132	23	29	2	4	0	7	24	8	0	1	62	11	3	.295	.370
Kelly, Carson	R-R	6-2	200	7-14-94	.235	.313	.200	56	213	24	48	10	0	9	25	10	1	1	0	33	0	0	.399	.263
Knox, Mike	R-R	6-4	230	4-18-89	.161	.109	.179	31	87	14	14	7	0	4	13	7	4	0	2	33	0	0	.379	.250
Lizcano, Ricardo	R-R	5-11	190	8-29-90	.262	.286	.257	22	42	5	11	0	1	1	6	8	0	0	0	12	0	0	.381	.380
Martin, Trevor	R-R	6-0	190	8-3-91	.250	.053	.299	31	96	13	24	6	0	5	15	9	3	0	0	27	2	1	.469	.333
Mateo, Leandro	B-R	5-11	170	3-17-90	.406	.000	.419	17	32	8	13	1	0	0	2	3	0	0	0	6	5	2	.438	.486
McElroy Jr., C.J.	R-R	5-10	180	5-29-93	.271	.327	.255	61	247	40	67	11	2	0	22	15	1	4	1	42	24	5	.332	.314
Schaffer, Jeremy	R-R	6-1	205	1-16-90	.272	.269	.272	62	232	32	63	20	3	10	51	16	6	0	4	47	0	0	.513	.329
Tuivailala, Sam	R-R	6-3	195	10-19-92	.250	.000	.333	1	4	1	1	0	0	1	1	0	0	0	0	2	0	0	1.000	.250
Valera, Cesar	R-R	6-1	180	3-8-92	.226	.297	.207	54	177	20	40	10	0	0	16	14	4	3	2	42	6	3	.282	.294
Vargas, Ildemaro	R-R	6-0	170	7-16-91	.322	.377	.305	59	230	42	74	15	2	4	28	17	7	2	2	24	8	6	.457	.383
Velazco, Gerwuins	R-R	6-1	190	10-7-91	.343	.269	.367	31	105	12	36	5	0	0	8	4	0	1	2	22	0	0	.390	.360

Pitching	B-T	HT	WT	DOB	W	L	ERA	G	GS	CG	SV	IP	H	R	ER	HR	BB	SO	AVG	vLH	vRH	K/9	BB/9
Aguilar, Cesar	R-R	6-3	250	5-15-92	2	1	4.13	14	0	0	1	28	33	13	13	1	6	23	.292	.357	.254	7.31	1.91
Aldrete, Mike	R-R	5-10	165	9-30-89	1	0	7.03	15	0	0	0	24	32	22	19	1	7	24	.320	.412	.273	8.88	2.59
Bautista, Juan	R-R	5-11	195	6-16-93	2	5	5.60	11	11	0	0	55	60	37	34	6	26	36	.274	.313	.244	5.93	4.28
Booden, Jacob	R-R	6-7	235	8-14-90	0	0	3.49	16	0	0	0	28	29	15	11	5	12	29	.259	.216	.280	9.21	3.81
Brand, Cole	R-R	6-2	225	5-19-92	0	0	6.39	6	0	0	0	13	18	10	9	1	6	12	.327	.412	.289	8.53	4.26
Canache, Roberto	R-R	6-5	180	5-12-90	0	0	0.73	8	0	0	0	12	10	3	1	0	3	13	.217	.337	.156	9.49	2.19
De Leon, Victor	R-R	6-2	190	4-19-92	3	0	3.25	10	10	0	0	44	39	19	16	1	20	42	.236	.222	.245	8.53	4.06
Donofrio, Joey	R-R	6-3	185	5-10-89	4	2	1.26	13	0	0	0	29	22	11	4	0	10	31	.218	.195	.233	9.73	3.14
Gallardo, Steven	R-R	5-11	180	10-28-92	0	1	4.50	2	2	0	0	6	4	3	3	1	1	6	.241	.000	.353	6.00	1.50
Garcia, Silfredo	R-R	6-2	170	7-19-91	4	2	2.93	7	7	1	0	43	38	19	14	3	4	45	.226	.203	.239	9.42	0.84
Gillung, Nick	R-L	6-1	185	2-25-89	2	0	3.77	3	3	0	0	14	21	7	6	0	7	12	.333	.313	.340	7.53	4.40
Jones, Cory	R-R	6-5	225	9-20-91	0	2	7.27	5	5	0	0	17	21	15	14	3	11	15	.296	.154	.378	7.79	5.71
Lee, Thomas	R-R	6-1	190	10-20-89	4	4	4.03	16	5	0	0	51	60	27	23	3	9	57	.291	.400	.235	9.99	1.58
Llorens, Dixon	R-R	5-10	170	11-18-92	2	0	0.00	8	0	0	2	16	5	0	0	0	6	28	.098	.211	.031	16.09	3.45
Lopez, Stalyn	L-L	5-9	160	12-28-91	3	4	4.43	10	1	0	0	43	43	29	21	2	33	43	.262	.176	.285	9.07	6.96
Martinez, Bryan	R-R	6-3		3-1-91	1	2	11.37	4	4	0	0	13	19	16		2	5	6	.393	.400	.382	4.26	3.53
Nuernberg, Dyllon	R-R	6-1	220	5-28-91	0	0	2.35	3	0	0	0	8	5	3	2	0	1	10	.179	.000	.263	11.74	1.17
Paulino, Willy	R-R	6-3	172	6-21-90	1	1	5.09	5	3	0	0	18	18	15	10	4	9	18	.257	.375	.222	9.17	4.58
Petrick, Zach	R-R	6-3	195	7-29-89	5	0	2.17	13	7	0	0	46	33	12	11	2	9	50	.195	.221	.178	9.85	1.77
Rauh, Jeff	R-R	6-2	200	1-24-90	3	2	5.18	18	0	0	0	24	32	16	14	2	14	20	.327	.320	.329	7.40	5.18
Sabatino, Steve	L-L	6-2	190	3-8-90	0	0	4.91	4	0	0	0	7	8	4	4	0	2	7	.276	.250	.286	8.59	2.45
Shaban, Ronnie	L-R	6-1	195	3-8-90	0	1	3.05	20	0	0	16	21	19	8	7	2	7	31	.244	.214	.260	13.50	3.05
Springer, Jared	R-R	6-2	210	7-17-88	0	1	13.50	4	0	0	0	3	5	4	4	1	7	1	.417	.333	.444	3.38	23.63

Fielding

Catcher	PCT	G	PO	A	E	DP	PB
Bean	.980	23	181	20	4	0	5
Ehrlich	1.000	16	146	13	0	1	2
Lizcano	1.000	1	2	0	0	0	0
Velazco	.981	30	231	24	5	1	6

First Base	PCT	G	PO	A	E	DP
Knox	.992	18	113	5	1	7
Martin	1.000	4	24	0	0	1
Schaffer	.982	53	425	24	8	41

Second Base	PCT	G	PO	A	E	DP
Caldwell	.952	3	9	11	1	2

	PCT/..	G	PO	A	E	DP
Martin	.920	9	6	17	2	2
Mateo	.824	3	9	5	3	1
Vargas	.986	56	118	167	4	38

Third Base	PCT	G	PO	A	E	DP
Caldwell	1.000	10	2	24	0	1
Kelly	.880	48	23	65	12	6
Martin	.889	12	4	12	2	1
Mateo	1.000	3	0	4	0	0

Shortstop	PCT	G	PO	A	E	DP
Caldwell	.892	14	13	45	7	9
Mateo	—	1	0	0	0	0

	PCT/..	G	PO	A	E	DP
Valera	.940	54	68	153	14	25
Vargas	1.000	1	2	3	0	1

Outfield	PCT	G	PO	A	E	DP
Bryant	1.000	3	9	0	0	0
Caldwell	—	1	0	0	0	0
Castillo	.937	53	71	3	5	0
Deol	1.000	35	34	1	0	0
Jeffries	.962	42	73	3	3	0
Lizcano	1.000	13	10	0	0	0
Martin	1.000	1	2	0	0	0
Mateo	.750	4	3	0	1	0
McElroy Jr.	.984	61	121	4	2	2

GCL CARDINALS

GULF COAST LEAGUE

ROOKIE

ST. LOUIS CARDINALS

Batting	B-T	HT	WT	DOB	AVG	vLH	vRH	G	AB	R	H	2B	3B	HR	RBI	BB	HBP	SH	SF	SO	SB	CS	SLG	OBP
Acevedo, Jhohan	R-R	6-1	173	3-28-93	.317	.406	.286	45	123	21	39	2	2	0	19	11	3	1	6	26	5	2	.366	.371
Ahmady, Alan	R-R	5-11	200	12-14-87	.250	.000	.250	2	4	1	1	0	0	1	3	2	1	0	0	0	0	0	1.000	.571
Almaraz, Joe	L-R	6-3	185	5-6-92	.246	.286	.233	20	57	7	14	3	0	2	9	9	3	0	0	15	0	0	.404	.377
Argenal, Jem	L-L	5-11	180	9-19-91	.242	.189	.258	45	157	21	38	5	2	3	22	3	3	0	1	27	1	0	.357	.268
Barbuena, Daniel	B-R	6-0	160	3-23-93	.217	.211	.220	26	60	9	13	4	0	0	1	4	2	0	0	21	0	1	.283	.288
Bean, Steve	L-R	6-2	190	9-15-93	.320	.400	.286	15	50	8	16	4	0	0	7	8	1	0	0	11	0	0	.400	.424
Bryant, Anthony	L-R	6-3	215	1-13-92	.277	.179	.308	38	119	21	33	7	0	4	19	19	1	0	1	36	18	8	.437	.379
Capellan, Amaury	R-R	5-11	190	9-30-92	.233	.259	.224	36	103	17	24	4	0	2	13	13	6	0	1	25	2	2	.330	.350
Dodd, Corderious	R-R	6-2	230	2-21-92	.190	.056	.220	37	100	7	19	3	0	1	8	9	5	0	1	43	0	0	.250	.287
Ehrlich, Adam	L-R	6-1	200	12-13-92	.284	.313	.276	22	74	12	21	4	1	0	6	12	0	1	0	17	0	0	.365	.384
Garcia, Ronnierd	R-R	6-1	185	3-8-90	.211	.200	.215	31	95	11	20	4	0	2	12	12	3	1	0	36	1	1	.316	.318
Gomez, Jose	R-R	5-11	183	1-30-92	.193	.188	.195	23	57	6	11	2	0	0	7	6	1	0	1	14	0	1	.228	.277
Gonzalez, Yoenny	B-R	5-9	170	1-31-92	.227	.107	.260	41	132	22	30	4	0	0	6	13	3	1	0	28	14	3	.258	.311
Luna, Aaron	R-R	5-11	200	3-28-87	.375	.667	.200	3	8	3	3	1	0	0	1	2	2	0	0	2	0	0	.500	.583
Medina, Rafael	R-R	6-2	170	10-24-91	.261	.185	.286	36	111	14	29	5	0	1	14	11	1	0	0	22	1	0	.333	.333
Peoples, Kenny	R-R	6-1	185	8-20-92	.260	.425	.200	43	150	19	39	4	3	2	21	7	6	0	1	35	4	5	.367	.317
Perez, Luis	R-R	5-10	160	7-24-91	.309	.333	.302	41	149	21	46	11	4	4	24	11	2	1	3	25	7	1	.517	.358
Popkins, David	L-R	6-3	215	11-16-89	.353	.375	.349	21	51	6	18	5	1	0	7	3	4	0	0	11	0	2	.490	.431
Stanley, Cody	L-R	5-10	190	12-21-88	.300	.000	.333	3	10	1	3	2	0	0	0	0	0	0	0	4	0	0	.500	.300
Stienstra, Danny	R-R	6-2	200	3-1-89	.333	.000	.400	3	6	0	2	1	0	0	0	0	0	0	0	0	0	0	.500	.333
Swinson, Mike	L-R	6-2	185	9-24-89	.200	.500	.000	2	5	1	1	0	0	1	2	1	0	0	1	1	0	0	.800	.286
Walsh, Colin	B-R	6-0	190	9-26-89	.125	.000	.200	2	8	1	1	0	0	0	1	0	0	0	0	1	0	0	.125	.125
Wick, Rowan	L-R	6-2	215	11-9-92	.156	.227	.127	23	77	9	12	4	1	1	8	5	3	0	1	21	1	1	.273	.233
Wiley, Brett	L-R	5-10	175	11-24-91	.300	.263	.314	40	140	20	42	11	3	1	16	19	2	0	1	27	3	0	.443	.389

Pitching	B-T	HT	WT	DOB	W	L	ERA	G	GS	CG	SV	IP	H	R	ER	HR	BB	SO	AVG	vLH	vRH	K/9	BB/9
Additon, Nick	L-L	6-5	215	12-16-87	0	0	0.00	2	2	0	0	6	3	0	0	0	0	7	.143	.000	.188	10.50	0.00
Aguilar, Cesar	R-R	6-3	250	5-15-92	0	0	0.00	4	0	0	0	7	5	0	0	0	1	8	.192	.000	.263	10.29	1.29
Blair, Seth	R-R	6-2	185	3-3-89	0	0	0.00	2	1	0	0	3	1	0	0	0	2	1	.167	.000	.333	3.00	6.00
Brand, Cole	R-R	6-2	225	5-19-92	2	0	0.51	15	0	0	3	18	12	2	1	0	2	10	.182	.167	.188	5.09	1.02
Caballero, Juan	R-R	6-4	175	8-20-92	2	0	3.05	16	0	0	0	21	19	9	7	2	8	20	.247	.292	.226	8.71	3.48
Canache, Roberto	R-R	6-5	180	5-12-90	0	0	0.00	2	0	0	0	2	1	0	0	0	0	0	.167	.000	.200	0.00	0.00
Copeland, Ryan	R-L	5-11	180	6-10-88	0	1	13.50	2	0	0	0	2	4	3	3	1	0	2	.400	.500	.375	9.00	0.00
De Los Santos, Hansel	R-R	6-3	160	8-7-91	4	3	4.57	8	8	0	0	41	39	22	21	2	15	29	.258	.270	.254	6.31	3.27
Delgado, Ramon	R-R	6-3	195	9-3-86	0	0	3.00	3	0	0	0	3	3	1	1	0	1	1	.273	.667	.125	3.00	3.00
Donofrio, Joey	R-R	6-3	185	5-10-89	0	0	0.00	1	0	0	0	1	0	0	0	0	2	2	.000	.000	.000	27.00	27.00
Flores, Fidencio	R-R	6-0	160	9-10-91	3	1	1.56	12	6	0	0	40	27	9	7	2	10	40	.186	.195	.183	8.93	2.23
Foody, Max	L-L	6-3	220	6-11-93	0	2	11.57	8	6	0	0	16	26	22	21	0	16	18	.356	.400	.345	9.92	8.82
Fuentes, Brian	L-L	6-4	230	8-9-75	0	0	0.00	2	2	0	0	2	1	0	0	0	0	1	.167	.000	.250	4.50	0.00
Garcia, Jaime	L-L	6-2	215	7-8-86	0	0	0.00	1	1	0	0	2	4	0	0	0	1	1	.400	.333	.429	3.86	0.00
Garcia, Silfredo	R-R	6-2	170	7-19-91	2	0	1.54	4	4	0	0	23	12	4	4	1	0	27	.143	.138	.145	10.41	0.00
Gerdel, Anderson	R-R	6-4	204	7-19-91	4	2	1.23	17	0	0	1	22	13	4	3	0	3	18	.169	.286	.125	7.36	1.23
Heyer, Kurt	L-R	6-2	185	1-23-91	0	0	0.00	2	0	0	0	2	1	0	0	0	0	4	.125	.000	.143	18.00	0.00
Machuca, Javier	L-L	6-3	200	11-21-92	3	0	5.16	17	0	0	0	30	31	19	17	0	9	22	.265	.391	.234	6.67	2.73
Mitchem, Burny	R-R	6-6	260	4-9-89	3	0	2.53	14	1	0	0	32	29	13	9	1	5	20	.238	.229	.241	5.63	1.41
Paredes, Norge	R-R	6-3	171	2-12-91	1	2	0.75	17	0	0	4	24	15	5	2	0	7	24	.176	.222	.155	9.00	2.63
Perdomo, Luis	R-R	6-2	159	5-9-93	1	1	5.00	2	2	0	0	9	11	6	5	0	3	5	.324	.364	.304	5.00	5.00
Polanco, Jhonny	R-R	6-3	191	4-28-92	1	3	1.91	15	7	0	4	33	27	12	7	1	13	38	.227	.108	.280	10.36	3.55
Renfro, Josh	L-L	6-0	182	8-31-89	0	1	0.36	20	0	0	2	25	19	4	1	0	5	31	.202	.091	.236	11.16	1.80
Russell, Zach	R-R	6-2	185	7-27-89	0	0	0.00	2	1	0	0	3	1	0	0	0	1	4	.111	.000	.143	6.00	0.00
Thomas, Chris	R-R	6-2	200	3-16-88	1	0	0.68	12	0	0	4	13	6	1	1	0	5	15	.133	.176	.107	10.13	3.38
Ulacio, Ramon	R-R	6-1	190	3-17-91	2	4	6.81	15	3	0	0	40	60	38	30	0	26	29	.364	.407	.340	6.58	5.90
Villegas, Kender	R-R	6-2	170	6-8-93	4	4	6.28	11	11	1	0	53	72	42	37	3	15	39	.324	.339	.319	6.62	2.55
Wacha, Michael	R-R	6-6	195	7-1-91	0	0	1.80	3	2	0	0	5	4	1	1	0	2	7	.222	.125	.300	12.60	0.00
Whiting, Boone	R-R	6-1	175	8-20-89	0	0	7.71	4	0	0	0	7	10	6	6	1	1	11	.323	.200	.381	14.14	1.29
Wilson, Josh	R-R	6-0	180	9-6-86	1	0	18.00	1	0	0	0	1	3	2	2	0	0	0	.500	1.000	.400	0.00	0.00

Fielding

Catcher	PCT	G	PO	A	E	DP	PB
Bean	1.000	12	92	11	0	3	7
Ehrlich	.975	19	147	9	4	0	7
Gomez	.992	17	100	21	1	2	7
Stanley	1.000	2	15	1	0	0	0
Wick	.957	12	82	7	4	1	12

First Base	PCT	G	PO	A	E	DP
Almaraz	.948	15	100	10	6	5
Argenal	.974	40	280	18	8	25
Medina	.985	9	62	4	1	11

Second Base	PCT	G	PO	A	E	DP
Barbuena	.952	8	18	22	2	5

Perez	.948	25	48	43	5	13
Walsh	.714	2	2	3	2	1
Wiley	.975	29	53	64	3	14

Third Base	PCT	G	PO	A	E	DP
Ahmady	1.000	2	0	4	0	1
Barbuena	1.000	1	0	2	0	0
Garcia	.908	30	25	44	7	7
Medina	.893	28	18	49	8	4
Stiensta	1.000	3	3	5	0	0
Wiley	.800	3	2	6	2	0

Shortstop	PCT	G	PO	A	E	DP
Barbuena	.915	13	21	22	4	6

Peoples	.918	42	46	88	12	24
Wiley	.875	7	6	15	3	2

Outfield	PCT	G	PO	A	E	DP
Acevedo	.971	44	94	8	3	3
Argenal	1.000	4	4	0	0	0
Bryant	.977	31	42	0	1	0
Capellan	.980	34	46	3	1	1
Dodd	.976	29	40	1	1	0
Gonzalez	.949	39	52	4	3	2
Luna	1.000	2	1	0	0	0
Perez	1.000	6	6	1	0	1
Popkins	.923	12	12	0	1	0
Swinson	1.000	2	4	0	0	0

DSL CARDINALS

ROOKIE

DOMINICAN SUMMER LEAGUE

Batting	B-T	HT	WT	DOB	AVG	vLH	vRH	G	AB	R	H	2B	3B	HR	RBI	BB	HBP	SH	SF	SO	SB	CS	SLG	OBP
Agustin, Jose	R-R	6-3	160	4-2-93	.162	.190	.149	43	136	12	22	9	0	0	10	14	3	2	1	45	0	4	.228	.253
Alvarez, Eliezer	B-R	5-11	165	10-15-94	.205	.208	.203	53	176	33	36	5	2	2	15	27	4	3	0	35	10	7	.290	.324
Araujo, George	L-L	6-2	170	11-26-93	.140	.151	.135	53	164	12	23	8	2	0	16	18	9	2	3	48	1	2	.213	.258
Celestino, Eduardo	L-R	6-2	175	9-8-92	.115	.150	.094	21	52	5	6	0	2	0	1	3	1	0	0	20	1	0	.192	.179
Cerdas, Jeffry	B-R	6-0	160	1-12-95	.159	.200	.145	47	113	10	18	2	0	0	6	24	4	1	1	25	1	4	.177	.324
Cruz, Luis	R-R	6-2	180	5-26-93	.316	.280	.333	65	234	40	74	11	2	5	32	23	6	0	2	36	5	3	.444	.389
Franco, Bladimil	R-R	6-0	170	10-29-93	.245	.239	.248	55	184	15	45	7	1	0	20	20	0	2	1	28	2	4	.293	.317
Godoy, Jose	L-R	5-11	180	10-13-94	.239	.205	.255	46	142	15	34	4	1	0	15	32	4	0	3	22	0	2	.282	.387
Mejia, Alejandro	R-R	6-4	195	3-10-93	.217	.216	.218	50	184	19	40	7	0	2	22	14	2	0	1	28	1	1	.288	.279
Pena, Jose	R-R	6-2	190	5-26-92	.200	.333	.000	1	5	0	1	1	0	0	0	0	0	0	0	1	0	0	.400	.200
Pina, Leobaldo	R-R	6-2	160	6-29-94	.296	.221	.329	66	250	39	74	13	2	0	25	32	2	4	3	37	16	6	.364	.376
Reyes, Robelys	B-R	5-9	150	7-25-90	.250	.215	.270	56	216	36	54	6	4	0	16	16	1	5	2	24	15	5	.315	.302
Ripoll, Sergio	R-R	6-0	180	4-16-94	.202	.222	.190	34	94	9	19	4	0	0	11	11	4	0	1	16	2	1	.245	.309
Sanchez, Domingo	R-R	6-0	182	1-11-94	.097	.235	.066	47	93	13	9	1	0	0	9	16	1	4	1	39	7	2	.108	.234
Torres, Carlos	R-R	6-3	160	10-1-92	.258	.211	.278	66	229	36	59	9	1	1	33	37	11	5	1	45	11	4	.319	.385

Pitching	B-T	HT	WT	DOB	W	L	ERA	G	GS	CG	SV	IP	H	R	ER	HR	BB	SO	AVG	vLH	vRH	K/9	BB/9
Brito, Ismael	L-L	5-11	170	3-23-93	1	0	1.57	20	0	0	14	34	21	6	6	0	12	42	.188	.000	.194	11.01	3.15
De La Rosa, Luis	R-R	5-11	180	12-18-92	0	0	5.40	8	0	0	0	15	17	11	9	0	14	18	.279	.235	.295	10.80	8.40
Escudero, Jhonatan	R-R	6-1	165	7-7-93	7	1	2.88	13	6	0	0	50	40	24	16	2	24	49	.216	.184	.224	8.82	4.32
Fresa, Juan	R-R	6-3	160	3-10-92	0	0	7.11	8	0	0	0	6	6	7	5	0	12	4	.273	.250	.278	5.68	17.05
Gonzalez, Fernando	R-R	6-4	175	4-22-94	1	0	3.38	4	0	0	1	5	7	2	2	1	0	5	.280	.200	.333	8.44	0.00
Lara, Jose	R-R	6-2	175	3-26-94	2	1	8.10	13	0	0	1	27	34	31	24	2	11	13	.301	.200	.323	4.39	3.71
Martinez, Dailyn	R-R	6-2	170	4-19-93	1	5	3.18	11	11	0	0	57	48	31	20	2	18	41	.227	.239	.224	6.51	2.86
Negrette, Alirio	L-L	5-11	176	3-29-95	1	2	3.24	13	0	0	0	17	13	8	6	0	12	13	.206	.200	.207	7.02	6.48
Parra, Frederis	R-R	6-3	162	10-22-94	4	2	2.21	15	1	0	0	37	30	11	9	0	10	21	.238	.180	.255	5.15	2.45
Perdomo, Luis	R-R	6-2	159	5-9-93	3	3	2.27	9	9	1	0	48	42	20	12	0	8	47	.230	.273	.224	8.87	1.51
Perez, Dewen	L-L	6-0	175	9-29-94	1	4	3.06	8	8	0	0	35	27	16	12	1	13	38	.206	.200	.207	9.68	3.31
Perez, Juan	R-R	6-2	195	7-22-95	2	5	4.33	12	12	0	0	52	43	29	25	2	34	55	.230	.103	.253	9.52	5.88
Rodriguez, Jorge L.	R-R	6-2	175	3-18-94	1	1	4.26	13	0	0	1	19	14	13	9	0	16	22	.209	.167	.213	10.42	7.58
Salazar, Hector	R-R	6-2	165	6-29-94	2	5	3.38	10	10	0	0	51	42	25	19	1	15	46	.232	.220	.236	8.17	2.66
Santos, Ramon	R-R	6-2	160	9-20-94	1	2	1.52	16	1	0	3	30	18	7	5	0	11	24	.171	.000	.194	7.28	3.34
Silva, Isaac	L-L	6-2	190	9-12-92	3	1	2.59	11	11	0	0	49	40	18	14	0	19	52	.229	.333	.223	9.62	3.51
Vallejo, Esteban	R-R	6-4	190	12-9-93	0	0	1.85	12	1	0	1	24	24	7	5	1	8	22	.264	.200	.276	8.14	2.96

Fielding

Catcher	PCT	G	PO	A	E	DP	PB
Cruz	.953	23	177	26	10	1	10
Godoy	.978	38	307	50	8	1	7
Ripoll	.960	18	85	10	4	0	2

First Base	PCT	G	PO	A	E	DP
Agustin	.667	1	1	1	1	1
Cruz	.968	29	231	10	8	16
Godoy	1.000	2	10	1	0	1
Mejia	.987	36	286	16	4	23
Ripoll	.966	9	56	1	2	7

Second Base	PCT	G	PO	A	E	DP
Alvarez	.921	10	17	18	3	7
Cerdas	.937	46	92	71	11	18
Reyes	.973	27	53	54	3	12

Third Base	PCT	G	PO	A	E	DP
Agustin	.898	41	39	84	14	7
Mejia	.917	5	2	9	1	0
Pina	.941	23	13	67	5	9
Reyes	.923	5	6	6	1	0

Shortstop	PCT	G	PO	A	E	DP
Alvarez	.825	23	37	48	18	7
Pina	.910	35	50	101	15	19
Reyes	.930	21	31	49	6	12

Outfield	PCT	G	PO	A	E	DP
Araujo	.928	51	60	4	5	1
Celestino	1.000	17	16	2	0	1
Franco	.959	53	66	5	3	0
Reyes	1.000	4	3	0	0	0
Sanchez	.918	40	44	1	4	0
Torres	.986	66	136	6	2	2

San Diego Padres

SEASON IN A SENTENCE: A young Padres team (with an average age of about 27.5 years) on the lowest budget in baseball (approximately $55.2 million) lived down to expectations with an 86-loss season—though the club showed fight by going 47-36 (.566) from July 1 to the end of the season.

HIGH POINT: Third baseman Chase Headley enjoyed a career year, batting .286/.376/.498 with 31 homers and a National League-leading 115 RBIs. He ranked third in the league with 86 walks and fifth with 301 total bases, while winning the Silver Slugger and Gold Glove awards. Headley led all big league third basemen with 315 assists.

LOW POINT: Arm injuries to top young pitchers such as lefties Cory Luebke and Robbie Erlin and righties Casey Kelly and Joe Wieland necessitated that the Padres turn to a random cast of 30-somethings—Jason Marquis (15 starts), Eric Stults (14), Ross Ohlendorf (nine), Kip Wells (seven) and Jeff Suppan (six)—to round out the rotation beyond Clayton Richard and Edinson Volquez. They produced a 4.49 ERA in 303 innings.

NOTABLE ROOKIES: The Padres broke in the majority of their rookies on the pitching side, but the club's two most productive rookies were first baseman Yonder Alonso and catcher Yasmani Grandal, a pair of first-rounders from the University of Miami whom the Padres acquired from the Reds in December for Mat Latos. Alonso led all rookies with 39 doubles and hit .285/.352/.430 in the second half as he adjusted to Petco Park. Grandal faces a 50-game drug suspension in 2013, but he showed promise by batting .297/.394/.469 with eight homers in 192 at-bats. Rookie relievers such as Brad Boxberger, Brad Brach, Cory Burns, Miles Mikolas and Nick Vincent got their feet in the door, while Kelly returned from elbow trouble in late August to make six starts.

KEY TRANSACTIONS: A busy offseason for incoming general manager Josh Byrnes yielded Alonso, Grandal, Boxberger, Volquez, Huston Street, Carlos Quentin and Andrew Cashner in trades at the expense of, among others, Latos, Anthony Rizzo and Simon Castro.

DOWN ON THE FARM: A talented low Class A Fort Wayne club advanced to the Midwest League finals, but in terms of overall domestic minor league winning percentage, the Padres' .455 mark ranked near the bottom.

OPENING DAY PAYROLL: $55.2 million (30th)

PLAYERS OF THE YEAR

MAJOR LEAGUE	MINOR LEAGUE
Chase Headley	**Jedd Gyorko**
3b	**2b/3b**
.286/.376/.498	(Double-A/Triple-A)
115 RBIs led NL	.311/.373/.547
Won first Gold Glove	30 HR, 100 RBIs

ORGANIZATION LEADERS

BATTING		*Minimum 250 AB
MAJORS		
* AVG	Chase Headley	.286
* OPS	Chase Headley	.874
HR	Chase Headley	31
RBI	Chase Headley	115
MINORS		
* AVG	Tommy Medica, Lake Elsinore	.330
* OBP	Tommy Medica, Lake Elsinore	.406
* SLG	Tommy Medica, Lake Elsinore	.623
R	Nate Freiman, San Antonio	80
	Jedd Gyorko, San Antonio/Tucson	80
H	Jedd Gyorko, San Antonio/Tucson	155
TB	Jedd Gyorko, San Antonio/Tucson	273
2B	Tommy Medica, Lake Elsinore	37
3B	Jace Peterson, Fort Wayne	9
HR	Jedd Gyorko, San Antonio/Tucson	30
RBI	Nate Freiman, San Antonio	105
BB	Dean Anna, San Antonio	66
SO	Rico Noel, Lake Elsinore	151
SB	Rico Noel, Lake Elsinore	90

PITCHING		#Minimum 75 IP
MAJORS		
W	Clayton Richard	14
# ERA	Clayton Richard	3.99
SO	Edinson Volquez	174
SV	Huston Street	23
MINORS		
W	Matthew Andriese, Lake Elsinore	10
	Jorge Reyes, Tucson	10
L	Matt Lollis, San Antonio/Tucson/Lake Elsinore	13
# ERA	Matthew Wisler, Fort Wayne	2.53
G	Erik Hamren, San Antonio/Tucson	58
GS	Josh Geer, Tucson/San Antonio	28
SV	Kevin Quackenbush, Lake Elsinore	27
IP	Josh Geer, Tucson/San Antonio	160
BB	Adys Portillo, Fort Wayne/San Antonio	70
SO	Burch Smith, Lake Elsinore	137
# AVG	Adys Portillo, Fort Wayne/San Antonio	.193

General Manager: Josh Byrnes. **Farm Director:** Randy Smith. **Scouting Director:** Jaron Madison.

Class	Team	League	W	L	PCT	Finish	Manager
Majors	San Diego Padres	National	76	86	.469	11th (16)	Bud Black
Triple-A	Tucson Padres	Pacific Coast	56	88	.389	15th (16)	Terry Kennedy
Double-A	San Antonio Missions	Texas	60	80	.429	7th (8)	John Gibbons
High A	Lake Elsinore Storm	California	69	71	.493	6th (10)	Shawn Wooten
Low A	Fort Wayne TinCaps	Midwest	69	71	.493	8th (16)	Jose Valentin
Short-season	Eugene Emeralds	Northwest	47	29	.618	1st (8)	Pat Murphy
Rookie	AZL Padres	Arizona	16	40	.286	13th (13)	Jim Gabella
Overall 2012 Minor League Record			317	379	.455	28th (30)	

ORGANIZATION STATISTICS

SAN DIEGO PADRES

NATIONAL LEAGUE

Batting	B-T	HT	WT	DOB	AVG	vLH	vRH	G	AB	R	H	2B	3B	HR	RBI	BB	HBP	SH	SF	SO	SB	CS	SLG	OBP
Alonso, Yonder	L-R	6-2	240	4-8-87	.273	.261	.278	155	549	47	150	39	0	9	62	62	3	1	4	101	3	0	.393	.348
Amarista, Alexi	L-R	5-7	150	4-6-89	.240	.266	.232	105	275	35	66	15	5	5	32	17	0	6	2	42	8	4	.385	.282
Baker, John	L-R	6-1	220	1-20-81	.238	.229	.241	63	193	17	46	8	0	0	14	20	0	1	0	41	2	1	.280	.310
Bartlett, Jason	R-R	6-0	190	10-30-79	.133	.160	.121	29	83	8	11	5	0	0	4	12	0	2	1	27	0	0	.193	.240
Blanks, Kyle	R-R	6-6	270	9-11-86	.200	.333	.000	4	5	0	1	0	0	0	0	1	0	0	0	2	0	0	.200	.333
Cabrera, Everth	B-R	5-10	175	11-17-86	.246	.195	.267	115	398	49	98	19	3	2	24	43	3	5	0	110	44	4	.324	.324
Darnell, James	R-R	6-2	195	1-19-87	.235	.111	.375	7	17	1	4	0	1	1	2	0	0	0	0	2	0	0	.471	.316
Denorfia, Chris	R-R	6-0	195	7-15-80	.293	.337	.247	130	348	56	102	19	6	8	36	27	2	2	3	52	13	5	.451	.345
Forsythe, Logan	R-R	6-1	205	1-14-87	.273	.384	.222	91	315	45	86	13	3	6	26	28	6	0	1	57	8	2	.390	.343
Grandal, Yasmani	B-R	6-2	210	11-8-88	.297	.308	.293	60	192	28	57	7	1	8	36	31	1	0	2	39	0	0	.469	.394
Guzman, Jesus	R-R	6-1	215	6-14-84	.247	.303	.206	120	287	32	71	18	2	9	48	29	2	1	2	71	3	3	.418	.319
Headley, Chase	B-R	6-2	200	5-9-84	.286	.265	.296	161	604	95	173	31	2	31	115	86	4	0	5	157	17	6	.498	.376
Hermida, Jeremy	L-R	6-3	220	1-30-84	.250	.500	.227	13	24	2	6	1	1	0	2	3	0	0	0	7	1	0	.375	.333
Hudson, Orlando	B-R	6-0	190	12-12-77	.211	.316	.165	35	123	11	26	0	5	1	11	8	0	0	0	27	3	2	.317	.260
Hundley, Nick	R-R	6-1	205	9-8-83	.157	.098	.197	58	204	14	32	7	1	3	22	15	2	1	3	56	0	3	.245	.219
Kotsay, Mark	L-L	6-0	210	12-2-75	.259	.250	.260	82	143	9	37	8	0	2	14	11	1	0	1	24	0	2	.357	.314
Maybin, Cameron	R-R	6-3	210	4-4-87	.243	.240	.244	147	507	67	123	20	5	8	45	44	4	3	3	110	26	7	.349	.306
Parrino, Andy	B-R	6-0	180	10-31-85	.207	.214	.203	55	116	9	24	5	0	1	6	17	2	2	1	35	1	0	.276	.316
Quentin, Carlos	R-R	6-2	235	8-28-82	.261	.329	.233	86	284	44	74	21	0	16	46	36	17	0	3	41	0	1	.504	.374
Rodriguez, Eddy	R-R	6-0	205	12-1-85	.200	.000	.250	2	5	1	1	0	0	1	1	2	0	0	0	3	0	0	.800	.429
Solis, Ali	R-R	6-0	175	9-29-87	.000	.000	.000	5	4	0	0	0	0	0	0	0	0	0	0	2	0	0	.000	.000
Tekotte, Blake	L-R	5-11	180	5-24-87	.133	.500	.077	11	15	0	2	0	0	0	0	0	0	0	0	4	1	0	.133	.133
Venable, Will	L-L	6-2	200	10-29-82	.264	.231	.270	148	417	62	110	26	8	9	45	41	5	5	2	94	24	6	.429	.335

Pitching	B-T	HT	WT	DOB	W	L	ERA	G	GS	CG	SV	IP	H	R	ER	HR	BB	SO	AVG	vLH	vRH	K/9	BB/9
Bass, Anthony	R-R	6-2	190	11-1-87	2	8	4.73	24	15	1	1	97	89	59	51	10	39	80	.243	.251	.234	7.42	3.62
Boxberger, Brad	R-R	6-2	200	5-27-88	0	0	2.60	24	0	0	0	28	22	12	8	3	18	33	.222	.239	.200	10.73	5.86
Brach, Brad	R-R	6-6	210	4-12-86	2	4	3.78	67	0	0	0	67	50	28	28	11	33	75	.207	.239	.188	10.13	4.46
Burns, Cory	R-R	6-0	205	10-9-87	0	1	5.50	17	0	0	0	18	26	11	11	1	10	18	.321	.325	.317	9.00	5.00
Cashner, Andrew	R-R	6-6	200	9-11-86	3	4	4.27	33	5	0	0	46	42	23	22	5	19	52	.244	.197	.281	10.10	3.69
Frieri, Ernesto	R-R	6-2	200	7-19-85	1	0	2.31	11	0	0	0	12	9	5	3	2	4	18	.205	.222	.192	13.89	3.09
Gregerson, Luke	L-R	6-3	200	5-14-84	2	0	2.39	77	0	0	9	72	57	19	19	7	21	72	.215	.214	.216	9.04	2.64
Hinshaw, Alex	L-L	6-2	175	10-31-82	1	1	4.50	31	0	0	0	28	23	14	14	5	20	36	.217	.196	.233	11.57	6.43
2-team total (2 Chicago)					1	1	6.04	33	0	0	0	28	27	19	19	8	21	36	—	—	—	11.44	6.67
Kelly, Casey	R-R	6-3	195	10-4-89	2	3	6.21	6	6	0	0	29	39	23	20	5	10	26	.322	.318	.327	8.07	3.10
Layne, Tommy	L-L	6-3	185	11-2-84	2	0	3.24	26	0	0	2	17	9	6	6	0	3	25	.148	.083	.240	13.50	1.62
Luebke, Cory	R-L	6-4	205	3-4-85	3	1	2.61	5	5	0	0	31	28	10	9	1	8	23	.233	.259	.226	6.68	2.32
Marquis, Jason	L-R	6-1	220	8-21-78	6	7	4.04	15	15	1	0	94	94	53	42	14	28	79	.258	.269	.249	7.59	2.69
Mikolas, Miles	R-R	6-5	220	8-23-88	2	1	3.62	25	0	0	0	32	32	15	13	4	15	23	.256	.231	.274	6.40	4.18
Moseley, Dustin	R-R	6-4	215	12-26-81	0	0	9.00	1	1	0	0	5	5	5	5	1	2	4	.263	.231	.333	7.20	3.60
Ohlendorf, Ross	R-R	6-4	240	8-8-82	4	4	7.77	13	9	0	0	49	62	44	42	7	24	39	.304	.286	.321	7.21	4.44
Owings, Micah	R-R	6-5	220	9-28-82	0	2	2.79	6	0	0	0	10	8	4	3	1	5	7	.229	.286	.190	6.52	4.66
Palmer, Matt	R-R	6-2	235	3-21-79	0	0	9.00	3	0	0	0	2	2	2	2	1	2	2	.286	.000	.400	9.00	9.00
Richard, Clayton	L-L	6-5	245	9-12-83	14	14	3.99	33	33	1	0	219	228	110	97	31	42	107	.267	.241	.275	4.40	1.73
Spence, Josh	L-L	6-1	190	1-22-88	0	1	4.35	11	0	0	0	10	13	5	5	1	5	10	.302	.158	.417	8.71	4.35
Stauffer, Tim	R-R	6-1	225	6-2-82	0	0	5.40	1	1	0	0	5	7	4	3	1	3	5	.333	.286	.429	9.00	5.40
Street, Huston	R-R	6-0	190	8-2-83	2	1	1.85	40	0	0	23	39	17	8	8	2	11	47	.130	.127	.132	10.85	2.54
Stults, Eric	L-L	6-0	225	12-9-79	8	3	2.92	18	14	0	0	92	86	36	30	7	23	51	.249	.286	.197	4.97	2.24
Suppan, Jeff	R-R	6-2	225	1-2-75	2	3	5.28	6	6	0	0	31	34	19	18	4	13	7	.281	.340	.243	2.05	3.82
Thatcher, Joe	L-L	6-2	230	10-4-81	1	4	3.41	55	0	0	1	32	30	13	12	2	14	39	.250	.175	.333	11.08	3.98
Thayer, Dale	R-R	6-0	195	12-17-80	2	2	3.43	64	0	0	7	58	53	24	22	4	12	47	.248	.253	.244	7.34	1.87
Vincent, Nick	R-R	6-0	175	7-12-86	2	0	1.71	27	0	0	0	26	19	5	5	2	7	28	.198	.139	.233	9.57	2.39
Volquez, Edinson	R-R	6-0	225	7-3-83	11	11	4.14	32	32	1	0	183	160	88	84	14	105	174	.236	.230	.240	8.57	5.17

SAN DIEGO PADRES

SAN DIEGO PADRES

	B-T	HT	WT	DOB	W	L	ERA	G	GS	CG	SV	IP	H	R	ER	HR	BB	SO	AVG	vLH	vRH	K/9	BB/9
Wells, Kip	R-R	6-3	205	4-21-77	2	4	4.58	7	7	0	0	37	41	23	19	6	20	19	.283	.279	.286	4.58	4.82
Werner, Andrew	L-L	6-2	215	2-25-87	2	3	5.58	8	8	0	0	40	45	26	25	5	14	35	.285	.205	.316	7.81	3.12
Wieland, Joe	R-R	6-3	195	1-21-90	0	4	4.55	5	5	0	0	28	26	16	14	5	9	24	.245	.250	.241	7.81	2.93

Fielding

Catcher	PCT	G	PO	A	E	DP	PB
Baker	.990	56	368	23	4	0	7
Grandal	.988	55	386	38	5	2	8
Hundley	.992	56	426	48	4	1	3
Rodriguez	1.000	2	20	1	0	0	0
Solis	.889	2	8	0	1	0	0

First Base	PCT	G	PO	A	E	DP
Alonso	.991	149	1269	96	12	77
Blanks	1.000	1	6	0	0	0
Guzman	1.000	19	116	12	0	8
Headley	—	1	0	0	0	0
Kotsay	1.000	5	26	0	0	2

Second Base	PCT	G	PO	A	E	DP
Amarista	.984	52	80	99	3	15
Cabrera	1.000	6	6	11	0	0
Forsythe	.967	81	166	187	12	35
Guzman	1.000	4	0	1	0	0
Hudson	.987	33	68	82	2	16
Parrino	1.000	15	18	20	0	5

Third Base	PCT	G	PO	A	E	DP
Amarista	—	1	0	0	0	0
Cabrera	1.000	1	0	2	0	0
Darnell	.667	1	1	1	0	0
Forsythe	1.000	4	0	2	0	0
Headley	.976	159	100	315	10	20
Parrino	1.000	2	0	4	0	0

Shortstop	PCT	G	PO	A	E	DP
Amarista	.973	12	8	28	1	6
Bartlett	.952	27	32	68	5	12
Cabrera	.966	111	140	315	16	34
Forsythe	1.000	5	4	7	0	1
Parrino	.940	26	26	68	6	11

Outfield	PCT	G	PO	A	E	DP
Amarista	1.000	34	32	1	0	1
Blanks	—	1	0	0	0	0
Darnell	1.000	4	2	0	0	0
Denorfia	.993	118	140	4	1	0
Guzman	.978	58	85	4	2	1
Hermida	1.000	7	11	0	0	0
Kotsay	.977	27	41	2	1	2
Maybin	.991	145	330	4	3	1
Parrino	—	1	0	0	0	0
Quentin	.970	72	96	2	3	0
Tekotte	1.000	4	3	0	0	0
Venable	.968	135	209	1	7	0

TUCSON PADRES   TRIPLE-A

PACIFIC COAST LEAGUE

Batting	B-T	HT	WT	DOB	AVG	vLH	vRH	G	AB	R	H	2B	3B	HR	RBI	BB	HBP	SH	SF	SO	SB	CS	SLG	OBP
Altman, Bryan	R-R	6-1	170	8-12-87	.000	.000	.000	3	5	2	0	0	0	0	0	1	0	0	0	1	0	0	.000	.167
Amarista, Alexi	L-R	5-7	150	4-6-89	.286	.250	.303	11	49	6	14	1	0	1	6	1	0	1	0	6	3	0	.367	.300
2-team total (18 Salt Lake)					.278	—	—	29	126	17	35	7	2	1	18	4	0	1	3	12	4	0	.389	.293
Belnome, Vince	L-R	5-11	205	3-11-88	.275	.233	.288	80	258	28	71	11	1	5	33	43	1	0	1	72	5	1	.384	.380
Cabrera, Everth	B-R	5-10	175	11-17-86	.333	.357	.328	34	144	27	48	9	1	0	15	12	1	2	0	28	15	0	.410	.389
Cabrera, Felix	R-R	6-0	170	7-14-89	.667	1.000	.600	2	3	1	2	0	0	0	0	0	0	0	0	1	3	0	.667	.667
Carroll, Sawyer	L-R	6-4	215	5-9-86	.263	.250	.286	112	372	46	98	15	6	8	56	42	0	0	2	69	10	6	.401	.337
Clark, Matt	L-R	6-5	215	12-10-86	.290	.248	.304	121	445	75	129	26	2	22	77	57	1	0	7	113	0	0	.506	.367
Contreras, Anthony	L-R	5-11	185	9-26-83	.280	.186	.300	123	407	51	114	28	3	7	51	12	0	3	1	61	6	2	.415	.300
Darnell, James	R-R	6-2	195	1-19-87	.267	.520	.198	31	116	22	31	6	0	7	21	16	3	0	2	25	1	1	.500	.365
Davis, Brad	R-R	6-1	190	12-29-82	.155	.269	.126	39	129	14	20	7	1	2	12	10	0	0	1	34	4	0	.271	.214
2-team total (7 New Orleans)					.146	—	—	46	144	15	21	8	1	2	12	11	0	0	1	37	4	0	.257	.205
Decker, Cody	R-R	5-11	220	1-17-87	.215	.258	.197	32	107	12	23	7	0	4	13	11	0	2	0	27	0	0	.393	.298
Forsythe, Logan	R-R	6-1	205	1-14-87	.259	.467	.186	16	58	12	15	2	3	1	9	13	3	0	0	18	3	0	.448	.419
Gale, Rocky	R-R	6-0	180	2-22-88	.171	.206	.157	41	123	12	21	6	0	0	11	6	0	2	0	22	0	0	.220	.209
Grandal, Yasmani	B-R	6-2	210	11-8-88	.335	.275	.357	56	194	40	65	18	0	6	35	37	2	0	2	35	0	0	.521	.443
Gyorko, Jedd	R-R	5-10	195	9-23-88	.328	.354	.319	92	369	62	121	24	0	24	83	34	0	0	5	68	4	3	.588	.380
Hermida, Jeremy	L-R	6-3	220	1-30-84	.252	.152	.295	44	151	21	38	7	0	3	22	15	1	0	3	43	1	0	.358	.318
Hundley, Nick	R-R	6-1	205	9-8-83	.190	.200	.188	13	42	4	8	1	1	0	7	4	0	0	1	9	0	1	.262	.255
Kral, Robert	L-R	5-9	190	3-28-89	.385	.500	.364	6	13	5	5	1	0	0	5	5	0	0	0	6	0	0	.462	.556
Merchan, Jesus	R-R	5-11	180	3-26-81	.366	.333	.386	45	145	18	53	7	2	3	16	7	0	1	1	8	2	3	.503	.392
Na, Kyung-Min	L-L	5-10	170	12-12-91	.000	.000	.000	3	4	0	0	0	0	0	0	1	0	0	0	2	0	0	.000	.000
Padilla, Jorge	R-R	6-2	205	8-11-79	.220	.300	.194	17	41	4	9	0	0	0	3	5	1	0	0	7	0	0	.220	.319
Parrino, Andy	B-R	6-0	180	10-31-85	.328	.348	.319	65	235	43	77	23	3	1	32	25	4	0	1	49	6	2	.464	.400
Quentin, Carlos	R-R	6-2	235	8-28-82	.286	.400	.222	5	14	5	4	0	0	1	4	2	1	0	0	3	0	0	.500	.412
Robertson, Dan	R-R	5-8	175	9-30-85	.302	.320	.296	129	490	70	148	28	4	2	38	48	6	8	1	58	18	8	.388	.371
Rodriguez, Eddy	R-R	6-0	205	12-1-85	.180	.240	.120	14	50	3	9	4	0	1	6	3	0	0	0	10	0	0	.320	.226
Roof, Jonathan	R-R	6-1	165	1-23-89	.250	.316	.220	49	120	17	30	2	0	0	11	15	3	0	0	19	1	1	.267	.348
Stokes, Mykal	R-R	6-4	190	6-2-90	.333	—	.333	2	3	1	1	1	0	0	1	2	0	0	1	0	0	0	.667	.500
Tekotte, Blake	L-R	5-11	180	5-24-87	.243	.224	.249	89	321	38	78	20	2	9	26	18	1	6	1	92	9	8	.402	.284
Weems, Beamer	R-R	5-10	175	7-28-87	.241	.231	.246	72	245	33	59	12	0	5	26	20	3	1	1	57	0	1	.351	.305
Zazueta, Amadeo	B-R	5-10	160	1-31-86	.183	.282	.132	46	115	8	21	4	1	0	5	1	1	3	1	19	0	0	.235	.195

Pitching	B-T	HT	WT	DOB	W	L	ERA	G	GS	CG	SV	IP	H	R	ER	HR	BB	SO	AVG	vLH	vRH	K/9	BB/9
Bass, Anthony	R-R	6-2	190	11-1-87	0	0	5.63	3	3	0	0	8	8	6	5	0	0	9	.250	.250	.250	10.13	0.00
Bay, Bear	R-R	6-3	170	7-8-83	4	9	4.63	25	18	0	0	117	139	67	60	12	28	73	.298	.305	.292	5.63	2.16
Boxberger, Brad	R-R	6-2	200	5-27-88	2	2	2.70	37	0	0	5	43	37	14	13	0	19	62	.233	.213	.250	12.88	3.95
Brach, Brad	R-R	6-6	210	4-12-86	2	1	2.79	10	0	0	3	10	11	3	3	0	1	5	.306	.333	.278	4.66	0.93
Burns, Cory	R-R	6-0	205	10-9-87	1	2	3.14	54	0	0	3	66	49	25	23	1	17	78	.205	.214	.199	10.64	2.32
Cashner, Andrew	R-R	6-6	220	9-11-86	0	1	3.00	3	3	0	0	9	8	3	3	2	3	8	.242	.273	.227	8.00	2.00
Franklin, Chris	R-R	6-1	200	11-10-87	0	1	23.14	3	0	0	0	5	17	12	12	3	4	2	.607	.600	.611	3.86	7.71
Geer, Josh	R-R	6-3	195	6-2-83	3	7	7.81	8	8	0	0	40	60	37	35	8	16	25	.353	.416	.301	5.58	3.57
Gonzalez, Greg	R-R	5-11	190	9-9-88	0	1	23.14	1	1	0	0	2	8	6	6	1	5	1	.571	.500	.750	3.86	0.00
Hamburger, Mark	R-R	6-4	195	2-5-87	0	2	7.50	5	1	0	0	12	17	12	10	2	3	11	.340	.450	.267	8.25	2.25
3-team total (17 Oklahoma City, 21 Round Rock)					1	5	6.20	43	4	0	2	78	104	57	54	11	36	63	—	—	—	7.24	4.14
Hamren, Erik	R-R	6-1	195	8-21-86	2	5	4.40	46	0	0	9	47	52	25	23	4	23	54	.284	.348	.210	10.34	4.40
Haney, Chris	R-R	5-11	185	2-13-89	0	0	5.63	4	0	0	0	8	9	5	5	1	2	7	.281	.222	.304	7.88	2.25
Hinshaw, Alex	L-L	6-2	175	10-31-82	0	0	3.72	14	0	0	0	19	14	8	8	0	10	18	.206	.222	.195	8.38	4.66
Hynes, Colt	L-L	5-11	200	6-28-85	9	5	5.76	30	21	0	0	127	190	93	81	11	29	74	.352	.342	.356	5.26	2.06
Jackson, Matt	R-R	6-4	190	12-18-87	2	0	0.00	2	2	0	0	12	7	0	0	0	2	7	.163	.045	.286	5.25	1.50

	B-T	HT	WT	DOB	W	L	ERA	G	GS	CG	SV	IP	H	R	ER	HR	BB	SO	AVG	vLH	vRH	K/9	BB/9
Kelly, Casey	R-R	6-3	195	10-4-89	0	0	2.25	2	2	0	0	12	12	3	3	0	0	14	.261	.267	.258	10.50	0.00
Kelly, Ryan	R-R	6-2	180	10-30-87	0	0	7.04	6	0	0	0	8	15	7	6	0	2	4	.405	.368	.444	4.70	2.35
Kunz, Eddie	R-R	6-6	260	4-8-86	3	2	6.35	21	1	1	0	40	51	32	28	4	20	12	.329	.388	.284	2.72	4.54
Lara, Alexis	R-R	6-0	150	3-23-87	0	0	16.88	3	0	0	0	3	8	5	5	0	0	0	.533	.333	.667	0.00	0.00
Layne, Tommy	L-L	6-3	185	11-2-84	0	3	7.77	5	5	0	0	22	28	20	19	4	15	19	.311	.219	.362	7.77	6.14
2-team total (5 Reno)					0	5	9.00	10	9	0	0	42	58	44	42	8	24	33	—	—	—	7.07	5.14
Lollis, Matt	R-R	6-9	250	9-11-90	0	1	8.10	2	2	0	0	7	11	7	6	2	3	6	.367	.429	.348	8.10	4.05
Mikolas, Miles	R-R	6-5	220	8-23-88	2	1	3.20	17	0	0	0	20	20	8	7	1	8	17	.260	.222	.293	7.78	3.66
Needy, James	R-R	6-6	205	3-30-91	0	0	3.00	3	0	0	0	3	4	1	1	0	2	0	.308	.000	.571	0.00	6.00
Ohlendorf, Ross	R-R	6-4	240	8-8-82	1	1	4.24	3	0	0	0	17	19	8	8	2	3	17	.288	.286	.290	9.00	1.59
Palmer, Matt	R-R	6-2	235	3-21-79	6	9	5.66	21	20	0	0	99	120	69	62	3	42	64	.305	.285	.322	5.84	3.83
Pope, Mark	R-R	6-2	203	8-29-89	0	1	7.20	1	1	0	0	5	9	8	4	1	1	4	.409	.500	.400	7.20	1.80
Ray, Jason	R-R	5-11	195	7-14-84	1	3	3.57	40	0	0	3	45	47	23	18	7	18	46	.275	.263	.284	9.13	3.57
Reyes, Anthony	R-R	6-2	230	10-16-81	0	4	6.75	7	4	0	1	21	33	19	16	2	8	20	.347	.431	.250	8.44	3.38
Reyes, Jorge	R-R	6-3	195	12-7-87	10	11	5.09	34	24	1	1	152	194	95	86	15	45	99	.315	.365	.266	5.86	2.66
Scott, Will	R-R	6-2	191	9-2-90	0	1	9.39	3	1	0	0	8	12	8	8	1	7	6	.364	.333	.381	7.04	8.22
Spence, Josh	L-L	6-1	190	1-22-88	4	2	4.20	31	4	0	0	49	48	27	23	4	20	36	.249	.239	.254	6.57	3.65
Stange, Daniel	R-R	6-1	229	12-22-85	0	0	0.00	2	0	0	0	1	1	0	0	1	1	1	.167	.000	.250	6.75	20.25
2-team total (3 Reno)					0	0	15.75	5	0	0	0	4	9	9	7	0	8	3	—	—	—	6.75	18.00
Stauffer, Tim	R-R	6-1	225	6-2-82	0	1	3.38	2	2	0	0	8	10	3	3	1	1	2	.333	.273	.368	2.25	1.13
Stults, Eric	L-L	6-0	225	12-9-79	0	0	5.40	2	2	0	0	7	7	5	4	0	4	10	.241	.091	.333	13.50	5.40
Suppan, Jeff	R-R	6-2	225	1-2-75	0	1	12.15	2	2	0	0	7	17	9	9	0	3	2	.486	.467	.500	2.70	4.05
Tallet, Brian	L-L	6-6	220	9-21-77	0	2	8.44	11	0	0	0	16	22	15	15	5	10	13	.344	.462	.263	7.31	5.63
Thayer, Dale	R-R	6-0	195	12-17-80	0	0	0.00	7	0	0	0	8	2	0	0	0	2	5	.074	.063	.091	5.40	2.16
Vincent, Nick	R-R	6-0	175	7-12-86	1	1	5.82	23	0	0	2	22	27	14	14	2	11	19	.314	.278	.340	7.89	4.57
Wagner, Neil	R-R	6-0	195	1-1-84	3	1	5.44	31	0	0	0	43	57	30	26	2	17	32	.320	.324	.317	6.70	3.56
2-team total (15 Sacramento)					4	2	5.46	46	0	0	1	63	77	43	38	3	23	56	—	—	—	8.04	3.30
Weber, Thad	R-R	6-2	205	9-28-84	1	0	4.42	3	3	0	0	18	22	9	9	1	3	14	.310	.343	.278	6.87	1.47
Wells, Kip	R-R	6-3	205	4-21-77	2	4	4.80	10	8	0	0	51	60	38	27	4	26	22	.306	.359	.260	3.91	4.62
Werner, Andrew	L-L	6-2	215	2-25-87	1	2	5.79	4	4	1	0	23	26	18	15	1	6	20	.271	.292	.264	7.71	2.31
Wieland, Joe	R-R	6-3	195	1-21-90	0	1	3.52	2	2	0	0	8	10	3	3	0	2	11	.313	.167	.400	12.91	2.35

Fielding

Catcher	PCT	G	PO	A	E	DP	PB
Davis	.988	33	222	19	3	3	4
Gale	.992	39	237	19	2	2	0
Grandal	.986	45	333	19	5	1	8
Hundley	.959	13	61	10	3	2	0
Kral	1.000	6	33	5	0	1	0
Rodriguez	.961	14	90	8	4	1	0

First Base	PCT	G	PO	A	E	DP
Belnome	.991	25	206	6	2	22
Carroll	1.000	9	82	1	0	7
Clark	.991	110	902	72	9	95
Decker	1.000	6	32	4	0	4
Owings	1.000	1	5	0	0	1

Second Base	PCT	G	PO	A	E	DP
Amarista	1.000	5	10	12	0	4
Belnome	.973	24	43	64	3	20
Cabrera	1.000	4	10	11	0	3
Contreras	.987	49	97	133	3	37
Forsythe	1.000	3	6	10	0	1
Gyorko	.994	30	62	117	1	23
Merchan	1.000	14	28	26	0	8

	PCT	G	PO	A	E	DP
Parrino	.982	11	22	33	1	6
Roof	1.000	1	2	5	0	1
Weems	1.000	1	4	6	0	0
Zazueta	.984	16	21	41	1	7

Third Base	PCT	G	PO	A	E	DP
Amarista	1.000	2	3	1	0	1
Belnome	.833	1	0	5	1	1
Cabrera	1.000	10	5	18	0	4
Contreras	.917	21	16	39	5	4
Darnell	.905	19	16	41	6	1
Forsythe	.909	7	5	15	2	2
Gyorko	.960	56	37	107	6	11
Merchan	.934	24	14	43	4	4
Parrino	.875	4	2	5	1	2
Weems	1.000	5	8	8	0	2

Shortstop	PCT	G	PO	A	E	DP
Altman	1.000	1	3	2	0	1
Amarista	1.000	3	4	11	0	1
Cabrera	.926	17	25	38	5	10
Cabrera	1.000	2	1	7	0	0
Contreras	.978	8	15	29	1	7

	PCT	G	PO	A	E	DP
Forsythe	1.000	5	5	14	0	2
Parrino	.964	39	44	115	6	20
Weems	.955	62	83	170	12	43
Zazueta	.926	18	24	63	7	11

Outfield	PCT	G	PO	A	E	DP
Cabrera	1.000	7	7	2	0	1
Carroll	.965	96	160	6	6	2
Clark	—	1	0	0	0	0
Contreras	1.000	27	57	3	0	0
Darnell	1.000	13	32	3	0	0
Decker	1.000	18	21	0	0	0
Hermida	.952	38	54	5	3	0
Na	—	2	0	0	0	0
Padilla	.957	12	20	2	1	0
Parrino	.917	6	9	2	1	0
Quentin	1.000	2	3	0	0	0
Robertson	.987	126	270	23	4	3
Roof	.944	36	48	3	3	0
Stokes	1.000	2	2	0	0	0
Tekotte	.989	83	172	11	2	3

SAN ANTONIO MISSIONS — DOUBLE-A

TEXAS LEAGUE

Batting	B-T	HT	WT	DOB	AVG	vLH	vRH	G	AB	R	H	2B	3B	HR	RBI	BB	HBP	SH	SF	SO	SB	CS	SLG	OBP
Altman, Bryan	R-R	6-1	170	8-12-87	.242	.211	.256	33	62	10	15	2	0	1	7	7	1	0	0	13	1	0	.323	.329
Anna, Dean	L-R	5-11	180	11-24-86	.271	.250	.276	129	425	75	115	16	3	10	47	66	11	1	7	76	6	4	.393	.377
Blackwood, Jake	R-R	6-0	195	9-14-85	.219	.169	.232	87	283	26	62	10	1	5	29	10	2	1	2	67	5	1	.314	.249
Cabrera, Felix	R-R	6-0	170	7-14-89	.400	.500	.000	4	5	3	2	1	0	0	0	1	0	0	0	0	0	0	.600	.500
Decker, Cody	R-R	5-11	220	1-17-87	.263	.211	.278	104	346	54	91	19	1	25	68	54	4	0	2	100	1	4	.540	.367
Decker, Jaff	L-L	5-10	190	2-23-90	.184	.108	.209	47	147	30	27	3	2	3	9	40	2	1	0	37	6	2	.293	.365
Freiman, Nate	R-R	6-7	225	12-31-86	.298	.348	.285	137	516	80	154	31	1	24	105	49	12	0	4	95	0	2	.502	.370
Fuentes, Reymond	L-L	6-0	160	2-12-91	.218	.200	.223	136	473	53	103	20	4	4	34	52	6	7	3	133	35	9	.302	.301
Gale, Rocky	R-R	6-0	180	2-22-88	.200	—	.200	3	5	0	1	0	0	0	0	0	0	0	0	1	0	0	.200	.200
Galvez, Jonathan	R-R	6-2	175	1-18-91	.292	.333	.276	82	312	47	91	20	2	6	35	31	5	1	1	70	12	3	.426	.364
Gyorko, Jedd	R-R	5-10	195	9-23-88	.262	.133	.300	34	130	18	34	4	0	6	17	17	2	0	0	27	1	1	.431	.356
Hagerty, Jason	B-R	6-3	220	9-13-87	.248	.311	.227	72	246	30	61	12	0	7	30	35	3	0	2	51	0	0	.382	.346
Kometani, Zach	R-R	6-0	200	11-26-89	.556	.333	.667	4	9	0	5	1	0	0	0	2	0	0	0	2	0	0	.667	.636
Kral, Robert	L-R	5-9	190	3-28-89	.160	.000	.160	14	25	6	4	1	0	0	1	9	0	1	1	8	0	0	.200	.371
Liriano, Rymer	R-R	6-0	210	6-20-91	.251	.211	.262	53	183	24	46	10	2	3	20	20	3	0	0	50	10	1	.377	.335

	B-T	HT	WT	DOB	AVG	vLH	vRH	G	AB	R	H	2B	3B	HR	RBI	BB	HBP	SH	SF	SO	SB	CS	SLG	OBP
Na, Kyung-Min	L-L	5-10	170	12-12-91	.209	.286	.194	29	43	1	9	1	0	0	1	4	0	0	0	20	2	2	.233	.277
Rincon, Edinson	R-R	6-1	185	8-11-90	.291	.378	.266	134	494	45	144	30	0	10	48	22	1	0	4	78	1	6	.413	.321
Rodriguez, Jeremy	B-R	5-8	185	8-30-89	.600	.333	.667	5	15	4	9	0	0	0	1	2	0	0	0	3	0	0	.600	.647
Solis, Ali	R-R	6-0	175	9-29-87	.283	.247	.296	87	329	26	93	25	1	6	40	11	1	1	1	77	1	1	.419	.307
Sosa, Carlos	L-R	6-1	195	5-19-83	.159	.143	.161	32	63	7	10	1	1	2	4	10	0	0	0	21	0	0	.302	.274
Steele, T.J.	R-R	6-3	205	9-21-86	.250	.286	.243	26	84	8	21	3	1	0	10	5	2	0	0	17	3	3	.310	.308
2-team total (26 Corpus Christi)					.200	—	—	52	155	18	31	4	2	2	17	9	2	2	1	44	5	3	.290	.251
Valdez, Jeudy	R-R	5-10	185	5-5-89	.225	.240	.221	128	462	52	104	24	2	12	46	21	12	5	7	126	13	7	.364	.273
Wing, Michael	R-R	6-1	180	10-25-88	.100	.000	.167	5	10	0	1	0	0	0	0	0	0	0	0	1	1	0	.100	.100

Pitching	B-T	HT	WT	DOB	W	L	ERA	G	GS	CG	SV	IP	H	R	ER	HR	BB	SO	AVG	vLH	vRH	K/9	BB/9
Beard, Hayden	R-R	6-1	175	1-22-85	6	5	5.58	31	19	0	0	119	144	76	74	12	40	69	.299	.330	.277	5.20	3.02
Broadway, Mike	R-R	6-5	215	3-30-87	0	2	6.35	33	0	0	0	40	51	32	28	4	13	45	.302	.317	.292	10.21	2.95
Cashner, Andrew	R-R	6-6	200	9-11-86	2	0	1.88	3	3	0	0	14	10	3	3	0	3	22	.196	.211	.188	13.81	1.88
Cropper, Daniel	R-R	6-4	200	1-13-88	0	0	3.86	5	0	0	0	7	7	4	3	0	3	5	.269	.200	.313	6.43	3.86
Erlin, Robbie	L-L	5-11	190	10-8-90	3	1	2.92	11	11	0	0	52	53	21	17	6	14	72	.255	.309	.235	12.38	2.41
Franklin, Chris	R-R	6-1	200	11-10-87	0	0	5.40	3	0	0	0	3	4	2	2	0	1	1	.308	.400	.250	2.70	2.70
Geer, Josh	R-R	6-3	195	6-2-83	5	7	4.44	20	20	0	0	120	145	68	59	8	20	79	.296	.313	.281	5.94	1.50
Gigliotti, Jeremy	L-L	6-1	190	1-16-88	0	0	4.50	2	0	0	0	2	3	1	1	0	0	1	.333	.000	.429	4.50	0.00
Hamren, Erik	R-R	6-1	195	8-21-86	0	1	1.80	12	0	0	1	15	6	4	3	0	11	21	.133	.077	.156	12.60	6.60
Hardy, Mark	L-L	6-6	195	8-21-86	1	1	2.65	6	3	0	0	17	17	6	5	0	6	17	.250	.296	.220	9.00	3.18
Ibarra, Jeff	L-L	6-6	180	8-18-87	0	0	0.75	20	0	0	0	24	22	5	2	0	5	24	.227	.128	.293	9.00	1.88
Jackson, Matt	R-R	6-4	190	12-18-87	2	1	3.73	7	7	0	0	41	39	19	17	3	5	33	.247	.246	.247	7.24	1.10
Jones, James	R-R	6-3	210	12-16-88	0	1	4.50	6	0	0	0	8	7	4	4	1	4	9	.250	.273	.235	10.13	4.50
Kelly, Casey	R-R	6-3	195	10-4-89	0	1	3.78	3	3	0	0	17	11	8	7	1	3	18	.190	.250	.115	9.72	1.62
Kelly, Ryan	R-R	6-2	180	10-30-87	4	1	2.66	39	0	0	1	47	39	20	14	2	15	47	.222	.338	.153	8.94	2.85
Kunz, Eddie	R-R	6-6	260	4-8-86	3	4	5.29	17	7	0	1	48	50	30	28	3	19	27	.263	.275	.255	5.10	3.59
Lara, Alexis	R-R	6-0	150	3-23-87	0	0	3.86	7	0	0	0	9	6	4	4	1	5	8	.188	.231	.158	7.71	4.82
Lara, Robert	R-R	6-2	190	11-25-86	5	1	3.23	36	0	0	0	53	49	22	19	3	31	48	.249	.183	.296	8.15	5.26
Layne, Tommy	L-L	6-3	185	11-2-84	0	5	3.28	32	2	0	1	36	31	15	13	2	16	36	.235	.182	.288	9.08	4.04
Lazzaroni, Dan	R-R	6-0	195	7-23-88	0	1	4.50	2	0	0	0	2	1	1	1	0	1	1	.286	.250	.333	4.50	0.00
Lollis, Matt	R-R	6-9	250	9-11-90	1	5	5.86	25	1	0	0	35	39	30	23	4	15	36	.277	.255	.289	9.17	3.82
Marquis, Jason	L-R	6-1	220	8-21-78	1	0	1.29	1	1	0	0	7	5	1	1	0	2	5	.208	.154	.273	6.43	2.57
McBryde, Jeremy	R-R	6-2	225	5-1-87	0	4	3.57	49	0	0	13	53	44	28	21	3	16	65	.228	.250	.215	11.04	2.72
Mejia, Ruben	R-R	6-1	175	2-23-92	0	0	0.00	1	0	0	0	1	0	0	0	0	2	0	.000	.000	.000	27.00	0.00
Mikolas, Miles	R-R	6-5	220	8-23-88	1	1	2.92	12	0	0	4	12	16	6	4	0	3	11	.320	.421	.258	8.03	2.19
Needy, James	R-R	6-6	205	3-30-91	0	0	1.69	2	0	0	0	5	4	1	1	0	2	6	.222	.500	.143	10.13	3.38
Oramas, Juan	L-L	5-10	215	5-11-90	3	4	6.37	8	8	0	0	35	39	28	25	5	16	33	.267	.258	.270	8.41	4.08
Pease, Dustin	B-L	5-11	170	10-4-85	3	2	3.94	52	0	0	0	64	61	33	28	8	25	56	.251	.200	.290	7.88	3.52
Portillo, Adys	R-R	6-2	185	12-21-91	2	5	7.20	8	8	0	0	35	34	33	28	4	25	26	.250	.191	.309	6.69	6.43
Ray, Jason	R-R	5-11	195	7-14-84	1	0	4.50	9	0	0	0	8	7	5	4	0	4	17	.233	.600	.160	19.13	4.50
Roach, Donn	R-R	6-1	200	12-14-89	1	1	1.59	4	3	0	0	17	9	4	3	0	8	5	.155	.174	.143	2.65	4.24
Sampson, Keyvius	R-R	6-0	185	1-6-91	8	11	5.00	26	25	0	0	122	108	70	68	11	57	122	.233	.212	.252	8.98	4.19
Stange, Daniel	R-R	6-1	229	12-22-85	3	6	3.35	46	0	0	6	54	50	23	20	3	12	64	.242	.274	.220	10.73	2.01
Vincent, Nick	R-R	6-0	175	7-12-86	1	0	1.86	9	0	0	0	10	4	2	2	0	0	15	.121	.154	.100	13.97	0.00
Werner, Andrew	L-L	6-2	215	2-25-87	4	8	3.23	18	18	0	0	103	107	46	37	6	25	89	.272	.253	.276	7.78	2.18
Wilkes, Chris	R-R	6-4	235	9-26-89	0	1	0.00	1	1	0	0	6	4	2	0	0	2	6	.190	.167	.200	9.00	3.00

Fielding

Catcher	PCT	G	PO	A	E	DP	PB
Gale	1.000	2	9	1	0	0	0
Hagerty	.977	55	438	38	11	4	8
Kral	.967	10	58	0	2	0	1
Rodriguez	.971	5	31	2	1	0	0
Solis	.991	80	616	58	6	6	12

First Base	PCT	G	PO	A	E	DP
Decker	1.000	9	76	5	0	2
Freiman	.996	129	1056	82	4	71
Kometani	1.000	1	12	1	0	1
Solis	1.000	1	2	0	0	0
Sosa	1.000	7	41	2	0	3

Second Base	PCT	G	PO	A	E	DP
Altman	.867	5	5	8	2	0
Anna	.979	57	100	131	5	25

Blackwood	1.000	3	7	5	0	0
Cabrera	1.000	3	1	2	0	0
Galvez	.968	66	116	222	11	28
Gyorko	.974	17	31	43	2	8
Wing	1.000	2	5	6	0	2

Third Base	PCT	G	PO	A	E	DP
Altman	1.000	2	1	1	0	0
Anna	.963	20	7	19	1	0
Blackwood	.972	33	17	53	2	4
Gyorko	.939	17	12	34	3	4
Rincon	.872	90	41	116	23	8
Solis	—	1	0	0	0	0
Wing	.800	2	1	3	1	1

Shortstop	PCT	G	PO	A	E	DP
Anna	.935	25	25	47	5	7

Blackwood	1.000	2	2	8	0	0
Valdez	.953	127	148	336	24	42

Outfield	PCT	G	PO	A	E	DP
Altman	.938	14	15	0	1	0
Anna	.975	35	37	2	1	0
Blackwood	1.000	45	56	2	0	0
Decker	.967	67	82	5	3	2
Decker	.938	42	70	5	5	1
Fuentes	.985	134	315	6	5	2
Galvez	1.000	9	19	0	0	0
Liriano	.961	52	91	7	4	1
Na	.931	23	27	0	2	0
Rincon	.958	27	21	2	1	0
Sosa	1.000	12	12	1	0	0
Steele	.957	24	45	0	2	0

LAKE ELSINORE STORM   HIGH CLASS A

CALIFORNIA LEAGUE

Batting	B-T	HT	WT	DOB	AVG	vLH	vRH	G	AB	R	H	2B	3B	HR	RBI	BB	HBP	SH	SF	SO	SB	CS	SLG	OBP
Altman, Bryan	R-R	6-1	170	8-12-87	.182	.143	.200	6	22	2	4	1	0	1	2	0	0	0	0	5	1	0	.364	.182
Belnome, Vince	L-R	5-11	205	3-11-88	.571	1.000	.455	4	14	2	8	3	0	1	7	3	0	0	0	2	0	0	1.000	.647
Bisson, Chris	L-R	5-11	185	8-14-89	.288	.311	.280	112	472	76	136	17	5	3	46	35	0	4	5	91	43	13	.364	.334
Carmon, Stephen	L-R	5-7	155	2-19-90	.167	.000	1.000	3	6	1	1	0	0	0	1	1	0	0	0	2	0	0	.167	.375
Domoromo, Luis	L-L	6-1	185	2-4-92	.219	.241	.212	95	351	34	77	16	2	3	36	22	2	0	3	89	9	2	.302	.267
Gabella, Cody	R-R	6-1	175	12-5-91	.333	.500	.000	1	3	0	1	0	0	0	0	0	0	0	0	1	0	0	.333	.333

Player	B-T	HT	WT	DOB	AVG	vLH	vRH	G	AB	R	H	2B	3B	HR	RBI	BB	HBP	SH	SF	SO	SB	CS	OBP	SLG
Gale, Rocky	R-R	6-0	180	2-22-88	.180	.000	.214	14	50	3	9	1	0	1	6	1	0	1	0	8	1	0	.260	.196
Gomez, Jairo	R-R	6-0	170	1-16-92	.400	.000	.667	5	5	0	2	0	0	0	1	0	1	1	0	1	0	0	.400	.500
Grandal, Yasmani	B-R	6-2	210	11-8-88	.000	.000	.000	2	7	0	0	0	0	0	0	1	0	0	0	3	0	0	.000	.125
Guinn, Brian	B-R	5-11	165	4-4-89	.227	.000	.303	14	44	4	10	0	0	0	2	2	1	0	0	7	0	2	.227	.277
Kotsay, Mark	L-L	6-0	210	12-2-75	.000	—	.000	1	4	0	0	0	0	0	0	0	0	0	0	0	0	0	.000	.000
Kral, Robert	L-R	5-9	190	3-28-89	.315	.222	.361	22	54	6	17	5	0	3	9	11	1	0	2	13	0	1	.574	.426
Liriano, Rymer	R-R	6-0	210	6-20-91	.298	.288	.301	74	282	41	84	22	2	5	41	21	8	0	3	69	22	7	.443	.360
McElroy, Casey	L-R	5-8	180	12-28-89	.327	.218	.363	58	226	44	74	13	1	5	36	27	2	2	1	32	1	1	.460	.402
Medica, Tommy	R-R	6-1	190	4-9-88	.330	.448	.291	93	355	65	117	37	5	19	87	41	7	0	3	86	1	1	.623	.406
Miller, Justin	R-R	5-9	190	12-14-88	.311	.369	.293	92	360	64	112	15	4	12	71	40	7	0	6	81	17	7	.475	.385
Noel, Rico	R-R	5-9	175	1-11-89	.270	.306	.256	134	514	79	139	14	2	0	30	62	8	8	1	151	90	23	.305	.357
O'Dowd, Chris	B-R	5-11	175	10-4-90	.310	.167	.348	8	29	4	9	1	0	0	2	1	0	0	0	8	2	0	.345	.333
Powers, Connor	R-R	6-2	220	12-21-87	.239	.287	.223	96	343	38	82	18	1	10	50	30	3	0	3	102	3	0	.385	.303
Quentin, Carlos	R-R	6-2	235	8-28-82	.429	.667	.364	4	14	3	6	1	0	1	5	0	1	0	0	2	0	0	.714	.467
Rodriguez, Eddy	R-R	6-0	205	12-1-85	.223	.217	.225	87	328	37	73	13	0	13	36	19	3	0	3	100	2	1	.381	.269
Rodriguez, Jeremy	R-R	5-8	185	8-30-89	.220	.400	.175	20	50	5	11	0	0	0	2	8	0	1	0	9	1	0	.220	.328
Roof, Jonathan	R-R	6-1	165	1-23-89	.333	.333	.333	6	21	3	7	2	0	0	1	1	0	0	0	1	0	0	.429	.364
Spangenberg, Cory	L-R	6-0	185	3-16-91	.271	.234	.285	98	384	53	104	12	8	1	40	26	6	6	4	72	27	9	.352	.324
Stubblefield, Tyler	R-R	5-10	185	11-19-87	.135	.154	.125	13	37	6	5	1	0	1	5	2	1	5	2	2	0	0	.243	.220
Tate, Donavan	R-B	6-3	200	9-27-90	.247	.265	.240	55	178	28	44	6	2	0	7	38	4	1	0	56	11	9	.303	.391
Williams, Everett	L-R	5-10	200	10-1-90	.242	.196	.258	105	397	38	96	25	4	5	50	28	0	2	5	112	9	4	.363	.288
Wing, Michael	R-R	6-1	180	10-25-88	.228	.202	.240	91	311	35	71	21	5	5	37	12	6	3	4	69	2	3	.376	.267

Pitching	B-T	HT	WT	DOB	W	L	ERA	G	GS	CG	SV	IP	H	R	ER	HR	BB	SO	AVG	vLH	vRH	K/9	BB/9
Andriese, Matt	R-R	6-3	180	8-28-89	10	8	3.58	27	26	0	0	146	140	72	58	9	38	131	.252	.284	.223	8.08	2.34
Branham, Matt	R-R	6-5	220	9-28-87	8	3	3.72	41	14	0	1	111	103	51	46	9	32	102	.246	.273	.213	8.25	2.59
Carvajal, Yefri	R-R	5-11	225	1-22-89	1	3	6.97	34	0	0	0	52	58	49	40	11	26	26	.282	.278	.284	4.53	4.53
Fetter, Chris	R-R	6-8	230	12-23-85	0	2	4.35	3	3	0	0	10	13	8	5	2	6	6	.295	.227	.364	5.23	5.23
Franklin, Chris	R-R	6-1	200	11-10-87	4	3	4.71	27	0	0	0	42	48	25	22	3	21	37	.284	.284	.284	7.93	4.50
Gigliotti, Jeremy	L-L	6-1	190	1-16-88	1	1	3.38	14	0	0	0	16	21	6	6	2	3	12	.333	.250	.385	6.75	1.69
Gonzalez, Greg	R-R	5-11	190	9-19-88	0	1	3.15	39	0	0	0	54	42	19	19	7	23	62	.212	.247	.178	10.27	3.81
Haney, Chris	R-R	5-11	185	2-13-89	1	1	5.30	22	0	0	0	36	44	30	21	3	9	30	.297	.382	.208	7.57	2.27
Hardy, Mark	L-L	6-4	195	5-3-88	2	5	5.62	13	7	0	0	50	70	42	31	10	9	47	.320	.259	.342	8.52	1.63
Ibarra, Jeff	L-L	6-6	180	8-18-87	0	0	1.74	9	0	0	0	10	11	3	2	0	0	12	.262	.200	.353	10.45	0.00
Jackson, Matt	R-R	6-4	190	12-18-87	5	4	5.08	16	16	0	0	85	105	54	48	10	14	49	.305	.316	.298	5.19	1.48
Lara, Alexis	R-R	6-0	150	3-23-87	1	1	2.25	12	0	0	0	16	9	4	4	1	4	4	.164	.188	.130	8.44	2.25
Lara, Robert	R-R	6-2	190	11-25-86	1	0	1.72	10	0	0	0	16	13	7	3	1	5	11	.228	.273	.200	6.32	2.87
Lazzaroni, Dan	R-R	6-0	195	7-23-88	0	0	20.25	3	0	0	0	4	5	3	3	1	0	5	.500	.800	.200	6.75	6.75
Lollis, Chris	R-R	6-9	250	9-11-90	0	7	6.83	12	11	0	0	58	77	51	44	8	29	50	.329	.293	.383	7.76	4.50
O'Grady, Dennis	R-R	5-10	200	5-17-89	3	1	3.38	19	0	0	0	27	23	14	10	2	13	31	.232	.233	.232	10.46	4.39
Paz, Uber	R-R	6-4	194	5-4-91	0	0	4.50	1	0	0	0	2	4	4	1	1	0	3	.364	.500	.333	13.50	4.50
Pope, Mark	R-R	6-2	203	8-29-89	7	8	6.13	30	20	0	0	112	133	82	76	18	34	58	.295	.256	.332	4.67	2.74
Quackenbush, Kevin	R-R	6-3	207	11-28-88	3	2	0.94	52	0	0	27	58	42	9	6	1	22	70	.205	.194	.210	10.92	3.43
Quigley, Ryan	R-R	6-2	205	4-11-85	4	6	4.58	51	0	0	3	79	62	44	40	9	31	90	.215	.219	.213	10.30	3.55
Roach, Donn	R-R	6-1	200	12-14-89	5	1	1.74	8	7	0	0	47	41	15	9	1	11	44	.233	.264	.212	8.49	2.12
2-team total (6 Inland Empire)					10	1	1.94	14	13	0	0	88	77	26	19	2	14	73	—			7.44	1.43
Smith, Burch	R-R	6-4	215	4-12-90	9	6	3.85	26	26	0	0	129	127	62	55	11	27	137	.256	.248	.263	9.58	1.89
Stauffer, Tim	R-R	6-1	225	6-2-82	0	1	3.38	4	4	0	0	13	15	5	5	0	2	11	.283	.320	.250	7.43	1.35
Street, Huston	R-R	6-0	190	8-2-83	0	0	9.00	2	2	0	0	2	1	2	2	1	1	1	.143	.333	.000	4.50	4.50
Sullivan, Jerry	R-R	6-4	220	1-18-88	4	5	4.20	49	3	0	2	81	86	42	38	8	12	82	.275	.257	.290	9.07	1.33
Thatcher, Joe	L-L	6-2	230	10-4-81	0	0	0.00	1	1	0	0	1	0	0	0	0	1	1	.000	.000	.000	9.00	0.00
Wilkes, Chris	R-R	6-4	235	9-26-89	0	2	10.13	4	0	0	0	5	10	6	6	0	1	5	.435	.625	.333	8.44	1.69

Fielding

Catcher	PCT	G	PO	A	E	DP	PB
Gale	.976	14	112	11	3	0	0
Gomez	1.000	3	8	2	0	0	0
Grandal	1.000	1	6	3	0	0	1
Kral	.982	21	151	17	3	1	6
Medica	1.000	1	9	3	0	1	0
O'Dowd	.971	8	58	8	2	0	8
Rodriguez	.984	85	641	88	12	9	5
Rodriguez	1.000	20	106	13	0	2	3

First Base	PCT	G	PO	A	E	DP
Kral	1.000	1	1	0	0	0
Medica	.988	39	310	27	4	22
Miller	.900	3	2	7	1	0
Powers	.995	76	693	42	4	65
Stubblefield	.964	3	26	1	1	1
Wing	1.000	25	210	15	0	15

Second Base	PCT	G	PO	A	E	DP
Belnome	1.000	1	2	1	0	2
Gabella	1.000	1	0	1	0	0
Guinn	.958	5	11	12	1	2
McElroy	.972	29	52	85	4	13
Miller	1.000	3	6	9	0	0
Powers	1.000	1	0	1	0	0
Spangenberg	.977	96	138	290	10	59
Stubblefield	1.000	1	1	6	0	1
Wing	.953	8	13	28	2	9

Third Base	PCT	G	PO	A	E	DP
Altman	.933	4	1	13	1	1
Belnome	1.000	3	1	1	0	0
Bisson	1.000	2	0	8	0	2
Guinn	1.000	4	3	1	0	0
McElroy	.853	18	14	15	5	1
Miller	.943	54	45	87	8	10
Powers	.893	14	2	23	3	2
Roof	1.000	5	4	7	0	2
Stubblefield	.750	3	2	1	1	0
Wing	.927	46	34	68	8	8

Shortstop	PCT	G	PO	A	E	DP
Altman	1.000	1	0	2	0	0
Bisson	.944	128	191	346	32	67
Carmon	1.000	3	3	5	0	0
Guinn	.957	5	7	15	1	3
McElroy	.955	6	9	12	1	3
Miller	1.000	2	2	4	0	1
Wing	.895	7	3	14	2	3

Outfield	PCT	G	PO	A	E	DP
Carvajal	—	1	0	0	0	0
Domoromo	.942	80	108	5	7	0
Liriano	.975	68	115	1	3	0
Miller	.952	30	56	3	3	0
Noel	.978	130	306	12	7	3
Quentin	1.000	3	4	0	0	0
Stubblefield	1.000	3	2	0	0	0
Tate	.947	50	86	3	5	1
Williams	.968	70	120	2	4	2

MIDWEST LEAGUE

SAN DIEGO PADRES

Batting	B-T	HT	WT	DOB	AVG	vLH	vRH	G	AB	R	H	2B	3B	HR	RBI	BB	HBP	SH	SF	SO	SB	CS	SLG	OBP
Adamson, Corey	L-R	6-2	185	2-23-92	.111	.111	.111	29	81	7	9	1	0	1	5	15	0	2	2	17	2	5	.160	.245
Alcantara, Yoan	R-R	6-1	175	11-14-89	.323	.386	.303	92	350	47	113	21	4	8	61	16	4	1	7	38	7	6	.474	.353
Cabrera, Felix	R-R	6-0	170	7-14-89	.209	.100	.304	18	43	4	9	2	0	1	4	2	0	1	0	10	7	1	.326	.244
Colantonio, Matt	L-R	6-0	195	5-17-89	.255	.188	.264	44	141	13	36	5	1	0	11	20	3	1	0	24	1	0	.305	.360
Dore, Jose	L-R	6-1	170	2-9-92	.333	.667	.222	3	12	0	4	0	0	0	1	0	0	0	0	7	0	1	.333	.385
Gaedele, Kyle	R-R	6-3	220	11-1-89	.258	.239	.263	129	407	59	105	28	7	5	51	53	7	6	3	118	23	6	.398	.351
Gallic, Mike	R-R	6-2	210	4-25-89	.273	.380	.240	82	300	43	82	15	2	3	32	20	5	0	4	68	21	2	.367	.325
Guinn, Brian	B-R	5-11	165	4-24-89	.210	.133	.234	19	62	4	13	0	1	0	3	4	0	2	1	18	6	0	.242	.254
Hedges, Austin	R-R	6-1	190	8-18-92	.279	.200	.308	96	337	44	94	28	0	10	56	23	7	2	4	62	14	9	.451	.334
Jankowski, Travis	L-R	6-2	190	6-15-91	.282	.286	.281	59	238	32	67	10	4	1	23	13	1	1	3	44	17	7	.370	.318
Jones, Duanel	R-R	6-3	195	5-11-93	.226	.250	.219	113	394	51	89	26	0	5	41	37	2	2	8	99	4	4	.330	.290
Kometani, Zach	R-R	6-0	200	11-26-89	.227	.353	.190	20	75	5	17	5	0	1	13	3	0	1	1	16	1	0	.333	.253
Martinez, Alberth	R-R	6-1	170	1-23-91	.129	.176	.111	20	62	8	8	4	0	0	3	4	2	1	0	14	3	0	.194	.206
McElroy, Casey	L-R	5-8	180	12-28-89	.237	.130	.270	59	228	19	54	13	2	5	30	20	4	2	4	42	1	0	.377	.305
Miller, Justin	R-R	5-9	190	12-14-88	.274	.385	.232	26	95	12	26	5	2	0	9	6	1	1	0	19	2	3	.368	.324
Murphy, Clark	L-L	6-2	190	12-18-89	.164	.167	.163	17	61	9	10	0	0	1	4	5	1	1	0	24	2	0	.213	.239
Na, Kyung-Min	L-L	5-10	170	12-12-91	.130	.000	.150	20	69	6	9	2	2	0	5	6	1	4	1	20	0	2	.217	.208
O'Dowd, Chris	B-R	5-11	175	10-4-90	.167	.000	.200	3	6	1	1	0	0	0	0	3	0	0	0	1	0	0	.167	.444
Orr, Lee	R-R	6-3	205	10-23-88	.211	.257	.195	79	270	41	57	17	3	11	41	32	3	0	2	112	14	5	.419	.300
Peterson, Jace	L-R	6-0	200	5-9-90	.286	.347	.268	117	444	78	127	23	9	2	48	62	5	8	2	63	51	13	.392	.378
Powers, Connor	R-R	6-2	220	12-21-87	.048	.000	.059	6	21	2	1	0	0	0	2	0	0	0	0	6	0	1	.048	.130
Rodriguez, Jeremy	B-R	5-8	185	8-30-89	.000	.000	.000	2	4	1	0	0	0	0	1	0	0	0	0	1	0	0	.000	.200
Stokes, Mykal	R-R	6-4	170	6-2-90	.182	.333	.125	4	11	0	2	0	0	0	0	1	0	1	0	2	0	0	.182	.250
Stubblefield, Tyler	R-R	5-10	185	11-19-87	.252	.200	.271	84	278	38	70	16	1	5	29	42	11	3	2	50	17	4	.371	.369
Tate, Donavan	R-R	6-3	200	9-27-90	.207	.235	.197	52	193	26	40	6	0	1	21	22	2	1	1	62	10	5	.254	.294
Whitmore, Travis	R-R	6-1	190	7-5-88	.277	.194	.295	115	411	56	114	22	7	4	47	48	3	5	2	94	8	6	.394	.356

Pitching	B-T	HT	WT	DOB	W	L	ERA	G	GS	CG	SV	IP	H	R	ER	HR	BB	SO	AVG	vLH	vRH	K/9	BB/9
Barbato, Johnny	R-R	6-2	185	7-11-92	6	1	1.84	48	0	0	3	73	52	23	15	4	31	84	.195	.262	.139	10.31	3.80
Cabrera, Erik	R-R	6-1	180	8-15-90	2	2	3.33	45	5	0	0	24	17	15	9	3	10	20	.183	.235	.119	7.40	3.70
Cropper, Daniel	R-R	6-4	200	1-13-88	5	1	4.28	43	0	0	8	48	53	25	23	4	12	49	.279	.352	.216	9.12	2.23
De La Cruz, Luis	R-R	6-6	195	6-15-89	5	5	3.78	48	0	0	0	69	51	36	29	3	37	52	.212	.220	.203	6.78	4.83
Eisenbach, R.L.	L-L	6-0	180	4-5-88	0	3	5.33	25	0	0	1	27	29	20	16	1	19	18	.266	.235	.293	6.00	6.33
Fetter, Chris	R-R	6-8	230	12-23-85	0	1	2.20	6	3	0	0	16	17	7	4	0	6	13	.283	.276	.290	7.16	3.31
Garces, Frank	L-L	5-11	155	1-11-90	9	6	2.81	25	25	0	0	122	102	51	38	3	55	112	.233	.252	.223	8.28	4.07
Gigliotti, Jeremy	L-L	6-1	190	1-16-88	0	0	0.00	2	0	0	0	1	0	0	0	0	1	1	.000	.000	.000	9.00	9.00
Hancock, Justin	R-R	6-4	185	10-28-90	0	4	6.95	13	2	0	0	34	44	31	26	3	20	23	.312	.299	.324	6.15	5.35
Haney, Chris	R-R	5-11	185	2-13-89	0	2	15.75	3	0	0	0	4	9	8	7	1	4	8	.429	.556	.333	18.00	9.00
Hebner, Cody	R-R	5-11	175	11-21-90	7	7	5.01	25	20	0	1	110	108	63	61	5	50	110	.258	.238	.279	9.03	4.10
Jones, James	R-R	6-3	210	12-16-88	4	5	3.98	28	0	0	0	54	56	26	24	7	15	43	.268	.208	.319	7.12	2.48
Kelly, Mike	R-R	6-4	185	9-6-92	0	2	7.53	7	0	0	0	14	18	14	12	0	18	14	.316	.211	.368	8.79	11.30
Mejia, Ruben	R-R	6-1	175	2-24-89	2	6	4.29	22	15	1	0	80	83	40	38	7	33	61	.268	.242	.294	6.89	3.73
Needy, James	R-R	6-6	205	3-30-91	6	3	1.75	32	4	1	1	87	71	20	17	1	25	68	.220	.236	.207	7.01	2.58
O'Grady, Dennis	R-R	5-10	200	5-17-89	4	1	4.73	24	0	0	0	51	54	32	27	4	23	49	.277	.303	.255	8.59	4.03
Portillo, Adys	R-R	6-2	185	12-21-91	6	6	1.87	18	18	0	0	92	54	30	19	3	45	81	.169	.159	.181	7.95	4.42
Rea, Colin	R-R	6-5	225	7-1-90	5	10	4.11	31	19	0	0	103	106	61	47	9	47	80	.268	.282	.250	6.99	4.11
Ross, Joe	R-R	6-3	185	5-21-93	0	2	6.26	6	6	0	0	27	33	21	19	2	11	27	.297	.349	.229	8.89	3.62
Sarria, Daniel	R-R	6-1	190	1-31-88	0	0	10.45	10	0	0	1	10	15	12	12	2	2	10	.341	.300	.375	8.71	1.74
Stites, Matt	R-R	5-11	170	5-28-90	2	0	0.74	42	0	0	13	49	25	7	4	4	3	60	.148	.135	.163	11.10	0.55
Wisler, Matt	R-R	6-3	175	9-12-92	5	4	2.53	24	23	1	0	114	95	39	32	1	28	113	.227	.220	.233	8.92	2.21

Fielding

Catcher	PCT	G	PO	A	E	DP	PB
Colantonio	.992	44	324	49	3	3	7
Hedges	.986	94	763	88	12	7	16
O'Dowd	1.000	3	12	0	0	0	0
Rodriguez	.889	2	8	0	1	0	0

First Base	PCT	G	PO	A	E	DP
Dore	.962	3	21	4	1	0
Kometani	.979	14	88	7	2	2
Murphy	.994	16	136	18	1	11
Orr	.984	48	364	15	6	34
Powers	.981	6	52	0	1	2
Stubblefield	1.000	1	1	0	0	0
Whitmore	.993	59	401	31	3	28

Second Base	PCT	G	PO	A	E	DP
Cabrera	.936	16	26	18	3	3
Guinn	.973	18	22	49	2	6
McElroy	.964	47	69	117	7	16
Miller	.889	6	8	8	2	0
Stubblefield	.957	45	79	121	9	22
Whitmore	.969	17	25	38	2	6

Third Base	PCT	G	PO	A	E	DP
Jones	.866	109	80	133	33	15
McElroy	.500	1	1	0	1	0
Stubblefield	.909	8	3	7	1	0
Whitmore	.960	27	14	34	2	1

Shortstop	PCT	G	PO	A	E	DP
Guinn	1.000	1	1	0	0	0

	PCT	G	PO	A	E	DP
McElroy	.960	5	5	19	1	1
Peterson	.938	107	185	241	28	47
Stubblefield	.968	33	55	65	4	15

Outfield	PCT	G	PO	A	E	DP
Adamson	1.000	28	54	1	0	0
Alcantara	.970	88	170	21	6	3
Gaedele	.989	126	256	20	3	5
Gallic	.973	34	68	4	2	2
Jankowski	.986	58	136	0	2	0
Martinez	1.000	20	32	0	0	0
Miller	1.000	3	1	0	0	0
Na	.980	20	46	2	1	2
Orr	1.000	14	15	0	0	0
Stokes	1.000	4	11	1	0	0
Tate	.943	43	75	8	5	2

EUGENE EMERALDS

SHORT-SEASON

NORTHWEST LEAGUE

Batting	B-T	HT	WT	DOB	AVG	vLH	vRH	G	AB	R	H	2B	3B	HR	RBI	BB	HBP	SH	SF	SO	SB	CS	SLG	OBP
Adams, Brian	R-R	6-4	215	2-28-91	.321	.500	.273	12	28	7	9	2	0	3	7	4	0	0	0	12	4	1	.714	.406
Adamson, Corey	L-R	6-2	185	2-23-92	.240	.250	.239	66	233	26	56	9	4	1	24	25	5	4	0	48	15	9	.326	.327
Baltz, Jeremy	R-R	6-3	195	9-17-90	.281	.208	.298	70	263	44	74	16	2	5	43	33	7	2	1	43	12	2	.414	.375
Blanco, Felipe	R-R	6-1	175	12-9-93	.000	.000	.000	3	6	0	0	0	0	0	0	0	0	0	0	3	0	0	.000	.000
Burke, Chris	R-R	6-1	205	4-25-90	.231	.194	.244	41	121	11	28	5	1	1	9	17	3	1	3	36	5	3	.314	.333
Cabrera, Felix	R-R	6-0	170	7-14-89	.243	.333	.235	15	37	6	9	3	0	2	10	2	1	0	0	9	0	0	.486	.300
Carmon, Stephen	L-R	5-7	155	2-19-90	.275	.300	.272	49	167	28	46	6	4	1	9	27	2	5	0	21	9	3	.377	.383
Charles, Eric	R-R	5-10	180	12-18-88	.185	.083	.267	10	27	1	5	0	0	0	2	1	2	0	0	7	0	2	.185	.267
Colon, Alexi	L-L	5-8	175	10-10-89	.182	.111	.193	32	66	9	12	4	0	2	14	13	1	0	0	20	1	0	.333	.325
Daal, Rodney	R-R	5-11	190	3-23-94	.288	.250	.300	21	66	5	19	3	1	0	8	7	0	2	1	8	1	0	.364	.351
Del Castillo, Miguel	R-R	5-10	170	10-14-91	.043	.000	.053	9	23	2	1	0	0	0	1	1	0	0	0	0	0	0	.043	.083
Dore, Jose	L-R	6-1	170	2-9-92	.143	1.000	.000	2	7	0	1	0	0	0	0	0	0	0	0	4	0	0	.143	.250
Gabella, Cody	R-R	6-1	175	12-5-91	.000	.000	.000	7	10	1	0	0	0	0	0	0	0	1	0	4	0	0	.000	.000
Gomez, Jairo	R-R	6-0	170	1-16-92	.091	.200	.000	8	11	1	1	1	0	0	2	2	1	0	1	0	0	0	.182	.267
Guinn, Brian	B-R	5-11	165	4-4-89	.184	.222	.172	13	38	2	7	0	0	0	7	8	0	0	1	7	1	1	.184	.319
Hagerty, Jason	B-R	6-3	220	9-13-87	.250	.500	.167	5	16	3	4	1	0	1	2	6	0	0	0	7	0	0	.500	.455
Kallunki, Goose	R-R	6-5	230	10-30-89	.254	.265	.250	53	138	12	35	10	0	2	13	13	3	3	0	41	1	0	.370	.331
Lopez, Yair	R-R	6-3	150	9-9-91	.429	.400	.500	2	7	0	3	2	0	0	2	0	0	0	0	1	1	0	.714	.429
Martinez, Alberth	R-R	6-1	170	1-23-91	.254	.245	.257	66	232	37	59	11	1	0	20	23	1	3	0	38	9	4	.310	.324
Moreno, Edwin	L-L	6-1	190	10-27-93	.067	.000	.083	6	15	1	1	0	0	1	2	2	0	1	0	4	0	0	.067	.176
Murphy, Clark	L-L	6-2	190	12-18-89	.267	.000	.308	23	60	8	16	3	0	2	9	7	2	0	0	23	0	0	.417	.362
O'Dowd, Chris	B-R	5-11	175	10-4-90	.104	.182	.075	26	48	3	5	0	1	0	2	11	0	1	1	16	0	0	.146	.267
Phillips, Dane	L-R	6-1	195	12-18-90	.226	.286	.216	69	234	33	53	17	0	4	30	38	0	2	6	53	4	2	.350	.327
Quintana, Gabriel	R-R	6-2	190	9-7-92	.230	.111	.250	16	61	2	14	2	0	1	8	1	0	0	2	18	0	0	.311	.234
Richardson, Ronnie	B-R	5-6	171	5-5-90	.233	.241	.231	52	159	29	37	9	2	2	16	27	16	5	0	40	10	2	.352	.396
Roof, Jonathan	R-R	6-1	165	1-23-89	.205	.190	.209	26	88	8	18	1	0	0	6	13	2	0	1	9	1	3	.216	.317
Smith, Mallex	L-R	5-9	155	5-6-93	.188	.429	.120	10	32	6	6	0	0	1	5	6	1	2	0	8	4	1	.281	.333
Stevens, River	L-R	6-0	165	1-10-92	.241	.185	.252	49	170	23	41	7	0	0	17	15	1	0	4	22	3	2	.282	.303
Tissenbaum, Maxx	B-R	5-10	185	7-25-91	.296	.290	.297	47	169	26	50	5	0	3	29	27	6	2	4	14	2	1	.379	.403

Pitching	B-T	HT	WT	DOB	W	L	ERA	G	GS	CG	SV	IP	H	R	ER	HR	BB	SO	AVG	vLH	vRH	K/9	BB/9
Alger, Brandon	L-L	6-2	180	7-4-91	4	1	2.32	15	5	0	0	43	39	12	11	0	6	36	.242	.310	.218	7.59	1.27
Chabot, Matt	R-R	6-2	190	9-11-91	0	0	2.17	25	0	0	2	29	23	7	7	0	11	23	.219	.242	.208	7.14	3.41
Church, Joe	R-R	6-2	190	9-29-89	4	2	3.54	25	0	0	0	28	24	15	11	0	15	35	.226	.242	.219	11.25	4.82
Fetter, Chris	R-R	6-8	230	12-23-85	0	0	2.08	6	6	0	0	17	13	5	4	2	5	11	.200	.190	.205	5.71	2.60
Guerrero, Tayron	R-R	6-7	189	1-9-91	0	1	3.38	4	4	0	0	13	10	6	5	0	12	11	.227	.278	.192	7.43	8.10
Hancock, Justin	R-R	6-4	185	10-28-90	5	2	1.61	15	14	0	0	73	52	17	13	3	23	66	.203	.207	.200	8.17	2.85
Haney, Chris	R-R	5-11	185	2-13-89	1	0	3.60	9	0	0	0	10	8	4	4	0	4	9	.216	.250	.200	8.10	3.60
Hardy, Mark	L-L	6-4	195	5-3-88	0	0	3.00	2	0	0	0	3	5	1	1	0	2	3	.357	.500	.167	9.00	6.00
Kelly, Ryan	R-R	6-2	180	10-30-87	0	0	0.00	2	0	0	2	3	1	0	0	0	1	4	.100	.000	.125	12.00	0.00
Lara, Alexis	R-R	6-0	150	3-23-87	0	0	5.40	4	0	0	0	3	3	4	2	0	4	4	.231	.200	.250	10.80	5.40
Madrid, Roman	R-R	6-0	185	2-26-91	7	0	2.89	31	0	0	13	37	26	12	12	0	11	44	.193	.154	.217	10.61	2.65
Marcano, Juan	L-L	6-1	165	8-24-90	4	5	3.03	16	9	0	0	65	72	36	22	4	13	62	.280	.348	.255	8.54	1.79
Nunn, Chris	L-L	6-5	200	10-5-90	3	0	0.57	24	0	0	3	31	18	2	2	0	19	45	.159	.111	.182	12.93	5.46
Ottoson, Kyle	L-L	6-3	150	7-11-90	0	2	4.82	9	5	0	0	28	33	19	15	3	7	21	.289	.333	.274	6.75	2.25
Paz, Uber	R-R	6-4	194	5-4-91	0	1	20.25	2	0	0	0	1	2	4	3	1	2	2	.333	.333	.333	13.50	13.50
Picca, Mark	L-L	6-2	200	5-31-89	4	2	4.19	25	0	0	0	43	40	25	20	3	12	36	.247	.273	.237	7.53	2.51
Reyes, Genison	R-R	6-5	190	9-19-91	3	2	2.61	16	3	0	0	38	28	18	11	3	22	38	.206	.275	.165	9.00	5.21
Reynolds, Collin	R-R	6-4	235	6-27-90	4	0	4.41	13	0	0	1	16	17	11	8	1	7	13	.262	.261	.262	7.16	3.86
Rodriguez, Bryan	R-R	6-5	180	7-6-91	0	1	8.31	2	2	0	0	4	7	10	4	0	3	3	.304	.143	.375	6.23	6.23
Ross, Joe	R-R	6-3	185	5-21-93	0	2	2.03	8	8	0	0	27	16	6	6	1	9	28	.178	.057	.255	9.45	3.04
Sarria, Daniel	R-R	6-1	190	1-31-88	0	0	0.00	3	0	0	0	3	1	0	0	0	1	5	.091	.000	.143	13.50	2.70
Schrader, Adam	R-R	6-3	210	3-10-89	0	0	0.00	1	0	0	0	4	1	0	0	0	3	6	.154	.000	.250	7.36	4.91
Scott, Will	R-R	6-2	191	9-2-90	2	4	5.20	14	12	0	0	54	59	39	31	6	17	39	.273	.256	.283	6.54	2.85
Shepherd, Matt	R-R	6-3	185	5-2-90	4	2	2.70	31	1	0	1	40	37	21	12	2	17	42	.239	.218	.250	9.45	3.83
Watt, Michael	L-R	6-1	185	2-24-89	0	0	19.29	3	1	0	0	2	5	7	5	0	2	0	.417	1.000	.364	0.00	7.71
Wieber, Tony	R-R	6-0	200	2-10-91	1	0	1.34	32	0	0	1	40	23	8	6	0	14	43	.167	.271	.111	9.60	3.12
Wilkes, Chris	R-R	6-4	235	9-26-89	1	2	3.80	10	6	0	0	21	17	10	9	2	19	14	.224	.194	.244	5.91	8.02

Fielding

Catcher	PCT	G	PO	A	E	DP	PB
Daal	.989	12	76	18	1	1	5
Del Castillo	.981	9	46	6	1	0	1
Gomez	1.000	8	41	4	0	1	4
Hagerty	1.000	3	32	3	0	0	0
O'Dowd	.990	21	91	11	1	1	5
Phillips	.997	45	344	34	1	3	4

First Base	PCT	G	PO	A	E	DP
Colon	.982	11	53	1	1	5
Dore	1.000	2	12	0	0	0
Gabella	1.000	4	13	1	0	2

	PCT	G	PO	A	E	DP
Kallunki	.977	51	359	23	9	35
Murphy	1.000	17	125	5	0	9
Phillips	.982	6	51	4	1	5
Roof	1.000	4	29	1	0	1
Tissenbaum	1.000	5	38	5	0	2

Second Base	PCT	G	PO	A	E	DP
Cabrera	1.000	1	3	0	0	0
Charles	.947	9	8	10	1	2
Gabella	.875	4	1	6	1	0
Guinn	.818	3	4	5	2	1
Stevens	.949	26	35	59	5	12

	PCT	G	PO	A	E	DP
Tissenbaum	.995	43	85	110	1	30
Third Base	**PCT**	**G**	**PO**	**A**	**E**	**DP**
Burke	.893	39	25	75	12	9
Cabrera	.857	7	7	5	2	1
Guinn	.882	5	6	9	2	0
Quintana	.861	13	5	26	5	1
Roof	1.000	1	0	4	0	2
Stevens	.891	19	10	31	5	3
Tissenbaum	—	1	0	0	0	0
Shortstop	**PCT**	**G**	**PO**	**A**	**E**	**DP**
Blanco	.909	3	3	7	1	0

SAN DIEGO PADRES

	PCT	G	PO	A	E	DP
Cabrera	.917	2	5	6	1	0
Carmon	.941	49	64	143	13	26
Guinn	.810	5	3	14	4	2
Roof	.944	17	23	45	4	12
Stevens	.897	7	10	16	3	3

Outfield	PCT	G	PO	A	E	DP
Adams	1.000	7	11	0	0	0
Adamson	.944	58	100	1	6	0
Baltz	.978	60	87	1	2	0
Colon	.875	7	6	1	1	0

	PCT	G	PO	A	E	DP
Lopez	1.000	2	4	0	0	0
Martinez	.992	65	123	8	1	2
Moreno	.500	1	1	0	1	0
Richardson	.969	37	61	1	2	1
Smith	.923	9	12	0	1	0

AZL PADRES   ROOKIE

ARIZONA LEAGUE

SAN DIEGO PADRES

Batting	B-T	HT	WT	DOB	AVG	vLH	vRH	G	AB	R	H	2B	3B	HR	RBI	BB	HBP	SH	SF	SO	SB	CS	SLG	OBP
Belnome, Vince	L-R	5-11	205	3-11-88	.400	.500	.375	3	10	1	4	1	1	1	5	2	0	0	0	0	0	0	1.000	.500
Bernard, Wynton	R-R	6-2	195	9-24-90	.232	.200	.244	23	56	14	13	3	0	1	9	7	1	0	1	14	4	0	.339	.323
Blanco, Felipe	R-R	6-1	175	12-9-93	.250	.136	.288	31	88	12	22	4	0	0	6	18	0	2	1	33	0	0	.295	.374
Brito, Malquiel	L-R	6-1	187	8-24-93	.248	.241	.250	29	113	19	28	2	1	0	14	7	1	1	1	27	3	1	.283	.295
Burke, Chris	R-R	6-1	205	4-25-90	.270	.125	.310	10	37	3	10	1	1	0	6	4	0	0	0	11	1	0	.351	.341
Charles, Henry	L-L	6-1	174	1-3-94	.276	.190	.307	43	156	30	43	8	2	1	22	16	3	1	3	26	2	2	.372	.348
Colon, Alexi	L-L	5-8	175	10-10-89	.364	.400	.353	6	22	5	8	1	2	0	6	3	0	0	0	7	0	0	.591	.440
Daal, Rodney	R-R	5-11	190	3-23-94	.306	.357	.281	21	85	15	26	9	3	2	11	9	2	0	0	15	2	1	.553	.385
Decker, Jaff	L-L	5-10	190	2-23-90	.296	.333	.292	9	27	5	8	1	2	1	7	4	1	0	1	3	0	0	.593	.394
Del Castillo, Miguel	R-R	5-10	170	10-14-91	.364	.308	.400	20	66	12	24	4	0	0	14	7	1	1	1	10	0	0	.424	.427
Dore, Jose	L-R	6	170	2-9-92	.214	.167	.250	4	14	1	3	0	1	0	0	1	0	0	1	6	0	0	.357	.313
Filpo, Fabel	B-R	6-1	180	9-28-92	.257	.304	.234	23	70	7	18	3	1	1	8	5	1	0	0	19	0	1	.371	.307
Ford, Adam	R-R	5-11	170	2-4-94	.257	.158	.291	21	74	11	19	2	0	4	11	0	1	0	13	0	1	.338	.353
Gabella, Cody	R-R	6-1	175	12-5-91	.200	.176	.211	18	55	5	11	2	0	0	5	10	0	0	0	26	0	0	.236	.323
Gomez, Jairo	R-R	6-0	170	1-16-92	.246	.400	.231	20	57	10	14	2	1	1	9	11	1	0	1	11	2	0	.368	.371
Goree, Jalen	R-R	5-10	195	6-15-93	.270	.333	.244	30	111	24	30	3	1	1	13	11	2	0	1	30	1	0	.342	.344
Jankowski, Travis	L-R	6-2	190	6-15-91	.250	.000	.286	2	8	1	2	0	0	0	0	4	0	0	1	1	0	0	.250	.222
Kreuter, Cade	R-R	6-5	205	4-27-91	.200	.333	.171	15	50	9	10	2	1	2	8	6	2	0	1	21	0	0	.400	.305
Lopez, Yair	R-R	6-3	150	9-9-91	.173	.158	.182	34	104	15	18	4	1	0	7	8	1	0	0	27	0	2	.231	.239
Moreno, Edwin	L-L	6-1	190	10-27-93	.298	.306	.295	42	178	35	53	15	4	2	36	7	0	0	3	31	4	0	.461	.319
Munoz, Christian	L-R	5-10	190	7-12-94	.343	.444	.308	14	35	6	12	5	0	0	8	9	1	0	1	9	0	0	.486	.478
Perez, Fernando	L-R	6-2	190	9-13-93	.273	.263	.278	14	55	6	15	2	1	2	16	2	0	0	0	17	1	0	.455	.298
Quintana, Gabriel	R-R	6-2	190	9-7-92	.291	.268	.300	37	151	25	44	10	2	5	36	6	5	0	1	37	2	1	.483	.337
Renteria, Anthony	L-R	6-0	180	8-30-89	.269	.273	.268	17	52	11	14	3	1	3	9	9	3	0	1	20	1	1	.538	.400
Rodriguez, Jeremy	R-R	5-8	185	8-30-89	.556	.500	.571	3	9	4	5	0	1	0	3	2	0	1	0	0	0	0	.778	.636
Smith, Mallex	L-R	5-9	155	5-6-93	.344	.296	.362	25	96	23	33	2	1	1	10	5	1	2	1	19	13	3	.417	.379
Tejada, Luis	R-R	6-3	175	10-12-92	.293	.340	.273	46	181	34	53	8	3	0	19	16	1	0	1	40	10	3	.370	.352
Tissenbaum, Maxx	B-R	5-10	185	7-25-91	.000		.000																.000	.000

Pitching	B-T	HT	WT	DOB	W	L	ERA	G	GS	CG	SV	IP	H	R	ER	HR	BB	SO	AVG	vLH	vRH	K/9	BB/9
Bostjancic, Cory	R-R	6-0	180	7-14-92	0	2	7.64	16	0	0	1	18	24	20	15	2	13	9	.300	.333	.277	4.58	6.62
Brasoban, Yimmi	R-R	6-1	185	6-22-94	0	0	8.10	2	0	0	0	3	7	3	3	0	1	4	.438	.500	.417	10.80	2.70
Corpas, Jean	R-R	6-2	170	3-9-91	0	0	6.00	22	0	0	1	27	40	27	18	2	5	28	.331	.388	.292	9.33	1.67
De La Cruz, Vladimir	R-R	6-3	174	9-23-90	1	5	5.67	14	3	0	0	40	38	34	25	3	28	44	.245	.315	.228	9.98	6.35
Diaz, Malcom	R-R	6-2	185	3-2-94	0	2	9.68	17	0	0	0	18	28	31	19	1	27	16	.354	.483	.280	8.15	13.75
Eflin, Zach	R-R	6-4	200	4-8-94	0	1	7.71	4	3	0	0	7	9	6	6	0	3	4	.300	.421	.091	5.14	3.86
Erlin, Robbie	L-L	5-11	190	10-8-90	0	2	2.16	3	3	0	0	8	7	7	2	0	2	8	.206	.143	.222	8.64	2.16
Fried, Max	L-L	6-4	185	1-18-94	0	1	3.57	10	9	0	0	18	14	9	7	1	6	17	.215	.250	.208	8.66	3.06
Guerrero, Tayron	R-R	6-7	189	1-9-91	1	0	1.50	5	3	0	0	12	7	2	2	0	2	6	.175	.053	.286	4.50	1.50
Hardy, Mark	L-L	6-4	195	5-3-88	0	0	0.00	1	0	0	0	1	1	1	0	0	0	1	.250	.000	.333	9.00	0.00
Harrelson, Drew	L-L	6-6	185	8-18-87	0	0	5.73	10	0	0	0	11	14	9	7	0	6	8	.304	.615	.182	6.55	4.91
Ibarra, Jeff	L-L	6-6	180	8-18-87	0	0	0.00	2	0	0	0	2	1	1	0	0	0	1	.143	—	.143	0.00	0.00
Kelly, Casey	R-R	6-3	195	10-4-89	0	1	4.00	3	3	0	0	9	10	8	4	0	0	7	.250	.304	.176	7.00	0.00
Kelly, Mike	R-R	6-4	185	9-6-92	0	5	7.11	13	6	0	0	44	54	48	35	2	25	37	.302	.280	.317	7.51	5.08
Kimber, Corey	R-R	6-1	175	3-7-94	2	1	3.38	8	0	0	0	5	6	5	2	0	7	3	.273	.111	.385	5.06	11.81
Lazzaroni, Dan	R-R	6-0	195	7-23-88	2	1	5.40	13	0	0	5	18	24	12	11	2	3	16	.312	.364	.273	7.85	1.47
Lockett, Walker	R-R	6-5	225	5-3-94	0	1	4.34	10	3	0	0	19	25	11	9	2	4	13	.329	.308	.340	6.27	1.93
Miller, Christian	L-L	6-1	190	3-5-94	2	3	9.95	16	1	0	0	25	35	39	28	1	27	12	.330	.455	.274	4.26	9.59
Nunn, Chris	L-L	6-5	200	10-5-90	1	0	4.50	1	0	0	0	2	2	1	1	0	0	4	.250	.500	.167	18.00	0.00
Ottoson, Kyle	L-L	6-3	150	7-11-90	0	0	1.80	3	0	0	0	5	3	1	1	0	0	9	.158	.333	.125	16.20	0.00
Paz, Uber	R-R	6-4	194	5-4-91	0	1	5.14	9	4	0	1	35	39	27	20	1	9	22	.277	.308	.265	5.66	2.31
Reynolds, Collin	R-R	6-4	235	6-27-90	0	2	7.94	5	0	0	0	6	8	5	5	1	3	4	.320	.500	.200	9.53	4.76
Rodriguez, Bryan	R-R	6-5	180	7-6-91	3	3	6.26	11	3	0	0	42	54	43	29	2	18	31	.298	.278	.307	6.70	3.89
Ross, Joe	R-R	6-3	185	5-21-93	0	0	13.50	1	1	0	0	3	2	1	1	0	2	1	.500	.333	1.000	13.50	27.00
Russell, Griffin	L-L	6-0	190	3-5-94	1	1	6.99	16	0	0	0	28	39	31	22	1	27	18	.322	.400	.291	5.72	8.58
Sarria, Daniel	R-R	6-1	190	1-31-88	0	0	3.00	2	1	0	0	3	3	3	1	0	1	1	.250	.333	.167	3.00	3.00
Schrader, Adam	R-R	6-3	210	3-10-87	0	1	10.80	2	2	0	0	5	6	6	6	0	3	6	.300	.600	.200	5.40	10.80
Stauffer, Tim	R-R	6-1	225	6-2-82	0	0	0.00	1	1	0	0	1	0	0	0	0	1	1	.250	1.000	.000	9.00	0.00
Stewart, Cam	L-R	6-2	220	9-9-94	1	2	6.75	13	1	0	0	31	38	27	23	0	22	14	.314	.371	.254	4.11	6.46
Weickel, Walker	R-R	6-6	195	11-14-93	1	3	4.50	9	6	0	0	14	16	17	7	0	6	12	.262	.158	.310	7.71	3.86
Wilkes, Chris	R-R	6-4	235	9-26-89	1	2	2.00	4	3	0	0	18	23	9	4	0	18		.295	.342	.250	9.00	2.00

Fielding

Catcher	PCT	G	PO	A	E	DP	PB
Daal	.986	17	115	21	2	2	6
Del Castillo	.993	20	113	20	1	0	6
Gomez	.963	18	109	21	5	1	7
Munoz	1.000	4	9	1	0	0	2
Rodriguez	1.000	2	14	1	0	0	1

First Base	PCT	G	PO	A	E	DP
Dore	.950	2	17	2	1	1
Gabella	1.000	3	25	2	0	0
Kreuter	.940	10	70	9	5	5
Tejada	.981	45	377	30	8	37

Second Base	PCT	G	PO	A	E	DP
Belnome	1.000	3	5	5	0	1
Brito	.795	22	40	61	26	8
Ford	.825	10	18	15	7	5
Gabella	.900	11	11	16	3	3
Gomez	1.000	1	1	2	0	0
Goree	.952	14	36	44	4	10

Tissenbaum	1.000	1	3	2	0	0

Third Base	PCT	G	PO	A	E	DP
Burke	.852	9	8	15	4	2
Kreuter	.667	3	1	3	2	1
Perez	.838	11	8	23	6	1
Quintana	.840	35	24	65	17	1

Shortstop	PCT	G	PO	A	E	DP
Blanco	.883	31	40	88	17	15
Ford	.881	10	13	24	5	5
Gabella	.957	5	10	12	1	3
Gomez	.750	1	1	2	1	0
Goree	.907	17	24	44	7	8

Outfield	PCT	G	PO	A	E	DP
Bernard	.956	20	42	1	2	1
Charles	.958	40	63	5	3	1
Colon	.667	3	2	0	1	0
Decker	1.000	6	1	0	0	0
Filpo	.957	17	22	0	1	0
Jankowski	1.000	1	2	0	0	0
Lopez	.955	28	41	1	2	0
Moreno	.923	41	70	2	6	0
Renteria	1.000	8	9	0	0	0
Smith	.963	24	50	2	2	0

DSL PADRES

ROOKIE

SAN DIEGO PADRES

DOMINICAN SUMMER LEAGUE

Batting	B-T	HT	WT	DOB	AVG	vLH	vRH	G	AB	R	H	2B	3B	HR	RBI	BB	HBP	SH	SF	SO	SB	CS	SLG	OBP
Barahona, Luis	B-R	5-11	170	11-27-93	.217	.152	.242	48	166	33	36	9	3	0	11	14	1	3	0	34	10	3	.307	.282
Bravo, Daniel	R-R	6-0	160	2-16-95	.242	.231	.245	38	120	22	29	5	2	0	14	20	4	1	1	34	7	1	.317	.366
Brugeura, Reynaldo	B-R	5-10	170	11-5-91	.272	.259	.277	60	217	38	59	10	5	2	20	38	4	2	0	51	15	7	.392	.390
Castillo, Fabian	R-R	6-1	175	9-26-93	.202	.182	.208	25	99	14	20	3	0	2	15	4	1	0	0	19	1	0	.293	.240
Cordero, Franchy	L-R	6-3	175	9-2-94	.270	.302	.260	61	230	39	62	9	6	1	38	37	1	1	1	73	14	4	.374	.372
Diaz, Yorky	R-R	6-2	185	6-18-93	.246	.200	.258	39	114	14	28	6	0	1	11	8	1	3	0	32	8	3	.325	.301
Jimenez, Miguel	L-L	6-3	175	10-17-93	.271	.319	.258	61	229	28	62	9	1	3	36	14	2	1	1	40	8	1	.358	.317
Lantigua, Jonas	L-R	6-5	205	12-15-94	.198	.174	.207	46	167	8	33	10	1	0	14	1	3	0	2	45	1	0	.269	.214
Lendor, Moises	B-R	6-1	170	6-25-93	.213	.182	.226	35	75	10	16	3	1	0	8	2	2	2	0	32	9	6	.280	.253
Martinez, Cristhofer	B-R	6-1	175	11-23-92	.228	.304	.201	52	180	45	41	8	8	3	32	33	1	3	6	43	9	2	.411	.347
Pomare, Derwin	R-R	5-11	160	5-11-95	.350	.167	.429	7	20	4	7	2	0	0	1	2	0	0	0	8	0	0	.450	.409
Reyes, Franmil	R-R	6-4	200	7-5-95	.267	.286	.262	67	243	32	65	16	4	4	37	30	5	0	0	56	12	4	.416	.360
Ruiz, Jose	R-R	6-1	190	10-21-94	.176	.113	.199	55	204	13	36	5	0	1	11	6	2	0	0	41	1	1	.216	.208
Urena, Jose	R-R	6-3	180	1-14-95	.285	.245	.298	57	214	37	61	13	3	6	33	28	8	0	4	58	3	6	.458	.382
Valenzuela, Ricardo	R-R	6-0	189	8-4-90	.275	.194	.303	42	120	14	33	6	0	1	15	15	2	0	0	12	1	4	.350	.365

Pitching	B-T	HT	WT	DOB	W	L	ERA	G	GS	CG	SV	IP	H	R	ER	HR	BB	SO	AVG	vLH	vRH	K/9	BB/9
Andujar, Rudi	R-R	6-2	190	5-14-91	2	0	6.82	30	0	0	0	30	27	24	23	1	29	25	.243	.333	.194	7.42	8.60
Beltre, Jacob	R-R	6-3	234	10-11-92	2	4	4.15	30	0	0	15	30	35	17	14	0	10	30	.287	.356	.247	8.90	2.97
Brasoban, Yimmi	R-R	6-1	185	6-22-94	1	2	1.50	11	11	0	0	54	43	24	9	2	15	39	.219	.265	.184	6.50	2.50
Cabrera, Erik	R-R	6-1	180	8-15-90	1	2	2.12	10	10	0	0	47	33	20	11	2	14	56	.189	.227	.165	10.80	2.70
Carrillo, Jhonathan	L-L	6-1	170	2-2-94	3	1	4.97	21	2	0	0	38	34	28	21	3	30	42	.234	.240	.233	9.95	7.11
Constanza, Alexander	L-L	6-3	190	7-27-94	0	3	18.00	6	1	0	0	6	10	14	12	0	11	2	.385	.250	.409	3.00	16.50
Corpas, Juan	R-R	6-0	180	10-28-94	4	2	3.03	25	1	0	1	39	45	24	13	0	12	18	.287	.328	.263	4.19	2.79
Garcia, Joel	L-L	6-2	180	8-7-92	0	0	3.66	14	0	0	0	20	19	12	8	0	17	15	.253	.357	.230	6.86	7.78
Gonzalez, Manuel	R-R	6-4	195	10-21-94	0	1	6.75	3	0	0	0	4	6	4	3	0	1	2	.333	.167	.417	4.50	2.25
Liriano, Elvin	L-L	6-3	190	10-17-92	0	7	5.27	14	14	0	0	55	49	43	32	2	31	47	.236	.167	.245	7.74	5.10
Marcano, Ivan	R-R	6-3	218	6-1-91	5	1	2.57	13	13	0	0	67	50	26	19	1	28	57	.213	.263	.187	7.70	3.78
Martinez, Deninson	L-L	6-0	180	2-1-94	0	1	2.25	4	0	0	0	4	2	3	1	0	2	3	.154	.000	.222	6.75	4.50
Pena, Arturo	R-R	6-4	200	5-13-94	4	4	6.55	20	0	0	0	33	50	44	24	2	28	29	.342	.357	.333	7.91	7.64
Pimentel, Carlos	R-R	6-2	175	10-24-91	1	2	9.64	12	0	0	0	9	13	17	10	1	12	8	.325	.273	.345	7.71	11.57
Reyes, Manuel	R-R	6-4	195	6-8-93	1	2	10.54	16	3	0	0	27	31	42	32	1	35	24	.290	.341	.254	7.90	11.52
Sanchez, Alejandro	R-R	6-2	170	9-7-92	0	0	3.38	4	0	0	0	5	5	3	2	0	3	7	.217	.143	.250	11.81	5.06
Santos, Wilson	R-R	6-2	200	10-20-91	0	3	5.46	25	0	0	1	31	32	32	19	0	22	22	.258	.353	.192	6.32	6.32
Severino, Miguel	R-R	6-3	180	5-30-93	0	3	4.23	11	8	0	0	38	30	23	18	2	24	26	.227	.333	.167	6.10	5.63
Solano, Leonardo	R-R	6-4	200	1-18-92	1	0	2.45	11	7	0	0	40	25	21	11	1	30	40	.177	.214	.153	8.93	6.69
Suero, Vladimil	R-R	6-1	180	3-22-90	0	0	13.50	2	0	0	0	1	2	3	2	0	4	1	.333	.333	.333	6.75	27.00

Fielding

Catcher	PCT	G	PO	A	E	DP	PB
Castillo	.987	19	137	18	2	0	7
Ruiz	.958	40	298	70	16	2	14
Valenzuela	.979	15	80	12	2	1	3

First Base	PCT	G	PO	A	E	DP
Jimenez	.970	30	236	24	8	19
Lantigua	.945	34	277	15	17	21
Martinez	1.000	1	4	1	0	0
Reyes	1.000	1	8	1	0	1
Valenzuela	1.000	14	110	3	0	8

Second Base	PCT	G	PO	A	E	DP
Bravo	.909	18	36	44	8	6

Brugeura	.955	4	10	11	1	0
Lendor	.917	10	17	27	4	3
Martinez	.925	40	80	104	15	18
Pomare	.895	3	9	8	2	4

Third Base	PCT	G	PO	A	E	DP
Bravo	.918	18	14	42	5	3
Brugeura	.892	46	51	98	18	8
Lendor	.833	2	2	3	1	2
Martinez	.833	1	2	3	1	2
Valenzuela	.950	7	6	13	1	0

Shortstop	PCT	G	PO	A	E	DP
Brugeura	.875	3	2	5	1	1

Cordero	.836	56	85	139	44	22
Lendor	.943	13	17	33	3	5
Pomare	.889	3	1	7	1	1

Outfield	PCT	G	PO	A	E	DP
Barahona	.956	47	85	2	4	0
Brugeura	—	1	0	0	0	0
Castillo	—	1	0	0	0	0
Diaz	.925	38	59	3	5	1
Jimenez	.947	31	33	3	2	0
Lantigua	—	1	0	0	0	0
Lendor	—	2	0	0	0	0
Reyes	.923	60	87	9	8	5
Urena	.943	47	56	10	4	0

San Francisco Giants

SEASON IN A SENTENCE: San Francisco swept Detroit to win the World Series, giving the team two championships in the past three years.

HIGH POINT: The Giants lost the first two games of the National League Division Series against the Reds—at home—but came back to win three straight. They fell down 3-1 to the Cardinals in the NL Championship Series and again roared back. So they came into the World Series and just continued their roll, outscoring the Tigers 16-6 in four games to win the ninth championship in franchise history. Pablo Sandoval was the World Series MVP after hitting three home runs in the first game, two off Justin Verlander, and going 8-for-16 in the series. On an individual level, Buster Posey hit .336/.408/.549 after missing most of 2011 with a broken leg, and Matt Cain threw first perfect game in Giants history on June 13.

LOW POINT: Outfielder Melky Cabrera was the All-Star Game MVP and was batting .346/.390/.516 when he was suspended 50 games for testing positive for high levels of testosterone. Cabrera was eligible to return for the postseason, but the Giants did not add him to their roster. He entered the 2013 offseason as a free agent.

NOTABLE ROOKIES: Backup catcher Hector Sanchez was the Giants' only notable rookie. The 22-year-old hit .280/.295/.390 over 218 at-bats.

KEY TRANSACTIONS: The biggest move heading into the season was sending Jonathan Sanchez and Ryan Verdugo to the Royals for Cabrera. Even with Cabrera's suspension, the move was a clear win for the Giants, as Sanchez imploded and went 1-6, 7.76 for the Royals before they sent him packing to Colorado. The Giants were active at the trading deadline, first by sending Charlie Culberson to the Rockies for second baseman Marco Scutaro. Four days later, the team shipped Nate Schierholtz, minor league righthander Seth Rosin and minor league catcher Tommy Joseph to the Phillies for Hunter Pence. Pence hit .219/.287/.384 with seven home runs for the Giants but provided energy. Scutaro seemed revitalized after the trade and was a playoff hero, hitting .328 in the playoffs.

DOWN ON THE FARM: Outfielder Gary Brown continued to hit in Double-A, posting a .279 batting average, but his power dipped after leaving the hitter-friendly California League. Shortstop Joe Panik posted a .297/.368/.402 line for a high Class A San Jose team that was one of the best in the Cal League.

OPENING DAY PAYROLL: $117.6 million (8th)

PLAYERS OF THE YEAR

BARRY COLLA

MAJOR LEAGUE	MINOR LEAGUE
Buster Posey	**Adam Duvall**
c	3b
.336/.408/.549	(High Class A)
24 HR, 103 RBIs	.258/.327/.487
NL batting champion	30 HR, 100 RBIs

ORGANIZATION LEADERS

BATTING		*Minimum 250 AB
MAJORS		
* AVG	Buster Posey	.336
* OPS	Buster Posey	.957
HR	Buster Posey	24
RBI	Buster Posey	103
MINORS		
* AVG	Brock Bond, Fresno	.332
* OBP	Brock Bond, Fresno	.422
* SLG	Adam Duvall, San Jose	.487
R	Adam Duvall, San Jose	101
H	Joe Panik, San Jose	159
TB	Adam Duvall, San Jose	260
2B	Gary Brown, Richmond	32
3B	Francisco Peguero, Fresno	10
HR	Adam Duvall, San Jose	30
RBI	Adam Duvall, San Jose	100
BB	Jarrett Parker, San Jose	70
SO	Jarrett Parker, San Jose	175
SB	Shawn Payne, Augusta/San Jose	53

PITCHING		#Minimum 75 IP
MAJORS		
W	Matt Cain	16
	Madison Bumgarner	16
# ERA	Matt Cain	2.79
SO	Matt Cain	193
SV	Santiago Casilla	25
MINORS		
W	Eric Hacker, Fresno	12
	Taylor Rogers, San Jose	12
L	Jason Stevenson, Richmond/Fresno	12
# ERA	Chris Heston, Richmond	2.24
G	Phil McCormick, San Jose	61
GS	Four tied at	28
SV	Cody Hall, Augusta/San Jose	21
IP	Yusmeiro Petit, Fresno	166.2
BB	Michael Kickham, Richmond	75
SO	Yusmeiro Petit, Fresno	153
# AVG	Michael Kickham, Richmond	.219

General Manager: Brian Sabean. **Farm Director:** Fred Stanley. **Scouting Director:** John Barr.

Class	Team	League	W	L	PCT	Finish	Manager
Majors	San Francisco Giants	National	94	68	.580	t-3rd (16)	Bruce Bochy
Triple-A	Fresno Grizzlies	Pacific Coast	74	70	.514	9th (16)	Bob Mariano
Double-A	Richmond Flying Squirrels	Eastern	70	71	.496	7th (12)	Dave Machemer
High A	San Jose Giants	California	75	65	.536	2nd (10)	Andy Skeels
Low A	Augusta GreenJackets	South Atlantic	69	70	.496	8th (14)	Lipso Nava
Short-season	Salem-Keizer Volcanoes	Northwest	32	44	.421	t-6th (8)	Tom Trebelhorn
Rookie	AZL Giants	Arizona	32	24	.571	5th (13)	Derin McMains
Overall 2012 Minor League Record			352	344	.506	13th (30)	

ORGANIZATION STATISTICS

SAN FRANCISCO GIANTS

NATIONAL LEAGUE

Batting	B-T	HT	WT	DOB	AVG	vLH	vRH	G	AB	R	H	2B	3B	HR	RBI	BB	HBP	SH	SF	SO	SB	CS	SLG	OBP
Arias, Joaquin	R-R	6-1	170	9-21-84	.270	.303	.240	112	319	30	86	13	5	5	34	13	5	2	5	44	5	1	.389	.304
Belt, Brandon	L-L	6-5	220	4-20-88	.275	.242	.290	145	411	47	113	27	6	7	56	54	3	0	4	106	12	2	.421	.360
Blanco, Gregor	L-L	5-11	185	12-24-83	.244	.248	.242	141	393	56	96	14	5	5	34	51	2	5	2	104	26	6	.344	.333
Burriss, Manny	B-R	6-0	205	1-17-85	.213	.094	.250	60	136	15	29	1	0	0	7	10	1	2	1	25	5	3	.221	.270
Cabrera, Melky	B-L	6-0	200	8-11-84	.346	.395	.327	113	459	84	159	25	10	11	60	36	0	1	5	63	13	5	.516	.390
Christian, Justin	R-R	6-1	195	4-3-80	.125	.121	.130	34	56	6	7	1	0	0	2	5	0	0	0	3	2	1	.143	.197
Crawford, Brandon	L-R	6-2	215	1-21-87	.248	.254	.246	143	435	44	108	26	3	4	45	33	3	2	3	95	1	4	.349	.304
Culberson, Charlie	R-R	6-1	200	4-10-89	.136	.250	.000	6	22	0	3	0	0	0	1	0	0	1	0	7	0	0	.136	.136
Gillaspie, Conor	L-R	6-1	195	7-18-87	.150	.000	.200	6	20	2	3	1	0	0	2	0	0	0	0	2	0	0	.200	.150
Huff, Aubrey	L-R	6-4	225	12-20-76	.192	.111	.203	52	78	7	15	4	0	1	7	16	0	0	1	12	0	0	.282	.326
Nady, Xavier	R-R	6-2	215	11-14-78	.240	.292	.192	19	50	6	12	3	1	1	7	6	1	0	0	13	0	0	.400	.333
2-team total (40 Washington)					.184	—	—	59	152	12	28	6	1	4	13	13	1	0	0	37	1	0	.316	.253
Pagan, Angel	B-R	6-2	200	7-2-81	.288	.271	.296	154	605	95	174	38	15	8	56	48	0	2	4	97	29	7	.440	.338
Peguero, Francisco	R-R	5-11	195	6-1-88	.188	.182	.200	17	16	6	3	0	0	0	0	0	0	0	0	7	3	0	.188	.188
Pence, Hunter	R-R	6-4	220	4-13-83	.219	.221	.219	59	219	28	48	11	2	7	45	19	4	1	5	60	1	0	.384	.287
2-team total (101 Philadelphia)					.253	—	—	160	617	87	156	26	4	24	104	56	7	1	7	145	5	2	.425	.319
Pill, Brett	R-R	6-4	225	9-9-84	.210	.200	.233	48	105	10	22	3	0	4	11	6	2	1	0	19	1	0	.352	.265
Posey, Buster	R-R	6-1	220	3-27-87	.336	.433	.292	148	530	78	178	39	1	24	103	69	2	0	9	96	1	1	.549	.408
Sanchez, Hector	B-R	5-11	225	11-17-89	.280	.304	.266	74	218	22	61	15	0	3	34	5	1	0	3	52	0	0	.390	.295
Sandoval, Pablo	B-R	5-11	240	8-11-86	.283	.299	.275	108	396	59	112	25	2	12	63	38	1	0	7	59	1	1	.447	.342
Schierholtz, Nate	L-R	6-1	205	2-15-84	.251	.152	.287	77	175	15	44	4	5	5	16	18	1	0	2	36	3	2	.417	.321
2-team total (37 Philadelphia)					.257	—	—	114	241	20	62	8	5	6	21	23	1	1	3	46	3	2	.407	.321
Scutaro, Marco	R-R	5-10	185	10-30-75	.362	.352	.368	61	243	40	88	16	1	3	44	13	0	6	6	14	2	1	.473	.385
2-team total (95 Colorado)					.306	—	—	156	620	87	190	32	4	7	74	40	4	10	9	49	9	4	.405	.348
Theriot, Ryan	R-R	5-11	185	12-7-79	.270	.272	.269	104	352	45	95	16	1	0	28	24	1	4	3	47	13	5	.321	.316
Whiteside, Eli	R-R	6-2	220	10-22-79	.091	.000	.111	12	11	3	1	1	0	0	2	1	0	1	0	4	0	0	.182	.214

Pitching	B-T	HT	WT	DOB	W	L	ERA	G	GS	CG	SV	IP	H	R	ER	HR	BB	SO	AVG	vLH	vRH	K/9	BB/9
Affeldt, Jeremy	L-L	6-4	230	6-6-79	1	2	2.70	67	0	0	3	63	57	23	19	1	23	57	.241	.236	.244	8.10	3.27
Blackley, Travis	L-L	6-3	205	11-4-82	0	0	9.00	4	0	0	0	5	7	6	5	0	2	2	.333	.375	.308	3.60	3.60
Bumgarner, Madison	R-L	6-5	235	8-1-89	16	11	3.37	32	32	2	0	208	183	87	78	23	49	191	.234	.208	.241	8.25	2.12
Cain, Matt	R-R	6-3	230	10-1-84	16	5	2.79	32	32	2	0	219	177	73	68	21	51	193	.222	.257	.191	7.92	2.09
Casilla, Santiago	R-R	6-0	220	7-25-80	7	6	2.84	73	0	0	25	63	55	24	20	8	22	55	.224	.265	.197	7.82	3.13
Edlefsen, Steve	B-R	6-2	195	6-27-85	0	1	4.70	14	0	0	0	15	20	8	8	1	6	9	.317	.316	.318	5.28	3.52
Hacker, Eric	B-R	6-1	230	3-26-83	0	1	5.59	4	1	0	0	10	14	6	6	2	2	8	.333	.368	.304	7.45	1.86
Hensley, Clay	R-R	5-11	190	8-31-79	4	5	4.62	60	0	0	3	51	50	30	26	5	30	42	.258	.241	.270	7.46	5.33
Kontos, George	R-R	6-3	225	6-12-85	2	1	2.47	44	0	0	0	44	34	15	12	3	12	44	.209	.167	.229	9.07	2.47
Lincecum, Tim	L-R	5-11	175	6-15-84	10	15	5.18	33	33	0	0	186	183	111	107	23	90	190	.257	.232	.282	9.19	4.35
Lopez, Javier	L-L	6-4	220	7-11-77	3	0	2.50	70	0	0	7	36	37	13	10	1	14	28	.270	.191	.417	7.00	3.50
Loux, Shane	R-R	6-2	225	8-31-79	1	0	4.97	19	0	0	0	25	32	15	14	3	9	9	.314	.302	.322	3.20	3.20
Machi, Jean	R-R	6-0	260	2-1-82	0	0	6.75	8	0	0	0	7	7	5	5	2	1	4	.259	.143	.385	5.40	1.35
Mijares, Jose	L-L	6-0	230	10-29-84	1	0	2.55	27	0	0	0	18	14	5	5	0	8	20	.215	.205	.231	10.19	4.08
Mota, Guillermo	R-R	6-6	240	7-25-73	0	1	5.23	26	0	0	0	21	24	13	12	3	8	24	.300	.375	.268	10.45	3.48
Otero, Danny	R-R	6-3	215	2-19-85	0	0	5.84	12	0	0	0	12	19	11	8	0	2	8	.358	.389	.343	5.84	1.46
Penny, Brad	R-R	6-4	230	5-24-78	0	1	6.11	22	0	0	0	28	42	22	19	4	9	10	.344	.392	.310	3.21	2.89
Petit, Yusmeiro	R-R	6-1	250	11-22-84	0	0	3.86	1	1	0	0	5	7	2	2	0	4	1	.412	.385	.500	1.93	7.71
Romo, Sergio	R-R	5-10	185	3-4-83	4	2	1.79	69	0	0	14	55	37	11	11	5	10	63	.185	.167	.192	10.25	1.63
Runzler, Dan	L-L	6-4	235	3-30-85	0	0	0.00	6	0	0	0	4	1	0	0	0	3	5	.100	.000	.250	12.27	7.36
Vogelsong, Ryan	R-R	6-4	215	7-22-77	14	9	3.37	31	31	0	0	190	171	76	71	17	62	158	.242	.254	.230	7.50	2.94
Wilson, Brian	R-R	6-2	205	3-16-82	0	0	9.00	2	0	0	1	2	4	2	2	0	2	2	.400	.333	.429	9.00	9.00
Zito, Barry	L-L	6-2	205	5-13-78	15	8	4.15	32	32	1	0	184	186	91	85	20	70	114	.263	.209	.281	5.57	3.42

Fielding

Catcher	PCT	G	PO	A	E	DP	PB
Posey	.991	114	855	69	8	9	2
Sanchez	.982	56	350	26	7	4	3
Whiteside	1.000	11	32	5	0	0	0

First Base	PCT	G	PO	A	E	DP
Belt	.992	139	913	73	8	85
Huff	.989	15	83	7	1	3
Pill	.988	24	157	13	2	15
Posey	.991	29	204	6	2	13
Sandoval	1.000	3	10	1	0	1

Second Base	PCT	G	PO	A	E	DP
Arias	.929	4	6	7	1	1
Burriss	.982	37	42	65	2	13
Culberson	1.000	6	9	11	0	1

	PCT	G	PO	A	E	DP
Huff	1.000	1	1	0	0	0
Scutaro	.989	46	91	96	2	27
Theriot	.975	91	152	202	9	53

Third Base	PCT	G	PO	A	E	DP
Arias	.967	74	26	90	4	8
Burriss	.875	6	1	6	1	0
Gillaspie	.857	5	3	9	2	0
Pill	—	1	0	0	0	0
Sandoval	.954	102	63	207	13	13
Scutaro	.962	15	14	36	2	3

Shortstop	PCT	G	PO	A	E	DP
Arias	.972	50	41	98	4	16
Burriss	.923	6	6	6	1	1
Crawford	.970	139	195	394	18	74

Outfield	PCT	G	PO	A	E	DP
Belt	1.000	4	4	0	0	0
Blanco	.989	125	181	3	2	0
Burriss	—	1	0	0	0	0
Cabrera	.981	112	198	7	4	3
Christian	.933	18	28	0	2	0
Huff	1.000	5	7	0	0	0
Nady	1.000	16	20	1	0	0
Pagan	.987	151	377	7	5	2
Peguero	1.000	10	14	1	0	0
Pence	.982	58	110	2	2	0
Pill	1.000	7	9	0	0	0
Schierholtz	.988	52	79	0	1	0
Theriot	1.000	2	1	0	0	0

FRESNO GRIZZLIES   TRIPLE-A
PACIFIC COAST LEAGUE

Batting	B-T	HT	WT	DOB	AVG	vLH	vRH	G	AB	R	H	2B	3B	HR	RBI	BB	HBP	SH	SF	SO	SB	CS	SLG	OBP
Arias, Joaquin	R-R	6-1	170	9-21-84	.400	.417	.391	18	70	14	28	5	0	2	17	3	1	0	0	11	0	1	.557	.432
Bond, Brock	B-R	5-11	185	9-11-85	.332	.333	.332	106	337	59	112	15	2	1	31	48	6	2	2	41	3	2	.398	.422
Burriss, Manny	B-R	6-0	205	1-17-85	.274	.318	.262	29	106	12	29	7	2	0	11	10	2	1	2	12	5	0	.377	.342
Christian, Justin	R-R	6-1	195	4-3-80	.343	.321	.352	72	303	58	104	23	3	7	35	28	6	1	0	32	12	5	.508	.409
Ciriaco, Juan	R-R	6-0	160	8-15-83	.260	.289	.250	56	150	20	39	6	2	5	34	20	2	4	2	30	7	2	.427	.351
Culberson, Charlie	R-R	6-1	200	4-10-89	.236	.244	.234	91	351	53	83	14	6	10	53	20	4	2	3	76	8	2	.396	.283
2-team total (30 Colorado Springs)					.263	—		121	476	70	125	25	7	12	65	21	5	2	4	94	14	4	.420	.298
Dominguez, Chris	R-R	6-5	235	11-22-86	.247	.256	.244	43	174	15	43	11	0	3	25	2	2	0	0	47	1	2	.362	.264
Gillaspie, Conor	L-R	6-1	195	7-18-87	.281	.283	.280	108	413	60	116	18	3	14	49	41	2	4	5	54	0	0	.441	.345
Graham, Tyler	R-R	6-0	185	1-25-84	.263	.000	.278	5	19	3	5	1	0	0	1	0	0	0	0	1	1	0	.316	.300
2-team total (26 Reno)					.150	—		31	60	8	12	1	2	1	6	9	2	1	0	13	2	1	.250	.253
Harris, Devin	R-R	6-3	225	4-23-88	.000	—	.000	1	1	0	0	0	0	0	0	0	0	0	0	1	0	0	.000	.000
Huff, Aubrey	L-R	6-4	225	12-20-76	.154	1.000	.083	4	13	1	2	0	0	1	0	0	0	0	0	1	0	0	.154	.214
Kieschnick, Roger	L-R	6-3	220	1-21-87	.306	.303	.308	55	222	49	68	13	4	15	40	24	2	0	2	68	0	2	.604	.376
La Torre, Tyler	L-R	6-0	219	4-22-83	.278	.118	.313	42	97	14	27	6	0	2	15	15	1	2	0	18	0	0	.402	.381
Linden, Todd	B-R	6-2	225	6-30-80	.280	.270	.284	127	425	63	119	27	6	11	66	53	7	0	2	99	3	3	.449	.368
Lollis, Ryan	L-L	6-2	185	12-16-86	.309	.138	.342	50	175	27	54	9	2	3	21	25	0	3	1	26	2	3	.434	.393
Lormand, Ryan	R-R	6-0	165	10-30-85	.500	.500	—	2	2	1	1	0	0	0	0	0	0	0	0	0	0	0	.500	.500
Nady, Xavier	R-R	6-2	215	11-14-78	.270	.308	.263	25	89	13	24	5	0	6	18	7	3	0	0	20	0	0	.528	.343
Noonan, Nick	L-R	6-1	170	5-4-89	.296	.305	.293	129	490	65	145	26	3	9	62	40	1	5	5	84	7	3	.416	.347
Page, Jarrad	B-R	6-1	205	10-19-84	.000	.000	.000	4	2	0	0	0	0	0	0	0	1	0	0	1	0	0	.000	.000
Peguero, Francisco	R-R	5-11	195	6-1-88	.272	.317	.255	105	449	46	122	20	10	5	68	15	3	4	5	82	1	0	.394	.297
Pill, Brett	R-R	6-4	225	9-9-84	.285	.319	.276	60	246	35	70	18	1	11	45	13	7	0	2	36	0	0	.500	.336
Sanchez, Hector	B-R	5-11	225	11-17-89	.067	.200	.000	4	15	0	1	0	0	0	0	0	0	0	0	1	0	0	.067	.067
Sandoval, Pablo	B-R	5-11	240	8-11-86	.273	.000	.375	3	11	3	3	1	0	2	1	2	1	0	0	0	0	0	.909	.333
Sim, Eric	R-R	6-2	215	1-3-89	.500	.000	.667	2	4	2	2	0	0	0	1	0	0	0	0	1	0	0	.500	.600
Stromsmoe, Skyler	R-R	5-10	175	3-30-84	.249	.338	.213	72	229	27	57	14	1	3	17	29	8	8	0	46	13	3	.358	.353
Villegas, Ydwin	B-R	5-10	180	9-1-90	.143	.111	.167	9	21	3	3	2	0	0	0	0	0	0	1	7	0	0	.238	.143
Whiteside, Eli	R-R	6-2	220	10-22-79	.224	.254	.209	60	201	27	45	11	1	1	20	17	5	3	3	43	0	1	.303	.296
Williams, Jackson	R-R	5-11	200	5-14-86	.247	.227	.253	86	295	34	73	15	1	11	40	13	2	1	3	62	0	0	.417	.281

Pitching	B-T	HT	WT	DOB	W	L	ERA	G	GS	CG	SV	IP	H	R	ER	BB	SO	AVG	vLH	vRH	K/9	BB/9
Blackley, Travis	L-L	6-3	205	11-4-82	3	0	0.39	4	3	0	1	23	13	1	1	1	3	19	.163	.190	.153	7.33	1.16
Bonser, Boof	R-R	6-4	265	10-14-81	0	3	4.50	11	7	0	0	34	38	17	17	4	13	23	.288	.268	.303	6.09	3.44
Burres, Brian	L-L	6-1	175	4-8-81	4	6	5.40	19	19	0	0	98	107	62	59	13	42	63	.279	.262	.286	5.77	3.84
Edlefsen, Steve	B-R	6-2	195	6-27-85	1	3	3.79	35	0	0	0	38	33	19	16	3	18	29	.228	.212	.241	6.87	4.26
Hacker, Eric	B-R	6-1	230	3-26-83	12	6	4.01	26	25	0	0	150	149	70	67	12	43	103	.264	.237	.293	6.17	2.57
Hembree, Heath	R-R	6-4	210	1-13-89	1	1	4.74	39	0	0	15	38	29	24	20	2	20	36	.207	.258	.167	8.53	4.74
Kontos, George	R-R	6-3	225	6-12-85	2	0	1.71	23	0	0	1	32	24	9	6	1	7	26	.209	.240	.185	7.39	1.99
Kown, Andrew	L-R	6-7	210	10-7-82	6	8	5.60	23	22	1	0	119	138	80	74	14	44	66	.293	.288	.298	4.99	3.33
Lively, Mitch	R-R	6-5	240	9-7-85	8	4	2.99	47	0	0	0	78	65	35	26	5	23	69	.220	.248	.198	7.93	2.64
Loux, Shane	R-R	6-2	225	8-31-79	4	1	1.41	23	0	0	0	32	23	6	5	0	5	22	.209	.192	.224	6.19	1.41
Machi, Jean	R-R	6-0	260	2-1-82	2	1	3.97	53	0	0	15	57	67	29	25	7	17	44	.288	.295	.283	6.99	2.70
Mota, Guillermo	R-R	6-6	240	7-25-73	0	0	4.26	4	0	0	0	6	8	3	3	1	2	3	.333	.200	.429	4.26	2.84
Munter, Scott	R-R	6-6	260	3-7-80	4	1	4.99	31	0	0	0	40	50	26	22	4	16	30	.314	.304	.322	6.81	3.63
Otero, Danny	R-R	6-3	215	2-19-85	5	5	2.90	48	0	0	9	62	70	26	20	4	8	45	.293	.330	.268	6.53	1.16
Penny, Brad	R-R	6-4	230	5-24-78	1	0	4.82	8	0	0	0	9	10	8	5	0	3	8	.270	.333	.227	2.89	2.89
Petit, Yusmeiro	R-R	6-1	250	11-22-84	7	7	3.46	28	28	1	0	167	178	88	64	14	36	153	.271	.300	.246	8.26	1.94
Rodriguez, Wilmin	L-L	6-2	215	5-13-85	5	5	5.92	37	3	0	0	62	90	46	41	7	31	34	.344	.323	.355	4.91	4.48
Runzler, Dan	L-L	6-4	235	3-30-85	0	2	6.00	29	0	0	1	27	36	21	18	14	33	.333	.308		11.00	4.67
Sanford, Shawn	R-R	6-0	210	8-28-88	0	3	4.74	4	0	0	0	19	20	12	10	12	12	.278	.286	.270	4.74	5.68
Stevenson, Jason	L-L	6-1	175	8-8-81	6	7	6.21	19	17	0	0	91	115	67	63	20	35	51	.308	.345	.291	5.03	3.45
Tanner, Clayton	R-L	6-2	205	12-5-87	0	2	8.40	12	4	0	0	30	50	31	28	3	12	19	.370	.381	.366	5.70	3.60
Vogelsong, Ryan	R-R	6-4	215	7-22-77	1	0	1.80	2	2	0	0	10	9	2	2	0	4	12	.243	.174	.357	10.80	3.60

SAN FRANCISCO GIANTS

Name	B-T	HT	WT	DOB	W	L	ERA	G	GS	CG	SV	IP	H	R	ER	HR	BB	SO	AVG	vLH	vRH	K/9	BB/9
Whitaker, Craig	R-R	6-4	210	11-19-84	0	0	9.28	18	0	0	0	21	19	22	22	2	25	20	.235	.216	.250	8.44	10.55
Yourkin, Matt	R-L	6-3	235	7-4-81	2	5	9.25	17	10	0	0	49	74	53	50	16	16	36	.347	.276	.387	6.66	2.96

Fielding

Catcher	PCT	G	PO	A	E	DP	PB
La Torre	1.000	13	64	10	0	0	1
Sanchez	1.000	4	20	0	0	0	0
Sim	1.000	1	6	1	0	0	1
Whiteside	.995	56	376	40	2	3	5
Williams	.995	79	505	39	3	9	12

First Base	PCT	G	PO	A	E	DP
Gillaspie	.979	20	169	19	4	11
Huff	.900	3	17	1	2	4
La Torre	1.000	3	23	0	0	3
Linden	.991	58	513	42	5	40
Nady	.988	9	77	8	1	10
Pill	.992	54	449	43	4	51

Second Base	PCT	G	PO	A	E	DP
Bond	.956	31	52	77	6	16
Burriss	.983	14	20	38	1	86
Ciriaco	1.000	1	1	2	0	0
Culberson	.975	88	174	254	11	67

	PCT	G	PO	A	E	DP
Noonan	1.000	6	9	9	0	3
Stromsmoe	.914	6	15	17	3	5
Villegas	1.000	1	2	4	0	2

Third Base	PCT	G	PO	A	E	DP
Bond	.921	27	20	50	6	4
Burriss	.750	1	1	2	1	0
Ciriaco	1.000	10	6	9	0	2
Dominguez	1.000	1	2	1	0	0
Gillaspie	.946	81	45	146	11	15
La Torre	1.000	1	0	1	0	0
Noonan	.864	13	9	29	6	2
Sandoval	1.000	3	1	5	0	1
Stromsmoe	.923	13	10	26	3	2

Shortstop	PCT	G	PO	A	E	DP
Arias	.919	16	22	46	6	12
Burriss	.950	4	10	9	1	2
Ciriaco	.958	7	7	16	1	1
Noonan	.961	97	155	289	18	73

	PCT	G	PO	A	E	DP
Stromsmoe	.956	19	27	59	4	12
Villegas	1.000	4	4	11	0	2

Outfield	PCT	G	PO	A	E	DP
Bond	—	1	0	0	0	0
Burriss	1.000	5	11	0	0	0
Christian	.994	72	164	5	1	2
Ciriaco	.941	27	47	1	3	0
Dominguez	.946	41	75	13	5	1
Graham	1.000	4	14	0	0	0
Harris	1.000	1	1	0	0	0
Kieschnick	1.000	49	101	5	0	1
Linden	.988	47	76	3	1	1
Lollis	.973	49	140	3	4	0
Nady	.957	14	22	0	1	0
Page	1.000	2	2	0	0	0
Peguero	.993	104	272	5	2	0
Pill	1.000	2	6	0	0	0
Stromsmoe	.979	26	43	4	1	0
Villegas	—	1	0	0	0	0

RICHMOND FLYING SQUIRRELS — DOUBLE-A
EASTERN LEAGUE

Batting	B-T	HT	WT	DOB	AVG	vLH	vRH	G	AB	R	H	2B	3B	HR	RBI	BB	HBP	SH	SF	SO	SB	CS	SLG	OBP
Adrianza, Ehire	B-R	6-0	170	8-21-89	.220	.227	.217	127	451	52	99	22	5	3	32	41	4	13	3	90	16	4	.310	.289
Anders, Luke	L-L	6-6	225	10-2-86	.202	.217	.197	30	89	3	18	4	0	2	9	3	0	0	1	23	0	0	.315	.226
Brown, Gary	R-R	6-1	190	9-28-88	.279	.319	.264	134	538	73	150	32	2	7	42	40	19	7	6	87	33	18	.385	.347
Cavan, Ryan	B-R	5-10	180	6-28-87	.228	.168	.249	129	426	44	97	13	2	10	40	32	3	3	5	89	3	3	.338	.283
Ciriaco, Juan	R-R	6-0	160	8-15-83	.204	.310	.156	33	93	7	19	1	1	1	11	7	0	0	1	12	4	1	.269	.257
Dominguez, Chris	R-R	6-5	235	11-24-86	.223	.211	.229	49	188	17	42	9	0	2	19	7	1	0	1	50	3	0	.303	.254
Eshleman, John	R-R	6-0	185	4-8-89	—	.000	.000	3	0	1	0	0	0	0	0	0	0	0	0	0	0	0	—	1.000
Fairley, Wendell	L-R	6-2	195	3-17-88	.220	.214	.221	47	109	6	24	5	0	0	9	13	1	2	1	33	1	1	.266	.306
Flores, Jose	B-R	5-11	175	8-17-87	.231	.263	.212	26	52	7	12	2	0	0	2	4	2	0	1	7	2	0	.269	.305
Hodges, Wes	R-R	6-2	205	9-14-84	.266	.222	.277	41	139	14	37	10	1	3	15	5	1	0	1	26	1	0	.417	.295
Joseph, Tommy	R-R	6-1	215	7-16-91	.260	.338	.232	80	304	32	79	16	0	8	38	25	1	0	5	64	0	3	.391	.313
2-team total (28 Reading)					.257	—	—	108	404	44	104	24	0	11	48	34	4	1	6	96	0	4	.399	.317
Liles, Nick	R-R	6-0	165	7-23-87	.259	.290	.241	90	259	28	67	5	2	0	20	23	2	9	0	42	6	4	.293	.324
Mayora, Daniel	R-R	5-11	175	7-27-85	.281	.302	.272	137	495	48	139	25	1	4	57	43	11	3	11	78	14	9	.360	.345
Minicozzi, Mark	R-R	6-1	210	2-11-83	.284	.230	.308	81	282	35	80	19	0	8	45	32	3	0	6	64	1	2	.436	.356
Mitchell, Russ	R-R	5-11	200	2-15-85	.207	.205	.208	47	140	21	29	10	0	2	12	25	2	2	1	41	0	2	.321	.333
Monell, Johnny	L-R	5-11	205	3-19-86	.257	.209	.274	108	323	39	83	27	1	11	50	41	5	0	5	84	2	2	.449	.345
Perez, Juan	R-R	5-11	185	11-13-86	.302	.318	.296	126	483	65	146	26	4	11	53	22	6	2	0	85	18	15	.441	.341
Weeks, Joel	L-R	5-9	185	11-30-84	.233	.222	.236	58	146	14	34	4	0	2	19	16	0	4	1	34	0	1	.301	.307
Zambrano, Eliezer	B-R	5-11	195	9-16-86	.238	.000	.294	13	21	2	5	0	0	0	3	4	1	0	0	6	0	0	.238	.385

Pitching	B-T	HT	WT	DOB	W	L	ERA	G	GS	CG	SV	IP	H	R	ER	HR	BB	SO	AVG	vLH	vRH	K/9	BB/9
Bochy, Brett	R-R	6-2	192	8-27-87	7	3	2.53	44	0	0	14	53	29	15	15	3	18	69	.161	.165	.158	11.64	3.04
Dunning, Jake	R-R	6-4	190	8-12-88	5	2	4.10	44	0	0	0	68	74	36	31	2	22	53	.285	.346	.242	7.01	2.91
Dunnington, Jake	L-R	6-2	160	2-2-91	0	0	1.76	13	0	0	0	15	12	3	3	0	8	18	.222	.316	.171	10.57	4.70
Fitzgerald, Justin	R-R	6-5	230	4-3-86	7	8	3.22	28	28	0	0	165	134	68	59	8	60	130	.225	.208	.238	7.11	3.28
Fleet, Austin	R-R	6-2	200	4-17-87	2	3	3.83	41	0	0	4	56	72	26	24	0	21	54	.320	.360	.300	8.63	3.36
Gloor, Chris	L-L	6-6	255	3-7-87	4	5	2.81	32	13	1	0	106	99	36	33	7	29	74	.255	.253	.256	6.30	2.47
Heston, Chris	R-R	6-4	185	4-10-88	9	8	2.24	25	25	1	0	149	124	43	37	2	40	135	.230	.208	.249	8.17	2.42
Kickham, Mike	L-L	6-4	205	12-12-88	11	10	3.05	28	28	1	0	151	119	57	51	8	75	137	.219	.212	.221	8.18	4.48
Maday, Daryl	R-R	6-2	225	8-12-85	3	6	3.11	43	3	0	13	84	81	36	29	7	16	73	.253	.218	.274	7.82	1.71
Quirarte, Edwin	R-R	6-2	185	12-20-86	3	1	3.18	39	0	0	2	45	41	23	16	1	14	24	.240	.268	.226	4.76	2.78
Reichard, Andy	R-R	6-4	230	12-4-84	1	3	5.65	12	7	0	0	37	41	24	23	1	14	20	.275	.254	.289	4.91	3.44
Ronick, Ari	L-L	6-4	205	3-25-86	1	2	7.93	35	1	0	1	36	45	35	32	5	21	23	.302	.225	.330	5.70	5.20
Stevenson, Jason	L-L	6-1	175	8-8-81	1	5	5.81	9	9	0	0	48	56	34	31	4	15	30	.298	.297	.298	5.63	2.81
Vessella, Tom	R-L	6-6	205	10-12-85	3	4	4.10	42	0	0	2	53	48	28	24	2	28	45	.247	.203	.269	7.69	4.78
Westcott, Craig	R-R	6-4	225	3-1-86	11	10	4.09	28	28	1	0	165	181	85	75	6	57	68	.290	.313	.274	3.71	3.11
Wilson, Chris	R-R	6-2	205	11-27-86	2	1	2.66	12	0	0	0	20	15	6	6	1	11	13	.214	.174	.234	5.75	4.87

Fielding

Catcher	PCT	G	PO	A	E	DP	PB
Joseph	.991	50	295	45	3	3	8
Monell	.995	73	501	54	3	2	15
Weeks	.992	23	116	14	1	0	3
Zambrano	1.000	10	32	5	0	0	1

First Base	PCT	G	PO	A	E	DP
Anders	.989	11	87	3	1	14

	PCT	G	PO	A	E	DP
Ciriaco	—	1	0	0	0	0
Flores	.988	12	82	3	1	5
Hodges	1.000	12	283	22	0	34
Joseph	.992	14	121	9	1	11
Liles	1.000	3	17	0	0	1
Mayora	1.000	1	12	0	0	2
Minicozzi	.992	43	368	23	3	33

	PCT	G	PO	A	E	DP
Mitchell	1.000	19	146	13	0	12
Monell	.993	21	144	8	1	19
Weeks	1.000	9	50	8	0	3

Second Base	PCT	G	PO	A	E	DP
Cavan	.994	124	278	402	4	99
Ciriaco	1.000	5	9	9	0	0
Flores	1.000	7	11	7	0	0

Mayora	1.000	4	5	13	0	2
Minicozzi	1.000	12	11	21	0	2
Weeks	.944	7	15	19	2	7

Third Base	PCT	G	PO	A	E	DP
Dominguez	.833	3	1	4	1	1
Flores	1.000	3	0	2	0	0
Mayora	.924	127	73	254	27	26
Minicozzi	1.000	4	0	8	0	0

Mitchell	1.000	7	3	13	0	3
Weeks	1.000	4	1	6	0	1

Shortstop	PCT	G	PO	A	E	DP
Adrianza	.969	127	180	359	17	84
Cavan	1.000	2	0	1	0	0
Ciriaco	.900	10	9	27	4	8
Weeks	.918	13	9	36	4	4

Outfield	PCT	G	PO	A	E	DP
Brown	.994	133	301	10	2	2
Ciriaco	1.000	13	12	0	0	0
Dominguez	.962	44	70	6	3	1
Fairley	.955	35	61	2	3	0
Liles	.983	76	109	6	2	0
Minicozzi	.880	19	22	0	3	0
Mitchell	.952	16	19	1	1	0
Perez	.981	115	239	13	5	5

SAN JOSE GIANTS

HIGH CLASS A

CALIFORNIA LEAGUE

Batting	B-T	HT	WT	DOB	AVG	vLH	vRH	G	AB	R	H	2B	3B	HR	RBI	BB	HBP	SH	SF	SO	SB	CS	SLG	OBP
Anders, Luke	L-L	6-6	225	10-2-86	.282	.228	.301	64	213	22	60	12	1	5	29	23	3	0	1	53	0	0	.418	.358
Arnold, Jeff	R-R	6-2	205	1-13-88	.429	.231	.545	12	35	6	15	4	0	0	8	1	2	0	1	9	1	0	.543	.462
Burg, Alex	R-R	6-0	190	8-9-87	.252	.278	.241	100	345	49	87	27	2	10	43	41	7	1	3	77	1	2	.429	.341
Burkhart, Dan	L-R	5-11	215	3-6-89	.298	.222	.322	34	114	14	34	6	2	2	19	12	1	0	3	27	1	1	.439	.362
Duvall, Adam	R-R	6-1	205	9-4-88	.258	.283	.249	134	534	101	138	24	4	30	100	47	10	1	6	116	8	2	.487	.327
Haney, Bobby	L-R	6-1	165	8-16-88	.310	.244	.325	64	210	28	65	16	0	0	22	17	1	1	3	41	3	1	.386	.359
Harris, Devin	R-R	6-3	225	4-23-88	.185	.220	.168	53	178	22	33	3	2	4	20	21	2	0	1	62	0	2	.292	.277
Huff, Aubrey	L-R	6-4	225	12-20-76	.250	.167	.300	5	16	3	4	1	0	1	3	3	0	0	0	4	0	0	.500	.368
Jurica, Carter	R-R	5-11	185	9-23-88	.300	.295	.302	108	403	68	121	19	3	6	56	43	3	2	8	74	6	4	.407	.365
La Torre, Tyler	L-R	6-0	219	4-22-83	.000	—	.000	1	3	1	0	0	0	0	1	0	0	0	0	0	0	0	.000	.250
Lofton, Chris	L-R	6-1	175	5-20-90	.245	.282	.233	96	347	67	85	14	1	5	30	38	1	13	1	103	22	7	.334	.320
Lollis, Ryan	L-L	6-2	185	12-16-86	.296	.288	.299	75	318	49	94	18	3	5	39	27	0	0	4	53	5	6	.418	.347
Metzger, Brennan	R-R	5-11	180	12-15-89	.400	.000	.500	9	10	4	4	1	0	1	5	1	4	0	0	3	0	1	.800	.600
Oropesa, Ricky	L-R	6-3	225	12-15-89	.263	.217	.281	134	518	70	136	30	3	16	98	59	2	0	4	150	1	1	.425	.338
Page, Jarrad	B-R	6-1	205	10-19-84	.182	.143	.191	30	110	16	20	3	2	1	9	9	0	0	1	41	5	1	.273	.242
2-team total (8 R. Cucamonga)					.156	—		38	135	16	21	3	2	1	10	10	0	0	2	47	6	2	.230	.211
Panik, Joe	L-R	6-1	190	10-30-90	.297	.299	.296	130	535	93	159	27	4	7	76	58	5	2	5	54	10	4	.402	.368
Parker, Jarrett	L-L	6-4	210	1-1-89	.247	.185	.265	122	409	71	101	21	7	15	67	70	8	2	2	175	28	6	.443	.366
Payne, Shawn	R-R	6-1	190	7-13-89	.333	.000	.500	2	9	1	3	1	0	0	2	0	0	0	0	2	0	0	.444	.333
Sanchez, Freddy	R-R	6-0	200	12-21-77	.400	.333	.500	3	10	1	4	0	0	0	3	0	0	0	1	0	0	0	.400	.400
Sandoval, Pablo	B-R	5-11	240	8-11-86	.273	.200	.294	6	22	1	6	2	0	1	1	1	0	0	0	5	0	0	.500	.304
Stromsmoe, Skyler	B-R	5-10	175	3-30-84	.267	.353	.241	22	75	7	20	3	1	0	8	15	1	2	1	16	1	1	.333	.391
Susac, Andrew	R-R	6-2	210	3-22-90	.244	.208	.259	102	361	58	88	16	3	9	52	55	6	2	2	100	1	1	.380	.351
Villegas, Ydwin	B-R	5-10	180	9-1-90	.235	.143	.300	13	34	3	8	1	0	0	0	0	1	0	0	8	0	0	.265	.250

Pitching	B-T	HT	WT	DOB	W	L	ERA	G	GS	CG	SV	IP	H	R	ER	HR	BB	SO	AVG	vLH	vRH	K/9	BB/9
Beacom, Mitchell	L-L	6-8	260	7-4-89	0	1	6.75	9	0	0	0	9	10	7	7	1	7	7	.286	.300	.280	6.75	6.75
Bowlin, Drew	R-R	6-1	190	12-28-86	3	1	3.97	36	0	0	1	34	30	16	15	2	21	39	.238	.267	.222	10.32	5.56
Bradley, Ryan	B-L	6-1	180	7-15-88	10	7	4.90	28	28	1	0	152	183	94	83	13	58	94	.296	.268	.304	5.55	3.43
Concepcion, Edward	R-R	6-3	190	10-3-88	4	3	6.10	46	1	0	2	49	41	38	33	2	37	51	.218	.227	.212	9.43	6.84
Correa, Hector	R-R	6-3	175	3-18-88	1	2	7.50	8	3	0	1	18	17	17	15	1	15	23	.262	.179	.324	11.50	7.50
Hall, Cody	R-R	6-4	220	1-6-88	1	1	3.24	9	0	0	1	8	12	6	3	0	4	10	.333	.000	.522	10.80	4.32
Harrold, Stephen	R-R	6-1	200	3-12-89	3	6	5.19	47	0	0	3	76	81	49	44	5	30	62	.272	.244	.291	7.31	3.54
Hembree, Heath	R-R	6-4	210	1-13-89	0	0	0.00	5	0	0	0	5	0	0	0	1	0	7	.000	.000	.000	12.60	1.80
Marte, Kelvin	R-R	6-0	180	11-24-87	2	1	3.47	10	7	0	0	36	36	15	14	2	8	27	.259	.250	.263	6.69	1.98
McCormick, Phil	L-L	6-1	184	9-7-88	3	1	3.48	61	0	0	1	52	46	21	20	1	20	54	.242	.177	.288	9.41	3.48
Osich, Josh	L-L	6-3	235	9-3-88	0	2	3.62	27	2	0	1	32	34	14	13	1	11	34	.272	.308	.256	9.46	3.06
Penny, Brad	R-R	6-4	230	5-24-78	0	0	0.00	2	1	0	0	2	2	1	0	0	1	1	.250	.400	.000	4.50	4.50
Rogers, Taylor	R-R	6-4	200	6-5-87	12	11	4.13	28	27	0	0	153	169	82	70	11	57	118	.280	.331	.245	6.96	3.36
Rojas, Luis	R-R	5-10	185	7-29-89	0	0	3.38	6	0	0	0	8	7	3	3	1	8	9	.219	.273	.190	10.13	9.00
Rosin, Seth	R-R	6-6	250	11-2-88	2	1	4.31	34	5	0	10	56	49	29	27	6	18	68	.228	.174	.268	10.86	2.88
Runzler, Dan	L-L	6-4	235	3-30-85	0	2	6.00	3	2	0	0	3	3	3	2	1	1	1	.250	.000	.375	3.00	3.00
Sandbrink, Danny	R-R	6-2	190	6-23-89	2	0	3.67	12	3	0	0	34	35	20	14	1	17	26	.259	.208	.293	6.82	4.46
Sanford, Shawn	R-R	6-0	210	8-28-88	6	8	5.15	40	12	0	2	101	113	64	58	12	28	65	.280	.297	.269	5.77	2.49
Schumer, Justin	R-R	6-0	180	8-2-88	7	4	4.87	27	23	1	0	140	152	81	76	16	36	88	.277	.269	.284	5.64	2.31
Snodgrass, Jack	L-L	6-6	216	12-10-87	10	8	4.62	27	26	0	0	146	159	84	75	7	57	92	.284	.287	.284	5.67	3.51
Valdez, Jose	R-R	6-7	250	8-1-88	6	4	2.83	53	0	0	7	57	52	18	18	4	28	78	.242	.243	.241	12.24	4.40
Whitaker, Craig	R-R	6-4	210	11-19-84	0	0	3.52	13	0	0	0	15	11	7	6	2	5	22	.193	.211	.184	12.91	2.93
Wilson, Chris	R-R	6-2	205	11-27-86	3	2	3.27	36	0	0	3	41	29	15	15	5	18	42	.199	.208	.194	9.15	3.92

Fielding

Catcher	PCT	G	PO	A	E	DP	PB
Arnold	.954	12	76	7	4	1	0
Burg	1.000	4	25	6	0	0	0
Burkhart	.996	33	222	16	1	2	3
La Torre	.900	1	9	0	1	0	1
Susac	.982	97	705	56	14	6	0

First Base	PCT	G	PO	A	E	DP
Anders	1.000	11	89	7	0	7
Burg	1.000	9	68	0	0	3
Burkhart	1.000	2	7	0	0	0

Duvall	—	1	0	0	0	0
Huff	1.000	2	19	0	0	5
Oropesa	.990	121	1048	79	11	106

Second Base	PCT	G	PO	A	E	DP
Burg	1.000	2	4	4	0	0
Haney	.985	42	75	118	3	28
Jurica	.964	96	180	244	16	51
Villegas	1.000	6	9	19	0	7

Third Base	PCT	G	PO	A	E	DP
Burg	.750	6	2	7	3	1

Duvall	.918	117	63	260	29	20
Haney	1.000	12	10	16	0	3
Jurica	1.000	3	2	1	0	0
Sandoval	1.000	4	0	1	0	0
Stromsmoe	1.000	1	0	5	0	0
Villegas	1.000	4	0	8	0	0

Shortstop	PCT	G	PO	A	E	DP
Haney	.886	12	13	26	5	8
Jurica	1.000	2	3	5	0	0
Panik	.972	122	177	423	17	79

Stromsmoe	.946	6	13	22	2	5
Villegas	.833	2	1	4	1	0
Outfield	**PCT**	**G**	**PO**	**A**	**E**	**DP**
Burg	.982	59	100	7	2	1

Harris	.950	46	73	3	4	0
Lofton	.981	89	208	4	4	2
Lollis	.986	73	135	6	2	0
Metzger	1.000	6	3	0	0	0

Page	.981	25	52	1	1	1
Parker	.977	115	210	7	5	0
Payne	1.000	2	5	0	0	0
Stromsmoe	.967	15	28	1	1	0

AUGUSTA GREENJACKETS   LOW CLASS A
SOUTH ATLANTIC LEAGUE

Batting	B-T	HT	WT	DOB	AVG	vLH	vRH	G	AB	R	H	2B	3B	HR	RBI	BB	HBP	SH	SF	SO	SB	CS	SLG	OBP
Arnold, Jeff	R-R	6-2	205	1-13-88	.238	.210	.247	75	240	26	57	19	1	3	23	23	8	4	0	72	1	1	.363	.325
Blair, Elliott	R-R	6-1	181	2-3-88	.204	.182	.211	76	240	29	49	14	0	3	19	19	11	1	2	62	11	2	.300	.290
Buechele, Garrett	R-R	6-0	200	10-23-89	.251	.197	.272	75	267	19	67	10	1	3	27	13	10	1	3	42	1	1	.330	.307
Cuevas, Jose	R-R	6-2	185	4-5-88	.212	.250	.202	99	344	46	73	20	0	6	33	29	5	4	3	58	18	7	.323	.281
Eshleman, John	R-R	6-0	185	4-8-89	.211	.154	.227	17	57	6	12	2	0	0	3	5	0	1	0	11	0	0	.246	.274
Flores, Jose	B-R	5-11	175	8-17-87	.269	.355	.242	85	324	44	87	21	1	2	37	29	0	1	6	53	4	5	.358	.323
Galindo, Jesus	B-R	5-11	175	8-23-90	.252	.264	.249	66	250	39	63	8	3	0	23	24	7	9	1	49	40	11	.308	.333
Harris, Devin	R-R	6-3	225	4-23-88	.245	.318	.222	50	188	22	46	8	4	8	39	22	1	0	1	56	2	3	.457	.325
Hodges, Wes	R-R	6-2	205	9-14-84	.227	.143	.254	23	88	10	20	5	0	2	7	2	0	0	0	21	0	0	.352	.244
Jones, Chuckie	R-R	6-4	235	7-28-92	.093	.095	.092	23	86	7	8	3	0	1	7	5	2	0	0	44	0	0	.163	.161
Krill, Brett	R-R	6-1	220	1-24-89	.288	.291	.287	122	448	53	129	26	2	5	53	20	12	2	0	79	8	6	.388	.335
Mergenthaler, Mike	L-L	6-4	210	1-6-89	.170	.222	.159	30	106	7	18	3	0	1	9	9	1	1	2	36	3	0	.226	.237
Minicozzi, Mark	R-R	6-1	210	2-11-83	.250	.500	.217	15	52	4	13	4	0	2	10	6	0	0	2	15	0	0	.442	.317
Payne, Shawn	R-R	6-1	190	7-13-89	.309	.235	.328	116	405	66	125	19	6	6	57	61	12	2	2	71	53	3	.430	.413
Relaford, Travius	R-R	5-11	160	5-13-92	.143	—	.143	2	7	0	1	0	0	0	0	0	0	0	0	3	0	0	.143	.143
Robles, Alberto	R-R	5-11	155	9-14-90	.167	.182	.161	13	42	4	7	0	0	0	1	1	1	1	0	8	2	0	.167	.205
Schroder, Myles	R-R	5-11	180	8-1-87	.177	.167	.180	24	62	10	11	1	0	1	3	6	2	2	0	25	2	1	.242	.271
Sim, Eric	R-R	6-2	215	1-3-89	.196	.091	.225	17	51	8	10	2	0	1	6	7	1	0	0	15	1	0	.294	.305
Staley, Joe	B-R	6-1	235	5-8-89	.230	.268	.221	71	213	26	49	13	2	2	23	42	4	2	1	66	5	0	.338	.365
Thomas, Ben	L-L	6-2	240	6-3-89	.243	.162	.262	100	379	36	92	14	1	5	49	20	2	0	4	71	2	0	.325	.281
Tomlinson, Kelby	R-R	6-2	180	6-16-90	.224	.149	.244	123	450	57	101	9	4	1	36	53	5	6	6	105	36	11	.269	.309
Willoughby, Carlos	B-R	5-10	170	11-12-88	.212	.174	.224	71	198	18	42	5	3	0	18	32	2	13	2	48	10	5	.268	.325

Pitching	B-T	HT	WT	DOB	W	L	ERA	G	GS	CG	SV	IP	H	R	ER	HR	BB	SO	AVG	vLH	vRH	K/9	BB/9
Arnold, Demondre	R-R	6-3	208	3-18-92	5	2	5.43	32	0	0	0	56	55	34	34	1	48	45	.259	.237	.272	7.19	7.67
Bandilla, Bryce	L-L	6-4	235	1-17-90	2	4	3.05	11	9	0	0	44	44	26	15	1	28	48	.256	.217	.270	9.74	5.68
Berger, Andrew	R-R	6-3	210	11-24-87	1	3	5.11	28	0	0	1	37	39	22	21	2	22	36	.271	.286	.263	8.76	5.35
Biagini, Joe	R-R	6-4	215	5-29-90	0	4	7.41	9	9	0	0	34	36	33	28	4	29	36	.267	.212	.301	9.53	7.68
Bilodeau, Keith	R-R	6-0	165	9-17-89	1	1	8.87	19	0	0	1	23	38	23	23	4	12	24	.358	.335	.379	9.26	4.63
Blackburn, Clayton	L-R	6-3	220	1-6-93	8	4	2.54	22	22	0	0	131	116	47	37	3	18	143	.232	.243	.224	9.80	1.23
Couture, Kevin	R-R	6-0	170	4-20-88	2	7	2.74	37	9	0	1	82	85	34	25	6	24	54	.266	.215	.296	5.93	2.63
Crick, Kyle	L-R	6-4	220	11-30-92	7	6	2.51	23	22	0	0	111	75	39	31	1	67	128	.193	.213	.180	10.35	5.42
Davis, Paul	R-R	6-2	210	1-29-90	6	8	3.69	30	15	0	1	115	130	59	47	5	20	87	.281	.242	.307	6.83	1.57
Dunnington, Jake	L-R	6-2	160	2-2-91	1	0	4.50	11	0	0	0	10	8	5	5	1	5	14	.216	.231	.208	12.60	4.50
Escobar, Edwin	L-L	6-1	185	4-22-92	7	8	2.96	22	22	0	0	131	121	57	43	7	32	122	.241	.207	.253	8.40	2.20
Hall, Cody	R-R	6-4	220	1-6-88	3	0	1.60	36	0	0	0	20	39	36	7	7	0	12	54	.247	.246	.247	12.36	2.75
Hess, Tyler	R-R	6-5	240	8-29-88	0	0	0.00	4	0	0	0	6	2	0	0	0	0	6	.100	.111	.091	8.53	0.00
Law, Derek	R-R	6-3	218	9-14-90	5	2	2.91	32	0	0	2	56	45	20	18	6	23	67	.216	.216	.216	10.83	3.72
Marlowe, Chris	R-R	6-0	175	10-26-89	1	9	4.20	30	14	0	2	84	66	47	39	5	59	86	.216	.237	.203	9.25	6.35
Mejia, Adalberto	L-L	6-3	195	6-20-93	10	7	3.97	30	14	1	0	107	122	57	47	4	21	79	.284	.333	.266	6.67	1.77
Neff, Steven	L-L	6-2	195	2-24-89	5	1	3.81	45	0	0	1	76	82	37	32	4	29	86	.283	.213	.316	10.23	3.45
Sandbrink, Danny	R-R	6-2	190	6-23-89	0	0	1.35	3	3	0	0	13	7	2	2	0	1	6	.265	.233	.167	2.70	0.68
Vazquez, Kyle	R-R	6-3	175	6-29-88	5	4	4.94	29	0	0	9	27	26	17	15	0	14	28	.255	.233	.271	9.22	4.61
Walker, Scotty	L-L	6-1	195	3-26-89	0	0	2.53	7	0	0	0	11	6	5	3	1	12	13	.154	.083	.185	10.97	10.13

Fielding

Catcher	PCT	G	PO	A	E	DP	PB
Arnold	.994	73	605	60	4	6	3
Schroder	.949	5	30	7	2	0	2
Sim	.980	17	133	16	3	2	2
Staley	.986	50	386	32	6	2	6

First Base	PCT	G	PO	A	E	DP
Blair	.974	5	38	0	1	1
Buechele	.993	32	255	16	2	25
Flores	.975	5	34	5	1	2
Hodges	.989	10	85	6	1	7
Minicozzi	1.000	3	25	0	0	2
Schroder	1.000	1	2	0	0	0
Staley	1.000	1	9	1	0	0
Thomas	.985	87	660	45	11	52

Second Base	PCT	G	PO	A	E	DP
Cuevas	.976	52	105	136	6	25

	PCT	G	PO	A	E	DP
Flores	.967	27	43	74	4	15
Minicozzi	1.000	4	4	8	0	1
Robles	1.000	5	8	7	0	2
Schroder	1.000	1	3	0	0	0
Willoughby	.976	56	90	151	6	24

Third Base	PCT	G	PO	A	E	DP
Buechele	.926	38	23	64	7	6
Cuevas	.916	42	19	57	7	3
Eshleman	.846	4	1	10	2	0
Flores	.905	41	27	59	9	6
Minicozzi	1.000	5	1	5	0	1
Robles	—	2	0	0	0	0
Schroder	.857	12	8	16	4	2

Shortstop	PCT	G	PO	A	E	DP
Cuevas	.909	4	2	8	1	0
Eshleman	1.000	1	1	0	1	

	PCT	G	PO	A	E	DP
Flores	.946	14	19	34	3	9
Relaford	.800	1	5	3	2	1
Robles	1.000	4	9	11	0	1
Tomlinson	.960	120	162	364	22	60

Outfield	PCT	G	PO	A	E	DP
Blair	1.000	64	116	3	0	1
Eshleman	.600	6	3	0	2	0
Galindo	.956	64	143	10	7	3
Harris	.986	37	64	4	1	1
Jones	.980	23	49	0	1	0
Krill	.983	94	175	2	3	0
Mergenthaler	.933	27	41	1	3	1
Payne	.953	94	119	4	6	0
Schroder	1.000	1	1	0	0	0
Willoughby	.923	9	12	0	1	0

SAN FRANSISCO GIANTS

SALEM-KEIZER VOLCANOES
NORTHWEST LEAGUE

SHORT-SEASON

Batting	B-T	HT	WT	DOB	AVG	vLH	vRH	G	AB	R	H	2B	3B	HR	RBI	BB	HBP	SH	SF	SO	SB	CS	SLG	OBP
Branca, Stephen	R-R	6-1	170	4-10-89	.248	.263	.246	40	153	15	38	7	0	3	14	11	0	1	0	34	3	0	.353	.299
Brown, Trevor	R-R	6-2	195	11-15-91	.221	.176	.229	33	122	10	27	8	0	0	12	13	1	1	2	16	1	1	.287	.297
Cain, Andrew	R-R	6-6	220	3-24-90	.243	.216	.252	44	140	19	34	6	1	2	13	18	2	1	0	49	5	1	.343	.338
Delfino, Mitch	R-R	6-2	210	1-13-91	.269	.242	.276	41	167	15	45	12	0	0	19	9	2	0	0	34	2	0	.341	.315
Delgado, Jean	R-R	5-11	150	2-5-93	.150	.125	.167	7	20	1	3	0	0	0	1	2	0	0	0	5	0	1	.150	.227
Duffy, Matt	R-R	6-2	170	1-15-91	.247	.262	.243	47	182	31	45	4	0	1	16	26	7	0	1	22	10	1	.286	.361
Eberle, Sam	R-R	6-0	215	2-1-90	.248	.313	.236	36	105	10	26	4	0	0	12	17	0	1	3	22	0	1	.286	.344
Hill, Kentrell	R-R	6-0	180	10-27-90	.283	.225	.297	55	198	33	56	8	0	0	8	40	1	2	1	50	8	10	.323	.404
Jones, Chuckie	R-R	6-3	235	7-28-92	.242	.176	.259	67	236	42	57	13	0	6	31	37	5	0	4	68	4	0	.373	.351
Jones, Ryan	R-R	5-10	175	9-8-90	.227	.400	.190	60	198	20	45	8	0	1	20	22	2	3	3	35	2	3	.283	.307
Mergenthaler, Mike	L-L	6-4	210	1-6-89	.223	.385	.206	39	139	27	31	7	2	3	19	16	1	2	0	25	0	0	.367	.308
Metzger, Brennan	R-R	5-11	180	12-15-89	.210	.154	.217	38	105	20	22	6	0	1	6	21	11	2	0	15	6	2	.295	.394
Nicholson, Bryan	L-L	6-2	225	10-31-89	.222	.000	.222	3	9	0	2	0	0	0	1	2	0	0	0	4	0	0	.222	.364
Rapp, Joey	R-R	6-2	225	11-27-89	.272	.231	.283	64	239	34	65	11	1	11	42	33	7	0	1	73	1	1	.464	.375
Rodriguez, Rafael	R-R	6-5	198	7-13-92	.235	.263	.226	43	162	9	38	10	1	3	20	9	3	2	0	31	7	7	.364	.287
Williamson, Mac	R-R	6-4	240	7-15-90	.342	.267	.354	29	114	22	39	8	0	7	26	6	4	0	1	19	0	3	.596	.392
Yarrow, Stephen	L-R	6-3	210	11-30-88	.199	.259	.188	53	171	17	34	6	1	3	12	16	0	1	3	49	0	3	.298	.263

Pitching	B-T	HT	WT	DOB	W	L	ERA	G	GS	CG	SV	IP	H	R	ER	HR	BB	SO	AVG	vLH	vRH	K/9	BB/9
Biagini, Joe	R-R	6-4	215	5-29-90	2	4	4.27	14	12	0	0	59	54	32	28	5	18	63	.248	.290	.216	9.61	2.75
Bilodeau, Keith	R-R	6-0	165	9-17-89	1	1	3.60	22	0	0	2	40	40	21	16	6	15	37	.270	.179	.326	8.33	3.38
Bucardo, Jorge	R-R	6-4	190	10-18-89	0	0	6.55	8	0	0	0	11	14	10	8	1	2	7	.304	.227	.375	5.73	1.64
Flores, Kendry	R-R	6-2	175	11-24-91	0	3	4.46	10	8	0	0	42	44	26	21	4	11	34	.257	.259	.256	7.23	2.34
Gardeck, Ian	R-R	6-2	215	11-21-90	2	2	4.20	19	0	0	0	30	22	19	14	0	24	45	.196	.277	.138	13.50	7.20
Graham, Matt	R-R	6-4	225	5-1-90	4	0	2.60	22	0	0	0	28	19	10	8	1	21	21	.200	.130	.265	6.83	6.83
Gregorio, Joan	R-R	6-7	180	1-12-92	7	7	5.54	16	16	0	0	76	85	49	47	9	23	69	.272	.255	.285	8.14	2.71
Johnson, Chris	R-R	6-4	205	8-24-91	2	4	6.84	16	6	0	0	49	56	40	37	7	11	47	.289	.329	.257	8.69	2.03
Johnson, Stephen	R-R	6-4	205	2-21-91	0	2	4.66	17	0	0	2	19	19	11	10	2	12	19	.257	.345	.200	8.84	5.59
Kurrasch, Joe	L-L	6-0	205	5-19-91	0	2	10.80	3	0	0	0	5	7	6	6	0	3	3	.350	.500	.250	5.40	5.40
Lamb, Cameron	R-R	6-3	195	5-29-89	2	1	2.42	9	3	0	0	22	17	8	6	0	6	16	.213	.114	.289	6.45	2.42
McVay, Mason	L-L	6-7	230	8-15-90	1	0	1.19	18	0	0	1	30	23	4	4	0	13	43	.207	.313	.165	12.76	3.86
Mendoza, Lorenzo	R-R	5-10	190	8-6-91	0	4	4.96	14	10	0	1	49	64	27	27	5	9	45	.325	.340	.317	8.27	1.65
Mizenko, Tyler	R-R	6-1	200	4-9-90	3	0	1.99	24	0	0	13	32	27	9	7	0	5	29	.229	.255	.206	8.24	1.42
Montero, Raymundo	R-R	6-2	185	9-20-89	3	4	4.38	11	11	0	0	49	58	28	24	5	17	38	.293	.333	.259	6.93	3.10
Noel, Franklin	L-L	6-1	175	12-20-88	1	1	5.40	7	0	0	0	12	14	9	7	1	5	9	.292	.263	.310	6.94	3.86
Okert, Steven	L-L	6-3	210	7-9-91	2	0	2.36	15	0	0	0	27	26	9	7	0	11	22	.255	.143	.313	7.43	3.71
Paniagua, Armando	R-R	5-11	155	1-11-90	1	1	4.78	19	0	0	0	26	34	18	14	2	16	32	.324	.260	.382	10.94	5.47
Rodriguez, Mario	L-L	6-2	190	8-21-88	0	3	7.94	4	0	0	0	17	26	15	15	3	4	8	.361	.300	.385	4.24	2.12
Santiago, Gaspar	L-L	6-0	200	9-23-89	0	0	1.59	15	0	0	0	23	14	4	4	1	16	22	.179	.148	.196	8.74	6.35
Stratton, Chris	R-R	6-3	186	8-22-90	0	1	2.76	8	5	0	0	16	14	6	5	1	10	16	.237	.167	.286	8.82	5.51
Zeigler, Randy	L-L	6-1	183	8-30-89	0	4	8.53	14	1	0	0	19	24	21	18	2	14	21	.320	.304	.327	9.95	6.63

Fielding

Catcher	PCT	G	PO	A	E	DP	PB
Brown	.992	14	115	10	1	2	2
Eberle	.978	29	209	18	5	2	10
Ricardo	.977	46	326	52	9	8	4

First Base	PCT	G	PO	A	E	DP
Brown	1.000	7	63	2	0	5
Mergenthaler	.950	3	16	3	1	3
Nicholson	1.000	3	27	2	0	3
Rapp	.991	63	540	32	5	31
Yarrow	1.000	5	34	2	0	1

Second Base	PCT	G	PO	A	E	DP
Branca	.967	17	18	40	2	5

	PCT	G	PO	A	E	DP
Delgado	1.000	4	4	7	0	1
Jones	.968	60	101	143	8	22
Yarrow	1.000	1	2	0	0	0

Third Base	PCT	G	PO	A	E	DP
Branca	.833	1	3	2	1	0
Delfino	.912	39	18	75	9	7
Delgado	1.000	1	1	5	0	0
Eberle	—	3	0	0	0	0
Yarrow	.959	39	39	77	5	5

Shortstop	PCT	G	PO	A	E	DP
Branca	.968	22	29	61	3	12
Delgado	.857	2	4	8	2	1

	PCT	G	PO	A	E	DP
Duffy	.935	45	61	127	13	12
Yarrow	.935	9	10	19	2	5

Outfield	PCT	G	PO	A	E	DP
Cain	1.000	38	60	5	0	2
Hill	.972	45	65	4	2	0
Jones	.984	60	119	4	2	0
Mergenthaler	.933	23	26	2	2	1
Metzger	.981	32	52	1	1	0
Rodriguez	1.000	22	31	0	0	0
Williamson	.976	23	37	3	1	2

AZL GIANTS
ARIZONA LEAGUE

ROOKIE

Batting	B-T	HT	WT	DOB	AVG	vLH	vRH	G	AB	R	H	2B	3B	HR	RBI	BB	HBP	SH	SF	SO	SB	CS	SLG	OBP
Barnett, Eldred	R-R	6-1	190	5-2-89	.240	.250	.238	10	25	3	6	3	0	0	4	0	0	1	0	13	1	1	.360	.240
Benusa, Gus	L-L	6-1	190	1-30-91	.000	—	.000	5	7	2	0	0	0	0	2	3	0	0	2	1	0	0	.000	.250
Branca, Stephen	R-R	6-1	170	4-10-89	.300	.000	.333	3	10	3	3	2	0	0	1	1	0	0	0	2	0	0	.500	.364
Cornier, Gabriel	B-R	6-0	190	6-10-92	.319	.375	.307	31	91	10	29	8	1	0	11	12	0	0	1	26	0	1	.429	.394
Delfino, Mitch	R-R	6-2	210	1-13-91	.208	.286	.195	12	48	7	10	6	0	0	2	4	1	0	0	6	2	0	.333	.283
Delgado, Jean	R-R	5-11	150	2-5-93	.300	.375	.273	9	30	5	9	4	0	0	2	6	0	1	0	4	0	1	.433	.417
Diaz, Christian	L-L	6-1	170	7-15-93	.129	.000	.154	16	31	6	4	1	0	1	4	2	2	2	0	11	1	0	.258	.270
Duran, Rey	R-R	6-0	200	7-31-89	.273	.000	.313	13	33	3	9	1	0	1	6	2	0	0	0	8	1	1	.394	.314
Fairley, Wendell	R-R	6-2	195	3-17-88	.192	.235	.171	13	52	7	10	4	1	0	7	3	0	1	0	14	1	0	.308	.236
Fuentes, Leonardo	R-R	6-4	215	11-29-92	.088	.000	.108	27	80	6	7	5	0	0	5	6	2	0	2	47	1	1	.150	.167
Hollick, Tyler	L-R	6-1	185	9-16-92	.301	.318	.297	32	113	22	34	4	2	0	14	28	1	0	1	27	21	2	.372	.441

Name	B-T	HT	WT	DOB	AVG	vLH	vRH	G	AB	R	H	2B	3B	HR	RBI	BB	HBP	SH	SF	SO	SB	CS	OBP	SLG
Honeycutt, Ryan	L-R	6-0	195	9-6-88	.289	.250	.300	27	90	14	26	5	0	2	21	9	1	0	2	9	1	0	.411	.353
Houck, Shayne	R-R	6-1	210	5-29-90	.291	.316	.286	34	110	18	32	6	2	4	22	20	3	0	1	21	0	0	.491	.410
Jones, Jonathan	R-R	6-4	205	2-15-92	.282	.462	.248	44	163	27	46	13	1	6	29	11	7	0	0	54	1	0	.485	.354
Kieschnick, Roger	L-R	6-3	220	1-21-87	.083	—	.083	3	12	0	1	1	0	0	4	0	0	0	1	5	0	0	.167	.077
McCall, Shilo	R-R	6-1	210	6-2-94	.246	.083	.281	39	138	22	34	7	1	3	20	25	1	0	0	43	6	2	.377	.366
Mercedes, Hector	R-R	6-3	185	10-5-91	.256	.139	.292	42	156	20	40	11	4	0	21	14	1	0	1	49	3	3	.378	.320
Nicholson, Bryan	L-L	6-2	225	10-31-89	.000	—	.000	3	4	0	0	0	0	0	0	0	0	0	0	2	0	0	.000	.000
Ortiz, Randy	R-R	5-11	170	6-15-93	.247	.195	.262	50	182	41	45	7	4	0	22	15	9	4	2	47	30	7	.330	.332
Otero, Cristian	R-R	6-0	168	3-30-93	.215	.333	.194	26	79	8	17	2	0	0	5	6	0	1	0	30	3	1	.241	.271
Paulino, Cristian	R-R	5-10	168	9-4-91	.247	.368	.218	30	97	13	24	5	1	0	10	6	1	2	0	24	11	2	.320	.298
Polonius, John	R-R	6-2	170	1-13-91	.300	.286	.304	32	120	25	36	5	4	0	7	12	3	1	0	19	7	0	.408	.378
Relaford, Travious	R-R	5-11	160	5-13-92	.331	.333	.330	39	130	34	43	13	4	0	18	19	1	1	3	17	2	1	.492	.412
Robles, Alberto	R-R	5-11	155	9-14-90	.380	.300	.400	19	50	8	19	2	0	0	5	5	0	4	1	7	4	0	.420	.429
Rojas, Leo	R-R	5-11	182	6-11-90	.250	.250	.250	21	44	4	11	3	1	0	9	6	0	1	1	10	0	1	.364	.333
Sim, Eric	R-R	6-2	215	1-3-89	.000	.000	.000	3	4	0	0	0	0	0	0	0	0	0	0	3	0	0	.000	.000
Stiner, Drew	R-R	6-1	200	9-5-92	.231	.000	.250	8	13	2	3	1	0	0	1	1	0	0	0	5	0	0	.308	.286
Williamson, Mac	R-R	6-4	240	7-15-90	.176	.250	.154	4	17	4	3	0	0	2	7	2	0	0	0	5	0	0	.529	.263

Pitching	B-T	HT	WT	DOB	W	L	ERA	G	GS	CG	SV	IP	H	R	ER	HR	BB	SO	AVG	vLH	vRH	K/9	BB/9
Agosta, Martin	R-R	6-1	180	4-7-91	0	0	4.22	5	5	0	0	11	8	5	5	0	9	19	.205	.071	.280	16.03	7.59
Allen, Brandon	R-R	6-6	190	8-15-91	1	2	5.95	14	6	0	0	39	48	28	26	1	10	26	.304	.333	.277	5.95	2.29
Angeles, Luis	R-R	6-0	165	12-15-89	1	0	6.41	10	3	0	0	20	36	23	14	1	4	14	.379	.300	.467	6.41	1.83
Bandilla, Bryce	L-L	6-4	235	1-17-90	0	0	1.93	4	4	0	0	14	7	3	3	1	2	20	.143	.133	.147	12.86	1.29
Bonser, Boof	R-R	6-4	265	10-14-81	1	1	3.38	6	2	0	0	5	2	3	2	0	4	3	.105	.143	.083	5.06	6.75
Burres, Brian	L-L	6-1	175	4-8-81	0	0	1.29	3	3	0	0	7	5	1	1	0	0	10	.208	.167	.222	12.86	0.00
Christman, Tyler	R-R	6-2	180	8-26-89	1	0	1.29	15	0	0	0	14	7	7	2	0	12	19	.140	.074	.217	12.21	7.71
De Jesus, Enmanuel	L-L	6-0	175	1-6-94	1	0	5.91	13	0	0	0	11	10	7	7	1	8	8	.238	.250	.233	6.75	6.75
Edgington, Zak	R-L	6-0	190	12-21-89	0	2	3.25	12	5	0	0	28	19	11	10	1	6	32	.188	.273	.147	10.41	1.95
Encinosa, E.J.	R-R	6-5	225	8-5-91	2	2	2.19	13	0	0	4	12	10	4	3	2	4	14	.204	.222	.194	10.22	2.92
Farley, Brandon	R-R	6-2	215	8-1-90	2	1	1.19	23	0	0	1	23	19	4	3	0	7	20	.224	.148	.259	7.94	2.78
Fern, Chris	L-L	6-4	215	8-22-91	1	0	2.70	11	0	0	1	10	15	4	3	0	5	5	.349	.313	.370	4.50	4.50
Ferrer, Miguel	R-R	6-3	168	8-7-90	0	0	9.95	7	0	0	0	6	10	9	7	1	4	8	.323	.462	.222	11.37	5.68
Forjet, Jason	R-R	6-2	185	1-4-90	0	1	1.93	7	1	0	2	9	7	2	2	0	2	6	.233	.300	.200	5.79	1.93
Freite, Renzo	R-R	6-1	170	1-3-93	1	1	12.34	11	0	0	0	12	18	20	16	0	15	7	.340	.346	.333	5.40	11.57
Hernandez, Ariel	R-R	6-3	180	3-2-92	1	0	4.50	11	0	0	0	12	8	7	6	1	13	19	.170	.182	.160	14.25	9.75
Hess, Tyler	R-R	6-5	240	8-29-88	1	1	3.00	15	0	0	1	18	18	7	6	1	5	20	.265	.250	.275	10.00	2.50
Johnson, Stephen	R-R	6-4	205	2-21-91	0	0	4.50	2	0	0	0	2	1	1	1	0	2	2	.167	.250	.000	9.00	9.00
Kurrasch, Joe	L-L	6-0	205	6-19-91	0	0	0.00	3	0	0	0	3	3	1	0	0	2	3	.300	.000	.333	9.00	6.00
Lamb, Cameron	R-R	6-3	195	5-29-89	0	0	0.00	3	0	0	0	3	1	1	0	0	1	3	.077	.000	.111	8.10	2.70
Leenhouts, Drew	L-L	6-3	195	3-28-90	3	1	4.38	16	6	0	0	37	41	24	18	2	14	60	.277	.341	.252	14.59	3.41
Loux, Shane	R-R	6-2	225	8-31-79	0	0	0.00	1	1	0	0	1	0	0	0	0	0	1	.000	.000	.000	9.00	0.00
Lujan, Matthew	L-L	6-1	210	8-23-88	4	1	1.95	11	7	0	0	37	24	8	8	3	11	35	.185	.086	.221	8.51	2.68
Marte, Kelvin	R-R	6-0	180	11-24-87	0	2	7.50	7	3	0	0	12	21	17	10	1	3	10	.389	.217	.516	7.50	2.25
McVey, Cameron	R-R	6-5	205	10-18-88	1	1	5.40	12	0	0	0	10	9	6	6	0	7	8	.257	.231	.273	7.20	6.30
Moronta, Reyes	R-R	6-0	175	1-6-93	3	0	3.06	17	0	0	0	18	16	9	6	2	9	18	.242	.263	.234	9.17	4.58
Mota, Guillermo	R-R	6-6	240	7-25-73	0	0	23.63	2	1	0	0	3	8	7	7	1	0	2	.500	.364	.800	6.75	0.00
Noel, Franklin	L-L	6-1	175	12-20-88	0	1	6.35	10	0	0	0	11	16	9	8	0	5	15	.320	.467	.257	11.91	3.97
Okert, Steven	L-L	6-3	210	7-9-91	0	0	0.00	2	0	0	0	2	2	0	0	0	1	6	.250	.333	.200	27.00	4.50
Penny, Brad	R-R	6-4	230	5-24-78	0	1	18.00	1	1	0	0	1	3	2	2	0	1	1	.400	.667	.000	9.00	9.00
Reichard, Andy	R-R	6-4	230	12-4-84	0	1	18.00	1	1	0	0	1	3	2	2	0	0	1	.600	1.000	.500	9.00	0.00
Reyes, Jose	R-R	6-1	184	1-3-91	6	3	4.53	16	7	0	0	48	49	31	24	2	18	41	.259	.284	.246	7.74	3.40
Roibal, Reinier	R-R	6-2	215	1-19-89	1	0	0.00	5	0	0	0	4	0	0	0	0	2	4	.000	.000	.000	8.31	4.15
Rojas, Luis	R-R	5-10	185	7-29-89	0	0	0.00	4	0	0	0	4	0	0	0	0	5	2	.000	.000	.000	4.50	11.25
Shadle, Jake	R-R	6-2	175	4-25-90	0	0	2.78	19	0	0	2	23	22	8	7	1	10	21	.268	.250	.278	8.34	3.97
Smith, Jake	R-R	6-4	190	6-2-90	0	0	0.00	6	0	0	0	9	5	2	0	0	2	13	.156	.063	.250	13.50	2.08
Walker, Scotty	L-L	6-1	195	3-26-89	0	1	7.20	12	0	0	1	10	12	9	8	0	6	13	.300	.111	.355	11.70	5.40
Zeigler, Randy	L-L	6-1	183	8-30-89	1	2	2.45	4	0	0	0	7	6	4	2	0	3	6	.207	.286	.182	7.36	3.68

Fielding

Catcher	PCT	G	PO	A	E	DP	PB
Cornier	1.000	30	205	27	0	2	7
Duran	1.000	13	73	13	0	1	6
Honeycutt	1.000	11	53	11	0	0	7
Rojas	.979	21	120	17	3	0	8
Sim	.909	3	9	1	1	0	0
Stiner	.962	7	25	0	1	0	1

First Base	PCT	G	PO	A	E	DP
Fuentes	.933	13	81	2	6	6
Houck	1.000	7	45	5	0	2
Jones	.984	42	347	34	6	26

Second Base	PCT	G	PO	A	E	DP
Delfino	—	1	0	0	0	0
Delgado	1.000	6	12	14	0	2

	PCT	G	PO	A	E	DP
Otero	.952	12	19	21	2	2
Paulino	.942	10	25	24	3	7
Relaford	.930	27	44	76	9	10
Robles	.929	5	4	9	1	4

Third Base	PCT	G	PO	A	E	DP
Delfino	.975	11	14	25	1	1
Houck	.841	22	12	25	7	2
Jones	1.000	1	1	0	0	0
Paulino	.981	19	15	38	1	3
Relaford	.900	4	1	8	1	0
Robles	.960	12	6	18	1	1

Shortstop	PCT	G	PO	A	E	DP
Branca	.800	3	3	5	2	1
Delgado	.750	3	2	10	4	1

	PCT	G	PO	A	E	DP
Otero	.891	13	19	30	6	7
Polonius	.928	31	47	81	10	13
Relaford	.844	10	14	24	7	4
Robles	—	2	0	0	0	0

Outfield	PCT	G	PO	A	E	DP
Barnett	1.000	6	8	1	0	0
Benusa	1.000	4	1	0	0	0
Diaz	.905	16	17	2	2	0
Fairley	.889	10	7	1	1	0
Hollick	1.000	29	38	3	0	1
McCall	.917	35	53	2	5	0
Mercedes	.864	39	54	3	9	1
Nicholson	—	1	0	0	0	0
Ortiz	.949	47	70	5	4	1
Williamson	1.000	2	5	0	0	0

DOMINICAN SUMMER LEAGUE

Batting

Batting	B-T	HT	WT	DOB	AVG	vLH	vRH	G	AB	R	H	2B	3B	HR	RBI	BB	HBP	SH	SF	SO	SB	CS	SLG	OBP
Almeida, Alexis	R-R	6-3	215	2-16-93	.153	.167	.149	32	59	6	9	3	0	0	3	3	1	0	0	26	0	1	.203	.206
Astacio, Royel	B-R	6-2	197	9-27-93	.244	.286	.237	55	197	31	48	12	2	2	26	28	1	0	1	50	1	3	.355	.339
Cartagena, Carlos	R-R	6-2	190	12-22-93	.194	.375	.169	23	67	9	13	2	0	0	5	11	3	0	2	21	4	2	.224	.325
Gomez, Anthony	R-R	6-3	200	11-23-94	.191	.400	.155	25	68	12	13	2	0	2	7	16	5	0	1	19	0	2	.309	.378
Gomez, Miguel	B-R	5-10	185	12-17-92	.231	.217	.235	37	121	17	28	6	2	1	17	11	4	0	0	25	2	1	.339	.316
Guzman, Marco	R-R	6-0	170	8-7-94	.174	.200	.167	47	121	19	21	7	1	0	16	22	4	0	1	26	5	3	.248	.318
Hernandez, Emmanuel	R-R	6-1	185	11-2-93	.292	.364	.279	26	72	11	21	7	0	1	13	6	0	0	0	24	1	0	.431	.346
Matamoros, Franklin	R-R	6-1	190	6-14-93	.229	.200	.237	19	48	4	11	3	1	0	6	5	3	0	1	13	0	0	.333	.333
Medina, Hengerber	R-R	5-11	158	10-12-94	.313	.625	.268	40	128	28	40	4	0	0	10	26	7	5	0	16	7	3	.344	.453
Mesa, Herody	R-R	5-11	185	4-10-91	.333	.583	.281	24	69	11	23	4	1	1	12	6	4	0	0	21	2	2	.464	.418
Moreno, Rando	R-R	5-11	164	6-6-92	.267	.304	.259	66	243	39	65	8	0	0	26	41	5	2	2	33	23	11	.300	.381
Parra, Nicoll	L-L	5-9	160	7-28-94	.230	.161	.245	65	178	32	41	5	3	0	13	59	8	5	2	43	21	12	.292	.437
Pena, Julio	R-R	6-0	185	12-13-92	.213	.205	.214	66	235	28	50	5	2	9	37	23	5	0	1	78	3	5	.366	.295
Pujadas, Fernando	R-R	6-1	179	1-2-92	.273	.276	.273	54	172	26	47	11	1	3	23	36	8	1	0	34	1	0	.401	.421
Rivas, Kleiber	L-R	5-11	200	6-22-95	.156	.000	.192	18	32	5	5	0	0	0	3	14	4	1	0	13	1	0	.156	.460
Rodriguez, Richard	R-R	6-1	170	10-3-92	.248	.304	.239	50	157	29	39	5	0	0	10	12	1	2	0	20	14	5	.280	.306
Sotelo, Ronny	R-R	5-10	180	11-13-93	.000	.000	.000	12	22	2	0	0	0	0	3	3	4	0	0	8	0	0	.000	.241
Valdez, Carlos	R-R	5-11	180	6-22-94	.232	.214	.235	59	211	27	49	7	5	4	27	24	5	1	1	58	4	4	.370	.324
Villalona, Angel	R-R	6-3	255	8-13-90	.303	.292	.305	44	155	32	47	9	0	7	34	23	1	0	0	40	0	0	.497	.430

Pitching

Pitching	B-T	HT	WT	DOB	W	L	ERA	G	GS	CG	SV	IP	H	R	ER	HR	BB	SO	AVG	vLH	vRH	K/9	BB/9
Alvarado, Carlos	R-R	6-4	175	10-22-89	4	2	1.02	17	0	0	4	44	37	14	5	0	10	47	.226	.226	.225	9.54	2.03
Castillo, Luis	R-R	6-2	170	12-12-92	1	3	3.31	19	0	0	2	54	47	25	20	1	22	47	.240	.190	.263	7.79	3.64
Diaz, Carlos	L-L	6-2	176	11-18-93	8	2	2.91	15	14	0	0	80	64	35	26	2	20	68	.225	.212	.226	7.62	2.24
Diaz, Noel	R-R	6-1	180	9-23-93	2	0	5.79	12	1	0	0	37	43	29	24	2	9	26	.285	.273	.290	6.27	2.17
Flores, Alejandro	R-R	6-0	180	9-25-93	6	4	2.04	12	12	0	0	62	50	21	14	3	9	44	.220	.096	.292	6.42	1.31
Gomez, Shawn	R-R	6-4	180	8-24-94	2	1	3.60	10	0	0	0	25	30	14	10	0	8	21	.288	.244	.322	7.56	2.88
Guzman, Eber	R-R	6-3	195	4-8-93	4	3	3.98	15	11	0	0	63	68	35	28	1	18	56	.272	.274	.271	7.96	2.56
Mateo, Diomedes	L-L	6-2	180	10-26-89	3	0	1.62	18	0	0	6	61	33	12	11	2	18	76	.159	.194	.152	11.21	2.66
Mella, Keury	R-R	6-2	200	8-2-93	3	3	2.47	14	14	0	0	69	59	22	19	3	28	75	.225	.211	.231	9.74	3.63
Morel, Jose	R-R	6-2	190	9-6-93	0	1	8.71	6	2	0	0	10	8	13	10	0	13	7	.222	.316	.118	6.10	11.32
Nova, Juan	R-R	6-3	190	10-7-91	3	2	3.28	12	11	0	0	47	32	24	17	0	32	37	.198	.208	.193	7.14	6.17
Pino, Luis	R-R	6-0	175	11-4-94	2	2	3.54	6	5	0	0	28	26	14	11	0	9	28	.250	.167	.294	9.00	2.89
Sanchez, Eury	R-R	5-10	170	11-8-92	4	4	1.23	23	0	0	7	29	27	20	4	1	14	36	.233	.297	.203	11.05	4.30
Sierra, Juan	R-R	6-4	185	3-2-91	0	1	9.47	13	0	0	0	19	24	23	20	2	23	10	.324	.393	.283	4.74	10.89

Fielding

Catcher	PCT	G	PO	A	E	DP	PB
Gomez	.974	25	157	34	5	1	3
Pujadas	.988	45	353	47	5	2	6
Rivas	.981	10	44	8	1	0	3
Sotelo	.952	5	18	2	1	0	0

First Base	PCT	G	PO	A	E	DP
Almeida	.975	31	145	11	4	16
Astacio	.968	13	83	8	3	8
Hernandez	1.000	4	43	0	0	4
Matamoros	.980	15	94	6	2	8
Villalona	.992	32	240	24	2	18

Second Base	PCT	G	PO	A	E	DP
Guzman	.970	36	89	74	5	21

Medina	.984	16	31	32	1	8	
Rodriguez	.933	26	49	48	7	14	

Third Base	PCT	G	PO	A	E	DP
Astacio	.872	38	25	70	14	4
Gomez	.806	12	6	19	6	1
Hernandez	.917	7	9	13	2	0
Matamoros	1.000	1	1	0	0	0
Medina	.894	20	16	43	7	3
Rodriguez	.862	13	10	15	4	3
Villalona	.333	1	0	1	2	0

Shortstop	PCT	G	PO	A	E	DP
Medina	.852	9	4	19	4	2
Moreno	.956	64	106	197	14	30

	PCT	G	PO	A	E	DP
Rodriguez	.800	2	1	7	2	1

Outfield	PCT	G	PO	A	E	DP
Cartagena	.923	22	23	1	2	0
Guzman	1.000	2	2	0	0	0
Mesa	.947	18	17	1	1	0
Moreno	1.000	1	4	0	0	0
Parra	.980	61	92	8	2	1
Pena	.981	65	99	4	2	1
Rodriguez	1.000	5	5	0	0	0
Valdez	.932	58	67	2	5	0

Seattle Mariners

SEASON IN A SENTENCE: The Mariners finished last in the American League West for the third straight season, but continue to make marginal improvements in the Jack Zduriencik era.

HIGH POINT: Ace Felix Hernandez threw the first perfect game in Mariners history on Aug. 15 against the Rays. Hernandez's 12 strikeouts were the fourth-most for any perfect game, behind Sandy Koufax (14 in 1965), Randy Johnson (13, 2004) and Matt Cain (14, 2012).

LOW POINT: The Mariners limped to the end of the season by going 9-17 in September, only scoring more than five runs in a game just three times in the month. The Mariners ranked last in the American League in runs, batting, on-base percentage and slugging percentage. The team announced it will move in the fences at Safeco Field for 2013.

NOTABLE ROOKIES: Jesus Montero hit .260/.298/.386 and was the youngest player to hit 15 home runs for the Mariners since Alex Rodriguez in 1998. Japanese righthander Hisashi Iwakuma was a solid mid-rotation starter, going 9-5, 3.16 with 101 strikeouts and 43 walks over 125 innings.

KEY TRANSACTIONS: The Mariners made one of the biggest trades in the offseason by shipping righthanders Michael Pineda and Jose Campos to the Yankees for Montero and righthander Hector Noesi. Both teams were dealing from areas of strength, but the Mariners got better early returns as both pitchers shipped to New York got injured. The Mariners continued with their youth movement in late July by sending franchise icon Ichiro Suzuki to the Yankees for righthanders in Danny Farquhar and D.J. Mitchell. The Mariners had one of the youngest rosters in baseball after the trade, with few players over 30 years old, several of whom won't be back for 2013.

DOWN ON THE FARM: Double-A Jackson led the Southern League in ERA (3.37) thanks in part to having the Mariners' top pitching prospects—righthanders Taijuan Walker, Carter Capps and Stephen Pryor and lefthanders Danny Hultzen and James Paxton—at some point in the season. Second baseman Stefan Romero had a breakthrough season (.352/.391/.599). Shortstop Brad Miller recorded the second-most hits (186) in the minor leagues and catcher Mike Zunino had a stellar debut (.360/.447/.689) after signing for $4 million as the third overall pick in the draft.

OPENING DAY PAYROLL: $82.0 million (18th)

PLAYERS OF THE YEAR

MAJOR LEAGUE	MINOR LEAGUE
Felix Hernandez rhp	**Stefen Romero** 2b
13-9, 3.06	(High A/Double-A)
223 SO/56 BB	.352/.391/.599
Led AL in HR/9	23 HR, 101 RBIs

ORGANIZATION LEADERS

BATTING   *Minimum 250 AB

MAJORS

* AVG	Jesus Montero	.260
* OPS	Kyle Seager	.739
HR	Kyle Seager	20
RBI	Kyle Seager	86

MINORS

* AVG	Stefen Romero, High Desert/Jackson	.352
* OBP	Brad Miller, High Desert/Jackson	.410
* SLG	Stefen Romero, High Desert/Jackson	.599
R	Brad Miller, High Desert/Jackson	110
H	Brad Miller, High Desert/Jackson	186
TB	Brad Miller, High Desert/Jackson	285
2B	Brad Miller, High Desert/Jackson	40
3B	Timothy Lopes, AZL/High Desert	13
HR	Steven Proscia, Jackson/High Desert	28
RBI	Steven Proscia, Jackson/High Desert	103
BB	Brad Miller, High Desert/Jackson	74
SO	Joseph Dunigan, Jackson	175
SB	Jamal Austin, Clinton	36

PITCHING   #Minimum 75 IP

MAJORS

W	Jason Vargas	14
# ERA	Felix Hernandez	3.06
SO	Felix Hernandez	223
SV	Tom Wilhelmsen	29

MINORS

W	Roenis Elias, High Desert	11
L	Ambioris Hidalgo, Clinton/Everett/High Desert	13
# ERA	Danny Hultzen, Jackson/Tacoma	3.05
G	Tyler Burgoon, High Desert	53
GS	James Gillheeney, High Desert/Jackson	28
SV	Carter Capps, Jackson/Tacoma	19
IP	Anthony Fernandez, High Desert/Jackson	164
BB	Danny Hultzen, Jackson/Tacoma	75
SO	James Gillheeney, High Desert/Jackson	148
# AVG	Danny Hultzen, Jackson/Tacoma	.197

General Manager: Jack Zduriencik. **Farm Director:** Chris Gwynn. **Scouting Director:** Tom McNamara.

Class	Team	League	W	L	PCT	Finish	Manager
Majors	Seattle Mariners	American	75	87	.463	9th (14)	Eric Wedge
Triple-A	Tacoma Rainiers	Pacific Coast	63	81	.438	13th (16)	Daren Brown
Double-A	Jackson Generals	Southern	79	61	.564	1st (10)	Jim Pankovits
High A	High Desert Mavericks	California	83	57	.593	1st (10)	Pedro Grifol
Low A	Clinton LumberKings	Midwest	71	67	.514	5th (16)	Eddie Menchaca
Short-season	Everett AquaSox	Northwest	46	30	.605	t-2nd (8)	Rob Mummau
Rookie	AZL Mariners	Arizona	31	25	.554	t-6th (13)	Mike Kinkade
Rookie	Pulaski Mariners	Appalachian	29	38	.433	8th (10)	Jose Moreno
Overall 2012 Minor League Record			402	359	.528	4th (30)	

ORGANIZATION STATISTICS

SEATTLE MARINERS
AMERICAN LEAGUE

Batting	B-T	HT	WT	DOB	AVG	vLH	vRH	G	AB	R	H	2B	3B	HR	RBI	BB	HBP	SH	SF	SO	SB	CS	SLG	OBP
Ackley, Dustin	L-R	6-1	190	2-26-88	.226	.246	.215	153	607	84	137	22	2	12	50	59	0	1	1	124	13	3	.328	.294
Carp, Mike	L-R	6-2	210	6-30-86	.213	.310	.180	59	164	17	35	6	0	5	20	21	3	0	1	46	1	0	.341	.312
Figgins, Chone	B-R	5-8	180	1-22-78	.181	.183	.179	66	166	18	30	5	2	2	11	19	0	7	2	48	4	1	.271	.262
Gutierrez, Franklin	R-R	6-2	190	2-21-83	.260	.400	.153	40	150	18	39	10	1	4	17	9	2	1	1	31	3	1	.420	.309
Jaso, John	L-R	6-2	205	9-19-83	.276	.119	.302	108	294	41	81	19	2	10	50	56	5	1	5	51	5	0	.456	.394
Jimenez, Luis	L-L	6-3	280	5-7-82	.059	.000	.091	7	17	0	1	0	0	0	0	0	0	0	0	4	0	0	.059	.111
Kawasaki, Munenori	L-R	5-10	165	6-3-81	.192	.105	.212	61	104	13	20	1	0	0	7	8	1	2	0	18	2	2	.202	.257
Liddi, Alex	R-R	6-4	230	8-14-88	.224	.197	.255	38	116	8	26	4	1	3	10	9	0	0	1	49	2	1	.353	.278
Montero, Jesus	R-R	6-3	235	11-28-89	.260	.322	.228	135	515	46	134	20	0	15	62	29	2	0	7	99	0	2	.386	.298
Olivo, Miguel	R-R	6-0	230	7-15-78	.222	.221	.223	87	315	27	70	14	0	12	29	7	0	1	0	85	3	6	.381	.239
Peguero, Carlos	L-L	6-5	245	2-22-87	.179	.000	.238	17	56	2	10	2	1	2	7	1	0	0	0	28	0	0	.357	.193
Robinson, Trayvon	L-R	5-10	200	9-1-87	.221	.192	.237	46	145	16	32	4	1	3	12	14	1	4	0	43	6	3	.324	.294
Ryan, Brendan	R-R	6-2	195	3-26-82	.194	.234	.169	141	407	39	79	19	3	3	31	44	5	8	6	98	11	5	.278	.277
Saunders, Michael	L-R	6-4	215	11-19-86	.247	.261	.239	139	507	71	125	31	3	19	57	43	1	1	1	132	21	4	.432	.306
Seager, Kyle	L-R	6-0	195	11-3-87	.259	.237	.272	155	594	62	154	35	1	20	86	46	5	2	4	110	13	5	.423	.316
Smoak, Justin	B-L	6-4	230	12-5-86	.217	.235	.208	132	483	49	105	14	0	19	51	49	1	0	2	111	1	0	.364	.290
Suzuki, Ichiro	L-R	5-11	170	10-22-73	.261	.236	.278	95	402	49	105	15	5	4	28	17	0	0	4	40	15	2	.353	.288
2-team total (67 New York)					.283	—	—	162	629	77	178	28	6	9	55	22	2	5	5	61	29	7	.390	.307
Thames, Eric	L-R	6-0	205	11-10-86	.220	.125	.242	40	123	10	27	5	2	6	14	6	0	1	0	47	1	0	.439	.256
2-team total (46 Toronto)					.232	—	—	86	271	27	63	12	3	9	25	15	1	1	2	87	1	1	.399	.273
Triunfel, Carlos	R-R	5-11	200	2-27-90	.227	.300	.167	10	22	2	5	2	0	0	3	1	0	1	0	4	0	0	.318	.261
Wells, Casper	R-R	6-2	220	11-23-84	.228	.267	.195	93	285	42	65	12	3	10	36	26	4	1	0	80	3	0	.396	.302

Pitching	B-T	HT	WT	DOB	W	L	ERA	G	GS	CG	SV	IP	H	R	ER	HR	BB	SO	AVG	vLH	vRH	K/9	BB/9
Beavan, Blake	R-R	6-7	240	1-17-89	11	11	4.43	26	26	0	0	152	168	76	75	23	24	67	.281	.304	.258	3.96	1.42
Capps, Carter	R-R	6-5	220	8-7-90	0	0	3.96	18	0	0	0	25	25	11	11	0	11	28	.260	.318	.212	10.08	3.96
Delabar, Steve	R-R	6-5	220	7-17-83	2	1	4.17	34	0	0	0	37	23	17	17	9	11	46	.177	.089	.243	11.29	2.70
2-team total (27 Toronto)					4	3	3.82	61	0	0	0	66	46	29	28	12	26	92	—	—	—	12.55	3.55
Furbush, Charlie	L-L	6-5	215	4-11-86	5	2	2.72	48	0	0	0	46	28	15	14	3	16	53	.174	.147	.198	10.29	3.11
Hernandez, Felix	R-R	6-3	230	4-8-86	13	9	3.06	33	33	5	0	232	209	84	79	14	56	223	.241	.248	.231	8.65	2.17
Iwakuma, Hisashi	R-R	6-3	190	4-12-81	9	5	3.16	30	16	0	2	125	117	49	44	17	43	101	.248	.246	.251	7.25	3.09
Kelley, Shawn	R-R	6-2	220	4-26-84	2	4	3.25	47	0	0	0	44	43	20	16	5	15	45	.256	.265	.252	9.14	3.05
Kinney, Josh	R-R	6-1	215	3-31-79	0	3	3.94	35	0	0	1	32	24	14	14	3	15	36	.209	.205	.211	10.13	4.22
League, Brandon	R-R	6-2	210	3-16-83	0	5	3.63	46	0	0	9	45	48	20	18	1	19	27	.281	.337	.224	5.44	3.83
Luetge, Lucas	L-L	6-4	205	3-24-87	2	2	3.98	63	0	0	2	41	37	20	18	3	24	38	.248	.193	.318	8.41	5.31
Millwood, Kevin	R-R	6-4	230	12-24-74	6	12	4.25	28	28	1	0	161	168	86	76	13	56	107	.271	.255	.286	5.98	3.13
Noesi, Hector	R-R	6-3	200	1-26-87	2	12	5.82	22	18	0	0	107	107	71	69	21	39	68	.266	.278	.253	5.74	3.29
Perez, Oliver	L-L	6-3	210	8-15-81	1	3	2.12	33	0	0	0	30	27	7	7	1	10	24	.243	.281	.204	7.28	3.03
Pryor, Stephen	R-R	6-4	245	7-23-89	3	1	3.91	26	0	0	0	23	22	13	10	5	13	27	.253	.243	.260	10.57	5.09
Ramirez, Erasmo	R-R	5-11	205	5-2-90	1	3	3.36	16	8	0	0	59	47	26	22	6	12	48	.217	.207	.226	7.32	1.83
Sherrill, George	L-L	6-0	225	4-19-77	0	0	27.00	2	0	0	0	1	6	4	4	2	1	0	.667	1.000	.400	0.00	6.75
Vargas, Jason	L-L	6-0	215	2-2-83	14	11	3.85	33	33	2	0	217	201	94	93	35	55	141	.245	.239	.247	5.84	2.28
Wilhelmsen, Tom	R-R	6-6	230	12-16-83	4	3	2.50	73	0	0	29	79	59	24	22	5	29	87	.202	.223	.181	9.87	3.29

Fielding

Catcher	PCT	G	PO	A	E	DP	PB
Jaso	1.000	43	263	15	0	1	5
Montero	.993	56	409	22	3	3	7
Olivo	.991	73	505	46	5	5	8

First Base	PCT	G	PO	A	E	DP
Ackley	.982	11	51	4	1	5
Carp	1.000	23	188	13	0	15
Liddi	.980	5	45	3	1	3
Smoak	.997	131	1094	70	4	119

Second Base	PCT	G	PO	A	E	DP
Ackley	.989	142	238	394	7	91
Kawasaki	1.000	10	6	13	0	3
Seager	1.000	18	40	52	0	17
Triunfel	1.000	2	1	8	0	1

Third Base	PCT	G	PO	A	E	DP
Figgins	1.000	10	6	17	0	0
Kawasaki	—	1	0	0	0	0
Liddi	.932	23	8	33	3	4
Seager	.962	138	99	226	13	20

Shortstop	PCT	G	PO	A	E	DP
Kawasaki	1.000	38	50	65	0	13

	PCT	G	PO	A	E	DP
Ryan	.985	138	196	396	9	104
Triunfel	.963	7	11	15	1	5
Outfield	**PCT**	**G**	**PO**	**A**	**E**	**DP**
Carp	.955	24	41	1	2	0

	PCT	G	PO	A	E	DP
Figgins	.987	47	72	2	1	1
Gutierrez	.990	38	98	1	1	0
Liddi	.900	7	9	0	1	0
Peguero	1.000	12	28	0	0	0
Robinson	.980	46	100	0	2	0

	PCT	G	PO	A	E	DP
Saunders	.988	136	315	4	4	1
Suzuki	.995	93	198	3	1	0
Thames	.974	36	73	1	2	0
Wells	1.000	87	151	8	0	2

TACOMA RAINIERS

TRIPLE-A

PACIFIC COAST LEAGUE

Batting	B-T	HT	WT	DOB	AVG	vLH	vRH	G	AB	R	H	2B	3B	HR	RBI	BB	HBP	SH	SF	SO	SB	CS	SLG	OBP
Bantz, Brandon	R-R	6-1	211	1-7-87	.229	.250	.224	34	109	11	25	7	0	2	14	5	1	4	4	28	1	1	.349	.261
Bonilla, Leury	R-R	6-3	170	2-8-85	.277	.286	.273	17	47	10	13	4	1	1	10	1	0	1	0	6	1	0	.468	.292
Carp, Mike	L-R	6-2	210	6-30-86	.223	.281	.206	35	139	13	31	8	0	2	17	12	1	0	2	31	1	3	.324	.286
Catricala, Vinnie	R-R	6-3	220	10-31-88	.229	.186	.243	122	463	58	106	23	1	10	60	37	5	1	1	88	4	2	.348	.292
Chiang, Chih-Hsien	L-R	6-2	195	2-21-88	.245	.163	.282	40	159	14	39	6	0	2	11	5	0	2	2	21	0	2	.321	.265
Ford, Darren	R-R	5-9	190	10-1-85	.273	.324	.258	70	304	39	83	16	3	4	33	23	1	1	0	61	26	14	.385	.326
Franklin, Nick	R-R	6-1	180	3-2-91	.243	.206	.255	64	267	39	65	15	5	7	29	24	2	2	1	68	3	2	.416	.310
Gutierrez, Franklin	R-R	6-2	190	2-21-83	.258	.143	.292	17	62	11	16	5	0	2	8	8	0	0	2	13	0	1	.435	.333
Henriquez, Ralph	B-R	6-1	205	4-7-87	.200	.000	.214	5	15	2	3	1	0	1	2	0	0	0	0	3	0	0	.467	.200
Jimenez, Luis	L-L	6-3	280	5-7-82	.310	.273	.324	125	471	64	146	32	2	20	81	64	1	0	0	97	3	0	.514	.394
Liddi, Alex	R-R	6-4	230	8-14-88	.270	.311	.257	76	296	39	80	18	2	11	30	24	1	0	2	75	9	6	.456	.325
Limonta, Johan	L-L	6-0	205	8-4-83	.279	.100	.325	41	147	24	41	9	0	3	18	10	1	0	2	29	1	0	.401	.325
Moore, Adam	R-R	6-3	220	5-8-84	.209	.313	.186	24	86	10	18	5	0	3	11	5	0	1	2	14	0	0	.372	.247
2-team total (35 Omaha)					.259	—		59	201	28	52	13	0	6	33	19	3	2	4	38	2	0	.413	.326
Olivo, Miguel	R-R	6-0	230	7-15-78	.231	.200	.250	3	13	3	3	0	0	1	1	0	0	0	0	6	0	0	.462	.231
Peguero, Carlos	L-L	6-5	245	2-22-87	.285	.352	.254	76	281	47	80	13	1	21	54	29	9	0	3	103	2	2	.562	.366
Quiroz, Guillermo	R-R	6-1	215	11-29-81	.278	.315	.266	89	302	45	84	15	1	15	52	36	5	2	2	70	0	0	.483	.362
Robinson, Trayvon	B-R	5-10	200	9-1-87	.265	.271	.263	83	340	50	90	18	2	9	41	34	1	3	3	85	19	5	.409	.331
Rodriguez, Luis	R-R	5-9	190	6-27-80	.296	.333	.286	102	361	49	107	16	1	12	51	50	6	3	2	41	5	3	.452	.389
Savastano, Scott	R-R	6-1	190	6-12-86	.259	.277	.252	72	224	35	58	15	2	2	19	19	5	2	0	57	1	1	.371	.331
Smoak, Justin	B-L	6-4	230	12-5-86	.242	.353	.204	20	66	10	16	6	1	0	4	16	0	0	0	16	1	0	.364	.390
Triunfel, Carlos	R-R	5-11	200	2-27-90	.260	.344	.233	131	496	74	129	31	2	10	62	23	13	7	4	89	3	2	.391	.308
Wells, Casper	R-R	6-2	220	11-23-84	.239	.263	.231	22	71	18	17	7	2	2	14	20	2	1	1	17	2	1	.479	.415
Wilson, Mike	R-R	6-2	245	6-29-83	.239	.305	.216	71	230	43	55	13	0	12	37	34	3	0	1	62	2	0	.452	.343
Yepez, Mario	B-R	6-1	184	6-15-88	.182	.000	.222	6	11	1	2	0	0	0	1	0	0	0	1	2	0	0	.182	.167

Pitching	B-T	HT	WT	DOB	W	L	ERA	G	GS	CG	SV	IP	H	R	ER	HR	BB	SO	AVG	vLH	vRH	K/9	BB/9
Beavan, Blake	R-R	6-7	240	1-17-89	4	0	2.61	6	6	0	0	38	39	12	11	3	9	15	.265	.217	.308	3.55	2.13
Capps, Carter	R-R	6-5	220	8-7-90	0	0	0.00	1	0	0	0	0	0	0	0	0	0	3	.000	.000	.000	20.25	0.00
Carraway, Andrew	R-R	6-2	200	9-4-86	5	7	4.66	20	20	1	0	112	114	63	58	15	30	69	.265	.242	.288	5.54	2.41
Delabar, Steve	R-R	6-5	220	7-17-83	0	1	3.75	9	0	0	1	12	11	10	5	0	12	12	.239	.130	.348	9.00	9.00
Farquhar, Danny	R-R	5-9	180	2-17-87	1	0	0.54	12	0	0	4	17	9	1	1	0	5	16	.158	.167	.148	8.64	2.70
2-team total (5 Sacramento)					2	2	3.65	17	0	0	4		19	10	10	1	11	22	—	—		8.03	4.01
Fox, Matt	R-R	6-3	190	12-4-82	0	3	5.11	3	3	0	0	12	14	8	7	1	4	12	.275	.269	.280	8.76	2.92
Furbush, Charlie	L-L	6-5	215	4-11-86	1	0	3.60	7	0	0	0	10	7	4	4	1	3	13	.189	.286	.130	11.70	2.70
Garrison, Steve	B-L	6-1	195	9-12-86	1	4	5.86	7	7	0	0	43	54	29	28	10	4	20	.302	.258	.325	4.19	0.84
Grube, Jarrett	R-R	6-4	220	11-5-81	0	5	9.26	16	8	0	0	47	86	53	48	8	20	43	.391	.385	.397	8.29	3.86
Henn, Sean	R-L	6-3	235	4-23-81	3	0	3.64	15	0	0	0	30	36	14	12	1	11	29	.298	.242	.318	8.80	3.34
Hensley, Steven	R-R	6-3	180	12-27-86	2	4	6.27	24	0	0	0	37	37	27	26	5	20	22	.250	.290	.221	5.30	4.82
Hultzen, Danny	L-L	6-3	200	11-28-89	1	4	5.92	12	12	0	0	49	49	35	32	2	43	57	.258	.293	.242	10.54	7.95
Jimenez, Cesar	L-L	5-11	220	11-12-84	2	2	5.75	23	0	0	0	41	53	28	26	3	19	38	.308	.349	.284	8.41	4.20
Jimenez, Jose	L-L	6-0	180	3-23-87	0	0	20.25	1	0	0	0	1	4	3	3	0	2	2	.571	.750	.333	13.50	13.50
Kelley, Shawn	R-R	6-2	220	4-26-84	2	0	0.90	14	0	0	6	20	9	2	2	0	4	25	.138	.200	.098	11.25	1.80
Kinney, Josh	R-R	6-1	215	3-31-79	1	0	2.70	27	0	0	3	37	37	13	11	0	11	38	.268	.246	.286	9.33	2.70
LaFromboise, Bobby	L-L	6-4	190	6-25-86	5	2	1.59	27	0	0	4	40	30	7	7	1	16	38	.214	.185	.240	8.62	3.63
Marquez, Jeff	R-R	6-2	190	8-10-84	4	8	6.69	17	14	0	0	77	108	62	57	10	34	45	.329	.353	.309	5.28	3.99
2-team total (2 Colorado Springs)					5	8	6.69	19	14	0	0	79	113	64	59	11	36	47	—	—		5.33	4.08
Mitchell, D.J.	R-R	6-0	160	5-13-87	3	2	2.96	8	8	0	0	49	41	19	16	4	19	33	.223	.252	.185	6.10	3.51
Moran, Brian	L-L	6-3	185	9-30-88	3	3	3.89	23	0	0	2	37	23	17	16	6	12	53	.178	.218	.149	12.89	2.92
Noesi, Hector	R-R	6-3	200	1-26-87	2	6	5.74	11	11	0	0	64	80	46	41	7	22	55	.303	.338	.257	7.69	3.08
Patterson, Scott	R-R	6-7	225	6-20-79	1	3	2.89	26	0	0	4	28	25	10	9	4	10	25	.236	.233	.238	8.04	3.21
Pauley, David	R-R	6-2	215	6-17-83	1	2	3.14	11	2	1	0	29	35	11	10	3	8	20	.310	.333	.286	6.28	2.51
2-team total (9 Salt Lake)					3	2	2.43	20	7	1	0	59	62	19	16	7	15	41	—	—		6.22	2.28
Perez, Oliver	L-L	6-3	210	8-15-81	2	2	4.65	22	0	0	1	31	33	16	16	4	19	42	.250	.290	.219	12.19	5.52
Pryor, Stephen	R-R	6-4	245	7-23-89	0	0	0.00	16	0	0	0	20	11	0	0	0	11	20	.159	.167	.152	9.00	4.95
Ramirez, Erasmo	R-R	5-11	205	5-2-90	6	3	3.72	15	15	0	0	77	81	45	32	5	18	58	.261	.253	.270	6.75	2.09
Robles, Mauricio	L-L	5-10	190	3-5-89	0	3	9.86	6	5	0	0	21	22	23	23	3	22	19	.275	.273	.276	8.14	9.43
Ruffin, Chance	R-R	6-1	185	9-8-88	0	5	5.99	50	0	0	1	71	75	55	47	8	35	54	.268	.294	.247	6.88	4.46
Sena, Jandy	L-R	6-6	245	8-10-89	0	0	7.59	5	1	0	0	18	11	9	2	6	8		.409	.440	.368	6.75	5.06
Snow, Forrest	R-R	6-6	220	12-30-88	1	4	8.42	13	11	0	0	57	69	55	53	8	38	56	.303	.308	.298	8.89	6.04
Sweeney, Brian	R-R	6-2	200	6-13-74	6	4	4.63	27	10	0	1	95	91	53	49	13	24	55	.253	.244	.260	5.19	2.27
Vasquez, Anthony	L-L	6-0	190	9-19-86	5	4	6.53	11	11	1	0	61	79	45	44	4	21	31	.319	.254	.341	4.60	3.12

SEATTLE MARINERS

Fielding

Catcher	PCT	G	PO	A	E	DP	PB
Bantz	1.000	34	238	22	0	1	2
Henriquez	1.000	5	29	3	0	0	0
Moore	.989	22	167	11	2	1	4
Olivo	1.000	2	11	1	0	0	0
Quiroz	.992	88	609	28	5	4	11

First Base	PCT	G	PO	A	E	DP
Carp	.967	10	86	3	3	10
Catricala	1.000	3	26	1	0	2
Jimenez	.985	44	309	19	5	34
Liddi	.995	23	172	16	1	22
Limonta	.949	7	34	3	2	5
Rodriguez	1.000	15	97	4	0	7
Savastano	.997	36	269	16	1	33
Smoak	.972	19	129	10	4	14

Second Base	PCT	G	PO	A	E	DP
Bonilla	1.000	8	11	12	0	5
Franklin	.992	34	52	73	1	13
Rodriguez	.988	76	126	213	4	50
Savastano	.970	10	12	20	1	6
Triunfel	.970	22	64	67	4	22

Third Base	PCT	G	PO	A	E	DP
Bonilla	.714	3	2	3	2	0
Catricala	.932	104	72	187	19	25
Liddi	.946	30	23	47	4	4
Rodriguez	1.000	6	2	8	0	1
Savastano	.667	3	1	1	1	0

Shortstop	PCT	G	PO	A	E	DP
Bonilla	.917	3	4	7	1	2
Franklin	.953	30	42	79	6	25
Rodriguez	1.000	4	5	4	0	1

	PCT	G	PO	A	E	DP
Triunfel	.948	108	178	295	26	64

Outfield	PCT	G	PO	A	E	DP
Bonilla	1.000	2	3	0	0	0
Carp	1.000	3	6	0	0	0
Catricala	.903	15	27	1	3	1
Chiang	.977	40	82	2	2	0
Ford	.986	70	217	2	3	0
Gutierrez	1.000	10	29	1	0	1
Liddi	.984	24	58	3	1	0
Limonta	.983	27	56	3	1	0
Peguero	.952	72	137	2	7	0
Robinson	.982	82	217	6	4	4
Savastano	.941	22	32	0	2	0
Wells	.980	22	48	2	1	0
Wilson	.952	53	79	1	4	0
Yepez	1.000	4	4	0	0	0

JACKSON GENERALS

DOUBLE-A

SOUTHERN LEAGUE

Batting	B-T	HT	WT	DOB	AVG	vLH	vRH	G	AB	R	H	2B	3B	HR	RBI	BB	HBP	SH	SF	SO	SB	CS	SLG	OBP
Almonte, Denny	B-R	6-2	187	9-24-88	.249	.248	.249	124	434	50	108	20	5	12	53	52	3	7	4	135	24	10	.401	.331
Bonilla, Leury	R-R	6-3	170	2-8-85	.257	.273	.250	64	210	22	54	5	3	1	19	18	1	5	1	54	3	6	.324	.317
Campbell, Eric	R-R	6-0	205	8-6-85	.245	.333	.222	59	200	29	49	9	1	5	20	23	2	3	3	34	0	1	.375	.325
Carroll, Dan	R-R	6-1	175	1-6-89	.224	.238	.218	32	76	10	17	4	0	1	5	9	2	0	1	19	7	2	.316	.322
Chavez, Johermyn	R-R	6-3	225	1-26-89	.232	.189	.250	75	246	39	57	12	1	8	26	35	5	2	0	62	2	4	.386	.339
Chiang, Chih-Hsien	L-R	6-2	195	2-21-88	.252	.259	.250	77	290	27	73	18	3	5	37	17	0	0	4	57	3	2	.386	.289
DeJesus, Jharmidy	R-R	6-3	185	8-30-89	.241	.429	.182	11	29	5	7	1	0	0	0	2	1	1	0	4	0	0	.276	.313
Dunigan, Joe	L-L	6-1	240	3-29-86	.254	.189	.276	115	426	64	108	25	3	25	72	38	4	0	1	175	15	5	.502	.320
Franklin, Nick	B-R	6-1	180	3-2-91	.322	.196	.369	57	205	25	66	17	4	4	26	24	1	8	1	38	9	2	.502	.394
Giobbi, Andrew	R-R	6-2	194	10-25-86	.077	.000	.083	4	13	0	1	0	0	0	1	0	0	0	0	4	0	1	.077	.143
Henriquez, Ralph	B-R	6-1	205	4-7-87	.229	.269	.220	45	144	15	33	8	0	2	17	9	1	0	4	35	2	0	.326	.272
Martinez, Francisco	R-R	6-2	210	9-1-90	.227	.167	.246	95	352	55	80	16	1	2	23	43	2	5	0	85	27	7	.295	.315
Miller, Brad	L-R	6-2	185	10-18-89	.320	.310	.324	40	147	21	47	7	2	4	12	22	0	0	2	26	4	1	.476	.406
Noriega, Gabriel	R-R	6-2	170	9-13-90	.208	.268	.192	84	269	24	56	4	0	0	16	18	3	14	0	62	2	2	.223	.266
Pettit, Chris	R-R	6-0	200	8-15-84	.279	.250	.287	63	215	30	60	16	4	4	26	23	5	3	0	61	7	2	.447	.362
Phillips, Anthony	R-R	5-9	160	4-11-90	.000	.000	.000	3	2	0	0	0	0	0	0	1	0	0	0	0	0	0	.000	.333
Poythress, Rich	R-R	6-4	235	8-11-87	.304	.318	.298	86	303	39	92	21	1	6	45	50	2	1	1	33	4	0	.439	.404
Proscia, Steve	R-R	6-2	210	6-26-90	.211	.118	.237	21	76	10	16	2	0	4	9	4	1	2	0	16	0	2	.395	.259
Romero, Stefen	R-R	6-3	225	10-17-88	.347	.339	.350	56	216	38	75	15	4	12	50	14	5	0	5	37	6	3	.620	.392
Sams, Kalian	R-R	6-2	248	8-25-86	.242	.270	.231	76	256	35	62	11	4	11	35	23	1	1	1	81	13	0	.445	.306
Sucre, Jesus	R-R	6-0	225	4-30-88	.271	.318	.254	90	321	27	87	11	0	1	30	20	3	4	1	39	1	1	.315	.319
Tenbrink, Nate	L-R	6-2	202	12-21-86	.283	.125	.325	46	152	29	43	9	3	8	23	23	6	1	3	56	5	3	.539	.396
Yepez, Mario	B-R	6-1	184	6-15-88	.250	.500	.200	5	12	1	3	0	0	0	3	0	0	1	0	0	0	0	.250	.231
Zunino, Mike	R-R	6-2	220	3-25-91	.333	.421	.281	15	51	6	17	4	0	3	8	5	0	0	1	7	0	0	.588	.386

Pitching	B-T	HT	WT	DOB	W	L	ERA	G	GS	CG	SV	IP	H	R	ER	HR	BB	SO	AVG	vLH	vRH	K/9	BB/9
Arias, Jonathan	R-R	6-3	190	2-8-88	1	4	2.97	22	0	0	0	33	18	12	11	5	19	23	.165	.163	.167	6.21	5.13
Bawcom, Logan	R-R	6-2	200	11-2-88	2	1	1.88	12	0	0	6	14	6	3	3	1	15	15	.128	.143	.105	9.42	9.42
2-team total (27 Chattanooga)					5	3	2.39	39	0	0	19	49	36	13	13	2	31	51	—	—	—	9.37	5.69
Capps, Carter	R-R	6-5	220	8-7-90	2	3	1.26	38	0	0	19	50	40	8	7	2	12	72	.212	.256	.178	12.96	2.16
Carraway, Andrew	R-R	6-2	200	9-4-86	4	0	2.61	7	7	0	0	38	37	11	11	1	7	32	.257	.246	.265	7.58	1.66
Fernandez, Anthony	L-L	6-4	180	6-8-90	4	3	3.32	13	13	2	0	76	74	29	28	6	24	55	.259	.247	.264	6.51	2.84
Fox, Matt	R-R	6-3	190	12-4-82	0	1	5.63	2	2	0	0	8	8	5	5	0	3	0	.258	.286	.235	0.00	3.38
Garrison, Steve	B-L	6-1	195	9-14-86	5	5	4.74	17	14	0	0	82	100	47	43	9	20	38	.307	.227	.341	4.19	2.20
Gillheeney, Jimmy	L-L	6-1	200	11-8-87	0	1	3.81	5	5	0	0	28	31	16	12	3	12	27	.279	.323	.263	8.58	3.81
Hensley, Steven	R-R	6-3	180	12-27-86	2	2	3.24	20	0	0	2	33	22	16	12	3	19	36	.188	.304	.113	9.72	5.13
Hernandez, Moises	R-R	6-1	168	3-18-84	5	2	6.66	32	0	0	0	50	63	39	37	5	31	17	.325	.351	.308	3.06	5.58
Hultzen, Danny	L-L	6-3	200	11-28-89	8	3	1.19	13	13	0	0	75	38	14	10	2	32	79	.151	.094	.170	9.44	3.82
Jimenez, Jose	L-L	6-0	180	3-23-87	1	2	4.55	20	0	0	0	28	30	16	14	2	11	32	.270	.271	.270	10.41	3.58
Kittredge, Andrew	R-R	6-1	200	3-17-90	0	0	1.80	4	0	0	0	5	5	3	1	2	4	2	.263	.273	.250	3.60	7.20
Kohlscheen, Stephen	R-R	6-6	223	9-20-88	0	0	0.00	1	0	0	0	1	2	1	0	0	1	1	.333	.000	.500	9.00	9.00
LaFromboise, Bobby	L-L	6-4	190	6-25-86	1	0	1.01	20	0	0	2	27	15	4	3	0	5	32	.158	.087	.224	10.80	1.69
Maurer, Brandon	R-R	6-5	200	7-3-90	9	2	3.20	24	24	1	0	138	133	54	49	4	48	117	.260	.271	.249	7.65	3.14
Medina, Yoervis	R-R	6-3	245	7-27-88	5	5	3.25	46	1	0	5	69	63	25	25	5	35	77	.245	.271	.227	10.00	4.54
Mieses, George	R-R	6-2	180	5-3-91	0	0	0.00	1	0	0	0	1	0	0	0	0	0	1	.000	—	.000	0.00	0.00
Moran, Brian	L-L	6-3	185	9-30-88	1	2	1.14	24	0	0	0	32	30	5	4	1	6	29	.248	.235	.257	8.24	1.71
Paxton, James	L-L	6-4	220	11-6-88	9	4	3.05	21	21	0	0	106	96	43	36	5	54	110	.244	.222	.254	9.31	4.57
Pryor, Stephen	R-R	6-4	245	7-27-89	1	0	1.13	11	0	0	7	16	7	3	2	0	5	24	.125	.182	.088	13.50	2.81
Robles, Mauricio	L-L	5-10	215	3-5-89	2	2	4.09	37	1	0	0	51	36	24	23	2	41	50	.199	.185	.210	8.88	7.28
Sena, Jandy	L-R	6-6	245	8-10-89	3	2	2.88	30	1	0	1	50	42	19	16	2	17	26	.227	.211	.239	4.68	3.06
Snow, Forrest	R-R	6-6	220	12-30-88	4	5	4.43	19	9	0	0	61	61	35	30	4	29	43	.263	.295	.233	6.34	4.28
Stanton, Taylor	R-R	6-2	230	1-15-88	3	2	5.53	8	4	0	0	28	35	19	17	2	11	30	.302	.286	.313	4.23	3.58
Walker, Taijuan	R-R	6-4	210	8-13-92	7	10	4.69	25	25	0	0	127	124	70	66	12	50	118	.258	.286	.230	8.38	3.55

Fielding

Catcher	PCT	G	PO	A	E	DP	PB
Giobbi	1.000	4	34	1	0	0	2
Henriquez	.993	43	258	30	2	4	2
Sucre	1.000	88	690	79	0	4	11
Zunino	1.000	12	81	9	0	1	2

First Base	PCT	G	PO	A	E	DP
Bonilla	.957	2	20	2	1	4
Campbell	.988	21	156	15	2	13
DeJesus	.988	11	79	2	1	13
Pettit	.968	2	27	3	1	2
Poythress	.997	83	690	33	2	68
Proscia	.994	21	164	11	1	18
Tenbrink	1.000	7	44	2	0	6

Second Base	PCT	G	PO	A	E	DP
Bonilla	.962	19	25	51	3	8
Campbell	.950	29	34	61	5	10
Franklin	1.000	14	28	49	0	15
Noriega	.985	30	54	80	2	21
Phillips	1.000	2	0	2	0	0
Romero	.980	54	104	147	5	33

Third Base	PCT	G	PO	A	E	DP
Bonilla	.960	32	23	73	4	8
Campbell	.875	4	1	6	1	1
Martinez	.965	78	50	144	7	14
Tenbrink	.944	31	25	59	5	2

Shortstop	PCT	G	PO	A	E	DP
Bonilla	.923	11	17	31	4	6

Franklin	.949	39	59	90	8	27
Miller	.969	37	59	96	5	28
Noriega	.970	55	106	156	8	42

Outfield	PCT	G	PO	A	E	DP
Almonte	.986	121	265	10	4	2
Campbell	1.000	1	2	0	0	0
Carroll	.968	19	29	1	1	0
Chavez	.986	72	133	5	2	1
Chiang	.972	65	99	7	3	1
Dunigan	.966	23	28	0	1	0
Martinez	1.000	11	24	0	0	0
Pettit	.990	57	97	6	1	0
Sams	.967	65	114	5	4	1
Yepez	1.000	4	12	1	0	1

HIGH DESERT MAVERICKS
CALIFORNIA LEAGUE

HIGH CLASS A

Batting	B-T	HT	WT	DOB	AVG	vLH	vRH	G	AB	R	H	2B	3B	HR	RBI	BB	HBP	SH	SF	SO	SB	CS	SLG	OBP
Bantz, Brandon	R-R	6-1	211	1-7-87	.000	.000	.000	1	3	0	0	0	0	0	0	1	0	0	0	1	0	0	.000	.250
Brady, Patrick	R-R	5-10	176	2-5-88	.297	.295	.298	40	128	24	38	4	1	3	19	7	1	0	2	24	3	2	.414	.333
Carp, Mike	L-R	6-2	210	6-30-86	.667	.750	.600	2	9	2	6	1	0	1	4	2	0	0	0	1	0	1	1.111	.727
Coleman, Trevor	B-R	6-1	205	1-19-88	.182	.000	.200	5	11	5	2	0	0	1	1	5	0	0	0	2	0	0	.455	.438
Franca, Gabriel	R-R	5-11	160	9-11-93	.500	—	.500	1	2	0	1	1	0	0	1	0	0	0	0	0	0	0	1.000	.500
Giobbi, Andrew	R-R	6-2	194	10-25-86	.067	.167	.000	4	15	2	1	0	0	1	1	1	0	0	0	1	0	0	.267	.125
Hicks, John	R-R	6-2	190	8-31-89	.312	.281	.322	121	506	87	158	32	2	15	79	28	3	0	1	73	22	8	.472	.351
Jones, James	L-L	6-4	193	9-24-88	.306	.250	.327	126	493	109	151	28	12	14	76	54	5	3	4	124	26	17	.497	.378
Landry, Leon	L-R	5-11	185	9-20-89	.385	.462	.359	24	104	25	40	8	3	5	25	5	1	0	1	14	7	2	.663	.414
2-team total (80 R. Cucamonga)					.341	—	—	104	449	88	153	34	18	13	76	19	6	7	6	66	27	11	.584	.371
Lopes, Timmy	R-R	5-11	180	6-24-94	.250	.167	.333	4	12	2	3	0	1	0	1	0	0	0	0	1	0	0	.417	.250
Marder, Jack	R-R	5-11	185	2-21-90	.360	.329	.371	65	278	68	100	24	4	10	56	21	13	4	3	44	16	6	.583	.425
Martinez, Mario	R-R	6-3	200	11-13-89	.283	.288	.282	120	467	63	132	24	4	21	80	13	6	1	5	97	3	3	.486	.308
McGee, Mike	R-R	6-0	185	3-7-89	.276	.275	.277	118	445	86	123	24	5	17	58	47	6	5	2	82	11	5	.467	.352
Melendres, Nathan	R-R	5-10	187	4-4-90	.286	.200	.304	8	28	4	8	2	1	1	3	0	1	0	0	8	0	1	.536	.310
Miller, Brad	L-R	6-2	185	10-18-89	.339	.263	.370	97	410	89	139	33	5	11	56	52	2	4	5	79	19	6	.524	.412
Morban, Julio	L-L	6-1	190	2-13-92	.313	.333	.307	76	300	56	94	16	2	17	52	21	3	3	3	67	5	1	.550	.361
Noriega, Gabriel	R-R	6-2	170	9-13-90	.271	.318	.260	31	118	16	32	8	2	0	15	5	0	2	1	23	1	2	.373	.298
Proscia, Steve	R-R	6-2	210	6-26-90	.333	.372	.317	106	436	88	145	24	3	24	94	25	3	1	6	97	12	2	.567	.368
Raben, Dennis	L-L	6-3	200	7-31-87	.271	.224	.285	66	258	52	70	16	2	9	44	36	7	2	0	63	3	0	.453	.375
Ramirez, Carlos	B-R	5-11	145	12-2-88	.175	.125	.192	33	97	11	17	2	0	0	6	14	1	2	0	25	2	1	.196	.286
Rivers, Kevin	L-R	6-2	210	8-24-88	.224	.225	.224	47	147	22	33	8	3	6	25	19	3	1	1	42	1	2	.442	.324
Romero, Stefen	R-R	6-3	225	10-17-88	.357	.397	.342	60	258	47	92	19	3	11	51	13	3	0	2	35	6	2	.581	.391
Tanabe, Carlton	R-R	6-0	190	10-28-91	.295	.364	.268	23	78	13	23	0	0	1	10	6	0	3	1	16	1	0	.333	.333
Wiswall, Mickey	L-R	6-1	200	11-25-88	.280	.226	.298	123	497	80	139	33	4	21	98	31	4	0	3	115	8	6	.489	.325

Pitching	B-T	HT	WT	DOB	W	L	ERA	G	GS	CG	SV	IP	H	R	ER	HR	BB	SO	AVG	vLH	vRH	K/9	BB/9
Alsup, Wes	R-R	6-2	205	11-25-86	1	0	10.80	15	0	0	0	13	12	17	16	2	28	18	.245	.346	.130	12.15	18.90
Arias, Jonathan	R-R	6-3	190	2-8-88	4	3	5.40	24	0	0	7	35	38	21	21	7	13	36	.288	.275	.296	9.26	3.34
Blandford, Tyler	R-R	6-3	165	1-25-88	1	0	6.05	16	0	0	0	19	17	13	13	3	20	25	.233	.216	.250	11.64	9.31
Boyce, Tim	R-R	6-2	193	2-6-87	2	4	4.38	17	0	0	2	25	23	13	12	4	10	22	.235	.190	.268	8.03	3.65
Burgoon, Tyler	R-R	5-10	160	4-25-89	8	2	3.25	53	0	0	3	64	54	28	23	5	31	80	.230	.264	.208	11.31	4.38
DeJesus, Yunior	R-R	6-3	210	9-22-88	0	0	6.75	2	0	0	0	3	4	3	2	0	3	3	.333	.250	.375	10.13	10.13
Elias, Roenis	L-L	6-2	178	8-1-88	11	6	3.76	26	26	0	0	148	136	80	62	19	41	128	.245	.212	.262	7.77	2.49
Fernandez, Anthony	L-L	6-4	180	6-8-90	2	5	3.68	14	14	1	0	88	89	43	36	6	14	79	.263	.274	.258	8.08	1.43
Gillheeney, Jimmy	L-L	6-1	200	11-8-87	8	4	5.39	23	23	1	0	120	140	84	72	19	48	121	.290	.274	.295	9.05	3.59
Griffin, Tim	B-R	6-1	200	3-1-88	1	0	7.47	19	0	0	0	31	43	31	26	9	8	20	.316	.321	.313	5.74	2.30
Hidalgo, Ambioris	R-R	6-2	196	2-4-91	0	1	4.35	2	2	0	0	10	7	5	5	1	1	3	.200	.182	.231	2.61	0.87
Hobson, Cameron	L-L	6-0	190	4-16-89	9	4	5.63	19	19	0	0	109	143	82	68	17	32	61	.324	.328	.321	5.05	2.65
Hudson, Austin	R-R	6-4	175	1-6-88	3	2	6.32	22	0	0	2	37	53	32	26	4	5	31	.338	.392	.289	7.54	1.22
Jimenez, Jose	L-L	6-0	180	3-23-87	1	0	4.78	28	0	0	0	26	31	21	14	4	11	28	.284	.320	.254	9.57	3.76
Kesler, Willy	R-R	6-0	225	8-11-87	2	2	6.75	19	0	0	0	28	40	29	21	5	9	22	.325	.396	.271	7.07	2.89
Kittredge, Andrew	R-R	6-1	200	3-17-90	2	1	5.81	16	0	0	0	26	32	17	17	4	9	25	.314	.383	.255	8.54	3.08
Kohlscheen, Stephen	R-R	6-6	223	9-20-88	3	2	3.27	29	0	0	3	44	46	20	16	6	23	60	.266	.373	.184	12.27	4.70
Mieses, George	R-R	6-2	180	5-3-91	1	3	5.21	7	7	0	0	38	48	27	22	4	8	27	.316	.358	.282	6.39	1.89
Miller, Trevor	R-R	6-3	190	6-13-91	1	2	2.73	5	5	0	0	30	29	11	9	0	7	29	.269	.315	.222	8.80	2.12
Pryor, Stephen	R-R	6-4	245	7-23-89	0	0	6.75	2	1	0	0	3	0	2	2	0	3	3	.000	.000	.000	10.13	10.13
Raga, Angel	R-R	6-1	168	7-25-89	4	4	6.00	31	7	0	0	60	80	44	40	6	34	57	.324	.302	.340	8.55	5.10
Sena, Jandy	L-R	6-6	245	8-10-89	1	0	2.25	3	0	0	0	4	4	1	1	0	3	4	.250	.429	.111	9.00	6.75
Shankin, Brett	R-R	6-5	205	10-30-89	7	3	6.28	14	13	0	0	77	94	57	54	8	34	47	.305	.352	.265	5.47	3.96
Smith, Carson	R-R	6-6	200	10-19-89	5	1	2.90	49	0	0	15	62	54	22	20	2	28	77	.234	.272	.203	11.18	4.06
Sorce, Chris	R-R	6-0	190	10-28-87	1	2	7.11	8	8	0	0	38	50	32	30	2	13	28	.318	.308	.326	6.63	3.08
Stanton, Taylor	R-R	6-2	230	1-15-88	6	5	5.17	24	15	1	0	108	132	67	62	14	21	79	.303	.302	.305	6.58	1.75

Fielding

Catcher	PCT	G	PO	A	E	DP	PB
Bantz	1.000	1	2	2	0	0	
Coleman	.980	5	47	2	1	0	1
Giobbi	1.000	4	25	4	0	0	
Hicks	.991	98	763	92	8	11	20
Marder	1.000	15	120	7	0	1	2
Tanabe	.978	22	154	22	4	1	3

First Base	PCT	G	PO	A	E	DP
Jones	1.000	1	10	0	0	1
Martinez	.993	16	126	11	1	9
Proscia	.981	23	189	14	4	16
Raben	.984	35	300	17	5	26
Wiswall	.989	67	591	34	7	57

Second Base	PCT	G	PO	A	E	DP
Brady	.971	23	46	56	3	12
Franca	—	1	0	0	0	0
Lopes	.750	2	0	3	1	1

	PCT	G	PO	A	E	DP
Marder	.973	29	56	88	4	22
Martinez	.750	2	1	2	1	0
Melendres	.857	3	5	7	2	2
Noriega	1.000	2	3	6	0	0
Proscia	.962	15	30	46	3	4
Ramirez	.977	19	37	49	2	8
Romero	.970	53	114	144	8	40

Third Base	PCT	G	PO	A	E	DP
Martinez	.930	100	69	184	19	18
Proscia	.950	40	30	83	6	10
Ramirez	1.000	2	0	1	0	0
Wiswall	1.000	1	0	1	0	0

Shortstop	PCT	G	PO	A	E	DP
Brady	.857	2	2	4	1	0
Lopes	1.000	1	0	1	0	0
Melendres	1.000	2	4	4	0	1
Miller	.936	97	144	306	31	66

	PCT	G	PO	A	E	DP
Noriega	.970	29	46	85	4	13
Ramirez	.906	11	21	27	5	6

Outfield	PCT	G	PO	A	E	DP
Brady	1.000	14	20	0	0	0
Jones	.980	123	231	8	5	2
Landry	.980	22	48	0	1	0
Marder	1.000	10	14	1	0	1
Martinez	1.000	1	1	1	0	1
McGee	.987	115	214	7	3	0
Melendres	1.000	3	4	0	0	0
Morban	.936	61	97	5	7	1
Raben	.750	4	3	0	1	0
Ramirez	1.000	1	2	0	0	0
Rivers	.967	44	56	3	2	0
Wiswall	.933	37	65	5	5	0

CLINTON LUMBERKINGS — LOW CLASS A

MIDWEST LEAGUE

Batting	B-T	HT	WT	DOB	AVG	vLH	vRH	G	AB	R	H	2B	3B	HR	RBI	BB	HBP	SH	SF	SO	SB	CS	SLG	OBP
Acevedo, Jean	R-R	6-0	185	12-5-90	.189	.364	.143	18	53	5	10	3	0	0	6	6	3	2	3	9	0	0	.245	.292
Austin, Jamal	R-R	5-9	170	8-26-90	.283	.321	.271	110	449	72	127	14	3	2	33	29	3	10	6	66	36	12	.341	.326
Baron, Steve	R-R	6-0	205	12-7-90	.241	.286	.223	64	249	29	60	18	2	4	30	13	2	3	4	49	10	1	.378	.280
Blash, Jabari	R-R	6-5	224	7-4-89	.245	.270	.235	113	400	71	98	20	5	15	50	60	9	0	2	134	13	7	.433	.355
Brady, Patrick	R-R	5-10	176	2-5-88	.251	.319	.226	46	171	21	43	12	1	2	15	16	3	4	0	24	2	6	.368	.326
Brito, Bryan	R-R	6-2	170	2-16-92	.145	.214	.125	18	62	10	9	3	0	1	6	3	2	0	1	20	1	2	.242	.206
Choi, Ji-Man	L-R	6-1	195	5-19-91	.298	.258	.311	66	242	43	72	14	1	8	43	39	12	1	0	55	0	2	.463	.420
DeJesus, Jharmidy	R-R	6-3	185	8-30-89	.220	.260	.203	76	259	27	57	17	1	6	29	23	4	0	2	58	1	0	.363	.292
DeMello, Toby	R-R	6-2	220	1-3-90	.188	.000	.231	6	16	3	3	0	0	0	1	2	0	0	1	6	0	0	.188	.263
Dowd, Mike	R-R	5-8	205	4-10-90	.294	.292	.295	78	279	28	82	15	1	2	43	20	6	0	7	32	3	2	.376	.346
Hazlett, Dillon	R-R	6-1	190	1-22-89	.266	.341	.238	95	331	52	88	19	3	7	27	25	10	8	1	77	11	10	.405	.335
Marte, Ketel	B-R	6-1	180	10-12-93	.286	.200	.333	4	14	3	4	0	0	0	2	0	1	0	0	3	1	0	.286	.375
Melendres, Nathan	R-R	5-10	187	4-4-90	.233	.231	.233	11	43	4	10	0	0	1	7	4	0	2	0	3	8	0	.302	.298
Morales, Alfredo	R-R	6-2	210	11-6-92	.200	.273	.172	13	40	6	8	2	0	0	3	6	0	0	0	13	0	2	.250	.304
Morla, Ramon	R-R	6-1	203	11-20-89	.278	.320	.264	102	410	63	114	27	7	13	68	17	7	0	8	102	7	1	.473	.312
Paolini, Dan	R-R	6-0	190	10-11-89	.299	.333	.286	111	418	68	125	29	0	18	73	49	3	2	1	63	5	2	.493	.376
Phillips, Anthony	R-R	5-9	160	4-11-90	.214	.250	.202	118	370	44	79	15	2	5	24	40	7	22	3	87	11	8	.305	.300
Pimentel, Guillermo	L-L	6-1	206	10-5-92	.245	.184	.263	105	372	37	91	18	0	9	51	19	5	0	2	115	5	2	.366	.289
Ramirez, Carlos	B-R	5-11	145	12-2-88	.190	.000	.190	6	21	3	4	0	0	0	3	1	0	0		2	0	0	.190	.320
Rivers, Kevin	L-R	6-2	210	8-24-88	.287	.261	.295	49	178	22	51	15	1	4	32	26	6	0	4	45	4	2	.449	.388
Tanabe, Carlton	R-R	6-0	190	10-28-91	.308	1.000	.250	5	13	0	4	1	0	0	1	1	0	0	0	3	0	0	.385	.357
Taylor, Chris	R-R	6-0	170	8-29-90	.304	.200	.317	12	46	5	14	0	0	0	4	2	3	2	0	4	4	1	.304	.373
Villasuso, David	R-R	5-10	195	12-31-89	.294	.500	.231	13	34	6	10	3	0	2	5	0	2	0	2	9	0	0	.559	.316
Yepez, Mario	B-R	6-1	184	6-15-88	.219	.235	.214	44	146	21	32	4	1	2	20	14	2	2	2	33	1	0	.301	.293
Zamarripa, James	L-L	5-10	190	9-17-93	.273	.286	.267	12	44	7	12	1	1	0	6	2	0	2	0	10	0	0	.341	.304
Zorrilla, Janelfry	R-R	6-3	205	9-2-90	.200	.000	.500	2	5	1	1	0	0	1	1	0	0	0	0	1	0	0	.800	.200

Pitching	B-T	HT	WT	DOB	W	L	ERA	G	GS	CG	SV	IP	H	R	ER	HR	BB	SO	AVG	vLH	vRH	K/9	BB/9
Alsup, Wes	R-R	6-2	205	11-25-86	0	3	6.14	9	0	0	0	7	8	5	0	11	9		.250	.200	.278	11.05	13.50
Brazis, Matt	R-R	6-3	205	9-6-89	1	0	0.93	11	0	0	5	19	10	3	2	1	5	32	.152	.190	.133	14.90	2.10
Colvin, David	R-R	6-3	215	1-7-89	5	3	3.15	32	1	0	4	69	62	28	24	4	16	61	.244	.209	.262	8.00	2.10
Cornwell, Ben	R-R	6-3	220	11-2-88	0	1	7.11	4	0	0	0	6	5	5	5	0	7	5	.238	.143	.286	7.11	9.95
Corrales, Josh	R-R	6-2	205	5-25-90	4	4	4.09	37	0	0	2	55	55	35	25	0	40	54	.270	.407	.220	8.84	6.55
DeJesus, Yunior	R-R	6-3	210	9-22-88	0	0	0.00	2	0	0	0	2	3	0	0	0	1	2	.300	.333	.250	7.71	3.86
Diaz, Nolan	R-R	6-1	175	3-28-91	0	0	0.00	1	0	0	0	1	0	0	0	0	0	0	.000	.000	.000	0.00	0.00
Dobbs, Jeremy	L-L	6-3	185	10-12-89	5	2	4.99	23	9	0	1	74	84	53	41	5	31	41	.279	.288	.276	4.99	3.77
Griffin, Tim	B-R	6-1	200	3-1-88	3	1	2.87	18	0	0	1	38	28	12	12	1	11	26	.204	.224	.193	6.21	2.63
Guaipe, Mayckol	R-R	6-3	175	8-11-90	5	0	3.39	11	11	0	0	58	60	31	22	4	15	34	.269	.244	.284	5.25	2.31
Hidalgo, Ambioris	R-R	6-2	196	2-4-91	2	9	5.67	15	15	0	0	73	76	51	46	9	32	38	.267	.289	.247	4.68	3.95
Hobson, Cameron	L-L	6-0	190	4-10-89	1	6	4.36	8	8	0	0	43	41	26	21	4	13	32	.244	.262	.238	6.65	2.70
Hunter, Kyle	L-L	6-3	205	6-18-89	4	5	2.98	39	0	0	3	85	81	36	28	5	11	71	.256	.229	.267	7.55	1.17
Kim, Seon Gi	R-R	6-2	185	9-1-91	4	4	4.59	14	14	0	0	69	74	41	35	8	30	49	.280	.337	.245	6.42	3.93
Kittredge, Andrew	R-R	6-1	200	3-17-90	1	0	0.84	5	0	0	1	11	8	1	1	1	1	16	.211	.211	.211	13.50	0.84
Kohlscheen, Stephen	R-R	6-6	223	9-20-88	1	1	3.96	12	0	0	0	25	29	13	11	2	12	30	.296	.357	.250	10.80	4.32
Landazuri, Steve	R-R	6-0	175	1-6-92	3	2	3.06	9	7	0	1	47	38	16	16	1	11	39	.222	.188	.245	7.47	2.11
Miller, Trevor	R-R	6-3	190	6-13-91	7	7	3.36	22	17	1	0	121	120	60	45	11	17	84	.255	.259	.252	6.27	1.27
Pries, Jordan	R-R	6-1	190	1-27-90	4	0	3.49	7	7	0	0	39	27	16	15	2	7	33	.190	.255	.154	7.68	1.63
Shackleford, Stephen	R-R	6-1	185	5-5-89	6	2	1.47	28	0	0	11	43	36	8	7	1	16	42	.226	.246	.214	8.79	3.35
Shankin, Brett	R-R	6-0	200	10-30-89	1	3	4.22	14	11	1	1	64	71	33	30	3	15	40	.287	.389	.229	5.63	2.11
Shellhorn, Rusty	R-R	5-10	170	2-25-90	3	1	3.60	4	4	0	0	25	15	11	10	0	11	18	.181	.160	.190	6.48	3.96
Shipers, Jordan	R-L	5-10	168	6-27-91	4	5	3.89	23	23	2	0	118	123	61	51	9	31	64	.273	.221	.289	4.88	2.36

	B-T	HT	WT	DOB	W	L	ERA	G	GS	CG	SV	IP	H	R	ER	HR	BB	SO	AVG	vLH	vRH	K/9	BB/9
Shore, Bobby	R-R	6-1	170	1-27-89	4	3	1.94	17	10	0	0	70	52	21	15	4	19	69	.208	.191	.221	8.91	2.45
Taylor, John	R-R	5-10	175	3-27-89	3	5	5.79	35	0	0	3	47	53	45	30	1	24	28	.293	.274	.303	5.40	4.63
Vargas, Richard	R-R	6-3	170	4-19-91	0	0	4.02	10	1	0	2	16	14	7	7	1	5	13	.230	.318	.179	7.47	2.87

Fielding

Catcher	PCT	G	PO	A	E	DP	PB
Baron	.981	53	315	52	7	2	9
DeMello	1.000	6	30	7	0	0	1
Dowd	.993	68	460	70	4	2	11
Tanabe	1.000	5	26	8	0	1	1
Villasuso	.965	13	79	4	3	0	1
Hazlett	.974	83	154	215	10	48	
Melendres	1.000	1	5	1	0	1	
Paolini	.961	30	64	84	6	19	
Phillips	1.000	4	9	6	0	1	
Marte	.879	4	12	17	4	5	
Morla	—	1	0	0	0	0	
Phillips	.976	110	164	375	13	69	
Taylor	1.000	8	13	17	0	5	

First Base	PCT	G	PO	A	E	DP
Choi	.986	35	318	23	5	21
DeJesus	.989	48	397	35	5	40
Dowd	1.000	1	2	0	0	0
Morla	.970	4	30	2	1	5
Paolini	.981	59	494	25	10	40

Second Base	PCT	G	PO	A	E	DP
Acevedo	.964	15	29	52	3	10
Brady	.978	7	21	24	1	3
Brito	.971	6	20	13	1	5

Third Base	PCT	G	PO	A	E	DP
Acevedo	1.000	4	2	7	0	1
Brady	.864	11	5	14	3	1
Brito	1.000	3	0	3	0	0
DeJesus	.863	20	11	33	7	1
Morla	.893	98	78	206	34	12
Phillips	.889	3	1	7	1	0
Ramirez	.882	6	5	10	2	1

Shortstop	PCT	G	PO	A	E	DP
Brady	.976	10	17	23	1	7
Brito	.963	9	22	30	2	6
Hazlett	.800	1	1	3	1	0

Outfield	PCT	G	PO	A	E	DP
Austin	.988	109	243	7	3	3
Blash	.973	90	205	8	6	0
Brady	.978	20	41	3	1	1
Hazlett	1.000	12	29	2	0	0
Melendres	1.000	8	8	2	0	0
Morales	.950	12	18	1	1	0
Phillips	1.000	2	3	0	0	0
Pimentel	.967	84	109	8	4	1
Rivers	.952	37	55	5	3	0
Yepez	.987	44	75	3	1	0
Zamarripa	.970	12	31	1	1	1
Zorrilla	1.000	2	1	1	0	0

EVERETT AQUASOX   SHORT-SEASON
NORTHWEST LEAGUE

Batting	B-T	HT	WT	DOB	AVG	vLH	vRH	G	AB	R	H	2B	3B	HR	RBI	BB	HBP	SH	SF	SO	SB	CS	SLG	OBP
Acevedo, Jean	R-R	6-0	185	12-5-90	.250	.250	.250	20	72	14	18	5	0	1	9	5	2	0	1	13	3	0	.361	.313
Ard, Taylor	R-R	6-2	230	1-31-90	.284	.203	.304	75	296	44	84	21	3	12	58	28	7	0	3	54	3	1	.497	.356
Carmichael, Christian	R-R	5-11	190	4-25-92	.231	.111	.294	8	26	3	6	2	0	0	0	0	0	0	0	8	0	0	.308	.231
Faulkner, Mike	L-L	5-9	150	6-28-91	.255	.349	.228	56	188	26	48	1	0	0	12	19	3	8	0	22	15	5	.261	.333
Hebert, Brock	R-R	5-10	180	5-11-90	.246	.316	.232	33	118	25	29	2	2	0	7	24	1	2	2	31	11	2	.297	.372
Henry, Jabari	R-R	6-0	198	11-11-90	.333	.000	.400	3	6	0	2	0	0	0	1	1	0	0	0	1	0	0	.333	.500
Kivlehan, Patrick	R-R	6-2	210	12-22-89	.301	.344	.290	72	282	46	85	17	3	12	52	19	13	2	0	93	14	1	.511	.373
Littlewood, Marcus	R-R	6-3	205	3-18-92	.262	.188	.283	62	214	36	56	10	0	9	37	44	1	0	0	72	2	2	.435	.390
Marlette, Tyler	R-R	5-11	195	1-23-93	.400	—	.400	2	5	0	2	1	0	0	0	0	0	0	0	0	0	0	.600	.400
Marte, Ketel	B-R	6-1	180	10-12-93	.247	.236	.250	65	251	36	62	4	2	0	22	12	0	6	0	35	14	4	.279	.281
McGruder, Jamodrick	L-R	5-8	155	8-4-91	.237	.204	.246	65	249	35	59	9	1	0	20	39	6	3	1	37	30	5	.281	.353
Morales, Alfredo	R-R	6-2	210	11-6-92	.234	.219	.239	70	265	31	62	13	3	5	35	24	0	0	4	88	5	2	.362	.294
Palase, Richard	R-R	5-11	195	8-17-90	.094	.167	.077	12	32	2	3	0	0	0	0	5	1	0	0	17	1	0	.094	.237
Pizzano, Dario	L-R	5-11	200	4-25-91	.333	.333	.333	6	21	1	7	3	0	1	4	0	0	0	0	2	0	0	.476	.440
Tanabe, Carlton	R-R	6-0	190	10-28-91	.160	.000	.182	8	25	1	4	2	0	0	2	1	0	0	0	5	0	0	.240	.192
Taylor, Chris	R-R	6-0	190	8-29-90	.328	.281	.343	37	137	26	45	12	1	2	18	21	5	0	2	18	13	5	.474	.430
Villasuso, David	R-R	5-10	195	12-31-89	.179	.100	.193	19	67	5	12	6	0	2	9	3	1	1	1	19	0	0	.358	.222
Werman, Keith	L-R	5-7	150	10-1-89	.000	—	.000	4	11	1	0	0	0	0	1	0	0	0	0	2	1	0	.000	.000
Zamarripa, James	L-L	5-10	190	9-17-93	.226	.200	.231	9	31	4	7	1	0	0	2	3	0	1	0	9	1	0	.258	.294
Zorrilla, Janelfry	R-R	6-3	205	9-2-90	.244	.200	.258	61	201	24	49	11	0	5	20	17	0	2	0	54	5	3	.373	.303
Zunino, Mike	R-R	6-2	220	3-25-91	.373	.409	.364	29	110	29	41	10	0	10	35	18	4	0	1	26	1	0	.736	.474

Pitching	B-T	HT	WT	DOB	W	L	ERA	G	GS	CG	SV	IP	H	R	ER	HR	BB	SO	AVG	vLH	vRH	K/9	BB/9
Bordonaro, Mark	R-R	6-0	170	8-17-90	3	4	5.76	18	0	0	0	30	36	21	19	6	17	20	.310	.280	.333	6.07	5.16
DeCecco, Scott	R-L	6-0	175	5-8-91	2	4	5.95	16	9	0	0	56	65	41	37	6	22	54	.293	.340	.278	8.68	3.54
DeJesus, Yunior	R-R	6-3	210	9-22-88	2	0	1.71	14	0	0	3	21	14	6	4	1	7	16	.184	.237	.132	6.86	3.00
Ewing, Steve	L-L	6-1	220	8-8-91	4	2	4.53	14	12	0	0	60	58	33	30	2	33	42	.261	.279	.253	6.34	4.98
Garcia, Oliver	R-R	6-2	205	12-7-90	2	0	3.80	19	0	0	5	24	25	13	10	0	15	24	.260	.195	.309	9.13	5.70
Guaipe, Mayckol	R-R	6-3	175	8-11-90	0	0	4.50	2	2	0	0	12	13	6	6	1	6	2	.295	.296	.294	4.50	1.50
Hauser, Blake	R-R	6-2	180	4-14-91	3	1	3.75	15	0	0	1	24	19	12	10	3	13	26	.213	.229	.204	9.75	4.88
Hidalgo, Ambioris	R-R	6-2	196	2-4-91	2	3	4.74	10	6	0	0	38	40	23	20	4	22	31	.286	.277	.290	7.34	5.21
Holman, David	R-R	6-6	220	5-31-90	0	0	6.00	1	0	0	1	3	3	2	2	1	1	2	.273	.250	.286	6.00	3.00
Holovach, Blake	L-L	6-5	195	3-27-91	0	0	15.00	1	1	0	0	3	4	5	5	0	5	0	.308	.000	.400	0.00	15.00
Kim, Seon Gi	R-R	6-2	185	9-1-91	2	0	0.75	2	2	0	0	12	4	1	1	1	2	16	.100	.200	.000	12.00	1.50
Leone, Dominic	R-R	5-11	185	10-26-91	3	0	1.36	19	0	0	5	33	20	6	5	0	19	39	.177	.267	.118	10.64	5.18
Plotz, Brandon	R-R	6-3	205	3-29-90	2	3	3.00	19	0	0	3	33	31	15	11	2	15	36	.242	.200	.269	9.82	4.09
Reyna, Marcos	R-R	6-1	195	11-4-89	0	3	3.67	18	3	0	2	42	34	20	17	2	29	37	.227	.292	.176	7.99	6.26
Sanchez, Victor	R-R	6-0	255	1-30-95	2	6	3.18	15	15	0	0	85	69	37	30	5	27	69	.223	.250	.192	7.31	2.86
Shellhorn, Rusty	R-R	5-10	170	2-25-90	3	2	2.76	6	0	0	0	33	29	15	10	3	7	32	.232	.214	.237	8.82	1.93
Shore, Bobby	R-R	6-1	170	1-27-89	0	0	3.00	1	0	0	0	3	2	1	1	0	2	2	.200	.250	.167	6.00	6.00
Unsworth, Dylan	R-R	6-1	175	9-23-92	7	2	3.90	14	14	0	0	85	76	40	37	9	19	67	.235	.228	.241	7.07	2.00
Valdivia, Jose	R-R	6-4	235	3-19-92	0	2	6.15	6	6	0	0	26	33	24	18	3	12	14	.306	.292	.317	7.18	4.10
Vedo, Matt	L-R	6-3	205	1-12-90	1	3	3.92	16	0	0	4	21	23	13	9	0	15	31	.264	.303	.241	13.50	6.53
Wood, Grady	R-R	6-2	195	5-18-90	4	0	2.17	17	0	0	2	37	29	12	9	0	15	35	.210	.269	.174	8.44	3.62

Fielding

Catcher	PCT	G	PO	A	E	DP	PB
Carmichael	.975	6	35	4	1	0	2
Littlewood	.994	41	309	38	2	3	7
Marlette	.875	1	7	0	1	0	0
Tanabe	.958	3	20	3	1	0	1
Villasuso	1.000	9	68	4	0	1	0
Zunino	.980	19	173	19	4	2	7

First Base	PCT	G	PO	A	E	DP
Acevedo	1.000	1	9	1	0	2
Ard	.986	69	586	29	9	54
Littlewood	.974	4	32	6	1	3
Villasuso	.955	2	18	3	1	2
Zorrilla	1.000	1	2	0	0	0

Second Base	PCT	G	PO	A	E	DP
Acevedo	.900	2	4	5	1	4
Hebert	.969	24	59	67	4	15
Marte	.981	25	34	67	2	12
McGruder	.945	19	44	59	6	15

Taylor	.963	6	7	19	1	4
Werman	1.000	3	5	4	0	2

Third Base	PCT	G	PO	A	E	DP
Acevedo	1.000	3	6	6	0	1
Ard	.750	1	1	2	1	0
Hebert	1.000	2	0	4	0	0
Kivlehan	.911	69	52	111	16	8
Taylor	1.000	1	2	3	0	0

Shortstop	PCT	G	PO	A	E	DP
Hebert	.946	7	8	27	2	5
Marte	.940	41	62	110	11	25

Taylor	.937	30	49	84	9	18

Outfield	PCT	G	PO	A	E	DP
Acevedo	1.000	2	4	0	0	0
Faulkner	.990	55	98	1	1	0
Henry	—	2	0	0	0	0
McGruder	.972	36	65	4	2	0
Morales	.972	68	99	6	3	1
Palase	.941	9	15	1	1	0
Pizzano	.800	3	4	0	1	0
Zamarripa	1.000	9	28	1	0	0
Zorrilla	.940	59	102	7	7	2

PULASKI MARINERS — ROOKIE
APPALACHIAN LEAGUE

Batting	B-T	HT	WT	DOB	AVG	vLH	vRH	G	AB	R	H	2B	3B	HR	RBI	BB	HBP	SH	SF	SO	SB	CS	SLG	OBP
Brito, Bryan	R-R	6-2	170	2-16-92	.186	.029	.236	48	140	17	26	3	2	1	14	6	1	4	3	64	7	1	.257	.220
Burin, Felipe	R-R	5-10	170	2-10-92	.214	.200	.217	43	145	21	31	4	1	0	17	23	1	2	3	29	2	0	.255	.320
Castillo, Phillips	R-R	6-2	190	2-2-94	.209	.178	.218	56	201	23	42	10	0	6	23	13	9	1	1	60	0	1	.348	.286
DeMello, Toby	R-R	6-2	220	1-3-90	.350	.600	.267	8	20	2	7	1	0	1	3	0	0	0	0	6	0	0	.550	.350
Diaz, Franklin	B-R	6-1	170	7-20-90	.200	.154	.213	24	60	14	12	2	0	0	9	4	3	2	1	13	1	1	.233	.279
Hebert, Brock	R-R	5-10	180	5-11-91	.288	.286	.289	30	111	18	32	5	0	1	16	13	5	0	1	21	8	4	.360	.385
Henry, Jabari	R-R	6-0	198	11-11-90	.247	.292	.264	58	207	35	56	15	3	8	42	27	3	1	4	46	5	2	.488	.357
Jones, Tyler	R-R	6-1	195	8-24-89	.269	.250	.273	11	26	3	7	1	0	0	1	6	1	0	0	6	0	0	.308	.424
Lampe, Reginald	R-R	6-3	185	3-1-90	.224	.278	.209	52	170	28	38	8	1	1	19	23	4	3	3	45	3	1	.300	.325
Lara, Jordy	R-R	6-3	180	5-21-91	.243	.224	.249	63	239	26	58	14	2	8	41	18	5	1	3	48	1	0	.418	.306
Lawson, Reggie	R-R	6-4	235	8-14-91	.246	.333	.247	55	193	22	51	4	2	6	14	23	2	0	1	63	3	0	.399	.347
Marlette, Tyler	R-R	5-11	195	1-23-93	.284	.250	.295	56	208	23	59	14	0	5	23	6	0	0	0	46	3	1	.423	.304
Palase, Richard	R-R	5-11	195	8-17-90	.200	.091	.263	11	30	5	6	3	0	0	2	4	1	1	0	9	0	1	.300	.314
Peguero, Martin	R-R	6-1	185	11-3-93	.231	.246	.227	60	238	30	55	11	2	0	24	12	1	3	2	32	3	1	.294	.269
Pizzano, Dario	L-R	5-11	200	4-25-91	.356	.308	.369	53	188	34	67	15	1	4	28	26	6	1	4	35	3	0	.511	.442
Werman, Keith	L-R	5-7	150	10-1-89	.359	.364	.357	13	39	13	14	0	0	0	2	7	0	1	0	5	5	2	.359	.457
Zamarripa, James	L-L	5-10	190	9-17-93	.221	.231	.218	20	68	8	15	7	1	0	5	7	0	1	0	21	2	2	.353	.293

Pitching	B-T	HT	WT	DOB	W	L	ERA	G	GS	CG	SV	IP	H	R	ER	HR	BB	SO	AVG	vLH	vRH	K/9	BB/9
Brazis, Matt	R-R	6-2	205	9-6-89	1	0	0.00	7	0	0	2	8	1	0	0	0	0	19	.036	.000	.053	20.52	0.00
Brazoban, Domingo	R-R	6-3	190	8-8-89	0	2	9.00	16	0	0	1	25	40	31	25	2	8	14	.339	.268	.377	5.04	2.88
Chen, Min-Sih	R-R	6-3	205	12-6-89	2	0	6.07	13	5	0	1	43	54	41	29	5	21	34	.293	.302	.289	7.12	4.40
Dean, Levi	R-R	6-4	225	12-15-89	1	2	6.37	15	2	0	0	30	37	24	21	3	11	24	.308	.355	.292	7.28	3.34
Diaz, Nolan	R-R	6-1	175	3-28-91	1	0	4.18	13	0	0	0	24	22	14	11	0	15	28	.244	.194	.271	10.65	5.70
Garcia, Rigoberto	R-R	6-5	202	9-23-93	5	4	5.37	13	13	0	0	60	66	41	36	9	20	54	.274	.200	.314	8.06	2.98
Gonzalez, Isliexel	R-R	6-3	185	5-10-91	5	4	2.32	16	2	0	2	50	36	23	13	1	20	43	.198	.263	.168	7.69	3.58
Holman, David	R-R	6-6	220	5-31-90	3	3	3.27	18	0	0	8	33	36	15	12	6	33	.283	.222	.308	9.00	1.64
Holovach, Blake	L-L	6-5	195	3-27-91	1	5	3.91	14	10	0	0	48	49	29	21	3	22	30	.261	.237	.267	5.59	4.10
Huijer, Lars	R-R	6-4	183	9-22-93	1	2	3.86	21	0	0	2	33	39	16	14	1	14	21	.302	.212	.333	5.79	3.86
Kaalekahi, Charles	B-R	6-2	175	5-13-92	4	4	3.19	13	13	0	0	68	66	34	24	7	18	65	.254	.242	.261	8.65	2.39
Koneski, Nate	R-L	6-0	175	3-11-90	1	0	4.05	14	0	0	2	20	18	12	9	3	3	24	.225	.125	.250	10.80	1.35
Marte, Wander	L-L	6-4	180	6-30-92	1	6	4.94	10	9	0	0	31	32	20	17	2	19	35	.267	.278	.265	10.16	5.52
Ogando, Jochi	R-R	6-5	210	5-27-93	2	3	4.17	12	12	0	0	50	49	27	23	2	23	39	.262	.333	.217	7.07	4.17
Pereira, Ricardo	B-R	6-3	150	4-18-91	1	2	6.21	18	0	0	1	33	38	27	23	6	17	25	.284	.256	.295	6.75	4.59
Valenza, Nick	R-L	5-10	180	3-31-93	0	0	5.68	17	0	0	0	25	32	19	16	4	14	23	.314	.200	.351	8.17	4.97
Zaragoza, Ernesto	R-R	6-1	175	9-26-92	0	1	5.23	8	1	0	0	10	12	7	6	1	7	8	.293	.300	.290	6.97	6.10

Fielding

Catcher	PCT	G	PO	A	E	DP	PB
DeMello	1.000	5	22	4	0	2	0
Diaz	.979	21	120	17	3	0	8
Jones	1.000	5	35	2	0	0	3
Marlette	.992	46	322	42	3	2	14

First Base	PCT	G	PO	A	E	DP
DeMello	1.000	1	5	0	0	0
Lampe	.982	43	362	16	7	29
Lara	.988	28	232	10	3	28

Second Base	PCT	G	PO	A	E	DP
Brito	1.000	1	2	5	0	3
Burin	.944	19	24	43	4	12

Hebert	.975	14	30	47	2	12
Peguero	.955	36	71	99	8	22
Werman	1.000	3	7	0	1	

Third Base	PCT	G	PO	A	E	DP
Brito	.833	10	5	15	4	3
Burin	.742	14	1	22	8	2
Hebert	.750	1	1	2	1	0
Lara	.922	37	29	65	8	7
Peguero	.950	8	8	11	1	2

Shortstop	PCT	G	PO	A	E	DP
Brito	.936	32	46	100	10	20
Hebert	.932	13	16	39	4	6

Peguero	.900	18	22	50	8	10
Werman	1.000	10	13	30	0	7

Outfield	PCT	G	PO	A	E	DP
Burin	.857	4	5	1	1	1
Castillo	.959	44	69	2	3	0
Henry	.967	56	112	5	4	0
Lampe	1.000	4	13	0	0	0
Lawson	.966	43	83	2	3	1
Palase	1.000	11	17	1	0	1
Pizzano	.966	34	56	0	2	0
Zamarripa	.967	13	27	2	1	1

AZL MARINERS — ROOKIE
ARIZONA LEAGUE

Batting	B-T	HT	WT	DOB	AVG	vLH	vRH	G	AB	R	H	2B	3B	HR	RBI	BB	HBP	SH	SF	SO	SB	CS	SLG	OBP
Brito, Kristian	R-R	6-5	240	12-20-94	.193	.269	.169	29	109	13	21	1	2	1	12	4	1	0	1	37	2	1	.266	.226
Carmichael, Christian	R-R	5-11	190	4-25-92	.319	.222	.348	31	116	18	37	9	2	2	23	16	4	0	1	20	4	0	.483	.416
Carroll, Dan	R-R	6-1	175	1-6-89	.143	.000	.200	3	7	1	1	0	1	0	0	1	0	0	0	2	0	0	.429	.250

	B-T	HT	WT	DOB	AVG	OBP	SLG	G	AB	R	H	2B	3B	HR	RBI	BB	SO	SB	CS	HP	SH	SF	vLH	vRH
Chavez, Johermyn	R-R	6-3	225	1-26-89	.368	.286	.417	6	19	6	7	4	0	2	8	2	1	0	2	4	0	0	.895	.417
Cohoes, Cavan	R-R	6-2	185	5-3-93	.000	.000	.000	2	4	0	0	0	0	0	0	0	0	0	0	2	0	0	.000	.000
DeCarlo, Joe	R-R	5-10	205	9-13-93	.236	.143	.271	53	182	29	43	12	3	4	31	31	8	0	2	47	0	2	.401	.368
DeMello, Toby	R-R	6-2	220	1-3-90	.222	.000	.333	4	9	1	2	1	0	0	1	0	0	1	0	2	0	0	.333	.300
Franca, Gabrial	R-R	5-11	160	9-11-93	.254	.333	.224	48	185	37	47	13	2	2	15	27	3	0	1	37	19	3	.378	.356
Guarnaccia, Luke	B-R	5-11	210	7-11-92	.257	.200	.278	29	109	16	28	3	5	1	14	3	0	0	0	25	3	0	.404	.277
Guerrero, Gabriel	R-R	6-3	190	12-11-93	.333	.409	.302	18	75	17	25	5	0	4	18	3	0	0	2	13	0	0	.560	.350
Jimenez, Charles	R-R	6-3	225	5-19-93	.224	.222	.225	24	58	8	13	5	1	0	8	8	3	0	0	30	3	4	.345	.348
Jones, Tyler	R-R	6-1	195	8-24-89	.250	.500	.167	3	8	2	2	0	0	0	0	1	0	0	0	0	0	0	.250	.333
Leal, Jose	R-R	6-3	215	2-16-95	.078	.167	.038	27	77	5	6	0	0	0	4	8	3	0	0	44	1	1	.078	.193
Lopes, Timmy	R-R	5-11	180	6-24-94	.316	.228	.348	53	215	42	68	11	12	0	32	24	1	0	4	29	7	3	.479	.381
Martinez, Francisco	R-R	6-2	210	9-1-90	.286	.200	.304	8	28	7	8	2	2	0	7	1	1	0	1	6	1	0	.500	.323
Martinez, Jose	R-R	6-1	180	7-22-92	.150	.000	.188	8	20	1	3	1	0	0	1	2	0	0	0	10	0	0	.200	.227
Melendres, Nathan	R-R	5-10	187	4-9-94	.529	.333	.571	4	17	3	9	1	2	0	5	0	1	0	0	2	1	0	.824	.556
Michel, Rashynol	B-R	6-2	175	11-30-92	.202	.190	.205	39	104	16	21	1	1	0	11	9	0	0	0	39	8	2	.231	.265
Morban, Julio	L-L	6-1	190	2-13-92	.238	.286	.214	6	21	2	5	0	0	0	3	0	0	0	1	3	0	0	.238	.227
Palase, Richard	R-R	5-11	195	8-17-90	.200	.000	.333	3	10	1	2	0	0	0	1	2	0	0	0	3	1	0	.200	.333
Poythress, Rich	R-R	6-4	235	8-11-87	.385	.000	.556	5	13	7	5	1	0	3	7	7	0	0	0	3	0	0	1.154	.600
Sanchez, Miguel	R-R	6-2	180	9-27-91	.256	.280	.245	28	78	13	20	5	1	0	7	16	1	0	0	15	0	0	.346	.389
Scammell, Cory	L-R	6-5	205	7-28-93	.266	.271	.264	48	173	21	46	5	3	0	26	17	3	0	0	45	4	2	.329	.342
Tenbrink, Nate	L-R	6-2	202	12-21-86	1.000	1.000	1.000	1	1	4	2	4	0	1	0	2	0	0	0	0	0	0	1.500	1.000
Velasquez, Roberto	B-R	5-11	160	2-14-90	.133	.200	.120	11	30	6	4	1	0	0	3	10	0	0	0	7	1	1	.167	.350
Werman, Keith	L-R	5-7	150	10-1-89	.239	.176	.260	23	67	10	16	0	0	0	4	10	1	2	1	13	1	3	.239	.342
Yates, Isaiah	R-L	5-9	185	8-31-94	.240	.255	.234	48	171	37	41	10	6	2	23	30	4	1	1	49	6	2	.404	.364

Pitching	B-T	HT	WT	DOB	W	L	ERA	G	GS	CG	SV	IP	H	R	ER	HR	BB	SO	AVG	vLH	vRH	K/9	BB/9
Alsup, Wes	R-R	6-2	205	11-25-86	1	0	4.50	1	0	0	0	2	1	1	1	1	2	4	.125	.000	.200	18.00	9.00
Anderson, Matt	R-R	6-1	210	11-18-91	2	0	0.00	6	0	0	0	9	2	0	0	0	2	12	.074	.125	.053	12.46	2.08
Brooks, Aaron	R-R	6-6	210	5-15-92	0	1	4.00	17	0	0	10	18	19	10	8	0	3	21	.264	.192	.304	10.50	1.50
Chang, Yao Wen	R-R	6-2	202	10-31-90	0	0	9.00	1	0	0	0	1	1	1	1	0	1	0	.250	.000	.333	0.00	9.00
Copping, Cameron	R-R	6-6	220	4-24-90	0	1	5.94	15	0	0	1	17	20	14	11	2	5	22	.274	.188	.341	11.88	2.70
De Meyer, Dylan	R-R	6-4	165	9-16-92	3	2	4.12	12	9	0	1	55	71	31	25	3	14	39	.314	.333	.301	6.42	2.30
Diaz, Edwin	R-R	6-2	165	3-22-94	2	1	5.21	9	1	0	0	19	12	13	11	2	17	20	.176	.171	.182	9.47	8.05
Flores, Jose	R-R	6-2	190	12-31-92	3	5	6.60	13	7	0	1	45	58	37	33	2	15	37	.314	.321	.307	7.40	3.00
Fox, Matt	R-R	6-3	190	12-4-82	0	0	1.50	3	0	0	0	6	4	1	1	0	0	5	.174	.222	.143	7.50	0.00
Hill, Nick	L-L	6-0	190	1-30-85	0	0	3.00	2	0	0	0	3	2	1	1	0	2	2	.222	.333	.167	6.00	6.00
Jimenez, Cesar	L-L	5-11	220	11-12-84	0	0	0.00	3	0	0	0	4	1	0	0	0	1	6	.083	.143	.000	13.50	2.25
Landazuri, Steve	R-R	6-0	175	1-6-92	0	1	3.00	3	0	0	0	6	7	1	1	0	0	5	.318	.308	.333	7.50	0.00
Mata, Daniel	R-R	6-2	180	7-3-93	5	0	5.32	18	0	0	0	24	27	17	14	0	11	11	.297	.278	.309	4.18	4.18
Mieses, George	R-R	6-2	180	5-3-91	0	0	3.00	4	0	0	0	3	3	2	1	0	2	2	.250	.000	.273	6.00	6.00
Pike, Tyler	L-L	6-0	180	1-26-94	2	1	1.78	11	11	0	0	51	34	13	10	1	21	57	.193	.273	.157	10.13	3.73
Pina, Luis	L-L	6-2	178	12-6-93	0	2	6.60	7	5	0	0	15	19	15	11	1	5	6	.302	.429	.238	3.60	3.00
Pries, Jordan	B-R	6-1	195	1-27-90	0	0	0.75	3	3	0	0	12	5	1	1	0	3	18	.125	.222	.045	13.50	2.25
Ronnenbergh, Scott	L-L	6-2	170	1-11-92	0	3	7.59	14	0	0	0	21	26	18	18	1	21	15	.317	.231	.357	6.33	8.86
Roy, Alex	L-L	6-2	170	7-28-95	0	0	11.12	6	0	0	1	6	4	7	7	0	11	5	.364	.235	.472	7.94	17.47
Saquilon, Gabe	R-R	6-0	180	6-7-93	3	2	4.06	12	5	0	1	44	45	23	20	1	17	34	.269	.333	.221	6.90	3.45
Seifrit, Logan	B-R	5-11	165	8-25-94	1	0	9.00	7	0	0	0	6	9	6	6	0	2	5	.375	.333	.400	7.50	3.00
Shellhorn, Rusty	R-R	5-10	170	2-25-90	1	0	1.53	4	3	0	0	18	8	3	3	1	3	26	.138	.158	.128	13.25	1.53
Sterling, Zach	R-R	6-2	195	2-11-90	0	0	0.00	2	0	0	0	2	1	0	0	0	0	1	.167	.333	.000	4.50	0.00
Taylor, Luke	R-R	6-6	200	7-14-92	1	1	2.70	9	1	0	1	23	16	13	7	1	6	20	.182	.244	.128	7.71	2.31
Thieben, Daniel	R-R	6-4	195	9-18-93	3	1	4.02	15	1	0	1	31	36	20	14	0	21	18	.308	.333	.295	5.17	6.03
Torres, Jose	R-R	6-4	165	9-1-93	1	3	6.86	9	3	0	0	21	24	20	16	0	19	15	.308	.310	.306	6.43	8.14
Weiss, Cody	R-R	5-10	195	8-14-90	1	0	22.24	6	0	0	1	6	8	16	14	0	12	3	.364	.333	.385	4.76	19.06
White, Richard	R-R	5-11	170	2-1-93	2	1	5.40	16	0	0	0	23	19	22	14	2	15	22	.209	.270	.167	8.49	5.79

Fielding

Catcher

Catcher	PCT	G	PO	A	E	DP	PB
Carmichael	.977	17	106	22	3	2	4
DeMello	1.000	3	5	6	0	0	2
Guarnaccia	.971	21	173	28	6	1	4
Sanchez	.980	20	136	13	3	1	6
Melendres	.800	1	2	2	1		
O Palase	.778	1	3	4	2	1	
Tenbrink	.833	1	3	2	1	1	
Velasquez	.933	3	6	8	1	2	
Werman	.971	8	13	21	1	5	

First Base

First Base	PCT	G	PO	A	E	DP
Brito	.978	28	246	17	6	22
Carmichael	.969	11	91	4	3	10
Guarnaccia	.979	6	44	3	1	5
Martinez	1.000	5	37	2	0	5
Poythress	1.000	4	25	0	0	1
Sanchez	.960	4	23	1	1	2
Scammell	1.000	7	41	3	0	1

Second Base

Second Base	PCT	G	PO	A	E	DP
Franca	.750	2	4	2	2	1
Lopes	.966	41	78	123	7	22

Third Base

Third Base	PCT	G	PO	A	E	DP
DeCarlo	.917	45	31	79	10	8
Martinez	1.000	5	5	4	0	0
Martinez	1.000	2	1	6	0	1
Velasquez	.909	5	2	8	1	0
Werman	.895	8	6	11	2	1

Shortstop

Shortstop	PCT	G	PO	A	E	DP
Franca	.955	43	78	114	9	25
Lopes	.960	5	9	15	1	2
Melendres	1.000	1	0	2	0	0
Velasquez	1.000	3	1	16	0	1
Werman	.950	6	12	26	2	7

Outfield

Outfield	PCT	G	PO	A	E	DP
Carroll	1.000	3	3	0	0	0
Chavez	.833	6	5	0	1	0
Cohoes	—	2	0	0	0	0
Guerrero	.912	15	27	4	3	1
Jimenez	1.000	22	25	3	0	0
Leal	.909	22	19	1	2	0
Martinez	1.000	4	4	0	0	0
Melendres	1.000	1	2	0	0	0
Michel	.931	39	47	7	4	0
Morban	1.000	4	3	0	0	0
Palase	.833	2	5	0	1	0
Scammell	.979	37	45	2	1	1
Yates	.926	44	83	5	7	2

DSL MARINERS

DOMINICAN SUMMER LEAGUE

Batting	B-T	HT	WT	DOB	AVG	vLH	vRH	G	AB	R	H	2B	3B	HR	RBI	BB	HBP	SH	SF	SO	SB	CS	SLG	OBP
Alcantara, Ismael	R-R	6-0	185	12-15-93	.261	.240	.273	67	218	28	57	8	2	6	25	26	12	1	1	50	6	8	.399	.370
Berro, Noe	L-R	6-3	180	8-21-93	.282	.254	.293	65	238	38	67	13	5	1	22	17	4	2	0	66	6	6	.391	.340
Brea, Ivan	R-R	6-2	190	7-5-88	.230	.154	.250	26	61	3	14	2	0	0	3	0	1	1	0	10	1	1	.262	.242
Caballero, Luis	R-R	6-1	157	7-8-92	.176	.120	.200	58	170	30	30	6	0	0	13	21	12	7	2	49	13	6	.212	.307
Capriata, Alexander	R-R	5-11	190	8-3-92	.200	.333	.136	46	120	11	24	5	0	0	9	10	8	1	2	9	3	3	.242	.300
Franco, Joshua	R-R	5-11	193	9-10-93	.237	.250	.230	33	93	10	22	3	2	0	11	12	7	0	0	23	1	2	.312	.366
Gonzalez, Ricardo	R-R	6-0	206	3-25-92	.206	.194	.212	38	97	16	20	4	0	3	9	14	3	1	0	32	0	1	.340	.325
Guerrero, Gabriel	R-R	6-3	190	12-11-93	.355	.364	.352	50	200	38	71	9	4	11	54	21	0	0	4	28	4	6	.605	.409
Jimenez, Angel	R-R	6-1	180	9-8-94	.238	.268	.225	44	130	20	31	7	1	3	13	24	2	1	1	32	7	2	.377	.363
Martinez, Hersin	R-R	6-5	220	2-27-95	.222	.321	.186	61	198	18	44	10	1	4	32	26	8	0	0	72	1	2	.343	.336
Martinez, Wilton	R-R	6-4	195	12-11-93	.251	.293	.232	66	243	30	61	9	1	10	37	20	6	2	3	36	9	1	.420	.321
Matias, Luis	R-R	6-2	180	8-27-90	.225	.275	.207	50	151	37	34	6	2	1	10	23	5	3	1	24	9	7	.311	.344
Mejia, Erick	B-R	5-11	155	11-9-94	.182	.125	.214	13	44	9	8	2	2	0	8	8	0	0	0	7	3	2	.318	.308
Mina, Diego	R-R	5-11	181	10-13-92	.167	.214	.143	26	42	13	7	1	1	0	2	15	1	1	0	22	3	1	.238	.397
Morales, Estarlyn	R-R	6-3	180	10-28-92	.255	.284	.242	68	216	31	55	11	2	4	26	34	1	3	3	29	14	5	.380	.354
Perez, Randy	R-R	6-3	180	2-23-89	.115	.143	.105	18	26	11	3	0	0	1	4	4	2	0	1	11	2	1	.231	.273
Rosa, Jose	R-R	6-0	175	3-7-94	.158	.125	.182	12	19	1	3	2	0	0	3	0	0	0	0	4	0	0	.263	.158

Pitching	B-T	HT	WT	DOB	W	L	ERA	G	GS	CG	SV	IP	H	R	ER	HR	BB	SO	AVG	vLH	vRH	K/9	BB/9
Asencio, Oliver	L-L	6-2	199	1-18-93	0	2	4.50	7	7	0	0	22	25	15	11	2	16	14	.287	.400	.280	5.73	6.55
Brito, Frankely	R-R	6-0	170	11-1-92	0	0	81.00	1	0	0	0	0	3	3	0	3	0	0	.000	.000	.000	0.00	81.00
Cleto, Joaquin	R-R	6-2	155	3-10-91	2	0	2.49	14	0	0	2	22	16	10	6	0	15	18	.203	.278	.180	7.48	6.23
Cleto, Ramire	R-R	6-0	190	4-4-93	6	4	2.33	14	13	2	0	70	78	45	18	2	17	26	.280	.236	.295	3.36	2.20
Cortoreal, Leonel	L-L	6-5	175	9-6-92	0	0	4.11	10	0	0	0	15	13	9	7	0	13	9	.245	.250	.245	5.28	7.63
De La Cruz, Noel	R-R	6-2	180	12-17-91	8	2	1.92	13	13	1	0	80	68	20	17	2	22	46	.234	.203	.242	5.20	2.49
Dominguez, Ronald	R-R	6-2	180	1-13-94	5	0	0.94	18	0	0	8	38	20	5	4	1	5	37	.161	.118	.178	8.69	1.17
Franco, Arismendy	R-R	6-1	165	4-15-94	1	1	4.97	8	0	0	0	13	8	13	7	0	9	14	.154	.091	.171	9.95	6.39
Garcia, Andres	R-R	6-4	170	3-11-92	1	1	3.72	13	0	0	1	19	19	14	8	2	4	24	.241	.412	.194	11.17	1.86
Gonzalez, Yeuri	R-R	6-2	170	12-22-92	4	1	1.48	14	3	2	2	61	51	13	10	0	8	25	.232	.222	.234	3.69	1.18
Julio, Ivan	R-R	6-3	175	8-19-91	6	2	3.11	13	12	1	0	72	65	31	25	2	13	49	.244	.236	.247	6.10	1.62
Munoz, Leoncio	L-L	6-4	170	8-18-90	6	2	2.01	15	7	1	0	63	55	22	14	1	16	49	.234	.267	.232	7.04	2.30
Nunez, Junior	R-R	6-3	210	3-1-92	3	1	3.09	10	1	0	1	23	24	19	8	1	11	8	.270	.235	.278	3.09	4.24
Paulino, Darel	R-R	6-6	225	11-24-92	0	0	9.00	3	0	0	0	2	2	2	2	0	4	1	.286	.500	.200	4.50	18.00
Pedie, Raul	R-R	6-0	175	8-14-92	4	2	1.30	23	0	0	12	42	29	10	6	0	11	52	.195	.158	.207	11.23	2.38
Tamarez, Albert	R-R	6-1	185	11-30-93	0	0	4.96	10	1	0	1	16	19	12	9	0	14	12	.279	.238	.298	6.61	7.71

Fielding

Catcher	PCT	G	PO	A	E	DP	PB
Brea	.975	25	103	14	3	1	1
Capriata	.986	46	234	57	4	2	6
Gonzalez	1.000	18	67	19	0	0	1
Perez	1.000	1	1	0	0	0	0
Rosa	.946	11	32	3	2	0	3

First Base	PCT	G	PO	A	E	DP
Alcantara	.992	41	338	21	3	28
Brea	—	1	0	0	0	0
Caballero	.973	5	34	2	1	0
Capriata	1.000	1	3	0	0	0
Franco	.955	8	64	0	3	4
Gonzalez	1.000	21	155	9	0	12
Matias	1.000	5	47	1	0	3

	PCT	G	PO	A	E	DP
Mina	1.000	1	10	0	0	0
Morales	.938	1	15	0	1	2
Second Base	PCT	G	PO	A	E	DP
Berro	.938	43	109	119	15	24
Caballero	1.000	6	8	16	0	0
Matias	.968	14	20	40	2	8
Mejia	.900	4	4	5	1	0
Mina	.944	13	25	26	3	4
Third Base	PCT	G	PO	A	E	DP
Alcantara	.800	21	19	33	13	3
Caballero	.950	35	32	64	5	2
Cortoreal	1.000	1	2	1	0	1
Jimenez	.900	4	1	8	1	0
Matias	.905	24	14	53	7	5

Shortstop	PCT	G	PO	A	E	DP
Berro	.865	23	29	48	12	8
Caballero	.868	9	15	18	5	4
Jimenez	.878	38	54	112	23	18
Matias	.857	5	2	10	2	0
Mejia	.808	9	16	26	10	4
Morales	1.000	1	0	2	0	0
Outfield	PCT	G	PO	A	E	DP
Caballero	1.000	14	9	1	0	0
Guerrero	.960	47	67	5	3	0
Martinez	.897	48	57	4	7	1
Martinez	.984	58	115	6	2	2
Morales	.963	60	118	13	5	3
Perez	1.000	6	5	0	0	0

VSL MARINERS

VENEZUELAN SUMMER LEAGUE

Batting	B-T	HT	WT	DOB	AVG	vLH	vRH	G	AB	R	H	2B	3B	HR	RBI	BB	HBP	SH	SF	SO	SB	CS	SLG	OBP
Brito, Miguel	R-R	6-3	228	9-11-92	.262	.245	.267	63	229	26	60	18	1	4	37	15	1	1	4	28	3	1	.402	.305
Calderon, Yordi	R-R	6-2	185	2-15-94	.210	.209	.210	64	205	33	43	11	2	6	34	25	5	2	3	66	9	4	.371	.307
Coronel, Ramon	R-R	5-11	155	2-2-92	.287	.259	.294	37	136	21	39	8	0	1	23	7	1	4	1	15	8	3	.368	.324
Fernandez, Rafael	B-R	5-10	180	4-21-94	.214	.156	.230	50	145	23	31	8	0	1	17	17	2	6	0	23	6	3	.290	.305
Guedez, Jose	R-R	6-2	175	9-6-94	.300	.750	.136	20	30	2	9	1	0	0	3	4	4	0	0	9	3	3	.333	.447
Morales, Jhonbaker	R-R	6-0	170	7-17-94	.208	.091	.243	18	48	8	10	2	0	1	7	6	2	0	0	7	0	2	.313	.321
Nieto, Arturo	R-R	6-2	195	12-9-92	.140	.167	.135	17	43	6	6	2	1	0	4	7	1	1	0	8	0	0	.233	.275
Okuda, Pedro	L-R	5-10	160	4-20-90	.274	.250	.278	56	190	34	52	11	4	0	19	31	2	5	0	34	4	7	.374	.381
Palma, Alexy	R-R	6-3	195	12-24-92	.275	.371	.246	51	149	28	41	13	2	6	25	29	2	1	4	29	7	1	.510	.391
Perez, Georvic	B-R	6-0	198	4-15-95	.253	.211	.263	32	95	9	24	4	0	1	9	5	3	2	0	8	2	0	.326	.311
Quevedo, Johan	R-R	6-1	212	11-6-93	.318	.387	.291	35	110	15	35	4	0	3	15	5	1	0	0	8	1	4	.436	.353
Ramirez, Ivan	R-R	6-0	210	7-25-92	.329	.265	.346	51	170	25	56	6	0	2	35	18	4	2	4	14	1	4	.400	.398
Sojo, Danilo	R-R	6-4	211	4-29-95	.225	.125	.255	32	71	11	16	1	0	3	9	7	9	0	0	20	1	0	.366	.368
Talos, Felipe	L-R	5-11	170	2-3-95	.283	.600	.255	25	60	9	17	1	2	0	5	8	0	1	0	8	1	2	.367	.368
Ugueto, Jesus	R-R	6-0	170	5-30-91	.388	.345	.399	71	276	72	107	16	6	6	49	35	6	0	6	38	22	8	.554	.458

	B-T	HT	WT	DOB																		
Velasquez, Alberto	L-L	6-5	240	3-7-94	.273	.292	.269	41	132	15	36	6	1	2	20	9	1 1 3	12	2 0	.379	.317	
Villa, Hilario	R-R	6-3	167	7-1-92	.163	.100	.181	39	92	20	15	5	0	2	7	13	1 1 0	23	3 1	.283	.274	
Wawoe, Gianfranco	B-R	5-11	170	7-25-94	.253	.179	.276	50	166	28	42	9	1	0	10	20	2 0 0	25	8 4	.319	.340	

Pitching	B-T	HT	WT	DOB	W	L	ERA	G	GS	CG	SV	IP	H	R	ER	HR	BB	SO	AVG	vLH	vRH	K/9	BB/9
Breto, Liarvis	L-L	5-11	175	4-10-93	2	2	2.03	16	0	0	5	27	17	6	6	0	13	30	.181	.167	.182	10.13	4.39
Carrera, Rafael	R-R	6-0	190	10-29-92	7	2	3.86	14	14	0	0	72	92	42	31	4	12	41	.317	.361	.291	5.10	1.49
Gomez, Erick	L-L	6-1	165	1-16-93	1	0	7.32	10	0	0	0	20	26	17	16	2	10	16	.329	.385	.318	7.32	4.58
Hidalgo, Hector	R-R	6-1	182	9-21-92	3	0	1.31	9	0	0	0	21	19	3	3	3	3	17	.244	.217	.255	7.40	1.31
Jimenez, Jonathan	R-R	6-1	196	2-14-92	1	2	7.77	11	2	0	0	22	40	19	19	1	6	15	.404	.325	.458	6.14	2.45
Marruffo, Wladimir	R-R	6-0	173	5-29-93	1	0	3.57	11	1	0	1	23	18	11	9	0	7	9	.222	.250	.208	3.57	2.78
Medina, Jefferson	R-R	6-2	184	5-31-94	2	3	4.81	11	4	0	1	39	58	29	21	1	9	18	.333	.339	.330	4.12	2.06
Mendoza, Jose	R-R	6-2	193	9-29-92	3	2	2.48	12	0	0	2	33	29	12	9	3	9	25	.244	.350	.190	6.89	2.48
Miliani, Eduardo	R-R	5-11	178	7-8-93	0	1	4.44	12	1	0	2	26	26	15	13	2	9	15	.260	.313	.235	5.13	3.08
Morales, Osmel	R-R	6-3	196	10-30-92	0	0	2.08	10	0	0	0	17	21	7	4	1	6	13	.300	.240	.333	6.75	3.12
Osorio, Neritzon	R-R	6-1	180	12-29-93	9	2	1.92	14	13	0	0	75	54	21	16	3	19	40	.201	.168	.224	4.80	2.28
Pereira, Cruz	L-L	5-10	175	12-18-90	4	1	2.19	13	0	0	0	37	38	22	9	2	12	22	.252	.333	.241	5.35	2.92
Quintanilla, Kevin	R-R	6-0	174	5-21-92	2	6	2.96	12	11	0	0	46	39	22	15	1	13	26	.229	.262	.211	5.12	2.56
Rodriguez, Carlos	R-R	6-0	190	5-23-95	0	0	6.91	8	1	0	0	14	21	16	11	0	9	7	.323	.348	.310	4.40	5.65
Urbina, Ugueth	R-R	6-1	185	10-28-94	3	0	2.44	14	11	0	0	59	55	21	16	3	17	32	.251	.200	.281	4.88	2.59
Vieira, Thyago	R-R	6-2	210	1-7-93	3	5	6.05	13	13	0	0	55	67	40	37	2	17	35	.310	.434	.243	5.73	2.78
Ynfantes, Maykel	R-R	6-0	190	12-6-90	3	1	1.73	21	0	0	11	26	24	10	5	0	5	19	.245	.257	.238	6.58	1.73

Fielding

Catcher	PCT	G	PO	A	E	DP	PB
Nieto	.978	15	71	17	2	3	4
Palma	—	1	0	0	0	0	0
Perez	.994	31	151	29	1	1	3
Quevedo	.979	30	129	13	3	0	2
Ramirez	.962	6	20	5	1	0	1
Talos	1.000	2	9	1	0	0	0

First Base	PCT	G	PO	A	E	DP
Brito	.995	40	365	14	2	30
Coronel	1.000	1	2	0	0	0
Quevedo	.926	3	21	4	2	3
Ramirez	1.000	1	13	0	0	2
Sojo	.929	7	35	4	3	4
Velasquez	.975	35	307	11	8	27

Second Base	PCT	G	PO	A	E	DP
Calderon	1.000	1	3	2	0	0

	PCT	G	PO	A	E	DP
Coronel	.982	23	51	57	2	15
Fernandez	1.000	7	8	14	0	1
Guedez	1.000	1	0	1	0	0
Morales	1.000	1	0	1	0	0
Okuda	.989	47	93	167	3	34

Third Base	PCT	G	PO	A	E	DP
Brito	.894	24	15	44	7	3
Calderon	.905	31	17	78	10	3
Coronel	.826	8	5	14	4	1
Fernandez	.933	22	18	38	4	3
Okuda	—	1	0	0	0	0

Shortstop	PCT	G	PO	A	E	DP
Coronel	.882	7	11	19	4	4
Fernandez	1.000	7	10	26	0	7
Morales	.932	17	19	49	5	10
Nieto	—	1	0	0	0	0

	PCT	G	PO	A	E	DP
Wawoe	.912	49	79	139	21	28

Outfield	PCT	G	PO	A	E	DP
Brito	1.000	3	1	0	0	0
Calderon	.978	34	44	0	1	0
Coronel	—	1	0	0	0	0
Fernandez	.944	21	15	2	1	0
Guedez	.950	17	18	1	1	0
Okuda	.600	5	3	0	2	0
Palma	.977	21	41	1	1	1
Ramirez	1.000	9	9	0	0	0
Sojo	.840	19	21	0	4	0
Talos	.871	22	23	4	4	0
Ugueto	.970	71	147	12	5	8
Villa	.957	37	41	3	2	0

Tampa Bay Rays

SEASON IN A SENTENCE: The Rays fell three games short of making their fourth playoff appearance in five years, but they continued to serve as the template for small-revenue success.

HIGH POINT: Tampa Bay led the American League in ERA (3.19) and opponent average (.229) and set an AL record for strikeouts (1,383). David Price won his 20th game, best in the AL, on Sept. 30 against the White Sox as the Rays continued to fight for the playoffs. Fernando Rodney took over as closer and converted 48 of 50 save opportunities while establishing a major league relief record with a 0.60 ERA.

LOW POINT: Tampa Bay won 90 games despite baseball's sixth-lowest Opening Day payroll and a string of injuries, most notably to Evan Longoria and Kyle Farnsworth, as well as Jeff Niemann. The truly low moments came in the stands, however. The club's Opening Day payroll represented a 56 percent increase from 2011, but its efforts have not been reciprocated by its fan base. Tampa Bay ranked last in the majors in attendance at 1.6 million—an average of 19,255 per game—which commissioner Bud Selig called inexcusable. A four-game series against the Red Sox in mid-September drew a total of 48,895 fans.

NOTABLE ROOKIES: Most of the organization's young talent is at the lower levels of the minor leagues now, so lefthander Matt Moore was the only rookie to play a significant role. After his amazing 2011 season, when he was dominant in the minor leagues, came up late in the year and even got a Division Series win, Moore's 2012 performance was merely good, as he went 11-11, 3.81 and made 31 starts.

KEY TRANSACTIONS: Signing Rodney as a free agent before the season proved to be an essential move, and Carlos Pena and Luke Scott were important parts of the lineup. But Tampa Bay made no significant moves during the year.

DOWN ON THE FARM: The Rays are the only club that hasn't graduated a single pick from the last five drafts to the majors, so there could be a lull in their talent production over the next year or so. Tampa Bay's more recent drafts show promise, especially a 2011 crop that included 12 picks in the first two rounds. Double-A Montgomery and low Class A Bowling Green were two of the best teams in their respective leagues, and short-season Hudson Valley completed a strong season to win its first New York-Penn League title since 1999.

OPENING DAY PAYROLL: $64.2 million (25th)

PLAYERS OF THE YEAR

MAJOR LEAGUE	MINOR LEAGUE
David Price	**Todd Glaesmann**
lhp	of
20-5, 2.56	(Low A/High A)
205 SO/59 BB	.285/.336/.493
Led AL in W, ERA	21 HR, 25 2B

ORGANIZATION LEADERS

BATTING		*Minimum 250 AB
MAJORS		
* AVG	Ben Zobrist	.270
* OPS	Ben Zobrist	.848
HR	B.J. Upton	28
RBI	B.J. Upton	78
MINORS		
* AVG	Omar Luna, Montgomery	.315
* OBP	Cameron Seitzer, Bowling Green	.386
* SLG	Todd Glaesmann, Bowling Green/Charlotte	.493
R	Drew Vettleson, Bowling Green	80
H	Omar Luna, Montgomery	148
TB	Todd Glaesmann, Bowling Green/Charlotte	242
2B	Henry Wrigley, Montgomery/Durham	37
3B	Three tied at	10
HR	Todd Glaesmann, Bowling Green/Charlotte	21
RBI	Henry Wrigley, Montgomery/Durham	79
BB	Jeff Malm, Bowling Green	62
SO	Kyeong Kang, Montgomery	135
SB	Ryan Brett, Bowling Green	48

PITCHING		#Minimum 75 IP
MAJORS		
W	David Price	20
# ERA	David Price	2.56
SO	James Shields	223
SV	Fernando Rodney	48
MINORS		
W	Matt Torra, Durham	12
L	Jim Paduch, Montgomery/Durham	12
	Jacob Thompson, Montgomery	12
# ERA	Roberto Gomez, Bowling Green	2.48
G	Dane De La Rosa, Durham	54
GS	Ryan Carpenter, Bowling Green	28
SV	Austin Hubbard, Bowling Green	23
IP	Matt Buschmann, Durham/Montgomery	151.1
BB	Enny Romero, Charlotte	76
SO	Chris Archer, Durham	139
# AVG	Enny Romero, Charlotte	.201

General Manager: Andrew Friedman. Farm Director: Mitch Lukevics. Scouting Director: R.J. Harrison.

Class	Team	League	W	L	PCT	Finish	Manager
Majors	Tampa Bay Rays	American	90	72	.556	5th (14)	Joe Maddon
Triple-A	Durham Bulls	International	66	78	.458	11th (14)	Charlie Montoyo
Double-A	Montgomery Biscuits	Southern	74	63	.540	2nd (10)	Billy Gardner
High A	Charlotte Stone Crabs	Florida State	55	79	.410	12th (12)	Jim Morrison
Low A	Bowling Green Hot Rods	Midwest	80	60	.571	2nd (16)	Brady Williams
Short-season	Hudson Valley Renegades	New York-Penn	52	24	.684	1st (14)	Jared Sandberg
Rookie	Princeton Rays	Appalachian	36	32	.529	t-5th (10)	Mike Johns
Rookie	GCL Rays	Gulf Coast	28	32	.467	10th (14)	Paul Hoover
Overall 2012 Minor League Record			391	368	.515	10th (30)	

ORGANIZATION STATISTICS

TAMPA BAY RAYS
AMERICAN LEAGUE

Batting	B-T	HT	WT	DOB	AVG	vLH	vRH	G	AB	R	H	2B	3B	HR	RBI	BB	HBP	SH	SF	SO	SB	CS	SLG	OBP
Allen, Brandon	L-R	6-2	235	2-12-86	.154	—	.154	7	13	3	2	0	0	1	3	2	0	0	0	4	0	0	.385	.267
2-team total (3 Oakland)					.100	—	—	10	20	3	2	0	0	1	3	2	0	0	0	9	0	0	.250	.182
Brignac, Reid	L-R	6-3	190	1-16-86	.095	.200	.063	16	21	1	2	0	0	0	1	1	0	0	0	5	0	0	.095	.136
Conrad, Brooks	B-R	5-10	190	1-16-80	.172	.222	.129	24	58	4	10	5	0	2	9	3	0	0	0	27	0	0	.362	.213
Francisco, Ben	R-R	6-1	185	10-23-81	.228	.176	.304	24	57	4	13	5	0	2	8	4	0	0	2	16	0	0	.421	.270
2-team total (27 Toronto)					.234	—	—	51	107	9	25	10	1	2	10	8	0	0	2	26	0	1	.402	.282
Fuld, Sam	L-L	5-10	175	11-20-81	.255	.250	.258	44	98	14	25	3	2	0	5	8	1	0	0	14	7	2	.327	.318
Gimenez, Chris	R-R	6-2	220	12-27-82	.260	.357	.136	42	100	10	26	4	0	1	9	8	0	1	0	24	0	0	.330	.315
Guyer, Brandon	R-R	6-2	210	1-28-86	.143	.143	—	3	7	2	1	0	0	1	1	0	0	0	0	1	0	0	.571	.143
Jennings, Desmond	R-R	6-2	200	10-30-86	.246	.246	.245	132	505	85	124	19	7	13	47	46	5	6	1	120	31	2	.388	.314
Johnson, Elliot	B-R	6-1	190	3-9-84	.242	.175	.275	123	297	32	72	10	2	6	33	24	3	5	2	84	18	6	.350	.304
Joyce, Matt	L-R	6-2	205	8-3-84	.241	.209	.250	124	399	55	96	18	3	17	59	55	6	1	1	102	4	3	.429	.341
Keppinger, Jeff	R-R	6-0	185	4-21-80	.325	.376	.302	115	385	46	125	15	1	9	40	24	4	1	4	31	1	0	.439	.367
Lobaton, Jose	B-R	6-0	210	10-21-84	.222	.310	.174	69	167	16	37	10	0	2	20	24	2	2	2	46	0	1	.317	.323
Longoria, Evan	R-R	6-2	210	10-7-85	.289	.318	.280	74	273	39	79	14	0	17	55	33	3	0	3	61	2	3	.527	.369
Matsui, Hideki	L-R	6-2	210	6-12-74	.147	.222	.102	34	95	7	14	1	0	2	7	8	0	0	0	22	0	0	.221	.214
Molina, Jose	R-R	6-2	250	6-3-75	.223	.170	.235	102	251	27	56	9	0	8	32	20	2	1	0	60	3	1	.355	.286
Pena, Carlos	L-L	6-2	225	5-17-78	.197	.176	.206	160	497	72	98	17	2	19	61	87	13	0	3	182	2	3	.354	.330
Rhymes, Will	L-R	5-9	155	4-1-83	.228	.000	.272	47	123	11	28	2	1	1	8	10	3	0	1	17	1	2	.285	.299
Roberts, Ryan	R-R	5-11	185	9-19-80	.214	.175	.234	60	187	23	40	10	0	6	18	18	1	1	2	47	4	3	.364	.284
Rodriguez, Sean	R-R	6-0	200	4-26-85	.213	.228	.205	112	301	36	64	14	1	6	32	27	3	8	3	75	5	0	.326	.281
Scott, Luke	L-R	6-0	205	6-25-78	.229	.149	.260	96	314	35	72	22	1	14	55	21	5	0	4	80	5	0	.439	.285
Sutton, Drew	B-R	6-3	200	6-30-83	.271	.273	.269	18	48	2	13	4	0	0	6	2	1	0	0	16	0	0	.354	.314
Thompson, Rich	L-R	6-3	185	4-23-79	.091	.154	.000	23	22	5	2	0	0	0	1	0	2	0	0	5	6	2	.091	.167
Upton, B.J.	R-R	6-3	185	8-21-84	.246	.238	.249	146	573	79	141	29	3	28	78	45	1	4	8	169	31	6	.454	.298
Vogt, Stephen	L-R	6-0	215	11-1-84	.000	.000	.000	18	25	0	0	0	0	0	0	2	0	0	0	2	0	0	.000	.074
Zobrist, Ben	B-R	6-3	210	5-26-81	.270	.308	.253	157	560	88	151	39	7	20	74	97	3	2	6	103	14	9	.471	.377

Pitching	B-T	HT	WT	DOB	W	L	ERA	G	GS	CG	SV	IP	H	R	ER	HR	BB	SO	AVG	vLH	vRH	K/9	BB/9
Archer, Chris	R-R	6-3	200	9-26-88	1	3	4.60	6	4	0	0	29	23	17	15	3	13	36	.215	.300	.164	11.05	3.99
Badenhop, Burke	R-R	6-5	220	2-8-83	3	2	3.03	66	0	0	0	62	63	24	21	6	12	42	.259	.300	.239	6.06	1.73
Cobb, Alex	R-R	6-2	195	10-7-87	11	9	4.03	23	23	2	0	136	130	67	61	11	40	106	.254	.256	.252	7.00	2.64
Davis, Wade	R-R	6-5	225	9-7-85	3	0	2.43	54	0	0	0	70	48	20	19	5	29	87	.189	.161	.211	11.13	3.71
De La Rosa, Dane	R-R	6-7	245	2-1-83	0	0	12.60	5	0	0	0	5	7	7	7	2	2	5	.350	.375	.333	9.00	3.60
Farnsworth, Kyle	R-R	6-4	230	4-14-76	1	6	4.00	34	0	0	0	27	22	13	12	1	14	25	.225	.210	8.33	4.67	
Gomes, Brandon	R-R	5-11	185	7-15-84	2	2	5.09	15	0	0	0	18	16	12	10	2	12	15	.235	.333	.171	7.64	6.11
Hellickson, Jeremy	R-R	6-1	190	4-8-87	10	11	3.10	31	31	0	0	177	163	68	61	25	59	124	.244	.241	.247	6.31	3.00
Howell, J.P.	L-L	6-0	190	4-25-83	1	0	3.04	55	0	0	0	50	39	17	17	7	22	42	.223	.200	.244	7.51	3.93
Lueke, Josh	R-R	6-5	235	12-5-84	0	0	18.90	3	0	0	0	3	7	7	7	0	3	2	.563	.667	.429	5.40	8.10
McGee, Jake	L-L	6-3	230	8-6-86	5	2	1.95	69	0	0	0	55	33	13	12	3	11	73	.168	.259	.098	11.87	1.79
Moore, Matt	L-L	6-2	205	6-18-89	11	11	3.81	31	31	0	0	177	158	85	75	18	81	175	.238	.243	.237	8.88	4.12
Niemann, Jeff	R-R	6-9	285	2-28-83	2	3	3.08	8	8	0	0	38	30	17	13	2	12	34	.213	.280	.119	8.05	2.84
Peralta, Joel	R-R	5-11	205	3-23-76	2	6	3.63	76	0	0	2	67	49	28	27	9	17	84	.200	.173	.229	11.28	2.28
Price, David	L-L	6-6	220	8-26-85	20	5	2.56	31	31	2	0	211	173	63	60	16	59	205	.226	.205	.232	8.74	2.52
Ramos, Cesar	L-L	6-2	205	6-22-84	1	0	2.10	17	1	0	0	30	19	7	7	2	10	29	.176	.222	.130	8.70	3.00
Rodney, Fernando	R-R	5-11	220	3-18-77	2	2	0.60	76	0	0	48	75	43	9	5	2	15	76	.167	.166	.168	9.16	1.81
Shields, James	R-R	6-4	215	12-20-81	15	10	3.52	33	33	3	0	228	208	103	89	25	58	223	.239	.232	.248	8.82	2.29

Fielding																		

Catcher	PCT	G	PO	A	E	DP	PB
Gimenez	.989	39	262	12	3	2	0
Lobaton	.992	66	448	28	4	3	0
Molina	.994	102	657	41	4	8	6

Vogt	1.000	7	19	2	0	0	0
First Base	**PCT**	**G**	**PO**	**A**	**E**	**DP**	
Gimenez	1.000	1	2	0	0	1	
Keppinger	.994	27	157	7	1	13	

Pena	.995	153	1182	95	7	119
Scott	1.000	6	28	2	0	3
Sutton	1.000	3	8	0	0	1

Second Base	PCT	G	PO	A	E	DP
Brignac	1.000	1	0	1	0	0
Conrad	1.000	9	9	10	0	2
Johnson	.978	13	20	25	1	5
Keppinger	1.000	27	32	52	0	12
Rhymes	.961	31	40	83	5	27
Roberts	1.000	46	76	117	0	26
Rodriguez	1.000	37	40	63	0	15
Sutton	1.000	6	3	5	0	1
Zobrist	.968	58	73	107	6	27

Third Base	PCT	G	PO	A	E	DP
Brignac	1.000	4	0	0	0	0
Conrad	.923	14	7	17	2	1
Gimenez	—	1	0	0	0	0

	PCT	G	PO	A	E	DP
Johnson	.895	6	5	12	2	0
Keppinger	.976	50	23	59	2	10
Longoria	.937	50	37	81	8	7
Rhymes	.889	15	3	21	3	1
Roberts	.943	18	3	30	2	0
Rodriguez	.894	49	23	70	11	8
Sutton	.906	11	7	22	3	0

Shortstop	PCT	G	PO	A	E	DP
Brignac	.971	11	13	20	1	11
Johnson	.965	100	102	204	11	50
Rodriguez	.959	47	50	115	7	18
Zobrist	.979	47	46	139	4	27

Outfield	PCT	G	PO	A	E	DP
Allen	1.000	3	4	0	0	0

	PCT	G	PO	A	E	DP
Brignac	—	1	0	0	0	0
Francisco	1.000	18	11	0	0	0
Fuld	.981	33	51	2	1	0
Gimenez	1.000	1	1	0	0	0
Guyer	.667	3	2	0	1	0
Jennings	1.000	129	220	4	0	0
Johnson	1.000	3	2	0	0	0
Joyce	.989	115	181	2	2	0
Matsui	1.000	15	14	0	0	0
Thompson	1.000	12	8	0	0	0
Upton	.990	142	290	10	3	4
Vogt	1.000	2	1	0	0	0
Zobrist	.983	71	113	6	2	1

DURHAM BULLS   TRIPLE-A
INTERNATIONAL LEAGUE

Batting	B-T	HT	WT	DOB	AVG	vLH	vRH	G	AB	R	H	2B	3B	HR	RBI	BB	HBP	SH	SF	SO	SB	CS	SLG	OBP
Acosta, Mayobanex	R-R	6-1	205	11-20-87	.190	.000	.235	9	21	3	4	0	0	1	2	2	0	0	1	4	0	0	.333	.250
Albernaz, Craig	R-R	5-8	195	10-30-82	.156	.138	.171	23	64	2	10	3	0	0	3	5	1	2	0	23	1	0	.203	.229
Allen, Brandon	L-R	6-2	235	2-12-86	.262	.324	.235	29	122	17	32	9	1	4	14	4	2	0	1	32	0	0	.451	.295
Anderson, Leslie	L-L	6-5		3-30-82	.309	.260	.327	116	444	63	137	21	0	14	56	26	8	0	4	56	0	3	.450	.355
Ashley, Nevin	R-R	6-1	215	8-14-84	.245	.283	.219	35	110	18	27	6	1	5	13	15	4	1	0	25	1	1	.455	.357
Beckham, Tim	R-R	6-0	190	1-27-90	.256	.209	.278	72	285	40	73	10	1	6	28	29	2	3	4	71	6	0	.361	.325
Brignac, Reid	L-R	6-3	190	1-16-86	.231	.222	.235	99	346	45	80	14	2	8	46	45	3	4	2	79	3	3	.353	.323
Conrad, Brooks	B-R	5-10	190	1-16-80	.265	.323	.231	25	83	10	22	5	0	4	12	18	0	0	1	34	0	3	.470	.392
Feliciano, Jesus	L-L	5-10	190	6-6-79	.270	.189	.303	125	429	46	116	19	1	1	46	25	3	4	5	43	8	3	.326	.312
Figueroa, Cole	L-R	5-10	180	6-30-87	.286	.320	.270	88	311	32	89	17	4	2	42	26	3	4	3	22	3	2	.386	.344
Fuld, Sam	L-L	5-10	175	11-20-81	.167	.400	.077	5	18	0	3	1	0	0	3	0	0	0	3	0	1	.222	.286
Gimenez, Chris	R-R	6-2	220	12-27-82	.310	.375	.273	71	261	39	81	15	0	10	49	33	3	0	4	57	0	3	.483	.389
Guyer, Brandon	R-R	6-2	210	1-28-86	.294	.286	.296	22	85	9	25	3	1	3	13	7	3	1	1	15	2	0	.459	.365
Hudson, Kyle	L-L	5-11	175	1-7-87	.291	.244	.319	31	110	16	32	1	1	0	8	15	1	6	1	20	7	4	.318	.378
2-team total (78 Lehigh Valley)					.264	—		109	406	48	107	5	2	0	25	43	1	11	1	74	22	11	.286	.335
Jennings, Desmond	R-R	6-2	200	10-30-86	.167	.000	.286	3	12	1	2	0	0	0	2	0	0	0	0	1	0	0	.167	.167
Joyce, Matt	L-R	6-2	205	8-3-84	.000	—	.000	1	2	0	0	0	0	0	0	1	0	0	0	0	0	1	.000	.333
Keppinger, Jeff	R-R	6-0	185	4-21-80	.286	.333	.250	6	21	4	6	1	0	0	1	4	0	0	0	2	0	0	.333	.400
Kiermaier, Kevin	L-R	6-1	200	4-22-90	.333	1.000	.250	4	9	2	3	0	0	1	3	0	0	0	1	0	0	0	.333	.500
Lobaton, Jose	B-R	6-0	210	10-21-84	.067	—	.067	4	15	0	1	1	0	0	0	0	0	0	0	5	0	0	.133	.067
Longoria, Evan	R-R	6-2	210	10-7-85	.200	.333	.111	10	30	0	6	0	0	0	3	7	1	0	1	9	0	0	.200	.359
Mangini, Matt	L-R	6-4	230	12-21-85	.273	.188	.305	82	300	28	82	15	0	5	32	25	4	0	0	84	2	1	.373	.337
Matsui, Hideki	L-R	6-2	210	6-12-74	.170	.000	.190	13	47	3	8	2	0	0	4	4	0	0	1	10	0	0	.213	.231
Miranda, Juan	L-L	6-0	220	4-25-83	.187	.182	.189	44	150	20	28	7	0	2	8	23	3	0	0	42	1	0	.273	.307
O'Malley, Shawn	R-R	5-11	160	12-28-87	.245	.295	.211	67	216	32	53	4	2	2	18	17	3	7	4	49	11	1	.310	.304
Price, Robby	L-R	5-10	188	4-20-88	.500	.000	.600	2	6	1	3	0	0	0	0	0	0	0	1	0	0	0	.500	.500
Rhymes, Will	L-R	5-9	155	4-1-83	.256	.230	.270	46	172	19	44	5	3	4	21	18	1	1	2	19	2	3	.390	.326
Rodriguez, Sean	R-R	6-0	200	4-26-85	.500	.500	.500	2	6	3	3	2	0	1	4	1	0	1	0	2	0	0	1.333	.571
Salazar, Jeff	L-L	6-0	195	11-24-80	.216	.242	.204	68	208	21	45	8	0	5	22	20	1	4	1	48	4	2	.327	.287
Scott, Luke	L-R	6-0	205	6-25-78	.375	.333	.500	2	8	3	3	0	0	2	4	0	1	0	1	0	0	0	1.125	.400
Thompson, Rich	L-R	6-3	185	4-23-79	.311	.306	.314	63	251	41	78	13	5	2	19	20	3	8	0	35	22	5	.426	.369
2-team total (30 Lehigh Valley)					.310	—	—	93	339	47	105	17	7	3	20	30	7	9	0	53	29	7	.419	.376
Vogt, Stephen	L-R	6-0	215	11-1-84	.272	.209	.303	94	349	48	95	18	4	9	43	42	1	2	2	61	1	0	.424	.350
Wrigley, Henry	R-R	6-3	180	8-9-86	.285	.208	.316	94	354	39	101	25	1	13	52	21	1	0	4	78	0	1	.472	.324

Pitching	B-T	HT	WT	DOB	W	L	ERA	G	GS	CG	SV	IP	H	R	ER	HR	BB	SO	AVG	vLH	vRH	K/9	BB/9
Archer, Chris	R-R	6-3	200	9-26-88	7	9	3.66	25	25	0	0	128	99	54	52	6	62	139	.216	.250	.192	9.77	4.36
Augenstein, Bryan	R-R	6-6	230	7-11-86	2	1	3.59	23	1	0	3	43	43	18	17	2	12	40	.261	.296	.226	8.44	2.53
Buschmann, Matt	R-R	6-2	210	2-13-84	0	0	5.23	2	2	0	0	10	13	6	6	3	5	9	.325	.368	.286	7.84	4.35
Cobb, Alex	R-R	6-2	195	10-7-87	1	4	4.14	8	8	0	0	41	44	21	19	1	18	44	.267	.242	.283	9.58	3.92
Colome, Alex	R-R	6-2	185	12-31-88	0	1	3.24	3	3	0	0	17	12	6	6	1	9	15	.207	.231	.188	8.10	4.86
De La Rosa, Dane	R-R	6-7	245	2-1-83	4	4	2.79	54	0	0	20	68	36	22	21	2	42	87	.158	.173	.146	11.57	5.59
De Los Santos, Frank	L-L	6-0	165	11-17-87	3	1	2.18	27	0	0	1	33	32	12	8	2	10	25	.250	.268	.236	6.82	2.73
Dyer, Shane	R-R	6-3	185	3-9-88	1	3	7.34	9	8	0	0	42	66	35	34	4	13	25	.382	.402	.360	5.40	2.81
Farnsworth, Kyle	R-R	6-4	230	4-14-76	0	0	0.00	2	1	0	0	2	2	0	0	0	0	4	.250	.400	.000	18.00	0.00
Fleming, Marquis	R-R	6-1	180	9-11-86	0	0	9.00	7	0	0	0	13	17	13	13	2	10	6	.315	.231	.393	4.15	6.92
Gaub, John	R-L	6-2	210	4-28-85	1	0	4.32	16	0	0	1	17	10	8	8	0	12	21	.167	.185	.152	11.34	6.48
Gomes, Brandon	R-R	5-11	185	7-15-84	5	4	3.09	40	0	0	9	55	44	19	19	5	14	73	.218	.209	.224	11.87	2.28
Liberatore, Adam	L-L	6-3	239	5-12-87	1	1	1.29	16	0	0	1	21	18	3	3	0	8	21	.225	.200	.236	9.00	3.43
Lueke, Josh	R-R	6-5	235	12-5-84	2	6	5.59	42	0	0	2	68	85	45	42	6	17	71	.305	.284	.319	9.44	2.25
Niemann, Jeff	R-R	6-9	285	2-28-83	0	0	7.56	2	2	0	0	8	17	7	7	1	2	4	.459	.500	.429	4.32	2.16
Nunez, Jhonny	L-R	6-3	215	11-26-85	2	2	6.57	22	3	0	0	37	45	29	27	8	26	39	.306	.321	.297	7.05	6.32
Paduch, Jim	R-R	6-2	190	11-2-82	6	10	5.65	23	21	1	0	107	128	76	67	13	39	63	.297	.310	.284	5.32	3.29
Patterson, Jimmy	R-L	6-0	190	2-9-89	0	0	0.00	1	0	0	0	3	2	0	0	0	0	4	.182	.333	.125	10.80	0.00
Pendleton, Lance	L-R	6-3	225	9-10-83	8	7	4.81	26	23	1	0	129	139	72	69	14	55	104	.272	.304	.248	7.26	3.84
Ramos, Cesar	L-L	6-2	205	6-22-84	5	5	3.77	25	7	0	1	62	58	30	26	10	16	46	.245	.125	.289	6.68	2.32

	B-T	HT	WT	DOB	W	L	ERA	G	GS	CG	SV	IP	H	R	ER	HR	BB	SO	AVG	vLH	vRH	K/9	BB/9
Reid, Ryan	L-R	5-11	215	4-24-85	6	3	3.52	46	3	0	1	79	75	36	31	8	28	79	.248	.285	.220	8.96	3.18
Sanchez, Romulo	R-R	6-5	270	4-28-84	2	2	6.31	34	0	0	0	51	56	37	36	9	21	45	.289	.269	.302	7.89	3.68
Torra, Matt	R-R	6-3	225	6-29-84	12	7	4.10	26	23	0	0	147	148	70	67	25	26	78	.261	.282	.241	4.78	1.59
Torres, Alex	L-L	5-10	175	12-8-87	3	7	7.30	26	14	0	0	69	70	58	56	6	63	91	.261	.280	.253	11.87	8.22

Fielding

Catcher	PCT	G	PO	A	E	DP	PB
Acosta	1.000	9	64	5	0	0	1
Albernaz	.989	22	170	16	2	1	1
Ashley	.996	33	255	9	1	1	4
Gimenez	.998	47	375	29	1	4	7
Lobaton	.976	4	39	1	1	0	0
Vogt	.996	37	234	14	1	3	1

First Base	PCT	G	PO	A	E	DP
Allen	.980	6	47	3	1	9
Anderson	1.000	24	172	12	0	15
Conrad	1.000	10	70	2	0	8
Gimenez	1.000	1	8	1	0	0
Keppinger	1.000	1	3	0	0	0
Mangini	1.000	8	50	0	0	5
Miranda	.977	35	262	31	7	28
Vogt	1.000	16	105	10	0	12
Wrigley	.995	53	386	21	2	42

Second Base	PCT	G	PO	A	E	DP
Beckham	.962	25	51	50	4	14

	PCT	G	PO	A	E	DP
Brignac	1.000	21	43	56	0	17
Figueroa	.982	42	79	89	3	23
O'Malley	.963	34	60	96	6	23
Price	1.000	2	3	4	0	1
Rhymes	.973	28	43	64	3	20
Rodriguez	1.000	1	2	1	0	0

Third Base	PCT	G	PO	A	E	DP
Conrad	.969	11	10	21	1	1
Figueroa	.952	51	28	72	5	11
Gimenez	.667	2	0	2	1	0
Keppinger	1.000	2	1	3	0	1
Mangini	.918	70	49	97	13	11
O'Malley	1.000	3	2	5	0	1
Rhymes	.933	13	7	21	2	1
Wrigley	—	1	0	0	0	0

Shortstop	PCT	G	PO	A	E	DP
Beckham	.946	48	70	121	11	34
Brignac	.968	74	119	188	10	42
O'Malley	.977	22	30	56	2	12

	PCT	G	PO	A	E	DP
Rodriguez	1.000	1	2	3	0	1

Outfield	PCT	G	PO	A	E	DP
Allen	.977	22	40	2	1	0
Anderson	.989	49	87	4	1	3
Feliciano	1.000	123	239	10	0	2
Fuld	1.000	4	12	1	0	0
Gimenez	1.000	20	41	1	0	0
Guyer	1.000	20	43	0	0	0
Hudson	.983	31	58	1	1	0
Jennings	1.000	2	3	0	0	0
Joyce	1.000	1	3	0	0	0
Kiermaier	1.000	4	8	0	0	0
Matsui	1.000	4	7	1	0	1
O'Malley	1.000	9	8	1	0	1
Rhymes	1.000	6	7	0	0	0
Salazar	.990	63	98	4	1	1
Thompson	.981	62	148	7	3	1
Vogt	1.000	35	52	3	0	1
Wrigley	1.000	6	6	0	0	0

MONTGOMERY BISCUITS   DOUBLE-A
SOUTHERN LEAGUE

Batting	B-T	HT	WT	DOB	AVG	vLH	vRH	G	AB	R	H	2B	3B	HR	RBI	BB	HBP	SH	SF	SO	SB	CS	SLG	OBP
Acosta, Mayobanex	R-R	6-1	205	11-20-87	.264	.290	.250	30	91	14	24	6	0	5	13	13	1	2	1	18	0	0	.495	.358
Albernaz, Craig	R-R	5-8	195	10-30-82	.000	—	.000	1	2	0	0	0	0	0	0	2	0	0	0	2	0	0	.000	.500
Bortnick, Tyler	R-R	5-11	185	7-3-87	.253	.287	.238	95	348	46	88	18	8	4	48	46	7	3	0	61	23	3	.385	.352
Coon, Brad	L-L	6-0	175	12-11-82	.227	.222	.229	90	278	31	63	8	3	2	30	46	2	4	0	58	13	5	.299	.340
Dietrich, Derek	L-R	6-1	200	7-18-89	.271	.241	.293	34	133	22	36	7	1	4	17	7	1	1	1	36	0	1	.429	.324
Figueroa, Cole	L-R	5-10	180	6-30-87	.314	.250	.339	25	86	17	27	6	1	3	12	17	0	0	2	9	1	2	.512	.419
Garko, Ryan	R-R	6-2	225	1-2-81	.297	.297	.297	61	229	33	68	9	0	8	40	28	7	0	3	50	0	0	.441	.386
Kang, K.D.	L-L	6-2	200	2-6-88	.243	.111	.290	104	345	58	84	18	4	14	53	51	6	0	2	135	4	2	.441	.349
Lee, Hak-Ju	L-R	6-2	170	11-4-90	.261	.231	.278	116	475	68	124	15	10	4	37	51	3	4	1	102	37	9	.360	.336
Lobaton, Jose	B-R	6-0	210	10-21-84	.154	.167	.143	4	13	1	2	1	0	0	1	3	0	0	0	3	0	0	.231	.313
Luna, Omar	R-R	5-11	165	12-13-86	.315	.311	.317	122	470	63	148	20	3	3	57	38	4	0	3	42	19	7	.389	.369
Mahtook, Mikie	R-R	6-1	200	11-30-89	.248	.250	.247	39	153	17	38	10	1	4	25	11	3	0	2	31	4	3	.405	.308
Morrison, Ty	L-R	6-2	170	7-22-90	.269	.272	.268	102	405	56	109	17	8	3	35	35	10	7	1	88	20	8	.373	.341
Nommensen, Brett	L-L	5-11	190	10-6-86	.255	.241	.262	50	157	19	40	10	0	3	25	25	2	0	2	33	2	3	.376	.360
O'Malley, Shawn	R-R	5-11	160	12-28-87	.231	.234	.230	35	121	22	28	3	3	0	5	17	2	3	1	24	7	3	.306	.333
Salem, Emeel	L-L	6-0	180	2-11-85	.238	.100	.264	26	63	11	15	1	1	0	8	8	3	2	1	16	0	2	.286	.347
Sexton, Greg	R-R	6-2	205	2-8-85	.235	.184	.268	79	247	29	58	6	0	5	30	34	1	2	2	39	0	1	.377	.327
Sheridan, Mike	L-L	6-2	205	8-8-87	.246	.191	.272	129	464	61	114	24	4	10	58	38	1	3	5	69	3	4	.379	.301
Thomas, Mark	R-R	6-1	180	5-5-88	.254	.305	.228	93	311	37	79	19	3	5	42	29	4	2	3	78	4	0	.383	.323
Upton, B.J.	R-R	6-3	185	8-21-84	.200	—	.200	3	10	1	2	0	0	0	1	1	0	0	0	1	0	0	.200	.273
Velasquez, Isaias	R-R	5-11	155	5-7-88	.242	.364	.182	10	33	4	8	2	0	0	1	1	1	0	0	5	0	2	.303	.286
Wendt, David	R-R	6-5	205	1-2-87	.276	.250	.283	18	58	9	16	1	3	0	5	2	3	0	0	9	0	0	.397	.333
Wrigley, Henry	R-R	6-3	180	8-9-86	.270	.261	.273	32	122	17	33	12	0	7	27	15	0	0	0	25	3	0	.541	.350

Pitching	B-T	HT	WT	DOB	W	L	ERA	G	GS	CG	SV	IP	H	R	ER	HR	BB	SO	AVG	vLH	vRH	K/9	BB/9
Barnese, Nick	R-R	6-2	170	1-11-89	3	1	5.72	13	12	0	0	57	65	41	36	5	25	30	.295	.281	.305	4.76	3.97
Buschmann, Matt	R-R	6-3	210	2-13-84	7	8	3.89	24	22	1	0	141	136	69	61	12	48	111	.260	.320	.203	7.09	3.06
Colome, Alex	R-R	6-2	185	12-31-88	8	3	3.48	14	14	1	0	75	69	30	29	2	34	75	.252	.286	.226	9.00	4.08
Cruz, Joe	R-R	6-4	190	7-20-88	6	6	4.60	18	15	0	0	78	64	42	40	7	54	64	.225	.209	.235	7.35	6.20
De Los Santos, Frank	L-L	6-0	175	11-17-87	4	1	2.06	24	2	0	4	48	45	11	11	1	15	26	.268	.231	.284	4.88	2.81
Dyer, Shane	R-R	6-3	185	3-9-88	4	3	2.85	23	9	0	0	66	55	31	21	2	25	34	.224	.194	.245	4.61	3.39
Fleming, Marquis	R-R	6-1	180	9-11-86	4	5	3.55	41	0	0	0	63	49	28	25	6	34	72	.218	.219	.217	10.23	4.83
Kelly, Merrill	R-R	6-1	170	10-14-88	8	3	3.57	32	9	0	0	88	84	41	35	4	28	61	.251	.263	.242	6.22	2.85
Koronis, Alex	R-R	6-2	187	1-4-88	1	2	4.12	24	0	0	0	39	29	18	18	2	30	37	.204	.246	.176	8.47	6.86
Liberatore, Adam	L-L	6-3	239	5-12-87	3	4	2.94	33	0	0	8	52	53	18	17	4	20	27	.275	.180	.318	4.67	3.46
Lobstein, Kyle	L-L	6-3	200	8-12-89	8	7	4.06	27	27	0	0	144	140	73	65	12	69	129	.260	.272	.257	8.06	4.31
Nevarez, Matt	R-R	6-4	220	8-6-86	0	0	3.38	3	0	0	1	3	2	1	1	1	5		.200	.167	.250	16.88	3.38
Paduch, Jim	R-R	6-2	190	11-2-82	0	2	4.05	6	1	0	2	13	11	6	6	0	4	11	.224	.208	.240	7.43	2.70
Patterson, Jimmy	R-L	6-0	190	2-9-89	0	0	2.70	1	0	0	0	3	5	2	1	0	1	0	.357	.500	.250	0.00	2.70
Quate, Zach	R-R	6-1	200	9-12-87	1	0	0.00	1	0	0	0	2	3	0	0	0	2	3	.375	.000	.429	9.00	9.00
Rearick, Chris	L-L	6-3	190	12-5-87	2	1	4.38	15	0	0	2	25	22	14	12	4	8	26	.234	.231	.236	9.49	2.92
Riefenhauser, C.J.	L-L	6-0	180	1-30-90	1	1	3.44	9	1	0	0	18	15	7	7	4	8	15	.224	.105	.271	7.36	3.93
Schenk, Neil	L-L	6-3	220	6-17-86	3	1	2.97	42	0	0	1	61	61	21	20	7	20	42	.268	.320	.242	6.23	2.97
Shuman, Scott	R-R	6-3	205	3-28-88	0	1	8.83	29	0	0	0	35	32	40	34	4	47	54	.239		.224	14.02	12.20
Thompson, Jake	R-R	6-3	225	8-8-89	7	12	5.56	25	25	0	0	125	162	90	77	12	56	90	.314	.305	.322	6.50	4.04
Yates, Kirby	R-R	5-10	170	3-25-87	4	2	2.65	50	0	0	16	68	48	21	20	4	39	94	.200	.225	.185	12.44	5.16

Fielding

Catcher	PCT	G	PO	A	E	DP	PB
Acosta	.992	29	207	27	2	4	3
Albernaz	1.000	1	7	3	0	0	0
Garko	1.000	1	10	1	0	0	0
Lobaton	1.000	3	18	2	0	0	0
Thomas	.988	93	672	78	9	12	2
Wendt	.977	18	115	10	3	0	2

First Base	PCT	G	PO	A	E	DP
Garko	1.000	9	75	5	0	7
Sexton	.981	8	49	3	1	3
Sheridan	.994	123	988	46	6	97
Wrigley	1.000	3	17	0	0	3

Second Base	PCT	G	PO	A	E	DP
Bortnick	.981	94	178	231	8	68

	PCT	G	PO	A	E	DP
Dietrich	.960	34	71	97	7	23
Figueroa	1.000	1	4	1	0	1
Luna	1.000	7	4	7	0	1
O'Malley	1.000	5	8	10	0	1

Third Base	PCT	G	PO	A	E	DP
Figueroa	.968	22	22	39	2	2
Luna	.960	60	44	122	7	13
O'Malley	—	1	0	0	0	0
Sexton	.938	60	37	113	10	10

Shortstop	PCT	G	PO	A	E	DP
Lee	.954	115	191	302	24	68
Luna	1.000	5	5	4	0	3
O'Malley	.971	22	19	47	2	10

Outfield	PCT	G	PO	A	E	DP
Coon	.994	84	151	8	1	1
Kang	1.000	47	72	2	0	0
Luna	.977	53	78	7	2	1
Mahtook	.985	34	64	3	1	2
Morrison	.996	101	254	4	1	3
Nommensen	1.000	43	87	1	0	0
O'Malley	1.000	8	17	2	0	0
Salem	.978	23	44	1	1	0
Upton	1.000	2	5	0	0	0
Velasquez	.960	10	22	2	1	0
Wrigley	1.000	25	37	6	0	0

CHARLOTTE STONE CRABS　　　　　HIGH CLASS A

FLORIDA STATE LEAGUE

Batting	B-T	HT	WT	DOB	AVG	vLH	vRH	G	AB	R	H	2B	3B	HR	RBI	BB	HBP	SH	SF	SO	SB	CS	SLG	OBP
Acosta, Mayobanex	R-R	6-1	205	11-20-87	.278	.300	.262	22	72	11	20	8	0	3	15	7	1	1	1	19	1	0	.514	.346
Allen, Brandon	L-R	6-2	235	2-12-86	.255	.294	.235	14	51	8	13	3	0	2	4	9	0	0	1	14	0	0	.431	.361
Bailey, Luke	R-R	6-0	198	3-11-91	.231	.241	.224	67	234	33	54	15	1	7	28	8	8	3	3	67	0	2	.393	.277
Castillo, Keith	B-R	6-4	215	7-10-87	.218	.150	.257	16	55	1	12	2	0	0	3	2	0	0	0	14	0	0	.255	.283
Dietrich, Derek	L-R	6-1	200	7-18-89	.282	.245	.308	98	372	49	105	21	9	10	58	25	12	3	5	78	4	2	.468	.343
Estrada, Robi	B-R	5-10	170	10-8-88	.253	.309	.226	75	249	32	63	15	1	3	25	22	0	5	3	43	6	1	.357	.310
Fuld, Sam	L-L	5-10	175	11-20-81	.154	.111	.250	5	13	0	2	0	0	0	2	0	0	0		3	0	1	.154	.267
Glaesmann, Todd	R-R	6-4	220	10-24-90	.295	.440	.213	36	139	20	41	8	2	8	22	8	0	1	0	35	0	0	.554	.333
Guevara, Hector	R-R	5-11	170	10-7-91	.234	.247	.223	100	367	35	86	12	1	3	35	24	2	8	5	44	6	6	.297	.281
Jennings, Desmond	R-R	6-2	200	10-30-86	.333	—	.333	1	3	1	1	0	0	0	0	0	0	0	0	0	0	0	.667	.333
Joyce, Matt	R-R	6-2	205	8-3-84	.250	.200	.333	2	8	2	2	1	0	0	2	1	0	0	1	0	0	0	.375	.333
Kiermaier, Kevin	L-R	6-1	200	4-22-90	.260	.257	.262	57	177	16	46	7	6	0	12	26	2	7	0	38	10	4	.367	.361
Lobaton, Jose	B-R	6-0		10-21-84	.000	.000	.000	2	5	0	0	0	0	0	0	1	0	0	0	1	0	0	.000	.167
Lyerly, Craige	R-R	5-11	175	8-24-88	.194	.133	.250	14	31	5	6	1	0	0	1	2	0	0	0	17	3	0	.226	.242
Mahtook, Mikie	R-R	6-1	200	11-30-89	.290	.264	.308	92	341	49	99	15	7	5	37	29	10	6	0	71	19	6	.419	.358
Morrison, Ty	L-R	6-2	170	7-22-90	.281	.288	.277	32	135	15	38	8	2	0	14	9	3	4	0	29	11	2	.370	.340
Murrill, Chris	L-L	6-2	190	6-5-88	.239	.500	.167	15	46	2	11	0	0	0	4	1	0	1	0	17	1	0	.239	.255
Nommensen, Brett	L-L	5-11	190	10-6-86	.216	.333	.111	13	51	5	11	1	0	0	3	4	0	0	1	9	3	1	.235	.273
Price, Robby	L-R	5-10	188	4-20-88	.265	.296	.252	110	389	51	103	14	3	3	30	45	22	9	1	36	5	9	.339	.372
Rogers, Cody	L-R	6-2	175	9-13-88	.244	.206	.264	112	361	39	88	12	6	4	38	30	8	9	5	99	22	4	.343	.312
Scott, Luke	L-R	6-0	205	6-25-78	.308	.333	.286	8	26	6	8	1	0	2	6	6	0	0	0	7	0	0	.577	.438
Tinoco, Steve	R-R	6-0	200	4-11-88	.281	.256	.300	83	303	30	85	8	1	1	27	16	2	0	3	24	3	1	.323	.318
Torres, Alejandro	R-R	6-1	178	9-30-88	.286	.320	.267	21	70	9	20	3	0	0	7	8	0	0	1	17	0	3	.329	.354
Torrez, Riccio	R-R	6-0	205	10-14-89	.219	.237	.208	123	442	52	97	18	3	9	50	27	16	3	2	86	7	2	.335	.287
Upton, B.J.	R-R	6-3	185	8-21-84	.100	.200	.000	4	11	1	1	0	0	0	1	1	0	0	0	1	2	0	.091	.167
Wendt, David	R-R	6-5	205	1-2-87	.185	.152	.208	24	81	4	15	2	0	0	3	3	0	2	0	15	0	0	.210	.214
Wunderlich, Phil	L-R	6-0	225	11-4-88	.230	.209	.240	109	404	47	93	21	2	9	47	21	7	0	4	75	2	0	.359	.278

Pitching	B-T	HT	WT	DOB	W	L	ERA	G	GS	CG	SV	IP	H	R	ER	HR	BB	SO	AVG	vLH	vRH	K/9	BB/9
Andujar, Chris	R-R	6-2	180	8-24-87	1	0	4.40	14	0	0	1	31	30	16	15	3	12	19	.259	.262	.255	5.58	3.52
Butler, Zach	R-R	6-3	200	7-28-89	0	0	0.00	1	0	0	0	0	0	0	0	0	0	0	.500	.000	1.000	0.00	0.00
Carlson, Kris	R-R	6-3	190	10-30-89	0	0	13.50	1	0	0	0	1	1	1	1	0	3	1	.333	.000	.500	13.50	40.50
Farnsworth, Kyle	R-R	6-4	230	4-14-76	0	0	2.25	4	4	0	0	4	3	1	1	0	0	2	.214	.143	.286	4.50	0.00
Garcia, Nate	R-R	6-1	190	5-9-88	0	3	3.58	17	0	0	1	33	35	14	13	3	14	28	.287	.346	.243	7.71	3.86
Garvin, Grayson	L-L	6-6	225	10-27-89	2	4	5.05	11	10	0	0	46	45	29	26	0	19	37	.259	.229	.270	7.13	3.69
Geith, T.J.	L-L	6-5	175	6-27-89	0	3	2.98	31	0	0	2	54	48	19	18	2	11	49	.241	.276	.227	8.12	1.82
Jensen, George	R-R	6-4	215	4-12-90	3	6	5.83	34	2	0	0	83	101	56	54	9	34	50	.298	.296	.299	5.40	3.67
Koronis, Alex	R-R	6-2	187	1-4-88	3	3	6.23	14	0	0	1	30	36	21	21	6	14	23	.305	.413	.236	6.82	4.15
Lara, Braulio	L-L	6-1	180	12-20-88	6	10	5.71	25	21	0	0	112	123	81	71	11	58	82	.276	.308	.260	6.59	4.66
Linsky, Lenny	R-R	6-2	220	3-4-90	1	2	3.07	18	0	0	2	29	28	13	10	2	19	12	.277	.378	.196	3.68	5.83
Mateo, Victor	R-R	6-5	180	7-27-89	6	5	4.31	30	16	0	1	117	115	66	56	9	43	72	.260	.242	.277	5.54	3.31
Nevarez, Matt	R-R	6-4	220	2-26-87	1	1	0.57	9	0	0	1	16	3	1	1	1	3	18	.063	.100	.036	10.34	1.72
Niemann, Jeff	R-R	6-9	285	2-28-83	0	0	6.00	2	2	0	0	6	9	5	4	0	3	6	.346	.364	.250	9.00	4.50
Patterson, Jimmy	R-L	6-0	190	2-9-89	8	4	2.82	37	1	0	2	73	56	26	23	4	17	48	.211	.228	.201	5.89	2.09
Rearick, Chris	L-L	6-3	190	12-5-87	2	3	1.79	35	0	0	20	45	35	12	9	1	15	59	.207	.133	.250	11.71	2.98
Riefenhauser, C.J.	L-L	6-0	180	1-30-90	7	8	4.76	23	14	0	1	96	98	55	51	11	32	103	.264	.168	.306	9.62	2.99
Rodriguez, Wilking	R-R	6-1	180	3-2-90	0	4	5.56	7	7	0	0	34	26	22	21	3	15	29	.213	.157	.288	7.68	3.97
Romero, Enny	L-L	6-3	165	1-24-91	5	7	3.93	25	23	1	0	126	89	67	55	5	76	107	.201	.228	.189	7.64	5.43
Suarez, Albert	R-R	6-2	235	10-8-89	5	9	4.08	25	25	1	0	126	132	74	57	11	30	62	.269	.266	.272	4.44	2.15
Suero, Eliazer	R-R	6-4	170	6-7-89	5	7	5.81	30	9	0	1	91	89	65	59	10	63	61	.259	.298	.228	6.01	6.21

Fielding

Catcher	PCT	G	PO	A	E	DP	PB
Acosta	.995	22	178	17	1	1	2
Bailey	.961	64	389	50	18	1	11
Castillo	.988	12	79	4	1	1	1
Lobaton	1.000	2	15	1	0	0	0
Torres	.972	18	127	11	4	1	3
Wendt	.974	18	104	9	3	0	2

First Base	PCT	G	PO	A	E	DP
Allen	1.000	5	38	2	0	5
Castillo	.857	1	6	0	1	0
Scott	1.000	2	14	2	0	1
Tinoco	.996	33	260	12	1	20
Wunderlich	.990	97	762	47	8	65

Second Base	PCT	G	PO	A	E	DP
Dietrich	1.000	17	36	35	0	13
Estrada	.951	21	31	47	4	9
Guevara	.974	74	115	181	8	34
Price	.992	29	48	72	1	16
Tinoco	1.000	2	2	7	0	0

Third Base	PCT	G	PO	A	E	DP
Price	.947	20	10	26	2	0
Tinoco	.500	2	1	0	1	0
Torrez	.942	118	73	217	18	16

Shortstop	PCT	G	PO	A	E	DP
Dietrich	.964	75	109	187	11	37
Estrada	.936	50	55	135	13	31
Guevara	.940	10	15	32	3	6

Outfield	PCT	G	PO	A	E	DP
Allen	1.000	6	6	0	0	0
Estrada	1.000	4	7	0	0	0
Fuld	1.000	5	8	0	0	0
Glaesmann	.955	36	62	2	3	1

	PCT	G	PO	A	E	DP
Jennings	1.000	1	2	0	0	0
Joyce	1.000	1	1	0	0	0
Kiermaier	.975	57	152	4	4	0
Lyerly	1.000	13	17	1	0	0
Mahtook	.980	91	237	10	5	4
Morrison	.973	30	69	3	2	0
Murrill	1.000	12	22	0	0	0
Nommensen	.962	11	23	2	1	0
Price	.974	22	38	0	1	0
Rogers	.964	108	256	10	10	2
Tinoco	1.000	26	54	2	0	0
Upton	1.000	4	5	0	0	0
Wendt	1.000	1	1	0	0	0

BOWLING GREEN HOT RODS
MIDWEST LEAGUE

LOW CLASS A

TAMPA BAY RAYS

Batting	B-T	HT	WT	DOB	AVG	vLH	vRH	G	AB	R	H	2B	3B	HR	RBI	BB	HBP	SH	SF	SO	SB	CS	SLG	OBP
Argo, Willie	R-R	6-1	220	10-15-89	.125	.200	.091	5	16	1	2	1	0	0	1	0	0	0	0	3	0	0	.188	.176
Brett, Ryan	R-R	5-9	180	10-9-91	.285	.188	.306	100	410	77	117	20	3	6	35	37	4	2	3	73	48	8	.393	.348
Caminero, Joel	R-R	6-1	185	10-24-89	.209	.138	.235	39	134	12	28	4	0	1	12	5	1	1	0	27	1	0	.261	.243
Carter, Kes	L-L	6-2	205	3-3-90	.228	.136	.248	37	127	16	29	5	2	2	16	23	5	1	2	34	9	4	.346	.363
Castillo, Keith	B-R	6-4	215	7-10-87	.250	.000	.273	8	24	5	6	1	0	0	2	6	0	0	0	5	0	0	.292	.400
Glaesmann, Todd	R-R	6-4	220	10-24-90	.281	.200	.299	91	352	57	99	17	5	13	53	22	11	1	6	89	8	3	.469	.338
Goeddel, Tyler	R-R	6-4	180	10-20-92	.246	.283	.238	103	329	52	81	19	2	6	46	38	7	3	2	94	30	5	.371	.335
Hager, Jake	R-R	6-1	170	3-4-93	.281	.329	.272	114	442	63	124	22	3	10	72	40	7	6	6	60	17	11	.412	.345
Kline, Ben	R-R	6-3	200	12-2-88	.281	.455	.190	9	32	2	9	2	0	1	4	2	1	1	0	9	0	1	.438	.343
Malm, Jeff	L-L	6-3	225	10-31-90	.263	.329	.251	128	464	67	122	36	3	13	61	62	8	0	6	127	6	3	.438	.356
Motter, Taylor	R-R	6-1	190	9-18-89	.244	.375	.219	99	303	41	74	17	2	5	37	50	3	5	0	60	24	12	.363	.357
Querecuto, Juniel	B-R	5-9	155	9-19-92	.249	.290	.241	106	386	53	96	17	2	0	32	38	1	9	2	79	13	6	.303	.316
Rice, Matt	R-R	6-3	195	5-8-89	.301	.244	.307	74	246	26	74	9	2	4	33	34	4	3	3	38	2	1	.402	.390
Sale, Josh	L-R	6-0	215	7-5-91	.264	.258	.264	74	239	35	63	10	4	10	44	51	2	0	5	62	7	6	.464	.391
Segovia, Alejandro	R-R	6-0	185	4-27-90	.269	.282	.267	70	245	43	66	14	2	15	45	29	7	2	1	36	2	0	.527	.362
Seitzer, Cameron	L-R	6-5	220	11-9-90	.307	.288	.313	118	424	50	130	36	2	4	54	55	3	1	5	83	1	1	.429	.386
Torres, Alejandro	R-R	6-1	178	9-30-88	.150	.000	.273	6	20	1	3	0	0	0	1	3	1	0	0	8	0	0	.150	.292
Vettleson, Drew	L-R	6-1	185	7-19-91	.275	.307	.269	132	505	80	139	24	5	15	69	51	1	0	5	117	20	11	.432	.340

Pitching	B-T	HT	WT	DOB	W	L	ERA	G	GS	CG	SV	IP	H	R	ER	HR	BB	SO	AVG	vLH	vRH	K/9	BB/9
Bellatti, Andrew	R-R	6-1	170	8-5-91	7	3	2.97	40	1	0	5	91	74	33	30	9	30	99	.221	.216	.225	9.79	2.97
Bierman, Sean	L-L	6-0	195	10-20-88	1	1	8.68	2	2	0	0	9	15	10	9	2	4	9	.349	.231	.400	8.68	3.86
Carpenter, Ryan	L-L	6-5	235	8-22-90	11	8	4.09	29	28	0	0	150	153	76	68	15	23	113	.265	.264	.265	6.80	1.38
Cononie, Charlie	R-R	6-7	210	2-25-89	2	4	4.20	34	0	0	5	60	45	34	28	1	45	69	.205	.244	.181	10.35	6.75
Crawford, Shay	L-L	6-2	190	12-12-87	0	0	4.50	7	0	0	0	10	9	5	5	1	4	10	.231	.125	.304	9.00	3.60
Floethe, Jake	R-R	6-3	205	5-29-89	10	3	3.31	24	24	0	0	122	104	56	45	4	31	92	.227	.239	.214	6.77	2.28
Gomez, Roberto	R-R	6-5	178	8-3-89	9	3	2.48	28	22	0	0	120	110	43	33	3	42	79	.248	.208	.279	5.93	3.15
Hubbard, Austin	R-R	6-2	206	6-14-88	2	6	4.11	49	0	0	23	57	53	28	26	7	25	72	.247	.270	.226	11.37	3.95
Lopez, Reinaldo	R-R	6-2	221	4-27-91	1	1	5.40	2	1	0	0	10	12	6	6	1	4	6	.286	.263	.304	5.40	3.60
Markel, Parker	R-R	6-4	220	9-15-90	11	5	3.53	24	24	0	0	120	117	55	47	6	34	96	.249	.229	.267	7.20	2.55
McEachern, Jason	R-R	6-2	160	10-12-90	2	2	2.80	28	0	0	2	61	46	24	19	2	31	68	.202	.153	.231	10.03	4.57
Partridge, Jacob	L-L	6-3	200	12-21-90	5	1	2.51	34	3	0	5	97	76	33	27	2	38	93	.217	.263	.188	8.66	3.54
Rivero, Felipe	L-L	6-0	151	7-5-91	8	8	3.41	27	21	0	0	113	115	56	43	5	29	98	.266	.259	.270	7.78	2.30
Sawyer, Nick	R-R	5-11	175	9-23-91	1	0	0.00	2	0	0	0	3	1	0	0	0	2	3	.111	.000	.200	9.00	6.00
Shull, Trevor	R-R	6-4	180	8-7-90	5	7	5.05	28	13	0	1	82	87	54	46	3	48	55	.278	.297	.262	6.04	5.27
Thomas, Stayton	R-R	5-11	180	10-28-89	1	4	3.62	39	0	0	5	75	77	46	30	1	20	44	.258	.274	.245	5.30	2.41
Wilson, Jason	R-R	6-1	195	8-6-90	1	0	8.22	4	0	0	0	8	11	7	7	2	3	4	.333	.333	.333	4.70	3.52
Woodall, Justin	L-L	6-2	210	11-6-87	3	4	4.76	30	1	0	4	59	58	36	31	3	36	52	.260	.215	.285	7.98	5.52

Fielding

Catcher	PCT	G	PO	A	E	DP	PB
Castillo	1.000	2	18	5	0	0	1
Rice	.993	72	533	49	4	8	8
Segovia	.979	69	499	61	12	14	6
Torres	1.000	3	28	2	0	0	4

First Base	PCT	G	PO	A	E	DP
Malm	.996	81	653	48	3	53
Motter	1.000	2	7	1	0	0
Seitzer	.988	68	594	44	8	49

Second Base	PCT	G	PO	A	E	DP
Brett	.949	88	156	218	20	43

Motter	.938	3	7	8	1	2
Querecuto	.991	52	83	130	2	30

Third Base	PCT	G	PO	A	E	DP
Goeddel	.899	93	70	187	29	20
Kline	.839	9	7	19	5	0
Motter	.912	25	17	66	8	8
Querecuto	.918	16	8	37	4	4
Seitzer	—	1	0	0	0	0

Shortstop	PCT	G	PO	A	E	DP
Hager	.957	105	161	266	19	44
Querecuto	.944	38	55	98	9	17

Outfield	PCT	G	PO	A	E	DP
Argo	1.000	4	6	0	0	0
Caminero	.947	38	72	0	4	0
Carter	.962	36	73	2	3	1
Glaesmann	.976	86	163	3	4	0
Malm	.951	22	33	6	2	1
Motter	.990	53	89	8	1	2
Sale	.919	70	109	4	10	1
Seitzer	1.000	1	1	0	0	0
Vettleson	.963	128	216	20	9	7

HUDSON VALLEY RENEGADES

SHORT-SEASON

NEW YORK-PENN LEAGUE

TAMPA BAY RAYS

Batting	B-T	HT	WT	DOB	AVG	vLH	vRH	G	AB	R	H	2B	3B	HR	RBI	BB	HBP	SH	SF	SO	SB	CS	SLG	OBP
Caminero, Joel	R-R	6-1	185	10-24-89	.226	.250	.218	58	217	25	49	10	0	2	21	4	1	2	0	53	6	4	.300	.243
Coyle, Tommy	L-R	5-7	170	10-24-90	.265	.203	.288	67	253	46	67	13	2	5	31	42	3	0	2	50	20	4	.391	.373
DePew, Jake	R-R	6-1	220	3-1-92	.204	.194	.207	46	147	11	30	4	0	1	16	18	0	3	1	24	3	0	.252	.289
Dixon, Deshun	R-L	6-0	190	9-20-91	.193	.139	.212	38	140	14	27	5	1	1	14	17	1	1	1	48	5	1	.264	.283
Dunn, Ryan	R-R	5-10	180	10-28-88	.278	.281	.277	61	223	32	62	16	0	1	36	27	5	0	2	25	8	2	.363	.366
Epperson, Charles	R-R	6-2	205	6-30-90	.194	.194	.194	32	103	13	20	4	1	1	9	8	3	0	0	34	4	4	.282	.272
Gantt, Marty	R-L	5-9	170	2-11-90	.204	.140	.222	63	235	37	48	10	2	2	21	29	1	3	3	52	6	4	.289	.291
Gonzalez, Felix	B-R	5-10	165	4-4-90	.150	.087	.175	27	80	6	12	1	0	0	3	0	1	0	27	1	1	.163	.181
Maile, Luke	R-R	6-3	195	2-6-91	.278	.381	.253	61	216	30	60	10	3	3	41	31	4	0	1	36	3	1	.394	.377
O'Conner, Justin	R-R	6-0	190	3-31-92	.223	.125	.247	59	238	39	53	18	1	5	29	18	0	0	1	73	2	0	.370	.276
Reardon, Pat	L-R	6-3	225	10-23-87	.000	.000	—	1	1	0	0	0	0	0	0	0	0	0	0	0	0	0	.000	.000
Reginatto, Leonardo	R-R	6-2	180	4-10-90	.276	.185	.303	65	232	22	64	8	0	1	29	16	3	2	1	26	8	4	.323	.329
Rickard, Joey	R-L	6-1	180	5-21-91	.279	.265	.284	47	183	35	51	11	0	2	14	16	12	0	2	32	11	3	.372	.371
Rowan, Geoff	R-R	5-9	190	10-30-89	.167	.000	.200	7	12	0	2	1	0	0	3	1	0	0	0	3	0	0	.250	.231
Shaffer, Richie	R-R	6-3	210	3-15-91	.308	.290	.314	33	117	25	36	5	2	4	26	16	4	0	1	31	0	0	.487	.406
Williams, Michael	R-R	6-2	210	4-30-90	.221	.150	.244	46	163	12	36	9	1	0	18	14	3	0	1	34	0	2	.288	.293

Pitching	B-T	HT	WT	DOB	W	L	ERA	G	GS	CG	SV	IP	H	R	ER	HR	BB	SO	AVG	vLH	vRH	K/9	BB/9
Ames, Jeff	R-R	6-4	225	1-31-91	6	1	1.96	14	13	0	0	64	44	21	14	1	20	70	.195	.236	.168	9.79	2.80
Bierman, Sean	L-L	6-0	195	10-20-88	4	2	2.75	11	11	0	0	52	55	20	16	2	5	36	.278	.267	.281	6.19	0.86
Carlson, Kris	R-R	6-3	190	10-30-89	1	2	3.74	17	0	0	1	22	20	11	9	1	12	15	.244	.314	.191	6.23	4.98
Crawford, Shay	L-L	6-2	190	12-12-87	1	0	2.76	14	0	0	3	16	14	7	5	1	5	12	.250	.176	.282	6.61	2.76
Finneran, Rob	R-R	6-3	215	9-18-89	0	0	3.70	19	0	0	0	24	24	13	10	2	14	21	.240	.250	.231	7.77	5.18
Floro, Dylan	L-R	6-2	175	12-27-90	4	1	2.40	18	0	0	2	30	26	11	8	0	4	21	.230	.211	.230	6.30	1.20
Garton, Ryan	R-R	5-11	170	12-5-89	4	0	2.00	21	0	0	7	27	19	9	6	0	8	31	.190	.225	.167	10.33	2.67
Guerrieri, Taylor	R-R	6-3	195	12-1-92	1	2	1.04	12	12	0	0	52	35	7	6	0	5	45	.186	.207	.168	7.79	0.87
Hahn, Jesse	R-R	6-5	182	7-30-89	2	2	2.77	14	14	0	0	52	38	18	16	0	15	55	.199	.220	.180	9.52	2.60
Harrison, Jordan	R-L	6-1	180	4-9-91	0	1	4.00	4	0	0	1	9	7	4	4	0	3	9	.212	.000	.280	9.00	3.00
Henderson, Brandon	L-L	6-3	175	4-19-92	5	2	2.06	18	1	0	0	48	35	12	11	3	7	41	.200	.161	.218	7.69	1.31
Kendall, Ian	R-R	6-0	205	11-11-91	1	0	6.21	17	1	0	0	42	46	34	29	3	27	41	.274	.265	.280	8.79	5.79
Lopez, Reinaldo	R-R	6-2	221	4-27-91	2	1	3.00	13	5	0	0	39	36	19	13	2	11	22	.231	.219	.241	5.08	2.54
Molina, Jose	L-L	5-11	160	6-26-91	3	1	1.41	22	0	0	3	32	27	5	5	0	12	26	.220	.237	.212	7.31	3.38
Moshier, Alex	R-R	5-11	200	2-19-89	0	0	0.00	3	0	0	0	5	2	0	0	0	4	.118	.250	.000	7.20	0.00
Proctor, Marcus	R-R	6-3	170	8-21-91	6	1	3.58	22	0	0	6	33	25	15	13	3	12	32	.224	.209	.203	8.82	3.31
Quinonez, Eduar	R-R	6-3	182	8-9-89	7	3	4.04	15	5	0	0	62	58	34	28	6	21	52	.246	.306	.192	7.51	3.03
Spann, Matt	L-L	6-7	185	2-17-91	5	5	3.59	16	14	0	0	73	71	40	29	5	28	39	.255	.273	.250	4.83	3.47

Fielding

Catcher	PCT	G	PO	A	E	DP	PB
DePew	.994	42	304	27	2	4	6
Maile	1.000	33	237	25	0	0	2
Rowan	.889	5	15	1	2	1	0
Williams	1.000	3	20	1	0	0	0

First Base	PCT	G	PO	A	E	DP
DePew	—	1	0	0	0	0
Dunn	.967	8	78	9	3	5
Maile	.989	28	256	10	3	29

	PCT	G	PO	A	E	DP
Williams	.976	43	382	23	10	34

Second Base	PCT	G	PO	A	E	DP
Coyle	.959	66	115	211	14	40
Dunn	1.000	2	3	4	0	0
Gonzalez	.957	10	19	25	2	7

Third Base	PCT	G	PO	A	E	DP
Gonzalez	.892	17	6	27	4	1
Reginatto	.912	39	18	85	10	9
Shaffer	.927	24	14	37	4	2

Shortstop	PCT	G	PO	A	E	DP
Dunn	.943	51	81	167	15	41
Reginatto	.903	28	48	73	13	12

Outfield	PCT	G	PO	A	E	DP
Caminero	.973	56	107	2	3	0
Dixon	.984	38	59	3	1	0
Epperson	.913	31	41	1	4	0
Gantt	.983	63	116	2	2	0
Rickard	.988	44	84	0	1	0

PRINCETON RAYS

ROOKIE

APPALACHIAN LEAGUE

Batting	B-T	HT	WT	DOB	AVG	vLH	vRH	G	AB	R	H	2B	3B	HR	RBI	BB	HBP	SH	SF	SO	SB	CS	SLG	OBP
Alexander, John	L-L	6-5	200	4-25-93	.230	.175	.241	62	235	23	54	15	1	4	33	9	1	0	1	39	5	3	.353	.260
Antunez, Ismel	L-R	5-7	166	6-17-91	.254	.000	.281	31	71	12	18	4	0	0	5	7	4	0	0	22	8	3	.310	.354
Argo, Willie	R-R	6-1	220	10-15-89	.301	.333	.291	64	209	41	63	15	1	2	24	31	7	2	3	49	17	6	.411	.404
Duran, Daniel	R-R	6-0	195	9-8-88	.238	.143	.265	19	63	4	15	3	0	0	9	3	0	1	0	4	0	0	.286	.273
George, Darryl	R-R	6-1	213	3-14-93	.260	.238	.268	50	169	19	44	10	0	2	28	13	1	1	2	27	6	0	.355	.314
Goetzman, Granden	R-R	6-4	200	11-14-92	.298	.333	.276	12	47	10	14	5	0	1	8	4	0	0	1	7	7	1	.468	.346
Harris, James	R-R	6-1	180	8-7-93	.182	.119	.203	58	170	20	31	6	4	1	16	22	2	2	0	38	6	8	.282	.284
Hernandez, Oscar	R-R	6-0	196	7-9-93	.231	.400	.184	49	160	25	37	9	1	5	24	23	8	0	4	31	0	1	.394	.349
Martin, Brandon	R-R	5-11	185	8-24-93	.209	.264	.194	63	254	46	53	11	4	10	32	21	2	0	2	73	8	1	.402	.272
Morillo, Julian	B-R	5-11	167	12-10-91	.303	.269	.312	38	119	15	36	3	4	1	20	2	3	1	1	18	2	2	.420	.328
Nacapoy, Chad	R-R	5-7	220	7-28-89	.244	.071	.323	22	45	4	11	1	0	0	2	9	1	0	1	11	0	0	.267	.375
Narvaez, Omar	B-R	5-10	172	2-10-92	.305	.136	.333	43	151	24	46	7	1	1	16	17	2	2	1	19	4	2	.384	.349
Redman, Reid	R-R	6-0	180	11-22-88	.265	.213	.279	60	226	40	60	15	2	2	26	21	0	3	3	46	6	4	.376	.324
Soriano, Ariel	R-R	5-11	160	11-24-90	.255	.171	.277	52	200	32	51	10	3	2	28	11	0	0	2	34	19	0	.365	.291
Toles, Andrew	L-R	5-10	185	5-24-92	.281	.258	.286	51	199	31	56	13	3	7	33	12	2	0	1	36	14	5	.482	.327

Pitching	B-T	HT	WT	DOB	W	L	ERA	G	GS	CG	SV	IP	H	R	ER	HR	BB	SO	AVG	vLH	vRH	K/9	BB/9
Brandt, Kevin	R-L	6-1	195	11-24-89	2	2	2.25	12	4	0	0	36	34	9	9	3	6	43	.245	.000	.286	10.75	1.50
Bream, Dan	R-R	6-6	185	8-16-88	1	1	3.60	17	0	0	0	35	30	17	14	2	18	29	.238	.243	.236	7.46	4.63

310 · Baseball America 2013 Almanac

BaseballAmerica.com

Name	B-T	HT	WT	DOB	W	L	ERA	G	GS	CG	SV	IP	H	R	ER	HR	BB	SO	AVG	vLH	vRH	K/9	BB/9
Butler, Zach	R-R	6-3	200	7-28-89	3	0	2.20	22	0	0	7	33	27	10	8	1	12	31	.223	.227	.221	8.54	3.31
Davis, R.J.	R-R	6-3	230	10-11-89	4	0	2.63	19	0	0	0	27	21	12	8	0	14	23	.206	.267	.181	7.57	4.61
Duarte, Hugo	R-R	6-1	169	1-7-90	1	3	8.53	14	2	0	0	32	49	30	30	2	10	29	.358	.333	.371	8.24	2.84
Echarry, Eli	R-R	6-1	150	7-1-92	1	3	6.05	13	10	0	0	55	65	45	37	9	14	36	.291	.338	.270	5.89	2.29
Faria, Jacob	R-R	6-3	175	7-30-93	3	4	5.14	13	5	0	0	42	44	25	24	6	9	34	.272	.347	.239	7.29	1.93
Gabay, Willie	R-R	6-0	180	7-3-91	2	1	7.77	15	1	0	0	22	30	19	19	5	15	23	.326	.321	.328	9.41	6.14
Guerrero, Joan	L-L	6-2	170	1-22-91	1	0	5.47	14	1	0	0	25	26	19	15	3	16	19	.263	.316	.250	6.93	5.84
James, Kevin	L-L	6-4	190	10-1-90	1	1	3.03	11	11	0	0	39	40	20	13	5	12	30	.272	.273	.272	6.98	2.79
Keudell, Alex	R-R	6-3	205	2-25-90	3	4	2.28	16	6	0	3	43	35	13	11	3	11	42	.226	.304	.193	8.72	2.28
Kirsch, Chris	L-L	6-2	185	11-15-91	2	2	8.10	10	0	0	0	17	24	17	15	2	9	15	.343	.294	.358	8.10	4.86
Rodriguez, Jorge	R-R	5-11	187	12-15-91	0	0	4.15	1	1	0	0	4	2	2	1	1	3	6	.316	.375	.273	6.23	2.08
Sawyer, Nick	R-R	5-11	175	9-23-91	2	1	0.37	15	0	0	5	24	6	5	1	0	10	50	.074	.150	.049	18.49	3.70
Silvestre, Pedro	R-R	6-2	185	10-23-89	1	0	3.27	12	0	0	1	22	23	10	8	3	4	20	.280	.308	.268	8.18	1.64
Snell, Blake	L-L	6-4	180	12-4-92	5	1	2.09	11	11	1	0	47	34	12	11	4	17	53	.202	.100	.216	10.08	3.23
Suero, Bruedlin	L-L	6-4	170	2-28-90	4	3	4.20	14	13	0	0	64	73	34	30	6	12	44	.285	.381	.266	6.16	1.68
Weaver, Jon	R-R	6-3	185	5-20-90	0	6	5.85	19	3	0	2	32	39	27	21	4	16	30	.302	.290	.306	8.35	4.45

Fielding

Catcher	PCT	G	PO	A	E	DP	PB
Hernandez	.988	46	369	34	5	3	6
Nacapoy	1.000	6	31	0	0	0	2
Narvaez	.989	21	163	15	2	0	2

First Base	PCT	G	PO	A	E	DP
Alexander	.987	61	527	20	7	49
George	.986	9	63	5	1	6

Second Base	PCT	G	PO	A	E	DP
Morillo	.932	17	29	39	5	11
Redman	.980	52	78	114	4	32

	PCT	G	PO	A	E	DP
Soriano	1.000	4	9	8	0	3
Third Base	PCT	G	PO	A	E	DP
Duran	.833	19	15	40	11	6
George	.915	35	24	62	8	5
Morillo	.636	4	2	5	4	0
Redman	.900	6	6	12	2	1
Soriano	.923	13	6	30	3	0
Shortstop	PCT	G	PO	A	E	DP
Martin	.951	63	78	194	14	37
Morillo	—	1	0	0	0	0

	PCT	G	PO	A	E	DP
Soriano	.963	11	5	21	1	2
Outfield	PCT	G	PO	A	E	DP
Antunez	1.000	28	35	2	0	0
Argo	.972	56	95	8	3	1
George	1.000	2	3	0	0	0
Goetzman	1.000	12	19	1	0	0
Harris	.957	53	88	2	4	1
Morillo	1.000	3	3	0	0	0
Nacapoy	—	1	0	0	0	0
Soriano	.943	18	28	5	2	1
Toles	.971	48	97	3	3	1

GCL RAYS   ROOKIE

GULF COAST LEAGUE

Batting	B-T	HT	WT	DOB	AVG	vLH	vRH	G	AB	R	H	2B	3B	HR	RBI	BB	HBP	SH	SF	SO	SB	CS	SLG	OBP
Araiza, Jesus	R-R	5-11	185	6-19-93	.284	.364	.264	34	109	13	31	5	1	0	10	11	1	0	3	22	0	2	.349	.347
Araujo, Yoel	R-R	6-0	190	12-3-92	.286	.421	.256	30	105	9	30	6	2	1	11	6	3	1	1	35	4	3	.410	.339
Ashley, Nevin	R-R	6-1	215	8-14-84	.333	.250	.364	15	45	6	15	3	0	1	5	7	1	0	0	6	2	0	.467	.434
Beltran, Miguel	L-L	6-3	225	3-2-90	.176	.111	.196	25	74	6	13	0	0	0	6	9	2	1	0	17	0	0	.176	.279
Carter, Kes	L-L	6-2	205	3-9-91	.381	.333	.417	7	21	5	8	1	1	0	3	4	2	0	0	7	0	3	.524	.519
Correa, Leopoldo	L-R	6-0	186	12-3-91	.256	.231	.263	39	121	6	31	5	1	0	15	7	0	2	1	29	1	1	.314	.336
Dominguez, Wilmer	R-R	5-10	182	6-19-90	.275	.263	.279	25	80	2	22	1	1	0	7	1	0	0	0	17	0	0	.313	.284
Duran, Douglas	B-R	5-10	150	11-17-92	.164	.095	.180	40	110	10	18	2	0	0	8	16	0	4	1	34	4	0	.182	.268
Edwards, Spencer	R-R	6-0	170	4-7-93	.188	.179	.190	33	128	14	24	5	2	1	7	9	2	1	1	42	8	4	.281	.250
Eierman, Johnny	R-R	6-1	195	8-23-92	.231	.259	.226	46	160	16	37	10	2	0	10	14	2	5	1	32	6	4	.319	.299
Hawkins, Taylor	R-R	5-11	188	9-17-93	.182	.100	.200	16	55	5	10	2	0	0	5	2	0	2	0	24	1	0	.218	.211
Henning, Clayton	L-L	6-3	180	11-9-93	.168	.316	.138	37	113	12	19	1	0	0	7	14	1	2	2	38	1	2	.177	.262
Jackson, Bralin	R-L	6-2	183	12-2-93	.253	.225	.264	39	146	16	37	5	4	0	11	6	1	0	1	39	5	3	.342	.286
Kiermaier, Kevin	L-R	6-1	200	4-22-90	.167	.000	.500	2	6	0	1	0	0	0	0	0	0	0	0	2	0	0	.167	.167
Kline, Ben	R-R	6-3	200	12-2-88	.347	.367	.340	36	124	14	43	6	0	1	16	7	3	0	1	15	10	5	.419	.393
McChesney, Ryan	L-R	6-0	200	2-3-90	.205	.000	.225	17	44	4	9	2	0	0	3	9	0	0	1	7	0	0	.250	.333
Natera, Jiminson	R-R	6-0	180	4-10-92	.247	.152	.271	49	162	20	40	6	5	3	17	12	3	0	0	64	7	4	.401	.311
Perez, Cesar	R-R	6-1	187	11-27-90	.175	.227	.160	33	103	7	18	6	0	0	12	8	0	2	2	27	0	2	.233	.230
Quinonez, Jonathan	R-R	6-1	187	11-27-90	.250	.500	.214	8	16	4	4	0	0	0	2	1	0	0	1	1	1	0	.250	.368
Rosa, Adderly	B-R	6-0	167	7-4-91	.228	.267	.215	40	123	14	28	4	1	0	10	10	0	1	0	22	2	1	.276	.286
Rowan, Geoff	R-R	5-9	190	10-30-89	.167	—	.167	2	6	0	1	0	0	0	0	0	0	0	0	0	0	0	.167	.167
Velasquez, Isaias	R-R	5-11	155	5-7-88	.290	.167	.368	9	31	4	9	3	0	0	0	2	0	0	0	8	0	1	.387	.333

Pitching	B-T	HT	WT	DOB	W	L	ERA	G	GS	CG	SV	IP	H	R	ER	HR	BB	SO	AVG	vLH	vRH	K/9	BB/9
Andujar, Chris	R-R	6-2	180	8-24-87	0	0	0.00	2	1	0	0	5	2	0	0	0	2	3	.118	.000	.250	5.40	3.60
Armenta, Oscar	R-L	5-11	170	10-15-93	0	1	0.00	5	4	0	0	21	14	2	0	0	2	21	.184	.250	.172	8.86	0.84
Barnese, Nick	R-R	6-2	170	1-11-89	1	0	1.80	1	1	0	0	5	2	2	1	0	1	5	.105	.167	.000	9.00	1.80
Blaise, Brett	L-L	6-3	180	6-19-90	1	1	8.36	8	0	0	0	14	17	14	13	2	12	16	.321	.167	.366	10.29	7.71
Cabrera, Luis	R-R	6-2	185	8-14-90	3	3	3.30	11	7	0	0	46	44	21	17	0	11	30	.254	.250	.256	5.83	2.14
Carlson, Kris	R-R	6-3	190	10-30-89	0	0	0.00	1	0	0	1	1	0	0	0	0	0	0	.000	.000	.000	0.00	0.00
Carroll, Damion	R-R	6-3	198	1-31-94	1	0	2.33	10	2	0	0	19	13	7	5	0	19	20	.197	.160	.220	9.31	8.84
Cedeno, Carlos	R-R	6-2	187	7-19-90	0	2	3.82	12	4	0	0	33	35	20	14	2	9	28	.261	.327	.224	7.64	2.45
De La Cruz, Geisel	L-L	6-0	139	4-11-93	2	5	4.20	10	10	0	0	45	46	24	21	0	11	35	.275	.375	.252	7.00	2.20
Gannon, Nolan	R-R	6-5	195	11-3-93	2	2	3.00	11	8	0	0	27	17	12	9	2	13	29	.175	.216	.150	9.67	4.33
Gil, Isaac	R-R	6-5	230	10-8-91	4	1	2.38	12	2	0	1	34	25	11	9	0	11	29	.216	.270	.190	7.68	2.91
Goodgion, Luke	L-L	6-4	220	7-8-89	0	1	1.80	12	0	0	2	25	19	6	5	0	8	22	.211	.333	.192	7.92	2.88
Harrison, Jordan	R-L	6-1	180	4-9-91	1	2	1.52	10	5	0	0	30	28	8	5	0	6	29	.250	.313	.240	8.80	1.82
Havlicek, Stepan	R-L	6-1	160	2-25-93	3	2	2.25	11	3	0	0	36	26	13	9	1	8	28	.202	.207	.200	7.00	2.00
Linsky, Lenny	R-R	6-2	180	3-4-90	0	0	0.00	2	0	0	1	2	0	0	1	0	0	0	.222	.400	.000	3.60	0.00
Moshier, Alex	R-R	5-11	200	2-19-89	1	3	2.82	14	0	0	4	22	20	9	7	1	10	16	.253	.391	.196	6.45	4.03
Pelchy, Kyle	R-R	6-0	210	9-26-89	0	2	5.25	12	0	0	0	24	32	16	14	0	5	19	.327	.390	.281	7.13	1.88

Name	B-T	HT	WT	DOB	W	L	ERA	G	GS	CG	SV	IP	H	R	ER	HR	BB	SO	AVG	vLH	vRH	K/9	BB/9
Quist, Dayne	R-L	5-10	180	1-20-89	1	2	2.55	11	0	0	0	18	14	5	5	0	1	17	.222	.000	.255	8.66	0.51
Ramsey, Matt	R-R	5-11	205	9-24-89	2	1	1.98	11	5	0	0	14	12	4	3	0	2	9	.218	.120	.300	5.93	1.32
Rodriguez, Jorge	R-R	5-11	187	12-15-91	2	3	3.54	11	8	0	0	48	54	27	19	0	7	26	.289	.329	.263	4.84	1.30
Sawyer, Nick	R-R	5-11	175	9-23-91	1	0	0.00	3	0	0	0	5	3	0	0	0	2	6	.231	.000	.300	11.57	3.86
Torres, Alex	L-L	5-10	175	12-8-87	0	1	3.18	4	4	0	0	11	7	4	4	0	4	17	.175	.000	.184	13.50	3.18
Wilson, Jason	R-R	6-1	195	8-6-90	3	0	3.15	13	0	0	5	20	20	9	7	3	1	22	.253	.348	.214	9.90	0.45

Fielding

Catcher	PCT	G	PO	A	E	DP	PB
Araiza	.983	32	215	22	4	0	7
Ashley	.960	5	21	3	1	0	1
Dominguez	.976	14	69	12	2	0	1
Hawkins	.982	14	92	16	2	2	5
McChesney	1.000	3	18	2	0	1	1
Rowan	1.000	2	15	0	0	0	1

First Base	PCT	G	PO	A	E	DP
Beltran	.995	22	168	14	1	21
Dominguez	1.000	6	47	6	0	5
Kline	1.000	9	79	6	0	6
McChesney	.971	9	61	6	2	10
Perez	.970	19	150	10	5	13
Rosa	—	1	0	0	0	0

Second Base	PCT	G	PO	A	E	DP
Duran	.986	19	28	45	1	8
Kline	1.000	8	16	16	0	8
Rosa	.965	36	80	85	6	30

Third Base	PCT	G	PO	A	E	DP
Correa	.935	39	22	93	8	11
Kline	.917	7	6	16	2	1
Perez	.891	16	8	33	5	6
Rosa	.900	4	1	8	1	0

Shortstop	PCT	G	PO	A	E	DP
Duran	.942	22	25	56	5	13
Edwards	.917	32	47	86	12	19
Kline	1.000	9	4	13	0	1

Outfield	PCT	G	PO	A	E	DP
Araujo	.943	22	32	1	2	0
Carter	1.000	4	13	1	0	1
Dominguez	1.000	3	3	1	0	0
Eierman	.968	42	58	3	2	0
Henning	.970	34	62	2	2	0
Jackson	.949	34	69	5	4	0
Kiermaier	.000	1	0	0	1	0
Kline	.889	5	7	1	1	1
Natera	.973	44	70	3	2	2
Velasquez	1.000	5	6	0	0	0

DSL RAYS — ROOKIE

DOMINICAN SUMMER LEAGUE

Batting	B-T	HT	WT	DOB	AVG	vLH	vRH	G	AB	R	H	2B	3B	HR	RBI	BB	HBP	SH	SF	SO	SB	CS	SLG	OBP
Adolfo, Roberto	R-R	6-1	175	3-31-91	.237	.302	.212	51	156	19	37	2	0	1	14	12	6	1	0	24	6	6	.269	.316
Aguero, Ismael	R-R	6-0	185	6-19-93	.274	.306	.262	60	226	29	62	23	2	5	34	13	4	0	0	36	0	3	.460	.325
Herrera, Julio	R-R	5-9	184	10-9-92	.219	.167	.231	41	128	15	28	5	0	1	10	8	2	1	3	19	0	1	.281	.270
Infante, Jhancarlos	R-R	6-0	180	10-12-89	.250	—	.250	5	8	1	2	0	0	0	2	1	0	0	0	0	0	0	.250	.333
Jumes, Joel	L-R	6-1	192	1-24-93	.150	.184	.138	58	187	14	28	4	0	0	10	22	1	0	0	45	3	4	.171	.243
Maria, Eric	R-R	6-0	180	6-30-94	.217	.214	.217	18	60	3	13	2	0	0	6	6	0	0	0	5	0	0	.250	.288
Marte, Luis	R-R	6-3	180	2-23-91	.167	.222	.155	31	102	9	17	1	0	3	9	5	0	1	0	26	3	1	.265	.206
Mojica, Anthony	B-R	5-9	178	7-12-92	.206	.077	.236	32	68	10	14	2	0	0	7	18	2	4	3	21	6	6	.265	.374
Paulino, Enmanuel	R-R	6-1	175	11-28-93	.239	.291	.223	59	230	39	55	9	5	2	25	13	4	1	2	51	5	3	.348	.289
Pujols, Bill	R-R	5-11	160	7-19-94	.286	.214	.300	48	168	28	48	12	1	1	20	20	7	2	1	23	6	7	.387	.383
Ramirez, Rolman	R-R	6-0	174	1-9-92	.191	.087	.225	37	94	15	18	0	2	0	3	9	5	1	0	36	5	2	.234	.296
Rojas, Jose	R-R	6-0	175	3-11-93	.256	.121	.304	61	219	28	56	16	3	2	35	32	1	1	0	36	0	0	.384	.348
Rosario, Francisco	R-R	6-1	175	1-26-91	.045	.000	.053	11	22	0	1	0	0	0	0	2	0	0	0	7	0	0	.045	.125
Simon, Alexander	B-R	6-2	182	9-8-94	.328	.403	.300	66	247	42	81	16	6	5	46	32	2	1	1	55	12	7	.502	.408
Tapia, Juan	B-R	6-0	156	3-1-92	.215	.154	.231	20	65	9	14	0	1	0	5	5	3	1	0	23	1	1	.246	.301
Toribio, Cristian	R-R	5-11	170	9-13-94	.284	.302	.277	55	208	34	59	10	3	1	25	18	4	2	4	43	13	3	.375	.346
Torres, Elias	R-R	6-1	176	2-22-92	.273	.333	.256	44	154	26	42	7	0	3	24	19	2	2	4	24	9	9	.377	.352

Pitching	B-T	HT	WT	DOB	W	L	ERA	G	GS	CG	SV	IP	H	R	ER	HR	BB	SO	AVG	vLH	vRH	K/9	BB/9
Almonte, Yomelbin	R-R	6-0	202	2-22-93	1	2	5.67	17	3	0	0	33	24	26	21	1	26	21	.209	.233	.200	5.67	7.02
Alonzo, Jose	R-R	6-4	191	2-24-93	2	6	5.92	14	14	0	0	62	73	52	41	6	23	29	.299	.300	.299	4.19	3.32
Arguila, Nelson	R-R	6-0	180	9-4-88	2	3	3.89	19	0	0	4	39	29	22	17	3	35	34	.201	.074	.231	7.78	8.01
Cano, Joselito	L-L	6-5	190	9-16-92	1	4	2.53	18	10	0	1	53	41	19	15	1	25	47	.209	.167	.212	7.93	4.22
Castillo, Eddy	L-L	6-1	165	1-2-94	3	1	8.57	13	0	0	0	21	26	26	20	0	23	9	.310	.400	.304	3.86	9.86
Castillo, Erodis	R-R	6-1	173	11-29-93	0	1	6.62	14	0	0	0	18	15	15	13	0	8	9	.259	.400	.209	4.58	14.26
Cordova, Rafael	R-R	6-2	175	11-16-94	1	0	1.00	8	0	0	0	9	8	5	1	0	2	5	.222	.333	.200	5.00	2.00
Crisostomo, Christopher	L-L	6-2	177	3-8-94	1	3	3.66	14	14	0	0	52	42	31	21	2	24	34	.220	.067	.233	5.92	4.18
De La Cruz, Dionicio	L-L	6-1	170	4-1-92	2	3	4.89	20	0	0	1	35	46	22	19	1	14	22	.329	.286	.331	5.66	3.60
De La Cruz, Geisel	L-L	6-0	139	4-11-93	0	2	2.33	4	4	0	0	19	12	8	5	0	6	16	.176	.000	.194	7.45	2.79
Feliz, Junior	R-R	6-0	160	1-17-94	0	1	4.20	8	2	0	0	15	11	9	7	0	10	8	.193	.000	.262	4.80	6.00
Garcia, Carlos	R-R	6-2	218	12-1-90	2	1	2.89	19	0	0	2	37	28	21	12	3	16	17	.197	.103	.221	4.10	3.86
Gracia, Ariel	L-L	5-11	173	9-17-94	2	4	4.38	15	9	0	0	51	53	30	25	1	16	23	.264	.250	.265	4.03	2.81
Gutierrez, Danilo	R-R	6-5	156	6-2-91	0	1	10.80	13	0	0	0	14	18	14	11	1	13	4	.286	.286	.286	3.09	10.03
Hernandez, Wilmer	R-R	6-3	175	8-29-91	4	4	4.20	14	14	0	0	71	73	43	33	6	7	53	.258	.175	.279	6.75	0.89
Mercedes, Luis	L-L	5-11	170	3-30-92	2	3	5.01	21	0	0	1	32	43	23	18	1	13	23	.328	.083	.353	6.40	3.62
Ortiz, Roquely	R-R	5-11	179	1-21-94	1	0	10.50	4	0	0	0	6	7	9	7	0	6	2	.280	.000	.292	3.00	9.00
Ortiz, Willy	R-R	6-1	174	7-20-95	0	0	9.00	1	0	0	0	1	2	1	1	0	0	0	.400	—	.400	0.00	0.00
Paredes, Ruben	R-R	6-1	180	9-21-93	4	2	2.14	19	0	0	4	42	34	19	10	3	12	28	.221	.129	.244	6.00	2.57
Ruiz, Luis	R-R	6-0	170	10-8-89	0	1	6.35	4	0	0	0	6	13	8	4	0	2	4	.433	.200	.480	6.35	3.18

Fielding

Catcher	PCT	G	PO	A	E	DP	PB
Herrera	.975	34	156	37	5	3	12
Infante	.857	14	9	3	2	0	0
Maria	.928	14	66	11	6	2	10
Rojas	.945	29	152	37	11	4	19
Rosario	1.000	1	2	0	0	0	1

First Base	PCT	G	PO	A	E	DP
Aguero	.993	31	288	8	2	22
Rojas	.976	26	227	13	6	15
Rosario	1.000	10	59	2	0	7
Simon	1.000	12	103	6	0	8

Second Base	PCT	G	PO	A	E	DP
Mojica	.810	3	10	7	4	2
Paulino	.958	25	46	46	4	13
Pujols	.953	30	64	79	7	20
Tapia	1.000	2	4	2	0	1
Toribio	.939	17	37	40	5	7

Third Base	PCT	G	PO	A	E	DP
Paulino	1.000	5	3	7	0	0
Pujols	.934	16	14	8	1	0
Simon	.849	53	46	134	32	8
Tapia	.875	3	1	6	1	0

Shortstop	PCT	G	PO	A	E	DP
Paulino	.962	25	38	87	5	14
Pujols	.960	6	8	16	1	4
Tapia	.870	10	7	33	6	4
Toribio	.933	34	64	118	13	18

Outfield	PCT	G	PO	A	E	DP
Adolfo	.968	47	86	5	3	1
Jumes	.972	58	99	5	3	2
Marte	.942	31	47	2	3	2
Mojica	.971	23	30	3	1	2
Ramirez	.915	32	51	3	5	2
Tapia	1.000	1	1	1	0	0
Torres	.972	43	97	7	3	2

VSL RAYS

ROOKIE

VENEZUELAN SUMMER LEAGUE

Batting	B-T	HT	WT	DOB	AVG	vLH	vRH	G	AB	R	H	2B	3B	HR	RBI	BB	HBP	SH	SF	SO	SB	CS	SLG	OBP
Aldazoro, Gianfranco	R-R	6-1	205	4-5-94	.241	.185	.259	34	112	8	27	3	1	3	16	12	3	0	2	28	3	2	.366	.326
Auciello, Kreiber	R-R	5-10	176	2-23-95	.143	.000	.179	19	49	4	7	1	0	0	1	4	0	0	0	14	1	0	.163	.208
Barrios, Kevin	R-R	6-1	190	2-28-95	.228	.176	.241	44	167	13	38	8	0	4	28	7	2	0	2	31	2	2	.347	.264
Colina, David	R-R	6-1	173	3-20-94	.248	.200	.259	44	165	17	41	3	1	3	23	5	5	0	2	22	7	3	.333	.288
Hernandez, Cesar	R-R	6-0	174	4-24-95	.194	.167	.200	42	144	17	28	4	0	5	10	5	5	0	0	50	0	2	.326	.247
Hernandez, Jose	B-R	6-0	191	11-9-92	.252	.375	.235	34	131	10	33	5	0	0	13	5	4	1	0	18	4	1	.290	.300
Maestre, Roni	R-R	6-3	170	4-22-95	.265	.259	.266	49	166	18	44	2	0	0	14	12	3	0	3	25	12	6	.277	.321
Paez, Jose	B-R	6-0	165	8-11-93	.364	.344	.367	61	250	41	91	13	9	4	29	24	5	0	0	41	12	9	.536	.430
Reyes, Keiverson	R-R	5-9	152	2-7-91	.264	.174	.280	46	148	25	39	12	2	5	19	7	5	0	1	22	5	1	.473	.317
Rivero, Nohisglin	R-R	6-0	180	1-26-90	.306	.000	.338	42	147	30	45	2	3	3	21	7	2	0	2	26	12	3	.422	.342
Suarez, Norly	R-R	5-11	156	9-17-93	.251	.320	.239	50	167	21	42	6	1	1	14	13	6	0	0	34	3	6	.317	.328
Teran, Jhonnathan	R-R	5-10	161	12-13-94	.242	.138	.261	57	186	13	45	8	0	1	7	11	3	2	0	20	3	4	.301	.295
Vaamonde, Carlos	R-R	6-1	195	11-21-94	.208	.067	.226	39	130	10	27	4	0	0	8	10	1	1	1	40	5	3	.238	.268
Vasquez, Erick	R-R	6-1	186	9-27-93	.267	.231	.273	67	255	40	68	13	2	8	25	26	6	0	1	80	24	9	.427	.347

Pitching	B-T	HT	WT	DOB	W	L	ERA	G	GS	CG	SV	IP	H	R	ER	HR	BB	SO	AVG	vLH	vRH	K/9	BB/9
Alvarado, Jose	L-L	6-0	180	5-21-95	2	3	3.81	12	0	0	0	26	20	14	11	0	17	20	.211	.267	.200	6.92	5.88
Alvarez, Freddy	R-R	6-1	170	9-10-93	3	4	4.91	15	13	0	0	51	57	32	28	6	20	31	.289	.325	.263	5.44	3.51
Bastardo, Armando	R-R	6-0	172	7-11-94	1	1	3.57	13	0	0	2	35	39	20	14	2	8	23	.279	.277	.280	5.86	2.04
Casanas, Alberto	R-R	6-2	158	11-27-93	0	0	4.91	7	1	0	0	15	11	9	8	3	5	2	.200	.278	.162	1.23	3.07
Cazorla, Marvin	R-R	6-2	190	10-14-93	1	4	5.50	9	9	0	0	38	45	30	23	4	13	18	.296	.333	.276	4.30	3.11
Centeno, Henry	R-R	6-2	174	8-24-94	0	5	4.31	13	13	0	0	48	61	34	23	3	23	33	.308	.284	.323	6.19	4.31
Duarte, Jorman	R-R	6-2	190	11-16-94	1	0	1.93	5	1	0	0	9	9	2	2	1	2	4	.257	.333	.231	3.86	1.93
Fernandez, Mario	R-R	6-0	206	9-7-93	0	6	4.75	14	12	0	0	61	72	36	32	5	18	36	.294	.299	.290	5.34	2.67
Guzman, Luis	R-R	6-3	222	7-21-91	0	0	5.00	9	0	0	0	18	14	15	10	1	18	6	.222	.240	.211	3.00	9.00
Hurtado, Jhefferson	R-R	6-0	181	12-19-91	1	5	6.41	11	5	0	0	27	34	26	19	3	24	11	.324	.342	.313	3.71	8.10
Lopez, Hector	R-R	6-4	192	6-15-95	0	0	7.27	13	0	0	0	17	16	16	14	2	21	14	.250	.190	.279	7.27	10.90
Marquez, German	R-R	6-1	184	2-22-95	0	2	6.82	15	6	0	0	34	43	32	26	4	20	29	.307	.283	.319	7.60	5.24
Marval, Johan	R-R	6-1	195	11-24-93	2	3	5.66	17	0	0	1	35	43	28	22	5	8	24	.299	.352	.267	6.17	2.06
Medina, Eduardo	R-R	6-0	170	2-24-92	0	2	3.76	19	0	0	3	26	31	12	11	0	9	32	.298	.333	.271	10.94	3.08
Molina, Benjamin	L-L	6-0	144	11-18-94	2	4	3.38	13	2	0	0	37	41	21	14	5	8	23	.268	.250	.270	5.54	1.93
Orasmo, Carlos	L-L	5-9	154	12-13-91	2	2	3.35	14	0	0	0	43	38	16	16	5	10	39	.250	.313	.243	8.16	2.09
Rodriguez, Abrahan	R-R	6-2	182	4-20-95	1	5	5.59	14	7	0	0	48	67	37	30	3	13	23	.332	.342	.325	4.28	2.42
Rosal, Gregory	R-R	6-1	207	9-24-92	3	5	4.24	20	0	0	3	40	44	25	19	2	17	24	.267	.246	.280	5.36	3.79
Sanchez, Yerwin	R-R	6-1	258	5-5-93	0	1	22.50	4	1	0	0	4	5	10	10	0	8	3	.294	.125	.444	6.75	18.00
Wilches, Luis	L-L	6-1	200	10-1-91	0	0	11.81	5	1	0	0	5	16	12	7	2	1	2	.485	.400	.500	3.38	1.69

Fielding

Catcher	PCT	G	PO	A	E	DP	PB
Aldazoro	.981	31	174	33	4	0	9
Auciello	.988	15	72	13	1	0	4
Barrios	1.000	11	47	11	0	0	5
Rivero	.979	21	122	19	3	1	1

First Base	PCT	G	PO	A	E	DP
Colina	1.000	4	33	3	0	4
Hernandez	.977	21	160	10	4	13
Januario	.979	40	362	13	8	23
Rivero	1.000	10	95	7	0	6

Second Base	PCT	G	PO	A	E	DP
Hernandez	.960	4	11	13	1	4
Reyes	.970	15	30	35	2	10
Suarez	.979	47	94	140	5	18
Teran	1.000	11	22	23	0	6

Third Base	PCT	G	PO	A	E	DP
Colina	.909	36	35	105	14	13
Reyes	.876	25	28	50	11	6
Rivero	.842	10	7	25	6	1
Teran	.909	6	5	15	2	1

Shortstop	PCT	G	PO	A	E	DP
Hernandez	.877	29	39	82	17	11
Reyes	.850	4	6	11	3	0
Suarez	.667	2	1	3	2	0
Teran	.953	41	63	99	8	19

Outfield	PCT	G	PO	A	E	DP
Hernandez	.923	14	22	2	2	0
Maestre	.932	45	77	5	6	0
Paez	.972	57	135	5	4	2
Reyes	.833	3	5	0	1	0
Vaamonde	.914	39	50	3	5	1
Vasquez	.941	63	121	6	8	1

TAMPA BAY RAYS

Texas Rangers

SEASON IN A SENTENCE: The Rangers looked unstoppable in the first half, going 50-29 (.633) through June—and so did outfielder Josh Hamilton, who hit .319/.385/.652 with 25 homers—but a disappointing second half for both parties left Texas well short of its third straight American League pennant.

HIGH POINT: The Rangers punctuated a stellar first half with a best-in-baseball eight all-stars in Kansas City, including starters Adrian Beltre, Hamilton and Mike Napoli. Meanwhile, shortstop Jurickson Profar (solo home run) and third baseman Mike Olt (RBI double) shined in the Futures Game.

LOW POINT: The Rangers led the Athletics by five games with nine to play, but they lost seven of those games. Hamilton misplayed a routine flyball in center field in Game No. 162 that helped key the A's to an AL West-clinching 12-5 victory. The Rangers found themselves in the AL Wild Card Game with the Orioles, and a quiet 5-1 loss brought their season to a sudden end.

NOTABLE ROOKIES: Profar and Olt, the organization's top two prospects, made late-summer cameos, but a pair of pitchers made the most impact in Arlington. Righthander Yu Darvish lived up to his $60 million deal, going 16-9, 3.90 in 29 starts and ranking second in the majors with 10.4 strikeouts per nine innings. Lefty reliever Robbie Ross made the team with a strong spring training, and he held lefties to a .225 average while leading all rookie relievers with a 65 percent groundball rate. Righty Justin Grimm and lefty Martin Perez picked up spot starts, while righthanders Wilmer Font and Tanner Scheppers put in bullpen time.

KEY TRANSACTIONS: Texas signed Darvish in January after winning his negotiating rights with a $51.7 million posting fee. At the trade deadline the Rangers dealt from prospect depth—notably, third baseman Christian Villanueva and righty Kyle Hendricks—to acquire righthander Ryan Dempster and catcher Geovany Soto from the Cubs in separate deals. The former went 7-3, 5.09 in 12 starts, while the latter hit .196/.253/.338 in 148 at-bats.

DOWN ON THE FARM: Rangers domestic affiliates finished with a winning record for a third consecutive season, while Double-A Frisco, led by Profar and Olt, made the playoffs for the second year in a row only to lose to Springfield in the Texas League championship series.

OPENING DAY PAYROLL: $120.5 (6th)

PLAYERS OF THE YEAR

MAJOR LEAGUE	MINOR LEAGUE
Adrian Beltre	**Jurickson Profar**
3b	ss
.321/.359/.561	(Double-A)
36 HR, 102 RBIs	.281/.368/.452
4th career Gold Glove	Youngest in TL

ORGANIZATION LEADERS

BATTING		*Minimum 250 AB
MAJORS		
* AVG	Adrian Beltre	.321
* OPS	Josh Hamilton	.931
HR	Josh Hamilton	43
RBI	Josh Hamilton	128
MINORS		
* AVG	Julio Borbon, Round Rock	.304
* OBP	Drew Robinson, Hickory	.409
* SLG	Mike Olt, Frisco	.579
R	Joey Butler, Round Rock	93
H	Julio Borbon, Round Rock	162
TB	Brad Nelson, Round Rock	245
2B	Brett Nicholas, Myrtle Beach	33
3B	Engel Beltre, Frisco	17
HR	Mike Olt, Frisco	28
RBI	Mike Olt, Frisco	82
BB	Drew Robinson, Hickory	86
SO	Jordan Akins, Hickory	162
SB	Engel Beltre, Frisco	36

PITCHING		#Minimum 75 IP
MAJORS		
W	Matt Harrison	18
# ERA	Matt Harrison	3.29
SO	Yu Darvish	221
SV	Joe Nathan	37
MINORS		
W	Barret Loux, Frisco	14
L	Zach Jackson, Round Rock	13
	Neil Ramirez, Round Rock/Frisco	13
# ERA	Cody Buckel, Myrtle Beach/Frisco	2.49
G	Joe Ortiz, Frisco/Round Rock	51
GS	Neil Ramirez, Round Rock/Frisco	27
	Greg Reynolds, Round Rock	27
SV	Ben Rowen, Myrtle Beach	19
IP	Greg Reynolds, Round Rock	163
BB	Luke Jackson, Hickory/Myrtle Beach	65
SO	Cody Buckel, Myrtle Beach/Frisco	159
# AVG	Cody Buckel, Myrtle Beach/Frisco	.206

General Manager: Jon Daniels. **Farm Director:** Tim Purpura. **Scouting Director:** Kip Fagg.

Class	Team	League	W	L	PCT	Finish	Manager
Majors	Texas Rangers	American	93	69	.574	t-3rd (14)	Ron Washington
Triple-A	Round Rock Express	Pacific Coast	69	75	.479	11th (16)	Bobby Jones
Double-A	Frisco RoughRiders	Texas	80	60	.571	2nd (8)	Steve Buechele
High A	Myrtle Beach Pelicans	Carolina	74	65	.532	2nd (8)	Jason Wood
Low A	Hickory Crawdads	South Atlantic	74	65	.532	5th (14)	Bill Richardson
Short-season	Spokane Indians	Northwest	28	48	.368	8th (8)	Tim Hulett
Rookie	AZL Rangers	Arizona	34	22	.607	4th (13)	Corey Ragsdale
Overall 2012 Minor League Record			359	335	.517	9th (30)	

ORGANIZATION STATISTICS

TEXAS RANGERS

AMERICAN LEAGUE

Batting	B-T	HT	WT	DOB	AVG	vLH	vRH	G	AB	R	H	2B	3B	HR	RBI	BB	HBP	SH	SF	SO	SB	CS	SLG	OBP
Andrus, Elvis	R-R	6-0	200	8-26-88	.286	.265	.294	158	629	85	180	31	9	3	62	57	5	17	3	96	21	10	.378	.349
Beltre, Adrian	R-R	5-11	220	4-7-79	.321	.269	.339	156	604	95	194	33	2	36	102	36	5	0	9	82	1	0	.561	.359
Cruz, Nelson	R-R	6-2	240	7-1-80	.260	.309	.244	159	585	86	152	45	0	24	90	48	5	0	4	140	8	4	.460	.319
Gentry, Craig	R-R	6-2	190	11-29-83	.304	.343	.277	121	240	31	73	12	3	1	26	14	10	5	0	41	13	7	.392	.367
Gonzalez, Alberto	R-R	5-10	195	4-18-83	.241	.227	.250	24	54	7	13	2	1	0	4	0	0	1	0	9	0	0	.315	.241
Hamilton, Josh	L-L	6-4	240	5-21-81	.285	.291	.282	148	562	103	160	31	2	43	128	60	5	0	9	162	7	4	.577	.354
Hernandez, Luis	B-R	5-10	190	6-26-84	.000	—	.000	2	2	0	0	0	0	0	0	0	0	0	0	0	0	0	.000	.000
Kinsler, Ian	R-T	6-0	200	6-22-82	.256	.350	.226	157	655	105	168	42	5	19	72	60	10	1	5	90	21	9	.423	.326
Martin, Leonys	L-R	6-2	190	3-6-88	.174	.125	.184	24	46	6	8	5	2	0	6	4	0	1	1	12	3	0	.370	.235
Martinez, Luis	R-R	6-0	210	4-3-85	.111	.000	.125	10	18	1	2	0	0	0	0	1	0	0	0	4	0	0	.111	.158
Moreland, Mitch	L-L	6-2	230	9-6-85	.275	.239	.281	114	327	41	90	18	0	15	50	23	1	2	4	71	1	1	.468	.321
Murphy, David	L-L	6-4	205	10-18-81	.304	.347	.296	147	457	65	139	29	3	15	61	54	4	0	4	74	10	5	.479	.380
Napoli, Mike	R-R	6-0	215	10-31-81	.227	.179	.250	108	352	53	80	9	2	24	56	56	7	0	2	125	1	0	.469	.343
Olt, Mike	R-R	6-2	210	8-27-88	.152	.176	.125	16	33	2	5	1	0	0	5	5	0	0	2	13	1	1	.182	.250
Profar, Jurickson	B-R	6-0	165	2-20-93	.176	.000	.231	9	17	2	3	2	0	1	2	0	0	0	0	4	0	0	.471	.176
Snyder, Brandon	R-R	6-2	215	11-23-86	.277	.318	.190	40	65	11	18	2	0	3	9	3	0	1	0	26	0	0	.446	.309
Soto, Geovany	R-R	6-1	220	1-20-83	.196	.243	.180	47	148	19	29	6	0	5	25	11	1	2	2	41	1	0	.338	.253
Torrealba, Yorvit	R-R	5-11	200	7-19-78	.236	.197	.267	49	161	16	38	8	0	3	12	14	2	3	2	31	1	1	.342	.302
2-team total (10 Toronto)					.233	—	—	59	189	19	44	8	0	4	14	16	2	3	2	38	1	1	.339	.297
Young, Michael	R-R	6-1	200	10-19-76	.277	.333	.257	156	611	79	169	27	3	8	67	33	1	0	6	70	2	2	.370	.312

Pitching	B-T	HT	WT	DOB	W	L	ERA	G	GS	CG	SV	IP	H	R	ER	HR	BB	SO	AVG	vLH	vRH	K/9	BB/9
Adams, Mike	R-R	6-5	195	7-29-78	5	3	3.27	61	0	0	1	52	56	21	19	4	17	45	.269	.290	.248	7.74	2.92
Darvish, Yu	R-R	6-5	215	8-16-86	16	9	3.90	29	29	0	0	191	156	89	83	14	89	221	.220	.231	.207	10.40	4.19
Dempster, Ryan	R-R	6-2	215	5-3-77	7	3	5.09	12	12	0	0	69	74	43	39	10	25	70	.276	.242	.327	9.13	3.26
Feldman, Scott	L-R	6-6	230	2-7-83	6	11	5.09	29	21	0	0	124	139	79	70	14	32	96	.279	.276	.283	6.99	2.33
Feliz, Neftali	R-R	6-3	215	5-2-88	3	1	3.16	8	7	1	0	43	28	15	15	5	23	37	.187	.173	.203	7.80	4.85
Font, Wilmer	R-R	6-4	210	5-24-90	0	0	9.00	3	0	0	0	2	0	2	2	0	4	1	.000	.000	.000	4.50	18.00
Grimm, Justin	R-R	6-3	195	8-16-88	1	1	9.00	5	2	0	0	14	22	14	14	1	3	13	.367	.406	.321	8.36	1.93
Harrison, Matt	L-L	6-4	240	9-16-85	18	11	3.29	32	32	4	0	213	210	82	78	22	59	133	.258	.209	.276	5.61	2.49
Holland, Derek	B-L	6-2	195	10-9-86	12	7	4.67	29	27	0	0	175	162	100	91	32	52	145	.243	.243	.243	7.44	2.67
Kirkman, Michael	L-L	6-4	195	9-18-86	1	2	3.82	28	0	0	0	35	24	16	15	5	17	38	.182	.216	.160	9.68	4.33
Lewis, Colby	R-R	6-4	230	8-2-79	6	6	3.43	16	16	2	0	105	99	48	40	16	14	93	.245	.252	.236	7.97	1.20
Lowe, Mark	L-R	6-3	210	6-7-83	0	2	3.43	36	0	0	0	39	35	15	15	5	13	28	.240	.239	.240	6.41	2.97
Nathan, Joe	R-R	6-4	225	11-22-74	3	5	2.80	66	0	0	37	64	55	23	20	7	13	78	.231	.232	.229	10.91	1.82
Ogando, Alexi	R-R	6-4	195	10-5-83	2	0	3.27	58	1	0	3	66	49	26	24	9	17	66	.203	.234	.179	9.00	2.32
Oswalt, Roy	R-R	6-0	190	8-29-77	4	3	5.80	17	9	0	0	59	79	41	38	11	11	59	.320	.306	.331	9.00	1.68
Perez, Martin	L-L	6-0	180	4-4-91	1	4	5.45	12	6	0	0	38	47	26	23	3	15	25	.297	.240	.324	5.92	3.55
Ross, Robbie	L-L	5-11	185	6-24-89	6	0	2.22	58	0	0	0	65	55	21	16	3	23	47	.232	.225	.237	6.51	3.18
Scheppers, Tanner	R-R	6-4	220	1-17-87	1	1	4.45	39	0	0	1	32	47	18	16	6	9	30	.343	.302	.369	8.35	2.51
Tateyama, Yoshinori	R-R	5-10	165	12-26-75	1	0	9.00	14	0	0	0	17	18	19	17	4	6	18	.257	.300	.225	9.53	3.18
Uehara, Koji	R-R	6-1	190	4-3-75	0	0	1.75	37	0	0	1	36	20	7	7	4	3	43	.160	.188	.125	10.75	0.75

Fielding

Catcher	PCT	G	PO	A	E	DP	PB
Martinez	1.000	10	54	1	0	0	0
Napoli	.993	72	511	37	4	1	8
Snyder	1.000	1	0	0	0		0
Soto	.997	44	358	12	1	1	1
Torrealba	.995	49	377	18	2	1	4

First Base	PCT	G	PO	A	E	DP
Moreland	.996	95	691	57	3	68

	PCT	G	PO	A	E	DP
Napoli	.984	28	174	15	3	13
Olt	.981	8	46	6	1	2
Snyder	1.000	11	67	6	0	5
Young	.995	41	358	24	2	37

Second Base	PCT	G	PO	A	E	DP
Gonzalez	1.000	5	4	7	0	2
Kinsler	.970	144	203	386	18	81
Profar	1.000	5	3	5	0	1

	PCT	G	PO	A	E	DP
Young	.965	16	24	31	2	8

Third Base	PCT	G	PO	A	E	DP
Beltre	.974	129	95	209	8	23
Gonzalez	1.000	8	4	11	0	2
Hernandez	—	1	0	0	0	0
Kinsler	—	1	0	0	0	0
Olt	.889	5	0	8	1	0
Snyder	1.000	7	0	1	0	0

	PCT	G	PO	A	E	DP
Young	.966	25	18	38	2	3
Shortstop	**PCT**	**G**	**PO**	**A**	**E**	**DP**
Andrus	.976	153	233	414	16	91
Gonzalez	.923	9	7	17	2	2
Hernandez	1.000	1	1	2	0	0
Profar	1.000	3	0	3	0	0

	PCT	G	PO	A	E	DP
Young	1.000	4	6	6	0	0
Outfield	**PCT**	**G**	**PO**	**A**	**E**	**DP**
Cruz	.987	151	288	9	4	2
Gentry	1.000	116	190	7	0	2
Hamilton	.975	138	273	5	7	2
Martin	1.000	17	39	1	0	1

	PCT	G	PO	A	E	DP
Moreland	1.000	3	3	0	0	0
Murphy	.995	133	197	4	1	2
Olt	.750	2	3	0	1	0
Snyder	1.000	10	10	0	0	0

ROUND ROCK EXPRESS   *TRIPLE-A*

PACIFIC COAST LEAGUE

Batting	B-T	HT	WT	DOB	AVG	vLH	vRH	G	AB	R	H	2B	3B	HR	RBI	BB	HBP	SH	SF	SO	SB	CS	SLG	OBP
Bianucci, Mike	R-R	6-1	225	6-26-86	.268	.319	.248	84	325	43	87	14	0	14	51	17	7	0	2	79	2	1	.440	.316
Borbon, Julio	L-L	6-0	195	2-20-86	.304	.305	.304	126	533	78	162	23	8	10	56	37	3	6	5	69	20	8	.433	.349
Brown, Dusty	R-R	6-0	195	6-19-82	.220	.214	.222	47	141	18	31	10	0	5	20	30	1	0	3	35	0	0	.397	.354
Butler, Joey	R-R	6-2	210	3-12-86	.290	.243	.311	137	493	93	143	28	1	20	78	79	7	0	5	128	6	4	.473	.392
Diaz, Robinzon	R-R	5-11	215	9-19-83	.320	.500	.263	7	25	3	8	2	0	0	2	1	0	0	0	1	0	0	.400	.346
2-team total (46 Salt Lake)					.290	—		53	183	28	53	12	1	4	33	6	1	1	1	0	2	1	.432	.314
Gonzalez, Alberto	R-R	5-10	195	4-18-83	.314	.636	.225	14	51	5	16	2	0	2	6	0	1	1	0	11	0	0	.471	.327
Hernandez, Luis	R-R	5-10	190	6-26-84	.262	.244	.270	129	519	64	136	23	6	8	70	30	5	8	10	80	9	3	.376	.303
Hill, Koyie	B-R	6-1	210	3-9-79	.236	.273	.227	15	55	4	13	1	0	1	3	4	1	0	0	16	0	0	.309	.300
Kata, Matt	B-R	6-1	185	3-14-78	.284	.255	.284	109	412	57	113	20	3	9	62	20	14	3	2	60	4	1	.403	.328
Majewski, Val	L-L	6-2	220	6-19-81	.316	.000	.400	6	19	3	6	4	0	0	5	2	0	0	0	2	0	0	.526	.381
Martin, Leonys	L-R	6-2	190	3-6-88	.359	.289	.394	55	231	48	83	18	2	12	42	24	2	2	1	39	10	9	.610	.422
Martinez, Luis	R-R	6-0	210	4-3-85	.270	.258	.275	65	215	27	58	15	2	2	22	26	2	1	3	45	0	0	.386	.350
Mendonca, Tommy	L-R	6-1	200	4-12-88	.208	.208	.208	63	231	27	48	7	0	7	31	9	5	2	4	84	0	0	.329	.249
Miclat, Greg	B-R	5-8	180	7-23-87	.275	.333	.243	37	109	17	30	10	0	1	13	12	1	6	1	28	6	2	.394	.350
Moreland, Mitch	L-L	6-2	230	9-6-85	.167	.167	—	2	6	0	1	0	0	0	0	0	0	0	0	2	0	0	.167	.167
Nelson, Brad	R-L	6-2	260	12-23-82	.279	.221	.305	132	502	85	140	31	1	24	81	70	1	0	6	123	2	1	.488	.364
Rodriguez, Guilder	B-R	6-0	160	7-24-83	.259	.188	.286	19	58	5	15	0	0	0	8	8	0	2	2	7	1	2	.259	.338
Sarmiento, Elio	R-R	5-11	200	6-20-86	.200	.226	.186	27	90	9	18	4	0	1	12	7	0	0	0	29	0	0	.278	.258
Snyder, Brandon	R-R	6-2	215	11-23-86	.253	.211	.265	23	87	12	22	7	0	2	9	4	0	1	0	30	0	0	.402	.286
Solarte, Yangervis	B-R	5-11	195	7-7-87	.288	.302	.281	130	518	69	149	28	0	11	54	41	3	0	6	44	3	1	.405	.340
Spilborghs, Ryan	R-R	6-1	200	9-5-79	.295	.252	.312	103	383	52	113	24	2	8	56	38	6	2	7	85	7	2	.431	.362

Pitching	B-T	HT	WT	DOB	W	L	ERA	G	GS	CG	SV	IP	H	R	ER	HR	BB	SO	AVG	vLH	vRH	K/9	BB/9
Bell, Chad	R-L	6-3	200	2-28-89	5	5	4.15	14	14	0	0	80	84	39	37	5	37	58	.274	.294	.263	6.50	4.15
Castillo, Fabio	R-R	6-1	235	2-19-89	2	0	4.82	14	0	0	0	19	17	10	10	2	14	13	.250	.250	.250	6.27	6.75
Cotts, Neal	L-L	6-1	200	3-25-80	2	1	4.55	25	0	0	3	32	32	16	16	2	15	41	.262	.275	.254	11.65	4.26
Eyre, Willie	R-R	6-0	235	7-21-78	1	2	4.09	24	0	0	1	33	29	20	15	2	8	32	.234	.282	.212	8.73	2.18
Feliz, Neftali	R-R	6-3	215	5-2-88	0	1	1.93	2	2	0	0	5	4	4	1	0	3	4	.211	.364	.000	7.71	5.79
Gaub, John	R-L	6-2	210	4-28-85	0	0	0.00	5	0	0	0	4	3	0	0	0	2	4	.200	.167	.222	8.31	4.15
2-team total (33 Memphis)					0	3	5.89	38	0	0	1	37	43	24	24	5	15	36	—	—		8.84	3.68
Green, Sean	R-R	6-6	230	4-20-79	2	2	5.60	19	0	0	0	27	35	20	17	1	23	25	.324	.431	.200	8.23	7.57
Grimm, Justin	R-R	6-3	195	8-16-88	2	3	4.59	9	8	0	0	51	53	27	26	2	16	30	.273	.265	.283	5.29	2.82
Hamburger, Mark	R-R	6-4	195	2-5-87	0	2	6.55	21	3	0	2	45	66	33	33	7	21	37	.353	.374	.325	7.35	4.17
3-team total (17 Oklahoma City, 5 Tucson)					1	5	6.20	43	4	0	2	78	104	57	54	11	36	63	—	—		7.24	4.14
Hankins, Derek	R-R	6-4	195	7-1-83	6	7	4.99	35	10	0	0	83	101	47	46	11	29	50	.301	.273	.328	5.42	3.14
Heilman, Aaron	R-R	6-5	230	11-12-78	2	1	4.02	34	0	0	8	47	45	23	21	4	16	43	.257	.207	.313	8.23	3.06
Holland, Derek	B-L	6-2	195	10-9-86	0	2	6.00	2	2	0	0	9	11	6	6	4	2	5	.324	.273	.348	5.00	2.00
Jackson, Zach	L-L	6-5	235	5-13-83	7	13	5.17	27	25	0	0	158	187	103	91	18	62	75	.303	.271	.319	4.26	3.52
Kirkman, Michael	L-L	6-4	195	9-18-86	5	1	5.25	15	8	0	0	48	47	29	28	5	31	48	.266	.267	.265	9.00	5.81
Lowe, Mark	L-R	6-3	210	6-11-83	0	0	0.00	2	0	0	0	2	0	0	0	0	0	4	.000		.000	18.00	0.00
Ogando, Alexi	R-R	6-4	195	10-5-83	0	0	0.00	2	1	0	0	3	1	0	0	0	0	5	.100	.000	.333	15.00	0.00
Ortiz, Joseph	L-L	5-7	175	8-13-90	1	1	1.97	24	0	0	2	32	31	7	7	6	3	23	.254	.196	.303	6.47	0.84
Oswalt, Roy	R-R	6-0	190	8-29-77	1	1	5.25	3	3	0	0	12	15	7	7	1	3	10	.306	.240	.375	7.50	2.25
Perez, Martin	L-L	6-0	180	4-4-91	7	6	4.25	22	21	2	0	127	122	70	60	10	56	69	.258	.230	.272	4.89	3.97
Ramirez, Neil	R-R	6-4	190	5-25-89	6	8	7.66	15	15	0	0	74	78	65	63	12	31	63	.271	.310	.217	7.66	3.77
Reynolds, Greg	R-R	6-7	225	7-3-85	11	9	5.30	27	27	0	0	163	208	108	96	22	46	69	.316	.315	.316	3.81	2.54
Scheppers, Tanner	R-R	6-4	220	1-17-87	1	2	3.48	27	0	0	11	31	30	12	12	2	4	31	.256	.254	.259	9.00	1.16
Snyder, Ben	L-L	6-2	225	7-20-85	3	6	4.19	43	5	0	0	86	84	45	40	11	26	65	.253	.222	.274	6.80	2.72
Tateyama, Yoshinori	R-R	5-10	165	12-26-75	4	0	1.13	32	0	0	6	40	29	8	5	2	7	45	.203	.191	.213	10.21	1.59
Tufts, Tyler	R-R	6-3	200	12-5-86	2	1	6.30	12	0	0	0	20	24	15	14	3	3	6	.300	.292	.313	2.70	1.35
Uehara, Koji	R-R	6-1	190	4-3-75	0	0	0.00	3	0	0	0	3	3	0	0	0	0	4	.273	.400	.167	12.00	0.00
Wolf, Ross	R-R	6-0	180	10-18-82	0	0	4.76	7	0	0	0	11	12	9	6	2	5	7	.250	.250	.250	5.56	3.97
Yan, Johan	R-R	6-3	185	9-27-88	1	1	5.03	28	0	0	1	34	35	22	19	3	17	24	.271	.364	.203	6.35	4.50

Fielding

Catcher	PCT	G	PO	A	E	DP	PB
Brown	.987	47	275	30	4	8	3
Diaz	1.000	7	49	5	0	0	0
Hill	1.000	15	88	10	0	2	0
Martinez	.989	65	398	35	5	1	2
Mendonca	1.000	1	10	1	0	0	0
Sarmiento	.978	16	82	8	2	0	1

First Base	PCT	G	PO	A	E	DP
Bianucci	.996	82	715	39	3	89
Gonzalez	—	1	0	0	0	0
Kata	.900	2	8	1	1	3
Moreland	1.000	1	6	1	0	0
Nelson	.996	54	510	30	2	52
Sarmiento	1.000	1	5	1	0	3

	PCT	G	PO	A	E	DP
Snyder	.982	5	51	3	1	12
Solarte	1.000	1	7	1	0	0
Second Base	**PCT**	**G**	**PO**	**A**	**E**	**DP**
Gonzalez	.833	1	1	4	1	1
Hernandez	.988	15	43	41	1	7
Kata	.961	17	38	61	4	17

Miclat	.939	11	15	31	3 5
Rodriguez	.943	13	25	41	4 10
Solarte	.976	91	185	269	11 93

Third Base	PCT	G	PO	A	E	DP
Gonzalez	1.000	4	0	13	0	1
Kata	.935	56	37	107	10	15
Mendonca	.938	61	41	124	11	12
Rodriguez	1.000	1	0	3	0	0
Snyder	.947	14	7	29	2	4

Solarte	.902	13	9	28	4	4

Shortstop	PCT	G	PO	A	E	DP
Gonzalez	.971	9	15	19	1	4
Hernandez	.980	113	194	337	11	99
Kata	.824	3	6	8	3	2
Miclat	.971	21	27	75	3	12
Rodriguez	1.000	1	7	4	0	2

Outfield	PCT	G	PO	A	E	DP
Borbon	.993	126	284	6	2	0

Butler	.996	133	254	12	1	0
Kata	1.000	11	22	0	0	0
Majewski	1.000	6	10	2	0	0
Martin	.962	55	144	7	6	1
Rodriguez	1.000	2	1	0	0	0
Sarmiento	1.000	2	4	0	0	0
Snyder	1.000	4	3	0	0	0
Solarte	.970	21	31	1	1	0
Spilborghs	.989	80	167	6	2	0

FRISCO ROUGHRIDERS

DOUBLE-A

TEXAS LEAGUE

Batting	B-T	HT	WT	DOB	AVG	vLH	vRH	G	AB	R	H	2B	3B	HR	RBI	BB	HBP	SH	SF	SO	SB	CS	SLG	OBP
Beltre, Engel	L-L	6-2	180	11-1-89	.261	.306	.245	133	564	80	147	17	17	13	55	26	13	8	3	118	36	10	.420	.307
Buchholz, Alex	R-R	6-0	185	9-30-87	.247	.289	.228	84	299	32	74	9	4	7	41	19	5	3	5	55	4	2	.375	.299
Felix, Jose	R-R	5-10	200	6-28-88	.260	.185	.282	82	292	34	76	11	1	7	41	5	1	3	5	25	3	0	.377	.271
Garcia, Leury	B-R	5-7	153	3-18-91	.292	.317	.282	100	377	55	110	12	11	2	30	22	5	9	3	79	31	7	.398	.337
Hawpe, Brad	L-L	6-3	210	6-22-79	.260	.125	.347	35	123	14	32	6	0	3	12	25	1	0	1				.382	.382
Hoying, Jared	L-R	6-3	190	5-18-89	.276	.255	.282	64	246	39	68	7	3	4	25	18	3	4	2	50	9	5	.378	.331
Majewski, Val	L-L	6-2	220	6-19-81	.221	.196	.229	68	235	27	52	9	3	1	21	21	2	1	1	37	3	1	.298	.290
McGuiness, Chris	L-L	6-1	210	4-11-88	.268	.252	.273	123	456	65	122	25	0	23	77	69	3	0	2	107	0	1	.474	.366
Mendonca, Tommy	L-R	6-1	200	4-12-88	.277	.259	.284	28	101	13	28	3	0	5	20	10	1	0	2	37	0	0	.455	.342
Moreland, Mitch	L-L	6-2	230	9-6-85	.308	.000	.364	3	13	4	4	2	0	0	1	0	1	0	0	2	0	0	.462	.357
Olt, Mike	R-R	6-2	210	8-27-88	.288	.272	.294	95	354	65	102	17	1	28	82	61	4	0	1	101	4	0	.579	.398
Prince, Jared	R-R	6-3	220	5-25-86	.234	.250	.226	106	385	46	90	14	0	12	45	19	19	2	2	54	0	0	.364	.301
Profar, Jurickson	B-R	6-0	165	2-20-93	.281	.328	.264	126	480	76	135	26	7	14	62	66	5	2	9	79	16	4	.452	.368
Rodriguez, Guilder	B-R	6-1	160	7-24-83	.208	.203	.209	65	207	24	43	2	0	0	13	25	0	6	0	27	13	4	.217	.293
Strausborger, Ryan	R-R	6-0	180	3-4-88	.247	.184	.270	116	433	62	107	15	11	6	46	33	7	6	3	101	25	0	.374	.309
Zaneski, Zach	R-R	6-2	215	6-27-86	.282	.318	.266	61	209	25	59	14	1	4	32	21	3	1	2	40	0	1	.416	.353

Pitching	B-T	HT	WT	DOB	W	L	ERA	G	GS	CG	SV	IP	H	R	ER	HR	BB	SO	AVG	vLH	vRH	K/9	BB/9
Bell, Chad	R-L	6-3	200	2-28-89	2	2	2.84	13	7	0	2	51	32	17	16	3	13	40	.182	.103	.204	7.11	2.31
Bleier, Richard	L-L	6-3	195	4-16-87	0	2	3.94	22	0	0	1	32	34	15	14	3	7	17	.274	.256	.284	4.78	1.97
Boscan, Wilfredo	R-R	6-2	187	10-26-89	7	5	3.75	34	9	0	0	98	92	45	41	10	28	89	.249	.293	.224	8.15	2.56
Brigham, Jake	R-R	6-3	210	2-10-88	5	5	4.28	21	21	0	0	124	122	65	59	19	46	116	.260	.287	.244	8.42	3.34
Buckel, Cody	R-R	6-1	170	6-18-92	5	5	3.78	13	10	0	0	69	56	31	29	7	23	68	.228	.256	.213	8.87	3.00
Castillo, Fabio	R-R	6-1	235	2-19-89	2	1	2.89	21	0	0	0	37	28	15	12	1	12	28	.199	.211	.194	6.75	2.89
De Los Santos, Miguel	L-L	6-1	170	7-10-88	3	2	5.22	26	4	0	0	59	54	34	34	8	34	70	.241	.254	.236	10.74	5.22
Edwards, Jon	R-R	6-5	230	1-8-88	0	0	4.50	1	0	0	0	2	2	1	1	0	3	3	.250	.500	.167	13.50	13.50
Feliz, Neftali	R-R	6-3	215	5-2-88	0	1	0.00	1	1	0	0	2	1	1	0	0	2	4	.143	.000	.200	18.00	9.00
Font, Wilmer	R-R	6-4	210	5-24-90	2	0	3.00	10	0	0	1	15	9	5	5	1	7	29	.170	.154	.175	17.40	4.20
Grimm, Justin	R-R	6-3	195	8-16-88	9	3	1.72	16	14	0	0	84	70	21	16	3	14	73	.227	.198	.243	7.85	1.51
Hurley, Trevor	R-R	6-3	215	7-28-87	0	0	3.62	18	0	0	0	27	26	15	11	2	15	24	.248	.345	.211	7.90	4.94
Loux, Barret	R-R	6-5	215	4-6-89	14	1	3.47	25	25	0	0	127	120	56	49	10	41	100	.251	.258	.247	7.09	2.91
Lowe, Mark	L-R	6-3	210	6-7-83	0	1	9.00	3	0	0	0	4	4	4	4	2	2	6	.250	.200	.273	13.50	4.50
Mendez, Roman	R-R	6-2	190	7-25-90	2	0	1.46	5	0	0	1	12	8	3	2	4	9	.174	.100	.194	6.57	2.92
Murphy, Tim	L-L	6-2	190	5-7-87	4	8	6.31	32	14	0	1	83	104	60	58	7	31	50	.312	.237	.335	5.44	3.38
Ortiz, Joseph	L-L	5-7	175	8-13-90	1	2	2.35	27	0	0	4	31	26	10	8	2	6	29	.226	.238	.219	8.51	1.76
Osborne, Zach	R-R	6-5	205	5-9-88	1	1	13.20	16	0	0	0	15	32	22	22	4	5	14	.432	.455	.423	8.40	3.00
Oswalt, Roy	R-R	6-0	190	8-29-77	0	0	8.10	1	1	0	0	3	5	3	3	0	1	3	.313	.000	.417	8.10	2.70
Pimentel, Carlos	R-R	6-3	180	12-1-89	8	3	2.55	35	8	0	1	88	58	29	25	4	52	92	.188	.178	.192	9.37	5.30
Ramirez, Neil	R-R	6-4	190	5-25-89	2	5	4.20	13	12	0	0	49	47	26	23	6	16	45	.258	.200	.291	8.21	2.92
Rodebaugh, Ryan	L-R	6-0	165	3-30-89	3	5	2.44	37	0	0	0	52	45	15	14	4	10	62	.233	.200	.252	10.80	1.74
Tepesch, Nick	R-R	6-4	225	10-12-88	6	3	4.28	16	14	0	0	90	97	47	43	10	26	68	.280	.266	.288	6.77	2.59
Tufts, Tyler	R-R	6-3	200	12-5-86	0	0	4.35	7	0	0	2	10	13	5	5	1	4	9	.310	.316	.304	7.84	3.48
Van Meter, Joe	R-R	6-2	195	10-18-88	0	0	11.81	3	0	0	0	5	7	7	7	1	2	6	.292	.300	.286	10.13	3.38
Wolf, Ross	R-R	6-0	180	10-18-82	3	1	2.09	36	0	0	9	43	36	10	10	1	8	44	.232	.305	.188	9.21	1.67
Yan, Johan	R-R	6-3	185	9-27-88	0	0	2.00	17	0	0	10	18	15	6	4	2	11	12	.221	.182	.239	6.00	5.50
Young, Corey	L-L	6-2	185	12-30-86	1	1	5.59	17	0	0	0	19	23	12	12	2	11	11	.319	.292	.333	5.12	5.12

Fielding

Catcher	PCT	G	PO	A	E	DP	PB
Felix	.994	82	656	62	4	7	0
Zaneski	.994	61	472	37	3	5	8

First Base	PCT	G	PO	A	E	DP
Majewski	.941	2	15	1	1	1
McGuiness	.993	115	961	71	7	116
Moreland	1.000	2	13	0	0	1
Olt	1.000	13	120	7	0	9
Rodriguez	1.000	10	78	8	0	9

Second Base	PCT	G	PO	A	E	DP
Buchholz	.976	21	40	43	2	14

Garcia	.979	57	103	179	6	39
Profar	.992	25	53	68	1	25
Rodriguez	1.000	34	70	104	0	27
Strausborger	.974	13	12	25	1	4

Third Base	PCT	G	PO	A	E	DP
Buchholz	.938	37	27	78	7	10
Mendonca	.912	28	15	37	5	11
Olt	.950	78	46	161	11	14
Profar	1.000	1	3	1	0	0
Strausborger	—	1	0	0	0	0

Shortstop	PCT	G	PO	A	E	DP

Garcia	.955	39	52	116	8	25
Profar	.950	97	154	268	22	72
Rodriguez	.938	8	7	23	2	4

Outfield	PCT	G	PO	A	E	DP
Beltre	.997	120	307	12	1	4
Buchholz	.667	4	2	0	1	0
Garcia	.833	4	5	0	1	0
Hawpe	1.000	16	26	0	0	0
Hoying	.983	60	108	6	2	2
Majewski	.932	26	39	2	3	0
Olt	1.000	3	11	0	0	0

TEXAS RANGERS

| Prince | 1.000 | 89 | 129 | 6 | 0 | 1 | | Rodriguez | .923 | 11 | 10 | 2 | 1 | 0 | | Strausborger | .988 | 98 | 157 | 13 | 2 | 0 |

MYRTLE BEACH PELICANS

HIGH CLASS A

CAROLINA LEAGUE

Batting	B-T	HT	WT	DOB	AVG	vLH	vRH	G	AB	R	H	2B	3B	HR	RBI	BB	HBP	SH	SF	SO	SB	CS	SLG	OBP
Alberto, Hanser	R-R	5-11	175	10-17-92	.265	.318	.249	66	279	36	74	11	2	4	34	2	3	1	5	27	9	3	.362	.273
Castillo, Yefry	R-R	5-11	175	4-22-90	.215	.189	.229	45	149	18	32	8	0	0	12	5	5	1	2	17	4	1	.268	.261
Chirino, Santiago	R-R	5-10	154	2-11-91	.218	.157	.239	103	357	27	78	9	1	4	27	17	4	5	4	37	3	1	.283	.259
Clark, Andrew	L-L	6-2	220	8-12-87	.167	.000	.200	2	6	0	1	0	0	0	0	1	0	0	0	2	0	0	.167	.286
DiFazio, Vin	R-R	6-0	215	5-15-86	.209	.217	.206	98	326	38	68	20	0	5	38	53	12	0	2	75	2	2	.316	.338
Garcia, Edwin	B-R	6-0	150	3-1-91	.240	.266	.229	79	254	20	61	10	0	1	24	25	4	2	3	34	5	3	.291	.315
Gomez, Jhonny	R-R	5-11	190	12-21-89	.215	.111	.246	22	79	7	17	1	0	1	3	6	0	1	0	23	0	1	.266	.271
Grayson, Chris	L-L	6-2	195	9-15-89	.178	.091	.206	27	90	14	16	3	0	3	7	16	1	1	0	25	7	0	.311	.308
Herrera, Odubel	L-R	5-11	165	12-29-91	.284	.326	.269	126	500	72	142	22	6	5	46	33	7	7	4	99	27	7	.382	.335
Hoying, Jared	L-R	6-3	190	5-18-89	.275	.270	.277	58	218	37	60	12	2	4	17	21	5	4	0	52	8	4	.404	.352
Martinez, Teodoro	R-R	5-11	155	3-16-92	.271	.345	.241	113	409	49	111	18	1	6	42	22	7	6	5	62	12	11	.364	.316
Nicholas, Brett	L-R	6-2	210	7-18-88	.285	.307	.278	122	446	49	127	33	0	8	63	44	6	0	8	84	5	1	.413	.351
Richmond, Josh	R-R	6-3	205	6-14-89	.178	.198	.169	88	264	32	47	11	2	5	22	22	5	1	3	80	8	3	.292	.252
Skole, Jake	L-R	6-1	190	1-17-92	.185	.188	.184	68	227	18	42	8	0	3	18	31	3	3	3	72	2	2	.260	.288
Telis, Tomas	B-R	5-8	175	6-18-91	.247	.248	.246	117	450	45	111	24	1	4	43	17	7	7	3	53	9	2	.331	.283
Villanueva, Christian	R-R	5-11	160	6-19-91	.285	.258	.294	100	375	45	107	19	1	10	59	24	20	1	5	83	9	9	.421	.356
Williams, Jeremy	R-R	6-2	220	4-1-87	.237	.310	.215	51	177	27	42	6	0	5	17	10	3	0	1	57	3	1	.356	.288

Pitching	B-T	HT	WT	DOB	W	L	ERA	G	GS	CG	SV	IP	H	R	ER	HR	BB	SO	AVG	vLH	vRH	K/9	BB/9
Bell, Chad	R-L	6-3	200	2-28-89	1	0	1.59	4	0	0	0	11	7	2	2	0	4	12	.184	.000	.194	9.53	3.18
Buckel, Cody	R-R	6-1	170	6-18-92	5	3	1.31	13	13	0	0	76	49	12	11	2	25	91	.186	.143	.215	10.82	2.97
Devore, Kyle	R-R	6-4	225	12-23-90	3	3	3.50	23	8	0	0	72	80	39	28	7	20	43	.283	.224	.308	5.38	2.50
Edwards, Jon	R-R	6-5	230	1-8-88	0	0	3.60	4	0	0	0	5	4	2	2	0	3	7	.235	1.000	.188	12.60	5.40
Font, Wilmer	R-R	6-4	210	5-24-90	2	5	4.21	23	19	0	0	83	58	41	39	10	37	109	.198	.206	.194	11.77	4.00
Hendricks, Kyle	R-R	6-3	190	12-7-89	5	8	2.82	20	20	2	0	131	123	49	41	8	15	112	.253	.353	.215	7.71	1.03
Henry, Ben	R-R	6-4	190	4-9-89	4	1	3.83	28	1	0	1	47	32	21	20	2	24	42	.199	.149	.219	8.04	4.60
Henry, Randy	R-R	6-3	190	5-10-90	5	9	3.35	29	11	0	7	83	88	42	31	7	33	65	.272	.281	.269	7.02	3.56
Jackson, Luke	R-R	6-2	185	8-24-91	5	2	4.39	13	13	0	0	66	67	35	32	2	32	74	.273	.361	.245	10.14	4.39
Klein, Phil	R-R	6-7	240	4-30-89	0	0	0.87	7	0	0	0	10	2	1	1	2	14	.063	.125	.042	12.19	1.74
Lopez, Daniel	R-R	6-1	170	5-16-87	0	0	5.06	5	0	0	0	5	8	4	3	0	3	3	.348	.333	.350	5.06	5.06
McBride, Nick	R-R	6-4	180	5-13-91	2	3	3.76	9	6	0	0	41	44	25	17	1	12	16	.286	.311	.275	3.54	2.66
McElwee, Josh	R-R	6-4	220	6-12-89	0	0	0.00	3	0	0	0	4	5	0	0	0	1	8	.294	1.000	.250	16.62	2.08
Mendez, Roman	R-R	6-2	190	7-25-90	4	6	5.14	18	12	0	1	70	69	43	40	7	25	71	.260	.311	.234	9.13	3.21
Mendoza, Francisco	R-R	6-0	175	12-7-87	3	4	4.88	34	0	0	0	48	51	26	26	4	28	34	.274	.333	.254	6.38	5.25
Monegro, Jose	R-R	6-3	200	9-19-89	1	0	6.60	6	0	0	0	15	17	11	11	3	4	10	.279	.304	.263	6.00	2.40
Osborne, Zach	R-R	6-5	205	5-9-88	5	1	1.94	28	0	0	2	56	47	14	12	3	10	54	.234	.254	.223	8.73	1.62
Reyes, Jimmy	L-L	5-10	195	3-7-89	6	3	2.44	41	0	0	3	66	61	23	18	5	16	71	.246	.274	.237	9.63	2.17
Rojas, Randol	R-R	6-0	160	9-28-90	9	6	3.73	26	16	0	0	113	120	59	47	7	37	76	.273	.223	.291	6.04	2.94
Rowen, Ben	R-R	6-4	190	11-15-88	5	7	1.57	38	0	0	19	57	41	10	10	2	3	52	.201	.153	.221	8.16	0.47
Tepesch, Nick	R-R	6-4	225	10-12-88	5	3	2.89	12	12	1	0	72	68	27	23	3	18	59	.253	.266	.247	7.41	2.26
Van Meter, Joe	R-R	6-2	195	10-18-88	4	5	2.06	25	8	0	3	74	55	21	17	5	22	74	.208	.198	.213	8.96	2.66
West, Matt	R-R	6-1	200	11-21-88	0	3	6.64	17	0	0	0	20	18	16	15	1	16	14	.240	.250	.235	6.20	7.08
Williams, Greg	L-L	6-4	205	12-30-89	0	0	9.00	1	0	0	0	1	2	1	1	0	0	0	.400	—	.400	0.00	0.00

Fielding

Catcher	PCT	G	PO	A	E	DP	PB
Castillo	.950	4	16	3	1	0	0
DiFazio	.993	46	386	30	3	5	2
Nicholas	.975	11	71	7	2	0	2
Telis	.984	79	630	91	12	8	13

First Base	PCT	G	PO	A	E	DP
Castillo	.983	19	159	14	3	15
Clark	1.000	2	10	1	0	1
Garcia	1.000	4	24	0	0	1
Gomez	.982	13	105	4	2	14
Nicholas	.989	106	926	66	11	96

Second Base	PCT	G	PO	A	E	DP
Chirino	.983	63	116	178	5	47

	PCT	G	PO	A	E	DP
Garcia	1.000	26	55	64	0	21
Herrera	.940	50	97	107	13	23
Villanueva	1.000	4	4	13	0	1

Third Base	PCT	G	PO	A	E	DP
Castillo	1.000	5	1	6	0	1
Chirino	.953	20	11	30	2	3
Garcia	.972	25	18	51	2	4
Villanueva	.938	90	64	164	15	25

Shortstop	PCT	G	PO	A	E	DP
Alberto	.972	65	104	240	10	49
Garcia	.969	14	25	37	2	10
Herrera	.909	60	85	196	28	40

Outfield	PCT	G	PO	A	E	DP
Castillo	1.000	14	18	3	0	0
Chirino	1.000	18	22	6	0	3
Garcia	1.000	9	7	0	0	0
Gomez	1.000	8	8	2	0	0
Grayson	.927	27	38	0	3	0
Hoying	.961	52	92	6	4	2
Martinez	.995	107	202	6	1	2
Richmond	.971	82	160	9	5	3
Skole	.980	64	96	0	2	0
Williams	.956	48	64	1	3	0

HICKORY CRAWDADS

LOW CLASS A

SOUTH ATLANTIC LEAGUE

Batting	B-T	HT	WT	DOB	AVG	vLH	vRH	G	AB	R	H	2B	3B	HR	RBI	BB	HBP	SH	SF	SO	SB	CS	SLG	OBP
Adams, Trever	R-R	6-0	200	9-30-88	.286	.246	.305	111	413	44	118	25	2	9	67	29	1	1	4	73	10	5	.421	.331
Akins, Jordan	R-R	6-3	192	4-19-92	.199	.184	.206	120	427	57	85	14	3	11	39	12	3	1	4	162	14	3	.323	.224
Alberto, Hanser	R-R	5-11	175	10-17-92	.337	.318	.348	62	246	37	83	17	1	4	38	18	3	2	3	22	15	4	.463	.385
Alfaro, Jorge	R-R	6-2	185	6-11-93	.261	.224	.282	74	272	40	71	21	5	5	34	16	9	0	3	84	7	3	.430	.320

Name	B-T	HT	WT	DOB	AVG	vLH	vRH	G	AB	R	H	2B	3B	HR	RBI	BB	HBP	SH	SF	SO	SB	CS	SLG	OBP
Cone, Zach	R-R	6-2	205	12-14-89	.262	.253	.267	112	432	66	113	27	4	17	64	39	3	0	1	110	10	0	.461	.326
Deglan, Kellin	L-R	6-2	195	5-3-92	.234	.198	.252	92	320	46	75	25	2	12	41	32	5	1	4	96	4	4	.438	.310
Garcia, Edwin	B-R	6-0	150	3-1-91	.700	.667	.714	2	10	2	7	2	0	0	2	0	0	0	0	2	0	0	.900	.700
Gomez, Jhonny	R-R	5-11	190	12-14-89	.227	.190	.242	51	141	27	32	5	0	3	20	27	3	1	1	33	3	1	.326	.360
Grayson, Chris	L-L	6-2	195	9-15-89	.266	.282	.258	99	364	73	97	25	6	10	47	54	10	1	4	92	27	8	.451	.373
Maloney, Joe	R-R	6-2	190	7-27-90	.158	.167	.154	5	19	4	3	0	0	1	3	0	1	0	0	9	0	0	.316	.200
Odor, Rougned	L-R	5-11	170	2-3-94	.259	.239	.269	109	432	60	112	23	4	10	47	25	10	2	2	65	19	10	.400	.313
Onaka, Hirotoshi	B-R	5-10	175	7-11-88	.233	.125	.273	12	30	5	7	1	0	0	4	6	0	0	1	9	1	0	.267	.351
Robinson, Drew	L-R	6-1	185	4-20-92	.273	.212	.304	123	410	72	112	23	4	13	67	86	9	1	1	123	10	7	.444	.409
Sardinas, Luis	B-R	6-1	150	5-16-93	.291	.295	.289	96	374	65	109	14	2	2	30	29	4	2	3	52	32	9	.356	.346
Selen, Alejandro	R-R	5-10	175	3-20-89	.313	.397	.273	55	195	29	61	12	3	11	46	11	2	0	2	51	0	0	.574	.352
Torres, Kevin	L-R	6-3	195	2-24-90	.236	.288	.216	64	212	21	50	10	0	1	24	12	2	2	5	41	0	0	.297	.277
Urbanus, Nick	B-R	6-1	175	3-29-92	.231	.224	.234	46	143	23	33	6	0	0	11	15	1	3	0	34	3	1	.273	.308
Williams, Jeremy	R-R	6-2	220	4-1-87	.304	.263	.325	64	237	35	72	18	0	8	42	9	5	1	2	65	3	2	.481	.340

Pitching

Name	B-T	HT	WT	DOB	W	L	ERA	G	GS	CG	SV	IP	H	R	ER	HR	BB	SO	AVG	vLH	vRH	K/9	BB/9
Alvarez, Richard	R-R	6-2	180	8-14-92	0	0	3.00	1	1	0	0	3	1	1	1	1	2	3	.111	.000	.250	9.00	6.00
Blackwell, Shawn	R-R	6-1	195	11-15-90	0	0	5.14	4	0	0	0	7	7	4	4	0	5	9	.259	.111	.333	11.57	6.43
Cowgill, Coby	R-R	6-1	200	3-23-91	0	1	2.16	7	0	0	0	8	5	2	2	0	6	7	.192	.125	.222	7.56	6.48
Dennis, Taylor	R-R	6-1	175	3-31-89	3	0	2.12	21	0	0	4	34	31	9	8	1	12	21	.254	.255	.254	5.56	3.18
Eickhoff, Jerad	R-R	6-4	200	7-2-90	13	7	4.69	26	25	0	0	127	132	75	66	22	38	90	.267	.252	.278	6.39	2.70
Faulkner, Andrew	R-L	6-3	180	9-12-92	5	5	4.31	29	10	0	0	94	97	56	45	2	44	74	.262	.238	.271	7.09	4.21
Hanna, Chris	R-L	6-1	180	3-7-92	1	0	4.62	16	0	0	2	39	47	22	20	6	9	30	.301	.362	.275	6.92	2.08
2-team total (7 Kannapolis)					3	3	4.46	23	5	0	2	77	86	43	38	10	17	57	—	—	—	6.69	2.00
Jackson, Luke	R-R	6-2	185	8-24-91	5	5	4.92	13	13	1	0	64	63	37	35	4	33	72	.259	.223	.286	10.13	4.64
Klein, Phil	R-R	6-7	240	4-30-89	6	0	1.90	33	0	0	8	52	37	12	11	2	21	53	.203	.159	.227	9.17	3.63
Lamb, Will	L-L	6-6	180	9-9-90	6	8	4.15	27	21	0	0	108	95	63	50	13	57	80	.234	.250	.228	6.65	4.74
Lopez, Daniel	R-R	6-1	170	5-16-87	0	2	3.96	16	0	0	2	25	21	11	11	1	11	25	.226	.297	.179	9.00	3.96
Martinez, Nick	L-R	6-1	175	8-5-90	8	6	4.83	31	20	0	1	117	121	66	63	8	37	109	.265	.271	.261	8.36	2.84
Matthews, Kevin	R-L	5-11	180	11-29-92	3	4	4.38	19	15	0	1	74	65	44	36	2	64	66	.239	.241	.238	8.03	7.78
Mavare, Jose	R-R	6-0	175	2-19-90	5	5	3.57	40	0	0	5	81	66	34	32	6	27	102	.222	.264	.198	11.38	3.01
McBride, Nick	R-R	6-4	180	5-13-91	3	1	2.41	24	1	0	2	52	39	21	14	2	15	52	.200	.227	.183	8.94	2.58
Monegro, Jose	R-R	6-3	200	9-19-89	2	1	4.32	16	0	0	2	25	18	13	12		4	26	.198	.250	.164	9.36	1.44
Payano, Victor	L-L	6-5	185	10-17-92	6	8	4.63	25	20	1	1	105	97	61	54	8	62	97	.243	.293	.230	8.31	5.31
Perez, Santo	R-R	6-5	200	11-22-88	4	10	5.38	30	13	0	1	99	109	72	59	7	39	72	.279	.293	.270	6.57	3.56
Rojas, Randol	R-R	6-0	160	9-28-90	1	0	0.71	4	0	0	0	13	6	1	1	0	5	13	.150	.100	.200	9.24	3.55
Schwendel, Paul	R-R	6-5	220	8-9-89	1	2	2.73	10	0	0	1	26	18	13	8	2	16	35	.188	.184	.190	11.96	5.47
Sossamon, Chance	R-R	6-2	185	10-19-89	0	0	9.22	10	0	0	0	14	20	17	14	1	15	11	.328	.263	.357	7.24	9.88
Williams, Greg	L-L	6-4	205	12-30-89	2	0	3.49	20	0	0	4	28	26	13	11	2	8	25	.248	.250	.247	7.94	2.54

Fielding

Catcher	PCT	G	PO	A	E	DP	PB
Alfaro	.975	29	209	23	6	0	5
Deglan	.989	77	590	66	7	8	12
Maloney	1.000	5	47	3	0	0	3
Torres	.987	32	210	22	3	1	3

First Base	PCT	G	PO	A	E	DP
Adams	.982	66	474	31	9	60
Alfaro	.977	17	119	10	3	14
Gomez	.994	42	291	23	2	30
Torres	.985	24	193	10	3	22

Second Base	PCT	G	PO	A	E	DP
Odor	.975	85	179	219	10	56
Robinson	.964	15	29	24	2	5

	PCT	G	PO	A	E	DP
Sardinas	.964	14	20	34	2	12
Selen	.969	15	24	39	2	10
Urbanus	1.000	22	37	66	0	17

Third Base	PCT	G	PO	A	E	DP
Adams	.853	17	3	26	5	1
Alberto	.930	17	10	30	3	3
Robinson	.899	104	69	181	28	24
Torres	—	1	0	0	0	0
Urbanus	.947	9	2	16	1	2

Shortstop	PCT	G	PO	A	E	DP
Alberto	.924	35	57	113	14	23
Garcia	1.000	2	2	5	0	1
Odor	.908	15	31	38	7	13

	PCT	G	PO	A	E	DP
Sardinas	.944	76	111	209	19	46
Urbanus	.968	17	20	40	2	9

Outfield	PCT	G	PO	A	E	DP
Adams	.968	31	59	1	2	0
Akins	.988	117	240	5	3	1
Cone	.995	93	197	5	1	2
Gomez	1.000	5	7	0	0	0
Grayson	.978	92	177	4	4	0
Onaka	.929	12	13	0	1	0
Selen	.955	30	40	2	2	0
Williams	.970	49	62	2	2	1

TEXAS RANGERS

SPOKANE INDIANS
SHORT-SEASON
NORTHWEST LEAGUE

Batting	B-T	HT	WT	DOB	AVG	vLH	vRH	G	AB	R	H	2B	3B	HR	RBI	BB	HBP	SH	SF	SO	SB	CS	SLG	OBP
Beck, Preston	L-R	6-2	190	10-26-90	.251	.259	.249	66	247	24	62	10	3	3	29	25	5	1	2	39	6	0	.352	.330
Bolinger, Royce	R-R	6-2	190	8-12-90	.301	.293	.303	66	266	25	80	15	1	1	26	12	5	1	2	37	3	2	.376	.340
Cantwell, Pat	R-R	6-2	190	4-10-90	.255	.318	.237	53	200	24	51	11	1	1	22	16	12	1	3	37	1	3	.335	.342
Edmonds, Guy	R-R	6-2	180	3-16-93	.154	.105	.174	21	65	7	10	3	1	0	4	3	0	0	2	27	0	0	.231	.186
Gallo, Joey	L-R	6-5	205	11-19-93	.214	.200	.220	16	56	9	12	2	0	4	9	11	0	0	0	26	0	0	.464	.343
Garcia, Brandon	L-R	6-1	195	6-26-90	.231	.333	.200	18	52	4	12	3	0	1	9	5	5	0	3	14	0	0	.346	.338
Garia, Christopher	R-R	6-0	165	12-16-90	.246	.222	.253	47	195	31	48	7	3	1	16	17	4	3	0	45	18	9	.328	.319
Johnson, Saquan	R-R	6-2	175	2-26-93	.161	.077	.197	30	87	10	14	2	2	2	12	7	1	2	1	45	1	0	.299	.229
Lantigua, Smerling	R-R	6-2	180	2-3-94	.212	.282	.188	42	151	17	32	4	4	0	9	3	1	2	0	47	0	0	.291	.232
Maloney, Joe	R-R	6-2	190	7-27-90	.251	.275	.245	53	183	26	46	16	1	6	26	25	5	0	2	66	0	0	.448	.347
Onaka, Hirotoshi	B-R	5-10	175	7-11-88	.333	.417	.315	20	36	6	12	3	0	0	4	11	2	1	0	17	3	1	.389	.463
Roa, Gabriel	R-R	5-8	165	3-26-92	.261	.264	.260	65	257	39	67	5	1	1	28	21	10	8	6	32	4	4	.300	.333
Rua, Ryan	R-R	6-2	180	3-11-90	.293	.281	.296	74	280	40	82	16	1	7	43	29	6	2	3	64	4	1	.432	.368
Schiller, Cam	B-R	6-0	195	11-30-89	.281	.152	.307	52	196	23	55	11	2	3	22	21	4	2	1	31	0	0	.403	.360

	B-T	HT	WT	DOB	AVG	vLH	vRH	G	AB	R	H	2B	3B	HR	RBI	BB	HBP	SH	SF	SO	SB	CS	SLG	OBP
Serrato, Barrett	L-R	6-2	185	9-1-90	.182	.333	.154	48	154	15	28	5	0	1	14	35	1	2	0	47	0	2	.234	.337
Skole, Jake	L-R	6-1	190	1-17-92	.229	.167	.261	10	35	2	8	0	1	0	2	12	0	0	0	17	3	3	.286	.426
Urbanus, Nick	B-R	6-1	175	3-29-92	.258	1.000	.233	7	31	5	8	3	0	0	2	2	0	1	0	3	0	0	.355	.303
Vickerson, Nick	R-R	5-11	205	7-8-89	.132	.174	.113	30	76	6	10	2	0	0	3	11	3	4	1	27	3	2	.158	.264

Pitching

	B-T	HT	WT	DOB	W	L	ERA	G	GS	CG	SV	IP	H	R	ER	HR	BB	SO	AVG	vLH	vRH	K/9	BB/9
Alvarez, Richard	R-R	6-2	180	8-14-92	2	2	2.61	18	0	0	0	48	47	19	14	3	9	40	.246	.308	.204	7.45	1.68
Asher, Alec	R-R	6-4	218	10-4-91	2	3	3.09	20	0	0	5	35	29	12	12	4	11	50	.221	.211	.230	12.86	2.83
Blackwell, Shawn	R-R	6-5	195	11-15-90	1	2	3.55	18	2	0	0	46	42	23	18	6	13	27	.241	.195	.278	5.32	2.56
Brooks, Eric	R-R	6-1	195	8-29-90	2	3	3.68	15	13	0	0	51	55	27	21	2	13	48	.263	.244	.276	8.42	2.28
Burns, Joe	L-L	6-0	200	8-3-89	1	1	2.25	20	0	0	2	32	23	9	8	2	7	24	.204	.242	.188	6.75	1.97
Cowgill, Coby	R-R	6-1	200	3-23-91	0	0	9.00	1	0	0	0	1	1	2	1	0	3	0	.200	.500	.000	0.00	27.00
De Los Santos, Abel	R-R	6-2	180	11-21-92	3	5	5.81	16	11	0	0	62	67	46	40	7	22	54	.280	.240	.308	7.84	3.19
Dennis, Taylor	R-R	6-1	175	3-31-89	0	1	1.35	4	0	0	0	7	3	6	1	0	3	8	.120	.077	.167	10.80	4.05
Edwards, C.J.	R-R	6-2	155	9-3-91	2	3	2.11	10	10	0	0	47	26	13	11	0	19	60	.160	.177	.149	11.49	3.64
Edwards, Jon	R-R	6-5	230	1-8-88	0	0	1.47	11	0	0	0	18	7	8	3	1	24	22	.115	.115	.114	10.80	11.78
Harvey, Ryan	L-R	6-2	220	1-31-91	1	1	6.21	19	0	0	0	33	41	29	23	3	10	44	.287	.370	.236	11.88	2.70
Kendall, Cody	R-R	6-2	210	12-12-89	3	5	2.31	19	0	0	0	39	34	15	10	1	18	20	.239	.197	.272	4.62	4.15
Kukuruda, John	R-R	6-4	180	6-9-92	4	4	4.50	14	9	0	0	56	61	43	28	6	16	31	.280	.202	.333	4.98	2.57
McElwee, Josh	R-R	6-4	220	6-12-89	1	2	3.67	20	0	0	7	27	26	13	11	1	6	35	.255	.310	.217	11.67	2.00
Melo, Carlos	R-R	6-3	180	2-27-91	1	3	3.77	19	0	0	0	29	30	16	12	1	21	30	.263	.182	.314	9.42	6.59
Monegro, Jose	R-R	6-2	200	9-19-89	0	1	1.32	6	0	0	0	14	6	3	2	0	3	14	.130	.059	.172	9.22	1.98
Peralta, Denny	R-R	6-4	170	12-11-89	0	0	6.75	1	0	0	0	1	4	4	1	0	3	0	.444	.500	.400	0.00	20.25
Perez, David	R-R	6-5	200	12-20-92	1	1	13.00	3	1	0	0	9	12	13	13	1	11	11	.324	.125	.476	11.00	11.00
Sadzeck, Connor	R-R	6-5	195	10-1-91	1	4	4.06	15	15	0	0	62	44	38	28	2	47	58	.200	.186	.209	8.42	6.82
Valdespina, Jose	R-R	6-6	220	3-22-92	3	6	5.58	15	15	0	0	60	67	40	37	3	34	54	.290	.343	.250	8.15	5.13

Fielding

Catcher	PCT	G	PO	A	E	DP	PB
Cantwell	.993	29	241	25	2	6	3
Edmonds	.980	17	138	10	3	1	7
Maloney	.972	34	256	24	8	5	10
Vickerson	1.000	1	4	0	0	0	0

First Base	PCT	G	PO	A	E	DP
Cantwell	.984	14	112	13	2	12
Lantigua	.977	16	126	2	3	12
Maloney	1.000	1	4	0	0	0
Rua	.983	14	105	11	2	7
Serrato	.985	35	301	21	5	35

Second Base	PCT	G	PO	A	E	DP
Rua	.980	11	21	29	1	10
Schiller	.954	46	93	133	11	21
Urbanus	1.000	1	3	2	0	2
Vickerson	.899	22	25	55	9	13

Third Base	PCT	G	PO	A	E	DP
Gallo	.909	16	11	39	5	4
Lantigua	.774	23	11	30	12	2
Rua	.882	38	25	57	11	3
Vickerson	1.000	1	1	2	0	2

Shortstop	PCT	G	PO	A	E	DP
Roa	.950	65	104	198	16	45

	PCT	G	PO	A	E	DP
Rua	.957	7	11	11	1	7
Schiller	.889	3	1	7	1	2
Urbanus	1.000	4	13	7	0	2
Outfield	PCT	G	PO	A	E	DP
Beck	.932	61	97	12	8	3
Bolinger	.969	60	88	7	3	1
Cantwell	1.000	3	8	0	0	0
Garcia	.909	9	10	0	1	0
Garia	.983	46	110	4	2	1
Johnson	1.000	29	23	1	0	0
Onaka	.958	17	22	1	1	0
Serrato	.750	5	2	1	1	0
Skole	.958	10	23	0	1	0

AZL RANGERS   ROOKIE

ARIZONA LEAGUE

Batting	B-T	HT	WT	DOB	AVG	vLH	vRH	G	AB	R	H	2B	3B	HR	RBI	BB	HBP	SH	SF	SO	SB	CS	SLG	OBP
Bianucci, Mike	R-R	6-1	225	6-26-86	.500	.400	.556	5	14	3	7	4	0	1	4	3	1	0	0	4	0	0	1.000	.611
Brinson, Lewis	R-R	6-3	170	5-8-94	.283	.333	.263	54	237	54	67	22	7	7	42	21	3	1	3	74	14	2	.523	.345
Castro, Janluis	B-R	5-9	165	1-4-94	.350	.100	.454	37	137	17	48	11	1	1	23	16	1	1	0	22	4	4	.467	.422
Gallo, Joey	L-R	6-5	205	11-19-93	.293	.410	.252	43	150	44	44	10	1	18	43	37	3	0	3	52	6	0	.733	.435
Guzman, Ronald	L-L	6-5	205	10-20-94	.321	.358	.308	52	212	29	68	15	3	1	33	19	1	0	3	42	7	1	.434	.374
Harlin, Rashad	R-R	6-0	185	2-7-93	.214	.000	.243	14	42	3	9	2	0	0	6	1	0	0	0	8	2	0	.262	.233
Henry, Desmond	R-R	6-1	175	7-7-93	.000	.000	.000	2	4	1	0	0	0	0	0	2	0	0	0	3	0	0	.000	.333
Jarmon, Jamie	R-R	6-1	190	6-21-94	.183	.063	.222	39	131	26	24	2	2	1	11	23	5	0	1	45	6	3	.252	.325
Lyon, David	B-R	5-11	190	1-19-90	.218	.174	.236	24	78	8	17	4	1	0	5	12	1	0	0	18	0	1	.295	.330
Marte, Luis	R-R	6-1	170	12-15-93	.187	.225	.176	44	171	28	32	9	2	0	17	8	1	1	3	31	5	1	.263	.224
Mazara, Nomar	L-L	6-4	195	4-26-95	.264	.224	.280	54	201	40	53	13	3	6	39	37	3	0	2	70	5	2	.448	.383
Mendez, Luis	B-R	5-9	165	1-1-93	.258	.235	.265	23	66	15	17	2	3	0	8	10	5	1	1	11	8	2	.379	.390
Moorman, Chuck	R-R	5-11	200	1-9-94	.207	.167	.217	19	58	8	12	2	0	0	7	10	2	0	0	10	0	0	.241	.343
Sarmiento, Elio	R-R	5-11	200	6-20-86	.412	.600	.379	8	34	6	14	4	1	2	9	1	1	1	1	5	1	1	.765	.432
Triunfel, Alberto	R-R	5-11	160	2-1-94	.224	.188	.235	42	147	23	33	8	2	2	19	16	5	5	5	25	6	4	.347	.312
Vivili, Fernando	R-R	6-3	210	1-9-94	.194	.200	.192	21	67	13	13	6	1	0	8	5	6	0	1	17	0	2	.313	.304
Williams, Nick	L-L	6-3	195	9-8-93	.313	.370	.297	48	201	34	63	9	6	2	27	16	5	0	2	50	15	2	.448	.375

Pitching	B-T	HT	WT	DOB	W	L	ERA	G	GS	CG	SV	IP	H	R	ER	HR	BB	SO	AVG	vLH	vRH	K/9	BB/9
Bores, Ryan	R-R	6-3	190	10-10-90	0	0	1.26	10	0	0	0	14	8	2	2	0	4	12	.167	.300	.071	7.53	2.51
Claudio, Alexander	L-L	6-3	160	1-31-92	4	0	1.79	14	3	0	1	45	36	11	9	1	5	54	.222	.133	.256	10.72	0.99
Cowgill, Coby	R-R	6-1	200	3-23-91	1	0	3.86	6	0	0	0	7	6	3	0	5	5	.167	.222	.133	6.43	6.43
De Jesus, Jorge	R-R	6-0	205	1-17-92	1	1	6.00	13	0	0	1	15	14	10	10	2	7	12	.241	.280	.212	7.20	4.20
Edwards, C.J.	R-R	6-2	155	9-3-91	3	0	0.00	4	3	0	0	20	6	0	0	0	6	25	.094	.091	.095	11.25	2.70
Edwards, Jon	R-R	6-5	230	1-8-88	1	0	0.00	3	0	0	1	5	3	0	0	0	2	5	.176	.125	.222	9.64	3.86
Kela, Keone	R-R	6-1	190	4-16-93	0	1	1.59	9	0	0	0	11	4	4	2	0	4	15	.105	.143	.083	11.91	3.18
Kuter, Brandon	R-R	6-7	220	10-13-90	0	0	2.04	12	0	0	1	18	15	6	4	1	10	17	.231	.200	.257	8.66	5.09
Leclerc, Angelo	R-R	6-0	170	10-9-91	3	1	2.96	14	7	0	1	49	49	21	16	1	11	52	.262	.241	.279	9.62	2.03

Name	B-T	HT	WT	DOB	W	L	ERA	G	GS	CG	SV	IP	H	R	ER	HR	BB	SO	AVG	vLH	vRH	K/9	BB/9
Lopez, Frank	L-L	6-1	175	2-18-94	4	3	5.19	14	11	0	1	52	50	33	30	1	14	53	.243	.241	.243	9.17	2.42
Mendez, Roman	R-R	6-2	190	7-25-90	0	1	3.00	3	3	0	0	9	7	3	3	1	1	7	.219	.231	.211	7.00	1.00
Niggli, John	R-R	6-4	185	5-2-90	0	1	7.71	8	1	0	0	9	17	9	8	1	2	4	.415	.250	.455	3.86	1.93
Parra, Luis	L-L	6-2	160	11-21-91	5	6	3.79	13	13	0	0	59	60	29	25	5	18	53	.260	.260	.260	8.04	2.73
Peralta, Denny	R-R	6-4	170	12-11-89	3	2	5.67	13	1	0	1	27	31	19	17	2	10	25	.290	.395	.232	8.33	3.33
Perez-Lobo, Andres	R-R	5-11	184	3-3-92	0	1	16.88	2	0	0	1	3	7	5	5	0	3	4	.467	.500	.429	13.50	10.13
Schwendel, Paul	R-R	6-5	220	8-9-89	1	1	3.00	6	0	0	1	12	10	5	4	0	2	19	.244	.190	.300	14.25	1.50
Shiver, Casey	R-R	6-2	175	10-21-90	1	0	2.22	14	0	0	7	24	19	6	6	3	4	23	.213	.188	.228	8.51	1.48
Slack, Ryne	L-L	6-2	210	7-22-92	6	1	5.34	13	1	0	0	32	38	22	19	2	12	37	.295	.267	.303	10.41	3.38
Smith, Tyler	R-R	6-3	195	2-3-92	0	0	27.00	1	0	0	0	1	2	2	2	0	2	2	.500	.500	.500	27.00	27.00
Sossamon, Chance	R-R	6-2	185	10-19-89	0	0	2.45	8	0	0	0	11	13	4	3	0	1	11	.283	.444	.179	9.00	0.82
Thompson, Matt	R-R	6-3	210	2-10-90	0	0	6.75	2	0	0	0	1	0	4	1	0	3	4	.000	.000	.000	20.25	20.25
Thrailkill, Austen	L-L	6-4	210	2-1-92	0	1	10.57	9	0	0	0	8	3	10	9	0	16	14	.120	.000	.188	16.43	18.78
Tirado, Pedro	L-L	6-2	170	12-18-90	0	1	5.50	9	0	0	0	18	22	13	11	1	5	18	.314	.389	.288	9.00	2.50
Weibley, Brett	R-R	6-3	195	1-3-89	0	0	12.60	6	0	0	0	5	6	8	7	1	8	1	.316	.333	.308	1.80	14.40
Wiles, Collin	R-R	6-4	187	5-30-94	1	1	6.87	14	12	0	0	37	48	30	28	3	12	25	.310	.292	.318	6.14	2.95
Williams, Greg	L-L	6-4	205	12-30-89	0	0	5.14	7	1	0	0	7	8	4	4	0	6	9	.276	.111	.350	11.57	7.71

Fielding

Catcher	PCT	G	PO	A	E	DP	PB
Lyon	.986	24	188	29	3	4	3
Moorman	.982	19	137	24	3	1	8
Sarmiento	1.000	4	46	2	0	0	2
Vivili	.978	16	117	18	3	4	5

First Base	PCT	G	PO	A	E	DP
Bianucci	1.000	4	37	1	0	2
Guzman	.983	49	443	26	8	36
Mendez	1.000	2	7	1	0	2
Sarmiento	1.000	3	27	2	0	1
Vivili	1.000	1	11	0	0	1

Second Base	PCT	G	PO	A	E	DP
Castro	.980	22	37	59	2	14
Marte	1.000	3	6	8	0	1
Mendez	1.000	6	9	16	0	2
Triunfel	.945	27	44	93	8	22

Third Base	PCT	G	PO	A	E	DP
Castro	1.000	8	0	14	0	0
Gallo	.872	40	28	54	12	5
Marte	.750	2	3	3	2	0
Mendez	.875	10	4	10	2	1

Shortstop	PCT	G	PO	A	E	DP
Marte	.927	40	62	115	14	24

	PCT	G	PO	A	E	DP
Mendez	.923	3	3	9	1	1
Triunfel	.958	15	22	46	3	8

Outfield	PCT	G	PO	A	E	DP
Brinson	.958	49	86	5	4	0
Guzman	1.000	1	1	0	0	0
Harlin	1.000	13	7	0	0	0
Henry	—	1	0	0	0	0
Jarmon	1.000	24	29	0	0	0
Mazara	.975	51	77	2	2	1
Triunfel	1.000	2	1	0	0	0
Williams	.979	34	45	2	1	0

DSL RANGERS

ROOKIE

DOMINICAN SUMMER LEAGUE

Batting	B-T	HT	WT	DOB	AVG	vLH	vRH	G	AB	R	H	2B	3B	HR	RBI	BB	HBP	SH	SF	SO	SB	CS	SLG	OBP
Adames, Crisford	B-R	6-1	160	1-26-95	.167	—	.167	7	6	1	1	1	0	0	1	0	0	0	0	3	0	0	.333	.167
Ayarza, Rodrigo	B-R	5-8	145	2-20-95	.205	.125	.225	55	161	24	33	5	3	0	22	23	1	3	1	17	1	4	.273	.306
Campos, Belarmino	B-R	5-10	165	6-19-93	.225	.226	.225	58	204	35	46	13	4	2	29	33	7	2	1	30	3	3	.358	.351
Caraballo, Oliver	R-R	6-1	180	8-25-94	.188	.111	.205	28	48	13	9	3	2	0	9	9	4	0	0	11	1	1	.333	.361
Castillo, Elio	R-R	6-1	160	3-1-94	.272	.230	.288	65	217	43	59	8	2	1	29	32	13	8	4	31	8	1	.341	.391
Cedeno, Diego	L-L	5-11	160	5-19-92	.256	.284	.245	69	258	47	66	9	4	0	42	43	3	3	3	32	6	3	.322	.365
Garay, Carlos	R-R	6-0	178	10-5-94	.318	.360	.303	58	192	23	61	7	2	0	35	20	1	2	3	16	1	3	.375	.380
Gonzalez, Alex	R-R	5-11	165	7-7-91	.266	.270	.265	64	233	56	62	6	5	1	35	42	1	2	5	44	13	7	.348	.385
Gonzalez, Jesus	R-R	6-1	180	9-12-94	.160	.286	.111	12	25	7	4	1	0	0	2	9	3	0	1	11	1	0	.200	.421
Gonzalez, Jose	B-R	6-1	175	3-16-94	.263	.382	.220	69	259	39	68	12	3	0	51	47	6	2	2	50	8	2	.332	.385
Jesus, Anderson	R-R	6-2	168	2-19-94	.227	.310	.182	42	119	14	27	5	2	1	9	7	2	1	0	30	1	2	.328	.281
Pinto, Eduard	L-L	5-11	150	10-23-94	.396	.351	.412	56	222	47	88	13	1	1	29	31	5	1	3	13	8	6	.477	.475
Santos, Jose	B-R	6-0	170	11-12-93	.233	.324	.202	50	146	36	34	4	0	0	11	19	5	6	1	41	4	2	.260	.339
Urias, Ramon	R-R	5-10	150	6-3-94	.268	.288	.261	56	190	28	51	11	0	1	36	14	10	6	3	16	3	3	.342	.346
Valencia, Ricardo	R-R	6-0	185	1-13-93	.246	.250	.244	28	61	11	15	2	0	0	9	11	4	2	1	11	0	0	.279	.390

Pitching	B-T	HT	WT	DOB	W	L	ERA	G	GS	CG	SV	IP	H	R	ER	HR	BB	SO	AVG	vLH	vRH	K/9	BB/9
Beltre, Dario	R-R	6-3	170	11-19-92	1	0	5.19	10	0	0	0	9	7	5	5	0	12	15	.212	.000	.233	15.58	12.46
Carvallo, Felix	L-L	6-0	175	10-5-93	8	1	3.35	21	0	0	0	46	44	21	17	1	13	47	.253	.250	.253	9.26	2.56
De Jesus, Jorge	R-R	6-0	205	1-17-92	2	0	1.23	4	0	0	0	7	3	1	1	0	2	11	.111	.000	.158	13.50	2.45
De La Cruz, Alex	R-R	5-11	170	10-7-94	4	2	1.93	18	0	0	9	37	25	8	8	0	2	29	.203	.171	.216	6.99	0.48
Decena, Albert	R-R	6-3	185	5-12-91	2	0	3.21	8	4	0	0	28	17	10	10	1	9	31	.172	.160	.176	9.96	2.89
Fandino, Jesus	R-R	6-1	160	1-27-94	0	2	5.90	10	4	0	0	29	34	21	19	0	16	19	.298	.167	.323	5.90	4.97
Fracchiolla, Gionny	L-L	5-7	156	9-10-91	0	0	4.05	6	0	0	0	7	7	10	3	0	8	8	.241	.250	.240	10.80	10.80
Gomez, Jose	R-R	6-1	155	10-4-93	2	0	3.32	8	1	0	0	22	16	9	8	2	5	11	.205	.105	.237	4.57	2.08
Leclerc, Jose	R-R	6-0	165	12-19-93	3	1	1.54	19	0	0	1	47	32	15	8	1	18	41	.193	.170	.204	7.91	3.47
Mendez, Yohander	L-L	6-5	175	1-17-95	2	1	1.99	14	13	0	0	45	36	13	10	1	13	35	.226	.235	.225	6.95	2.58
Mendoza, Anyenil	R-R	6-2	185	12-9-89	0	1	9.00	2	0	0	0	1	2	1	1	0	2	1	.000	.000	.000	9.00	18.00
Morel, Luis	R-R	6-2	188	9-14-93	0	0	9.45	3	0	0	0	7	11	7	7	0	1	7	.393	.500	.385	9.45	1.35
Nunez, Nerfy	L-L	6-0	210	8-12-92	0	3	5.88	17	9	0	1	49	60	38	32	3	21	42	.306	.167	.315	7.71	3.86
Payano, Pedro	R-R	6-2	170	9-27-94	2	3	5.53	12	9	0	0	42	44	28	26	1	18	26	.272	.265	.273	5.53	3.83
Pena, Richelson	R-R	6-1	170	9-29-93	2	3	4.85	15	6	0	1	39	34	23	21	1	13	29	.239	.212	.248	6.69	3.00
Rodriguez, Ricardo	R-R	6-2	220	8-31-92	3	3	2.87	26	0	0	2	47	46	19	15	0	13	54	.253	.205	.266	10.34	2.49
Solano, Stanley	R-R	6-1	165	5-20-92	1	0	4.91	15	0	0	0	22	25	13	12	1	11	19	.291	.273	.297	7.77	4.50
Sosa, Kevin	R-R	6-1	192	1-6-95	3	3	3.99	13	11	0	0	50	52	28	22	1	22	46	.267	.192	.311	8.34	3.99
Vargas, Daris	R-R	6-3	195	8-12-92	0	0	3.86	4	0	0	0	5	3	2	2	0	5	3	.200	.500	.091	5.79	9.64
Vasquez, Kelvin	R-R	6-4	180	4-6-93	2	3	3.42	16	13	0	0	55	56	29	21	1	15	51	.256	.235	.265	8.30	2.44

Fielding

Catcher	PCT	G	PO	A	E	DP	PB
Caraballo	1.000	18	90	5	0	0	2
Garay	.992	36	225	26	2	0	5
Gonzalez	1.000	10	54	18	0	0	1
Valencia	.994	28	153	21	1	0	3

First Base	PCT	G	PO	A	E	DP
Adames	1.000	2	5	0	0	0
Caraballo	1.000	4	8	0	0	0
Castillo	.958	15	111	3	5	8
Cedeno	.991	34	312	16	3	29
Garay	.985	22	182	10	3	17
Pinto	1.000	1	10	1	0	1

Second Base	PCT	G	PO	A	E	DP
Ayarza	.983	46	86	91	3	16

	PCT	G	PO	A	E	DP
Campos	.970	23	47	50	3	9
Gonzalez	1.000	4	2	11	0	0
Urias	.966	12	8	20	1	8

Third Base	PCT	G	PO	A	E	DP
Campos	.800	4	1	3	1	0
Caraballo	1.000	1	0	1	0	0
Castillo	.975	39	30	88	3	7
Gonzalez	.914	7	12	20	3	2
Urias	.926	29	26	62	7	2

Shortstop	PCT	G	PO	A	E	DP
Adames	—	1	0	0	0	0
Campos	.894	22	38	46	10	13
Caraballo	.750	1	0	3	1	0
Castillo	.981	13	16	36	1	2

	PCT	G	PO	A	E	DP
Gonzalez	.915	43	51	121	16	22

Outfield	PCT	G	PO	A	E	DP
Cedeno	.971	34	61	5	2	2
Gonzalez	.818	12	8	1	2	0
Gonzalez	1.000	1	3	0	0	0
Gonzalez	.978	69	130	5	3	2
Jesus	.905	17	18	1	2	0
Pinto	.953	49	75	6	4	0
Santos	.968	45	60	1	2	0

Toronto Blue Jays

SEASON IN A SENTENCE: With some solid young contributors in the big leagues and talent developing in the minors, Toronto looked to take a step forward in the American League East, but injuries depleted the big league roster and the Jays finished in fourth for the fifth straight season.

HIGH POINT: Edwin Encarnacion continued to provide exceptional offense in the middle of the lineup, even with Jose Bautista limited to 92 games and Brett Lawrie missing about a month. Encarnacion hit .280/.384/.557 with 42 home runs. The Blue Jays signed him to an extension in July through 2015 for $29 million and a club option for 2016.

LOW POINT: Injuries gutted the Blue Jays' rotation and lineup throughout the season. Most notably, righthanders Drew Hutchison and Kyle Drabek had Tommy John surgery and will be expected to miss much of the 2013 season. Bautista hit 27 home runs in 92 games, but left wrist surgery cut his season short.

NOTABLE ROOKIES: Though they didn't really have a choice, the Blue Jays weren't shy about throwing rookies into the fire when big leaguers hit the disabled list. Outfielders Anthony Gose (.223/.303/.319 in 59 games) and Moises Sierra (.224/.274/.374 in 49 games) saw significant playing time, while shortstop Adeiny Hechavarria was asked to switch to third base to fill in for Lawrie. Hechavarria hit .254/.280/.365 in 126 at-bats while showing good defense.

KEY TRANSACTIONS: Toronto made a 10-player trade with Houston at midseason to acquire righthanders David Carpenter and Brandon Lyon and lefthander J.A. Happ. The Blue Jays gave up righthanders Asher Wojciechowski, David Rollins, Joe Musgrove, Kevin Comer and Francisco Cordero as well as outfielder Ben Francisco and catcher Carlos Perez. They also sent Travis Snider to the Pirates in a deal that marked the end of the tenure of a player once expected to be a franchise building block. Toronto extracted Mike Aviles from the Red Sox when John Farrell departed for Boston's managerial opening, then used Aviles in a trade to get righthander Esmil Rogers from the Indians.

DOWN ON THE FARM: High Class A Dunedin and low Class A Lansing both made it to the postseason, and short-season Vancouver won the Northwest League championship. After the season, Toronto was able to move its Triple-A affiliation from Las Vegas to Buffalo.

OPENING DAY PAYROLL: $75.5 million (23rd)

PLAYERS OF THE YEAR

MAJOR LEAGUE	MINOR LEAGUE
Edwin Encarnacion	**Kevin Pillar**
3b	**of**
.280/.384/.557	(Low A/High A)
42 HR, 110 RBIs	.323/.374/.439
3rd in AL in OPS, RBIs	Midwest Lg. MVP

ORGANIZATION LEADERS

BATTING		*Minimum 250 AB
MAJORS		
* AVG	Edwin Encarnacion	.280
* OPS	Edwin Encarnacion	.941
HR	Edwin Encarnacion	42
RBI	Edwin Encarnacion	110
MINORS		
* AVG	Kevin Pillar, Lansing/Dunedin	.323
* OBP	Kevin Pillar, Lansing/Dunedin	.374
* SLG	Ryan Schimpf, Dunedin/New Hampshire	.500
R	Kenny Wilson, Lansing/Dunedin	92
H	Kevin Pillar, Lansing/Dunedin	161
TB	Ryan Schimpf, Dunedin/New Hampshire	236
2B	K.C. Hobson, Lansing	43
3B	Anthony Gose, Las Vegas	10
	Jake Marisnick, Dunedin/New Hampshire	10
HR	Ryan Schimpf, Dunedin/New Hampshire	22
RBI	Kevin Pillar, Lansing/Dunedin	91
BB	Jonathan Diaz, New Hampshire/Las Vegas	75
SO	Marcus Knecht, Dunedin	146
SB	Kenny Wilson, Lansing/Dunedin	55

PITCHING		#Minimum 75 IP
MAJORS		
W	Brandon Morrow	10
# ERA	Henderson Alvarez	4.85
SO	Ricky Romero	124
SV	Casey Janssen	22
MINORS		
W	Marcus Walden, Lansing/Dunedin	14
L	Deck McGuire, New Hampshire	15
# ERA	Justin Nicolino, Lansing	2.46
G	Jerry Gil, Las Vegas	58
GS	Deck McGuire, New Hampshire	28
SV	Danny Barnes, New Hampshire/Dunedin	34
IP	Casey Lawrence, New Hampshire/Dunedin	151.1
BB	Deck McGuire, New Hampshire	62
SO	Javier Avendano, Lansing/Vancouver	130
# AVG	Marcus Walden, Lansing/Dunedin	.222

2012 PERFORMANCE

General Manager: Alex Anthopoulos. **Farm Director:** Charlie Wilson. **Scouting Director:** Andrew Tinnish.

Class	Team	League	W	L	PCT	Finish	Manager
Majors	Toronto Blue Jays	American	73	89	.451	10th (14)	John Farrell
Triple-A	Las Vegas 51s	Pacific Coast	79	64	.552	5th (16)	Marty Brown
Double-A	New Hampshire Fisher Cats	Eastern	61	81	.430	11th (12)	Sal Fasano
High A	Dunedin Blue Jays	Florida State	78	55	.586	2nd (12)	Mike Redmond
Low A	Lansing Lugnuts	Midwest	82	55	.599	1st (16)	John Tamargo
Short-season	Vancouver Canadians	Northwest	46	30	.605	t-2nd (8)	Clayton McCullough
Rookie	Bluefield Blue Jays	Appalachian	29	37	.439	7th (10)	Dennis Holmberg
Rookie	GCL Blue Jays	Gulf Coast	22	38	.367	13th (14)	Omar Malave/John Schneider
Overall 2012 Minor League Record			397	360	.524	7th (30)	

ORGANIZATION STATISTICS

TORONTO BLUE JAYS

AMERICAN LEAGUE

Batting	B-T	HT	WT	DOB	AVG	vLH	vRH	G	AB	R	H	2B	3B	HR	RBI	BB	HBP	SH	SF	SO	SB	CS	SLG	OBP
Arencibia, J.P.	R-R	6-0	205	1-5-86	.233	.244	.230	102	347	45	81	16	0	18	56	18	3	1	3	108	1	0	.435	.275
Bautista, Jose	R-R	6-0	190	10-19-80	.241	.200	.255	92	332	64	80	14	0	27	65	59	4	0	4	63	5	2	.527	.358
Cooper, David	L-L	6-0	200	2-12-87	.300	.294	.302	45	140	16	42	11	0	4	11	4	1	0	0	22	0	1	.464	.324
Davis, Rajai	R-R	5-9	195	10-19-80	.257	.285	.243	142	447	64	115	24	3	8	43	29	6	1	4	102	46	13	.378	.309
Encarnacion, Edwin	R-R	6-2	230	1-7-83	.280	.301	.273	151	542	93	152	24	0	42	110	84	11	0	7	94	13	3	.557	.384
Escobar, Yunel	R-R	6-2	210	11-2-82	.253	.258	.251	145	558	58	141	22	1	9	51	35	4	7	4	70	5	1	.344	.300
Francisco, Ben	R-R	6-1	185	10-23-81	.240	.273	.176	27	50	5	12	5	1	0	2	4	0	0	0	16	0	1	.380	.296
2-team total (24 Tampa Bay)					.234	—	—	51	107	9	25	10	1	2	10	8	0	0	2	26	0	1	.402	.282
Gomes, Yan	R-R	6-2	215	7-19-87	.204	.217	.192	43	98	9	20	4	0	4	13	6	3	1	3	32	0	0	.367	.264
Gose, Anthony	L-L	6-1	190	8-10-90	.223	.290	.207	56	166	25	37	7	3	1	11	17	2	4	0	59	15	3	.319	.303
Hechavarria, Adeiny	R-R	5-11	180	4-15-89	.254	.234	.266	41	126	10	32	8	0	2	15	4	1	5	1	32	0	0	.365	.280
Johnson, Kelly	L-R	6-1	200	2-22-82	.225	.201	.234	142	507	61	114	19	2	16	55	62	5	2	4	159	14	2	.365	.313
Lawrie, Brett	R-R	6-0	215	1-18-90	.273	.319	.256	125	494	73	135	26	3	11	48	33	5	2	2	86	13	8	.405	.324
Lind, Adam	L-L	6-2	210	7-17-83	.255	.202	.276	93	321	28	82	14	2	11	45	29	0	0	3	61	0	0	.414	.314
Mathis, Jeff	R-R	6-0	200	3-31-83	.218	.219	.218	70	211	25	46	13	0	8	27	9	0	6	1	68	1	0	.393	.249
McCoy, Mike	R-R	5-9	175	4-2-81	.173	.150	.188	32	52	10	9	1	1	0	5	7	0	4	0	6	2	1	.250	.232
Rasmus, Colby	L-L	6-2	200	8-11-86	.223	.182	.238	151	565	75	126	21	5	23	75	47	7	2	4	149	4	3	.400	.289
Sierra, Moises	R-R	6-0	225	9-24-88	.224	.286	.187	49	147	14	33	4	0	6	15	8	2	0	0	44	1	0	.374	.274
Snider, Travis	L-L	6-0	235	2-2-88	.250	.385	.174	10	36	6	9	2	0	3	8	3	0	0	1	14	0	0	.556	.300
Thames, Eric	L-R	6-0	205	11-10-86	.243	.286	.233	46	148	17	36	7	1	3	11	9	1	0	2	40	0	1	.365	.288
2-team total (40 Seattle)					.232	—	—	86	271	27	63	12	3	9	25	15	1	1	2	87	1	1	.399	.273
Torrealba, Yorvit	R-R	5-11	200	7-19-78	.214	.400	.174	10	28	3	6	0	0	1	2	2	0	0	0	7	0	0	.321	.267
2-team total (49 Texas)					.233	—	—	59	189	19	44	8	0	4	14	16	2	3	2	38	1	1	.339	.297
Vizquel, Omar	B-R	5-9	180	4-24-67	.235	.217	.243	60	153	13	36	5	1	0	7	7	0	1	2	17	3	2	.281	.265

Pitching	B-T	HT	WT	DOB	W	L	ERA	G	GS	CG	SV	IP	H	R	ER	HR	BB	SO	AVG	vLH	vRH	K/9	BB/9
Alvarez, Henderson	R-R	6-1	210	4-18-90	9	14	4.85	31	31	1	0	187	216	110	101	29	54	79	.290	.312	.265	3.80	2.59
Beck, Chad	R-R	6-4	255	1-17-85	0	0	6.32	14	0	0	0	16	21	12	11	2	5	9	.318	.310	.324	5.17	2.87
Carpenter, Drew	R-R	6-3	230	5-18-85	0	0	5.00	6	0	0	0	9	7	5	5	4	6	9	.206	.214	.200	9.00	6.00
Carpenter, David	R-R	6-2	215	7-15-85	0	0	30.38	3	0	0	0	3	8	10	9	1	2	4	.471	.625	.333	13.50	6.75
Carreno, Joel	R-R	6-2	220	3-7-87	0	2	6.14	11	2	0	0	22	22	15	15	7	14	16	.265	.231	.295	6.55	5.73
Cecil, Brett	R-L	6-1	215	7-2-86	2	4	5.72	21	9	0	0	61	70	40	39	11	23	51	.294	.214	.319	7.48	3.38
Chavez, Jesse	R-R	6-2	160	8-21-83	1	1	8.44	9	2	0	0	21	25	22	20	6	10	27	.281	.343	.241	11.39	4.22
2-team total (4 Oakland)					1	1	9.85	13	2	0	0	25	34	29	27	7	11	30	—	—	—	10.95	4.01
Coello, Robert	R-R	6-5	250	11-23-84	0	1	12.79	6	0	0	0	6	10	9	9	2	4	11	.357	.364	.353	15.63	5.68
Cordero, Francisco	R-R	6-3	245	5-11-75	3	5	5.77	41	0	0	2	34	48	24	22	7	14	26	.340	.352	.329	6.82	3.67
Crawford, Evan	R-L	6-2	190	9-2-86	0	0	6.75	10	0	0	0	8	10	6	6	3	4	5	.333	.118	.615	5.63	4.50
Delabar, Steve	R-R	6-5	220	7-17-83	2	2	3.38	27	0	0	0	29	23	12	11	3	15	46	.213	.265	.169	14.11	4.60
2-team total (34 Seattle)					4	3	3.82	61	0	0	0	66	46	29	28	12	26	92	—	—	—	12.55	3.55
Drabek, Kyle	R-R	6-1	230	12-8-87	4	7	4.67	13	13	0	0	71	67	41	37	10	47	47	.250	.199	.307	5.93	5.93
Dyson, Sam	R-R	6-2	205	5-7-88	0	0	40.50	2	0	0	0	1	4	3	3	0	2	1	.667	1.000	.600	13.50	27.00
Frasor, Jason	R-R	5-9	180	8-9-77	1	1	4.12	50	0	0	0	44	42	20	20	6	22	53	.256	.273	.245	10.92	4.53
Happ, J.A.	L-L	6-6	195	10-19-82	3	2	4.69	10	6	0	0	40	35	21	21	2	17	46	.236	.237	.236	10.26	3.79
Hill, Shawn	R-R	6-2	225	4-28-81	1	0	0.00	1	0	0	0	3	0	0	0	0	2	0	.000	.000	.000	0.00	6.00
Hutchison, Drew	L-R	6-2	195	8-22-90	5	3	4.60	11	11	0	0	59	59	31	30	8	20	49	.257	.254	.259	7.52	3.07
Igarashi, Ryota	R-R	5-11	200	5-28-79	0	0	36.00	2	0	0	0	1	5	4	4	0	2	2	.625	.500	.667	18.00	18.00
2-team total (2 New York)					0	0	18.00	4	0	0	0	4	9	8	8	0	5	5	—	—	—	11.25	11.25
Janssen, Casey	R-R	6-3	225	9-17-81	1	1	2.54	62	0	0	22	64	44	18	18	7	11	67	.195	.172	.218	9.47	1.55
Jenkins, Chad	R-R	6-4	230	12-22-87	1	3	4.50	13	3	0	0	32	32	16	16	5	11	16	.260	.283	.238	4.50	3.09
Korecky, Bobby	R-R	5-11	185	9-16-79	0	0	18.00	1	0	0	0	1	2	2	2	1	1	0	.250	.500	.000	0.00	9.00
Laffey, Aaron	L-L	6-0	200	4-15-85	4	6	4.56	22	16	0	0	101	100	56	51	17	37	48	.260	.239	.269	4.29	3.31
Lincoln, Brad	L-R	6-0	210	5-25-85	1	0	5.65	24	0	0	0	29	29	18	18	6	10	28	.264	.208	.306	8.79	3.14

Name	B-T	HT	WT	DOB	W	L	ERA	G	GS	CG	SV	IP	H	R	ER	HR	BB	SO	AVG	vLH	vRH	K/9	BB/9
Loup, Aaron	L-L	5-11	205	12-19-87	0	2	2.64	33	0	0	0	31	26	10	9	0	2	21	.232	.207	.259	6.16	0.59
Lyon, Brandon	R-R	6-1	200	8-10-79	4	0	2.88	30	0	0	1	25	19	8	8	2	9	28	.207	.161	.230	10.08	3.24
Morrow, Brandon	R-R	6-3	200	7-26-84	10	7	2.96	21	21	3	0	125	98	45	41	12	41	108	.214	.188	.246	7.80	2.96
Oliver, Darren	R-L	6-2	200	10-6-70	3	4	2.06	62	0	0	2	57	43	13	13	3	15	52	.214	.234	.196	8.26	2.38
Pauley, David	R-R	6-2	215	6-17-83	0	0	9.95	5	0	0	0	6	11	7	7	1	2	2	.393	.500	.313	2.84	2.84
2-team total (5 Los Angeles)					0	1	6.48	10	0	0	0	17	27	13	12	2	5	6	—	—	—	3.24	2.70
Perez, Luis	L-L	6-0	210	1-20-85	2	2	3.43	35	0	0	0	42	38	16	16	3	16	39	.244	.194	.277	8.36	3.43
Richmond, Scott	R-R	6-5	220	8-30-79	0	0	6.00	3	0	0	0	3	5	2	2	1	0	2	.357	.143	.571	6.00	0.00
Romero, Ricky	R-L	6-0	220	11-6-84	9	14	5.77	32	32	1	0	181	198	122	116	21	105	124	.282	.310	.268	6.17	5.22
Santos, Sergio	R-R	6-3	240	7-4-83	0	1	9.00	6	0	0	2	5	6	5	5	1	4	4	.316	.182	.500	7.20	7.20
Villanueva, Carlos	R-R	6-2	235	11-28-83	7	7	4.16	38	16	0	0	125	113	59	58	23	46	122	.242	.239	.246	8.76	3.30

Fielding

Catcher	PCT	G	PO	A	E	DP	PB
Arencibia	.994	94	622	57	4	1	9
Gomes	1.000	9	35	0	0	0	0
Mathis	.996	66	433	38	2	5	6
Torrealba	1.000	9	52	3	0	1	0

First Base	PCT	G	PO	A	E	DP
Bautista	1.000	4	8	2	0	1
Cooper	.996	29	217	25	1	22
Encarnacion	.995	68	602	32	3	61
Gomes	.991	20	106	7	1	7
Lind	.991	61	545	37	5	64
Torrealba	1.000	1	2	0	0	0
Vizquel	1.000	2	6	0	0	0

Second Base	PCT	G	PO	A	E	DP
Hechavarria	1.000	8	17	20	0	4

	PCT	G	PO	A	E	DP
Johnson	.983	136	247	386	11	100
McCoy	1.000	8	6	12	0	2
Vizquel	1.000	24	32	52	0	13

Third Base	PCT	G	PO	A	E	DP
Bautista	—	1	0	0	0	0
Encarnacion	.667	1	2	0	1	0
Gomes	1.000	8	7	12	0	2
Hechavarria	.980	18	8	40	1	5
Lawrie	.955	123	84	273	17	23
McCoy	1.000	6	2	12	0	1
Vizquel	.932	18	10	31	3	3

Shortstop	PCT	G	PO	A	E	DP
Escobar	.982	143	240	431	12	100
Hechavarria	.959	17	15	32	2	12
Lawrie	1.000	1	1	0	0	0

	PCT	G	PO	A	E	
McCoy	—	1	0	0	0	
Vizquel	1.000	10	10	20	0	3

Outfield	PCT	G	PO	A	E	DP
Bautista	.988	90	155	11	2	4
Davis	.965	135	211	8	8	1
Encarnacion	1.000	3	3	0	0	0
Francisco	1.000	9	3	0	0	0
Gomes	—	4	0	0	0	0
Gose	.991	54	106	2	1	2
McCoy	1.000	9	8	1	0	0
Rasmus	.981	145	304	7	6	1
Sierra	1.000	39	67	3	0	0
Snider	.950	10	19	0	1	0
Thames	.986	43	72	0	1	0
Vizquel	—	1	0	0	0	0

LAS VEGAS 51S · TRIPLE-A

PACIFIC COAST LEAGUE

Batting	B-T	HT	WT	DOB	AVG	vLH	vRH	G	AB	R	H	2B	3B	HR	RBI	BB	HBP	SH	SF	SO	SB	CS	SLG	OBP
Bailli, Kenen	L-L	6-0	190	1-25-85	.323	.500	.296	12	31	5	10	1	0	1	3	4	0	1	0	6	0	0	.452	.400
Bocock, Brian	R-R	5-11	185	3-9-85	.211	.217	.208	20	76	9	16	5	1	0	9	5	0	0	0	13	1	0	.303	.259
Cooper, David	L-L	6-0	200	2-12-87	.314	.329	.309	68	261	45	82	27	1	10	52	37	1	0	5	34	0	1	.540	.395
Cust, Jack	L-R	6-1	247	1-7-79	.200	.235	.182	16	50	7	10	1	0	0	6	16	1	0	1	21	3	0	.220	.397
d'Arnaud, Travis	R-R	6-2	195	2-10-89	.333	.297	.344	67	279	45	93	21	2	16	52	19	3	0	2	59	1	1	.595	.380
Diaz, Jonathan	R-R	5-9	170	4-10-85	.240	.293	.222	95	312	58	75	11	2	3	31	62	7	15	4	56	12	4	.317	.374
Eigsti, Ryan	R-R	6-1	205	8-24-85	.154	.222	.118	10	26	0	4	1	0	0	3	2	0	0	0	7	0	0	.192	.214
2-team total (11 Omaha)					.158	—	—	21	38	1	6	1	0	0	3	3	0	2	0	10	0	0	.184	.220
Galarraga, Joel	R-R	5-11	185	3-20-82	.320	.167	.368	9	25	3	8	1	1	0	3	4	0	0	0	5	1	0	.440	.414
2-team total (3 Sacramento)					.306	—	—	12	36	4	11	1	1	0	3	4	0	0	0	8	1	0	.389	.375
Gomes, Yan	R-R	6-2	215	7-19-87	.328	.344	.324	79	305	44	100	29	1	13	59	25	2	0	2	72	4	0	.557	.380
Gose, Anthony	L-L	6-1	190	8-10-90	.286	.176	.313	102	420	87	120	21	10	5	43	49	5	4	1	101	34	12	.419	.366
Gosewisch, Tuffy	R-R	5-11	180	8-17-83	.277	.214	.309	24	83	9	23	8	1	1	8	3	1	1	0	17	0	1	.434	.365
Gotay, Ruben	B-R	5-11	175	12-8-82	.346	.278	.367	22	78	14	27	3	0	0	14	13	0	0	1	19	3	0	.385	.435
Guerrero, Vladimir	R-R	6-3	235	2-9-75	.303	.462	.200	8	33	5	10	2	1	0	4	0	1	0	1	4	0	0	.424	.314
Hechavarria, Adeiny	R-R	5-11	180	4-15-89	.312	.385	.289	102	443	78	138	20	6	6	63	38	1	3	5	86	8	2	.424	.363
Howard, Kevin	L-R	6-2	210		.311	.172	.356	35	119	14	37	6	1	4	16	12	0	0	0	19	3	1	.479	.374
Hughes, Luke	R-R	5-11	205	8-2-84	.314	.400	.271	28	105	20	33	9	3	3	13	13	1	1	1	32	1	0	.543	.392
2-team total (35 Sacramento)					.275	—	—	63	207	36	57	15	3	5	26	27	3	1	4	60	2	2	.449	.361
Hurtado, Luis	R-R	5-11	175	11-4-88	.167	.000	.333	4	12	0	2	0	0	0	0	0	0	0	0	2	0	0	.167	.167
Lind, Adam	L-L	6-2	210	7-17-83	.392	.429	.381	32	125	24	49	10	0	8	29	15	0	0	3	26	1	0	.664	.448
McCoy, Mike	R-R	5-9	175	4-2-81	.263	.235	.271	85	278	46	73	13	1	3	31	58	1	7	5	51	21	10	.349	.386
McDade, Mike	B-R	6-1	250	5-8-89	.338	.417	.298	18	71	9	24	3	1	2	18	7	0	0	1	11	0	0	.493	.392
Nanita, Ricardo	R-L	6-0	205	6-12-81	.306	.253	.320	93	333	49	102	17	0	12	62	23	4	1	5	39	3	3	.465	.353
Perales, Danny	L-L	6-0	195	3-18-85	.279	.258	.286	72	262	39	73	18	2	6	39	15	1	1	1	41	4	2	.431	.319
Phillips, Paul	R-R	5-11	200	4-15-77	.333	.400	.318	17	54	5	18	2	0	0	4	5	1	3	0	5	0	1	.370	.400
2-team total (14 Nashville)					.278	—	—	31	97	7	27	2	0	0	6	9	1	3	1	12	0	1	.299	.343
Sierra, Moises	R-R	6-0	225	9-24-88	.289	.302	.285	100	377	62	109	16	1	17	63	39	4	0	2	86	7	6	.472	.360
Snider, Travis	L-L	6-0	235	2-2-88	.335	.283	.350	56	209	49	70	16	0	13	56	34	0	0	3	42	2	4	.598	.423
Sobolewski, Mark	R-R	6-0	195	12-24-86	.188	.115	.222	23	80	12	15	4	0	2	8	6	0	0	0	12	1	0	.313	.244
Thames, Eric	R-R	6-0	205	11-10-86	.330	.316	.333	54	197	31	65	15	3	6	32	26	3	0	5	42	1	1	.528	.407
Woodward, Chris	R-R	6-0	190	6-27-76	.285	.309	.274	88	309	39	88	25	1	2	34	21	5	4	2	58	4	2	.392	.338

Pitching	B-T	HT	WT	DOB	W	L	ERA	G	GS	CG	SV	IP	H	R	ER	HR	BB	SO	AVG	vLH	vRH	K/9	BB/9
Abreu, Juan	R-R	6-0	185	4-8-85	0	0	2.70	4	0	0	0	3	4	1	1	1	2	5	.286	.000	.333	13.50	5.40
2-team total (38 Oklahoma City)					2	3	6.80	42	0	0	5	49	50	38	37	13	36	59	—	—	—	10.84	6.61
Beck, Chad	R-R	6-4	205	1-17-85	2	0	1.31	43	0	0	18	48	39	7	7	2	13	24	.218	.331	.152	4.50	2.44
Carpenter, Drew	R-R	6-3	230	5-18-85	6	3	3.38	21	12	0	0	75	83	31	28	10	19	56	.284	.297	.274	6.75	2.29
Carpenter, David	R-R	6-2	215	7-15-85	0	1	3.57	16	0	0	0	18	15	8	7	1	7	19	.221	.226	.216	9.68	3.57
2-team total (7 Oklahoma City)					1	1	3.08	23	0	0	4	26	22	10	9	2	7	25	—	—	—	8.54	2.39
Carreno, Joel	R-R	6-2	220	3-7-87	2	5	8.92	10	8	0	0	36	50	41	36	7	27	30	.336	.347	.325	7.43	6.69
Cecil, Brett	R-L	6-1	215	7-2-86	1	2	2.50	6	6	0	0	40	36	11	11	1	7	33	.248	.293	.231	7.49	1.59

TORONTO BLUE JAYS

Pitching	B-T	HT	WT	DOB	W	L	ERA	G	GS	CG	SV	IP	H	R	ER	HR	BB	SO	AVG	vLH	vRH	K/9	BB/9
Chavez, Jesse	R-R	6-2	160	8-21-83	8	5	3.98	19	17	1	1	95	90	45	42	10	20	86	.246	.272	.220	8.15	1.89
2-team total (2 Sacramento)					8	5	3.77	21	18	1	2	105	98	47	44	10	22	95	—	—	—	8.14	1.89
Coello, Robert	R-R	6-5	250	11-23-84	4	1	3.00	19	3	0	0	42	31	16	14	4	18	43	.208	.184	.233	9.21	3.86
Crawford, Evan	R-L	6-2	190	9-2-86	1	4	6.83	26	0	0	0	28	38	22	21	2	12	20	.328	.346	.313	6.51	3.90
Everts, Clint	B-R	6-2	195	8-10-84	3	2	3.10	37	0	0	2	61	53	23	21	2	32	53	.236	.247	.227	7.82	4.72
Gil, Jerry	R-R	6-3	210	10-14-82	7	1	4.92	58	0	0	9	64	68	36	35	8	20	51	.268	.270	.265	7.17	2.81
Hill, Shawn	R-R	6-2	225	4-28-81	9	2	4.52	15	15	0	0	90	115	49	45	10	22	52	.312	.353	.276	5.22	2.21
Hoey, Jim	R-R	6-6	205	12-30-82	0	3	4.60	46	0	0	1	61	59	36	31	5	42	45	.261	.257	.265	6.68	6.23
Igarashi, Ryota	R-R	5-11	200	5-28-79	1	1	1.29	19	0	0	4	21	10	3	3	0	3	28	.139	.128	.152	12.00	1.29
Jakubauskas, Chris	R-R	6-2	215	12-22-78	0	0	13.50	3	0	0	0	3	4	4	4	0	2	0	.400	.200	.600	0.00	6.75
2-team total (18 Reno)					2	3	4.64	21	7	0	0	54	61	35	28	2	16	28	—	—	—	4.64	2.65
Korecky, Bobby	R-R	5-11	185	9-16-79	3	4	3.44	46	2	0	0	86	89	40	33	10	19	47	.266	.305	.235	4.90	1.98
Laffey, Aaron	L-L	6-0	200	4-15-85	3	5	4.52	11	11	1	0	64	77	41	32	6	20	38	.298	.329	.284	5.37	2.83
Moyer, Jamie	L-L	6-0	185	11-18-62	1	1	8.18	2	2	0	0	11	17	10	10	3	3	9	.340	.333	.343	7.36	2.45
Murphy, Bill	L-L	5-11	195	5-9-81	8	5	4.38	28	15	0	0	101	109	56	49	7	47	59	.276	.285	.272	5.27	4.20
O'Sullivan, Sean	R-R	6-1	240	9-1-87	9	3	2.72	14	14	0	0	89	77	39	27	5	23	44	.239	.212	.263	4.43	2.32
2-team total (17 Omaha)					14	7	4.23	31	19	0	1	143	153	82	67	11	46	70	—	—	—	4.42	2.90
Pino, Yohan	R-R	6-2	190	12-26-83	0	2	22.18	3	3	0	0	9	29	23	22	1	3	8	.518	.650	.444	7.71	2.29
Redding, Tim	R-R	5-11	230	2-12-78	0	5	8.66	23	7	0	1	62	94	64	60	15	25	38	.364	.392	.336	5.49	3.61
Richmond, Scott	R-R	6-5	220	8-30-79	11	7	5.61	27	25	0	0	135	163	93	84	21	43	112	.302	.296	.308	7.49	2.87
Robertson, Nate	R-L	6-2	225	9-3-77	0	1	8.00	9	2	0	0	18	20	9	8	2	4	5	.351	.176	.500	5.00	4.00
2-team total (14 Iowa)					0	3	8.07	23	2	0	0	29	43	28	26	8	8	20	—	—	—	6.21	2.48
Schwinden, Chris	R-R	6-3	215	9-22-86	0	1	21.00	1	1	0	0	3	8	8	7	1	1	2	.471	.600	.417	6.00	3.00
Uviedo, Ronald	R-R	6-1	160	10-7-86	0	0	3.00	3	0	0	0	6	5	3	2	0	2	5	.227	.143	.267	7.50	3.00

Fielding

Catcher	PCT	G	PO	A	E	DP	PB
d'Arnaud	.991	55	383	37	4	0	6
Eigsti	1.000	8	31	5	0	1	3
Galarraga	.983	9	55	2	1	0	1
Gomes	.983	35	204	22	4	3	3
Gosewisch	.994	23	145	15	1	0	1
Hurtado	1.000	4	16	0	0	0	0
Phillips	.989	16	79	7	1	1	5

First Base	PCT	G	PO	A	E	DP
Cooper	.996	54	491	37	2	54
d'Arnaud	1.000	2	16	0	0	3
Eigsti	1.000	2	13	0	0	0
Gomes	.987	17	139	13	2	14
Howard	1.000	7	59	7	0	9
Lind	.985	25	240	16	4	28
McDade	.980	16	137	7	3	20
Nanita	.987	8	71	6	1	12
Woodward	.974	21	145	7	4	19

Second Base	PCT	G	PO	A	E	DP
Diaz	.990	80	162	329	5	79

	PCT	G	PO	A	E	DP
Gotay	.977	22	53	77	3	20
Hechavarria	1.000	8	13	34	0	5
Howard	1.000	2	10	8	0	2
Hughes	1.000	1	1	4	0	1
McCoy	.977	27	47	79	3	16
Woodward	1.000	5	9	13	0	6

Third Base	PCT	G	PO	A	E	DP
Bocock	1.000	1	0	2	0	1
Diaz	1.000	6	4	8	0	1
Gomes	.905	24	11	46	6	12
Howard	.932	16	6	35	3	1
Hughes	1.000	5	3	4	0	1
McCoy	.909	26	11	39	5	7
Sobolewski	.838	15	10	21	6	5
Woodward	.948	60	36	109	8	12

Shortstop	PCT	G	PO	A	E	DP
Bocock	.935	19	30	57	6	12
Diaz	.959	9	14	33	2	10
Hechavarria	.961	95	144	304	18	90
Hughes	.929	3	4	9	1	2

	PCT	G	PO	A	E	DP
McCoy	.988	17	28	51	1	11
Woodward	1.000	1	1	4	0	2

Outfield	PCT	G	PO	A	E	DP
Bailli	.967	11	27	2	1	1
Cust	.933	8	14	0	1	0
Gomes	1.000	1	1	0	0	0
Gose	.975	102	222	8	6	2
Gosewisch	—	1	0	0	0	0
Guerrero	1.000	2	2	0	0	0
Howard	—	1	0	0	0	0
Hughes	1.000	21	40	1	0	0
McCoy	.980	18	46	4	1	2
Nanita	.975	47	77	1	2	0
Perales	.983	63	114	5	2	0
Sierra	.980	99	188	10	4	5
Snider	.986	45	72	1	1	0
Thames	1.000	33	64	3	0	0

NEW HAMPSHIRE FISHER CATS

DOUBLE-A

EASTERN LEAGUE

Batting	B-T	HT	WT	DOB	AVG	vLH	vRH	G	AB	R	H	2B	3B	HR	RBI	BB	HBP	SH	SF	SO	SB	CS	SLG	OBP
Bailli, Kenen	L-L	6-0	190	1-25-85	.310	.200	.330	36	129	14	40	7	2	1	13	4	1	0	0	35	5	2	.419	.336
Bautista, Jose	R-R	6-0	190	10-19-80	.500	1.000	.333	1	4	2	2	0	0	2	5	1	0	0	0	1	0	0	2.000	.600
Bocock, Brian	R-R	5-11	185	3-9-85	.244	.282	.229	73	270	36	66	17	1	2	25	23	2	4	3	42	17	3	.337	.305
Clemens, Koby	R-R	5-11	210	12-4-86	.218	.297	.184	41	124	17	27	9	1	5	17	17	3	0	1	46	5	4	.427	.324
Diaz, Jonathan	R-R	5-9	170	4-10-85	.179	.161	.184	39	145	18	26	2	0	1	9	13	2	2	1	28	6	2	.214	.255
Francisco, Ben	R-R	6-1	185	10-23-81	.222	.625	.107	9	36	2	8	3	0	0	2	3	0	0	0	4	0	0	.306	.282
Galarraga, Joel	R-R	5-11	185	3-20-82	.351	.357	.348	16	37	6	13	2	0	0	5	5	2	0	0	9	2	1	.405	.455
Glenn, Brad	R-R	6-2	220	4-2-87	.239	.280	.223	112	423	50	101	28	0	19	63	29	4	0	5	122	8	4	.440	.291
Goins, Ryan	L-R	5-10	185	2-13-88	.289	.265	.299	136	546	66	158	33	4	7	61	47	0	19	6	78	15	9	.403	.342
Howard, Kevin	L-R	6-2	210	6-25-81	.283	.315	.275	65	247	25	70	11	1	6	37	13	0	1	1	30	7	2	.409	.318
Jackson, Justin	R-R	6-2	190	12-11-88	.225	.193	.238	66	204	24	46	7	3	0	15	23	2	2	0	61	11	4	.289	.310
Jacobo, Gabe	R-R	6-3	200	4-14-87	.330	.343	.321	25	91	13	30	8	0	2	9	6	0	0	0	17	1	0	.484	.371
Jeroloman, Brian	L-R	5-11	195	5-10-85	.195	.276	.167	37	113	7	22	0	0	0	9	15	4	4	1	25	3	2	.195	.308
Jimenez, A.J.	R-R	6-0	210	5-1-90	.257	.250	.259	27	105	14	27	4	1	2	16	5	1	1	1	14	2	3	.371	.295
Lind, Adam	L-L	6-2	210	7-17-83	.545	.750	.429	3	11	2	6	0	0	1	1	2	0	0	0	4	0	0	.818	.615
Marisnick, Jake	R-R	6-4	200	3-30-91	.233	.256	.221	55	223	25	52	11	3	2	15	11	7	2	4	45	14	4	.336	.286
McDade, Mike	B-R	6-2	250	5-8-89	.275	.212	.297	100	378	44	104	16	0	15	49	43	5	0	3	85	1	0	.437	.354
McElroy, Brad	L-R	5-11	195	4-24-86	.196	.148	.207	56	148	11	29	2	0	1	7	9	3	5	0	36	10	4	.230	.256
Murphy, Jack	B-R	6-4	235	4-6-88	.333	.125	.438	8	24	5	8	1	0	2	4	3	0	0	1	7	0	0	.625	.393
Ochinko, Sean	R-R	5-11	205	10-21-87	.264	.321	.245	59	216	26	57	11	1	8	29	8	5	1	1	40	0	0	.435	.304
Rankin, Pierce	R-R	6-1	190	4-26-89	.000	.000	.000	1	4	0	0	0	0	0	0	0	0	0	0	4	0	0	.000	.000
Schimpf, Ryan	L-R	5-9	181	4-11-88	.279	.146	.357	33	111	21	31	8	0	8	15	23	2	1	0	32	3	1	.568	.412
Sobolewski, Mark	R-R	6-0	195	12-24-86	.262	.215	.281	94	374	57	98	17	1	18	51	17	1	0	1	86	2	2	.457	.295

	B-R	5-11	190	10-7-88	.250	.267	.243	116	436	62	109	27	3	12	42	53	1	6	1	82	20	13	.408	.332
Tolisano, John	B-R	5-11	190	10-7-88	.250	.267	.243	116	436	62	109	27	3	12	42	53	1	6	1	82	20	13	.408	.332
Torrealba, Yorvit	R-R	5-11	200	7-19-78	.417	—	.417	4	12	1	5	0	0	0	1	3	0	0	0	1	1	0	.417	.533
Van Kirk, Brian	R-R	6-1	200	8-10-85	.273	.310	.256	115	399	46	109	28	0	7	44	42	6	0	3	70	12	6	.396	.349

Pitching	B-T	HT	WT	DOB	W	L	ERA	G	GS	CG	SV	IP	H	R	ER	HR	BB	SO	AVG	vLH	vRH	K/9	BB/9
Barnes, Dan	L-R	6-1	195	10-21-89	0	1	16.20	1	0	0	0	2	2	3	3	1	2	2	.333	.500	.000	10.80	10.80
Boone, Randy	R-R	6-0	200	8-6-84	0	2	10.24	3	3	0	0	10	19	13	11	5	1	4	.413	.500	.375	3.72	0.93
Carreno, Joel	R-R	6-2	220	3-7-87	2	4	3.86	17	7	0	0	54	43	25	23	4	19	58	.218	.284	.172	9.73	3.19
Cecil, Brett	R-L	6-1	215	7-2-86	3	2	3.38	9	9	0	0	43	44	18	16	2	14	34	.267	.414	.235	7.17	2.95
Crawford, Evan	R-L	6-2	190	9-2-86	0	0	0.00	3	0	0	0	4	3	1	0	0	2	5	.200	.000	.214	11.25	4.50
Daly, Matt	R-R	5-11	185	8-14-86	2	4	4.52	47	0	0	0	70	70	35	35	8	35	51	.264	.241	.281	6.59	4.52
Dubee, Michael	R-R	6-3	185	1-12-86	2	1	3.68	16	0	0	0	22	19	10	9	3	7	26	.229	.220	.238	10.64	2.86
2-team total (26 Trenton)					4	4	4.07	42	0	0	0	55	63	28	25	5	29	53	—	—	—	8.62	4.72
Dyson, Sam	R-R	6-2	205	5-7-88	2	2	2.38	33	0	0	9	45	38	20	12	2	15	22	.233	.167	.278	4.37	2.98
Englebrook, Evan	R-R	6-8	255	4-28-82	1	0	6.52	7	0	0	2	10	11	7	7	0	8	9	.282	.200	.333	8.38	7.45
Everts, Clint	B-R	6-2	195	8-10-84	2	1	4.19	12	1	0	1	19	21	9	9	0	12	23	.276	.333	.239	10.71	5.59
Farquhar, Danny	R-R	5-9	180	2-17-87	0	1	2.97	20	0	0	1	30	28	14	10	2	10	33	.237	.321	.169	9.79	2.97
2-team total (6 Trenton)					1	1	2.18	26	0	0	5	41	30	14	10	2	10	47	—	—	—	10.23	2.18
Gracey, Scott	R-R	6-2	190	10-15-86	0	0	3.81	12	0	0	0	26	26	11	11	1	14	18	.265	.318	.222	6.23	4.85
Hernandez, Fernando	R-R	5-11	215	7-31-84	5	8	4.34	36	13	0	0	106	129	58	51	8	29	85	.302	.267	.323	7.24	2.47
Hutchison, Drew	L-R	6-2	195	8-22-90	2	1	2.16	3	3	0	0	17	16	4	4	1	3	12	.262	.207	.313	6.48	1.62
Jakubauskas, Chris	R-R	6-2	215	12-22-78	0	2	2.53	6	1	0	0	11	8	4	3	1	6	8	.200	.200	.200	6.75	5.06
Jenkins, Chad	R-R	6-4	230	12-22-87	5	9	4.96	20	20	0	0	114	145	67	63	17	31	57	.310	.319	.303	4.49	2.44
Lawrence, Casey	R-R	6-2	170	10-28-87	0	1	6.39	3	2	0	0	13	20	9	9	1	5	6	.392	.308	.480	4.26	3.55
Loup, Aaron	L-L	5-11	185	12-19-87	0	3	2.78	37	0	0	3	45	46	19	14	4	14	43	.263	.255	.267	8.54	2.78
Magnuson, Trystan	L-R	6-7	220	6-6-85	0	1	1.95	25	0	0	5	32	26	10	7	1	7	24	.215	.120	.282	6.68	1.95
Marek, Stephen	L-R	6-2	240	9-3-83	1	1	6.94	9	0	0	0	12	9	9	9	1	7	13	.205	.235	.185	10.03	5.40
McGuire, Deck	R-R	6-6	235	6-23-89	5	15	5.88	28	28	0	0	144	162	103	94	22	62	97	.286	.282	.288	6.06	3.88
Morrow, Brandon	R-R	6-3	200	7-26-84	1	0	2.51	3	3	0	0	14	11	4	4	0	3	12	.200	.250	.154	7.53	1.88
Nolin, Sean	L-L	6-5	235	12-26-89	1	0	1.20	3	3	0	0	15	9	3	2	0	6	18	.170	.125	.189	10.80	3.60
Pino, Yohan	R-R	6-2	190	12-26-83	10	8	3.56	25	22	2	0	134	122	58	53	17	29	111	.238	.273	.213	7.46	1.95
Spoone, Chorye	R-R	6-1	215	9-16-85	0	2	3.18	16	1	0	0	23	14	9	8	1	15	15	.182	.212	.159	5.96	5.96
2-team total (12 Portland)					2	3	3.65	28	1	0	0	44	33	21	18	2	29	32	—	—	—	6.50	5.89
Stilson, John	R-R	6-3	200	7-28-90	2	4	5.04	17	9	0	1	50	54	33	28	6	23	44	.277	.253	.295	7.92	4.14
Stroman, Marcus	R-R	5-9	185	5-1-91	2	0	3.38	8	0	0	0	8	8	3	3	1	6	8	.258	.400	.190	9.00	6.75
Tepera, Ryan	R-R	6-1	190	11-3-87	7	3	4.84	16	15	0	0	74	82	44	40	4	37	57	.280	.314	.257	6.90	4.48
Uviedo, Ronald	R-R	6-1	160	10-7-86	5	3	2.97	43	0	0	7	58	51	23	19	4	25	57	.231	.241	.225	8.90	3.90
Walrond, Les	L-L	6-3	205	11-7-76	0	0	2.25	3	0	0	0	4	3	4	1	0	4	3	.200	.000	.375	6.75	9.00
Wright, Matt	L-L	5-10	170	5-7-87	1	2	3.96	27	2	0	2	52	39	24	23	9	18	58	.204	.200	.209	9.97	3.10

Fielding

Catcher	PCT	G	PO	A	E	DP	PB
Clemens	1.000	11	68	3	0	0	2
Galarraga	1.000	16	88	9	0	1	4
Jeroloman	.997	37	285	24	1	3	2
Jimenez	.981	27	188	22	4	2	3
Murphy	1.000	8	61	5	0	0	1
Ochinko	.992	49	328	28	3	3	5
Rankin	1.000	1	10	0	0	0	0
Torrealba	1.000	2	13	0	0	0	1

First Base	PCT	G	PO	A	E	DP
Bocock	.750	1	2	1	1	1
Clemens	.989	11	88	2	1	8
Howard	.992	26	238	16	2	21
Jacobo	1.000	16	118	8	0	9
Lind	1.000	1	7	1	0	1
McDade	.989	87	747	48	9	71
Ochinko	.977	5	40	2	1	3

Second Base	PCT	G	PO	A	E	DP
Bocock	.966	50	85	139	8	39
Diaz	.972	21	42	63	3	11
Goins	.972	23	59	82	4	19
Howard	1.000	6	6	14	0	3
Schimpf	1.000	4	2	11	0	2
Tolisano	.970	41	57	102	5	18

Third Base	PCT	G	PO	A	E	DP
Bocock	.969	12	10	21	1	1
Clemens	.667	2	1	1	1	0
Diaz	1.000	2	4	4	0	0
Howard	.896	20	11	32	5	5
Jacobo	.667	2	0	2	1	0
Schimpf	.936	16	16	28	3	4
Sobolewski	.951	92	58	157	11	8

Shortstop	PCT	G	PO	A	E	DP
Bocock	.986	12	26	46	1	13

Diaz	.975	17	18	61	2	12
Goins	.976	114	146	339	12	68

Outfield	PCT	G	PO	A	E	DP
Bailli	.944	22	33	1	2	0
Bautista	—	1	0	0	0	0
Clemens		1	0	0	0	0
Francisco	1.000	5	12	0	0	0
Glenn	.968	105	209	3	7	2
Jackson	.955	64	124	4	6	1
Jacobo	1.000	2	5	0	0	0
Marisnick	.980	55	142	5	3	0
McElroy	.977	40	82	2	2	0
Schimpf	1.000	12	18	3	0	0
Tolisano	.971	74	133	3	4	0
Van Kirk	.992	62	113	4	1	0

DUNEDIN BLUE JAYS   HIGH CLASS A

FLORIDA STATE LEAGUE

Batting	B-T	HT	WT	DOB	AVG	vLH	vRH	G	AB	R	H	2B	3B	HR	RBI	BB	HBP	SH	SF	SO	SB	CS	SLG	OBP
Ahrens, Kevin	B-R	6-1	195	4-26-89	.240	.273	.220	120	409	59	98	17	1	8	53	60	3	0	5	87	1	1	.345	.338
Arencibia, J.P.	R-R	6-0	205	1-5-86	.200	—	.200	1	5	0	1	0	0	0	1	0	0	0	0	0	0	0	.400	.333
Bailli, Kenen	L-L	6-0	190	1-25-85	.267	.222	.288	26	86	15	23	8	1	1	18	6	1	0	1	19	0	1	.419	.319
Berti, Jon	R-R	5-10	175	1-22-90	.190	.164	.204	50	174	28	33	7	5	0	13	26	3	0	3	49	8	3	.287	.301
Clemens, Koby	R-R	5-11	210	1-3-87	.299	.281	.314	23	67	7	20	4	0	3	7	11	0	0	0	22	0	0	.493	.397
Contreras, Ivan	B-R	5-9	155	1-3-87	.056	.000	.167	7	18	2	1	0	0	0	0	1	0	0	0	3	2	1	.056	.056
Crouse, Michael	R-R	6-4	215	11-22-90	.203	.131	.234	59	202	42	41	9	1	6	26	26	2	0	1	73	9	5	.347	.299
Dominguez, Oliver	B-R	5-9	156	4-23-89	.253	.278	.238	82	265	40	67	19	2	4	34	30	3	5	1	73	4	1	.385	.334
Francisco, Ben	R-R	6-1	185	10-23-81	.000	.000	.000	2	6	0	0	0	0	0	1	0	0	0	1	0	0	0	.000	.143
Guerrero, Vladimir	R-R	6-3	235	2-9-75	.450	.667	.357	4	20	7	9	1	0	4	8	0	0	0	0	1	0	0	1.100	.450
Jackson, Justin	R-R	6-2	190	12-11-88	.212	.255	.186	44	137	15	29	6	1	0	8	15	0	1	2	43	5	3	.270	.286
Jacobo, Gabe	R-R	6-3	200	4-14-87	.338	.471	.253	31	130	28	44	14	0	6	27	12	2	0	2	20	2	0	.585	.397

TORONTO BLUE JAYS

Name	B-T	HT	WT	DOB	AVG	vLH	vRH	G	AB	R	H	2B	3B	HR	RBI	BB	HBP	SH	SF	SO	SB	CS	SLG	OBP
Jeroloman, Brian	L-R	5-11	195	5-10-85	.000	—	.000	3	11	0	0	0	0	0	0	0	0	0	0	6	0	0	.000	.000
Jones, Jonathan	R-R	5-11	185	8-2-89	.266	.306	.245	90	320	50	85	16	1	0	28	34	11	7	0	54	25	4	.322	.356
Knecht, Marcus	R-R	6-1	200	6-21-90	.210	.228	.201	126	452	63	95	32	5	13	59	50	11	0	3	146	5	1	.389	.302
Lawrie, Brett	R-R	6-0	215	1-18-90	.000	—	.000	3	0	0	0	0	0	0	0	0	0	0	0	0	0	0	.000	.000
Marisnick, Jake	R-R	6-4	200	3-30-91	.263	.313	.234	65	266	41	70	18	7	6	35	26	10	2	2	55	10	5	.451	.349
Munoz, Aaron	R-R	5-9	185	12-24-88	—	—	—	1	0	0	0	0	0	0	0	0	0	0	0	0	0	0	—	—
Murphy, Jack	B-R	6-4	235	4-6-88	.223	.172	.251	86	278	31	62	13	1	10	51	35	3	2	5	67	0	0	.385	.312
Nolan, Kevin	R-R	6-2	200	12-31-87	.316	.365	.287	78	310	54	98	23	5	5	40	34	2	0	3	43	12	4	.471	.384
Ochinko, Sean	R-R	5-11	205	10-21-87	.306	.342	.286	28	108	21	33	12	0	1	13	10	1	0	0	16	0	0	.444	.370
Pillar, Kevin	R-R	6-0	200	1-4-89	.323	.328	.321	42	164	16	53	8	2	1	34	5	2	1	6	17	16	3	.415	.339
Rankin, Pierce	R-R	6-1	190	4-26-89	.292	.167	.367	17	48	7	14	4	0	1	7	6	1	0	0	18	0	1	.438	.382
Rodriguez, Alexys	R-R	5-10	200	11-23-88	.000	.000	.000	3	5	0	0	0	0	0	0	0	0	0	0	3	0	0	.000	.000
Schimpf, Ryan	L-R	5-9	181	4-11-88	.266	.228	.289	96	361	59	96	29	3	14	61	48	4	0	6	89	4	2	.479	.353
Snider, Travis	L-L	6-0	235	2-2-88	.227	.231	.222	5	22	3	5	1	0	0	1	1	0	0	0	5	2	0	.273	.261
Talley, Jon	L-R	6-3	220	2-18-89	.259	.215	.282	111	410	55	106	27	1	9	68	48	5	0	5	105	2	1	.395	.340
Wilson, Kenny	B-R	5-10	160	1-30-90	.282	.324	.263	29	117	24	33	6	0	1	13	14	2	2	0	22	14	4	.359	.368
Zazueta, Amadeo	B-R	5-10	160	1-31-86	.429	.571	.357	6	21	2	9	2	1	1	5	0	0	0	2	3	0	0	.762	.391

Pitching	B-T	HT	WT	DOB	W	L	ERA	G	GS	CG	SV	IP	H	R	ER	HR	BB	SO	AVG	vLH	vRH	K/9	BB/9
Antolin, Dustin	R-R	6-2	195	8-9-89	7	3	4.58	48	0	0	1	59	72	31	30	3	25	47	.305	.356	.267	7.17	3.81
Barnes, Dan	L-R	6-1	195	10-21-89	1	2	1.40	50	0	0	34	51	37	8	8	3	16	63	.198	.213	.188	11.05	2.81
Boone, Randy	R-R	6-0	200	8-6-84	2	1	4.08	18	3	0	1	35	35	21	16	2	7	27	.246	.263	.235	6.88	1.78
Collazo, Willie	L-L	5-8	180	11-7-79	0	0	2.25	2	0	0	0	4	4	1	1	0	0	4	.250	.250	.250	9.00	0.00
Copeland, Scott	R-R	6-3	210	12-15-87	4	1	2.70	7	6	1	0	37	35	15	11	1	14	32	.246	.317	.195	7.85	3.44
Dyson, Sam	R-R	6-2	205	5-7-88	2	0	4.08	6	6	0	0	29	35	16	13	1	5	16	.297	.263	.328	5.02	1.57
Englebrook, Evan	R-R	6-8	255	4-28-82	0	1	2.08	17	0	0	0	17	13	6	4	0	7	14	.197	.290	.114	7.27	3.63
Escalante, Alesone	B-R	6-4	180	8-29-88	0	0	5.40	4	0	0	1	8	14	6	5	0	2	1	.368	.385	.360	1.08	2.16
Evans, Cody	R-R	6-5	190	9-3-83	1	2	6.91	10	2	0	0	14	18	12	11	2	4	13	.310	.280	.333	8.16	2.51
Farina, Alan	R-R	5-11	190	8-9-86	1	2	5.18	24	0	0	1	24	28	18	14	1	14	24	.289	.243	.317	8.88	5.18
Frasor, Jason	R-R	5-9	180	8-9-77	0	0	0.00	2	0	0	0	2	0	0	0	0	0	4	.000	.000	.000	18.00	0.00
Gailey, Frank	L-L	5-9	190	11-18-85	3	0	1.04	8	3	0	0	26	19	3	3	0	5	27	.204	.233	.190	9.35	1.73
2-team total (4 Clearwater)					3	0	2.45	12	3	0	0	29	26	9	8	0	7	32	—	—	—	9.82	2.15
Ghysels, Chuck	R-R	5-11	200	11-28-89	0	0	0.00	2	0	0	0	3	2	0	0	0	0	6	.182	.250	.143	18.00	0.00
Gracey, Scott	R-R	6-2	190	10-15-86	2	3	3.81	17	0	0	1	28	27	14	12	3	11	42	.248	.200	.281	13.34	3.49
Griffith, Shawn	R-R	5-10	180	5-24-87	4	3	6.31	27	2	0	0	41	41	33	29	3	26	42	.263	.308	.213	9.15	5.66
Hernandez, Jesse	R-R	6-1	200	8-23-88	1	5	6.61	17	0	0	0	48	55	37	35	7	12	38	.293	.322	.265	7.17	2.27
Jensen, Tucker	R-R	6-2	205	8-3-89	0	1	14.54	1	1	0	0	4	9	7	7	0	2	1	.450	.286	.538	2.08	4.15
Kaye, Brandon	R-R	6-4	200	8-16-88	0	1	2.16	4	0	0	0	8	4	2	2	1	1	3	.143	.125	.150	3.24	1.08
Lawrence, Casey	R-R	6-2	170	10-28-87	9	6	3.63	24	23	1	0	139	149	60	56	9	21	90	.277	.288	.267	5.84	1.36
Longpre, Bryan	R-R	6-2	195	7-13-87	1	0	1.04	7	0	0	0	9	5	1	1	0	2	7	.167	.067	.267	7.27	2.08
Magnuson, Trystan	L-R	6-7	220	6-6-85	0	4	5.40	13	0	0	0	18	25	14	11	4	3	26	.305	.324	.292	12.76	1.47
Marek, Stephen	L-R	6-2	240	9-3-83	1	0	3.60	7	0	0	0	10	7	4	4	1	11	11	.189	.158	.222	9.90	9.90
Marze, Dayton	R-R	6-2	185	1-1-89	2	1	2.82	46	0	0	1	70	66	26	22	4	25	37	.256	.256	.255	4.73	3.20
Morrow, Brandon	R-R	6-3	200	7-26-84	0	0	1.50	2	2	0	0	6	8	2	1	0	3	6	.348	.500	.182	9.00	4.50
Nolin, Sean	L-L	6-5	235	12-26-89	9	0	2.19	17	15	0	0	86	72	26	21	7	21	90	.226	.248	.217	9.38	2.19
Permison, Drew	R-R	5-10	170	2-24-89	0	0	0.00	1	0	0	0	1	1	0	0	0	0	0	.250	.500	.000	0.00	0.00
Potts, Jared	L-L	6-3	210	7-4-85	0	1	3.34	36	0	0	1	32	21	12	12	3	23	35	.186	.115	.269	9.74	6.40
Smith, Egan	L-L	6-5	200	3-16-89	8	7	3.49	23	15	0	1	98	94	42	38	4	34	70	.247	.226	.259	6.43	3.12
Stilson, John	R-R	6-3	200	7-28-90	3	1	2.82	13	13	0	0	54	56	22	17	2	19	47	.265	.257	.273	7.79	3.15
Tepera, Ryan	R-R	6-1	190	11-3-87	1	3	7.71	5	5	1	0	21	27	19	18	3	12	14	.310	.366	.261	6.00	5.14
Walden, Marcus	R-R	6-0	195	9-13-88	9	2	2.85	13	12	0	0	73	58	26	23	0	18	42	.216	.267	.165	5.20	2.23
Wojciechowski, Asher	R-R	6-4	235	12-21-88	7	3	3.57	18	18	0	0	93	91	40	37	3	22	76	.261	.243	.278	7.33	2.12
Wright, Matt	L-L	5-10	170	5-7-87	0	0	0.00	7	0	0	0	6	7	0	0	0	1	7	.292	.300	.286	9.95	1.42

Fielding

Catcher	PCT	G	PO	A	E	DP	PB
Clemens	1.000	16	89	13	0	1	4
Jeroloman	1.000	2	10	1	0	0	1
Munoz	1.000	1	2	0	0	0	0
Murphy	.994	84	627	48	4	6	3
Ochinko	1.000	23	155	10	0	5	0
Rankin	.989	14	86	5	1	0	1
Rodriguez	1.000	3	6	0	0	0	0

First Base	PCT	G	PO	A	E	DP
Ahrens	.992	18	121	7	1	14
Clemens	.957	4	19	3	1	2
Jacobo	1.000	18	158	15	0	15
Murphy	1.000	1	3	0	0	0
Talley	.985	96	889	65	15	85

Second Base	PCT	G	PO	A	E	DP
Berti	.987	48	79	141	3	29
Contreras	1.000	6	6	18	0	3
Dominguez	.962	13	25	25	2	9
Jones	1.000	1	2	0	0	0
Schimpf	.955	69	82	192	13	39

Third Base	PCT	G	PO	A	E	DP
Ahrens	.951	98	61	193	13	17
Clemens	.500	1	0	1	1	0
Dominguez	.760	19	3	16	6	1
Lawrie	1.000	1	0	4	0	1
Schimpf	1.000	16	7	29	0	1
Zazueta	1.000	3	2	6	0	1

Shortstop	PCT	G	PO	A	E	DP
Dominguez	.918	20	24	54	7	10
Jackson	.971	37	53	116	5	31
Nolan	.955	77	118	224	16	50
Zazueta	.923	3	1	11	1	1

Outfield	PCT	G	PO	A	E	DP
Bailli	.972	17	33	2	1	0
Crouse	.962	53	94	6	4	1
Francisco	1.000	1	2	0	0	0
Guerrero	1.000	1	0	0	0	0
Jackson	1.000	6	15	0	0	0
Jacobo	1.000	5	7	0	0	0
Jones	1.000	65	128	7	0	2
Knecht	.961	121	193	5	8	0
Marisnick	.994	63	155	5	1	3
Pillar	1.000	38	70	3	0	2
Rankin	1.000	1	1	0	0	0
Schimpf	1.000	3	3	0	0	0
Snider	1.000	3	5	0	0	0
Wilson	.950	28	56	1	3	0

LANSING LUGNUTS

MIDWEST LEAGUE

Batting	B-T	HT	WT	DOB	AVG	vLH	vRH	G	AB	R	H	2B	3B	HR	RBI	BB	HBP	SH	SF	SO	SB	CS	SLG	OBP
Baligod, Nick	L-R	5-11	190	9-28-87	.291	.381	.271	29	117	20	34	8	0	3	7	16	1	0	1	20	1	0	.436	.378
Berti, Jon	R-R	5-10	175	1-22-90	.281	.260	.287	60	224	35	63	8	2	2	27	34	7	1	1	41	26	8	.362	.391
Brisker, Markus	R-R	6-3	210	8-21-90	.192	.195	.191	48	156	23	30	6	2	1	14	19	5	2	1	46	18	3	.276	.298
Burns, Andy	R-R	6-2	190	8-7-90	.248	.306	.231	78	278	57	69	25	4	9	37	38	7	0	2	75	15	2	.464	.351
Crouse, Michael	R-R	6-4	215	11-22-90	.194	.192	.194	36	124	18	24	3	0	4	15	15	1	0	1	44	6	2	.315	.284
Fermin, Andy	L-R	6-0	180	7-27-89	.258	.192	.270	55	178	31	46	7	3	1	17	28	1	1	0	28	0	1	.348	.362
Hawkins, Chris	L-R	6-2	195	8-17-91	.269	.303	.260	123	491	67	132	17	4	2	43	46	0	3	1	78	11	0	.332	.331
Hobson, K.C.	L-L	6-2	205	8-22-90	.276	.190	.299	128	490	57	135	43	2	10	86	56	1	0	9	85	2	1	.433	.345
Leblebijian, Jason	R-R	6-1	190	5-13-91	.222	.000	.256	12	45	7	10	1	0	0	1	7	2	0	0	13	1	1	.244	.352
Munoz, Aaron	R-R	5-9	185	12-24-88	.223	.174	.236	34	112	11	25	4	0	0	7	11	2	3	0	31	1	0	.259	.304
Namba, Bryson	R-R	6-2	210	1-31-91	.667	.500	1.000	1	3	1	2	0	0	0	1	0	0	0	0	0	0	0	.667	.750
Opitz, Shane	L-R	6-1	180	1-10-92	.225	.242	.221	90	315	42	71	19	2	2	37	25	1	10	3	65	3	1	.317	.282
Patterson, Kevin	L-R	6-4	220	9-28-88	.245	.276	.238	108	387	48	95	22	3	19	79	52	6	0	5	124	2	0	.465	.340
Perez, Carlos	R-R	5-11	195	10-27-90	.275	.368	.250	71	273	48	75	22	5	5	40	35	3	3	5	38	3	2	.447	.358
Peters, Chris	R-R	6-0	175	12-29-88	.274	.333	.254	28	95	13	26	7	1	0	9	15	1	1	2	21	2	0	.368	.372
Pierre, Gustavo	R-R	6-2	183	12-28-91	.252	.172	.273	76	278	35	70	14	8	5	28	16	4	5	0	79	8	7	.414	.302
Pillar, Kevin	R-R	6-0	200	1-4-89	.322	.286	.333	86	335	49	108	20	4	5	57	35	3	1	1	53	35	6	.451	.390
Pompey, Dalton	B-R	6-1	170	12-11-92	.227	.000	.263	5	22	1	5	0	1	0	3	1	0	1	0	5	1	1	.318	.261
Rankin, Pierce	R-R	6-1	190	4-26-89	.162	.100	.185	10	37	6	6	1	0	1	3	1	1	0	0	12	0	0	.270	.205
Schaeffer, Chris	R-R	5-10	195	11-19-87	.209	.357	.181	28	86	14	18	6	0	2	19	9	5	2	1	17	0	0	.349	.317
Schutz, Kipp	L-L	6-4	205	3-21-88	.227	.000	.259	19	66	7	15	4	1	0	6	4	2	0	0	22	0	0	.318	.292
Sweeney, Kellen	L-R	6-1	190	5-14-91	.179	.148	.186	43	140	13	25	2	1	0	12	23	1	0	1	30	1	2	.207	.297
Vega-Rosado, Jorge	R-R	5-8	175	12-5-91	.091	.000	.125	6	22	1	2	0	0	0	1	0	0	0	0	12	1	0	.091	.130
Wilson, Kenny	B-R	5-10	185	1-30-90	.252	.261	.249	94	349	68	88	13	6	4	40	44	17	7	4	75	41	8	.358	.360

Pitching	B-T	HT	WT	DOB	W	L	ERA	G	GS	CG	SV	IP	H	R	ER	HR	BB	SO	AVG	vLH	vRH	K/9	BB/9
Avendano, Javier	R-R	6-3	180	9-6-90	2	3	1.48	19	0	0	2	30	20	8	5	0	18	39	.182	.180	.183	11.57	5.34
Beck, Casey	R-R	6-1	215	3-28-87	0	1	0.00	2	0	0	0	2	2	1	0	0	2	2	.286	.500	.200	9.00	9.00
Berl, Brandon	R-R	6-0	185	4-9-88	4	7	3.02	46	0	0	1	63	67	29	21	2	15	46	.275	.274	.275	6.61	2.15
Brechbuehler, Tim	R-R	6-8	205	10-21-89	0	0	19.80	3	0	0	0	5	11	11	11	1	3	2	.423	.455	.400	3.60	5.40
Brown, Eric	L-R	6-1	185	2-23-89	2	0	3.52	8	0	0	0	15	13	6	6	0	4	17	.224	.120	.303	9.98	2.35
Brua, Phil	L-R	6-2	185	4-3-89	3	1	5.36	24	0	1	0	40	61	26	24	3	13	27	.365	.406	.337	6.02	2.90
Champlin, Kramer	R-R	6-6	200	3-8-90	4	1	4.09	29	3	0	1	70	75	38	32	7	19	77	.266	.257	.276	9.85	2.43
DeSclafani, Anthony	R-R	6-2	195	4-18-90	11	3	3.37	28	21	0	0	123	145	55	46	3	25	92	.307	.324	.286	6.73	1.83
Escalante, Alesone	R-R	6-2	180	8-29-88	1	2	6.16	32	0	0	0	57	79	45	39	11	19	43	.320	.286	.348	6.79	3.00
Griffith, Shawn	R-R	5-10	180	5-24-87	2	1	3.16	11	0	0	0	26	19	10	9	5	13	23	.202	.231	.167	8.06	4.56
Hernandez, Jesse	R-R	6-1	180	8-23-88	4	5	2.26	16	15	2	0	96	82	30	24	2	19	61	.234	.227	.240	5.74	1.79
Kadish, Ian	R-R	6-0	200	8-29-88	1	1	4.00	15	0	0	2	18	14	9	8	0	9	21	.209	.214	.205	10.50	4.50
Longpre, Bryan	R-R	6-2	195	7-13-87	0	2	7.08	11	0	0	0	20	30	25	16	2	9	10	.349	.190	.500	4.43	3.98
McFarland, Blake	R-R	6-5	230	2-2-88	5	6	5.68	36	7	0	2	90	116	58	57	5	27	73	.320	.325	.315	7.27	2.69
Meyer, Ajay	L-R	6-6	185	7-19-87	3	3	3.67	54	0	0	33	56	47	28	23	7	13	57	.224	.229	.219	9.11	2.08
Nicolino, Justin	L-L	6-3	160	11-22-91	10	4	2.46	28	22	0	0	124	112	41	34	6	21	119	.241	.283	.221	8.61	1.52
Rollins, David	L-L	6-1	195	12-21-89	6	1	2.78	18	18	0	0	78	64	29	24	2	36	75	.227	.189	.246	8.69	4.17
Sanchez, Aaron	R-R	6-4	190	7-1-92	8	5	2.49	25	18	0	0	90	64	33	25	3	51	97	.204	.106	.287	9.66	5.08
Syndergaard, Noah	R-R	6-5	200	8-29-92	8	5	2.60	27	19	0	1	104	81	41	30	3	31	122	.212	.219	.205	10.59	2.69
Walden, Marcus	R-R	6-0	195	9-13-88	5	2	3.11	14	14	0	0	67	54	24	23	4	30	40	.220	.210	.250	5.40	4.05
Ybarra, Tyler	L-L	6-2	170	12-11-89	3	2	2.27	26	0	0	2	44	38	16	11	2	26	57	.229	.250	.214	11.75	5.36

Fielding

Catcher	PCT	G	PO	A	E	DP	PB
Munoz	.993	34	251	32	2	6	4
Perez	.991	71	575	74	6	4	13
Rankin	.965	8	75	7	3	0	0
Schaeffer	1.000	27	201	18	0	0	3

First Base	PCT	G	PO	A	E	DP
Fermin	.875	2	14	0	2	1
Hobson	.985	118	1134	77	18	102
Namba	.938	1	13	2	1	0
Patterson	.992	17	113	16	1	16

Second Base	PCT	G	PO	A	E	DP
Berti	.982	58	87	181	5	33
Burns	1.000	12	12	41	0	5

Third Base	PCT	G	PO	A	E	DP
Burns	.792	10	6	13	5	3
Fermin	.909	12	9	21	3	0
Pierre	.918	75	51	129	16	14
Sweeney	.902	43	22	79	11	5

Shortstop	PCT	G	PO	A	E	DP
Burns	.958	55	69	161	10	36
Leblebijian	.778	2	1	5	2	1
Opitz	.961	77	122	245	15	56

	PCT	G	PO	A	E	DP
Fermin	.987	37	59	95	2	27
Leblebijian	.969	11	26	37	2	9
Opitz	1.000	14	24	47	0	10
Peters	.958	13	29	39	3	8

	PCT	G	PO	A	E	DP
Peters	1.000	3	5	4	0	0
Vega-Rosado	.889	5	10	14	3	2

Outfield	PCT	G	PO	A	E	DP
Baligod	.952	29	58	2	3	1
Brisker	.922	39	44	3	4	2
Crouse	.947	36	69	3	4	0
Hawkins	.983	120	163	14	3	1
Hobson	1.000	1	1	0	0	0
Peters	1.000	12	18	3	0	0
Pillar	.973	74	138	4	4	2
Pompey	1.000	5	11	0	0	0
Schutz	1.000	13	10	0	0	0
Wilson	.959	91	152	10	7	4

VANCOUVER CANADIANS

NORTHWEST LEAGUE

Batting	B-T	HT	WT	DOB	AVG	vLH	vRH	G	AB	R	H	2B	3B	HR	RBI	BB	HBP	SH	SF	SO	SB	CS	SLG	OBP
Arcila, Daniel	L-R	6-1	170	7-4-90	.176	.133	.186	43	148	17	26	6	1	3	13	11	2	1	0	50	4	2	.291	.242
Baligod, Nick	L-R	5-11	190	9-28-87	.259	.313	.246	42	158	24	41	8	2	1	25	26	3	0	0	19	2	0	.354	.374
Charles, Art	L-L	6-6	221	11-10-90	.236	.286	.222	33	127	19	30	10	1	7	18	13	1	0	1	41	0	1	.496	.310
Chung, Derrick	R-R	5-10	180	2-23-88	.241	.158	.258	34	108	12	26	7	1	0	12	13	5	3	3	25	0	1	.324	.341

	B-T	HT	WT	DOB	AVG	vLH	vRH	G	AB	R	H	2B	3B	HR	RBI	BB	HBP	SH	SF	SO	SB	CS	SLG	OBP
Davis, D.J.	L-L	6-1	180	7-25-94	.167	.286	.091	5	18	3	3	0	0	0	0	5	0	0	0	6	1	1	.167	.348
Flores, Jorge	R-R	5-5	160	11-25-91	.265	.319	.250	60	215	31	57	14	1	3	19	19	11	6	0	45	11	9	.381	.355
Frawley, Tucker	R-R	6-0	185	6-1-89	.185	.263	.161	26	81	8	15	0	0	0	8	8	3	1	1	20	2	0	.185	.280
Fuenmayor, Balbino	R-R	6-3	235	11-26-89	.282	.222	.298	67	259	35	73	20	1	9	52	14	5	0	5	82	1	0	.471	.325
Hernandez, Leonardo	R-R	5-10	195	2-22-90	.104	.286	.073	16	48	3	5	0	0	0	3	1	0	1	0	13	1	0	.104	.122
Johnson, Matt	R-R	6-3	210	5-26-88	.313	.333	.308	9	16	2	5	0	0	0	2	6	2	0	0	6	5	0	.313	.542
Klein, Dan	R-R	5-10	185	8-29-90	.207	.273	.200	37	116	16	24	5	0	4	15	17	3	0	2	40	1	2	.353	.319
Leblebijian, Jason	R-R	6-1	190	5-13-91	.291	.179	.330	37	148	24	43	9	1	2	20	10	0	0	2	44	6	1	.405	.331
Leyland, Jordan	R-R	6-4	205	9-6-89	.235	.133	.258	23	81	11	19	4	1	1	13	13	0	0	1	18	0	0	.346	.337
Lopes, Christian	R-R	6-0	185	10-1-92	.270	.222	.286	10	37	4	10	1	1	0	4	2	1	0	1	6	0	0	.351	.317
Melendez, Ronnie	R-R	5-10	170	9-29-89	.000	—	.000	1	1	0	0	0	0	0	0	0	0	0	0	0	0	0	.000	.000
Nessy, Santiago	R-R	6-2	230	12-8-92	.091	.125	.071	6	22	4	2	1	0	1	3	3	0	0	0	7	0	0	.273	.200
Newman, Matt	L-L	5-10	170	9-20-88	.262	.277	.259	61	221	34	58	16	5	6	41	30	2	0	3	61	6	2	.462	.352
Parmley, Ian	L-L	5-11	175	12-19-89	.201	.222	.197	58	209	42	42	9	1	0	12	52	0	2	1	44	12	5	.254	.359
Phillips, Eric	R-R	6-2	195	7-16-90	.182	.000	.211	8	22	3	4	0	0	0	2	2	1	0	0	6	0	1	.182	.280
Pompey, Dalton	R-B	6-1	170	12-11-92	.294	.143	.333	11	34	11	10	3	1	0	4	9	0	1	0	7	3	0	.441	.442
Ramirez, Carlos	R-R	6-3	172	4-24-91	.245	.324	.221	42	159	17	39	5	6	2	19	4	0	1	0	45	7	2	.390	.264
Smith Jr., Dwight	L-R	5-11	180	10-26-92	.175	.083	.196	18	63	5	11	3	1	0	8	6	1	0	1	11	0	0	.254	.254
Sweeney, Kellen	L-R	6-0	180	9-14-91	.229	.229	.228	67	245	35	56	15	2	5	29	35	4	0	4	47	5	0	.367	.330

Pitching	B-T	HT	WT	DOB	W	L	ERA	G	GS	CG	SV	IP	H	R	ER	HR	BB	SO	AVG	vLH	vRH	K/9	BB/9
Anderson, Kyle	R-L	6-2	205	5-24-90	4	2	4.81	13	8	0	0	49	56	27	26	4	12	25	.296	.318	.290	4.62	2.22
Avendano, Javier	R-R	6-3	180	9-6-90	8	1	1.27	16	14	0	0	78	53	13	11	3	25	91	.193	.214	.174	10.50	2.88
Breault, Zack	R-R	6-2	220	12-6-88	2	2	3.93	18	2	0	0	34	28	15	15	1	18	21	.222	.326	.169	5.50	4.72
Brosnahan, Bobby	L-L	6-0	155	6-2-89	2	2	4.50	10	4	0	0	32	34	17	16	2	8	16	.279	.269	.281	4.50	2.25
Brown, Eric	L-R	6-1	185	2-23-89	2	5	7.09	19	9	0	1	46	62	40	36	9	17	43	.310	.269	.336	8.47	3.35
Browning, Wil	R-R	6-3	175	9-8-88	0	0	1.50	5	0	0	0	6	7	1	1	0	0	5	.304	.667	.176	7.50	0.00
Brua, Phil	L-R	6-2	185	4-3-89	2	0	1.23	5	0	0	0	7	2	1	1	0	2	3	.087	.222	.000	3.68	2.45
Cole, Taylor	R-R	6-1	180	8-20-89	6	0	0.81	12	11	0	0	66	36	6	6	0	17	57	.161	.173	.151	7.73	2.31
Delatte, Brad	L-L	6-0	175	1-13-90	0	0	27.00	1	0	0	0	0	2	1	0	0	0	0	.667	.500	1.000	0.00	0.00
Donahue, Tucker	R-R	6-2	200	8-27-90	3	2	5.26	22	0	0	1	26	29	16	15	2	14	21	.282	.217	.333	7.36	4.91
Kadish, Ian	L-R	6-0	200	8-29-88	1	1	1.59	15	0	0	5	23	10	5	4	1	11	36	.130	.139	.122	14.29	4.37
Longpre, Bryan	R-R	6-2	195	7-13-87	0	1	8.00	7	0	0	0	9	14	8	8	1	3	8	.341	.182	.400	8.00	3.00
Lucas, Jon	R-R	5-10	205	12-12-87	1	1	3.35	27	0	0	1	40	46	17	15	0	20	27	.299	.267	.319	6.02	4.46
Murphy, Griffin	R-L	6-3	200	1-16-91	0	0	3.86	2	0	0	0	2	2	1	1	0	0	2	.222	.500	.000	7.71	0.00
Norris, Daniel	L-L	6-2	180	4-25-93	0	1	10.57	2	2	0	0	8	14	9	9	0	5	5	.400	.556	.346	5.87	5.87
Osuna, Roberto	R-R	6-2	230	2-7-95	1	0	3.20	5	5	0	0	20	14	9	7	1	9	25	.192	.043	.260	11.44	4.12
Permison, Drew	R-R	5-10	170	2-24-89	0	0	0.79	12	0	0	5	11	9	1	1	0	2	10	.220	.313	.160	7.94	1.59
Purdy, Nick	R-R	6-5	205	10-2-89	2	3	3.96	19	2	0	0	39	40	19	17	3	22	33	.263	.293	.245	7.68	5.12
Sikula, Arik	R-R	6-1	195	12-21-88	2	1	2.45	29	0	0	10	37	25	10	10	3	10	31	.189	.153	.219	7.61	2.45
Stroman, Marcus	R-R	5-9	185	5-1-91	1	0	3.18	7	0	0	0	11	8	5	4	0	3	15	.190	.200	.185	11.91	2.38
Turner, Colton	L-L	6-3	185	1-17-91	4	0	1.57	14	4	0	0	34	23	6	6	0	17	29	.200	.136	.215	7.60	4.46
White, Ben	R-R	6-2	185	5-10-89	4	7	5.73	15	15	0	0	77	76	52	49	7	31	50	.255	.229	.275	5.84	3.62

Fielding

Catcher	PCT	G	PO	A	E	DP	PB
Chung	.857	1	6	0	1	1	0
Frawley	.990	26	177	21	2	1	1
Hernandez	.989	13	79	9	1	0	0
Klein	.987	35	259	39	4	1	2
Nessy	.974	6	34	4	1	0	2

First Base	PCT	G	PO	A	E	DP
Charles	.980	12	89	10	2	12
Chung	1.000	1	11	0	0	0
Fuenmayor	.991	51	417	25	4	33
Johnson	—	1	0	0	0	0
Leyland	1.000	13	112	6	0	8

Second Base	PCT	G	PO	A	E	DP
Arcila	.972	42	78	98	5	22
Chung	.975	22	34	45	2	4
Leblebijian	1.000	6	10	14	0	3
Lopes	.981	10	23	28	1	6

Third Base	PCT	G	PO	A	E	DP
Chung	1.000	5	3	11	0	2
Johnson	1.000	1	1	1	0	0
Leblebijian	1.000	8	8	14	0	0
Sweeney	.948	63	51	114	9	9

Shortstop	PCT	G	PO	A	E	DP
Flores	.945	54	64	143	12	26

	PCT	G	PO	A	E	DP
Johnson	1.000	5	13	13	0	4
Leblebijian	.918	14	20	36	5	3
Phillips	.895	5	7	10	2	3
Outfield	PCT	G	PO	A	E	DP
Baligod	.966	40	83	1	3	1
Chung	1.000	4	2	0	0	0
Davis	1.000	5	19	1	0	1
Melendez	—	1	0	0	0	0
Newman	.984	57	112	13	2	2
Parmley	1.000	58	125	1	0	0
Pompey	.960	10	24	0	1	0
Ramirez	.972	41	102	2	3	0
Smith Jr.	1.000	17	21	2	0	0

BLUEFIELD BLUE JAYS   ROOKIE

APPALACHIAN LEAGUE

Batting	B-T	HT	WT	DOB	AVG	vLH	vRH	G	AB	R	H	2B	3B	HR	RBI	BB	HBP	SH	SF	SO	SB	CS	SLG	OBP
Alvarez, Hector	R-R	5-11	170	2-14-91	.083	.000	.095	20	48	1	4	0	0	0	2	2	1	2	1	12	0	0	.083	.135
Anderson, Jake	R-R	6-4	190	11-22-92	.194	.105	.216	57	191	25	37	10	1	3	13	11	10	1	2	72	3	3	.304	.271
Arce, Eric	L-R	5-9	205	11-29-91	.236	.125	.262	47	127	26	30	5	1	8	27	27	4	0	1	55	0	0	.480	.384
Atkinson, Justin	R-R	6-1	205	7-24-93	.300	—	.300	3	10	2	3	1	0	0	1	0	1	0	0	1	0	1	.400	.364
Azor, Alex	L-L	5-11	190	11-21-88	.250	.091	.310	14	40	5	10	1	0	0	1	3	0	2	0	5	0	1	.275	.302
Charles, Art	L-L	6-6	221	11-10-90	.235	.136	.270	31	85	18	20	5	3	6	16	33	4	0	1	33	2	0	.576	.463
Conner, Seth	R-R	6-2	205	1-29-92	.296	.324	.287	49	142	23	42	8	2	2	28	24	9	1	3	33	0	0	.423	.421
Davis, D.J.	L-L	6-1	180	7-25-94	.340	.250	.349	12	47	9	16	3	1	1	6	2	0	0	0	10	6	2	.511	.415
Dean, Matt	R-R	6-3	190	12-22-92	.222	.250	.211	49	167	22	37	8	4	2	24	12	2	1	0	60	3	2	.353	.282
Frias, Christian	B-R	5-10	170	7-19-89	.229	.000	.256	18	48	7	11	1	1	0	3	6	0	1	0	12	0	0	.292	.315
Guerrero, Emilio	R-R	6-4	170	8-21-92	.185	.400	.163	16	54	6	10	1	1	0	8	2	0	2	2	17	1	0	.241	.207
Jones, Dennis	R-R	6-3	185	9-4-92	.192	.158	.212	18	52	6	10	2	0	0	6	1	1	2	0	17	7	0	.231	.222

Name	B-T	HT	WT	DOB	AVG	vLH	vRH	G	AB	R	H	2B	3B	HR	RBI	BB	HBP	SH	SF	SO	SB	CS	SLG	OBP
Leblebijian, Jason	R-R	6-1	190	5-13-91	.194	.167	.200	9	31	3	6	3	0	0	3	5	2	0	1	8	1	0	.290	.333
Leyland, Jordan	R-R	6-4	205	9-6-89	.235	.250	.229	16	51	3	12	3	0	1	4	1	1	0	0	12	0	1	.353	.264
Lopes, Christian	R-R	6-0	185	10-1-92	.280	.231	.293	49	186	33	52	16	5	4	29	15	3	1	0	34	6	1	.484	.343
Nessy, Santiago	R-R	6-2	230	12-8-92	.256	.295	.241	45	160	26	41	8	0	8	23	13	3	0	2	47	0	0	.456	.320
Peters, Chris	R-R	6-0	175	12-29-88	.267	.333	.250	11	15	5	4	2	0	0	4	4	0	2	0	2	1	0	.400	.421
Pompey, Dalton	B-R	6-1	170	12-11-92	.357	—	.357	4	14	2	5	1	1	0	1	0	0	0	0	2	1	0	.571	.357
Ramirez, Carlos	R-R	6-3	172	4-24-91	.273	.111	.333	10	33	4	9	2	0	1	6	2	1	0	0	6	0	1	.424	.333
Smith Jr., Dwight	L-R	5-11	180	10-26-92	.226	.178	.246	41	159	20	36	6	0	4	21	11	3	0	0	22	1	1	.340	.289
Taylor, Nico	R-R	6-4	215	2-9-90	.268	.220	.285	49	164	21	44	9	1	1	14	13	1	1	1	49	5	3	.354	.324
Thon, Dickie Joe	R-R	6-2	185	11-16-91	.221	.185	.230	48	149	18	33	5	1	2	14	19	6	1	1	34	7	3	.309	.331
Vega-Rosado, Jorge	R-R	5-8	175	12-5-91	.275	.348	.243	41	149	20	41	4	2	1	8	12	6	3	2	40	7	4	.369	.355

Pitching

Name	B-T	HT	WT	DOB	W	L	ERA	G	GS	CG	SV	IP	H	R	ER	HR	BB	SO	AVG	vLH	vRH	K/9	BB/9
Broussard, Colby	R-R	6-4	220	5-8-89	0	4	7.04	17	0	0	3	23	28	22	18	3	16	27	.295	.417	.254	10.57	6.26
Browning, Wil	R-R	6-3	175	9-8-88	0	1	0.82	10	0	0	4	11	6	3	1	0	3	16	.146	.273	.100	13.09	2.45
Carmona, Julio	R-R	6-1	205	10-10-90	0	4	2.83	17	0	0	2	29	22	13	9	0	15	34	.208	.321	.167	10.67	4.71
Comer, Kevin	R-R	6-3	205	8-1-92	3	3	3.95	10	7	0	0	43	43	25	19	4	8	29	.249	.214	.265	6.02	1.66
2-team total (2 Greenville)					3	4	4.56	12	8	0	0	49	53	31	25	6	10	34	—	—		6.20	1.82
Davis, Shane	R-L	6-0	195	4-19-88	0	2	4.84	13	0	0	0	22	24	17	12	1	12	20	.279	.263	.284	8.06	4.84
Dorsett, Brandon	R-R	6-3	200	11-1-89	3	2	1.71	18	0	0	4	32	26	16	6	0	6	19	.211	.282	.179	5.40	1.71
Estrada, Deivy	R-R	5-11	178	8-22-92	3	6	4.29	13	12	0	0	57	62	48	27	7	15	49	.267	.301	.252	7.78	2.38
Gabryszwski, Jeremy	R-R	6-4	195	3-16-93	3	0	2.35	11	9	0	0	46	44	13	12	5	4	22	.253	.283	.242	4.30	0.78
Gonzalez, Alonzo	L-L	6-5	200	1-15-92	2	0	0.00	2	2	0	0	12	3	0	0	0	3	9	.077	.000	.088	6.75	2.25
James, Justin	R-R	6-1	195	3-17-90	2	4	7.36	12	5	0	0	26	37	27	21	2	11	24	.339	.484	.282	8.42	3.86
Jensen, Tucker	R-R	6-2	205	8-3-89	3	1	3.83	12	8	0	1	49	45	29	21	5	10	42	.230	.225	.232	7.66	1.82
Kaye, Brandon	R-R	6-4	200	8-16-88	0	0	0.00	5	3	0	0	5	3	0	0	0	0	3	.167	.000	.231	5.40	0.00
Murphy, Griffin	R-L	6-3	200	1-16-91	1	2	1.70	15	2	0	1	37	24	13	7	1	13	42	.180	.217	.173	10.22	3.16
Musgrove, Joe	R-R	6-5	230	12-4-92	0	0	1.13	2	1	0	0	8	5	1	1	0	0	9	.179	.143	.190	10.13	0.00
2-team total (4 Greenville)					0	1	4.24	6	1	0	0	17	19	8	8	0	4	19	—	—		10.06	2.12
Norris, Daniel	L-L	6-2	180	4-25-93	2	3	7.97	11	10	0	0	35	44	35	31	4	13	38	.301	.407	.277	9.77	3.34
Osuna, Roberto	R-R	6-2	230	2-7-95	1	0	1.50	7	4	0	0	24	18	5	4	1	6	24	.209	.375	.171	9.00	2.25
Robson, Tom	R-R	6-4	200	6-27-93	0	2	4.09	3	3	0	0	11	10	6	5	2	0	7	.238	.412	.120	5.73	0.00
Spano, Joe	L-L	5-10	175	10-27-89	1	1	5.00	17	0	0	1	27	29	16	15	0	20	33	.282	.105	.321	11.00	6.67
Tirado, Alberto	R-R	6-1	177	12-10-94	2	0	2.45	3	3	0	0	11	4	3	3	1	5	11	.121	.250	.080	4.09	4.09
Valdez, Denny	R-R	6-3	188	5-8-90	1	1	5.03	16	0	0	0	20	14	13	11	3	18	20	.192	.083	.245	9.15	8.24
Williams, Les	R-R	6-2	220	3-2-89	2	1	5.40	13	0	0	0	23	22	15	14	3	6	17	.239	.042	.309	6.56	2.31

Fielding

Catcher	PCT	G	PO	A	E	DP	PB
Alvarez	.985	19	115	17	2	2	3
Conner	.992	17	101	18	1	2	6
Nessy	.963	38	251	33	11	1	5

First Base	PCT	G	PO	A	E	DP
Arce	.931	3	27	0	2	3
Charles	.993	29	267	16	2	14
Conner	.990	23	180	13	2	12
Leyland	1.000	13	138	3	0	8

Second Base	PCT	G	PO	A	E	DP
Atkinson	1.000	3	3	8	0	1
Frias	.959	14	31	40	3	7
Leblebijian	1.000	2	9	5	0	3
Lopes	.948	33	53	92	8	13

	PCT	G	PO	A	E	DP
Peters	1.000	1	2	1	0	0
Vega-Rosado	.938	15	34	42	5	12

Third Base	PCT	G	PO	A	E	DP
Conner	1.000	4	1	8	0	0
Dean	.858	47	26	119	24	8
Guerrero	.852	8	2	21	4	0
Leblebijian	.667	0	2	1	0
Peters	.800	4	1	3	1	0
Vega-Rosado	.714	5	2	8	4	1

Shortstop	PCT	G	PO	A	E	DP
Guerrero	.946	9	12	23	2	4
Leblebijian	1.000	3	5	7	0	1
Lopes	.911	10	9	32	4	3
Thon	.917	41	56	109	15	17

	PCT	G	PO	A	E	DP
Vega-Rosado	.813	6	3	10	3	0

Outfield	PCT	G	PO	A	E	DP
Anderson	.986	46	71	2	1	1
Arce	.857	20	12	0	2	0
Azor	1.000	13	11	0	0	0
Davis	1.000	12	20	0	0	0
Jones	1.000	18	23	1	0	0
Peters	1.000	5	2	0	0	0
Pompey	1.000	4	10	1	0	1
Ramirez	.955	10	21	0	1	0
Smith Jr.	.970	39	63	2	2	0
Taylor	.985	48	66	0	1	0
Vega-Rosado	1.000	3	4	0	0	0

GCL BLUE JAYS   ROOKIE
GULF COAST LEAGUE

Batting	B-T	HT	WT	DOB	AVG	vLH	vRH	G	AB	R	H	2B	3B	HR	RBI	BB	HBP	SH	SF	SO	SB	CS	SLG	OBP
Alford, Anthony	R-R	6-1	193	7-20-94	.167	.000	.214	5	18	1	3	0	0	1	1	2	0	0	0	4	4	0	.333	.250
Almonte, Josh	R-R	6-3	193	1-28-94	.159	.235	.135	20	69	5	11	1	1	0	2	2	0	0	0	30	0	1	.203	.183
Atkinson, Justin	R-R	6-0	205	7-24-93	.259	.255	.261	52	185	14	48	1	0	1	23	13	4	1	0	29	1	2	.281	.322
Bartlett, Cody	R-R	6-5	180	7-22-88	.130	.143	.128	14	46	5	6	2	0	0	2	3	0	0	0	7	0	0	.174	.184
Bautista, Jose	R-R	6-0	190	10-19-80	.000	.000	.000	1	3	0	0	0	0	0	0	0	0	0	0	1	0	0	.000	.250
Becerra, Wuilmer	R-R	6-4	190	10-11-94	.250	.500	.333	11	32	5	8	4	0	0	4	4	2	0	1	7	0	1	.375	.359
Carroll, George	R-R	6-2	210	4-17-88	.182	.067	.210	26	77	9	14	5	0	0	4	7	2	1	0	17	1	1	.247	.267
Cenas, Gabriel	R-R	6-1	155	10-16-93	.192	.162	.200	49	172	15	33	7	0	2	15	13	6	0	1	46	3	1	.267	.271
Conner, Seth	R-R	6-2	205	1-29-92	.250	.667	.154	5	16	2	4	1	0	0	2	2	1	0	1	3	0	0	.313	.350
Davis, D.J.	L-L	6-1	180	7-25-94	.233	.154	.258	43	163	30	38	7	2	4	12	18	8	1	0	54	18	7	.374	.339
DeSouza, Nathan	L-R	6-0	185	7-13-94	.241	.000	.318	9	29	7	7	0	1	1	3	3	0	0	0	6	0	0	.414	.313
Devonshire, Daniel	L-R	6-1	220	3-30-92	.148	.000	.174	11	27	4	4	0	0	1	5	2	0	0	0	12	0	0	.148	.324
Dupont, Will	L-R	6-0	170	12-19-91	.214	.222	.212	15	42	9	9	1	1	0	3	8	2	0	0	15	4	1	.286	.365
Gonzalez, Jesus	R-R	6-0	180	1-11-95	.206	.222	.201	51	194	16	40	8	1	3	19	14	1	0	0	58	3	2	.304	.263
Guerrero, Emilio	R-R	6-4	170	8-21-92	.244	.238	.246	24	82	14	20	7	1	2	9	12	1	0	0	20	3	3	.427	.347
Jacobo, Gabe	R-R	6-3	200	4-14-87	.333	.000	.500	5	18	0	6	3	0	0	1	0	0	1	2	0	0	.500	.350
Jeroloman, Brian	L-R	5-11	195	5-10-85	.286	.000	.333	3	7	1	2	0	0	0	0	0	0	0	0	0	.286	.286
Jones, Dennis	R-R	6-3	185	9-4-92	.192	.231	.183	24	73	8	14	3	0	0	4	9	3	0	0	29	5	8	.314	

Batting	B-T	HT	WT	DOB	AVG	vLH	vRH	G	AB	R	H	2B	3B	HR	RBI	BB	HBP	SH	SF	SO	SB	CS	SLG	OBP
Lawrie, Brett	R-R	6-0	215	1-18-90	.000	.000	—	1	1	0	0	0	0	0	0	0	0	0	0	0	0	0	.000	.000
Loveless, Derrick	L-R	6-1	200	3-7-93	.165	.111	.175	37	115	15	19	5	4	1	11	16	2	0	0	38	2	0	.304	.278
Lugo, Dawel	R-R	6-0	188	12-13-94	.224	.267	.208	47	170	20	38	2	5	2	20	7	5	1	0	25	5	1	.329	.275
Pascazi, Trey	B-R	6-1	175	8-7-93	.161	.167	.160	14	31	3	5	1	0	0	4	5	0	0	0	19	0	0	.194	.278
Rodriguez, Alexys	R-R	5-10	200	11-23-88	.056	.000	.071	7	18	1	1	0	0	0	0	5	0	0	0	4	0	1	.056	.261
Saez, Jorge	R-R	5-10	185	8-28-90	.200	.174	.207	36	110	19	22	5	0	3	21	23	0	0	1	19	4	1	.327	.336
Schaeffer, Chris	R-R	5-10	195	11-19-87	.000	.000	.000	3	7	2	0	0	0	0	0	2	0	0	0	1	0	0	.000	.222
Silviano, John	L-R	5-11	190	7-11-94	.164	.115	.178	39	116	11	19	4	2	2	17	22	1	0	2	21	0	3	.284	.298
Valeriote, Shaun	R-R	6-1	200	1-22-90	.227	.125	.250	27	88	17	20	4	0	2	12	12	1	0	0	25	0	1	.341	.327
Vega-Rosado, Jorge	R-R	5-8	175	12-5-91	.143	.200	.125	9	21	3	3	2	0	0	2	4	1	0	0	3	4	1	.238	.308

Pitching	B-T	HT	WT	DOB	W	L	ERA	G	GS	CG	SV	IP	H	R	ER	HR	BB	SO	AVG	vLH	vRH	K/9	BB/9
Adams, Zak	L-L	6-2	190	3-19-92	1	1	13.06	6	1	0	0	10	21	18	15	2	11	8	.412	.400	.417	6.97	9.58
Anderson, John	L-L	6-2	200	11-9-88	0	1	9.00	2	2	0	0	4	3	4	4	0	1	4	.214	.500	.100	9.00	2.25
Anderson, Kyle	R-L	6-2	205	5-24-90	0	0	1.80	2	0	0	0	5	6	1	1	0	1	2	.286	.333	.250	3.60	1.80
Beck, Casey	R-R	6-1	215	3-28-87	1	0	0.00	3	0	0	0	4	0	0	0	0	1	6	.000	.000	.000	13.50	2.25
Biggs, Mark	R-R	6-3	205	5-10-93	1	4	5.93	11	4	0	0	27	32	20	18	4	9	20	.291	.316	.278	6.59	2.96
Borucki, Ryan	L-L	6-4	175	3-31-94	1	0	3.00	4	0	0	0	6	4	2	2	1	0	10	.182	.200	.167	15.00	0.00
Brechbuehler, Tim	R-R	6-8	205	10-21-89	1	0	3.71	21	0	0	2	27	28	13	11	0	18	29	.269	.211	.303	9.79	6.08
Browning, Wil	R-R	6-3	175	9-8-88	0	0	1.35	7	0	0	0	7	2	1	1	0	1	2	.087	.286	.000	16.20	1.35
Cabrera, Oscar	L-L	6-2	215	5-22-94	0	1	5.40	2	1	0	0	5	6	3	3	0	2	5	.286	.200	.313	9.00	3.60
Cardona, Adonys	R-R	6-1	170	1-16-94	0	1	6.32	8	2	0	0	16	15	11	11	1	10	20	.246	.227	.256	11.49	5.74
Collazo, Willie	L-L	5-8	180	11-7-79	0	0	4.50	2	0	0	0	2	2	1	1	0	1	3	.250	.000	.500	13.50	4.50
D'Alessandro, Justin	R-R	6-4	190	9-27-89	1	0	3.07	14	0	0	0	15	16	5	5	0	8	12	.281	.235	.300	7.36	4.91
Dawson, Shane	R-L	6-1	180	9-9-93	2	1	2.35	10	3	0	0	31	33	13	8	2	10	35	.282	.323	.267	10.27	2.93
DeJong, Chase	L-R	6-4	185	12-29-93	1	0	1.50	6	0	0	0	12	7	2	2	0	1	15	.171	.250	.152	11.25	0.75
Del Rosario, Yeyfry	R-R	6-2	182	4-27-94	1	5	3.63	13	12	0	0	45	37	18	18	1	12	52	.292	.168		10.48	2.42
Dragmire, Brady	R-R	6-1	180	2-5-93	0	3	1.14	15	0	0	1	24	17	10	3	0	5	14	.215	.242	.196	5.32	1.90
Ghysels, Chuck	R-R	5-11	200	11-28-89	0	3	3.86	25	0	0	7	26	22	11	11	4	8	41	.232	.333	.177	14.38	2.81
Gonzales, Tyler	R-R	6-2	175	1-22-93	1	1	8.40	9	3	0	0	15	20	14	14	1	7		.328	.269	.371	4.20	2.40
Gonzalez, Alonzo	L-L	6-5	200	1-15-92	3	3	5.15	10	7	0	0	37	34	26	21	3	12	22	.272	.243	.283	5.40	2.95
Gracesqui, Francisco	L-L	6-0	175	11-26-91	3	2	2.88	22	0	0	0	34	24	14	11	1	26	46	.195	.286	.168	12.06	6.82
Kaye, Brandon	R-R	6-4	200	8-16-88	0	2	3.55	13	0	0	0	25	24	10	10	0	4	28	.258	.171	.310	9.95	1.42
Kelly, Adaric	R-R	5-10	180	12-1-92	2	0	1.48	14	0	0	1	24	20	8	4	2	7	22	.220	.067	.295	8.14	2.59
Labourt, Jairo	L-L	6-4	204	3-7-94	0	3	3.79	12	12	0	0	38	38	20	16	2	23	39	.253	.167	.294	9.24	5.45
Lara, Wilmin	R-R	6-2	175	6-5-94	0	0	6.23	3	0	0	0	4	4	3	3	0	5	2	.235	.400	.167	4.15	10.38
Mendez, Luis	R-R	6-7	250	10-14-89	1	1	8.38	9	0	0	0	10	19	10	9	0	3	3	.413	.375	.433	2.79	2.79
Ramirez, Alex	R-R	6-2	200	2-11-90	0	0	13.50	1	0	0	0	1	2	1	1	0	2	0	.667	.500	1.000	0.00	27.00
Tinoco, Jesus	R-R	6-4	190	4-30-95	1	1	6.00	2	0	0	0	6	7	4	4	0	1	8	.280	.100	.400	12.00	1.50
Tirado, Alberto	R-R	6-1	177	12-10-94	1	2	2.68	11	11	0	0	37	28	12	11	0	12	34	.217	.245	.200	8.27	2.92
Wasilewski, Zak	L-L	6-1	190	6-16-93	0	3	7.89	10	2	0	0	22	30	21	19	1	19	21	.333	.385	.313	8.72	7.89

Fielding

Catcher	PCT	G	PO	A	E	DP	PB
Carroll	.988	11	75	8	1	0	2
Conner	1.000	4	26	6	0	0	0
Jeroloman	1.000	3	15	1	0	0	0
Rodriguez	.983	7	54	5	1	1	1
Saez	.978	31	246	23	6	3	3
Schaeffer	1.000	2	7	1	0	0	0
Silviano	.991	15	101	11	1	2	4

First Base	PCT	G	PO	A	E	DP
Carroll	.976	15	112	9	3	11
Cenas	1.000	20	152	11	0	10
Conner	1.000	1	9	0	0	0
Jacobo	1.000	3	23	1	0	0
Valeriote	.975	25	186	13	5	13

Second Base	PCT	G	PO	A	E	DP
Atkinson	.986	38	50	87	2	16
Bartlett	.966	8	10	18	1	1
Dupont	.977	15	20	23	1	5
Pascazi	1.000	4	3	5	0	1
Vega-Rosado	1.000	6	6	9	0	1

Third Base	PCT	G	PO	A	E	DP
Atkinson	1.000	11	7	16	0	2
Bartlett	.786	5	5	6	3	1
Cenas	.940	29	19	59	5	4
Guerrero	.898	18	18	26	5	1
Lawrie	1.000	1	0	1	0	0

Shortstop	PCT	G	PO	A	E	DP
Bartlett	.600	1	1	2	2	0
Guerrero	.933	5	7	7	1	0
Lugo	.948	47	76	123	11	25
Pascazi	.958	8	7	16	1	1
Vega-Rosado	1.000	2	3	4	0	1

Outfield	PCT	G	PO	A	E	DP
Alford	.923	5	12	0	1	0
Almonte	.952	20	35	5	2	0
Becerra	1.000	9	9	2	0	0
Davis	.961	43	71	2	3	0
DeSouza	1.000	8	8	0	0	0
Gonzalez	.939	46	73	4	5	2
Jones	.949	23	33	4	2	1
Loveless	.980	35	47	3	1	1

DSL BLUE JAYS   ROOKIE
DOMINICAN SUMMER LEAGUE

Batting	B-T	HT	WT	DOB	AVG	vLH	vRH	G	AB	R	H	2B	3B	HR	RBI	BB	HBP	SH	SF	SO	SB	CS	SLG	OBP
Barazarte, Cesar	R-R	6-1	195	4-19-93	.258	.143	.292	59	217	34	56	10	1	0	31	20	5	1	5	36	15	1	.313	.328
Barreto, Deiferson	R-R	5-10	165	5-19-95	.292	.297	.291	46	171	18	50	7	1	0	9	12	5	3	1	23	4	3	.345	.354
De Aza, Andres	R-R	6-4	200	11-17-94	.227	.167	.241	28	97	11	22	3	1	3	17	6	4	0	2	26	0	0	.371	.294
Demorizi, Ronniel	B-R	6-0	170	7-19-95	.178	.156	.186	43	129	16	23	1	0	2	12	11	2	3	1	38	4	4	.233	.282
Fuentes, Edwin	R-R	6-0	170	8-14-94	.260	.244	.264	54	181	21	47	5	2	0	20	36	4	5	4	34	11	5	.309	.387
Garcia, Leudy	R-R	6-4	195	4-18-95	.277	.282	.276	36	137	15	38	6	1	0	12	14	2	0	0	39	2	2	.336	.353
Kelly, Juan	L-R	5-10	155	7-16-94	.170	.172	.169	37	100	10	17	3	0	0	8	14	1	1	1	19	2	1	.200	.276
Martin, Luis	R-R	6-4	210	2-12-94	.214	.110	.246	51	154	21	33	5	0	2	20	13	5	1	5	65	5	1	.286	.288
Perinan, Gustavo	L-R	5-11	185	1-2-95	.287	.321	.277	40	122	20	35	6	1	0	20	10	4	0	1	24	3	2	.352	.401
Rojas, Angel	R-R	5-11	160	4-7-93	.271	.250	.277	63	218	32	59	7	3	0	21	28	6	8	3	50	11	6	.330	.365
Santiago, Kervin	R-R	5-11	185	4-5-93	.257	.310	.236	40	101	11	26	0	0	1	11	19	3	4	0	16	5	2	.257	.390
Segovia, Rolando	B-R	5-11	165	10-26-94	.299	.354	.276	44	164	33	49	12	2	1	18	22	5	3	0	33	18	6	.415	.398
Sotillo, Andres	R-R	5-11	180	12-28-93	.305	.200	.347	43	105	17	32	5	0	1	14	10	9	0	0	23	8	4	.381	.411

	B-T	HT	WT	DOB	AVG	vLH	vRH	G	AB	R	H	2B	3B	HR	BB	SO	SB	CS					AVG	OBP
Tejada, Juan	R-R	6-3	180	2-13-94	.236	.262	.229	58	182	25	43	8	0	1	12	20	4	0	2	66	16	12	.297	.322
Vahlis, Roberto	R-R	5-10	190	11-19-93	.149	.278	.069	21	47	1	7	1	0	1	3	5	2	0	0	13	1	0	.234	.259

Pitching	B-T	HT	WT	DOB	W	L	ERA	G	GS	CG	SV	IP	H	R	ER	HR	BB	SO	AVG	vLH	vRH	K/9	BB/9
Bobonagua, Wilfredo	R-R	6-0	195	2-1-94	0	0	0.00	1	0	0	0	1	1	0	0	0	0	0	.167	.000	.250	0.00	0.00
Brito, Jose	R-R	6-2	185	12-19-94	0	1	5.23	4	2	0	0	10	10	7	6	0	3	8	.244	.400	.194	6.97	2.61
Burgos, Miguel	L-L	5-9	155	6-16-95	2	1	5.34	15	0	0	0	30	34	25	18	1	12	27	.274	.174	.297	8.01	3.56
Cabrera, Oscar	L-L	6-2	215	5-22-94	0	2	2.12	9	7	0	0	34	26	8	8	0	15	40	.224	.429	.196	10.59	3.97
Calatayud, Edgar	R-R	6-1	185	6-10-92	0	0	13.50	1	0	0	0	1	3	2	2	0	0	0	.429	1.000	.333	0.00	0.00
Castro, Miguel	R-R	6-5	190	12-24-94	3	2	4.87	8	3	0	0	20	16	13	11	1	11	20	.232	.136	.277	8.85	4.87
Conde, Greylor	R-R	6-4	195	6-25-94	1	3	3.57	12	2	0	0	35	43	17	14	1	12	13	.323	.333	.319	3.31	3.06
Contreras, Jorge	R-R	6-2	190	10-7-92	3	3	2.55	13	13	1	0	60	51	22	17	1	24	44	.238	.243	.236	6.60	3.60
Cordero, Jimmy	R-R	6-3	195	10-19-91	1	3	5.60	7	3	0	0	18	13	14	11	3	11	18	.203	.217	.195	9.17	5.60
De La Rosa, Luis	R-R	6-2	170	8-11-93	2	1	8.38	10	4	0	0	19	22	21	18	2	14	11	.286	.269	.294	5.12	6.52
Eduardo, Francis	R-R	6-2	190	5-24-94	3	2	6.39	12	3	0	0	31	26	25	22	2	17	33	.243	.325	.194	9.58	4.94
Fernandez, Jose	L-L	6-3	170	2-13-93	2	0	1.52	9	4	0	0	30	25	7	5	1	2	34	.234	.188	.242	10.31	0.61
Guerrero, Eyerys	R-R	6-3	208	10-14-92	0	1	6.75	7	0	0	1	12	17	13	9	0	6	11	.340	.400	.314	8.25	4.50
Gutierrez, Osman	R-R	6-4	185	12-15-94	1	0	4.50	7	2	0	0	14	17	9	7	0	9	10	.309	.278	.324	6.43	5.79
Lara, Wilmin	R-R	6-2	175	6-5-94	0	3	5.13	13	1	0	0	26	23	19	15	1	22	22	.264	.458	.190	7.52	7.52
Lopez, Manuel	R-R	6-2	182	3-2-91	2	3	2.36	19	1	0	7	42	24	13	11	1	19	37	.175	.173	.176	7.93	4.07
Paulino, Simon	R-R	6-6	200	10-20-89	3	2	5.08	20	2	0	4	28	36	20	16	1	5	23	.305	.244	.338	7.31	1.59
Perdomo, Angel	L-L	6-6	200	5-7-94	0	0	5.40	7	0	0	0	12	2	7	7	0	13	13	.059	.167	.036	10.03	10.03
Rodriguez, Carlos	L-L	6-0	185	1-29-95	3	2	4.19	13	4	0	0	34	29	19	16	0	12	33	.232	.143	.243	8.65	3.15
Solarte, Alejandro	L-L	6-4	180	9-22-94	3	0	1.53	9	2	0	0	29	10	6	5	0	10	25	.104	.167	.095	7.67	3.07
Tinoco, Jesus	R-R	6-4	190	4-30-95	0	4	4.14	12	7	0	0	37	37	24	17	0	12	26	.266	.357	.227	6.32	2.92
Torres, Jonathan	L-L	6-4	190	12-31-94	0	1	4.29	11	4	0	0	21	17	11	10	0	21	24	.243	.000	.254	10.29	9.00
Vielma, Gilberto	R-R	6-4	220	11-23-93	1	1	3.68	10	1	0	1	22	23	16	9	0	10	19	.256	.281	.241	7.77	4.09

Fielding

Catcher	PCT	G	PO	A	E	DP	PB
Kelly	.986	10	67	6	1	0	2
Santiago	.972	38	211	35	7	3	6
Sotillo	.980	26	178	21	4	1	14
Vahlis	.982	6	50	4	1	1	3

First Base	PCT	G	PO	A	E	DP
Barazarte	.988	19	155	10	2	5
Kelly	.957	11	42	2	2	5
Perinan	1.000	7	60	4	0	2
Rojas	.992	40	332	19	3	23
Santiago	1.000	2	15	1	0	0

Second Base	PCT	G	PO	A	E	DP
Barreto	.934	14	20	37	4	7
Demorizi	.966	25	33	52	3	5
Perinan	.833	2	2	3	1	0
Rojas	1.000	2	1	3	0	0
Segovia	.949	30	50	62	6	15

Third Base	PCT	G	PO	A	E	DP
Barreto	.933	23	16	54	5	1
Fuentes	.923	6	4	8	1	2
Kelly	1.000	3	1	4	0	0
Perinan	.877	20	13	44	8	5
Rojas	.929	12	13	13	2	0
Segovia	.800	6	4	8	3	0

Shortstop	PCT	G	PO	A	E	DP
Barreto	—	1	0	0	0	0
Demorizi	1.000	2	3	7	0	3
Fuentes	.957	46	68	112	8	17
Rojas	.931	12	21	33	4	6
Segovia	.925	12	13	24	3	2

Outfield	PCT	G	PO	A	E	DP
Barazarte	.987	43	68	6	1	3
De Aza	.920	17	19	4	2	2
Demorizi	1.000	4	5	0	0	0
Garcia	.953	36	40	1	2	0
Martin	.929	50	95	9	8	4
Perinan	—	1	0	0	0	0
Rojas	—	3	0	0	0	0
Tejada	.950	56	90	5	5	1

TORONTO BLUE JAYS

Washington Nationals

SEASON IN A SENTENCE: Not only did the Nationals post their first winning season since moving to Washington in 2005, but they also led the majors with 98 wins to snap the franchise's 31-year postseason drought.

HIGH POINT: When the Braves lost 2-1 at Pittsburgh on Oct. 1, the Nationals clinched the National League East, launching a frenzied celebration at Nationals Park. Minutes later, the Nats dropped a 2-0 decision to the Phillies, but nothing could put a damper on the party, as players literally rolled on the floor with laughter in a champagne-soaked clubhouse, and the 35,387 fans in attendance roared. It was the first division title for a Washington baseball club since 1933.

LOW POINT: Washington's dream season had a nightmarish ending. After splitting the first four games of the Division Series against the Cardinals, the Nationals built a 6-0 lead through three innings in the decisive fifth game, with ace Gio Gonzalez on the mound. St. Louis fought back within a run by the eighth, but the Nationals added an insurance run and led 7-5 with two outs in the ninth inning. But closer Drew Storen could not get the final out, as the Cardinals rallied for four runs to complete the stunning comeback.

NOTABLE ROOKIES: Bryce Harper's rookie season was one of the most anticipated in baseball history, and the 19-year-old phenom did not disappoint. After getting called up on April 28, Harper held down a starting outfield job for the rest of the season, earning a trip to the All-Star Game en route to hitting .270/.340/.477 with 22 home runs, 59 RBIs and 18 stolen bases. His bazooka arm dazzled fans as much as his powerful bat, and he compiled eight outfield assists.

KEY TRANSACTIONS: The Nationals traded four of their best prospects (Derek Norris, Brad Peacock, A.J. Cole and Tommy Milone) to the Athletics land Gonzalez in December, and he rewarded them by going 21-8, 2.89. Stephen Strasburg had a sterling first full season back after Tommy John surgery (15-6, 3.16), but the Nationals shut him down after 159 innings in order to protect his arm—a decision that spawned a cacophony of controversy.

DOWN ON THE FARM: The Gonzalez trade and the graduation of Harper left the farm system diminished, but outfielder Brian Goodwin and righthander Alex Meyer took steps forward to lead the organization's next wave of top prospects.

OPENING DAY PAYROLL: $81.3 million (20th)

PLAYERS OF THE YEAR

MAJOR LEAGUE	MINOR LEAGUE
Gio Gonzalez lhp	**Matt Skole** 3b
21-8, 2.89	(Low A/High A)
207 SO/76 BB	.291/.426/.559
Led NL in W, SO/9	SAL MVP

ORGANIZATION LEADERS

BATTING		*Minimum 250 AB
MAJORS		
* AVG	Ian Desmond	.292
* OPS	Adam LaRoche	.853
HR	Adam LaRoche	33
RBI	Adam LaRoche	100
MINORS		
* AVG	Billy Burns, Hagerstown	.322
* OBP	Billy Burns, Hagerstown	.432
* SLG	Steven Souza Jr., Hagerstown/Potomac	.572
R	Jason Martinson, Hagerstown/Potomac	104
H	Eury Perez, GCL Nationals/Harrisburg/Syracuse	167
TB	Corey Brown, Syracuse	253
2B	Michael Taylor, Potomac	33
3B	Caleb Ramsey, Hagerstown	10
HR	Matthew Skole, Hagerstown/Potomac	27
RBI	Jason Martinson, Hagerstown/Potomac	106
BB	Matthew Skole, Hagerstown/Potomac	99
SO	Jason Martinson, Hagerstown/Potomac	167
SB	Eury Perez, GCL Nationals/Harrisburg/Syracuse	51

PITCHING		#Minimum 75 IP
MAJORS		
W	Gio Gonzalez	21
# ERA	Gio Gonzalez	2.89
SO	Gio Gonzalez	207
SV	Tyler Clippard	32
MINORS		
W	Zach Duke, Syracuse	15
L	Tanner Roark, Syracuse	17
# ERA	Nathan Karns, Hagerstown/Potomac	2.17
G	Patrick McCoy, Harrisburg	50
GS	Yunesky Maya, Syracuse	28
SV	Christian Garcia, Harrisburg/Syracuse	21
IP	Yunesky Maya, Syracuse	167
BB	Paul Demny, Harrisburg	61
SO	Nathan Karns, Hagerstown/Potomac	148
# AVG	Nathan Karns, Hagerstown/Potomac	.174

General Manager: Mike Rizzo. **Farm Director:** Bob Boone. **Scouting Director:** Kris Kline.

Class	Team	League	W	L	PCT	Finish	Manager
Majors	Washington Nationals	National	98	64	.605	1st (16)	Davey Johnson
Triple-A	Syracuse Chiefs	International	70	74	.486	9th (14)	Tony Beasley
Double-A	Harrisburg Senators	Eastern	64	78	.451	10th (12)	Matthew LeCroy
High A	Potomac Nationals	Carolina	64	75	.460	6th (8)	Brian Rupp
Low A	Hagerstown Suns	South Atlantic	82	55	.599	2nd (14)	Brian Daubach
Short-season	Auburn Doubledays	New York-Penn	46	30	.605	3rd (14)	Gary Cathcart
Rookie	GCL Nationals	Gulf Coast	27	33	.450	11th (14)	Tripp Keister
Overall 2012 Minor League Record			353	345	.506	14th (30)	

ORGANIZATION STATISTICS

WASHINGTON NATIONALS

NATIONAL LEAGUE

Batting	B-T	HT	WT	DOB	AVG	vLH	vRH	G	AB	R	H	2B	3B	HR	RBI	BB	HBP	SH	SF	SO	SB	CS	SLG	OBP
Ankiel, Rick	L-L	6-1	210	7-19-79	.228	.174	.237	68	158	15	36	10	2	5	15	12	0	1	0	59	1	3	.411	.282
Bernadina, Roger	L-L	6-2	215	6-12-84	.291	.417	.276	129	227	25	66	11	0	5	25	28	2	3	1	53	15	3	.405	.372
Brown, Corey	L-L	6-1	210	11-26-85	.200	.250	.190	19	25	4	5	2	0	1	3	1	0	1	0	9	0	0	.400	.231
Carroll, Brett	R-R	5-11	210	10-3-82	.000	.000	.000	5	2	2	0	0	0	0	0	0	0	0	0	0	0	0	.000	.000
DeRosa, Mark	R-R	6-1	215	2-26-75	.188	.225	.156	48	85	13	16	5	0	0	6	14	0	1	1	18	1	0	.247	.300
Desmond, Ian	R-R	6-2	205	9-20-85	.292	.303	.289	130	513	72	150	33	2	25	73	30	3	0	1	113	21	6	.511	.335
Espinosa, Danny	B-R	6-0	195	4-25-87	.247	.281	.234	160	594	82	147	37	2	17	56	46	13	3	2	189	20	6	.402	.315
Flores, Jesus	R-R	6-1	210	10-26-84	.213	.189	.225	83	277	22	59	12	1	6	26	13	1	2	3	59	1	2	.329	.248
Harper, Bryce	L-R	6-3	215	10-16-92	.270	.240	.286	139	533	98	144	26	9	22	59	56	2	3	3	120	18	6	.477	.340
Izturis, Cesar	B-R	5-9	180	2-10-80	.500	.500	.500	5	4	4	2	1	0	0	0	0	0	0	0	0	0	0	.750	.500
2-team total (57 Milwaukee)					.241	—	—	62	166	13	40	7	2	2	11	3	0	4	0	13	1	1	.343	.254
LaRoche, Adam	L-L	6-3	210	11-6-79	.271	.268	.273	154	571	76	155	35	1	33	100	67	0	0	9	138	1	1	.510	.343
Leon, Sandy	B-R	5-11	220	3-13-89	.267	.500	.182	12	30	2	8	2	0	0	2	4	2	0	0	11	0	0	.333	.389
Lombardozzi, Steve	B-R	6-0	195	9-20-88	.273	.231	.287	126	384	40	105	16	3	3	27	19	6	6	1	46	5	3	.354	.317
Maldonado, Carlos	R-R	6-2	290	1-3-79	.000	.000	.000	4	9	0	0	0	0	0	0	1	2	0	1	0	4	0	0	.000	.182
Moore, Tyler	R-R	6-2	215	1-30-87	.263	.247	.286	75	156	20	41	9	0	10	29	14	1	0	0	46	3	0	.513	.327
Morse, Michael	R-R	6-5	245	3-22-82	.291	.290	.291	102	406	53	118	17	1	18	62	16	4	0	4	97	0	1	.470	.321
Nady, Xavier	R-R	6-2	215	11-14-78	.157	.176	.137	40	102	6	16	3	0	3	6	7	0	0	0	24	1	0	.275	.211
2-team total (19 San Francisco)					.184	—	—	59	152	12	28	6	1	4	13	13	1	0	0	37	1	0	.316	.253
Perez, Eury	R-R	6-0	180	5-30-90	.200	.500	.000	13	5	3	1	0	0	0	0	0	0	0	0	0	3	0	.200	.200
Ramos, Wilson	R-R	6-0	250	8-10-87	.265	.300	.260	25	83	11	22	2	0	3	10	12	0	0	1	19	0	0	.398	.354
Solano, Jhonatan	R-R	5-9	205	8-12-85	.314	.444	.269	12	35	6	11	3	0	2	6	2	0	0	0	5	1	0	.571	.351
Suzuki, Kurt	R-R	5-11	195	10-4-83	.267	.273	.266	43	146	17	39	5	0	5	25	11	2	2	3	20	1	0	.404	.321
Tracy, Chad	L-R	6-1	220	5-22-80	.269	.333	.262	73	93	7	25	7	0	3	14	10	1	0	1	15	0	0	.441	.343
Werth, Jayson	R-R	6-5	225	5-20-79	.300	.395	.268	81	300	42	90	21	3	5	31	42	1	0	1	57	8	2	.440	.387
Zimmerman, Ryan	R-R	6-3	230	9-28-84	.282	.307	.273	145	578	93	163	36	1	25	95	57	2	0	4	116	5	2	.478	.346

Pitching	B-T	HT	WT	DOB	W	L	ERA	G	GS	CG	SV	IP	H	R	ER	HR	BB	SO	AVG	vLH	vRH	K/9	BB/9
Burnett, Sean	L-L	6-1	180	9-17-82	1	2	2.38	70	0	0	2	57	58	16	15	4	12	57	.262	.211	.298	9.05	1.91
Clippard, Tyler	R-R	6-3	200	2-14-85	2	6	3.72	74	0	0	32	73	55	32	30	7	29	84	.204	.170	.239	10.40	3.59
Detwiler, Ross	R-L	6-5	190	3-6-86	10	8	3.40	33	27	0	0	164	149	75	62	15	52	105	.241	.170	.263	5.75	2.85
Duke, Zach	L-L	6-1	205	4-19-83	1	0	1.32	8	0	0	0	14	11	2	2	0	4	10	.212	.267	.189	6.59	2.63
Garcia, Christian	R-R	6-5	215	8-24-85	0	0	2.13	13	0	0	0	13	8	3	3	2	2	15	.186	.267	.143	10.66	1.42
Gonzalez, Gio	L-R	6-0	200	9-19-85	21	8	2.89	32	32	2	0	199	149	69	64	9	76	207	.206	.231	.199	9.35	3.43
Gonzalez, Mike	R-L	6-2	215	5-23-78	0	0	3.03	47	0	0	0	36	31	14	12	2	16	39	.237	.179	.297	9.84	4.04
Gorzelanny, Tom	L-L	6-2	205	7-12-82	4	2	2.88	45	1	0	1	72	65	27	23	7	30	62	.242	.237	.245	7.75	3.75
Jackson, Edwin	R-R	6-3	210	9-9-83	10	11	4.03	31	31	1	0	190	173	90	85	23	58	168	.243	.249	.236	7.97	2.75
Lannan, John	L-L	6-4	235	9-27-84	4	1	4.13	6	6	0	0	33	33	15	15	0	14	17	.270	.281	.267	4.68	3.86
Lidge, Brad	R-R	6-5	210	12-23-76	0	1	9.64	11	0	0	2	9	12	10	10	1	11	10	.308	.545	.214	9.64	10.61
Mattheus, Ryan	R-R	6-3	205	11-10-83	5	3	2.85	66	0	0	0	66	57	22	21	8	19	41	.241	.241	.240	5.56	2.58
Perry, Ryan	R-R	6-4	215	2-18-87	1	0	10.13	7	0	0	0	8	12	9	9	2	3	3	.364	.333	.400	3.38	2.25
Rodriguez, Henry	R-R	6-1	225	2-25-87	1	3	5.83	35	0	0	9	29	19	20	19	4	22	31	.181	.208	.158	9.51	6.75
Stammen, Craig	R-R	6-4	225	3-9-84	6	1	2.34	59	0	0	1	88	70	27	23	7	36	87	.215	.198	.224	8.86	3.67
Storen, Drew	B-R	6-2	190	8-11-87	3	1	2.37	37	0	0	4	30	22	8	8	0	8	24	.210	.289	.164	7.12	2.37
Strasburg, Stephen	R-R	6-4	220	7-20-88	15	6	3.16	28	28	0	0	159	136	62	56	15	48	197	.230	.271	.185	11.13	2.71
Wang, Chien-Ming	R-R	6-4	225	3-31-80	2	3	6.68	10	5	0	0	32	50	24	24	5	15	15	.376	.413	.343	4.18	4.18
Zimmermann, Jordan	R-R	6-2	220	5-23-86	12	8	2.94	32	32	0	0	196	186	69	64	18	43	153	.251	.234	.268	7.04	1.98

Fielding

Catcher	PCT	G	PO	A	E	DP	PB
Flores	.994	80	648	52	4	5	6
Leon	.987	12	73	5	1	1	3
Maldonado	1.000	4	24	0	0	0	0
Ramos	.995	24	189	14	1	1	2

	PCT	G	PO	A	E	DP	PB
Solano	1.000	11	55	10	0	2	2
Suzuki	.991	42	324	24	3	3	2

First Base	PCT	G	PO	A	E	DP	
DeRosa	1.000	3	4	0	0	1	

	PCT	G	PO	A	E	DP
LaRoche	.995	153	1260	100	7	113
Moore	1.000	14	70	6	0	7
Morse	1.000	1	8	1	0	0
Tracy	.986	14	64	4	1	6

Second Base	PCT	G	PO	A	E	DP
DeRosa	—	1	0	0	0	0
Espinosa	.989	126	192	329	6	67
Izturis	—	1	0	0	0	0
Lombardozzi	.992	51	95	141	2	27

Third Base	PCT	G	PO	A	E	DP
DeRosa	1.000	11	5	5	0	0
Izturis	1.000	1	1	0	0	0
Lombardozzi	.917	13	3	19	2	2
Tracy	1.000	10	3	13	0	0

	PCT	G	PO	A	E	DP
Zimmerman	.950	145	76	284	19	28
Shortstop	PCT	G	PO	A	E	DP
DeRosa	.889	1	3	5	1	1
Desmond	.970	128	171	306	15	65
Espinosa	.956	36	43	110	7	23
Izturis	—	1	0	0	0	0
Lombardozzi	1.000	1	0	2	0	0
Outfield	PCT	G	PO	A	E	DP
Ankiel	.983	62	115	2	2	0
Bernadina	1.000	94	117	3	0	1

	PCT	G	PO	A	E	DP
Brown	1.000	11	14	0	0	0
Carroll	—	3	0	0	0	0
DeRosa	1.000	16	15	1	0	0
Harper	.979	138	311	8	7	3
Lombardozzi	1.000	41	48	2	0	0
Moore	1.000	41	29	1	0	0
Morse	.993	92	146	3	1	0
Nady	.971	35	32	1	1	0
Perez	1.000	7	1	0	0	0
Werth	.994	79	166	4	1	1

SYRACUSE CHIEFS   TRIPLE-A
INTERNATIONAL LEAGUE

Batting	B-T	HT	WT	DOB	AVG	vLH	vRH	G	AB	R	H	2B	3B	HR	RBI	BB	HBP	SH	SF	SO	SB	CS	SLG	OBP
Ankiel, Rick	L-L	6-1	210	7-19-79	.333	.333	—	1	3	1	1	0	0	0	0	0	1	0	0	2	0	0	.333	.500
Brown, Corey	L-L	6-1	210	11-26-85	.285	.270	.291	126	484	83	138	22	9	25	71	59	4	3	4	139	18	7	.523	.365
Bynum, Seth	R-R	6-0	185	12-19-80	.205	.224	.200	94	278	36	57	11	2	6	34	26	4	4	1	89	3	2	.324	.282
Carroll, Brett	R-R	5-11	210	10-3-82	.250	.210	.265	111	364	55	91	23	2	10	50	44	3	2	4	97	7	5	.407	.333
Harper, Bryce	L-R	6-3	215	10-16-92	.243	.190	.264	21	74	8	18	4	1	1	3	9	0	1	0	14	1	1	.365	.325
Higley, J.R.	R-R	6-3	190	6-21-88	.100	.250	.000	4	10	1	1	0	0	0	0	0	0	1	0	1	0	0	.100	.100
Hill, Koyie	B-R	6-1	210	3-9-79	.163	.300	.149	31	104	14	17	1	0	2	9	9	0	2	2	26	1	0	.231	.226
Hoffpauir, Jarrett	R-R	5-9	190	6-18-83	.280	.255	.289	106	336	45	94	16	2	3	44	32	2	2	6	41	4	0	.366	.340
Howell, Jeff	R-R	6-0	205	4-1-83	.211	.269	.188	30	90	6	19	2	0	0	11	3	0	0	2	16	0	1	.233	.232
Johnson, Josh R.	B-R	5-11	170	1-11-86	.231	.278	.217	76	234	35	54	8	0	0	18	35	1	7	0	30	6	7	.265	.333
Komatsu, Erik	L-L	5-10	175	10-1-87	.269	.263	.271	31	104	16	28	4	0	3	14	13	2	2	2	13	2	5	.394	.355
Leon, Sandy	B-R	5-11	220	3-13-89	.346	.462	.231	19	52	8	18	5	0	2	4	12	0	0	0	10	0	0	.558	.469
Maldonado, Carlos	R-R	6-2	290	1-31-79	.210	.212	.210	51	157	20	33	7	0	6	11	27	0	3	0	42	0	0	.369	.326
Marrero, Chris	R-R	6-3	220	7-2-88	.244	.364	.202	37	127	13	31	6	1	0	12	16	1	0	0	28	0	0	.307	.333
Mayorson, Manny	R-R	5-9	195	3-10-83	.225	.300	.200	17	40	4	9	1	0	0	1	2	0	0	0	2	0	0	.250	.262
McConnell, Chris	R-R	5-9	190	12-15-86	.235	.000	.333	6	17	1	4	2	0	0	0	0	0	0	0	6	0	0	.353	.235
Michaels, Jason	R-R	6-0	215	5-4-76	.202	.355	.137	35	104	11	21	3	0	2	12	9	0	0	0	19	0	0	.288	.265
Moore, Tyler	R-R	6-2	215	1-30-87	.307	.423	.267	29	101	15	31	6	1	9	26	12	0	0	2	26	1	0	.653	.374
Negrych, Jim	L-R	5-10	180	3-2-85	.264	.309	.253	91	276	31	73	9	1	8	39	40	1	5	2	41	2	4	.391	.357
Paul, Xavier	L-R	5-9	200	2-25-85	.315	.244	.331	60	213	30	67	16	5	4	29	19	2	3	0	41	6	3	.512	.376
2-team total (6 Louisville)					.332	—	—	66	238	34	79	18	1	9	48	20	2	3	0	46	9	3	.529	.388
Perez, Eury	R-R	6-0	180	5-30-90	.333	.339	.330	40	159	21	53	7	1	0	10	8	2	4	0	26	20	5	.390	.373
Rivero, Carlos	R-R	6-3	215	5-20-88	.303	.353	.286	126	455	57	138	28	1	10	64	33	1	3	6	87	6	5	.435	.347
Skelton, James	L-R	5-11	165	10-28-85	.280	.273	.282	17	50	9	14	4	0	0	7	10	1	0	0	10	1	0	.360	.410
Solano, Jhonatan	R-R	5-9	205	8-12-85	.250	.444	.147	13	52	8	13	2	0	2	3	1	0	1	0	6	0	0	.288	.298
Teahen, Mark	L-R	6-3	220	9-6-81	.260	.278	.255	124	450	60	117	28	4	3	63	45	2	0	3	102	9	3	.360	.328
Tracy, Chad	L-R	6-1	220	5-22-80	.474	1.000	.444	6	19	2	9	0	0	1	3	1	0	0	0	2	0	0	.632	.500
Valdez, Jesus	R-R	6-2	170	11-2-84	.263	.325	.241	48	156	21	41	6	1	6	31	9	1	0	2	29	0	0	.429	.304
Walters, Zach	B-R	6-2	195	9-5-89	.214	.226	.209	29	98	9	21	4	0	1	6	6	0	1	0	28	0	0	.286	.260
Werth, Jayson	R-R	6-5	225	5-20-79	.238	.000	.238	7	21	4	5	2	0	0	4	6	0	0	0	5	0	0	.333	.407

Pitching	B-T	HT	WT	DOB	W	L	ERA	G	GS	CG	SV	IP	H	R	ER	HR	BB	SO	AVG	vLH	vRH	K/9	BB/9
Arnesen, Erik	R-R	6-3	260	3-19-84	3	4	3.53	33	3	0	2	64	65	27	25	6	21	46	.269	.290	.252	6.50	2.97
Atkins, Mitch	R-R	6-3	230	10-1-85	6	9	4.87	28	20	1	0	118	133	73	64	12	39	91	.283	.291	.275	6.92	2.97
Bibens-Dirkx, Austin	R-R	6-1	210	4-29-85	0	3	5.59	29	2	0	1	47	57	31	29	4	16	41	.298	.361	.250	7.91	3.09
Davis, Erik	R-R	6-4	200	10-8-86	1	0	4.15	8	0	0	0	9	10	5	4	1	3	5	.278	.200	.333	5.19	2.08
Duke, Zach	L-L	6-1	205	4-19-83	15	5	3.51	26	26	2	0	164	178	69	64	16	39	91	.276	.243	.293	4.98	2.14
Garcia, Christian	R-R	6-5	215	8-24-85	1	1	0.56	27	0	0	14	32	18	4	2	0	11	38	.157	.170	.147	10.58	3.06
Gonzalez, Mike	R-L	6-2	215	5-23-78	0	0	0.00	1	0	0	0	1	0	0	0	0	0	2	.000	.000	.000	13.50	0.00
Holland, Neil	R-R	6-0	190	8-14-88	0	0	0.00	1	0	0	0	1	0	0	0	0	0	0	.000	—	.000	0.00	0.00
Lannan, John	L-L	6-4	235	9-27-84	9	11	4.30	24	24	3	0	149	164	77	71	16	50	86	.283	.250	.295	5.21	3.03
Lehman, Pat	R-R	6-3	210	10-18-86	1	1	3.32	37	0	0	1	43	42	18	16	3	17	29	.247	.261	.238	6.02	3.53
MacDougal, Mike	B-R	6-4	180	3-5-77	1	1	4.22	12	0	0	2	11	9	5	5	1	8	14	.237	.368	.105	11.81	6.75
Mandel, Jeff	B-R	6-3	190	4-30-85	6	5	2.58	19	11	1	1	84	78	26	24	6	16	48	.251	.278	.222	5.16	1.72
Martin, Rafael	R-R	6-3	215	5-16-84	0	0	7.13	13	0	0	0	18	16	14	14	2	11	15	.232	.303	.167	7.64	5.60
Maya, Yunesky	R-R	5-11	210	8-28-81	11	10	3.88	28	28	0	0	167	158	79	72	20	40	89	.248	.243	.253	4.80	2.16
Pena, Hassan	R-R	6-2	210	3-25-85	3	5	3.81	42	0	0	4	57	53	26	24	6	22	36	.250	.228	.267	5.72	3.49
Perry, Ryan	R-R	6-4	215	2-13-87	1	1	4.50	11	0	0	2	12	16	6	6	0	7	14	.356	.368	.346	10.50	5.25
Pucetas, Kevin	R-R	6-4	225	11-27-84	1	0	3.86	1	1	0	0	7	7	3	3	1	1	5	.269	.294	.222	6.43	1.29
Roark, Tanner	R-R	6-2	220	10-5-86	6	17	4.39	28	26	1	0	148	161	89	72	14	47	130	.281	.273	.290	7.92	2.86
Rodriguez, Henry	R-R	6-1	225	2-25-87	0	0	0.00	4	0	0	2	4	0	0	0	0	3	6	.000	.000	.000	6.75	9.00
Severino, Atahualpa	L-L	5-9	225	11-6-84	3	0	2.81	46	0	0	3	48	37	20	15	5	36	43	.218	.273	.159	8.06	6.75
VanAllen, Cory	L-L	6-3	180	12-24-84	0	0	8.50	17	0	0	1	18	24	19	17	1	13	14	.320	.375	.294	7.00	6.50
Wang, Chien-Ming	R-R	6-4	225	3-31-80	2	0	4.35	3	3	0	0	21	26	10	10	1	5	8	.321	.327	.310	3.48	2.18
Wilkie, Josh	R-R	6-2	190	7-22-84	0	2	4.76	18	0	0	3	17	12	9	9	1	5	14	.314	.240	.356	7.41	2.65

Fielding						
Catcher	PCT	G	PO	A	E	DP	PB
Hill	.995	30	175	17	1	2	0
Howell	.989	28	167	13	2	1	5

	PCT	G	PO	A	E	DP	PB
Leon	.992	19	115	15	1	1	0
Maldonado	.996	45	250	20	1	2	4
Skelton	.974	16	108	5	3	3	0

	PCT	G	PO	A	E	DP
Solano	.978	12	76	11	2	2	0
First Base	PCT	G	PO	A	E	DP
Maldonado	1.000	2	2	0	0	0

Marrero	.990	31	279	18	3 30
Moore	1.000	24	187	18	0 21
Negrych	1.000	2	11	3	0 2
Rivero	1.000	16	74	4	0 7
Teahen	.992	83	729	41	6 70
Tracy	1.000	3	28	0	0 3

Second Base	PCT	G	PO	A	E	DP
Bynum	.992	30	46	84	1	22
Hoffpauir	.981	51	71	132	4	24
Johnson	.980	22	38	59	2	16
Mayorson	.979	7	19	27	1	7
Negrych	.981	54	83	125	4	26
Teahen	.778	1	2	5	2	1

Third Base	PCT	G	PO	A	E	DP
Hoffpauir	.960	40	21	74	4	6

Mayorson	—	1	0	0	0 0
Rivero	.953	98	57	208	13 22
Teahen	.973	15	8	28	1 2
Tracy	1.000	1	0	1	0 0

Shortstop	PCT	G	PO	A	E	DP
Bynum	.961	58	80	141	9	35
Johnson	.967	46	76	132	7	28
McConnell	.958	6	7	16	1	4
Rivero	.986	17	25	43	1	12
Walters	.964	29	39	95	5	14

Outfield	PCT	G	PO	A	E	DP
Ankiel	—	1	0	0	0	0
Brown	.970	120	258	5	8	1
Carroll	.978	104	207	17	5	6
Harper	.920	21	43	3	4	1

Higley	1.000	3	5	0	0 0
Johnson	1.000	5	6	0	0 0
Komatsu	1.000	27	41	4	0 0
Mayorson	1.000	1	2	0	0 0
Michaels	1.000	13	18	0	0 0
Moore	1.000	4	5	0	0 0
Negrych	1.000	5	10	0	0 0
Paul	.951	45	77	1	4 0
Perez	.989	39	90	3	1 1
Roark	1.000	1	1	0	0 0
Teahen	1.000	22	41	0	0 0
Valdez	1.000	37	60	2	0 0
Werth	1.000	7	7	0	0 0

HARRISBURG SENATORS
DOUBLE-A
EASTERN LEAGUE

Batting	B-T	HT	WT	DOB	AVG	vLH	vRH	G	AB	R	H	2B	3B	HR	RBI	BB	HBP	SH	SF	SO	SB	CS	SLG	OBP
Ankiel, Rick	L-L	6-1	210	7-19-79	.333	.500	.200	4	9	3	3	0	0	2	3	2	0	0	0	2	0	0	1.000	.455
Bloxom, Justin	R-B	6-1	205	4-29-88	.251	.259	.247	68	243	26	61	11	1	9	24	21	0	0	0	65	0	2	.416	.311
Bynum, Seth	R-R	6-0	185	12-19-80	.236	.286	.213	28	89	10	21	6	0	3	13	7	1	0	0	30	2	0	.404	.299
Goodwin, Brian	L-L	6-1	195	11-2-90	.223	.178	.240	42	166	17	37	8	1	5	14	18	2	0	0	50	3	3	.373	.306
Higley, J.R.	R-R	6-3	190	6-21-88	.143	.250	.000	8	7	2	1	0	0	0	0	1	0	0	1	1	1	0	.143	.333
Hood, Destin	R-R	6-1	225	4-3-90	.245	.272	.234	94	355	45	87	20	3	3	45	24	6	0	4	89	6	1	.344	.301
Howell, Jeff	R-R	6-0	205	4-1-83	.364	.200	.500	3	11	2	4	1	0	0	2	2	0	0	0	3	0	0	.455	.462
Ivany, Devin	R-R	6-2	185	7-27-82	.212	.263	.195	49	156	17	33	6	2	3	13	10	2	3	1	28	1	0	.333	.266
Johnson, Josh R.	B-R	5-11	170	1-11-86	.395	.222	.448	11	38	7	15	5	1	1	7	5	0	0	0	5	2	1	.658	.465
King, Stephen	R-R	6-2	195	10-2-87	.185	.205	.176	47	124	12	23	2	1	0	9	5	0	2	1	42	1	0	.218	.215
Kobernus, Jeff	R-R	6-2	210	6-30-88	.282	.319	.268	82	330	41	93	10	2	1	19	19	4	9	4	57	42	11	.333	.325
Leon, Sandy	B-R	5-11	220	3-13-89	.311	.295	.319	40	135	15	42	12	0	1	19	9	2	1	2	16	1	0	.422	.358
Lozada, Jose	B-R	6-0	180	12-29-85	.241	.206	.251	99	286	36	69	11	1	5	28	27	10	4	3	56	2	3	.339	.325
Marrero, Chris	R-R	6-3	220	7-2-88	.273	.500	.143	5	22	2	6	2	0	1	3	0	1	0	0	3	0	0	.500	.304
Mayo, Jeremy	R-R	5-10	194	6-17-88	.500	—	.500	1	2	0	1	0	0	0	0	1	0	0	0	0	0	0	.500	.667
Mayorson, Manny	R-R	5-9	195	3-10-83	.244	.233	.247	33	123	10	30	5	1	0	9	2	0	0	0	8	0	1	.285	.256
McConnell, Chris	R-R	5-9	170	12-18-85	.169	.179	.167	44	124	9	21	4	1	0	9	8	3	2	1	30	2	2	.218	.235
Morse, Michael	R-R	6-5	245	3-22-82	.375	.500	.333	3	8	1	3	2	0	1	4	1	0	0	0	3	0	0	1.000	.444
Negrych, Jim	L-R	5-10	180	3-2-85	.600	1.000	.500	3	5	0	3	2	0	0	5	3	0	0	1	0	0	0	1.000	.667
Nicol, Sean	R-R	5-10	175	9-25-86	.256	.197	.283	79	242	24	62	11	2	3	26	18	1	5	2	55	3	1	.355	.308
Pahuta, Tim	L-R	6-4	225	5-3-83	.226	.182	.239	121	421	55	95	24	3	15	49	40	4	0	3	106	2	0	.404	.297
Perez, Eury	R-R	6-0	180	5-30-90	.299	.316	.293	82	351	34	105	11	2	0	30	7	7	7	1	53	26	10	.342	.325
Rahl, Chris	R-R	5-10	185	12-5-83	.291	.395	.254	92	330	55	96	18	2	12	50	19	6	1	2	84	26	4	.467	.339
Rendon, Anthony	R-R	6-0	195	6-6-90	.162	.200	.146	21	68	14	11	3	1	3	11	3	11	0	0	16	0	0	.368	.305
Seabury, Beau	R-R	6-1	195	6-13-85	.300	.500	.269	11	30	4	9	2	0	1	5	2	0	0	0	6	0	0	.467	.344
Skelton, James	L-R	5-11	165	10-28-85	.292	.100	.342	24	48	4	14	2	0	0	5	14	2	1	2	9	0	0	.333	.455
Solano, Jhonatan	R-R	5-9	205	8-12-85	.195	.182	.200	11	41	4	8	1	0	1	7	0	1	1	0	12	0	0	.293	.209
Tucker, Jonny	R-R	5-8	180	7-2-83	.136	.130	.139	22	59	3	8	0	0	0	3	8	2	0	0	13	2	2	.136	.261
Valdez, Jesus	R-R	6-2	170	11-2-84	.294	.377	.269	72	269	31	79	19	3	4	29	11	4	0	4	40	2	1	.431	.326
VanOstrand, Jimmy	R-R	6-4	210	8-7-84	.310	.276	.326	80	271	37	84	12	0	10	30	16	11	0	2	33	0	0	.465	.370
Walters, Zach	B-R	6-2	195	9-5-89	.293	.245	.315	43	164	23	48	11	4	6	19	8	0	0	0	38	1	0	.518	.326
Watts, Kris	L-R	6-1	210	7-15-84	.156	.143	.160	39	109	6	17	6	0	1	7	15	3	0	2	24	0	0	.239	.271

Pitching	B-T	HT	WT	DOB	W	L	ERA	G	GS	CG	SV	IP	H	R	ER	HR	BB	SO	AVG	vLH	vRH	K/9	BB/9
Ballard, Michael	R-L	6-2	180	2-6-84	1	5	4.31	12	12	0	0	65	81	35	31	10	17	56	.300	.245	.324	7.79	2.37
Barthmaier, Jimmy	R-R	6-5	205	1-6-84	0	2	3.77	11	0	0	1	14	12	7	6	1	9	10	.240	.313	.206	6.28	5.65
Bibens-Dirkx, Austin	R-R	6-1	210	4-29-85	1	0	2.25	3	2	0	0	12	9	3	3	1	2	12	.209	.261	.150	9.00	1.50
Broderick, Brian	R-R	6-6	205	9-1-86	2	0	3.99	8	3	0	0	29	37	14	13	3	5	13	.303	.308	.300	3.99	1.53
Davis, Erik	R-R	6-4	200	10-8-86	7	3	2.52	40	0	0	5	64	61	18	18	5	18	69	.253	.264	.244	9.65	2.52
Demny, Paul	R-R	6-2	200	8-3-89	6	8	5.46	28	23	0	0	124	138	80	75	13	61	97	.285	.281	.288	7.06	4.44
Frias, Marcos	R-R	6-2	190	12-19-88	4	4	4.82	47	0	0	0	65	77	41	35	3	31	64	.304	.358	.272	8.82	4.27
Garcia, Christian	R-R	6-5	215	8-24-85	1	0	1.35	18	0	0	7	20	13	6	3	0	6	28	.181	.148	.200	12.60	2.70
Gilliam, Rob	R-R	6-1	195	11-29-87	3	7	6.38	20	13	0	0	85	94	62	60	9	37	75	.280	.298	.265	7.97	3.93
Holder, Trevor	R-R	6-2	185	1-8-87	4	3	3.78	10	9	0	0	52	55	24	22	3	11	23	.274	.231	.301	3.96	1.89
Kimball, Cole	R-R	6-4	250	8-1-85	0	0	0.00	1	0	0	0	1	0	0	0	1	0	1	.500	1.000	.000	0.00	27.00
Lehman, Pat	R-R	6-3	210	10-18-86	0	0	1.17	8	0	0	0	8	4	1	1	1	2	9	.000		.133	10.57	2.35
Mandel, Jeff	B-R	6-3	190	4-30-85	4	4	4.66	11	11	0	0	66	73	40	34	4	20	38	.285	.295	.276	5.21	2.74
Martin, Rafael	R-R	6-3	215	5-16-84	0	0	7.41	15	0	0	0	17	21	15	14	4	12	14	.313	.409	.267	7.41	6.35
Mattheus, Ryan	R-R	6-3	205	11-10-83	0	0	4.50	2	0	0	0	2	1	1	1	0	1	3	.000		.000	13.50	4.50
McCoy, Patrick	L-L	6-4	200	8-3-88	7	3	3.70	50	0	0	2	58	65	29	24	9	18	60	.279	.256	.291	9.26	2.78
Nelo, Hector	R-R	6-1	200	11-5-86	1	6	2.73	47	0	0	16	53	44	21	16	4	29	63	.229	.233	.227	10.77	4.96
Olbrychowski, Adam	R-R	6-3	205	9-7-86	0	1	5.79	1	1	0	0	5	5	3	3	0	2	5	.294	.500	.182	9.64	3.86
Perry, Ryan	R-R	6-4	215	2-13-87	2	4	2.84	13	13	1	0	73	59	28	23	3	22	46	.229	.239	.221	5.67	2.71
Pucetas, Kevin	R-R	6-4	225	11-27-84	7	6	3.69	28	12	0	0	98	94	45	40	9	20	67	.249	.256	.243	6.17	1.84

	B-T	HT	WT	DOB	W	L	ERA	G	GS	CG	SV	IP	H	R	ER	HR	BB	SO	AVG	vLH	vRH	K/9	BB/9
Rodriguez, Henry	R-R	6-1	225	2-25-87	0	0	0.00	3	0	0	0	3	0	0	0	0	1	4	.000	.000	.000	12.00	3.00
Rosenbaum, Danny	R-L	6-1	210	10-10-87	8	10	3.94	26	26	2	0	155	164	79	68	8	39	99	.278	.210	.297	5.74	2.26
Selik, Cameron	R-R	6-2	235	8-25-87	0	0	27.00	1	0	0	0	0	0	1	1	0	1	0	.000	—	.000	0.00	27.00
Storen, Drew	B-R	6-2	190	8-11-87	0	0	54.00	1	0	0	0	1	3	4	4	1	1	0	.750	1.000	.667	0.00	13.50
Tatusko, Ryan	R-R	6-5	200	3-27-85	4	5	3.50	27	8	0	1	82	71	33	32	4	35	78	.237	.257	.225	8.53	3.83
Testa, Joe	L-L	5-10	175	12-18-85	0	0	8.31	5	0	0	0	4	4	4	4	0	5	6	.250	.000	.364	12.46	10.38
VanAllen, Cory	L-L	6-3	180	12-24-84	0	0	3.21	11	0	0	0	14	10	6	5	2	8	16	.196	.176	.206	10.29	5.14
Wang, Chien-Ming	R-R	6-4	225	3-31-80	1	5	6.75	9	9	1	0	45	59	36	34	7	9	33	.321	.397	.281	6.55	1.79
Zinicola, Zech	R-R	6-1	220	3-2-85	1	2	2.30	21	0	0	3	27	24	8	7	2	4	27	.240	.171	.277	8.89	1.32

Fielding

Catcher	PCT	G	PO	A	E	DP	PB
Howell	1.000	3	22	0	0	1	1
Ivany	.978	43	324	27	8	3	6
Leon	.991	39	307	32	3	0	5
Mayo	.875	1	5	2	1	0	0
Seabury	1.000	11	59	10	0	1	0
Skelton	.979	6	46	1	1	1	0
Solano	.982	9	48	7	1	0	0
Watts	.984	37	215	28	4	0	2

First Base	PCT	G	PO	A	E	DP
Bloxom	1.000	43	396	30	0	37
King	1.000	2	14	0	0	1
Lozada	1.000	3	20	3	0	5
Marrero	1.000	3	23	2	0	2
Pahuta	.995	94	818	61	4	93
VanOstrand	1.000	2	15	1	0	1

Second Base	PCT	G	PO	A	E	DP
Kobernus	.982	81	156	220	7	49

	PCT	G	PO	A	E	DP
Lozada	.957	22	46	64	5	19
Mayorson	.962	10	14	36	2	8
Nicol	.985	29	53	78	2	24
Tucker	.946	6	12	23	2	4

Third Base	PCT	G	PO	A	E	DP
Bloxom	.333	1	0	1	2	0
King	.947	31	18	54	4	6
Lozada	.934	30	19	52	5	6
Mayorson	.942	20	7	42	3	2
Negrych	1.000	1	0	1	0	0
Nicol	.964	42	18	89	4	10
Pahuta	.952	11	4	16	1	1
Rendon	.964	18	9	44	2	6
VanOstrand	—	1	0	0	0	0

Shortstop	PCT	G	PO	A	E	DP
Bynum	.962	27	41	87	5	25
Johnson	.981	11	16	37	1	4
Lozada	.971	33	38	96	4	22

	PCT	G	PO	A	E	DP
McConnell	.969	39	51	105	5	28
Nicol	1.000	1	0	4	0	0
Walters	.958	43	56	127	8	29

Outfield	PCT	G	PO	A	E	DP
Ankiel	1.000	2	1	0	0	0
Bloxom	1.000	13	15	1	0	0
Goodwin	.976	42	78	3	2	1
Higley	1.000	5	5	1	0	0
Hood	.980	88	147	2	3	0
Ivany	1.000	2	2	0	0	0
Lozada	1.000	8	8	1	0	0
Morse	1.000	1	2	0	0	0
Nicol	1.000	4	3	0	0	0
Perez	.991	82	204	9	2	1
Rahl	.970	77	126	3	4	0
Skelton	1.000	6	9	2	0	0
Tucker	.957	11	22	0	1	0
Valdez	.973	54	101	9	3	2
VanOstrand	.984	48	59	3	1	0

POTOMAC NATIONALS   HIGH CLASS A

CAROLINA LEAGUE

Batting	B-T	HT	WT	DOB	AVG	vLH	vRH	G	AB	R	H	2B	3B	HR	RBI	BB	HBP	SH	SF	SO	SB	CS	SLG	OBP
Bloxom, Justin	R-B	6-1	205	4-29-88	.259	.205	.272	65	224	35	58	13	0	12	34	23	2	0	2	64	0	0	.478	.331
Curran, Chris	L-R	5-9	170	12-21-87	.000	—	.000	2	3	0	0	0	0	0	0	0	1	0	0	2	0	0	.000	.250
DeRosa, Mark	R-R	6-1	215	2-26-75	.091	—	.091	4	11	1	1	0	0	0	2	4	0	0	0	3	0	0	.091	.333
Fernandez, Erick	R-R	5-11	190	11-30-88	.237	.300	.221	36	97	11	23	1	0	0	7	10	1	2	1	20	0	0	.247	.312
Freitas, David	R-R	6-3	225	3-18-89	.271	.277	.270	78	273	37	74	22	0	5	46	39	7	0	2	52	0	0	.407	.374
Greer, Brent	R-R	6-0	185	10-16-87	.200	.250	.182	4	15	1	3	0	0	0	1	1	0	0	0	5	0	0	.200	.250
Hague, Rick	R-R	6-2	190	9-18-88	.258	.289	.251	105	395	58	102	20	3	6	48	28	4	3	3	93	20	5	.370	.312
Higley, J.R.	R-R	6-3	190	6-21-88	.100	.000	.167	4	10	2	1	0	0	0	1	0	2	0	0	5	0	0	.100	.250
Howell, Jeff	R-R	6-0	205	4-1-83	.225	.182	.233	20	71	5	16	1	0	1	4	2	3	0	0	15	1	1	.282	.276
Kelso, David	R-R	5-10	170	3-28-89	.231	.257	.225	106	381	51	88	11	4	0	31	40	3	11	2	49	27	6	.281	.308
Keyes, Kevin	R-R	6-3	225	3-15-89	.223	.227	.222	114	390	47	87	27	1	21	78	33	6	0	6	108	4	2	.459	.290
King, Stephen	R-R	6-2	195	10-2-87	.283	.316	.276	64	219	26	62	22	1	1	23	10	3	1	2	57	4	3	.406	.321
Maldonado, Carlos	R-R	6-2	290	1-3-79	.111	—	.111	3	9	0	1	0	0	0	2	0	0	0	0	4	0	0	.111	.273
Marrero, Chris	R-R	6-3	220	7-2-88	.462	.500	.455	4	13	1	6	1	0	1	4	0	0	0	0	2	0	0	.769	.462
Martinson, Jason	R-R	6-1	190	10-15-88	.215	.250	.208	66	237	36	51	2	4	12	43	21	2	0	5	79	7	2	.409	.279
Moore, Wade	L-R	6-1	215	12-27-87	.207	.182	.211	26	82	7	17	3	1	2	9	8	2	0	1	30	2	1	.341	.290
Morse, Michael	R-R	6-5	245	3-22-82	.333	—	.333	3	9	0	3	1	0	0	1	1	0	0	0	2	0	0	.444	.400
Nady, Xavier	R-R	6-2	215	11-14-78	.158	.286	.129	12	38	2	6	1	0	0	1	3	0	0	0	9	0	0	.184	.220
Nicol, Sean	R-R	5-10	175	9-25-86	.286	.417	.233	13	42	8	12	2	0	1	3	4	0	0	0	15	0	0	.405	.348
Oduber, Randolph	R-L	6-3	190	3-18-89	.252	.423	.212	80	274	35	69	13	4	5	27	14	1	7	3	77	14	3	.383	.288
Palace, Sam	R-R	6-1	210	6-3-86	.000	—	.000	3	3	0	0	0	0	0	0	0	0	0	0	2	0	0	.000	.000
Ramirez, J.P.	L-L	5-10	185	9-29-89	.275	.129	.296	76	247	23	68	6	1	0	16	7	3	2	1	41	3	1	.308	.302
Rendon, Anthony	R-R	6-0	195	6-6-90	.333	.250	.348	9	27	5	9	2	3	0	5	0	0	0	0	4	0	0	.630	.438
Sanchez, Adrian	R-R	6-4	215	8-16-90	.269	.169	.295	101	375	46	101	20	3	3	32	11	5	8	1	59	25	16	.363	.298
Seabury, Beau	R-R	6-1	195	6-13-85	.176	.000	.188	7	17	0	3	0	0	0	1	3	0	0	0	1	0	0	.176	.333
Skelton, James	L-R	5-11	165	10-28-85	.333	.000	.500	4	9	2	3	0	0	0	3	4	0	0	0	3	0	0	.333	.538
Skole, Matt	L-R	6-4	230	7-30-89	.314	.300	.317	18	70	11	22	10	1	0	12	5	0	0	1	17	1	0	.486	.355
Soriano, Francisco	B-R	5-11	169	6-16-87	.270	.161	.300	87	256	44	69	11	6	0	28	40	2	1	3	53	12	8	.359	.369
Souza, Steven	R-R	6-3	220	4-24-89	.319	.429	.299	27	91	16	29	2	1	6	13	13	3	0	0	25	7	1	.560	.421
Taylor, Michael	R-R	6-2	190	3-26-91	.242	.181	.256	109	384	51	93	33	2	3	37	40	3	3	1	113	19	9	.362	.318
Tracy, Chad	L-R	6-1	220	5-22-80	.222	.000	.267	6	18	3	4	0	0	0	2	1	0	0	3	4	0	0	.222	.250
Walters, Zach	B-R	6-2	195	9-5-89	.269	.189	.288	54	193	24	52	8	1	5	24	10	1	0	3	43	6	3	.399	.304
Werth, Jayson	R-R	6-5	225	5-20-79	.500	—	.500	2	6	2	3	1	0	0	1	2	0	0	0	1	0	0	.667	.625

Pitching	B-T	HT	WT	DOB	W	L	ERA	G	GS	CG	SV	IP	H	R	ER	HR	BB	SO	AVG	vLH	vRH	K/9	BB/9
Applebee, Paul	L-L	6-3	195	5-17-88	2	1	5.00	13	1	0	0	36	38	23	20	8	6	19	.270	.282	.265	4.75	1.50
Barrett, Aaron	R-R	6-4	215	1-2-88	0	0	1.06	11	0	0	1	17	9	2	2	0	3	21	.153	.000	.191	11.12	1.59
Barthmaier, Jimmy	R-R	6-5	205	1-6-84	0	1	1.83	14	0	0	3	20	10	4	4	1	5	12	.154	.150	.156	5.49	2.29
Carr, Adam	R-R	6-2	220	4-1-84	0	1	4.15	19	0	0	1	30	24	16	14	3	13	14	.226	.333	.190	4.15	3.86
Demmin, Ryan	L-L	6-1	210	4-5-88	1	2	4.57	29	2	0	1	63	77	40	32	11	25	65	.297	.196	.319	9.29	3.57

Name	B-T	HT	WT	DOB	W	L	ERA	G	GS	CG	SV	IP	H	R	ER	HR	BB	SO	AVG	vLH	vRH	K/9	BB/9
Eusebio, Wilson	R-R	6-0	170	8-20-88	1	0	9.42	11	0	0	0	14	18	16	15	2	10	10	.305	.333	.293	6.28	6.28
Gilliam, Rob	R-R	6-1	195	11-29-87	1	2	4.25	7	6	0	0	36	39	24	17	5	8	30	.273	.320	.247	7.50	2.00
Grace, Matt	L-L	6-3	190	12-14-88	9	12	4.84	26	24	2	0	141	178	95	76	10	48	83	.310	.304	.311	5.29	3.06
Hansen, Bobby	L-L	6-6	235	12-17-89	2	2	5.85	9	6	0	0	32	39	21	21	4	14	14	.312	.258	.330	3.90	3.90
Hill, Taylor	R-R	6-3	233	3-12-89	1	1	4.80	3	3	1	0	15	17	11	8	2	3	11	.283	.100	.320	6.60	1.80
Holder, Trevor	R-R	6-2	185	1-8-87	5	3	4.01	18	10	0	0	76	83	39	34	4	20	54	.272	.264	.276	6.37	2.36
Holland, Neil	R-R	6-0	190	8-14-88	7	1	1.64	39	0	0	4	60	44	15	11	3	14	44	.211	.228	.204	6.56	2.09
Karns, Nate	R-R	6-5	230	11-25-87	8	4	2.26	13	13	1	0	72	47	23	18	1	26	87	.190	.211	.180	10.93	3.27
Kimball, Cole	R-R	6-4	250	8-1-85	0	1	10.80	3	2	0	0	3	6	7	4	3	0	2	.333	.000	.353	5.40	0.00
Lidge, Brad	R-R	6-5	210	12-23-76	0	1	6.75	2	1	0	0	1	2	1	1	0	1	3	.333	.667	.000	20.25	6.75
Mattheus, Ryan	R-R	6-3	205	11-10-83	0	1	18.00	1	0	0	0	1	2	2	2	2	0	0	.400	.000	.667	0.00	0.00
McCatty, Shane	R-R	6-3	205	5-18-87	1	1	8.83	13	0	0	0	17	23	19	17	3	15	11	.338	.421	.306	5.71	7.79
Meyer, Alex	R-R	6-9	220	1-3-90	3	2	2.31	7	7	0	0	39	29	11	10	2	11	32	.213	.211	.214	7.38	2.54
Olbrychowski, Adam	R-R	6-3	205	9-7-86	5	10	6.24	26	16	1	0	101	120	76	70	15	50	74	.304	.313	.299	6.59	4.46
Ray, Robbie	L-L	6-2	170	10-1-91	4	12	6.56	22	21	0	0	106	122	85	77	14	49	86	.292	.260	.299	7.32	4.17
Selik, Cameron	R-R	6-2	235	8-25-87	2	1	3.68	18	0	0	8	22	20	11	9	1	3	34	.230	.233	.228	13.91	1.23
Smoker, Josh	L-L	6-2	195	11-26-88	0	0	10.80	2	0	0	0	2	2	2	2	0	1	2	.286	.000	.500	10.80	5.40
Storen, Drew	B-R	6-2	190	8-11-87	1	0	3.00	5	1	0	0	6	4	3	2	1	1	8	.190	.333	.133	12.00	1.50
Swynenberg, Matt	R-R	6-5	215	2-16-89	7	5	4.92	27	16	2	0	115	147	70	63	10	38	72	.313	.254	.346	5.62	2.97
Testa, Joe	L-L	5-10	175	12-18-85	1	1	5.17	29	0	0	0	38	32	25	22	3	31	31	.229	.143	.250	7.28	7.28
Wang, Chien-Ming	R-R	6-4	225	3-31-80	0	1	4.50	2	2	0	0	8	7	4	4	0	2	4	.226	.375	.174	4.50	2.25
Winters, Kyle	R-R	6-4	190	4-22-87	1	5	7.02	8	8	0	0	42	56	35	33	7	12	40	.322	.362	.295	8.50	2.55
Wort, Rob	R-R	6-2	170	2-7-89	2	4	2.38	40	0	0	13	57	42	16	15	2	19	95	.204	.257	.174	15.09	3.02

Fielding

Catcher	PCT	G	PO	A	E	DP	PB
Fernandez	.988	36	219	23	3	3	4
Freitas	.996	76	519	42	2	2	6
Howell	.994	20	153	15	1	2	0
Maldonado	1.000	3	16	0	0	0	2
Seabury	1.000	6	30	3	0	0	0
Skelton	1.000	3	15	5	0	0	0
Kelso	1.000	12	27	29	0	6	
Sanchez	.972	76	155	186	10	58	
Soriano	.989	19	35	58	1	20	
Kelso	1.000	6	13	20	0	5	
Martinson	.940	43	54	134	12	21	
Soriano	.909	10	10	30	4	8	
Walters	.902	33	47	100	16	26	

First Base	PCT	G	PO	A	E	DP
Bloxom	.983	59	487	32	9	56
DeRosa	1.000	1	8	0	0	1
Freitas	1.000	1	4	0	0	0
King	.987	61	503	29	7	51
Marrero	1.000	2	16	0	0	3
Nady	1.000	2	20	2	0	3
Nicol	1.000	2	18	0	0	3
Soriano	.972	17	98	8	3	12
Tracy	1.000	2	16	0	0	1

Second Base	PCT	G	PO	A	E	DP
Hague	.983	35	82	93	3	25

Third Base	PCT	G	PO	A	E	DP
DeRosa	1.000	2	1	5	0	1
Greer	.857	2	1	5	1	0
Kelso	.968	82	60	181	8	21
King	.889	4	2	6	1	0
Martinson	.833	11	5	20	5	2
Nicol	1.000	10	4	20	0	0
Rendon	.842	6	4	12	3	3
Sanchez	1.000	6	2	12	0	1
Skole	.895	12	7	27	4	3
Soriano	.800	3	0	4	1	0
Tracy	1.000	1	2	1	0	1
Walters	.913	9	7	14	2	2

Shortstop	PCT	G	PO	A	E	DP
Greer	.833	1	1	4	1	2
Hague	.936	49	79	142	15	35

Outfield	PCT	G	PO	A	E	DP
Curran	1.000	1	2	0	0	0
DeRosa	1.000	1	2	0	0	0
Higley	1.000	4	5	0	0	0
Keyes	.981	99	149	8	3	1
Moore	.929	17	25	1	2	0
Morse	—	1	0	0	0	0
Nady	1.000	5	4	0	0	0
Oduber	.986	76	141	3	2	1
Ramirez	.918	68	76	2	7	0
Skelton	—	1	0	0	0	0
Soriano	.935	25	28	1	2	0
Souza	.962	25	45	5	2	0
Taylor	.973	108	267	21	8	7
Walters	1.000	1	2	0	0	0
Werth	1.000	2	5	0	0	0

HAGERSTOWN SUNS

LOW CLASS A

SOUTH ATLANTIC LEAGUE

Batting	B-T	HT	WT	DOB	AVG	vLH	vRH	G	AB	R	H	2B	3B	HR	RBI	BB	HBP	SH	SF	SO	SB	CS	SLG	OBP
Alvarez, Carlos	B-R	5-11	175	11-25-85	.171	.091	.200	20	41	3	7	1	1	0	2	8	1	1	0	11	0	1	.244	.320
Ankiel, Rick	L-L	6-1	210	7-19-79	.500	1.000	.429	3	8	2	4	1	0	1	4	3	0	0	0	2	0	0	1.000	.636
Burns, Billy	B-L	5-9	180	8-30-89	.322	.324	.320	113	398	83	128	14	5	0	41	65	13	8	1	68	38	9	.382	.432
Curran, Chris	L-R	5-9	170	12-21-87	.333	.000	.364	5	12	3	4	0	1	0	1	2	0	1	0	1	0	0	.500	.429
Dykstra, Cutter	R-R	5-11	180	6-29-89	.291	.277	.298	110	436	62	127	28	1	7	64	43	10	0	3	83	32	3	.408	.366
Goodwin, Brian	L-L	6-1	195	11-2-90	.324	.282	.351	58	216	47	70	18	1	9	38	43	3	1	3	39	15	4	.542	.438
Higley, J.R.	R-R	6-3	190	6-21-88	.231	.238	.227	38	130	19	30	6	0	2	12	16	0	1	1	38	1	2	.323	.313
Jimenez, Hendry	B-R	5-10	160	12-30-89	.205	.244	.173	65	190	22	39	9	2	3	19	12	2	2	1	38	2	1	.321	.259
Leonida, Cole	R-R	6-2	220	12-25-88	.191	.130	.218	56	178	17	34	7	2	4	24	20	3	2	1	61	1	1	.320	.282
Marrero, Chris	R-R	6-3	220	7-2-88	.250	.000	.333	2	4	1	1	0	0	0	1	1	0	0	0	2	0	0	.500	.500
Martinson, Jason	R-R	6-1	190	10-15-88	.272	.310	.248	69	265	68	72	11	3	10	63	47	6	1	2	88	23	3	.449	.391
Mayo, Jeremy	R-R	5-10	194	6-17-88	.182	.222	.171	17	44	5	8	4	0	0	2	10	0	1	0	20	3	0	.273	.333
Mesa, Narciso	R-R	5-11	175	11-16-91	.000	.000	.000	6	10	1	0	0	0	0	0	1	0	0	0	5	0	0	.000	.091
Miller, Justin	R-R	6-0	180	11-28-88	.245	.236	.250	116	420	67	103	25	4	10	67	36	10	0	8	101	13	4	.395	.314
Montilla, Angelberth	R-R	6-1	180	4-11-89	.154	.161	.150	28	91	7	14	6	0	0	3	4	1	0	1	21	2	2	.220	.196
Morse, Michael	R-R	6-5	245	3-22-82	.500	.500	.500	1	4	1	2	0	0	0	0	0	0	0	0	0	0	0	.500	.500
Newsome, Brett	L-L	6-2	210	8-24-86	.267	.261	.270	109	352	47	94	27	1	9	43	34	3	1	2	89	2	0	.426	.335
Nieto, Adrian	L-R	6-1	185	11-12-89	.257	.273	.247	70	257	32	66	17	0	6	39	35	2	1	4	64	4	2	.393	.346
Norfork, Khayyan	R-R	5-10	190	1-19-89	.286	.278	.288	19	70	10	20	7	1	0	7	8	1	0	4		4	1	.429	.367
Ortega, Bryce	R-R	5-11	170	9-22-88	.258	.304	.232	78	260	54	67	8	5	1	27	39	4	2	1	42	15	4	.338	.362
Palace, Sam	R-R	6-1	210	6-3-86	.194	.071	.294	8	31	1	6	0	0	0	3	1	0	0	0	9	0	0	.194	.219
Ramirez, J.	L-L	5-10	185	9-29-88	.285	.317	.270	35	130	15	37	7	0	2	16	6	5	0	2	22	4	2	.385	.336
Ramsey, Caleb	L-R	6-2	215	10-7-88	.294	.307	.288	127	462	78	136	17	10	7	66	37	5	4	2	46	22	10	.420	.352
Skole, Matt	L-R	6-4	230	7-30-89	.286	.288	.284	101	343	73	98	18	0	27	92	94	4	1	6	116	10	0	.574	.438
Souza, Steven	R-R	6-3	220	4-24-89	.290	.222	.320	70	262	48	76	20	2	17	72	22	3	1	5	49	7	7	.576	.346

Pitching	B-T	HT	WT	DOB	W	L	ERA	G	GS	CG	SV	IP	H	R	ER	HR	BB	SO	AVG	vLH	vRH	K/9	BB/9
Anderson, Dixon	R-R	6-5	225	7-2-89	1	1	2.79	3	3	0	0	10	7	6	3	0	6	11	.194	.077	.261	10.24	5.59
Barrett, Aaron	R-R	6-4	215	1-2-88	3	2	2.60	31	0	0	16	35	25	12	10	2	11	52	.197	.205	.193	13.50	2.86
Bates, Colin	R-R	6-1	175	3-10-88	8	3	2.79	29	0	0	6	52	48	23	16	3	18	36	.244	.275	.227	6.27	3.14
Dupra, Brian	R-R	6-3	200	12-15-88	3	4	7.17	11	8	0	0	38	47	34	30	7	15	20	.303	.288	.313	4.78	3.58
Encarnacion, Pedro	R-R	6-4	175	6-26-91	0	1	6.06	6	2	0	0	16	14	12	11	3	9	8	.226	.227	.225	4.41	4.96
Estevez, Wirkin	R-R	6-1	170	3-15-92	5	2	5.76	12	12	0	0	59	57	40	38	6	25	49	.254	.289	.231	7.43	3.79
Eusebio, Wilson	R-R	6-0	170	8-20-88	1	0	6.75	18	0	0	2	28	40	24	21	3	10	15	.325	.313	.333	4.82	3.21
Hansen, Bobby	L-L	6-6	235	12-17-89	3	4	4.55	11	11	0	0	55	74	37	28	3	32	28	.332	.383	.313	4.55	5.20
Hawkins, Ben	L-L	6-2	175	11-4-89	3	3	3.55	30	0	0	1	58	50	27	23	3	30	57	.224	.230	.221	8.79	4.63
Henke, Travis	R-R	6-6	241	7-9-88	0	1	12.00	2	0	0	0	3	7	4	4	0	1	1	.438	.556	.286	3.00	3.00
Hill, Taylor	R-R	6-3	233	3-12-89	10	6	4.92	24	20	0	0	124	144	80	68	12	31	60	.283	.319	.260	4.34	2.24
Hollins, L.J.	R-R	6-3	185	7-31-91	2	0	4.50	11	0	0	1	18	18	13	9	0	7	8	.257	.320	.222	4.00	3.50
Holt, Greg	R-R	6-2	205	6-19-89	5	2	4.12	41	0	0	3	79	66	45	36	11	29	49	.233	.245	.227	5.61	3.32
Jordan, Taylor	R-R	6-3	190	1-17-89	3	4	4.05	9	9	0	0	40	52	22	18	2	9	28	.319	.217	.379	6.30	2.03
Karns, Nate	R-R	6-5	230	11-25-87	3	0	2.03	11	5	1	2	44	23	11	10	1	21	61	.148	.196	.121	12.38	4.26
Kimball, Cole	R-R	6-4	250	8-1-85	0	0	0.00	1	1	0	0	1	0	0	0	0	2	.250	.500	.000	18.00	0.00
Kreis, Alex	R-R	6-1	210	5-30-89	0	0	5.88	19	0	0	3	26	40	21	17	3	7	13	.351	.350	.351	4.50	2.42
Lucas, Bobby	L-L	6-4	220	8-12-87	2	0	7.67	24	0	0	2	29	24	27	25	3	31	36	.220	.225	.217	11.05	9.51
McKenzie, Chris	R-R	6-3	185	12-6-89	2	3	8.64	26	8	0	0	50	66	53	48	5	42	35	.322	.360	.300	6.30	7.56
Meyer, Alex	R-R	6-9	220	1-3-90	7	4	3.10	18	18	1	0	90	68	33	31	4	34	107	.210	.189	.227	10.70	3.40
Meza, Christian	L-L	6-0	185	8-3-90	8	1	2.97	36	3	0	2	88	65	35	29	4	37	94	.208	.269	.183	9.61	3.78
Mirowski, Richie	R-R	6-2	190	4-30-89	4	0	2.00	16	0	0	3	27	19	6	6	1	15	28	.190	.108	.238	9.33	5.00
Purke, Matt	L-L	6-4	205	7-17-90	0	2	5.87	3	3	0	0	15	15	11	10	1	12	14	.263	.313	.244	8.22	7.04
Rauh, Brian	R-R	6-2	200	7-23-91	3	3	4.76	9	8	0	0	40	36	23	21	3	18	29	.247	.316	.202	6.58	4.08
Schwartz, Blake	R-R	6-3	200	10-9-89	1	1	3.05	7	7	0	0	38	39	13	13	3	11	41	.271	.209	.297	9.63	2.58
Simko, Todd	L-L	6-5	220	12-5-88	0	1	2.37	11	0	0	1	19	14	10	5	0	15	15	.200	.242	.152	7.11	7.11
Smith, Jason	R-R	6-3	180	8-7-90	0	1	27.00	1	1	0	0	2	4	5	5	1	2	1	.500	.667	.400	5.40	10.80
Smoker, Josh	L-L	6-2	195	11-26-88	0	1	15.00	2	0	0	1	3	5	5	5	1	4	1	.300	.333	.286	3.00	12.00
Turnbull, Kylin	R-L	6-5	205	9-12-89	4	5	5.16	18	17	0	0	89	104	53	51	6	30	51	.292	.247	.307	5.16	3.03
Wang, Chien-Ming	R-R	6-4	225	3-31-80	1	0	1.50	1	1	0	0	6	3	2	1	1	1	7	.136	.000	.188	10.50	1.50

Fielding

Catcher	PCT	G	PO	A	E	DP	PB
Leonida	.977	55	376	46	10	1	6
Mayo	.949	15	64	10	4	0	7
Nieto	.990	65	439	59	5	4	14
Palace	.984	8	58	4	1	1	0

First Base	PCT	G	PO	A	E	DP
Marrero	.923	2	12	0	1	1
Miller	.993	80	645	51	5	49
Newsome	.986	76	606	33	9	50

Second Base	PCT	G	PO	A	E	DP
Alvarez	.893	9	14	11	3	4
Dykstra	.958	81	120	202	14	38
Jimenez	.959	48	79	110	8	28
Miller	1.000	4	2	5	0	1
Norfork	1.000	3	7	10	0	1

Ortega	.917	11	16	28	4	4

Third Base	PCT	G	PO	A	E	DP
Alvarez	1.000	7	0	10	0	0
Dykstra	1.000	6	3	11	0	3
Jimenez	—	2	0	0	0	0
Miller	.938	21	18	42	4	5
Norfork	.956	16	9	34	2	0
Ortega	1.000	1	0	1	0	0
Skole	.923	95	62	165	19	17

Shortstop	PCT	G	PO	A	E	DP
Alvarez	.800	2	1	3	1	0
Dykstra	.953	18	29	53	4	10
Martinson	.954	62	82	189	13	30
Ortega	.954	61	87	180	13	36

Outfield	PCT	G	PO	A	E	DP
Ankiel	1.000	2	3	0	0	0
Burns	.986	106	201	10	3	4
Curran	1.000	5	8	0	0	0
Dykstra	1.000	2	2	0	0	0
Goodwin	.985	55	129	3	2	0
Higley	1.000	37	70	1	0	0
Mesa	1.000	4	6	0	0	0
Miller	1.000	20	27	2	0	0
Montilla	1.000	23	28	4	0	0
Morse	.500	1	1	0	1	0
Ortega	—	1	0	0	0	0
Ramirez	.882	28	29	1	4	0
Ramsey	.979	109	180	6	4	1
Souza	.968	44	90	1	3	0

AUBURN DOUBLEDAYS
NEW YORK-PENN LEAGUE

SHORT-SEASON

Batting	B-T	HT	WT	DOB	AVG	vLH	vRH	G	AB	R	H	2B	3B	HR	RBI	BB	HBP	SH	SF	SO	SB	CS	SLG	OBP
Alvarez, Carlos	B-R	5-11	175	11-25-85	.229	.333	.194	25	83	12	19	5	0	1	17	5	2	0	6	13	2	0	.325	.271
Brooks, James	R-R	6-0	185	10-12-88	.031	.071	.000	10	32	2	1	1	0	0	1	0	1	2	1	14	0	0	.063	.059
Higley, J.R.	R-R	6-3	190	6-21-88	.320	.000	.333	7	25	7	8	1	1	2	9	2	3	0	0	5	0	0	.680	.433
Hood, Destin	R-R	6-1	225	4-3-90	.176	.000	.231	5	17	3	3	1	0	0	2	1	0	0	0	7	0	0	.235	.300
Johnson, Josh R.	B-R	5-11	170	1-11-86	.333	.333	.333	2	9	3	3	1	0	0	2	0	0	0	0	1	1	0	.444	.333
Kieboom, Spencer	R-R	6-0	199	3-16-91	.258	.262	.256	41	128	13	33	6	0	0	20	19	2	6	0	24	0	0	.305	.362
Leon, Sandy	B-R	5-11	220	3-13-89	.333	.000	.385	5	15	3	5	2	0	0	3	3	0	0	0	2	0	0	.467	.444
Lopez, Carlos	R-R	6-2	220	1-18-90	.253	.364	.200	45	170	24	43	10	1	3	27	20	1	2	2	50	2	0	.376	.332
Manuel, Craig	L-R	6-1	205	5-22-90	.266	.208	.277	47	154	23	41	2	1	0	10	19	6	1	1	13	3	1	.292	.367
Marrero, Chris	R-R	6-3	220	7-2-88	.357	.250	.400	5	14	4	5	1	0	1	3	2	0	0	0	6	0	0	.643	.438
Martinez, Estarlin	R-R	6-1	185	3-8-92	.319	.360	.302	66	257	43	82	16	2	5	44	26	3	0	2	43	13	4	.455	.385
McQuillan, Mike	L-R	5-11	175	10-2-89	.268	.500	.237	41	149	33	40	8	5	2	23	21	2	3	2	27	4	1	.430	.362
Mesa, Narciso	R-R	5-11	175	11-16-91	.343	.286	.368	32	105	24	36	6	0	0	13	7	0	1	2	3	1	22	11	2	.400	.391
Miller, Brandon	R-R	6-2	215	10-8-89	.292	.314	.282	29	113	20	33	11	3	4	21	10	2	0	2	36	0	0	.549	.354
Montilla, Angelberth	R-R	6-1	180	4-11-89	.297	.320	.288	24	91	16	27	2	0	2	8	9	1	0	1	18	4	0	.385	.363
Norfork, Khayyan	R-R	5-10	190	11-19-89	.255	.242	.260	33	106	17	27	6	0	1	17	11	3	0	1	21	4	0	.340	.339
Perez, Stephen	B-R	5-11	175	12-16-90	.231	.200	.241	21	78	11	18	5	2	1	12	3	0	0	0	30	3	1	.385	.259
Pleffner, Shawn	L-R	6-5	225	8-17-89	.329	.472	.282	55	216	34	71	17	1	3	34	22	2	0	1	38	6	2	.458	.394
Poole, Jordan	R-R	6-3	210	9-11-91	.196	.037	.250	31	107	17	21	6	1	1	9	9	0	2	1	47	0	1	.299	.256
Ramirez, Andruth	R-R	5-11	180	3-10-89	.152	.286	.115	14	33	3	5	2	0	0	1	5	0	1	0	6	0	0	.212	.263
Ramos, Wander	R-R	6-3	192	4-26-90	.275	.309	.262	67	236	38	65	16	2	7	45	36	5	3	4	74	5	4	.449	.377

	B-T	HT	WT	DOB	AVG	vLH	vRH	G	AB	R	H	2B	3B	HR	RBI	BB	HBP	SH	SF	SO	SB	CS	SLG	OBP
Renda, Tony	R-R	5-10	170	1-24-91	.264	.221	.282	71	295	47	78	9	0	0	32	31	5	0	3	33	15	3	.295	.341
Rendon, Anthony	R-R	6-0	195	6-6-90	.259	.222	.278	8	27	7	7	2	0	1	3	4	1	0	0	6	0	0	.444	.375
Schill, Wes	R-R	5-9	170	11-22-89	.246	.217	.259	60	207	28	51	7	0	1	25	18	0	3	5	30	9	3	.295	.300

Pitching	B-T	HT	WT	DOB	W	L	ERA	G	GS	CG	SV	IP	H	R	ER	HR	BB	SO	AVG	vLH	vRH	K/9	BB/9
Baez, Gregori	L-L	6-3	185	5-5-92	1	1	9.64	3	3	0	0	9	18	11	10	1	3	7	.409	.100	.500	6.75	2.89
Benincasa, Robert	R-R	6-2	180	9-5-90	2	0	3.09	16	0	0	3	23	27	10	8	0	3	32	.278	.270	.283	12.34	1.16
Boyden, Mike	R-R	6-0	180	6-18-90	3	0	1.44	13	0	0	0	25	18	4	4	0	17	22	.205	.161	.228	7.92	6.12
Davis, Cody	R-R	5-9	170	7-21-90	4	1	3.64	21	0	0	3	42	33	18	17	4	15	50	.219	.183	.242	10.71	3.21
Encarnacion, Pedro	R-R	6-4	175	6-26-91	5	1	4.20	13	12	0	0	64	68	39	30	4	23	51	.260	.282	.245	7.13	3.22
Fischer, David	R-R	6-5	175	4-10-90	3	3	4.96	12	8	0	0	49	56	34	27	5	14	31	.280	.279	.281	5.69	2.57
Harper, Bryan	L-L	6-5	205	12-29-89	0	1	10.59	15	0	0	0	17	34	21	20	1	11	21	.420	.348	.448	11.12	5.82
Henke, Travis	R-R	6-6	241	7-9-88	7	2	2.78	23	0	0	0	45	40	15	14	3	13	42	.230	.197	.252	8.34	2.58
Hudgins, Will	R-R	6-4	200	2-12-90	0	0	2.25	3	1	0	0	8	6	3	2	0	3	6	.207	.182	.222	6.75	3.38
Jordan, Taylor	R-R	6-3	190	1-17-89	0	3	8.16	6	6	0	0	14	19	15	13	0	2	17	.302	.240	.342	10.67	1.26
Lee, Nick	L-L	5-11	185	1-13-91	3	1	3.77	13	11	0	0	62	63	29	26	2	21	62	.267	.250	.271	9.00	3.05
McGeary, Jack	L-L	6-3	195	3-19-89	0	1	7.04	6	0	0	0	8	6	7	6	0	9	5	.207	.333	.174	5.87	10.57
Medina, Silvio	R-R	6-1	190	6-6-89	1	4	4.98	16	4	0	0	47	41	35	26	6	20	47	.218	.243	.203	9.00	3.83
Mendez, Gilberto	R-R	6-0	165	11-17-92	0	1	16.20	4	0	0	0	3	6	6	6	0	3	4	.400	.286	.500	10.80	8.10
Mirowski, Richie	R-R	6-2	190	4-30-89	1	0	1.29	7	0	0	0	7	7	1	1	0	2	8	.259	.188	.364	10.29	2.57
Monar, Blake	L-L	6-2	198	6-16-89	2	3	3.29	12	12	0	0	55	50	21	20	1	32	54	.237	.298	.220	8.89	5.27
Mooneyham, Brett	L-L	6-5	235	1-24-90	2	2	2.55	10	9	0	0	42	36	18	12	2	16	29	.225	.178	.243	6.17	3.40
Pena, Ronald	R-R	6-4	195	9-19-91	1	0	2.84	2	0	0	0	6	3	3	2	0	0	4	.136	.077	.222	5.68	0.00
Peters, John	R-R	6-3	225	6-15-89	0	0	4.00	6	0	0	0	9	13	5	4	1	3	7	.361	.357	.364	7.00	3.00
Pineyro, Ivan	R-R	6-1	198	9-29-91	3	2	5.50	8	8	0	0	34	49	21	21	2	8	27	.345	.397	.310	7.08	2.10
Rauh, Brian	R-R	6-2	200	7-23-91	0	0	2.37	5	1	0	0	19	13	5	5	0	8	14	.194	.150	.213	6.63	3.79
Self, Derek	R-R	6-3	205	1-14-90	1	3	3.27	26	0	0	14	33	32	13	12	0	8	25	.260	.294	.236	6.82	2.18
Smith, Jason	R-R	6-3	180	8-7-90	4	1	7.94	11	1	0	0	23	32	22	20	4	10	12	.333	.255	.422	4.76	3.97
Wall, Andrew	L-L	6-3	210	4-10-89	1	0	5.59	9	0	0	0	10	13	7	6	2	2	11	.333	.500	.276	10.24	1.86
Waterman, Elliott	L-L	6-5	230	11-24-90	2	1	4.97	19	0	0	0	25	31	15	14	3	22	24	.307	.250	.329	8.53	7.82

Fielding

Catcher	PCT	G	PO	A	E	DP	PB
Kieboom	1.000	39	300	29	0	0	9
Leon	1.000	3	15	2	0	0	0
Manuel	.991	29	201	23	2	0	6
Ramirez	.959	14	84	10	4	0	6

First Base	PCT	G	PO	A	E	DP
Lopez	.993	14	127	9	1	15
Marrero	1.000	3	16	0	0	0
Martinez	.983	14	107	12	2	8
Pfeffer	.988	51	439	37	6	27

Second Base	PCT	G	PO	A	E	DP
McQuillan	.949	6	19	18	2	4
Norfork	.750	1	2	1	1	0

	PCT	G	PO	A	E	DP
Renda	.966	66	132	213	12	33
Schill	1.000	3	5	7	0	2

Third Base	PCT	G	PO	A	E	DP
Alvarez	.871	11	5	22	4	3
Lopez	.857	27	27	51	13	1
McQuillan	.900	3	3	6	1	0
Norfork	.911	30	16	56	7	6
Rendon	.909	5	1	9	1	1
Schill	.889	7	2	14	2	1

Shortstop	PCT	G	PO	A	E	DP
Alvarez	.947	5	3	15	1	2
Brooks	.956	10	14	29	2	6
Johnson	1.000	2	4	6	0	0

		G	PO	A	E	DP
McQuillan	.920	13	21	25	4	5
Perez	.936	19	27	61	6	9
Schill	.932	33	32	77	8	15

Outfield	PCT	G	PO	A	E	DP
Higley	1.000	5	8	0	0	0
Hood	1.000	4	6	0	0	0
Martinez	.963	44	74	3	3	1
McQuillan	1.000	16	17	0	0	0
Mesa	.966	31	57	0	2	0
Miller	.955	20	38	4	2	0
Montilla	.931	23	27	0	2	0
Poole	.974	27	37	0	1	0
Ramos	.971	64	88	13	3	1
Schill	1.000	16	39	0	0	1

GCL NATIONALS   ROOKIE
GULF COAST LEAGUE

Batting	B-T	HT	WT	DOB	AVG	vLH	vRH	G	AB	R	H	2B	3B	HR	RBI	BB	HBP	SH	SF	SO	SB	CS	SLG	OBP
Albaladejo, Mike	R-R	5-7	170	2-26-90	.234	.273	.222	17	47	5	11	0	0	0	4	3	1	1	0	7	2	0	.234	.294
Bailey, Hunter	R-R	6-0	180	5-17-89	.247	.133	.276	26	73	12	18	6	0	0	4	8	3	0	0	12	1	0	.329	.345
Brooks, James	R-R	6-0	185	10-12-88	.273	.313	.265	28	99	14	27	4	2	0	13	8	3	3	0	25	1	0	.354	.345
Chubb, Austin	R-R	6-1	200	4-17-89	.209	.400	.154	23	67	4	14	5	0	2	12	3	2	0	1	11	0	0	.373	.260
Difo, Wilmer	R-R	6-0	175	4-2-92	.263	.190	.282	54	198	33	52	7	3	0	13	34	2	0	1	35	19	5	.328	.374
Eusebio, Diomedes	R-R	6-0	185	9-8-92	.277	.219	.294	43	141	7	39	11	2	0	18	5	3	2	0	27	1	6	.383	.315
Foat, Matt	R-R	6-0	185	3-20-90	.333	.364	.326	43	162	20	54	6	1	1	20	14	6	0	1	18	2	2	.401	.404
Jennings, Hayden	L-L	6-0	170	10-16-92	.192	.139	.208	47	156	18	30	2	2	0	3	11	2	1	0	70	17	2	.231	.254
Leonida, Cole	R-R	6-2	220	5-30-90	.154	.000	.222	4	13	2	2	0	0	0	1	0	0	0	0	4	0	0	.154	.214
Lippincott, Bryan	L-R	6-3	210	9-26-89	.281	.233	.294	43	139	9	39	11	1	0	18	16	2	2	1	29	5	2	.374	.361
McQuillan, Mike	L-R	5-11	175	10-2-89	.375	.600	.326	19	56	6	21	1	1	0	5	11	0	1	0	10	0	3	.429	.478
Mesa, Narciso	R-R	5-11	175	11-16-91	.229	.333	.202	32	118	15	27	6	1	0	12	4	8	2	1	21	5	4	.297	.262
Nieto, Adrian	B-R	6-0	200	11-12-89	.154	.333	.100	8	26	3	4	1	0	1	3	5	0	0	0	7	0	0	.308	.290
Nix, Tony	R-R	5-11	185	2-3-89	.215	.217	.214	38	121	14	26	9	0	2	12	6	4	4	0	18	5	1	.339	.275
Ortega, Bryce	R-R	5-11	170	9-22-88	.000	—	.000	1	3	0	0	0	0	0	0	0	0	0	0	1	0	0	.000	.000
Perez, Eury	R-R	6-0	180	5-30-90	.409	.333	.409	5	22	4	9	1	0	0	2	1	0	0	0	5	0	0	.455	.435
Perez, Stephen	B-R	5-11	175	12-16-90	.190	.000	.235	7	21	1	4	2	0	0	1	0	1	0	0	10	0	2	.286	.227
Piwnica-Worms, Will	R-R	6-3	215	4-1-90	.229	.268	.216	46	166	24	38	9	1	1	18	23	4	0	1	27	5	0	.313	.335
Poole, Jordan	R-R	6-3	210	9-11-91	.240	.143	.278	8	25	2	6	1	0	0	1	0	0	1	0	11	0	1	.280	.296
Rendon, Anthony	R-R	6-0	195	6-6-90	.364	.667	.250	5	11	2	4	1	0	2	6	3	0	0	0	3	0	0	1.000	.500
Rodriguez, Wilman	R-R	6-1	175	6-7-91	.200	.000	.231	5	15	1	3	1	0	0	0	1	1	0	0	5	1	0	.267	.294
Ruiz, Adderling	R-R	6-1	175	5-3-91	.200	.000	.238	11	25	3	5	0	0	0	2	1	0	0	6	0	0	.200	.286
Severino, Pedro	R-R	6-1	180	7-20-93	.220	.174	.233	38	109	9	24	3	1	0	8	9	4	2	1	9	0	0	.266	.301
Solano, Jhonatan	R-R	5-9	205	8-12-85	.333	—	.333	2	3	1	1	0	0	0	1	0	0	0	1	0	0	0	.667	.250

	B-T	HT	WT	DOB	AVG	vLH	vRH	G	AB	R	H	2B	3B	HR	RBI	BB	HBP	SH	SF	SO	SB	CS	SLG	OBP
Valdez, Jean Carlos	R-R	6-2	190	3-14-93	.224	.250	.216	44	147	12	33	9	0	0	14	11	7	2	1	34	1	0	.286	.307
Williams, Deion	R-R	6-3	190	11-11-92	.000	—	.000	4	7	0	0	0	0	0	0	0	0	0	0	5	0	0	.000	.000

Pitching

Pitching	B-T	HT	WT	DOB	W	L	ERA	G	GS	CG	SV	IP	H	R	ER	HR	BB	SO	AVG	vLH	vRH	K/9	BB/9
Anderson, Dixon	R-R	6-5	225	7-2-89	0	1	3.18	6	4	0	0	17	19	6	6	2	2	13	.297	.375	.219	6.88	1.06
Barrientos, Joel	L-L	6-2	145	8-16-93	4	1	3.00	14	4	0	0	45	46	19	15	2	17	42	.263	.234	.273	8.40	3.40
Boyden, Mike	R-R	6-0	180	6-18-90	0	0	0.00	6	0	0	1	9	6	0	0	0	0	12	.188	.273	.143	12.46	0.00
Carr, Adam	R-R	6-2	220	4-1-84	1	0	0.00	1	0	0	0	2	0	0	0	0	0	1	.000	.000	.000	4.50	0.00
Dicharry, Austin	R-R	6-4	200	11-27-89	4	1	2.84	16	0	0	4	25	19	8	8	0	4	22	.211	.258	.186	7.82	1.42
Estevez, Wirkin	R-R	6-1	170	3-15-92	0	0	0.00	3	3	0	0	9	3	0	0	0	2	10	.103	.188	.000	10.00	2.00
Eusebio, Wilson	R-R	6-0	170	8-20-88	0	0	5.40	5	0	0	1	5	4	3	3	0	1	2	.222	.182	.286	3.60	1.80
Giolito, Lucas	R-R	6-6	225	7-14-94	0	0	4.50	1	1	0	0	2	2	1	1	0	0	1	.286	.333	.250	4.50	0.00
Heredia, Inocencio	R-R	5-11	172	12-11-91	2	2	2.61	16	0	0	2	31	28	13	9	1	4	27	.237	.264	.215	7.84	1.16
Hicks, Graham	L-L	6-5	170	2-9-94	0	0	0.00	1	0	0	0	2	1	0	0	0	2	2	.167	1.000	.000	9.00	9.00
Hollins, L.J.	R-R	6-3	185	7-31-91	1	0	0.00	1	0	0	0	9	0	0	0	0	3	8	.000	.000	.000	8.00	3.00
Hudgins, Will	R-R	6-4	200	2-12-90	4	3	2.21	10	6	0	0	37	35	15	9	2	3	25	.250	.286	.231	6.14	0.74
Kimball, Cole	R-R	6-4	250	8-1-85	0	0	0.00	1	1	0	0	1	1	0	0	0	0	1	.250	.000	.333	9.00	0.00
Kreis, Alex	R-R	6-1	210	5-30-89	0	0	0.00	3	0	0	0	5	5	0	0	0	1	5	.278	.429	.182	9.64	1.93
Lucas, Bobby	L-L	6-2	180	8-12-87	0	0	2.53	7	0	0	0	11	10	3	3	0	3	14	.263	.333	.241	11.81	2.53
Marcelino, Anthony	R-R	6-3	175	1-21-93	0	0	6.75	1	0	0	0	4	7	4	3	0	2	4	.389	.000	.636	9.00	4.50
Martin, Rafael	R-R	6-3	215	5-16-84	1	0	0.00	2	0	0	0	3	1	0	0	0	0	4	.100	.000	.000	12.00	0.00
McCatty, Shane	R-R	6-3	205	5-18-87	0	0	0.00	3	0	0	0	4	4	0	0	0	0	3	.286	.333	.250	6.75	0.00
McGeary, Jack	L-L	6-3	195	3-19-89	0	0	5.40	2	0	0	0	2	1	1	1	0	4	1	.167	.000	.250	5.40	21.60
McKenzie, Chris	R-R	6-3	185	12-6-89	0	0	0.00	1	0	0	0	1	0	0	0	0	0	1	.000	.000		13.50	0.00
Mendez, Gilberto	R-R	6-0	165	11-17-92	2	1	3.24	14	1	0	0	33	29	14	12	3	4	34	.228	.292	.190	9.18	1.08
Mieses, Adalberto	R-R	6-3	190	1-1-90	1	5	5.05	13	6	0	0	41	56	30	23	3	10	25	.318	.273	.354	5.49	2.20
Mudron, Mike	L-R	6-0	185	2-4-90	0	1	3.75	10	0	0	1	24	16	14	10	3	8	27	.178	.176	.179	10.13	3.00
Pena, Ronald	R-R	6-4	195	9-19-91	0	1	3.00	3	3	0	0	6	2	2	2	0	1	5	.100	.250	.000	7.50	1.50
Peters, John	R-R	6-3	225	6-15-89	1	0	2.08	6	0	0	1	9	9	2	2	0	3	7	.290	.182	.350	7.27	3.12
Pineyro, Ivan	R-R	6-1	198	9-29-91	0	0	2.38	5	5	0	0	23	13	7	6	2	7	23	.163	.222	.132	9.13	2.78
Santana, Andy	R-R	6-2	187	12-5-90	1	4	6.46	13	2	0	0	24	25	21	17	2	12	22	.260	.367	.212	8.37	4.56
Schultz, Mike	R-R	6-7	220	11-28-89	0	0	0.00	1	0	0	0	1	0	0	0	0	0	1	.000	.000		9.00	0.00
Schwartz, Blake	R-R	6-3	200	10-9-89	0	2	5.06	5	5	0	0	16	24	10	9	0	1	12	.353	.320	.372	6.75	0.56
Selsor, Casey	L-L	6-2	185	2-23-90	4	6	6.10	14	6	0	0	41	50	32	28	5	15	34	.298	.273	.310	7.40	3.27
Smoker, Josh	L-L	6-2	195	11-26-88	1	0	1.80	2	0	0	0	5	3	1	1	0	1	3	.188	.250	.167	5.40	1.80
Turnbull, Kylin	R-L	6-5	205	9-12-89	0	1	2.89	4	0	0	0	9	11	3	3	0	0	9	.282	.400	.241	8.68	0.00
Vasquez, Daury	R-R	6-4	170	11-21-92	4	6	4.10	11	9	0	0	53	49	34	24	4	33	29	.251	.247	.255	4.96	5.64

Fielding

Catcher

Catcher	PCT	G	PO	A	E	DP	PB
Albaladejo	.973	6	34	2	1	2	1
Chubb	1.000	11	58	4	0	0	3
Leonida	1.000	3	17	1	0	0	0
Nieto	1.000	5	18	0	0	0	1
Ruiz	.973	9	62	9	2	1	1
Severino	.993	38	236	44	2	5	6
Solano	1.000	2	2	0	0	0	0

First Base

First Base	PCT	G	PO	A	E	DP
Chubb	1.000	1	3	0	0	0
Foat	1.000	8	47	5	0	4
Lippincott	.995	21	192	12	1	14
Valdez	.974	38	282	16	8	20

Second Base

Second Base	PCT	G	PO	A	E	DP
Bailey	.959	21	25	46	3	5
Brooks	1.000	2	4	2	0	0
Difo	1.000	5	8	10	0	4
Foat	.991	25	50	62	1	18
McQuillan	.930	12	29	24	4	5

Third Base

Third Base	PCT	G	PO	A	E	DP
Bailey	1.000	3	1	6	0	1
Brooks	.934	18	16	41	4	7
Eusebio	.875	1	1	6	1	0
McQuillan	.750	1	0	3	1	0
Rendon	.750	3	1	2	1	1
Valdez	1.000	1	0	4	0	0
Williams	1.000	3	2	6	0	0

Shortstop

Shortstop	PCT	G	PO	A	E	DP
Bailey	.909	2	3	7	1	1
Brooks	.941	6	7	9	1	1
Difo	.925	51	58	138	16	19
Ortega	1.000	1	0	3	0	1
Perez	1.000	5	3	9	0	4

Outfield

Outfield	PCT	G	PO	A	E	DP
Albaladejo	1.000	1	5	0	0	0
Foat	1.000	2	4	0	0	0
Jennings	.987	44	75	2	1	0
Lippincott	.960	12	24	0	1	0
McQuillan	1.000	1	0	0	0	0
Mesa	.970	30	60	4	2	2
Nix	.953	33	56	5	3	2
Perez	1.000	5	7	0	0	0
Piwnica-Worms	.973	44	70	1	2	0
Poole	1.000	8	10	0	0	0
Rodriguez	.875	5	7	0	1	0
Selsor	—	1	0	0	0	0

DSL NATIONALS   ROOKIE
DOMINICAN SUMMER LEAGUE

Batting	B-T	HT	WT	DOB	AVG	vLH	vRH	G	AB	R	H	2B	3B	HR	RBI	BB	HBP	SH	SF	SO	SB	CS	SLG	OBP
Abreu, Osvaldo	R-R	6-0	170	6-13-94	.279	.364	.250	59	215	38	60	14	2	0	26	27	9	2	1	49	22	14	.363	.381
Aguero, Younaifred	R-R	6-2	170	4-10-93	.254	.286	.243	52	138	26	35	3	1	2	17	29	2	1	3	20	7	5	.333	.384
Alvarez, Thomas	R-R	6-1	165	2-15-95	.222	.500	.188	18	18	7	4	1	0	1	3	5	0	1	0	6	2	0	.444	.391
Atencio, Miguel	R-R	6-0	165	5-3-95	.247	.150	.275	33	89	13	22	6	1	0	14	10	1	1	1	24	2	0	.337	.327
Bautista, Rafael	R-R	6-2	165	3-8-93	.329	.340	.325	67	210	38	69	8	3	0	25	27	8	6	3	39	47	7	.395	.419
Cerda, Kevin	R-R	6-0	190	6-11-93	.206	.222	.200	52	189	27	39	9	0	4	24	20	0	0	2	31	4	4	.317	.280
De Los Santos, Juan	R-R	5-11	170	1-11-94	.224	.217	.227	48	143	26	32	8	0	0	12	28	10	1	2	36	8	6	.280	.383
Echenique, Armando	R-R	6-0	180	1-7-95	.211	.111	.229	26	57	8	12	4	0	0	4	5	3	0	0	27	0	0	.281	.308
Marmolejos-Diaz, Jose	L-L	6-1	185	1-2-93	.298	.232	.317	69	255	33	76	21	8	4	39	23	3	0	1	34	1	2	.490	.362
Martinez, Andres	R-R	6-1	170	7-7-95	.248	.231	.254	42	157	22	39	7	2	1	23	22	4	1	1	42	5	3	.338	.353
Mejia, Bryan	R-R	6-1	170	3-2-94	.239	.179	.253	55	201	27	48	10	8	0	27	11	1	1	2	45	8	4	.368	.279
Mercedes, Yermin	R-R	5-11	175	2-14-93	.327	.333	.324	36	110	22	36	6	3	1	19	13	4	0	1	11	3	1	.398	.412
Novas, Randy	R-R	6-3	180	7-31-94	.271	.294	.265	60	221	32	60	19	1	4	26	18	5	0	2	54	25	6	.421	.337
Ramirez, Algenis	R-R	6-3	175	4-11-94	.256	.273	.250	14	39	9	10	2	0	0	5	7	1	0	1	11	0	1	.308	.375
Read, Raudy	R-R	6-0	170	10-29-93	.251	.270	.244	62	227	33	57	16	0	9	47	18	8	0	3	33	3	3	.441	.324

	B-T	HT	WT	DOB																				
Serrata, Brayan	R-R	6-3	175	6-17-94	.500	—	.500	2	2	0	1	0	0	0	0	0	0	0	0	1	0	0	.500	.500
Suarez, Wester	L-L	6-2	195	11-10-94	.130	.200	.122	24	46	10	6	1	0	0	3	11	2	0	0	22	0	0	.152	.322
Tillero, Jorge	R-R	5-11	160	12-21-93	.200	.158	.211	29	90	10	18	1	0	0	5	8	3	1	0	15	1	2	.211	.287

Pitching	B-T	HT	WT	DOB	W	L	ERA	G	GS	CG	SV	IP	H	R	ER	HR	BB	SO	AVG	vLH	vRH	K/9	BB/9
Acevedo, Miguel	R-R	6-2	180	3-7-94	0	2	6.06	16	0	0	0	33	37	26	22	4	20	21	.289	.371	.258	5.79	5.51
Aquino, Jonathan	R-R	6-1	185	3-28-95	2	0	3.48	5	0	0	0	10	7	5	4	0	4	7	.200	.231	.182	6.10	3.48
Benitez, Juan	R-R	6-6	180	12-16-91	3	2	6.96	12	3	0	2	32	32	32	25	2	24	36	.269	.342	.235	10.02	6.68
Berrio, Jorge	R-R	6-0	145	2-8-95	0	1	8.38	7	0	0	0	10	12	10	9	1	6	12	.293	.000	.333	11.17	5.59
Chavez, Jose	R-R	6-3	165	12-1-91	2	0	3.28	13	0	0	0	25	24	11	9	1	17	24	.264	.333	.230	8.76	6.20
De La Cruz, Emmanuel	R-R	6-4	180	4-16-92	0	0	1.23	8	6	0	0	15	8	5	2	0	8	6	.163	.091	.184	3.68	4.91
De Los Santos, Jesus	R-R	6-4	190	11-28-92	0	0	13.50	2	0	0	0	3	3	4	4	1	6	3	.333	.667	.167	10.13	20.25
Dilone, Angelo	R-R	6-5	188	12-15-92	2	1	4.25	14	0	0	0	30	31	17	14	0	19	20	.277	.238	.300	6.07	5.76
Gomez, Elisaul	L-L	6-1	165	3-26-92	7	3	3.31	17	8	0	1	71	49	31	26	2	35	54	.202	.129	.212	6.88	4.46
Lopez, Reynaldo	R-R	6-0	185	1-4-94	1	1	3.38	5	0	0	1	11	12	5	4	1	5	9	.333	.333	.333	7.59	4.22
Martinez, Anderson	R-R	6-3	180	2-22-93	0	1	7.50	2	1	0	0	6	3	5	5	0	7	10	.150	.000	.231	15.00	10.50
Moscat, Felix	R-R	6-2	160	12-2-90	0	1	6.75	4	1	0	0	8	5	6	6	0	7	10	.185	.556	.000	11.25	7.88
Navarro, Miguel	R-R	6-2	180	3-4-93	0	0	94.50	1	0	0	0	1	2	7	7	0	3	1	.500	1.000	.333	13.50	40.50
Ramos, David	R-R	6-0	175	9-13-91	1	2	4.97	8	0	0	1	13	15	8	7	0	8	6	.294	.077	.368	4.26	5.68
Rodriguez, Jefry	R-R	6-5	185	7-26-93	0	2	2.93	10	9	0	0	43	28	24	14	2	33	35	.185	.267	.132	7.33	6.91
Rodriguez, Kelvin	R-R	6-0	190	11-6-91	5	2	3.86	28	0	0	8	47	44	23	20	4	21	41	.259	.250	.264	7.91	4.05
Ruiz, Raul	L-L	5-10	160	12-4-90	0	0	1.77	4	4	0	0	20	21	8	4	1	2	10	.269	.267	.270	4.43	0.89
Salazar, Melvi	R-R	6-1	175	12-17-94	0	0	7.00	6	0	0	0	9	9	7	7	0	8	1	.257	.364	.208	1.00	8.00
Sanchez, Mario	R-R	6-1	166	10-31-94	0	2	5.79	8	0	0	1	14	14	10	9	1	7	10	.269	.278	.265	6.43	4.50
Silvestre, Hector	L-L	6-3	180	12-14-92	5	3	3.20	15	13	0	0	76	67	32	27	3	24	69	.241	.257	.239	8.17	2.84
Suero, Wander	R-R	6-3	175	9-15-91	4	2	3.41	9	8	0	0	37	29	19	14	3	12	34	.207	.196	.213	8.27	2.92
Valdez, Phillip	R-R	6-2	160	11-16-91	2	2	5.40	14	5	0	0	48	65	43	29	1	30	32	.327	.284	.348	5.96	5.59
Valerio, Maximo	R-R	6-2	175	7-22-95	3	5	3.55	15	12	0	0	63	62	39	25	2	17	37	.258	.227	.270	5.26	2.42

Fielding

Catcher	PCT	G	PO	A	E	DP	PB
Mercedes	.933	9	57	13	5	1	3
Read	.997	44	307	44	1	6	12
Serrata	—	1	0	0	0	0	0
Tillero	.973	26	141	39	5	1	7

First Base	PCT	G	PO	A	E	DP
Aguero	1.000	1	5	0	0	0
Cerda	.980	31	236	14	5	27
Marmolejos-Diaz	.972	45	297	21	9	23
Mercedes	.970	6	32	0	1	4
Serrata	1.000	1	4	0	0	0
Suarez	1.000	1	1	0	0	0

Second Base	PCT	G	PO	A	E	DP
Abreu	.963	5	13	13	1	3
Alvarez	.333	2	0	1	2	0
Cerda	1.000	1	3	1	0	0
De Los Santos	.941	32	56	72	8	18
Martinez	.857	2	4	2	1	0

Third Base	PCT	G	PO	A	E	DP
Mejia	.955	40	96	75	8	19
Aguero	.902	27	30	44	8	8
Cerda	.886	10	7	24	4	1
Martinez	—	1	0	0	0	0
Martinez	.935	26	22	36	4	2
Mejia	.890	17	29	36	8	8

Shortstop	PCT	G	PO	A	E	DP
Abreu	.912	54	93	113	20	17
Alvarez	.875	9	11	10	3	3
Martinez	1.000	1	0	1	0	1
Martinez	.935	15	15	28	3	6
Mejia	1.000	1	3	3	0	1
Ramirez	1.000	1	2	1	0	1

Outfield	PCT	G	PO	A	E	DP
Abreu	—	1	0	0	0	0
Aguero	.947	24	33	3	2	2
Atencio	.917	32	32	1	3	1
Bautista	.951	63	127	9	7	4
De Los Santos	1.000	4	5	1	0	1
Echenique	.964	24	26	1	1	1
Marmolejos-Diaz	1.000	29	51	2	0	1
Novas	.990	59	91	6	1	2
Ramirez	.941	13	15	1	1	1

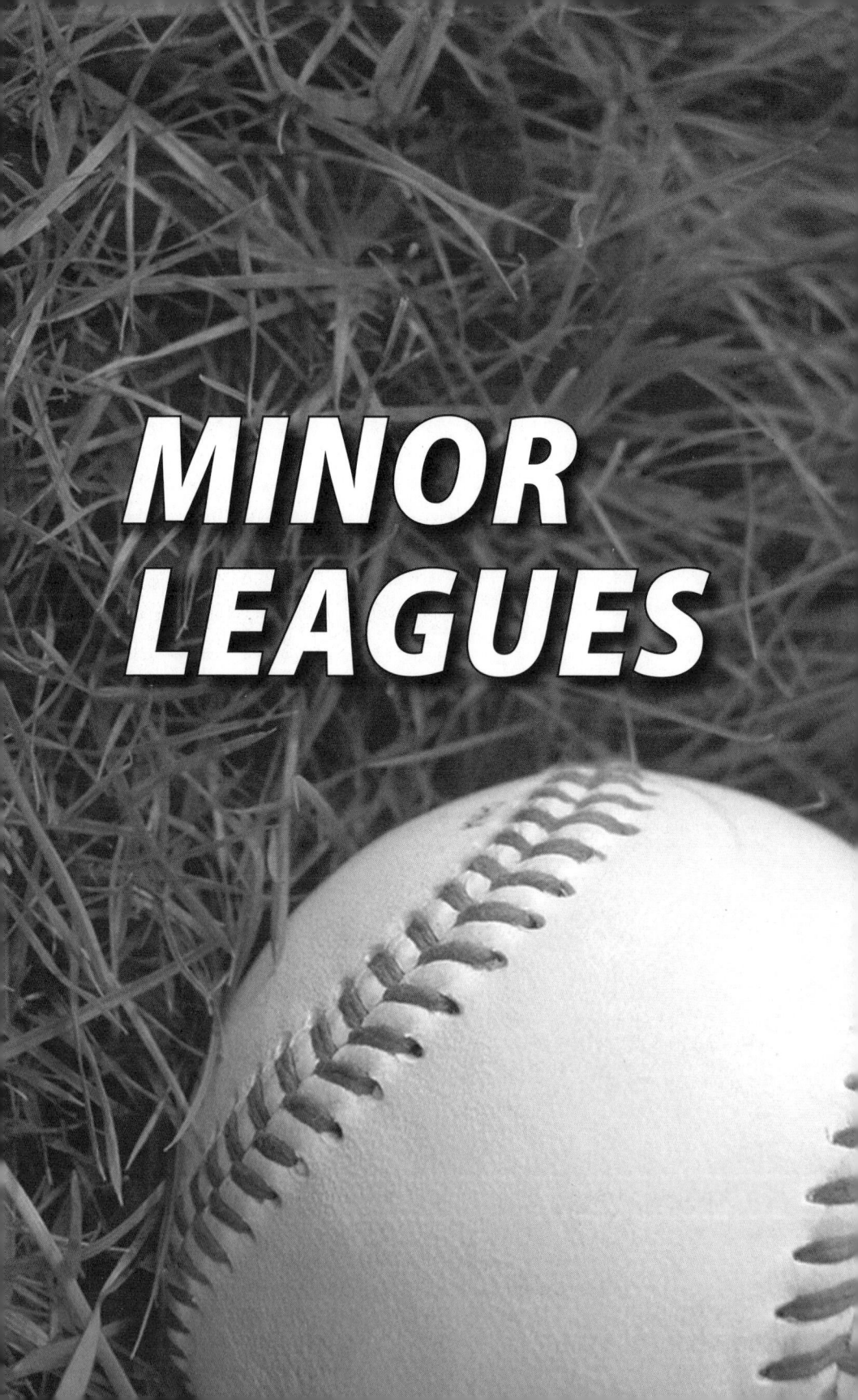

MINOR LEAGUES

Billy Hamilton stole the show in 2012 by setting a minor league record with 155 stolen bases

Historic season offers hope for minor leagues

BY JOSH LEVENTHAL

Minor league baseball records don't break easily.

In fact, the record book filled with feats accomplished in a distant and much different era of baseball barely bends and rarely breaks under the weight of today's most prolific achievements.

Joe Bauman's 72 home runs in 1954 dwarf the 44 Phil Hiatt hit in 2001—the most by a minor leaguer this century. Amarillo West slugger Bob Crues and his record 254 RBIs in 1948 are not in jeopardy of being trumped any time soon, neither are Grover Lowdermilk's 465 strikeouts in 1907.

In fact, no minor league record had been broken in 27 years before Reds speedster Billy Hamilton managed to slide his way into the exclusive club this season with the figure below, which kicks off our by-the-numbers review of the 2012 minor league baseball season.

155

Stolen bases by Billy Hamilton, topping the record of 145 steals set by Vince Coleman in 1985.

Hamilton made history while splitting his fourth professional season between high Class A

Bakersfield and Double-A Pensacola in the Reds system. He led the California League in steals with 104 in 82 games and remarkably needed just 50 games to top the Southern League with 51 steals—10 more than runner-up Josh Prince. He impressed his stolen-base predecessor along the way.

"I am excited for this young man," Coleman said. "From what I hear, he has all the dynamics that a basestealer should have."

Hamilton, who turned 22 after the season and will make the transition from shortstop to center field next season, set the new record in dramatic fashion. He needed just two at-bats and three innings to procure the necessary steals to set the record on Aug. 21. Hamilton tied and eclipsed the record in three pitches, stealing second base and then third, following his two-out single in the third inning against Double-A Montgomery.

At the request of Major League Baseball, both the tying and record-setting bases were removed after time was called.

"It's a bunch of relief," Hamilton said after setting the record. "Now, I feel a little better, like I can get on with my game and finish out the season strong."

A second-round pick in 2009 out of Taylorsville (Miss.) High, Hamilton topped the minors in steals for a second straight season after swiping 103 bags in 123 attempts last season while playing for low Class A Dayton (Midwest).

While Hamilton is soft-spoken and humble off the field, his feats of speed on it have turned him into a modern-day baseball folk hero. There was the time he scored the game-winning run from third base on a sacrifice fly to second. He scored from second base on a groundout and made a catch in deep left field—while playing shortstop.

20

Home runs hit by Double-A Reading Phillies first baseman Darin Ruf in August.

Ruf's home-run outburst over 31 late-season games propelled the 2009 20th-round pick to a total of 38 homers, edging Minor League Player of the Year Wil Myers for the most in the minors. And while his August binge may not have landed him in the record book, he did eclipse Reading's single-season mark of 37 set by Ryan Howard in 2004.

The unheralded 26-year-old earned a promotion to Philadelphia after the minor league season and added three more home runs in 33 at-bats with the Phillies, only adding to the legend of the player his Reading teammates dubbed "Babe Ruf."

"In the minors you don't get that buzz when a guy walks to the plate often," Reading manager Dusty Wathan said. "There is a buzz when he walks to the plate. People are disappointed when he doesn't hit a home run."

19 of 32

Number of first-round picks from the 2011 draft to rank among the top five prospects in their respective leagues in 2012.

The 2011 draft was projected to be among the best and deepest in the 47-year history of the event. It did not take long to prove those lofty projections correct, as the Class of '11 made quite a debut in '12.

In fact, 49 of the first 60 picks ranked in a league Top 20—a feat made even more impressive considering two players did not sign and No. 6 overall selection Anthony Rendon (Nationals) missed most of the season with an injury.

And, as you would expect, there were plenty of memorable individual performances from the Class of '11. For example . . .

4

Pitchers from the 2011 draft class to rank in the top six in strikeouts.

Unheralded Athletics righthander Dan Straily, a 2009 24th-round pick, took over for Matt Moore as the minors strikeout king with 190, but several members of the 2011 draft class trailed closely.

Reds third-round lefty Tony Cingrani ranked second in the minors with 172 strikeouts between Bakersfield and Pensacola and had three more whiffs than fellow third-round lefty Adam Morgan (Phillies). A's righthander Drew Granier finished fourth with 167 and Astros righthander Nick Tropeano rounded out the top six with 166.

Marlins phenom Jose Fernandez registered 158 strikeouts between low Class A Greensboro and high Class A Jupiter, one more than third overall pick Trevor Bauer tallied between Double-A Mobile and Triple-A Reno.

0

Runs yielded by Dylan Bundy in his eight starts with low Class A Delmarva.

No player from the 2011 draft made a bigger splash in 2012 than the Orioles righthander. The fourth overall pick out of Owasso (Okla.) High, Bundy overwhelmed South Atlantic League hitters in his professional debut. He walked just two, yielded five hits, and registered 40 strikeouts in 30 innings before earning a promotion to high Class A Frederick—where he would rank as the Carolina League's top prospect.

"He looked like a No. 1 major league starter who came down to pitch a Carolina League game," Wilmington manager Vance Wilson said of Bundy following the season.

Bundy moved on to Double-A Bowie in August and earned a late-September callup to Baltimore to aid a weary Orioles pitching staff. He could still begin next season in the minors, but he wasn't the only one from the class who looked like he belonged in the big leagues . . .

0.07 %

Increase in overall minor league attendance compared to the 2011 season.

That figure may seem insignificant, but it marks a big win for the industry, as it brings to an end three straight years of declining attendance figures.

Minor League Baseball announced after the season that its teams had attracted a total of 41,279,382 spectators, a tick above the 41,252,053 they drew in 2011. It marks the second straight year that the sport's attendance has held relatively steady, and the 2011 total was just 0.4 percent off 2010, prompting Minor League Baseball president Pat O'Conner to proclaim that "flat is the new up" during such challenging financial times.

The same appears true this year, though a bigger

finish appeared possible early in the season.

An improving economy combined with picture-perfect springtime weather had minor league baseball on pace to shatter last year's number. Attendance was up 11.2 percent in April, and the 6,401,632 fans who visited minor league ballparks that month was the second-highest total since 2000. The minors remained 6.3 percent ahead of pace after May and up 901,800 through June. That number dipped to 500,000 after July, as the hottest month on record cooled baseball's early season pace.

"We had such a good April weather-wise compared to a year ago that we came out of the gate almost 11 or 12 percent higher," O'Conner said. "We have gradually given up some of that increase and played back to being flat. But this has been a good year regardless of the attendance numbers. Clubs are reporting good (sales) activity in the ballpark. It's a new environment . . . Our goal is to increase activity in the ballpark and not give up ground on attendance."

7

New ballparks scheduled to open over the next two seasons, compared to five during the past three years.

There may be no better sign that the industry is headed toward better days than teams finding ways to build new ballparks, even amid challenging financial circumstances. For it was the ballpark building boom that propelled the minor leagues to five consecutive attendance records from 2004-08, and the success of the sport's newest venue gave it a boost in 2012.

The Pensacola Blue Wahoos debuted this season and led the Southern League in attendance with 328,147 fans, for a 4,826 average. Pensacola also proved to be a marked improvement over the Kinston Indians, the franchise it essentially replaced. (Pensacola had purchased the Carolina Mudcats franchise in the Southern League in December 2010, while the Mudcats bought the Kinston franchise in the Carolina League.)

The Blue Wahoos drew 215,966 more fans than Kinston did in 2011, and Pensacola's average attendance was a 170 percent higher than the Indians' 1,781 average.

The minors could expect similar returns from three new ballparks in 2013. The Scranton/Wilkes-Barre Yankees (International) sent its team on the road for all of 2012 so that it's home could be overhauled in time for the start of next season. The Birmingham Barons (Southern) are leaving Regions Field in suburban Birmingham for a new $64 million downtown venue. And the Hillsboro Hops (Northwest) will debut in a new ballpark in

2013 after relocating the franchise from Yakima, Wash.

Four additional teams are expected to open new ballparks in 2014, including a new franchise in El Paso that has played the past two seasons in Tucson. The other teams scheduled to open new ballparks are the Triple-A Charlotte Knights (International), high Class A Bakersfield Blaze (California) and high Class A Potomac Nationals (Carolina).

ORGANIZATION STANDINGS

Cumulative domestic farm club records for major league organizations, with winning percentages going back five years. Most organizations have six affiliates.

	2012						
	W	L	PCT	2011	2010	2009	2008
1. Houston	417	347	.546	.408	.436	.426	.376
2. Colorado	386	329	.540	.495	.480	.513	.499
3. N.Y. Yankees	366	326	.529	.494	.538	.554	.586
4. Seattle	402	359	.528	.483	.530	.528	.472
L.A. Dodgers	366	327	.528	.543	.508	.498	.484
6. Minnesota	360	326	.525	.490	.434	.535	.532
7. Toronto	397	360	.524	.515	.506	.467	.511
Miami	361	328	.524	.495	.490	.502	.530
9. Texas	359	335	.517	.565	.522	.495	.556
10. Tampa Bay	391	368	.515	.497	.534	.502	.475
11. N.Y. Mets	355	343	.509	.498	.511	.466	.453
12. Cleveland	352	343	.506	.515	.504	.501	.506
San Francisco	352	344	.506	.539	.524	.603	.553
Washington	353	345	.506	.511	.501	.501	.481
15. St. Louis	383	375	.505	.518	.569	.498	.525
Pittsburgh	353	346	.505	.512	.511	.499	.430
17. Boston	351	346	.504	.490	.491	.505	.518
Chi. White Sox	353	348	.504	.500	.489	.551	.503
19. Arizona	385	387	.499	.488	.489	.476	.426
20. Philadelphia	343	346	.498	.522	.508	.507	.462
21. Oakland	343	348	.496	.514	.527	.494	.520
22. Kansas City	374	386	.492	.494	.492	.482	.442
23. Detroit	333	358	.482	.467	.485	.492	.448
24. Chi. Cubs	321	362	.470	.507	.542	.487	.488
25. Atlanta	315	368	.461	.471	.457	.503	.506
26. Milwaukee	316	373	.459	.466	.493	.488	.469
27. Baltimore	319	380	.456	.487	.463	.475	.468
28. San Diego	317	379	.455	.515	.485	.501	.517
29. Cincinnati	311	381	.449	.503	.466	.453	.476
30. L.A. Angels	312	383	.449	.507	.507	.514	.542

POSTSEASON RESULTS

LEAGUE	CHAMPION	RUNNER-UP
International	Pawtucket	Charlotte
Pacific Coast	Reno	Omaha
Eastern	Akron	Trenton
Southern	Mobile	Jackson
Texas	Springfield	Frisco
California	Lancaster	Modesto
Carolina	Lynchburg	Winston-Salem
Florida State	Lakeland	Jupiter
Midwest	Wisconsin	Fort Wayne
South Atlantic	Asheville	Greensboro
New York-Penn	Hudson Valley	Tri-City
Northwest	Vancouver	Boise
Appalachian	Elizabethton	Burlington
Pioneer	Missoula	Ogden
Arizona	Rangers	Athletics
Gulf Coast	Pirates	Red Sox

BRIAN BUTLER

Pensacola's picturesque ballpark helped the minors to its first attendance increase since 2008

2,534

Miles between Citi Field and Cashman Field, the new home of the Mets' Triple-A Las Vegas affiliate.

Just four years ago the Mets were the hot commodity during the minors' bi-annual renewal of affiliations. After parting ways with Triple-A New Orleans following the 2008 season, New York had its choice of International League affiliates in Buffalo and Syracuse.

Times sure have changed.

After four years in Buffalo, the Mets are on the move for the third time in six seasons. And this time there were no suitors stepping forward to bring New York to town. The Mets will spend the next two seasons in Las Vegas, swapping affiliations with the Blue Jays, whom Buffalo welcomed with open arms.

Eager to put a winning team on the field and boost sagging attendance figures, Bisons management opted not to renew their player-development contract with the Mets and instead sign on with Toronto—where the Rogers Centre is just a two-hour drive north. Buffalo general manager Mike Buczkowski insisted that there was no strife with the Mets, but rather they sought a change after fielding losing teams in three of the past four years.

"We want to be here for years," Blue Jays owner Paul Beeston said. "This is the start of not a two-year deal. Hopefully it's the start of a 42-year deal."

6 of 16

Number of Midwest League teams to change major league affiliates following the season.

Stability was the watchword at the minor league's higher levels as teams went through the affiliation shuffle this offseason. Just two Triple-A teams swapped places while no Double-A or high

AFFILIATION SHUFFLE

Which teams changed affiliations this offseson

TEAM	NEW AFFILIATE	OLD AFFILIATE
INTERNATIONAL LEAGUE (AAA)		
Buffalo	Blue Jays	Mets
PACIFIC COAST LEAGUE (AAA)		
Las Vegas	Mets	Blue Jays
MIDWEST LEAGUE (LO A)		
Beloit	Athletics	Twins
Burlington	Angels	Athletics
Cedar Rapids	Twins	Angels
Kane County	Cubs	Royals
Peoria	Cardinals	Cubs
Quad Cities	Astros	Cardinals
SOUTH ATLANTIC LEAGUE (LO A)		
Lexington	Royals	Astros
NEW YORK-PENN LEAGUE (SS)		
Batavia	Marlins	Cardinals
Jamestown	Pirates	Marlins
State College	Cardinals	Pirates

Class A teams made a move.

But change is coming to low Class A, in particular the Midwest League, where six franchises will welcome new partners in 2013. The Cedar Rapids Kernels split from the Angels after 20 years and signed a four-year player-development contract with the Twins, who will leave Beloit after eight years. The Kane County Cougars, who two years ago signed on with the Royals, confirmed a rumor that leaked out during the season by affiliating with the hometown Cubs through 2014.

The Peoria Chiefs were the losers when the Cubs left for Kane County, but they salvaged things by reuniting with the Cardinals, their affiliate before the Cubs came to town in 2005. The Cardinals had spent the previous eight seasons with Quad Cities, which becomes an Astros affiliate in 2013.

CONTINUED ON PAGE 350

New approach suits Myers

BY J.J. COOPER

Wil Myers had never struck out more than 100 times before this season. As he'll quickly point out, he had never hit 15 home runs in a season, either.

Myers, and the Royals, see him as a middle-of-the-order hitter, not a tablesetter. Middle-of-the-order hitters don't settle for line-drive singles and doubles. So Myers decided to do something about that. Like a chef tweaking a recipe, Myers decided to alter his approach. He stood more upright at the plate, which enabled him to get more backspin on the ball, and he took more aggressive swings later in at-bats.

The change led Myers to strike out at a higher rate than before, but with a significant payoff: launching balls over fences night after night. Myers finished second in the minors with 37 home runs, which were 23 more than his previous high for a season. Despite the strikeouts, he hit .313/.387/.600 between Double-A Northwest Arkansas and Triple-A Omaha. Game-changing power as a 21-year-old rounded Myers' game out perfectly.

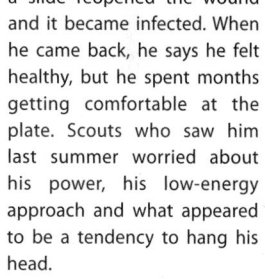

Wil Myers

Myers was the second-youngest regular in the Pacific Coast League. Still, he ranked among the league's top 10 in slugging percentage, on-base-plus-slugging and home runs. He didn't join the league until May 17, after hitting 13 home runs in just over a month with Northwest Arkansas.

To boost his power, Myers made sacrifices. His 137 strikeouts this season are a career high. But he and the Royals are quite willing to make that trade. And as the season's grind reached August, he showed that Wil Myers, middle-of-the-order slugger, still grasps the value of knowing the strike zone—though he has seen fewer pitches to hit.

"At the beginning of the year, I'd get a fast-ball or at least a hanging breaking ball early in the count to get a good swing on," Myers said. "Now, they aren't throwing anything really over the plate."

With fewer pitches to drive, Myers hit just two home runs in the first 25 games of August. But he also cut his strikeout rate back to his traditional 21 percent.

Learning has come much easier for Myers this year. At the same time last year, he was finishing up a miserable 2011 season that saw him slug less than .400 in his first trip through the Texas League.

That season got off to an awful start when Myers slipped and fell at his apartment complex, cutting his left knee on bricks. He missed time because of the fall, then missed significantly more after a slide reopened the wound and it became infected. When he came back, he says he felt healthy, but he spent months getting comfortable at the plate. Scouts who saw him last summer worried about his power, his low-energy approach and what appeared to be a tendency to hang his head.

The Royals were concerned enough with his struggles that they gave Myers the option of heading to the Arizona Fall League or going home to clear his head. The front office was happy to hear Myers say he wanted to play in the AFL. He went there and hit .360/.481/.674.

"We feel like that year will help him down the road" Royals assistant general manager J.J. Picollo said. "The quicker he's receptive to adjustments, the faster he'll get out of (slumps). Now he knows he can deal with adversity and pull himself out of it."

MINOR LEAGUES

The Northwest leader

Bob Richmond is leaving the Northwest League in a much better state than when he first took over as its president in 1973.

Richmond has spent a total of 30 years on the job—he left his post in 1980 only to return in 1991—and is stepping down from a league now considered among the most stable in the minors.

"Bob has done a great job stabilizing the Northwest League," said Minor League Baseball president Pat O'Conner, who looked up to Richmond as a mentor when he first broke into the business in the early 1990s.

The league once considered the wild west of minor league baseball has indeed benefitted from Richmond's steady hand. Much of his early duties focused on helping keep teams afloat. Along with longtime business partner Bob Freitas, with whom Richmond launched the consulting firm Baseball Opportunities, Richmond would often field phone calls from frustrated teams owners threatening to close up shop in midseason only to talk them off the

ledge. Remarkably, the Northwest League now features three franchises playing in ballparks built within the past 15 years, while four of its eight franchises attracted more than 100,000 fans in 2012.

A baseball lifer, Richmond will continue serve as president of the Arizona League, a post he has held since the Rookie-level circuit debuted in 1988. He is also a co-owner of the Midland RockHounds (Texas League).

CONTINUED FROM PAGE 348

When the Royals got squeezed out of Kane County, they decided to move to the South Atlantic League rather than reunite with their previous Midwest League affiliate in Burlington. The Lexington Legends, the lone team in the South Atlantic League that was on the market, inked a four-year PDC with the Royals and promptly unveiled new logos and jerseys.

That left the Midwest League's smallest franchises—Beloit and Burlington—as the last two standing. Burlington, which had been a Royals affiliate for 10 years before partnering with the A's two years ago, signed on with the Angels through 2014, leaving Beloit and Oakland to partner.

1st

Lori Webb became the first female league president in minor league history when she took over the reins of the Southern League.

The Southern League board of trustees turned to a familiar face when it appointed Lori Webb president. She served as the league's vice president of operations since 2000, and she played a key behind-the-scenes role in recent years as her former boss, Don Mincher, battled health issues before

dying in March.

Webb, 56, replaces a figure beloved throughout the sport. Mincher helped save Organized Baseball in his hometown of Huntsville, Ala., before bringing the rare perspective of a former big leaguer to the post of league president. Mincher spent 13 years in the majors, retiring after the 1972 season with 200 home runs, more than 1,000 hits and two All-Star Game appearances. In 1965 with the Twins, he homered off of Don Drysdale in his first World Series at-bat.

108

Number of players suspended in 2012 (through early November) as part of Major League Baseball's drug prevention and treatment program.

The 2012 tally is the most since 118 players were suspended in 2005, when the Players Association and MLB agreed to expand drug testing, and brings the overall number to 622 (including 40 major leaguers) in eight years.

Of the 102 minor leaguers suspended in 2012, 17 were playing in Latin American rookie leagues and 30 were free agents at the time of their suspensions. But the list also included several notable players, including Triple-A Durham shortstop Tim Beckham, whom the Rays selected with the No.

Miley overcomes all odds

BY GEORGE KING

By all accounts baseball lifer Dave Miley is well respected by players, bosses and opponents. He has been a big league manager and led clubs in Cedar Rapids and Greensboro.

The 50-year-old recently completed his 26th season as a minor league manager by leading Triple-A Scranton/Wilkes-Barre to the International League Northern Division title without playing a home game. Through all the minor league stops the Tampa native has understood the basic tenant of being a manager not working in the big leagues: make the players better.

"He knows the drill. He understands the organization's objectives," Yankees minor league head Mark Newman said of Miley's blending development with winning. "And he does it with poise and a very level head."

This past summer may have been Miley's best managing job. Forced to play every game on the road while Scranton's PNC Field was renovated, Miley's Yankees posted an 84-60 record

MANAGER OF THE YEAR

en route to winning the division by five games.

Playing a full season on the road presented a rare challenge. Miley firmly believes if the character of the players wasn't so strong, it could have been a miserable five months.

"No home games and win the division, that's pretty unbelievable," Newman said. "He is a really good person and very good at his job."

---

1 overall pick in the 2008 draft. Also receiving a 50-game suspension was Rays outfielder Josh Sale, one of four members of the low Class A Bowling Green Hot Rods to be suspended after testing positive for methamphetamine and an amphetamine.

The Orioles essentially cut ties with Billy Rowell, the maligned ninth overall pick in 2006, after he was suspended 50 games for a second positive test for a drug of abuse.

.546

Winning percentage of Astros domestic minor league affiliates, the best in baseball.

That's notable because over the previous five years, the Astros easily had the losingest farm system in baseball. Houston finished last in organization standings in 2011, 29th in 2010, last in 2009, last in 2008 and 26th in 2007. No other team has come close to matching the Astros' recent run of futility.

But Houston is a team in transition, on the field and off. First-year general manager Jeff Luhnow overhauled the front office and traded veterans for prospects who have helped turn the Astros into winners in the minor leagues. The high Class A Lancaster JetHawks won their first-ever California League title, and the short-season Tri-City Valley

Cats lost in the New York-Penn League finals. The Astros' Double-A Corpus Christi affiliate lost in the first round of the Texas League playoffs.

2,642

Combined career victories by Tom Kotchman and Joe Mikulik, the longest-tenured managers in the minors who won't be back with their teams in 2013.

Kotchman had served as a scout and manager for the Angels the past 29 years but resigned abruptly after the season when Angels general manager Jerry Dipoto requested he abandon his role as manager and focus solely on his duties as an area scout in Florida.

Kotchman had accumulated a 1,704-1,435 (.543) record over 34 years as a minor league manager—including five with the Red Sox and Tigers—and he had mentored such players as Troy Percival, Garret Anderson, Erick Aybar, Alberto Callaspo and Roger Clemens.

His imprint is all over the Angels organization, as much as any area scout's in the industry. Four Kotchman-signed lefthanded pitchers debuted in the majors this season alone: Nick Maronde (Angels), Will Smith (Royals), Pat Corbin (Diamondbacks) and Barret Browning (Cardinals). He also signed such big leaguers as second baseman

MINOR LEAGUES

TRIPLE-A

Pos	Player, Team (Org)	League	AVG	OBP	SLG	AB	R	H	2B	3B	HR	RBI	BB	SO	SB	CS
C	Travis d'Arnaud, Las Vegas (Blue Jays)	PCL	.333	.380	.595	279	45	93	21	2	16	52	19	59	1	1
1B	* Anthony Rizzo, Iowa (Cubs)	PCL	.342	.405	.696	257	48	88	18	2	23	62	23	52	2	2
2B	Alex Castellanos, Albuquerque (Dodgers)	PCL	.328	.420	.590	344	74	113	25	7	17	52	46	85	16	8
3B	Jedd Gyorko, Tucson (Padres)	PCL	.325	.377	.585	369	62	120	24	0	24	83	34	68	4	3
SS	Jake Elmore, Reno (Diamondbacks)	PCL	.344	.442	.465	419	95	144	30	9	1	73	74	54	32	8
CF	* Adam Eaton, Reno (Diamondbacks)	PCL	.381	.456	.539	488	119	186	46	5	7	45	53	68	38	10
OF	* Corey Brown, Syracuse (Nationals)	IL	.285	.365	.523	484	83	138	22	9	25	71	59	139	18	7
OF	Wil Myers, Omaha (Royals)	PCL	.304	.378	.554	388	66	118	15	5	24	79	45	98	2	2
DH	* Chris Parmelee, Rochester (Twins)	IL	.338	.457	.645	228	45	77	17	1	17	49	51	52	1	1

Pos	Pitcher, Team (Org)	League	W	L	ERA	G	GS	SV	IP	H	HR	BB	SO	G/F	WHIP	AVG
SP	Chris Archer, Durham (Rays)	IL	7	9	3.66	25	25	0	128	99	6	62	139	1.36	1.26	.214
SP	Trevor Bauer, Reno (Diamondbacks)	PCL	5	1	2.85	14	14	0	82	74	8	35	97	1.35	1.33	.237
SP	John Ely, Albuquerque (Dodgers)	PCL	14	7	3.20	27	27	0	169	149	18	36	165	1.48	1.10	.232
SP	Matt Harvey, Buffalo (Mets)	IL	7	5	3.68	20	20	0	110	97	9	48	112	1.28	1.32	.232
RP	J.J. Hoover, Louisville (Reds)	IL	4	0	1.22	30	0	13	37	15	1	12	55	0.49	0.73	.120

Player of the Year: Wil Myers, Omaha (Royals). **Pitcher of the Year:** John Ely, Albuquerque (Dodgers).
Manager of the Year: Lorenzo Bundy, Albuquerque (Dodgers).

DOUBLE-A

Pos	Player, Team (Org)	League	AVG	OBP	SLG	AB	R	H	2B	3B	HR	RBI	BB	SO	SB	CS
C	Evan Gattis, Mississippi (Braves)	SL	.258	.343	.522	182	24	47	13	4	9	37	20	29	1	1
1B	* Jonathan Singleton, Corpus Christi (Astros)	TL	.284	.396	.497	461	94	131	27	4	21	79	88	131	7	2
2B	* Logan Watkins, Tennessee (Cubs)	SL	.281	.383	.422	488	93	137	20	11	9	52	76	97	28	7
3B	Mike Olt, Frisco (Rangers)	TL	.288	.398	.579	354	65	102	17	1	28	82	61	101	4	0
SS	# Jurickson Profar, Frisco (Rangers)	TL	.281	.368	.452	480	76	135	26	7	14	62	66	79	16	4
CF	# Aaron Hicks, New Britain (Twins)	EL	.285	.382	.459	473	100	135	21	11	13	61	78	115	32	11
OF	* Marc Krauss, Mobile/C.C. (ARI/HOU)	SL/TL	.291	.421	.544	375	86	109	31	2	20	77	79	96	7	4
OF	* Oscar Taveras, Springfield (Cardinals)	TL	.321	.380	.572	477	83	153	37	7	23	94	42	56	11	1
DH	Darin Ruf, Reading (Phillies)	EL	.317	.408	.620	489	93	155	32	1	38	104	65	102	2	0

Pos	Pitcher, Team (Org)	League	W	L	ERA	G	GS	SV	IP	H	HR	BB	SO	G/F	WHIP	AVG
SP	Justin Grimm, Frisco (Rangers)	TL	9	3	1.72	16	14	0	84	70	3	14	73	1.18	1.00	.227
SP	Chris Heston, Richmond (Giants)	EL	9	8	2.24	25	25	0	149	123	2	40	135	1.63	1.10	.223
SP	Dan Straily, Midland (Athletics)	TL	3	4	3.38	14	14	0	85	70	6	23	108	1.07	1.09	.219
SP	Zack Wheeler, Binghamton (Mets)	EL	10	6	3.26	19	19	0	116	92	2	43	117	1.16	1.16	.219
RP	Carter Capps, Jackson (Mariners)	SL	2	3	1.29	37	0	19	49	39	2	12	71	0.73	1.04	.210

Player of the Year: Oscar Taveras, Springfield (Cardinals). **Pitcher of the Year:** Chris Heston, Richmond (Giants).
Manager of the Year: Steve Buechele, Frisco (Rangers).

HIGH CLASS A

Pos	Player, Team (Org)	League	AVG	OBP	SLG	AB	R	H	2B	3B	HR	RBI	BB	SO	SB	CS
C	Josmil Pinto, Fort Myers (Twins)	FSL	.295	.361	.473	349	45	103	22	2	12	51	39	63	0	0
1B	* Travis Shaw, Salem (Red Sox)	CAR	.305	.411	.545	354	69	108	31	3	16	73	59	81	10	2
2B	* Ty Kelly, Frederick (Orioles)	CAR	.346	.460	.513	263	47	91	17	0	9	41	54	41	2	3
3B	Miles Head, Stockton (Athletics)	CAL	.382	.433	.715	267	57	102	23	6	18	56	23	55	3	0
SS	* Billy Hamilton, Bakersfield (Reds)	CAL	.323	.413	.439	337	79	109	18	9	1	30	50	70	104	21
CF	* Jackie Bradley, Salem (Red Sox)	CAR	.357	.479	.523	235	53	84	26	2	3	34	52	40	15	6
OF	Kyle Parker, Modesto (Rockies)	CAL	.308	.415	.562	390	86	120	18	6	23	73	66	88	1	2
OF	* Christian Yelich, Jupiter (Marlins)	FSL	.330	.404	.519	397	76	131	29	5	12	48	49	85	20	6
DH	Tommy Medica, Lake Elsinore (Padres)	CAL	.330	.406	.623	355	65	117	37	5	19	86	41	86	1	1

Pos	Pitcher, Team (Org)	League	W	L	ERA	G	GS	SV	IP	H	HR	BB	SO	G/F	WHIP	AVG
SP	Matt Barnes, Salem (Red Sox)	CAR	5	5	3.58	20	20	0	93	85	6	25	91	1.00	1.18	.243
SP	Cody Buckel, Myrtle Beach (Rangers)	CAR	5	3	1.31	13	13	0	76	49	2	25	91	1.61	0.98	.183
SP	* Adam Morgan, Clearwater (Phillies)	FSL	4	10	3.29	21	20	0	123	103	7	28	140	0.94	1.07	.224
SP	Yordano Ventura, Wilmington (Royals)	CAR	3	5	3.30	16	16	0	76	66	7	28	98	0.87	1.23	.225
RP	Mark Montgomery, Tampa (Yankees)	FSL	4	1	1.34	31	0	14	40	23	0	16	61	1.71	0.97	.163

Player of the Year: Christian Yelich, Jupiter (Marlins). **Pitcher of the Year:** Cody Buckel, Myrtle Beach (Rangers).
Manager of the Year: Tommy Thompson, Winston-Salem (White Sox).

Howie Kendrick, catchers Jeff Mathis and Bobby Wilson, and righthanders Bobby Cassevah, David Herndon, Bobby Mosebach and Darren O'Day. Of those, only Mathis was a premium draft pick (supplemental first round), and O'Day was a non-drafted free agent.

Mikulik did not have his contract renewed by the Rockies after he completed his 13th season—

LOW CLASS A

Pos	Player, Team (Org)	League	AVG	OBP	SLG	AB	R	H	2B	3B	HR	RBI	BB	SO	SB	CS
C	Will Swanner, Asheville (Rockies)	SAL	.302	.385	.529	325	60	98	24	1	16	61	38	101	3	2
1B	O'Koyea Dickson, Great Lakes (Dodgers)	MWL	.272	.366	.479	386	63	105	27	1	17	48	46	65	11	6
2B	Delino DeShields Jr., Lexington (Astros)	SAL	.298	.401	.436	440	96	131	23	4	10	52	70	108	84	14
3B	Miguel Sano, Beloit (Twins)	MWL	.258	.373	.521	457	75	118	28	4	28	100	80	144	8	3
SS	# Alen Hanson, West Virginia (Pirates)	SAL	.307	.379	.526	489	99	150	33	13	16	62	55	105	35	19
CF	* Gregory Polanco, West Virginia (Pirates)	SAL	.323	.386	.519	437	84	141	26	6	16	85	44	64	40	15
OF	Tyler Austin, Charleston (Yankees)	SAL	.320	.405	.598	266	69	85	22	5	14	54	38	68	17	2
OF	* Keury de la Cruz, Greenville (Red Sox)	SAL	.308	.352	.536	474	71	146	35	8	19	81	26	101	19	7
DH	* Matt Skole, Hagerstown (Nationals)	SAL	.286	.438	.574	343	73	98	18	0	27	92	94	116	10	0

Pos	Pitcher, Team (Org)	League	W	L	ERA	G	GS	SV	IP	H	HR	BB	SO	G/F	WHIP	AVG
SP	Clayton Blackburn, Augusta (Giants)	SAL	8	4	2.54	22	22	0	131	116	3	18	143	2.32	1.02	.230
SP	Jose Fernandez, Greensboro (Marlins)	SAL	7	0	1.59	14	14	0	79	50	2	18	99	0.98	0.86	.182
SP	* Justin Nicolino, Lansing (Blue Jays)	MWL	10	4	2.46	28	22	0	124	111	6	21	119	1.64	1.06	.237
SP	Noah Syndergaard, Lansing (Blue Jays)	MWL	8	5	2.60	27	19	1	104	80	3	31	122	2.16	1.07	.207
RP	Matt Stites, Fort Wayne (Padres)	MWL	2	0	0.74	42	0	13	48	25	4	3	60	0.56	0.58	.146

Player of the Year: Delino DeShields Jr., Lexington (Astros). **Pitcher of the Year:** Clayton Blackburn, Augusta (Giants).
Manager of the Year: Jose Valentin, Fort Wayne (Padres).

SHORT-SEASON

Pos	Player, Team (Org)	League	AVG	OBP	SLG	AB	R	H	2B	3B	HR	RBI	BB	SO	SB	CS
C	Mike Zunino, Everett (Mariners)	NWL	.373	.474	.736	110	29	41	10	0	10	35	18	26	1	0
1B	* Dan Vogelbach, Boise (Cubs)	NWL	.322	.423	.608	143	23	46	9	1	10	31	23	34	0	1
2B	Gioskar Amaya, Boise (Cubs)	NWL	.298	.381	.496	272	61	81	6	12	8	33	33	65	15	5
3B	Patrick Kivlehan, Everett (Mariners)	NWL	.301	.373	.511	282	46	85	17	3	12	52	19	93	14	1
SS	# Roman Quinn, Williamsport (Phillies)	NYP	.281	.370	.408	267	56	75	9	11	1	23	28	61	30	6
CF	* Andrew Aplin, Tri-City (Astros)	NYP	.348	.441	.537	164	38	57	9	5	4	25	24	22	20	7
OF	Jesus Solorzano, Jamestown (Marlins)	NYP	.314	.374	.519	210	36	66	13	3	8	27	17	49	7	6
OF	* Preston Tucker, Tri-City (Astros)	NYP	.321	.390	.509	165	32	53	7	0	8	38	18	16	1	2
DH	* Saxon Butler, Staten Island (Yankees)	NYP	.296	.370	.620	142	29	42	14	1	10	36	14	32	0	0

Pos	Pitcher, Team (Org)	League	W	L	ERA	G	GS	SV	IP	H	HR	BB	SO	G/F	WHIP	AVG
SP	Jeff Ames, Hudson Valley (Rays)	NYP	6	1	2.10	14	13	0	64	44	1	20	70	0.60	0.99	.191
SP	Taylor Cole, Vancouver (Blue Jays)	NWL	6	0	0.81	12	11	0	66	36	0	17	57	1.13	0.80	.161
SP	Taylor Guerrieri, Hudson Valley (Rays)	NYP	1	2	0.87	12	12	0	52	35	0	5	45	2.76	0.77	.185
SP	Luis Mateo, Brooklyn (Mets)	NYP	4	5	2.45	12	12	0	73	57	2	9	85	1.05	0.90	.209
RP	Robert Benincasa, Auburn (Nationals)	NYP	2	0	3.09	16	0	3	23	27	0	3	32	2.00	1.29	.276

Player of the Year: Mike Zunino, Everett (Mariners). **Pitcher of the Year:** Taylor Guerrieri, Hudson Valley (Rays).
Manager of the Year: Jared Sandberg, Hudson Valley (Rays).

ROOKIE

Pos	Player, Team (Org)	League	AVG	OBP	SLG	AB	R	H	2B	3B	HR	RBI	BB	SO	SB	CS
C	Clint Coulter, AZL Brewers	AZL	.302	.439	.444	169	37	51	3	3	5	33	37	40	3	5
1B	* Dan Vogelbach, AZL Cubs	AZL	.324	.391	.686	102	16	33	12	2	7	31	12	14	1	0
2B	Dilson Herrera, GCL Pirates	GCL	.281	.341	.482	199	41	56	11	4	7	28	18	41	11	4
3B	* Joey Gallo, AZL Rangers	AZL	.293	.435	.733	150	44	44	10	1	18	43	37	52	5	0
SS	Addison Russell, AZL Athletics	AZL	.415	.488	.717	106	29	44	4	5	4	29	14	23	9	1
CF	* David Dahl, Grand Junction (Rockies)	PIO	.379	.423	.625	280	62	106	22	10	9	57	21	42	12	7
OF	Lewis Brinson, AZL Rangers	AZL	.283	.345	.523	237	54	67	22	7	7	42	21	74	14	2
OF	* Max Kepler, Elizabethton (Twins)	APP	.297	.387	.539	232	40	69	16	5	10	49	27	33	7	0
DH	Dorssys Paulino, AZL Indians	AZL	.355	.404	.610	172	42	61	14	6	6	30	15	31	9	1

Pos	Pitcher, Team (Org)	League	W	L	ERA	G	GS	SV	IP	H	HR	BB	SO	G/F	WHIP	AVG
SP	* Tony Cingrani, Billings (Reds)	PIO	3	2	1.75	13	13	0	51	35	1	6	80	1.30	0.80	.190
SP	J.R. Graham, Danville (Braves)	APP	5	2	1.72	13	8	0	58	52	0	13	52	2.30	1.13	.245
SP	Tyrell Jenkins, Johnson City (Cardinals)	APP	4	2	3.86	11	11	0	56	63	3	13	55	1.83	1.36	.296
SP	* Scott Snodgress, Great Falls (White Sox)	PIO	3	3	3.34	16	12	0	59	61	5	17	68	1.55	1.31	.262
RP	Edwin Carl, Idaho Falls (Royals)	PIO	3	1	1.36	21	0	5	33	17	0	3	71	2.00	0.61	.145

Player of the Year: Eddie Rosario, Elizabethton (Twins). **Pitcher of the Year:** Tony Cingrani, Billings (Reds).
Manager of the Year: Dennis Holmberg, Bluefield (Blue Jays).

and arguably his best—managing the low Class A Asheville Tourists (South Atlantic). Mikulik was named SAL manager of the year in 2012 for the fourth time in his career after guiding the Tourists to their first league championship since 1984. He was inducted into the league's hall of fame in 2010 and had a career record of 938-860 (.522) in Asheville.

MINOR LEAGUES

Trevor Bauer helped Triple-A Reno claim the Pacific Coast League crown

BILL MITCHELL

Double-A Reading slugger Darin Ruf topped the minors with 38 home runs

ANDREW WOOLLEY

FIRST TEAM

Pos	Player, Level (Organization)	Age	AVG	OBP	SLG	G	AB	R	H	2B	3B	HR	RBI	BB	SO	SB
C	Gary Sanchez, LoA/HiA (Yankees)	19	.290	.344	.485	116	435	65	126	29	1	18	85	32	106	15
1B	* Jonathan Singleton, AA (Astros)	20	.284	.396	.497	131	461	94	131	27	4	21	79	88	131	7
2B	Delino DeShields Jr., LoA/HiA (Astros)	20	.287	.389	.428	135	537	113	154	24	8	12	61	83	131	101
3B	Mike Olt, AA (Rangers)	24	.288	.398	.579	95	354	65	102	17	1	28	82	61	101	4
SS	# Jurickson Profar, AA (Rangers)	19	.281	.368	.452	126	480	76	135	26	7	14	62	66	79	16
CF	* Adam Eaton, AAA (Diamondbacks)	23	.375	.456	.523	130	528	130	198	47	5	7	48	59	76	44
OF	Wil Myers, AAA/AA (Royals)	21	.314	.387	.600	134	522	98	164	26	6	37	109	61	140	6
OF	* Oscar Taveras, AA (Cardinals)	20	.321	.380	.572	124	477	83	153	37	7	23	94	42	56	10
DH	# Billy Hamilton, HiA/AA (Reds)	21	.311	.410	.420	132	512	112	159	22	14	2	45	86	113	155

Pos	Pitcher, Level (Organization)	Age	W	L	ERA	G	GS	SV	IP	H	HR	BB	SO	G/F	AVG	WHIP
SP	Trevor Bauer, AAA/AA (Diamondbacks)	21	12	2	2.42	22	22	0	130	107	9	61	157	1.23	.223	1.29
SP	Dylan Bundy, HiA/LoA/AA (Orioles)	19	9	3	2.08	23	23	0	104	67	6	28	119	0.89	.186	0.92
SP	* Tony Cingrani, AA/HiA (Reds)	23	10	4	1.73	26	25	0	146	98	9	52	172	0.99	.191	1.03
SP	Jose Fernandez, LoA/HiA (Marlins)	20	14	1	1.75	25	25	0	134	89	2	35	158	0.98	.191	0.93
SP	Dan Straily, AA/AAA (Athletics)	23	9	7	2.78	25	25	0	152	110	9	42	190	1.02	.202	1.00
RP	Carter Capps, AA/AAA (Mariners)	22	2	3	1.23	39	0	19	51	40	2	12	75	0.72	.207	1.01

SECOND TEAM

Pos	Player, Level (Organization)	Age	AVG	OBP	SLG	G	AB	R	H	2B	3B	HR	RBI	BB	SO	SB
C	Will Swanner, LoA (Rockies)	20	.302	.385	.529	88	325	60	98	24	1	16	61	38	101	3
1B	Darin Ruf, AA (Phillies)	26	.317	.408	.620	139	489	93	155	32	1	38	104	65	102	2
2B	Stefen Romero, HiA/AA (Mariners)	23	.352	.391	.599	116	474	85	167	34	7	23	101	27	72	12
3B	Miguel Sano, LoA (Twins)	19	.258	.373	.521	129	457	75	118	28	4	28	100	80	144	9
SS	Xander Bogaerts, HiA/AA (Red Sox)	19	.307	.373	.523	127	476	71	146	37	3	20	81	44	106	5
CF	* Jackie Bradley, HiA/AA (Red Sox)	22	.315	.430	.482	128	463	90	146	42	4	9	63	87	89	24
OF	Kyle Parker, HiA (Rockies)	22	.308	.415	.562	102	390	86	120	18	6	23	73	66	88	1
OF	* Christian Yelich, HiA (Marlins)	20	.330	.404	.519	106	397	76	131	29	5	12	48	49	85	20
DH	* Oswaldo Arcia, AA/HiA (Twins)	21	.320	.388	.539	124	469	76	150	36	8	17	98	51	107	4

Pos	Pitcher, Level (Organization)	Age	W	L	ERA	G	GS	SV	IP	H	HR	BB	SO	G/F	AVG	WHIP
SP	Matt Barnes, HiA/LoA (Red Sox)	22	7	5	2.86	25	25	0	120	97	6	29	133	1.14	.225	1.05
SP	Clayton Blackburn, LoA (Giants)	19	8	4	2.54	22	22	0	131	116	3	18	143	2.32	.232	1.02
SP	Cody Buckel, HiA/AA (Rangers)	20	10	8	2.49	26	23	0	145	105	9	48	159	1.15	.206	1.06
SP	* Adam Morgan, HiA/AA (Phillies)	22	8	11	3.35	27	26	0	159	137	9	39	169	0.91	.235	1.11
SP	Zack Wheeler, AA/AAA (Mets)	22	12	8	3.26	25	25	0	149	115	4	59	148	1.20	.221	1.17
RP	Bruce Rondon, HiA/AA/AAA (Tigers)	21	2	1	1.53	52	0	29	53	32	3	26	66	1.57	.172	1.09

Springfield rallies to a title

BY KARY BOOHER

It was mid-November 2011—just weeks after the surprise retirement of Tony La Russa began to be felt in the high minors—when the Double-A Springfield Cardinals called for a news conference to introduce their new manager.

Nobody expected a curveball.

Into the room and, thus, into the managerial role walked Mike Shildt, promoted all the way from the Rookie-level Appalachian League, where he was fresh off winning back-to-back league titles for Johnson City. But he had never played in the minor leagues, nor had he ever coached for a full-season club.

"I remember everybody's reaction was, 'Who is this guy?'," Shildt said before breaking into a laugh.

By year's end, no one had to ask. Not after Shildt, 43, led Springfield to a club-record 77 wins and to its first Texas League pennant.

Second baseman Kolten Wong (2011 first round), righthander Trevor Rosenthal and a then-19-year-old Oscar Taveras jumped straight from low Class A Quad Cities out of spring training and then played starring roles. Taveras won his second consecutive batting title, and Rosenthal reached St. Louis in July. Wong batted .287/.348/.405.

But the storylines also included the key additions of three seasoned minor leaguers in May and June, a steady bullpen that supported a rotation whose names were completely different in mid-July than on Opening Day, and the late-season arrival of first-round pick Michael Wacha—a Texas A&M stalwart who reached Double-A just 66 days after signing.

By the time Springfield blitzed Frisco in the championship series in four games—even receiving a surprise clubhouse visit from La Russa after a dramatic Game Two victory—one story had long been forgotten.

That is, a 10-game losing streak in April.

"That was very trying. I had never experienced anything close to that," Shildt said, noting that he received encouraging calls from the front office and fellow coaches in the system. "That meant a lot for them to say, 'Hey, just keep plugging.' It also reinforced that it's not about the winning and losing.

"We're obviously keeping score and competitive. But through adversity comes growth, and we were able to grow during those 10 games."

Within the losing streak, Springfield suffered six one-run losses that could have torpedoed the youngest team in the league (with an average age of 23). However, the narrative slowly changed over the next nine weeks.

Kolten Wong

In May and June, the additions of infielder Jermaine Curtis, outfielder Chris Swauger (who would blast three postseason homers) and outfielder/first baseman Jamie Romak from Triple-A Memphis proved valuable. Wong moved fully into the leadoff role, while Curtis and Romak flanked Taveras in a lineup that often alternated between lefthanded and righthanded hitters throughout. Springfield finished with a .268 average, tied with Corpus Christi (Astros) atop the league—the second year in a row the Cardinals led the circuit with batting coach Phillip Wellman. Curtis not only led the league in on-base percentage (.416) but almost wrestled away the batting title, hitting .313 to Taveras' .321.

"We knew we were dealing with a ton of inexperience going into the season," Shildt said. "It was an adjustment period for all of us at the beginning, but it was a real character-builder."

PREVIOUS 10 WINNERS

2002: Akron/Eastern (Indians)
2003: Sacramento/Pacific Coast (Athletics)
2004: Lancaster/California (Diamondbacks)
2005: Jacksonville/Southern (Dodgers)
2006: Tucson/Pacific Coast (Diamondbacks)
2007: San Antonio/Texas (Padres)
2008: Frisco/Texas (Rangers)
2009: Akron/Eastern (Indians)
2010: Northwest Arkansas/Texas (Royals)
2011: Mobile BayBears/Southern (Diamondbacks)
Full list: BaseballAmerica.com/awards

MINOR LEAGUES

BY JIM CALLIS

KANSAS CITY, MO.

Advance billing for the Futures Game centered around pitching. Thirteen of the 20 hurlers selected were first- or supplemental first-round draft picks, including all 10 members of the pitching staff.

But it was the hitters who took center stage. The United States won 17-5, scoring the most runs in the event's 14-year history. The U.S. offense tallied nine runs in the sixth inning, matching the previous single-game record. Thirteen different U.S. players collected hits in a 17-hit attack, with DH Nick Castellanos (Tigers) earning MVP honors by going 3-for-4 with a walk. He capped the sixth-inning outburst with a three-run homer off Julio Rodriguez (Phillies).

Castellanos was visibly moved after the game when the Baseball of Hall of Fame requested his bat for the museum.

"That's probably the coolest thing ever," Castellanos said. "That's right up there with performing in this game. I don't think I've even taken it in yet that the bat I used today is going to Cooperstown."

The World took an early 3-0 lead on a solo homer in the first from Jurickson Profar (Rangers) off Jake Odorizzi (Royals), and a two-run, opposite-field blast in the second from Jae-Hoon Ha (Cubs) off 2011 No. 1 overall pick Gerrit Cole (Pirates) in the second. The World didn't let up in the third against last year's No. 2 overall pick, Danny Hultzen (Mariners), putting runners on the corners with leadoff singles from Jean Segura (Angels) and Profar.

Oscar Taveras (Cardinals) then scorched a shot to deep center field, where Anthony Gose (Blue Jays) showed off his plus-plus speed by running the ball down and making a diving catch, turning what looked like a sure extra-base hit into merely a sacrifice fly. Hultzen escaped without further damage.

In the bottom half, the U.S. got on the scoreboard when Billy Hamilton (Reds) provided a two-run triple off Chris Reed (Dodgers). Kolten Wong (Cardinals) followed with a comebacker to Reed, who looked Hamilton back to third base but rushed his throw to first, apparently worried that the minors' fastest player would try to score. Wong raced to third on the error and scored on a groundout by Wil Myers (Royals).

The U.S. took the lead for good on an RBI double from Tommy Joseph (Giants) in the fourth,

scoring an additional run on the play thanks to an errant throw by Tavares. It salted the game away with its sixth-inning barrage, doing most of the damage against Ariel Pena (Angels).

Though the pitchers didn't dominate as expected, several did stand out. Yordano Ventura (Royals) hit 100 mph three times and needed just 11 pitches to work a perfect first inning. Cole also reached triple digits. Bruce Rondon (Tigers) won radar-gun honors by throwing 102 mph on his first pitch in the eighth and then firing three consecutive 101-mph fastballs. The U.S. pitching staff settled down after Dylan Bundy (Orioles) got through a dicey fourth inning without allowing a run despite surrendering three hits.

FUTURES GAME BOX SCORE

JULY 8
UNITED STATES 17, WORLD 5

WORLD	AB	R	H	BI	U.S.	AB	R	H	BI
Segura, 2b	3	1	2	0	Hamilton, ss	3	1	1	2
a-Pan, 2b	2	0	0	0	a-Machado	3	1	1	2
Profar, ss	3	1	2	1	Wong, 2b	2	1	0	0
b-Lindor, ss	1	0	1	0	b-Gennett, 2b	3	2	1	0
Taveras, rf-cf	3	0	1	1	Myers, rf-cf	4	1	2	3
Marte, lf	3	0	0	0	Olt, 3b-1b	5	1	1	1
c-Liriano	1	0	0	0	Singleton, 1b-lf	4	2	3	1
Bogaerts, dh	4	0	1	0	Choice, lf	2	0	0	0
Flores, 3b	2	0	0	0	c-Arenado, 3b	3	1	1	0
d-Sanchez, 3b	2	1	1	0	Castellanos, dh	4	3	3	3
Aguilar, 1b	3	1	1	0	Joseph, c	1	1	1	1
Ha, cf	2	1	2	2	e-Brantly, c	3	1	1	1
e-Arcia, rf	2	0	1	1	Gose, cf	1	1	1	0
Bethancourt, c	3	0	0	0	d-Yelich, rf	2	1	1	0
f-Solis, c	1	0	0	0					
Totals	**34**	**5**	**12**	**5**	**Totals**	**40**	**17**	**17**	**14**

```
WORLD    121 001 000 — 5
U.S.     004 209 20X — 17
```

LOB: World 5, U.S. 6. **2B:** Sanchez, Arcia, Joseph, Brantly, Machado, Olt, Gennett. **3B:** Hamilton. **HR:** Profar, Ha, Castellanos. **GIDP:** Hamilton. **SB:** None. **CS:** Taveras, Singleton.

WORLD	IP	H	R	ER	BB	SO	U.S.	IP	H	R	ER	BB	SO
Ventura	1	0	0	0	0	0	Odorizzi	1	1	1	1	0	1
Fernandez	1	1	0	0	0	2	Cole	1	1	2	2	1	2
Reed	1	2	4	2	1	1	Hultzen	1	3	1	1	0	1
Rivero	1	1	2	1	3	0	Bundy	1	3	0	0	0	0
Romero	1	2	0	0	0	0	Skaggs	1	1	0	0	0	1
Pena	$\frac{1}{3}$	7	8	8	1	0	Taillon	1	2	1	1	0	0
Rodriguez	1	3	3	2	1	0	Walker	1	1	0	0	0	1
Lotzkar	1	1	0	0	0	0	Meyer	$\frac{2}{3}$	0	0	0	0	1
Rondon	$\frac{2}{3}$	0	0	0	0	0	Wheeler	$\frac{2}{3}$	0	0	0	0	0
							Barnes	$\frac{2}{3}$	0	0	0	0	0
Totals	**8**	**17**	**17**	**13**	**6**	**3**	**Totals**	**9**	**12**	**5**	**5**	**1**	**7**

Umpires: HP—Kolin Kline. 1B—Tom Woodring. 2B—Nick Bailey. 3B—Spencer Flynn.

TRIPLE-A: The Pacific Coast League has a well-deserved reputation as a hitter's paradise, but league pitchers served notice in front of 18,035 at Buffalo's Coca-Cola Field that they can control a game as well. Eleven PCL hurlers combined to shut out the host International League 3-0 in a game in which the first two batters of the game came around to score.

Omaha left fielder Wil Myers (Royals) finished with a pair of hits four days after tallying three RBIs in the Futures Game in Kansas City. Buffalo Bisons ace Matt Harvey (Mets) earned the IL's star of stars award for tossing two scoreless innings in front of the hometown crowd. Myers earned the same honor for the PCL, which snapped a three-game losing streak in the event.

A pair of Reno Aces kicked off the excitement, as center fielder Adam Eaton led off the game with a single into short left-center field. Second baseman Jake Elmore then drilled a grounder through the hole into shallow left, moving Eaton to third. That hustle play paid off one out later when Oklahoma City first baseman Mike Hessman scored him on a sacrifice fly.

Adam Eaton

EASTERN LEAGUE: Binghamton first baseman Eric Campbell delivered the game-winning hit in the bottom of the ninth by stroking a two-out single to right field to score Reading shortstop Troy Hanzawa and lift the Eastern Division to a 5-4 victory before 9,477 at FirstEnergy Stadium in Reading, Pa. East DH Mike McDade of New Hampshire went 4-for-4 with two RBIs. Erie first baseman Jordan Lennerton went 2-for-3 and drove in three runs for the West. His sacrifice in the sixth tied the score at four, just as his two-run homer in the fourth made it 3-3.

SOUTHERN LEAGUE: Diamondbacks right fielder Alfredo Marte added to a breakout campaign by earning MVP honors after he went 2-for-2 with a double, an RBI and a run scored in the South Division's 6-2 win against the North at Smokies Park in Knoxville, Tenn. The victory was the South's first in the all-star game in the past eight seasons.

TEXAS LEAGUE: Springfield center fielder Oscar Taveras went 3-for-4 with a home run and two RBIs to earn MVP honors as the North topped the South 3-1 at Tulsa's ONEOK Field. Drillers third baseman Nolan Arenado (Rockies) added an RBI single and eight North pitchers combined for a two-hitter.

CALIFORNIA/CAROLINA LEAGUE: The Carolina League overwhelmed the Cal League as a core of less-heralded prospects turned in elite performances en route to a 9-1 rout at BB&T Ballpark in Winston-Salem, N.C. Salem first baseman Travis Shaw (Red Sox) was named the Carolina League's star of the game for going 1-for-2 with two runs scored and two RBIs. He struck a massive two-run home run that landed high up on the walkway beyond the right-field fence.

FLORIDA STATE LEAGUE: The South Division ousted their North counterparts by scoring three runs in both the seventh and eighth innings to win 6-3 at Charlotte Sports Park. St. Lucie third baseman Wilmer Flores (Mets) went 3-for-4 with a walk, a run scored and three RBIs to win MVP honors for the game. He drove in one run on a single up the middle in the seventh, and then knocked home two on a single in the eighth against Lakeland righthander Bruce Rondon.

MIDWEST LEAGUE: The East Division scored 13 runs in the first two innings and went on to rout the West 18-2 at Kane County's Fifth Third Bank Ballpark. The second hitter of the game, South Bend second baseman Gerson Montilla (Diamondbacks), hit a solo home run off West starter Drew Granier (Athletics). Two hitters later, Great Lakes first baseman O'Koyea Dickson (Dodgers) pulled a two-run blast that went deep beyond the left-field fence. The East scored five runs in the first and then tallied eight times in the second.

SOUTH ATLANTIC LEAGUE: Delmarva first baseman Nicky Delmonico went 2-for-4 with a double and two runs scored as the game's MVP led the North to a 3-2 victory over the South at Charleston's Riley Park.

DEPARTMENT LEADERS

(*Full-season teams only)

TEAM

WINS
Indianapolis (International)	89
Asheville (South Atlantic)	88
Winston-Salem (Carolina)	87
Sacramento (Pacific Coast)	86
Scranton/Wilkes-Barre (International)	84

LONGEST WINNING STREAK*
Rome (South Atlantic)	13
Bakersfield (California)	11
6 teams tied at	10

LOSSES
Louisville (International)	93
Tucson (Pacific Coast)	88
Iowa (Pacific Coast)	87
Cedar Rapids (Midwest)	86
Delmarva (South Atlantic)	86

LONGEST LOSING STREAK*
Stockton (California)	16
Gwinnett (International)	15
Durham (International)	13
Rome (South Atlantic)	13
Delmarva (South Atlantic)	12

BATTING AVERAGE*
High Desert (California)	.303
Las Vegas (Pacific Coast)	.298
Albuquerque (Pacific Coast)	.298
Reno (Pacific Coast)	.297
Colorado Springs (Pacific Coast)	.291

RUNS
High Desert (California)	951
Reno (Pacific Coast)	856
Lancaster (California)	843
Albuquerque (Pacific Coast)	842
Sacramento (Pacific Coast)	833

HOME RUNS
High Desert (California)	189
Sacramento (Pacific Coast)	171
Trenton (Eastern)	162
Stockton (California)	160
Lancaster (California)	158

STOLEN BASES
Bakersfield (California)	266
Lake Elsinore (California)	242
Fort Wayne (Midwest)	206
Daytona (Florida State)	201
Augusta (South Atlantic)	199

EARNED RUN AVERAGE*
Akron (Eastern)	3.30
Charlotte (International)	3.15
Indianapolis (International)	3.15
Myrtle Beach (Carolina)	3.28
Savannah (South Atlantic)	3.33

STRIKEOUTS
Visalia (California)	1291
Pensacola (Southern)	1190
Chattanooga (South Atlantic)	1177
Stockton (California)	1169
Clearwater (Florida State)	1161

INDIVIDUAL BATTING

BATTING AVERAGE*
Adam Eaton (Mobile/Reno)	.375
Mike O'Neill (Palm Beach/Springfield)	.359
Stefen Romero (High Desert/Jackson)	.352
Ryan Wheeler (Reno)	.351
Matt McBride (Colorado Springs)	.344

RUNS
Adam Eaton (Mobile/Reno)	130
Delino DeShields Jr. (Lexington/Lancaster)	113
Billy Hamilton (Bakersfield/Pensacola)	112
Brad Miller (High Desert/Jackson)	110
James Jones (High Desert)	109
George Springer (Lancaster/Corpus Christi)	109

HITS
Adam Eaton (Mobile/Reno)	198
Brad Miller (High Desert/Jackson)	186
Nick Castellanos (Lakeland/Erie)	172
Carlos Sanchez (Winston-Salem/Birmingham/Charlotte)	169
Cody Asche (Clearwater/Reading)	168

TOP HITTING STREAKS
Jake Elmore (Reno)	31
Tommy Medica (Lake Elsinore)	29
Jurickson Profar (Frisco)	29
David Dahl (Grand Junction)	27
Josmar Cordero (DSL Dodgers)	26

MOST HITS (ONE GAME)
Michael Freeman (Visalia)	7
5 players tied at	6

TOTAL BASES
Wil Myers (Northwest Arkansas/Omaha)	313
Darin Ruf (Reading)	303
Hunter Morris (Huntsville)	294
Brad Miller (High Desert/Jackson)	285
Stefen Romero (High Desert/Jackson)	284

EXTRA-BASE HITS
Hunter Morris (Huntsville)	74
Darin Ruf (Reading)	71
Corey Dickerson (Modesto/Tulsa)	69
Wil Myers (Northwest Arkansas/Omaha)	69
Trevor Story (Asheville)	67
Oscar Taveras (Springfield)	67

DOUBLES
Adam Eaton (Mobile/Reno)	47
Travis Shaw (Salem/Portland)	44
Taylor Harbin (Reno)	43
K.C. Hobson (Lansing)	43
Jim Murphy (Clearwater)	43
Trevor Story (Asheville)	43

TRIPLES
Leon Landry (Rancho Cucamonga/High Desert)	18
Engel Beltre (Frisco)	17
Billy Hamilton (Bakersfield/Pensacola)	14
Rubi Silva (Daytona/Tennessee)	14
Alen Hanson (West Virginia)	13
Timmy Lopes (AZL Mariners/High Desert)	13
Starling Marte (Indianapolis/State College)	13
Jared Mitchell (Birmingham/Charlotte)	13

HOME RUNS
Darin Ruf (Reading)	38
Wil Myers (Northwest Arkansas/Omaha)	37
Mike Hessman (Oklahoma City)	35
Adam Duvall (San Jose)	30
Jedd Gyorko (San Antonio/Tucson)	30

RUNS BATTED IN
C.J. Cron (Inland Empire)	123
Hunter Morris (Huntsville)	113
Justin Bour (Tennessee)	110
Wil Myers (Northwest Arkansas/Omaha)	109
Erik Castro (Lancaster)	108
Zach Johnson (Lexington)	108

MOST RBIS (ONE GAME)
Jared Goedert (Columbus)	9
Steven Souza (Hagerstown)	9
13 players tied at	8

WALKS
Conner Crumbliss (Midland)	120
Matt Skole (Hagerstown/Potomac)	99
Brenden Webb (Delmarva/Frederick)	98
Jack Cust (Scranton/Wilkes-Barre/Las Vegas)	97
Dan Johnson (Charlotte)	94

STRIKEOUTS
Telvin Nash (Lancaster)	198
Dusty Coleman (Midland)	182
Jared Mitchell (Birmingham/Charlotte)	179
James Baldwin (Great Lakes)	177
Joe Dunigan (Jackson)	175
Jarrett Parker (San Jose)	175

STOLEN BASES
Billy Hamilton (Bakersfield/Pensacola)	155
Delino DeShields Jr. (Lexington/Lancaster)	101
Rico Noel (Lake Elsinore)	90
Theo Bowe (Dayton/Bakersfield)	70
Keenyn Walker (Kannapolis/Winston-Salem)	56

CAUGHT STEALING
Billy Hamilton (Bakersfield/Pensacola)	37
Theo Bowe (Dayton/Bakersfield)	29
Rico Noel (Lake Elsinore)	23
John Andreoli (Daytona)	20
Delino DeShields Jr. (Lexington/Lancaster)	19
Alen Hanson (West Virginia)	19
Reggie Keen (Brevard County)	19

ON BASE PERCENTAGE*
Mike O'Neill (Palm Beach/Springfield)	.458
Adam Eaton (Mobile/Reno)	.456
Jake Elmore (Reno)	.442
Billy Burns (Hagerstown)	.432
Jackie Bradley (Salem/Portland)	.430

SLUGGING PERCENTAGE*
Tommy Medica (Lake Elsinore)	.623
Darin Ruf (Reading)	.620
Wil Myers (Northwest Arkansas/Omaha)	.600
Stefen Romero (High Desert/Jackson)	.599
Andrew Brown (Colorado Springs)	.597

ON BASE PLUS SLUGGING (OPS)*
Tommy Medica (Lake Elsinore)	1.029
Darin Ruf (Reading)	1.028
Alex Castellanos (Albuquerque)	1.010
Stefen Romero (High Desert/Jackson)	.991
Wil Myers (Northwest Arkansas/Omaha)	.987

HIT BY PITCH
Matt Duffy (Lexington)	41
Cyle Hankerd (Kannapolis/Winston-Salem)	28
Nate Roberts (Beloit)	23
Robby Price (Charlotte/Durham)	22
Brandon Macias (Wisconsin)	21
Josh Parr (South Bend/Yakima)	21
Brady Shoemaker (Winston-Salem/Birmingham)	21
Christian Villanueva (Myrtle Beach/Daytona)	21

SACRIFICE BUNTS
Anthony Phillips (Jackson/Clinton)	22
Wilson Soriano (DSL Rockies)	21
Reggie Keen (Brevard County)	20
Nick Buss (Chattanooga)	19
Ryan Goins (New Hampshire)	19

SACRIFICE FLIES
Zach Johnson (Lexington)	14
Jackie Bradley (Salem/Portland)	11
Daniel Mayora (Richmond)	11
Darin Ruf (Reading)	11
Max Stassi (Stockton)	11
Andy Workman (Cedar Rapids)	11

BATTING AVERAGE*

CATCHERS
Austin Barnes (Greensboro)	.318
John Hicks (High Desert)	.312
Camden Maron (Savannah)	.300
Max Ramirez (Omaha)	.300
Rob Brantly (Erie/Toledo/New Orleans)	.298

FIRST BASEMEN
Matt McBride (Colorado Springs)	.344
Miles Head (Stockton/Midland)	.333
Tommy Medica (Lake Elsinore)	.330
Dean Green (West Michigan/Lakeland)	.322
Chris Duffy (Lakewood/Clearwater)	.322

SECOND BASEMEN
Brock Holt (Altoona/Indianapolis)	.344
Jake Elmore (Reno)	.344
Brock Bond (Fresno)	.332
Irving Falu (Omaha)	.329
Johnny Giavotella (Omaha)	.323

THIRD BASEMEN
Stefen Romero (High Desert/Jackson)	.352
Ryan Wheeler (Reno)	.351
Mike Cervenak (New Orleans)	.340
Ty Kelly (Norfolk/Frederick/Bowie)	.327
Cody Asche (Clearwater/Reading)	.324

SHORTSTOPS
Brad Miller (High Desert/Jackson)	.334
T.J. Rivera (Savannah/St. Lucie)	.320
Angel Sanchez (Oklahoma City)	.320

Adeiny Hechavarria (Las Vegas)	.312
Billy Hamilton (Bakersfield/Pensacola)	.311

OUTFIELDERS

Adam Eaton (Mobile/Reno)	.375
Mike O'Neill (Palm Beach/Springfield)	.359
Leon Landry (Rancho Cucamonga/High Desert)	.341
Brent Keys (Greensboro)	.335
Christian Yelich (Jupiter)	.330

DESIGNATED HITTERS

Colin Walsh (Quad Cities)	.314
Luis Jimenez (Tacoma)	.310
Jermaine Curtis (Memphis/Springfield)	.310
Erik Castro (Lancaster)	.285
Reynaldo Rodriguez (Portland/Pawtucket)	.249

INDIVIDUAL PITCHING

EARNED RUN AVERAGE*

Tony Cingrani (Bakersfield/Pensacola)	1.73
Jose Fernandez (Greensboro/Jupiter)	1.75
Hiram Burgos (Brevard County/Huntsville/Nashville)	1.95
Nate Karns (Hagerstown/Potomac)	2.17
Chris Heston (Richmond)	2.24

WORST ERA*

Max Russell (Inland Empire)	7.11
Shawn Teufel (Toledo/Lakeland/West Michigan)	6.62
Angel Sanchez (Rancho Cucamonga)	6.58
Dellin Betances (Scranton/Wilkes-Barre/Trenton)	6.44
Noel Arguelles (Northwest Arkansas)	6.41

Jose Fernandez

BRIAN WESTERHOLT

WINS

Christian Bergman (Modesto)	16
T.J. McFarland (Akron/Columbus)	16
Zach Clark (Bowie/Norfolk)	15
Tyler Cloyd (Reading/Lehigh Valley)	15
Zach Duke (Syracuse)	15
Jake Odorizzi (Northwest Arkansas/Omaha)	15

LOSSES

Tanner Roark (Syracuse)	17
Seth McClung (Nashville/Iowa)	15
Deck McGuire (New Hampshire)	15
Noel Arguelles (Northwest Arkansas)	14
Fabio Castro (Sacramento/Midland)	14
Ryan Crowley (Inland Empire/Cedar Rapids)	14
Parker Frazier (Tulsa)	14
Pedro Villarreal (Pensacola/Louisville)	14

GAMES

Phil McCormick (San Jose)	61
Coty Woods (Tulsa/Colorado Springs)	61
Josh Sullivan (Tulsa)	60
Jerry Gil (Las Vegas)	58
Erik Hamren (San Antonio/Tucson)	58
Adam Reifer (Memphis)	58

GAMES STARTED

Barry Enright (Reno/Salt Lake)	29
Jake Petricka (Winston-Salem/Birmingham)	29
Rob Scahill (Colorado Springs)	29
Ross Seaton (Oklahoma City/Corpus Christi)	29
Matt Shoemaker (Salt Lake)	29

COMPLETE GAMES

Jose Alvarez (Jacksonville)	3
Anthony Fernandez (High Desert/Jackson)	3
Sean Gilmartin (Mississippi/Gwinnett)	3
Phil Irwin (Bradenton/Altoona/Indianapolis)	3
John Lannan (Syracuse)	3
Tyler Lyons (Springfield/Memphis)	3
Zack Von Rosenberg (West Virginia)	3
Adam Wilk (Toledo)	3

SHUTOUTS

Anthony Fernandez (High Desert/Jackson)	2
John Lannan (Syracuse)	2
Jordan Shipers (Clinton)	2
Zack Wheeler (Binghamton/Buffalo)	2
95 players tied at	1

SAVES

Danny Barnes (New Hampshire/Dunedin)	34
Ajay Meyer (Lansing)	33
Bruce Rondon (Lakeland/Erie/Toledo)	29
Josh Wall (Albuquerque)	28
Kevin Quackenbush (Lake Elsinore)	27
Jason Stoffel (Corpus Christi)	27
Coty Woods (Tulsa/Colorado Springs)	27

INNINGS PITCHED

Matt Shoemaker (Salt Lake)	176.2
David Holmberg (Visalia/Mobile)	173.1
Greg Smith (Arkansas/Salt Lake)	173.1
Hiram Burgos (Brevard County/Huntsville/Nashville)	171
Charlie Shirek (Charlotte)	170.1

WALKS

Dellin Betances (Scranton/Wilkes-Barre/Trenton)	99
Tyler Matzek (Modesto)	95
Andy Oliver (Toledo)	88
Alex Burgos (Lakeland)	88
Archie Bradley (South Bend)	84

STRIKEOUTS

Dan Straily (Midland/Sacramento)	190
Tony Cingrani (Bakersfield/Pensacola)	172
Adam Morgan (Clearwater/Reading)	169
Matt Magill (Chattanooga)	168
Drew Granier (Burlington)	167

HITS ALLOWED

Matt Shoemaker (Salt Lake)	229
Greg Reynolds (Round Rock)	208
Joe Martinez (Reno)	206
Josh Geer (Tucson/San Antonio)	205
Max Russell (Inland Empire)	200

HOME RUNS ALLOWED

Charles Brewer (Mobile/Reno)	28
Stalin Gerson (Dayton/Bakersfield)	27
Ray Hernandez (Visalia)	27
David Huff (Akron/Columbus)	27
Max Russell (Inland Empire)	26
Angel Sanchez (Rancho Cucamonga)	26

STRIKEOUTS PER NINE INNINGS (STARTERS)*

Andrew Chafin (Visalia)	11.30
Dan Straily (Midland/Sacramento)	11.25
Trevor Bauer (Mobile/Reno)	10.84
Jose Fernandez (Greensboro/Jupiter)	10.61
Shelby Miller (Memphis)	10.54

STRIKEOUTS PER NINE INNINGS (RELIEVERS)*

Rob Wort (Potomac)	15.09
John Cornely (Rome/Lynchburg)	14.42
Jack Leathersich (Savannah/St. Lucie)	14.13
Michael Olmsted (Salem/Portland)	13.96
Mark Montgomery (Tampa/Trenton)	13.85

OPPONENT BATTING AVERAGE (STARTERS)*

Archie Bradley (South Bend)	.181
Justin Wilson (Indianapolis)	.189
Jose Fernandez (Greensboro/Jupiter)	.191
Tony Cingrani (Bakersfield/Pensacola)	.192
Adys Portillo (Fort Wayne/San Antonio)	.193

OPPONENT BATTING AVERAGE (RELIEVERS)*

A.J. Ramos (Jacksonville)	.151
Mark Montgomery (Tampa/Trenton)	.157
Dane de la Rosa (Durham)	.158
Tom Kahnle (Tampa/Trenton)	.162
Santos Rodriguez (Birmingham/Charlotte)	.164

MOST STRIKEOUTS/ONE GAME

Chris Devenski (Lexington)	16
Tony Cingrani (Pensacola)	15
Isaac Silva (DSL Cardinals)	15
Dan Straily (Midland)	15
5 players tied at	14

WILD PITCHES

Jeff Gibbs (Yakima/AZL Diamondbacks)	28
Willy Paulino (Quad Cities/Johnson City)	25
Jairo Diaz (Cedar Rapids/Orem)	24
Kyle Blair (Lake County/Carolina)	22
Jose Encarnacion (DSL Mets 2/DSL Mets 1)	22
Jim Hoey (Las Vegas)	22

BALKS

Roenis Elias (High Desert)	8
David Goforth (Wisconsin)	8
Danny Rosenbaum (Harrisburg)	8
Malcom Diaz (AZL Padres)	7
Ramon Garcia (Toledo/Erie)	7

HIT BATTERS

Danny Winkler (Asheville)	22
Julio Rodriguez (Reading)	21
Michael Goodnight (Carolina)	19
Allen Webster (Chattanooga/Portland)	19
Brody Colvin (Clearwater/Reading)	18

INDIVIDUAL FIELDING

MOST ERRORS

Orlando Calixte (Kane County/Wilmington)	46
Franchy Cordero (DSL Padres)	44
Edward Salcedo (Lynchburg)	42
Miguel Sano (Beloit)	42
Odubel Herrera (Myrtle Beach)	41

MINOR LEAGUES

MINOR LEAGUES

	INTERNATIONAL LEAGUE	PACIFIC COAST LEAGUE	EASTERN LEAGUE	SOUTHERN LEAGUE	TEXAS LEAGUE	CALIFORNIA LEAGUE	CAROLINA LEAGUE	FLORIDA STATE LEAGUE	MIDWEST LEAGUE	SOUTH ATLANTIC LEAGUE
Best Batting Prospect	Starling Marte, Indianapolis	Anthony Rizzo, Iowa	Nick Castellanos, Erie	Hunter Morris, Huntsville	Oscar Taveras, Springfield	Miles Head, Stockton	Jackie Bradley, Salem	Nick Castellanos, Lakeland	Kevin Pillar, Lansing	Tyler Austin, Charleston
Best Power Prospect	Ernesto Mejia, Gwinnett	Wil Myers, Omaha	Cody Johnson, Trenton	Matt Davidson, Mobile	Mike Olt, Frisco	C.J. Cron, Inland Empire	Trayce Thompson, Winston-Salem	Marcell Ozuna, Jupiter	Miguel Sano, Beloit	Gary Sanchez, Charleston
Best Strike-Zone Judgment	Alex Hassan, Pawtucket	Jake Elmore, Reno	Robbie Grossman, Altoona	Tyler Saladino, Birmingham	Jermaine Curtis, Springfield	Brad Miller, High Desert	Jackie Bradley, Salem	Mike O'Neill, Palm Beach	Nick Martin, Quad Cities	Matt Skole, Hagerstown
Best Baserunner	Luis Durango, Gwinnett	Anthony Gose, Las Vegas	Abe Almonte, Trenton	Billy Hamilton, Pensacola	Jonathan Villar, Corpus Christi	Billy Hamilton, Bakersfield	Jackie Bradley, Salem	Alonzo Harris, St. Lucie	Jace Peterson, Fort Wayne	Delino DeShields Jr., Lexington
Fastest Baserunner	Luis Durango, Gwinnett	Adam Eaton, Reno	Gary Brown, Richmond	Billy Hamilton, Pensacola	Jean Segura, Arkansas	Billy Hamilton, Bakersfield	Nick Ahmed, Lynchburg	Matt Szczur, Daytona	James Baldwin III, Great Lakes	Delino DeShields Jr., Lexington
Best Pitching Prospect	Matt Harvey, Buffalo	Trevor Bauer, Reno	Zack Wheeler, Binghamton	Danny Hultzen, Jackson	Trevor Rosenthal, Springfield	Donn Roach, Lake Elsinore	Jameson Taillon, Bradenton	Jameson Taillon, Bradenton	Aaron Sanchez, Lansing	Dylan Bundy, Delmarva
Best Fastball	Jose Ortega, Toledo	Tanner Scheppers, Round Rock	Zack Wheeler, Binghamton	Carter Capps, Jackson	Carlos Martinez, Springfield	Tony Cingrani, Bakersfield	Dylan Bundy, Frederick	Gerrit Cole, Bradenton	Archie Bradley, South Bend	Dylan Bundy, Delmarva
Best Breaking Pitch	Corey Kluber, Columbus	Tyler Skaggs, Reno	Zack Wheeler, Binghamton	Tyler Skaggs, Mobile	Ariel Pena, Arkansas	Garrett Gould, Rancho Cucamonga	Cody Buckel, Myrtle Beach	Jameson Taillon, Bradenton	Archie Bradley, South Bend	Kyle Crick, Augusta
Best Changeup	Adam Wilk, Toledo	Cory Burns, Tucson	Brett Marshall, Trenton	Danny Hultzen, Jackson	Edwar Cabrera, Tulsa	Daniel Renken, Bakersfield	Kyle Hendricks, Myrtle Beach	Adam Morgan, Clearwater	Justin Nicolino, Lansing	Nick Tropeano, Lexington
Best Control	Tyler Cloyd, Lehigh Valley	Graham Godfrey, Sacramento	Chris Heston, Richmond	Sean Gilmartin, Mississippi	Dan Straily, Midland	Donn Roach, Lake Elsinore	Kyle Hendricks, Myrtle Beach	Seth Maness, Palm Beach	Trevor Miller, Clinton	Dylan Bundy, Delmarva
Best Reliever	Tim Wood, Indianapolis	Cory Burns, Tucson	Bruce Rondon, Erie	Carter Capps, Jackson	Sean Doolittle, Midland	Kevin Quackenbush, Lake Elsinore	Michael Olmsted, Salem	Bruce Rondon, Lakeland	Ajay Meyer, Lansing	Cody Hall, Augusta
Best Defensive Catcher	Ryan Lavarnway, Pawtucket	Tim Federowicz, Albuquerque	Roberto Perez, Akron	Christian Bethancourt, Mississippi	Audry Perez, Springfield	Tucker Barnhart, Bakersfield	Christian Vazquez, Salem	J.T. Realmuto, Jupiter	Austin Hedges, Fort Wayne	Cory Brownsten, Rome
Best Defensive First Baseman	Lars Anderson, Pawtucket	Efren Navarro, Salt Lake	Jordan Lennerton, Erie	Hunter Morris, Huntsville	Anthony Aliotti, Midland	Connor Powers, Lake Elsinore	Travis Shaw, Salem	Alex Dickerson, Bradenton	Jerrud Sabourin, Lake County	Zach Johnson, Lexington
Best Defensive Second Baseman	Pedro Ciriaco, Pawtucket	Charlie Culberson, Fresno/Colo. Springs	Cesar Hernandez, Reading	Scooter Gennett, Huntsville	Kolten Wong, Springfield	Cory Spangenberg, Lake Elsinore	Carlos Sanchez, Winston-Salem	Starlin Rodriguez, Palm Beach	Jose Ramirez, Lake County	Roughned Odor, Hickory
Best Defensive Third Baseman	Carlos Rivero, Syracuse	Matt Dominguez, New Orleans/OKC	Mark Sobolewski, New Hampshire	Joe Leonard, Mississippi	Nolan Arenado, Tulsa	C.J. Retherford, Rancho Cucamonga	Christian Villanueva, Myrtle Beach	Cody Asche, Clearwater	Kaleb Cowart, Cedar Rapids	Sam Mende, Asheville
Best Defensive Shortstop	Jose Iglesias, Pawtucket	Adeiny Hechavarria, Las Vegas	Manny Machado, Bowie	Didi Gregorius, Pensacola	Jurickson Profar, Frisco	Joe Panik, San Jose	Nick Ahmed, Lynchburg	Gift Ngoepe, Bradenton	Francisco Lindor, Lake County	Trevor Story, Asheville
Best Infield Arm	Pedro Florimon, Rochester	Adeiny Hechavarria, Las Vegas	Manny Machado, Bowie	Andrelton Simmons, Mississippi	Jonathan Villar, Corpus Christi	Chris Owings, Visalia	Ronny Rodriguez, Carolina	Arismendy Alcantara, Daytona	Miguel Sano, Beloit	Garin Cecchini, Greenville
Best Defensive Outfielder	Starling Marte, Indianapolis	Anthony Gose, Las Vegas	Gary Brown, Richmond	Ryan LaMarre, Pensacola	Engel Beltre, Frisco	George Springer, Lancaster	Jackie Bradley, Salem	Mel Rojas Jr., Bradenton	Todd Glaesmann, Bowling Green	Mason Williams, Charleston
Best Outfield Arm	Greg Golson, Charlotte	Moises Sierra, Las Vegas	Bryce Brentz, Portland	Ryan LaMarre, Pensacola	Jeremy Barfield, Midland	Rafael Ortega, Modesto	Jackie Bradley, Salem	Marcell Ozuna, Jupiter	Drew Vettleson, Bowling Green	Gregory Polanco, West Virginia
Most Exciting Player	Starling Marte, Indianapolis	Adam Eaton, Reno	Manny Machado, Bowie	Billy Hamilton, Pensacola	Oscar Taveras, Springfield	Billy Hamilton, Bakersfield	Jackie Bradley, Salem	Christian Yelich, Jupiter	Javier Baez, Peoria	Alan Hansen, West Virginia
Best Manager Prospect	Mike Sarbaugh, Columbus	Lorenzo Bundy, Albuquerque	Matthew LeCroy, Harrisburg	Andy Barkett, Jacksonville	Steve Buechele, Frisco	Pedro Grifol, High Desert	Jason Wood, Myrtle Beach	Ryan Ellis, St. Lucie	Brady Williams, Bowling Green	Brian Daubach, Hagerstown

Awards highlight long-term success

TRIPLE-A
Lehigh Valley IronPigs (International)

"Laugh. Cheer. Oink.""Go Hog Wild!"

The IronPigs have turned a pair of their slogans into reality since debuting in 2008. The International League affiliate of the Phillies has become minor league baseball's most successful franchise.

Lehigh Valley has topped the minors in attendance each of the past three seasons, with 622,421 fans visiting Coca-Cola Field in 2012. The IronPigs were the only team in the minors to average more than 9,000 spectators per game.

Creativity has been key to the team's success, and it shows in every facet of its operation. The name, which creatively pays tribute to the region's ties to steel production, led to a unique logo and long line of off-the-wall marketing slogans and promotions. Their ballpark—the first in the minors to land Coca-Cola as a title sponsor—has become a model for other teams. It includes unique seating options—like dugout suites that put fans closer to home plate than the pitcher, two party porches and an open-air concourse.

DOUBLE-A
Northwest Arkansas Naturals (Texas)

A key component to minor league baseball's success has been replacing failing markets with thriving ones. Northwest Arkansas is an example of that model, as it took over Wichita's spot in the Texas League and has become one of the minors' steadiest franchises over the past five years.

The Naturals averaged 5,200 fans in their 2008 debut, and tripled Wichita's attendance by drawing 358,792 spectators. Despite challenging weather in recent years and playing in one of the Texas League's smallest markets, the Naturals have held relatively steady at the gate while becoming active members of the community. The team has helped local programs raise more than $250,000 through ticket fundraisers while creating a family-friendly atmosphere at Arvest Park.

"It seems like they have battled Mother Nature more than most teams and just shake it off and keep going," Minor League Baseball president Pat O'Conner said.

CLASS A
Greenville Drive (South Atlantic)

Greenville became the hottest market in the minors when the Braves decided to leave town for a new ballpark in Pearl, Miss., after the 2004 season. In fact, there was so much interest in Greenville that Minor League Baseball changed its protocol for dealing with future open territories.

Ultimately, MiLB ruled in favor of the Columbia (S.C.) Bombers relocating to Greenville, and the team's owners quickly struck a deal for a new downtown ballpark. Fluor Field is designed after the big league affiliate's Fenway Park and includes its own 30-foot-tall Green Monster. It has also been a boon for the city's once-blighted area.

"They are the poster child for how a stadium can drive downtown development," South Atlantic League president Eric Krupa said.

SHORT-SEASON
Billings Mustangs (Pioneer)

O'Conner describes Billings as one of the steadiest franchises in the minors. The Mustangs have served as a Reds affiliate since 1974. And since 2008, when the team debuted new-but-not-extravagant Dehler Park, average attendance has held steady around the 3,000 mark. The ballpark is a significant improvement on the team's previous home, Cobb Field, where they played since 1948.

"They define hometown baseball," O'Conner said of Billings, noting the team's involvement in the local American Legion program, which also plays at Dehler Park.

MINOR LEAGUES

PREVIOUS WINNERS

TRIPLE-A	DOUBLE-A	CLASS A	SHORT-SEASON
2002: Memphis (Pacific Coast)	**2002:** Chattanooga (Southern)	**2002:** Fort Myers (Florida State)	**2002:** Ogden (Pioneer)
2003: Pawtucket (International)	**2003:** New Britain (Eastern)	**2003:** Modesto (California)	**2003:** Spokane (Northwest)
2004: Sacramento (Pacific Coast)	**2004:** Round Rock (Texas)	**2004:** Dayton (Midwest)	**2004:** Burlington (Appalachian)
2005: Toledo (International)	**2005:** Tulsa (Texas)	**2005:** Lakewood (South Atlantic)	**2005:** Brooklyn (New York-Penn)
2006: Durham (International)	**2006:** Altoona (Eastern)	**2006:** Daytona (Florida State)	**2006:** Aberdeen (New York-Penn)
2007: Albuquerque (Pacific Coast)	**2007:** Frisco (Texas)	**2007:** Lake Elsinore (California)	**2007:** Missoula (Pioneer)
2008: Columbus (International)	**2008:** Birmingham (Southern)	**2008:** Greensboro (South Atlantic)	**2008:** Greeneville (Appalachian)
2009: Iowa (Pacific Coast)	**2009:** New Hamshire (Eastern)	**2009:** San Jose (California)	**2009:** Tri-City (New York-Penn)
2010: Louisville (International)	**2010:** Corpus Christi (Texas)	**2010:** Lynchburg (Carolina)	**2010:** Idaho Falls (Pioneer)
2011: Colo. Springs (Pacific Coast)	**2011:** Harrisburg (Eastern)	**2011:** Fort Wayne (Midwest)	**2011:** Vancouver (Northwest)

MINOR LEAGUES

BY JOHN MANUEL

The Scranton/Wilkes-Barre Yankees didn't win the International League's Governors' Cup in 2012; that went to Pawtucket after beating Charlotte in the championship series. But the story of the season was the Yankees, who won the North Division despite having to play "home" games in six different parks.

Dave Miley earned league manager of the year honors as well as BA's Manager of the Year Award for steering the team to a title despite playing no games at PNC Field, which was in the midst of a rebuilding and renovation project expected to cost more than $50 million.

The parent Yankees tried to move their Triple-A affiliate to Newark, N.J., for the year, but the Mets blocked the move, citing territorial rights infringement. So Scranton went on the road and played home games at six parks, most in upstate New York. That led the team to rebrand itself the Empire State Yankees for the season, as the club played in Rochester's Frontier Field as well as in Batavia, home of a New York-Penn League team operated by the Rochester franchise. The Yankees also played home dates in Buffalo and Syracuse plus Pawtucket and Lehigh Valley.

The Yankees also had several on-field setbacks. Prospects such as catcher Austin Romine (back) and Manny Banuelos (elbow) got hurt; the Yankees traded rotation stalwart D.J. Mitchell for Ichiro Suzuki; and prospect Dellin Betances flopped and was sent back to Double-A.

Nevertheless, Miley steered the team to 84 wins behind a staff that relied on veterans such as Ramon Ortiz and Nelson Figueroa. The lineup included more vets, like team home run leader Jack Cust and Cuban import Ronnier Mustelier.

TOP 20 PROSPECTS

1. Matt Harvey, rhp, Buffalo Bisons (Mets)
2. Starling Marte, of, Indianapolis Indians (Pirates)
3. Chris Archer, rhp, Durham Bulls (Rays)
4. Julio Teheran, rhp, Gwinnett Braves
5. Chris Parmelee, 1b, Rochester Red Wings (Twins)
6. Ryan Lavarnway, c, Pawtucket Red Sox
7. Didi Gregorius, ss, Louisville Bats (Reds)
8. Jacob Turner, rhp, Toledo Mud Hens (Tigers)
9. Jeff Locke, lhp, Indianapolis Indians (Pirates)
10. Tim Beckham, ss, Durham Bulls (Rays)
11. Jose Iglesias, ss, Pawtucket Red Sox
12. Cory Kluber, rhp, Columbus Clippers (Indians)
13. Cody Allen, rhp, Columbus Clippers (Indians)
14. Jeurys Familia, rhp, Buffalo Bisons (Mets)
15. L.J. Hoes, of, Norfolk Tides (Orioles)
16. Zach McAllister, rhp, Columbus Clippers (Indians)
17. Jenrry Mejia, rhp, Buffalo Bisons (Mets)
18. Casey Crosby, lhp, Toledo Mud Hens (Tigers)
19. Tyler Cloyd, rhp, Lehigh Valley IronPigs (Phillies)
20. Christian Garcia, rhp, Syracuse Chiefs (Nationals)

Figueroa wound up with Pawtucket after being released in July, and was a crucial piece of the PawSox's postseason push. He won both of his playoff starts, striking out 13 in 14 innings as the PawSox won a four-game set with Scranton and then swept Charlotte. Pawtucket won despite the September promotion of league MVP Mauro Gomez, who hit .310/.371/.589 with 24 homers.

The Yankees were emblematic of a league that skewed older and was thin on prospects. Indianapolis had the league's top record and one of its younger rosters, especially on the mound with a left-leaning rotation that included Jeff Locke, Rudy Owens and Justin Wilson. Wilson was part of two unusual no-hitters. He started an April one at Durham, striking out nine in 7 ⅓ innings before Jose Diaz and Doug Slaten wrapped up. Then in August, he no-hit visiting Charlotte for eight innings before the game was called due to rain.

OVERALL STANDINGS

Team (Organization)	W	L	PCT	GB	Manager(s)	Attendance	Average	Last Pennant
Indianapolis Indians (Pirates)	89	55	.618	—	Dean Treanor	595,043	8,501	2000
* Scranton/Wilkes-Barre Yankees (Yankees)	84	60	.583	5	Dave Miley	272,168	3,944	2008
Charlotte Knights (White Sox)	83	61	.576	6	Joel Skinner	282,117	4,030	1999
Pawtucket Red Sox (Red Sox)	79	65	.549	10	Arnie Beyeler	521,023	7,551	2012
Lehigh Valley IronPigs (Phillies)	75	68	.524	13 ½	Ryne Sandberg	622,421	9,153	1995
Columbus Clippers (Indians)	75	69	.521	14	Mike Sarbaugh	611,223	8,732	2010
Norfolk Tides (Orioles)	74	70	.514	15	Ron Johnson	389,188	5,560	1985
Rochester Red Wings (Twins)	72	72	.500	17	Gene Glynn	414,398	6,094	1997
Syracuse Chiefs (Nationals)	70	74	.486	19	Tony Beasley	349,027	5,288	1976
Buffalo Bisons (Mets)	67	76	.469	21 ½	Wally Backman	515,898	7,370	2004
Durham Bulls (Rays)	66	78	.458	23	Charlie Montoyo	483,593	6,811	2009
Gwinnett Braves (Braves)	62	82	.431	27	Dave Brundage	327,584	4,680	2007
Toledo Mud Hens (Tigers)	60	84	.417	29	Phil Nevin	550,900	7,870	2006
Louisville Bats (Reds)	51	93	.354	38	David Bell	570,003	8,143	2001

* Played entire home schedule on the road

Semifinals: Pawtucket defeated Scranton/Wilkes-Barre 3-1 and Charlotte defeated Indianapolis 3-1 in best-of-five series. **Finals:** Pawtucket defeated Charlotte 3-0 in best-of-five series.

CLUB BATTING

	AVG	G	AB	R	H	2B	3B	HR	RBI	BB	SO	SB	OBP	SLG
Columbus	.269	144	4832	709	1302	296	23	150	665	506	1003	70	.342	.433
Durham	.267	144	4845	604	1292	225	27	103	564	459	931	74	.334	.388
Pawtucket	.266	144	4855	654	1290	257	27	133	606	485	1008	91	.336	.412
Indianapolis	.260	144	4863	662	1263	256	44	91	619	513	1108	123	.334	.387
Scranton/Wilkes-Barre	.260	144	4869	667	1264	263	25	128	625	598	1113	101	.344	.403
Syracuse	.259	144	4725	632	1224	227	27	107	597	494	1020	88	.331	.386
Gwinnett	.258	144	4819	600	1241	258	29	89	570	457	1011	141	.327	.379
Lehigh Valley	.257	143	4690	551	1203	235	19	84	509	349	851	93	.311	.368
Charlotte	.254	144	4834	626	1228	274	24	105	592	467	1056	84	.323	.386
Buffalo	.252	143	4780	640	1205	236	25	130	584	566	1211	88	.333	.394
Rochester	.251	144	4816	568	1208	250	27	101	525	421	1031	90	.315	.377
Norfolk	.250	144	4831	586	1208	240	29	111	544	495	1091	76	.324	.381
Toledo	.249	144	4766	606	1188	224	29	115	563	521	1100	154	.330	.381
Louisville	.241	144	4837	552	1167	249	14	116	516	443	1092	68	.310	.370

CLUB PITCHING

	ERA	G	CG	SHO	SV	IP	H	R	ER	HR	BB	SO	AVG
Charlotte	3.15	144	4	13	37	1273	1142	524	446	95	457	1111	.241
Indianapolis	3.15	144	4	16	44	1293	1119	500	452	102	425	1123	.233
Norfolk	3.41	144	7	11	38	1281	1175	564	485	80	441	1036	.243
Pawtucket	3.43	144	5	10	42	1268	1160	553	483	124	481	1074	.243
Lehigh Valley	3.77	143	3	12	42	1242	1198	590	520	108	470	1047	.254
Scranton/Wilkes-Barre	3.86	144	5	11	40	1276	1240	601	547	112	486	1052	.256
Syracuse	3.95	144	8	14	36	1238	1274	611	544	117	410	862	.267
Buffalo	3.99	143	4	7	34	1259	1242	650	558	110	515	1046	.256
Rochester	4.06	144	4	10	48	1261	1284	638	569	112	454	1003	.266
Columbus	4.14	144	6	12	34	1252	1257	637	576	142	414	1045	.261
Toledo	4.23	144	7	5	27	1261	1237	673	592	107	577	1067	.258
Gwinnett	4.41	144	5	9	29	1252	1330	707	614	103	557	1044	.274
Durham	4.59	144	2	11	39	1257	1271	684	641	130	509	1125	.263
Louisville	4.71	144	1	3	34	1273	1354	725	666	121	578	991	.276

CLUB FIELDING

	PCT	PO	A	E	DP		PCT	PO	A	E	DP
Scranton/Wilkes-Barre	.983	3829	1442	92	135	Columbus	.979	3756	1436	109	135
Pawtucket	.982	3805	1423	96	119	Lehigh Valley	.979	3726	1356	109	142
Rochester	.982	3783	1431	98	141	Louisville	.979	3819	1479	114	143
Charlotte	.981	3818	1447	102	139	Norfolk	.977	3842	1454	122	137
Durham	.981	3771	1277	96	133	Toledo	.977	3782	1461	122	135
Indianapolis	.981	3880	1418	101	113	Buffalo	.974	3776	1399	136	106
Syracuse	.980	3715	1540	107	145	Gwinnett	.974	3755	1359	135	139

INDIVIDUAL BATTING LEADERS (Minimum 2.7 PA/Team Game)

	AVG	G	AB	R	H	2B	3B	HR	RBI	BB	SO	SB
Constanza, Jose, Gwinnett	.314	88	344	54	108	10	4	1	27	36	43	14
Gomez, Mauro, Pawtucket	.310	100	387	65	120	34	1	24	74	35	88	1
Anderson, Leslie, Durham	.309	116	444	63	137	21	0	14	56	26	56	0
Rivero, Carlos, Syracuse	.303	126	455	57	138	28	1	10	64	33	87	6
Frandsen, Kevin, Lehigh Valley	.302	99	391	38	118	34	0	1	33	14	31	2
Perez, Felix, Louisville	.301	116	392	46	118	25	1	4	35	23	63	5
Henry, Justin, Toledo	.300	131	476	72	143	14	5	1	38	54	65	22
Rottino, Vinny, Buffalo/Columbus	.297	96	374	60	111	28	2	9	66	34	53	14
Mejia, Ernesto, Gwinnett	.296	133	514	73	152	31	1	24	92	34	132	10
Carrera, Ezequiel, Columbus	.294	97	394	65	116	19	6	6	42	29	60	26

INDIVIDUAL PITCHING LEADERS (Minimum 0.8 IP/Team Game)

	W	L	ERA	G	GS	CG	SV	IP	H	R	HR	BB	SO
Cloyd, Tyler, Lehigh Valley	12	1	2.35	22	22	1	0	142	105	39	14	38	93
Leesman, Charles, Charlotte	12	10	2.47	26	26	0	0	135	129	54	8	52	103
Locke, Jeff, Indianapolis	10	5	2.48	24	24	0	0	142	126	42	9	43	131
Wilk, Adam, Toledo	7	11	2.77	24	24	3	0	150	123	61	13	28	128
van den Hurk, Rick, Indianapolis	13	5	2.92	21	19	0	0	123	112	46	8	35	113
Owens, Rudy, Indianapolis	8	5	3.14	19	19	1	0	117	112	42	12	25	85
Schwinden, Chris, Col./Scranton/Buffalo	9	9	3.21	25	23	2	0	126	126	54	11	37	99
Seddon, Chris, Columbus	11	5	3.44	20	20	1	0	123	112	55	16	27	108
Ortiz, Ramon, Scranton/WB	13	6	3.45	27	27	1	0	169	167	75	18	37	104
Berken, Jason, Norfolk	5	6	3.5	26	26	1	0	144	160	73	10	39	98

ALL-STAR TEAM

C: Ryan Lavarnway, Pawtucket. **1B:** Ernesto Mejia, Gwinnett. **2B:** Cord Phelps, Columbus. **3B:** Carlos Rivero, Syracuse. **SS:** Jose Iglesias, Pawtucket. **OF:** Leslie Anderson, Durham; Corey Brown, Syracuse; Starling Marte, Indianapolis. **DH:** Mauro Gomez, Pawtucket. **UT:** Dan Johnson, Charlotte. **SP:** Tyler Cloyd, Lehigh Valley. **RP:** Tim Wood, Indianapolis.

Most Valuable Player: Mauro Gomez, Pawtucket. **Most Valuable Pitcher:** Tyler Cloyd, Lehigh Valley. **Rookie of the Year:** Ernesto Mejia, Gwinnett. **Manager of the Year:** Dave Miley, Scranton/Wilkes-Barre.

DEPARTMENT LEADERS

BATTING

OBP	Cust, Jack, Scranton/WB	.400
SLG	Gomez, Mauro, Pawtucket	.589
OPS	Gomez, Mauro, Pawtucket	.960
R	Brown, Corey, Syracuse	83
H	Mejia, Ernesto, Gwinnett	152
TB	Mejia, Ernesto, Gwinnett	258
XBH	Canzler, Russ, Columbus	61
2B	Canzler, Russ, Columbus	36
3B	Marte, Starling, Indianapolis	13
HR	Johnson, Dan, Charlotte	28
RBI	Mejia, Ernesto, Gwinnett	92
SAC	Durango, Luis, Gwinnett	14
BB	Johnson, Dan, Charlotte	94
HBP	Cervelli, Francisco, Scranton/WB	15
SO	Pascucci, Valentino, Buffalo	148
SB	Durango, Luis, Gwinnett	46
CS	Durango, Luis, Gwinnett	16
AB/SO	Frandsen, Kevin, Lehigh Valley	12.6

PITCHING

G	Cabrera, Fernando, Buffalo	57
GS	Familia, Jeurys, Buffalo	28
	Maya, Yunesky, Syracuse	28
GF	Cabrera, Fernando, Buffalo	49
SV	Cabrera, Fernando, Buffalo	22
W	Duke, Zach, Syracuse	15
L	Roark, Tanner, Syracuse	17
IP	Shirek, Charles, Charlotte	170.1
H	Duke, Zach, Syracuse	178
R	Elarton, Scott, Lehigh Valley	93
ER	Elarton, Scott, Lehigh Valley	82
HB	Teheran, Julio, Gwinnett	15
BB	Oliver, Andrew, Toledo	88
SO	Archer, Chris, Durham	139
SO/9	Archer, Chris, Durham	9.8
SO/9 (RP)	De La Rosa, Dane, Durham	11.6
BB/9	Shirek, Charles, Charlotte	1.5
WP	Oliver, Andrew, Toledo	18
BK	Betances, Dellin, Scranton/WB	3
	Wilson, Alex, Pawtucket	3
HR	Huff, David, Columbus	27
AVG	Wilson, Justin, Indianapolis	.189

FIELDING

C	FPCT	Phegley, Josh, Charlotte	.996
	PO	Phegley, Josh, Charlotte	772
	A	Rivera, Rene, Rochester	62
	E	Rivera, Rene, Rochester	10
	DP	Boscan, J.C., Gwinnett	13
	PB	Cervelli, Francisco, Scranton/WB	15
1B	FPCT	Mahoney, Joe, Norfolk	.998
	PO	Mahoney, Joe, Norfolk	1086
	A	Soto, Neftali, Louisville	88
	E	Soto, Neftali, Louisville	11
	DP	Mahoney, Joe, Norfolk	105
2B	FPCT	Phelps, Cord, Columbus	.991
	PO	Phelps, Cord, Columbus	254
	A	Phelps, Cord, Columbus	322
	E	Adams, Ryan, Norfolk	14
	DP	Phelps, Cord, Columbus	88
3B	FPCT	Rivero, Carlos, Syracuse	.953
	PO	Rivero, Carlos, Syracuse	57
	A	Rivero, Carlos, Syracuse	208
	E	Terdoslavich, Joey, Gwinnett	22
	DP	Rivero, Carlos, Syracuse	22
SS	FPCT	Davis, Blake, Norfolk	.985
	PO	Blanco, Andres, Lehigh Valley	149
	A	Blanco, Andres, Lehigh Valley	333
	E	Rodriguez, Josh, Buffalo	20
	DP	Blanco, Andres, Lehigh Valley	79
OF	FPCT	Feliciano, Jesus, Durham	.100
	PO	Durango, Luis, Gwinnett	282
	A	Carroll, Brett, Syracuse	17
	E	Brown, Corey, Syracuse	8
	DP	Carroll, Brett, Syracuse	6

MINOR LEAGUES

MINOR LEAGUES

BY NATHAN RODE

Sticking with the typical strength of the Pacific Coast League, the Reno Aces hit their way to the league title and Triple-A National Championship. Three Aces finished among the top five in batting average—outfielder Adam Eaton (.381), third baseman Ryan Wheeler (.351) and second baseman Jake Elmore (.344)—and got a boost on the bases as Eaton and Elmore combined for 70 steals.

Eaton, who also scored 119 runs and stole 38 bases, earned league MVP honors. Omaha Storm Chaser outfielder/third baseman Wil Myers was the league's top prospect and lived up to expectations, hitting .304/.378/.554 with 24 home runs in 388 games.

The Diamondbacks had one of the top farm systems entering the season and it showed on the offensive side, but Reno had a few aces on the mound as well. Righthander Trevor Bauer and lefthanders Tyler Skaggs and Pat Corbin each got at least nine starts for the Aces and held their own in an unforgiving environment for pitchers. Bauer went 5-1, 2.85 in 82 innings (14 starts) but didn't qualify for the ERA title. Skaggs tossed 53 innings and went 4-2, 2.91 while Corbin went 3-2, 3.44 in 52 innings.

Sacramento led the league in wins with an 86-58 record on the way to a sixth consecutive Pacific South Division title. The River Cats took on Reno—winners of the Pacific North Division—in the first round of the playoffs and lost in five games. On the other side, Omaha needed five games to knock off Albuquerque. Reno took the championship series in four games, outscoring Omaha 29-12.

Oklahoma City third baseman Mike Hessman

TOP 20 PROSPECTS

1. Wil Myers, of/3b, Omaha Storm Chasers (Royals)
2. Travis D'Arnaud, c, Las Vegas 51s (Blue Jays)
3. Trevor Bauer, rhp, Reno Aces (Diamondbacks)
4. Tyler Skaggs, lhp, Reno Aces (Diamondbacks)
5. Anthony Rizzo, 1b, Iowa Cubs
6. Shelby Miller, rhp, Memphis Redbirds (Cardinals)
7. Danny Hultzen, lhp, Tacoma Rainiers (Mariners)
8. Anthony Gose, of, Las Vegas 51s (Blue Jays)
9. Yasmani Grandal, c, Tucson Padres
10. Jedd Gyorko, 3b/2b, Tucson Padres
11. Jake Odorizzi, rhp, Omaha Storm Chasers (Royals)
12. Adam Eaton, of, Reno Aces (Diamondbacks)
13. Dan Straily, rhp, Sacramento River Cats (Athletics)
14. Adeiny Hechavarria, ss, Las Vegas 51s (Blue Jays)
15. Brett Jackson, of, Iowa Cubs
16. Nick Franklin, 2b/ss, Tacoma Rainiers (Mariners)
17. Leonys Martin, of, Round Rock Express (Rangers)
18. Derek Norris, c, Sacramento River Cats (Athletics)
19. Matt Adams, 1b, Memphis Redbirds (Cardinals)
20. Patrick Corbin, lhp, Reno Aces (Diamondbacks)

has been a prolific home run hitter in the minor leagues and belted 35 in 123 games this season to boost his career total to 364 in 17 seasons. Righthander John Ely (Albuquerque) topped the league in ERA (3.20) and strikeouts (165).

New Orleans finished in third in the American South Division, but had a disappointing end to the season. The Zephyrs were forced to cancel their final series of the season against Iowa due to damage at their home ballpark from Hurricane Isaac. The Zephyrs had played their previous home series at Round Rock because of the storm, and decided to cancel their final four games after being eliminated from postseason play.

The offseason affiliation shuffle resulted in a pair of teams swapping big league affiliates. The Blue Jays left Las Vegas to ink a player-development contract with the Buffalo Bisons. The Mets, after four years in Buffalo, will spend the next two years in Vegas.

OVERALL STANDINGS

Team (Organization)	W	L	PCT	GB	Manager(s)	Attendance	Average	Last Pennant
Sacramento River Cats (Athletics)	86	58	.597	—	Darren Bush	586,090	8,140	2008
Omaha Storm Chasers (Royals)	83	61	.576	3	Mike Jirschele	415,650	5,938	2011
Reno Aces (Diamondbacks)	81	63	.563	5	Brett Butler	389,860	5,415	2012
Albuquerque Isotopes (Dodgers)	80	64	.556	6	Lorenzo Bundy	568,417	8,120	1994
Las Vegas 51s (Blue Jays)	79	64	.552	6½	Marty Brown	311,516	4,388	1998
Oklahoma City Redhawks (Astros)	78	65	.545	7½	T. DeFrancesco/T. Lawless	399,965	5,633	1965
New Orleans Zephyrs (Marlins)	73	67	.521	11	Ron Hassey	329,942	4,999	2001
Colorado Springs Sky Sox (Rockies)	75	69	.521	11	Stu Cole	334,245	4,915	1995
Fresno Grizzlies (Giants)	74	70	.514	12	Bob Mariano	471,686	6,551	Never
Salt Lake Bees (Angels)	73	71	.507	13	Keith Johnson	515,633	7,162	1979
Round Rock Express (Rangers)	69	75	.479	17	Bobby Jones	595,584	8,389	Never
Nashville Sounds (Brewers)	67	77	.465	19	Mike Guerrero	321,042	4,792	2005
Tacoma Rainiers (Mariners)	63	81	.438	23	Daren Brown	352,032	4,889	2010
Memphis Redbirds (Cardinals)	57	87	.396	29	Ron Warner	493,706	6,954	2009
Tucson Padres (Padres)	56	88	.389	30	Terry Kennedy	200,991	2,956	2006
Iowa Cubs (Cubs)	53	87	.379	31	Dave Bialas	509,798	7,283	Never

Semifinals: Omaha defeated Albuquerque 3-2 and Reno defeated Sacramento 3-2 in best-of-five series. **Finals:** Reno defeated Omaha 3-1 in best-of-five series.

CLUB BATTING

	AVG	G	AB	R	H	2B	3B	HR	RBI	BB	SO	SB	OBP	SLG
Albuquerque	.298	144	5020	842	1495	309	58	148	793	484	1088	80	.362	.471
Las Vegas	.298	143	4954	808	1474	305	39	133	755	557	964	115	.370	.455
Reno	.297	144	5081	856	1507	339	40	116	791	507	983	155	.363	.448
Colorado Springs	.291	144	4991	808	1452	348	43	103	752	394	902	88	.344	.440
Omaha	.290	144	5032	796	1460	253	41	132	742	496	861	124	.356	.435
Oklahoma City	.282	143	4898	764	1379	264	22	147	710	456	1081	119	.349	.434
Salt Lake	.279	144	4966	795	1384	296	58	143	747	438	991	129	.338	.448
Round Rock	.278	144	5003	719	1392	271	25	137	681	459	997	70	.342	.425
Fresno	.276	144	5051	710	1395	267	48	122	671	435	947	64	.339	.421
Sacramento	.276	144	5018	833	1384	285	41	171	784	657	1110	120	.363	.451
Tucson	.271	144	4925	684	1336	273	30	112	629	467	1036	91	.337	.407
Iowa	.270	140	4729	613	1277	275	34	112	563	437	999	108	.334	.414
New Orleans	.265	140	4770	638	1265	223	19	153	605	470	992	81	.336	.416
Tacoma	.264	144	4960	709	1307	285	26	152	640	479	1082	84	.333	.423
Nashville	.259	144	4753	561	1233	257	29	119	507	380	964	97	.318	.401
Memphis	.257	144	4888	629	1255	244	21	120	590	493	1060	83	.328	.389

CLUB PITCHING

	ERA	G	CG	SHO	SV	IP	H	R	ER	HR	BB	SO	AVG
New Orleans	3.96	140	2	12	40	1242	1234	603	547	121	446	1053	.261
Sacramento	4.10	144	3	9	34	1305	1266	649	594	124	460	1134	.254
Omaha	4.24	144	3	7	42	1290	1368	681	607	137	501	1082	.274
Nashville	4.29	144	4	12	29	1249	1264	646	596	119	552	1058	.267
Las Vegas	4.59	143	2	7	37	1261	1379	721	643	135	437	912	.280
Memphis	4.59	144	3	2	24	1263	1340	720	644	144	447	1100	.273
Fresno	4.60	144	2	6	33	1293	1415	757	661	137	449	949	.279
Iowa	4.67	140	1	7	22	1219	1273	711	632	126	513	994	.269
Round Rock	4.74	144	2	4	34	1280	1386	745	674	137	480	890	.280
Reno	4.87	144	5	3	45	1283	1442	798	695	164	445	992	.285
Oklahoma City	4.89	143	2	5	39	1259	1441	758	684	144	457	974	.289
Tacoma	4.97	144	3	4	30	1274	1380	777	703	131	512	1026	.275
Albuquerque	5.01	144	1	8	45	1264	1415	804	703	148	456	945	.284
Colorado Springs	5.06	144	3	4	36	1247	1435	795	701	108	511	1083	.289
Tucson	5.13	144	3	8	27	1248	1520	801	711	105	439	949	.304
Salt Lake	5.18	144	2	6	35	1273	1437	799	733	140	504	916	.287

CLUB FIELDING

	PCT	PO	A	E	DP		PCT	PO	A	E	DP
Nashville	.983	3747	1426	89	155	Reno	.978	3850	1491	120	124
Salt Lake	.980	3820	1521	108	144	Sacramento	.978	3914	1360	117	139
Omaha	.979	3869	1403	112	145	Fresno	.976	3880	1502	135	139
Round Rock	.979	3839	1562	117	171	Albuquerque	.975	3792	1567	139	140
Las Vegas	.978	3782	1614	122	176	Colorado Springs	.975	3741	1461	135	130
Memphis	.978	3788	1359	115	140	Iowa	.975	3656	1421	129	118
New Orleans	.978	3726	1313	114	124	Tucson	.975	3744	1566	136	145
Oklahoma City	.978	3776	1488	121	127	Tacoma	.974	3821	1296	139	135

INDIVIDUAL BATTING LEADERS (Minimum 2.7 Pa/Team Game)

	AVG	G	AB	R	H	2B	3B	HR	RBI	BB	SO	SB
Eaton, Adam, Reno	.381	119	488	119	186	46	5	7	45	53	68	38
Wheeler, Ryan, Reno	.351	93	362	56	127	27	4	15	90	26	67	3
McBride, Matt, Colo. Springs	.344	108	439	73	151	42	6	10	87	19	47	0
Elmore, Jake, Reno	.344	108	419	95	144	30	9	1	73	74	54	32
Cervenak, Mike, New Orleans	.340	101	371	61	126	22	0	13	57	43	49	1
Bond, Brock, Fresno	.332	106	337	59	112	15	2	1	31	48	41	3
Falu, Irving, Omaha	.329	88	365	69	120	22	3	7	50	28	41	21
Castellanos, Alex, Albuquerque	.328	94	344	74	113	25	7	17	52	46	85	16
Gyorko, Jedd, Tucson	.328	92	369	62	121	24	0	24	83	34	68	4
Van Slyke, Scott, Albuquerque	.327	95	358	68	117	34	1	18	67	46	64	5

INDIVIDUAL PITCHING LEADERS (Minimum 0.8 IP/Team Game)

	W	L	ERA	G	GS	CG	SV	IP	H	R	HR	BB	SO
Ely, John, Albuquerque	14	7	3.20	27	27	1	0	169	150	68	18	36	165
Petit, Yusmeiro, Fresno	7	7	3.46	28	28	1	0	167	178	88	14	36	153
Dickson, Brandon, Memphis	5	11	3.63	23	23	0	0	141	151	67	17	27	104
Verdugo, Ryan, Omaha	12	4	3.75	27	24	0	0	137	114	60	19	67	118
Banwart, Travis, Sacramento	9	5	3.85	32	18	0	2	129	132	59	15	37	99
Smith, Greg, Salt Lake	9	10	3.97	22	21	0	0	138	136	67	18	38	83
Billings, Bruce, Sacramento	7	6	3.98	25	25	0	0	133	126	63	15	39	117
Hand, Brad, New Orleans	11	7	4.00	27	27	0	0	148	129	72	15	75	141
Hacker, Eric, Fresno	12	6	4.01	26	25	0	0	150	149	70	12	43	103
Koehler, Tom, New Orleans	12	11	4.17	28	27	0	0	151	154	80	15	61	138

ALL-STAR TEAM

C: Tim Federowicz, Albuquerque. **1B:** Matt McBride, Colorado Springs. **2B:** Jake Elmore, Reno. **3B:** Ryan Wheeler, Reno. **SS:** Adeiny Hechavarria, Las Vegas. **OF:** Andrew Brown, Colorado Springs; Adam Eaton, Reno; Wil Myers, Omaha. **DH:** Jerry Sands, Albuquerque. **RHP:** John Ely, Albuquerque. **LHP:** Ryan Verdugo, Omaha. **RP:** Josh Wall, Albuquerque.
Most Valuable Player: Adam Eaton, Reno. **Pitcher of the Year:** John Ely, Albuquerque. **Rookie of the Year:** Adam Eaton, Reno. **Manager of the Year:** Lorenzo Bundy, Albuquerque.

DEPARTMENT LEADERS

BATTING

OBP	Eaton, Adam, Reno	.456
SLG	Brown, Andrew, Colorado Springs	.597
OPS	Castellanos, Alex, Albuquerque	.101
R	Eaton, Adam, Reno	119
H	Eaton, Adam, Reno	186
TB	Eaton, Adam, Reno	263
XBH	Brown, Andrew, Colorado Springs	61
2B	Eaton, Adam, Reno	46
3B	Jackson, Brett, Iowa	12
HR	Hessman, Mike, Oklahoma City	35
RBI	Sands, Jerry, Albuquerque	107
SAC	Diaz, Jonathan, Las Vegas	15
BB	Taylor, Michael, Sacramento	86
HBP	Eaton, Adam, Reno	15
SO	Jackson, Brett, Iowa	158
SB	Eaton, Adam, Reno	38
CS	Ford, Darren, Tacoma	14
AB/SO	Sanchez, Angel, Oklahoma City	13.8

PITCHING

G	Gil, Jerry, Las Vegas	58
	Reifer, Adam, Memphis	58
GS	Three tied at	29
GF	Brasier, Ryan, Salt Lake	48
	Wall, Josh, Albuquerque	48
SV	Wall, Josh, Albuquerque	28
W	Ely, John, Albuquerque	14
	O'Sullivan, Sean, Omaha/Las Vegas	14
L	McClung, Seth, Nashville/Iowa	15
IP	Shoemaker, Matt, Salt Lake	176.2
H	Shoemaker, Matt, Salt Lake	229
R	Shoemaker, Matt, Salt Lake	123
ER	Shoemaker, Matt, Salt Lake	111
HB	Miller, Shelby, Memphis	11
BB	Peralta, Wily, Nashville	78
SO	Ely, John, Albuquerque	165
SO/9	Miller, Shelby, Memphis	10.5
SO/9 (RP)	Burns, Cory, Tucson	10.6
BB/9	Martin, J.D., New Orleans	1.2
WP	Hoey, Jim, Las Vegas	22
BK	Loop, Derrick, Albuquerque	4
HR	Brewer, Charles, Reno	26
AVG	Verdugo, Ryan, Omaha	.227

FIELDING

C	FPCT	Williams, Jackson, Fresno	.995
	PO	Anderson, Bryan, Nashville	722
	A	Federowicz, Tim, Albuquerque	101
	E	Federowicz, Tim, Albuquerque	12
	DP	Williams, Jackson, Fresno	9
	PB	Williams, Jackson, Fresno	12
1B	FPCT	Navarro, Efren, Salt Lake	.997
	PO	Navarro, Efren, Salt Lake	1215
	A	Navarro, Efren, Salt Lake	93
	E	Robinson, Clint, Omaha	13
	DP	Navarro, Efren, Salt Lake	120
2B	FPCT	Farris, Eric, Nashville	.988
	PO	Culberson, Charlie, Fresno/Colo. Springs	233
	A	Culberson, Charlie, Fresno/Colo. Springs	353
	E	Paredes, Jimmy, Okla. City	20
	DP	Solarte, Yangervis, Round Rock	93
3B	FPCT	Jimenez, Luis, Salt Lake	.947
	PO	Jimenez, Luis, Salt Lake	90
	A	Jimenez, Luis, Salt Lake	264
	E	Vitters, Josh, Iowa	21
	DP	Jimenez, Luis, Salt Lake	29
SS	FPCT	Hernandez, Luis, Round Rock	.980
	PO	Hernandez, Luis, Round Rock	194
	A	Hernandez, Luis, Round Rock	337
	E	Triunfel, Carlos, Tacoma	26
	DP	Hernandez, Luis, Round Rock	99
OF	FPCT	Angle, Matt, Albuquerque	1.000
		Gindl, Caleb, Nashville	1.000
	PO	Lough, David, Omaha	313
	A	Robertson, Daniel, Tucson	23
	E	Brown, Andrew, Colo. Springs	9
	DP	Sierra, Moises, Las Vegas	5

MINOR LEAGUES

BY MATT EDDY

The Akron Aeros defeated the Trenton Thunder in four games to win the Eastern League title for the fourth time in the past 10 seasons, but to do so the Aeros needed a furious first-round comeback.

Akron dropped the first two games of their opening best-of-five series in Bowie before pulling out a pair of one-run wins in Games Three and Four at home. Game Five didn't feature as much drama. The Aeros opened up a 4-0 lead after two innings and went on to win 5-2 behind 6 ⅔ strong innings from righthander Brett Brach.

Akron righthander Paolo Espino tossed seven shutout innings in the opener of the finals against Trenton, a 3-0 Aeros win. Akron took Game Two as well before Trenton extended the series with an 11-7 rout in Game Three. Akron closed out the series in Game Four with a 6-1 win behind 6 ⅓ quality innings from Japanese righthander Toru Murata and a 2-for-2 showing by third baseman Ryan Rohlinger.

But despite the success of Akron and Trenton, neither featured a player who ranked among the Top 20 Prospects in the league. Thunder righthander Brett Marshall went 13-7, 3.52 in 27 starts and came closest to cracking the list. The 22-year-old struck out 120 and walked 53 in 158 innings, though he went just 0-2, 4.85 in two postseason starts.

Reading first baseman Darin Ruf won the EL MVP award, almost took the league's triple crown and led the minors with 38 homers (including 20 in August). He smacked three homers in 12 big league games for the Phillies in September.

Ruf just missed making the EL Top 20—his age and lack of athleticism hurt him—but a surge of second-half promotions strengthened the overall quality of the league. Most of the circuit's 12 clubs added a rising star midway through the year.

Among those who joined the EL midstream were

TOP 20 PROSPECTS

1. Manny Machado, ss, Bowie Baysox (Orioles)
2. Zack Wheeler, rhp, Binghamton Mets
3. Gerrit Cole, rhp, Altoona Curve (Pirates)
4. Nick Castellanos, 3b/of, Erie Seawolves (Tigers)
5. Jackie Bradley, of, Portland Sea Dogs (Red Sox)
6. Oswaldo Arcia, of, New Britain Rock Cats (Twins)
7. Brian Goodwin, of, Harrisburg Senators (Nationals)
8. Aaron Hicks, of, New Britain Rock Cats (Twins)
9. Jake Marisnick, of, New Hampshire Fisher Cats (Blue Jays)
10. Tommy Joseph, c, Richmond (Giants)/Reading Phillies
11. Avisail Garcia, of, Erie Seawolves (Tigers)
12. Bruce Rondon, rhp, Erie Seawolves (Tigers)
13. Mike Kickham, lhp, Richmond Flying Squirrels (Giants)
14. Jonathan Schoop, 2b/ss, Bowie Baysox (Orioles)
15. Rob Brantly, c, Erie Seawolves (Tigers)
16. Gary Brown, of, Richmond Flying Squirrels (Giants)
17. Cody Asche, 3b, Reading Phillies
18. Wilmer Flores, 3b/2b, Binghamton Mets
19. Jon Pettibone, rhp, Reading Phillies
20. Drake Britton, lhp, Portland Sea Dogs (Red Sox)

2011 draft picks who raced to Double-A such as Pirates righthander Gerrit Cole (Altoona), Red Sox center fielder Jackie Bradley (Portland), Nationals center fielder Brian Goodwin (Harrisburg) and Phillies third baseman Cody Asche (Reading).

A fourth-rounder from Nebraska, Asche surprised even the Phillies by reaching Double-A in his full-season debut. He hit .300/.360/.513 with 10 homers in 283 at-bats for Reading, then went 6-for-14 (.429) with two doubles in the playoffs.

Four of the EL's finest prospects signed out of Venezuela in 2007 and came to the league during the season: Twins right fielder Oswaldo Arcia (New Britain), Tigers right fielder Avisail Garcia (Erie), Tigers reliever Bruce Rondon (Erie) and Mets third baseman Wilmer Flores (Binghamton).

Garcia hit .312/.345/.465, made his big league debut in late August and then earned starts in right field for the Tigers during the playoffs. Several other high-profile prospects joined the EL in August—including righthanders Dylan Bundy (Bowie) and Jameson Taillon (Altoona) and shortstop Xander Bogaerts (Portland)—but they didn't play enough to qualify for our prospect list.

OVERALL STANDINGS

Team (Organization)	W	L	PCT	GB	Manager	Attendance	Average	Last Pennant
Akron Aeros (Indians)	82	59	.582	—	Chris Tremie	256,473	3,772	2012
Trenton Thunder (Yankees)	79	63	.556	3 ½	Tony Franklin	373,355	5,411	2008
Bowie Baysox (Orioles)	78	64	.549	4 ½	Gary Kendall	248,210	3,650	Never
Reading Phillies (Phillies)	76	66	.535	6 ½	Dusty Wathan	426,623	6,368	2001
New Britain Rock Cats (Twins)	75	67	.528	7 ½	Jeff Smith	339,100	5,061	2001
Altoona Curve (Pirates)	72	70	.507	10 ½	P.J. Forbes	270,613	4,295	2010
Richmond Flying Squirrels (Giants)	70	71	.496	12	Dave Machemer	438,002	6,257	2002
Portland Sea Dogs (Red Sox)	68	73	.482	14	Kevin Boles	374,930	5,434	2006
Binghamton Mets (Mets)	68	74	.479	14 ½	Pedro Lopez	196,929	2,984	1994
Harrisburg Senators (Nationals)	64	78	.451	18 ½	Matt LeCroy	280,964	4,132	1999
New Hampshire Fisher Cats (Blue Jays)	61	81	.430	21 ½	Sal Fasano	377,317	5,549	2011
Erie SeaWolves (Tigers)	57	84	.404	25	Chris Cron	208,725	3,025	Never

Semifinals: Trenton defeated Reading 3-1 and Akron defeated Bowie 3-2 in best-of-five series. **Finals:** Akron defeated Trenton 3-1 in best-of-five series.

MINOR LEAGUES

CLUB BATTING

	AVG	G	AB	R	H	2B	3B	HR	RBI	BB	SO	SB	OBP	SLG
Reading	.274	142	4727	634	1295	256	42	109	591	318	961	73	.325	.415
Bowie	.265	142	4741	697	1258	266	26	125	640	584	972	117	.350	.412
New Britain	.262	142	4745	669	1244	236	33	109	620	468	978	84	.333	.395
Binghamton	.261	142	4652	619	1216	230	42	90	563	502	1048	91	.338	.387
Erie	.261	141	4654	577	1213	250	27	94	527	430	914	113	.328	.387
Akron	.260	141	4588	605	1192	263	24	83	540	555	998	87	.345	.382
Trenton	.260	142	4835	653	1255	261	22	162	605	445	1050	104	.327	.423
Altoona	.259	142	4510	605	1170	254	42	72	561	500	1019	84	.339	.382
New Hampshire	.259	142	4810	588	1244	252	21	121	538	418	992	145	.322	.395
Portland	.255	141	4689	583	1196	272	24	112	546	451	1084	105	.326	.395
Richmond	.255	145	4675	519	1191	233	19	76	491	393	957	104	.318	.361
Harrisburg	.253	142	4752	554	1204	226	31	91	497	338	1023	125	.311	.371

CLUB PITCHING

	ERA	G	CG	SHO	SV	IP	H	R	ER	HR	BB	SO	AVG
Akron	3.03	141	5	9	43	1231	1088	481	415	79	433	1057	.240
Richmond	3.51	141	4	15	36	1253	1174	556	489	64	450	967	.252
Altoona	3.65	142	3	9	34	1211	1162	569	491	85	427	939	.253
Trenton	3.74	142	0	8	36	1264	1291	619	525	95	463	1030	.266
Bowie	3.79	142	2	9	51	1249	1208	611	526	90	403	1019	.256
New Britain	4.00	142	5	10	30	1238	1281	604	551	114	401	930	.271
Reading	4.01	142	2	8	45	1225	1169	630	545	119	540	1051	.253
Portland	4.06	141	2	7	33	1225	1227	617	553	104	459	1013	.263
Binghamton	4.13	142	7	8	27	1228	1239	630	564	114	428	994	.264
New Hampshire	4.14	142	2	8	31	1260	1277	654	579	128	469	1013	.263
Harrisburg	4.15	142	4	7	39	1244	1281	645	574	106	428	1015	.269
Erie	4.71	141	7	4	30	1212	1281	687	634	146	501	968	.274

CLUB FIELDING

	PCT	PO	A	E	DP		PCT	PO	A	E	DP
Erie	.984	3637	1331	83	114	New Hampshire	.977	3779	1451	121	126
Akron	.982	3692	1487	96	143	Portland	.977	3676	1506	123	143
New Britain	.981	3715	1432	100	125	Reading	.977	3674	1341	117	152
Richmond	.981	3758	1610	104	150	Bowie	.976	3747	1548	132	146
Harrisburg	.980	3731	1567	110	150	Trenton	.974	3791	1493	141	123
Binghamton	.977	3683	1329	119	115	Altoona	.972	3632	1493	145	140

INDIVIDUAL BATTING LEADERS (Minimum 2.7 PA/Team Game)

	AVG	G	AB	R	H	2B	3B	HR	RBI	BB	SO	SB
Holt, Brock, Altoona	.322	102	382	52	123	24	6	2	43	40	51	11
Ruf, Darin, Reading	.317	139	489	93	155	32	1	38	104	65	102	2
Widlansky, Robbie, Bowie	.316	128	469	71	148	35	1	8	83	64	74	11
Neal, Thomas, Akron	.314	117	405	77	127	24	1	12	51	46	71	11
Chen, Chun-Hsiu, Akron	.308	108	399	62	123	30	1	5	43	56	101	6
Adams, David, Trenton	.306	86	327	44	100	23	0	8	48	38	53	3
Hernandez, Cesar, Reading	.304	103	411	50	125	26	11	2	51	27	67	16
Perez, Juan, Richmond	.302	126	483	65	146	26	4	11	53	22	85	18
Romero, Niuman, Erie	.300	135	523	73	157	28	4	9	67	54	65	19
Campbell, Eric, Binghamton	.297	115	394	53	117	25	2	9	50	58	76	10

INDIVIDUAL PITCHING LEADERS (Minimum 0.8 IP/Team Game)

	W	L	ERA	G	GS	CG	SV	IP	H	R	HR	BB	SO
Heston, Chris, Richmond	9	8	2.24	25	25	1	0	149	124	43	2	40	135
Wright, Steven, Akron, Portland	10	6	2.44	21	21	1	0	122	91	45	8	64	103
Nuno, Vidal, Trenton	9	5	2.45	20	20	0	0	114	109	40	10	27	100
Kickham, Michael, Richmond	11	10	3.05	28	27	1	0	151	119	57	8	75	137
Espino, Paolo, Akron	7	3	3.09	22	20	0	0	116	116	42	7	34	106
Clark, Zach, Bowie	10	5	3.19	20	19	1	0	121	112	47	8	38	66
Hermsen, B.J., New Britain	11	6	3.22	22	22	1	0	140	145	59	12	25	75
Fitzgerald, Justin, Richmond	7	8	3.22	28	28	0	0	165	134	68	8	60	130
Wheeler, Zack, Binghamton	10	6	3.26	19	19	1	0	116	92	46	2	43	117
Pettibone, Jonathan, Reading	9	7	3.30	19	19	1	0	117	115	52	9	27	81

ALL-STAR TEAM

C: Tommy Joseph, Reading. **1B:** Darin Ruf, Reading. **2B:** Cesar Hernandez, Reading. **3B:** Deibinson Romero, New Britain. **SS:** Niuman Romero, Erie. **OF:** Zoilo Almonte, Trenton; Aaron Hicks, New Britain; Thomas Neal, Akron. **DH:** Chris Colabello, New Britain. **UT:** Brock Holt, Altoona. **RHP:** Chris Heston, Richmond. **LHP:** Mike Kickham, Richmond. **RP:** Preston Guilmet, Akron.
Most Valuable Player: Darin Ruf, Reading. **Pitcher of the Year:** Chris Heston, Richmond. **Rookie of the Year:** Darin Ruf, Reading. **Manager of the Year:** Tony Franklin, Trenton.

DEPARTMENT LEADERS

BATTING

OBP	Ruf, Darin, Reading	.408
SLG	Ruf, Darin, Reading	.620
OPS	Ruf, Darin, Reading	1.028
R	Hicks, Aaron, New Britain	100
H	Goins, Ryan, New Hampshire	158
TB	Ruf, Darin, Reading	303
XBH	Ruf, Darin, Reading	71
2B	Colabello, Chris, New Britain	37
3B	Hernandez, Cesar, Reading	11
	Hicks, Aaron, New Britain	11
HR	Ruf, Darin, Reading	38
RBI	Ruf, Darin, Reading	104
SAC	Goins, Ryan, New Hampshire	19
BB	Hicks, Aaron, New Britain	79
	Lennerton, Jordan, Erie	79
HBP	Brown, Gary, Richmond	19
SO	Lennerton, Jordan, Erie	141
SB	Kobernus, Jeff, Harrisburg	42
CS	Brown, Gary, Richmond	18
AB/SO	Abreu, Miguel, Reading	11.8

PITCHING

G	Black, Vic, Altoona	51
GS	Five tied at	28
GF	Guilmet, Preston, Akron	39
SV	Friend, Justin, Reading	24
	Guilmet, Preston, Akron	24
W	Marshall, Brett, Trenton	13
L	McGuire, Deck, New Hampshire	15
IP	Westcott, Craig, Richmond	165
H	Darnell, Logan, New Britain	193
R	McGuire, Deck, New Hampshire	103
ER	McGuire, Deck, New Hampshire	94
HB	Rodriguez, Julio, Reading	21
BB	May, Trevor, Reading	78
SO	May, Trevor, Reading	151
SO/9	Rodriguez, Julio, Reading	9.1
SO/9 (RP)	Black, Vic, Altoona	12.8
BB/9	Hermsen, B.J., New Britain	1.6
WP	Fitzgerald, Justin, Richmond	18
BK	Rosenbaum, Daniel, Harrisburg	8
HR	Three tied at	22
AVG	Wright, Steven, Akron, Portland	.208

FIELDING

C	FPCT	Valle, Sebastian, Reading	1.000
	PO	Perez, Roberto, Akron	699
	A	Perez, Roberto, Akron	92
	E	Ivany, Devin, Harrisburg	8
		Perez, Roberto, Akron	8
	DP	Herrmann, Chris, New Britain	8
	PB	Perez, Roberto, Akron	25
1B	FPCT	Lennerton, Jordan, Erie	.998
	PO	Lennerton, Jordan, Erie	1000
	A	Colabello, Chris, New Britain	82
	E	Murton, Luke, Trenton	12
	DP	Colabello, Chris, New Britain	98
2B	FPCT	Cavan, Ryan, Richmond	.994
	PO	Cavan, Ryan, Richmond	278
	A	Cavan, Ryan, Richmond	402
	E	Hernandez, Cesar, Reading	15
	DP	Cavan, Ryan, Richmond	99
3B	FPCT	Romero, Deibinson, New Britain	.945
	PO	Romero, Deibinson, New Britain	77
	A	Mayora, Daniel, Richmond	254
	E	Mayora, Daniel, Richmond	27
	DP	Mayora, Daniel, Richmond	26
SS	FPCT	Romero, Niuman, Erie	.977
	PO	Romero, Niuman, Erie	191
	A	Adrianza, Ehire, Richmond	359
	E	Holt, Brock, Altoona	23
	DP	Adrianza, Ehire, Richmond	84
OF	FPCT	Neal, Thomas, Akron	.996
	PO	Lagares, Juan, Binghamton	353
	A	Lagares, Juan, Binghamton	17
	E	Latimore, Quincy, Altoona	12
	DP	Perez, Juan, Richmond	5

MINOR LEAGUES

BY JOHN MANUEL

The Mobile BayBears won the 2011 Southern League championship with a roster full of top prospects. The playoff rotation alone featured Trevor Bauer, Patrick Corbin, Jarrod Parker and Tyler Skaggs, while the lineup included league MVP Paul Goldschmidt, Adam Eaton and Ryan Wheeler. All those former BayBears played in the majors in 2012, and many helped the Reno Aces win the Triple-A national championship.

None of that turnover kept manager Turner Ward and the 2012 BayBears from repeating as league champs. Neither did a slew of promotions (including Bauer and Skaggs) that prompted Mobile to finish just 29-41 in the second half. Mobile became the first outright Southern League champ since Birmingham in 1987 to win the league with a losing overall record.

Nonetheless, the BayBears regrouped in the playoffs behind a group of prospects promoted from high Class A Visalia and holdovers such as third baseman Matt Davidson and outfielder Alfredo Marte, who combined to hit 43 home runs. Davidson had one of the biggest hits of the postseason, a two-run, walk-off homer in the 10th inning of Game Three of the championship series that gave Mobile a 4-2 victory and 2-1 series lead.

It also found a new slew of postseason aces, such as righthander Mike Bolsinger, who won both his playoff starts. He tossed seven scoreless in the 1-0 clincher against Jackson in Game Four, and independent league signee Bo Schultz got the save, retiring Mike Zunino—the Mariners' 2012 first-round pick—for the final out.

Jackson had the league's most talented team, with six Generals placing on BA's Top 20 Prospects list, even without Zunino having enough at-bats to qualify. Righthander Taijuan Walker and lefthander James Paxton spent the whole season in Jackson, and both pitched well in the playoffs. Zunino went 11-for-29 with three homers in the playoffs.

Pensacola didn't make the playoffs, but the Blue Wahoos made a splash in their debut season. The Reds affiliate relocated from Zebulon, N.C., where the Carolina Mudcats became a member of the Carolina League (replacing the Kinston Indians). The Blue Wahoos went 34-35 in each half but still led the league in attendance by more than 500 fans per game at 328,147 total fans. Many came out for the newness, but some came out for shortstop Billy Hamilton, who joined the team after the all-star break and led it in stolen bases with 51 in just 50 games. Hamilton set the new single-season steals record for all of professional baseball with 155.

TOP 20 PROSPECTS

1. Trevor Bauer, rhp, Mobile (Diamondbacks)
2. Taijuan Walker, rhp, Jackson (Mariners)
3. Tyler Skaggs, lhp, Mobile (Diamondbacks)
4. Danny Hultzen, lhp, Jackson (Mariners)
5. Billy Hamilton, ss, Pensacola (Reds)
6. Andrelton Simmons, ss, Mississippi (Braves)
7. Nick Franklin, ss/2b, Jackson (Mariners)
8. Hak-Ju Lee, ss, Montgomery (Rays)
9. Allen Webster, rhp, Chattanooga (Dodgers)
10. James Paxton, lhp, Jackson (Mariners)
11. Tony Cingrani, lhp, Pensacola (Reds)
12. Matt Davidson, 3b, Mobile (Diamondbacks)
13. Zach Lee, rhp, Chattanooga (Dodgers)
14. Brad Miller, ss, Jackson (Mariners)
15. Didi Gregorius, ss, Pensacola (Reds)
16. Tyler Thornburg, rhp, Huntsville (Brewers)
17. Daniel Corcino, rhp, Pensacola (Reds)
18. Christian Bethancourt, c, Mississippi (Braves)
19. Carter Capps, rhp, Jackson (Mariners)
20. Sean Gilmartin, lhp, Mississippi (Braves)

STANDINGS: SPLIT SEASON

FIRST HALF					SECOND HALF				
NORTH	**W**	**L**	**PCT**	**GB**	**NORTH**	**W**	**L**	**PCT**	**GB**
Jackson	42	28	.600	—	Chattanooga	41	29	.586	—
Huntsville	35	35	.500	7	Jackson	37	33	.529	4
Tennessee	35	35	.500	7	Tennessee	37	33	.529	4
Chattanooga	32	38	.471	9	Birmingham	33	37	.471	8
Birmingham	30	39	.435	11½	Huntsville	30	39	.435	10½
SOUTH	**W**	**L**	**PCT**	**GB**	**SOUTH**	**W**	**L**	**PCT**	**GB**
Mobile	40	30	.571	—	Montgomery	38	31	.551	—
Montgomery	36	32	.529	3	Jacksonville	37	33	.529	1½
Pensacola	34	35	.493	5½	Pensacola	34	35	.493	4
Jacksonville	33	37	.471	7	Mississippi	32	37	.464	6
Mississippi	30	40	.429	10	Mobile	29	41	.414	9½

Semifinals: Jackson defeated Chattanooga 3-1 and Mobile defeated Montgomery 3-1 in best-of-five series. **Finals:** Mobile defeated Jackson 3-1 in best-of-five series.

OVERALL STANDINGS

Team (Organization)	W	L	PCT	GB	Manager	Attendance	Average	Last Pennant
Jackson Generals (Mariners)	79	61	.564	—	Jim Pankovits	133,352	2,052	2000
Montgomery Biscuits (Rays)	74	63	.540	3½	Billy Gardner Jr.	244,976	3,769	2007
Chattanooga Lookouts (Dodgers)	73	65	.529	5	Carlos Subero	243,051	3,522	1998
Tennessee Smokies (Cubs)	72	68	.514	7	Buddy Bailey	251,112	3,748	2004
Jacksonville Suns (Marlins)	70	70	.500	9	Andy Barkett	293,013	4,309	2010
Mobile Baybears (Diamondbacks)	69	71	.493	10	Turner Ward	133,062	2,112	2012
Pensacola Blue Wahoos (Reds)	68	70	.493	10	Jim Riggleman	328,147	4,826	2003
Huntsville Stars (Brewers)	65	74	.468	13½	Darnell Coles	130,231	1,973	2001
Birmingham Barons (White Sox)	63	76	.453	15½	Bobby Magallanes	204,269	3,004	2002
Mississippi Braves (Braves)	62	77	.446	16½	Aaron Holbert	191,639	2,904	2008

CLUB BATTING

	AVG	G	AB	R	H	2B	3B	HR	RBI	BB	SO	SB	OBP	SLG
Jackson	.261	140	4645	601	1211	235	39	118	555	473	1120	134	.333	.404
Montgomery	.261	137	4615	636	1204	227	53	84	570	518	935	140	.342	.388
Huntsville	.260	139	4567	558	1188	225	22	90	508	491	1002	112	.336	.378
Birmingham	.254	139	4641	629	1181	234	38	84	576	561	1038	118	.341	.374
Tennessee	.253	140	4552	595	1152	237	36	99	549	552	1015	97	.336	.386
Chattanooga	.251	138	4591	621	1153	262	42	91	569	557	1020	127	.338	.386
Pensacola	.249	138	4478	529	1117	192	35	73	485	478	986	129	.326	.357
Mississippi	.247	139	4581	555	1131	225	30	53	505	475	941	124	.324	.344
Mobile	.244	140	4467	583	1092	210	20	101	540	520	950	101	.330	.368
Jacksonville	.237	140	4527	606	1073	223	26	108	565	548	1181	59	.326	.369

CLUB PITCHING

	ERA	G	CG	SHO	SV	IP	H	R	ER	HR	BB	SO	AVG
Jackson	3.37	140	3	10	42	1230	1117	522	461	76	514	1068	.244
Chattanooga	3.57	138	0	6	45	1233	1101	554	489	61	554	1177	.241
Mississippi	3.65	139	7	9	27	1222	1116	569	495	77	498	1031	.245
Pensacola	3.69	138	1	11	40	1207	1035	542	495	116	567	1190	.234
Jacksonville	3.92	140	5	14	41	1222	1236	601	533	101	381	975	.264
Tennessee	3.92	140	3	7	48	1208	1188	615	526	109	507	898	.258
Montgomery	3.98	137	2	6	34	1207	1151	604	533	92	568	1004	.255
Huntsville	3.99	139	3	2	39	1206	1173	624	535	85	557	962	.259
Mobile	4.13	140	0	9	36	1205	1238	637	553	105	437	997	.267
Birmingham	4.22	139	2	6	32	1210	1147	645	568	79	590	886	.252

CLUB FIELDING

	PCT	PO	A	E	DP		PCT	PO	A	E	DP
Jackson	.980	3689	1431	106	141	Jacksonville	.976	3667	1343	122	118
Pensacola	.980	3620	1241	100	98	Tennessee	.975	3623	1510	132	113
Montgomery	.979	3620	1329	106	129	Birmingham	.974	3630	1449	135	125
Chattanooga	.978	3699	1442	117	134	Huntsville	.974	3617	1468	137	131
Mississippi	.978	3666	1480	115	152	Mobile	.972	3614	1354	145	113

INDIVIDUAL BATTING LEADERS *(MINIMUM 2.7 PA/TEAM GAME)*

	AVG	G	AB	R	H	2B	3B	HR	RBI	BB	SO	SB
Luna, Omar, Montgomery	.315	122	470	63	148	20	3	3	57	38	42	19
Fellhauer, Josh, Pensacola	.314	117	338	50	106	20	2	4	41	54	54	6
Cunningham, Todd, Mississippi	.309	120	466	77	144	23	6	3	51	38	51	24
Morris, Hunter, Huntsville	.303	136	522	77	158	40	6	28	113	40	117	2
Marte, Alfredo, Mobile	.294	113	398	68	117	25	3	20	75	34	72	6
Gennett, Scooter, Huntsville	.293	133	533	66	156	30	2	5	44	28	71	11
Krauss, Marc, Mobile	.283	104	346	75	98	29	2	15	61	73	91	6
Bour, Justin, Tennessee	.283	138	506	64	143	36	0	17	110	62	115	4
Watkins, Logan, Tennessee	.281	133	488	93	137	20	11	9	52	76	97	28
Lake, Junior, Tennessee	.279	103	405	56	113	26	3	10	50	35	105	21

INDIVIDUAL PITCHING LEADERS *(MINIMUM 0.8 IP/TEAM GAME)*

	W	L	ERA	G	GS	CG	SV	IP	H	R	HR	BB	SO
Moran, Gary, Mississippi	5	10	2.91	29	23	2	1	161	153	73	7	42	117
Corcino, Daniel, Pensacola	8	8	3.01	26	26	0	0	143	111	61	9	65	126
Stinson, Josh, Huntsville	11	9	3.16	29	24	1	1	145	167	70	7	71	91
Struck, Nick, Tennessee	14	10	3.18	28	26	0	0	156	140	69	14	44	123
Maurer, Brandon, Jackson	9	2	3.20	24	24	1	0	138	133	54	4	48	117
Gilmartin, Sean, Mississippi	5	8	3.54	20	20	3	0	119	111	49	9	26	86
Webster, Allen, Chattanooga	6	8	3.55	27	22	0	0	122	120	63	1	57	117
Martin, Ethan, Chattanooga	8	6	3.58	20	20	0	0	118	89	48	5	61	112
Spruill, Zeke, Mississippi	9	11	3.67	27	27	1	0	162	158	81	8	46	106
Magill, Matt, Chattanooga	11	8	3.75	26	26	0	0	146	127	71	8	61	168

ALL-STAR TEAM

C: Jesus Sucre, Jackson. **1B:** Hunter Morris, Huntsville. **2B:** Scooter Gennett, Huntsville. **3B:** Matt Davidson, Mobile. **SS:** Hak-Ju lee, Montgomery. **OF:** Todd Cunningham, Mississippi; Josh Fellhauer, Pensacola; Marc Krauss, Mobile; Alfredo Marte, Mobile. **DH:** Justin Bour, Tennessee. **UT:** Omar Luna, Montgomery. **RHSP:** Brandon Maurer, Jackson. **LHSP:** Sean Gilmartin, Mississippi. **RP:** Carter Capps, Jackson.
Most Valuable Player: Hunter Morris, Huntsville. **Most Outstanding Pitcher:** Brandon Maurer, Jackson. **Manager of the Year:** Billy Gardner Jr., Montgomery.

DEPARTMENT LEADERS

BATTING

OBP	Krauss, Marc, Mobile	.416
SLG	Morris, Hunter, Huntsville	.563
OPS	Krauss, Marc, Mobile	.924
R	Watkins, Logan, Tennessee	93
H	Morris, Hunter, Huntsville	158
TB	Morris, Hunter, Huntsville	294
XBH	Morris, Hunter, Huntsville	74
2B	Wise, J.T., Chattanooga	41
3B	Mitchell, Jared, Birmingham	12
HR	Morris, Hunter, Huntsville	28
RBI	Morris, Hunter, Huntsville	113
SAC	Buss, Nick, Chattanooga	19
BB	Smolinski, Jake, Jacksonville	78
HBP	Gran, Paul, Jacksonville	19
SO	Dunigan, Joseph, Jackson	175
SB	Hamilton, Billy, Pensacola	51
CS	Prince, Josh, Huntsville	18
AB/SO	Luna, Omar, Montgomery	11.2

PITCHING

G	Freeman, Justin, Pensacola	57
GS	Five tied at	27
GF	Ramos, A.J., Jacksonville	46
SV	Batista, Frank, Tennessee	24
W	Struck, Nick, Tennessee	14
L	Thompson, Jacob, Montgomery	12
IP	Spruill, Zeke, Mississippi	161.2
H	Taylor, Graham, Jacksonville	169
R	Rhee, Dae-Eun, Tennessee	93
ER	Thompson, Jacob, Montgomery	77
HB	Webster, Allen, Chattanooga	17
BB	Miller, Aaron, Chattanooga	71
	Stinson, Josh, Huntsville	71
SO	Magill, Matt, Chattanooga	168
SO/9	Magill, Matt, Chattanooga	10.3
SO/9 (RP)	Yates, Kirby, Montgomery	12.4
BB/9	Alvarez, Jose, Jacksonville	1.7
WP	Paxton, James, Jackson	13
BK	Three tied at	3
HR	Rhee, Dae-Eun, Tennessee	18
	Taylor, Graham, Jacksonville	18
AVG	Martin, Ethan, Chattanooga	.214

FIELDING

C	FPCT	Sucre, Jesus, Jackson	.100
	PO	Skipworth, Kyle, Jacksonville	725
	A	Perez, Rossmel, Mobile	95
	E	Fleury, Mark, Pensacola	12
	DP	Thomas, Mark, Montgomery	12
	PB	De La Rosa, Anderson, Huntsville	15
1B	FPCT	Morris, Hunter, Huntsville	.995
	PO	Morris, Hunter, Huntsville	1198
	A	Bour, Justin, Tennessee	67
	E	Bour, Justin, Tennessee	18
	DP	Morris, Hunter, Huntsville	112
2B	FPCT	Watkins, Logan, Tennessee	.987
	PO	Gennett, Scooter, Huntsville	239
	A	Gennett, Scooter, Huntsville	377
	E	Gennett, Scooter, Huntsville	19
	DP	Gennett, Scooter, Huntsville	81
		Gosselin, Philip, Mississippi	81
3B	FPCT	Vidal, David, Pensacola	.986
	PO	Davidson, Matt, Mobile	101
	A	Davidson, Matt, Mobile	227
	E	Davidson, Matt, Mobile	28
	DP	Leonard, Joe, Mississippi	24
SS	FPCT	Lee, Hak-Ju, Montgomery	.954
	PO	Lee, Hak-Ju, Montgomery	191
	A	Lee, Hak-Ju, Montgomery	302
	E	Three tied at	24
	DP	Lee, Hak-Ju, Montgomery	68
OF	FPCT	Morrison, Ty, Montgomery	.996
	PO	LaMarre, Ryan, Pensacola	274
	A	LaMarre, Ryan, Pensacola	20
	E	Mitchell, Jared, Birmingham	12
	DP	Jensen, Kyle, Jacksonville	6

MINOR LEAGUES

BY WILL LINGO

It would be hard to imagine a better year for talent in the Texas League.

With eight teams, the Double-A circuit sometimes gets premium prospects or offers decent depth, but rarely both. In 2012 there was clearly talent at the top, starting with the three best position prospects in the minors: Northwest Arkansas outfielder/third baseman Wil Myers—who was Baseball America's Minor League Player of the Year after hitting 37 home runs between Double-A and Triple-A—Frisco shortstop Jurickson Profar, and Springfield outfielder Oscar Taveras.

Frisco, with Profar and third baseman Mike Olt on the left side of its infield, and Springfield, led by Taveras and righthanders Carlos Martinez and Trevor Rosenthal, were the TL's most talented squads. So it was fitting that they met in the league finals, with the Cardinals winning the first title in franchise history 3-1 in a best-of-five series.

With manager Mike Shildt at the helm after jumping all the way from the Rookie-level Appalachian League, Springfield won the second-half title in the Northern Division and beat Tulsa in the full five games in the semifinals.

Corpus Christi actually had the league's best record, but the Hooks were swept by Frisco in the other semifinal. Olt and Profar had moved on to the majors, but the RoughRiders got contributions from less heralded players like Guilder Rodriguez and Chris McGuiness to power to the finals.

Taveras was still with the Cardinals, and he contributed four doubles during the playoffs (on top of his .321/.380/.572 regular season when he led the league in batting and total bases), but the Cardinals too leaned on more obscure players like Xavier Scruggs and Chris Swauger during their playoff run. Scott Gorgen, who has spent the better part of his last three seasons in Springfield, won the clincher for the Cardinals.

Shildt led the team to a franchise-record 77 regular-season wins and his third straight title, after he managed Johnson City to back-to-back Appalachian League championships.

"This is really an organizational championship,"

he told MLB.com. "A lot of times people get left off, but from the scouts to the player development people to everyone in St. Louis, it's a really well-run organization.

"It was very sweet to get the first one for the franchise, and the team was very conscious of that. They made it part of the team goal this year to win it for the front office, who have treated us like gold all year. We wanted this one to take care of them and our fans."

Taveras won the league MVP in postseason award voting, and Frisco righthander Barret Loux was named the league's top pitcher after going 14-1, 3.47.

STANDINGS: SPLIT-SEASON

FIRST HALF

NORTH	W	L	PCT	GB
Tulsa	40	30	.571	—
NW Arkansas	37	33	.529	3
Springfield	35	35	.500	5
Arkansas	27	43	.386	13

SOUTH	W	L	PCT	GB
Frisco	41	29	.586	—
Corpus Christi	37	33	.529	4
Midland	35	35	.500	6
San Antonio	28	42	.400	13

SECOND HALF

NORTH	W	L	PCT	GB
Springfield	42	26	.618	—
Tulsa	35	34	.507	7½
Arkansas	35	35	.500	8
NW Arkansas	21	48	.304	21½

SOUTH	W	L	PCT	GB
Corpus Christi	44	26	.629	—
Frisco	39	31	.557	5
San Antonio	32	38	.457	12
Midland	29	39	.426	14

Playoffs—Semifinals: Frisco defeated Corpus Christi 3-0 and Springfield defeated Tulsa 3-2 in best-of-five series. **Finals:** Springfield defeated Frisco 3-1 in a best-of-five series.

OVERALL STANDINGS

Team (Organization)	W	L	PCT	GB	Manager(s)	Attendance	Average	Last Pennant
Corpus Christi Hooks (Astros)	81	59	.579	—	Keith Bodie	388,927	5,556	2006
Frisco Roughriders (Rangers)	80	60	.571	1	Steve Buechele	488,224	7,076	2004
Springfield Cardinals (Cardinals)	77	61	.558	3	Mike Shildt	352,674	5,111	2012
Tulsa Drillers (Rockies)	75	64	.540	5½	Duane Espy	372,624	5,323	1998
Midland Rockhounds (Athletics)	64	74	.464	16	Steve Scarsone	301,110	4,562	2009
Arkansas Travelers (Angels)	62	78	.443	19	Mike Micucci	308,109	4,531	2008
San Antonio Missions (Padres)	60	80	.429	21	John Gibbons	301,942	4,440	2007
NW Arkansas Naturals (Royals)	58	81	.417	22½	Brian Poldberg	321,254	4,656	2010

MINOR LEAGUES

CLUB BATTING

	AVG	G	AB	R	H	2B	3B	HR	RBI	BB	SO	SB	OBP	SLG
Corpus Christi	.268	140	4769	736	1280	240	32	123	665	480	1054	132	.342	.410
Springfield	.268	138	4772	671	1277	229	25	125	624	481	998	87	.341	.405
Frisco	.262	140	4774	661	1249	189	59	129	603	440	951	144	.331	.407
Northwest Arkansas	.257	139	4656	564	1198	217	27	109	517	394	1033	122	.321	.386
San Antonio	.256	140	4770	604	1220	237	22	124	559	470	1111	97	.329	.393
Midland	.253	138	4668	652	1180	233	29	105	605	554	1239	66	.338	.383
Tulsa	.252	139	4645	562	1171	226	21	122	511	329	1029	82	.307	.389
Arkansas	.235	140	4636	525	1089	201	20	82	482	370	927	123	.299	.340

CLUB PITCHING

	ERA	G	CG	SHO	SV	IP	H	R	ER	HR	BB	SO	AVG
Tulsa	3.36	139	0	7	39	1236	1142	517	462	122	365	982	.247
Arkansas	3.81	140	4	13	31	1248	1216	598	528	112	446	1031	.258
Springfield	3.83	138	1	8	36	1248	1175	591	531	118	398	1041	.250
Frisco	3.86	140	0	13	37	1255	1177	591	538	118	436	1123	.249
Corpus Christi	4.06	140	3	7	35	1249	1256	628	563	120	408	1055	.261
San Antonio	4.13	140	0	9	27	1243	1227	658	570	90	430	1141	.256
Midland	4.38	138	1	6	24	1218	1265	671	593	98	477	993	.270
Northwest Arkansas	4.78	139	0	6	35	1210	1206	721	643	141	558	976	.261

CLUB FIELDING

	PCT	PO	A	E	DP		PCT	PO	A	E	DP
Tulsa	.982	3709	1583	95	145	Arkansas	.977	3744	1402	120	126
Frisco	.980	3764	1458	105	149	Northwest Arkansas	.976	3630	1425	122	135
Corpus Christi	.979	3747	1467	114	137	Midland	.973	3654	1474	140	139
Springfield	.978	3744	1643	123	163	San Antonio	.972	3729	1426	147	87

INDIVIDUAL BATTING LEADERS (MINIMUM 2.7 PA/TEAM GAME)

	AVG	G	AB	R	H	2B	3B	HR	RBI	BB	SO	SB
Taveras, Oscar, Springfield	.321	124	477	83	153	37	7	23	94	42	56	10
Curtis, Jermaine, Springfield	.313	96	368	61	115	19	1	1	24	47	51	6
Rutledge, Josh, Tulsa	.306	87	356	57	109	27	3	13	35	14	69	14
Goebbert, Jake, Corpus Christi	.304	114	368	71	112	23	6	9	53	55	57	5
Wates, Austin, Corpus Christi	.304	95	359	58	109	16	4	7	48	31	71	17
Martinez, Jose, Corpus Christi	.304	107	425	75	129	21	4	13	75	36	40	3
Freiman, Nate, San Antonio	.298	137	516	80	154	31	1	24	105	49	95	0
Simunic, Andrew, Corpus Christi	.297	106	391	59	116	11	1	2	37	29	65	15
Segura, Jean, Arkansas	.294	94	374	50	110	10	5	7	40	23	57	33
Aliotti, Anthony, Midland	.292	123	455	72	133	29	1	10	76	68	129	0

INDIVIDUAL PITCHING LEADERS (MINIMUM 0.8 IP/TEAM GAME)

	W	L	ERA	G	GS	CG	SV	IP	H	R	HR	BB	SO
Schugel, A.J., Arkansas	6	8	2.89	27	27	0	0	140	117	54	9	55	109
Pena, Ariel, Arkansas	6	6	2.99	19	19	1	0	114	95	43	14	42	111
Maness, Seth, Springfield	11	3	3.27	20	20	1	0	124	122	50	13	9	83
Hellweg, Johnny, Arkansas	5	10	3.38	21	21	1	0	120	105	52	8	60	93
Mariot, Michael, NW Arkansas	6	3	3.4	31	14	0	1	114	111	48	12	30	81
Loux, Barret, Frisco	14	1	3.47	25	25	0	0	127	120	56	10	41	100
Houston, Dan, Tulsa	10	10	3.74	27	27	0	0	161	174	75	16	38	96
Oye, Matt, Arkansas	4	6	3.85	34	15	0	4	112	113	57	10	40	75
Frazier, Parker, Tulsa	5	14	3.88	27	27	0	0	167	182	79	19	40	93
Gardner, Joe, Tulsa	8	8	3.97	28	23	0	1	138	129	68	13	39	99

ALL-STAR TEAM

C: Lars Davis, Tulsa; Ali Solis, San Antonio. **1B:** Nate Freiman, San Antonio. **2B:** Kolten Wong, Springfield. **3B:** Mike Olt, Frisco. **SS:** Jurickson Profar, Frisco. **OF:** Engel Beltre, Frisco; Oscar Taveras, Springfield; Austin Wates, Corpus Christi. **DH:** Jonathan Singleton, Corpus Christi. **UT:** Jose Martinez, Corpus Christi. **P:** Keith Butler, Springfield; Edwar Cabrera, Tulsa; Barret Loux, Frisco; Seth Maness, Springfield; Trevor Rosenthal, Springfield; A.J. Schugel, Arkansas; Jason Stoffel, Corpus Christi; Dan Straily, Midland.
Player of the Year: Oscar Taveras, Springfield. **Pitcher of the Year:** Barret Loux, Frisco. **Manager of the Year:** Keith Bodie, Corpus Christi. **Coach of the Year:** Terry Bradshaw, Northwest Arkansas.

DEPARTMENT LEADERS

BATTING

OBP	Curtis, Jermaine, Springfield	.416
SLG	Olt, Mike, Frisco	.579
OPS	Olt, Mike, Frisco	.977
R	Crumbliss, Conner, Midland	94
	Singleton, Jon, Corpus Christi	94
H	Freiman, Nate, San Antonio	154
TB	Taveras, Oscar, Springfield	273
XBH	Taveras, Oscar, Springfield	67
2B	Taveras, Oscar, Springfield	37
3B	Beltre, Engel, Frisco	17
HR	Olt, Mike, Frisco	28
RBI	Freiman, Nate, San Antonio	105
SAC	Garcia, Leury, Frisco	9
	Navarro, Rey, NW Arkansas	9
BB	Crumbliss, Conner, Midland	120
HBP	Curtis, Jermaine, Springfield	19
	Prince, Jared, Frisco	19
SO	Coleman, Dusty, Midland	182
SB	Villar, Jonathan, Corpus Christi	39
CS	Mitchell, Michael, Tulsa	13
	Segura, Jean, Arkansas	13
AB/SO	Martinez, Jose, Corpus Christi	10.6

PITCHING

G	Sullivan, Josh, Tulsa	60
GS	Three tied at	27
GF	Stoffel, Jason, Corpus Christi	49
SV	Stoffel, Jason, Corpus Christi	27
W	Loux, Barret, Frisco	14
L	Arguelles, Noel, NW Arkansas	14
	Frazier, Parker, Tulsa	14
IP	Frazier, Parker, Tulsa	167
H	Frazier, Parker, Tulsa	182
R	Arguelles, Noel, NW Arkansas	95
ER	Arguelles, Noel, NW Arkansas	85
HB	Haviland, Shawn, Midland	14
BB	Daley, Gary, Midland	71
SO	Sampson, Keyvius, San Antonio	122
SO/9	Sampson, Keyvius, San Antonio	9.0
SO/9 (RP)	Lafferty, Brendan, NW Arkansas	10.6
BB/9	Maness, Seth, Springfield	0.7
WP	Daley, Gary, Midland	20
BK	Rondon, Jorge, Springfield	4
HR	Brigham, Jacob, Frisco	19
	Frazier, Parker, Tulsa	19
AVG	Pena, Ariel, Arkansas	.222

FIELDING

C	FPCT	Davis, Lars, Tulsa	.999
	PO	Felix, Jose, Frisco	656
	A	Ramirez, Carlos, Arkansas	68
	E	Hagerty, Jason, San Antonio	11
	DP	Davis, Lars, Tulsa	10
	PB	Davis, Lars, Tulsa	14
		Rodriguez, Julio, NW Arkansas	14
1B	FPCT	Freiman, Nate, San Antonio	.996
	PO	Scruggs, Xavier, Springfield	1180
	A	Aliotti, Anthony, Midland	87
	E	Scruggs, Xavier, Springfield	15
	DP	Scruggs, Xavier, Springfield	140
2B	FPCT	Martinez, Jose, Corpus Christi	.988
	PO	Wong, Kolten, Springfield	262
	A	Wong, Kolten, Springfield	370
	E	Wong, Kolten, Springfield	17
	DP	Wong, Kolten, Springfield	111
3B	FPCT	Arenado, Nolan, Tulsa	.952
	PO	Arenado, Nolan, Tulsa	90
	A	Arenado, Nolan, Tulsa	362
	E	Arenado, Nolan, Tulsa	23
		Rincon, Edinson, San Antonio	23
	DP	Arenado, Nolan, Tulsa	36
SS	FPCT	Coleman, Dusty, Midland	.971
	PO	Coleman, Dusty, Midland	191
	A	Garcia, Greg, Springfield	425
	E	Valdez, Jeudy, San Antonio	24
		Villar, Jonathan, Corpus Christi	24
	DP	Garcia, Greg, Springfield	92
OF	FPCT	Beltre, Engel, Frisco	.997
	PO	Fuentes, Reymond, San Antonio	315
	A	Barfield, Jeremy, Midland	17
	E	Barfield, Jeremy, Midland	9
	DP	Three tied at	4

MINOR LEAGUES

BY JIM SHONERD

Any discussion of the California League's 2012 season has to begin with one name: Billy Hamilton.

For three months, Hamilton was appointment viewing every night he stepped on the field for Bakersfield. The Reds' shortstop prospect began his historic dash toward Vince Coleman's minor league stolen base record with a steal on Opening Day and rarely slowed down. Hamilton stole four bases in a game four times.

Along with Hamilton, Lancaster center fielder George Springer was the Cal League's other top blue-chip prospect. The Astros' 2011 first-round pick, Springer came to Lancaster for his first full season and flourished. Showing off superb athleticism and five-tool potential, Springer hit .316/.398/.557 with 22 homers for the JetHawks, helping them capture a playoff berth.

Springer wasn't around for the postseason though, having been promoted to Double-A in early August. But while they lost Springer, the JetHawks boasted other impact players. Talented outfielder Domingo Santana was a fixture, hitting .302 with 23 homers of his own, and the team got a boost from the in-season callups of shortstop Delino DeShields Jr. and righthander Nick Tropeano. Tropeano went 6-3, 3.31 down the stretch and DeShields stole 18 bases in 24 games, finishing second to Hamilton with a total of 101 steals between his two Class A stops.

Lancaster's playoff run got off to an inauspicious start with a loss to Lake Elsinore, but the JetHawks came back to win a pair of do-or-die games and didn't look back. Lancaster dispatched High Desert, which finished with the league's best record, in four games in the division finals and then swept Modesto in the title series. DeShields led the way, collecting 14 hits in 10 playoff games, and won the playoff MVP award. It was Lancaster's first title since joining the league in 1996.

Inland Empire first baseman C.J. Cron led the minors in RBIs with 123 and San Jose third

baseman Adam Duvall was one of just five minor leaguers to hit 30 home runs. Modesto righthander Christian Bergman tied for the minor league wins lead (16), while minor league ERA champ Tony Cingrani began his season in Bakersfield. Cingrani braved the Cal League's hitters' paradises to the tune of a 5-1, 1.11 mark before moving up to Double-A.

STANDINGS: SPLIT SEASON

FIRST HALF

NORTH	W	L	PCT	GB
Bakersfield	41	29	.586	—
San Jose	38	32	.543	3
Modesto	34	36	.486	7
Visalia	31	39	.443	10
Stockton	28	42	.400	13

SOUTH	W	L	PCT	GB
High Desert	37	33	.529	—
Rancho Cuca.	37	33	.529	—
Lancaster	37	33	.529	—
Lake Elsinore	36	34	.514	1
Inland Empire	31	39	.443	6

SECOND HALF

NORTH	W	L	PCT	GB
Modesto	39	31	.557	—
San Jose	37	33	.529	2
Visalia	33	37	.471	6
Bakersfield	31	39	.443	8
Stockton	28	42	.400	11

SOUTH	W	L	PCT	GB
High Desert	46	24	.657	—
Lancaster	37	33	.529	9
Inland Empire	35	35	.500	11
Lake Elsinore	33	37	.471	13
Rancho Cuca.	31	39	.443	15

PLAYOFFS—Division Series: Lancaster defeated Lake Elsinore 2-1 and Modesto defeated San Jose 2-1 in best-of-three series. **Semifinals:** Lancaster defeated High Desert 3-1 and Modesto defeated Bakersfield 3-2 in best-of-five series; **Finals:** Lancaster defeated Modesto 3-0 in best-of-five series.

OVERALL STANDINGS

Team (Organization)	W	L	PCT	GB	Manager(s)	Attendance	Average	Last Pennant
High Desert Mavericks (Mariners)	83	57	.593	—	Pedro Grifol	122,906	1,756	1997
San Jose Giants (Giants)	75	65	.536	8	Andy Skeels	210,895	3,101	2010
Lancaster JetHawks (Astros)	74	66	.529	9	Rodney Linares	151,558	2,196	2012
Modesto Nuts (Rockies)	73	67	.521	10	Lenn Sakata	175,918	2,550	2004
Bakersfield Blaze (Reds)	72	68	.514	11	Ken Griffey	43,969	637	1989
Lake Elsinore Storm (Padres)	69	71	.493	14	Shawn Wooten	227,000	3,243	2011
Rancho Cucamonga Quakes (Dodgers)	68	72	.486	15	Juan Bustabad	160,715	2,296	1994
Inland Empire 66ers (Angels)	66	74	.471	17	Bill Haselman	171,986	2,493	2006
Visalia Rawhide (Diamondbacks)	64	76	.457	19	Jason Hardtke	118,625	1,771	1978
Stockton Ports (Athletics)	56	84	.400	27	Webster Garrison	198,602	2,878	2008

CLUB BATTING

	AVG	G	AB	R	H	2B	3B	HR	RBI	BB	SO	SB	OBP	SLG
High Desert	.303	140	5100	951	1547	307	57	189	855	407	1033	147	.359	.497
Lancaster	.283	140	4946	843	1398	248	47	158	760	499	1232	136	.353	.448
Visalia	.276	140	4849	721	1338	236	27	150	657	409	1031	108	.335	.429
Bakersfield	.270	140	4801	734	1296	265	39	127	665	503	1109	266	.346	.421
Modesto	.270	140	4855	782	1312	278	58	121	726	581	1124	105	.351	.426
Rancho Cucamonga	.269	140	4792	728	1288	256	49	144	661	420	1080	128	.336	.433
Inland Empire	.267	140	4876	682	1303	237	53	99	616	383	863	105	.327	.398
Lake Elsinore	.267	140	4862	671	1299	244	41	89	610	432	1181	242	.332	.389
San Jose	.267	140	4809	755	1285	249	38	118	694	543	1176	93	.345	.408
Stockton	.259	140	4843	695	1254	246	31	160	645	529	1226	76	.335	.422

CLUB PITCHING

	ERA	G	CG	SHO	SV	IP	H	R	ER	HR	BB	SO	AVG
Lake Elsinore	4.31	140	0	8	33	1260	1306	709	603	129	375	1124	.267
Modesto	4.39	140	1	7	34	1258	1326	711	613	104	523	1041	.273
San Jose	4.47	140	2	10	32	1231	1272	684	611	94	486	1018	.267
Bakersfield	4.59	140	1	5	37	1246	1290	731	636	158	525	1151	.267
Inland Empire	4.77	140	2	5	31	1257	1374	771	666	121	486	1034	.277
Stockton	4.84	140	1	5	20	1235	1365	799	665	165	370	1169	.276
Visalia	4.89	140	0	4	23	1224	1265	779	665	142	548	1291	.264
High Desert	4.98	140	3	6	33	1248	1400	802	690	152	457	1114	.285
Lancaster	5.00	140	2	7	35	1252	1399	786	695	154	426	987	.284
Rancho Cucamonga	5.06	140	0	3	41	1233	1323	790	693	136	510	1126	.274

CLUB FIELDING

	PCT	PO	A	E	DP		PCT	PO	A	E	DP
Lancaster	.976	3755	1530	132	141	High Desert	.971	3744	1506	158	128
Modesto	.974	3773	1404	138	140	Lake Elsinore	.971	3781	1499	156	118
San Jose	.973	3692	1507	143	133	Visalia	.970	3673	1411	155	125
Inland Empire	.972	3770	1473	151	104	Bakersfield	.966	3738	1458	183	108
R. Cucamonga	.972	3699	1460	148	115	Stockton	.966	3706	1272	174	101

INDIVIDUAL BATTING LEADERS (MINIMUM 2.7 PA/TEAM GAME)

	AVG	G	AB	R	H	2B	3B	HR	RBI	BB	SO	SB
Landry, Leon, Rancho/High Desert	.341	104	449	88	153	34	18	13	76	19	66	27
Miller, Brad, High Desert	.339	97	410	89	139	33	5	11	56	52	79	19
Proscia, Steven, High Desert	.333	106	436	88	145	24	3	24	94	25	97	12
Medica, Tommy, Lake Elsinore	.330	93	355	65	117	37	5	19	87	41	86	1
Hamilton, Billy, Bakersfield	.323	82	337	79	109	18	9	1	30	50	70	104
Springer, George, Lancaster	.316	106	433	101	137	18	10	22	82	56	131	28
Bowe, Theo, Bakersfield	.314	96	373	65	117	13	2	3	39	45	72	58
Pederson, Joc, Rancho Cucamonga	.313	110	434	96	136	26	4	18	70	51	81	26
Hicks, John, High Desert	.312	121	506	87	158	32	2	15	79	28	73	22
Miller, Justin, Lake Elsinore	.311	92	360	64	112	15	4	12	71	40	81	17

INDIVIDUAL PITCHING LEADERS (MINIMUM 0.8 IP/TEAM GAME)

	W	L	ERA	G	GS	CG	SV	IP	H	R	HR	BB	SO
Andriese, Matthew, Lake Elsinore	10	8	3.58	27	26	0	0	146	140	72	9	38	131
Bowman, Josh, Stockton	6	10	3.62	25	25	0	0	147	157	76	14	33	127
Bergman, Christian, Modesto	16	5	3.65	27	27	0	0	163	161	73	16	37	121
Elias, Roenis, High Desert	11	6	3.76	26	26	0	0	148	136	80	19	41	128
Smith, Josh, Bakersfield	9	8	3.8	27	27	1	0	147	143	71	15	46	140
Batista, Lay, Inland Empire	6	7	3.82	29	16	0	0	113	111	61	12	53	80
Smith, Burch, Lake Elsinore	9	6	3.85	26	25	0	0	129	127	62	11	27	137
Meo, Anthony, Visalia	9	8	4.11	26	25	0	0	140	134	78	15	71	153
Rogers, Taylor, San Jose	12	11	4.13	28	27	0	0	153	169	82	11	57	118
Correa, Manny, Inland Empire	9	10	4.31	31	25	1	0	165	191	85	13	26	111

ALL-STAR TEAM

C: John Hicks, High Desert. **1B:** C.J. Cron, Inland Empire. **2B:** Taylor Lindsey, Inland Empire. **3B:** Adam Duvall, San Jose. **SS:** Billy Hamilton, Bakersfield. **OF:** Leon Landry, High Desert; Kyle Parker, Modesto; George Springer, Lancaster. **DH:** Tommy Medica, Lake Elsinore. **UT:** Steve Proscia, High Desert. **P:** Matt Andriese, Lake Elsinore; Christian Bergman, Modesto; Roenis Elias, High Desert; Kevin Quackenbush, Lake Elsinore.

Most Valuable Player: Billy Hamilton, Bakersfield. **Pitcher of the Year:** Christian Bergman, Modesto. **Rookie of the Year:** C.J. Cron, Inland Empire. **Manager of the Year:** Pedro Grifol, High Desert. **Coach of the Year:** Roy Howell, High Desert.

DEPARTMENT LEADERS

BATTING

OBP	Parker, Kyle, Modesto	.415
SLG	Medica, Tommy, Lake Elsinore	.623
OPS	Medica, Tommy, Lake Elsinore	.102
R	Jones, James, High Desert	109
H	Freeman, Michael, Visalia	166
TB	Cron, C.J., Inland Empire	271
XBH	Landry, Leon, Rancho/High Desert	65
2B	Medica, Tommy, Lake Elsinore	37
3B	Landry, Leon, Rancho/High Desert	18
HR	Duvall, Adam, San Jose	30
RBI	Cron, C.J., Inland Empire	123
SAC	Lofton, Chris, San Jose	13
BB	Clark, Jared, Modesto	89
HBP	Three tied at	15
SO	Nash, Telvin, Lancaster	198
SB	Hamilton, Billy, Bakersfield	104
CS	Bowe, Theo, Bakersfield	28
AB/SO	Panik, Joe, San Jose	9.9

PITCHING

G	McCormick, Phil, San Jose	61
GS	Three tied at	28
GF	Quackenbush, Kevin, Lake Elsinore	46
SV	Quackenbush, Kevin, Lake Elsinore	27
W	Bergman, Christian, Modesto	16
L	Gonzalez, Juan, Modesto	13
IP	Correa, Manny, Inland Empire	165
H	Russell, Max, Inland Empire	200
R	Russell, Max, Inland Empire	131
ER	Russell, Max, Inland Empire	105
HB	Schumer, Justin, San Jose	16
BB	Matzek, Tyler, Modesto	95
SO	Matzek, Tyler, Modesto	153
	Meo, Anthony, Visalia	153
SO/9	Chafin, Andrew, Visalia	11.0
SO/9 (RP)	Valdez, Jose, San Jose	12.2
BB/9	Correa, Manny, Inland Empire	1.4
WP	Three tied at	17
BK	Elias, Roenis, High Desert	8
HR	Hernandez, Raymond, Visalia	27
AVG	Chafin, Andrew, Visalia	.241

FIELDING

C	FPCT	O'Brien, Chris, R. Cucamonga	.994
	PO	Hicks, John, High Desert	763
	A	Hicks, John, High Desert	92
	E	Susac, Andrew, San Jose	14
	DP	Hicks, John, High Desert	11
	PB	Hicks, John, High Desert	20
1B	FPCT	Griffin, Jonathan, Visalia	.991
	PO	Oropesa, Ricky, San Jose	1048
	A	Oropesa, Ricky, San Jose	79
	E	Cron, C.J., Inland Empire	19
	DP	Oropesa, Ricky, San Jose	106
2B	FPCT	Spangenberg, Cory, Lake Elsinore	.977
	PO	Lindsey, Taylor, Inland Empire	226
	A	Lindsey, Taylor, Inland Empire	388
	E	Wingo, Scott, Rancho Cucamonga	21
	DP	Hernandez, Enrique, Lancaster	71
3B	FPCT	Meyer, Jonathan, Lancaster	.954
	PO	Meyer, Jonathan, Lancaster	102
	A	Duvall, Adam, San Jose	260
	E	Duvall, Adam, San Jose	29
	DP	Meyer, Jonathan, Lancaster	24
SS	FPCT	Panik, Joe, San Jose	.972
	PO	Bisson, Chris, Lake Elsinore	191
	A	Panik, Joe, San Jose	423
	E	Bisson, Chris, Lake Elsinore	32
	DP	Panik, Joe, San Jose	79
OF	FPCT	Ortega, Rafael, Modesto	.993
	PO	Noel, Rico, Lake Elsinore	306
	A	Ortega, Rafael, Modesto	19
	E	Duran, Juan, Bakersfield	12
	DP	Garcia, Jonathan, R. Cucamonga	4

MINOR LEAGUES

BY JOSH LEVENTHAL

A 10-game win streak at the end of April propelled Winston-Salem into first place in the South Division. It's a spot the Dash would not relinquish for the rest of the season.

Winston-Salem rolled to first- and second-half titles and finished 13 ½ games ahead of second-place Myrtle Beach, whom the Dash dispatched in the first round of the playoffs en route to making their second championship appearance in three years. But like in 2010, Winston-Salem went home without the Mills Cup, this time falling to North Division champ Lynchburg in four games.

The Dash went into the postseason without much of its regular season firepower. Switch-hitting infielder Carlos Sanchez, whom veteran Winston-Salem manager Tommy Thompson proclaimed "one of the best defenders I've been around in 30 years," moved on to Double-A Huntsville in late July before finishing the season with Triple-A Charlotte. Outfielder Trayce Thompson belted 22 homers for the Dash while playing stellar defense in center field, but was also promoted by the time the postseason started. Top pick Courtney Hawkins joined Winston-Salem late and hit a pair of postseason home runs.

The Hillcats ended an up-and-down season—they claimed the North's first-half title before sinking to the cellar in the second half—with a walk-off win in Game Four of the finals for their second title in four years. Adam Milligan, who had gone 1-for-13 in the championship round, hit a sacrifice fly to drive home the winning run in the bottom of the 11th inning. Lynchburg shortstop Nick Ahmed earned MVP honors after going 4-for-5 with three doubles in the decisive game.

"It was Nick Ahmed Night," Lynchburg manager Luis Salazar said.

Dylan Bundy arrived to Frederick with high expectations after beginning his pro career with seven weeks of near-perfect baseball in the low Class A South Atlantic League. The 19-year-old hit a few bumps in the road with Frederick but still was the league's most complete pitcher and best prospect. Lynchburg righthander J.R.

Graham made a case for best pitcher honors after breezing through the Carolina League with a 9-1, 2.63 mark and earning a midseason promotion to Double-A Mississippi.

Salem fielded three of the league's top four prospects, as shortstop Xander Bogaerts and center fielder Jackie Bradley packed a punch atop the Red Sox's lineup before moving on to Double-A. Like Bundy, Salem righthander Barnes is a 2011 first-rounder who made quick work of the South Atlantic League at the start of his pro debut. He overwhelmed CL hitters before tiring down the stretch.

TOP 20 PROSPECTS

1. Dylan Bundy, rhp, Frederick Keys (Orioles)
2. Xander Bogaerts, ss, Salem Red Sox
3. Matt Barnes, rhp, Salem Red Sox
4. Jackie Bradley Jr., of, Salem Red Sox
5. Cody Buckel, Myrtle Beach Pelicans (Rangers)
6. Carlos Sanchez, ss/2b, Winston-Salem Dash (White Sox)
7. J.R. Graham, rhp, Lynchburg Hillcats (Braves)
8. Yordano Ventura, rhp, Wilmington Blue Rocks (Royals)
9. Christian Villanueva, 3b, Myrtle Beach Pelicans (Rangers)
10. Orlando Calixte, ss, Wilmington Blue Rocks (Royals)
11. Erik Johnson, rhp, Winston-Salem Dash (White Sox)
12. Hanser Alberto, ss, Myrtle Beach Pelicans (Rangers)
13. Nick Ahmed, ss, Lynchburg Hillcats (Braves)
14. Edward Salcedo, 3b, Lynchburg Hillcats (Braves)
15. Nathan Karns, rhp, Potomac Nationals
16. Luke Jackson, rhp, Myrtle Beach Pelicans (Rangers)
17. Christian Vazquez, c, Salem Red Sox
18. Trayce Thompson, of, Winston-Salem Dash (White Sox)
19. Ronny Rodriguez, ss/2b, Carolina Mudcats (Indians)
20. Cheslor Cuthbert, 3b, Wilmington Blue Rocks (Royals)

STANDINGS: SPLIT SEASON

FIRST HALF

NORTH	W	L	PCT	GB
Lynchburg	39	31	.557	—
Potomac	31	39	.443	8
Wilmington	29	41	.414	10
Frederick	27	43	.386	12

SOUTH	W	L	PCT	GB
W-S	44	25	.638	—
Salem	41	28	.594	3
Myrtle Beach	36	34	.514	8 ½
Carolina	32	38	.457	12 ½

SECOND HALF

NORTH	W	L	PCT	GB
Wilmington	37	33	.529	—
Frederick	35	34	.507	1 ½
Potomac	33	36	.478	3 ½
Lynchburg	33	37	.471	4

SOUTH	W	L	PCT	GB
W-S	43	26	.623	—
Myrtle Beach	38	31	.551	5
Carolina	31	39	.443	12 ½
Salem	27	41	.397	15 ½

PLAYOFFS—Semifinals: Lynchburg defeated Wilmington 2-1 and Winston-Salem defeated Myrtle Beach 2-1 in best-of-three series. **Finals:** Lynchburg defeated Winston-Salem 3-1 in a best-of-five series.

OVERALL STANDINGS

Team (Organization)	W	L	PCT	GB	Manager(s)	Attendance	Average	Last Pennant
Winston-Salem Dash (White Sox)	87	51	.630	—	Tommy Thompson	305,515	4,428	2003
Myrtle Beach Pelicans (Rangers)	74	65	.532	13 ½	Jason Wood	219,273	3,273	2000
Lynchburg Hillcats (Braves)	72	68	.514	16	Luis Salazar	155,261	2,426	2012
Salem Red Sox (Red Sox)	68	69	.496	18 ½	Billy McMillon	178,730	2,628	2001
Wilmington Blue Rocks (Royals)	66	74	.471	22	Vance Wilson	287,992	4,235	1999
Potomac Nationals (Nationals)	64	75	.460	23 ½	Brian Rupp	191,928	2,953	2010
Carolina Mudcats (Indians)	63	77	.450	25	Edwin Rodriguez	225,577	3,418	2006
Frederick Keys (Orioles)	62	77	.446	25 ½	Orlando Gomez	311,805	4,724	2011

CLUB BATTING

	AVG	G	AB	R	H	2B	3B	HR	RBI	BB	SO	SB	OBP	SLG
Winston-Salem	.278	139	4736	796	1318	296	41	135	743	458	1027	131	.350	.444
Salem	.270	138	4573	672	1234	311	32	94	615	487	1050	180	.348	.414
Carolina	.257	140	4561	613	1174	268	41	105	565	381	1060	97	.321	.403
Lynchburg	.254	140	4546	590	1155	268	32	103	537	432	1031	144	.328	.395
Frederick	.253	139	4501	579	1140	242	19	99	521	463	1046	129	.329	.381
Potomac	.253	139	4489	590	1136	233	36	84	531	383	1061	152	.317	.377
Myrtle Beach	.247	139	4606	534	1136	215	16	68	472	349	882	113	.310	.345
Wilmington	.246	140	4565	553	1125	205	28	86	489	408	1095	110	.315	.360

CLUB PITCHING

	ERA	G	CG	SHO	SV	IP	H	R	ER	HR	BB	SO	AVG
Myrtle Beach	3.28	139	3	13	36	1228	1116	524	447	80	390	1111	.245
Lynchburg	3.54	140	5	9	34	1224	1193	585	481	74	412	1107	.258
Winston-Salem	3.71	139	2	15	39	1227	1127	596	506	87	469	1106	.244
Wilmington	3.74	140	1	10	29	1204	1160	575	500	94	399	1072	.253
Frederick	4.19	139	3	11	35	1195	1217	601	557	126	399	977	.264
Salem	4.21	138	3	10	36	1192	1190	633	558	113	349	1005	.261
Carolina	4.31	140	2	8	31	1189	1174	654	570	82	511	916	.262
Potomac	4.65	139	7	11	31	1174	1241	700	606	118	432	958	.273

CLUB FIELDING

	PCT	PO	A	E	DP		PCT	PO	A	E	DP
Myrtle Beach	.973	3683	1507	142	147	Wilmington	.971	3613	1343	147	115
Salem	.973	3576	1428	139	123	Lynchburg	.970	3672	1518	160	139
Carolina	.971	3569	1450	151	132	Potomac	.970	3522	1510	155	146
Frederick	.971	3586	1493	151	130	Winston-Salem	.970	3681	1431	157	113

INDIVIDUAL BATTING LEADERS *(MINIMUM 2.7 PA/TEAM GAME)*

	AVG	G	AB	R	H	2B	3B	HR	RBI	BB	SO	SB
Sanchez, Carlos, Winston-Salem	.315	92	365	58	115	14	6	1	42	31	64	19
Black, Dan, Winston-Salem	.315	129	499	82	157	29	2	17	88	64	92	5
Shaw, Travis, Salem	.305	99	354	69	108	31	3	16	73	59	81	11
Bogaerts, Xander, Salem	.302	104	384	59	116	27	3	15	64	43	85	4
Almanzar, Michael, Salem	.300	124	454	62	136	36	0	12	54	33	77	10
Earley, Michael, Winston-Salem	.291	124	454	76	132	27	7	13	73	34	73	7
Villanueva, Christian, Myrtle Beach	.285	100	375	45	107	19	1	10	59	24	83	9
Nicholas, Brett, Myrtle Beach	.285	122	446	49	127	33	0	8	63	44	84	5
Garcia, Chris, Lynchburg	.285	125	411	56	117	25	1	11	59	85	92	3
Herrera, Odubel, Myrtle Beach	.284	126	500	72	142	22	6	5	46	33	99	27

INDIVIDUAL PITCHING LEADERS *(MINIMUM 0.8 IP/TEAM GAME)*

	W	L	ERA	G	GS	CG	SV	IP	H	R	HR	BB	SO
Hendricks, Kyle, Myrtle Beach	5	8	2.82	20	20	2	0	131	123	49	8	15	112
McCray, Stephen, Winston-Salem	9	3	3.23	25	17	0	0	117	97	53	11	43	91
Schlosser, Gus, Lynchburg	13	7	3.38	27	27	1	0	165	156	73	9	33	139
Workman, Brandon, Salem	7	7	3.4	20	20	0	0	114	104	47	10	20	107
Couch, Keith, Salem	11	9	3.46	28	22	2	0	146	152	65	9	34	109
Adam, Jason, Wilmington	7	12	3.53	27	27	0	0	158	148	73	18	36	123
Rojas, Randol, Myrtle Beach	9	6	3.73	26	16	0	0	113	120	59	7	37	76
Delgado, Dimasther, Lynchburg	7	7	3.92	24	24	0	0	129	144	63	7	39	80
Northcraft, Aaron, Lynchburg	10	11	3.98	27	27	2	0	152	143	83	4	53	160
Collop, Justin, Winston-Salem	9	4	4.17	31	16	0	0	121	131	59	14	38	80

ALL-STAR TEAM

C: Braeden Schlehuber, Lynchburg; Christian Vazquez, Salem. **1B:** Dan Black, Winston-Salem. **2B:** Ronny Rodriguez, Carolina; Carlos Sanchez, Winston-Salem. **3B:** Michael Almanzar, Salem. **SS:** Xander Bogaerts, Salem. **OF:** Jackie Bradley, Winston-Salem; Michael Earley, Winston-Salem; Trayce Thompson, Winston-Salem. **DH:** Travis Shaw, Salem. **UT IF:** Nick Ahmed, Lynchburg. **UT OF:** Brady Shoemaker, Winston-Salem. **SP:** Gus Schlosser, Lynchburg. **RP:** Ben Rowen, Myrtle Beach.
Most Valuable Player: Dan Black, Winston-Salem. **Pitcher of the Year:** Gus Schlosser, Lynchburg.
Manager of the Year: Tommy Thompson, Winston-Salem.

DEPARTMENT LEADERS

BATTING

OBP	Shaw, Travis, Salem	.411
SLG	Shaw, Travis, Salem	.545
OPS	Shaw, Travis, Salem	.957
R	Ahmed, Nick, Lynchburg	84
H	Black, Dan, Winston-Salem	157
TB	Black, Dan, Winston-Salem	241
XBH	Thompson, Trayce, Winston-Salem	55
2B	Ahmed, Nick, Lynchburg	36
	Almanzar, Michael, Salem	36
3B	Wolters, Tony, Carolina	8
HR	Baker, Aaron, Frederick	22
	Thompson, Trayce, Winston-Salem	22
RBI	Thompson, Trayce, Winston-Salem	90
SAC	Franco, Angel, Wilmington	18
BB	Garcia, Chris, Lynchburg	85
HBP	Hankerd, Cyle, Winston-Salem	25
SO	Eibner, Brett, Wilmington	165
SB	Ahmed, Nick, Lynchburg	40
CS	Sanchez, Adrian, Potomac	16
AB/SO	Chirino, Santiago, Myrtle Beach	9.7

PITCHING

G	Chaffee, Matt, Lynchburg	45
	Walters, David, Frederick	45
GS	Five tied at	27
GF	Jaime, Juan, Lynchburg	37
SV	Rowen, Ben, Myrtle Beach	19
W	Schlosser, Gus, Lynchburg	13
L	Goodnight, Michael, Carolina	13
IP	Schlosser, Gus, Lynchburg	165.1
H	Grace, Matthew, Potomac	178
R	Grace, Matthew, Potomac	95
ER	Ray, Robbie, Potomac	77
	Roberts, Will, Carolina	77
HB	Goodnight, Michael, Carolina	19
BB	Goodnight, Michael, Carolina	76
SO	Northcraft, Aaron, Lynchburg	160
SO/9	Northcraft, Aaron, Lynchburg	9.5
SO/9 (RP)	Wort, Rob, Potomac	15.1
BB/9	Hendricks, Kyle, Myrtle Beach	1.0
WP	Blair, Kyle, Carolina	20
	Goodnight, Michael, Carolina	20
BK	Rojas, Randol, Myrtle Beach	4
HR	Adam, Jason, Wilmington	18
	Celestino, Miguel, Salem	18
AVG	McCray, Stephen, Winston-Salem	.226

FIELDING

C	FPCT	Freitas, David, Potomac	.996
	PO	Telis, Tomas, Myrtle Beach	630
	A	Vazquez, Christian, Salem	110
	E	Telis, Tomas, Myrtle Beach	12
	DP	Telis, Tomas, Myrtle Beach	8
	PB	Telis, Tomas, Myrtle Beach	13
1B	FPCT	Aguilar, Jesus, Carolina	.996
	PO	Black, Dan, Winston-Salem	1018
	A	Black, Dan, Winston-Salem	108
	E	Black, Dan, Winston-Salem	12
	DP	Nicholas, Brett, Myrtle Beach	96
2B	FPCT	Coyle, Sean, Salem	.967
	PO	Coyle, Sean, Salem	177
	A	Coyle, Sean, Salem	290
	E	Coyle, Sean, Salem	16
		Wolters, Tony, Carolina	16
	DP	Coyle, Sean, Salem	67
3B	FPCT	Urshela, Giovanny, Carolina	.964
	PO	Salcedo, Edward, Lynchburg	79
	A	Salcedo, Edward, Lynchburg	265
	E	Salcedo, Edward, Lynchburg	42
	DP	Almanzar, Michael, Salem	26
SS	FPCT	Ahmed, Nick, Lynchburg	.963
	PO	Ahmed, Nick, Lynchburg	211
	A	Ahmed, Nick, Lynchburg	457
	E	Herrera, Odubel, Myrtle Beach	28
		Rodriguez, Ronny, Carolina	28
	DP	Ahmed, Nick, Lynchburg	99
OF	FPCT	Wilkerson, Shannon, Salem	.996
	PO	Taylor, Michael, Potomac	267
	A	Taylor, Michael, Potomac	21
	E	Beltre, Geulin, Wilmington	8
		Taylor, Michael, Potomac	8
	DP	Beltre, Geulin, Wilmington	7
		Taylor, Michael, Potomac	7

MINOR LEAGUES

BY J.J. COOPER

Outfielder Avisail Garcia began the season in Lakeland and ended it by playing in the World Series for the Tigers. Third baseman Nick Castellanos was promoted out of Lakeland after hitting .405 in 55 games.

But even without the team's top two players, the Flying Tigers still had enough to knock off Jupiter for the Florida State League title. It was Lakeland's first in 20 years.

The championship series truly went down to the wire. In the deciding Game Five, Hernan Perez stole third and then scored on a throwing error by catcher J.T. Realmuto. Tyler Collins followed up with an RBI single, giving Lakeland all the runs it needed in a 2-0 win. Two games earlier, Jupiter had taken a 2-1 lead in the best-of-five series with a 2-0 win of its own. Lakeland came from behind to win Game Four 5-3 and force a winner-takes-all finale.

Winning high-stakes games was a normal part of the Flying Tigers' 2012 season. Lakeland only made it to the playoffs because it won its final three games of the regular season. That proved just enough to edge Clearwater for the North Division second-half title by one game.

Dunedin and St. Lucie had the league's best records in the regular season but were each knocked out in the first round of the playoffs. The Marlins hired Dunedin manager Mike Redmod as their big league manager after the season.

By playoff time, Lakeland wasn't exactly a prospect-laden club, but there were plenty of prospects sprinkled around the Florida State League. Between Bradenton's Gerrit Cole and Jameson Taillon and Jupiter's Jose Fernandez, the FSL had three of the best pitching prospects in the game. The league wasn't lacking for center fielders either, as Jupiter's Christian Yelich, Dunedin's Jake Marisnick and Tampa's Mason Williams and Slade Heathcott all impressed.

Palm Beach Cardinals outfielder Mike O'Neill won the league's batting title with a .342 average,

but his 70 walks compared to just 24 strikeouts was even more impressive.

There were a couple of games to remember as well. Palm Beach's Chris Corrigan held Port Charlotte hitless in an easy 8-0 win on Aug. 29 for the league's only no-htter. Jupiter's Marcel Ozuna, the league's home run champion with 24, had a three home run game on June 10.

STANDINGS: SPLIT SEASON

FIRST HALF					SECOND HALF				
North	W	L	PCT	GB	**North**	W	L	PCT	GB
Dunedin	42	25	.627	—	Lakeland	37	29	.561	—
Lakeland	36	29	.554	5	Clearwater	36	30	.545	1
Clearwater	36	30	.545	5½	Dunedin	36	30	.545	1
Tampa	30	37	.448	12	Tampa	35	33	.515	3
Daytona	30	38	.441	12½	Brevard Co.	34	33	.507	3½
Brevard Co.	29	39	.426	13½	Daytona	29	36	.446	7½
South	W	L	PCT	GB	**South**	W	L	PCT	GB
St. Lucie	49	19	.721	—	Jupiter	38	28	.576	—
Jupiter	36	34	.514	14	St. Lucie	34	33	.507	4½
Palm Beach	31	36	.463	17½	Palm Beach	33	36	.478	6½
Charlotte	29	38	.433	19½	Fort Myers	32	36	.471	7
Fort Myers	28	39	.418	20½	Bradenton	31	36	.463	7½
Bradenton	29	41	.414	21	Charlotte	26	41	.388	12½

PLAYOFFS—Semifinals: Lakeland defeated Dunedin 2-0 and Jupiter defeated St. Lucie 2-1 in best-of-three series. **Finals:** Lakeland defeated Jupiter 3-2 in a best-of-five series.

OVERALL STANDINGS

Team (Organization)	W	L	PCT	GB	Manager	Attendance	Average	Last Pennant
St. Lucie Mets (Mets)	83	52	.615	—	Ryan Ellis	92,044	1,509	2006
Dunedin Blue Jays (Blue Jays)	78	55	.586	4	Mike Redmond	53,091	830	Never
Lakeland Flying Tigers (Tigers)	73	58	.557	8	Dave Huppert	59,589	1,027	2012
Clearwater Threshers (Phillies)	72	60	.545	9½	Chris Truby	177,297	2,570	2007
Jupiter Hammerheads (Marlins)	74	62	.544	9½	Andy Haines	73,337	1,128	1991
Tampa Yankees (Yankees)	65	70	.481	18	Luis Sojo	112,668	1,817	2010
Palm Beach Cardinals (Cardinals)	64	72	.471	19½	Johnny Rodriguez	73,954	1,121	2005
Brevard County Manatees (Brewers)	63	72	.467	20	Joe Ayrault	101,528	1,515	2001
Fort Myers Miracle (Twins)	60	75	.444	23	Jake Mauer	121,452	1,840	1985
Daytona Cubs (Cubs)	59	74	.444	23	Brian Harper	143,131	2,346	2011
Bradenton Marauders (Pirates)	60	77	.438	24	Carlos Garcia	101,528	1,515	1963
Charlotte Stone Crabs (Rays)	55	79	.410	27½	Jim Morrison	117,417	1,925	1990

CLUB BATTING

	AVG	G	AB	R	H	2B	3B	HR	RBI	BB	SO	SB	OBP	SLG
Lakeland	.267	131	4327	582	1154	232	35	66	528	382	884	135	.331	.382
Jupiter	.265	136	4540	623	1204	237	28	71	567	443	908	99	.336	.377
Daytona	.263	133	4374	602	1149	224	51	66	544	418	874	201	.331	.382
Clearwater	.257	133	4496	569	1157	235	30	84	530	352	996	91	.318	.379
Dunedin	.255	133	4415	669	1125	277	37	94	609	499	1041	121	.336	.398
St. Lucie	.255	135	4417	613	1128	251	28	106	552	476	954	167	.336	.397
Tampa	.254	135	4476	538	1135	228	38	75	493	382	984	115	.317	.372
Palm Beach	.253	136	4469	528	1130	219	26	50	471	437	926	92	.324	.347
Charlotte	.252	134	4436	518	1120	197	44	69	472	338	860	105	.316	.363
Fort Myers	.250	135	4483	598	1119	212	33	89	551	494	1006	61	.329	.371
Bradenton	.245	138	4487	583	1099	194	46	71	505	457	1023	130	.319	.356
Brevard County	.242	135	4319	538	1047	210	27	66	509	438	1019	157	.320	.349

CLUB PITCHING

	ERA	G	CG	SHO	SV	IP	H	R	ER	HR	BB	SO	AVG
St. Lucie	3.34	135	2	11	43	1170	1092	511	434	61	378	1027	.247
Jupiter	3.51	136	0	11	30	1181	1156	556	461	68	415	1013	.255
Dunedin	3.59	133	3	7	42	1158	1135	524	462	66	356	962	.256
Palm Beach	3.71	136	4	9	35	1180	1122	574	487	76	430	920	.250
Clearwater	3.74	133	2	8	39	1186	1102	570	493	80	431	1161	.246
Tampa	3.77	135	3	14	32	1170	1110	565	490	62	498	1086	.251
Lakeland	3.79	131	1	10	39	1120	1045	539	472	59	470	897	.252
Brevard County	3.86	135	4	11	34	1153	1140	587	495	79	421	937	.258
Daytona	4.12	133	1	5	25	1133	1090	602	518	84	438	874	.252
Bradenton	4.15	138	5	9	32	1200	1182	631	553	92	400	830	.259
Fort Myers	4.23	135	1	5	31	1179	1286	655	554	90	397	899	.277
Charlotte	4.42	134	2	7	33	1159	1107	647	569	90	482	869	.253

CLUB FIELDING

	PCT	PO	A	E	DP		PCT	PO	A	E	DP
Lakeland	.978	3360	1376	109	110	Tampa	.973	3510	1329	133	105
Bradenton	.977	3600	1513	122	148	Clearwater	.972	3559	1310	140	107
Dunedin	.975	3473	1397	124	134	St. Lucie	.972	3511	1269	137	90
Fort Myers	.975	3543	1292	124	107	Daytona	.970	3398	1296	147	93
Brevard County	.973	3459	1363	133	99	Palm Beach	.970	3541	1413	153	105
Charlotte	.973	3476	1261	132	105	Jupiter	.969	3543	1292	156	101

INDIVIDUAL BATTING LEADERS *(MINIMUM 2.7 PA/TEAM GAME)*

	AVG	G	AB	R	H	2B	3B	HR	RBI	BB	SO	SB
O'Neill, Mike, Palm Beach	.342	108	386	56	132	19	5	0	35	70	24	12
Yelich, Christian, Jupiter	.330	106	397	76	131	29	5	12	48	49	85	20
Silva, Rubi, Daytona	.302	111	420	48	127	15	11	3	61	13	75	7
Flores, Ramon, Tampa	.302	131	517	83	156	29	7	6	39	54	85	24
Rodriguez, Starlin, Palm Beach	.300	114	430	66	129	25	6	8	48	37	90	16
Pinto, Josmil, Fort Myers	.295	93	349	45	103	22	2	12	51	39	63	4
Dickerson, Alex, Bradenton	.295	129	488	65	144	31	3	13	90	39	93	12
Canha, Mark, Jupiter	.293	114	406	65	119	24	3	6	68	54	75	1
Mahtook, Mikie, Charlotte	.290	92	341	44	99	15	7	5	37	29	71	19
Collins, Tyler, Lakeland	.290	126	473	68	137	35	5	7	66	58	64	20

INDIVIDUAL PITCHING LEADERS *(MINIMUM 0.8 IP/TEAM GAME)*

	W	L	ERA	G	GS	CG	SV	IP	H	R	HR	BB	SO
Turley, Nik, Tampa	9	5	2.89	23	21	1	0	112	97	38	7	44	116
Kirk, Austin, Daytona	7	3	3.13	22	21	0	0	129	120	50	3	48	78
Biddle, Jesse, Clearwater	10	6	3.22	26	26	1	0	143	129	64	10	54	151
Morgan, Adam, Clearwater	4	10	3.29	21	20	1	0	123	103	46	7	28	140
Sanz, Luis Angel, Lakeland	11	3	3.46	23	16	0	0	114	107	53	9	40	91
Wright, Austin, Clearwater	11	5	3.47	27	25	0	0	148	147	73	11	60	133
Jungmann, Taylor, Brevard County	11	6	3.53	26	26	1	0	153	159	70	7	46	99
Navarro, Eliecer, Bradenton	5	8	3.62	31	13	1	1	112	112	51	9	27	88
Lawrence, Casey, Dunedin	9	6	3.63	24	23	1	0	139	149	60	9	21	90
Sadler, Casey, Bradenton	4	6	3.73	32	17	0	2	130	125	63	7	35	93

ALL-STAR TEAM

C: Josmil Pinto, Fort Myers; Cameron Rupp, Clearwater. **1B:** Alex Dickerson, Bradenton. **2B:** Starlin Rodriguez, Palm Beach. **3B:** Mike Walker, Brevard County. **SS:** Kevin Nolan, Dunedin. **OF:** Mike O'Neill, Palm Beach; Marcell Ozuna, Jupiter; Christian Yelich, Jupiter. **DH:** Kyle Roller, Tampa. **UT IF:** Danny Black, Jupiter. **UT OF:** John Andreoli, Daytona. **SP:** Matt Loosen, Daytona; Adam Morgan, Clearwater; Nik Turley, Tampa; Austin Wright, Clearwater. **RP:** Dan Barnes, Dunedin; Adam Kolarek, St. Lucie.

DEPARTMENT LEADERS

BATTING

OBP	O'Neill, Mike, Palm Beach	.442
SLG	Yelich, Christian, Jupiter	.519
OPS	Yelich, Christian, Jupiter	.922
R	Ozuna, Marcell, Jupiter	89
H	Flores, Ramon, Tampa	156
TB	Ozuna, Marcell, Jupiter	233
XBH	Murphy, Jim, Clearwater	61
2B	Murphy, Jim, Clearwater	43
3B	Rojas, Mel, Bradenton	12
HR	Ozuna, Marcell, Jupiter	24
RBI	Ozuna, Marcell, Jupiter	95
SAC	Keen, Reggie, Brevard County	20
BB	Andreoli, John, Daytona	75
HBP	Price, Robby, Charlotte	22
SO	Robbins, James, Lakeland	171
SB	Andreoli, John, Daytona	55
CS	Andreoli, John, Daytona	20
AB/SO	O'Neill, Mike, Palm Beach	16.1

PITCHING

G	Three tied at	50
GS	Dean, Pat, Fort Myers	28
GF	Barnes, Danny, Dunedin	47
SV	Barnes, Danny, Dunedin	34
W	Four tied at	11
L	Eight tied at	10
IP	Dean, Pat, Fort Myers	153.1
H	Dean, Pat, Fort Myers	177
R	Boer, Madison, Fort Myers	88
ER	Boer, Madison, Fort Myers	79
	Teufel, Shawn, Lakeland	79
HB	Four tied at	12
BB	Burgos, Alex, Lakeland	88
SO	Biddle, Jesse, Clearwater	151
SO/9	Morgan, Adam, Clearwater	10.2
SO/9 (RP)	Kolarek, Adam, St. Lucie	11.1
BB/9	Lawrence, Casey, Dunedin	1.4
WP	Wright, Austin, Clearwater	17
BK	Burgos, Alex, Lakeland	6
HR	Boer, Madison, Fort Myers	15
AVG	Romero, Enny, Charlotte	.201

FIELDING

C	FPCT	Murphy, Jack, Dunedin	.994
	PO	Rupp, Cameron, Clearwater	869
	A	Rupp, Cameron, Clearwater	104
	E	Bailey, Lucas, Charlotte	18
	DP	Murphy, JR, Tampa	8
	PB	De La Cruz, Luis, Palm Beach	13
1B	FPCT	Roller, Kyle, Tampa	.994
	PO	Robbins, James, Lakeland	1063
	A	Roller, Kyle, Tampa	89
	E	Lucas, Richard, St. Lucie	18
	DP	Dickerson, Alex, Bradenton	107
2B	FPCT	Perez, Hernan, Lakeland	.979
	PO	Vucinich, Shea, Brevard County	217
	A	Vucinich, Shea, Brevard County	298
	E	Three tied at	16
	DP	Vucinich, Shea, Brevard County	63
3B	FPCT	Ahrens, Kevin, Dunedin	.951
	PO	Torrez, Riccio, Charlotte	73
	A	Torrez, Riccio, Charlotte	217
	E	Fisher, Ryan, Jupiter	22
	DP	Ahrens, Kevin, Dunedin	17
SS	FPCT	Machado, Dixon, Lakeland	.966
	PO	Ngoepe, Gift, Bradenton	188
	A	Ngoepe, Gift, Bradenton	351
	E	Gil, Ronny, Palm Beach	32
	DP	Ngoepe, Gift, Bradenton	71
OF	FPCT	Lavin, Peter, Clearwater	.100
	PO	Morales, Angel, Fort Myers	303
	A	Andreoli, John, Daytona	13
		Silva, Rubi, Daytona	13
	E	Hewitt, Anthony, Clearwater	20
	DP	Mahtook, Mikie, Charlotte	4

MINOR LEAGUES

BY J.J. COOPER

Like it is most years, the Midwest League was a must-see stop for propsect watchers in 2012. There were plenty of pitchers to watch, led by Archie Bradley, Noah Syndergaard, ERA champ Justin Nicolino and Aaron Sanchez, and there was a power prodigy in third baseman Miguel Sano.

But the most interesting debate for scouts and fans watching the league was deciding which shortstop prospect has the brightest long-term future. On one side, there was Lake County's Francisco Lindor, a smooth-fielding shortstop with plenty of potential to hit as well.

In Peoria, Javier Baez was impressing scouts with his potential at the plate. Baez didn't start the season in Peoria (he was held back in extended spring training), and he didn't finish the year there either (he was promoted to high Class A Daytona), but in between, he hit .333/.383/.596 and showed that he was a better shortstop than his high school scouting reports projected.

Baez ended up as our No. 1 prospect in our end of season league prospect list, but it was Lindor's Lake County club that did more during the 2012 season. The Captains made it to the Midwest League semifinals.

The Wisconsin Timber Rattlers won the title, knocking off Fort Wayne three games to one in the championship series. The Timber Rattlers won the title despite seeing 11 members of their first-half West Division title promoted. In the deciding game, first baseman Nick Ramirez came through with a two-run double and propelled the Brewers affiliate to a championship-clinching 4-2 win. The final game heroics were part of a great playoffs for Ramirez. He led the way for the Timber Rattlers with four doubles and four home runs.

TOP 20 PROSPECTS

1. Javier Baez, ss, Peoria Chiefs (Cubs)
2. Miguel Sano, 3b, Beloit Snappers (Twins)
3. Francisco Lindor, ss, Lake County Captains (Indians)
4. Archie Bradley, rhp, South Bend Silver Hawks (Dbacks)
5. Noah Syndergaard, rhp, Lansing Lugnuts (Blue Jays)
6. Aaron Sanchez, rhp, Lansing Lugnuts (Blue Jays)
7. Austin Hedges, c, Fort Wayne TinCaps (Padres)
8. Kaleb Cowart, 3b, Cedar Rapids Kernels (Angels)
9. Matt Wisler, rhp, Fort Wayne TinCaps (Padres)
10. A.J. Cole, rhp, Burlington Bees (Athletics)
11. Justin Nicolino, lhp, Lansing Lugnuts (Blue Jays)
12. Eddie Rosario, 2b/of, Beloit Snappers (Twins)
13. Jorge Bonifacio, of, Kane County Cougars (Royals)
14. Tyrell Jenkins, rhp, Quad Cities River Bandits (Cardinals)
15. Drew Vettleson, of, Bowling Green Hot Rods (Rays)
16. Kyle Smith, rhp, Kane County Cougars (Royals)
17. Travis Jankowski, of, Fort Wayne TinCaps (Padres)
18. Adys Portillo, rhp, Fort Wayne TinCaps (Padres)
19. Jace Peterson, ss, Fort Wayne TinCaps (Padres)
20. Stephen Piscotty, 3b, Quad Cities River Bandits (Cardinals)

STANDINGS: SPLIT SEASON

FIRST HALF

EAST	W	L	PCT	GB
Lansing	47	22	.681	—
Bowling Green	38	33	.543	9 ½
W. Michigan	36	35	.514	11 ½
South Bend	35	35	.500	12 ½
Great Lakes	34	36	.486	13 ½
Lake County	31	38	.449	16
Fort Wayne	31	39	.443	16 ½
Dayton	30	40	.429	17 ½

WEST	W	L	PCT	GB
Wisconsin	44	25	.638	—
Beloit	39	31	.557	5 ½
Peoria	35	34	.507	9
Quad Cities	35	34	.507	9
Kane County	34	36	.486	10 ½
Burlington	32	37	.464	12
Cedar Rapids	32	38	.457	12 ½
Clinton	23	45	.338	20 ½

SECOND HALF

EAST	W	L	PCT	GB
Bowling Green	42	28	.600	—
Lake County	40	30	.571	2
Fort Wayne	38	32	.543	4
Lansing	35	33	.515	6
W. Michigan	36	34	.514	6
Great Lakes	33	37	.471	9
South Bend	32	38	.457	10
Dayton	30	38	.441	11

WEST	W	L	PCT	GB
Clinton	48	22	.686	—
Beloit	38	32	.543	10
Burlington	35	35	.500	13
Kane County	34	36	.486	14
Wisconsin	34	36	.486	14
Quad Cities	33	37	.471	15
Peoria	28	41	.406	19 ½
Cedar Rapids	21	48	.304	26 ½

Division Series: Fort Wayne defeated Lansing 2-0, Lake County defeated Bowling Green 2-0, Wisconsin defeated Burlington 2-1 and Clinton defeated Beloit 2-1 in best-of-three series; **Semifinals:** Wisconsin defeated Clinton 2-0 and Fort Wayne defeated Lake County 2-1 in best-of-three series; **Finals:** Wisconsin defeated Fort Wayne 3-1 in a best-of-five series.

OVERALL STANDINGS

Team (Organization)	W	L	PCT	GB	Manager(s)	Attendance	Average	Last Pennant
Lansing Lugnuts (Blue Jays)	82	55	.599	—	John Tamargo Jr.	345,763	5,239	2003
Bowling Green Hot Rods (Rays)	80	60	.571	3 ½	Brady Williams	233,208	3,430	Never
Wisconsin Timber Rattlers (Brewers)	78	61	.561	5	Matt Erickson	240,509	3,590	2012
Beloit Snappers (Twins)	77	63	.550	6 ½	Nelson Prada	68,867	1,013	1995
Clinton LumberKings (Mariners)	71	67	.514	11 ½	Eddie Menchaca	111,760	1,644	1991
West Michigan Whitecaps (Tigers)	72	68	.514	11 ½	Ernie Young	362,554	5,179	2007
Lake County Captains (Indians)	71	68	.511	12	David Wallace	248,114	3,596	2010
Fort Wayne TinCaps (Padres)	69	71	.493	14 ½	Jose Valentin	396,531	5,747	2009
Quad Cities River Bandits (Cardinals)	68	71	.489	15	Luis Aguayo	240,008	3,582	2011
Kane County Cougars (Royals)	68	72	.486	15 ½	Brian Buchanan	391,102	5,587	2001
Burlington Bees (Athletics)	67	72	.482	16	Aaron Nieckula	58,195	856	2008
Great Lakes Loons (Dodgers)	67	73	.479	16 ½	John Shoemaker	259,160	3,702	2000
South Bend Silver Hawks (Diamondbacks)	67	73	.479	16 ½	Mark Haley	189,575	2,747	2005
Peoria Chiefs (Cubs)	63	75	.457	19 ½	Casey Kopitzke	190,244	2,798	2002
Dayton Dragons (Reds)	60	78	.435	22 ½	Delino DeShields	588,689	8,532	Never
Cedar Rapids Kernels (Angels)	53	86	.381	30	Jamie Burke	160,064	2,320	1994

CLUB BATTING

	AVG	G	AB	R	H	2B	3B	HR	RBI	BB	SO	SB	OBP	SLG
Bowling Green	.269	140	4698	681	1262	254	37	105	616	547	1004	188	.350	.405
Lake County	.265	139	4796	657	1269	233	40	75	579	478	989	144	.335	.377
Quad Cities	.261	139	4714	717	1228	269	32	109	649	458	1050	92	.333	.401
Beloit	.260	140	4681	694	1216	254	37	102	616	565	1045	140	.349	.395
Clinton	.259	138	4665	650	1208	248	29	102	580	421	1023	123	.329	.390
South Bend	.258	140	4833	668	1245	261	45	69	609	415	1033	108	.323	.373
Wisconsin	.257	139	4656	644	1195	255	35	107	577	415	1187	118	.323	.395
Lansing	.254	137	4623	672	1174	252	49	75	588	532	1014	178	.338	.378
Fort Wayne	.252	140	4593	606	1157	249	45	64	535	461	1031	206	.325	.368
Cedar Rapids	.251	139	4678	622	1172	220	34	94	557	386	924	108	.315	.372
Kane County	.250	140	4720	601	1182	225	47	80	536	368	1005	99	.310	.369
Dayton	.249	138	4675	598	1166	234	42	81	548	383	1026	184	.311	.369
West Michigan	.249	140	4768	610	1187	256	35	81	554	459	946	92	.320	.368
Peoria	.248	138	4653	598	1156	212	48	77	530	489	1085	164	.315	.368
Burlington	.240	139	4639	619	1114	235	40	90	549	510	1110	142	.321	.366
Great Lakes	.238	140	4676	616	1114	241	41	99	547	413	1073	189	.309	.371

CLUB PITCHING

	ERA	G	CG	SHO	SV	IP	H	R	ER	HR	BB	SO	AVG
Lansing	3.45	137	2	16	45	1219	1194	563	467	68	403	1100	.258
Beloit	3.53	140	2	9	38	1245	1217	625	488	92	404	1136	.255
West Michigan	3.53	140	2	10	36	1263	1224	576	496	67	377	1007	.257
Bowling Green	3.59	140	6	50	1246	1163	602	497	66	449	1062	.246	
Fort Wayne	3.59	140	3	11	28	1225	1111	592	489	72	499	1101	.242
Peoria	3.70	138	0	7	35	1231	1160	658	506	81	460	1033	.247
Clinton	3.71	138	4	6	35	1224	1172	621	504	77	392	930	.253
Wisconsin	3.83	139	1	9	47	1242	1149	598	528	97	487	1019	.247
Burlington	3.86	139	1	12	37	1228	1201	635	526	109	419	1037	.259
Lake County	3.91	139	3	6	32	1240	1129	641	538	104	454	1005	.243
Quad Cities	3.93	139	2	3	33	1224	1211	672	535	88	431	1058	.257
Kane County	3.97	140	2	6	34	1232	1243	674	543	89	436	1117	.260
Dayton	4.14	138	0	2	30	1233	1245	704	567	116	459	959	.259
Great Lakes	4.16	140	1	6	42	1241	1158	683	573	95	579	1041	.246
South Bend	4.31	140	0	6	30	1244	1221	690	596	85	535	1002	.258
Cedar Rapids	4.78	139	1	8	23	1205	1247	720	640	104	516	938	.272

CLUB FIELDING

	PCT	PO	A	E	DP		PCT	PO	A	E	DP
Wisconsin	.976	3726	1460	125	115	Bowling Green	.967	3739	1477	179	125
Cedar Rapids	.975	3615	1519	129	144	Fort Wayne	.966	3676	1271	173	96
West Michigan	.975	3789	1493	136	118	Beloit	.965	3735	1475	191	131
Burlington	.973	3683	1450	142	137	Dayton	.964	3699	1486	191	117
Lake County	.972	3719	1428	148	127	Great Lakes	.964	3722	1507	194	98
Lansing	.972	3656	1557	150	138	Quad Cities	.964	3672	1608	197	147
South Bend	.971	3731	1637	158	145	Kane County	.961	3695	1433	209	96
Clinton	.969	3671	1563	169	117	Peoria	.960	3671	1541	216	98

INDIVIDUAL BATTING LEADERS *(MINIMUM 2.7 PA/TEAM GAME)*

	AVG	G	AB	R	H	2B	3B	HR	RBI	BB	SO	SB
Asencio, Yeison, Fort Wayne	.323	92	350	47	113	21	4	8	61	16	38	7
Smith, Jordan, Lake County	.316	116	468	70	148	23	7	9	74	35	52	9
Walsh, Colin, Quad Cities	.314	97	353	69	111	18	5	16	68	60	65	4
Seitzer, Cameron, Bowling Green	.307	118	424	50	130	36	2	4	54	55	83	1
Paolini, Daniel, Clinton	.299	111	418	68	125	27	0	18	73	49	63	5
Sabourin, Jerrud, Lake County	.297	130	472	60	140	26	2	3	66	51	77	4
Rosario, Eddie, Beloit	.296	95	392	60	116	32	4	12	70	31	69	11
Myles, Bryson, Lake County	.290	102	369	40	107	20	2	3	59	33	85	20
Macias, Brandon, Wisconsin	.288	127	468	83	135	35	2	8	63	58	73	11
Suarez, Eugenio, West Michigan	.288	135	511	82	147	34	5	6	67	65	116	21

INDIVIDUAL PITCHING LEADERS *(MINIMUM 0.8 IP/TEAM GAME)*

	W	L	ERA	G	GS	CG	SV	IP	H	R	HR	BB	SO
Nicolino, Justin, Lansing	10	4	2.46	28	22	0	0	124	112	41	6	21	119
Gomez, Roberto, Bowling Green	9	3	2.48	28	22	0	0	120	110	43	3	42	79
Wisler, Matthew, Fort Wayne	5	4	2.53	24	23	1	0	114	95	39	1	28	113
Collier, Thomas, West Michigan	9	8	2.74	24	24	1	0	125	112	44	5	37	84
Garces, Frank, Fort Wayne	9	6	2.81	25	25	0	0	122	102	51	3	55	112
Granier, Drew, Burlington	11	10	3.21	28	28	1	0	163	149	71	12	53	167
Carreno, Marcelo, West Michigan	9	8	3.23	27	27	0	0	139	129	55	5	28	119
Floethe, Jake, Bowling Green	10	3	3.31	24	24	0	0	122	104	56	4	31	92
Miller, Trevor, Clinton	7	7	3.36	22	17	1	0	121	120	60	11	17	84
DeSclafani, Anthony, Lansing	11	3	3.37	28	21	0	0	123	145	55	3	25	92

ALL-STAR TEAM

C: Austin Hedges, Fort Wayne. **1B:** Cameron Seitzer, Bowling Green. **2B:** Ryan Brett, Bowling Green. **3B:** Miguel Sano, Beloit. **SS:** Francisco Lindor, Lake County. **OF:** Anthony Garcia, Quad Cities; Kevin Pillar, Lansing; Drew Vettleson, Bowling Green. **DH:** Colin Walsh, Quad Cities. **RHSP:** Adys Portillo, Fort Wayne. **LHSP:** Justin Nicolino, Lansing. **RHRP:** Ajay Meyer, Lansing. **LHRP:** Corey Williams, Beloit. **Most Valuable Player:** Kevin Pillar, Lansing. **Prospect of the Year:** Miguel Sano, Beloit. **Manager of the Year:** John Tamargo Jr., Lansing.

DEPARTMENT LEADERS

BATTING

OBP	Walsh, Colin, Quad Cities	.419
SLG	Walsh, Colin, Quad Cities	.530
OPS	Walsh, Colin, Quad Cities	.949
R	Ellison, Chris, South Bend	90
H	Smith, Jordan, Lake County	148
TB	Sano, Miguel, Beloit	238
XBH	Sano, Miguel, Beloit	60
2B	Hobson, K.C., Lansing	43
3B	McMahan, Ben, Wisconsin	11
HR	Sano, Miguel, Beloit	28
RBI	Sano, Miguel, Beloit	100
SAC	Phillips, Anthony, Clinton	22
BB	DeVoss, Zeke, Peoria	82
HBP	Roberts, Nate, Beloit	23
SO	Baldwin, James, Great Lakes	177
SB	Baldwin, James, Great Lakes	53
CS	DeVoss, Zeke, Peoria	16
AB/SO	Arredondo, Jesus, Great Lakes	9.6

PITCHING

G	Wyatt, Heath, Quad Cities	55
GS	Five tied at	28
GF	Meyer, Ajay, Lansing	50
	Wyatt, Heath, Quad Cities	50
SV	Meyer, Ajay, Lansing	33
W	Wheeler, Jason, Beloit	14
L	Brooks, Aaron, Kane County	12
	Wood, Austin, Cedar Rapids	12
IP	Granier, Drew, Burlington	162.2
H	Brooks, Aaron, Kane County	191
R	Brooks, Aaron, Kane County	99
ER	Brooks, Aaron, Kane County	85
HB	Bradley, Archie, South Bend	15
	Jensen, Michael, Peoria	15
BB	Bradley, Archie, South Bend	84
SO	Granier, Drew, Burlington	167
SO/9	Bradley, Archie, South Bend	10.1
SO/9 (RP)	Hubbard, Austin, Bowling Green	11.4
BB/9	Miller, Trevor, Clinton	1.3
WP	Paulino, Willy, Quad Cities	22
BK	Goforth, David, Wisconsin	8
HR	Gerson, Stalin, Dayton	21
AVG	Bradley, Archie, South Bend	.181

FIELDING

C	FPCT	Rice, Matt, Bowling Green	.993
	PO	Hedges, Austin, Fort Wayne	763
	A	Castillo, Juan, Quad Cities	91
	E	Aguila, Roidany, South Bend	13
	DP	Segovia, Alejandro, Bowling Green	14
	PB	Castillo, Juan, Quad Cities	23
1B	FPCT	Sabourin, Jerrud, Lake County	.993
	PO	Hobson, K.C., Lansing	1134
	A	Sabourin, Jerrud, Lake County	89
	E	Hoilman, Paul, Peoria	19
	DP	Sabourin, Jerrud, Lake County	108
2B	FPCT	Mateo, Luis, Quad Cities	.980
	PO	DeVoss, Zeke, Peoria	255
	A	Mateo, Luis, Quad Cities	325
	E	DeVoss, Zeke, Peoria	28
	DP	Mateo, Luis, Quad Cities	76
3B	FPCT	Macias, Brandon, Wisconsin	.957
	PO	Castillo, Leonardo, Lake County	84
	A	Sano, Miguel, Beloit	249
	E	Sano, Miguel, Beloit	42
	DP	Goeddel, Tyler, Bowling Green	20
SS	FPCT	Phillips, Anthony, Clinton	.976
	PO	Suarez, Eugenio, West Michigan	257
	A	Williams, Matt, Quad Cities	442
	E	Williams, Matt, Quad Cities	36
	DP	Williams, Matt, Quad Cities	91
OF	FPCT	Wright, Chad, West Michigan	.997
	PO	Wright, Chad, West Michigan	331
	A	Asencio, Yeison, Fort Wayne	21
	E	Baldwin, James, Great Lakes	10
	E	Sale, Joshua, Bowling Green	10
	DP	Vettleson, Drew, Bowling Green	7

MINOR LEAGUES

MINOR LEAGUES

BY JOHN MANUEL

While the big league Rockies endured the Rockies of seasons, their Asheville Tourists affilate had one for the ages.

The Tourists won their first South Atlantic League championship since 1984, capping an 88-win season with a dominant championship series performance against Greensboro.

The league's most potent offensive team in the regular season (.278, 812 runs), Asheville won its first title for 13-year manager Joe Mikulik by scoring 29 runs in its three victories against the Grasshoppers. The Tourists won with prospects as well, getting strong efforts from shortstop Trevor Story (.310, two homers) and 2011 first-round pick Tyler Anderson (2-0, 0.69) in the postseason. Anderson had won the league's ERA title in the regular season. The Tourists also got a boost from new closer Seth Willoughby, a fourth-round pick out of Xavier who notched a pair of playoff saves.

Mikulik was let go by the Rockies after the season. He had a 938-860 record as Tourists manager, and he has lived in the city since 1985, when he played there as an Astros farmhand.

The Grasshoppers, league champions in 2011, were somewhat surprising finalists. They went 46-24 in the first half, but phenom righthander Jose Fernandez was promoted in July. Without its ace, Greensboro stumbled to a 34-35 mark. The team got a new ace in 2012 first-rounder Andrew Heaney, who struck out 17 in 12 innings and gave up just three runs (two earned) in two starts.

Asheville had to beat Rome in the South Division playoffs, and the Braves engineered one of the biggest turnarounds in the minors. Rome went just 18-52 in the first half, but after adding players from the 2012 draft such as second baseman Ross Heffley, lefthander Alex Wood and outfielder Chase Anselment, the Braves went 44-24 to win the second-half title.

TOP 20 PROSPECTS

1. Jose Fernandez, rhp, Greensboro Grasshoppers (Marlins)
2. Trevor Story, ss/3b, Asheville Tourists (Rockies)
3. Gregory Polanco, of, West Virginia Power (Pirates)
4. Tyler Austin, of, Charleston Riverdogs (Yankees)
5. Gary Sanchez, c, Charleston Riverdogs (Yankees)
6. Alen Hanson, ss, West Virgjnia Power (Pirates)
7. Kyle Crick, rhp, Augusta Greenjackets (Giants)
8. Brian Goodwin, of, Hagerstown Suns (Nationals)
9. Mason Williams, of, Charleston Riverdogs (Yankees)
10. Alex Meyer, rhp, Hagerstown Suns (Nationals)
11. Michael Foltynewicz, rhp, Lexington Legends (Astros)
12. Delino DeShields Jr., 2b, Lexington Legends (Astros)
13. Michael Fulmer, rhp, Savannah Sand Gnats (Mets)
14. Adam Conley, lhp, Greensboro Grasshoppers (Marlins)
15. Garin Cecchini, 3b, Greenville Drive (Red Sox)
16. Maikel Franco, 3b, Lakewood BlueClaws (Phillies)
17. Blake Swihart, c, Greenville Drive (Red Sox)
18. Domingo Tapia, rhp, Savannah Sand Gnats (Mets)
19. Matt Skole, 3b, Hagerstown Suns (Nationals)
20. Rougned Odor, 2b/ss, Hickory Crawdads (Rangers)

STANDINGS: SPLIT SEASON

FIRST HALF

NORTH	W	L	PCT	GB
Greensboro	46	24	.657	—
Hagerstown	42	27	.609	3½
Hickory	36	33	.522	9½
Kannapolis	33	37	.471	13
Delmarva	28	41	.406	17½
Lakewood	26	43	.377	19½
West Virginia	23	47	.329	23

SOUTH	W	L	PCT	GB
Asheville	47	23	.671	—
Savannah	41	26	.612	4½
Charleston	39	28	.582	6½
Lexington	39	30	.565	7½
Greenville	34	36	.486	13
Augusta	32	37	.464	14½
Rome	18	52	.257	29

SECOND HALF

NORTH	W	L	PCT	GB
Hagerstown	40	28	.588	—
Hickory	38	32	.543	3
West Virginia	38	32	.543	3
Lakewood	36	33	.522	4½
Greensboro	34	35	.493	6½
Kannapolis	28	41	.406	12½
Delmarva	24	45	.348	16½

SOUTH	W	L	PCT	GB
Rome	44	24	.647	—
Asheville	41	29	.586	4
Augusta	37	33	.529	8
Charleston	34	35	.493	10½
Greenville	32	37	.464	12½
Lexington	30	39	.435	14½
Savannah	28	41	.406	16½

PLAYOFFS—Semifinals: Greensboro defeated Hagerstown 2-0 and Asheville defeated Rome 2-1 in best-of-three series. **Finals:** Asheville defeated Greensboro 3-1 in a best-of-five series.

Lexington's Chris Devenski struck out 16 in a complete-game no-hitter against Rome on Sept. 1. It was just his fifth start in the Astros organization after being acquired from the White Sox in the Brett Myers trade in August.

OVERALL STANDINGS

Team (Organization)	W	L	PCT	GB	Manager	Attendance	Average	Last Pennant
Asheville Tourists (Rockies)	88	52	.629	—	Joe Mikulik	155,760	2,291	2012
Hagerstown Suns (Nationals)	82	55	.599	4½	Brian Daubach	87,429	1,366	Never
Greensboro Grasshoppers (Marlins)	80	59	.576	7½	Dave Berg	367,077	5,479	2011
Charleston Riverdogs (Yankees)	73	63	.537	13	Carlos Mendoza	254,002	3,791	Never
Hickory Crawdads (Rangers)	74	65	.532	13½	Bill Richardson	132,696	2,011	2004
Savannah Sand Gnats (Mets)	69	67	.507	17	Luis Rojas	117,372	1,863	1996
Lexington Legends (Astros)	69	69	.500	18	Ivan DeJesus	295,937	4,352	2001
Augusta GreenJackets (Giants)	69	70	.496	18½	Lipso Nava	182,124	2,846	2008
Greenville Drive (Red Sox)	66	73	.475	21½	Carlos Febles	347,042	5,104	1998
Lakewood BlueClaws (Phillies)	62	76	.449	25	Mickey Morandini	410,113	6,031	2010
Rome Braves (Braves)	62	76	.449	25	Randy Ingle	184,983	2,803	2003
Kannapolis Intimidators (White Sox)	61	78	.439	26½	Julio Vinas	132,493	2,007	2005
West Virginia Power (Pirates)	61	79	.436	27	Rick Sofield	157,875	2,356	1990
Delmarva Shorebirds (Orioles)	52	86	.377	35	Ryan Minor	231,194	3,303	2001

CLUB BATTING

	AVG	G	AB	R	H	2B	3B	HR	RBI	BB	SO	SB	OBP	SLG
Asheville	.278	140	4740	812	1319	335	42	127	729	469	1074	149	.351	.447
Greensboro	.272	139	4793	669	1304	250	26	101	614	494	901	58	.345	.398
Hagerstown	.269	137	4614	766	1243	252	38	116	705	586	1023	195	.358	.416
Charleston	.268	136	4597	672	1230	252	36	85	596	412	979	174	.334	.394
Hickory	.265	139	4677	706	1240	268	36	117	626	420	1123	158	.332	.413
Greenville	.263	139	4678	666	1229	270	31	75	601	519	1118	188	.343	.382
West Virginia	.263	140	4679	672	1231	250	44	102	601	389	968	165	.322	.401
Kannapolis	.257	139	4719	654	1213	237	37	78	582	478	1113	141	.333	.373
Lexington	.252	138	4653	691	1174	247	24	99	623	573	1062	198	.344	.380
Lakewood	.251	138	4539	612	1141	257	31	73	545	465	1047	138	.329	.370
Savannah	.244	136	4508	575	1102	242	29	85	542	486	1030	98	.324	.368
Rome	.243	138	4453	562	1080	230	29	77	509	410	1040	125	.313	.359
Augusta	.240	139	4497	536	1080	206	28	52	483	428	1010	199	.316	.333
Delmarva	.240	138	4516	567	1082	232	18	67	511	507	1031	130	.324	.343

CLUB PITCHING

	ERA	G	CG	SHO	SV	IP	H	R	ER	HR	BB	SO	AVG
Savannah	3.33	136	2	13	32	1194	1108	526	441	62	329	1073	.244
Augusta	3.55	139	1	13	38	1194	1145	573	471	55	476	1160	.251
Greensboro	3.70	139	2	8	36	1229	1132	595	505	94	474	1123	.245
Asheville	3.82	140	5	8	30	1222	1182	601	518	92	370	915	.253
Hickory	4.19	139	2	9	34	1195	1121	648	557	94	530	1072	.247
Charleston	4.22	136	0	7	32	1197	1176	632	561	75	502	1117	.257
Lexington	4.24	138	1	10	40	1238	1266	664	584	123	452	1144	.265
Lakewood	4.28	138	2	9	31	1198	1199	673	570	90	497	926	.260
Delmarva	4.36	138	4	2	27	1186	1184	700	575	89	507	931	.261
Kannapolis	4.38	139	0	6	32	1225	1257	711	597	78	507	1008	.266
Hagerstown	4.50	137	2	8	43	1184	1173	687	592	92	514	957	.258
West Virginia	4.58	140	5	4	29	1204	1239	738	612	122	484	946	.265
Rome	4.62	138	3	5	34	1183	1236	707	607	75	534	1059	.267
Greenville	4.71	139	0	6	33	1206	1250	705	631	113	460	1088	.268

CLUB FIELDING

	PCT	PO	A	E	DP		PCT	PO	A	E	DP
Asheville	.975	3665	1587	133	120	Hagerstown	.969	3552	1463	160	112
Charleston	.973	3590	1418	138	124	Lakewood	.969	3593	1340	159	113
Greensboro	.972	3687	1462	146	126	Hickory	.968	3584	1377	164	135
Augusta	.971	3581	1368	148	103	Kannapolis	.967	3676	1495	178	119
Greenville	.971	3618	1393	150	128	Rome	.967	3549	1438	168	121
Savannah	.971	3581	1478	147	94	Delmarva	.965	3558	1446	179	120
Lexington	.970	3715	1478	162	115	West Virginia	.964	3611	1443	188	91

INDIVIDUAL BATTING LEADERS (MINIMUM 2.7 PA/TEAM GAME)

	AVG	G	AB	R	H	2B	3B	HR	RBI	BB	SO	SB
Keys, Brent, Greensboro	.335	95	370	72	124	21	3	5	51	34	30	18
Polanco, Gregory, West Virginia	.325	116	437	84	142	26	6	16	85	44	64	40
Burns, Billy, Hagerstown	.322	113	398	83	128	14	5	0	41	65	68	38
Barnes, Austin, Greensboro	.318	123	478	76	152	36	3	12	65	59	61	9
Hanson, Alen, West Virginia	.309	124	489	99	151	33	13	16	62	55	105	35
Payne, Shawn, Augusta	.309	116	405	66	125	19	6	6	57	61	71	53
De La Cruz, Keury, Greenville	.308	116	474	71	146	35	8	19	81	26	101	19
Gamel, Ben, Charleston	.306	110	444	56	136	23	5	2	61	23	71	19
Haddow, Mark, Kannapolis	.306	108	392	69	120	21	4	7	57	51	85	6
Cecchini, Garin, Greenville	.305	118	455	84	139	38	4	4	62	61	90	51

INDIVIDUAL PITCHING LEADERS (MINIMUM 0.8 IP/TEAM GAME)

	W	L	ERA	G	GS	CG	SV	IP	H	R	HR	BB	SO
Anderson, Tyler, Asheville	12	3	2.47	20	20	2	0	120	102	43	5	28	81
Blackburn, Clayton, Augusta	8	4	2.54	22	22	0	0	131	116	47	3	18	143
Escobar, Edwin, Augusta	7	8	2.96	22	22	0	0	131	121	57	7	32	122
Foltynewicz, Michael, Lexington	14	4	3.14	27	27	0	0	152	145	65	11	62	125
Urena, Jose, Greensboro	9	6	3.38	27	22	1	2	138	143	67	13	29	101
Alsup, Ben, Asheville	14	5	3.63	24	24	1	0	156	150	68	9	46	90
Hodges, Josh, Greensboro	8	10	3.65	27	26	1	0	148	147	72	14	56	98
Gillingham, Alex, Asheville	6	6	3.66	19	19	1	0	123	122	58	5	28	83
Davis, Paul, Augusta	6	8	3.69	30	15	0	1	115	130	59	5	20	87
Davies, Zachary, Delmarva	5	7	3.86	25	17	0	1	114	109	52	11	46	91

ALL-STAR TEAM

C: Austin Barnes, Greensboro. **1B:** Harold Riggins, Asheville. **2B:** Delino DeSheilds Jr., Lexington. **3B:** Matt Skole, Hagerstown. **SS:** Alen Hanson, West Virginia. **OF:** Keury de la Cruz, Greenville; Brent Keys, Greensboro; Gregory Polanco, West Virginia. **DH:** Zach Johnson, Lexington. **UT IF:** Trevor Story, Asheville. **UT OF:** Shawn Payne, Augusta. **RHP:** Mike Foltynewicz, Lexington. **LHP:** Tyler Anderson, Asheville.

Most Valuable Player: Matt Skole, Hagerstown. **Most Outstanding Pitcher:** Mike Foltynewicz, Lexington. **Most Outstanding Prospect:** Gregory Polanco, West Virginia. **Manager of the Year:** Joe Mikulik, Asheville. **Coach of the Year:** Josh Bonifay, Lexington.

DEPARTMENT LEADERS

BATTING

OBP	Skole, Matt, Hagerstown	.438
SLG	Skole, Matt, Hagerstown	.574
OPS	Skole, Matt, Hagerstown	.101
R	Hanson, Alen, West Virginia	99
H	Barnes, Austin, Greensboro	152
TB	Hanson, Alen, West Virginia	258
XBH	Story, Trevor, Asheville	67
2B	Story, Trevor, Asheville	43
3B	Hanson, Alen, West Virginia	13
HR	Skole, Matt, Hagerstown	27
RBI	Johnson, Zachary, Lexington	108
SAC	Barnes, Austin, Greensboro	17
	Mueller, Tony, Rome	17
BB	Skole, Matt, Hagerstown	94
HBP	Duffy, Matt, Lexington	41
SO	Akins, Jordan, Hickory	162
SB	DeShields, Delino, Lexington	83
CS	Hanson, Alen, West Virginia	19
AB/SO	Keys, Brent, Greensboro	12.3

PITCHING

G	Hernandez, Jefri, Asheville	53
GS	Three tied at	27
GF	Hernandez, Jefri, Asheville	42
SV	Hernandez, Jefri, Asheville	21
W	Alsup, Ben, Asheville	14
	Foltynewicz, Michael, Lexington	14
L	Mitchell, Bryan, Charleston	11
IP	Alsup, Ben, Asheville	156
H	Cruz, Luis, Lexington	152
	Winkler, Daniel, Asheville	152
R	Dufek, Jonas, Lexington	89
ER	Garcia, Jason, Greenville	79
HB	Winkler, Daniel, Asheville	22
BB	Mitchell, Bryan, Charleston	72
SO	Blackburn, Clayton, Augusta	143
SO/9	Blackburn, Clayton, Augusta	9.8
SO/9 (RP)	Nappo, Gregory, Greensboro	11.6
BB/9	Blackburn, Clayton, Augusta	1.2
WP	Mitchell, Bryan, Charleston	18
	Rowland, Robby, West Virginia	18
BK	Three tied at	4
HR	Eickhoff, Jerad, Hickory	22
AVG	Blackburn, Clayton, Augusta	.232

FIELDING

C	FPCT	Arnold, Jeff, Augusta	.994
	PO	Gimenez, Wilfredo, Greensboro	717
	A	Diaz, Elias, West Virginia	86
	E	Lino, Gabriel, Delmarva/Lakewood	9
	DP	Deglan, Kellin, Hickory	8
		Lino, Gabriel, Delmarva/Lakewood	8
	PB	Lino, Gabriel, Delmarva/Lakewood	28
1B	FPCT	Johnson, Zachary, Lexington	.988
	PO	Johnson, Zachary, Lexington	1038
	A	Johnson, Zachary, Lexington	77
	E	Pangilinan, Leighton, Kannapolis	17
	DP	Moanaroa, Boss, Greenville	78
2B	FPCT	Barnes, Austin, Greensboro	.981
	PO	Gamache, Dan, West Virginia	211
	A	Barnes, Austin, Greensboro	311
	E	Gamache, Dan, West Virginia	21
	DP	Barnes, Austin, Greensboro	73
3B	FPCT	Cecchini, Garin, Greenville	.944
	PO	Bichette Jr., Dante, Charleston	85
	A	Adams, Josh, Greensboro	230
		Bichette, Dante Jr., Charleston	230
	E	Robinson, Drew, Hickory	28
	DP	Adams, Josh, Greensboro	27
SS	FPCT	Tomlinson, Kelby, Augusta	.960
	PO	Culver, Cito, Charleston	194
	A	Tomlinson, Kelby, Augusta	364
	E	Hanson, Alen, West Virginia	40
	DP	Culver, Cito, Charleston	80
OF	FPCT	Altherr, Aaron, Lakewood	.996
	PO	Altherr, Aaron, Lakewood	253
	A	Simon, Jared, Asheville	20
	E	Four tied at	9
	DP	Davis, Glynn, Delmarva	7

MINOR LEAGUES

BY AARON FITT

The championship series between Hudson Valley and Tri-City was a thrilling back-and-forth affair. The two teams traded late-innings heroics in the first two games, but the resilient Renegades got off to a big early lead in the decisive third game and held on for an 8-3 win, clinching their first league title in 13 years.

"We knew we were ready for a dog fight—the two best teams in the league, both resilient teams. It was a dog fight from the beginning to the end," Hudson Valley manager Jared Sandberg said.

The Renegades, who edged the ValleyCats by one game for the league's best regular season record, forced extra innings in the championship series opener when shortstop Leonardo Reginatto hit a solo homer in the ninth inning. But Tri-City won it in the 10th on three consecutive singles and a sacrifice fly.

In Game Two, Hudson Valley's Richie Shaffer broke a 2-2 tie with a game-winning three-run homer in the eighth inning. "There's no bigger stage at this level, and he rose to occasion," Sandberg said of Shaffer, a first-round pick out of Clemson.

In the third game, Ryan Dunn's two-run single in the first inning sparked a four-run rally, and the Renegades never looked back. The ValleyCats made things interesting in the ninth, loading the bases with one out, but reliever Ryan Garton got a pair of groundball outs to preserve the win.

The Renegades won with a roster full of prospects. Shaffer (No. 4) was one of four Renegades to make the league's Top 20 Prospects list. Young righthander Taylor Guerrieri, a second-year prep product, topped the list, and fellow righties Jeff Ames (No. 8) and Jesse Hahn (No. 13) also cracked the rankings.

TOP 20 PROSPECTS

1. Taylor Guerrieri, rhp, Hudson Valley Renegades (Rays)
2. Luis Heredia, rhp, State College Spikes (Pirates)
3. Roman Quinn, ss, Williamsport Crosscutters (Phillies)
4. Richie Shaffer, 3b, Hudson Valley Renegades (Rays)
5. Luis Mateo, rhp, Brooklyn Cyclones (Mets)
6. Patrick Wisdom, 3b, Batavia Muckdogs (Cardinals)
7. Deven Marrero, ss, Lowell Spinners (Red Sox)
8. Jeff Ames, rhp, Hudson Valley Renegades (Rays)
9. Danry Vasquez, of, Connecticut Tigers
10. Barrett Barnes, of, State College Spikes (Pirates)
11. Brandon Nimmo, of, Brooklyn Cyclones (Mets)
12. Hansel Robles, rhp, Brooklyn Cyclones (Mets)
13. Jesse Hahn, rhp, Hudson Valley Renegades (Rays)
14. Vincent Velasquez, rhp, Tri-City ValleyCats (Astros)
15. Clay Holmes, rhp, State College Spikes (Pirates)
16. Tyler Naquin, of, Mahoning Valley Scrappers (Indians)
17. Pat Light, rhp, Lowell Spinners (Red Sox)
18. Phillip Evans, ss, Brooklyn Cyclones (Mets)
19. Tim Cooney, lhp, Batavia Muckdogs (Cardinals)
20. Breyvic Valera, 2b/ss, Batavia Muckdogs (Cardinals)

Brooklyn, which led the league with a 2.62 staff ERA, also landed four players on the list, and several of its other power arms were in contention. The Cyclones finished second behind Hudson Valley in the McNamara Division to earn the league's wild-card spot. Tri-City, which led the league in batting (.271) and homers (50), topped Brooklyn in the first round of the playoffs, while Hudson Valley bested Pinckney Division champion Auburn in the first round.

The new Collective Bargaining Agreement made negotiations with drafted players a simpler process, causing many college draftees to sign earlier than usual and get started on their pro careers in the NY-P. First-rounders like Shaffer, Deven Marrero and Tyler Naquin might not have signed until mid-August under the old system. There was a solid collection of college talent in the league, but young power pitchers like Guerrieri, Luis Heredia and Ames stood out most against older competition.

OVERALL STANDINGS

Team (Organization)	W	L	PCT	GB	Manager	Attendance	Average	Last Pennant
Hudson Valley Renegades (Rays)	52	24	.684	—	Jared Sandberg	161,811	4,373	2012
Tri-City ValleyCats (Astros)	51	25	.671	1	Stubby Clapp	159,966	4,210	2010
Auburn Doubledays (Nationals)	46	30	.605	6	Gary Catchart	55,810	1,469	2007
Brooklyn Cyclones (Mets)	45	31	.592	7	Rich Donnelly	249,009	6,553	2001
Batavia Muckdogs (Cardinals)	44	32	.579	8	Dan Bilardelo	33,443	904	2008
Lowell Spinners (Red Sox)	36	40	.474	16	Bruce Crabbe	168,239	4,547	Never
Connecticut Tigers (Tigers)	35	40	.467	16½	Andrew Graham	58,086	1,660	1998
Jamestown Jammers (Marlins)	35	40	.467	16½	Angel Espada	36,078	1,031	1991
State College Spikes (Pirates)	35	41	.461	17	Dave Turgeon	129,588	3,502	1994
Vermont Lake Monsters (Oakland)	33	43	.434	19	Rick Magnante	89,977	2,499	1996
Mahoning Valley Scrappers (Indians)	30	45	.400	21½	Ted Kubiak	109,956	3,054	2004
Staten Island Yankees (Yankees)	30	45	.400	21½	Justin Pope	141,163	3,715	2011
Williamsport Crosscutters (Phillies)	30	46	.395	22	Andy Tracy	62,901	1,700	2003
Aberdeen Ironbirds (Orioles)	28	48	.368	24	Gary Allenson	244,974	6,447	1983

PLAYOFFS—Semifinals: Hudson Valley defeated Brooklyn 2-1 and Tri-City defeated Auburn 2-1 in best-of-three series. **Finals:** Hudson Valley defeated Tri-City 2-1 in a best-of-three series.

CLUB BATTING

	AVG	G	AB	R	H	2B	3B	HR	RBI	BB	SO	SB	OBP	SLG
Auburn	.271	76	2667	432	722	143	19	35	381	284	566	82	.346	.378
Tri-City	.271	76	2538	414	688	109	23	50	361	288	500	119	.355	.391
Batavia	.260	76	2608	342	678	150	23	43	302	208	603	43	.320	.385
Williamsport	.249	76	2608	337	650	137	25	21	300	241	617	66	.320	.345
Jamestown	.245	76	2468	293	604	116	16	30	261	208	466	54	.309	.341
Vermont	.243	76	2497	281	607	118	16	21	243	234	569	45	.313	.328
Hudson Valley	.241	76	2560	347	617	125	13	28	308	260	548	77	.319	.333
Mahoning Valley	.241	75	2530	294	610	124	19	27	266	222	626	54	.310	.337
Staten Island	.239	75	2538	317	607	119	14	39	274	263	594	51	.321	.343
State College	.237	76	2431	295	577	110	22	19	251	209	545	83	.310	.324
Aberdeen	.234	76	2544	301	595	114	27	30	273	237	553	83	.308	.335
Lowell	.231	76	2538	297	586	99	14	33	251	243	624	106	.305	.320
Brooklyn	.230	76	2552	288	586	116	11	44	251	310	539	23	.321	.335
Connecticut	.227	75	2469	284	561	105	20	30	231	192	594	73	.291	.322

CLUB PITCHING

	ERA	G	CG	SHO	SV	IP	H	R	ER	HR	BB	SO	AVG
Brooklyn	2.62	76	0	10	27	686	565	240	200	30	158	650	.222
Tri-City	2.75	76	1	6	25	670	583	251	205	33	201	602	.231
Hudson Valley	2.91	76	0	9	23	683	582	280	221	29	209	572	.228
Batavia	3.08	76	1	6	24	674	622	274	231	32	143	584	.247
Jamestown	3.15	75	0	3	21	656	568	301	230	26	291	589	.232
Lowell	3.40	76	0	4	17	677	580	314	256	25	283	545	.233
Connecticut	3.55	75	0	5	16	660	588	309	260	30	232	527	.238
State College	3.62	76	0	7	17	658	643	318	265	18	222	478	.258
Vermont	3.65	76	0	4	15	661	600	334	268	40	270	674	.238
Mahoning Valley	3.78	75	1	1	14	662	648	347	278	39	248	513	.255
Aberdeen	4.07	76	0	1	17	671	624	382	303	28	337	574	.245
Staten Island	4.16	75	0	4	19	667	665	384	308	42	292	505	.256
Auburn	4.29	76	0	5	23	682	715	378	325	41	269	613	.266
Williamsport	4.42	76	0	2	15	670	705	410	329	37	244	518	.269

CLUB FIELDING

	PCT	PO	A	E	DP		PCT	PO	A	E	DP
Brooklyn	.977	2058	774	67	49	Auburn	.966	2046	845	102	52
Batavia	.973	2022	842	79	76	Aberdeen	.965	2012	812	102	70
Lowell	.970	2030	761	86	69	State College	.965	1974	867	102	76
Tri-City	.970	2011	762	86	57	Vermont	.964	1982	777	102	46
Connecticut	.967	1980	849	97	78	Mahoning Valley	.960	1987	749	115	68
Hudson Valley	.967	2048	822	99	71	Staten Island	.959	2000	847	121	64
Jamestown	.967	1969	846	95	72	Williamsport	.957	2011	750	125	61

INDIVIDUAL BATTING LEADERS (MINIMUM 2.7 PA/TEAM GAME)

	AVG	G	AB	R	H	2B	3B	HR	RBI	BB	SO	SB
Heineman, Tyler, Tri-City	.358	55	193	33	69	14	0	0	26	26	12	6
Pleffner, Shawn, Auburn	.329	55	216	34	71	17	1	3	34	22	38	6
Wendle, Joseph, Mahoning Valley	.327	61	245	32	80	15	4	4	37	15	25	4
Martinez, Estarlin, Auburn	.319	66	257	43	82	16	2	5	44	26	43	13
Valera, Breyvic, Batavia	.316	69	282	39	89	18	4	1	33	18	27	10
Solorzano, Jesus, Jamestown	.314	59	210	36	66	13	3	8	27	17	49	7
Vasquez, Danry, Connecticut	.311	72	289	36	90	16	2	2	35	13	45	6
Dugas, Taylor, Staten Island	.306	59	209	38	64	9	1	1	15	51	35	5
Perkins, Cameron, Williamsport	.304	67	270	31	82	23	1	1	38	14	41	5
Snyder, Matt, Staten Island	.299	52	187	18	56	13	1	3	34	26	19	0

INDIVIDUAL PITCHING LEADERS (MINIMUM 0.8 IP/TEAM GAME)

	W	L	ERA	G	GS	CG	SV	IP	H	R	HR	BB	SO
Robles, Hansel, Brooklyn	6	1	1.11	12	12	0	0	73	47	14	0	10	66
Cuevas, William, Lowell	8	2	1.40	15	6	0	0	77	55	12	4	15	72
Ames, Jeff, Hudson Valley	6	1	1.96	14	13	0	0	64	44	21	1	20	70
Taveras, Francisco, Lowell	6	3	1.99	15	1	0	0	68	46	21	0	31	59
Melling, Tyler, Batavia	3	1	2.01	13	13	0	0	67	67	23	2	4	46
DeJesus, Luis, Mahoning Valley	4	2	2.02	14	14	1	0	80	57	24	5	17	52
West, Aaron, Tri-City	6	2	2.04	12	12	0	0	62	50	15	3	9	59
Ynoa, Gabriel, Brooklyn	5	2	2.23	13	13	0	0	77	61	25	1	10	64
Mateo, Luis, Brooklyn	4	5	2.45	12	12	0	0	73	57	22	2	9	85
Cessa, Luis, Brooklyn	5	4	2.49	13	13	0	0	72	64	21	4	13	44

DEPARTMENT LEADERS

BATTING

OBP	Dugas, Taylor, Staten Island	.465
SLG	Solorzano, Jesus, Jamestown	.519
OPS	Solorzano, Jesus, Jamestown	.894
R	Quinn, Roman, Williamsport	56
H	Vasquez, Danry, Connecticut	90
TB	Serritella, Christopher, Williamsport	131
XBH	Serritella, Christopher, Williamsport	30
2B	Serritella, Christopher, Williamsport	24
3B	Quinn, Roman, Williamsport	11
HR	Butler, Saxon, Staten Island	10
	O'Brien, Peter, Staten Island	10
RBI	Serritella, Christopher, Williamsport	47
SAC	Three tied at	9
BB	Dugas, Taylor, Staten Island	51
HBP	Gaffney, Tyler, State College	20
SO	Greene, Tyler, Williamsport	85
SB	Quinn, Roman, Williamsport	30
CS	Aplin, Andrew, Tri-City	7
	Johnson, Neiko, Tri-City	7
AB/SO	Gomez, Anthony, Jamestown	19.3

PITCHING

G	Pazos, James, Staten Island	28
GS	Four tied at	15
GF	Ford, Blake, Tri-City	23
	Vanderheiden, Tyler, Brooklyn	23
SV	Ford, Blake, Tri-City	14
	Self, Derek, Auburn	14
W	Cuevas, William, Lowell	8
	Lara, Rainy, Brooklyn	8
L	Menna, J.C., Vermont	9
IP	Warner, Josh, Williamsport	81.2
H	Warner, Josh, Williamsport	86
R	Warner, Josh, Williamsport	52
ER	Sisco, Jake, Mahoning Valley	43
HB	Ames, Jeff, Hudson Valley	10
BB	Velette, Raynel, Lowell	41
SO	Mateo, Luis, Brooklyn	85
SO/9	Mateo, Luis, Brooklyn	10.4
SO/9 (RP)	Creath, Brandon, Batavia	13.0
BB/9	Melling, Tyler, Batavia	0.5
WP	Encinas, Gabriel, Staten Island	17
BK	De La Rosa, Edgar, Connecticut	4
HR	Encinas, Gabriel, Staten Island	8
AVG	Holmes, Brian, Tri-City	.165

FIELDING

C	FPCT	Kieboom, Spencer, Auburn	.100
	PO	Maxwell, Bruce, Vermont	332
	A	Perez, Oscar, Lowell	46
	E	Pickar, Bennett, Connecticut	7
	DP	Three tied at	4
	PB	Maxwell, Bruce, Vermont	18
1B	FPCT	Wierzbicki, Jesse, Tri-City	.995
	PO	Aguasvivas, Juaner, Connecticut	579
	A	Wierzbicki, Jesse, Tri-City	47
	E	Three tied at	10
	DP	Aguasvivas, Juaner, Connecticut	53
2B	FPCT	Betts, Mookie, Lowell	.969
	PO	Renda, Tony, Auburn	132
	A	Renda, Tony, Auburn	213
	E	Coyle, Tommy, Hudson Valley	14
	DP	Coyle, Tommy, Hudson Valley	40
3B	FPCT	Wisdom, Patrick, Batavia	.969
	PO	Three tied at	52
	A	Walding, Mitch, Williamsport	133
	E	Duran, Matthew, Staten Island	21
	DP	Wisdom, Patrick, Batavia	14
SS	FPCT	Reaves, Phillip, Brooklyn	.966
	PO	Evans, Phillip, Brooklyn	115
	A	Evans, Phillip, Brooklyn	223
	E	Quinn, Roman, Williamsport	27
	DP	Hutter, Joel, Aberdeen	42
OF	FPCT	Nimmo, Brandon, Brooklyn	.994
	PO	Three tied at	152
	A	Ramos, Wander, Auburn	13
	E	Nine tied at	5
	DP	Vasquez, Danry, Connecticut	4

MINOR LEAGUES

BY CONOR GLASSEY

For the second year in a row, Vancouver won the Northwest League championship. While last year's edition of the Canadians featured Blue Jays No. 1 prospect Justin Nicolino, this year's club was an older team highlighted by the No. 20 prospect in the league, righthander Taylor Cole.

The Canadians became the league's first repeat champion since Salem Keizer did it in 2006-07. Vancouver knocked off Boise, which placed a league-high seven players on the Top 20 list.

The best performer of the Boise group was Stephen Bruno, who played every position during the season except first base and catcher. Bruno led the league in hits (91) and recorded the highest batting average (.361) and on-base percentage (.442), which was partly aided by the fact that he also led the league by being hit by 20 pitches.

Even with Boise's talented infield, the talk of the league was Everett catcher Mike Zunino, the Mariners' No. 3 pick in the 2012 draft. Zunino started his pro career in Everett and torched NWL pitchers to the tune of .373/.474/.736 before being promoted to Double-A without skipping a beat.

Zunino's teammate, third baseman Patrick Kivlehan, was also one of the league's best stories. After playing defensive back on Rutgers' football team for four years, Kivlehan got the itch to play baseball again this spring for the first time since high school. He became the first Scarlet Knight honored as the Big East Conference player of the year since Todd Frazier in 2007, then encored by winning MVP honors in the NWL. He led the league in homers (12) and slugging (.511).

Another Everett masher, first baseman Taylor Ard, matched Kivlehan with 12 home runs, and topped the circuit in doubles (21), RBIs (58), total bases (147) and extra-base hits (36).

On the pitching side, Cole was the top performer, going 6-0 with a league-leading 0.81 ERA. One of the best stories was the emergence of Spokane (Rangers) righthander C.J. Edwards, a 48th-round pick from 2011 who used his 90-95 mph fastball and solid secondary stuff to go 2-3, 2.11 with 60

strikeouts and 19 walks over 47 innings.

While most Rookie-level and short-season leagues greatly benefited from the earlier draft signing deadline, NWL talent was just average this summer. The top half of this list would have been much stronger had several other notable 2012 draft picks played enough to qualify, such as Boise center fielder Albert Almora, Salem-Keizer righthander Chris Stratton and Spokane third baseman Joey Gallo as well as Vancouver righthander Roberto Osuna (2011 international sign).

The Yakima Bears were on the move after the season and will open next season as the Hillsboro Hops at a new ballpark in Hillsboro, Ore.

TOP 20 PROSPECTS

1. Mike Zunino, c, Everett AquaSox (Mariners)
2. Dan Vogelbach, 1b, Boise Hawks (Cubs)
3. Victor Sanchez, rhp, Everett AquaSox (Mariners)
4. Joe Ross, rhp, Eugene Emeralds (Padres)
5. Tom Murphy, c, Tri-City Dust Devils (Rockies)
6. Marco Hernandez, ss, Boise Hawks (Cubs)
7. Jeimer Candelario, 3b, Boise Hawks (Cubs)
8. C.J. Edwards, rhp, Spokane Indians (Rangers)
9. Gioskar Amaya, 2b, Boise Hawks (Cubs)
10. Patrick Kievlehan, 3b, Everett AquaSox (Mariners)
11. Mac Williamson, of, Salem-Keizer Volcanoes (Giants)
12. Rosell Herrera, ss/3b, Tri-City Dust Devils (Rockies)
13. Jose Valdespina, rhp, Spokane Indians (Rangers)
14. Dane Phillips, c, Eugene Emeralds (Padres)
15. Stephen Bruno, inf, Boise Hawks (Cubs)
16. Trey Martin, of, Boise Hawks (Cubs)
17. Tayler Scott, rhp, Boise Hawks (Cubs)
18. Jeremy Baltz, of, Eugene Emeralds (Padres)
19. Ketel Marte, ss/2b, Everett Aqua Sox (Mariners)
20. Taylor Cole, rhp, Vancouver Canadians (Blue Jays)

STANDINGS: SPLIT SEASON

FIRST HALF	W	L	PCT	GB	SECOND HALF	W	L	PCT	GB
EAST					**EAST**				
Yakima	21	17	.553	–	Boise	24	14	.632	–
Tri-City	18	20	.474	3	Spokane	16	22	.421	8
Boise	13	25	.342	8	Yakima	15	23	.395	9
Spokane	12	26	.316	9	Tri-City	14	24	.368	10
WEST	**W**	**L**	**PCT**	**GB**	**WEST**	**W**	**L**	**PCT**	**GB**
Everett	28	10	.737	–	Vancouver	24	15	.615	–
Eugene	24	13	.649	3 ½	Eugene	23	16	.590	1
Vancouver	22	15	.595	5 ½	Salem-Keizer	19	19	.500	4 ½
Salem-Keizer	13	25	.342	15	Everett	18	20	.474	5 ½

PLAYOFFS—Semifinals: Vancouver defeated Everett 2-0 and Boise defeated Yakima 2-1 in best-of-three series. **Finals:** Vancouver defeated Boise 2-1 in a best-of-three series.

OVERALL STANDINGS

Team (Organization)	W	L	PCT	GB	Manager	Attendance	Average	Last Pennant
Eugene Emeralds (Padres)	47	29	.618	—	Pat Murphy	115,569	3,041	1980
Everett AquaSox (Mariners)	46	30	.605	1	Rob Mummau	95,929	2,665	2010
Vancouver Canadians (Blue Jays)	46	30	.605	1	Clayton McCullough	164,461	4,445	2012
Boise Hawks (Cubs)	37	39	.487	10	Mark Johnson	91,167	2,399	2004
Yakima Bears (Diamondbacks)	36	40	.474	11	Audo Vicente	61,895	1,629	2000
Salem-Keizer Volcanoes (Giants)	32	44	.421	15	Tom Trebelhorn	101,785	2,679	2009
Tri-City Dust Devils (Rockies)	32	44	.421	15	Freddie Ocasio	86,095	2,266	Never
Spokane Indians (Rangers)	28	48	.368	19	Tim Hulett	179,880	4,734	2008

CLUB BATTING

	AVG	G	AB	R	H	2B	3B	HR	RBI	BB	SO	SB	OBP	SLG
Boise	.278	76	2638	410	733	140	29	64	368	216	585	44	.342	.426
Everett	.261	76	2607	389	681	130	15	58	340	288	607	119	.343	.389
Spokane	.249	76	2597	320	647	118	21	31	280	264	621	46	.330	.347
Salem-Keizer	.247	76	2622	338	648	123	7	43	288	302	585	49	.333	.349
Eugene	.241	76	2533	334	610	117	16	32	297	329	525	83	.338	.338
Yakima	.241	76	2561	304	618	114	19	33	266	222	549	63	.315	.339
Tri-City	.240	76	2533	313	608	105	20	21	280	248	619	86	.320	.322
Vancouver	.236	76	2536	360	599	136	26	44	322	299	643	67	.324	.362

CLUB PITCHING

	ERA	G	CG	SHO	SV	IP	H	R	ER	HR	BB	SO	AVG
Eugene	3.00	76	0	2	23	683	588	306	228	32	263	647	.230
Yakima	3.17	76	1	6	16	676	621	305	238	34	270	534	.243
Vancouver	3.54	76	0	8	23	671	607	291	264	37	251	570	.241
Everett	3.84	76	0	2	26	680	627	346	290	49	297	606	.245
Spokane	3.94	76	0	6	14	678	627	382	297	44	296	631	.243
Tri-City	3.94	76	0	3	18	674	660	348	295	30	240	556	.255
Salem-Keizer	4.38	76	0	2	19	682	701	382	332	55	266	646	.266
Boise	4.50	76	0	6	20	671	713	408	336	45	285	544	.270

CLUB FIELDING

	PCT	PO	A	E	DP		PCT	PO	A	E	DP
Vancouver	.976	2013	740	69	58	Tri-City	.967	2023	811	96	54
Salem-Keizer	.968	2045	802	95	52	Eugene	.966	2049	807	99	69
Yakima	.968	2027	803	94	58	Boise	.959	2014	821	120	51
Everett	.967	2040	769	96	68	Spokane	.957	2033	792	128	79

INDIVIDUAL BATTING LEADERS (MINIMUM 2.7 PA/TEAM GAME)

	AVG	G	AB	R	H	2B	3B	HR	RBI	BB	SO	SB
Bruno, Stephen, Boise	.361	67	252	51	91	19	3	3	37	18	47	2
Medrano, Kevin, Hillsboro	.341	64	264	33	90	8	4	0	24	14	30	13
Kivlehan, Patrick, Everett	.301	72	282	46	85	17	3	12	52	19	93	14
Bolinger, Royce, Spokane	.301	66	266	25	80	15	1	1	26	12	37	3
Amaya, Gioskar, Boise	.298	69	272	61	81	6	12	8	33	33	65	15
Tissenbaum, Maxx, Eugene	.296	47	169	26	50	5	0	3	29	27	14	2
Rua, Ryan, Spokane	.293	74	280	40	82	16	1	7	43	29	64	4
Murphy, Tom, Tri-City	.288	55	212	26	61	13	3	6	38	14	52	1
Hernandez, Marco, Boise	.286	67	269	39	77	12	4	5	38	10	36	8
Ard, Taylor, Everett	.284	75	296	44	84	21	3	12	58	28	54	3

INDIVIDUAL PITCHING LEADERS (MINIMUM 0.8 IP/TEAM GAME)

	W	L	ERA	G	GS	CG	SV	IP	H	R	HR	BB	SO
Cole, Taylor, Vancouver	6	0	0.81	12	11	0	0	66	36	6	0	17	57
Avendano, Javier, Vancouver	8	1	1.27	16	14	0	0	78	53	13	3	25	91
Hancock, Justin, Eugene	5	2	1.61	15	14	0	0	73	52	17	3	23	66
Watts, Daniel, Hillsboro	4	5	2.23	15	15	0	0	77	72	31	2	16	52
Perry, Blake, Hillsboro	5	1	2.37	13	12	1	0	68	52	22	4	17	58
Scott, Tayler, Boise	5	1	2.52	15	15	0	0	71	66	30	0	29	43
Carreras, Alexander, Hillsboro	8	5	2.96	15	15	0	0	82	79	36	5	36	55
Marcano, Juan, Eugene	4	5	3.03	16	9	0	0	65	72	36	4	13	62
Sanchez, Victor, Everett	6	2	3.18	15	15	0	0	85	69	37	5	27	69
Arias, Jose, Boise	4	2	3.25	14	13	0	0	64	61	26	3	19	46

ALL-STAR TEAM

C: Mike Zunino, Everett. **1B:** Taylor Ard, Everett. **2B:** Gioskar Amaya, Boise. **3B:** Patrick Kivlehan, Everett. **SS:** Jorge Flores, Vancouver. **OF:** Royce Bolinger, Spokane; Francisco Sosa, Tri-City; Kyle Von Tungeln, Tri-City. **DH:** Taylor Ard, Everett. **SP:** Javier Avendano, Vancouver; Alexander Carreras, Yakima. **RP:** Roman Madrid, Eugene; Chris Nunn; Eugene.
Player of the Year: Patrick Kivlehan, Everett. **Manager of the Year:** Clayton McCullough, Vancouver.

DEPARTMENT LEADERS

BATTING

OBP	Bruno, Stephen, Boise	.442
SLG	Kivlehan, Patrick, Everett	.511
OPS	Bruno, Stephen, Boise	.938
R	Amaya, Gioskar, Boise	61
H	Bruno, Stephen, Boise	91
TB	Ard, Taylor, Everett	147
XBH	Ard, Taylor, Everett	36
2B	Ard, Taylor, Everett	21
3B	Amaya, Gioskar, Boise	12
HR	Ard, Taylor, Everett	12
	Kivlehan, Patrick, Everett	12
RBI	Ard, Taylor, Everett	58
SAC	Martin, Darien, Boise	9
BB	Parmley, Ian, Vancouver	52
HBP	Bruno, Stephen, Boise	20
SO	Kivlehan, Patrick, Everett	93
SB	McGruder, Jamodrick, Everett	30
CS	Hill, Kentrell, Salem-Keizer	10
AB/SO	Tissenbaum, Maxx, Eugene	12.1

PITCHING

G	Wieber, Tony, Eugene	32
GS	Gregorio, Joan, Salem-Keizer	16
GF	Madrid, Roman, Eugene	24
SV	Madrid, Roman, Eugene	13
	Mizenko, Tyler, Salem-Keizer	13
W	Avendano, Javier, Vancouver	8
	Carreras, Alexander, Yakima	8
L	Three tied at	7
IP	Unsworth, Dylan, Everett	85.1
H	Gregorio, Joan, Salem-Keizer	85
R	White, Ben, Vancouver	52
ER	White, Ben, Vancouver	49
HB	Sadzeck, Connor, Spokane	12
BB	Sadzeck, Connor, Spokane	47
SO	Avendano, Javier, Vancouver	91
SO/9	Avendano, Javier, Vancouver	10.5
SO/9 (RP)	Nunn, Christopher, Eugene	12.9
BB/9	Broyles, Shane, Tri-City	1.5
WP	Sadzeck, Connor, Spokane	13
BK	Valdespina, Jose, Spokane	6
HR	Three tied at	9
AVG	Cole, Taylor, Vancouver	.161

FIELDING

C	FPCT	Phillips, Dane, Eugene	.997
	PO	Phillips, Dane, Eugene	344
	A	Ricardo, Dashenko, Salem-Keizer	52
	E	Ricardo, Dashenko, Salem-Keizer	9
	DP	Ricardo, Dashenko, Salem-Keizer	8
	PB	Eberle, Sam, Salem-Keizer	10
		Maloney, Joe, Spokane	10
1B	FPCT	Rapp, Joseph, Salem-Keizer	.991
	PO	Ard, Taylor, Everett	586
	A	Shoulders, Rock, Boise	34
	E	Mateo, Wagner, Yakima	10
	DP	Ard, Taylor, Everett	54
2B	FPCT	Amaya, Gioskar, Boise	.968
	PO	Amaya, Gioskar, Boise	110
	A	Amaya, Gioskar, Boise	165
	E	Schiller, Cam, Spokane	11
	DP	Amaya, Gioskar, Boise	30
		Tissenbaum, Maxx, Eugene	30
3B	FPCT	Sweeney, Kellen, Vancouver	.948
	PO	Kivlehan, Patrick, Everett	52
	A	Candelario, Jeimer, Boise	124
	E	Candelario, Jeimer, Boise	20
	DP	Candelario, Jeimer, Boise	11
SS	FPCT	Roa, Gabriel, Spokane	.950
	PO	Roa, Gabriel, Spokane	104
	A	Roa, Gabriel, Spokane	198
	E	Hernandez, Marco, Boise	22
	DP	Roa, Gabriel, Spokane	45
OF	FPCT	Parmley, Ian, Vancouver	1.000
		Poma, Daniel, Yakima	1.000
	PO	Lang, Michael, Yakima	128
	A	Newman, Matt, Vancouver	13
	E	Beck, Preston, Spokane	8
		Sosa, Francisco, Tri-City	8
	DP	Beck, Preston, Spokane	3

BY MATT EDDY

Predictably, the new mid-July signing date instituted for the 2012 draft had a positive impact on the talent levels of the six domestic short-season and Rookie leagues. More top draft picks signed in time to suit up and play enough to qualify for our prospect lists.

Perhaps no league benefited more than the Appalachian League, where No. 2 overall draft pick Byron Buxton, a center fielder with the Twins, ranked as the circuit's top prospect and helped drive Elizabethton to a league title. The 18-year-old Buxton earned a promotion from the Gulf Coast League to Elizabethton on Aug. 8, and his bat came alive in the final 10 regular-season games when he went 15-for-38 (.395) with five extra-base hits, six walks and six steals in six tries.

Three other first-rounders—Bristol center fielder Courtney Hawkins (White Sox, No. 13 overall), Danville righthander Luke Sims (Braves, No. 21) and Kingsport shortstop Gavin Cecchini (Mets, No. 12)—made our top 20 list. So did Johnson City third baseman Carson Kelly, a Cardinals second-rounder who signed for $1.6 million.

Greeneville shortstop Carlos Correa, whom the Astros drafted first overall, batted .371/.450/.600 but his 41 plate appearances weren't enough to qualify for our list. Other premium 2012 picks who didn't qualify included Bluefield center fielder D.J. Davis, taken 17th overall by the Blue Jays, and three supplemental first-rounder: Elizabethton righthander J.O. Berrios (Twins), Greeneville righty Lance McCullers Jr. (Astros) and Bristol first baseman Keon Barnum (White Sox).

Burlington and Elizabethton won their divisions and met in the finals. The Royals led all clubs with 66 homers, thanks largely to a middle-of-the-order featuring center fielder Bubba Starling, the fifth pick in the 2011 draft, and third baseman Patrick Leonard, a fifth-rounder from the same draft who tied for the Appy League lead with 14 homers.

The Twins led the league in runs scored and

TOP 20 PROSPECTS

1. Byron Buxton, of, Elizabethton Twins
2. Courtney Hawkins, of, Bristol White Sox
3. Bubba Starling, of, Burlington Royals
4. Blake Snell, lhp, Princeton Rays
5. Mauricio Cabrera, rhp, Danville Braves
6. Luke Sims, rhp, Danville Braves
7. Max Kepler, of, Elizabethton Twins
8. Roberto Osuna, rhp, Bluefield Blue Jays
9. Victor DeLeon, rhp, Johnson City Cardinals
10. Santiago Nessy, c, Bluefield Blue Jays
11. Brandon Martin, ss, Princeton Rays
12. Gavin Cecchini, ss, Kingsport Mets
13. Carson Kelly, 3b, Johnson City Cardinals
14. Daniel Norris, lhp, Bluefield Blue Jays
15. Andrew Toles, of, Princeton Rays
16. Patrick Leonard, 3b, Burlington Royals
17. Adrian Houser, rhp, Greeneville Astros
18. Jose Peraza, ss, Danville Braves
19. Jochi Ogando, rhp, Pulaski Mariners
20. Cameron Gallagher, c, Burlington Royals

ERA, boasting a pitching staff featuring prospects such as Berrios (2-0, 1.29 in three starts) and righthanders Hudson Boyd (2011 sandwich pick; 2-5, 2.95 in 13 starts) and Angel Mata (Venezuela, 2010; 4-3, 3.38 in 13 starts).

In addition to Buxton, the Twins featured a potent lineup that included Max Kepler, the German-born left fielder who led the league in slugging (.539) and total bases (125) while ranking second with 31 extra-base hits and 49 RBIs. Right fielder Adam Brett Walker, a third-rounder in June from Jacksonville, smacked 14 homers. Shortstop Niko Goodrum (2010 second round) led the league with 38 walks and eight triples, and third baseman Travis Harrison (2011 supplemental first) hit .301/.383/.461 in 219 at-bats.

But even with that firepower, the Twins trailed the Royals 6-1 in the bottom of the ninth inning of the deciding Game Three. That's when Kepler drew a two-out walk and Royals closer John Walter surrendered successive runs on a bases-loaded hit-by-pitch and wild pitch. Walker followed with a game-tying three-run homer, and the Twins won it all on a D.J. Hicks grand slam in the bottom of the 12th. Final score: Elizabethton 10, Burlington 6.

STANDINGS

Team (Organization)	W	L	PCT	GB	Manager(s)	Attendance	Average	Last Penn.
Elizabethton (Twins)	43	22	.662	—	Ray Smith	25,430	877	2012
Burlington (Royals)	41	25	.620	12½	Tommy Shields	33,501	1,015	1993
Johnson City (Cardinals)	39	28	.582	5	Oliver Marmol	24,827	801	2011
Danville (Braves)	36	28	.563	6½	Jonathan Schuerholz	27,628	891	2009
Greeneville (Astros)	36	32	.529	8½	Omar Lopez	42,303	1,322	2004
Princeton (Rays)	36	32	.529	8½	Mike Johns	26,110	816	1994
Bluefield (Blue Jays)	29	37	.439	14½	Dennis Holmberg	23,890	853	2001
Pulaski (Mariners)	29	38	.433	15	Jose Moreno	25,301	791	Never
Kingsport (Mets)	23	43	.348	20½	Jose Leger	26,408	911	1995
Bristol (White Sox)	19	46	.292	24	Pete Rose Jr.	23,387	835	2002

PLAYOFFS—Semifinals: Elizabethton defeated Danville 2-1 and Burlington defeated Johnson City 2-1 in best-of-three series. **Finals:** Elizabethton defeated Burlington 2-1 in a best-of-three series.

CLUB BATTING

	AVG	G	AB	R	H	2B	3B	HR	RBI	BB	SO	SB	OBP	SLG
Elizabethton	.279	65	2231	401	623	131	32	61	352	259	521	53	.360	.449
Johnson City	.263	67	2234	326	587	124	17	43	271	185	505	64	.328	.391
Greeneville	.262	68	2315	339	607	124	10	42	297	209	515	53	.328	.379
Danville	.257	64	2165	346	556	121	14	42	302	236	525	70	.339	.384
Princeton	.254	68	2318	346	589	127	24	38	304	205	454	102	.321	.379
Burlington	.252	66	2181	337	550	107	21	66	296	249	520	85	.339	.411
Pulaski	.252	67	2283	322	576	117	15	41	283	218	549	46	.325	.371
Bluefield	.242	66	2122	307	513	106	23	45	266	224	583	51	.328	.377
Kingsport	.236	66	2104	255	497	90	21	23	223	196	564	47	.304	.332
Bristol	.234	65	2049	234	480	98	25	24	201	188	577	36	.313	.342

CLUB PITCHING

	ERA	G	CG	SHO	SV	IP	H	R	ER	HR	BB	SO	AVG
Elizabethton	3.13	65	0	9	14	561	467	244	195	42	223	589	.223
Burlington	3.69	66	0	4	18	573	537	273	235	41	155	455	.247
Greeneville	3.76	68	2	5	15	596	543	297	249	35	233	642	.239
Bluefield	3.87	66	0	6	16	551	513	321	237	41	184	489	.241
Danville	3.98	64	0	4	18	565	558	301	250	36	182	497	.255
Johnson City	4.08	67	2	5	19	576	594	317	261	41	228	580	.263
Princeton	4.14	68	1	3	18	600	606	326	276	59	206	554	.263
Pulaski	4.55	67	0	1	19	592	627	380	299	52	238	519	.269
Bristol	4.96	65	4	3	8	532	557	358	293	35	246	492	.266
Kingsport	5.31	66	0	4	16	550	576	396	325	43	274	496	.266

CLUB FIELDING

	PCT	PO	A	E	DP		PCT	PO	A	E	DP
Burlington	.973	1719	719	68	55	Bristol	.961	1595	607	90	46
Greeneville	.972	1789	663	71	51	Pulaski	.961	1775	711	100	66
Elizabethton	.966	1684	669	84	55	Danville	.959	1694	695	102	65
Johnson City	.965	1727	683	88	54	Bluefield	.957	1652	726	107	45
Princeton	.964	1799	704	93	63	Kingsport	.950	1651	631	119	41

INDIVIDUAL BATTING LEADERS (MINIMUM 2.7 PA/TEAM GAME)

	AVG	G	AB	R	H	2B	3B	HR	RBI	BB	SO	SB
Pizzano, Dario, Pulaski	.356	53	188	34	67	15	1	4	28	26	35	3
Pimentel, Candido, Elizabethton	.330	56	215	45	71	10	3	1	22	26	42	16
Vargas, Ildemaro, Johnson City	.322	59	230	42	74	15	2	4	28	17	24	8
Batista, Jean, Greeneville	.321	51	196	30	63	19	2	6	36	7	31	6
Blasik, Brian, Greeneville	.318	55	217	29	69	14	3	1	43	11	25	6
Polanco, Jorge, Elizabethton	.318	51	173	35	55	15	2	5	27	20	26	6
Argo, Willie, Princeton	.301	64	209	41	63	15	1	2	24	31	49	17
Harrison, Travis, Elizabethton	.301	60	219	39	66	12	4	5	27	24	51	3
Kepler, Max, Elizabethton	.297	59	232	40	69	16	5	10	49	27	33	7
Castillo, Ronard, Johnson City	.295	55	200	28	59	11	2	0	26	11	30	2

INDIVIDUAL PITCHING LEADERS (MINIMUM 0.8 IP/TEAM GAME)

	W	L	ERA	G	GS	CG	SV	IP	H	R	HR	BB	SO
Minor, Daniel, Greeneville	3	2	2.75	11	11	0	0	59	51	23	3	10	48
Kibby, Todd, Bristol	5	4	2.79	11	11	2	0	71	59	30	2	21	69
Boyd, Hudson, Elizabethton	2	5	2.95	13	13	0	0	58	63	33	7	23	36
Cabrera, Mauricio, Danville	2	2	2.97	12	12	0	0	57.7	45	23	2	23	48
Kaalekahi, Charles, Pulaski	4	4	3.19	13	13	0	0	67.7	66	34	7	18	65
Caramo, Yender, Burlington	5	3	3.33	11	11	0	0	71	72	30	5	5	47
Silva, Ernesto, Danville	5	1	3.8	11	11	0	0	64	64	32	7	9	23
Lafreniere, Frank, Danville	5	2	4.02	12	12	0	0	65	79	34	5	17	39
Conroy, Patrick, Burlington	5	2	4.13	13	11	0	1	61	59	31	6	22	43
Perez, Williams, Danville	4	3	4.15	13	9	0	1	56.3	54	31	5	9	54

ALL-STAR TEAM

C: Tyler Marlette, Pulaski. 1B: Jeremy Schaffer, Johnson City. 2B: Eric Grabe, Bristol. 3B: Patrick Leonard, Burlington. SS: Jean Batista, Greeneville. OF: Max Kepler, Elizabethton; Candido Pimentel, Elizabethton; Dario Pizzano, Pulaski. DH: Mark Threlkeld, Burlington. UT IF: Brian Blasik, Greeneville. UT OF: Bubba Starling, Burlington. RHP: Jeremy Gabryszwski, Bluefield. LHP: Blake Snell, Princeton. RP: Ronnie Shaban, Johnson City.
Player of the Year: Candido Pimentel, Elizabethton. Pitcher of the Year: Blake Snell, Princeton. Manager of the Year: Tommy Shields, Burlington.

DEPARTMENT LEADERS

BATTING

OBP	Pizzano, Dario, Pulaski	.442
SLG	Kepler, Max, Elizabethton	.539
OPS	Pizzano, Dario, Pulaski	.953
R	Gore, Terrance, Burlington	50
H	Vargas, Ildemaro, Johnson City	74
TB	Kepler, Max, Elizabethton	125
XBH	Schaffer, Jeremy, Johnson City	33
2B	Schaffer, Jeremy, Johnson City	20
3B	Goodrum, Niko, Elizabethton	8
HR	Leonard, Patrick, Burlington	14
	Walker, Adam Brett, Elizabethton	14
RBI	Schaffer, Jeremy, Johnson City	51
SAC	Arteaga, Humberto, Burlington	10
BB	Goodrum, Niko, Elizabethton	38
	Kaupe, Branden, Kingsport	38
HBP	Kiser, Kale, Bristol	15
SO	Ford, Fred, Burlington	83
SB	Gore, Terrance, Burlington	36
CS	Harris, James, Princeton	8
AB/SO	Vargas, Ildemaro, Johnson City	9.6

PITCHING

G	Jankowski, Jordan, Greeneville	23
GS	Six tied at	13
GF	Shaban, Ronald, Johnson City	19
SV	Shaban, Ronald, Johnson City	16
W	Burris, Joshua, Elizabethton	7
L	Seven tied at	6
IP	Caramo, Yender, Burlington	71
	Kibby, Todd, Bristol	71
H	Lafreniere, Frank, Danville	79
R	Estrada, Deivy, Bluefield	48
ER	Echarry, Eli, Princeton	37
HB	Huijer, Lars, Pulaski	8
BB	Olacio, Jefferson, Bristol	38
SO	Kibby, Todd, Bristol	69
SO/9	Cose, Jake, Bristol	9.3
SO/9 (RP)	Jankowski, Jordan, Greeneville	14.8
BB/9	Caramo, Yender, Burlington	0.6
WP	Diaz, Miller, Kingsport	14
BK	Three tied at	3
HR	Echarry, Eli, Princeton	9
	Garcia, Rigoberto, Pulaski	9
AVG	Cabrera, Mauricio, Danville	.213

FIELDING

C	FPCT	Marlette, Tyler, Pulaski	.992
	PO	Genoves, Ernesto, Greeneville	401
	A	Marlette, Tyler, Pulaski	42
	E	Nessy, Santiago, Bluefield	11
	PB	Three tied at	3
	DP	Barraza, Jose, Bristol	17
1B	FPCT	Threlkeld, Mark, Burlington	.993
	PO	Alexander, John, Princeton	527
		Threlkeld, Mark, Burlington	527
	A	Threlkeld, Mark, Burlington	30
	E	Schaffer, Jeremy, Johnson City	8
	DP	Alexander, John, Princeton	49
2B	FPCT	Vargas, Ildemaro, Johnson City	.986
	PO	Vargas, Ildemaro, Johnson City	118
	A	Vargas, Ildemaro, Johnson City	167
	E	Kaupe, Branden, Kingsport	12
	DP	Vargas, Ildemaro, Johnson City	38
3B	FPCT	Leonard, Patrick, Burlington	.929
	PO	Leonard, Patrick, Burlington	37
	A	Leonard, Patrick, Burlington	145
	E	Dean, Matthew, Bluefield	24
		Harrison, Travis, Elizabethton	24
	DP	Franco, Carlos, Danville	15
SS	FPCT	Arteaga, Humberto, Burlington	.965
	PO	Martin, Brandon, Princeton	78
	A	Martin, Brandon, Princeton	194
	E	Basto, Nicholas, Bristol	24
	DP	Martin, Brandon, Princeton	37
OF	FPCT	Kepler, Max, Elizabethton	.989
	PO	Gore, Terrance, Burlington	142
	A	Argo, Willie, Princeton	8
	E	Tuschak, Joe, Kingsport	7
	DP	Starling, Bubba, Burlington	3

MINOR LEAGUES

BY J.J. COOPER

David Dahl was one of the youngest players in the Pioneer League. He was also its best. There was little question about Dahl's domination in 2012. The Grand Junction outfielder led the league in batting average (.379) by more than 40 points. He also topped the Pioneer in hits (106), slugging percentage (.625) and extrabase hits (41), putting on the kind of show that left scouts wondering how he slipped all the way to the 10th pick in the 2012 draft.

Dahl was an easy choice as the league's MVP.

"When you combine his mechanics with his mental approach, you get an impact-type player," Grand Junction manager Tony Diaz said. "I feel like he can be a Grady Sizemore or some type of player like that."

Dahl wasn't the only young star in the Pioneer League in 2012. Fellow 18-year-old Jesse Winker, a fixture in Billings lineup, hit .338. Another Billings teenager, righthander Robert Stephenson, showed a high 90s fastball while giving up just seven earned runs in seven starts.

Compared to Idaho Falls shortstop Aldaberto Mondesi, the 18-year-olds seemed like veterans. Only 16, Mondesi showed good range in the field and plenty of ability at the plate.

"He might have the highest ceiling in the league because of his youth," Diaz said. "This guy may show up in three years hitting 30 bombs in the big leagues."

Come playoff time, the prospects had to step aside. Missoula put only one player, catcher Michael Perez, on the league's Top 20 Prospects list, but they had plenty of postseason success. After knocking off Great Falls in the semifinals, the Osprey eliminated all of the drama early in the deciding game of the championship series against Grand Junction.

Missoula scored five runs in the top of the first against Ogden, then kept adding additional insurance runs while righthander Yoimer Camacho and three Missoula relievers shut out the Ogden lineup.

The final score was 10-0, as Missoula's players had plenty of time to plan their dogpile. Third baseman Jake Lamb hit his second home run of the playoffs as part of a 3-for-5 night for Missoula. Designated hitter Yosbel Gutierrez added another home run and right fielder Socrates Brito went 2-for-4 with a triple.

Ogden finished the regular season with the league's best record. Billings had the best record in the North Division, but because of the league's split-schedule format, they failed to make the playoffs.

TOP 20 PROSPECTS

1. David Dahl, of, Grand Junction Rockies
2. Robert Stephenson, rhp, Billings (Reds)
3. Adalberto Mondesi, ss, Idaho Falls Chukars (Royals)
4. Corey Seager, ss, Ogden Raptors (Dodgers)
5. Jesse Winker, of, Billings Mustangs (Reds)
6. Eddie Butler, Grand Junction Rockies
7. Michael Perez, c, Missoula Osprey (Diamondbacks)
8. Sam Selman, lhp, Idaho Falls Chukars (Royals)
9. Mark Sappington, rhp, Orem Owlz (Angels)
10. Dan Langfield, rhp, Billings Mustangs (Reds)
11. Jeff Gelalich, of, Billings Mustangs (Reds)
12. Chris Beck, rhp, Great Falls Voyagers (White Sox)
13. Wilfredo Rodriguez, rhp, Grand Junction Rockies
14. Julian Yan, of, Grand Junction Rockies
15. Ross Stripling, rhp, Ogden Raptors (Dodgers)
16. Brandon Brennan, rhp, Great Falls Voyagers (White Sox)
17. Jayson Aquino, lhp, Grand Junction Rockies
18. Seth Mejias-Brean, 3b, Billings Mustangs (Reds)
19. Wendell Soto, ss, Orem Owlz (Angels)
20. Ismael Guillon, lhp, Billings Mustangs (Reds)

STANDINGS: SPLIT SEASON

FIRST HALF

NORTH	W	L	PCT	GB
Great Falls	24	14	.632	—
Billings	21	17	.553	3
Missoula	18	20	.474	6
Helena	13	25	.342	11

SOUTH	W	L	PCT	GB
Ogden	21	17	.553	—
Grand Junc.	21	17	.553	—
Idaho Falls	17	21	.447	4
Orem	17	21	.447	4

SECOND HALF

NORTH	W	L	PCT	GB
Missoula	23	15	.605	—
Billings	21	17	.553	2
Great Falls	16	22	.421	7
Helena	11	27	.289	12

SOUTH	W	L	PCT	GB
Ogden	23	15	.605	—
Grand Junc.	22	16	.579	1
Idaho Falls	18	20	.474	5
Orem	18	20	.474	5

PLAYOFFS—Semifinals: Missoula defeated Great Falls 2-1 and Ogden defeated Grand Junction 2-1 in best-of-three series. **Finals:** Missoula defeated Ogden 2-1 in a best-of-three series.

OVERALL STANDINGS

Team (Organization)	W	L	PCT	GB	Manager	Attendance	Average	Last Pennant
Ogden Raptors (Dodgers)	44	32	.579	—	Damon Berryhill	123,625	3,434	Never
Grand Junction Rockies (Rockies)	43	33	.566	1	Tony Diaz	101,496	2,671	Never
Billings Mustangs (Reds)	42	34	.553	2	Pat Kelly	112,602	3,043	2001
Missoula Osprey (Diamondbacks)	41	35	.539	3	Andy Green	89,812	2,363	2012
Great Falls Voyagers (White Sox)	40	36	.526	4	Ryan Newman	56,869	1,497	2011
Idaho Falls Chukars (Royals)	35	41	.461	9	Omar Ramirez	89,828	2,428	2000
Orem Owlz (Angels)	35	41	.461	9	Tom Kotchman	87,392	2,300	2009
Helena Brewers (Brewers)	24	52	.316	20	Jeff Isom	33,428	880	2010

CLUB BATTING

	AVG	G	AB	R	H	2B	3B	HR	RBI	BB	SO	SB	OBP	SLG
Orem	.296	76	2678	500	792	177	32	70	445	357	550	63	.383	.464
Ogden	.292	76	2652	510	774	164	26	55	442	321	624	125	.378	.436
Missoula	.288	76	2726	454	786	154	37	51	393	272	657	83	.361	.428
Grand Junction	.283	76	2631	466	744	141	28	68	395	250	650	85	.352	.435
Billings	.275	76	2628	448	723	148	40	54	396	236	575	86	.345	.424
Helena	.269	76	2619	367	704	133	23	38	321	232	677	98	.333	.381
Idaho Falls	.268	76	2688	429	720	133	41	49	373	209	578	59	.327	.403
Great Falls	.261	76	2597	420	677	142	32	29	356	333	666	41	.351	.374

CLUB PITCHING

	ERA	G	CG	SHO	SV	IP	H	R	ER	HR	BB	SO	AVG
Great Falls	4.11	76	0	3	19	674	764	385	308	30	216	593	.286
Billings	4.52	76	0	5	22	666	687	413	335	40	285	676	.265
Missoula	4.68	76	0	5	18	685	693	418	356	68	281	683	.264
Ogden	4.93	76	1	3	20	669	736	470	367	58	275	566	.276
Grand Junction	4.97	76	0	4	19	673	745	439	372	70	278	561	.279
Idaho Falls	5.36	76	0	1	25	672	773	472	400	46	280	715	.286
Orem	5.62	76	0	3	16	666	752	484	416	43	272	580	.285
Helena	5.89	76	0	1	12	666	770	513	436	59	323	603	.291

CLUB FIELDING

	PCT	PO	A	E	DP		PCT	PO	A	E	DP
Missoula	.964	2056	875	108	69	Grand Junction	.959	2019	875	124	80
Idaho Falls	.963	2016	832	110	59	Helena	.955	1998	869	134	74
Orem	.962	1998	837	112	78	Billings	.954	1999	812	136	69
Great Falls	.960	2023	885	120	82	Ogden	.953	2008	849	142	76

INDIVIDUAL BATTING LEADERS *(MINIMUM 2.7 PA/TEAM GAME)*

	AVG	G	AB	R	H	2B	3B	HR	RBI	BB	SO	SB
Dahl, David, Grand Junction	.379	67	280	62	106	22	10	9	57	24	42	12
Hinkle, Wade, Orem	.338	72	266	62	90	21	0	15	57	43	52	1
Winker, Jesse, Billings	.338	62	228	42	77	16	3	5	35	40	50	1
Smith, Eric, Ogden	.336	63	256	55	86	17	7	3	55	33	32	2
Capote, Joel, Orem	.335	56	224	45	75	16	5	4	33	35	33	8
Snyder, Michael, Orem	.332	70	277	42	92	25	3	8	59	28	53	3
Marzilli, Evan, Missoula	.332	51	211	40	70	10	1	0	15	21	35	6
Soto, Wendell, Orem	.329	59	234	45	77	18	5	4	37	20	51	8
Lamb, Jake, Missoula	.329	67	280	47	92	22	5	9	57	24	51	8
Robinson, Kyle, Great Falls	.326	49	187	30	61	18	3	2	44	24	43	1

INDIVIDUAL PITCHING LEADERS *(MINIMUM 0.8 IP/TEAM GAME)*

	W	L	ERA	G	GS	CG	SV	IP	H	R	HR	BB	SO
Butler, Eddie, Grand Junction	7	1	2.13	13	12	0	0	68	59	18	1	13	55
Casey, Jonathan, Great Falls	4	7	3.46	15	15	0	0	75	81	39	3	26	55
Ray, Jared, Missoula	3	5	4.10	13	12	0	0	64	57	34	4	22	58
Frias, Carlos, Ogden	7	4	4.15	15	15	0	0	78	83	49	5	21	67
Carasiti, Matthew, Grand Junction	3	4	4.37	14	14	0	0	68	80	45	6	20	34
Linza, Keegan, Great Falls	5	3	4.78	16	16	0	0	79	99	50	3	6	57
Camacho, Yoimer, Missoula	3	4	4.91	13	13	0	0	62	70	43	5	25	61
Gerdeman, Ross, Missoula	5	5	5.06	16	15	0	0	89	97	58	6	35	62
Perez, Gabriel, Orem	8	1	5.06	15	15	0	0	80	80	45	4	25	78
Diaz, Jairo, Orem	5	6	5.30	14	14	0	0	75	93	57	5	23	61

ALL-STAR TEAM

C: Michael Perez, Missoula. **1B:** Wade Hinkle, Orem. **2B:** Micah Johnson, Great Falls. **3B:** Seth Mejias-Brean, Billings. **SS:** Wendell Soto, Orem. **OF:** Joel Capote, Orem; David Dahl, Grand Junction; Jeremy Rathjen, Ogden. **DH:** Mike Snyder, Orem. **P:** Eddie Butler, Grand Junction; Ismael Guillon, Billings; Scott Oberg, Grand Junction; Gabriel Perez, Orem; Sam Selman, Idaho Falls.
Player of the Year: David Dahl, Grand Junction. **Pitcher of the Year:** Sam Selman, Idaho Falls.
Manager of the Year: Pat Kelly, Billings.

DEPARTMENT LEADERS

BATTING

OBP	Winker, Jesse, Billings	.443
SLG	Dahl, David, Grand Junction	.625
OPS	Dahl, David, Grand Junction	.104
R	Rathjen, Jeremy, Ogden	67
H	Dahl, David, Grand Junction	106
TB	Dahl, David, Grand Junction	175
XBH	Dahl, David, Grand Junction	41
2B	Snyder, Michael, Orem	25
3B	Sanchez, Carlos, Billings	12
HR	Yan, Julian, Grand Junction	16
RBI	Valdez, Jesus, Ogden	62
SAC	Ozuna, Ruben, Helena	10
BB	Holland, Malcolm, Ogden	54
HBP	Hinkle, Wade, Orem	11
SO	Mondesi, Jr., Raul, Helena	87
SB	Holland, Malcolm, Ogden	44
CS	Capote, Joel, Orem	10
	Rodriguez, Alfredo, Helena	10
AB/SO	Pulfer, Daniel, Missoula	8.7

PITCHING

G	Fernandez, Raul, Grand Junction	30
GS	Linza, Keegan, Great Falls	16
GF	Oberg, Scott, Grand Junction	22
SV	Oberg, Scott, Grand Junction	13
W	Nishijima, Kazuki, Ogden	8
	Perez, Gabriel, Orem	8
L	Four tied at	7
IP	Gerdeman, Ross, Missoula	89
H	Linza, Keegan, Great Falls	99
R	Gerdeman, Ross, Missoula	58
ER	Gerdeman, Ross, Missoula	50
HB	Perez, Gabriel, Orem	14
BB	Gerdeman, Ross, Missoula	35
SO	Selman, Sam, Idaho Falls	89
SO/9	Lorenzo, Leonard, Helena	9.0
SO/9 (RP)	Stevens, Chase, Missoula	15.8
BB/9	Linza, Keegan, Great Falls	0.7
WP	Diaz, Jairo, Orem	17
	Schulz, Clayton, Idaho Falls	17
BK	Four tied at	3
HR	Pack, Chris, Missoula	10
	Schaub, Michael, Helena	10
AVG	Butler, Eddie, Grand Junction	.230

FIELDING

C	FPCT	Capellan, Jose, Ogden	.987
	PO	Perez, Michael, Missoula	433
	A	Perez, Michael, Missoula	62
	E	Gomez, Wagner, Billings	11
	DP	Perez, Michael, Missoula	8
	PB	Gomez, Wagner, Billings	13
1B	FPCT	Sanchez, Carlos, Billings	.991
	PO	Giacalone, Adam, Helena	650
	A	Giacalone, Adam, Helena	53
	E	Hinkle, Wade, Orem	14
	DP	Hinkle, Wade, Orem	64
2B	FPCT	Johnson, Sherman, Orem	.976
	PO	McFarland, Chris, Helena	100
	A	Ciriaco, Juan, Grand Junction	185
	E	McFarland, Chris, Helena	18
	DP	Ciriaco, Juan, Grand Junction	43
3B	FPCT	Lamb, Jake, Missoula	.963
	PO	Lamb, Jake, Missoula	43
	A	Lamb, Jake, Missoula	141
	E	Bolaski, Michael, Orem	22
	DP	Graeter, Ashley, Grand Junction	15
SS	FPCT	Soto, Wendell, Orem	.942
	PO	Rodriguez, Alfredo, Helena	112
	A	Rodriguez, Alfredo, Helena	232
	E	Ruiz, Pedro, Missoula	30
	DP	Rodriguez, Alfredo, Helena	51
OF	FPCT	Capote, Joel, Orem	.991
	PO	Chapman, Ethan, Idaho Falls	127
	A	Chapman, Ethan, Idaho Falls	12
		Yan, Julian, Grand Junction	12
	E	Hernandez, Elier, Idaho Falls	11
	DP	Amaral, Beau, Billings	4

BY BILL MITCHELL

The Rangers captured their first Arizona League championship by defeating the Athletics in a one-game playoff and dominated the Top 20 with five of the league's best prospects.

The marquee star of that group was third baseman Joey Gallo. The Rangers paid a well above-slot $2.25 million to sign Gallo in the supplemental first round. Some scouts questioned whether his top-of-the-scale raw power would translate to pro ball because he swings and misses a lot, but he emphatically answered the doubters by shattering the AZL record with 18 homers in just 43 games and earning league MVP honors.

Other Rangers hitters also had standout seasons. Outfielder Lewis Brinson (the team's 2012 first-round pick) led the league in hits (68), doubles (22), extra-base hits (36) and runs (54).

The Rangers also had a few nice surprises, most notably from righthander C.J. Edwards, a 48th-round pick in 2011. Edwards ranked as one of the league's top prospects after showing a mid-90s fastball. Second baseman Janluis Castro, a 2012 16th-rounder from Puerto Rico, had an exceptional debut, hitting .350/.422/.467 over 137 at-bats.

But Gallo wasn't the only star in the league, as the earlier signing deadline for draft picks had an obvious effect on the caliber of talent in the AZL. This summer's crop of prospects arguably was deeper than any group in the league's 25-year history. Unlike in past years when Latin American players dominated this list, the 2012 Top 20 features several draft choices from June, starting with the top three prospects: Athletics shortstop Addison Russell, Cubs outfielder Albert Almora and Gallo.

Russell and Almora were two of the six 2012 first-rounders who qualified for this list, along with

TOP 20 PROSPECTS

1. Addison Russell, ss, Athletics
2. Albert Almora, of, Cubs
3. Joey Gallo, 3b, Rangers
4. Jorge Soler, of, Cubs
5. Dorssys Paulino, ss, Indians
6. Lewis Brinson, of, Rangers
7. Stryker Trahan, c, Diamondbacks
8. C.J. Edwards, rhp, Rangers
9. Daniel Robertson, ss/3b, Athletics
10. Clint Coulter, c, Brewers
11. Nomar Mazara, of, Rangers
12. Ronald Guzman, 1b, Rangers
13. Renato Nunez, 3b, Athletics
14. Dan Vogelbach, 1b, Cubs
15. Mitch Brown, rhp, Indians
16. Nick Travieso, rhp, Reds
17. Gabriel Guerrero, of, Mariners
18. Tyler Pike, lhp, Mariners
19. Zach Bird, rhp, Dodgers
20. Matt Olson, 1b, Athletics

Brinson, Diamondbacks catcher Stryker Trahan, Brewers catcher Clint Coulter and Reds righthander Nick Travieso. Padres lefthander Max Fried fell one inning short of making the cut, while Royals righty Kyle Zimmer authored the AZL's lone complete-game shutout but worked just 10 innings in the AZL. By contrast, only one first-rounder was eligible for this Top 20 in the previous two years combined.

Even though the Athletics lost the championship, it's no surprise that the team had the best record during the regular season. The team featured more than $7 million in signing bonuses with the club's first three picks in 2012—Russell, third baseman Daniel Robertson and first baseman Matt Olson—along with 2010 international signee, third baseman Renato Nunez.

The presence of two high-profile Cuban outfielders, Jorge Soler (Cubs) and Yasiel Puig (Dodgers), also bolstered the league, though Puig fell just short of having enough playing time to make the top prospect list list.

OVERALL STANDINGS

Team (Organization)	W	L	PCT	GB	Manager	Last Pennant
Athletics	37	17	.685	—	Marcus Jensen	2001
Cubs	37	19	.661	1	Bobby Mitchell	2002
Dodgers	34	21	.618	3½	Matt Martin	2011
Rangers	34	22	.607	4	Corey Ragsdale	2012
Giants	32	24	.571	6	Derin McMains	2008
Indians	31	25	.554	7	Anthony Medrano	Never
Mariners	31	25	.554	7	Mike Kinkade	2009
Diamondbacks	27	29	.482	11	Hector de la Cruz	Never
Royals	23	32	.418	14½	Darryl Kennedy	2003
Angels	23	33	.411	15	Brenton Del Chiaro	Never
Brewers	19	37	.339	19	Tony Diggs	2010
Reds	18	38	.321	20	Jose Nieves	Never
Padres	16	40	.286	22	Jim Gabella	2006

PLAYOFFS—Semifinals: Rangers defeated Dodgers and Athletics defeated Cubs in one-game playoffs. **Finals:** Rangers defeated Athletics in a one-game playoff.

CLUB BATTING

	AVG	G	AB	R	H	2B	3B	HR	RBI	BB	SO	SB	OBP	SLG
Athletics	.294	54	1934	393	569	138	34	47	335	206	427	54	.367	.474
Cubs	.285	56	1943	352	553	108	27	26	288	236	398	79	.366	.408
Padres	.275	56	1962	343	540	97	33	24	295	196	473	46	.346	.395
Royals	.274	55	1901	328	521	96	27	19	268	205	407	58	.349	.383
Rangers	.267	56	1950	352	521	123	33	41	301	236	490	79	.355	.427
Indians	.266	56	1917	341	510	113	26	38	301	251	528	67	.356	.412
Reds	.265	56	1902	292	504	93	29	27	245	153	381	100	.324	.387
Dodgers	.261	55	1862	341	486	96	22	37	277	226	470	71	.345	.396
Giants	.260	56	1929	314	501	119	26	19	259	220	509	96	.343	.378
Brewers	.255	56	1921	318	490	74	32	25	278	210	453	73	.335	.366
Diamondbacks	.255	56	1839	315	469	79	31	15	242	260	527	108	.354	.356
Mariners	.254	56	1909	321	484	91	44	21	266	233	487	62	.343	.380
Angels	.248	56	1940	265	482	93	25	10	210	192	442	51	.324	.338

CLUB PITCHING

	ERA	G	CG	SHO	SV	IP	H	R	ER	HR	BB	SO	AVG
Cubs	3.28	56	0	4	11	491	449	248	179	19	192	465	.240
Giants	4.08	56	0	2	12	496	488	287	225	22	212	515	.253
Rangers	4.11	56	0	7	16	499	480	265	228	25	173	505	.252
Dodgers	4.23	55	0	2	16	483	511	294	227	36	167	453	.266
Athletics	4.24	54	0	2	19	476	451	265	224	27	211	479	.250
Mariners	4.61	56	0	2	18	494	492	316	253	19	231	432	.261
Angels	4.63	56	0	0	12	501	532	332	258	21	187	421	.268
Diamondbacks	4.76	56	1	1	14	482	489	330	255	24	227	490	.260
Indians	4.81	56	0	0	15	488	493	344	261	35	243	508	.259
Reds	5.23	56	0	1	8	482	544	366	280	36	227	453	.277
Brewers	5.57	56	0	1	7	484	573	389	300	37	232	428	.291
Royals	5.60	55	1	2	11	476	549	394	296	26	265	470	.286
Padres	5.91	56	0	1	8	477	579	445	313	22	257	373	.293

CLUB FIELDING

	PCT	PO	A	E	DP		PCT	PO	A	E	DP
Athletics	.968	1427	569	66	60	Angels	.951	1504	666	111	51
Rangers	.962	1497	607	82	51	Royals	.951	1427	586	104	59
Dodgers	.960	1448	557	84	38	Reds	.945	1445	557	117	59
Cubs	.957	1473	619	95	52	Brewers	.943	1453	583	124	44
Mariners	.956	1481	643	98	53	Indians	.943	1464	617	126	45
Diamondbacks	.952	1445	594	102	45	Padres	.927	1430	591	160	47
Giants	.952	1489	616	106	40						

INDIVIDUAL BATTING LEADERS (MINIMUM 2.7 PA/TEAM GAME)

	AVG	G	AB	R	H	2B	3B	HR	RBI	BB	SO	SB
Hoenecke, Paul, Dodgers	.382	41	165	29	63	21	4	5	38	11	22	2
Paulino, Dorssys, Indians	.355	41	172	42	61	14	6	6	30	15	31	3
Carhart, Ben, Cubs	.353	35	136	28	48	9	1	1	21	15	14	1
Castro, Janluis, Rangers	.350	37	137	17	48	11	1	1	23	16	22	4
Martinez, Jorge, Indians	.347	46	190	31	66	14	3	7	39	16	44	4
Rivera, Alexis, Royals	.341	48	176	35	60	7	4	3	34	23	29	9
Relaford, Travious, Giants	.331	39	130	34	43	13	4	0	18	19	17	2
Nunez, Renato, Athletics	.325	42	160	31	52	18	3	4	42	17	32	4
Guzman, Ronald, Rangers	.321	52	212	29	68	15	3	1	33	19	42	7
Lopes, Timothy, Mariners	.316	53	215	42	68	11	12	0	32	24	29	7

INDIVIDUAL PITCHING LEADERS (MINIMUM 0.8 IP/TEAM GAME)

	W	L	ERA	G	GS	CG	SV	IP	H	R	HR	BB	SO
Pike, Tyler, Mariners	2	1	1.78	11	11	0	0	51	34	13	1	21	57
Claudio, Alexander, Rangers	4	0	1.79	14	3	0	1	45	36	11	1	5	54
Sulbaran, Miguel, Dodgers	6	3	2.51	11	11	0	0	57	57	23	2	9	62
LeBarron, Zach, Angels	4	3	2.70	14	13	0	0	67	63	32	2	20	53
Leclerc, Angelo, Rangers	3	1	2.96	14	7	0	1	49	49	21	1	11	52
Martinez, Jonathan, Dodgers	3	0	3.05	13	12	0	0	59	59	28	3	16	59
Parra, Luis, Rangers	5	6	3.79	13	13	0	0	59	60	29	5	18	53
De Meyer, Dylan, Mariners	3	2	4.12	12	9	0	1	55	71	31	3	14	39
Eckels, Ben, Diamondbacks	4	3	4.13	11	9	0	0	52	50	31	1	23	56
Torres, Jose, Athletics	3	1	4.33	12	12	0	0	52	52	29	2	29	41

ALL-STAR TEAM

C: Stryker Trahan, Diamondbacks. 1B: Dan Vogelbach, Cubs. 2B: Jorge Martinez, Indians. 3B: Joey Gallo, Rangers. SS: Dorssys Paulino, Indians; Addison Russell, Athletics. OF: Lewis Brinson, Rangers; Jonathan Reynoso, Reds; Alexis Rivera, Royals. DH: Renato Nunez, Athletics. RHSP: Carlos Martinez-Pumarino, Cubs; Jonathan Martinez, Dodgers. LHSP: Tyler Pike, Mariners. RHRP: Dakota Bacus, Athletics. LHRP: Alexander Claudio, Rangers.
Most Valuable Player: Joey Gallo, Rangers. Manager of the Year: Marcus Jensen, Athletics.

DEPARTMENT LEADERS

BATTING

OBP	Coulter, Clint, Brewers	.439
SLG	Gallo, Joey, Rangers	.733
OPS	Gallo, Joey, Rangers	1.116
R	Brinson, Lewis, Rangers	54
H	Guzman, Ronald, Rangers	68
	Lopes, Timothy, Mariners	68
TB	Brinson, Lewis, Rangers	124
XBH	Brinson, Lewis, Rangers	36
2B	Brinson, Lewis, Rangers	22
3B	Lopes, Timothy, Mariners	12
HR	Gallo, Joey, Rangers	18
RBI	Gallo, Joey, Rangers	43
SAC	Torres, Ramon, Royals	9
BB	Trahan, Stryker, D-backs	40
HBP	Ortiz, Randy, Giants	9
SO	Brinson, Lewis, Rangers	74
SB	Ortiz, Randy, Giants	30
	Reynoso, Jonathan, Reds	30
CS	Reynoso, Jonathan, Reds	9
AB/SO	Carhart, Ben, Cubs	9.7

PITCHING

G	Farley, Brandon, Giants	23
GS	LeBarron, Zach, Angels	13
	Parra, Luis, Rangers	13
GF	Brooks, Aaron, Mariners	15
SV	Brooks, Aaron, Mariners	10
W	Three tied at	6
L	Howard, Dillon, Indians	7
IP	LeBarron, Zach, Angels	66.2
H	Keller, Daniel, Brewers	76
R	Keller, Daniel, Brewers	58
ER	Keller, Daniel, Brewers	47
HB	Lovvorn, Zachary, Royals	11
BB	Gibbs, Jeff, D-backs	35
SO	Sulbaran, Miguel, Dodgers	62
SO/9	Claudio, Alexander, Rangers	10.7
SO/9 (RP)	Nervis, Joshua, Indians	12.9
BB/9	Claudio, Alexander, Rangers	1.0
WP	Gibbs, Jeff, D-backs	22
BK	Diaz, Malcom, Padres	7
HR	Araujo, Victor, Dodgers	9
AVG	Pike, Tyler, Mariners	.193

FIELDING

C	FPCT	Cornier, Gabriel, Giants	1.000
	PO	Trahan, Stryker, D-backs	328
	A	Trahan, Stryker, D-backs	56
	E	Trahan, Stryker, D-backs	11
	DP	Five tied at	4
	PB	Coulter, Clint, Brewers	21
1B	FPCT	Donato, Mark, Royals	.991
	PO	Guzman, Ronald, Rangers	443
	A	Sharkey, Alan, Brewers	35
	E	Whitley, Jackson, Angels	11
	DP	Donato, Mark, Royals	42
2B	FPCT	Lopes, Timothy, Mariners	.966
	PO	Lopes, Timothy, Mariners	78
	A	Lopes, Timothy, Mariners	123
	E	Brito, Malquiel, Padres	26
	DP	Three tied at	22
3B	FPCT	DeCarlo, Joseph, Mariners	.917
	PO	Rahier, Tanner, Reds	45
	A	Rahier, Tanner, Reds	98
	E	Rahier, Tanner, Reds	18
	DP	DeCarlo, Joseph, Mariners	8
		Ramos, Mauricio, Royals	8
SS	FPCT	Franca, Gabriel, Mariners	.955
	PO	Three tied at	78
	A	Penalver, Carlos, Cubs	141
		Rondon, Jose, Angels	141
	E	Munoz, Jose, D-backs	25
	DP	Torres, Ramon, Royals	33
OF	FPCT	Santander, Anthony, Indians	1.000
	PO	Reynoso, Jonathan, Reds	102
	A	Pena, Jose, Brewers	8
	E	Mercedes, Hector, Giants	9
	DP	Allen, Jerrell, Royals	3
		Pena, Jose, Brewers	3

MINOR LEAGUES

BY BEN BADLER

Righthander Tyler Glasnow didn't throw a pitch in pro ball the year the Pirates drafted him, but he made a major imprint in 2012.

With the Pirates having won the first game of a best-of-three series in the Gulf Coast League finals against the Red Sox, Glasnow threw four shutout innings with a career-high seven strikeouts, two walks and only one hit allowed to lead the Pirates to a 5-2 victory and clinch the GCL title. It was the Pirates' first GCL championship since they joined the league in 1968.

Glasnow, a fifth-round pick in 2011 who signed for $600,000, ranked as the top pitching prospect in the GCL. The Pirates, who tied with the Tigers for the league's best regular-season record, were a prospect-laden team. Catchers Wyatt Mathisen and Jin-De Jhang both ranked among the league's Top 20 prospects, as did second baseman Dilson Herrera, who led the league in runs and total bases and ranked second in slugging and home runs. Herrera helped propel the Pirates in Game One, going 3-for-5 with a homer, a triple and a double in a 5-2 victory over the Red Sox.

The Red Sox made it to the championship series despite losing center fielder Jeremias Pineda, the league MVP, in an Aug. 5 trade to the Twins that brought Danny Valencia to Boston. Pineda hit .421/.447/.534 in 36 games for the Red Sox, though he cooled down to a .237/.318/.322 line in 16 games with the Twins and didn't garner much attention from scouts for his long-term potential. Pineda led the league in batting average (.365), on-base percentage (.406) and stolen bases (23) while ranking second to Herrera in total bases (90).

The league was significantly richer in prospects than in previous years thanks to the new Collective Bargaining Agreement that pushed the draft sign-

ing deadline up a month. The top two picks in the 2012 draft—Astros shortstop Carlos Correa and Twins center fielder Byron Buxton—both played in the league before earning late promotions to the Rookie-level Appalachian League. They ranked as the top two prospects in the league, with Buxton getting the edge over Correa for the top spot. Neither prospect dominated the league, but their tools and upside were evident to those around the GCL. Blue Jays first-round pick D.J. Davis ranked as the league's No. 3 prospect in large part because of his elite speed and athleticism.

In addition to Herrera, the league also featured its usual array of intriguing international talent. Phillies center fielder Carlos Tocci spent most of the season in the league as a 16-year-old. Despite his youth, Tocci hit .278 with nine steals in 11 attempts and played quality defense in center field. Tzu-Wei Lin, a Taiwanese shortstop the Red Sox signed for $2.05 million in June, also made an impression on both sides of the ball.

TOP 20 PROSPECTS

1. Byron Buxton, of, Twins
2. Carlos Correa, ss, Astros
3. D.J. Davis, of, Blue Jays
4. Rio Ruiz, 3b, Astros
5. Wyatt Mathisen, c, Pirates
6. Carlos Tocci, of, Phillies
7. Dilson Herrera, 2b, Pirates
8. Tzu-Wei Lin, ss, Red Sox
9. Tyler Glasnow, rhp, Pirates
10. Jose Peraza, ss, Braves
11. Steve Bean, c, Cardinals
12. Alberto Tirado, rhp, Blue Jays
13. Luis Merejo, lhp, Braves
14. Jake Thompson, rhp, Tigers
15. Austin Schotts, of, Tigers
16. Kolby Copeland, of, Marlins
17. Avery Romero, 3b/2b, Marlins
18. Harold Castro, 2b, Tigers
19. Jin-De Jhang, c, Pirates
20. Francellis Montas, rhp, Red Sox

OVERALL STANDINGS

Team (Organization)	W	L	PCT	GB	Manager	Last Pennant
Pirates	36	24	.600	—	Tom Prince	2012
Tigers	36	24	.600	—	Basillio Cabrera	Never
Cardinals	34	24	.586	1	Steve Turco	Never
Yankees	35	25	.583	1	Tom Nieto	2011
Red Sox	34	26	.567	2	George Lombard	2006
Twins	33	27	.550	3	Ramon Borrego	Never
Marlins	29	30	.492	6½	Jorge Hernandez	Never
Phillies	28	30	.483	7	Rolando de Armas	2010
Astros	28	31	.475	7½	Ed Romero	Never
Rays	28	32	.467	8	Paul Hoover	Never
Nationals	27	33	.450	9	Tripp Keister	2009
Orioles	25	35	.417	11	Romon Sambo	Never
Blue Jays	22	38	.367	14	Omar Malave/John Schneider	Never
Braves	21	37	.362	14	Rocket Wheeler	2003

Semifinals: Red Sox defeated Tigers and Pirates defeated Cardinals in one-game playoffs. **Finals:** Pirates defeated Red Sox 2-0 in a best-of-three series.

CLUB BATTING

	AVG	G	AB	R	H	2B	3B	HR	RBI	BB	SO	SB	OBP	SLG
Pirates	.263	60	1971	303	518	95	25	32	259	196	433	90	.340	.385
Cardinals	.257	58	1846	258	475	90	17	25	226	180	448	57	.337	.365
Phillies	.254	58	1856	230	472	108	19	24	202	139	407	55	.317	.372
Nationals	.249	60	1976	223	492	97	15	9	186	181	407	69	.326	.327
Red Sox	.248	60	1926	277	477	110	17	8	243	217	510	63	.328	.335
Marlins	.247	59	1906	238	470	88	16	21	198	192	414	42	.327	.343
Astros	.244	59	1901	227	464	93	18	19	197	149	437	47	.307	.342
Yankees	.244	60	1936	254	473	100	17	32	215	213	499	43	.326	.363
Twins	.239	60	1850	228	442	91	16	20	188	158	447	73	.310	.338
Rays	.238	60	1882	187	448	73	20	7	155	164	483	56	.304	.309
Braves	.237	58	1855	221	440	67	14	19	176	178	490	67	.318	.319
Tigers	.234	60	1932	262	453	105	17	20	205	199	490	84	.315	.337
Orioles	.223	60	1837	186	409	78	13	15	155	139	412	37	.291	.304
Blue Jays	.204	60	1930	236	394	73	18	24	196	209	499	57	.296	.298

CLUB PITCHING

	ERA	G	CG	SHO	SV	IP	H	R	ER	HR	BB	SO	AVG
Twins	2.75	60	0	6	22	503	413	198	154	6	179	459	.224
Rays	2.97	60	0	3	14	507	452	214	167	11	145	428	.241
Yankees	3.09	60	0	8	23	513	439	224	176	19	148	482	.229
Red Sox	3.11	60	0	4	15	512	457	213	177	21	163	460	.240
Marlins	3.27	59	0	4	13	504	467	238	183	17	206	457	.243
Phillies	3.28	58	1	1	13	494	428	220	180	22	186	449	.235
Tigers	3.32	60	0	8	19	521	433	217	192	21	179	505	.227
Cardinals	3.42	58	1	8	18	486	459	225	185	15	151	430	.249
Nationals	3.44	60	0	4	10	510	480	243	195	29	145	428	.248
Astros	3.45	59	1	4	13	501	495	240	192	13	200	391	.258
Pirates	3.68	60	0	3	13	528	451	261	216	35	222	408	.232
Orioles	3.76	60	0	5	13	500	454	253	209	12	191	505	.243
Blue Jays	4.13	60	0	3	11	517	504	277	237	25	217	520	.256
Braves	4.32	58	0	2	13	490	495	307	235	29	182	454	.258

CLUB FIELDING

	PCT	PO	A	E	DP		PCT	PO	A	E	DP
Orioles	.971	1499	556	62	35	Yankees	.964	1539	592	80	35
Pirates	.970	1583	678	71	50	Red Sox	.963	1535	592	82	58
Tigers	.970	1562	630	68	56	Rays	.962	1520	635	85	62
Twins	.970	1510	586	64	53	Astros	.956	1503	598	97	69
Blue Jays	.967	1551	586	73	41	Marlins	.956	1513	603	98	53
Phillies	.965	1482	601	75	37	Cardinals	.955	1459	529	93	50
Nationals	.964	1529	612	79	46	Braves	.951	1469	543	103	38

INDIVIDUAL BATTING LEADERS (MINIMUM 2.7 PA/TEAM GAME)

	AVG	G	AB	R	H	2B	3B	HR	RBI	BB	SO	SB
Pineda, Jeremias, Red Sox/Twins	.365	52	192	28	70	9	4	1	25	11	38	23
Foat, Matt, Nationals	.333	43	162	20	54	6	1	1	20	14	18	2
Mejia, Aderlin, Twins	.324	48	170	27	55	13	0	1	20	14	13	11
Lopez, Jerison, Yankees	.321	48	159	26	51	13	1	0	15	15	26	3
Castro, Harold, Tigers	.311	51	193	24	60	14	2	1	21	10	25	15
Rivera, Darwin, Astros	.310	57	200	24	62	14	0	4	29	19	44	0
Schotts, Austin, Tigers	.310	40	155	31	48	11	1	3	21	12	41	15
Perez, Luis, Cardinals	.309	41	149	21	46	11	4	4	24	11	25	7
Wiley, Brett, Cardinals	.300	40	140	20	42	11	3	1	16	19	27	3
Mathisen, Wyatt, Pirates	.295	45	139	24	41	8	0	1	15	16	19	10

INDIVIDUAL PITCHING LEADERS (MINIMUM 0.8 IP/TEAM GAME)

	W	L	ERA	G	GS	CG	SV	IP	H	R	HR	BB	SO
Lopez, Yorfrank, Tigers	5	3	2.32	15	7	0	0	54	44	15	3	12	57
Gomez, Sergio, Red Sox	5	4	2.83	12	8	0	0	57	44	22	4	10	56
Beltre, Andy, Marlins	1	5	2.96	12	9	0	0	49	46	21	1	19	41
Barrios, Agapito, Astros	1	5	3.28	11	5	0	0	49	51	25	1	8	26
Rodriguez, Jorge, Rays	2	3	3.54	11	8	0	0	48	54	27	0	7	26
Ubiera, Andry, Braves	2	2	4.04	12	9	0	0	49	54	24	2	17	48
Vasquez, Daury, Nationals	4	6	4.10	11	9	0	0	53	49	34	4	33	29
Franco, Enderson, Astros	3	2	4.86	10	7	1	0	50	69	31	2	8	37
Villegas, Kender, Cardinals	4	4	6.28	11	11	1	0	53	72	42	3	15	39

ALL-STAR TEAM

C: Wyatt Mathisen, Pirates. **1B:** Ben Kline, Rays. **2B:** Matt Foat, Nationals. **3B:** Darwin Rivera, Astros. **SS:** Aderlin Mejia, Twins. **OF:** Kolby Copeland, Marlins; Jeremias Pineda, Twins; Andrew Pullin, Phillies; Austin Schotts, Tigers. **DH:** Yeicok Calderon, Yankees. **UT IF:** Luis Perez, Cardinals. **SP:** Sergio Gomez, Red Sox; Yorfrank Lopez, Tigers. **RP:** Chuck Ghysels, Blue Jays; Jose Valdez, Tigers.
Most Valuable Player: Jeremias Pineda, Twins. **Manager of the Year:** Tom Prince, Pirates.

DEPARTMENT LEADERS

BATTING

OBP	Pineda, Jeremias, Red Sox/Twins	.406
SLG	Perez, Luis, Cardinals	.517
OPS	Pineda, Jeremias, Red Sox/Twins	.875
R	Herrera, Dilson, Pirates	41
H	Pineda, Jeremias, Red Sox/Twins	70
TB	Herrera, Dilson, Pirates	96
XBH	Herrera, Dilson, Pirates	22
	Oliberto, Mikeson, Yankees	22
2B	Colorado, Jose, Red Sox	17
3B	Four tied at	6
HR	Calderon, Yeicok, Yankees	8
RBI	Copeland, Kolby, Marlins	34
SAC	Escobar, Elvis, Pirates	10
	Herrera, Dilson, Pirates	10
BB	Difo, Wilmer, Nationals	34
HBP	Lien, Connor, Braves	10
SO	Jennings, Hayden, Nationals	70
SB	Pineda, Jeremias, Red Sox, Twins	23
CS	Pineda, Jeremias, Red Sox, Twins	9
AB/SO	Mejia, Aderlin, Twins	13.1

PITCHING

G	Ghysels, Chuck, Blue Jays	25
GS	Three tied at	12
GF	Valdez, Jose, Tigers	23
SV	Valdez, Jose, Tigers	15
W	Nine tied at	5
L	Espinosa, Abraham, Braves	6
	Vasquez, Daury, Nationals	6
IP	Gomez, Sergio, Red Sox	57.1
H	Villegas, Kender, Cardinals	72
R	Villegas, Kender, Cardinals	42
ER	Villegas, Kender, Cardinals	37
HB	Spalding, Matt, Red Sox	10
BB	Alcantara, Mario, Red Sox	35
SO	Lopez, Yorfrank, Tigers	57
SO/9	Lopez, Yorfrank, Tigers	9.4
SO/9 (RP)	Ghysels, Chuck, Blue Jays	14.4
BB/9	Rodriguez, Jorge, Rays	1.3
WP	Severino, Janser, Orioles	17
BK	Four tied at	3
HR	Lopez, Cesar, Pirates	5
	Selsor, Casey, Nationals	5
AVG	Gomez, Sergio, Red Sox	.210

FIELDING

C	FPCT	Jhang, Jin-De, Pirates	.100
	PO	Longley, Andrew, Tigers	263
	A	Sopilka, David, Red Sox	45
	E	De La Rosa, Bryan, Braves	9
	DP	Severino, Pedro, Nationals	5
	PB	De La Rosa, Bryan, Braves	13
1B	FPCT	Ustariz, Jesus, Tigers	.993
	PO	Ustariz, Jesus, Tigers	393
	A	Jones, Austin, Yankees	32
	E	Mejia, Yonathan, Astros	9
	DP	Ustariz, Jesus, Tigers	37
2B	FPCT	Lopez, Jerison, Yankees	.981
	PO	Herrera, Dilson, Pirates	95
	A	Herrera, Dilson, Pirates	141
	E	Castro, Harold, Tigers	9
	DP	Rosa, Adderly, Rays	30
3B	FPCT	Andujar, Miguel, Yankees	.907
	PO	Moore, Nick, Red Sox	37
	A	Andujar, Miguel, Yankees	104
	E	Eusebio, Diomedes, Nationals	16
		Moore, Nick, Red Sox	16
	DP	Rivera, Darwin, Astros	18
SS	FPCT	Rondon, Cleuluis, Red Sox	.949
	PO	Lugo, Dawel, Blue Jays	76
	A	Difo, Wilmer, Nationals	138
	E	Difo, Wilmer, Nationals	16
	DP	Lugo, Dawel, Blue Jays	25
		Rondon, Cleuluis, Red Sox	25
OF	FPCT	Salgado, Ismael, Tigers	.100
	PO	Phillips, Brett, Astros	117
	A	Hernandez, Teoscar, Astros	12
	E	Calderon, Yeicok, Yankees	6
	DP	Hernandez, Teoscar, Astros	5

DOMINICAN SUMMER LEAGUE

In the decisive Game Five of the Dominican Summer League championship series, the Pirates edged the Angels 4-3 to claim their first DSL title since 2003.

The Pirates reached the championship series after sweeping the Mariners 2-0 in the semifinals to knock out the team with the league's best regular season record.

Rangers outfielder Eduard Pinto, who signed on July 2, 2011 for $300,000, won the batting title (.396) in his first pro season. Mets outfielder Vicente Lupo, who repeated the league after signing for $350,000 on July 2, 2010, led the league with a .500 on-base percentage. Rockies righthander Antonio Senzatela, who signed for $250,000 shortly after July 2 in 2011, won the ERA title (0.72) in 63 innings in his pro debut. Yankees righthander Rafael DePaula, who signed for $500,000 in November 2010 and had to wait until this past season to get his contract approved, finished seventh in the league in ERA at 1.46 in 62 innings.

STANDINGS

BOCA CHICA NORTH

TEAM	W	L	PCT	GB
Mets2	44	26	.629	–
Pirates1	44	26	.629	–
Rangers	42	28	.600	2
Red Sox	41	29	.586	3
Marlins	22	48	.314	22
Yankees2	17	53	.243	27

BOCA CHICA SOUTH

TEAM	W	L	PCT	GB
Yankees1	49	21	.700	–
Giants	42	28	.600	7
Nationals	38	32	.543	11
Pirates2	34	34	.500	14
Cubs2	33	36	.478	15 ½
Mets1	33	37	.471	16
Phillies	32	36	.471	16
D-backs/Reds	16	53	.232	32 ½

BOCA CHICA NORTHWEST

TEAM	W	L	PCT	GB
Mariners	50	20	.714	–
Royals	41	27	.603	8
Dodgers	38	32	.543	12
Cardinals	37	33	.529	13

TEAM	W	L	PCT	GB
Indians	35	35	.500	15
Rays	28	42	.400	22
Athletics	26	41	.388	22 ½
Astros	22	47	.319	27 ½

BOCA CHICA BASEBALL CITY

TEAM	W	L	PCT	GB
D-backs	43	27	.614	–
Rockies	42	28	.600	1
Reds	40	29	.580	2 ½
Orioles	34	36	.486	9
Cubs1	33	37	.471	10
Twins	31	39	.443	12
White Sox	28	41	.406	14 ½
Padres	28	42	.400	15

SAN PEDRO DE MACORIS

TEAM	W	L	PCT	GB
Angels	40	24	.625	–
Braves	35	29	.547	5
Tigers	30	34	.469	10
Blue Jays	30	35	.462	10 ½
Brewers	26	39	.400	14 ½

INDIVIDUAL BATTING LEADERS

PLAYER, TEAM	AVG	G	AB	R	H	2B	3B	HR	RBI	BB	SO	SB
Pinto, Eduard, Rangers	.396	56	222	47	88	13	1	1	29	31	13	8
Figueroa, Jose, Yankees1	.382	58	186	44	71	12	11	3	39	18	25	4
Rivera, Maximo, Pirates	.367	57	199	47	73	7	1	4	31	19	26	34
Cordero, Josmar, Dodgers	.362	60	229	50	83	19	1	6	47	14	20	9
Guerrero, Gabriel, Mariners	.355	50	200	38	71	9	4	11	54	21	28	4
Soriano, Wilson, Rockies	.354	66	229	39	81	14	4	0	24	21	13	27
Camargo, Johan, Braves	.343	59	198	38	68	14	1	2	26	25	27	6
Lupo, Vicente, Mets	.343	65	204	58	70	18	3	10	45	46	45	12
Ledesma, Ronarsy, Orioles	.343	68	245	35	84	18	8	2	41	26	43	19
Tamarez, Christopher, Yankees1	.338	56	228	41	77	18	1	6	35	21	40	2

INDIVIDUAL PITCHING LEADERS

PLAYER, TEAM	W	L	ERA	G	GS	CG	SV	IP	H	R	BB	SO
Vizcaya, Anthony, Indians	3	2	0.94	13	12	0	0	67	38	13	19	33
Torrez, Daury, Cubs2	6	3	1.21	14	13	0	0	75	57	14	4	50
Canela, Erick, Yankees1	7	1	1.29	14	14	0	0	70	37	13	13	70
Navas, Carlos, Athletics	4	5	1.38	14	12	0	0	65	51	21	11	54
Subero, Junior, Twins	5	3	1.43	12	12	1	0	63	50	16	9	54
De Paula, Rafael, Yankees1	8	2	1.46	14	14	1	0	62	35	18	18	85
Gonzalez, Yeuri, Mariners	4	1	1.48	14	3	2	2	61	51	13	8	25
Diaz, Jose Agusto, Dodgers	4	1	1.49	15	10	2	2	73	54	15	6	59
Aquino, Jayson, Rockies	6	1	1.52	9	9	2	0	65	45	12	9	74
Mateo, Diomedes, Giants	3	0	1.62	18	0	0	6	61	33	12	18	76

VENEZUELAN SUMMER LEAGUE

With the Venezuelan Summer League down to just four teams as clubs continue to pull out of their Venezuelan academies, the Phillies captured the VSL title by beating the Mariners 4-0 in the decisive Game Three of the championship series.

The Phillies, who finished with a league-best 48-22 record, had a starting rotation that featured the pitchers who ranked first and second in the league in ERA with righthander Severino Gonzalez (1.65 in 93 innings) and lefthander Douglas Parada (1.82 in 79 innings). As a team, the Phillies led the league in team ERA (2.51) and strikeouts (449) while issuing the fewest walks (165) in the circuit.

The Mariners, the only other team in the VSL to finish above .500, were led by outfielder Jesus Ugueto, who batted .388/.458/.554 in 71 games. In his fourth season in the VSL, Ugueto ranked first in average, on-base percentage and slugging.

STANDINGS

TEAM	W	L	PCT	GB	TEAM	W	L	PCT	GB
Phillies	48	22	.686	–	Tigers	30	40	.429	18
Mariners	44	27	.620	4 ½	Rays	19	52	.268	29 ½

INDIVIDUAL BATTING LEADERS

PLAYER, TEAM	AVG	G	AB	R	H	2B	3B	HR	RBI	BB	SO	SB
Ugueto, Jesus, Mariners	.388	71	276	72	107	16	6	6	49	35	38	22
Paez, Jose, Rays	.364	61	250	41	91	13	9	4	29	24	41	12
Garcia, Wilson, Phillies	.353	56	201	21	71	18	1	4	38	12	12	1
Olivera, Deiber, PhilWlies	.350	57	200	35	70	17	2	1	32	13	22	5
Zambrano, Jose, Tigers	.342	60	225	37	77	12	0	1	34	20	16	12
Ramirez, Ivan, Mariners	.329	51	170	25	56	6	0	2	35	18	14	1
Herrera, Francisco, Phillies	.324	53	182	37	59	13	0	5	33	23	25	1
Navarro, Franklin, Tigers	.315	62	241	31	76	19	1	4	33	16	51	2
Martinez, Gustavo, Phillies	.313	60	227	40	71	5	4	1	26	17	22	27
Oberto, Wilmer, Phillies	.295	66	217	44	64	16	1	7	35	31	38	6

INDIVIDUAL PITCHING LEADERS

PITCHER, TEAM	W	L	ERA	G	GS	CG	SV	IP	H	R	BB	SO
Gonzalez, Severino, Phillies	7	3	1.65	14	14	2	0	93	59	26	6	86
Parada, Douglas, Phillies	8	2	1.82	14	14	1	0	79	53	17	10	73
Osorio, Neritzon, Mariners	9	2	1.92	14	13	0	0	75	54	21	19	40
Urbina, Ugueth, Mariners	3	0	2.44	14	11	0	0	59	55	21	17	32
Pinto, Ricardo, Phillies	7	3	2.74	15	10	0	1	69	70	34	20	39
Carrera, Rafael, Mariners	7	2	3.86	14	14	0	0	72	92	42	12	41
Fernandez, Mario, Rays	0	6	4.75	14	12	0	0	61	72	36	18	36
Belisario, Johan, Tigers	1	7	4.91	13	13	0	0	62	85	43	10	43

BY BILL MITCHELL

This year's Arizona Fall League championship resembled a close political election, with the result being contested and a subsequent delay until a winner was finally declared. Twenty minutes after the last out, the Peoria Javelinas were confirmed as the 2012 AFL champs by defeating the Salt River Rafters, 4-3, at Scottsdale Stadium.

The controversial play occurred in the bottom of the seventh inning with Salt River trailing by a run. Rafters leadoff hitter Brian Goodwin (Nationals) smoked a line-drive triple to the right-center gap. Chris Owings (Diamondbacks) then flew out to right field, with Goodwin beating a strong throw to home by Rymer Liriano (Padres) for what looked like the tying run. The home plate umpire signaled the runner safe after Peoria catcher Mike Zunino (Mariners) stepped on home in case Goodwin had missed the plate, and that call was followed by an appeal at third base arguing that the runner tagged up before the ball was caught.

The umpires conferred before correctly declaring Goodwin out for leaving third early, which brought a protest by Salt River manager Matt Williams, arguing that two different appeals could not be made on the same play. After arguing his point, Williams notified the umpires that he was playing the game under protest.

The umpires conferred after the game with Steve Palermo, Major League Baseball's supervisor of umpires, who was in attendance, and it was ruled that multiple appeals can be made on the same play. AFL director Steve Cobb finally announced to both teams and the remaining crowd that the protest was not upheld.

The Rafters also came close to tying the game in the bottom of the eighth with another leadoff triple, this time by Anthony Rendon (Nationals) on a ball nearly caught by Peoria center fielder Billy Hamilton (Reds), who was injured on the play. Rendon was thrown out at home plate on the next at-bat on Carlos Sanchez's (White Sox) soft grounder back to pitcher Curtis Partch (Reds).

"To win a championship or to win a league title, it takes the ball to bounce your way," Javelinas manager Dusty Wathan said. "The ball bounced our way the last couple of innings."

All seven runs came in the game's first three innings, with Peoria jumping out to an early 2-0 lead that it never lost. The Rafters' first big threat came in the bottom of the second, when they scored one run but left the bases loaded after Owings was called out on strikes.

Hamilton, whose injury turned out to be back spasms sustained when he hit the wall, was one of three offensive catalysts at the top of Peoria order. The switch-hitting outfielder, who set a minor league record with 155 stolen bases during the regular season, tripled to lead off the game, scoring the game's first run two batters later on Zunino's RBI single. Hamilton also reached first base in his second at-bat, with a bunt single in which he was timed at 3.45 seconds down the line.

Zunino, the Mariners' first-round draft choice, had an especially long season that started in mid-February with his junior year at Florida, where he earned College Player of the Year honors. In addition to the AFL championship game, Zunino also played in the College World Series and later in the Double-A Southern League playoffs.

Fall League Superlatives

Surprise Saguaros first baseman Chris McGuiness (Rangers) won the AFL MVP award. The lefthanded slugger batted .283/.370/.474, and led the league with 27 RBIs.

"I always wanted to come out here and play in the Fall League," McGuiness said. "To be lucky enough to win an MVP trophy, it's a great honor."

Nate Roberts (Twins) led all AFL hitters in the slash categories, batting .446/.565/.662.

"I was definitely seeing the ball well," Roberts said. "I played the last two years in Beloit and some of the ballparks are kind of difficult to see. Here, great batter's eyes, great places to hit, and pitchers throw strikes here, so I was able to see a lot of strikes and hit a lot of strikes."

While most observers expected Hamilton to lead the AFL in stolen bases, he came up one short, with the title going to Salt River infielder Carlos Sanchez (White Sox) with 11. The Venezuela native said through an interpreter that he worked with Rafters hitting coach Jon Nunnally on getting better leads and studying pitchers.

TOP 10 PROSPECTS

1. Javier Baez, ss, Solar Sox (Cubs)
2. Jonathan Singleton, 1b, Solar Sox (Astros)
3. Christian Yelich, of, Desert Dogs (Marlins)
4. Kyle Gibson, rhp, Javelinas (Twins)
5. George Springer, of, Solar Sox (Astros)
6. Slade Heathcott, of, Scorpions (Yankees)
7. Mike Zunino, c, Javelinas (Mariners)
8. Nick Castellanos, of, Solar Sox (Tigers)
9. Rymer Liriano, of, Javelinas (Padres)
10. Billy Hamilton, of, Javelinas (Reds)

MINOR LEAGUES

STANDINGS

EAST	W	L	PCT	GB	WEST	W	L	PCT	GB
Salt River Rafters	17	13	.567	—	Peoria Javelinas	19	13	.594	—
Scottsdale Scorpions	15	16	.484	2 ½	Surprise Saguaros	17	14	.548	1 ½
Mesa Solar Sox	10	20	.333	7	Phoenix Desert Dogs	3	15	.464	4

INDIVIDUAL BATTING LEADERS
(Minimum 2 Plate Appearances/League Games)

Player, Team	AVG	G	AB	R	H	HR	RBI
Roberts, Nate, Peoria	.446	19	65	15	29	3	15
Prince, Josh, Phoenix	.404	25	89	23	36	1	14
Alberto, Hanser, Surprise	.397	17	63	10	25	0	7
Heathcott, Slade, Scottsdale	.388	18	67	13	26	1	15
Collier, Zach, Peoria	.371	19	62	12	23	0	10
Pillar, Kevin, Salt River	.371	15	62	13	23	1	7
O'Neill, Mike, Surprise	.368	18	68	12	25	0	7
Dickerson, Corey, Salt River	.364	17	66	11	24	1	11
Kiermaier, Kevin, Phoenix	.348	23	69	16	24	0	7
Rendon, Anthony, Salt River	.338	22	77	17	26	0	11

INDIVIDUAL PITCHING LEADERS
(Minimum .4 Innings Pitched/League Games)

Player, Team	W	L	ERA	IP	H	BB	SO
Reyes, Jimmy, Surprise	1	0	0.68	13	7	2	9
McGough, Scott, Phoenix	0	0	1.13	16	12	6	8
Kaminska, Kyle, Scottsdale	3	1	1.61	28	22	4	21
Buchter, Ryan, Phoenix	2	0	1.84	15	10	9	14
Huntzinger, Brock, Surprise	0	1	1.93	14	7	6	12
Hellweg, Johnny, Phoenix	0	1	2.08	13	11	7	8
Blair, Seth, Surprise	2	1	2.25	20	17	14	22
Erlin, Robbie, Peoria	2	1	2.28	24	18	6	31
Siegrist, Kevin, Surprise	2	1	2.37	19	15	6	27
Smith, Carson, Peoria	1	1	2.40	15	11	4	18

MESA SOLAR SOX

BATTERS	AVG	AB	R	H	2B	3B	HR	RBI	BB	SO	SB
Baez, Javier	.211	57	9	12	2	0	4	16	2	14	3
Borchering, Bobby	.158	38	6	6	2	0	2	5	5	13	0
Castellanos, Nick	.242	99	8	24	6	0	1	11	10	31	2
Erickson, Gorman	.268	41	7	11	3	0	0	4	9	10	1
Hoes, L.J.	.257	70	11	18	2	0	0	6	7	14	4
McCann, James	.195	41	3	8	0	0	0	3	2	7	0
Mier, Jiovanni	.297	64	10	19	8	0	0	7	4	15	0
Pederson, Joc	.096	52	4	5	0	0	1	6	3	6	3
Schoop, Jonathan	.270	63	12	17	4	0	2	10	16	18	2
Silva, Rubi	.206	68	8	14	0	2	0	3	5	21	3
Singleton, Jonathan	.226	93	18	21	4	2	3	8	17	24	0
Springer, George	.286	70	17	20	4	3	4	14	13	20	5
Szczur, Matt	.264	91	13	24	2	1	1	13	14	10	9
Ward, Brian	.297	37	3	11	1	0	0	4	6	5	2
Watkins, Logan	.219	32	8	7	1	0	1	3	8	3	0
Westlake, Aaron	.194	72	8	14	2	0	3	7	2	17	0
Ynoa, Rafael	.330	97	11	32	4	4	2	20	8	14	7
PITCHERS	W	L	ERA	G	GS	SV	IP	H	BB	SO	AVG
Belfiore, Mike	1	1	4.38	12	0	1	12	14	4	13	.286
Clark, Tyler	0	0	10.13	9	0	1	8	12	6	11	.343
Cosart, Jarred	0	3	6.50	6	6	0	18	25	9	15	.313
Eadington, Eric	0	0	5.11	12	0	1	12	15	8	15	.288
Garcia, Onelki	0	1	2.25	2	2	0	4	4	2	2	.250
Hoffman, Matt	0	0	4.97	13	0	0	13	14	5	14	.286
Lo, Chia-Jen	1	0	2.40	14	0	3	15	14	4	11	.255
Morrison, Michael	0	0	2.79	8	0	0	10	5	4	5	.152
Patterson, Red	1	1	5.40	11	0	0	12	19	4	4	.380
Petrini, Chris	0	1	7.15	12	0	0	11	15	8	8	.319
Putkonen, Luke	1	1	5.06	6	6	0	21	19	7	11	.238
Reed, Chris	1	0	7.20	11	0	0	10	17	7	12	.362
Rhee, Dae-Eun	0	2	6.27	6	6	0	19	26	8	12	.333
Rhoderick, Kevin	0	1	4.82	9	0	0	9	7	2	14	.212
Santiago, Andres	1	2	6.86	6	4	0	20	24	12	18	.304
Schrader, Clay	0	1	9.28	11	0	0	11	14	12	7	.318
Sogard, Alex	2	1	11.12	11	0	0	11	18	9	8	.367
Struck, Nick	1	0	5.51	12	0	0	16	12	12	11	.207
Tropeano, Nick	0	0	3.00	11	1	0	15	10	5	18	.189
Wright, Mike	0	5	6.43	7	7	0	21	37	7	15	.389
Zych, Tony	1	3	3.86	13	0	1	14	18	2	4	.327

PEORIA JAVELINAS

BATTERS	AVG	AB	R	H	2B	3B	HR	RBI	BB	SO	SB
Asche, Cody	.281	89	14	25	11	0	1	12	8	16	0
Bigley, Tyler	.242	62	11	15	4	2	0	9	7	16	0
Catricala, Vinnie	.279	68	5	19	3	0	2	13	6	18	1
Collier, Zach	.371	62	12	23	4	3	0	10	12	10	3
Franklin, Nick	.338	77	13	26	6	1	2	22	12	15	3

	AVG	AB	R	H	2B	3B	HR	RBI	BB	SO	SB
Freiman, Nate	.266	79	13	21	5	0	1	14	9	12	0
Gregorius, Didi	.284	74	12	21	3	1	1	8	6	4	2
Hamilton, Billy	.234	64	11	15	1	1	1	9	7	12	10
Herrmann, Chris	.500	10	3	5	1	0	0	0	2	1	0
Joseph, Tommy	.204	49	5	10	1	0	0	5	6	8	1
Liriano, Rymer	.319	91	23	29	5	0	4	15	6	21	6
Lutz, Donald	.395	43	10	17	3	1	1	4	1	7	2
Mattair, Travis	.188	32	5	6	1	0	0	3	2	10	0
Roberts, Nate	.446	65	15	29	5	0	3	15	12	7	6
Rohlfing, Dan	.333	18	3	6	0	0	0	5	3	4	0
Romero, Stefen	.333	45	7	15	2	0	2	9	1	10	1
Spangenberg, Cory	.345	29	6	10	1	0	1	3	8	5	2
Valdez, Jeudy	.303	66	18	20	10	1	2	11	10	13	3
Zunino, Mike	.288	80	10	23	4	2	2	15	5	20	1
PITCHERS	W	L	ERA	G	GS	SV	IP	H	BB	SO	AVG
Bawcom, Logan	1	0	5.27	11	0	0	14	16	5	11	.308
Crabbe, Tim	1	1	4.26	6	6	0	19	19	9	11	.260
Darnell, Logan	2	0	2.45	9	2	0	18	18	5	17	.257
Erlin, Robbie	2	1	2.28	7	7	0	24	18	6	31	.212
Gibson, Kyle	3	2	5.40	6	6	0	23	31	8	28	.326
Hayes, Drew	2	0	4.50	11	1	0	14	13	8	11	.232
Johnson, Jay	0	0	10.13	11	0	0	8	13	9	14	.361
Kim, Seon Gi	0	1	20.25	2	0	0	1	3	2	3	.429
Knigge, Tyler	1	1	7.50	10	0	0	12	13	5	10	.277
LaFromboise, Bobby	0	0	5.54	13	0	1	13	13	4	17	.250
Partch, Curtis	0	0	3.55	12	0	1	13	8	6	14	.178
Paxton, James	1	1	5.68	5	5	0	13	14	6	16	.275
Quackenbush, Kevin	0	0	2.45	11	0	6	11	4	3	16	.105
Ravin, Josh	0	1	6.97	9	0	0	10	10	7	10	.270
Shreve, Colby	0	1	4.50	9	0	0	10	8	5	6	.211
Simon, Kyle	2	2	9.00	5	5	0	12	21	3	8	.382
Smith, Carson	1	1	2.40	11	0	0	15	11	4	18	.212
Spence, Josh	0	1	9.00	7	0	0	7	10	5	5	.345
Stites, Matt	1	0	3.21	12	0	2	14	12	3	15	.245
Thielbar, Caleb	1	0	11.08	11	0	0	13	21	8	12	.375
Tonkin, Michael	1	0	2.45	10	0	0	15	8	3	7	.163

PHOENIX DESERT DOGS

BATTERS	AVG	AB	R	H	2B	3B	HR	RBI	BB	SO	SB
Ahmed, Nick	.288	73	13	21	3	3	1	10	9	11	5
Beckham, Tim	.244	78	9	19	2	2	1	10	5	13	3
Brownstein, Cory	.400	25	3	10	1	0	0	7	1	4	0
Cabrera, Yordy	.286	63	8	18	1	0	1	6	2	15	0
Davis, Khris	.226	53	6	12	2	0	0	6	10	11	0
Green, Grant	.273	66	8	18	2	1	2	11	10	19	1
Head, Miles	.000	3	0	0	0	0	0	0	0	2	0
Jensen, Kyle	.330	91	15	30	7	1	5	19	6	23	1
Kennelly, Matt	.111	9	0	1	0	0	0	1	1	1	0
Kiermaier, Kevin	.348	69	16	24	6	2	0	7	12	12	7
Kjeldgaard, Brock	.385	26	7	10	0	0	4	9	3	10	0
Lee, Hak-Ju	.247	81	8	20	1	0	6	11	21	3	
Morris, Hunter	.256	86	7	22	6	0	7	8	7	20	2
Prince, Josh	.404	89	23	36	8	2	1	14	15	14	10
Realmuto, Jake	.222	36	2	8	2	0	1	4	7	10	1
Salcedo, Edward	.140	86	7	12	6	1	1	5	5	22	5
Shaffer, Richie	.259	54	10	14	4	1	0	2	6	19	0
Stassi, Max	.271	48	4	13	3	0	1	11	3	12	1
Yelich, Christian	.301	93	13	28	6	1	0	11	5	17	3
PITCHERS	W	L	ERA	G	GS	SV	IP	H	BB	SO	AVG
Brady, Michael	1	1	2.25	9	0	0	12	9	3	9	.209
Bucci, Nick	2	2	9.00	6	6	0	18	26	9	23	.345
Buchter, Ryan	2	0	1.84	10	0	0	15	10	9	14	.185
Daley, Gary	1	0	6.75	11	0	1	12	16	12	8	.327
Dayton, Grant	0	0	3.75	10	0	0	12	8	7	18	.186
Flynn, Brian	1	3	3.63	7	7	0	22	21	7	18	.250
Haviland, Shawn	0	0	5.19	3	3	0	9	10	3	8	.313
Heckathorn, Kyle	1	0	6.75	10	0	0	13	17	6	9	.304
Hellweg, Johnny	0	1	2.08	9	0	2	13	11	7	8	.239
Hunter, Brett	0	0	4.66	10	0	0	9	10	11	5	.225
Jones, Chris	0	0	4.60	10	0	0	16	14	7	11	.250
Linsky, Lenny	0	1	5.56	9	0	0	11	20	7	7	.377
Manzanillo, Santo	0	1	31.50	3	0	0	2	6	4	1	.545
McGough, Scott	0	0	1.13	9	2	0	16	12	6	8	.222
Nelson, Jimmy	2	3	4.91	7	6	0	22	22	14	23	.262
Rasmus, Cory	0	0	7.53	10	0	0	14	18	5	11	.321
Rearick, Chris	1	1	3.77	10	0	0	14	18	7	13	.300
Riefenhauser, C.J.	0	0	2.19	9	1	0	12	6	5	14	.146
Simmons, James	0	0	1.59	12	0	0	11	2	3	8	.059
Spruill, Zeke	2	2	3.63	7	7	0	22	22	7	13	.250
Yates, Kirby	0	0	2.45	10	0	2	11	7	5	12	.175

SALT RIVER RAFTERS

BATTERS	AVG	AB	R	H	2B	3B	HR	RBI	BB	SO	SB
Bortnick, Tyler	.267	45	12	12	2	1	0	5	8	10	4
Davidson, Matt	.200	40	7	8	0	0	2	6	2	18	0
Davis, Lars	.310	42	5	13	3	0	1	8	2	11	0
Dickerson, Corey	.364	66	11	24	3	2	1	11	1	13	8
Goins, Ryan	.133	45	4	6	1	0	0	5	4	9	0
Gonzalez, Jose	.167	36	7	6	2	0	0	5	5	9	1
Goodwin, Brian	.238	80	16	19	6	2	3	6	12	25	2
Marisnick, Jake	.314	70	9	22	3	2	1	8	3	20	5
Martinson, Jason	.189	37	5	7	4	0	1	8	5	16	2
Matthes, Kent	.235	85	15	20	5	0	5	18	11	19	2
Ochinko, Sean	.277	47	6	13	2	0	1	7	2	7	0
Owings, Chris	.275	91	12	25	9	1	1	9	0	17	4
Pillar, Kevin	.371	62	13	23	1	0	1	7	3	13	8
Rendon, Anthony	.338	77	17	26	10	1	0	11	15	14	6
Sanchez, Carlos	.299	87	12	26	4	1	0	16	9	18	11
Skole, Matt	.305	59	9	18	4	0	3	15	13	18	1
Thompson, Trayce	.208	48	10	10	0	0	2	7	17	17	2
Wilkins, Andy	.270	89	14	24	4	0	3	15	8	22	2

PITCHERS	W	L	ERA	G	GS	SV	IP	H	BB	SO	AVG
Anderson, Chase	3	1	3.47	6	6	0	23	19	9	26	.218
Barrett, Aaron	0	0	3.27	10	0	0	11	15	2	10	.333
Chatwood, Tyler	1	1	4.60	4	4	0	16	15	10	15	.273
Demny, Paul	0	0	3.94	10	1	0	16	18	8	12	.310
Dyson, Sam	0	0	7.04	7	0	0	8	12	1	8	.353
Froneberger, Isaiah	1	1	8.25	11	0	0	12	16	5	10	.314
Kadish, Ian	0	1	7.00	10	0	0	9	14	4	6	.350
Kimball, Cole	0	0	4.80	11	0	0	15	18	9	10	.290
Marbry, Mike	0	0	2.70	3	0	0	3	3	0	3	.250
Marshall, Evan	0	1	2.19	11	0	2	12	15	0	6	.294
McGuire, Deck	2	1	3.95	11	1	0	14	9	7	11	.191
Munson, Kevin	0	0	6.75	11	0	1	9	13	6	12	.310
Perry, Ryan	2	0	4.98	6	6	0	22	17	8	16	.213
Rienzo, Andre	1	1	4.74	6	6	0	25	21	15	24	.241
Riordan, Cory	3	1	5.65	11	2	0	14	21	3	11	.344
Rodriguez, Santos	0	1	4.76	11	0	0	11	11	10	13	.262
Sanchez, Salvador	0	1	2.31	11	0	0	12	9	12	9	.220
Smith, Eric	1	1	3.46	11	0	1	13	16	7	4	.302
Tepera, Ryan	1	2	6.75	6	6	0	17	29	8	20	.367
Thompson, Taylor	1	0	3.38	10	0	0	13	16	4	10	.314
Woods, Coty	1	0	3.18	10	0	2	11	7	4	9	.171

SCOTTSDALE SCORPIONS

BATTERS	AVG	AB	R	H	2B	3B	HR	RBI	BB	SO	SB
Adams, David	.286	84	13	24	7	2	3	15	14	13	1
Brown, Gary	.313	64	7	20	2	1	0	5	5	14	2
Cowart, Kaleb	.200	60	7	12	2	0	1	8	6	16	0
Curry, Matt	.253	79	10	20	4	0	1	6	13	23	4
Dominguez, Chris	.317	41	6	13	2	0	3	8	2	17	1
Grichuk, Randal	.228	57	9	13	1	0	2	5	4	18	2
Heathcott, Slade	.388	67	13	26	6	3	1	15	12	14	5
Holt, Tyler	.300	60	8	18	0	0	0	8	5	10	4
Moncrief, Carlos	.167	42	6	7	2	0	1	6	1	19	3
Monsalve, Alex	.340	47	8	16	5	0	0	6	2	8	2
Ngoepe, Gift	.261	46	8	12	2	1	1	5	7	15	2
Oropesa, Ricky	.234	47	6	11	0	0	2	6	11	16	0
Panik, Joe	.205	78	11	16	0	1	1	8	10	7	4
Ramirez, Carlos	.250	24	4	6	0	0	0	4	3	3	0
Rodriguez, Ronny	.239	67	8	16	3	3	0	7	2	17	6
Romine, Austin	.222	63	9	14	4	0	0	6	12	13	0
Santos, Adalberto	.299	77	15	23	7	1	1	11	14	14	9
Witherspoon, Travis	.219	73	10	16	3	1	3	11	6	28	6

PITCHERS	W	L	ERA	G	GS	SV	IP	H	BB	SO	AVG
Armstrong, Shawn	0	0	0.00	5	0	0	6	2	4	3	.105
Betances, Dellin	1	3	5.25	8	0	0	12	13	4	15	.271
Black, Vic	1	1	11.81	12	0	1	11	17	11	11	.370
Boshers, Buddy	0	1	10.12	5	0	0	3	7	3	3	.467
Bradley, Ryan	0	0	9.00	2	0	0	2	4	2	2	.444
Burawa, Dan	0	0	11.57	11	0	0	12	19	13	6	.388
Cassevah, Bobby	2	0	3.13	6	6	0	23	22	8	18	.253
Chaffee, Ryan	0	0	11.37	8	0	0	6	11	6	9	.393
Cumpton, Brandon	0	0	2.57	11	0	0	14	11	7	6	.229
Dunnington, Jacob	0	1	6.75	10	0	0	9	13	4	14	.333
Gloor, Chris	2	2	2.70	7	7	0	30	28	11	22	.264
Haley, Trey	0	0	1.64	8	0	0	11	2	4	3	.065
Hembree, Heath	0	0	3.00	9	0	2	9	8	3	12	.229
House, T.J.	3	1	3.00	6	6	0	27	20	9	26	.208
Johnson, Kevin	1	1	3.75	10	0	0	12	15	1	7	.306
Kaminska, Kyle	3	1	1.61	6	6	0	28	22	4	21	.208
Montgomery, Mark	0	0	2.61	9	0	1	10	5	5	19	.143
Nuding, Zach	1	3	5.82	7	7	0	22	31	10	12	.344
Packer, Matt	0	1	4.05	8	0	0	13	16	5	10	.327
Runzler, Dan	1	1	3.38	10	0	1	8	6	7	11	.222
Waldron, Tyler	0	0	3.14	10	0	0	14	8	6	11	.167

SURPRISE SAGUAROS

BATTERS	AVG	AB	R	H	2B	3B	HR	RBI	BB	SO	SB
Alberto, Hanser	.397	63	10	25	2	2	0	7	2	4	4
Almanzar, Michael	.185	81	12	15	4	0	0	8	7	19	0
Brentz, Bryce	.297	64	10	19	1	1	2	11	6	19	2
Calixte, Orlando	.275	40	5	11	0	0	1	2	2	14	1
Ceciliani, Darrell	.258	66	10	17	3	0	1	9	9	13	5
Deglan, Kellin	.171	35	5	6	0	0	1	3	3	12	0
Fletcher, Brian	.203	69	9	14	4	1	1	9	17	24	0
Lawley, Dustin	.268	41	7	11	4	0	1	9	1	9	0
McClure, Alex	.216	37	7	8	2	0	0	4	2	11	2
McGuiness, Chris	.283	92	5	26	5	0	4	27	13	16	0
Merrifield, Whit	.250	68	15	17	1	0	1	8	10	8	9
Muno, Daniel	.226	31	6	7	2	0	0	1	6	7	0
Nicholas, Brett	1.000	1	0	1	0	0	0	0	1	0	0
O'Neill, Mike	.368	68	12	25	2	0	0	7	11	11	2
Puello, Cesar	.247	85	12	21	1	1	0	9	8	29	10
Sardinas, Luis	.318	44	7	14	3	0	1	4	4	9	1
Stanley, Cody	.208	48	7	10	1	0	3	5	6	13	1
Vazquez, Christian	.257	35	4	9	3	0	1	3	8	9	0
Walsh, Colin	.281	57	11	16	6	0	1	14	13	20	0
Wong, Kolten	.324	74	12	24	2	0	1	12	2	11	5

PITCHERS	W	L	ERA	G	GS	SV	IP	H	BB	SO	AVG
Blair, Seth	2	1	2.25	6	6	0	20	17	14	22	.236
Carl, Edwin	0	1	2.77	10	0	0	13	9	3	8	.188
Culver, Malcom	0	1	6.35	5	0	0	6	6	0	3	.286
Fraser, Ryan	1	1	5.79	9	0	0	14	16	5	10	.286
Freeman, Sam	0	0	3.86	7	0	0	7	11	1	8	.333
Henry, Ben	0	1	11.57	4	4	0	7	10	9	4	.357
Huchingson, Chase	1	0	5.73	9	0	0	11	12	10	6	.273
Huntzinger, Brock	0	1	1.93	10	0	0	14	17	6	12	.315
Keck, Jon	0	0	5.59	10	0	0	10	15	5	7	.357
Kolarek, Adam	0	0	2.92	9	0	0	12	19	5	8	.365
Marks, Justin	5	1	2.59	7	7	0	24	24	5	22	.253
Martin, Chris	1	0	3.38	7	0	0	11	8	1	12	.195
Peavey, Greg	1	1	3.86	9	0	0	14	11	7	7	.224
Pressly, Ryan	0	0	3.86	10	0	1	14	18	1	18	.300
Reyes, Jimmy	1	0	0.68	9	0	1	13	7	2	9	.152
Rodebaugh, Ryan	0	1	2.63	10	0	0	14	10	5	12	.208
Rowen, Ben	0	0	3.21	14	0	0	14	9	6	13	.176
Ruiz, Pete	0	1	8.25	10	0	1	12	17	5	16	.315
Siegrist, Kevin	2	1	2.37	6	5	0	19	15	6	27	.214
Sulbaran, J.C.	0	0	6.00	1	1	0	3	4	0	2	.308
Van Meter, Joe	0	0	6.00	2	2	0	6	9	4	4	.360
Whiting, Boone	3	2	4.62	7	7	0	25	30	8	33	.303

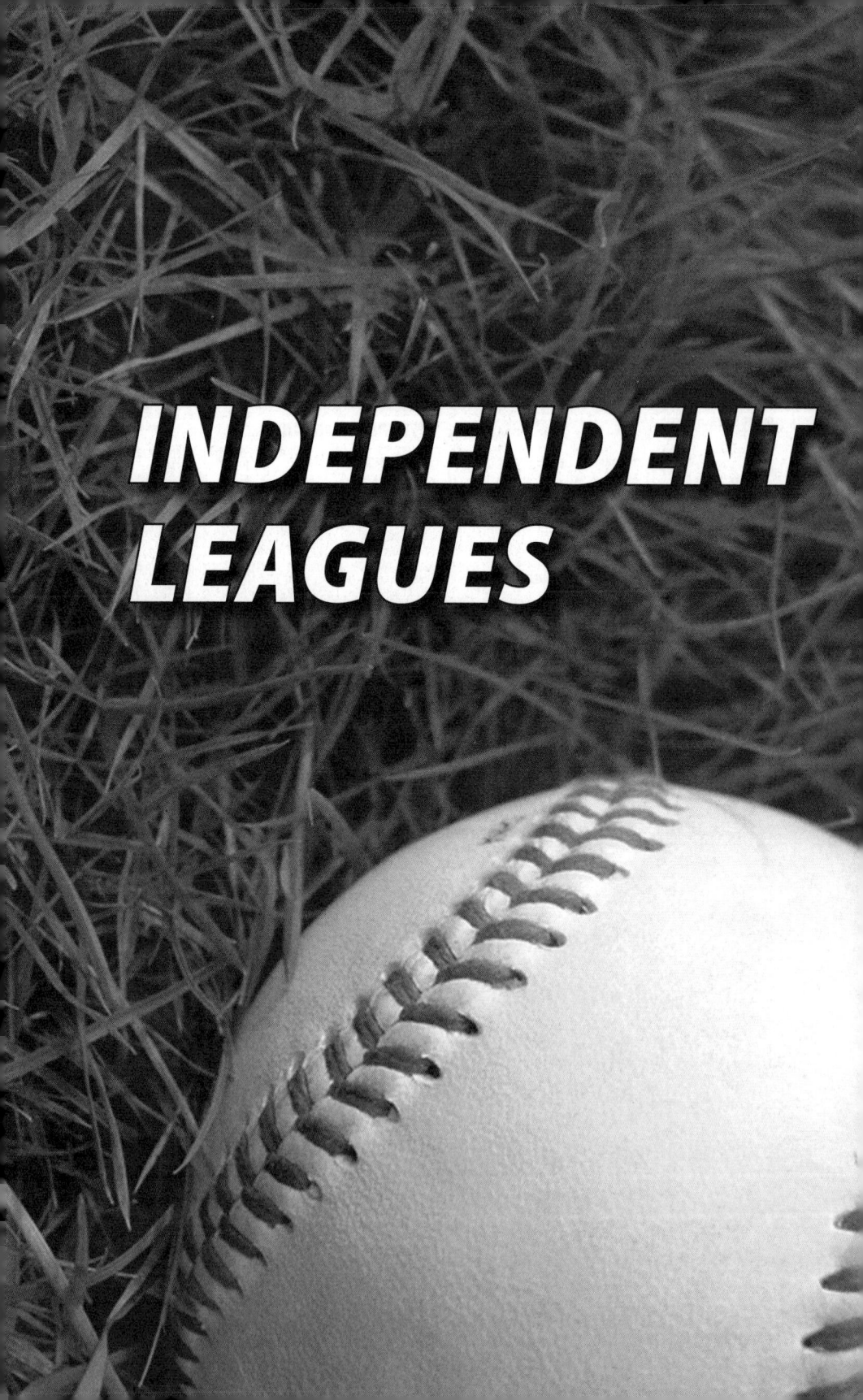

INDEPENDENT LEAGUES

Shrinking number of teams has some leagues struggling

J.J. COOPER

With the 20th anniversary of modern, independent minor league baseball just one year away, indy ball is well established as a part of the baseball landscape.

But when you look on a league-by-league level or a team-by-team level, it's clear stability isn't always part of the game.

The Atlantic League, American Association and Frontier League are the AAA-rated bonds of the independent leagues. While each league will occasionally have a team or two that hits financial trouble, the leagues themselves are rock solid, with large footprints, plenty of cornerstone franchises and the attendance to show for it.

But once you get past those three leagues, there is still a lot of instability, a couple of years after the financial crisis and resulting recession began pruning the number of leagues.

The Can-Am League, formerly the Northeast League, has been around for quite a while, but with the Atlantic League, multiple affiliated leagues and summer college leagues sharing its geographic footprint, the Can-Am League has been in survival mode for several years. It has been able to add enough new cities to stay afloat after several franchises have gone under, but it has not been able to find enough solid markets to ever buy any breathing space. As it was planning for 2013, at least in the fall the Can-Am was down to a five-team league, with one new expansion club (Trois-Rivieres) filling the spot left when the league had to take over the Worcester club at the end of the 2012 season.

Portions of the North American League might gladly swap problems with the Can-Am League. What was at one point a robust, if attendance-challenged California-based league saw itself reduced to four teams in 2012—two in Hawaii and two in California. Despite crippling travel costs and attendance struggles, the league did manage to make it through the season, but heading into 2013, the league will have to fight the new American West League, which has announced plans to set up shop in some of the North American League's old cities.

Because of the smaller number of leagues and clubs, independent baseball drew just over seven millions fans in announced attendance in 2012,

Blake Gailen's success in the Atlantic League helped him sign with the Rockies

down more than one million fans from just two seasons ago. More than 87 percent of those fans attended American Association, Atlantic League or Frontier League games.

On the field, the caliber of play around independent ball has continued to improve. In part because of the reduced number of teams, the talent on the average team has improved, especially on the mound. Teams have also continued to become more an more innovative to unearth talent. This year saw teams try a number of conversion projects. Ben Klafczynski, a former minor league outfielder, converted to pitching with Lake Erie (Frontier) and parlayed that into a contract with the Red Sox. Chuck Lofgren, a former Indians pitcher, tried hitting.

The indy leagues also were not averse to bringing back an aging star. While Jose Canseco's never-ending independent league road trip continued, new Atlantic League franchise Sugar Land managed to land Roger Clemens for a couple of late-season starts that drew sellout crowds and national attention.

INDEPENDENT LEAGUES

Gailen proves he can hit anywhere

Blake Gailen has seen all that independent baseball can offer.

Through six seasons, Gailen has played in a league that went under. He played in another that has since changed its name. One year he was summarily released at the end of spring training along with all of his teammates when his team was sold.

He has manned center field behind the knuckleball princess, Eri Yoshida, and has been pulled off the field to the cheers of the crowd when it was announced that his contract had been sold to the Los Angeles Angels.

"Sometimes, I think adversity is my middle name," Gailen said.

But wherever he's gone, Gailen has always hit. He proved that once again in 2012, making the jump to the Atlantic League's Lancaster Barnstormers, where he hit .338/.415/.534 with a career-high 22 home runs and 25 stolen bases. That actually lowered his career independent league batting average to .348. For his consistent success, the 27-year-old Gailen is our 2012 Independent League Player of the Year.

Coming out of college, Gailen latched on with the fledgling South Coast League—a first-year league that ended up not having a second year. On the lowest rung of independent ball, Gailen was signed largely because of his versatility and good attitude.

Gailen provided leadership—on a team with almost no one over the age of 25, a 23-year-old could be a leader—and proved he could hit. He batted .368/.455/.526 that season, good enough that when his manager got a job as the manager of the American Association's Wichita Wingnuts the next season, he brought Gailen along with him.

Gailen has had to pack lightly. He's been

moving around ever since.

With the Golden League's Chico club, Gailen established himself as one of the better hitters in indy ball. He hit over .350 in both of his two seasons in Chico. He then asked and received a trade back to the American Association, hoping that a change of scenery would help him get noticed by more scouts.

It worked, and it didn't hurt that he hit .406 with a 1.100 on-base plus slugging percentage in 69 games with the Lincoln Saltdogs. Once known most for his do-anything-for-the-team attitude, Gailen was now known as one of the toughest outs in independent ball. The Angels, who had brought Gailen to a tryout camp before the season, purchased his contract on July 29, 2011, and assigned him to Double-A Arkansas, where he would replace a teenager who had just been promoted to the big leagues: Mike Trout.

Gailen hit .208/.322/.366 in 101 at-bats with the Travelers before the season ended. For a top prospect, a bad 100 at-bat stretch would be written off as adjusting to a new league or a small sample size. For Gailen, it would prove to be his only taste of affiliated ball up to now. After the season, he was released.

But that time in Double-A did help him get to the Atlantic League this year, as it beefed up his resume to jump to the most veteran-heavy independent league of them all. Coming to Lancaster, the longtime leadoff hitter expected to continue to be a spark plug, but when the season began, he found himself hitting fifth. Before long, he was the No. 3 hitter on the Barnstormers team that set an Atlantic League record for most wins in a season.

Gailen's size has been a hurdle to overcome in the eyes of scouts. He has made it to affiliated ball, briefly, one time. Now he's getting another shot, after the Rockies purchased his contract following the season.

PREVIOUS WINNERS

1996: Darryl Motley, of, Fargo-Moorhead (Northern)
1997: Mike Meggers, of, Winnipeg/Duluth (Northern)
1998: Morgan Burkhart, 1b, Richmond (Frontier)
1999: Carmine Cappucio, of, New Jersey (Northeast)
2000: Anthony Lewis, 1b, Duluth-Superior (Northern)
2001: Mike Warner, of, Somerset (Atlantic)
2002: Bobby Madritsch, lhp, Winnipeg (Northern)
2003: Jason Shelley, rhp, Rockford (Frontier)

2004: Victor Rodriguez, ss, Somerset (Atlantic)
2005: Eddie Lantigua, 3b, Quebec (Can-Am)
2006: Ian Church, of, Kalamazoo (Frontier)
2007: Darryl Brinkley, of, Calgary (Northern)
2008: Patrick Breen, of, Orange County (Golden)
2009: Greg Porter, of, Wichita (American Association)
2010: Beau Torbert, of, Sioux Falls (American Association)
2011: Chris Collabello, 1b, Worcester (Can-Am League)

AMERICAN ASSOCIATION

The Winnipeg Goldeyes picked the perfect time to go on a run.

In the regular season, Winnipeg barely earned a playoff spot by edging Grand Prairie for the American Association wild card berth. But when the playoffs began, the Goldeyes suddenly became invincible. Winnipeg swept Fargo-Moorhead, owners of the league's best regular season record, then swept Wichita, owners of the league's second-best record, to pick up the city's first title since 1994. It was Winnipeg's first six-game winning streak of the season.

Goldeyes' closer Brian Beuning saved four of the six postseason wins and won another as he appeared in all six games. Beuning, a Minnesota state trooper, was on unpaid leave so he could pitch in the playoffs.

CENTRAL	W	L	PCT	GB
Wichita Wingnuts	59	41	.590	—
Kansas City T-Bones	51	49	.510	8
Gary SouthShore RailCats	50	50	.500	9
Sioux City Explorers	45	55	.450	14
Lincoln Saltdogs	41	59	.410	18

NORTH	W	L	PCT	GB
Fargo-Moorhead Redhawks	65	35	.650	—
*Winnipeg Goldeyes	55	45	.550	10
St. Paul Saints	52	48	.520	13
Sioux Falls Pheasants	45	55	.450	20

SOUTH	W	L	PCT	GB
Laredo Lemurs	54	46	.540	—
Grand Prairie AirHogs	53	47	.530	1
El Paso Diablos	47	53	.470	7
Amarillo Sox	46	54	.460	8

*Wild Card

PLAYOFFS: Semifinals—Winnipeg defeats Fargo-Moorhead 3-0 and Wichita defeats Laredo 3-0 in best-of-five series. **Finals**—Wichita defeats Winnipeg 3-0 in best-of-five series.
ATTENDANCE: Winnipeg 285,263; Kansas City 260,620; St Paul 240,616; Laredo 187,845; Fargo-Moorhead 187,438; El Paso 181,122; Lincoln 160,986; Gary SouthShore 159,837; Wichita 152,727; Amarillo 133,380; Sioux Falls 130,541; Grand Prairie 108,236; Sioux City 55,627.
MANAGERS: Amarillo—John Harris; **El Paso**—Jorge Alvarez/Tim Johnson; **Fargo-Moorhead**—Doug Simunic; **Gary**—Greg Tagert; **Grand Prairie**—Ricky Van Asselberg; **Kansas City**—Kenny Hook; Laredo-Pete Incaviglia; **Lincoln**—Chris Miyake; **St. Paul**—George Tsamis; **Sioux City**—Stan Cliburn; **Sioux Falls**—Steve Shirley; **Wichita**—Kevin Hooper; **Winnipeg**—Rick Forney.
ALL-STAR TEAM: C—Chris McMurray (Grand Prairie/Lincoln). **1B**—Brian Myrow (Grand Prairie). **2B**—Jake Kahaulelio (Wichita). **3B**—Cesar Nicolas (Sioux Falls). **SS**—Zach Penprase (Fargo-Moorhead). **OF**—Nic Jackson (Fargo-Moorhead); Chris Roberson (Winnipeg); Adam Buschini (Amarillo). **DH**—Ryan Delgado (Fargo-Moorhead). **SP**—Josh Lowey (Wichita). **RP**—Tom Boleska (Fargo-Moorhead).
PLAYER OF THE YEAR: Nic Jackson (Fargo-Moorhead). **MANAGER OF THE YEAR:** Tim Johnson (El Paso).

BATTING LEADERS

PLAYER	TEAM	AVG	G	AB	R	H	HR	RBI
Welington Dotel	EP	.405	58	247	46	100	2	44
Jake Kahaulelio	WCH	.372	59	239	60	89	6	39
Brian Myrow	GP	.364	92	316	65	115	12	63
Adam Buschini	AMA	.354	96	395	87	140	14	70
Jimmy Mojica	LAR	.339	93	389	72	132	9	61
Cesar Nicolas	SF	.335	99	373	62	125	12	82
Brandon Newton	SC	.332	89	352	67	117	1	32
David Peralta	WIC	.332	98	377	65	125	3	70
John Rodriguez	WIC	.332	94	373	67	124	16	81
Jimmy Rohan	LIN/EP	.332	72	271	39	90	4	42
John Allen	LAR	.331	92	359	63	119	11	59

PITCHING LEADERS

PLAYER	TEAM	W	L	ERA	IP	H	BB	K
Matt Rusch	WIN	10	4	2.40	139	117	31	113
Lucas Irvine	KC	4	2	2.59	104	105	42	107
Robert Coe	STP	12	5	2.91	139	124	59	87
Paul Burnside	FM	9	6	3.20	115	101	62	91
Stephen Hiscock	GARY	6	6	3.22	126	120	37	69
Jared Simon	WIC	3	6	3.25	64	66	18	53
Tyler Herron	FMH	12	3	3.29	123	113	30	105
Devin Anderson	KC	7	6	3.36	112	136	28	70
Shaun Garceau	KC	9	6	3.47	106	106	27	75
Alex Caldera	FM	10	4	3.50	123	126	44	88
Josh Lowey	WIC	15	4	3.57	134	126	43	96

AMARILLO SOX

PLAYER	P	AVG	OBP	SLG	AB	R	H	HR	RBI	SB
Adam Buschini	OF	.354	.410	.562	395	87	140	14	70	34
*Jonathan Cisneros	IF	.338	.375	.471	68	10	23	2	11	0
#Matthew Tucker	OF	.319	.380	.487	238	46	76	5	39	4
Tim Alberts	OF	.319	.397	.510	408	70	130	14	73	10
Cyle Hankerd	OF	.304	.385	.478	23	3	7	1	4	0
*Jake Opitz	IF	.303	.386	.522	228	48	69	7	40	5
*Jerry Verastegui	C	.292	.320	.333	24	3	7	0	1	0
Tyler Goodro	C	.290	.339	.410	100	9	29	1	15	0
Van Pope	3B	.281	.370	.352	196	22	55	2	24	3
Derrick Pyles	RF	.280	.316	.304	125	12	35	0	12	6
Garrett Rau	IF	.268	.329	.345	325	54	87	3	33	13
*Jason White	SS	.265	.369	.380	234	36	62	3	27	14
Mitch Abeita	C	.260	.381	.422	154	29	40	5	33	1
Alberto Espinosa	C	.246	.280	.415	248	32	61	8	35	0
Chuck Lofgren	P	.245	.352	.350	200	30	49	3	25	0
Harrison Kain	OF	.238	.312	.371	302	47	72	3	44	17
#Kevin Lusson	IF	.231	.231	.231	26	3	6	0	1	0
Danny Gallinot	OF	.227	.286	.227	44	3	10	0	4	0
Patrick Arlis	C	.226	.303	.302	106	12	24	1	10	2
*Jake Luce	RF	.211	.257	.263	95	7	20	0	4	3

PLAYER	W	L	ERA	G	SV	IP	H	BB	SO
Garrett Rau	0	0	0.00	3	0	3	2	1	4
Chad Povich	4	1	3.20	38	2	53	49	20	41
Wes Littleton	4	3	3.21	53	4	56	54	19	48
Chase Johnson	5	5	3.66	44	11	47	43	22	46
Justin Garcia	9	3	3.99	22	0	135	148	28	101
Matt Lackie	0	2	4.01	17	0	49	42	22	54
*Chuck Lofgren	4	6	4.36	21	0	120	123	58	68
Ryan Mitchell	8	5	5.64	23	0	118	162	31	91
*Trent Lare	2	5	5.92	40	0	52	70	22	52
*Cliff Springston	2	3	5.93	9	0	44	57	14	17
*Jack Spradlin	5	7	6.18	28	0	83	107	34	60
*Andrew Bowman	1	2	6.30	21	0	20	17	22	15
Philip Bartleski	0	7	6.98	22	0	67	98	20	35
Derek Christensen	2	4	7.24	22	0	50	66	38	34
Marcus Limon	0	1	9.52	3	0	6	11	3	4
*Paul Montalbano	0	0	27.00	4	0	2	8	3	2

EL PASO DIABLOS

PLAYER	P	AVG	OBP	SLG	AB	R	H	HR	RBI	SB
Welington Dotel	OF	.405	.436	.518	247	46	100	2	44	23
Jimmy Rohan	IF	.368	.467	.553	38	11	14	2	8	0
*Zane Chavez	C	.336	.374	.427	143	18	48	0	22	0
Kory Drew	OF	.333	.385	.450	60	11	20	2	5	3
Maikol Gonzalez	IF	.330	.405	.403	427	83	141	5	50	40
#Jermy Acey	IF	.330	.431	.518	191	39	63	5	40	2
*Fernando Valenzuela	IF	.326	.343	.411	95	9	31	1	17	0
Derrick Pyles	OF	.314	.314	.343	35	6	11	0	4	0
Scott Hodsdon	P	.313	.421	.375	16	3	5	0	0	0
Nelson Teilon	IF	.312	.347	.384	138	22	43	1	21	6
Patrick Arlis	C	.302	.373	.367	199	28	60	0	33	0

INDEPENDENT LEAGUES

Jordan Marks	IF	.298	.339	.421	114	18	34	1	18	2
Mitch Einertson	OF	.297	.344	.430	279	54	83	7	43	5
*Reid Fronk	OF	.291	.390	.434	258	51	75	4	37	2
Bryan Frichter	IF	.286	.351	.345	84	13	24	0	11	4
Scott Clement	C	.277	.309	.462	65	10	18	3	14	0
Enrique Cruz	3B	.274	.318	.435	62	12	17	1	5	2
Brian Joynt	OF	.272	.351	.437	151	25	41	4	26	2
#Dan Nelson	IF	.272	.378	.497	151	23	41	5	30	2
*Jonathan Cisneros	IF	.268	.344	.407	231	38	62	4	33	1
J.J. Muse	OF	.263	.299	.350	320	35	84	1	35	7
#Uriak Marquez	IF	.258	.294	.305	128	13	33	1	11	3
Ryan Lauer	C	.250	.250	.250	4	0	1	0	0	0
Palmer Karr	OF	.228	.262	.380	79	12	18	2	8	0
Javier Brito	IF	.218	.291	.372	78	12	17	0	9	0
Brian Ramirez	IF	.200	.200	.200	5	1	1	0	0	0

PLAYER	W	L	ERA	G	SV	IP	H	BB	SO
Jordan Marks	0	0	0.00	1	0	1	0	0	0
*T.J. Wink	0	0	0.00	1	0	0	1	1	1
Luis Chirinos	5	2	3.10	7	0	46	43	17	35
Marcel Prado	2	3	3.37	44	15	51	48	20	43
Reyes Dorado	1	5	3.70	29	0	68	77	37	33
Reymond Cruz	4	3	3.81	12	0	66	74	17	57
Scott Hodsdon	9	2	3.91	21	0	143	161	41	80
Ronny Morla	5	7	5.30	48	0	56	77	15	43
Justin Harper	4	3	4.28	25	2	27	26	14	14
Freddy Flores	3	2	5.29	12	1	66	92	15	39
Kevin Cooper	1	0	5.29	3	0	17	20	5	11
David Casillas	6	2	5.46	11	0	56	52	32	39
Tim Adleman	0	2	5.94	29	0	33	40	8	30
Kyle Cremers	3	3	6.33	32	0	38	47	25	29
Edgar Garcia	0	3	6.53	4	0	21	35	9	10
*Grafton Kent	0	0	6.75	2	0	1	2	2	1
Ramon Garcia	1	4	6.81	7	0	34	42	13	16
*Steve Evarts	0	1	6.93	18	0	25	38	23	11
Juan Peralta	0	1	8.04	3	0	16	19	11	10
*Marc Gomez	0	0	8.30	6	0	4	6	5	3
Colin Allen	0	4	8.37	7	0	29	43	11	13
Drew Graham	1	1	8.62	19	0	24	40	9	19
Eric Blackwell	0	2	8.67	2	0	9	18	1	4
Geivy Garcia	1	3	9.25	11	1	12	17	5	16
*Kyle Kriech	0	0	10.19	5	0	15	25	8	6
Osvaldo Rodriguez	1	3	10.47	5	0	22	37	12	11
Cody Railsback	0	0	10.80	7	0	10	14	13	4
Drew Graham	0	0	11.25	2	0	4	6	7	0
*Blake Cull	0	0	15.42	4	0	2	4	3	1
*Brandon Godfrey	0	0	54.00	1	0	0	2	0	0

FARGO-MOORHEAD REDHAWKS

PLAYER	P	AVG	OBP	SLG	AB	R	H	HR	RBI	SB
Eric Campbell	3B	.354	.424	.655	206	49	73	13	55	2
*Buddy Sosnoskie	OF	.339	.357	.484	192	35	65	2	31	9
Max Casper	IF	.333	.417	.333	21	1	7	0	4	0
Ryan Delgado	C	.312	.363	.551	365	66	114	20	86	1
Zach Penprase	SS	.311	.424	.416	380	95	118	6	46	47
*Nic Jackson	CF	.309	.377	.522	404	77	125	17	89	19
*Marcos Rodriguez	1B	.296	.351	.383	389	54	115	1	40	5
Ryan Stovall	IF	.290	.338	.426	303	44	88	7	52	25
*Jon Gaston	RF	.277	.350	.484	256	45	71	12	41	5
*Aharon Eggleston	LF	.277	.371	.374	155	29	43	2	14	10
*Sergio Pedroza	OF	.266	.379	.457	94	19	25	6	24	3
Todd Jennings	C	.239	.304	.297	327	42	78	3	38	3
Carlo Cota	2B	.219	.295	.333	333	47	73	3	40	6
Enrique Cruz	3B	.215	.287	.278	79	10	17	0	12	2
Dale Cornstubble	C	.167	.167	.167	6	0	1	0	1	0
Jorge Delgado	1B	.143	.294	.143	14	1	2	0	0	0
Zach Wentz	3B	.143	.143	.143	7	0	1	0	0	0

PLAYER	W	L	ERA	G	SV	IP	H	BB	SO
Tom Boleska	2	1	1.76	46	29	46	37	11	58
*Ethan Opsahl	1	0	1.86	8	0	19	16	5	11
Eric Massingham	0	0	2.25	4	0	4	2	0	5
*Joe Harris	1	3	2.64	43	0	51	35	19	44
Paul Burnside	9	6	3.19	20	0	115	101	62	91
Tyler Herron	12	3	3.29	23	0	123	113	30	105
Kevin Fuqua	2	1	3.33	47	1	57	59	16	46
Kyle Dahman	3	1	3.40	36	1	37	31	11	20

Alex Caldera	10	4	3.50	20	0	123	126	44	88
*Daniel Morari	1	1	3.68	27	0	22	25	6	15
*Jake Laber	7	7	5.02	20	0	115	135	57	57
Aaron Shafer	10	5	5.06	20	0	112	131	47	97
Kenn Kasparek	1	1	5.40	2	0	12	14	3	6
Mike Zenko	3	1	5.40	25	0	30	37	15	27
*Tony Davis	2	0	6.75	5	0	4	4	4	2
Alex Rivers	1	1	7.00	9	0	18	27	8	8
*Tony Butler	0	0	27.00	1	0	1	4	3	1

GARY SOUTHSHORE RAILCATS

PLAYER	P	AVG	OBP	SLG	AB	R	H	HR	RBI	SB
Sergio Miranda	3B	.750	.750	1.250	4	0	3	0	1	0
Eric Suttle	OF	.382	.523	.441	34	6	13	0	7	4
*Mike Massaro	OF	.325	.372	.467	415	76	135	6	63	17
*Rico Washington	IF	.301	.366	.398	83	10	25	1	17	5
Mike Coles	OF	.300	.393	.396	273	40	82	3	43	19
Sean Smith	CF	.298	.339	.368	57	9	17	0	5	6
Chase Tucker	IF	.297	.333	.351	37	3	11	0	7	1
Brian Kolb	IF	.297	.369	.328	293	41	87	0	32	10
*Adam Klein	OF	.285	.410	.359	376	72	107	0	49	30
*Trevor Willis	OF	.283	.411	.391	46	9	13	0	2	2
*David Cooper	IF	.266	.396	.332	271	42	72	0	32	30
Chris Carrara	IF	.261	.335	.296	253	36	66	1	30	12
#Kyle Haines	IF	.258	.361	.355	124	13	32	3	13	0
*Mike Rohde	IF	.257	.333	.383	303	40	78	5	42	14
Ryan Babineau	C	.257	.386	.342	187	27	48	2	31	5
*Tomochika Tsuboi	OF	.250	.286	.350	20	4	5	0	2	0
*Zac Mitchell	IF	.247	.357	.247	93	17	23	0	11	2
#K.C. Judge	IF	.242	.324	.242	33	3	8	0	1	0
*Craig Maddox	C	.235	.310	.380	221	23	52	5	40	2
Sean Henry	OF	.221	.280	.360	86	9	19	2	11	4
Matt Forgatch	OF	.216	.250	.431	51	6	11	3	9	1
Zach Tanner	IF	.200	.333	.200	5	0	1	0	0	0
*Jason James	OF	.192	.214	.231	26	4	5	0	1	0
*Kenny Bryant	IF	.167	.245	.250	48	5	8	0	6	0
*Cody Coffman	C	.000	.000	.000	4	0	0	0	0	0
*Asif Shah	RF	.000	.000	.000	5	0	0	0	0	0

PLAYER	W	L	ERA	G	SV	IP	H	BB	SO
*Justin Roelle	0	0	0.00	4	0	6	2	3	5
Dexter Carter	2	0	1.58	9	0	11	9	4	12
*David Quinowski	3	1	2.07	20	1	17	10	6	19
*T.J. Wohlever	2	0	2.40	15	0	15	11	3	12
*Jon Gulbransen	4	1	3.13	10	0	52	48	15	39
Stephen Hiscock	6	6	3.22	25	0	126	120	37	69
Nolan Nicholson	4	3	3.24	39	0	61	58	36	34
Chris Allen	4	5	3.32	31	6	43	40	6	38
Will Krout	4	5	3.57	30	6	128	154	15	59
*Estevan Uriegas	1	0	3.69	22	0	24	19	13	27
Marco Gonzalez	4	3	4.28	41	10	42	51	11	17
*Chuck Lukanen	2	0	4.29	18	0	29	28	10	27
Mike Perconte	0	1	4.65	2	0	9.2	14	2	4
Marshall Schuler	2	3	5.10	21	1	25	24	10	23
Andrew Johnston	0	3	5.25	9	0	24	34	3	16
Morgan Coombs	6	9	5.44	22	0	114	134	40	72
Nick Polsinelli	0	0	6.23	5	0	4	7	1	0
*Tyler Deetjen	2	2	6.82	12	0	32	48	9	9
Derek Drage	2	3	7.15	6	0	28	34	16	13
Kyle Wilson	1	3	7.48	10	0	55	78	26	24
Alberto Rolon	1	1	8.69	4	0	20	29	14	11
Steve Matre	0	0	11.57	5	0	2	7	1	2
Tyler Vaske	0	0	13.50	2	0	3	4	2	5
Chad Rhoades	0	1	28.92	6	0	5	16	3	2
Derek Johnson	0	0	32.40	1	0	2	5	4	1

GRAND PRAIRIE AIRHOGS

PLAYER	P	AVG	OBP	SLG	AB	R	H	HR	RBI	SB
*Brian Myrow	IF	.364	.490	.608	316	65	115	12	63	0
*Zane Chavez	C	.343	.370	.598	102	21	35	4	29	1
Chris McMurray	C	.332	.401	.623	220	36	73	12	39	1
Scott Clement	C	.323	.338	.477	65	10	21	1	5	0
*Keanon Simon	CF	.308	.359	.412	403	76	124	2	39	26
Kenny Held	OF	.300	.340	.520	100	21	30	4	19	2
Alberto Espinosa	C	.291	.391	.382	55	4	16	0	6	0
Andres Rodriguez	IF	.282	.351	.466	373	51	105	15	81	1

		AVG	OBP	SLG	AB	R	H	HR	RBI	SB
*Yasutsugu Nishimoto	IF	.280	.371	.304	296	41	83	0	30	6
Mike Brownstein	IF	.278	.381	.333	18	4	5	0	4	0
Jonny Kaplan	OF	.277	.341	.429	119	22	33	3	15	3
*Trent Lockwood	IF	.274	.382	.485	340	55	93	15	64	2
Jairo Perez	IF	.274	.298	.419	117	16	32	2	18	2
*Greg Porter	RF	.262	.291	.380	271	40	71	7	33	2
#David Thomas	OF	.252	.332	.424	238	39	60	5	28	5
Bryan Frichter	IF	.228	.291	.333	246	39	56	5	31	2
*James McOwen	OF	.222	.211	.222	18	2	4	0	3	0
John Alonso	IF	.217	.309	.233	60	8	13	0	9	0
Bridger Hunt	IF	.185	.224	.241	54	5	10	0	2	0
Daniel Evatt	OF	.167	.167	.167	6	0	1	0	0	0
Jorge Alvarez	IF	.071	.071	.071	14	1	1	0	2	0
Thomas McAlpine	C	.000	.000	.000	4	0	0	0	0	0

PLAYER	W	L	ERA	G	SV	IP	H	BB	SO
Kenny Held	0	0	0.00	2	0	2	1	1	2
*Justin Dowdy	2	1	2.27	31	17	32	15	21	39
*Ronnie Morales	5	4	2.96	55	0	58	48	16	50
Derrick Miramontes	7	1	3.12	43	2	58	60	20	45
John Brownell	8	7	3.64	21	0	148	154	41	99
Lance Day	2	0	3.75	4	0	24	23	2	16
Jakob Cunningham	0	0	3.93	34	0	34	34	12	25
Josh Strawn	7	5	4.13	20	0	126	134	21	75
Lance Janke	0	3	4.19	4	0	19	22	10	24
Nick DeBarr	12	7	4.34	22	0	141	149	46	93
Mark Herrera	0	0	4.76	5	0	11	17	7	2
Adam Miller	2	2	4.76	16	0	17	21	8	17
Griffin Bailey	3	3	5.06	26	0	27	32	7	12
*Teddy Nowell	1	0	5.10	3	0	12	9	10	10
*Cody White	0	3	5.44	17	0	45	63	16	30
*Alain Quijano	2	1	5.45	5	0	31	34	7	14
Ray Silva	1	1	6.13	6	0	7	10	2	5
Reymond Cruz	0	3	6.63	3	0	19	22	8	12
Jake Cowan	1	2	7.26	5	0	26	33	12	21
Will Irvin	1	2	7.57	4	0	19	28	6	12
Adrian DeMar	0	0	7.71	2	0	2	5	0	2
Ramon Garcia	0	2	7.90	3	0	14	18	5	7
Mike Hart	0	0	27.00	3	0	2	5	3	3

KANSAS CITY T-BONES

PLAYER	P	AVG	OBP	SLG	AB	R	H	HR	RBI	SB
Lee Cruz	1B	.354	.388	.569	181	29	64	7	28	2
*Beau Stoker	3B	.345	.424	.517	29	7	10	1	3	0
Bridger Hunt	IF	.333	.333	.333	9	3	3	0	0	1
*Brandon Jones	OF	.326	.393	.524	393	74	128	14	73	2
Bubby Williams	C	.311	.330	.567	90	15	28	4	26	3
Jose Duran	IF	.302	.333	.365	192	25	58	1	20	14
#Justin Bass	2B	.301	.374	.400	385	70	116	3	53	21
*Hunter Mense	OF	.291	.338	.457	175	23	51	6	30	0
Sean Henry	OF	.288	.362	.365	52	9	15	1	8	3
Devin Goodwin	IF	.287	.349	.509	348	68	100	18	57	14
*Aric Weinberg	IF	.286	.375	.286	7	1	2	0	2	0
Ray Sadler	RF	.278	.335	.475	345	53	96	16	63	7
Enrique Cruz	3B	.268	.333	.377	239	30	64	4	31	2
#Spiker Helms	IF	.268	.336	.392	97	16	26	3	12	3
*Reid Fronk	OF	.265	.426	.429	98	17	26	3	14	0
#Trevor Coleman	C	.262	.370	.366	317	47	83	5	38	2
Gus Milner	OF	.258	.337	.348	233	44	60	5	16	10
Adam De La Garza	2B	.245	.277	.302	106	15	26	1	11	8
Kala Ka'aihue	C	.235	.340	.412	85	15	20	4	15	0
*Kris Sanchez	1B	.200	.254	.327	55	5	11	1	4	0
Pat Trettel	C	.188	.247	.362	69	9	13	3	10	0
*Jonathan Cisneros	1B	.000	.000	.000	1	0	0	0	0	0
Matthew Garza	OF	.000	.000	.000	4	0	0	0	0	0

PLAYER	W	L	ERA	G	SV	IP	H	BB	SO
*Brad Furnish	1	0	1.58	13	0	11	9	4	12
Matt Foust	1	0	2.25	6	0	4	7	2	3
Lucas Irvine	4	2	2.58	30	1	104	105	42	107
Drew Graham	0	0	2.70	1	0	3	5	2	2
Drew Bailey	0	1	2.81	13	0	16	11	11	15
Sean Toler	1	2	2.97	29	2	33	40	8	26
Mike Mehlich	1	2	3.27	23	9	22	23	16	21
*Devin Anderson	7	6	3.36	19	0	112	136	28	70
Shaun Garceau	9	6	3.47	17	0	106	106	27	75
Brian Grening	10	5	3.69	22	0	146	149	30	113

Jacob Wiley	1	5	3.85	24	7	23	18	19	17
*Steven Kent	4	4	4.56	41	1	47	45	17	67
Josh Rainwater	6	11	4.78	22	0	137	161	18	77
Nick Singleton	4	1	5.31	7	0	42	54	8	35
Matt Mitchell	2	2	5.53	6	0	26	28	9	10
Dustin Loggins	0	1	5.82	13	0	17	20	9	14
Dan Kickham	0	0	6.95	12	0	22	26	11	10
Justin Ziegler	0	0	9.00	2	0	3	6	2	1
Eric Schaler	0	0	9.00	2	0	2	4	4	1
Griffin Bailey	2	2	12.46	5	1	4	8	1	5
*Christian Kowalchuk	0	0	40.50	1	0	1	4	0	0
*Greg Denton	0	0	135.00	2	0	0	1	6	1

LAREDO LEMURS

PLAYER	P	AVG	OBP	SLG	AB	R	H	HR	RBI	SB
*J.B. Brown	IF	.421	.429	.579	19	2	8	1	4	0
Ernie Banks	OF	.343	.393	.474	137	17	47	3	25	0
Jimmy Mojica	SS	.339	.391	.486	389	72	132	9	61	14
Palmer Karr	OF	.337	.403	.542	273	45	92	12	50	1
John Allen	OF	.331	.389	.515	359	63	119	11	59	4
Javier Brito	IF	.307	.372	.460	313	48	96	9	47	1
*Steve Pearson	OF	.296	.335	.417	362	54	107	5	53	6
Luis Uribe	OF	.289	.341	.368	38	5	11	0	5	2
Brian Peterson	C	.284	.381	.377	292	43	83	4	36	3
*Jeff Vincent	OF	.271	.386	.339	59	10	16	0	3	2
#Uriak Marquez	IF	.258	.305	.397	194	33	50	5	27	8
*Anthony Scelfo	2B	.253	.333	.361	360	60	91	4	38	12
Matt Forgatch	OF	.250	.364	.389	36	6	9	1	4	3
*Stephen Douglas	OF	.249	.300	.387	253	37	63	6	37	9
Yunesky Sanchez	IF	.232	.274	.319	69	11	16	1	5	0
Kevin Butler	C	.228	.264	.250	136	19	31	0	17	0
Jorge Delgado	1B	.222	.364	.222	27	1	6	0	1	2
#Matthew Tucker	OF	.133	.125	.133	15	0	2	0	0	1
Philip Incaviglia	OF	.115	.169	.115	61	13	7	0	3	4
Kyle Nichols	OF	.032	.063	.129	31	3	1	1	4	0
Chris Murrill	OF	.000	.000	.000	8	0	0	0	0	0

PLAYER	W	L	ERA	G	SV	IP	H	BB	SO
Chaz Roe	3	2	1.47	49	1	55	47	7	69
Bradley Blanks	3	1	1.57	29	0	40	35	11	25
Kyle Wilson	0	1	2.31	10	0	23	23	14	16
Mike Benacka	2	2	2.39	43	12	53	33	35	92
*Edwin Walker	5	1	3.35	30	0	46	37	21	57
*Ryan Sasaki	6	3	3.83	12	0	70	92	15	46
*Matthew Way	10	7	3.98	21	0	129	116	61	112
*Todd Privett	1	2	4.05	8	0	40	55	11	23
Stephen Kahn	1	1	4.07	9	0	18	24	8	7
Osvaldo Rodriguez	3	2	4.22	9	0	38	42	21	33
Chris Chavez	4	4	4.38	9	0	53	45	11	34
Leonard Giammanco	5	4	4.69	25	0	79	93	27	36
Garrett Sherrill	3	1	4.70	17	0	29	27	8	16
Mark Haynes	4	7	5.18	21	0	108	119	47	95
Jon Hunton	1	0	5.40	8	1	8	13	4	4
Alex Jones	0	0	5.40	2	0	5	5	7	3
*Tony Butler	0	2	6.00	6	0	21	23	17	12
Manny Ayala	2	4	7.80	7	0	28	44	9	19
Gabriel Zavala	1	1	9.56	10	0	16	18	15	15
*Jesus Martinez	0	1	9.81	16	0	15	25	8	12
Robert Romero	0	1	15.00	9	0	9	18	9	12

LINCOLN SALTDOGS

PLAYER	P	AVG	OBP	SLG	AB	R	H	HR	RBI	SB
Kevin Flynn	C	1.000	1.000	1.000	1	0	1	0	0	0
Leivi Ventura	3B	.337	.396	.511	92	18	31	3	9	3
Jimmy Rohan	IF	.326	.407	.395	233	28	76	2	34	2
#David Espinosa	IF	.313	.425	.467	259	50	81	7	35	12
John Alonso	IF	.313	.348	.504	230	27	72	9	59	0
*Jared McDonald	IF	.304	.361	.429	56	8	17	0	6	1
Joe Spiers	IF	.297	.360	.385	195	31	58	2	12	18
Matt Forgatch	OF	.295	.356	.492	132	18	39	3	20	7
*Asif Shah	OF	.288	.383	.407	236	38	68	3	20	3
*Stephen Holdren	OF	.279	.363	.405	380	52	106	9	71	1
Mike Provencher	IF	.275	.339	.407	378	62	104	9	45	21
Sean Smith	CF	.274	.349	.400	135	20	37	1	15	14
Salomon Manriquez	C	.256	.302	.322	90	8	23	1	5	0
Brad Payne	IF	.252	.312	.315	127	14	32	0	4	6

INDEPENDENT LEAGUES

Leugim Barroso	IF	.250	.250	.292	24	4	6	0	1	2
Tom Collaro	OF	.236	.272	.403	144	13	34	6	15	0
#C.J. Beatty	OF	.217	.327	.326	46	8	10	0	3	2
Bryan Pounds	IF	.212	.302	.271	85	9	18	0	7	1
Wilberto Ortiz	IF	.212	.288	.442	52	12	11	4	9	1
#Miguel Chacoa	IF	.210	.273	.225	138	13	29	0	7	6
*A.J. Miller	C	.210	.317	.307	176	22	37	3	29	0
*Alan Rick	C	.208	.301	.347	72	8	15	1	12	0
Chris McMurray	C	.206	.311	.540	63	13	13	6	14	0
Derek Coverstone	C	.182	.357	.182	11	2	2	0	2	0
#D'Angelo Jimenez	IF	.167	.286	.167	18	1	3	0	1	1
*Nate Wilder	IF	.162	.195	.311	74	9	12	3	7	0
#Victor Mercedes	IF	.111	.111	.222	9	1	0	0	1	0
Alberto Espinosa	C	.111	.111	.111	9	1	1	0	0	0

PLAYER	W	L	ERA	G	SV	IP	H	BB	SO
Walker McKinven	0	0	0.00	1	0	0	0	0	1
Brad Payne	0	0	2.25	5	0	4	5	0	1
Brandon Sinnery	5	1	2.62	7	0	48	43	10	27
Pete Parise	6	6	3.60	41	1	67	70	12	44
*Moises Melendez	0	2	3.82	21	0	40	36	24	30
Tim Adleman	0	0	3.85	5	0	7	8	4	8
*Conor Spink	1	1	3.90	31	0	25	23	9	21
Ryan Sheldon	7	4	4.09	21	0	121	133	39	108
*Tony Butler	2	4	4.10	13	0	37	48	26	27
Wade Mackey	6	4	4.93	23	0	104	129	32	63
Justin Edwards	4	8	5.23	21	0	122	152	31	90
P.J. Zocchi	1	3	5.26	43	24	41	46	15	55
Ricardo Estevez	0	1	5.40	3	0	13	16	12	8
*Aaron Odom	0	0	5.78	3	0	5	6	3	5
Travis Parker	1	0	5.96	14	0	26	37	12	17
Yohan Gonzalez	1	1	6.13	7	0	7	10	3	5
*David Quinowski	0	1	6.23	12	0	13	13	7	14
Tycen Povey	0	2	6.30	17	0	30	37	13	26
Brandon Cooney	4	2	6.48	26	0	25	31	23	14
*Justin Roelle	0	0	6.96	7	0	10	7	14	5
David Slovak	0	1	7.10	5	0	6	14	1	4
*Tommy Palica	2	8	7.67	13	0	70	101	30	68
Chandler Barnard	0	2	8.59	3	0	15	23	7	7
Drew Graham	0	0	9.00	4	0	5	8	2	5
*Mike Zoellner	0	0	9.44	4	0	7	8	6	5
Ronny Morla	0	3	11.57	3	0	5	9	3	2
*Jino Gonzalez	0	3	12.21	5	0	14	25	9	16
Alberto Rolon	0	0	16.20	2	0	7	18	4	1
Brandon Hedrick	2	3	30.00	2	0	3	8	9	4

SIOUX CITY EXPLORERS

PLAYER	P	AVG	OBP	SLG	AB	R	H	HR	RBI	SB
Michael Lang	OF	.405	.452	.612	121	28	49	4	25	6
Jorge Delgado	1B	.404	.430	.596	99	13	40	4	23	0
*Brandon Newton	OF	.332	.406	.415	352	67	117	1	32	12
Mike Murphy	IF	.304	.339	.373	263	26	80	1	24	4
Ray Serrano	C	.303	.335	.455	389	49	118	9	47	3
*Wally Backman	IF	.292	.369	.386	363	49	106	2	31	5
Yusuke Inoguchi	OF	.287	.342	.391	366	57	105	4	40	8
Peter Barrows	OF	.284	.346	.534	236	34	67	11	48	4
Adrian Martinez	C	.266	.310	.358	173	20	46	3	25	0
Brian Bistagne	IF	.257	.290	.398	261	41	67	6	29	2
Michael Glantz	SS	.250	.250	.250	4	0	1	0	0	0
*Kris Sanchez	1B	.242	.303	.429	310	35	75	14	65	0
Ryan Priddy	IF	.239	.283	.369	314	38	75	8	38	6
Tyler Goodro	C	.225	.296	.270	89	10	20	0	6	1
*Mike Bisenius	OF	.215	.282	.252	135	15	29	0	7	2

PLAYER	W	L	ERA	G	SV	IP	H	BB	SO
*Alain Quijano	3	6	3.37	10	0	81	76	20	42
Jon Plefka	1	3	3.96	33	1	48	54	17	43
*Richard Salazar	8	7	4.07	20	0	139	148	32	87
Chris Bodishbaugh	6	4	4.12	39	17	52	58	12	55
Jason Jarvis	9	8	4.13	21	0	146	168	32	69
Andrew Snowdon	2	3	4.88	32	2	63	78	16	39
Max Whieldon	2	2	5.22	16	0	21	24	11	12
Ty Marotz	2	2	5.53	16	0	83	114	27	39
Nick Schumacher	5	8	5.56	17	0	108	112	38	85
*Chuck Lukanen	1	4	6.00	19	0	15	28	9	10
Eddie De La Cruz	2	2	6.23	35	1	39	46	15	28
Geno Glynn	0	1	6.33	13	0	27	34	9	18

*Aaron Correa	2	4	8.61	14	0	39	61	15	21
Colin Allen	0	1	9.14	7	0	21	32	10	7

SIOUX FALLS PHEASANTS

PLAYER	P	AVG	OBP	SLG	AB	R	H	HR	RBI	SB
Reggie Abercrombie	OF	.336	.360	.595	131	24	44	8	31	5
Cesar Nicolas	IF	.335	.426	.528	373	62	125	12	82	3
Jonny Kaplan	OF	.325	.405	.519	212	50	69	7	25	8
*Mark Shorey	OF	.307	.339	.416	166	14	51	4	20	2
Al Quintana	C	.305	.351	.377	334	39	102	2	41	3
*Jared Bolden	1B	.293	.331	.388	423	66	124	7	56	23
Cory Morales	IF	.292	.329	.413	380	60	111	9	51	8
Jake Taylor	C	.268	.316	.401	269	34	72	3	27	1
Trevor Lawhorn	IF	.257	.314	.369	366	53	94	7	39	2
Cristian Guerrero	OF	.249	.318	.444	358	54	89	15	59	5
*Joe Anthonsen	IF	.248	.371	.290	314	39	78	0	22	3
*Rob Lind	IF	.222	.263	.222	18	2	4	0	0	1
*Ridge Carpenter	OF	.221	.274	.485	68	14	15	5	13	1
*Nick Judkins	IF	.132	.179	.132	53	5	7	0	3	0
Max Casper	IF	.111	.226	.111	27	2	3	0	0	0
*Dan Barbero	IF	.083	.214	.083	24	0	2	0	1	0

PLAYER	W	L	ERA	G	SV	IP	H	BB	SO
Kyle Mertins	4	1	1.00	45	4	54	36	14	54
Cody Evans	1	0	1.66	22	8	22	14	2	14
*Jack Van Leur	3	1	3.78	39	0	33	37	7	23
Daniel Cooper	1	6	4.13	43	1	46	45	21	29
Rod Scurry	6	7	4.23	23	0	115	127	34	86
*Mitchell Clegg	9	6	4.99	20	0	124	148	51	63
Thomas Heithoff	1	1	5.40	32	0	48	53	26	44
Alan DeRatt	4	7	5.44	26	5	89	108	27	53
Barry Fowler	1	3	5.44	8	0	40	56	12	13
*Pete Gehle	6	10	5.50	18	0	105	138	36	54
Mark Michael	7	7	6.60	20	0	109	128	47	74
Jordan Wellander	0	0	6.75	6	0	8	14	2	6
Dusty Gober	1	2	6.75	27	0	49	71	19	30
Matt Sommo	1	1	8.64	6	0	25	37	16	13
Andrew Liebel	0	3	20.03	3	0	10	28	11	6

ST. PAUL SAINTS

PLAYER	P	AVG	OBP	SLG	AB	R	H	HR	RBI	SB
Jose Hernandez	OF	.316	.349	.468	376	50	119	10	51	12
Joe Spiers	IF	.314	.357	.359	156	22	49	0	17	15
Willie Cabrera	OF	.313	.354	.475	284	48	89	11	56	7
Jon Townsend	IF	.291	.313	.435	230	32	67	3	34	3
Adam Frost	SS	.289	.331	.398	329	47	95	3	32	24
*Jim Rapoport	OF	.289	.361	.388	325	51	94	4	34	10
*Ron Bourquin	IF	.284	.375	.458	349	56	99	11	53	1
Ole Sheldon	IF	.279	.339	.493	383	55	107	20	69	1
*Shane Costa	OF	.264	.361	.296	125	14	33	0	8	1
Jake Krause	IF	.260	.318	.340	100	16	26	1	8	4
Miles Durham	OF	.249	.299	.404	193	31	48	6	31	11
Tanner Townsend	IF	.242	.311	.398	256	39	62	8	27	6
Jon Hurst	C	.235	.381	.471	17	4	4	1	2	0
Benji Johnson	C	.210	.262	.333	138	19	29	3	9	0
Alex Garabedian	C	.203	.254	.245	212	17	43	2	17	0

PLAYER	W	L	ERA	G	SV	IP	H	BB	SO
Daniel Sattler	1	0	0.00	3	3	7	1	2	5
Benji Johnson	0	0	0.00	1	0	1	1	1	2
Wes Roemer	2	0	2.60	4	0	28	29	3	18
Kyle Ruwe	4	2	2.68	9	0	67	75	12	23
Billy Spottiswood	1	3	2.72	24	0	50	47	10	33
Robert Coe	12	5	2.90	22	0	139	124	59	87
Nick Carr	1	1	3.17	15	1	17	17	8	6
Luke Anderson	5	3	3.28	14	0	71	59	38	46
Dustin Klabunde	2	1	3.42	34	10	42	47	21	22
Christopher Odegaard	3	8	3.85	37	2	77	79	37	64
Danny Gutierrez	1	1	3.92	4	0	18	20	6	15
*Brian Gump	0	2	4.61	4	0	14	17	8	14
*Taylor Sinclair	1	1	4.69	13	0	8	6	7	4
*Kyle Carr	0	2	4.83	31	1	22	18	15	19
Matt Schuld	1	1	4.90	3	0	15	18	8	9
Anthony Claggett	7	4	5.04	22	2	77	89	27	57
Bret Severtson	3	1	5.66	32	1	48	57	18	31
Kyle Hurst	0	1	5.68	4	0	19	20	8	8

Reid Mahon	4	5	5.76	27	0	30	36	15	17
Josh Cephas	1	0	6.27	6	0	14	12	13	10
Alberto Rolon	2	4	6.63	11	0	57	68	31	30
Todd Mathison	1	2	6.70	8	0	51	71	17	26
*T.J. Wink	1	1	7.29	3	0	12	15	7	4
Ben Kincaid	0	0	21.00	2	0	3	8	3	1

WICHITA WINGNUTS

PLAYER	P	AVG	OBP	SLG	AB	R	H	HR	RBI	SB
*Steve Stanley	OF	.429	.515	.464	28	1	12	0	6	1
Jake Kahaulelio	2B	.372	.448	.536	239	60	89	6	39	11
Jairo Perez	IF	.358	.424	.547	53	10	19	1	8	3
*David Peralta	OF	.332	.392	.462	377	65	125	3	70	25
*John Rodriguez	OF	.332	.400	.515	373	67	124	16	81	5
Juan Richardson	3B	.321	.409	.436	78	19	25	2	15	5
C.J. Ziegler	IF	.320	.408	.631	222	46	71	18	61	0
Salomon Manriquez	C	.317	.349	.366	41	6	13	0	6	1
*Gerardo Avila	IF	.296	.324	.437	71	7	21	2	12	1
Jessie Mier	C	.292	.341	.351	154	17	45	0	19	3
*Mike Conroy	OF	.287	.369	.414	307	45	88	2	28	21
Wilberto Ortiz	2B	.286	.338	.524	63	9	18	3	14	5
*Greg Porter	RF	.278	.356	.426	115	21	32	3	17	2
#Wilson Batista	3B	.258	.319	.371	62	9	16	0	8	3
Ryan Khoury	IF	.256	.360	.347	398	79	102	4	38	37
Mark Wagner	3B	.256	.330	.372	78	14	20	1	15	1
Mitch Einertson	OF	.252	.301	.358	123	21	31	2	23	2
*Zac Mitchell	IF	.250	.357	.250	12	2	3	0	0	0
Blake Bergeron	IF	.250	.318	.425	40	4	10	2	4	0
Steve Carrillo	IF	.247	.314	.390	154	19	38	3	17	2
*Jared McDonald	IF	.236	.293	.354	246	34	58	5	31	16
Taylor Freeman	IF	.231	.250	.356	104	12	24	2	14	3
Justin Tellam	C	.231	.281	.423	52	7	12	2	8	0
Mason Morioka	C	.226	.333	.258	31	3	7	0	2	0
*Tom Fitzgerald	IF	.222	.300	.222	9	2	2	0	0	0
Sean Smith	CF	.194	.333	.250	36	5	7	0	2	3
Patrick Murphy	PH	.000	.000	.000	1	0	0	0	0	0
*Kevin Whitehead	C	.000	.125	.000	7	0	0	0	1	0

PLAYER	W	L	ERA	G	SV	IP	H	BB	SO
*Nate Robertson	0	0	0.00	3	0	8	4	1	6
*Nick Walters	2	2	1.73	57	2	52	22	27	53
Jamie Baker	0	2	2.48	24	0	25	16	8	23
James Hoyt	2	0	2.61	11	1	10	9	5	15
Josh Dew	3	0	2.70	16	9	17	12	7	20
Matt Nevarez	3	2	3.07	25	7	26	17	11	45
Jared Simon	3	6	3.25	57	2	64	66	18	53
Josh Lowey	15	4	3.56	23	0	134	126	43	96
Andrew Aizenstadt	1	0	3.76	10	0	14	18	2	7
Derek Blacksher	10	5	4.55	23	0	144	168	35	84
Ben Graham	2	2	4.71	6	0	34	36	13	15
Edgar Martinez	2	1	4.75	43	1	42	48	19	29
*Ryan Hinson	9	8	4.84	24	0	137	154	39	93
Nick Schreiber	1	1	4.90	2	0	7	4	5	7
*Anthony Capra	3	2	4.99	11	0	58	62	38	54
Jose Perez	2	1	5.20	5	0	28	36	9	17
*Jeff Nadeau	0	2	5.25	22	0	50	56	38	31
*Chris Cummins	0	1	6.00	1	0	6	9	0	3
*Dillon Wilson	0	0	9.00	4	0	4	7	2	2
Robert Roth	1	0	9.52	6	0	6	7	2	4
Dumas Garcia	0	1	11.67	3	0	12	23	6	14
*Shawn Lewick	0	1	16.20	1	0	5	11	1	2
*Moises Melendez	0	0	36.00	2	0	2	8	4	1

WINNIPEG GOLDEYES

PLAYER	P	AVG	OBP	SLG	AB	R	H	HR	RBI	SB
Barbaro Canizares	1B	.364	.419	.455	55	5	20	1	10	0
Yurendell de Caster	IF	.327	.398	.478	343	52	112	10	68	15
Luis Alen	IF	.317	.394	.413	375	59	119	5	50	2
#Chris Roberson	OF	.317	.360	.490	394	75	125	11	59	36
Josh Mazzola	IF	.308	.364	.541	364	69	112	18	74	7
Price Kendall	IF	.283	.362	.334	407	69	115	0	34	21
*Jon Weber	LF	.281	.357	.376	306	38	86	4	42	1
Amos Ramon	IF	.281	.348	.421	242	28	68	4	35	7
*Kyle Day	C	.275	.329	.395	258	33	71	4	31	1
*Matt Cusick	2B	.273	.347	.386	44	7	12	1	10	1
*Dan Barbero	IF	.250	.386	.324	68	8	17	1	8	1

Jose Duran	IF	.232	.289	.272	125	13	29	0	8	7
Mike Coles	OF	.221	.281	.269	104	14	23	0	7	0
*Ridge Carpenter	OF	.218	.311	.273	165	25	36	0	14	6
*Gabby Martinez	IF	.211	.268	.526	38	6	8	3	8	0
David Narodowski	IF	.194	.224	.245	155	14	30	0	16	1

PLAYER	W	L	ERA	G	SV	IP	H	BB	SO
Brian Beuning	5	2	0.99	28	6	63	29	14	64
Matt Rusch	10	4	2.39	21	0	139	117	31	113
Alex Jones	2	0	2.72	26	0	33	32	19	24
*Barrett Phillips	0	0	3.52	11	0	8	9	6	2
*Fabian Williamson	2	4	3.63	8	0	40	35	17	41
Andrew Walker	9	5	3.73	22	0	140	141	28	81
*Chris Salamida	5	7	3.76	20	0	117	138	25	80
Dexter Carter	1	3	3.99	31	6	38	45	18	44
*Todd Privett	4	5	4.37	13	0	72	86	21	51
Kaohi Downing	4	2	4.50	37	2	48	52	13	34
Craig James	2	1	4.70	29	2	29	33	15	19
Nick Carr	1	0	5.06	11	4	11	13	5	11
Chris Allen	1	0	5.78	12	0	9	15	2	9
Chris Bodishbaugh	0	1	6.00	9	2	9	12	6	11
*Tony Butler	1	1	6.09	2	0	10	10	8	3
*Zach Baldwin	2	3	6.40	38	0	32	41	15	20
*Jack Van Leur	1	0	6.75	12	0	5	8	2	6
Denver Wynn	0	1	7.26	2	0	9	11	4	3
*Rich Hawkins	3	1	7.82	8	0	36	47	11	13
Billy Spottiswood	1	2	8.67	12	0	9	15	3	8
Chris Kaminski	1	1	9.00	7	0	8	11	4	4
Griffin Bailey	0	1	10.50	6	0	6	14	1	3
Brian Leach	0	0	11.73	3	0	8	11	8	2
Stephen Kahn	0	0	11.81	6	0	5	11	4	6
*Chris Zbin	0	1	15.18	3	0	5	9	4	5

ATLANTIC LEAGUE

During the regular season, the Atlantic League has never seen anything like the Lancaster Barnstormers. The Barnstormers set a league record with 88 wins. Led by batting champ Blake Gailen and ERA champ Dwayne Pollok, Lancaster and the Freedom Division dominated the Atlantic League in 2012. In fact, no Liberty Division club finished the season with a winning record.

But when the playoffs arrived, the Liberty Division's Long Island Ducks took home the trophy. In a nail-biting five-game series, Long Island edged Lancaster 5-4 in the deciding Game Five when Dan Lyons' bunt scored Matt Esquivel with the game-winning run in the bottom of the ninth.

In the playoffs, Lancaster knocked off the York Revolution in the first round of the playoffs, ending York manager Andy Etchebarren's 51 years in the game. Etchebarren announced before the season ended that he was retiring.

FIRST HALF

FREEDOM DIVISION	W	L	PCT	GB
Lancaster Barnstormers	45	25	.643	—
York Revolution	36	34	.514	9
Somerset Patriots	35	35	.500	10
Sugar Land Skeeters	29	41	.414	16

LIBERTY DIVISION	W	L	PCT	GB
Long Island Ducks	39	30	.565	—
Camden Riversharks	34	35	.493	5
Bridgeport Bluefish	31	39	.443	8.5
Southern Maryland Blue Crabs	30	40	.429	9.5

SECOND HALF

FREEDOM DIVISION	W	L	PCT	GB
Lancaster Barnstormers	43	27	.614	—
York Revolution	43	27	.614	—
Sugar Land Skeeters	35	35	.500	8

INDEPENDENT LEAGUES

	W	L	PCT	GB
Somerset Patriots	30	39	.435	12.5

LIBERTY DIVISION	W	L	PCT	GB
Southern Maryland Blue Crabs	39	31	.557	—
Bridgeport Bluefish	36	33	.522	2.5
Camden Riversharks	28	42	.400	11
Long Island Ducks	24	44	.353	14

PLAYOFFS: Semfinals—Lancaster defeated York 3-0 and Long Island defeated Southern Maryland 3-2 in best-of-five series. **Finals**—Long Island defeated Lancaster 3-2 in best-of-five series.

ATTENDANCE: Sugar Land 465,511; Long Island 377,473; Somerset 350,295; Lancaster 307,431; York 273,648; Camden 231,987; Southern Maryland 229,094; Bridgeport 132,139.

MANAGERS: Bridgeport—Willie Upshaw; **Camden**—Jeff Scott; **Lancaster**—Butch Hobson; **Long Island**—Kevin Baez; **Somerset**—Sparky Lyle; **Southern Maryland**—Pat Osborn; **Sugar Land**—Gary Gaetti; **York**—Andy Etchebarren.

ALL-STAR TEAM: C—Emerson Frostad (Lancaster); **1B**—Brian Burgamy (Camden); **2B**—Andres Perez (York); **3B**—Chris Nowak (York); **SS**—Dan Lyons (Long Island); **Utility**—Ray Navarrete (Long Island); **OF**—Blake Gailen (Lancaster); Fehlandt Lentini (Lancaster); Prentice Redman (Bridgeport); Adam Godwin (Lancaster); **DH**—Ryan Harvey (Lancaster). **RHS**—Dwayne Pollok (Lancaster); **LHS**—Paul Oseguera (Bridgeport); **RP**—Rommie Lewis (Bridgeport); **Closer**—Tim Hamulack (Lancaster). **PLAYER OF THE YEAR:** Blake Gailen (Lancaster). **PITCHER OF THE YEAR:** Dwayne Pollock (Lancaster). **MANAGER OF THE YEAR:** Butch Hobson (Lancaster).

BATTING LEADERS

PLAYER	TEAM	G	AB	R	H	HR	RBI	SB
Blake Gailen	LAN	134	500	94	169	22	89	25
Adam Godwin	LAN	125	532	93	174	2	44	39
Fehlandt Lentini	LAN	136	539	98	172	19	92	32
Andres Perez	YORK	132	512	86	161	23	86	4
Brian Barton	SML	130	495	69	153	8	60	23
Ray Navarrete	LGI	131	518	76	160	18	90	1
Michael Hernandez	YOR	105	402	56	122	13	55	3
Ryan Harvey	LNC	109	398	65	120	27	79	3
Brian Burgamy	CAM	126	456	84	134	20	81	8

PITCHING LEADERS

PITCHER	TEAM	W	L	ERA	IP	H	BB	K
Dwayne Pollok	LAN	14	4	2.30	145	127	29	113
Paul Oseguera	BRDG	12	6	2.52	147	129	36	146
Ryan Feierabend	YORK	9	5	2.71	113	122	18	75
John Halama	LAN	13	9	3.15	189	203	41	113
Roy Merritt	SOM	8	8	3.22	154	138	52	118
Justin Cassel	SOM	6	11	3.43	152	152	39	115
Nick Green	SM	9	10	3.58	174	177	42	122
Corey Thurman	YORK	14	3	3.82	153	157	52	79
Keith Weiser	CAM	7	8	3.91	115	137	41	70
Mark Brackman	LAN	9	10	4.29	151	175	35	119

BRIDGEPORT BLUEFISH

PLAYER	P	AVG	OBP	SLG	AB	R	H	HR	RBI	SB
*Collin DeLome	OF	.368	.430	.678	87	22	32	5	22	5
Elio Ayala	IF	.339	.379	.383	115	19	39	1	14	2
#Sergio Miranda	IF	.333	.500	.333	3	0	1	0	0	0
Brock Peterson	IF	.293	.376	.563	341	62	100	21	68	2
James Simmons	OF	.289	.351	.486	329	47	95	13	45	12
Peter Barrows	OF	.286	.409	.343	35	0	10	0	2	0
Eddie Rogers	IF	.283	.323	.383	509	78	144	8	67	21
Prentice Redman	OF	.282	.366	.489	503	79	142	21	82	4
Willis Otanez	IF	.278	.347	.429	133	17	37	5	20	0
#Luis Figueroa	IF	.277	.310	.333	213	26	59	1	21	0
Pedro Lopez	IF	.272	.404	.296	125	17	34	0	11	4
Luis Lopez	IF	.265	.353	.386	472	54	125	11	73	0
*Brad Boyer	IF	.263	.317	.338	133	14	35	2	16	1
*Kennard Jones	OF	.263	.324	.319	467	60	123	0	47	28
Luis Rodriguez	C	.255	.296	.363	364	37	93	9	43	1
*Ramon Vazquez	IF	.243	.355	.272	103	9	25	0	10	2
*Joey Gathright	OF	.242	.323	.315	260	46	63	2	22	14
Edgardo Baez	OF	.226	.222	.302	53	5	12	1	3	1
Angel Flores	C	.223	.322	.236	148	15	33	0	11	1
Brett Dowdy	IF	.211	.333	.237	38	4	8	0	2	0

#Norberto Susini	IF	.200	.294	.289	45	8	9	0	1	0
Shea Hillenbrand	IF	.194	.272	.330	103	9	20	3	9	1
Michael Moras	C	.143	.143	.143	7	0	1	0	0	0
Daryl Jones	IF	.095	.136	.095	21	2	2	0	1	0
#Norm Hutchins#	OF	.059	.105	.059	17	0	1	0	1	0
Joe Poletsky	IF	.043	.083	.087	23	1	1	0	2	0

PLAYER	W	L	ERA	G	SV	IP	H	BB	SO
Juan Rincon	1	0	1.87	20	11	24	19	13	27
*Rommie Lewis	3	1	2.01	48	7	54	56	11	47
Mike Ness	2	0	2.07	2	0	13	12	5	12
*Mike Tarsi	1	0	2.07	13	0	35	33	6	25
Daniel Stange	0	0	2.25	3	0	4	3	4	6
*Paul Oseguera	12	6	2.51	24	0	147	129	36	146
Pat Bresnehan	1	1	2.70	5	0	7	3	7	2
Julio DePaula	1	2	3.02	31	2	36	34	13	38
*Jesse English	3	0	3.47	42	0	54	46	20	57
Brad Thompson	6	5	3.53	11	0	76	78	10	38
Wynn Pelzer	0	0	3.76	11	0	14	20	11	10
*Dan Serafini	5	3	4.01	17	0	81	74	33	46
*Gilbert De La Vara	11	9	4.41	27	0	153	183	56	100
Kyle Zaleski	5	3	4.61	49	0	68	81	28	71
Jonah Bayliss	4	9	4.88	39	2	101	96	43	76
Matt Pike	4	9	5.87	31	0	87	116	34	47
Raymar Diaz	3	9	6.23	18	0	78	103	37	56
Jorge Julio	0	1	6.26	19	8	19	25	13	13
*Isaac Hess	2	3	6.40	8	0	45	59	17	34
Tobi Stoner	1	8	7.43	11	0	59	78	21	38
Joe Bateman	2	0	7.62	22	0	28	34	12	34
Chris Hayes	0	3	9.14	6	0	21	38	5	8
Wanel Mesa	0	0	9.44	3	0	7	6	8	7
*Brad Furnish	0	0	19.28	3	0	2	5	9	3

CAMDEN RIVERSHARKS

PLAYER	P	AVG	OBP	SLG	AB	R	H	HR	RBI	SB
Chris Berroa	OF	.500	.500	1.000	2	0	1	0	0	0
Marquez Smith	3B	.363	.422	.593	91	20	33	3	20	2
*Felix Pie	OF	.353	.386	.608	51	12	18	3	12	1
*Bill Rice	OF	.300	.344	.483	60	11	18	0	3	1
#Brian Burgamy	3B	.294	.409	.493	456	84	134	20	81	8
Pedro Feliz	3B	.285	.335	.426	305	41	87	9	38	0
Paddy Matera	IF	.274	.347	.409	208	38	57	5	21	3
#Eduardo Perez	IF	.268	.346	.387	426	46	114	7	69	3
*Raul Padron	C	.267	.319	.410	315	33	84	10	45	0
Jake Eigsti	IF	.257	.316	.368	421	44	108	5	46	7
Steve Doetsch	OF	.251	.328	.340	371	41	93	5	31	16
Alvin Colina	C	.244	.297	.333	270	23	66	4	26	0
Lloyd Turner	IF	.242	.324	.311	392	48	95	2	38	7
*Chris Walker	OF	.237	.307	.359	510	72	121	12	44	42
Reid Gorecki	OF	.236	.281	.348	89	9	21	1	10	6
Juan Martinez	IF	.222	.250	.481	27	5	6	2	6	0
*Drew Macias	OF	.216	.330	.386	176	26	38	5	24	4
Danny Santiesteban	OF	.212	.250	.242	99	8	21	0	17	1
Chris Caves	C	.208	.387	.375	24	4	5	1	5	0
Scott Knazek	C	.198	.266	.291	86	9	17	1	7	0
#Delwyn Young	OF	.192	.302	.267	120	14	23	2	5	1
*Colin Roberson	OF	.162	.241	.270	74	8	12	2	10	4
Shea Harris	C	.153	.238	.181	72	6	11	0	5	0
*Bryan Goelz	IF	.000	.125	.000	7	0	0	0	0	0

PLAYER	W	L	ERA	G	SV	IP	H	BB	SO
Jon Velasquez	0	0	0.00	1	0	1	0	0	1
Jason Bergmann	0	0	0.80	22	1	22	11	10	33
Stephen Fox	1	0	1.20	3	0	15	12	3	11
Leo Rosales	3	2	1.52	34	5	41	24	13	30
Adrian Martin	0	1	1.92	5	0	5	4	3	2
Ricky Brooks	6	1	2.43	10	0	52	45	17	23
Santo Hernandez	0	0	3.00	11	1	15	12	6	20
Zach Hammes	2	4	3.24	62	3	67	61	35	51
*Keith Weiser	7	8	3.91	22	0	115	137	41	70
*James Houser	3	0	4.01	25	0	25	30	4	24
Blake King	3	5	4.03	42	0	58	51	53	46
*Eddie Camacho	0	5	4.13	19	0	61	72	26	46
Jon Velasquez	1	0	3.86	5	0	7	7	1	5
Mike McGuire	9	10	4.30	28	0	165	176	75	122
*Spencer Steedley	3	1	4.63	44	0	45	39	29	23
John Lujan	2	5	4.74	54	23	55	65	28	46

Player	W	L	ERA	G	SV	IP	H	BB	SO
Josh Walter	0	4	5.56	45	0	55	65	38	33
Bryan Corey	8	10	5.91	25	0	126	152	35	65
Sean Jarrett	5	5	5.92	14	0	68	68	18	33
Kevin Reese	4	10	6.09	29	0	130	171	32	72
Jeff Farnsworth	0	2	6.46	21	0	24	27	15	25
*Mariano Gomez	3	2	6.48	23	0	25	33	11	16
Mike Mehlich	1	0	7.16	13	0	16	17	9	14
Joe D'Alessandro	0	0	12.00	8	0	9	10	7	13
Humberto Sanchez	1	1	14.40	3	0	5	9	9	4
Chris Rollins	0	0	15.00	3	0	3	3	8	1
*Alex Smith	0	1	15.18	7	0	11	20	18	4

LANCASTER BARNSTORMERS

PLAYER	P	AVG	OBP	SLG	AB	R	H	HR	RBI	SB
Jesus Merchan	SS	.391	.440	.478	115	15	45	0	11	0
*Blake Gailen	OF	.338	.415	.534	500	94	169	22	89	25
Bridger Hunt	IF	.333	.393	.434	159	20	53	1	20	2
Adam Godwin	OF	.327	.369	.412	532	93	174	2	44	39
Fehlandt Lentini	OF	.319	.359	.499	539	98	172	19	92	32
#Gilberto Mejia	IF	.312	.388	.452	186	41	58	4	18	17
*Jaime Pedroza	IF	.310	.398	.565	232	39	72	14	50	3
Ryan Harvey	OF	.302	.342	.563	398	65	120	27	79	3
Travis Denker	2B	.297	.369	.571	175	36	52	11	35	2
#Terry Tiffee	3B	.297	.346	.472	269	30	80	11	46	1
*Emerson Frostad	C	.295	.406	.429	312	51	92	7	35	4
Kody Kirkland	3B	.263	.334	.530	304	51	80	17	53	3
#Francisco Hernandez	C	.258	.291	.387	217	24	56	6	29	0
Tommy Everidge	1B	.255	.316	.404	385	38	103	9	46	1
#Kyle Haines	C	.239	.328	.292	113	12	27	1	0	0
*Brad Boyer	IF	.233	.285	.327	275	41	64	4	25	4
*Brandon Haveman	OF	.182	.182	.182	33	2	6	0	3	0
#Danny Gonzalez	SS	.130	.355	.304	23	4	3	1	5	0

PLAYER	W	L	ERA	G	SV	IP	H	BB	SO
*Ronnie Morales	0	0	0.00	6	0	5	3	1	3
Joe Gannon	0	0	0.00	1	0	1	2	1	0
Josh Dew	0	0	0.00	2	0	2	2	0	3
*Horacio Ramirez	2	0	1.96	12	0	37	37	6	22
*Tim Hamulack	2	1	2.15	48	33	46	38	14	53
Dwayne Pollok	14	4	2.29	34	0	145	127	29	113
Jason Urquidez	0	2	2.29	15	0	16	11	8	14
*Ross Peeples	1	0	2.77	38	0	36	36	10	13
*Rich Rundles	2	1	3.02	8	0	48	40	11	40
*John Halama	13	9	3.14	28	0	189	203	41	113
Beau Vaughan	5	0	3.24	52	1	53	44	13	51
*Les Walrond	3	1	3.32	21	0	24	15	11	24
Jeff Bennett	4	8	3.42	54	2	50	48	17	33
*Mike Johnston	1	1	4.12	27	0	24	26	12	18
Mark Brackman	9	10	4.29	29	1	151	175	35	119
J.D. Durbin	14	9	4.47	28	0	181	182	73	116
Alan Johnson	14	6	4.56	27	0	138	157	49	79
Ching Lung Lo	1	0	5.35	37	0	42	41	9	28
Joe Bateman	1	2	5.65	30	0	29	27	9	40

LONG ISLAND DUCKS

PLAYER	P	AVG	OBP	SLG	AB	R	H	HR	RBI	SB
Ryan Garko	IF	.450	.535	.683	60	9	27	4	16	0
Lew Ford	OF	.333	.398	.627	75	16	25	4	14	4
Brandon Pinckney	IF	.310	.323	.345	29	3	9	0	5	0
Ray Navarrete	IF	.309	.372	.510	518	76	160	18	90	1
*Timo Perez	OF	.292	.346	.380	171	20	50	3	14	0
Brandon Sing	IF	.284	.367	.527	457	78	130	26	78	3
#Joash Brodin	OF	.282	.333	.371	170	31	48	3	24	3
Reid Gorecki	OF	.281	.386	.441	306	55	86	10	41	21
#Shawn Williams	IF	.272	.353	.374	353	47	96	6	46	18
Matt Esquivel	OF	.269	.338	.357	238	26	64	4	29	2
*Bry Nelson	IF	.265	.322	.402	520	72	138	13	80	6
Kraig Binick	OF	.264	.357	.325	458	60	121	3	33	32
*Mitch Canham	C	.253	.310	.371	178	28	45	3	21	6
Dan Lyons	IF	.248	.321	.334	443	60	110	3	56	14
Wilberto Ortiz	IF	.245	.312	.367	98	15	24	2	14	1
*James McOwen	OF	.244	.296	.345	238	34	58	4	25	7
Lee Cruz	1B	.244	.287	.549	82	10	20	7	16	1
Matt Fleishman	OF	.238	.304	.262	42	0	10	0	3	0
Josh Johnson	C	.207	.304	.320	275	32	57	6	25	2

PLAYER		AVG	OBP	SLG	AB	R	H	HR	RBI	SB
Paul Karmas	OF	.000	.000	.000	2	0	0	0	1	0
*Colin Roberson	OF	.000	.000	.000	7	0	0	0	0	0

PLAYER	W	L	ERA	G	SV	IP	H	BB	SO
Leo Rosales	0	0	0.00	2	1	3	2	2	2
Nick DeBarr	0	0	0.00	2	0	3	2	1	1
*Matthew Way	2	0	0.00	2	0	13	4	4	19
Jon Meloan	4	0	0.98	23	11	27	23	8	36
Bobby Blevins	1	0	2.42	6	0	26	22	8	16
*Randy Keisler	5	3	2.63	13	0	82	89	19	60
Jared Lansford	0	2	2.98	47	0	54	65	18	40
Jason Monti	7	4	3.21	27	0	78	69	27	64
Jeremy Hill	5	7	3.49	63	1	67	63	17	49
Chris Hayes	3	1	3.51	10	0	56	55	6	25
*Eric Niesen	3	2	3.89	57	0	69	69	28	64
*Gustavo Chacin	2	2	3.93	9	0	50	48	17	32
Rob Zimmermann	6	10	4.32	29	0	179	193	74	126
Connor Graham	2	2	4.35	51	0	64	63	44	66
Josh Lansford	0	1	4.73	31	1	38	45	20	33
Nick Singleton	3	4	4.84	9	0	48	49	18	53
Mike Loree	5	7	4.91	18	0	104	117	26	89
Armando Benitez	2	1	5.23	32	2	33	38	10	20
Jon Hunton	2	1	5.72	22	8	22	26	9	15
*Jino Gonzalez	0	2	6.15	5	0	19	19	11	8
John Brownell	2	2	6.61	4	0	16	21	10	15
*Dan Meyer	2	6	7.02	18	0	41	45	40	28
Joe Esposito	2	3	7.25	8	0	36	38	24	21
Chris McCoy	1	3	7.39	5	0	28	41	5	15
*Adam Rowe	0	3	11.84	6	0	19	41	8	12
Jeff Lyman	2	2	12.96	9	0	8	10	10	5
Chris Flinn	0	4	13.20	7	0	15	28	9	6
Reid Gorecki	0	0	14.72	3	0	4	8	0	2
Wynn Pelzer	1	0	17.05	5	0	6	9	5	5
Bubbie Buzachero	1	1	20.25	4	0	7	20	3	4
Matt Lyons	0	1	162.0	1	0	0	4	2	1

SOMERSET PATRIOTS

PLAYER	P	AVG	OBP	SLG	AB	R	H	HR	RBI	SB
Jake Fox	IF	.388	.433	.750	80	15	31	7	20	0
*Colin Curtis	IF	.308	.368	.391	156	15	48	1	18	2
Jesse Hoorelbeke	IF	.279	.364	.494	358	45	100	20	53	0
*Freddie Bynum	IF	.276	.339	.375	421	58	116	2	43	26
Yunesky Sanchez	IF	.274	.284	.401	307	34	84	7	38	0
*Joe Holden	OF	.268	.347	.336	321	40	86	1	25	22
Corey Smith	IF	.263	.333	.514	175	25	46	11	30	3
Adam Donachie	C	.257	.320	.353	269	27	69	3	22	1
*Jon Drennen	OF	.256	.322	.402	246	29	63	8	23	6
Dan Hennigan	IF	.253	.383	.274	95	16	24	0	5	3
Jonny Tucker	OF	.252	.335	.310	365	50	92	2	31	16
Aaron Mathews	OF	.252	.284	.348	250	21	63	4	32	1
*Freddy Sandoval	IF	.250	.321	.359	192	30	48	2	25	3
Jeff Nettles	IF	.249	.321	.344	497	46	124	9	73	0
Daniel DeGeorge	IF	.239	.290	.341	264	34	63	2	18	2
*Rian Kiniry	OF	.233	.325	.252	103	11	24	0	5	8
Rex Rundgren	IF	.216	.234	.255	102	11	22	0	12	2
#Yusuf Carter	C	.209	.267	.384	263	33	55	12	38	7
Lou Santangelo	C	.207	.263	.239	92	7	19	1	5	1
*DeAngelo Mack	OF	.136	.208	.295	44	5	6	1	3	2

PLAYER	W	L	ERA	G	SV	IP	H	BB	SO
Corey Smith	0	0	0.00	1	0	1	0	2	2
Brian Anderson	0	1	1.50	6	0	6	4	0	9
Brandon Braboy	2	0	2.27	22	3	28	22	7	31
*Keith Ramsey	0	0	2.34	9	0	15	12	12	5
Mike Solbach	1	2	2.48	21	0	33	27	9	26
Josh Rupe	2	4	2.72	28	15	33	25	8	25
*Andrew Dobies	2	4	2.74	39	0	39	41	5	29
Paul Phillips	8	2	3.09	12	0	73	65	21	57
*Roy Merritt	8	8	3.22	27	0	154	138	52	118
*Andy Sisco	3	0	3.37	24	0	35	21	12	44
Justin Cassel	6	11	3.42	25	0	152	152	39	115
Travis Bowyer	0	1	3.46	15	1	13	15	6	15
T.J. Hose	1	4	3.58	31	1	33	24	12	29
Mike MacDonald	3	4	3.60	13	0	70	67	27	37
Carlton Smith	3	4	4.03	46	0	67	70	32	41
Sean Green	4	6	4.15	12	0	65	90	20	52

INDEPENDENT LEAGUES

PLAYER	W	L	ERA	G	SV	IP	H	BB	SO
*Douglas Arguello	6	8	4.35	24	0	128	113	67	98
Derell McCall	10	6	4.52	28	2	121	.146	31	60
*Jon Kibler	0	1	4.95	15	0	36	38	18	26
*Chase Wright	5	3	5.26	45	0	65	72	31	33
*David Quinowski	0	0	6.09	11	0	10	11	4	6
Tobi Stoner	1	0	7.20	1	0	5	6	3	9
*Adam Champion	0	2	9.58	3	0	10	17	8	3
*Taylor Sinclair	0	1	11.25	4	0	4	6	6	2
Anthony Claggett	0	2	16.87	10	0	11	27	4	9

SOUTHERN MARYLAND BLUE CRABS

PLAYER	P	AVG	OBP	SLG	AB	R	H	HR	RBI	SB
Javier Colina	IF	.360	.346	.800	25	5	9	3	6	1
Brian Barton	OF	.309	.375	.432	495	69	153	8	60	23
Jesse Gutierrez	IF	.307	.359	.538	277	46	85	14	49	1
Chin-lung Hu	IF	.296	.351	.402	189	23	56	2	19	1
Pat Osborn	3B	.280	.379	.280	25	1	7	0	0	1
Richard Mercado	C	.273	.321	.408	267	33	73	8	40	0
Paco Figueroa	IF	.264	.337	.342	269	40	71	2	29	7
*Mike Daniel	OF	.263	.345	.363	490	66	129	5	37	17
Jeremy Owens	OF	.260	.348	.465	493	81	128	22	65	17
*Casey Benjamin	LF	.260	.365	.490	431	61	112	21	85	4
*Matt Padgett	1B	.251	.335	.394	439	56	110	12	54	2
Cesar Nicolas	3B	.250	.381	.404	52	7	13	1	8	0
Kevin Rios	PR	.246	.290	.342	260	29	64	3	23	0
Christian Lopez	C	.242	.297	.356	281	26	68	4	23	10
#David Espinosa	2B	.225	.331	.338	151	20	34	1	12	5
James Shanks	OF	.220	.276	.308	91	8	20	2	9	2
Eddy Martinez-Esteve	PH	.200	.333	.400	5	0	1	0	0	0
#Richard Giannotti	OF	.196	.268	.340	209	27	41	3	22	1
Travis Garcia	3B	.193	.237	.352	145	12	28	5	18	2
*Sergio Pedroza	1B	.165	.265	.329	85	8	14	4	10	3
Cory Morales	IF	.063	.118	.063	16	0	1	0	1	0

PLAYER	W	L	ERA	G	SV	IP	H	BB	SO
*Chris Russ	0	0	0.00	2	0	2	2	2	0
Eddie Morlan	3	2	1.76	43	0	46	30	14	38
Chris Mobley	5	2	1.89	52	11	52	45	11	41
Kevin Hart	1	1	2.25	21	1	24	14	13	22
Richard Giannotti	0	1	2.25	5	0	4	4	3	3
*Charlie Manning	5	6	2.49	56	0	65	59	40	60
Chris McCoy	1	0	2.57	1	0	7	11	1	2
Gaby Hernandez	5	1	2.76	7	0	39	31	20	45
Daryl Thompson	2	2	2.93	11	0	49	42	16	55
Ryan Speier	0	0	3.00	3	0	3	6	1	1
Ben Moore	3	2	3.05	8	0	53	42	11	48
Nick Green	9	10	3.57	28	0	174	177	42	122
*Bryan Dumesnil	0	1	3.72	32	1	39	37	18	39
Virgil Vasquez	10	9	4.43	30	0	193	196	48	120
Deinys Suarez	5	6	4.47	35	0	117	118	45	83
Dan Reichert	6	7	4.52	20	0	117	120	51	72
*David Jones	3	5	4.65	19	0	87	98	31	68
Jamie Baker	1	0	4.76	11	0	11	12	6	14
*Ricky Barrett	0	1	4.97	26	0	25	21	14	32
Jim Ed Warden	6	8	5.31	51	11	64	77	25	53
Rayner Oliveros	2	2	5.60	8	1	18	26	9	13
*Jared Locke	1	1	6.94	14	0	23	28	17	20
Joe Gannon	1	2	6.98	5	0	19	28	9	8
Michael Schlact	0	2	11.57	3	0	7	8	7	3

SUGAR LAND SKEETERS

PLAYER	P	AVG	OBP	SLG	AB	R	H	HR	RBI	SB
Jimmy Van Ostrand	IF	.368	.447	.568	95	14	35	3	20	0
*Jason Botts	OF	.348	.413	.639	155	27	54	9	33	2
*Miguel Negron	OF	.310	.425	.394	71	15	22	0	6	4
Ofilio Castro	IF	.306	.376	.389	468	66	143	4	56	4
Kade Johnson	C	.300	.417	.600	10	3	3	1	4	0
*Bubba Bell	OF	.289	.317	.384	461	52	133	1	53	11
Drew Locke	OF	.285	.339	.406	165	28	47	4	24	4
Ben Harrison	OF	.282	.378	.563	103	24	29	8	19	3
Manny Mejia	C	.278	.358	.394	216	23	60	4	24	0
Jason Lane	P	.275	.345	.463	229	29	63	9	31	1
*Josh Pressley	IF	.275	.363	.439	433	53	119	16	74	0
*Carlos Sosa	OF	.263	.300	.316	19	4	5	0	2	0
Octavio Martinez	C	.259	.311	.296	297	25	77	0	20	2

PLAYER	P	AVG	OBP	SLG	AB	R	H	HR	RBI	SB
Dominic Ramos	IF	.257	.313	.443	393	57	101	12	30	9
Steve Moss	OF	.254	.324	.400	295	35	75	9	44	11
#Dionys Cesar	OF	.250	.290	.355	152	23	38	3	10	6
Koby Clemens	C	.250	.250	.500	4	1	1	0	0	0
Colt Morton	C	.250	.368	.563	16	2	4	1	2	0
Matt Hagen	IF	.236	.300	.380	258	29	61	6	25	8
Aaron Bates	IF	.233	.282	.359	206	17	48	5	26	1
Vic Gutierrez	IF	.219	.219	.281	32	4	7	0	4	0
#Amadeo Zazueta	IF	.214	.236	.359	103	10	22	2	10	1
Iggy Suarez	IF	.212	.289	.321	349	39	74	6	35	1
Alex Cintron#	IF	.167	.167	.167	30	3	5	0	3	0
Deybis Benitez	IF	.139	.158	.139	36	2	5	0	3	0
Ryde Rodriguez	OF	.110	.161	.122	82	9	9	0	2	1
#Luis Figueroa	IF	.103	.200	.103	29	2	3	0	4	0
Marcos Cabral	IF	.087	.250	.087	23	1	2	0	0	0

PLAYER	W	L	ERA	G	SV	IP	H	BB	SO
Matt Hagen	0	0	0.00	1	0	1	3	1	2
Roger Clemens	0	0	0.00	2	0	8	3	0	3
Jusef Frias	0	1	2.07	9	0	9	5	7	6
Roberto Giron	1	3	2.17	34	2	37	18	13	49
Saul Rivera	2	0	2.19	18	1	29	20	10	17
Matt Wright	2	0	2.20	8	0	49	38	9	47
Pedro Liriano	8	3	2.42	30	0	78	55	31	52
*Will Startup	3	3	3.08	31	0	47	39	17	34
Eric Krebs	1	1	3.11	20	0	26	20	9	28
*Jason Lane	9	5	3.17	18	0	111	99	18	77
Gary Majewski	5	3	3.37	56	25	67	69	18	41
*Dustin Richardson	1	0	3.77	17	0	31	25	14	31
Tim Redding	3	2	4.28	5	0	27	27	4	14
Garrett Parcell	1	2	4.32	24	0	33	32	17	21
Trey Rackel	0	0	4.35	6	0	10	9	3	5
*Bobby Livingston	9	2	4.37	16	0	93	90	37	68
*Heath Phillips	1	7	4.72	20	0	67	87	26	36
Michael Nix	4	11	4.88	32	1	109	110	44	88
Ryan McKeller	2	4	4.96	26	0	74	82	34	43
Sean Morgan	0	0	5.14	29	0	42	50	19	21
*Scott Kazmir	3	6	5.34	14	0	64	74	33	51
Jeff Farnsworth	2	5	5.44	21	3	41	46	18	31
*Kelvin Villa	4	8	5.44	28	0	78	89	30	62
*Derrick Gordon	1	4	6.43	15	0	57	65	21	40
Duniesky Flores	1	1	6.75	5	0	11	13	7	7
Ryan Houston	1	2	13.03	13	1	10	14	14	9
*Ryan Ketchner	0	3	20.00	4	0	9	20	7	9

YORK REVOLUTION

PLAYER	P	AVG	OBP	SLG	AB	R	H	HR	RBI	SB
#Liu Rodriguez	IF	.327	.364	.432	220	34	72	3	39	0
Andres Perez	2B	.314	.373	.529	512	86	161	23	86	4
*Joe Thurston	IF	.314	.391	.528	229	46	72	8	28	2
*Jeff Fiorentino	OF	.311	.401	.426	244	49	76	4	27	4
Michael Hernandez	OF	.303	.353	.483	402	56	122	13	55	3
*Brandon Haveman	OF	.290	.316	.386	482	68	140	6	48	21
Ramon Castro	IF	.288	.359	.449	403	61	116	14	67	0
Salomon Manriquez	C	.287	.346	.400	115	17	33	2	16	1
Joe Spiers	IF	.286	.444	.429	7	1	2	0	1	0
Chris Nowak	IF	.285	.391	.570	463	81	132	34	107	10
*Johan Limonta	OF	.277	.321	.381	155	20	43	1	15	0
#Danny Gonzalez	SS	.249	.364	.336	229	39	57	3	20	3
James Shanks	OF	.249	.285	.388	289	37	72	9	41	2
Scott Grimes	OF	.241	.338	.409	394	63	95	13	54	20
*Travis Scott	C	.228	.288	.358	285	38	65	7	38	1
Salvador Paniagua	C	.227	.299	.402	132	13	30	5	18	0
*Stephen Douglas	IF	.221	.253	.291	86	6	19	2	6	1
#Bobby Kielty	OF	.221	.329	.382	68	13	15	3	8	0
#Kyle Haines	IF	.217	.308	.261	23	2	5	0	2	1
*Rian Kiniry	IF	.182	.250	.273	11	0	2	0	1	0
#David Espinosa	IF	.133	.328	.289	45	7	6	2	7	0

PLAYER	W	L	ERA	G	SV	IP	H	BB	SO
*Ian Thomas	1	0	0.96	7	0	9	9	5	12
R.J. Rodriguez	2	3	2.02	55	13	53	49	20	48
*Wade Korpi	4	0	2.26	18	0	40	25	16	30
Shawn Hill	2	0	2.42	7	0	30	26	9	21
Ricardo Gomez	4	1	2.66	46	17	47	25	23	60
*Ryan Feierabend	9	5	2.70	18	0	113	122	18	75

*Kris Regas	3	2	2.78	44	0	42	35	18	42
Mike Benacka	1	0	3.00	6	1	6	3	3	6
Stephen Penney	2	1	3.13	62	1	60	64	15	47
Adam Thomas	8	2	3.65	67	4	64	71	15	42
Corey Thurman	14	3	3.81	27	0	153	157	52	79
*Derrick Gordon	5	3	4.02	12	0	63	69	25	28
*Chris Cody	10	14	4.38	28	0	164	191	29	112
Santo Luis	0	0	4.50	3	0	4	4	2	4
*Chris Waters	6	8	4.53	19	0	95	114	31	63
*Yunior Novoa	2	6	4.71	38	0	78	84	20	66
*Victor Garate	0	0	5.40	1	0	2	4	0	1
*James Houser	2	1	5.50	33	0	34	44	8	31
Omar Javier	1	6	5.66	22	0	60	74	38	28
Dumas Garcia	1	0	6.00	27	0	33	41	18	35
*Jesus Sanchez	1	3	6.49	10	0	26	38	23	13
*Matt Chico	1	3	7.50	6	0	24	33	13	11
Shaun Garceau	0	0	7.71	3	0	2	1	2	0
Chris Nowak	0	0	9.00	1	0	1	1	0	1
Andy Wells	0	0	16.61	3	0	4	8	9	3

CAN-AM LEAGUE

The Can-Am League has seen its ups and downs over the years, but there is one thing about the league you can count on. More than likely, when the season is complete, the Quebec Capitales will be celebrating another title.

Quebec won its fourth consecutive Can-Am League title and its fifth in seven years with a 4-1 series win over the New Jersey Jackals. Quebec was also the class of the league during the regular season, finishing with the best record in the league, seven games up on New Jersey.

Quebec's dominance was the bright spot of a rough year for the rest of the league. Worcester was locked out of the team's offices and had its uniforms repossessed, forcing the team to finish the season wearing league-supplied hand-me-down jerseys for the defunct Grays. The league eventually took over the franchise at the end of the season. The league was already down to five teams before the Tornadoes' struggles became public.

STANDINGS
	W	L	PCT	GB
Quebec Capitales	66	34	.660	—
New Jersey Jackals	59	41	.590	7
Rockland Boulders	48	52	.480	18
Newark Bears	35	65	.350	31
Worcester Tornadoes	29	71	.290	37

PLAYOFFS: Finals—Quebec defeated New Jersey 4-1 in best-of-seven series.
ATTENDANCE: Rockland 161,375; Quebec 152,663; New Jersey 87,206; Worcester 61,398; Newark 32,056.
MANAGERS: Newark—Ken Oberkfell/Chuck Stewart; **New Jersey**—Joe Calfapietra; **Quebec**—Pat Scalabrini; **Rockland**—Dave LaPoint; **Worcester**—Chip Plante
ALL-STAR TEAM: C—Josue Peley (Quebec); **1B**—Francisco Caraballo (New Jersey); **2B**—Angel Berroa (New Jersey); **3B**—Nick Giarraputo (New Jersey); **SS**—Jeff Helps (Quebec); **OF**—Bryan Sabatella (New Jersey); Sebastien Boucher (Quebec); Keith Brachold (Rockland); **DH**—Rene Leveret (Quebec). **SP**—Jeff Duda (Quebec); **RP**—Jorge L. Vasquez (Newark).
PLAYER OF THE YEAR: Nick Giarraputo (New Jersey). **ROOKIE OF THE YEAR:** Tucker Nathans (Newark).

BATTING LEADERS
PLAYER	TEAM	AVG	G	AB	R	H	HR	RBI
Rene Leveret	QC	.361	77	316	42	114	9	59
Brandon Pinckney	ROCK	.333	74	285	45	95	4	37
Sebastien Boucher	QC	.325	94	366	78	119	14	76
Chris Torres	ROCK	.317	81	284	36	90	12	35

Nick Giarraputo	NJ	.316	92	358	62	113	22	71
Francisco Caraballo	NJ	.314	88	347	63	109	19	77
Ryan Mollica	ROCK	.313	94	364	50	114	12	65
Angel Berroa	NJ	.310	88	342	63	106	18	62
Ryan Scoma	ROCK	.310	99	387	61	120	13	59
Qualon Millender	ROCK	.302	91	318	61	96	2	19

PITCHING LEADERS
PLAYER	TEAM	W	L	ERA	IP	H	BB	SO
Jeff Duda	QC	15	1	2.10	116	90	26	120
Karl Gelinas	QC	9	4	2.66	132	125	16	101
Mike Ness	NEW	11	3	3.15	143	135	32	97
Isaac Pavlik	NJ	12	2	3.21	132	139	25	114
Steve Fox	NJ	13	3	3.57	126	103	40	129
Bobby Blevins	ROC	8	9	3.65	136	137	30	86
Pat Moran	ROC	6	7	3.82	139	132	45	108
John Mariotti	QC	10	1	4.03	98	105	25	59
Dan Jurik	ROC	5	4	4.14	83	85	34	69
Bryan Rembisz	QC	10	4	4.17	125	130	34	56

NEW JERSEY JACKALS
PLAYER	P	AVG	OBP	SLG	AB	R	H	HR	RBI	SB
*Matt Cusick	2B	.328	.397	.529	204	40	67	5	24	9
*Chris Curran	CF	.321	.358	.364	165	26	53	0	15	14
Nick Giarraputo	IF	.316	.366	.567	358	62	113	22	71	0
Francisco Caraballo	OF	.314	.362	.550	347	63	109	19	77	0
Matt Nandin	IF	.312	.366	.457	186	25	58	3	23	10
Angel Berroa	SS	.310	.398	.544	342	63	106	18	62	5
Bryan Sabatella	OF	.294	.369	.422	398	72	117	10	69	42
#Carlos Guzman	OF	.288	.376	.427	358	54	103	11	51	3
Nick Salotti	IF	.281	.339	.386	171	20	48	5	27	1
#Roberto Ramos	IF	.278	.316	.389	18	2	5	0	4	1
*Chris Henderson	C	.276	.374	.387	217	37	60	2	32	0
Edgard Clemente	LF	.264	.264	.415	53	4	14	1	4	0
Jeff Lanning	C	.262	.329	.461	141	24	37	6	22	0
Danny Santiesteban	OF	.245	.314	.372	94	19	23	3	10	3
#Gaetano Giunta	IF	.238	.301	.271	269	46	64	1	17	11
*Steven Caseres	1B	.236	.335	.345	148	17	35	2	18	0

PLAYER	W	L	ERA	G	SV	IP	H	BB	SO
*Jeff Gogal	6	2	1.56	46	3	58	45	16	54
Marc Rutledge	0	0	1.80	2	0	5	6	2	5
Keith Cantwell	2	1	1.88	38	17	48	35	8	44
Jake Hale	1	1	2.23	29	0	40	36	16	31
Jacob Wiley	0	1	2.51	15	0	14	13	7	9
Mike Ness	2	1	2.57	3	0	21	19	4	13
*Isaac Pavlik	12	2	3.21	21	0	132	139	25	114
Zach Woods	2	1	3.21	32	1	42	43	11	70
Stephen Fox	13	3	3.57	20	0	126	103	40	129
Kyle Greenwalt	8	3	4.21	19	0	117	122	40	89
Jimmer Kennedy	0	2	4.32	42	0	44	48	11	47
*Craig Clark	6	7	5.22	15	0	81	93	35	53
*Dustin Birosak	3	6	6.19	20	0	65	84	22	48
Mike Zenko	0	1	6.23	8	1	9	11	5	9
*Jon Kibler	4	5	6.54	10	0	54	71	20	35
*Matt Chico	0	4	9.78	5	0	23	39	12	13
*T.J. Wink	0	1	17.18	6	0	7	14	7	5

NEWARK BEARS
PLAYER	P	AVG	OBP	SLG	AB	R	H	HR	RBI	SB
*Quentin Davis	OF	.335	.358	.480	173	26	58	4	20	18
*Tucker Nathans	IF	.307	.362	.457	199	28	61	5	30	6
#D'Angelo Jimenez	3B	.297	.359	.441	118	14	35	4	18	5
Mike Richard	IF	.294	.356	.385	296	46	87	3	14	29
*Daryle Ward	1B	.290	.357	.475	217	28	63	10	39	2
Billy Alvino	C	.282	.357	.363	124	18	35	1	10	1
James Roche	OF	.278	.345	.406	133	19	37	3	15	4
Eric McGee	C	.274	.330	.469	179	24	49	7	19	0
Dan Coury	C	.273	.312	.484	161	23	44	7	20	1
Orlando Mercado	IF	.273	.340	.391	128	17	35	3	23	1
Bryce Lane	OF	.270	.343	.381	252	32	68	6	34	7
Ryde Rodriguez	OF	.255	.287	.314	137	13	35	0	11	2
Juan Martinez	IF	.254	.309	.389	311	38	79	7	36	7
*Pat Reardon	C	.252	.333	.308	159	15	40	2	16	2
#Alex Bardeguez	IF	.250	.300	.301	176	21	44	0	9	2

Burt Reynolds	OF	.246	.281	.402	199	24	49	7	20	4
Danny Santiesteban	OF	.233	.304	.383	60	8	14	2	9	5
#McFarlin Kellon	OF	.222	.222	.222	18	1	4	0	0	1
*Nick Santomauro	OF	.196	.229	.196	46	4	9	0	1	0
#Norberto Susini	C	.185	.353	.185	27	3	5	0	2	0
Matt Tomczyk	IF	.169	.210	.182	77	4	13	0	7	0
Courtney Billingslea	IF	.161	.224	.323	62	7	10	3	5	0
*Charlie Stewart	OF	.154	.207	.346	26	3	4	1	3	1
#Glen Johnson	IF	.151	.215	.291	86	10	13	2	3	2
#Alex Bardeguez	3B	.125	.263	.125	16	1	2	0	0	0

PLAYER	W	L	ERA	G	SV	IP	H	BB	SO
Jorge Vasquez	1	2	2.18	41	22	45	33	15	71
Mike Ness	9	2	3.24	17	0	122	116	28	84
Rob Swift	0	1	3.60	3	0	5	4	6	5
Omar Javier	2	2	3.74	6	0	34	33	18	36
Damian Seguen	1	0	4.05	5	0	7	4	4	6
*Sergio Espinosa	1	0	4.10	14	0	26	25	12	22
Kyle Morrison	0	1	4.60	16	0	29	27	15	33
Pedro Rivera	5	11	4.76	21	0	117	130	55	63
Brian Parker	1	6	4.99	13	0	79	96	17	51
Anthony Pluta	4	5	5.35	38	0	42	37	44	57
*Matt Fitton	3	3	5.54	14	0	50	56	29	42
Greg Lane	3	3	6.12	23	0	65	90	19	25
Mike Petrowski	0	3	7.20	9	0	25	43	16	10
Caleb Cuevas	2	5	7.32	26	0	63	79	33	51
Zac Goyer	1	2	7.41	9	0	17	19	21	12
*Victor Gonzalez	0	2	8.30	7	0	17	24	9	10
Marc Rutledge	0	1	8.48	6	0	12	17	7	8
Julian Sampson	1	7	9.06	10	0	44	65	33	31
*Sean Campbell	0	4	11.07	5	0	13	17	21	5
Luis Garcia	0	1	11.57	9	0	16	26	12	14
*Alex Smith	0	3	12.96	4	0	17	38	9	11
Matt Lyons	1	1	18.00	10	0	8	15	10	4

QUEBEC CAPITALES

PLAYER	P	AVG	OBP	SLG	AB	R	H	HR	RBI	SB
Rene Leveret	1B	.361	.413	.494	316	42	114	9	59	0
Thomas Di Benedetto	IF	.333	.333	.333	3	0	1	0	0	0
Douglas Toro	IF	.333	.600	.667	3	0	1	0	0	0
*Sebastien Boucher	CF	.325	.425	.519	366	78	119	14	76	18
*Ivan Naccarata	SS	.325	.349	.525	40	7	13	1	9	0
Josue Peley	C	.299	.330	.439	408	46	122	10	79	10
*Jeff Helps	IF	.294	.384	.372	384	72	113	2	45	12
Jonathan Malo	3B	.288	.354	.448	406	80	117	12	63	9
*Seth Boyd	3B	.273	.273	.273	11	1	3	0	1	0
Steve Brown	OF	.257	.334	.409	362	51	93	13	54	29
*Josh Garton	LF	.241	.368	.438	112	20	27	4	9	1
Josh Colafemina	2B	.240	.356	.293	304	65	73	0	35	28
Rony Rodriguez	OF	.233	.323	.438	146	23	34	6	15	2
*Bobby Wagner	OF	.220	.340	.348	164	32	36	4	20	6
James Roche	OF	.218	.232	.291	55	7	12	1	5	1
*Normand Gosselin	OF	.213	.280	.333	75	10	16	0	9	4
Patrick D'Aoust	C	.213	.329	.325	249	46	53	4	28	5
Paul Karmas	1B	.200	.278	.306	85	12	17	2	8	4

PLAYER	W	L	ERA	G	SV	IP	H	BB	SO
*Tony Davis	2	0	1.05	20	0	17	11	6	16
Jamie Richmond	2	0	1.72	3	0	16	13	3	9
T.J. Stanton	3	2	1.73	34	18	36	21	7	46
Jeff Duda	15	1	2.09	20	1	116	90	26	120
Roque Mercedes	1	0	2.54	18	0	18	12	12	16
Karl Gelinas	9	4	2.65	19	0	132	125	16	101
Chad Jones	3	4	2.97	22	0	76	59	26	48
Chris Cox	2	3	3.45	36	1	44	49	27	38
Guillaume Duguay	3	5	3.72	41	1	58	49	14	47
John Mariotti	10	1	4.02	16	0	98	105	25	59
Bryan Rembisz	10	4	4.16	21	0	125	130	34	56
Dustin Crenshaw	2	1	4.42	3	0	20	24	3	8
Normand Gosselin	0	0	4.50	4	0	4	5	3	2
Guillaume Leduc	2	6	4.93	26	1	55	55	22	31
*Justin Wiley	1	0	5.68	1	0	6	5	4	3
*Shawn Joy	1	0	7.90	3	0	14	23	4	5
*Dexter Bobo	1	0	8.01	21	1	21	29	15	22
*Adam Kudryk	0	3	8.37	4	0	19	30	6	10
Josue Peley	0	0	9.00	1	0	1	2	0	0

Max St. Pierre	1	0	10.80	11	0	12	13	10	12
Jack Crawford	0	0	40.50	1	0	1	6	0	0

ROCKLAND BOULDERS

PLAYER	P	AVG	OBP	SLG	AB	R	H	HR	RBI	SB
John Smith	LF	.462	.462	.923	13	5	6	2	2	0
Brandon Pinckney	IF	.313	.370	.358	67	9	21	0	12	1
*Ryan Mollica	IF	.313	.367	.492	364	50	114	12	65	1
*Ryan Scoma	IF	.310	.364	.486	387	61	120	13	59	13
#Qualon Millender	OF	.302	.398	.381	318	61	96	2	19	15
#Phillip Cuadrado	3B	.280	.333	.530	200	33	56	12	46	4
Matt Nandin	IF	.278	.363	.415	176	28	49	4	23	6
Landis Wilson	C	.270	.306	.443	115	16	31	4	13	0
*Keith Brachold	OF	.259	.339	.538	390	80	101	29	84	5
#Melvin Falu	IF	.257	.250	.314	35	6	9	0	4	0
*Chris Valencia	OF	.256	.307	.329	371	58	95	3	40	22
*Jon Smith	OF	.246	.360	.516	126	18	31	8	26	3
*Cole Kraft	IF	.240	.291	.329	334	46	80	3	36	7
*Gabby Martinez	1B	.204	.291	.388	49	4	10	2	7	1
Billy Alvino	C	.201	.295	.236	144	12	29	1	19	1
Jose Reyes	2B	.197	.250	.211	71	8	14	0	2	2
#Norm Hutchins	OF	.164	.258	.182	55	4	9	0	4	0
*Todd Gossage	IF	.161	.161	.387	31	2	5	2	2	0
Orlando Mercado	C	.148	.276	.261	88	5	13	1	8	0
Scott Clement	C	.125	.192	.229	48	6	6	1	4	0
#Glen Johnson	IF	.091	.259	.091	22	5	2	0	1	1

PLAYER	W	L	ERA	G	SV	IP	H	BB	SO
Landis Wilson	0	0	0.00	1	0	2	1	0	
Adrian Martin	6	3	1.26	46	19	50	48	1	38
*Garrett Johnson	3	3	3.49	47	0	49	51	19	55
MacKenzie King	3	2	3.54	30	1	53	56	15	44
Bobby Blevins	8	9	3.64	21	0	136	137	30	86
Julio Santana	0	1	3.75	9	0	12	7	5	8
Pat Moran	6	7	3.82	21	0	139	132	45	108
Dan Jurik	5	4	4.13	30	1	83	85	34	69
Julian Sampson	3	3	4.90	10	0	48	45	34	24
Jon Velasquez	6	7	4.95	21	0	129	125	60	85
*Gustavo Chacin	3	5	5.42	12	0	66	91	12	52
Chris Rubio	2	4	7.00	27	0	27	33	16	15
Nicolas Blanco	0	1	7.71	13	0	16	30	10	12
Will Hassett	2	2	7.82	12	0	46	61	32	32
*Rob Savarese	0	1	13.50	2	0	1	2	1	1
*Andy Suiter	0	0	14.21	6	0	6	12	5	4
Eric Federico	1	0	16.20	8	0	10	18	4	4

WORCESTER TORNADOES

PLAYER	P	AVG	OBP	SLG	AB	R	H	HR	RBI	SB
Brandon Pinckney	IF	.339	.399	.459	218	36	74	4	25	1
Chris Torres	C	.317	.347	.486	284	36	90	12	35	1
*Alex Nunez	OF	.295	.377	.401	217	27	64	1	17	16
*Alex Trezza	IF	.281	.366	.485	167	28	47	8	29	1
*Mike Gedman	P	.276	.336	.459	98	20	27	4	16	7
Cameron Monger	OF	.261	.348	.349	295	46	77	2	22	11
*Jimmy Best	C	.260	.291	.340	50	4	13	1	11	0
*Jerod Edmondson	OF	.255	.311	.433	411	54	105	14	59	22
Nick Salotti	IF	.251	.285	.466	191	18	48	9	34	0
John Welch	IF	.242	.312	.484	244	38	59	15	42	2
Cam Kneeland	IF	.236	.320	.376	157	19	37	5	25	4
Ryan Brockett	IF	.232	.305	.246	224	23	52	0	12	2
Brendon Kelliher	IF	.207	.287	.290	290	30	60	5	24	3
Jose Canseco	1B	.194	.310	.250	72	5	14	1	7	3
Mike Samela	C	.186	.314	.302	43	4	8	1	3	1
Tony Patane	IF	.181	.221	.258	287	17	52	4	21	4
Matt Jacobs	OF	.150	.239	.233	60	7	9	0	1	1
Kyle Nisson	C	.143	.250	.143	14	0	2	0	3	0
*J.B. Brown	IF	.095	.156	.095	42	5	4	0	1	0

PLAYER	W	L	ERA	G	SV	IP	H	BB	SO
Sean Keeler	2	2	2.88	19	0	25	16	15	19
Matt McDonald	2	4	3.56	36	3	35	36	13	27
*Nick Serino	4	4	3.60	37	11	40	38	18	55
*Kyle Regnault	1	6	3.79	31	0	43	37	23	46
Chris Torres	0	0	4.26	5	0	13	10	5	6
*Mike Gedman	3	7	4.67	24	0	102	114	45	63
Dan Sausville	7	10	4.97	21	0	130	165	44	74

PLAYER	W	L	ERA	G	SV	IP	H	BB	SO
Mike Dicato	0	1	5.14	1	0	7	11	1	0
Phil Negus	1	4	5.33	12	0	59	60	26	55
Mike Mullen	2	2	5.59	35	0	37	48	24	26
Kevin Cooper	4	9	5.63	17	0	107	117	46	73
Ryan Bicondoa	1	6	5.98	9	0	56	63	14	42
*Zach Zuercher	1	5	6.08	9	0	58	76	18	38
Walker McKinven	1	6	6.43	9	0	43	51	29	12
Tony Patane	0	0	7.50	5	0	6	10	3	4
*Eric Katzman	0	1	7.61	8	0	13	18	8	7
Michael Bourdon	1	0	8.75	11	0	12	15	8	10
Bryan Leigh	0	0	9.32	15	0	18	29	18	12
Conner Hulse	0	5	9.49	8	0	43	66	23	20
Cam Kneeland	0	1	15.42	3	0	2	8	0	2

FRONTIER LEAGUE

It wasn't exactly a walk-off home run, but the Southern Illinois Miners were quite happy with their walk-off walk. With Game Four of the championship tied 3-3 in the 12th inning, Jake Kaase walked with the bases loaded to score Chad Maddox, giving the Miners their first Frontier League title.

The Miners have been one of the best teams in the Frontier League in recent years. They had a 20-game winning streak in 2010, three playoff appearances in the past four years and had a winning record every year since the team was founded in 2007.

The Miners' win capped off a topsy-turvy year for the league. The league welcomed back the Rockford RiverHawks, who had jumped to the Northern League only to watch that league disintegrate. The league also had to shut down the London Rippers two months into their first season. The awfully named club was replaced by a travel team, the Road Warriors. The league announced that it will field a travel team again in 2013.

EASTERN DIVISION	W	L	PCT	GB
Traverse City Beach Bums	64	32	.667	—
Florence Freedom	57	39	.594	7
Southern Illinois Miners	55	39	.585	8
Lake Erie Crushers	53	42	.558	10 ½
Evansville Otters	45	50	.474	18 ½
Washington WildThings	44	52	.458	20
London Rippers/Road Warriors	34	62	.354	30

WESTERN DIVISION	W	L	PCT	GB
Gateway Grizzlies	57	39	.594	—
Schaumburg Boomers	54	42	.563	3
Windy City ThunderBolts	54	42	.563	3
River City Rascals	45	50	.474	11 ½
Rockford RiverHawks	41	55	.427	16
Joliet Slammers	37	58	.389	19 ½
Normal CornBelters	29	67	.302	28

PLAYOFFS: Semifinals—Southern Illinois defeated Traverse City 3-0 and Florence defeated Gateway 3-2 in best-of-five series. **Finals**—Southern Illinois defeated Florence 3-1 in best-of-five series.
ATTENDANCE: Traverse City 175,284; Gateway 150,745; Southern Illinois 129,936; Schaumburg 128,287; Lake Erie 127,124; Evansville 120,819; Normal 119,936; Joliet 104,019; River City 107,986; Rockford 97,453; Florence 97,382; Windy City 86,178; Washington 76,829; London 21,985.
MANAGERS: Evansville—Andy McCauley; **Florence**—Fran Riordan; **Gateway**—Phil Warren; **Joliet**—Bart Zeller; **Lake Erie**—John Massarelli; **London/Road Warriors**—David Martin/Frank DeSmit; **Normal**—Chad Parker; **River City**—Steve Brook; **Rockford**—Richard

Austin; **Schaumburg**—Jamie Bennett; **Southern Illinois**—Mike Pinto; **Traverse City**—Gregg Langbehn; **Washington**—Chris Bando; **Windy City**—Morgan Burkhart.
ALL-STARS: C—Landon Hernandez, (Gateway); **1B**—Chase Burch, (Traverse City); **2B**—Ryan Still, (Traverse City); **3B**—Jose Vargas, (Traverse City); **SS**—Junior Arrojo, (Florence); **OF**—Javier Herrera, (Southern Illinois); Chad Mozingo, (Schaumburg); Jeff Flagg (Traverse City); **DH**—Chad Cregar, (Windy City). **SP**—Mike Recchia, (Windy City). **RP**—Jonathan Kountis, (Lake Erie).
MOST VALUABLE PLAYER: Jose Vargas, (Traverse City). **PITCHER OF THE YEAR:** Mike Recchia, (Windy City). **ROOKIE OF THE YEAR:** Zac Treece, (Gateway). **MANAGER OF THE YEAR:** Gregg Langbehn (Traverse City).

INDIVIDUAL BATTING LEADERS

PLAYER	TEAM	AVG	G	AB	R	H	HR	RBI
Joash Brodin	LON	.370	59	238	49	88	11	54
Abel Nieves	JOL	.320	89	322	56	103	8	44
Javier Herrera	SI/ROCK	.319	93	348	61	111	14	78
Chad Mozingo	SCH	.313	83	319	69	100	11	54
Andrew Heck	WAS	.310	67	252	42	78	2	27
Jeremy Synan	RC	.307	90	339	56	104	7	50
Frank Pfister	SCH	.306	96	395	58	121	13	58
Curran Redal	RC	.305	77	256	49	78	4	28
Chase Burch	TC	.304	96	358	66	109	17	76

INIDVIDUAL PITCHING LEADERS

PLAYER	TEAM	W	L	ERA	IP	H	BB	SO
Tim Brown	GAT	12	2	2.28	150	139	40	66
Mike Recchia	WIN	11	3	2.51	150	107	56	177
Tyson Corley	WIN	5	8	2.52	100	73	34	69
Daniel Calhoun	SI	7	4	2.52	86	69	12	62
Jamie Richmond	LON	6	3	2.61	90	85	16	68
Cody Hall	SI	9	1	2.63	79	72	30	39
Gary Lee	WASH	7	5	2.90	115	93	27	60
Chris Smith	WASH	9	6	2.92	129	106	52	116
Jacob Clem	TC	7	4	3.02	128	103	35	59
David Harden	SI	10	5	3.05	136	137	20	78

EVANSVILLE OTTERS

PLAYER	P	AVG	OBP	SLG	AB	R	H	HR	RBI	SB
Stephen Marino	IF	.302	.342	.436	179	21	54	5	23	1
Brent Walters	C	.300	.462	.400	10	0	3	0	0	0
*Billy Killian	C	.297	.366	.359	128	19	38	0	9	1
Luis Uribe	OF	.279	.325	.453	179	28	50	7	22	0
Greg Fontenot	IF	.271	.384	.284	155	23	42	0	12	12
Taylor Black	IF	.264	.309	.395	258	27	68	6	35	15
Matt Sheely	OF	.255	.340	.351	282	36	72	4	20	11
*Nick Schwaner	1B	.254	.317	.434	350	46	89	12	52	14
*Luis Parache	IF	.250	.296	.358	288	36	72	4	25	24
*DeAngelo Mack	OF	.249	.343	.392	293	37	73	7	50	9
Brett Chamberlain	C	.238	.310	.368	193	22	46	5	28	0
#Frank Martinez	IF	.226	.294	.315	124	13	28	1	16	5
*Nick Farnsworth	1B	.222	.333	.222	18	1	4	0	0	1
Runey Davis	OF	.216	.272	.363	171	25	37	3	21	4
Alex Foltz	OF	.203	.309	.253	79	10	16	1	9	4
Andrew Kuhn	C	.194	.259	.262	103	11	20	2	7	0
Steven Garcia	C	.189	.271	.321	53	5	10	1	3	0
*Dan Killian	DH	.180	.333	.262	61	6	11	1	6	0
Jon Karcich	IF	.169	.279	.254	59	8	10	1	2	4
*Nick Colwell	OF	.148	.207	.148	27	2	4	0	0	0
Kevin Lovelace	IF	.130	.259	.130	23	2	3	0	0	0
Troy Frazier	OF	.121	.194	.152	33	3	4	0	0	0
Jeff Hulett	IF	.048	.130	.048	21	1	1	0	0	0

PLAYER	W	L	ERA	G	SV	IP	H	BB	SO
Dan Blewett	2	1	1.06	7	0	42	22	28	51
Eric Massingham	4	2	2.85	33	21	35	29	15	40
*Patrick Crider	2	2	2.91	36	3	34	32	25	41
*Adam Champion	8	5	3.06	23	0	100	96	40	69
*Garrett Bullock	3	6	3.73	11	0	65	55	29	61
David Kubiak	1	1	3.90	19	2	30	35	10	39
*Matt Zielinski	7	7	3.96	18	0	111	106	32	84
Bryce Morrow	8	8	3.97	19	0	111	104	32	78
Tyree Hayes	2	3	4.17	21	0	37	35	24	28

*Matt Crim	4	9	4.47	19	0	109	114	46	73
Wynn Pelzer	1	4	4.50	10	0	54	53	30	30
Dan Marcacci	2	1	4.76	25	0	45	50	20	46
Kevin Christy	0	0	4.90	3	0	4	4	4	4
Nick Montgomery	0	0	5.14	12	0	14	13	6	10
Patrick Dolan	0	0	5.40	3	0	7	7	11	7
*Todd Hughson	0	0	7.71	3	0	2	3	3	0
Cory Trudell	0	1	9.00	4	0	4	3	10	2
D.J. Ponder	1	0	9.00	7	0	9	13	7	7
Sean Woolard	0	0	10.80	2	0	2	4	3	3
John Holley	0	0	31.50	2	0	2	6	4	1

FLORENCE FREEDOM

PLAYER	P	AVG	OBP	SLG	AB	R	H	HR	RBI	SB
Chris Curley	IF	.356	.387	.611	180	35	64	10	44	7
Junior Arrojo	IF	.302	.420	.378	331	76	100	5	30	28
Eddie Rodriguez	C	.300	.380	.495	313	51	94	15	56	17
#Cole Miles	OF	.299	.397	.343	67	13	20	0	5	12
*Peter Fatse	IF	.284	.369	.449	352	58	100	8	69	17
Kyle Bluestein	OF	.277	.365	.338	65	16	18	0	7	4
#David Harris	OF	.275	.384	.472	324	61	89	10	50	2
Stephen Cardullo	IF	.250	.352	.341	88	11	22	1	9	5
Jimmy Jacquot	C	.244	.307	.370	357	39	87	10	54	2
Ryan Skellie	OF	.239	.286	.370	92	13	22	2	12	4
*John Malloy	OF	.233	.302	.457	300	50	70	15	48	10
Victor Gomez	C	.225	.311	.300	40	4	9	0	5	0
Pierre LePage	IF	.222	.276	.282	252	27	56	2	34	9
*Drew Rundle	OF	.215	.355	.404	223	34	48	10	40	7
Junior Rodriguez	IF	.203	.291	.275	69	8	14	1	9	0
Edwin Padua	IF	.175	.235	.317	63	14	11	2	7	1
Esteban Meletiche	IF	.167	.167	.167	12	2	2	0	0	0
*Tucker Nathans	IF	.164	.311	.213	61	9	10	1	4	5

PLAYER	W	L	ERA	G	SV	IP	H	BB	SO
Chad Sheppard	0	0	0.00	2	0	2	0	1	2
Brad Allen	4	1	1.06	8	0	34	25	3	21
Ian Durham	1	2	2.30	19	0	27	22	16	21
Andy Clark	2	1	2.40	5	0	34	23	3	22
Jose Velazquez	6	0	2.40	46	1	52	41	24	37
Jorge Marban	1	4	2.43	36	16	44	29	24	38
*Mike Hanley	1	0	3.04	20	0	24	26	7	14
Matt Kline	3	3	3.29	38	6	41	26	20	29
Brennan Flick	7	2	3.51	40	4	41	34	29	23
Brandon Mathes	4	0	3.61	35	4	95	88	38	78
*Andres Caceres	7	3	3.90	20	0	111	100	52	71
Sean Gregory	6	6	4.34	16	0	79	86	21	43
*Brent Choban	3	1	4.50	9	0	26	31	11	17
Alec Lewis	5	7	4.99	18	0	101	104	22	55
Daniel DeSimone	2	5	5.11	9	0	44	54	17	25
Maxx Catapano	4	2	5.52	10	0	59	51	22	36
Scott Moviel	0	1	8.82	4	0	17	27	14	9
Stephen Shackleford	1	0	9.00	2	0	2	2	2	2
Kevin Asselin	0	1	10.80	1	0	5	4	4	5

GATEWAY GRIZZLIES

PLAYER	P	AVG	OBP	SLG	AB	R	H	HR	RBI	SB
*Sam Mahoney	C	.350	.481	.550	20	4	7	1	3	0
Rogelio Noris	OF	.313	.352	.579	240	45	75	18	60	3
*John Johnson	IF	.295	.445	.395	352	79	104	3	38	20
*Chris McClendon	IF	.288	.383	.426	312	53	90	8	49	7
#Vladimir Frias	IF	.283	.384	.400	120	16	34	3	11	5
*Antone DeJesus	OF	.270	.359	.391	348	55	94	5	46	11
*Jerod Yakubik	IF	.269	.349	.346	335	52	90	4	56	3
Jon Myers	OF	.257	.338	.497	350	65	90	20	57	2
Alex Guthrie	IF	.256	.340	.402	82	11	21	2	11	0
*Mike Schwartz	IF	.250	.250	.250	20	1	5	0	1	0
Landon Hernandez	IF	.247	.354	.479	263	32	65	16	49	1
Justin Dunning	C	.245	.357	.298	94	14	23	0	9	0
John Shelby	OF	.239	.309	.430	330	45	79	14	55	12
Richie Jimenez	IF	.230	.370	.303	178	34	41	2	23	7
Aaron Conway	OF	.196	.288	.348	46	8	9	1	3	0
Case Rigby	IF	.151	.235	.233	73	7	11	1	4	1
Kenton Parmley	IF	.143	.182	.143	21	1	3	0	0	0
Ben Ives	IF	.130	.163	.174	46	5	6	0	4	2
Casey Allison	OF	.063	.286	.125	16	3	1	0	0	0

PLAYER	W	L	ERA	G	SV	IP	H	BB	SO
*Kolby Moore	0	0	1.08	5	0	8	2	6	5
Zac Treece	2	1	1.21	36	4	52	31	16	54
Phillip Reamy	5	2	2.18	33	0	45	28	27	42
Jordan Cudney	1	1	2.21	20	3	24	14	8	19
Tim Brown	12	2	2.27	20	0	150	139	40	66
*Logan Mahon	2	1	2.52	33	0	36	30	21	25
Richard Barrett	1	4	2.58	36	17	38	33	11	40
Brett Kennedy	0	2	3.17	5	0	6	4	1	5
Paul Tremlin	7	4	3.72	25	1	97	75	34	68
Alex Kaminsky	10	5	3.73	18	0	108	94	39	93
JaVaun West	5	2	3.77	20	0	48	49	12	50
Brett Zawacki	2	2	4.69	8	0	38	38	20	25
Patrick Arnold	3	2	5.11	7	0	32	35	23	18
Chris Enourato	5	4	5.12	20	0	72	68	34	40
*Jonathan Gonzalez	1	2	5.45	7	0	31	30	17	13
Cale Johnson	0	2	5.46	5	0	26	32	21	12
Max Whieldon	1	0	5.53	5	0	26	33	6	13
*Gil Rehwinkel	0	1	5.87	6	0	8	11	4	5
Maurice Bankston	0	0	7.71	2	0	2	3	3	1
*Zach Robertson	0	2	12.37	2	0	8	12	8	4

JOLIET SLAMMERS

PLAYER	P	AVG	OBP	SLG	AB	R	H	HR	RBI	SB
Abel Nieves	IF	.320	.421	.466	322	56	103	8	44	3
Andrew Brauer	OF	.295	.340	.386	44	2	13	0	5	0
*Trey Manz	C	.292	.433	.333	24	3	7	0	2	0
Brad Netzel	SS	.272	.312	.363	353	33	96	2	27	5
Chretien Matz	OF	.270	.270	.432	37	2	10	1	1	1
*Erik Lis	1B	.261	.335	.383	345	40	90	8	45	2
David Fox	LF	.258	.324	.409	198	29	51	5	44	4
Hector Pellot	2B	.258	.368	.363	240	46	62	3	20	9
#Ben Hewett	C	.253	.391	.280	75	9	19	0	5	2
David Christensen	OF	.248	.314	.411	141	25	35	5	12	8
Kyle Maunus	1B	.232	.309	.396	293	37	68	12	45	2
Matt Mirabal	C	.222	.282	.259	108	9	24	0	8	1
#Patrick Norris	OF	.217	.300	.311	180	20	39	2	13	11
*Jimmy Waters	OF	.208	.361	.292	106	19	22	1	8	3
*Zach Mandelblatt	OF	.197	.314	.310	142	15	28	4	23	4
Sean Estand	3B	.194	.220	.216	134	7	26	0	6	1
*Josh Lyon	C	.190	.260	.301	153	18	29	3	17	1
Kyle Zimmerman	IF	.189	.231	.189	37	2	7	0	0	0
Eric McGee	C	.160	.232	.267	75	7	12	2	9	0
*Trevor Willis	C	.146	.255	.188	48	3	7	0	3	2
Tony Sanchez	C	.143	.240	.190	21	2	3	0	1	0
William Hill	OF	.074	.194	.074	27	2	2	0	0	0

PLAYER	W	L	ERA	G	SV	IP	H	BB	SO
Gaby Hernandez	0	1	0.00	1	0	6	8	3	3
Amalio Diaz	1	1	2.59	34	19	35	25	10	40
Chase Doremus	2	4	2.76	41	0	52	46	30	49
Jacob Sanchez	5	2	2.89	11	0	65	67	15	45
Daniel Carela	2	2	3.00	36	1	36	21	23	41
*Geoff Brown	1	3	3.67	44	0	42	45	21	46
Steven Maxwell	6	8	3.85	18	0	112	104	32	77
Tyler Ware	0	0	3.85	3	0	7	9	4	3
*Justin Albert	1	1	3.85	5	0	12	12	4	8
Tommy Mendoza	5	7	3.99	20	0	115	118	33	72
Alex Thieroff	0	0	4.50	2	0	2	3	0	2
*Chuck Lukanen	0	0	4.50	2	0	2	3	3	0
Jim Schult	5	8	4.85	25	0	102	95	41	93
Eric Binder	2	2	4.90	4	0	18	17	10	15
*Dustin Quattrocchi	0	0	5.19	12	0	17	21	11	15
Brian Smith	1	2	5.65	34	0	35	39	8	19
Rey Cotilla	0	2	5.90	8	0	11	11	7	8
Jake Renshaw	1	2	6.23	5	0	22	20	7	23
Jeremy Tietze	0	2	6.96	4	0	21	23	12	9
Wander Alvino	1	3	7.20	5	0	20	21	15	16
Mike Barsotti	2	1	7.33	19	0	31	33	15	19
Seth Hobbs	0	0	7.71	2	0	7	11	5	3
Mike Perconte	0	3	8.14	5	0	21	22	17	19
Matt Sommo	2	4	8.22	7	0	35	41	19	30

LAKE ERIE CRUSHERS

PLAYER	P	AVG	OBP	SLG	AB	R	H	HR	RBI	SB
Rich Witten	C	.323	.405	.355	31	2	10	0	2	2

INDEPENDENT LEAGUES

	P	AVG	OBP	SLG	AB	R	H	HR	RBI	SB
Daniel Bowman	OF	.312	.386	.450	202	39	63	5	37	13
Jason Taylor	IF	.290	.418	.477	279	60	81	12	35	18
*Russell Moldenhauer	IF	.285	.380	.460	337	55	96	9	51	1
#Andrew Davis	IF	.277	.358	.468	361	52	100	14	67	1
*J.C. Figueroa	IF	.260	.332	.302	235	28	61	1	22	8
Rogelio Noris	OF	.250	.253	.425	80	7	20	3	14	0
Wally Correa	IF	.250	.344	.336	220	28	55	2	21	3
*Adrian Ortiz	OF	.246	.279	.330	382	51	94	4	31	21
Brian Erie	C	.246	.318	.304	240	23	59	2	32	1
*Kellen Kulbacki	OF	.234	.303	.323	167	20	39	3	16	2
Robby Kuzdale	IF	.230	.353	.397	282	44	65	6	38	17
*Brandon Decker	IF	.225	.297	.264	129	14	29	0	12	0
*Kyle Weldon	IF	.222	.268	.244	90	4	20	0	7	0
Kyle Shaffer	C	.169	.279	.237	59	7	10	0	4	1
Aaron Klinec	IF	.125	.125	.125	16	2	2	0	0	0
*Gered Mochizuki	IF	.102	.254	.119	59	3	6	0	2	1

PLAYER	W	L	ERA	G	SV	IP	H	BB	SO
Andrew Heston	0	0	0.00	2	0	2	1	3	0
Russell Moldenhauer	0	0	0.00	1	0	1	0	1	1
Matthew Smith	1	0	0.64	4	0	14	13	2	14
Jonathan Kountis	6	2	1.05	40	18	60	31	19	68
Ben Klafczynski	4	1	2.21	31	1	45	29	31	40
*Sam Strickland	0	1	2.25	2	0	12	10	3	5
Mickey Jannis	1	4	2.53	34	6	75	65	14	46
Trevor Longfellow	11	3	3.35	28	0	99	80	34	75
Brad Duffy	1	0	3.37	7	0	16	14	12	13
Patrick Arnold	0	0	3.37	10	0	43	41	25	28
*Paul Fagan	7	9	3.39	22	0	133	122	43	94
Jeff Neptune	0	0	3.85	2	1	7	9	2	5
*Randy Sturgill	2	0	3.96	31	1	50	58	9	35
Kelyn Schellenberg	1	1	3.97	13	0	11	16	0	4
Alex Loftin	4	2	4.38	9	0	41	45	14	26
*Josh Hungerman	0	1	4.39	4	0	14	12	10	23
Eric Gonzalez-Diaz	7	10	4.56	22	0	118	131	26	80
*Joshua Rickards	2	2	4.69	11	0	38	49	15	25
Travis Risser	6	4	5.44	31	0	45	51	14	24
*Chance Gilmore	0	2	6.00	11	1	15	14	15	14
Mike Inselmann	0	1	17.18	4	0	4	10	1	2

LONDON RIPPERS

PLAYER	P	AVG	OBP	SLG	AB	R	H	HR	RBI	SB
*Ben Magsig	DH	.375	.375	.500	8	2	3	0	0	0
#Joash Brodin	OF	.370	.446	.592	238	49	88	11	54	10
Justino Cuevas	IF	.285	.305	.398	123	13	35	0	11	3
Jim Vahalik	C	.282	.326	.362	174	21	49	2	24	2
Brad Agustin	IF	.280	.379	.350	100	11	28	1	14	5
*Mark Samuelson	IF	.278	.376	.443	194	24	54	7	33	0
Stephen Cardullo	IF	.268	.350	.388	224	35	60	2	26	10
Shane Bagley	IF	.267	.323	.350	60	5	16	1	6	5
David Christensen	OF	.250	.307	.469	196	32	49	9	29	12
Zach Larson	C	.239	.284	.375	88	9	21	3	15	0
Tony Delmonico	P	.190	.354	.302	63	13	12	2	6	2
Clifton Thomas	IF	.188	.282	.215	144	26	27	1	5	10
*J-C Paquin	C	.156	.308	.250	32	6	5	1	4	1
Josh Federico	IF	.125	.176	.188	16	0	2	0	1	0

PLAYER	W	L	ERA	G	SV	IP	H	BB	SO
David Francis	0	3	2.38	16	6	23	17	6	21
Jamie Richmond	6	3	2.61	12	0	90	85	16	68
David Triplet	0	0	2.70	3	0	3	2	4	4
Matt Sommo	0	2	3.04	7	1	24	23	12	17
Andrew Chilcoat	1	0	3.05	10	1	18	15	5	16
Brandon Sinnery	4	1	3.47	8	0	54	45	9	35
Sheng-An Kuo	0	5	3.60	8	0	40	27	25	27
Yohan Gonzalez	4	4	3.78	9	0	50	51	16	41
*Rob Cooper	1	0	4.29	11	0	15	16	9	9
Tony Delmonico	0	3	4.86	15	2	20	23	7	24
Charles Wooten	1	1	5.25	13	0	12	11	5	7
*Eric Katzman	1	4	6.42	11	0	42	45	35	30
Denver Wynn	0	0	6.75	3	0	3	3	1	2
Justin Mazur	1	1	7.02	6	0	17	19	12	7
Matt Brennan	0	0	9.81	6	0	7	5	9	9
Adam Arnold	1	2	10.60	16	0	19	28	9	12
Matt Schimpf	0	0	11.57	1	0	2	5	0	2
Robert Chamra	0	0	32.40	3	0	2	6	4	2

NORMAL CORNBELTERS

PLAYER	P	AVG	OBP	SLG	AB	R	H	HR	RBI	SB
Andrew Cohn	IF	.311	.377	.370	135	17	42	0	6	3
Ernie Banks	OF	.302	.338	.445	182	15	55	4	23	4
Sam Judah	OF	.298	.374	.396	225	19	67	2	19	4
Bobby Rinard	OF	.283	.344	.343	166	21	47	1	13	9
Pat McKenna	IF	.281	.378	.497	199	32	56	9	25	7
*Alvaro Ramirez	CF	.273	.350	.329	161	24	44	0	18	12
Justin Clark	OF	.269	.296	.308	26	2	7	0	2	0
Yasel Gomez	IF	.268	.316	.415	164	15	44	3	17	6
*Steve Felix	OF	.268	.332	.410	351	41	94	11	48	16
#K.C. Judge	LF	.265	.306	.353	34	4	9	0	4	1
*Ty Wiesemeyer	OF	.241	.344	.353	224	30	54	4	25	13
Pat Trettel	C	.240	.293	.389	167	18	40	5	19	1
Randy Wells	IF	.227	.268	.364	66	9	15	2	8	0
Brantley Meier	CF	.208	.321	.250	24	5	5	0	1	1
Bubby Williams	DH	.200	.204	.232	95	4	19	0	5	2
Jordan Stouffer	IF	.198	.327	.296	81	8	16	2	10	2
#Jason Thompson	IF	.195	.250	.293	82	6	16	1	7	0
*Trey Manz	C	.191	.274	.237	131	7	25	0	10	0
Sean Wilson	IF	.182	.250	.205	44	6	8	0	2	3
Jovan Rosa	IF	.179	.238	.308	39	3	7	1	2	0
#Derrick Fox	IF	.160	.300	.160	25	1	4	0	0	1
Jesse Olivar	IF	.157	.295	.235	51	6	8	0	0	2
*Derek Luciano	IF	.149	.268	.149	47	4	7	0	3	2
Pat Dockendorf	IF	.143	.221	.151	119	8	17	0	5	3
*J.B. Brown	IF	.136	.161	.153	59	4	8	0	2	0
Robert Brooks	IF	.133	.258	.229	105	11	14	2	7	2
Matt Mirabal	C	.130	.130	.130	23	1	3	0	1	1
#Norberto Susini	IF	.125	.222	.125	16	1	2	0	1	1
Mitch Rider	C	.118	.118	.118	17	1	2	0	2	0
*Ruben Sierra	OF	.063	.059	.063	16	0	1	0	1	0
Daniel Cayton	IF	.048	.091	.048	21	2	1	0	0	1
Trace Voshell	C	.000	.235	.000	13	0	0	0	1	0

PLAYER	W	L	ERA	G	SV	IP	H	BB	SO
Stephen Adkins	0	0	0.00	1	0	1	1	0	2
Ross Davis	1	1	1.00	6	0	27	18	7	31
*Estevan Uriegas	1	0	2.07	4	0	4	1	4	5
*Rich Mascheri	0	0	2.29	26	10	35	33	14	47
Ryan Krumlauf	3	2	3.00	13	0	45	41	16	25
Drew Provence	5	3	3.52	10	0	61	61	23	43
*Justin Albert	1	2	3.79	5	0	21	28	6	8
Marshall Schuler	1	2	4.00	18	5	18	21	6	16
Mike Lebo	0	0	4.50	8	0	10	14	4	7
Mitch Mormann	0	0	4.50	15	1	14	14	7	13
Kyle DiMartino	1	3	4.54	32	0	32	32	17	40
Josh Joseph	1	4	4.58	37	0	51	62	22	24
Tyler Lavigne	5	10	4.71	21	0	124	125	63	126
*Jacob Liedka	2	13	5.15	23	0	119	123	49	94
Brendon Smith	2	8	5.22	23	0	62	62	37	37
Elio Briones	0	2	5.65	7	0	14	14	11	11
*Tyler Stovall	2	9	5.70	22	0	84	68	91	92
Dan Britt	3	7	6.31	12	0	61	80	13	40
Austin Bailey	0	1	8.18	7	0	11	11	2	8
*Kaleb Engelke	1	0	12.00	8	1	6	6	5	5
Bobby Hillier	0	0	12.10	7	0	9.2	18	8	4
Richard Ruff	0	0	16.20	8	0	7	9	12	5
Sam Judah	0	0	22.50	2	0	2	5	1	0

RIVER CITY RASCALS

PLAYER	P	AVG	OBP	SLG	AB	R	H	HR	RBI	SB
Caleb Curry	C	.333	.500	.333	6	1	2	0	0	0
Corey Amerson	IF	.333	.333	.333	3	0	1	0	1	0
*Jeremy Synan	OF	.307	.381	.448	339	56	104	7	50	11
*Curran Redal	OF	.305	.356	.398	256	49	78	4	28	8
*Josh Workman	IF	.295	.413	.429	156	31	46	3	23	3
*Jason Patton	OF	.292	.351	.421	342	47	100	8	53	6
#Ben Hewett	C	.288	.338	.398	118	14	34	1	20	2
*Gerardo Avila	IF	.286	.352	.366	161	20	46	3	27	4
Doug Sanders	2B	.273	.342	.351	242	37	66	3	28	10
Matt Serna	IF	.270	.346	.308	237	32	64	0	33	6
*Kyle Jones	IF	.265	.490	.441	34	7	9	1	8	0
*Chris Andreas	1B	.261	.391	.385	234	32	61	6	29	3
*Eric Williams	OF	.251	.455	.312	279	61	70	1	22	13

		AVG	OBP	SLG	AB	R	H	HR	RBI	SB
Ryan Kaup	IF	.250	.375	.250	20	0	5	0	3	0
Charlie Lisk	IF	.246	.331	.443	309	47	76	14	55	7
*Corey LeVier	IF	.225	.360	.350	40	8	9	1	4	1
Zach Deutscher	C	.183	.294	.296	115	10	21	3	14	1
Bobby Burk	SS	.171	.233	.293	164	21	28	4	18	5
Keli'i Zablan	P	.138	.194	.172	29	2	4	0	1	1
Jareck West	OF	.125	.286	.188	16	0	2	0	1	2
Erik Wetzel	IF	.000	.000	.000	9	0	0	0	0	0

PLAYER	W	L	ERA	G	SV	IP	H	BB	SO
Max Rusch	0	0	0.00	3	0	3	0	1	4
Dustin Umberger	5	2	0.93	22	7	29	15	9	48
David Haselden	0	0	1.50	1	0	6	4	0	7
Brad Stillings	1	0	1.63	2	0	11	7	3	12
Brandon Cunniff	2	0	1.83	28	4	34	31	11	55
Alex Sunderland	0	1	2.53	19	0	21	20	17	34
Tony Marsala	5	7	3.26	15	0	91	90	34	58
Dan Lazzaroni	0	0	3.60	6	0	10	8	2	3
Nick Kennedy	5	4	3.68	38	3	90	98	24	77
Justin Gill	4	3	4.40	38	2	45	43	25	62
Jason Sullivan	3	2	4.43	33	1	45	44	22	30
*Cory Caruso	0	2	4.44	29	0	28	22	22	25
Keli'i Zablan	4	4	4.68	20	0	73	76	33	44
Preston Vancil	7	10	4.75	21	0	117	129	38	80
Justin Sarratt	2	4	4.92	8	0	46	43	15	45
*Justin Edwards	1	2	5.26	5	0	26	34	16	22
Adam Worthington	0	1	5.40	2	0	5	7	4	0
Doug Shields	5	1	5.76	20	0	64	62	28	59
Albert Ayala	0	0	6.51	11	1	9.2	11	8	10
Chandler Barnard	1	7	7.36	3	0	15	19	7	8
*Aaron King	0	0	7.71	2	0	2	2	4	3
Don Lisi	0	1	8.61	9	0	16	29	5	15
Liam Ohlmann	1	4	9.26	5	0	22	26	13	24
*Matt Costello	0	0	9.81	5	0	4	6	2	3
Nick Schreiber	0	0	12.70	4	0	6	12	5	6
Blaine O'Brien	0	1	30.85	2	0	2	7	5	2

ROCKFORD RIVERHAWKS

PLAYER	P	AVG	OBP	SLG	AB	R	H	HR	RBI	SB
Carlos Luciano	IF	.343	.397	.463	67	13	23	2	11	2
Javier Herrera	OF	.338	.414	.522	278	47	94	8	64	7
*Trevor Whyte	IF	.325	.384	.442	77	7	25	1	8	1
Matt Greener	IF	.306	.364	.444	340	51	104	5	44	0
*Jimmy Parque	OF	.304	.448	.333	69	7	21	0	7	2
Michael Hur	OF	.298	.352	.474	369	56	110	15	57	0
#Ted Obregon	SS	.286	.348	.357	255	42	73	2	19	26
Justino Cuevas	IF	.282	.328	.410	117	16	33	1	9	3
#Jet Butler	IF	.278	.342	.417	345	53	96	10	55	5
*Evan Button	IF	.268	.355	.409	340	66	91	10	43	18
Danny Gonzalez	IF	.268	.328	.330	112	14	30	0	4	3
Devin Shepherd	IF	.252	.310	.328	131	10	33	2	16	2
#Brandon Anderson	OF	.250	.349	.328	256	41	64	0	19	25
Greg Van Horn	OF	.243	.343	.301	173	24	42	1	20	4
Elvin Millan	C	.233	.233	.333	30	2	7	0	3	0
Michael Thomas	C	.216	.318	.276	185	14	40	1	23	0
*Rudy Wilson	OF	.189	.259	.230	74	11	14	0	8	0
Steve Anderson	LF	.171	.239	.171	41	5	7	0	4	0
Jeremy Richter	OF	.167	.286	.167	6	0	1	0	1	0
Elliot Hagburg	C	.158	.158	.158	19	2	3	0	3	0

PLAYER	W	L	ERA	G	SV	IP	H	BB	SO
Greg Van Horn	0	0	0.00	1	0	0	1	0	0
Mike Lee	3	1	2.19	13	1	41	30	14	59
Garrett Granitz	3	2	2.93	39	12	46	39	21	28
Drew Rucinski	7	4	3.12	22	1	104	96	26	91
Kyle Schepel	4	7	3.66	16	0	79	67	43	72
Mickey Cassidy	3	2	3.98	36	1	50	46	10	35
Joey Gradney	0	1	4.50	11	0	16	14	15	19
Cody Hallahan	6	8	4.55	20	0	105	111	47	70
Jordan Goldschmidt	0	1	4.74	23	0	25	26	19	15
*Alex Szymanski	0	2	5.14	2	0	7	9	2	10
Brett Scarpetta	0	0	5.14	4	1	7	8	2	8
Nick Sarianides	1	2	5.22	4	0	21	28	14	22
Nelson Curry	0	1	5.25	29	0	38	40	20	35
Kyle Lindquist	0	1	5.46	11	0	28	33	5	20
*Ziggie Vanderwall	7	6	5.69	18	0	87	103	63	65

	W	L	ERA	G	SV	IP	H	BB	SO
*Andrew Armstrong	2	2	6.23	40	0	30	28	24	24
Dylan Brammer	0	0	6.48	7	0	8	12	7	9
Cory Trudell	0	1	6.75	2	0	7	9	7	2
Tyree Hayes	1	0	6.90	10	0	14	16	8	12
*Theron Minium	1	0	7.20	14	0	15	21	13	13
Nick Anderson	1	4	7.71	7	0	33	42	21	20
Jordan Stern	1	0	8.10	5	0	13	24	5	12
Cliff Archibald	1	1	9.00	7	1	6	5	8	7
*Kevin Patterson	0	2	10.12	3	0	11	18	9	6
Jordan Liette	0	2	12.46	3	0	9	13	10	4
Rob Currie	0	0	12.60	6	0	5	5	6	4
Eric Rohe	0	1	12.82	4	0	13	25	3	5
Artie Clyde	0	0	13.50	2	0	1	3	2	0
*Kasey Kiker	0	2	17.55	3	0	7	8	17	8
Blake Drake	0	0	18.00	6	0	4	4	10	2
*Brad Schnitzer	0	1	18.56	2	0	5	12	5	2
Scott Kelley	0	1	20.25	1	0	3	4	3	4
Jack Crawford	0	0	45.00	1	0	1	5	1	1

SCHAUMBURG BOOMERS

PLAYER	P	AVG	OBP	SLG	AB	R	H	HR	RBI	SB
*Chad Mozingo	OF	.313	.385	.530	319	69	100	11	54	23
Frank Pfister	3B	.306	.347	.468	395	58	121	13	58	8
*Chase Fontaine	IF	.295	.371	.475	61	10	18	2	10	3
Nate Baumann	OF	.283	.326	.424	304	44	86	9	50	12
#Gerard Hall	SS	.275	.341	.388	80	12	22	1	12	5
Mike Valadez	C	.254	.286	.309	256	29	65	1	28	2
Steve McQuail	IF	.251	.345	.521	263	47	66	20	57	2
*Sean Mahley	IF	.246	.341	.334	293	46	72	3	31	5
*Nick Kuroczko	IF	.245	.377	.328	192	28	47	1	15	3
*J.B. Brown	IF	.238	.273	.286	21	0	5	0	1	0
#K.C. Judge#	LF	.235	.297	.294	34	6	8	0	0	0
Ty Nelson	C	.232	.331	.259	112	13	26	0	11	1
Jereme Milons	OF	.232	.308	.350	323	38	75	6	47	4
Brandon Gregorich	IF	.222	.326	.333	36	5	8	1	7	0
Drew Heithoff	IF	.221	.323	.238	172	14	38	0	15	7
Andrew Cohn	IF	.217	.308	.290	69	7	15	0	7	5
*Karexon Sanchez	IF	.215	.359	.317	284	47	61	5	29	9
*Brandon Hairston	IF	.154	.207	.154	26	0	4	0	2	0
Marty Coyle	C	.000			0	0	0	0	0	0

PLAYER	W	L	ERA	G	SV	IP	H	BB	SO
Patrick Lala	0	0	0.00	2	0	0	3	2	0
Kirk Clark	0	0	0.00	10	1	9	7	2	4
Joe Parsons	3	1	1.57	37	0	51	34	28	56
Cody Griebling	6	2	2.48	10	0	65	62	19	41
Patrick Mincey	4	1	2.77	34	17	36	22	17	57
Tyler Ware	0	0	3.00	4	1	6	8	2	4
Tyler Watkins	3	4	3.21	9	0	56	50	15	29
Dave Whigham	0	3	3.29	9	1	14	13	4	10
Robby Donovan	11	5	3.44	19	0	123	108	55	86
*Cameron Roth	8	10	3.74	20	0	130	135	56	82
Jason Braun	4	1	3.77	31	2	31	32	16	29
*Sam Robinson	2	0	3.85	15	1	12	10	10	5
*Jose Rodriguez	1	1	4.01	16	0	25	21	16	13
Alex Thieroff	0	0	4.05	8	2	7	4	4	7
Matt Kuna	3	5	4.51	15	0	76	95	23	47
*Adam Tollefson	1	1	4.54	36	2	34	31	10	34
Robbie Penny	2	4	5.00	8	0	45	50	20	32
*Thomas Nelson	0	1	5.40	6	0	5	3	3	3
Alex Rivers	4	4	5.49	11	0	59	65	9	41
*Eric Holmes	0	0	5.71	10	0	17	19	7	9
Shane Prance	1	1	6.23	8	0	26	35	13	14
*Kaleb Engelke	0	0	6.75	13	0	11	9	6	13
Tony Delmonico	0	0	6.75	9	1	11	13	6	10
*Andy Weeks	0	1	13.03	2	0	9.2	22	4	4

SOUTHERN ILLINOIS MINERS

PLAYER	P	AVG	OBP	SLG	AB	R	H	HR	RBI	SB
*Gerardo Avila	IF	.441	.486	.765	34	7	15	2	8	0
Phillip Butler	C	.407	.448	.481	27	3	11	0	2	0
Sean Wilson	IF	.313	.313	.313	16	3	5	0	0	0
Ryan Eigsti	C	.300	.500	.600	10	3	3	1	1	0
Jason Ganek	IF	.293	.394	.449	198	36	58	8	27	4
*Cory Harrilchak	OF	.284	.340	.375	88	11	25	1	14	1

PLAYER		AVG	OBP	SLG	AB	R	H	HR	RBI	SB
Carlos Mendez	IF	.278	.335	.369	352	38	98	3	47	5
*Ken Gregory	OF	.277	.338	.410	307	43	85	6	43	6
Chris Anderson	C	.273	.356	.416	77	15	21	1	12	0
*Jacob Kaase	IF	.271	.351	.444	351	53	95	13	47	9
Cannon Lester	IF	.262	.324	.369	187	29	49	3	27	3
#Matt Fields	1B	.261	.363	.565	115	20	30	9	24	3
Chad Maddox	OF	.256	.318	.430	351	49	90	11	67	3
#Darian Sandford	OF	.256	.353	.325	246	57	63	1	14	45
*Alvaro Ramirez	CF	.256	.326	.346	156	19	40	2	11	10
*Cody Coffman	C	.250	.250	.250	8	1	2	0	0	0
Sean Harrell	OF	.250	.324	.360	100	18	25	2	8	3
Javier Herrera	OF	.243	.329	.529	70	14	17	6	14	0
Elliot Hagburg	C	.238	.304	.262	42	3	10	0	7	1
Will Block	2B	.223	.338	.359	220	30	49	5	30	2
*Sean Coughlin	C	.205	.314	.331	151	15	31	4	15	1
Matt Soderlund	C	.154	.241	.154	26	1	4	0	1	0
Taye Larry	OF	.111	.111	.111	9	0	1	0	1	0
Josh Haley	OF	.063	.211	.063	16	2	1	0	1	1

PLAYER	W	L	ERA	G	SV	IP	H	BB	SO
Jason Ganek	0	0	0.00	1	0	1	3	0	1
*Nick Cicio	0	0	0.71	10	0	13	3	1	12
Steve Grife	0	0	0.81	11	0	11	6	3	14
*Max Peterson	0	1	1.10	17	12	16	12	1	25
Albert Ayala	0	0	1.90	30	8	33	19	14	20
*Anthony Collazo	3	0	2.28	17	1	24	21	13	27
*Daniel Calhoun	7	4	2.52	13	0	86	69	12	62
Cody Hall	9	1	2.63	14	0	79	72	30	39
Brandon Cunniff	1	0	2.70	9	4	10	7	6	10
Reese McGraw	0	0	2.89	7	0	9	6	1	11
David Harden	10	5	3.05	19	0	136	137	20	78
Gabriel Shaw	1	2	3.13	39	1	46	46	5	45
*Shawn Gilblair	11	5	3.84	19	0	117	117	36	93
*Brian Fowler	6	10	4.12	19	0	105	117	31	68
Ross Davis	1	0	4.61	9	0	14	16	6	16
*Darrin Tew	2	2	4.61	23	0	51	52	23	33
*Ryan Quigley	1	2	4.62	23	0	23	28	9	22
Ian Campbell	3	1	6.88	7	0	17	25	6	9
Jimmy Albury	0	1	8.10	1	0	3	6	4	3
Dave Whigham	0	2	8.37	11	0	9.2	15	4	8
Thomas Campbell	0	2	9.22	4	0	14	22	7	7
Ben Shivers	0	1	10.38	8	0	9	9	7	3
*Casey Fry	0	0	14.72	4	0	4	7	5	6

TRAVERSE CITY BEACH BUMS

PLAYER	P	AVG	OBP	SLG	AB	R	H	HR	RBI	SB
Chase Burch	1B	.304	.423	.497	358	66	109	17	76	6
*Ryan Still	IF	.301	.510	.420	276	82	83	4	34	12
Kyle Colligan	OF	.290	.339	.423	397	49	115	7	56	19
Jose Vargas	3B	.290	.346	.576	410	78	119	29	100	4
*Sean Gusrang	IF	.266	.406	.509	293	52	78	15	50	2
*Brian Heere	OF	.264	.345	.353	394	68	104	5	40	7
Jeff Flagg	IF	.249	.309	.452	398	63	99	20	83	3
Chris Kay	C	.247	.303	.506	81	11	20	4	10	0
Marcus Nidiffer	C	.241	.347	.409	257	37	62	9	38	0
Travis Higgs	C	.239	.352	.304	46	6	11	1	4	0
Matt Howard	OF	.222	.300	.378	45	8	10	1	7	2
Kyle Eveland	SS	.203	.313	.297	320	50	65	5	32	4
Jon Hurst	C	.083	.214	.333	12	1	1	1	2	0

PLAYER	W	L	ERA	G	SV	IP	H	BB	SO
Jake Sabol	2	0	0.71	6	1	13	8	2	8
*Nick Capito	6	0	1.58	39	3	57	36	17	67
Matt Miller	6	4	2.25	41	12	64	53	6	38
Michael Devine	0	0	2.84	5	3	13	11	0	11
Jacob Clem	7	4	3.01	20	0	128	103	35	59
Reid Kelly	10	3	3.27	18	0	110	84	28	106
Scott Dunn	5	4	3.32	29	3	73	62	23	63
Jason Mattila	1	2	3.33	18	0	30	28	15	15
Brooks Belter	10	3	3.52	20	0	107	88	59	86
Sam Brown	1	1	3.60	21	0	25	22	12	17
*Bennett Whitmore	6	4	4.32	20	1	94	88	37	47
Kurt Wunderlich	3	0	4.35	6	0	31	26	12	23
Scott Mueller	2	5	4.43	41	14	45	35	23	32
*David Deminsky	5	2	6.17	13	0	51	60	18	31
Cody Baker	0	0	6.58	5	0	14	16	5	11

Maxx Catapano	0	0	8.30	2	0	4	7	4	0	

ROAD WARRIORS

PLAYER	P	AVG	OBP	SLG	AB	R	H	HR	RBI	SB
*Mike Schwartz	IF	.311	.446	.473	74	13	23	2	8	1
Tyler Hall	OF	.276	.398	.395	76	11	21	0	8	2
Doug Thennis	OF	.254	.333	.339	118	13	30	1	12	0
*David Roney	C	.250	.283	.273	44	5	11	0	6	0
Ryan Kaup	IF	.243	.322	.272	103	12	25	0	14	3
*Cody Coffman	C	.243	.378	.297	37	7	9	0	6	0
*Ben Magsig	IF	.225	.391	.297	138	20	31	1	15	2
*Matt Wright	OF	.224	.300	.371	259	30	58	2	30	6
Jacob Daniel	OF	.224	.339	.265	49	5	11	0	4	2
Wesley Jones	OF	.216	.262	.297	111	14	24	2	12	6
Will Arnold	C	.214	.389	.286	42	4	9	1	7	0
Aaron Glaum	IF	.205	.316	.251	263	41	54	1	13	26
*Tanner Leighton	IF	.204	.306	.301	93	9	19	0	9	3
Taylor Oldham	IF	.170	.260	.239	88	6	15	1	7	0
*T.J. McManus	IF	.000	.091	.000	10	1	0	0	0	0

PLAYER	W	L	ERA	G	SV	IP	H	BB	SO
Aaron Glaum	0	0	0.00	1	0	1	2	0	1
Cutler Ruby	0	0	0.00	1	0	1	0	0	0
Michael Jahns	0	1	3.79	15	0	21	20	21	10
Tyler Vaske	2	2	3.85	5	0	26	24	13	7
*Shawn Marquardt	2	5	4.32	7	0	42	42	12	19
Chris Kaminski	2	5	5.09	24	7	30	34	14	26
*Jared Christensen	3	1	5.22	13	1	21	21	9	21
*Kevin McGovern	1	2	5.26	23	0	26	30	9	13
Sheng-An Kuo	0	5	6.08	8	0	37	42	32	28
Matt Schimpf	4	8	6.28	20	0	96	128	31	52
*Matt Faiman	0	0	6.35	4	0	6	8	6	3
*Scott Foster	0	1	6.38	13	0	18	25	11	9
Stephen Corbett	0	1	8.67	10	0	9	9	8	0
*Greg Hendrix	0	3	8.80	10	0	15	22	16	13
*Jon Jones	0	2	9.44	9	0	20	24	23	15
Max Rusch	0	0	27.00	3	0	2	7	4	1

WASHINGTON WILD THINGS

PLAYER	P	AVG	OBP	SLG	AB	R	H	HR	RBI	SB
Andrew Heck	OF	.310	.399	.413	252	42	78	2	27	20
Jovan Rosa	IF	.308	.379	.474	78	6	24	2	12	0
Coley Crank	C	.269	.321	.308	26	3	7	0	3	0
*Gus Benusa	OF	.260	.310	.370	154	26	40	1	13	7
Orlando Santos	P	.250	.250	.250	8	0	2	0	0	0
Mark Samuelson	IF	.250	.383	.383	120	20	30	2	19	0
Shain Stoner	IF	.249	.353	.415	301	43	75	10	58	2
*AJ Nunziato	IF	.238	.332	.448	181	35	43	6	32	4
*Jeriel Waller	OF	.237	.293	.237	38	3	9	0	0	0
*Rick Devereaux	C	.237	.283	.337	270	37	64	4	33	5
#Darian Sandford	OF	.236	.346	.273	110	13	26	0	11	26
Will Arnold	C	.234	.347	.281	64	7	15	0	4	0
*Matthew McConnell	IF	.228	.331	.267	101	13	23	0	5	0
Luis Rivera	OF	.227	.370	.273	22	3	5	0	0	0
#Michael Mooney	OF	.226	.281	.262	84	6	19	0	9	3
Doug Thennis	OF	.222	.301	.296	162	13	36	1	11	5
*Allan Boyer	OF	.221	.338	.221	68	10	15	0	9	5
*Robbie Garvey	OF	.216	.274	.295	190	26	41	2	13	18
*Johnathan Erb	OF	.212	.276	.288	52	5	11	0	7	1
Taylor Oldham	IF	.202	.267	.365	104	12	21	4	16	0
#Davis Page	3B	.200	.556	.200	5	1	1	0	0	0
*Tanner Leighton	IF	.197	.269	.295	61	5	12	0	5	2
Nick Lockwood	IF	.192	.222	.308	26	5	5	0	1	0
*Mitch Dening	OF	.191	.328	.319	47	4	9	1	5	0
Brad Agustin	IF	.183	.302	.268	82	12	15	2	6	3
James Simmons	OF	.176	.333	.294	17	3	3	0	0	1
Chris Lloyd	OF	.174	.240	.174	23	3	4	0	1	2
Michael Bando	IF	.172	.255	.244	180	23	31	1	14	3
*Trevor Pippin	OF	.171	.190	.268	41	3	7	1	4	0
Jim Vahalik	C	.163	.212	.217	92	5	15	1	9	0
Joel Carranza	C	.138	.257	.345	29	4	4	2	7	0
Tim Leary	IF	.130	.176	.217	46	1	6	1	5	0
David Peters	C	.111	.111	.111	9	0	1	0	1	0
Eric Blackwell	P	.111	.200	.222	9	1	1	0	2	0
Vinnie Fayard	OF	.083	.313	.083	12	3	1	0	0	0

| Chris Anderson | C | .000 | .222 | .000 | 13 | 1 | 0 | 0 | 2 | 0 |
| Aaron Guinn | OF | .000 | .000 | .000 | 6 | 0 | 0 | 0 | 0 | 0 |

PLAYER	W	L	ERA	G	SV	IP	H	BB	SO
Kyle Wahl	0	0	0.00	1	0	0	1	0	1
Andrew Heck	0	0	0.00	1	0	1	0	1	1
Orlando Santos	1	1	1.20	22	11	22	20	8	14
Nathan Striz	2	1	1.45	9	3	12	10	1	17
Chandler Barnard	1	4	2.47	25	2	40	31	12	46
*Alfonso Yevoli	1	2	2.62	28	0	34	25	11	34
Gary Lee	7	5	2.89	17	0	115	93	27	60
Chris Smith	9	6	2.92	19	0	129	106	52	116
*Shawn Smith	3	4	2.94	25	0	58	53	32	47
Alan Gatz	1	0	3.37	8	0	13	12	4	8
Casey Barnes	6	7	3.66	19	0	118	109	31	66
Jhonny Montoya	3	3	3.91	23	0	62	53	31	66
Justin Hall	6	7	4.11	18	0	112	122	20	82
*Nick Cicio	0	4	4.24	22	1	30	25	11	30
Steve Grife	0	2	4.79	19	6	21	19	13	20
Ross Gusky	1	2	5.40	11	0	13	14	7	7
Nick Schreiber	0	0	5.78	4	0	5	3	3	3
Eric Blackwell	3	4	7.92	19	0	50	51	40	45
Mickey Cassidy	0	0	9.81	4	0	4	6	1	5
Ryan Thomas	0	0	10.80	3	0	5	7	5	2
*Anthony Collazo	0	0	13.50	3	0	2	4	3	2

WINDY CITY THUNDERBOLTS

PLAYER	P	AVG	OBP	SLG	AB	R	H	HR	RBI	SB
Chris Wade	SS	.301	.375	.383	345	48	104	5	37	20
Mike Torres	IF	.296	.363	.369	388	60	115	1	36	36
*Chad Cregar	1B	.291	.363	.599	374	64	109	31	93	6
*Brandon Decker	1B	.288	.357	.544	316	46	91	18	54	11
Brandon Pearl	C	.276	.330	.367	98	18	27	1	11	8
#C.J. Gillman	IF	.246	.328	.318	211	28	52	1	25	1
Travis Weaver	IF	.240	.293	.267	225	23	54	0	18	6
*Ryan Cuneo	1B	.236	.297	.362	127	11	30	1	16	0
Bob Glover	OF	.236	.301	.356	250	44	59	4	23	11
Zach Aakhus	C	.234	.321	.311	334	40	78	4	35	14
*T.J. McManus	IF	.231	.302	.359	39	3	9	1	3	0
Jareck West	OF	.225	.291	.377	244	29	55	7	30	12
Billy Nowlin	LF	.213	.290	.258	89	9	19	0	6	0
Mike Mobbs	OF	.212	.250	.231	52	5	11	0	3	0
*Bryan Burke	OF	.182	.325	.212	66	6	12	0	6	0
Bruce Alter	IF	.167	.250	.278	18	3	3	0	1	0
Travis Shreve	IF	.143	.143	.143	7	1	1	0	0	0
Andy Chriscaden	IF	.125	.182	.225	40	5	5	1	2	0
*Matt Grosso	OF	.111	.226	.148	27	1	3	0	3	0
Greg Bachman	IF	.000	.154	.000	11	1	0	0	1	0

PLAYER	W	L	ERA	G	SV	IP	H	BB	SO
Andy Mee	3	3	2.28	38	3	39	34	19	40
Willy Kesler	2	3	2.51	13	4	14	11	4	17
Mike Recchia	11	3	2.51	24	1	150	107	56	177
Tyson Corley	5	8	2.52	31	8	100	73	34	69
*Shane Zegarac	2	1	2.92	46	8	40	32	17	44
*Matt Costello	1	1	3.04	28	0	21	27	5	17
Andrew Chilcoat	1	1	3.48	19	0	21	18	9	7
*Paul Montalbano	0	0	3.52	11	0	8	10	9	8
Michael Click	3	1	3.65	45	3	44	40	23	61
Donovan Drake	1	1	3.76	3	0	14	13	8	20
*Matt Jernstad	0	0	3.85	2	0	2	3	1	4
Duke Dykeman	0	2	4.24	16	0	30	29	14	23
Stephen Sauer	8	7	4.28	21	0	126	140	39	104
Blayne Weller	5	3	4.59	21	0	96	96	48	108
Dustin Williams	11	6	4.78	20	0	115	109	57	101
*Mark Kuzma	1	0	6.45	18	0	15	17	12	16
Michael Jahns	0	0	7.71	3	0	2	1	5	2
Ricky Szeligo	0	1	9.00	1	0	3	4	2	3
Ryan Carr	0	1	9.52	5	0	6	8	7	5
Rye Davis	0	0	12.78	7	0	6	11	8	10

NORTH AMERICAN LEAGUE

Calling the North American League a league is not really accurate. Viewing it as two leagues operating under a cooperation agreement would be a better description. On the West Coast, you had four teams trying to make a league work with regular travel between two Hawaii clubs and two Northern California clubs.

And thousands of miles away, the clubs of the former United League ran their own league, with their own championship series and their own schedule.

After finishing the regular season with the league's best record, the Northern Division's San Rafael defeated Maui 6-5 in the deciding Game Three, as division most valuable player Maikel Jova drove in two runs.

In Texas, that division's best record was also rewarded as Edinburg won all five of its playoff games to win the club's first title since the then-named Edinburg Coyotes won the Central League crown in 2004.

NORTHERN DIVISION	W	L	PCT	GB
San Rafael Pacifics	34	26	.567	—
Maui Na Koa Ikaika	36	30	.545	1
Hawaii Stars	25	29	.463	6
Sonoma County Grapes	19	29	.396	9

UNITED LEAGUE DIVISION	W	L	PCT	GB
Edinburg Roadrunners	60	36	.625	—
Fort Worth Cats	52	44	.542	8
Rio Grande Valley WhiteWings	51	44	.537	8 ½
San Angelo Colts	51	45	.531	9
Abilene Prairie Dogs	34	53	.391	21 ½
McAllen Thunder	31	57	.352	25

PLAYOFFS: North Division—San Rafael defeated Maui 2-1 in best-of-three series. **United Division Semifinals**—Edinburg defeated Rio Grande Valley 2-0 and Fort Worth defeated San Angelo 2-0 in best-of-three series. **Finals**—Edinburg defeated Fort Worth 3-0 in best-of-five series.
ATTENDANCE: San Angelo Colts 115,735; Edinburg Roadrunners 86,947; Fort Worth Cats 57,596; Rio Grande Valley Whitewings 47,520; San Rafael Pacifics 31,411; McAllen Thunder 29,082; Abilene Prairie Dogs 17,979.
MANAGERS: Abilene—Bobby Brown; Edinburg—Vince Moore; Fort Worth—Curt Wilkerson; Hawaii—Garry Templeton; Maui—Jamie Vermilyea; McAllen—Al Gallagher; Rio Grande Valley—Eddie Dennis; San Angelo—Doc Edwards; San Rafael—Mike Marshall; Sonoma County—Joe Morello;
ALL-STAR TEAM (NORTH DIVISION): C—Nick Valdez (Maui). **IF**—Johnny Woodward (San Rafael); Jose Sanchez (Maui); Arnoldo Ponce (Hawaii); Kalaika Kahoohalahala (Maui). **OF**—Maikel Jova (San Rafael); Keoni Manago (Hawaii); Steve Tedesco (Hawaii). **DH**—Anthony Lopez (Hawaii). **RHSP**—Jesse Smith (Maui). **LHSP**—Brian Gump (San Rafael). **RHRP**—Victor Ferrante (Maui). **LHRP**—Matthew Stabelfeid (San Rafael). **MOST VALUABLE PLAYER:** Maikel Jova (San Rafael). **PITCHER OF THE YEAR:** Jesse Smith (Maui).

INDIVIDUAL BATTING LEADERS

PLAYER	TEAM	AVG	G	AB	R	H	HR	RBI
Chad Gabriel	FtW	.363	86	344	52	125	3	46
Ruddy Yan	RGV	.356	76	303	58	108	1	30
Jose Ruiz	FtW	.347	90	349	55	121	9	54
J.J. Sherrill	SA	.345	70	287	62	99	3	27
Maikel Jova	SR	.341	60	252	35	86	7	45
Joe Weik	EDN/ABL	.340	91	356	67	121	12	67
Ronnie Gaines	SA	.339	71	313	55	106	9	36
Chuck Caufield	FtW	.335	84	310	55	104	4	45
Jason Martin	SA/ABL	.332	92	383	71	127	7	41
Carlos Hereaud	EDIN	.330	95	361	59	119	7	58

INDIVIDUAL PITCHING LEADERS

PLAYER	TEAM	W	L	ERA	IP	H	BB	SO
Jesse Smith	MAU	10	2	1.33	108	73	28	85
Celson Polanco	RGV	12	4	1.83	123	108	20	108
Dustin Crenshaw	SCG	5	4	2.17	75	73	19	54
Jake Rasner	SRP	7	1	2.71	70	69	15	56
Adam Rowe	APD	2	4	2.75	79	78	21	57
Blake Nation	FTW	10	3	2.77	123	103	48	83
Brian Gump	SRP	5	2	2.78	71	70	19	64
Logan Williamson	SAN	9	3	2.88	128	121	50	94
Tyler Pearson	SRP	4	1	2.98	48	46	6	36
Brian Murphy	MCA	5	7	2.99	108	128	35	63

ABILENE PRAIRIE DOGS

PLAYER	P	AVG	OBP	SLG	AB	R	H	HR	RBI	SB
#K.C. Judge	OF	.400	.455	.400	10	1	4	0	1	0
*Austin Newell	OF	.375	.545	.375	8	2	3	0	1	0
*Braden Embry	OF	.368	.409	.579	19	4	7	0	7	0
Clint Stroud	IF	.359	.444	.385	39	7	14	0	4	0
Joe Weik	OF	.347	.405	.549	317	59	110	12	61	8
Jason Martin	IF	.337	.405	.440	350	61	118	6	40	18
#Wilson Batista	IF	.309	.369	.498	301	52	93	12	52	9
Gunner Glad	P	.304	.407	.348	23	2	7	0	1	0
Danny Gonzalez	IF	.294	.361	.344	163	23	48	0	19	2
Geraldo Valentin	SS	.292	.349	.415	195	35	57	3	21	10
*Reggie Williams	IF	.288	.333	.346	52	6	15	0	4	2
K.C. Judge	IF	.286	.375	.286	7	0	2	0	0	0
Dan Pembroke	OF	.280	.367	.320	25	1	7	0	2	0
Zach Welch	C	.278	.355	.292	216	33	60	0	19	14
Case Rigby	DH	.273	.393	.273	22	4	6	0	2	0
Bryan Fogle	OF	.266	.355	.394	94	21	25	3	9	0
Kyle Nichols	1B	.263	.332	.438	308	27	81	11	57	0
Eddie Browne	IF	.255	.325	.276	192	22	49	0	23	1
Adam De La Garza	IF	.252	.347	.292	226	31	57	0	15	5
Zach Crosswhite	C	.227	.292	.409	22	2	5	1	1	0
Nick Ochoa	1B	.223	.267	.321	112	6	25	1	10	2
Logan Lotti	RF	.222	.417	.222	9	2	2	0	0	0
#Davis Page	IF	.222	.326	.222	36	7	8	0	2	1
Chris Caves	C	.205	.293	.347	176	19	36	6	24	1
*Angel Sierra	OF	.200	.375	.200	25	5	5	0	0	0
Jessie Mier	C	.194	.342	.226	31	3	6	0	1	0
Levi Tapia	DH	.158	.304	.158	19	0	3	0	2	0
*Tylor Prudhomme	3B	.143	.143	.143	14	1	2	0	3	0
Jason Venya	IF	.133	.188	.133	15	0	2	0	0	0
Todd Alls	1B	.125	.125	.125	8	0	1	0	0	0
Alex Guthrie	IF	.120	.214	.240	25	2	3	1	2	0

PLAYER	W	L	ERA	G	SV	IP	H	BB	SO
Karson Robinson	0	0	0.00	4	0	5	2	5	5
*Steve Merslich	0	0	0.00	7	0	5	8	1	5
Tommy Hoenshell	1	0	2.25	2	0	8	10	0	8
Todd Weldon	0	3	2.50	15	1	18	16	10	10
*Adam Rowe	2	4	2.74	12	0	79	78	21	57
Matt Larkins	4	1	2.87	12	0	56	70	9	35
Jeremy Tietze	3	3	2.95	24	0	43	40	32	20
*Kevin Gelinas	4	2	3.13	22	2	23	20	5	29
Ray Silva	0	1	4.28	20	7	21	16	10	13
Billy Petrick	5	3	4.34	18	1	85	95	17	61
Derrick Dingeman	0	2	4.56	14	1	24	27	6	14
David Slovak	2	0	5.25	11	0	12	14	0	9
Woods Fines	5	10	5.27	18	0	102	105	51	56
Gunner Glad	0	1	5.55	21	1	23	32	17	22
Freddy Flores	1	1	5.74	5	0	31	43	8	20
*Brian Smith	3	4	5.86	8	0	43	57	14	25
Scott Vander Weg	1	8	6.13	39	2	51	80	20	43
*David Phillips	0	0	6.75	1	0	1	2	0	0
Braden Tullis	2	4	6.78	12	0	65	93	30	42
Erik Gonsalves	1	1	7.07	3	0	14	19	5	5
Ben Tootle	0	2	8.73	4	0	11	14	15	8
*Casey Fry	0	0	9.00	2	0	2	3	1	2
Wade Morrison	0	0	9.00	5	0	4	4	8	5
Kyle Nichols	0	1	9.64	2	0	5	13	2	3
Shawn Kale	0	0	9.81	1	0	4	4	4	5
*Sean White	0	1	11.57	2	0	7	16	0	2
Chris Peacock	0	1	11.57	2	0	2	6	0	1

PLAYER	W	L	ERA	G	SV	IP	H	BB	SO
Mitch Mormann	0	0	16.87	1	0	3	7	1	2
Eric Schaler	0	0	16.87	3	0	3	3	7	1
Reese McGraw	0	0	18.00	4	0	2	7	1	2

EDINBURG ROADRUNNERS

PLAYER	P	AVG	OBP	SLG	AB	R	H	HR	RBI	SB
Carlos Hereaud	IF	.330	.401	.474	361	59	119	7	58	25
*Derrek Perren	OF	.327	.407	.413	339	45	111	2	50	10
Wilmer Pino	IF	.322	.370	.418	366	63	118	4	51	31
Stantrel Smith	OF	.304	.325	.363	369	55	112	1	41	59
Joe Weik	OF	.282	.388	.282	39	8	11	0	6	1
Cristobal Santana	IF	.279	.359	.316	190	25	53	0	21	4
Osiel Flores	C	.276	.375	.333	246	34	68	1	23	6
Tim Battle	OF	.273	.369	.408	267	46	73	5	25	29
*Vincent Blue	OF	.267	.387	.328	344	60	92	1	37	32
#Felix Molina	SS	.264	.329	.330	261	30	69	1	33	10
Eric Bloom	C	.259	.379	.306	85	14	22	0	12	0
*Tony Phillips	IF	.231	.355	.327	52	7	12	0	8	2
Pascual Del Real	IF	.212	.309	.243	189	18	40	1	20	6
Luis Sumoza	OF	.200	.242	.341	85	12	17	2	14	1
*Rusty Jones	P	.111	.143	.222	27	2	3	1	2	0
Jose Mendoza	IF	.059	.111	.059	17	0	1	0	1	0

PLAYER	W	L	ERA	G	SV	IP	H	BB	SO
Billy Petrick	0	0	0.00	1	0	0	0	0	1
Eric Bloom	0	0	0.00	1	1	4	2	0	2
Jose Oyervidez	2	0	0.78	4	0	23	16	11	14
James Hoyt	0	0	1.03	12	1	17	13	10	19
Osvaldo Rodriguez	4	0	1.30	8	0	41	28	13	42
Robert Roth	2	0	2.10	21	4	26	28	13	24
Paul Koss	3	2	2.10	38	9	43	37	13	52
Julio Castro	4	1	2.12	27	13	42	27	16	43
Tetsuya Iwasaki	5	0	2.19	22	0	41	42	8	23
*Rusty Jones	4	1	2.43	32	1	52	41	17	41
*Miguel Martinez	11	4	3.19	19	0	130	131	40	89
Aaron Tullo	6	4	3.31	23	0	100	86	56	99
*Kirk Wetmore	0	2	3.64	9	0	12	12	8	11
David Dinelli	5	8	4.10	17	0	105	108	63	88
Matison Smith	9	6	4.28	19	0	124	136	54	89
Ryan Smith	3	7	5.61	21	0	75	87	28	53
Josh Walker	1	0	7.36	4	0	4	5	1	2
Ruben De La Rosa	0	1	9.39	6	0	8	9	6	7
Stefan Comeaux	1	0	16.20	1	0	2	3	1	1

FORT WORTH CATS

PLAYER	P	AVG	OBP	SLG	AB	R	H	HR	RBI	SB
Chad Gabriel	IF	.363	.381	.439	344	52	125	3	46	9
*Jose Ruiz	1B	.347	.388	.484	349	55	121	9	54	3
Chuck Caufield	RF	.335	.395	.461	310	55	104	4	45	16
Benji Gil	AC	.333	.333	.667	3	1	1	0	0	0
Antoin Gray	IF	.309	.371	.436	94	21	29	2	12	0
#Shelby Ford	SS	.299	.359	.422	154	27	46	1	19	3
#C.J. Beatty	IF	.292	.376	.447	295	46	86	8	47	14
Jonathan Dziomba	IF	.291	.341	.369	309	45	90	1	30	9
Derek Marshall	C	.274	.297	.348	270	30	74	3	37	7
#Brandon Jones	3B	.272	.311	.478	356	63	97	18	64	1
*Gabe Memmert	1B	.264	.316	.283	53	4	14	0	5	0
*Jason Diaz	IF	.259	.355	.259	27	6	7	0	1	2
*R.J. Harris	OF	.254	.357	.349	252	44	64	2	30	11
Randall Thorpe	OF	.233	.311	.320	150	19	35	0	6	9
Scott Dalrymple	C	.226	.295	.321	168	21	38	3	27	3
*Kenny Gilbert	1B	.212	.313	.259	85	10	18	0	11	1
Adam Gordon	IF	.176	.364	.176	17	3	3	0	1	1
Luis Blanco	IF	.154	.154	.231	13	1	2	0	0	0

PLAYER	W	L	ERA	G	SV	IP	H	BB	SO
Jeff Jamnik	0	0	1.12	33	20	32	31	12	22
T.J. Bozeman	2	3	2.15	34	3	38	24	16	36
Blake Nation	10	3	2.77	18	0	123	103	48	83
Trevor Harden	10	4	3.18	18	0	116	111	35	78
Tim Haines	2	3	3.40	7	0	37	39	14	17
*Mace Thurman	2	3	3.41	22	0	26	30	9	35
Brandon Wilkerson	5	1	3.65	33	0	44	36	19	28
Rick Bauer	0	0	3.75	9	0	12	16	7	14
Cameron Dullnig	0	0	4.00	4	0	9	7	7	7
Casey Russell	2	4	4.43	9	0	43	49	16	13

INDEPENDENT LEAGUES

PLAYER	W	L	ERA	G	SV	IP	H	BB	SO
Steve Barnes	6	6	4.46	21	0	97	106	57	72
Kane Holbrooks	3	5	4.84	25	0	65	98	15	50
Blake Parry	6	5	4.86	19	0	78	101	19	31
*James Giulietti	4	7	5.26	17	0	94	132	38	56
*R.J. Harris	0	0	6.00	1	0	3	4	2	2

HAWAII STARS

PLAYER	P	AVG	OBP	SLG	AB	R	H	HR	RBI	SB
Keoni Manago	LF	.333	.368	.423	123	18	41	1	17	0
*Anthony Lopez	OF	.316	.374	.353	190	24	60	0	20	7
*Bam Davis	IF	.309	.404	.372	94	11	29	1	13	3
Steven Tedesco	OF	.300	.400	.357	140	28	42	0	13	15
#Arnoldo Ponce	SS	.280	.382	.382	186	32	52	1	19	6
Jenzen Torres	DH	.276	.323	.586	29	6	8	2	8	0
Matt Hibbert	OF	.264	.353	.303	208	35	55	0	15	22
#Jason Thomas	2B	.261	.318	.370	119	12	31	2	11	6
Reece Alnas	OF	.245	.271	.296	159	13	39	1	19	3
#Dion Pouncil	2B	.236	.302	.264	106	17	25	1	9	13
Adam Jacobs	C	.231	.342	.340	156	20	36	2	18	4
Jose Sanchez	IF	.184	.283	.233	103	14	19	0	14	16
Keith Kendel	IF	.182	.250	.273	11	3	2	0	5	1
Logan Kanamu	PH	.179	.273	.214	28	4	5	0	3	0
Anthony Williams	IF	.175	.245	.198	126	11	22	0	4	8
Reggie York	RF	.161	.188	.226	31	2	5	0	2	1
Brandon Young	2B	.105	.150	.158	19	3	2	0	0	1

PLAYER	W	L	ERA	G	SV	IP	H	BB	SO
Reece Alnas	0	0	0.00	1	0	1	1	0	0
Andrew Miller	1	2	2.53	5	0	32	34	11	15
Steve Raburn	4	2	2.86	6	0	38	26	8	28
*Dallas Mahan	0	7	3.53	10	0	69	67	12	39
Roman Martinez	1	3	3.93	16	2	32	28	14	33
Michael Kenui	3	1	4.08	20	1	29	22	10	25
Ronnie Loeffler	6	3	4.39	10	0	70	58	23	40
*Bryan Herrera	4	3	4.63	10	0	56	52	38	38
Josh Larson	0	1	5.19	4	0	9	8	5	10
John Holly	0	3	5.27	7	0	43	38	34	30
Cortney Arruda	1	1	5.40	17	2	25	18	17	27
Ryan Screnar	2	1	7.16	12	1	33	42	19	18
Paul Jinkens	3	2	7.67	14	0	32	26	22	14

MAUI NA KOA IKAIKA

PLAYER	P	AVG	OBP	SLG	AB	R	H	HR	RBI	SB
Jose Sanchez	IF	.318	.429	.400	220	44	70	3	29	10
Kalaika Kahoohalahala	IF	.291	.350	.355	220	39	64	2	22	12
Nick Valdez	C	.273	.353	.364	231	30	63	2	42	6
*Gered Mochizuki	IF	.270	.360	.396	159	29	43	1	27	8
*Waylen Sing Chow	OF	.266	.365	.352	233	45	62	2	28	15
#Danny Sandoval	SS	.263	.359	.362	232	33	61	5	40	9
Keith Kandel	2B	.234	.309	.289	197	29	46	1	11	12
Victor Ferrante	P	.222	.364	.667	9	2	2	1	3	0
Logan Kanamu	C	.179	.244	.256	78	5	14	1	12	1
*Mark Okano	OF	.174	.288	.239	109	15	19	1	17	6
Joseph Kala	IF	.171	.304	.193	140	12	24	0	19	1
AJ Alexander	OF	.168	.246	.181	155	17	26	0	12	8
*Alan Rick	1B	.155	.248	.255	110	11	17	2	8	0
Eric Rodriguez	OF	.067	.176	.067	15	0	1	0	0	1

PLAYER	W	L	ERA	G	SV	IP	H	BB	SO
Jesse Smith	10	2	1.32	16	0	108	73	28	85
Josh Larson	2	0	2.02	20	0	44	35	13	25
Victor Ferrante	1	0	2.29	28	9	31	31	11	40
Chad Blackwell	9	1	3.12	15	0	98	110	11	75
*Yoshihiro Doi	1	1	3.72	17	0	19	25	3	8
*Mike Williams	2	6	3.91	13	0	71	74	32	38
Matt Walker	3	5	4.06	12	0	73	87	19	34
Mike Koons	2	3	4.15	32	9	30	40	9	29
Vinnie St. John	2	3	4.90	28	0	29	25	24	17
Eri Yoshida	4	6	5.55	11	0	45	41	28	12
*Dave Jensen	0	2	7.10	27	0	19	34	17	16
Kalaika Kahoohalahala	0	1	13.50	1	0	1	2	3	1
Randy Castillo	0	0	14.40	3	0	5	11	3	1

McALLEN THUNDER

PLAYER	P	AVG	OBP	SLG	AB	R	H	HR	RBI	SB
*Yasser Gomez	OF	.332	.409	.377	199	38	66	0	16	5
Cristobal Santana	IF	.308	.379	.365	52	8	16	0	6	4
Fidel Hernandez	IF	.298	.355	.333	57	2	17	0	4	2
Manny Osborne	OF	.286	.375	.286	7	0	2	0	3	0
*Roberto Rodriguez	IF	.275	.354	.291	182	23	50	0	11	16
*Mike Goss	OF	.274	.297	.301	113	7	31	0	10	0
*Craig Hertler	OF	.273	.382	.321	308	54	84	0	31	18
Nick Mahin	OF	.271	.351	.332	199	28	54	2	26	4
Miguel Alfonzo	IF	.269	.336	.406	212	31	57	5	33	9
Antoin Gray	IF	.265	.350	.462	117	16	31	5	29	0
Michael Demperio	IF	.263	.370	.342	114	23	30	2	11	6
Luis Blanco	IF	.259	.328	.362	58	2	15	1	9	0
*Gianison Rosa	IF	.251	.384	.311	235	30	59	0	32	7
*Henry Gonzalez	1B	.250	.292	.294	68	6	17	0	6	0
#Davis Page	IF	.237	.297	.288	59	7	14	0	5	2
Henry Abad	IF	.231	.286	.231	26	5	6	0	2	0
Michael Lewis	IF	.227	.346	.242	66	15	15	0	7	6
*Nathan Tomaszewski	IF	.225	.291	.285	253	25	57	1	23	1
Lyndon Poole	IF	.208	.311	.221	77	11	16	0	5	7
*Brian Nichols	IF	.207	.273	.307	150	16	31	3	15	0
Adam Gordon	IF	.200	.455	.333	15	4	3	0	0	1
Nelson Teilon	IF	.192	.247	.315	146	16	28	4	19	7
Matt Redding	IF	.189	.266	.234	111	6	21	1	13	1
Terrence McClain	OF	.140	.178	.140	43	2	6	0	1	1
Carl Johnson	C	.000	.364	.000	7	2	0	0	0	1
Chris Brown	OF	.000	.000	.000	7	0	0	0	0	0

PLAYER	W	L	ERA	G	SV	IP	H	BB	SO
Scott Sobczak	1	1	2.59	3	0	17	12	5	4
Brian Murphy	5	7	2.99	18	0	108	128	35	63
Yunier Colon	2	2	3.27	20	0	33	28	13	15
Chad Robinson	4	0	3.48	27	14	31	32	22	30
*Alex Smith	3	4	3.98	11	0	61	72	26	26
*Jason Moody	0	0	4.05	15	0	20	33	12	14
Jeff Sakowski	0	4	4.14	16	0	54	61	22	27
Kurt Houck	2	3	4.32	30	4	50	58	19	42
Adrian Garza	0	1	4.50	4	0	6	8	2	4
Alexi Perez	5	5	4.59	14	0	82	93	33	48
*Kedrick Martin	1	3	4.88	7	0	31	40	13	13
*Frank James	5	7	5.13	16	0	100	123	38	49
*Demetrius Banks	3	5	5.58	12	0	58	57	30	28
Quinn Bright	0	3	6.15	5	0	19	30	8	13
Evan Cunningham	0	0	6.75	5	0	7	10	2	3
*Sean McGrath	0	1	7.50	4	0	6	9	6	4
Baron Short	0	4	9.14	7	0	21	36	15	15
Spencer Trygg	0	3	9.67	10	0	18	28	13	12
Sean Keeler	0	2	11.25	9	0	16	26	12	13
Eugene Smith	0	0	18.00	2	0	2	6	2	2
Rex Garner	0	1	21.00	2	0	3	10	0	2
Toro Trevino	0	1	23.62	1	0	3	10	4	0
Jamel Mann	0	0	23.62	3	0	3	2	6	1
Roberto Rodriguez	0	0	27.00	1	0	2	2	0	0

RIO GRANDE VALLEY WHITEWINGS

PLAYER	P	AVG	OBP	SLG	AB	R	H	HR	RBI	SB
#Ruddy Yan	OF	.356	.418	.419	303	58	108	1	30	13
Romulo Ruiz	IF	.322	.377	.493	205	34	66	5	40	5
Leugim Barroso	SS	.321	.351	.369	355	56	114	0	37	12
Bryan Marquez	3B	.311	.420	.363	251	36	78	0	25	6
Welinson Baez	1B	.309	.427	.468	94	17	29	3	14	3
#Miguel Chacoa	SS	.308	.379	.346	26	2	8	0	1	0
Mario Mercedes	C	.300	.361	.352	290	34	87	1	44	1
Fidel Hernandez	IF	.295	.347	.353	258	35	76	2	44	3
Miguel Alfonzo	OF	.291	.368	.359	103	19	30	1	8	3
Leivi Ventura	3B	.290	.364	.439	262	40	76	6	38	6
*Roberto Rodriguez	IF	.282	.330	.329	85	15	24	0	7	3
*Robert Moron	1B	.275	.310	.400	80	14	22	1	12	1
*Francisco Santana	OF	.270	.322	.349	189	31	51	0	17	8
*James Mays	OF	.260	.321	.356	73	16	19	1	13	2
Luis Sumoza	CF	.255	.350	.307	153	18	39	0	23	6
Salvador Paniagua	C	.238	.304	.444	63	9	15	3	14	0
Juan Fuentes	C	.230	.254	.246	61	4	14	0	9	0
Nick Lenzendorf	P	.230	.296	.257	74	8	17	0	7	1

PLAYER		AVG	OBP	SLG	AB	R	H	HR	RBI	SB
Jacinto Cipriota	IF	.215	.229	.280	93	9	20	2	11	2
*Tomochika Tsuboi	OF	.200	.273	.267	30	6	6	0	0	0
Nestor Castillo	IF	.178	.208	.267	45	7	8	0	5	1
Jose Rivero	OF	.163	.241	.184	49	4	8	0	8	0
John Sciullo	1B	.125	.176	.125	16	1	2	0	0	0
#Michael Pair	C	.118	.118	.176	17	1	2	0	0	0
Ernesto Manzarillo	2B	.111	.111	.111	18	1	2	0	1	0
Jhonaldo Pozo	C	.107	.167	.107	28	0	3	0	1	0
Jordan Price	CF	.059	.238	.059	17	2	1	0	1	0

PLAYER	W	L	ERA	G	SV	IP	H	BB	SO
*Robert Moron	0	0	0.00	1	0	2	3	0	0
Leivi Ventura	0	0	0.00	1	0	1	0	0	0
*Wander Perez	3	1	1.58	24	3	34	26	12	35
Celson Polanco	12	4	1.83	18	1	123	108	20	108
Rey Cotilla	0	0	2.84	6	4	6	2	4	7
*Henry Garcia	1	3	3.02	11	0	45	45	6	23
Alberto Reyes	2	2	3.10	21	0	38	35	7	37
Luis Chirinos	7	4	3.16	11	0	68	68	20	58
Nick Lenzendorf	3	2	3.33	22	12	27	22	13	22
Eddie Dennis	2	2	3.75	25	0	48	54	33	24
Luis Noel	8	3	3.80	18	0	102	108	33	79
*James Mays	0	1	3.93	6	0	16	16	5	6
Julio Santana	0	2	3.98	27	1	41	41	19	32
Reymond Cruz	1	2	4.11	4	0	20	21	6	19
Yobanny Reyes	2	3	4.24	5	0	23	27	8	9
Clint Bowker	1	4	4.35	20	1	70	86	17	44
Coleman Stephens	6	7	5.43	18	0	94	121	21	48
Erinzon Bautista	2	2	5.94	21	1	50	59	33	34
Ricardo Estevez	1	2	6.38	8	0	18	24	10	11
Jhonaldo Pozo	0	0	9.00	2	0	3	4	1	0

SAN ANGELO COLTS

PLAYER	P	AVG	OBP	SLG	AB	R	H	HR	RBI	SB
*Mark Ramos	IF	.352	.423	.374	91	12	32	0	10	2
#J.J. Sherrill	OF	.345	.405	.498	287	62	99	3	27	22
Ronnie Gaines	OF	.339	.385	.492	313	55	106	9	36	24
Salvador Paniagua	C	.333	.364	.617	81	14	27	4	19	0
*Jamar Walton	OF	.296	.339	.404	307	37	91	2	43	5
Daryl Jones	IF	.293	.371	.420	379	77	111	10	63	29
*Cory Patton	OF	.287	.358	.421	380	61	109	7	70	2
Landon Camp	IF	.280	.352	.445	375	57	105	14	60	1
Ryan Hutson	IF	.276	.379	.345	87	10	24	0	11	1
Jason Martin	OF	.273	.368	.394	33	10	9	1	3	0
Collin Janssen	C	.273	.333	.273	11	1	3	0	1	0
*David Phillips	P	.267	.313	.333	15	1	4	0	0	0
#K.C. Judge	IF	.250	.250	.250	4	0	1	0	0	0
Danny Gonzalez	IF	.240	.259	.240	25	2	6	0	5	0
Jason Crosland	IF	.236	.299	.376	271	30	64	7	41	2
*Davis Page	IF	.234	.368	.362	47	11	11	1	4	1
Danny Hernandez	IF	.232	.256	.292	168	16	39	1	13	1
Joshua Banda	C	.231	.325	.454	108	20	25	6	22	1
*Jason Diaz	IF	.220	.404	.254	118	22	26	0	12	12
*Andrew Caron	IF	.186	.239	.233	43	2	8	0	4	0
#Michael Pair	C	.173	.263	.216	139	13	24	1	6	0
Lyndon Poole	OF	.111	.273	.111	9	0	1	0	0	0
*Justin McDavid	IF	.000	.000	.000	1	0	0	0	0	0
Eddie Browne	IF	.000	.167	.000	5	0	0	0	0	0

PLAYER	W	L	ERA	G	SV	IP	H	BB	SO
*Demetrius Banks	4	0	1.82	4	0	25	26	9	22
*Cory Patton	0	1	1.83	19	0	20	18	6	20
*Ryan Riddle	1	0	2.25	2	0	12	12	1	8
Erik Draxton	5	1	2.41	38	23	41	29	15	32
Alfredo Caballero	0	0	2.53	11	1	11	7	2	15
*Logan Williamson	9	3	2.88	20	0	128	121	50	94
Russell Johns	1	2	3.32	17	0	24	22	11	17
*Kyle Boggio	2	3	3.52	20	0	46	38	16	33
Ryan Hanna	1	3	3.75	3	0	12	16	3	11
Mark Willinsky	9	6	4.36	19	0	118	146	33	74
Mike Hart	6	4	4.41	16	0	84	97	25	51
*Michael Hacker	4	5	4.50	36	0	38	51	16	24
Brian Henschel	7	9	4.53	21	0	143	169	29	61
Chris Weast	1	2	4.82	22	2	28	36	9	19
Reece Cross	0	0	6.23	3	0	4	4	3	3
*David Phillips	1	2	6.62	24	0	37	45	26	34

*Jose Sanchez	1	3	7.64	13	0	58	73	27	30
Stephen Nikonchik	0	1	11.57	3	0	5	5	5	5
Chris Peacock	0	1	12.46	2	0	4	10	3	4
Ronnie Gaines	0	1	18.00	1	0	1	3	1	1
Chad Nading	0	2	19.28	4	0	7	11	11	5

SAN RAFAEL PACIFICS

PLAYER	P	AVG	OBP	SLG	AB	R	H	HR	RBI	SB
Maikel Jova	RF	.341	.362	.468	252	35	86	7	45	1
Jon Hurst	C	.306	.421	.403	62	9	19	1	11	0
*Chase Fontaine	IF	.294	.404	.429	170	35	50	4	25	11
Bunyu Maeda	IF	.294	.400	.529	17	3	5	1	2	0
Chad Bunting	OF	.292	.346	.417	24	6	7	0	2	1
*Tomochika Tsuboi	OF	.282	.390	.353	85	17	24	0	8	2
*Darrick Hal	SS	.279	.377	.397	229	35	64	5	33	4
Johnny Woodard	1B	.275	.373	.511	229	41	63	10	36	2
Will Wright	IF	.267	.351	.362	116	14	31	0	14	6
#Steve Boggs	OF	.245	.332	.294	204	27	50	1	23	6
*Zack Pace	OF	.243	.355	.320	169	30	41	0	22	15
Steve Detwiler	OF	.223	.356	.357	112	19	25	3	13	1
Henry Calderon	IF	.217	.278	.303	175	23	38	3	22	1
Matt Alton	C	.216	.293	.321	134	14	29	2	14	0
*D.J. Dixon	IF	.211	.238	.316	19	0	4	0	5	0
Matt Soderlund	IF	.143	.357	.286	21	4	3	1	4	0
Ernie Munoz	C	.000	.000	.000	5	0	0	0	0	0

PLAYER	W	L	ERA	G	SV	IP	H	BB	SO
Vinny Pacchetti	0	0	0.00	1	0	1	1	0	0
*Matthew Stabelfeld	3	3	2.22	29	4	32	30	10	35
*Jesse Garcia	2	2	2.25	8	0	28	26	11	27
Jake Rasner	7	1	2.71	11	0	70	69	15	56
*Brian Gump	5	2	2.77	11	0	71	70	19	64
Tyler Pearson	4	1	2.97	11	0	48	46	6	34
Tyler Graham	2	3	3.08	31	4	35	25	18	38
Julian Arballo	5	3	3.85	28	3	37	42	11	58
*Bill Lee	1	0	4.00	1	0	9	8	0	0
Tyler Topp	2	1	4.15	6	0	30	29	9	20
Will Krasne	0	1	4.37	14	1	25	15	23	24
*Andrew Pevsner		1	5.27	18	0	43	43	20	34
Michael Hebert		1	5.47	9	0	23	19	20	26
Chondell Jones	0	0	7.20	3	0	10	19	2	10
Matt Durkin	3	6	7.89	16	1	51	48	38	57
Jason Roenicke	0	0	12.60	5	0	5	7	7	4
Will Wright	0	0	13.50	1	0	2	4	0	2
Steve Detwiler	0	1	15.42	3	0	7	14	5	2

SONOMA COUNTY GRAPES

PLAYER	P	AVG	OBP	SLG	AB	R	H	HR	RBI	SB
Mark Micowski	OF	.319	.410	.407	182	24	58	2	22	15
Brandon Gregorich	IF	.319	.390	.446	166	20	53	3	23	2
*D.J. Dixon	IF	.286	.349	.399	168	18	48	3	21	1
Bunyu Maeda	IF	.280	.373	.422	161	25	45	4	15	11
Samuel Perry	SS	.265	.365	.361	166	32	44	0	20	12
Michael Johnson	IF	.254	.275	.403	67	5	17	1	7	0
Chris De Biasi	2B	.246	.306	.263	118	12	29	0	11	3
Frederick Atkins	OF	.245	.294	.324	188	23	46	2	13	12
George Ban	OF	.220	.298	.298	168	28	37	1	22	5
#Colin Bryan	IF	.206	.289	.252	107	9	22	0	12	5
*Javan Williams	OF	.200	.333	.200	5	0	1	0	0	0
Tyler Finley	C	.184	.276	.224	76	14	14	0	7	1
*Joey Lewis	1B	.183	.253	.232	82	7	15	1	10	0
Tayler Cresswell	OF	.143	.250	.143	7	2	1	0	0	0
Liepman, Ben	C	.000	.167	.000	5	0	0	0	0	0

PLAYER	W	L	ERA	G	SV	IP	H	BB	SO
Michael Hebert	0	0	0.00	2	0	11	5	6	9
Dustin Crenshaw	5	4	2.17	12	0	75	73	19	54
Joey Lewis	0	0	3.00	9	0	12	11	7	11
Vinny Pacchetti	1	5	3.30	18	0	33	42	11	29
Michael Johnson	1	1	4.15	7	0	22	21	10	7
*Ross Pomerantz	2	3	4.20	11	0	51	47	24	31
Jeffrey Lyons	2	3	4.44	20	2	26	25	17	20
Marquis Pettis	0	0	4.50	7	2	8	6	7	9
Daniel March	2	3	4.73	8	0	38	47	22	29
*Javan Williams	0	1	4.76	1	0	6	5	3	3
*Rob Savarese	0	0	4.83	20	1	22	30	7	14

INDEPENDENT LEAGUES

INTERNATIONAL

Amateurs, expanded WBC highlight slate

BY JOHN MANUEL

For the first time since 1980 in Moscow, the world held the Olympics and didn't invite baseball.

A new era of international baseball began with the expanded World Baseball Classic replacing the Olympics as the sport's top-level international tournament. Four WBC qualifying tournaments were held in 2012—two in September and two scheduled for November as the Almanac went to press—that would whittle the WBC field down from 28 nations to 16.

The 2013 Classic will wrap up at the end of March in San Francisco, home of the World Series champions. For the first time, the International Baseball Federation will call the WBC winner its World Champion, another sign of the Classic's new primacy in international baseball.

IBAF hasn't given up totally on the Olympics, however. The governing body and the International Softball Federation moved toward a joint Olympic bid, which the ISF passed at the end of October, to try to get both sports back into the Olympics in 2020.

Under the proposal, baseball and softball would share a facility and be considered two disciplines of the same sport. One sport's athletes would march in the Opening Ceremonies, play a one-week event, then leave the Games while the other sport's athletes take over their spots in the Olympic Village and at the athletic venue. After the conclusion of their event, the other sport's athletes would march in the Closing Ceremonies, so both disciplines would have an Olympic experience.

"We applaud and congratulate our friends from the ISF for their courage and determination in this decision," said IBAF President Riccardo Fraccari. "But also for putting the interest of their athletes and their sport before politics."

The International Olympic Committee is considering several other sports in addition to baseball and softball for the 2020 Games, which will be played in either Tokyo, Madrid or Istanbul. It is scheduled to vote on the 28-sport program on Sept. 7, 2013. The sports competing with baseball and softball to join the Olympics include karate, roller sports, sport climbing, squash, wakeboarding, wushu (Chinese martial arts) and beach soccer.

The World Baseball Classic overcame several

With a team heavy with Cubans, Spain upset Israel to win its WBC qualifier

previous impediments in 2012. The IBAF vote formally declaring the WBC, and not the Baseball World Cup, as deciding its world champion was made just prior to the 2011 Winter Meetings. WBC Inc.—the corporate partnership of MLB and the union that operates the classic—successfully negotiated with Nippon Professional Baseball and its players union to get two-time defending champion Japan back in the games.

And the first two WBC qualifiers went off without a significant hitch. One was held in Jupiter, Fla., while the other took place in Regensberg, Germany. Neither was a commercial hit, and Canada completely dominated the field in Germany, beating the Czech Republic, Great Britain and host Germany by a combined score of 38-9, belting nine home runs in three games.

"We came here knowing that we had to win three games and we accomplished our goal," Canada manager Ernie Whitt said. "I can't say enough about this team. They're gamers, they're guys that play hard with pride and passion."

For Canada, the result means a large group of Canadian major leaguers will be returning to the WBC. That list likely includes Justin Morneau, who contacted members of Team Canada to encourage them in the run-up to the qualifier, along with Joey Votto, Ryan Dempster, John Axford, Brett Lawrie and Russell Martin. Several members of the qualifying squad will also be included in the final WBC roster, Whitt said.

One player who made an argument for inclusion was Van Ostrand, who went 7-for-13 with four home runs, 10 RBIs and nine runs. Other standouts included Robinson, who went 5-for-11; Tyson Gillies (Phillies) and Loewen each went 7-for-14.

Meanwhile, the Jupiter event was considered more wide open, with Israel the favorite over Spain, France and South Africa. The Israel team drew its roster almost exclusively from Americans of Jewish extraction, including retired big leaguer Shawn Green. First baseman Nate Freiman (Padres) hit .417 with four homers and seven RBIs as Israel made it to the championship game, a one-game final that followed a double-elimination preliminary round. But he didn't have enough help, as Spain rallied to a 9-7, 10-inning victory to earn its WBC berth with a team that featured one native of Spain and thrived with Americans of Spanish origin as well as plenty of Cubans.

Had Israel won and advanced to the 16-team main draw in March, they would have added at least one major league veteran to their roster in Kevin Youkilis, who had already committed to play. Other Jewish stars such as Braun, Ike Davis and Ian Kinsler were also on Israel's radar.

It seemed likely that Braun would now play for Team USA instead of Israel.

Meanwhile, Spain advanced to the main draw, and manager Mauro Mazzotti said his team will try to bring in major league reinforcements. They will be needed because the step up in class in March will be steep. Instead of facing minor leaguers, Spain will now try to keep from getting awed by American, Puerto Rican, Dominican and Venezuelan rosters loaded with major league stars. And that's not to mention two-time WBC champion Japan.

Mazzotti said his team will use the time between the qualifier and the main even to look for players with a parent or grandparent who has Spain citizenship.

"We have (a lot) of research to do," he said. "We could try to reach out to Cuban players (who have left Cuba) as well . . . MLB has helped us out a bit."

Cubans with Spanish ancestry played a major role for Spain, such as shortstop Yunesky Sanchez, who hit the game-winning two-run single in the 10th in the championship game. Another was the 29-year-old Cuban-American Figueroa, who reached as high as Triple-A with the Orioles and is now playing independent ball. He said he welcomes any reinforcements.

"They will make our team more powerful," he said. "There are going to be some players on our (current) team who will lose their (roster) spots (to

OVERALL STANDINGS

TEAM	W	L	PCT	TEAM	W	L	PCT
U.S.A.	7	2	.778	Panama	3	3	.500
Chinese Taipei	6	2	.750	Colombia	4	5	.444
Canada	6	3	.667	Venezuela	2	4	.333
South Korea	5	3	.625	Italy	1	4	.200
Japan	5	4	.556	Netherlands	1	4	.200
Australia	3	3	.500	Czech Republic	0	6	.000

Gold Medal Game: USA 6, Canada 2. **Bronze Medal Game:** Chinese Taipei 4, Colombia 1.

LEADERS
(Min 2.0 AB/Team game)

IND. BATTING	G	AVG	AB	R	H	2B	3B	HR	RBI	BB
Phillippi, Marciano, NED	5	.500	10	4	5	1	2	0	0	5
Hodges, Jesse, CAN	9	.484	31	6	15	4	0	1	5	5
Jun, Yoo-young, KOR	8	.478	23	4	11	0	0	0	1	1
McGuire, Reese, USA	9	.462	26	7	12	4	0	0	11	8
Takahashi, Hiroki, JPN	8	.455	22	4	10	2	1	0	2	3
Mineo, Alberto, ITA	5	.450	20	2	9	3	0	0	5	0
Song, Jun-sik, KOR	8	.448	29	2	13	2	2	0	6	4
Vykoukal, Michal, CZE	6	.400	20	2	8	0	0	0	3	1
Arroyo, Christian, USA	9	.387	31	7	12	4	0	0	10	2
Pimentel, Ivan, PAN	5	.385	13	0	5	0	0	0	3	0
Tamura, Tatsuhiro, JPN	9	.364	33	5	12	0	0	0	3	7
Hargreaves, Elliott, AUS	6	.357	28	3	10	2	0	0	3	1
Kim, In-tae, KOR	7	.348	23	6	8	1	0	0	2	7
Martinez, Jeremy, USA	9	.344	32	6	11	2	1	0	9	4
Cano, Cristian, COL	9	.333	33	4	11	3	2	0	7	3

(Min 0.8 IP/Team game)

IND. PITCHING	G	W-L	ERA	SV	IP	H	R	ER	BB	SO
Williams, Garrett, USA	2	1-0	0.00	0	11.2	9	0	0	5	13
Olson, Ryan, USA	2	1-0	0.00	0	10	2	0	0	2	9
Johma, Ryuhei, JPN	3	1-0	0.00	0	9.2	7	1	0	1	3
Indriago, Carlos, VEN	2	0-0	0.00	0	8.1	8	0	0	2	5
Perez, Dewin, COL	3	1-0	0.00	0	7.1	6	0	0	6	3
Dedek, Vojtech, CZE	4	0-0	0.00	0	6.2	5	1	0	2	4
Lee, Geon-wook, KOR	5	1-0	0.48	0	18.2	9	1	1	3	20
Dykxhoorn, Brock, CAN	3	2-0	0.73	0	12.1	6	1	1	4	8
Guzman, Omar, PAN	3	1-1	0.77	0	11.2	9	1	1	5	7
Jang, Hyun-sik, KOR	4	1-0	0.77	0	11.2	9	2	1	3	12

USA 18U OVERALL STATISTICS

BATTERS	AVG	AB	R	H	HR	RBI	SB
Keegan Thompson	1.000	1	0	1	0	1	0
Reese McGuire	.462	26	7	12	0	11	3
Christian Arroyo	.387	31	7	12	0	10	2
Jeremy Martinez	.344	32	6	11	0	8	2
Chris Okey	.333	27	6	9	0	4	2
Cavan Biggio	.323	31	1	10	0	3	3
Garrett Williams	.286	7	1	2	0	1	1
Ryan Boldt	.250	32	11	8	0	3	12
Dom Nunez	.241	29	7	7	0	3	3
Bryson Brigman	.214	14	3	3	0	2	3
Willie Abreu	.200	30	5	6	0	3	4
Connor Heady	.200	5	1	1	0	1	0
Andy McGuire	.176	17	5	3	0	0	2

PITCHERS	W-L	ERA	G	SV	IP	H	BB	SO
Ryan Olson	1-0	0.58	3	0	12	6	3	9
Stephen Gonsalves	2-0	0.74	3	0	19	15	7	12
Keegan Thompson	0-2	0.88	4	0	8	7	4	8
Garrett Williams	1-0	1.26	4	0	16.2	16	9	18
Connor Heady	0-0	1.31	4	0	5.1	3	5	6
Ian Clarkin	1-0	1.70	4	0	12.1	8	6	9
Dominic Taccolini	1-0	2.47	3	0	11.1	5	6	10
Carson Sands	1-1	4.77	3	0	7.1	6	7	5
Kevin Davis	1-0	4.94	5	1	11.1	11	10	13
John Kilichowski	0-0	5.25	3	0	2.2	2	4	0

a major leaguer). That's part of the business side of baseball, but I'm confident I will keep my spot."

Figueroa, who hit .438 at Jupiter's Roger Dean Stadium as his team went 3-1, called Spain's 9-7, 10-inning win over Israel in the final "one of the most exciting games I've ever played."

Israel manager Brad Ausmus, who had an 18-year big league career as a catcher, said Spain was deserving of the title. "No sour grapes," Ausmus said. "We knew the format coming in."

Mazzotti said that with the Netherlands winning the World Cup in 2011 and now Spain advancing to the WBC main draw, he is no longer being asked if baseball is played in Europe.

International Amateur

While USA Baseball's College National Team had a summer without a major international tournament, IBAF staged World Championships at both the 18-and-under and 15-and-under levels. It was the first for the 15-and-under level after IBAF reorganized its amateur levels during its December 2011 congress, with demarcations at 12, 15, 18 and 21 years old.

Due to security concerns, the U.S. did not participate in the 15-and-under event held in Chihuahua, Mexico, which Venezuela won by upsetting Cuba 10-2.

"We have a close relationship with Major League Baseball and their security department," USA Baseball's Jeff Singer said. "We looked into Chihuahua and weren't really comfortable, security-wise, especially considering the State Department's travel advisory to that region of Mexico."

In order to provide a competitive international experience for the players, USA Baseball worked with Major League Baseball to set up a four-game series against some of the best young talent in the Caribbean, with two teams from the Dominican Republic's newly formed MLB Amateur Prospect League (with the talent split up along geographic lines) and one traveling in from Puerto Rico.

The 18-and-under team was able to play in the World Championships and made the most of its trip. USA Baseball's 18-and-under team, managed by former big leaguer Scott Brosius, capped off its 10-day stay in Seoul, South Korea, with a gold medal as it defeated Canada 6-2.

The win gives the 18-and-under team its first gold medal in a world championship tournament since 1999, a team led by future big leaguers such as Joe Mauer, Carlos Quentin and Jeff Baker.

"To be able to come home with the gold medal was great," Brosius said. "We were thrilled for the players, coaches, and all of USA Baseball to be able to have gold medal back here in this country."

After going 4-1 in pool play, Team USA dropped the first of its three crossover games, as it fell 1-0 to Canada. Some players thought that they had blown their shot at the gold medal until Brosius—the head coach at Division III Linfield (Ore.)—spoke with them.

"My biggest message after that game was, 'Don't go to bed losing hope,' " Brosius said. "Possibilities still existed for us to get back to the gold medal game, but all of those possibilities required us to win our final two games. Essentially the message was, 'We have to be the aggressors.' We wanted to be the ones that went out and earned it instead of waiting for something to fall in our laps."

"We actually thought we were done," said shortstop Christian Arroyo (Hernando HS, Brooksville, Fla.). "When Coach Brosius told us we had a chance to get back in there we were pumped."

Just three days after Brosius' speech, the two sides met again in the championship game, and Team USA never looked back after it scored three runs in the bottom of the third to break a 1-1 tie.

Arroyo, who played every inning at shortstop, was named the tournament's MVP, but the Brookville, Fla., native was quick to deflect his personal accolades.

"I was just happy to get a gold medal in the first place," Arroyo said. "Personally, I think my buddy Reese McGuire played better than I did. That kid was one of the most clutch kids that I've ever played with."

Jeremy Martinez also joined Arroyo on the all-tournament team. Reese McGuire and outfielder/lefthander Garrett Williams both had tremendous tournaments but were not included in any awards. McGuire hit .456/.583/.615 (12-for-26) and Williams finished with the tournament's best ERA, as the lefthander did not allow a run and struck out 13 over 11⅔ innings.

After a series of long flights back to their respective hometowns, the players, coaches, and staff members couldn't help but to reflect upon their historic achievement.

"It still hasn't hit me," Arroyo said. "It was absolutely the most incredible experience of my life. It takes a group of 20 special young men to come together and form a brotherhood and that is exactly what we did."

"You don't know what you are going to get in international play," team director Brant Ust said. "There are a lot of variables and factors that can come in to play in these tournaments and it is quite an accomplishment for the players and coaches to be a part of that—to be recognized as the group that brought the gold back to the U.S."

INTERNATIONAL

Barcelo turns hero in Veracruz championship

Lorenzo Barcelo was a key piece of the 1997 white flag trade, when the Chicago White Sox traded three big league pitchers to the San Francisco Giants for six prospects.

Barcelo was one of the prospects and wound up spending parts of three seasons in the majors with the White Sox before injuries seemingly ended his career. But after five arm surgeries, Barcelo—who had not pitched since 2003—returned to the game as a 31-year-old in 2009, and he has become a regular in the Mexican League.

In 2012, Barcelo put himself back on the big league map by pitching Veracruz to the Mexican League championship. He was 6-5, 3.56 in the regular season for Puebla before being sold to Veracruz in July. He become the Red Eagles' playoff ace, winning all six of his playoff starts, including a Game Seven victory against Aguascalientes.

Barcelo, who five years ago was working at a Home Depot in Tucson, Ariz., while trying to work his way back into baseball, went 6-0, 1.06 in the postseason, including a pair of wins in the seven-game finals. He pitched seven innings in the final, giving up six hits, one walk and one run while striking out five. He was named series MVP as he led Veracruz to its first Mexican League championship in 42 years.

As a reward, Barcelo signed with the Dodgers in September, pitching one game for Triple-A Albuquerque. He became a minor league free agent again in November.

Catcher Humberto Sosa was the team's top offensive force, hitting .309 with four homers and 14 RBIs, while outfielder Jorge Guzman contributed a team-high 19 postseason RBIs.

Veracruz finished the regular season with the league's second-best winning percentage, just behind fellow Southern Division foe Quintana Roo. The Red Eagles led the league with a 3.69 ERA and 12 shutouts during the regular season, and complemented the pitching with an offense that belted 127 home runs in 112 games, good for fifth in the league.

Cuban expatriate Michel Abreu, who previously played in both the Mets and Marlins farm systems, narrowly missed winning the Mexican League triple crown during a monster season. Abreu won the "modern" triple crown, leading in batting, on-base and slugging percentage while hitting .371/.474/.678. He ranked second in home runs with 29—three behind 30-year-old catcher Carlos Rodriguez of Aguascalientes—and led the league with 106 RBIs. His Monterrey club won the Northern Division in the regular season and swept its first-round playoff series before losing to Aguascalientes in six games.

Aguascalientes had relied on power all season, from Rodriguez to 38-year-old ex-big leaguer Mendy Lopez (27 homers), but also had a shutdown bullpen in the postseason, led by former Astros righty Sammy Gervacio.

STANDINGS & LEADERS

NORTH	W	L	PCT	GB
Sultanes de Monterrey	67	45	.598	—
Rieleros de Aguascalientes	59	49	.546	6 ½
Saraperos de Saltillo	59	50	.541	6 ½
Diablos Rojos del Mexico	61	52	.540	6 ½
Acereros del Norte	57	56	.504	10 ½
Pericos de Puebla	52	57	.477	13 ½
Vaqueros de la Laguna	48	63	.432	18 ½
Broncos de Reynosa	44	68	.393	23

SOUTH	W	L	PCT	GB
Tigres de Quintana Roo	70	42	.625	—
Rojos del Aguila de Veracruz	67	44	.604	2 ½
Olmecas de Tabasco	59	50	.541	9 ½
Guerreros de Oaxaca	56	52	.519	12
Piratas de Campeche	51	60	.459	18 ½
Delfines de Ciudad del Carmen	51	60	.459	18 ½
Leones de Yucatan	46	66	.411	24
Petroleros de Minatitlan	40	73	.354	30 ½

INDIVIDUAL BATTING LEADERS

PLAYER, TEAM	AVG	AB	R	H	2B	3B	HR	RBI	BB	SO	SB
Abreu, Michel, MTY	.371	367	81	136	26	0	29	106	72	75	0
Gastelum, Carlos, TIG	.363	435	94	158	23	1	9	52	42	61	6
#Valdez, Alex, CDC	.359	390	76	140	22	7	19	78	38	62	11
*Valenzuela, Mario, MEX	.357	375	72	134	23	0	22	77	35	65	2
*Romero, Alex, TIG	.349	415	79	145	20	0	14	74	40	35	6
Canizares, Barbaro, OAX	.348	382	85	133	36	0	28	103	74	64	2
*Harper, Brett, MVA	.343	321	58	110	16	0	27	77	40	71	1
Lindsey, John, LAG	.341	287	58	98	20	0	21	64	27	67	1
*Rivera, Carlos, VER	.340	385	56	131	25	0	17	76	47	58	2
Orantes, Ramon, TAB	.338	361	48	122	18	2	6	53	28	42	4
Lamas, Antonio, MVA	.336	455	81	153	34	3	15	81	28	71	9
*Terrazas, Ivan, MEX	.334	374	62	125	25	5	13	60	39	61	4
*Garcia, Karim, MTY	.334	380	73	127	23	3	22	80	30	86	8
Salas, Issmael, SAL	.333	339	78	113	23	1	19	61	28	59	4
Aguilar, Jose, REY	.332	298	45	99	13	8	4	35	27	48	13

PITCHER, TEAM	W	L	ERA	G	SV	IP	H	R	ER	BB	SO
Ruiz, Miguel, CAM	9	8	2.42	22	0	130	114	44	35	26	84
Castillo Ripalda, Jesus, REY	6	3	2.43	18	0	93	80	30	25	20	62
Corcoran, Tim, CDC	7	4	2.50	16	0	94	80	32	26	24	74
Ramirez, Miguel, TIG	9	2	2.53	19	0	103	87	37	29	26	52
*Rodriguez, Daniel, SAL	11	5	2.54	20	0	117	101	38	33	46	135
*Solis, Tomas, VER	14	4	3.05	22	0	130	111	46	44	36	99
Negrin, Yoanner, TAB	7	6	3.12	24	1	104	101	45	36	51	78
*Rivera, Oscar, YUC	10	8	3.12	22	0	133	130	56	46	40	91
Ramirez, Ramon A., YUC	9	9	3.25	26	2	136	124	59	49	43	123
Barcelo, Lorenzo, VER	7	5	3.34	20	0	119	122	48	44	30	72

Yomiuri claims 22nd Japan Series

BY WAYNE GRACZYK

The Central League's Tokyo Yomiuri Giants won the 2012 Japan Series, defeating the Pacific League's Hokkaido Nippon-Ham Fighters. It marked the 22nd time the team known as "Japan's Yankees" has won the championship of Japanese professional baseball. Victory came in Game Six of the series.

Managed by Tatsunori Hara, regular season pennant winner Yomiuri advanced to the Japan Series by beating the second-place Chunichi Dragons of Nagoya in the final stage of the Central League Climax Series, coming back from a 3-1 deficit to take the final three games. Chunichi had knocked off the third-place Tokyo Yakult Swallows in the Climax Series' first stage.

The Fighters, led by rookie manager Hideki Kuriyama, got to the Japan Series by beating the regular season third-place Fukuoka SoftBank Hawks in the Pacific League Climax Series final stage. The Hawks advanced by winning over the second-place Saitama Seibu Lions in the Climax Series first stage.

A total of 76 foreigners played in the Japanese leagues in a season again dominated by pitching. Yakult Swallows fence-buster Wladimir Balentien won the Central League home run crown for the second straight year, belting 31 out of the parks. However, the former Seattle Mariners major leaguer did not qualify for listing among the CL leading hitters because, due to injury, he did not have the required number of minimum plate appearances.

Other foreign standouts included Balentien's Yakult teammate, closer Tony Barnette, who tied for the Central League lead in saves with 33. Korean slugger Dae Ho Lee led the Pacific League with 91 RBIs. Yakult's Lastings Milledge batted .300 with 21 homers, while Wily Mo Pena also hit 21 home runs for the Fukuoka SoftBank Hawks. Both were playing their first seasons in Japan.

American pitchers D.J. Houlton of Yomiuri and Seth Greisinger of the Chiba Lotte Marines both logged 12-8 records, and Hiroshima Carp closer Kam Mickolio racked up 21 saves.

Attendance in Japanese baseball was down slightly from 2011, with the Central League drawing 11,790,536 fans, a decrease of 0.02 percent. The Pacific League attracted 9,579,690 spectators, down about two percent.

Three all-star games were played in July, with the Central League winning games at Osaka Dome and Matsuyama, and the Pacific League triumphant at Morioka in Iwate Prefecture, an area hard hit by the devastating earthquake and tsunami in March 2011. The Pacific League continues to lead the series, 78-73, with nine mile games since 1950.

Three pitchers threw no-hitters in Japan in 2012: Hiroshima Carp ace Kenta Maeda blanked the Yokohama DeNA Baystars April 4; Giants lefty Toshiya Sugiuchi no-hit the Rakuten Eagles in an inter-league game May 30; and Orix Buffaloes righthander Yuuki Nishi tossed the first no-hitter in the Pacific League since 2000, beating the SoftBank Hawks on Oct. 8.

A trio of Japanese hitters reached 2,000 career hits during the season to join the *Meikyukai*, or Golden Players Club, for batters who reach 2,000 hits or pitchers who accumulate 200 lifetime victories. The new members are Yakult infielder Shinya Miyamoto, Nippon-Ham first baseman-outfielder Atsunori Inaba and SoftBank slugger Hiroki Kokubo, who retired after the season.

Another notable retirement in 2012 was that of Hanshin Tigers outfielder Tomoaki Kanemoto. The 44-year-old, 21-year veteran holds the world record of 1,492 consecutive games played without missing an inning during his time with the Hiroshima Carp and Hanshin. Kanemoto's career stats include 2,539 hits, 476 home runs and 1,521 RBIs, ranking him high among the all-time leaders in most offensive categories in Japanese baseball. He was a 10-time Central League all-star and the league MVP in 2005.

Just missing the career 2,000-hit mark in 2012 was 12-year Japan pro baseball veteran Alex Ramirez, who hit .300 with 19 home runs but finished the year with 1,993 career hits since coming to Japan in 2001. The Venezuelan played seven years with the Yakult Swallows and four with the Yomiuri Giants before transferring to the Baystars this year. He expects to become the first foreigner to join the GPC during the 2013 season.

Free-agent Japanese players possibly headed for the major leagues in 2013 include two Hanshin Tigers: closer Kyuji Fujikawa and shortstop Takashi Toritani. Another is Seibu shortstop Hiroyuki Nakajima, who was posted by the Lions following the 2012 season. The Yankees had made the highest bid for Nakajima but could not reach a contract agreement, so he returned for another year with Seibu. He has now reached the nine-year overseas free-agent qualification.

INTERNATIONAL

CENTRAL LEAGUE

	W	L	T	PCT.	GB
Yomiuri Giants	86	43	15	.667	—
Chunichi Dragons	75	53	16	.586	10 ½
Tokyo Yakult Swallows	68	65	11	.511	20
Hiroshima Carp	61	71	12	.462	26 ½
Hanshin Tigers	55	75	14	.423	31 ½
Yokohama DeNA Baystars	46	85	13	.351	41

CLIMAX SERIES PLAYOFFS—First Stage: Chunichi defeated Tokyo Yakult 2-1 in best-of-three series. **Final Stage:** Yomiuri defeated Chunichi 4-3 in best-of-seven series.

INDIVIDUAL BATTING LEADERS
(MINIMUM 446 PLATE APPEARANCES)

	AVG.	AB	R	H	2B	3B	HR	RBI	SB
Abe, Shinnosuke, Giants	.340	467	72	159	22	1	27	104	0
Sakamoto, Hayato, Giants	.311	557	87	173	35	2	14	69	16
Oshima, Yohei, Dragons	.310	555	83	172	19	5	1	13	32
Chono, Hisayoshi, Giants	.301	574	84	173	29	2	14	60	20
Milledge, Lastings, Swallows	.300	476	73	143	23	1	21	65	9
Ramirez, Alex, Baystars	.300	476	40	143	25	0	19	76	0
Kawabata, Shingo, Swallows	.298	453	52	135	15	5	4	49	3
Wada, Kazuhiro, Dragons	.285	508	52	145	32	2	9	63	2
Ibata, Hirokazu, Dragons	.284	489	35	139	17	0	2	35	4
Nakamura, Norihiro, Baystars	.274	442	50	121	24	1	11	61	1
Tanaka, Hiroyasu, Swallows	.274	486	48	133	16	1	2	40	1
Aranami, Sho, Baystars	.268	504	53	135	16	7	1	25	24
Hatakeyama, Kazuhiro, Swallows	.266	455	49	121	21	1	13	55	2
Toritani, Takashi, Tigers	.262	515	62	135	22	6	8	59	15
Murton, Matt, Tigers	.260	453	39	118	18	2	5	38	2

REMAINING NORTH AMERICAN AND LATIN PLAYERS

	AVG.	AB	R	H	2B	3B	HR	RBI	SB
Balentien, Wladimir, Swallows	.272	353	58	96	13	0	31	81	1
Eldred, Brad, Carp	.262	225	22	59	10	0	11	35	0
Blanco, Tony, Dragons	.248	311	44	77	10	0	24	65	2
Stavinoha, Nick, Carp	.238	181	19	43	8	0	9	24	0
Gonzalez, Edgar, Giants	.236	174	13	41	12	0	4	19	0
Brazell, Craig, Tigers	.233	275	21	64	11	0	12	43	0
Salazar, Oscar, Baystars	.222	27	1	6	1	0	0	1	0
Ruiz, Randy, Baystars	.210	62	5	13	2	0	2	5	0
Bowker, John, Giants	.196	184	12	36	5	0	3	10	2
Diaz, Victor, Dragons	.174	23	1	4	0	0	0	1	0

INDIVIDUAL PITCHING LEADERS
(MINIMUM 144 INNINGS)

	W	L	ERA	G	SV	IP	H	BB	SO
Maeda, Kenta, Carp	14	7	1.53	29	0	206	161	44	171
Nomura, Yusuke, Carp	9	11	1.98	27	0	173	143	52	103
Utsumi, Tetsuya, Giants	15	6	1.98	28	0	186	173	40	121
Sugiuchi, Toshiya, Giants	12	4	2.04	24	0	163	116	43	172
Tateyama, Shohei, Swallows	12	8	2.25	25	0	168	141	45	119
Otake, Kan, Carp	11	5	2.36	24	0	145	144	43	85
Nomi, Atsushi, Tigers	10	10	2.42	29	0	182	157	37	172
Yamauchi, Soma, Dragons	10	7	2.43	24	0	148	128	32	68
Houlton, D.J., Giants	8	8	2.45	25	0	158	116	44	132
Messenger, Randy, Tigers	10	11	2.52	30	0	197	165	65	166
Standridge, Jason, Tigers	7	12	2.69	25	0	150	134	45	102
Miura, Daisuke, Baystars	9	9	2.86	25	0	183	160	48	107
Sawamura, Hirokazu, Giants	10	10	2.86	27	0	170	172	54	138
Roman, Orlando, Swallows	9	11	3.04	26	0	166	152	69	96
Takasaki, Kentaro, Baystars	7	10	3.20	24	0	152	155	40	97
Bullington, Bryan, Carp	7	14	3.23	29	0	176	166	44	137

REMAINING U.S., CANADIAN AND LATIN PLAYERS

	W	L	ERA	G	SV	IP	H	BB	SO
Romero, Levi, Giants	0	0	0.00	1	0	1	0	1	1
Mathieson, Scott, Giants	2	0	1.71	40	10	42	30	11	48
Barnette, Tony, Swallows	1	2	1.82	57	33	54	44	11	52
Sosa, Jorge, Dragons	5	1	1.85	53	4	63	54	19	50
Soto, Enyelbert, Dragons	4	1	2.17	18	0	62	45	21	48
Mickolio, Kam, Carp	3	5	2.79	61	21	58	42	14	54
Sarfate, Dennis, Carp	2	5	2.90	47	9	50	43	24	44
Gonzalez, Dicky, Giants	4	1	3.20	11	0	45	57	22	26
Mann, Brandon, BayStars	2	8	5.32	16	0	69	66	29	42

PACIFIC LEAGUE

	W	L	T	PCT.	GB
Hokkaido Nippon Ham Fighters	74	59	11	.556	—
Saitama Seibu Lions	72	63	9	.533	3
Fukuoka SoftBank Hawks	67	65	12	.508	6 ½
Tohoku Rakuten Golden Eagles	67	67	10	.500	7 ½
Chiba Lotte Marines	62	67	15	.481	10
Orix Buffaloes	57	77	10	.425	17 ½

CLIMAX SERIES PLAYOFFS—First Stage: Fukuoka SoftBank defeated Saitama Seibu 2-1 in best-of-three series. **Final Stage:** Hokkaido Nippon Ham defeated Fukuoka SoftBank 4-0 in best-of-seven series.

INDIVIDUAL BATTING LEADERS
(MINIMUM 446 PLATE APPEARANCES)

	AVG.	AB	R	H	2B	3B	HR	RBI	SB
Kakunaka, Katsuya, Marines	.312	477	51	149	30	5	3	61	8
Nakajima, Hiroyuki, Lions	.311	499	69	155	29	1	13	74	7
Itoi, Yoshio, Fighters	.304	510	72	155	21	3	9	48	22
Uchikawa, Seiichi, Hawks	.300	523	44	157	21	3	7	53	6
Tanaka, Kensuke, Fighters	.300	457	49	137	14	3	3	32	13
Akiyama, Shogo, Lions	.293	403	50	118	17	8	4	37	10
Inaba, Atsunori, Fighters	.290	449	46	130	23	3	10	61	0
Kuriyama, Takumi, Lions	.289	394	57	114	17	1	2	33	3
Yo, Daikan, Fighters	.287	533	71	153	28	5	7	55	17
Lee, Dae Ho, Buffaloes	.286	525	54	150	25	2	24	91	0
Akaminai, Ginji, Eagles	.280	432	37	121	16	2	4	45	8
Pena, Wily Mo, Hawks	.280	461	52	129	30	2	21	76	2
Nemoto, Shunichi, Marines	.279	512	58	143	25	4	9	41	6
Hasegawa, Yuya, Hawks	.278	403	41	112	15	3	4	37	16
German, Esteban, Lions	.270	507	55	137	20	4	3	60	41

REMAINING U.S. AND LATIN PLAYERS

	AVG.	AB	R	H	2B	3B	HR	RBI	SB
Whitesell, Josh, Marines	.309	223	24	69	13	0	9	43	0
Carter, Chris, Lions	.294	126	9	37	8	0	4	27	0
Ortiz, Jose, Lions	.286	199	20	57	8	0	9	21	0
Baldiris, Aarom, Buffaloes	.264	503	37	133	31	2	10	55	1
Scales, Bobby, Buffaloes	.262	305	42	80	16	3	5	28	4
Hoffpauir, Micah, Fighters	.247	296	28	73	13	0	14	37	1
Sledge, Terrmel, Fighters	.232	138	12	32	7	1	5	23	0
Garcia, Luis, Eagles	.227	269	20	61	12	0	7	30	0
Terrero, Luis, Eagles	.153	111	8	17	2	0	1	7	2

INDIVIDUAL PITCHING LEADERS
(MINIMUM 144 INNINGS)

	W	L	ERA	G	SV	IP	H	BB	SO
Yoshikawa, Mitsuo, Fighters	14	5	1.71	25	0	174	108	45	158
Tanaka, Masahiro, Eagles	10	4	1.87	22	0	173	160	19	189
Settsu, Tadashi, Hawks	17	5	1.91	27	0	193	148	54	153
Otonari, Kenji, Hawks	12	8	2.03	25	0	177	147	46	134
Greisinger, Seth, Marines	12	8	2.24	25	0	169	144	24	112
Takeda, Masaru, Fighters	11	7	2.36	28	0	183	159	30	90
Makita, Kazuhisa, Lions	13	9	2.43	27	0	178	175	36	108
Kishi, Takayuki, Lions	11	12	2.45	26	0	188	141	40	150
Kisanuki, Hiroshi, Buffaloes	5	9	2.60	24	0	152	138	42	96
Wolfe, Brian, Fighters	10	9	2.66	26	0	149	155	40	83

REMAINING U.S., ITALIAN AND LATIN PLAYERS

	W	L	ERA	G	SV	IP	H	BB	SO
Falkenborg, Brian, Hawks	0	1	1.57	23	13	23	14	8	26
Williams, Randy, Lions	4	3	1.70	55	4	42	30	23	41
Maestri, Alessandro, Buffaloes	4	3	2.17	8	0	50	45	12	40
Rasner, Darrell, Eagles	1	3	2.79	46	6	42	36	12	32
Jimenez, Kelvin, Eagles	5	10	3.15	18	0	109	102	39	63
Heuser, Jim, Eagles	1	2	3.17	58	1	48	33	15	29
Duckworth, Brandon, Eagles	3	1	3.22	6	0	36	32	8	22
Mollebon, Dustin, Fighters	2	1	3.27	23	0	22	20	8	18
Doyle, Terry, Hawks	1	1	3.55	3	0	13	14	9	7
MacLane, Evan, Buffaloes	5	4	3.91	18	0	69	74	26	28
Penn, Hayden, Marines	1	2	3.98	4	0	20	21	7	15
Rosa, Carlos, Marines	0	1	6.00	16	0	15	24	6	13
Mathis, Doug, Marines	1	4	6.49	6	0	26	41	8	14
Gonzalez, Enrique, Lions	2	5	7.04	16	3	23	40	12	16
Pinto, Renyel, Hawks	1	1	7.36	2	0	7	9	7	6
Keppel, Bobby, Fighters	0	1	9.00	2	0	6	12	2	2

INTERNATIONAL

Lions Repeat

The Samsung Lions won only one Korean Baseball Organization championship prior to 2002. But in the last decade, the Lions have become Korea's premier franchise. In 2012, the Lions repeated as champions for the second time since 2005, beating the SK Wyverns.

This was a rematch of the 2011 championship series, and Samsung had a key leg up by earning a bye all the way to the Korean Series by virtue of a first-place regular-season finish. The Wyverns, who played in their sixth consecutive Korean Series, finished second in the regular season and beat the Lotte Giants in the playoffs in five games to advance to the championship series.

The Lions won the Game Six clincher 7-0 as Lee Seung-yeop was named series MVP. Lee, who played for the Lions from 1995-2003 before an eight-season stint in Japan, hit .348 with a home run and seven RBIs in the series.

Korea's top talent, Hanwha lefthander Ryu Hyun-jin, went 9-9, 2.66 overall in 2012, his seventh season and his first with fewer than 11 victories. The Dodgers paid $25.7 million for the rights to sign Ryu, who Ryu 27 complete games in seven seasons in the KBO and is 98-52, 2.80 overall.

STANDINGS & LEADERS

Team	W	L	T	Pct	GB
Samsung Lions	80	51	2	.611	—
SK Wyverns	71	59	3	.546	8 ½
Doosan Bears	68	62	3	.523	11 ½
Lotte Giants	65	62	6	.512	13
KIA Tigers	62	65	6	.488	16
Nexen Heroes	61	69	3	.469	18 ½
LG Twins	57	72	4	.442	22
Hanwha Eagles	53	77	3	.408	26 ½

INDIVIDUAL BATTING LEADERS

PLAYER, TEAM	AVG	AB	R	H	2B	3B	HR	RBI	BB	SO
Kim Tae-kyun, HAN	.363	416	61	151	24	0	16	80	81	69
Son Ah-seop, LOT	.314	503	61	158	26	0	5	58	41	79
Kang Jung-ho, NEX	.314	436	77	137	32	0	25	82	71	78
Park Suk-min, SAM	.312	443	79	138	19	3	23	91	72	83
Jung Sung-hoon, LG	.310	365	50	113	27	3	12	53	65	62
Lee Jin-young, LG	.307	365	39	112	18	0	4	55	44	41
Lee Seung-yeop, SAM	.307	488	84	150	28	2	21	85	59	101
Jin Gap-yong, SAM	.307	313	27	96	15	1	6	57	17	46

INDIVIDUAL PITCHING
Minimum 70 Innings

PITCHER, TEAM	W	L	ERA	G	SV	IP	H	BB	SO	AVG
Park Hee-soo, SK	8	1	1.32	65	6	82	52	27	93	.189
Yoo Won-sang, LG	4	2	2.19	58	3	74	70	13	43	.249
Brandon Knight, Nexen	16	4	2.20	30	0	209	180	53	102	.240
Noh Kyung-eun, Doosan	12	6	2.53	42	0	146	106	69	133	.204
Shane Youman, Lotte	13	7	2.55	29	0	180	156	56	142	.239
Seo Jae-Weong, KIA	9	8	2.59	29	0	160	143	51	97	.242
Ryu Hyun-Jin, Hanwha	9	9	2.66	27	0	183	153	46	210	.232
Yoon Sung-hwan, Samsung	9	6	2.84	19	0	114	112	26	81	.264

Lin's homers power Lamigo

Behind shortstop Lin Chih-sheng's 8-for-17 championship series performance that included three home runs in five games, the Lamigo Monkeys cruised to the Taiwan Series championship, their second Chinese Professional Baseball League title in team history.

Lin had seven RBIs as he earned series MVP honors in helping the franchise, formerly known as the La New Bears, win its first title since 2006. Lin went just 3-for-21 in last year's Taiwan Series, a loss to the Uni-President Lions. In this year's rematch, Lin showed the power that allowed him to hit a league-high 24 regular-season homers in a .317/.413/.579 season that also included 82 RBIs in 99 games.

He had support in the series from a newer teammate in outfielder Chen Guan-ren, whose lefthanded bat was acquired during the season from the Brother Elephants. The combination of the two proved too much in the title series as Chen went 7-for-21 with four RBIs, after batting .369 following his midseason trade.

American pitchers figured prominently in the league leaders as Jon Leicester led the CPBL in ERA, while righthander Matt DeSalvo was Lamigo's ace, leading the league in strikeouts.

STANDINGS & LEADERS

Team	W	L	T	Pct	GB
Lamigo Monkeys	67	49	4	.575	—
Uni-President Lions	65	52	3	.554	2 ½
Brother Elephants	53	57	10	.463	11
Sinon Bulls	44	68	8	.383	21

INDIVIDUAL BATTING LEADERS

PLAYER, TEAM	AVG	AB	R	H	2B	3B	HR	RBI
Pan Wu-xiong, Uni	.388	312	62	121	28	5	9	57
Lin Yi-quan, Sinon	.371	450	72	167	46	3	13	92
Chou Szu-Chi, Brother	.365	433	74	158	27	3	21	91
Zhang Zheng-wei, Brother	.362	489	91	172	26	15	0	50
Chang Tai-shan, Uni	.333	448	75	149	36	0	17	96
Chan Chi-Yao, Lamigo	.329	422	67	139	21	2	2	51
Kao Chih-Kang, Uni	.322	339	37	109	15	3	2	37
Peng Cheng-min, Brother	.320	440	78	141	28	0	14	88
Lin Chih-sheng, Lamigo	.317	363	87	115	21	1	24	82
Chung Cheng-yu, Lamigo	.304	441	80	134	30	7	9	72

INDIVIDUAL PITCHING LEADERS

PITCHER, TEAM	W	L	ERA	G	SV	IP	WHIP	BB	SO
Jon Leicester, Uni	12	5	2.48	27	0	167	1.19	43	111
Matt DeSalvo, Lamigo	11	6	2.77	22	0	146	1.31	63	137
Kamada Yuya, Brother	16	7	3.15	25	0	171	1.14	26	119
Lin Yu-Ching, Brother	8	11	3.91	26	0	147	1.47	56	111
Lin Chen-hua, Sinon	7	10	3.96	21	0	125	1.37	44	77

INTERNATIONAL

ITALY: Bologna, San Marino Share Spoils

BY HARVEY SAHKER

San Marino defeated Rimini in the Italy Series in six games. It was the team's third Italian Baseball League title and fourth finals appearance in the last five years.

San Marino second baseman Francesco Imperiali was chosen as series MVP. Imperiali hit .364 in the Series and ended Game Six with a walk-off double in the bottom of the ninth inning. He hit a three-run homer earlier in the game.

San Marino also benefited from the addition of lefthander Chris Cooper, who joined the club in 2012 after spending the previous four seasons with Grosseto. Owner of a 7-16, 4.53 record between 2009 and 2011, the former minor leaguer had his best year in Italy (7-2, 2.27).

Takahiko "G.G." Sato

Bologna won the pennant when it beat San Marino on the final day of the regular season. The teams finished with the same record, but Bologna was awarded first because it took four of the six games in which the two clubs went head to head. The Bologna offense was bolstered by the addition of Japanese outfielder Takahiko "G.G." Sato. A former Phillies farmhand who spent three seasons in the U.S. minor leagues, reaching the low Class A South Atlantic League in 2003, Sato played for the Seibu Lions for seven years. He hit .319 for Bologna and finished in the IBL top 10 in hits, runs and total bases.

Nineteen-year IBL veteran Fabio Betto (10-0, 2.35) extended his regular-season winning streak to 19 games. The Bologna righthander's last regular-season defeat was on the final day of the 2010 season. Betto turned 40 a month after the Italy Series ended.

Bologna also won the European Cup, beating IBL opponent and host Nettuno in the final, which attracted an estimated 4,500 spectators. It was the fifth straight year that an IBL team won the European club title.

Lefty Massimiliano Masin played his 25th season for Nettuno, going 3-1, 1.97 in his spot-starting and relieving roles. Opponents hits just .136 against the intrepid 43-year old.

Former Braves farmhand Osman Marval had a standout season for Parma and finished within two home runs of winning the triple crown. But the accomplishments of the Venezuelan slugger were not enough to earn a post-season berth for the club. Parma hired Marval's countryman and former IBL star player Orlando Munoz as its new manager in October.

Italy also won the European Championship, played in the Netherlands in September. The national team went 9-0 in the competition and outscored opponents 63-10, batting .388 as a team. Former Giants farmhand Tyler LaTorre went 8-for-12 with a home run and six RBIs to help lead the way. It was Italy's 10th continental title and second in a row.

STANDINGS & LEADERS

REGULAR SEASON	W	L	Pct	GB
Unipol Bologna	31	11	.738	—
T&A San Marino	31	11	.738	—
Danesi Caffe' Nettuno	28	14	.667	3
Rimini	28	14	.667	3
Cariparma Parma	21	21	.500	10
Godo Knights	14	28	.333	17
Grosseto	11	31	.262	20
Novara	4	38	.095	27

PLAYOFF ROUND ROBIN	W	L	GB
San Marino	6	3	—
Rimini	5	4	1
Nettuno	5	4	1
Bologna	2	7	4

INDIVIDUAL BATTING LEADERS

PLAYER, TEAM	AVG	AB	R	H	2B	3B	HR	RBI
Osman Marval, PAR	.384	159	33	61	8	1	8	40
Ray Sadler, NET	.265	96	21	35	7	1	4	19
Gabriele Ermini, BOL	.363	146	23	53	7	2	0	18
Rolexis Molina, GRS	.363	160	19	58	14	1	1	23
Alessandro Vaglio, BOL	.340	159	25	54	8	3	1	27
Joe Pereschina, RIM	.335	167	29	56	14	0	1	32
Danilo Sanchez, GOD	.333	141	24	47	7	0	10	40
Juan Carlos Infante, BOL	.327	171	39	56	15	1	4	35
Giuseppe Mazzanti, NET	.326	129	22	42	14	1	1	23
Daniel Bittar, SM	.322	183	36	59	14	2	1	32

INDIVIDUAL PITCHING LEADERS

PITCHER, TEAM	W	L	ERA	G	SV	IP	H	R	ER	BB	SO
Cody Cillo, BOL	2	2	1.19	17	1	38	22	7	5	19	33
Marcos Tabata, RIM	3	0	1.23	14	1	37	26	5	5	11	44
Darwin Cubillan, SM	2	0	1.23	14	5	37	28	11	5	11	34
Matteo d'Angelo, BOL	2	1	1.79	14	5	40	25	9	8	12	39
Juan Figueroa, NET	7	3	1.87	14	1	77	61	19	16	23	79
Santo Hernandez, NET	1	2	1.90	14	3	43	22	10	9	20	73
Pete Sikara, GRS	1	5	1.97	17	6	64	51	20	14	17	87
Tiago da Silva, SM	6	1	2.09	13	0	82	87	26	19	15	72
Jesus Matos, BOL	7	2	2.13	14	0	84	57	26	20	15	81
Ricardo Hernandez, NET	9	3	2.22	14	0	89	67	29	22	25	90

NETHERLANDS: Kinheim Comeback

Kinheim rose up from the brink of elimination in the Dutch Major League semifinals and went on to sweep Neptunus in four games in the Holland Series. It was Kinheim's third national title in seven years.

Veteran righthander Dave Bergman was voted Holland Series MVP after winning Games One and Game Four. Bergman, 31, logged 13 strikeouts in the series finale.

The Dutch semifinals have a triple round robin format and include the four top clubs in the regular-season standings. Defeated by Neptunus in its first three games of the semis, Kinheim fired manager Eelco Jansen and replaced him with assistant Hans Lemmink. Former big leaguer Ralph Milliard was also dropped from the coaching staff. The Haarlem-based club then won four of its final six to finish in a tie for second with the Amsterdam Pirates. Kinheim qualified for the Holland Series because it beat the Pirates in two of their three head-to-head semi-final contests. The Pirates dropped four games by one run in the semis.

Amsterdam hurler Rob Cordemans pitched eight shutout innings in a 1-0 European Cup semifinal loss to Italian club Nettuno. The Pirates then defeated the Rouen Huskies 8-7 to claim the bronze medal in the continental club championship. Cordemans, 38, had a spectacular DML regular season, going 10-1, 0.22 as he allowed just two earned runs in over eighty innings of work. On July 1, Cordemans broke the DML record for most career victories when he picked up win number 151 in a 6-2 decision against Sparta/Feyenoord 6-2 in Rotterdam.

Sparta/Feyenoord fared better against Cordemans than they did in many other games. They were shut out 14 times in the regular season. Sparta/Feyenoord lost its first 11 games and last ten games. During the latter streak, they were shut out six times and were outscored 102-7. The team hit .193 and had an 8.93 ERA. Sparta/Feyenoord were blanked three more times in the promotion-relegation playoffs and lost the best-of-five final to the Dordrecht Hawks three games to two.

Mika de Lincel of the Hoofddorp Pioniers threw the only no-hitter of the DML season, a rain-short-ened, five-inning 3-0 win over HCAW. He issued five free passes in the game.

AROUND EUROPE

■ C.B. Barcelona beat the Valencia Astros three games to one in the Spanish finals. The Astros had reeled off 11- and 14-game winning streaks during the regular season and won the pennant with a 32-4 record. Former Angels farmhand Larry Infante won the triple crown in Spain. The Venezuelan infielder batted .471 with 14 homers and 50 RBIs for Valencia.

■ The Rouen Huskies won their eighth consecutive French title. Rouen defeated the Senart Templars three games to one in the best-of-five finals.

■ Buchbinder Legionäre of Regensburg swept the Paderborn Untouchables in three games in the German Bundesliga finals. Regensburg has won three straight national championships and four in the last five years.

■ One year after they were dethroned as champions of the Czech Republic, Draci Brno reclaimed the title that they had previously won 16 straight times. Draci Brno defeated the Prague Eagles three games to one in the finals.

STANDINGS & LEADERS

REGULAR SEASON	W	L	Pct	GB
Amsterdam Pirates	34	7	.893	—
Neptunus	33	9	.786	1½
Kinheim	27	15	.643	7½
Hoofddorp Pioniers	26	15	.631	8
UVV	25	16	.607	9
HCAW	8	33	.202	26
ADO	8	34	.190	26½
Sparta/Feyenoord	5	37	.119	29½

Standings do no include ties

PLAYOFF ROUND ROBIN	W	L	GB
Neptunus	7	2	—
Kinheim	4	5	3
Amsterdam	4	5	3
Hoofddorp	3	6	4

INDIVIDUAL BATTING LEADERS

PLAYER, TEAM	AVG	AB	R	H	2B	3B	HR	RBI	BB	SO	SB
Bas de Jong, AMS	.370	135	28	50	11	0	3	29	9	23	1
Danny Rombley, UVV	.359	156	28	56	8	1	1	32	24	25	7
Kody Hightower, HCAW	.357	112	20	40	6	1	2	15	11	11	16
Philip Ortez, ADO	.355	166	20	59	13	0	2	30	8	10	7
Rashid Gerard, AMS	.352	122	22	43	2	0	1	22	10	18	1
Zerzinho Croes, HDP	.349	152	29	53	3	0	0	20	10	7	
4 Austin Weymouth, UVV	.344	163	28	56	14	1	0	30	16	8	1
Bryan Engelhardt, KIN	.340	100	18	34	5	0	8	33	19	17	2
Mike Duursma, HDP	.333	144	30	48	8	0	0	27	27	14	4
Mervin Gario, KIN	.333	132	39	44	7	1	0	17	34	23	11

INDIVIDUAL PITCHING LEADERS

PITCHER, TEAM	W	L	ERA	G	SV	IP	H	R	ER	BB	SO
Rob Cordemans, AMS	10	1	0.22	12	0	81	53	6	2	5	94
Derek Tarapacki, UVV	3	0	0.64	27	7	42	20	6	3	7	59
Ben Grover, AMS	9	0	0.86	13	0	94	52	12	9	18	69
Diegomar Markwell, NEP	11	1	1.34	12	0	81	62	15	12	19	62
David Bergman, KIN	9	3	1.52	15	0	101	79	26	17	12	101
Tim Roodenburg, NEP	3	1	1.55	9	0	41	31	11	7	9	17
Kevin Heijstek, NEP	8	3	1.71	13	0	84	66	26	16	20	64
Luke Sommer, KIN	10	2	2.05	14	0	92	76	30	21	10	76
Orlando Yntema, UVV	6	7	2.15	14	0	88	75	33	21	29	60
Joey Evans, HDP	9	2	2.29	14	0	102	72	30	26	18	101

Home run mark falls again

Cuba's 51st Serie Nacional season started with a startling change—the loss of the La Habana team. The national capital's province was split in two, resulting in two teams, Mayabeque and Artemisa.

The awkward 17-team league also instituted other changes that affected play, such as allowing 1960s-style 15-inch-high pitcher's mounds to combat rampant offensive inflation in recent years. Nevertheless, with expansion came another assault on the league's home run record.

Alfredo Despaigne

Outfielders Alexei Bell, Yoenis Cespedes and Alfredo Despaigne and first baseman Jose Abreu have each set the single-season home run record in the last four seasons. With Cespedes gone to the United States and starring for the Athletics, Bell, Granma's Despaigne and Cienfuegos' Abreu duked it out in 2011-12, with Bell trailing.

Bell hit 31 in 2007-2008; Despaigne homered in six straight games in 2008-09 en route to setting the league record with 32; Cespedes and Abreu hit 33 in 2010-2011; then Despaigne and Abreu went back and forth in spring 2012.

Despaigne was first to break the record, but Abreu tied him with 35 entering the season's final day. Despaigne set the new record with No. 36 coming on an inside-the-park homer against Isla de la Juventud.

The home run record helped the 5-foot-9 26-year-old win his third league MVP award, tying a post-Cuban Revolution record held by Wilfredo Sanchez and Omar Linares.

Despite their tremendous power displays, Despaigne and Abreu weren't able to lead their teams to championships. Both of their clubs, Granma in the East and Cienfuegos in the West, finished 54-42. West champ Matanzas and East winner Villa Clara had the league's top records at 58-48, but second-place Industriales beat

Matanzas in the West playoffs while third-place Ciego de Avila won the East playoffs.

Ciego de Avila then beat Industriales 4-1 to win its first championship, winning 4-3 in 11 innings. Yander Guevara pitched into the 11th inning for Ciego before reliever Lazaro Santana got the final two outs. Ricardo Bordon drove in the game-winner with an RBI single to end the championship drought for the 35-year-old franchise.

STANDINGS & LEADERS

WEST	Record	GB
Matanzas	58-38	—
Industriales	55-41	3
Cienfuegos	54-42	4
Sancti Spíritus	49-46	8 ½
Pinar del Rio	47-49	9
Isla de la Juventud	39-57	19
Metropolitanos	38-58	20
Artemisa	36-60	22
Mayabeque	33-63	25

EAST	Record	GB
Villa Clara	58-38	—
Las Tunas	54-41	3 ½
Ciego de Ávila	54-42	4
Granma	54-42	4
Santiago de Cuba	53-43	5
Guantánamo	45-49	12
Holguín	44-52	14
Camagüey	43-53	15

Playoffs

Ciego de Ávila 4, Las Tunas 3   Ciego de Ávila 4, Granma 2
Granma 4, Villa Clara 3   Industriales 4, Matanzas 3
Matanzas 4, Sancti Spíritus 3   Ciego de Ávila 4, Industriales 1
Industriales 4, Cienfuegos 1

INDIVIDUAL BATTING LEADERS

PLAYER, TEAM	AVE	AB	R	H	2B	3B	HR	RBI	BB	SO	SB
J. Dariel Abreu, CFG	.394	282	71	111	18	1	35	99	75	40	1
D. Castro, LTU	.370	316	50	117	12	0	15	73	45	36	3
Y. Samon, GRA	.363	366	63	133	21	2	15	82	43	42	17
R. Reyes, IND	.353	317	54	112	17	2	9	60	45	20	8
Y. Manduley, HOL	.351	370	50	130	14	1	6	58	18	17	8
G. Heredia, MTZ	.343	364	91	125	19	9	10	52	51	38	3
H. Olivera, SCU	.341	214	48	73	10	0	17	42	44	22	0
Y. Mendoza, SSP	.340	291	44	99	18	3	3	43	16	20	0
R. Carlos Ramirez, MET	.339	380	49	129	19	1	4	48	28	36	8
L. Yander La 0, SCU	.335	263	55	88	12	2	2	29	19	20	13
Y. Leyva, CFG	.335	349	58	117	11	5	2	40	47	31	22
A. Ayala, CMG	.333	351	60	117	16	0	12	52	33	35	0
R. Castillo, CAV	.332	376	80	125	28	2	16	66	32	42	22
Y. Hernandez, MTZ	.330	297	66	98	23	6	8	67	80	46	1
S. Perez, IND	.330	312	40	103	12	1	12	66	21	20	1

INDIVIDUAL PITCHING LEADERS

PITCHER, TEAM	W	L	ERA	G	IP	R	ER	BB	SO
Pablo Fernandez Rojas, HOL	7	4	1.52	35	95	25	16	23	70
Vladimir Garcia, CAV	14	5	1.71	22	174	39	33	68	101
Ismel Jimenez, SSP	17	5	2.48	26	185	64	51	39	119
Erlis Casanova, PRI	10	7	2.50	24	112	40	31	35	79
Odrisamer Despaigne, IND	13	8	2.60	24	169	56	49	66	128
Leandro Martinez, GRA	11	4	2.62	15	113	36	33	22	43
Yadier Pedroso, ART	10	6	2.64	20	129	47	38	34	128
Alain Sanchez, VCL	12	3	2.69	18	114	35	34	19	67
Frank Madan, CMG	8	6	2.78	32	110	43	34	40	47
Angel Pena Garcia, SSP	11	4	2.88	20	128	48	41	50	64

Bryan LaHair hit 53 homers in 2011 between Triple-A and winter ball in Venezuela

ANDREW WOOLLEY

Dominican sweeps to Caribbean Series crown

Escogido of the host Dominican Republic won the Caribbean Series, going 4-2 to edge Puerto Rico and Venezuela (3-3 each) and Mexico (2-4) in the round robin tournament.

Righgthander Lorenzo Barcelo, who pitched in the Mexican League in 2011, and Blue Jays right-hander Jerry Gil each threw five shutout innings in their starts for the Dominican squad, while free agent infielder Pablo Ozuna led the Dominican hitters by going 8-for-18 with a .421/.476/.421 batting line.

Escogido won the first four games of the Caribbean Series to quickly clinch the crown. The Caribbean Series championship is the second title in three years for Escogido.

Tigers outfielder Andy Dirks was a standout for Escogido in the clutch, coming through with the game-winning hit in the final game of the Dominican League playoffs to send Escogido to the Caribbean Series.

The 2013 series is scheduled for Hermosillo, Mexico.

First baseman Bryan LaHair won Baseball America's Winter Player of the Year award after slamming 15 home runs to lead the Venezuelan League. That followed LaHair's 2011 season when he led the minor leagues with 38 homers. LaHair went on to a successful season with the Cubs in the major leagues, earning an all-star berth and hitting .259/.334/.450 with 16 home runs.

AUSTRALIAN BASEBALL LEAGUE

TEAM	W	L	PCT	GB
Perth Heat	34	11	.756	—
Melbourne Aces	21	24	.467	13
Adelaide Bite	20	25	.444	14
Brisbane Bandits	20	25	.444	14
Canberra Cavalry	20	25	.444	14
Sydney Blue Sox	20	25	.444	14

PLAYOFFS: Perth defeated Melbourne in best-of-three finals 2-1.

PLAYER, TEAM	AVG	AB	R	H	2B	3B	HR	RBI	BB	SO	SB
Burgamy, Brian, CAN	.409	164	41	67	8	0	12	34	34	20	2
Kennelly, Tim, PER	.374	174	34	65	10	0	10	39	16	22	10
Hightower, Kody, CAN	.361	122	26	44	11	1	6	25	19	17	4
Givens, Mychal, PER	.352	159	32	56	13	0	5	18	6	22	15
Huber, Justin, MEL	.348	155	39	54	7	0	6	26	28	28	3
Barnes, Brandon, SYD	.322	118	23	38	7	0	6	30	9	19	1
Weichard, Paul, MEL	.313	147	33	46	7	0	11	30	20	37	0
Biddle, Elliot, MEL	.310	168	33	52	14	0	13	42	8	41	4
Roberts, Joshua, BRI	.308	182	28	56	15	1	7	31	11	35	3
Jones, James, ADE	.307	166	29	51	11	2	8	25	20	34	6

PITCHER, TEAM	W	L	ERA	G	SV	IP	H	R	ER	BB	SO
Saupold, Warwick, PER	5	3	1.41	10	0	70	43	18	11	22	53
Brown, Geoff, PER	5	0	1.88	8	0	38	33	8	8	8	31
Beard, Hayden, CAN	5	3	2.82	10	0	54	50	25	17	16	42
Oxspring, Chris, SYD	4	4	3.08	11	0	50	52	33	17	17	45
McGuire, Mike, CAN	4	4	3.21	14	1	56	51	20	20	28	63
Maestri, Alex, BRI	4	4	3.25	11	1	64	50	25	23	24	53
Grening, Brian, CAN	1	2	3.50	23	1	44	46	23	17	13	43
Mildren, Paul, ADE	4	3	3.94	11	0	62	74	33	27	11	51

| Schmidt, Daniel, PER | 6 | 2 | 4.08 | 10 | 0 | 57 | 62 | 33 | 26 | 15 | 34 |
| Ungs, Nic, MEL | 3 | 3 | 4.18 | 9 | 0 | 52 | 48 | 31 | 24 | 11 | 33 |

DOMINICAN LEAGUE

TEAM	W	L	PCT	GB
Aguilas Cibaenas	30	20	.600	—
Tigres del Licey	26	24	.520	4
Leones del Escogido	26	24	.520	4
Gigantes del Cibao	25	26	.490	5 ½
Toros del Este	24	27	.471	6 ½
Estrellas Oriente	20	30	.400	10

LIDOM Championship: Escogiodo defeated Aguilas 5-4.

PLAYER, TEAM	AVG	AB	R	H	2B	3B	HR	RBI	BB	SO	SB
Joaquin Arias, AGU	.387	150	19	58	6	4	0	30	9	16	10
Alexi Casilla, GIG	.336	119	22	40	7	1	0	7	15	21	6
Brian Bogusevic, AGU	.317	120	26	38	8	1	4	12	27	28	4
Herrera, Elian, AGU	.311	132	25	41	7	2	1	8	15	23	5
Ciriaco, Audy, AGU	.310	126	10	39	4	2	3	16	9	23	0
Hernandez, Anderso, LIC	.305	190	27	58	8	2	2	18	19	23	2
Francisco, Juan, LIC	.300	180	25	54	7	2	5	26	17	41	0
Nanita, Ricardo, TOR	.299	117	16	35	7	0	6	20	17	12	1
Perez, Juan, AGU	.290	162	23	47	10	3	0	12	8	38	13
Hernandez, Diory, TOR	.287	174	13	50	11	1	2	26	11	36	3

PITCHER, TEAM	W	L	ERA	G	SV	IP	H	R	ER	BB	SO
Youman, Shane, AGU	5	1	0.88	7	0	41	30	4	4	10	30
Baez, Manauris, EST	2	1	1.66	11	0	49	28	10	9	25	30
Bueno, Francisley, LIC	4	2	1.90	11	0	43	28	12	9	11	28
DiNardo, Lenny, GIG	3	5	2.22	11	0	53	52	25	13	16	23
Castro, Angel, AGU	5	3	2.53	21	2	43	35	12	12	8	40
Santiago, Mario, LIC	2	0	2.62	9	0	45	40	19	13	12	35
Noesi, Hector, LIC	3	3	2.70	10	0	47	45	22	14	10	27
Barcelo, Lorenzo, AGU	6	2	3.14	12	0	66	60	23	23	7	47
Sosa, Jorge, ESC	2	4	3.56	11	0	48	44	20	19	16	43
Halama, John, GIG	4	3	4.29	8	0	42	50	21	20	10	23

MEXICAN PACIFIC LEAGUE

TEAM	W	L	PCT	GB
Culiacan	41	27	.603	—
* Mexicali	40	28	.588	1
Obregon	37	31	.544	4
Hermosillo	36	32	.529	5
Los Mochis	31	37	.456	10
Navojoa	31	37	.456	10
^ Guasave	29	39	.426	12
Mazatlan	27	41	.397	14

*first-half champion; ^second-half champion

MPL Championship: Obregon def. Guasave 4-0.

PLAYER, TEAM	AVG	AB	R	H	2B	3B	HR	RBI	BB	SO	SB
Madera, Sandy, MOC	.366	213	39	78	14	1	13	44	24	32	0
Binick, Kraig, NAV	.354	189	28	67	9	2	2	17	24	19	20
Cruz, Luis, CUL	.340	244	41	83	17	0	17	47	9	26	1
Vazquez, Jorge, CUL	.330	212	34	70	7	0	18	60	21	66	0
Leon, Maxwell, CUL	.318	198	42	63	16	0	6	22	18	32	9
Arredondo, Eduardo, GSV	.318	214	30	68	5	0	1	14	14	25	10
Canizares, Barbaro, OBR	.312	234	46	73	9	0	20	55	44	37	0
Morejon, Oswaldo, MAZ	.311	196	30	61	14	0	5	21	16	18	1
Robles, Oscar, MXC	.305	236	31	72	7	0	8	37	29	16	0
Cota, Humberto, HER	.305	187	23	57	14	0	11	45	28	38	1

PITCHER, TEAM	W	L	ERA	G	SV	IP	H	R	ER	BB	SO
Solis, Tomas, MOC	4	2	2.31	14	0	78	62	27	20	24	41
Meza, Andres, CUL	8	1	2.54	13	0	85	73	25	24	22	60
Carrillo, Marco, OBR	5	3	2.72	14	0	76	76	25	23	23	39
Keisler, Randy, OBR	7	3	3.33	13	0	73	56	30	27	32	61
Delgadillo, Juan, HER	4	1	3.61	14	0	82	83	34	33	32	48
Campillo, Jorge, MXC	6	5	3.84	13	0	68	67	30	29	19	29
Campos, Francisco, CUL	8	3	3.84	14	0	82	74	36	35	22	69
Armenta, Alejandro, CUL	4	6	3.93	13	0	76	64	43	33	32	51
Castellanos, Jonathan, HER	4	5	4.11	14	0	70	70	35	32	34	34
Ortega, Pablo, MAZ	3	10	4.16	15	0	89	106	49	41	16	35

PUERTO RICAN LEAGUE

TEAM	W	L	PCT	GB
Caguas	23	19	.548	—
Ponce	21	20	.512	1 ½
Mayaguez	20	21	.488	2 ½
Carolina	19	23	.452	4

ROUND ROBIN: Mayaguez def. Ponce 3-2. **FINALS:** Mayaguez def. Caguas, 5-3.

PLAYER, TEAM	AVG	AB	R	H	2B	3B	HR	RBI	BB	SO	SB
Padilla, Jorge, CAG	.391	128	18	50	11	0	4	24	24	18	0
Ruiz, Randy, MAY	.336	110	13	37	7	1	3	17	10	26	0
De Jesus, Ivan, PON	.328	125	13	41	8	4	0	13	10	20	2
Dominguez, Jeff, CAR	.324	142	24	46	6	0	5	21	18	21	3
Baez, Edgardo, CAG	.323	130	16	42	4	0	3	16	15	34	0
Bocachica, Hiram, CAR	.297	118	16	35	6	2	4	21	22	22	1
Falu, Irving, MAY	.284	162	21	46	3	4	0	13	24	21	6
Maldonado, Martin, MAY	.271	118	17	32	5	0	4	15	10	26	1
Rodriguez, John, PON	.270	126	14	34	3	1	7	17	13	21	1
Negron, Miguel, MAY	.263	156	15	41	5	1	2	16	13	22	1

PITCHER, TEAM	W	L	ERA	G	SV	IP	H	R	ER	BB	SO
Schlichting, Travis, MAY	2	0	0.92	8	0	39	30	6	4	8	30
Marti, Yadel, PON	1	1	1.93	10	0	56	49	13	12	14	37
Kim, Mu-Young, CAG	5	1	2.18	8	0	41	39	13	10	13	25
Alvarado, Giancarlo, PON	2	2	2.28	10	0	51	33	18	13	23	55
DeSalvo, Matt, CAR	2	1	2.36	9	0	46	38	16	12	12	32
Ono, Jumpei, CAR	2	3	3.53	7	0	36	30	15	14	11	24
Cruz, Luis, CAG	0	3	4.31	11	0	48	53	24	23	20	27
Antonini, Michael, MAY	2	3	4.38	9	0	37	36	20	18	9	16
Kasahara, Shoki, CAR	1	2	4.76	10	0	34	31	20	18	16	26

VENEZUELA

TEAM	W	L	PCT	GB
La Guaira	37	26	.587	—
Caribes	33	30	.524	4
Magallanes	33	30	.524	4
Zulia	32	30	.516	4 ½
Aragua	32	30	.516	4 ½
Lara	31	32	.492	6
Caracas	28	35	.444	9
Margarita	25	38	.397	12

ROUND ROBIN: Aragua 10-6; La Guaira 10-7; Magallanes 10-8; Caribes 9-8; Zulia 3-13. FINALS: Aragua def. La Gaira, 4-2.

PLAYER, TEAM	AVG	AB	R	H	2B	3B	HR	RBI	IBB	SO	SB
Suarez, Cesar, LAG	.347	216	35	75	20	0	6	40	0	20	9
Sanchez, Hector, LAG	.339	177	29	60	10	0	9	39	3	37	0
Altuve, Jose, MAG	.339	242	32	82	18	2	2	35	0	26	10
Blanco, Gregor, LAG	.337	196	47	66	14	5	4	23	4	46	18
Flores, Jesus, MAG	.330	218	28	72	16	0	8	39	2	42	1
Henry, Justin, ZUL	.328	198	31	65	9	1	0	20	1	25	6
Lopez, Jose, LAR	.310	168	24	52	12	0	5	24	2	15	1
Pirela, Jose, ZUL	.301	236	25	71	8	4	3	36	3	29	4
Jimenez, Luis, LAR	.300	220	42	66	12	0	10	33	7	47	1
Gonzalez, Marwin, CAR	.292	168	19	49	7	0	0	17	3	24	3

PITCHER, TEAM	W	L	ERA	G	GS	SV	IP	H	R	ER	BB	SO
Junge, Eric, MAG	4	1	1.59	11	10	0	57	45	13	10	13	50
Parisi, Mike, MAR	1	3	2.09	9	8	0	52	41	15	12	5	39
Bibens-Dirkx, Austin, ZUL	7	3	2.19	14	13	0	78	56	20	19	22	51
Baldwin, Andrew, ORI	5	3	2.29	13	13	0	83	70	30	21	27	38
Perez, Sergio, ARA	3	1	2.47	14	14	0	66	65	24	18	30	50
Pinto, Renyel, ORI	6	1	2.55	13	13	0	78	55	26	22	32	72
Petit, Yusmeiro, MAR	5	4	2.98	14	13	0	82	85	33	27	11	74
Pollok, Dwayne, ZUL	6	4	3.05	14	14	0	80	86	29	27	18	34
Sanchez, Jose, MAG	2	3	3.56	13	13	0	56	53	31	22	25	35
Herrera, Alex, ORI	3	5	3.57	18	11	0	58	55	29	23	29	43

432 · Baseball America 2013 Almanac

BaseballAmerica.com

INTERNATIONAL

COLLEGE

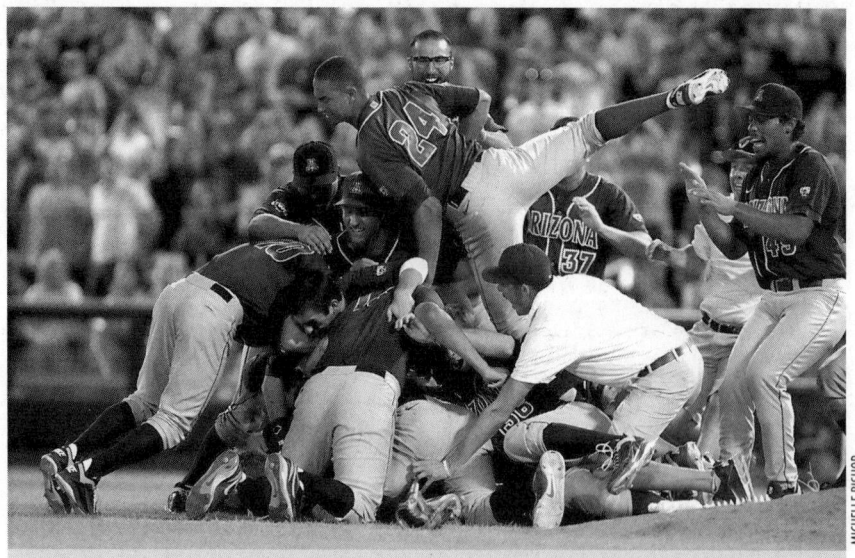

MICHELLE BISHOP

After playing well in all phases, Arizona dogpiled to celebrate a 10-0 run through the CWS

Arizona storms Omaha, wins first title since '86

BY AARON FITT

As two of Arizona's great leaders, Alex Mejia and Robert Refsnyder, posed together for a postgame photo, Mejia grinned at the photographer and shook his head.

"Brandon Dixon—that's all you need to say," Mejia blurted. "Brandon Dixon! He saved us all."

Arizona's core veterans—led by Mejia, Refsnyder, Kurt Heyer and Konner Wade—might have carried the Wildcats to the CWS Finals, but unlikely heroes such as Dixon led them to a 4-1 win against South Carolina, clinching the fourth national championship in school history, and the first since 1986.

Dixon, a sophomore part-time first baseman, entered the game as a defensive replacement in the sixth inning, when the Wildcats led 1-0. The Gamecocks tied the game in the seventh, and the score remained 1-1 until the ninth, when Dixon doubled down the left-field line to drive in the go-ahead run against South Carolina closer Matt Price—the all-time wins leader at the CWS.

"Oh, ye of little faith—I was going to pinch-hit for him," Arizona coach Andy Lopez said of

Dixon's ninth-inning at-bat. "I was going to pinch-hit for him, and coach (Matt) Siegel looked at me and shook his head no. OK, I'll go with the guy's gut. Please forgive me, Brandon—but he obviously came through."

Dixon's double put runners at second and third with one out and knocked Price out of the game. Two batters later, another less-heralded Wildcat provided crucial insurance. Freshman second baseman Trent Gilbert, the No. 9 hitter, lined a two-run single into right field against Tyler Webb to give Arizona its final margin of victory.

"I think it's no secret the juniors, they're the main contributors throughout the season," said Gilbert, a slick defender who carried a .268 average into the final game, but had come up with his share of big hits in the postseason. "But I mean, with me and some of the other younger guys, I think we feel just as confident in those situations."

The two-time defending champion Gamecocks, inevitably, fought back in the bottom of the ninth to make Arizona sweat, and Gilbert had a big hand in stifling their rally. South Carolina loaded the bases with one out against freshman closer Mathew Troupe, and Tanner English hit a line

COACHING CAROUSEL

SCHOOL	NEW COACH (PREVIOUS SCHOOL/JOB)	FORMER COACH (REASON FOR DEPARTURE)
Appalachian State	Billy Jones (Oklahoma State assistant)	Chris Pollard (Duke head coach)
Ball State	Rich Maloney (Michigan head coach)	Alex Marconi (fired)
Brigham Young	Mike Littlewood (Dixie State, Utah, head coach)	Vance Law (fired)
Bucknell	Scott Heather (Bucknell assistant)	Gene Depew (retired)
Chicago State	Steve Joslyn (N. Illinois associate head coach)	Michael Caston (fired)
Duke	Chris Pollard (Appalachian State head coach)	Sean McNally (resigned)
George Washington	Gregg Ritchie (Pittsburgh Pirates hitting coach)	Steve Mrowka (fired)
Harvard	Bill Decker (Trinity, Conn., head coach)	Joe Walsh (died)
Maryland	John Szefc (Kansas State assistant)	Erik Bakich (Michigan head coach)
Maryland-Eastern Shore	Pedro Swann (private insructor)	Will Gardner (resigned)
Middle Tenn. State	Jim McGuire (MTSU associate head coach)	Steve Peterson (retired)
Michigan	Erik Bakich (Maryland head coach)	Rich Maloney (fired)
Morehead State	Mike McGuire (Louisburg, N.C., JC head coach)	Jay Sorg (resigned)
New York Tech	Bob Malvagna (Adelphi, N.Y., assistant)	Mike Mac Millan (served as interim coach)
UNC Greensboro	Link Jarrett (Auburn assistant)	Mike Gaski (fired)
Northwestern State	Lane Burroughs (Mississippi State assistant)	J.P. Davis (fired)
Ohio	Rob Smith (Creighton assistant)	Joe Carbone (retired)
Oklahoma State	Josh Holliday (Vanderbilt assistant)	Frank Anderson (fired)
Oral Roberts	Ryan Folmar (ORU assistant)	Rob Walton (Oklahoma State assistant)
San Jose State	Dave Nakama (Washington assistant)	Sam Piraro (retired)
South Carolina	Chad Holbrook (South Carolina assoc. head coach)	Ray Tanner (South Carolina athletic director)
Southeast Mo. State	* Steve Bieser (SEMO assistant)	Mark Hogan (retired)
Texas-San Antonio	Jason Marshall (UTSA assistant)	Sherman Corbett (resigned)
Texas Tech	Tim Tadlock (Texas Tech assistant)	Dan Spencer (fired)
Va. Commonwealth	* Shawn Stiffler (VCU assistant)	Paul Keyes (died)
West Virginia	Randy Mazey (TCU assistant)	Greg Van Zant (fired)
Western Illinois	Ryan Brownlee (Iowa assistant)	Mike Villano (resigned)
William & Mary	Jamie Pinzino (William & Mary assistant)	Frank Leoni (resigned)
Youngstown State	Steve Gillispie (Jacksonville State assistant)	Rich Pasquale (fired)

*Interim

drive up the middle that Gilbert read perfectly. He snared it and lunged toward second base, where he just missed doubling off the baserunner. The next batter, Grayson Greiner, flew out to right to end the game and set off a dogpile around Troupe just behind the mound.

James Farris was the big story on the mound for Arizona in the finale, and although he was a weekend starter all season long, he still qualified as an unlikely hero. The righthander threw only one inning as a freshman in 2011 and entered 2012 with a career ERA of 36.00. He had a solid sophomore year, going 7-3, 4.18 in 99 innings, but his last appearance before the CWS Finals came 22 days earlier in regionals. The Wildcats hadn't needed him since because they won their super regional in two games and their CWS bracket in three, bringing Heyer back on five days' rest to win the bracket clincher against Florida State.

Lopez had debated bringing Heyer back again on three days' rest to start the second game of the Finals, especially because South Carolina was planning to start lefthander Michael Roth—whom Lopez later called "a legend." Eventually, he decid-

ed that it was wiser to get Heyer an extra day of rest for a potential third game. Lopez reasoned that Farris' intense bullpen sessions would have him ready to go, but he admitted that doubts lingered.

"Against Michael Roth—against Michael Roth," Lopez said, shaking his head. "Listen: someone's going to get mad at me, so go ahead and get mad at me. When I woke up this morning, I went, 'Farris against Roth. We're probably going to be playing (Game Three).' "

When freshman first baseman Joseph Maggi led off the third with a double to left, it ended a streak of 28 consecutive batters retired by Roth, dating back to his start against Kent State three days earlier. That led to Arizona's first run.

That was all the scoring Arizona would do against Roth, who left the mound for the final time in his brilliant collegiate career to a standing ovation with two outs in the sixth.

But Farris more than matched Roth, holding the Gamecocks scoreless on one hit through the first six innings. They manufactured a run in the seventh, and Farris wound up taking a no-decision, but the Wildcats could not have asked for more from Farris, who allowed just two hits and two walks while striking out four over 7⅔ innings.

A night earlier, Lopez had asked his two veteran leaders—Mejia and Refsnyder—who they thought he should start. Neither of them hesitated: Farris, they said.

"Because I know how hard Farris has worked," explained Refsnyder, who won CWS Most Outstanding Player honors by hitting .476/.542/.762 with two homers and five RBIs. "Farris, honestly, a lot of people thought he wasn't going to be back in the program (this season). He didn't really have the maturity and poise a lot of people look for. But when he came back, he was determined. He started lifting with Kurt, and really motivated himself. I didn't hesitate because I knew Farris would be ready, I knew how hard he's worked."

So maybe Farris and the rest were unlikely heroes to the world. But the men in the Arizona dugout believed in them.

When the on-field celebration had finally died down, Lopez led three players to the interview dais: Gilbert, Dixon and Refsnyder, who clutched the national championship trophy tight. Near the end of the press conference, a reporter asked Refsnyder if he was ever going to let the trophy go.

A few moments later, as Gilbert and Dixon were answering another question, Refsnyder silently picked up the huge trophy and set it down between the two. He gave a satisfied nod, and returned to his seat.

Heroes To Spare

But the Wildcats would not have been in position to win that final game without Refsnyder, who was the only player to hit two home runs at the 2012 CWS. He led the CWS in runs (six) and tied for the lead in RBIs (five).

Refsnyder's biggest impact came in the first game of the Finals, when he hit a two-run, opposite-field homer in the first to ignite the offense, then curtailed South Carolina's best chance to rally by throwing out Adam Matthews trying to go first to third on a single to right field in the seventh.

"That's why he's one of the better players in the country—he's able to do things like that," Gamecocks coach Ray Tanner said.

Arizona's other star in that game was sophomore righthander Konner Wade, who allowed one run on six hits in a complete game, leading the Wildcats to a 5-1 win. It was his second straight complete game in Omaha; he threw a five-hit shutout in Arizona's second CWS game against UCLA.

Wade and Heyer formed the backbone of

COLLEGE WORLD SERIES

STANDINGS

BRACKET ONE	W	L
Arizona	3	0
Florida State	2	2
UCLA	1	2
Stony Brook	0	2

BRACKET TWO	W	L
South Carolina	4	1
Arkansas	2	2
Kent State	1	2
Florida	0	2

CWS FINALS (BEST OF THREE)

June 24: Arizona 5, South Carolina 1
June 25: Arizona 4, South Carolina 1

ALL-TOURNAMENT TEAM

C: Riley Moore, Arizona. **1B:** Christian Walker, South Carolina. **2B:** Devon Travis, Florida State. **3B:** Sherman Johnson, Florida State. **SS:** Alex Mejia, Arizona. **OF:** Evan Marzilli, South Carolina; *Robert Refsnyder, Arizona; Joey Rickard, Arizona. **DH:** Bobby Brown, Arizona. **P:** Michael Roth, South Carolina; Konner Wade, Arizona.
*Named Most Outstanding Player.

BATTING
(Minimum 10 PA)

PLAYER	AVG	AB	R	H	2B	3B	HR	RBI	SB
Devon Travis, FSU	.563	16	4	9	2	0	1	4	0
Robert Refsnyder, Ariz.	.476	21	6	10	0	0	2	5	2
Riley Moore, Ariz.	.412	17	1	7	0	0	0	0	0
Sherman Johnson, FSU	.412	17	5	7	3	0	1	3	0
Justin Gonzalez, FSU	.412	17	1	7	2	0	1	5	0
Sawyer Polen, KSU	.400	10	0	4	0	0	0	1	0
Joe Serrano, Ark.	.385	13	0	5	0	0	0	1	0
Bo Bigham, Ark.	.385	13	2	5	1	0	0	0	1
Christian Walker, SC	.381	21	4	8	1	0	0	1	1
Preston Tucker, UF	.375	8	0	3	1	0	0	2	0

PITCHING
(Minimum 6 IP)

PITCHER	W-L	ERA	G	SV	IP	H	BB	SO
Tyler Webb, SC	0-0	0.00	4	0	11	5	4	8
Brandon Moore, Ark.	0-0	0.00	2	1	8	3	1	1
Jordan Montgomery, SC	1-0	0.00	1	0	8	3	1	6
David Berg, UCLA	0-0	0.00	3	0	6	1	1	2
Konner Wade, Ariz.	2-0	0.50	2	0	18	11	1	7
James Farris, Ariz.	0-0	1.17	1	0	8	2	2	4
Adam Plutko, UCLA	1-0	1.29	1	0	7	5	2	7
Scott Sitz, FSU	1-0	1.35	1	0	7	5	1	8
Ryne Stanek, Ark.	1-0	1.50	1	0	6	3	3	3
Kurt Heyer, Ariz.	1-0	1.80	2	0	15	15	6	11

Arizona's pitching staff in 2012, combining to throw just about half of the team's innings (289 of 586) and claim exactly half of its 48 wins. Heyer went 13-2, 2.24 with seven complete games en route to second-team All-America honors; Wade went 11-3, 3.96 with six complete games.

Lopez became the second coach to win a national championship with two schools, having won in 1992 at Pepperdine. (Augie Garrido, won has five titles between Cal State Fullerton and with

COLLEGE WORLD SERIES CHAMPIONS

*Undefeated

YEAR	CHAMPION	COACH	RECORD	RUNNER-UP	MOST OUTSTANDING PLAYER
1948	Southern California	Sam Barry	40-12	Yale	None selected
1949	Texas*	Bibb Falk	23-7	Wake Forest	Charles Teague, 2b, Wake Forest
1950	Texas	Bibb Falk	27-6	Washington State	Ray VanCleef, of, Rutgers
1951	Oklahoma*	Jack Baer	19-9	Tennessee	Sid Hatfield, 1b-p, Tennessee
1952	Holy Cross	Jack Barry	21-3	Missouri	Jim O'Neill, p, Holy Cross
1953	Michigan	Ray Fisher	21-9	Texas	J.L. Smith, p, Texas
1954	Missouri	Hi Simmons	22-4	Rollins	Tom Yewcic, c, Michigan State
1955	Wake Forest	Taylor Sanford	29-7	Western Michigan	Tom Borland, p, Oklahoma State
1956	Minnesota	Dick Siebert	33-9	Arizona	Jerry Thomas, p, Minnesota
1957	California*	George Wolfman	35-10	Penn State	Cal Emery, 1b-p, Penn State
1958	Southern California	Rod Dedeaux	35-7	Missouri	Bill Thom, p, Southern California
1959	Oklahoma State	Toby Greene	27-5	Arizona	Jim Dobson, 3b, Oklahoma State
1960	Minnesota	Dick Siebert	34-7	Southern California	John Erickson, 2b, Minnesota
1961	Southern California*	Rod Dedeaux	43-9	Oklahoma State	Littleton Fowler, p, Oklahoma State
1962	Michigan	Don Lund	31-13	Santa Clara	Bob Garibaldi, p, Santa Clara
1963	Southern California	Rod Dedeaux	37-16	Arizona	Bud Hollowell, c, Southern California
1964	Minnesota	Dick Siebert	31-12	Missouri	Joe Ferris, p, Maine
1965	Arizona State	Bobby Winkles	54-8	Ohio State	Sal Bando, 3b, Arizona State
1966	Ohio State	Marty Karow	27-6	Oklahoma State	Steve Arlin, p, Ohio State
1967	Arizona State	Bobby Winkles	53-12	Houston	Ron Davini, c, Arizona State
1968	Southern California*	Rod Dedeaux	45-14	Southern Illinois	Bill Seinsoth, 1b, Southern California
1969	Arizona State	Bobby Winkles	56-11	Tulsa	John Dolinsek, of, Arizona State
1970	Southern California	Rod Dedeaux	51-13	Florida State	Gene Ammann, p, Florida State
1971	Southern California	Rod Dedeaux	53-13	Southern Illinois	Jerry Tabb, 1b, Tulsa
1972	Southern California	Rod Dedeaux	50-13	Arizona State	Russ McQueen, p, Southern California
1973	Southern California*	Rod Dedeaux	51-11	Arizona State	Dave Winfield, of-p, Minnesota
1974	Southern California	Rod Dedeaux	50-20	Miami	George Milke, p, Southern California
1975	Texas	Cliff Gustafson	56-6	South Carolina	Mickey Reichenbach, 1b, Texas
1976	Arizona	Jerry Kindall	56-17	Eastern Michigan	Steve Powers, dh-p, Arizona
1977	Arizona State	Jim Brock	57-12	South Carolina	Bob Horner, 3b, Arizona State
1978	Southern California*	Rod Dedeaux	54-9	Arizona State	Rod Boxberger, p, Southern California
1979	Cal State Fullerton	Augie Garrido	60-14	Arkansas	Tony Hudson, p, Cal State Fullerton
1980	Arizona	Jerry Kindall	45-21	Hawaii	Terry Francona, of, Arizona
1981	Arizona State	Jim Brock	55-13	Oklahoma State	Stan Holmes, of, Arizona State
1982	Miami	Ron Fraser	57-18	Wichita State	Dan Smith, p, Miami
1983	Texas	Cliff Gustafson	66-14	Alabama	Calvin Schiraldi, p, Texas
1984	Cal State Fullerton	Augie Garrido	66-20	Texas	John Fishel, of, Cal State Fullerton
1985	Miami*	Ron Fraser	64-16	Texas	Greg Ellena, dh, Miami
1986	Arizona	Jerry Kindall	49-19	Florida State	Mike Senne, of, Arizona
1987	Stanford	Mark Marquess	53-17	Oklahoma State	Paul Carey, of, Stanford
1988	Stanford	Mark Marquess	46-23	Arizona State	Lee Plemel, p, Stanford
1989	Wichita State	Gene Stephenson	68-16	Texas	Greg Brummett, p, Wichita State
1990	Georgia	Steve Webber	52-19	Oklahoma State	Mike Rebhan, p, Georgia
1991	Louisiana State*	Skip Bertman	55-18	Wichita State	Gary Hymel, c, Louisiana State
1992	Pepperdine*	Andy Lopez	48-11	Cal State Fullerton	Phil Nevin, 3b, Cal State Fullerton
1993	Louisiana State	Skip Bertman	53-17	Wichita State	Todd Walker, 2b, Louisiana State
1994	Oklahoma*	Larry Cochell	50-17	Georgia Tech	Chip Glass, of, Oklahoma
1995	Cal State Fullerton*	Augie Garrido	57-9	Southern California	Mark Kotsay, of-p, Cal State Fullerton
1996	Louisiana State*	Skip Bertman	52-15	Miami	Pat Burrell, 3b, Miami
1997	Louisiana State*	Skip Bertman	57-13	Alabama	Brandon Larson, ss, Louisiana State
1998	Southern California	Mike Gillespie	49-17	Arizona State	Wes Rachels, 2b, Southern California
1999	Miami*	Jim Morris	50-13	Florida State	Marshall McDougall, 2b, Florida State
2000	Louisiana State*	Skip Bertman	52-17	Stanford	Trey Hodges, rhp, Louisiana State
2001	Miami*	Jim Morris	53-12	Stanford	Charlton Jimerson, of, Miami
2002	Texas*	Augie Garrido	57-15	South Carolina	Huston Street, rhp, Texas
2003	Rice	Wayne Graham	58-12	Stanford	John Hudgins, rhp, Stanford
2004	Cal State Fullerton	George Horton	47-22	Texas	Jason Windsor, rhp, Cal State Fullerton
2005	Texas*	Augie Garrido	56-16	Florida	David Maroul, 3b, Texas
2006	Oregon State	Pat Casey	50-16	North Carolina	Jonah Nickerson, rhp, Oregon State
2007	Oregon State*	Pat Casey	49-18	North Carolina	Jorge Reyes, rhp, Oregon State
2008	Fresno State	Mike Batesole	47-31	Georgia	Tommy Mendonca, 3b, Fresno State
2009	Louisiana State	Paul Mainieri	56-17	Texas	Jared Mitchell, of, Louisiana State
2010	South Carolina	Ray Tanner	54-16	UCLA	Jackie Bradley Jr., of, South Carolina
2011	South Carolina*	Ray Tanner	55-14	Florida	Scott Wingo, 2b, South Carolina
2012	Arizona*	Andy Lopez	48-17	South Carolina	Robert Refsnyder, of, Arizona

COLLEGE

Texas, is the other.) He has earned a reputation for developing standout bullpens, but he quickly realized his starters were the strength of his staff in 2012, and he made a concerted decision to ride them as deep as he could.

Workhorse starting pitching, slick defense and an explosive offense were all hallmarks of this Arizona team, which ranked fourth in the nation in batting (.329) and seventh in scoring (7.4 runs per game). It also ranked third with 35 triples and ninth with 132 doubles, figures that reflect the cavernous dimensions of Arizona's new home, Hi Corbett Field. The Wildcats were accustomed to driving the gaps rather than swinging for the fences, so they were well suited for spacious TD Ameritrade Park.

Few players are more fun to watch than the flashy Mejia, who dazzled at shortstop through the Series and the 2012 season. Refsnyder insisted in Omaha that Mejia is Arizona's heart and soul. His leadership and defense are his defining characteristics, but he also hit in Arizona's No. 3 hole. The entire package made him the Pac-12 player of the year.

Star power, a strong supporting cast that came up big when it mattered most, and one of the premier coaches in college baseball—Arizona had it all. No wonder the consistent Wildcats shared the Pac-12 title with UCLA and then ran through the postseason unbeaten—a perfect 10-0.

"I'm extremely, extremely fortunate to have coached this group this year," Lopez said. "They really, really were easy to work with, and for three years they've been this way. They've just been a joy."

Gamecocks Fall Short Of Three-peat

Ray Tanner stood silently in front of the third-base dugout at TD Ameritrade Park, watching Arizona celebrate its College World Series Finals sweep of his South Carolina team.

Finally, Tanner ducked into the tunnel and made his way toward the postgame press conference.

"Golly," he said wistfully, as he walked up the tunnel for what would be the final time in his illustrious coaching career (he became South Carolina's athletic director in the summer). "If we'd just gotten a couple of hits, we'd have evened this thing up."

The Gamecocks had their chances in the late innings of Game Two of the Finals, but they failed to get the timely hits that were the hallmarks of their 2010 and 2011 national titles.

RPI RANKINGS

The Ratings Percentage Index is an important tool used by the NCAA in selecting at-large teams for the 64-team Division I regional tournament. The NCAA now releases its RPI rankings during the season. These were the top 100 finishers for 2012. A team's rank in the final Baseball America Top 25 is indicated in parentheses, and College World Series teams are in bold.

1. **UCLA** (5)	48-16	51. Michigan State	37-23
2. **Florida** (3)	47-20	52. Texas	30-22
3. **Florida State** (4)	50-17	53. Auburn	31-28
4. **Arizona** (1)	48-17	54. Indiana State	41-19
5. Baylor (10)	49-17	55. Washington	30-25
6. Oregon (11)	46-19	56. Elon	33-26
7. **South Carolina** (2)	49-20	57. Georgia	31-26
8. North Carolina (17)	46-16	58. Illinois State	33-19
9. **Arkansas** (6)	46-22	59. California	29-25
10. Louisiana State (9)	47-18	60. Texas-Arlington	36-25
11. Stanford (13)	41-18	61. Stetson	35-23
12. Purdue (23)	45-14	62. Southeastern La.	39-21
13. N.C. State (12)	43-20	63. New Mexico	37-24
14. Virginia (25)	39-19	64. Liberty	41-19
15. Arizona State	36-20	65. Tulane	38-20
16. Texas A&M (19)	43-18	66. Cal Poly	36-20
17. Miami	36-23	67. Belmont	39-24
18. Kentucky (20)	45-18	68. Utah Valley	47-10
19. Rice (18)	41-19	69. Long Beach State	28-27
20. Cal State Fullerton (21)	36-21	70. Texas Tech	29-26
21. Central Florida	45-17	71. South Florida	38-22
22. Mississippi State (22)	40-24	72. Ohio State	33-27
23. Dallas Baptist	41-19	73. Texas State	32-24
24. Oklahoma (14)	42-25	74. Missouri	33-28
25. Vanderbilt	35-28	75. Nevada	32-25
26. Mississippi	37-26	76. Kennesaw State	34-25
27. Oregon State (24)	40-20	77. Connecticut	31-27
28. Georgia Tech	38-26	78. Memphis	31-28
29. Pepperdine	36-23	79. Indiana	32-28
30. Clemson	35-28	80. Washington State	28-28
31. Texas Christian (16)	40-22	81. Mercer	38-21
32. Maryland	32-24	82. Florida Atlantic	32-22
33. Appalachian State	41-18	83. Fresno State	31-28
34. St. John's (15)	40-23	84. Illinois	28-25
35. East Carolina	36-24	85. Evansville	32-27
36. San Diego	40-17	86. Georgia Southern	33-27
37. Missouri State	40-22	87. Oral Roberts	38-25
38. Virginia Tech	34-21	88. Hawaii	30-25
39. Wake Forest	33-24	89. UC Irvine	31-25
40. New Mexico State	35-24	90. Southern Miss.	32-24
41. Coastal Carolina	42-19	91. Western Carolina	32-24
42. Louisville	41-22	92. S.C.-Upstate	33-20
43. UNC Wilmington	39-23	93. Nebraska	35-23
44. Samford	41-23	94. Florida Gulf Coast	26-31
45. **Kent State** (8)	47-20	95. Campbell	41-18
46. Wichita State	35-25	96. Notre Dame	31-27
47. Gonzaga	34-22	97. Boston College	22-33
48. Col. of Charleston	38-22	98. Va. Commonwealth	34-25
49. **Stony Brook** (7)	52-15	99. Southern California	23-32
50. Sam Houston State	40-22	100. Oklahoma State	32-25

"In the end, if you had to put your finger on one thing, it's run output," Tanner said. "We just didn't get enough runs on the board."

In seven CWS games, South Carolina hit .205 as a team and averaged 2.7 runs per game. Arizona hit .282 during its 5-0 run to the title, averaging 5.4 runs per game.

Considering South Carolina's lack of offensive

ALL-AMERICA TEAM

FIRST TEAM

POS.	NAME	YEAR	AVG	OBP	SLG	AB	R	H	HR	RBI	BB	SO	SB
C	Mike Zunino, Florida	Jr.	.322	.390	.678	239	53	77	19	31	31	47	9
1B	Chris Serritella, Southern Illinois	Jr.	.389	.461	.667	234	56	91	13	61	34	51	6
2B	Alex Yarbrough, Mississippi	Jr.	.380	.437	.508	250	43	95	3	43	22	24	4
3B	Kris Bryant, San Diego	So.	.366	.483	.671	213	59	78	14	57	39	38	9
SS	Jimmy Rider, Kent State	Sr.	.359	.425	.529	295	70	106	6	58	33	41	3
OF	Jeff Gelalich, UCLA	Jr.	.351	.444	.535	245	56	86	11	48	34	45	16
OF	Travis Jankowski, Stony Brook	Jr.	.414	.475	.620	266	79	110	5	46	24	22	36
OF	James Ramsey, Florida State	Sr.	.378	.513	.652	233	78	88	13	58	63	42	11
DH	Josh Ludy, Baylor	Sr.	.362	.455	.634	232	41	84	16	71	32	41	1
UT	Marco Gonzales, Gonzaga	So.	.325	.372	.430	151	23	49	2	29	11	21	0

POS.	NAME	YEAR	W	L	ERA	G	CG	SV	IP	H	BB	SO	AVG
SP	Andrew Heaney, Oklahoma State	Jr.	8	2	1.60	15	6	0	118	74	22	140	.180
SP	Nick Petree, Missouri State	So.	10	4	1.01	16	3	0	115	85	36	114	.203
SP	Carlos Rodon, North Carolina State	Fr.	9	0	1.57	17	2	0	115	71	41	135	.176
SP	Chris Stratton, Mississippi State	Jr.	11	2	2.38	17	1	1	110	84	25	127	.211
RP	Robert Benincasa, Florida State	Jr.	4	2	1.32	32	0	16	41	24	7	58	.163
UT	Marco Gonzales, Gonzaga	So.	8	2	1.55	12	3	0	93	63	23	92	.201

SECOND TEAM

POS.	NAME	YEAR	AVG	OBP	SLG	AB	R	H	HR	RBI	BB	SO	SB
C	Kevin Plawecki, Purdue	Jr.	.359	.445	.578	223	54	80	7	47	26	8	3
1B	D.J. Hicks, Central Florida	Jr.	.316	.438	.560	225	52	71	14	72	56	52	0
2B	Jamodrick McGruder, Texas Tech	Jr.	.358	.500	.503	193	54	69	2	27	45	35	39
3B	D.J. Peterson, New Mexico	So.	.419	.490	.734	248	57	104	17	78	33	29	1
SS	Alex Mejia, Arizona	Jr.	.357	.392	.478	272	54	97	3	54	14	22	8
OF	Michael Conforto, Oregon State	Fr.	.349	.438	.601	218	45	76	13	76	24	37	1
OF	Mitch Haniger, Cal Poly	Jr.	.346	.438	.626	211	48	73	13	64	36	32	6
OF	Brandon Miller, Samford	Sr.	.301	.395	.650	246	58	74	23	65	37	52	1
DH	William Carmona, Stony Brook	Jr.	.395	.464	.691	256	62	101	12	73	35	39	7
UT	Brian Johnson, Florida	Jr.	.314	.377	.419	194	24	61	6	41	11	34	0

POS.	NAME	YEAR	W	L	ERA	G	CG	SV	IP	H	BB	SO	AVG
SP	Mark Appel, Stanford	Jr.	10	2	2.56	16	5	0	123	97	30	130	.213
SP	Kevin Gausman, Louisiana State	So.	12	2	2.77	18	2	0	124	106	28	135	.229
SP	Kurt Heyer, Arizona	Jr.	13	2	2.24	19	7	0	153	151	28	113	.256
SP	Michael Wacha, Texas A&M	Jr.	9	1	2.06	16	2	0	113	95	20	116	.228
RP	Jimmie Sherfy, Oregon	So.	5	3	2.20	36	0	19	61	36	34	93	.172
UT	Brian Johnson, Florida	Jr.	8	5	3.90	17	1	0	90	87	18	73	.251

THIRD TEAM

POS.	NAME	YEAR	AVG	OBP	SLG	AB	R	H	HR	RBI	BB	SO	SB
C	Mitchell Garver, New Mexico	Jr.	.377	.438	.612	268	68	101	10	57	25	28	6
1B	Goose Kallunki, Utah Valley	Sr.	.419	.481	.734	229	61	96	18	86	27	29	1
2B	Brock Hebert, Southeastern La.	Jr.	.374	.474	.511	227	58	85	2	37	30	34	36
3B	Trenton Moses, Southeast Mo. State	Jr.	.408	.531	.761	213	58	87	19	61	42	37	3
SS	Matt Wessinger, St. John's	Sr.	.348	.435	.486	247	62	86	6	48	34	30	34
OF	Tyler Naquin, Texas A&M	Jr.	.380	.458	.541	242	56	92	3	49	25	37	21
OF	Danny Poma, Hofstra	Sr.	.430	.500	.654	237	78	102	7	48	22	16	29
OF	Raph Rhymes, Louisiana State	Jr.	.431	.489	.530	232	44	100	4	53	22	13	2
DH	Patrick Kivlehan, Rutgers	Jr.	.392	.480	.693	189	47	74	14	50	22	40	24
UT	Stephen Piscotty, Stanford	Jr.	.329	.415	.467	246	44	81	5	56	30	23	4

POS.	NAME	YEAR	W	L	ERA	G	CG	SV	IP	H	BB	SO	AVG
SP	Tyler Johnson, Stony Brook	Sr.	12	2	2.52	16	5	0	100	90	29	49	.251
SP	Adam Plutko, UCLA	So.	12	3	2.48	18	2	0	120	91	47	99	.215
SP	Marcus Stroman, Duke	Jr.	6	5	2.39	14	1	0	98	83	26	136	.231
SP	Josh Turley, Baylor	Jr.	9	1	1.96	17	2	0	110	95	21	79	.227
RP	Michael Morin, North Carolina	Jr.	6	4	1.40	38	0	19	58	38	19	55	.191
UT	Stephen Piscotty, Stanford	Jr.	6	2	3.05	12	0	1	41	46	9	20	.280

firepower, it's a testament to the quality of its pitching, defense and leadership that it was able to return to the CWS Finals for the third straight year. No team has had a better three-year run in the last three decades. South Carolina went 30-4 in the NCAA tournament over the last three years, including a 22-game postseason winning streak that encompassed a pair of national titles.

But when a reporter asked Tanner if the accomplishments of the past three years soothed the disappointment of losing at all, Roth vigorously shook his head no.

Roth and Price were the pillars of South Carolina's three-year run, and they left their names all over the CWS record book. Maybe the Gamecocks will find their way back to Omaha in 2013, but even if they do, 2012 marked the end of an era—and not just for South Carolina, but for all of college baseball. The final year of the Rosenblatt Stadium/BESR bat era and the first year of the TD Ameritrade Park/BBCOR bat era will always be identified with Roth, Price and Tanner more than anyone else. They captivated the college baseball world for three years, and they elevated South Carolina's program to remarkable heights.

"The players come and go. But then you have guys that have tremendous roots in your program, and these guys do," said Tanner, who was replaced as head coach by former assistant Chad Holbrook. "There's a tremendous void."

CWS NOTES

■ The Wildcats were one of the nation's best offensive teams in 2012, but their pitching was superb during the NCAA tournament. During their perfect 10-0 run through the postseason, Arizona pitchers posted a 1.91 ERA in 94 innings. They put up a team ERA of 1.13 in 48 innings over five games in Omaha. Arizona became just the third team to win the national title without ever trailing in the CWS. The other two were Texas (in three games in 1949) and LSU (in four games in 1991).

■ Roth finished with CWS records for career innings (60 1/3), starts (eight) and hit batsmen (seven). His 1.49 career ERA in Omaha is the fifth-lowest among pitchers with at least 30 CWS innings.

■ Another Gamecocks star, **Christian Walker**, tied a significant CWS record. He finished with 28 career hits in Series play, knotting him with North Carolina's Dustin Ackley for first all-time. Walker also tied a single-Series record with eight walks.

■ The combination of BBCOR bats and configuration of the new ballpark, where the wind generally blows in, has suppressed offense in Omaha to an extreme degree. The combined batting average of all eight 2012 CWS teams was .234, the lowest at the CWS since 1974 (.227). And the loser has scored four runs or fewer in each of the last 36 games at the CWS, dating back to June 24, 2010. That streak easily surpassed the previous longest in CWS history—24 straight games, set in 1954-55 and equaled in 1973-75.

■ The average attendance in year two of TD Ameritrade declined to 21,782 per game, down from 22,977 a year earlier. The final game drew 23,872, nearly 3,000 fewer than the final game in 2011 (26,721).

OTHER TOP STORIES OF 2012

■ Calling 2012 a banner year for Northern baseball is an understatement. No team from Ohio or further Northeast had

been to Omaha since Maine in 1986, and the 2012 CWS field included two such teams. Kent State was the first team from the Buckeye State to reach Omaha since Ohio University in 1970, and the first Mid-American Conference team to make it since Eastern Michigan in 1976. Stony Brook, which won a regional at Miami as the No. 4 seed before stunning Louisiana State in the Baton Rouge Super Regional, was the first team from the Empire State to make it since St. John's in 1980.

The warmest winter and spring that many Northerners can remember certainly made a difference, allowing cold-weather teams to practice outside in February—a prospect that is ordinarily impossible. The weather certainly contributed to the great Northern baseball renaissance of 2012, which also included a trip to super regionals by St. John's and a banner season for Purdue, which ended a centurylong Big Ten title drought and hosted a regional in Gary, Ind. But attributing the success of the Northern teams to the weather is a major oversimplification.

"I think it shows that parity in college baseball does exist," said Kent State coach **Scott Stricklin**, whose team eliminated top-seeded Florida in Omaha. "And that's something that we talked about a few years ago as coaches, with the scholarships, with the roster limits, with all those things that are put into play—we wanted this to be a national game."

■ The first weekend of regional play was full of highlights. Florida righthander **Jonathon Crawford** spun the first no-hitter in tournament play since 1991. The sophomore, who pitched just four innings all year for the Gators last year, needed just 98 pitches against Bethune-Cookman. In the second-longest game in tournament history, Kent State upset Kentucky 7-6 in a 21-inning thriller. Both teams combined for 47 strikeouts and 43 men left on base. And each of the three games between Vanderbilt and North Carolina State were decided in the final at-bat. The Wolfpack got the last hurrah, scoring six runs in the last two innings to come back from a four-run deficit.

■ Kentucky opened the season by winning its first 22 games, the longest winning streak in school history. But two teams actually authored longer winning streaks. Baylor ran its winning streak up to 24 games, a school and Big 12 record, while winning its first 18 league games. Utah Valley's run at NCAA history fell short after 32 straight wins, two shy of the all-time D-I record held by Texas (1977) and Florida Atlantic (1999). The Wolverines fell short of an at-large bid despite winning 40 of their last 41.

■ Missouri State sophomore righthander **Nick Petree** went 73 consecutive innings without giving up an earned run during a 12-game stretch from early March until mid-May, a run that included 38 straight shutout innings. Petree, the Missouri Valley Conference pitcher of the year, led the nation with a 1.01 ERA.

■ Southeast Missouri senior third baseman **Trenton Moses** entered the year carrying a 20-game on-base streak and reached base in all 59 games for the Redhawks in 2012. Moses finished the year batting .395/.502/.672 with 11 homers and 53 RBIs in 177 at-bats, leading the nation in on-base and slugging percentage. His teammate, junior shortstop **Kenton Parmley**, compiled a 47-game hitting streak that tied for the third-longest in Division I history.

REGIONALS

JUNE 1-4
64 teams, 16 four-team, double-elimination tournaments. Winners advance to super regionals.

GAINESVILLE, FLA.
Host: Florida (No. 1 national seed).
Participants: No. 1 Florida (42-18), No. 2 Georgia Tech (36-24), No. 3 College of Charleston (37-20), No. 4 Bethune Cookman (34-25)
Champion: Florida (3-0)
Runner-up: Georgia Tech (2-2)
Outstanding player: Casey Turgeon, 2b, Florida.

RALEIGH, N.C.
Host: North Carolina State.
Participants: No. 1 North Carolina State (39-17), No. 2 Vanderbilt (33-26), No. 3 UNC Wilmington (38-21), No. 4 Sacred Heart (25-30).
Champion: North Carolina State (4-1).
Runner-up: Vanderbilt (2-2).
Outstanding player: Ryan Mathews, of, North Carolina State.

CHARLOTTESVILLE, VA.
Host: Virginia
Participants: No. 1 Virginia (38-17-1), No. 2 Oklahoma (38-22), No. 3 Appalachian State (39-16), No. 4 Army (41-13).
Champion: Oklahoma (4-1).
Runner-up: Appalachian State (2-2).
Outstanding player: Matt Oberste, dh, Oklahoma.

COLUMBIA, S.C.
Host: South Carolina (No. 8 national seed).
Participants: No. 1 South Carolina (40-17), No. 2 Clemson (33-26), No. 3 Coastal Carolina (41-17), No. 4 Manhattan (33-25).
Champion: South Carolina (3-0).
Runner-up: Clemson (2-2).
Outstanding player: Adam Matthews, of, South Carolina.

EUGENE, ORE.
Host: Oregon (No. 5 national seed).
Participants: No. 1 Oregon (42-17), No. 2 Cal State Fullerton (35-19), No. 3 Indiana State (41-17), No. 4 Austin Peay (38-22).
Champion: Oregon (3-0).
Runner-up: Austin Peay (2-2).
Outstanding player: Ryan Hambright, 3b, Oregon.

GARY, IND.
Host: Purdue.
Participants: No. 1 Purdue (44-12), No. 2 Kentucky (43-16), No. 3 Kent State (41-17), No. 4 Valparaiso (35-23).
Champion: Kent State (3-0).
Runner-up: Kentucky (2-2).
Outstanding player: George Roberts, 1b, Kent State.

HOUSTON, TEXAS
Host: Rice.
Participants: No. 1 Rice (40-17), No. 2 Arkansas (39-19), No. 3 Sam Houston State (38-20), No. 4 Prairie View (28-23).
Champion: Arkansas (3-0).
Runner-up: Sam Houston State (2-2).
Outstanding player: Ryne Stanek, rhp, Arkansas.

WACO, TEXAS
Host: Baylor (No. 4 national seed).
Participants: No. 1 Baylor (44-14), No. 2 Dallas Baptist (39-17), No. 3 UT Arlington (36-23), No. 4 Oral Roberts (37-23).
Champion: Baylor (4-1).
Runner-up: Dallas Baptist (2-2).
Outstanding player: Dan Evatt, of, Baylor.

LOS ANGELES
Host: UCLA (No. 2 national seed).
Participants: No. 1 UCLA (42-14), No. 2 San Diego (40-15), No. 3 New Mexico (36-22), No. 4 Creighton (26-28).
Champion: UCLA (3-0).
Runner-up: Creighton (2-2).
Outstanding player: Jeff Gelalich, of, UCLA.

COLLEGE STATION, TEXAS
Host: Texas A&M.
Participants: No. 1 Texas A&M (42-16), No. 2 Texas Christian (36-19), No. 3 Mississippi (35-24), No. 4 Dayton (31-28).
Champion: Texas Christian (4-1).
Runner-up: Mississippi (2-2).
Outstanding player: Justin Scharf, rhp, Texas Christian.

CORAL GABLES, FLA.
Host: Miami.
Participants: No. 1 Miami (36-21), No. 2 Central Florida (43-15), No. 3 Missouri State (39-20), No. 4 Stony Brook (46-11).
Champion: Stony Brook (3-0).
Runner-up: Central Florida (2-2).
Outstanding player: William Carmona, 3b, Stony Brook.

BATON ROUGE, LA.
Host: Louisiana State (No. 7 national seed).
Participants: No. 1 Louisiana State (43-16), No. 2 Oregon State (38-18), No. 3 Belmont (39-22), No. 4 Louisiana Monroe (31-28).
Champion: Louisiana State (3-0).
Runner-up: Oregon State (2-2).
Outstanding player: Austin Nola, ss, Louisiana State.

CHAPEL HILL, N.C.
Host: North Carolina (No. 6 national seed).
Participants: No. 1 North Carolina (44-14), No. 2 East Carolina (35-22-1), No. 3 St. Johns (37-21), No. 4 Cornell (31-15-1).
Champion: St. Johns (3-0).
Runner-up: North Carolina (2-2).
Outstanding player: Jeremy Baltz, of, St. Johns

TUCSON, ARIZ.
Host: Arizona.
Participants: No. 1 Arizona (38-17), No. 2 New Mexico State (35-22), No. 3 Louisville (39-20), No. 4 Missouri (32-26).
Champion: Arizona (3-0).
Runner-up: Louisville (2-2).

Outstanding player: Johnny Field, of, Arizona.

STANFORD, CALIF.
Host: Stanford.
Participants: No. 1 Stanford (38-16), No. 2 Pepperdine (34-21), No. 3 Michigan State (37-21), No. 4 Fresno State (30-26).
Champion: Stanford (3-0).
Runner-up: Pepperdine (2-2).
Outstanding player: Mark Appel, rhp, Stanford.

TALLAHASSEE, FLA.
Host: Florida State (No. 3 national seed).
Participants: No. 1 Florida State (43-15), No. 2 Mississippi State (39-22), No. 3 Samford (39-21), No. 4 University of Alabama Birmingham (32-28).
Champion: Florida State (3-0).
Runner-up: Samford (2-2).
Outstanding player: James Ramsey, of, Florida State.

SUPER REGIONALS
June 8-11
16 teams, best-of-three series.
Winners advance to College World Series.

NORTH CAROLINA STATE
AT FLORIDA
Site: Gainesville, Fla.
Florida wins 2-0, advances to CWS.

OKLAHOMA
AT SOUTH CAROLINA
Site: Columbia, S.C.
South Carolina wins 2-0, advances to CWS.

KENT STATE
AT OREGON
Site: Eugene, Ore.
Kent State wins 2-1, advances to CWS.

ARKANSAS
AT BAYLOR
Site: Waco, Texas
Arkansas wins 2-1, advances to CWS.

TEXAS CHRISTIAN
AT UCLA
Site: Los Angeles
UCLA wins 2-0, advances to CWS.

STONY BROOK AT
LOUISIANA STATE
Site: Baton Rouge, La.
Stony Brook wins 2-1, advances to CWS.

ST. JOHNS AT ARIZONA
Site: Tucson, Ariz.
Arizona wins 2-0, advances to CWS.

STANFORD AT
FLORIDA STATE
Site: Tallahassee, Fla.
Florida State wins 2-0, advances to CWS.

Leadership sets Zunino apart

Few players have had more of an impact on college baseball over the last three years than Florida catcher Mike Zunino.

His offensive numbers in 2012 were robust: He tied for fourth in the nation with 19 home runs, ranked 10th with 67 RBIs, third with 28 doubles, 11th with a .669 slugging percentage and fifth with 164 total bases. He finished the year hitting .322/.394/.669, and he did it while playing rock-solid defense behind the plate—baseball's most physically demanding position.

His combination of offensive production, quality defense, superb leadership and remarkable durability (he started all 66 of Florida's games, including 62 at catcher) made Zunino the No. 3 overall pick in the draft, and it made him the 2012 Baseball America College Player of the Year.

Here's what Zunino's coach and some of those who coached against him had to say about him, and what Zunino himself said about his standout season and collegiate carer.

■ **Florida coach Kevin O'Sullivan:** "He's been a tremendous leader, both on and off the field. He's been a major reason why this program has taken the next step. Obviously he's improved each year, and I'm awfully proud of what he's been able to accomplish on the field, and off the field as well.

"(His leadership ability) didn't start when he got to Florida—it started well before that. He comes from a baseball family, and they've obviously done a really good job

Mike Zunino

helping prepare him for this. I think it's just the want. He wants to be a leader . . . The success we've had on the mound certainly starts with Mike."

■ **Georgia coach David Perno:** "He's almost like a good umpire—you don't notice him, other than he hits the ball out of the yard, makes every throw, blocks every ball. It's just amazing. Through the years, while he's been at Florida, you just have had to earn everything you got. You weren't getting any gifts from him. You could just tell the respect he commands. They just don't come around like him very often. He makes everybody better, no question about it."

■ **Mississippi State coach John Cohen:** "I think the neat thing about that kid is, and I'm not taking anything away from his physical skills, but what makes him special to me is he is like having a coach on the field. He is such a game changer just between the ears, the way he plays the game. Yeah, he's got some power and some feel to hit, but he can make an impossible block. He's not the best thrower I've ever seen, but everything is around the bag. He's just a winner, man."

■ **Mike Zunino:** "It's been the best three years of my life playing here. I'm just grateful for it. Coming in here out of high school, I was just raw. They saw potential in me, and they got the best out of it. I bought into what they were saying. I'm just grateful for what they did. Obviously we didn't win the national championship, but I hope we laid the groundwork for what (O'Sullivan) wants to have in years to come."

PREVIOUS WINNERS

1982: Jeff Ledbetter, of/lhp, Florida State	**1992:** Phil Nevin, 3b, Cal State Fullerton	**2002:** Khalil Greene, ss, Clemson
1983: Dave Magadan, 1b, Alabama	**1993:** Brooks Kieschnick, dh/rhp, Texas	**2003:** Rickie Weeks, 2b, Southern
1984: Oddibe McDowell, of, Arizona State	**1994:** Jason Varitek, c, Georgia Tech	**2004:** Jered Weaver, rhp, Long Beach State
1985: Pete Incaviglia, of, Oklahoma State	**1995:** Todd Helton, 1b/lhp, Tennessee	**2005:** Alex Gordon, 3b, Nebraska
1986: Casey Close, of, Michigan	**1996:** Kris Benson, rhp, Clemson	**2006:** Andrew Miller, lhp, North Carolina
1987: Robin Ventura, 3b, Oklahoma State	**1997:** J.D. Drew, of, Florida State	**2007:** David Price, lhp, Vanderbilt
1988: John Olerund, 1b/lhp, Washington St.	**1998:** Jeff Austin, rhp, Stanford	**2008:** Buster Posey, c/rhp, Florida State
1989: Ben McDonald, rhp, Louisiana State	**1999:** Jason Jennings, rhp, Baylor	**2009:** Stephen Strasburg, rhp, San Diego State
1990: Mike Kelly, of, Arizona State	**2000:** Mark Teixeira, 3b, Georgia Tech	**2010:** Anthony Rendon, 3b, Rice
1991: David McCarthy, 1b, Stanford	**2001:** Mark Prior, rhp, Southern California	**2011:** Trevor Bauer, rhp, UCLA

FSU's Martin has magic touch

Back in January, first-year Florida State pitching coach Mike Bell admitted he had no idea how his staff would shake out. The Seminoles had to replace ace Sean Gilmartin and closer Daniel Bennett, and they lacked any proven starters or shutdown relievers.

But Bell expressed confidence that his new boss, longtime FSU coach Mike Martin, would figure it out.

Around the start of February, as Martin recalls it, he summoned his assistants and asked them a simple question: Who is the best pitcher on the team? Everyone gave the same answer: junior righthander Robert Benincasa.

"And I looked at them all and said, 'Why isn't he closing?' Because he was not figured in the rotation or in the closer role at that time, he was in the middle," Martin said. "At that point, we made the decision to go with Benincasa as our closer. The rest is history."

Mike Martin

CLIFF WELCH

Martin wanted his best arms anchoring the bullpen, which meant trusting freshmen Brandon Leibrandt and Mike Compton for the top two spots in the rotation.

"He said it, golly, probably two or three days into spring training: 'This is what we're going to do, and it's going to work. This is our best club—put these freshmen here, put our experienced guys on the back end,'" assistant Mike Martin Jr. recalled. "Mike (Bell) and I looked at each other like, 'Oh my gosh, I'm going to have trouble sleeping, throwing these two freshmen guys into the ACC.'

He makes guys better because of his trust in them, his faith in them. They love that."

Martin Jr. has served as an assistant on his father's staff for the last 15 years, and he said 2012 should go down as one of his dad's best coaching jobs. The uncertainty in the pitching staff caused the Seminoles to rank No. 20 in BA's preseason Top 25, but they reached the top of the rankings by April and stayed there for seven weeks, en route to a 50-17 record, runaway ACC title and a trip to the College World Series.

It was Florida State's 15th trip to Omaha under Martin, who has led the 'Noles to 44 or more wins and trips to regionals every year since he became head coach in 1980. Because he has maintained such a high level of performance year in and year out, Martin gets taken for granted by the college baseball world. But he shouldn't. For his long-term consistency and this year's national semifinals club, Martin is Baseball America's Coach of the Year, for the first time in his illustrious career.

But more than his .744 winning percentage (second among active coaches), his 1,723 wins (third-most in Division I history), or his 24 seasons of 50 or more wins, Martin's lasting legacy will be the impact he makes on his players.

"I don't even look to him as a coach; I look to him as a father," junior shortstop Justin Gonzalez said. "He's old school, and a lot of people don't appreciate that. These 27 guys on this team appreciate every moment they've spent with coach Martin."

PREVIOUS WINNERS

1982: Gene Stephenson, Wichita State	**1992:** Andy Lopez, Pepperdine	**2002:** Augie Garrido, Texas
1983: Barry Shollenberger, Alabama	**1993:** Gene Stephenson, Wichita State	**2003:** George Horton, Cal State Fullerton
1984: Augie Garrido, Cal State Fullerton	**1994:** Jim Morris, Miami	**2004:** David Perno, Georgia
1985: Ron Polk, Mississippi State	**1995:** Pat Murphy, Arizona State	**2005:** Rick Jones, Tulane
1986: Skip Bertman, LSU/Dave Snow, LMU	**1996:** Skip Bertman, Louisiana State	**2006:** Pat Casey, Oregon State
1987: Mark Marquess, Stanford	**1997:** Jim Wells, Alabama	**2007:** Dave Serrano, UC Irvine
1988: Jim Brock, Arizona State	**1998:** Pat Murphy, Arizona State	**2008:** Mike Fox, North Carolina
1989: Dave Snow, Long Beach State	**1999:** Wayne Graham, Rice	**2009:** Paul Mainieri, Louisiana State
1990: Steve Webber, Georgia	**2000:** Ray Tanner, South Carolina	**2010:** Ray Tanner, South Carolina
1991: Jim Hendry, Creighton	**2001:** Dave Van Horn, Nebraska	**2011:** Kevin O'Sullivan, Florida

Rodon matures into ace for Pack

Anyone who has seen Carlos Rodon pitch will tell you the first thing that stands out about the southpaw—perhaps other than his blazing fastball—is his fierce competitiveness on the mound.

After putting on roughly 20 pounds of muscle over the course of six months at North Carolina State, Rodon transformed himself from a very promising but inconsistent pitcher into a dominant ace. That transformation made Rodon the winner of Baseball America's 2012 Freshman of the Year Award.

Carlos Rodon

"His demeanor and the way he goes about his business on the mound reminds me a lot of Bob Gibson," N.C. State coach Elliott Avent said. "He's got two plus pitches in the fastball and slider, but the biggest thing that sells you about Rodon is his competitiveness."

FRESHMAN OF THE YEAR

Rodon earned first-team All-America honors by going 9-0, 1.57 with 135 strikeouts and 41 walks in 115 innings. He was also the Atlantic Coast Conference pitcher of the year and freshman of the year after leading the Wolfpack to a super regional.

The 6-foot-3, 234-pounder was one of the headliners of the Wolfpack's fourth-ranked recruiting class. While Avent admitted he and his coaching staff were "a little shocked" to see Rodon make it to campus, they were even more surprised by how quickly he developed.

Learning to harness his famous competitiveness was a key part of his maturation process.

"I can get a little too amped up at times," Rodon said. "When I cross the white line, it's my mound and my field and I'm going to protect it. It's a sense of pride. But if there's one thing this game does teach you, it's humility. I'm trying to become more of a quiet assassin."

PREVIOUS WINNERS

1982: Cory Snyder, 3b, Brigham Young
1983: Rafael Palmeiro, of, Mississippi State
1984: Greg Swindell, lhp, Texas
1985: Jack McDowell, rhp, Stanford
1986: Robin Ventura, 3b, Oklahoma State
1987: Paul Carey, of, Stanford
1988: Kirk Dressendorfer, rhp, Texas
1989: Alex Fernandez, rhp, Miami
1990: Jeffrey Hammonds, of, Stanford
1991: Brooks Kieschnick, rhp-dh, Texas
1992: Todd Walker, 2b, Louisiana State
1993: Brett Laxton, rhp, Louisiana State
1994: R.A. Dickey, rhp, Tennessee
1995: Kyle Peterson, rhp, Stanford
1996: Pat Burrell, 3b, Miami
1997: Brian Roberts, ss, North Carolina
1998: Xavier Nady, 2b, California
1999: James Jurries, 2b, Tulane
2000: Kevin Howard, 3b, Miami
2001: Michael Aubrey, of/lhp, Texas
2002: Stephen Drew, ss, Florida State
2003: Ryan Braun, ss, Miami
2004: Wade LeBlanc, lhp, Alabama
2005: Joe Savery, lhp, Rice
2006: Pedro Alvarez, 3b, Vanderbilt
2007: Dustin Ackley, 1b, North Carolina
2008: Chris Hernandez, lhp, Miami
2009: Anthony Rendon, 3b, Rice
2010: Matt Purke, lhp, Texas Christian
2011: Colin Moran, 3b, North Carolina

FRESHMAN ALL-AMERICA TEAMS

FIRST TEAM

		AVG	OBP	SLG	AB	R	H	HR	RBI	SB
C	Riley Moore, Arizona	.301	.385	.379	219	40	66	1	38	2
1B	Sam Travis, Indiana	.319	.397	.509	232	41	74	9	50	4
2B	Pat Kelly, Nebraska	.313	.345	.521	163	27	51	8	37	5
3B	Trea Turner, N.C. State	.336	.432	.459	259	72	87	5	43	57
SS	Andrew Daniel, San Diego	.339	.394	.487	230	37	78	4	45	3
OF	Michael Conforto, Oregon State	.349	.438	.601	218	45	76	13	76	1
OF	Austin Cousino, Kentucky	.319	.408	.515	260	61	83	9	41	15
OF	Rhys Hoskins, Sacramento State	.353	.411	.567	215	44	76	10	53	1
DH	Derek Fisher, Virginia	.288	.375	.507	219	44	63	7	50	4
UT	A.J. Reed, Kentucky	.300	.378	.405	200	29	60	4	43	0

		W	L	ERA	G	SV	IP	H	BB	SO	BAA
SP	Brandon Leibrandt, Florida State	8	3	2.82	19	0	99	89	29	83	.243
SP	Preston Morrison, Texas Christian	9	2	2.08	22	1	113	88	12	72	.216
SP	Benton Moss, North Carolina	7	2	1.94	17	0	79	65	23	83	.218
SP	Carlos Rodon, N.C. State	9	0	1.57	17	0	115	71	41	135	.176
RP	David Berg, UCLA	5	3	1.46	50	1	74	42	17	63	.165
UT	A.J. Reed, Kentucky	5	3	2.52	16	0	54	54	9	51	.267

SECOND TEAM

C—Chase Griffin (.320-10-42). **1B**—Kevin Cron, Texas Christian (.338-6-34). **2B**—Casey Turgeon, Florida (.281-4-30). **3B**—Jose Trevino, Oral Roberts (.317-13-57). **SS**—Cole Peragine, Stony Brook (.304-0-39). **OF**—Jake Fincher, North Carolina State (.300-1-23); Steven Goldstein, Stony Brook (.337-4-34); Ryan Padilla, New Mexico (.353-5-49). **DH**—Alex Blandino, Stanford (.294-8-40). **UT**—Mason Robbins, Southern Mississippi (.330-3-38; 1-0, 4.01, 34 IP/17 SO). **SP**—Mike Compton, Florida State (12-2, 2.87, 91 IP/64 SO); Jace Fry, Oregon State (5-3, 2.45, 88 IP/53 SO); Aaron Nola, Louisiana State (7-4, 3.61, 90 IP/89 SO); Jake Reed, Oregon (8-4, 2.92, 114 IP/67 SO). **RP**—Jonathan Holder, Mississippi State (2-1, 0.32, 9 SV, 28 IP/30 SO).

Minimum 120 plate appearances, 3.0 plate appearances per team game

BATTING AVERAGE

RANK NAME, TEAM	YEAR	G	AB	H	AVG
1. Raph Rhymes, Louisiana State	Jr.	61	232	100	.431
2. Danny Poma, Hofstra	Sr.	56	237	102	.430
3. Albert Carpen, Chicago State	Sr.	53	183	78	.426
4. Michael Felton, Campbell	Jr.	59	243	103	.424
5. D.J. Peterson, New Mexico	So.	61	248	104	.419
6. Goose Kallunki, Utah Valley	Sr.	58	229	96	.419
7. Roger Bernal, Texas-Pan American	Sr.	52	222	92	.414
8. Travis Jankowski, Stony Brook	Jr.	66	266	110	.414
9. Thomas Brown, Grambling	So.	42	173	71	.410
10. Trenton Moses, Southeast Mo. State	Sr.	59	213	87	.408
11. Daniel Bowman, Coastal Carolina	Sr.	61	237	95	.401
12. Jake Carlson, Dartmouth	Sr.	40	131	52	.397
13. Billy Burgess, Utah Valley	Sr.	57	222	88	.396
14. Matt Honchel, Miami (Ohio)	Fr.	59	233	92	.395
15. William Carmona, Stony Brook	Jr.	66	256	101	.395
16. Andrew Deeds, Morehead State	Sr.	54	221	87	.394
17. Royce Bolinger, Gonzaga	Sr.	56	237	93	.392
18. Adam T. McClain, Memphis	Sr.	58	232	91	.392
19. Patrick Kivlehan, Rutgers	Sr.	51	189	74	.392
20. Mike Garza, Georgetown	Jr.	53	220	86	.391
21. Eric Phillips, Ga. Southern	Sr.	60	238	93	.391
22. Joey Cujas, VCU	So.	59	223	87	.390
23. Maxx Tissenbaum, Stony Brook	Jr.	65	241	94	.390
24. Chris Serritella, Southern Illinois	Jr.	58	234	91	.389
25. Michael Pritchard, Nebraska	So.	57	212	82	.387
26. Matt Ford, Hofstra	Jr.	53	219	84	.384
27. Mike Martinez, Fla. International	Sr.	54	201	77	.383
28. Adam Hilker, Northern Colo.	Sr.	57	225	86	.382
29. Brett Vertigan, UC Santa Barbara	Jr.	56	236	90	.381
30. Nick Backlund, Mercer	So.	59	223	85	.381
31. Tim Colwell, North Dakota State	So.	60	244	93	.381
32. Jake Rickenbach, Utah Valley	Sr.	59	239	91	.381
33. Tyler Naquin, Texas A&M	Jr.	61	242	92	.380
34. Alex Yarbrough, Mississippi	Jr.	62	250	95	.380
35. Kevin McKague, Army	Sr.	55	198	75	.379
36. James Ramsey, Florida State	Sr.	67	233	88	.378
37. Richie Rodriguez, Eastern Ky.	Sr.	54	212	80	.377
38. Mitchell Garver, New Mexico	Jr.	61	268	101	.377
39. Jayce Boyd, Florida State	Jr.	66	255	96	.376
40. Justin Lacy, Longwood	Jr.	47	173	65	.376
41. Gaither Bumgardner, S.C.-Upstate	Jr.	50	205	77	.376
42. Jared Hammer, Hofstra	Jr.	55	213	80	.376
Ryan Lindemuth, William & Mary	So.	56	213	80	.376
44. Boomer Collins, Dallas Baptist	Jr.	60	235	88	.374
45. Brock Hebert, Southeastern La.	Jr.	60	227	85	.374
46. Ryan Ashe, Wright State	Sr.	57	222	83	.374
47. Marty Gantt, Col. of Charleston	Sr.	60	236	88	.373
48. Jared King, Kansas State	So.	56	220	82	.373
49. Rick Devereaux, Pittsburgh	Sr.	56	231	86	.372
Thomas Pope, UNC Wilmington	Sr.	59	231	86	.372
51. Adam Frazier, Mississippi State	So.	64	245	91	.371
52. Ryan Kresky, Fairleigh Dickinson	Sr.	54	186	69	.371
53. Brian Ruby, Binghamton	Fr.	37	116	43	.371
54. Stephen Bruno, Virginia	Jr.	58	238	88	.370
Brig Tison, George Mason	Sr.	57	238	88	.370
56. Johnny Field, Arizona	So.	65	257	95	.370
57. Bryan Aanerud, Liberty	Jr.	60	220	81	.368
58. Zach Stephens, Tennessee Tech	So.	53	204	75	.368
59. Jeremy Hill, Nicholls State	Sr.	50	185	68	.368
60. George Roberts, Kent State	Jr.	66	264	97	.367
61. Andrew Kubuski, Bowling Green	So.	51	196	72	.367
Corey LeVier, San Diego	Sr.	51	196	72	.367
63. Kris Bryant, San Diego	So.	57	213	78	.366
64. Justin Glass, Cincinnati	So.	56	227	83	.366
65. Clinton Freeman, East Tenn. State	So.	55	222	81	.365
66. Shane Brown, Charlotte	Sr.	49	192	70	.365
67. Robert Refsnyder, Arizona	Jr.	65	258	94	.364
68. Justin Guidry, Middle Tenn.	Sr.	59	239	87	.364
69. Erik Hink, Niagara	Sr.	48	198	72	.364
70. Kenton Parmley, Southeast Mo. State	Sr.	58	245	89	.363
71. Jensen Park, Northern Colo.	Fr.	58	212	77	.363
72. Jordan Steranka, Penn State	Sr.	56	226	82	.363
73. Chesny Young, Mercer	Fr.	59	215	78	.363
74. Ryan McCauley, Niagara	Jr.	47	185	67	.362
75. Eric Charles, Purdue	Sr.	57	232	84	.362
Josh Ludy, Baylor	Sr.	63	232	84	.362
77. Joe Sever, Pepperdine	Jr.	59	235	85	.362
78. Bob Donato, Bucknell	Sr.	46	177	64	.362
79. Alex Maruri, Delaware	Jr.	50	155	56	.361
80. Brandon Bayardi, UNLV	Jr.	55	205	74	.361
81. Brian Billigen, Cornell	Sr.	43	158	57	.361
82. Cole McInturff, James Madison	Jr.	51	186	67	.360
83. Brandon Thomas, Georgia Tech	Jr.	56	211	76	.360
84. Ryan Tella, Auburn	So.	59	236	85	.360
85. Jon Eisen, Columbia	Sr.	41	150	54	.360
Dario Pizzano, Columbia	Jr.	44	150	54	.360
Ryan Walker, Texas-Arlington	So.	61	250	90	.360
88. Ryan Haas, Delaware State	Jr.	56	203	73	.360
89. Brian Klukowicz, Md.-Baltimore County	Sr.	42	153	55	.359
90. Jimmy Rider, Kent State	Jr.	67	295	106	.359
91. Tanner Mathis, Mississippi	Jr.	63	245	88	.359
92. Tyler Sciacca, Villanova	Sr.	55	220	79	.359
93. Sam Eberle, Jacksonville State	Sr.	55	209	75	.359
94. Kevin Plawecki, Purdue	Jr.	59	223	80	.359
95. Claude Johnson, Arkansas State	So.	51	184	66	.359
96. Mike Albaladejo, Florida Atlantic	Sr.	54	212	76	.358
97. Jimmy Yezzo, Delaware	So.	50	187	67	.358
98. Josh Scheffert, Nebraska	Jr.	50	179	64	.358
99. Jamodrick McGruder, Texas Tech	Jr.	53	193	69	.358
T.J. McManus, Eastern Illinois	Sr.	53	193	69	.358

ON-BASE PERCENTAGE

RANK NAME, TEAM	OBP
1. Trenton Moses, Southeast Mo. State	.531
2. Albert Carpen, Chicago State	.522
3. James Ramsey, Florida State	.513
4. Jamodrick McGruder, Texas Tech	.500
Danny Poma, Hofstra	.500
6. Billy Burgess, Utah Valley	.491
7. D.J. Peterson, New Mexico	.490
8. Ryan Kresky, Fairleigh Dickinson	.489
9. Mike McQuillan, Iowa	.489
10. Raph Rhymes, Louisiana State	.489
11. Mike Martinez, Fla. International	.488
12. Parker Hipp, New Mexico State	.488
13. Forrestt Allday, Central Arkansas	.486
14. Juluis Green, Savannah State	.483
Michael Sterling, Southern Miss.	.483
16. Kris Bryant, San Diego	.483
17. Jake Rickenbach, Utah Valley	.483
18. Marty Gantt, Col. of Charleston	.483
19. Zac Mitchell, Belmont	.482
20. Wade Hinkle, Kansas State	.482
21. Adam Frazier, Mississippi State	.482
22. Goose Kallunki, Utah Valley	.481
23. Eddie Sorondo, Delaware State	.481
24. Brandon Thomas, Georgia Tech	.481
25. Patrick Kivlehan, Rutgers	.480
26. Richie Shaffer, Clemson	.480
27. Ronnie Richardson, Central Florida	.480
28. Jared Hammer, Hofstra	.479
29. Daniel Bowman, Coastal Carolina	.478
30. Ben Magsig, Eastern Mich.	.478
31. Johnny Field, Arizona	.476
32. Zach Stephens, Tennessee Tech	.476
33. Joey Cujas, VCU	.476
34. Kevin McKague, Army	.475
35. Travis Jankowski, Stony Brook	.475
36. Brock Hebert, Southeastern La.	.474
37. Michael Felton, Campbell	.474
38. Shane Zimmer, Canisius	.473
39. Chris Wolfe, Grambling	.473
40. Tanner Waite, New Mexico State	.472
41. Nick Backlund, Mercer	.471
42. Bryan Aanerud, Liberty	.471
43. Jimmy Brenneman, Campbell	.470
44. Matt Ford, Hofstra	.469
Richie Rodriguez, Eastern Ky.	.469
46. Casey Coy, Northern Colo.	.469
47. Sam Eberle, Jacksonville State	.469
48. Dario Pizzano, Columbia	.468
49. Justin Lacy, Longwood	.468
50. Ryan Haas, Delaware State	.468

SLUGGING PERCENTAGE

RANK NAME, TEAM	SLG
1. Trenton Moses, Southeast Mo. State	.761
2. D.J. Peterson, New Mexico	.734
3. Goose Kallunki, Utah Valley	.734
4. Sean Bignall, Ark.-Little Rock	.696
5. Zach Stephens, Tennessee Tech	.696
6. Patrick Kivlehan, Rutgers	.693
7. William Carmona, Stony Brook	.691
8. Richie Rodriguez, Eastern Ky.	.689
9. Ryan McCauley, Niagara	.676
10. Kris Bryant, San Diego	.671
11. Mike Zunino, Florida	.669
12. Nick Backlund, Mercer	.668
13. Chris Serritella, Southern Illinois	.667
14. Robby Newman, Longwood	.663
15. Ben Waldrip, Jacksonville State	.660
16. Greg Zebrack, Penn	.657
17. Danny Poma, Hofstra	.654
18. James Ramsey, Florida State	.652
19. Brandon Miller, Samford	.650
20. Boomer Collins, Dallas Baptist	.647
21. Jon Leroux, Northeastern	.647
22. Chris Cowell, Richmond	.643
23. Brian Klukowicz, Md.-Baltimore Co.	.641
24. Matt Pollock, Buffalo	.638
25. Daniel Kassouf, Appalachian State	.635
26. Josh Ludy, Baylor	.634
27. Zach Kirksey, Mississippi	.631
28. Ryan Mathews, North Carolina State	.628
29. Mitch Haniger, Cal Poly	.626
30. Travis Jankowski, Stony Brook	.620
31. Royce Bolinger, Gonzaga	.620
32. Chris Burke, Iona	.620
33. Preston Beck, Texas-Arlington	.619
Kendall Logan, Jackson State	.619
35. Tom Murphy, Buffalo	.616
36. Jordan Steranka, Penn State	.615
37. Jacob Wilson, Memphis	.615
38. Marty Gantt, Col. of Charleston	.614
39. Ryan Deitrich, Penn	.614
40. Mike Garza, Georgetown	.614
41. Mitchell Garver, New Mexico	.612
42. Scott Burkett, Longwood	.611
43. T.J. McManus, Eastern Illinois	.606
44. Andy Chriscaden, Kennesaw State	.606
45. Zach Helgeson, George Mason	.605
46. Austin Elkins, Dallas Baptist	.602
47. Michael Conforto, Oregon State	.601
48. Mac Doyle, Wofford	.600
49. Trevor Edwards, UNC Greensboro	.599
50. Brooks Klein, Nevada	.598

HOME RUNS

RANK NAME, TEAM	HR
1. Brandon Miller, Samford	23
2. Chris Cowell, Richmond	20
Matthew Scruggs, East Tenn. State	20
4. Trenton Moses, Southeast Mo. State	19
Mike Zunino, Florida	19
6. Sean Bignall, Ark.-Little Rock	18
Goose Kallunki, Utah Valley	18
Zach Stephens, Tennessee Tech	18
Ben Waldrip, Jacksonville State	18
10. Daniel Kassouf, Appalachian State	17
Ryan Mathews, North Carolina State	17
D.J. Peterson, New Mexico	17
Mac Williamson, Wake Forest	17
Jacob Wilson, Memphis	17
15. Greg Bachman, Austin Peay	16
Nick Backlund, Mercer	16
Josh Ludy, Baylor	16
Tyler Molinaro, UNC Wilmington	16
Dylan Pratt, East Tenn. State	16
Ben Thoma, Eastern Illinois	16
Preston Tucker, Florida	16
22. Saxon Butler, Samford	15
Zack Helgeson, George Mason	15
Tyler Horan, Virginia Tech	15
25. Preston Beck, Texas-Arlington	14
Kris Bryant, San Diego	14
Andy Chriscaden, Kennesaw State	14
Alex Close, Liberty	14
Jake Davies, Georgia Tech	14
Trevor Edwards, UNC Greensboro	14
D.J. Hicks, Central Florida	14
Patrick Kivlehan, Rutgers	14
Jensen Painter, Ohio	14
Richie Rodriguez, Eastern Ky.	14
Bryan Soloman, Eastern Ky.	14
36. Boomer Collins, Dallas Baptist	13
Michael Conforto, Oregon State	13
Mac Doyle, Wofford	13
Mitch Haniger, Cal Poly	13
Eric Jagielo, Notre Dame	13
Mason Katz, Louisiana State	13
Zach Kirksey, Mississippi	13
Trent Miller, Middle Tenn.	13
Tom Murphy, Buffalo	13
Robby Newman, Longwood	13
Kenton Parmley, Southeast Mo. State	13
James Ramsey, Florida State	13
Abe Ruiz, Arizona State	13
Jared Schlehuber, Oral Roberts	13
Chris Serritella, Southern Illinois	13
Jordan Sivertsen, Southern Illinois	13
Jose Trevino, Oral Roberts	13

RUNS BATTED IN

RANK NAME, TEAM	RBI
1. Goose Kallunki, Utah Valley	86
2. D.J. Peterson, New Mexico	78
3. Michael Conforto, Oregon State	76
4. William Carmona, Stony Brook	73
Jake Davies, Georgia Tech	73
6. D.J. Hicks, Central Florida	72
Joel Hutter, Dallas Baptist	72
8. Josh Ludy, Baylor	71
9. Preston Beck, Texas-Arlington	70
10. Greg Bachman, Austin Peay	67
Mike Zunino, Florida	67
12. Jared Hammer, Hofstra	66
Jordan Hankins, Austin Peay	66
Daniel Kassouf, Appalachian State	66
Robert Refsnyder, Arizona	66
George Roberts, Kent State	66
Rich Witten, Coastal Carolina	66
18. Billy Burgess, Utah Valley	65
Stewart Ijames, Louisville	65
Brandon Miller, Samford	65
21. Sean Bignall, Ark.-Little Rock	64
Mitch Haniger, Cal Poly	64
Jacob Wilson, Memphis	64
24. Johnny Coy, Wichita State	63
C.J. Gillman, Dayton	63
Matt Snyder, Mississippi	63
27. Jake Gonzalez, Houston Baptist	62
Ryan Mathews, North Carolina State	62
29. Jayce Boyd, Florida State	61
Saxon Butler, Samford	61
Seth Mejias-Brean, Arizona	61
Trenton Moses, Southeast Mo. State	61
Cameron Perkins, Purdue	61
Chris Serritella, Southern Illinois	61
Ben Waldrip, Jacksonville State	61
36. Andy Chriscaden, Kennesaw State	60
Zac Fisher, New Mexico State	60
Ryan Haas, Delaware State	60
39. Bobby Brown, Arizona	59
Kendall Logan, Jackson State	59
Boone Shear, Troy	59
42. Nick Backlund, Mercer	58
Jeff Cammans, Rhode Island	58
Boomer Collins, Dallas Baptist	58
Chris Cowell, Richmond	58
Austin Heaps, Utah Valley	58
Michael Katz, William & Mary	58
Phil Pohl, Clemson	58
James Ramsey, Florida State	58
Jimmy Rider, Kent State	58

DOUBLES

RANK NAME, TEAM	2B
1. Danny Poma, Hofstra	32
2. Jimmy Rider, Kent State	30
3. Mike Zunino, Florida	28
4. Mitchell Garver, New Mexico	27
5. William Carmona, Stony Brook	26
6. Bill Cullen, VCU	25
Chris Diaz, North Carolina State	25
8. Eric Phillips, Ga. Southern	24
George Roberts, Kent State	24
Chris Serritella, Southern Illinois	24
Jacob Stallings, North Carolina	24
Devon Travis, Florida State	24
Logan Vick, Baylor	24
14. Stephen Bruno, Virginia	23
Jeff Cammans, Rhode Island	23
Boomer Collins, Dallas Baptist	23
Matt Frazer, West Virginia	23
Spiker Helms, Missouri State	23
19. Hunter Dozier, Stephen F. Austin	22
Eduardo Gonzalez, Alcorn State	22
Ryan Haas, Delaware State	22
Seth Mejias-Brean, Arizona	22
Chad Pinder, Virginia Tech	22
Jake Rickenbach, Utah Valley	22
Austin Wynns, Fresno State	22
26. Brian Blasik, Dayton	21
Jayce Boyd, Florida State	21
James Brooks, Utah	21
Joey Cujas, VCU	21
Will Fadness, Milwaukee	21
Alex Friedrich, Central Florida	21
Mike Garza, Georgetown	21
Justin Glass, Cincinnati	21
Zack Haley, Liberty	21
Brock Hebert, Southeastern La.	21
Taylor Johnson, Furman	21
Alex Jones, Northern Illinois	21
D.J. Long, Delaware	21
Jeff McVaney, Texas State	21
D.J. Peterson, New Mexico	21
Richie Shaffer, Clemson	21
42. Jimmy Allen, Cal Poly	20
Evan Boyd, Mercer	20
Chris Burke, Iona	20
Evan Campbell, Kent State	20
Austin Cousino, Kentucky	20
Marty Gantt, Col. of Charleston	20
Conrad Gregor, Vanderbilt	20
Jake Gronsky, Monmouth	20
Jordan Hagel, Maryland	20
Travis Isaak, Murray State	20
Michael Lorenzen, Cal State Fullerton	20
Thomas McCarthy, Kentucky	20
Ryan McCauley, Niagara	20
Tom Murphy, Buffalo	20
David Olson, Campbell	20
Kevin Plawecki, Purdue	20
Matt Reynolds, Arkansas	20
Jordan Steranka, Penn State	20
Richard Stock, Nebraska	20
Maxx Tissenbaum, Stony Brook	20

TRIPLES

RANK NAME, TEAM	3B
1. Travis Jankowski, Stony Brook	11

2. Jake Arrington, Sam Houston State 10
3. Nathan Burns, Fla. International 9
   Tim Colwell, North Dakota State 9
   Bill Cullen, VCU 9
   Nolan Gaige, Albany 9
   Jake Gonzalez, Houston Baptist 9
   Josh Melendez, New Mexico 9
   Brett Vertigan, UC Santa Barbara 9
10. Thomas Brittle, Clemson 8
    Austin Elkins, Dallas Baptist 8
    Derek Fisher, Virginia 8
    Tony Kemp, Vanderbilt 8
    Jamodrick McGruder, Texas Tech 8
    Adrian Schenk, Northern Colo. 8
    Casey Selsor, Texas-San Antonio 8
    Ty Wiesemeyer, Illinois State 8
18. Daniel Aldrich, Col. of Charleston 7
    Thomas Brown, Grambling 7
    Bobby Brown, Arizona 7
    Byron Campbell, Md.-Eastern Shore 7
    William Carmona, Stony Brook 7
    Casey Coy, Northern Colo. 7
    Jacob Daniel, Eastern Ky. 7
    Joey DeMichele, Arizona State 7
    Taylor Dugas, Alabama 7
    Johnny Field, Arizona 7
    Austin Liput, S.C.-Upstate 7
    Aaron Nardone, Delaware State 7
    Jensen Park, Northern Colo. 7
    Thomas Pope, UNC Wilmington 7
    Jeremy Sy, Louisiana-Monroe 7
    Will Walsh, Seton Hall 7
34. Ryan Ashe, Wright State 6
    Barrett Barnes, Texas Tech 6
    Hunter Burton, Furman 6
    Eric Cain, South Dakota State 6
    Tommy Coyle, North Carolina 6
    Greg Dupell, Navy 6
    Jake Fincher, North Carolina State 6
    Chaz Frank, North Carolina 6
    Dominic Fratantuono, Towson 6
    Andrew Hahn, Navy 6
    Jesse Kelso, Canisius 6
    Jeff Kemp, Radford 6
    Brooks Klein, Nevada 6
    Joe Kohan, Nevada 6
    Trey Massenberg, Missouri State 6
    Alex Mejia, Arizona 6
    Tyler Naquin, Texas A&M 6
    Cole Norton, St. Mary's 6
    Jordan Owen, Tennessee-Martin 6
    Cole Peragine, Stony Brook 6
    James Ramsey, Florida State 6
    Cody Reine, Oklahoma 6
    Tyler Sciacca, Villanova 6
    Stephen Talbott, Purdue 6
    Luke Tendler, N.C. A&T 6
    Kyle Wren, Georgia Tech 6

STOLEN BASES

RANK NAME, TEAM	SB	CS
1. Trea Turner, North Carolina State	57	4
2. Michael Faulkner, Arkansas State	41	1
3. Jonathan Murphy, Jacksonville	40	6
4. Jamodrick McGruder, Texas Tech	39	5
5. Adam Engel, Louisville	37	2
6. Richard Amion, Alabama State	36	6
Brian Blasik, Dayton	36	3
Brock Hebert, Southeastern La.	36	8
Travis Jankowski, Stony Brook	36	6
10. Glen Walker, Jackson State	35	8
11. Ian Miller, Wagner	34	7
Matt Wessinger, St. John's	34	2
13. Wynton Bernard, Niagara	32	7
Patrick Biondi, Michigan	32	12

	SB	CS
Anthony Vega, Manhattan	32	3
16. Shane Brown, Charlotte	31	2
E. Cheatham, Mississippi Val.	31	6
Kirby Pellant, Ohio State	31	6
19. Jimmy Brenneman, Campbell	30	2
Hector Crespo, Appalachian State	30	3
Brandyn Crutcher, Alabama A&M	30	8
Jay Gonzalez, Auburn	30	4
Ian Parmley, Liberty	30	4
Eric Stamets, Evansville	30	7
25. Marty Gantt, Col. of Charleston	29	9
Eric Phillips, Ga. Southern	29	4
Danny Poma, Hofstra	29	9
Chris Wolfe, Grambling	29	4
29. Josh Johnson, Bethune-Cookman	27	4
Michael Lowe, Mississippi Val.	27	6
Jacob May, Coastal Carolina	27	5
Ben McQuown, Campbell	27	5
33. Ryan Cowhey, Western Illinois	26	3
Aaron Dobbs, Kennesaw State	26	11
Dalton Rouleau, Hofstra	26	7
Tim Ryan, Oakland	26	9
37. Larry Cornelia, Fairfield	25	4
Ross Kivett, Kansas State	25	4
Justin Mackert, Citadel	25	6
John Murphy, Sacred Heart	25	5
Austin Nyman, Hofstra	25	5
Creede Simpson, Auburn	25	9
43. Les Aulds, La.-Monroe	24	10
Ben Crumpton, Ark.-Little Rock	24	1
Billy Ferriter, Connecticut	24	5
Patrick Kivlehan, Rutgers	24	4
Justin Maffei, San Francisco	24	5
Ronnie Richardson, Central Florida	24	8
Ali Rodriguez, NYIT	24	4
Jamison Wells, Northern Illinois	24	8

RUNS

RANK NAME, TEAM	R
1. Travis Jankowski, Stony Brook	79
2. Danny Poma, Hofstra	78
James Ramsey, Florida State	78
4. Billy Burgess, Utah Valley	73
Troy Drummond, Delaware State	73
6. Johnny Field, Arizona	72
Trea Turner, North Carolina State	72
8. Jimmy Rider, Kent State	70
9. Marty Gantt, Col. of Charleston	68
Mitchell Garver, New Mexico	68
Sean Moysh, Utah Valley	68
12. Jake Rickenbach, Utah Valley	67
13. Jimmy Brenneman, Campbell	66
Ian Parmley, Liberty	66
15. Jeremy Baltz, St. John's	65
Mason Katz, Louisiana State	65
Zac Mitchell, Belmont	65
18. Sherman Johnson, Florida State	64
Josh Melendez, New Mexico	64
Nick Ratajczak, Louisville	64
Robert Refsnyder, Arizona	64
22. Beau Amaral, UCLA	63
Hector Crespo, Appalachian State	63
Austin Heaps, Utah Valley	63
Devon Travis, Florida State	63
26. Daniel Bowman, Coastal Carolina	62
William Carmona, Stony Brook	62
Boomer Collins, Dallas Baptist	62
Tim Colwell, North Dakota State	62
Bill Cullen, VCU	62
Jordan Dean, Central Mich.	62
Matt Wessinger, St. John's	62
33. Evan Campbell, Kent State	61
Cameron Cecil, Delaware State	61
Austin Cousino, Kentucky	61
Austin Elkins, Dallas Baptist	61

	R
Goose Kallunki, Utah Valley	61
Nathan Orf, Baylor	61
39. Sean Bignall, Ark.-Little Rock	60
Joey Rickard, Arizona	60
41. Pat Blair, Wake Forest	59
Kris Bryant, San Diego	59
Andrew Cain, UNC Wilmington	59
Aaron Dobbs, Kennesaw State	59
Nolan Fontana, Florida	59
Michael Fransoso, Maine	59
Ronnie Richardson, Central Florida	59
Richie Rodriguez, Eastern Ky.	59
Jeff Roy, Rhode Island	59
50. Bobby Glover, Dayton	58
Brock Hebert, Southeastern La.	58
Brandon Miller, Samford	58
Trenton Moses, Southeast Mo. State	58
Kenton Parmley, Southeast Mo. State	58
Christian Stringer, Rice	58

HITS

RANK NAME, TEAM	H
1. Travis Jankowski, Stony Brook	110
2. Jimmy Rider, Kent State	106
3. D.J. Peterson, New Mexico	104
4. Michael Felton, Campbell	103
5. Danny Poma, Hofstra	102
6. William Carmona, Stony Brook	101
Mitchell Garver, New Mexico	101
8. Raph Rhymes, Louisiana State	100
9. Alex Mejia, Arizona	97
George Roberts, Kent State	97
11. Jayce Boyd, Florida State	96
Jordan Dean, Central Mich.	96
Goose Kallunki, Utah Valley	96
14. Daniel Bowman, Coastal Carolina	95
Johnny Field, Arizona	95
Alex Yarbrough, Mississippi	95
17. Seth Mejias-Brean, Arizona	94
Robert Refsnyder, Arizona	94
Maxx Tissenbaum, Stony Brook	94
20. Greg Bachman, Austin Peay	93
Royce Bolinger, Gonzaga	93
Tim Colwell, North Dakota State	93
Eric Phillips, Ga. Southern	93
24. Roger Bernal, Texas-Pan American	92
Matt Honchel, Miami (OH)	92
Ryan Jones, Michigan State	92
Tyler Naquin, Texas A&M	92
28. Chris Diaz, North Carolina State	91
Adam Frazier, Mississippi State	91
Adam T. McClain, Memphis	91
Jake Rickenbach, Utah Valley	91
Chris Serritella, Southern Illinois	91
33. Bill Cullen, VCU	90
Anthony Gomez, Vanderbilt	90
Brett Vertigan, UC Santa Barbara	90
Ryan Walker, Texas-Arlington	90
37. Jordan Keur, Michigan State	89
Kenton Parmley, Southeast Mo. State	89
39. Stephen Bruno, Virginia	88
Billy Burgess, Utah Valley	88
Saxon Butler, Samford	88
Boomer Collins, Dallas Baptist	88
Marty Gantt, Col. of Charleston	88
Tanner Mathis, Mississippi	88
James Ramsey, Florida State	88
Brig Tison, George Mason	88
47. Brian Blasik, Dayton	87
Joey Cujas, VCU	87
Andrew Deeds, Morehead State	87
Justin Guidry, Middle Tenn.	87
Reed Harper, Austin Peay	87
Mike Miller, Cal Poly	87
Trenton Moses, Southeast Mo. State	87

Devon Travis, Florida State	87
Trea Turner, North Carolina State	87

TOTAL BASES

RANK NAME, TEAM	TB
1. D.J. Peterson, New Mexico	182
2. William Carmona, Stony Brook	177
3. Goose Kallunki, Utah Valley	168
4. Travis Jankowski, Stony Brook	165
5. Mitchell Garver, New Mexico	164
Mike Zunino, Florida	164
7. Trenton Moses, Southeast Mo. State	162
8. Brandon Miller, Samford	160
9. Greg Bachman, Austin Peay	157
10. Jimmy Rider, Kent State	156
Chris Serritella, Southern Illinois	156
12. Danny Poma, Hofstra	155
13. Preston Tucker, Florida	153
14. Boomer Collins, Dallas Baptist	152
James Ramsey, Florida State	152
16. Nick Backlund, Mercer	149
Sean Bignall, Ark.-Little Rock	149
Saxon Butler, Samford	149
19. Bill Cullen, VCU	148
Daniel Kassouf, Appalachian State	148
21. Royce Bolinger, Gonzaga	147
Josh Ludy, Baylor	147
George Roberts, Kent State	147
24. Richie Rodriguez, Eastern Ky.	146
25. Marty Gantt, Col. of Charleston	145
Robert Refsnyder, Arizona	145
27. Kris Bryant, San Diego	143
Kenton Parmley, Southeast Mo. State	143
29. Zach Stephens, Tennessee Tech	142
Jacob Wilson, Memphis	142
31. Matt Pollock, Buffalo	141
Jose Trevino, Oral Roberts	141
33. Ryan Mathews, North Carolina State	140
Ben Waldrip, Jacksonville State	140
35. Tyler Molinaro, UNC Wilmington	139
Jordan Steranka, Penn State	139
37. Daniel Bowman, Coastal Carolina	137
Andy Chriscaden, Kennesaw State	137
39. Johnny Field, Arizona	136
Jordan Hankins, Austin Peay	136
Thomas Pope, UNC Wilmington	136
42. Evan Campbell, Kent State	135
Chris Cowell, Richmond	135
Hunter Dozier, Stephen F. Austin	135
Phillip Ervin, Samford	135
Mike Garza, Georgetown	135
Tom Murphy, Buffalo	135
Devon Travis, Florida State	135
49. Austin Cousino, Kentucky	134
Jordan Dean, Central Mich.	134
Eric Phillips, Ga. Southern	134

WALKS

RANK NAME, TEAM	BB
1. Sherman Johnson, Florida State	69
Tanner Waite, New Mexico State	69
3. James Ramsey, Florida State	63
Richie Shaffer, Clemson	63
5. Stephen McGee, Florida State	61
6. Forrestt Allday, Central Arkansas	57
Parker Hipp, New Mexico State	57
8. D.J. Hicks, Central Florida	56
9. Brendan Norton, La Salle	55
10. Malcolm White, IPFW	54
Shane Zimmer, Canisius	54
12. Ben Magsig, Eastern Mich.	53
Ty Stetson, Murray State	53
14. Jared King, Virginia	51
Christian Walker, South Carolina	51
16. Adam Frazier, Mississippi State	50
David Lyon, Kent State	50

18. Chris Wolfe, Grambling	49
19. Danny Canela, North Carolina State	48
Nolan Fontana, Florida	48
Wade Hinkle, Kansas State	48
Aaron Judge, Fresno State	48
23. Pat Blair, Wake Forest	46
Chaz Frank, North Carolina	46
Jensen Painter, Ohio	46
Myles Parma, Ark.-Little Rock	46
Scott Wilcox, Western Ky.	46
28. Michael Blanchard, Austin Peay	45
Hector Crespo, Appalachian State	45
Marty Gantt, Col. of Charleston	45
Matt Lowenstein, Loyola Marymount	45
Jamodrick McGruder, Texas Tech	45
Evan Richard, Prairie View	45
Logan Uxa, Arkansas State	45
35. Jimmy Brenneman, Campbell	44
Spiker Helms, Missouri State	44
Brad Moss, Samford	44
Austin Nola, Louisiana State	44
Tim Wetzel, Ohio State	44
Ryan Yamane, Northern Colo.	44
41. Isaac Ballou, Marshall	43
Torsten Boss, Michigan State	43
Johnny Field, Arizona	43
Logan Pierce, Troy	43
Logan Vick, Baylor	43
46. Evan Boyd, Mercer	42
Marco DiRoma, Saint Louis	42
Josh Elander, Texas Christian	42
Trenton Moses, Southeast Mo. State	42
Michael Ratterree, Rice	42

TOUGHEST TO STRIKE OUT

RANK NAME, TEAM	AB/SO
1. Kyle Nisson, Quinnipiac	34.2
2. Kevin Plawecki, Purdue	27.9
3. Nick Ratajczak, Louisville	27.2
4. Maxx Tissenbaum, Stony Brook	26.8
5. Marquis Riley, N.C. A&T	24.1
6. Kai Hatch, Utah Valley	21.5
7. Joe Corfman, Toledo	21.4
8. Michael Pritchard, Nebraska	21.2
9. Pat Cantwell, Stony Brook	20.4
10. Darian Johnson, Lamar	19.3
11. Zac Mitchell, Belmont	18.6
12. Alex Swim, Elon	18.5
13. Zach Osborne, Tennessee	18
14. Matt Honchel, Miami (OH)	17.9
15. Raph Rhymes, Louisiana State	17.8
16. Andrew Aplin, Arizona State	17.7
17. Derek Hagy, Texas-Pan American	17.6
18. Zach Shank, Marist	17.3
19. Billy Urban, St. Bonaventure	17.1
20. Anthony Gomez, Vanderbilt	17
21. Preston Morrow, Texas-Arlington	16.9
22. J.J. Altobelli, Oregon	16.7
23. Ross Heffley, Western Carolina	16.5
Matt Miller, Northeastern	16.5
Gabe Guerino, Quinnipiac	16.5

HIT BY PITCH

RANK NAME, TEAM	HBP
1. Scott Davis, Delaware State	37
2. Nathan Orf, Baylor	35
Ronnie Richardson, Central Florida	35
4. Zac Mitchell, Belmont	30
5. Nick Ratajczak, Louisville	28
Michael Sterling, Southern Miss.	28
7. Jimmy Brenneman, Campbell	27
Pat Cantwell, Stony Brook	27
Juluis Green, Savannah State	27
10. Ryan Lindemuth, William & Mary	26
11. Bryan Conway, Richmond	25
Aaron Payne, Oregon	25

13. Marlon Calbi, Villanova	24
Chris Cook, George Mason	24
Paul Nice, VCU	24
16. Nick Camastro, Manhattan	23
17. Sean Bignall, Ark.-Little Rock	22
Tanner Vavra, Valparaiso	22
19. Cameron Cecil, Delaware State	21
Judd Edwards, La.-Monroe	21
Mike Levine, Saint Louis	21
Austin Wulf, Tennessee Tech	21
Ty Young, Louisville	21
Zac Zellers, Kentucky	21
25. James Alfonso, Hartford	20
Brendan Butler, Towson	20
Landon Curry, Indiana State	20
Jake Mahon, Evansville	20

SACRIFICE BUNTS

RANK NAME, TEAM	SH
1. Keith Werman, Virginia	28
2. Joe Meggs, Washington	24
3. Tanner Vavra, Valparaiso	23
4. Ben Hernandez, Southeastern La.	22
5. Zach Thoma, Western Mich.	21
6. Jon Clinard, Austin Peay	20
Scott Davis, Delaware State	20
Maxx Garrett, Gonzaga	20
Ben McQuown, Campbell	20
10. Kevin Cho, Oral Roberts	19
11. Nick Colwell, North Dakota State	18
Carlos Delgado, Bethune-Cookman	18
Drew Farber, UNC Wilmington	18
Mike Genovese, Seton Hall	18
Colin Harrington, Virginia	18
Tyler Heineman, UCLA	18
Jason Mahood, San Francisco	18
Aaron Payne, Oregon	18
John Tommasini, Oregon State	18
Chesny Young, Mercer	18
21. Pat Cantwell, Stony Brook	17
Cole Peragine, Stony Brook	17
Tyler Smith, Oregon State	17
24. Corey Davis, Wright State	16
Duran Elmore, Morehead State	16
Mark Elwell, Xavier	16
Brock Niggebrugge, Delaware	16
Lance Roenicke, UC Santa Barbara	16

SACRIFICE FLIES

RANK NAME, TEAM	SH
1. Mike Zunino, Florida	11
2. Brett Austin, North Carolina State	10
C.J. Gillman, Dayton	10
D.J. Hicks, Central Florida	10
Andrew Parker, Towson	10
6. Stephen Bruno, Virginia	9
Cody Gougler, Southeastern La.	9
Michael Katz, William & Mary	9
George Roberts, Kent State	9
Alfredo Rodriguez, Maryland	9
11. Brian Blasik, Dayton	8
Kyle Bluestein, Jacksonville State	8
Jonathan Carpen, Chicago State	8
Parker Hipp, New Mexico State	8
Casey Kalenkosky, Texas State	8
Evan Marzilli, South Carolina	8
Stephen McGee, Florida State	8
Alex Mejia, Arizona	8
Riley Moore, Arizona	8
Jessie Plumlee, Sam Houston State	8
Jeremy Rathjen, Rice	8
Brian Rowry, Southern	8
Tucker Rubino, Eastern Mich.	8
Justin Shafer, Florida	8
Eric Stamets, Evansville	8

PITCHING

Minimum 50 IP, 1 IP per team game

EARNED RUN AVERAGE

RANK NAME, TEAM	YEAR	G	IP	R	ER	ERA
1. Nick Petree, Missouri State	So.	16	115	22	13	1.01
2. David Berg, UCLA	Fr.	50	74	14	12	1.46
3. Marco Gonzales, Gonzaga	So.	12	93	18	16	1.55
4. Carlos Rodon, North Carolina State	Fr.	17	115	29	20	1.57
5. Aaron Burke, Coastal Carolina	Jr.	35	80	22	14	1.58
6. Andrew Heaney, Oklahoma State	Jr.	15	118	23	21	1.60
7. Joe Popielarczyk, Massachusetts	Sr.	12	87	26	16	1.66
8. Matt Davenport, William & Mary	Sr.	17	109	32	21	1.73
9. Joe Spring, Oral Roberts	Sr.	28	76	20	15	1.78
10. Alex Cruz, Georgia Tech	So.	30	74	20	15	1.83
11. Blake Mascarello, Purdue	Sr.	29	73	23	15	1.86
12. Cory Kent, Lehigh	Sr.	15	62	17	13	1.88
13. Andy Smithmyer, East Carolina	Jr.	22	61	21	13	1.92
14. Benton Moss, North Carolina	Fr.	17	79	25	17	1.94
15. Drew Bowen, Oral Roberts	Sr.	14	88	27	19	1.95
16. Kent Emanuel, North Carolina	So.	17	110	33	24	1.96
Josh Turley, Baylor	Jr.	17	110	31	24	1.96
18. Andrew Pierce, Southern Miss.	Jr.	15	99	23	22	1.99
19. Kyle Kraus, Portland	Sr.	16	111	38	25	2.03
20. Andrew Vasquez, UC Santa Barbara	Fr.	15	89	31	20	2.03
21. Trevor Williams, Arizona State	So.	16	110	33	25	2.05
22. Joe Kurrasch, Penn State	Jr.	16	88	26	20	2.05
23. Will Hudgins, Notre Dame	Sr.	15	96	44	22	2.06
24. Michael Wacha, Texas A&M	Jr.	16	113	31	26	2.07
25. Ryan Van Spronsen, Wagner	Sr.	12	100	25	23	2.07
26. Jerry Keel, Cal State Northridge	Fr.	16	91	26	21	2.07
27. Corey Knebel, Texas	So.	27	74	20	17	2.08
28. Duke von Schamann, Texas Tech	So.	12	87	28	20	2.08
29. Preston Morrison, Texas Christian	Fr.	22	113	29	26	2.08
30. Travis Radke, Portland	Fr.	15	86	23	20	2.09
31. Ryan Connolly, Coastal Carolina	Jr.	35	77	24	18	2.10
32. Kevin Brandt, East Carolina	Sr.	16	106	37	25	2.12
33. James Pazos, San Diego	Jr.	29	63	17	15	2.14
34. Rayan Gonzalez, Bethune-Cookman	Sr.	15	92	27	22	2.15
35. Tyler Moore, North Florida	So.	18	79	29	19	2.16
36. Reed Garrett, VMI	Fr.	25	54	18	13	2.17
37. John Niggli, Liberty	Sr.	16	104	28	25	2.17
38. Martin Agosta, St. Mary's	Jr.	14	103	34	25	2.18
39. Abe Bobb, San Francisco	So.	14	87	24	21	2.18
40. Braden Shipley, Nevada	So.	15	98	26	24	2.20
41. Daniel Minor, A&M-Corpus Christi	Jr.	16	110	35	27	2.20
42. Eddie Butler, Radford	Jr.	14	98	29	24	2.20
43. Trent Blank, Baylor	Sr.	19	105	30	26	2.23
44. Kyle Heyer, Arizona	Jr.	19	153	55	38	2.24
45. Kyle Crockett, Virginia	So.	32	60	22	15	2.25
46. Brady Rodgers, Arizona State	Jr.	15	115	36	29	2.27
47. Jonny Hoffman, Indiana	Jr.	29	63	23	16	2.27
48. Ryan Billo, Evansville	So.	13	75	23	19	2.28
49. Jonathan Sa, Texas-Pan American	Sr.	17	63	20	16	2.29
50. Alex Gonzalez, Oral Roberts	So.	17	86	31	22	2.30
51. Justin Amlung, Louisville	Jr.	16	109	34	28	2.31
52. T.J. Oakes, Minnesota	Jr.	14	97	30	25	2.31
53. Joey Wagman, Cal Poly	Jr.	15	108	35	28	2.33
54. Desmond Russell, Jackson State	So.	17	108	33	28	2.34
55. Ricky Knapp, Fla. Gulf Coast	So.	15	111	31	29	2.35
56. Pat Lowery, Columbia	Sr.	9	54	22	14	2.35
57. Taylor Haydel, Western Ky.	Jr.	25	65	22	17	2.35
58. Jordan Egan, Norfolk State	Jr.	19	57	27	15	2.36
59. Chris Stratton, Mississippi State	Jr.	17	110	33	29	2.38
60. Alex Keudell, Oregon	Sr.	18	125	42	33	2.38
61. Marcus Stroman, Duke	Jr.	14	98	31	26	2.39
62. Pat Light, Monmouth	Jr.	14	101	35	27	2.40
63. Chris Rowley, Army	Jr.	15	97	30	26	2.40
64. Michael Roth, South Carolina	Sr.	20	137	41	37	2.43
65. Brandon Moore, Arkansas	So.	29	81	28	22	2.44
66. Shawn Stuart, Long Beach State	Sr.	14	92	30	25	2.44
67. Jordan John, Oklahoma	So.	27	122	41	33	2.44
68. Joe Pistorese, Washington State	Fr.	15	66	24	18	2.44
69. Jace Fry, Oregon State	Fr.	13	88	35	24	2.45
70. Chase Brookshire, Belmont	Jr.	16	110	33	30	2.45
Vince Voiro, Penn	Sr.	10	66	29	18	2.45
72. James Buckelew, Belmont	So.	14	73	27	20	2.46
73. Colton Turner, Texas State	Jr.	14	88	38	24	2.46
74. Adam Plutko, UCLA	So.	18	120	35	33	2.48
David Starn, Kent State	Sr.	19	120	39	33	2.48
76. Francis Brooke, Northwestern	Sr.	15	97	45	27	2.51
77. David Randall, Mercer	Jr.	16	82	30	23	2.52
78. Michael Oros, Sam Houston State	Sr.	25	79	31	22	2.52
79. Tyler Johnson, Stony Brook	Sr.	16	100	35	28	2.52
80. Pierce Johnson, Missouri State	Jr.	14	100	35	28	2.53
81. Mike Hoekstra, Eastern Illinois	Sr.	16	110	46	31	2.53
82. Aaron West, Washington	Jr.	17	96	29	27	2.53
83. Matt Fyffe, Eastern Ky.	Sr.	22	71	28	20	2.54
84. Kevin Brady, Clemson	Jr.	14	64	22	18	2.54
85. Nate Koneski, Holy Cross	Sr.	14	74	28	21	2.54
86. Bobby Wahl, Mississippi	So.	17	99	36	28	2.55
87. Tom Jameson, Nevada	Jr.	15	95	37	27	2.55
88. Anthony Marzi, Connecticut	So.	15	99	42	28	2.55
89. Josh Cotham, Lipscomb	Sr.	13	81	24	23	2.56
90. John Simms, Rice	So.	25	63	21	18	2.56
91. Mark Appel, Stanford	Jr.	16	123	39	35	2.56
92. Zak Sterling, Richmond	Fr.	13	77	23	22	2.57
93. Michael Wagner, San Diego	So.	31	59	20	17	2.58
94. Hudson Randall, Florida	Jr.	16	94	28	27	2.59
95. Scott Warwick, Fairfield	Sr.	12	73	29	21	2.60
96. Tyler Herb, Coastal Carolina	So.	17	97	46	28	2.61
97. Matt Kuna, Toledo	Sr.	16	79	28	23	2.61
98. John Straka, North Dakota State	Jr.	15	110	37	32	2.61
99. A.J. Vanegas, Stanford	So.	21	65	22	19	2.62
100. Jose De Leon, Southern	So.	13	82	28	24	2.62

WINS

RANK NAME, TEAM	W	L
1. Kurt Heyer, Arizona	13	2
2. Mike Compton, Florida State	12	2
Kevin Gausman, Louisiana State	12	2
Tyler Johnson, Stony Brook	12	2
Josh Martin, Samford	12	2
Trevor Williams, Arizona State	12	2
Adam Plutko, UCLA	12	3
Lance Day, Texas-Arlington	12	4
9. Ryan Arrowood, Appalachian State	11	0
Trent Blank, Baylor	11	1
Joe Haase, Purdue	11	1
Chris Rowley, Army	11	1
Taylor Sewitt, Manhattan	11	2
Chris Stratton, Mississippi State	11	2
Tyler Skulina, Kent State	11	3
Michael Trionfo, Towson	11	3
Konner Wade, Arizona	11	3
Travis Ballew, Texas State	11	4
Quintavious Drains, Jackson State	11	4
David Starn, Kent State	11	4
Alex Keudell, Oregon	11	5
22. Kyle Anderson, Cal Poly	10	1
Mark Appel, Stanford	10	2
Charles Basford, Samford	10	2
Jordan Elliott, Delaware State	10	2
Matt Pegler, Col. of Charleston	10	2
Desmond Russell, Jackson State	10	2
Ryan Bores, Kent State	10	3
Jeremy Gendlek, Utah Valley	10	3
Daniel Minor, A&M-Corpus Christi	10	3
Brady Rodgers, Arizona State	10	3
Dlan Floro, Cal State Fullerton	10	4
Nick Petree, Missouri State	10	4
Ross Stripling, Texas A&M	10	4
Nick Vander Tuig, UCLA	10	4
Aaron Burke, Coastal Carolina	10	5
37. Carlos Rodon, North Carolina State	9	0
Matt Fyffe, Eastern Ky.	9	1
Jacob Lee, Arkansas State	9	1
Michael Roth, South Carolina	9	1
Derrick Stultz, South Fla.	9	1
Josh Turley, Baylor	9	1
Michael Wacha, Texas A&M	9	1
Martin Agosta, St. Mary's	9	2
Stefan Crichton, Texas Christian	9	2
Rayan Gonzalez, Bethune-Cookman	9	2
Shane Halley, Virginia	9	2
Tyler Herb, Coastal Carolina	9	2
Corey Littrell, Kentucky	9	2
Ben Lively, Central Florida	9	2
Jordan Marker, Wright State	9	2
Preston Morrison, Texas Christian	9	2
Grant Watson, UCLA	9	2
Josh Carr, Kennesaw State	9	3
Ryan Garton, Florida Atlantic	9	3
Jon Prosinski, Seton Hall	9	3
Hudson Randall, Florida	9	3
Sam Selman, Vanderbilt	9	3

Name, Team		
Joey Wagman, Cal Poly	9	3
Justin Amlung, Louisville	9	4
Alex Byo, Tulane	9	4
Dylan Clark, Elon	9	4
Chance Cleveland, Ark.-Little Rock	9	4
Casey Delgado, Austin Peay	9	4
Dylan Hills, Southeastern La.	9	4
Justin Jackson, Sam Houston State	9	4
Ricky Knapp, Fla. Gulf Coast	9	4
Taylor Massey, Dallas Baptist	9	4
Matt McClain, Delaware State	9	4
Tyler McSwain, UNC Wilmington	9	4
John Niggli, Liberty	9	4
Christian Powell, Col. of Charleston	9	4
Braden Shipley, Nevada	9	4
Jeff Thompson, Louisville	9	4
Troy Barton, Eastern Illinois	9	5
Steven Okert, Oklahoma	9	8

SAVES

RANK NAME, TEAM	SV
1. Stefan Lopez, Southeastern La.	20
2. Michael Wagner, San Diego	19
Jimmie Sherfy, Oregon	19
Michael Morin, North Carolina	19
5. Robbie Powell, Stetson	18
6. Michael Lorenzen, Cal State Fullerton	16
Nathan Hyatt, Appalachian State	16
Owen Jones, Portland	16
Robert Benincasa, Florida State	16
10. Scott Griggs, UCLA	15
11. Chris O'Grady, George Mason	14
12. Matt Gardner, Nevada	13
Matt Duncan, Morehead State	13
Michael Gomez, Fla. International	13
Matt Price, South Carolina	13
Joe Rogers, Central Florida	13
Dan Slania, Notre Dame	13
18. Eric Snyder, Fairleigh Dickinson	12
Chad Sobotka, S.C.-Upstate	12
Seth Willoughby, Xavier	12
Travis Parker, Saint Louis	12
DJ Ponder, Tulane	12
Michael Dimock, Wake Forest	12
Michael Schum, Wright State	12
Kenny Long, Illinois State	12
Todd Hornsby, Jacksonville State	12
Austin Maddox, Florida	12
Justin Thompson, Virginia	12
Tyler Rogers, Austin Peay	12
30. Bradley Roney, Southern Miss.	11
Nate Young, Elon	11
Jon Fitzsimmons, Canisius	11
Tyler Burgess, Missouri State	11
Bret Dahlson, Loyola Marymount	11
Taylor Garrison, Fresno State	11
John Koch, Arkansas State	11
John Colella, Holy Cross	11
Garrett Fanchier, Belmont	11
Jake Barrett, Arizona State	11
Kyle Glancy, Northern Illinois	11
Barrett Astin, Arkansas	11
Jordan Dailey, Bethune-Cookman	11
Ryan Connolly, Coastal Carolina	11
Nick Goody, Louisiana State	11
45. Lee Sosa, Binghamton	10
Brett Huber, Mississippi	10
Drew Reynolds, East Carolina	10
Max Garner, Baylor	10
Nick Blount, Tennessee	10
Russell Luxton, Oakland	10
Leif Sorenson, Massachusetts	10
Matt Rosinski, Miami (OH)	10
Kyle Bartsch, South Ala.	10

Name, Team	
Mike Bradstreet, Rhode Island	10
Ryan Mattes, Campbell	10
Nick Wittgren, Purdue	10
Chase Byerly, Butler	10
Kyle Friedrichs, Long Beach State	10
Preston Hatcher, Western Carolina	10
Blake Hauser, VCU	10
C.K. Irby, Samford	10
Michael Burchett, Sam Houston State	10
David Peterson, Col. of Charleston	10

STRIKEOUTS

RANK NAME, TEAM	SO
1. Andrew Heaney, Oklahoma State	140
2. Marcus Stroman, Duke	136
3. Kevin Gausman, Louisiana State	135
Carlos Rodon, North Carolina State	135
5. Mark Appel, Stanford	130
6. David Starn, Kent State	127
Chris Stratton, Mississippi State	127
8. Dillon Overton, Oklahoma	126
9. Ross Stripling, Texas A&M	120
10. Travis Ballew, Texas State	119
Pierce Johnson, Missouri State	119
12. Michael Wacha, Texas A&M	116
13. Chris Beck, Ga. Southern	115
Buck Farmer, Georgia Tech	115
Sean Manaea, Indiana State	115
16. Nick Petree, Missouri State	114
17. Joe Bircher, Bradley	113
Kurt Heyer, Arizona	113
19. Matthew Vedo, UC Santa Barbara	112
20. Dan Langfield, Memphis	111
Randy Zeigler, La.-Monroe	111
22. Andrew Barbosa, South Fla.	110
Daniel Minor, A&M-Corpus Christi	110
24. Kyle Hansen, St. John's	109
25. Brandon Yarusi, Wofford	107
26. Dustin Hunter, Western Illinois	106
Jordan John, Oklahoma	106
Eddie Orozco, UC Riverside	106
Tyler Skulina, Kent State	106
30. Justin Amlung, Louisville	105
Jonathan Gray, Oklahoma	105
Konner Wade, Arizona	105
33. Andrew Vasquez, UC Santa Barbara	104
Bobby Wahl, Mississippi	104
Kyle Zimmer, San Francisco	104
36. Jose De Leon, Southern	103
37. Pat Light, Monmouth	102
38. Andrew Mitchell, Texas Christian	101
39. Frank Duncan, Kansas	100
Kent Emanuel, North Carolina	100
Alex Wood, Georgia	100
42. Adam Plutko, UCLA	99
Matthew Reckling, Rice	99
44. Chance Cleveland, Ark.-Little Rock	98
Zach Cooper, Central Mich.	98
R.J. Hively, Mississippi	98
47. Ryan Beck, New Mexico State	97
48. DJ Baxendale, Arkansas	96
Andrew Pierce, Southern Miss.	96
Cody Schumacher, Missouri State	96

STRIKEOUTS PER NINE INNINGS

RANK NAME, TEAM	SO/9
1. Tyler Austin, Towson	12.66
2. Dustin Hunter, Western Illinois	12.55
3. Marcus Stroman, Duke	12.49
4. Matthew Vedo, UC Santa Barbara	12.25
5. Andrew Mitchell, Texas Christian	11.81
6. Chase Stevens, Oklahoma State	11.28
7. Jose De Leon, Southern	11.26
8. Jamie Gilley, Louisiana Tech	11.01
9. Matt Milroy, Illinois	10.98
10. Gera Sanchez, New Mexico	10.92
11. Matt Price, South Carolina	10.89
12. Dan Tobik, Tennessee-Martin	10.8
13. Pierce Johnson, Missouri State	10.74
14. Brandon Bixler, Fla. Gulf Coast	10.68
15. Dan Langfield, Memphis	10.66
16. Andrew Heaney, Oklahoma State	10.65
17. Drew Steckenrider, Tennessee	10.61
18. Kyle Zimmer, San Francisco	10.6
19. Carlos Rodon, North Carolina State	10.59
20. R.J. Hively, Mississippi	10.59
21. Andrew Vasquez, UC Santa Barbara	10.55
22. Ryan Harvey, Seton Hall	10.52
23. Travis Ballew, Texas State	10.47
24. Andrew Barbosa, South Florida	10.42
25. Chris Stratton, Mississippi State	10.42

FEWEST HITS PER NINE INNINGS

RANK NAME, TEAM	BB/9
1. Brandon Bixler, Florida Gulf Coast	5.03
2. David Berg, UCLA	5.11
3. James Pazos, San Diego	5.43
4. Carlos Rodon, North Carolina State	5.57
5. Alex Cruz, Georgia Tech	5.62
6. Andrew Heaney, Oklahoma State	5.63
7. Zak Sterling, Richmond	5.73
8. Andrew Vasquez, UC Santa Barbara	5.89
9. Chris Rowley, Army	5.92
10. Matthew Reckling, Rice	5.95
11. Travis Radke, Portland	5.97
12. Drew Steckenrider, Tennessee	6.04
13. Andrew Barbosa, South Florida	6.06
14. Corey Knebel, Texas	6.11
15. Marco Gonzales, Gonzaga	6.12
16. Jordan Hymel, Southeastern La.	6.17
17. Jose De Leon, Southern	6.23
18. Andrew Thurman, UC Irvine	6.24
19. Matt Milroy, Illinois	6.25
20. Chase Stevens, Oklahoma State	6.31
21. Brian Hunter, Hartford	6.37
22. Matt Price, South Carolina	6.37
23. Michael Oros, Sam Houston State	6.4
24. Andrew Mitchell, Texas Christian	6.43
25. Alex Gonzalez, Oral Roberts	6.59

FEWEST WALKS PER NINE INNINGS

RANK NAME, TEAM	BB/9
1. Adam Norton, Notre Dame	0.64
2. Aaron Nola, Louisiana State	0.7
3. Mike Augliera, Binghamton	0.76
4. Tyler Deetjen, Valparaiso	0.82
5. Hudson Randall, Florida	0.96
6. Preston Morrison, Texas Christian	0.96
7. Kerry Doane, East Tenn. State	0.96
8. Eric Erickson, Miami	1.02
9. Dylan Floro, Cal State Fullerton	1.02
10. Brian Connolly, UNC Asheville	1.04
11. Trevor Williams, Arizona State	1.07
12. Koby Gauna, Cal State Fullerton	1.09
13. Matthew Sisto, Hawaii	1.09
14. Kyle Kraus, Portland	1.14
15. Matt Gwaltney, Longwood	1.14
16. A.J. Ladwig, Wichita State	1.14
17. Jaron Long, Ohio State	1.15
18. Tyler Joyner, East Carolina	1.17
19. Justin Ziegler, Bradley	1.17
20. Seth Cutler-Voltz, VCU	1.18
21. Tom Briner, UC Davis	1.19
22. Jordan Montgomery, South Carolina	1.2
23. Matt Flemer, California	1.21
24. Brandon Moore, Arkansas	1.22
25. Seth Webster, Nicholls State	1.23

BATTING

SCORING

RANK TEAM	G	R	R/G
1. Utah Valley	59	532	9
2. Delaware State	58	475	8.2
3. New Mexico State	59	473	8
4. Hofstra	56	447	8
5. New Mexico	61	468	7.7
6. Arkansas-Little Rock	54	400	7.4
7. Arizona	65	478	7.4
8. Nebraska	58	413	7.1
9. Appalachian State	59	417	7.1
10. Stony Brook	67	471	7
11. Campbell	59	410	6.9
12. Illinois State	52	361	6.9
13. North Carolina State	63	437	6.9
14. Virginia	59	409	6.9
15. Florida State	67	459	6.9
16. Liberty	60	411	6.9
17. Southern	49	335	6.8
18. Dallas Baptist	60	410	6.8
19. Samford	64	436	6.8
20. Louisville	63	427	6.8
21. Wright State	58	390	6.7
22. Stanford	59	395	6.7
23. Eastern Ky.	54	361	6.7
24. Grambling	48	319	6.6
25. Kent State	67	445	6.6
26. Purdue	59	390	6.6
27. Central Florida	62	409	6.6
28. Nevada-Las Vegas	57	374	6.6
29. Mercer	59	384	6.5
30. Baylor	66	427	6.5
31. Austin Peay	64	414	6.5
32. South Carolina-Upstate	53	342	6.5
33. Buffalo	56	361	6.4
34. Texas-Pan American	52	335	6.4
35. Troy	58	373	6.4
36. Southern Illinois	59	378	6.4
37. Northern Colorado	60	383	6.4
38. St. John's	63	400	6.3
39. Georgia Tech	64	405	6.3
40. UNC Wilmington	62	392	6.3
41. Western Carolina	56	353	6.3
42. James Madison	53	332	6.3
Texas Southern	53	332	6.3
44. William & Mary	56	350	6.3
Maine	56	350	6.3
46. College of Charleston	60	374	6.2
Indiana State	60	374	6.2
48. Princeton	39	242	6.2
49. Rhode Island	59	366	6.2
50. Morehead State	55	341	6.2

BATTING AVERAGE

RANK TEAM	AVG
1. Utah Valley	.350
2. Hofstra	.334
3. Stony Brook	.331
4. Arizona	.329
5. New Mexico	.326
6. Northern Colorado	.319
7. Purdue	.316
8. Nebraska	.315
9. Campbell	.314
10. Wright State	.311

HOME RUNS

RANK, TEAM	HR
1. Florida	75
2. Arkansas-Little Rock	66
Samford	66
Eastern Kentucky	66
5. Col. of Charleston	65
Mercer	65
7. Dallas Baptist	63
8. Austin Peay	61
Southeast Missouri State	61
Richmond	61

DOUBLES

RANK, TEAM	2B
1. Kent State	164
2. North Carolina State	151
3. Hofstra	145
4. Stony Brook	143
5. Florida State	139
6. Buffalo	135
7. Appalachian State	134
8. New Mexico	133
9. Arizona	132
10. New Mexico State	130

TRIPLES

RANK, TEAM	3B
1. Northern Colorado	39
2. Stony Brook	36
3. Arizona	35
4. Virginia	32
5. Utah Valley	30
New Mexico	30
7. Nevada	28
8. Navy	27
9. Sam Houston State	26
10. North Carolina	25
Seton Hall	25

SLUGGING PERCENTAGE

RANK, TEAM	SLG
1. Utah Valley	.523
2. Stony Brook	.478
3. Arkansas-Little Rock	.477
4. Eastern Kentucky	.477
5. Dallas Baptist	.476
6. Buffalo	.476
7. Hofstra	.475
8. New Mexico	.472
9. Mercer	.461
10. Samford	.457

STOLEN BASES

RANK, TEAM	SB	CS
1. Dayton	164	34
2. Hofstra	157	58
3. Alabama State	132	38
4. Texas A&M	129	43
5. Rhode Island	122	33
6. Campbell	114	30
7. Auburn	113	38
8. Miss. Vallley State	110	28
Jackson State	110	28
10. Army	109	30

WALKS

RANK, TEAM	BB
1. Florida State	386
2. New Mexico State	347
3. Austin Peay	312
4. North Carolina	304
5. Baylor	296
6. Arkansas State	281
Ohio State	281
8. South Carolina	280
9. Coastal Carolina	279
Rice	279

PITCHING

EARNED RUN AVERAGE

RANK TEAM	ERA
1. Missouri State	2.57
2. Mississippi State	2.58
3. Coastal Carolina	2.65
4. North Carolina	2.66
5. Arkansas	2.83
6. Rice	2.85
7. Portland	2.89
8. Florida	2.92
9. Texas A&M	2.92
10. Gonzaga	2.95
11. South Carolina	2.97
12. Oregon	2.99
13. Oral Roberts	3.03
14. William & Mary	3.03
15. Liberty	3.04
16. Texas State	3.04
17. Long Beach State	3.08
18. Oklahoma State	3.08
19. Baylor	3.08
20. Saint Louis	3.08
21. Belmont	3.14
22. UCLA	3.15
23. Stony Brook	3.15
24. Minnesota	3.16
25. Cal State Fullerton	3.17
26. Purdue	3.17
27. Arizona State	3.19
28. Miami	3.20
29. Col. of Charleston	3.21
30. Maryland	3.21
31. Army	3.25
32. Indiana State	3.25
33. Louisiana State	3.25
34. San Francisco	3.27
35. Michigan State	3.28
36. UC Irvine	3.28
37. Hawaii	3.29
38. Mercer	3.32
39. Oklahoma	3.32
40. Sam Houston State	3.35
41. San Diego	3.35
42. Texas Christian	3.35
43. East Carolina	3.37
44. North Dakota State	3.38
45. Tulane	3.38
46. Kentucky	3.41
47. St. Mary's	3.42
48. Valparaiso	3.42
49. Texas	3.43
50. Creighton	3.44

STRIKEOUTS PER NINE INNINGS

RANK, TEAM	SO/9
1. Rice	9.1
2. Oklahoma State	8.7
3. Missouri State	8.7
4. Louisiana State	8.7
5. Florida International	8.7
6. Mississippi	8.6
7. North Carolina	8.5
8. Texas State	8.5
9. North Carolina State	8.4
10. Fresno State	8.3

FEWEST WALKS PER NINE INNINGS

RANK, TEAM	BB/9
1. Cal State Fullerton	1.87
2. Florida	2.07
3. Purdue	2.18
4. Hawaii	2.24
5. Texas A&M	2.27
6. Valparaiso	2.29
7. Binghamton	2.31
8. Dartmouth	2.33
9. Arizona State	2.33
10. William & Mary	2.33

FIELDING

FIELDING PERCENTAGE

RANK TEAM	PCT
1. Evansville	.981
2. Louisiana State	.980
3. Oklahoma State	.980
4. South Carolina	.980
5. Sacramento State	.979
6. Illinois State	.979
7. Oregon	.978
8. Creighton	.978
9. Georgia	.978
10. Stony Brook	.978
11. Tulane	.978
12. Washington	.978
13. Radford	.978
14. Washington State	.978
15. Cal Poly	.978
16. Florida	.977
17. Dartmouth	.977
18. Kansas	.977
19. Mississippi	.976
20. Minnesota	.976
21. UCLA	.976
22. Kentucky	.976
23. San Francisco	.976
24. Santa Clara	.976
25. Baylor	.975

DOUBLE PLAYS PER NINE INNINGS

RANK TEAM	DP/G
1. Illinois	1.3
2. Nevada	1.19
3. Hofstra	1.16
4. Washington State	1.13
5. Eastern Ky.	1.11
6. Mississippi State	1.11
7. Texas Christian	1.1
8. North Florida	1.07
9. Ohio State	1.07
10. Murray State	1.05

Batters: 10 or more at-bats. **Pitchers:** 5 or more innings.

1. ARIZONA

Coach: Andy Lopez. **Record:** 48-17.

PLAYER, POS., YEAR	AVG	AB	R	H	2B	3B	HR	RBI	SB
Johnny Field, of, So.	.370	257	72	95	18	7	3	44	11
Robert Refsnyder, of, Jr.	.364	258	64	94	19	4	8	66	14
Alex Mejia, ss, Jr.	.357	272	54	97	12	6	3	54	8
Seth Mejias-Brean, 3b, Jr.	.355	265	57	94	22	4	1	61	10
Bobby Brown, of, Sr.	.348	207	44	72	13	7	5	59	7
Joseph Maggi, of, Fr.	.326	144	19	47	5	1	0	19	3
Joey Rickard, of, Jr.	.320	259	60	83	17	2	1	33	18
Riley Moore, c, Fr.	.301	219	40	66	10	2	1	38	2
Trent Gilbert, 2b, Fr.	.272	235	34	64	7	2	0	42	4
Brandon Dixon, 1b, So.	.245	155	30	38	9	0	1	14	8
Jordan Berger, c, Fr.	.200	10	2	2	0	0	0	1	0

PLAYER, POS., YEAR	W	L	ERA	G	SV	IP	H	BB	SO
Kurt Heyer, rhp, Jr.	13	2	2.24	19	0	153	151	28	113
Tyler Crawford, lhp, Fr.	1	1	3.05	15	2	38	36	7	18
Mathew Troupe, rhp, Fr.	6	1	3.47	24	6	36	38	19	44
Konner Wade, rhp, So.	11	3	3.96	21	0	136	121	37	105
James Farris, rhp, So.	7	3	3.97	17	0	106	108	20	73
Tyler Hale, rhp, Jr.	2	0	4.05	12	0	20	19	16	23
Stephen Manthei, rhp, Jr.	6	4	4.29	23	2	36	32	16	25
Vincent Littleman, lhp, Jr.	0	1	6.26	9	0	23	25	10	15
Lucas Long, rhp, Fr.	2	2	7.20	9	0	25	34	10	18
Bill Augey, lhp, Jr.	0	0	0.00	5	0	7	2	1	7

2. SOUTH CAROLINA

Coach: Ray Tanner. **Record:** 49-20.

PLAYER, POS., YEAR	AVG	AB	R	H	2B	3B	HR	RBI	SB
Christian Walker, 1b, Jr.	.321	240	48	77	12	2	11	55	3
Tanner English, of, Fr.	.298	248	43	74	6	4	0	23	12
Evan Marzilli, of, Jr.	.284	268	51	76	14	4	2	32	13
Joey Pankake, ss, Fr.	.264	239	42	63	15	3	2	27	3
LB Dantzler, 3b, Jr.	.262	263	37	69	15	0	10	48	0
Chase Vergason, 2b, Jr.	.258	128	17	33	8	0	1	13	2
Adam Matthews, of, Sr.	.236	225	30	53	6	0	5	26	7
Grayson Greiner, c, Fr.	.222	194	26	43	13	1	6	32	0
Kyle Martin, 1b, Fr.	.295	78	11	23	5	0	1	12	0
TJ Costen, of, Fr.	.275	51	13	14	4	1	1	2	1
Erik Payne, 2b, So.	.265	98	10	26	5	3	3	19	2
Connor Bright, dh, Fr.	.228	79	8	18	1	0	0	9	1
Brison Celek, 1b, So.	.224	58	3	13	5	0	0	8	0
Michael Roth, lhp, Sr.	.211	19	0	4	2	0	0	2	0
Dante Rosenberg, c, Jr.	.209	67	7	14	3	0	0	7	0
Sean Sullivan, of, Jr.	.161	31	3	5	0	1	0	5	0

PLAYER, POS., YEAR	W	L	ERA	G	SV	IP	H	BB	SO
Michael Roth, lhp, Sr.	9	1	2.43	20	0	137	101	41	93
Colby Holmes, rhp, Jr.	7	2	3.05	16	0	80	66	17	65
Matt Price, rhp, Jr.	5	5	3.48	28	13	78	55	31	94
Jordan Montgomery, lhp, Fr.	6	1	3.62	15	0	75	69	10	57
Ethan Carter, rhp, Jr.	1	0	0.00	5	0	10	3	2	10
Tyler Webb, lhp, Jr.	6	1	1.56	39	3	58	44	18	58
Hunter Privette, rhp, Jr.	1	0	1.86	15	0	10	9	2	14
Nolan Belcher, lhp, Jr.	4	2	2.12	19	2	30	22	13	35
Joel Seddon, rhp, Fr.	2	0	2.76	9	1	16	9	6	13
Adam Westmoreland, lhp, Jr.	2	1	2.86	7	0	22	20	4	14
Patrick Sullivan, rhp, Jr.	0	0	3.52	13	0	23	25	11	16
Evan Beal, rhp, Fr.	4	4	3.81	28	5	52	39	32	55
Logan Munson, lhp, Sr.	0	0	4.50	11	0	8	8	2	8
Forrest Koumas, rhp, So.	2	3	4.82	18	3	28	31	17	31

3. FLORIDA

Coach: Kevin O'Sulivan. **Record:** 47-20.

PLAYER, POS., YEAR	AVG	AB	R	H	2B	3B	HR	RBI	SB
Mike Zunino, c, Jr.	.322	245	53	79	28	0	19	67	9
Preston Tucker, of, Sr.	.321	262	57	84	17	2	16	50	6

PLAYER, POS., YEAR	AVG	AB	R	H	2B	3B	HR	RBI	SB
Daniel Pigott, of, Sr.	.318	255	49	81	13	2	8	41	12
Brian Johnson, 1b, Jr.	.307	202	24	62	13	0	6	41	0
Nolan Fontana, ss, Jr.	.284	243	59	69	10	1	9	30	13
Casey Turgeon, 2b, Fr.	.281	231	35	65	11	3	4	30	10
Tyler Thompson, of, Sr.	.319	47	12	15	0	0	2	9	4
Justin Shafer, of, Fr.	.284	162	11	46	8	0	0	27	3
Vickash Ramjit, 1b, Sr.	.273	128	21	35	6	0	5	20	3
Connor Mitchell, of, Fr.	.273	11	4	3	0	0	0	1	0
Austin Maddox, c, Jr.	.265	65	5	18	2	0	0	5	0
Josh Tobias, 3b, Fr.	.252	135	26	34	5	2	0	10	3
Taylor Gushue, c, Fr.	.206	141	21	29	8	1	5	21	1
Cody Dent, 3b, Jr.	.134	82	9	11	0	0	0	4	1
Jeff Moyer, 3b, Sr.	.115	26	4	3	1	0	0	2	1

PLAYER, POS., YEAR	W	L	ERA	G	SV	IP	H	BB	SO
Greg Larson, rhp, Sr.	6	0	1.33	35	0	54	38	12	38
Steven Rodriguez, lhp, Jr.	3	2	2.18	34	4	62	49	13	81
Austin Maddox, rhp, Jr.	3	3	2.44	32	12	55	41	11	57
Hudson Randall, rhp, Jr.	9	3	2.59	16	0	94	86	10	62
Jonathon Crawford, rhp, So.	6	2	3.13	19	0	78	75	24	73
Brian Johnson, lhp, Jr.	8	5	3.90	17	0	90	87	18	73
Johnny Magliozzi, rhp, Fr.	4	3	5.03	16	0	34	45	5	21
Keenan Kish, rhp, So.	0	0	1.98	13	1	27	19	5	28
Daniel Gibson, lhp, So.	1	1	2.96	23	1	24	24	11	17
Bobby Poyner, lhp, Fr.	1	1	3.18	21	0	23	26	4	16
Ryan Harris, rhp, Fr.	2	0	3.38	16	0	16	12	4	12
Karsten Whitson, rhp, So.	4	0	3.51	14	0	33	37	18	20
Justin Shafer, rhp, Fr.	0	0	4.50	6	0	6	9	1	7

4. FLORIDA STATE

Coach: Mike Martin. **Record:** 50-17.

PLAYER, POS., YEAR	AVG	AB	R	H	2B	3B	HR	RBI	SB
James Ramsey, of, Sr.	.378	278	78	88	13	6	13	58	11
Jayce Boyd, 1b, Jr.	.376	255	47	96	21	0	4	61	8
Devon Travis, 2b, Jr.	.325	268	63	87	24	0	8	44	7
Sherman Johnson, 3b, Sr.	.283	247	64	70	18	0	5	38	4
Josh Delph, of, Fr.	.267	131	19	35	10	0	0	20	3
Justin Gonzalez, ss, Jr.	.256	211	42	54	11	0	9	42	13
John Nogowski, dh, Fr.	.250	140	21	35	5	0	2	23	2
Stephen McGee, c, So.	.230	204	35	47	9	0	0	41	2
Jose Brizuela, of, Fr.	.226	221	34	50	12	2	2	38	6
Seth Miller, of, Jr.	.212	146	20	31	7	2	3	29	4
Stephen Spradling, of, Jr.	.262	42	11	11	1	0	0	4	0
John Holland, dh, Jr.	.243	74	17	18	8	0	0	10	1
Giovanny Alfonzo, ss, Fr.	.107	28	7	3	0	0	0	4	2
Lee Howard, c, Fr.	.000	12	0	0	0	0	0	0	0
Sean O'Brien, of, So.	.000	12	1	0	0	0	0	0	0

PLAYER, POS., YEAR	W	L	ERA	G	SV	IP	H	BB	SO
Robert Benincasa, rhp, Jr.	4	2	1.32	32	16	41	24	7	58
Brandon Leibrandt, lhp, Fr.	8	3	2.82	19	0	99	89	29	83
Mike Compton, rhp, Fr.	12	2	2.87	18	0	91	89	28	64
Gage Smith, rhp, So.	5	0	2.89	39	3	53	53	17	32
Scott Sitz, rhp, Jr.	4	3	3.72	17	1	65	65	21	50
Hunter Scantling, rhp, Sr.	5	1	3.81	31	0	50	47	15	40
Peter Miller, rhp, So.	5	2	3.89	14	0	42	41	30	36
Luke Weaver, rhp, Fr.	1	0	5.93	16	1	41	31	21	40
Mack Waugh, rhp, Sr.	3	2	2.33	18	0	27	27	11	22
Brandon Johnson, lhp, So.	1	0	2.87	16	0	16	10	2	9
Bryant Holtmann, lhp, So.	2	0	3.20	24	0	25	24	9	17
Brian Busch, lhp, Sr.	0	1	5.04	28	0	25	32	17	20
Kyle Bird, lhp, Fr.	0	1	7.15	22	0	23	25	20	27

5. UCLA

Coach: John Savage. **Record:** 48-16.

PLAYER, POS., YEAR	AVG	AB	R	H	2B	3B	HR	RBI	SB
Jeff Gelalich, of, Jr.	.351	245	56	86	10	1	11	48	16
Cody Keefer, of, Jr.	.333	240	44	80	12	1	0	37	7
Tyler Heineman, c, Jr.	.332	211	42	70	7	1	1	27	3

	AVG	AB	R	H	2B	3B	HR	RBI	SB
Trevor Brown, 1b, Jr.	.321	246	41	79	13	2	3	52	4
Beau Amaral, of, Jr.	.313	268	63	84	10	5	4	46	13
Kevin Williams, 2b, So.	.302	159	28	48	6	0	2	21	4
Kevin Kramer, 3b, Fr.	.281	121	18	34	5	0	0	13	1
Pat Valaika, ss, Jr.	.266	229	37	61	11	4	1	39	5
Cody Regis, 3b, Jr.	.239	188	31	45	4	1	1	25	3
Shane Zeile, dh, Fr.	.371	62	12	23	3	1	0	10	1
Chris Keck, dh, Fr.	.293	41	3	12	3	0	0	5	0
Brenton Allen, of, So.	.286	14	5	4	2	0	0	2	0
Eric Filia-Snyder, of, Fr.	.245	53	6	13	1	0	0	8	3
Matt Giovinazzo, 1b, So.	.238	21	1	5	0	0	0	7	1
Brian Carroll, of, So.	.225	17	7	4	2	0	0	2	1
Pat Gallagher, 1b, So.	.100	20	0	2	0	0	0	5	0

PLAYER, POS., YEAR	W	L	ERA	G	SV	IP	H	BB	SO
Ryan Deeter, rhp, So.	1	0	0.89	36	0	30	20	18	26
David Berg, rhp, Fr.	5	3	1.46	50	1	74	42	17	63
Adam Plutko, rhp, So.	12	3	2.48	18	0	120	91	47	99
Scott Griggs, rhp, Jr.	3	1	2.65	36	15	37	23	31	64
Zack Weiss, rhp, So.	3	3	4.28	17	0	69	73	32	44
Nick Vander Tuig, rhp, So.	10	4	4.43	18	0	110	121	25	77
Grant Watson, lhp, Fr.	9	2	4.45	35	0	89	94	34	46
Eric Jaffe, rhp, Fr.	1	0	0.00	8	0	8	8	10	3
Chase Brewer, rhp, Jr.	2	0	1.69	15	0	16	13	11	6
Zack Ortiz, rhp, Fr.	2	0	2.92	12	0	12	16	9	6

6. ARKANSAS

Coach: Dave Van Horn. Record: 46-22.

PLAYER, POS., YEAR	AVG	AB	R	H	2B	3B	HR	RBI	SB
Matt Reynolds, 3b, Jr.	.323	235	48	76	20	0	7	45	16
Tim Carver, ss, Sr.	.299	264	38	79	15	0	2	30	15
Dominic Ficociello, 1b, So.	.290	252	45	73	15	1	6	41	4
Bo Bigham, 2b, Sr.	.269	216	30	58	10	0	1	18	9
Joe Serrano, of, Fr.	.333	69	13	23	1	1	0	7	4
Brian Anderson, of, Fr.	.283	120	23	34	4	0	2	11	2
John Clay Reeves, c, Fr.	.281	57	5	16	3	0	0	4	1
Jimmy Bosco, of, Jr.	.262	122	17	32	7	0	4	28	1
Jacob Mahan, 2b, Jr.	.257	144	15	37	3	0	0	18	2
Derrick Bleeker, of, Jr.	.250	160	22	40	10	3	6	23	2
Michael Gunn, of, Fr.	.250	24	1	6	1	0	0	5	0
Jake Wise, c, So.	.244	164	27	40	10	0	2	25	2
Sam Bates, of, Sr.	.240	129	23	31	6	0	6	25	3
Jacob Morris, of, So.	.236	140	27	33	9	3	3	23	5
Matt Vinson, of, Jr.	.217	120	16	26	5	1	0	13	2
Conor Costello, of, Fr.	.176	17	1	3	0	0	0	3	0
David Masters, ss, Fr.	.071	14	0	1	0	0	0	0	0

PLAYER, POS., YEAR	W	L	ERA	G	SV	IP	H	BB	SO
Brandon Moore, rhp, So.	5	2	2.43	29	3	81	68	11	36
Ryne Stanek, rhp, So.	8	4	2.82	17	0	93	75	36	83
DJ Baxendale, rhp, Jr.	8	5	3.11	20	0	107	97	29	96
Colby Suggs, rhp, So.	7	1	1.38	30	0	39	26	19	36
Barrett Astin, rhp, So.	3	5	1.99	32	11	59	46	25	61
Cade Lynch, lhp, Jr.	3	1	2.11	21	2	47	29	17	46
Nolan Sanburn, rhp, So.	4	1	2.43	20	0	41	29	22	49
Michael Gunn, lhp, Fr.	1	0	2.57	14	0	14	6	10	19
Tyler Wright, lhp, Jr.	1	0	2.60	16	0	17	15	12	19
Randall Fant, lhp, Jr.	2	3	3.27	15	0	52	59	11	39
Chris Oliver, rhp, Fr.	1	0	3.86	11	0	14	17	6	14
Trent Daniel, lhp, Jr.	2	0	5.06	21	1	32	32	15	25
Mark Reyes, lhp, Fr.	1	0	9.30	6	0	8	8	4	8

7. STONY BROOK

Coach: Matt Senk. Record: 52-15.

PLAYER, POS., YEAR	AVG	AB	R	H	2B	3B	HR	RBI	SB
Travis Jankowski, of, Jr.	.414	266	79	110	18	11	5	46	36
William Carmona, 1b, Jr.	.395	256	62	101	26	7	12	73	7
Maxx Tissenbaum, 2b, Jr.	.390	241	44	94	20	1	3	51	0
Steven Goldstein, of, Fr.	.337	166	36	56	8	3	4	34	14
Kevin Krause, dh, Jr.	.330	209	38	69	12	0	3	40	6
Tanner Nivins, of, Jr.	.306	206	35	63	11	3	2	34	4
Cole Peragine, ss, Fr.	.304	214	42	65	11	6	0	39	8
Kevin Courtney, 1b, So.	.293	174	32	51	14	0	4	38	1
Patrick Cantwell, c, Sr.	.290	224	57	65	11	4	2	34	10

	AVG	AB	R	H	2B	3B	HR	RBI	SB
Joshua Mason, of, So.	.300	10	4	3	1	0	0	3	0
Sal Intagliata, of, Sr.	.270	126	22	34	7	0	2	16	7
Anthony Italiano, c, So.	.238	42	4	10	0	0	0	5	0
Michael Roehrig, of, Fr.	.229	35	4	8	1	0	0	6	0
Luke Alba, ss, Fr.	.200	10	2	2	1	0	0	1	0
Michael Hubbard, of, So.	.192	26	4	5	1	0	1	2	0
Gabriel Pena, 2b, So.	.175	40	6	7	1	1	0	5	0

PLAYER, POS., YEAR	W	L	ERA	G	SV	IP	H	BB	SO
Frankie Vanderka, rhp, So.	3	3	2.33	21	5	66	39	23	47
Matt Gallup, rhp, Fr.	4	0	2.35	11	0	23	22	4	13
Tyler Johnson, rhp, Sr.	12	2	2.52	15	0	100	90	29	49
Brandon McNitt, rhp, So.	8	4	2.76	17	0	104	96	27	63
Joshua Mason, rhp, So.	3	1	3.23	20	3	39	30	16	32
Evan Stecko-Haley, rhp, Sr.	7	3	3.47	15	0	80	74	13	63
James Campbell, rhp, Jr.	5	0	3.47	19	3	57	42	17	42
Jasvir Rakkar, rhp, So.	6	2	3.68	20	3	51	41	20	41
G.C. Yerry, lhp, Jr.	1	0	3.31	8	1	16	22	9	14
Josh Barry, lhp, So.	1	0	5.62	6	0	8	10	5	6
Bryan Tatelman, rhp, So.	1	0	6.75	9	0	12	15	8	9
Zachary Uher, lhp, So.	0	0	7.04	9	0	8	13	3	11

8. KENT STATE

Coach: Scott Stricklin. Record: 47-20.

PLAYER, POS., YEAR	AVG	AB	R	H	2B	3B	HR	RBI	SB
George Roberts, 1b, Jr.	.364	264	45	96	23	1	8	66	2
Jimmy Rider, ss, Sr.	.359	295	70	106	30	1	6	58	3
Nick Hamilton, dh, Jr.	.337	178	20	60	12	2	1	35	1
Evan Campbell, of, Jr.	.312	279	61	87	20	4	7	40	5
T.J. Sutton, of, So.	.300	20	32	60	12	3	0	30	0
David Lyon, c, Sr.	.282	245	51	69	17	4	10	42	3
Sawyer Polen, 3b, Fr.	.278	198	39	55	8	4	4	31	3
Alex Miklos, of, So.	.250	156	23	39	8	4	2	21	5
Derek Toadvine, 2b, So.	.244	225	35	55	5	0	0	15	8
Tommy Monnot, c, Jr.	.324	71	9	23	8	0	0	11	0
Jason Bagoly, 1b, Jr.	.277	94	10	26	9	0	3	24	0
Cody Koch, 1b, So.	.273	22	4	6	1	0	0	0	0
Jeff Revesz, c, Fr.	.265	34	7	9	2	0	0	6	0
Troy Summers, of, So.	.217	83	23	18	4	0	0	10	2
Joe Koch, of, Sr.	.179	95	15	17	4	0	0	10	2

PLAYER, POS., YEAR	W	L	ERA	G	SV	IP	H	BB	SO
David Starn, lhp, Sr.	11	4	2.48	19	0	120	95	51	127
Ryan Bores, rhp, Jr.	10	2	3.33	18	0	111	116	18	68
Tyler Skulina, rhp, So.	11	3	3.77	18	0	107	97	45	106
Tim Faix, lhp, Fr.	1	0	1.98	7	0	14	18	6	11
Brian Clark, lhp, Fr.	5	0	2.08	22	4	30	19	10	28
Josh Pierce, rhp, Fr.	1	0	2.83	20	3	29	23	17	26
Eric Dorsch, rhp, Fr.	1	1	3.15	21	2	20	21	10	11
Casey Wilson, rhp, Jr.	1	0	3.53	30	7	36	31	10	27
Ryan Mace, rhp, Sr.	2	3	3.61	16	4	57	62	19	45
John Birkbeck, rhp, Fr.	1	0	3.77	12	0	14	10	6	7
Dan Kopcak, rhp, Fr.	0	0	5.27	10	0	13	11	8	17
Michael Clark, lhp, Fr.	3	4	5.40	17	0	33	32	29	48
Dan Slavik, rhp, So.	0	2	9.78	12	0	23	33	15	18

9. LOUISIANA STATE

Coach: Paul Mainieri. Record: 47-18.

PLAYER, POS., YEAR	AVG	AB	R	H	2B	3B	HR	RBI	SB
Raph Rhymes, of, Jr.	.431	232	44	100	11	0	4	53	2
Mason Katz, of, Jr.	.320	241	65	77	15	1	13	52	8
Austin Nola, ss, Sr.	.299	221	47	66	16	1	4	43	3
Ty Ross, c, So.	.292	185	19	54	6	1	3	41	2
Tyler Hanover, 3b, Jr.	.281	224	34	63	13	0	1	28	3
Tyler Moore, 1b, Fr.	.261	134	14	35	4	0	4	27	1
JaCoby Jones, 2b, Jr.	.253	245	42	62	13	1	4	29	11
Arby Fields, of, Jr.	.203	133	27	27	3	4	0	12	4
Jordy Snikeris, c, Sr.	.303	89	16	27	3	0	3	17	1
Jackson Slaid, of, So.	.271	48	10	13	1	1	1	8	0
Grant Dozar, dh, Sr.	.265	117	23	31	7	2	3	19	0
Chris Sciambra, of, Fr.	.246	61	10	15	2	1	0	11	2
Alex Edward, of, Jr.	.243	74	6	18	3	0	0	5	0
Jared Foster, of, Fr.	.218	110	21	24	5	0	1	13	4
Casey Yocom, 2b, Jr.	.211	57	11	12	2	0	0	4	0

PLAYER, POS., YEAR	AVG	AB	R	H	2B	3B	HR	RBI	SB
Beau Didier, ss, Sr.	.167	24	5	4	1	0	1	2	0
Evan Powell, c, Fr.	.143	14	3	2	1	0	0	4	0

PLAYER, POS., YEAR	W	L	ERA	G	SV	IP	H	BB	SO
Kevin Gausman, rhp, So.	12	2	3.77	18	0	123	106	28	135
Aaron Nola, rhp, Fr.	7	4	3.61	19	0	90	88	7	89
Ryan Eades, rhp, So.	5	3	3.83	17	0	94	107	28	63
Chris Cotton, lhp, Jr.	7	0	1.59	36	1	45	30	7	40
Joey Bourgeois, rhp, Jr.	3	2	2.38	26	0	34	22	14	37
Nick Goody, rhp, Jr.	1	2	2.67	35	11	34	28	12	26
Kevin Berry, rhp, Jr.	0	0	3.09	16	0	12	8	9	10
Brent Bonvillain, lhp, Jr.	4	0	3.49	22	0	28	27	12	26
Nick Rumbelow, rhp, So.	0	0	3.65	29	0	25	22	14	34
Joe Broussard, rhp, So.	4	1	3.73	19	0	41	37	12	45
Kurt McCune, rhp, So.	3	4	4.04	12	1	42	42	14	24
Cody Glenn, lhp, Fr.	1	0	5.62	11	0	16	24	6	16

10. BAYLOR
Coach: Steve Smith. Record: 49-17.

PLAYER, POS., YEAR	AVG	AB	R	H	2B	3B	HR	RBI	SB
Josh Ludy, c, Sr.	.362	232	41	84	15	0	16	71	1
Logan Vick, of, Jr.	.345	232	50	80	25	0	4	43	19
Dan Evatt, of, Sr.	.329	158	27	52	5	2	8	30	4
Max Muncy, 1b, Jr.	.322	255	55	82	17	3	7	56	7
Nathan Orf, c, Jr.	.303	234	61	71	10	2	2	31	17
Lawton Langford, 2b, So.	.301	206	43	62	7	2	0	20	7
Cal Towey, 3b, Jr.	.295	224	43	66	13	4	6	51	9
Adam Toth, of, Fr.	.286	154	28	44	8	1	1	18	18
Jake Miller, ss, Jr.	.278	234	33	65	13	2	1	31	3
Wes Mercurio, of, Jr.	.308	13	1	4	0	0	0	3	3
Steve DalPorto, 2b, Jr.	.306	36	6	11	1	0	0	6	0
Michael Howard, of, Fr.	.298	94	20	28	2	1	1	12	4
Logan Brown, of, Fr.	.269	52	12	14	1	0	0	4	7
Nate Goodwin, 2b, So.	.267	15	3	4	0	0	0	3	0
Joey Hainsfurther, c, Sr.	.136	22	3	3	0	0	0	5	0

PLAYER, POS., YEAR	W	L	ERA	G	SV	IP	H	BB	SO
Josh Turley, lhp, Jr.	9	1	1.96	17	0	110	95	21	79
Trent Blank, rhp, Sr.	11	1	2.23	10	0	105	92	25	61
Crayton Bare, lhp, So.	2	0	1.25	24	2	22	13	7	23
Dillon Newman, rhp, So.	4	4	2.40	21	2	45	39	11	44
Kolt Browder, rhp, Jr.	1	1	2.57	18	1	212	14	7	21
Tyler Bremer, rhp, Sr.	7	1	2.61	15	1	59	47	14	50
Ryan Smith, rhp, Fr.	3	1	3.14	14	1	29	30	6	15
Trae Davis, rhp, So.	0	0	3.65	9	0	12	10	6	6
Brad Kuntz, lhp, So.	4	2	4.20	19	1	41	32	21	40
Landry Miles, rhp, Jr.	0	0	4.26	6	0	6	2	5	2
Austin Stone, rhp, Fr.	3	1	4.60	12	0	31	27	16	21
Joey Hainsfurther, rhp, Sr.	2	1	4.62	14	1	37	50	13	29
Doug Ashby, lhp, So.	0	1	4.76	5	0	6	6	3	2
Max Garner, rhp, Jr.	3	3	4.89	22	10	46	45	19	43
Joe Kirkland, rhp, Fr.	0	0	6.14	7	0	7	5	5	9

11. OREGON
Coach: George Horton. Record: 46-19.

PLAYER, POS., YEAR	AVG	AB	R	H	2B	3B	HR	RBI	SB
Brett Thomas, of, So.	.313	201	22	63	14	4	1	25	9
Ryon Healy, 1b, So.	.312	253	35	79	13	1	4	42	3
Aaron Jones, of, So.	.303	208	38	63	13	2	6	39	7
Kyle Garlick, of, So.	.287	202	28	58	11	4	6	41	9
Aaron Payne, 2b,So.	.277	235	42	65	8	4	1	27	16
J.J. Altobelli, ss, Jr.	.265	200	32	53	12	1	0	14	6
Connor Hofmann, of, So.	.239	142	19	34	2	1	3	14	9
Brett Hambright, c, Sr.	.217	157	16	34	6	0	1	15	1
Vernell Warren, of, Sr.	.343	35	5	12	2	0	0	2	0
Ryan Hambright, 3b, Jr.	.265	102	11	27	2	1	1	12	0
Thomas Walker, 3b, Fr.	.227	66	10	15	3	0	1	4	0
Andrew Mendenhall, of, Jr.	.218	55	7	12	1	0	1	6	3
Kevin Shepherd, 3b, Sr.	.193	57	9	11	0	0	0	4	3
Scott Heineman, 3b, Fr.	.189	90	16	17	3	1	1	9	7
Shaun Chase, c, Jr.	.178	73	10	13	5	1	2	9	0
Jordan Spencer, 1b, Jr.	.111	18	1	2	0	0	0	0	0
Daniel Pardini, c, So.	.100	10	2	1	0	0	1	2	0
Billy Flamion, of, Fr.	.091	11	0	1	0	0	0	1	0

PLAYER, POS., YEAR	W	L	ERA	G	SV	IP	H	BB	SO
Alex Keudell, rhp, Sr.	11	5	2.38	18	0	125	103	30	74
Jake Reed, rhp, Fr.	8	4	2.92	17	0	114	91	42	67
Jeff Gold, rhp, So.	8	4	3.66	19	0	76	75	24	46
Joey Housey, rhp, Jr.	2	0	1.72	22	1	37	29	16	27
Thomas Thorpe, lhp, Fr.	2	0	2.11	35	1	43	24	20	48
Jimmie Sherfy, rhp, So.	5	3	2.20	36	19	61	36	34	93
Brando Tessar, rhp, So.	4	1	3.42	11	0	53	44	33	37
Jordan Spencer, lhp, Fr.	4	2	4.26	12	0	38	31	18	19
Billy Flamion, lhp, Fr.	1	0	4.85	11	0	13	4	11	12
David Wylie, rhp, Jr.	1	0	5.30	9	1	19	19	11	12

12. NORTH CAROLINA STATE
Coach: Elliott Avent. Record: 43-20.

PLAYER, POS., YEAR	AVG	AB	R	H	2B	3B	HR	RBI	SB
Danny Canela, c, Jr.	.348	227	46	79	18	9	6	46	0
Chris Diaz, ss, Jr.	.346	263	55	91	25	2	2	56	8
Trea Turner, 3b, Fr.	.336	259	72	87	13	2	5	43	57
Ryan Mathews, of, Sr.	.327	223	48	73	16	0	17	62	1
Jake Fincher, of, Jr.	.300	210	35	63	7	6	1	23	16
Brett Austin, c, Fr.	.284	243	49	69	17	1	0	37	6
Andrew Ciencin, 1b, Sr.	.278	223	41	62	14	1	5	36	5
Logan Ratledge, of , Fr.	.261	142	25	37	11	0	1	21	4
Tarran Senay, of, Jr.	.222	171	26	38	15	0	6	32	2
Matt Bergquist, 2b, Jr.	.222	144	19	32	8	1	1	21	2
Grant Clyde, of, Jr.	.316	19	4	6	2	0	0	4	0
Bryan Adametz, of, Jr.	.250	24	10	6	1	2	0	1	0
John Gianis, of, Sr.	.242	66	6	16	2	0	0	7	0

PLAYER, POS., YEAR	W	L	ERA	G	SV	IP	H	BB	SO
Carlos Rodon, lhp, Fr.	9	0	1.57	17	0	115	71	41	135
Ethan Ogburn, rhp, Jr.	5	4	3.38	19	2	91	89	19	71
Anthony Tzamtzis, rhp, So.	5	5	4.38	18	0	64	50	39	63
Travis Orwig, lhp, Jr.	1	1	2.19	18	0	12	12	5	11
Dillon Frye, rhp, Jr.	3	0	2.70	14	1	23	17	14	17
Chris Overman, rhp, Jr.	0	1	2.91	28	6	34	27	14	43
Danny Healey, rhp, Jr.	4	0	3.29	13	0	27	24	12	12
Vance Williams, rhp, Sr.	4	4	3.70	22	2	56	52	18	42
Ryan Wilkins, rhp, Jr.	5	2	5.09	25	1	53	59	18	49
D.J. Thomas, lhp, So.	2	2	5.59	21	1	39	47	16	29
Logan Jernigan, rhp, Fr.	5	1	5.71	14	0	52	39	35	57

13. STANFORD
Coach: Mark Marquess. Record: 41-18.

PLAYER, POS., YEAR	AVG	AB	R	H	2B	3B	HR	RBI	SB
Dominic Jose, of, Fr.	.375	40	8	15	3	1	1	11	2
Danny Diekroeger, 2b, So.	.354	96	16	34	4	1	3	10	1
Brian Ragira, 1b, So.	.329	252	41	83	15	0	5	50	3
Stephen Piscotty, 3b, So.	.329	246	44	81	13	3	5	56	4
Eric Smith, c, Jr.	.321	187	35	60	11	1	2	32	1
Alex Blandino, ss, Fr.	.294	153	26	45	9	1	8	40	4
Jake Stewart, of, Jr.	.294	194	40	57	16	0	7	27	3
Austin Wilson, of, So.	.285	221	56	63	12	2	10	54	7
Lonni Kauppila, ss, So.	.280	100	16	28	5	1	0	13	0
Kenny Diekroeger, ss, Jr.	.275	222	32	61	16	0	2	31	3
Tyler Gaffney, of, Jr.	.245	188	48	46	10	1	2	17	8
Brett Michael Doran, 2b, Jr.	.242	62	14	15	4	0	0	9	1
Brian Guymon, of, Jr.	.211	19	1	4	0	0	0	1	0
Christian Griffiths, dh, Jr.	.200	60	12	12	4	0	1	7	0
Justin Ringo, 1b, Jr.	.190	21	2	4	0	0	1	2	0
Wayne Taylor, c, Fr.	.152	33	4	5	2	1	0	1	1

PLAYER, POS., YEAR	W	L	ERA	G	SV	IP	H	BB	SO
Mark Appel, rhp, Jr.	10	2	2.56	16	0	123	97	30	130
A.J. Vanegas, rhp, So.	4	0	2.62	21	5	65	56	37	53
A.J. Talt, rhp, Sr.	0	0	2.84	6	0	6	6	2	3
Stephen Piscotty, rhp, Jr.	6	2	3.05	12	1	41	46	9	29
Garrett Hughes, lhp, So.	3	1	3.20	15	0	25	22	13	22
Sahil Bloom, rhp, Jr.	2	0	3.56	21	2	48	46	8	17
Dean McArdle, rhp, Jr.	3	3	3.97	24	0	48	48	19	38
David Schmidt, rhp, Fr.	3	1	3.98	25	3	32	34	17	14
John Hochstatter, lhp, Jr.	3	3	4.53	12	0	44	52	18	15
Brett Mooneyham, lhp, Jr.	7	6	4.75	15	0	83	79	39	90
Spenser Linney, lhp, Jr.	0	0	5.68	10	0	6	6	5	5

Sam Lindquist, rhp, So. 0 0 7.36 9 1 11 16 6 6

14. OKLAHOMA

Coach: Sunny Golloway. **Record:** 42-25.

PLAYER, POS., YEAR	AVG	AB	R	H	2B	3B	HR	RBI	SB
Max White, of, Jr.	.337	252	39	85	17	2	2	55	7
Matt Oberste, dh, So.	.312	125	28	39	10	0	6	22	6
Jack Mayfield, 2b, Jr.	.280	236	43	66	15	3	3	34	10
Brian Brightwell, of, Fr.	.270	37	5	10	1	0	0	4	1
Evan Mistich, of, Sr.	.267	187	30	50	9	1	3	35	4
Erik Ross, of, Sr.	.266	229	33	61	10	2	0	19	20
Cody Reine, of, Sr.	.263	213	45	56	10	6	6	33	5
Caleb Bushyhead, ss, Sr.	.260	250	33	65	7	1	1	17	9
Chase Simpson, dh, So.	.250	52	7	13	2	2	0	4	0
Hunter Lockwood, c, Fr.	.249	185	29	46	7	2	11	39	6
Dillon Yeaman, of, Jr.	.231	13	2	3	0	0	1	3	0
Garrett Carey, 3b, Jr.	.209	206	21	43	8	0	2	24	2
Tanner Toal, c, Sr.	.196	92	8	18	1	0	1	8	2
Dylan Neal, c, So.	.153	59	6	9	1	0	0	7	0
Dustin Dishman, 2b, Jr.	.077	13	1	1	0	0	0	0	0

PLAYER, POS., YEAR	W	L	ERA	G	SV	IP	H	BB	SO
Drew Krittenbrink, rhp, So.	1	0	0.00	2	0	10	6	3	1
Cale Coshow, rhp, Fr.	2	0	2.08	3	0	13	10	7	7
Jake Fisher, lhp, Jr.	1	0	2.08	9	1	13	12	4	14
Jordan John, lhp, So.	8	8	2.44	27	4	122	104	32	106
Drew Harrison, rhp, Jr.	1	0	2.93	6	1	15	11	9	12
Steven Okert, lhp, Jr.	9	8	3.07	30	5	85	72	37	78
Dillon Overton, lhp, So.	6	3	3.15	22	0	123	127	24	126
Jonathan Gray, rhp, Jr.	8	4	3.16	18	0	103	100	42	104
Damien Magnifico, rhp, So.	3	1	3.68	21	2	51	56	25	34
Kindle Ladd, rhp, So.	0	1	4.68	16	2	25	27	13	20
Ty Taylor, lhp, So.	0	0	6.97	5	0	10	12	4	3
Jacob Rhame, rhp, Fr.	1	0	7.20	10	0	15	15	2	7
Steven Bruce, rhp, So.	2	0	7.91	12	0	19	21	15	8

15. ST. JOHN'S

Coach: Ed Blankmeyer. **Record:** 40-23.

PLAYER, POS., YEAR	AVG	AB	R	H	2B	3B	HR	RBI	SB
Matt Wessinger, ss, Sr.	.348	247	62	86	14	1	6	48	34
Jeremy Baltz, of, Jr.	.344	241	65	83	13	4	8	52	18
Sean O'Hare, 3b, Jr.	.341	220	42	75	15	1	3	43	8
Frank Schwindel, 1b, So.	.332	202	33	67	5	1	4	30	0
Bret Dennis, 2b, Fr.	.298	104	20	31	3	0	0	14	1
Kyle Richardson, of, Sr.	.297	148	25	44	3	0	0	15	7
Pat Talbut, 1b, Jr.	.265	170	30	45	2	0	0	24	3
Danny Bethea, c, Jr.	.263	167	16	44	5	0	3	20	1
Zach Lauricella, 3b, Fr.	.263	175	29	46	4	1	2	32	6
Martin Kelly, of, So.	.232	142	29	33	7	1	0	17	4
Jimmy Brennan, of, Jr.	.207	135	13	28	3	2	0	19	1
Robert Case, c, Jr.	.250	52	10	13	3	0	0	5	1
Eric Peterson, 1b, Fr.	.208	48	7	10	2	0	0	8	1
Kevin Grove, of, So.	.200	15	2	3	0	0	0	1	0
Anthony Iacomini, 2b, So.	.150	60	11	9	0	2	1	5	5
Kyle Lombardo, 3b, So.	.111	18	6	2	0	1	0	1	2

PLAYER, POS., YEAR	W	L	ERA	G	SV	IP	H	BB	SO
Stephen Rivera, rhp, Sr.	5	0	1.79	27	4	55	42	16	53
Sean Hagan, lhp, Jr.	8	3	2.90	16	0	109	98	30	68
Brendan Lobban, lhp, Sr.	5	3	3.51	14	0	56	51	17	42
Kyle Hansen, rhp, Jr.	5	5	3.62	17	0	99	98	30	109
Matt Carasiti, rhp, Jr.	7	5	3.98	18	0	84	89	31	64
James Lomangino, rhp, So.	2	1	4.34	25	6	29	35	11	38
Kevin Kilpatrick, lhp, So.	3	3	4.96	28	5	49	46	16	29
Eddie Medina, rhp, Sr.	3	2	4.97	16	0	38	39	25	33
Jerome Werniuk, rhp, Jr.	1	1	7.11	13	0	13	13	11	7
Jake Woodward, lhp, So.	1	0	8.31	13	0	13	15	10	6
Brad Bellinger, rhp, Fr.	0	0	8.68	8	0	9	6	12	8

16. TEXAS CHRISTIAN

Coach: Jim Schlossnagle. **Record:** 40-22.

PLAYER, POS., YEAR	AVG	AB	R	H	2B	3B	HR	RBI	SB
Jason Coats, of, Sr.	.326	193	36	63	13	2	6	45	7

PLAYER, POS., YEAR	AVG	AB	R	H	2B	3B	HR	RBI	SB
Josh Elander, c, Jr.	.314	223	56	70	12	1	11	43	14
Kyle Von Tungeln, of, Jr.	.304	227	54	69	10	5	3	25	12
Derek Odell, 2b, Fr.	.276	174	30	48	5	4	4	26	6
Brance Rivera, of, So.	.229	175	42	40	9	0	4	26	7
Keaton Jones, ss, Fr.	.166	169	26	28	4	0	0	17	7
Kevin Cron, 1b, Fr.	.338	151	20	51	7	0	6	34	0
Jantzen Witte, 3b, Jr.	.315	162	21	51	12	0	3	22	1
Jerrick Suiter, dh, Jr.	.310	145	19	45	4	3	0	20	4
Josh Gonzales, 2b, Jr.	.250	60	9	15	3	0	1	7	1
Davy Wright, 3b, Jr.	.239	117	19	28	8	0	0	7	0
Brett Johnson, 1b, So.	.228	101	13	23	7	0	1	10	2
Braden Mattson, c, So.	.190	63	5	12	3	1	0	7	1
Zac Jordan, of, Sr.	.180	89	7	16	1	0	0	14	1
Axel Johnson, of, Fr.	.118	17	1	2	0	0	0	3	0
Michael Resnick, 1b, So.	.083	12	0	1	1	0	0	4	0

PLAYER, POS., YEAR	W	L	ERA	G	SV	IP	H	BB	SO
Preston Morrison, rhp, Fr.	9	2	2.08	22	1	113	88	12	72
Stefan Crichton, rhp, So.	9	2	3.41	19	0	95	103	18	53
Brandon Finnegan, lhp, Fr.	4	5	3.47	23	0	62	51	30	56
Andrew Mitchell, rhp, So.	5	3	3.74	17	0	77	55	46	101
Tyler Duffie, rhp, So.	1	0	0.00	5	0	9	3	5	8
Kevin Allen, rhp, Jr.	5	3	2.97	28	5	26	18	17	43
Kaleb Merck, rhp, Jr.	1	1	3.12	24	5	26	18	10	25
Justin Scharf, rhp, Jr.	4	2	3.23	38	4	47	49	14	30
Jerrick Suiter, rhp, Fr.	0	1	3.60	6	0	10	10	4	7
Travis Evans, lhp, Fr.	1	0	4.05	7	0	7	6	3	9
Trey Teakell, rhp, Fr.	1	2	4.70	19	0	46	52	10	25
Nick Frey, rhp, So.	0	1	4.81	10	0	24	32	11	15
Chris Murphy, rhp, So.	0	0	7.71	5	0	7	12	3	1

17. NORTH CAROLINA

Coach: Mike Fox. **Record:** 46-16.

PLAYER, POS., YEAR	AVG	AB	R	H	2B	3B	HR	RBI	SB
Colin Moran, 3b, So.	.365	170	30	62	11	1	3	35	1
Jacob Stallings, c, Sr.	.294	238	44	70	24	0	1	24	5
Chaz Frank, of, Jr.	.293	242	45	71	14	6	0	39	16
Jordan Parks, of, So.	.270	189	29	51	7	4	0	31	7
Michael Russell, of, Fr.	.269	223	40	60	14	1	0	24	14
Cody Stubbs, 1b, Jr.	.258	233	39	60	19	0	5	35	6
Mike Zolk, 2b, Fr.	.255	161	20	41	6	2	0	26	2
Tommy Coyle, ss, Sr.	.244	246	53	60	7	6	4	29	14
Grayson Atwood, 1b, Fr.	.353	17	6	6	1	0	1	5	0
Brian Holberton, c, So.	.297	118	22	35	5	2	1	15	1
Tom Zengel, dh, So.	.286	91	19	26	7	2	0	19	2
Adam Griffin, of, Fr.	.267	86	14	23	1	1	0	20	3
Shell McCain, 2b, Fr.	.235	81	9	19	3	0	2	14	0
Matt Roberts, c, Fr.	.111	27	1	3	1	0	0	3	0

PLAYER, POS., YEAR	W	L	ERA	G	SV	IP	H	BB	SO
Benton Moss, rhp, Fr.	7	2	1.94	17	0	79	65	23	83
Kent Emanuel, lhp, So	8	4	1.96	17	0	110	91	23	100
Michael Morin, rhp, Jr.	6	4	1.40	38	19	58	38	19	55
Hobbs Johnson, lhp, So.	7	1	1.56	22	0	58	37	24	69
Chris McCue, rhp, Fr.	1	0	2.10	25	0	26	22	9	17
R.C. Orlan, lhp, Jr.	8	1	2.21	38	0	57	55	11	66
Tate Parrish, lhp, So.	1	0	2.89	25	0	9	11	5	13
Chris O'Brien, lhp, Fr.	1	2	3.46	14	0	26	30	11	16
Shane Taylor, rhp, So.	5	1	3.48	26	0	41	38	17	34
Chris Munnelly, rhp, So.	2	0	3.61	15	0	47	43	27	24
Mason McCullough, rhp, Fr.	0	0	3.86	16	0	9	9	8	8
Luis Paula, rhp, Fr.	0	1	5.95	13	0	20	25	11	21
Cody Penny, rhp, Jr.	0	0	6.61	18	0	16	19	9	19

18. RICE

Coach: Wayne Graham. **Record:** 41-19.

PLAYER, POS., YEAR	AVG	AB	R	H	2B	3B	HR	RBI	SB
Christian Stringer, 2b, Jr.	.343	236	58	81	12	3	3	36	6
Jeremy Rathjen, of, Jr.	.329	219	39	72	14	1	9	42	6
J.T. Chargois, 1b, Jr.	.323	189	26	61	10	0	0	31	1
Micheal Fuda, of, Sr.	.298	245	36	73	12	3	8	45	9
Ford Stainback, ss, Fr.	.289	142	30	41	8	0	0	17	2
Craig Manuel, c, Sr.	.275	171	19	47	6	0	2	25	1
Shane Hoelscher, 3b, So.	.244	217	36	53	9	1	4	30	5

PLAYER, POS., YEAR	AVG	AB	R	H	2B	3B	HR	RBI	SB
Michael Ratterree, of, Jr.	.233	189	39	44	13	1	6	32	6
Ryan Lewis, 1b, Jr.	.225	151	14	34	7	1	2	28	4
Michael Aquino, of, So.	.324	37	1	12	2	0	0	3	0
Keenan Cook, of, So.	.304	46	9	14	2	0	0	3	3
Geoff Perrott, c, Jr.	.289	38	10	11	5	0	0	2	0
Chase McDowell, of, So.	.243	37	6	9	2	0	1	5	0
Syler Ewing, c, Fr.	.182	11	0	2	0	0	0	0	1
Derek Hamilton, ss, So.	.151	86	10	13	4	0	0	4	5

PLAYER, POS., YEAR	W	L	ERA	G	SV	IP	H	BB	SO
John Simms, rhp, So.	6	0	2.56	25	0	63	47	22	59
Austin Kubitza, rhp, So.	6	5	2.69	16	0	80	60	38	73
Andrew Benak, rhp, Jr.	7	2	2.70	16	0	67	63	18	72
Matthew Reckling, rhp, Jr.	8	3	2.98	17	0	88	58	36	99
Taylor Wall, lhp, Sr.	6	4	3.08	29	1	61	50	24	51
Evan Rutter, rhp, Fr.	0	0	0.00	6	0	7	6	0	3
Tyler Duffey, rhp, Jr.	1	1	1.93	36	7	51	33	21	68
J.T. Chargois, rhp, Jr.	4	1	2.15	25	8	38	28	12	38
Zech Lemond, rhp, Jr.	1	0	2.52	15	1	36	27	15	32
Jordan Stephens, rhp, Fr.	2	3	4.38	14	0	39	30	25	40
Chase McDowell, rhp, So.	0	0	4.50	9	0	10	13	1	9

19. TEXAS A&M
Coach: Rob Childress. Record: 43-18.

PLAYER, POS., YEAR	AVG	AB	R	H	2B	3B	HR	RBI	SB
Tyler Naquin, of, Jr.	.380	242	56	92	18	6	3	49	21
Jacob House, 1b, Sr.	.308	234	40	72	14	0	8	56	10
Mikey Reynolds, ss, Jr.	.306	216	55	66	12	3	1	23	21
Troy Stein, c, So.	.304	158	16	48	12	0	2	25	1
Matt Juengel, dh, Sr.	.292	236	31	69	8	1	2	46	17
Scott Arthur, 2b, Sr.	.273	165	36	45	4	1	0	20	18
Brandon Wood, of, Jr.	.258	178	30	46	10	1	5	25	10
Krey Bratsen, of, So.	.226	199	34	45	5	2	1	25	21
Jace Statum, of, So.	.289	45	11	13	3	0	0	7	3
Chance Bolcerek, of, Fr.	.289	97	18	28	2	3	0	7	3
Blake Allemand, ss, Fr.	.289	149	16	43	3	2	0	14	4
Daniel Mengden, c, Fr.	.222	18	1	4	0	0	1	4	0
Mitchell Nau, c, Fr.	.217	60	7	13	2	0	0	13	0
Charlie Curl, 2b, So.	.154	13	2	2	0	0	0	2	0
Cole Lankford, c, Fr.	.146	48	1	7	0	0	0	6	0

PLAYER, POS., YEAR	W	L	ERA	G	SV	IP	H	BB	SO
Michael Wacha, rhp, Jr.	9	1	2.06	16	0	113	95	20	116
Rafael Pineda, rhp, So.	5	1	2.71	15	0	83	75	16	44
Ross Stripling, rhp, Sr.	10	4	3.08	16	0	126	105	19	120
Parker Ray, rhp, So.	2	1	1.29	16	0	14	9	6	16
Estevan Uriegas, lhp, Sr.	4	0	1.69	39	0	21	15	8	17
Kyle Martin, rhp, Jr.	6	5	3.20	38	7	56	57	21	52
Corey Ray, rhp, Fr.	2	0	3.52	12	0	31	27	10	17
Daniel Mengden, rhp, Fr.	3	4	3.83	22	3	47	48	8	41
Gandy Stubblefield, rhp, Fr.	0	0	3.86	10	0	21	19	15	15
Jason Freeman, rhp, Fr.	1	1	4.13	28	0	28	26	11	22
Derrick Hadley, rhp, So.	1	1	5.40	4	0	10	14	5	3

20. KENTUCKY
Coach: Gary Henderson. Record: 45-18.

PLAYER, POS., YEAR	AVG	AB	R	H	2B	3B	HR	RBI	SB
Austin Cousino, of, Fr.	.319	260	61	83	20	2	9	41	15
Luke Maile, c, Jr.	.319	229	48	73	13	0	12	51	9
Zac Zellers, of, Jr.	.311	177	36	55	12	1	5	19	7
Thomas McCarthy, 3b, Sr.	.310	242	42	75	20	0	5	33	4
A.J. Reed, 1b, Fr.	.300	200	29	60	9	0	4	43	0
Michael Williams, 1b, Sr.	.290	214	22	62	10	0	3	36	0
J.T. Riddle, 2b, Jr.	.279	226	44	63	12	1	5	38	3
Cameron Flynn, of, Jr.	.268	194	29	52	9	0	9	36	2
Matt Reida, ss, So.	.239	213	31	51	8	1	2	22	4
Thomas Bernal, c, Fr.	.370	27	3	10	0	0	0	4	1
Jeff Boehm, of, Fr.	.357	14	5	5	2	0	0	1	0
Paul McConkey, 2b, Sr.	.323	31	4	10	1	0	0	2	0
Lucas Witt, of, So.	.319	69	14	22	1	0	0	9	5
Brian Adams, of, Jr.	.250	44	6	11	2	0	1	7	1
Michael Thomas, c, So.	.250	20	6	5	3	0	1	4	0

PLAYER, POS., YEAR	W	L	ERA	G	SV	IP	H	BB	SO
Corey Littrell, lhp, So.	9	2	2.74	16	0	99	104	25	87

PLAYER, POS., YEAR	W	L	ERA	G	SV	IP	H	BB	SO
Jerad Grundy, lhp, Jr.	6	3	3.78	16	0	86	79	36	63
Taylor Rogers, lhp, Jr.	6	4	4.53	17	1	89	103	21	84
Trevor Gott, rhp, So.	3	0	2.16	23	9	25	17	7	38
Tim Peterson, rhp, Jr.	3	0	2.42	28	1	26	24	4	28
A.J. Reed, rhp, Fr.	5	3	2.52	16	0	54	54	9	51
Sam Mahar, lhp, Fr.	3	3	2.79	22	2	39	36	11	33
Alex Phillips, lhp, Sr.	5	2	3.03	30	8	59	43	18	50
Chandler Shepherd, rhp, Sr.	3	1	3.83	18	1	56	60	16	33
Walter Wijas, rhp, Jr.	2	0	5.57	20	0	21	22	7	17

21. CAL STATE FULLERTON
Coach: Rick Vanderhook. Record: 36-21.

PLAYER, POS., YEAR	AVG	AB	R	H	2B	3B	HR	RBI	SB
Richy Pedroza, 2b, Jr.	.324	213	34	69	10	1	0	21	1
Carlos Lopez, 1b, Sr.	.317	218	32	69	18	0	1	35	7
Michael Lorenzen, of, Jr.	.297	232	38	69	20	3	2	43	14
Matt Chapman, 3b, Fr.	.286	189	25	54	10	0	2	23	1
Anthony Hutting, of, Jr.	.279	129	23	36	6	3	1	27	3
Ivory Thomas, of, Jr.	.258	132	27	34	3	1	0	19	12
Matt Orloff, 2b, Jr.	.396	53	12	21	3	1	0	7	1
Austin Diemer, of, Fr.	.370	27	10	10	1	0	0	4	0
Jared Deacon, c, So.	.302	53	9	16	0	1	0	6	0
Keegan Dale, 3b, So.	.290	31	8	9	1	1	0	5	1
Anthony Trajano, ss, Sr.	.258	97	18	25	4	0	0	6	1
Austin Kingsolver, of, Jr.	.232	82	12	19	2	1	0	7	3
J.D. Davis, dh, Fr.	.229	118	12	27	6	0	4	20	2
Clay Williamson, of, Fr.	.229	35	5	8	0	1	0	9	0
Greg Velazuez, of, So.	.210	62	8	13	1	0	0	6	0
Chad Wallach, c, So.	.206	68	7	14	4	0	0	7	1
Derek Legg, 2b, Sr.	.193	88	9	17	2	0	0	6	1
Casey Watkins, c, Jr.	.185	65	6	12	3	0	0	4	2

PLAYER, POS., YEAR	W	L	ERA	G	SV	IP	H	BB	SO
Michael Lorenzen, rhp, So.	2	0	1.23	20	16	22	16	5	17
Tyler Peitzmeier, lhp, Fr.	1	0	2.75	16	0	20	19	7	15
Dylan Floro, rhp, Jr.	10	4	2.83	17	0	114	111	13	70
Koby Gauna, rhp, Fr.	5	3	2.85	19	0	66	70	8	31
Christian Coronado, rhp, So.	1	0	2.87	9	0	15	16	2	10
Grahamm Wiest, rhp, Fr.	5	5	3.12	16	1	87	65	18	57
Dave Birosak, lhp, Jr.	1	0	3.38	13	0	8	5	1	5
Dimit DeLaFuente, rhp, Jr.	1	1	3.52	22	0	31	28	11	18
J.D. Davis, rhp, Fr.	2	0	3.52	5	0	23	29	3	9
Kenny Mathews, lhp, Fr.	6	2	3.68	15	0	78	68	16	60
Willie Kuhl, rhp, Fr.	2	4	3.71	18	1	27	26	15	36
Jose Cardona, rhp, Fr.	0	2	6.92	8	0	13	17	4	7

22. MISSISSIPPI STATE
Coach: John Cohen. Record: 40-24.

PLAYER, POS., YEAR	AVG	AB	R	H	2B	3B	HR	RBI	SB
Adam Frazier, ss, So.	.371	245	45	91	16	1	0	26	9
Wes Rea, 1b, Fr.	.300	20	1	6	4	0	0	3	0
Daryl Norris, 3b, So.	.273	139	17	38	6	1	1	25	2
Trey Porter, 1b, Jr.	.259	205	26	53	9	0	5	24	1
C.T. Bradford, of, So.	.258	124	19	32	2	1	2	17	3
Hunter Renfroe, of, So.	.252	230	24	58	16	0	4	25	7
Demarcus Henderson, 3b, Fr.	.245	102	17	25	3	0	0	10	6
Taylor Stark, of, So.	.245	49	8	12	0	1	0	4	2
Mitch Slauter, c, Jr.	.232	220	35	51	10	1	3	23	0
Tyler Fullerton, 3b, Jr.	.215	93	12	20	5	0	0	7	1
Sam Frost, 3b, Jr.	.214	140	18	30	8	0	0	20	8
Phillip Casey, 2b, Fr.	.206	34	6	7	1	0	1	7	1
Brent Brownlee, of, Sr.	.204	98	12	20	3	0	0	11	1
Matthew Britton, 2b, Fr.	.177	124	17	22	1	0	0	9	3
Brayden Jones, 3b, Fr.	.174	23	3	4	1	0	0	2	1
Brandon Woodruff, rhp, Fr.	.105	19	0	2	0	0	0	1	0
Nick Ammirati, c, Jr.	.250	12	0	3	0	0	0	2	0
Luis Pollorena, lhp, Jr.	.182	11	3	2	0	0	0	1	0

PLAYER, POS., YEAR	W	L	ERA	G	SV	IP	H	BB	SO
Jonathan Holder, rhp, So.	2	1	0.32	24	9	28	17	5	30
Ben Bracewell, rhp, So.	0	0	0.93	9	0	19	13	10	19
Tanner Gaines, rhp, Fr.	1	0	1.08	6	0	8	5	2	8
Ross Mitchell, lhp, Fr.	3	0	1.18	24	0	38	24	8	24
Luis Pollorena, lhp, Jr.	4	0	1.85	16	0	34	24	6	24

PLAYER, POS., YEAR	W	L	ERA	G	SV	IP	H	BB	SO
Chris Stratton, rhp, Jr.	11	2	2.38	17	1	110	84	25	127
Brandon Woodruff, rhp, Fr.	1	2	2.38	12	0	34	25	17	37
Caleb Reed, rhp, Sr.	1	5	2.47	31	9	58	51	22	52
Kendall Graveman, rhp, Jr.	4	4	2.81	16	0	90	84	21	59
Jacob Lindgren, lhp, Fr.	2	2	3.18	14	1	28	31	7	24
Trevor Fitts, rhp, Fr.	3	0	3.29	8	0	14	17	3	14
Evan Mitchell, rhp, So.	2	1	3.52	13	0	38	31	28	43
Taylor Stark, rhp, So.	1	0	3.68	8	1	7	11	5	5
Nick Routt, lhp, Jr.	3	5	3.80	18	0	45	58	15	39
Will Cox, rhp, Fr.	2	1	4.64	7	0	21	22	3	22
Chad Girodo, lhp, Jr.	0	1	5.87	11	0	8	13	6	7

23. PURDUE

Coach: Doug Schreiber. Record: 45-14.

PLAYER, POS., YEAR	AVG	AB	R	H	2B	3B	HR	RBI	SB
Eric Charles, 2b, Sr.	.362	232	51	84	13	1	0	33	16
Kevin Plawecki, c, Jr.	.359	223	54	80	20	4	7	47	3
Cameron Perkins, 3b, Jr.	.355	242	53	86	15	0	9	61	8
Stephen Talbott, of, Jr.	.347	173	32	60	4	6	1	18	15
Barrett Serrato, of, Jr.	.325	234	39	76	13	1	6	49	4
Andrew Dixon, of, Sr.	.322	149	23	48	2	0	0	17	5
David Miller, ss, Sr.	.312	205	35	64	12	1	3	32	5
Tyler Spillner, of, Sr.	.261	230	43	60	12	1	1	25	5
Angelo Cianfrocco, 1b, Jr.	.235	153	18	36	8	0	2	25	0
Sean McHugh, 1b, So.	.317	82	17	26	4	3	3	24	0
Ryan Bridges, 1b, Sr.	.282	110	14	31	4	0	2	13	0
Chris Antonelli, of, Sr.	.235	17	5	4	1	0	0	3	0
Bennett Oliver, ss, Fr.	.227	22	1	5	0	0	0	5	0
Kyle Upp, c, Fr.	.167	12	1	2	0	0	0	1	0
Brandon Krieg, 2b, Fr.	.077	13	2	1	0	0	0	0	1

PLAYER, POS., YEAR	W	L	ERA	G	SV	IP	H	BB	SO
Blake Mascarello, lhp, Jr.	8	1	1.86	29	3	73	58	12	49
Joe Haase, rhp, Sr.	11	1	3.26	16	0	102	100	21	59
Lance Breedlove, rhp, Sr.	8	6	3.33	16	0	97	86	16	76
Pat Gannon, lhp, Jr.	1	0	1.35	9	0	13	13	7	13
Nick Wittgren, rhp, Jr.	3	0	1.76	26	10	41	35	12	39
Sean Collins, rhp, Sr.	1	0	2.75	13	0	20	25	4	12
Robert Ramer, rhp, Jr.	6	1	2.86	12	0	50	44	2	30
Calvin Gunter, lhp, Sr.	2	1	3.80	15	0	43	52	24	23
Jack DeAno, lhp, So.	2	1	4.02	10	0	16	15	11	14
Brett Andrzejewski, rhp, Jr.	1	0	4.72	13	0	13	16	5	5
Connor Podkul, rhp, Fr.	2	3	4.84	12	0	45	42	9	28

24. OREGON STATE

Coach: Pat Casey. Record: 40-20.

PLAYER, POS., YEAR	AVG	AB	R	H	2B	3B	HR	RBI	SB
Michael Conforto, of, Fr.	.349	218	45	76	14	1	13	76	1
Tyler Smith, ss, Jr.	.343	213	46	73	11	2	1	39	9
Danny Hayes, dh, Jr.	.307	114	23	35	10	1	5	27	0
Ryan Gorton, c, Sr.	.303	119	20	36	4	0	0	15	0
Jake Rodriguez, c, So.	.290	176	23	51	8	0	2	28	4
Ryan Dunn, 3b, Sr.	.286	224	41	64	19	0	7	36	1
Ryan Barnes, of, Jr.	.284	201	39	57	13	0	2	24	11
Joey Matthews, of, Jr.	.267	90	24	24	6	2	1	9	1

PLAYER, POS., YEAR	AVG	AB	R	H	2B	3B	HR	RBI	SB
Max Gordon, of, Jr.	.257	113	24	29	5	1	0	11	2
Dylan Davis, of, Fr.	.247	166	20	41	12	1	3	30	4
Kavin Keyes, 1b, So.	.226	177	23	40	8	2	0	18	3
John Tommasini, 2b, Sr.	.219	137	28	30	3	0	0	14	2
Nate Esposito, c, Fr.	.167	12	3	2	0	0	0	2	0
Jordan Dunatov, of, Fr.	.125	16	2	2	0	0	0	2	0
Ryan Dettman, of, Jr.	.091	11	8	1	0	0	0	1	2
Sam Montgomery, of, Sr.	.077	13	1	1	0	0	0	1	0

PLAYER, POS., YEAR	W	L	ERA	G	SV	IP	H	BB	SO
Jace Fry, lhp, Fr.	5	3	2.45	13	0	88	68	35	53
Scott Schultz, rhp, So.	3	1	2.56	24	2	46	34	9	32
Dan Child, rhp, So.	6	4	2.95	17	1	107	108	25	79
Ben Wetzler, lhp, So.	8	2	3.10	16	0	102	94	42	75
Matt Boyd, lhp, Jr.	4	0	3.41	31	3	37	33	13	31
Tony Bryant, rhp, Jr.	6	2	3.82	24	9	31	33	8	35
Dylan Davis, rhp, Fr.	1	1	4.32	10	1	8	5	7	9
Taylor Starr, rhp, Sr.	5	2	4.37	18	0	45	51	19	26
Ryan Gorton, rhp, Sr.	1	1	4.82	9	0	9	11	1	10
Cole Brocker, rhp, Jr.	0	3	4.88	25	0	24	30	9	26
Carlos Rodriguez, lhp, Fr.	0	0	5.14	8	0	7	5	12	4
Riley Wilkerson, rhp, Fr.	1	0	5.68	6	0	13	16	8	7
Zack Reser, lhp, Fr.	0	0	6.75	10	0	5	7	4	4
Cole Baylis, rhp, So.	0	1	8.10	5	0	10	13	9	7

25. VIRGINIA

Coach: Brian O'Connor. Record: 39-19.

PLAYER, POS., YEAR	AVG	AB	R	H	2B	3B	HR	RBI	SB
Stephen Bruno, 3b, So.	.370	238	49	88	23	2	6	54	11
Colin Harrington, of, So.	.305	167	29	51	5	2	1	28	2
Derek Fisher, of, Fr.	.288	219	44	63	11	8	7	50	4
Chris Taylor, ss, Jr.	.284	236	57	67	13	5	5	47	12
Nate Irving, c, Fr.	.279	154	33	43	7	1	0	35	4
Keith Werman, 2b, Sr.	.274	157	37	43	4	2	0	24	5
Jared King, 1b, Jr.	.263	205	41	54	12	5	4	44	13
Reed Gragnani, of, Jr.	.362	69	7	25	2	0	0	9	0
Nick Howard, 3b, Fr.	.346	52	11	18	1	1	0	6	1
Brandon Downes, of, Fr.	.321	106	20	34	7	2	1	22	3
Kenny Towns, dh, Fr.	.294	51	6	15	5	0	0	12	1
Mike Papi, of, Fr.	.283	106	24	30	8	0	1	17	5
Mitchell Shifflett, of, So.	.263	99	22	26	3	0	0	14	9
Branden Cogswell, ss, Fr.	.260	100	28	26	2	4	0	15	2

PLAYER, POS., YEAR	W	L	ERA	G	SV	IP	H	BB	SO
Kyle Crockett, lhp, So.	5	2	2.25	32	0	60	44	12	57
Branden Kline, rhp, Jr.	7	3	3.56	16	0	94	85	43	94
Artie Lewicki, rhp, So.	4	3	3.82	16	0	78	69	22	50
Scott Silverstein, lhp, Jr.	2	5	4.48	15	0	64	59	32	43
Shane Halley, rhp, Jr.	9	2	2.15	22	0	50	32	19	46
Justin Thompson, rhp, Sr.	4	3	2.27	34	12	40	34	14	37
Nick Howard, rhp, Jr.	3	0	2.81	19	0	42	34	12	37
Whit Mayberry, rhp, Jr.	2	0	3.67	5	0	27	31	6	24
Joel Effertz, rhp, Jr.	0	0	4.50	9	0	12	12	8	14
Austin Young, rhp, So.	1	1	4.86	21	0	33	31	8	30
Nathaniel Abel, lhp, Fr.	0	0	5.06	7	0	5	5	4	4
Barrett O'Neill, rhp, Fr.	2	0	5.23	10	0	21	30	5	15

CONFERENCE STANDINGS & LEADERS

NCAA regional teams in bold. Conference category leaders in bold.
*Team won conference's automatic regional bid. #Category leader who did not qualify for batting or pitching title.

AMERICA EAST CONFERENCE

Team	Conference		Overall	
	W	**L**	**W**	**L**
* **Stony Brook**	21	3	52	15
Albany	16	8	22	32
Binghamton	13	9	23	26
Maine	11	11	28	28
Hartford	7	17	16	40
Maryland-Baltimore County	2	22	10	42

ALL-CONFERENCE TEAM: C—Pat Cantwell, Sr., Stony Brook. **1B**—Max Himmelstein, Sr., UMBC. **2B**—Maxx Tissenbaum, Jr., Stony Brook. **SS**—Mike Fransoso, Jr., Maine. **3B**—William Carmona, Jr., Stony Brook. **OF**—Nolan Gaige, Jr. Albany; Travis Jankowski, Jr., Stony Brook; Tanner Nivins, Jr., Stony Brook. **DH**—Mike Tirri, Sr., Albany. **SP**—Mike Augliera, Sr., Binghamton; Sean Coughlin, So., Maine; Tyler Johnson, Sr., Stony Brook; Brandon McNitt, So., Stony Brook. **RP**—Lee Sosa, Jr., Binghamton.
Player of the Year: Travis Jankowski, Stony Brook. **Pitcher of the Year:** Tyler Johnson, Stony Brook. **Rookie of the Year:** Cole Peragine, Stony Brook. **Coach of the Year:** Matt Senk, Stony Brook.

INDIVIDUAL BATTING LEADERS
(Minimum 2.5 at-bats per team game)

	AVG	AB	R	H	2B	3B	HR	RBI	SB
Jankowski, Travis, Stony Brook	**.414**	266	79	110	18	**11**	5	46	**36**
Carmona, William, Stony Brook	.395	256	62	101	26	7	**12**	**73**	7
Tissenbaum, Max, Stony Brook	.390	241	44	94	**20**	1	3	51	0
Klukowicz, Brian, UMBC	.359	153	31	55	12	2	9	47	1
Kudernatsch, Simon, Hartford	.352	179	35	63	14	3	3	38	10
Nevares, Daniel, Binghamton	.343	143	32	49	11	0	2	17	0
Black, Troy, Maine	.338	157	30	53	5	0	0	21	17
Fransoso, Michael, Maine	.327	223	59	73	18	4	5	26	19
Krause, Kevin, Stony Brook	.327	308	37	68	12	0	3	40	3
Hoagboon, D.J., Albany	.318	151	29	48	7	2	1	29	3
Nethaway, Josh, Albany	.313	163	27	51	12	1	2	30	1
Tirri, Mike, Albany	.310	200	30	62	16	0	6	42	0
Schinkner, Curtis, UMBC	.307	163	28	50	7	0	0	22	8
Nivins, Tanner, Stony Brook	.306	206	35	63	11	3	2	34	4
Peragine, Cole, Stony Brook	.304	214	42	65	11	6	0	39	8
Gatto, Anthony, UMBC	.303	155	29	47	14	2	2	22	6
Gaige, Nolan, Albany	.302	222	42	67	11	9	1	28	14
Gay, Colin, Maine	.299	214	34	64	7	0	1	28	14
Thomas, Jake, Binghamton	.296	135	17	40	6	0	3	24	1
Himmelstein, Max, UMBC	.296	179	37	53	9	2	9	33	4
Glassman, Ian, UMBC	.295	176	30	52	10	0	1	15	3
Courtney, Kevin, Stony Brook	.293	174	32	51	14	0	4	38	1
Heath, Scott, Maine	.293	147	26	43	11	1	2	22	3
Tracy, Joey, Albany	.291	148	29	43	5	2	1	19	4
Whitten, Fran, Maine	.290	186	33	54	11	1	3	32	3
Cantwell, Pat, Stony Brook	.290	224	57	65	11	4	2	34	10
Alfonso, James, Hartford	.290	183	28	53	14	0	2	19	2
DiResta, Pete, Albany	.288	208	35	60	12	2	5	35	3
Hunter, Brian, Hartford	.288	170	22	49	13	2	2	21	5
Calbick, Alex, Maine	.287	209	40	60	18	0	5	43	0

INDIVIDUAL PITCHING LEADERS
(Minimum 1 IP per team game)

	W	L	ERA	G	SV	IP	H	BB	SO
#Sosa, Lee, Binghamton	0	0	2.50	18	**10**	18	15	8	18
Johnson, Tyler, Stony Brook	**12**	2	**2.52**	16	0	100	90	38	49
McNitt, Brandon, Stony Brook	8	4	2.76	17	0	**104**	96	27	63
Augliera, Mike, Binghamton	6	7	3.16	13	0	83	69	7	**83**
Stecko-Haley, Evan, Stony Brook	7	3	3.47	15	0	80	74	13	63
Lambert, Jake, Binghamton	6	4	3.79	13	0	78	83	12	33
Perakslis, Steve, Maine	5	5	3.81	15	0	87	109	19	48
Coughlin, Shaun, Maine	4	5	3.98	17	2	84	91	19	51
Chase, Austin, Albany	4	1	4.24	14	1	74	76	13	41
Hunter, Brian, Hartford	3	4	4.71	16	0	65	46	46	55
Kraham, Zach, Albany	4	6	4.96	14	0	78	87	43	54

Lynch, Jay, Binghamton	2	5	5.05	11	0	52	64	9	39
Lucas, Sean, Albany	4	6	5.19	14	0	76	77	37	53
Graham, Kasciem, Albany	2	5	5.37	13	0	64	82	26	26
Connolly, Mike, Maine	5	6	5.40	25	3	65	64	34	52
Miller, Steve, UMBC	1	9	6.29	25	0	69	90	33	36
Vlasic, Shane, UMBC	2	8	6.62	13	0	69	96	27	29
Englehart, Hunter, Hartford	1	9	7.65	12	0	60	77	33	12
Gill, Mac, UMBC	1	8	8.39	13	0	54	91	22	26
Gibbs, Jeffrey, Maine	3	4	8.40	14	0	60	66	42	56

ATLANTIC COAST CONFERENCE

	Conference		Overall	
ATLANTIC	**W**	**L**	**W**	**L**
Florida State	24	6	50	17
North Carolina State	19	11	43	20
Clemson	16	14	35	28
Wake Forest	13	17	33	24
Maryland	10	20	32	24
Boston College	10	20	21	34
COASTAL	**W**	**L**	**W**	**L**
North Carolina	22	8	46	16
Virginia	18	12	40	18
Miami	16	14	36	23
* **Georgia Tech**	12	18	38	26
Virginia Tech	11	19	34	21
Duke	9	21	21	34

ALL-CONFERENCE TEAM: C—Peter O'Brien, Sr., Miami. **1B**—Jayce Boyd, Jr., Florida State. **2B**—Devon Travis, Jr., Florida State. **3B**—Richie Shaffer, Jr., Clemson. **SS**—Chris Diaz, Jr., North Carolina State. **OF**—Brandon Thomas, Jr., Georgia Tech; James Ramsey, Sr., Florida State; Ryan Mathews, Sr., North Carolina State; Mac Williamson, Jr., Wake Forest. **DH/UT**—Phil Pohl, Sr. Clemson. **SP**—Marcus Stroman, Jr., Duke; Buck Farmer, Jr., Georgia Tech; Kent Emanuel, So., North Carolina; Carlos Rodon, Fr., North Carolina State. **RP**—Robert Benicasa, Jr., Florida State; Michael Morin, Jr., North Carolina.
Player of the Year: James Ramsey, Florida State. **Pitcher of the Year:** Carlos Rodon, North Carolina State. **Freshman of the Year:** Carlos Rodon, North Carolina State. **Coach of the Year:** Mike Martin, Florida State.

INDIVIDUAL BATTING LEADERS
(Minimum 2.5 at-bats per team game)

	AVG	AB	R	H	2B	3B	HR	RBI	SB
Ramsey, James, Florida State	**.378**	233	78	88	13	6	13	64	9
Boyd, Jayce, Florida State	.376	255	37	**96**	21	0	4	61	8
Bruno, Stephen, Virginia	.370	238	49	88	23	2	6	54	11
Moran, Colin, North Carolina	.365	238	30	62	11	1	3	55	1
Thomas, Brandon, Georgia Tech	.360	211	57	76	15	5	5	44	12
Canela, Danny, N.C. State	.348	227	46	79	18	0	6	46	0
Diaz, Chris, N.C. State	.346	263	55	91	**25**	2	2	56	8
Zagunis, Mark, Virginia Tech	.344	189	35	65	13	2	5	34	17
O'Brien, Peter, Miami	.340	147	31	50	12	0	10	40	1
Dove, Sam, Georgia Tech	.340	253	54	86	15	1	3	30	12
Shaffer, Richie, Clemson	.336	232	49	78	21	2	10	46	8
Turner, Trea, N.C. State	.336	259	72	87	13	2	5	43	**57**
Hayden, Brendon, Virginia Tech	.336	131	16	44	10	1	2	21	1
Mathews, Ryan, N.C. State	.327	223	48	73	16	0	**17**	62	1
Davies, Jake, Georgia Tech	.326	239	43	78	11	0	14	**73**	0
Pinder, Chad, Virginia Tech	.325	212	36	69	22	1	7	37	6
Travis, Devon, Florida State	.325	**268**	63	87	24	0	8	44	7
Bourdon, Tom, Boston College	.324	244	38	79	18	1	10	37	4
Downes, Brandon, Virginia	.321	106	20	34	7	2	1	22	3
Cleary, Jack, Maryland	.319	116	9	37	8	0	0	15	2
Hagel, Jordan, Maryland	.317	205	33	65	20	2	3	24	15
Rosenfeld, Mike, Duke	.312	170	21	53	10	3	3	31	7
Melchionda, Anthony, B.C.	.310	210	39	65	17	0	6	35	4
Hockaday, K.J., Maryland	.305	203	35	62	10	2	2	27	4
Harrington, Colin, Virginia	.305	167	29	51	5	2	1	29	2
Palka, Daniel, Georgia Tech	.303	238	44	72	19	2	12	47	6

	AVG	AB	R	H	2B	3B	HR	RBI	SB
Smith, Thomas, Georgia Tech	.302	126	18	38	6	0	0	12	5
Fincher, Jake, N.C. State	.300	210	35	63	7	6	1	23	16
Brittle, Thomas, Clemson	.298	228	43	68	9	**8**	2	36	15
Evans, Zane, Georgia Tech	.295	224	34	66	17	1	4	51	1
#Fisher, Derek, Virginia	.288	219	44	63	11	**8**	7	50	4
#Williamson, Mac, Wake Forest	.286	192	42	55	7	0	**17**	52	12

INDIVIDUAL PITCHING LEADERS
(Minimum 1 IP per team game)

	W	L	ERA	G	SV	IP	H	BB	SO
#Morin, Michael, North Carolina	6	4	1.40	38	**19**	58	38	19	55
Rodon, Carlos, N.C. State	9	0	**1.57**	17	0	**115**	71	41	135
Cruz, Alex, Georgia Tech	8	3	1.83	30	0	74	46	23	47
Moss, Benton, North Carolina	7	2	1.94	17	0	79	46	23	83
Emanuel, Kent, North Carolina	8	4	1.97	17	0	110	91	23	100
Crockett, Kyle, Virginia	5	2	2.25	32	0	60	44	12	57
Stroman, Marcus, Duke	6	5	2.39	14	0	98	83	26	136
Whaley, Eric, Miami	4	4	2.68	15	0	91	95	20	63
Reed, Jimmy, Maryland	1	3	2.70	20	0	60	49	16	52
Leibrandt, Brandon, Florida St.	8	3	2.82	19	0	99	89	29	83
Holmes, Brian, Wake Forest	7	3	2.83	14	0	83	62	49	81
Fischer, Jack, Wake Forest	5	4	2.87	22	1	63	55	30	34
Compton, Mike, Florida State	12	2	2.87	18	0	91	89	28	64
Erickson, Eric, Miami	8	6	2.88	16	0	97	99	11	66
Harman, Brett, Maryland	6	4	3.04	13	0	83	78	17	73
Mantiply, Joe, Virginia Tech	5	6	3.53	13	0	82	84	19	52
Farmer, Buck, Georgia Tech	8	4	3.54	16	0	107	100	37	115
Kline, Branden, Virginia	7	3	3.56	16	0	94	85	43	94
Pohle, Kevin, Clemson	7	4	3.66	16	0	76	80	32	40
Cooney, Tim, Wake Forest	6	7	3.82	15	0	99	99	38	90
Lewicki, Artie, Virginia	4	3	3.82	16	0	78	69	22	50

ATLANTIC SUN CONFERENCE

	Conference		Overall	
	W	L	W	L
* Belmont	17	10	39	24
South Carolina-Upstate	16	10	33	20
Kennesaw State	15	11	34	25
Mercer	15	12	38	21
Stetson	15	12	35	23
Florida Gulf Coast	15	12	26	31
Lipscomb	14	13	25	30
North Florida	12	15	31	24
East Tennessee	8	19	23	32
Jacksonville	7	20	18	38

ALL-CONFERENCE TEAM: C—Ronnie Freeman, Jr., Kennesaw State. **1B**—Adam Brett Walker, Jr., Jacksonville. **2B**—Zac Mitchell, Sr., Belmont. **SS**—Mark Jones, Sr., Stetson. **3B**—Aaron Dobbs, Sr., Kennesaw State. **OF**—Derrick Workman, So., Mercer; Gaither Bumgardner, Jr, USC Upstate; Dan Gulbransen, Jr., Jacksonville. **DH**—Nate Woods, Sr., Belmont. **SP**—Chase Brookshire, Jr., Belmont; Josh Carr, Sr., Kennesaw State; Ricky Knapp, So., Fla. Gulf Coast. **RP**—Robbie Powell, Sr., Stetson. **Player of the Year:** Gaither Bumgardner, USC Upstate. **Pitcher of the Year:** Ricky Knapp, Florida Gulf Coast. **Freshman of the Year:** Chesny Young, Mercer. **Coach of the Year:** Matt Fincher, USC Upstate.

INDIVIDUAL BATTING LEADERS
(Minimum 2 at-bats per team game)

	AVG	AB	R	H	2B	3B	HR	RBI	SB
Nick Backlund, Mercer	**.381**	223	51	**85**	16	0	16	58	3
Bumgardner, Gaither, S.C.-Upstate	.376	205	43	77	12	3	0	32	5
Young, Chesny, Mercer	.367	215	42	79	16	1	3	37	5
Freeman, Clinton, ETSU	.365	222	33	81	14	3	7	50	1
Mitchell, Zac, Belmont	.350	223	**65**	78	16	4	5	37	20
Freeman, Ronnie, Kennesaw	.348	224	42	80	13	0	6	54	0
Dobbs, Aaron, Kennesaw	.343	236	59	81	18	3	4	35	26
Walker, Adam Brett, Jacksonville	.341	211	44	72	14	0	12	42	19
Carhart, Ben, Stetson	.339	236	40	80	17	1	4	37	2
Akers, Judah, Belmont	.336	241	37	81	17	2	3	36	6
Boyd, Evan, Mercer	.335	200	46	67	**20**	1	5	38	6
Workman, Derrick, Mercer	.333	210	42	70	12	2	7	34	6
Chriscaden, Andy, Kennesaw	.332	226	46	75	16	2	14	**60**	1
Marincov, Tyler, North Florida	.332	205	41	68	10	3	9	40	9

	AVG	AB	R	H	2B	3B	HR	RBI	SB
Wielbruda, Joe, North Florida	.332	199	26	66	6	2	0	22	4
Kimmel, Sam, Stetson	.327	226	41	74	11	2	11	26	9
Gulbransen, Dan, Jacksonville	.324	207	27	67	12	1	6	33	5
Liput, Austin, S.C.-Upstate	.318	195	43	62	6	**7**	5	36	8
Guers, Greg, S.C.-Upstate	.309	175	37	54	11	1	4	36	1
Pratt, Dylan, ETSU	.307	205	34	63	9	0	16	38	1
Jones, Mark, Stetson	.306	222	41	68	11	0	5	36	11
Crews, Robert, Stetson	.306	232	35	71	5	2	3	29	8
Bednar, Brandon, Fla. Gulf Coast	.306	216	29	66	5	1	1	33	2
Weber, Luke, USC-U	.302	205	31	62	9	1	2	38	0
Johnson, D.J., Mercer	.302	189	29	57	8	0	1	23	3
#Scruggs, Matthew, ETSU	.257	222	44	57	8	2	**20**	46	11
#Murphy, Jonathan, Jacksonville	.248	218	33	54	11	2	4	26	**41**

INDIVIDUAL PITCHING LEADERS
(Minimum 1 IP per team game)

	W	L	ERA	G	SV	IP	H	BB	SO
#Powell, Robbie, Stetson	1	1	2.05	**30**	**18**	44	36	15	46
Moore, Tyler, North Florida	7	3	**2.16**	18	3	79	58	24	**88**
Knapp, Ricky, Fla. Gulf Coast	**9**	4	2.34	15	0	111	100	19	61
Buckelew, James, Belmont	7	1	2.45	14	0	73	66	36	30
Brookshire, Chase, Belmont	8	4	2.45	16	0	110	87	26	81
Randall, David, Mercer	4	4	2.51	16	0	82	80	28	76
Cotham, Josh, Lipscomb	5	5	2.56	13	0	81	70	21	72
Westwood, Kyle, North Florida	6	4	2.84	13	0	86	81	19	73
Sinclair, Connor, Lipscomb	6	4	2.99	14	0	90	83	33	72
Forjet, Jason, Fla. Gulf Coast	2	4	3.01	16	0	96	90	22	83
Kyle, Kevin, Kennesaw	3	4	3.23	15	0	75	72	26	57
Love, Brandon, Mercer	7	3	3.36	16	0	88	90	31	75
Roseboom, David, S.C.-Upstate	7	3	3.40	16	0	82	77	28	64
Barker, Brandon, Mercer	7	3	3.47	22	2	73	73	21	57
Ludwig, Dan, Belmont	5	5	3.49	17	1	67	64	14	51
Augenstein, Ben, S.C.-Upstate	4	1	3.49	20	1	57	63	16	43
McRae, Alex, Jacksonville	4	7	3.63	16	0	87	98	27	42
Long, John, ETSU	7	6	3.73	20	1	**113**	111	29	70
Hamann, Matt, Belmont	4	6	3.82	17	1	101	95	26	74
Lee, Brandon, S.C.-Upstate	7	4	3.83	15	4	82	84	19	59
Caughel, Lindsey, Stetson	7	3	3.86	16	0	89	104	18	80
Kourtis, Dimitri, Mercer	6	2	3.90	25	2	65	67	19	38
#Carr, Josh, Kennesaw	**9**	3	3.91	14	0	90	85	33	70

ATLANTIC 10 CONFERENCE

	Conference		Overall	
	W	L	W	L
Saint Louis	17	7	41	18
* Dayton	17	7	31	30
Rhode Island	16	8	33	25
Richmond	14	10	30	26
Massachusetts	14	10	22	22
St. Joseph's	13	10	25	32
Xavier	13	11	28	28
Fordham	12	12	22	34
St. Bonaventure	10	14	23	25
Charlotte	9	14	21	32
LaSalle	7	17	20	33
Temple	7	17	19	34
George Washington	6	18	20	35

ALL-CONFERENCE TEAM: C—Chris Cowell, Sr., Richmond. **1B**—Kevin Taylor, Sr., Saint Joseph's. **2B**—Pat Fortunato, Jr. Rhode Island. **3B**—Steve Nikorak, Sr. Temple. **SS**—Brian Blasick, Sr., Dayton. **OF**—Jeff Roy, So. Rhode Island; Bobby Glover, Sr., Dayton; Shane Brown, Sr. Charlotte. **DH**—Jacob Mayers, Jr., Richmond. **SP**—Joe Popielarczyk, Sr., Massachusetts; Kyle Mullen, Jr., Saint Joseph's. **RP**—Travis Parker, Sr., Saint Louis.. **Player of the Year:** Jeff Roy, Rhode Island. **Pitcher of the Year:** Joe Popielarczyk, Massachussets. **Rookie of the Year:** Zak Sterling, Richmond. **Coach of the Year:** Darin Hendrickson, Saint Louis.

INDIVIDUAL BATTING LEADERS
(Minimum 2.5 at-bats per team game)

	AVG	AB	R	H	2B	3B	HR	RBI	SB
Brown, Shane, Charlotte	**.365**	192	46	70	7	3	0	16	31
Roy, Jeff, Rhode Island	.356	236	**59**	84	15	5	2	38	22
Blasik, Brian, Dayton	.343	254	50	**87**	21	3	3	48	**36**

	AVG	AB	R	H	2B	3B	HR	RBI	SB
Urban, Billy, St. Bonaventure	.340	188	38	64	13	1	1	38	1
Mayers, Jacob, Richmond	.339	186	38	63	16	0	10	48	3
Radwan, Jason, St. Bonaventure	.337	193	42	65	11	4	1	26	1
Graef, Rich, Massachusetts	.333	138	23	46	1	0	0	17	6
Ruzbarsky, Phil, Richmond	.332	205	45	68	13	1	10	39	7
Elwell, Mark, Massachusetts	.329	164	22	54	6	0	0	29	11
Basen, Shane, Charlotte	.327	199	32	65	11	5	2	45	6
Kelly, Alex, Saint Louis	.326	230	43	75	13	0	8	41	4
Mauri, Mike, Fordham	.325	200	26	65	6	2	2	32	9
Glover, Bobby, Dayton	.322	255	58	82	16	3	9	41	23
Hundley, Ian, Dayton	.319	135	25	43	3	1	2	12	17
Maghini, Ryan, Fordham	.318	214	29	68	14	0	5	28	9
Stewart, Zach, Dayton	.317	202	31	64	12	1	3	21	10
Nelson, Grant, Saint Louis	.314	210	35	66	14	2	2	34	2
Skellie, Ryan, St. Bonaventure	.313	182	24	57	6	3	5	31	5
Cammans, Jeff, Rhode Island	.313	246	38	77	23	2	1	58	20
Shive, Corbin, Charlotte	.309	181	30	56	9	1	7	27	3
Beighton, Owen, GW	.309	181	30	56	10	1	5	19	4
Gillman, C.J., Dayton	.306	245	42	75	7	0	5	63	19
Roland, Justin, Charlotte	.306	196	32	60	14	0	0	18	14
#Cowell, Chris, Richmond	.271	210	47	57	18	0	20	58	0

INDIVIDUAL PITCHING LEADERS
(Minimum 1 inning pitched per team game)

	W	L	ERA	G	SV	IP	H	BB	SO
#Parker, Travis, Saint Louis	3	1	0.00	27	12	38	19	16	32
Popielarczyk, Joe, Massachusetts	6	2	1.66	12	0	87	75	29	65
Sterling, Zak, Dayton	7	1	2.57	13	0	77	49	30	59
Smith, Clay, Saint Louis	7	2	2.62	15	0	96	80	26	65
O'Brien, Kenny, GW	5	4	2.76	20	6	59	52	20	52
Alemann, Alex, Saint Louis	7	2	2.84	15	0	98	80	23	78
Donahue, Ryan, LaSalle	3	3	2.91	24	0	65	65	34	62
Christy, Kevin, LaSalle	2	5	2.95	14	0	88	82	17	85
#Vice, Alex, Xavier	5	3	3.00	31	2	36	36	9	17
Mullen, Kyle, St. Joseph's	6	4	3.07	15	0	106	100	21	90
Furney, Sean, Rhode Island	5	1	3.33	17	0	70	62	24	58
Torres, Dennis, Massachusetts	4	4	3.34	12	0	89	106	22	54
Charest, Joseph, Fordham	5	8	3.43	15	0	105	97	33	53
Yermal, Joe, Charlotte	6	5	3.48	13	0	72	74	18	40
Peterson, Patrick, Temple	3	4	3.51	15	1	85	74	28	68
Van Wyk, Eric, LaSalle	3	8	3.52	14	0	95	97	20	63
Bury, Tim, Dayton	8	2	3.52	19	0	107	109	29	77
Weisberg, Aaaron, GW	2	7	3.56	14	0	83	76	42	50
Carter, Jordan, St. Joseph's	0	6	3.62	16	1	72	89	28	31
Pracher, Alex, St. Joseph's	5	9	3.79	16	0	95	100	27	80
Brockett, Andrew, Richmond	3	8	3.79	26	6	59	62	20	64
Maffett, Alex, Richmond	5	3	3.86	22	3	61	89	25	35
Nittoli, Vinny, Xavier	4	5	3.95	14	0	78	90	32	43
Crane, Jordan, St. Bonaventure	5	2	3.95	13	0	84	95	28	44
Mitchem, Burny, Dayton	6	8	4.00	26	7	81	76	32	72
Gray, Eddie, St. Bonaventure	4	3	4.04	13	0	94	96	33	70
#Hauschild, Mike, Dayton	7	3	4.26	18	0	120	132	30	92

BIG EAST CONFERENCE

	Conference		Overall	
	W	L	W	L
Louisville	18	9	41	22
*St. John's	18	9	40	23
South Florida	17	10	38	22
Seton Hall	17	10	34	24
Rutgers	16	11	31	25
Connecticut	16	11	31	27
Notre Dame	14	13	31	27
Villanova	10	17	28	27
Pittsburgh	10	17	28	28
Georgetown	10	17	24	29
West Virginia	9	18	33	18
Cincinnati	7	20	18	38

ALL-CONFERENCE TEAM: C—Jeff Melillo, Sr., Rutgers. 1B—Rick Deveraux, Sr., Pittsburgh. 2B—L.J. Mazilli, Jr., Connecticut. 3B—Kivlehan, Patrick, Jr., Rutgers. SS—Mike Garza, Jr., Georgetown. OF— Jeremy Baltz, Jr., St. John's; Justin Glass, So. Cincinnati; Billy Ferriter, Jr., Connecticut. DH—Matt Fleishman, Sr., Villanova. P—Justin Amlung, Jr., Louisville;

Sean Hagan, Jr., St. John's; Jon Prosinski, Jr., Seton Hall; Andrew Barbosa, Sr., USF. RP—Scott Oberg, Jr., Connecticut.
Player of the Year: Patrick Kivlehan, Jr., Rutgers. Pitcher of the Year: Justin Amlung, Jr., Louisville. Rookie of the Year: Jared Ruxer, Louisville. Coach of the Year: Ed Blankmeyer, St. John's.

INDIVIDUAL BATTING LEADERS
(Minimum 2.5 at-bats per team game)

	AVG	AB	R	H	2B	3B	HR	RBI	SB
Garza, Mike, Georgetown	.393	219	40	86	21	2	8	44	10
Kivlehan, Patrick, Rutgers	.392	189	47	74	11	2	14	50	24
Devereaux, Rick, Pittsburgh	.372	231	37	86	15	1	7	54	3
Glass, Justin, Cincinnati	.366	227	39	83	21	1	3	26	15
Sciacca, Tyler, Villanova	.359	220	43	79	16	1	6	39	27
Wagner, Kevin, Villanova	.350	226	36	79	11	1	0	47	8
Wessinger, Matt, St. John's	.348	247	62	86	13	1	6	48	34
Young, Ty, Louisville	.344	180	42	62	9	4	6	42	15
Baltz, Jeremy, St. John's	.344	241	65	83	13	4	8	53	18
Ratajczak, Nick, Louisville	.343	245	64	84	1	1	0	25	6
O'Hare, Sean, St. John's	.341	220	42	75	15	1	3	43	8
Mazzilli, L.J., Connecticut	.339	243	43	81	19	2	9	38	16
Favatella, Nick, Rutgers	.333	222	54	74	12	3	5	42	8
Hudson, Joe, Notre Dame	.332	202	39	67	14	1	6	39	3
Schwindel, Frank, St. John's	.332	202	33	67	5	1	4	30	0
Bielek, Joey, Cincinnati	.330	230	28	78	16	1	1	31	5
Ramsay, James, South Florida	.328	238	33	78	9	0	2	32	14
Vazquez, Boo, Pittsburgh	.327	159	25	52	7	4	1	22	4
Martin, Tim, Connecticut	.327	196	26	64	11	1	3	23	5
Leeson, Justin, Georgetown	.325	212	40	69	8	5	2	21	18
Ravnaas, Rand, Georgetown	.325	194	37	65	12	1	2	37	14
Roche, Casey, Pittsburgh	.322	202	37	65	17	3	3	45	4
Sturgeon, Cole, Louisville	.321	221	42	71	11	5	1	45	8
Fleishman, Matt, Villanova	.320	222	45	71	17	4	5	42	2
Boyd, Bobby, West Virginia	.320	194	40	62	7	1	2	20	23
Ferriter, Billy, Connecticut	.319	234	43	76	6	2	1	31	24
DeFabio, Anthony, Pittsburgh	.317	205	53	65	16	2	4	34	9
Mancini, Trey, Notre Dame	.317	202	47	64	10	0	12	45	3
Melillo, Jeff, Rutgers	.311	183	35	57	10	0	4	30	0
#Engel, Adam, Louisville	.308	214	43	66	4	0	1	19	37
#DeSico, Frank, Notre Dame	.302	248	42	75	9	0	0	23	13
#Frazer, Matt, West Virginia	.294	197	27	58	23	0	6	31	0
#Walsh, Will, Seton Hall	.280	225	32	63	9	7	4	33	13
#Ijames, Stewart, Louisville	.259	239	48	62	15	0	12	65	6

INDIVIDUAL PITCHING LEADERS
(Minimum 1 IP per team game)

	W	L	ERA	G	SV	IP	H	BB	SO
#Slania, Dan, Notre Dame	3	0	2.03	31	12	31	36	12	37
Hudgins, Will, Notre Dame	5	3	2.06	15	0	96	85	24	90
Amlung, Justin, Louisville	9	4	2.31	16	0	109	83	26	105
Marzi, Anthony, Connecticut	3	8	2.55	15	0	99	76	20	64
Barbosa, Andrew, South Florida	7	7	2.75	17	0	95	64	24	110
Reed, Matt, South Florida	5	3	2.76	13	0	78	70	19	16
Harris, Will, Georgetown	5	4	2.85	13	0	76	80	18	38
Hagan, Sean, St. John's	8	3	2.90	16	0	109	98	30	68
Harvey, Ryan, Seton Hall	6	4	3.04	17	2	77	65	43	90
Morris, Zach, Cincinnati	3	4	3.11	14	0	75	72	24	53
Gentile, Thomas, Cincinnati	2	3	3.22	23	1	67	57	26	60
Stultz, Derrick, South Florida	9	1	3.29	17	0	88	71	23	60
Fasano, Ryan, Rutgers	6	5	3.34	16	0	97	92	17	59
Ruxer, Jared, Louisville	8	3	3.38	16	0	77	78	15	32
Smorol, Rob, Rutgers	8	4	3.46	15	0	94	91	27	53
Fischer, David, Connecticut	5	6	3.47	16	0	80	76	27	68
Prosinski, John, Seton Hall	9	3	3.52	15	0	95	108	19	73
Hansen, Kyle, St. John's	5	5	3.62	17	0	99	98	30	109
Mildren, Ethan, Pittsburgh	6	6	3.76	14	0	96	106	17	72
Fitzgerald, Sean, Notre Dame	7	3	3.82	27	0	71	72	14	57
Iannazzo, Matt, Pittsburgh	7	4	3.95	16	0	100	122	22	76
Carasiti, Matt, St. John's	7	5	3.98	18	0	84	89	31	64
Thompson, Jeff, Louisville	9	4	4.00	15	0	79	77	38	73

BIG SOUTH CONFERENCE

	Conference		Overall	
	W	**L**	**W**	**L**
* Coastal Carolina	18	5	42	19
Campbell	15	9	41	18
Liberty	14	10	41	19
Gardner-Webb	12	12	32	28
Radford	12	12	29	28
UNC Asheville	12	12	25	30
High Point	11	13	28	31
Charleston Southern	11	13	20	36
Presbyterian	10	14	24	31
Winthrop	9	14	17	35
Virginia Military Institute	7	17	16	36

ALL-CONFERENCE TEAM: C—Tucker Frawley, Sr., Coastal Carolina. **1B**—Kenny Bryant, Sr., Presbyterian. **2B**—Michael Felton, Jr., Campbell. **3B**—Rich Witten, Sr., Coastal Carolina. **SS**—Jeff Kemp, Jr., Radford. **DH**—Jake Kirkland, Jr., Campbell. **OF**—Daniel Bowman, Sr. Coastal Carolina; Matt Hillsinger, Sr., Radford; Ian Pamley, Sr., Liberty. **SP**—Eddie Butler, Jr., Radford; John Niggli, Sr., Liberty; Matt Sergey, Sr., Campbell. **RP**—Aaron Burke, Jr. Coastal Carolina.
Player of the Year: Daniel Bowman, Coastal Carolina. **Pitcher(s) of the Year:** Eddie Butler, Jr. Radford; Aaron Burke, Jr., Coastal Carolina. **Freshman of the Year:** Alex Close, Liberty. **Coach of the Year:** Gary Gilmore, Coastal Carolina.

INDIVIDUAL BATTING LEADERS
(Minimum 2.5 at-bats per team game)

	AVG	AB	R	H	2B	3B	HR	RBI	SB
Felton, Michael, Campbell	**.424**	243	52	**103**	12	3	1	45	11
Bowman, Daniel, Coastal Caro.	.401	237	62	95	14	5	6	40	15
Aanderud, Bryan, Liberty	.368	220	42	81	9	2	2	53	5
Olson, David, Campbell	.350	214	41	75	20	1	5	55	2
Kirkland, Jake, Campbell	.350	226	47	79	19	2	7	55	5
Witten, Chase, Coastal Caro.	.346	228	39	79	17	0	5	**66**	10
Shelton, Chase, Charleston So.	.342	193	29	66	13	1	4	29	5
Ison, Bobby, Charleston So.	.332	217	32	72	7	1	1	16	10
Mack, Matt, Radford	.332	193	26	64	7	0	5	40	7
Rush, Ryne, High Point	.330	218	32	72	17	1	3	37	6
Kemp, Jeff, Radford	.328	192	41	63	16	**6**	4	48	9
Smith, Andy, Liberty	.322	183	50	59	4	5	8	36	10
Mollenhauer, Brett, Radford	.321	224	43	72	10	1	1	24	3
Hillsinger, Matt, Radford	.321	184	43	59	10	0	8	37	7
Dickinson, Rob, VMI	.320	181	25	58	11	3	6	32	7
Morley, Jacob, WMI	.318	198	32	63	14	4	11	32	2
Hodge, Ryan, Gardner-Webb	.315	213	46	67	11	2	1	23	16
McQuown, Ben, Campbell	.315	213	43	67	6	1	1	37	27
Bryant, Kenny, Presbyterian	.313	208	30	65	16	1	10	36	6
Buccilli, Aaron, Coastal Caro.	.313	192	32	60	11	0	3	43	10
Coleman, Scott, Gardner-Webb	.312	221	38	69	15	0	4	30	8
Parmley, Ian, Liberty	.312	**250**	**66**	78	10	2	0	26	**30**
Motroni, Billy, Presbyterian	.311	196	30	61	7	0	0	14	2
Lizanich, Jay, Presbyterian	.311	190	19	59	7	0	0	16	5
Medina, Willie, High Point	.310	197	34	61	11	1	0	26	19
Buch, Cody, UNC-Asheville	.307	176	25	54	8	0	4	16	0
Creighton, Billy, UNC-Asheville	.306	160	22	49	10	5	6	32	0
May, Jacob, Coastal Carolina	.306	209	43	64	7	4	2	18	27
Close, Alex, Liberty	.304	207	36	63	8	2	**14**	47	3
Piccirilli, George, VMI	.303	188	30	57	14	0	5	23	3
Bryant, Hunter, UNC-Asheville	.303	165	8	50	10	0	0	19	1
Haley, Zack, Liberty	.303	208	45	63	**21**	2	2	25	11

INDIVIDUAL PITCHING LEADERS
(Minimum 1 IP per team game)

	W	L	ERA	G	SV	IP	H	BB	SO
Burke, Aaron, Coastal Carolina	**10**	5	**1.58**	**35**	7	80	68	24	40
Connolly, Ryan, Coastal Carolina	5	2	2.10	**35**	**11**	77	68	22	55
Garrett, Reed, VMI	2	3	2.17	25	1	54	47	21	41
Niggli, John, Liberty	9	4	2.17	16	1	**104**	103	30	68
Butler, Eddie, Radford	7	4	2.20	14	0	98	78	23	**95**
Herb, Tyler, Coastal Carolina	9	2	2.61	17	0	97	78	40	70
Kemmerer, Jacob, Liberty	4	4	2.90	20	3	62	56	19	32
Knox, Chandler, Presbyterian	5	2	3.02	14	0	89	96	19	48

Eckelbarger, Patrick, Liberty	7	1	3.09	15	0	76	59	31	62
Hilton, Beau, Gardner-Webb	7	3	3.14	15	0	77	76	33	45
McCready, Charlie, Charleston So.	4	6	3.29	13	0	79	77	22	49
Klitsch, Tyler, Winthrop	4	7	3.32	22	0	87	92	17	46
Sergey, Matt, Campbell	7	0	3.38	15	0	91	82	33	75
Fraudin, Matt, Gardner-Webb	1	5	3.41	18	0	71	76	28	47
Zier, Frank, Campbell	4	3	3.48	15	0	93	95	22	58
Dull, Ryan, UNC-Asheville	5	5	3.55	14	0	84	93	13	84
Costello, Tyler, Radford	7	3	3.81	14	0	85	95	28	39
Roland, Dean, UNC-Asheville	5	6	3.92	16	0	96	93	29	61
Barnett, Andrew, Gardner-Webb	4	4	4.15	17	0	87	102	27	69
Retz, Ryan, High Point	6	5	4.16	13	0	80	72	19	47
Gunther, Ryan, Charleston So.	0	8	4.25	15	0	83	96	23	64

BIG TEN CONFERENCE

	Conference		Overall	
	W	**L**	**W**	**L**
* Purdue	17	7	45	14
Indiana	16	8	32	28
Penn State	15	9	29	27
Nebraska	14	10	35	23
Michigan State	13	11	37	23
Ohio State	11	13	33	27
Illinois	11	13	29	27
Minnesota	11	13	23	27
Iowa	10	14	23	27
Michigan	8	16	22	34
Northwestern	6	18	18	36

ALL-CONFERENCE TEAM: C—Kevin Plawecki, Jr., Purdue. **1B**—Jordan Steranka, Sr., Penn State. **2B**—Eric Charles, Sr., Purdue. **SS**—Chad Christensen, Jr., Nebraska. **3B**—Cameron Perkins, Jr., Purdue. **OF**—Willie Argo, Sr., Illinois; Jordan Keur, Jr., Michigan State; Rich Sanguinetti, Jr., Nebraska. **DH**—Michael Pritchard, So., Nebraska. **SP**—T.J. Oakes, Jr., Minnesota; Jaron Long, So., Ohio State; Joe Haase, Sr., Purdue. **RP**—Jonny Hoffman, Sr., Indiana
Player of the Year: Kevin Plawecki, Jr., Purdue. **Pitcher of the Year:** Joe Haase, Sr., Purdue. **Freshman of the Year:** Sam Travis, Indiana. **Coach of the Year:** Doug Schreiber, Purdue.

INDIVIDUAL BATTING LEADERS
(Minimum 2.5 at-bats per team game)

	AVG	AB	R	H	2B	3B	HR	RBI	SB
Pritchard, Michael, Nebraska	.387	212	51	82	10	0	0	22	6
Steranka, Jordan, Penn State	.363	226	35	82	**20**	2	11	40	2
Charles, Eric, Purdue	.362	232	51	84	13	1	0	33	16
Plawecki, Kevin, Purdue	.359	223	**54**	80	**20**	4	7	47	3
Scheffert, Josh, Nebraska	.358	179	37	64	12	0	8	41	5
Perkins, Cameron, Purdue	.355	242	53	86	15	0	9	**61**	8
McQuillan, Mike, Iowa	.354	178	44	63	8	2	1	24	14
Keur, Jordan, Michigan State	.353	252	47	89	14	0	1	34	8
Jones, Ryan, Michigan State	.351	**261**	52	**92**	16	3	3	39	8
Stock, Richard, Nebraska	.351	211	40	74	**20**	3	4	45	1
Parr, Jordan, Illinois	.348	201	37	70	13	3	5	45	6
Talbott, Stephen, Purdue	.347	173	32	60	4	**6**	1	18	15
Keppler, Phil, Iowa	.345	145	24	50	6	1	1	22	2
O'Neill, Michael, Michigan	.327	162	31	53	12	1	6	31	19
Serrato, Barrett, Purdue	.325	234	39	76	13	1	6	49	4
Sanguinetti, Rich, Nebraska	.321	218	44	70	11	2	2	43	7
Travis, Sam, Indiana	.319	232	41	74	17	0	9	50	4
Olinger, Dan, Minnesota	.318	201	25	64	11	2	2	27	7
Argo, Willie, Illinois	.318	195	47	62	13	0	0	34	22
Henkemeyer, Andy, Minnesota	.314	207	31	65	11	2	2	24	7
Kelly, Pat, Nebraska	.313	163	27	51	6	2	8	37	5
Miller, David, Purdue	.312	205	35	65	12	1	3	32	5
Christensen, Chad, Nebraska	.311	228	49	71	9	2	10	48	8
Hallberg, Brad, Ohio State	.311	209	40	65	15	2	2	34	1
Kalkowski, Kash, Nebraska	.310	174	25	54	8	0	4	37	7
Juan, Bobby, Minnesota	.307	153	17	47	10	3	3	20	1
Halloran, Matt, Minnesota	.307	150	19	46	5	2	2	23	0
Martinez, John, Michigan St.	.306	186	24	57	8	2	3	32	2
Dezse, Josh, Ohio State	.306	216	31	66	9	1	5	33	1
Biondi, Patrick, Michigan	.303	221	44	67	11	3	2	17	**32**
#Crank, Coley, Michigan	.251	191	35	48	7	0	**12**	45	1

#Deegan, Sean, Penn State .241 237 37 57 10 4 **12** 42 3

INDIVIDUAL PITCHING LEADERS
(Minimum 1 IP per team game)

	W	L	ERA	G	SV	IP	H	BB	SO
#Wittgren, Nick, Purdue	3	0	1.76	26	**10**	41	35	12	39
Mascarello, Blake, Purdue	8	1	**1.86**	16	0	73	58	12	49
Kurrasch, Joe, Penn State	4	2	2.05	16	0	88	68	46	78
Hoffman, Jonny, Indiana	8	2	2.27	29	5	63	57	17	35
Oakes, T.J., Minnesota	7	3	2.31	14	0	97	93	15	78
Brooke, F., Northwestern	2	7	2.51	15	0	97	105	14	61
Long, Jaron, Ohio State	6	2	2.66	16	1	101	108	13	63
Kubel, Sasha, Iowa	6	0	2.67	13	0	88	79	15	36
Waszak, Andrew, Michigan St.	4	4	2.96	16	0	106	92	27	50
Bucciferro, Tony, Michigan St.	6	4	3.07	16	0	111	105	22	**94**
Hart, Kyle, Indiana	5	5	3.21	15	0	84	91	30	53
Joey DeNato, Indiana	7	3	3.22	15	0	92	96	31	76
Snelten, D.J., Minnesota	4	4	3.24	16	0	86	70	33	55
Haase, Joe, Purdue	11	1	3.26	16	0	102	100	21	59
Garner, David, Michigan State	6	3	3.28	20	0	74	64	31	75
Breedlove, Lance, Michigan St.	8	6	3.33	16	0	97	86	16	76
Morton, Northwestern	1	10	3.46	14	0	83	89	26	49
Hill, Steven, Penn State	5	4	3.84	15	0	100	107	22	60
Lubinsky, Austin, Minnesota	4	4	3.87	14	0	79	94	14	51
Milroy, Matt, Illinois	2	6	3.88	20	0	53	37	44	65
Sinnery, Brandon, Michigan	5	5	3.91	14	0	101	107	24	58

BIG 12 CONFERENCE

	Conference		Overall	
	W	L	W	L
Baylor	20	4	49	17
Texas A&M	16	8	43	18
Texas	14	10	30	22
Oklahoma	13	10	42	25
Oklahoma State	13	11	32	25
* **Missouri**	10	14	33	28
Kansas	7	16	24	34
Texas Tech	7	17	29	26
Kansas State	7	17	27	31

ALL-CONFERENCE TEAM: C—Josh Ludy, Sr., Baylor. **IF**—Lawton Langford, So., Baylor; Max Muncy, Jr., Baylor; Erich Weiss, So. Texas; Jacob House, Sr., Texas A&M; Jamodrick McGruder, Texas Tech. **OF**—Barrett Barnes, Jr., Texas Tech; Logan Vick, Sr., Baylor; Tyler Naquin, Jr., Texas A&M. **DH**—Nathan Orf, Jr., Baylor. **UT**—Max White, Jr. Oklahoma. **SP**—Josh Turley, Jr. Baylor; Andrew Heaney, Jr., Oklahoma State; Ross Stripling, Sr., Texas A&M; Michael Wacha, Jr., Texas A&M. **RP**—Max Garner, Jr., Baylor; Corey Knebel, So., Texas.
Player of the Year: Josh Ludy, Sr. Baylor. **Pitcher of the Year:** Andrew Heaney, Jr., Oklahoma State. **Newcomer of the Year:** Nathan Orf, Jr., Baylor. **Freshman of the Year:** Parker French, Texas. **Coach of the Year:** Steve Smith, Baylor.

INDIVIDUAL BATTING LEADERS
(Minimum 2.5 at-bats per team game)

	AVG	AB	R	H	2B	3B	HR	RBI	SB
Naquin, Tyler, Texas A&M	.380	242	56	**92**	18	6	3	49	21
King, Jared, Kansas State	.377	220	49	83	15	4	7	47	16
Ludy, Josh, Baylor	.362	232	41	84	15	0	**16**	**71**	1
McGruder, Jamodric, Texas Tech	.358	193	54	69	6	8	2	27	**39**
Weiss, Erich, Texas	.350	203	39	71	17	4	5	38	10
Altobelli, Bo, Texas Tech	.346	205	31	71	12	0	3	33	5
Vick, Logan, Baylor	.345	232	50	80	**25**	0	4	43	19
White, Max, Oklahoma	.337	252	39	85	17	2	2	55	8
Hinkle, Wade, Kansas State	.330	191	44	63	8	0	10	49	3
Barnes, Barrett, Texas Tech	.325	206	53	67	17	6	9	49	19
Rea, Robbie, Oklahoma State	.324	222	33	72	18	0	5	38	1
Payton, Mark, Texas	.322	208	40	67	13	4	5	29	8
Muncy, Max, Baylor	.322	255	55	82	17	3	7	56	7
Sommerfeld, Scott, Missouri	.312	189	25	59	8	1	2	29	5
Witt, Tanner, Kansas State	.310	187	48	58	9	3	0	21	20
#Orf, Nathan, Baylor	.303	234	**61**	71	10	2	2	31	17

INDIVIDUAL PITCHING LEADERS
(Minimum 1 IP per team game)

	W	L	ERA	G	SV	IP	H	BB	SO
Heaney, Andrew, Oklahoma St.	8	2	**1.60**	15	0	118	74	22	**140**
#Uriegas, Estevan, Texas A&M	4	0	1.69	**39**	0	21	15	8	17
Turley, Josh, Baylor	9	1	1.96	17	0	110	95	21	79
Wacha, Michael, Texas A&M	9	1	2.06	30	0	113	95	20	116
Von Schamann, Duke, Texas Tech	6	4	2.08	16	0	87	66	12	60
Knebel, Corey, Texas	4	5	2.08	27	9	74	50	20	68
Blank, Trent, Baylor	**11**	1	2.23	19	0	105	92	25	61
John, Jordan, Oklahoma	8	8	2.44	27	4	122	104	32	106
Milner, Hoby, Texas	7	4	2.64	34	3	72	55	19	68
Emens, Jeff, Missouri	4	1	2.71	32	3	86	90	15	65
Pineda, Rafael, Texas A&M	5	1	2.71	15	0	83	75	16	44
French, Parker, Texas	6	2	2.84	21	2	67	58	19	30
Okert, Steven, Oklahoma	9	8	3.07	30	5	85	72	37	78
Stripling, Ross, Texas A&M	10	4	3.08	16	0	**126**	105	19	120
Overton, Dillon, Oklahoma	6	3	3.15	22	0	123	127	24	126
Gray, Jonathan, Oklahoma	8	4	3.16	18	0	103	100	42	104
#Garner, Max, Baylor	3	3	4.89	22	**10**	46	45	19	43

BIG WEST CONFERENCE

	Conference		Overall	
	W	L	W	L
* **Cal State Fullerton**	17	7	36	21
Cal Poly	16	8	36	20
Long Beach State	15	9	28	27
UC Irvine	13	11	31	25
UC Davis	12	12	27	30
UC Santa Barbara	10	14	28	28
Cal State Northridge	9	15	23	30
UC Riverside	9	15	22	32
Pacific	6	18	16	40

ALL-CONFERENCE TEAM: C—Chris Hoo, So., Cal Poly. **1B**—Carlos Lopez, Jr., Cal State Fullerton. **2B**—Richy Pedroza, Jr., Cal State Fullerton. **3B**—Jimmy Allen, So., Cal Poly. **SS**—Mike Miller, Sr. Cal Poly. **OF**—Mitch Haniger, Jr. Cal Poly; Brennan Metzger, Sr. Long Beach State; Brett Vertigan, Jr., UC Santa Barbara. **DH**—Tim Wise, So., Cal Poly. **UT**—Michael Lorenzen, So., Cal State Fullerton. **SP**—Joey Wagman, Jr., Cal Poly; Dylan Floro, Jr,. Cal State Fullerton; Andrew Thurman, Fr., UC Irvine. **RP**—Reed Riley, Fr., Cal Poly. **CP**—Michael Lorenzen, So., Cal State Fullerton.
Player of the Year: Mitch Haniger, Cal Poly. **Pitcher of the Year:** Dylan Floro, Cal State Fullerton. **Defensive Player of the Year:** D.J. Crumlich, UC Irvine. **Freshman Player of the Year:** Matt Chapman, Cal State Fullerton. **Freshman Pitcher of the Year:** Jerry Keel, Cal State Northridge. **Coach of the Year:** Rick Vanderhook, Cal State Fullerton.

INDIVIDUAL BATTING LEADERS
(Minimum 2.5 at-bats per team game)

	AVG	AB	R	H	2B	3B	HR	RBI	SB
Vertigan, Brett, UCSB	.381	236	54	**90**	14	**9**	1	30	**17**
Miller, Mike, Cal Poly	.354	**246**	**56**	87	16	4	3	35	5
Lockwood, Erik, Pacific	.352	165	22	58	12	0	1	26	2
Gonzalez, Vince, UC Riverside	.351	211	21	74	11	2	0	32	3
Mahle, Greg, UCSB	.347	190	26	66	6	0	0	35	0
Trinkwon, Brandon, UCSB	.347	202	42	70	16	4	2	32	7
Haniger, Mitch, Cal Ploy	.346	211	48	73	18	1	**13**	64	6
Politi, Paul, UC Davis	.345	229	24	79	13	0	3	32	3
Allen, Jimmy, Cal Poly	.345	229	32	79	**20**	4	3	44	9
Crumlich, D.J., UC Irvine	.324	222	39	72	16	1	0	19	8
Ramirez, Christian, UC Irvine	.324	179	26	58	9	4	0	21	3
Pedroza, Richy, CS Fullerton	.324	213	34	69	10	1	0	21	1
Fox, Jordan, UC Irvine	.322	211	31	68	11	5	0	37	10
Lopez, Carlos, CS Fullerton	.317	218	32	69	18	0	1	35	7
Simms, Josh, Pacific	.316	212	30	67	15	2	1	25	11
Armendariz, David, Cal Poly	.312	230	30	63	12	2	4	36	13
Roenicke, Lance, UC Santa Barbara	.310	210	38	65	18	1	4	35	7
Wise, Tim, Cal Ploy	.308	182	28	56	10	1	3	28	11
Lipson, Alex, UC Davis	.306	160	18	49	4	1	0	17	3
Spencer, Connor, UC Irvine	.306	170	19	52	3	5	0	30	1
Metzger, Brennan, Long Beach St.	.302	189	37	57	12	1	2	37	11
Barker, Kevin, UC Davis	.300	170	30	51	15	2	2	19	4
Lorenzen, Michael, CS Fullerton	.297	232	38	69	**20**	3	2	43	14

Torchio, Dustin, Pacific	.296	159	23	47	9	0	0	22	2
Young, Eddie, UC Riverside	.295	193	35	57	9	0	1	24	2
Prestridge, Clayton, UC Riverside	.292	171	27	50	9	1	0	24	9
Reyes, Tommy, UC Irvine	.291	185	36	54	13	2	2	31	9
Bekakis, Johnny, Long Beach St.	.290	169	25	49	9	1	0	16	7
Stephens, Jeff, UC Irvine	.288	156	22	45	8	0	0	20	2
Avila, Juan, Long Beach State	.288	198	32	57	10	0	2	30	7

INDIVIDUAL PITCHING LEADERS
(Minimum 1 IP per team game)

	W	L	ERA	G	SV	IP	H	BB	SO
Vasquez, Andrew, UC Santa Barbara	6	4	**1.93**	15	0	89	58	63	104
Keel, Jerry, CS Northridge	6	3	2.07	16	0	91	88	25	48
Wagman, Joey, Cal Poly	9	3	2.33	15	0	108	94	20	79
Stuart, Shawn, Long Beach St.	7	1	2.44	14	0	92	70	32	69
Thurman, Andrew, UC Irvine	8	3	2.66	15	0	98	68	23	69
Anderson, Matt, Long Beach St.	4	3	2.74	15	0	85	72	36	60
Kupbens, Anthony, UC Davis	5	4	2.83	14	0	95	109	19	49
Floro, Dylan, CS Fullerton	**10**	4	2.83	17	0	**114**	111	13	70
Orozco, Eddie, UC Riverside	5	7	2.84	14	0	98	105	23	106
Gauna, Koby, CS Fullerton	5	3	2.85	19	0	66	70	8	31
Strufing, Ryan, Long Beach St.	7	3	2.99	15	0	90	74	31	52
Wiest, Grahamm, CS Fullerton	5	5	3.12	16	1	87	65	18	57
Quist, Dayne, UC Davis	6	3	3.15	13	0	86	69	13	95
Benson, Michael, Pacific	3	9	3.34	14	0	94	99	28	46
Edgington, Zak, UCSB	3	4	3.35	20	1	81	74	35	56
Anderson, Kyle, Cal Poly	**10**	1	3.40	15	0	93	107	16	61
Briner, Tom, UC Davis	5	6	3.56	14	0	99	98	13	56
Slaught, Crosby, UC Irvine	7	7	3.63	18	0	79	62	39	57
Mathews, Kenny, CS Fullerton	6	2	3.68	15	0	78	68	16	60
Ferragamo, Phillip, UC Irvine	3	5	3.72	19	1	65	64	16	40
Stuart, Dylan, UC Riverside	7	7	4.00	15	0	99	108	21	56
#Vedo, Matthew, UCSB	5	5	4.59	28	3	82	62	57	**112**
#Litchfield, Jimmy UC Irvine	3	2	3.60	**29**	1	45	44	13	30

COLONIAL ATHLETIC ASSOCIATION

	Conference		Overall	
	W	L	W	L
* UNC Wilmington	24	6	39	23
Hofstra	20	10	34	22
Delaware	17	13	31	27
George Mason	16	14	33	24
Virginia Commonwealth	15	15	34	25
Towson	15	15	27	31
Georgia State	14	16	24	31
Northeastern	13	17	23	28
William & Mary	12	18	31	25
James Madison	10	20	16	35
Old Dominion	9	21	19	34

ALL-CONFERENCE TEAM: C—Jon Leroux, Jr., Northeastern. **1B**—Jared Hammer, Jr., Hofstra. **2B**—Matt Ford, Jr., Hofstra. **3B**—Joey Cujas, So., VCU. **SS**—Dalton Rouleau, Jr., Hofstra. **OF**—Andrew Cain, Sr., UNCW; Thomas Pope, Sr., UNCW; Danny Poma, Sr., Hofstra. **UT**—Brig Tison, Sr., George Mason. **DH**—Kevin Flynn, Sr. Hofstra. **SP**—Matt Davenport, Sr., William & Mary; Tyler McSwain, Sr., UNCW. **RP**—Chris O'Grady, Jr., George Mason.
Player of the Year: Danny Poma, Hofstra. **Pitcher of the Year:** Matt Davenport, William & Mary. **Defensive Player of the Year:** Matt Ford, Hofstra. **Rookie of the Year:** Jason Vosler, Northeastern. **Coach of the Year:** Mark Scalf, UNCW.

INDIVIDUAL BATTING LEADERS
(Minimum 125 at-bats)

	AVG	AB	R	H	2B	3B	HR	RBI	SB
Poma, Danny, Hofstra	**.430**	237	**78**	**102**	32	0	7	48	**29**
Cujas, Joey, VCU	.390	223	43	87	21	2	3	49	2
Ford, Matt, Hofstra	.384	219	50	84	10	0	2	38	20
Lindemuth, Ryan, William & Mary	.376	213	54	80	17	4	5	48	14
Hammer, Jared, Hofstra	.376	213	47	80	18	0	4	**66**	12
Pope, Thomas, UNCW	.372	231	49	86	18	7	6	46	16
Tison, Brig, George Mason	.370	238	44	88	26	0	0	34	13
Maruri, Alex, Delaware	.361	155	30	56	13	2	3	28	0
McInturff, Cole, James Madison	.360	186	35	67	10	2	0	25	14

Yezzo, Jimmy, Delaware	.358	187	38	67	13	1	8	46	0
Barbosa, Aaron, Northeastern	.349	215	38	75	6	4	1	20	14
Cullen, Bill, VCU	.347	259	62	90	25	**9**	5	40	11
Leroux, Jon, Northeastern	.347	167	41	58	12	1	12	50	1
Jackson, Kenny, Hofstra	.344	215	33	74	12	1	4	51	8
Ridge, Hunter, UNCW	.340	228	40	81	16	1	4	42	3
Brown, Conner, James Madison	.338	148	31	50	10	2	3	33	2
Fisher, Zach, Towson	.333	162	25	54	10	3	2	27	5
Schafferman, Dan, George Mason	.332	217	37	72	10	1	5	39	8
Rouleau, Dalton, Hofstra	.328	195	51	64	14	2	5	30	26
Flynn, Kevin, Hofstra	.326	175	29	57	15	1	1	28	13
Bass, Michael, UNCW	.324	222	33	72	9	3	0	33	20
Puttress, John, Northeastern	.323	192	30	62	9	0	0	29	1
Cain, Andrew, UNCW	.322	239	59	77	10	1	12	43	23
Nutter, Kevin, William & Mary	.321	209	45	67	8	1	0	16	11
Allen, Nick, George Mason	.319	160	36	51	8	3	1	28	5
Katz, Michael, William & Mary	.316	212	42	67	10	0	10	58	6
Powell, Tyler, Delaware	.316	187	19	59	9	0	0	27	4
Bailey, Caden, Georgia State	.315	181	28	57	3	1	0	16	1
Ferdinand, Nick, Delaware	.313	208	38	65	19	1	4	47	4
Vosler, Jason, Northeastern	.308	182	40	56	5	2	1	34	14
#Molinaro, Tyler, UNCW	.273	**264**	49	72	17	1	**16**	48	6

INDIVIDUAL PITCHING LEADERS
(Minimum 50 IP)

	W	L	ERA	G	SV	IP	H	BB	SO
#O'Grady, Chris, George Mason	2	0	1.22	25	**14**	37	20	20	51
Davenport, Matt, William & Mary	7	5	**1.73**	17	0	**109**	82	16	**90**
Pearson, Devon, Delaware	6	1	1.76	27	0	56	51	25	41
Secrest, Kelly, UNCW	5	2	2.12	30	0	51	34	17	45
Holden, Ricky, UNCW	3	0	2.28	26	0	59	49	15	30
Ali, Dean, ODU	3	4	2.32	24	2	50	41	24	60
Batts, Mat, UNCW	6	5	3.04	16	0	101	109	20	90
McSwain, Tyler, UNCW	9	4	3.18	17	0	105	106	24	67
Koehler, Brett, William & Mary	6	2	3.21	13	0	70	64	10	55
Trionfo, Michael, Towson	**11**	3	3.35	15	0	83	86	31	52
Montefusco, Anthony, George Mason	4	3	3.61	14	0	85	84	22	62
Farrar, Ryan, VCU	4	3	3.67	14	0	88	87	33	64
Pelchy, Kyle, VCU	4	4	3.70	18	0	58	69	14	36
Ferguson, Kevin, Northeastern	6	4	3.78	12	0	79	80	20	66
Marshall, Ben, Georgia State	5	6	3.82	14	0	92	90	42	53
Wainman, Matt, William & Mary	3	4	3.92	14	0	57	57	19	44
Leenhouts, Andrew, Northeastern	6	3	3.93	13	0	92	90	35	87
Shain, Cole, William & Mary	4	3	3.97	17	0	68	67	19	44
Pfaeffle, Ryan, George Mason	5	6	4.25	14	4	72	82	29	42
Cutler-Voltz, Seth, VCU	7	3	4.29	19	0	84	94	11	67
Schmitz, Max, Georgia State	2	3	4.35	13	0	52	46	38	34
#Austin, Tyler, Towson	2	5	5.06	**32**	6	64	58	39	**90**

CONFERENCE USA

	Conference		Overall	
	W	L	W	L
Rice	17	7	41	19
Central Florida	16	8	45	17
Tulane	14	10	38	20
Southern Mississippi	14	10	32	24
Memphis	14	10	31	28
East Carolina	13	10	36	24
* Alabama-Birmingham	9	15	32	30
Houston	5	18	18	35
Marshall	5	19	17	37

ALL-CONFERENCE TEAM: C—Jeremy Schaffer, Sr., Tulane. **IF**—D.J. Hicks, Jr. UCF; Christian Stringer, Jr., Rice; Jacob Wilson, Sr., Memphis; John Wooten, Jr., East Carolina. **OF**—Brandon Boudreaux, Jr. Tulane; Adam McClain, Sr., Memphis; Jeremy Rathjen, Jr., Rice. **DH/UT**—J.T. Chargois, Jr., Rice. **P**—Kevin Brandt, Sr. East Carolina; Dan Langfield, Jr., Memphis; Andrew Pierce, Jr., Southern Mississippi; Matthew Reckling, Sr., Rice. **RP**—Joe Rogers, Jr. UCF.
Player of the Year—Jacob Wilson, Memphis. **Pitcher of the Year**—Matthew Reckling, Rice. **Freshman of the Year**—Mason Robbins, Southern Mississippi. **Newcomer of the Year**—Andrew Pierce, Southern Mississippi. **Coach of the Year**—Wayne Graham, Rice.

INDIVIDUAL BATTING LEADERS
(Minimum 150 at-bats)

	AVG	AB	R	H	2B	3B	HR	RBI	SB
McClain, Adam, Memphis	**.392**	232	49	**91**	13	0	3	36	13
Middleton, Brennan, Tulane	.357	196	45	70	10	2	0	19	14
Hynes, Eli, Memphis	.352	233	43	82	17	0	11	47	2
Schreve, Travis, UCF	.351	202	38	71	13	0	0	26	15
Graeter, Ashley, Southern Miss	.346	214	45	74	15	1	1	30	6
Schneeberger, Nick, Tulane	.345	226	42	78	12	3	3	36	12
Stringer, Chris, Rice	.343	236	58	81	12	3	3	36	6
Wooten, John, East Carolina	.338	237	50	80	10	1	9	40	2
Robbins, Mason, Southern Miss	.330	215	36	71	11	**5**	3	38	7
Reynolds, Drew, East Carolina	.330	209	31	69	8	0	3	24	0
Boudreaux, Brandon, Tulane	.330	209	56	69	14	3	8	36	10
Rathjen, Jeremy, Rice	.329	219	39	72	14	1	9	42	6
Schaffer, Jeremy, Tulane	.326	218	41	71	19	0	9	49	5
Appling, Landon, Houston	.324	188	32	61	5	0	3	26	10
Chargois, J.T., Rice	.323	189	26	61	10	0	0	31	1
Wilson, Jacob, Memphis	.320	231	47	74	17	0	**17**	64	7
Crohan, Blake, Tulane	.319	172	28	55	11	1	2	21	6
Friedrich, Alex, UCF	.316	232	45	74	**21**	3	4	39	16
Hicks, D.J., UCF	.316	225	52	71	13	0	14	**72**	0
Gomez, Nathan, Marshall	.316	206	35	65	17	0	3	39	0
Thompson, Corey, East Caro.	.315	241	40	76	13	0	4	40	0
Younger, Tim, East Carolina	.313	217	38	68	10	0	0	27	2
Potkay, Sean, Tulane	.313	150	25	47	9	0	5	29	3
Lueneburg, Jacob, Houston	.309	181	17	56	4	1	1	23	13
Ballou, Isaac, Marshall	.308	195	40	60	5	4	2	24	21
Cannizaro, Garrett, Tulane	.305	226	42	69	12	1	4	42	6
Richardson, Ronnie, UCF	.305	220	**59**	67	14	1	9	34	**24**
DePew, Keith, UAB	.304	181	31	55	5	1	0	21	5
Leon, Sergio, Marshall	.302	169	20	51	9	0	1	20	7
Cannon, John, Houston	.302	179	21	54	7	0	1	19	0
#Taladay, Chris, UCF	.298	**262**	42	78	8	1	5	49	1

INDIVIDUAL PITCHING LEADERS
(Minimum 1 IP per team game)

Player, team	W	L	ERA	G	SV	IP	H	BB	SO
#Ponder, D.J., Tulane	2	1	1.10	27	**12**	49	31	27	35
#Rogers, Joe, UCF	5	1	1.47	31	**12**	43	32	7	47
#Duffey, Tyler, Rice	1	1	1.93	**36**	7	51	33	21	68
Smithmyer, East Carolina	5	2	**1.92**	22	1	61	50	25	67
Pierce, Andrew, Southern Miss	7	4	1.99	15	0	99	88	16	96
Brandt, Kevin, East Carolina	7	6	2.12	16	0	**106**	93	27	68
Simms, John, Rice	6	0	2.56	25	0	63	47	22	59
Kubitza, Austin, Rice	6	5	2.69	16	0	80	60	38	73
Benak, Andrew, Rice	7	2	2.70	16	0	67	63	18	72
Langfield, Dan, Memphis	7	6	2.79	15	0	94	70	47	**111**
Napoli, David, Tulane	7	3	2.86	15	0	88	81	39	57
Bullard, Ben, UAB	5	5	2.96	14	0	82	72	19	79
Reckling, Matthew, Rice	8	3	2.98	17	0	88	58	36	99
Lively, Ben, UCF	**9**	2	3.00	19	0	81	67	45	84
Joyner, Tyler, East Carolina	6	2	3.01	17	0	93	88	12	68
Wall, Taylor, Rice	6	4	3.08	29	0	61	50	24	51
Byo, Alex, Tulane	**9**	4	3.38	14	0	91	87	19	50
Moll, Sam, Memphis	5	5	3.48	16	1	96	91	44	59
Mallard, Chase, UAB	4	4	3.50	24	2	64	56	26	45
Drehoff, Jake, So.n Mississippi	6	2	3.51	15	0	95	85	35	57
Cotton, Jharel, East Carolina	8	3	3.65	15	0	74	65	24	62
Hoffman, Jeff, East Carolina	3	2	3.67	19	0	74	60	21	55
Matulis, Chris, UCF	7	0	3.69	20	1	73	69	40	62
Busby, Michael, UAB	5	5	3.77	18	1	98	97	26	59
Blair, Aaron, Marshall	5	5	3.98	14	0	84	76	28	82

GREAT WEST CONFERENCE

	Conference		Overall	
	W	L	W	L
Utah Valley	28	0	47	12
Texas-Pan American	16	12	30	22
New Jersey Tech	16	12	25	27
Houston Baptist	15	13	28	33
Northern Colorado	15	13	27	33
North Dakota	10	18	19	37
Chicago State	9	19	13	40

New York Tech	3	25	5	46

ALL-CONFERENCE TEAM: C—Mike McCarthy, Sr., Texas-Pan American. 1B—Goose, Kallunki, Sr., Utah Valley. 2B—Willie Pratt, Jr., Utah Valley. 3B—Jake Rickenbach, Sr., Utah Valley. SS—Kai Hatch, Sr., Utah Valley. DH—Austin Heaps, Sr., Utah Vally. OF—Billy Burgess, Sr., Utah Valley; Albert Carpen, Sr., Chicago State; Sean Moysh, Jr., Utah Valley. UT—Jeff Campbell, Fr., North Dakota. P—Tripp Davis, Jr., New Jersey Tech; Jeremy Gendlek, Sr., Utah Valley; Adam Gunn, Jr., Utah Valley. RP—Jonathan Sa, Sr., UTPA.

Player of the Year: Goose Kallunki, Utah Valley. Pitcher of the Year: Adam Gunn, Utah Valley. Newcomer of the Year: Jeff Campbell, North Dakota. Coach of the Year: Eric Madsen, Utah Valley.

INDIVIDUAL BATTING LEADERS
(Minimum 125 at-bats)

	AVG	AB	R	H	2B	3B	HR	RBI	SB
Carpen, Albert, Chicago State	**.429**	183	54	78	10	3	1	23	13
Kallunki, Goose, Utah Valley	.419	229	61	**96**	16	1	**18**	**86**	1
Bernal, Roger, UTPA	.412	216	52	89	14	3	1	31	9
Burgess, Billy, Utah Valley	.396	222	**73**	88	16	3	7	65	4
Hilker, Adam, No. Colorado	.382	225	40	86	8	3	3	49	8
Rickenbach, Jake, Utah Valley	.381	239	67	91	22	2	4	54	0
Park, Jensen, No. Colorado	.363	212	33	77	10	7	0	38	5
#Rodriguez, Ali, NYIT	.357	115	21	53	8	0	0	16	**25**
Schenk, Adrian, No.Colorado	.354	209	40	74	7	8	1	40	6
Exon, Alex, Utah Valley	.353	170	36	60	15	1	4	31	4
Follis, Tyler, North Dakota	.352	210	49	74	13	1	0	29	2
Heaps, Austin, Utah Valley	.347	231	63	81	12	2	8	58	1
Ratajczyk, Jeremy, Chicago St.	.346	185	27	64	17	2	4	42	1
Hatch, Kai, Utah Valley	.342	237	44	81	12	5	3	42	12
Moysh, Sean, Utah Valley	.339	236	68	80	9	5	4	44	15
Ibanzez, Angel, UTPA	.337	202	37	68	5	4	3	37	12
Pratt, Willie, Utah Valley	.333	144	39	48	14	4	2	50	4
Malhotra, Ryan, Chicago State	.333	135	21	45	9	0	2	24	0
Roche, D.J., NJIT	.329	146	26	48	10	0	2	24	5
Crudo, Tony, Northern Colorado	.328	192	39	63	7	2	3	30	4
Gonzalez, Jake, Houston Baptist	.328	238	39	78	19	**9**	5	63	6
Hagy, Marcus, NJIT	.327	205	45	67	7	0	0	34	5
Campell, Jeff, North Dakota	.326	224	43	73	14	2	12	47	5
Jones, Curtis, Houston Baptist	.319	204	26	65	13	2	0	31	3
Yamane, Ryan, N. Colorado	.316	190	45	60	13	3	0	31	5
Charlton, Ed, NJIT	.315	197	39	62	15	2	2	31	15
Kwak, Kris, North Dakota	.313	208	42	65	10	2	4	32	1
Weckerle, Matt, NJIT	.313	208	31	65	10	3	3	34	5
Romanin, Mattingly, Chicago St.	.311	206	41	64	14	1	2	22	6
Bolander, Kyle, North Dakota	.310	174	31	54	9	1	9	43	5
Torres, Chris, UTPA	.306	134	19	41	3	1	0	22	0

INDIVIDUAL PITCHING LEADERS
(Minimum 50 IP)

	W	L	ERA	G	SV	IP	H	BB	SO
Sa, Jonathan, UTPA	5	2	**2.23**	16	2	61	45	26	64
Hoelscher, Tyler, Houston Baptist	5	4	2.97	14	0	88	104	19	34
Olson, Preston, Utah Valley	8	0	3.15	16	0	71	61	33	71
Davis, Tripp, NJIT	5	2	3.29	14	0	98	89	30	82
Thome, Andrew, North Dakota	5	5	3.58	14	0	93	83	20	65
Leiter, Mark, NJIT	5	7	3.65	14	0	94	95	43	**95**
Shulle, Michael, NJIT	2	4	3.67	25	2	61	75	14	29
#Swenson, Josh, Utah Valley	3	0	3.69	22	**6**	39	42	11	25
Zouzalik, Michael, Houston Baptist	4	1	3.81	13	0	52	46	29	28
Vanmeerbeke, Bill, NJIT	2	5	3.81	10	0	59	63	14	39
Jones, Curtis, Houston Baptist	6	5	4.10	14	0	59	77	20	37
Gunn, Adam, Utah Valley	8	3	4.10	17	1	86	93	24	75
Hammer, Chris, No. Colorado	6	2	4.83	17	0	60	87	10	47
Gendlek, Jeremy, Utah Valley	**10**	3	4.89	17	0	96	115	24	54
Lower, Ryan, Houston Baptist	2	3	4.90	12	0	61	61	33	33
Schafer, Dalton, Houston Baptist	5	9	4.98	16	0	**116**	154	17	52
Knight, Dusten, UTPA	3	4	5.10	14	0	67	76	33	69
Willman, Joe, No. Colorado	5	7	5.13	16	0	79	96	31	41
Hall, Eric, Chicago State	1	6	5.79	18	0	56	88	21	27
Kennell, Ross, Houston Baptist	5	4	5.86	13	0	55	76	26	36
Steinmetz, Nate, No. Colorado	4	6	6.22	18	0	64	102	19	57
Campbell, Jeff, North Dakota	4	7	6.30	12	0	76	96	29	41
Amedee, Jess, No. Colorado	4	6	6.34	12	0	60	80	28	38
#Tallman, Cameron, No. Colorado	0	2	7.16	**26**	3	43	64	27	34

HORIZON LEAGUE

	Conference		Overall	
	W	L	W	L
*Valparaiso	22	8	35	25
Wright State	20	10	37	21
Wisconsin-Milwaukee	18	11	27	27
Illinois-Chicago	12	17	23	34
Butler	10	20	22	34
Youngstown State	7	23	11	44

ALL-CONFERENCE TEAM: C—Corey Davis, Sr., Wright State. **1B**—Jake Hibberd, Sr., Wright State. **2B**—Tanner Vavra, Jr., Valparaiso. **3B**—Drew Dosch, So., Youngstown State. **SS**—Spencer Mahoney, Fr., Valparaiso. **OF**—Luke Meeteer, Fr., Wisconsin-Milwaukee; Ryan Ashe, Sr. Wright State; Tristan Moore, Sr., Wright State. **DH**—Jeremy Banks, Sr. Youngstown State. **UT**—Paul Hoenecke, Sr., Wisconsin-Milwaukee. **P**—Kevin Wild, Sr., Valparaiso; Cale Tassi, Jr., Wisconsin-Milwaukee.
Player of the Year: Tristan Moore, Wright State. **Pitcher of the Year:** Kevin Wild, Valparaiso. **Relief Pitcher of the Year:** Michael Schum, Wright State. **Co-Newcomers of the Year:** Jimmy Risi, Butler; Jyle Wormington, Valparaiso. **Coach of the Year:** Tracy Woodson, Valparaiso.

INDIVIDUAL BATTING LEADERS
(Minimum 125 at-bats)

	AVG	AB	R	H	2B	3B	HR	RBI	SB
Banks, Jeremy, YSU	.385	161	24	62	16	0	5	44	2
Ashe, Ryan, Wright State	.374	222	51	83	10	6	2	46	6
Moore, Tristan, Wright State	.358	229	56	82	14	2	7	51	9
Gray, Garrett, Wright State	.354	164	27	58	17	0	3	36	0
Dosch, Drew, YSU	.353	224	36	79	13	1	8	42	5
Grunenwald, Alex, UIC	.345	197	36	68	13	2	5	39	1
Gelwicks, Pat, Butler	.337	199	48	67	12	1	5	37	2
Hibberd, Jake, Wright State	.336	250	50	84	18	1	9	47	3
Vavra, Tanner, Valparaiso	.332	229	52	76	8	4	1	20	15
Meeteer, Luke, Milwaukee	.331	172	35	57	5	2	1	15	16
Tanner, Zach, Wright State	.324	179	26	58	13	4	1	30	1
Bain, Andrew, Valparaiso	.318	261	39	83	2	1	0	20	6
Fadness, Will, Milwaukee	.316	190	26	60	21	0	4	30	1
Betcher, Joe, UIC	.311	209	36	65	9	3	4	37	7
Hoenecke, Paul, Milwaukee	.306	216	42	66	18	0	3	41	2
Ryan, Jon, UIC	.302	215	37	65	13	2	6	50	3
Shirley, Jason, YSU	.301	196	31	59	7	1	0	16	9
Martin, Elliot, Valparaiso	.301	236	36	71	6	0	2	50	5
Koenig, Sam, Milwaukee	.300	190	35	57	13	1	1	28	7
De LaRosa, Alex, UIC	.298	225	35	67	12	2	0	30	4
Haddad, Radley, Butler	.295	166	25	49	12	1	0	16	0
Davis, Corey, Wright State	.295	227	40	67	18	1	4	32	3
Hagel, Will, Valparaiso	.294	231	37	68	10	3	2	42	0
Capasso, Jonathan, Milwaukee	.290	210	28	61	14	1	3	35	6
Scoby, Steven, Valparaiso	.286	231	26	66	6	2	1	20	7
Hoscheit, Mike, Butler	.286	182	26	52	12	0	5	34	0
Richeson, Griffin, Butler	.286	175	34	50	7	0	0	15	5
Manning, Chris, Valparaiso	.283	244	44	69	7	2	2	35	11
Risi, Jimmy, Butler	.282	156	28	44	4	0	12	46	1
Kopale, Justin, Wright State	.281	203	30	57	13	1	4	45	1
Loeffler, John, Valparaiso	.279	201	33	56	18	0	2	37	0

INDIVIDUAL PITCHING LEADERS
(Mimimum 50 IP)

	W	L	ERA	G	SV	IP	H	BB	SO
Tassi, Cale, Milwaukee	6	5	2.74	15	0	95	87	28	69
#Schum, Michael, Wright State	4	2	3.00	29	12	48	45	15	42
Deetjen, Tyler, Valparaiso	6	3	3.12	17	0	121	136	11	65
Elliot, Andrew, Wright State	1	1	3.15	18	1	54	61	13	29
Wild, Kevin, Valparaiso	6	4	3.16	16	0	111	104	34	60
Marker, Jordan, Wright State	9	2	3.18	29	2	62	50	18	47
Wormington, Kyle, Valparaiso	6	6	3.33	16	0	103	100	19	58
Semmelhack, Eric, Milwaukee	5	7	3.77	15	0	88	90	39	72
Schneider, Mike, Milwaukee	2	5	4.55	13	0	63	63	31	42
Evak, Brian, UIC	5	6	4.66	17	0	93	100	31	35
Braun, Taylor, Wright State	6	2	4.97	12	0	63	68	20	47
Schnitzer, Brad, Butler	3	4	5.07	24	0	60	80	21	47
McCulloh, Kevin, YSU	1	2	5.07	32	0	55	63	24	52
Harless, Russ, YSU	3	7	5.15	22	0	80	89	12	50
Kopilchack, Cody, Wright State	4	4	5.20	14	0	55	42	51	52
Begel, Joey, UIC	7	7	5.38	17	0	99	112	33	46
Silvestri, Dom, Butler	4	6	6.00	14	0	69	89	22	39
Valencheck, Lee, Wright State	2	3	6.29	14	0	54	72	21	36
Hoelzel, Joey, Wright State	5	5	6.62	17	0	53	59	20	29
Aquandro, Blake, YSU	3	9	7.11	21	0	86	120	33	37

IVY LEAGUE

	Conference		Overall	
GEHRIG	W	L	W	L
*Cornell	14	6	31	17
Princeton	13	7	20	19
Columbia	12	8	21	24
Pennsylvania	8	12	17	23
ROLFE	**W**	**L**	**W**	**L**
Dartmouth	14	6	24	18
Harvard	8	12	12	30
Brown	6	14	9	35
Yale	5	15	13	31

ALL-CONFERENCE TEAM: C—Sam Mulroy, Sr., Princeton. **1B**—Dustin Selxer, So., Dartmouth. **2B**—Jeff Reynolds, Sr., Harvard. **3B**—Joe Eisen, Sr., Columbia. **SS**—Joe Sclafani, Sr., Dartmouth. **OF**—Dario Pizzano, Jr., Columbia; Jake Carlson, Sr., Dartmouth; Greg Zebrack, Sr., Pennsylvania. **DH**—Ennis Coble, Jr., Dartmouth. **UT**—Alex Keller, So., Princeton. **SP**—Zak Hermans, Jr., Princeton; Pat Lowery, Sr., Columbia; Connor Kaufmann, So., Cornell. **RP**—Keller Urbon, Fr., Cornell.
Player of the Year: Dario Pizzano, Columbia. **Pitcher of the Year:** Zak Hermans, Princeton. **Freshman of the Year:** Kellen Urbon, Cornell.

INDIVIDUAL BATTING LEADERS
(Minimum 2.5 at-bats per team game)

	AVG	AB	R	H	2B	3B	HR	RBI	SB
Carlson, Jake, Dartmouth	.397	131	30	52	4	3	2	19	3
Billigen, Brian, Cornell	.361	158	35	57	10	3	6	40	13
Pizzano, Dario, Columbia	.360	150	37	54	16	0	4	36	3
Eisen, Jon, Columbia	.360	150	37	54	9	0	0	12	13
McGuiggan, Jake, Harvard	.352	122	17	43	11	0	2	21	2
Keller, Jeff, Dartmouth	.352	122	26	43	8	0	5	26	3
Mulroy, Sam, Princeton	.351	148	37	52	8	1	8	32	11
Deitrich, Ryan, Pennsylvania	.350	140	24	49	17	4	4	22	2
Keller, Alec, Princeton	.346	136	22	47	4	1	0	18	6
Zebrack, Greg, Pennsylvania	.343	137	34	47	18	2	7	28	10
Hanson, Cale, Yale	.340	162	21	55	8	0	0	8	11
Reynolds, Jeff, Harvard	.333	162	21	54	13	1	3	24	3
Fornaca, Nick, Brown	.326	138	19	45	9	3	0	18	2
Selzer, Dustin, Dartmouth	.324	142	30	46	11	2	5	41	0
Slaughter, Cody, Brown	.318	129	23	41	8	0	5	32	0
Colton, Jack, Harvard	.316	155	16	49	4	0	1	14	7
Lee, Brandon, Cornell	.314	153	21	48	13	0	0	20	0
Marcal, Will, Brown	.311	167	32	52	11	1	5	26	2
Coble, Ennis, Dartmouth	.311	135	24	42	4	1	0	16	3
Ferraresi, Nick, Columbia	.310	142	27	44	15	1	4	32	2
Bowman, Matt, Princeton	.308	133	26	41	2	1	1	15	1
Toups, David, Yale	.306	147	14	45	5	1	1	15	3
Tatum, Kevin, Cornell	.300	140	26	42	5	0	0	18	1
Hager, Frank, Cornell	.296	176	31	52	15	1	3	10	6
Vigoa, Derek, Pennsylvania	.292	137	15	40	2	0	0	17	5
Sclafani, Joe, Dartmouth	.288	163	32	47	13	3	2	24	4
Brenner, Ryan, Yale	.288	153	26	44	8	0	0	10	6
Peters, Brenton, Cornell	.286	161	36	46	7	2	2	20	5
Rumpke, Billy, Columbia	.283	152	22	43	6	2	1	25	8
Franco, J.J., Brown	.281	153	24	43	5	1	0	14	2
#Cruz, Chris	.258	178	33	46	7	2	12	35	8
#Yanzick, Marshall, Cornell	.258	194	27	50	7	0	0	26	4

INDIVIDUAL PITCHING LEADERS
(Minimum 1 IP per team game)

	W	L	ERA	G	SV	IP	H	BB	SO
#Urbon, Kellen, Cornell	3	1	0.48	22	9	37	22	13	20
Lowery, Pat, Columbia	4	4	2.35	9	0	54	49	19	46
#Shultz, Eric, Yale	5	2	2.37	25	2	38	46	22	29
Voiro, Vince, Pennsylvania	5	3	2.45	16	0	66	70	14	59
Ludwig, Pat, Yale	1	5	2.73	9	0	63	60	23	64

Hermans, Zak, Princeton	6	2	3.00	9	0	63	57	22	60
McAfee, Brian, Cornell	6	1	3.38	11	0	67	74	10	41
Marks, Rich, Cornell	4	5	3.43	12	0	63	62	24	28
Ford, Mike, Princeton	4	4	3.60	9	0	50	58	17	26
Thomson, Cody, Pennsylvania	2	4	3.63	14	2	52	57	23	36
Olson, Stefan, Columbia	4	5	3.65	9	0	49	49	12	38
Giel, Tim, Columbia	3	3	3.83	9	0	55	55	13	34
Kaufmann, Connor, Cornell	7	2	3.90	11	0	55	56	18	32
Concato, Louis, Dartmouth	4	1	4.15	13	0	43	52	12	20
Suter, Brent, Harvard	2	6	4.36	11	1	54	52	15	45
Johnson, Michael, Harvard	4	1	4.37	8	0	47	49	13	32
Becker, Nolan, Yale	2	4	4.44	12	0	51	46	25	56
Frank, Adam, Dartmouth	4	1	4.47	10	0	48	49	15	18
O'Hare, Christopher, Yale	1	5	4.63	12	0	47	55	24	38
Bowman, Matt, Princeton	4	2	4.66	9	0	56	63	17	58
Speer, David, Columbia	3	1	4.91	10	0	48	53	13	40
Cerfolio, Rob, Yale	0	4	4.98	10	0	47	65	17	19
Lower, Pat, Columbia	1	5	4.62	9	0	49	52	31	37
Horacek, Mitch, Dartmouth	4	3	5.47	9	0	54	72	10	47
Mayo, Heath, Brown	2	3	5.53	11	0	54	58	38	32
Link, Kevin, Princeton	3	3	5.73	9	0	49	66	12	26
Hunter, Kyle, Dartmouth	3	4	5.76	10	0	55	70	13	29
Galan, Anthony, Brown	3	4	7.02	10	0	58	86	20	42

	AVG	AB	R	H	2B	3B	HR	RBI	SB
Trymbiski, Ted, Siena	.295	146	17	43	6	1	0	8	0
McQuail, Nick, Marist	.292	178	25	52	5	1	1	24	4
Cornelia, Larry, Fairfield	.291	223	36	65	11	0	0	21	25
Metzler, Ryan, Siena	.291	172	22	50	4	0	0	19	2
Welsh, Pat, Marist	.284	134	17	38	9	0	3	26	1
Galan, Yoandry, Manhattan	.283	187	32	53	9	0	0	22	8
Grimes, Chris, St. Peter's	.283	138	19	39	14	0	4	30	3
Zimmer, Shane, Canisius	.282	163	35	46	10	1	0	38	3
#Kelso, Jesse, Canisius	.257	148	19	38	6	6	0	30	5

INDIVIDUAL PITCHING LEADERS
(Minimum 50 IP)

	W	L	ERA	G	SV	IP	H	BB	SO
#Fitzsimmons, Jon, Canisius	3	2	1.42	25	11	25	16	17	34
Warwick, Scott, Fairfield	3	4	2.60	12	0	73	65	30	57
Sewitt, Taylor, Manhattan	11	2	2.62	23	1	96	71	25	86
Ashworth, E.J., Fairfield	5	6	2.97	16	0	58	53	21	46
Murphy, Mike, Rider	4	5	3.09	14	0	96	98	26	55
Soldinger, John, Manhattan	6	5	3.43	16	1	94	90	38	58
Mancini, Matt, St. Peter's	5	3	3.48	13	0	72	80	27	40
Hopf, Zack, St. Peter's	4	8	3.49	14	0	90	88	33	71
Cortright, Garrett, Canisius	6	6	3.50	16	0	98	91	37	76
Smith, Tyler, Rider	5	5	3.72	23	3	77	87	16	62
Bielak, Chris, Marist	2	2	3.73	12	1	63	63	25	53
Stewart, Devon, Canisius	6	4	3.80	15	0	95	96	31	60
Gallagher, Chad, Marist	6	4	3.90	12	0	81	79	17	48
Houseal, Brett, Marist	4	6	4.00	13	0	72	80	14	42
Yuhas, Matthew, St. Peter's	5	7	4.52	13	0	72	81	22	36
Soule, Jeremy, Fairfield	4	3	4.53	12	0	56	51	24	29
Pierce, Rohn, Canisius	2	3	4.63	20	0	68	70	17	51
Martin, Billy, Canisius	6	4	4.67	15	0	96	112	22	40
Sowa, Kurt, Rider	5	4	4.78	14	0	75	71	43	50
Macaluso, Dom, St. Peter's	1	8	4.84	19	7	58	62	16	24
Macaluso, Eddie, Iona	4	7	5.42	14	0	83	91	37	42
McClennan, Scott, Manhattan	2	6	5.47	16	1	76	100	20	28
#Soja, Geoff, Niagara	2	6	5.90	27	2	40	40	15	38

METRO ATLANTIC ATHLETIC CONFERENCE

	Conference		Overall	
	W	L	W	L
*Manhattan	18	6	33	27
Canisius	16	8	33	27
Fairfield	14	10	27	28
Rider	13	11	22	34
Marist	11	12	25	25
Iona	10	14	21	33
St. Peter's	10	14	20	34
Siena	8	16	18	37
Niagara	7	16	19	29

ALL-CONFERENCE TEAM: C—Ramon Ortega, Jr., Manhattan. 1B—Ryan McCauley, Jr., Niagara. 2B—Nick Camastro, Jr., Manahattan. 3B—Chris Burke, Sr., Iona. SS—Yoandry Galan, So., Manhattan. OF—Anthony Vega, Jr., Manhattan; Wynton Bernard, Sr., Niagara; Brandon Cotten, Sr., Rider. DH—Ian Lindsay, Jr., Rider. UT—Eric Hink, Sr., Niagara. P—John Soldinger, Jr., Manhattan; Mike Murphy, So., Rider. **Player of the Year:** Chris Burke, Iona. **Pitcher of the Year:** Mike Murphy, Rider. **Relief Pitcher of the Year:** Jon Fitzsimmons, Canisius. **Rookie of the Year:** Devon Stewart, Canisius. **Coach of the Year:** Bill Currier, Fairfield.

INDIVIDUAL BATTING LEADERS
(Minimum 125 at-bats)

	AVG	AB	R	H	2B	3B	HR	RBI	SB
Hink, Eric, Niagara	.364	198	40	72	12	1	5	39	1
McCauley, Ryan, Niagara	.362	185	36	67	20	1	12	51	0
Burke, Chris, Iona	.351	205	44	72	20	1	11	50	23
Lindsay, Ian, Rider	.339	174	29	59	7	0	2	25	9
Carter, Justyn, St. Peter's	.331	136	23	45	4	0	1	12	21
Plourde, Ryan, Fairfield	.328	186	32	61	10	2	6	35	2
Vega, Anthony, Manhattan	.326	227	41	74	11	4	5	31	32
Berry, Jake, Marist	.323	189	36	61	5	4	0	21	7
Hajjar, Anthony, Fairfield	.322	202	35	65	10	2	1	36	2
Shank, Zach, Marist	.321	190	36	61	8	0	2	24	7
Rooney, John, Siena	.316	193	25	61	10	2	0	27	9
Orefice, Mike, Marist	.316	171	35	54	11	0	4	27	0
Chiaravalloti, Michael, Iona	.315	162	26	51	17	0	4	27	2
Camastro, Nick, Manhattan	.314	210	38	66	16	1	0	28	20
Bernard, Wynton, Niagara	.314	172	34	54	12	2	3	24	32
Cotten, Brandon, Rider	.313	195	33	61	9	4	3	32	16
Kriss, Matthew, Iona	.304	181	30	55	13	0	1	25	9
Wosleger, Tyler, Fairfield	.301	143	28	43	7	2	0	17	7
Pettit, Drew, Canisius	.298	198	30	59	4	1	3	39	2
Klock, Joel, Niagara	.297	158	34	47	11	1	1	25	5
Wayman, Adam, Rider	.297	212	36	63	13	0	1	30	6
Guiliano, Jimmy, Iona	.297	155	33	46	8	1	0	13	12

MID-AMERICAN CONFERENCE

	Conference		Overall	
EAST	W	L	W	L
*Kent State	24	3	47	20
Ohio	16	11	28	29
Miami (OH)	12	15	30	29
Buffalo	10	16	20	36
Akron	10	17	17	38
Bowling Green	9	18	20	33
WEST	**W**	**L**	**W**	**L**
Toledo	19	8	30	27
Central Michigan	17	10	34	29
Western Michigan	14	12	26	29
Eastern Michigan	14	13	25	31
Ball State	9	18	14	36
Northern Illinois	7	20	15	40

ALL-CONFERENCE TEAM: C—Tom Murphy, Jr., Buffalo. 1B—George Roberts, Jr., Kent State 2B—Joe Corfman, Sr., Toledo. 3B—Ryan McMillan, Sr., Western Michigan. SS—Jimmy Rider, Sr., Kent State. OF—Matt Pollock, Buffalo; Brent Ohrman, Sr., Eastern Michigan; Matt Honchel, Fr., Miami (OH). DH—Sam Ott, So., Eastern Michigan. SP—Zach Cooper, Sr., Central Michigan; David Starn, Sr., Kent State; Jason Moulton, Sr., Ohio; Matt Kuna, Toledo. RP—Lincoln Rassi, Sr., Toledo
Player of the Year: George Roberts, Kent State. **Pitcher of the Year:** David Starn, Kent State. **Freshman of the Year:** Matt Honchel, Miami (OH). **Coach of the Year:** Scott Stricklin, Kent State.

INDIVIDUAL BATTING LEADERS
(Minimum 125 at-bats)

	AVG	AB	R	H	2B	3B	HR	RBI	SB
Honchel, Matt, Miami (OH)	.395	233	43	92	7	2	0	26	10
Roberts, George, Kent State	.368	253	44	93	23	1	8	64	2
Rider, Jimmy, Kent State	.364	283	66	103	29	1	5	56	3
Pollock, Matt, Buffalo	.357	221	56	79	18	4	12	44	1
Bower, Kevin, Miami (OH)	.352	210	35	74	14	1	3	52	0
Dean, Jordan, Ct. Michigan	.349	275	62	96	13	2	7	46	10

Hamilton, Nick, Kent State	.347	173	20	60	12	2	1	35	1
Forton, Troy, W. Michigan	.346	133	11	46	6	1	2	23	0
Kanzler, Jason, Buffalo	.345	223	50	77	13	5	8	40	17
Bien, Brian, Bowling Green	.345	168	26	58	8	1	0	19	7
Madsen, Jake, Ohio	.344	221	32	76	13	0	1	32	1
Ohrman, Brent, Ea. Michigan	.344	227	49	78	12	5	1	41	21
Gaertner, Cody, Ohio	.338	151	25	51	8	0	1	24	4
Williams, Arnold, Ct. Michigan	.335	218	46	73	10	0	6	52	2
Corfman, Joe, Toledo	.333	234	52	78	16	1	3	21	22
McMillin, Ryan, W. Michigan	.333	216	46	72	19	1	7	52	5
Scanlon, Jack, W. Michigan	.330	188	36	62	9	2	4	37	3
Hall, Tyler, Central Michigan	.327	168	52	55	9	2	3	30	3
Campbell, Evan, Kent State	.327	266	61	87	20	4	7	40	5
Jones, Alex, Northern Illinois	.322	211	33	68	21	4	1	33	8
Duncan, Patrick, W. Michigan	.321	218	37	70	15	0	3	39	0
Losby, T.J., Bowling Green	.319	182	27	58	9	2	3	37	1
Wells, Tyler, Ohio	.315	200	36	63	13	3	5	24	2
Huffman, Jordan, N. Illinois	.312	170	26	53	6	0	0	14	4
Thomas, Jake, Bowling Green	.311	177	28	55	5	4	0	19	2
Murphy, Tom, Buffalo	.311	219	46	68	20	4	13	51	6
Thoma, Zach, W. Michigan	.309	194	34	60	9	1	0	23	4
Lancaster, Pan, Bowling Green	.309	149	19	46	5	0	0	18	6
Winkle, Wes, Ball State	.307	189	30	58	7	2	0	13	12
Delewski, Matt, Toledo	.306	173	16	53	11	0	0	20	2
#Painter, Jensen, Ohio	.281	210	44	59	14	1	14	44	4
#Wells, Jamsion, N. Illinois	.238	214	26	51	6	0	0	11	25

INDIVIDUAL PITCHING LEADERS
(Minimum 50 IP)

	W	L	ERA	G	SV	IP	H	BB	SO
Starn, Kyle, Kent State	11	3	2.21	18	0	114	89	45	123
Enns, Dietrich, Ct. Michigan	4	2	2.34	17	2	58	47	23	43
Kuna, Matt, Toledo	7	1	2.61	16	2	79	67	17	59
Moulton, Jason, Ohio	6	3	2.66	13	0	91	102	28	55
Thoreson, Mac, Miami (Ohio)	6	4	2.22	16	0	101	89	20	71
Cooper, Zach, Central Michigan	7	5	2.82	15	0	108	82	44	98
Choban, Brett, Ohio	7	6	2.95	15	0	110	129	38	60
Wilkinson, Ryan, Toledo	7	4	2.99	19	0	78	86	18	50
Kaminska, Patrick, Ct. Michigan	5	4	3.05	18	0	74	76	19	42
Foster, Scott, Akron	3	5	3.09	18	0	55	50	20	34
Loftin, Alex, Akron	3	4	3.12	15	0	75	75	28	50
Brown, Andrew, Akron	6	8	3.19	14	0	99	94	28	67
Singer, Ben, Bowling Green	2	2	3.27	27	0	55	56	12	23
Mace, Ryan, Kent State	2	3	3.27	15	0	55	58	18	44
Bores, Ryan, Kent State	9	3	3.35	17	0	105	110	16	67
Marquardt, Shawn, Miami (OH)	7	5	3.43	15	0	102	97	19	66
Laudicina, Steve, W. Michigan	7	4	3.51	15	0	85	94	34	50
Skulina, Tyler, Kent State	11	2	3.63	17	0	102	91	41	97
Nimke, Will, Western Michigan	4	4	3.74	15	0	67	73	20	31
Butara, Neil, Eastern Michigan	4	5	3.84	16	0	80	76	35	58
#Glancy, Kyle, Northern Illinois	0	4	7.96	31	11	32	39	19	30

MID-EASTERN ATHLETIC CONFERENCE

	Conference		Overall	
NORTH	W	L	W	L
Delaware State	22	2	40	17
Norfolk State	15	9	22	28
Maryland-Eastern Shore	11	13	14	39
Coppin State	0	24	1	53
SOUTH	W	L	W	L
* Bethune-Cookman	18	5	34	27
North Carolina Central	13	10	19	32
North Carolina A&T	12	12	20	36
Savannah State	11	13	19	34
Florida A&M	5	19	7	45

ALL-CONFERENCE TEAM: C—Eddie Sorondo, So., Delaware State. **1B**—Ryan Haas, Jr., Delaware State. **2B**—Marquis Riley, Sr., North Carolina A&T. **3B**—Cameron Cecil, So., Delaware State. **SS**—Brashad Johnson, Sr., Bethune-Cookman. **OF**—Luis Diaz, Jr., North Carolina Central; Cameron Day, So., Norforlk State; David Lee, Jr., Bethune-Cookman. **P**—Rayan Gonzalez, Sr., Bethune-Cookman; Jordan Elliot, Sr. Delaware State. **RP**—Jordan Dailey, Jr., Bethune-Cookman.
Player of the Year: Ryan Haas, Delaware State. **Pitcher of the Year:**

Rayan Gonzalez, Bethune-Cookman. **Rookie of the Year:** Rexford Davis, Savannah State. **Coach of the Year:** JP Blandin, Delaware State.

INDVIDUAL BATTING LEADERS
(Minimum 2 at-bats per team game)

	AVG	AB	R	H	2B	3B	HR	RBI	SB
Haas, Ryan, Delaware State	.360	203	46	73	22	0	1	60	1
Frey, J.P., Delaware State	.357	196	40	70	7	2	0	40	10
Day, Cameron, Norfolk State	.356	146	30	52	7	4	1	24	9
Diaz, Luis, N.C. Central	.351	185	45	65	9	4	4	30	7
Riley, Marquis, N.C. A&T	.346	217	44	75	10	1	2	43	11
Freeman, Kelvin, N.C. A&T	.338	216	32	73	14	1	2	33	4
Johnson, Brashad, B-CU	.336	211	40	71	11	2	2	34	20
Green, Julius, Delaware State	.331	136	31	45	8	0	2	17	17
Cecil, Cameron, Delaware St.	.327	199	61	65	12	0	2	44	9
Nardone, Aaron, Delaware St.	.322	183	49	59	6	7	5	46	20
Drummond, Troy, Delaware St.	.320	219	73	70	8	4	3	32	22
Newsome, James, UMES	.319	185	27	59	14	3	2	24	4
Johnson, Tre-von, UMES	.318	201	31	64	12	1	1	23	12
Sorondo, Eddie, Delaware St.	.318	154	47	49	8	0	1	42	2
West, Dylan, Florida A&M	.315	143	12	45	7	0	1	16	2
Marrow, Troy, N.C. Central	.313	176	36	55	9	2	0	44	0
Lee, David, B-CU	.306	222	40	68	14	2	3	47	13
Tendler, Luke, N.C. A&T	.305	220	38	67	10	6	6	55	2
Warren, Chris, Norfolk State	.303	145	31	44	11	3	1	20	6
Campbell, Byron, UMES	.302	199	29	60	13	7	1	20	4
Radford, Michael, N.C. A&T	.301	196	32	59	13	1	0	26	12
McKoy, Andre, N.C. A&T	.298	191	45	57	11	3	3	31	13
Turner, Brandon, B-CU	.292	219	45	64	5	2	0	23	23
Johnson, Josh, B-CU	.291	227	37	66	9	1	1	26	27
Simpson, Tyson, N.C. Central	.291	172	26	50	10	0	2	28	1
Hagen, Todd, Savannah State	.290	183	31	53	10	1	1	20	12
Drayton, Dylan, N.C. Central	.287	178	40	51	3	2	0	19	8
McCrary, Joseph, Savannah St.	.286	196	26	56	11	5	1	28	11
Johnson, Nick, B-CU	.285	186	30	53	9	2	2	16	5
Oglesby, Matthew, Savannah St.	.285	172	18	49	8	1	0	25	2
#Stokes, Anthony, B-CU	.261	157	28	41	7	0	10	35	2

INDIVIDUAL PITCHING LEADERS
(Minimum 1 IP per team game)

	W	L	ERA	G	SV	IP	H	BB	SO
Gonzalez, Ryan, B-CU	9	2	2.15	15	0	92	80	21	82
Egan, Jordan, Norfolk State	2	3	2.35	19	3	57	58	20	48
Adkins, Zach, Delaware State	8	1	2.73	16	0	69	58	29	45
Horne, Chris, Norfolk State	7	5	2.75	18	1	79	81	24	70
Hernandez, Gabriel, B-CU	6	3	2.92	16	0	77	68	35	45
Elliot, Jordan, Delaware State	10	2	2.92	17	0	92	91	29	65
McClain, Matt, Delaware State	9	4	2.95	15	0	92	88	19	55
Moore, Brent, N.C. A&T	5	6	3.01	12	0	75	81	17	37
#Dailey, Jordan, B-CU	4	6	3.30	34	11	46	43	9	29
McGowin, Kyle, Savannah State	6	5	3.43	16	0	97	94	14	91
Paulino, Estarlin, N.C. A&T	7	5	3.47	15	0	96	94	33	58
Durapau, Montana, B-CU	4	7	3.86	17	0	91	83	27	70
Bhatti, Justin, Norfolk State	4	7	3.94	14	0	78	86	26	67
Vanassche, Ryan, Norfolk State	4	7	4.08	15	0	82	90	33	79
Rivera, Bryan, B-CU	3	3	4.08	25	0	57	48	26	41
Boone, Tyler, N.C. A&T	5	6	4.68	14	0	77	87	42	51
Frye, Glenn, N.C. Central	4	6	4.72	15	0	74	89	29	56
Fulmer, Sam, N.C. Central	4	5	5.17	16	0	78	99	16	53
Romano, Michael, N.C. Central	3	3	5.24	15	1	57	80	15	31

MISSOURI VALLEY CONFERENCE

	Conference		Overall	
	W	L	W	L
Indiana State	14	7	41	19
Missouri State	13	7	40	22
Wichita State	12	9	35	25
Illinois State	10	9	33	19
Evansville	10	11	32	27
Southern Illinois	9	12	31	28
Bradley	8	13	27	27
* Creighton	6	14	28	30

ALL-CONFERENCE TEAM: C—Jeremy Lucas, Jr., Indiana State. **1B**—Chris

Serritella, Jr., Southern Illinois. **2B**—Kevin Medrano, Sr., Missouri State. **SS**—Eric Stamets, Jr., Evansville. **3B**—Zac Johnson, Jr. Illinois State. **OF**—Eric Aguilera, Jr., Illinois State Rob Ort, Jr., Indiana State; Jordan Sivertsen, Sr., Southern Illinois. **DH**—Johnny Coy, Jr., Wichita State. **UT**—Austin Montgomery, Jr., Southern Illinois. **SP**—Dakota Bacus, Jr., Indiana State; Joe Bircher, Sr., Bradley; Nick Petree, So., Missouri State. **RP**—Tyler Burgess, Fr., Missouri State; Kenny Long, Sr., Illinois State.
Player of the Year: Jeremy Lucas, Indiana State. **Pitcher of the Year:** Nick Petree, Missouri State. **Newcomer of the Year:** Dakota Bacus, Indiana State. **Freshman of the Year:** Tyler Burgess, Missouri State. **Coach of the Year:** Rick Heller, Indiana State.

INDIVIDUAL BATTING LEADERS
(Minimum 2.5 at-bats per team game)

	AVG	AB	R	H	2B	3B	HR	RBI	SB
Serritella, Chris, So. Illinois	.389	234	56	91	24	1	13	61	6
Lucas, Jeremy, Indiana State	.345	226	53	78	13	2	9	52	5
Coy, Johnny, Wichita State	.344	227	43	78	17	2	9	63	0
Montgomery, Austin, So. Ill.	.332	241	34	80	16	0	7	55	7
Aguilera, Eric, Illinois State	.330	203	41	67	8	1	7	36	0
Wiesemeyer, Ty, Illinois State	.329	207	37	68	14	8	4	45	9
Medrano, Kevin, Missouri St.	.327	248	39	81	19	0	0	24	12
Mirabal, Matt, Illinois State	.326	190	37	62	11	2	3	25	7
Maddox, Keenen, Missouri St.	.324	182	29	59	10	0	8	36	2
Johnson, Zac, Illinois State	.323	192	37	62	15	2	6	43	3
Curry, Landon, Indiana State	.322	211	49	68	6	0	1	27	16
Burnam, Kyle, Indiana State	.321	212	36	68	5	1	1	32	3
Godinez, Chris, Bradley	.320	169	33	54	6	0	4	18	11
Stamets, Eric, Evansville	.316	225	41	71	19	1	1	27	30
Judkins, Nick, Creighton	.313	227	38	71	9	2	1	31	5
Welch, Jake, Southern Illinois	.308	237	48	73	14	5	2	33	16
Chaffin, Brock, Missouri State	.307	215	28	66	11	1	2	42	3
Hockemeyer, Jason, Evansville	.306	209	26	64	9	5	1	29	5
Stanton, Kyle, Illinois State	.305	167	31	51	12	0	1	35	1
Tauchman, Mike, Bradley	.305	164	27	50	11	1	1	23	5
Hedges, Jon, Indiana State	.305	233	29	71	13	1	7	43	0
Kaczmarski, Kevin, Evansville	.303	201	38	61	13	5	1	33	13
Troggio, Rennie, So. Illinois	.303	155	30	47	5	1	0	21	8
Ross, Chance, Creighton	.301	246	48	74	14	3	3	36	14
Tokarski, Kevin, Illinois State	.300	190	42	57	11	1	3	37	14
Hollenbeck, Mike, Illinois St.	.299	177	31	53	10	1	3	39	1
Voit, Luke, Missouri State	.298	248	40	74	14	2	6	46	9
Lambert, Don, Wichita State	.293	181	39	53	9	2	3	26	18
Ort, Rob, Indiana State	.291	237	43	69	20	1	7	54	6
Harding, Brock, So. Illinois	.286	182	26	52	8	1	1	20	2

INDIVIDUAL PITCHING LEADERS
(Minimum 1 IP per team game)

	W	L	ERA	G	SV	IP	H	BB	SO
Petree Nick, Missouri State	10	4	1.01	16	0	115	85	36	114
Murphy, Clay, Missouri State	5	1	1.37	10	1	59	55	19	55
Billo, Ryan, Evansville	8	1	2.28	13	0	75	67	15	42
Long, Kenny, Illinois State	2	1	2.29	30	13	51	35	11	69
Johnson, Pierce, Missouri State	4	6	2.53	14	0	100	85	28	119
#Winkleman, Mark, Creighton	2	1	2.57	37	0	49	45	21	27
Rupe, Kyle, Indiana State	6	1	2.63	15	0	62	62	17	32
Gardner, Wichita State	5	2	2.66	14	0	71	60	16	34
Blach, Ty, Creighton	6	6	2.69	21	0	120	94	28	83
Bacus, Dakota, Indiana State	7	4	2.70	17	0	117	103	32	89
Bircher Joe, Bradley	7	3	2.70	15	0	110	93	21	113
Mattingly, Erik, Creighton	3	4	2.75	17	0	69	58	21	35
Lloyd, Kyle, Evansville	6	3	3.01	14	0	87	75	23	58
Torgerson, Ryan, Indiana State	8	3	3.03	14	0	86	96	14	51
Forsythe, Cody, Southern Ill.	5	4	3.10	16	0	104	97	30	84
Smith, Josh, Wichita State	6	4	3.10	16	0	96	84	32	77
Ladwig, A.J., Wichita State	4	1	3.14	17	1	63	71	8	32
Manaea, Sean, Indiana State	5	3	3.34	17	0	105	94	37	115
Liska, Shane, Creighton	3	4	3.44	20	0	55	42	23	54
Schumacher, Cody, Missouri St.	8	1	3.71	17	0	99	93	33	96
Minnis, Albert, Wichita State	4	4	3.82	16	0	66	63	26	52
Mormann, Mitch, Wichita State	3	3	3.91	15	0	53	45	31	28
Dorris, Nathan, Southern Ill.	7	4	4.17	16	0	82	97	35	80
Sorkin, Brad, Illinois State	4	3	4.31	14	0	79	85	31	44
Razo, Chris, Illinois State	7	4	4.50	16	0	88	88	40	73

MOUNTAIN WEST CONFERENCE

	Conference		Overall	
	W	L	W	L
* Texas Christian	18	6	40	22
New Mexico	18	6	37	24
San Diego State	12	12	26	34
Nevada-Las Vegas	7	17	26	31
Air Force	5	19	14	39

ALL-CONFERENCE TEAM: C—Mitchell Garver, Jr., New Mexico. **1B**—Trent Cook, Sr., UNLV. **2B**—Blair Roberts, Sr., Air Force. **3B**—D.J. Peterson, So., New Mexico. **SS**—Alex Allbritton, Jr., New Mexico. **OF**—Josh Melendez, Jr., New Mexico; Jason Coats, Sr., Texas Christian; Brandon Bayardi, Jr., UNLV. **DH/UT**—Ben Woodchick, Sr., New Mexico. **P**—Austin House, Jr., New Mexico; Andrew Mitchell, So. Texas Christian; Preston Morrison, Fr., Texas Christian. **RP**—Zach Hartman, So., UNLV
Co-Players of the Year: Mitchell Garver, New Mexico; D.J. Peterson, New Mexico. **Pitcher of the Year:** Preston Morrison, Texas Christian. **Freshman of the Year:** Preston Morrison, Texas Christian. **Coach of the Year:** Ray Birmingham, New Mexico.

INDIVIDUAL BATTING LEADERS
(Minimum 125 at-bats)

	AVG	AB	R	H	2B	3B	HR	RBI	SB
Peterson, D.J., New Mexico	.419	248	57	104	21	3	17	78	1
Garver, Mitchell, New Mexico	.377	268	68	101	27	3	10	32	5
Bayardi, Brandon, UNLV	.365	203	43	74	16	1	7	54	12
Kirk, Trevor, UNLV	.354	212	51	75	13	4	5	34	5
Padilla, Ryan, New Mexico	.353	221	49	78	19	2	5	49	4
Melendez, Josh, New Mexico	.347	236	64	82	13	9	3	44	23
Higa, Danny, UNLV	.342	196	38	67	15	1	3	36	6
Woodchick, Ben, New Mexico	.342	243	54	83	13	4	0	31	9
Cron, Kevin, TCU	.338	151	20	51	7	0	6	34	3
Coats, Jason, TCU	.326	193	36	63	13	2	6	45	7
Porras, Trey, New Mexico	.324	173	35	56	8	0	1	35	2
Zier, Tim, San Diego State	.318	211	31	67	11	1	0	31	10
Custons, Garrett, Air Force	.316	171	34	54	16	2	4	20	7
Witte, Jantzen, TCU	.315	162	21	51	12	0	3	22	1
Elander, Josh, TCU	.314	223	56	70	12	1	11	44	14
Shannon, Mark, UNLV	.313	233	50	73	18	3	6	42	5
Suiter, Jerrick, TCU	.310	145	19	45	4	3	0	20	4
Swanner, Joe, UNLV	.309	162	28	50	7	2	0	16	2
Muno, Ryan, San Diego State	.308	185	32	57	11	0	4	20	5
Allen, Greg, San Diego State	.306	232	44	71	11	2	2	31	11
Bast, Alex, Air Force	.305	197	30	60	12	5	4	31	7
Von Tungeln, Kyle, TCU	.304	227	57	69	10	5	3	26	12
Stiner, Kyle, New Mexico	.304	237	46	72	12	4	1	37	8
Cook, Trent, UNLV	.302	232	34	70	15	0	2	42	3
Thorton, Spencer, San Diego St.	.295	156	26	46	4	3	0	27	4
Romanski, Jake, San Diego St.	.289	142	21	41	9	0	0	23	2
Odell, Derek, TCU	.276	174	30	48	4	4	4	26	6
Wilson, Chris, San Diego State	.259	193	26	50	7	1	10	37	2
Roberts, Blair, Air Force	.258	194	25	50	8	1	1	12	9
Allbritton, Alex, New Mexico	.251	207	30	52	4	3	1	31	2

INDIVIDUAL PITCHING LEADERS
(Minimum 50 IP)

	W	L	ERA	G	SV	IP	H	BB	SO
Morrison, Preston, TCU	9	2	2.08	22	1	113	88	12	72
House, Austin, New Mexico	8	5	2.74	16	0	112	103	36	91
Sanchez, Gera, New Mexico	8	3	2.76	21	0	78	63	23	95
#Scharf, Justin, TCU	4	2	3.23	38	4	47	49	14	30
Crichton, Stefan, TCU	9	2	3.41	19	0	95	103	18	53
Hepner, Justin, San Diego State	5	3	3.46	22	7	52	54	20	50
Finnegan, Brandon, TCU	4	5	3.47	23	0	62	51	30	56
Fedde, Erick, UNLV	6	5	3.59	15	0	90	90	33	66
Mitchell, Andrew, TCU	4	3	3.70	13	0	77	55	46	101
Cederoth, Michael, San Diego St.	4	4	4.01	15	0	67	57	48	62
Walker, Josh, New Mexico	8	3	4.19	18	1	82	108	14	66
Doran, Ryan, San Diego State	3	6	4.50	16	0	88	110	22	53
Abrecht, Evan, Air Force	5	4	4.81	13	0	95	101	24	65
Borden, Buddy, UNLV	2	5	4.94	16	1	55	56	34	63
Ceci, Michael, Air Force	2	7	5.10	14	0	65	83	21	33
White, Cameron, Air Force	3	9	5.16	14	0	82	111	18	63

	W	L	ERA	G	SV	IP	H	BB	SO
Pitcher, Travis, San Diego State	3	4	5.31	17	1	58	60	44	51
Robinson, Joe, UNLV	2	6	5.37	16	0	54	68	30	23
Qualls, Zak, UNLV	4	6	5.71	15	0	76	91	39	48
Jaramillo, Rudy, New Mexico	5	3	6.75	16	0	56	87	11	39
Bertelson, Ben, Air Force	1	10	7.88	14	0	64	86	37	66

NORTHEAST CONFERENCE

	Conference		Overall	
	W	L	W	L
Bryant	24	8	33	21
Monmouth	21	11	35	24
Central Connecticut State	19	13	28	24
* Sacred Heart	19	13	25	32
Fairleigh Dickinson	18	14	25	28
Wagner	15	17	22	33
Long Island	13	19	22	33
Quinnipiac	8	24	9	38
Mount St. Mary's	7	25	14	40

ALL-CONFERENCE TEAM: C—Tyler Jones, Jr., Long Island. 1B—Tyler McIntyre, Jr., Central Connecticut State. 2B—Jake Gronsky, So., Monmouth. 3B—Zak Palmer, So., Quinnipiac. SS—Ryan Kresky, Sr., Fairleigh Dickinson. OF—J.P. Sportman, So., Central Connecticut State; Kevin Brown, Jr., Bryant; Pete Leonello, Sr., Long Island. DH—Dan Perez, So., Sacred Heart. UT—Matt Holsman, Sr., Farleigh Dickinson. SP—Peter Kelich, Sr., Bryant; Pat Light, Jr., Monmouth. RP—Sal Lisanti, So., Bryant. **Player of the Year:** Ryan Kresky, Fairleigh Dickinson. **Pitcher of the Year:** Peter Kelich, Bryant. **Rookie of the Year:** Kevin McAvoy, Bryant. **Coach of the Year:** Steve Owens, Bryant.

INDIVIDUAL BATTING LEADERS
(Minimum 125 at-bats)

	AVG	AB	R	H	2B	3B	HR	RBI	SB
Kresky, Ryan, FDU	.371	186	40	69	18	1	5	38	6
Sportman, J.P., CCSU	.353	190	36	67	14	2	7	33	2
Murphy, John, Sacred Heart	.347	170	38	59	11	4	1	34	24
Palmer, Zak, Quinnipiac	.342	158	24	54	6	0	1	22	6
Quaranta, Mount St. Mary's	.328	192	30	63	12	0	4	34	3
Leonello, Pete, Long Island	.327	217	41	71	13	3	1	31	12
Delacruz, Dylan, CCSU	.326	190	39	62	19	3	2	25	2
Carignan, Connor, CCSU	.325	160	31	52	11	1	1	14	15
Perez, Dan, Sacred Heart	.320	169	23	54	14	1	1	36	1
Wells, Mitch, CCSU	.318	201	35	64	14	1	2	31	2
Nisson, Kyle, Quinnipiac	.316	171	26	54	8	0	0	17	0
Brown, Eddie, Wagner	.314	169	31	53	15	0	3	36	22
Gronsky, Jake, Monmouth	.313	**227**	36	**71**	**20**	1	2	35	4
Miller, Ian, Wagner	.312	205	39	64	7	2	1	17	**34**
Jones, Tyler, Long Island	.312	199	34	62	10	4	6	34	4
Walsh, Drew, Long Island	.303	201	30	61	8	2	2	31	6
Winter, Mount St. Mary's	.302	202	27	61	13	1	8	44	0
Anderson, Eric, FDU	.300	180	17	54	6	0	8	40	0
Greve, Brad, Long Island	.299	197	37	59	10	1	0	13	9
Skagerlind, Jamie, Bryant	.298	188	25	56	16	0	5	29	1
Rosekranz, Jamie, Monmouth	.293	225	**43**	66	15	1	3	28	7
Dini, Nick, Wagner	.293	198	25	58	8	**5**	1	30	6
McIntyre, Tyler, CCSU	.291	172	29	50	9	1	**10**	38	0
Muscatello, Dan, Bryant	.290	193	37	56	6	1	0	17	2
Avella, Danny, Monmouth	.288	208	34	60	17	0	8	**45**	0
Perret, Chris, Monmouth	.288	170	18	49	10	0	1	27	2
Matuszak, Jake, CCSU	.286	203	30	58	5	3	2	25	13
Brown, Kevin, Bryant	.281	196	40	55	16	2	9	35	8
Holsman, Matt, FDU	.279	183	31	51	9	0	2	13	9

INDIVIDUAL PITCHING LEADERS
(Minimum 50 IP)

	W	L	ERA	G	SV	IP	H	BB	SO
Kelich, Peter, Bryant	8	3	1.81	13	0	94	74	26	74
Van Spronsen, Ryan, Wagner	8	1	2.07	12	0	100	82	23	65
Light, Pat, Monmouth	8	3	2.40	14	0	**101**	84	16	**102**
Schlitter, Craig, Bryant	6	6	2.70	13	1	73	65	20	55
Wilcox, Jordan, Long Island	3	1	2.81	14	0	64	48	22	32
McAvoy, Kevin, Bryant	5	1	2.94	14	0	70	75	20	41
Glynne, Harry, CCSU	3	4	3.25	11	0	69	58	25	48
Greenhouse, Jack, CCSU	4	1	3.58	10	0	55	65	13	34

	W	L	ERA	G	SV	IP	H	BB	SO
Franzese, Chris, Long Island	3	7	3.63	16	0	94	74	49	57
Michaud, Joseph, Bryant	8	4	3.73	13	0	70	66	33	57
Maguire, Robbie, Sacred Heart	1	4	3.88	12	0	56	55	24	36
McCormick, Matt, Long Island	6	5	3.91	14	0	71	82	26	52
Warner, Craig, FDU	3	5	3.96	15	0	75	82	15	29
Scribner, Troy, Sacred Heart	7	5	4.04	13	0	85	88	17	65
Leiningen, Nick. Sacred Heart	6	5	4.12	14	0	87	82	24	38
Brown, Casey, CCSU	4	4	4.33	11	0	52	49	17	39
Eliasen, Mike, FDU	8	4	4.33	14	1	98	91	19	66
Brown, Cody, CCSU	5	4	4.41	11	0	67	70	15	37
McGee, Andrew, Monmouth	7	4	4.58	17	0	77	80	24	61
Kane, Spencer, Quinnipiac	4	6	4.71	12	0	63	61	23	44
#Snyder, Eric, FDU	2	2	5.20	22	**12**	28	25	14	13
#Perline, Yonah, FDU	1	0	6.49	**27**	1	26	40	12	18

OHIO VALLEY CONFERENCE

	Conference		Overall	
Team	W	L	W	L
* Austin Peay State	19	7	40	24
Eastern Kentucky	19	7	31	23
Jacksonville State	17	10	28	30
Eastern Illinois	15	11	29	29
Morehead State	13	14	28	27
Southern Illinois-Edwardsville	13	14	27	28
Southeast Missouri State	12	15	23	36
Tennessee Tech	10	16	21	32
Murray State	8	19	23	33
Tennessee-Martin	7	20	13	41

ALL-CONFERENCE TEAM: C—Ben Burgess, Sr., Tennessee Tech. 1B—Ben Waldrip, Sr., Jacksonville State. 2B—Jordan Hankins, So., Austin Peay State. SS—Richie Rodriguez, Sr., Eastern Kentucky. 3B—Trenton Moses, Sr., Southeast Missouri State. OF—Jacob Daniel, Sr., Eastern Kentucky; Kyle Bluestein, Sr., Jacksonville State; Derek Gibson, So., Southeast Missouri State. DH—Ben Thoma, Sr. Eastern Illinois. UT—Travis Isaak, Sr., Murray State. SP—Zach Toney, Sr., Austin Peay State; Mike Hoekstra, Sr., Eastern Illinois; Matt Fyffe, Sr., Eastern Kentucky. RP—Dustin Quattrocchi, Sr., Southern Illinois-Edwardsville. **Player of the Year:** Trenton Moses, Southeast Missouri State. **Pitcher of the Year:** Matt Fyfe, Eastern Kentucky. **Rookie of the Year:** Brant Valach, Eastern Illinois. **Coach of the Year:** Jason Stein, Eastern Kentucky.

INDIVIDUAL BATTING LEADERS
(Minimum 2.5 at-bats per team game)

	AVG	AB	R	H	2B	3B	HR	RBI	SB
Moses, Trenton, SE Mo.	.408	213	58	87	16	1	**19**	61	3
Deeds, Andrew Morehead St.	.394	221	42	87	13	3	7	42	14
Rodriguez, Richie, E. Kentucky	.377	212	**59**	80	18	3	14	46	12
Stephens, Zach, Tenn. Tech	.368	204	44	75	13	0	18	52	0
Parmley, Kenton, SE Mo.	.363	245	58	89	13	1	13	40	13
Eberle, Sam, Jacksonville St.	.359	209	49	75	18	2	8	28	2
McManus, T.J., Eastern Illinois	.358	193	34	69	19	1	9	49	0
Bachman, Greg, Austin Peay	.351	265	45	93	14	1	16	**67**	4
Gibson, Derek, Southeast Mo.	.338	195	32	66	12	3	7	38	0
Highland, Matt, SI-Edwardsville	.338	157	21	53	6	0	3	21	0
Greenwell, Chase, Morehead St.	.336	217	37	73	16	1	0	27	5
Bluestein, Kyle, Jacksonville St.	.336	220	39	74	12	1	10	46	8
Hankins, Jordan, Austin Peay	.336	250	52	84	16	3	10	66	3
Dineen, Ryan, Eastern Illinois	.335	206	37	69	9	1	7	36	15
Owen, Jordan, Tenn.-Martin	.332	199	33	66	11	6	8	28	7
Waldrip, Ben, Jacksonville St.	.330	212	40	70	14	1	18	61	1
Pickens, Taylor, Morehead St.	.330	206	43	68	10	2	5	25	11
Morris, Michael, Tenn. Tech	.328	195	34	64	15	1	3	29	0
Harper, Austin Peay	.327	**266**	49	87	17	2	3	36	9
Abraham, James, Tenn. Tech	.326	181	32	59	10	1	1	24	8
Burgess, Ben, Tennessee Tech	.321	187	31	60	9	0	6	29	0
Grisham, Austin, E. Kentucky	.320	231	38	74	8	1	3	31	16
Dunlop, Dustin, E. Kentucky	.316	177	36	56	11	4	3	21	9
Howell, Caleb, Eastern Illinois	.316	206	37	65	9	0	0	20	4
Duff, Nick, Morehead State	.315	178	47	56	8	2	6	34	1
Valach, Brant, Eastern Illinois	.314	207	17	65	10	0	1	28	1
Wulf, Austin, Tennessee Tech	.314	220	37	69	5	2	4	25	9
Isaak, Travis, Murray State	.311	190	39	59	**20**	1	6	41	0
Daniel, Jacob, E. Kentucky	.311	219	42	68	15	**7**	6	48	11

	AVG	AB	R	H	2B	3B	HR	RBI	SB
Kozlowski, Mike, Murray State	.306	222	42	68	13	3	2	39	
#Hudson, Cody, Austin Peay	.300	213	39	64	12	2	6	36	**21**

INDIVIDUAL PITCHING LEADERS
(Minimum 1 IP per team game)

	W	L	ERA	G	SV	IP	H	BB	SO
#Duncan, Matt, Morehead State	2	1	2.45	27	**13**	33	26	19	30
Hoekstra, Mike, Eastern Illinois	5	4	**2.53**	16	0	110	111	23	83
Fyffe, Matt, Eastern Kentucky	9	1	2.54	22	2	71	59	21	62
Tobik, Dan, Tennessee-Martin	3	2	2.78	27	5	55	44	22	66
Toney, Zach, Austin Peay	5	3	3.10	17	1	93	72	45	86
Grimm, Shane, E. Kentucky	6	4	3.14	13	0	77	83	26	38
Barton, Troy, Eastern Illinois	9	5	3.20	17	0	79	68	38	52
Elias, Aaron, Jacksonville State	2	9	3.67	15	0	96	102	27	69
Mills, Alec, Tennessee-Martin	4	6	3.94	14	0	89	104	26	74
Archer, Tristan, Tennessee Tech	4	4	4.04	14	0	89	92	33	76
Goe, Aaron, Morehead State	6	5	4.20	16	0	96	119	17	63
Watts, Daniel, Jacksonville St.	6	6	4.35	15	0	89	86	23	87
Rivers, Hunter, Jacksonville St.	6	3	4.41	16	0	65	68	19	62
Simmons, Shae, Southeast Mo.	7	4	4.50	15	0	82	88	52	**89**
Slazinik, Christian, E. Illinois	6	6	4.50	15	0	80	74	43	68
Quick, Ryan, Austin Peay	5	2	4.63	16	0	84	81	37	58
Hull, Christian, Southeast Mo.	4	7	5.01	19	4	70	77	36	61
Worman, Darin, Eastern Illinois	5	4	5.12	**38**	0	58	64	29	42
Smallwood, Noah, Morehead St.	3	4	5.30	16	0	90	109	34	57
Delgado, Casey, Austin Peay	9	4	5.59	20	0	103	113	43	61
Harris, Matt, Eastern Kentucky	5	5	5.65	15	0	94	111	32	55
Babin, Bryan, Murray State	5	5	5.82	19	0	73	92	26	38

PACIFIC-12 CONFERENCE

	Conference		Overall	
	W	L	W	L
* UCLA	20	10	48	16
Arizona	20	10	48	17
Oregon	19	11	46	19
Stanford	18	12	41	18
Oregon State	18	12	40	20
Arizona State	18	12	36	20
Washington	13	17	30	25
California	12	18	29	25
Washington State	12	18	28	28
Southern California	8	22	23	32
Utah	7	23	14	42

ALL-CONFERENCE TEAM: C—Tyler Heineman, Jr. UCLA. 1B—Taylor Ard, Jr., Washington State; 2B—Joey DeMichele, Jr. Arizona State; Tony Renda, Jr., California. SS—Alex Mejia, Jr., Arizona; Devin Marrero, Jr., Arizona State; Tyler Smith, Jr., Oregon State. 3B—Stephen Piscotty, Jr., Stanford; Alex Mejias-Brean, Jr., Arizona. DH—Bobby Brown, Sr., Arizona. OF—Beau Amaral, Jr., UCLA; Robert Refsnyder, Jr., Arizona; Joey Rickard, Jr., Arizona; Derek Jones, Sr., Washington State; Jeff Gelalich, Jr.; Michael Conforto, Fr. Oregon State. RHP—Mark Appel, Jr., Stanford; Scot Griggs, Jr., UCLA; Alex Keudell, Sr. Oregon; Kurt Heyer, Jr., Arizona; Brady Rodgers, Jr., Arizona State; Adam Plutko, So., UCLA; Jimmie Sherfy, So. **Player of the Year:** Alex Mejia, Arizona. **Pitcher of the Year:** Alex Keudell, Oregon. **Defensive Player of the Year:** Alex Mejia, Arizona. **Freshman of the Year:** Michael Conforto, Oregon State. **Coach of the Year:** Andy Lopez, Arizona.

INDIVIDUAL BATTING LEADERS
(Minimum 2.5 at-bats per team game)

	AVG	AB	R	H	2B	3B	HR	RBI	SB
Field, Johnny, Arizona	**.370**	257	72	95	18	7	3	44	11
Refsnyder, Robert, Arizona	.364	258	64	94	19	4	8	66	14
Mejia, Alex, Arizona	.357	272	54	**97**	12	6	3	54	8
Mejias-Brean, Seth, Arizona	.356	264	57	94	**22**	4	1	61	10
Delfino, Mitch, California	.353	201	28	71	11	0	5	38	0
Gelalich, Jeff, UCLA	.351	245	56	86	10	1	11	48	16
Conforto, Michael, Oregon St.	.349	218	45	76	14	1	**13**	**76**	1
Brown, Bobby, Arizona	.348	207	44	72	13	**7**	5	59	7
Smith, Tyler, Oregon State	.343	213	46	73	11	2	1	39	9
Renda, Tony, California	.338	219	41	74	16	5	0	27	16
DeMichele, Joey, Arizona St.	.336	217	50	73	14	**7**	6	47	12
Jones, Derek, Washington St.	.335	209	43	70	17	3	9	45	11
Keefer, Cody, UCLA	.333	240	44	80	12	1	0	37	7

	AVG	AB	R	H	2B	3B	HR	RBI	SB
Ard, Taylor, Washington St.	.332	220	41	73	16	1	12	50	3
Heineman, Tyler, UCLA	.332	211	42	70	7	1	1	27	3
Ragira, Brian, Stanford	.329	252	41	83	15	0	5	50	3
Piscotty, Stephen, Stanford	.329	246	44	81	13	3	5	56	4
Landecker, Adam, USC	.329	152	31	50	4	0	0	12	4
Bruno, Vince, California	.323	198	37	64	6	2	1	24	5
Brown, Trevor, UCLA	.321	246	41	79	13	2	3	52	4
Lamb, Jacob, Washington	.321	190	32	61	12	3	3	30	4
Smith, Eric, Stanford	.321	187	35	60	11	1	2	32	1
Rickard, Joey, Arizona	.320	259	60	83	17	2	1	33	**18**
Foat, Matt, USC	.318	201	33	64	13	0	3	27	3
Morin, Parker, Utah	.314	220	23	69	11	1	3	35	1
Amaral, Beau, UCLA	.313	268	63	84	10	5	4	46	13
Thomas, Brett, Oregon	.313	201	22	63	14	4	1	25	9
Aplin, Andrew, Arizona State	.313	230	52	72	16	4	6	30	8
Healy, Ryon, Oregon	.312	253	35	79	13	1	4	42	3
Ray, Jayce, Washington	.311	206	38	64	11	3	0	18	6

INDIVIDUAL PITCHING LEADERS
(Minimum 1 IP per team game)

	W	L	ERA	G	SV	IP	H	BB	SO
Berg, David, UCLA	5	3	**1.46**	**50**	1	74	42	17	63
Williams, Trevor, Arizona State	12	2	2.05	16	0	110	90	13	59
#Sherfy, Jimmie, Oregon	5	3	2.20	36	**19**	61	36	34	93
Heyer, Kurt, Arizona	**13**	2	2.24	19	0	**153**	151	28	113
Rodgers, Brady, Arizona State	10	3	2.27	15	0	115	94	16	79
Keudell, Alex, Oregon	11	5	2.38	18	0	125	103	30	74
Pistorese, Joe, Washington St.	4	3	2.44	15	0	66	61	29	39
Fry, Jayce, Oregon State	5	3	2.45	13	0	88	68	35	53
Plutko, Adam, UCLA	12	3	2.48	18	0	120	91	47	99
West, Aaron, Washington	6	5	2.53	17	1	96	89	18	65
Appel, Mark, Stanford	10	2	2.56	16	0	123	97	30	**130**
Vanegas, A.J., Stanford	4	0	2.62	21	5	65	56	37	53
Flemer, Matt, California	7	5	2.74	16	0	112	99	15	66
Reed, Jake, Oregon	8	4	2.92	17	0	114	91	42	67
Child, Dan, Oregon State	6	4	2.95	17	0	107	108	25	79
Wetzler, Ben, Oregon State	8	2	3.10	16	0	102	94	42	75
Tarpley, Stephen, USC	5	3	3.22	14	0	78	72	29	67
Watrous, Mitch, Utah	2	5	3.48	21	1	62	69	17	32
Triggs, Andrew, USC	5	9	3.49	16	1	106	112	20	85
Davis, Tyler, Washington	2	4	3.57	19	0	71	56	16	40
Gold, Jeff, Oregon	8	4	3.66	19	0	76	75	24	46

PATRIOT LEAGUE

	Conference		Overall	
	W	L	W	L
* Army	18	2	41	15
Holy Cross	13	7	33	22
Navy	9	11	23	29
Bucknell	7	13	21	28
Lafayette	7	13	14	37
Lehigh	6	14	18	31

ALL-CONFERENCE TEAM: C—J.T. Watkins, Sr., Army. 1B—Kevin McKague, Sr., Army. 2B—Zach Price, Sr., Army. 3B—Mike Ahmed, So. Holy Cross. SS—Alex Maldonado, Jr., Holy Cross. OF—Bob Donato, Sr., Bucknell; Patrick Puentes, Jr., Holy Cross; Alex Azor, Sr., Navy. DH—Mark McCants, Fr., Army. SP—Chris Rowley, Jr., Army; Nate Koneski, Sr., Holy Cross. RP—John Colella, Jr., Holy Cross. **Player of the Year:** Kevin McKague, Army. **Pitcher of the Year:** Chris Rowley, Army. **Rookie of the Year:** Harold Earls, Army. **Coach of the Year:** Joe Sottolano, Army.

INDIVIDUAL BATTING LEADERS
(Minimum 2.5 at-bats per team game)

	AVG	AB	R	H	2B	3B	HR	RBI	SB
McKague, Kevin, Army	**.379**	198	38	**75**	**16**	0	5	**45**	13
Dontao, Bob, Bucknell	.362	177	32	64	**16**	1	6	31	8
Puentes, Patrick, Holy Cross	.343	134	28	46	6	0	3	22	6
Earls, Harold, Army	.341	179	27	61	8	1	0	22	**23**
Price, Zach, Army	.324	**216**	**51**	70	8	3	0	25	20
Cipolla, Brandon, Holy Cross	.323	161	31	52	10	1	5	28	3
Azor, Alex, Navy	.322	152	37	49	4	3	1	21	3
Dupell, Greg, Navy	.319	185	38	59	14	**6**	5	44	3
Duffett, David, Bucknell	.319	185	23	59	10	5	0	30	4

	AVG	AB	R	H	2B	3B	HR	RBI	SB
Watkins, J.T., Army	.316	158	25	50	9	1	5	31	5
McGaheran, Brendan, Lehigh	.305	187	39	57	9	0	4	21	18
Enos, Jordan, Holy Cross	.305	151	22	46	11	0	2	23	0
Ahmed, Mike, Holy Cross	.295	207	39	61	13	3	7	26	7
Clark, Travis, Bucknell	.293	174	27	51	12	3	2	25	5
Maldonado, Holy Cross	.292	212	38	62	6	4	0	23	14

INDIVIDUAL PITCHING LEADERS
(Minimum 1 IP per team game)

	W	L	ERA	G	SV	IP	H	BB	SO
Kent, Cory, Lehigh	4	3	1.88	15	5	62	55	15	53
#Colella, John, Holy Cross	7	3	2.32	29	11	54	39	29	53
Rowley, Chris, Army	11	1	2.40	15	0	97	64	22	80
Koneski, Nate, Holy Cross	7	3	2.54	14	0	74	61	26	82
Weigel, Dan, Bucknell	6	4	3.01	11	0	72	67	13	32
Murray, Donny, Holy Cross	4	1	3.12	17	1	58	58	9	43
Lee, Logan, Army	8	2	3.13	15	0	92	81	21	64
Gainey, Preston, Navy	3	3	3.25	10	0	55	51	31	54
Marra, Tommy, Holy Cross	4	3	3.27	11	0	66	52	17	39
Dignacco, Nick, Army	7	2	3.38	13	0	67	62	18	58
Hough, Bryson, Bucknell	2	7	3.63	11	0	57	63	12	33
Nelson, Ben, Navy	3	3	3.72	13	0	77	74	20	67
Croglio, Matt, Holy Cross	3	4	4.42	13	0	55	62	27	37
Schoberl, Johnny, Navy	5	4	4.45	11	0	63	70	19	45
Gentile, John, Lafayette	1	10	5.80	16	0	68	87	15	36
Ebner, Ryan, Bucknell	3	6	6.18	12	0	55	65	32	47

SOUTHEASTERN CONFERENCE

	Conference		Overall	
EAST	**W**	**L**	**W**	**L**
South Carolina	18	11	49	20
Kentucky	18	12	45	18
Florida	18	12	47	20
Vanderbilt	16	14	35	28
Georgia	14	15	31	26
Tennessee	8	22	24	31
WEST	**W**	**L**	**W**	**L**
Louisiana State	19	11	47	18
Arkansas	16	14	46	22
* **Mississippi State**	16	14	40	24
Mississippi	14	16	37	26
Auburn	13	17	31	28
Alabama	9	21	21	34

ALL-CONFERENCE TEAM: C—Mike Zunino, Jr., Florida. **1B**—Christian Walker, Jr., South Carolina. **2B**—Alex Yarbrough, Jr., Mississippi. **3B**—Matt Reynolds, Jr., Arkansas. **SS**—Anthony Gomez, Jr., Vanderbilt. **OF**—Raph Rhymes, Jr., Louisiana State; Taylor Dugas, Sr., Auburn; Preston Tucker, Sr., Florida. **DH/UT**—Brian Johnson, Jr., Florida. **P**—Chris Stratton, Jr., Mississippi State; Kevin Gausman, Jr., Louisiana State. **RP**—Steven Rodriguez, Jr., Florida.
Player of the Year: Raph Rhymes, Louisiana State. **Pitcher of the Year:** Chris Stratton, Mississippi State. **Freshman of the Year:** Austin Cousino, Kentucky. **Coach of the Year:** Gary Henderson, Kentucky.

INDIVIDUAL BATTING LEADERS
(Minimum 3 plate appearances per team game)

	AVG	AB	R	H	2B	3B	HR	RBI	SB
Rhymes, Raph, LSU	.431	232	44	100	11	0	4	53	3
Yarbrough, Alex, Mississippi St.	.380	250	43	95	17	3	3	43	4
Frazier, Adam, Mississippi St.	.371	245	45	91	16	1	0	26	9
Tella, Ryan, Auburn	.360	236	41	85	12	4	5	34	17
Mathis, Tanner, Mississippi	.359	245	50	88	12	1	0	23	8
Powell, Curt, Georgia	.355	203	45	72	11	1	2	20	12
Gomes, Anthony, Vanderbilt	.353	255	37	90	12	2	1	57	11
Wacker, Cullen, Auburn	.350	157	31	55	11	5	1	27	4
Dugas, Taylor, Alabama	.343	207	41	71	12	7	2	28	8
Moore, Ben, Alabama	.342	199	33	68	10	1	2	31	10
Snyder, Matt, Mississippi	.332	238	37	79	17	0	12	63	1
Gregor, Conrad, Vanderbilt	.328	229	37	75	20	1	3	35	10
Cooper, Garrett, Auburn	.324	173	35	56	9	0	5	31	1
Reynolds, Matt, Arkansas	.323	235	48	76	20	0	7	45	16
Zunino, Mike, Florida	.322	245	53	79	28	0	19	67	9
Walker, Christian, S. Carolina	.321	240	48	77	12	2	11	55	3

	AVG	AB	R	H	2B	3B	HR	RBI	SB
Tucker, Preston, Florida	.321	262	57	84	17	2	16	50	6
Katz, Mason, LSU	.320	241	65	77	15	1	13	52	8
Glevenvak, Dan, Auburn	.319	191	34	61	13	1	1	28	13
Cousino, Austin, Kentucky	.319	260	61	83	20	2	9	41	15
Maile, Luke, Kentucky	.319	229	48	73	13	0	12	51	9
Pigott, Daniel, Florida	.318	255	49	81	13	2	8	41	12
Reaves, Jared, Alabama	.316	215	29	68	9	1	4	34	3
Simpson, Creede, Auburn	.316	235	42	74	18	0	3	40	25
Zellers, Zac, Kentucky	.311	177	36	55	12	1	5	19	7
McCarthy, Thomas, Kentucky	.310	242	42	75	20	0	5	33	4
Gonzalez, Jay, Auburn	.308	221	48	68	13	5	0	29	30
Johnson, Brian, Florida	.307	202	24	62	13	0	6	41	0
Verdin, Peter, Georgia	.307	176	21	54	4	3	0	24	15
DeLoach, Brett, Georgia	.303	175	28	53	12	1	1	21	6
#Marzilli, Evan, South Carolina	.284	268	51	76	14	4	2	32	13
#Kemp, Tony, Vanderbilt	.261	241	55	63	11	8	1	31	21

INDIVIDUAL PITCHING LEADERS
(Minimum 1 IP per team game)

	W	L	ERA	APP	SV	IP	H	BB	SO
#Webb, Tyler, South Carolina	6	1	1.56	39	3	58	44	18	58
Stratton, Chris, Mississippi St.	11	2	2.38	17	1	110	84	25	127
Roth, Michael, South Carolina	9	1	2.43	20	0	137	101	41	93
Moore, Brandon, Arkansas	5	2	2.43	29	3	81	68	11	36
Wahl, Bobby, Mississippi	7	4	2.55	17	0	99	76	32	104
Randall, Hudson, Florida	9	3	2.59	16	0	94	86	10	62
Wood, Alex, Georgia	7	3	2.73	16	0	102	95	21	100
Littrell, Corey, Kentucky	9	2	2.74	16	0	99	104	25	87
Gausman, Kevin, LSU	12	2	2.77	18	0	124	106	28	135
Graveman, Kendall, Miss. St.	4	4	2.81	16	0	90	84	21	59
Stanek, Ryne, Arkansas	8	4	2.82	17	0	93	75	36	83
Hively, R.J., Mississippi	5	6	3.02	19	4	83	70	20	98
Holmes, Colby, South Carolina	7	2	3.05	16	0	80	66	17	65
Baxendale, D.J., Arkansas	8	5	3.11	20	0	107	97	29	96
Crawford, Jonathon, Florida	6	2	3.13	19	0	78	75	24	73
Koger, Daniel, Auburn	4	5	3.19	15	0	79	74	28	33
Steckenrider, Drew, Tennessee	4	6	3.36	27	1	67	45	40	79
Price, Matt, South Carolina	5	5	3.48	28	13	78	55	31	94
Mayers, Mike, Mississippi	6	3	3.50	17	0	93	75	30	71
VerHagen, Drew, Vanderbilt	6	3	3.50	27	2	69	64	28	37
Godley, Zack, Tennessee	4	2	3.50	12	0	69	66	18	53

SOUTHERN CONFERENCE

	Conference		Overall	
	W	**L**	**W**	**L**
Appalachian State	21	9	41	18
College of Charleston	21	9	38	22
Elon	20	10	33	26
* **Samford**	19	11	41	23
Western Carolina	16	14	32	24
Georgia Southern	15	15	33	27
Furman	13	17	28	31
The Citadel	13	17	25	33
UNC Greensboro	10	20	25	27
Wofford	9	21	22	32
Davidson	8	22	17	31

ALL-CONFERENCE TEAM: C—Alex Swim, Jr., Elon. **1B**—Saxon Butler, Sr., Samford. **2B**—Ross Hefley, Sr., Western Carolina. **3B**—Eric Phillips, Sr., Georgia Southern. **SS**—Will Callaway, Sr., Appalachian State. **OF**—Marty Gantt, Sr., College of Charleston; Phillip Ervin, So., Samford; Brandon Miller, Sr., Samford. **DH**—Danniel Kassouf, Sr., Appalachian State. **SP**—Josh Martin, Sr., Samford; Christian Powell, Jr., College of Charleston. **RP**—Preston Hatcher, Jr., Western Carolina.
Player of the Year: Marty Gantt, College of Charleston. **Pitcher of the Year:** Christian Powell, College of Charleston. **Freshman of the Year:** Chase Griffin, Georgia Southern. **Coach of the Year:** Chris Pollard, Appalachian State.

INDIVIDUAL BATTING LEADERS
(Minimum 2.5 at-bats per team game)

	AVG	AB	R	H	2B	3B	HR	RBI	SB
Phillips, Eric, Ga. Southern	.391	238	47	93	24	1	5	54	29

Player	AVG	AB	R	H	2B	3B	HR	RBI	SB
Gantt, Marty, Col. of Charleston	.373	236	**68**	88	20	2	11	46	29
Tewell, Tyler, Appalachian St.	.357	221	47	79	17	4	6	45	4
Swim, Alex, Elon	.357	241	39	86	11	1	3	45	7
White, Tyler, Western Caro.	.354	212	41	75	16	0	1	30	3
Heffley, Ross, Western Caro.	.346	231	47	80	12	1	9	43	16
Richards, Kris, UNCG	.342	184	34	63	15	0	5	28	8
Doyle, Mac, Wofford	.341	205	37	70	10	2	13	47	13
Butler, Saxon, Samford	.340	259	55	88	14	1	15	61	1
Irby, C.K., Samford	.340	215	28	73	14	4	5	49	4
Kassouf, Daniel, Appalachian St.	.339	233	51	79	16	1	17	**66**	0
Zupcic, Tyler, Appalachian St.	.338	210	56	71	17	4	2	34	12
Owens, Will, Furman	.338	237	50	80	11	1	2	29	11
Ridings, Julian, W. Carolina	.331	160	24	53	8	1	3	21	12
Murray, Brandon, Col. of Charleston	.330	200	45	66	10	1	12	42	4
Ervin, Phillip, Samford	.327	260	55	85	18	1	10	52	16
Gadaire, Drew, Davidson	.322	177	27	57	18	1	0	31	11
Johnson, Taylor, Furman	.322	230	49	74	21	0	5	31	5
Stone, Zeth, Samford	.321	**262**	57	84	14	4	1	34	8
Moss, Brad, Samford	.321	234	48	75	9	0	2	44	4
Griffin, Chase, Ga. Southern	.320	197	35	63	10	1	10	42	2
Callaway, Will, Ga. Southern	.320	241	54	77	12	3	4	53	23
Kinsella, Ryan, Elon	.316	212	43	67	11	2	8	54	0
Luce, Jake, Elon	.316	187	25	59	14	5	1	31	4
Leach, Zach, UNCG	.315	165	29	52	8	3	2	28	6
Glazer, Brandon, Col. of Charleston	.313	128	22	40	3	0	7	25	4
Jones, Cody, Western Carolina	.312	199	40	62	5	0	3	23	11
Miller, Will, Furman	.310	242	54	75	15	0	10	44	21
Hoyle, Jacob, Western Carolina	.308	185	22	57	14	0	4	45	2
Davis, T.D., Ga. Southern	.308	211	35	65	14	0	5	34	7
Crespo, Hector, Appalachian St.	.308	234	63	72	16	0	3	23	30
Strong, Bradley, W. Carolina	.305	177	27	54	8	3	1	24	8
#Miller, Brandon, Samford	.301	246	58	74	17	0	**23**	65	1
#Aldrich, Daniel, Col. of Charleston	.287	216	47	62	15	**7**	11	46	4

INDIVIDUAL PITCHING LEADERS
(Minimum 1 IP per team game)

Player	W	L	ERA	G	SV	IP	H	BB	SO
Powell, Christian, Col. of Charleston	9	4	**2.69**	17	0	94	88	29	77
Pegler, Matt, Col. of Charleston	10	2	2.83	15	0	89	73	20	66
Yarusi, Brandon, Wofford	5	7	3.10	14	0	99	88	33	107
Pritcher, Austin, The Citadel	6	5	3.19	15	0	99	101	30	61
Hathcock, Dylan, UNCG	4	4	3.32	21	2	60	57	20	32
Medick, Spencer, Elon	2	3	3.35	15	0	75	86	21	72
Martin, Josh, Samford	**12**	3	2.35	17	0	**110**	111	34	95
Renfro, Josh, Col. of Charleston	6	8	3.44	19	0	84	95	20	73
Smith, Jordan, Western Carolina	4	5	3.48	16	0	96	91	45	78
Grant, Seth, Appalachian State	7	3	3.49	16	0	101	96	34	69
#Hines, Ryan, The Citadel	3	1	3.51	**36**	6	41	36	12	21
Middour, Will, Ga. Southern	3	3	3.60	15	0	60	60	20	36
Basford, Charles, Samford	10	2	3.65	16	0	106	106	30	58
West, Ryan, Col. of Charleston	4	3	3.73	17	0	60	54	18	53
McKinney, Morgan, W. Carolina	6	3	3.74	15	0	84	76	41	68
Hollstegge, Tyler, UNCG	6	6	3.75	17	0	60	68	26	37
Clark, Dylan, Elon	9	4	3.76	15	0	89	82	18	64
Hess, Justin, Ga. Southern	5	3	3.76	17	0	79	85	24	85
Arrowood, Ryan, Appalachian St.	11	0	3.81	16	0	99	91	39	93
Beck, Chris, Ga. Southern	6	7	3.91	17	1	104	117	29	**115**
Webb, Kyle, Elon	4	4	4.18	12	0	65	69	18	49
#Hyatt, Nathan, Appalachian State	1	0	4.28	28	**16**	27	22	24	29

SOUTHLAND CONFERENCE

	Conference		Overall	
	W	L	W	L
Sam Houston State	24	9	40	22
Southeastern Louisiana	20	13	39	21
*Texas-Arlington	19	14	36	25
Texas State	19	14	32	24
McNeese State	17	16	24	30
Central Arkansas	16	17	25	30
Stephen F. Austin	16	17	26	33
Lamar	14	19	22	30
Texas A&M-Corpus Christi	14	19	24	33
Northwestern State	14	19	19	32
Nicholls State	13	29	26	28
Texas-San Antonio	11	21	22	32

ALL-CONFERENCE TEAM: C—Travis Snider, Sr., Central Arkansas. **1B**—Jonathan Pace, Sr., Southeastern Louisana. **2B**—Brock Herbert, Jr., Southeastern Louisiana. **3B**—Kevin Miller, Jr., Sam Houston State. **SS**—Hunter Dozier, So., Stephen F. Austin. **OF**—Preston Beck, Jr., Texas-Arlington; Jeff McVaney, Sr., Texas State; Seth Granger, Sr., McNeese State. **DH**—Anthony Azar, So., Sam Houston State. **P**—Daniel Minor, Jr., Texas A&M-Corpus Christi; Travis Ballew, Jr., Texas State; Stefan Lopez, Jr., Southeastern Louisiana.

Player of the Year: Brock Hebert, Southeastern Louisiana. **Pitcher of the Year:** Travis Bellew, Texas State. **Relief Pitcher of the Year:** Stefan Lopez, Southeastern Louisiana. **Freshman of the Year:** Andro Cutura, Southeastern Louisiana. **Newcomer of the Year:** Daniel Minor, Texas A&M-Corpus Christi. **Coach of the Year:** David Pierce, Sam Houston State.

INDIVIDUAL BATTING LEADERS
(Minimum 125 At-bats)

Player	AVG	AB	R	H	2B	3B	HR	RBI	SB
Herbert, Brock, SE La.	**.374**	227	**58**	85	21	2	2	37	**36**
Hill, Jeremy, Nicholls State	.368	185	30	68	8	1	4	40	6
Walker, Ryan, Texas-Arlington	.360	**250**	56	**90**	10	1	0	31	14
Dozier, Hunter, Stephen F. Austin	.357	227	43	81	**22**	1	10	37	8
Azar, Anthony, Sam Houston St.	.354	175	24	62	10	3	3	38	1
Pace, Jonathan, SE La.	.350	234	32	82	16	1	1	42	5
Johnson, Darian, Lamar	.344	212	34	73	13	2	4	25	6
McVaney, Jeff, Texas State	.338	222	46	75	21	2	10	48	16
Watson, Will, Northwestern St.	.335	179	32	60	10	2	0	20	23
Lyons, Philip, Nicholls State	.335	212	40	71	5	2	1	36	16
Beck, Preston, Texas-Arlington	.333	222	45	74	9	4	**14**	**71**	4
Davis, Jonathan, C. Arkansas	.333	153	35	51	11	2	0	29	17
Lee, Jordan, Texas A&M-CC	.333	144	23	48	5	2	2	18	5
Granger, Seth, McNeese State	.327	211	35	69	13	4	4	20	14
Allday, Forrestt, C. Arkansas	.324	188	49	61	8	4	1	34	7
Picha, Brad, Lamar	.320	181	23	58	17	0	1	38	2
Helenihi, Drew, NW State	.319	188	38	60	5	0	0	14	19
Atwood, Colt, Sam Houston St.	.316	244	37	77	10	2	0	20	11
Miller, Kevin, Sam Houston St.	.315	219	38	69	9	0	2	33	1
Dornak, Seth, Lamar	.310	187	23	58	6	0	3	22	1
Willson, Bryan, C. Arkansas	.308	211	31	65	13	0	4	40	3
LeGrange, Michael, Nicholls St.	.308	211	28	65	16	2	3	29	11
Dalton, Ryan, UTSA	.307	202	33	62	11	0	9	42	1
O'Hearn, Ryan, Sam Houston St.	.304	227	34	69	9	2	2	30	5
Selsor, Casey, UTSA	.302	172	32	52	10	8	1	29	17
Bear, Colin, Northwestern St.	.301	153	16	46	12	0	2	30	0
Brown, Garrett, C. Arkansas	.301	153	31	46	7	1	2	17	3
Arrington, Jake, Sam Houston St.	.300	200	33	60	8	**10**	3	37	7
Autrey, Garret, Lamar	.299	204	25	61	11	3	4	29	5
Gonzalez, Jonathan, Texas A&M-CC	.299	174	25	52	5	0	9	33	2

INDIVIDUAL PITCHING LEADERS
(Minimum 50 IP)

Player	W	L	ERA	G	SV	IP	H	BB	SO
#Lopez, Stefan, Southeastern La.	2	1	0.61	28	**20**	29	19	5	42
Minor, Daniel, Texas A&M-CC	10	3	**2.20**	16	0	110	100	23	110
Greenleaf, Jason, SE La.	3	2	2.44	26	0	52	40	24	43
Turner, Colton, Texas State	5	3	2.46	14	0	88	96	34	87
Oros, Michael, Sam Houston St.	8	1	2.52	25	2	79	56	35	61
Gann, Cameron, Stephen F. Austin	7	3	2.62	17	0	72	72	25	34
Hymel, Jordan, Southeastern La.	6	3	2.64	14	0	82	56	33	55
Jackson, Justin, Sam Houston St.	9	4	2.69	16	2	97	90	29	65
Ballew, Travis, Texas State	11	4	2.73	16	4	102	91	29	**119**
Scanio, Joe, Northwestern St.	5	4	2.96	31	3	67	52	22	72
Ware, Blake, McNeese State	7	7	3.16	16	0	100	114	41	56
Day, Lance, Texas-Arlington	**12**	4	3.18	18	0	**122**	126	33	69
McDonald, Tyler, McNeese State	4	4	3.21	18	2	81	88	22	25
Smith, Caleb, Texas State	8	6	3.23	17	0	98	79	39	82
Dickson, Cody, Sam Houston St.	5	4	3.25	18	0	72	68	38	46
Finnegan, Kyle, Texas State	5	6	3.28	15	0	93	86	26	75
Cutura, Andro, Southeastern La.	6	1	3.30	15	0	76	68	16	38
#Burchett, Michael, Sam Houston St.	4	3	3.35	**32**	10	48	56	14	27
Clemens, Michael, McNeese St.	3	3	3.43	20	6	63	52	22	50
Dziedzic, Jonathan, Lamar	5	4	3.47	13	0	73	68	34	68
Melotakis, Mason, NW State	4	4	3.63	23	7	62	47	18	70

Bergen, Brandon, Sam Houston St.	3	2	3.72	24	3	51	49	12	26
Shreve, Patrick, Nicholls State	4	7	3.87	14	0	88	104	30	63
Janway, Josh, Southeastern La.	3	3	3.93	16	0	51	50	21	26

SOUTHWESTERN ATHLETIC CONFERENCE

	Conference		Overall	
EAST	**W**	**L**	**W**	**L**
Jackson State	21	3	34	17
Alabama State	14	10	20	36
Alcorn State	14	10	18	37
Mississippi Valley State	10	14	17	39
Alabama A&M	1	23	8	42
WEST	**W**	**L**	**W**	**L**
Southern	17	7	33	16
* **Prairie View A&M**	15	8	28	25
Grambling State	13	11	22	26
Texas Southern	8	15	26	28
Arkansas-Pine Bluff	7	17	8	38

ALL-CONFERENCE TEAM: C—Evan Richard, Sr., Prairie View A&M. **1B**—Brian Rowry, So., Southern. **2B**—Elias Todman, Jr., Grambling State. **3B**—Thomas Brown III, So., Grambling State. **SS**—Chris Wolfe, Sr., Grambling State. **OF**—D.J. Wallace, Fr., Southern; Eduardo Gonzalez, Sr. Alcorn State; Kendall Logan, Sr., Jackson State. **DH**—Derrick Hopkins, Jr., Southern. **SP**—Quintavious Drains, Sr., Jackson State; Jose De Leon, So., Southern. **RP**—Josh Powell, Jr., Southern

Player of the Year: Kendall Logan, Jackson State. **Hitter of the Year:** Thomas Brown III, Grambling State. **Pitcher of the Year:** Quintavious Drains, Jackson State. **Freshman of the Year:** D.J. Wallace, Southern.

INDIVIDUAL BATTING LEADERS
(Minimum 100 at-bats)

	AVG	AB	R	H	2B	3B	HR	RBI	SB
Brown, Thomas, Grambling	.416	169	36	70	17	**7**	0	32	3
Todman, Elias, Grambling	.344	180	34	62	9	3	2	43	3
Hopkins, Derrick, Southern	.344	129	29	44	12	1	5	29	0
Wallace, Stephen, Southern	.340	141	30	48	9	0	7	37	1
Longoria, Jose, Grambling	.340	153	24	52	11	0	1	33	2
Gonzalez, Eduardo, Alcorn St.	.335	**215**	41	**72**	**22**	0	8	52	7
Hernandez, Ray, Texas So.	.333	180	39	60	10	1	3	36	17
McGriff, Cameron, Southern	.330	188	45	62	16	1	6	43	8
Butler, Jann, Alcorn State	.329	167	29	55	9	4	2	22	14
Logan, Kendall, Jackson State	.328	189	42	62	11	4	**12**	**59**	10
Solis, Frank, Jackson State	.324	173	32	56	7	2	0	29	15
Wolfe, Chris, Grambling	.321	187	**46**	60	8	3	0	29	29
Harris, Dominiq, Prairie View	.315	165	28	52	14	1	2	31	2
Epperson, Charles, Jackson St.	.314	188	29	59	7	2	4	36	8
Farmer, Darren, Grambling	.314	185	41	58	13	2	6	39	5
Logan, Cameron, Texas So.	.313	150	23	47	8	3	4	32	4
Warren, Rodney, Alcorn State	.307	189	36	58	8	0	9	37	5
Benes, Brad, Prairie View A&M	.306	186	27	57	12	1	1	24	3
Jackson, Lacy, Texas Southern	.303	142	25	43	10	2	5	38	1
Cheatham, Edmund, Miss. Valley	.301	209	35	63	6	0	0	17	31
Samsa, Sean, Ark.-Pine Bluff	.297	155	34	46	9	5	1	16	9
Pedro, Darrion, Alcorn State	.296	159	25	47	11	2	2	22	9
Flenoy, Anthony, Texas State	.293	140	31	41	3	1	0	21	19
Gonzalez, Richard, Texas So.	.292	212	32	62	9	4	0	32	7
Rosa, Angel, Alcorn State	.292	171	23	50	10	2	4	30	5
Amion, Richard, Alcorn State	.288	153	40	44	6	0	0	22	**36**
Rowry, Brian, Southern	.287	174	27	50	15	1	5	36	1
Walker, Glenn, Jackson State	.287	171	41	49	6	3	0	18	35

INDIVIDUAL PITCHING LEADERS
(Minimum 50 IP)

	W	L	ERA	G	SV	IP	H	BB	SO
Russell, Desmond, Jackson St.	10	2	**2.34**	17	1	108	88	28	86
Deleon, Jose, Southern	8	3	2.62	18	0	82	57	34	**103**
Drains, Quintavious, Jackson St.	**11**	4	2.85	19	0	**117**	90	44	86
Mitchell, Derrick, Prairie View	5	5	3.06	15	1	94	88	37	58
Holliday, Jesse, Southern	7	3	3.09	13	0	76	61	32	59
Foster, Brian, Southern	8	2	3.21	12	0	67	62	22	52
Mitchell, Matt, Grambling	6	4	3.35	13	0	83	66	44	47
Parker, Cody, Miss. Valley State	3	0	3.54	**41**	3	69	73	29	57

Bautista, Richard, Grambling	4	2	3.69	13	1	100	102	27	59
Easter, Steve, Alcorn State	4	6	3.69	14	0	93	95	26	67
Alvira, Joel, Alcorn State	4	5	3.86	13	0	77	82	41	65
#Powell, Josh, Southern	1	1	3.93	19	**7**	34	37	17	29
Hernandez, Stef, Prairie View	7	4	4.00	13	0	74	62	25	50
Renda, T.J., Alcorn State	4	5	4.04	12	0	76	84	20	48
Flores, Abel, Texas Southern	2	6	4.29	18	2	65	51	33	59
Freeman, Josh, Alabama A&M	2	9	4.48	12	0	76	68	39	25
Cruz IV, Frank, Texas Southern	4	3	4.61	19	0	55	49	21	40
Garcia, Daniel, Southern	3	2	4.76	15	3	51	62	19	22
Stady, Kameron, Miss. Valley St.	2	10	4.98	21	0	108	116	42	76
Jackson, E., Ark.-Pine Bluff	4	3	5.04	23	0	70	78	45	53
Broadway, Chris, Miss. Valley St.	4	7	5.19	22	2	85	98	39	34
Listi, Michael, Prairie View	3	7	5.31	13	0	72	75	31	39
Garcia, Jose, Jackson State	4	5	5.69	18	0	87	72	59	88
Williams, Troy, Alcorn State	6	5	5.84	15	0	86	100	30	39

SUMMIT LEAGUE

	Conference		Overall	
	W	**L**	**W**	**L**
* **Oral Roberts**	17	6	38	25
Oakland	15	6	25	31
North Dakota State	14	10	40	20
Southern Utah	12	11	18	36
South Dakota State	7	14	18	33
IUPU-Fort Wayne	8	16	16	40
Western Illinois	7	17	17	35

ALL-CONFERENCE TEAM: . C—Bennett Pickar, Jr., Oral Roberts. **1B**—Jared Schlehuber, Sr., Oral Roberts. **2B**—Cam Schiller, Jr., Oral Roberts. **3B**—Jose Trevino, Fr., Oral Roberts. **SS**—Bo Cuthbertson, Sr., Southern Utah. **OF**—Tim Colwell, So., North Dakota State; Beau Hanowski, Jr., South Dakota State; Tim Ryan, Sr., Oakland. **DH**—Kevin Kline, Fr., Southern Utah. **UT**—Chase Rezac, Jr., Southern Utah. **SP**—Drew Bowen, Jr., Oral Roberts; Kurt Giller, Jr., Oral Roberts; John Straka, Jr., North Dakota State. **RP**—Joe Spring, Sr., Oral Roberts

Player of the Year: Jared Schlehuber, Oral Roberts. **Pitcher of the Year:** Drew Roberts, Oral Roberts. **Freshman of the Year:** Jose Trevino, Oral Roberts. **Coach of the Year:** Joe Musachio, Oakland.

INDIVIDUAL BATTING LEADERS
(Minimum 2.5 plate appearances per team game)

	AVG	AB	R	H	2B	3B	HR	RBI	SB
Colwell, Tim, N. Dakota State	.381	244	**62**	**93**	11	**9**	1	35	12
Romero, Marcus, S. Utah	.349	152	23	53	10	3	3	32	13
Dispensa, Dan, W. Illinois	.344	192	37	66	12	3	2	28	7
Ryan, Tim, Oakland	.339	224	56	76	10	0	1	24	**26**
Colwell, Nick, N. Dakota State	.333	234	42	78	**18**	2	2	43	2
Hanowski, Beau, S. Dakota St.	.326	132	19	43	5	2	0	16	3
Cowen, Austin, Western Illinois	.317	189	24	60	9	2	4	41	0
Wentz, Zach, N. Dakota State	.317	227	31	72	13	0	5	41	8
Trevino, Jose, Oral Roberts	.317	246	44	78	**18**	3	**13**	**57**	3
Schlehuber, Jared, Oral Roberts	.316	225	43	71	15	0	**13**	56	1
Jacoby, Nolan, Oakland	.312	154	22	48	4	0	2	17	0
Demonico, Logan, Oral Roberts	.312	138	40	43	8	0	0	16	1
Anderson, Nick, N. Dakota St.	.308	195	34	60	12	5	5	41	5
Schiller, Cam, Oral Roberts	.306	255	43	78	14	0	8	51	6
Satzinger, Wes, N. Dakota St.	.305	210	42	64	15	1	1	31	6
Carson, Mike, Oakland	.303	188	32	57	14	2	6	46	1
Macbitz, Aaron, S. Dakota St.	.302	159	28	48	11	2	4	27	0
Casper, Max, N. Dakota State	.300	203	29	61	9	1	0	20	2
Pickar, Bennett, Oral Roberts	.296	199	25	59	9	0	2	33	0
Cain, Eric, S. Dakota State	.295	183	32	54	9	6	2	34	4
Cieslak, Aaron, Oakland	.292	212	33	62	16	0	7	42	5
Paquette, Phil, S. Dakota St.	.290	186	21	54	10	1	1	28	4
Marra, Daniel, S. Dakota State	.290	162	22	47	6	1	2	22	3
Phelan, Andrew, S. Dakota St.	.285	193	31	55	9	2	0	20	5
Cuthbertson, Bo, S. Utah	.283	191	36	54	11	2	6	34	11
Neuhart, Justin, S. Utah	.280	132	16	37	7	1	3	20	3
Marentette, Spencer, Oakland	.278	151	15	42	3	0	0	20	14
Cowhey, Ryan, W. Illinois	.277	184	31	51	12	0	2	24	**26**
Morton, Jake, Oakland	.274	201	35	55	5	1	0	16	12
Hathaway, Clay, IPFW	.274	212	39	58	12	2	4	21	10
King, Brandon, Oral Roberts	.273	227	44	62	15	1	1	29	2

INDIVIDUAL PITCHING LEADERS
(Minimum 1 IP per team game)

	W	L	ERA	G	SV	IP	H	BB	SO
Spring, Joe, Oral Roberts	6	2	**1.78**	28	3	76	68	17	55
Bowen, Drew, Oral Roberts	7	5	1.95	14	1	88	78	21	68
Gonzalez, Alex, Oral Roberts	6	3	2.30	17	0	86	63	24	66
#Liguori, Lars, Oral Roberts	0	3	2.33	**29**	1	19	16	7	14
Straka, John, N. Dakota State	7	4	2.61	15	0	**110**	103	18	92
Gorecki, Jeff, Oakland	5	5	3.10	15	0	96	102	18	51
Mascheri, Rich, Western Illinois	3	8	3.39	14	0	90	87	32	72
Giller, Kurt, Oral Roberts	6	4	3.42	16	0	84	64	36	79
#Russell, Luxton, Oakland	3	5	3.49	23	**10**	49	45	26	30
Anderson, Luke, N. Dakota St.	**8**	3	3.58	15	0	98	84	29	69
Outram, Kelsey, Southern Utah	3	10	3.97	16	0	95	108	39	52
Bougher, Stephen, S. Dakota St.	6	5	4.01	13	0	76	85	34	50
Weaver, Charles, IPFW	4	7	4.30	14	0	98	91	40	87
Bray, Adam, S. Dakota State	3	3	4.31	12	0	65	78	24	48
Hager, Jason, Oakland	5	3	4.34	16	0	64	73	21	65
Hunter, Dustin, Western Illinois	4	6	4.38	14	0	76	68	52	**106**
Torrence, Mike, Oral Roberts	5	6	4.52	19	0	78	79	30	63
Somsen, Layne, S. Dakota State	1	6	4.53	12	0	56	45	36	53
Russell, Dan, Western Illinois	3	6	4.57	16	1	63	71	21	37
Smith, Nick, Western Illinois	3	6	4.98	14	0	69	75	40	60
Neubauer, Justin, S. Utah	6	5	5.01	13	0	83	102	18	37
Wentz, Zach, N. Dakota State	2	6	5.50	13	0	69	92	30	28
Fox, Hayden, Oakland	2	7	6.13	15	0	62	83	32	63
Karlik, Joe, Southern Utah	2	3	6.47	12	0	57	80	26	20
Adamek, Brady, Oakland	2	5	6.63	13	0	56	68	41	34
Rezac, Chase, Southern Utah	3	6	6.88	15	0	69	91	30	42

SUN BELT CONFERENCE

	Conference		Overall	
	W	L	W	L
Florida Atlantic	19	8	32	22
Arkansas State	19	9	34	23
Florida International	15	14	31	26
* Lousiana-Monroe	15	15	32	30
South Alabama	15	15	23	34
Middle Tennessee State	14	16	31	28
Troy	14	16	28	30
Western Kentucky	13	17	25	33
Arkansas-Little Rock	12	18	26	28
Louisiana-Lafayette	11	19	23	30

ALL-CONFERENCE TEAM: C—Blake Johnson, Jr., Arkansas-Little Rock. **1B**—Troy Pierce, Jr., Troy. **2B**—Mike Albaladejo, Sr., Florida Atlantic. **3B**—Mike Martinez, Sr., Florida International. **SS**—Jeremy Sy, Sr., Louisiana-Monroe. **OF**—Sean Bignall, Sr., Arkansas-Little Rock; Jabari Henry, Jr., Florida International; Justin Guidry, Sr., Middle Tennessee State. **DH**—Whitt Dorsey, Jr., South Alabama. **SP**—Chance Cleveland, Jr., Arkansas-Little Rock; Jacob Lee, Sr., Arkansas State; Ryan Garton, Sr., Florida Atlantic. **RP**—R.J. Alvarez, Jr., Florida Atlantic. **UT**—Myles Parma, Jr., Arkansas-Little Rock. **Player of the Year:** Jeremy Sy, Louisiana-Monroe. **Pitcher of the Year:** Jacob Lee, Arkansas State. **Freshman of the Year:** Johnathan Frebis, rhp, Middle Tennessee State. **Coach of the Year:** Tommy Raffo, Arkansas State.

INDIVIDUAL BATTING LEADERS
(Minimum 2.5 at-bats per team game)

	AVG	AB	R	H	2B	3B	HR	RBI	SB
Martinez, Mike, FIU	**.383**	201	42	77	16	1	7	46	7
Guidry, Justin, MTSU	.364	239	51	**87**	10	4	4	34	12
Johnson, Claude, App. St.	.359	184	28	66	**19**	0	1	27	1
Albaladejo, Mike, Fla. Atlantic	.358	212	43	76	13	2	2	30	3
Bignall, Sean, UALR	.346	214	**60**	74	13	**4**	**18**	**64**	9
Miller, Trent, MTSU	.345	226	39	78	15	1	13	49	1
Pierce, Logan, Troy	.341	226	51	77	18	1	5	47	0
Bentley, Cameron, UALR	.339	227	42	77	17	4	6	35	22
LaRue, Hank, MTSU	.338	222	34	75	15	1	5	39	5
Dorsey, Whitt, South Alabama	.337	205	34	69	12	0	2	31	3
Sy, Jeremy, Louisiana-Monroe	.329	222	51	73	14	6	4	35	14
Compton, Chase, La.-Lafayette	.328	195	26	64	12	5	1	25	2
Leonards, Ryan, La.-Lafayette	.327	165	29	54	9	3	0	22	10
Rapp, Joey, Louisiana-Monroe	.325	234	44	76	18	2	9	51	6

Patterson, Jordan, S. Alabama	.323	217	41	70	15	1	8	44	2
Shear, Boone, Troy	.319	226	51	72	14	0	9	59	7
Collins, Danny, Troy	.318	233	41	74	17	2	12	52	3
Earley, Nolan, South Alabama	.318	211	44	67	14	1	6	35	5
Burns, Nathan, FIU	.317	221	45	70	12	**9**	3	48	9
Johnson, Blake, UALR	.315	165	30	52	14	2	6	33	3
Newton, Kyle, Florida Atlantic	.311	219	37	68	13	1	7	34	2
Bermudez, Pablo, FIU	.310	213	47	66	14	0	4	25	12
Vaughn, Tyler, Troy	.305	174	23	53	13	0	0	18	0
Clowers, Caleb, La.-Monroe	.303	**251**	38	76	10	1	0	33	9
Keller, Corey, Florida Atlantic	.302	205	36	62	8	1	7	28	5
Henry, Jabari, FIU	.301	183	38	55	8	2	12	45	4
Shantz, T.J., FIU	.294	235	41	69	9	1	5	33	6
Crumpton, Ben, UALR	.292	154	40	45	8	3	3	19	24
Edwards, Judd, La.-Monroe	.292	216	43	63	12	1	4	27	10
Parma, Myles, UALR	.292	192	41	56	10	1	4	31	5
Faulkner, Michael, Ark. State	.291	223	46	65	6	2	0	34	**41**

INDIVIDUAL PITCHING LEADERS
(Minimum 1 IP per team game)

	W	L	ERA	G	SV	IP	H	BB	SO
Haydel, Taylor, Western Kentucky	4	5	**2.35**	25	3	65	68	12	74
Lee, Jacob, Arkansas State	**9**	1	2.77	16	0	97	88	36	86
Austin, Thomas, Troy	3	5	2.80	32	3	64	63	14	52
Garton, Ryan, Florida Atlantic	**9**	3	3.09	15	0	93	78	30	84
Ellis, Michael, FIU	3	2	3.13	15	0	83	76	45	88
Thamm, Kendall, La.-Monroe	6	3	3.18	28	2	65	59	25	47
Alexander, Kevin, Florida Atlantic	5	1	3.29	12	1	55	64	11	40
McVay, Mason, FIU	2	3	3.36	17	0	64	59	41	72
Sisco, Jonathan, MTSU	5	4	3.49	16	0	70	56	36	45
Griffitt, Chris, Louisiana-Lafayette	6	3	3.52	14	0	69	70	21	63
Hill, Nate, Troy	7	2	3.53	**35**	4	79	75	33	75
Zeigler, Randy, Louisiana-Monroe	5	6	3.65	17	0	**106**	92	55	**108**
Frebis, Johnathan, MTSU	6	3	3.65	15	0	81	67	36	61
#Gomez, Michael, FIU	1	4	3.76	28	**13**	38	28	26	40
Gomber, Austin, Florida Atlantic	3	4	3.82	14	0	61	58	33	63
Wine, Cale, Louisiana-Monroe	6	4	3.93	16	0	94	93	41	54
Cleveland, Chance, UALR	**9**	4	3.93	14	0	92	87	33	98
Bado, Tim, Western Kentucky	4	7	4.31	14	0	86	88	27	76
Kyle, Cory, Arkansas State	3	4	4.34	18	1	66	65	32	56
Nicholoson, Jordan, La.-Lafayette	3	7	4.35	14	0	83	91	14	59
Clay, Austin, Western Kentucky	4	4	4.74	23	0	74	88	19	39
Aulds, Shelby, Louisiana-Monroe	3	2	4.77	21	0	60	66	22	44

WEST COAST CONFERENCE

	Conference		Overall	
	W	L	W	L
*Pepperdine	16	8	36	23
San Diego	15	9	40	17
Gonzaga	14	10	34	22
Loyola Marymount	14	10	27	27
San Francisco	14	10	29	30
Portland	12	12	27	25
Brigham Young	10	14	22	27
St. Mary's	8	16	24	29
Santa Clara	5	19	25	28

ALL-CONFERENCE TEAM: C—Colton Plaia, Jr., Loyola Marymount. **1B**—Nik Balog, Sr., San Francisco. **2B**—Joe Sever, Jr., Pepperdine; Greg Harisis. So., Santa Clara. **3B**—Kris Bryant, So., San Diego. **SS**—Andrew Daniel, Fr., San Diego; Zach Vincej, Jr., Pepperdine. **IF**—Alex Stanford, Sr., Gonzaga. **OF**—Royce Bolinger, Sr., Gonzaga; Kelton Caldwell, So., BYU; Turner Gill, So., Portland; Brenden Kalfus, Jr., Saint Mary's; Matt Lowenstein, Jr., Loyola Marymount; Justin Maffei, Jr., San Francisco; Pat Stover, Jr., Santa Clara; Corey LeVier, Sr., San Diego. **DH**—Clayton Eslick, Jr., Gonzaga. **P**—Martin Agosta, Jr., St. Mary's; Marco Gonzales, So., Gonzaga; Abe Bobb, So., San Diego; Kyle Kraus, Sr., Portland; Jon Moscot, Jr., Pepperdine; James Pazos, Jr., San Diego; Paul Sewald, Sr., San Diego; Kyle Zimmer, Jr., San Francisco. **Player of the Year:** Joe Sever, Pepperdine. **Pitcher of the Year:** Marco Gonzales, Gonzaga. **Defensive Player of the Year:** Zach Vincej, Pepperdine. **Freshman of the Year:** Travis Radke, Portland. **Coach of the Year:** Steve Rodriguez, Pepperdine.

INDIVIDUAL BATTING LEADERS
(Minimum 3 plate appearances per team game)

	AVG	AB	R	H	2B	3B	HR	RBI	SB
Bollinger, Royce, Gonzaga	.392	237	46	93	15	3	11	51	3
LeVier, Corey, San Diego	.367	196	29	72	15	0	3	31	2
Bryant, Kris, San Diego	.366	213	59	78	17	3	14	57	9
Sever, Joe, Pepperdine	.351	235	48	86	16	0	6	53	9
Herbst, Lucas, Santa Clara	.351	151	29	53	7	4	2	26	6
Eslick, Clayton, Gonzaga	.340	197	41	67	9	2	2	23	0
Daniel, Andrew, San Diego	.339	230	37	78	18	2	4	45	3
Vincej, Zach, Pepperdine	.339	242	56	82	18	0	2	23	11
Plaia, Colton, LMU	.326	193	28	63	8	0	6	38	5
Gonzales, Marco, Gonzaga	.325	151	23	49	10	0	2	29	0
Ferguson, Collin, St. Mary's	.315	184	21	58	16	0	2	18	0
Maffei, Justin, San Francisco	.315	200	46	63	13	1	4	16	24
Gill, Turner, Portland	.314	185	24	58	14	1	5	30	2
Lane, Eric, Gonzaga	.313	166	26	52	6	0	0	15	3
Cooper, Tony, Pepperdine	.313	179	25	56	2	2	0	29	6
Lechich, Louie, San Diego	.311	225	39	70	10	2	1	39	7
Stanford, Alex, Gonzaga	.309	188	29	58	12	3	2	31	6
Clear, Adam, San Francisco	.303	198	24	60	14	0	0	14	7
Balog, Nik, San Francisco	.302	202	20	61	15	1	5	44	8
Halcomb, Steven, Gonzaga	.297	219	32	65	8	0	1	30	4
Haar, Bryan, San Diego	.296	199	32	59	17	1	2	34	12
Stover, Pat, Santa Clara	.296	196	31	58	10	0	5	37	13
Lowenstein, Matt, LMU	.293	191	36	56	10	3	0	28	1
Hall, Austin, BYU	.293	165	23	48	13	2	1	19	8
Mahood, Jason, San Francisco	.284	201	27	57	13	1	1	28	1
Haupt, Dillon, San Diego	.279	179	37	50	7	4	5	31	3
Brugman, Jaycob, BYU	.279	172	25	48	4	5	2	30	12
Mahoney, Cullen, LMU	.277	173	31	48	8	0	3	24	4
Guthrie, Alex, LMU	.277	202	30	56	15	0	4	26	4
#Norton, Cole, St. Mary's	.262	187	24	49	9	6	1	18	1

INDIVIDUAL PITCHING LEADERS
(Minimum 1 IP per team game)

	W	L	ERA	G	SV	IP	H	BB	SO
Gonzales, Marco, Gonzaga	8	2	1.55	12	0	93	63	23	92
Kraus, Kyle, Portland	7	6	2.03	16	0	111	103	14	61
Radke, Travis, Portland	7	4	2.09	15	0	86	57	29	85
Pazos, James, San Diego	5	1	2.14	29	4	63	38	21	63
Agosta, Martin, St. Mary's	9	2	2.18	14	0	103	87	27	95
Bobb, Abe, San Francisco	8	4	2.18	14	0	87	79	12	66
Wagner, Michael, San Diego	5	2	2.58	31	19	59	57	20	53
Olson, Tyler, Gonzaga	5	4	2.77	15	0	110	107	27	90
Zimmer, Kyle, San Francisco	5	3	2.85	13	0	88	75	17	104
Moscot, Jon, Pepperdine	7	5	2.90	15	0	115	113	24	95
Capper, Chris, BYU	3	6	2.97	10	0	67	75	21	50
Johnson, Chris, Portland	4	4	3.08	14	0	76	81	21	57
Sewald, Paul, San Diego	8	4	3.09	15	0	84	75	27	75
Griffin, Aaron, LMU	3	5	3.29	32	1	65	69	16	61
Covey, Dylan, San Diego	6	3	3.32	17	0	81	74	43	50
Miller, Corey, Pepperdine	8	3	3.38	18	0	101	98	28	67
Hunter, Andy, Gonzaga	5	2	3.38	15	0	99	91	27	73
Drummond, Calvin, San Diego	8	6	3.43	17	0	87	98	34	80
Balog, Alex, San Francisco	4	4	3.43	15	0	79	62	31	57
#Twining, Paul, Santa Clara	6	6	3.55	33	8	51	47	16	42
Maurer, Matt, Pepperdine	6	1	3.56	17	0	66	65	32	35
Megill, Trevor, LMU	5	8	3.57	15	0	91	83	24	82
Welmon, Colin, LMU	7	4	3.87	15	0	95	101	14	66
Poulson, Desmond, BYU	1	3	3.91	13	0	76	86	20	50
Frazier, Scott, Pepperdine	7	5	3.93	15	0	103	104	31	69
Barraclough, Kyle, St. Mary's	2	9	3.95	14	0	84	81	50	80
Fansler, Powell, Santa Clara	5	5	4.06	18	0	69	77	15	26
Couch, Mike, Santa Clara	1	5	4.08	9	0	57	63	14	39
Nance, Tommy, Santa Clara	4	6	4.20	16	0	94	107	29	48

WESTERN ATHLETIC CONFERENCE

	Conference		Overall	
	W	L	W	L
New Mexico State	11	7	35	24
Nevada	11	7	32	25
Sacramento State	11	7	31	28
Hawaii	10	8	30	25
* Fresno State	8	10	31	28
Louisiana Tech	7	11	27	28
San Jose State	6	18	19	39

ALL-CONFERENCE TEAM: C—Derrick Chung, Sr., Sacramento State; Zac Fisher, Jr., New Mexico State; Carlos Escobar, Jr., Nevada. **INF**—Andrew Ayers, Jr., Sacramento State; Pi'kea Kitamura, Jr., Hawaii; Ryan Gebhardt, So., Louisiana Tech; Zach Voight, Sr., New Mexico State. **OF**—Aaron Judge, So., Fresno State; Brooks Klein, Jr., Nevada; Tanner Waite, Sr., New Mexico State; Justin Higley, So., Sacramento State. **DH**—Kenny Wise, Sr., Fresno State. **SP**—Bradey Shipley, So., Nevada; Tom Jameson, Jr., Nevada; Adam Mott, Jr., New Mexico State. **RP**—Scott Coffman, Sr., New Mexico State. **Player of the Year:** Andrew Ayers, Sacramento State. **Pitcher of the Year:** Bradey Shipley, Nevada. **Freshman of the Year:** Rhys Hoskins, Sacramento State. **Coach of the Year:** Reggie Christiansen, Sacramento State.

INDIVIDUAL BATTING LEADERS
(Minimum 2.5 at-bats per team game)

	AVG	AB	R	H	2B	3B	HR	RBI	SB
Fisher, Zac, New Mexico State	.355	231	39	82	18	0	6	60	2
Hoskins, Rhys, Sacramento St.	.353	215	44	76	16	0	10	53	1
Hipp, Parker, New Mexico St.	.349	209	51	73	17	1	1	49	4
Gebhardt, Ryan, La. Tech	.341	223	44	76	14	0	1	27	5
Chung, Derrick, Sacramento St.	.340	235	42	80	14	2	2	31	7
Ayers, Andrew, Sacramento St.	.336	220	36	74	16	2	3	31	3
Snowley, Kurt, New Mexico St.	.335	176	51	59	9	2	1	27	1
Klein, Brooks, Nevada	.335	203	33	68	16	6	8	42	2
Garrison, Trent, Fresno State	.333	195	29	65	12	0	2	39	0
Williams, Alex, Louisiana Tech	.332	217	38	72	11	0	12	46	5
Bennett, Collin, Hawaii	.328	180	30	59	7	3	3	33	5
Meyer, Kewby, Nevada	.324	182	23	59	9	2	1	34	1
Wise, Kenneth, Fresno State	.318	173	23	55	8	1	4	40	1
Phillips, Kyle, New Mexico St.	.311	193	42	60	12	0	6	39	3
Kitamura, Pi'kea, Hawaii	.311	206	30	64	9	1	0	29	4
Judge, Aaron, Fresno State	.308	201	47	62	14	2	4	27	13
Paine, Trevor, Sacramento St.	.308	182	23	56	13	0	3	32	1
Voight, Zach, New Mexico St.	.305	203	40	62	10	2	8	56	0
Kohan, Joe, Nevada	.305	177	22	54	8	6	1	32	4
Cederquis, Clay, Sacramento St.	.304	184	18	56	4	0	2	32	4
Waite, Tanner, New Mexico St.	.301	209	55	63	14	4	1	30	2
Hedges, Austin, Louisiana Tech	.296	189	27	56	8	0	2	26	8
Ventimilia, Stephen, Hawaii	.293	208	42	61	3	1	0	14	14
Karraker, Bryan, New Mexico St.	.292	219	53	64	18	0	3	48	2
Hutcheson, Patrick, Fresno St.	.290	231	37	67	10	1	5	30	13
Swasey, Zack, Hawaii	.288	205	16	59	10	2	1	26	11
Yrigoyen, Garrett, Nevada	.288	160	31	46	11	3	0	18	11
Anderson, Jay, Nevada	.286	203	36	58	5	5	0	19	10
Schulz, Nick, San Jose State	.286	140	22	40	9	0	4	21	3
Wynns, Austin, Fresno State	.284	194	35	55	22	0	0	30	1
Escobar, Jr., Carlos, Nevada	.283	173	28	49	14	1	5	38	2

INDIVIDUAL PITCHING LEADERS
(Minimum 1 IP per team game)

	W	L	ERA	G	SV	IP	H	BB	SO
Shipley, Bradey, Nevada	9	4	2.20	15	0	98	73	40	88
Jameson, Tom, Nevada	7	2	2.55	15	0	95	103	38	41
Harlan, Thomas, Fresno State	7	7	2.78	21	1	107	103	16	85
Arakawa, Jarrett, Hawaii	7	6	2.88	15	0	97	99	18	70
Maton, Phil, Louisiana Tech	8	5	2.93	18	0	89	78	22	79
Melero, Johnny, San Jose State	2	7	3.03	13	0	74	74	18	47
Haley, Justin, Fresno State	7	4	3.18	22	0	93	96	39	94
Sisto, Matt, Hawaii	8	4	3.46	14	0	91	94	11	45
Squier, Scott, Hawaii	3	4	3.50	15	0	64	64	30	55
Linehan, Tyler, Fresno State	4	5	3.58	15	0	83	95	30	82
Russo, David Wayne, San Jose St.	2	3	3.97	16	0	59	62	19	41
Gilley, Jamie, Louisiana Tech	3	4	4.03	25	3	67	67	21	82
Beck, Ryan, New Mexico State	5	7	4.24	17	0	98	113	38	97
Jones, Zack, San Jose State	3	4	4.50	19	7	54	51	17	60
#Hoelzen, Tyler, Sacramento St.	3	2	4.50	31	0	34	32	16	35
Mendonca, Tanner, Sacramento St.	6	8	4.74	17	0	89	93	40	55
Hennessey, Andy, San Jose State	3	4	4.73	16	0	72	78	35	59
Jameson, Tom, Nevada	6	6	4.84	15	0	84	103	35	41
Cole, Jeremy, Nevada	4	5	4.90	15	0	64	80	21	26

	W	L	ERA	G	SV	IP	H	BB	SO
Petersen, Trevor, Louisiana Tech	6	4	5.08	18	1	83	90	49	45
Mendonca, Tanner, Sacramento St.	2	6	5.73	14	1	66	75	31	33
Mott, Adam, New Mexico State	6	3	4.80	19	1	86	94	41	78
Job, Stefan, Louisiana Tech	2	7	4.89	16	1	85	86	40	81
Kendall, Cody, Fresno State	7	5	5.00	18	0	86	104	22	45
#Gardner, Matt, Nevada	0	1	5.40	24	**13**	27	22	19	22

	AVG	AB	R	H	2B	3B	HR	RBI	SB
Waldron, Mark, Nebraska-Omaha	.272	184	24	50	8	0	1	21	0
Morales, Marcelin, Seattle	.271	144	17	39	4	0	1	10	13
Dickason, Matt, Longwood	.271	199	31	54	14	0	1	26	4
McAlphine, Duncan	.267	210	34	56	9	2	9	42	1
Owens, Alex, Longwood	.265	132	22	35	9	0	4	28	3
Tompkins, Riley, Seattle	.263	137	14	36	8	0	3	20	0
Oleszczuk, Trent, Seattle	.262	191	29	50	11	0	0	13	8
Varaksa, Joey, Longwood	.252	155	18	39	6	1	1	14	2
Biddix, Travis, Longwood	.250	168	30	42	4	0	0	14	1
Palensky, Caleb, Nebraska-Omaha	.250	180	24	45	9	2	2	17	3
Legg, D.C., CS Bakersfield	.244	160	25	39	14	1	3	25	2
Roberts, Nate, Seattle	.233	172	19	40	8	0	1	18	5
Hein, Jordie, CS Bakersfield	.228	180	31	41	6	5	0	8	6
Ecklund, Bryndon, Seattle	.226	137	12	31	3	0	1	16	2
Kincaid, Doug, Seattle	.225	129	14	29	10	1	1	14	1
Donner, Scotty, Nebraska-Omaha	.211	147	16	31	2	2	1	14	2

INDEPENDENTS

Overall

	W	L
Dallas Baptist	41	19
Longwood	27	21
Cal State Bakersfield	25	30
Seattle	23	30
Nebraska-Omaha	12	36

INDIVIDUAL BATTING LEADERS
(Minimum 125 at-bats)

	AVG	AB	R	H	2B	3B	HR	RBI	SB
Behmanesh, Ryan, Dallas Baptist	**.391**	128	31	50	12	0	9	34	6
Lacy, Justin, Longwood	.376	157	28	56	15	2	7	35	**15**
McCord, Colby, Nebraska-Omaha	.366	172	27	63	18	1	3	20	3
Collins, Boomer, Dallas Baptist	.374	**235**	**62**	**88**	**23**	1	**13**	**58**	**15**
Burkett, Scott, Longwood	.357	157	28	56	15	2	7	35	4
Elkins, Austin, Dallas Baptist	.344	221	61	76	14	**8**	9	44	7
Hutter, Joel, Dallas Baptist	.338	234	45	79	16	1	11	**72**	8
Newman, Robby, Longwood	.331	175	41	58	17	1	**13**	47	7
Sanay, Oscar, CS Bakersfield	.312	205	31	64	5	0	0	25	7
Anderson, Landon, Dallas Baptist	.310	232	48	72	14	3	3	38	**15**
Delk, Brandon, Longwood	.303	145	20	44	6	1	3	20	8
Hohl, Brady, Nebraska-Omaha	.297	209	24	62	12	0	2	22	14
Mitchell, Ronnie, Dallas Baptist	.296	189	42	56	12	4	3	27	6
Mortensen, Alex, Nebraska-Omaha	.292	161	19	47	9	1	4	26	1
Brockmeyer, Cael, CS Bakersfield	.285	200	34	57	11	3	6	32	0
Chryock, Tyler, CS Bakersfield	.276	185	24	51	5	4	2	29	2
Olson, Brian, Seattle	.276	152	17	42	8	0	2	18	1
Letourneau, Andrew, CS Bakersfield	.274	186	21	51	4	2	0	25	8

INDIVIDUAL PITCHING LEADERS
(Minimum 50 IP)

	W	L	ERA	G	SV	IP	H	BB	SO
McKenzie, Jeff, CS Bakersfield	6	5	**2.67**	15	0	**108**	106	37	69
Messmore, Spenser, CS Bakersfield	4	7	2.95	22	2	92	103	24	60
Massey, Taylor, Dallas Baptist	**9**	4	3.10	15	0	87	78	33	**76**
Aikenhead, Taylor, CS Bakersfield	6	3	3.20	10	0	59	56	11	31
Howe, Seafth, Seattle	4	5	3.21	14	0	84	86	22	30
Smith, Michael, Dallas Baptist	4	1	3.51	30	**6**	67	66	17	57
Kizer, Brandon, Seattle	5	4	3.59	16	0	93	84	25	42
Morgan, Kyler, Longwood	6	6	3.87	14	0	74	82	20	43
Elkins, Andrew, Dallas Baptist	4	1	3.86	15	0	61	55	17	32
Vick, Brandon, Longwood	6	2	4.00	14	0	54	67	20	40
Reck, Andrew, Nebraska-Omaha	1	7	4.30	12	0	61	69	26	38
Sneed, Cy, Dallas Baptist	8	5	4.45	17	0	85	91	27	71
Gwaltney, Matt, Longwood	3	4	4.55	15	2	87	97	11	55
Dalton, Bryan, Seattle	1	4	4.57	23	3	56	56	30	31
Brattvet, Scott, CS Bakersfield	6	5	4.75	15	0	91	105	38	66
Tew, Mark, Nebraska-Omaha	1	6	5.60	14	0	63	61	39	48
Anderson, Garrett, Seattle	6	6	5.66	23	3	56	56	30	31

NCAA DIVISION II

CARY, N.C.

After West Chester (Pa.) finished in last place in the Pennsylvania State Athletic Conference East a year ago, first-year coach Jad Prachniak completed an amazing turnaround by guiding the school to its first Division II World Series title, pummeling Delta State 9-0 to punctuate a 12-game winning streak.

When Prachniak, who had been the pitching coach at William & Mary, was asked how he planned on following up a national title in his first season at the helm, the 30-year-old facetiously said, "I'm going to retire. It was a good run and there's not much left."

Winners of 15 of their last 16 postseason games, the Golden Rams (46-10) came to the USA Baseball Complex with plenty of momentum. From the first pitch of their opening-round game, they were the best team in the tournament. Led by sophomore righthander Joe Gunkle (10-1, 2.07), the Rams went a perfect 4-0 with wins over Chico State (Calif.), Southern New Hampshire, Catawba (N.C.) and Delta State (Miss.).

Gunkle, the tournament's Most Outstanding Player, pitched two shutouts, allowing just six hits combined in both starts. He took a no-hitter into the ninth inning against Chico State and elicited weak contact from Delta State hitters by getting good leverage out of his 6-foot-6, 210-pound frame, pitching ahead in the count and filling up the strike zone with an 88-91 mph fastball.

"What makes it even more impressive is I don't think he had his best stuff in either start," Prachniak said. "He didn't really command his breaking ball very well. He missed some spots, but that just speaks to the type of competitor he is. He doesn't need his best stuff to win."

West Chester ended Delta State's Cinderella story abruptly. The Statesmen (49-15) were coming off a dramatic win in an elimination game against Minnesota State-Mankato the day before, where they came back from five runs down in the eighth inning to win on a walk-off single by junior first baseman Michael Vinson.

The Rams came into the title game following an off day, which might have been a bad thing for any other team. The Rams came out of the gates by putting up a five-spot in the first inning, knocking out Delta State righthander Colton Mitchell before he could record an out.

"Baseball is a tough sport to grunt through," Prachniak said. "We play over 50 games a year and the games are long. The first three innings felt like forever (against Delta State), so you can't always be amped up all the time. There are spots for that, but you have to digest what's happening and (the team) did a good job analyzing each situation."

Before sweeping their way through the Atlantic Regional in the opening-round games of the NCAA tournament, West Chester edged out Shippensburg (Pa.) by one game in the PSAC regular season and went 5-1 to win the conference tournament. In three championship games for the Rams, they outscored their opponents 25-0. Prachniak attributes his team's success to the quality of play within its conference. In fact, nine of the Rams' 10 losses came against PSAC opponents.

West Chester tied a school record for most wins in a season and became the first team from the Northeast to win a title. Senior second baseman Joe Wendle (.399/.479/.768, 12 HR and 59 RBI in 198 AB) admitted the difference between the Rams' last trip to Cary in 2009 and this year's title run was a change in leadership and attitude.

"This year, we had a different mentality, and it comes from the coaching staff," Wendle said. "Just from being here three years ago and seeing the teams we played, we left there with a bitter taste. We knew if we executed well and hit at the right time this year, that we'd have a good chance."

—*Pat Hickey*

DIVISION II WORLD SERIES

Site: Cary, N.C.
Participants: West Chester, Pa. (46-10); Chico State, Calif. (40-19); Minnesota State-Mankato (51-12); Southern New Hampshire (43-15); Catawba, N.C. (45-17); Indianapolis (46-16); St. Mary's, Texas (49-11); Delta State, Miss. (49-15).
Champion: West Chester.
Runner-up: Delta State.
Outstanding player: Joe Gunkle, rhp, West Chester.

PRELIMINARIES
West Chester 4, Chico State 0
Southern New Hampshire 3, Minnesota State-Mankato 2
Catawba 2, Indianapolis 1
Delta State 4, St. Mary's 1
West Chester 13, Southern New Hampshire 7
Minnesota-State Mankato 6, Chico State 5 (Chico State eliminated)
Delta State 6, Catawba 5
St. Mary's 13, Indianapolis 2 (Indianapolis eliminated)
Minnesota State-Mankato 6, Southern New Hampshire 0 (Southern New Hampshire eliminated)
Catawba 5, St. Mary's 4 (St. Mary's eliminated)
West Chester 2, Catawba 1 (Catawba eliminated)
Minnesota State-Mankato 1, Delta State 0
Delta State 6, Minnesota State-Mankato 5 (Minnesota State-Mankato eliminated)
West Chester 9, Delta State 0 (Delta State eliminated)

NCAA DIVISION III

For the first time in 33 years there is a repeat champion in Division III, as Marietta (Ohio) beat Wheaton (Mass.) in the championship game of the D-III College World Series in Appleton, Wis. The Pioneers become the first team to repeat since Glassboro (N.J.) State, now known as Rowan, did it in 1979.

This year's title run did not come without its share of suspense, as Marietta twice came out of the losers' bracket. The Pioneers lost the second game of their regional, then won five straight to reach Appleton. Once there, they faced a similar situation after losing their second game to St. Thomas (Minn.). Playing for its tournament life, Marietta once again came back by winning three elimination games before beating Wheaton in the championship game 7-2.

Marietta senior shortstop Tim Saunders was named the tournament's Most Outstanding Player. Saunders batted .458 in the tournament (11-for-24) and finished the season with a .441 average.

"There was never any doubt with us," Saunders said. "We did it in the regionals and we knew if we came out here and played like we did in the regionals we'd be able to win . . . Our pitchers just stepped up huge."

That they did. Mike Mahaffey pitched eight shutout innings for Marietta against St. Thomas to put the Pioneers into the championship game. Then Brian Gasser pitched eight innings of his own in the championship game against Wheaton that afternoon, giving up two runs in the win. Most impressive of all is that the Pioneers won their final two games without their ace Austin Blaski, who had thrown more than 13 innings in the tournament up to that point.

"I don't know how many team could have done it," Marietta coach Brian Brewer said after the win. "Hitting a baseball's the hardest thing to do in sports. Winning back-to-back national championships is probably a close second."

This is Brewer's third championship, having won his first back in 2006 when Marietta beat the same opponent, Wheaton, by the same score, 7-2. It's the program's sixth title.

—*John Sandberg*

DIVISION III WORLD SERIES

Site: Appleton, Wis.
Participants: Webster, Mo. (35-12); Wheaton, Mass. (41-11); Cortland State, N.Y. (41-9-1); Kean, N.J. (37-12); St. Thomas, Minn. (41-10); Christopher Newport, Va. (34-10); Marietta, Ga. (48-8); Whitworth, Wash. (31-16-1).
Champion: Marietta.

Runner-up: Wheaton.
Outstanding player: Tim Saunders, ss, Marietta.
PRELIMINARIES
Cortland State 10, Kean 5
St. Thomas 12, Christopher Newport 7
Marietta 13, Whitworth 2
Wheaton 3, Webster 2
Webster 8, Kean 7 (Kean eliminated)
Wheaton 6, Cortland State 1
Whitworth 7, Christopher Newport 2 (Christopher Newport eliminated)
St. Thomas 3, Marietta 1
Marietta 12, Webster 7 (Webster eliminated)
Wheaton 13, St. Thomas 9
Cortland State 5, Whitworth 4 (Whitworth eliminated)
Marietta 6, Wheaton 5 (10 innings)
St. Thomas 7, Cortland State 6 (Cortland State eliminated)
Marietta 7, Wheaton 2 (Wheaton eliminated)
Marietta 5, St. Thomas 0 (St. Thomas eliminated)

NAIA

In front of a crowd that had three times as many spectators as Tennessee Wesleyan has students, the Bulldogs captured their first NAIA championship, defeating Rogers (Okla.) State 10-6 in the title game after going winless in their previous two World Series appearances in Lewiston, Idaho.

"I think the most important thing for us this year was that familiarity aspect of being back in Lewiston," coach Billy Berry said. "It really helped us understand where we needed to improve in the offseason and the areas we needed the most help in."

Tennessee Wesleyan (53-12) came into the tournament as the No. 4 seed and beat No. 9 Rogers State in the opening game 8-6 followed by No. 2 Lee (Tenn.) 13-3. In a decisive elimination game in the semifinals against top-seeded Louisiana State-Shreveport, the Bulldogs outslugged the Pilots 17-10 behind senior right fielder Jordan Guida's three home runs, which tied for the most in a game in NAIA tournament history. The last player to hit three home runs in the World Series was Beau Mills of Lewis-Clark State (Idaho) in 2007.

Guida, the tournament's MVP, hit .440/.481/1.280 with seven homers and 14 RBIs in 25 at-bats in the tournament.

"We kept teasing him every day that he would go to the phone booth before the game and change his clothes from Clark Kent into Superman," Berry said.

In the seven years under Berry, the Bulldogs have averaged 8.3 runs a game. Over six games in eight days at Harris Field, TWC averaged more than 11 runs per game by clubbing 17 home runs, a Series record.

Tennessee Wesleyan capped off an impressive late-season run, winning 19 of their last 20 games. The Bulldogs were crowned Appalachian Athletic Conference regular-season and tournament champions and swept through the Kingsport bracket.

"A lot of NAIA schools are seen as a second chance for guys that have had academic problems or otherwise," Berry said. "We've really sold that and the fact that we've advanced deep in the post-season these past few years. We have a unique mix of players from different backgrounds that really clicked together this year."

—Pat Hickey

NAIA WORLD SERIES

Site: Lewiston, Idaho
Participants: Louisiana State-Shreveport (54-6); Lee, Tenn. (56-11-1); Oklahoma City (48-12); Tennessee Wesleyan (53-12); Embry-Riddle, Fla. (43-18); Lewis-Clark State, Idaho (42-14); Point Park, Pa. (53-11); South Carolina Beaufort (41-19); Rogers State, Okla. (49-16); College of Idaho (41-21).
Champion: Tennessee Wesleyan.
Runner-up: Rogers State.
Outstanding player: Jordan Guida, of, Tennessee Wesleyan.

NJCAA DIVISION I

For the second time in three seasons, Iowa Western defeated San Jacinto (Texas) to win the NJCAA Division I Junior College World Series. This time, the victory was a 6-5 squeaker, as Iowa Western scored two in the ninth, the final run coming in on a balk. Brett Bass had the game-tying hit earlier in the inning, following up his brother Brandon's heroics in 2010, when Brandon produced the game-winning hit.

The Rievers set a school record with their 62nd victory in the game and remain the only Northern district team to win an NJCAA championship.

Keaton Steele earned tournament MVP honors after hitting .389 with a home run and four RBIs while also earning two saves as Iowa Western's closer. He went 2-for-2 with a homer and three RBIs in the title game and struck out two in the ninth for the save.

Site: Grand Junction, Colo.
Participants: San Jacinto, Texas (41-25); Iowa Western (62-6); Neosho County, Kan. (49-16); Spartanburg Methodist, S.C. (45-18); Polk State, Fla. (46-12); Western Nevada (48-17); Jefferson, Mo. (53-12); Cisco, Texas (48-15).
Champion: Iowa Western.
Runner-up: San Jacinto.
Outstanding player: Keaton Steele, Iowa Western.

NJCAA DIVISION II

Louisiana State-Eunice battled back through the loser's bracket to win their fourth title in seven years by defeating Western Oklahoma State 7-3 at David Allen Memorial Ballpark. Bengals catcher Stuart Turner hit .400 for the tournament to earn MVP honors. Left-hander Cody Boutte, who pitched seven innings of seven-hit, three-run ball while striking out 11 in the title game, was named the tournament's top pitcher.

Site: Enid, Okla.
Participants: Heartland, Ill. (54-8); Catawba Valley, N.C. (38-17); Madison, Wis. (45-13); Rhode Island (33-13); Scottsdale, Ariz. (39-24); Lackawanna, Pa. (47-12); Western Oklahoma State (48-17); Grand Rapids, Mich. (39-24); Des Moines Area, Iowa (51-14); Louisiana State-Eunice (57-5).
Champion: Louisiana State-Eunice.
Runner-up: Western Oklahoma State.
Outstanding player: Stuart Turner, Louisiana State-Eunice.

NJCAA DIVISION III

Joliet (Ill.) JC scored two runs in the bottom of the 10th inning to defeat Niagara (N.Y.) CC 6-5 to capture its third national championship. Luke Andrade hit a sacrifice fly to score the winning run and also earned MVP honors at Mike Carter Field in Tyler, Texas.

Site: Tyler, Texas
Participants: Niagara County, N.Y. (39-22); Joliet, Ill. (37-29); Tyler, Texas (38-20); Montgomery-Germantown, Md. (30-28); St. Cloud, Minn. (43-8); Nassau, N.Y. (26-18); Gloucester, N.J. (47-11); Northern Essex, Mass. (30-9).
Champion: Joliet
Runner-up: Niagara
Outstanding player: Luke Andrade, Joliet.

CALIFORNIA CC ATHLETIC ASSOCIATION

Cosumnes River CC won its first California Community College Athletic Association title, defeating third-ranked Rio Hondo 8-6 in 12 innings at Bakersfield College.

The Hawks' freshman right-hander Austin Ales (11-2, 1.09) was named the tournament's MVP after going 1-0 with a save in 10 innings. Ales allowed one run in a complete-game effort against Rio Hondo in the opening-round game–snapping the Roadrunners 33-game winning streak–and came in to earn his fifth save of the year in the championship.

Cosumnes River (28-16) had just 19 players on their active roster and played their home games at three different fields as they build a new ballpark set to open next season.

—Pat Hickey

Site: Bakersfield, Calif.
Participants: Orange Coast (36-7-1); Sierra (26-18-1); Cosumnes River (28-16); Rio Hondo (40-5).
Champion: Cosumnes River.
Runner-up: Rio Hondo.
Outstanding player: Austin Ales, Cosumnes River.

NORTHWEST ATHLETIC ASSOCIATION OF CCS

Pierce College defeated Mt. Hood CC 10-8 at David Story Field in Longview, Wash. to earn its first NWAACC title. Josh Potter hit .426 for the weekend, and was named the tournament MVP.

Site: Longview, Wash.
Participants: Columbia Basin, Wash. (25-23); Chemeketa, Ore. (25-21); Yakima Valley, Wash. (34-16); Bellevue, Wash. (35-12); Pierce, Calif. (33-13); Mt. Hood, Ore. (39-11); Lower Columbia, Wash. (31-15); Everett, Wash. (30-12).
Champion: Pierce.
Runner-up: Mt. Hood.
Outstanding player: Josh Potter, Pierce.

Team USA and Cuba could hardly have been more evenly matched.

After splitting the first six meetings against each other this summer, USA Baseball's Collegiate National Team faced Cuba's national team a seventh time in the semifinals of Haarlem Honkbal Week in the Netherlands, with a trip to the gold-medal game on the line.

After nine innings in that final matchup, the score was tied, 3-3. Not only that, but the cumulative run total for both teams in the seven games was also dead even: 33 apiece.

International tiebreaker rules went into effect in the 10th, and Cuba scored twice to win 5-3. Team USA had to settle for a white-knuckle 4-3 win against the Netherlands the next day in the bronze-medal game, ending its summer at 12-5.

While the Americans were disappointed to lose the series to Cuba and to come up short of the gold medal in Haarlem, they could feel good about holding their own against a Cuban team loaded with veteran international stars, such as Alfredo Despaigne, Yulieski Gourriel and Ariel Pestano. And the first five meetings took place in Cuba, with the host winning three of them.

"From my perspective, obviously we wanted to win it all at Honkbal, but I thought this was a pretty grueling tour for this group," Team USA coach Dave Serrano said. "This team went to Cuba and played five games on their soil, with their umpires and their crowd. I thought we went in there and stood toe-to-toe with them in every game we played.

"Knowing what I do know about that (Cuban) team and the professionalism of those players—the age and strength of those players, the ability of those players, the amount of time those guys have played together for years and years—I was very proud of our group."

Eric Campbell, USA Baseball's general manager of national teams, said the summer proved that American collegians belong on the same field with Cuba's best players, and he hopes the series with Cuba becomes a regular staple of the summer program, starting with a return trip next year.

And if Team USA's bullpen had been able to hold late leads in three of its four losses against Cuba, Campbell and Serrano would be celebrating a wildly successful summer against a challenging schedule. Instead, Cuba rallied from behind one last time in the final meeting.

Jonathon Crawford (Florida) held Cuba scoreless for seven innings and carried a 3-0 lead into the eighth. Serrano said his pitch count was just 71 heading into the frame, so Crawford went back to the mound to start the eighth. But he hit the leadoff man and walked the next batter on four pitches, and suddenly Cuba was in business.

COLLEGIATE NATIONAL TEAM STATS

Year indicates 2012-13 class standing

PLAYER, POS.	YEAR	SCHOOL	AVG	OBP	SLG	G	AB	R	H	2B	3B	HR	RBI	BB	SO	SB
Austin Cousino, of	So.	Kentucky	.351	.479	.459	16	37	10	13	4	0	0	5	8	8	3
Trea Turner, if	So.	North Carolina State	.320	.493	.380	17	50	17	16	3	0	0	3	16	16	10
Kris Bryant, 1b/of	Jr.	San Diego	.271	.368	.508	17	59	7	16	3	1	3	10	8	17	0
Jose Trevino, 3b	So.	Oral Roberts	.263	.275	.368	11	38	0	10	2	1	0	7	0	5	0
Johnny Field, of	Jr.	Arizona	.261	.300	.370	13	46	5	12	0	1	9	2	9	1	
Kyle Farmer, ss	Sr.	Georgia	.250	.333	.346	17	52	6	13	5	0	0	8	2	10	0
Marco Gonzales, dh	Jr.	Gonzaga	.250	.382	.286	12	28	2	7	1	0	0	4	4	3	1
D.J. Peterson, 1b	Jr.	New Mexico	.241	.329	.483	16	58	15	14	2	0	4	14	8	8	1
Jordan Hankins, 2b	Jr.	Austin Peay State	.214	.421	.214	8	14	2	3	0	0	0	3	4	2	1
Michael Conforto, dh	So.	Oregon State	.213	.296	.362	13	47	6	10	1	0	2	10	5	17	0
Michael Lorenzen, of	Jr.	Cal State Fullerton	.171	.341	.171	14	35	7	6	0	0	0	1	6	7	1
Brett Hambright, c	Gr.	Oregon	.150	.370	.150	13	20	4	3	0	0	0	2	6	5	1
Colton Plaia, c	Sr.	Loyola Marymount	.130	.200	.130	12	23	2	3	0	0	0	1	2	9	1
Adam Frazier, ss	Jr.	Mississippi State	.059	.158	.059	9	17	3	1	0	0	0	0	1	4	0

PITCHER, POS.	YEAR	SCHOOL	W	L	ERA	G	SV	IP	H	R	ER	BB	SO	AVG
Zack Godley, rhp	Jr.	Tennessee	1	0	0.00	3	0	4	4	0	0	3	6	.235
Michael Lorenzen, rhp	Jr.	Cal State Fullerton	1	1	0.00	3	1	3	0	0	0	4	1	.000
Bobby Wahl, rhp	Jr.	Mississippi	0	0	1.17	6	2	8	6	1	1	5	9	.222
Carlos Rodon, lhp	So.	North Carolina State	2	0	1.42	5	0	19	17	3	3	7	21	.243
Trevor Williams, rhp	Jr.	Arizona State	0	1	1.80	5	0	10	11	6	2	5	5	.268
Jake Reed, rhp	So.	Oregon	1	0	2.08	4	0	9	10	3	2	3	8	.312
Jonathon Crawford, rhp	Jr.	Florida	3	0	2.10	6	0	26	14	7	6	11	13	.157
Adam Plutko, rhp	Jr.	UCLA	0	0	2.63	3	0	14	9	4	4	5	12	.188
Marco Gonzales, lhp	Jr.	Gonzaga	3	0	2.82	4	0	22	14	7	7	5	29	.182
Dan Child, rhp	Jr.	Oregon State	0	0	3.00	6	2	9	8	4	3	4	8	.235
David Berg, rhp	So.	UCLA	0	1	3.72	8	2	10	13	5	4	4	10	.310
Ryne Stanek, rhp	Jr.	Arkansas	0	2	4.09	2	0	11	10	6	5	7	9	.263
Tommy Thorpe, lhp	So.	Oregon	0	0	12.27	3	0	4	4	5	5	4	4	.267

Bobby Wahl (Mississippi) entered and gave up three hits and a walk, allowing three runs to score and erasing the USA lead.

Team USA intended for Wahl, a starter for Ole Miss in the spring, to be its power-armed closer at the back of the bullpen, but his cumulative workload limited him in the summer. Sidewinder David Berg (UCLA) picked up much of the slack, working 9 2/3 innings over eight appearances, but Team USA could have used a full-strength Wahl.

Team USA had envisioned Oregon's Jimmie Sherfy in the closer role, but he was injured in super regionals, forcing improvisation. Ultimately, the bullpen proved to be the Achilles' heel.

The bullpen nearly relinquished another lead in the bronze-medal game against the Netherlands. Team USA carried a 4-1 lead into the ninth behind Marco Gonzales (Gonzaga), who struck out nine without issuing a walk and scattering six hits over eight strong innings. Gonzales, dubbed "college baseball's Tom Glavine" by Serrano, had also struck out 10 over seven strong innings earlier in the tournament to beat Japan.

But after Gonzales exited in that final game, the Dutch bats got going against Berg in the ninth, pushing two runs across and sending the tying run to third base. Child took over for Berg and ended the game with a strikeout on a 3-and-2 slider.

"I told our guys it was going to be a character game," Serrano said. "Everyone was disappointed after losing to Cuba, but we were going to show up the next day and represent our country. When it was 4-3 in the ninth, we showed a lot of character."

Offense Rules In Cape

The Wareham Gatemen won their sixth Cape Cod League title—and their first since 2002—in improbable fashion.

The Gatemen trailed Yarmouth-Dennis 5-2 in the ninth inning of the final game of the championship series, but they stormed back with three in the ninth and three more in the 10th to claim a stunning 8-6 win. Kyle Schwarber (Indiana) hit a solo homer in the ninth and added a tie-breaking two-run shot in the 10th to earn series MVP honors. Mott Hyde (Georgia Tech) followed Schwarber with a two-run homer to tie the game with two outs, forcing extra innings.

"It didn't look good for us in the ninth did it?" Wareham manager Cooper Ferris said. "But I told the guys that I felt good in this park (at Y-D). We've been down seven runs and five runs this year and come back to win."

It was appropriate that home runs decided the final game (which featured seven long balls

in all), because balls flew out of Cape League parks at a record clip in 2012. Cape teams hit 159 home runs in 2011 and 158 in 2010, but in 2012 the league total was 382, an increase of 140 percent. Harwich's 64 homers broke the single-season record set with metal bats in 1981, while Wareham's Tyler Horan (Virginia Tech) tied the league record with 16 homers. Hitting (.247 in 2011 to .260 this year) and scoring (more than 500 more runs than a year ago) also spiked dramatically.

The story was the same across much of college baseball, as offensive records fell from the Coastal Plain to the New England Collegiate League to the Prospect League and beyond. Prospect League commissioner Dave Chase cited four main reasons that he believes apply across summer college ball: lively balls, record heat (July 2012 was the hottest month on record in the United States), expansion that has sapped the pitching pool and the cyclical nature of baseball.

SUMMER LEAGUE ROUNDUP

■ The Santa Barbara Foresters beat the Seattle Studs 6-2 in the championship game of the National Baseball Congress World Series. The Foresters became the first team to repeat as NBC World Series champions since Kenai of the Alaska League in 1993-94. In the championship game, **John Beck** (Texas-Arlington) struck out 10 and allowed just one unearned run in 6⅔ innings. Tournament MVP **Zach Fish** (Oklahoma State) led the offense, going 3-for-4 with a home run.

■ For the second straight year, a team swept the Mankato MoonDogs to win the Northwoods League championship in a best-of-three series. In 2012, it was the La Crosse Loggers who were victorious, winning 12-2 in the first game and then 8-1 in the second game..

■ Behind stout starting pitching and a potent offense, the Newport Gulls swept the Danbury Westerners for their fifth New England Collegiate League championship. **Daniel Wright** (Arkansas State) and **Pete Kelich** (Bryant) combined to pitch 16 innings in the best-of-three series, allowing just three runs on seven hits while striking out 24 to keep Danbury at bay. **Jeff Melillo** (Rutgers) and **Kasey Coffman** (Vanderbilt) went a combined 9-for-19 as Newport banged out 27 total hits.

■ Managed by ex-big leaguer **Brian Buscher**, Columbia beat Fayetteville in the best-of-three finals of the Petit Cup tournament, rallying after losing the first game to win its first Coastal Plain League title. The finals matched the league's No. 2 and 4 seeds, with Fayetteville rallying despite a preseason ballpark explosion that sidelined team manager **Darrell Handelsman** for much of the season.

■ For the second time in five years, the Anchorage Glacier Pilots won the Alaska League title, with a league record of 26-14 (27-19 overall). The Peninsula Oilers and Anchorage Bucs finished tied for second place at 21-19.

COLLEGE — sidebar

COLLEGE *SUMMER LEAGUES*

For players who played for multiple teams: 1: Stats with first team. 2: Stats with second team. 3: Stats with third team. T: combined stats.

CAPE COD LEAGUE

EAST	W	L	T	PCT	PTS
Harwich	27	16	1	.614	55
Yarmouth-Dennis	25	19	0	.568	50
Orleans	22	22	0	.500	44
Chatham	21	21	2	.477	44
Brewster	17	26	1	.386	35

WEST	W	L	T	PCT	PTS
Cotuit	30	14	0	.681	60
Wareham	21	23	0	.477	42
Falmouth	21	23	0	.477	42
Bourne	17	27	0	.386	34
Hyannis	17	27	0	.386	34

PLAYOFFS—Semifinals: Wareham defeated Bourne 2-0 and Yarmouth-Dennis defeated Orleans 2-0 in best-of-three series. Finals: Wareham defeated Yarmouth-Dennis 2-1 in best-of-three series.
TOP 30 PROSPECTS: 1. Sean Manaea, lhp, Hyannis (Jr., Indiana State). **2.** Colin Moran, 3b, Bourne (Jr., North Carolina). **3.** Phil Ervin, of, Harwich (Jr., Samford). **4.** Austin Wilson, of, Harwich (Jr., Stanford). **5.** Kevin Ziomek, lhp, Cotuit (Jr., Vanderbilt). **6.** Aaron Judge, of, Brewster (Jr., Fresno State). **7.** Jeff Hoffman, rhp, Hyannis (So., East Carolina). **8.** Colby Suggs, rhp, Wareham (Jr., Arkansas). **9.** Jacoby Jones, of/2b, Harwich (Jr., Louisiana State). **10.** A.J. Vanegas, rhp, Yarmouth-Dennis (Jr., Stanford). **11.** Tom Windle, lhp, Brewster (Jr., Minnesota). **12.** Dan Slania, rhp, Cotuit (Jr., Notre Dame). **13.** Chad Pinder, 3b, Chatham (Jr., Virginia Tech). **14.** Eric Jagielo, 3b, Harwich (Jr., Notre Dame). **15.** Mason Robbins, of, Bourne (So., Southern Mississippi). **16.** Trey Masek, rhp, Falmouth (Jr., Texas Tech). **17.** Mike Mayers, rhp, Bourne (Jr., Mississippi). **18.** Michael O'Neill, of, Falmouth (Jr., Michigan). **19.** Aaron Blair, rhp, Yarmouth-Dennis (Jr., Marshall). **20.** Michael Wagner, rhp, Chatham (Jr., San Diego). **21.** Alex Blandino, ss, Yarmouth-Dennis (So., Stanford). **22.** Corey Littrell, lhp, Harwich (Jr., Kentucky). **23.** Matt Boyd, lhp, Orleans (Sr., Oregon State). **24.** Conrad Gregor, 1b, Orleans (Jr., Vanderbilt). **25.** Jared King, of, Falmouth (Jr., Kansas State). **26.** Dylan Covey, rhp, Orleans (Jr., San Diego). **27.** Aaron Brown, lhp/of, Chatham (So., Pepperdine). **28.** Hawtin Buchanan, rhp, Bourne (So., Mississippi). **29.** Daniel Aldrich, of, Orleans/ Cotuit (SIGNED: Yankees). **30.** Tyler Horan, of, Wareham (Jr., Virginia Tech).

INDIVIDUAL BATTING LEADERS
(MINIMUM 2.7 PLATE APPEARANCES PER TEAM GAME)

	AVG	G	AB	R	H	HR	RBI
Biondi, Patrick, Cotuit	.388	41	134	37	52	0	19
Aldrich, Daniel, Cotuit	.350	27	117	27	41	10	26
Schwarber, Kyle, Wareham	.343	44	172	30	59	8	38
Kemp, Tony, Cotuit	.343	35	108	27	37	3	29
Horan, Tyler , Wareham	.342	41	152	32	52	16	40
Travis, Sam, Yarmouth-Dennis	.339	44	168	32	57	4	35
Blair, Zak, Wareham	.338	44	148	29	50	2	20
Phel, Robert, Yarmouth-Dennis	.329	44	158	29	52	6	28
Gregor, Conrad, Orleans	.329	44	149	29	49	8	21
Dosch, Drew, Falmouth	.326	44	175	23	57	8	30

INDIVIDUAL PITCHING LEADERS
(MINIMUM 0.8 INNINGS PITCHED PER TEAM GAME)

	W	L	ERA	IP	H	BB	SO
Blair, Aaron, Yarmouth-Dennis	6	0	1.17	38	27	12	44
Manaea, Sean, Hyannis	5	1	1.22	52	21	7	85
Reed, A.J., Harwich	3	0	2.21	37	42	7	38
Connolly, Ryan, Cotuit	8	0	2.28	51	38	15	56
Windle, Tom, Brewster	3	2	2.35	38	29	7	47
Schlitter, Craig, Falmouth	5	2	2.72	43	36	8	41
Whitehead, David, Harwich	5	2	2.81	42	44	8	28
Ruxer, Jared, Wareham	1	4	2.95	37	52	15	34
Knapp, Rick, Yarmouth-Dennis	2	0	2.95	40	38	9	27
Green, Chad, Bourne	4	0	3.00	36	30	9	41

BOURNE

BATTING	AVG	AB	R	H	2B	3B	HR	RBI	SB
Hankins, Jordan	.600	5	0	3	1	0	0	0	0
Payne, Aaron	.340	47	9	16	4	0	0	7	4
Robbins, Mason	.316	117	14	37	8	1	7	19	1
Moran, Colin	.314	159	25	50	8	2	6	42	0
Murphy, John	.308	104	18	32	3	0	4	16	6

	AVG	AB	R	H	2B	3B	HR	RBI	SB
Reinheimer, Jack	.296	159	30	47	7	1	1	19	4
Mazzilli, LJ	.275	40	4	11	1	0	1	7	0
McDonald, Chase	.274	117	12	32	5	0	5	15	0
Patterson, Jordan	.263	133	10	35	5	0	1	8	3
Goldstein, Steve	.250	28	5	7	1	0	0	0	1
Leeson, Justin	.248	125	16	31	7	0	0	5	2
Ahmed, Mike	.236	157	29	37	1	1	5	16	2
Jackson, Joe	.213	89	16	19	4	1	1	8	0
Wynns, Austin	.207	82	10	17	4	0	0	4	0
Dezse, Josh	.205	39	5	8	1	0	2	8	0

PITCHING	W	L	ERA	G	SV	IP	H	BB	SO
Farrell, John	2	0	2.25	15	3	24	23	2	27
Young, Patrick	1	0	2.74	14	0	23	22	9	18
Giel, Timothy	1	1	2.79	11	1	29	23	7	25
Green, Chad	4	0	3.00	7	0	36	30	9	41
Taylor, Shane	0	2	3.00	9	0	18	16	10	20
Dezse, Josh	0	1	3.18	5	2	6	4	5	6
Long, Jaron	3	0	3.47	7	0	36	37	5	32
King, Tyler	1	2	3.57	13	0	23	18	10	23
Buchanan, Hawtin	1	2	3.78	14	3	17	8	17	23
Thompson, Jeff	2	3	4.11	8	0	35	34	11	33
Mayers, Mike	0	2	4.82	6	0	28	28	7	42
Donohue, Ryan	0	3	5.02	11	0	14	21	7	20
Keller, Jon	0	3	5.08	8	0	34	41	15	35
Moore, Brandon	1	3	5.73	9	0	22	24	10	21
Jones, Justin	0	0	8.04	9	0	16	25	6	13

BREWSTER

BATTING	AVG	AB	R	H	2B	3B	HR	RBI	SB
Healy, Ryon	.310	116	15	36	9	2	4	20	1
McNeil, Jeff	.301	136	22	41	7	2	0	13	5
Mitsui, Trevor	.298	141	20	42	11	0	5	26	0
Judge, Aaron	.270	100	18	27	3	0	5	16	6
Olinger, Dan	.265	113	10	30	3	1	0	14	2
Campbell, Derek	.250	112	15	28	6	1	4	8	7
Files, J.T.	.246	57	5	14	4	0	0	7	1
Forgione, Erik	.243	70	9	17	3	0	1	8	3
Monda, Jason	.240	104	19	25	6	0	2	9	5
Navin, Spencer	.233	60	12	14	2	0	3	9	1
Davis, James	.226	31	2	7	2	1	1	4	0
Kalish, Jake	.213	47	3	10	3	0	2	5	2
Williams, Kevin	.211	71	6	15	2	0	2	7	2
Smith, Tyler	.206	34	4	7	3	0	0	1	2
Nivins, Tanner	.203	64	5	13	1	0	2	6	2
Booth, Brett	.176	34	6	6	0	0	0	1	1
Lorenzen, Mike	.161	31	3	5	0	0	1	4	2
McDowell, Chase	.077	13	1	1	0	0	0	0	0

PITCHING	W	L	ERA	G	SV	IP	H	BB	SO
Windle, Tom	3	2	2.35	7	0	38	29	7	47
Moll, Sam	1	2	2.76	9	0	33	37	2	43
Rutter, Evan	1	0	3.03	17	0	30	23	6	36
Burchett, Michael	1	1	3.27	18	0	22	24	2	17
Kirkpatrick, Brady	1	2	3.51	8	0	33	34	15	20
Voth, Austin	1	3	4.29	7	0	36	27	20	52
Schoenrock, Erik	0	1	4.50	10	0	18	18	16	26
McCasland, Jake	0	0	4.77	15	1	17	24	3	12
Weaver, Luke	1	2	5.70	7	1	24	35	9	23
McDowell, Chase	2	1	5.82	10	0	17	17	7	17
Theofanopoulos, Michael	0	2	5.88	9	1	34	30	26	30
Leckenby, James	3	3	6.19	12	1	16	22	11	21
Kalish, Jake	2	3	6.87	8	1	18	22	3	17
Davis, Dylan	0	2	7.04	9	2	15	19	18	15
Spezial, Niko	1	1	8.49	13	0	23	30	15	18

CHATHAM

BATTING	AVG	AB	R	H	2B	3B	HR	RBI	SB
Knapp, Andrew	.293	140	27	41	13	0	8	29	1
Fransoso, Michael	.268	127	21	34	8	0	0	13	12
Lechich, Louie	.258	66	4	17	1	0	0	2	0
Valaika, Pat	.258	120	16	31	5	0	1	12	1
Carey, Dale	.240	121	18	29	7	1	1	11	7
Bourdon, Tom	.238	80	9	19	4	0	0	5	3
Engel, Adam	.229	157	24	36	2	3	1	14	15

	AVG	AB	R	H	2B	3B	HR	RBI	SB
Calbick, Alex	.210	138	17	29	6	0	5	19	0
Morgan, Chad	.208	77	6	16	2	1	1	8	0
Hennessy, John	.182	11	2	2	0	0	0	2	0
Martinez, John	.180	111	16	20	1	0	4	16	0
Brown, Aaron	.169	65	8	11	3	0	1	7	0
Flores, Dante	.154	52	8	8	2	0	0	3	0
Chittenden, Alex	.135	89	6	12	0	0	0	6	0

PITCHING	W	L	ERA	G	SV	IP	H	BB	SO
Wagner, Michael	2	2	1.57	7	0	34	26	14	38
Powers, Alex	0	0	1.69	10	0	11	7	7	11
Brown, Aaron	2	0	1.69	8	0	21	10	13	25
Atwood, Ryan	0	1	1.80	10	0	10	5	8	15
Parrish, Tate	1	3	2.46	12	0	15	14	8	18
Schultz, Jaime	2	0	2.82	15	1	22	15	11	40
Joyce, Jake	2	0	3.38	15	6	19	15	12	35
Lawrence, Thomas	2	1	3.55	10	0	38	42	7	35
Thompson, Ryan	1	3	3.86	7	0	33	33	9	31
Lechich, Louie	1	2	4.55	9	0	32	32	12	31
Litchfield, Jimmy	1	2	4.63	10	0	23	28	6	15
Kime, Dace	1	0	4.97	11	1	25	23	18	28
Stevens, Eric	1	4	5.16	9	0	30	29	9	26

COTUIT

BATTING	AVG	AB	R	H	2B	3B	HR	RBI	SB
Biondi, Patrick	.388	134	37	52	6	1	0	19	14
Aldirch, Daniel	.350	117	27	41	6	0	10	26	1
Kemp, Tony	.343	108	27	37	7	5	3	29	18
Roberts, James	.306	124	16	38	3	0	1	25	2
Valdez, Jacob	.295	78	15	23	3	1	2	17	0
Nelubowich, Adam	.288	170	25	49	14	1	4	20	4
May, Jacob	.283	159	23	45	5	0	1	8	14
Brockmeyer, Cael	.278	79	14	22	5	0	5	13	0
Kiene, Tim	.271	59	7	16	2	1	1	12	2
Smith, Derek	.167	60	5	16	3	0	0	5	2
Ford, Mike	.252	103	22	26	4	0	2	17	1
Garcia, Aramis	.250	100	13	25	6	0	3	14	1
Rhymes, Raph	.234	47	6	11	2	0	2	12	0
Rosa, Angel	.211	57	9	12	2	0	1	8	2
Bereszniewicz, Billy	.208	24	2	5	0	0	0	4	0

PITCHING	W	L	ERA	G	SV	IP	H	BB	SO
Ziomek, Kevin	3	0	1.27	5	0	28	22	6	36
Slania, Dan	2	0	1.52	21	10	30	18	4	39
Isaacs, Dusty	2	1	1.82	9	0	25	13	8	28
Broussard, Joe	1	0	1.83	8	0	20	14	10	23
Connolly, Ryan	8	0	2.28	23	4	51	38	15	56
Gomez, Mike	0	0	3.00	3	0	3	2	4	3
Stone, Jacob	4	1	3.64	13	2	17	22	7	18
Bixler, Brandon	0	0	3.98	11	0	20	13	19	36
Ramsey, Jordan	2	0	4.36	11	1	31	30	7	19
Griffin, Cameron	2	2	5.40	15	0	20	23	17	21
McCreery, Aadam	1	1	5.46	10	0	30	38	12	37
Bargeron, Zach	0	0	5.68	2	0	6	9	0	4

FALMOUTH

BATTING	AVG	AB	R	H	2B	3B	HR	RBI	SB
Colton, Jack	.600	5	1	3	0	0	0	3	0
Dosch, Drew	.326	175	23	57	13	0	8	30	3
King, Jared	.308	107	18	33	10	0	3	7	5
McGibbon, Jonathan	.280	157	18	44	13	1	2	20	3
Rodriguez, Jake	.273	121	15	33	8	1	4	17	4
O'Neill, Michael	.262	164	30	43	6	3	4	17	16
Turgeon, Casey	.261	111	18	29	5	0	3	16	1
Blanchard, Coty	.257	136	16	35	6	1	0	15	8
Ruchim, Kyle	.235	17	1	4	0	1	0	3	0
Ferriter, Billy	.229	153	22	35	2	0	2	8	15
Anderson, Austin	.214	112	19	24	6	0	5	21	0
Maldonado, Alex	.210	81	12	17	1	0	0	7	5
Eldredge, Kaiana	.205	78	14	16	3	0	3	16	3

PITCHING	W	L	ERA	G	SV	IP	H	BB	SO
Ruchim, Kyle	1	1	1.47	15	0	18	13	10	33
Paterson, Sam	0	0	1.48	19	0	24	13	11	34
Colella, John	0	2	2.16	19	2	25	19	7	30
Scribner, Troy	1	0	2.25	1	0	4	2	4	6
Marks, Bret	0	0	2.25	3	0	4	3	2	3
Wetzler, Ben	1	1	2.35	3	0	15	13	8	17

	W	L	ERA	G	SV	IP	H	BB	SO
Magliozzi, Johnny	0	2	2.60	13	2	17	12	9	25
Pohle, Kevin	1	1	2.70	2	0	10	8	4	9
Gonzales, Marco	1	0	2.70	2	0	10	9	0	13
Schlitter, Craig	5	2	2.72	8	0	43	36	8	41
Masek, Trey	3	3	3.18	7	0	40	37	15	47
Dziedzic, Jonathan	2	1	3.62	5	0	27	28	11	23
Simms, John	1	3	4.05	11	4	27	22	12	31
Farrell, Luke	1	0	4.91	6	0	7	8	4	9
Elam, Cale	0	0	6.61	13	2	16	26	4	11

HARWICH

BATTING	AVG	AB	R	H	2B	3B	HR	RBI	SB
Ervin, Phil	.323	130	29	42	5	1	11	31	10
Wilson, Austin	.312	77	18	24	4	1	6	20	3
Sciacca, Tyler	.293	75	16	22	2	1	3	12	6
Jagielo, Eric	.291	158	27	46	4	2	13	29	1
Austin, Brett	.276	98	18	27	9	0	3	13	4
Jones, Jacoby	.266	139	27	37	5	2	5	17	7
Reida, Matt	.258	155	17	40	4	2	3	16	8
Ragira, Brian	.235	155	17	40	4	2	3	16	8
Dove, Sam	.218	142	25	31	5	2	4	12	9
Connolly, Mike	.188	64	6	12	0	0	2	8	1
Irby, C.K.	.188	16	2	3	1	0	1	3	0
Reed, A.J.	.176	34	1	6	0	0	0	2	0
Hageman, Justin	.167	6	1	0	0	0	1	0	0
Smith, Austen	.163	123	14	20	0	0	2	13	1
VanBoom, Wes	.150	20	1	3	1	0	0	1	0
Evans, Zane	.128	47	3	6	1	0	1	4	1

PITCHING	W	L	ERA	G	SV	IP	H	BB	SO
Connolly, Mike	1	0	0.00	2	0	3	1	2	4
Ervin, Phil	1	0	0.00	1	0	3	3	0	3
Gordon, Grant	1	0	0.50	12	0	18	15	4	26
Burgess, Tyler	0	0	2.16	15	4	17	12	8	24
Reed, A.J.	3	0	2.21	7	0	27	42	7	38
Camacho, Vladimir	0	0	2.31	10	2	12	9	7	12
Meurer, Matt	0	0	2.35	3	0	8	9	3	2
Whitehead, David	5	2	2.81	8	0	42	44	8	28
Woodruff, Brandon	4	2	3.38	10	0	32	31	9	30
Irby, C.K.	2	4	3.51	16	2	26	20	13	41
Campbell, Eddie	3	2	4.50	8	0	36	33	12	44
Evans, Zane	1	0	4.66	10	4	10	6	5	14
Littrell, Corey	1	2	5.06	7	0	32	34	11	45
Nuss, Garrett	0	0	5.28	7	0	15	20	7	14
Labitan, Clark	2	1	5.66	14	0	21	23	8	20
Mitchell, Evan	0	0	5.79	12	0	9	5	13	14
Bourgeois, Joey	0	0	6.00	2	0	3	5	0	2
Skoglund, Eric	2	0	6.30	11	0	20	22	11	15
Hageman, Justin	0	2	6.87	12	0	18	27	9	22
Pitts, Cole	0	0	8.25	9	0	12	17	6	17

HYANNIS

BATTING	AVG	AB	R	H	2B	3B	HR	RBI	SB
Torres, Daniel	.400	5	1	2	0	0	0	0	0
Wilkerson, Steve	.308	26	2	8	2	0	0	2	4
Zebedis, Brad	.303	165	20	50	8	0	4	23	3
Trinkwon, Brandon	.301	166	27	50	10	0	6	33	3
Garver, Mitchell	.298	151	19	45	12	0	4	28	3
Doran, Brett-Michael	.294	119	22	35	9	0	2	21	8
Jose, Dominic	.272	125	29	34	6	1	6	12	12
Zeutenhorst, Taylor	.247	93	11	23	5	0	0	8	5
Callaway, Will	.247	73	9	18	4	1	1	13	5
Alvord, Zach	.236	106	9	25	6	0	1	8	0
Fortunato, Pat	.225	40	5	9	2	0	1	4	3
Austin, Blake	.225	138	14	31	4	0	4	16	2
Fultz, Ben	.222	9	1	2	0	0	0	0	0
Zellers, Zac	.217	69	15	15	1	0	2	6	9

PITCHING	W	L	ERA	G	SV	IP	H	BB	SO
Wijas, Walter	1	0	0.92	16	1	20	12	6	13
Manaea, Sean	5	1	1.22	9	0	52	21	7	85
Hoffman, Jeff	2	1	2.40	6	0	30	21	10	30
Silverstein, Scott	0	1	2.53	3	0	21	22	3	11
Eck, Eric	1	1	2.57	3	0	7	4	0	7
Garner, David	2	4	3.12	10	0	43	37	12	41
Smithmyer, Andrew	0	2	3.12	13	2	26	23	13	34
Maurer, Matt	1	1	4.15	11	0	17	17	8	13

	W	L	ERA	G	SV	IP	H	BB	SO
Walker, Josh	2	1	5.14	5	0	21	23	6	15
Firth, Scott	0	1	5.59	2	0	10	8	8	11
Smith, Gage	1	1	5.92	20	0	24	36	3	17
Miller, Peter	1	1	7.00	10	0	18	25	6	23
Barnette, Tyler	1	4	7.14	8	0	29	39	18	14

ORLEANS

BATTING	AVG	AB	R	H	2B	3B	HR	RBI	SB
Gregor, Conrad	.329	149	29	49	7	1	8	21	7
Gragnani, Reed	.291	127	14	37	4	1	1	13	3
LaBruna, Angelo	.260	123	13	32	3	1	5	16	1
Hernandez, Jake	.260	100	17	26	5	0	5	18	0
Kitamura, Piikea	.250	172	25	43	4	0	1	23	2
Toadvine, Derek	.243	111	14	27	4	0	5	5	9
Kulp, Cody	.234	128	19	30	2	0	6	26	1
Gonzalez, Jay	.233	90	15	21	2	1	0	3	8
Riddle, J.T.	.232	151	27	35	7	2	2	15	1
Rossiter, Max	.208	96	9	20	3	0	1	11	1
Ficociello, Dominic	.196	51	3	10	0	0	1	5	0
Wise, Jake	.188	16	0	3	0	0	0	0	0
Brown, Kevin	.171	82	6	14	4	0	1	11	2
Montville, Michael	.165	85	14	14	3	0	7	14	2

PITCHING	W	L	ERA	G	SV	IP	H	BB	SO
Troupe, Matt	0	0	0.00	2	0	3	2	2	5
Crockett, Kyle	1	1	0.75	17	6	24	18	3	28
Arakawa, Jarrett	3	2	1.82	7	0	35	22	2	28
Clark, Dylan	3	0	1.93	10	0	23	15	3	21
Christensen, Pat	2	1	1.98	23	0	27	25	6	37
Whitson, Karsten	0	0	2.70	2	0	3	3	0	5
Reed, Jimmy	2	1	3.32	8	0	41	41	11	43
Covey, Dylan	3	1	3.86	13	0	26	27	11	16
Johnson, Chase	2	1	3.98	20	1	20	23	7	23
Boyd, Matt	2	1	4.33	11	0	27	23	7	39
Grundy, Jerad	1	2	4.45	7	0	30	27	9	32
Kubitza, Austin	1	3	5.06	11	0	27	28	12	17
McNitt, Brandon	1	3	5.21	8	0	28	30	8	19
Pfeifer, Philip	1	2	5.95	19	0	20	19	12	24
Hunter, Kyle	0	2	6.18	10	0	28	34	9	28
Farris, James	0	1	6.92	4	0	13	14	3	12

WAREHAM

BATTING	AVG	AB	R	H	2B	3B	HR	RBI	SB
Schwarber, Kyle	.343	172	30	59	10	2	8	38	4
Horan, Tyler	.342	152	32	52	7	1	16	40	3
McFarland, Tyler	.309	81	14	25	1	1	1	9	1
Sturgeon, Cole	.297	182	38	54	8	2	5	15	6
Hyde, Mott	.281	160	29	45	9	0	6	26	8
Palka, Daniel	.272	158	25	43	6	0	11	35	4
Sullivan, Ryan	.237	38	11	9	2	0	0	4	0
Gross, Ethan	.230	139	21	32	6	2	0	13	6
Ross, Tyler	.226	124	9	28	4	0	1	14	0
Johnson, Claude	.224	58	3	13	4	0	1	9	1
Sheridan, John	.200	5	1	1	0	0	0	2	0
Uxa, Logan	.188	69	7	13	3	0	1	2	0
DeMuth, Dustin	.187	75	4	14	4	0	0	4	0
Bishop, Andrew	.160	25	3	4	1	0	0	2	1

PITCHING	W	L	ERA	G	SV	IP	H	BB	SO
Palka, Daniel	1	0	0.00	1	0	3	1	3	1
Huffman, Chris	0	0	0.00	3	0	6	7	1	7
Suggs, Colby	1	0	1.37	13	2	20	9	8	30
Sturgeon, Cole	2	0	1.69	7	1	11	7	4	11
Holder, Jonathan	3	1	1.99	14	2	23	23	11	33
Stoops, Dylan	0	0	2.08	1	0	4	1	7	4
Camacho, Vladimir	0	0	2.08	5	0	4	1	2	8
Graveman, Kendall	2	1	2.22	6	0	24	29	4	26
Ruxer, Jared	1	4	2.95	8	0	37	52	15	34
Rumbelow, Nicholas	1	0	3.51	17	0	26	19	12	43
Kuntz, Brad	1	2	3.86	7	0	37	40	13	42
Chapman, Clay	2	2	4.93	18	1	35	38	18	27
Wade, Konnor	0	1	4.97	8	1	13	12	3	6
Milewski, Ryan	0	0	5.19	5	0	9	12	1	4
Shepard, Frederick	2	3	5.35	8	0	34	32	19	33

YARMOUTH-DENNIS

BATTING	AVG	AB	R	H	2B	3B	HR	RBI	SB
Mickan, Morgan	.438	32	8	14	3	0	2	9	3

	AVG	AB	R	H	2B	3B	HR	RBI	SB
Travis, Sam	.339	168	32	57	12	0	4	35	5
Blair, Aaron	.338	148	29	50	5	1	2	20	8
Pehl, Robert	.329	158	29	52	12	0	6	38	3
Mathis, Tanner	.316	114	20	36	5	1	0	8	9
Shafer, Justin	.315	73	13	23	4	0	2	16	4
Blandino, Alex	.312	138	30	43	8	1	3	24	1
McHugh, Sean	.292	65	16	19	3	0	2	8	0
Taylor, Wayne	.292	89	15	26	3	1	2	13	1
Asuaje, Carlos	.280	175	35	49	12	2	2	26	5
Tobias, Josh	.250	48	6	12	2	0	1	7	1
Dwyer, Sean	.243	103	16	25	4	1	4	12	1
Diekroger, Danny	.200	20	1	4	2	0	1	2	1
Campbell, Robby	.167	6	3	1	0	0	0	0	1
McGovern, Matt	.138	29	5	4	1	0	0	3	1

PITCHING	W	L	ERA	G	SV	IP	H	BB	SO
Blair, Aaron	6	0	1.17	8	1	38	27	12	44
Denato, Joey	3	1	2.15	11	1	29	20	12	34
Knapp, Rick	2	0	2.95	10	1	40	38	9	27
Hatcher, Preston	0	1	3.00	14	0	15	10	8	18
Bowen, Andrew	0	0	3.21	5	1	14	10	2	9
Thurman, Andrew	3	3	3.23	7	0	39	35	11	49
Verbitsky, Bryan	1	2	4.15	15	4	22	16	10	35
Lively, Ben	0	2	4.15	6	0	30	28	10	43
Gonzalez, Alex	3	2	5.28	7	0	29	40	9	25
Anderson, Chris	0	2	6.34	8	0	33	43	12	42
Gilbert, Brian	2	1	6.58	13	1	26	28	5	31
Hoffman, Johnny	2	1	7.02	12	1	17	24	7	11
Lopez, Jose	1	1	10.8	3	0	3	6	0	3
Linney, Spenser	0	0	10.8	8	0	12	13	11	10

ALASKA LEAGUE

FINAL STANDINGS	W	L	PCT	GB
Anchorage Glacier Pilots	26	14	.650	—
Anchorage Bucs	21	19	.525	5
Peninsula Oilers	21	19	.525	5
Alaska Goldpanners	18	21	.462	7 ½
Chugiak Chinooks	17	22	.436	8 ½
Matsu Miners	16	24	.400	10

TOP 10 PROSPECTS: 1. Braden Shipley, rhp, Anchorage Bucs (Jr., Nevada). **2.** Kyle Freeland, lhp, Anchorage Glacier Pilots (So., Evansville). **3.** Nigel Nootbaar, rhp, Peninsula (So., Southern California). **4.** Trey Teakell, rhp, Anchorage Glacier Pilots (R-So., Texas Christian). **5.** Tyler Spoon, of, Anchorage Glacier Pilots (R-Fr., Arkansas). **6.** Ian Miller, of, Mat-Su (Jr., Wagner). **7.** Jordan Luplow, of, Anchorage Glacier Pilots (So., Fresno State). **8.** Jon Maciel, rhp, Peninsula (Jr., Long Beach State). **9.** Chase Compton, 1b, Anchorage Bucs (Jr., Louisiana-Lafayette). **10.** Jordan Mills, lhp, Peninsula (Jr., St. Mary's)

INDIVIDUAL BATTING LEADERS
(MINIMUM 2.7 PLATE APPEARANCES PER TEAM GAME)

	AVG	AB	R	H	2B	3B	HR	RBI	SB
Freeman, Clint, Miners	.379	145	26	55	14	1	3	24	4
Compton, Chase, Bucs	.377	130	31	49	9	2	7	19	3
Miller, Blake, Goldpanners	.365	115	24	42	7	0	5	27	3
Casey, Kevin, Goldpanners	.356	101	23	36	12	2	6	26	0
Kremer, Jeff, Glacier Pilots	.347	95	13	33	3	2	1	16	3
Boyd, B.J., Miners	.340	106	18	36	4	1	0	11	24
Kwak, Kris, Chinooks	.338	139	24	47	9	0	6	26	0
Shyrock, Tyler, Chinooks	.336	107	21	36	11	1	0	5	2
Susdorf, Danny, Bucs	.329	143	27	47	7	2	3	26	18
Ferguson, Collin, Bucs	.319	116	23	37	7	0	6	24	1

INDIVIDUAL PITCHING LEADERS
(MINIMUM 0.8 INNINGS PITCHED PER TEAM GAME)

	W	L	ERA	G	SV	IP	ER	BB	SO
Freeland, Kyle, Pilots	5	0	0.72	7	0	38	3	13	35
Calhoun, Jay, Miners	3	0	1.38	6	0	33	5	7	15
Grist, Scott, Bucs	4	0	1.91	9	0	42	9	11	33
Rhame, Jacob, Bucs	3	0	2.06	6	0	35	8	7	32
Maciel, Jon, Oilers	4	2	2.14	8	0	46	11	6	36
Johns, Sam, Pilots	3	2	2.46	7	0	33	9	11	24
Theodore, Mike, Bucs	1	2	2.79	7	0	42	13	8	30
Wilson, Garrett, Goldpanners	4	1	2.96	10	0	46	15	10	18
Mills, Jordan, Oilers	3	3	3.20	8	0	45	16	13	37
Teakell, Trey, Pilots	3	0	3.89	8	0	46	20	10	47

ATLANTIC COLLEGIATE LEAGUE

WOLFF	W	L	PCT	GB
Trenton Generals	27	11	.705	—
Quakertown Blazers	21	19	.525	7
North Jersey Eagles	19	20	.487	8 ½
Allentown Railers	18	22	.450	10
Jersey Pilots	17	22	.438	10 ½
Lehigh Valley Catz	16	24	.400	12

KAISER	W	L	PCT	GB
Staten Island Tide	27	10	.730	—
New York Atlantics	24	14	.632	3 ½
Long Island Shamrocks	13	21	.382	12 ½
Nassau Collegians	7	26	.212	18

HAMPTON	W	L	PCT	GB
Shelter Island Bucks	23	17	.575	—
North Fork Ospreys	22	17	.564	½
Southampton Breakers	21	18	.538	1 ½
Riverhead Tomcats	21	19	.525	2
C. Moriches Battlecats	20	20	.500	3
Westhampton Aviators	18	22	.450	5
Sag Habor Whalers	14	26	.350	9

PLAYOFFS—North Jersey defeated New York in championship game. **TOP 10 PROSPECTS: 1.** Paul Paez, lhp, Southampton (So., Rio Hondo, Calif., JC). **2.** Kyle McGowin, rhp, Sag Harbor (Jr., Savannah State). **3.** Esteban Gomez, 1b, Westhampton (Jr., St. Thomas, Fla.). **4.** Patrick Peterson, lhp, Southampton (So., Temple). **5.** Eric Peterson, rhp, Southampton (So., Temple). **6.** Trevor Simms, rhp, Shelter Island (So., Weatherford, Texas, JC). **7.** Brenton Allen, of, Southampton (Jr., UCLA). **8.** Thomas Roulis, 2b/ss, Shelter Island (So., Dartmouth). **9.** Steven Goldstein, of, Long Island (So., Stony Brook). BCharlie Curl, 2b/ss, Sag Harbor (Jr., Texas A&M).

INDIVIDUAL BATTING LEADERS
(MINIMUM 74 PLATE APPEARANCES)

BATTING	AVG	AB	R	H	2B	3B	HR	RBI	SB
Solomeno, Joe, C. Moriches	.421	145	27	61	14	0	7	53	1
Kelso, Jesse, Allentown	.404	99	25	40	13	2	1	28	5
Kerr, Daniel, North Fork	.404	104	24	42	5	0	3	19	5
Roulis, Thomas, Shelter Island	.399	148	41	59	10	1	2	29	24
Iturrey, Daniel, Lehigh	.389	95	22	37	5	1	0	19	10
Smith, Josh, Riverhead	.381	97	30	37	10	0	1	9	18
Selden, Chris, Staten Island	.380	129	30	49	8	3	2	39	9
Lepre, Craig, Quakertown	.377	77	17	29	5	0	0	14	1
Kelly, Scott, Trenton	.376	125	32	47	6	3	1	15	24
Brantley, Cliff, Staten Island	.376	125	38	47	12	0	1	16	18

INDIVIDUAL PITCHING LEADERS
(MINIMUM 35 INNINGS)

PITCHING	W	L	ERA	G	SV	IP	H	BB	SO
Paez, Paul, Southampton	7	2	1.65	14	1	60	35	5	23
Anastasi, Rich, North Jersey	7	0	2.11	16	2	43	33	13	57
Maguire, Robert, Staten Island	5	1	2.52	7	0	36	26	14	34
St. Lawrence, David, North Fork	5	1	2.53	7	0	46	38	9	57
Singer, Jeff, Trenton	4	1	2.62	9	0	45	43	16	32
McGowin, Kyle, Sag Harbor	3	2	2.73	8	0	56	50	9	65
Martin, Mike, New York	3	2	2.83	9	2	35	30	12	49
England, Chris, Shelter Island	3	3	2.85	10	0	47	52	18	26
Klever, Scott, Riverhead	3	3	3.09	9	0	47	53	16	27
Jensen, Josh, Trenton	5	1	3.21	8	0	42	50	20	43

CAL RIPKEN COLLEGIATE LEAGUE

FINAL STANDINGS	W	L	PCT	GB
Rockville Express	30	11	.732	—
Baltimore Redbirds	28	13	.683	2
Bethesda Big Train	25	16	.610	5
Vienna River Dogs	23	18	.561	7
Youses Orioles	20	20	.50	9 ½
Alexandria Aces	20	21	.488	10
D.C. Grays	18	21	.462	11
Herndon Braves	15	24	.385	14
Southern Maryland Nationals	15	26	.366	15
Silver Spring Takoma Thunderbolts	9	33	.214	21 1/2

PLAYOFFS— Baltimore defeated Bethesda in the championship of a four-team, double-elimination tournament. **TOP 10 PROSPECTS: 1.** K.J. Hockaday, 3b, Youse's Orioles (So.,

Maryland). **2.** Mark Zagunis, c, Baltimore (So., Virginia Tech). **3.** Hunter Renfroe, of, Bethesda (Jr., Mississippi State). **4.** Pat Blair, ss/2b, Baltimore (Sr., Wake Forest). **5.** Kevin Mooney, rhp, Youse's Orioles (Fr., Maryland). **6.** Luke Lowery, c, Vienna (Fr., East Carolina). **7.** Joe Harvey, rhp, Baltimore (R-So., Pittsburgh). **8.** Mike Costello, rhp, Herndon (R-So., Radford). **9.** John-Austin Sheppard, rhp, Southern Maryland (Jr., Tusculum, Tenn.). **10.** Joey Donino, rhp, D.C. (Jr., Columbia).

INDIVIDUAL BATTING LEADERS
(MINIMUM 2.7 PLATE APPEARANCES PER TEAM GAME)

	AVG	AB	R	H	2B	3B	HR	RBI	SB
Williams, Bret, Vienna	.433	141	29	61	12	0	6	38	2
Vasquez, James, Herndon	.418	110	33	46	11	0	12	42	2
Hendriks, Brendan, Bethesda	.400	160	38	64	17	2	6	40	1
Bzozowski, Chris, Silver Spring	.377	146	30	55	15	0	7	30	0
Beaubien, John, D.C.	.366	134	47	49	11	4	16	53	4
Renfroe, Hunter, Bethesda	.366	134	47	49	11	4	16	53	7
Cole, Johnny, Rockville	.362	141	24	51	11	1	4	43	1
Higginbotham, Trent, Vienna	.349	126	31	44	15	2	6	37	0
Hockaday, K.J., Youses	.346	133	22	46	11	1	1	36	6

INDIVIDUAL PITCHING LEADERS
(MINIMUM 0.8 INNINGS PITCHED PER TEAM GAME)

	W	L	ERA	G	SV	IP	H	BB	SO
Taylor, Corey, Baltimore	6	1	2.76	9	0	49	38	15	51
Doran, Ryan, Bethesda	3	2	2.79	8	1	42	35	8	44
Logan, Bo, Bethesda	5	1	3.13	7	0	37	32	13	32
Vanderplas, Joseph, Vienna	6	0	3.23	9	0	39	36	13	35
Poretz, Austin, S. Maryland	3	3	3.23	7	0	39	37	15	26
McHale, Bryan, S. Maryland	0	4	3.71	10	0	53	58	20	41
Park, D.J., Youses	4	1	3.79	11	2	40	40	11	36
Bowie, Michael, S. Maryland	2	1	3.92	9	0	44	44	24	51
Milon, Colin, Alexandria	2	4	4.01	8	0	43	50	15	49
Louscher, Blake, D.C.	4	1	4.02	20	0	31	35	19	29

CALIFORNIA COLLEGIATE LEAGUE

FINAL STANDINGS	W	L	PCT	GB
Santa Barbara Foresters	20	10	.667	—
San Luis Obispo Blues	20	10	.667	—
Academy Barons	14	16	.467	6
Conejo Oaks	12	18	.400	8
Orange County Brewers	12	18	.400	8
Team Vegas Baseball Club	12	18	.400	8

TOP 10 PROSPECTS: 1. Cody Dickson, lhp, Santa Barbara (Jr., Sam Houston State). **2.** Daniel Mengden, rhp/c, San Luis Obispo (So., Texas A&M). **3.** Gandy Stubblefield, rhp, San Luis Obispo (So., Texas A&M). **4.** John Beck, rhp, Santa Barbara (Jr., Texas-Arlington). **5.** Nick Palewicz, rhp, Santa Barbara (Jr., Washington). **6.** Dylan Munger, lhp, San Luis Obispo (So., Alabama-Birmingham). **7.** Albert Minnis, lhp, Santa Barbara (Jr., Wichita State). **8.** Matt Shortall, of, San Luis Obispo (Jr., Texas-Arlington). **9.** Jacob Felts, c, Santa Barbara (Jr., Texas). **10.** Marvin Campbell, 1b/of, Team Vegas (Sr., Hawaii Pacific).

INDIVIDUAL BATTING LEADERS
(MINIMUM 85 AT-BATS)

	AVG	AB	R	H	2B	3B	HR	RBI	SB
Martin, Michael, Team Vegas	.426	141	36	60	9	3	0	22	21
Campbell, Marvin, Team Vegas	.396	91	25	36	6	2	5	29	2
Hansen, Taylor, Conejo	.358	120	26	43	10	3	0	23	4
O'Neal, Austin, Orange County	.349	109	25	38	6	1	4	19	3
Shortall, Matt, SLO	.336	116	23	39	13	2	4	25	3
Ocello, Evan, Conejo	.320	103	22	33	3	2	1	17	16
Greager, Bryce, Team Vegas	.319	119	25	38	8	2	4	25	2
Sewald, John, Team Vegas	.316	95	19	30	2	1	0	20	11
Micken, Morgan, Orange County	.312	93	28	29	5	0	3	18	17
Grisham, Austin, SLO	.309	181	39	56	4	2	1	33	24

INDIVIDUAL PITCHING LEADERS
(MINIMUM 23 INNINGS PITCHED)

	W	L	ERA	SV	IP	H	BB	SO
McGreevy, T.J., Santa Barbara	3	1	0.75	0	24	24	6	19
Girodo, Chad, SLO	1	0	0.99	1	27	16	3	44
Bellow, Kirby, Santa Barbara	1	1	1.48	0	24	17	13	26
Lemke, Hunter, Santa Barbara	1	0	1.48	12	24	21	4	34
Ray, Parker, SLO	1	2	1.82	5	30	15	21	58
Rieser, Chad, Orange County	1	0	1.84	1	24	18	8	20
Munger, Dylan, SLO	4	0	1.91	0	38	29	9	38

McCarthy, Ian, Santa Barbara	4	2	1.93	0	42	33	11	39
Minnis, Albert, Santa Barbara	1	0	2.10	0	26	20	6	32
Delange, Kory, SLO	4	2	2.16	0	50	45	20	59

COASTAL PLAIN LEAGUE

East	W	L	PCT	GB
Edenton Steamers	36	17	.679	—
Fayetteville SwampDogs	33	20	.623	3
Wilmington Sharks	29	23	.558	6 ½
Peninsula Pilots	26	28	.482	10 ½
Morehead City Marlins	25	30	.455	12
Petersburg Generals	22	33	.400	15
Wilson Tobs	21	34	.382	16

WEST	W	L	PCT	GB
Forest City Owls	34	22	.607	—
Columbia Blowfish	32	23	.582	1 ½
Asheboro Copperheads	27	27	.500	6
Florence RedWolves	25	30	.455	8 ½
Thomasville HiToms	24	30	.444	9
Martinsville Mustangs	24	31	.436	9 ½
Gastonia Grizzlies	23	33	.411	11

PLAYOFFS— Columbia defeated Fayetteville 2-1 in a best-of-three championship series of an eight-team tournament.
TOP 10 PROSPECTS: 1. Andrew Istler, rhp, Wilson (So., Duke). **2.** Reed Harper, ss, Fayetteville (Sr., Austin Peay State). **3.** Jake Stone, 3b, Martinsville (Sr., Tennessee Wesleyan). **4.** Chris McCue, rhp, Thomasville (So., North Carolina). **5.** Nathan Chong, of, Forest City (Jr., Presbyterian). **6.** Andrew Brockett, rhp, Wilmington (Jr., Richmond). **7.** Zack Houchins, ss/3b, Wilson (Jr., East Carolina). **8.** Dale Innes, rhp, Gastonia (Jr., UNC Pembroke). **9.** Blaze Tart, rhp, Wilmington (R-Jr., UNC Wilmington). **10.** Gunnar Heidt, ss, Forest City (So., College of Charleston).

INDIVIDUAL BATTING LEADERS
(MINIMUM 149 PLATE APPEARANCES)

	AVG	AB	R	H	2B	3B	HR	RBI	SB
Stone, Jake, Martinsville	.375	120	19	45	13	1	3	19	5
Kraemer, Koby, Edenton	.371	124	26	46	9	0	6	24	8
Harper, Reed, Fayetteville	.370	154	26	57	8	2	2	31	12
Tauchman, Mike, Fayetteville	.351	148	38	52	5	2	3	30	35
Camporeale, Michael, Edenton	.340	162	33	55	19	0	9	42	11
Close, Alex, Forest City	.329	155	26	51	13	0	4	30	0
White, Tyler, Gastonia	.319	191	36	61	13	0	5	38	2
Toole, Eric, Petersburg	.317	145	18	46	2	1	0	20	17
Chong, Nathan Forest City	.317	183	38	58	10	1	5	32	16
Crowe, J.D., Florence	.316	174	23	55	9	1	0	16	3

INDIVIDUAL PITCHING LEADERS
(MINIMUM 42 INNINGS)

	W	L	ERA	G	SV	IP	H	BB	SO
Istler, Andrew, Wilson	3	0	0.78	6	0	46	19	12	39
Gardner, Mike, Asheboro	5	0	1.28	12	0	42	28	16	35
Vaughn, Derek, Florence	1	3	1.29	10	3	42	30	12	31
Somsen, Layne, Fayetteville	5	0	1.29	7	0	42	18	15	47
Caravella, Alex, Petersburg	4	2	1.62	9	0	50	34	21	57
Wainman, Matt, Morehead City	2	3	1.78	10	0	51	49	6	56
Lomascolo, Nick, Forest City	5	1	1.80	8	0	50	36	20	43
Tuttle, John, Asheboro	2	4	1.83	17	3	44	35	15	37
Smith, Danny, Fayetteville	6	0	1.95	7	0	51	44	7	20
Whitley, Ross, Wilmington	5	3	2.14	9	0	46	26	28	39

FLORIDA COLLEGIATE SUMMER LEAGUE

	W	L	T	PCT	GB
Leesburg Lightning	26	15	0	.634	—
Winter Park Diamond Dawgs	25	15	0	.625	1/2
DeLand Suns	23	17	0	.575	2 ½
Orlando Monarchs	19	21	0	.475	6 ½
Sanford River Rats	17	23	0	.425	8 ½
Orlando Freedom	10	29	0	.256	15

PLAYOFFS— DeLand defeated Leesburg in championship of a five-team playoff.
TOP 10 PROSPECTS: 1. Nick Gonzalez, lhp, Sanford (Jr., South Florida). **2.** Daniel Sweet, of, Winter Park (Fr., Polk State JC, Fla.). **3.** David Lee, of, Orlando (Sr., Bethune-Cookman). **4.** Trey Norris, of, Leesburg (So., Polk State JC, Fla.). **5.** Darryl Knight, c, Orlando (So., Seminole State JC, Fla.). **6.** Drew Jackson, rhp, DeLand (So., Stetson). **7.** Mike Danner, 1b/lf,

Winter Park (Jr., Tampa). **8.** Mike Sylvestri, rhp, Winter Park (Sr., Florida Atlantic). **9.** Cary Baxter, rhp, Winter Park (R-So., Alabama). **10.** Mike Compton, rhp, DeLand (So., Florida State).

INDIVIDUAL BATTING LEADERS
(MINIMUM 2.7 PLATE APPEARANCES PER TEAM GAME)

	AVG	AB	R	H	2B	3B	HR	RBI	SB
Nelson, Mark, Orlando Freedom	.370	135	29	50	16	3	3	28	2
Teaf, Kyle, Leesburg	.354	127	40	45	8	2	0	25	11
Danner, Michael, Winter Park	.349	149	39	52	7	3	8	29	32
Curcio, Keith, Sanford	.339	121	22	41	11	1	4	31	4
Adametz, Bryan, DeLand	.336	110	23	37	9	0	3	16	9
Rocklein, Tyler, Winter Park	.331	139	28	46	9	3	4	41	23
Hindmon, Erik, Leesburg	.325	117	28	38	7	0	4	16	0
Lemon, Jeff, DeLand	.322	146	27	47	13	0	0	20	4
Stewart-Pagani, A., Orlando Mon.	.319	119	26	38	3	0	0	10	4
Durham, Chase, Leesburg	.314	121	28	38	8	1	4	27	1

INDIVIDUAL PITCHING LEADERS
(MINIMUM 0.8 INNINGS PITCHED PER TEAM GAME)

	W	L	ERA	G	SV	IP	H	BB	SO
Incinelli, Evan, Winter Park	5	1	1.66	10	0	38	24	14	31
Monkman, Reily, DeLand	1	1	1.95	22	6	37	36	12	37
Davis, Jonah, Leesburg	5	1	2.57	21	1	35	39	10	18
Sylvestri, Michael, Winter Park	4	1	2.65	8	0	34	34	10	38
Kovacs, Nic, Leesburg	6	1	3.13	10	0	55	55	10	40
Gay, Drew, Orlando Monarchs	5	2	3.43	8	0	42	40	18	31
Meiers, Jake, DeLand	4	1	3.45	9	0	44	48	13	31
Mueller, Brett, DeLand	3	2	3.66	10	0	32	33	14	30
Hukari, Harrison, Sanford	0	3	3.93	9	0	37	44	20	33
Baxter, Cary, Winter Park	3	2	3.97	9	0	48	42	25	55

FUTURES COLLEGE BASEBALL LEAGUE

FINAL STANDINGS	W	L	PCT	GB
Nashua Silver Knights	39	13	.750	—
North Shore Navigators	32	20	.615	7
Torrington Titans	29	22	.569	9 ½
Brockton Rox	30	23	.566	9 ½
Pittsfield Suns	27	25	.519	12
Martha's Vineyard Sharks	26	27	.491	13 ½
Old Orchard Beach Raging Tide	23	30	.434	16 ½
Seacoast Mavericks	20	33	.377	19 ½
Wachusett Dirt Dawgs	9	42	.176	29 ½

PLAYOFFS—Nashua defeated North Shore in championship of a four-team, double-elimination tournament.
TOP 10 PROSPECTS: 1. Rhett Wiseman, of, Brockton (Fr., Vanderbilt). **2.** Tyler Bashlor, rhp, Torrington (So., South Georgia JC). **3.** Chris Shaw, 1b, Nashua (Fr., Boston College). **4.** Mike Joseph, rhp, Torrington (SIGNED: Orioles). **5.** Corey Stump, lhp, North Shore (So., Florida). **6.** Donnie Hissa, rhp, Seacoast (Jr., Notre Dame). **7.** Bryan Langlois, of, Seacoast (R-So., Pepperdine). **8.** Saige Jenco, of, Old Orchard Beach (Fr., Virginia Tech). **9.** Conor Bierfeldt, of, Torrington (Sr., Western Connecticut State). **10.** Jon Minucci, of, Nashua (Sr., Southern New Hampshire).

INDIVIDUAL BATTING LEADERS
(MINIMUM 2.7 PLATE APPEARANCES PER TEAM GAME)

	AVG	AB	R	H	2B	3B	HR	RBI	SB
Stenhouse, Kevin, Seacoast	.393	163	40	64	13	0	5	29	10
Ryan, Sean, Brockton	.356	180	25	64	10	6	0	25	19
Vosler, Jason, Old Orchard	.343	172	22	59	12	0	3	23	0
Gillis, Logan, Nashua	.333	201	43	67	8	0	6	32	12
Bierfeldt, Conor, Torrington	.329	152	29	50	15	1	9	39	3
Katsiroubas, James, Nashua	.329	158	38	52	8	1	4	25	4
Jensen, Eric, Martha's Vineyard	.327	156	23	51	8	0	1	23	13
Serino, Tony, North Shore	.325	154	25	50	6	0	0	19	8
Hendricks, Tim, North Shore	.323	155	28	50	7	2	1	24	6
Perna, Vito, Brockton	.320	147	18	47	5	0	3	23	0

INDIVIDUAL PITCHING LEADERS
(MINIMUM 0.8 INNINGS PITCHED PER TEAM GAME)

	W	L	ERA	G	SV	IP	H	BB	SO
Dierke, Tyler, Torrington	7	1	0.61	9	0	59	38	8	47
Palioca, Alec, Torrington	5	2	1.07	9	0	59	41	14	57
Poore, Nick, Nashua	6	1	1.28	9	0	49	43	12	44
Good, Christopher, Nashua	5	2	1.58	9	0	51	37	19	33
Rey, Lamarre Nashua	4	1	1.60	9	0	45	37	22	30
Hissa, Donald, Seacoast	4	0	1.62	8	0	50	39	17	35

Morency, Alek, Nashua	4	1	1.69	10	0	48	35	17	53
Gruntkosky, Joe, North Shore	3	1	1.85	9	0	54	46	14	37
Brockett, Ryan, Martha's Vineyard	3	2	2.02	11	0	58	46	19	56
Bradstreet, Mike, Martha's Vineyard	7	2	2.14	11	0	76	59	13	59

GREAT LAKES LEAGUE

NORTH	W	L	PCT	GB
Cincinnati Steam	24	15	.615	—
Lima Locos	24	15	.615	—
Licking County Settlers	24	15	.615	—
Southern Ohio Copperheads	22	17	.564	2
Stark County Terriers	21	18	.538	3
Lake Erie Monarchs	21	19	.525	3 ½
Dayton Docs	17	22	.436	7
Lexington Hustlers	16	21	.432	7
Xenia Scouts	17	23	.425	7 ½
Grand Lake Mariner	15	23	.395	8 ½
Hamilton Joes	13	26	.333	11

PLAYOFFS—Licking County defeated Cincinnati in championship of a six-team, double-elimination tournament.

TOP 10 PROSPECTS: 1. Ryan Cordell, of, Licking Co. (Jr., Liberty). **2.** Ivan De Jesus, of, Lima (Jr., Alabama-Birmingham). **3.** Brian Clark, lhp, Lima (So., Kent State). **4.** Matt Glomb, ss, So. Ohio (So., Santa Clara). **5.** Max Murphy, of, Stark Co. (So., Bradley). **6.** Justin Glass, of, Cincinnati (Jr., Cincinnati). **7.** Justin Brantley, rhp, So. Ohio (Sr. Siena). **8.** Collin Radack, of, Xenia (Jr., Hendrix, Ark.). **9.** Jake Madsen, 1b, Cincinnati (So., Ohio). **10.** Justin McCalvin, rhp, Lima (So., Kennesaw State).

INDIVIDUAL BATTING LEADERS
(MINIMUM 2.7 PLATE APPEARANCES PER TEAM GAME)

	AVG	AB	R	H	2B	3B	HR	RBI	SB
Pollock, Kyle, Stark County	.424	99	29	42	7	0	8	20	0
Madsen, Jake, Cincinnati	.396	106	27	42	7	1	3	21	7
Radack, Collin, Xenia	.393	112	14	44	13	0	2	19	6
de Jesus, Ivan, Lima	.373	102	24	38	7	1	4	18	12
Murphy, Max, Stark County	.369	168	39	62	14	2	9	34	8
Glass, Justin, Cincinnati	.364	99	16	36	5	0	4	22	5
Calderon, Marcos, Licking Co.	.363	102	24	37	9	0	0	12	4
Tubbs, Tucker, Hamilton	.359	145	28	52	9	2	4	23	6
Harris, Buck, Xenia	.356	101	18	36	3	0	1	11	5
Simmons, David, Lexington	.342	114	31	39	8	1	3	7	11

INDIVIDUAL PITCHING LEADERS
(MINIMUM 0.8 INNINGS PITCHED PER TEAM GAME)

	W	L	ERA	G	SV	IP	H	BB	SO
Gooding, Jeremy, Lima	3	1	1.70	7	0	42	39	9	51
Korte, Brian, Cincinnati	2	0	2.12	6	0	34	30	12	26
Botjer, Zach, Lima	5	1	2.28	8	0	47	45	15	54
Cook, Matt, Lima	2	1	2.65	6	0	34	28	8	30
McKinney, Brett, Hamilton	1	2	2.65	6	0	34	24	17	37
Koll, David, Licking County	3	0	3.14	8	0	43	36	11	48
Clay, Austin, Lexington	3	0	3.21	9	0	34	38	11	23
Zachrich, Preston, Grand Lake	4	3	3.47	8	0	47	49	15	37
Szkutni, Trenton, Dayton	4	2	3.57	7	0	35	31	13	42
Fasola, Johnny, Stark County	3	1	3.72	9	1	36	39	22	41

HAWAII COLLEGIATE LEAGUE

FINAL STANDINGS	W	L	PCT	GB
Kamuela Paniolos	19	15	.557	
Oahu Paddlers	18	16	.529	1
Hawaii Aliis	18	16	.529	1
Waikiki Surfers	14	22	.389	6

PLAYOFFS—Hawaii defeated Waikiki 8-3 in championship game.

TOP 5 PROSPECTS: 1. David Hickey, lhp, Waikiki (Jr., Yale). **2.** Mick VanVossen, rhp, Oahu (So., Michigan State). **3.** Ben McQuown, cf, Waikiki (Sr., Campbell). **4.** Robert Kahana, rhp, Oahu (So., Kansas). **5.** Alec Keller, of, Waikiki (Jr., Princeton).

INDIVIDUAL BATTING LEADERS
(MINIMUM 3.1 PLATE APPEARANCES PER TEAM GAME)

	AVG	AB	R	H	2B	3B	HR	RBI	SB
Keller, Alec, Waikiki	.420	112	25	47	3	2	0	14	6
Gentili, Nicholas, Waikiki	.377	106	21	40	8	2	1	19	4
Poulos, Nicholas, Waikiki	.349	146	22	51	4	2	0	22	6
Meyer, Kewby, Kamuela	.343	105	14	36	7	1	1	22	3
Nolden, William, Hawaii	.343	108	25	37	3	6	0	19	9
McQuown, Ben, Waikiki	.326	135	28	44	6	1	1	15	23

Kamoe, Kaden, Hawaii	.318	107	21	34	4	0	0	14	19
Saenz, Austin, Hawaii	.315	89	28	28	7	1	1	18	6
Gerig, Brad, Hawaii	.306	108	25	33	10	1	1	27	7
Angerer, Eric, Hawaii	.284	102	32	29	6	2	1	12	23

INDIVIDUAL PITCHING LEADERS
(MINIMUM 0.8 INNINGS PITCHED PER TEAM GAME)

	W	L	ERA	G	SV	IP	H	BB	SO
Hickey, David, Waikiki	2	1	1.80	5	0	35	33	5	29
Holt, Harley, Oahu	2	2	2.34	8	0	50	46	17	25
Van Vossen, Mick, Oahu	3	2	2.93	7	0	31	31	9	21
Wood, Tyler, Oahu	3	1	3.00	7	0	33	39	5	25
Franklin, John, Hawaii	3	2	3.12	8	0	40	41	8	23
Barto, Jeff, Hawaii	4	0	3.31	9	0	52	58	8	33
McNamara, Joseph, Hawaii	3	0	3.71	12	0	34	39	16	13
Herd, David, Kamuela	4	1	3.81	10	0	52	60	11	30
Yoneshige, Seamus, Kamuela	4	2	3.96	10	1	50	67	18	30
Cornett, Kyle, Waikiki	3	2	4.08	7	0	40	40	22	41

JAYHAWK LEAGUE

FINAL STANDINGS	W	L	PCT	GB
Hays Larks	23	11	.676	—
Dodge City A's	19	15	.559	4
Liberal BeeJays	19	15	.559	4
Derby Twins	16	18	.471	7
El Dorado Broncos	14	20	.412	9
Haysville Heat	11	23	.324	12

TOP 10 PROSPECTS: 1. Jonathan Youngblood, of, Dodge City (So., Meridian, Miss., CC). **2.** Tim Anderson, ss, Dodge City (So., East Central, Miss., CC). **3.** Austin Darby, of, Hays (So., Nebraska). **4.** Derek Thompson, lhp, Derby (So., John A. Logan, III., CC). **5.** Dayne Parker, 2b, Liberal (Jr., Wichita State). **6.** Chad Nack, rhp, Liberal (So., Texas-Arlington). **7.** Tyler Baker, c, Liberal (So., Wichita State). **8.** Jake Barrios, ss, Liberal (Jr., Texas Tech). **9.** Aaron Cornell, of, Hays (Jr., Oklahoma State). **10.** Taylor Drake, 3b, Dodge City (Jr., McNeese State).

INDIVIDUAL BATTING LEADERS
(MINIMUM 80 PLATE APPEARANCES)

	AVG	AB	H	2B	3B	HR	RBI
Drake, Taylor, Dodge City	.421	107	45	9	0	6	35
Diaz, Luis, Dodge City	.380	92	35	5	1	3	18
Darby, Austin, Hays	.374	139	52	12	1	4	33
Harris, David, El Dorado	.365	85	31	6	1	1	17
Davidson, Walker, Haysville	.359	128	46	7	0	0	11
Becherer, Travis, Derby	.347	124	43	6	0	1	7
McCormick, Adam, Haysville	.337	104	35	2	0	0	15
Anderson, Tim, Dodge City	.328	134	44	12	2	5	29
Parker, Dayne, Liberal	.324	136	44	10	1	2	19
Baptista, Daniel, El Dorado	.321	84	27	9	0	0	17

INDIVIDUAL PITCHING LEADERS
(MINIMUM 20 INNINGS)

	W	L	ERA	IP	H	SO
Johnston, Blake, Hays	3	0	1.13	24	18	16
Royal, Matt, Haysville	3	0	1.63	40	34	24
Stone, Josh, El Dorado	2	1	1.74	48	32	44
Lewick, Shawn, Hays	1	0	1.93	23	24	20
Nack, Chad, Liberal	4	2	2.08	49	43	28
McKaskie, Dakota, El Dorado	3	0	2.65	51	47	34
Begel, Joey, Hays	3	2	2.79	42	28	24
Ziegler, Justin, Hays	5	1	2.81	51	39	47
Hamer, Tyler, Derby Twins	0	1	2.84	25	25	21
Schnedler, Justin, Liberal	2	1	2.89	28	25	14

MINK LEAGUE

NORTH	W	L	PCT	GB
St. Joseph Mustangs	28	17	.622	—
Chillicothe Mudcats	23	19	.548	3 ½
Clarinda A's	19	23	.452	7 ½
Omaha Diamond Spirit	17	25	.405	9 ½
SOUTH	**W**	**L**	**PCT**	**GB**
Sedalia Bombers	24	21	.533	—
Ozark Generals	22	20	.524	0 ½
Nevada Griffons	21	21	.500	1 ½
Joplin Outlaws	17	25	.405	5 ½

PLAYOFFS—St. Joseph defeated Sedalia 2-1 in best-of-three series.

COLLEGE

TOP 10 PROSPECTS: 1. Robert Greco, rhp, Sedalia (Jr., Bellevue, Neb.). **2.** Dylan Nelson, rhp, Omaha (So., California)**. 3.** Mark Robinette, rhp, St. Joseph (Jr., Oklahoma State). **4. C**ody Cunningham, rhp, St. Joseph (So., West Texas JC). **5.** Matt Sinclair, c, Clarinda (So., Angelina, Texas, JC). **6.** Nick Billinger, if/of, Ozark (Sr., Regis, Colo.). **7.** Jeff Gacke, rhp, Clarinda (Sr., Morningside, Iowa). **8.** Robert Preito, ss, Ozark (Sr., Freed-Hardeman, Tenn.). **9.** Aaron Baker, rhp, St. Joseph (Sr., Central Missouri). **10.** Ethan Opsahl, lhp, Sedalia (SIGNED: Fargo-Moorhead Redhawks).

INDIVIDUAL BATTING LEADERS
(MINIMUM 2.7 PLATE APPEARANCES PER TEAM GAME)

	AVG	AB	R	H	2B	3B	HR	RBI	SB
Billinger, Nick, Ozark	.388	147	21	57	6	0	1	30	14
Busch, Ryan, Chillicotte	.370	146	24	54	9	2	1	25	10
Preito, Robert, Ozark	.369	149	29	55	5	1	2	23	20
Duplantis, Tyler, Chillicotte	.353	133	25	47	8	2	0	22	6
Eaves, Taylor, Joplin	.340	144	19	44	14	3	0	19	6
Peebles, Koby, Sedalia	.331	136	22	45	7	1	0	17	3
Segovia, Shane, St. Joseph	.331	118	18	39	6	2	0	21	4
McComack, Travis, Sedalia	.326	138	22	45	6	0	0	11	4
Simpson, Kyle, St. John's	.325	157	31	51	14	1	0	38	2
Robinette, Mark, St. John's	.312	173	37	54	11	2	1	30	4

INDIVIDUAL PITCHING LEADERS
(MINIMUM 0.8 INNINGS PITCHED PER TEAM GAME)

	W	L	ERA	G	SV	IP	H	BB	SO
Gacke, Jeff, Clarinda	4	2	2.00	9	0	54	39	8	39
Ochoa, Roland, Nevada	3	1	2.02	12	2	36	28	22	27
Butler, Zac, Ozark	4	1	2.02	9	0	49	34	16	30
Woodcock, Jon, Joplin	3	1	2.03	9	0	40	24	22	24
Cunningham, Cody, St. John's	7	0	2.13	9	0	63	45	19	45
Opshl, Ethen, Sedalia	4	1	2.31	11	2	39	27	14	48
Adkins, Steve, Chillicotte	5	1	2.33	8	0	50	46	12	42
Isom, Cole, Chillicotte	3	2	2.37	6	0	38	31	16	24
Baker, Aaron, St. John's	5	2	2.38	7	0	53	52	13	34
Watson, Trey, Ozark	3	3	2.52	9	0	39	34	14	28

NEW ENGLAND COLLEGIATE LEAGUE

EASTERN	W	L	PCT	GB
Newport Gulls	31	10	.756	—
New Bedford Bay	25	17	.595	6 ½
Laconia Muskrats	17	24	.415	14
Sanford Mainers	15	26	.366	16
Mystic Schooners	9	31	.225	21 ½
WESTERN	**W**	**L**	**PCT**	**GB**
Keene Swamp Bats	29	13	.690	—
Danbury Westerners	23	18	.561	5 ½
North Adams SteepleCats	22	20	.524	7
Vermont Mountaineers	18	23	.439	10 ½
Holyoke Blue Sox	17	24	.415	11 ½

PLAYOFFS—Newport defeated Danbury 2-0 in best-of-three series.
TOP 10 PROSPECTS: 1. Alex Haines, lhp, Vermont (Jr., Seton Hill, Pa.). **2.** Danny Collins, 3b, Laconia (Jr., Troy). **3.** Yale Rosen, of, Newport (So., Washington State). **4.** Grant Kay, 2b, Keene (So., Iowa Western CC). **5.** Scott Squier, lhp, Holyoke (So., Hawaii). **6.** Vince Conde, 3b, Laconia (So., Vanderbilt). **7.** Max Pentecost, c, Holyoke (So., Kennesaw State). **8.** Cole Peragine, ss/2b, Vermont (So., Stony Brook). **9.** Nic Manuppelli, rhp, Laconia (Jr., Youngstown). **10.** Artie Lewicki, rhp, Keene (Jr., Virginia).

INDIVIDUAL BATTING LEADERS
(MINIMUM 2.7 PLATE APPEARANCES PER TEAM GAME)

	AVG	AB	R	H	2B	3B	HR	RBI	SB
Melillo, Jeff, Newport	.404	94	34	38	12	0	5	30	1
Collins, Danny, Laconia	.390	159	37	62	9	1	9	37	2
Schwindel, Frank, Keene	.380	137	24	52	5	1	9	30	1
Stone, Zeth, New Bedford	.374	171	45	64	14	0	4	32	0
Kay, Grant, Keene	.360	139	34	50	6	0	11	32	6
McConkey, Paul, Holyoke	.358	120	22	43	11	1	4	22	4
Hagel, Jordan, Sanford	.356	104	21	37	8	1	4	21	7
Kelly, Rob, Vermont	.356	149	32	53	13	1	9	45	6
Sportman, J.P., Keene	.355	152	27	54	6	41	2	34	11
DelaCruz, Dylan, Keene	.352	159	35	56	10	0	7	31	6

INDIVIDUAL PITCHING LEADERS
(MINIMUM 0.8 INNINGS PITCHED PER TEAM GAME)

	W	L	ERA	G	SV	IP	H	BB	SO
Haines, Alex, Vermont	5	2	0.90	9	0	40	24	6	54

Derner, Brian, New Bedford	3	1	1.91	7	0	38	29	12	47
Kelich, Pete, Newport	2	1	2.20	12	4	41	31	11	49
Simon, Scott, Keene	4	0	2.52	6	0	36	32	10	27
Pierce, Rohn, Sanford	2	3	2.74	9	0	43	39	13	27
Murray, Donald, New Bedford	3	2	3.06	7	0	35	35	11	29
Catalina, Stephen, Danbury	4	3	3.16	8	0	37	42	11	27
Speer, David, Holyoke	3	3	3.21	7	0	48	51	7	33
Delgado, Casey, Vermont	2	4	3.22	9	0	36	38	12	38
Houseal, Brett, Danbury	6	1	3.25	9	0	64	51	14	37

NEW YORK COLLEGIATE LEAGUE

EAST	W	L	PCT	GB
Syracuse Junior Chiefs	28	12	0.700	—
Adirondack Trail Blazers	22	18	0.550	6
Utica Brewers	19	21	0.475	9
Geneva Red Wings	18	22	0.450	10
Syracuse Salt Cats	17	23	0.425	11
Sherrill Silversmiths	16	24	0.400	12
WEST	**W**	**L**	**PCT**	**GB**
Hornell Dodgers	25	15	0.625	—
Niagara Power	24	17	0.585	1 ½
Olean Oilers	23	18	0.561	2 ½
Geneva Twins	18	22	0.450	7
Rochester (AIA)	16	24	0.400	9
Wellsville Nitros	15	25	0.375	10

PLAYOFFS—Syracuse Jr. Chiefs defeated Niagara 2-0 in best-of-three series.
TOP 10 PROSPECTS: 1. Eric Eck, rhp, Hornell (Jr., Wofford). **2.** Grant Heyman, of/1b, Red Wings (Fr., Miami). **3.** Jon Leroux, c/1b, Red Wings (SIGNED: Mets). **4.** Jon Kemmer, of/lhp, Olean (Sr., Clarion, Pa.). **5.** Dan Fiorito, ss/3b, Syracuse (Sr., Manhattanville, N.Y.). **6.** Marcus Crescentini, rhp, Utica (So., Indian River, Fla., State JC). **7.** Leon Stimpson, of, Red Wings (Sr., Alvernia, Pa.). **8.** Cody Walker, c, Twins (So., Chattahoochee Valley, Ga., CC,). **9.** Adam Taylor, of, Niagara (Sr., North Greenville, S.C.). **10.** Eric Baker, of, Adirondack, (Sr., Rogers State, Okla.).

INDIVIDUAL BATTING LEADERS
(MINIMUM 2.0 PLATE APPEARANCES PER TEAM GAME)

	AVG	AB	R	H	2B	3B	HR	RBI	SB
Sanchez, Alex, SJC	.444	151	47	67	14	1	0	42	2
Kemmer, Jon, Olean	.441	152	51	67	12	3	9	53	18
Salerno, Frank, SJC	.401	142	47	57	8	1	3	29	20
Dezzi, Stephen, Utica	.391	151	35	59	11	1	4	31	3
May, K., Adirondack	.385	130	34	50	12	1	3	21	9
Campbell, Byron, Sherrill	.379	145	31	55	8	2	8	44	8
Morton, Bud, Syr. Salt Cats	.378	98	24	37	1	1	1	11	14
Baker, Eric, Adirondack	.375	136	29	51	11	2	9	31	10
Stevenson, Cody, Hornell	.371	124	44	46	6	5	0	20	17
Belk, Joel, Rochester	.364	121	28	44	6	2	5	21	1

INDIVIDUAL PITCHING LEADERS
(MINIMUM 0.8 INNINGS PITCHED PER TEAM GAME)

	W	L	ERA	G	SV	IP	H	BB	SO
Beckham, Steven, Niagara	4	0	1.84	8	1	44	30	17	46
Menke, Jon, Twins	4	1	1.85	7	0	39	24	16	42
Wilson, Tyler, Hornell	3	1	2.16	17	0	33	25	12	19
Basso, Alex, SJC	5	0	2.19	7	0	37	32	8	33
Ratte, Justin, Geneva Twins	5	3	2.31	8	0	39	34	9	30
Galan, Anthony, Wellsville	3	5	2.60	9	0	55	59	13	31
Meleski, Mike, Sherrill	4	1	2.68	6	0	37	29	18	36
Williams, Sean, SSC	3	1	2.75	9	0	52	48	13	66
Harris, Nate, Geneva Twins	2	1	2.78	15	3	36	27	11	26
Hockenberry, Matt, Geneva Red Wings	4	0	2.84	8	0	38	37	15	30

NORTHWOODS LEAGUE

NORTH	W	L	PCT	GB
Willmar Stingers	21	13	.618	—
Alexandria Beetles	20	15	.571	1 ½
St. Cloud Rox	20	16	.556	2
Duluth Huskies	19	17	.528	3
Thunder Bay Border Cats	16	18	.471	5
Waterloo Bucks	15	19	.441	6
Mankato MoonDogs	14	20	.412	7
Rochester Honkers	14	21	.400	7 ½

SOUTH	W	L	PCT	GB
Wisconsin Woodchucks	26	9	.743	—
La Crosse Loggers	23	12	.657	3
Madison Mallards	23	12	.657	3
Lakeshore Chinooks	18	17	.514	8
Eau Claire Express	15	21	.417	11 ½
Battle Creek Bombers	12	22	.357	13 ½
Green Bay Bullfrogs	12	23	.343	14
Wisconsin Rapid Rafters	11	24	.319	15

PLAYOFFS—La Crosse defeated Mankato 2-0 in best-of-three series.
TOP 10 PROSPECTS: 1. Derek Fisher, of, Madison (So., Virginia). **2.** Matt Chapman, ss, La Crosse (So., Cal State Fullerton). **3.** Richard Prigatano, of, La Crosse (So., Long Beach State). **4.** Michael Suchy, of, Willmar (So., Florida Gulf Coast). **5.** Casey Gillaspie, 1b, Eau Claire (So., Wichita State). **6.** Jerrick Suiter, of/rhp, Thunder Bay (So., Texas Christian). **7.** Justin Topa, rhp, Madison (Jr., Long Island). **8.** Wes Parsons, rhp, Thunder Bay (SIGNED: Braves). **9.** Anthony Bazzani, rhp, Alexandria (Sr., Eastern Kentucky). **10.** Eric Filia-Snyder, of, Wisconsin (So., UCLA).

INDIVIDUAL BATTING LEADERS
(MINIMUM 2.7 PLATE APPEARANCES PER TEAM GAME)

	AVG	AB	R	H	2B	3B	HR	RBI	SB
Ramsay, James, Duluth	.381	247	45	94	11	10	3	41	19
Vavra, Tanner, Alexandria	.381	231	58	88	9	2	4	40	7
Parr, Justin, Rochester	.370	243	48	90	18	0	8	44	26
Aguilera, Eric, Lakeshore	.369	187	31	69	21	0	4	28	3
Pickens, Jimmy, Alexandria	.365	181	37	66	14	1	5	29	21
Kaczmarski, Kevin, Waterloo	.361	219	50	79	14	4	10	55	14
Campbell, Luke, Duluth	.350	163	39	57	18	1	5	35	10
Suchy, Michael, Willmar	.349	241	57	84	13	1	8	62	17
Twichell, John Michael, Mankato	.347	176	35	61	14	4	8	36	8
Karmeris, Paul, Duluth	.344	209	39	72	15	1	1	23	2

INDIVIDUAL PITCHING LEADERS
(MINIMUM 0.8 INNINGS PITCHED PER TEAM GAME)

	W	L	ERA	G	SV	IP	H	BB	SO
Fisher, Jack, Wisconsin	6	1	1.76	9	0	56	40	14	61
Bellin, Bryce, Green Bay	5	3	2.61	13	0	59	53	16	63
Mott, Adam, Mankato	5	3	3.14	10	0	66	56	15	42
Novak, Joey, Duluth	7	3	3.18	13	0	74	62	22	77
Guillen, James, La Crosse	5	2	3.20	12	0	59	48	17	36
Kent, Matt, Rochester	3	6	3.43	11	0	79	96	14	50
Holiday, Jesse, La Crosse	5	2	3.44	12	0	65	62	28	42
LaMothe, Matt, Madison	5	4	3.46	11	0	65	61	19	69
Lieser, Scott, Willmar	8	1	3.47	19	2	57	68	13	53
Glenn, Cody, Lakeshore	3	4	3.51	14	2	59	49	30	45

PERFECT GAME COLLEGIATE LEAGUE

EAST	W	L	PCT	GB
Amsterdam Mohawks	35	12	.745	—
Glens Falls Golden Eagles	27	20	.574	8
Newark Pilots	26	20	.565	8 ½
Mohawk Valley DiamondDawgs	25	21	.543	9 ½
Oneonta Outlaws	25	22	.532	10
Albany Dutchmen	22	24	.478	12 ½
Watertown Wizards	18	27	.400	16
Elmira Pioneers	17	29	.370	17 ½
Cooperstown Hawkeyes	12	32	.273	21 ½

PLAYOFFS—Amsterdam defeated Glens Falls 2-0 in best of three series.
TOP 10 PROSPECTS: 1. Chandler Shepherd, rhp, Amsterdam (So., Ky.). **2.** Rocky McCord, rhp, Amsterdam (So., Auburn). **3.** Zach Remillard, 3b, Albany (Fr., Coastal Carolina). **4.** James Yacabonis, rhp, Elmira (Jr., St. Joe's). **5.** Chris Cruz, of, Mohawk (Jr., Cornell). **6.** Morgan Phillips, of, Albany (So., Charleston). **7.** Zach Lucas, ss, Oneonta (So., Louisville). **8.** Ben Mordini, rhp, Oneonta (Jr., Utah). **9.** Taylor Martin, rhp, Amsterdam (So., Kentucky). **10.** Ross Kivett, 2b, Glens Falls (Jr., Kansas State).

INDIVIDUAL BATTING LEADERS
(MINIMUM 132 PLATE APPEARANCES)

	AVG	AB	R	H	2B	3B	HR	RBI
Kivett, Ross, Glens Falls	.401	152	41	61	10	3	3	29
Colby, Zak, Amsterdam	.375	152	31	57	19	0	1	25
Remillard, Zach, Albany	.369	141	33	52	12	0	4	31
Perez, Josh, Newark	.356	149	32	53	5	1	0	19
Charlton, Ed, Amsterdam	.353	139	31	49	6	3	7	30
Rodrigue, Casey, Glens Falls	.347	121	27	42	7	6	0	18

Enos, Jordan, Watertown	.339	124	18	42	15	2	1	28
Walter, Donald, Watertown	.338	157	43	53	11	2	5	24
Green, Chase, Amsterdam	.336	143	27	48	9	2	3	20
Crowdus, Josh, Newark	.333	159	35	53	6	1	0	16

INDIVIDUAL PITCHING LEADERS
(MINIMUM 1.0 INNINGS PITCHED PER TEAM GAME)

	W	L	ERA	G	SV	IP	H	BB	SO
Shepherd, Chandler, Amsterdam	7	0	1.31	8	0	55	29	12	50
Solis, Rene, Watertown	4	1	1.31	7	0	48	29	10	49
McCord, Rocky, Amsterdam	4	0	1.71	8	0	37	29	16	50
Lee, Sheldon, Oneonta	7	1	2.72	9	0	53	54	11	42
Abel, Nathaniel, Oneonta	3	2	2.79	9	0	52	50	17	40
Dallas, Derek, Newark	2	2	2.93	12	0	46	41	15	33
Stagg, David, Albany	5	3	3.08	8	0	50	50	18	61
Thorpe, Daniel, Newark	6	1	3.20	8	0	56	48	25	51
Lisle, Brett, Oneonta	2	3	3.55	9	0	51	46	20	30
Martin, Taylor, Amsterdam	3	2	3.71	9	0	51	51	19	49

PROSPECT LEAGUE

EAST	W	L	PCT	GB
West Virginia Miners	19	10	.655	—
Richmond RiverRats	18	11	.621	1
Chillicothe Paints	18	12	.600	1 ½
Butler Blue Sox	15	14	.517	4
Slippery Rock Sliders	10	20	.333	9 ½
Lorain County Ironmen	8	21	.276	11

WEST	W	L	PCT	GB
Terre Haute Rex	22	9	.710	—
Quincy Gems	16	14	.533	5 ½
Dubois County Bombers	16	15	.516	6
Hannibal Cavemen	15	15	.500	6 ½
Springfield Sliders	13	17	.433	8 ½
Danville Dans	9	21	.300	12 ½

PLAYOFFS—West Va. defeated Dubois Co. 2-0 in best-of-three series.
TOP 10 PROSPECTS: 1. Elliot Caldwell, of, Butler (So., Spartanburg, S.C., Methodist JC). **2.** Nick Blount, rhp, Terre Haute (So., Southern Polytechnic State, Ga.). **3.** Jake Johansen, rhp, West Virginia (Jr., Dallas Baptist). **4.** Matt Tellor, 1b, Springfield (Jr., SE Missouri State). **5.** George Roberts, 1b/3b, Butler (Sr., Kent State). **6.** Nick Johnson, ss, Terre Haute (So., Mesa, Ariz., CC). **7.** Kris Gardner, lhp, Hannibal (R-So., Wichita State). **8.** Radley Haddad, c, Slippery Rock (Sr., Butler). **9.** Giancarlo Brugnoni, 1b, Chillicothe (Jr., Grand Valley State, Mich.). **10.** Sam Lewis, rhp, West Virginia (SIGNED: Royals).

INDIVIDUAL BATTING LEADERS
(MINIMUM 2.7 PLATE APPEARANCES PER TEAM GAME)

	AVG	AB	R	H	2B	3B	HR	RBI	SB
Prestridge, Clayton, W. Va.	.393	145	41	57	14	1	5	44	14
Caldwell, Elliott, Butler	.388	255	65	99	17	7	7	47	27
Pearson, Justin, Richmond	.376	202	66	76	11	3	3	29	12
Kempf, Kyle, Terry Haute	.365	219	38	80	12	2	2	44	24
Earley, Nolan, Richmond	.364	217	50	79	21	0	4	47	7
Strong, Bradley, W. Va.	.359	217	57	78	10	6	1	37	29
Williams, Joseph, W. Va.	.358	201	41	72	13	2	1	38	16
George, Zach, Quincy	.350	206	45	72	15	3	2	51	11
Nichols, Zach, Hannibal	.350	183	46	64	15	3	8	60	2
Koch, Cody, Lorain County	.348	198	35	69	12	1	5	29	3

INDIVIDUAL PITCHING LEADERS
(MINIMUM 0.8 INNINGS PITCHED PER TEAM GAME)

	W	L	ERA	G	SV	IP	H	BB	SO
Britt, Alex, Dubois County	5	1	1.85	8	0	58	47	27	46
Gardner, Kris, Hannibal	7	1	2.37	9	0	57	49	7	45
Blalock, Will, West Virginia	5	3	2.39	10	0	49	45	20	40
Lewis, Sam, West Virginia	8	1	2.70	12	0	70	38	27	71
Strunc, Tommy, Terre Haute	5	2	2.99	13	0	66	52	39	72
Terrell, Dylan, Hannibal	6	2	3.09	10	0	58	63	17	35
Johansen, Jacob, West Virginia	5	3	3.18	10	2	51	40	19	56
Candelmo, Joe, West Virginia	5	2	3.31	14	0	52	49	19	40
Tinnon, Josh, Slippery Rock	3	2	3.36	11	2	56	53	17	35
Smith, Bronson, Quincy	4	1	3.47	25	5	49	54	13	29

TEXAS COLLEGIATE LEAGUE

FINAL STANDINGS	W	L	PCT	GB
East Texas PumpJacks	41	23	.651	—

Brazos Valley Bombers	39	22	.639	1
Victoria Generals	38	24	.613	2 ½
Acadiana Cane Cutters	27	31	.466	11 ½
Alexandria Aces	27	32	.458	12
Woodlands Strykers	22	37	.281	17
McKinney Marshalls	15	41		

PLAYOFFS—East Texas defeated Victoria 2-1 in best-of-three series.
TOP 10 PROSPECTS: 1. Jason Jester, rhp, East Texas (Jr., Texas A&M).
2. Kyle Martin, rhp, Brazos Valley (Sr., Texas A&M). **3.** Braden Mattson, c, Brazos Valley (So., San Jacinto, Texas, JC). **4.** Jacob Lindgren, lhp, East Texas (So., Mississippi State). **5.** Kyle Kubat, lhp, East Texas (So., Nebraska). **6.** Dillon Newman, rhp, Victoria (Jr., Baylor). **7.** Trae Davis, rhp, Victoria (Jr., Baylor). **8.** Nathan Sorenson, lhp, Brazos Valley (Jr., Texas A&M). **9.** Krey Bratsen, of, McKinney (Jr., Texas A&M). **10.** R.J. Santigate, 3b, East Texas (Jr., Kansas State).

INDIVIDUAL BATTING LEADERS
(MINIMUM 2.7 PLATE APPEARANCES FOR TEAM GAME)

	AVG	AB	R	H	2B	3B	HR	RBI	SB
Aquino, Michael, Woodlands	.327	165	25	54	7	3	10	36	5
Alexander, K.J., McKinney	.322	143	22	46	13	2	2	24	9
Moreda, Rene, Alexandria	.320	175	36	56	12	1	1	35	12
Vidrine, Jude, Victoria	.317	164	28	52	9	0	4	28	3
Wharton, James, Brazos Valley	.308	143	26	44	15	0	6	35	2
Rodriguez, Isaac, Acadiana	.304	168	32	51	10	0	1	23	10
Sanchez, Ricardo, Woodlands	.297	212	38	63	17	2	2	26	6
Lozano, Garrett, Woodlands	.295	139	22	41	2	0	0	6	10
Kruse, Chad, Victoria	.294	245	28	72	13	1	2	36	13
Weiss, Eric, Victoria	.293	164	33	48	7	2	6	30	3

INDIVIDUAL PITCHING LEADERS
(MINIMUM 0.8 IP PER TEAM GAME)

	W	L	ERA	G	SV	IP	H	BB	SO
Langston, Kelby, Acadiana	2	1	1.32	21	2	48	44	15	36
Kubat, Kyle, East Texas	7	1	1.57	11	0	69	57	14	58
Pacheco, Jordan, Victoria	7	2	1.84	11	0	73	57	21	59
Vail, Tyler, Alexandria	4	3	2.01	9	0	49	35	16	38
Manual, Kaleb, Acadiana	6	4	3.25	11	0	69	66	27	48
Easterling, Brannon, Brazos Valley	4	4	3.52	10	0	64	62	24	37
Schlottmann, Ty, East Texas	3	5	3.88	12	0	65	66	14	43
Morrow, Covey, Victoria	5	4	3.88	12	0	56	58	9	32
Mathis, William, Acadiana	2	4	3.95	9	0	55	49	27	39
Kennel, Sean, Acadiana	3	7	4.02	10	0	52	53	21	25

VALLEY LEAGUE

NORTH	W	L	PCT	GB
Winchester Royals	36	16	.692	—
Haymarket Senators	21	24	.466	11 ½
Woodstock River Bandits	22	26	.458	12
Front Royal Cardinals	17	27	.386	15
Luray Wranglers	16	26	.380	15
Strasburg Express	17	28	.378	15 ½
SOUTH	**W**	**L**	**PCT**	**GB**
Waynesboro Generals	34	15	.694	—
Harrisonburg Turks	34	18	.654	1 ½
New Market Rebels	22	24	.478	10 ½
Rockbridge Rapids	22	24	.478	10 ½
Staunton Braves	21	23	.477	11 ½
Covington Lumberjacks	16	27	.372	15

PLAYOFFS—Harrisonburg def. Winchester 3-1 in best-of-five series.
TOP 10 PROSPECTS: 1. Chad Kuhl, rhp, New Market, (Jr., Delaware). **2.** Jake McWhirter, lhp, Front Royal (Jr., Tennessee Tech). **3.** Julian Ridings, of, Waynesboro (Jr., Western Carolina). **4.** Janson Carr, rhp, Winchester (Jr., Southern Arkansas). **5.** Jimmy Yezzo, if, Winchester (Jr., Delaware). **6.** Trey Cochran-Gill, rhp, Harrisonburg (So., Auburn). **7.** Josh Bullock, rhp, Waynesboro (Jr., Nebraska-Omaha). **8.** Seth Lucio, rhp, Waynesboro (So., Tennessee Tech). **9.** Shay Maltese, rhp, Haymarket (Sr., Cal State Stanislaus). **10.** Leo Rojas, 2b, Winchester (So., Alabama State).

INDIVIDUAL BATTING LEADERS
(MINIMUM 2.5 PLATE APPEARANCES PER TEAM GAME)

	AVG	AB	R	H	2B	3B	HR	RBI	SB
Ridings, Julian, Waynesboro	.419	172	45	72	14	3	7	39	15
Sipe, Blake, Staunton	.396	149	38	59	11	1	0	26	20

	AVG	AB	R	H	2B	3B	HR	RBI	SB
Campbell, Robby, Luray	.387	124	19	48	10	1	5	24	3
Dolan, Cody, Rockbridge	.378	164	27	62	10	0	4	33	7
Sullivan, Ryan, Covington	.375	136	35	51	9	1	10	44	5
Williams, Ethan, Woodstock	.373	134	21	50	8	0	0	26	3
Palensky, Caleb, Waynesboro	.371	159	26	59	11	4	1	26	4
Picha, Bradley, Winchester	.370	181	38	67	14	1	12	36	4
Yezzo, Jimmy, Winchester	.362	218	51	79	21	0	16	62	0
Rojas, Leo, Winchester	.357	213	59	76	14	2	7	34	11

INDIVIDUAL PITCHING LEADERS
(MINIMUM 1.0 INNINGS PITCHED PER TEAM GAME)

	W	L	ERA	G	SV	IP	H	BB	SO
O'Neill, Shawn, Harrisonburg	4	1	1.40	16	5	64	45	25	69
Justice, Derek, Staunton	4	2	2.09	9	0	52	50	23	50
Ortman, Dillon, Harrisonburg	7	2	2.26	10	0	64	45	12	50
Bargeron, Zach, Front Royal	3	3	2.70	8	0	50	47	12	50
Carr, Janson, Winchester	6	2	3.00	12	0	60	51	8	69
Herget, Kevin, Strasburg	3	1	3.18	10	1	51	36	22	77
Lucio, Seth, Waynesboro	5	2	3.27	11	1	52	52	18	56
Cochran-Gill, Trey, Harrisonburg	6	0	3.62	11	1	60	59	31	48
Williams, John, Haymarket	3	3	3.67	11	0	61	61	15	56
Volpe, Mike, Woodstock	5	2	3.75	10	0	50	50	12	52

WEST COAST LEAGUE

EAST	W	L	PCT	GB
Wenatchee AppleSox	37	17	.685	—
Bellingham Bells	32	22	.593	5
Kelowna Falcons	28	26	.519	9
Walla Walla Sweets	24	30	.444	13
WEST				
Corvallis Knights	32	22	.593	—
Cowlitz Black Bears	26	28	.481	6
Klamath Falls Gems	26	28	.481	6
Bend Elks	24	30	.444	8
Kitsap BlueJackets	14	40	.259	18

PLAYOFFS—Wenatchee defeated Corvallis 2-1 in best-of-three series.
TOP 10 PROSPECTS: 1. Taylor Sparks, 3b/of, Wenatchee (So., UC Irvine). **2.** Hunter Virant, lhp, Walla Walla (Fr., UCLA). **3.** James Kaprielian, rhp, Wenatchee (Fr., UCLA). **4.** Felipe Perez, rhp, Cowlitz (SIGNED: Diamondbacks). **5.** Cole Irvin, lhp, Cowlitz (Fr., Oregon). **6.** Shane Zeile, 3b, Walla Walla (So., UCLA). **7.** Darin Gillies, rhp, Bend (So., Arizona State). **8.** Tyler Kane, rhp, Wenatchee (Jr., Washington). **9.** Derek Callahan, lhp, Wenatchee (So., Gonzaga). **10.** Thomas Eshelman, rhp, Klamath Falls (Fr., Cal State Fullerton).

INDIVIDUAL BATTING LEADERS
(MINIMUM 2.7 PLATE APPEARANCES PER TEAM GAME)

	AVG	AB	R	H	2B	3B	HR	RBI	SB
Sparks, Will, Bend	.392	158	20	62	13	0	2	23	5
Sparks, Taylor, Wenatchee	.388	134	31	52	12	2	9	30	6
Wong, Joshua, Klamath Falls	.371	197	37	73	15	1	7	46	4
Gunsolus, Mitchell, Wenatchee	.371	213	47	79	8	4	3	48	10
Firth, Andrew, Kelowna	.331	142	23	47	9	0	2	21	1
Pearson, Kyle, Kelowna	.326	181	37	59	11	1	7	33	8
Walter, Bo, Bend	.325	191	26	62	5	2	2	20	15
Byler, Austin, Klamath Falls	.325	163	33	53	14	4	8	35	0
Ely, Andrew, Bellingham	.324	173	26	56	5	1	1	20	9
Gallegos, Marc, Corvallis	.316	155	33	49	7	2	0	19	21

INDIVIDUAL PITCHING LEADERS
(MINIMUM 0.8 INNINGS PER TEAM GAME)

	W	L	ERA	G	SV	IP	H	BB	SO
Dittrick, Rob, Corvallis	4	1	1.10	10	0	49	31	9	29
Reyes, Arturo, Walla Walla	4	1	2.05	10	0	53	43	14	37
Chew, Lawrence, Wenatchee	2	2	2.25	8	2	44	35	8	35
Cockrell, Cord, Kelowna	7	3	2.30	14	0	70	67	15	32
Merten, Mitch, Klamath Falls	5	1	2.36	14	0	50	45	11	47
Irvin, Cole, Cow	5	1	2.56	11	1	56	53	19	47
Kerns, Beau, Wenatchee	4	2	2.56	14	1	63	61	16	43
Callahan, Derek, Wenatchee	6	2	2.59	12	0	63	56	20	56
Coshow, Cale, Kelowna	3	4	2.74	15	0	62	64	33	38
Perez, Jorge, Corvallis	3	3	2.78	8	0	45	47	5	30

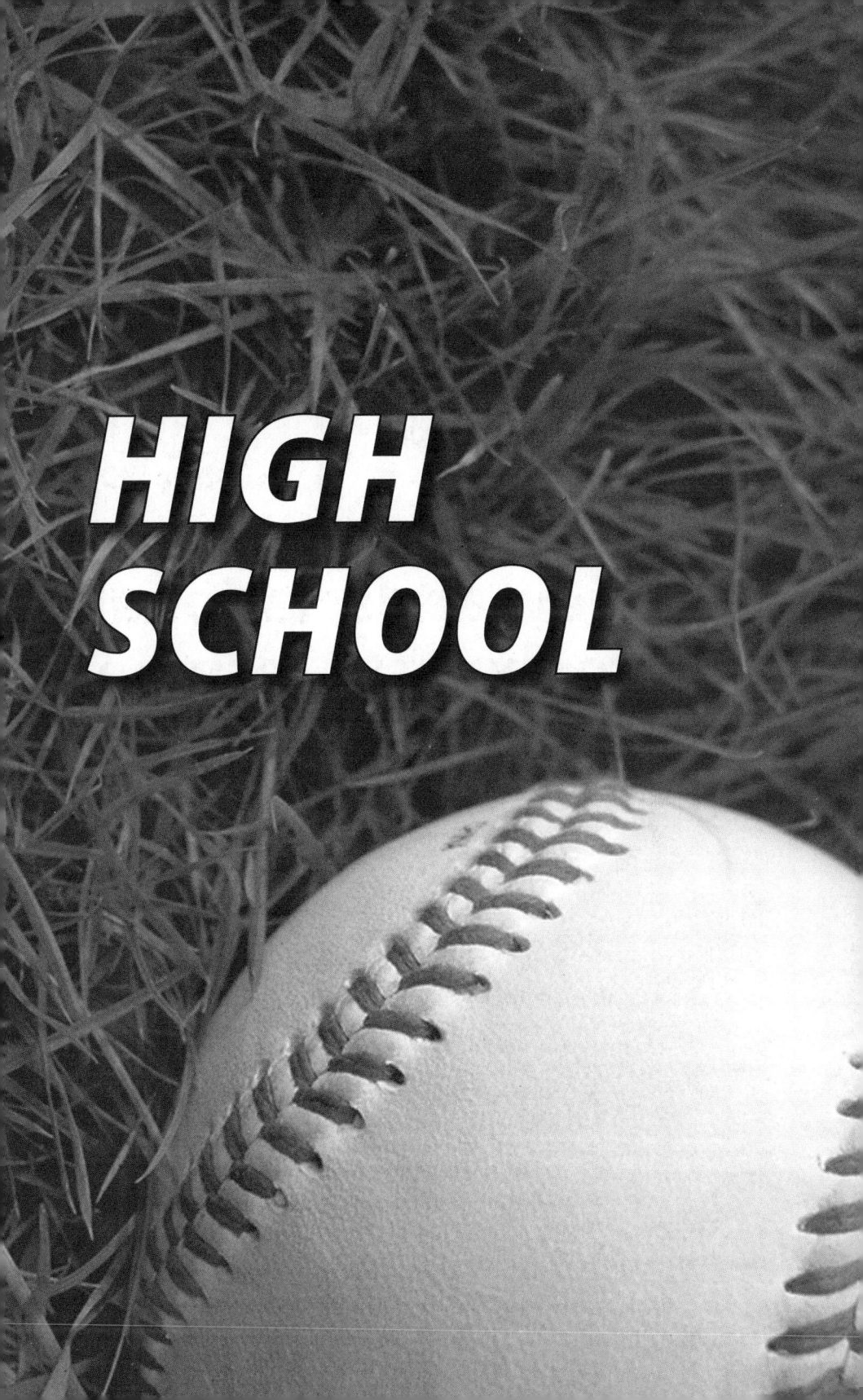

HIGH
SCHOOL

Senior Matt Olson (left) and junior Josh Hart led Parkview High to a state and national title

BOYER RODE

Parkview adds national title to dynasty resume

BY NATHAN RODE

Before each season begins, Chan Brown hosts a dinner at his house for the seniors on the Parkview High (Lilburn, Ga.) baseball team. It's a time for the head coach to meet with his most experienced players and discuss goals and expectations before the first pitch is thrown.

With a strong group of players back after winning the Georgia 5-A title in 2011, the 2012 seniors had their sights set high. Matt Olson, a slugging first baseman and the staff ace, stood up and said it straight.

"Anything less than a region and state title would be a disappointment," he recalled. "The whole national thing would be a cherry on top. It's crazy that all three worked out."

Parkview spent the entire season in the Baseball America/High School Baseball Coaches Association Top 25, fluctuating up and down as the season went on, but finished with a second consecutive 5-A state championship—beating rival Brookwood High (Snellville, Ga.) in the finals—and is Baseball America's 2012 High School Team of the Year.

Parkview opened the season as the top-ranked team in Georgia, and Brown knew teams would be targeting his team. But he also believed his team was good enough to be there in the end and focused on keeping his players positive during a difficult early-season schedule.

"Early on, with our out-of-region schedule, we try to challenge our kids," Brown said. "We put everybody through a test to see how we would do down the road. We've taken some losses because of that, but it makes us better. We felt good and were playing good ball going into the National High School Invitational."

Several teams traveled to Cary, N.C., for the NHSI at the end of March, knowing that going 4-0 would give them a good shot at finishing atop the Top 25. Parkview dropped two games before the event to good teams in Cartersville (Ga.) High and Columbus (Ga.) High, but blew past New York's Washington High in the opening round. That set up a tilt between the Panthers and Harvard-Westlake High of Studio City, Calif.

The Wolverines were without righthander Lucas Giolito, the top righthanded pitching prospect in the country. But Parkview still had to face Max Fried, the top lefthanded pitching prospect in the country and eventual seventh overall pick in the draft. Parkview battled early and Olson even homered off Fried, but lefty Mac Marshall had to exit the game with an injury and Harvard-Westlake

Rank	School	Record	Season conclusion
1	Parkview HS, Lilburn, Ga.	31-6	Georgia 5-A Champion
2	Columbus (Ga.) HS	33-4	Georgia 3-A Champion
3	Bishop Gorman HS, Las Vegas	40-3	Nevada 4-A Champion
4	American Heritage HS, Plantation, Fla.	28-4	Florida 5-A Champion
5	Archbishop McCarthy HS, Southwest Ranches, Fla.	27-4	Florida 6-A Champion
6	Campolindo HS, Moraga, Calif.	23-4	CIF North Coast Section Div. II Champion
7	Chaparral HS, Scottsdale, Ariz.	28-7	Arizona Div. I Champion
8	Spruce Creek HS, Port Orange, Fla.	28-4	Florida 8-A Champion
9	Columbus HS, Miami	27-5	Florida 8-A Runner-up
10	Vista (Calif.) HS	31-4	CIF San Diego Section Div. I Champion
11	Jesuit HS, Tampa	28-2	Florida 5-A Runner-up
12	Olympia HS, Orlando	32-2	Florida 8-A Region Finalist
13	Oak Grove HS, Hattiesburg, Miss.	34-3	Mississippi 6-A Champion
14	Barbe HS, Lake Charles, La.	35-6	Louisiana 5-A Champion
15	Newbury Park HS, Thousand Oaks, Calif.	21-7	CIF Southern Section Div. I Champion
16	Orange (Calif.) Lutheran HS	23-5	CIF Southern Section Div. I Quarterfinalist
17	Mater Dei HS, Santa Ana, Calif.	24-6	CIF Southern Section Div. I Semifinalist
18	Cy-Ranch HS, Houston	32-8	Texas 5-A Champion
19	Rockwall-Heath HS, Heath, Texas	36-9	Texas 4-A Champion
20	Carroll HS, Corpus Christi, Texas	33-5	Texas 5-A Semifinalist
21	Martin HS, Arlington	36-6	Texas 5-A Semifinalist
22	Calallen HS, Corpus Christi, Texas	33-2	Texas 4-A Region Semifinalist
23	Loganville (Ga.) HS	31-5	Georgia 4-A Champion
24	Pacifica HS, Garden Grove, Calif.	28-5	CIF Southern Section Div. II Champion
25	Venice (Fla.) HS	24-8	Florida 7-A Champion
26	Harvard-Westlake HS, Studio City, Calif.	24-5	Southern Section Div. II Second Round
27	Cherry Creek HS, Greenwood Village, Colo.	24-3	Colorado 5-A Champion
28	Bonita HS, La Verne, Calif.	32-2	CIF Southern Section Div. III Champion
29	Oxford (Ala.) HS	39-13	Alabama 6-A Champion
30	Pensacola (Fla.) Catholic HS	27-3	Florida 4-A Champion
31	Lake Braddock HS, Burke, Va.	26-3	Virginia 3-A Champion
32	A&M Consolidated HS, College Station, Texas	29-12	Texas 5-A Runner-up
33	Providence School, Jacksonville	28-4	Florida 3-A Champion
34	Appling County HS, Baxley, Ga.	35-4	Gerogia 2-A Champion
35	Edmond (Okla.) North HS	21-14	Oklahoma 6-A Champion
36	Arlington (Tenn.) HS	34-11	Tennessee 3-A Champion
37	Glocester Catholic HS, Gloucester City, N.J.	23-4	New Jersey Non-Public A Champion
38	Kentwood HS, Convington, Wash.	25-2	Washington 4-A Champion
39	Creighton Prep, Omaha	34-4	Nebraska A Champion
40	Middle Creek HS, Apex, N.C.	25-6	North Carolina 4-A Champion
41	North HS, Riverside, Calif.	25-6	CIF Southern Section Div. I Second Round
42	Broken Arrow (Okla.) HS	35-5	Oklahoma 6-A Runner-up
43	Woodford County HS, Versailles, Ky.	34-6	Kentucky Champion
44	Archbishop Moeller HS, Cincinnati	26-5	Ohio Div. I Champion
45	Malvern (Pa.) Prep	31-5	Pennsylvania Independent Schools Champion
46	Pace (Fla.) HS	25-7	Florida 6-A Runner-up
47	Grand Street Campus HS, New York	20-1	PSAL A Champion
48	Owasso (Okla.) HS	30-5	Oklahoma 6-A Semifinalist
49	Gainesville (Ga.) HS	32-2	Georgia 3-A Semifinalist
50	Lake Central HS, Saint John, Ind.	32-1	Indiana 4-A Champion

jumped all over the bullpen and won 10-3.

"We really didn't know what to expect in Cary, but the kids' excitement was very high," Brown added. "When we lost to Harvard-Westlake, that was a huge disappointment, but a huge motivator too. The kids turned it on after that."

Parkview won 10 of its next 12 games, losing only to Brookwood, which twice started right-hander Luke Sims, who went on to be the Braves' first-round pick. A win over South Gwinnett High (Snellville, Ga.) gave the Panthers their third straight region championship, and they followed it with a win over Columbus, avenging an earlier loss, and had a 21-5 record as the playoffs began.

They swept the first two rounds, but got a tough draw in the third having to travel to Hillgrove High (Powder Springs, Ga.), the team they beat for the state title in 2011. And for a second straight year, Parkview dropped the opening game of the best-of-three series.

"Both series mirrored each other," Brown said. "We were in a lull, but turned back into the team we have been and took the momentum from them."

It was smooth sailing from there as Parkview swept Mill Creek High (Hochston) and Brookwood in the next two series to capture a second straight state championship.

Continuing Legacy

Parkview has developed into one of the strongest programs in a talent-rich state after winning five Georgia championships in the last 16 years. The Panthers also won titles in 1996, 2001 and 2002, and the tradition of the program has carried through to the latest group of players.

"I like to think we left a legacy around this community," Olson said. "The Parkview tradition is one that I don't think can be matched. There's a lot of pride associated with Parkview that you take strongly in."

Ten years ago, Parkview was celebrating back-to-back titles and had four players go on to play professionally, including Jeff Francouer. Hugh "Buck" Buchanan, now a member of the BCA Hall of Fame and a scout for the Braves, was the head coach then and saw parallels between his teams and the past two Parkview squads.

"There were some similarities, if nothing else both played very difficult schedules," he said. "That was something we believed in and had to do. Coach Brown has continued to do that. We played anybody, anywhere, anytime. You feel like that's going to prepare the youngsters down the road. That proved to help us then and it helped them this year."

Buchanan added that they had to bounce back from Game One losses and were ranked highly too. The latest Parkview team also had its own high-profile prospect in Olson. Also a first team All-American, Olson was committed to Vanderbilt and the 47th overall pick in the draft by the Athletics. He was drafted as a first baseman and signed for $1,079,700 thanks to his potent bat and hit .385 with nine home runs and 47 RBIs in 96 at-bats in the spring.

He was also a key leader for the Panthers. After that senior dinner, he and fellow righthander Jesse Foster stood at their cars for an hour talking about the season and how it was going to be based on them setting the tempo with their pitching.

"Olson, when he needed to, he spoke," Brown said. "And our bulldog was Jesse Foster. Our second game against Hillgrove, he was lights out. That whole senior class, they've been special since they came in."

The Panthers' mantra all season was "Teamwork makes the dream work" and they persevered through challenges to bring home another state championship and new accomplishment to put in a trophy case.

"They're together over 300 days a year," Brown said. "They love each other like I've never seen. The chemistry this group brings, there's no quit in them."

NHSI Debuts With A Bang

Scouts spend the spring running to see high school players all over the country, usually seeing one player at a time, two if they're lucky. There are high school tournaments every spring that attract a large contingent of talent evaluators, but the National High School Invitational took things to a new level.

The event was put on by USA Baseball at its National Training Complex in Cary with the help of Baseball America and had a field of some of the best teams in the country. Seven players in the 16-team field made BA's Draft Top 200—eight if you count Giolito, who didn't play due to an injury. Five of those players, Giolito included, went in the first 60 picks. And 11 teams were in Baseball America's preseason rankings.

The level of competition did not disappoint as there were upsets, dominant pitching performances, explosive offenses and walk-off wins. Mater Dei High of Santa Ana, Calif., made the biggest statement, taking down three teams in the top 10 on its way to winning the NHSI championship.

The Monarchs faced Harvard-Westlake High in the final game and needed a seventh-inning home run from righthander/first baseman Davis Tominaga to tie the score before getting a walk-off single from left fielder Ryan Barr to win 3-2.

Other standouts in the event included Carroll High (Corpus Christi, Texas) outfielder/right-hander Courtney Hawkins, Bishop Gorman High (Las Vegas) third baseman/righthander Joey Gallo, Brookwood High righty Luke Sims and Fried.

Hawkins, who went on to become a first-round pick of the White Sox, boosted his draft stock with a home run against Gulliver Prep (Miami)—an important run in a 1-0 shutout in which he pitched and sat 91-93 mph with his fastball. Gallo struggled at the plate, but made one start on the mound and touched 98 mph and sat 93-96 with relative ease. Fried allowed a home run to Parkview's slugger in Olson (who was celebrating his 18th birthday), but buckled down to beat the eventual national champions. Sims had a marquee matchup against righthander Ryan Burr (Highlands Ranch, Colo., HS) and stole the show, taking a no-hitter into the sixth inning.

Dynamic Duo Short Lived

It was supposed to be a rotation to remember. Like having Roy Halladay and Cliff Lee pitching for the same high school. It was supposed to be Harvard-Westlake High's year. After winning its first league title last season, the California school had higher expectations for 2012.

It just wasn't meant to be.

Circumstances put two premium draft prospects, Fried and Giolito, on the same Harvard-Westlake team. Since the draft began in 1965, high school teammates have been selected in the first round six times, with the Giolito and Fried being the first since Mike Moustakas and Matt Dominguez of Chatsworth (Calif.) High in 2007.

Fried and Giolito certainly expected to join that fraternity, but their path to the draft took an unexpected turn when Giolito went out with an elbow strain in March, knocking him out of action for the rest of the spring.

The Wolverines had the core of their 2011 team returning, and excitement for the 2012 season grew when they made the high school equivalent of a free-agent signing.

Just a nine-mile drive down the 101 and the 405 freeways from Harvard-Westlake is Van Nuys' Montclair College Prep, which had Fried—a projectable lefty with a commitment to UCLA and first-round aspirations—as its staff ace. News spread during the summer that Montclair Prep was going to cut its entire athletic program to satisfy budget concerns, however, and all athletes would be allowed to transfer to another school with no restrictions. His family began looking for options, and Fried had his sights set on Harvard-Westlake.

"It really came down to Montclair's field was right next door," Fried said. "Seeing them play and the program, the academics. I know a lot of the guys from playing and having that sort of relationship, I thought it was a perfect fit."

Transferring to Harvard-Westlake would mean one of the top lefthanded prospects in the country would join a pitching staff that already had the top righthanded prospect in Lucas Giolito, also a UCLA signee. But it wasn't that easy.

"First and foremost, Max had to go through the application process like everyone else," Wolverines head coach Matt LaCour said. "People don't get that. It's not, 'You're a good athlete.' You have to fit academically. Max passed that test. He has shown in previous years that he was a good student and maintained high-end grades."

Fried also went through several interviews, none of which included the athletics director or members of the coaching staff. Once Fried was accepted, LaCour was ecstatic but knew the transition wasn't complete.

"Obviously, there's excitement," he said. "You want to coach great players. But there's a hesitation. The fabric of a team is very delicate at times. Bringing in someone that isn't a part of the program can cause conflict."

But if Fried's transition were a baseball, it would be too smooth for Fried to spin his trademark curveball.

"It was the most seamless transition I've ever made," Fried said. "My teammates embraced me. The coaches and I really took the time to understand each other and my philosophy on pitching."

Giolito and Fried were poised to challenge 2002 draftees Clint Everts and Scott Kazmir of Cypress Falls High (Houston) as the highest-drafted duo in draft history, and there is the relation of righty-lefty combination as well. In spite of the excitement, the pitchers were trying to stay grounded.

"It feels really good," Giolito said in January. "Max is an unbelievable player. Acquiring him through the chance we got, it's fantastic. We're really looking forward to it. Max is my best friend so we're going to have a good time."

The feeling was mutual.

"It's great," Fried said. "Lucas has been a great support for me. He's helped me transition into the school. This program has become an elite one over the past couple of years and to have the recognition nationwide would be big."

The Tweak

Harvard-Westlake's season got off to a solid start, with wins in its first four games. For the No. 4 team in Baseball America's preseason rankings, excitement was building as the calendar got closer to the National High School Invitational, where Giolito, Fried and several other top draft picks would compete for their schools in front of dozens of scouting directors and crosscheckers.

That's when the master plan fell apart. In a start against Valencia High (Santa Clarita, Calif.), Fried got tagged for eight runs on 10 hits. It was unexpected, but part of the learning process.

Then a week after touching triple digits and coming within two outs of a no-hitter, Giolito was facing league rival Bishop Alemany High (Mission Hills, Calif.) and struggling with his command. He had given up two runs on five hits, three walks and three hit batters while striking out four in 6 1/3 innings and knew something didn't feel right.

Giolito felt something grab at his elbow and knew that he should come out of the game. He removed himself and an MRI the next morning revealed a sprained ulnar collateral ligament. Just like that, Giolito's season and Harvard-Westlake's one-two punch were gone. While the early outlook had him avoiding surgery, rest and rehab meant he was unable to throw until May at the earliest, erasing any hope a return.

Giolito took a day off to wrap his head around it all. He was understandably downcast but said

HIGH SCHOOL

USA BASEBALL

Event	Site	Champion	Runner-up
Tournament of Stars (18U)	Cary, N.C.	Pony	Babe Ruth
USA Baseball 17U—East	Palm Beach Co., Fla.	Palm Beach PAL	Columbus Explorers
USA Baseball 17U—West	Goodyear, Ariz.	Trombley Baseball	2014 Rawlings
USA Baseball 15U—East	Fort Myers, Fla.	Impact	A-Team
USA Baseball 15U—West	Goodyear, Ariz.	SGV Arsenal	Norcal 2016
USA Baseball 14U—East	Cary, N.C.	EvoShield Canes	Frozen Ropes Rampage
USA Baseball 14U—West	Goodyear, Ariz.	Norcal Black	No Fear

ALL-AMERICAN AMATEUR BASEBALL ASSOCIATION (AAABA) · Headquarters: Zanesville, Ohio

Event	Site	Champion	Runner-up
World Series (21-and-Under)	Johnstown, Pa.	New Brunswick	Cleveland

AMATEUR ATHLETIC UNION (AAU) · Headquarters: Lake Buena Vista, Fla.

Event	Site	Champion	Runner-up
10-and-Under Diamond (60-foot)	Orlando	Team MVP	CBC Riverhawks Black
10-and-Under Gold (60-foot)	Orlando	Miami Bulldogs	Oakleaf R Knights
11-and-Under Diamond (70-foot)	Orlando	Team MVP	Orlando Tigers
11-and-Under Gold (70-foot)	Orlando	Boca Bombers	Jupiter Cardinals
12-and-Under Diamond (70-foot)	Orlando	Texas	Team MVP
12-and-Under Gold (70-foot)	Orlando	Dirtdawgs Elite	Winter Park Blaze
13-and-Under Diamond (90-foot)	Orlando	Tampa Titans	Homeplate Chili Dogs
13-and-Under Gold (90-foot)	Orlando	Rawlings, N.C.	Western Mass Storm
14-and-Under Diamond (90-foot)	Viera, Fla.	Lamorinda Monarchs	Western Mass Storm
14-and-Under Gold (90-foot)	Viera, Fla.	Connecticut Wolfpack	Maryland Express
Underclassmen Diamond	Fort Myers, Fla.	East Cobb Titans	New Jersey Tigers
Underclassmen Gold	Acadiana, La.	South Shore Hurricanes	South Florida Stingers
Upperclassmen Diamond	Acadiana, La.	Brazos Valley Renegades	Tallahassee Baseball Club

AMERICAN AMATEUR BASEBALL CONGRESS (AABC) · Headquarters: Farmington, N.M.

Event	Site	Champion	Runner-up
Gil Hodges	Surprise, Ariz.	Diamondbacks	Fuel
Pee Wee Reese (12 & U)	Toa Baja, P.R.	Outlaws Black	San Diego Show
Sandy Koufax (13 & U)	Vero Beach, Fla.	South Troy Dodgers	Mich. Blue Jays-Elite
Sandy Koufax (14 & U)	Vero Beach, Fla.	Aguilas Arrevica	South Troy Dodgers
Ken Griffey, Jr. (15 & U)	Surprise, Ariz.	Rockford Travelers	Texas Blacksox
Mickey Mantle (16 & U)	McKinney, Texas	Dallas Tigers-Hernandez	Frozen Ropes
Don Mattingly (17 & U)	Port St. Lucie, Fla.	Cherry Creek	Oakland
Connie Mack (18 & U)	Farmington, N.M.	So Cal Renegades	Midland Redskins
Stan Musial (open)	Port St. Lucie, Fla.	Albany Athletics	Tampa Elite Rays

AMERICAN LEGION BASEBALL · Headquarters: Indianapolis

Event	Site	Champion	Runner-up
World Series (19 & U)	Shelby, N.C.	New Orleans	Brooklawn, N.J.

BABE RUTH BASEBALL · Headquarters: Trenton, N.J.

Event	Site	Champion	Runner-up
Cal Ripken (10 & U)	Bentonville, Ark.	Northwest Bakersfield, Calif.	Willamette Valley, Ore.
Cal Ripken 12-year-old (60 feet)	Winchester, Mass.	Visalia, Calif.	Burlington, Mass.
Cal Ripken 13-year-old (70 feet)	Aberdeen, Md.	Japan	Maryland
13-year-old	Kitsap County, Wash.	Bryant, Ark.	Greenville, N.C.
14-year-old	Murray, Utah	Branchburg, N.J.	Jacksonville, Fla.
13-15-year-olds	Van Buren, Ark.	SE Lexington, Ky.	Brazowswood, Texas
16-18-year-old	Weimar, Texas	Onondaga, N.Y.	Texas Tri-Counties

CONTINENTAL AMATEUR BASEBALL ASSOCIATION (CABA) · Headquarters: Westerville, Ohio

Event	Site	Champion	Runner-up
8-and-Under	Sylvania, Ohio	Detroit Bees	Michigan Blue Jays
9-and-Under	East Cobb, Ga.	Atlanta Angels	Brecksville Bees
10-and-Under	Westfield, Ind.	Windy City Travelers	Indiana Mustangs Blue
11-and-Under	East Cobb, Ga.	East Cobb Astros	643 DP Cougars

he wasn't dwelling on the injury. He said he was focused on supporting his teammates while getting stronger and better in other areas.

"One of the things I wanted to express to them was even though I'm gone, we're still really good," Giolito said. "We still have Max and Jack Flaherty."

Flaherty was the No. 2 starter behind Giolito last season as a freshman. A good athlete who has seen time on the left side of the infield, in the outfield and on the mound, Flaherty hit .355 with 18 RBIs and 21 runs in 76 at-bats while going 6-2, 2.51 in 47 innings last season. Harvard-Westlake will miss Giolito, but Flaherty's presence makes for a softer landing.

"Jack Flaherty is ready to be a guy," LaCour

12-and-Under	Sylvania, Ohio	British Columbia	Wisconsin RiverCats
13-and-Under	Westfield, Ind.	East Cobb Astros	Kentucky Blue
14-and-Under (60x90)	Lebanon, Tenn.	Bergen Beach	East Cobb Reebok
15-and-Under (Aluminum)	South Bend, Ind.	Gravel	School of Hard Knocks Landsharks
15-and-Under (Wood)	Charleston, S.C.	GC Diamondbacks	Upstate Mavericks
16-and-Under	East Cobb, Ga.	East Cobb Astros	North Alabama Vipers
17-and-Under/HS (Aluminum)	Euclid, Ohio	Heat	Ohio Elite
17-and-Under/HS (Wood)	Charleston, S.C.	Knoxville Stars	East Cobb Rangers
18-and-Under (Aluminum)	Charleston, S.C.	Georgia	Diamond Devils
18-and-Under (Wood)	Struthers, Ohio	Astro Falcons	Ohio Yankees

LITTLE LEAGUE BASEBALL · Headquarters: Williamsport, Pa.

Event	Site	Champion	Runner-up
Little League (11-12)	Williamsport, Pa.	Japan	Goodlettsville, Tenn.
Junior League (13-14)	Taylor, Mich.	Rockledge, Fla.	Aruba
Senior League (15-16)	Bangor, Maine	Guatemala	Lemon Grove, Calif.
Big League (17-18)	Easley, S.C	San Juan, P.R. District 1	S.C. District 1

NATIONAL AMATEUR BASEBALL FEDERATION (NABF) · Headquarters: Bowie, Md.

Event	Site	Champion	Runner-up
Sophomore (14 & U)	Youngstown, Ohio	Maryland Monarchs	Ohio Glaciers
Junior (16 & U)	Northville, Mich.	Creekside Fitness	SAYO Grays
High School (17 & U)	Knoxville, Tenn.	Top Tier Baseball of Chicago	Allen Baseball
Senior (18 & U)	Struthers, Ohio	Astro Falcons	Houston Raiders

PERFECT GAME/BCS FINALS · Headquarters: Cedar Rapids, Iowa

Event	Site	Champion	Runner-up
14-and-Under	Fort Myers, Fla.	Dallas Patriots/EvoShield Canes co-champions (weather)	
15-and-Under	Fort Myers, Fla.	East Cobb Astros	Elite Baseball
16-and-Under	Fort Myers, Fla.	SWFL	Dulins Dodgers
17-and-Under	Fort Myers, Fla.	Orlando Scorpions	East Cobb Astros
18-and-Under	Fort Myers, Fla.	East Cobb Braves	Marlins Scout Team/Storm

PERFECT GAME/WORLD WOOD BAT ASSOCIATION SUMMER CHAMPIONSHIPS · Headquarters: Cedar Rapids, Iowa

Event	Site	Champion	Runner-up
14-and-Under	Marietta, Ga.	San Diego Show	Dallas Patriots
15-and-Under	Marietta, Ga.	East Cobb Astros	Elite Baseball
16-and-Under	Marietta, Ga.	Georgia Blue	South Charlotte Panthers 2014
17-and-Under	Marietta, Ga.	Houston Banditos Black	Alabama Seminoles
18-and-Under	Marietta, Ga.	East Cobb Yankees	Marlins Scout Team

PONY BASEBALL · Headquarters: Washington, Pa.

Event	Site	Champion	Runner-up
Mustang (9-10)	Burleson, Texas	Blossom Valley, Calif.	San Lorenzo, P.R.
Bronco (11-12)	Chesterfield, Va.	Miami (Tamiami), Fla.	Chesterfield (CBC), Va.
Pony (13)	Fullerton, Calif.	Irvine, Calif.	Miami (Tamiami), Fla.
Pony (13-14)	Washington, Pa.	Tournament not complete before press time	
Colt (15-16)	Lafayette, Ind.	Los Gatos, Calif.	San Juanita Bayamon, P.R.
Palomino (17-18)	Compton, Calif.	Chinese Taipei, Taiwan	Urban Youth Academy, Calif.

REVIVING BASEBALL IN INNER CITIES (RBI) · Headquarters: New York

Event	Site	Champion	Runner-up
Junior (13-15)	Minneapolis	Dominican RBI	Chicago White Sox RBI
Senior (16-18)	Minneapolis	Jackie Robinson RBI	Brandenton (Fla.)

U.S. SPECIALTY SPORTS ASSOCIATION (USSSA) · Headquarters: Petersburg, Va.

Event	Site	Champion	Runner-up
10-and-Under/Majors Elite	Orlando	Central Florida Wolverines	BPA Rawlings Elite
11-and-Under/Majors Elite	Orlando	Oakley Stingrays	SY Titans
12-and-Under/Majors Elite	Orlando	Team Phenom	Next Level Tornadoes
13-and-Under/Majors Elite	Orlando	Bandits	South Florida Giants
14-and-Under/Majors Elite	Orlando	Winter Park Diamond Dawgs	Reivers Elite, P.R.

said after Giolito's injury. "A No. 2 is the least of our worries."

With Flaherty playing an important role, the Wolverines held onto a stellar season. They fell short of a section title in California, but reached the championship game of the NHSI, only to lose to Mater Dei High in extra innings.

And with all the trials and tribulations, the duo still became first-round teammates.

Fried was taken by the Padres with the seventh overall pick and received a $3 million signing bonus. Giolito went to the Nationals nine picks later and signed for $2.925 million. He pitched two innings in his pro debut, but eventually learned he would need Tommy John surgery and miss the 2013 season.

Buxton's Talent, Character Shine

Byron Buxton is a young man of very few words, but those who know him and have seen him play have no shortage of stories to tell. Some of those tales illustrate his character while others sound like folklore. He was considered the best position player in the country in the 2012 draft class and his on-field performance reflected that. He hit .513 with 68 runs scored, 17 doubles, 35 RBIs, 38 stolen bases. He was caught stealing once and struck out just five times in his 117 at-bats He also went 10-1, 1.90 on the mound with five saves and 154 strikeouts in 81 innings while walking just 29 batters. Opponents managed only 36 hits against him.

Those numbers alone would net all kinds of accolades, but he led Appling County High (Baxley, Ga.) to its first state championship in a male sport. After losing Game One of the final series with Buxton on the mound, the Pirates bounced back in Game Two before a tropical storm delayed the deciding game. The wait worked out well, as Buxton was rested enough to pitch again.

"Byron took the first loss personal," head coach Jeremy Smith said. "So in Game Three, he came to me and said, 'I want the ball. I got you coach.'"

Buxton made good on his promise with a complete-game, 18-strikeout victory to lift the Pirates to the Georgia 2-A title.

Baseball America engaged in a spirited debate about its 2012 High School Player of the Year, but Buxton's season, state championship performance and status as a prospect sealed the deal. Buxton is extremely humble and quiet, rarely touting his athletic exploits or giving answers with more than a few words. Not long before finding out he was named the High School Player of the Year—and after signing a pro contract for a $6 million dollar bonus—he was in his football coach's office just catching up and said he had to head out to mow the lawn at home. The people of South Georgia love Buxton about as much as he loves them so after featuring him in the Draft Preview, we let others tell their favorite stories this time.

Jack Powell, Area Scout, Minnesota Twins: "The first time I saw him play was two years ago in the World Wood Bat tournament in Atlanta. He wasn't physical at all, but he had

PLAYER OF THE YEAR

PREVIOUS WINNERS

1992: Preston Wilson, of/rhp, Bamberg-Ehrhardt (S.C.) HS
1993: Trot Nixon, of/lhp, New Hanover HS, Wilmington, N.C.
1994: Doug Million, lhp, Sarasota (Fla.) HS
1995: Ben Davis, c, Malvern (Pa.) Prep
1996: Matt White, rhp, Waynesboro Area (Pa.) HS
1997: Darnell McDonald, of, Cherry Creek HS, Englewood, Colo.
1998: Drew Henson, 3b/rhp, Brighton (Mich.) HS
1999: Josh Hamilton, of/lhp, Athens Drive HS, Raleigh, N.C.
2000: Matt Harrington, rhp, Palmdale (Calif.) HS
2001: Joe Mauer, c, Cretin-Derham Hall HS, St. Paul, Minn.
2002: Scott Kazmir, lhp, Cypress Falls HS, Houston
2003: Jeff Allison, rhp, Veterans Memorial HS, Peabody, Mass.
2004: Homer Bailey, rhp, LaGrange (Texas) HS
2005: Justin Upton, ss, Great Bridge HS, Chesapeake, Va.
2006: Adrian Cardenas, ss/2b, Mons. Pace HS, Opa Locka, Fla.
2007: Mike Moustakas, ss, Chatsworth (Calif.) HS
2008: Ethan Martin, rhp/3b, Stephens County HS, Toccoa, Ga.
2009: Bryce Harper, c, Las Vegas HS
2010: Kaleb Cowart, rhp/3b, Cook HS, Adel, Ga.
2011: Dylan Bundy, rhp, Owasso (Okla.) HS

that really good body and you knew it was going get really good. The thing that was really impressive about him then was how easy the game was for him. There was no effort. He would glide in the outfield. When you watched him run, you knew that he could really run easy. He had a really good run stride, was strong. Watching his arm work, everything was just loose, fluid and easy. Then when he got into the batter's box, the first time I saw him swing, I said 'Whoa!' For the amount of bat speed that he had, he had that ability to keep the bat in zone a long time."

Greg Gay, Head Coach, Pierce County High: "We've played first-round picks before. Byron is different. Some of the other guys one or two tools. This guy is a five-tool guy. That's what is impressive about him. I don't know Byron well, but he's a very humble kid. Knowing his parents the little bit I know them, they live by modest means and are very humble people. He's just a great kid. That's the first time we had the opportunity to play for a state championship. Of course, we go to Game Three and lose 6-4. The only thing that can console this is knowing who you lost to. Appling had a good team even without Byron. With Byron they were practically unbeatable."

ALL-AMERICA TEAM

Byron Buxton

ALYSON BOYER RODE

Lance McCullers

MIKE JANES

HIGH SCHOOL

FIRST TEAM

Pos.	Name	School	Yr.	AVG	AB	R	H	2B	3B	HR	RBI	SB	DRAFTED
C	Alex Jackson	Rancho Bernardo HS, San Diego	So.	.400	95	37	38	5	1	17	36	6	Not eligible
IF	Austin Aune	Argyle (Texas) HS	Sr.	.463	82	39	38	10	5	8	41	20	Yankees (2)
IF	Joey Gallo	Bishop Gorman HS, Las Vegas	Sr.	.509	114	66	58	8	2	21	80	13	Rangers (1s)
IF	Matt Olson	Parkview HS, Lilburn, Ga.	Sr.	.385	96	27	37	13	2	9	47	2	Athletics (1s)
IF	Corey Seager	Northwest Cabarrus HS, Concord, N.C.	Sr.	.532	77	12	41	32	1	10	37	10	Dodgers (1)
OF	Albert Almora	Mater Academy, Hialeah Gardens, Fla.	Sr.	.603	73	42	44	13	5	6	34	24	Cubs (1)
OF	Clint Frazier	Loganville (Ga.) HS	Jr.	.424	118	55	50	7	2	24	58	14	Not eligible
OF	Courtney Hawkins	Carroll HS, Corpus Christi, Texas	Sr.	.452	84	50	38	4	4	10	36	16	White Sox (1)
DH	Dylan Cozens	Chaparral HS, Scottsdale, Ariz.	Sr.	.520	100	44	52	11	2	19	52	5	Phillies (2)
UT	Byron Buxton	Appling County HS, Baxley, Ga.	Sr.	.513	117	68	60	17	4	3	35	38	Twins (1)

Pos.	Name	School	Yr.	W	L	ERA	G	SV	IP	H	BB	K	DRAFTED
RHP	Luke Eubank	Newbury Park HS, Thousand Oaks, Calif.	Sr.	11	0	0.98	14	2	83	34	12	85	Undrafted
RHP	Carson Fulmer	All Saints Academy, Winter Haven, Fla.	Sr.	10	1	0.25	14	0	84	36	19	167	Red Sox (15)
RHP	Justin Garza	Bonita HS, La Verne, Calif.	Sr.	12	1	0.72	16	3	88	55	12	101	Indians (26)
RHP	Lance McCullers Jr.	Jesuit HS, Tampa	Sr.	13	0	0.18	14	0	77	28	30	140	Astros (1s)
RHP	Collin Wiles	Blue Valley West HS, Stilwell, Kan.	Sr.	9	0	0.12	9	0	56	29	9	87	Rangers (1s)
UT	Byron Buxton	Appling County HS, Baxley, Ga.	Sr.	10	1	1.90	22	5	81	36	29	154	Twins (1)

SECOND TEAM

Pos.	Name	School	Yr.	AVG	AB	R	H	2B	3B	HR	RBI	SB	DRAFTED
C	Chris Chinea	Gulliver Prep, Miami	Sr.	.542	72	29	39	12	1	9	38	7	Undrafted
IF	Austin Dean	Klein-Collins HS, Spring, Texas	Sr.	.379	95	44	36	10	0	12	45	12	Marlins (4)
IF	Scott Kingery	Mountain Pointe HS, Phoenix	Sr.	.495	101	38	50	13	2	8	36	12	Undrafted
IF	Wyatt Mathisen	Calallen HS, Corpus Christi, Texas	Sr.	.453	86	37	39	14	1	3	38	12	Pirates (2)
IF	A.J. Simcox	Farragut HS, Knoxville	Sr.	.460	150	60	69	13	4	9	45	12	Rockies (32)
OF	Spencer Edwards	Rockwall (Texas) HS	Sr.	.440	100	45	44	13	5	4	14	17	Rays (2)
OF	Sam Gillikin	Hoover (Ala.) HS	Sr.	.453	158	55	58	15	3	6	36	25	Braves (33)
OF	Timmy Robinson	Ocean View HS, Huntington Beach, Calif.	Sr.	.523	86	30	45	9	1	12	37	2	Twins (31)
DH	Mitch Nay	Hamilton HS, Chandler, Ariz.	Sr.	.380	92	33	35	9	0	11	33	6	Blue Jays (1s)
UT	Ty Hensley	Santa Fe HS, Edmond, Okla.	Sr.	.447	94	27	42	10	1	10	41	0	Yankees (1)

Pos.	Name	School	Yr.	W	L	ERA	G	SV	IP	H	BB	K	DRAFTED
RHP	Jamie Callahan	Dillon (S.C.) HS	Sr.	7	1	0.89	9	0	55	23	15	113	Red Sox (2)
LHP	Rob Kaminsky	St. Joseph Regional HS, Montvale, N.J	Jr.	8	2	0.20	10	0	53	12	15	103	Not eligible
RHP	Jackson Stephens	Oxford (Ala.) HS	Sr.	14	1	0.96	17	2	85	47	12	117	Reds (18)
RHP	Jake Thompson	Rockwall-Heat HS, Heath, Texas	Sr.	12	1	0.73	17	0	96	63	27	165	Tigers (2)
RHP	Keegan Thompson	Cullman (Ala.) HS	Jr.	7	2	0.94	16	4	67	42	5	119	Not eligible
UT	Ty Hensley	Santa Fe HS, Edmond, Okla.	Sr.	10	0	1.52	11	0	55	23	28	111	Yankees (1)

DRAFT

Teams feel their way through 2012 draft after CBA changes

BY CONOR GLASSEY

Most drafts are remembered for specific players.

Nationals fans will surely remember the 2009 and 2010 drafts for righthander Stephen Strasburg and outfielder Bryce Harper. The 2005 first round is memorable for producing a number of young stars, including Justin Upton, Alex Gordon, Ryan Zimmerman, Ryan Braun, Ricky Romero, Troy Tulowitzki, Cameron Maybin, Andrew McCutchen, Jay Bruce, Jacoby Ellsbury, Matt Garza and Colby Rasmus. The 1999 draft was a battle between two high school players named Josh—Hamilton and Beckett—for who would go first overall, and years like 1993 (Alex Rodriguez), 1990 (Chipper Jones) and 1987 (Ken Griffey) stand out for having Hall of Famers picked at the top.

While there will surely be players from the latest crop who go on to have notable careers, the 2012 draft reflected what may have been the most significant changes to the process since the beginning of the draft in 1965.

After years of labor peace, negotiators were able to make the draft a focus of baseball's newest Collective Bargaining Agreement. Baseball officials had long considered changes to the process and had made piecemeal tweaks over the years, but

TOMASSO DeROSA

The Astros made shortstop Carlos Correa the first Puerto Rican to be drafted No. 1

FIRST-ROUND BONUS PROGRESSION

Even with new draft rules designed to curtail spending, teams paid an average of $2,475,167 in bonuses to first-round picks in 2012. That's the second-highest amount ever, trailing only the $2,653,375 average from 2011.
After the first draft in 1965, first-round bonuses rose by an average of just 0.6 percent annually for the rest of the 1960s and 5.2 percent per year in the 1970s. Bonus inflation started to pick up in the 1980s, averaging 10.2 percent annually, and soared to 26.9 percent per year in the 1990s. When MLB instituted an informal slotting system from 2000-11, first-round bonuses rose by an average of 3.8 percent.
Below are the annual averages for first-round bonuses since the draft started in 1965.

YEAR	AVERAGE	CHANGE	YEAR	AVERAGE	CHANGE	YEAR	AVERAGE	CHANGE
1965	$42,516	—	1981	$78,573	+6.1%	1997	$1,325,536	+40.4%
1966	$44,430	+4.5%	1982	$82,615	+5.1%	1998	$1,637,667	+23.1%
1967	$42,898	-3.4%	1983	$87,236	+5.6%	1999	$1,809,767	+10.5%
1968	$43,850	+2.2%	1984	$105,391	+20.8%	2000	$1,872,586	+3.5%
1969	$43,504	-0.8%	1985	$118,115	+12.1%	2001	$2,154,280	+15.0%
1970	$45,230	+3.9%	1986	$116,300	-1.6%	2002	$2,106,793	-2.2%
1971	$45,197	-0.1%	1987	$128,480	+10.5%	2003	$1,765,667	-16.2%
1972	$44,952	-0.5%	1988	$142,540	+10.9%	2004	$1,958,448	+10.9%
1973	$48,832	+8.6%	1989	$176,008	+23.5%	2005	$2,018,000	+3.0%
1974	$53,333	+9.2%	1990	$252,577	+43.5%	2006	$1,933,333	-4.2%
1975	$49,333	-7.5%	1991	$365,396	+44.7%	2007	$2,098,083	+8.5%
1976	$49,631	+0.6%	1992	$481,893	+31.9%	2008	$2,458,714	+17.2%
1977	$48,813	-1.6%	1993	$613,037	+27.2%	2009	$2,434,800	-1.0%
1978	$67,892	+39.1%	1994	$790,357	+28.9%	2010	$2,220,966	-8.8%
1979	$68,094	+0.2%	1995	$918,019	+16.1%	2011	$2,653,375	+19.5%
1980	$74,025	+8.7%	1996*	$944,404	+2.9%	2012	$2,475,167	-6.7%

comprehensive change had been forestalled by more significant issues.

Major League Baseball went into labor negotiations with the draft at the top of its list this time, however, with the idea that significant changes could result in more equitable distribution of talent.

The biggest change in that regard was the establishment of aggregate signing bonus pools for each team's picks in the first 10 rounds of the draft. Each pick in the first 10 rounds now has a predetermined bonus value, which in 2012 ranged from $7.2 million for the No. 1 choice to $125,000 for pick No. 300 and those that followed.

The pools ranged from $12,368,200 for the Twins (who owned the No. 2 choice and added three selections for the loss of free agents Michael Cuddyer and Jason Kubel) to $1,645,700 for the Angels (who forfeited their first two picks to sign free agents Albert Pujols and C.J. Wilson). The sum of all the pools was $189,903,500, a slight reduction from the $191,876,250 clubs spent on the first 10 rounds of the loaded 2011 draft.

Teams had been under similar recommendations since 2000, but the commissioner's office lacked an enforcement mechanism. So some teams followed the recommendations, but many did not, giving them an advantage in stockpiling talent from the draft.

Under the new system, however, the penalties for exceeding the aggregate limit are significant. Any team that exceeds its bonus pool by as much as 5 percent must pay a 75 percent tax on the overage. The penalties escalate, with a 75 percent tax and the loss of a first-round pick in the next draft for a 5-10 percent overage; a 100 percent tax and the loss of first- and second-rounders for a 10-15 percent overage; and a 100 percent tax and the loss of two first-rounders for an overage of 15 percent or more.

The budget applies only to picks in the first 10 rounds, unless a player after the 10th round (including nondrafted free agents) signs for more than $100,000. Anything beyond the $100,000 is applied to the overall budget as well. Teams were also encouraged to sign players in the first 10 rounds, because failing to sign a player in the top 10 rounds subtracted that pick value from the team's overall bonus pool.

Because the budget is applied to the aggregate spending and not individual picks, some teams saved money by signing certain players for below-slot deals and applying the savings to bonuses for tougher signs. This led to an unusual run on college seniors—the easiest, cheapest draft demo-

DRAFT EXPENDITURES BY CLUB

Teams spent $207.9 million on draft bonuses in 2012, the second-highest total ever. The record was set in 2011, when clubs combined to spend $228 million on bonuses and another $8.1 million on guaranteed salaries as part of major league contracts.

With new draft rules allocating specific bonus pools and prescribing harsh draft-pick penalties to teams that exceeded them by more than 5 percent, several clubs changed their shopping patterns. The Pirates and Nationals were the two biggest draft spenders under the old Collective Bargaining Agreement, which covered the 2007-11 seasons. Pittsburgh plummeted from a record $17 million in 2011 to $3.8 million this year, while Washington dropped from $15 million (and another $2.6 million in salary guarantees) to $4.9 million.

On the other side of the spectrum, both the Twins and Astros had ranked in the bottom third in bonus spending under the old CBA. With the top two draft slots and bonus pools this year, Minnesota and Houston led all clubs by paying $12.6 million and $12.1 million in bonuses, respectively.

TEAM	2012	2011	2007-11
Twins	$12,602,400	$5,902,300	$4,720,740
Astros	$12,074,200	$5,545,800	$5,032,526
Padres	$10,993,000	$11,020,600	$7,153,620
Blue Jays	$10,486,000	$10,996,500	$7,685,920
Cardinals	$9,909,490	$4,554,000	$5,363,640
Mariners	$9,325,200	$11,330,500	$7,211,180
Cubs	$9,164,700	$11,994,550	$6,481,420
Athletics	$8,300,600	$3,067,300	$5,042,100
Red Sox	$7,908,000	$10,978,700	$8,819,450
Royals	$7,573,000	$14,066,000	$9,040,980
Reds	$7,450,400	$6,378,900	$5,533,770
Orioles	$7,433,200	$8,432,100	$8,243,940
Rangers	$7,394,400	$4,193,000	$6,276,860
Brewers	$7,200,100	$7,509,300	$5,870,300
Mets	$7,007,400	$6,782,500	$4,983,860
Rockies	$6,978,700	$3,967,900	$4,900,780
White Sox	$6,450,100	$2,786,300	$3,665,490
Dodgers	$6,277,300	$3,509,300	$4,721,610
Marlins	$5,755,700	$4,135,000	$4,342,210
Indians	$5,330,000	$8,225,000	$6,635,860
Yankees	$4,898,400	$6,324,500	$6,739,800
Nationals	$4,880,500	$15,002,100	$10,216,920
Phillies	$4,787,800	$4,689,800	$4,560,540
Braves	$4,758,000	$3,735,700	$4,402,210
Giants	$4,630,500	$6,266,000	$6,632,480
Diamondbacks	$4,594,800	$11,930,000	$7,052,200
Rays	$4,427,300	$11,482,900	$8,116,440
Pirates	$3,830,700	$17,005,700	$10,411,480
Tigers	$3,172,300	$2,878,700	$6,253,840
Angels	$2,289,800	$3,318,100	$4,538,880
Total	**$207,883,990**	**$228,009,050**	**$190,651,046**
Average	**$6,929,466**	**$7,600,302**	**$6,355,035**

graphic to sign—in rounds six through 10.

Overall, 57 seniors were drafted in the top 10 rounds of the 2012 draft—significantly more than in 2011 (30), 2010 (29), 2009 (33) or 2008 (29).

At the end of the day, every team stayed below the 5 percent threshold in 2012. There were 11 teams that exceeded their bonus pools by up to 5 percent, so the tax on that spending will amount to about $1.7 million. It will be divided among the 11 teams that receive revenue-sharing money and did not exceed their bonus pools this year: the Athletics, Brewers, Indians, Marlins, Orioles,

Padres, Pirates, Rays, Reds, Rockies and Tigers.

More Changes

The changes weren't limited to budgets, however. The draft has been reduced from 50 to 40 rounds, the signing deadline moved up to mid-July rather than mid-August, and major league contracts are no longer an option for teams when signing drafted players.

There were also significant changes to the free-agent compensation system that will result in fewer compensation and supplemental picks in future drafts.

The familiar Type A and Type B free agents, which were based on the Elias ranking system, will be eliminated. Now the only free agents subject to compensation will be those who are offered contracts equal to the average salary of the 125 highest-paid players in the game as they enter the free-agent process. Players also have to be with a team for an entire season to be subject to compensation, so pending free agents who are traded at midseason will not generate extra picks for the teams that acquire them.

A team that signs one of those free agents will give up its first-round pick. Unlike before, when the top 15 overall picks were protected, now only

ALYSON BOYER RODE

Rockies outfielder David Dahl hit .379/.423/.625 in the Pioneer League

the top 10 are protected. In those cases, the team will lose its second-highest selection (not necessarily its second-round pick, as before). And unlike before, the forfeited pick will no longer go to the team that lost the free agent; now the pick is simply eliminated. The team that lost the free agent receives a supplemental pick after the first round.

The new rules have also added a lottery for six supplemental picks following both the first and second rounds, labeled as competitive balance selections. Teams that are in the bottom 10 in revenue and/or market size go into a pool for six picks after the first round, with odds of winning based on the prior season's winning percentage. Teams that don't get one of those picks—and any other team that receives money from revenue sharing—then goes into another lottery for six picks after the second round. The odds of winning are based on prior season winning percentage and the lottery picks can be traded.

The Royals won the first competitive-balance lottery, meaning they'll get a pick after the first-round and free-agent compensation choices. They were followed by the Pirates, Diamondbacks, Orioles, Reds and Marlins. The competitive-balance selections after the second round were won by the Padres, Indians, Rockies, Athletics, Brewers and Tigers.

HIGHEST BONUSES EVER

Three of the five highest bonuses in draft history were paid in 2011, including a record $8 million to No. 1 overall pick Gerrit Cole by the Pirates. This year, the largest bonus went to No. 2 overall choice Byron Buxton, whose $6 million from the Twins tied for the 11th-most ever.

PLAYER, POS.	TEAM, YEAR (PICK)	BONUS
Gerrit Cole, rhp	Pirates, 2011 (No. 1)	$8,000,000
Stephen Strasburg, rhp	Nationals, 2009 (No. 1)	*$7,500,000
Bubba Starling, of	Royals, 2011 (No. 5)	+$7,500,000
Jameson Taillon, rhp	Pirates, 2010 (No. 2)	$6,500,000
Danny Hultzen, lhp	Mariners, 2011 (No. 2)	*$6,350,000
Donavan Tate, of	Padres, 2009 (No. 3)	+$6,250,000
Bryce Harper, of	Nationals, 2010 (No. 1)	*$6,250,000
Buster Posey, c	Giants, 2008 (No. 5)	$6,200,000
Tim Beckham, ss	Rays, 2008 (No. 1)	+$6,150,000
Justin Upton, ss	D'backs, 2005 (No. 1)	+$6,100,000
Matt Wieters, c	Orioles, 2007 (No. 5)	$6,000,000
Pedro Alvarez, 3b	Pirates, 2008 (No. 2)	*$6,000,000
Eric Hosmer, 1b	Royals, 2008 (No. 3)	$6,000,000
Dustin Ackley, of	Mariners, 2009 (No. 2)	*$6,000,000
Anthony Rendon, 3b	Nationals, 2011 (No. 6)	*$6,000,000
Byron Buxton, of	Twins, 2012 (No. 2)	$6,000,000
David Price, lhp	Devil Rays, 2007 (No. 1)	*$5,600,000
Joe Borchard, of	White Sox, 2000 (No. 12)	+$5,300,000
Manny Machado, ss	Orioles, 2010 (No. 3)	$5,250,000
Zach Lee, rhp	Dodgers, 2010 (No. 28)	+$5,250,000
Joe Mauer, c	Twins, 2001 (No. 1)	+$5,150,000
Archie Bradley, rhp	Diamondbacks, 2011 (No. 7)	+$5,000,000
Josh Bell, of	Pirates, 2011 (No. 61)	$5,000,000

*Part of major league contract.
+Bonus spread over multiple years under MLB provisions for two-sport athletes.

The Marlins and Tigers then made history by trading their competitive-balance picks as part of a trade-deadline deal centered around Anibal Sanchez, Omar Infante and Jacob Turner. So in 2013 the Tigers will pick after the first round, and the Marlins will pick after the second. The picks can be traded only once.

2012 Class Muddled At The Top

With the new rules in place, combined with a draft class that didn't have a Strasburg or Harper kind of talent at the top, teams went into the draft tight-lipped about how their board shaped up at the top.

But at the end of the day, things played out pretty true to form. The top picks ranked by Baseball America were still picked at the top of the draft, even if the order was a little different.

The Astros provided a mild surprise off the bat as they picked Puerto Rican high school shortstop Carlos Correa with the first-overall selection. Correa, as expected, easily eclipsed Ramon Castro's record, set in 1994, for being the highest-drafted player ever out of Puerto Rico, which became part of the draft in 1989 while becoming the first Puerto Rican ever drafted first overall.

Houston scouting director Bobby Heck said the team had a pool of five players it was considering with the top pick and did not settle on Correa until the afternoon of the draft.

But Correa still has star potential. At 6-foot-3 and 185 pounds he's big for a shortstop, but he's agile with soft hands and smooth actions. He is an above-average runner and has premium arm strength, allowing him to play deep in the infield. He has a smooth righthanded swing with excellent balance and bat speed, and the overall package reminds scouts of Troy Tulowitzki.

"He's a power-hitting shortstop and that's a pretty good separator," Heck said. "All of the players we considered had strong profiles as well, but it was tough to walk away from the shortstop with power potential."

In addition to his tools, Correa also has many other enviable qualities scouts love. He is bilingual and has excellent work ethic.

The Astros made another splash in the supplemental round by taking righthander Lance McCullers Jr. from Jesuit High in Tampa. McCullers has big league bloodlines and his fastball has been clocked as high as 98 mph. He was expected to go in the middle of the first round.

There were only a few surprises on the first day of the draft. Overall, only a few players taken in the first 60 picks could be considered reaches based on BA's predraft rankings. The first eight

NO. 1 OVERALL PICKS

YEAR	TEAM: PLAYER, POS., SCHOOL	BONUS
1965	Athletics: Rick Monday, of, Arizona State	$100,000
1966	Mets: Steve Chilcott, c, Antelope Valley HS, Lancaster, Calif.	$75,000
1967	Yankees: Ron Blomberg, 1b, Druid Hills HS, Atlanta	$65,000
1968	Mets: Tim Foli, ss, Notre Dame HS, Sherman Oaks, Calif.	$74,000
1969	Senators: Jeff Burroughs, of, Centennial HS, Long Beach	$88,000
1970	Padres: Mike Ivie, c, Walker HS, Atlanta	$75,000
1971	White Sox: Danny Goodwin, c, Peoria (Ill.) HS	Did Not Sign
1972	Padres: Dave Roberts, 3b, Oregon	$70,000
1973	Rangers: David Clyde, lhp, Westchester HS, Texas	*$65,000
1974	Padres: Bill Almon, ss, Brown	*$90,000
1975	Angels: Danny Goodwin, c, Southern	*$125,000
1976	Astros: Floyd Bannister, lhp, Arizona State	$100,000
1977	White Sox: Harold Baines, of, St. Michaels (Md.) HS	$32,000
1978	Braves: Bob Horner, 3b, Arizona State	*$162,000
1979	Mariners: Al Chambers, 1b, Harris HS, Harrisburg, Pa.	$60,000
1980	Mets: Darryl Strawberry, of, Crenshaw HS, Los Angeles	$152,500
1981	Mariners: Mike Moore, rhp, Oral Roberts	$100,000
1982	Cubs: Shawon Dunston, ss, Jefferson HS, New York	$135,000
1983	Twins: Tim Belcher, rhp, Mount Vernon Nazarene (Ohio)	Did Not Sign
1984	Mets: Shawn Abner, of, Mechanicsburg (Pa.) HS	$150,500
1985	Brewers: B.J. Surhoff, c, North Carolina	$150,000
1986	Pirates: Jeff King, 3b, Arkansas	$180,000
1987	Mariners: Ken Griffey Jr., of, Moeller HS, Cincinnati	$160,000
1988	Padres: Andy Benes, rhp, Evansville	$235,000
1989	Orioles: Ben McDonald, rhp, Louisiana State	*$350,000
1990	Braves: Chipper Jones, ss, The Bolles School, Jacksonville	$275,000
1991	Yankees: Brien Taylor, lhp, East Carteret HS, Beaufort, N.C.	$1,550,000
1992	Astros: Phil Nevin, 3b, Cal State Fullerton	$700,000
1993	Mariners: Alex Rodriguez, ss, Westminster Christian HS, Miami	*$1,000,000
1994	Mets: Paul Wilson, rhp, Florida State	$1,550,000
1995	Angels: Darin Erstad, of, Nebraska	$1,575,000
1996	Pirates: Kris Benson, rhp, Clemson	$2,000,000
1997	Tigers: Matt Anderson, rhp, Rice	$2,505,000
1998	Phillies: Pat Burrell, 3b, Miami	*$3,150,000
1999	Devil Rays: Josh Hamilton, of, Athens Drive HS, Raleigh	$3,960,000
2000	Marlins: Adrian Gonzalez, 1b, Eastlake HS, Chula Vista, Calif.	$3,000,000
2001	Twins: Joe Mauer, c, Cretin-Derham Hall, St. Paul	$5,150,000
2002	Pirates: Bryan Bullington, rhp, Ball State	$4,000,000
2003	Devil Rays: Delmon Young, of, Camarillo (Calif.) HS	*$3,700,000
2004	Padres: Matt Bush, ss, Mission Bay HS, San Diego	$3,150,000
2005	Diamondbacks: Justin Upton, ss, Great Bridge HS, Chesapeake, Va.	$6,100,000
2006	Royals: Luke Hochevar, rhp, Fort Worth (American Association)	*$3,500,000
2007	Devil Rays: David Price, lhp, Vanderbilt	*$5,600,000
2008	Rays: Tim Beckham, ss, Griffin (Ga.) HS	$6,150,000
2009	Nationals: Stephen Strasburg, rhp, San Diego State	*$7,500,000
2010	Nationals: Bryce Harper, of, JC of Southern Nevada	*$6,250,000
2011	Pirates: Gerrit Cole, rhp, UCLA	$8,000,000
2012	Astros: Carlos Correa, ss, Puerto Rico Baseball Academy, Gurabo, P.R.	$4,800,000

*Part of major league contract.

picks in the draft were all ranked in the top eight and there wasn't a player selected in the first round who wasn't on the top 50.

"I think the board played out more to the talent," Heck said. "I think players getting ridden down, that seems less evident. I think players are going where they're supposed to be going, closer to the order of their talent."

Overall, the top 60 picks consisted of 25 college players and 35 high schoolers.

"For the most part what we saw today, not every team has the same board and every team's order is different," Red Sox general manager Ben Cherington said. "But the picks that went today, a lot of the best players were taken today. Not necessarily in the order that they might have been for us, but in aggregate. . . There are still talented players, but most of the top players were taken today."

Seventeen of the 31 first-round picks were taken out of high school. Three of the high school picks—Florida shortstop Addison Russell, California third baseman Daniel Robertson and Georgia first baseman Matt Olson—were taken by the Athletics. It's the first time the team has used back-to-back-to-back picks on high school players since 1978 when Oakland drafted Mike Morgan, Tim Conroy and Keith Atherton.

"I think it was just a reflection of what was available to us in this draft," A's scouting director Eric Kubota said. "We just took the best guys on our board, it just turned out they were high school guys. With Russell, we love his athleticism and his now baseball skills. He has a chance to be a five-tool player in the middle of the diamond."

Righthander Lucas Giolito was one of the top high school players in the class—a physical athlete with a fastball in the upper 90s—but slipped to the Nationals with the 16th overall pick after missing most of the spring with an elbow injury.

It was a risky move for the Nationals, as their

FIRST-ROUND TRENDS

Year	College	HS	Hitters	Pitchers	Average Bonus	Change
2000	12	18	13	17	$1,872,586	+3.5%
2001	18	12	10	*20	$2,154,280	+15.0%
2002	14	16	14	16	$2,106,793	-2.2%
2003	18	12	*20	10	$1,765,667	*-16.2%
2004	17	13	11	19	$1,958,448	+10.9%
2005	19	10	17	13	$2,018,000	+3.0%
2006	16	13	12	18	$1,933,333	-4.2%
2007	13	17	13	17	$2,098,083	+8.5%
2008	*21	9	11	19	$2,458,714	+17.2%
2009	15	16	16	16	$2,434,800	-1.0%
2010	15	17	18	14	$2,220,966	-8.8%
2011	19	14	14	19	*$2,653,375	+19.5%
2012	14	17	18	13	$2,457,167	-6.7%

*Draft record.

bonus pool was one of the smallest at $4.4 million. After picking Giolito, the team was conservative with the rest of its picks and signed the righthander away from his UCLA commitment for $2.925 million. Giolito started one game for the Nationals Rookie-level Gulf Coast League affiliate before re-injuring his elbow, requiring Tommy John surgery.

Pirates Fail To Sign Appel

In general, the new draft rules had the effect of getting players to sign much more quickly. In 2011, 23 first-round choices were unsigned when deadline day began, and teams spent $132.1 million on bonuses and another $7 million in guarantees that day to get them signed. In 2012, however, just 17 of the first 338 choices in the first 10 rounds had not come to terms when deadline day started, and clubs wound up signing 23 players

LARRY GOREN

The Pirates did not sign their first-round pick, Stanford righthander Mark Appel

from all rounds for $16.9 million.

Commissioner Bud Selig got the reduction in draft spending he wanted, with teams spending about $208 million on bonuses, down from a record $228 million in 2011. That was still the second-most spending on the draft ever, though.

The one exception to the quick signing trend was Stanford righthander Mark Appel, who had been the leading candidate to go with the No. 1 pick heading into the draft.

With the Astros taking Correa with the first pick (and their decision coming down to the last minute), it created a bit of a domino effect for Appel. The teams drafting behind the Astros had already lined up their selections, and because Appel is advised by the Boras Corp. and teams couldn't be sure how he would fit into their budgets, he fell to the Pirates with the No. 8 pick.

The Pirates have spent more aggressively than any team in the draft in recent years. In Neal Huntington's first four years as general manager from 2008-11, Pittsburgh paid $47.6 million in bonuses, including a record $17 million in 2011.

But the new draft rules limited the team in 2012. The Pirates decided they could not incur a draft pick penalty, and Appel didn't come off his bonus demands, so ultimately Appel did not sign and will go back into the 2013 draft. The Pirates' final offer was reportedly $3.8 million. They will receive a compensation pick in 2013 for failing to sign Appel.

"The knee-jerk reaction as a scout is that you want to sign the player," Pirates assistant GM Greg Smith said. "When you step back from it, you say he slid and you knew it was a risk going in. We have the ninth pick next year, plus our own pick, so we're good with it.

"With the new CBA, you can just keep going. Teams are not going to give up draft picks. If the landscape were different, sure, things might have worked out."

Big League Bloodlines

As usual, plenty of players with famous relatives were taken in the draft. Most notably, Lance McCullers Jr., was taken 41st overall, the exact same spot his father was picked 30 years prior.

The Orioles drafted Cal Ripken's son, Ryan, in the 20th round, but he didn't sign and now attends South Carolina. The Mariners took Mike Yastrzemski—Carl's grandson—out of Vanderbilt in the 30th round, but he didn't sign, either. The Braves signed Craig Kimbrel's brother, Matt, in the 31st round and the Pirates' seventh-round pick, catcher Jacob Stallings, is the son of Kevin Stallings, the head coach of Vanderbilt's basketball team.

Righthander Kevin Gausman became the highest pick from Louisiana State since 1989

ANDREW WOOLLEY

DRAFT

TEAM. PLAYER, POS., SCHOOL	BONUS	TEAM. PLAYER, POS., SCHOOL	BONUS
1. Astros. Carlos Correa, ss, HS—Gurabo, P.R.	$4,800,000	51. Dodgers. Jesmuel Valentin, 2b, HS—Gurabo, P.R.	$984,700
2. Twins. Byron Buxton, of, HS—Baxley, Ga.	$6,000,000	52. Cardinals. Patrick Wisdom, 3b, St. Mary's	$678,790
3. Mariners. Mike Zunino, c, Florida	$4,000,000	53. Rangers. Collin Wiles, rhp, HS—Stilwell, Kan.	$975,000
4. Orioles. Kevin Gausman, rhp, Louisiana State	$4,320,000	54. Phillies. Mitch Gueller, rhp, HS—Chehalis, Wash.	$940,200
5. Royals. Kyle Zimmer, rhp, San Francisco	$3,000,000	55. Padres. Walker Weickel, rhp, HS—Orlando	$2,000,000
6. Cubs. Albert Almora, of, HS—Hialeah Gardens, Fla.	$3,900,000	56. Cubs. Paul Blackburn, rhp, HS—Brentwood, Calif.	$911,700
7. Padres. Max Fried, lhp, Studio City, Calif.	$3,000,000	57. Reds. Jeff Gelalich, of, UCLA	$825,000
8. Pirates. Mark Appel, rhp, Stanford.	Did not sign	58. Blue Jays. Mitch Nay, 3b, HS—Chandler, Ariz.	$1,000,000
9. Marlins. Andrew Heaney, lhp, Oklahoma State	$2,800,000	59. Cardinals. Steve Bean, c, HS—Rockwall, Texas	$700,000
10. Rockies. David Dahl, of, HS—Birmingham	$2,600,000	60. Blue Jays. Tyler Gonzales, rhp, HS—San Antonio	$750,000
11. Athletics. Addison Russell, ss, HS—Pace, Fla.	$2,625,000	61. Astros. Nolan Fontana, ss, Florida	$875,000
12. Mets. Gavin Cecchini, ss, HS—Barbe, La.	$2,550,000	62. Athletics. Bruce Maxwell, c/1b, Birmingham-Southern	$700,000
13. White Sox. Courtney Hawkins, of, HS—Corpus Christi, Texas	$2,475,000	63. Twins. Mason Melotakis, lhp, Northwestern State	$750,000
14. Reds. Nick Travieso, rhp, HS—Southwest Ranches, Fla.	$2,375,000	64. Mariners. Joe DeCarlo, 3b, HS—Glen Mills, Pa.	$1,300,000
15. Indians. Tyler Naquin, of, Texas A&M	$2,250,000	65. Orioles. Branden Kline, rhp, Virginia	$793,700
16. Nationals. Lucas Giolito, rhp, HS—Studio City, Calif.	$2,925,000	66. Royals. Sam Selman, lhp, Vanderbilt	$750,000
17. Blue Jays. D.J. Davis, of, HS—Wiggins, Miss.	$1,750,000	67. Cubs. Duane Underwood, rhp, HS—Marietta, Ga.	$1,050,000
18. Dodgers. Corey Seager, 3b, HS—Concord, N.C.	$2,350,000	68. Padres. Jeremy Baltz, of, St. John's	$625,000
19. Cardinals. Michael Wacha, rhp, Texas A&M	$1,900,000	69. Pirates. Wyatt Mathisen, c, HS—Corpus Christi, Texas	$746,300
20. Giants. Chris Stratton, rhp, Mississippi State	$1,850,000	70. Padres. Dane Phillips, c/1b, Oklahoma City	$450,000
21. Braves. Luke Sims, rhp, HS—Snellville, Ga.	$1,825,000	71. Mets. Matt Reynolds, 3b, Arkansas	$525,000
22. Blue Jays. Marcus Stroman, rhp, Duke	$1,650,000	72. Twins. J.T. Chargois, rhp, Rice	$712,600
23. Cardinals. James Ramsey, of, Florida State	$1,775,000	73. Rockies. Max White, of, HS—Williston, Fla.	$1,000,000
24. Red Sox. Deven Marrero, ss, Arizona State	$1,750,000	74. Athletics. Nolan Sanburn, rhp, Arkansas	$691,000
25. Rays. Richie Shaffer, 3b, Clemson	$1,725,000	75. Mets. Teddy Stankiewicz, rhp, HS—Richland Hills, Texas	Did not sign
26. Diamondbacks. Stryker Trahan, c/of, HS—Lafayette, La.	$1,700,000	76. White Sox. Chris Beck, rhp, Georgia Southern	$600,000
27. Brewers. Clint Coulter, c, HS—Camas, Wash.	$1,675,000	77. Phillies. Dylan Cozens, of, HS—Scottsdale, Ariz.	$659,800
28. Brewers. Victor Roache, of, Georgia Southern	$1,650,000	78. Reds. Tanner Rahier, ss, HS—Palm Desert, Calif.	$649,700
29. Rangers. Lewis Brinson, of, HS—Coral Springs, Fla.	$1,625,000	79. Indians. Mitch Brown, rhp, HS—Rochester, Minn.	$800,000
30. Yankees. Ty Hensley, rhp, HS—Edmond, Okla.	$1,200,000	80. Nationals. Tony Renda, 2b, California	$500,000
31. Red Sox. Brian Johnson, lhp, Florida	$1,575,000	81. Blue Jays. Chase DeJong, rhp, HS—Long Beach	$860,000
32. Twins. J.O. Berrios, rhp, HS—Bayamon, P.R.	$1,550,000	82. Dodgers. Paco Rodriguez, lhp, Florida	$610,800
33. Padres. Zach Eflin, rhp, HS—Oviedo, Fla.	$1,200,000	83. Rangers. Jamie Jarmon, of, HS—Dagsboro, Del.	$601,500
34. Athletics. Daniel Robertson, 3b, HS—Upland, Calif.	$1,500,000	84. Giants. Martin Agosta, rhp, St. Mary's	$612,500
35. Mets. Kevin Plawecki, c, Purdue	$1,400,000	85. Braves. Alex Wood, lhp, Georgia	$700,000
36. Cardinals. Stephen Piscotty, of/3b, Stanford	$1,430,400	86. Cardinals. Carson Kelly, 3b, HS—Portland, Ore.	$1,600,000
37. Red Sox. Pat Light, rhp, Monmouth	$1,000,000	87. Red Sox. Jamie Callahan, rhp, HS—Dillon, S.C.	$600,000
38. Brewers. Mitch Haniger, of, Cal Poly	$1,200,000	88. Rays. Spencer Edwards, of, HS—Rockwall, Texas	$554,400
39. Rangers. Joey Gallo, 3b, HS—Las Vegas	$2,250,000	89. Yankees. Austin Aune, of, HS—Argyle, Texas	$1,000,000
40. Phillies. Shane Watson, rhp, HS—Lakewood, Calif.	$1,291,300	90. Diamondbacks. Joe Munoz, 3b, HS—Hacienda Heights, Calif.	$540,000
41. Astros. Lance McCullers Jr., rhp, HS—Tampa	$2,500,000	91. Tigers. Jake Thompson, rhp, HS—Heath, Texas	$531,800
42. Twins. Luke Bard, rhp, Georgia Tech	$1,227,000	92. Brewers. Tyrone Taylor, of, HS—Torrance, Calif.	$750,000
43. Cubs. Pierce Johnson, rhp, Missouri State	$1,196,000	93. Rangers. Nick Williams, of, HS—Galveston, Texas	$500,000
44. Padres. Travis Jankowski, of, Stony Brook	$975,000	94. Yankees. Peter O'Brien, c, Miami	$460,000
45. Pirates. Barrett Barnes, of, Texas Tech	$1,000,000	95. Phillies. Alec Rash, rhp, HS—Adel, Iowa	Did not sign
46. Rockies. Eddie Butler, rhp, Radford	$1,000,000	96. Astros. Brady Rodgers, rhp, Arizona State	$495,200
47. Athletics. Matt Olson, 1b, HS—Lilburn, Ga.	$1,079,700	97. Twins. Adam Brett Walker, 1b, Jacksonville	$490,400
48. White Sox. Keon Barnum, 1b, HS—Tampa	$950,000	98. Mariners. Edwin Diaz, rhp, HS—Caguas, P.R.	$300,000
49. Reds. Jesse Winker, of, HS—Orlando	$1,000,000	99. Orioles. Adrian Marin, ss, HS—Miami	$481,100
50. Blue Jays. Matt Smoral, lhp, HS—Solon, Ohio	$2,000,000	100. Royals. Colin Rodgers, lhp, HS—Baton Rouge	$700,000

ORDER OF SELECTION IN PARENTHESES PLAYERS SIGNED IN BOLD

ARIZONA DIAMONDBACKS (25)

1. **Stryker Trahan, c/of, Acadiana HS, Lafayette, La.**
2. **Joe Munoz, 3b, Los Altos HS, Hacienda Heights, Calif.**
3. **Jake Barrett, rhp, Arizona State**
4. **Charles Taylor, of, Timberview HS, Mansfield, Texas**
5. **Ronnie Freeman, c, Kennesaw State**
6. **Jake Lamb, 3b, Washington**
7. **Andrew Velazquez, ss, Fordham Prep, New York**
8. **Evan Marzilli, of, South Carolina**
9. **Jeff Gibbs, rhp, Maine**
10. **Danny Poma, of, Hofstra**
11. **Ben Eckels, rhp, Davis (Calif.) HS**
12. **Alex Glenn, of, Henry County HS, McDonough, Ga.**
13. **Phildrick Llewellyn, c, Trinity Christian Academy, Lake Worth, Fla.**
14. **Derrick Stultz, rhp, South Florida**
15. **Blake Forslund, rhp, Liberty**
16. Landon Lassiter, ss, North Davidson HS, Lexington, N.C.
17. **Yogey Perez-Ramos, of, Miami Dade JC**
18. **Kevin Medrano, 2b, Missouri State**
19. **R.J. Hively, rhp, Mississippi**
20. **Jacob House, 1b, Texas A&M**
21. **Rudy Flores, 1b, Florida International**
22. **Holden Helmink, rhp, Willis (Texas) HS**
23. Matt Dermody, lhp, Iowa
24. **Mark Ginther, 3b, Oklahoma State**
25. **Vince Spilker, rhp, Lee (Tenn.)**
26. **Chris Capper, rhp, Brigham Young**
27. **Damion Smith, of, Holy Names Catholic HS, Windsor, Ont.**
28. Max Schrock, 2b, Cardinal Gibbons HS, Raleigh
29. **Adam McConnell, ss, Richmond**
30. **Chase Stevens, rhp, Oklahoma State**
31. **Andrew Potter, rhp, Eastside HS, Lancaster, Calif.**
32. **Daniel Watts, lhp, Jacksonville State**
33. **Jonathan Pulley, rhp, Spartanburg Methodist (S.C.) JC**
34. **Jared Ray, rhp, Houston**
35. **Robbie Buller, rhp, Houston Baptist**
36. **Andrew Barbosa, lhp, South Florida**
37. **Breland Almadova, of, Hawaii**
38. Cam Gibson, of, Grosse Point (Mich.) South HS
39. **Rafael Garcia, c, Gilroy (Calif.) HS**
40. Zane Hemond, rhp, Montrose (Colo.) HS

ATLANTA BRAVES (21)

1. **Lucas Sims, rhp, Brookwood HS, Snellville, Ga.**
2. **Alex Wood, lhp, Georgia**
3. **Bryan de la Rosa, c, Bucky Dent Academy, Delray Beach, Fla.**
4. **Justin Black, of, Billings (Mont.) West HS**
5. **Blake Brown, of, Missouri**
6. **Josh Elander, c, Texas Christian**
7. **David Starn, lhp, Kent State**
8. **David Peterson, rhp, College of Charleston**
9. **Steven Schils, rhp, Florida Tech**
10. **Mike Dodig, 3b, Columbia-Greene (N.Y.) CC**
11. Levi Borders, c, Winter Haven (Fla.) HS
12. **Connor Lien, of, Olympia HS, Orlando**
13. **Nathan Hyatt, rhp, Appalachian State**
14. **Tyler Tewell, c, Appalachian State**
15. **Alex Wilson, rhp, Wofford**
16. **Fernelys Sanchez, of, Washington HS, New York**
17. **Chase Anselment, c/of, Washington**
18. **Ross Heffley, 2b, Western Carolina**
19. **Levi Hyams, 2b, Georgia**
20. **Eric Garcia, ss, Missouri**
21. **Jeremy Fitzgerald, rhp, Tennessee Wesleyan**
22. **Shae Simmons, rhp, Southeast Missouri State**
23. **Kevin McKague, rhp, Army**
24. **Michael Flores, rhp, Grossmont (Calif.) JC**
25. **Brandon Rohde, lhp, Central Washington**

26. **Trenton Moses, 3b, Southeast Missouri State**
27. **Chris Barczycowski, rhp, Niagara County (N.Y.) CC**
28. **Kraig Clabough, ss, Florida Tech**
29. **Jaden Dillon, rhp, Texas A&M-Kingsville**
30. **Casey Kalenkosky, 1b, Texas State**
31. **Matt Kimbrel, rhp, Southern Polytechnic State (Ga.)**
32. **Adam Grantham, rhp, Kennett (Mo.) HS**
33. Sam Gillikin, of, Hoover (Ala.) HS
34. Ben Johnson, of, Westwood HS, Austin
35. Matt Creech, ss, Colquitt County HS, Moultrie, Ga.
36. Braden Bishop, of, St. Francis HS, Mountain View, Calif.
37. Giovanni Brusa, of, St. Mary's HS, Stockton, Calif.
38. Sean McLaughlin, rhp, Northview HS, Johns Creek, Ga.
39. Cullen O'Dwyer, of, El Dorado HS, Albuquerque
40. Jimmy Herget, rhp, Jefferson HS, Tampa

BALTIMORE ORIOLES (4)

1. **Kevin Gausman, rhp, Louisiana State**
2. **Branden Kline, rhp, Virginia**
3. **Adrian Marin, ss, Gulliver Prep, Miami**
4. **Christian Walker, 1b, South Carolina**
5. Colin Poche, lhp, Marcus HS, Flower Mound, Texas
6. **Lex Rutledge, lhp, Samford**
7. **Matt Price, rhp, South Carolina**
8. **Torsten Boss, 3b, Michigan State**
9. **Brady Wager, rhp, Grand Canyon (Ariz.)**
10. **Joel Hutter, ss, Dallas Baptist**
11. **Kevin Grendell, lhp, San Pasqual HS, Escondido, Calif.**
12. Billy Waltrip, lhp, Seminole State (Okla.) JC
13. Wade Wass, c, Meridian (Miss.) CC
14. **Sean McAdams, rhp, Cardinal Mooney HS, Sarasota, Fla.**
15. Derick Velasquez, rhp, Merced (Calif.) JC
16. **Luc Rennie, rhp, Torrey Pines (Calif.) HS**
17. **Nick Grim, rhp, Cal Poly**
18. **Sammy Kimmel, c, Stetson**
19. **Josh Hader, lhp, Old Mill HS, Millersville, Md.**
20. Ryan Ripken, 1b, Gilman School, Baltimore
21. Julian Service, of, Sinclair SS, Whitby, Ont.
22. **Will Howard, of, Kennesaw State**
23. **Gene Escat, rhp, Fresno State**
24. **Tommy Richards, 2b, Washington State**
25. **Creede Simpson, 2b, Auburn**
26. **Lucas Herbst, of, Santa Clara**
27. **Anthony Caronia, ss, Tampa**
28. **Dennis Torres, rhp, Massachusetts**
29. **Jake Pintar, rhp, San Juan Hill HS, Cota de Coza, Calif.**
30. **Anthony Vega, of, Manhattan**
31. Anthony Bazzani, rhp, Eastern Kentucky
32. **Steel Russell, c, Midland (Texas) JC**
33. Colton Plaia, c, Loyola Marymount
34. Jim Sewald, of, Bishop Gorman HS, Las Vegas
35. **Charles Porter, lhp, Miami (No school)**
36. Peter Irvin, lhp, Skagit Valley (Wash.) CC
37. **Derrick Bleeker, of/rhp, Arkansas**
38. **Jack Graham, c, Kenyon (Ohio)**
39. Scott Kalush, c, UC Davis
40. **Ray Hunnicutt, of, Central HS, Hampshire, Ill.**

BOSTON RED SOX (23)

1. **Deven Marrero, ss, Arizona State**
1. **Brian Johnson, lhp, Florida** (Pick from Phillies for loss of Type A free agent Jonathan Papelbon)
1. **Pat Light, rhp, Monmouth** (Supplemental pick—37th—for loss of Papelbon)
2. **Jamie Callahan, rhp, Dillon (S.C.) HS**
3. **Austin Maddox, rhp, Florida**
4. **Ty Buttrey, rhp, Providence HS, Charlotte**
5. **Mike Augliera, rhp, Binghamton**
6. **Justin Haley, rhp, Fresno State**
7. **Kyle Kraus, rhp, Portland**

8. **Nathan Minnich, 1b, Shepherd (W.Va.)**
9. **Mike Miller, ss, Cal Poly**
10. **J.T. Watkins, c, Army**
11. Jamal Martin, of, Dwyer HS, West Palm Beach, Fla.
12. **Mike Meyers, ss, Silverado HS, Las Vegas**
13. **J.B. Wendelken, rhp, Middle Georgia JC**
14. **Dylan Chavez, lhp, Mississippi**
15. Carson Fulmer, rhp, All Saints Academy, Winter Haven, Fla.
16. **Stephen Williams, rhp, Seminole State (Okla.) JC**
17. **Willie Ethington, rhp, Mountain View HS, Mesa, Ariz.**
18. **Shaq Thompson, of, Grant HS, Sacramento**
19. **Iseha Conklin, ss, Iowa Western CC**
20. **Greg Larson, rhp, Florida**
21. **Jake Davies, 1b, Georgia Tech**
22. Joe Greenfield, rhp, South Suburban (Ill.) JC
23. **Brandon Magee, of, Arizona State**
24. **Keaton Briscoe, 2b, British Columbia**
25. **Khiry Cooper, of, Nebraska**
26. Jake Nelson, rhp, Lake Stevens (Wash.) HS
27. Quinn Carpenter, rhp, Goshen (N.Y.) HS
28. Wes Rogers, of, Mann HS, Greenville, S.C.
29. Alex Bregman, 2b, Albuquerque Academy
30. Justin Taylor, rhp, Farmville (N.C.) Central HS
31. Austin Davis, rhp, Southern Mississippi
32. Hunter Wood, rhp, Rogers (Ark.) Heritage HS
33. Chris Carlson, of, Orange Coast (Calif.) CC
34. Xavier Turner, 3b, Sandusky (Ohio) HS
35. Pat Delano, rhp, Braintree (Mass.) HS
36. **Miguel Rodriguez, c, UNC Charlotte**
37. Jonathan Dziedzic, lhp, Lamar
38. Donald Smith, c, Claflin (S.C.)
39. Kurt Schluter, rhp, Stetson
40. Kevin Heller, of, Amherst (Mass.)

CHICAGO CUBS (6)

1. **Albert Almora, of, Mater Academy, Hialeah Gardens, Fla.**
1. **Pierce Johnson, rhp, Missouri State** (Supplemental pick—43rd—for loss of Type B free agent Aramis Ramirez)
1. **Paul Blackburn, rhp, Heritage HS, Brentwood, Calif.** (Supplemental pick—56th—for loss of Type B free agent Carlos Pena)
2. **Duane Underwood, rhp, Pope HS, Marietta, Ga.**
3. **Ryan McNeil, rhp, Nipomo (Calif.) HS**
4. **Josh Conway, rhp, Coastal Carolina**
5. **Anthony Prieto, lhp, Americas HS, El Paso, Texas**
6. **Trey Lang, rhp, Gateway (Ariz.) CC**
7. **Stephen Bruno, 2b, Virginia**
8. **Michael Heesch, lhp, South Carolina-Beaufort**
9. **Chadd Krist, c, California**
10. **Chad Martin, rhp, Indiana**
11. **Rashad Crawford, of, Mundy's Mill HS, Clayton, Ga.**
12. **Justin Amlung, rhp, Louisville**
13. **Bijan Rademacher, of, Orange Coast (Calif.) CC**
14. **Corbin Hoffner, rhp, St. Petersburg (Fla.) JC**
15. **Carlos Escobar, c, Nevada**
16. **Mike Hamann, rhp, Toledo**
17. **Nathan Dorris, lhp, Southern Illinois**
18. **David Bote, ss, Neosho County (Kan.) CC**
19. Damek Tomscha, 3b, Iowa Western CC
20. Blake Hickman, c/rhp, Simeon HS, Chicago
21. **Steve Perakslis, rhp, Maine**
22. **Eddie Orozco, rhp, UC Riverside**
23. Jake Drossner, lhp, Council Rock North HS, Newton, Pa.
24. Jameson Fisher, c, Zachary (La.) HS
25. Rhett Wiseman, of, Buckingham Browne & Nichols HS, Cambridge, Mass.
26. **Jasvir Rakkar, rhp, Stony Brook**
27. **Tyler Bremer, rhp, Baylor**
28. **Lance Rymel, c, Rogers State (Okla.)**
29. Austin Pentecost, rhp, Lewis-Clark State (Idaho)
30. **Izaac Garsez, of, College of Idaho**
31. Bryan Bonnell, rhp, Centennial HS, Las Vegas
32. **Tim Saunders, ss, Marietta (Ohio)**
33. Tom Pannone, of, Bishop Hendricken HS, Warwick, R.I.

34. Christian Botnick, rhp, Notre Dame SS, Brampton, Ont.
35. **Ben Carhart, 3b, Stetson**
36. Sly Edwards, of, St. Brendan HS, Miami
37. Clayton Crum, rhp, Howard (Texas) JC
38. Hassan Evans, rhp, Herkimer County (N.Y.) CC
39. Rustin Sveum, 3b, Desert Mountain HS, Scottsdale, Ariz.
40. **Jacob Rogers, 1b, Mount Olive (N.C.)**

CHICAGO WHITE SOX (13)

1. **Courtney Hawkins, of, Carroll HS, Corpus Christi, Texas**
1. **Keon Barnum, 1b, King HS, Tampa** (Supplemental pick—48th—for loss of Type B free agent Mark Buehrle)
2. **Chris Beck, rhp, Georgia Southern**
3. **Joey DeMichele, 2b, Arizona State**
4. **Brandon Brennan, rhp, Orange Coast (Calif.) CC**
5. **Nick Basto, ss, Archbishop McCarthy HS, Southwest Ranches, Fla.**
6. **Kyle Hansen, rhp, St. John's**
7. **Jose Barraza, c, Sunnyside HS, Fresno**
8. **Zach Isler, rhp, Cincinnati**
9. **Micah Johnson, 2b, Indiana**
10. **Brandon Hardin, rhp, Delta State (Miss.)**
11. **Eric Jaffe, rhp, UCLA**
12. **Zach Stoner, 1b, Boylan HS, Rockford, Ill.**
13. Derek Thompson, lhp, John A. Logan (Ill.) CC
14. **Tony Bucciferro, rhp, Michigan State**
15. **Jordan Guerrero, lhp, Moorpark (Calif.) HS**
16. **Abe Ruiz, 1b, Arizona State**
17. **Sammy Ayala, c, La Jolla (Calif.) Country Day HS**
18. **Thomas McCarthy, 3b, Kentucky**
19. **Alex Williams, 1b, Louisiana Tech**
20. **Zach Voight, ss, New Mexico State**
21. **Adam Lopez, rhp, Virginia Military Institute**
22. **Cory McGinnis, rhp, Auburn-Montgomery (Ala.)**
23. **Kale Kiser, of, Nebraska**
24. **Eric Grabe, 2b, Tampa**
25. **Storm Throne, rhp, Morningside (Iowa)**
26. **Zach Toney, lhp, Austin Peay State**
27. **Zac Fisher, c, New Mexico State**
28. **James Hudelson, rhp, Delta State (Miss.)**
29. Jason Coats, of, Texas Christian
30. **Jake Brown, ss, Kansas State**
31. **Corey Thompson, 3b, East Carolina**
32. **Steve Nikorak, 3b, Temple**
33. Jon Savarise, lhp, Stevenson HS, Lincolnshire, Ill.
34. Ryan Castellanos, rhp, Archbishop McCarthy HS, Southwest Ranches, Fla.
35. Kyle Martin, rhp, Texas A&M
36. Mitch Patishall, rhp, Pendleton (Ind.) Heights HS
37. **Thurman Hall, of, Western Texas CC**
38. DeJohn Suber, ss, Morgan Park HS, Chicago
39. Mitch Glasser, 2b, Macalester (Minn.)
40. Sam Mason, rhp, Beverly Hills (Calif.) HS

CINCINNATI REDS (14)

1. **Nick Travieso, rhp, Archbishop McCarthy HS, Southwest Ranches, Fla.**
1. **Jesse Winker, of, Olympia HS, Orlando** (Supplemental pick—49th—for loss of Type B free agent Ramon Hernandez)
1. **Jeff Gelalich, of, UCLA** (Supplemental pick—57th—for loss of Type B free agent Francisco Cordero)
2. **Tanner Rahier, ss, Palm Desert (Calif.) HS**
3. **Dan Langfield, rhp, Memphis**
4. **Jon Moscot, rhp, Pepperdine**
5. **Mason Felt, lhp, Hebron Christian Academy, Dacula, Ga.**
6. **Joe Hudson, c, Notre Dame**
7. **Beau Amaral, of, UCLA**
8. **Seth Mejias-Brean, 3b, Arizona**
9. **Daniel Pigott, of, Florida**
10. **Jeremy Kivel, rhp, Spring (Texas) HS**
11. **Nolan Becker, lhp, Yale**
12. **Brent Peterson, ss, Bakersfield (Calif.) JC**
13. Matt Boyd, lhp, Oregon State
14. **Luke Moran, rhp, Grayson County (Texas) CC**

15. Ben Klimesh, rhp, Trinity (Texas)
16. Nick Routt, lhp, Mississippi State
17. Jose Ortiz, c, Colon HS, Comerio, P.R.
18. Jackson Stephens, rhp/3b, Oxford (Ala.) HS
19. Austin Muehring, rhp, Palomar (Calif.) CC
20. Brock Dykxhoorn, rhp, St. Anne's SS, Clinton, Ont.
21. Jordan Remer, lhp, San Francisco
22. Avain Rachal, rhp, Cy-Fair HS, Cypress, Texas
23. Daniel Sweet, of, Northwest Rankin HS, Brandon, Miss.
24. Mike Saunders, rhp, Saginaw Valley State (Mich.)
25. Sean Lucas, lhp, Albany
26. Chase Rezac, rhp, Southern Utah
27. Joey Housey, rhp, Oregon
28. Mo Wiley, rhp, Houston
29. Adam Matthews, of, South Carolina
30. Kyle Wren, of, Georgia Tech
31. Austin Salter, rhp, Cisco (Texas) JC
32. Christian McElroy, rhp, Cincinnati
33. Justin Topa, rhp, Long Island
34. Richard McCaffrey, lhp, UC Santa Barbara
35. Mike Sheppard, rhp, Seton Hall Prep, West Orange, N.J.
36. Jarvis Flowers, 2b, Cy-Ranch HS, Cypress, Texas
37. Zach Vincej, ss, Pepperdine
38. Daniel Ponce de Leon, rhp, Cypress (Calif.) JC
39. Jacob Stone, rhp, Weatherford (Texas) JC
40. Rafael Pineda, rhp, Texas A&M

CLEVELAND INDIANS (15)

1. Tyler Naquin, of, Texas A&M
2. Mitch Brown, rhp, Century HS, Rochester, Minn.
3. Kieran Lovegrove, rhp, Mission Viejo (Calif.) HS
4. D'Vone McClure, of, Jacksonville (Ark.) HS
5. Dylan Baker, rhp, Western Nevada JC
6. Joe Wendle, 2b, West Chester (Pa.)
7. Josh Schubert, of, Calhoun (Ga.) HS
8. Caleb Hamrick, rhp, Cedar Hill (Texas) HS
9. Jacob Lee, rhp, Arkansas State
10. Josh Martin, rhp, Samford
11. Logan Vick, of, Baylor
12. Jeremy Lucas, c, Indiana State
13. Tyler Booth, of, Central Arizona JC
14. Scott Peoples, rhp, Western Oklahoma State JC
15. Nelson Rodriguez, 1b, Washington HS, New York
16. Cody Penny, rhp, North Carolina
17. Andrew Calica, of, Eastlake HS, Chula Vista, Calif.
18. Louis Head, rhp, Texas State
19. Colyn O'Connell, rhp, Dunedin (Fla.) HS
20. Nick Pasquale, rhp, Diablo Valley (Calif.) JC
21. Joe Sever, 2b, Pepperdine
22. Jim Stokes, rhp, Elon
23. Richard Stock, c/1b, Nebraska
24. Walker White, rhp, South Georgia JC
25. Cameron Cox, rhp, Weatherford (Texas) JC
26. Justin Garza, rhp, Bonita HS, La Verne, Calif.
27. Ray Castillo, rhp, Russell County HS, Seale, Ala.
28. Josh Pigg, 3b/rhp, Franklin HS, Elk Grove, Calif.
29. Randall Fant, lhp, Arkansas
30. Josh Lester, ss, Columbus (Ga.) HS
31. Danny Holst, of, Parkway South HS, Manchester, Mo.
32. Paul Hendrix, ss, Howard (Texas) JC
33. Cory Raley, ss, Uvalde (Texas) HS
34. Matt Fultz, c, Lee's Summit (Mo.) West HS
35. Nick Hamilton, ss, Kent State
36. Benny Suarez, rhp, Hill (Texas) JC
37. Jacob Morris, of/c, Arkansas
38. Joshua Nervis, rhp, Sonoma State (Calif.)
39. D.J. Brown, rhp, James Madison
40. Anthony Hawkins, of, Fresno HS

COLORADO ROCKIES (10)

1. David Dahl, of, Oak Mountain HS, Birmingham
1. Eddie Butler, rhp, Radford (Supplemental pick—46th—for loss of Type B free agent Mark Ellis)
2. Max White, of, Williston (Fla.) HS

---

3. Tom Murphy, c, Buffalo
3. Ryan Warner, rhp, Pine Creek HS, Colorado Springs, Colo. (Supplemental pick—128th—for failure to sign 2011 third-round pick Peter O'Brien)
4. Seth Willoughby, rhp, Xavier
5. Matt Wessinger, ss, St. John's
6. Matt Carasiti, rhp, St. John's
7. Wilfredo Rodriguez, c, Puerto Rico Baseball Academy, Gurabo, P.R.
8. Derek Jones, of, Washington State
9. Zach Jemiola, rhp, Great Oak HS, Temecula, Calif.
10. Ben Waldrip, 1b, Jacksonville State
11. T.J. Oakes, rhp, Minnesota
12. Correlle Prime, 1b, Manatee HS, Bradenton, Fla.
13. Kyle Von Tungeln, of, Texas Christian
14. Shane Broyles, rhp, Texas Tech
15. Scott Oberg, rhp, Connecticut
16. Jeff Popick, of, Colorado Mesa
17. Jason Stolz, 2b, Clemson
18. Aaron Jones, c, Oregon
19. Kyle Newton, 3b, Florida Atlantic
20. Anthony Seise, lhp, West Orange HS, Winter Garden, Fla.
21. Rayan Gonzalez, rhp, Bethune-Cookman
22. Jordan Mejia, rhp, Riverside (Calif.) CC
23. Andrew Brown, rhp, Akron
24. Mike Mason, lhp, Marshall
25. Alec Mehrten, ss, Fresno Pacific
26. Adam Paulencu, rhp, Embry-Riddle (Fla.)
27. Matt Flemer, rhp, California
28. Ryan Arrowood, rhp, Appalachian State
29. Pat Hutcheson, 2b, Fresno State
30. Trent Blank, rhp, Baylor
31. Shawn Stuart, rhp, Long Beach State
32. A.J. Simcox, ss, Farragut HS, Knoxville
33. Ryan Garvey, of, Riverside (Calif.) CC
34. Chris Cowell, c, Richmond
35. Justin Solomon, 2b, Piedra Vista HS, Farmington, N.M.
36. Kevin Bradley, ss, Hopewell Valley Central HS, Pennington, N.J.
37. Casey Burns, 3b, Grand Junction (Colo.) HS
38. Dansby Swanson, ss, Marietta (Ga.) HS
39. Justin Dillon, rhp, El Dorado HS, Placentia, Calif.
40. Brandon Montalvo, c, Langham Creek HS, Houston

DETROIT TIGERS (26)

1. (Pick to Brewers as compensation for Type A free agent Prince Fielder)
2. Jake Thompson, rhp, Rockwall-Heath HS, Heath, Texas
3. Austin Schotts, ss, Centennial HS, Frisco, Texas
4. Drew Verhagen, rhp, Vanderbilt
5. Joe Rogers, lhp, Central Florida
6. Jordan John, lhp, Oklahoma
7. Hudson Randall, rhp, Florida
8. Jeff McVaney, of/lhp, Texas State
9. Jake Stewart, of, Stanford
10. Charlie Gillies, rhp, The Masters (Calif.)
11. Bennett Pickar, c, Oral Roberts
12. Julio Felix, rhp, Pima (Ariz.) CC
13. Devon Travis, 2b, Florida State
14. Hunter Scantling, rhp, Florida State
15. Jordan Dean, ss, Central Michigan
16. Josh Turley, lhp, Baylor
17. Slade Smith, rhp, Auburn
18. Dylan LaVelle, 3b, Lake Stevens (Wash.) HS
19. Will Clinard, rhp, Vanderbilt
20. Logan Ehlers, lhp, Howard (Texas) JC
21. Alex Phillips, lhp, Kentucky
22. D.J. Driggers, of, Middle Georgia JC
23. Drew Harrison, rhp, Oklahoma
24. Nick Carmichael, rhp, Palomar (Calif.) CC
25. Jared Reaves, ss, Alabama
26. Rashad Brown, of, Westlake HS, Atlanta
27. Miguel Paulino, of, Choctawhatchee HS, Fort Walton Beach, Fla.
28. Josh Carr, rhp, Kennesaw State

29. Zach Kirksey, of, Mississippi
30. Preston Jamison, lhp, South Mountain (Ariz.) CC
31. Connor Harrell, of, Vanderbilt
32. Blake McFadden, rhp, Savannah (Mo.) HS
33. Tyler Hanover, 2b, Louisiana State
34. Matt Davenport, rhp, William & Mary
35. Jacob Kapstein, c, Tiverton (R.I.) HS
36. Clate Schmidt, rhp, Allatoona HS, Acworth, Ga.
37. Charlie Neil, c, Yale
38. Alex Minter, lhp, Brook Hill HS, Bullard, Texas
39. John Sansone, ss, Neshannock HS, New Castle, Pa.
40. Ryan Longstreth, lhp, Central Michigan

HOUSTON ASTROS (1)

1. Carlos Correa, ss, Puerto Rico Baseball Academy, Gurabo, P.R.
1. Lance McCullers Jr., rhp, Jesuit HS, Tampa (Supplemental pick—41st—for loss of Type B free agent Clint Barmes)
2. Nolan Fontana, ss, Florida
3. Brady Rodgers, rhp, Arizona State
4. Rio Ruiz, 3b, Bishop Amat HS, La Puente, Calif.
5. Andrew Aplin, of, Arizona State
6. Brett Phillips, of, Seminole (Fla.) HS
7. Preston Tucker, of, Florida
8. Tyler Heineman, c, UCLA
9. Daniel Minor, rhp, Texas A&M-Corpus Christi
10. Joe Bircher, lhp, Bradley
11. Hunter Virant, lhp, Camarillo (Calif.) HS
12. Terrell Joyce, of, Florida State JC
13. Brian Holmes, lhp, Wake Forest
14. Joe Sclafani, ss, Dartmouth
15. Erick Gonzalez, rhp, Gateway (Ariz.) CC
16. Dan Gulbransen, of, Jacksonville
17. Aaron West, rhp, Washington
18. Ricky Gingras, c, Point Loma Nazarene (Calif.)
19. Austin Elkins, 2b, Dallas Baptist
20. Michael Clark, lhp, Kent State
21. Marc Wik, of, Chabot (Calif.) JC
22. Kenny Long, lhp, Illinois State
23. Travis Ballew, rhp, Texas State
24. Pat Blair, ss, Wake Forest
25. Ryan Dineen, ss, Eastern Illinois
26. C.J. Hinojosa, ss, Klein Collins HS, Spring, Texas
27. Tanner Mathis, of, Mississippi
28. Angel Ibanez, 3b, Texas-Pan American
29. Christian Garcia, rhp, Florence-Darlington Tech (S.C.) JC
30. John Neely, rhp, Texas Tech
31. M.P. Cokinos, c, St. Mary's (Texas)
32. Tyler Manez, lhp, Plainedge HS, North Massapequa, N.Y.
33. Mike Hauschild, rhp, Dayton
34. Jordan Jankowski, rhp, Catawba (N.C.)
35. Jimmy Sinatro, c, Skyline HS, Sammamish, Wash.
36. Mike Martinez, 3b, Florida International
37. Michael Dimock, rhp, Wake Forest
38. Zach Remillard, 3b, LaSalle Institute, Troy, N.Y.
39. Mitchell Traver, rhp, Houston Christian HS
40. Joseph Shaw, rhp, Ennis (Texas) HS

KANSAS CITY ROYALS (5)

1. Kyle Zimmer, rhp, San Francisco
2. Sam Selman, lhp, Vanderbilt
3. Colin Rodgers, lhp, Parkview Baptist HS, Baton Rouge
4. Kenny Diekroeger, 2b, Stanford
5. Chad Johnson, c, Galesburg (Ill.) HS
6. Zach Lovvorn, rhp, Oxford (Ala.) HS
7. Fred Ford, of, Jefferson (Mo.) CC
8. Alfredo Escalera-Maldonado, of, Pendleton School, Bradenton, Fla.
9. Daniel Stumpf, lhp, San Jacinto (Texas) JC
10. Alexis Rivera, of/1b, Montverde Academy, Kissimmee, Fla.
11. Zeb Sneed, rhp, Northwest Nazarene (Idaho)
12. Jackson Willeford, 2b, Ramona (Calif.) HS
13. Hunter Haynes, lhp, Mexico (Mo.) HS
14. Parker Morin, c, Utah

15. Dylan Sons, lhp, Halifax County HS, South Boston, Va.
16. Austin Fairchild, lhp, St. Thomas HS, Houston
17. Ariel Estades, of, Puerto Rico Baseball Academy, Gurabo, P.R.
18. Justin Alleman, rhp, Holt (Mich.) HS
19. Andrew Triggs, rhp, Southern California
20. Shane Halley, of, Virginia
21. Matt Strahm, lhp, Neosho County (Kan.) CC
22. Alec Mills, rhp, Tennessee-Martin
23. Kevin Allen, rhp, Texas Christian
24. Beau Maggi, c, Arizona State
25. Matt Tenuta, lhp, Apex (N.C.) HS
26. Mark Donato, 1b, Indian River (Fla.) JC
27. Ashton Goudeau, rhp, Maple Woods (Mo.) CC
28. Sam Bates, 1b, Arkansas
29. John Walter, rhp, Penn State
30. Ethan Chapman, of, Cal State San Bernardino
31. Hayden Edwards, rhp, Blue Valley HS, Stilwell, Kan.
32. Patrick Conroy, lhp, Marin (Calif.) CC
33. Evan Phillips, rhp, Clayton (N.C.) HS
34. Marsalis Holloway, of, Columbia State (Tenn.) CC
35. Tyler Joyner, lhp, East Carolina
36. Raphael Andrades, of, Lincoln HS, Tallahassee, Fla.
37. Jake Newberry, rhp, Mira Mesa HS, San Diego
38. Carlos Urena, of, Whitehall (Pa.) HS
39. Justin Leeson, of, Georgetown
40. Taylor Kaczmarek, rhp, South Mountain (Ariz.) CC

LOS ANGELES ANGELS (19)

1. (Pick to Cardinals as compensation for Type A free agent Albert Pujols)
2. (Pick to Rangers as compensation for Type A free agent C.J. Wilson)
3. R.J. Alvarez, rhp, Florida Atlantic
4. Alex Yarbrough, 2b, Mississippi
5. Mark Sappington, rhp, Rockhurst (Mo.)
6. Eric Stamets, ss, Evansville
7. Andrew Patterson, c, Montgomery HS, Semmes, Ala.
8. Austin Adams, rhp, South Florida
9. Michael Roth, lhp, South Carolina
10. Chris O'Grady, lhp, George Mason
11. Jonathan Walsh, c, Texas
12. Zach Wright, c, East Carolina
13. Mike Morin, rhp, North Carolina
14. Sherman Johnson, 3b, Florida State
15. Reid Scoggins, rhp, Howard (Texas) JC
16. Kody Eaves, 2b, Pasadena Memorial (Texas) HS
17. Yency Almonte, rhp, Columbus HS, Miami
18. Ryan Dalton, 3b, Texas-San Antonio
19. Aaron Newcomb, rhp, Delta State (Miss.)
20. Quintin Davis, of, McLennan (Texas) CC
21. Pat Lowery, rhp, Columbia
22. Anthony Bemboom, c, Creighton
23. Mike Snyder, 3b, Florida Southern
24. Garrett Bush, rhp, Flagler (Fla.)
25. Kyle Johnson, of, Washington State
26. Tyler DeLoach, lhp, UNC Wilmington
27. Wade Hinkle, 1b, Kansas State
28. Joel Capote, of, St. Thomas (Fla.)
29. Caleb Bushyhead, ss, Oklahoma
30. Nic Dellatorre, lhp, St. John's River (Fla.) JC
31. Jeff Kemp, ss, Radford
32. Robbie Powell, rhp, Stetson
33. Sam Mulroy, c, Princeton
34. Zac Livingston, c, Arizona Christian
35. Pedro Pizarro, c, Byrd HS, Shreveport, La.
36. Kenny Hatcher, rhp, Dallas Baptist
37. Matt Collins, rhp, Central Florida
38. Jake Boyd, rhp, Stetson
39. Justin Morhardt, c, Gilbert School, Winsted, Conn.
40. Blake Amaral, of, Hawaii Pacific

LOS ANGELES DODGERS (18)

1. Corey Seager, 3b, Northwest Cabarrus HS, Concord, N.C.
1. Jesmuel Valentin, 2b, Puerto Rico Baseball Academy,

Gurabo, P.R. (Supplemental pick—51st—for loss of Type B free agent Rod Barajas)
2. **Paco Rodriguez, lhp, Florida**
3. **Onelki Garcia, lhp, Los Angeles (no school)**
4. **Justin Chigbogu, 1b, Raytown (Mo.) South HS**
5. **Ross Stripling, rhp, Texas A&M**
6. **Joey Curletta, 1b/rhp, Mountain Pointe HS, Phoenix**
7. **Theo Alexander, of, Lake Washington HS, Kirkland, Wash.**
8. **Scott Griggs, rhp, UCLA**
9. **Zachary Bird, rhp, Murrah HS, Jackson, Miss.**
10. **Zach Babitt, 2b, Academy of Art (Calif.)**
11. **Jeremy Rathjen, of, Rice**
12. **James Campbell, rhp, Stony Brook**
13. **Darnell Sweeney, ss, Central Florida**
14. **Matthew Reckling, rhp, Rice**
15. **Duke von Schamann, rhp, Texas Tech**
16. **Josh Henderson, of, First Baptist Christian School, Suffolk, Va.**
17. Kevin Maxey, of, Long Beach Poly HS
18. **Eric Smith, c, Stanford**
19. **Owen Jones, rhp, Portland**
20. **Jharel Cotton, rhp, East Carolina**
21. **Jacob Scavuzzo, of, Villa Park HS, Orange, Calif.**
22. **Alan Garcia, rhp, Azusa Pacific (Calif.)**
23. **Lindsey Caughel, rhp, Stetson**
24. **Paul Hoenecke, 1b, Wisconsin-Milwaukee**
25. **Danny Coulombe, lhp, Texas Tech**
26. Jordan Parr, 1b, Illinois
27. **Justin Gonzalez, ss, Florida State**
28. **Jake Hermsen, lhp, Northern Illinois**
29. **John Cannon, c, Houston**
30. Trent Giambrone, ss, King HS, Metairie, La.
31. David Graybill, rhp, Brophy Prep, Phoenix
32. **Alfredo Unzue, lhp, Los Angeles (no school)**
33. C.J. Saylor, c, South Hills HS, West Covina, Calif.
34. **Jordan Hershiser, rhp, Southern California**
35. **Austin Cowen, c, Western Illinois**
36. Jose Vizcaino, 3b, Parker HS, San Diego
37. **John Sgromolo, 1b, Flagler (Fla.)**
38. **Corey Embree, of, Maple Woods (Mo.) CC**
39. Korey Dunbar, c, Nitro (W.Va.) HS
40. **Pat Stover, of, Santa Clara**

MIAMI MARLINS (9)

1. **Andrew Heaney, lhp, Oklahoma State**
2. (Pick to Mets as compensation for Type A free agent Jose Reyes)
3. **Avery Romero, 3b, Menendez HS, St. Augustine, Fla.**
3. **Kolby Copeland, of, Parkway HS, Bossier City, La.** (Supplemental pick—127th—for failure to sign 2011 third-round pick Connor Barron)
4. **Austin Dean, 2b, Klein Collins HS, Spring, Texas**
5. **Austin Nola, ss, Louisiana State**
6. **Anthony Gomez, ss, Vanderbilt**
7. **Ryan Newell, rhp, Shorter (Ga.)**
8. **Drew Steckenrider, rhp, Tennessee**
9. **Nick Wittgren, rhp, Purdue**
10. **Ron Miller, 1b, JSerra HS, Gardena, Calif.**
11. **Matt Milroy, rhp, Illinois**
12. **Christian Rivera, ss, Nueva Superior Vocacional HS, Loiza, P.R.**
13. **Blake Logan, rhp, Eastern Oklahoma State JC**
14. **Michael Vaughn, c, Fresno Pacific**
15. **Cody Keefer, of, UCLA**
16. **Brian Ellington, rhp, West Florida**
17. **Bubba Keene, of, Brookhaven (Miss.) Academy**
18. **Patrick Merkling, lhp, Lee (Tenn.)**
19. Cody Gunter, 3b, Flower Mound (Texas) HS
20. Jordan Hillyer, rhp, Hebron Christian Academy, Dacula, Ga.
21. **Hayden Fox, lhp, Oakland**
22. **Robert Ravago, rhp, Arizona State**
23. **Cameron Flynn, of, Kentucky**
24. **Matt Juengel, 3b, Texas A&M**
25. **Dane Stone, rhp, St. Thomas (Fla.)**
26. Seth Grant, rhp, Appalachian State

27. **Justin Jackson, rhp, Sam Houston State**
28. **Casey McCarthy, rhp, Cal State San Bernardino**
29. **Blake Barnes, rhp, Oklahoma State**
30. **David Cruz, c, Miami (no school)**
31. Lucas Hunter, ss, Central Catholic HS, Portland, Ore.
32. Ty Williams, rhp, Sulphur (Okla.) HS
33. Steve Weber, rhp, Eastern Michigan
34. **Patrick Claussen, 3b, Washington State**
35. Chad Christensen, of, Nebraska
36. Kendall Graveman, rhp, Mississippi State
37. **Eddie Sappelt, of, Southern Alamance HS, Graham, N.C.**
38. **Chipper Smith, lhp, Cumberland (Tenn.)**
39. Marcus Greene, c, Vista Del Lago HS, Moreno Valley, Calif.
40. Alex Polston, ss, Albert HS, Midwest City, Okla.

MILWAUKEE BREWERS (27)

1. **Clint Coulter, c, Union HS, Camas, Wash.** (Pick from Brewers as compensation for Type A free agent Prince Fielder)
1. **Victor Roache, of, Georgia Southern**
1. **Mitch Haniger, of, Cal Poly** (Supplemental pick—38th—for loss of Fielder)
2. **Tyrone Taylor, of, Torrance (Calif.) HS**
3. **Zach Quintana, rhp, Arbor View HS, Las Vegas**
4. **Tyler Wagner, rhp, Utah**
5. **Damien Magnifico, rhp, Oklahoma**
6. **Angel Ortega, ss, International Baseball Academy, Ceiba, P.R.**
7. **David Otterman, lhp, British Columbia**
8. **Edgardo Rivera, of, Inzarry de Puig HS, Toa Baja, P.R.**
9. **Alex Lavandero, rhp, Belen Jesuit Prep, Miami**
10. **Anthony Banda, lhp, San Jacinto (Texas) JC**
11. **Preston Gainey, rhp, Navy**
12. **Eric Semmelhack, rhp, Wisconsin-Milwaukee**
13. **Alan Sharkey, 1b, Coral Springs (Fla.) HS**
14. **Ryan Gibbard, rhp, Lynn (Fla.)**
15. Buck Farmer, rhp, Georgia Tech
16. **Adam Giacalone, 1b, Neosho County (Kan.) CC**
17. **Alfredo Rodriguez, ss, Maryland**
18. Hunter Adkins, rhp, Middle Tennessee State
19. Carlos Garmendia, 3b, South Miami HS
20. **Mike Garza, ss, Georgetown**
21. **Austin Blaski, rhp, Marietta (Ohio)**
22. **Taylor Wall, lhp, Rice**
23. **Paul Eshleman, c, Cal State San Bernardino**
24. **Michael Turay, c, Cal State Stanislaus**
25. **Lance Roenicke, of, UC Santa Barbara**
26. Mark McCoy, lhp, Barnegat (N.J.) HS
27. Tyler Duffie, rhp, Texas Christian
28. **Martin Viramontes, rhp, Southern California**
29. Bryan Saucedo, 1b, Vaughan Road Academy, Toronto
30. **Jonathan Armold, lhp, Flagler (Fla.)**
31. **Brent Suter, lhp, Harvard**
32. Nick Anderson, rhp, Mayville State (N.D.)
33. **Austin Hall, rhp, Brigham Young**
34. Tommy Burns, rhp, Don Bosco Prep, Ramsey, N.J.
35. **Jose Sermo, ss, Bethany (Kan.)**
36. Alex Mangano, c, Southwest Miami HS
37. **Taylor Brennan, ss, Edmonds (Wash.) CC**
38. Chris Shaw, c, Trinity Academy, Okotoks, Alb.
39. Derek Jones, of, St. Marguerite d'Youville SS, Brampton, Ont.
40. Chucky Vazquez, c, American Senior HS, Miami

MINNESOTA TWINS (2)

1. **Byron Buxton, of, Appling County HS, Baxley, Ga.**
1. **J.O. Berrios, rhp, Papa Juan XXIII HS, Bayamon, P.R.** (Supplemental pick—32nd—for loss of modified Type A free agent Michael Cuddyer)
1. **Luke Bard, rhp, Georgia Tech** (Supplemental pick—42nd—for loss of Type B free agent Jason Kubel)
2. **Mason Melotakis, lhp, Northwestern State**
2. **J.T. Chargois, rhp, Rice** (Supplemental pick—72nd—for loss of Cuddyer)
3. **Adam Brett Walker, 1b, Jacksonville**
4. **Zach Jones, rhp, San Jose State**

5. Tyler Duffey, rhp, Rice
6. Andre Martinez, lhp, Archbishop McCarthy HS, Southwest Ranches, Fla.
7. Jorge Fernandez, c, International Baseball Academy, Ceiba, P.R.
8. Christian Powell, rhp, College of Charleston
9. L.J. Mazzilli, 2b, Connecticut
10. D.J. Baxendale, rhp, Arkansas
11. Taylor Rogers, lhp, Kentucky
12. Alex Muren, rhp, Cal State Northridge
13. Erich Knab, rhp, Carolina Forest HS, Myrtle Beach, S.C.
14. Jake Proctor, of, Cincinnati
15. Jarret Leverett, lhp, Georgia Southern
16. Will Hurt, ss, Lexington (Ky.) Catholic HS
17. D.J. Hicks, 1b, Central Florida
18. Will LaMarche, rhp, Chabot (Calif.) JC
19. Jonathan Murphy, of, Jacksonville
20. Zach Larson, of, Lakewood Ranch HS, Bradenton, Fla.
21. Bo Altobelli, c, Texas Tech
22. Josh Graham, c, Roseburg (Ore.) HS
23. Travis Huber, rhp, Nebraska
24. Jose Favela, c, Franklin (Texas) HS
25. Joel Licon, ss, Orange Coast (Calif.) CC
26. Justin Jones, lhp, California
27. Jerad Grundy, lhp, Kentucky
28. Carson Goldsmith, rhp, Northwestern State
29. Sean Hagan, lhp, St. John's
30. Bryan Santy, c, Washington
31. Timmy Robinson, of, Ocean View HS, Huntington Beach, Calif.
32. Andrew Ferreira, lhp, Harvard
33. Kaleb Merck, rhp, Texas Christian
34. Bryan Haar, of, San Diego
35. Jared Wilson, rhp, UC Santa Barbara
36. Brandon Bayardi, of, Nevada-Las Vegas
37. James Marvel, rhp, Campolindo HS, Moraga, Calif.
38. Austin Rel, c, Campolindo HS, Moraga, Calif.
39. Alex Liquori, of, Whitewater HS, Fayetteville, Ga.
40. Brad Schreiber, rhp, Purdue

NEW YORK METS (12)

1. Gavin Cecchini, ss, Barbe HS, Lake Charles, La.
1. Kevin Plawecki, c, Purdue (Supplemental pick—35th—for loss of Type A free agent Jose Reyes)
2. Matt Reynolds, 3b, Arkansas (Pick from Marlins for loss of Reyes)
2. Teddy Stankiewicz, rhp, Fort Worth Christian HS, North Richland Hills, Texas
3. Matt Koch, rhp, Louisville
4. Branden Kaupe, ss, Baldwin HS, Wailuku, Hawaii
5. Brandon Welch, rhp, Palm Beach State (Fla.) JC
6. Jayce Boyd, 1b, Florida State
7. Corey Oswalt, rhp, Madison HS, San Diego
8. Tomas Nido, c, Orangewood Christian HS, Maitland, Fla.
9. Richie Rodriguez, 2b, Eastern Kentucky
10. Paul Sewald, rhp, San Diego
11. Logan Taylor, rhp, Eastern Oklahoma State JC
12. Rob Whalen, rhp, Haines City (Fla.) HS
13. Matt Bowman, rhp, Princeton
14. Chris Flexen, rhp, Newark (Calif.) Memorial HS
15. Nicholas Grant, rhp, Milford (Del.) HS
16. Myles Smith, rhp, Miami Dade JC
17. Stefan Sabol, c, Orange Coast (Calif.) CC
18. Paul Paez, lhp, Rio Hondo (Calif.) CC
19. Tyler Vanderheiden, rhp, Samford
20. Tim Peterson, rhp, Kentucky
21. Gary Ward, lhp, Bethel (Tenn.)
22. Tejay Antone, rhp, Legacy HS, Mansfield, Texas
23. Connor Baits, rhp, Point Loma HS, San Diego
24. Andrew Massie, rhp, Dyer County (Tenn.) HS
25. Leon Byrd, ss, Cy-Ranch HS, Cypress, Texas
26. Chris Shaw, 1b, Lexington (Mass.) HS
27. Zach Arnold, c, Franklin County HS, Frankfort, Ky.
28. Jake Marks, rhp, St. Clair SS, Sarnia, Ont.
29. Austin Barr, c, Camas (Wash.) HS
30. Dustin Cook, rhp, Hargrave HS, Huffman, Texas

31. Vance Vizcaino, ss, Wakefield HS, Raleigh
32. Jon Leroux, 1b, Northeastern
33. Jared Price, rhp, Twin Valley HS, Elverson, Pa.
34. Mikey White, of, Spain Park HS, Hoover, Ala.
35. Brad Markey, rhp, Santa Fe (Fla.) JC
36. Donovan Walton, ss, Bishop Kelley HS, Tulsa
37. Benny Distefano, c, Elkins HS, Missouri City, Texas
38. Jeff Reynolds, 3b, Harvard
39. Patrick Ervin, 2b, Pace (Fla.) HS
40. David Gonzalez, rhp, Gainesville (Ga.) HS

NEW YORK YANKEES (29)

1. Ty Hensley, rhp, Santa Fe HS, Edmond, Okla.
2. Austin Aune, of, Argyle (Texas) HS (Supplemental pick—89th—for failure to sign 2011 second-round pick Sam Stafford)
2. Peter O'Brien, c, Miami
3. Nathan Mikolas, 1b, Bradford HS, Kenosha, Wis.
4. Corey Black, rhp, Faulkner (Ala.)
5. Robert Refsnyder, 2b, Arizona
6. Nick Goody, rhp, Louisiana State
7. Taylor Garrison, rhp, Fresno State
8. Taylor Dugas, of, Alabama
9. Derek Varnadore, rhp, Auburn
10. Matt Snyder, 1b, Mississippi
11. Caleb Frare, lhp, Custer County HS, Miles City, Mont.
12. Chris Breen, c, Winter Springs (Fla.) HS
13. James Pazos, lhp, San Diego
14. Andrew Benak, rhp, Rice
15. Dayton Dawe, rhp, Lucas SS, London, Ont.
16. Stefan Lopez, rhp, Southeastern Louisiana
17. Tim Flight, lhp, Southern New Hampshire
18. Brady Lail, rhp, Bingham HS, South Jordan, Utah
19. Dietrich Enns, lhp, Central Michigan
20. Mikey Reynolds, ss, Texas A&M
21. Jimmy Reed, lhp, Maryland
22. Brett Marks, rhp, Wallace State (Ala.) CC
23. Vincent Jackson, of, Luella HS, McDonough, Ga.
24. Jose Mesa Jr., rhp, Flanagan HS, Pembroke Pines, Fla.
25. Ty Moore, of, Mater Dei HS, Santa Ana, Calif.
26. Charlie Haslup, rhp, Maryland
27. Danny Oh, of, California
28. D.J. Stewart, of, Bolles School, Jacksonville, Fla.
29. Jose Diaz, lhp, Advantage Learning Institute, Ponce, P.R.
30. Raph Rhymes, of, Louisiana State
31. Kevin Johnson, rhp, Illinois
32. Garrett Cannizaro, ss, Tulane
33. Saxon Butler, 1b/c, Samford
34. Eric Erickson, lhp, Miami
35. Kyle Farmer, ss, Georgia
36. Dalton Smith, c, University City HS, San Diego
37. Charles Basford, rhp, Samford
38. David Thompson, of, Westminster Christian School, Miami
39. Bo Decker, of, East Ridge HS, Clermont, Fla.
40. Sherman LaCrus, of/c, Western Oklahoma State JC

OAKLAND ATHLETICS (11)

1. Addison Russell, ss, Pace (Fla.) HS
1. Daniel Robertson, 3b, Upland (Calif.) HS (Supplemental pick—34th—for loss of modified Type A free agent Josh Willingham)
1. Matt Olson, 1b, Parkview HS, Lilburn, Ga. (Supplemental pick—47th—for loss of Type B free agent David DeJesus)
2. Bruce Maxwell, c/1b, Birmingham-Southern (Supplemental pick—62nd—for loss of Willingham)
2. Nolan Sanburn, rhp, Arkansas
3. Kyle Twomey, lhp, El Dorado HS, Placentia, Calif.
4. B.J. Boyd, of, Palo Alto (Calif.) HS
5. Max Muncy, 1b, Baylor
6. Seth Streich, rhp, Ohio
7. Cody Kurz, rhp, Oxnard (Calif.) JC
8. Kris Hall, rhp, Lee (Tenn.)
9. Dakota Bacus, rhp, Indiana State
10. Brett Vertigan, of, UC Santa Barbara
11. Matt Gonzalez, ss/c, Harrison HS, Kennesaw, Ga.
12. John Caputo, 3b, Toronto (no school)

13. Stuart Pudenz, rhp, Dallas Baptist
14. Austin House, rhp, New Mexico
15. Vince Voiro, rhp, Pennsylvania
16. Melvin Mercedes, ss, JC of Central Florida
17. Tyler Olson, lhp, Gonzaga
18. Derek DeYoung, rhp, Oakton (Ill.) CC
19. Robert Martinez, of, Quinones Medina HS, Yabucoa, P.R.
20. Boog Powell, of, Orange Coast (Calif.) CC
21. Tyler Hollstegge, rhp, UNC Greensboro
22. Matt Hillsinger, of, Radford
23. Tucker Healy, rhp, Ithaca (N.Y.)
24. Kayvon Bahramzadeh, rhp, Kansas State
25. Derek Hansen, rhp/3b, Augustana (S.D.)
26. Lee Sosa, rhp, Binghamton
27. Ryan Mathews, of, North Carolina State
28. Phil Pohl, c, Clemson
29. Taylor Massey, lhp, Dallas Baptist
30. Chris Wolfe, ss, Grambling State
31. Ryan Gorton, c, Oregon State
32. Ryan Dull, rhp, UNC Asheville
33. Tyler Johnson, rhp, Stony Brook
34. Devon Gradford, ss, Downey (Calif.) HS
35. Brett Sunde, c, Bishop Foley HS, Madison Heights, Mich.
36. Conor Williams, rhp/of, Bingham HS, South Jordan, Utah
37. John Wooten, 1b/of, East Carolina
38. Calvin Drummond, rhp, San Diego
39. Dalton Blaser, of, Roseville (Calif.) HS
40. David Olmedo-Barrera, ss, St. Francis HS, Mountain View, Calif.

PHILADELPHIA PHILLIES (30)

1. (Pick to Red Sox as compensation for Type A free agent Jonathan Papelbon)
1. Shane Watson, rhp, Lakewood (Calif.) HS (Supplemental pick—40th—for loss of modified Type A free agent Ryan Madson)
1. Mitch Gueller, rhp, West HS, Chehalis, Wash. (Supplemental pick—54th—for loss of Type B free agent Raul Ibanez)
2. Dylan Cozens, of, Chaparral HS, Scottsdale, Ariz. (Supplemental pick—77th—for loss of Madson)
2. Alec Rash, rhp, Adel DeSoto Minburn HS, Adel, Iowa
3. Zach Green, 3b, Jesuit HS, Sacramento
4. Chris Serritella, 1b, Southern Illinois
5. Andrew Pullin, of, Centralia (Wash.) HS
6. Cameron Perkins, 3b, Purdue
7. Hoby Milner, lhp, Texas
8. Josh Ludy, c, Baylor
9. Jordan Guth, rhp, Wisconsin-Milwaukee
10. Kevin Brady, rhp, Clemson
11. William Carmona, 1b, Stony Brook
12. Zach Taylor, of, Armstrong Atlantic State (Ga.)
13. Steven Golden, of, San Lorenzo (Calif.) HS
14. Ricky Bielski, rhp, Servite HS, Anaheim
15. Zach Cooper, rhp, Central Michigan
16. Nic Hanson, rhp, Golden West (Calif.) JC
17. David Hill, rhp, El Modena HS, Orange, Calif.
18. Tony Blanford, rhp, Boulder Creek HS, Phoenix
19. Tim Carver, ss, Arkansas
20. Matt Sisto, rhp, Hawaii
21. Drew Anderson, rhp, Galena HS, Reno, Nev.
22. Jeb Stefan, rhp, Louisiana Tech
23. Geoff Broussard, rhp, Cal Poly Pomona
24. Chad Carman, c, Oklahoma City
25. Brennan Henry, lhp, Northeastern (Colo.) JC
26. Evan Van Hoosier, 2b, Green Valley HS, Henderson, Nev.
27. Fernando Fernandez, lhp, Montpetit HS, Montreal
28. Joe Mantiply, lhp, Virginia Tech
29. Brad Wieck, lhp, Frank Phillips (Texas) JC
30. Jordan Kipper, rhp, Central Arizona JC
31. Chris Nichols, rhp, Sioux Falls (S.D.)
32. Scott Firth, rhp, Clemson
33. Kyle Cody, rhp, Chippewa Falls (Wis.) HS
34. Darrell Miller Jr., c, Servite HS, Anaheim
35. Steven Wilson, rhp, Dakota Ridge HS, Littleton, Colo.
36. Charles Galiano, c, Commack (N.Y.) HS
37. Daniel Starwalt, rhp, Granite Hills HS, El Cajon, Calif.

38. Geordy Smith, 1b, Highlands Ranch (Colo.) HS
39. Austin Norris, rhp, Trenton (Mo.) HS
40. Eric Hanhold, rhp, East Lake HS, Palm Harbor, Fla.

PITTSBURGH PIRATES (8)

1. Mark Appel, rhp, Stanford
1. Barrett Barnes, of, Texas Tech (Supplemental pick—45th—for loss of Type B free agent Ryan Doumit)
2. Wyatt Mathisen, c, Calallen HS, Corpus Christi, Texas
3. Jon Sandfort, rhp, Winter Springs (Fla.) HS
4. Brandon Thomas, of, Georgia Tech
5. Adrian Sampson, rhp, Bellevue (Wash.) CC
6. Eric Wood, 3b, Blinn (Texas) JC
7. Jacob Stallings, c, North Carolina
8. Kevin Ross, 3b, Niles West HS, Skokie, Ill.
9. D.J. Crumlish, ss, UC Irvine
10. Pat Ludwig, rhp, Yale
11. Chris Diaz, ss, North Carolina State
12. Dalton Friend, lhp, Jefferson (Mo.) CC
13. Tom Harlan, of/lhp, Fresno State
14. Walker Buehler, rhp, Clay HS, Lexington, Ky. 15.Jon Youngblood, of, Meridian (Miss.) CC
16. Max Moroff, ss, Trinity Prep, Winter Park, Fla.
17. Hayden Hurst, rhp, Bolles School, Jacksonville, Fla
18. John Kuchno, rhp, Ohio State
19. Michael Peterson, rhp, St. Francis HS, Mountain View, Calif.
20. Kyle Haynes, rhp, Virginia Commonwealth
21. Jordan Steranka, 3b, Penn State
22. Taylor Hearn, lhp, Royse City (Texas) HS
23. Lance Breedlove, rhp, Purdue
24. Tyler Gaffney, of, Stanford
25. Josh Smith, lhp, Wichita State
26. Jimmy Rider, ss, Kent State
27. Jake Johansen, rhp, Dallas Baptist
28. Tommy Mirabelli, 2b, St. Edward HS, Lakewood, Ohio
29. Jake Post, rhp, Chesterton (Ind.) HS
30. Chase McDowell, rhp, Rice
31. Jack Moffit, rhp, Flower Mound (Texas) HS
32. Max Rossiter, c, Arizona State
33. Carlos Leal, c, East Central (Miss.) CC
34. Ryan Rand, of, Langham Creek HS, Houston
35. Jackson McClelland, rhp, East Valley HS, Redlands, Calif.
36. Brody Russell, 2b, Centennial HS, Bakersfield, Calif.
37. Jacob Waguespack, rhp, Dutchtown HS, Geismar, La.
38. Matt Pope, rhp, Science Hill (Tenn.) HS
39. Jared West, lhp, North DeSoto HS, Stonewall, La.
40. Zarley Zalewski, of, Valley HS, New Kensington, Pa.

ST. LOUIS CARDINALS (22)

1. Michael Wacha, rhp, Texas A&M (Pick from Angels as compensation for Type A free agent Albert Pujols)
1. James Ramsey, of, Florida State
1. Stephen Piscotty, of/3b, Stanford (Supplemental pick—36th—for loss of Pujols)
1. Patrick Wisdom, 3b, St. Mary's (Supplemental pick—52nd—for loss of Type B free agent Octavio Dotel)
1. Steve Bean, c, Rockwall (Texas) HS (Supplemental pick—59th—for loss of Type B free agent Edwin Jackson)
2. Carson Kelly, 3b/rhp, Westview HS, Portland, Ore.
3. Tim Cooney, lhp, Wake Forest
4. Alex Mejia, ss, Arizona
5. Cory Jones, rhp, JC of the Canyons (Calif.)
6. Kurt Heyer, rhp, Arizona
7. Kyle Barraclough, rhp, St. Mary's
8. Yoenny Gonzalez, of, Central Florida JC
9. Rowan Wick, c, Cypress (Calif.) JC
10. Jacob Wilson, 2b, Memphis
11. Trey Williams, 3b, Valencia (Calif.) HS
12. Max Foody, lhp, Pendleton School, Bradenton, Fla.
13. Brett Wiley, ss, Jefferson (Mo.) CC
14. Anthony Melchionda, ss, Boston College
15. Bruce Caldwell, 2b, Spartanburg Methodist (S.C.) JC
16. Joe Scanio, rhp, Northwestern State
17. Chris Perry, rhp, Methodist (N.C.)

18. Jeremy Schaffer, 1b, Tulane
19. Steven Gallardo, rhp, Long Beach CC
20. Matt Young, of/rhp, Cal State Dominguez Hills
21. Joe Almaraz, 1b, Angelina (Texas) JC
22. Casey Schroeder, c, Ottawa-Glandorf HS, Ottawa, Ohio
23. Tate Matheny, of, Westminster Christian Academy, St. Louis
24. Lee Stoppelman, lhp, Central Missouri State
25. Dixon Llorens, rhp, Miami Dade JC
26. Steve Sabatino, lhp, Notre Dame
27. Joey Cuda, rhp, Eckerd (Fla.)
28. Dodson McPherson, of, Wingate (N.C.)
29. Andy Hillis, rhp, Lee (Tenn.)
30. Kyle Helisek, lhp, Villanova
31. Joey Donofrio, rhp, California
32. Eduardo Oquendo, ss, Olney Central (Ill.) CC
33. Ronnie Shaban, rhp, Virginia Tech
34. Mark Trentacosta, lhp, UC Irvine
35. Ben O'Shea, lhp, Tampa
36. Alex Swim, c, Elon
37. Derrick May, of, Tattnall School, Wilmington, Del.
38. Javier Machuca, lhp, Turabo (P.R.) JC
39. Mike Aldrete, rhp, San Jose State
40. Ian Rice, c, Madison Academy, Huntsville, Ala.

SAN DIEGO PADRES (7)

1. Max Fried, lhp, Harvard-Westlake HS, Studio City, Calif.
2. Zach Eflin, rhp, Hagerty HS, Oviedo, Fla. (Supplemental pick—33rd—for loss of modified Type A free agent Heath Bell)
1. Travis Jankowski, of, Stony Brook (Supplemental pick—44th—for loss of Type B free agent Aaron Harang)
1. Walker Weickel, rhp, Olympia HS, Orlando (Supplemental pick—55th—for failure to sign 2011 supplemental first-round pick Brett Austin)
2. Jeremy Baltz, of, St. John's
2. Dane Phillips, c/1b, Oklahoma City (Supplemental pick—70th—for loss of Bell)
3. Fernando Perez, 3b, Central Arizona JC
4. Walker Lockett, rhp, Providence HS, Jacksonville, Fla.
5. Mallex Smith, of, Santa Fe (Fla.) JC
6. Jalen Goree, 2b, Bibb County HS, Centreville, Ala.
7. Roman Madrid, rhp, Central Florida
8. Brian Adams, of, Kentucky
9. River Stevens, 2b, Allan Hancock (Calif.) JC
10. Stephen Carmon, ss, South Carolina-Aiken
11. Maxx Tissenbaum, 2b, Stony Brook
12. Drew Harrelson, lhp, Berrien County HS, Nashville, Ga.
13. Malcolm Diaz, rhp, International Baseball Academy, Ceiba, P.R.
14. Andrew Sopko, rhp, Loyola Sacred Heart HS, Missoula, Mont.
15. Cory Bostjancic, rhp, Marin (Calif.) CC
16. Ronnie Richardson, of, Central Florida
17. Joe Church, rhp, Marshall
18. Chris Burke, 3b, Iona
19. Christian Miller, lhp, Loganville (Ga.) HS
20. Cam Stewart, rhp, Valley Christian HS, San Jose
21. Matt Chabot, rhp, Riverside (Calif.) CC
22. Kevin McCanna, rhp, The Woodlands (Texas) HS
23. Chris O'Dowd, c, Dartmouth
24. Chris Nunn, lhp, Lipscomb
25. Corey Kimber, rhp, Dudley HS, Greensboro, N.C.
26. Brandon Alger, lhp, Indiana Tech
27. Goose Kallunki, 1b, Utah Valley
28. Griffin Russell, lhp, Wichita Falls (Texas) HS
29. Eric Charles, 2b, Purdue
30. Jacob Robson, of, Massey SS, Windsor, Ont.
31. Matt Shepherd, rhp, Tennessee Tech
32. Alexi Colon, of, Tusculum (Tenn.)
33. Tony Wieber, rhp, Michigan State
34. Kyle Ottoson, lhp, Oklahoma State
35. Wynton Bernard, of, Niagara
36. Mac Seibert, 2b, Tate HS, Cantonment, Fla.
37. Christian Munoz, c, Colegio Hector Udraneta, Ceiba, P.R.
38. Adam Ford, ss, Trousdale County (Tenn.) HS
39. Anthony Renteria, of, Cal State San Marcos

40. Terrance Owens, lhp, Toledo

SAN FRANCISCO GIANTS (20)

1. Chris Stratton, rhp, Mississippi State
2. Martin Agosta, rhp, St. Mary's
3. Mac Williamson, of, Wake Forest
4. Steven Okert, lhp, Oklahoma
5. Ty Blach, lhp, Creighton
6. Stephen Johnson, rhp, St. Edward's (Texas)
7. E.J. Encinosa, rhp, Miami
8. Joe Kurrasch, lhp, Penn State
9. Shilo McCall, of, Piedra Vista HS, Farmington, N.M.
10. Trevor Brown, c, UCLA
11. Ryan Tella, of, Auburn
12. Jeremy Sy, ss, Louisiana-Monroe
13. Ryan Jones, 2b, Michigan State
14. Tyler Hollick, of, Chandler-Gilbert (Ariz.) CC
15. Leo Rojas, c, Miami Dade JC
16. Ian Gardeck, rhp, Alabama
17. Chris Johnson, rhp, Portland
18. Matt Duffy, ss, Long Beach State
19. Randy Zeigler, lhp, Louisiana-Monroe
20. Mitch Delfino, inf/rhp, California
21. Ben Turner, c, Missouri
22. Brennan Metzger, of, Long Beach State
23. Drew Leenhouts, lhp, Northeastern
24. Andrew Cain, of, UNC Wilmington
25. Sam Eberle, 3b/c, Jacksonville State
26. Mason McVay, lhp, Florida International
27. Chris Fern, lhp, Union (Ky.)
28. Joey Rapp, 1b/of, Louisiana-Monroe
29. Shayne Houck, of, Kutztown (Pa.)
30. Michael Blanchard, of, Austin Peay State
31. Jason Forjet, rhp, Florida Gulf Coast
32. Chris Pickering, lhp, Rhode Island
33. Brandon Farley, rhp, Arkansas State
34. Zach Edgington, lhp, UC Santa Barbara
35. Danny Grazzini, rhp, San Mateo (Calif.) JC
36. Clint Terry, lhp, San Mateo (Calif.) JC
37. Drew Jackson, ss, Miramonte HS, Orinda, Calif.
38. Nolan Long, rhp, Waterford (Conn.) HS
39. Kevin Fagan, 2b, North Broward Prep, Coconut Creek, Fla.
40. Tyler Ferguson, rhp, Clovis (Calif.) West HS

SEATTLE MARINERS (3)

1. Mike Zunino, c, Florida
2. Joe DeCarlo, 3b, Garnet Valley HS, Glen Mills, Pa.
3. Edwin Diaz, rhp, Naguabo (P.R.) HS
3. Tyler Pike, lhp, Winter Haven (Fla.) HS (Supplemental pick—126th—for failure to sign 2011 third-round pick Kevin Cron)
4. Patrick Kivlehan, 3b, Rutgers
5. Chris Taylor, ss, Virginia
6. Timmy Lopes, 2b, Edison HS, Huntington Beach, Calif.
7. Taylor Ard, 1b, Washington State
8. Nick Halamandaris, 1b, Stevenson HS, Carmel, Calif.
9. Jamodrick McGruder, 2b, Texas Tech
10. Grady Wood, rhp, Western Oregon
11. Kristian Brito, 1b, Quinones Medina HS, Yabucoa, P.R.
12. Mike Faulkner, of, Arkansas State
13. Blake Hauser, rhp, Virginia Commonwealth
14. Brock Hebert, ss, Southeastern Louisiana
15. Dario Pizzano, of, Columbia
16. Dominic Leone, rhp, Clemson
17. Isaiah Yates, of, Clovis (Calif.) East HS
18. Jabari Henry, of, Florida International
19. Nate Koneski, lhp, Holy Cross
20. Steve Ewing, lhp, Miami
21. Scott DeCecco, lhp, South Carolina-Upstate
22. Gabrial Franca, ss, North HS, Riverside, Calif.
23. Levi Dean, rhp, Tennessee Wesleyan
24. Matt Vedo, rhp, UC Santa Barbara
25. Mark Bordonaro, rhp, Fairfield
26. Aaron Brooks, rhp, Edmonds (Wash.) CC
27. Blake Holovach, lhp, Missouri

28. Matt Brazis, rhp, Boston College
29. Toby DeMello, c, St. Mary's
30. Mike Yastrzemski, of, Vanderbilt
31. **Rusty Shellhorn, lhp, Texas Tech**
32. **Richard Palase, 2b, Lynchburg (Va.)**
33. **Logan Seifrit, rhp, Vauxhall (Alb.) HS**
34. Alex Ross, c, Bellevue (Wash.) CC
35. Tyler Krieger, ss, Northview HS, Johns Creek, Ga.
36. Trey Wingenter, rhp, Jones HS, Madison, Ala.
37. Brett Lilek, lhp, Marion Catholic HS, Chicago Heights, Ill.
38. Richie Martin, ss, Bloomingdale (Fla.) HS
39. Grayson Long, rhp, Barbers Hill HS, Mont Belvieu, Texas
40. James Kaprielian, rhp, Beckman HS, Irvine, Calif.

TAMPA BAY RAYS (24)

1. **Richie Shaffer, 3b, Clemson**
2. **Spencer Edwards, of, Rockwall (Texas) HS**
3. **Andrew Toles, of, Chipola (Fla.) JC**
4. **Nolan Gannon, rhp, Santa Fe Christian HS, Solana Beach, Calif.**
5. **Bralin Jackson, of, Raytown (Mo.) South HS**
6. **Damion Carroll, rhp, King George (Va.) HS**
7. **Marty Gantt, of, College of Charleston**
8. **Luke Maile, c/1b, Kentucky**
9. **Joey Rickard, of, Arizona**
10. **Sean Bierman, lhp, Tampa**
11. **Clayton Henning, of, St. Thomas Aquinas HS, Overland Park, Kan.**
12. **Taylor Hawkins, c, Albert HS, Midwest City, Okla.**
13. **Dylan Floro, rhp, Cal State Fullerton**
14. **Chris Kirsch, lhp, Lackawanna (Pa.) JC**
15. **Willie Gabay, rhp, Herkimer County (N.Y.) CC**
16. **Tommy Coyle, 2b, North Carolina**
17. **Ryan Dunn, 3b, Oregon State**
18. **Kevin Brandt, lhp, East Carolina**
19. **Miguel Beltran, 1b, Oklahoma City**
20. **R.J. Davis, rhp, Sacramento State**
21. **Jon Weaver, rhp, Central Michigan**
22. **Willie Argo, of, Illinois**
23. **Reid Redman, 3b, Texas Tech**
24. **Daniel Duran, 3b, Cal State Los Angeles**
25. **Jordan Harrison, lhp, Louisiana-Lafayette**
26. **Jason Wilson, rhp, Western Oregon**
27. **Alex Keudell, rhp, Oregon**
28. **Dayne Quist, lhp, UC Davis**
29. Keaton Steele, rhp, Iowa Western CC
30. **Michael Williams, c, Kentucky**
31. Taylor Ward, c, Shadow Hills HS, Indio, Calif.
32. **Ben Kline, ss, Embry-Riddle (Fla.)**
33. **Luke Goodgion, rhp, Lewis-Clark State (Idaho)**
34. **Ryan Garton, rhp, Florida Atlantic**
35. **Kris Carlson, rhp, Colorado Mesa**
36. Brett McAfee, ss, Panola (Texas) JC
37. **Rob Finneran, rhp, Bentley (Mass.)**
38. **Chad Nacapoy, c, Cal State Los Angeles**
39. **Geoff Rowan, c, Northwestern**
40. **Nick Sawyer, rhp, Howard (Texas) JC**

TEXAS RANGERS (29)

1. **Lewis Brinson, of, Coral Springs (Fla.) HS**
1. **Joey Gallo, 3b/rhp, Bishop Gorman HS, Las Vegas** (Supplemental pick—39th—for loss of Type A free agent C.J. Wilson)
1. **Collin Wiles, rhp, Blue Valley West HS, Stilwell, Kan.** (Supplemental pick—53rd—for loss of Type B free agent Darren Oliver)
2. **Jamie Jarmon, of, Indian River HS, Dagsboro, Del.** (Pick from Angels for loss of Wilson)
2. **Nick Williams, of, Ball HS, Galveston, Texas**
3. **Pat Cantwell, c, Stony Brook**
4. **Alec Asher, rhp, Polk County (Fla.) JC**
5. **Preston Beck, of, Texas-Arlington**
6. **Royce Bollinger, of, Gonzaga**
7. **Cam Schiller, 2b, Oral Roberts**

8. Cody Kendall, rhp, Fresno State
9. **John Niggli, rhp, Liberty**
10. **Casey Shiver, rhp, Southern Polytechnic State (Ga.)**
11. **Eric Brooks, rhp, McLennan (Texas) CC**
12. **Keone Kela, rhp, Everett (Wash.) CC**
13. **Sam Stafford, lhp, Texas**
14. Kwinton Smith, of, Dillon (S.C.) HS
15. Jameis Winston, of, Hueytown (Ala.) HS
16. **Janluis Castro, 2b, Colegio Hector Urdaneta, Ceiba, P.R.**
17. **Chuck Moorman, c, El Capitan HS, Lakeside, Calif.**
18. **Ryan Harvey, rhp, Seton Hall**
19. **Tyler Smith, rhp, South Carolina-Sumter JC**
20. **Josh McElwee, rhp, Newberry (S.C.)**
21. Jake Lemoine, rhp, Bridge City (Texas) HS
22. Travis Dean, rhp, Kennesaw State
23. **Coby Cowgill, rhp, Virginia Military Institute**
24. Chase Mullins, lhp, Bourbon County HS, Paris, Ky.
25. **Gabriel Roa, ss, Wabash Valley (Ill.) CC**
26. **Austen Thrailkill, lhp, St. Petersburg (Fla.) JC**
27. **Ryan Bores, rhp, Kent State**
28. **Joseph Burns, lhp, Samford**
29. **Brandon Kuter, rhp, George Mason**
30. **Barrett Serrato, of, Purdue**
31. **Zach Brill, lhp, Morris HS, Longview, Wash.**
32. Alex Young, lhp, Carmel Catholic HS, Mundelein, Ill.
33. Ryan Burr, rhp, Highlands Ranch (Colo.) HS
34. **David Lyon, c, Kent State**
35. Brad Stone, lhp, Ardrey Kell HS, Charlotte
36. Sterling Wynn, lhp, China Spring (Texas) HS
37. Matt Withrow, rhp, Midland (Texas) Christian HS
38. Zack Fields, 1b, Annapolis (Mich.) HS
39. Tevin Johnson, of, Henry County HS, McDonough, Ga.
40. **Paul Schwendel, rhp, Emory (Ga.)**

TORONTO BLUE JAYS (17)

1. **D.J. Davis, of, Stone HS, Wiggins, Miss.**
1. **Marcus Stroman, rhp, Duke** (Supplemental pick—22nd—for failure to sign 2011 first-round pick Tyler Beede)
1. **Matt Smoral, lhp, Solon (Ohio) HS** (Supplemental pick—50th—for loss of Type B free agent Frank Francisco)
1. **Mitch Nay, 3b, Hamilton HS, Chandler, Ariz.** (Supplemental pick—58th—for loss of Type B free agent Jon Rauch)
1. **Tyler Gonzales, rhp, Madison HS, San Antonio** (Supplemental pick—60th—for loss of Type B free agent Jose Molina)
2. **Chase DeJong, rhp, Wilson HS, Long Beach**
3. **Anthony Alford, of, Petal (Miss.) HS**
4. **Tucker Donahue, rhp, Stetson**
5. **Brad Delatte, lhp, Nicholls State**
6. **Eric Phillips, 2b, Georgia Southern**
7. **Ian Parmley, of, Liberty**
8. **Tucker Frawley, c, Coastal Carolina**
9. **Jordan Leyland, 1b, Azusa Pacific (Calif.)**
10. **Alex Azor, of, Navy**
11. Grant Heyman, of, Pittsford (N.Y.) Sutherland HS
12. Ryan Kellogg, lhp, Street HS, Whitby, Ont.
13. **John Silviano, c, Summit Christian School, West Palm Beach, Fla.**
14. **Zak Wasilewski, lhp, Tazewell (Va.) HS**
15. **Ryan Borucki, rhp, Mundelein (Ill.) HS**
16. **William DuPont, 2b, Lafayette HS, Wildwood, Mo.**
17. **Shane Dawson, lhp, Lethbridge (Alb.) JC**
18. **Alonzo Gonzalez, lhp, Glendale (Calif.) JC**
19. **Jorge Flores, ss, Central Arizona JC**
20. **Dennis Jones, of, Hillsborough (Fla.) CC**
21. **Colton Turner, lhp, Texas State**
22. **Josh Almonte, of, Long Island City (N.Y.) HS**
23. **Trey Pascazi, ss, East Rochester (N.Y.) HS**
24. Matt Rose, rhp, Palm Bay (Fla.) HS
25. **Jason Leblebijian, ss, Bradley**
26. **Nathan DeSouza, of, Drury HS, Milton, Ont.**
27. Daniel Zamora, lhp, Bishop Amat HS, La Puente, Calif.
28. **Dan Klein, c, Kansas State**
29. Cole Irvin, lhp, Servite HS, Anaheim
30. Devin Pearson, of, Carmel (Calif.) HS

31. Derrick Chung, ss, Sacramento State
32. Jorge Saez, c, Lee (Tenn.)
33. Jonathan Harris, rhp, Hazelwood Central HS, Florissant, Mo.
34. Brandon Lopez, ss, American Heritage HS, Plantation, Fla.
35. Devyn Rivera, rhp, California Baptist
36. Brian Cruz, ss, Galveston (Texas) JC
37. Daniel Devonshire, 1b, Colby (Kan.) CC
38. Nick Lovullo, ss, Newbury Park (Calif.) HS
39. Shaun Valeriote, 3b, Brock (Ont.)
40. Jose Cuas, ss, Grand Street Campus HS, Brookyln

WASHINGTON NATIONALS (16)

1. Lucas Giolito, rhp, Harvard-Westlake HS, Studio City, Calif.
2. Tony Renda, 2b, California
3. Brett Mooneyham, lhp, Stanford
4. Brandon Miller, of, Samford
5. Spencer Kieboom, c, Clemson
6. Hayden Jennings, of, Evangel Christian Academy, Shreveport, La.
7. Robert Benincasa, rhp, Florida State
8. Stephen Perez, ss, Miami
9. Derek Self, rhp, Louisville
10. Craig Manuel, c, Rice
11. Brian Rauh, rhp, Chapman (Calif.)
12. Carlos Lopez, 1b, Wake Forest
13. Elliot Waterman, lhp, San Francisco

14. Jordan Poole, rhp, Chipola (Fla.) JC
15. Brandon Smith, of, Woodbridge HS, Irvine, Calif.
16. Ronald Pena, rhp, Palm Beach State (Fla.) JC
17. Blake Schwartz, rhp, Oklahoma City
18. Dave Fischer, rhp, Connecticut
19. Bryan Lippincott, 3b, Concordia (Minn.)
20. James Brooks, ss, Utah
21. Austin Chubb, c, Florida Southern
22. Will Hudgins, rhp, Notre Dame
23. Casey Selsor, lhp, Texas-San Antonio
24. Austin Dicharry, rhp, Texas
25. Freddy Avis, rhp, Menlo School, Atherton, Calif.
26. Skye Bolt, of, Holy Innocents' HS, Atlanta
27. Cody Poteet, rhp, Christian HS, El Cajon, Calif.
28. Hunter Bailey, ss, Oklahoma State
29. L.J. Hollins, rhp, Chipola (Fla.) JC
30. R.C. Orlan, lhp, North Carolina
31. Mike Boyden, rhp, Maryland
32. Mike Mudron, lhp, Cal State San Bernardino
33. Mike McQuillan, 2b, Iowa
34. Jake Jeffries, 2b, Foothill HS, Santa Ana, Calif.
35. Cory Bafidis, lhp, Texas Wesleyan
36. Max Ungar, c, Smith Jewish Day School, Bethesda, Md.
37. Tyler Watson, lhp, Georgetown (Texas) HS
38. Jared Messer, rhp, Malone (Ohio)
39. Mitchell Williams, c, Coosa HS, Rome, Ga.
40. Ricky Gutierrez, of, American Senior HS, Miami

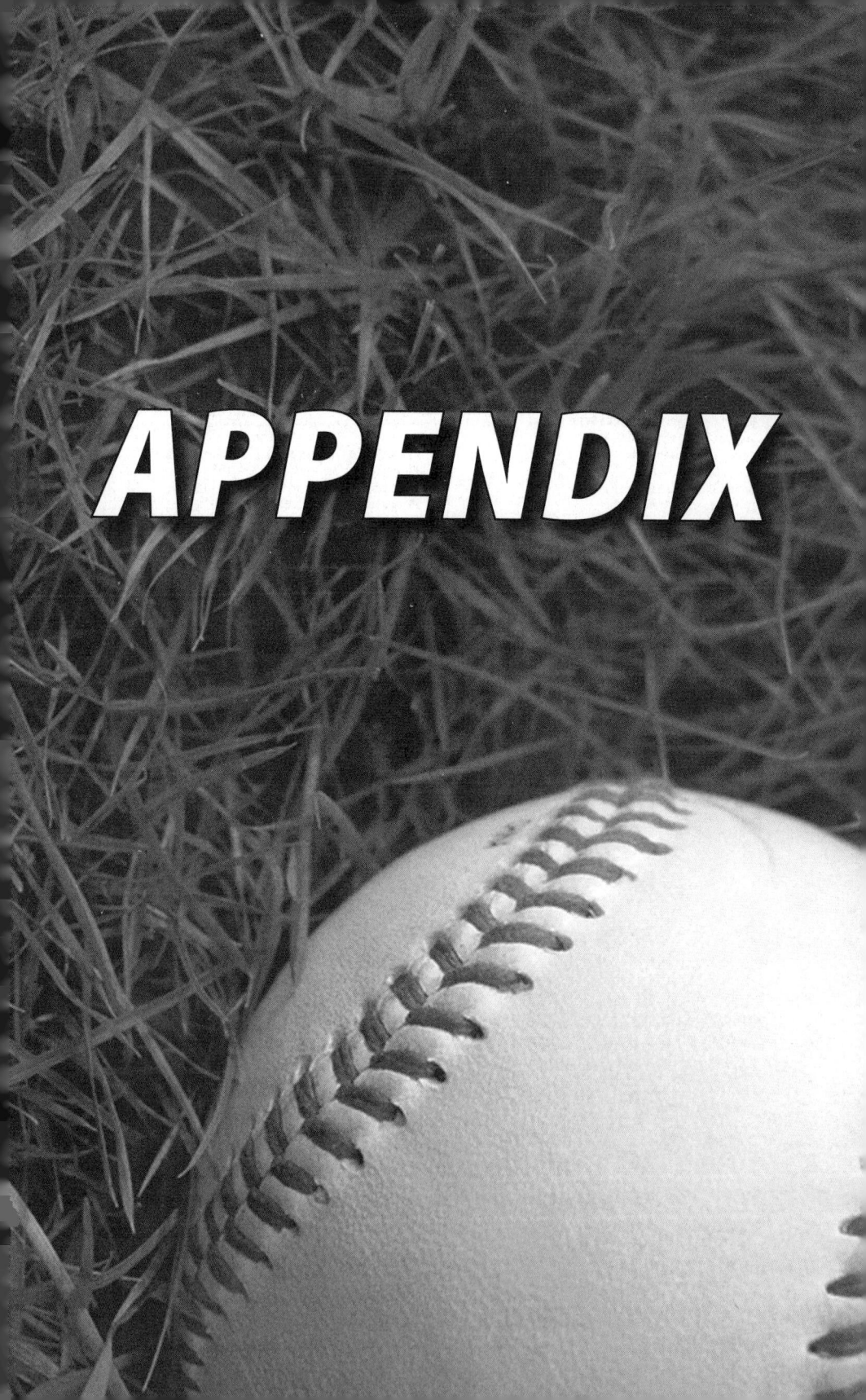

APPENDIX

Herb Adams, an outfielder who played in parts three seasons with the White Sox, died Feb. 1 in Tulsa. He was 83.

Adams received his first big league callup at the end of the 1948 season, when he was coming off winning the batting title in the Cotton States League by hitting .375 with Hot Springs. He appeared in five games for the White Sox in September 1948 and went 3-for-11. Adams was a reserve with the 1949 White Sox, appearing in 56 games and hitting .293. He got into another 34 games for Chicago in 1950 but hit just .203. He missed the next two seasons to serve in the military, and while he resumed his pro career in 1953, he never got back to the majors.

Darrel Akerfelds, a righthander who pitched five seasons in the majors and who served as the Padres' big league bullpen coach since 2001, died June 24 in Phoenix. He was 50.

Akerfelds pitched for four different teams over five big league seasons between 1986-91. He was primarily a reliever but did make 13 starts for the 1987 Indians, going 2-6, 6.75. His best big league season came in 1990 with the Phillies, when he logged 93 innings, all in relief, and went 5-2, 3.77 with three saves. He continued pitching in the minors through 1995, and he joined the Padres organization as a coach two years later in 1997.

Matty Alou, an outfielder who played 15 seasons in the majors and was a two-time all-star, died Nov. 3, 2011, in Miami. He was 72.

Matty was the second of the three Alou brothers to come up with the Giants in the late 1950s and early '60s, following older brother Felipe and preceding younger brother Jesus. Alou was traded to the Pirates after the 1965 season, and he immediately blossomed in Pittsburgh. A .260 career hitter up to that point, Alou changed his approach and went out and won the National League batting title in 1966, hitting .342 in 535 at-bats in his first year in Pittsburgh. In a stretch of years dominated by pitching, Alou batted at least .330 for four straight years from 1966 to '69. He made the All-Star Game in 1968 and '69, leading the NL in both hits (231) and doubles (41) in '69.

Hub Andrews, a righthander who pitched in the major leagues for the New York Giants in 1947 and '48, died March 11 in Dodge City, Kan. He was 89.

Andrews, who pitched professionally in 1942 and from 1946-49, was a reliever for the Giants, making 8 appearances over his two seasons in the majors. He pitched 11 2/3 total innings and finished his big league career with a 4.63 ERA.

Ted Beard, an outfielder who played in parts of seven seasons in the majors, died Dec. 30, 2011, in Fishers, Ind. He was 90.

Beard saw action as a part-time outfielder for the Pirates from 1948-52. His busiest and most successful big league season came in 1950, when he appeared in 61 games for Pittsburgh and hit .232 with four homers in 177 at-bats. After 1952, Beard didn't get back to the majors until 1957, appearing in 57 games for the White Sox from 1957-58.

Rick Behenna, a righthander who pitched for the Braves and Indians in the mid-80s, died Jan. 31 in Newnan, Ga. He was 51.

Behenna, a professional pitcher from 1978-85, made his major league debut with Atlanta in 1983, going 3-3, 4.58. The Braves traded him late in 1983 to the Indians, and he pitched the next two seasons in Cleveland. Behenna was 3-10, 6.12 in his three-year big league career, going 0-7 with the Indians.

Dennis Bennett, a lefthander who pitched in the major leagues from 1962-68 as part of a 16-year professional career, died March 23 in Klamath Falls, Ore. He was 72.

Bennett, who made 127 starts over his seven-year big league career, went 43-47 with a 3.69 ERA. He also had six saves. Bennett pitched for the Phillies from 1962-64, going 12-14 in '64 with a 3.68 ERA. He pitched for the Red Sox from 1965-67, splitting the '67 season between the Red Sox and the Mets. Bennett finished up his major league career with the California Angels in 1968.

Clyde "Bud" Bloomfield, a shortstop who played briefly in two big league seasons, died Dec. 21, 2011, in Huntsville, Ark. He was 75.

Bloomfield broke into pro ball in 1956 and made his big league debut at the end of the 1963 season, appearing in one game for the Cardinals. He went to the Twins in 1964 and made seven big league appearances, going 1-for-7 at the plate.

Fred Bradley, a righthander who pitched in parts of two big league seasons, died April 24 in Pico Rivera, Calif. He was 91.

Bradley played five seasons in the minors before making his big league debut with the White Sox in 1948. He made eight appearances for Chicago and posted a 4.50 ERA in 16 innings. He made only one appearance with the White Sox in 1949.

Pedro Borbon, a righthander who pitched 12 seasons in the major leagues mostly with the Reds, died June 4 in Pharr, Texas. He was 65.

Borbon was best known for his time in Cincinnati, where he was one of the mainstays

APPENDIX

APPENDIX

in the bullpen for the Big Red Machine, a team that won back-to-back World Seires in 1975 and '76. Borbon had his breakout year in 1972, when he went 8-3, 3.17 with 11 saves and logged 122 innings over 62 appearances. The 1973 season was his best, as he won 11 games and saved 14 while posting a 2.16 ERA over 121 innings, all out of the bullpen. He had a 3.02 cumulative ERA from 1972-77.

■ **Dave Boswell**, a righthander who pitched eight seasons in the majors, mostly with the Twins, died June 11 in Joppa, Md. He was 67.

Boswell got his first big league callup with the Twins as a 19-year-old in September 1964, and he became a full-time member of the rotation in '66 at age 21. Boswell went 12-5, 3.14 that season and went on to finish in the top 10 in the American League in strikeouts three times, highlighted by his 204-whiff season in 1967.

Boswell won 20 games with a 3.23 ERA in 1969, but he infamously got into a bar fight with Billy Martin, his manager, that August. Two months later, Boswell injured himself during his start in Game Two of the AL Championship Series against the Orioles, a game in which he pitched 10 2/3 innings. Never the same after that, Boswell lasted just two more seasons in the majors, ending his career at age 26 in 1971 with a 68-56, 3.52 record.

■ **Al Brancato**, a shortstop who played four seasons with the Philadelphia Athletics, died June 14 in Media, Pa. He was 93.

Brancato reached the majors in just his second year of pro ball, appearing in 21 games as a 20-year-old in September 1939 and hitting .206 with one homer in 68 at-bats. The A's primary shortstop for the next two seasons, Brancato peaked in 1941 when he hit .234 with two homers in 530 at-bats. He left baseball to join the Navy during World War II and didn't get back on the field until the tail end of the 1945 season, when he made 10 appearances for the A's. He never played in the big leagues again after 1945, though he continued playing in the minors through 1953.

■ **Bud Byerly**, a righthander who pitched in 11 major league seasons between 1943 and 1960, died Jan. 26 in St. Louis. He was 91.

Bylery, who pitched for the Cardinals, Reds, Washington Senators, Red Sox and Giants, made 17 starts out of 237 big league appearances, going 22-22 with a 3.70 ERA and 14 career saves. In 1944, when the Cardinals won the World Series, Byerly was 2-2, 3.40 for the season.

■ **Andy Carey**, a third baseman who played 11 seasons in the major leagues, died Dec. 15, 2011,

in Costa Mesa, Calif. He was 80.

Carey was one of the lesser-known players with the powerful 1950s Yankees squads. He broke into the majors as a 20-year-old with the Yankees in 1952 and became New York's regular third baseman in 1954. He had one of his best years at the plate at age 22 in 1954, batting .302 with eight homers in 411 at-bats. He led the American League with 11 triples in 1955, but otherwise his offensive production fell off over the next few seasons. Nonetheless, Carey helped the Yankees reach four straight World Series from 1955-58, winning in 1956 and '58. His hitting bounced back somewhat in 1958, when he batted .286 with 12 homers, but he lost his everyday job in 1959 and was traded to the Kansas City Athletics in 1960. Carey played two more seasons with the A's, White Sox and Dodgers, ending his career in 1962 as a .260 lifetime hitter with 64 homers.

■ **Gary Carter**, a Hall of Fame catcher who played 19 seasons in the major leagues, died Feb. 16 in West Palm Beach, Fla., after a 10-month battle with cancer. He was 57.

Carter, an exuberant player who was nicknamed "The Kid," was inducted into the Hall of Fame in 2003 after retiring in 1992. An 11-time all-star who spent most of his career with the Montreal Expos and Mets but also played one season each for the Giants and Dodgers, Carter finished with a .262 average, 324 homers and 1,225 RBIs.

Carter had many highlights in his storied career, but he is most remembered for a crucial hit in the 1986 World Series. With the Mets trailing the Red Sox 5-3 in the 10th inning of Game 6 and New York down to its last out in the Series, Carter started a winning rally with a single. Kevin Mitchell and Ray Knight followed with singles, and Carter scampering home on Knight's hit. A wild pitch tied the score, and Bill Buckner's infamous error followed, giving the Mets a 6-5 victory.

■ **Art Ceccarelli**, a lefthander who pitched five seasons in the majors from 1955-60, died July 11 in Orange, Conn. He was 82.

Ceccarelli made his big league debut in May 1955 with the Kansas City Athletics, who had acquired him in the Rule 5 draft the previous winter. He made 31 appearances, including 16 starts, for the A's that summer though he went just 4-7, 5.31. He went back and forth between the majors and minors over the next few seasons, seeing big league time with the Orioles and Cubs. He did see significant big league time for the Cubs in 1959, going 5-5, 4.76 in 102 innings, making 15 starts.

■ **Cliff Chambers**, a lefthander who pitched

six seasons in the majors, died Jan. 21 in Eagle, Idaho. He was 90.

Chambers is best remembered for throwing a no-hitter for the Pirates against the Boston Braves on May 6, 1951, in the second game of a doubleheader. He overcame some wildness that day, issuing eight walks and recording just four strikeouts, to hold the Braves hitless. Chambers pitched in the majors from 1948-53, debuting with the Cubs and going on to pitch for the Pirates and Cardinals. He won a career-high 14 games in 1951, a season during which he was traded from Pittsburgh to St. Louis, but his best year might have come in 1949, when he went 13-7, 3.96 for Pittsburgh. Chambers compiled a 48-53, 4.29 career record in 897 big league innings.

■ **Dave Cheadle,** a lefthander who pitched for the Atlanta Braves in 1973, died Feb. 25 in St. Augustine, Fla. He was 60.

Cheadle, who pitched professionally from 1970-78, made two relief appearances for the Braves in 1973, going 0-1. He pitched a total of two innings, giving up four runs.

■ **Allie Clark,** an outfielder who played in the major leagues from 1947-53, died April 2 in Morgan, N.J. He was 88.

Clark, one of the last New York Yankees to wear No. 3 before Babe Ruth's number was retired in 1948, broke into the majors on Aug. 5, 1947 with the Yankees, hitting .373 in 24 games in a World Series championship season for New York. Clark went to Cleveland the next season, hitting .310 as the Indians won the 1948 World Series. Clark stayed with the Indians until 1951, splitting that season between Cleveland and the Philadelphia Athletics. He finished his big league career in 1953, splitting the season between the A's and the White Sox. Clark compiled a .262 career average in 358 games, hitting 32 homers and driving in 149 runs as a part-time player.

■ **Danny Clyburn,** an outfielder who played in three big league seasons, died Feb. 7 in Lancaster, S.C., the victim of a shooting. He was 37.

Clyburn was the Pirates' second-round pick, No. 47 overall, in the 1992 draft out of Lancaster (S.C.) High. He was traded twice, to the Reds and then the Orioles, before making his big league debut with Baltimore at the tail end of the 1997 season. Clyburn earned another late season callup in 1998 and hit .280 in 25 big league at-bats. He was traded to the Devil Rays before the 1999 season and made Tampa Bay's Opening Day roster, though he hit just .198 in 28 games before being sent down. He went on to play three seasons with

independent Newark (Atlantic) before leaving pro ball in 2004.

■ **Glenn Cox,** a righthander who pitched four seasons in the majors in the 1950s, died Jan. 8 in Los Molinos, Calif. He was 80.

After four seasons in the minors, Cox made his big league debut in September 1955 with the Kansas City Athletics. He continued to spend most of his time in the minors in coming seasons but made 17 big league appearances, all with the A's, from 1955-58, compiling a 1-4, 6.39 record.

■ **Bill Cutler,** who served as Pacific Coast League president from 1979 to 1997 as part of 50 distinguished years in baseball, died March 24 in Mesa, Ariz. He was 92.

Cutler purchased the PCL franchise in Portland, Ore., and relocated it to Spokane, Wash., in 1973. He served as general manager for the franchise in both locations. Cutler sold the Spokane club in 1978 and ascended to PCL president the following year.

A press release issued by the PCL credits Cutler, the longest-tenured president in league history, with expanding the circuit into Canadian cities Edmonton (1981) and Calgary (1985). During Cutler's tenure as president, Colorado Springs, Edmonton, Las Vegas, Phoenix and Salt Lake City all built new ballparks, a sign of league prosperity.

Cutler got his start in baseball when hired as an administrative assistant for the American League in 1946.

■ **Bob DiPietro,** an outfielder who played in one major league season, died Sept. 3 in Yakima, Wash. He was 85.

DiPietro played 13 seasons of pro ball from 1947-59, but his only big league experience came at the tail end of the '51 season. Called up by the Red Sox that September, DiPietro appeared in four major league games and went 1-for-11 at the plate.

■ **Don Erickson,** a righthander who pitched in one season for the Phillies, died Aug. 1 in Springfield, Ill. He was 80.

Erickson pitched 10 seasons in pro ball between 1951-62, missing two seasons to serve in the military, but his only big league experience came in 1958. After posting a 2.96 ERA for Tulsa (Texas) that season, the Phillies made him a September callup and he got into nine big league games, all in relief, going 0-1, 4.50 in 12 innings.

■ **Bob Forsch,** a righthander who won 168 games in a 16-year major-league career that included 15-plus seasons with the Cardinals, died Nov. 2, 2011, in Weeki Wachee, Fla. He has 61.

Forsch, who began his professional career in

1968, broke in with the Cardinals in 1974 and was a solid St. Louis starter for the next 15 seasons. A 20-game winner in 1977 when he went 20-7, Forsch finished 168-136 with a career ERA of 3.76. He pitched in the World Series in 1982, '85 and '87, going 1-3, 7.36. Forsch pitched 15 seasons for the Cardinals, notching 163 of his career victories. St. Louis traded him to the Astros during the 1988 season, and he retired following the '89 season for Houston.

■ **Rosman Garcia,** a righthander who pitched for the Rangers in 2003 and '04, died Dec. 29, 2011, in Aragua, Venezuela, as the result of an automobile accident. He was 32.

Garcia, a native of Venezuela, pitched professionally from 1996-2011. In the major leagues, Garcia made 50 relief appearances with the Rangers, going 1-2, 5.94 with no saves.

■ **Bob Hale,** a first baseman who played seven seasons in the majors from 1955-61, died Sept. 8 in Park Ridge, Ill. He was 78.

Hale broke into the majors with a bang, hitting .357 with 29 RBIs in 67 games for the 1955 Orioles, but he hit just .237 in 85 games the next year. Hale spent most of the remainder of his big league career being used as a pinch-hitter, making just 27 appearances in the field over the next five years. Hale's best offensive season in that stretch came in 1960, after he'd been picked up on waivers by the Indians, when he hit .300 in 70 at-bats. Hale finished his big league career with the Yankees in 1961.

■ **Greg Halman,** an outfielder with the Mariners and their former No. 1 prospect, died Nov. 21, 2011, in Rotterdam, Netherlands. He was 24.

A native of Haarlem, Netherlands, Halman established himself as a premium prospect thanks to his outstanding athleticism and power. Halman was ranked as the Mariners' No. 1 prospect entering the 2009 season, and he hit 25 home runs that year for Double-A West Tenn. He finished second in the Triple-A Pacific Coast League with 33 homers for Tacoma in 2010 and made his big league debut that September. Ranked as Seattle's No. 11 prospect entering 2011, Halman hit .299/.358/.441 with 15 homers in 177 at-bats for Tacoma and appeared in 35 games with the Mariners, hitting .230. He hit his first career major league homer on June 15 against the Angels and added one more against Toronto on July 19.

■ **Troy "Dutch" Herriage,** a pitcher who spent the 1956 season with the Kansas City Athletics during a seven-year professional career, died Jan.

21 in Atlanta. He was 81.

Promoted to the majors after a 15-win season in Montgomery (South Atlantic) in 1955, the righthander went 1-13, 6.64 for the A's in 1956.

■ **Kevin Hickey,** a lefthander who pitched six seasons in the major leagues, died May 16 in Chicago. He was 56.

A Chicago native, Hickey came up with the White Sox in 1981 and spent three seasons working out of their bullpen, highlighted by his 1982 campaign when he appeared in 60 games and went 4-4, 3.00 with six saves. Hickey was back in the minors in 1984 when he was traded to the Yankees, and he bounced between several organizations before making it back to the majors with the Orioles in 1989. He spent three seasons pitching out of Baltimore's bullpen before his big league career came to an end in 1991. He made 231 career appearances, all in relief, and put together a 9-14, 3.91 record with 17 saves.

■ **Mike Hershberger,** an outfielder who played 11 seasons in the major leagues, died July 1 in Massillon, Ohio. He was 72.

Hershberger made his big league debut in 1961 with the White Sox and took over as their everyday right fielder in 1962. He hit .262 with four homers in his first full big league season and played three years for Chicago before being traded to the Kansas City Athletics prior to the 1965 season. Hershberger was best known for his outstanding throwing arm, and he led the American League in outfield assists twice, in 1965 and '67. His best offensive season came in 1968, the A's first season in Oakland, when he hit .272 with five homers.

■ **Lloyd Hittle,** a lefthander who pitched in two big league seasons, died March 3 in Lodi, Calif. He was 88.

Hittle pitched four seasons in the minors before making his big league debut with the Washington Senators in June 1949. He went on to log 109 innings for the Senators, going 5-7, 4.21 in 36 games (nine starts). He returned to the minors for most of the 1950 season but did pitch 43 innings for Washington, going 2-4, 4.98.

■ **Stan Johnson,** an outfielder who played in the major leagues in 1960 and '61, died April 17 in San Francisco. He was 75.

Johnson, who played professionally from 1957-69, played five games for the White Sox in 1960, batting .167 with his only hit in six at-bats a solo home run. He played three games for the Kansas City Athletics in 1961.

■ **Roger Jongewaard,** a former minor league catcher and longtime Mariners scouting director, died June 11. He was 86.

Jongewaard ran the Mariners' drafts from 1985-2004, landing two of the most successful No. 1 overall picks ever in Ken Griffey Jr. (1987) and Alex Rodriguez (1993). He was the 2004 recipient of Baseball America's Roland Hemond Award for his longtime contributions to scouting and player development.

■ **Hal Keller,** a catcher who played three seasons in the majors and later became Mariners general manager, died June 5 in Sequim, Wash. He was 84.

Keller played in the majors with the Washington Senators between 1949 and 1952. He worked in the front offices of the Senators and Rangers before joining the Mariners as farm director in 1979. He was elevated to GM in 1984 and spent two seasons in the role before retiring in 1985.

■ **Charles "Chick" King,** an outfielder who played in parts of five big league seasons in the 1950s, died July 9 in Paris, Tenn. He was 81.

The first major leaguer ever to come out of the University of Memphis, King saw limited action at the big league level between 1954 and '59, playing for the Tigers, Cubs and Cardinals. He had 76 career at-bats in the majors and hit .237 with five RBIs.

■ **Jack Kralick,** a lefthander who pitched nine seasons in the majors and made one all-star team, died Sept. 18 in San Bias, Mexico. He was 77.

Kralick came up with the Washington Senators in 1959 and became a mainstay in the rotation in 1961, the first season after the Senators' relocation to Minnesota. Kralick logged more than 220 innings in three straight seasons for the Twins from 1961-63, winning 39 games with a 3.51 ERA over those three years.

Kralick, who was traded from the Twins to the Indians in May 1963, made the American League all-star team in 1964, a season in which he went 12-7, 3.21 in 191 innings. His numbers fell off sharply in subsequent seasons, and he lost his place in the Indians' rotation in 1965. He was out of the majors after the 1967 season, the end hastened by injuries he suffered in an automobile accident earlier that year.

■ **Howie Koplitz,** a righthander who pitched in five major league seasons, died Jan. 2 in Oshkosh, Wis. He was 73.

Koplitz got his first major league callup to the Tigers in September 1961, making four appearances. He made 10 appearances for Detroit in 1962 but remained in the minors throughout 1963. The Washington Senators grabbed Koplitz in the Rule 5 draft after the '63 season, and he went on to make a career-high 33 big league appearances, including 11 starts, for the Senators in 1965, going 4-7, 4.05. He last pitched in the majors in 1966, ending his career with a 4.21 ERA in 175 big league innings.

■ **Charlie Lea,** a righthander who pitched in the major leagues from 1980-84 and 1987-88 with the Montreal Expos and Twins, died Nov. 11, 2011, in Collierville, Tenn. He was 54.

Lea made 144 starts in a seven-year big league career, finishing 62-48, 3.54. Lea pitched for the Expos in all but the 1988 season when he went 7-7 for the Twins. He was one of the few French-born pitchers in the major leagues and the only one to pitch a no-hitter, accomplishing the feat on May 10, 1981, in a 4-0 victory against the Giants. Lea was a front-line starter until 1984 when he began to have arm problems that kept him on the sidelines for both the 1985 and '86 seasons.

■ **Don Leshnock,** a lefthander who made one big league appearance for the Tigers, died May 5 in Raleigh, N.C. He was 65.

Leshnock's lone game in the majors came on June 7, 1972, when he pitched a scoreless inning for the Tigers against the California Angels. His minor league career spanned from 1968-75.

■ **Jerry Lynch,** an outfielder in the major leagues from 1954-1966, died April 1 in Atlanta. He was 81.

Lynch split his career between Pittsburgh (1954-56 and 1963-66) and Cincinnati (1957-63), posting a career .277 average with 115 homers and 470 RBIs. He hit .300 twice for Cincinnati (.312 in 1958 and .315 in 19961).

■ **Terry Mathews,** a righthander who pitched in the major leagues for eight seasons from 1991-99, died Feb. 24 in Alexandria, La. He was 47.

Mathews, who pitched professionally from 1987-2000, made his major league debut with the Rangers in 1991. He also pitched for the Marlins, Orioles and Royals. Mathews, who made just five starts in 324 big league appearances, had a career record of 22-21, 4.25 with 10 saves.

■ **Benny McCoy,** a second baseman who played two seasons each for the Tigers and Philadelphia Athletics from 1938-41, died Nov. 9, 2011, in Grandville, Mich. He was 96.

McCoy, who played professionally from 1934-41, made it to the big leagues in 1938 with the Tigers as a late-season callup. He was signed by the A's before the 1940 season and spent two seasons in Philadelphia. McCoy finished with a career big league average of .269 with 16 homers and 156

APPENDIX

RBIs in 337 games.

■ **Jerry McMorris,** a former owner, CEO and president of the Rockies, died May 8 in Denver. He was 71.

McMorris was a key figure in the early days of the Rockies, rallying together a local ownership group to take over the expansion franchise in 1992 after its original ownership group fell apart. He went on to serve as the team's president and chief executive officer through 2001. He sold his ownership stake in the team in 2005.

■ **Don Mincher,** a first baseman in the major leagues from 1960-72, died March 4 in Huntsville, Ala. He was 73.

Mincher made two American League all-star teams, in 1967 with the California Angels and '69 with the Seattle Pilots, and he finished his 13-year career with 200 homers and 643 RBIs while batting .249. Mincher made his big league debut in 1960 with the Washington Senators and also played for the Twins, Angels, Pilots, Athletics and Rangers. He hit 20 or more homers five times in his career, belting a career-high 27 in 1970 for Oakland. Mincher went on to become a minor league executive and served as President of the Southern League from 2000-2011.

■ **Don Mueller,** an outfielder who played in the major leagues from 1948-59 with the New York Giants and the White Sox, died Dec. 28, 2011, in Maryland Heights, Mo. He was 84.

Mueller was on base after a single when Bobby Thomson belted his famous pennant-winning home run against the Brooklyn Dodgers in 1951. Mueller, an all-star in 1954 and '55, finished second in the NL in batting in '54 with a .342 average. He played with the Giants from 1948-57 and finished his career by playing two seasons with the White Sox. Mueller finished his big league career with a .296 average, 65 homers and 520 RBIs.

■ **Les Moss,** a catcher who played 13 seasons in the major leagues, died Aug. 29 in Longwood, Fla. He was 87.

Moss spent the bulk of his big league career playing for the St. Louis Browns/Baltimore Orioles, playing in parts of 10 seasons there from 1946-55. He put up some quality offensive seasons early in his career, hitting 14 home runs for the Browns in 1948 and batting .291 with 10 homers in 1949. He was mostly a part-time player though, topping 100 games played in a season only once, in 1948. The Orioles traded him to the White Sox in June 1955 and he finished out his playing career with Chicago. He went on to a scouting and coaching career, including short tenures as the White Sox's

interim manager for 36 games in 1968 and 53 games as manager of the Tigers in 1979.

■ **Ray Narleski,** a righthander who pitched in the majors from 1954-59, died March 29 in Clementon, N.J. He was 73.

Used primarily as a reliever who notched 58 career saves, Narleski made two all-star teams while with the Indians (1956 and '58). He led the AL with 60 appearances and (retroactively, at least) 19 saves in 1955, a season in which he also went 9-1. Narleski had a career-best 1.52 ERA one year later in '56, his first all-star campaign. He made a combined 39 starts in 1957 and '58 with Cleveland, going 24-15, 3.62 with 195 strikeouts and 161 walks in 338 innings. Narleski spent his final season, 1959, with the Tigers, finishing with a career record of 43-33, 3.60.

■ **Howie Nunn,** a righthander who pitched for the Cardinals in 1959 and the Reds from 1961-62, died Feb. 17 in Winston-Salem, N.C. He was 76.

Nunn made 46 relief appearances in his career without a start, posting a 4-3 record with a 5.11 ERA and no saves.

■ **John O'Neil,** a shortstop who played for the Phillies in 1946 during a 15-year pro career, died April 18 in Jamestown, N.Y. He was 91.

O'Neil played 46 games for the Phillies in 1946, hitting .266 with no homers and nine RBIs. His best season as a minor leaguer was in 1945, when he hit .315 with 13 triples and 88 RBIs for Portland (Pacific Coast).

■ **Jim Obradovich,** a first baseman who played for the Astros in 1978 during a 14-year pro career, died March 3 in Lancaster, Ky. He was 62.

Obradovich played 10 games for the Astros during the '78 season, hitting 3-for-17 (.176) with one triple and two RBIs in 17 at-bats.

■ **Mel Parnell,** a lefthander who pitched for the Red Sox from 1947-56, died March 20 in New Orleans. He was 89.

Parnell, who spent his entire big league career with in Boston, was an all-star in 1949 and '51. He led the American League in victories in 1949 when he went 25-7 and in innings pitched that season with 295. Parnell finished his career with a 123-75 record and a 3.50 ERA.

■ **Johnny Pesky,** a shortstop who played 10 seasons in the majors mostly with the Red Sox, died Aug. 13 in Danvers, Mass. He was 92.

Pesky broke into the majors with Boston at age 22 in 1942 and hit .331 as a rookie. He would miss the next three seasons while serving in the Navy but returned to hit .335 in 1946. He made his only All-Star Game that year and the Red Sox captured their first AL pennant since 1918.

Though Pesky never captured a batting title, he led the AL in hits three times and finished in the top 10 in the AL in average five times. He was traded to the Tigers in June 1952 as injuries started slowing him down. He kept playing through the 1954 season, ending his career with a .307 lifetime average. In all, Pesky spent 61 seasons as a member of the Red Sox organization as a player, coach, manager and broadcaster.

■ **Dave Philley,** who played 18 seasons in the major leagues from 1941-62, died March 15 in Paris, Texas. He was 91.

Philley played seven games for the White Sox in 1941. After a season in the minors and three years in the military, he made it back to the majors in '46 and stayed there through '62. Philley played for the White Sox, Philadelphia Athletics, the Phillies, Indians, Orioles, Tigers, Giants and Red Sox. He compiled a .270 career average with 84 homers and 729 RBIs in 1,904 games.

■ **Jack Pierce,** a first baseman who played in parts of three major league seasons, died Sept. 13 in Monterrey, Mexico. He was 63.

Pierce played in a total of 70 major league games from 1973-75 with the Braves and Tigers, hitting .211 with eight homers in 189 at-bats. However, he was a prolific power hitter in the minors, his career spanning from 1970-87. He had nine 20-homer seasons in pro ball, including four 30-homer seasons. Unable to stick in the major leagues, Pierce played one season in Japan and 11 in Mexico, where he set a Mexican League record with 54 homers for Leon in 1986.

■ **Andy Replogle,** a righthander who pitched for the Brewers in 1978 and '79, died April 10 in Fort Myers, Fla. He was 58.

Replogle, who pitched professionally from 1975-81, made 32 appearances for the Brewers in 1978, starting 18 games. He went 9-5, 3.92 and had two shutouts. Replogle made three relief appearances for the Brewers in 1979, getting no decisions and posting a 5.63 ERA.

■ **Roberto Rodriguez,** a righthander who pitched in parts of two seasons in the majors in 1967 and 1970, died Sept. 27 in Maracay, Venezuela. He was 70.

■ **George Rorer,** a sportswriter who had a long career covering minor league baseball and other sports in Louisville, died June 27 in Covington, Ky. He was 79.

Rorrer also authored the book "The Redbirds: A Love Affair," documenting the return of minor league baseball to Louisville in 1982.

■ **Tom Saffell,** an outfielder who played four seasons in the majors in the 1940s and '50s, died Sept. 10 in Sarasota, Fla. He was 91.

Saffell came up to the majors for the first time in July 1949 with the Pirates. He went on to hit .322 with with two homers in 205 at-bats over the rest of the '49 season, but he continued shuttling back and forth between the majors and minors over the next two seasons. He returned to the majors again in 1955, appearing in 82 games with the Pirates and Kansas City Athletics and hitting a combined .180. Saffell later embarked on a long career as a minor league manager and executive. He was president of the Gulf Coast League for 30 years until his retirement in 2009.

■ **Bill "Moose" Skowron,** a first baseman in the majors from 1954-67, died April 27 in Arlington Heights, Ill. He was 81.

Skowron, a six-time all-star, broke into the majors in 1954 and hit .340 for the Yankees in 87 games. He finished his career with a .282 average, 211 homers and 888 RBIs. Skowron hit 20-plus homers four times in his career, slugging a career-high 28 in 1961. He played in eight World Series, winning titles with the Yankees in 1956, '58, '61 and '62 and with the Dodgers in '63. In 1963, he helped Los Angeles sweep his old team, hitting .385 with a homer against New York.

■ **Randy Stein,** a righthander who pitched in the major leagues with the Brewers, Mariners and Cubs, from 1978-82, died Dec. 12, 2011, in Rancho Cucamonga, Calif. He was 58.

Stein pitched professionally from 1971-83 and made his big league debut with the Brewers in 1978. He pitched for the Mariners in 1979 and '81, and the Cubs in 1982. Stein, who made just two starts in 65 big league appearances, had a career record of 5-6, 5.72 with one save.

■ **Nick Strincevich,** a righthander who pitched in the major leagues for eight seasons in the 1940s with the Boston Braves, Pirates and Phillies, died Nov. 11, 2011, in Valparaiso, Ind. He was 96.

Strincevich pitched professionally from 1935-50 and made his big league debut with Boston in 1940, going 4-8. He was a Pirate for most of his major league career after being traded to Pittsburgh early in the 1941 season. Strincevich finished his career in 1948, a season he split between Pittsburgh and Philadelphia. Used primarily as a starter, he was 46-49 for his big league career with a 4.05 ERA. From 1944-46, he went 40-32 for the Pirates—winning 16 games in '45.

■ **Ed Stroud,** and outfielder who played in parts of six major league seasons, died July 2 in

Cleveland. He was 72.

Stroud was 26 years old by the time he made his big league debut as a September callup for the 1966 White Sox. Chicago traded him to the Washington Senators in June 1967, and he spent the rest of the 1967-70 seasons as a regular in Washington's outfield. He finished third in the American League with 10 triples in 1968, though he was a .237 career hitter. Traded back to the White Sox shortly before the 1971 season, Stroud appeared in 53 games for Chicago that year, the final season of his career.

■ **John "Champ" Summers,** an outfielder who played in 11 major league seasons from 1974-84, died Oct. 12 in Ocala, Fla. He was 66.

Summers was mostly a part-time player in his 11-year big league career, during which he played for six teams. He saw the most action with the Tigers from 1979-81, hitting .293 over those three seasons, including a .297 average over a career-high 347 at-bats in 1980.

■ **Robert "Hawk" Taylor,** a catcher who played in parts of 11 big league seasons, died June 9 in Paducah, Ky. He was 73.

Taylor broke into the majors in 1957 and spent the bulk of his career as a reserve with the Milwaukee Braves, the Mets, Angels and Royals. Although he hit .218 in the majors, Taylor was fairly productive in the one season he received significant playing time, hitting .240 with four homers over 225 at-bats for the 1964 Mets. But he had only one other season ('66) in which he received more than 100 at-bats, and he ended his career in the minors in 1971.

■ **Thad Tillotsen,** a righthander who pitched two seasons with the Yankees, died May 16 in Merced, Calif. He was 71.

Tillotsen made his big league debut at age 26 in 1967. He made 43 appearances for the Yankees in '67, including five starts, going 3-9, 4.03 in 98 innings. He spent most of the 1968 season back in the minors but did get into seven games for New York, going 1-0, 4.35.

■ **Tom Umphlett,** an outfielder who played three seasons in the majors from 1953-55, died Sept. 21 in Norfolk, Va. He was 82.

Umphellt burst onto the scene, making the majors as a 22-year-old in 1953 with the Red Sox and batting .283 with three homers and 59 RBIs in 495 at-bats. He was traded to the Washington Senators after the '53 season and his production fell off quickling, as he hit .219 in 1954 and .217 in 1955. Umphlett was sent back to the minors in 1956 and never made it back to the big leagues,

though he continued playing through 1967.

■ **Bruce Von Hoff,** a righthander who pitched in two big league seasons, died Sept. 11 in Gulfport, Fla. He was 68.

Von Hoff was just 21 when he made his big league debut with the Astros in September 1965 at the tail end of his second pro season. He made three appearances for the Astros, all in relief, and allowed three runs in three innings of work. He wasn't called up to the majors again until August 1967, and he made 10 starts for the Astros down the stretch that season, going 0-3, 4.83 in 50 innings. Von Hoff was never summoned to the majors again, though he kept pitching in the minors through the 1970 season.

■ **Jay Ward,** an infielder who played two seasons for the Twins and one for the Reds during a 16-year professional career, died Feb. 24 in Kalispell, Mont. He was 73.

Ward appeared in nine games for the Twins in 1963 and 12 in 1964, combining to hit .174 with four RBIs. He resurfaced in the majors in 1970, when he played in six games for the Reds, going 0-for-3. He hit 20-plus homers in six of his minor league seasons and hit 241 homers in the minors in his 16 seasons.

■ **Harry Wendelstedt,** a former National League umpire who worked 33 years in the majors from 1966-1998 and in five World Series, died March 9 in Daytona Beach, Fla. He was 73.

■ **Frank Wills,** a righthander who pitched nine seasons in the big leagues with four different teams, died May 11 in New Orleans. He was 53.

Wills got his first big league callup in July 1983 with the Royals and went 2-1, 4.15 in six appearances. He saw his most extensive big league action two years later with the Mariners, getting into 24 games (including 18 starts) and going 5-11, 6.00 in 123 innings. He made 27 starts over his first three big league seasons but was primarily a reliever for the rest of his career, pitching for the Indians (1986-87) and Blue Jays (1988-91). His best big league season came in 1989 with Toronto, when he went 3-1, 3.66 in 71 innings.

■ **Eddie Yost,** a third baseman who played in 18 big league seasons from 1944-62, died Oct. 16 in Weston, Mass. He was 86.

Yost spent the bulk of his career with the Washington Senators, taking over as their regular third baseman in 1947 and holding down the job until 1958. A patient hitter, Yost led the American League in walks six times during his career and led it in on-base percentage twice. He was an all-star in 1952 and hit 139 career home runs.

APPENDIX